Schroeder's
ANTIQUES
Price Guide

Twenty-seventh Edition

FULL COLOR!

OUR #1 BEST-SELLER!

2009

cb
COLLECTOR BOOKS
A Division of Schroeder Publishing Co., Inc.

JACKSON COUNTY LIBRARY SERVICES
MEDFORD OREGON 97501

Identification & Values of Over 50,000 Antiques & Collectibles

COLLECTOR BOOKS
P.O. Box 3009
Paducah, Kentucky 42002-3009

www.collectorbooks.com

The current values in this book should be used only as a guide. They are not
intended to set prices, which vary from one section of the country to another.
Auction prices as well as dealer prices vary greatly and are affected by condition
as well as demand. Neither the editors nor the publisher assumes responsibility
for any losses that might be incurred as a result of consulting this guide.

Searching for a Publisher?

We are always looking for people knowledgeable within their fields. If you
feel that there is a real need for a book on your collectible subject and
have a large comprehensive collection, contact Collector Books.

Proudly printed and bound in the
United States of America

Introduction

Another year has gone by and we are still trying to sort out the latest collecting trends for this edition of *Schroeder's*. We have streamlined the book a bit. Some of the categories formerly found both in this book and *Garage Sale and Flea Market Annual* are now found in one volume only. The older antiques and collectibles remained in *Schroeder's*, while other items are now exclusively in its companion book *Garage Sale and Flea Market Annual*. In this way we can make better use of space in both books and provide as much accurate background and pricing information possible. We still depend largely on our advisory board, which provides us with so much knowledge. With hundreds of advisors currently taking part in the production of our book, we can't say enough about how we appreciate their assistance. It is their special expertise and experience in their specific fields that enables us to offer with confidence what we feel are useful, accurate evaluations that provide a sound understanding of the dealings in the marketplace today. Correspondence with so large an advisory panel adds months of extra work to an already monumental task, but we feel that to a very large extent this is the foundation that makes *Schroeder's* the success it has become today. Encompassing nearly 500 categories, many of which you will not find in other price guides, we carefully edit and revise categories each year to bring the latest information to publication. Our sources are greatly varied. We use auction results, dealer lists, and (of course) the internet. We consult with national collectors' clubs, recognized authorities (including other Collector Book authors), researchers, and appraisers. We have by far the largest advisory board of any similar publication on the market. With the addition of new advisors each year, nearly all of our categories are covered by an expert who goes over our computer print-outs each year, checking each listing line by line, deleting those listings that are somewhat vague or misleading. Many of these advisors often send background information and photos. In sharing their knowledge with us, we are able to pass it on and share it with you. We appreciate their assistance very much. In this way we can offer with confidence what we believe to be useful and accurate evaluations that provide a sound understanding of the dealings in the marketplace today.

Our Directory, which you will find in the back of the book, lists each contributor by state or country. These are people who have given us advice on various antiques and collectibles, sent us pricing information, or in any way contributed to this year's book. If you happen to be traveling, consult the Directory for shops along your way. Don't forget that we also list clubs who have worked with us as well as auction houses who have agreed to permit us to use the lovely colored photographs from their catalogs. We send a special thanks to liveauctioneers.com for their generous willingness to work with us on this project.

Our Advisory Board lists only names and partial addresses, so check the Directory for addresses and telephone numbers should you want to correspond with one of our experts. We list an international advisory board; so remember, when you do contact them, *always* enclose a self-addressed, stamped envelope (SASE). Thousands of people buy our guide, and hundreds contact our advisors. The only agreement we have with our advisors is that they edit their categories. They are in no way obligated to answer mail. Many of these people are very busy, spending much time on the road. Time at home is always precious, and they may not be open to contacts. There's no doubt that the reason behind the success of our book is their assistance. We regret seeing them becoming more and more burdened by phone and mail inquiries. We have lost some of our good advisors for this reason, and when we do, the book suffers and consequently, so do our readers. Many of our listed reference sources report that they constantly receive long distance calls (at all hours) that are really valuation requests. If they are registered appraisers, they make their living at providing such information and expect a fee for their service and expertise. If you are aware of a new interest in a collectible, please feel free to contact us and make us aware so that we can research the subject and possibly add a new category to the book.

Since *Schroeder's* cannot provide all available information on antiques and collectibles, there are other sources available that you may want to pursue. The local library is always a good place to start. Check their section on reference books. I'm sure you will find many Collector Books there. Museums are public facilities that are willing and able help you establish the origin and possibly even the value of your particular treasure. A more recent source of information includes the world of e-commerce, where many websites provide pertinent, up-to-date information. Another alternative is the yellow pages of your phone book. Other cities' phone books are available from either your library or from the telephone company office. The Antique Dealers heading in the yellow pages is a good place to start. Look for qualified appraisers (this may be mentioned in their advertisement). Always remember that a dealer buying your merchandise will set a price low enough that he will be able to make a reasonable profit when the item is sold. Once you decide to contact one of these appraisers, unless you intend to see them directly, you'll need to take photographs. Don't send photos that are under- or over-exposed, out of focus, or shot against a background that detracts from important details you want to emphasize. It is almost impossible for them to give you a value judgement on items they've not seen when your photos are of poor quality. Shoot the front, top, and the bottom; describe any marks and numbers (or send a pencil rubbing), explain how and when you acquired the article, and give accurate measurements and any further background information that may be helpful.

The section of the Directory titled Auction Houses includes auctions houses whose catalogs have been used for pricing information. Nearly all have appraisal experts on staff. If the item you're attempting to research is of the caliber of items they deal with, they can offer extremely accurate evaluations. Be sure to send them only professional-quality photographs and expect to pay a fee. Let the auction house know if you expect to consign your item. You will be under no obligation to do so, especially if you disagree with the value they suggest.

We have tried to use simple logic in the organization of this book. With nearly 500 categories included, topics are listed alphabetically, using either manufacturer or type of product. Sometimes listings may fall in several sections of the book. For example furniture may be listed under several major headings by specific manufacturers or types. Please consult the index. It is as complete as we know how to make it, with many cross-references. It will save you much time. We are constantly doing research on background information and have devoted more space to sharing it with our readers than any other publication of this type. The positive feedback from this tells us that we are on the right track. In order to provide this information, we have a single-line format, wherein we describe the items to the fullest extent possible by using several common-sense abbreviations; they will be easy to read and understand if you will first take the time to quickly scan through them.

The Editors

Editorial Staff

Senior Editor
Sharon Huxford

Layout
Terri Hunter and Heather Carvell

Editors
Loretta Suiters and Donna Newnum

Scanning
Donna Ballard and Kelly Dowdy

Research and Editorial Staff
Kimberly Vincent

Cover Design
Beth Summers

On the Cover

Front: Clock, Ansonia "La Vergne," Royal Bonn, porcelain, 11¾", $1,350.00; Napkin ring, Dachshund, 3" $895.00; Sugar bowl, Mayfair, pink, $28.50; Doll, Tete Jumeau, 16½", $4,000.00; Parlor chair, American Rococo, laminated rosewood, 45", $6,000.00 to $8,000.00; Firkin, covered, 10", $860.00; Jardiniere and pedestal, Roseville, Bittersweet, $750.00.

Back: Sculpture, Chiparus, "Friends Forever," bronze and ivory, 25x26", $26,500.00.

Listing of Standard Abbreviations

The following is a list of abbreviations that have been used throughout this book in order to provide you with the most detailed descriptions possible in the limited space available. No periods are used after initials or abbreviations. When two dimensions are given, height is noted first. If only one dimension is listed, it will be height, except in the case of bowls, dishes, plates, or platters, when it will be diameter. The standard two-letter state abbreviations apply.

For glassware, if no color is noted, the glass is clear. Hyphenated colors, for example blue-green, olive-amber, etc., describe a single color tone; colors divided by a slash mark indicate two or more colors, i.e. blue/white. Biscuit jars, teapots, sugar bowls, and butter dishes are assumed to be 'with cover.' Condition is extremely important in determining market value. Common sense suggests that art pottery, china, and glassware values would be given for examples in pristine, mint condition, while suggested prices for utility wares such as Redware, Mocha, and Blue and White Stoneware, for example, reflect the probability that since such items were subjected to everyday use in the home they may show minor wear (which is acceptable) but no notable damage. Values for other categories reflect the best average condition in which the particular collectible is apt to be offered for sale without the dealer feeling it necessary to mention wear or damage. A basic rule of thumb is that an item listed as VG (very good) will bring 40% to 60% of its mint price — a first-hand, personal evaluation will enable you to make the final judgement; EX (excellent) is a condition midway between mint and very good, and values would correspond.

AD....after dinner
Am....American
appl....applied
att....attributed to
bbl....barrel
bk....back
bl....blue
blk....black
brd....board
brn....brown
bulb....bulbous
bsk....bisque
b3m....blown 3-mold
C....century
c....copyright
ca....circa
cb....cardboard
Chpndl....Chippendale
CI....cast iron
compo....composition
cr/sug....creamer and sugar
c/s....cup and saucer
cvd....carved
cvg....carving
dbl....double
dc....die cut
decor....decoration
demi....demitasse
dk....dark
dmn....diamond
Dmn Quilt....Diamond Quilted
drw....drawer
dtd....dated
dvtl....dovetail
emb....embossed, embossing
embr....embroidered
Emp....Empire
eng....engraved, engraving
EPNS....electroplated nickel silver
EX....excellent

Fed....Federal
fr....frame, framed
Fr....French
ft, ftd....foot, feet, footed
G....good
gr....green
grad....graduated
grpt....grain painted
H....high, height
Hplwht....Hepplewhite
hdl, hdld....handle, handled
HP....hand painted
illus....illustration, illustrated by
imp....impressed
ind....individual
int....interior
Invt T'print....Inverted Thumbprint
irid....iridescent
jtd....jointed
L....length, long
lav....lavender
ldgl....leaded glass
litho....lithograph
lt....light
M....mint
mahog....mahogany
mc....multicolor
MIB....mint in box
MIG....Made in Germany
MIP....mint in package
mk....mark
MOC....mint on card
MOP....mother-of-pearl
mt, mtd....mount, mounted
NE....New England
NM....near mint
NRFB....never removed from box
NP....nickel plated
opal....opalescent
orig....original

o/l....overlay
o/w....otherwise
Pat....patented
pc....piece
ped....pedestal
pk....pink
pnt....paint
porc....porcelain
prof....professional
QA....Queen Anne
re....regarding
rfn....refinished
rnd....round
rpl....replaced
rpr....repaired
rpt....repainted
rstr....restored
rtcl....reticulated
rvpt....reverse painted
s&p....salt and pepper
sgn....signed
SP....silverplated
sq....square
std....standard
str....straight
sz....size
trn....turned, turning
turq....turquoise
uphl....upholstered
VG....very good
Vict....Victorian
vnr....veneer
W....width
wht....white
w/....with
w/o....without
X, Xd....cross, crossed
x....times (i.e. 4x)
yel....yellow
(+)....has been reproduced

A B C Plates

Children's china featuring the alphabet as part of the design has been made from the late eighteenth century up to the present day. The earliest creamware items, plates, and mugs were often decorated with embossed or printed letters and prim, moralistic verses or illustrations and were made in Staffordshire, England. In later years they were made by American potters as well, and varied pictures of animals, events, famous people, and childhood activities became popular design themes. All were decorated by the transfer method, and many had colors brushed on for added interest.

Be sure to inspect these plates carefully for damage, since condition is a key price-assessing factor, and aside from obvious chips and hairlines, even wear can substantially reduce their values. Another problem for collectors is the fact that there are current reproductions of glass and tin plates, particularly the glass plate referred to as Emma (child's face in center) and a tin plate showing children with hoops. These plates are so common as to be worthless as collectibles. Our advisor for this category is Dr. Joan George; she is listed in the Directory under New Jersey.

Ceramic

Aesop's Fable, cock & fox, mc transfer, unmk Staffordshire, 5½".. 135.00
April, figure between roses, mc transfer, unmk, 6¾" 150.00
Baseball - Caught on the Fly, blk transfer 450.00
Baseball - Running to First Base, blk transfer, 8", EX 565.00
Bible Pictures - Elijah Fed by the Ravens, mc transfer, 7¼" 225.00
Bible scene, At 12 Years Old..., mc transfer, J&G Meakin, 5½"... 125.00
Birds of Paradise, red transfer, Edge & Malkin, ca 1840, 7¼" 110.00
Boys playing marbles, mc transfer, unmk Staffordshire, 5½".........225.00
Children w/rabbit, red transfer, unmk Staffordshire, 7½" 125.00
Civil War scene, red transfer, Staffordshire, 7½" 350.00

Crusoe Finding the Foot Prints, polychrome, B.P. Co., Rd. #69963, 8", from $140.00 to $250.00. (Photo courtesy Ralph and Irene Lindsay)

Farmer loading hay wagon, mc transfer, unmk Staffordshire, 6"..... 90.00
Feeding the Donkey, blk transfer, Powell & Bishop, 7" 110.00
Franklin's Proverbs, He That by Plow..., mc transfer, Meakin, 5½".175.00
Franklin's Proverbs, Keep Thy Shop..., mc, Staffordshire, 5½".....175.00
Game dog among grasses, brn transfer, Staffordshire, 7"............... 127.50
Guardian, dog & sleeping boy, mc transfer, Elsmore & Foster (sic), 7".225.00
Hush My Dear..., mc transfer, Staffordshire, 6⅛" 125.00
Kestrel, mc transfer, unmk Staffordshire, 7" 130.00
Nations of the World, Japanese, couple in mc transfer, BP, 7¼"... 175.00
Not To Oversee Workmen Is To Leave Your Purse Open, mc, 5".. 150.00
Nursery Tales, Whittington & His Cat, Staffordshire, 8" 350.00
Nursery Tales - Old Mother Hubbard, mc transfer, Tunstall, 7½"..225.00
Organ grinder & children, bl transfer, unmk Staffordshire, 6¾" .. 110.00
Robinson Crusoe at Work, mc transfer, Staffordshire, 7½"........... 225.00
Spelling Bee, mc transfer, unmk Staffordshire, 5½" 175.00
Stag (deer) in heart, red transfer, Staffordshire, 6½".................... 125.00
T Is for Tulip..., mc transfer, Staffordshire, stain, 6"..................... 175.00
Their First Day, chicks in basket, mc transfer, Staffordshire, 6⅛"... 60.00

Three Men in a tub, mc transfer, gr ABCs along rim, Wood & Sons...45.00
Tulip & Butterfly..., children in garden, mc transfer, Meakin, 5½"..100.00
Wild Animal Series, leopard, mc transfer, BPCo, 7½" 350.00

Glass

Clock, ABCs, Roman & standard numerals, scalloped rim, vaseline, 7".. 45.00
Clock, ABCs, Roman & standard numerals, scalloped rim, 7"....... 40.00
Dog's head etched in clear, emb rim, Higbee, 6½" (+).................. 125.00
Emma (child's face), ABC rim, vaseline, Clay's Crystal Works, 8"...35.00
Milk glass, ABC rim w/beaded edge, 7".. 22.00
President Garfield, ABC rim, clear & frosted 80.00
President Garfield, smooth rim, 6" 80.00

Sancho Panza and Dapple, 6", from $50.00 to $60.00. (Photo courtesy Irene and Ralph Lindsay)

Stork, marigold carnival, 7½" 95.00
Stork among rushes, clear & frosted, 6", NM................................ 85.00

Tin

Geo Washington, 13 stars, 5⅝", VG 50.00
Geometric center, emb ABC rim, 2¼" 55.00
Lion, emb ABC rim, ca 1860s, 2¾" 40.00
Victorian girl on swing, mc litho, Ohio Art, early 1900s, 8" 35.00
Who Killed Cock Robin?, unmk, 7¾" 55.00

Abingdon

From 1934 until 1950, the Abingdon Pottery Co. of Abingdon, Illinois, made a line of art pottery with a white vitrified body decorated with various types of glazes in many lovely colors. Novelties, cookie jars, utility ware, and lamps were made in addition to several lines of simple yet striking art ware. Fern Leaf, introduced in 1937, featured molded vertical feathering. La Fleur, in 1939, consisted of flowerpots and flower-arranger bowls with rows of vertical ribbing. Classic, 1939 – 1940, was a line of vases, many with evidence of Chinese influence. Several marks were used, most of which employed the company name. In 1950 the company reverted to the manufacture of sanitary ware that had been their mainstay before the art ware division was formed.

Highly decorated examples and those with black, bronze, or red glaze usually command at least 25% higher prices.

For further information we recommend *Abingdon Pottery Artware 1934 – 1950, Stepchild of the Great Depression,* by Joe Paradis (Schiffer).

#30, vase, Chan, bronze.. 225.00
#84, vase, What Not, 5" 60.00
#101, vase, Alpha, 10".. 25.00
#113, water jug.. 95.00
#116, vase, Classic, 10"... 27.50
#149, flowerpot, La Fleur, 3" 15.00
#158, candleholder, La Fleur, 2x3½", ea...................................... 12.50
#258, lamp base, fluted shaft, 23" 75.00

#305, bookends, Sea Gull, 6" 85.00
#308D, jar, Coolie, 11" 90.00
#322, goblet, Swedish, 6½" 60.00
#324, vase, Rope, 6¼" 20.00
#336, bowl, sq, 9" 35.00
#360, candleholders, Quatrain, sq, 3", pr 40.00
#365, jar, Dart Candy, 6¼" dia 65.00
#377, wall pocket, Morning Glory, 7½" 32.50
#412, floor vase, Volute, 15" 55.00
#424, bowl, Fern Leaf, 8½" 75.00
#426, flower boat, Fern Leaf, 4x13" 90.00
#432, fruit boat, Fern Leaf, 6½x15" 15.00
#463, vase, Star, 7½", from $20 to 25.00

#513, vase, Double Cornucopia, 8¾", $32.00. (Photo courtesy Tom Harris Auctions/ LiveAuctioneers.com)

#539, urn, Regency, 7" 22.00
#542, vase, Bali, 9" 75.00
#550, vase, Fluted, 11" 25.00
#568, mint compote, pk, 6" dia 25.00
#591, vase, Pleat, 10" 28.00
#610, bowl, Shell, deep, 9" 42.50
#615, ashtray, Chic, 4" dia 22.50
#672, planter, Fawn, 5" 38.00
#690D, range set, Daisy, 3-pc 45.00
#705, vase, Modern, 8" 20.00
Cookie jar, #471, Old Lady, plaid apron, minimum value 400.00
Cookie jar, #495, Fat Boy, from $250 to 300.00
Cookie jar, #549, Hippo, decor, 1942, from $250 to 300.00
Cookie jar, #588, Money Bag, from $45 to 50.00
Cookie jar, #602, Hobby Horse, from $200 to 250.00
Cookie jar, #611, Jack-in-the-Box, from $300 to 325.00
Cookie jar, #622, Miss Muffet, from $275 to 325.00
Cookie jar, #651, Choo Choo (Locomotive), blk/yel decor, from $150 to ... 200.00
Cookie jar, #653, Clock, 1949, from $65 to 75.00
Cookie jar, #663, Humpty Dumpty, decor, from $200 to ... 250.00
Cookie jar, #664, Pineapple, from $65 to 75.00
Cookie jar, #665, Wigwam, decor, minimum value 400.00
Cookie jar, #674, Pumpkin, 1949, minimum value 300.00
Cookie jar, #677, Daisy, 1949, from $35 to 45.00
Cookie jar, #678, Windmill, from $125 to 150.00
Cookie jar, #692, Witch, minimum value 1,000.00
Cookie jar, #693, Little Girl, from $80 to 95.00
Cookie jar, #694, Bo Peep (must have serial # & ink stamp) 300.00
Cookie jar, #695, Mother Goose, minimum value 350.00
Cookie jar, #696, Three Bears, from $90 to 115.00

Adams, Matthew Catlin

In the 1950s a trading post in Alaska contacted Sascha Brastoff to design a line of porcelain with scenes of Eskimos, Alaskan motifs, and animals indigenous to that area. These items were to be sold in Alaska to the tourist trade.

Brastoff selected Matthew Adams, born in April 1915, to design the Alaska series. Pieces from the line he produced have the Sascha B mark on the front; some have a pattern number on the reverse. They did not have the rooster backstamp. (See the Sascha Brastoff category for information on this mark.)

After the Alaska series was introduced and proved to be successful, Matthew Adams left the employment of Sascha Brastoff (working three years there in all) and opened his own studio. Pieces made in his studio are signed Matthew Adams in script and may have the word Alaska on the front. Mr. Adams's studio is now located in Los Angeles, but at this time, due to his age, he has ceased production.

Our advisor for this category is Marty Webster; his is listed in the Directory under Michigan. He welcomes new information on this subject.

Ashtray, Eskimo family, 8½" 20.00
Ashtray, walrus on gr, boomerang shape, 6x11" 65.00
Ashtray, walrus on turq, hooded, 5½" 65.00
Bowl, Eskimo girl w/igloo, #150, 11½" 100.00
Bowl, ram on gr, freeform, 7" 45.00
Bowl, seal on blk, freeform, w/lid, #145, 7½" L 55.00
Bowl, walrus on blk, freeform, #104, 6½" L 50.00
Bowl, walrus on yel, w/lid, 7" 75.00
Charger, caribou on dk bl, 18" 150.00
Charger, Eskimo crawling on snow w/igloo beyond, #101, 18" 200.00
Charger, Eskimo w/harpoon, 16" 135.00
Cigarette lighter, cabin on stilts, 5x5" 50.00
Coffeepot, ram on gr, 11½", +6 4½" mugs 180.00
Compote, grizzly bear on brn, tall, 8½" dia 70.00
Cookie jar, Eskimo mother & child on brn, w/lid, 8" 75.00
Creamer, polar bear on blk, 4¾" 30.00
Creamer & sugar bowl, Eskimo child, #3144 & #144a 65.00
Cup & saucer, sled on bl 25.00
Dish, cabin on stilts, #163, freeform, 6x6½" 40.00
Dish, caribou, #099, 2x6½x7½" 45.00
Dish, Eskimo child w/2 igloos, #170, 6x12¾" 130.00
Dish, wolf on snow w/cobalt sky, sq, #012, 6½x6½" 40.00
Ginger jar, walrus on turq, w/lid, 6½" 90.00
Jar, Eskimo on ice bl, 6" 30.00
Mug, Husky dog, #112A, 4½x4¾" 40.00
Pitcher, Eskimo mother & child, 13", +6 5½" mugs 200.00
Pitcher, Eskimo w/fishing pole on turq, 11½" 130.00
Pitcher, husky dog, wht on teal, bulbous, 5" 35.00
Plate, Eskimo girl, #162, 7½" 45.00

Plate, Eskimo mother and child, 10½", $60.00. (Photo courtesy Marianne Keil)

Plate, moose standing in water, #161, 11½" 100.00
Plate, seal on ice, 12" 60.00
Shakers, Eskimo child on gray, pr 35.00
Tankard, polar bear on blk, w/lid, 13" 200.00
Teapot, walrus on ice bl, 6½" 75.00
Tile, igloo & sled on cobalt, 8½x9¾" 85.00
Tray, walrus on ice floe on cobalt, sq, #122, 12½" 90.00
Tumbler, cabin 20.00

Vase, Eskimo w/fishing pole on turq, 12x5" dia............................ 125.00
Vase, glacier on gray, #143, 5½"... 50.00
Vase, house on yel, 11½".. 70.00
Vase, polar bear on gr, 10" 100.00
Vase, sea lion & seaweed, oval, #128, 8" 95.00

Advertising

The advertising world has always been a fiercely competitive field. In an effort to present their product to the customer, every imaginable gimmick was put into play. Colorful and artfully decorated signs and posters, thermometers, tape measures, fans, hand mirrors, and attractive tin containers (all with catchy slogans, familiar logos, and often-bogus claims) are only a few of the many examples of early advertising memorabilia that are of interest to today's collectors.

Porcelain signs were made as early as 1890 and are highly prized for their artistic portrayal of life as it was then… often allowing amusing insights into the tastes, humor, and way of life of a bygone era. As a general rule, older signs are made from a heavier gauge metal. Those with three or more fired-on colors are especially desirable.

Tin containers were used to package consumer goods ranging from crackers and coffee to tobacco and talcum. After 1880 can companies began to decorate their containers by the method of lithography. Though colors were still subdued, intricate designs were used to attract the eye of the consumer. False labeling and unfounded claims were curtailed by the Pure Food and Drug Administration in 1906, and the name of the manufacturer as well as the brand name of the product had to be printed on the label. By 1910 color was rampant with more than a dozen hues printed on the tin or on paper labels. The tins themselves were often designed with a second use in mind, such as canisters, lunch boxes, even toy trains. As a general rule, tobacco-related tins are the most desirable, though personal preference may direct the interest of the collector to peanut butter pails with illustrations of children or talcum tins with irresistible babies or beautiful ladies. Coffee tins are popular, as are those made to contain a particularly successful or well-known product.

Perhaps the most visual of the early advertising gimmicks were the character logos, the Fairbank Company's Gold Dust Twins, the goose trademark of the Red Goose Shoe Company, Nabisco's ZuZu Clown and Uneeda Kid, the Campbell Kids, the RCA dog Nipper, and Mr. Peanut, to name only a few. Many early examples of these bring high prices on the market today.

Our listings are alphabetized by product name or, in lieu of that information, by word content or other pertinent description. Items are evaluated according to condition as stated in the line descriptions. When no condition code is present, assume items are in at least near mint condition. Remember that condition greatly affects value (especially true for tin items). For instance, a sign in excellent to near mint condition may bring twice as much as the same one in only very good condition, sometimes even more. On today's market, items in good to very good condition are slow to sell unless they are extremely rare.

We have several advertising advisors; see specific subheadings. For further information we recommend *Hake's Price Guide to Character Toys, 3rd Edition,* by Ted Hake; and *Antique & Contemporary Advertising Memorabilia, Collectible Soda Pop Memorabilia,* and *Value Guide to Gas Station Memorabilia,* all by B.J. Summers. *Garage Sale and Flea Market Annual* is another good reference. All of these books are available at your local bookstore or from Collector Books. See also Advertising Dolls; Advertising Cards; Automobilia; Coca-Cola; Banks; Calendars; Cookbooks; Paperweights; Posters; Sewing Items; Thermometers.

Key:
cb — cardboard	ps — porcelain sign
cl — celluloid	tc — tin container
dc — diecut	tm — trademark
gs — glass sign	ts — tin sign
sf — self-framed	

A-1 Beer, sign, tin litho, barbershop scene, 25x37", EX 375.00
Acme Beer, tray, cowgirl enameled on aluminum, 1940s, 17x9", EX . 70.00
Advance - Rumely Oilpull, paperweight, tractor form, metal, 4" L, EX . 160.00
Agfa Photo Goods, ps, lady sits on fence, 48x21", VG 425.00

American Seal Paint, poster, Uncle Sam and Lady Liberty, Donaldson Litho Co. for Troy Paint & Color Works, 55x42", $10,825.00. (Photo courtesy James D. Julia Inc.)

Anheuser Busch, charger, tin litho, Say When, couple, 16", EX.... 90.00
Bagdad Coffee, Middle-Eastern figures, tc, 5-lb pail, EX.............. 110.00
Bartholomay Brewing, tip tray, girl in winged wheel, 4¼" dia, EX+ . 350.00
Berry Bros' Varnishes, pocket mirror, cl, children, 2" dia 300.00
Berry Bros Varnishes, pocket mirror, cl, boy, dog in wagon, 3", EX .190.00
Betsy Ross Cigars, sf ts, lady in oval reserve, 27x22", G 360.00
Big Ben Smoking Tobacco, pocket tin, blk horse, 4½", EX+ 100.00
Bireley's Orange Drink, thermometer, tin litho, bottle, 16x4½", EX+ .. 350.00
Black Bass 10¢ Cigar, box, wooden, bass graphics, 9", EX+............ 50.00
Black Duck Dust Cloth, tc, duck reserve, 1924, 4½x3x2", EX+ ... 130.00
Black Hawk Cigars, wooden box, Indian label inside, 8" L, EX ... 275.00
Block Bros' Mail Pouch, cb sign, methods of delivery, 13x11", EX..240.00
Buckingham Bright Smoking Tobacco, tc, 1926, unopened, 4x3x¾", EX. 50.00
Bull Durham Smoking Tobacco, sign, Royal Victor, orig fr, 23x35", EX+ . 1,100.00
Burkholder's Potato Chips, tc, red & wht, 2-lb, EX 30.00

Buster Brown

Buster Brown was the creation of cartoonist Richard Felton Outcault; his comic strip first appeared in the *New York Herald* on May 4, 1902. Since then Buster and his dog Tige (short for Tiger) have adorned sundry commercial products but are probably best known as the trademark for the Brown Shoe Company established early in the twentieth century. Today hundreds of Buster Brown premiums, store articles, and advertising items bring substantial prices from many serious collectors.

Balloon blower, Fiberglas head w/orig pnt, 1960s, 24x21", EX 350.00
Bank, pnt CI, BB & Tige, 5¼", EX 480.00
Bank, pnt CI, horse in horseshoe w/BB & Tige, gold & blk, 4¼", EX. 240.00
Bank, pnt plaster, BB & Tige, 5x5x3", EX 300.00
Banner, cloth, BB Shoes, BB & Tige, fringed bottom, 1900s, 12x9", EX . 180.00
Bowl, porc, BB running w/Tige transfer on wht, Elkins NY, EX 95.00
Candy container, compo, BB, HP, bl sailor suit, red pants, 4½", EX . 180.00
Comic book, BB's Antics, full color, Outcault, 1906, G 100.00
Croquet set, 4 wood mallets/5 balls, J Pressman #890, BB logo, VGIB..48.00
Cup, china, BB & Tige decal on wht, ca 1910 .... 45.00
Door plate, blk & brass, BB & Tige above text, 5½x11¼", EX 125.00
Game, BB & Tige Ball Toss, Bliss, 10x24", VG 375.00
Hobby horse, pnt wood, BB & Tige decal on pnt saddle, EX 240.00
Humidor, bsk, BB & bag mk Good Luck, pnt, mk JM C3505, 1920s, 8½"..160.00
Mug, silver, emb BB & Tige/sunburst, mk Sterling, 3¼", VG 275.00

Pennant, felt, BB Guaranteed Hosiery, BB & Tige w/sock, 29", EX . 240.00
Poster, BB & Tige, Felton/Outcault/Selchow & Righter, 24x18", EX. 1,325.00
Rocking chair, pnt wood, BB Shoes on bk rail, slat seat, 22", VG . 60.00

Sign, cardboard, early images, 14x14" including frame, VG+, $2,100.00. (Photo courtesy Wm. Morford Auctions)

Sign, rvpt in wood fr, BB Shoes, lights up, 10½x24½", VG 210.00
Statuette, pnt chalkware, BB & Tige, dtd 1972, 19x11", VG 85.00
String holder, pnt compo, BB & Tige, Wiehl c 1938, 7½", EX..... 360.00
Target, litho paper on wood beanbag toss, BB graphics, 24" W, VG+. 540.00
Target, paper litho on wood, BB graphics, Bliss, 10x24", G.......... 250.00
Toy, CI, Tige pulls BB in cart, EX pnt, 7" L 210.00
Toy, HP tin, BB & Tige on seesaw, clockwork, Germany, 8½" L, EX.1,550.00
Waffle press, CI, Buster Waffles, BB & Tige, Pat 1906, 14", EX ... 155.00

Cameo Hot Point, doll, pnt wood man in red, decal on ft, EX..1,560.00
Campbell Brand Coffee, tc, camel scene, 4-lb pail, 8x7½", EX 50.00
Castle Brand Pure Whiskies, paperweight, glass, Pyro Art Co, 4" L. 110.00
Chamberlain's Cough Remedy, door push, tin litho, Norton, 5½x3".675.00
Cherry Blossom Perfume, emb cb dc sign, nun & flowers, sq, 9½" . 90.00
City Club, ts, bottle on blk, Schmidt Brewing, 40x14", EX+ 525.00
Clabber Girl Baking Powder, ts, dbl-sided, 12x34" 80.00
Cliquot Club Ginger Ale, cb dc display, child w/bottle, easel-bk, 21".170.00
Clysmic King of Table Waters, tray, draped nude, Meek, 13x10½", EX..550.00
Cobbs Creek Drink-O-Meter, thermometer, tin litho, 39x18", EX.130.00
Colgate's Borated Baby Powder, tc, smiling baby, 3¼x1¾" dia, EX...50.00
Colgate's Dactylis Talc, tc, girl reserve, sample sz, 2x1¼x⅝", EX ... 50.00
Continental Insurance, ts, Continental soldier, 31x21", VG 480.00
Counsellor 5¢ Cigars, rvpt sign, convex, bk-lit, 5x18" dia, VG ... 625.00
Cruwell-Tabak, countertop cb litho sign, Indian chief, 15x9½", EX.50.00
Cupid Bouquet Little Cigars, pocket tin, thoughtful Cupid, 3½", EX..50.00
Curtiss Baby Ruth Gum, ts, red & cream, 10x27", EX+ 150.00
Dad's Root Beer, thermometer, tin litho, bright mc on wht, 27x18", EX+..120.00
DeKalb Profit Pullets, ts, chicken among eggs, 12½x28", VG 300.00

De Laval, sign, two-sided tin flange type, 28x18", EX, $4,500.00. (Photo courtesy Wm. Morford Auctions)

DeLaval Separators, ts, lady w/cow/scenes, 1920s, 33x22", VG ... 275.00
Delaware Punch, thermometer, tin litho, Am's Soft..., 16x6½", VG+..100.00

Dold Quality Hams & Bacon, bill clip w/1¾" cl button, EX 50.00
Dorothy Vernon Perfumed Talcum, tc, stylish lady, weekend sz, 2", EX.160.00
Dotterweich Brewing, tray, bottle & foaming mug, 12" dia, EX ... 600.00
Dr LeGear, ts, Giant Horse, 14½x17½", EX................................. 480.00

Dr. Pepper

A young pharmacist, Charles C. Alderton, was hired by W.B. Morrison, owner of Morrison's Old Corner Drug Store in Waco, Texas, around 1884. Alderton, an observant sort, noticed that the drugstore's patrons could never quite make up their minds as to which flavor of extract to order. He concocted a formula that combined many flavors, and Dr. Pepper was born. The name was chosen by Morrison in honor of a beautiful young girl with whom he had once been in love. The girl's father, a Virginia doctor by the name of Pepper, had discouraged the relationship due to their youth, but Morrison had never forgotten her. On December 1, 1885, a U.S. patent was issued to the creators of Dr. Pepper. Our advisor for this category is Craig Stifter; he is listed in the Directory under Colorado. See also Soda Fountain Collectibles.

Bottle, Baylor, Cotton Bowl Champs, unopened 42.50
Calendar, lady w/glass, full pad, 1937, 32x15¼", EX..................... 180.00
Can, red/wht/bl cone top, Dallas TX, 6-oz, 4½", EX..................... 450.00
Clock, convex glass front, 10-2-4, dmn shape, Pam, 15½", EX 195.00
Clock, Dr Pepper in red banner, 10-2-4 in red, GE, electric, rnd, VG .72.50
Clock, glass front, Drink a Bite To Eat, 1950s, 15" dia, EX 550.00
Clock, mc numbers on wht face, lights up, sq, 1960s, 15¾", EX .. 165.00
Clock, neon-lit, octagonal, chrome bezel, 18", VG 525.00
Clock, oak, mirrored glass w/logo, pendulum, Roman numerals, 35x15".325.00
Clock, printed paper dial, Telechron, electric, gr fr, 14" dia, EX ..220.00
Clock, rvpt Drink Dr P...Thanks Call Again, EX........................3,600.00
Cooler, aluminum ice chest, w/decal, EX 30.00
Cooler, metal, hand holds bottle on gr chest, rstr 120.00
Door push, Dr Pepper on red rectangle mtd to aluminum bars, 5x31", EX..275.00
Match holder, pnt tin, dk gr print on lt gr, wall mt, PHCo, 1940s, EX...72.50
Menu sign, chalkboard, logo at top, 1960s, 27x19", EX.................. 48.00
Seltzer bottle, pk glass, Dr Pepper spigot top, Czech, 1920s, 12"..425.00
Sign, cb, girl w/bottle, The Friendly Pepper-Upper, fr, 17x27", EX.170.00
Sign, cb, Smart Lift, blond lady, 1940s-50s, fr, 21x33½", VG....... 180.00
Sign, flange; metal dc, bottle at right, 1939, 15x24", EX...........1,200.00
Sign, flange; tin, Dr Pepper on brick ground, 10-2-4 below, 16x24", VG ..480.00
Sign, metal bottle cap, 10-2-4, red & wht, unknown age, EX 24.00
Sign, paper litho, girl w/fishing gear, wood fr, 1940s, 28x34", VG. 155.00
Sign, porc, Dr Pepper Bottling Co, red/wht, triangular, 23x18", EX.1,080.00
Sign, porc, Dr Pepper on brick design, 10½x26¼", EX 275.00
Sign, porc, Drink...Good for Life, Texlite/Dallas, 10½x26", EX ... 300.00
Sign, tin litho, bottle, 10-2-4 on yel, 54x18¼", VG 240.00
Thermometer, bubble glass front, Pam, 12" dia, VG..................... 145.00
Thermometer, tin, bottle on yel, faded/weathered, 1940s, 17½", G .85.00
Thermometer, tin, bottle on yel, 1940s, 25x10", EX...................... 360.00
Thermometer, tin litho, Drink...Frosty Cold, 1950s, 26x9½", VG ..215.00
Tray, tin litho, Drink...King of Beverages, 13x10½", VG........... 1,200.00
Tray, tin litho, Free From Caffein..., Shonk, 13½x16½", EX 900.00

Dutch Boy Paints, lamp, Dutch boy figural, pnt compo base, 15", VG.180.00
Dutch Cleanser, ps, Dutch girl on yel, 20x14", EX 375.00
Elgin Ice Cream, tray, Victorian boy & girl w/sweets, 13½", VG . 360.00
Ex-Ha-Fe Hay Fever Relief, cb sign, man sneezing, easel-bk, 28x18", EX .825.00
Fairy Soap, tip tray, girl on bar, Am Art Works, 4¼" dia, EX 50.00
Farquhar Ironage Farm Machinery, porc sign, yel & blk, 15x58", EX. 1,200.00
Federal Hi-Power Shells, cb sign, lg shell, 22x8" 480.00
Fire Chief Gasoline, ps, star logo, 1953, 18x12", EX 540.00

Fireman's Fund Ins, card holder, Christmas greeting, 3" L............ 475.00
Flor De General Arthur Cigars, rvpt sign, flakes, 14x25", EX 275.00
Flycasters Tobacco Mixture, tc, man casting, 4x5" dia, EX+ 550.00
Folger's Coffee, tc, sailing ship reserve, key-wind, 1931, 2-lb, EX .. 50.00
Forest & Stream Tobacco, pocket tin, men in canoe, 4¼x3", EX. 400.00
Frimousse D'or Paris Powder, box, lady among flowers, 2x1½x1" ... 50.00
Garden Co Confectioners, bucket, tin litho beach scenes, 2½x3", EX... 50.00
Ghirardelli's Chocolate, dc cb hanger, parrot/perch, 1940-50s, 20", EX.525.00
Goebel Beer, tip tray, man drinking, Meyer & Lavensen, 4½" dia, EX.170.00

Gold Dust, trolley car sign, Black twins, cardboard, 11x21", $400.00.
(Photo courtesy Wm. Morford Auctions)

Golden Cup Coffee, tc, children playing, 3-lb, 9x6" dia, EX........ 110.00
Golden West Coffee, dripolator, aluminum, blk hdl, 10", EX+ 300.00
Golden West Coffee, tc, cowgirl on red, key-wind, 1927, 3-lb, EX+..450.00
Golden West Coffee, tc, girl drinking coffee on red, 1937, 2-lb, EX+. 200.00
Goodrich Rubber Footwear, ts, 3 styles shown, 14x39" 190.00
Governor Coffee, tc, governor reserve on red, 6x4" dia, EX........... 90.00
Grapette, trolley sign, cb, blond girl w/bottle, fr, 11¼x23", EX 210.00
Green River Whiskey, tray, Black man stands w/horse, 24", G 180.00
Hadensa, ps, red/wht/bl, 12x17¾", VG 600.00
Hanley's Peerless Ale, tin tray, man w/glass, 1937, 11½" dia, EX ... 70.00
Hazle Club Cream Soda, cl sign, foaming mug on red & cream, 9" dia, EX..50.00
Heinz Soups, menu brd, pnt wood, bowl at top, 13x26¾", EX 60.00
Heptol Splits, tip tray, Russell Western scene, Shonk, 4¼", EX...375.00
Hi-Plane Tobacco, pocket tin, plane on red, 4½x3x1", EX 110.00

Hires

    Charles E. Hires, a drugstore owner in Philadelphia, became interested in natural teas. He began experimenting with roots and herbs and soon developed his own special formula. Hires introduced his product to his own patrons and began selling concentrated syrup to other soda fountains and grocery stores. Samples of his 'root beer' were offered for the public's approval at the 1876 Philadelphia Centennial. Today's collectors are often able to date their advertising items by observing the Hires boy on the logo. From 1891 to 1906, he wore a dress. From 1906 until 1914, he was shown in a bathrobe; and from 1915 until 1926, he was depicted in a dinner jacket. The apostrophe may or may not appear in the Hires name; this seems to have no bearing on dating an item. Our advisor for this category is Craig Stifter; he is listed in the Directory under Colorado.

Bottle, rvpt label, aluminum top, sm ding/clouding, 12", EX 150.00
Carrier, stenciled wood, cut-out hdls, tall sides, 1950s, EX............. 20.00
Clock, glass face, Drink..., red/wht/bl, 15" dia, EX........................ 215.00
Cooler, metal, Hires emb on wht (2 sides), 1940s, 10x19x16", VG . 120.00
Dispenser, Drink It's Pure, ceramic, orig pump, Germany 1,200.00
Dispenser, hourglass shape, w/spigot & pump, EX 1,300.00
Dispenser, marble base, Munimaker #8049, 35x16", EX............ 7,900.00

Dispenser, wht Vitrolite base, rnd milk glass ball top, 23", EX ..4,800.00
Dispenser, wooden bbl, metal bands, 1930s, 27", EX 660.00
Elgin Watches, wooden sign, boy in straw hat, Myercord, 22x25", EX. 180.00
Malt mixer, porc base, hand-crank, orig metal container, 13", EX ..850.00
Mug, ceramic, bbl form, Hires boy, Mettlach 225.00
Mug, ceramic, Hires boy, Villeroy & Boch, 5" 425.00
Mug, ceramic, Hires boy pointing, Cauldon Ware, England, 4"... 125.00
Mug, ceramic, ped ft, Hires boy/Hires, ca 1900, 4" 2,400.00
Mug, stoneware, bl & gray, bark hdl, 5½", EX............................. 300.00
Mug, stoneware, Hires on hourglass form, 6" 24.00
Pocket mirror, cl, lady w/flowers & mug, ca 1905-10, EX 480.00
Pocketknife, enamel on silver-tone, boy pointing, ca 1915, EX ... 425.00
Sign, cb, lady in yel dress by sign, rpl easel bk, 1940s, 12x7", G... 150.00
Sign, cb standup, lady w/Hires ribbon & tray, 1910-15, 58", VG . 150.00
Sign, glass front, light-up bubble in metal fr, 16" dia, EX 725.00
Sign, metal over cb, brunette in evening gown, 1920s, 9x6½", EX .325.00
Sign, paper, dc foaming glass, ca 1910-15, 11x5½" 600.00
Sign, paper, Got a Minute?, lady w/tray, 1940s-50s, 28x16", EX.. 1,325.00
Sign, porc, Drink...It Is Pure, blk on yel, 1908, 15x36", EX.......... 400.00
Sign, porc, Hires boy as cop, Stop!..., ca 1900, 3x15", G.............. 180.00
Sign, tin, Enjoy...Helpful & Delicious, 9½x27½", VG.................. 840.00
Sign, tin, flapper lady w/glass on orange, 20" W, VG................... 415.00
Sign, tin, Have a...& Refresh, mc, 9x18", G 155.00
Sign, tin, Hires Delicious in Bottles, 1948, 11½x35½", EX 120.00
Sign, tin, Hires in Bottles & bottle, 1930s, 9¾x27½", EX 480.00
Sign, tin, Hires Milkshake a Frosted Delight, 6x9", VG 240.00
Sign, tin, Hires R-J Root Beer, 24" dia, VG 170.00
Sign, tin bottle cap, Drink...in Bottles, 1950s, 35" dia, EX.......... 240.00
Straw dispenser, CI, Hires on 4 panels, dtd 1911, 5½x10", EX..3,600.00
Straw dispenser, CI w/ruby glass inserts, dtd 1911, 5½x10", EX .4,550.00
Thermometer, dc tin bottle, 29x8", EX+..................................... 130.00
Thermometer, tin, Hires Refreshes Right, bottle at bottom, 27x8", EX.. 95.00
Tray, tin litho, lady in oval, Haskell Coffin, Beach, 13x10½", EX. 290.00
Tray, tin litho, 2 ladies w/glasses, much rstr, 19½x23½"................. 180.00
Wrigley's Soap, tip tray, tin litho, cat on soap bars on yel, EX...... 330.00

Hoffman Bicycles, door push, emb tin litho, bl & wht 480.00
Hotel Majestic, tip tray, After the Barndance...1914, 6" dia 80.00
Humboldt Beer, tray, lady w/goblet, Beach, 13" dia, EX+.......... 1,050.00
Hyroler Whiskey, tip tray, well-dressed man, blk & wht, Shonk, EX ...50.00
Ideal Ear Stopples, cb countertop sign, beach scene, 7½x8"........... 50.00
Imperial Sporting Powder, tc, paper label w/game bird, 1-lb, EX. 2,100.00
Incandescent Light & Stove, tip tray, Make Home Home Like, 4½", EX.170.00

Indian Crown 10¢ Cigar, sign, embossed tin in wooden frame, 15x21", EX+, $1,700.00. (Photo courtesy Wm. Morford Auctions)

Internat'l Beer, tray, figures in rowboat, 12" dia, G 480.00
Iroquois Brewing, tray, Indian chief in profile, Shonk, 12", EX . 1,020.00
J&P Coats Spool Thread, ts, lg wht spool, 14x19¾", VG 480.00
Jap Rose Talcum Powder, tc, lady reserve, sample sz, 2x1¼x¾", EX . 60.00
John Deere, thermometer, tin litho, yel & gr, 1950s, 13x3" 50.00
JP Primley's...Chewing Gum, display case, glass & oak, 18x20x12", EX . 625.00
Juno Cream Tartar, spice tin, tin litho, 3x2x1", EX+ 50.00
Ken-L-Ration, dc metal sign, dog w/red tongue, 21x14", EX+ 350.00
Kenny's Teas & Coffees, tip tray, lady w/flowers in hair, 4¼", EX... 70.00
Keystone Overalls, cl pocket mirror, Masquerader, 2¾x1¾", EX . 250.00
Kik Soda, carrier, wooden, football player logo, 11x9", EX 150.00
King Cole Coffee, tin, king being served, screw top, 5¾x4", EX .. 130.00
Lion Brand Confections, tin, paper label w/lion reserve, 5-lb sz, EX . 70.00
Lipe-Walrath, page turner/calendar, tin litho, brunette, 13½x3¾" . 1,100.00
Log Cabin Syrup, display, wood, Country Store log cabin, 34x41x25", VG . 3,400.00
Log Cabin Syrup, glass, bottle, Ben Franklin molded on side, 8", EX . 35.00
Log Cabin Syrup, syrup tin, Log Cabin Express, w/wheels, 6x5½", EX . 480.00
Los Angeles Brewing, cl pocket mirror, Whitehead & Hoag, 1¾x2¾" . 240.00
Lucky Strike Roll Cut Tobacco, pocket tin, mc on gr, 1917, 4x3x1", EX . 50.00
Mail Pouch Tobacco, thermometer, tin, Treat Yourself..., 9x3", EX . 250.00
Maple Lane Dairy, cream pitcher, spongeware, Home of Better..., 6" . 50.00
Mennen's Borated Talcum Powder, tc, baby reserve, 1910, 4½", EX . 50.00
Mission Brand Cayenne, spice tin, paper label, unopened, 4x2½" . 60.00
Mission Coffee, tc, CA mission on red & blk, 1930s, 2-lb, EX 50.00
Morton's Salt, dc cb sign, girl w/umbrella, easel-bk, 12", EX 100.00

Moxie

The Moxie Company was organized in 1884 by George Archer of Boston, Massachusetts. It was at first touted as a 'nerve food' to improve the appetite, promote restful sleep, and in general to make one 'feel better'! Emphasis was soon shifted, however, to the good taste of the brew, and extensive advertising campaigns rivaling those of such giant competitors as Coca-Cola and Hires resulted in successful marketing through the 1930s. Today the term Moxie has become synonymous with courage and audacity, traits displayed by the company who dared compete with such well-established rivals. Our advisor for this category is Craig Stifter; he is listed in the Directory under Colorado. See also Soda Fountain Collectibles.

Ashtray holder, CI male figure, Moxie pnt ea side, 34", VG 1,800.00
Blackboard, sf tin, It's Always a Pleasure..., 28" H, VG 125.00
Dispenser, glass bottle sits in glass receiver on ceramic base, 18" . 275.00
Display, plaster, man on horse in Moxiemobile, 1920s, 8x9x4", EX . 480.00
Fan, hand; cb, Francis Prichard w/glass, 1916, EX 65.00
Fan, hand; cl, folding, ca 1900-10, 6½" (closed), VG 60.00
Postcard, Drink Moxie, man & horse in Moxiemobile, 1916, G.... 55.00
Shade, ldgl, Moxie lettering, 14x16" dia 150.00
Sign, cb, mc man delivering case of bottles, 7x3" 180.00
Sign, cb, Try Our Soda Syrups 5¢, fr under glass, 18x13", EX 900.00
Sign, flange; tin, Moxie in red oval, 2-sided, 9x18", VG 685.00
Sign, rvpt, lady w/glass, easel bk, minor flaking, 10x8", G............ 360.00

Sign, self-framed tin, cardboard backing, dated 1933, 13x19", VG+, $450.00.
(Photo courtesy Pettigrew Auctions)

Sign, sf tin, Drink... & bottle cap, red & wht, Donaldson, 20x17", EX . 395.00
Sign, sf tin, man pointing, 1930-40s, 41½x15", EX 660.00
Sign, tin, Drink Moxie & Soda Syrups, listing products, 19x13", VG . 1,325.00
Sign, tin, Drink Moxie in oval, rolled edge, 19x27", EX 325.00
Sign, tin, girl pours from bottle, ca 1905, 17x19"+fr, G............. 1,000.00
Sign, tin, lady on horse in Moxiemobile, 19x27"+wood fr, VG ... 850.00
Sign, tin, Yes! We Sell..., oval, Kaufmann & Strauss, 28x10", VG . 425.00
Thermometer, tin, man pointing, early, 25x10", VG 900.00
Tip tray, lady w/glass on flower background, 1906, 6" 425.00
Tip tray, Moxie among flowers, 6" dia, G 215.00
Tray, girl w/Moxie glass, red ribbon in hair, 9¾", VG 780.00

My Baby's Talcum, tc, cherubs on bl, Sears Roebuck & Co, 6" 275.00
National Beer, tray, Good Judge, man pouring, Meek, 1908, 13" dia, EX+ . 500.00
Nehi, ts, We Serve Nehi Ice Cold, 3½x19" 120.00
Nesco Royal Granite Enameled Cookware, pot & pan scraper, 3¼x3", EX . 150.00
Northwestern Nat'l Bank, tip tray, bank building, 6x4½", VG+ 60.00

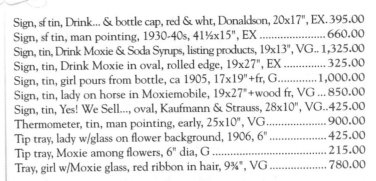

NuGrape, sign, embossed tin litho, 14x5", $475.00.
(Photo courtesy Wm. Morford Auctions)

Nylotis Talcum, tc, peacock on red, triangular, 6", EX+ 60.00
O'San Cigars, ts, Cigar of Smiles, yel & blk, 10x28", EX 60.00
Oilzum Motor Oil, clock, electric, convex glass, Telechrom, 15" dia . 1,400.00
Ojibwa Cut Plug, plaster bust, Indian brave, mc details, 20" 3,000.00
Old Commonwealth, clock, crow at right, lights up, 1960s, 10x19", VG . 155.00
Old Commonwealth, display, plastic figural, 1950s, 30x22x10", EX . 235.00
Old Commonwealth, sign, rvpt, distillery scene, 31½x51½", EX .. 3,400.00
Old Gold Cigarettes, ts, Not a Cough... on yel, 10x29", EX........... 70.00
Old Master Coffee, tc, man in reserve, Blodgett & Beckley, 6x4", EX... 50.00
Old Master Coffee, tc, man in reserve, key-wind, 3½x5" dia, EX+ .. 70.00
Orange Crush, ts, bottle, rolled edge, 1920, 12x3", EX................ 190.00
Owl Drugs, plaque, plaster owl in relief, glass eyes, 12½" dia, EX . 275.00
P Lorillard Century Tobacco..., cb sign, nude/animals, 10x8½", EX . 1,050.00
Page Baby Talc, tc, mother & baby front & bk, 4½", EX.............. 190.00
Peerless Washing Machine, ps, red/wht/bl shield, 8¾", EX 475.00
Pendleton, ashtray, cast metal, man on bucking horse by tray, 8", NM . 550.00
Pendleton Shirts, window display, wood figure w/sign+orig shirt, EX . 275.00

Pepsi-Cola

Pepsi-Cola was first served in the early 1890s to customers of Caleb D. Bradham, a young pharmacist who touted his concoction to be medicinal as well as delicious. It was first called 'Brad's Drink' but was renamed Pepsi-Cola in 1898. Various logos have been registered over the years. The familiar oval was first used in the early 1940s. At about the same time, the two 'dots' (indicated in our listings by '=') between the words Pepsi and Cola became one, though more recent items may carry the double-dot logo as well, especially when they're designed to be reminiscent of the old ones. The bottle cap logo came along in 1943 and with variations was used through the early 1960s. Our advisor for this category is Craig Stifter; he is listed in the Directory under Colorado. See also Soda Fountain Collectibles.

Beach towel, red/wht/bl terrycloth, 57x34", EX.............................. 12.50
Bottle opener, cast brass, old patina, 5¼" 48.00
Cap, tin, emb bottle & cap, 48x18", EX.. 300.00
Carrier, tin, worn pnt, holds 8 bottles, G 24.00
Chalk board, Have a Pepsi & bottle cap on yel, at top................... 24.00
Cigarette lighter, Drink... on chrome, Wind Master, EX................. 12.50
Clock, back-lit bubble, Be Sociable, Have a ..., 16" dia, EX......... 375.00
Clock, bubble glass front, lights up, bottle cap on yel, 16" dia, EX..375.00
Clock, glass front, Say Pepsi Please, lights up, sq,. 16x16".......... 125.00
Clock, molded plastic, Say Pepsi Please, 1963, 12x12½", EX......... 65.00
Cooler, aluminum, red lettering on wht, ca 1940-50s, 18" H, EX . 150.00
Cooler, metal, red lettering on gray enamel, 19x17½", EX.......... 300.00
Cooler, metal chest, wht lettering on bl enamel, G....................... 85.00
Fan, hand; cb, Drink P=C, red/wht/bl, fading, VG....................... 12.50
Menu board, Have a Pepsi & bottle cap at top, 30x19½", EX....... 70.00
Miniature, carton & 6 bottles, 2½x2½".. 30.00
Sign, cl on cb button, P=C, ca 1945, 9", EX.............................. 175.00
Sign, emb metal, Drink 5¢ Pepsi=Cola, 1940s, 10x30", EX+ 595.00
Sign, metal bottle cap, 39" dia, VG... 250.00
Sign, neon bottle cap, 1960s, 30" dia 495.00
Sign, steel, comic cop character, P=C logo, 14x10", G+ 132.50
Sign, tin, bottle cap, More Bounce... on gold, 9" dia, VG 72.50
Sign, tin, Drink P=C 5¢ Bigger-Better, 3-color, 22x40", EX........ 425.00
Sign, tin, logo on left, red/wht/bl/yel, 18x54", EX 60.00
Sign, tin, Say Pepsi Please & bottle cap on yel, 12x31", VG........ 150.00
Sign, tin, Say Pepsi Please & bottle on yel, 1969, 47x17", NM ... 575.00
Syrup drum, metal, P=C logo, red & wht, 18x16" dia, VG 85.00
Thermometer, tin, Say Pepsi Please, sq, 9", EX............................ 42.50
Thermometer, tin, Say Pepsi Please & bottle cap on yel, 27x7¼", EX..110.00
Tip tray, lady w/glass on gr, oval, 6", VG+...................................825.00
Toy biplane, Pepsi & Pete, diecast, Arch Inc, MIB 12.50
Toy boxing gloves, Everlast, Diet Pepsi on red, NMIB 24.00
Toy train car, Lionel #7800, G... 78.00
Toy truck, Ford Model T, blk fenders, Matchbox Y12C33, NMIB. 48.00
Toy truck, metal, w/accessories, Nylint #5500, 16", MIB 600.00
Toy truck, pressed steel, w/3 cases of Pepsi & dolly, Nylint, 21", EX ..120.00
Tray, Enjoy P=C Hits the Spot, red/wht/bl, 13¾x10½", EX 60.00
Vending machine, logo on bl enameling, 10¢ bottle, VG 1,800.00

Planters Peanuts

The Planters Peanut Co. was founded in 1906. Mr. Peanut, the dashing peanut man with top hat, spats, monocle, and cane, has represented Planters since 1916. He took on his modern-day appearance after the company was purchased by Standard Brands in November 1960. He remains perhaps the most highly recognized logo of any company in the world. Mr. Peanut has promoted the company's products by appearing in ads; on product packaging; on or as store displays, novelties, and premiums; and even in character at promotional events (thanks to a special Mr. Peanut costume).

Among the favorite items of collectors today are the glass display jars which were sent to retailers nationwide to stimulate 'point-of-sale' trade. They come in a variety of shapes and styles. The first, distributed in the early 1920s, was a large universal candy jar (round covered bowl on a pedestal) with only a narrow paper label affixed at the neck to identify it as 'Planters.' In 1924 an octagonal jar was produced, all eight sides embossed, with Mr. Peanut on the narrow corner panels. On a second octagon jar, only seven sides were embossed, leaving one of the large panels blank to accommodate a paper label.

In late 1929 a fishbowl jar was introduced, and in 1932 a beautiful jar with a blown-out peanut on each of the four corners was issued. The football shape was also made in the 1930s, as were the square jar, the large barrel jar, and the hexagon jar with yellow fired-on designs alternating on each of the six sides. All of these early jars had glass lids which after 1930 had peanut finials.

In 1937 jars with lithographed tin lids were introduced. The first of these was the slant-front streamline jar, which is also found with screened yellow lettering. Next was a squat version, the clipper jar, then the upright rectangular 1940 leap year jar, and last, another upright rectangular jar with a screened, fired-on design similar to the red, white, and blue design on the cellophane 5¢ bags of peanuts of the period. This last jar was issued again after WWII with a plain red tin lid.

In 1959 Planters first used a stock Anchor Hocking one-gallon round jar with a 'customer-special' decoration in red. As the design was not plainly evident when the jar was full, the decoration was modified with a white under-panel. The two jars we've just described are perhaps the rarest of them all due to their limited production. After Standard Brands purchased Planters, they changed the red-on-white panel to show their more modern Mr. Peanut and in 1963 introduced this most plentiful, thus very common, Planters jar. In 1966 the last counter display jar was distributed: the Anchor Hocking jar with a fired-on large four-color design such as that which appeared on peanut bags of the period. Prior to this, a plain jar with a transfer decal in an almost identical but smaller design was used.

Some Planters jars have been reproduced: the octagon jar (with only seven of the sides embossed), a small version of the barrel jar, and the four peanut corner jar. Some of the first were made in clear glass with 'Made in Italy' embossed on the bottom, but most have been made in Asia, many in various colors of glass (a dead giveaway) as well as clear, and carrying only small paper stickers, easily removed, identifying the country of origin. At least two reproductions of the Anchor Hocking jar with a four-color design have been made, one circa 1978, the other in 1989. Both, using the stock jar, are difficult to detect, but there are small differences between them and the original that will enable you to make an accurate identification. With the exception of several of the earliest and the Anchor Hocking, all authentic Planters jars have 'Made in USA' embossed on the bottom, and all, without exception, are clear glass. Unfortunately, several paper labels have also been reproduced, no doubt due to the fact that an original label or decal will greatly increase the value of an original jar. Jar prices continue to remain stable in today's market.

In the late 1920s, the first premiums were introduced in the form of story and paint books. Late in the 1930s, the tin nut set (which was still available into the 1960s) was distributed. A wood jointed doll was available from Planters Peanuts stores at that time. Many post-WWII items were made of plastic: banks, salt and pepper shakers, cups, cookie cutters, small cars and trucks, charms, whistles, various pens and mechanical pencils, and almost any other item imaginable. Since 1981 the company, as a division of Nabisco (NGH) has continued to distribute a wide variety of novelties. In late 2000 NGH was sold to Philip Morris Cos. and Nabisco was combined with its Kraft Foods unit. With the increased popularity of Mr. Peanut memorabilia, more items surface, and the value of common items decrease.

Note that there are many unauthorized Planters/Mr. Peanut items. Although several are reproductions or 'copycats,' most are fantasies and fakes. Our advisor for this category is Anthony Scola; he is listed in the Directory under Pennsylvania.

Key: MrP. — Mr. Peanut

Alarm clock, MrP on yel, glass front, 2 bells, Lux, EX................... 60.00
Award pin, 14k gold MrP in wreath w/sm dmn & blk enameling . 125.00
Badge, employee; silver-tone metal w/red lettering, 1950s, EX 195.00

Bag, brn paper, Packed by Planters Nut & Chocolate Co, 58x20", EX+ . 132.50
Bank, MrP head shape, yel w/can top, peanut vendor, 1950s, 8x5", EX . 575.00
Bank/dispenser, MrP figural, plastic, mc, 10x6" 30.00
Bowl, metal, NFL Football stadium form, 3½x10x5¾" 5.00
Box, cb, Salted Peanuts, WWII airplanes, w/diecut, 3x9x6", EX . 600.00
Box, cb, Salted Peanuts, WWII airplanes, w/o diecut, 3x9x6", EX . 200.00
Can, Ali D'Italia (oil), tin w/plane graphics, '40s, full, 1-gal..... 1,150.00
Can, High Grade Confections, bl/gold, 10-lb, 1920s-30s, 9½x8", G..5,175.00
Can, Pennant Brand, Made in Canada, worn lid, 10-lb, 9½x8", EX ..145.00
Can, Pennant Brand, red band, orig lid, 1930s, 10½x8", VG+ 145.00
Can, Popcorn Seasoning (oil), tin w/MrP popping corn, '40s, 1-gal, EX..2,875.00
Can, Sal-In-Shell, MrP, 1930s, 20-lb, 17x11", VG 9,200.00
Cocktail glass, bl plastic, MrP at stem, 1960s, 5", from $50 to 60.00
Cocktail glass box (only), MrP Plastic Cocktail Glasses, 1950s ... 115.00
Cookie cutters, plastic, 1950s, 5", 5½", MOC, pr from $60 to 75.00
Cookie cutters, plastic, 1950s, 5", 5½", pr 10.00
Costume, MrP, Fiberglas, strong mc w/some rpt, 1930s, 50x20" ... 800.00
Cruet, MrP figural, ceramic, V on hat 37.50
Display, cb, 3-tiered, for sale of cocktail peanuts, 1930s, 18x18" . 2,300.00
Display, cb diecut of seated girl, yel, 1930s, 25x10" 2,185.00
Display, MrP figure (pnt metal) stands by Clipper jar, 1930s, 13"..9,200.00
Display, MrP figure, pnt resin/light-up blinker, 1930s-40s, 24", NMIB....5,175.00
Figure, MrP, jtd wood, mc pnt, 1930s, 9", EX................................ 110.00
Game, Planters Peanut Party Game, printed paper, undtd, 18x18" EX..50.00
Golf putter, peanut shell shape, Grip Rite hdl, Victory..., EX......... 85.00
Jar, bbl shape w/peanut finial, running MrPs, worn decal, 12x8".. 350.00
Jar, bbl shape w/running MrPs in silver pnt, w/label, 12x8", EX... 400.00
Jar, clear glass, Streamline w/boy decal, gr tin lid, 1930s, 10x8" . 1,955.00
Jar, football shape, emb lid, 8x8" 260.00
Jar, rnd, 5 lines of products listed in red pyro, 1940s, 10x7", EX .. 345.00
Jar, 4-cornered peanut shape, peanut finial, 12½" 150.00
Mask, MrP, cl, sm tear at hat brim, strong mc, 11x7" 175.00
Mask, MrP as Santa, cl, strong mc, 1940s, 10x7" 260.00
Mold, chocolate; MrP (2), metal, hinged/2-pc, 1930s, 7x8"......2,075.00

Pail, Circus Peanut Butter, tin litho, professionally restored, one pound, $525.00. (Photo courtesy Morford Auctions/LiveAuctioneers.com)

Pail, High Grade Peanut Butter, orig lid, bail hdl, 1930s, 9x10", EX..400.00
Pail, Peanut Butter, orange w/paper label, bail hdl, 1910s-20s, 4" .1,150.00
Puppet, hand; MrP, rubber, normal wear, 1930s-40s, 6", EX......... 635.00
Roaster rider, MrP, Fiberglas, sm pnt touchup, 1930s, 53x33" .10,350.00
Shakers, MrP, gr plastic figural, 3", pr, MIB..................................... 35.00
Sign, early products decal/pnt on Masonite/wood, 1930s, 40x69", VG ..2,875.00
Sign, MrP & red candy apples, paper, 1950s, 45x29".................... 175.00
Sign, Presidents of US/pnt book, paper, 1940s-50s, 12½x27", VG+ ..175.00
Sign, trolley; maid w/tray, cb, 1930s, 10x20½", EX....................... 515.00
Sign, trolley; Peanut Butter, cb, strong mc, 1930s, 10x20½" 515.00
Sign, trolley; Planters Fall Fiesta, 1930s-40s, 11x21", EX............. 465.00
Tin, Planters Cocktail Peanuts, MrP, full/unopened/attached key, 8-oz .. 42.50
Tin, Planters Crunchy Cashew...Candy, paper label, unopened, 5½-oz .. 42.50
Tin, pocket; Pennant Salted Peanuts, MrP, 1930s, 3½" 8,000.00
Toy car, bl plastic peanut car, Souvenir of Atlanta, 1950s, 5" H..460.00
Toy train car, Planters Peanut hopper car, Lionel #9115, MIB....... 15.00

Tray, MrP, Planters Peanut Co...Roasted Daily, 1970s, 14x12", EX+. 15.00
Whistle, orange & blk plastic (scarce color), 3½", EX................. 100.00

Poll Parrot Shoes, display, plaster parrot on base, mc, 12", EX+... 150.00
Poll Parrot Shoes, rvpt sign, parrot before moon on blk, 24x12", EX.325.00
Popsicle, ts, Everybody Likes..., mc, 12x36".................................. 180.00
President Suspenders, tip tray, lady w/flowing hair, 4¼", EX+ 90.00
Prichard & Constance Amami Bath Powder, tc, girl, 1921, 6½", EX+.100.00
Pureoxia Ginger Ale, ts, mc, 7x23", EX+...................................... 110.00
Ramsey's Agent Paints, ps, 2-sided, 1940s, 30x36" 840.00

RCA Victor

Nipper, the RCA Victor trademark, was the creation of Francis Barraud, an English artist. His pet's intense fascination with the music of the phonograph seemed to him a worthy subject for his canvas. Although he failed to find a publishing house who would buy his work, the Gramophone Co. in England saw its potential and adopted Nipper to advertise their product. The painting was later acquired and trademarked in the United States by the Victor Talking Machine Co., which was purchased by RCA in 1929. The trademark is owned today by EMI in England and by General Electric in the U.S. Nipper's image appeared on packages, accessories, ads, brochures, and in three-dimensional form. You may find a life-size statue of him, but all are not old. They have been manufactured for the owner throughout RCA history and are marketed currently by licensees, BMG Inc. and Thomson Consumer Electronics (dba RCA). Except for the years between 1968 and 1976, Nipper has seen active duty, and with his image spruced up only a bit for the present day, the ageless symbol for RCA still listens intently to 'His Master's Voice.' Many of the items have been reproduced in recent years. Exercise care before you buy. The true Nipper collectible is one which has been authorized by either Victor or RCA Victor as an advertising aid. This includes items used in showrooms, billboards, window dressings, and customer give-aways. The showroom items included three-dimensional Nippers first in papier-maché, later in spun rubber, and finally in plastic. Some were made in chalk. Throughout the years these items were manufactured largely by one company, Old King Cole, but often were marketed through others who added their names to the product. The key to collecting Nipper is to look for those items which were authorized and to overlook those items that were copied or made without permission of the copyright/trademark owner. Some of the newer but unauthorized items, however, are quite good and have become collectible notwithstanding their lack of authenticity.

The recent phenomenon of internet auctions has played havoc with prices paid for Victor and RCA Victor collectibles. Often prices paid for online sales bear little resemblance to the true value of the item. Reproductions are often sold as old on the internet and bring prices accordingly. Auction prices, more often than not, are inflated over sales made through traditional sales outlets. The internet has exacerbated the situation by focusing a very large number of buyers and sellers through the narrow portal of a modem. The prices here are intended to reflect what one might expect to pay through traditional sales.

Our advisor for RCA Victor is Roger R. Scott; he is listed in the Directory under Oklahoma.

Armchair, chrome, vinyl & wood, blk stenciled logo, 33", EX..... 150.00
Clock, RCA Victor Radio, bk-lit bubble, PAM, 19½" dia, EX..... 350.00
Clock, RCA Victor Television, bk-lit bubble, 16" dia, EX 325.00
Nipper, chalkware, 14", VG+ 165.00
Nipper, chalkware, 4", EX.. 45.00
Nipper, crystal, Fenton, VG 50.00
Nipper, papier-maché, 11", VG 200.00

Nipper, papier-maché, 14", VG 400.00
Nipper, papier-maché, 14", VG 300.00
Nipper, papier-maché, 18" 300.00
Nipper, papier-maché, 36" 600.00
Nipper, plastic, 11" 75.00
Nipper, plastic, 18" 100.00
Nipper, plastic, 36" 350.00
Nipper, Visco 125.00
Nipper, zinc, glass eyes, studded collar, pnt touchups, 18" 3,600.00
Nipper bank, pot metal, flocked, VG 75.00
Shakers, Nipper, ceramic, 4", pr 85.00
Sign, dog & Victrola, lights up, 13x12", VG.................... 180.00
Sign, porc, His Master's Voice, Nipper & player, oval, 26" L, EX. 350.00
Sign, porc, His Master's Voice, Nipper & player, 4-color, 12", VG+ ..515.00
Sign, porc, vertical, Radio, HMV 800.00
Stickpin, cl, VG 100.00
Tray, Nipper, mixed wood inlay, glass covered, 8-sided, 1930s, 18" dia . 125.00

Red Goose Shoes

Realizing that his last name was difficult to pronounce, Herman Giesecke, a shoe company owner, resolved to give the public a modified, shortened version that would be better suited to the business world. The results suggested the use of the goose trademark with the last two letters, 'ke,' represented by the key that this early goose held in his mouth. Upon observing an employee casually coloring in the goose trademark with a red pencil, Giesecke saw new advertising potential and renamed the company Red Goose Shoes. Although the company has changed hands down through the years, the Red Goose emblem has remained. Collectors of this desirable fowl increase in number yearly, as do prices. Beware of reproductions; new chalkware figures are prevalent.

Bank, CI goose, squatty version, orig pnt, rare, EX+ 1,925.00
Bank, CI goose figural, 3¾", EX...................................... 400.00
Bank, NP goose, 3¾" 1,300.00
Bench, pnt wood, red goose stencil ea end, 72", VG 360.00
Clock, goose on face, glass front, 8-sided, windup, EX 400.00
Clock, goose on face, Kohnop's Shoes, replaced #s, windup alarm, EX. 325.00
Clock, goose on face (lg), lights up, electric, 14" dia 725.00
Display, chalkware goose w/neck extended, 10½x16x5½", EX 150.00
Marbles, yel clay & 1 steelie, EX, in yel cloth pouch w/red goose .. 60.00

Sign, die-cut tin, 60x42", EX, $700.00. (Photo courtesy Don and Carol Raycraft)

Sign, porc, red goose, red neon, 1940s, 36" 1,925.00
Sign, tin, goose on yel, 13x9", EX 155.00
String holder, tin goose above wire holder, G...................... 545.00
Thermometer, tin, red goose on yel, 13x4", EX 25.00
Red Raven, tip tray, raven on blk, Shonk, 1905, 4⅜", EX 150.00
Red Raven, tray, Ask the Man, nude child, Shonk, 12" dia, EX+ . 775.00
Red Rose Tea, ts, ...Is Good Tea, red/wht/bl, 17x11", EX 50.00
Red Top Beer, ts, red top shape, 21x14", EX+............................. 250.00
Reinken's Havana Plantation Cigars, ts, Griselda, 13½" dia, EX+ . 1,350.00

Rheingold Extra Dry Lager Beer, accessory holder, Bakelite, 8" L. 120.00
Rigby's Toco Havana Cigars, tip tray, brunette & cherubs, 4¼", VG .200.00

Roly Poly

The Roly Poly tobacco tins were patented on November 5, 1912, by Washington Tuttle and produced by Tindeco of Baltimore, Maryland. There were six characters in all: Satisfied Customer, Storekeeper, Mammy, Dutchman, Singing Waiter, and Inspector. Four brands of tobacco were packaged in selected characters; some tins carry a printed tobacco box on the back to identify their contents. Mayo and Dixie Queen Tobacco were packed in all six; Red Indian and U.S. Marine Tobacco in only Mammy, Singing Waiter, and Storekeeper. Of the set, the Inspector is considered the rarest and in near mint condition may fetch more than $1,000.00 on today's market.

Dutchman, red neckscarf, wht belt, Mayo, VG 300.00
Mammy, Mayo, EX... 720.00
Satisfied Customer, man w/pipe, tooth on watch chain, Mayo, EX.420.00
Singing Waiter, Dixie Queen Cut Plug, 7x6", EX........................ 450.00
Singing Waiter, Mayo, VG+.. 425.00
Storekeeper, bald man smoking pipe, Mayo, G- 300.00

Roth's Hy Quality Coffee, dc cb sign, lady in swing, 35x16", EX+ ...1,650.00
Rough Rider Baking Powder, cb container, Roosevelt reserve, 4½", EX. 80.00
Roundup Ginger Spice, tc, man on bucking bronco, 3x2x1", EX .. 50.00
Royal Corona Coffee, tc, man w/burro, Seattle, 1925, 15-lb, EX ... 50.00
Ruhstaller's Gilt Edge Lager, tray, lady w/flowers, 12" dia, EX+.... 215.00
S&H Green Trading Stamps, tip tray, brunette, Shonk litho, 4¼", EX..80.00
Sander's Satin Candy, tin pail, children at table, 5½x5" 50.00
Satin Finish Typewriter Ribbons, tc, Black man reserve, 2½" L 50.00
Savage Arms, booklet, Tenderfoot's Turn, 24-pg, 6½x4½", EX+ .. 150.00
Schultze Gunpowder, tc, blk/gold paper label, Du Pont, 5½", EX .. 60.00

Seven-Up

The Howdy Company of St. Louis, Missouri, was founded in 1920 by Charles L. Grigg. His first creation was an orange drink called Howdy. In the late 1920s Howdy's popularity began to wane, so in 1929 Grigg invented a lemon-lime soda called Seven-Up as an alternative to colas. Grigg's Seven-Up became a widely accepted favorite. Our advisor for this category is Craig Stifter; he is listed in the Directory under Colorado. See also Soda Fountain Collectibles.

Clock, 7-Up on red in center, sq gold fr, EX 48.00
Cooler, metal, logo on wht, Progress Refr Co..., 1955, 19x16x13", EX. 175.00
Door push, porc, 7-Up in red sq on wht, 34½", EX........................ 72.50
Figure, Fresh Up Freddie, vinyl, logo on shirt, 1959, EX 120.00
Sign, cl button, 7-Up & bubbles, 9" dia 180.00
Sign, tin, Fresh Up, hand holds bottle on gr, wood fr, 59x35", EX ..525.00
Sign, tin, Fresh Up & bottle, on yel, 54x18", VG......................... 120.00
Sign, tin, hand holds bottle on wht, 42x13", EX 240.00
Sign, tin, Nothing Does It Like..., red/wht/gr, 18¾x13", EX 48.00
Sign, tin, 7Up (no hyphen) & bubbles on red, 13x11", EX.......... 110.00
Thermometer, rising sun, Made in USA, 12¼" dia, EX................. 70.00
Thermometer, tin, 7-Up on blk, 20x5", EX................................. 90.00

Sheboygan Mineral Water, ts, Black waiters, 1904, 12x10", EX+ . 750.00
Sherwin Williams Paints..., paperweight, Cover the Earth, 5", EX+ ..350.00
Sight Draft 5¢ Cigar, clock, CI cherubs/flowers, Lux, 10x8x2½", EX.450.00

Speckled Trout 5¢ Cigars, wooden box, fish graphics, 8½", EX...... 70.00
Squirt, bank, compo boy, mc, 1948, 7½" 170.00
Squirt, thermometer, tin litho, gr bottle, 196s, 13½x6" 190.00
Star Egg Carriers & Tray, bill clip w/cl button, EX 90.00
Star Naptha Washing Powder, ts, star border, Shonk, 4x19", EX+..240.00
Star Tobacco, ps, 4-color, 12x24", EX 300.00
Starlight Marshmallows, tc, Cracker Jack Co, 2-color, 6x10" dia, EX..50.00
Stegmaier Beer, tip tray, factory scene, 6¼x4¼", EX 50.00

Stein Club Havana Cigars, litho tin sign, Kaufmann & Strauss lithographers, early, 20x28", EX, $3,700.00.

(Photo courtesy Wm. Morford Auctions)

Stickney & Poor's Pure Mustard, display box, litho on wood, 15" L, EX..325.00
Stokely VanCamp, figure, uniformed boy, porc, mc, 1950s, 8x5½" .150.00
Sweet Girl Peanut Butter, pail, tin litho, blond girl, 16-oz, VG ...425.00
Sykes Comfort Powder, tc, children reserve, Bay Co, 4¼", EX....... 80.00
Talc Francoise, tc, exotic bird on branch, 6x2x1¼", EX 60.00
Talmage Bros Hardware Horse Blankets, tin sign, wood fr, 29x21", G..425.00
Teaberry Gum, tin sign, A Happy Thought! & package on yel, 9x12", EX.275.00
Three Crow Black Pepper, tc, birds reserve on yel, 3x2¼x1" 70.00
Tiger Brand Tobacco, pocket tin, tiger in grasses, 1x4¾x2¾", EX .. 50.00
Trailing Arbutus Talcum Powder, lady reserve, dome lid, 5½", EX+...130.00
Uncle Sam's Kisses, candy box, cb, Uncle Sam graphics, 3x8x7", EX. 425.00
Uncle Sam Shirts, cb box, Uncle Sam graphics, 1923, 3x15x11", EX..110.00
Velvet Tobacco, tc, smoke from pipe spells Velvet, 3½x3½x1", EX....150.00
Ver-ba, sign, tin litho on cb, lady w/glass & roses, 18x12", G....... 850.00
Vouiliue's Sandalwood Talcum Powder, tc, scenic litho, 2", EX 80.00
War Eagle Cigars, tc, eagle on red, slip lid, 5x5", EX 200.00
Watkins Egyptian Bouquet Talcum Powder, tc, Sphinx scene, 5½", EX. 80.00
White King Washing Machine Soap, ts, Crown litho, 14x10", NM..180.00
White Rock, tip tray, nymph at water's edge, Shonk, 4¼" dia, EX. 90.00
Whitmoyer Feeds, paperweight, CI chicken, mc pnt, 2⅜x2¼"..... 480.00
Wonder Bread, puppet, dc cb Howdy Doody, 1950s, 13x7", EX+. 110.00
Wonder Enriched Bread, steel sign, bread loaf, 12½x20", EX+ 250.00
Wrigley's Double Mint Gum, sign, tin litho on cb, clown, 6x13", VG ..70.00
Yellow Cab, ink blotter, Thinking Fellow Calls..., dc foil, 6" L....160.00
Yellow Cab 5¢ Cigars, box, yel cabs, 7" L....................................... 500.00
Yengling Lager Ale Beer, tray, lady in plumed hat, rnd, EX.......1,450.00
Zingo Sweets, candy tin, racecar graphics, peacock on lid, 10-lb, VG+ .160.00

Advertising Cards

Advertising trade cards enjoyed great popularity during the last quarter of the nineteenth century when the chromolithography printing process was refined and put into common use. The purpose of the trade card was to acquaint the public with a business, product, service, or event. Most trade cards range in size from 2" x 3" to 4" x 6"; however, many are found in both smaller and larger sizes.

There are two classifications of trade cards: 'private design' and 'stock.' Private design cards were used by a single company or individual; the images on the cards were designed for only that company. Stock cards were generics that any individual or company could purchase from a printer's inventory. These cards usually had a blank space on the front for the company to overprint with their own name and product information.

Four categories of particular interest to collectors are:

Mechanical — a card which achieves movement through the use of a pull tab, fold-out side, or movable part.

Hold-to-light — a card that reveals its design only when viewed before a strong light.

Die-cut — a card in the form of something like a box, a piece of clothing, etc.

Metamorphic — a card that by folding down a flap shows a transformed image, such as a white beard turning black after use of a product.

For a more thorough study of the subject, we recommend *Reflections 1* and *Reflections 2* by Kit Barry; his address can be found in the Directory under Vermont. Values are given for cards in near-mint condition.

AMCo Wringer, woman, 2 children, cat w/oversz tub................. 10.00
AST Shoes, girl w/boy painting at easel...7.00
Ayer's Ague Cure, log cabin in swamp, alligator & 2 frogs.................7.00
Ayer's Cherry Pectoral, woman w/cherry basket & 2 birds 6.00

Ayer's Cherry Pectoral, 5½x8¼", EX, $40.00. (Photo courtesy Past Tyme Pleasures)

Ayer's Sarsaparilla, 2 women, 2 children w/dog outdoors 6.00
Babbitt Soap, man by soap box sled w/baby in it 8.00
Babbitt Soap, man in 18th-C attire giving soap to women 8.00
Baum's Castorine Axle Oil, driver & Maude S 2:08¾ 25.00
Borax Soap, man holding woman by stream 6.00
Burdox Bitters, baby boy holding bottle..8.00
Burt & Co Shoes, 1 wht cat in basket, 1 beside 8.00
Clark's ONT Thread, boy on street sewing his pants.........................5.00
Clark's ONT Thread, boy playing spool drum 5.00
Clark's ONT Thread, diecut spool, lady & walking baby 8.00
Clark's ONT Thread, 2 boys flying kite...6.00
Cox & Bros Fine Shoes, 2 shoemakers & customer 9.00
Eagle Pencils, Statue of Liberty, mechanical 35.00
Estey Organ, Brownie band w/instruments 12.00
Fairbanks & Cole, banjo & girl w/doll picking flower 25.00
Fisher & Fairbanks, man w/packages under ea arm...........................5.00
Fleischmann Yeast, man on stage, woman & 3 children................. 10.00
Hind's Radical Corn Remover, pig running w/corn stalk................ 15.00
Hood's Sarsaparilla, child in fox hunt dress w/7 hounds 7.00
Horsford's Acid Phosphate, red capped, curly-haired boy.................9.00
JP Coats Thread, woman & dog, mountain beyond 5.00
Kilmer's Female Remedy, 2 women, baby girl, envelope................. 15.00
McLaughlin Coffee, A Maly Family, lg 8.00
McLaughlin Coffee, girl on floor, dog, spilled pnt, lg.................... 12.00
McLaughlin Coffee, Landing of Columbus, lg 12.00
New Home Sewing Machine, 'What are the wild waves...'.................5.00
Niagara Corn Starch, girl holding kitten w/bl ribbon.......................5.00
Rock Hall Clothing, 4 kids in woods looking at rock 12.00
Sapanule, int barn scene w/man by horse, 2 boys 45.00

Sollers Co Shoes, boy (right) w/hand on shoulder of boy (left) 6.00
Sollers Co Shoes, girl w/doll (right) & girl (left) points to 2nd doll .6.00
Standard Tip Shoe, 4 kids in marching band w/banner 10.00
Standard Tip Shoe, 6 kids dancing around banner 10.00
Universal Wringer, barefoot woman lying on ground 6.00
Universal Wringer, boy in sailor suit lying on ground, sea beyond....6.00
Universal Wringer, 3 women & girl ironing shirt 12.00
Universal Wringer, 3 women in kitchen, Baking Day 12.00
Van Haagen Soap, formally dressed woman w/fan in right hand.... 16.00
Van Stan's Stratena Cement, man stuck in chair, woman, child.......8.00
Van Stan's Stretena Cement, 2 men w/jackets stuck together...........8.00
Wanamaker Store, 4 kids: jump rope, leap frog, balloon 12.00
White Mountain Ice Cream Freezer, pretty girls looking right..........8.00
Willimantic Thread, boy w/peacock feather in hat 5.00
Wool Soap, 2 sm girls, 1 w/bare bottom, oval card 6.00

Agata

Agata is New England peachblow (the factory called it 'Wild Rose') with an applied metallic stain which produces gold tracery and dark blue mottling. The stain is subject to wear, and the amount of remaining stain greatly affects the value. It is especially valuable (and rare) on satin-finish items when found on peachblow of intense color. Caution! Be sure to use only gentle cleaning methods.

Currently rare types of art glass have been realizing erratic prices at auction; until they stabilize, we can only suggest an average range of values. In the listings that follow, examples are glossy unless noted otherwise. A condition rating of 'EX' indicates that the stain shows a moderate amount of wear. To evaluate an item with very worn stain, deduct from 60% to 75% from these prices. When 'color' is included in the condition assessment, it will refer to the intensity of the glass itself.

Bowl, hemisperical w/tightly crimped rim, EX color & stain, 3x8" .500.00
Bowl, pinched rim, deep, EX color & stain, 3x4½"........................ 360.00
Bowl, 10-crimp rim, flared rim, EX stain, 2½x5"........................... 550.00
Celery, EX stain, 6⅜" 750.00
Creamer & sugar bowl, loop hdls, 3x6" 3,750.00
Cruet, alabaster stopper & hdl, EX color & stain, 6" 1,300.00
Pitcher, sq mouth, reed hdl, lt stain, 6½" 2,500.00
Pitcher, tankard; outstanding color & stain, 8" 5,700.00
Punch cup, EX stain, 2½" 495.00
Spittoon, ruffled/petal rim, G stain, w/label, 5" dia....................1,300.00
Toothpick holder, cylindrical w/sq rim, EX color & stain, 2¼" 900.00
Toothpick holder, cylindrical w/sq rim, lt stain, +SP holder: 6½" . 400.00
Toothpick holder, tricorner, EX stain, 2⅜", from $525 to............. 625.00
Tumbler, lemonade; w/hdl, EX stain, 5" 1,750.00
Tumbler, M stain, 3½", minimum value 500.00
Vase, bud; dimpled bulbous bottom, EX color & stain, 6½" 600.00
Vase, lily; EX gold & stain, intense color, 6¾" 1,250.00

Vase, lily; 3-fold rim, EX color & stain, 8" 1,500.00
Vase, lily; 3-fold rim, VG stain, 10½"..1,100.00
Vase, Morgan; lt stain, amber satin griffin holder 10" 3,850.00
Vase, pinched body, crimped rim, EX stain, 6"............................ 800.00
Vase, slightly shouldered, tight crimped rim, EX color & stain, 6x4" .850.00
Vase, 4-sided body w/lg rnd depressions, flared/crimped rim, 4½"..1,400.00

Agate Ware

Clays of various natural or artificially dyed colors were combined to produce agate ware, a procedure similar to the methods used by Niloak in potting their Mission Ware. It was made by many Staffordshire potteries from about 1740 until about 1825.

Bowl, ivory/mocha swirl, scalloped rim, 5¾" 850.00
Casolette, appl swags/laurel hdls, Wedgwood & Bentley, 1775, 9⅜"..3,000.00
Cup, coffee; bl/brn/cream, hexagonal, mid-18th C, 3" 2,600.00

Akro Agate

The Akro Agate Company operated in Clarksburg, West Virginia, from 1914 until 1951. In addition to their famous marbles, they also produced children's dishes and a general line consisting of vases, planters, and flowerpots in the garden line. They made ashtrays, bathroom fixtures, lamps, powder jars, bells, baskets, and candlesticks as well. Akro made a number of novelty items which were distributed in 5 & 10¢ stores such as Woolworth. Though many pieces are not marked, you will find some that bear their distinctive logo: a crow flying through the letter 'A' holding an Aggie in its beak and one in each claw. Some novelty items may instead carry one of these trademarks: 'J.V. Co., Inc.,' 'Braun & Corwin,' 'N.Y.C. Vogue Merc Co. U.S.A.,' 'Hamilton Match Co.,' and 'Mexicali Pickwick Cosmetic Corp.'

Color is a very important worth-assessing factor. Some pieces may be common in one color but rare in others. Occasionally an item will have exceptionally good multicolors, and this would make it more valuable than an example with only average color. When buying either marbles or juvenile tea sets in original boxes, be sure the box contains its original contents.

Note: Recently unearthed original written information has discounted the generally accepted attribution of the Chiquita and J.P. patterns to the Akro company, proving instead that they were made by the Alley Agate Company.

Due to the influence of eBay and other online auctions, the prices of children's dishes have fallen considerably over the past few years, with only the rare boxed sets retaining their higher values.

For more information we recommend *The Complete Line of the Akro Agate Co.* by our advisors, Roger and Claudia Hardy (available from the authors); they are listed in the Directory under West Virginia. Our advisor for miscellaneous Akro Agate is Albert Morin, who is listed in the Directory under Massachusetts. See also Marbles.

Concentric Rib

Creamer, dk gr or wht, 1 5/16" ... 15.00
Plate, canary yel, 3¼" ... 25.00
Saucer, wht, 2¾" ... 3.00
Teapot, dk gr, 2⅜" ... 18.00
Teapot lid, dk gr, wht or canary yel, 2 5/16" ... 5.00
Tumbler, dk gr or canary yel, 2" ... 7.00

Concentric Ring

Creamer, bl & wht marbleized, 1 9/16" ... 75.00
Creamer, bl transparent, 1 9/16" ... 40.00
Creamer, med or royal bl, 1⅜" ... 2.00
Cup, ivory or wht, 1⅜" ... 45.00
Cup, orange, 1 9/16" ... 40.00
Cup, purple, 1 9/16" ... 65.00
Plate, canary yel, 3 5/16" ... 30.00
Plate, purple, 3 5/16" ... 45.00
Sugar bowl, apple or dk gr, 1⅜" ... 20.00
Sugar bowl, bl/wht marbleized, 1 9/16" ... 75.00
Teapot, royal bl, 2⅜" ... 65.00

Interior Panel

Cereal, med bl (lustre), 16 panels, 3⅜" ... 40.00
Cereal, pk (lustre), 16 panels, 3⅜" ... 35.00
Creamer, gr transparent, 18 panels, 1 5/16" ... 45.00
Creamer, topaz transparent, 16 panels, 1½" ... 35.00
Plate, dk gr lustre, 18 panels, 3 5/16" ... 10.00
Plate, gr transparent, 16 panels, 4¼" ... 15.00
Plate, lemonade & oxblood, 16 panels, 4¼" ... 40.00
Plate, topaz transparent, 18 panels, 3 5/16" ... 12.00
Sugar bowl, canary yel, 18 panels, 1 5/16" ... 45.00
Teapot, gr transparent, 16 panels, 2¾" ... 30.00
Teapot lid, lemon & oxblood marbleized, 16 panels, 2 11/16" ... 75.00
Teapot lid, topaz transparent, 16 panels, 2 11/16" ... 20.00

Miss America

Boxed set, gr transparent, 8-pc ... 900.00
Boxed set, wht, 8-pc ... 400.00
Creamer, gr transparent, 1 9/16" ... 125.00
Cup, red transparent, 1 9/16" ... 175.00
Plate, wht, 4½" ... 28.00
Saucer, gr transparent, 3⅝" ... 40.00
Saucer, red transparent, 3⅝" ... 75.00
Sugar bowl, gr transparent, 1 9/16" ... 125.00
Teapot, red, 2½" ... 150.00

Octagonal

Cereal, dk gr, wht or ivory, 3⅜" ... 18.00
Cereal, dk gr, 3⅜" ... 18.00
Cereal, pk, 3⅜" ... 20.00
Creamer, med or dk bl, open hdl, 1½" ... 30.00
Cup, dk gr, 1½" ... 15.00
Cup, lemonade & oxblood, 1½" ... 65.00
Cup, turq or lt bl, 1½" ... 30.00
Pitcher, pale bl, open hdl, 3" ... 40.00
Sugar bowl, canary yel, closed hdls, 1½" ... 25.00
Teapot, dk gr, closed hdl, 3⅝" ... 25.00
Teapot, lemonade & oxblood, closed hdl, 3⅝" ... 175.00
Tumbler, apple gr, 2" ... 15.00

Raised Daisy

Creamer, dk turq or dk bl, 1 5/16" ... 75.00
Creamer, lt or dk yel, 1 5/16" ... 40.00
Cup, dk turq or dk bl, 1 5/16" ... 60.00
Pitcher/teapot, plain, dk gr, 2⅜" ... 80.00
Plate, dk turq or dk bl, 3" ... 28.00
Saucer, dk ivory, 2½" ... 20.00
Sugar bowl, lt or dk yel, 1 5/16" ... 35.00
Teapot, dk turq or dk bl, w/lid, 2½" ... 60.00
Tumbler, Daisy, dk turq or dk bl, 2" ... 75.00
Tumbler, Daisy, lt or dk yel, 2" ... 25.00

Stacked Disk

Creamer, med or dk bl, 1 5/16" ... 15.00
Creamer, orange, 1 5/16" ... 40.00
Cup, canary yel, 1 5/16" ... 60.00
Cup, med or dk bl, 1 5/16" ... 10.00
Sugar bowl, dk gr, wht or canary yel, 1 5/16" ... 15.00
Sugar bowl, pk, 1 5/16" ... 25.00
Teapot, purple or orange, 2⅜" ... 60.00
Tumbler, dk gr, 2" ... 9.00

Stacked Disk and Interior Panel

Creamer, bl transparent, 1⅜" ... 50.00
Cup, orange, 1⅜" ... 30.00
Pitcher, bl transparent, 2⅞" ... 60.00
Pitcher, gr transparent, 2⅞" ... 50.00
Teapot, bl/wht marbleized, 2⅜" ... 120.00
Teapot, gr transparent, 2⅜" ... 50.00
Tumbler, bl transparent, 2" ... 25.00

Stippled Band

Creamer, azure bl transparent, 1½" ... 45.00
Creamer, gr transparent, 1½" ... 28.00
Cup, gr or topaz transparent, 1½" ... 20.00
Saucer, gr transparent, 2¾" ... 8.00
Saucer, topaz transparent, 2¾" ... 6.00
Sugar bowl, gr or topaz transparent, 1¼" ... 60.00
Teapot lid, gr transparent, 2⅝" ... 50.00
Teapot lid, topaz transparent, 2⅝" ... 40.00

Miscellaneous

Ashtray, marbleized, 5" sq, from $60 to ... 90.00
Ashtray, oxblood marbleized, rectangular, no tab, 3½" ... 125.00
Basket, bl marbleized, single high arched hdl ... 375.00
Basket, gr/wht marbleized, 2 hdls, 4" ... 25.00
Bell, dk gr (forest gr) ... 450.00
Bowl, ftd, marbleized ... 500.00
Candlestick, inkwell type 1, bl, ea ... 30.00
Candlestick, Tall Ribbed, orange ... 275.00
Cigarette holder, any color, from $10 to ... 15.00
Finger bowl ... 200.00
Flowerpot, Ribs & Flutes, solid color, #307, 5½", from $25 to ... 30.00
Jar, powder; Ivy, marbleized, #323 ... 75.00
Jar, powder; Ribbed, solid color ... 25.00
Jardiniere, No 306 Type 1 or Type 2, any color ... 65.00
Planter, Japanese, solid color other than blk, #650, 11¼" ... 425.00
Puff box, Colonial lady, lt bl ... 100.00
Puff box, Scottie dog, lt pk ... 80.00

Tray, Victory Safety, 6".. 400.00
Vase, Hand (holding vase), any color, 3¼", from $20 to................ 30.00
Vase, Lily, any color, 4¼", from $10 to.. 15.00
Vivaudou, apothecary jar, pk... 95.00
Vivaudou, mortar & pestle, 2-tone... 200.00
Vivaudou, shaving mug, blk... 45.00
Wall lamp, from $25 to... 40.00

Alexandrite

Alexandrite is a type of art glass introduced around the turn of the twentieth century by Thomas Webb and Sons of England. It is recognized by its characteristic shading, pale yellow to rose and blue at the edge of the item. Although other companies (Moser, for example) produced glass they called Alexandrite, only examples made by Webb possess all the described characteristics and command premium prices. Amount and intensity of blue determines value. Our prices are for items with good average intensity, unless otherwise noted.

Compote, Honeycomb, scalloped, 4½" dia................................. 1,150.00
Cordial, bl rim to amber bowl, stem & ft, lt ribbing, 3"............... 635.00

Finger bowl, Webb, 5", with 6" underplate, $1,850.00. (Photo courtesy Early Auction Co.)

Vase, cylindrical w/ruffled top, 2½" 1,095.00
Vase, Dmn Quilt, petal rim, 3" 2,500.00
Vase, Honeycomb, ovoid w/6-sided rim, 2¾" 1,200.00
Wine, amber stem & ped, 4½".. 2,000.00

Almanacs

The earliest evidence indicates that almanacs were used as long ago as Ancient Egypt. Throughout the Dark Ages they were circulated in great volume and were referred to by more people than any other book except the Bible. *The Old Farmer's Almanac* first appeared in 1793 and has been issued annually since that time. Usually more of a pamphlet than a book (only a few have hard covers), the almanac provided planting and harvesting information to farmers, weather forecasts for seamen, medical advice, household hints, mathematical tutoring, postal rates, railroad schedules, weights and measures, 'receipts,' and jokes. Before 1800 the information was unscientific and based entirely on astrology and folklore. The first almanac in America was printed in 1639 by William Pierce Mariner; it contained data of this nature. One of the best-known editions, Ben Franklin's *Poor Richard's Almanac*, was introduced in 1732 and continued to be printed for 25 years.

By the nineteenth century, merchants saw the advertising potential in a publication so widely distributed, and the advertising almanac evolved. These were distributed free of charge by drugstores and mercantiles and were usually somewhat lacking in information, containing simply a calendar, a few jokes, and a variety of ads for quick remedies and quack cures.

Today their concept and informative, often amusing text make almanacs popular collectibles that may usually be had at reasonable prices. Because they were printed in such large numbers and often saved from year to year, their prices are still low. Most fall within a range of $4.00 to $15.00. Very common examples may be virtually worthless; those printed before 1860 are especially collectible. Quite rare and highly prized are the Kate Greenaway 'Almanacks,' printed in London from 1883 to 1897. These are illustrated with her drawings of children, one for each calendar month. See also Kate Greenaway.

1799, Farmer's Almanac, Robert B Thomas, VG............................ 40.00
1829, Almanach de Gotha, G 50.00
1840, Harrison Almanac, JP Giffing, G- 45.00
1841, New England Anti-Slavery Almanac, JA Collins, VG 55.00
1845, Whig Almanac & United States Register, Greeley & McElrath, VG..115.00
1846, Boston Almanac, VG 48.00
1847, General Taylor Old Rough & Ready Almanac, G 32.00
1847, Liberty Almanac, 48-pg, very rare, VG.............................. 260.00
1849, Agricultural & Family Almanac, EX..................................... 30.00
1850, VB Palmer's Business-Men's Almanac, EX........................ 48.00
1870, Frank Leslie's Comic Almanac for the Year..., 30-pg, VG .. 115.00
1884, Ayer's American Almanac, Dr JC Ayer & Co, 7½x5", G... 130.00
1892, Warner's Safe Cure Almanac, EX.. 25.00
1897, World Almanac & Encyclopedia, VG.................................... 40.00
1898, Seven Barks Almanac, EX.. 75.00
1908, Green's Almanac/August Flower & German Syrup, EX....... 35.00
1912, IHC Almanac & Encyclopedia, about 100 pgs, VG 90.00

1913, Swamp Root, Dr. Kilmer & Co., Binghampton, N.Y., $15.00.

1917, Cirencester Almanac & Directory, VG................................. 50.00
1934, Wilkes-Barre Record Almanac & Year Book, G.................. 70.00
1941, Wilkes-Barre Record Almanac & Yearbook, VG................. 85.00
1966, Drag World...Drag Racing Almanac, EX.............................. 45.00

Aluminum

Aluminum, though being the most abundant metal in the earth's crust, always occurs in combination with other elements. Before a practical method for its refinement was developed in the late nineteenth century, articles made of aluminum were very expensive. After the process for commercial smelting was perfected in 1916, it became profitable to adapt the ductile, nontarnishing material to many uses.

By the late '30s, novelties, trays, pitchers, and many other tableware items were being produced. They were often handcrafted with elaborate decoration. Russel Wright designed a line of lovely pieces such as lamps, vases, and desk accessories that are becoming very collectible. Many who crafted the ware marked it with their company logo, and these signed pieces are attracting the most interest. Wendell August Forge (Grove City, Pennsylvania) is a mark to watch for; this firm was the first to produce hammered aluminum (it is still made there today), and some of their examples are particularly nice. Upwardly mobile market values reflect their popularity with today's collectors. In general, 'spun' aluminum is from the '30s or early '40s, and 'hammered' aluminum is from the '30s to the '60s.

Basket, palm leaves, rnd w/flat-sided grip inserted on hdl, Everlast..10.00
Basket, rnd hammered bowl w/beaded rim, dbl hdl w/twists, Buenilum. 5.00
Basket, sq w/rolled-up rims, finger-wave hdl, Continental, 6x8".... 35.00
Bowl, deep w/plain flat flared rim, no decor, Kensington, 7x11" 15.00
Bowl, dogwood pattern, plain fluted rim, Wendell A Forge, 2x7".. 45.00
Buffet server/bun warmer, 3-ftd w/tulip inserts, II Farberware, 9"... 25.00
Butter dish, bamboo design w/bamboo finial, Everlast, 4x4x7" L .. 10.00
Cake stand, band of shields decor, serrated, ped ft, Wilson, 8x12". 15.00
Candy dish, fruits, rnd w/3 indents, fluted rim, scrolled hdl, 9" dia ...5.00
Candy dish, 2 leaves w/looped stems, serrated, Buenilum, 6" 10.00
Casserole, bamboo w/bamboo finial & hdls, Everlast, 7" dia 10.00
Cigarette box, 4 pine cones on hammered hinged lid, Town, 5x3x2"..75.00
Coaster set, bamboo, 4 in ftd trivet-type folder, Everlast................ 20.00
Coaster set, mnt lion/duck/2 turkeys, Wendell A Forge, 3", w/cb box .45.00
Compote, deep hammered bowl, short flared ped ft, unmk, 5x6"... 10.00

Condiment stand, three removable baskets, Everlast, from $60.00 to $80.00.

Creamer/sugar, hammered, elbow hdls, flower finial, World Hand Forged..5.00
Creamer/sugar/tray, plain/beaded rims, scrolled hdl/finial, Buenilum . 15.00
Gravy boat, hammered w/mums, long hdl, attached tray, Continental .25.00
Hurricane lamps, grapes, loop hdls, glass chimneys, Everlast, 9", pr.45.00
Ice bucket, hammered int, beaded rim, twisted hdl, Buenilum, 6" . 10.00
Lazy Susan, fruits/flowers, 2-tiered, upturned rims, 13" H, Cromwell. 10.00
Matchbox covers, pine cone or bittersweet, Wendell A Forge, ea . 65.00
Mint dish, dogwood, flat rim, 3-part glass insert, Wendell Forge, 12"...45.00
Napkin holder, flower/ribbons pattern, fan shape, 4-leaf ft, 6" L 15.00
Pitcher, acorn & leaf, bulbous, coiled hdl, Continental, 8"............ 25.00
Pitcher, bamboo, rolled rim w/ice lip, Everlast, 8" 35.00
Relish tray, flying geese in 4 compartments, tab hdls, A Armour, 5x16" .. 75.00
Tray, bar; ducks in flight & cattail, tab hdls, unmk, 9x16".............. 30.00
Tray, bread; tulips, applied tulip & ribbon hdls, R Kent, 8x13" 25.00
Tray, bread; wild rose, tab hdls, serrated, Continental, 6x13" 15.00
Tray, sandwich; crane/bamboo, rnd w/applied hdls, Hand Forged, 9". 35.00
Tray, serving; hammered w/deer/geese, appl hdls, Continental, 12x16".75.00
Tray, serving; larkspur, plain upturned rim, Wendell A Forge, 13x20" .85.00

AMACO, American Art Clay Co.

AMACO is the logo of the American Art Clay Co. Inc., founded in Indianapolis, Indiana, in 1919, by Ted O. Philpot. They produced a line of art pottery from 1931 through 1938. The company is still in business but now produces only supplies, implements, and tools for the ceramic trade.

Values for AMACO have risen sharply, especially those for figurals, items with Art Deco styling, and pieces with uncommon shapes. Our advisors for this category are Suzanne Perrault and David Rago; they are listed in the Directory under New Jersey.

Bust, woman's head, hair drawn at nape, ivory gloss, 7" 395.00
Bust, woman's head, long str hair, bl gloss, paper label, 7" 395.00
Vase, bl w/uneven texture, bulbous, 4"... 15.00
Vase, trees scenic, blk/bl on red, shouldered, #31, 7", EX............. 150.00
Vase, yel matt, organic form w/4 sides, 13¼"................................. 360.00

Amberina

Amberina, one of the earliest types of art glass, was developed in 1883 by Joseph Locke of the New England Glass Company. The trademark was registered by W.L. Libbey, who often signed his name in script within the pontil.

Amberina was made by adding gold powder to the batch, which produced glass in the basic amber hue. Part of the item, usually the top, was simply reheated to develop the characteristic deep red or fuchsia shading. Early amberina was mold blown, but cut and pressed amberina was also produced. The rarest type is plated amberina, made by New England for a short time after 1886. It has been estimated that less than 2,000 pieces were ever produced. Other companies, among them Hobbs and Brockunier, Mt. Washington Glass Company, and Sowerby's Ellison Glassworks of England, made their own versions, being careful to change the name of their product to avoid infringing on Libbey's patent. Prices realized at auction seem to be erratic, to say the least, and dealers appear to be 'testing the waters' with prices that start out very high only to be reduced later if the item does not sell at the original asking price. Lots of amberina glassware is of a more recent vintage — look for evidence of an early production, since the later wares are worth much less than glassware that can be attributed to the older makers. Generic amberina with hand-painted flowers will bring lower prices as well. Our values are taken from auction results and dealer lists, omitting the extremely high and low ends of the range.

Basket, swirled w/rigaree rim, thorny hdl w/rasberry prunts, 7" H. 450.00
Bowl, Dmn Quilt, ovoid w/inverted scalloped rim, 8" 225.00
Celery vase, Dmn Optic, cylinder w/crimped sq rim, NE, 6½" 225.00
Celery vase, Dmn Quilt, cylinder w/tight ruffled rim, NE, 4½" 175.00

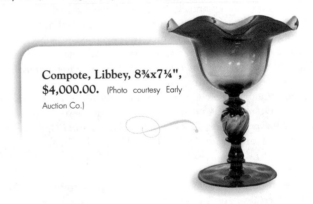

Compote, Libbey, 8¾x7¼", $4,000.00. (Photo courtesy Early Auction Co.)

Condiment set, cruet/2 shakers/mustard, Coinspot, Pairpoint caddy .600.00
Epergne, 1-lily, crimped everted rim, ruffled base, Mt WA, 9"...2,600.00
Punch cup, Dmn Quilt & thorn pattern, amber reed hdl, 2½"........ 75.00
Spittoon, Dmn Quilt, rose ruffled rim, Mt WA, 5" dia 225.00
Toothpick holder, cylindrical cup in swan-hdld Tufts holder, 3½"...550.00
Vase, diagonal swirls, bulbous urn, amber rigaree rim, Harach, 10".250.00
Vase, Dmn Quilt, ovoid, ruffled rim w/amber rigaree collar, 6" 400.00
Vase, jack-in-pulpit; optic ribs, fuchsia rim, Libbey, 5" 450.00
Vase, jack-in-pulpit; ruby rim, amber stem w/ruby ft, NE, 10" 275.00
Vase, optic ribs, ft lily form w/trifold rim, Libbey, 9".................... 350.00
Vase, swirl ribbed trumpet form w/amber ruffled rim & ft, 20" 515.00
Vinegar jar, Coinspot, fuchsia around top, metal spout, NE, 4" ... 425.00

Plated Amberina

Bowl, bulbous w/inverted rim, 3x5"..7,800.00
Bowl, 6-pinch rim, outstanding color, minor mfg anomalies, 3¼x8"..9,000.00
Creamer, wide spout, amber hdl, minor mfg anomalies, 2½"...10,800.00
Cruet, swirled/ribbed neck, amber stopper/hdl, 7", EX 10,800.00

Cup, bulbous, amber hdl, 2½"..4,500.00
Mug, slightly incurvate sides, amber ring hdl, 2⅝" 225.00
Pitcher, tankard, amber ear hdl, 5½" 18,000.00
Pitcher, tankard; 8¾" 17,000.00

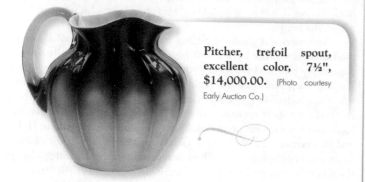

Pitcher, trefoil spout, excellent color, 7½", $14,000.00. (Photo courtesy Early Auction Co.)

Shaker, pillar form, strong color, 4" 4,500.00
Sugar bowl, 2 appl amber hdls, 3¾x5¾".................................15,600.00
Toothpick holder, hexagonal rim, star pontil, minor rim wear, 2½"..10,800.00
Tumbler, lemonade; appl hdl, 5"..4,000.00
Tumbler, 3¾", from $2,100 to..2,900.00
Vase, 4 lg dents to body, flared/crimped rim, minor mfg flaws, 4¾"..19,200.00

American Indian Art

That time when the American Indian was free to practice the crafts and culture that was his heritage has always held a fascination for many. They were a people who appreciated beauty of design and colorful decoration in their furnishings and clothing; and because instruction in their crafts was a routine part of their rearing, they were well accomplished. Several tribes developed areas in which they excelled. The Navajo were weavers and silversmiths, the Zuni, lapidaries. Examples of their craftsmanship are very valuable. Today even the work of contemporary Indian artists — weavers, silversmiths, carvers, and others — is highly collectible. Unless otherwise noted, values are for items with no obvious damage or excessive wear (EX/NM). For more information we recommend *Ornamental Indian Artifacts; Rare & Unusual Indian Artifacts; Antler, Bone & Shell Artifacts;* and *Indian Trade Relics,* all by Lar Hothem.

Key:
bw — beadwork
COA — Certificate of Authenticity
dmn — diamond
p-h — prehistoric
s-s — sinew sewn

Apparel and Accessories

Before the white traders brought the Indian women cloth from which to sew their garments and beads to use for decorating them, clothing was made from skins sewn together with sinew, usually made of animal tendon. Porcupine quills were dyed bright colors and woven into bags and armbands and used to decorate clothing and moccasins. Examples of early quillwork are scarce today and highly collectible.

Early in the nineteenth century, beads were being transported via pony pack trains. These 'pony' beads were irregular shapes of opaque glass imported from Venice. Nearly always blue or white, they were twice as large as the later 'seed' beads. By 1870 translucent beads in many sizes and colors had been made available, and Indian beadwork had become commercialized. Each tribe developed its own distinctive methods and preferred decorations, making it possible for collectors today to determine the origin of many items. Soon after the turn of the twentieth century, the craft of beadworking began to diminish.

Bandolier, Chippewa, floral bw on wht, early 1900s, 40x16".....1,400.00
Bandolier, Chippewa, floral/zigzag bw on red tradecloth, 1890s, 40x16".1,200.00
Belt, Chippewa, bw on satin w/red tradecloth trim, 1900s, 42x10"..1,900.00
Belt, Chippewa, geometric bw on dk wool w/red satin trim, 1900s, 45x5"...400.00
Cuffs, Chippewa, floral bw w/cloth trim, 1900s, 7x6"+9" fringe...250.00
Cuffs, Plateau, bw roses on wht buckskin, long fringe, 5¼x11", pr..350.00
Cuffs, Sioux, geometric bw, s/s buckskin, 1900s, 5½x5"+5" fringe...275.00
Dress, Apache, wht buckskin w/cone dangles/bw/fringe, 1970s ...400.00
Dress, Cheyenne child's, s/s bw on buckskin w/shells/tin cones, 1880s. 5,000.00
Dress, S Plains, wht buckskin, bw accents, waist tabs, fringe, 1980s. 450.00
Leggings, Assiniboine, wht-selvaged red stroud w/bw, 1900s, 30x13". 950.00
Leggings, Blackfoot, striped buckskin, bw/horsehair trim, 1950s, 40". 350.00
Moccasins, Arapaho, bw on buffalo hide, s/s, 1880s, 10½"........1,300.00
Moccasins, Arapaho baby's, full bw, s/s buffalo calf hide, 1900s, 4".700.00
Moccasins, Cheyenne, full bw on elk hide, 1880s, 10¼" 2,500.00
Moccasins, Cheyenne, partial bw, hard soles, yel/red ochre, 1950s, 12". 200.00
Moccasins, Cheyenne, s/s ochered buffalo hide, 1880s, 11" 3,250.00
Moccasins, Chippewa, puckered toes, floral bw vamps, cuffs, 1900s, 8"..160.00
Moccasins, Plateau, buckskin w/floral bw/brass buttons, 1950s, 10x10".550.00
Moccasins, Plateau, geometric bw, high-top, 1900s, 7x10" 1,000.00
Moccasins, Seneca child's, bw tops & cuffs on buckskin, 1890s, 9"..1,800.00
Moccasins, Sioux lady's, gr ochre high-top, bw, s/s, 1890s, 14x9"..2,500.00
Tunic, Woodlands, floating bw forms on blk velvet, 1900s, 23x19".275.00
Yoke, Plateau child's, mc bw stars & cowry shells, early 1900s, 12x15".650.00

Bags and Cases

The Indians used bags for many purposes, and most display excellent form and workmanship. Of the types listed below, many collectors consider the pipe bag to be the most desirable form. Pipe bags were long, narrow, leather and bead or quillwork creations made to hold tobacco in a compartment at the bottom and the pipe, with the bowl removed from the stem, in the top. Long buckskin fringe was used as trim and complemented the quilled and beaded design to make the bag a masterpiece of Indian art.

Arapaho, strike-a-lite, s/s bw on leather w/tin cones/fringe, 1890s..750.00
Blackfoot, parfleche, classic pnt design, 1870s, 24x14"..............2,750.00
Chippewa, bandolier, floral bw on cloth, velvet trim, 1890s, 45x16".. 2,000.00
Crow, awl case, full bw, bw drops, s/s rawhide, 1950s, bone awl...475.00
Crow, parfleche, mineral pnt, late 1800s, 17½x9"......................1,500.00
Crow, Tobacco Society, buffalo hide w/bw cloth top, 19th C, 8½x6".. 700.00
Nez Perce, corn husk, dmns/sqs, vegetal dyes, 1950s, 11¾x10½". 375.00
Nez Perce, corn husk, spools/butterflies, mc yarns, 1890s, 18x13". 550.00
Ojibway, bandolier, full bw, 1860-70, 37x11"............................2,750.00
Plateau, geometric bw, red felt trim, 1950s, 16x15" 350.00
Plateau, lady's, floral bw front, buckskin fringe/hdl, 1950s, 10x8" . 250.00
Plateau, pictorial bw of Jesus on water, mid-1900s, 12x10" 900.00
Prairie, tobacco bag, native buckskin w/full bw, 12x7"+4" fringe. 400.00
Ute, medicine, full bw on buckskin, s/s, long fringe, 1890s, 12x5" . 2,250.00
Ute, strike-a-lite, full bw on antelope hide w/tin cones, 1890s, 8" ..600.00
Ute chief's, tobacco, buckskin, s/s, much bw, 1900s, 29"+6" drop.1,800.00
Yakima, pipe, bw on tanned buckskin, 1930s-40s, 21"..................500.00

Baskets

In the following listings, examples are coil built unless noted otherwise.

Apache, bowl, dbl 5-point stars, ticked rim, 1950s, 2x5¼"..........225.00
Apache, bowl, squash blossom amid 5 eagles, early 1900s, 2½x9".1,800.00
Apache, burden, fine-weave cone, buckskin trim & fringe, 1980s, 6x7"..110.00
Apache, tray, triangles/dmns extending from center, 1940s, 4x12"..1,000.00
Chemehuevi, olla, wide mouth, modified squash blossom, 1940s, 6x8"..1,300.00

Cherokee, carrying, ash splint, faded colors, 1900s, 13x8"+12" hdl ...275.00
Choctaw, herringbone twill weave, faded dyed bands, 1900s, 8x8x8". 525.00
Choctaw, market basket, natural dyed bands, lacks hdls, 12x13x10" .525.00
Choctaw, natural dyed cane (completely faded), 1910s, 13x11x11" ..650.00
Hopi 2nd Mesa, tray, 6-point central rosette, 1950s, 14" dia........ 650.00
Hopi 3rd Mesa, bowl, 2 faces parted by squash blossom, 1970s, 3x12"..325.00
Hopi 3rd Mesa, 5 sq kachina faces/geometrics, 1950s, 7x11½" 425.00
Iroquois, birchbark w/deer/trees in dyed quills, 1970s, 2½x7" 200.00
Iroquois, quilled bark, moose on lid, dmns on sides, 1950s, 4x8" . 325.00
Mission, bowl, radiating triangles/steps, polychrome, 1930s, 2x12" . 650.00
Paiute, bowl, tight weave, repeating brn/orange arrows, 1900s, 3x8" .550.00
Papago, bowl, hooked butterflies, flared w/flat base, 1950s, 4x16". 300.00
Papago, doll, female figure, 3-section, 1950s, 28x12", +hat.......... 550.00
Papago, olla, long neck, dog figures, 1930s, 11x10" 750.00
Pima, olla, stylized geometrics, flat base, 1930s, 13x14" 2,200.00
Pima, tray, radiating stepped geometrics, early 1900s, 4x15"........ 650.00
Pima, tray, traditional maze design, EX patina, 1920s, 11" 400.00
Pit River, covered bottle, blk serrated decor, w/cap, 1950s, 9x4" . 375.00
Pomo, cradle, traditional-style open weave, toy, mid-1900s, 14½x7".. 260.00
Pomo, fine weave, gr & yel feathers, shell disk trim, 1900s, 1x2" ..1,100.00

Blades and Points

Relics of this type usually display characteristics of a general area, time period, or a particular location. With study, those made by the Plains Indians are easily discerned from those of the West Coast. Because modern man has imitated the art of the Indian by reproducing these artifacts through modern means, use caution before investing your money in 'too good to be authentic' specimens. For a more thorough study we recommend *Authenticating Ancient Indian Artifacts: How to Recognize Reproduction and Altered Artifacts* and *Ancient Indian Artifacts, Volume I Introduction to Collecting* by Jim Bennett; and *Indian Artifacts of the Midwest, Book V; Indian Artifacts: The Best of the Midwest; Paleo-Indian Artifacts;* and *Arrowhead & Projectile Points*, all by Lar Hothem.

Agate Basin, Burlington flint, late Paleo, 3¼" 400.00
Clovis, creamy flint w/dk specks, early Paleo, IL, 2½" 650.00
Clovis, hornstone, fluted, early Paleo, IN, 3½x1⅛" 2,000.00
Clovis, translucent flint, fluted, rstr ear, early Paleo, 2¾" 400.00
Dalton, wht chert, serrated edges, MO, 3⅝x1⅛" 1,000.00
Dvtl, dk hornstone, beveled & serrated, sm rstr, KY, 4" 125.00
Dvtl, pale hornstone, notched base, KY, 3x1½"........................... 750.00
Hardaway, bl Coshocton w/lightning lines, Archaic, OH, 1⅞".... 250.00
Holland, tan flint, chipped/streamlined, late Paleo, 4¾x1⅜" 1,700.00
Kirk, gray & blk flint, corner notches, resharpened, Archaic, 3¼"..225.00
Lanceolate, pk flint, KY, 3⅜".. 225.00
Pine tree, gray w/cream quartz inclusions, Archaic, 2¾" 425.00
Sq base, tan Burlington chert, late Paleo, IL, 5½x1¼".................. 800.00
Stilwell, mixed Burlington chert, Archaic, OH, 5¼" 850.00

Ceremonial Items

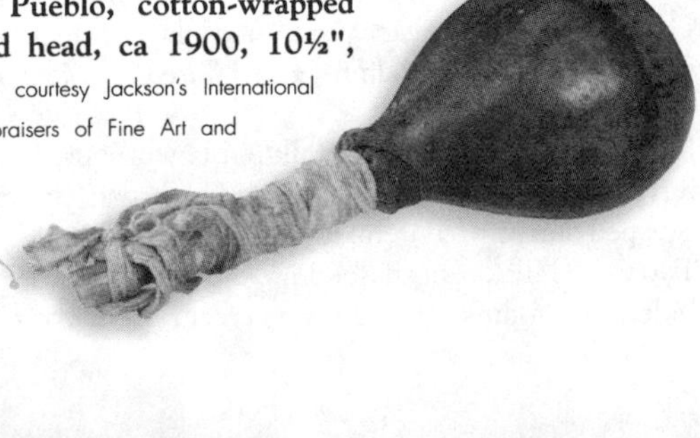

Gourd rattle, Pueblo, cotton-wrapped handle, painted head, ca 1900, 10½", $320.00. (Photo courtesy Jackson's International Auctioneers and Appraisers of Fine Art and Antiques)

Dance cuffs, harness leather covered w/sm shells, 1930s, 9½x3" .. 110.00
Dance roach, Plains, porcupine hair w/mc ornaments, 1950s, 15" ..225.00
Dance roach, Prairie, porcupine & deer hair, 11" woven base, 1900s ...550.00
Dance wand, Sioux, hide bound, wrapped w/2 mtd buffalo horns, 9x22"..190.00
Drum, Pueblo, rawhide on cottonwood, mc pnt, mid-1900s, 7x11". 325.00
Flute, Woodlands, cvd cylinder w/bird-head end, 6-hole, 1890s, 26".2,750.00
Headdress, Hopi, 2 corrugated cb layers, earth pigments, 1950s, 13x12"..325.00
Mask, Mexican, hand cvd & colored, early 1900s, 10½x6½" 60.00
Medicine necklace, Crow, dog teeth/trade beads, attached bag, 19th C..450.00
Rattle, Plains, rawhide w/wood hdl, s/s, X on face, 1870s, 10x5" . 500.00
Rattle, Sioux, rawhide 'doughnut,' wrapped bw hdl, 1930s, 10x5"+fringe.800.00
Spoon, NW Coast, wrought silver w/human figural hdl, 1950s, 12" ..140.00
Spoon, Ojibway, cvd w/eagle effigy hdl, late 1800s, 14x5½"......... 325.00
Staff, Cheyenne Peyote, cvd pipestone w/cvd feather, 1900s, 19". 400.00
Staff, Peyote, cvd wood w/3 2" beaded bands, ca 1910, 43".......... 225.00
Staff, speaker's; owl effigy, cvd from branch, dk patina, 1900s, 34"..250.00

Dolls

Hopi, kachina, Eagle Dancer, R Allison, 1990, 14½" 250.00
Hopi, kachina, OTA Skirt Man, dtd 1937, 10¼".......................... 800.00
Hopi, kachina, Road Runner, 1950s, 11" 425.00
Hopi, kachina, Shalako, 1-pc, 1980s, 20" 225.00
Hopi, kachina, Shalako Mana, EX cvg & detail, 1950s, 11" 110.00
Sioux, buckskin & cloth, human hair, fringed leggings, 1950s, 12".650.00
Zuni, kachina, Sipikne, jtd arms, 1920s, 10½" 1,300.00

Domestics

Blanket, Navajo chief, 2nd Phase, stripes/steps/dmns, 1900s, 60x51". 7,000.00
Canteen, tobacco; Navajo, wrought & stamped silver, 1960s, 3" dia .375.00
Cradle cover, bw on buckskin, s/s, early heavy muslin, 1890s, 27x8" .4,250.00
Cradleboard, Menominee, pine w/bentwood sunshade, plain, 1900s, 17".550.00
Rug, tanned buffalo hide, late 1900s, 84x80"..............................1,100.00
Saddle, Cheyenne, buffalo rawhide w/wooden sides/horn trees, 19th C..900.00
Saddle, Crow child, dbl horn, bw on stirrups/horns, 15x16" 2,000.00
Spoon, Ojibway, cvd wood, stepped neck, bird effigy finial, 1890s, 9". 275.00

Jewelry and Adornments

As early as 500 A.D., Indians in the Southwest drilled turquoise nuggets and strung them on cords made of sinew or braided hair. The Spanish introduced them to coral, and it became a popular item of jewelry; abalone and clamshells were favored by the Coastal Indians. Not until the last half of the nineteenth century did the Indians learn to work with silver. Each tribe developed its own distinctive style and preferred design, which until about 1920 made it possible to determine tribal origin with some degree of accuracy. Since that time, because of modern means of communication and travel, motifs have become less distinct.

Quality Indian silver jewelry may be antique or contemporary. Age, though certainly to be considered, is not as important a factor as fine workmanship and good stones. Pre-1910 silver will show evidence of hammer marks, and designs are usually simple. Beads have sometimes been shaped from coins. Stones tend to be small; when silver wire was used, it is usually square. To insure your investment, choose a reputable dealer.

Belt, Navajo, 8 silver conchos ea w/natural turq cabochon, 3x39"..325.00
Belt, Navajo, 9 silver & turq conchos & buckle on blk leather, 1970s . 550.00
Bolo, Navajo, eagle dancer figural, silver/turq/coral, 1980s, 7"..... 275.00
Bolo, Zuni, chanel inlay Sun Face, jet/MOP/coral, matching tips, 21". 160.00
Bolo, Zuni, inlay eagle, jet/turq/MOP, sgn, 1970s, 18".................. 425.00
Bracelet, Navajo, coral cabochons set in silver, late 1900s, ⅝" W. 275.00
Bracelet, Navajo, wrought silver w/lg turq stone, 1980s, 3" W..... 110.00

Bracelet, Zuni, ca 1940s, many stones now green, 2" wide, $200.00. (Photo courtesy R. G. Munn Auction LLC)

Bracelet, Zuni, wrought silver w/3 rows of turq, 1980s, 1" W 200.00
Breast collar, Sioux, 4" hairpipe bone beads/trade beads, 1950s, 54" ..275.00
Earrings, Navajo, wrought silver & turq cluster, late 1900s, 1½".. 120.00
Hair ties, Sioux, quilled, tin cones, 19th C, 11", pr 300.00
Hat band, Navajo, silver w/turq cabochons, narrow, 1940s, 26" .. 140.00
Necklace, Navajo, 4-strands Blue Gem turq nuggets, 18", +earrings .160.00
Necklace, Pueblo, turq heshi w/pr of jaclas, late 1900s, 38" 110.00
Necklace, Pueblo, 4-strand heshi w/uniform turq stones, 1970s, 29"..130.00
Pendant, Navajo, Kings Manassa turq w/silver leaf decor, hallmk, 2x1". 130.00
Pendant, Navajo, 6 turq cabochons, 12k gold-filled flute player, 1980.. 225.00
Squash blossom, Navajo, silver, 12-segment/lg turq stone, 3" naja, 24".. 350.00
Watch bracelet, Navajo, 6 lt turq stones, 2" W 130.00

Pipes

Pipe bowls were usually carved from soft stone, such as catlinite or red pipestone, an argilaceous sedimentary rock composed mainly of hardened clay. Steatite was also used. Some ceremonial pipes were simply styled, while others were intricately designed naturalistic figurals, sometimes in bird or frog forms called effigies. Their stems, made of wood and often covered with leather, were sometimes nearly a yard in length.

Chippewa, catlinite & steatite w/bone stem, glass beads, 1½x7½" ..500.00
Disk, catlinite, well cvd, late p-h, 2⅝x3⅞" 550.00
Elbow, brn-grit tempered ceramic, 1000-1500 AD, 2⅞" L 600.00
Elbow, sandstone w/brn patina, made w/flint drill, IL, 2⅝x3" 450.00
Hopewell, stone effigy of wolf pulling snake from ground, p-h, 2¼" ...800.00
Jersey Bluff elbow, grit-tempered pottery w/smooth finish, 2x3" .. 550.00
Lady's, snouted hardstone bowl, cvd/pnt stem w/duck-head tip, 1900s. 500.00
Plains type, catlinite, IL, 4¼x8½" 700.00
Sioux, catlinite, quill-wrapped ash stem/horsehair dangles, 1800s, 31" ..4,000.00
Sioux, catlinite w/produding bands/ridges, cvd stem, 1950s, 20" . 300.00
Tomahawk, Great Lakes, iron head, wood haft, brass tacks, 1800s, 22" ..2,750.00
Tomahawk, iron head, brass tacks, file-burned haft, 1900s, 16x9". 550.00
Tomahawk, iron head, brass tacks, file-burned haft, 1900s, 24x8". 600.00

Pottery

Indian pottery is nearly always decorated in such a manner as to indicate the tribe that produced it or the pueblo in which it was made. For instance, the designs of Cochiti potters were usually scattered forms from nature or sacred symbols. The Zuni preferred an ornate repetitive decoration of a closer configuration. They often used stylized deer and bird forms, sometimes in dimensional applications.

Acoma, jar, birds w/in arched frames, sq prayer boxes, 1890s, 10x14" .. 3,500.00
Acoma, olla, curvilinear forms, concave base, 1920s, 10½x11" ... 800.00
Anasazi, bowl, blk-on-wht w/geometrics, p-h, as found, 3½x8¾". 450.00
Anasazi, bowl, Salado Gila deer w/geometrics, p-h, rpr, 7x13" 475.00
Anasazi, jar, olla form w/busy geometrics, rstr, 12x18" 1,600.00
Anasazi, ladle, blk on wht curvilinear decor, p-h, rstr, 3x11x6" .. 500.00
Anasazi, pitcher, blk-on-wht geometrics, crude hdl, p-h, 9x6" ..450.00
Anasazi, pitcher, blk-on-wht geometrics, p-h, rstr, 5½x5¾" 225.00
Casas Grandes, effigy pot, rabbits/lines, lizard on top, Quesada, 10".2,500.00

Hopi, jar, effigy; full face, necklace/earrings/brow band, 1900s, 6x5"..1,800.00
Hopi, jar, mc bird-tail decor at shoulder, mid-1900s, 2½x5" 110.00
Hopi, jar, stylized avian/geometric forms, buff slip, Frog Woman, 4x6".275.00
Hopi, wedding vase, polished blkware, swirl form, Komalestawa, 6"..650.00
Matsaki, bowl, birds/feathers, mc, p-h, rstr/over-pnt, 5x12" 275.00
Santa Clara, basket, Yei figures/bugs/etc, mc, Margaret & Luther, 7".425.00
Santa Clara, bowl, redware w/cvd motif revealing buff core, 4x8".. 1,100.00
Santa Clara, jar, blkware, repeating feathers/serpents, 1970s, 9x10" .600.00
Santa Clara, jar, blkware, serpents, M Tafoya, w/lid, 7⅝x8" 3,000.00
Santa Clara, jar, blkware, stylized kachina/chief heads, Tafoya, 8x10"..900.00
Santa Clara, vase, blkware, serpents, Margaret (Tafoya), 14x11"..7,500.00
Zuni, canteen, mc floral medallion ea side, ca 1960, 4x6¾" 350.00
Zuni, jar, birds/foliage/classic figures, high shoulder, 1890s, 8x11".. 1,700.00
Zuni, jar, X-hatched bands/geometrics/etc, 1890s, 8¾x12" 6,000.00

Pottery, San Ildefonso

The pottery of the San Ildefonso pueblo is especially sought after by collectors today. Under the leadership of Maria Martinez and her husband Julian, experiments began about 1918 which led to the development of the 'black-on-black' design achieved through exacting methods of firing the ware. They discovered that by smothering the fire at a specified temperature, the carbon in the smoke that ensued caused the pottery to blacken. Maria signed her work (often 'Marie') from the late teens to the sixties; she died in 1980. Today examples with her signature may bring prices in the $500.00 to $4,500.00 range.

Bowl, blkware, birds along rim, Marie & Julian, ca 1954, 4x8", NM .2,040.00
Figure, heartline bear, 2-color, turq eyes, Tony Da, 1970s, 3x5".. 16,000.00
Jar, blkware, curvilinear designs in 4 panels, Marie & Julian, 7x10".3,250.00
Jar, blkware, feathers, early 1900s, 7x6" 300.00

Jar, blackware, Marie and Santana, mid-1950s, 7" diameter, $1,500.00. (Photo courtesy Jackson's International Auctioneers & Appraisers of Fine Art & Antiques)

Jar, blkware, traditional/non-traditional forms, C Dunlap, '78, 11x16" ...2,750.00
Jar, blkware in gunmetal finish, no decor, long neck, Maria, 9x9".. 6,000.00
Jar, high polish, raindrop lip, Maria Poveka, mid-1900s, 8½x9". 7,500.00
Olla, blkware, sienna spiders w/turq cabochons, B Gonzales, 6x5"... 400.00
Plate, blkware, lg 10-leg serpent, Rose, 1977, 11¾" 5,000.00
Plate, buff & red slip, feathers, Blue Corn, 1974, 4½" 950.00
Seed jar, sgraffito zoomorphic figure on marbleized slip, Sanchez, 5"..650.00

Rugs, Navajo

Classic geometrics, blk/red/wht/gray, 1950s, 51x84" 850.00
Dmn eye dazzler w/serrated bands, 3-color border, 1940s, 84x52" .1,600.00
Dmns, 4 swastika & 4 sm dmns, brn/wht/red/wht, 1940s, 60x40". 600.00
Dmns (3) & fancy zigzags, 1940s, 63x40½" 1,100.00
Figures (2) in Klagetoh-style dmn, red/blk/gray/wht, 1940s, 53x31"..1,400.00
Ganado area, dmns & zigzag bands, red/blk/gray/wht, G age, 92x64". 1,500.00
Ganado area, terraced dmns, gray/blk/red/brn, 1920s, 96x55"...1,100.00
Klagetoh classic, natural & vegetal dyes, 1960s, 57x35".............. 550.00
Pictorial, 3 Yei figures/cornstalk/rainbow, 1950s, 46x36"............. 350.00
Revival chief's, dmn figures/bands, HM Johnson, ca 1991, 85x64"..4,000.00
Stepped deisgn w/central lozenge, red/gray/blk, 1930s, 64x40" .. 900.00
Two Gray Hills, central dbl dmn, 3-color border, 1980s, 36x25".. 400.00
Valero stars/dmns/stepped sqs on cream, 1930s, 60x37" 600.00

Shaped Stone Artifacts

Amulet, polished limestone, bar form, undrilled, KY, 1⅛x3x1" ... 250.00
Bannerstone, winged, dk gray steatite, NC, 6⅜" 2,500.00
Bead, hematite, IL,¾x2" 100.00
Discoidal, blk steatite w/much polish, Mississippian, 1¼x4¼" 400.00
Discoidal, gray-brn hardstone, not polished, 1⅜x2⅞" 175.00
Discoidal, hardstone, 1⅛x2⅝" 75.00
Disk gamestone, hardstone, Woodland or later,½x¾" dia 20.00
Gorget, banded slate, bi-concave, early Woodland, 2x5½" 450.00
Gorget, dk red pipestone, polished, tally mks, 1¼x3⅛" 500.00
Gorget, steatite, oval, Woodland, 1½x3⅛" 200.00
Pendant, gr banded slate, anchor shape, IN, 4x2" 350.00
Pendant, gray banded glacial slate, 4¼x2½" 425.00
Pendant, slate, bell shaped w/horizontal lines, late p-h, 1⅜" 100.00
Plummet, gray hematite, grooved top, well polished, 3¼x¾" 400.00
Plummet, hematite, IL, 4⅝" 75.00
Plummet, patinated hardstone, grooved top, 2¼x1½" 50.00

Tools

Awl, needle; bone splinter w/EX patina/polish, OH, 2⅜" 30.00
Awl, needle; split bird bone, Late Woodland, 3½" 200.00
Awl, split deer bone, tip has abrupt taper, OH, 3⅞" 30.00
Awl, trigger; raccoon bone, 3½" 45.00
Axe, ¾-groove w/facial effigy on heel, p-h, 4x6" 325.00
Fishhook, deer bone, U-shape, Midwest, 1⁵⁄₁₆" 100.00
Gouge, beaver tooth w/wood hdl, leather wrap, 1x3⅜" 175.00
Needle, split bird bone, glossy, Woodland, OH, 4⅞" 75.00

Trade Relics

Arrow point, brass, long stem, 1¾" 40.00
Arrow point, brass, triangular, 1600s, 1⅞" 40.00
Axe head, iron, rnd eye, 6½" 375.00
Axe head, iron, rnd eye w/tapered hole, ca 1800, 5¼x4" 150.00
Beads, amber, varied shapes, 23" strand 135.00
Beads, bl glass, ea ¼x⅜", 28" strand 150.00
Beads, emerald gr glass, 24" strand 175.00
Fishhook, iron, ca 1800, 2¼" 50.00
Gun flint, gray translucent English flint, 1" W 10.00
Hatchet, iron, rnd eye, mk NR, ca 1750, 3⅜x5⅜", +rpl haft 200.00
Kettle, feast; hammered brass, Wolcottville Brass Co, 12x20" 175.00
Knife, Marsh Bros & Co on 7" blade, horn (?) hdl 200.00
Spear head, iron, smithy made, 8¾" 200.00
Spike axe head, iron, rnded reinforcing eyes, 2x8" 200.00
Teakettle, copper, gooseneck, dvtl, 10x7½" 198.00

Weapons

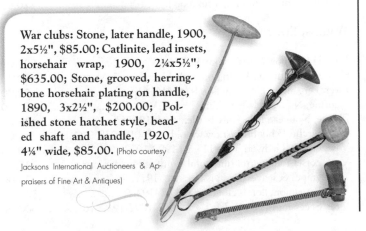

War clubs: Stone, later handle, 1900, 2x5½", $85.00; Catlinite, lead insets, horsehair wrap, 1900, 2¼x5½", $635.00; Stone, grooved, herringbone horsehair plating on handle, 1890, 3x2½", $200.00; Polished stone hatchet style, beaded shaft and handle, 1920, 4¼" wide, $85.00. (Photo courtesy Jacksons International Auctioneers & Appraisers of Fine Art & Antiques)

Bow & arrow, Sioux, cvd wood, 19th C, 47", +arrow w/sinew-bound point ... 400.00
War club, Cheyenne, stone head, rawhide-wrapped hdl, 19th C, 15" .. 650.00
War club, Great Lakes, hardwood head w/cvd otter effigy, 1900s, 26" .. 300.00
War club, stone w/pewter inlay, bw hdl, late 1800s, 23½" 800.00

Miscellaneous

Birchbark canoe model, ca 1940, 23" long, $345.00. (Photo courtesy Jacksons International Auctioneers & Appraisers of Fine Art & Antiques)

Aquatint, Wahktageli Yankton Sioux, K Bodmer, mid-1900s, 17x12"+fr. 700.00
Book, Song of Hiawatha, HW Longfellow, 1st ed, 68 lithographs, 1911 .. 350.00
Charcoal drawing, Iowa Chief w/war club, N Jacob, ca 1973, 24x14"+fr. 300.00
Multi-media art, Navajo landscape w/hogan, R Draper, 10x24"+fr. 225.00
Peace medal, JQ Adams, silver, on ornate presentation collar, 1825 .. 425.00
Peace medal, Millard Fillmore, S Ellis hallmk, 1859, 3" 400.00
Silkscreen, Navajo on horse lights cigarette, Chee, 1959, 13x18"+fr. 325.00
Tempera painting, Long Journey, figures in robes, D O'leary, 22x30"+fr. 300.00
Watercolor, Horse Tail Dancers, JE Pena, 1950s, 10x11"+fr 375.00
Watercolor, mtn lion in tree waiting for deer, Tahoma, '45, 26x20"+fr .. 3,750.00
Watercolor, Navajo, Yeibeichai figure, R Chee, ca 1970, 14x11"+fr .. 550.00
Watercolor, Navajo dancer w/lg torches, Tahoma, 1941, 6x4"+fr . 1,400.00
Watercolor, Pocano Painted Pony, J Martinez, 1950s, 28x23"+fr .. 5,000.00
Watercolor, 2 horses & lg Ponderosa pine, Tahoma, '45, 17x13"+fr .. 3,000.00

American Painted Porcelain

    The American china-painting movement can be traced back to an extracurricular class attended by art students at the McMicken School of Design in Cincinnati. These students, who were the wives and daughters of the city's financial elite, managed to successfully paint numerous porcelains for display in the Woman's Pavilion of the 1876 United States Centennial Exposition held in Philadelphia — an amazing feat considering the high technical skill required for proficiency, as well as the length of time and multiple firings necessary to finish the ware. From then until 1917 when the United States entered World War I, china painting was a profession as well as a popular amateur pursuit for many people, particularly women. In fact, over 25,000 people were involved in this art form at the turn of the last century.

    Collectors and antique dealers have discovered American hand-painted porcelain, and they have become aware of its history, beauty, and potential value. For more information on this subject, *Antique Trader's Comprehensive Guide to American Painted Porcelain* and *Painted Porcelain Jewelry and Buttons: Collector's Identification & Value Guide* by Dorothy Kamm are the culmination of a decade of research; we recommend them highly for further study.

    Though American pieces are of high quality and commensurate with their European counterparts, they are much less costly today. Generally, you will pay as little as $20.00 for a 6" plate and less than $75.00 for many other items. Values are based on aesthetic appeal, quality of the workmanship, size, rarity of the piece and of the subject matter, and condition. Age is the least important factor, because most American painted porcelains are not dated. (Factory backstamps are helpful in establishing the approximate time period an item was decorated, but they aren't totally reliable.)

Bar pin, brass-plated bezel, 1½" W, from $25 to 55.00
Bowl, 4¾", from $50 to 75.00
Brooch, gold-plated bezel, 1½" dia, from $35 to 55.00
Cake plate, from $35 to 75.00
Celery tray, from $35 to 75.00
Cup & saucer 45.00
Cup & saucer, bouillon; from $35 to 55.00
Gravy boat, from $55 to 75.00
Mug, from $40 to 75.00
Pin tray, from $30 to 50.00

Plate, blank: C.T. Altwasser, Germany, 1875, from $25.00 to $50.00. (Photo courtesy Dorothy Kamm)

Plate, 6", from $10 to 35.00
Plate, 8", from $45 to 75.00
Salt cellar, from $20 to 40.00
Scarf pin, medallion, brass-plated bezel & shank, 1¼", from $35 to.65.00
Shakers, pr, from $25 to 40.00
Shirtwaist button, 1" dia, from $20 to 40.00

Amphora

The Amphora Porcelain Works in the Teplitz-Turn area of Bohemia produced Art Nouveau-styled vases and figurines during the latter part of the 1800s through the first few decades of the twentieth century. They marked their wares with various stamps, some incorporating the name and location of the pottery with a crown or a shield. Because Bohemia was part of the Austro-Hungarian empire prior to WWI, some examples are marked Austria; items marked with the Czechoslovakia designation were made after the war.

Teplitz was a town where most of the Austrian pottery was made. There are four major contributors to this pottery. One was Amphora, also known as RStK (Reissner, Stellmacher & Kessel). This company was the originator of the Amphora line. Edward Stellmacher, who was a founding member, went out on his own, working from 1905 until 1910. During this same time, Ernst Wahliss often used Amphora molds for his wares. He did similar work and was associated with the Amphora line. Turn Teplitz was never a pottery line. It was a stamp used to signify the towns where the wares were made. There were four lines: Amphora, Paul Dachsel, Edward Stellmacher, and Ernst Wahliss. More information can be found by referring to *Monsters and Maidens, Amphora Pottery of the Art Nouveau Era*, by Byron Vreeland, and *The House of Amphora* by Richard L. Scott. All decoration described in the listings that follow is hand painted unless otherwise indicated.

Our advisor for this category is John Cobabe; he is listed in the Directory under California.

Amphora

Vase, appl flower heads, 4 upswept scrolled supports, #3581, 14x6" ...295.00
Vase, floral panels w/gold, gourd shape, #G3730, ca 1900, 16½", NM . 3,600.00
Vase, frog (3D) on lily pads on rim, mc, sm rstr, #4099/52, 10x7" .7,200.00
Vase, lady in landscape w/gold, RStK, 8½x5½" 6,600.00
Vase, lady's emb profile, 3D flowers, mc swirls/pk, #0607, 17x12" .. 1,650.00
Vase, lady's portrait, gold hdls, w/lid, #321, 7x5½", EX 6,600.00
Vase, lady's portrait, waisted neck/wide base, RStK, 5¾x5½" 5,150.00
Vase, lady's portrait (great detail) w/much gold, #468, 10½x6" . 14,500.00
Vase, lady's portrait in landscape, #464, RStK, ca 1900, 15x6" .3,350.00
Vase, lady's portrait w/much gold, bottle form, #525, 6¾", NM.. 4,250.00
Vase, lady's portrait/moth/thistles, shouldered, RStK, 12x5½" ..6,600.00
Vase, lady's portrait/water/sun setting, ovoid, RStK, 8½x4½"....6,600.00
Vase, maiden w/flowers in long hair, cylindrical, RStK, 9¾x5¾". 5,500.00
Vase, moth/flowers/garlands w/gold, slim, ftd, RStK, 15⅜"........3,000.00

Vase, portrait of Joan of Arc, #1K, red ink stamp, 6x4", $2,600.00. (Photo courtesy David Rago Auctions)

Vase, Summer Queen, #478/#999, 4⅜" 2,950.00
Vase, tiger/flowers/leaves w/gold (VG), RStK, drilled, 10¾" 950.00

Dachsel, Paul

Compote, organic/geometric designs, ivory/gr/gold, #9848, 7½x10" ..4,250.00
Jug, mushrooms w/red caps/forest scene w/lustre, #1110 6, 6⅝", NM.. 850.00
Vase, artichoke form w/faux jewels, #103/10, 6" 1,950.00
Vase, elk in landscape, circle borders w/gold, 17½" 1,550.00
Vase, invt fern fronds in relief, bl, ca 1907, 6½" 2,350.00
Vase, mushrooms w/pearlescent stems/birch trees, 5½" 1,325.00
Vase, mushrooms w/pearlescent stems/birch trees, 15¾", NM.26,500.00
Vase, pines w/appl red pine cones, 6" 1,175.00
Vase, sunrise w/gold, organic hdls, 14x6½" 6,600.00
Vase, tree trunks/leaves/berries, bl/tan/gold, cylindrical, 6", EX... 775.00
Vase, trees, emb, gr matt, #1071/10, 7¾"............................ 2,650.00
Water jug, roses/foliage/gold, 2-spout, arched hdls, #1165, 8⅛"..2,150.00

Stellmacher, Edward

Bust, lady w/ribboned hat, gold trim, sm chips, 20x16" 2,400.00
Vase, Bedouin on horsebk, mc on blk, 4 sm loop hdls, 10½"........ 150.00
Vase, cactus form w/ornate hdls/blossoms, ftd, 18" 1,550.00
Vase, roses, mc on mottle, 4 sm loop hdls, 10½" 120.00

Wahliss, Ernst

Bust, lady w/bow & sash, #4393, 15½x13" 600.00
Centerpc, 2 cherubs kissing on curled leaf form, NM 1,450.00
Ewer, Pergamon, Nouveau florals, #2416, 6⅜" 150.00
Figurine, Nouveau lady holding bird, 11½" 150.00
Plaque, Nouveau lady, leafy border, oval, 19x16" 1,325.00
Vase, birches/3 blk birds/snow w/gold, #5530II/9028, 9½" 480.00
Vase, classical lady on blk, #113, ca 1900-10, 7½" 480.00
Vase, corset form w/rtcl rim, floral w/unfired gold, 6", pr 235.00
Vase, grapes & leaves, Serapis Fayence, 1911, 5¾" 75.00
Vase, Pergamon, florals/clouds, #5639/24194, 9" 500.00
Vase, Secessionist, birds, 3-ftd, #309IIG, 1892-1910, 10"............ 600.00

Animal Dishes with Covers

Covered animal dishes have been produced for nearly two centuries and are as varied as their manufacturers. They were made in many types of glass (slag, colored, clear, and milk glass) as well as china and pottery. On bases of nests and baskets, you will find animals and birds of every sort. The most common was the hen.

Some of the smaller versions made by McKee, Indiana Tumbler and Goblet Company, and Westmoreland Specialty Glass of Pittsburgh, Pennsylvania, were sold to food-processing companies who filled them with prepared mustard, baking powder, etc. Occasionally one will be found with the paper label identifying the product and processing company still intact.

Many of the glass versions produced during the latter part of the nineteenth century have been recently reproduced. In the 1960s, the Kemple Glass Company made the rooster, fox, lion, cat, lamb, hen, horse, turkey, duck, dove, and rabbit on split-ribbed or basketweave bases. They were made in amethyst, blue, amber, and milk glass, as well as a variegated slag. Kanawha, L.G. Wright, and Imperial made several as well. It is sometimes necessary to compare items in question to verified examples of older glass in order to recognize reproductions. Reproduction is continued today.

For more information, we recommend *Collector's Encyclopedia of Milk Glass* by Betty and Bill Newbound. In the listings below, when only one dimension is given, it is the greater one, usually length. See also Greentown and other specific companies. For information on modern Westmoreland issues, we recommend *Garage Sale and Flea Market Annual* (Collector Books).

Bambi, carnival glass powder jar, Jeannette, 1950s 25.00
Cat, lacy base, blk carnival, Westmoreland, 5x8" 175.00
Cat, lacy base, vaseline, appl glass eyes, Westmoreland, 8" 550.00
Cat, wide-rib base, wht w/opaque bl head, Westmoreland 65.00
Chick on Eggs, basketweave base, frosted bl w/HP decor 40.00
Deer on Fallen Trees, milk glass w/some opal, Flaccus, 6½" L 240.00
Dog, recumbent, head & tail up, ribbed base, milk glass, McKee. 110.00
Dog, recumbent, ribbed base, milk glass, Westmoreland, 4x5½" 75.00
Dolphin, sawtooth edge, milk glass, Challinor Taylor, 8" 135.00
Dromedary Camel, recumbent, opaque custard, Vallerysthal, 7½" L..515.00
Duck, ribbed base, caramel slag w/dk amber eyes, Westmoreland .. 30.00
Duck, wavy base, milk glass, Challinor Taylor, 8" 135.00
Elephant w/Circus Blanket, ribbed base, milk glass, McKee 710.00
Elephant w/Rider, opaque bl w/mc details, Vallerysthal, 7" L....... 165.00
Fish, flat w/tail on base, milk glass, Atterbury, 8" L 200.00
Frog, eyes/upper bk on lid, frosted crystal, Co-Operative Flint, 4x6"..225.00
Hen on Nest, coral w/HP, Westmoreland, 1982, 7½x6" (+)......... 100.00
Hen on Nest, dmn basketweave base, bl, Greentown................... 300.00

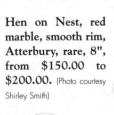

Hen on Nest, red marble, smooth rim, Atterbury, rare, 8", from $150.00 to $200.00. (Photo courtesy Shirley Smith)

Horse, recumbent, ribbed base, milk glass, McKee 55.00
Jackrabbit, ribbed base, milk glass, att Flaccus, 6¼" L................... 200.00
Lamb, picket base, milk glass, Westmoreland Specialty, 5½" 50.00

Lovebirds, brn marble, Westmoreland, 1980, 6½x5¼" 150.00
Monkey, fleur-de-lis base, milk glass, Flaccus, 6¼" 1,800.00
Mouse on Toadstool, opaque cream, Vallerysthal, ca 1908, 6" dia...660.00
Pig, recumbent, ribbed base, milk glass, McKee............................ 365.00
Quail, scroll base, milk glass, 5½" 85.00
Robin on Nest, milk glass, att Greentown, 6½" 165.00
Rooster Standing, milk glass w/red comb, yel ft, Westmoreland, 8½" ..50.00
Squirrel, split-rib base, unmk McKee, 5½" 185.00
Turkey, pebbled base, crystal, LE Smith, 1973, 7¾" 45.00
Turtle, milk glass, 2-hdld, Westmoreland, 4¼x7¼" 200.00
Water Buffalo, recumbent, milk glass, 1900s................................ 250.00
Water Buffalo w/Rider, caramel w/pnt traces, Vallerysthal, 10" L..1,450.00

Appliances, Electric

Antique electric appliances represent a diverse field and are always being sought after by collectors. There were over 100 different companies manufacturing electric appliances in the first half of the twentieth century; some were making over ten different models under several different names at any given time in all fields: coffeepots, toasters, waffle irons, etc., while others were making only one or two models for extended periods of time. Today collectors and decorators alike are seeking those items to add to a collection or to use as accent pieces in a period kitchen. Refer to *Toasters and Small Kitchen Appliances* published by L-W Book Sales for more information.

Always check the cord before use and make sure the appliance is in good condition, free of rust and pitting. Unless noted otherwise, our values are for appliances in excellent condition. Prices may vary around the country.

Broiler, Farberware Open Hearth #4550 Smokeless, stainless steel ..90.00
Coffee urn, Farberware, chrome w/red-stained wood hdls, ca 1933..30.00
Coffeepot, Farberware Superfast, chrome/blk Bakelite, 12-cup 32.50
Coffeepot, General Electric #A3P15, chrome w/glass finial, 11½". 40.00
Coffeepot, Sunbeam Vacuum Drip #C30A, chrome, 1939-44, 12x6½". 80.00
Fan, Century S3 Model #15, 4-blade, 5-speed, Pat Dec 20 1914, 20½"..385.00
Fan, Emerson #2010, 6 brass blades & cage, 1908 .... 750.00
Fan, Emerson #29646, 4 Parker blades, 1922-1925, rstr, 12" dia ..615.00
Fan, General Electric, 4-blade, CI base, 1903, 12" dia.................. 645.00
Fan, General Electric, 4-blade pancake model, 5-speed, 1905, 12" dia. 375.00
Fan, General Electric #C106576, 4-blade, oscillates, ca 1915, 12" dia..315.00
Griddle, Farberware #260, cast aluminum, immersible, 12x18" 95.00
Griddle, Farberware #260, cast aluminum, immersible, 12x18", MIB. 245.00
Heater, Arvin, Deco styling, cream enamel w/red lettering, 1940s ..20.00
Heater/fan, Arvin, heating coil surrounds blades, late 1940s 65.00
Kettle, General Electric, stainless w/cream-pnt metal hdl, 1940s, 9" . 25.00
Kettle, General Electric #4002-12, chrome, Deco styling, NMIB.. 45.00
Mixer, KitchenAid Model G, brn, 1929...................................... 435.00

Mixer, KitchenAid Model 3C, with attachments (not shown), ca. 1950s, from $25.00 to $35.00. (Photo courtesy C. Diane Zweig)

Percolator, Royal Robeston Rochester Royalite, birds/flowers, +cr/sug..95.00
Percolator, Royal Rochester, bl/wht lustre, Deco style, 1924, +cr/sug ..52.50
Percolator, Universal #E9637, chrome w/blk hdl & glass lid, 1920s, 10".. 50.00
Skillet, Farberware #344, stainless, domed lid, 12" dia 75.00
Skillet, Miracle Maid Lektro, aluminum w/blk hdls & base 175.00
Toaster, Delta Pop-Down Automatic, red w/chrome sides.............. 85.00
Toaster, Hot Point, chrome, side drops, July 28 1914 .... 57.50
Toaster, Samson Trimatic, chrome & Bakelite, 3-slot.................. 150.00
Toaster, Toast-O-Lator Model J, Deco style, blk base & hdls 150.00
Toaster, Universal #9410, 2 side buttons, needs replated, 1920s .. 235.00
Toaster oven, General Electric, Deco, chrome w/blk hdls, 10x12x7". 50.00
Vacuum cleaner, Electrolux Silverado, gray canister, +accessories ..265.00
Vacuum cleaner, General Electric, Deco-style upright, 2-speed ... 125.00
Vacuum cleaner, Vaquette, Scott & Fetzer CO...OH, upright...... 215.00
Waffle iron, Dominion #1208A, w/griddles, thermometer in lid.... 65.00

Arequipa

Following the example of the Marblehead sanatorium and pottery, the director of the Arequipa sanatorium turned to the craft of pottery as a curative occupation for his patients. In 1911 Dr. Philip K. Brown asked Frederick Hurten Rhead and his wife Agnes to move to Fairfax, California, to organize such a department. Rhead had by then an impressive resume, having worked at Vance/Avon, Weller, Roseville, Jervis, and University City. The Rheads' stay at Arequipa would be short-lived, and by 1913 they were replaced by Albert Solon, another artist from a renowned pottery family. That same year, the pottery was incorporated as a separate entity from the sanatorium and would greatly expand in the following few years. It distinguished itself with two medals at the Pan-Pacific Exposition in 1915. A third Englishman, Frederick H. Wilde, replaced Solon in 1916 and remained at the helm of the pottery until its closing in 1918.

The finest pieces produced at Arequipa were done during the Rhead years, decorated in squeeze-bag or slip-trail. Others were embossed with floral patterns and covered in single-color glazes. Early vases are marked with a hand-painted Arequipa in blue on applied white glaze or incised in the clay. Our advisors for this category are Suzanne Perrault and David Rago; they are listed in the Directory under New Jersey.

Bowl, stylized trees (squeeze-bag), ink mark, #269, 6¼" diameter, $20,400.00. (Photo courtesy David Rago Auctions/LiveAuctioneers. com)

Bowl, medallion emb, wht on plum matt, #37, 1912, rstr, 2¾x7". 900.00
Vase, cinquefoils cvd under dk gr crystalline, CH 11 77 16, 4¼x6"..2,400.00
Vase, floral band cvd under, bl-gray frothy matt, MMKW 1624, 3½" . 960.00
Vase, Greek keys/quatrefoils cvd under gr matt, NN 11 76 15, 5x3½" . 1,450.00
Vase, leaves (squeeze-bag), yel on gr, ca 1912, glaze bubbles, 8x4" . 9,600.00
Vase, quatrefoils/leaves cvd under gr/brn mottled lustre, 3x4¼", NM. 1,300.00
Vase, spade leaves in slip trails, brn/gr/dk gr, 1912, 2½x5½"......2,525.00
Vase, stylized blossoms HP in brn on gray-brn, 3½x3"............... 1,200.00

Argy-Rousseau, G.

Gabriel Argy-Rousseau produced both fine art glass and quality commercial ware in Paris, France, in 1918. He favored Art Nouveau as well as Art Deco and in the '20s produced a line of vases in the Egyptian manner, made popular by the discovery of King Tut's tomb. One of the most important types of glass he made was pate-de-verre. Most of his work is signed. Items listed below are pate-de-verre unless noted otherwise.

Box, hydrangea, purple w/wht & blk centers, 3¾" dia...............5,750.00
Box, mask (laughint) orange red on mc geometrics, 6" dia 7,000.00
Jar, honesty leaves, golden/brn tones, 3¼x3½ dia 4,200.00
Pendant, butterfly, burgundy, sq, 2¼", on gold silk cord............1,900.00
Pendant, cicada, purple & red, 2½x1¾", on purple silk cord.....1,700.00
Pendant, dogwood blossoms, 2½" dia, on bl silk cord 1,450.00
Pendant, moth, purple & fuchsia on frost w/lav, 2½" L 1,435.00
Pendant, peony blossom, 2½" dia, on ivory silk cord 1,550.00
Pendant, thistle-like blossom, red & gr, 2½" dia, on red silk cord..1,150.00
Vase, bud; eagles support cone, clear w/raspberry on purple ft, 5¼"..4,000.00

Vase, Le Jardin Des Hesperides, maiden in apple orchard, pale red, pale orange, slate gray, and ivory, 9½", $27,600.00. (Photo courtesy Skinner Inc. Auctioneers & Appraisers of Antiques & Fine Art)

Vase, stacked triangles, grs & purple, flared, ftd, 8½x5"...........12,000.00
Vase, 2 male masks/ivy, 4x2¾"...3,250.00
Veilleuse, lg moths on shade; ftd metal base, 5½" 15,800.00
Veilleuse, shade w/3 masks in vivid coral/earth-tone sqs; ftd base, 6".. 8,400.00
Veilleuse lamp shade, lg roses, bl/purples, 6x3¼" 5,000.00
Veilleuse lamp shade, spade-shaped leaves, rose garlands, 6x3¼" ..5,700.00

Art Glass Baskets

Popular novelty and gift items during the Victorian era, these one-of-a-kind works of art were produced in just about any type of art glass in use at that time. They were never marked. Many were not true production pieces but 'whimsies' made by glassworkers to relieve the tedium of the long work day. Some were made as special gifts. The more decorative and imaginative the design, the more valuable the basket. For more information we recommend *The Collector's Encyclopedia of American Art Glass* by John A. Shuman, III (Collector Books).

Note: Prices on art glass baskets have softened due to the influence of the internet which has made them much more accessible.

Cranberry to clear ft, ruffled rim, clear hdl, 12½x8" 42.50
Cranberry w/HP floral, lt gr twist hdl w/thorns, 5x6" 55.00
Crystal w/pressed pattern & etched flowers, 14x7x6½" 85.00
Pk & wht 'peppermint' stripes, swirl ribs, ruffled, clear twig hdl, 7".. 170.00
Pk opaque w/appl floral, clear rim & hdl, 8½"................................ 75.00
Pk shaded, wht int, ruffled/crimped rim w/clear edge, 1890s 72.50
Ruby cased in yel opaque, clear thorn hdl.................................... 130.00
Spatter, mc w/wht int, crimped sq top, clear thorn hdl, 1880s, 7½". 130.00
Spatter, pk w/milk glass lining, ruffled/crimped, clear thorn hdl, 4".50.00
Yel to pk scallops at pleated rim, vaseline twisted hdl, 6½x5x4" 55.00

Arts and Crafts

The Arts and Crafts movement began in England during the last quarter of the nineteenth century, and its influence was soon felt in this country. Among its proponents in America were Elbert Hubbard (see Roycroft) and Gustav Stickley (see Stickley). They rebelled against the mechanized mass production of the Industrial Revolution and against the cumulative influence of hundreds of years of man's changing taste. They subscribed to a theory of purification of style: that designs be geared strictly to necessity. At the same time they sought to elevate these basic ideals to the level of accepted 'art.' Simplicity was their virtue; to their critics it was a fault.

The type of furniture they promoted was squarely built, usually of heavy oak, and so simple was its appearance that as a result many began to copy the style which became known as 'Mission.' Soon various manufacturers' factories had geared production toward making cheap copies of the designs. In 1915 Stickley's own operation failed, a victim of changing styles and tastes. Hubbard lost his life that same year on the ill-fated *Lusitania*. By the end of the decade the style had lost its popularity.

Metalware was produced by numerous crafts people, from experts such as Dirk van Erp and Albert Berry to unknown novices. Metal items or hardware should not be scrubbed or scoured; to do so could remove or damage the rich, dark patina typical of this period. Collectors have become increasingly fussy, rejecting outright pieces with damage or alteration to their original condition (such as refinishing, patina loss, repairs, and replacements). As is true for other categories of antiques and collectibles, premium prices have been paid for objects in mint original and untouched condition. Our advisor for this category is Bruce Austin; he is listed in the Directory under New York. See also Heintz; Jewelry; Limbert; Roycroft; Silver; Stickley; van Erp; specific manufacturers.

Note: When no condition is noted within the description lines, assume that values are given for examples in excellent condition. That is, metal items retain their original patina and wooden items are still in their original finish. Values for examples in conditions other than excellent will be indicated in the descriptions with appropriate condition codes.

Key: h/cp — hammered copper

Armchair, Cortland, 3 vertical slats at bk/under arms, rfn, 35".... 450.00
Armchair, Old Hickory, caned seat & bk, 44x29x25", +caned footstool . 1,200.00

Armchair, Shop of the Crafters, inlaid with mixed woods, paper label, 39x30x30", $11,400.00. (Photo courtesy David Rago Auctions)

Bookcase, 2 door w/divided glass at top, recoated finish, 55x42x14"..1,300.00
Box, E Burton, copper w/abalone inserts, hinged clasp, 2x6¾x4"..3,500.00
Box, G Twichell (att), h/cp & enamel, maiden & deer, 2x4¾x3¾".. 10,800.00
Box, Rohlfs, cvd wood, h/cp hinges, velvet lined, 1901, 9" L..23,000.00
Brooch, Harry Dixon, hammered sterling w/citrine, #9259, 1933, 1x2". 500.00
Buttons, Liberty, Cymric silver, emb ship/orange sky, 1", 6 in box.. 2,000.00
Cabinet, Lifetime, Puritan Line, 2-shelf, panel door, 28x13x21"... 1,200.00
Candle snuffer, Kalo, hammered silver, Sterling mk, 2¼x10".... 1,000.00
Candlestick, Jarvie, bronze, emb spade-shaped leaves, unmk, 14", ea. 5,000.00
Candlesticks, Jarvie, Beta, bronze, rpl bobeches, new patina, 12", pr.1,500.00
Candlesticks, Jarvie-style, bronze, disk ft, 5½", pr........................ 350.00

Candlesticks, Liberty, SP, leaves & berries, #0530, 11x9½", VG . 2,650.00
Chair, Morris; Lifetime, reuphl w/brn leather, slat sides, 41x32x36" ..2,650.00
Chair, Morris; Shop of Crafters, leather uphl, label, 38¼"......... 9,600.00
Chair, side; Shop of Crafters, geometric inlay bk/leather seat, 43" . 1,200.00
Chairs, dining; Lifetime, #116, T-bk, reuphl seat, 5 side+1 arm.1,200.00
Chalice, Bruckmann, silver w/hardstone cabochons, gilt int, 11¼x7".. 2,500.00
Chandelier, ldgl panels w/stylized flowers, orig cap, 14x25" dia..2,200.00
Chandelier, wrought-iron geometric shade over gr & yel slag, 15x19x18"...500.00
Charger, Onondaga Metal Shops, h/cp, organic design at rim, 19" . 1,100.00
China cabinet, Lifetime, 1-pane door/sides, 3-shelf, Paine, 56x32x16"....960.00
China cabinet, Michigan Chair Co, 1-pane doors, glass sides, 56x44x16"...850.00
China cabinet, Prairie School style, 1-pane doors, glass sides, 60x52" .. 1,000.00
Clock, Liberty, pewter w/enameled face, #0721, 4¾x3¼x2½"...4,200.00
Costumer, Barber Bros, dbl posts, iron hooks, missing drip pan, 67" ..475.00
Desk, Lifetime, Puritan Line drop-front, slatted sides, 43x32x16".1,550.00
Desk, partners; McHugh (att), 2 blind drw ea side, shelf, 72" ... 1,100.00
Etching, WM Rice, CA Foothills, 6¾x8¼"+mat & fr 800.00
Fireplace surround, sailing ship/floral tiles on brn field, 50x67"..1,100.00
Footstool, Lakeside Crafters, cutouts, leather seat, 16x22x16"..1,000.00
Frame, Rohlfs, eagle shape, rustic, branded R, 1904, 11x9¾"....1,100.00
Lamp, floor; Yellin, wrought-iron twisted tripod, 19" mica shade, 60".. 4,800.00
Lamp, twisted iron base & chain, gr glass shade, 19x15x15"........ 325.00
Lantern, ldgl pk blossoms on caramel slag, 25x10½" 1,325.00
Lantern, pierced brass w/mc jewels, hanging, 14x8x11" 350.00
Linen press, English, dbl doors, 4-shelf/3-drw int, 49x43x20" .. 2,150.00
Magazine stand, unmk, cut-out sides, 4-shelf, 44⅛x13x13".......2,000.00
Mirror, hall; dmn-shape in sq fr, thru-tenons, iron hooks, rfn, 27x27" ..375.00
Mirror, hall; paneled splayed sides, pyramidal caps, hooks, 26x37" .250.00
Nightstand, Lifetime (att), shelf inside, 27½x14x14" 1,300.00
Painting, V Toothaker, mtn scene, watercolor/gouache/ink, 7¼x3"+fr...1,440.00
Pastel on paper, PJ de Lemos, Castle de Lemos...Spain, 1934, 13x10"+fr.1,325.00
Pitcher, Wm Hutton & Sons, sterling, emb/HP tulips, 5¼x5" ..1,800.00
Plate, Linossier, h/cp w/silver inlay, 6" 200.00
Plate rack, McHugh (att), dbl-X details at sides, 14x38x6".......... 300.00
Plate stand, Rohlfs, ebonized, branded R, 1901, 9x6x5"............. 1,800.00
Poker, Yellin, wrought iron/brass, 41".. 2,500.00
Rocker, arm; Barber Bros, high bk, leather cushions, label, 42" ... 550.00
Rocker, Old Hickory #37, bentwood curved bk, ash seat, re-caned, 39" ..600.00
Rocker, Plail, slatted bbl form, reuphl seat, 32x25x32" 900.00
Rug, Wm Morris style, delicate floral, rust/amber tones, 108x72". 600.00
Rug, Wm Morris style, delicate leaves, grs, 174x120"................... 800.00
Rug, Wm Morris style, Iznik pattern on emerald gr, 144x108"..1,450.00
Rug, Wm Morris style, leafy patterns, gold/dk red, 96x61"........1,440.00
Rug, Wm Morris style, leaves, cinnamon on blk, 142x111"......... 850.00
Server, gallery over 2 open shelves divided by 2 drw, 41x46x21"...1,100.00
Settee & armchair, Old Hickory, caned bks/seats, curved arms, child's...1,200.00
Settle, even-arm, canted sides, drop-in cushion, unmk, 38x74".2,275.00
Settle, JM Young, box type, reuphl burgundy leather, 34x79x30" .1,450.00
Shaker, Guild of Handicrafts, hammered sterling, jade cabochons, 3" . 1,300.00
Shaker, Liberty, sterling w/enameled leaf bands, 3½x2" 700.00
Sideboard, mirror bk/3 drw/4 doors/long drw, 55x60x22".......... 1,100.00
Spoon, Liberty, Cymric hammered sterling, #394, 8x2½" 1,200.00
Stool, folding; Rose Valley, cvd rosettes, 25x25x17" 6,000.00
Table, dining; Hastings, rnd top, ped base w/4 ft, 5 10" leaves ..1,900.00
Table, library; Michigan Chair Co, oval top, 2-shelf, 29x44x28" . 600.00
Table, Lifetime, Puritan, gate-leg extension, rfn, label, 31x48".1,675.00
Table, Rose Valley, butterflies on sq top, cvd apron, 32x24x24" .. 9,000.00
Tray, Jarvie, h/cp, rectangular, 11" L... 1,500.00
Tray, unmk, h/cp w/tooled florals/leaves, 10½"........................... 300.00
Umbrella stand, Benedict Studios, h/cp w/emb monogram, 24¾".1,800.00
Vase, Harry Dixon, h/cp, med patina, incurvate rim, 7¾x4½"..2,400.00
Vase, Iowa State, bachelor buttons, celadon gr, M Yancy, 1930, 6½"..4,500.00
Vase, Iowa State, bl-gr mottle, paneled cylinder neck, 7¼x6"..1,020.00
Vase, Tudric, hammered pewter, organic hdls, 9¾" 600.00

Vase, Jarvie, hammered copper with embossed 'TR,' riveted base, old cleaning, 12x7", $4,500.00. (Photo courtesy David Rago Auctions)

Vase, unmk R Crook, lions HP on blk & cobalt salt glaze, 9½x7½"...6,000.00
Window screen, 4-panel, acorn/leaves cvgs, ea panel: 30x6⅝"..1,300.00
Woodblock print, G Baumann, Point Lobos, 9x9"+mat & fr....8,500.00
Woodblock print, G Baumann, Woodland Meadows, 9¼x11"+mat & fr..6,500.00
Woodblock print, G Baumann, 3 Pines, 10½x9¼"+mat & fr....9,000.00
Woodblock print, JB Judson, Gorge of Genessee River..., 6x8"+mat & fr. 2,000.00
Woodblock print, M Patterson, Morning Glories, '30, 10x7¼"+mat & fr...4,200.00

Austrian Glass

Many examples of fine art glass were produced in Austria during the times of Loetz and Moser that cannot be attributed to any glasshouse in particular, though much of it bears striking similarities to the products of both artists.

Vase, bl & gold irid, pleated rim, ca 1905, 8¼"..............................215.00
Vase, bl w/mc irid, shaped rim, long stem, disk ft, 10½"...............120.00
Vase, bl w/oilspot irid, Nouveau flared cylinder w/flared ft, 11¾".275.00
Vase, brn mottle, incurvate rim, bulbous body, flared ft, 7"..........280.00
Vase, fuchsia w/strings & oil spots, ruffled rim, att Palme-Konig, 13 ..360.00
Vase, gold w/mc irid, Nouveau shape w/brass mts, ca 1904, 13¼" .1,675.00
Vase, gold-bl satin, rnd w/short neck, appl 'worm' under hdls, WMT, 5".450.00
Vase, gr irid w/platinum tendrils, vertical ribs, ruffled rim, 5½"....115.00
Vase, gr/purple lustre, swollen stick neck, fancy pewter sgn/#d mt, 7". 585.00

Vase, iridescent purple tones, Heliosine, 6", $275.00. (Photo courtesy Morphy Auctions/LiveAuctioneers.com)

Vase, irid w/random vines, in hdld bronze Nouveau shoulder mt, 11x3" .540.00
Vase, peachblow, gold pheasant, cup-top stick neck, #1122 V429, 10" ..385.00
Vase, purple w/threading, ruffled rim, att Palme-Konig, 6½"........540.00
Vase, ruby w/floral o/l, gourd shape w/3 twisted hdls, Kralik, 9" .2,300.00
Vase, sapphire bl w/dk ribs & EX irid, Kralik, ca 1900, 21".......1,250.00
Vase, wine irid, notched rim/folded-bk hdls, Palme-Konig & Habel, 9" ..265.00

Autographs

Autographs can be as simple as signatures on cards or album pages, signed photos, signed documents, or letters, but they can also be signed balls, bats, T-shirts, books, and a variety of other items.

Simple signatures are the most common form and thus are usually of lesser value than signed photos, letters, or anything else. But as with any type of collectible, the condition of the autograph is paramount to value. If the signature is in pencil, value drops automatically by one-half or more. If the item signed is torn, creased, stained, laminated or is a menu, bus ticket, magazine page, or something unusual, many collectors will avoid buying these because they are less desirable than a nice dark ink signature on an undamaged card or autograph album page.

When pricing signed photos, many variables come into play. Size is important (all things being equal, the larger the photo, the more it's worth), as is condition (wrinkles, tape stains, tears, or fading will all have a negative impact). If the signature is signed over a dark area, making it difficult to see, the photo's value can drop by 90%. Finally, the age of the signed photo will cause the value to increase or decrease. Generally speaking, if the photo is signed when the celebrity was young and not well known, it will be worth more than those signed in later years. For example, the photos signed by Shirley Temple as a child are worth hundreds of dollars, whereas her adult-signed photos can be purchased for as little as $20.00.

The savvy autograph buyer or antique/collectibles dealer needs to know that since the 1950s, many U.S. Presidents, politicians, and astronauts commonly used (and still do) a machine known as the 'autopen,' a mechanical device that 'signs' photos and letters for fans requesting an autograph through the mail. The tip-off to an auto-penned signature is that each one will be identical.

Autopens aren't so common with movie and television stars, however. If you were to write to a famous entertainer asking for a signed photo, the chances are extremely high you'll either receive a photo signed by a secretary or one bearing a 'machine-imprinted' signature which will appear as real ink on the photo.

Yes, there are authentic and valuable autographs out there, but make sure you are buying from a reputable autograph dealer or from a seller who has convincing evidence that what his offering is genuine. The internet is full of autograph auction sites that sell forgeries, so always beware of a deal with a price that's too good to be true — you might be getting conned!

Most reputable autograph dealers belong to one of several autograph organizations: the UACC (The Universal Autograph Collectors Club) or The Manuscript Society. If you buy from a dealer, make sure the autograph has a lifetime guarantee of authenticity. If you buy from a private party, then as the old saying goes, '...let the buyer beware!' Just because the autograph listed for sale says it comes with a 'COA' (Certificate of Authenticity) doesn't mean it's authentic if the seller is a forger or unscrupulous dealer. Our advisor for autographs is Tim Anderson; he listed in the Directory under Utah.

Key:
ALS — handwritten letter	ISP — inscribed signed photo
ANS — handwritten note signed	LH — Letterhead
AQS — autographed quotation signed	LS — signed letter, typed or written by someone else
COA — certificate of authenticity	sig — signature
DS — document signed	SP — signed photo
ins — inscription	

Ali, Muhammed; SP, color, 8x10"...145.00
Aniston, Jennifer; SP, topless portrait, color, 8x10", +COA..........40.00
Armstrong, Louis (Sachmo); sig in gr ink on wht pg....................150.00
Armstrong, Neil; sig (bold) on cover of Apollo 11, 20th Anniv program. 1,200.00
Astaire, Fred; sig on clipped pg, matted w/blk & wht 9x7" photo ...215.00
Ball, Lucille; SP, color, 8x10", +COA...150.00
Berlin, Irving; sig on clipped paper, w/blk & wht picture...............36.00
Bird, Larry; sig on basketball, +COA...180.00
Brooks, Garth; sig on cover of Rolling Stone magazine, 1993, +COA ..95.00

Buffalo Bill (Wm. F. Cody), cabinet card inscribed 'True to Friend and Foe,' 4x2¼" on 6x4" mount, minor wear and restoration, $1,800.00.

(Photo courtesy Early American History Auctions/LiveAuctioneers.com)

Cagney, James; sig on pg, matted w/early blk & wht photo 95.00
Clark, Will; sig on baseball 85.00
Coolidge, Grace; sig (4" L)on clipped paper, 2½x4½" 55.00
Dangerfield, Rodney; sig on clipped pg, matted w/blk & wht 9x7" photo. 180.00
Davis, Bette; sig on clipped pg, matted w/early blk & wht photo... 95.00
Day, Doris; SP, color, 8x10", +mat & fr 120.00
Dietrich, Marlene; SP, blk & wht, 9x7"+mat & fr 150.00
DiMaggio, Joe; sig on baseball, +COA 545.00
Duvall, Robert; SP, from Apocalypse Now, 8x10", +COA 62.50
Earnhardt, Dale; SP, color, matted w/2 sm photos, +fr 65.00
Ellington, Duke; SP, blk & wht, 8x10" 120.00
Esposito, Phil; sig on Espo Line poster 120.00
Frost, Robert; sig on clipped pg mtd w/blk & wht 8x10" photo.... 240.00
Gable, Clark; SP, sepia, 11x14" 2,500.00
Gershwin, George; sig on card, w/newspaper clipping 240.00
Goldwater, Barry; SP, blk & wht, 8x10" 45.00
Griffith, Andy; SP, blk & wht, 7x9" 25.00
Harpo (Marx), ins sig on Harpo Speaks! 1st edition book 480.00
Hayes, Rutherford B; sig on card dtd 1881, 3x5¼" 235.00
Hepburn, Katharine; sig on playbill from Colonial 145.00
Hodges, Gil; sig on baseball, 1966 .... 30.00
Hoover, Herbert; sig on Hoover...Documented Narrative, 1st edition... 60.00
Jackson, Janet; SP, blk & wht, 8x10" 30.00
Jagger, Mick; sig on Rolling Stones Love You Live LP album cover, +COA. 65.00
Johnson, London B; SP (not autopen), blk & wht, 8x10" 750.00
Jolie, Angelina; SP, color, 8x10", +COA 60.00
Jones, Catherine Zeta; SP, color, 8x10", +COA 37.50
Jordan, Michael; sig on photo cover of ESPN magazine, 1990 .... 60.00
Lincoln, Abraham; sig on alum pg 4,000.00
Loy, Myrna; SP, color, w/COA 30.00
Madison, James; ALS, 1-pg, dtd 1805 .... 1,650.00
Mantle, Mickey; sig on baseball cap 275.00
Marshall, George C; sig on card 50.00
Mays, Willie; sig on baseball bat, Cooperstown Bat Co logo, +COA . 175.00

McDaniel, Hattie; inscribed signed photo, dated 1945, 8x10", $900.00.

Nicholson, Jack; SP, from The Shining, color, 8x10", +COA 40.00
Ride, Sally; SP, in bl NASA shirt, color, 8x10", +COA 36.00
Rogers, Will; ins sig on clipped pg, w/blk & wht picture 300.00

Rutherford, Ann; SP, from Gone w/Wind, blk & wht 8x10", +COA .. 35.00
Smith, Anna Nicole; SP, sexy, color, 8x10", +COA 165.00
Stewart, James; SP, blk & wht, 8x10" 30.00
Swarzenegger, Arnold; sig on Last Action Hero poster, +COA 75.00
Truman, Harry; TLS, 1-pg, dtd Dec 1948, +fr 325.00
Westmoreland, General William C; sig on banquet program 24.00
Williams, Ted; SP, blk & wht, in uniform, bl ink, 8x10" 240.00
Wood, Natalie; ISP, blk & wht, as child, 8x10" 150.00
Woods, Tiger; SP, golf action, color, 8x10", +COA 155.00
Young, Loretta; ISP, blk & wht close-up portrait, 8x10" 115.00

Automobilia

While some automobilia buffs are primarily concerned with restoring vintage cars, others concentrate on only one area of collecting. For instance, hood ornaments were often quite spectacular. Made of chrome or nickel plate on brass or bronze, they were designed to represent the 'winged maiden' Victory, flying bats, sleek greyhounds, soaring eagles, and a host of other creatures. Today they often bring prices in the $75.00 to $200.00 range. R. Lalique glass ornaments go much higher!

Horns, radios, clocks, gear shift knobs, and key chains with company emblems are other areas of interest. Generally, items pertaining to the classics of the '30s are most in demand. Paper advertising material, manuals, and catalogs in excellent condition are also collectible.

License plate collectors search for the early porcelain-on-cast-iron examples. First year plates (e.g., Massachusetts, 1903; Wisconsin, 1905; Indiana, 1913) are especially valuable. The last of the states to issue regulation plates were South Carolina and Texas in 1917, and Florida in 1918. While many northeastern states had registered hundreds of thousands of vehicles by the 1920s making these plates relatively common, those from the southern and western states of that period are considered rare. Naturally, condition is important. While a pair in mint condition might sell for as much as $100.00 to $125.00, a pair with chipped or otherwise damaged porcelain may sometimes be had for as little as $25.00 to $30.00. Unless noted otherwise our values are for examples in excellent to near mint condition. Our advisor for this category is Leonard Needham; he is listed in the Directory under California. See also Gas Globes and Panels.

Badge, hat; Yellow Cab, enamel over nickel silver, 2½" 60.00
Bank, 1951 Styleline Deluxe Club Coupe Chevrolet promo, PMC, 7¾".. 65.00
Book, Buick Facts 1946, red/wht/bl cover, 114-pg, 6½x5" 95.00
Book, Chevrolet America's Most Popular Car, for showroom, 1947, 29-pg..155.00
Book, 70 Years of Buick, Crestline Publishing, 1973, VG 32.50
Booklet, Dodge Brothers Brief History of Great Achievement, 1928 ..50.00
Booklet, Studebaker, Pathfinding for the Glidden Tour, 1909, 6x4¾".. 155.00
Booklet, Studebaker a Story of Contests, 1909, 7¾x9¾" 45.00
Brochure, Buick, full-pg views of 1934 models, 50+pgs, 10x14" 90.00
Brochure, Cadillac Deville, Eldorado, Fleetwood & Series 62, 1956.. 25.00
Brochure, Chevrolet, 1958 models, opens to 14½x20½" 15.00
Brochure, Dodge Power Wagon, blk/wht/bl cover, 1949 .... 48.00
Brochure, Edsel, 1958 models in color, opens to 50x24" 32.00
Brochure, Oldsmobile 6 & 8, Prices - Terms..., 1934, unfolds: 12x8", M.. 45.00
Cap, Yellow Cab, worsted fabric w/leather brim, cello badge 80.00
Car vase, Ford, etched glass, ca 1915 .... 62.50
Catalog, Chevrolet Truck Parts, 1955-65, 804-pg, GG 20.00
Catalog, Lil' 500 America's No 1 Kart & Scooter Linc, 1960s, G.. 25.00
Catalog, Mr Bug Street & Off Road Parts, illus, 1980, 122-pg 40.00
Catalog, Studebaker Modern Accessories, blk & wht illus, 1941... 50.00
Catalog, The White Steam Car, Models K&L, 1908, 26-pg, 6x9", VG . 75.00
Catalog, Western Auto Supply Co, 1928 Auto Owner's Supply Book ..20.00
Catalog, World Car 1970, 439-pg 55.00
Chalkboard, Chevrolet, Chalk Talk, ca 1960s, 28x17" 100.00
Clock, Chrysler, glass bubble face, lights up, Telechron, NM....... 535.00

Clock, Packard, yellow neon, ca. 1950s, 26", NM, $1,800.00. (Photo courtesy Morphy Auctions/ LiveAuctioneers.com)

Coin, Ford Thunderbird 35th ltd ed, silver, w/holder & booklet, M .. 65.00
Emblem, radiator; Chevrolet, cloisonnè, 1931, 3x3", VG+ 60.00
Emblem, trunk; Dodge Brothers, enameled metal shield w/wings, 1930s. 80.00
Gauge, tire pressure; Studebaker, US Gauge Co 120.00
Handbook, Hand Book of Gasoline Automobiles 1912, 200+pgs, VG .65.00
Hood ornament, Buick, goddess figural, NP diecast zinc, 1928 .... 415.00
Hood ornament, Cadillac, Deco nude figural, chrome, 1936, rare ..295.00
Hood ornament, Cadillac emblem, chrome w/mc enameling 32.50
Hood ornament, Chevrolet, bird figural, chrome plated, 1953-54 . 80.00
Hood ornament, Chevrolet, Deco bird, chrome w/blk stripes, 1937 ..115.00
Hood ornament, Chevrolet, gazelle, gold pnt, ca 1951, 14½" L... 170.00
Hood ornament, Chevrolet, Viking figural, silver-tone metal, 1931-32 . 90.00
Hood ornament, Chrysler, gazelle figural, cast metal, 1932, 2½x5" .235.00
Hood ornament, Dodge, goddess figural, chrome plated, ca 1950, 17" L.. 90.00
Hood ornament, Dodge, ram figural, chrome, 1946-47, 14¼" L..... 80.00
Hood ornament, Oldsmobile, winged creature, pitted chrome, 15" L, G. 42.50
Hood ornament, Packard, Lady of Speed figural, chrome, 1929-31.. 145.00
Hood ornament, Packard, swan w/wings up, chrome, ca 1949, 8x6½". 88.00
Hood ornament, Studebaker, 'dog bone' shape, chrome, Boyce, 1920s-30s.. 150.00
Hubcap part, Packard, enamel on metal, ca 1932-33, 4½" dia 215.00
Hubcaps, Cadillac, spoke wheel, 16½", 4 for................................ 215.00
Jacket, Corvette 25th Anniversary, silver/blk/red, zip front, 1978, M ..80.00
Key holder, Hupmobile, emb metal, scarce 70.00
Lapel pin, Edsel Ford Registered Mechanic, gold & bl enamel 40.00
Lapel pin, Studebaker Star Honor Club, red enamel on silver..... 125.00
License plate topper, Pontiac & Cadillac emblems, 1930s-40s, 4x5" . 25.00
Lighter, Buick Retirement Club, Zippo, 1950s, MIB 165.00
Manual, Buick Chassis Service All Series, 1972 .... 40.00
Manual, Ford, Lincoln, Mercury & Edsel Special Tools, 1958 .... 25.00
Manual, Motor's Auto Repair Manual, 18th ed, 1955, VG 10.00
Manual, owner's; Buick, 1955, w/insert, M in VG envelope 55.00
Manual, owner's; Chrysler Imperial, 1962...................................... 35.00
Manual, owner's; Studebaker Champion, 48-pg, 1949 .... 32.50
Manual, salesman's; Studebaker Inside Facts, 1954 .... 275.00
Motometer, Buick, Boyce, missing glass lens, 5x3⅞" dia 40.00
Motometer, Ford Model T, brass w/wings, Boyce, ca 1924, 2¼x6¾".. 95.00
Pennant, Buick 1916 in bl on gr & pk felt, 9x28"........................... 75.00
Pennant, Harley-Davidson, blk on orange, 12x5½" 190.00
Pin-bk, Chevrolet, Watch the Leader, band leader, ¾" 20.00
Pin-bk, Chrysler Desoto 2 for 1 in '41, red/yel/bl, 2½" 37.50
Pin-bk, Yellow Cab, No 1 Safe Driver, enamel on gold-tone shield . 240.00
Pin-bk, Yellow Cab, orange cello, Maier Lavaty, 2¼" 50.00
Postcard, Best Buick Yet, 1941 red sedan 30.00
Postcard, Chevrolet dealership photo located on Route 66 in CA, 1950s. 57.50
Poster, Cadillac Has Earned..., red/wht/bl, 1943, 38x25".............. 115.00
Press kit, Cadillac Seville Eldorado Convertible, 1976 .... 40.00
Promo record, Ford the Going Thing, 1969, 33⅓ LP...................... 75.00
Promotional car, Buick Reatta, pewter, 1½x4¾x2" 240.00
Promotional car, Buick Roadmaster, pnt metal, Brooklin, 1994, MIB. 58.00
Promotional car, Buick Skylark 1954 convertible, red & cream, 8½" .. 55.00
Promotional car, Buick Wildcat, diecast metal, 1964, 8", VG...... 120.00
Promotional car, Cadillac Eldorado Brougham 1957, Franklin Mint, MIB..62.50
Promotional car, Cadillac Eldorado 1976 convertible, Privelege, MIB. 615.00

Promotional car, Chevrolet 1956 Convertible, Franklin Mint, MIB . 60.00
Promotional car, Edsel Tu-Tone Hardtop 1958, friction type 50.00
Promotional car, Oldsmobile Cutlass, Cypress Green, Jo-Han, 1974, MIB..37.50
Promotional car, Studebaker 1962 convertible, blk 50.00
Promotional car, Yellow Cab, tin litho, friction, Japan, 1950s, 6".. 80.00
Promotional car/bank, Dodge sedan, pot metal, Banthrico, 1950s, 8", VG .100.00
Repair kit, tire tube; GM Chevrolet, blk/yel can w/contents 135.00
Rule, Studebaker, wood, folding, early 1900s, 12" 55.00
Shift knob, Dodge Brothers, butterscotch Bakelite & NP brass ... 225.00
Sign, Chevrolet Super Service, tin litho, 60x56", G 525.00
Sign, GM Chevrolet Genuine Parts, tin litho, 1950s-60s, 23x18" ..535.00
Sign, Studebaker...Service, pnt porc, 31½x48", G 850.00
Speedometer, Ford Special, Stewart-Warner Co, magnetic type, ca 1914 . 90.00
Watch fob, Dodge Brothers, blk/bl/gray enamel on metal, leather strap. 30.00

Autumn Leaf

In 1933 the Hall China Company designed a line of dinnerware for the Jewel Tea Company, who offered it to their customers as premiums. Although you may hear the ware referred to as 'Jewel Tea,' it was officially named 'Autumn Leaf' in the 1940s. In addition to the dinnerware, frosted Libbey glass tumblers, stemware, and a melmac service with the orange and gold bittersweet pod were available over the years, as were tablecloths, plastic covers for bowls and mixers, and metal items such as cake safes, hot pads, coasters, wastebaskets, and canisters. Even shelf paper and playing cards were made to coordinate. In 1958 the International Silver Company designed silver-plated flatware in a pattern called 'Autumn' which was to be used with dishes in the Autumn Leaf pattern. A year later, a line of stainless flatware was introduced. These accessory lines are prized by collectors today.

One of the most fascinating aspects of collecting the Autumn Leaf pattern has been the wonderful discoveries of previously unlisted pieces. Among these items are two different bud-ray lid one-pound butter dishes; most recently a one-pound butter dish in the 'Zephyr' or 'Bingo' style; a miniature set of the 'Casper' salt and pepper shakers; coffee, tea, and sugar canisters; a pair of candlesticks; an experimental condiment jar; and a covered candy dish. All of these china pieces are attributed to the Hall China Company. Other unusual items have turned up in the accessory lines as well and include a Libbey frosted tumbler in a pilsner shape, a wooden serving bowl, and an apron made from the oilcloth (plastic) material that was used in the 1950s tablecloth. These latter items appear to be professionally done, and we can only speculate as to their origin. Collectors believe that the Hall items were sample pieces that were never meant to be distributed.

Hall discontinued the Autumn Leaf line in 1978. At that time the date was added to the backstamp to mark ware still in stock in the Hall warehouse. A special promotion by Jewel saw the reintroduction of basic dinnerware and serving pieces with the 1978 backstamp. These pieces have made their way into many collections. Additionally, in 1979 Jewel released a line of enamel-clad cookware and a Vellux blanket made by Martex which were decorated with the Autumn Leaf pattern. They continued to offer these items for a few years only, then all distribution of Autumn Leaf items was discontinued.

It should be noted that the Hall China Company has produced several limited edition items for the National Autumn Leaf Collectors Club (NALCC): a New York-style teapot (1984); an Edgewater vase (1987, different than the original shape); candlesticks (1988); a Philadelphia-style teapot, creamer, and sugar set (1990); a tea-for-two set and a Solo tea set (1991), a donut jug, and a large oval casserole. Later came the small ball jug, one-cup French teapot, and a set of four chocolate mugs. Other special items over the past few years made for them by Hall China include a sugar packet holder, a chamberstick, and an oyster cocktail. Additional items are scheduled for production. All of these are plainly marked as having been made for the NALCC and are appropriately dated. A few other pieces have been made by Hall as limited editions for China Specialties, but these are easily identified: the Airflow teapot and the Norris refrigerator pitcher (neither of which was previously decorated with the Autumn Leaf decal), a square-handled beverage mug, and the new-style Irish mug. A production problem with the square-handled mugs halted their production. Additional items available now are a covered onion soup, tall bud vase, china kitchen memo board, canisters, and egg drop-style salt and pepper shakers with a mustard pot. They have also issued a deck of playing cards and Libbey tumblers. See *Garage Sale & Flea Market Annual* (Collector Books) for suggested values for club pieces. Our advisor for this category is Gwynneth Harrison; she is listed in the Directory under California. For more information we recommend *Collector's Encyclopedia of Hall China, Third Edition,* by Margaret and Kenn Whitmyer.

Baker, cake; Heatflow clear glass, Mary Dunbar, 1½-qt, from $65 to..85.00
Baker, French, 3-pt 25.00
Blanket, Autumn Leaf color, Vellux, twin sz, from $100 to.......... 175.00
Bowl, cereal; 6", from $8 to 12.00
Bowl, cream soup; hdls.. 40.00
Bowl, fruit; 5½", from $3 to 6.00
Bowl, mixing; New Metal, 3-pc set 325.00
Bowl, Royal Glas-Bake, set of 4, from $300 to............................ 450.00
Bowl, vegetable; divided, oval 125.00
Bowl, vegetable; oval, Melmac, from $40 to 50.00
Bowl, vegetable; oval, w/lid, from $50 to 70.00
Bowl cover set, plastic, 8-pc, 7 assorted covers in pouch 100.00
Bread box, metal, from $400 to 800.00
Butter dish, 1-lb, regular, ruffled top...................................... 500.00
Butter dish, ¼-lb, regular, ruffled top, from $175 to 250.00
Cake safe, metal, motif on top or sides, 5", ea................................ 50.00
Calendar, 1920s to 1930s, from $100 to 200.00
Candlesticks, metal, Douglas, pr from $70 to........................... 100.00
Candy dish, metal base, from $500 to 600.00
Canisters, sq, 4-pc set, from $295 to....................................... 350.00
Casserole, rnd, w/lid, 2-qt, from $30 to 45.00
Coaster, metal, 3⅛" 8.00
Coffee percolator, electric, all china, 4-pc, from $325 to.............. 400.00
Coffeepot, all china, 4-pc, from $275 to 350.00
Cooker, waterless, metal, Mary Dunbar, from $50 to 75.00
Cookie jar, Tootsie, Rayed... 310.00
Cookware, New Metal, 7-pc set, from $450 to............................. 700.00
Creamer & sugar bowl, Ruffled-D, 1940s style, from $40 to 65.00
Custard cup, Radiance 10.00
Fondue set, complete, from $200 to 300.00

Gravy boat, $25.00.

Gravy boat w/underplate (pickle dish)............................... 55.00
Hot pad, metal, oval, 10¾", from $12 to 15.00
Marmalade, 3-pc, from $100 to 125.00
Mug, conic 65.00
Mustard, 3-pc, from $100 to 120.00
Napkin, ecru muslin, 16" sq... 50.00

Place mat, paper, scalloped, set of 8, from $150 to........................ 325.00
Plate, 6", from $5 to...8.00
Plate, 7¼", from $5 to... 10.00
Platter, oval, 13½"... 28.00
Saucepan, metal, w/lid, 2-qt 100.00
Shakers, Casper, ruffled, regular, pr...................................... 30.00
Teapot, Rayed, long spout, 1935, from $75 to........................ 95.00
Teapot, Rayed, long spout, 1978, rare, from $800 to................. 1,600.00
Tidbit tray, 3-tier.. 100.00
Tin, fruitcake; wht or tan... 10.00
Toaster cover, plastic, Mary Dunbar 50.00
Towel, tea; cotton, 16x33"... 60.00
Toy, Jewel Truck, gr, from $350 to 425.00
Toy, Jewel Van, brn, Buddy L, from $400 to........................... 650.00
Tray, glass, wood hdl 140.00
Tray, metal, oval.. 100.00
Tumbler, Brockway, 9-oz, 13-oz or 16-oz, ea............................. 45.00
Tumbler, Libbey, frosted, 9-oz, 3¾"....................................... 32.00

Aviation

Aviation buffs are interested in any phase of flying, from early developments with gliders, balloons, airships, and flying machines to more modern innovations. Books, catalogs, photos, patents, lithographs, ad cards, and posters are among the paper ephemera they treasure alongside models of unlikely flying contraptions, propellers and rudders, insignia and equipment from WWI and WWII, and memorabilia from the flights of the Wright Brothers, Lindbergh, Earhart, and the Zeppelins. See also Militaria. Our advisor for this category is John R. Joiner; he is listed in the Directory under Georgia. Our values are for examples in near mint to mint condition unless noted otherwise.

Badge, hat; South African Airways pilot, type 1, 2½" W 160.00
Badge, hat; Transamerica Airlines, emb metal w/bl enamel........... 60.00
Badge, hat; Transcontinental & Western captain, brass chief's head .. 120.00
Bag, Pan Am crew, logo on dk bl canvas, shoulder strap, 11x16x6". 135.00
Bag, Pan Am messenger, bl logo on wht vinyl, shoulder strap, 11x12". 145.00
Book, Ozark Air Lines Contrails, pictorial history, hardbound, 1983.215.00
Brochure, Air-India 40 Yrs, 12-pg 55.00
Brochure, Graf Zeppelin Passenger Trips, 1928-30, 6-pg, 8x9"..... 215.00
Brochure, Pan Am World Airways Boeing 707, mc, ca 1958, 20-pg.. 60.00

Cachet for Graf Zeppelin First Flight, United States – Germany, October 1928, VG, $90.00. (Photo courtesy Jackson's International Auctioneers and Appraisers of Fine Art & Antiques)

Calendar, Alaska Northern..., Yard Antarctica plane, 1932, 20x13¼". 165.00
Cap, Braniff Airlines pilot, bl w/gold braid & badge, 1960s 125.00
Cart, serving; stainless steel/aluminum, hand brake, 40x12xx34". 250.00
Clock, travel alarm; Pan Am, windup, Sloan, 1950s, 3x3"............. 70.00

Cordials, Pan Am, stemmed, 1960s, 4", set of 12, MIB 145.00
Dispenser/coffee thermos, TWA Arrow, stainless steel, 1930s-40s, 17" .. 185.00
Flag, Braniff on wht nylon, Dura-Lite, 72x120" 140.00
Flatware, Air France Concorde, Art Moderne, 1965, 12-pc........... 85.00
Flatware, Japan Airlines, 1980s, 28-pc set.................................... 100.00
Hat, Pan Am attendant, navy wool, Escrello, 1980s...................... 85.00
Ice bucket, Pan Am, International Silver Co, 8¼" 60.00
Luggage label, Am Airlines, Airship Hindenburg, mc paper, 5¼" L.. 55.00
Luggage label, Pennsylvania Airlines, tri-motor plain, 1938, 3x4½". 65.00
Manual, flight; F-4 Phantom pilot's, 500+ pgs in 3-ring binder, 1975 . 315.00
Manual, TWA Boeing 727 flight handbook, 1980s, 12x11½" 85.00
Menu, Pan Am Airways System, 1935, unfolds to: 12x19", VG .. 260.00
Model, Airbus A-330, resin, removable wings, chrome stand, 1:50 scale . 750.00
Model, Boeing Model 314 Dixie Clipper Flying Boat, aluminum, 32" W. 365.00
Model, Boeing 747 SP, PacMin, 1:100 scale, MIB 650.00
Model, Continental Airlines A-300, resin, Atlantic, 1:100 scale, MIB.. 275.00
Model, NW Orient Boeing 707, PacMin, late 1960s, 1:100 scale . 485.00
Model, Republic F-105/FH-105 Thunderchief Fighter/bomber jet, aluminum.. 495.00
Model, TWA Boeing 707-320, pnt mahog, 1:100 scale, MIB........ 70.00
Pennant, Goodyear Zeppelin, Akron OH, felt, 30" 65.00
Photo, Boeing B-314 Pan Am Clipper, blk & wht, 1939, 8x10" 60.00
Pin, Am Airlines 15 Yr Service, 10k gold, full wreath, screw-bk . 140.00
Pin, lapel; Hughes Aircraft 25 Yr Service, 10k gold & dmn........... 80.00
Pin, Zeppelin airship form, silver, mk Sterling, 1x3½"................... 75.00
Pin-bk, Lindbergh portrait over plane silhouette, cello, 1¼" 55.00
Pin-bk, Pan Am 40 Year Service, 10k gold w/bl enamel logo, MIB.. 265.00

Platter, Graf Zeppelin, made by Heinrich & Co., Bavaria, 1928, 12x9", $2,000.00. (Photo courtesy Richard Wallin)

Propeller/prop, wood, US Propeller Inc, 43" 165.00
Propeller/prop, wood w/red pnt tips, 32", VG 120.00
Scarf, Braniff Airlines, printed silk (polyester), Pucci, 24x24" 215.00
Sign, Eastern Airlines...Silver Fleet, porc, red/wht/bl, 14" dia 110.00
Sign, Taylorcraft America's Most..., porc on steel, 1946, 14x10" . 200.00
Timetable, Aloha Airlines, columnar format, trifold, 1959 .... 55.00
Timetable, British Airways Ltd, 4-pg, 1935................................... 130.00
Timetable, Eastern Airlines, columnar format, route map, 1936.... 65.00
Timetable, Northwest Airways, columnar format, 1932 .... 100.00
Uniform, Pan Am attendant, Stonington USA, 1980s, 6-pc+badge+pins.. 260.00
Uniform, TWA captain, Thorngate Uniforms, w/gold wings, 1970s.. 275.00
Validation plate, Alaska Airlines, emb metal 85.00
Validation plate, Aloha Airlines, pressed metal, 2x3½" 60.00
Wings, Air Tanzania Airlines pilot, gold w/bl, clutch bk, 3" W ... 150.00
Wings, Darr Aero Tech Military Flight Commander, silver/enamel, 1940s.. 275.00
Wings, Saudia Airlines pilot, gold w/gr enameling, pin-bk, 3" W . 230.00
Wings, TWA Flight Service Manager, silver-tone, 1¼x2¾" 235.00
Wristwatch, Pan Am pilot, 2-tone, 24-hr dial, Gruen, 1943........ 235.00

Baccarat

The Baccarat Glass company was founded in 1765 near Luneville, France, and continues to this day to produce quality crystal tableware, vases, perfume bottles, and figurines. The firm became famous for the high-quality millefiori and caned paperweights produced there from 1845

until about 1860. Examples of these range from $300.00 to as much as several thousand. Since 1953 they have resumed the production of paperweights on a limited edition basis. Our advisors for this category are Randall Monsen and Rod Baer; their address is listed in the Directory under Virginia. See also Bottles, Commercial Perfume; Paperweights.

Box, cut crystal w/starburst base, brass mts, 4½x5x3½" 360.00
Campana urn, cut crystal w/bronze doré mts/rims, mid-20th C, 14x9", pr. 3,250.00
Candelabra, 5-light, crystal & bronze w/winged figures/swans, 23", pr.. 2,400.00
Candlesticks, swirled crystal, 9", pr 360.00
Chandelier, crystal/silver, 10 candle lights, ca 1860, 57x36".. 12,000.00
Chandelier, draped/cascading prisms, 26" doré ceiling mt, 72x40".. 30,000.00
Chandelier, foliate cast candle arms, 12-light, prisms, 32x28" .. 4,000.00
Chandelier, Louis XV style w/gilt fr, 8-light, crystal drops, 27x28".. 2,300.00
Chandelier, tiered vasiform std, rope-twist supports, 10-light, 36".. 3,200.00

Cologne bottles, Rose Tiente Swirl, 6", from $125.00 to $150.00 for the pair. (Photo courtesy Early Auction Co.)

Cornucopias, cut crystal w/bronze doré/marble bases, 11x7½", pr .6,600.00
Decanter, cut crystal, paneled sides, faceted stopper, +12 wines .. 425.00
Decanter, cut crystal, sq w/flattened stopper, 9½x4" 350.00
Decanter, Louis XIII Remi Martin, crystal fleur-de-lis, 11x7"....... 300.00
Decanter set, 6½" decanter+5 cordials in glass/gilt-mtd 12" box ... 1,200.00
Figurine, eagle w/wings wide, 7x9½", MIB.................................. 360.00
Figurine, hippo standing, 3x5¾", MIB 275.00
Figurine, jaguar crouching, 3½x10", MIB.................................... 360.00
Figurine, leopard sitting, blk, 6¼", MIB 300.00
Figurine, polar bear, 6½" L... 300.00
Goblet, wine; etched crystal w/gold lily-of-valley, 7", 12 for 2,400.00
Ice bucket, crystal w/gold hdls, box-pleat design, 9x8" 425.00
Ice bucket, crystal w/gold hdls, 9x11", MIB................................ 725.00
Ice bucket, cut crystal w/gold rim, bail hdl, 6x9" dia, +tongs 395.00
Inkwell, swirled crystal, Gorham silver cap, 6x4½" 480.00
Lamp, table; bronze/crystal column form w/Corinthian capital, 25" .. 1,650.00
Obelisk, crystal, 9⅞" 395.00
Obelisk, crystal, 18" 780.00
Punch bowl, cut crystal w/bronze doré acanthus leaves/mts, 1860, 17"... 5,500.00
Punch bowl, Deco cuttings, ftd, 8½x11¾" 550.00
Rose bowl, sunflower cuttings, 8½x8" 350.00
Vase, cut crystal w/gilt bronze mts & rim, 21¼".......................... 1,800.00
Vase, cut crystal w/gold ormulu mts, hdls w/cut beads, w/lid, 19" ... 1,950.00
Vase, Diane, thick cut crystal, 10x6"... 500.00
Vase, opal crystal w/floral sprays all over, bulbous, 9¾x8"............. 115.00
Vase, smoked glass w/etched/gilt swallows, bronze ft, 9½", pr.. 3,600.00
Vase, spiral cuttings, swollen cylinder, 9¾" 360.00
Washbowl & pitcher, flat-cut crystal, 14½", 11¼" 660.00

Badges

The breast badge came into general usage in this country about 1840. Since most are not marked and styles have changed very little to the present day, they are often difficult to date. The most reliable clue is the pin and catch. One of the earliest types, used primarily before the turn of the century, involved a 't-pin' and a 'shell' catch. In a second style, the pin was hinged with a small square of sheet metal, and the clasp was cylindrical. From the late 1800s until about 1940, the pin and clasp were made from one continuous piece of thin metal wire. The same type, with the addition of a flat back plate, was used a little later. There are exceptions to these findings, and other types of clasps were also used. Hallmarks and inscriptions may also help pinpoint an approximate age.

Badges have been made from a variety of materials, usually brass or nickel silver; but even solid silver and gold were used for special orders. They are found in many basic shapes and variations — stars with five to seven points, shields, disks, ovals, and octagonals being most often encountered. Of prime importance to collectors, however, is that the title and/or location appear on the badge. Those with designations of positions no longer existing (City Constable, for example) and names of early western states and towns are most valuable.

Badges are among the most commonly reproduced (and faked) types of antiques on the market. At any flea market, 10 fakes can be found for every authentic example. Genuine law badges start at $30.00 to $40.00 for recent examples (1950 – 1970); earlier pieces (1910 – 1930) usually bring $50.00 to $90.00. Pre-1900 badges often sell for more than $100.00. Authentic gold badges are usually priced at a minimum of scrap value (karat, weight, spot price for gold); fine gold badges from before 1900 can sell for $400.00 to $800.00, and a few will bring even more. A fire badge is usually valued at about half the price of a law badge from the same era and material. Our values have been gleaned from internet auctions and are actual selling prices.

Alturas Police, NP 6-point star, early 1900s, 2½" 515.00
Boston Special Police, scallops at edge of oval, 1930s, 1½x2¼" ... 195.00
CA State Board of Health Engineer, brass w/bl enamel, Shreve, 2¾x2".. 725.00
Chicago Police, NP/enamel, 2nd issue, SD Childs, ca 1899, 3x2¼".. 865.00
City Police, Oaks N Dak, ball-tipped 6-point star, Liepsner, 2" ... 235.00
Deputy Sheriff, Boston MA, NP shield, SM Spencer Mfg, ca 1900, 2¾"..275.00
Deputy Sheriff, Milwaukee WI, ball-tipped star w/bl enamel, 2¼" ... 225.00

Deputy Sheriff, Sachs & Lawyer, Denver CO, marked LS Coll., $265.00. (Photo courtesy Engel Auction Co./LiveAuctioneers.com)

Deputy Sheriff, Sacramento CA, NP 6-point star, HE Sleeper, 1950s.. 240.00
Deputy Sheriff, star in circle, emb metal, pitting, illegible mk, G. 275.00
Deputy Sheriff San Diego, 6-point star, Cal Stamp Co, ca 1910, 2⅝". 345.00
Deputy Warden, CT, State Board of Fisheries..., NP shield, 1⅞" . 260.00
Forest Fire Warden, CT, emb shield, Whitehead & Hoag, 1¾x2". 230.00
Jacksonville (FL) Police Dept, eagle on seal, NP/bl enamel, 2¾". 385.00
NY City Transit Police, silver-tone shield, lug bk, 2½" 180.00
Patrol Officer, Oak Park Police, 5-point star, CH Hanson, 1930s . 180.00
Police Constable, NP shield, tongue catch, AA White Co, 2¼x1¾" . 130.00
Registered Chauffeur IL Motor Vehicle Law, emb metal, 2x1½".. 360.00
Reporter Los Angeles Police, gold-tone & enamel, Entenmann.. 675.00
Reserve Captain Police Dept of NY, eagle on shield, gold-tone, 3".. 300.00
US Special Police, Inauguration of President, gold & bl shield, 1985. 215.00
WI State Traffic Police, eagle on shield, Schwaab, 1953, 3⅛x2¼" ..600.00

Banks

This has been a monumental year for raising the bar and establishing

higher prices for mechanical banks in outstanding condition. The Steve Steckbeck collection crossed the auction block on October 27, 2007, at Morphy Auctions in Denver, Pennsylvania. Record prices were achieved for many examples, and the strong showing represented the demand for quality specimens. The values in the listings that follow represent the selling prices for the mechanical banks that sold through that auction and include the buyer's premium. The 'Uncle Sam Bank' scenario mentioned in the paragraph below should have a 99%++ (condition)entry worth $64,350.00, that price having been achieved at the same Morphy auction!

To gain a better consensus of value and to factor in mechanical banks in lesser condition, price guides from previous years must be used. Whether or not lesser-condition banks will rise in value accordingly remains to be seen; however, there always seems to be some upward movement in those areas. In general, bank values are established on the auction block and sales between collectors and dealers, and condition is the driving force that determines the final price. The spread between the price of a bank in excellent condition and the identical model in only good condition continues to widen. In order to be a seasoned collector in the pursuit of wise investments, one must learn to carefully determine overall condition by assessing the amount and strength (depth) of the paint, and by checking for breaks, repairs, and replaced parts; all bear heavily on value. Paint and casting variations are other considerations the collector should become familiar with.

It's imperative that collectors understand the market. Let's take a look at the price variations possible on an Uncle Sam mechanical bank. If you find one with considerable paint missing but with some good color showing, the price would be around $1,000.00. If it has repairs or restoration, the value could drop to somewhere near $800.00 or less. Still another example with two thirds of its original paint and no repairs would probably bring $1,800.00. If it had only minor nicks, it could go as high as $3,500.00. Should you find one in 95% paint with no repairs, $5,000.00 would be a minimum value. (Morphy's 99%++ example, being near-pristine, brought more than ten times that.) After considering all of these factors, remember: The final price is always determined by what a willing buyer and seller agree on for a specific bank.

Mechanical banks are the 'creme de le creme' in the arena of cast-iron toy collecting. They are among the most outstanding products of the Industrial Revolution and are recognized as some of the most successful of the mass-produced products of the nineteenth century. The earliest mechanicals were made of wood or lead. In 1869 John Hall introduced Hall's Excelsior, made of cast iron. It was an immediate success. J. & E. Stevens produced the bank for Hall and as a result soon began to make their own designs. Several companies followed suit, most of which were already in the hardware business. They used newly developed iron-casting techniques to produce these novelty savings devices for the emerging toy market. The social mores and customs of the times, political attitudes, racial and ethnic biases, the excitement of the circus, and humorous everyday events all served as inspiration for the creation of hundreds of banks. Designers made the most of simple mechanics to produce models with captivating actions that served not only to amuse but promote the concept of thrift to the children. The quality and detail of the castings were truly remarkable. The majority of collectible banks were made from 1870 to 1910; however, they continued to be manufactured until the onset of WWII. J. & E. Stevens, Shepard Hardware, and Kyser and Rex were some of the most prolific manufacturers of mechanicals. They made still banks as well.

Still banks are widely collected. Various materials were used in their construction, and each material represents a subfield in still bank collections. No one knows exactly how many different banks were made, but upwards of 3,000 have been identified in the various books published on the subject. Cast-iron examples still dominate the market, but lead banks from Europe are growing in value. Tin and early pottery banks are drawing more interest as well. American pottery banks which were primarily collected by Americana collectors are becoming more important in the still bank field.

To increase your knowledge of banks, attend shows and auctions. Direct contact with collectors and knowledgeable dealers is a very good way to develop a feel for prices and quality. It will also help you in gaining the ability to judge condition, and you'll learn to recognize the more desirable banks as well.

Both mechanical and still banks have been reproduced. One way to detect a reproduction is by measuring. The dimensions of a reproduced bank will always be fractionally smaller, since the original bank was cast from a pattern while the reproduction was made from a casting of the original bank. As both values and interest continue to increase, it becomes even more important to educate ourselves to the fullest extent possible. We recommend these books for your library: *The Bank Book* by Norman, *The Dictionary of Still Banks* by Long and Pitman, *The Penny Bank Book* by Moore, *Penny Banks Around the World* by Don Duer, *Registering Banks* by Robert L. McCumber, and *Penny Lane* by Davidson, which is considered the most complete reference available. It contains a cross-reference listing of numbers from all other publications on mechanical banks.

All banks are assumed to be complete and original unless noted otherwise in the description. A number of banks are commonly found with a particular repair. When this repair is reflected in our pricing, it will be so indicated. When traps (typically key lock, as in Uncle Sam) are an integral part of the body of the bank, lack of such results is a severe reduction in the value of the bank. When the trap is underneath the bank (typically a twist trap, as in Eagle and Eaglets), reduction in value is minimal.

Still banks have maintained their value with higher values and greater demand leaning towards rarity and condition, although cast-iron painted building banks still seem to be the most sought after by collectors.

Another interesting 'bank' collectible which is quickly gaining momentum with collectors is the 'Banthrico' bank. Prices have risen dramatically for these banks that were 'giveaways' in the 1950s through the 1970s. For more information on these we recommend *Coin Banks by Banthrico*, written by collector James L. Redwine.

Our advisor for mechanical and still banks is Clive Devenish, who is listed in the Directory under California.

To most accurately represent current market values, we have used condition codes in some of our listings that correspond with guidelines developed by today's bank collectors.

NM — 98% paint	VG — 80% paint
PR (pristine) — 95% paint	G — 70% paint
EX — 90% paint	

Key:
CI — cast iron	RM — Robert McCumber Book:
M — Andy Moore Book:	*Registering Banks*
The Penny Bank Book	SM — sheet metal
N — Bill Norman Book:	WM — white metal
The Bank Book	

Book of Knowledge

Book of Knowledge banks were produced by John Wright (Pennsylvania) from circa 1950 until 1975. Of the 30 models they made during those years, a few continued to be made in very limited numbers until the late 1980s; these they referred to as the 'Medallion' series. (Today the Medallion banks command the same prices as the earlier Book of Knowledge series.) Each bank was a handcrafted, hand-painted duplicate of an original as was found in the collection of The Book of Knowledge, the first children's encyclopedia in this country. Because the antique banks are often priced out of the range of many of today's collectors, these banks are being sought out as affordable substitutes for their very expensive counterparts. It should also be noted that China has repro-

duced banks with the Book of Knowledge inscription on them. These copies are flooding the market, causing authentic Book of Knowledge banks to decline in value. Buyers should take extra caution when investing in Book of Knowledge banks and purchase them through a reputable dealer who offers a satisfaction guarantee as well as a guarantee that the bank is authentic. Our advisor for Book of Knowledge banks is Dan Iannotti; he is listed in the Directory under Michigan.

Always Did 'Spise a Mule, Boy on Bench, M	150.00
Artillery Bank, NM	135.00
Boy on Trapeze, M	225.00
Butting Buffalo, M	135.00
Cat & Mouse, NM	150.00
Cow (Kicking), NM	175.00
Creedmore Bank, M	175.00
Dentist Bank, EX	110.00
Eagle & Eaglets, M	175.00
Humpty Dumpty, M	150.00
Indian & Bear, M	195.00
Jonah & the Whale, M	150.00
Leap Frog, NM	175.00
Magician, MIB	150.00
Organ Bank (Boy & Girl), NM	125.00

Owl (Turns Head), NM, $150.00. (Photo courtesy Du Mouchelles/LiveAuctioneers.com)

Paddy & Pig, NM	175.00
Punch & Judy, NM	150.00
Teddy & the Bear, NM	125.00
Uncle Remus, M	150.00
US & Spain, M	150.00
William Tell, M	175.00

Mechanical

Acrobat, N-1010, CI, NM	24,750.00
Atlas, N-1080, CI & WM, NM+	49,725.00
Bank of Education, N-1170, CI, NM	2,340.00
Bear & Tree Stump, N-1210, CI, NM	1,638.00
Bill E Grin, N-1230, CI, NM	9,945.00
Bird on Roof, N-1270, CI, NM	5,558.00
Boy Robbing Bird's Nest, N-1360, CI, NM+	52,650.00
Bulldog - Standing, N-1450, CI, NM	1,170.00
Cat & Mouse (Cat Balancing), N-1700, CI, NM+	19,890.00
Creedmore, N-2000, CI, NM+	3,802.00
Dapper Dan, N-2070, tin, NM+	2,340.00
Darktown Battery, N-2080, CI, NM+	32,175.00
Dinah, N-2150, CI, NM+	2,925.00
Dog on Turntable, N-2170, CI, NM+	2,340.00
Elephant & 3 Clowns, N-2250, CI, NM	6,345.00
Elephant w/Howdah - Man Pops Out, N-2280, CI, NM	2,106.00
Girl Skipping Rope, N-2640, CI, NM+	93,600.00

Hold the Fort (5 Holes), N-2820, CI, NM................38,025.00
Indian & Bear, N-2980, CI, NM+............................32,175.00
Joe Socko Novelty Bank, N-3050, tin, NM+............. 263.00
Jonah & the Whale, N-3490, CI, NM+......................9,945.00

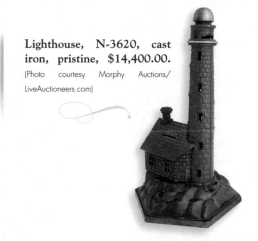

Lighthouse, N-3620, cast iron, pristine, $14,400.00.
(Photo courtesy Morphy Auctions/LiveAuctioneers.com)

Lion, N-3640, tin, NM+..4,972.00
Lion Hunter, N-3660, CI, NM...............................21,060.00
Magician, N-3760, CI, NM+IB...............................26,325.00
Mammy & Child, N-3790, CI, NM 64,350.00

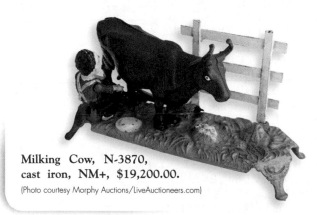

Milking Cow, N-3870, cast iron, NM+, $19,200.00.
(Photo courtesy Morphy Auctions/LiveAuctioneers.com)

Minstrel Bank, N-3880, tin, NM+ 585.00
Monkey & Parrot, N-3950, CI, NM+ 700.00
Mosque, N-4010, CI, NM+...................................11,700.00
Mule Entering Barn, N-4030, CI, NM+......................3,510.00
Musical Savings Bank - Regina, N-4100, wood, NM..............17,550.00
New Creedmore, N-4220, CI, NM 3,215.00
Novelty, N-4260, CI, NM+ 7,605.00
Organ Bank - Boy & Girl, N-4310, CI, NM 3,800.00
Organ Bank - Cat & Dog, N-4320, CI, NM 4,680.00
Organ Grinder & Performing Bear, N-4350, CI, NM+ 22,230.00
Owl Turns Head, N-4380, CI, NM...........................2,750.00
Paddy & the Pig, N-4400, CI, NM..........................10,530.00
Pelican - Mammy, N-4510, CI, NM..........................3,215.00
Popeye Knockout Bank, N-4620, tin, NM..................... 995.00
Punch & Judy, N-4740, CI, NMIB...........................11,700.00
Santa Claus, N-5010, CI, NM.................................4,972.00
Speaking Dog - Red Dress, N-5170, CI, NM 4,972.00
Tabby, N-5410, CI, NM...1,170.00
Teddy & the Bear, N-5460, CI, NM+ 6,435.00
Toad on Stump, N-5570, CI, NM+.............................5,265.00
Trick Dog, Hubley, bl, N-5630, CI, NM...................... 645.00
Trick Pony, N-5640, CI, NM+IB..............................19,890.00
Weeden's Plantation, N-5910, wood & tin, NM+IB 8,190.00

William Tell, N-5940, CI, NM+ 7,020.00
Wireless, N-5980, tin/iron/wood, NM+IB 585.00
World's Banker, N-6030, tin, NM 10,530.00
Zoo, N-6070, CI, NM+...8,190.00

Registering

Balfour Budget Bank, RM-249, tin, 3", EX................ 85.00
Beehive, NPCI, window on side, detailed, H&H, 1891, 5⅜", EX ...200.00
Bestmaid, tin, 4¾", EX.. 75.00
Captain Marvel, tin litho, dime register, Fawcett, '48, 2⅝", VG..115.00
Captain Marvel's Magic Dime Saver (pocket), RM-223, tin, EX. 275.00
Chein Mercury Dime (pocket), RM-227, tin, EX........... 60.00
Chein Thrifty Elf 'Dime a Day' Register, RM-127, tin, EX 85.00
Clock Face, 2 hands registering dollars & cents, ornate CI, VG . 1,450.00
Clown & Monkey Daily Dime (pocket), RM-224, tin, EX 60.00
Clown & Monkey Daily Dime Bank, RM-225, tin, EX................. 75.00
Coin Registering Bank, mid-Eastern building, Kayser & Rex, 1890s, NM.12,000.00
Columbian Recording Bank, RM-24, NPCI, EX 250.00
Dime a Day Thrifty Elf (pocket), RM-229, tin, EX 100.00
Donald Duck Bank (cash register), RM-97, tin, EX 225.00
Donald Duck Clock Vault, tin, Spanish sayings on drum, EX...... 140.00
Dopey Dime Register (pocket), RM-218, tin, EX............ 180.00
Elves Rolling Coins to Bank Dime Register, RM-126, tin, EX..... 125.00
Gem Registering, w/orig paper label, J&E Stevens, ca 1893, NM.4,500.00
George Washington Bank, RM-67, tin, EX................... 150.00
Imperial 3 Coin Bank, RM-16, bronze, EX.................. 400.00
Jackie Robinson (pocket), RM-234, tin, EX................. 500.00
Keene Savings Bank, tin, EX.................................... 350.00
Keep 'Em Sailing Dime Register (pocket), RM-220, tin, EX........ 440.00
Keep 'Em Smiling Dime Register, RM-124, tin, EX................... 250.00
Little Orphan Annie (pocket), RM-213, tin, EX 225.00
Penny Register Bank (pail), RM-22, CI, EX................. 225.00
Penny Saver, CI, 5⅛", VG..................................... 80.00
Popeye Daily Quarter, tin litho, USA, 4½", EX............ 150.00
Popeye Dime Register (pocket), M-1573, silver pnt on tin, 2½", EX. 75.00
Prince Valiant (pocket), RM-231, tin, EX 125.00
Prudential Registering Savings Bank (10¢), NPCI, 7¼", EX........ 350.00
Prudential Registering Savings Bank (25¢), RM-17, NPCI, EX .. 400.00
Sen Sen Gum, polished chrome, 1912, 2½x1¼", EX................... 135.00
Snow White Dime Register (pocket), M-1567, tin, 2½" sq, EX... 150.00
Superman Dime Register (pocket), RM-216, tin, EX........ 125.00
Time Clock, NPCI, Ives, Blakeslee & Williams, ca 1893, EX...2,750.00
Trunk Savings Bank, RM-35, NPCI, EX...................... 200.00
Uncle Sam's Nickel Register Bank, RM-79, SM cash register, EX ..125.00
United Nations Register (pocket), RM-236, tin, EX...................... 60.00
Vacation Daily Dime, tin litho, Kalon Mfg, 2⅝", NM................. 90.00
Woven Basket Dime Bank, RM-28, CI, EX................... 200.00

Still

$100,000 Money Bag, M-1262, CI, 3⅝", EX................. 440.00
Airplane Spirit of St Louis, M-1423, steel, EX............ 600.00
Amherst Buffalo, M-556, CI, 5¼", EX 525.00
Andy Gump, M-217, CI, EX....................................1,500.00
Arcade Steamboat, M-1460, CI, 2⅜" H, EX................. 500.00
Baby Bird, Arthur Shaw Co/England, hinged head, 3", EX.......... 515.00
Baby in Cradle, M-51, NPCI, EX..............................2,200.00
Baby in Egg (Black), M-261, lead, 7¼", EX................ 495.00
Baseball on 3 Bats, M-1608, CI, EX..........................1,500.00
Baseball Player, M-18, CI, 5¾", VG.......................... 160.00
Baseball Player, M-19, CI, 5¾", NM........................1,125.00
Battleship Maine, M-1439, CI, 6", EX.......................4,950.00

Battleship Oregon, M-1439, CI, EX......................................3,800.00
Bear Stealing Pig, M-693, CI, rpl screw, 5½", G 600.00
Bear w/Honey Pot, M-717, CI, 6½", EX......................195.00
Beehive Bank, M-683, CI, EX..225.00
Begging Rabbit, M-566, CI, 5⅛", EX 250.00
Billiken Bank, M-74, CI, EX...85.00
Billy Bounce (Give Billy a Penny), M-15, CI, 4¾", VG....385.00
Bird on Stump (Songbird), M-664, CI, EX..................400.00
Blackpool Tower, M-984, CI, partial rpt, rpl screw, 7⅜".....110.00
Boston Bull Terrier, M-421, CI, 5¼", EX....................220.00
Boy Scout, M-45, CI, EX...150.00
Buffalo, M-560, CI w/gold pnt, 3⅛", EX....................145.00
Bugs Bunny (Barrel), M-270, WM, EX.........................175.00
Bugs Bunny by the Tree, M-278, CI, 5½", EX.............140.00
Building w/Eagle Finial, M-1134, CI, 9¾", EX............935.00
Bulldog (Seated), M-396, CI, 3⅞", NM.......................440.00
Bulldog w/Sailor Cap, M-363, lead, 4⅜", EX.............440.00
Buster Brown & Tige, M-241, CI, gold & red pnt, 5½", VG........175.00
Buster Brown & Tige, M-242 variant, CI, 5½", NM........935.00
Cadet, M-8, CI, crack at slot, 5¾", VG.......................165.00
Camel (Kneeling), M-770, CI, 2½", EX........................825.00
Camel (Oriental), M-769, CI, EX...............................1,800.00
Camel (Oriental), M-769, CI, 3¾", G..........................360.00
Camel (Sm), M-768, CI, 4¾", EX.................................250.00
Campbell Kids, M-163, CI, gold pnt, 3¾", EX............330.00
Captain Kidd, M-38, CI, 5⅝", G..................................145.00
Cat on Tub, M-358, CI, gold pnt, 4⅛", EX..................175.00
Cat on Tub, M-358, CI, 4⅛", EX..................................195.00
Cat w/Ball, M-352, CI, EX...225.00
Cat w/Bowtie, M-350, CI, EX..175.00
Charles Russell, M-247, WM, gold pnt, 6¼", EX..........55.00
Charlie McCarthy on Trunk, M-207, compo, 5¼", M.............475.00
City Bank w/Chimney, M-1101, CI, old rpt, 6¾".......1,595.00
City Bank w/Teller, M-1097, CI, 5½", NM...................625.00
Clock 'Time Is Money,' M-1555, CI, EX........................350.00

Clown, blue costume, M-211, cast iron, EX, $325.00. (Photo courtesy Dunbar Galleries)

Colonial House, M-992, CI, 4", EX................................140.00
Columbia Bank, M-1070, CI, 5¾", EX..........................615.00
Columbia Tower, M-1118, CI, rpl turn pin, 6⅞", VG.......745.00
County Bank, M-1110, CI, 4¼", G.................................175.00
Crown Building, M-1225, CI, 5", NM..........................3,300.00
Crystal Bank, M-926, CI & glass, EX..............................70.00
Cupola, M-1146, CI, 4⅛", EX..375.00
Deer (Lg), M-737, CI, EX...200.00
Deer (Sm), M-736, CI, EX..100.00
Dime Bank, M-1183, CI, 4¾", EX.................................140.00
Dog (Cutie), M-414, CI, EX...250.00
Dog (Scottie Standing), M-435, CI, 3¾", VG..............155.00
Dog (Scottie), M-419, CI, EX..275.00

Dog (Spaniel), M-418, CI, EX..225.00
Dog by Ball, M-390, lead/tin, 2⅛", VG.......................255.00
Dog on Tub, M-359, CI, 4¹⁄₁₆", EX..............................195.00
Dog w/Pack (Lg), M-437, CI, EX..................................200.00
Dog w/Pack (Sm), M-439, EX...100.00
Dolphin, M-33, CI, gold pnt, 4½", EX.........................880.00
Donkey w/Saddle & Reins, M-497 variant, lead, 4", EX.......120.00
Double Decker Bus, M-1490, CI, bl pnt, 2¼", NM......1,130.00
Duck, M-624, CI, 4¾", EX..330.00
Duck on Tub, M-616, CI, 5⅜", EX.................................220.00
Dutch Boy, M-180, CI, EX...150.00
Dutch Girl w/Flowers, M-181, CI, 5¼", EX.................120.00
Elephant on Tub, M-483, CI, 5⅜", EX...........................195.00
Elephant on Wheels, M-446, CI, 4⅛", EX.....................365.00
Elmer at Barrel, M-306, WM, EX..................................150.00
Eureka Trust & Savings Safe, CI, 5¾", EX....................470.00
Every Copper Helps, M-71, CI, EX.................................900.00
Feed My Sheep (Lamb), M-596, lead, gold pnt, 2¾", VG......155.00
Fidelity Trust Vault, M-903, CI, EX...............................650.00
Fido, M-417, CI, 5", EX..140.00
Fido on Pillow, M-443, CI, 7⅜", EX..............................385.00
Flat Iron Building, M-1159, CI, 8¼", EX....................2,640.00
Flat Iron Building, M-1160, CI, no trap, 5¾", EX.........410.00
Football Player, M-11, CI, 5⅞", EX...............................440.00
Forlorn Dog, M-408, WM, 4¾", G...................................85.00
Fortune Ship, M-1457, CI, 4⅛", NM...........................1,760.00
Foxy Grandpa, M-320, CI, 5½", EX...............................375.00
Foxy Grandpa, M-320, CI, 5½", G.................................215.00
Frowning Face, M-12, CI, 5⅝", EX..............................1,815.00
Gas Pump, M-1485, CI, EX...250.00
General Butler, M-54, CI, 6½", EX..............................3,960.00
General Grant, M-115 variant, CI, Harper, 5⅝", EX.......3,740.00
Give Me a Penny, M-166, CI, EX....................................300.00
Globe, M-812, CI, 5", VG...275.00
Globe on Arc, M-789, CI, red pnt, 5¼", EX...................420.00
Globe on Arc, M-789, CI, 5¼", G..................................140.00
Globe Savings Fund, M-1199, CI, 7⅛", EX.................3,300.00
Golliwog, M-85, CI, 6¼", EX..550.00
Goose (Red Goose Shoes), M-628, CI, EX.....................175.00
Graf Zeppelin, M-1428, CI, 1¾" H, EX.........................245.00
Grizzly Bear, M-703, lead, pnt worn in bk, 2¾".............110.00
Hansel & Gretel, M-1016, tin, 2¼", EX..........................140.00
Harper Stork Safe, M-651, CI, hdl missing, 5½", EX........935.00
Hen on Nest, M-546, CI, EX..1,600.00
High Rise, M-1217, CI w/japanning, 5½", EX................330.00
High Rise, M-1219, CI, 4⅝", EX....................................430.00
High Rise Tiered, M-1215, CI, 5¾", EX.........................385.00
Home Savings, M-1126, CI, 5⅞", EX.............................320.00
Horse on Tub (decorated), M-509, CI, 5¼", VG............170.00
Horse on Wheels, M-512, CI, 5", EX.............................470.00
Horse Prancing, M-517, CI, EX..85.00
Horse Tally Ho, M-535, CI, EX......................................275.00
Horseshoe 'Good Luck,' M-508, CI, EX.........................300.00
Horseshoe Wire Mesh, M-524, CI/tin, G- Arcade label, 3¼", VG..110.00
Independence Hall, M-1244, CI, 8⅞", EX......................660.00
Independence Hall Tower, M-1205, CI, 9½", EX.........2,850.00
Indian w/Tomahawk, M-228, CI, EX..............................400.00
Iron Master's Cabin, M-1027, CI, 4¼", EX.................3,630.00
Jimmy Durante, M-259, WM, 6¾", EX...........................220.00
Junior Cash Register, M-930, NPCI, EX.........................200.00
Key, M-1616, CI, EX..800.00
King Midas, M-13, CI, EX..1,200.00
Labrador Retriever, M-412, CI, 4½", EX........................295.00
Lamb, M-595, CI, EX..150.00

Liberty Bell (Harper), M-780, CI, EX....................300.00
Lindbergh w/Goggles, M-125, lead, 5⅞", EX....................250.00
Lindy Bank, M-124, AL, 6½", EX....................200.00
Lion, M-765, CI, sm, 4", EX....................110.00
Lion (Lg, Tail Right), M-754, CI, 5¼", EX....................195.00
Lion (Sm, Tail Right), M-755, CI, 4", EX....................85.00
Lion on Tub, M-747, CI, 4⅛", EX....................165.00
Lion on Wheels, M-760, CI, 4½", EX....................330.00
Litchfield Cathedral, M-968, CI, 6⅝", EX....................495.00
Main Street Trolley (No People), M-1469, CI, gold pnt, 3", EX..330.00
Maine (Battleship), M-1439, CI, 6" H, NM....................4,400.00
Maine (Sm Battleship), M-1440, CI, 4⅝", EX....................440.00
Mammy w/Hands on Hips, M-176, CI, 5¼", EX....................165.00
Mammy w/Spoon, M-168, CI, 5⅞", EX....................250.00
Man on Bale of Cotton, M-37, CI, 4⅞", EX....................3,960.00
Mary & Lamb, M-164, CI, 4⅜", VG....................770.00
Mary & Lamb, M-164, CI, 4⅜" (ex Moore collection), NM.....4,180.00
Mascot Bank, M-3, CI, NM....................3,800.00
Metropolitan Safe, CI, 5⅞", NM....................2,420.00
Mickey Mouse Post Office, tin, cylindrical, 6", NM....................155.00
Middy, M-36, CI, w/clapper, 5¼", G....................150.00
Model T (2nd Version), M-1483, CI, 4", NM....................1,155.00
Monkey w/Removable Hat, M-740, brass, 3⅞", EX....................990.00
Mule 'I Made St Louis Famous,' M-489, CI, Harper, 4¾", EX...2,145.00
Mulligan, M-177, CI, 5¾", EX....................175.00
Mutt & Jeff, M-157, CI, gold pnt, 4¼", EX....................165.00
Newfoundland (Dog), M-440, CI, 3⅝", EX....................330.00
Ocean Liner, M-1444, lead, 2¾" H, VG....................155.00
Oregon (Battleship), M-1450, CI, rpl guns, 3⅞", G....................255.00
Oregon (Battleship), M-1452, CI, rpl turn pin, VG....................440.00
Oriental Boy on a Pillow (conversion), M-186, CI, 5½", EX.......275.00
Owl on Stump, M-598, CI, EX....................225.00
Pass Round the Hat (Derby), M-1381, CI, 1⅝", EX....................220.00
Peaceful Bill/Harper Smiling Jim, M-109, CI, 4", EX....................2,640.00
Pearl Street Building, M-1096, worn gold overpnt, 4¼"....................420.00
Pelican, M-679, CI, EX....................1,400.00
Pet Safe, M-866, CI, 4½", EX....................250.00
Pig 'I Made Chicago Famous,' M-629, CI, Harper, 2⅛", EX.........245.00
Pig 'I Made Chicago Famous,' M-631, CI, EX....................175.00
Pig (Standing), M-478, CI, 3", EX....................265.00
Pocahontas Bust, M-226, lead, 3⅛", EX....................195.00
Policeman, M-182, CI, Arcade, 5½", EX....................1,200.00
Polish Rooster, M-541, CI, 5½", EX....................1,375.00
Porky Pig, M-264, CI, 6", EX+....................440.00
Porky Pig, M-264, CI, 6", VG....................195.00
Porky Pig (Barrel), M-265, WM, EX....................150.00
Possum, M-561, CI, EX....................400.00
Potato Bank, M-1663, CI, EX....................900.00
Professor Pug Frog, M-311, CI, 3¼", EX....................365.00
Puppo, M-416, CI, 4⅞", VG....................170.00
Quilted Lion, M-758, CI, 3¾", EX....................330.00
Rabbit Begging, M-566, CI, EX....................150.00
Radio (Crosley), M-819, CI, 5⅛", EX....................745.00
Radio (Sm Crosley), M-820, CI, EX....................175.00
Reindeer, M-376, CI, 6¼", NM....................310.00
Retriever w/a Pack, M-436, CI, 4¹¹⁄₁₆", EX....................165.00
Rhino, M-721, CI, EX....................400.00
Rhino, M-721, CI, 2⅝", NM....................1,155.00
Roller Safe, M-880, CI, 3¹¹⁄₁₆", EX....................250.00
Roof Bank Building, M-1122, CI, 5¼", G....................330.00
Rooster, M-548, CI, 4¾", EX....................145.00
Rumplestiltskin, M-27, CI, 6", VG....................220.00
Sailor, M-27, CI, 5¼", G....................95.00
Sailor, M-28, CI, 5½", G....................140.00
Sailor, M-29, CI, 5⅝", NM....................880.00
Santa Claus, Ive's, M-56, CI, 7¼", EX....................770.00
Santa Claus w/Tree, M-61, CI, EX....................900.00
Save & Smile, M-1641, CI, 4¼", EX....................415.00
Saving Sam, M-158, AL, 5¼", EX....................935.00
Scotties (6 in Basket), M-427, WM, 4½", EX....................85.00
Seal on Rock, M-732, CI, 3½", EX....................660.00
Seated Rabbit, M-368, CI, 3⅝", EX....................165.00
Sharecropper, M-173, CI, 5½", EX....................305.00
Shell Out, M-1622, CI, EX....................500.00
Skyscraper, M-1238, CI, 3¾", EX....................110.00
Skyscraper, M-1239, CI, 4⅜", EX....................150.00
Skyscraper (6 Posts), M-1241, CI, 6½", EX....................330.00
Songbird on Stump, M-664, CI, 4¾", EX....................715.00
Squirrel w/Nut, M-660, CI, 4⅛", VG....................515.00
State Bank, M-1078, CI, w/key, 8", NM....................1,485.00
State Bank, M-1083, CI, 4⅛", EX....................275.00
State Bank, M-1085, CI, 3", EX....................330.00
Statue of Liberty (Lg), M-1166, CI, EX....................850.00
Statue of Liberty (Sm), M-1164, CI, EX....................150.00
Stop Sign, M-1479, CI, 4½", G....................240.00
Tank, M-1436, lead, 3", VG....................800.00
Tank Bank USA 1918 (Lg), M-1435, CI, 3", EX....................300.00
Tank Bank USA 1918 (Sm), M-1437, CI, 2⅜", EX....................250.00
Teddy Roosevelt, M-120, CI, EX....................350.00
Temple Bar Building, M-1163, CI, 4", EX....................660.00
Tower Bank, M-1208, CI, 9¼", EX....................440.00
Transvaal Money Box, M-1, CI, recast pipe, 6¼", VG..............3,500.00
Triangular Building w/Clock, M-1235, CI, 6", EX....................715.00
Trust Bank, The; M-154, CI, 7¼", EX....................4,950.00
Turkey (Lg), M-585, CI, 4¼", EX....................495.00
Turkey (Sm), M-587, CI, 3⅜", EX....................165.00
Two Kids (Goats), M-594, CI, EX....................900.00
Two-Faced Black Boy (Lg), M-83, CI, EX....................330.00
Two-Faced Black Boy (Sm), M-84, CI, 3⅛", EX....................220.00
Two-Faced Devil, M-31, CI, 4¼", EX....................770.00
US Army/Navy Safe, electroplated CI, 6⅛", EX....................1,320.00
US Mail, M-838, CI, sm, 3⅝", EX....................85.00

US Mail Mailbox With Eagle, M-850, CI, 4⅛", EX, $135.00. (Photo courtesy Dunbar Galleries)

USA Mail Mailbox w/Eagle, M-851, CI, 4⅛", EX....................85.00
Villa Bank, M-1179, CI, EX....................850.00
Watch Me Grow, M-279 variant, tin, 5¾", EX....................75.00
Westminster Abbey, M-973, CI, old gold pnt, 6¼"....................275.00
White City Barrel #1, M-908, NP, EX....................165.00
White City Barrel on Cart, M-907, CI, 4", EX....................580.00
Woolworth Building (Lg), M-1041, CI, 7⅞", EX....................330.00
Woolworth Building (Sm), M-1042, CI, 5¾", EX....................195.00
World Time Bank, M-1539, CI, orig paper, 4⅛", EX....................550.00
Yellow Cab, M-1493, CI, 4¼", EX....................2,000.00
Young Negro, M-170, CI, 4½", EX....................275.00
1882 Villa, M-959, CI, 5⅞", VG....................880.00
1890 Tower Bank, M-1198, CI, 6⅞", EX....................1,320.00
1893 World's Fair Administration Building, M-1072, CI, 6", EX. 715.00

Barbershop Collectibles

Even for the stranger in town, the local barbershop was easy to find, its location vividly marked with the traditional red and white striped barber pole that for centuries identified such establishments. As far back as the twelfth century, the barber has had a place in recorded history. At one time he not only groomed the beards and cut the hair of his gentlemen clients but was known as the 'blood-letter' as well, hence the red stripe for blood and the white for the bandages. Many early barbers even pulled teeth! Later, laws were enacted that divided the practices of barbering and surgery.

The Victorian barbershop reflected the charm of that era with fancy barber chairs upholstered in rich wine-colored velvet; rows of bottles made from colored art glass held hair tonics and shaving lotion. Backbars of richly carved oak with beveled mirrors lined the wall behind the barber's station. During the late nineteenth century, the barber pole with a blue stripe added to the standard red and white as a patriotic gesture came into vogue.

Today the barbershop has all but disappeared from the American scene, replaced by modern unisex salons. Collectors search for the barber poles, the fancy chairs, and the tonic bottles of an era gone but not forgotten. Our advisor for this category is Robert Doyle; he is listed in the Directory under New York. See also Bottles; Razors; Shaving Mugs.

Antiseptor, detachable clipper blade, Oster, plastic & glass, 1950s ..60.00
Antiseptor, wht porc, 1940s, 3½x3½x1½", M 30.00
Book, Young Men's Modern Hairstyles, Mastoianni, 1950s, 15-pg, 7x10". 27.50
Brush, ceramic dog figural hdl, gr brush fibers, Germany 30.00
Brush, Syroco German shepherd (head) figural hdl, pnt eyes, 1900s, 7". 38.00
Cabinet, chestnut/walnut/poplar, dvtl drw amid 16 slots, OH, 14x10x7".. 600.00
Chair, Buerger Bros, orig uphl, oak fr, ca 1900s, VG 550.00
Chair, Kochs, stainless steel/porc/leather, Pats 1909 & 1910, NM ... 850.00
Finger bowl, amethyst, emb ribs, mc floral, 2⅝", M 140.00
Hone, Barber's Razor Hone on stone, 5x2" 25.00
Jar, Burma Shave emb on clear glass, bl/yel tin lid, ½-lb sz 27.50
Jar, comb germicidal disinfectant, glass w/metal top, Marvy #3, NM. 27.50
Mirror, Burma Shave, pnt poles/foamy mug/etc on face, wood fr, 22x15".. 90.00
Pole, glass red/wht/bl stripes, chrome mts, lights up/spins, 12" 70.00
Pole, glass red/wht/bl stripes, lights up, Wm Marvy #55, 26x10" . 465.00
Pole, pnt porc, Look Better Feel Better, Wm Marvy #4812, 48x8" .300.00
Pole, tapered wood w/acorn finial, red/bl/wht pnt, metal stand, 70"...1,100.00
Pole, trn wood, red/wht/bl pnt & gesso w/yel & gold, splits, 27".. 800.00
Pole, trn wood, red/wht/bl stripes, cone/ball finial, 1890s, 68" 900.00
Postcard, barbershop street scene, blk & wht photo, IA, ca 1908.. 35.00

Sign, heavy milk glass globe, striped milk glass pole, cast-iron bracket, 31x12", $1,100.00. (Photo courtesy Morphy Auctions/LiveAuctioneers.com)

Sign, neon, shop name in red & gr, 1950s, 29x44" 175.00
Sign, porc, diagonal stripes & Barber Shop, Wm Marvy, 14x15½" .345.00

Sterilizer, razor/comb; chrome over brass w/glass front, w/key 115.00
Sterilizer, wood cabinet w/glass shelf, Deco style, 12½x12½x8" ... 145.00
Strop, 2 boar-skin straps joined by metal connector, 1940s, 24x2½".25.00
Tintype, barber cutting hair of well dressed man, 9th plate 100.00

Barometers

Barometers are instruments designed to measure the weight or pressure of the atmosphere in order to anticipate approaching weather changes. They have a glorious history. Some of the foremost thinkers of the seventeenth century developed the mercury barometer, as the discovery of the natural laws of the universe progressed. Working in 1644 from experiments by Galileo, Evangelista Torrecelli used a glass tube and a jar of mercury to create a vacuum and therefore prove that air has weight. Four years later, Rene Descartes added a paper scale to the top of Torrecelli's mercury tube and created the basic barometer. Blaise Pascal, working with Descartes, used it to determine the heights of mountains; only later was the correlation between changes in air pressure and changes in the weather observed and the term 'weather-glass' applied. Robert Boyle introduced it to England, and Robert Hook modified the form and designed the wheel barometer.

The most common type of barometer is the wheel or banjo, followed by the stick type. Modifications of the plain stick are the marine gimballed type and the laboratory, Kew, or Fortin type. Another style is the Admiral Fitzroy of which there are 12 or more variations. The above all have mercury contained either in glass tubing or wood box cisterns.

The aneroid is a variety of barometer that works on atmospheric pressure changes. These come in all sizes ranging from 1" in diameter to 12" or larger. They may be in metal or wood cases. There is also a barograph which records on a graph that rotates around a drum powered by a seven-day clock mechanism. Pocket barometers (altimeters) vary in sizes from 1" in diameter up to 6". One final type of barometer is the symphisometer, a modification of the stick barometer; these were used for a limited time as they were not as accurate as the conventional marine barometer. Our advisor for this category is Bob Elsner; he is listed in the Directory under Florida. Prices are subject to condition of wood, tube, etc.; number of functions; and whether or not they are signed.

American Stick Barometers

Chas Wilder, Peterboro, NH 1,250.00
DE Lent, Rochester, NY 1,250.00
EO Spooner, Storm King, Boston, MA 1,450.00
FD McKay Jr, Elmira, MA 3,100.00
Simmons & Sons, Fulton, NY 1,250.00

English Barometers

Note: The 10" mahogany wheel listed below is marked 'Royal Exchange London Optician to King George IV Prince of Wales.' It may be referenced in Goodison, page 85.

Admiral Fitzory, various kinds, ea from $500 to 4,500.00
Fortin type (Kew or Laboratory), metal on brd w/milk glass, $750 to. 1,250.00
Marine gimballed, sgn Walker, London 4,000.00
Right angle, sgn John Whitehurst, ca 1790 ....20,000.00
Stick, mahog bowfront w/urn-shaped cistern, S Mason, Dublin, 1824-30...5,000.00
Stick, rosewood, sgn L Casella, London 1,950.00
Stick, rosewood w/ivory scale, sgn Adie, dbl vernier, ca 1840 ...3,500.00
Symphisometer, sgn Adie 3,950.00
Wheel, mahog w/rosette inlay, A Artelli & Co, Birmingham, 38½"... 950.00
Wheel, 6", sgn Stanley, Peterborough 1,500.00
Wheel, 8", sgn F Molten, Norwich...1,450.00

Wheel, 10", mahog, J Smith Royal Exchange...Optican...Prince of Wales..1,950.00
Wheel, 10", MOP, sgn Spelizini, London....................................1,950.00

Other Types

Swiss, castle with fox greeting ducks, ca. 1890, 18x13", $1,250.00. (Photo courtesy Andre Ammelounx)

Aneroid, 4-6" dia in brass case w/half-rnd thermometer, $200 to.. 350.00
Mahog barograph (recording type), sgn Negretti & Zambra 950.00
Pocket barometer (altimeter), w/case, from $200 to.....................400.00

Barware

Back in the '30s when social soirees were very elegant affairs thanks to the influence of Hollywood in all its glamour and mystique, cocktails were often served up in shakers styled as miniature airplanes, zeppelins, skyscrapers, lady's legs, penguins, roosters, bowling pins, etc. Some were by top designers such as Norman Bel Geddes and Russel Wright. They were made of silver plate, glass, and chrome, often trimmed with colorful Bakelite handles. Today these are hot collectibles, and even the more common Deco-styled chrome cylinders are often priced at $25.00 and up. Ice buckets, trays, and other bar accessories are also included in this area of collecting.

For further information we recommend *Vintage Bar Ware Identification & Value Guide* by Stephen Visakay, our advisor for this category; he is listed in the Directory under New York. See also Bottle Openers.

Book, Authentic & Hilarious Bar Guide, True Magazine, 1950s ... 45.00
Book, Old Mr Boston...Bartender's Guide, hardbk, 1951 later edition. 35.00
Coaster, Queen's Surf, girl on surfboard, 1950s, 3½"....................... 32.50
Cocktail glass, amber w/pierced chrome holder, Farber Bros, 3½".. 30.00
Cocktail glass, rooster scenes, ftd, 1930s, 3½x3¼" 8.00
Cocktail glasses, conical top w/orange ball base, 1960s, 4⅝", 4 for...48.00
Ice bucket, chrome w/porc lining, Bakelite trim, Keystone Ware, 11".75.00
Ice bucket, musical pigs (3) in orange pyro on clear glass................45.00
Pick holder, bartender figural, pnt plastic/pot metal, 1930s, 6¼" ... 60.00
Picks, silver, fruit finial, mk Sterling, 3", set of 12, NMIB.............. 68.00
Pitcher, brass w/rattan woven hdl, thermos lined, M Phillip, 11" .. 95.00
Pitcher, chrome-plated w/red Bakelite hdl, blk-pnt stripes, 1930s . 45.00
Pitcher, pheasant decal on clear frost, clear hdl, 1960s, 8½" 15.00
Pitcher, polkadots w/gold fleur-de-lis on clear, slim, 11x3" 45.00
Pitcher, rainbow-colored rings on clear glass, 72-oz........................ 45.00
Pourer, dbl; chrome w/brn swirl Bakelite hdl, 4⅛x7" 55.00
Shaker, aluminum, anodized bl, cylindrical, 11¼" 75.00
Shaker, blk & red Oriental flowers on clear glass, aluminum top, 1930s.. 88.00
Shaker, blk & wht stripes on clear glass, chrome lid, 10¼" 48.00
Shaker, brushed aluminum w/red Bakelite trim, West Bend, 10". 140.00
Shaker, Cheers, red & orange on clear, chrome top, Irvinware, 9¼".. 25.00
Shaker, chrome, Krome Kraft/Farber Bros, 11x7½"+6 5½" stems... 60.00
Shaker, chrome, Manhattan, vertical ribs, Bell Geddes, 13" 800.00
Shaker, chrome, skyscraper, blk, enamel cap & base, 12¼" 95.00

Shaker, chrome bell shape, wood hdl removes, 1920s-30s............. 40.00
Shaker, chrome w/blk metal top, Soda King Syphon, 1938, 10" .. 100.00
Shaker, chrome w/butterscotch Bakelite, Farber Bros, 12½" 115.00
Shaker, Deco figures wave flags, red/bl on clear glass, SP lid 75.00
Shaker, elephants, pk on clear glass, Hazel-Atlas, chrome lid, 10"...68.00
Shaker, extinguisher form, red glass, Thirst Extinguisher, 1940s-50s.. 68.00
Shaker, fish & bubbles etched on gr glass, chrome lid, 8⅞", NM ... 80.00
Shaker, NP, hammered & plain, Expressware, 17½" 200.00
Shaker, SP, attached spout cover, Heinrichs...Pat...1910, 8½"........ 85.00
Shaker, SP, Deco-shaped top, CSG & Co, 1920s-30s, 10" 115.00
Shaker, SP, LCGC NY 1923 eng on top, 8" 195.00
Shaker, SP, penguin, Towle, 1997, MIB 50.00
Shaker, SP/frosted glass, lady's leg, 1930s, 15"............................. 700.00
Shaker, stainless steel, rocket shape, 1930s-40s, 11½" 65.00

Shakers: Blue barbell, from $375.00 to $450.00; Silver rooster, from $1,500.00 to $2,000.00; Ruby glass lady's leg with silver-plated high-heel sandal, from $900.00 to $1,200.00. (Photo courtesy Steven Visakay)

Shaker, Windmill, wht on cobalt glass/SP lid, Hazel-Atlas, +6 tumblers . 95.00
Shot glass, A Pick Up!, sexy girl leaning on lamppost, mc on clear.12.50
Shot glass, hunter thrown from horse, blk/red on clear 15.00
Stopper, horse head, Heisey, 13½", from $350 to.......................... 450.00
Stopper, silver w/emb decor, orig cork, Silver 800 mk, 3x1⅜"........ 25.00
Swizzle sticks, assorted colors of glass, 6", 6 for 12.00
Tallstirs, leaves on anodized aluminum, RJ Walthes, 1950s, 8", 8 for. 25.00
Traveling barn, NP shaker form, 9-pc, mk Germany, ca 1928, 8" .. 85.00
Tray, rvpt Deco design in rosewood fr, Fr, 1930s, 16½x11" 100.00
Tumbler, circus elephants on clear, ftd, Libbey, 5¼" 20.00
Tumblers, highball; Art Deco gold bands on clear, 1940s, 6 for 85.00
Tumblers, Manhattans w/backgammon decor on clear, Cassini, 6 for..65.00

Baskets

Basket weaving is a craft as old as ancient history. Baskets have been used to harvest crops, for domestic chores, and to contain the catch of fishermen. Materials at hand were utilized, and baskets from a specific region are often distinguishable simply by analyzing the natural fibers used in their construction. Early Indian baskets were made of corn husks or woven grasses. Willow splint, straw, rope, and paper were also used. Until the invention of the veneering machine in the late 1800s, splint was made by water-soaking a split log until the fibers were softened and flexible. Long strips were pulled out by hand and, while still wet and pliable, woven into baskets in either a cross-hatch or hexagonal weave.

Most handcrafted baskets on the market today were made between 1860 and the early 1900s. Factory baskets with a thick, wide splint cut by machine are of little interest to collectors. The more popular baskets are those designed for a specific purpose, rather than the more commonly found utility baskets that had multiple uses. Among the most costly forms are the Nantucket Lighthouse baskets, which were basically copied from those made there for centuries by aboriginal Indians. They were designed in the style of whale-oil barrels and named for the South Shoal Nantucket Lightship where many were made during the last half of the nineteenth century. Cheese baskets (used to separate curds from whey), herb-gathering baskets, and finely woven Shaker miniatures are other highly-prized examples of the basket-weaver's art.

In the listings that follow, assume that each has a center bentwood handle (unless handles of another type are noted) that is not included in the height. Unless another type of material is indicated, assume that each is made of splint. Prices are subjective and hinge on several factors: construction, age, color, and general appearance. Baskets rated very good (VG) will have minor losses and damage. See also American Indian; Eskimo; Sewing; Shaker.

Apple, with hand grips, late 1800s, bushel size, 14x18", $120.00; Potato stamped, red fruit and green leaves, New York, ca. 1860, VG, 9x12", $190.00; Feather or tow, with lid, ca. 1860, 17x13", $40.00. (Photo courtesy Aston Macek Auctions)

Baby, willow, wrapped rim, early 20th C, 30" L, VG 60.00
Baluster, buckled woven tape harness for carrying on bk, hdl, 25x16" . 90.00
Burl, natural freeform, 2 hdls, EX patina, 15x19x13" 515.00
Buttocks, minor splits, 8x16" 120.00
Buttocks, tight weave, varnished, 4½x9" 150.00
Buttocks, well defined form, some damage, 9x18½" 150.00
Buttocks, wide rim, 2½x4¼" 200.00
Buttocks, 2-tone, 9½x17½" 175.00
Cheese, wide splint, open weave, bentwood rim, 8x30", VG 125.00
Field, 1 rim hdl & buckled woven-tape harness, 25x16" 115.00
Gathering, rectangular, no hdl, 12x37x31" 360.00
Gathering, rnd on sq base, stamped flowers/bands, 5x10½" 250.00
Gathering, shallow, 1890s, 7¼x12¼" dia...................................... 175.00
Grape carrying, woven reeds, 42" L.. 25.00
Market, rectangular, 15x14½" 100.00
Melon, tight weave, 34-rib, EX patina, sm break, 16x18" 325.00
Mini, tight weave, 3x5" 270.00
Nantucket, curly maple bottom, branded 4¼x19" 725.00
Nantucket, paper label: Ferdinand Sylvaro, 4x10¼" 975.00
Nantucket, purse, oval w/ivory shells on lid, 1973, 7x10½" 3,300.00
Nantucket, rattan & splint, cvd swing hdl & ears, wood base, 7x9⅜".. 1,900.00
Oval, radiating ribs, wrapped rim, ca 1900, 10x10" 550.00
Oval, red pnt, rectangular base, cvd upright hdl, 10x16" 530.00
Oval, wide splint, dk red pnt, lt wear, 13½" 375.00
Oval w/sq bottom, 2 rim hdls, thick red pnt, 1900s, 3x8x7", VG.. 120.00
Picnic, Hawkeye Refrigerator, hickory & bamboo, 15x21" 60.00
Rectangular, bl/gr/red stripes, cvd hdls, minor rim loss, 5x14x12". 460.00
Rnd, ash splint, swing hdl, fine & tight weave, natural, NY, 8x12".. 660.00
Rnd, dk ash splint, dbl hdls, 13" 155.00
Rnd, orig gr pnt, 8x15", VG 325.00
Rnd, ribbed, fine/thin splints, cvd upright hdl, 1890s, 5½" 230.00
Rnd w/domed base, ash, swing hdl, NY, 11x14"........................... 345.00
Rnd w/domed center, tin reinforcement, HH Harris, 15x18"....... 265.00
Rnd w/flat bottom, wrapped rim, 8x12" 60.00
Rnd w/wrapped ft, ash w/mixed wood hdl, 14x11" 200.00
Sq to rnd, ash, G color, NY, 15x26" 400.00
Utility, 16x16" 110.00

Batchelder

Ernest A. Batchelder was a leading exponent of the Arts and Crafts movement in the United States. His influential book, *Design in Theory and Practice,* was originally published in 1910. He is best known, however, for his artistic tiles which he first produced in Pasadena, California, from 1909 to 1916. In 1916 the business was relocated to Los Angeles where it continued until 1932, closing because of the Depression.

In 1938 Batchelder resumed production in Pasadena under the name of 'Kinneola Kiln.' Output of the new pottery consisted of delicately cast bowls and vases in an Oriental style. This business closed in 1951. Tiles carry a die-stamped mark; vases and bowls are hand incised. For more information we recommend *Collector's Encyclopedia of California Pottery, Second Edition,* by Jack Chipman (Collector Books) and *American Art Tiles,* in four volumes by Norman Karlson (Schiffer, 2005). Our advisors for this category are Suzanne Perrault and David Rago; they are listed in the Directory under New Jersey.

Bowl, lav w/lt gr int, everted rim, sm ft, stepped body, 2½x5" 85.00
Chest, dk stained oak w/incised daffodil front panel, 14x28x15" ..8,400.00
Corbel, geometrics emb, bl-gr matt, sm chips, 6x3", pr 120.00
Fountain, children w/flutes beneath trees, 2-pc, wall mt, #F565, 31".8,350.00
Fountain, peacocks/grapes/angels, bl engobe on beige, 2-pc, 34x35".6,000.00
Planter, mosaic pattern tile border, acorn shape, hanging, att, 16x12"..600.00
Tile, castle scene, 12½x8", in dk oak fr 400.00

Triptych, pumpkin field, marked Batchelder Pasedena, 19½x63" long, $12,600.00. (Photo courtesy David Rago Auctions/LiveAuctioneers.com)

Vase, gr transparent on red clay, swollen cylinder, wide mouth, 14". 950.00
Vase, moss gr to warm beige, slim cylinder, Kinneloa mk, 9½"..... 250.00

Battersea

Battersea is a term that refers to enameling on copper or other metal. Though originally produced at Battersea, England, in the mid-eighteenth century, the craft was later practiced throughout the Staffordshire district. Boxes are the most common examples. Some are figurals, and many bear an inscription. Unless a condition is noted in the description, values are given for examples with only minimal damage, which is normal. Please note that items with printed Bilston labels are new. Our advisor for this category is John Harrigan; he is listed in the Directory under Minnesota

Box, courting couple/mtn scene, 2x2¾" dia, +Cartier gift box..... 660.00
Box, Fair Words Are Always... on seafoam gr, 1⅛x2", EX 235.00
Box, peach form, missing stem, 18th C, 1¾x1½" 1,550.00
Box, scenic reserves on pk w/gold, no-hinge lid, late 1700s, 3½" H . 900.00
Box, snuff; wrestling scene, 1¾" 270.00
Box, W/Grateful Heart This Trifle...Content, mc on lav enamel, sm, EX. 210.00
Candlesticks, floral on turq w/gold, 1750s, 10¾", pr 3,000.00
Candlesticks, floral on wht, petal bobeche removes, 1750s, 10", pr..2,350.00

Curtain ties, hot air balloon scene in grisaille, 1800s, 1¾", pr...... 425.00
Vase, potpourri; figures in landscape reserve on turq w/gold, 9¼" ..2,700.00

Bauer

The Bauer Pottery Company is one of the best known of the California pottery companies, noted for both its artware and its dinnerware. In the past 10 years, Bauer has become particularly collectible, and prices have risen accordingly. The pottery actually started in Kentucky in 1885. It moved to Los Angeles in 1910 where it remained in operation until 1962. The company produced several successful dinnerware lines, including La Linda, Monterey, and Brusche Al Fresco. Most popular and most significant was the Ringware line introduced in 1932, which preceded Fiesta as a popular solid-color everyday dinnerware. The earliest pieces are unmarked, although to collectors they are unmistakable, partly due to their distinctive glazes which have an almost primitive charm due to their drips, misses, and color variations.

Another dinnerware line favored by collectors is Speckleware, its name derived from the 1950s-era speckled glaze Bauer used on various products, including vases, flowerpots, kitchenware items, and dinnerware. Though not as popular as Ringware, Speckleware holds its value and is usually available at much lower prices than Ring. Keep an eye out for other flowerpots and mixing bowls as well.

Artware by Bauer is not so easy to find now, but it is worth seeking out because of its high values. So-called oil jars sell for upwards of $1,500.00, and Rebekah vases routinely fetch $400.00 or more. Matt Carlton is one of the most desirable designers of handmade ware.

After WWII a flood of foreign imports and loss of key employees drastically curtailed their sales, and the pottery began a steady decline that ended in failure in 1962. Prices listed below reflect the California market. For more information we recommend *California Pottery Scrapbook* and *Collector's Encyclopedia of California Pottery, Second Edition*, both by Jack Chipman (Collector Books).

In the lines of Ring and Plain ware, pricing depends to some extent on color. Low-end colors include light brown, Chinese yellow, orange-red, Jade green, red-brown, olive green, light blue, turquoise, and gray; the high-end colors are Delph blue, ivory, dusty burgundy, cobalt, chartreuse, papaya, and burgundy. In Monterey, Monterey blue, burgundy, and white are high-end colors; all others are considerably less. Black is highly collectible in all of these lines; to evaluate black, add at least 100% to an item's value in any other color. An in-depth study of colors may be found in the books referenced above.

Ring Ware

Bowl, mixing; bright yel, #18, 8¼" 65.00
Bowl, mixing; ivory, 6¾" 48.00
Bowl, mixing; pumpkin, #9, 5½x11" 85.00
Bowl, mixing; wht gloss (rare), 10¾" 420.00
Bowl, vegetable; gr, oval, 9½x6½" 48.00
Bowls, mixing; Chinese Yellow, nesting set of 6 .... 325.00
Bowls, mixing; mixed colors, nesting set of 5 .... 275.00
Candlesticks, orange, 2", pr 170.00
Casserole, blk, w/lid & metal fr 170.00
Chop plate, yel, 14" 150.00
Coffeepot, orange, 6¼" 450.00
Cookie jar, gr 445.00
Cookie jar, wht 545.00
Creamer, blk, 3¼" 85.00
Creamer, Jade Green, 1½-pt, 4¼" 95.00
Creamer & sugar bowl, yel & orange, w/lid, 2½", 3½" 250.00
Cup & saucer, bright yel 60.00
Cup & saucer, orange 60.00

Honey jar, 2-bee lid, complete 1,000.00
Pitcher, yel, 5" 45.00
Plate, orange, 9½" 55.00
Platter, blk gloss, 12½" 85.00
Platter, wht, 12½" 120.00
Refrigerator jar, Monterey Orange, w/lid 265.00
Shakers, orange, squat, pr 50.00
Sherbet, orange, ftd 50.00
Sugar bowl, orange, w/lid 65.00
Tumbler, Jade Green, metal hdl, 4½" 65.00
Tumbler, orange, 12-oz, 4½" 85.00
Vase, gr, #B7, 11" 75.00

Miscellaneous

Art pottery, vase, Matt Carlton's 'signature' style, 18½", in orange-red: minimum value, $1,800.00.

(Photo courtesy Jack Chipman)

Art pottery, vase, leaf-formed ball, wht, mk Bauer Atlanta, 7½".. 195.00
Art pottery, vase, Pinnacle, pk, #509, 10x6½" 170.00
Art pottery, vase, rectangular, gunmetal gray, 8¼x4½x3⅛" 55.00
Art pottery, vase, ribbed fan form, cobalt, Matt Carlton, 6" 460.00
Art pottery, vase, ruffled rim, orange, Matt Carlton, 6¼x3¾" 165.00
Art pottery, vase, Teardrop, lime gr speckled, Tracy Irwin, 8½" ...125.00
Art pottery, vase, Teardrop, wht speckled, Tracy Irwin, 10x4" 125.00
Cal-Art, bowl, tan satin, shallow, Tracy Irwin, 16½" L 60.00
Cal-Art, flowerpot, Swirl, pk speckled, #9 .... 65.00
Cal-Art, flowerpot, Swirl, turq, 6" 55.00
Cal-Art, flowerpot, Swirl, wht matt, 5" 40.00
Cal-Art, flowerpot, Swirl, yel, 7½x8" 65.00
Cal-Art, swan planter, bl, 12" L 55.00
Cal-Art, swan planter, chartreuse gr, 10" L 55.00
Cal-Art, swan planter, lt gr, 7" L 42.50
Cal-Art, vase, wht matt, low hdls, 5⅛" 80.00
Cal-Art, 3-Step pot, wht, 4" 40.00
Florist ware, Indian pot, unglazed terra cotta, 12x18", NM 150.00
Florist ware, Indian pot, unglazed terra cotta, 9¼x14¼" 165.00
Florist ware, Spanish pot, wht gloss, 5" 30.00
Florist ware, Spanish pot, yel, 3" 18.00
Florist ware, vase, Swirl, aqua, 8x9" 75.00
Florist ware, 3-Step pot, orange-red, 2¾x5¼" 380.00
Novelty, hippo w/open mouth, stands w/head up, wht, 3¼x4½" ..235.00
Plain ware, batter bowl, orange, NM 60.00
Plain ware, bowl, turq, no rings, 4¾x15" 140.00
Plain ware, carafe, chartreuse, wood hdl, 8" 80.00

Bellaire, Marc

Marc Bellaire, originally Donald Edmund Fleischman, was born in Toledo, Ohio, in 1925. He studied at the Toledo Museum of Art under Ernest Spring while employed as a designer for the Libbey Glass Company. During World War II while serving in the Navy, he traveled extensively throughout the Pacific, resulting in his enriched sense of design and color.

Marc settled in California in the 1950s where his work attracted the attention of national buyers and agencies who persuaded him to create ceramic lines of his own, employing hand-decorating techniques throughout. He built a studio in Culver City, and there he produced high-quality ceramics, often decorated with ultramodern figures or geometric patterns and executed with a distinctive flair. His most famous line was Mardi Gras, decorated with slim dancers in spattered and striped colors of black, blue, pink, and white. Other major patterns were Jamaica, Balinese, Beachcomber, Friendly Island, Cave Painting, Hawaiian, Bird Isle, Oriental, Jungle Dancer, and Kashmir. Kashmir usually has the name Ingle on the front and Bellaire on the reverse.

It is to be noted that Marc was employed by Sascha Brastoff during the 1950s. Many believe that he was hired for his creative imagination and style.

During the period from 1951 to 1956, Marc was named one of the top 10 artware designers by *Giftwares Magazine*. After 1956 he taught and lectured on art, design, and ceramic decorating techniques from coast to coast. Many of his pieces were one of a kind, commissioned throughout the United States.

During the 1970s he set up a studio in Marin County, California, and eventually moved to Palm Springs where he opened his final studio/ gallery. There he produced large pieces with a Southwestern style. Mr. Bellaire died in 1994. Our advisor for this category is Marty Webster; he is listed in the Directory under Michigan.

Ashtray, Balinese dancers, freeform, #B-47x14, 14" 60.00
Ashtray, Calypso, #7798, 1x10¾x8" 28.00
Ashtray, Clown, mc on cream, 8" 85.00
Ashtray, Mardi Gras, 2 men dancing, triangular, 14" 120.00
Ashtray, Still Life, matt fruits & leaves, 10x15" 100.00
Bowl, Mardi Gras, 2 men dancing, #B-18, 13x11" 120.00
Box, African figures on lid, 6" 95.00
Box, Cortillian, lady w/bl bird, 13x9" 125.00
Box, Mardi Gras, 10" dia 150.00
Box, Still Life, fruits & leaves on lid, 2x4½x3½" 75.00
Candlestick, Jamaican man, 10½" 125.00
Compote, Cave Painting, 4-ftd, 6x12" 100.00
Compote, Cortillian, 4-ftd, 8x17" 200.00
Dish, exotic plants & flowers, bl/red on yel, 13½" dia 70.00
Figurine, bird w/long neck, 17" 250.00
Figurine, horse, gray/gr/brn, 8x7½" 140.00
Figurine, Mardi Gras, female seated, 5½" 150.00
Figurines, Jamaican man w/guitar, 2nd w/bongos, tallest: 8", pr ... 425.00

Figurines, Mardi Gras, 24", 30" (on metal stand), from $700.00 to $900.00 each. (Photo courtesy Jack Chipman)

Jar, Stick People, conical w/wide top, w/lid, 5x5" 135.00
Plate, Jamaican men (3) on brn, sq, 5" 25.00
Platter, fisherman w/net, 16" dia 150.00

Platter, rectangles form chain, triangular, 16x9" 68.00
Switch plate, dancer on blk, #B-26, 3x4¾" 150.00
Tray, Balinese women, hourglass shape, 8" 100.00
Vase, Jungle Dancer, strong colors, flaring toward bottom, 7x8" .. 165.00
Vase, line figures on brn & beige, tapered cylinder, 8¾x3" 75.00
Vase, Polynesian woman, 9" 100.00
Vase, reindeer, 4½" 45.00

Belleek, American

From 1883 until 1930, several American potteries located in New Jersey and Ohio manufactured a type of china similar to the famous Irish Belleek soft-paste porcelain. The American manufacturers dentified their porcelain by using 'Belleek' or 'Beleek' in their marks. American Belleek is considered the highest achievement of the American porcelain industry. Production centered around artistic cabinet pieces and luxury tablewares. Many examples emulated Irish shapes and decor with marine themes and other naturalistic styles. While all are highly collectible, some companies' products are rarer than others. The best-known manufacturers are Ott and Brewer, Willets, The Ceramic Art Company (CAC), and Lenox. (Refer to the Lenox category for listings on CAC an Lenox.) You will find more detailed information in those specific categories. Our advisor for this category is Mary Frank Gaston; she is listed in the Directory under Texas.

Key:
AAC — American Art China   CAP — Columbian Art Pottery

Bowl, tiny flowers w/in & w/o, gold rim, AAC, 2½x5" 425.00
Cup & saucer, morning glories, Morgan 175.00

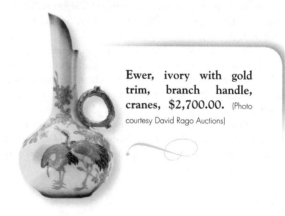

Ewer, ivory with gold trim, branch handle, cranes, $2,700.00. (Photo courtesy David Rago Auctions)

Mug, monk playing violin, CAP, 5" 150.00
Plate, mixed floral, bright mc on wht w/gold rim, Coxon, 5¾" 115.00
Salt cellar, sponged gold, scalloped, pk int, AAC, 2½" 145.00
Vase, floral on wht, gold emb hdls, AAC, 12" 1,200.00

Belleek, Irish

Belleek is a very thin translucent porcelain that takes its name from the village in Ireland where it originated in 1859. The glaze is a creamy ivory color with a pearl-like lustre. The tablewares, baskets, figurines, and vases that have always been made there are being crafted yet today. Shamrock, Tridacna, Echinus, and Thorn are but a few of the many patterns of tableware which have been made during some periods of the pottery's history. Throughout the years, their most popular pattern has been Shamrock.

It is possible to date an example to within 20 to 30 years of crafting by the mark. Pieces with an early stamp often bring prices nearly triple that of a similar but current item. With some variation, the marks have always incorporated the Irish wolfhound, Celtic round tower, harp, and shamrocks. The first three marks (usually in black) were used from 1863 to 1946. A series of green marks identified the pottery's offerings from 1946 until the seventh mark (in gold/brown) was introduced in 1980 (it was discontinued in 1992). The eighth mark was blue and closely resembled the gold mark. It was used from 1993 to 1996. The ninth, tenth, and eleventh marks went back to the simplicity of the first mark with only the registry mark (an R encased in a circle) to distinguish them from the original. The ninth mark, which was used from 1997 to 1999, was blue. A special black version of that mark was introduced for the year 2000 and a Millennium 2000 banner was added. The tenth or Millennium mark was retired at the end of 2000, and the current green mark was introduced as the eleventh mark. Belleek Collector's International Society limited edition pieces are designated with a special mark in red. In the listings below, numbers designated with the prefix 'D' relate to the book *Belleek, The Complete Collector's Guide and Illustrated Reference, Second Edition*, by Richard K. Degenhardt (published by Wallace-Homestead Book Company, One Chilton Way, Radnor, PA 19098-0230). The numbers designated with the prefix 'B' are current production numbers used by the pottery. Our advisor for this category is Liz Stillwell; she is listed in the Directory under California.

Key:

A — plain (glazed only)	I — 1863 – 1890
B — cob lustre	II — 1891 – 1926
C — hand tinted	III — 1926 – 1946
D — hand painted	IV — 1946 – 1955
E — hand-painted shamrocks	V — 1955 – 1965
F — hand gilted	VI — 1965 – 3/31/1980
G — hand tinted and gilted	VII — 4/1/1980 – 1992
H — hand-painted shamrocks and gilted	VIII — 1/4/1993 – 1996
	IX — 1997 – 1999
J — mother-of-pearl	X — 2000 only
K — hand painted and gilted	XI — 2001 – current
L — bisque and plain	
M — decalcomania	
N — special hand-painted decoration	
T — transfer design	

Further information concerning Periods of Crafting (Baskets):

1 — 1865 – 1890, BELLEEK (three-strand)

2 — 1865 – 1890, BELLEEK CO. FERMANAGH (three-strand)

3 — 1891 – 1920, BELLEEK CO. FERMANAGH IRELAND (three-strand)

4 — 1921 – 1954, BELLEEK CO. FERMANAGH IRELAND (four-strand)

5 — 1955 – 1979, BELLEEK® CO. FERMANAGH IRELAND (four-strand)

6 — 1980 – 1985, BELLEEK® IRELAND (four-strand)

7 — 1985 – 1989, BELLEEK® IRELAND 'ID NUMBER' (four-strand)

8 – 12 — 1990 to present (Refer to *Belleek, The Complete Collector's Guide and Illustrated Reference, 2nd Edition*, Chapter 5)

Aberdeen Tea Ware Tea & Saucer, D489-II, B	575.00
Aberdeen Vase, Flowered, D70-III, G, lg	750.00
Artichoke Tea Ware Teapot, D710-I, F	800.00
Bamboo Teapot, D516-I, A, sm	800.00
Basket Compote, D30-I, A	950.00
Bird's Nest Basket, D123-II, J	700.00
Blarney Tea Ware Tea & Saucer, D567-II, C	375.00
Bust of Queen of the Hops, D1130-III, L&B, 11½"	4,000.00
Cane Spill, D165-1, C, lg, 11"	700.00
Celtic Design Tea Ware Coffee & Saucer, D1428 & 1430-III, K	300.00
Cherry Blossom Plate, 3 Strand, Flowered, D1685-6, D	650.00

Cherub Font, D1110-III, A, lg	350.00
Chinese Tea Ware Teapot, D484-I, K	1,500.00
Cleary Mug, D218-II, B, 2½"	150.00
Cone Tea Ware Dejeuner Set, D437-II, C	4,250.00
Diamond Biscuit Jar, D600-IV, D	400.00
Earthenware Jelly Mould, D883-II, A, 9"	175.00
Earthenware Soup Plate, D888-II, A, 9"	175.00
Echinus Footed Bowl, D1521-VI, G	600.00
Echinus Tea Ware Dejeuner Set, D650-II, C	4,500.00
Egg Frame & 6 Cups, D621-VI, G	300.00
Egyptian Napkin Ring, D1551-I, F	600.00
Fan Tea Ware Tea & Saucer, D694-I, K	425.00
Flowered Crate, D268-II, J	475.00
Forget-Me-Not Box, D111 II, A, 2" H	650.00
Gospel Plates, Set of 4, D1811-VI/D1813-VII/D1815-VII/D1817-VII, M&F	650.00
Grass Mug, D214-III, B	190.00
Grass Tea Ware Teapot, D733-II, D, med	650.00
Harebell Vase, D180-V, K	105.00
Harp w/Applied Shamorcks, D1640-II, K	550.00
Hexagon Tea Ware Tea & Saucer, D622-II, N	450.00
Irish Harp, D77-V, E, sm	280.00
Irish Squirrel Wall Bracket, D1803-I, A	4,750.00
Ivy Sugar & Cream, D237-I & D238-I, B, lg	325.00
Ivy Tea Ware Bread Plate, D1410-III, B	325.00
Jack-'O-Lantern Votive, B2971-XI	55.00
Killarney Candlestick, D1982-VII, D, ea	85.00

Lace Tea Ware Teapot, D800-I, made during the first period, pink tinted with gold trim, scarce, **$2,250.00**. (Photo courtesy Richard Degenhardt)

Lily of the Valley Frame, D1720-I, J, sm	1,700.00
Lily Tea Ware Tea & Saucer & Side Plate, D536-II & D542-II, G	450.00
Mask Tea Ware Cream, tall, D1483-III, B, lg	195.00
Milk Maid Lithophane, B2436-XI, L&B, 9¼x11⅛"	175.00
Nautilus Cream, D279-II, A	325.00
Neptune Tea Ware Kettle, D431-VII, B, lg	275.00
Neptune Tea Ware Tea & Saucer, D414-III, C	150.00
Nickel Flowerpot, D209-III, B	275.00
Oak Flowerpot, ftd, D46-II, J	2,700.00
Pierced Spill, Flowered, D49-III, A, lg	350.00
Plain Heart Shape Basket, D1284-4, A	525.00
Prince Arthur Vase, D73-II, J	800.00
Rock Spill, D162-II, C, med	300.00
Rope Handle Mug, D215-II, B	250.00
Scroll Tea Ware Tea & Saucer, D502-II, G	425.00
Shamrock Flowerpot, D98-II, H, 8"	850.00
Shamrock Honey Pot on Stand, D530-II, E	600.00
Shamrock Mug, D216-II, E	150.00
Shamrock Tea Ware Covered Muffin Dish, D388-III, E	525.00
Shamrock Tea Ware Kettle, D386-II, E, lg	600.00
Shamrock Tea Ware Moustache & Saucer, D374-II, E	450.00
Shamrock Ware TV Set, D2017-VII, E	110.00
Shamrock Wedding Cup, 3-hdl, D2105-II, E	475.00
Single Henshall's Spill, Flowered, D61-IV, B	135.00
Single Hippiritus, D146-I, B, 7"	850.00
Single Root Spill, D151-II, D, 3"	550.00
Sydney Tea Ware Tea & Saucer, D607-II, C	425.00

Table Centre, D56-IV, D	1,200.00
Thistle Tea Ware Tea & Saucer, D779-I, G	425.00
Thorn Tea Ware Bread Plate, D767-II, K, 9" L	1,200.00
Thorn Ware Tea Stand, D2068-I, K	800.00
Tridacna Tea Ware Covered Muffin Dish, D479-II, A	425.00
Tridacna Tea Ware Milk Jug, D480-V, B	95.00
Undine Cream, D305-V, C	70.00
Victoria Shell, D128-II, B	550.00
Victoria Tea Ware Tea & Saucer, D593-II, G	550.00

Bells

Some areas of interest represented in the study of bells are history, religion, and geography. Since Biblical times, bells have announced morning church services, vespers, deaths, christenings, school hours, fires, and community events. Countries have used them en masse to peal out the good news of Christmas, New Year's, and the endings of World Wars I and II. They've been rung in times of great sorrow, such as the death of Abraham Lincoln.

For further information, we recommend *World of Bells* by Dorothy Malone Anthony (a series of 10 books). All have over 200 colored pictures covering many bell categories. See also Nodders; Schoolhouse Collectibles.

Brass, simple casting, 12"	110.00
Brass boxing ring type, Bevin, 8" dia	180.00
Brass dinner type, cylinder hangs from stand, 17x9x5"	65.00
Brass hotel type on CI base, 4½"	85.00
Brass lady figural, hands folded, legs as clapper, 19th C, 4¼"	48.00
Brass sleigh, varied szs, 16 on leather strap	120.00
Brass sleigh, 12 on leather strap	85.00
Brass sleigh, 8 on leather strap	55.00
Brass w/CI parrot figural hdl, mc pnt, 4⅞"	120.00
Bronze, cat w/bow tie as handle, England, 6½"	120.00
Bronze, cherub hdl, figures emb around body, 1920s, 6¼"	60.00
CI church tower type, ca 1880, 39" W	550.00
CI hotel type, Atlas supporting world figural, 1860s, 7"	275.00
CI turtle figural, orig pnt, Germany, 5¾" L	220.00
CI w/wrought-iron yoke, worn gilt, 24x20"	480.00
Metal lady figural, nodder head, Renaissance dress, EB, 4¾"	235.00

Plantation bell mounted on a frame, 1800s, height of bell: 28", $4,370.00. (Photo courtesy Neal Auction Co. Auctioneers & Appraisers of Fine Art)

Silver, Oriental figural hdl, bl enameled body, 4½"	150.00
Silver, repoussé w/Neoclassical figures, Cupid hdl, 5"	300.00

Bennett, John

Bringing with him the knowledge and experience he had gained at the Doulton (Lambeth) Pottery in England, John Bennett opened a studio in New York City around 1877, where he continued his methods of decorating faience under the glaze. Early wares utilized imported English biscuit, though subsequently local clays (both white and cream-colored) were also used. His first kiln was on Lexington Avenue; he built another on East Twenty-Fourth Street. Pieces are usually signed 'J. Bennett, N.Y.,' often with the street address and date. Later examples may be marked 'West Orange, N.J.,' where he retired. The pottery was in operation approximately six years in New York. Pieces signed with other initials are usually worth less. Our advisor for this category is Robert Tuggle; he is listed in the Directory under New York.

Vase, floral on cobalt mottle, signed, #101, 10", $5,500.00. (Photo courtesy David Rago Auctions/ LiveAuctioneers.com)

Bottle, chrysanthemums, mc w/cobalt on cadmium yel, rstr, 13½x6½"	5,400.00
Deep dish plate, Rockingham, 11", EX	60.00
Jar, dogwood & roses, mc on blk, floral inner lid, 1881, 15½"	66,000.00
Pitcher, Floral Nymphs, flint enamel, 6½", EX	60.00
Spittoon, flint enamel, 4½x8"	60.00
Vase, bud; quatrefoils, red on turq, bulbous, 11x5"	5,700.00
Vase, chrysanthemums, mc on dk ground, bulbous, rare red clay, 11x7"	3,600.00
Vase, daisies & butterflies, mc on turq, spherical, 1878, 8¼x5½"	5,280.00
Vase, dogwood branches on teal, bulbous, 10x6½", NM	2,040.00
Vase, floral/foliage, pk/gr on cobalt mottle, gourd shape, #102, 10"	5,750.00
Vase, hibiscus/leaves, mc on indigo, 1889, 12½x12", NM	6,345.00

Bennington

Although the term has become a generic one for the mottled brown ware produced there, Bennington is not a type of pottery, but rather a town in Vermont where two important potteries were located. The Norton Company, founded in 1793, produced mainly redware and salt-glazed stoneware; only during a brief partnership with Fenton (1845 – 1847) was any Rockingham attempted. The Norton Company endured until 1894, operated by succeeding generations of the Norton family. Fenton organized his own pottery in 1847. There he manufactured not only redware and stoneware, but more artistic types as well — graniteware, scroddled ware, flint enamel, a fine parian, and vast amounts of their famous Rockingham. Though from an esthetic standpoint his work rated highly among the country's finest ceramic achievements, he was economically unsuccessful. His pottery closed in 1858.

It is estimated that only one in five Fenton pieces were marked; and although it has become a common practice to link any fine piece of Rockingham to this area, careful study is vital in order to be able to distinguish Bennington's from the similar wares of many other American and Staffordshire potteries. Although the practice was without the permission of the proprietor, it was nevertheless a common occurrence for a potter to take his molds with him when moving from one pottery to the next, so particularly well-received designs were often reproduced at several locations. Of eight known Fenton marks, four are variations of the '1849' impressed stamp: 'Lyman Fenton Co., Fenton's Enamel Patented 1849, Bennington, Vermont.' These are generally found on examples of Rockingham and flint enamel. A raised, rectangular scroll with 'Fenton's

Works, Bennington, Vermont,' was used on early examples of porcelain. From 1852 to 1858, the company operated under the title of the United States Pottery Company. Three marks — the ribbon mark with the initials USP, the oval with a scrollwork border and the name in full, and the plain oval with the name in full — were used during that period.

Among the more sought-after examples are the bird and animal figurines, novelty pitchers, figural bottles, and all of the more finely modeled items. Recumbent deer, cows, standing lions with one forepaw on a ball, and opposing pairs of poodles with baskets in their mouths and 'coleslaw' fur were made in Rockingham, flint enamel, and occasionally in parian. Numbers in the listings below refer to the book *Bennington Pottery and Porcelain* by Barret. Our advisors for Bennington (except for parian and stoneware) are Barbara and Charles Adams; they are listed in the Directory under Massachusetts.

Key: c/s — cobalt on salt glaze

Book flask, Departed Spirits, flint enamel, 5¾x4x2" 795.00
Bottle, coachman, Rockingham, att Fenton Pottery, ca 1849, 10" ..900.00
Candlestick, flint enamel, ca 1849, 7", ea 695.00

Coffee urn, flint enamel, paneled form with pewter spigot, 21", EX, $3,450.00. (Photo courtesy Garth's Auctions Inc.)

Figurine, cow on base, recumbent, 1849 mk, 6x10", EX, from $12,000 to ..14,000.00
Figurine, dog on base, sitting, 10½", EX 600.00
Figurine, lion, flint enamel, tongue up, coleslaw mane, 10⅜" L .9,000.00
Kettle, croup; Rockingham, w/lid, ca 1850, 6½", NM 245.00
Pitcher, gr & cream mottle, ca 1850s, 9" 295.00
Pitcher, paneled, Rockingham, ca 1850s, 12" 465.00
Snuff jar, male figure sitting, flint enamel, hat lid, 1849 mk, 4¼". 960.00
Toby mug, gr & cream mottle, Lyman, Fenton & Co Enamel Pat 1849, 6"..950.00

Stoneware

Churn, #2/stylized flower, E&LP Norton, ca 1880, flaw, 14" 685.00
Churn, #6/flower bouquet, J&E Norton, 1960-61, w/lid, 19" ..10,000.00
Cooler, #4/dotted leaf, E&LP Norton, bbl form, ca 1880, 13½" ...600.00
Cooler, #5/floral bands, J&E Norton..., chips/lines, 15" 1,100.00
Cream pot, #2/flower, J&E Norton, ca 1880, prof rstr lines, 11" ..250.00
Cream pot, #2/flower (triple), Norton & Fenton, ca 1845, 11", EX.132.50
Cream pot, #3/flower bouquet, E&LP Norton, ca 1880, stain, 12"..440.00
Cream pot, #4/lg floral spray, J&E Norton, ca 1855, crack, 14".... 360.00
Cream pot, bird on twig, J&E Norton, ca 1855, staining, 8½" ..1,155.00
Crock, #2/chicken pecks corn, J Norton & Co, ca 1861, rstr, 9" . 1,485.00
Crock, #2/ribbed leaf, J Norton & Co, sm flakes, 11x9" 635.00
Crock, #3/flower basket (lg), J Norton & Co, ca 1861, hairline, 11" .1,155.00
Crock, #5/floral spray (lg), E&LP Norton, ca 1880, chip, 13" ...1,045.00
Crock, #6/bird on stump, E&LP Norton, ca 1880, crack, 13½"..1,925.00

Crock, cake; #2/flying hawk/fence, J&E Norton, ca 1855, hairline, 8" ...6,600.00
Jar, #3/bird (dbl), J Norton & Co, ca 1861, prof rstr, 13" 1,200.00
Jar, perserve; #2/stylized leaf, E&LP Norton, ca 1880, chips, 112" ..750.00
Jar, preserve; #1½/flower (Benny Blue), J&E Norton, ca 1855, 11"..385.00
Jar, preserve; #2/bird on plume, E&LP Norton, 1880s, 11½", EX.440.00
Jug, #1½/bud, Julius Norton, ca 1848, ping, 13½" 2,200.00
Jug, #1/bird on twig, J Norton & Bennington, ca 1861, 10½" 850.00
Jug, #1/bird on twig, J Norton & Co, ca 1861, 11" 635.00
Jug, #2/flower, Julius Norton, ca 1848, sm chip, 14" 775.00
Jug, #2/pheasant on stump, J&E Norton, ca 1855, lt stain, 14".2,650.00
Jug, #2/pheasant on stump, J&E Norton, ca 1855, rstr lines, 14"...1,540.00
Jug, #4/flower basket, J&E Norton, ca 1855, 16" 1,650.00

Beswick

In the early 1890s, James Wright Beswick operated a pottery in Longston, England, where he produced fine dinnerware as well as ornamental ceramics. Today's collectors are most interested in the figurines made since 1936 by a later generation Beswick firm, John Beswick, Ltd. They specialize in reproducing accurately detailed bone-china models of authentic breeds of animals. Their Fireside Series includes dogs, cats, elephants, horses, the Huntsman, and an Indian figure, which measure up to 14" in height. The Connoisseur line is modeled after the likenesses of famous racing horses. Beatrix Potter's characters and some of Walt Disney's are charmingly re-created and appeal to children and adults alike. Other items, such as character Tobys, have also been produced. The Beswick name is stamped on each piece. The firm was absorbed by the Doulton group in 1973.

Animaland, Loopy Hare, c GB - Animation Ltd Beswick..., 4⅛".. 325.00
Beatrix Potter, Benjamin Bunny, gold mk, 4" 165.00
Beatrix Potter, Duchess w/Flowers, gold mk, 3¾" 2,135.00
Beatrix Potter, Duchess w/Pie, BP-3B, 4" 350.00
Beatrix Potter, Ginger, BP-3B, c 1976, 3¾", MIB 255.00
Beatrix Potter, Mr Jackson, gr version, BP-3, 2¾" 225.00
Beatrix Potter, Mr Todd, #3091, BP-4, 1988, 4¾" 215.00
Beatrix Potter, Pickles, gold mk, BP-2, 4¾" 265.00
Beatrix Potter, Pig-Wig, blk version, 1972, 4" 200.00
Beatrix Potter, Pigling Bland, gold mk, 4½" 150.00
Beatrix Potter, Sir Isaac Newton, c 1973, 1981 edition, MIB....... 140.00
Beatrix Potter, Susan, BP-3C, 4", MIB....................................... 415.00
Bird, Bald Eagle, #1018, c 1945, 5x13½" 195.00
Bird, Dove, #1614, blk circle mk, 6" 475.00
Bird, Golden Eagle, #2062, 1966-74, 10x9½" 150.00

Bird, Lapwing, #2416B, late 1970s, 5½", $200.00.

Bird, Pheasants (cock & hen), #2078, 6¾" 425.00
Bird, Seagull on Rock, #768, 1939-54...................................... 1,285.00
Cat, Siamese seated, copper lustre, #1882, ca 1963 .... 465.00
Cow, Brahma Bull Champion of Champions, #3095, ca 1910, 7¾" L.. 175.00
Cow, Charolais, cream matt, #3075A, 1988 edition, 5" 390.00
Cow, Hereford, brn & wht gloss, #1360, 6¾" L............................ 340.00

Cow, Highland; #1740, 5¾".. 200.00
Cow, Polled Hereford Bull, brn & wht gloss, ringed nose, 5" 215.00
Fish, Large Mouthed Black Bass, 1952-68, 5x8" 625.00
Horse, Appaloosa in walking pose, 5¼" 560.00

Horse, chestnut, late 1950s, 5½", minimum value, $800.00.

Horse, Elizabeth II & Imperial Trooping the Colors, 10x10½", NM... 625.00
Horse, Mare, chestnut gloss, #1812, red label, 1962-67, 5¼" 875.00
Horse, Mare, facing left, chestnut gloss, #976, 1958-67, 6¾" 715.00
Walt Disney, Christopher Robin, gold mk, 4¾" 160.00
Wild Animal, Lion, facing right, #1506, 1957-67, 5¼x10" 165.00
Wild Animal, Tiger, attacking elephant, #1720, 12x16½" 750.00
Wild Animal, Tiger, 7½x13x3"...................................... 150.00

Bicycle Collectibles

Bicycles and related ephemera and memorabilia have been collected since the end of the nineteenth century, but for the last 20 years, they have been regarded as bonafide collectibles. Today they are prized not only for their charm and appearance, but for historical impact as well. Many wonderful items are now being offered through live and internet auctions, rare book sites, etc.

Hobby horse/draisienne bicycles were handmade between during circa 1818 and 1821. If found today, one of these would almost certainly be 'as found.' (Be suspect of any that look to be restored or are brightly painted; it would be very doubtful that it was authentic.)

Bicycle collectors are generally split as specializing in pre- and post-1920. Those specializing in pre-1920 might want only items from the hobby horse era (1816 – 1821), velocipede and manumotive era (1830 – 1872), high-wheel and hard-tired safety era (1873 – 1890), or the pneumatic safety era (post 1890). With the introduction of the pneumatic tire, the field was impacted both socially and technically. From this point, collector interest relates to social, sport, fashion, manufacturing, urbanization, financial, and technical history. Post 1920 collectors tend to be drawn to Art Deco and aerodynamic design, which forge prices. Many seek not only cycles but signage, prints and posters, watches, medals, photographs, porcelains, toys, and various other types of ephemera and memorabilia. Some prefer to specialize in items relating to military cycling, certain factories, racing, country of origin, type of bike, etc. All radiate from a common interest.

The bicycle has played an important role in the rapid developement of the twentieth century and onwards, impacting the airplane, motorcycle, and automobile, also the manufacture of drawn tubing, differentials, and spoked wheels. It has affected advertising, urbanization, women's lib, and the vote. There are still many treasures to be discovered.

AMF Spiderman Jr Roadmaster, boy's, 1978, EX 100.00
Cleveland Deluxe Roadmaster, boy's, prewar, 24", EX.................. 375.00
Colson Bullnose, boy's, 1939, front light, EX rstr 1,800.00
Columbia Air-Rider, boy's, 1940-42, EX 800.00
Elgin Bluebird, boy's, 1936, VG.. 7,000.00
Elgin Robin, boy's, 1937, G 1,600.00
High-wheeler, 1890s, leather seat, rpl #9 lamp, 60" w/54" front wheel. 2,415.00
Huffy Radio, boy's, 1955, EX 2,900.00

JC Higgins, boy's, Wonderide Spring Fork, EX, from $800 to 900.00
JC Higgins Flow Motion, girl's, 1948, G, from $100 to................ 150.00
Monarch Silver King Wingbar, girl's, 1939, EX 600.00
Murray Fire Cat, boy's, 1977, VG... 250.00
Raleigh Chopper, boy's, 1970s, EX, from $150 to 250.00
Schwinn Green Phantom, boy's, 1951, 26", EX............................ 700.00
Schwinn Mark IV Jaguar, boy's, West Wind tires, 1960s, VG...... 800.00

Schwinn Red Phantom, Bendix rear brake, front brake, speedometer, head and tail lights, luggage rack, springer front end, horn tank, exceptional restoration, ca 1950s, $1,500.00.

Sears Free Spirit, boy's, 1960s, EX, from $100 to 150.00
Shelby Traveler, boy's, 1938, G 175.00
Vista Banana 3-Speed, boy's, 1970s, 20", M, from $200 to 550.00

Campagnola

This company was founded in 1933 in the small town of Vicenza, Italy, by Tullio Campagnolo. His was a concept that focused on three fundamentals — performance, technological innovation, and high quality products. Campagnola had been an accomplished bicycle racer in the Italy of the 1920s, and he conceived of several innovative ideas while racing which he later turned into revolutionary fundamental cycling products such as the quick-release mechanism for bicycle wheels, derailleurs, and the patented 'rod' gear for gear changing. His early components such as the Cambio Corsa, Paris - Roubaix, and Gran Sport chargers are very sought after today. Now regarded as the most prestigious name in bicycle components, Campagnolo has equipped most of the greatest names in cycling and winners of the Tour de France such as Eddy Merckx. After decades of producing bicycles using steel tubes and Campagnolo componets made from aluminum alloy, in the late 1990s Campagnolo introduced carbon fiber as their main fabrication material in Record and most other groups. Because of this very shift in manufacturing, all of the earlier groups in alloy are now very sought after by collectors. In 1983 Campagnolo offered the Fiftieth Anniversary group to celebrate the company's half century and mark Tullio Campagnolo's passing on February 3 at the age of 81. In 1984 the company introduced its first group since Tullio's death; the 180 Record Corsa group with its sculpted and aerodynamic lines were a major departure from the dated but much celebrated Super Record group. From 1984 until 1994, the Record Corsa (or C-Record as it is also known) was refined and became well known for its sleek triangular-shaped Delta brakes and Century finish, which were offered only briefly. In 1987 Campagnolo ended production of the venerable Super Record road group, which had debuted in 1974. This was a blow to many, as it was seen as the demise of the components made great by the late Tullio Campagnolo. Today highly regarded for their beauty and old world craftsmanship, these components are collected not only for display but for use in the restoration of vintage bicycles.

In the listings that follow, some items are 'new old stock,' indicated by 'NOS' in the description. Our advisor for this category is David Weddington; he is listed in the Directory under Tennessee.

C-Record, sm flange q/r hubs 36/36, rear 130mm, OLN Century finish ..475.00
C-Record chain wheel set, Century finish, 172.5mm, 41/52 .... 595.00
C-Record Cobalto brakeset, w/levers & cables, NOS+box 525.00
C-Record Delta brakeset, w/levers & cables, NOS+box 750.00
C-Record front derailleur, brake on, early model as in catalog 18bis..189.00
C-Record PISTA lg flanges, hubs NJS Keirin approved, 36/36 .... 600.00
CdA brakeset, graphite, Powergrade aero brake levers, blk hoods, pr .575.00
Croce d'Aune 1st generation front & rear derailleurs in display box..250.00
Nouvo Record Hi-Lo hub set, 36-hole, front & rear, NOS+box .. 450.00
NR sm flange q/r hubs 32/32, 126.5mm, flat skewers, NOS in sealed box. 250.00
Nuovo Record front derailleur, band on, 3 cutouts in cage face ... 100.00
Nuovo Record rear derailleur, NOS 190.00
Record/NR Down tube band on dbl levers.. 75.00
Record/NR seat post, 2-bolt, 27.2x130mm 198.00
Regina ORO 5-speed freewheel 14-20, 14-22, 14-24, 15-19, 15-23..50.00
Regina Record ORO drilled chain 75.00
Regina TITANIO 5-speed freewheel, 5 titanium sprockets 14-22 ...250.00
SR Alloy freewheel, 7-speed 12-21, 12-23, 12-27, NOS 325.00
SR Alloy head set, Italian thread, NOS... 225.00
SR front derailleur, band on 105.00
SR Pista unfluted cranks w/dust caps, 170mm, late production.... 425.00
SR Rear derailleur, 1977, NOS... 435.00
SR Seat post 2nd generation, 1-bolt, 27.2x180mm 255.00
SR Strada chain set, 170mm 39/52 unfluted cranks, eng or etch blk logo. 400.00
Strada Superleggeri pedals, alloy body, blk alloy fr 200.00
50th Anniversary group set, NOS w/case & bag........................... 3,500.00

Big Little Books

The first Big Little Book was published in 1933 and copyrighted in 1932 by the Whitman Publishing Company of Racine, Wisconsin. Its hero was Dick Tracy. The concept was so well accepted that others soon followed Whitman's example; and though the 'Big Little Book' phrase became a trademark of the Whitman Company, the formats of his competitors (Saalfield, Goldsmith, Van Wiseman, Lynn, and World Syndicate) were exact copies. Today's Big Little Book buffs collect them all.

These hand-sized sagas of adventure were illustrated with full-page cartoons on the right-hand page and the story narration on the left. Colorful cardboard covers contained hundreds of pages, usually totaling over an inch in thickness. Big Little Books originally sold for 10¢ at the dime store; as late as the mid-1950s when the popularity of comic books caused sales to decline, signaling an end to production, their price had risen to a mere 20¢. Their appeal was directed toward the pre-teens who bought, traded, and hoarded Big Little Books. Because so many were stored in attics and closets, many have survived. Among the super heroes are G-Men, Flash Gordon, Tarzan, the Lone Ranger, and Red Ryder; in a lighter vein, you'll find such lovable characters as Blondie and Dagwood, Mickey Mouse, Little Orphan Annie, and Felix the Cat.

In the early to mid-'30s, Whitman published several Big Little Books as advertising premiums for the Coco Malt Company, who packed them in boxes of their cereal. These are highly prized by today's collectors, as are Disney stories and super-hero adventures.

For more information we recommend *Encyclopeida of Collectible Children's Books* by Diane McClure Jones and Rosemary Jones (Collector Books).

Note: At the present time, the market for these books is fairly stable — values for common examples are actually dropping. Only the rare, character-related titles are increasing somewhat.

Adventures of Huckleberry Finn, #1422, NM 40.00
Alice in Wonderland, #759, 1933, NM 100.00
Best of Tarzan, #1410, 1937, EX 30.00
Betty Boop in Snow White, #1119, 1934, EX.......................... 100.00

Billy the Kid, #773, 1935, EX.. 35.00
Brer Rabbit Tales by Uncle Remus, #704-10, 1949, EX.................. 30.00
Bringing Up Father, #1133, 1936, NM...................................... 60.00
Buck Rogers in the 25th Century AD, 1933, EX+........................ 70.00
Captain Midnight & the Moon Woman, #1452, VG...................... 60.00
Chester Gump Finds the Hidden Treasure, VG........................... 45.00
Cowboy Lingo, Boys Books of Western Facts, #1457, EX............... 30.00
Donald Duck Gets Fed Up, 1940, #1462, VG+........................... 35.00
Ellery Queen the Master Detective, #1472, 1942, NM 60.00
Felix the Cat, #1129, 1936, EX 125.00
Freckles & the Lost Diamond Mine, #1164, EX 35.00
G-man on the Crime Trail, 1936, VG....................................... 25.00
Gang Busters in Action, #1451, NM.. 50.00
Green Hornet Strikes, 1940, G.. 45.00
Jungle Jim & the Vampire Woman, #1139, EX............................ 45.00
Little Mary Mixup & the Grocery Robberies, 1940, EX................. 45.00
Little Orphan Annie & the Big Train Robbery, #1140, 1934, EX.. 45.00
Little Women, #757, EX... 40.00
Lone Ranger & the Menace of Murder Valley, #1465, 1938, EX ... 50.00

The Lone Ranger and the Secret Killer, Whitman #1431, 1937, EX, $50.00.

(Photo courtesy Larry Jacobs)

Mandrake the Magician, #1167, 1935, VG...................................... 45.00
Mickey Mouse & Bobo the Elephant, 1935, EX............................... 40.00
Mickey Mouse in Blaggard Castle, 1934, EX.................................. 45.00
Mutt & Jeff, 1936, VG+... 35.00
Og Son of Fire, #1115, NM... 50.00
Phantom, #1100, 1936, VG... 30.00
Popeye & Queen Olive Oyl, #1458, EX+ 40.00
Popeye & the Deep Sea Mystery, #1499, 1939, VG......................... 30.00
Punch Davis of the Aircraft Carrier, 1945, NM............................. 50.00
Roy Rogers at Crossed Feathers Ranch, 1945, EX 25.00
Scrappy, #1122, 1934, VG.. 30.00
Sir Lancelot, #1649, NM+.. 20.00
Story of Skippy, 1934, Phillips Dental Magnesia premium, EX 45.00
Tailspin Tommy the Dirigible Flight to the North Pole, #1124, 1934, VG..30.00
Tarzan the Untamed, #1452, 1942, EX 50.00
Three Little Pigs/Little Red Riding Hood, 2-in-1 version, 1933, EX+..175.00
Tom Mix in the Range War, 1937, EX+.. 32.00
Tom Swift & the Giant Telescope, 1939, VG+ 35.00
Two-Gun Montana, #1104, VG+... 25.00
Walt Disney's Mickey Mouse, #717, 1933, G................................ 55.00
Wimpy the Hamburger Eater, 1934, G.. 32.00
Wings of the USA, #1407, NM.. 35.00
Zane Grey's Tex Thorne Comes Out of the West, 1937, EX 25.00
Zip Sanders King of the Speedway, #1465, EX............................. 20.00

Bing and Grondahl

In 1853 brothers M.H. and J.H. Bing formed a partnership with Frederick Vilhelm Grondahl in Copenhagen, Denmark. Their early wares were porcelain plaques and figurines designed by the noted sculptor Thorvaldsen of Denmark. Dinnerware production began in 1863, and by 1889 their underglaze color 'Copenhagen Blue' had earned them worldwide acclaim. They are perhaps most famous today for their Christmas plates, the first of which was made in 1895. See also Limited Edition Plates.

Note: Prices for all figurines are auction values plus buyer's premium.

Blue Traditional, bowl, rimmed soup; 7½", from $40 to 45.00
Blue Traditional, creamer, 8-oz.. 60.00
Blue Traditional, cup & saucer 50.00
Blue Traditional, plate, dinner; 10" 60.00
Blue Traditional, plate, luncheon; 8½" 40.00
Blue Traditional, platter, 14" L 125.00
Christmas Rose, bowl, vegetable; rnd, w/lid............................... 195.00
Christmas Rose, cake plate, ftd.. 85.00
Christmas Rose, creamer, 4" 30.00
Christmas Rose, cup & saucer 30.00
Christmas Rose, plate, dinner; 9½" 50.00
Christmas Rose, plate, dinner; 10½" 55.00
Christmas Rose, plate, luncheon; 8½" 30.00
Christmas Rose, platter, 10" L 75.00
Figurine, antelope, recumbent, #1693, 9x7½"........................... 200.00
Figurine, baker holds tray w/lg pretzel, #2223, 11"................... 300.00
Figurine, ballerina kneeling, #2284, 8x9½"............................... 325.00

Figurine, borzoi, #2115, factory second, 8", $390.00. (Photo courtesy Skinner Inc. Auctioneers & Appraisers of Antiques & Fine Art/ LiveAuctioneers.com)

Figurine, boxer, #2212, retired in 1986, 6x8" 350.00
Figurine, boy sitting on book, #1742, 6x5½x2½" 165.00
Figurine, calf, recumbent, #2168/10, ca 1901-04, 3¾" L 70.00
Figurine, Children Playing, child in girl's lap, #1568, 4¾" 95.00
Figurine, First Kiss, #2162P, 7½" 175.00
Figurine, fledgling bird, #1852, 2¾x2½" 65.00
Figurine, girl reading, #2247KP, 4¾x4¼x2½" 180.00
Figurine, Hans Christian Anderson, #2037, 9⅛x5¾" 225.00
Figurine, lady w/guitar, #1684, 10x6" 165.00
Figurine, lion cub seated, #1923, 6x6" 225.00
Figurine, lioness & cub, #2268, 6x12" 545.00
Figurine, peacock, #1628, 7¼x15½x3¾" 275.00
Figurine, perch fish, #23174, ca 1902-04, 3¾" L 70.00
Figurine, Sea Captain, #2370, 8" 275.00
Figurine, Sealyham terrier, #2017, 2½x4" 150.00
Figurine, St Bernard pup, #1926, 1970-83, 4¾x4¼" 100.00
Figurine, Two Brothers, #1648, 7¾" 160.00
Figurine, Victor, boy w/cup, #1713, 5¼" 165.00
Seagull, bowl, rimmed soup; 9¾", from $25 to 30.00
Seagull, bowl, vegetable; sq, 8¾" 90.00
Seagull, bowl, vegetable; 9½" 90.00
Seagull, creamer, ind.. 38.00
Seagull, cup, oversz, 2⅝" 60.00
Seagull, cup & saucer 30.00
Seagull, plate, bread & butter; 6" 15.00
Seagull, plate, dinner; 9½" 50.00
Seagull, plate, dinner; 10½" 60.00

Seagull, platter, 10".. 42.50
Seagull, sandwich tray, 10½" 60.00
Seagull, sugar bowl, 3¾" 70.00
Seagull, vase, 5½".. 40.00
Tray, 2 mice at side, tails wrap circumference, #1562, 3x5"......... 325.00
Vase, doves, wht on bl, #720/5463, 1976, 6½" 120.00
Vase, lg flower, bl tones on wht, sgn, #681, ca 1960s, 5".............. 120.00
Vase, sailboat/port scene, #271, 12x10" 540.00
Vase, tree along river, sgn BS, 1950s, 9¼" 95.00
Vase, windmill scene, sgn EK, #8682-420, 1960s, 7½"................. 95.00

Binoculars

There are several types of binoculars, and the terminology used to refers to them is not consistent or precise. Generally, 'field glasses' refer to simple Galilean optics, where the lens next to the eye (the ocular) is concave and dished away from the eye. By looking through the large lens (the objective), it is easy to see that the light goes straight through the two lenses. These are lower power, have a very small field of view, and do not work nearly as well as prism binoculars. In a smaller size, they are opera glasses, and their price increases if they are covered with mother-of-pearl (fairly common but very attractive), abalone shell (more colorful), ivory (quite scarce), or other exotic materials. Field glasses are not valuable unless very unusual or by the best makers, such as Zeiss or Leitz. Prism binoculars have the objective lens offset from the eyepiece and give a much better view. This is the standard binocular form, called Porro prisms, and dates from around 1900. Another type of prism binocular is the roof prism, which at first resembles the straight-through field glasses, with two simple cylinders or cones, here containing very small prisms. These can be distinguished by the high quality views they give and by a thin diagonal line that can be seen when looking backwards through the objective. In general, German binoculars are the most desirable, followed by American, English, and finally French, which can be of good quality but are very common unless of unusual configuration. Japanese optics of WWII or before are often of very high quality. 'Made in Occupied Japan' binoculars are very common, but collectors prize those by Nippon Kogaku (Nikon). Some binoculars are center focus (CF), with one central wheel that focuses both sides at once. These are much easier to use but more difficult to seal against dirt and moisture. Individual focus (IF) binoculars are adjusted by rotating each eyepiece and tend to be cleaner inside in older optics. Each type is preferred by different collectors. Very large binoculars are always of great interest. All binoculars are numbered according to their magnifying power and the diameter of the objective in millimeters. Optics of 6x30 magnify six times and have 30 millimeter objectives.

Prisms are easily knocked out of alignment, requiring an expensive and difficult repair. If severe, this misalignment is immediately noticeable on use by the double-image scene. Minor damage can be seen by focusing on a small object and slowly moving the binoculars away from the eye, which will cause the images to appear to separate. Overall cleanliness should be checked by looking backwards (through the objective) at a light or the sky, when any film or dirt on the lenses or prisms can easily be seen. Pristine binoculars are worth far more than when dirty or misaligned, and broken or cracked optics lower the value far more. Cases help keep binoculars clean but do not add materially to the value.

As of 2008, any significant changes in value are due to internet sales. Some of the prices listed here are lower than would be reached at an online auction. Revisions of these values would be inappropriate at this point for these reasons: First, values are fluctuating wildly on the internet; 'auction fever' is extreme. Second, some common instruments can fetch a high price at an internet sale, and it is clear that the price will not be supported as more of them are placed at auction. In fact, an overlooked collectible like the binocular will be subject to a great increase in supply as they are retrieved from closets in response to the values people see at an online auction. Third, sellers who have access to these internet auctions can use them for price guides if they wish, but the values in this listing have to reflect what can be obtained at an average large antique show. The following listings assume a very good overall condition, with generally clean and aligned optics. Our advisor for this category is Jack Kelly; he is listed in the Directory under Washington.

Field Glasses

Fernglas 08, German WWI, 6x39, military gr, many makers.......... 50.00
Folding, modern, hinged flat case, oculars outside 10.00
Folding or telescoping, no bbls, old 125.00
Ivory covered, various sm szs & makers.. 200.00
LeMaire, bl leather/brass, various szs, other Fr same 25.00
Metal, emb hunting scene, various sm szs & makers......................... 45.00
Pearl covered, various sm szs & makers.. 90.00
Porc covered, delicate painting, various sm szs & makers.............. 200.00
US Naval Gun Factory Optical Shop 6x30 .... 75.00
Zeiss 'Galan' 2.5x34, modern design look, early 1920s................. 170.00

Prism Binoculars (Porro)

Barr & Stroud, 7x50, Porro II prisms, IF, WWII 120.00
Bausch & Lomb, 6x30, IF, WWI, Signal Corps 50.00
Bausch & Lomb, 7x50, IF, WWII, other makers same.................. 140.00
Bausch & Lomb Zephyr, 7x35 & other, CF.................................... 160.00
Bausch & Lomb/Zeiss, 8x17, CF, Pat 1897.................................... 140.00
Crown Optical, 6x30, IF, WWI, filters.. 50.00
France, various makers & szs, if not unusual 30.00
German WWII 10x80, eyepcs at 45 degrees 500.00
German WWII 6x30, 3-letter code for various makers.................... 60.00
Goertz Trieder Binocle, various szs, unusual adjustment............... 110.00
Huet, Paris 7x22, other sm szs, unusual shapes.............................. 80.00
Leitz 6x30 Dienstglas, IF, good optics 75.00
Leitz 8x30 Binuxit, CF, outstanding optics................................... 150.00
M19, US military 7x50, ca 1980 .... 180.00
Nikon 9x35, 7x35, CF, 1950s-70s.. 140.00
Nippon Kogaku, 7x50, IF, Made in Occupied Japan..................... 150.00
Ross Stepnada, 7x30, CF, wide angle, 1930s 250.00
Ross 6x30, standard British WWI issue.. 50.00
Sard, 6x42, IF, very wide angle, WWII... 900.00
Toko (Tokyo Opt Co) 7x50, IF, Made in Occupied Japan.............. 45.00
Universal Camera 6x30, IF, WWII, other makers same.................. 50.00
US Naval Gun Factory Optical Shop 6x30, IF, filters, WWI 70.00
US Naval Gun Factory Optical 10x45, IF, WWI.......................... 200.00
US Navy, 20x120, various makers, WWII & later.................... 2,200.00
Warner & Swasey (important maker) 8x20, CF, 1902................. 200.00
Wollensak 6x30, ca 1940 .... 50.00
Zeiss Deltrintem 8x30, CF, 1930s 95.00
Zeiss DF 95, 6x18, sq shoulder, very early 160.00
Zeiss Starmorbi 12/24/42x60, turret eyepcs, 1920s 2,500.00
Zeiss Teleater 3x13, CF, bl leather.. 120.00
Zeiss 15x60, CF or IF, various models.. 700.00
Zeiss 8x40 Delactis, CF or IF, 1930s 230.00

Roof Prism Binoculars

Hensoldt Dialyt, various szs, 1930s-80s.. 140.00
Hensoldt Universal Dialyt, 6x26, 3.5x26, 1920s............................ 120.00
Leitz Trinovid, 7x42 & other, CF, 1960s-80s, EX.......................... 500.00
Zeiss Dialyt, 8x30, CF, 1960s... 400.00

Bisque

Bisque is a term referring to unglazed earthenware or porcelain that has been fired only once. During the Victorian era, bisque figurines became very popular. Most were highly decorated in pastels and gilt and demonstrated a fine degree of workmanship in the quality of their modeling. Few were marked. See also Heubach; Nodders; Dolls; Piano Babies.

Black boy on chair, humidor, 10" 1,200.00
Black man playing accordion, seated on plinth, 11".................... 215.00
Black man playing banjo, fine attire, 6" 215.00
Boy w/glasses sits astride column, 16", NM 225.00

Child holding leaves, intaglio eyes, unmarked, 12", $150.00. (Photo courtesy McMasters Harris Auction Company)

Child seated, hands holding sm cup, Germany, ca 1900, 14" 600.00
Nude blond w/bird in perched on hand, lying on side, Germany, 6"... 275.00
18th-C lady w/1 hand raised, fine details, 16"............................... 215.00

Black Americana

Black memorabilia is without a doubt a field that encompasses the most widely exploited ethnic group in our history. But within this field there are many levels of interest: arts and achievements such as folk music and literature, caricatures in advertising, souvenirs, toys, fine art, and legitimate research into the days of their enslavement and enduring struggle for equality. The list is endless.

In the listings below are some with a derogatory connotation. Thankfully, these are from a bygone era and represent the mores of a culture that existed nearly a century ago. They are included only to convey the fact that they are a part of this growing area of collecting interest. Black Americana catalogs featuring a wide variety of items for sale are available; see the Directory under Clubs, Newsletters, and Catalogs for more information. We also recommend *African American Dolls* by Yvonne H. Ellis. Our advisor for this category is Judy Posner; she is listed in the Directory under Florida. See also Cookie Jars; Postcards; Posters; Salt Shakers; Sheet Music.

Ashtray, face w/open mouth & red tongue for rest, ceramic, Japan, 3" ..80.00
Ashtray, sq dish w/nude native figure reclining, Gilner, 1950s, 6", EX. 32.00
Birthday card, Golly/friends celebrating #4, Hooray, Mia Cards, unused . 15.00
Birthday card, Missed Yo' Birfday!, boy/8-ball, 1953, EX............... 12.00
Book, A Treasury of Stephen Foster, Random House, 1946, 225-pg, EX . 35.00
Book, Amos 'n Andy & Their Creators Correll & Gosden, 1930, EX. 30.00
Book, Black Mammy & Other Poems by Wm Lightfoot Visscher, 1886, G...275.00
Book, The Cotton Tots, Grace Johnston, 1926, VG 65.00
Book, Uncle Remus His Songs & Sayings, Joel C Harris, 1921, EX.50.00
Book, Well Done Noddy!, Enid Blyton, not dtd, EX 18.00
Bottle, King's Dairy Chocolate Milk, pyro picaninny head, 1-qt, EX. 20.00

Box, candy; Amos 'n Andy, cardboard, Williamson Candy Co., Chicago, Brooklyn, San Francisco, G, $100.00.

Brush, barber/dresser; Mammy figure, pnt wood, 6½", EX 35.00
Candy container, man standing/big smile, papier-maché, Germany, 6", EX . 150.00
Celluloid toy, porter w/luggage, windup, Occupied Japan, 4", EX . 125.00
Celluloid toy, 2 native boys w/nodding heads on alligator, Japan, EX .. 85.00
Charm, Mammy figure, mk Sterling, w/enameling, 1940s-50s, ¹¹⁄₁₆", EX.. 26.00
Clock, wall; Mammy figure w/rnd clock, ceramic, electric, Lanshire, EX .. 110.00
Condiment set, native Mustard/Catsup, ceramic, Nasco/Del Coronado, EX .135.00
Creamer, ceramic, wht w/Aunt Jemima head decal, no hdl, 2½", VG...26.00
Cup, boy in gr outfit, Brownie Downing Ceramics, 1960s, 3", EX.. 25.00
Doll, girl, compo/pnt features, Shirley Temple wig, dress, 11", VG+.50.00
Doll, golliwog, red/wht/bl/blk knit, 1950s-60s, 13", EX 30.00
Doll, nun in blk & wht habit, red lips, rnd eyes, 5", EX 35.00
Egg cup, porc w/HP golliwog & teddy bear on wht, 2¼", EX 65.00
Figurine, boy playing fiddle, porc, Occupied Japan, 2½", NM 42.00
Figurine, girl in pigtails w/fiddle, red lips/lg eyes, porc, 4", EX........ 32.00
Figurine, minstrel/palm tree, chenille w/wood base, 1940s-50s, 4", EX..10.00
Figurines, boy & girl seated, pnt CI, Hubley, 1930s, 1¼", EX, pr . 110.00
Game, Minstrel Show board game, Helmer & Sons/Germany, 1941, VGIB..90.00
Marbles, 6 wht marbles w/blk & red images, drawstring canvas bag, NM.. 36.00
Marionette, Lucifer, compo w/cloth outfit, Effanbee, 1937-39, 14", EX .230.00
Menu, Old Dixie Southern Barbecue/Savanna GA, die-cut Mammy, 10x5", EX... 58.00
Nodder, girl w/fruit, straw hat, St Augustine FL, 1950s-60s, 7", EX .35.00
Note pad & pencil holder, plastic Mammy figure, wall mt, 10½", G.52.00
Paperweight, boy (bust) eating watermelon slice, pnt CI, EX 36.00
Pincushion, chalkware picaninny head w/burlap ball body, 3", EX ..65.00
Postcard, Greetings From the Sunny South, bearded man fr by gators, VG ..68.00
Postcard, In the 'Land of the Sky' Demoralization, man/2 boys, unused. 28.00
Postcard, Look in My Eyes an' Say Goo!, die-cut pop-up couple, EX. 90.00
Postcard, Thanksgiving Greetings, boy w/lg corncob, smiling moon, EX .. 25.00
Poster, Messett's Musical Entertainers, Quigley Litho, 42x14", EX ..1,200.00
Poster, Uncle Tom's Cabin, Ackermann Quigley Litho, 1920s, 28x21", EX.1,500.00
Recipe book, Mandy's Favorite Lousiana Recipes, Natalie V Scott, EX. 28.00
Sampler, family scene w/trees, What Is Home..., 1880s, fr, 22x19", VG.115.00
Shakers, boy seated w/2 melon slices (shakers) on knees, 1950s, EX.. 85.00
Shakers, Mammy (Peppy)/Chef (Salty), cream/detail, 7", NM, 2-pc. 60.00
Shakers, man's head in beret/watermelon slice, 1940s, EX, 2-pc.... 85.00
Shakers, men in overalls/hats in hand, bl & yel/red & yel, 3", EX, pr..50.00
Sign, JP Alley's Hambone.., emb tin w/Black pilot in plane, 10x14", VG. 195.00

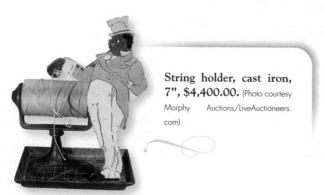

String holder, cast iron, 7", $4,400.00. (Photo courtesy Morphy Auctions/LiveAuctioneers.com)

Spoon rest, flat ceramic Mammy figure w/2 rests mk Spoon/Rest, 8", NM..125.00
String holder, Mammy head, gauze-type mask face w/cloth scarf, EX ..48.00
Tablecloth, circular plantation scene on wht, 1950s, 45x48", EX . 140.00
Tape measure, Mammy figure holding apple, plastic, Germany, 2", VG. 80.00
Teapot, plump clown figure on all 4s, red clay, coiled hdl, 8", EX .. 30.00
Thermometer, 'Diaper Dan' figure, Syroco, Multi Prod, 1949, 5½", EX.. 38.00
Tin, Rum Creoles, head image/tropics on lid, 1940s-50s, 4x6" dia, EX..32.00
Toaster cover, Mammy figure w/'Oh My' expression, 1950s, 17", EX . 42.00
Towel, Mammy w/cake embr on wht linen, 24x15", EX................ 25.00
Wall plaques, heads, eyes closed/red lips/gold hair, chalk, 6", NM, pr ..35.00
Whiskbroom, 3½" detailed pnt wood man figure w/4" bristles, EX...35.00

Blown Glass

Blown glass is rather difficult to date; eighteenth- and nineteenth-century examples vary little as to technique or style. It ranges from the primitive to the sophisticated, but the metallic content of very early glass caused tiny imperfections that are obvious upon examination, and these are often indicative of age.

In America, Stiegel introduced the English technique of using a patterned, part-size mold, a practice which was generally followed by many glasshouses after the Revolution. From 1820 to about 1850, glass was blown into full-size three-part molds. In the listings below, glass is assumed clear unless color is mentioned. Our advisor for this category is Mark Vuono; he is listed in the Directory under Connecticut. See also Bottles; Lamps, Whale Oil, Burning Fluid; specific manufactures.

Bottle, amber, 24 swirled ribs, ovoid, att Kent, broken blister, 7".. 260.00
Bottle, aqua, club shape w/24 broken-swirl ribs, blisters, 8" 250.00
Bottle, bar; bright yel gr, ribs swirled to right at neck, 12", pr 475.00

Bowl, deep amber, pontil scar, rolled rim, tooled spout, ca. 1850 – 1870, 3½x9½", $550.00. (Photo courtesy Glass-Works Auctions)

Bowl, folded rim, appl cobalt bands, 2¼x6¼", 4 for 880.00
Bowl, pale amethyst, 16 dainty ribs, folded rim, 2x5" 235.00
Bowl, yel olive, rolled rim, pontil scar, NE, 1820-60, 7⅛" 950.00
Candlestick, wht opaque petticoat type, clear hdl & socket, 7", ea .. 115.00
Canister, clear w/3 cobalt rings, cobalt wafer finial, 9¾x4" 575.00
Compote, peacock gr, clear stem, gallery rim, 5x5½" 515.00
Compote, ribbed, folded rim, hollow baluster stem, Pittsburgh, 9x8" . 800.00
Creamer, clear w/opal looping, appl hdl, S Jersey, 5½" 485.00
Creamer, cobalt, 14 horizontal ribs, pontil, 1850-70, 3⅛" 1,200.00
Creamer, cobalt, 20-Dmn, appl ft, solid hdl, Pittsburgh, 4⅛" 450.00
Creamer, Lily Pad decor at neck, aquamarine, 1840-50, 4⅝" 4,500.00
Jar, apothecary; appl ft, tooled rim, orig lid, pontil, 14¼" 150.00
Jar, golden amber, depressed shoulder, wide neck/mouth, 1830-60, 6x4" .475.00
Jar, lt yel olive, cylinder, tooled flared mouth, pontil, NE, 12" 700.00
Jar, yel olive, sheared mouth w/string rim, pontiled, 15¼x5⅛" 500.00
Pan, cobalt, flared/folded rim, domed base, 2¼x8¼" 65.00
Pan, golden yel amber, rolled rim, iron pontil, 3⅜x11¾", EX....... 700.00
Pitcher, amber, pronounced spout, appl hdl, S Jersey, 6½" 700.00
Pitcher, appl hdl & 4 rings, flint, 8½" 175.00
Pitcher, aquamarine w/appl threading, solid hdl, burst bubble, 6" .1,900.00
Pitcher, 12 swirl ribs, flint, Pittsburgh, 8¼" 435.00
Rolling pin, blk olive amber w/mc blotches, knob hdls, 1850s, 17".. 125.00
Rolling pin, fiery opal, knob hdls, pontil, late 19th C, 15".......... 150.00

Salt cellar, gr bottle glass, att S Jersey, early 1800s, 1½x2" 300.00
String holder, clear w/cobalt ring & finial, 4½x4¾" 285.00
Sugar bowl, clear w/opal streak, swirled ribs, gallery rim, 5x5" 350.00
Tumbler, gr aquamarine, 24 left-swirl ribs, Midwest, 1820-40, 4¾" ..1,500.00
Tumbler, smoky yel gr, 6 arched panels, pontil, 3⅝" 300.00
Vase, dk olive amber w/many wht flecks, flared mouth, ftd, NE, 6⅜" . 2,000.00

Blown Three-Mold Glass

A popular collectible in the 1920s, 1930s, and 1940s, blown three-mold glass has again gained the attention of many. Produced from approximately 1815 to 1840 in various New York, New England, and Midwestern glasshouses, it was a cheaper alternative to the expensive imported Irish cut glass.

Distinguishing features of blown three-mold glass are the three distinct mold marks and the concave-convex appearance of the glass. For every indentation on the inner surface of the ware, there will be a corresponding protuberance on the outside. Blown three-mold glass is most often clear with the exception of inkwells and a few known decanters. Any colored three-mold glass commands a premium price.

The numbers in the listings that follow refer to the book *American Glass* by George and Helen McKearin. Our advisor for this category is Mark Vuono; he is listed in the Directory under Connecticut.

Sugar bowl, GII-18, clear with light bluish tint, Sandwich, 6½", M, from $5,000.00 to $6,000.00. (Photo courtesy Conestoga Auction Company/LiveAuctioneers.com)

Decanter, GI-27, half-post pinch bottle w/etch castle, 12½" 300.00
Decanter, GI-29, dk cobalt, tooled mouth, pontil, tam stopper, 5½"..900.00
Decanter, GIII-09, faint aqua, tooled mouth, pontil, w/stopper, 5⅜" .350.00
Decanter, GIII-16, olive w/amber tone, 7¼" 300.00
Dish, GIII-20, folded rim, 1¼x5" 300.00
Inkwell, Dmn Quilt, dk amber, mid-19th C, Am, 2x2⅞" dia 275.00
Inkwell, GIII-29, olive amber, 1½x2¼" 300.00

Blue and White Stoneware

'Salt glaze' (slang term) or molded stoneware was most commonly produced in a blue and white coloration, much of which was also decorated with numerous 'in-mold' designs (some 150 plus patterns). It was made by practically every American pottery from the turn of the century until the mid-1930s. Crocks, pitchers, wash sets, rolling pins, and other household wares are only a few of the items that may be found in this type of 'country' pottery, now one of today's popular collectibles.

Logan, Brush-McCoy, Uhl Co., and Burley Winter were among those who produced it, but very few pieces were ever signed. Research and the availability of some manufacturers' sales catalogs has enabled collectors to attribute certain pattern lines to some companies. Naturally condition must be a prime consideration, especially if one is buying for resale; pieces with good, strong color and fully molded patterns bring premium prices. Be mindful that very good reproductions are on the market and are often misrepresented as the real thing. Normal wear and signs of age are to be expected, since this was utility ware and received heavy use in busy households.

In the listings that follow, crocks, salts, and butter holders are assumed to be without lids unless noted otherwise. Items are in near-mint condition unless noted otherwise. Though common pieces seem to have softened to some degree, scarce items and those in outstanding mint condition are stronger than ever. Nationwide internet sales such as eBay have stabilized and standardized prices that once fluctuated from region to region. They have also helped to determine what is really rare and what isn't. See also specific manufacturers.For information on the Blue & White Pottery Club, see the Clubs, Newsletters, and Catalogs, section of the Directory or visit their website at: www.blueandwhitepottery.org.

Bowl, Apricot, common 80.00
Bowl, Daisy on Lattice, 10¾" 115.00
Bowl, mixing; Flying Bird, 4x6" 200.00
Bowl, Wildflower (stenciled), 4½x8" 179.00
Butter crock, Apricot, appl wood & wire hdl, w/lid, 4x7" 275.00
Butter crock, Butterfly, w/lid & bail, 6½" 225.00
Butter crock, Daisy & Waffle, 4x8" 175.00
Butter crock, Draped Windows, 4½x8" 235.00
Butter crock, Eagle, w/lid & bail, M 1,000.00
Butter crock, Lovebirds, w/lid, 5½x6", M 535.00
Butter jar, Wildflower, appl wood & wire hdl, 5x7" 275.00
Canister, Basketweave, Crackers, w/lid 740.00
Canister, Basketweave, Put Your Fist In, w/lid, 7½" 760.00
Canister, Basketweave, Sugar, w/lid, 7½" 200.00
Chamberpot, Wildflower & Fishscale, w/lid 400.00
Coffeepot, Peacock, w/lid & insides 5,900.00
Coffeepot, Swirl, w/lid & metal base plate 900.00
Cooler, iced tea; Blue Band, flat lid, complete, 13x11" 295.00
Cooler, water; Cupid, brass spigot, patterned lid, 15x12" 700.00
Cuspidor, Basketweave & Morning Glory, 5x2½" 125.00
Egg storage crock, Barrel Staves, bail hdl, 5½x6" 225.00
Meat tenderizer, Wildflower, no chips, complete w/wood hdl 500.00
Mug, beer; advertising, Diffused Blue, sqd hdl 150.00
Mug, Flying Bird, 5x3" 130.00
Pie plate, Blue Walled Brick-Edge star-emb base, 10½" 200.00
Pitcher, Acorns, stenciled, 8x6½" 175.00

Pitcher, Apricots, 8", from $250.00 to $350.00.

Pitcher, Barrel, +6 mugs 395.00
Pitcher, Bluebird, 9x7" 450.00
Pitcher, Cattails, stenciled design, bulbous, 7" 225.00
Pitcher, Cherry Band, w/advertising, 8¼" 1,600.00
Pitcher, Cherry Cluster, scarce, 7½" 450.00
Pitcher, Columns & Arches, 8¾x5" 425.00
Pitcher, Eagle w/Shield & Arrows, rare, 8" 750.00
Pitcher, Garden Rose, 9" 500.00
Pitcher, Grape & Shield, common, 8½x5" 150.00
Pitcher, Grazing Cows, bl, very common, 8" 250.00
Pitcher, Indian Boy & Girl (Capt John Smith & Pocahontas), 6" ..300.00
Pitcher, Leaping Deer, 8½" 375.00
Pitcher, Lincoln, allover deep bl, 4¾x4¾" 250.00
Pitcher, Lincoln, allover deep bl, 7x5" 500.00

Pitcher, Lovebird, pale color, 8½"...300.00
Pitcher, Pine Cone, scarce, 9½"...1,500.00
Pitcher, Scroll & Leaf, Trade at IGA Store, Deshler, NE Phone 193, 8"..1,290.00
Pitcher, Swan, in oval, deep color, 8½", EX 400.00
Pitcher, Tulip, 8x4"...325.00
Pitcher, Wildflowers/Cosmos, w/advertising 2,100.00
Pitcher, Windy City (Fannie Flagg), Robinson Clay, 8½"..........450.00
Rolling pin, Blue Band, no advertising, 14x4".................375.00
Rolling pin, orange band w/advertising & dtd 1916 ....756.00
Rolling pin, Swirl, orig wooden hdls, 13".....................1,500.00
Rolling pin, Wildflower, plain 375.00
Salt crock, Butterfly, w/lid..350.00
Salt crock, Eagle, w/lid..800.00
Soap dish, Indian in War Bonnet (beware, highly reproduced) ...250.00
Vinegar cruet, rare, 4½x3"...375.00
Washboard, sponge 400.00

Blue Ridge

Blue Ridge dinnerware was produced by Southern Potteries of Erwin, Tennessee, from the late 1930s until 1956 in 12 basic styles and 2,000 different patterns, all of which were hand decorated under the glaze. Vivid colors lit up floral arrangements of seemingly endless variation, fruit of every sort from simple clusters to lush assortments, barnyard fowl, peasant figures, and unpretentious textured patterns. Although it is these dinnerware lines for which they are best known, collectors prize the artist-signed plates from the '40s and the limited line of character jugs made during the '50s most highly. Examples of the French Peasant pattern are valued at double the prices listed below; very simple patterns will bring 25% to 50% less.

Our advisors, Betty and Bill Newbound, have compiled four lovely books, *Blue Ridge Dinnerware, Revised Third Edition; The Collector's Encyclopedia of Blue Ridge, Volumes I and II; and Best of Blue Ridge*, all with beautiful color illustrations. They are listed in the Directory under North Carolina. For information concerning the National Blue Ridge Newsletter, see the Clubs, Newsletters, and Catalogs section of the Directory.

Ashtray, advertising, rnd, from $60 to...........................70.00
Baker, divided, 8x13", from $20 to 25.00
Bonbon, Charm House, china, from $150 to 175.00
Bonbon, divided, center hdl, china, from $85 to 95.00
Bowl, flat soup; from $15 to..25.00
Bowl, flat soup; Premium, from $25 to 35.00
Bowl, fruit; 5¼", from $6 to 8.00
Bowl, hot cereal; from $15 to 20.00
Bowl, mixing; lg, from $25 to 30.00
Bowl, mixing; sm, from $15 to..20.00
Box, Seaside, china, from $125 to 150.00
Butter pat/coaster, from $20 to 25.00
Cake lifter, from $25 to..30.00

Celery dish, Fox Grape, leaf shape, china, from $40.00 to $50.00. (Photo courtesy Betty and Bill Newbound; Bill Newbound photographer)

Child's cereal bowl, from $125 to 160.00
Child's feeding dish, divided, from $125 to......................150.00

Child's play tea set, from $300 to 350.00
Chocolate pot 225.00
Cigarette box, sq, from $85 to 90.00
Creamer, Charm House, from $70 to 85.00
Creamer, lg, Colonial, open, from $18 to 25.00
Creamer, ped ft, china, from $45 to....................................50.00
Cup & saucer, demi; earthenware, from $25 to....................30.00
Cup & saucer, Holiday, from $60 to 75.00
Cup & saucer, Turkey & Acorn, from $75 to.......................100.00
Deviled egg dish, from $50 to 60.00
Egg cup, dbl, from $25 to 35.00
Gravy boat, Premium, from $35 to.......................................55.00
Jug, character; Indian, from $600 to 700.00
Lamp, china, from $125 to 150.00
Marmite w/lid, Charm House, from $170 to 200.00
Pie baker, from $30 to 40.00
Pitcher, Betsy, gold decor, from $250 to 300.00

Pitcher, Charm House, from $190.00 to $220.00.
(Photo courtesy Betty and Bill Newbound; Bill Newbound photographer)

Pitcher, Clara, china, from $95 to 125.00
Pitcher, Grace, china, from $100 to 120.00
Pitcher, Spiral, earthenware, 7", from $45 to 55.00
Plate, aluminum edge, 12", from $40 to 45.00
Plate, Christmas Tree, from $75 to 85.00
Plate, dinner; Premium, 9¼", from $25 to 35.00
Plate, novelty patterns, sq, 6", from $65 to 75.00
Plate, sq, 8", from $20 to..25.00
Plate, 11½-12", from $50 to..65.00
Ramekin, w/lid, 7½", from $35 to 45.00
Relish, Palisades, from $40 to 50.00
Relish dish, Charm House, china, from $175 to 200.00
Relish dish, Loop Handle, china, from $65 to 75.00
Relish dish, T-hdl, from $65 to 75.00
Shakers, Good Housekeeping, pr from $125 to....................150.00
Shakers, Skyline, pr from $30 to 40.00
Sugar bowl, Colonial, eared, from $15 to 20.00
Sugar bowl, Woodcrest, w/lid, from $25 to 30.00
Teapot, Piecrust, from $150 to..200.00
Teapot, Skyline, from $110 to 125.00
Teapot, Snub Nose, china, from $175 to..............................200.00
Tidbit, 2-tier, from $30 to 40.00
Tray, demi; Colonial, 5½x7", from $150 to 175.00
Tray, from waffle set, 9½x13½", from $100 to 125.00
Tumbler, glass, from $15 to 20.00
Vase, ruffled top, china, 9½", from $95 to 125.00
Wall sconce, from $70 to..75.00

Blue Willow

Blue Willow, inspired no doubt by the numerous patterns of the blue and white Nanking imports, has been popular since the late eighteenth century and has been made in as many variations as there were manufacturers. English transfer wares by such notable firms as Allerton and Ridgway are the most sought after and the most expensive. Japanese potters have been producing Willow-patterned dinnerware since the late 1800s, and American manufacturers have followed suit. Although blue is the color most commonly used, mauve and black lines have also been made. For further study we recommend the book *Gaston's Blue Willow*, with full-color photos and current prices, by Mary Frank Gaston, our advisor for this category; she is listed in the Directory under Texas. In the listings, if no manufacturer is noted, the ware is unmarked. See also Buffalo.

Ashtray, Schweppes Table Waters, unmk English, from $50 to...... 65.00
Biscuit jar, cane hdl, octagonal, Gibson, 1912-30, 6½", $250 to .. 275.00
Bonbon, flat shell, from $55 to 65.00
Bowl, cereal; Johnson Bros, from $20 to 35.00
Bowl, lug soup; Homer Laughlin, from $25 to 30.00
Bowl, soup; fleur-de-lis, Barker, 1930-37, ea from $25 to 35.00
Bowl, soup/cereal; short ped ft, Japan, from $30 to 40.00
Bowl, vegetable; flow bl, Doulton, 1891-1902, from $120 to 140.00
Bowl, vegetable; w/lid, Japan, from $100 to 125.00
Bowl, vegetable; w/o Willow, Gibson, w/lid, from $225 to 275.00
Bowl & pitcher, Wedgwood 1,200.00
Box, egg-shaped, for trinkets or jewelry, Japan, from $125 to 150.00
Butter dish, Royal China, ¼-lb 45.00
Butter dish, w/drainer, Ridgways, 1927 & after, from $300 to 350.00
Butter warmer, burner in tripod stand, unmk Japan, from $100 to .. 120.00
Cake stand, Traditional pattern, unmk English, 4x10½" 325.00
Candleholders, no border, gold trim, Coalport, post-1960, 5½", pr .. 225.00

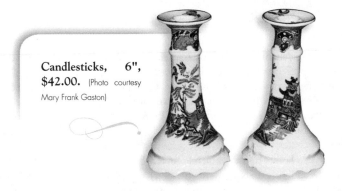

**Candlesticks, 6",
$42.00.** (Photo courtesy
Mary Frank Gaston)

Canisters, sq, tin, unmk, set of 4, from $400 to 500.00
Chamber pot, flow bl, Doulton, 1891-1902, from $350 to 400.00
Cheese dish, Wiltshaw & Robinson, Godden #4201, after 1894, $250 to .. 275.00
Coffeepot, Booths, gold trim, Real Old Willow, 8½" 210.00
Coffeepot, Victorian Porcelain Ltd, ca 1949-57, from $125 to 150.00
Condiment set, 3-pc on silver fr, Royal Worcester 285.00
Creamer, demi; china, from $75 to 85.00
Creamer & sugar bowl, John Steventon, 1923-36, from $80 to ... 100.00
Creamer & sugar bowl, w/lid, Steventon & Sons, 3", 4", from $70 to .. 80.00
Cup, chili; w/liner plate, Japan 75.00
Cup, mustache; gold trim, Minton, early 1900s+, from $200 to ... 225.00
Cup & saucer, Meakin for Nieman-Marcus, 1970s 30.00
Cupsidor, rnd, Doulton, 1891-1902, 7½", from $350 to 450.00
Egg cup, dbl, unmk English, from $40 to 50.00
Egg cup, dbl; Japan, 4", from $30 to 40.00
Gravy boat, Homer Laughlin, from $20 to 25.00
Gravy boat, Wood & Sons, ca 1971, from $55 to 65.00
Gravy boat & tray, scalloped, Allerton & Sons, 1929-42, 4x8", 9" .. 195.00
Horseradish dish, Doulton, 5½" 65.00
Jug, milk; Homer Laughlin, from $125 to 150.00
Lamp, kerosene; ceramic shade, Japan, 11½", from $125 to 150.00
Leaf dish, unmk English, 6" 175.00
Muffin bowl, w/lid, illegible English mk, from $175 to 225.00

Mustard pot, flared neck, hdl, unmk English, from $80 to 90.00
Napkin ring, unmk, from $80 to 100.00
Pie plate, Royal China, 10" 30.00
Pitcher, cylindrical, Doulton, ca 1891-1902, 7", from $250 to 275.00
Pitcher, scalloped, Allerton & Sons, 1929-42, 6", from $150 to .. 175.00
Pitcher, triangular, Doulton, 1891-1902, 6", from $250 to 275.00
Plate, dessert; sq, Traditional pattern, Washington Pottery, $15 to . 18.00
Plate, dinner; Imperial, 9¾" 27.00
Plate, dinner; Liner & Carter, 9½" 24.00
Plate, grill; Booth's center pattern, Bowknot border, 10¾" 35.00
Plate, grill; Made in Poland, 10" from $25 to 35.00
Plate, Royal China, ca 1949-60, 10", from $10 to 15.00
Plate, salad; red, Jackson China Restaurant Ware 8.00
Plate, smooth rim, Samuel Radford, 1928-38, 8", from $25 to 35.00
Platter, Allerton, 16x12" 275.00
Platter, on base, rtcl inner border, J&R Riley, 1802-28, 10" 550.00
Platter, rectangular, smooth edge, WM&S Edge, 1841-47, 14x11¼" . 325.00
Platter, Traditional center, 1912-27, 15½x12½" 225.00
Punch bowl, unmk, 7x9¼", from $300 to 400.00
Relish, divided; lug hdls, Adderly, 1929-47, 8" 130.00
Relish, scalloped, John Maddock, Gooden #2475, 11" L, from $55 to .. 65.00
Relish tray, Booth's center pattern, Bowknot border, Wood & Sons, 9". 30.00
Shakers, Japan, 3", pr from $30 to 40.00
Shakers, Royal China, pr 25.00
Spoon rest, dbl, Japan, 9", from $40 to 50.00
Sugar bowl, w/lid, Japan 15.00
Tea set, Japan, stacking 2-cup pot+cr/sug, from $150 to 175.00
Teapot, Doulton, 1882-90, from $250 to 300.00
Teapot, musical base, unmk Japan, from $130 to 150.00
Trivet, unmk English, 5½", from $75 to 100.00
Tumbler, ceramic, Japan, 3½", from $30 to 35.00
Tureen, soup; Traditional center, Ridgways, 1912-27 mk, 7¾x11" . 45.00

Bluebird China

The earliest examples of the pudgy little bluebird in the apple blossoms decal appear in the late 1890s. The craze apparently peaked during the early to mid-1920s and had all but died out by 1930. More than 50 manufacturers, most of whom were located in East Liverpool, Ohio, produced bluebird dinnerware. There are variations on the decal, and several are now accepted as 'bluebird china.' The larger china companies like Homer Laughlin and KT&K experimented with them all. One of the variations depicts larger, more slender bluebirds in flight. The latter variety is seen on pieces made by Knowles, Taylor, Knowles; W.S. George (Derwood); French Co.; Sterling Colonial; and Pope Gosser. The dinnerware was never expensive, and shapes varied from one manufacturer to another. Today, the line produced by Homer Laughlin is valued most highly. Besides the companies we've already mentioned, producers of Bluebird China include Limoges China of Sebring, Ohio; Salem; Taylor, Smith, Taylor; and there are others. Our advisor for this category is Kenna Rosen, author of a book on this subject (Schiffer); she is listed in the Directory under Texas.

Bone dish, Empress, Homer Laughlin 125.00
Bowl, berry; Cleveland, ind 20.00
Bowl, deep, Derwood, WS George, 4¾", from $40 to 50.00
Bowl, gravy; Hopewell China, w/saucer 100.00
Bowl, oatmeal; Newell pattern, Homer Laughlin 50.00
Bowl, salad; heavy, Chester Hotel China, dtd 1925, 5" 40.00
Bowl, soup; PMC Co, 8" 30.00
Bowl, vegetable; Cleveland, 9¾" 50.00
Butter dish, Empress, Homer Laughlin 200.00
Butter dish, Salem China 150.00
Butter dish, sq, Carrollton, 6¼" 100.00

Butter dish, Steubenville, 4½" holder w/in 7" dish 150.00
Butter dish, Victory, Knowles Taylor Knowles 150.00
Calendar plate, 1921 advertising pc, DE McNicol.................... 50.00
Canister set, rnd, unmk, 6½x5", 6 for.. 300.00
Casserole, Buffalo China, w/lid 150.00
Casserole, Empress, Homer Laughlin, w/lid, 8½" dia 150.00
Casserole, Pope Gosser, w/lid, 10½x10½" 100.00
Casserole, SPI Clinchfield China, w/lid 150.00
Casserole, Taylor Smith & Taylor, w/lid, 11x7½" 150.00
Casserole, Vodrey China, early 1900s, w/lid, 12x6" 100.00
Chamber pot, unmk, w/lid, late 1890s 150.00

Chocolate cup, no mark, 3½", $85.00.

Chocolate pot, Knowles Taylor & Knowles 200.00
Creamer, unmk, 4¼" 25.00
Creamer & sugar bowl, SP Co, w/lid.. 85.00
Cup, 2 hdls, unmk.. 40.00
Cup & saucer, Owen China, St Louis 40.00
Mug, baby's, Cleveland China.. 100.00
Pitcher, wash; Bennett China.. 400.00
Pitcher, water; Crown Pottery Co 200.00
Pitcher, water; Empress, Homer Laughlin 250.00
Pitcher, water; National China 200.00
Plate, Knowles Taylor Knowles, 9¾" 40.00
Plate, Steubenville, 9" 40.00
Plate, Wilmer Ware 20.00
Platter, Edwin M Knowles, 14½x11" 60.00
Platter, Pope Gosser, 17x13" 75.00
Platter, souvenir; gold leaves & stenciled initials, dtd 1923, 6" 65.00
Platter, Thompson Glenwood, 13x10" 50.00
Platter, West End Pottery Co, 15½x11" 60.00
Platter, 10 bluebirds, gold trim at rim, DE McNichol, 15¼x11¼" .. 75.00
Shakers, Art Deco styling, tall, unmk, extremely rare, pr............. 250.00
Shaving mug, The Potters Co-Op 65.00
Sugar bowl, Illinois China Co, w/lid, 7x6" 50.00
Syrup, Homer Laughlin, 6½" 175.00
Tea set, child's, CPCo, 21-pc 400.00
Tea set, child's, Summit China Co 800.00
Teacup, unmk... 15.00
Teapot, Carollton... 250.00
Teapot, ELP Co, 8½x8½" 250.00
Teapot, Homer Laughlin, Kwaker 500.00
Teapot, West Virginia Pottery Co, sm 150.00

Boch Freres

Founded in the early 1840s in La Louviere, Boch Freres Keramis became the foremost producer of art pottery in Belgium. Though primarily they served a localized market, in 1844 they earned worldwide recognition for some of their sculptural works on display at the International Exposition in Paris.

In 1907 Charles Catteau of France was appointed head of the art department. Before that time, the firm had concentrated on developing glazes and perfecting elegant forms. The style they pursued was tradition-

al, favoring the re-creation of established eighteenth-century ceramics. Catteau brought with him to Boch Freres the New Wave (or Art Nouveau) influence in form and decoration. His designs won him international acclaim at the Exhibition d'Art Decoratif in Paris in 1925, and it is for his work that Boch Freres is so highly regarded today. He occasionally signed his work as well as that of others who under his direct supervision carried out his preconceived designs. He was associated with the company until 1950 and lived the remainder of his life in Nice, France, where he died in 1966. The Boch Freres Keramis factory continues to operate today, producing bathroom fixtures and other utilitarian wares. A variety of marks have been used, most incorporating some combination of 'Boch Freres,' 'Keramis,' 'BFK,' or 'Ch Catteau.' A shield topped by a crown and flanked by a 'B' and an 'F' was used as well.

Box, Deco floral, mc on blk & gr stripes, La Louviere, 2⅞x4⅝" ... 300.00
Lamp base, Deco floral, mc on tan crackle, Catteau, 6½" 165.00
Pitcher, Deco style, yel w/gold, stylized hdl, La Louviere, 9½x7" . 900.00

Vase, birds and flowers, Julius Ernest Chaput, marked J 38/ BFK/UNIQUE/472 CB, 20x16", $18,000.00. (Photo courtesy David Rago Auctions/LiveAuctioneers.com)

Vase, birds (stylized) in panels, brn/cream crackle, Catteau/#931, 11".. 9,000.00
Vase, birds on branches, mc on wht crackle, D1322, 12x7½" 1,025.00
Vase, birds on branches form band on brn, Catteau, #1348, rstr, 7" ... 1,200.00
Vase, blk sphere w/fired-on parallel silver lines, #894, 9⅛"........... 600.00
Vase, Deco floral, 3-color, Catteau, La Louviere, #898C, 11"...... 2,400.00
Vase, Deco floral band, mc on wht crackle, Catteau, 5½x5½"... 1,985.00
Vase, Deco floral band atop vertical stripes, Catteau, 10½".......1,450.00
Vase, Deco floral on tan pebbled ground, #889, 8⅜"..................... 240.00
Vase, Deco linear design, bl on wht, silver wing-like hdls, 9"....... 150.00
Vase, deer in cuerda seca, turq/indigo on wht crackle, 9x8½" 800.00
Vase, deer in relief, fired-on silver accents on blk, #1221, 9½".....660.00
Vase, elk (stylized) leaping, brn tones, Catteau, #1291, 9⅛" 6,000.00
Vase, floral stripes on wht crackle, ovoid, Fabrication Belge, 20x11".5,250.00
Vase, geometric panels, bl & turq on wht crackle, 6-sided, 12⅜", NM. 1,800.00
Vase, nasturtiums/leaves, mc on crackle, unmk, 8⅞".................... 335.00
Vase, Nouveau floral on gr shading to bl, bulbous, 7".................. 265.00
Vase, penguins in cuerda seca, blk/mint/wht, #976, 14½x13½"..9,600.00
Vase, red w/gold spirals, La Louviere, #909, 12⅛"........................ 300.00
Vase, rows of lappets, bl/wht/blk/tan, Catteau, La Louviere, #986, 11". 5,750.00
Vase, squirrel reserves (3), blk & gold, #2237, 8¾", NM 360.00
Vase, stags leaping, ivory on terra cotta, spherical, DL339, 8x7½" ..540.00

Boehm

Boehm sculptures were the creation of Edward Marshall Boehm, a ceramic artist who coupled his love of the art with his love of nature to produce figurines of birds, animals, and flowers in lovely background settings accurate to the smallest detail. Sculptures of historical figures and those representing the fine arts were also made and along with many of the bird figurines, have established secondary-market values many times their original prices. His first pieces were made in the very early 1950s in Trenton, New Jersey, under the name of Osso Ceramics. Mr. Boehm died in 1969, and the firm has since been managed by his wife. Today known as Edward Marshall Boehm, Inc., the private family-held corporation produces not only porcelain sculptures but collector plates as well. Both limited and non-limited editions of their works have been issued. Examples are marked with various backstamps, all of which have incorporated the Boehm name since 1951. 'Osso Ceramics' in upper case lettering was used in 1950 and 1951. Our advisor for this category is Leon Reimert; he is listed in the Directory under Pennsylvania.

Bird of Paradise, Helen Boehm/FJ Cansentins, #58, 15x11x10". 1,025.00
Blue Grosbeak, #489, 11" 215.00

Bobolink on corn stalk, #475, 14¾", $400.00. (Photo courtesy Cincinnati Art Galleries)

Camellia, Helen Boehm, #300-25, 1978, 3x7" 240.00
Catbird among hyacinths, #483, 14" 480.00
Cymbidium Orchid, #30155, limited ed, 1984 .... 725.00
Fledgling Kingfisher, #449, 6" 72.50
Great Egret, Helen Boehm, #867/40221, 12x17" 660.00
Hummingbird & blooming cactus, #440, 8" 180.00
Hunter (horse), #203, 15" 480.00
Mallard w/wings wide, #406, 12" 95.00
Mockingbirds, #439, 12" 335.00
Mountain Bluebirds, #470, 12" 1,800.00
Mourning Dove, #40189, 15" 1,025.00
Mourning Doves on stump, #443, 14" 425.00
Mute Swan among cattails, #68, 19⅝" 900.00
Owl, winter plumage, #40122, 5" 150.00
Parrot Tulip, #186, 10" 75.00
Parula Warblers, #484, 16" 600.00
Robin beside daffodil, #472, 15" 900.00
Robin beside nest w/eggs, #143, 9" 840.00
Rufous Hummingbirds & yel flowers, #487, 15" 780.00
Sweet Pea, shell w/flowers, #25010, 6" 250.00
Tree Sparrow on log, #468, 8" 110.00
Tufted Titmice, #482, 13½" 600.00
Turtle, #40125, 3x4" 180.00
Tutenkhamen Sacred Cow, #513, 12¼" 135.00
Varied Buntings, #481, 23" 780.00
Woodcock, oval base, #413, 11" 300.00
Yel-Throated Warbler, #481, 9" 300.00

Bohemian Glass

The term 'Bohemian glass' has come to refer to a type of glass developed in Bohemia in the late sixteenth century at the Imperial Court of Rudolf II, the Hapsburg Emperor. The popular artistic pursuit of the day was stone carving, and it naturally followed to transfer familiar procedures to the glassmaking industry. During the next century, a

formula was discovered that produced a glass with a fine crystal appearance which lent itself well to deep, intricate engraving, and the art was further advanced.

Although many other kinds of art glass were made there, we are using the term 'Bohemian glass' to indicate glass overlaid or stained with color through which a design is cut or etched. (Unless otherwise described, the items in the listing that follows are of this type.) Red or yellow on clear glass is common, but other colors may also be found. Another type of Bohemian glass involves cutting through and exposing two layers of color in patterns that are often very intricate. Items such as these are sometimes further decorated with enamel and/or gilt work.

Beaker, amber, Rheinstein Castle scene, 1860s, 5" 225.00
Beaker, red stain, cut circles, 1900, 5½" 90.00
Beaker, ruby o/l, cameo cut knight w/sword, ca 1850-60, rare, 6" ... 2,000.00
Beaker, wht o/l, HP floral, stained/cut panels, 19th C, 5" 250.00
Goblet, amber stain, stags in landscape, ca 1870, 10x4¼" 400.00
Lustres, gr/milk glass, floral, prisms, 19th C, 14½", pr 1,200.00

Pokal, amber, paneled, spa scenes with German titles, nineteenth century, 10½", $600.00. (Photo courtesy Garth's Auctions Inc./LiveAuctioneers.com)

Pokal, red stain, woodland deer, ca 1900, 11½", pr 700.00
Pokal, ruby, o/l, stags in forest, fluted/faceted lid, 16" 3,750.00
Pokal, ruby o/l, stags/trees, bk: reducing lens, facet lid, 1860, 14" .. 1,725.00
Powder box, cranberry opaline w/HP foliage & gold, 2¼x4" 350.00
Stein, red stain, Steinbad scene, inlaid lid, ½-liter 350.00
Tumbler, bl stain, hunting dogs/trees, ca 1890, 4" 200.00
Vase, gr stain, deer & castle, ca 1930, 12" 125.00
Vase, red stain, hunting scenes, ca 1900, 13", pr 600.00

Bookends

Though a few were produced before 1880, bookends became a necessary library accessory and a popular commodity after the printing industry was revolutionized by Mergenthaler's invention, the linotype. Books became abundantly available at such affordable prices that almost every home suddenly had need for bookends. They were carved from wood; cast in iron, bronze, or brass; or cut from stone. Chalkware and glass were used as well. Today's collectors may find such designs as ships, animals, flowers, and children. Patriotic themes, art reproductions, and those with Art Nouveau and Art Deco styling provide a basis for a diverse and interesting collection.

Currently, figural cast-iron pieces are in demand, especially examples with good original polychrome paint. This has driven the value of painted cast-iron bookends up considerably.

For further information we recommend *Collector's Encyclopedia of Bookends* by Louis Kuritzky and Charles De Costa (Collector Books). Mr. Kuritzky is our advisor for this category; he is listed in the Directory under Florida. See also Arts and Crafts, Bradley and Hubbard.

Aesculapian Owl, CI, Germany mk, ca 1930, 5½" 50.00
Amish couple, CI, Wilton, ca 1925, 4" 50.00
Bear Frolic, CI, ca 1928, 4½" 90.00
Bedouin, CI, Hubley #418, polychrome finish, ca 1920, 5¾" 125.00
Boy & girl, resin, Alexander Backer Co, ca 1960, 9½" 35.00
Boy on world, gray metal, ca 1930, 6" 115.00
Brick fireplace, CI, ca 1925, 4¾" 75.00
Buccaneer, bronze-clad, Marion Bronze, ca 1965, 6¾" 125.00
Budda, bronze, Tiffany, ca 1920, 5¾" 450.00
Cameo girls, CI, 1926, 4¼" 125.00
Cat, playful, brass, ca 1932, 5½" (+) 100.00
Dante & Beatrice, bronze-clad, PM c 1915 mk, 1915, 8" 165.00
Duck, CI, Littco paper label, ca 1928, 5" 150.00
Eagle, brass, Virginia Metal Crafters, VM mk, ca 1986, 6" 95.00
Eagle landing, bronze, ca 1920, 4½" 175.00
Elephant Challenge, gray metal, Ronson #195M, ca 1926, 6" 175.00
Emancipator, CI, Connecticut Foundry, 1928 .... 75.00
End of the Trail, gray metal, Ronson, LV Aronson mk, 1925, 4¼". 95.00
English Stage Coach, CI, ca 1925, 4¼" 95.00
Gazelle feeding, gray metal, Ronson, ca 1930, 5" 95.00
Geisha, gray metal, Pompeian Bronze, ca 1925, 4¾" 90.00
German Shepherd, CI, ca 1928, 4¾" 45.00
Glass Lyre, glass, Fostoria Glass, 1943, 7" 150.00

Great Emancipator, gray metal, Pompeian Bronze, 1925, 5½", $175.00. (Photo courtesy Louis Kuritzky)

Guarding Pharaoh, CI, Judd #9743, ca 1926, 6¼" 225.00
Halloween cats, CI, Snead, 1925, 4½" 35.00
Hold Those Books, gray metal, Dodge Inc paper label, ca 1929, 7½".195.00
Horse, glass, Smith Glass, ca 1925, 8" 50.00
Hunter's Moon, CI, Acorn #603, ca 1930, 5¾" 165.00
Innocence, gray metal, Jennings Bro #1702, ca 1930, 7" 125.00
Knight in armor, CI, Robert Schwartz & Bro C-45 mk, ca 1930s, 7".175.00
Knights of Columbus, bronze, ca 1925, 6½" 125.00
Lincoln profile, CI, ca 1925, 5¼" 65.00
Lion, glass, Imperial Glass Co, 1978, 6" 125.00
Longtime Sweethearts, bronze-clad, Armor Bronze, ca 1925, 7".... 95.00
Nude on book, CI, Littco, ca 1929, 8" 175.00
Owl Family, gray metal, Weidlich Brothers #645, ca 1929, 6¼" 65.00
Pioneers, gray metal, Pompeian Bronze Co, 1925, 4¾" 150.00
Pirate Booty, CI, Littco, ca 1925, 6½" 75.00
Pony, CI, Littco, ca 1926, 6" 110.00
Proud Peacock, CI, ca 1925, 5½" 75.00
Ralph Waldo Emerson, bronze-clad, Galvano Bronze, ca 1925, 7½" .135.00
Sailfish, gray metal, PM Craftsman, ca 1965, 8" 65.00
Scotch Twins, CI, Art Colony Industries, ca 1925, 5¼" 90.00
Sower, CI, BFM mk, ca 1925, 4¾" 50.00
Sphinx face, iron, ca 1925, 6" 100.00
Springtime, gray metal, WB 638 c USA, ca 1930, 5" 95.00
Swan design, gray metal, Ronson #10817 paper label, ca 1930, 4¾".65.00
Thespian, CI, #140, ca 1925, 5½" 115.00
Tiger & snake, CI, Connecticut Foundry, 1928, 5" 65.00
Tom Sawyer, gray metal, PMC 4E, ca 1975, 5¼" 25.00
Tryst, CI, Hubley #301, ca 1924, 5½" 75.00
Water sprite, CI, Acorn #604, ca 1925, 5⅜" 195.00

Bootjacks and Bootscrapers

Bootjacks were made from metal or wood. Some were fancy figural shapes, others strictly business. Their purpose was to facilitate the otherwise awkward process of removing one's boots. Bootscrapers were handy gadgets that provided an effective way to clean the soles of mud and such. Our advisor for this category is Louis Picek; he is listed in the Directory under Iowa.

Bootjacks

Advertising for Musselman's Boot Jack Tobacco, cast iron, 9¾" long, $210.00. (Photo courtesy Wm. Morford Auctions)

Aluminum, bull's head, Ricardo, worn pnt 55.00
Brass, longhorn steer, 10" 15.00
Brass, sunflower, Musselman's Plug advertising 150.00
CI, American Bull Dog, pistol shape, Ricardo, worn pnt 55.00
CI, Baroque scrollwork set in marble block, 14" 95.00
CI, beetle, EX blk pnt, 11x4x2" 50.00
CI, Boss emb on shaft, lacy, 15" L 135.00
CI, cat silhouette, blk pnt, 10½x10" 295.00
CI, cricket, Harvest Bros & Co, Reading PA, 11x4¾" 110.00
CI, Labrador retriever, 3x10x4¾" 15.00
CI, lyre on oval scalloped base, 9x11" 125.00
CI, moose, 11x8" 15.00
CI, Naughty Nellie, nudy lady on bk, great old pnt, 9½", M 2,705.00
CI & wood, lever action, EX 150.00
Wood w/brass hinges, unfolds, att military, 19th C, 10¼x2" 1,200.00
Wrought iron, scrolled top, granite base, early 280.00

Bootscrapers

Brass, Scottie dogs (2) sit between wall (scraper), 4x10½" 85.00
CI, beetle form, orig pnt 85.00
CI, Black man sits above base, rust/soiling, 13x10", EX 225.00
CI, Black shoeshine boy atop, oval base, 13", VG 140.00
CI, cat w/long tail sticking up, 10x15" 35.00
CI, dachshund, tail forms ring, no pnt, 10½x7½x7" 185.00
CI, duck, full body, 14½" L 350.00
CI, eagle relief & classical lady in oval, Portland Foundry 300.00
CI, horseshoe mtd on rimmed base, 9x11x9" 2,500.00
CI, pan base w/flared rim & emb decor, pitting, 17x13x16" 195.00
CI, quatrefoil base, 5½x10½x11" 625.00
Wrought iron, scrolled finial (detailed), 21x24" 500.00
Wrought iron, scrolls, 19th C, 15¾x10" 760.00

Borsato, Antonio

Borsato was a remarkable artist/sculptor who produced some of the most intricately modeled and executed figurines ever made. He was born in Italy and at an early age enjoyed modeling wildlife from clay he dug from the river banks near his home. At age 11, he became an apprentice of Guido Cacciapuotti of Milan, who helped him develop his skills. During the late '20s and '30s, he continued to concentrate on wildlife studies. Because of his resistance to the fascist government, he was interred at Sardinia from 1940 until the end of the war, after which he returned to Milan where he focused his attention on religious subjects. He entered the export market in 1948 and began to design pieces featuring children and more romantic themes. By the 1960s his work had become very popular in this country. His talent for creating lifelike figures has seldom been rivaled. He contributed much of his success to the fact that each of his figures, though built from the same molded pieces, had its own personality, due the unique way he would tilt a head or position an arm. All had eyelashes, fingernails, and defined musculature; and each piece was painted by hand with antiquated colors and signed 'A. Borsato.' He made over 600 different models, with some of his groups requiring more than 160 components and several months of work to reach completion. Various pieces were made in two mediums, gres and porcelain, with porcelain being double the cost of gres. Borsato died in 1982. Today, some of his work is displayed in the Vatican Museum as well private collections.

The Wooden Shoe Maker, red mark, foil tag, 11x13", minimum value $1,000.00. (Photo courtesy Jackson's International Auctioneers & Appraisers of Fine Art & Antiques/ LiveAuctioneers.com)

Bullfighter, man on rearing horse charges bull, 13½x18½" 18,000.00
Chestnuts & Tales, girl sits on box by stove w/old man, 10½" ..1,400.00
Christ (head of), 6½" 485.00
Cobbler's Dilemma, man & boy at bench, 10½x7½x8½" 2,900.00
Coffee Counter, 3 figures surrounding coffee urn, 10x9" 4,000.00
Comfort & Love, courting people, lady & dog in interior, 12x22"..13,600.00
Cowboy w/guitar, man seated on saddle w/instrument, 6¼" 500.00
Dog Trainer, man working w/upright poodle, 6x9½" 1,600.00
Elegant Harmony, man at piano/2nd w/violin, lady beside, 13x15".9,600.00
Fagoters, man w/bundle on bk w/goat & dog, 11½x8½" 2,100.00
Fiddler's Revelry, man seated/playing fiddle, 6x10".....................2,140.00
Grandma, seated old lady w/knitting, chickens at ft, 6" 375.00
Gypsy Camp, gypsy around wagon w/horse & pony, 10x18x10" . 3,300.00
Lover's Lane, figures in horse-drawn carriage on base, 11x24" ..8,775.00
Man w/pipe, head of old man w/eyes closed smoking pipe, 7½" ... 250.00
Miss Fragrance, lady seated in chair w/legs crossed, 6½"............... 550.00
Mother & Child, mother wrapping baby in blanket, 6½x6".......... 650.00
Musketeer (bust of) in plumed hat, 9x12"..................................... 375.00
Psyche & Eros, classical couple on base, 7¾x8" 1,575.00
Rescue, man on horse lifting woman up by waist, 12x15" 6,800.00
Serenity, lady seated by sm tree w/birds, butterfly on finger, 9½" . 3,000.00
Siesta's Price, fruit cart, peddler asleep while case drw is robbed . 3,200.00
Wine Vendor, man & woman w/child on horse-drawn wagon, 12x8" . 2,500.00

Bossons Artware

The late William Henry Bossons founded Bossons in 1946. When he died in 1951, his son, W. Ray Bossons took charge and in 1958 designed the first 'character wall masks.' Jane Bossons Roberts, Ray's daughter, directed operations from 1994 until the company's closing in December 1996.

Ken Potts was the head mold maker and factory foreman. The principle sculptors/modelers of Bossons were (in chronological order): Fred Wright (FW), Alice Brindley (AB), and Ray Bossons (WRB), who oversaw all Bossons creations and made sure that they met the company's highest standards.

The last character masks (heads) were released in 1995 and 1996. Currently they are commanding unusually high prices when new and in original condition.

These final editions are pictured in full color on the last mini-folder leaflet from Bossons entitled 'Autumn 1996 Collection': Nuvolari, No. 243; Sinbad the Sailor, No. 250; Cossack, No. 251; and Evzon, No. 248.

One of the easiest ways to recognize an authentic Bossons is by viewing the reverse side. The back is most often silver, and the hanging mechanism may be protruding or recessed, a factor that is sometimes helpful in determining production dates. Though the recessed hook was used from the '60s through the '90s, some very early Bossons also have the recessed hook. During the period from 1946 to 1960, Bossons most often employed an exterior or protruding hook.

Though the mark has changed slightly over the years, an authentic Bossons will have the following copyright incision on the back: BOSSONS Congleton England World Copyright. Regardless of when they were produced or released, each Bossons has its own copyright date, so that date is not relative to value.

Though scarcity is a prime worth-assessing factor, condition is enormously important in determing value. Mint in the box examples can command several hundred dollars. Popular Bossons produced in mid-1960 to early 1990 are found in great numbers, and many can be readily purchased for under $100.00. But condition is critical; with only a few facial blemishes, even plentiful Bossons are not worth more than $10.00 to $20.00. As a general rule, early editions, those produced from 1957 to 1959, sell for the highest prices. Literature by Bossons such as large descriptive, colored brochures and the miniature folders that they published nearly every year is also collectible.

Bossons articles in previous editions of *Schroeder's Antiques Price Guide* contain many important details on Bossons; reviewing past issues will discolose many fluctuations in prices over the years.

Our advisor, Donald M. Hardisty, is a recognized authority in the field of Bossons. He has been recommended by Bossons since his official invitation from Ray Bossons to visit their facilities in Congleton, England, in 1984. Don has given many demonstrations/lectures for various collector organizations and meetings, spends countless hours advising buyers and sellers via the phone and the internet, offers official appraisals for dealers and insurance claimants, and has published numerous articles on this subject. He is listed in the Directory under New Mexico. For more information you may link to www.donsbossons.com or www.bossons.us.

Our values are for items that are in new condition and in their original boxes. (When dates are given they are release dates, not copyright dates.)

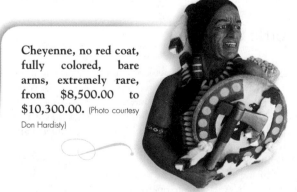

Cheyenne, no red coat, fully colored, bare arms, extremely rare, from $8,500.00 to $10,300.00. (Photo courtesy Don Hardisty)

Abduhl, from $45 to 85.00
Aruj Barbarossa (1994-96), from $185 to.....................................245.00
Betsy Trotwood, w/bl collar, from $150 to................................ 200.00
Birds & Sunflowers, from $475 to.. 750.00
Blackbeard (1993-96), from $125 to 150.00
Boatman, from $65 to... 85.00

Bossons Santa Claus, from $175 to..................................225.00
Boxed Mallards, pottery, from $350 to..........................450.00
Captain Pierre Le Grand, from $150 to..........................225.00
Carnival Annie, 1961-63, from $300 to..........................500.00
Carnival Joe, 1961-63, from $300 to..............................500.00
Cheyenne w/red coat, 1970-92, from $165 to..................200.00
Churchill (1988 for IBCS), must have gold name tag on reverse, $185 to ..225.00
Clipper Captain, from $125 to.....................................175.00
Coolie, 1964-70, from $125 to.....................................165.00
Cossack, from $200 to..250.00
Dickens Characters, 1964-96, ea from $85 to..................125.00
Evzon, from $185 to..275.00
Falcon, red head, from $385 to...................................600.00
Floral Plaque, Autumn Gold, 14", from $185 to..............250.00
Fly Fisherman, from $165 to.......................................185.00
Golfer, from $150 to..185.00
Highwayman, from $175 to...275.00
Indian Chief, 1961-64, from $300 to............................485.00
Jolly Tar, from $100 to...145.00
Karim, 1967-69, from $165 to.....................................185.00
King Henry VIII, 1986-94, from $175 to........................250.00
Kurd (1964-96), from $25 to...45.00
Lifeboat Man, 1966-96, from $75 to...............................85.00
Military Masks, w/o eyes, ea from $350 to.....................500.00
Nuvolari, 1996, from $225 to......................................300.00
Old Timer, 1977-92, from $125 to................................165.00
Paddy; blk hair, 1959, from $125 to..............................145.00
Paddy, issued for IBCS, must have sgn certificate, from $185 to ..200.00
Paddy, 1969, from $75 to...85.00
Parson, from $145 to...165.00
Persian, from $25 to...45.00
Rawhide, from $85 to..145.00
Rob Roy, 1995-96, from $175 to...................................200.00
Sea Hawk Bossons, from $500 to.................................650.00
Shepherd, 1995-96, from $100 to.................................150.00
Sherlock Holmes, from $150 to....................................175.00
Sindbad, from $285 to..350.00
Smuggler, from $25 to...45.00
Squire, from $125 to..165.00
Syrian (1960-96), from $50 to..75.00
Tecumseh, 1962-96, from $165 to.................................185.00
Tulip Time, from $175 to..225.00
White Swan, Fraser-Art, from $750 to...........................900.00
Winston Churchill, IBCS, must have gold emblem, from $185 to..215.00

Bottle Openers

At the beginning of the nineteenth century, manufacturers began to seal bottles with a metal cap that required a new type of bottle opener. Now the screw cap and the flip top have made bottle openers nearly obsolete. There are many variations, some in combination with other tools. Many openers were used as means of advertising a product. Various materials were used, including silver and brass.

A figural bottle opener is defined as a figure designed for the sole purpose of lifting a bottle cap. The actual opener must be an integral part of the figure itself. A base-plate opener is one where the lifter is a separate metal piece attached to the underside of the figure. The major producers of iron figurals were Wilton Products, John Wright Inc., Gadzik Sales, and L & L Favors. Openers may be free standing and three dimensional, wall hung or flat. They can be made of cast iron (often painted), brass, bronze, or aluminum.

Numbers within the listings refer to a reference book printed by the FBOC (Figural Bottle Opener Collectors) organization. Those seeking ad-

ditional information are encouraged to contact FBOC, whose address can be found in the Directory under Clubs, Newsletters, and Catalogs. The items below are all in excellent original condition unless noted otherwise.

Billy goat, brass, Made in Canada, 4x2½"..................... 38.00
Black caddy, NPCI & mc pnt, #F44, 5¾".......................275.00
Boy winking, CI, worn pnt, Wilton................................ 70.00
Clown, CI, mc pnt, 3 holes for wall mt, 4½x4", VG.......... 60.00
Cockatoo, CI, mc pnt, John Wright, #F121...................120.00

Cocker spaniel, John Wright, 3¾" long, $150.00. (Photo courtesy Morphy Auctions/LiveAuctioneers.com)

Drunken man hanging on to palm tree, CI, mc pnt, 4x2¾", NM .. 55.00
Elephant seated w/trunk up, CI, pnt traces, 3¾".............. 48.00
Elephant walking, trunk up, pnt CI, Wilton, 3¼" L.......... 75.00
Foundry man, CI, mc pnt, John Wright, #F-29................ 65.00
German shepherd, Syroco... 70.00
Goose, CI, mc pnt, Scott Products, 5¼x2¾x1½"............. 45.00
Greek lady, enamel on brass, Enamel Work on Solid Brass..., 5".... 25.00
Hockey player, Molson Ice, place bottle in mouth, cap tray at chest... 230.00
Hula girls & shaking palm tree, copper on metal w/mc enamel, 2x4¼".. 45.00
Kansas Jayhawk, CI, mc pnt, 4x1¾"............................. 75.00
Mallard duck, CI, mc pnt, John Wright, 1940s-50s, 2½"..... 58.00
Man at lamppost, Moosehead ME, CI, mc pnt, 4", NM...... 48.00
Modernist dog, Hagenauer style, shiny metal, Austria, 3x4½"....... 95.00
Nude lady, brass, Lions Illinois 1954, 5".......................... 60.00
Parrot on tall perch, CI, mc pnt...................................150.00
Pelican on base, CI, mc pnt, 3¼".................................. 60.00

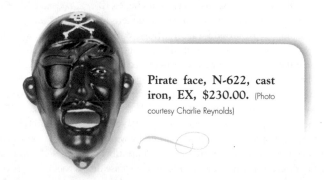

Pirate face, N-622, cast iron, EX, $230.00. (Photo courtesy Charlie Reynolds)

Pointer hunting dog, CI, blk & wht pnt 2½x4⅜"............. 50.00
Rooster, CI, mc pnt, #F100..235.00
Seagull on stump, CI, mc pnt, 3¼"............................... 48.00
Skunk, CI, mc pnt, 1940s, 2¼x3", NM..........................125.00
Squirrel, brass, 2x2¾".. 45.00
Timberjack on base, metal, 3"...................................... 75.00
4-eyed woman w/lg front teeth, CI, worn mc pnt............. 45.00

Bottles and Flasks

As far back as the first century B.C., the Romans preferred blown glass containers for their pills and potions. American business firms preferred glass bottles in which to package their commercial products and used them extensively from the late eighteenth century on. Bitters bottles contained 'medicine' (actually herb-flavored alcohol). Because of a heavy tax imposed on the sale of liquor in seventeenth-century England by King George, who hoped to curtail alcohol abuse among his subjects, bottlers simply added 'curative' herbs to their brew and thus avoided taxation. Since gin was taxed in America as well, the practice continued in this country. Scores of brands were sold; among the most popular were Dr. H.S. Flint & Co. Quaker Bitters, Dr. Kaufman's Anti-Cholera Bitters, and Dr. J. Hostetter's Stomach Bitters. Most bitters bottles were made in shades of amber, brown, and aquamarine. Clear glass was used to a lesser extent, as were green tones. Blue, amethyst, red-brown, and milk glass examples are rare. Color is a strong factor when pricing bottles.

Perfume or scent bottles were produced by companies all over Europe from the late sixteenth century on. Perfume making became such a prolific trade that as a result beautifully decorated bottles were fashionable. In America they were produced in great quantities by Stiegel in 1770 and by Boston and Sandwich in the early nineteenth century. Cologne bottles were first made in about 1830 and toilet-water bottles in the 1880s. Rene Lalique produced fine scent bottles from as early as the turn of the century. The first were one-of-a-kind creations done in the cire perdue method. He later designed bottles for the Coty Perfume Company with a different style for each Coty fragrance. (See Lalique.)

Spirit flasks from the nineteenth century were blown in specially designed molds with varied motifs including political subjects, railroad trains, and symbolic devices. The most commonly used colors were amber, dark brown, and green.

Pitkin flasks were the creation of the Pitkin Glass Works which operated in East Manchester, Connecticut, from 1783 to 1830. However, other glasshouses in New England and the Midwest copied the Pitkin flask style. All are known as Pitkins.

From the twentieth century, early pop and beer bottles are very collectible as is nearly every extinct commercial container. Dairy bottles are also desirable; look for round bottles in good condition with both city and state as well as a nice graphic relating to the farm or the dairy.

Bottles may be dated by the methods used in their production. For instance, a rough pontil indicates a date before 1845. After the bottle was blown, a pontil rod was attached to the bottom, a glob of molten glass acting as the 'glue.' This allowed the glassblower to continue to manipulate the extremely hot bottle until it was finished. From about 1845 until approximately 1860, the molten glass 'glue' was omitted. The rod was simply heated to a temperature high enough to cause it to afix itself to the bottle. When the rod was snapped off, a metallic residue was left on the base of the bottle; this is called an 'iron pontil.' (The presence of a pontil scar thus indicates early manufacture and increases the value of a bottle.) A seam that reaches from base to lip marks a machine-made bottle from after 1903, while an applied or hand-finished lip points to an early mold-blown bottle. The Industrial Revolution saw keen competition between manufacturers, and as a result, scores of patents were issued. Many concentrated on various types of closures; the crown bottle cap, for instance, was patented in 1892. If a manufacturer's name is present, consulting a book on marks may help you date your bottle. For more information we recommend *Bottle Pricing Guide, 3rd Edition*, by Hugh Cleveland.

Among our advisors for this category are Madeleine France (see the Directory under Florida), Mark Vuono (Connecticut), Monsen and Baer (Virginia), and Robert Doyle (New York). Values suggested below reflect hammer prices (plus buyer's premium) of bottles that were sold through cataloged auctions. See also Advertising, various companies; Blown Glass; Blown Three-Mold Glass; California Perfume Company; Czechoslovakia; De Vilbiss; Fire Fighting; Lalique; Steuben; Zanesville Glass.

Key:

am — applied mouth	GW — Glass Works
bbl — barrel	ip — iron pontil
bt — blob top	op — open pontil

b3m — blown 3-mold	ps — pontil scar
cm — collared mouth	rm — rolled mouth
fl — filigree	sb — smooth base
fm — flared mouth	sl — sloping
gm — ground mouth	sm — sheared mouth
gp — graphite pontil	tm — tooled mouth
grd — ground pontil	

Barber Bottles

Amethyst, mc geometric floral, rm, ps, mallet form, 7⅝"	80.00
Bl-gr, Mary Gregory girl w/twig, rm, ps, 8"	275.00
Canary yel opal, Hobnail, rm, ps, 6¾", EX	50.00
Clear, floral, mc on pk, tm, ps, 8⅛"	375.00
Clear frost, palm tree in gr & wht, tm, sb, 8"	1,100.00
Clear w/red flashing, yel & silver floral, ribs, ps, 7⅞"	375.00
Clear w/ruby flashed int, Hobnail, rm, ps, 7½", EX	70.00
Cobalt, Nouveau florals, tm, ps, 7⅝"	150.00
Cranberry opal, wht swirl, tm, ps, 7⅛"	450.00
Dk amethyst, Bay Rum/grist mill, ribs, ps, 7¾"	325.00
Dk amethyst, geometric mc floral, rm, 8"	100.00
Dk amethyst, Hair Tonic & windmill, emb ribs, ps, 7⅝"	475.00
Dk amethyst, Mary Gregory girl sitting, rm, ps, haze, 8"	110.00
Emerald gr, geometric wht enameling, emb ribs, ps, 7⅜"	100.00
Milk glass, Bay Rum & mc roses, tm, ps, 10⅜"	250.00
Milk glass, cherub & rose springs, mc on bl & yel, ps, 7¾"	200.00
Milk glass, Cologne, mc label under glass, sb, 7⅞"	300.00
Milk glass, cranes in mc, WT&Co on sb, tm, 9¼"	425.00
Milk glass, running horse in mc, sb, pewter cap, 9½"	425.00
Purple amethyst, fleur-de-lis in yel, tm, ps, 7½"	175.00
Turq, Hobnail, rm, ps, 6⅞"	125.00
Turq opal, wht swirl, tm, ps, 6⅞"	375.00
Turq w/gold & wht floral, emb ribs, tm, ps, 8"	325.00
Wht opal, Bay Rum in red, twisted swirl, tm, sb, 8¼"	200.00
Wht opal, Bay Rum/mc florals, am, ps, 8⅞"	150.00
Wht opal, Coinspot, rm, sb, 7⅛"	160.00
Wht opal, Hair Tonic in blk, mc tulips, rm, sb, 8⅝"	160.00
Wht opal, Sea Foam/swallows/roses, mc, tm, ps, 10⅜"	250.00
Wht opal, Stars & Stripes, rm, ps, 7⅛"	300.00
Wht opal, Swirl, tm, ps, 6¾"	300.00
Wht opal, Toilet Water/mc tulips, rm, sb, 8⅝"	100.00
Wht opal, Uno Tonique...Chicago Ill, gr letters on lt gr reserve, 8"	400.00
Yel amber, Hobnail, rm, ps, 6⅞", NM	110.00
Yel gr, Mary Gregory girl sitting, ribbed, ps, 7¾"	200.00
Yel gr, Mary Gregory girl w/twig, emb ribs, rm, ps, 8"	120.00
Yel olive, mc floral, emb ribs, rm, ps, 7⅝"	100.00

Bitters Bottles

African Stomach..., yel amber, tapered cm, sb, 9⅝"	160.00
Big Bill Best... (2 sides), amber, tm, sb, NM label, 12¼"	425.00
Bissell's Tonic...1868...Peoria Ill, med amber to yel amber, sb, 9"	300.00
Bitters Wild Cherry...Reading PA, med amber, am, semi-cabin, 10"	400.00
Brown's Celebrated Indian Herb...1867, dk amber, sb, princess, 12¼"	500.00
Brown's Celebrated Indian..., yel amber, sb, princess, 12¼"	1,700.00
Burdock Blood...Buffalo NY, aqua sample, tm, sb, open bubble, 4⅛"	140.00
California Fig...San Francisco Cal, med amber, tm, sb, 9¾"	50.00
Cooley's Anti-Dispeptic or Jaundice..., bl aqua, 8-panel roof, 6¼"	1,400.00
Dr CW Roback's...Cincinnati O, amber, tapered cm, sb, bbl, 9⅜"	275.00
DR CW Roback's...Cincinnati O, yel amber, sb, stain, 9½"	300.00
DR CW Roback's...Cincinnati O, yel olive amber, bbl, 9¼"	600.00
Dr Geo Pierce's Indian Restorative..., bl aqua, am, op, 7⅝"	350.00
Dr Henley's Wild Grape Root IXL..., med olive, am, sb, 12"	6,000.00
Dr Henley's Wild Grape Root..., bl aqua, sb, am, crude, 12¼"	200.00

Dr J Hostetter's Stomach..., med to dk olive gr, cm, sb, crude, 9½" .250.00
Dr Loew's Celebrated...Cleveland O, med yel lime gr, sb, 3⅞" 220.00
Dr Loew's Celebrated...Cleveland O, med yel lime gr, sb, 9½" 400.00
Dr Walkinshaw's Curative...NY, yel amber, tapered cm, sb, 10" ... 500.00
Dr XX Lovegood's Family..., deep amber, sb, cabin, 9⅜" 1,000.00
Drake's Plantation...Pat 1862, amber, sb, 4-log cabin, D-110, 10" . 150.00
Drake's Plantation...Pat 1862, dk copper puce, sb, 6-log cabin, 10" 180.00
Drake's Plantation...Pat 1862, dk strawberry puce, 6-log, D-105, 8" . 220.00
Drake's Plantation...Pat 1862, med strawberry puce, 6-log cabin, 10" . 750.00
Drake's Plantation...Pat 1862, med yel olive, 6-log cabin, D-105, 10" .. 2,750.00
Drake's Plantation...Pat 1862, yel amber, 4-log cabin, D-110, 10" .. 110.00
Drake's Plantation...Pat 1862, yel amber w/olive tone, 4-log, 10" . 475.00
Edw Wilder...(building)...Patented, amethyst tint, semi-cabin, 10½" .. 325.00
Established 1845 Schroeder's...Cincinnati, amber, lady's leg, 5¼" . 550.00
Established 1845 Schroeder's...Sole Owners, amber, lady's leg, 11⅜" .1,900.00
Great Tonic Caldwell's Herb, amber, am, ip, 12½" 300.00
Greeley's Bourbon Whiskey..., med apricot puce, bbl, sb, 9⅛" 700.00
Hall's...Established 1842, orange amber, sb, bbl, 9¼" 250.00
Hartwig Kantorowicz...Germanin, milk glass, case gin form, 3⅞" .. 80.00
Harvey's Prairie...Pat, med amber to yel amber, sl cm, sb, 9¾" . 19,000.00
Holtzermann's Pat Stomach..., med amber, NM label, cabin, 10" . 850.00
Hops & Malt..., med amber, sl cm, sb, semi-cabin, 9½" 400.00
John Moffat...Price $1.00, bl aqua, am, op, crude, 5⅝" 90.00
Kelly's Old Cabin...1863, dk tobacco amber, sb, 2-story cabin, 9" .. 2,750.00
Keystone..., orange amber, cm, sb, bbl, 9¾" 750.00
Khoosh..., yel olive, dbl cm, sb, 8¼" 100.00
Koehler & Hinrich's Red Star...Minn, yel amber, tm, sb, 11½" 600.00
Lediard's Celebrated Stomach..., bl gr, sl dbl cm, sb, 10⅛" 1,700.00
Litthauer Stomach...Berlin, milk glass, gin form, sb, 9½" 100.00
Malabac...M Cziner Chemist, yel amber, semi lady's leg, 11¾" 700.00
Mckeever's Army..., med amber, cm, sb, cannonballs on drum, 10⅝" . 2,750.00
Mishler's Herb...Graduation, yel olive, cm, sb, stain, 9¼" 275.00
Moulton's Olorosa...Trade (pineapple) Mark, bl aqua, sb, 11¼" ... 300.00
National..., yel w/amber tone, Pat 1867 on sb, ear of corn, 12¾" . 900.00

Old Sachem Bitters and Wigwam Tonic, amber-tone barrel, smooth base, applied mouth, 9½", $425.00. (Photo courtesy Glass-Works Auctions)

Old Sachem...& Wigwam Tonic, med copper puce, am, sb, 9½" .. 600.00
Old Sachem...& Wigwam Tonic, med pk puce, am, sb, bbl, 9¼" . 3,000.00
Parham's German...Dr C Parham Philada, aqua, am, op, 6⅜" ... 2,300.00
Pat'd 1884 Dr Petzold's...Incpt 1862, amber, tm, sb, semi cabin, 10" ... 180.00
Pat'd 1884 Dr Petzold's...Incpt 1862, yel amber, sb, semi-cabin, 8" . 300.00
Peruvian...W&K, med yel amber, crude am, sb, 9¼" 50.00
Sanborn's Kidney & Liver Laxative..., med amber, B on sb, 9¾" ... 80.00
Sanitarium...Rock Island Ill, yel olive gr, sb, triangular, 9¾" 350.00
Schroeder's...Louisville KY, med amber, SB&G Co on sb, lady's leg, 9" . 475.00
Simon's Centennial...Trade Mark, bl aqua, Geo Washington bust, 10" . 90.00
Smyrna Stomach...Dayton Ohio, med amber, NM label, sb, 9" ... 350.00
Solomon's Strengthening & Invigoration...Georgia, cobalt, am, sb, 10" .. 1,200.00
Suffolk...Philbrook & Tucker Boston, yel amber, sb, pig, 10¼" L. 950.00
Traveler's (man w/cane)...1834 1870, yel amber, open bubble, 10½" . 4,250.00
Warner's Safe...(safe)...Rochester NY, amber, A&DC on sb, 9½" . 950.00
Wr Wonser's USA Indian Root..., med yel amber to yel, sb, 11¼" .. 13,000.00
Zingari...F Rahter, med yel amber, sb, lady's leg, 11⅞" 400.00
1834 John Root's...Buffalo NY, aqua, tapered cm, sb, 10⅝" 600.00

Black Glass Bottles

Many early European and American bottles are deep, dark green, or amber in color. Collectors refer to such coloring as black glass. Before held to light, the glass is so dark it appears to be black.

Kidney shape, deep olive green with amber tone, pontil scar, applied string lip, Dutch, 1760 – 1790, 6¾", $700.00. (Photo courtesy Glass-Works Auctions)

Mallet, med yel olive gr, sm, ps, blown in dip mold, 7¼x4⅝" 325.00
Onion, med bl emerald gr, tm w/appl string lip, op, 1720-50, 7½" . 90.00
Onion, med bl gr, sm w/appl string lip, op, 1720-1750, 6½x5⅝" .. 150.00
Onion, med emerald gr, sm w/appl string lip, op, 1720-50, 6⅜x5⅝" . 130.00
Onion, med olive gr, sm w/appl string lip, op, haze, 7⅜x5¾" 100.00
Onion, med yel olive gr, sm w/appl string lip, op, 7¼x5½" 120.00
Onion, med yel olive w/amber tone, sm w/appl string lip, op, 7½" ... 80.00
Onion, yel gr, appl string lip, op, Dutch, chip, 5⅝x4⅝" 375.00
Seal: IC Hoffman, med olive gr, cylinder, ps, 8⅜" 325.00
Seal: Superfine Olive Oil...Clarified, med olive gr, op, 11" 180.00
Seal: V Led Giraudeao (snake & tree) Paris, yel olive gr, ps, 8⅜" .. 1,300.00
Wine/ale, dk olive amber, IV on shoulder, am, ps, 9" 475.00

Blown Glass Bottles and Flasks

Chestnut flask, dk teal gr, appl lip & hdl, 6⅜" 125.00
Chestnut flask, med emerald gr, am, op, crude/bubbles, 5¾" 1,100.00
Demi-john, gr, ovoid, early 19th C, flake, 10¼" 840.00
Globular, yel amber w/16 ribs, att Mantua, blisters/bruise, 5" 840.00
Paneled, cobalt, Pittsburgh area, 10½" 1,950.00
Pitkin flask, bright yel gr, 16 right-swirl ribs, sm, ps, Midwest, 7" . 850.00
Pitkin flask, sea gr, 32 left-swirl ribs, sm, ps, Midwest, 6½" 500.00
Pitkin flask, yel root beer amber, 36 broken left-swirl ribs, 6" 950.00
Pocket flask, dk amber, 24 left-swirl ribs, sm, ps, Midwest, 4¾" 750.00
Teardrop, med emerald gr, outward rm, ps, pebble mks, 9¾" 110.00

Cologne, Perfume, and Toilet Water Bottles

Atomizer, bl cut to clear pinwheels, unmk, 5½" 60.00
Blown, lady's hand w/wedding ring, unmk, 5¼" L 40.00
Cobalt, 12-sided w/sloped shoulders, ps, rm, 6" 325.00
Crown top, lady head, pk hat, pnt porc, Germany, #8051, 2¼" ... 200.00
Crown top, lady's head, long earring, pnt porc, Germany, 2⅜" 150.00
Crown top, Oriental lady's head, pnt porc, Germany, 3½" 250.00
Crown top, pirate's head, bl hat, pnt porc, Germany, #8057, 2⅜" . 200.00
Cut o/l, red/crystal geometric pyramidal form, Saks Fifth Ave, 5½" . 175.00
Dk grape amethyst, 12-sided w/sl shoulders, sb, rm, 4⅛" 145.00
Lundberg Studios, wht blossoms in dk bl, long dauber, 7¼" 195.00
Med pk amethyst, 12-sided, sb, rm, 6½" 115.00

Commercial Perfume Bottles

One of the most popular and growing areas of perfume bottle collecting is what are called 'commercial' perfume bottles. They are called commercial because they were sold with perfume in them — in a sense one pays for the perfume and the bottle is free. Collectors especially value bottles that retain their original label and box, called a perfume presentation. If the bottle is unopened, so much the better. Rare fragrances and those from the 1920s are highly prized. 'Tis a sweet, sweet hobby. Our advisors are Randy Monsen and Rod Baer; they are listed in the Directory under Virginia.

Annette, airplane w/bird pilot, blown w/mc HP, Germany, 1920s, 4⅜" .350.00
Caron, Infini, plastic stopper w/mirror image of bottle, 4⅜", MIB. 100.00
Caron, Royal Bain de Champagne, wine bottle form, 10½", MIB...200.00
Christian Dior, Dioring, amphora form w/wht enamel, 6½", MIB. 300.00
Chu Chin Chow, Oriental figure seated, mc, Bryenne, 1918, 2½" . 1,675.00
Ciro, Danger, clear w/gold cap, 2¼", +bag, MIB 100.00
Coty, Emeraude, clear w/gr cap, 2¼", +Air Spun powder, MIB.... 150.00
Coty, Le Vertige, clear w/gold cap, gold label, 2¼", MIB.............. 100.00
Fabergè, Woodhue, blk lettering, wooden cap, mini, 2½", +bag, MIB...45.00
Gai Montmartre, windmill, red w/pnt brass lid, 1926, to roof: 4¾" ..2,350.00
Gilbert Orcel, Coup de Chapeau, milk glass lady w/gold, 5" 300.00
H Rubinstein, Town, canteen form w/blk enameling, 3⅜", MIB.. 250.00
Houbigant, Chantilly, gold 17th-C figures, Baccarat, 7½", MIB .. 500.00
Hudnut, Tenfold Lily of Valley, clear w/frosted stopper, 3⅜", MIB. 70.00
J Patou, Amour Amour, gold & bl labels, Baccarat, 1924, 3½", MIB.. 450.00
Kaya Tokio, Narcis, oriental figure seated, w/label, 1920s, 2½" 120.00

Lucien Lelong, Jabot, clear and frosted, sealed, 3", in excellent original box, $850.00. (Photo courtesy Monsen and Baer)

L Lelong, Murmure, rectangular stopper, gold/wht label, 2", +box base .200.00
L Lelong, Parfum J, 4-sided, gold stopper, 2½", +atomizer, MIB... 200.00
L Lelong, Parfum N, urn form, sealed, 4", MIB............................. 200.00
Lentheric, Babana, rectangular, gold/wht label, 2¼", MIB 50.00
Lentheric, Pink Party, clear w/gold cap, yel label, 2⅜", MIB 50.00
Mary Chess, White Lilac, chess castle form, 3", MIB 150.00
Ming Toy, Oriental figure seated w/fan, mc, Baccarat, 1923, 4⅜"..3,250.00
R Hudnut, Extreme Violet, mc label, sealed, 4½", +floral/eagle box ..300.00
Rochambeau, cat figural, clear frost, Rochambeau, ca 1924, 3".... 600.00
Schiaparelli, Shocking Body Radiance, Dali art front, 5¼".......... 400.00
Schiaparelli, Snuff, pipe form w/amber stopper (stem), 5⅜", MIB...450.00
Vando, Julius Casear head, wht pottery, 5¼", NM 30.00

Dairy Bottles

Assoc Dairies Malvern Pty Ltd, Clotted Cream, emb letters, 1920s...115.00
Biltmore Dairy Farms, Asheville NC, blk pyro, rnd qt 230.00
Byron Pepper & Sons, Georgetown DE, emb lettering, rnd pt..... 120.00
Clark Dairy, West Haven CT, orange pyro front & bk, cream sz, 2"... 82.50
Creole Dairy Co, Genevieve MO, red pyro, rnd ½-gal 115.00
Cueman's Dairy Farm, Hackettstown NJ, cow, blk pyro, dmn rim, rnd qt.285.00
Dari-Maid Batavia Dairy Co, lady & windmill, orange pyro, gal.. 175.00
Exclusive Briggs Dairy Service, red pyro, cream top, 1940s, rnd qt ..65.00
Herlihy's Dairy Products, purple pyro, cream top, rnd qt, +spoon.. 60.00
Illiana, red pyro, ind cream sz, 2".. 100.00
Jones Dairy Grade A Milk, Thomasville NC, emb letters, rnd qt . 250.00

Keep 'Em Flying, aviator, red pyro, Pat Nov 22 27, rnd qt 135.00
Kona Dairy, Keauhou HI, red pyro, rnd qt 145.00
Munger's Dairy, Cassopolis MI, red & bl pyro, rnd qt.................. 215.00
Norfolk Creamer Co, Norfolk NE, emb letters, cream top, qt........ 70.00
Pet Milk, orange pyro, wire hdl, Duraglas, gal............................... 75.00
Prairie Farms Dairy...3 in 1 Concentrate, red pyro, sq qt 58.00
Purdue University Creamery, Lafayette IN, emb letters, rnd ½-pt . 70.00
Sanitary Creamery, Tonopah NV, orange pyro, Owens, 1948, rnd qt.. 125.00
Sibley Farms, Disney graphics (Mickey, Clarabelle), red pyro, '30s, pt.. 155.00
Sunshine Goat Milk, emb letters & goat, rnd ½-pt 55.00
Thatcher Dairy, Martinsburg WV, nursery rhyme, red pyro, sq qt . 110.00
Vern Tex Dairy, Keep 'Em Flying..., airplane, red pyro, rnd qt, EX..160.00
White Thorn Dairy Farm, New Alexandria PA, bl pyro, rnd qt..... 63.00

Flasks

Eagle/Cornucopia, GII-46, aqua, sm w/tooled lip, op, flake, ½-pt . 240.00
Eagle/Eagle, GII-40, emerald gr, sm, op, scarce, pt.....................3,000.00
Eagle/Eagle, GII-81, yel amber, tm, op, pt................................... 300.00
Eagle/Eagle, GII-101, yel olive gr, ringed cm, sb, flake, qt 375.00
Eagle/Eagle, GII-106, dk olive gr, ringed am, sb, pt 350.00
Eagle/Louisville..., GII-33, med amber, am, sb, dullness, ½-pt...... 200.00
Eagle/Man w/Bag, GII-140, pt, ringed am, sb, rare, pt...............1,200.00

Eagle/Masonic Arch, GIV-3, deep teal blue, tooled mouth, shallow chip, one-pint, $975.00. (Photo courtesy Pacific Glass Auctions)

Flag BBl & Plow/Log Cabin, GX-22, bl aqua, sm, op, pt.........10,000.00
Great Western Trapper/Deer, GX-30, aqua, am, C on sb, pt 550.00
Liberty/Willington..., GII-61, dk root beer, dbl cm, sb, potstone, qt...325.00
M'Carty & Torreyson/Sunburst, GIX-48, bl aqua, sm, ip, pebbly, pt..2,500.00
Masonic Arch/Eagle, GIV-18, yel olive amber, sm, op, chip, pt... 160.00
Scroll, GIX-34a, med yel gr, sm, ps, stress crack, ½-pt 275.00
Sunburst, GVIII-29, lt bl gr, melon ribs, ps, ½-pt........................ 450.00
Sunburst/Keen-P&W, GVIII-10, med olive gr w/amber tone, ps, ½-pt ..750.00
Traveler's Star Companion/Sheaf of Grain, GXIV-1, yel amber, sb, qt .400.00
Union/Eagle, GXII-25, med olive yel, ringed cm, sb, pt............3,500.00
W Ihmsens/Agriculture, GII-10, pale yel gr, sm, ps, pt 600.00
Washington/Taylor, GI-24, aqua, tm, ps, faint stain, pt............... 190.00
Washington/Taylor, GI-54, med to dk pk amethyst, tm, op, bold emb, qt. 4,750.00

Food Bottles and Jars

Demi-john, med yel 'old' amber, sl cm, ps, bubbles, 12¼x6½"...... 120.00
Demi-john storage, yel 'old' amber, cm, ps, crude, bubbles, 12½" .. 70.00
Peppersauce, gr aqua, 12-sided, rm, op, milky stain, 11"............... 120.00
Pickles, CP Sanborn & Son Union..., yel olive, sm, sb, 5" 110.00
Storage, dk yel olive, sm w/flared-out lip, ps, 12½" 600.00
Storage, gr aqua, thick 4" W rm, internal bubble, 1800-40, 10"... 190.00
Storage, med bl gr, cm, ps, stain, 1850-70, 20½"......................... 325.00
Storage, med bl gr, dbl ringed mouth, ps w/kick-up, bubbles, 12¾".475.00
Storage, med yel olive amber, sl cm, ps, 1770-80, 14"................... 250.00

Utility, dk tobaco amber, 2⅝" tm w/appl string lip, ps, 10½" 350.00
Utility, med olive amber, 3¼" W tm w/appl string lip, ps, 14¾" ... 325.00
Utility, yel olive gr, wide flared tm, ps, chip, 12⅛" 80.00

Ink Bottles

Cathedral, Carter, cobalt, 9¾", NM 55.00
Cone, Carter (on base), dk teal, crude, lt haze, 2½" 60.00
Cone, Carter's #77, dk amber, 2½x2½" 20.00
Cone, Carter's Made in USA, dk emerald gr, 2½x2⅜" 55.00
Cone w/rope twist, amber, 2¾x2⅞" 90.00
Conical, Carter's, bl aqua, tm, sb, whittled, 2⅜" 350.00
Cylinder, Harrison's Columbian, cobalt, am, op, flake, 5¾" 1,900.00
Geometric, GIII-29, med amber, ps, 1½" 240.00
Globe, J Raynald, The World, aqua, sb, 2¼" 135.00
Helmet, tin w/leather strap, traveling type, Fr, 1920s 220.00
Igloo, gr, J&IEM, chip, 1½" 125.00
Igloo, Harrison's Columbian, aqua, 1¾x2⅛" 265.00
Igloo, Kirkland's Ink W&H, aqua, sm, 2x2¼" 25.00
6-sided, Carter, ruby red, 2½x2" 15.00

Medicine Bottles

Trade Mark SparkS Perfect Health, For Kidney & Liver Diseases, Camden, N.J., medium amber, smooth base, tooled mouth, 9", $275.00.

(Photo courtesy Glass-Works Auctions)

Arthur's Elixer of Sulphur...Catarrh, bl aqua, oval w/panel, 8⅜" .. 210.00
Baker's Vegetable Blood & Liver...Tenn, med red amber, sb, 9⅝" . 450.00
Boston Lung Institute, wide mouth w/rm, ps, 2⅝" 270.00
Brown's Blood Cure Philadelphia, lime gr, tm, sb, stain, 6¼" 140.00
Butler & Son London...Toronto CW, bl aqua, am, op, bubbles, 5¾"..450.00
Chloride Calcium St Catharine's..., aqua, tapered cm, op, 5⅝".... 275.00
Dr Craig's (kidneys) Kidney Cure, med red amber, dbl cm, sb, 9⅝" .2,000.00
Dr Craig's Cough & Consumption Cure, yel amber, dbl cm, sb, 7⅞".4,000.00
Dr FS Hutchinson Co...Paralysis Cure, aqua, dbl cm, sb, 8½" 250.00
Dr Goers's Chaulmoogra East India...MD, red amber, tm, sb, 6".. 180.00
Dr JA Sherman's Rupture Curative...NY, med amber, am, sb, 8⅜"... 350.00
Dr Kelling's Per Herb..., aqua, cylinder, am, op, 6⅜" 150.00
Dr MM Fenner's People's Remedies...1872-1898, yel amber, tm, sb, 10"..200.00
Dr Seelye's Magic Cough & Consumption...Kansas, aqua, dbl cm, sb, 9"..600.00
Dr Seelye's Magic Cough...Chemists, aqua, dbl cm, sb, stain, 7⅛" ..400.00
Frog Pond Chill & Fever Cure, amber, tm, sb, 7" 425.00
Genuine Swaim's Panacea Philadelphia, aqua, tapered cm, op, 7⅝"..750.00
Gibbs Bone Liniment, med olive gr, 6-sided, tapered cm, op, 6⅜" . 1,900.00
GW Merchant Chemist...NY, bl gr, tapered cm, sb, flake, 7" 200.00
Hampton's V Tincture...Balto, dk copper puce, oval, sb, 6¼"....... 300.00
Juniper Berry Gin Diuretic Cures...KY, bl aqua, tm, sb, 9¾" 160.00
LQC Wishart's Pine Tree Tar..., emerald gr, crude am, sb, 9¾"..... 230.00
LQC Wishart's Pine Tree Tar..., teal, tm, sb, 10".......................... 230.00
Lucien Pratte Kidney & Ronova Liver...Conn, med amber, tm, sb, 9½"..300.00
Mizpah Cure for Weak Lungs...PA USA, tm, sb, lt haze, 10⅛" 300.00
Mrs Dr Secor Boston Mass, dk cobalt (vivid), tm, sb, 9½" 150.00
National Kidney & Liver Cure, red amber, tm, sb, 9¼" 90.00

NY Medical University (emb measure), dk cobalt, NM label, sb, 7⅜" .600.00
Parks Liver & Kidney Cure...NY, amber to yel amber, tm, sb, 9⅝"...250.00
Parks Liver & Kidney Cure...NY, aqua, tm, sb, 9⅝" 110.00
S Sines Genuine Philada PA...Oil, bl aqua, rm, op, haze, 5¼" 350.00
SparkS Kidney & Liver Cure...NJ, med yel amber, tm, sb, 9⅜".1,300.00
Warner's Safe Cure (safe) Frankfort A/Main, red amber, sb, 9½".400.00
Warner's Safe Cure (safe) Frankfurt A/M, med olive gr, sb, 9".....240.00
Warner's Safe Cure (safe) London, yel olive gr, am, sb, 11", NM ..1,900.00
Warner's Safe Nervine (safe) London, med yel topaz, bt, sb, chip, 9" . 100.00
WC Montgomery's Hair Restorer Philada, dk amethyst, sb, 7½" .325.00
Winans Bros...Indian Cure, bl aqua, tm, sb, 9¼" 450.00
Wm Johnson's Pure Herb...Malarial Diseases, yel amber, sb, 8¾".375.00

Mineral Water, Beer, and Soda Bottles

AG Van Norstrano...Bunker Hill Lager..., med amber, tm, sb, 9⅝"..110.00
August Reinig 2107...Philada..., yel w/olive tone, 1A on sb, 9½" .. 80.00
August Stoehr...Manchester NH...Sold, med yel olive, No 2 on sb, 9".130.00
Brownell & Wheaton New Bedford...Sold, sapphire bl, sb, 7⅜" ..425.00
C Andrae Port Huron...C&CO 2, med cobalt hutch, sb, chips, 6⅝".120.00
Central Bottling...C&CO Lim No 5, cobalt hutch, JJG on sb, chips, 7".100.00
City Bottling...Louisville Seltzer..., cobalt hutch, MIK on sb, 6⅝" ... 750.00
Claussen...Charleston SC, yel amber w/olive tone hutch, 6⅝" .2,100.00
Distilled Soda Water Co...SB&C, gr aqua hutch, 10-panel, flake, 7½"..800.00
E Wagner Trade W...Not Sold, med yel amber, tm, sb, 9⅜" 60.00
E Wagner Trade W...Not Sold, yel w/olive tone, tm, sb, 9⅛" 140.00
F Jacob Jockers 803-...12½ oz, lt to med cobalt, porc stopper, 9".275.00
FJ Kastner Newark NJ..., med golden yel w/amber tone, 9⅜"....... 140.00
Geo Schmuck's Ginger Ale...Lim, yel amber hutch, 12-sided, sb, 7¾".275.00
Gleason & Cole Pittsb..., yel olive, 10-sided, ip, chip, 7¾" 500.00
Guyette & Co...C&CO Lim No 5, cobalt hutch, G on sb, 6⅞" ... 110.00
GW Erandt Carlisle (in slug plate), emerald gr, ip, 7⅜" 400.00
H Clausen & Son Brewing...Phoenix..., med olive gr, tm, sb, 9⅛" ..550.00
H Koehler & Co Fidelio...NY, dk amber, tm, sb, porc stopper, 8⅝"..40.00
Hayes Bros...Chicago Ill MCC, cobalt hutch, 10-panel, sb, 7⅜"..140.00
J Gahm Trade (mug) Mark...Lager Beer, med yel amber, tm, sb, 9⅜"...30.00
J Ryder Mount Holly NJ, med bl gr, sb, 7⅜" 120.00
J Weilerbacher Pittsburgh PA...DCC 149, yel amber hutch, sb, 7⅝".300.00
James Ray Savannah Geo Ginger Ale, dk cobalt hutch, sb, 7¾" . 300.00
JG Bolton Lement Ills A&DHC, med cobalt hutch, sb, ding, 6¾".325.00
Lohrberg Bros's Bud Bell Ill, lt to med apple gr hutch, sb, 6¾"..... 400.00
Lynch Bros Plymouth PA...Sold, med citron, tm, sb, w/closure, 9¼"..230.00
MJ McNerney (in slug plate), bl gr, squat, dbl cm, ip, 6⅞" 150.00
Moriarity & Caroll...Conn, dk amber hutch, 10-panel, tm, sb, 7⅜"...375.00
Pensacola Bottling...Fla, dk bl aqua hutch, tm, sb, 6¾" 80.00
Phillips Bros Champion...Baltimore..., amber, tm, sb, chip, 9⅛".... 60.00
Registered C Norris...C&CO Lim, med cobalt hutch, CN&CO on sb, 6¾".100.00
Registered WH Cawley Co...Flemington..., lt gr, C on sb, bruise, 9".. 40.00
Robert Portner Brewing...VA..., dk olive gr, sb, flake, 9⅜" 160.00
S Smith...Water, med cobalt, 10-sided, bm, ip, 7⅜"....................... 600.00
Standard Bottling...Minn 8 5 ABC, dk amber hutch, HR on sb, 6¾". 150.00
Standard Bottling...SABCO, dk amber hutch, HR on sb, 6⅞"..... 140.00
Sullivan Bros Providence RI, aqua hutch, C/25 on sb, label, 6¾" .1,600.00
Twitchell T Philada..., teal, top-hat/m, ip, 7⅛" 100.00
Wm Heiss Jr...Philada, dk reddish puce, 8-sided, cm, ip, 7¼"....8,500.00

Poison Bottles

Dr Oreste Sinanide's..., dk cobalt, tm, sb, orig stopper, 4⅝" 275.00
Dr Oreste Sinanide's..., milk glass, tm, sb, orig stopper, 4½" 350.00
Not To Be Taken, cobalt, hexagonal, NM label, 4 on sb, 5½" 160.00
Poison, amber, hexagonal, EB& CO LO/5000 on sb, flake, 8⅜" .. 200.00
Poison, cobalt, HBCO on sb, scarce, 5⅝" 90.00
Poison Bowman's Drug..., cobalt, hexagonal, GLG & Co... on sb, 7½".1,200.00

Poison (star)/(skull and crossbones)/Poison, yellow amber, smooth base, tooled lip, scarce, 4⅝", $475.00. (Photo courtesy Glass-Works Auctions)

Skeleton (draped), porc, mk Shofu, Made in Japan, 7" 180.00
USPHS on sb, cobalt, wide tm, 5⅜" 230.00

Sarsaparilla Bottles

BF Williams Syrup of...& Iodid...Tenn, bl aqua, sl cm, ps, 9½" 950.00
Carl's...& Celery Comp Aurora Ill, yel amber, tm, sb, 9⅛" 475.00
Catlin's...For Blood St Louis, med amber, tm, sb, stain, 8¼" 210.00
Chas Cable & Son Po'Keepsie...Soda, med bl gr, bt, ip, 7" 475.00
Compound Syrup of...Cures Rheumatism...VA, gr aqua, tm, sb, 9½" . 3,500.00
Currier's..., lt aqua hutch, tm, sb, 6¾" 240.00
Custer's Extract..., lt aqua, tm, MCC on sb, 9" 200.00
Dana's... For the Blood Liver & Kidneys, bl aqua, tm, sb, 6⅝" 60.00
De Witt's...Chicago, lt aqua, tm, sb, 8⅞" 50.00
Dr AP Sawyer's (eclipsed sun) Eclipse..., bl aqua, tm, sb, stain, 9" ..180.00
Dr Clarke's..., dk olive gr, tm, sb, open bubble, 8½" 375.00
Dr Foster's Jamaica..., gr aqua, tm, sb, 9¾" 120.00
Dr Guysott's Compound Extract..., bl aqua, sb, dbl am, sb, 9½" ...375.00
Dr Guysott's Yel Dock...Cincinnati O, med gr aqua, oval, ip, 9⅝" ..400.00
Dr Morley's...& Iod Potas St Louis, tm, sb, EX label, 9⅜" 150.00
Dr Reinhauser's Hydriodated...NY, bl aqua, sl cm, op, 8⅝" 4,000.00
Dr Townsend's...NY, med gr aqua, lacks 'Old' emb, ip, 9⅞" 400.00
Dr Weiley's..., gr aqua, tapered cm, sb, whittled, 9" 240.00
Dr White's...Adrian Paradis...NY, bl aqua, am, sb, 8⅜" 130.00
Indian Vegetable &...Bitters...Goodwin Boston, aqua, ps, dbl cm, 8" . 1,000.00
IXL...& Iodide Potassium, gr aqua, tm, sb, 9⅛" 130.00
Jones's...CO Jones...Sole Proprietors...PA, bl aqua, tm, sb, 8⅞".... 600.00
Kennedy's...& Celery Compound, tm, sb, VG label, bruise, 9¾" . 175.00
Log Cabin...Rochester NY, med yel olive amber, Pat Sept 6/87, 9⅛".. 200.00
McBride Medicine Co..., tm, sb, 7¾" 50.00
Miner's...Henry a Miner Pharmacist..., bl aqua, dbl cm, sb, 9⅜" .. 750.00
Moroney's...Moroney Medicine...Indianapolis Ind, bl aqua, sb, chip, 9" ..250.00

Old Dr. Townsend's – Sarsaparilla – New York, blue green, smooth base, applied sloping collar mouth, variant with two rivet circles on one beveled corner panel, 9½", $140.00. (Photo courtesy Glass-Works Auctions)

Old Dr J Townsend's...NY, med yel gr, sb, tm, 10¼" 140.00
Post's..., bl aqua, dbl cm, sb, sm flake, 8⅜" 650.00
SB Goff...& Blood Purifier Camden NJ, tm, sb, NM label, 6¾" ... 215.00

Sheerer's..., ice bl, tm, sb, haze, 9" 140.00
Thos A Hurley's Compound Syrup...KY, bl aqua, sl cm, ip, 9½" .. 800.00
Tyler's Indian, bl aqua, tm, sb, stress crack, 9" 200.00
Vickery's...Dover NH, bl aqua, WT&Co on sb, 9⅝" 200.00
Walker's Vegetable..., aqua, tm, WT&Co USA on sb, haze, 9½". 160.00

Spirits Bottles

AM Binninger...NY, med yel amber, tm, sb, cannon, 12⅝" 1,100.00
Bininnger's Travelers' Guide...NY, med yel amber, sb, teardrop, 6⅞" .. 700.00
Chestnut Grove (sm crown) Whiskey CW, dk tobacco amber, ps, 8¾"...275.00
Chestnut Grove (sm crown) Whiskey CW, yel amber, hdl, op, 8⅝"..250.00
EG Booz's Old Cabin...Philadelphia, yel amber, cm, sb, cabin, 7⅝" .450.00
Griffith Hyatt & Co Baltimore, dk yel amber w/olive tone, op, 7¼"..650.00
Hopatkong Whiskey...Phila, dk cobalt, 12 fluted panels, sb, 10¼" ...3,750.00
Horse hoof onion, med yel olive amber, sm, op, 8⅜x5⅞" 160.00
Jacob A Wolford Chicago..., yel amber, am, sb, bbl w/stopper, 8⅝"....475.00
JT Gayen Altona, red amber, bt, cannon, bubbles, crude, 13⅝". 1,700.00
M Schwartzkopf Liquors...PA, bright yel olive, strap-sided, 9¾".. 1,100.00
Star Whiskey NY WB Crowell Jr, yel w/amber tone, ribs/hdl, ps, 8"..1,000.00
Wharton's...1850 Chestnut Grove, cobalt, am, sb, teardrop, 5¼" . 325.00

Boxes

Boxes have been used by civilized man since ancient Egypt and Rome. Down through the centuries, specifically designed containers have been made from every conceivable material. Precious metals, papier maché, Battersea, Oriental lacquer, and wood have held riches from the treasuries of kings, snuff for the fashionable set of the last century, China tea, and countless other commodities. In the following descriptions, when only one dimension is given, it is length. See also Toleware; specific manufacturers.

Band, thin poplar covered w/printed wallpaper, 12x18x14" 545.00
Bride's, bentwood w/laced seams, floral decor on ivory, 5½x15"... 460.00
Bride's, bentwood w/laced seams, HP flowers/couple/text, 6½x17" .700.00
Bride's, pnt pine/maple, cvd pinwheels/etc on domed lid, PA, 8x18x10".5,450.00
Candle, bl pnt pine w/chamfered sliding lid, 8x27x10" 1,050.00
Candle, curly maple, dvtl & chip cvd, sq nails, rfn, 4¾x13x6½".. 865.00
Candle, pine, slide lid w/thumb notch, old grpt, nailed, 6x16x7" . 175.00
Desk, cvd oak, slant front, butterfly hinges, 12x25x16" 435.00

Dome top, blue putty painted decoration with brown borders, attributed to Moses Eaton (1753 – 1833), 18" wide, $6,400.00. (Photo courtesy Skinner Inc. Auctioneers & Appraisers of Antiques & Fine Art)

Dome-top, dvtl pine w/sq nails, red grpt, iron bail hdls, 13x24x12".250.00
Dome-top, patterned putty pnt w/compass flower, 19th C, 16x17x17"...1,525.00
Dome-top, pine, fine mc grpt, pnt band on lid, att ME, 7x18x10"..290.00
Dome-top, pine/poplar w/blk & red grpt, lt wear, 7x15x7"........... 175.00
Dome-top, poplar, dvtl/appl molding, old pnt, 6¾x14x10" 460.00

Knife, mahog Hplwht style w/inlay, slip lid, 14⅞x8⅜".................. 700.00
Liquor, mahog vnr w/inlaid conch shell & gilt, 8x7x4".................. 765.00
Pantry, dk bl pnt, copper tacks, 2⅛x5½x4" 485.00
Pantry, pine top/bottom, bent ash lapped sides, rosehead nails, 8x11".. 645.00
Rnd w/lapped seams, pnt medallion on red, PA, 5x15½" dia..... 2,100.00
Rosewood & maple w/inlaid dmns, bone escutcheon, 19th C, 5x10x6".. 500.00
Spice, walnut, lift-lid, heart-shaped cutout on crest, 7x14x8"...... 460.00
Wall, pine, peaked crest/lift-lid & 2 open compartments, rfn, 24x13x6" . 345.00
Wallpaper, floral, oval w/additional paper around lid rim, 5x9" .. 515.00
Writing, mahog w/bow-tie inlay, fitted int, dvtl drw, 18th C, 7x19x10".975.00

Bradley and Hubbard

The Bradley and Hubbard Mfg. Company was a firm which produced metal accessories for the home. They operated from about 1860 until the early part of this century, and their products reflected both the Arts and Crafts and Art Nouveau influence. Their logo was a device with a triangular arrangement of the company name containing a smaller triangle and an Aladdin lamp. Our advisor is Bruce Austin; he is listed in the Directory under New York.

Lamps

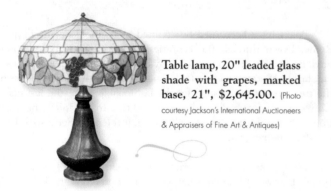

Table lamp, 20" leaded glass shade with grapes, marked base, 21", $2,645.00. (Photo courtesy Jackson's International Auctioneers & Appraisers of Fine Art & Antiques)

Banquet, floral ball shade; brass std w/wht metal foliage, 36½" 600.00
Boudoir, 5½" ldgl 6-panel shade; gilt std, 15"............................... 500.00
Piano, 7" ruby-to clear ruffled globe w/chimney; brass base, 30¼". 475.00
Student, 2 12" milk glass shades; center stem w/loop finial, 21½" . 950.00
Student, 2 5x6" faceted gr slag shades; mk gilt base, 16x15½" ..2,350.00
Table, 7" slag 6-panel umbrella shade w/metal o/l; owl std, 12".1,325.00
Table, 17" slag 6-panel shade w/copper o/l; mk std, 24"............. 1,650.00
Table, 17" slag 8-panel shade w/floral o/l; bronzed metal std, 21". 750.00
Table, 18" ldgl floral shade; 4-socket std w/brass wash, 24"........ 1,500.00
Table, 18" slag 6-panel shade w/acorn o/l; bronze std, 24"............ 850.00
Table, 18" slag 6-panel shade w/geometric o/l; bronzed std, 22" ... 600.00
Table, 18" slag 8-panel shade w/metal o/l; stick std, 22½" 1,375.00
Table, 20" slag 8-panel shade; 3-socket std w/4 stylized heads, 24" . 1,800.00

Miscellaneous

Andirons, dolphin form, CI, 14½x17" 235.00
Bookends, Boston terrier, pnt CI, 4⅞x5¼", EX............................ 450.00
Bookends, Egyptian masks/temple design, pnt CI, ca 1920, 6x4¾", EX .240.00
Bookends, King Tut's Tomb, pnt CI, 5⅛x4⅜", EX 335.00
Bookends, Lincoln Memorial, CI, ca 1925, 3⅝" 150.00
Bookends, Nouveau draped nude & dolphin, pnt metal, 1890-1900, 6½"..400.00
Bookends, Owl, Deco style, EX details, 6x4¾", EX...................... 1,175.00
Clock, John Bull, blinking eyes, ca 1880, 15½x8", EX 1,800.00
Desk set, Tree of Life, 2 blotters/wells+tray+knife+box+calendar+rack... 525.00
Doorstop, Boston terrier, pnt CI, 9⅝x12", EX.............................. 850.00
Doorstop, boy in waders stands/smokes pipe, pnt CI, #7903, 8½", EX.. 1,650.00

Doorstop, Old Woman, Victorian lady w/flower basket/parasol, 11x7", EX...1,200.00
Doorstop, owl on ped, pnt CI, #7797, 15⅝x5", NM 3,000.00
Doorstop, rabbit sitting, pnt CI, #7800, 15¼x8¼", NM 2,400.00
Doorstop, squirrel on log w/nut, EX pnt/details, 11½x9⅞" 4,000.00
Humidor, brass w/hammered/appl decor, wood lined, 3½x9½"....... 50.00
Parade lantern clock, pierced brass w/glass inserts, 30-hr, 13" 900.00

Plaque, three kittens, painted cast iron, #1640, 5x7", EX, $350.00. (Photo courtesy Morphy Auctions/LiveAuctioneers.com)

Plaques, lady w/flowers emb, bronzed w/mc pnt, #1810/#1811, 8", pr. 350.00
Spittoon, dragon, fancy CI, #3612, ca 1880, 5½x11½".............. 1,100.00

Brass

Brass is an alloy consisting essentially of copper and zinc in variable proportions. It is a medium that has been used for both utilitarian items and objects of artistic merit. Today, with the inflated price of copper and the popular use of plastics, almost anything made of brass is collectible, though right now, at least, there is little interest in items made after 1950. Our advisor, Mary Frank Gaston, has compiled a lovely book, *Antique Brass and Copper,* with full-color photos. Mrs. Gaston is listed in the Directory under Texas. See also Candlesticks.

Kettle stand, pierced design at top & front apron, 4-leg, hdls, 12x18" .. 485.00
Lighter, street lamp; ball-shaped font, trn wood hdl, 27½"........... 115.00
Statue, satyr by tree trunk holding child, bronze patina, 24".....1,375.00
Tie backs, pressed rosettes, English, ca 1825, 4" dia, 4 for 700.00

Brastoff, Sascha

The son of immigrant parents, Sascha Brastoff was encouraged to develop his artistic talents to the fullest, encouragement that was well taken, as his achievements aptly attest. Though at various times he was a dancer, sculptor, Hollywood costume designer, jeweler, and painter, it is his ceramics that are today becoming highly regarded collectibles.

Sascha began his career in the United States in the late 1940s. In a beautiful studio built for him by his friend and mentor, Winthrop Rockefeller, he designed innovative wares that even then were among the most expensive on the market. All designing was done personally by Brastoff; he also supervised the staff which at the height of production numbered approximately 150. Wares signed with his full signature (not merely backstamped 'Sascha Brastoff') were personally crafted by him and are valued much more highly than those signed 'Sascha B.,' indicating work done under his supervision. Until his death in 1993, he continued his work in Los Angeles, in his latter years producing 'Sascha Holograms,' which were distributed by the Hummelwerk Company.

Though the resin animals signed 'Sascha B.' were neither made nor designed by Brastoff, collectors of these pieces value them highly. After he left the factory in the 1960s, the company retained the use of the name to be used on reissues of earlier pieces or merchandise purchased at trade shows.

In the listings that follow, items are ceramic and signed 'Sascha B.' unless 'full signature' or another medium is indicated. For further information we recommend *Collector's Encyclopedia of California Pottery, Second Edition* by Jack Chipman, available from Collector Books or your local bookstore.

Ashtray, copper w/HP bl & wht flowers, ¾x5½" 35.00
Ashtray, Fancy Peacock, turq/gray/wht/gold, 2½x5½x5½" 20.00
Bowl, fish decor, mc, 3x13½x9½" 100.00
Bowl, Hawaiian Surfer, 4½x13" 140.00
Box, Rooftops, 1¾x7¼x4¾" 60.00
Candleholder, amber resin w/dmn-like geometric cvgs, 10", ea 35.00
Candleholder, red resin w/cvd dmn-shaped geometric cvgs, 7¾", ea 35.00

Cat head, Mosaic, 8", $475.00. (Photo courtesy www.lifeofrileycollectiques.com)

Charger, Star Steed, 15¼" 155.00
Dish/bowl, Minos line, modernist figure on blk, 3-ftd, 8¾" L 60.00
Ewer, brn w/orange Chinese characters, #068, 10½" 70.00
Figurine, elephant, wht resin w/HP decor, 7½x9" 400.00
Figurine, owl, bl resin, 7½", from $125 to 140.00
Figurine, owl, bl resin, 14⅝", from $300 to 350.00
Pitcher, fruit on rust-brn, 7¼x6" 250.00
Plaque, Sun Face, gr pnt plaster, 1970s, 6⅜" dia, NM 85.00
Sugar bowl, Surf Ballet, turq & silver, w/lid 35.00
Teapot, Surf Ballet, turq & silver, 10¼" L, NM 30.00
Tray, Rooftops, irregular shape, 15½" 125.00
Vase, horizontal mc bands w/gold, leaf band, teardrop shape, 10" .. 95.00
Vase, Rooftops, mc on blk gloss, 5½x4" .... 100.00.
Vase, stylized floral on creamy wht, irregular rim, 13½x4" 175.00
Wine coaster, orange resin w/grape leaf design, 2¼x5½" 25.00

Brayton Laguna

A few short years after Durlin Brayton married Ellen Webster Grieve, his small pottery, which he had opened in 1927, became highly successful. Extensive lines were created and all of them flourished. Hand-turned pieces were done in the early years; today these are the most difficult to find. Durlin Brayton hand incised ashtrays, vases, and dinnerware (plates in assorted sizes, pitchers, cups and saucers, and creamers and sugar bowls). These early items were marked 'Laguna Pottery,' incised on unglazed bases.

Brayton's children's series is highly collected today as is the Walt Disney line. Also popular are the Circus line, Calasia (art pottery decorated with stylized feathers and circles), Webton ware, the Blackamoor series, and the Gay Nineties line. Each seemed to prove more profitable than the lines before it. Both white and pink clays were utilized in production. At its peak, the pottery employed more than 150 people. After World War II when imports began to flood the market, Brayton Laguna was one of the companies that managed to hold their own. By 1968, however, it was necessary to cease production.

For more information on this as well as many other potteries in the state, we recommend *Collector's Encyclopedia of California Pottery* and *California Pottery Scrapbook*, both by Jack Chipman; he is listed in the Directory under California.

Bookends, skeleton key emb on orange, 8x6", pr, NM 40.00
Candy dish, Blackamoor, brn skin tones, gold trim, 8x5" 55.00
Cookie jar, Brayton Maid, blk stamp, 12½", minimum value 2,000.00
Cookie jar, Dutch Lady, arms Xd, appl flowers on apron, crazing, EX . 145.00
Cookie jar, Gingham Dog, 8½x7½x5¾" 120.00
Cookie jar, Granny Smith, #40-85, from $400 to 450.00
Cookie jar, Matilda, from $350 to 400.00
Creamer & sugar bowl, wheelbarrow & watering can, floral decor .. 20.00
Figure vase, girl w/bird, c 1940, 6½x3⅜x3¾" 27.50
Figure vase, Sally, girl in pk dress w/wht apron, 7" 25.00

Figurine, Blackamoor kneeling, 14½", $165.00.

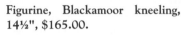

Figurine, Dutch boy & girl, c 1943, 8", 7½", pr 35.00
Figurine, fawn from Snow White, Disney, 1930s, 6⅜" 75.00
Figurine, Ferdinand the Bull, Disney, 1930s, 7x8¾", NM 415.00
Figurine, Franciscan friar in red robe, 9" 58.00
Figurine, Geppetto holds Pinocchio, Figaro on his head, Disney, 9" .. 2,585.00
Figurine, horse, oversz head, brn to wht w/blk mane & tail, 7x8" .. 35.00
Figurine, horse w/oversz head down, bell around neck, 4½x8" 32.00
Figurine, Kiki the Cat, pk & bl hat & shawl, 9½" 35.00
Figurine, King & Queen chess pcs, 1947, 14x5", 12x5", pr 225.00
Figurine, lady opera singer, red dress, c 1943 .... 85.00
Figurine, Maxwell, boy in bl outfit, 7", NM 30.00
Figurine, stylized birds, pk w/brn, 9x10x3½", pr 35.00
Planter, mini; Dutch shoe, floral on wht, 2x4½" 12.00
Planter, peasant lady w/baskets, bl skirt, 8x5" 75.00
Shakers, Black Chef & Mammy, 5¾", 5½", pr 50.00

Bread Plates and Trays

Bread plates and trays have been produced not only in many types of glass but in metal and pottery as well. Those considered most collectible were made during the last quarter of the nineteenth century from pressed glass with well-detailed embossed designs, many of them portraying a particularly significant historical event. A great number of these plates were sold at the 1876 Philadelphia Centennial Exposition by various glass manufacturers who exhibited their wares on the grounds. Among the themes depicted are the Declaration of Independence, the Constitution, McKinley's memorial 'It Is God's Way,' Remembrance of Three Presidents, the Purchase of Alaska, and various presidential campaigns, to mention only a few.

'L' numbers correspond with a reference book by Lindsey; 'S' refers to a book by Stuart. Our advisor for this category is Darlene Yohe; she is listed in the Directory under Arkansas.

Barley (Cable Edge & Stippled) 65.00
Be Industrious, oval 80.00
Beaded Grape 25.00
Bishop, L-201 .... 200.00
Cleopatra, rectangular 95.00
Columbia, shield shape, bl, 11½x9½" 165.00

Continental (Memorial Hall), hand & bar hdls, 12¾" 60.00
Daisy & Button (Hobbs) 25.00
Deer & Pine Tree, bl 65.00
Eagle, Constitution, motto, oval 60.00
Fleur-de-lis w/Pan Am (Buffalo) Exposition center 17.50
Flower Pot, We Trust in God 75.00
Frosted Lion, Give Us This Day, 12½x9" 175.00
Give Us Our Daily Bread, Dew Drop 65.00
Good Luck, dbl horseshoe hdls 120.00
In Remembrance, 3 Presidents, frosted 60.00
Jeweled Band (Scalloped Tape) 25.00
Let Us Have Peace, amber 65.00
Liberty Bell Signers 95.00
Memorial Hall 65.00
Merry Christmas, bells in center, shallow bowl shape 75.00
Mormon Tabernacle, stippled border, rare 425.00
Nelly Bly, L-136, 12" 200.00
Niagara Falls, L-489 .... 95.00
Pope Leo XIII, L-240, 10" 35.00
Santa Maria Variant 15.00
Sheaf of Wheat, Give Us This Day, 11" dia 40.00
Teddy Roosevelt, platter 185.00
Three Graces, Pat dtd 1865 .... 65.00

Transcontinental Railroad, 9x12", $95.00.

Volunteer, emerald gr, L-101 .... 575.00
Washington, First War/First Peace, L2-7, 12x8½" 100.00
William J Bryan, milk glass 45.00

Bretby

Bretby art pottery was made by Tooth & Co., at Woodville, near Burton-on-Trent, Derbyshire, from as early in 1884 until well into the twentieth century. Marks containing the 'Made in England' designation indicate twentieth-century examples.

Bust, boy smiling, bronzed look, blk sockle, 20¾" 425.00
Bust, Neapolitan fisherboy, bronzed earthenware, 20th C, 21" 400.00
Jar, apple form, gr w/touches of yel & red, #847, 3½" 100.00
Lamp base, bronzed look w/appl designs/stones, unmk, 32x12". 1,800.00
Ligna vessel, cvd/pnt, appl insects, hdl, #1517, very slim, 16" 600.00
Mug, Edward VII commemorative, cream, 4½" 50.00
Pitcher, sgraffito sailboats, gr, #359, 7" 24.00
Tankard, Japanese scene, bronzed-look base, 10" 180.00
Vase, bl heron by bamboo stalks, #917, 11½" 150.00
Vase, brn/gr/yel mottle, slim neck, bulbous body, #2455H, 10" 70.00
Vase, bronzed look w/appl stones, invt cone w/hdls, #1588E, 9", NM .. 600.00
Vase, bronzed look w/enameled stones, hdls, Solon, #1669, 12¼". 1,050.00
Vase, Clanta, sailboats/appl stones, hdls, Solon, #1811, 13¼", EX ..480.00

Bride's Baskets and Bowls

Victorian brides were showered with gifts, as brides have always

been; one of the most popular gift items was the bride's basket. Art glass inserts from both European and American glasshouses, some in lovely transparent hues with dainty enameled florals, others of Peachblow, Vasa Murrhina, satin, or cased glass, were cradled in complementary silverplated holders. While many of these holders were simply engraved or delicately embossed, others (such as those from Pairpoint and Wilcox) were wonderfully ornate, often with figurals of cherubs or animals or birds. The bride's basket was no longer in fashion after the turn of the century.

Watch for 'marriages' of bowls and frames. To warrant the best price, the two pieces should be the original pairing. If you can't be certain of this, at least check to see that the bowl fits snugly into the frame. Beware of later-made bowls (such as Fenton's) in Victorian holders and new frames being produced in Taiwan. In the listings that follow, if no frame is described, the price is for a bowl only.

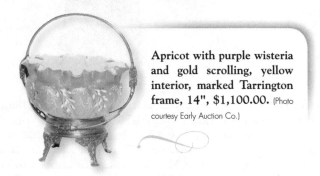

Apricot with purple wisteria and gold scrolling, yellow interior, marked Tarrington frame, 14", $1,100.00. (Photo courtesy Early Auction Co.)

Bl cased, HP floral, dbl-crimp rim w/clear edge; SP fr, 12x12" 240.00
Bl Coin Dot, dbl crimped w/wht edge, SP fr, 12x12" 215.00
Bl satin cased, HP floral, ruffled; Meriden SP fr, 1880s, 17x16"....660.00
Bl w/HP floral, ruffled/crimped rim; unmk SP fr, 13x11½" 175.00
Burmese, mums, ruffled/crimped, Mt WA; SP Pairpoint fr, rope hdls, 11". 3,750.00
Cranberry to wht w/HP floral, ruffles/pleats; SP fr, 14½x14" 240.00
Milk glass shaded to bl, ruffled/pleated rim; SP fr, 9x7" 150.00
Milk glass w/cranberry at rim, ruffled/crimped; SP fr, 9x7" 265.00
Pk cased, HP floral, ruffled; SP fr, ca 1870, 11½x12½" 335.00
Pk cased, ruffled rim; simple SP fr, 12x11" 150.00
Pk cased w/clear edge, ruffled/pleated; SP fr, 11x10x10¼" 135.00
Pk cased w/clear ruffle, HP floral; SP basket fr, 12x11" 335.00
Pk cased w/HP floral, 7-crimp rim; SP Pairpoint #2175 fr, 10x10" ..360.00
Pk opaque; ornate brass ftd fr, 9x9x8" 240.00
Pk/yel cased, coralene leaves/berries/gold trim; SP Meriden fr, 9". 725.00
Red to clear cased, HP floral, ruffled rim; SP fr, 12x11" 300.00
Ruby w/clear appl rigaree; SP stand w/hdl (worn) 135.00
Wht opal w/bl opaque rim, ruffled/crimped; SP fr, 9x7" 150.00
Wht opal w/HP floral, ruffled/crimped; SP fr, 12x10" 165.00
Wht w/pk ruffled edge, HP floral; SP fr, ca 1870, 11½x12½" 325.00

Bristol Glass

Bristol is a type of semi-opaque opaline glass whose name was derived from the area in England where it was first produced. Similar glass was made in France, Germany, and Italy. In this country, it was made by the New England Glass Company and to a lesser extent by its contemporaries. During the eighteenth and nineteenth centuries, Bristol glass was imported in large amounts and sold cheaply, thereby contributing to the demise of the earlier glasshouses here in America. It is very difficult to distinguish the English Bristol from other opaline types. Style, design, and decoration serve as clues to its origin; but often only those well versed in the field can spot these subtle variations.

Bottle, wht, floral, slender neck, flower stopper, 11", pr 80.00
Cheese dish, wht w/bl & gold Nouveau decor, gold finial, 6" 75.00

Epergne, bl w/floral, bronze ft, single lily, 11½"................................. 80.00
Jar, wht w/floral & gold, flower finial, 9".. 70.00
Vase, wht, landscape & bl foliage, ftd, trumpet neck, 8¼", pr 85.00
Vase, wht w/gold floral, slim, flared ft, 12", pr 85.00

Vases, portraits of Victorian ladies, minor wear to gold, 14", set of three, $350.00. (Photo courtesy James D. Julia Inc.)

British Royalty Commemoratives

Royalty commemoratives have been issued for royal events since Edward VI's 1547 coronation through modern-day occasions, so it's possible to start collecting at any period of history. Many collectors begin with Queen Victoria's reign, collecting examples for each succeeding monarch and continuing through modern events.

Some collectors identify with a particular royal personage and limit their collecting to that era, ie., Queen Elizabeth's life and reign. Other collectors look to the future, expanding their collection to include the heir apparents Prince Charles and his first-born son, Prince William.

Royalty commemorative collecting is often further refined around a particular type of collectible. Nearly any item with room for a portrait and a description has been manufactured as a souvenir. Thus royalty commemoratives are available in glass, ceramic, metal, fabric, plastic, and paper. This wide variety of material lends itself to any pocketbook. The range covers expensive limited edition ceramics to inexpensive souvenir key chains, puzzles, matchbooks, etc.

Many recent royalty headline events have been commemorated in a variety of souvenirs. Buying some of these modern commemoratives at the moderate issue prices could be a good investment. After all, today's events are tomorrow's history.

For further study we recommend *British Royal Commemoratives* by our advisor for this category, Audrey Zeder; she is listed in the Directory under Washington.

Key:
ann — anniversary
C/D — Charles and Diana
chr — christening
cor — coronation
ILN — Illustrated London News
inscr — inscription, inscribed
jub — jubilee
LE — limited edition
mem — memorial
Pr — prince
Prs — princess
QM — queen mother
wed — wedding

Album, Royal Family, 1983, 3-ring binder, 200 pictures................. 85.00
Baby dish, Geo VI, mc portrait, Baby Plate on rim, inscr............. 125.00
Beaker, Charles/Diana betrothal, mc portrait/decor, Caverswall.. 155.00
Beaker, Elizabeth II jub, mc, lion-head hdls, Caverswall 80.00
Beaker, Victoria 1897 jub, enamel w/portrait, 3¾" 195.00
Book, Elizabeth II cor, Her Majesty Queen..., child's book............. 25.00
Book, Royal Souvenirs by Geoffrey Warren, hardbk, 1977 .... 45.00
Booklet, Elizabeth II cor, Our Queen & Her Consort, Pitkins 15.00
Booklet, His Royal Highness Pr of Wales, Pitkins, 1958 .... 25.00
Booklet, Prs Margaret's Betrothal, Pitkins, 1960........................... 20.00

Bowl, Edward VIII 1937, mc portrait w/crown, Grindley, 1x5"....... 55.00
Bowl, Victoria 1887 jub, brn portrait w/mc decor, 1x8½"............. 175.00
Bust, Elizabeth II cor, wht bsk, rose dress, Foley, 6" 125.00
Coin, Prs Diana, 1999 5-pound, special pack, Royal Mint 30.00
Compact, Elizabeth II cor, mc portrait, unused in orig folder......... 55.00
Cup & saucer, Charles/Diana '81 wedding, mc portrait, Canada ... 65.00
Doll, Pr Phillip, vinyl, bl uniform, Nisbit, ca 1950, 8½" 150.00
Doll, Pr Wm birth, cloth, Nottingham lace gown, 3", MIB 50.00
Doll, Victoria, plastic, blk dress, modern mfg, 7½" 25.00
Egg cup, Geo VI cor, shaded portrait, gold rim, ftd........................ 35.00
Ephemera, Duchess of Windsor, unused letter paper/envelope....... 65.00
Ephemera, Geo V 1935 vis, invitation to watch procession........... 15.00
Glass, Edward VII 1937, beaker, frosted wht portrait, 4½" 30.00
Glass, George VI 1937 cor, basket, clear w/emb portrait/decor, 10".165.00
Horse brass, Elizabeth II jub, brass w/emb crown 20.00
ILN Record No, Elizabeth II jub, bl cover/silver decor, 14x10"...... 55.00
Jewelry, Elizabeth II cor, crown earrings, MOC 25.00
Jewelry, Geo VI stickpin, cut-out profile, brass 20.00
Loving cup, C/D wed, bl portrait, Adams, 3½x5¾" 50.00
Loving cup, Pr William '82 birth, Bunnykins decor, Doulton 60.00
Magazine, Country Life Royal Wedding Number, November 28, 1947 . 35.00
Magazine, Geo VI cor, Weekly Illustrated Cor Souvenir................. 25.00
Magazine, Hello, Charles/Harry in S Africa, 11/15/97 .... 12.00
Magazine, Sphere, Funeral of King Geo V, February 1, 1936.......... 45.00
Magazine, Star Weekly, Toronto, Geo VI Canada visit, 1939........ 25.00
Matchbox, Geo V jub, blk & wht portrait, inscr, unused 25.00
Medallion, Victoria/Albert 1858 visit w/Napoleon, brass, ⅞" 75.00
Miniature, photo album, of 1982 Royal Family, 1¼x2" 35.00
Miniature, Pr Wm 1st birthday plate, mc w/Diana, 2¼"................. 35.00
Mug, C/D wed, milk glass, mc portrait/decor 25.00
Mug, Charles/Diana engagement, blk line portrait, Carlton 75.00
Mug, Elizabeth II cor, pk w/emb portrait & floral decor, 4¼" 40.00
Mug, Pr Wm 25 birthday, LE 30, Chown.................................... 20.00
Mug, Prs Anne 50th birthday, portrait, LE 50, Chown.................. 75.00
Newspaper, QM 100 birthday, Daily Express, Tribute, July 19, 2000.. 15.00
Newspaper, The Queen, Edward VII funeral, 5-21-1910................. 30.00
Novelty, Edward VII cor letter opener, emb figure, ivory color 60.00
Novelty, Elizabeth II 1977 jub bedwarmer, copper w/ceramic insert .25.00
Novelty, Pr Albert document clip, relief portrait, 1860, 5x2" 55.00
Pin-bk button, Pr of Wales, blk/wht portrait, 1936, ¾" 30.00
Pitcher, Edward VII cor, mc portrait, pk lustre, 6" 150.00

Plate, King George and Queen Elizabeth 1939 Canada Visit, Royal Winton, 10½", $55.00.

Plate, Prs Anne 1973 wed, bl jasper, Wedgwood, 4½" 60.00
Playing cards, Charles/Diana wed, mc portrait/etc, 2-pack, unused .55.00
Postcard, Geo V at front, WWI, mc, Daily Mail, unused 15.00
Postcard, QM 100 birthday, set of 5 picturing royal postage stamps.20.00
Print, Sarah, Duchess of York, mc portrait, 11¾x8½" 10.00
Program, Windsor Castle, town & neighborhood guide, 1934....... 15.00
Puzzle, Royal Family, comic version, dbl-sided, Buffalo 75.00
Sheet music, Pr of Wales 1863 wed, mc wed scene, for piano 50.00
Sheet music, When the King Goes Riding By, 1937........................ 35.00
Spoon, Geo VI cor, annointing featured SP, 4½" 35.00

Teapot, Edward VII cor, mc portrait in red uniform, Doulton, 2-cup .210.00
Teapot, George VI cor, sepia King/Queen & 2 Prs, Shelley, 2-cup ..110.00
Teapot stand, Geo V jub, mc portrait/decor, silver rim, 6" 95.00
Textile, Elizabeth II jub place mat, hand embr, 19x13" 25.00
Thimble, Charles/Diana/Wm '83 New Zealand vis, mc, Caverswall.. 45.00
Thimble, Elizabeth II 1897 wed ann, silhouettes, appl ruby 40.00
Thimble, Pr William '83 1st birthday, mc portrait/decor, Fenton... 35.00
Tin, Edward VII cor, mc portrait on purple, angular 195.00
Tin, Elizabeth II cor, standing portrait in formal gown, 6x4x2"...... 45.00
Toby mug, Victoria, HP, L&S, 3"... 55.00
Trinket box, Charles/Diana wed, mc portrait, scalloped lid, Mason..85.00

Broadmoor

In October of 1933, the Broadmoor Art Pottery was formed and space rented at 217 East Pikes Peak Avenue, Colorado Springs, Colorado. Most of the pottery they produced would not be considered elaborate, and only a handful was decorated. Many pieces were signed by P.H. Genter, J.B. Hunt, Eric Hellman, and Cecil Jones. It is reported that this plant closed in 1936, and Genter moved his operations to Denver.

Broadmoor pottery is marked in several ways: a Greek or Egyptian-type label depicting two potters (one at the wheel and one at a tile-pressing machine) and the word Broadmoor; an ink-stamped 'Broadmoor Pottery, Colorado Springs (or Denver), Colorado'; and an incised version of the latter.

The bottoms of all pieces are always white and can be either glazed or unglazed. Glaze colors are turquoise, green, yellow, cobalt blue, light blue, white, pink, pink with blue, maroon red, black, and copper lustre. Both matt and high gloss finishes were used.

The company produced many advertising tiles, novelty items, coasters, ashtrays, and vases for local establishments around Denver and as far away as Wyoming. An Indian head was incised into many of the advertising items, which also often bear a company or a product name. A series of small animals (horses, dogs, elephants, lambs, squirrels, a toucan bird, and a hippo), each about 2" high, are easily recognized by the style of their modeling and glaze treatments, though all are unmarked.

Ashtray, pirate ship in nautical surround, matchbook slot, orange, 7" ..175.00
Bust of lady, 1 shoulder raised, looking upward, turq gloss, 5½x5". 425.00
Paperweight, scarab, burgundy, 1x3¼x2½"..................................... 135.00

Theatrical masks, signed HW Schwartz, Broadmoor Pottery Colorado Springs CO on bottom, 14½", $200.00 each.

Tile, bird & foliage, mc faience, flakes, 5¾x5¾" 285.00
Tray, 3-leaf form w/centered swirl knob, turq, 11" dia 35.00
Vase, gunmetal blk, JB Hunt, baluster, 7" 270.00
Vase, spherical, dk bl, w/paper label, 5"... 45.00

Bronzes

Thomas Ball, George Bessell, and Leonard Volk were some of the earliest American sculptors who produced figures in bronze for home decor during the 1840s. Pieces of historical significance were the most popular, but by the 1880s a more fanciful type of artwork took hold. Some of the fine sculptors of the day were Daniel Chester French, Augustus St. Gaudens, and John Quincy Adams Ward. Bronzes reached the height of their popularity at the turn of the century. The American West was portrayed to its fullest by Remington, Russell, James Frazier, Hermon Mac-Neil, and Solon Borglum. Animals of every species were modeled by A.P. Proctor, Paul Bartlett, and Albert Laellele, to name but a few.

Art Nouveau and Art Deco influenced the medium during the '20s, evidenced by the works of Allen Clark, Harriet Frismuth, E.F. Sanford, and Bessie P. Vonnoh.

Be aware that recasts abound. While often aesthetically satisfactory, they are not original and should be priced accordingly. In much the same manner as prints are evaluated, the original castings made under the direction of the artist are the most valuable. Later castings from the original mold are worth less. A recast is not made from the original mold. Instead, a rubber-like substance is applied to the bronze, peeled away, and filled with wax. Then, using the same 'lost wax' procedure as the artist uses on completion of his original wax model, a clay-like substance is formed around the wax figure and the whole fired to vitrify the clay. The wax, of course, melts away, hence the term 'lost wax.' Recast bronzes lose detail and are somewhat smaller than the original due to the shrinkage of the clay mold. Values in the listings that follow are prices realized at auction.

Aizelin, Eugene-Antoine; Nymphe de Diane, 17", $3,220.00. (Photo courtesy Jackson's International Auctioneers & Appriasers of Fine Arts & Antiques)

Aichele, Paul; nude female dancer on carpet, marble ped, 11½"..650.00
Alonzo, D; mother w/basket holds daughter's hand, 18"...............600.00
Alonzo, D; Rose Peddler, ivory head/arms, red rose in hand, 9¼" .2,875.00
Barye, AL; & Guillemin, E; Arabian huntsman w/gazelle & goose, 30"+ped.1,725.00
Barye, AL; bear raiding bird's nest, 4½x6"+base 5,600.00
Barye, AL; lion stands w/curved tail/open mouth, 5½"..............2,875.00
Boisseau, E; lute player, color-tinted patina, 31" 1,100.00
Bourron, Marie-Josephe; nude lying on tummy, ca 1967, 4½x10¾".1,200.00
Canova, Venus a la Pomme, 20th-C replica, 45½" 975.00
Cassel, S; man w/guitar, gilt & cold pnt, ca 1900, 13" 14,500.00
Chiurazzi Naples, fawn bound to gnarled tree, gilt surface, 26".2,650.00
Choppin, Paul-Francois; Call to Arms, soldier w/rifle, 35"......10,600.00
Dubucand, Alfred; Alert Stag, 19th C, 16¼x11½x4½" 1,000.00
Falconet, Etienne-Maurice; woman bather, brn patina, 1757, 23" ..700.00
Fatori, Deco lady dancer, ivory inlay, marble base, 1920s, 12"..18,000.00
Fayral, nude w/gazelle, verdigris, stone base, 8½x11"................1,550.00
Fratin, lion standing on base, detailed mane, 22" L...................3,850.00
Fremiet, E; Credo, knight in chain mail w/banner, 16¼x12¼"..1,375.00
Fremiet, E; horse w/military saddle/accessories, 12x13"............2,550.00
Gardet, G; lioness attacking snake, 2 dead cubs, 12x29"...........4,700.00
Italy, Narcissus after classical antiquity, nude warrior, 11x4"........550.00
Jaray, S; lady dancer w/castinet, ivory head/shoulders/arms, legs, 13".6,500.00
Landowski, PM; nude male on plinth, orig brn patina, 27¾" 4,600.00

Lemon, David; Applejack Pete, mountain man, late 1900s, 11¼" ..200.00
Lorenzl, Deco maiden w/arms spreading cape, silvered/HP, 16¼"..3,600.00
Lorenzl, lady dancer w/leg kicked bk, silvered, gr onyx base, 10"...1,950.00
Madrassi, Luca; Tree Nymph, sits on stump w/hands above head, 27" .3,165.00
Moigniez, J; pheasant on rocky plinth, 14x14" 3,165.00
Omerth, G; Madeleon, lady w/pitcher & jug, ivory inlay, 1920s, 10" .2,200.00
Pilanos, C; nude torso of woman, gr patina, 1979, 36¾" 1,650.00
Quinto (?), hunter w/bow on plinth, late 1800s, 30¼" 4,200.00
Remington, F; Bronco Buster, man on rearing horse, restrike, 22½" ... 1,600.00
Remington, F; Cheyenne, hunter w/spear on horse, restrike, 16x19" . 2,300.00
Remington, F; Rattlesnake, cowboy on rearing horse, restrike, 23¾" . 1,600.00
Russell, CM; Double Buffalo Hunt, ltd ed, 1906, 17x28x21" 1,300.00
Seger, Ernst; classical maiden of marble removing bronze robe, 24".5,000.00
Unmk, boxer fallen & sprawling on 1 knee, verdigris, 20th C, 9x12x9"..1,950.00
Unmk, fox prowling, pk marble base, 7½" L 115.00
Unmk, lion roaring, dk brn patina, red marble base, 8" L............. 285.00
Unmk, lion roaring, worn brn surface, bronze base, 9½" L 115.00
Varenne, HF; 18th-C lady w/arm extended behind her, 7⅛"........ 175.00
Vienna, Arab man praying on rug, cold pnt, 4" 725.00
Vienna, Banana Seller, cold pnt/brn patina, 19th C, 2¾x4x4" .1,450.00
Vienna, Bavarian peasant dancers, cold pnt, 19th C, 7½"........... 660.00
Vienna, horse, cold pnt, articulated reins/stirrups, 5½x6½"..........850.00
Vienna, parrot w/extended tail, cold pnt, onyx base, 6¼x12" 600.00
Vienna, rabbit seated w/ears bk, brn patina, 6¼x8x3½" 1,450.00
Waagen, Arthur; Standing Stallion, saddled, 18??, 19x22" 1,150.00

Brouwer

Theophilis A. Brouwer operated a one-man studio on Middle Lane in East Hampton, Long Island, from 1894 until 1903, when he relocated to West Hampton. He threw rather thin vessels of light, porous white clay which he fired at a relatively low temperature. He then glazed them and fired them in an open-flame kiln, where he manipulated them with a technique he later patented as 'flame painting.' This resulted in lustered glazes, mostly in the orange and amber family, with organic, free-form patterns. Because of the type of clay he used and the low firing, the wares are brittle and often found with damage. This deficiency has kept them undervalued in the art pottery market.

Brouwrer turned to sculpture around 1911. His pottery often carries the 'whalebone' mark, M-shaped for the Middle Lane Pottery, and reminiscent of the genuine whalebones Brouwer purportedly found on his property. Other pieces are marked 'Flame' or 'Brouwer.' Our advisors for this category are Suzanne Perrault and David Rago; they are listed in the Directory under New Jersey.

Vase, flame-pnt bronze, Chinese melon shape, 3¾x4½" 1,200.00
Vase, flame-pnt copper tones, flat shoulder, 4x4"..........................950.00
Vase, flame-pnt gold & burgundy, 5x5½" 1,100.00

Vase, flame-pnt orange & yel lustre, paper label, 4x4"...............1,325.00
Vase, flame-pnt yel & amber, flat shoulder, 4x4¾".....................1,325.00
Vase, flame-pnt yel/amber/gunmetal, flakes, 9¾x5¼".................1,500.00

Brownies by Palmer Cox

Created by Palmer Cox in 1883, the Brownies charmed children through the pages of books and magazines, as dolls, on their dinnerware, in advertising material, and on souvenirs. Each had his own personality, among them The Dude, The Cadet, The Policeman, and The Chairman. They represented many nations; one national character was Uncle Sam. But the oversized, triangular face with the startled expression, the protruding tummy, and the spindle legs were characteristics of them all. They were inspired by the Scottish legends related to Cox as a child by his parents, who were of English descent. His introduction of the Brownies to the world was accomplished by a poem called *The Brownies Ride*. Books followed in rapid succession, 13 in the series, all written as well as illustrated by Palmer Cox.

By the late 1890s, the Brownies were active in advertising. They promoted such products as games, coffee, toys, patent medicines, and rubber boots. 'Greenies' were the Brownies' first cousins, created by Cox to charm and to woo through the pages of the advertising almanacs of the G.G. Green Company of New Jersey. The Kodak Brownie camera became so popular and sold in such volume that the term became synonymous with this type of camera. (However, it was not endorsed by Cox. George Eastman named the camera but avoided royalty payment to Palmer Cox by doing his own version of them.)

Since the late 1970s a biography on Palmer Cox has been written, a major rock band had their concert T-shirts adorned with his Brownies, and a reproduction of the Uncle Sam candlestick is known to exist. Because of the resurging interest in Cox's Brownies, beware of other possible reproductions. Our advisors for this category are Don and Anne Kier; they are listed in the Directory under Ohio. Unless noted otherwise, our values are for items in at least near mint condition.

Ashtray, Brownie scene, RS Germany, 1913................................. 125.00
Book, A Fox Grows Old, 1946, EX 12.00
Book, Another Brownie Book, NY, 1890, 1st ed, w/dust jacket, VG ..250.00
Book, Another Brownie Book, 144 pgs, 1967, 9½x6¾", EX........... 10.00
Book, Brownies & Goblins, Grosset Dunlap, no date, VG............. 35.00
Book, Brownies & Other Stories, 1918, EX 40.00
Book, Brownies & the Farmer, 1902, 8¾x6¾", VG+ 40.00
Book, Brownies at Home, w/dust jacket, 1942, VG........................ 35.00
Book, Brownies in Fairyland, Century Co............................ 40.00
Book, Comic Yarns in Verse, Prose & Picture, 1898, 7½x5", VG .. 25.00
Book, Funny Stories About Funny People, 1905, EX 35.00
Book, Little Goody Two Shoes, 1903, EX 40.00
Book, Wit & Wisdom, 1890, 32 pgs, 7x4½", VG......................... 15.00
Bottle, soda; emb Brownies, M 30.00
Calendar, Brownies, color litho, 1898, EX 225.00
Camera, Eastman-Kodak Brownie 2A, EXIB (not endorsed by Cox) ..145.00

Vase, flame-painted lustred gold and amber, incised whalebone mark, 7½", $2,500.00. (Photo courtesy David Rago Auctions)

Candlesticks, majolica, continental: policeman, 8¾", $600.00; sailor, professional repair, 8¾", $275.00. (Photo courtesy Majolica Auctions, Strawser Auction Group)

Candy dish, 15 Brownies, ball ft, Tufts SP, 7x5½".........................265.00
Cigar box, wood w/Our Brownies emb inner on lid label, EX+....145.00
Comic book, The Brownies, Dell Four-Color, #398, 1952, VG......20.00
Creamer, Little Boy Blue verse & 4 Brownies, gold trim, china.....95.00
Cup, SP w/9 enameled Brownies, Middletown Plate Co, 3".........195.00
Cup & saucer, demi; comical action Brownies, Ceramic Art Co ...95.00
Figures, papier-maché w/stick legs, jtd arms, 1900s, 5", EX, 4 for...1,500.00
Fruit crate label, harvesting orange juice, 1930s, 10x11", EX.........20.00
Ice cream bag, Cox illus, 5¢ orig value, 1930s, M..........................35.00
Magazine page, Ladies' Home Journal, Cox illus, ca 1890..............15.00

Mug, silver-plate, Pairpoint, $385.00.

(Photo courtesy Dick Soulis Auctions/LiveAuctioneers.com)

Needle book, Brownies, 1892 World's Fair, rare..............................75.00
Nodder, Brownies (3) on donkey, bsk, German, 1890s, 6½x6¼"...1,950.00
Paperweight, Brownie figural, SP..145.00
Pencil box, rolling-pin shape, 15 Brownies in boat.........................70.00
Pin box, Brownies running across lid, SP, EX..................................125.00
Pitcher, china, Brownies playing golf on tan, 6" 150.00
Pitcher, china, 2 Brownies on front, 3 on bk, 4½"...........................110.00
Plate, SP, Brownies on rim, 8½"...85.00
Print, Brownies fishing, matted, 1895, 13½x15½"...........................55.00
Rubber stamp, set of 12..120.00
Shaker, opal glass w/Brownie, ovoid, Mt WA, 2⅝".........................275.00
Sign, emb Brownies on tin, Howell's Root Beer, EX.......................185.00
Sign, If You Like Chocolate Soda Drink Brownie, MCA Co, 59x21", G....230.00
Stationery, Ten Little Brownies, envelopes/note paper/box, 1930s, G...25.00
Table set, brass, emb Brownies, 6", in orig box...............................95.00
Toy, Movie Top, litho tin w/3 windows, ca 1927, 1⅞x4¾" dia 150.00
Trade card, Mitchell, Lewis & Stave Co, 3x5", VG..........................25.00
Trade card, Sheriff's Sale Segars, Brownies & product, 5x3" 25.00
Tray, tin, Brownies w/giant dish of ice cream, 13¼x10½", EX......185.00

Brush-McCoy, Brush

George Brush began his career in the pottery industry in 1901 working for the J.B. Owens Pottery Co. in Zanesville, Ohio. He left the company in 1907 to go into business for himself, only to have fire completely destroy his pottery less than one year after it was founded. In 1909 he became associated with J.W. McCoy, who had operated a pottery of his own in Roseville, Ohio, since 1899. The two men formed the Brush-McCoy Pottery in 1911, locating their headquarters in Zanesville. After the merger, the company expanded and produced not only staple commercial wares but also fine artware. Lines of the highest quality such as Navarre, Venetian, Oriental, and Sylvan were equal to that of their larger competitors. Because very little of the ware was marked, it is often mistaken for Weller, Roseville, or Peters and Reed.

In 1918 after a fire in Zanesville had destroyed the manufacturing portion of that plant, all production was contained in their Roseville (Ohio) plant #2. A stoneware type of clay was used there, and as a result the artware lines of Jewel, Zuniart, King Tut, Florastone, Jetwood, Krakle-Kraft, and Panelart are so distinctive that they are more easily recognizable. Examples of these lines are unique and very beautiful, also quite rare and highly prized!

After McCoy died, the family withdrew their interests, and in 1925 the name of the firm was changed to The Brush Pottery. The era of hand-decorated art pottery production had passed for the most part, having been almost completely replaced by commercial lines. The Brush-Barnett family retained their interest in the pottery until 1981 when it was purchased by the Dearborn Company.

For more information we recommend *The Collector's Encyclopedia of Brush-McCoy Pottery* by Sharon and Bob Huxford; and *Sanford's Guide to Brush-McCoy Pottery, Books I* and *II*, written by Martha and Steve Sanford, our advisors for this category, and edited by David P. Sanford. They are listed in the Directory under California.

Of all the wares bearing the later Brush script mark, their figural cookie jars are the most collectible, and several have been reproduced. Information on Brush cookie jars (as well as confusing reproductions) can be found in *The Ultimate Collector's Encyclopedia of Cookie Jars* by Joyce and Fred Roerig; they are listed in the Directory under South Carolina. Beware! Cookie jars marked Brush-McCoy are not authentic.

Cookie Jars

Antique Touring Car, from $850 to..1,000.00
Boy w/Balloons, minimum value 800.00
Chick in Nest, #W38 (+), from $275 to 375.00
Cinderella Pumpkin, #W32...200.00
Circus Horse, gr (+), from $700 to 750.00
Clown, yel pants, #W22..200.00
Clown Bust, #W49, from $200 to..250.00
Cookie House, #W31, from $60 to..75.00
Covered Wagon, dog finial, #W30, (+), from $400 to.....................450.00
Cow w/Cat on Bk, brn, #W10 (+), from $100 to...........................125.00

Cow With Cat on Back, purple, rare, minimum value, $900.00. (Watch for reproductions.) (Photo courtesy Ermagene Westfall)

Davy Crockett, no gold, mk USA (+), from $225 to....................250.00
Dog & Basket, from $250 to..275.00
Donkey Cart, ears down, gray, #W33, from $300 to.......................400.00
Donkey Cart, ears up, #W33 ....700.00
Elephant w/Ice Cream Cone, #W18 (+)...450.00
Elephant w/Monkey on Bk, rare...4,500.00
Fish, #W52 (+), from $400 to...450.00
Formal Pig, gold trim, #W7 Brush USA (+), from $350 to.........400.00
Formal Pig, no gold, gr hat & coat (+), from $225 to...................275.00
Gas Lamp, #K1, from $45 to...65.00
Granny, pk apron, bl dots on skirt, #W19, from $200 to.............250.00
Granny, plain skirt, from $250 to..275.00
Happy Bunny, wht, #W25, from $150 to 175.00
Hen on Basket, unmk, from $75 to 100.00
Hillbilly Frog, from $3,000 to...3,500.00
Humpty Dumpty, w/beany & bow tie (+), from $175 to 200.00
Humpty Dumpty, w/peaked hat & shoes, #W29.............................200.00
Laughing Hippo, #W27 (+), from $650 to.......................................750.00
Little Angel (+), from $650 to 700.00
Little Boy Blue, gold trim, #K25, sm, from $650 to 750.00
Little Boy Blue, no gold, #K24 Brush USA, lg (+), from $600 to .650.00
Little Girl, #017 (+), from $450 to...500.00
Little Red Riding Hood, gold trim, mk, lg, (+) minimum value ..800.00

Little Red Riding Hood, no gold, #K24 USA, sm, from $425 to.. 475.00
Night Owl, #W40, from $65 to 95.00
Old Clock, #W20, from $75 to.. 100.00
Old Shoe, #W23 (+), from $65 to.. 85.00
Panda, #W21 (+), from $175 to 200.00
Peter, Peter Pumpkin Eater, #W24, from $200 to 250.00
Peter Pan, gold trim, lg (+), from $725 to............................ 775.00
Peter Pan, no gold, sm, from $425 to 475.00
Puppy Police, #W8 (+), from $450 to 500.00
Raggedy Ann, #W16, from $400 to....................................... 450.00
Sitting Pig, #W37 (+) from $325 to...................................... 375.00
Smiling Bear, #W46 (+), from $225 to 275.00
Squirrel on Log, #W26, from $60 to...................................... 80.00
Squirrel w/Top Hat, blk coat & hat, #W15, from $225 to........... 300.00
Squirrel w/Top Hat, gr coat, from $200 to.............................. 225.00
Stylized Owl, from $250 to 300.00
Stylized Siamese, #W41, from $375 to 425.00
Teddy Bear, ft apart, from $175 to 225.00
Teddy Bear, ft together, #014 USA, from $125 to.................... 175.00
Treasure Chest, #W28, from $100 to..................................... 125.00

Miscellaneous

Bookends, Venetian, Indian chief, Ivotint, 1929, 5x5½".............. 300.00
Bowl, Moss Green, #01, 6", from $20 to................................ 30.00
Butter crock, Corn, w/lid, #60, from $300 to 350.00
Candlestick, Vogue, blk geometrics on wht, 12", ea 325.00
Casserole, Grape Ware, w/lid, #178, 1913, from $150 to.......... 200.00
Clock, Flapper, Onyx (gr), #336, 1926, 4½", from $75 to 150.00
Decanter, Onyx (bl), 7", from $100 to 150.00
Flower arranger, Princess Art Line, #560, 5½-6½", ea $30 to 40.00

Garden ornament, frog, 1933, 6½", from $70.00 to $85.00. (Photo courtesy Cincinnati Art Galleries)

Garden ornament, squirrel, #482, 8x8", from $100 to 125.00
Garden ornament, turtle, gr or brn, #487D, 6½", from $75 to...... 100.00
Hanging pot, #168, 1962, 8", from $24 to................................ 40.00
Jardiniere, Egyptian, bl, 1923, 5½" 200.00
Jardiniere, Fancy Blended, #202, 1910, 10½", from $150 to........ 175.00
Jardiniere, Modern Kolorkraft, #260, 1929, 10", from $125 to..... 175.00
Jardiniere, Woodland, #2230, 7", +7½" ped, from $300 to.......... 400.00
Jewelry caddy, mermaid.. 150.00
Jug, Decorated Ivory, #131, 1915, 2-qt, from $150 to 175.00
Lamp base, Kolorkraft, 1920s, 10½", from $125 to 175.00
Ornament, birdbath; wht, 2 frogs (standing/sitting), 7½"............ 200.00
Pitcher, Nurock, #351, 1916, 5-pt, 8½", from $165 to................ 200.00
Pitcher, Peacock, Bristol glaze, #351, from $900 to 1,500.00
Planter, penguin, #332A, from $30 to.................................... 40.00
Radio bug, 1927, 9½x3", from $500 to................................... 950.00
Umbrella stand, Liberty, #73, 1912, from $600 to 800.00
Urn, Onyx (gr), #699, 11½", from $125 to 175.00
Vase, Bronze Line, palette mk USA 720, 8", from $25 to............. 40.00

Vase, Cleo, #042, 11¾", from $750 to 900.00
Vase, Onyx (brn), shouldered, 4" 45.00
Vase, Vestal, #729, 10½", from $250 to... 300.00
Wall plaques, African Masks, mk USA, 10½", pr 300.00

Vases: Zuniart, 9½", $475.00; King Tut, with Egyptian scarab band, 12", $950.00. (Photo courtesy Martha and Steve Sanford)

Buffalo Pottery

The founding of the Buffalo Pottery in Buffalo, New York, in 1901, was a direct result of the success achieved by John Larkin through his innovative methods of marketing 'Sweet Home Soap.' Choosing to omit 'middle-man' profits, Larkin preferred to deal directly with the consumer and offered premiums as an enticement for sales. The pottery soon proved a success in its own right and began producing advertising and commemorative items for other companies, as well as commercial tableware. In 1905 they introduced their Blue Willow line after extensive experimentation resulted in the development of the first successful underglaze cobalt achieved by an American company. Between 1905 and 1909, a line of pitchers and jugs were hand decorated in historical, literary, floral, and outdoor themes. Twenty-nine styles are known to have been made.

Their most famous line was Deldare Ware, the bulk of which was made from 1908 to 1909. It was hand decorated after illustrations by Cecil Aldin. Views of English life were portrayed in detail through unusual use of color against the natural olive green cast of the body. Today the 'Fallowfield Hunt' scenes are more difficult to locate than 'Scenes of Village Life in Ye Olden Days.' A Deldare calendar plate was made in 1910. These are very rare and are highly valued by collectors. The line was revived in 1923 and dropped again in 1925. Every piece was marked 'Made at Ye Buffalo Pottery, Deldare Ware Underglaze.' Most are dated, though date has no bearing on the value. Emerald Deldare was made on the same olive body and on standard Deldare Ware shapes, featured historical scenes and Art Nouveau decorations. Most pieces are found with a 1911 date stamp. Production was very limited due to the intricate, time-consuming detail. Needless to say, it is very rare and extremely desirable.

Abino Ware, most of which was made in 1912, also used standard Deldare shapes, but its colors were earthy and the decorations more delicately applied. Sailboats, windmills, and country scenes were favored motifs. These designs were achieved by overpainting transfer prints and were often signed by the artist. The ware is marked 'Abino' in hand-printed block letters. Production was limited; and as a result, examples of this line are scarce today.

Commercial or institutional ware was another of Buffalo Pottery's crowning achievements. In 1917 vitrified china production began, and the firm produced for accounts worldwide. After 1956 all of their wares bore the name Buffalo China. In the early 1980s, the Oneida Company purchased Buffalo China and continued production of commercial and institutional ware. However, in 2004, Oneida divested itself of Buffalo China.

All items listed below are in near-mint to mint condition unless otherwise noted. Our advisor for this category is Lila Shrader; she is listed in the Directory under California. See also Bluebird China.

Key:
BC — Buffalo China
BC-Oneida — Buffalo China after 1983
BM — bottom mark
BS — bottom stamp
SL — side logo
SM — side mark
TL — top logo
TM — top mark

Abino

Matchbox holder w/attached ashtray, windmill scene, 3¾" H ... 1,180.00
Pitcher, windmill, harbor scene w/sm sailboats, Harris, 9" 710.00
Plate, seascape w/sailing ships, Harris, 9½" 268.00
Sugar bowl, sailing ships on choppy water, hdls, 3½" 440.00

Commercial China

All items listed below are of the heavy 'restaurant' weight china.

Bone dish, Blue Willow, oval, scalloped, 1922, 4½x6½" 12.00
Bowl, cereal; children's ware w/mc circus animals, 1926, 5" 22.00
Bowl, cereal; Natural Wood Design, 5½" 78.00
Bowl, cereal; US Forest Service, BC-Onieda, 5¾", from $11 to 25.00
Bowl, cereal; US Forest Service, 1926, 5½", from $38 to 59.00
Bowl, serving; Buffalo Athletic Club, TL, ftd, 2½x7½" 26.00
Bowl, vegetable; Indian Tree, flared base, 8½" 49.00
Bowl, vegetable; Natural Wood Design, 8½" 135.00
Butter pat, Blue Willow, 3½", from $9 to 26.00
Butter pat, Cecil's San Diego Calif, w/stylized cocktail glass, TL ... 49.00
Butter pat, golf balls & trees, TM, 3½" 45.00
Butter pat, Henry Ford Hospital, HFM in dmn, TM, 3¼" 49.00
Butter pat, pine trees & pine cones TM, 3¼" 29.00
Butter pat, stylized rooster silouette, blk pinstripe, 3¼" 42.00
Butter pat, TCC TL in script w/acorn border, 3¼" 62.00
Creamer, ind; crossed golf clubs, FCC, SL, no hdl, 3" 44.00
Creamer, ind; desert scene w/MCC, SL, hdl, 3¼" 28.00
Creamer, ind; Green Willow, hdl, 3¼" 10.00
Creamer, ind; Laramie (WY) Golf Club, SL Indian w/Golf Club, hdl, 3" . 66.00
Creamer, ind; mc band w/sailing ship, Hotel Commodore, hdl, BS, 3" .18.00
Creamer, ind; Trocadero Hotel, SL, hdl, 3" 44.00
Cup, 1939 NY World's Fair, Trylon & Perisphere SL, teacup style. 56.00
Cup & saucer, Airport Café, Akron OH, SL & TM of prop-type plane .. 110.00
Cup & saucer, Blue Willow, demi 31.00
Cup & saucer, demi; Ritz-Carlton, BM, demi 15.00
Cup & saucer, Mallard Seeds w/images of soaring mallard, SL, 1960s 18.00
Gravy boat, Multifleure Lamelle, 3½x6½" 98.00
Match holder (sm), Commonwealth Poultry, Boston, 3½x6½" 20.00
Match holder (sm), detailed lighthouse image, Lighthouse Inn, SL ... 46.00
Matchbox holder (sm) w/attached ashtray, Buffalo Trap & Field SL, 4" .. 46.00
Mug, gr stripe, heavy base, 1926, 3⅛" 12.00
Mug, US Army Medical Dept, SL, 3½" 14.00
Mustard pot, ivory w/gr bands, hdl, 1924, 3½" 18.00
Mustard pot, Patio Risoli, helmet & arrow SM, Rouge Ware, 3½" .. 29.00
Pitcher, Ahwahnee, Yosemite Park & Curry Co, BS, 1926, 6½" .. 100.00
Pitcher, detailed American Indian image, Plains, 5¾" 101.00
Pitcher, pelican in blk & wht SL, 7½" 120.00
Plate, Ahwahnee, Yosemite Park & Curry Co, BS, 1927, 10½" 49.00
Plate, Automobile Club of (buffalo image), TL, 1915, 9" 125.00
Plate, Benny's Bistro, Gardena, smiling man w/moustache TL, 1925, 10" .. 39.00
Plate, bl sailing ship/waves/moon, Gandy's, Made Especially BM, 7" ... 12.00
Plate, Bluebird Inn, bluebird TL, 7½" 32.00

Plate, Country Gardens, bl, 10¾" 12.00
Plate, grill; Blue Willow, w/4 sections, 1926, 10¼" 56.00
Plate, Howard Johnson's Pie Man, fluted edge, TL, 6½" 10.00
Plate, mallard soaring, Mallard Seeds, 1960s, 9½" 16.00
Plate, Masonic Temple, Orlando FL, TL, 1926, 9½" 15.00
Plate, Multifleure, 5½" 58.00
Plate, stylized grand piano w/musical notes, blk pinstripes, 10½" ... 95.00
Plate, Tahoe Tavern, TL, 1922, 5¾" 250.00
Plate, USSB (US Bureau of Fisheries), TL, 1926, 8¼" 68.00
Platter, Radcliffe pattern, WCC, 1925, 8x11" 272.00
Platter, USBS (US Bureau of Fisheries), TL, 1926, 8x11½" 155.00
Relish dish, floral border, Charlie's Café, Springfield OR, TL, 4x8" . 48.00
Relish dish, gold decor, shell shape, 5½x7½" 26.00
Spittoon, Edgemoor in script w/striping, SL, 1915, 7¾" 55.00
Teapot, Roycroft, BC - Oneida, 3½", from $26 to 65.00
Teapot, US Forest Service, BC - Oneida, SL, 3½" 88.00
Tray, pin; LAAC, Los Angeles Athletic Club, TL, 1928, 5x3½" ... 27.00

Deldare

Ashtray/matchholder, Fallowfield Hunt, A Lang, 3½x6" 790.00
Bowl, fruit; Ye Village Tavern, EB, 3¾x9", from $280 to 325.00
Bowl, nut; Ye Lion Inn, inward rolled rim, 3¼x8", from $380 to . 550.00

Calendar plate, 1910, by Evan Horn, 9¼", $1,430.00. (Photo courtesy Smith & Jones Inc.)

Candleholder/matchholder, untitled Village Scene, unmk, 5½" .. 489.00
Candlesticks, Ye Village Scene, drilled, 9", pr 650.00
Chamberstick, Fallowfield scenes, finger ring, 5¾" dia, ea 778.00
Chocolate pot, Ye Village Street, 6-sided, 9¼" 955.00
Creamer, Emerald Ware, Dr Syntax w/the Dairymaid, 3" 355.00
Cup & saucer, chocolate; Ye Village Street 409.00
Cup & saucer, Emerald Ware, Dr Syntax & Bookseller 339.00
Cup & saucer, Fallowfield Hunt, MHF 285.00
Egg cup, untitled Fallowfield scene, no horses, 4" 485.00
Hair receiver, Ye Village Street, w/lid, 4¼" 310.00
Humidor, Emerald Ware, Dr Syntax, lid vented for sponge, 7" 1,100.00
Humidor, There Was an Old Sailor..., vented lid, 8" 880.00

Humidor, Ye Village Tavern, 7", $400.00. (Photo courtesy Tom Harris Auctions/ LiveAuctioneers.com)

Mug, Scenes of Village Life in Ye Olden Days, 1924, 2½" 160.00
Mug, The Fallowfield Hunt, M Gerhardt, 2½" 350.00
Mug, The Fallowfield Hunt, M Gerhardt, 4½" 295.00

Mug, Ye Lion Inn, M Gerhardt, 4½" 185.00
Pitcher, Emerald Ware, Dr Sytax Setting Out to the Lakes, Stuart, 9". 1,000.00
Pitcher, Fallowfield Hunt, The Return, 8-sided, W Foster, 8" 765.00
Pitcher, Robin Hood (on Deldare body), 8¼" 955.00
Pitcher, To Advise Me in a Whisper..., 8-sided, 7" 415.00
Plate, bread & butter; Ye Olden Days, 6" 75.00
Plate, chop; Emerald Ware, Dr Syntax Sell's Grizzle, A Sauter, 13" .1,360.00
Plate, Emerald Ware, Dr Sytax Soliloquising, J Gerhardt, 7½" 795.00
Plate, Fallowfield Hunt, The Death, 1908, 9½" 265.00
Plate, Fallowfield Hunt, The Death, 1909, 8¼" 180.00
Plate, Hand Painted Deldare, salesman sample, 6½" 925.00
Plate, rim soup; Fallowfield Hunt, Breaking Cover, 9" 310.00
Plate, rim soup; Fallowfield Hunt, The Start, 6¼" 80.00
Powder jar, Ye Village Street, 4¼" 362.00
Punch bowl, Fallowfield Hunt, various scenes, ped ft, 9x14½" ..5,420.00
Relish tray, Ye Olden Times, W Foster, 6½x12" 305.00
Sugar bowl, Fallowfield Hunt, 6-sided, open, 3½" 388.00
Sugar bowl, Scenes of Village Life, 6-sided, open, 3¼" 260.00
Sugar bowl, Scenes of Village Life in Ye Olden Days, CD, 3¼" 195.00
Tankard, The Great Controversy, Steiner, 12½" 800.00
Tea tile, Fallowfield Hunt, Breaking Cover, 6" 435.00
Teapot, Scenes of Village Life in Ye Olden Days, 3¾" 390.00
Teapot, Scenes of Village Life in Ye Olden Days, 5¾" 485.00
Tray, calling card; Emerald Ware, Dr Syntax Robbed..., tab hdls, 7" ..500.00
Tray, calling card; Fallowfield Hunt, Breakfast, Sauter, tab hdls, 8" ..380.00
Tray, dresser; Dancing Ye Minuet, 9x12" 398.00
Tray, pin; Ye Olden Days, 6½x3½", from $105 to 200.00
Tray, relish; Fallowfield Hunt, The Dash, A Lang, 6½x12" 795.00
Tray, tea; Emerald Ware, Dr Syntax Mistakes a..., M Ramlin, 10x13½" .1,389.00
Vase, untitled Village Scene, fashionable man, 7" 218.00
Vase, untitled Village scene, fashionable man, 9" 410.00

Miscellaneous

In this section all items are marked Buffalo Pottery unless noted. It does not include any commerical (restaurant type) china or items marked Deldare.

Bowl, mixing; Geranium, metal rim, ped ft, 10½" 144.00
Bowl, vegetable; Bonrea, gr/bl floral & swags border, 9½" 17.00
Butter dish, Beverly, pk roses, gold trim, w/ice ring, domed lid, 6". 67.00
Butter dish, Bluebird, w/ice ring, w/knob, rnd, 8" 110.00
Butter pat, Blue Willow, 3¼", from $12 to 38.00
Butter pat, Bluebird, 3" 45.00
Butter pat, Bonrea, ornate bl/gr scroll border w/gold, 3" 12.00
Butter tub, Bluebird, mk Buffalo China, w/ice ring, tab hdls.......... 86.00
Canister, Cinnamon, bl floral on ivory, barrel shape, 4x2¾" 48.00
Canisters, Flour, Sugar, Coffee, Tea, roses on gingham band, 8¼".. 56.00
Chocolate pot, floral bouquet on gr shading w/gold, ornate hdl, 11"....88.00
Coaster, Blue Willow, 1913, 3½" 23.00
Creamer, Children's Ware, Dutch children, 4½" 39.00
Creamer, Vienna, Art Nouveau decor on cobalt w/gold, 3" 28.00
Creamer & sugar bowl, Bluebird, w/lid 85.00
Cup & saucer, Vienna, Art Nouveau decor on cobalt w/gold......... 55.00
Egg cup, Bluebird, very rare, 2½" 75.00
Feeding dish, Roosevelt Bears w/Model T, gold trim, 1½x7½" 260.00
Fruit set, natural fruit decor, bowl (8")+4 bowls (4½") 67.00
Gravy/sauceboat, Princess, gr floral w/gold.................................... 10.00
Mug, advertising; Bing & Nathan, mc monk image, 4½" 39.00
Mug, Anticipation, Celebration, Fascination...series, 4½", $32 to. 87.00
Pitcher, Blue Willow, rnd, 1905, 4½" 67.00
Pitcher, Geraniums, gr, 4¼" 43.00
Pitcher, Geraniums, mc w/gold accents, 4¼" 130.00
Pitcher, Geraniums, mc w/gold accents, 8" 265.00
Pitcher, John Paul Jones, battle scene, bl & wht, crazing, 9½" 389.00

Pitcher, Roosevelt Bears, 8", $1,800.00.
(Photo courtesy Smith & Jones Inc.)

Pitcher, water; Bluebird 100.00
Plate, advertising; stork image, Compliments...Home Furniture, 7"... 88.00
Plate, Automobiling, early car image, mc pnt, 9½" 675.00
Plate, Christmas, Ebenezer Scrooge reformed state of mind, 1957, 10"..66.00
Plate, Christmas, Master Peter Cratchit, mc, 1959, 10" 12.00
Plate, commemorative; Natatorium, Broadwater Hotel, Helena MT, 7½" ..46.00
Plate, commemorative; The White House, bl/gr border, Washington DC, 8"..54.00
Plate, Dr Syntax Disputing...Landlady, flow bl transfer, 1909, 9¼".....125.00
Plate, Gaudy Willow, cobalt, brick red & gold, scalloped rim, 10". 66.00
Plate, Historical Mt Vernon, bl/gr floral border, 10" 35.00
Plate, historical; White House, bl floral border, Washington DC, 10"..65.00
Plate, Maple Leaf, pk floral, gr maple leaf border w/gold, 9½" 32.00
Plate, Roosevelt Bears, 5 lg & 5 sm scenes, scalloped edge, 10¼" . 310.00
Plate, Two Roosevelt Bears Had a Home..., scalloped gold rim, 7½"..255.00
Plate, Wild Turkey (from fowl set), gold edge, 9½" 83.00
Platter, Blue Willow, 11x14"... 92.00
Platter, Bonrea, ornate bl & gr scroll border w/gold, 11x14" 125.00
Platter, Buffalo Hunt, teal gr, scalloped edge, 14x11" 110.00
Relish dish, lg rose clusters on gr/bl border, gold rim, open hdls 95.00
Salt box, Salt in blk block letters, hanging, hinged wood lid, 6".... 62.00
Slop jar, Cairo w/pk & yel roses, w/lid, 10" 161.00
Sugar bowl, Blue Willow, 8-sided, hdls, 6x5x6", from $66 to 119.00
Sugar bowl, Bluebird, Buffalo China, hdls 76.00
Tea & toast set, Lucerne, underplate(10½x6")+cup 47.00
Tea set, Baby Bunting, pot+cr/sug w/lid+2 plates (7"), child sz.... 188.00
Teapot, Argyle, bl on wht, vitreous body, w/orig infusor 88.00
Teapot, Blue Willow, sq, 1911, 4½x6¼" 101.00
Teapot, Blue Willow, sq, 1911, 6x9" 194.00
Teapot, child's, Bluebird 500.00
Tureen, vegetable; forget-me-not border, gold trim, 7½x9½" 119.00
Tureen, vegetable; pk floral w/gr leaves, gold trim, hdls, 7½x9½".. 119.00
Vase, Geraniums, mc, rose bowl shape, 3¾" 89.00
Vase, roses & violets w/gold, low ped, ornate hdls, 10½" 48.00
Warming dish, Bluebird, metal fr w/hdls, 8½"............................. 152.00

Burley-Winter

Located in Crooksville, Ohio, this family venture had its roots in a company started in 1872 by William Newton Burley and Wilson Winter. From 1885 it operated under the name of Burley, Winter and Brown, reverting back to Burley & Winter after Mr. Brown left the company in 1892. They merged with the Keystone Pottery about 1900 (its founders were brothers Z.W. Burley and S.V. Burley), and merged again in 1912 with the John G. Burley Pottery. This company was dissolved in the early 1930s. A variety of marks were used.

Ash receiver, frog figural, orange & gr mottle, 3¾"......................... 28.00
Vase, foliage at neck, rim-to-hip hdls, ftd, bl & wht mottle, 9"...... 50.00
Vase, geometrics at rim, rim-to-hip hdls, gr/brn/purple mottle, 20"..350.00
Vase, geometrics at shoulder, bulbous, pk/gr/cream mottle, chips, 9". 32.00
Vase, lion-head medallions on olive/turq/ivory mottle, 18x14" ...480.00

Vase, lion-head medallions on purple/rose mottle, 21x17".........550.00
Vase, yel, purple & gr mottle, flared rim, hdls, 7" 50.00

Vase, drip glaze on white clay, 20", $1,840.00.
(Photo courtesy Garth's Auctions Inc.)

Burmese

Burmese glass was patented in 1885 by the Mount Washington Glass Co. It is typically shaded from canary yellow to a rosy salmon color. The yellow is produced by the addition of uranium oxide to the mix. The salmon color comes from the addition of gold salts and is achieved by reheating the object (partially) in the furnace. It is thus called 'heat sensitive' glass. Thomas Webb of England was licensed to produce Burmese and often added more gold, giving an almost fuchsia tinge to the salmon in some cases. They called their glass 'Queen's Burmese,' and this is sometimes etched on the base of the object. This is not to be confused with Mount Washington's 'Queen's Design,' which refers to the design painted on the object. Both companies added decoration to many pieces. Mount Washington-Pairpoint produced some Burmese in the late 1920s and Gundersen and Bryden in the 1950s and 1970s, but the color and shapes are different. In the listings that follow, examples are assumed to have the satin finish unless noted 'shiny.' See also Lamps, Fairy.

Bowl, Mt WA, mums, rectangular top, 2x5x4¼" 260.00
Bowl, Mt WA, Queen's pattern, faint dmn quilt, 3-ftd, 5½x6"..5,175.00
Condiment set, Mt WA, cruet+shakers w/pillar ribs; SP Pairpoint fr....750.00
Cruet, Mt WA, mums, vertical ribs, ribbed stopper, 6½" 2,300.00
Jar, Mt WA, floral, lid w/gold enamel, 4x4¾"............................1,265.00
Jar, Mt WA, floral, plain lid, 4x5"..1,725.00
Pitcher, Mt WA, flowers/verse by Wordsworth, tankard, 9"....5,175.00
Pitcher, Mt WA, ivy in gr & brn, tankard, 9" 3,750.00

Pitcher, Mt. Washington, Thomas Hood poem, 5½x7½", $7,200.00. (Photo courtesy Early Auction Co.)

Rose bowl, Webb, floral, crimped incurvate rim, 3x3½" 465.00
Shade, Mt WA, fish/seaweed/gold net, 9¾" dia.........................3,395.00
Sugar bowl, Mt WA, floral w/gold, appl ft, 2¼x3"........................750.00
Sugar bowl, Mt WA, Queen's pattern, appl ft, 2x3½"...............1,375.00
Toothpick holder, Mt WA, floral, mold-blown, 2¼".....................485.00
Toothpick holder, Mt WA, floral, sq top, 2½" 435.00
Tumbler, Mt WA, Queen's pattern, 3¾" 900.00
Tumbler, Mt WA, violets/leaves/stems, 3¾"................................515.00
Vase, jack-in-pulpit; Mt WA, floral w/beading, crimped rim, 11¼"..1,265.00

Vase, Mt WA, barn swallows, gourd shape, 8" 4,600.00
Vase, Mt WA, daisies, long neck w/cup mouth, 6" 925.00
Vase, Mt WA, fish/seaweed/gold net, 7½x6" 9,775.00
Vase, Mt WA, floral w/gold, petticoat shape w/tri-fold top, 10" .2,000.00
Vase, Mt WA, flowers/berries/leaves, stick neck, 11¾", NM 1,150.00
Vase, Mt WA, gourd shape, 7¾" 345.00
Vase, Mt WA, pouch-like, flared rim w/8 scallops, 4½x4¾" 375.00
Vase, Mt WA, Queen's pattern, gold hdls/rim/ft, teardrop, 5½" .3,450.00
Vase, Mt WA, Queen's pattern, slightly conical, slender, 9" 2,000.00
Vase, Webb, pine cones/needles/branches, 6-sided neck, 3¼" 350.00

Butter Molds and Stamps

The art of decorating butter began in Europe during the reign of Charles II. This practice was continued in America by the farmer's wife who sold her homemade butter at the weekly market to earn extra money during hard times. A mold or stamp with a special design, hand carved either by her husband or a local craftsman, not only made her product more attractive but also helped identify it as hers. The pattern became the trademark of Mrs. Smith, and all who saw it knew that this was her butter. It was usually the rule that no two farms used the same mold within a certain area, thus the many variations and patterns available to the collector today. The most valuable are those which have animals, birds, or odd shapes. The most sought-after motifs are the eagle, cow, fish, and rooster. These works of early folk art are quickly disappearing from the market.

Molds

Beaver and maple leaf, notched border, excellent patina, 3¼", $2,000.00.
(Photo courtesy Morphy Auctions/ LiveAuctioneers.com)

Anchor w/rope border, tight hairline, ca 1860, 3½" 90.00
Cow grazing w/branch on her bk, notched border, 1880s, 1⅞".....180.00
Donkey standing in grass w/leaves overhead, minor chip, 1850s, 3¾"..1,800.00
Eagle & olive branch, rope border, 19th C, 4½" 215.00
Eagle facing left holds shield, worn hdl, 3½"...............................150.00
Fish (5) in folky style, EX details, notched border, 1840s, 3" 1,200.00
Fish over 3 fern leaves & seaweed, notched border, hairline, 3¼".270.00
Goat lying in grass, fence beyond, scalloped border, 1880s, 2⅛" ..120.00
Maple leaf, realistic details, notched border, 1880s, 3½" 120.00
Maple leaf thistle, dbl-sided, ca 1850, 4⅛x3¼" 1,980.00
Pheasant among foliage, rpl hdl, crack, 3¼".................................120.00
Rooster crowing & standing on branches, hairline, 1860s, 4⅝" ...180.00
Sheep in grass, facing left, notched border, 1860s, 2⅝" 480.00
Sheep in grass, notched border, EX detail & cvg, 1860s, 3⅛"....1,550.00
Sheep in grass w/head up, notched border, dry patina, 1880s, 3½"..265.00
Sunflower (lg), single line border, 1860s, 4⅜" 240.00
Swan, scalloped border, lightly scrubbed, 4" 75.00
Swan in rough water among reeds, rpl hdl, sm crack, 4"..............300.00
Turkey standing in grass, notched/sawtooth borders, EX patina, 4"..1,325.00
UNION letters circle geometric design, notched border, ca 1864, 4¼"..480.00

Stamps

Acorn (stylized), dk patina, w/hdl, 4" 120.00

Compass star w/X-hatched background, trn poplar, aged patina, 4½". 240.00
Cow facing left, branch over bk, scalloped edge, 1-pc hdl, 4¾" ... 120.00
Eagle (stylized), curly maple w/EX figure, lollipop form, rfn, 4".... 600.00
Eagle among grasses, sm snowflake at shoulder, coggled rim, 4⅛". 360.00
Heart & leaves, semicircular, 6¾x4½"..1,025.00
Heart & star on oval block, EX detail & cvg, 5½x3¼" 1,650.00
Horse/2 partridges, dbl-sided, dry patina, 1840s, 3¼" 725.00
Lyre, deep cvg, notched border, 1840s, EX patina, 5" 1,200.00
Quatrefoil flowers/ribbed leaves, dbl-sided, scrubbed, 3½x4½".....270.00
Radish w/wreath for border, rare subject, ca 1880, 3" 1,450.00
Sheaves of wheat, checked wood, 3½" 48.00
Sheep w/tree & foliage, geometric border, EX detail, 4" 960.00
Swirls/stars, dbl-sided lollipop, butternut wood, 1800s, 4½"......3,000.00
Tulip (stylized), serrated border, aged patina, flat, 3¾" 360.00

Buttonhooks

The earliest known written reference to buttonhooks (shoe hooks, glove hooks, or collar buttoners) is dated 1611. They became a necessary implement in the 1850s when tight-fitting high-button shoes became fashionable. Later in the nineteenth century, ladies' button gloves and men's button-on collars and cuffs dictated specific types of buttoners, some with a closed wire loop instead of a hook end. Both shoes and gloves used as many as 24 buttons each. Usage began to wane in the late 1920s following a fashion change to low-cut laced shoes and the invention of the zipper. There was a brief resurgence of use following the 1948 movie 'High Button Shoes.' For a simple, needed utilitarian device, buttonhook handles were made from a surprising variety of materials: natural wood, bone, ivory, agate and mother-of-pearl to plain steel, celluloid, aluminum, iron, lead and pewter, artistic copper, brass, silver, gold, and many other materials in lengths that varied from under 2" to over 20". Many designs folded or retracted, and buttonhooks were often combined with shoehorns and other useful implements. Stamped steel buttonhooks often came free with the purchase of shoes, gloves, or collars. Material, design, workmanship, condition, and relative scarcity are the primary market value factors. Prices range from $1.00 to over $500.00, with most being in the $10.00 to $100.00 range. Buttonhooks are fairly easy to find, and they are interesting to display.

See the Buttonhook Society listing in the Directory under Clubs, Newsletters, and Catalogs.

Buttonhook/penknife, ivory side plates, man's................................ 50.00
Collar buttoner, stamped steel, advertising, closed end, 3"............. 20.00
Glove hook, gold-plated, retractable, 3" 90.00
Glove hook, loop end, agate hdl, 2½" 60.00
Shoe hook, colored celluloid hdl, 8" 15.00
Shoe hook, lathe-trn hardwood hdl, dk finish, 8"............................ 15.00
Shoe hook, SP w/blade, repoussé hdl, Pat Jan 5 1892, 5" 40.00
Shoe hook, stamped steel, advertising, 5"..8.00
Shoe hook, sterling, floral & geometrics, 8"................................... 55.00
Shoe hook, sterling, Nouveau lady's face, 6½" 75.00
Shoe hook, sterling, W w/arrow, hammered Florentine decor, mk. 55.00
Shoe hook/shoehorn, combination, steel & celluloid, 9" 35.00

Bybee

The Bybee Pottery was founded in 1845 in the small town of Bybee, Kentucky, by the Cornelison family. Their earliest wares were primarily stoneware churns and jars. Today the work is carried on by sixth-generation Cornelison potters who still use the same facilities and production methods to make a more diversified line of pottery.

From a fine white clay mined only a few miles from the potting shed itself, the shop produces vases, jugs, dinnerware, and banks in a variety of colors, some of which are shipped to the larger cities to be sold in department stores and specialty shops. The bulk of their wares, however, is sold to the thousands of tourists who are attracted to the pottery each year.

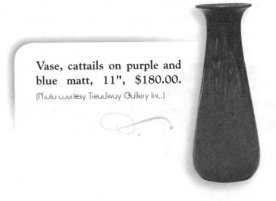

Vase, cattails on purple and blue matt, 11", $180.00.
(Photo courtesy Treadway Gallery Inc.)

Bean pot, brn matt, 1-hdl, 6-cup, 6x8"...................................... 28.00
Bowl, bl, fluted & scalloped rim, 7½".. 24.00
Jar, orange (uranium oxide) on stoneware, 3 strap hdls, 17½"...... 450.00
Teapot, mauve gloss, 6½".. 30.00
Vase, gr matt, Genuine Bybee sticker, 4¾x3½"............................ 135.00

Cabat

From its inception in New York City around 1940, through various types of clays, designs, and glazes, the Rose Cabat 'Feelie' evolved into present forms and glazes in the late 1950s, after a relocation to Arizona. Rose was aided and encouraged through the years by her late husband Erni. Their small 'weed pots' are readily recognizable by their light weight, tiny necks, and soft glazes. Pieces are marked with a hand-incised 'Cabat' on the bottom. Our advisor for this category is Suzanne Perrault; she is listed in the Directory under New Jersey.

Bottle, brn matt w/crystalline inclusions, sm chip, 6"................1,680.00
Vase, bl w/gr runs, #841 47, 4¼x1⅞" 600.00
Vase, cobalt, pear shape, #841 43, 3¼x2" 600.00
Vase, forest gr w/blk striations, 2¾x2¼" 630.00
Vase, gr w/brn streaks on brn clay, bulbous, 3x3" 480.00
Vase, gr w/gray streaks, #380, 4x1½" 630.00
Vase, gunmetal gray & turq matt on stoneware, bulbous, 5x3¾".. 780.00
Vase, lime gr & celadon, 5¼x4"... 780.00

Vase, mauve vellum crystalline flambé on turquoise ground, 9½x8", $2,800.00. (Photo courtesy David Rago Auctions)

Vase, streaky brn, onion form, 3x2¼".. 330.00
Vase, turq to olive gr, spherical, 3⅞" 840.00
Vase, turq w/tan drips on brn clay, gourd form, 5x3" 725.00

Calendar Plates

Calendar plates were advertising giveaways most popular from about 1906 until the late 1920s. They were decorated with colorful underglaze decals of lovely ladies, flowers, animals, birds and, of course, the twelve months of the year of their issue. During the 1950s they came into vogue again but never to the extent they were originally. Those with exceptional detailing or those with scenes of a particular activity are most desirable, so are any from before 1906.

1900, Round Oak Stoves, Doe-Wah-Jack featured, 9", $170.00. (Photo courtesy Past Tyme Pleasures)

1895, months in center w/floral & swirl border, 8"	270.00
1904, Happy New Year, Cupid & bell, 8"	50.00
1904, months surrounded by berries	65.00
1907, lady drinking from fountain of Roman god Pan	75.00
1908, pk rose border	30.00
1909, cherries & strawberry blossoms, Imperial, 7½"	60.00
1909, Gibson Girl, scalloped edge, 9¼", from $60 to	70.00
1909, monks drinking wine, 9"	55.00
1909, roses in center w/months around border w/flowers, Wedgwood	50.00
1910, dog (upright) holds months suspended from stick in mouth	60.00
1910, Indian chief, months on feathers of headdress, 7½"	65.00
1910, lady w/horse in center w/months surrounding, Princeton on border	68.00
1910, sailing scene, months w/pk & gr floral along rim, TB Colby, 9"	42.00
1910, Washington's Old Home at Mt Vernon, 9⅛"	50.00
1910, winter church scene & summer lakeside home, months in 3 groups	48.00
1911, Abraham Lincoln portrait, 9"	150.00
1911, Billiken portrait on wht, gold months on bl rim, 8"	40.00
1911, cherub & advertising in center, Kingburg Departmant Store, 8"	56.00
1911, ocean scene w/months & roses, emb/scalloped edge, 8¼", $45 to	55.00
1911, Salem Evangelical Church center w/floral & months border, 8¼"	45.00
1911, time-zone clocks & flowers, 8⅛"	50.00
1912, airplane/scenic view, fruit & flower border, 8½", EX	65.00
1912, floral w/months & cherubs border, Old Plantation Distilling, 8"	40.00
1912, mixed fruits, cherubs & months along border, gold trim, 8"	90.00
1913, Rainbow Falls, Yosemite Valley, 9⅜"	75.00
1914, Plymouth Rock center w/months at border, mk Carnation	35.00
1915, floral w/butterflies & months, scalloped rim, AC Lubenow, 8"	32.00
1915, strawberries, butterflies between months on border, 8"	50.00
1916, yel roses, months separated by bluebirds in border, 8¼"	35.00
1918, American flag center, months & birds along rim, DE McNicol, 8"	60.00
1919, fruit & peace dove, 9¼"	45.00
1922, hunting dogs & game, 9¼"	45.00
1945, English Setter, months along rim, Walter's Auction Gallery, 10"	55.00
1954, Indian chief in full headdress, months along rim	35.00
1967, fox terrier head, Walter's Auction Gallery, 9"	27.00

Calendars

Calendars are collected for their colorful prints, often attributed to a well recognized artist of the period. Advertising calendars from the turn of the century often have a double appeal when representing a company whose tins, signs, store displays, etc., are also collectible. Our advisor for

this category is Robert Doyle; he is listed in the Directory under New York. See also Parrish, Maxfield; Railroadiana; Winchester.

1904, Devers Golden West, girl w/basket, partial pad, 7x3½", EX+	300.00
1909, Metropolitan Life Ins, Victorian lady & child, 21x12", NM	275.00
1910, Kis-Me Chewing Gum, lady in oval on faux leather cb, 11x6", VG	150.00

1910, United States Cream Separators, 30x20", VG, $200.00.

1912, Wrigley's Spearmint Pepsin Gum, children w/dog, 9x5", EX	140.00
1915, Answering the Call, moose scene, full pad, 37x18", EX+	425.00
1918, Lehigh Nat'l Cement, lady w/hat, bow on shoulder, 15x9", EX	70.00
1919, North Ferguson & Co, Eager for the Hunt, dogs, 25x16", EX	210.00
1920, Conradi's Pharmacy, man on horse in water, Goodwin, 16x8", EX+	60.00
1922, Peters Cartridges, Lest We Forget, Forbes, 31½x12", NM	1,050.00
1928, US Shell Shots, boy w/mother dog & pups, 33x16", EX	1,200.00
1929, American Stores, children in landscape, full pad, 26x12", NM	100.00
1929, US Cartridge Co, man & dog in winter scene, 35x16", EX	975.00
1930, Western Ammunition, Veteran, canoe scene, Parsons, 27x14", EX+	625.00
1942, PA Railroad, Partners in Nat'l Defence, G Teller, 28x20", EX+	75.00
1943, Hercules Powder, Not This Trip Old Pal, Fuller, 30x13", EX+	350.00
1948, Hercules Powder, Veterans, Cronwell, full pad, 30x13", EX	90.00
1949, Burns Tool Co, Vision of Beauty, Elvgren nude, 46x22", EX	375.00
1953, Famous Mint, Who Killed the Bear, C Russell, 14x18½", EX+	60.00
1958, Grapette, blond lady in crocheted hat, 33x16", M	150.00

California Faience

California Faience was founded in 1913 as 'The Tile Shop' by Chauncey R. Thomas in Berkeley, California. He was joined by William V. Bragdon in 1915 who became sole owner in 1938. The product line was apparently always marked 'California Faience,' which became the company's legal name in 1924. Production was reduced after 1933, but the firm stayed in business as a studio and factory until it closed in 1959. Products consisted of hand-pressed tiles and slip-cast vases, bowls, flower frogs, and occasional figures. They are notable for high production quality and aesthetic simplicity. Items produced before 1934 were of dark brown or reddish brown clay. After that, tan clay was used. Later production consisted mainly of figurines made by local artists. The firm made many of the tiles used at Hearst Castle, San Simeon, California. From 1928 to 1930 a line marked 'California Porcelain' was produced in white porcelain at West Coast Porcelain Manufacturers in Millbrae.

The multicolored art tiles are especially popular with collectors. Generally speaking, matt glazes were in use mostly before 1921 and are rare. Prices continue to be depressed, especially for glossy glaze and low bowls. A few rare tiles and matt pieces have brought strong prices. Collectors are quite fussy about condition; impared pieces sell for very low prices. Almost all known pieces are marked. Unmarked pieces in a pale creamy clay were made from cast-off West Coast Porcelain molds by

Potlatch pottery in Seattle, Washington, from 1934 to 1941. Unmarked tiles are presently being made from original molds by Deer Creek Pottery, Grass Valley, California (deercreekpottery.com). They can be distinguished from the old tiles as they are thinner, and in each case there is a repetition of the raised design on the back. Our advisor for this category is Dr. Kirby William Brown; he is listed in the Directory under California. Dr. Brown is currently researching a book on this topic and welcomes input from collectors.

Ashtray, dog facing backward, porc, wht, 5¾" H 115.00
Bowl, dk bl gloss, Pueblo Indian form, incurvate rim, #21, 5" 190.00
Bowl, gray/cream gloss, incurvate rim, low, #39-a, 11½" 95.00
Bowl, oxblood gloss, scalloped, flared rim, #83, 6" 110.00
Bowl, turq gloss, incurvate rim, low, #32-a, 10½" 150.00
Desk set, turq gloss, lidded inkwell & 2 open jars, 3" H 460.00
Flower frog, turq gloss, rnd w/3 crabs, #8, 5" 85.00
Ginger jar, gr matt, globular, lid missing, K mk, #42, 3½" H 450.00
Planter box, bl/turq mottle gloss, rectangular, 3x7" 70.00
Temple jar, oxblood gloss, broad ovoid, flat-top lid, #71, 8½" 300.00
Tile, mc gloss, daisy in circle (Hearst Castle), sq, 7¼" 170.00
Tile, mc matt & gloss, galleon w/furled sails, sq, 5½" 300.00
Trivet, bird & flowers (by Marion Martin), mc gloss, rnd, 5½" 450.00
Trivet, flower basket, mc matt & gloss, rnd, 5½" 320.00
Trivet, peacock, mc matt & gloss, rnd, 5⅜" 335.00
Trivet, 3 chrysanthemums, mc gloss, rnd, 5½" 320.00
Tumbler, turq gloss, ribbed, 5" 170.00
Vase, crystalline ivory, porc, tapered bumpy gourd, 10¼" 1,350.00

**Vase, cuenca shoulder band on brown mottled matt, 8¼",
$2,750.00.** (Photo courtesy Dr. Kirby William Brown)

Vase, dk bl matt, club shape, #64, 9" 920.00
Vase, dk bl matt, Pueblo Indian form, very high lip, #55, 6" 350.00
Vase, gr matt, no lip, globular, #12, 3¼" 265.00
Vase, lt bl matt, raised flared lip, ovoid, #14, 5⅛" 320.00
Vase, oxblood gloss, pomegranate shape, #89, 10½" 420.00
Vase, rose gloss, raised straight lip, ovoid, #11, 5½" 250.00
Vase, shaded bl gloss, Pueblo Indian form, #23, 4" 165.00
Vase, turq gloss, raised flared lip, ovoid, #14, 5¼" 160.00
Vase, turq gloss, wide flared trumpet, #96, 4x10" 60.00

California Perfume Company

D.H. McConnell, Sr., founded the California Perfume Company (C.P. Company; C.P.C.) in 1886 in New York City. He had previously been a salesman for a book company, which he later purchased. His door-to-door sales usually involved the lady of the house, to whom he presented a complimentary bottle of inexpensive perfume. Upon determining his perfume to be more popular than his books, he decided that the manufacture of perfume might be more lucrative. He bottled toiletries under the name 'California Perfume Company' and a line of household products called 'Perfection.' In 1928 the name 'Avon' appeared on the label, and in 1939 the C.P.C. name was entirely removed from the product. The success of the company is attributed to the door-to-door sales approach and 'money back' guarantee offered by his first 'Depot Agent,' Mrs. P.F.E. Albee, known today as the 'Avon Lady.'

The company's containers are quite collectible today, especially the older, hard-to-find items. Advanced collectors seek 'go with' items labeled Goetting & Co., New York; Goetting's; or Savoi Et Cie, Paris. Such examples date from 1871 to 1896. The Goetting Company was purchased by D.H. McConnell; Savoi Et Cie was a line which they imported to sell through department stores. Also of special interest are packaging and advertising with the Ambrosia or Hinze Ambrosia Company label. This was a subsidiary company whose objective seems to have been to produce a line of face creams, etc., for sale through drugstores and other such commercial outlets. They operated in New York from about 1875 until 1954. Because very little is known about these companies and since only a few examples of their product containers and advertising material have been found, market values for such items have not yet been established. Other items sought by the collector include products marked Gertrude Recordon, Marvel Electric Silver Cleaner, Easy Day Automatic Clothes Washer, pre-1915 catalogs, California Perfume Company 1909 through 1914 calendars, and 1926 Calopad Sanitary Napkins.

There are local Avon Collector Clubs throughout the world that also have C.P.C. collectors in their membership. If you are interested in joining, locating, or starting a new club, contact the National Association of Avon Collectors, Inc., listed in the Directory under Clubs, Newsletters, and Catalogs. Inquiries concerning California Perfume Company items and the companies or items mentioned in the previous paragraphs should be directed toward our advisor, Dick Pardini, whose address is given under California. (Please send a large SASE and be sure to request clearly the information you are seeking; not interested in Avons, 'Perfection' marked C.P.C.'s, or Anniversary Keepsakes.) For more information we recommend *Bud Hastin's Avon Collector's Encyclopedia*.

Note: Our values are for items in mint condition. A very rare item or one in super mint condition might go for 10% more. Damage, wear, missing parts, etc., must be considered; items judged to be in only good to very good condition should be priced at up to 50% of listed values, with fair to good at 25% and excellent at 75%. Parts (labels, stoppers, caps, etc.) might be evaluated at 10% of these prices.

American Ideal Box 'C' Set, perfume+powder sachet, 1911, M... 310.00
Army & Navy Kit, 6 grooming items, 1918, MIB......................... 215.00
Atomizer Set, atomizer+3 perfumes, ca 1900, M 385.00
Baby Set, oil+powder+soap+boric acid, 1925, M in yel box 310.00
Baking Powder 'California,' 1915, 1-lb or 5-lb szs, M, ea............... 80.00
Bay Rum, came in 4-, 8- & 16-oz, 1890s, M, ea........................... 150.00
Daphne Set, 1-oz perfume, face power, rouge, 1918, M 205.00
Easy Day/Simplex Automatic Clothes Washer, 1918, MIB.......... 100.00
Flavoring Extract Set, 20 1-oz bottles in blk case, 1912, M....... 1,130.00
Gentleman's Shaving Set, 7 items, 1923, MIB 320.00
Gertrude Recordon's Facial Treatment Set, 4-pc, 1929, MIB....... 257.50
Gift Box Set #1, ½-oz perfume+powder sachet, 1915, MIB.......... 180.00
Holly Set, pr ½-oz perfumes, 1912, M in holly-pattern box.......... 265.00

Jack and Jill Jungle Jinks suitcase, tin litho, empty, VG, from $30.00 to $45.00. (Photo courtesy John Coker Ltd/LiveAuctioneers.com)

Little Folks Set, 4 sm perfumes, 1915, MIB..............110.00
Manicure Set, holds 8 different items, 1912, M..............255.00
Marvel Electric Silver Cleaner, 1918, MIB..............100.00
Memories That Linger Set, 3 different perfumes, 1913, M..........335.00
Mission Garden Perfume, Bavarian glass, 1½-oz, MIB..............415.00
Natoma Rose Talcum, triangular tin container, 1914, 4-oz, M.....590.00
Shoe White, 5-oz sack of powder, 1915, MIB 77.50
Supreme Huile D'Olive Oil, 1-pt or 1-qt can, 1923, M, ea 53.00
Trailing Arbutus Gift Box 'T,' 3-pc, 1915, M in mc box..............310.00
Vernafleur Threesome Gift Set, 3-pc, 1928, MIB 210.00
Violet Gift Set 'H,' 1-oz perfume+talc+sachet+atomizer, M 355.00

Camark

The Camden Art and Tile Company (commonly known as Camark) of Camden, Arkansas, was organized in the fall of 1926 by Samuel J. 'Jack' Carnes. Using clays from Arkansas, John Lessell, who had been hired as art director by Carnes, produced the initial lustre and iridescent Lessell wares for Camark ('CAM'den, 'ARK'ansas) before his death in December 1926. Before the plant opened in the spring of 1927, Carnes brought John's wife, Jeanne, and stepdaughter Billie to oversee the art department's manufacture of Le-Camark. Production by the Lessell family included variations of J.B. Owens' Soudanese and Opalesce and Weller's Marengo and Lamar. Camark's version of Marengo was called Old English. They also made wares identical to Weller's LaSa. Pieces made by John Lessell back in Ohio were signed 'Lessell,' while those made by Jeanne and Billie in Arkansas during 1927 were signed 'Le-Camark.' By 1928 Camark's production centered on traditional glazes. Drip glazes similar to Muncie Pottery were produced, in particular the green drip over pink. In the 1930s commercial castware with simple glossy and matt finishes became the primary focus and would continue so until Camark closed in the early 1960s. Between the 1960s and 1980s the company operated mainly as a retail store selling existing inventory, but some limited production occurred. In 1986 the company was purchased by the Ashcraft family of Camden, but no pottery has yet been made at the factory.

Our advisor for this category is Tony Freyaldenhoven; he is listed in the Directory under Arkansas.

Vase, Brown Stipple, 11", from $250.00 to $300.00; Vase, Green and Blue, 10¼", from $250.00 to $350.00.

Charger, bl & wht stipple, 1st block letter mk, 13¼"..............250.00
Flower bowl, Aztec Red mottle, die stamp, 5¼"..............180.00
Flower frog, Rose-Green Overflow, 1st block letter mk,¾x3".........30.00
Ginger jar, Ivory Crackle Matt, gold ink stamp, 9"..............350.00
Humidor, Sea Green, 6-sided, unmk, 6½"..............140.00
Lamp base, Aztec Red mottle, pinched body, sticker, 8"..............800.00
Lamp base, palm trees on lustre, Lessell, 13¾"..............1,200.00
Pig bottle, orange, 1st block letter mk, 3x9"..............250.00
Pitcher, bl & wht stipple, 1st block letter mk, 6"..............100.00
Pitcher, brn stipple, ball form, gold ink stamp, 6½"..............200.00
Pitcher, gr w/ivory cat handle, #088, USA mk, 7½"..............100.00

Pitcher, Rose-Green Overflow, 1st block letter mk, 9¾"..............250.00
Shot glass, Orange-Green Overflow, unmk, 2"..............30.00
Vase, Autumn, flower form, 1st block letter mk, 10"..............100.00
Vase, Aztec Red Mottle, shouldered, brn sticker, 6"..............200.00
Vase, Brown Stipple, baluster, unmk, 3"..............30.00
Vase, Celestial Blue, swollen cylinder, 1st block letter mk, 2¾".....30.00
Vase, Celestial Blue w/blk overflow, brn sticker, 6"..............140.00
Vase, Delphinium Blue, cylindrical neck, unmk, 5"..............20.00
Vase, evergreens, silver lustre on red, LeCamark, 9¾"..............1,100.00
Vase, Frosted Green, flower form, unmk, 13¼"..............250.00
Vase, Frosted Green, low hdls, flared rim, bl sticker, 4¼"..............20.00
Vase, Mulberry w/lt overflow, Deco shape, #405, 6¾"..............120.00
Vase, Old English Rose, Lessell, cylindrical, 11¾"..............1,000.00
Vase, orange crackle, gold ink stamp, 9½"..............400.00
Vase, Rose-Green Overflow, 4 buttressed ft, unmk, 8"..............250.00
Vase, Swirl, earthen tones, shouldered, 1st block letter mk, 4½" . 100.00
Vase, turq matt, fan shape, unmk, 5¾"..............60.00
Vase, wht w/blk overflow, ring hdls, unmk, 4½"..............140.00
Vase, yel & bl mottle, shouldered, gold ink stamp, 7"..............120.00
Vase, yel to bl matt, baluster, unmk, 8"..............450.00
Vase, Yellow Crackle Bright, emb ribs, sticker, 16¼"..............1,300.00
Vase, Yellow-Green Overflow, tricorner top, unmk, 4½"..............100.00

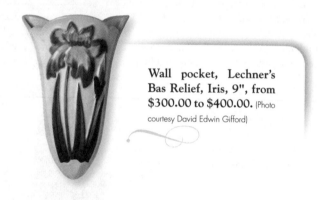

Wall pocket, Lechner's Bas Relief, Iris, 9", from $300.00 to $400.00. (Photo courtesy David Edwin Gifford)

Cambridge Glass

The Cambridge Glass Company began operations in 1901 in Cambridge, Ohio. Primarily they made crystal dinnerware and well-designed accessory pieces until the 1920s when they introduced the concept of color that was to become so popular on the American dinnerware market. Always maintaining high standards of quality and elegance, they produced many lines that became bestsellers; through the '20s and '30s they were recognized as the largest manufacturer of this type of glassware in the world.

Of the various marks the company used, the 'C in triangle' is the most familiar. Production stopped in 1958. For a more thorough study of the subject, we recommend Colors in Cambridge Glass by the National Cambridge Collectors, Inc.; their address may be found in the Directory under Clubs, Newsletters, and Catalogs. They are listed in the Directory under Illinois. See also Carnival Glass; Glass Animals.

Achilles, crystal, bowl, #3900/62, 4-toed, flared, 12"..............75.00
Achilles, crystal, celery/relish, #3900/126, 3-part, 12"..............75.00
Achilles, crystal, cocktail, #3121, 3-oz..............35.00
Achilles, crystal, cocktail icer, #968, w/liner..............85.00
Achilles, crystal, creamer, #3900/41..............25.00
Achilles, crystal, mayonnaise, #3900/11, 2-part..............35.00
Achilles, crystal, pitcher, #3400/38, ball jug, 80-oz..............265.00
Achilles, crystal, plate, #3900/166, rolled edge, 14"..............75.00

Achilles, crystal, sugar bowl, #3900/41 .... 25.00
Achilles, crystal, tumbler, water; #3121, ftd, 10-oz 40.00
Adonis, crystal, bonbon, #3900/130, ftd, w/hdls, 7½" 45.00
Adonis, crystal, candy dish, #3900/165, w/lid 135.00
Adonis, crystal, compote, #3500, w/hdls, 8" 125.00
Adonis, crystal, plate, luncheon; #3500, 8½" 16.00
Adonis, crystal, shakers, pr 85.00
Adonis, crystal, tumbler, juice; #3500, ftd, 5-oz 35.00
Apple Blossom, amber or yel, bowl, console; 12½" 75.00
Apple Blossom, amber or yel, cordial, #3130, 1-oz 90.00
Apple Blossom, amber or yel, cup, #3400/75 .... 28.00
Apple Blossom, amber or yel, vase, rippled sides, 6" 145.00
Apple Blossom, crystal, bowl, cereal; 6" 30.00
Apple Blossom, crystal, plate, dinner; 9½" 45.00
Apple Blossom, crystal, relish tray, w/hdls, 7" 25.00
Apple Blossom, gr or pk, bowl, cereal; 6" 50.00
Apple Blossom, gr or pk, candlestick, 2-light, keyhole, ea ... 50.00
Apple Blossom, gr or pk, plate, dinner; 9½" 100.00
Candlelight, crystal, bowl, #3400/48, 4-ftd, fancy edge, 11" ... 100.00
Candlelight, crystal, cake plate, #3900/35, w/hdls, 13½" ... 85.00
Candlelight, crystal, candlestick, #3900/74, 3-light, 6", ea ... 95.00
Candlelight, crystal, candy jar, #3500/41, 10" 195.00
Candlelight, crystal, cocktail, #3776, 3-oz 35.00
Candlelight, crystal, cup, #3900/17 .... 33.00
Candlelight, crystal, mayonnaise, #3900/19, ftd, 2-pc ... 75.00
Candlelight, crystal, saucer, #3900/17 .... 7.00
Candlelight, crystal, tumbler, iced tea; #3114, ftd, 12-oz ... 45.00
Candlelight, crystal, vase, bud; #274, 10" 95.00

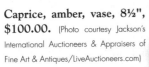

Caprice, amber, vase, 8½", $100.00. (Photo courtesy Jackson's International Auctioneers & Appraisers of Fine Art & Antiques/LiveAuctioneers.com)

Caprice, bl or pk, bonbon, #133, sq, ftd, 6" 40.00
Caprice, bl or pk, bowl, #49, 4-ftd 115.00
Caprice, bl or pk, bowl, salad; #84, shallow, 15" 175.00
Caprice, bl or pk, cigarette box, #208, w/lid, 4½x3½" ... 60.00
Caprice, bl or pk, mayonnaise, #127, 5" 45.00
Caprice, bl or pk, nut dish, #94, 2½" 400.00
Caprice, bl or pk, plate, salad; #23, 7½" 22.00
Caprice, bl or pk, tray, #42, oval, 9" 45.00
Caprice, bl or pk, tumbler, iced tea; #310, flat, 12-oz .. 110.00
Caprice, bl or pk, vase, #338, crimped top, 6½" 225.00
Caprice, crystal, ashtray, #216, 5" 8.00
Caprice, crystal, bowl, #52, crimped, 4-ftd, 9½" 45.00
Caprice, crystal, bowl, almond; #95, 4-ftd, 2" 25.00
Caprice, crystal, cake plate, #36, ftd, 13" 150.00
Caprice, crystal, candlestick, #1338, 3-light, ea 45.00
Caprice, crystal, candy dish, #165, 3-ftd, w/lid, 6" 42.50
Caprice, crystal, marmalade, #89, w/lid, 6-oz 75.00
Caprice, crystal, plate, luncheon; #22, 8½" 13.00
Caprice, crystal, shakers, #91, ball, pr 45.00
Caprice, crystal, tumbler, water; stem ft, #300, blown, 9-oz ... 18.00
Caprice, crystal, tumbler, whiskey; #300, 2½-oz 45.00
Chantilly, crystal, bowl, ftd, tab hdls, 11½" 55.00
Chantilly, crystal, butter dish, rnd 195.00

Chantilly, crystal, candy dish, ftd, w/lid 75.00
Chantilly, crystal, marmalade, w/lid 60.00
Chantilly, crystal, plate, dinner; 10½" 65.00
Chantilly, crystal, plate, salad; 8" 11.00
Chantilly, crystal, sherbet, #3600, 7-oz 16.00
Chantilly, crystal, tumbler, juice; #3775, ftd, 5-oz 16.00
Chantilly, crystal, tumbler, water; stem ft, #3779, 9-oz ... 28.00
Chantilly, crystal, vase, bud; 10" 95.00
Cleo, amber, gr, pk or yel, bowl, cranberry; 3½" 45.00
Cleo, amber, gr, pk or yel, bowl, vegetable; w/lid, 9" ... 295.00
Cleo, amber, gr, pk or yel, compote, #877, 12" 85.00
Cleo, amber, gr, pk or yel, platter, 12" 110.00
Cleo, amber, gr, pk or yel, tumbler, #3007, ftd, 5-oz .. 22.00
Cleo, amber, gr, pk or yel, tumbler, water; stem ft, #3115, 9 oz ... 25.00
Cleo, bl, bowl, cranberry; 3½" 65.00
Cleo, bl, bowl, oval, 11½" 125.00
Cleo, bl, bowl, 8½" 90.00
Cleo, bl, candlestick, 3-light, ea 150.00
Cleo, bl, creamer, #867, ftd 40.00
Cleo, bl, gravy boat, #917, 2-spout 185.00
Cleo, bl, ice tub, #394 .... 210.00
Cleo, bl, tumbler, #3077, ftd, 5-oz 60.00

Cleo, green, asparagus platter, from $250.00 to $300.00. (Photo courtesy Jackson's International Auctioneers & Appraisers of Fine Art & Antiques/LiveAuctioneers.com)

Daffodil, crystal, bonbon, #1181 .... 28.00
Daffodil, crystal, cake plate, #1495, 11½" 80.00
Daffodil, crystal, candlestick, #628, 3½", ea 50.00
Daffodil, crystal, compote, #533, ftd, 5½" 45.00
Daffodil, crystal, jug, #3400/140 .... 295.00
Daffodil, crystal, relish, #214, 3-part, 10" 65.00
Daffodil, crystal, shakers, #360, squatty, pr 65.00
Daffodil, crystal, sugar bowl, #254 .... 25.00
Daffodil, crystal, tumbler, iced tea; #3779, ftd, 12-oz .. 38.00
Daffodil, crystal, tumbler, water; stem ft, #3779, 9-oz . 35.00
Decagon, bl, bowl, berry; #1087, 10" 50.00
Decagon, bl, bowl, fruit; #1009, flat rim, 5¾" 10.00
Decagon, bl, plate, dinner; 9½" 60.00
Decagon, bl, sauceboat, #1091, w/underplate 110.00
Decagon, bl, tray, #1078, oval, 12" 45.00
Decagon, bl, tumbler, #3077, ftd, 12-oz 30.00
Decagon, pastels, bowl, cranberry; flat rim, 3¾" 30.00
Decagon, pastels, bowl, vegetable; #1085, rnd, 9" 30.00
Decagon, pastels, celery tray, #1083, 11" 30.00
Decagon, pastels, compote, #877, 9½" 35.00
Decagon, pastels, creamer, #979, ftd 10.00
Decagon, pastels, ice pail, #851 .... 45.00
Decagon, pastels, plate, grill; #1200, 10" 35.00
Decagon, pastels, shakers, #396, pr 40.00
Diane, crystal, bitters 210.00
Diane, crystal, bowl, cereal; 6" 35.00
Diane, crystal, bowl, 4-ftd, 12" 70.00
Diane, crystal, butter, rnd 150.00
Diane, crystal, candlestick, 5", ea 30.00
Diane, crystal, compote, 5½" 40.00
Diane, crystal, creamer, #3400, scroll hdl 22.00

Diane, crystal, goblet, water; #3122, 9-oz 30.00
Diane, crystal, pitcher, martini 795.00
Diane, crystal, plate, dinner; #3900/24, 10½" 75.00
Diane, crystal, platter, 13½" 100.00
Diane, crystal, saucer 5.00
Diane, crystal, sugar bowl, #3400, scroll hdl 18.00
Diane, crystal, tumbler, water; #1066, 9-oz 20.00
Diane, crystal, vase, bud; 10" 65.00
Elaine, crystal, bonbon, ftd, tab hdl, 7" 35.00
Elaine, crystal, candlestick, 3-light, 6", ea 50.00
Elaine, crystal, candy dish, #306, 6" 110.00
Elaine, crystal, candy jar, #3500/42, 12" 250.00
Elaine, crystal, creamer, various styles, ea 20.00
Elaine, crystal, cup 18.00
Elaine, crystal, goblet, #3104, 9-oz 175.00
Elaine, crystal, ice bucket, chrome hdl 110.00
Elaine, crystal, pickle/relish dish, 7" 30.00
Elaine, crystal, pitcher, ball; 80-oz 225.00
Elaine, crystal, plate, bread & butter; 6½" 10.00
Elaine, crystal, plate, dinner; 10½" 70.00
Elaine, crystal, plate, torte; 4-ftd, 13" 60.00
Elaine, crystal, shakers, flat or ftd, pr 40.00
Elaine, crystal, sherbet; #1402 .... 16.00
Elaine, crystal, tumbler, water; #3500, ftd, 10-oz 30.00
Elaine, crystal, vase, ftd, 8" 90.00
Gloria, crystal, bowl, cranberry; 3½" 35.00
Gloria, crystal, bowl, oval, 4-ftd, 12" 85.00
Gloria, crystal, butter dish, hdls, w/lid 225.00
Gloria, crystal, candy dish, tab hdls, 4-ftd, w/lid 145.00
Gloria, crystal, compote, 4-ftd, 6" 30.00
Gloria, crystal, cordial, #3130, 1-oz 65.00
Gloria, crystal, cup, sq, 4-ftd 50.00
Gloria, crystal, pitcher, w/lid, 64-oz 295.00
Gloria, crystal, plate, salad; #3400/62, 8½" 14.00
Gloria, crystal, plate, sandwich; tab hdls, 11½" 60.00
Gloria, crystal, platter, 11½" 75.00
Gloria, crystal, shakers, short, pr 45.00
Gloria, crystal, sugar bowl, #3400/16 .... 20.00
Gloria, crystal, tumbler, #3130, ftd, 12-oz 28.00
Gloria, crystal, vase, #1308, 6" 50.00
Gloria, gr, pk or yel, bowl, cereal; rnd, 6" 55.00
Gloria, gr, pk or yel, butter dish, hdls, w/lid 450.00
Gloria, gr, pk or yel, cake plate, sq, ftd, 11" 265.00
Gloria, gr, pk or yel, creamer, tall, ftd 35.00
Gloria, gr, pk or yel, oyster cocktail, #3035, 4½" 18.00
Gloria, gr, pk or yel, plate, dinner; sq 85.00
Gloria, gr, pk or yel, plate, w/hdls, 6" 18.00
Gloria, gr, pk or yel, relish, 4-part, center hdl 65.00
Gloria, gr, pk or yel, shakers, ftd, metal tops, pr 125.00
Gloria, gr, pk or yel, sherbet, #3135, 6-oz 22.00
Gloria, gr, pk or yel, tumbler, #3035, ftd, 10-oz 40.00
Gloria, gr, pk or yel, vase, 11" 225.00
Gloria, gr, pk or yel, wine, #3035, 2½-oz 55.00
Imperial Hunt Scene, colors, bowl, cereal; 6" 40.00
Imperial Hunt Scene, colors, cordial, #3075, 1-oz 175.00
Imperial Hunt Scene, colors, creamer, ftd 75.00
Imperial Hunt Scene, colors, plate, #224, 10" 30.00
Imperial Hunt Scene, colors, tumbler, #3075, ftd, 12-oz, 5⅜" 50.00
Imperial Hunt Scene, crystal, bowl, 8" 40.00
Imperial Hunt Scene, crystal, ice bucket, #851, scalloped edge 95.00
Imperial Hunt Scene, crystal, pitcher, #711, w/lid, 76-oz 195.00
Imperial Hunt Scene, crystal, plate, #244, 10½" 25.00
Imperial Hunt Scene, crystal, plate, #556, 8" 18.00
Imperial Hunt Scene, crystal, sugar bowl, #842, w/lid 50.00

Imperial Hunt Scene, crystal, tumbler, #3085, ftd, 8-oz 45.00
Marjorie, crystal, compote, #4404, 5" 70.00
Marjorie, crystal, cup 50.00
Marjorie, crystal, jug, #93, 3-pt 255.00
Marjorie, crystal, nappy, #4111, 8" 90.00
Marjorie, crystal, sugar bowl, #1917/10, flat, waisted 100.00
Marjorie, crystal, tumbler, #7606, ftd, w/hdl, 10-oz 45.00
Marjorie, crystal, wine, #7606, 2½-oz 55.00
Mt Vernon, amber or crystal, ashtray, #63, 3½" 8.00
Mt Vernon, amber or crystal, bowl, cereal; #32, 6" 12.50
Mt Vernon, amber or crystal, butter tub, #73, w/lid 60.00
Mt Vernon, amber or crystal, candelabrum, #38, 13½", ea 150.00
Mt Vernon, amber or crystal, celery, #79, 12" 20.00
Mt Vernon, amber or crystal, coaster, #60, plain, 3" 5.00
Mt Vernon, amber or crystal, compote, #96, bell shape, 6½" 22.50
Mt Vernon, amber or crystal, finger bowl, #23 .... 10.00
Mt Vernon, amber or crystal, mustard, #28, w/lid, 2½-oz 25.00
Mt Vernon, amber or crystal, plate, dinner; #40 .... 30.00
Mt Vernon, amber or crystal, relish, #103, 3-part, 8" 20.00
Mt Vernon, amber or crystal, shakers, #28, pr 22.50
Mt Vernon, amber or crystal, sugar bowl, #8, ftd 10.00
Mt Vernon, amber or crystal, tumbler, juice; #22, ftd, 3-oz 8.00
No 520 Byzantine, amber, gr or Peach Blo, bowl, fruit; #928, 5" 22.50
No 520 Byzantine, amber, gr or Peach Blo, cocktail, #3060, 2½-oz ...20.00
No 520 Byzantine, amber, gr or Peach Blo, compote, #531, 7¼" 40.00
No 520 Byzantine, amber, gr or Peach Blo, plate, dinner; #810, 9½" . 50.00
No 520 Byzantine, amber, gr or Peach Blo, platter, #903, 14½" L .. 75.00
No 520 Byzantine, amber, gr or Peach Blo, sauceboat, #917, dbl ... 95.00
No 520 Byzantine, amber, gr or Peach Blo, tumbler, #3060, ftd, 3-oz. 20.00
No 703 Florentine, gr, bowl, fruit; #928, 5¼" 12.50
No 703 Florentine, gr, candlestick, #625, ea 30.00
No 703 Florentine, gr, tray, sandwich; #173, oval, center hdl 35.00
No 703 Florentine, gr, tumbler, #3060, ftd, 8-oz 17.50
No 703 Florentine, gr, wine, #3060, 2½-oz 22.00
No 704 Windows Border, colors, bowl, fruit; 5¼" 18.00
No 704 Windows Border, colors, candlestick, #437, 9½", ea 45.00
No 704 Windows Border, colors, cup, #933 .... 12.00
No 704 Windows Border, colors, plate, dinner; 9½" 55.00
No 704 Windows Border, colors, tumbler, #3060, 10-oz 20.00
No 704 Windows Border, gr, cigarette box, #430 .... 50.00
No 704 Windows Border, gr, claret, #3075, 4½-oz 33.00
No 704 Windows Border, gr, jug, #955, flat, 64-oz 225.00
No 704 Windows Border, gr, plate, 7" 8.00
No 704 Windows Border, gr, sugar bowl, #137/#942/#943/#944, flat, ea .. 18.00
Nude Stem, Amber, compote, #3011/27, 5⅜" dia 350.00
Nude Stem, Carmen, compote, 7" 275.00
Nude Stem, Carmen, ivy ball, #3011/25 .... 300.00
Nude Stem, Crown Tuscan, candlestick, #3011, 9", ea 150.00
Nude Stem, Crown Tuscan, cigarette box, #3011 .... 1,250.00
Nude Stem, Pistachio, cocktail, #3011, 3-oz 275.00

Nude Stem, compote, emerald green on clear stem, 8", $265.00. (Photo courtesy T.W. Conroy/LiveAuctioneers.com)

Nude Stem, Royal Blue, goblet, banquet; #3011/1 .... 400.00
Nude Stem, Royal Blue, wine, #3011/12, 3-oz 325.00
Nude Stem, Smoke, goblet, #3011/2 .... 300.00
Nude Stem, Topaz, cocktail, #3011/11 .... 750.00
Portia, crystal, bonbon, ftd, tab hdls, 7" 30.00
Portia, crystal, bowl, #3500/28, hdls, 10" 60.00
Portia, crystal, bowl, grapefruit or oyster; 6" 33.00
Portia, crystal, cake plate, w/hdls, 13½" 60.00
Portia, crystal, candy dish, rnd, w/lid 135.00
Portia, crystal, cocktail shaker, w/glass stopper 195.00
Portia, crystal, cup, #3400/54, rnd 16.00
Portia, crystal, ice bucket, w/chrome hdl 110.00
Portia, crystal, plate, dinner; 10½" 75.00
Portia, crystal, plate, salad, 8" 15.00
Portia, crystal, tumbler, iced tea; #3124, 12-oz 30.00
Portia, crystal, vase, 11" 100.00
Portia, crystal, wine, #3126, 2½-oz 33.00
Rosalie, amber or crystal, bowl, fruit; 5½" 15.00
Rosalie, amber or crystal, bowl, soup; 8½" 30.00
Rosalie, amber or crystal, candlestick, #627, 4", ea 25.00
Rosalie, amber or crystal, candy dish, #864, w/lid, 6" 75.00
Rosalie, amber or crystal, compote, high ft, 6½" 30.00
Rosalie, amber or crystal, pitcher, #955, 62-oz 195.00
Rosalie, amber or crystal, plate, dinner; 9½" 40.00
Rosalie, amber or crystal, sugar bowl, #867, ftd 13.00
Rosalie, amber or crystal, tumbler, #3077, ftd, 12-oz 22.00
Rosalie, bk, gr or pk, bowl, rolled edge, 10" 75.00
Rosalie, bl, gr or pk, bowl, cream soup 30.00
Rosalie, bl, gr or pk, cheese & cracker, 11" 65.00
Rosalie, bl, gr or pk, cup 25.00
Rosalie, bl, gr or pk, platter, 15" 135.00
Rosalie, bl, gr or pk, relish, 2-part, 11" 50.00
Rosalie, bl, gr or pk, sugar bowl, #867, ftd 22.00
Rosalie, bl, gr or pk, tray, center hdl, 11" 38.00
Rosalie, bl, gr or pk, vase, ftd, 6½" 125.00
Rose Point, crystal, ashtray, #3500/128, 4½" 50.00
Rose Point, crystal, basket, #3500/52, 1-hdl, 6" 395.00
Rose Point, crystal, bonbon, #3400/204, 3½" 85.00
Rose Point, crystal, bowl, cereal; #3400/10, 6" 100.00
Rose Point, crystal, bowl, rimmed soup; #361, 8½" 250.00
Rose Point, crystal, butter dish, #3900/52, ¼-lb 450.00
Rose Point, crystal, candlestick, #3500/31, 6", ea 135.00
Rose Point, crystal, candy dish, #3900-165, w/lid 140.00
Rose Point, crystal, cheese dish, #980, w/lid, 5" 595.00
Rose Point, crystal, cocktail shaker, #101, w/glass stopper, 32-oz . 295.00
Rose Point, crystal, compote, #3500/111, 6" 175.00
Rose Point, crystal, ice bucket, #3900/671, chrome lid 175.00
Rose Point, crystal, mayonnaise, #3400/11, 3-pc 75.00
Rose Point, crystal, pitcher, #3400/100, ice lip, 76-oz 225.00
Rose Point, crystal, plate, #1397, rolled edge, 13½" 70.00
Rose Point, crystal, plate, dinner; #3400/64 or #3900/24, 10½", ea. 150.00
Rose Point, crystal, plate, luncheon; #3400/63, 9½" 30.00
Rose Point, crystal, relish, #3400/1093, 2-part, 6" 90.00
Rose Point, crystal, saucer, demi; #3400/69 .... 60.00
Rose Point, crystal, shakers, #1468, egg shape, pr 125.00
Rose Point, crystal, sugar bowl, #137, flat 135.00
Rose Point, crystal, tray, #3500/99, oval, w/hdls, 12" 250.00
Rose Point, crystal, tumbler, #498, str sides, 12-oz 75.00
Rose Point, crystal, tumbler, water; #3500, low ft, 10-oz 28.00
Rose Point, crystal, vase, #400, ball bottom, 10" 265.00
Tally Ho, amber or crystal, bowl, 8" 25.00
Tally Ho, amber or crystal, compote, 4½" H 17.50
Tally Ho, amber or crystal, relish, 3-part, w/hdls, 8" 25.00
Tally Ho, Carmen or Royal, cheese & cracker, w/hdls, 11½" 90.00

Tally Ho, Carmen or Royal, nappy, w/hdls, 6" 27.50
Tally Ho, Carmen or Royal, plate, dinner; 10½" 125.00
Tally Ho, Forest Green, celery dish, oval, 12" 35.00
Tally Ho, Forest Green, goblet, wine; #1402 .... 24.00
Tally Ho, Forest Green, plate, chop; 14" 50.00
Valencia, crystal, bowl, #1402/82, 10" 45.00
Valencia, crystal, creamer, #3500/14 .... 15.00
Valencia, crystal, nut dish, #3400/71, 4-ftd, 3" 50.00
Valencia, crystal, plate, #3500/67, 12" 35.00
Valencia, crystal, plate, sandwich; #1402, hdls, 11½" 28.00
Valencia, crystal, relish, #3500/71, 3-part, center hdl, 7½" 75.00
Valencia, crystal, sugar bowl, #3500/14 .... 14.00
Wildflower, crystal, bonbon, #3400/1180, w/hdls, 5¼" 32.50
Wildflower, crystal, bowl, #3900/1185, 10" 60.00
Wildflower, crystal, candlestick, #3400/646, 5", ea 45.00
Wildflower, crystal, cup, #3900/17 or #3400/54, ea 20.00
Wildflower, crystal, mayonnaise set, #3400/11, 3-pc 55.00
Wildflower, crystal, plate, crescent salad 140.00
Wildflower, crystal, plate, dinner; #3900/24, 10½" 75.00
Wildflower, crystal, sugar bowl, #3400/16 or #3400/68, ea 18.00
Wildflower, crystal, vase, #6004, ftd, 8" 75.00

Rose Point, crystal, relish, three-part, three-handle, 8", $40.00.

Cameo

The technique of glass carving was perfected 2,000 years ago in ancient Rome and Greece. The most famous ancient example of cameo glass is the Portland Vase, made in Rome around 100 A.D. After glass blowing was developed, glassmakers devised a method of casing several layers of colored glass together, often with a light color over a darker base, to enhance the design. Skilled carvers meticulously worked the fragile glass to produce incredibly detailed classic scenes. In the eighteenth and nineteenth centuries, Oriental and Near-Eastern artisans used the technique more extensively. European glassmakers revived the art during the last quarter of the nineteenth century. In France, Galle and Daum produced some of the finest examples of modern times, using as many as five layers of glass to develop their designs, usually scenics or subjects from nature. Hand carving was supplemented by the use of a copper engraving wheel, and acid was used to cut away the layers more quickly.

In England, Thomas Webb and Sons used modern machinery and technology to eliminate many of the problems that plagued early glass carvers. One of Webb's best-known carvers, George Woodall, is credited with producing over 400 pieces. Woodall was trained in the art by John Northwood, famous for reproducing the Portland Vase in 1876. Cameo glass became very popular during the late 1800s, resulting in a market that demanded more than could be produced, due to the tedious procedures involved. In an effort to produce greater volume, less elaborate pieces with simple floral or geometric designs were made, often entirely acid etched with little or no hand carving. While very little cameo glass was made in this country, a few pieces were produced by James Gillinder, Tiffany, and the Libbey Glass Company. Though some continued to be made on a limited scale into the 1900s (and until about 1920 in France), for the most part, inferior products caused a marked reduction in its manufacture by the turn of the century. Beware of new 'French' cameo glass from Romania and Taiwan. Some of it is very good and may be signed with 'old' signatures. Know your dealer! Our advisor for this category is Don Williams; he is listed in the Directory under Missouri. See also specific manufactures.

English

Bottle, scent; daffodils, wht on bl, lay down, silver lid, 3½" L ... 1,000.00
Bottle, scent; floral, wht on red to yel, silver lid, lay down, 3¾" . 1,600.00
Bottle, scent; floral, wht opal on citrine, silver lid, lay down, 4" .. 850.00
Pitcher, floral, wht on bl, appl bl hdl, 6½" 2,500.00
Vase, apple blossoms, wht on turq w/gray ft, 7¼" 1,500.00
Vase, berries & leaves, wht on lav, short neck, 9¾" 2,450.00
Vase, floral, wht on bl, stick neck, 11" 2,000.00
Vase, floral, wht on citron, baluster, 4¾" 650.00
Vase, floral, wht on red, bowling-pin shape, 12" 2,000.00
Vase, floral vines, wht on citron, bulbous, 5½" 480.00

Vase, flowers, white on rare amber-peach, 12", $9,000.00. (Photo courtesy Early Auction Co.)

Vase, fruited vines/butterfly, wht on citron, teardrop, 9½" 1,600.00
Vase, lilies, wht on cranberry, shouldered, 6", NM 1,000.00
Vase, morning glories, wht on chartreuse, slim neck, #519/5, 9" . 1,200.00
Vase, morning glories, wht on red, bulbous, 5½" 950.00
Vase, oak leaves & acorns, wht on red, 4½" 600.00
Vase, peach branch, wht on citron, 5¾" 500.00

French

Vase, bud; roses, rose red on lt gray frost, stick neck, Vessisere, 7" ... 300.00
Vase, floral, celery gr on frost, slim, Mercier, 13¾" 425.00
Vase, floral, gr on pale pk frost w/gold, hdls, att St Louis, 3⅛" 235.00
Vase, floral, peach/gr on pk to wht frost, Arsall, 10" 725.00
Vase, foliage, aqua/beige on frost, Cristallerie de Pantin, 4½" 335.00
Vase, grapes/leaves, brn & rust on orange, slim, ftd, Arsall, 12¼" . 600.00
Vase, irises, voilet on frost w/gold, Cristallerie de Pantin, 14" 450.00
Vase, leaves, brn/peach on frost, Degue, 19x8" 360.00
Vase, lotus/butterfly, bl on yel, flared body, Camila, 6" 270.00
Vase, thistle flowers/quote, purple to wht, Vessiere Nancy, 5x2½" .. 270.00
Vase, trees/lake/birds, brn on orange, slim neck, Michel, 6¼" 515.00

Canary Ware

Canary ware was produced from the late 1700s until about the mid-nineteenth century in the Staffordshire district of England. It was potted of yellow clay and the overglaze was yellow as well. More often than not, copper or silver lustre trim was added. Decorations were usually black-printed transfers, though occasionally hand-painted polychrome designs were also used.

Cup & saucer, woman & child playing harp, blk transfer, 2¾", 5" .. 350.00
Inkwell, shoe form w/mc pattern, 3½" L 2,000.00
Mug, LaFayette/Washington/eagle/stars, rust transfer, 2⅜" .. 1,175.00
Pepper shaker, vining tulips (later HP), dome-top, 4½", VG 2,100.00
Pitcher, eagle, bk: roses, roses at incurvate neck, ftd, 6x8" 1,900.00

Pitcher, Lafayette above an eagle, reverse: Revolutionary War, Cornwallis surrendering his sword, 3¾", EX, $570.00. (Photo courtesy Skinner Inc. Auctioneers & Appraisers of Antiques & Fine Art)

Pitcher, Peace & Plenty, blk transfer, silver lustre trim, 6½" 1,450.00
Plate, floral at rim (strong red/gr), brn edge, underside chip, 8¾".. 1,320.00
Vase, quintal; HP (King's Rose type) roses, 5-finger fan form, 8x9"..8,400.00

Candlewick

Candlewick crystal was made by the Imperial Glass Corporation, a division of Lenox Inc., Bellaire, Ohio. It was introduced in 1936, and though never marked except for paper labels, it is easily recognized by the beaded crystal rims, stems, and handles inspired by the tufted needlework called candlewicking, practiced by our pioneer women. During its production, more than 741 items were designed and produced. In September 1982 when Imperial closed its doors, 34 pieces were still being made.

Identification numbers and mold numbers used by the company help collectors recognize the various styles and shapes. Most of the pieces are from the #400 series, though other series numbers were also used. Stemware was made in eight styles — five from the #400 series made from 1941 to 1962, one from #3400 series made in 1937, another from #3800 series made in 1941, and the eighth style from the #4000 series made in 1947. In the listings that follow, some #400 items lack the mold number because that information was not found in the company files.

A few pieces have been made in color or with a gold wash. At least two lines, Valley Lily and Floral, utilized Candlewick with floral patterns cut into the crystal. These are scarce today. Other rare items include gifts such as the desk calendar made by the company for its employees and customers; the dresser set comprised of a mirror, clock, puff jar, and cologne; and the chip and dip set.

Ashtray, rnd, #400/19, 2 2/4" 8.00
Ashtray, 3-pc nesting, sq, #400/650 .... 105.00
Bowl, baked apple; rolled edge, #400/53X, 6" 35.00
Bowl, bouillon; w/hdls, #400/126 .... 45.00
Bowl, cupped edge, #400/75F, 10" 45.00
Bowl, fruit; #400/3F, 6" 12.00
Bowl, salad; #400/75B, 10½" 40.00
Bowl, shallow, #400/17F, 12" 47.50
Bowl, sq, #400/233, 7" 155.00
Bowl, vegetable; #400/65/1, w/lid, 8" 375.00
Butter & jam set, #400/204, 5-pc 495.00
Cake stand, low ft, #400/67D, 10" 60.00
Candleholder, 2-way, beaded base, #400/115, ea 135.00
Candleholder, 3-bead stem, #400/224, 5½", ea 150.00
Candy dish, w/lid, #400/259 .... 150.00
Celery, oval, w/hdls, #400/105, 13½" 35.00
Celery boat, oval, #400/46, 11" 65.00
Claret, #3400, 5-oz 55.00

Cocktail, #400/190, 4-oz 20.00
Compote, beaded stem, #400/220, 5" 90.00
Cordial, #400/190, 1-oz 90.00
Creamer, domed ft, #400/18 .... 125.00
Cup, coffee; #400/37 ....6.00
Egg cup, #400/19 .... 60.00
Goblet, #4000, 11-oz 32.00
Goblet, water; #3800, 9-oz 38.00
Ice tub, w/hdls, #400/168, 7" 250.00
Marmalade, w/spoon & lid, #400/79 .... 45.00
Mint dish, w/hdl, #400/51F, 6" 22.00
Nappy, 4-ftd, #400/74B, 8½" 75.00
Oil bottle, #400/177, 4-oz 55.00
Parfait, #3400, 6-oz 60.00
Pitcher, flat, #400/16, 16-oz 200.00
Pitcher, juice/cocktail; #400/19, 40-oz 215.00
Plate, cracker; #400/145, 13½" 40.00
Plate, crescent salad; #400/120, 8¼" 60.00
Plate, cupped edge, #400/20V, 17" 95.00
Plate, dinner; #400/10D, 10½" 42.00
Plate, oval, #400/124, 12½" 90.00
Plate, oval, #400/169, 8" 25.00
Plate, salad; #400/3D, 7" 8.00
Plate, service; #400/92D, 14" 50.00
Punch set, bowl on 18" plate, 12 cups & ladle, #400/102 .... 275.00
Relish, 2-part, #400/85, 6½" 25.00
Relish, 5-part, #400/102, 13" 65.00
Relish, 5-part, 5 hdls, #400/56 .... 75.00
Salt dip, #400/61, 2" 11.00
Sauceboat, #400/169 .... 115.00
Saucer, coffee or tea; #400/35 or #400/37, ea 2.50
Shakers, straight-sided, beaded ft, chrome top, #400/247, pr 20.00
Sherbet, low stem, #3800 .... 28.00
Sugar bowl, flat, beaded hdl, #400/126 .... 35.00
Tidbit, 2-tier, cupped, #400/2701 .... 60.00
Tray, center hdl, #400/68D, 11½" 65.00
Tray, hdls, #400/113E, 14" 95.00
Tumbler, #400/19, 10-oz 12.00
Tumbler, #400/19, 12-oz 22.00
Tumbler, juice; #400/18, 5-oz 60.00
Tumbler, old-fashioned; #400/18, 7-oz 70.00
Vase, bud; #400/28C, 8½" 110.00
Vase, crimped edge, flat, #400/287C, 6" 50.00
Vase, pitcher; #400/227, 8½" 595.00
Vase, rose bowl; #400/142K, 7" 300.00

Candy Containers

Figural glass candy containers were first created in 1876 when ingenious candy manufacturers began to use them to package their products. Two of the first containers, the Liberty Bell and Independence Hall, were distributed for our country's centennial celebration. Children found these toys appealing, and an industry was launched that lasted into the mid-1960s.

Figural candy containers include animals, comic characters, guns, telephones, transportation vehicles, household appliances, and many other intriguing designs. The oldest (those made prior to 1920) were usually hand painted and often contained extra metal parts in addition to the metal strip or screw closures. During the 1950s these metal parts were replaced with plastic, a practice that continued until candy containers met their demise in the 1960s. While predominately clear, they are found in nearly all colors of glass including milk glass, green, amber, pink, emerald, cobalt, ruby flashed, and light blue. Usually the color was

intentional, but leftover glass was used as well and resulted in unplanned colors. Various examples are found in light or ice blue, and new finds are always being discovered. Production of the glass portion of candy containers was centered around the western Pennsylvania city of Jeannette. Major producers include Westmoreland Glass, West Bros., Victory Glass, J.H. Millstein, J.C. Crosetti, L.E. Smith, Jack Stough, and T.H. Stough. While 90% of all glass candies were made in the Jeannette area, other companies such as Eagle Glass, Play Toy, and Geo. Borgfeldt Co. have a few to their credit as well.

Buyer beware! Many candy containers have been reproduced. Some, including the Camera and the Rabbit Pushing Wheelbarrow, come already painted from distributors. Others may have a slick or oily feel to the touch. The following list may also alert you to possible reproductions:

Amber Pistol, L #144 (first sold full in the 1970s, not listed in E&A)

Auto, D&P #173/E&A #33/L #377

Auto, D&P #163/E&A #60/L #356

Black and White Taxi, D&P #182/L #353 (Silk-screened metal roofs are being reproduced. They are different from originals in that the white section is more silvery in color than the original cream. These closures are put on original bases and often priced for hundreds of dollars. If the top is not original, the value of these candy containers is reduced by 80%.)

Camera, D&P #419/E&A #121/L #238 (original says 'Pat Apld For' on bottom, reproduction says 'B. Shakman' or is ground off)

Carpet Sweeper, D&P 296/E&A #133/L #243 (currently being sold with no metal parts)

Carpet Sweeper, E&A #132/L #242 (currently being sold with no metal parts)

Charlie Chaplin, D&P 195/E&A #137/L #83 (original has 'Geo. Borgfeldt' on base; reproduction comes in pink and blue)

Chicken on Nest, D&P #10/E&A #149/L #12

Display Case, D&P #422/E&A #177/L #246 (original should be painted silver and brown)

Dog, D&P #21/E&A #180/L #24 (clear and cobalt)

Drum Mug, D&P #431/E&A #543/L #255

Happifats on Drum, D&P #199/E&A #208/L #89 (no notches on repro for closure to hook into)

Fire Engine, D&P 258/E&A #213/L #386 (repros in green and blue glass)

Independence Hall, D&P #130/E&A #342/L #76 (original is rectangular; repro has offset base with red felt-lined closure)

Jackie Coogan, D&P #202/E&A #345/L #90 (marked inside 'B')

Kewpie, D&P #204/E&A #349/L #91 (must have Geo. Borgfeldt on base to be original)

Mailbox, D&P #216/E&A #521/L #254 (repro marked Taiwan)

Mantel Clock, D&P #483/E&A #162/L #114 (originally in ruby flashed, milk glass, clear, and frosted only)

Mule and Waterwagon, D&P #51/E&A #539/L #38 (original marked Jeannette, PA)

Naked Child, E&A 546/L #94

Owl, D&P #52/E&A #566/L #37, (original in clear only, often painted; repro found in clear, blue, green, and pink with a higher threaded base and less detail)

Peter Rabbit, D&P #60/E&A #618/L #55

Piano, D&P #460/E&A #577/L #289 (original in only clear and milk glass, both painted)

Rabbit Pushing Wheelbarrow, D&P #72/E&A #601/L #47 (eggs are speckled on the repro; solid on the original)

Rocking Horse, D&P #46/E&A #651/L #58 (original in clear only, repro marked 'Rocky')

Safe, D&P #311/E&A #661/L #268 (original in clear, ruby flashed, and milk glass only)

Santa, D&P 284/E&A #674/L #103 (original has plastic head; repro [1970s] is all glass and opens at bottom)

Santa's Boot, D&P #273/E&A #111/L #233

Scottie Dog, D&P #35/E&A #184/L #17 (repro has a ice-like color and is often slick and oily)

Station Wagon, D&P #178/E&A #56/L #378

Stough Rabbit, D&P #53/E&A #617/L #54

Uncle Sam's Hat, D&P #428/E&A #303/L #168

Wagon, U.S. Express D&P #530 (glass is being reproduced without any metal parts)

Others are possible. If in doubt, do not buy without a guarantee from the dealer and return privilege in writing. Also note that other reproductions are possible.

Our advisor for glass containers is Jeff Bradfield; he is listed in the Directory under Virginia. You may contact him with questions, if you will include an SASE. See Clubs, Newsletters, and Catalogs for the address of the Candy Container Collectors of America. A bimonthly newsletter offers insight into new finds, reproductions, updates, and articles from over 400 collectors and members, including authors of books on candy containers. Dues are $25.00 yearly. The club holds an annual convention in June in Lancaster, Pennsylvania, for collectors of candy containers.

'L' numbers used in this guide refer to a standard reference series, *An Album of Candy Containers, Vols. I* and *II*, by Jennie Long. 'E&A' numbers correlate with *The Compleat American Glass Candy Containers Handbook* by Eikelberner and Agadjanian, revised by Adele Bowden. D&P numbers refer to *Collector's Guide to Candy Containers* by Doug Dezso and Leon and Rose Poirier (out of print).

Airplane, Boyd; various colors, D&P 77 .... 28.00
Airplane, Patent 113053; tin propeller, D&P 81/E&A 4 .... 85.00
Airplane, Spirit of St Louis, amber body, D&P 85/E&A 9, $500 to . 700.00
Barney Google by Barrel, King Features Syndicate, D&P 188/E&A 71.1,500.00
Baseball Player by Barrel, G pnt, D&P 190/E&A 77/L 80 .... 800.00
Bell, Liberty w/Hanger; bl glass, wire bail, D&P 95/E&A 85 .... 60.00
Bird on Mound, no whistle, ca 1920, D&P 3/E&A 94 .... 600.00
Boat, Battleship; open base w/3 sections, D&P 99/E&A 97 .... 30.00
Bottle, Apothecary-Lg; 5¼", D&P 113 .... 80.00
Bottle, Dolly's Milk; VG Co, D&P 109/E&A 527/L 66 .... 60.00
Bottle, Maude Muller Candies, 4 in cb crate, D&P 110 .... 250.00
Bus, Victory Stages; 8 side windows, D&P 157/E&A 118-1 .... 425.00
Candleabrum, 2 glass shakers in metal stand, D&P 317/E&A 174/L 202 . 45.00
Cannon, US Defense Field Gun; tin bbl, D&P 387/E&A 128/L 142. 350.00
Car, Coupe-Long Hood w/Tin Wheels; D&P 160/E&A 50/L 357 ..175.00
Car, Four Door; mk West Bros Co, D&P 168/E&A 41/L 348 ...1,000.00
Car, Hearse #2, open top, D&P 165/E&A 40/L 360 .... 140.00
Car, Little Touring; Stough, D&P 172/E&A 32 .... 30.00
Carpet Sweeper, Baby; wire hdl, D&P 295/E&A 132/L 242 (+).. 475.00
Cash Register, open bottom, tin closure, D&P 420/E&A 135/L 244.450.00
Chick in Shell Auto w/Balloon Tires, tin closure, D&P 9............ 900.00
Clarinet, red/wht striped tube as mouthpc, D&P 448/E&A 316/L 285.35.00
Clock, Octagon; deep open base, paper dial, D&P 484/E&A 163 ..225.00
Clock Lynne Bank; 2-pc tin w/glass base, D&P 481/E&A 159 .... 600.00
Condiment Set, Rainbow Candy; metal base, D&P 297/E&A 174/L 503 ...50.00
Dog, Scottie, looking str ahead, D&P 35/E&A 184/L 17 (+) 25.00
Dog w/Umbrella, wide opening, D&P 37/E&A 194-2/L 29 .... 50.00
Fire Engine, Ladder Truck; Victory, orig wheels, D&P 254/E&A 216/L 384 ..250.00
Fire Engine, 1914 Stough, orig wheels, mk Pat Pending, D&P 262/E&A 223.175.00
Gun, Grooved Barrel; X-hatching on grip, D&P 392 .... 35.00
Gun, Medium w/Hook Grip; screw head in grip, D&P 396/E&A 259 ..25.00
Hansel & Gretel Fairy Pups Salt & Pepper, D&P 22/E&A 193/L 23, pr. 90.00
Horn, Musical Clarinet No 515a; whistle cap, D&P 452/E&A 315 ..175.00
Horn, Musical Clarinet No 55, cb tube/tin whistle cap, D&P 451/E&A 316.. 30.00
Jack o' Lantern, Big Straight Eyes; bail hdl, D&P 264/E&A 347/L 160.275.00
Jack O'Lantern, Slant Eyes; orig pnt, D&P 265/E&A 349 .... 225.00
Lamp, Library; mk Pat Pending on metal base, D&P 334/E&A 372..525.00
Lantern, Beaded #2; pnt clear or milk glass, D&P 348/E&A 405/L 180 .. 35.00

Lantern, Stough's All Glass; D&P 364/E&A 406 .... 25.00
Locomotive, Am Type 23; bl, 4-4-0 wheels/3 stacks, D&P 489/E&A 480..150.00
Locomotive, Man in Window 888; 4-4-0 wheels, D&P 497/E&A 486 .400.00
Mail Box, Letters US Mail; tin closure, Westmoreland, D&P 216/E&A 521 ..250.00
Nurser, Lynne Doll; rubber nipple mk Hygeia, D&P 122/E&A 550 .35.00
Nurser, Plain; rubber nipple, D&P 123/E&A 549 .... 30.00
Oil Can, Independence Bell; w/oil-can spout, D&P 435/E&A 556...550.00
Parlor Car, arched windows, D&P 516/E&A 169 .... 325.00
Pipe, Fancy Bowl; cut-glass pattern, Trade Mark, D&P 436/E&A 583. 125.00
Powder Horn, blown, mk Pat Appd For, D&P 411/E&A 589/L 265 . 95.00

Rabbit Family, D&P 56, 3½", from $900.00 to $1,200.00. (Photo courtesy Doug Dezso and Leon and Rose Poirier)

Racer, Plastic; clear w/gr wheels, D&P 472 .... 30.00
Racer, Stough's; wheels mtd on axles, D&P 473/E&A 640 .... 80.00
Racer, Stutz Bear Cat; 10-rib radiator, D&P 474/E&A 639 ......1,500.00
Racer #12, Victory Glass, D&P 476/E&A 642/L 432 .... 200.00
Racer #12, 2-vent sides, disk wheels, D&P 476/E&A 642/L 432 . 200.00
Rocking Horse w/Rider, pnt clown & horse, D&P 47/E&A 652 . 200.00
Rooster, Crowing; Victory Glass, G pnt, D&P 73/E&A 151....... 350.00
Safe, Dime; CD Kenny, D&P 312/E&A 661/L 268 .... 100.00
Santa Claus in Long Coat, gold-tone cap, REGDNO716934, D&P 279 .300.00
Santa Claus Leaving Chimney, Victory Glass, D&P 281/E&A 673/L 102 ..150.00
Settee, Rocking; gold edge/arms/risers, D&P 313/E&A 653/L 134 ..650.00
Snowman, Sears; styrofoam head, D&P 289/E&A 681-1 .... 18.00
Soldier, Doughboy; emb helmet/uniform, D&P 209/L 525........... 200.00
Table, emb drw w/center knob, D&P 316/E&A 714/L 136 .... 850.00
Tank, Man in Turret; emb treads/geared wheels, D&P 412/E&A 722...45.00
Tank, 2 Cannons; D&P 413/E&A 723 .... 35.00

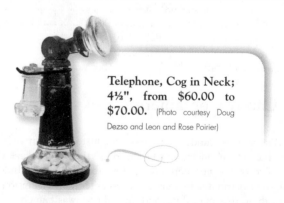

Telephone, Cog in Neck; 4½", from $60.00 to $70.00. (Photo courtesy Doug Dezso and Leon and Rose Poirier)

Telephone, Lynne-Sunken Dial; candlestick, complete, D&P 232/E&A 741 .50.00
Telephone, Pewter Top #1; blown, blk wood receiver, D&P 236/E&A 756.90.00
Telephone, Stough's Musical Toy; ringed base, D&P 246/E&A 732/L 310.45.00
Telephone, Wood Transmitter; D&P 251/E&A 751/L 308 .... 125.00
Tomahawk & Gun, wood hdl, cb head, glass gun, D&P 416.......... 50.00
Toonerville Trolley, Fontaine Fox, G pnt, D&P 214/E&A 767/L 111..800.00
Toy Assortment, Kiddies Candy Filled; 5 toys, D&P 470 .... 600.00
Train, Coal Car/No Couplers; tin wheels, D&P 518 .... 600.00
Village Bank, tin litho w/insert, D&P 133/E&A 804/L 76E......... 275.00
Village City Garage, tin w/insert, D&P 136/E&A 811/L 76G 140.00

Village Drug Store, w/liner, D&P 137/E&A 810 .... 135.00
Village School House, tin w/insert, D&P 143/E&A 808/L 76J 170.00
Wagon, US Express; metal wheels, wire hdl, D&P 530/E&A 821 ..750.00
Watch, Eagle; w/eagle fob, D&P 486/E&A 823/L 122 .... 450.00
Wheelbarrow, Victory Glass, tin snap-on closure, D&P 531/E&A 832/L 273.90.00
Windmill, Candy Guaranteed; tin blades, D&P 533/E&A 840 . 1,000.00
Windmill, Plastic Bank, D&P 536 .... 30.00
Windmill, TG Stough's 1915; D&P 538/E&A 842 .... 375.00
World Globe, mtd on pewter stand, D&P 445/E&A 860/L 276... 500.00

Miscellaneous

These types of candy containers are generally figural. Many are holiday related. Small sizes are common; larger sizes are in greater demand. Because of eBay's influence, prices have dropped and remain soft. Our prices reflect this trend. Our advisor for this category is Jenny Tarrant; she is listed in the Directory under Missouri. See also Christmas; Easter; Halloween.

Key: pm — papier-maché

Baseball player, compo, w/wood bat, early, 7½", EX...................... 780.00
Bulldog, compo, cream w/orange hat Germany, 4", VG 130.00
Cat, pm w/gesso, mc pnt, glass eyes, red ribbon, rpt 6" 225.00
Cat, seated, pm w/gesso, worn flocking, glass eyes, rpt 4" 200.00
Cat in shoe, compo & gesso w/mc pnt, rpr, 4" 175.00
Doll, bsk open dome head, crepe-paper/cb cylinder body, Germany, 6" ...120.00
Dove, compo w/gray pnt, pk-pnt metal fr, orange glass eyes, 4½x8" ...100.00
Elephant, pm, porc tusks, Germany, ca 1885-1920, 6" 155.00
English Bobby, pm, EX pnt, Pat No 28063, 5" 160.00
George Washington, compo, stands on rnd box w/silk flag, Germany, 5".. 150.00
George Washington bust, compo, bottom plug, 2-3" 75.00
George Washington bust, compo, bottom plug, 4-6" 150.00
George Washington w/tree stump, compo, Germany, 3-4" 150.00
George Washington w/tree stump, compo, Germany, 5-7" 225.00
Hen, compo w/metal fr, yel/red/brn pnt, lt ft wear, 4½x4¾" 75.00
Horse, pm, head removes, 4½", VG 155.00
Pig, pm, gr w/HP features, Made in Germany, 5¼x5½x3" 90.00
Pig, pm, sleeping, pk flocking, 5⅜" 90.00
Pigeon, comp w/metal fr, gray/wht/irid purple, 4½x6" 75.00
Rooster, compo, w/metal fr, yel/red/brn pnt, lt ft wear, 4½x4¾" 95.00
Rooster, pm, red/wht/blk pnt, metal legs, glass eyes, 9¼" 250.00
St Patrick's Day, Irishman bust, compo, w/plug, Germany, 3-4" 75.00
St Patrick's Day, Irishman bust, compo, w/plug, Germany, 5-6" ... 125.00
St Patrick's Day, Irishman on candy box, compo, Germany, 3½" . 125.00
St Patrick's Day, pig, flocked gr, wood legs, plug in tummy, 3" 95.00
St Patrick's Day, pig, flocked gr, wood legs, plug in tummy, 5" 125.00
St Patrick's Day, potato, compo, Germany, 3-4" 50.00
Stag, compo w/metal rack, brn flock, yel glass eyes, Germany, 5", VG .275.00
Stork w/baby, spun cotton & paper, lifts legs, Germany, 1930s, 6½" .. 75.00
Turkey, compo w/metal ft, head removes, Germany, 3½" 65.00
Turkey, compo w/metal ft, head removes, Germany, 5" 100.00

Turkey, compo w/metal ft, head removes, Germany, 10" 375.00
Turkey, compo w/metal ft, head removes, Germany, 12" 425.00
Watermelon w/face, molded cb w/celluloid body, Austria, 4¼".... 125.00

Canes

Fancy canes and walking sticks were once the mark of a gentleman. Hand-carved examples are collected and admired as folk art from the past. The glass canes that never could have been practical are unique whimseys of the glassblower's profession. Gadget and container sticks, which were produced in a wide variety, are highly desirable. Character, political, and novelty types are also sought after as are those with handles made of precious metals.

Our values reflect actual prices realized at auction. For more information we recommend *American Folk Art Canes, Personal Sculpture,* by George H. Meyer, Sandringham Press, 100 West Long Lake Rd., Suite 100, Bloomfield Hills, MI 48304. Other possible references are *Canes in the United States* by Catherine Dike and *Canes From the 17th – 20th Century* by Jeffrey Snyder. For information concerning the Cane Collectors Club, see the Directory under Clubs, Newsletters, and Catalogs.

Wood, laced boot handle with toes exposed, shaft with fraternal devices and an alligator labled 'High Price' attacking a snake labeled 'Low Price,' 37", $2,875.00; Ebony, boy's head as handle, 35", $300.00; Curly maple, bulldog face with collar and glass eyes and alligator on handle, 32", $200.00; Silver cap, shaft carved with dogs, a lion, a tiger, snake, sheaf of wheat, etc., refinished, minor damage to cap, 35", $260.00; Two intertwined snakes and ivory knob handle, black paint, 34", $230.00.

(Photo courtesy Garth's Auctions Inc.)

Bone hdl contains microscope/magnifier/spyglass/kaleidoscope, 1800s...2,000.00
Dagger w/in hardwood crook hdl, 8½" blade, wood shaft 215.00
Flashlight in L-shaped metal hdl (not working), hardwood shaft.. 120.00
Gold-cap hdl, whalebone w/gold mts, gold eyelets, ca 1840...... 1,000.00
Horn hdl w/gold collar, blk wooden shaft, ca 1900 .... 360.00
Horn knob hdl, whalebone shaft, 19th C..................................... 425.00
Ivory bulldog head hdl, quartz eyes, silver collar, wood shaft, 1880s...1,000.00
Ivory eagle-head hdl w/mechanical eyes, cvd shaft, eX 780.00
Ivory grapevines/leaves hdl, cherrywood shaft, ivory ferrule, 1870s.. 700.00
Ivory lady w/flowing hair/hat hdl, partridgewood stepped shaft, 1900s. 3,400.00
Ivory Mother Goose hdl, silver collar, snakewood shaft, 1880s.3,250.00
Ivory/wood Buddhist deity hdl, ivory collar, hardwood shaft, 1890s.1,100.00
Jade pc held by gold loops, rosewood shaft, brass/iron ferrule, 1895 .1,000.00
Leather-covered hdl w/gold hallmk matchsafe compartment, wood shaft. 360.00
Porc knob hdl w/HP Queen Victoria scene, hardwood shaft........ 240.00
Porc Royal Copenhagen hdl w/2 baby chicks, ebony shaft, ca 1880 ..650.00
Quartz purple top, silver mt, ebony shaft, brass ferrule, ca 1900... 750.00
Rock crystal hdl w/jewels/gold snake w/jewel eye, ebony shaft, 1900s .. 7,000.00
Silver Art Nouveau lady w/pheasant headdress hdl, ebony shaft, 1900s...650.00
Silver pheasant w/glass eyes, bamboo shaft, w/brass ferrule, 1890s...750.00
Silver swan's head hdl w/glass eyes, hardwood shaft 300.00
Silver/branch whistle hdl, mahog shaft, metal ferrule, Brigg London.. 350.00
Vertebrae, horn tip & end w/8 horn rings, curved hdl, 35" 220.00
Vertebrae, lg ivory knob top, horn tip, graduated, 34".................. 225.00

Turkey, composition with metal feet, head removes, Germany, 8", $300.00.

(Photo courtesy Morphy Auctions/ LiveAuctioneers.com)

Wood, cvd Am flag/spiraling banner/acorns/etc, mc stain............ 350.00
Wood dog head (2½" L) w/pull-down mouth, glass eyes, silver mts . 460.00
Wood dog's head hdl w/mechanical mouth to hold gloves, wood shaft.. 240.00

Canton

Canton is a blue and white porcelain that was first exported in the 1790s by clipper ships from China to the United States. Importation continued into the 1920s. Canton became very popular along the East Coast where the major ports were located. Its popularity was due to several factors: it was readily available, inexpensive, and due to the fact that it came in many different forms, appealing to homeowners.

The porcelain's blue and white color and simple motif (teahouse, trees, bridge, and a rain-cloud border) have made it a favorite of people who collect early American furniture and accessories. Buyers of Canton should shop at large outdoor shows and up-scale antique shows. Collections are regularly sold at auction and many examples may be found on eBay. However, be aware of reproductions and fantasy pieces being sold on eBay by sellers in Hong Kong and Shanghai. Collectors usually prefer a rich, deep tone rather than a lighter blue. Cracks, large chips, and major repairs will substantially affect values. Prices of Canton have escalated sharply over the last 20 years, and rare forms are highly sought after by advanced collectors. Our advisor for this category is Hobart D. Van Deusen; he is listed in the Directory under Connecticut.

Bowl, outside scenes and interior bottom scene, 1800s, 9½" dia., $1,200.00. (Photo courtesy James D. Julia Inc.)

Bowl, salad; notched corners, 19th C, 4¾x9¾"........................ 1,000.00
Bowl, vegetable; notched corners, scenic lid w/berry knop, 6x11x10".. 650.00
Candlesticks, tapered form, flat rim, 19th C, 11½", pr............... 3,000.00
Cider jug, mid-19th C, 8½".. 2,500.00
Ginger jar, mid-19th C, 7", pr.. 500.00
Platter, canted corners, 14½x11¾"................................... 300.00
Teapot, cylindrical, 19th C, 7½"..................................... 660.00
Teapot, good form, high dome lid, 9"................................ 500.00
Teapot, strap hdl, lg orig lid, 19th C, 7½"......................... 725.00
Tub, butter; rnd, w/underplate & lid, ca 1800, 3¼x6½"............... 780.00
Tureen, boar's head hdls, w/lid, 8½x12¾"+15" platter.............. 1,440.00

Capodimonte

The relief style, highly colored and defined porcelain pieces in this listing are commonly called and identified in our current marketplace as Capodimonte. It was King Ferdinand IV, son of King Charles, who opened a factory in Naples in 1771 and began to use the mark of the blue crown N (BCN). When the factory closed in 1834, the Ginori family at Doccia near Florence, Italy, acquired what was left of the factory and continued using its mark. The factory operated until 1896 when it was then combined with Societa Ceramica Richard of Milan which continues today to manufacture fine porcelain pieces marked with a crest and wreaths under a blue crown with R. Capodimonte.

Boxes and steins are highly sought after as they are cross collectibles. Figurines, figure groupings, flowery vases, urns, and the like are also very collectible, but most items on the market today are of recent manufacture. In the past several years, Europeans have been attending U.S. an-

tique shows and auctions in order to purchase Capodimonte items to take back home, since many pieces were destroyed during the two world wars. This has driven up prices of the older ware. Our advisor for this category is James Highfield; he is listed in the Directory under Indiana

Box, Cupid on gray goat, BCN France, 2x5¼x3"..................... 110.00
Box, Cupid w/swan on lid, BCN, 2½x5x3"............................ 100.00
Box, kissing couple next to ped stand, BCN France, 3x9x6"........ 430.00
Box, nude children writing on paper, BCN, 1¾x2¾x2¾............... 135.00
Casket, banquet beheading scene, BCN, 6x9½x5"..................... 1,065.00

Casket, multi-scene with bronze spire, handles, and lock, BCN, made in France, 7x14x14", $3,500.00. (Photo courtesy James Highfield)

Compote, angel w/sickle & wheat, BCN, 7½", pr......................... 65.00
Cup, cherubs, 4 seasons, BCN, 4¼"................................... 225.00
Ewer, nude maiden, rooster hdl, BCN, 10¼"........................... 380.00
Figurine, male peasant, long hair, Germany Erphila BCN, 3¼".... 10.00
Figurine, monk holding chicken & jug, BCN, 6"...................... 42.00
Figurine, monkey band trumpet player, BCN, 4⅜".................... 85.00
Pedestal & urn, nude & partially draped figures, BCN, 61"....... 2,900.00
Pitcher, nymphs in woods, BCN, 5".................................. 95.00
Planter, playful cherubs, wht ware, BCN........................... 55.00
Plate, toga scenes, floral int, BCN, 9"........................... 48.00
Platter, Roman scene w/circled cherubs, B Crown RE, 11x9"...... 300.00
Snuff box, winged cherubs, sq, BCN, 1½x1¾x1¾".................. 100.00
Urn, party scene, dbl mask hdls, BCN, 7½x5½"..................... 215.00
Urns, continuous putto bacchanal scene, BCN, 16¼"................ 750.00
Vase, musical procession, dbl mask hdls, BCN, 6½"................. 160.00
Vase, Olympic scenes, human & lion face hdls, BCN, 11¼"......... 200.00
Water font, Jesus, Mary & angels, R CAPO mk, 8½x4"................ 40.00

Carlton

Carlton Ware was the product of Wiltshaw and Robinson, who operated in the Staffordshire district of England from about 1890. During the 1920s, they produced ornamental ware with enameled and gilded decorations such as flowers and birds, often on a black background. From 1935 until about 1961, in an effort to thward the theft of their designs by Japanese potters, Carlton adapted the 'Registerd Australian Design' mark, taking advantage of the South East Asia Treaty Organization which prohibited such piracy. In 1958 the firm was renamed Carlton Ware Ltd. Their trademark was a crown over a circular stamp with 'W & R, Stoke on Trent,' surrounding a swallow. 'Carlton Ware' was sometimes added by hand.

Bowl, Oriental scene on yel, cartouches on blk w/gold rim, 1920s, 10".. 150.00
Bowl, pagoda scene on Rouge Royale, 2 lg gilt scrolls at rim, 12" L ... 125.00
Bowl, spider web & dragonfly on Rouge Royale, 12x7"............... 100.00
Box, Oak Tree, 4x4".. 95.00
Candlestick, Deco flowers on bl w/gold, disk ft, 4x5¾"........... 165.00
Coffeepot, Lily of the Valley on Rouge Lustre w/gold, 6¾"........ 180.00
Compote, wisteria & heron on Rouge Royale, ped ft, 9"............ 110.00
Creamer & sugar bowl, Foxglove, pre-1959, 2½", 3".............. 150.00
Cup & saucer, demitasse; heron/flowers/gold on Rouge Royale, 2¼" . 132.00

Cup & saucer, Wild Duck on wht w/gilt, 2¼", 4¼"...................... 230.00
Dish, butterfly & berries on Rouge Royale, gold hdls, 7x4¼"......... 48.00
Figurine, nude lady surrounded by hollyhocks, limited edition, 11½". 165.00
Ginger jar, bird/butterfly/floral on Rouge Royale, 8½".................. 185.00
Ginger jar, dragonfly & floral on gr w/gold, 1952-62, 7¼".......... 220.00
Ginger jar, Oriental scenic on blk w/orange bands, 11", pr......... 525.00
Ginger jar, pagoda scenes, gold on cobalt, domed lid, 10¼", pr.... 425.00
Jug, Anemone on yel, scalloped rim, 5½"................................... 150.00
Jug, Foxglove on gr, brn stem hdl, 10½".................................. 380.00
Leaf dish, floral on wht, 1x5x4"... 40.00
Platter, Willow on bl, ftd, oval, 11"....................................... 80.00
Teapot, Foxglove, brn stem hdl, pre-1958, 5½"......................... 200.00
Teapot, Wild Rose on cream, brn hdl, 4½".............................. 185.00
Teapot, 2 golliwogs dancing, 1980, 9".................................... 150.00
Vase, bird & floral, mc on bl w/gilt, bulbous, ped ft, ca 1910, 7".. 175.00
Vase, butterfly lustre, mottled ground, bulbous base, 6"............... 135.00
Vase, Deco flowers, blk/wht on red, hexagonal, ca 1935, w/lid, 12". 335.00
Vase, Deco flowers on Rouge Royale, waist-to-hip hdls, ca 1930, 4½".. 120.00
Vase, Deco poppies & hollyhocks on wht, 5 mc rings, ovoid, 6¾" 160.00
Vase, egrets in landscape on powder bl w/gold, w/lid, 7", pr......... 360.00
Vase, fairies & moon, orange & gold on blk, 8-sided rim, 1930, 9".. 300.00
Vase, floral on gray, flambé int, ovoid, #456, w/lid, 9¼", pr.......1,500.00
Vase, Forest Tree on bl w/gold, domed lid, early 20th C, 11½".....150.00

Vase, hollyhocks, Carlton Ware Made in England O Trade Mark transfer logo, 8", $360.00. (Photo courtesy Cincinnati Art Galleries)

Vase, hollyhocks on orange lustre, mushroom shape, ca 1935, 4¾".225.00
Vase, Kingfisher on Rouge Royale, w/sm gold hdls, 4½"............... 165.00
Vase, Medley, ftd, ca 1930, 7"... 125.00
Vase, Oak Tree, limb hdls, 8½", pr.. 375.00
Vase, Oriental scene on bl lustre w/gold, 1920s, 10½x4¾"......... 150.00
Vase, Oriental scene on yel, cylindrical neck, 10¼".................... 120.00
Vase, Rouge Royale w/gold ribbon-like hdls, 1930s, 5", pr............ 60.00
Vase, spider web/berries/foliage on bl & blk mottle, gold hdls, 4¾".. 170.00
Vase, tropical birds/butterflies on orange lustre, 5¼", pr............1,325.00
Vase, weeping willows/gold prunus tree on Rouge Royale, hdls, 10" ..600.00
Vase, Worcester Birds, blk & gold on orange panels, trumpet shape, 8".160.00

Carnival Collectibles

Carnival items from the early part of this century represent the lighter side of an America that was alternately prospering and sophisticated or devastated by war and domestic conflict. But whatever the country's condition, the carnival's thrilling rides and shooting galleries were a sure way of letting it all go by — at least for an evening.

In the shooting gallery target listings below, items are rated for availability from 1, commonly found, to 10, rarely found (these numbers appear just before the size), and all are made of cast iron. Our advisors for shooting gallery targets are Richard and Valerie Tucker; their address is listed in the Directory under Texas.

Chalkware Figures

Army girl, mc pnt, 1946, 9", EX+... 20.00
Bugs Bunny holding carrot, mc pnt, ca 1940, 14"...................... 240.00
Bugs Bunny standing by tree, mc pnt, 9½"................................. 42.00
Cowboy w/hat in left hand, gr shirt, red scarf, 1947, 8½", NM...... 30.00
Dale Evans, mc pnt, ca 1940s, 15"... 120.00
Donald Duck, bl jacket, mc pnt, 1940s, 13½", from $125 to........ 150.00
Donald Duck holding coin aloft, mc pnt, 7"............................... 60.00
Hopalong Cassidy, mc pnt, 1940s, 13"..................................... 275.00
Kewpie-like Black child w/hands raised, yel outfit, 12½", NM....... 45.00
King Kong, mc pnt, 1940s, 13".. 120.00
Lone Ranger, mc pnt, 1940s, 15"... 90.00
Mickey Mouse, blk w/red shorts & shoes, 10"........................... 100.00
Rabbit seated w/ears up, bank, mc pnt, 1940s, 12".................... 27.50
Snow White, bl dress w/glitter details, 15", NM........................ 175.00
Terrier dog seated, brn & yel w/red ribbon, 1948, 7x7x4¼", VG+ . 30.00

Shooting Gallery Targets

Battleship, worn wht pnt, Mangels, 5, 6¼x11⅜", from $200 to.... 300.00
Birds (8) on bar, worn pnt, Mangels, 9, 3½x41½", from $700 to.. 800.00
Bull's-eye w/pop-up duck, old pnt, Quackenbush, 7, 12" dia, $500 to. 600.00

Clown, with bull's eye, Emil R. Hoffman, Chicago, Illinois, rarity value: 9, 21", minimum value, $1,000.00. (Photo courtesy Richard and Valerie Tucker)

Clown, worn red/wht pnt, Mangels, 9, 19x19½"+movable arms, min. 1,000.00
Clown standing, bull's-eye, mc pnt, Evans or Hoffman, 10, 12", min. 1,000.00
Dog running, worn wht pnt, Smith or Evans, 6, 6x11", from $100 to. 200.00
Duck, detailed feathers, old pnt, Parker, 8, 3¾x5½", $100 to....... 200.00
Duck, detailed feathers, worn pnt, Evans, 4, 5½x8½", $100 to..... 200.00
Eagle w/wings wide, mc pnt, Smith or Evans, 6, 14¾", $650 to ... 750.00
Eagle w/wings wide, W Wurfflein Phila'd'a, old pnt/bullet holes, 33". 8,225.00
Elephant, wht pnt, flakes, 9½"... 250.00
Greyhound, bull's-eye, old patina, Parker, 8, 26" W, min.......... 1,000.00
Indian chief, worn mc pnt, Hoffmann or Smith, 10, 20x15", min ..100.00
Lion running, old wht pnt, 12½" L.. 220.00
Monkey standing, worn pnt, 10, 9¾x8½", from $300 to............... 400.00
Mountain goat leaping, worn wht pnt, 8¾"............................... 150.00
Owl, bull's-eye, wht traces, Evans, 6, 10¾x5⅛", from $400 to...... 500.00
Pipe, old patina, Smith, 1, 5¾x1¾", value less than...................... 50.00
Rabbit running, bull's-eye, old patina, Parker, 8, 12x25x1", min. 1,000.00
Rabbit standing, worn pnt, Smith or Mueller, 8, 18x10", from $900 to ..1,000.00
Reindeer (elk), wht pnt (worn/rusty), 7, 10x9", from $300 to...... 400.00
Saber-tooth tiger, old patina, Mangels, 7, 7¾x13", from $300 to . 400.00
Soldier w/rifle, pnt traces/old patina, Mueller, 5, 9x5", from $100 to .200.00
Squirrel running, old patina, Smith, 4, 5⅛x9¾", from $100 to 200.00
Stag running, worn blk pnt, hooves missing, 9½"........................ 220.00
Star spinner, dbl, worn mc pnt, Mangels, 6, 8x2¾", from $200 to. 300.00
Swan, worn pnt, Mueller, 7, 5¾x5", from $100 to 200.00

Carnival Glass

Carnival glass is pressed glass that has been coated with a sodium solution and fired to give it an exterior lustre. First made in America in 1905, it was produced until the late 1920s and had great popularity in the average American household, for unlike the costly art glass produced by Tiffany, carnival glass could be mass produced at a small cost. Colors most found are marigold, green, blue, and purple; but others exist in lesser quantities and include white, clear, red, aqua opalescent, peach opalescent, ice blue, ice green, amber, lavender, and smoke.

Companies mainly responsible for its production in America include the Fenton Art Glass Company, Williamstown, West Virginia; the Northwood Glass Company, Wheeling, West Virginia; the Imperial Glass Company, Bellaire, Ohio; the Millersburg Glass Company, Millersburg, Ohio; and the Dugan Glass Company (Diamond Glass), Indiana, Pennsylvania. In addition to these major manufacturers, lesser producers included the U.S. Glass Company, the Cambridge Glass Company, the Westmoreland Glass Company, and the McKee Glass Company.

Carnival glass has been highly collectible since the 1950s and has been reproduced for the last 25 years. Several national and state collectors' organizations exist, and many fine books are available on old carnival glass, including *Standard Encyclopedia of Carnival Glass*, *Collector's Companion to Carnival Glass*, and *Standard Companion to North American Carnival Glass*, all by Bill Edwards and Mike Carwile.

Acanthus (Imperial), bowl, marigold, 8-9½" 60.00
Acorn (Fenton), bowl, gr, 6¼-7½" 165.00
Angoori, tumbler, marigold 175.00
Apple Blossom (Diamond), bowl, bl, 6-7½" 150.00
Arcs (Imperial), compote, amethyst 90.00
Austral, jug, amber, 7¼" 125.00
Australian Diamond (Crystal), creamer, amethyst 80.00
Autumn Acorns (Fenton), bowl, gr, 8½" 110.00
Ball & Swirl, mug, marigold 120.00
Bamboo Spike (China), tumbler, marigold 75.00
Band of Stars, decanter, marigold 175.00
Banded Drape (Fenton), pitcher, bl 400.00
Banded Neck, vase, marigold 50.00
Basketweave (Northwood), compote, gr 95.00
Beaded Basket (Dugan), basket, gr, flared 275.00
Beaded Basket (Dugan), basket, marigold, flared 25.00
Beaded Shell (Dugan), butter dish, marigold 130.00
Beaded Stars (Fenton), banana boat, marigold 35.00
Bells & Beads (Dugan), nappy, peach opal 100.00
Berry Basket, shakers, marigold, pr 75.00
Big Basketweave (Dugan), basket, wht, lg 150.00
Birds & Cherries (Fenton), bonbon, amethyst 125.00
Blackberry Banded (Fenton), hat, irid moonstone 125.00
Blackberry Spray (Fenton), bonbon, bl 45.00
Blackberry Wreath (Millersburg), bowl, ice cream; marigold, 10" . 95.00
Blossom & Shell, bowl, Alaskan (marigold over gr), 9" 90.00
Blue Ring (Czech), decanter, marigold 200.00
Bordered Cosmos, hatpin, blk amethyst 125.00
Boutonniere (Millersburg), compote, amethyst 135.00
Brocaded Acorns, candleholder, lav, ea 65.00
Brocaded Acorns (Fostoria), ice bucket, ice bl 185.00
Brocaded Palms (Fostoria), cake plate, ice gr 150.00
Brocaded Roses (Fostoria), wine, ice gr 200.00
Broken Arches (Imperial), punch cup, marigold 20.00
Bull's Eye (US Glass), oil lamp, marigold 210.00
Bunny, bank, marigold 30.00
Butterflies (Fenton), bonbon, bl 65.00

Butterfly & Berry (Fenton), sugar bowl, gr 200.00
Butterfly & Fern (Fenton), pitcher, marigold 325.00
Buttermilk, Plain (Fenton), goblet, marigold 50.00
Buzz Saw (European), pitcher, marigold 100.00
Cambridge Hobstar (Cambridge), napkin ring, marigold 165.00
Cane (European), tankard, marigold 170.00
Cane & Scroll (English), rose bowl, bl 75.00
Capitol (Westmoreland), mug, marigold, sm 140.00
Cartwheel, #411 (Heisey), bonbon, marigold 60.00
Chain & Star (Fostoria), creamer, marigold 175.00
Charlie (Sweden), bowl, bl 200.00
Checkerboard Bouquet, plate, marigold, 8" 80.00
Cherry (Dugan), bowl, peach opal, ftd, 8½" 250.00

Cherry (Millersburg), bowl, amethyst, 10", $300.00. (Photo courtesy Bill Edwards and Mike Carwile)

Cherry (Millersburg), spooner, gr 200.00
Cherry Blossoms, pitcher, bl 150.00
Cherry Chain Variant (Fenton), plate, marigold, 9½" 225.00
Cherubs, toothpick holder, marigold, mini 200.00
Chesterfield (Imperial), candy dish, wht, tall, w/lid 95.00
Circle Scroll (Dugan), creamer, amethyst 175.00
Cloverleaf, bowl, goldfish; marigold, mini 45.00
Colonial (Imperial), goblet, lemonade; marigold 40.00
Columbia (Imperial), compote, smoke 100.00
Concave Diamonds (Northwood), pickle caster, vaseline, complete . 175.00
Corinth (Dugan), vase, marigold milk glass 260.00
Coronet, tumbler, marigold 30.00
Cosmos & Cane (US Glass), bowl, dessert; wht, stemmed 165.00
Cosmos & Cane (US Glass), butter dish, honey amber 165.00
Country Kitchen (Millersburg), sugar bowl, amethyst 400.00
Crackle (Imperial), salt shaker, aqua 60.00
Crown of India (Jain), tumbler, marigold 250.00
Curtain Optic (Fenton), pitcher, vaseline 450.00
Curved Star/Cathedral, flower holder, marigold 135.00
Cut Flowers (Jenkins), vase, smoke, 10" 140.00
Czech Flower, cruet, marigold 200.00
Dahlia (Dugan), bowl, wht, ftd, 10" 225.00
Daisy & Cane (Brockwitz), epergne, marigold 175.00
Daisy & Plume (Dugan), candy dish, peach opal, 3-ftd, w/lid 200.00
Daisy & Scroll, wine, marigold 75.00
Daisy Wreath (Westmoreland), bowl, aqua opal, 8-10" 300.00
Delores, bottle, scent; marigold 60.00
Dewhirst Berry Band, carafe, marigold, 7" 175.00
Diamond & Daisy, plate, marigold, 8" 95.00
Diamond & Fan, compote, peach opal 100.00
Diamond Cut (Crystal), banana bowl, amethyst 115.00
Diamond Point (Northwood), vase, ice bl, 7-14" 400.00
Diamond Ring (Imperial), bowl, fruit; smoke, 9½" 65.00
Diamond Top (English), spooner, marigold 40.00
Dimples, hatpin, amethyst 135.00
Diving Dolphins (English), bowl, amethyst, ftd, 7" 275.00
Double Daisy (Fenton), pitcher, gr, tankard style 385.00
Double Scroll (Imperial), candlesticks, red, pr 400.00
Dragonfly, lamp shade, amber 65.00

Drapery Variant (Finland), shot glass, marigold............................ 225.00
Dugan's #1013 (Dugan), vase, peach opal, 8-13"................. 85.00
Dutch Twins, ashtray, marigold 50.00
Early American (Duncan & Miller), plate, marigold..................... 75.00
Elektra, compote, bl, 4½"....................................... 65.00
Embroidered Panels, tumbler, marigold............................ 165.00
Enameled Chrystanthemum w/Prism Band, pitcher, ice gr... 265.00
Enameled Freesia, tumbler, bl.. 30.00
Enameled Periwinkle, tumbler, marigold........................ 25.00
English Flute & File (Sowerby), sugar bowl, lav 70.00
Estate (Westmoreland), bud vase, smoke, 6"..................... 75.00
Etched Deco (Standard), hat, marigold 45.00
Fanciful (Dugan), plate, wht, 9"... 225.00
Fashion (Imperial), punch bowl w/base, smoke 1,000.00
Feathered Lotus, jar, marigold 165.00
Fenton's #643, compote, celeste bl 70.00
Fenton's #847, vase, fan; bl... 70.00
Fenton's Smooth Rays, bowl, ice gr, 3-corner, 6½" 70.00
Fentonia (Fenton), bowl, gr, ftd, 5" 70.00
Fine Block (Imperial), lamp shade, gr 50.00
Fine Cut Rings (English), celery, marigold........................ 160.00
Fine Rib (Northwood), vase, horehound, 7-14" 145.00
Fishscales & Beads, bride's basket, peach opal, complete 150.00
Florabelle, tumbler, ice gr.. 175.00
Floral & Optic (Imperial), cake plate, marigold milk glass, ftd.... 180.00
Florentine (Imperial), vase, hat; clambroth 65.00
Fluffy Peacock (Fenton), pitcher, bl............................... 575.00
Flute (Northwood), sherbet, teal...................................... 80.00
Flute & Cane (Imperial), pickle dish, marigold 25.00
Forum (Finland), candlesticks, pk, pr............................... 250.00
Four Flowers (Dugan), plate, peach opal, 6½" 175.00
Four Garlands, vase, marigold, 7½" 225.00
Foxhunt, decanter, marigold.. 275.00
Frosted Block (Imperial), compote, clambroth 75.00
Fruits & Flowers (Northwood), bonbon, violet 125.00
Gaelic (Indiana Glass), butter dish, marigold.................... 165.00
Garden Path (Dugan), bowl, wht, ruffled rim, 8-9½"......... 350.00
Garland (Fenton), rose bowl, bl, ftd................................. 90.00
Gibson Girl, toothpick holder, marigold........................... 60.00
Golden Grapes (Dugan), bowl, gr, 7"................................ 50.00
Good Luck (Northwood), plate, amethyst, 9" 600.00
Grape & Cable (Fenton), bowl, bl, ball ft, 7-8½"............... 110.00
Grape & Cable (Northwood), pin tray, iridized custard 400.00
Grape & Cable (Northwood), plate, amethyst, w/handgrip......... 200.00
Grape & Cable Variant (Northwood), bowl, gr, 6-8"........... 90.00
Grape & Gothic Arches (Northwood), creamer, pearl opal......... 425.00
Grape Delight (Dugan), nut bowl, wht, ftd, 6" 95.00
Grecian Urn, bottle, scent; marigold, 6" 50.00
Greek Key Variant, hat pin, amethyst................................ 75.00
Halloween, spittoon, marigold 600.00
Hawaiian Lei, creamer, marigold...................................... 75.00
Heart Band Souvenir (McKee), mug, gr, lg........................ 165.00
Heavy Diamond (Imperial), vase, smoke 85.00
Heavy Grape (Imperial), punch bowl w/base, gr............... 525.00
Heavy Prisms (English), celery vase, amethyst, 6" 115.00
Heinz, bottle, clambroth.. 60.00
Helen's Star (India), vase, marigold 190.00
Hexagon Square, breakfast set, child's, lav, complete 60.00
Hobnail Soda Gold (Imperial), spittoon, gr, lg.................. 100.00
Hobstar (Imperial), pickle castor, marigold, complete.............. 750.00
Hobstar & Shield (European), tumbler, marigold................ 125.00
Hobstar Reversed (English), butter dish, bl 70.00
Holly (Fenton), hat, red 350.00
Holly Sprig (Millersburg), bonbon, lav 100.00

Holly Whirl (Millersburg), nappy, amethyst, 3-corner 95.00
Honeybee (Jeannette), honey pot, teal, w/lid.............................. 85.00
Horseshoe, shot glass, marigold 35.00
Illinois Daisy (English), cookie jar, marigold 60.00
Imperial #499, sherbet, wht... 95.00
Imperial Grape, nappy, gr.. 40.00
Imperial Jewels, hat, celeste bl.. 100.00
Indian Bangles, pitcher, marigold.. 325.00
Intaglio Ovals (US Glass), bowl, pastel marigold, 7"................. 75.00
Interior Swirl, spittoon, pearl opal 140.00
Inverted Feather (Cambridge), cracker jar, gr........................... 300.00
Inverted Strawberry (Cambridge), bowl, amethyst, 9-10½" 235.00
Ivy, wine, marigold... 75.00
Jacobean Ranger (Czech & English), tumbler, marigold 90.00
Jester's Cap (Dugan/Diamond), celeste bl 200.00
Jester's Cap (Dugan/Diamond), vase, peach opal...................... 100.00
Jewels (Diamond), candlesticks, red, pr 275.00
Keg, toothpick holder, gr 25.00
Knotted Beads (Fenton), vase, amber, 4-12"............................ 250.00
Laco, oil bottle, marigold... 80.00
Lacy Dewdrop (Westmoreland), cake plate, irid moonstone........ 200.00
Late Enameled Grape, goblet, marigold 100.00
Lattice & Daisy (Dugan), tumbler, wht..................................... 200.00
Lattice Heart, plate, blk amethyst, 7-8" 325.00
LBJ Hat, ashtray, marigold... 25.00
Leaf Swirl (Westmoreland), compote, yel.................................. 145.00
Leverne, bottle, scent; marigold 40.00
Lined Lattice (Dugan), vase, peach opal, squat, 5-7".................. 300.00
Little Beads, compote, aqua, sm 70.00

Little Stars (Millersburg), bowl, blue, scarce, 7½", $3,000.00. (Photo courtesy Bill Edwards and Mike Carwile)

Long Hobstar (Imperial), punch bowl w/base, clambroth 150.00
Long Thumbprint Variant, butter dish, marigold....................... 75.00
Lotus & Grape Variant (Fenton), bowl, bl, ftd, 6" 80.00
Lustre & Clear (Imperial), shakers, marigold, pr 75.00
Madonna (India), tumbler, marigold.. 95.00
Manhattan, wine, marigold 40.00
Many Fruits (Dugan), cup, punch; wht..................................... 70.00
Maple Leaf (Dugan), butter dish, bl... 150.00
May Basket (English), basket, gr, 7½" 95.00
Melon Rib, powder jar, marigold, w/lid.................................... 35.00
Miltered Block (European), lamp, marigold, scarce 195.00
Miltered Maze, vase, red, 12"... 300.00
Miniature Shell, candleholder, clear, ea.................................... 75.00
Minnesota (US Glass), toothpick holder, marigold.................... 60.00
Moonprint (Brockwitz), cordial, marigold 35.00
Mt Gambier (Crystal), mug, marigold....................................... 100.00
Nanna (Eda), jardiniere, bl.. 500.00
Napoli (Italy), wine, vaseline 25.00
Nell (Highbee), mug, marigold 75.00
Nippon (Northwood), bowl, ice bl, 8½" 400.00
No 270 (Westmoreland), compote, russet gr (olive) 140.00
Northwood #569, vase, vaseline.. 75.00

Northwood #699, cheese dish, vaseline 100.00
O'Hara (Loop), pitcher, marigold.. 120.00
Octagon (Imperial), butter dish, powder bl 325.00
Omera (Imperial), celery, clambroth, w/hdl 35.00
Optic Flute (Imperial), bowl, smoke, 5" 35.00
Orange Tree (Fenton), punch bowl w/base, gr 650.00
Orbit (India), vase, marigold, 9"... 180.00
Oriental Poppy (Northwood), tumbler, ice bl 175.00
Palm Beach (US Glass), banana bowl, honey amber 175.00
Paneled Dandelion (Fenton), pitcher, amethyst........................ 400.00
Paneled Smocking, sugar bowl, marigold 50.00
Pansy (Imperial), dresser tray, amber 150.00
Parquet, creâmer, marigold 70.00
Peach (Northwood), tumbler, bl 150.00
Peacock (Millersburg), bowl, ice cream; amethyst, 5" 300.00
Peacock & Urn & Variants, bowl, gr, ruffled rim, 6" 250.00

Peacock and Urn Variant (Millersburg) bowl, amethyst, 6", $150.00.
(Photo courtesy Bill Edwards and Mike Carwile)

Peacock at the Fountain (Northwood), spooner, ice bl 250.00
Peacock Tail (Fenton), compote, wht 55.00
Pebbles (Fenton), bowl, sauce; gr 30.00
Persian Garden (Dugan), bowl, wht, 5" 60.00
Persian Medallion (Fenton), hair receiver, bl 85.00
Pigeon, paperweight, marigold 200.00
Pine Cone (Fenton), plate, gr, 6¼" 375.00
Plain Jane (Imperial), bowl, gr, 10-12" 70.00
Plume Panels (Fenton), vase, amethyst, 7-12" 100.00
Pond Lily (Fenton), bonbon, vaseline....................................... 135.00
Poodle, powder jar, marigold, w/lid 20.00
Poppy (Northwood), pickle dish, wht, oval 325.00
Post Lantern, lamp shade, amber.. 95.00
Pretty Panels (Fenton), tumbler, ice gr, w/hdl 90.00
Prism, shakers, marigold, pr 60.00
Propeller (Imperial), compote, gr 85.00
Puzzle (Dugan), bonbon, peach opal 85.00
Queen's Jewel, goblet, marigold.. 55.00
Radiance, syrup, marigold.. 325.00
Ranger (Imperial), cracker jar, marigold 80.00
Ranger (Mexican), pitcher, milk; marigold................................ 150.00
Rays & Ribbons (Millersburg), bowl, amethyst, ruffled rim, 8½" . 225.00
Regal, jardinere, marigold...275.00
Ribbed Holly (Fenton), goblet, bl 110.00
Ribbed Swirl, tumbler, gr 80.00
Ribbon Tie (Fenton), plate, amethyst, ruffled rim, 9½" 250.00
Ripple (Imperial), vase, funeral; marigold, 15-21" 175.00
Rising Sun (US Glass), bowl, sauce; marigold, sm...................... 35.00
Rococo (Imperial), vase, lav, 5½" 235.00
Rolled Ribs (New Martinsville), bowl, marigold opal, 8-10"........ 200.00
Rose Ann, lamp shade, marigold 40.00
Rose Show (Northwood), plate, wht, 9½" 525.00
Rosette (Northwood), bowl, gr, ftd, 7-9"................................... 165.00
Royal Lustre (Dugan), bowl, console; ice gr.............................. 60.00
Royalty (Imperial), fruit bowl w/stand, smoke 100.00
S-Repeat (Dugan), tumbler, amethyst....................................... 125.00

Sailboats (Fenton), wine, bl 80.00
Scales (Westmoreland), plate, bl opal, 9" 250.00
Scroll Embossed Variant (English), ashtray, amethyst, w/hdl, 5" ... 60.00
Shell & Balls, bottle, scent; marigold, 2½" 65.00
Singing Birds (Northwood), sugar bowl, gr 300.00
Ski Star (Dugan), banana bowl, peach opal 225.00
Smooth Rays (Imperial), champagne, smoke 40.00
Smooth Rays (Westmoreland), bowl, bl opal, 6-9" 125.00
Sowerby Drape, vase, blk amethyst 225.00
Spicer Beehive (Spicer Studios), honey pot w/plate, amber......... 110.00
Spider, hatpin, marigold 250.00
Star & File (Imperial), cordial, clambroth 50.00
Star Medallion (Imperial), cup, custard; marigold 20.00
Starbright, vase, bl, 6½" 50.00
Stippled Diamond Swag (English), compote, gr 65.00
Stippled Rays (Fenton), bowl, amethyst, sq, ruffled rim, 8".......... 55.00
Stork & Rushes (Dugan), hat, bl 30.00
Stretch, punch bowl w/base, red...3,500.00
Sungold, epergne, amber.. 450.00
Swirl (Northwood), tumbler, gr.. 125.00
Swirl Variant (Imperial), cake plate, clear 85.00
Thistle & Thorn (English), nut bowl, marigold.......................... 75.00
Threaded Six Panel, bud vase, marigold, 7¾" 75.00
Tiger Lily (Imperial), tumbler, amethyst 145.00
Tobacco Leaf (US Glass), champagne, clear.............................. 100.00
Tree of Life, basket, marigold, hdl 25.00
Triple Alliance (Brockwitz), biscuit jar, bl 350.00
Two Forty Nine, candleholders, red, pr 700.00
Unpinched Rib, vase, marigold 85.00
US #310 (US Glass), cheese set, ice gr 90.00
Valentine, ring tray, marigold 80.00
Vining Twigs (Dugan), hat, wht 65.00
Vintage (Imperial), tray, smoke, center hdl.............................. 60.00
Voltec (McKee), butter dish, amethyst 150.00
Waffle Block (Imperial), nappy, marigold 40.00
Waffle Block & Hobstar (Imperial), basket, smoke 265.00
Water Lily & Cattails (Fenton), bonbon, bl 90.00
Whirling Star (Imperial), punch cup, marigold 10.00
Wide Panel (Imperial), bowl, marigold milk glass, 7-10"............ 125.00
Wildflower (Northwood), compote, gr, plain interior.................. 300.00

Wild Rose (Northwood), syrup pitcher, marigold, $600.00. (Photo courtesy Bill Edwards and Mike Carwile)

Windmill (Imperial), pickle dish, clambroth 75.00
Wine & Roses (Fenton), wine, aqua 145.00
Woodpecker (Dugan), wall vase, vaseline.................................. 120.00
Wreathed Cherry (Dugan), tumbler, wht 100.00
Zig Zag, hatpin, amber 125.00
Zig Zag (Fenton), tumbler, bl, decorated.................................. 80.00
Zip Zip (English), flower frog, marigold.................................... 60.00
Zipper Loop (Imperial), lamp, smoke, sm, rare, 7"................... 800.00
Zipper Variant, sugar bowl, lav, w/lid 50.00
Zippered Heart (Imperial), bowl, marigold, 9" 85.00

Carousel Figures

For generations of Americans, visions of carousel horses revolving majestically around lively band organs rekindle wonderful childhood experiences. These memories are the legacy of the creative talent from a dozen carving shops that created America's carousel art. Skilled craftsmen brought their trade from Europe and American carvers took the carousel animal from a folk art creation to a true art form. The golden age of carousel art lasted from 1880 to 1929.

There are two basic types of American carousels. The largest and most impressive is the 'park style' carousel built for permanent installation in major amusement centers. These were created in Philadelphia by Gustav and William Dentzel, Muller Brothers, and E. Joy Morris who became the Philadelphia Toboggan Company in 1902. A more flamboyant group of carousel animals was carved in Coney Island, New York, by Charles Looff, Marcus Illions, Charles Carmel, and Stein & Goldstein's Artistic Carousel Company. These park-style carousels were typically three, four, and even five rows with 45 to 68 animals on a platform. Collectors often pay a premium for the carvings by these men. The outside row animals are larger and more ornate and command higher prices. The horses on the inside rows are smaller, less decorated, and of lesser value.

The most popular style of carousel art is the 'country fair style.' These carousels were portable affairs created for mobility. The horses are smaller and less ornate with leg and head positions that allow for stacking and easy loading. These were built primarily for North Tonawanda, New York, near Niagara Falls, by Armitage Herschell Company, Herschell Spillman Company, Spillman Engineering Company, and Allen Herschell. Charles W. Parker was also well known for his portable merry-go-rounds. He was based in Leavenworth, Kansas. Parker and Herschell Spillman both created a few large park-style carousels as well, but they are better known for their portable models.

Horses are by far the most common figure found, but there are two dozen other animals that were created for the carousel platform. Carousel animals, unlike most other antiques, are oftentimes worth more in a restored condition. Figures found with original factory paint are extraordinarily rare and bring premium amounts. Typically, carousel horses are found in garish, poorly applied 'park paint' and are often missing legs or ears. Carousel horses are hollow. They were glued up from several blocks for greater strength and lighter weight. Bass and poplar woods were used extensively.

If you have an antique carousel animal you would like to have identified, send a clear photograph and description along with a LSASE to our advisor, William Manns, who is listed in the Directory under New Mexico. Mr. Manns is the author of *Painted Ponies*, containing many full-color photographs, guides, charts, and directories for the collector.

Key:
IR — inside row   OR — outside row
MR — middle row   PTC — Philadelphia Toboggan Company

Coney Island-Style Horses

Carmel, IR jumper, unrstr	4,500.00
Carmel, MR jumper, unrstr	7,300.00
Carmel, OR jumper w/cherub, rstr	16,000.00
Illions, IR jumper, rstr	4,500.00
Illions, MR stander, rstr	7,800.00
Looff, IR jumper unrstr	4,500.00
Looff, OR jumper, unrstr	14,000.00
Stein & Goldstein, IR jumper, unrstr	4,700.00
Stein & Goldstein, MR jumper, rstr	8,000.00
Stein & Goldstein, OR stander w/bells, unrstr	20,000.00

European Horses

Anderson, English, unrstr	3,500.00
Bayol, French, unrstr	2,500.00
Heyn, German, unrstr	3,200.00
Hubner, Belgian, unrstr	2,000.00
Savage, English, unrstr	2,500.00

Menagerie Animals (Non-Horses)

Charles W. Parker, cat with American flag, jumper, repaired, repainted, missing pole and base, 24x62", $1,600.00. (Photo courtesy Skinner Inc. Auctioneers & Appraisers of Fine Art)

Dentzel, bear, unrstr	20,000.00
Dentzel, cat, unrstr	22,000.00
Dentzel, deer, unrstr	16,000.00
Dentzel, lion, unrstr	30,000.00
Dentzel, pig, unrstr	9,500.00
E Joy Morris, deer, unrstr	10,000.00
Herschell Spillman, cat, unrstr	11,000.00
Herschell Spillman, chicken, portable, unrstr	5,500.00
Herschell Spillman, dog, portable, unrstr	6,500.00
Herschell Spillman, frog, unrstr	18,000.00
Looff, camel, unrstr	9,000.00
Looff, goat, rstr	13,500.00
Muller, tiger, rstr	32,000.00

Philadelphia-Style Horses

Dentzel, IR 'topknot' jumper, unrstr	5,500.00
Dentzel, MR jumper, unrstr	7,800.00
Dentzel, OR stander, female cvg on shoulder, rstr	20,000.00
Dentzel, prancer, rstr	8,000.00
Morris, IR prancer, rstr	4,500.00
Morris, MR stander, unrstr	7,000.00
Morris, OR stander, rstr	17,000.00
Muller, IR jumper, rstr	5,000.00
Muller, MR jumper, rstr	7,500.00
Muller, OR stander, rstr	23,000.00
Muller, OR stander w/military trappings	27,000.00
PTC, chariot (bench-like seat), rstr	7,500.00
PTC, IR jumper, rstr	4,000.00
PTC, MR jumper, rstr	8,500.00
PTC, OR stander, armored, rstr	25,000.00
PTC, OR stander, unrstr	17,000.00

Portable Carousel Horses

Allan Herschell, all aluminum, ca 1950	500.00
Allan Herschell, half & half, wood & aluminum head	1,100.00
Allan Herschell, IR Indian pony, unrstr	2,000.00
Allan Herschell, OR, rstr	3,200.00
Allan Herschell, OR Trojan-style jumper, rstr	3,500.00

Armitage Herschell, track-machine jumper.............................2,800.00
Dare, jumper, unrstr..3,000.00
Herschell Spillman, chariot (bench-like seat) 3,800.00
Herschell Spillman, IR jumper, unrstr.....................................2,400.00
Herschell Spillman, MR jumper, unrstr 2,900.00
Herschell Spillman, OR, eagle decor..4,300.00
Herschell Spillman, OR, park machine 7,500.00

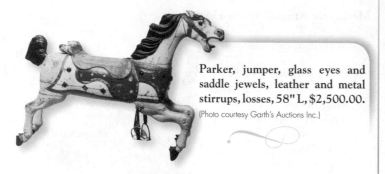

Parker, jumper, glass eyes and saddle jewels, leather and metal stirrups, losses, 58"L, $2,500.00.

(Photo courtesy Garth's Auctions Inc.)

Parker, MR jumper, unrstr 4,200.00
Parker, OR jumper, park machine, unrstr.................................6,500.00
Parker, OR jumper, rstr..5,800.00

Cartoon Art

Collectors of cartoon art are interested in many forms of original art — animation cels, sports, political or editorial cartoons, syndicated comic strip panels, and caricature. To produce even a short animated cartoon strip, hundreds of original drawings are required, each showing the characters in slightly advancing positions. Called 'cels' because those made prior to the 1950s were made from a celluloid material, collectors often pay hundreds of dollars for a frame from a favorite movie. Prices of Disney cels with backgrounds vary widely. Background paintings, model sheets, storyboards, and preliminary sketches are also collectible — so are comic book drawings executed in India ink and signed by the artist. Daily 'funnies' originals, especially the earlier ones portraying super heroes, and Sunday comic strips, the early as well as the later ones, are collected. Cartoon art has become recognized and valued as a novel yet valid form of contemporary art. In the listings below all cels are untrimmed and full size unless noted otherwise.

Cartoon, War Gardens, watercolor, 6 scenes, S Slippers, 14x22"+fr ..215.00
Cartoon page, Snoopy, printed, sgn C Schulz, 7x4"+mat & fr 275.00
Cel, Briar Rose, full bkground, Disney, 6½x10" 1,900.00
Cel, elephant baby (unidentified), Disney, 11x14"+mat & fr.......150.00
Cel, Flower the skunk, Courvoisier ground, Disney, 1937, 7x7⅞". 900.00
Cel, Grumpy (Snow White & 7 Dwarfs), WDE, c 1937, 5½x5¼"+fr.. 3,450.00
Cel, Ludwig Von Drake w/letter, full bkground, Disney, 8x10" 900.00
Cel, Malificent & Diablo w/bkground, Disney, 5½x8"...............3,000.00
Cel, Michelangelo Teenage Mutant Ninja Turtle w/bkground, 1980s, 8x10" .35.00
Cel, Mr Magoo dressed as monk, United Films, 10x12"+mat & fr..185.00
Cel, Pinocchio & Figaro, Courvoisier ground, Disney, 5½x6½" .1,800.00
Cel, Roger & Anita (101 Dalmatians), full bkground, Disney, 8x7" ...725.00
Cel, Smurf w/musical instrument, 10¼x12¼" 180.00
Cel, Super Chicken & Fred in desert, Jay Ward, 9x7" 515.00
Cel, Tramp (dog) walking, Disney, 5x4" 800.00
Concept art, Donald w/paintbrush, Darren Hunt, Disney, 7x8".....60.00
Concept art, Great Mouse Detective int, mc, Disney/Peraza, 11x14". 1,450.00
Concept art, Hamm's Bear scene, 6x8", from $400 to 600.00
Concept art, Minnie Mouse, Alex Maher, Disney, 6x8".................65.00
Drawing, Breakers Ahead, boat scene, pen/ink, T Brown, 1940, 9x17" . 48.00
Drawing, Centaurette, waist up, Disney, 7x2" image, 10x12".......275.00

Drawing, Chernabog in Night on Bald Mountain, Disney, black pencil, 1940, 9x11", $600.00. (Photo courtesy Morphy Auctions)

Drawing, Country Mouse, pencil, unsgn, 6x6"..............................195.00
Drawing, Katzenjammer Kids & Captain, color, Dirks, 1930, 6x8".300.00
Drawing, Kotik (seal) from White Seal, Chuck Jones, 1975, 8½x11"..55.00
Drawing, lady w/sign, charcoal/pencil, W Darrow Jr/New Yorker, 14x10"...215.00
Drawing, Mama Bear, bl pencil, Engel, Disney, 1940s, 9½x7½" ... 360.00
Drawing, Minnie mouse w/hat, full figure, 2x3" image, stain 275.00
Drawing, Red Riding Hood as nightclub singer, Blair, 1943, 8x4"...215.00
Drawing, Uncle Sam/Mateo Cagasta play chess, pen/ink, Corey, 1898..120.00
Model sheet, Sneezy & Bashful in varied poses, Disney, 10½x12½".1,000.00
Sericel, Aladdin characters hugged by Genie, Disney, 7½x10½" . 300.00
Sericel, Betty Boop on Parade, R Fleischer, 1991, 11½x8½"+fr ... 120.00
Sericel, Gift for Olive Oyl, Popeye & Olive, 1999, 16½x13½" 85.00
Sericel, Lion King's Simba & Nala as cubs, Disney, 5½x9" 180.00
Sericel, Mr Duck Steps Out, Donald & Daisy, Disney.................400.00

Story-drawing cel, Donald Duck, 1940, 6x8", VG+, $250.00.

(Photo courtesy Morphy Auctions)

Sunday page, Hagar the Horrible, D Browne, 1977, 11½x16"......600.00
Sunday page, Joe Palooka, Ham Fisher, 1930s, 18x24" 250.00
Sunday page, Mandrake the Magician, Falk & Davis, 1952, full pg.1,080.00

Cast Iron

In the mid-1800s, the cast-iron industry was raging in the United States. It was recognized as a medium extremely adaptable for uses ranging from ornamental architectural filigree to actual building construction. It could be cast from a mold into any conceivable design that could be reproduced over and over at a relatively small cost. It could be painted to give an entirely versatile appearance. Furniture with openwork designs of grapevines and leaves and intricate lacy scrollwork was cast for gardens as well as inside use. Figural doorstops of every sort, bootjacks, trivets, and a host of other useful and decorative items were made before the 'ferromania' had run its course. For more information, we recommend *Antique Iron*, by Kathryn McNerney (Collector Books). See also Kitchen, Cast-Iron Bakers and Kettles; and other specific categories. Values in the listings that follow are for items in excellent original condition unless noted otherwise.

Bench, serpentine crest rail forms dbl bk, pierced supports, 30x40" ...975.00
Bracket, grapevines, late 19th C, 20x33½" 230.00
Figure, lion, After A Canova, old ochre pnt, 1850s, 19x39x16", pr.9,695.00
Finials, pineapple forms, 18½x12", 4 for 880.00
Finials, pineapple in urn w/petal rim, pnt traces, 22", pr 400.00

Garden gate, archet top w/acanthus crest, rocaille elements, 48x47"..1,000.00
Kettle, sugar; wide lip, pitting, 19th C, 57" dia............................3,175.00
Kettle, sugar; wide lip, pitting, 28" dia 1,175.00
Lawn jockey, red & bl jacket, wht pants, blk boots, 46" 1,450.00
Lawn sprinkler, alligator facing upward, sprinkler head in mouth, 10" ...145.00
Lawn sprinkler, arrow on base, WD Allen Chicago emb on feathers, 11".690.00
Lawn sprinkler, frog facing upward, sprinkler head in mouth, 4" .200.00
Lawn sprinkler, mallard duck w/sprinkler atop head, mc rpt, 13".975.00
Lawn sprinkler, mermaid on rnd fluted base holding sprinker head, 14".1,090.00
Lawn sprinkler, turtle w/sprinkler head in mouth, blk & red, 9" L ...800.00
Paperweight, chicken, Whitmoyer Feed Myerstown on base, 2x2½", NM.450.00
Paperweight, quail pr, grassy base, Fred Everett/Hubley, 2½x2" ...345.00
Settee, grape clusters, set-in grill seat, wht pnt, 33x44", pr 345.00
Settee, Urn of Blossoms pattern, C&S Scrolls, old wht pnt, 42x46"..3,525.00
Settee & 2 armchairs, scrolled fern bks, openwork seats, old pnt, 3-pc. 1,250.00
Urn, campagna form on ped, scrolled foliage, 31x22½", pr 1,800.00
Urn, weathered gr pnt, 19th C, 6⅜x7⅛" 175.00

Castor Sets

Castor sets became popular during the early years of the eighteenth century and continued to be used through the late Victorian era. Their purpose was to hold various condiments for table use. The most common type was a circular arrangement with a center handle on a revolving pedestal base that held three, four, five, or six bottles. A few were equipped with a bell for calling the servant. Frames were made of silverplate, glass, or pewter. Though most bottles were of pressed glass, some of the designs were cut, and on rare occasion, colored glass with enameled decorations was used as well. To maintain authenticity and value, castor sets should have matching bottles. Prices listed below are for those with matching bottles and in frames with plating that is in excellent condition (unless noted otherwise). Note: Watch for new frames and bottles in clear, cranberry, cobalt, and vaseline Inverted Thumbprint as well as reproductions of Czechoslovakian cut glass bottles. These have recently been appearing on the market. Our advisor for this category is Barbara Aaronson; she is listed in the Directory under California.

1-bottle+pr shakers+jar; Wilcox compote-shaped ftd fr, 15x7", EX ...275.00
2-bottle, dmn-cut cruets; angel w/torch & dog cutouts in silver fr, 7" ...220.00
2-bottle+pr shakers, etched; simple Meriden fr.............................375.00
3-bottle, Am Shield; pewter fr w/eagle, mini, child sz 165.00
3-bottle, Daisy & Button; SP fr w/toothpick holder finial............275.00
3-bottle, paneled cylinder, mk fr w/loop hdl & triangle base........100.00
4-bottle, Bellflower, single vine; pewter fr.....................................400.00

4-bottle, English silver stand marked P&A Bateman, 1796, 9½x7¾", $1,500.00. (Photo courtesy James D. Julia Inc.)

4-bottle, King's Crown ruby stain, Adams; matching glass fr, NM ..575.00
4-bottle, Log & Star, amber; orig ped-base fr 145.00
4-bottle, milk glass w/HP insects; 8" dia glass stand w/metal hdl, NM..125.00
4-bottle, navette-shaped rtcl stand w/center loop hdl, 9½x7¾" ...700.00

5-bottle, Bristol glass, floral on pk; cherub SP fr, 15x5" 975.00
5-bottle, etched amberina, cut amberina stoppers; gilt fr...........2,200.00
5-bottle, etched floral w/cutting, much decor; Meriden ft 450.00
5-bottle, pressed glass; rstr Meriden fr w/cherub hdl revolves.......525.00
6-bottle, amber w/etched trees/deer; Rogers fr #116 (VG plating) ...636.00
6-bottle, etched; NP fr w/bell, ftd, 17" 175.00
6-bottle, pressed; 18" Simpson-Hall-Miller fr 550.00
7-bottle, cut crystal, w/stoppers; lg ped-ft Gleason fr w/doors....2,500.00
7-bottle, cut crystal; gadrooned/shell-border Geo III SP fr 495.00
8-bottle, cut crystal w/silver mts; cut/pierced Geo III silver fr...1,100.00

Catalina Island

Catalina Island pottery was made on the island of the same name, which is about 26 miles off the coast of Los Angeles. The pottery was started in 1927 at Pebble Beach, by Wm. Wrigley, Jr., who was instrumental in developing and using the native clays. Its principal products were brick and tile to be used for construction on the island. Garden pieces were first produced, then vases, bookends, lamps, ashtrays, novelty items, and finally dinnerware. The ware became very popular and was soon being shipped to the mainland as well.

Some of the pottery was hand thrown; some was made in molds. Most pieces are marked Catalina Island or Catalina with a printed incised stamp or handwritten with a pointed tool. Cast items were sometimes marked in the mold, a few have an ink stamp, and a paper label was also used. The most favored colors in tableware and accessories are 1) black (rare), 2) Seafoam and Monterey Brown (uncommon), 3) matt blue and green , 4) Toyon Red (orange), 5) other brights, and 6) pastels with a matt finish.

The color of the clay can help to identify approximately when a piece was made: 1927 to 1932, brown to red (Island) clay (very popular with collectors, tends to increase values); 1931 to 1932, an experimental period with various colors; 1932 to 1937, mainly white clay, though tan to brown clays were also used on occasion.

Items marked Catalina Pottery are listed in Gladding McBean. For further information we recommend *Catalina Island Pottery Collectors Guide* by Steven and Aisha Hoefs, and *Collector's Encyclopedia of California Pottery, Second Edition*, and *California Pottery Scrapbook*, both by Jack Chipman (Collector Books). Our advisor for this category is Steven Hoefs; he is listed in the Directory under Georgia.

Vase, Toyon Red, 6x8", $500.00. (Photo courtesy Brunk Auctions/ LiveAuctioneers.com)

Ashtray, cowboy hat form, yel 275.00
Bowl, serving; oval...125.00
Candlesticks, wht matt, 3½", pr 145.00
Casserole, w/lid, lg 275.00
Cup, demitasse; 2⅝" 35.00
Cup & saucer, gr matt, red clay cup, wht clay saucer, 2½x3¾" 45.00
Figurine, cat, bl, 4½"...600.00
Flower frog, bl, red clay, stepped, 1930, 2¼x5½" 52.00
Mug, matt gr over brn, flared ft, 5⅛x4" 35.00
Novelty hat, cowboy, wht, 6¼" dia...205.00
Pitcher, beverage; Mandarin Manchu Yellow, 7½" 375.00

Plate, chop; gr, 18" 160.00
Plate, dinner; Toyon Red, 9¼" 35.00
Plate, orange matt, 11" 45.00
Plate, Undersea Garden, mc scene w/bl border, 12½" 780.00
Tumbler, wht clay, 4" 50.00
Vase, bl, bulbous w/slim neck, #614, 6" 50.00
Vase, gourd shape w/hdls, 9" 425.00
Vase, Toyon Red over gr, flared rim, ftd, 8" 220.00
Wall pocket, basketweave, 9½" 525.00

Catalogs

Catalogs are not only intriguing to collect on their own merit, but for the collector with a specific interest, they are often the only remaining source of background information available, and as such they offer a wealth of otherwise unrecorded data. The mail-order industry can be traced as far back as the mid-1800s. Even before Aaron Montgomery Ward began his career in 1872, Laacke and Joys of Wisconsin and the Orvis Company of Vermont, both dealers in sporting goods, had been well established for many years. The E.C. Allen Company sold household necessities and novelties by mail on a broad scale in the 1870s. By the end of the Civil War, sewing machines, garden seed, musical instruments, even medicine, were available from catalogs. In the 1880s Macy's of New York issued a 127-page catalog; Sears and Spiegel followed suit in about 1890. Craft and art supply catalogs were first available about 1880 and covered such varied fields as china painting, stenciling, wood burning, brass embossing, hair weaving, and shellcraft. Today some collectors confine their interests not only to craft catalogs in general but often to just one subject. There are several factors besides rarity which make a catalog valuable: age, condition, profuse illustrations, how collectible the field is that it deals with, the amount of color used in its printing, its size (format and number of pages), and whether it is a manufacturer's catalog verses a jobber's catalog (the former being the most desirable).

Abbott's Magic Novelty Co Catalogue No 2, 64 pgs, EX 90.00
American Flyer Trains Erector & Other Gilbert Toys, 1953, EX+ . 22.00
Atwater Kent Radio, 1928, 30 pgs, 9x6", EX 35.00
Bennett Bros 1956 Blue Book of Quality Merchandise, hardbound, VG .. 95.00
Billy & Ruth Go A-Christmas Shopping! big-name toys, 1931, 16 pgs, EX. 105.00

Bristol Steel Fishing Rods, Horton Mfg. Co., Bristol, Conn., 1915, 32 pages, rare, EX, $550.00. (Photo courtesy Lang's Sporting Collectables)

Britains Ltd, lead toy soldiers, 1954, 125+ pgs, VG 75.00
Caterpillar Line Condensed Catalog, 1936, 43 pgs, EX 80.00
Charles Williams Stores, New York Styles, Fall/Winter 1917, 515 pgs, G. 15.00
Coleman Happier Vacations, camping equipment, 1965, EX 12.00
Crest Wedding Cake Ornaments, blk & wht illus, 1920s, 24+ pgs, VG... 70.00
Delta Quality Tools, Motor Driven, w/price list, 1935, 47 pgs, EX. 22.00
Dinky Toys, 1950s, 20 pgs, 6", EX 50.00
Dress Goods Silks & General Yard Goods, Spring/Summer 1916, 66 pgs, VG.. 175.00
Epiphone Recording Banjos, 1928, 22 pgs, EX 15.00
Estes Model Rocketry Catalog, 1975, w/Star Trek models, EX....... 15.00
Ethan Allen Treasury of American Traditional Interiors, 1971, EX. 15.00

Evinrude Outboard Motors, 1941, w/price list, EX 40.00
Fairmount Tools, 1940s, 25 pgs, EX....................................... 60.00
Firestone Extra Value Merchandise, car parts/toys.., 1947, 96 pgs, VG..15.00
Geo Master Garment Corp Catalog No 287, work clothes, 50+ pgs, EX.. 100.00
Gimbels Schuster, Christmas 1966, general, 91 pgs, EX 18.00
Guitars for Moderns by Gretsch, 1955, 16 pgs, EX 150.00
Harley-Davidson Accessories, 1940, 32 pgs, EX 65.00
Hawkes & Son Cornets, 20 pgs, G 110.00
His Master's Voice 1957-1958 Recording Entertainment, 704 pgs, VG . 20.00
Hobbies for Family Fun, 1960, 24 pgs, EX.............................. 15.00
International Harvester 1958 Farmer's Catalogue, 48 pgs, EX 55.00
JA Holland Bicycles, 1925, 5½x8½", G 75.00
JC Penney, Spring/Summer or Fall/Winter 1985, both EX, ea 35.00
John Deere Model 'T' General Purpose Tractor, 1940, 32 pgs, EX. 95.00
Lane Bryant Tall Girls Summer Fashion Sale, 1958, VG 100.00
Lionel, 1957, New 'O' Super Track, VG 25.00
Lone Star Carefreedom Line for '59, 32 pgs of boats, EX............ 45.00
Louie Miller Wholesale Millinery Jobber, 1951, VG 80.00
Lugwig Quality Percussion (Ludwig 64), 72 full-color pgs, rare, VG.. 80.00
Magnavox Annual Sale, Save Up to $100, radios, etc, 1960s, 23 pgs, EX. 18.00
Marshall Field & Co Chicago Holiday Goods No 203, 1912, 288 pgs, VG .105.00
Martin Guitar Catalogue, 1960s, 24 pgs, EX............................ 15.00
Mobile Life, mobile homes, 1955, 125 pgs, 11x8½", VG.............. 21.00
Montgomery Ward Spring & Summer 1938, general, 832 pgs, VG .30.00
Montgomery Ward Summer, 1942, 151 pgs, EX 60.00
Napa Tractor Parts, 1943, 256 pgs, EX 15.00
Neiman Marcus, Christmas 1966, VG 12.00
Proto Tools/Plomb Tool Co, No 5023, 1950, 64 pgs, VG 21.00
Radolek 1931 Catalog of Radio & Electrical Bargains, 98 pgs, VG .12.00
Randall Made Knives, 1950s, 20 pgs, EX 150.00
Rogers Drums w/Memriloc Hardware '76/'77, 8 pgs, EX............. 35.00
Rumely Cream Separaters Instructions for Size 14, 33 pgs, G 160.00
S&H Green Stamp Idea Book, 1960-61, 98 pgs, EX.................... 25.00
Samuel Kirk & Son Sterling Silver, 1940, 48 pgs, 6½x9", VG 20.00
Schlage Locks, 1936, binder cover, EX.................................. 105.00
Schwinn Hornet...(The Popular), various bike photos, 1940s-50s, EX... 50.00
Sears Christmas Book, 1952, VG 285.00
Sears Christmas Book, 1954, 437 pgs, VG 130.00
Sears Roebuck & Co Chicago Catalog No 122, 1911, 1,265 pgs, VG ..7.50
Sheaffer's Writing Instruments Featuring the Snorkel, 1950s, EX.. 80.00
Snap-On Blue Point/Snap-On Tools Inc, 1935, 96 pgs, VG 140.00
Spiegel Nation's Yardstick of Value, Spring/Summer 1941, 592 pgs, VG. 30.00
Spiegel The Golden Christmas Book, 1959, 403 pgs, EX.............. 55.00
Stanley Tools No 34, July 1, 1927, 192 pgs, w/Sweetheart logo, EX..38.00
Storrs & Harrison Co (Seed Catalog), Spring 1899, 168 pgs, VG ..145.00
Swimaster New for 1960, 8 pgs, VG....................................... 75.00
Topper Toys, ...Here Comes Johnny Express, insert booklet, 1965, EX..20.00
Vogue Pattern Catalog, 1959, EX 18.00
Wagner Fans, 1937, 18 pgs, G+ 35.00
Walter Field Co, Summer, 1953, general, 58 pgs, G 15.00
Yankee & Yankee Handyman Tools, 1942, 51 pgs, G 12.00
York Gas Engine, For Sale by Flinchbaugh Mfg Co York PA, VG...175.00

Caughley Ware

The Caughley Coalport Porcelain Manufactory operated from about 1775 until 1799 in Caughley, near Salop, Shropshire, in England. The owner was Thomas Turner, who gained his potting experience from his association with the Worcester Pottery Company. The wares he manufactured in Caughley are referred to as 'Salopian.' He is most famous for his blue-printed earthenwares, particularly the Blue Willow pattern, designed for him by Thomas Minton. For a more detailed history, see Coalport.

Jug, floral w/emb cabbage leaves, mask spout, ca 1785, 8½" 500.00
Mug, Chinese scenic vignettes, 7"... 800.00
Strainer, fisherman, S mk, ca 1780, 3"... 375.00
Sugar bowl, Willow w/gold, acorn finial, late 18th C 100.00
Tea bowl & saucer, birds on branches, 18th C............................ 175.00
Tea canister, fence pattern, bbl form, 18th C, rpl wooden lid, 4½" .180.00
Teapot, wht w/gold band, ear hdl on reeded bbl form, 1785, 6⅜", NM. 265.00

Cauldon

Formerly Brown-Westhead, Moore & Co., Cauldon Ltd. was a Staffordshire pottery that operated under that name from 1905 until 1920, producing dinnerware that was most often transfer decorated. They company operated under the title Cauldon Potteries Ltd. from 1920 until 1962.

Pitcher, milk; Candia, bl on wht w/gold, 5¾" 60.00
Plate, lady w/fan, Maurice, bl & gold rim, blk mk, 10⅛" 190.00
Plates, cobalt & gold rim, wht center, Ovington Bros, 10½", 12 for... 360.00
Plates, Fern, bl on wht, scalloped, 9¾", 10 for 275.00
Plates, morning glories on wht w/gold, scalloped, 8¾", 12 for 240.00
Platter, Sylvan, bl on wht, 17¾x14½", NM 50.00

Platter, turkey, blue transfer, 20" long, $650.00. (Photo courtesy Cowan's Auctions Inc./ LiveAuctioneers.com)

Platter, turkey scene, bl on wht, rectangular, 22x18½" 725.00
Tureen, flowers & butterflies, w/lid, sm, w/underplate 60.00
Vase, Cairo Ware, flowering foliage, baluster, Royal Couldon, 14"..150.00

Celluloid

In 1869 John Wesley Hyatt invented plastic in an attempt to devise a material that could be used to replicate the look of ivory. Eventually it became a substitute not only for ivory (which was protected by game preservation laws), but for tortoiseshell as well, epecially in the manufacture of combs. Many others filed patents to improve, decorate, and widen its uses. Today, the term celluloid is used to encompass all types of early plastic.

Lithographed works of famous artists were often added to the lids of celluloid boxes and the covers of photograph albums; other items had embossed patterns. (In the listings that follow, assume the decoration is lithographed unless noted 'in relief' or 'cvd'.)

Collectors should be critical of condition; avoid items that are cracked and peeling.

Box, Collars & Cuffs/flowers on cream, ftd, 6½x7½x7½" 90.00
Comb, cvd fleur-de-lis & filigree, amber, Continental, 11½x7"...... 35.00
Comb, fan shape, rhinestone studs on blk, 7" 40.00
Letter opener, cvd floral hdl, minor wear to blade, 11"................... 24.00
Painting, lady in finery, in cvd wood fr, 7½x5½" 195.00
Photo album (9x12") & box (13" L) set, Native Am in full headdress...2,300.00
Photo album cover, Native Am portrait, working clasp, 16x7½", VG..625.00

Vanity set, gr marbleized, mirror+2 boxes+brush............................ 40.00
Vanity set, tan marbleized, 9-pc in orig case, 3x11x10"................... 42.50
Vanity set, yel marbleized, mirror+2 boxes+buffer+shoehorn+file+hook.. 75.00

Ceramic Art Company

Johnathan Coxon, Sr., and Walter Scott Lenox established the Ceramic Art Company in 1889 in Trenton, New Jersey, where they introduced fine belleek porcelain. Both were experienced in its production, having previously worked for Ott and Brewer. They hired artists to hand paint their wares with portraits, scenes, and lovely florals. Today artist-signed examples bring the highest prices. Several marks were used, three of which contain the 'CAC' monogram. A green wreath surrounding the company name in full was used on special-order wares, but these are not often encountered. Coxon eventually left the company, and it was later reorganized under the Lenox name. Lenox beleek items are included in this listing. Our advisor for this category is Mary Frank Gaston; she is listed in the Directory under Texas.

Demitasse pot, couple reserve w/gold & turq trim, CAC mk, 8½" ..165.00
Mug, drunken taverners w/pk lustre, sgn EMS '04, 4½"............... 120.00
Mustache cup, floral w/gold, CAC palette mk, 1900s, 4" 180.00
Mustache mug, roses w/gold, 4x4½x3½" 180.00
Pitcher, grape clusters/vines w/gold, slender, 14½" 390.00
Pitcher, grapes & vines w/gold, cylindrical, CAC mk, 14½" 390.00
Pitcher, monk drinking/grapes, earth tones, gr CAC mk, 1901, 14½"..240.00
Vase, blueberries/autumn foliage, sgn AFS, Lenox, 1916, 9½" 165.00
Vase, bluebirds on stump, cylindrical, 16".................................... 250.00
Vase, chrysanthemums, gold rim, WH Morley, bulbous, 12x8½" ... 1,200.00
Vase, lg roses w/multi-tone gr leaves, uptrn hdls, 13" 540.00
Vase, peacocks, mc on gold, Lenox, #402, drilled, 14⅝"............... 515.00

Vase, poppies with silver overlay marked Gorham, artist signed Eva Gordery, 14½", $1,800.00. (Photo courtesy Jackson's International Auctioneers & Appraisers of Fine Art & Antiques/ LiveAuctioneers.com)

Vase, Queen Louise reserve, shouldered, CAC mk, 1889-1906, 13", NM...240.00
Vase, semi-nude w/Aladdin's lamp, w/gold, amphora shape, CAC mk, 15"..1,250.00
Vase, vines & leaves, gold on wht, rtcl neck & hdls, CAC mk, 9¼"..425.00
Vase, wht gloss w/cherub hdls, Lenox, 12" 240.00

Ceramic Arts Studio, Madison, Wisconsin

Although most figural ceramic firms of the 1940s and 1950s were located on the West Coast, one of the most popular had its base of operations in Madison, Wisconsin. Ceramic Arts Studio was founded in 1940 as a collaboration between entrepreneur Reuben Sand and potter Lawrence Rabbitt. Early ware consisted of hand-thrown pots by Rabbitt, but CAS came into its own with the 1941 arrival of Betty Harrington. A self-taught artist, Harrington served as the studio's principal designer until it closed in 1955. Her imagination and skill quickly brought Ceramic Arts Studio to the forefront of firms specializing in decorative ceramics. During its peak production period in the late 1940s, CAS turned out more than 500,000 figurines annually.

Harrington's themes were wide-ranging, from ethnic and theatrical subjects, to fantasy characters, animals, and even figural representations of such abstractions as fire and water. While the majority of the studio's designs were by Harrington, CAS also released a limited line of realistic and modernistic animal figures designed by 'Rebus' (Ulle Cohen). In addition to traditional figurines, the studio responded to market demand with such innovations as salt-and-pepper pairs, head vases, banks, bells, shelf sitters, and candleholders. Metal display shelves for CAS pieces were produced by Jon-San Creations, a nearby Reuben Sand operation. Most Jon-San designs were by Ceramic Art Studio's head decorator Zona Liberace, stepmother of the famed pianist.

Betty Harrington carved her own master molds, so the finished products are remarkably similar to her initial sketches. CAS figurines are prized for their vivid colors, characteristic high-gloss glaze, lifelike poses, detailed decoration, and skill of execution. Unlike many ceramics of the period, CAS pieces today show little evidence of crazing.

Most Ceramic Arts Studio pieces are marked, although in pairs only one piece may have a marking. While there are variants, including early paper stickers, one common base stamp reads 'Ceramic Arts Studio, Madison, Wis.' (The initials 'BH' which appear on many pieces do not indicate that the piece was personally decorated by Betty Harrington. This is simply a designer indicator.)

In the absence of a base stamp, a sure indicator of a CAS piece is the decorator 'color marking' found at the drain hole on the base. Each studio decorator had a separate color code for identification purposes, and almost any authentic CAS piece will display these tick marks.

Following the Madison Studio's closing in 1955, Reuben Sand briefly moved his base of operations to Japan. While perhaps a dozen master molds from Madison were also utilized in Japan, most of the Japanese designs were original ones and do not correlate to those produced in Madison. Additionally, about 20 master molds and copyrights were sold to Mahana Imports, which created its own CAS variations, and a number of molds and copyrights were sold to Coventry Ware for a line of home hobbyware. Pieces produced by these companies have their own individual stampings or labels. While these may incorporate the Ceramic Arts Studio name, the vastly different stylings and skill of execution are readily apparent to even the most casual observer, easily differentiating them from authentic Madison products. When the CAS building was demolished in 1959, all remaining molds were destroyed. Betty Harrington's artistic career continued after the studio's demise; and her later works, including a series of nudes and abstract figurals, are especially prized by collectors. Mrs. Harrington died in 1997. Her last assignment, the limited-edition *M'amselle* series was commissioned for the Ceramic Arts Studio Collectors Association Convention in 1996.

Our advisors for this category are BA Wellman (his address can be found under Massachusetts) and Donald-Brian Johnson (Nebraska). Both encourage collectors to email them with any new information concerning company history and/or production. Mr. Johnson, in association with Timothy J. Holthaus and James E. Petzold, is the co-author of *Ceramic Arts Studio: The Legacy of Betty Harrington* (Schiffer). See also Clubs, Newsletters, and Catalogs.

Bank, Drum Girl, 4½", from $220 to	250.00
Bank, Skunky, 4", from $260 to	280.00
Bank, Tony the Barber (blade bank), 4¾", from $75 to	100.00
Candleholders, Triad Girls, left & right, 7", center, 5", from $250 to.	340.00
Doll, Boy, rare, 12", from $1,200 to	1,400.00
Figurine, Adonis & Aphrodite, gr/gray, 9", 7", pr from $500 to ...	700.00
Figurine, Alice & March Hare (White Rabbit), 4½", 6", pr, $350 to.	450.00

Figurine, All Children's Orchestra, 5" boys/4½" girls, 5-pc, $700 to.	800.00
Figurine, Ancient Cat & Kitten, 4½", 2½", pr from $150 to	190.00
Figurine, Annie (baby elephant) and Benny, 3¼", 3¾", pr, $115 to.	160.00
Figurine, Bear Mother & Cub, realistic, 3¼", 2¼", pr, $320 to	380.00
Figurine, Bird of Paradise, A&B, 3", pr from $360 to	440.00
Figurine, Blythe & Pensive, 6½", 6", pr from $300 to	350.00

Figurine, Bride and Groom, 4¾", 5", pair from $250.00 to $300.00. (Photo by John Petzold from *Ceramic Arts Studio: The Legacy of Betty Harrington*, printed by Schiffer)

Figurine, Butch & Billy (boxer dogs), snugglers, 3", pr from $120 to .	160.00
Figurine, Chinese Girl w/umbrella, very rare, 5½", from $400 to.	500.00
Figurine, Colonial Boy & Girl, 5½", 5", pr from $200 to	250.00
Figurine, Dachshund, 3½" L, from $85 to	100.00
Figurine, Dawn, sandstone, 6½", from $175 to	200.00
Figurine, Donkey Mother & Young Donkey, 3¼", 3", pr from $320 to.	380.00
Figurine, Duck Mother & Duckling, 3¼", 2¼", pr from $80 to	125.00
Figurine, Fifi/Fufu poodle, stand/crouch, 3", 2½", pr, $180 to	240.00
Figurine, Frisky & Balky Colts, 3¾", pr from $200 to	250.00
Figurine, Giraffes, 5½", 4", pr from $150 to	200.00
Figurine, Gypsy Man & Woman, 6½", 7", pr from $80 to	100.00
Figurine, Hansel & Gretel (1-pc), 3", from $125 to	150.00
Figurine, Harem Trio, Sultan & 2 harem girls, from $320 to	395.00
Figurine, Isaac & Rebekah, 10", pr from $140 to	200.00
Figurine, King's Flutist & Lutist Jesters, 11½", 12", pr, $250 to	350.00
Figurine, Leopards A&B, fighting, 3½", 6¼" L, pr from $180 to .	250.00
Figurine, Lion & Lioness, 7¼", 5½" L, pr from $340 to	380.00
Figurine, Little Miss Muffet #1, 4½", from $50 to	75.00
Figurine, Love Trio, Lover Boy, Willing & Bashful girls, 3-pc, $300 to.	375.00
Figurine, Madonna w/Bible, 9½", from $235 to	350.00
Figurine, Mermaid Trio, 4" mother, 3" & 2½" babies, 3-pc, $475 to.	550.00
Figurine, Minnehaha & Hiawatha, 6½", 4½", pr from $480 to	540.00
Figurine, Modern Doe & Fawn, 3¾", 2", pr from $175 to	225.00
Figurine, Modern Fox, sandstone, 6½" L, from $120 to	150.00
Figurine, Mother Horse & Spring Colt, 4¼", 3½", pr from $425 to.	475.00
Figurine, Musical Trio, Accordion & Harmonica Boys/Banjo Girl, $420 to.	480.00
Figurine, Out Lady of Fatima, 9", from $260 to	285.00
Figurine, Peek-a-Boo Pixie, 2½", from $40 to	50.00
Figurine, Peter Pan & Wendy, 5¼", pr from $120 to	150.00
Figurine, Pied Piper Set, piper+running boy+praying girl, $380 to.	465.00
Figurine, Rhumba Man & Woman, 7¼", 7", pr from $80 to	120.00
Figurine, Saucy Squirrel w/Jacket, 2¼", from $175 to	200.00
Figurine, Seal Mother on Rock & Pup, 5", pr from $950 to	1,100.00
Figurine, Smi-Li & Mo-Pi, chubby man & woman, 6", pr from $60 to.	80.00
Figurine, St Agnes w/Lamb, 6", from $260 to	285.00

Figurine, Sultan and Harem Girls, from $320.00 to $395.00 for the set.

Figurine, Tembo Elephant & Tembino Baby, 6½", 2½", pr, $345 to ...**415.00**
Figurine, Thai & Thai Thai Siamese, snugglers, 4½"/5½" L, $70 to .. **90.00**
Figurine, Tom Cat standing, 5", from $75 to **95.00**
Figurine, tortoise w/wht hat crawling, 2½" L, from $150 to **175.00**
Figurine, Water Man & Woman, 11½", pr from $350 to **400.00**
Figurine, Wing-Sang & Lu-Tang, 6", pr from $90 to **110.00**
Figurine, Winter Willie, 4", from $90 to **120.00**
Figurine, Zulu Man & Woman #1, 5½", 7", pr from $1,100 to ..**1,400.00**
Head vase, Becky, 5¼", from $100 to **125.00**
Head vase, Manchu & Lotus, head vase plaques, 8½", pr from $400 to .**450.00**
Head vase, Mei-Ling, 5", from $150 to **175.00**

Head vases, Svea and Sven, from $350.00 to $400.00 for the pair. (Photo courtesy John Petzold from *Ceramic Arts Studio: The Legacy of Betty Harrington*, Schiffer Publishing)

Lamp, Fire Man (on base), very scarce, Moss Mfg, 19½", from $350 to..**375.00**
Miniature, Adam & Eve Autumn Pitcher, 3", from $40 to **50.00**
Miniature, Aladdin's Lamp Server, 2" L, from $65 to **85.00**
Miniature, Toby Mug, 3¼", from $75 to **95.00**
Mug, Barbershop Quartet (1949), 3½", from $650 to **750.00**
Pitcher, Lorelei on Shell, 6", from $250 to **300.00**
Pitcher, Pine Cone, mini, 3¾", from $65 to **85.00**
Plaque, Attitude & Arabesque, 9½", 9¼", pr from $70 to **100.00**
Plaque, Comedy & Tragedy masks, 5¼", pr from $180 to **220.00**
Plaque, Dutch Boy & Girl, 8½", 8", pr from $120 to **150.00**
Plaque, Goosey Gander, scarce, 4½", from $140 to **160.00**
Plaque, Greg & Grace, 9½", 9", pr from $50 to **70.00**
Plaque, Hamlet & Orphelia, 8", pr from $360 to **440.00**
Plaque, Jack Be Nimble, 5", from $400 to **450.00**
Shakers, Bear & Cub, snuggle, 4¼", 2¼", pr form $40 to **60.00**
Shakers, Blackamoors, 4¾", pr from $140 to **160.00**
Shakers, Calico Cat & Gingham Dog, 3", 2¾", pr from $90 to.... **100.00**
Shakers, Chihuahua & Doghouse, snugglers, 1½", 2" L, pr, $120 to .. **160.00**
Shakers, Children in chairs, boy & girl+2 chairs, from $240 to ...**320.00**
Shakers, Covered Wagon & Ox, 3" L, pr from $100 to **135.00**
Shakers, Fix Up on Tail, 4", pr from $40 to.................................... **70.00**
Shakers, Monkey Mother & Baby, snugglers, 4", 2½", pr, $40 to ... **60.00**
Shakers, Native Boy & Crocodile, 3", 4½" L, pr from $200 to.....**240.00**
Shakers, Paul Bunyan & Evergreen, 4½", 2½", pr from $200 to...**250.00**
Shakers, Sambo & Tiger, 3½", 5" L, from $500 to **575.00**
Shakers, Santa Claus & Evergreen, 2¼", 2½", pr from $325 to.....**375.00**
Shakers, Wee Scotch Boy & Girl, 3¼", 3", pr from $70 to **80.00**
Shelf sitter, Collie Mother, 5", from $75 to **100.00**
Shelf sitter, Little Jack Horner #1, from $50 to.............................. **75.00**
Shelf sitter, Maurice & Michelle, 7", pr from $130 t o **150.00**
Shelf sitter, Wally, ball up, 4½", from $220 to.............................. **250.00**
Shelf sitters, Canaries, sleeping/singing, 5", pr from $300 to........**350.00**
Shelf sitters, Cowboy & Cowgirl, 4½", pr from $250 to **300.00**
Shelf sitters, Dutch Boy & Girl, 4½", pr from $50 to..................... **70.00**
Shelf sitters, Young Love Couple (kissing boy & girl), 4½", $90 to..**100.00**
Snuggle pr, Thai & Thai Thai Siamese, 4½" L, 5½" L, pr, $70 to .. **90.00**
Teapot, appl swan, mini, 3", from $60 to.. **75.00**
Vase, Bamboo, 6", from $55 to **75.00**
Vase, Comedy/Tragedy, 4½", from $125 to **150.00**
Vase, Flying Duck, rnd, 2½", from $75 to....................................... **85.00**

Metal Accessories

Arched windows for religious figure, 6½", from $125 to **150.00**

Artist palette w/shelves, left & right, 12" W, pr from $200 to **250.00**
Circle bench w/crescent planter, 8¾" dia, from $200 to **245.00**
Corner spider web for Miss Muffet, flat bk, 4", from $175 to........**225.00**
Diamond shape, 15x13", from $45 to **55.00**
Garden shelf from Mary Contrary, 4x12", from $100 to **120.00**
Ladder for Jack, rare, 13", from $125 to..**150.00**
Musical score, flat bk, 14x12", from $85 to **100.00**
Parakeet cage, 13", from $125 to **150.00**
Rainbow arch w/shelf, blk, 13½x19", from $100 to **120.00**
Sofa for Maurice & Michelle, 7½" L, from $250 to **275.00**
Stairway to the Stars, 18½" from $100 to......................................**120.00**
Star for angel, flat bk, 9¾", from $65 to **75.00**
Triple ring, left or right, w/shelf, 15", from $110 to **130.00**

Chalkware

Chalkware was popular from 1860 until 1890. It was made from gypsum or plaster of Paris formed in a mold and then hand painted in oils or watercolors. Items such as animals and birds, figures, banks, toys, and religious ornaments modeled after more expensive Staffordshire wares were often sold door to door. Their origin is attributed to Italian immigrants. Today regarded as a form of folk art, nineteenth-century American pieces bring prices in the hundreds of dollars. Carnival chalkware from this century is also collectible, especially figures that are personality related. For those, see Carnival Collectibles.

Bouquet, mc pnt, rstr, late 19th C, 13¾" **150.00**
Carrier pigeon on rock, mc pnt, glass eyes, 13".............................**335.00**
Cat, recumbent w/tail curled around body, gray pnt, hollow, 7x15", VG.**100.00**
Cat seated on base, mc details, fine form, ca 1900, 6¼"............**3,800.00**
Dove on rock, mc pnt, ca 1900, 9½", VG **180.00**
Fruit garniture, mc pnt, wht plinth, 19th C, 13¾".....................**3,000.00**

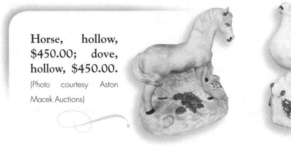

Horse, hollow, $450.00; dove, hollow, $450.00. (Photo courtesy Aston Macek Auctions)

Horse on rocky base, yel & blk pnt, hollow body, 10¼x8½".........**195.00**
Lamb reclining on book, mc pnt, detailed fleece, 19th C, 9x10½". **1,450.00**
Mother & Child, mc pnt, late 19th C, 16½", VG **515.00**
Owl, brn tones, inset eyes, 14", NM..**900.00**
Pug dog, free-standing, tan w/blk details, 7"..................................**300.00**
Rooster, bright mc, 19th C, 6¾", NM **2,275.00**
Spaniel seated, mc pnt, Staffordshire style, rprs, 8¾".....................**170.00**
Squirrel seated on base eating nut, mc pnt, 6½x4½x3", VG+ **550.00**

Champlevé

Champlevé, enameling on brass or other metal, differs from cloisonné in that the design is depressed or incised into the metal, rather than being built in with wire dividers as in the cloisonné procedure. The cells, or depressions, are filled in with color, and the piece is then fired.

Jardiniere, geometric band & reserves, 11x12½" **335.00**
Planter, floral bands w/foliage, shouldered, 9x12" **120.00**

Vase, Deco geometrics/florals, bulbous center, hdls, 12" 270.00
Vase, dragons, mc on gr, shouldered, bottle neck, 6", pr, NM 90.00
Vase, dragons on moon form, dragon hdls, 19th C, 13" 275.00
Vase, floral bands, shouldered, 10x6" 85.00
Vase, floral tendrils on turq, melon ribs, late 19th C, 14" 390.00

Chase Brass & Copper Company

Chase introduced this logo in 1928. The company was incorporated in 1876 as the Waterbury Manufacturing Company and was located in Waterbury, Connecticut. This location remained Chase's principal fabrication plant, and it was here that the 'Specialties' were made. In 1900 the company chose the name Chase Companies Inc., in honor of their founder, Augustus Sabin Chase. The name encompassed Chase's many factories. Only the New York City sales division was called Chase Brass and Copper Co., but from 1936 on, that name was used exclusively.

In 1930 the sales division invited people to visit their new Specialties Sales Showroom in New York City 'where an interesting assortment of decorative and utilitarian pieces in brass and copper in a variety of designs and treatments are offered for your consideration.' Like several other large companies, Chase hired well-known designers such as Walter Von Nessen, Lurelle Guild, the Gerths, Russel Wright, and Dr. A Reimann. Harry Laylon, an in-house designer, created much of the new line.

From 1930 to 1942 Chase offered lamps, smoking accessories, and housewares similar to those Americans were seeing on the Hollywood screen — generally at prices the average person could afford.

Besides chromium, Chase manufactured many products in a variety of finishes, some even in silver plate. Many objects were of polished or satin-finished brass and/or copper; other pieces were chromium plated.

After World War II Chase no longer made the Specialties line. It had represented only a tiny fraction of this huge company's production. Instead they concentrated on a variety of fabricated mill items. Some dedicated Chase collectors even have shower heads, faucet aerators, gutter pipe, and metal samples. Is anyone using Chase window screening?

Chase products are marked either on the item itself or on a screw or rivet. Because Chase sold screws, rivets, nails, etc. (all with their logo), not all items having these Chase-marked components were actually made at Chase. It should also be noted that during the 1930s, China produced good quality chromium copies; so when you're not absolutely positive an item is Chase, buy it because you like it, understanding that its authenticity may be in question. Remember that if a magnet sticks to it, it's not Chase. Brass and copper are not magnetic, and Chase did not use steel.

Prior to 1933 Chase made smoking accessories for the Park Sherman Co. Some are marked 'Park Sherman, Chicago, Illinois, Made of Chase Brass.' Others carry a Park Sherman logo. It is believed that the 'heraldic emblem' was also used during this period. Many items are identical or very similar to Chase-marked pieces. Produced in the 1950s, National Silver's 'Emerald Glo' wares look very similar to Chase pieces, but Chase did not make them. It is very possible that National purchased Chase tooling after the Chase Specialties line was discontinued.

Although Chase designer pieces and rarer items are still commanding good prices, the market has softened on the more common wares. This year's price guide will reflect this trend. The availability of Chase on the internet has helped the collector, but has also contributed to the leveling off of values.

For further study we recommend *Chase Complete, Chase Catalogs 1934 & 1935, 1930s Lighting — Deco & Traditional* by Chase, and *The Chase Era, 1933 and 1942 Catalogs of the Chase Brass & Copper Co.*, all by Donald-Brian Johnson and Leslie Piña (Schiffer); *Art Deco Chrome, The Chase Era*, by Richard Kilbride; and *Art Deco Chrome* by James Linz (Schiffer). Our advisors for this category are Donna and John Thorpe; they are listed in the Directory under Wisconsin.

Key:
Ac — Ackerman	LG — Laurelle Guild
Ge — Gerth	RK — Rockwell Kent
HD — Helen Bishop Dennis	RW — Russel Wright
HL — Harry Layton	VN — designed by Von Nessen

Arcadia Pitcher, Bakelite handle, 7¼", from $65.00 to $80.00.

Ashtray, Globe, chromium, #17068, from $50 to 60.00
Autumn Leaf Ash Receiver, chromium or copper, #28009, 5⅛" 35.00
Band Box, chromium, red plastic hdl, 3-compartment, #852, 7⅛" L.85.00
Bell, Ming, chromium, #13007, from $50 to.................................... 60.00
Bookends, Davy Jones, wheel, brass/walnut/Bakelite, #90142........ 50.00
Bookends, Horse, very stylized, polished brass, #17044, 6".......... 800.00
Bookends, Moderne, brass/copper w/rivets/panels, #11246, 6½", G.950.00
Box, Occasional, chromium w/plastic hearts, glass insert, #90144. 45.00
Canape plate, #27001, from $15 to.. 20.00
Candlesticks, Bubble, copper/orange Catalin, #17063, 1935, 2½", pr..75.00
Carefree Set, chromium, #8003, 4 cup holders+tray...................... 95.00
Cigarette Box, Bacchus, RK, bronze, #847...................................... 700.00
Cigarette Lighter, Automatic Table; chromium, #825, 3¼", $40 to.45.00
Circlet Tray, chromium & ivory compo, #90060, 7"..................... 175.00
Cocktail Set, Doric, chrome, 12½" shaker+6 3" cups+12" tray.... 350.00
Cocktail Shakers, Gaiety, chrome w/blk rings #90034, from $40 to... 45.00
Coffee Set, Continental, chrome/Bakelite, VN, #17052, 3-pc..... 250.00
Continental Sugar Bowl, chrome w/blk, VN, #17052 .... 25.00
Crumber Set, Tidy, moon shape, chromium, plastic hdls, #90092.. 35.00
Devonshire Pitcher, polished copper or chromium, RW, #90025, $65 to. 70.00
Dish, Tulip, polished chromium, scroll hdl, #90095 .... 35.00
Duplex Server, 2-tier, chromium or satin copper, #9005, 12", $85 to. 95.00
Flower Bowl, Diana, chromium on plastic base, #15005, 10"......... 65.00
Glow Lamp, #01001, copper & brass, cone shade, 8", M................ 50.00
Ice Bowl, chromium, w/tongs, #28002, from $65 to 75.00
Informal Tray, copper, #09012 .... 70.00
Jubilee Globe Mustard, copper or chrome w/wht, #90070, 4", from $45 to..55.00
Lamp, Binnacle; wired, 1933-34 Chicago Expo, #25002, from $75 to..100.00
Lamp, Desk, chrome w/pivoting socket on ribbed O shaft, 13½"x12".. 50.00
Lamp, Glow, #01001, copper w/wht, cone shade, 8", M................ 85.00
Light, Binnacle; #25002, wired, colored glass 45.00
Manchu Table Bell, chrome/Catalin, #13006, 1936, from $45 to .. 50.00
Marionette Ashtray, #304... 30.00
Meridian Tray, chromium w/wht hdls, #17078, 7⅞", from $35 to .. 40.00
Newspaper Rack, English bronze or brass & copper, #27027, from $35 to.45.00
Niagara Watering Can, Ge, #05004, 8⅜"... 75.00
Nob-Top Ashtray, chromium w/colored knob center, #810, 6½" dia .40.00
Pelican Smokers' Stand, English Bronze, VN, #17056, 21x8¼" dia.375.00
Piccadilly Cigarette Box, chromium-plate & wht, #867, ¾x8¾x3"..95.00
Savoy Creamer & Sugar Bowl, w/tray, #26008, 1936, from $45 to. 50.00
Smokeless Ashtray, polished brass w/mc enameling, #537, from $40 to. 50.00

Soldier Bookends, brass with red polymer jackets, on brass base with sphere, 7½", $375.00 for the pair. (Photo courtesy Skinner Inc. Auctioneers & Appraisers of Antiques & Fine Art)

Sparta Water Pitcher, chromium, wht plastic hdl, #90055, 8" 75.00
Spiral Bookends, blk & satin nickel, #17018, 1933, from $200 to ..250.00
Sugar Sphere, chromium, RW, #90078, 2⅞x2⅝", from $45 to........ 55.00
Sunday Supper Candleholders, blk nickel, #24002, 4 for 50.00
Sunshine Watering Can, brass & copper, Ge, #5003, 5x8½", $30 to . 40.00
Tarpon Fishbowl, amber bronze, HD, #90125, 8" 80.00
Three-Layer Candy Box, apple & leaves on lid, chromium, #90104, 5⅝". 60.00
Tripod Ashtray, copper & brass, 3-leg, VN, #301 .... 40.00
Trowel, brass w/blk hdl, VN, #90015, 10" 100.00

Chelsea Dinnerware

Made from about 1830 to 1880 in the Staffordshire district of England, this white dinnerware is decorated with lustre embossings in the grape, thistle, sprig, or fruit and cornucopia patterns. The relief designs vary from lavender to blue, and the body of the ware may be porcelain, ironstone, or earthenware. Because it was not produced in Chelsea as the name would suggest, dealers often prefer to call it 'Grandmother's Ware.' For more information we recommend *English China Patterns and Pieces* by Mary Frank Gaston, our advisor for this category. Mrs. Gaston is listed in the Directory under Texas.

Grape, bowl, 8" 35.00
Grape, cake plate, emb ribs, 10", from $25 to 30.00
Grape, cake plate, w/copper lustre, sq, 10", from $25 to 30.00
Grape, coffeepot, stick hdl, 2-cup, 7" 75.00
Grape, creamer, 5½" 55.00
Grape, cup & saucer, from $25 to 35.00
Grape, egg cup, 2¼", from $35 to 50.00
Grape, pitcher, milk; 40-oz 60.00
Grape, plate, 6", from $12 to 15.00
Grape, plate, 7" 18.00
Grape, plate, 8", from $22 to 25.00
Grape, plate, 9½" 22.50

Grape, sugar bowl with lid, Edward Walley's coat of arms mark, 8", from $100.00 to $125.00. (Photo courtesy Mark Frank Gaston)

Grape, teapot, octagonal, 8½", from $125 to 150.00
Grape, teapot, octagonal, 10" 165.00
Grape, teapot, 2-cup 75.00
Grape, waste bowl 40.00

Sprig, cake plate, 9" 40.00
Sprig, cup & saucer 40.00
Sprig, pitcher, milk 60.00
Sprig, plate, dinner 25.00
Sprig, plate, 7" 18.00
Thistle, butter pat 15.00
Thistle, cake plate, 8¾", from $25 to 30.00
Thistle, cup & saucer, from $30 to 35.00
Thistle, plate, 6", from $6 to 8.00
Thistle, plate, 7" 15.00
Thistle, sugar bowl, 8-sided, w/lid, 7½" 45.00

Chelsea Keramic Art Works

In 1866 fifth-generation Scottish potter Alexander Robertson started a pottery in Chelsea, Massachusetts, where his brother Hugh joined him the following year. Their father James left the firm he partnered to help his sons in 1872, teaching them techniques and pressing decorative tiles, an extreme rarity at that early date. Their early production consisted mainly of classical Grecian and Asian shapes in redware and stoneware, several imitating metal vessels. They then betrayed influences from Europe's most important potteries, such as Royal Doulton and Limoges, in underglaze and barbotine or Haviland painting. Hugh's visit to the Philadelphia Centennial Exposition introduced him to the elusive sang-de-boeuf or oxblood glaze featured on Ming porcelain, which he would strive to achieve for well over a decade at tremendous costs.

James passed away in 1880, and Alexander moved to California in 1884, leaving Hugh in charge of the pottery and his oxblood glaze experiments. The time and energy spent doing research were taken away from producing saleable artwares. Out of funds, Hugh closed the pottery in 1889.

Wealthy patrons supported the founding of a new company, the short-lived Chelsea Pottery U.S., where the emphasis became the production of Chinese-inspired crackleware, vases, and tableware underglaze-painted in blue with simplified or stylized designs. The commercially viable pottery found a new home in Dedham, Massachusetts, in 1896, whose name it adopted. Hugh died in 1908, and the production of crackleware continued until 1943.

The ware is usually stamped CKAW within a diamond or Chelsea Keramic Art Works/Robertson & Sons. Our advisors for this category are Suzanne Perrault and David Rago; they are listed in the Directory under New Jersey. See also Dedham Pottery.

Vase, oxblood red, marked CKAW, 7½", $4,800.00. (Photo courtesy David Rago Auctions)

Pilgrim flask, amber vellum w/appl rose, CKW, sm chips, 4¼" 500.00
Plate, glaze samples, Chelsea Keramic Art Works, Robertson & Sons, 6". 2,920.00
Plate, Lotus border w/rare gr leaves on crackleware, 1895, 10", ex . 3,000.00
Plate, 8 wedges of experimental colors, 1870-80, 5½" 3,100.00
Vase, brn & gr mottle, pinched rim, CKAW, 3¼x4" 120.00
Vase, brn-gr luster & oxblood, H Robertson, experimental, 3¼x3¼" ...850.00

Vase, bud; dk gr gloss, CKAW, 5x2½".....................................1,175.00
Vase, gr-brn & oxblood, ring hdls, att H Robertson, CKAW, 5" ..250.00
Vase, orange-peel oxblood, baluster, 8¾x4" 7,200.00
Vase, orange-peel oxblood, shouldered, CKAW, 4¼x3½"..........1,200.00
Vase, streaky brn & gr, 5-lobed ruffled rim, CKAW, 6⅝x5⅝" 350.00
Vase, wht crackle w/ash from firing, swollen body, 1880-99, 8¾"..550.00

Chicago Crucible

For only a few years during the 1920s, the Chicago (Illinois) Crucible Company made a limited amount of decorative pottery in addition to their regular line of architectural wares. Examples are very scarce today; they carry a variety of marks, all with the company name and location. Our advisors for this category are Suzanne Perrault and David Rago; they are listed in the Directory under New Jersey.

Vase, bud; frothy gr & lt amber, 8x4¼" 725.00
Vase, frothy gr, angle hdls, ca 1900, 7".......................................1,325.00
Vase, frothy gr, twisted body, unmk, 8x4¼"...................................500.00
Vase, grapevines emb, gr bottle form w/scalloped rim, 10½x6" .1,100.00
Vase, stylized floral, pk on dk gr, shouldered, 8¾"..........................725.00
Vase, vertical leaves emb, brn & gr, shouldered, 6½x5".................600.00

Children's Things

Nearly every item devised for adult furnishings has been reduced to child size — furniture, dishes, sporting goods, even some tools. All are very collectible. During the later seventeenth and early eighteenth centuries, miniature china dinnerware sets were made both in China and in England. They were not intended primarily as children's playthings, however, but instead were made to furnish miniature rooms and cabinets that provided a popular diversion for the adults of that period. By the nineteenth century, the emphasis had shifted, and most of the small-scaled dinnerware and tea sets were made for children's play.

Late in the nineteenth century and well into the twentieth, toy pressed glass dishes were made, many in the same patterns. Today these toy dishes often fetch prices in the same range or above those for the 'grown-ups'!

Children's books, especially those from the Victorian era, are charming collectibles. Colorful lithographic illustrations that once delighted little boys in long curls and tiny girls in long stockings and lots of ribbons and lace have lost none of their appeal. Some collectors limit themselves to a specific subject, while others may be far more interested in the illustrations. First editions are more valuable than later issues, and condition and rarity are very important factors to consider before making your purchase. For further information we recommend *Encyclopedia of Collectible Children's Books* by Diane McClure Jones and Rosemary Jones.

Our advisors for children's china and glassware are Margaret and Kenn Whitmyer; you will find their address in the Directory under Ohio.

In the following listings, unless otherwise noted, our values are for examples in excellent condition. See also A B C Plates; Blue Willow; Clothing; Stickley; etc.

Key:
ds — doll size   hc — hardcover
dj — dust jacket   pic brds — pictorial boards

Books

Alphabet Book, M Winter, Merill Publishing #3493, 1938, pic brds .35.00
Baby's Christmas, E Wilkin, Little Golden Book, 1959, 13th printing ..10.00
Barkley, Syd Hoff, Harper & Row, 1975, hc paper over brds.........17.50

Betty Lee Sophomore, HP Grove, AL Burt Co, 1931, cloth cover ..22.50
Big Little Kitty, Biggers, Whitman Tell-a-Tale, 1953, pic brds.......17.50
Bobbsey Twins & County Fair Mystery, Grosset & Dunlap #15, pic brds..7.50
Bugle Puppy in Old Yorktown, Elf Tip Top Rand McNally, 1958, pic brds..12.50
Buttons & Whirlybird, Benefit Press, 1960, pic brds, 64-pg 10.00
Cat That Would Be King, RM Woods, Saalfield Easy To Read Series, hc.15.00
Child's Book of Ballet, V La Mont, Maxton Books...Little People, 1964.5.00
Child's Garden of Verses, RL Stevenson, Saalfield, 1937 1st ed.....40.00
Child's Garden of Verses, RL Stevenson, Platt & Munk Deluxe, 1961 .37.50
Child Star: Shirley Temple Black, An Autobiography, paper bk....15.00
Corduroy, D Freeman, Viking Press, 1968, pic brds 22.00
David's Silver Dollar, EB Squires, Platt & Munk, hardbk, 1940.....12.00
Donna Parker Mystery at Arawak, M Martin, Whitman, 1962, hc..10.00

Dutch Courage and Other Stories, Jack London, Macmillan Co., New York, 1922, first edition hardcover, 8vo, 180 pages, VG, from $2,800.00 to $3,000.00.

Everyday Play for Children, CS Bailey, 1916 1st ed, w/dj............125.00
Fall of Fairy Prince, FC McElroy, Johnson Publishing, 1929, hc 50.00
Finnegan II: His Nine Lives, CS Bailey, Seredy illus, 1965, ex-library ...7.00
Honey Bunch: Just a Little Girl, Thorndyke, Grosset & Dunlap, hc .12.50
How the Grinch Stole Christmas, Seuss, Random House, 1985, pic brds.20.00
How To Tell Time, JW Watson, Little Golden Book, 1957, later printing...17.50
Jack & Beanstalk, M Winter, Whitman, 1939, linen-like cloth.....25.00
Jim Forest & Flood, Rambeau, Harr Wagner Publishing, 1959, pic brds..10.00
Jungle Book, R Kipling, Illus Jr Library, 1950 ....27.50
Kankie Kangaroo Who Couldn't Hop, Roselle/Braker Ross, Maxton, 1945.35.00
Klaas & Jansje Children of the Dike, Olcott, Burdette & Co, 1933, hc.15.00
Let's Go on Space Trip, M Chester, J Coggins Illus, 1963, hardbk, NM..6.00
Little Bear's Visit, Minarik, Harper Row, 1961, hc, w/dj 25.00
Little Boy Blue, McLoughlin Bros, 1920s, linen, 6-pg 40.00
Little Cub Scout, M Watts/Wm Timmins, Rand McNally Elf Book, 1964 .15.00
Little Duck, M Barrows, Grosset & Dunlap, 1931 1st ed, pic brds .20.00
Little Elephant, Brocerick/Ozone, Rand McNally Jr Elf Book, 1959, hc..15.00
Little Indian Hiawatha, CH Lawrence illus, MA Donohue, 1916, linen..150.00
Little Red Bicycle, DU King, Whitman, 1953 1st ed, pic brds.......20.00
Little Toot, Gramatky, GP Putnam's Sons, 1939, hc w/pic brds 35.00
Mary Jane's City Home, CI Judson, 1920, gr cloth cover w/medallion ..15.00
Minnow Vail, WE Wise, Whitman by Western Publishing, 1962, hc .12.50
Mistress Mary, Martin, Read Out Loud Book by Dodd Mead & Co, 1911 ..40.00
My Good Morning, Wilkin, Golden Sturdy Shape Book, 1983, later ed.12.00
My Name Is Aram, Saroyan/Freeman, Harcourt Brace & Co, 1940, w/dj...125.00
Mystery in Rainbow Valley, LJ Hunt, Funk & Wagnalls, 1961, pic brds ..10.00
One, Two, Three by Charlie; Whitman, 1953, pic brds..................16.00
Peter Rabbit the Magician, M Richards, Strathmore, spiral bound, 1942..10.00
Pets & Playmates, Vrendenburg/R Tuck, Germany, Victorian era .17.50
Pied Piper of Hamlin, R Browning, H Dunlap Illus, 1928, pic brds..60.00
Pinocchio, C Collodi, Grosset & Dunlap, undtd, hc.......................40.00
Pooh Story Book, AA Milne, EH Shepard, EP Dutton & Co, 1965, hc..22.00
Raggedy Ann & Tagalong Present, Schwalje, Golden Tell-a-Tale, 1971, hc...12.50
Raggedy Ann...Tunnel of Lost Toys, Bushnell, Bobbs-Merril, 1980, hc.12.50
Rose in Bloom, LM Alcock, Whitman, 1952 Modern Abridged Ed, EX.10.00
Shoelace Box, E Winthrop, Little Golden Book, 1984, 10th printing...12.00
Shy Little Kitten, C Schurr, Little Golden Book, 50th Anniversary Ed..7.50
Smokey Bear Saves Forest, Graham, Whitman Tell-a-Tale, 1971, pic brds ..8.00
So Big, Wilkin, Little Golden Book, red spine, 1st ed, NM 40.00

Southpaw Speed, J Archibald, Macrae Smith Co, 1965, pic brds .. 24.00
Stories of Indian Children, MH Husted, 1897 2nd ed, hc, 137-pg. 20.00
Surprising Pets of Billy Brown, Kitt, Wonder Books Easy Reader, 1962 . 10.00
Things That Go, Whitman by Western Publishing, thick cb, 1970..40.00
Tinka & His Friends, Downing & Mansfield, 1960 1st ed, w/dj 75.00
Troll Music, A Lobel, Weekly Reader Book Club, 1966, hc, w/dj.....5.00
Troy Nesbit: Diamond Cave Mystery, Whitman, 1964, pic brds 10.00
Uncle Wiggily Goes Swimming, HR Garis, CE Graham & Co, 1927, pic brds.. 40.00
Visit to Dentist, BJ Garn, L Wallace, Wonder Book, 1959, 1st printing. 25.00
Walt Disney's Donald Duck & His Cat Troubles, Whitman, 1948, pic brds.17.50
Waltons & Birthday Present, Little Golden Book, pic brds..............5.00
We Help Daddy, M Stein, Little Golden Book, 20th printing, pic brds.. 10.00
We Like Kindergarten, Cassidy/Wilkin, Little Golden Book, 1965, C ed . 20.00
Wee Gillis, Muro Leaf, Viking Press, 1964...................................... 45.00
Whitey & Colt Killer, G Rounds, Holiday House, 1962, hc 20.00
Wind in Willows, Grahame, Golden Anniversary Ed, 1960s, hc, w/dj, NM.... 27.50

China, Pottery, and Stoneware

Angel w/Shining Star, creamer, mc on wht, Germany 45.00
Angel w/Shining Star, cup, mc on wht, Germany 32.00
Angel w/Shining Star, sugar bowl, mc on wht, Germany, w/lid 48.00
Athens, gravy boat, bl & wht, Davenport, mid-1800s, 1¾"........... 38.00
Athens, platter, bl & wht, Davenport, mid-1800s, 4½" 30.00
Athens, tureen underplate, bl & wht, Davenport, mid-1800s, 5½"..16.50
Barnyard Animals, creamer, mc transfer, Germany, 3⅜" 15.00
Barnyard Animals, plate, mc transfer, Germany, 5½" 8.00
Blue Willow, casserole, Japan, 4¾" 52.50
Blue Willow, gravy boat, Japan... 30.00
Blue Willow, teapot, Japan, 2⅝"... 50.00
Bluebird, casserole, mc on wht, Noritake, w/lid, 6" 50.00
Bluebird, platter, mc on wht, Noritake, 7⅛" 27.50
Buster Brown, plate, mc transfer, Germany.................................. 30.00
Buster Brown, sugar bowl, mc transfer, Germany, w/lid, 3¾" 75.00
Butterfly, plate, mc on wht (brn dominant), England, 5" 7.50
Butterfly, teapot, mc on wht (brn dominant), England, 4¼" 60.00
Children w/Toy Animals, creamer, mc transfer, Germany, 3¼"...... 20.00
Children w/Toy Animals, sugar bowl, mc transfer, Germany 20.00
Dimity, bowl, soup; gr & cream, England, 4¼"............................ 12.00
Dimity, tray, gr & cream, rectangular, England, 5¾"..................... 21.50

Feeding dish, Czecho-slovakia, 1930s, 3¾", $65.00.

Flow Blue Dogwood, bowl, oval, Minton, 4⅜"............................. 60.00
Flow Blue Dogwood, plate, Minton, 4" 22.00
Flow Blue Dogwood, server, Minton, 1x3".................................. 36.00
Forget-Me-Not, casserole, bl & wht, England, 4¾" 110.00
Forget-Me-Not, platter, bl & wht, England, 4¾" 95.00
Forget-Me-Not, server, bl & wht, England, 1x2¾" 48.00
Forget-Me-Not, tureen, bl & wht, England, 7⅞" 150.00
Friends, cup & saucer, mc transfer, Germany, 1⅞", 4¼" 28.00
Friends, sugar bowl, mc transfer, Germany, w/lid, 3⅝" 28.00
Gaudy Ironstone, creamer, mc on wht, England, 2⅜" 48.00
Gaudy Ironstone, sugar bowl, mc on wht, England, w/lid, 4" 72.50

Girls w/Pets, creamer, brn transfer, Allerton, 3⅛"........................... 20.00
Girls w/Pets, teapot, brn transfer, Allerton, 5⅛" 55.00
Greek Key, bowl, fish form, Ridgway, Sparks & Ridgway, 3" 26.50
Greek Key, ladle, brn & wht, Ridgway, Sparks & Ridgway, 5" 12.00
Greek Key, platter, brn & wht, Ridgway, Sparks & Ridgway, 8"..... 32.50
Holly, creamer, mc on wht, Germany, 1900s.................................. 36.00
Holly, sugar bowl, mc on wht, Germany, w/lid............................... 42.50
Kite Fliers, bowl, vegetable; w/lid, England, 3½" 132.50
Kite Fliers, gravy boat, England, 3¼".. 120.00
Kite Fliers, plate, England, 3½" 48.00
Lady Standing by Urn, creamer, purple transfer, England 60.00
Lady Standing by Urn, waste bowl, purple transfer, England, 2⅞" . 48.00
Livesley Fern & Floral, bowl, gr floral, oval, mid-1800s, 3⅞" 36.00
Livesley Fern & Floral, platter, gr floral, mid-1800s, 5" 30.00
Livesley Fern & Floral, tureen w/stand, gr floral, 1885, 5½" 72.50
Mary Had a Little Lamb, plate, mc on wht, England, 3⅛" 8.00
Mary Had a Little Lamb, teapot, mc on wht, England, 3½" 65.00
Pagodas, casserole, mc on wht (bl dominant), w/lid, England, 5½"..65.00
Pagodas, platter, mc on wht (bl dominant), England, 5⅛" 34.00
Pembroke, casserole, red floral, Bistro England, 5¼"..................... 55.00
Pembroke, plate, red floral, Bistro England, 4½" 9.00
Pembroke, tureen, red floral, Bistro England, 6½" 78.00
Pink Lustre, creamer, hunt scene transfer, Germany..................... 32.00
Pink Lustre, pitcher, England, 3" 48.00
Pink Lustre, soap dish, England, 1½x2"....................................... 35.00
Pink Lustre, teapot, hunt scene transfer, Germany 115.00
Pink Open Rose, cup & saucer, mc on wht, England, 2", 3⅞" 12.00
Pink Open Rose, tray, mc on wht, England, 6" 12.00
Roman Chariots, cup & saucer, bl on wht, Cauldon England........ 40.00
Roman Chariots, sugar bowl, bl transfer, Cauldon England, 1½" ... 48.00
Scenes From England, bowl, soup; bl & wht, England, 3⅝" 60.00
Scenes From England, bowl, vegetable; bl & wht, w/lid, England, 3⅞"..175.00
Scenes From England, plate, bl & wht, England, 3¼" 35.00

Set: Japan, 1930s, MIB, from $150.00 to $250.00. (Photo courtesy Carol Bess White)

Silhouette, creamer, blk on wht, Noritake 18.00
Silhouette, teapot, blk on wht, Noritake, 3½" 70.00
Silhouette Children, creamer, Victoria/Czechoslovakia, 2¼"......... 14.50
Silhouette Children, sugar bowl, w/lid, Victoria/Czechoslovakia... 18.00
Silhouette Children, teapot, Victoria/Czechoslovakia, 3⅝" 38.00
Snow White, cup, mc on wht, WD Enterprises, Japan, 1937, 1½". 15.00
Snow White, teapot, mc on wht, WD Enterprises, Japan, 1937, 3¼" ..77.00
Spirit of Children, casserole, mc scene, 4½" 30.00
Spirit of Children, plate, mc scene, 4" 8.00
Spirit of Children, platter, mc scene, 5" 24.00
St Nicholas, plate, mc on wht, Germany, 5⅛" 15.00
St Nicholas, sugar bowl, mc on wht, Germany, 3" 48.00
Standing Pony, creamer, mc w/gr lustre, Germany, 3¼"................. 16.50
Standing Pony, teapot, mc transfer w/gr lustre, Germany, 6".......... 78.00
Tan & Gray Lustre, creamer, Phoenix China, Japan, 2¼" 10.00
Tan & Gray Lustre, saucer, Phoenix China, Japan, 2¾"...................2.50
Tan Lustre, creamer, mc dots, Made in Japan.................................3.50
Tan Lustre, teapot, mc dots, Made in Japan 13.50

Furniture

Armcair, 3-slat ladder-bk w/tulip & ball finials, rush seat, rpt, 26" ... 700.00
Armchair, maple, 2-slat bk, trn handholds, rfn, 21" 475.00
Baby tender, pnt pine, canted sides w/rails/extending tray, 22x18x11".700.00
Bassinette, walnut, scalloped splats/shoe ft, pnt traces, 22x31x19".700.00
Chair, mixed woods, trn stiles/legs/stretchers, cane seat, pnt, 15". 300.00
Chair, pnt peaches on curved crest & splat, gold stripes, rpr, 21".285.00
Chair, side; Windsor, bamboo w/pnt traces/crazing, Yardley, 28".175.00
Chair, side; Windsor pnt fan-bk w/serpentine crest, 18th C, 34"...2,600.00
Chair, 3-slat ladder-bk w/mushroom finials, string seat, 25" 100.00
Chest, cherry Sheraton, 3 grad drw w/inlay/paneled ends, 16x16x10". 2,415.00
Chest, cherry/poplar Sheraton, 4 dvtl drws, 38x25x16" 1,200.00
Chest, pnt pine, 6-brd, hinged lid, cut-out ends, NE, 1790s, 16x31x13". 3,300.00
Chest, walnut/poplar, 4 dvtl drws, trn legs, old rfn, 31x22x12" 800.00
Cradle, pine, orig gr/mustard pnt w/foliate borders, NH, 26x44x22"..700.00
Cradle, pine w/floral decor, rprs, 24x35x25" 150.00
Cradle, pine w/HP decor on red pnt, sq nails, ds, 10x16x14" 115.00
Cradle, redware w/molded lattice work, mc glaze, ds, 9x12"......... 115.00
Cradle, shallow hood w/scallops, pine w/worn bl pnt, 38x36x14". 460.00

Desk, Chippendale, New England, 1700s, restored finish, 29x24", $1,650.00.
(Photo courtesy Skinner Inc. Auctioneers & Appraisers of Antiques & Fine Art)

Dry sink, pnt poplar, china knobs, side drw/door, 17x20x10"....1,150.00
Dry sink, walnut/pine, red pnt, paneled door, cut-out ft, 26x24x15"..4,400.00
Highchair, 3-slat ladder-bk, trn arms/post, old bl pnt, 36"............ 200.00
Rocker, trn arms, cloth seat & bk, gold gr pnt over salmon, 22"....1,000.00

Button Panel No. 44 (with gold trim): Creamer, 2½", $70.00; Sugar bowl with lid, 4⅝", $100.00; Butter dish, 4", $125.00; Spooner, 2½", $70.00. (Photo courtesy Margaret and Kenn Whitmyer)

Glass

Acorn, creamer, 3⅜" 110.00
Acorn, spooner, frosted, 3⅛" 200.00
Acorn, table set, frosted, 4-pc, from $1,000 to......................... 1,100.00
Arched Panel, pitcher, amber, 3¾" 96.00
Austrian No 200, butter dish, canary, Greentown, 2¼"............... 350.00
Baby Thumbprint, cake stand, tall, US Glass, 3"........................ 110.00

Bead & Scroll, butter dish, dk gr or bl, 4" 300.00
Bead & Scroll, creamer, 3", from $84 to.................................... 96.00
Beaded Swirl, creamer, amber or cobalt, 2¾" 90.00
Beaded Swirl, sugar bowl, w/lid, 3¾" 42.00
Betty Jane, casserole, w/lid, #209, McKee Glass, from $36 to 40.00
Betty Jane, set, 6-pc, Mckee Glass, from $90 to 100.00
Block, spooner, 3", from $96 to 120.00
Braided Belt, butter dish, amber or lt gr, 2¼", from $365 to 385.00
Braided Belt, creamer, amber or lt gr, 2⅝" 140.00
Braided Belt, creamer, 2⅝", from $80 to 90.00
Bucket (aka Wooden Pail), creamer, 2½"................................... 60.00
Buzz Saw No 2697, butter dish, 2⅜" 35.00
Cherry Blossom, cup, pk, 1½", from $30 to 34.00
Cherry Blossom, saucer, Delphite, 4½".......................................5.00
Chimo, butter dish, 2⅜" 125.00
Chimo, cup, punch; 1⁷⁄₁₆" 20.00
Colonial Flute, pitcher, 3¼" 22.00
Colonial Flute, punch set, 7-pc, from $140 to 150.00
D&M No 42, butter dish, George Duncan & Sons, 4", from $180 to. 200.00
Diamond Ridge/D&M No 48, spooner, 2¾" 110.00
Doric & Pansy, plate, pk, Jeannette Glass Co, 5⅞".......................8.00
Doyle No 500, mug, amber, 2".. 37.00
Doyle No 500, spooner, Doyle & Co, 2¼", from $48 to 55.00
Drum, sugar bowl, w/lid, 3½", from $120 to 130.00
Dutch Boudoir, bowl, milk glass, 1¼"...................................... 90.00
Dutch Boudoir, candlestick, bl opaque, 3", ea.......................... 125.00
Dutch Boudoir, tray, milk glass, 3¼x6", from $150 to.................. 160.00
Flattened Diamond & Sunburst, creamer, Westmoreland, 2¼"...... 20.00
Grape Stein, tankard, Federal Glass Co, from $160 to 185.00
Grapevine w/Ovals, mug, amber, bl or yel, McKee, 1⅞".............. 50.00
Hawaiian Lei, sugar bowl, w/lid, JB Higbee, 3", from $32 to 36.00
Hobnail w/Thumbprint Base No 150, butter dish, bl or amber, 2"..120.00
Homespun, saucer, pk, Jeannette Glass Co, 3¼"...........................5.00
Homespun, tea set, 12-pc, Jeannette Glass Co 175.00
Horizontal Threads, butter dish, 1⅞"....................................... 90.00
Horizontal Threads, table set, 4-pc, from $250 to...................... 265.00
Inverted Strawberry, berry set, Cambridge Glass, from $210 to.... 235.00
Kidibake, ramekin, clear opal, Fry Glass Co, #1923, 2½", $24 to... 27.00
Kittens, bowl, cereal; marigold, Fenton, 3½", from $120 to 150.00
Kittens, cup, marigold, Fenton, 2⅛", from $100 to 110.00
Lamb, butter dish, 3⅛", from $180 to....................................... 210.00
Laurel, creamer, Scottie decal, McKee Glass Co, 2⅝", from $175 to..200.00
Lion, creamer, frosted, Gillinder & Sons, 3⅛", from $90 to 96.00
Michigan, stein set, 7-pc, US Glass, from $87 to....................... 110.00
Monk, tankard, 4", from $85 to 95.00
Nearcut, tumbler, Cambridge, 2"..6.50
Nursery Rhyme, punch bowl, bl opaque, US Glass, 3¼", from $360 to..420.00
Nursery Rhyme, table set, 4-pc, US Glass, from $295 to.............. 365.00
Nursery Rhyme, water set, 7-pc, from $250 to 290.00
Oval Star No 300, pitcher, Indiana Glass, 4", from $65 to............ 78.00
Palm Leaf Fan, banana stand.. 72.00
Pattee Cross, bowl, master berry; US Glass, 1¾" 40.00
Pattee Cross, tumbler, US Glass, 1¾", from $14 to........................ 16.00
Peacock Feather, creamer, US Glass, 2", from $54 to 60.00
Pert, butter dish, 2¾", from $145 to 150.00
Plain Pattern No 13, table set, King, 4-pc, from $365 to.............. 395.00
Pointed Jewel 'Long Diamond' No 15006, butter dish, US Glass, 2".170.00
Pointed Jewel 'Long Diamond' No 15006, spooner, US Glass, 2½". 100.00
Pyrexette, bakeware, boxed set, from $180 to 210.00
Rooster No 140, butter dish, King, 2¾", from $210 to................. 240.00
Rooster No 140, creamer, King, 3¼", from $132 to 155.00
Sandwich Ivy, creamer, amethyst, 2⅜", from $130 to 150.00
Sawtooth, butter dish, 3", from $56 to 60.00
Sawtooth Band No 1225, spooner, Heisey, 2½", from $78 to 90.00

Stippled Vines & Beads, butter dish, teal or amber, 2⅜" 140.00
Stippled Vines & Beads, sugar bowl, w/lid, 3⅛" 85.00
Sunbeam No 15139 (aka Twin Snowshoes), spooner, US Glass, 2⅛". 110.00
Tulip & Honeycomb, casserole, rnd or oval, w/lid, 3¼" 80.00
Tulip & Honeycomb, punch bowl, Federal, 4¼", from $30 to 36.00
Twist, butter dish, bl opal, Albany, 3⅝"................................... 200.00
Two Band, butter dish, Federal, 4¼", from $27 to.......................... 32.00
Wee Branches, saucer, 3", from $15 to 18.00
Wheat Sheaf No 500, bowl, master berry; 2¼" 45.00
Wheat Sheaf No 500, wine jug, Cambridge, 4⅛", from $70 to....... 85.00
Whirligig No 1501, butter dish, US Glass, 2½" 28.00
Wild Rose, candlestick, Greentown, 4⅛", ea 125.00
Wild Rose, table set, milk glass, Greentown, 4-pc, from $275 to . 300.00

Miscellaneous

Baby carriage, molded composition horse covered with hand-stitched horsehide, real horsehair tail and mane, English, ca 1875, 58" long, $2,300.00. (Photo courtesy Aston Macek)

Carriage, brn wicker w/wicker hood, spring steel chassis & wood wheels.. 120.00
Carriage, wht pnt on pewter, cloth hood, ds 240.00
Horse, wood w/old pnt on gesso, rpl bridle & tail, 30x40", VG ... 350.00
Noah's Ark, mc pnt wood, early, 13" +116 animals, people & bugs...1,100.00
Noah's Ark, mc pnt wood, Germany, ca 1900, 20x40", +42 animals. 4,560.00
Noah's Ark, stenciled/decoupage on wood, 6x13", +29 pnt wood animals..460.00
Rocking horse, wood, horsehair mane/tail, leather saddle, old rpt, 28". 1,100.00
Rocking horse, wood, horsehair mane/tail, leather saddle, 27x46". 1,300.00
Sled, G Welch 1889 in banner & horses on dk gr pnt, 4-person, 14x70".. 1,000.00
Sled, Reindeer in gold script on wood, pnt deer on gr, 19x32½" ...8,400.00
Sled, Wild Rover emb on CI, gr pnt, ds, 8" L.............................. 700.00
Sleigh, blk pnt w/yel pinstripes, pk int, NY, 1850s, 23x65x18".3,700.00

Chintz Dinnerware

'Chintz' is the generic name for English china with an allover floral transfer design. This eye-catching china is reminiscent of chintz dress fabric. It is colorful, bright, and cheery with its many floral designs and reminds one of an English garden in full bloom. It was produced in England during the first half of this century and stands out among other styles of china. Pattern names often found with the manufacturer's name on the bottom of pieces include Florence, Blue Chintz, English Roses, Delphinium, June Roses, Hazel, Eversham, Royalty, Sweet Pea, Summertime, and Welbeck, among others.

The older patterns tend to be composed of larger flowers, while the later, more popular lines can be quite intricate in design. And while the first collectors preferred the earthenware lines, many are now searching for the bone china dinnerware made by such firms as Shelley. You can concentrate on reassembling a favorite pattern, or you can mix two or more designs together for a charming, eclectic look. Another choice may be to limit your collection to teapots (the stacking ones are especially nice), breakfast sets, or cups and saucers.

Though the Chintz market remains very active, prices for some pieces have been significantly compromised due to their having been reproduced. For further information we recommend *Charlton Book of Chintz, I, II,* and *II,* by Susan Scott. Our advisor is Mary Jane Hastings; she is listed in the Directory under Illinois. See also Shelley.

Apple Blossom, nut dish, James Kent, 6½x6½"........................... 65.00
Bedale, plate, Ascot, sq, Royal Winton, 6" 45.00
Beeston, milk jug, Countess, Royal Winton, 3" 250.00
Beeston, mustard jar, Ascot, Royal Winton, 2⅛" 235.00
Blue Chintz, plate, Crown Ducal, 8" 60.00
DuBarry, creamer, James Kent, 2½" 40.00
DuBarry, jug, James Kent, 4½" 150.00
Eleanor, coffeepot, Albans, Royal Winton.. 725.00
Eleanor, cup & saucer, Royal Winton, 2¾x3½", 5¾" 75.00
Eleanor, pin dish, Royal Winton, 4⅜x3½" 48.00
Evesham, milk jug, Globe, Royal Winton, 3¾".............................. 275.00
Evesham, teapot, stacking; Royal Winton, 3-pc set...................... 500.00
Floral Feast, milk jug, Dutch, Royal Winton, 3¾" 350.00
Hazel, sugar shaker & underplate, Fife, Royal Winton, 4⅛".........675.00
Hazel, vase, bud; Clywd, Royal Winton 275.00
Hazel, water jug, Sexta, Royal Winton, w/lid, 7" 950.00
Julia, coffeepot, Albans, Royal Winton... 725.00
Julia, plate, Ascot, sq, Royal Winton, 6" 150.00
Julia, relish tray, 2-compartment, Royal Winton, 9⅛x5¼" 500.00
Majestic, nut dish, heart cutouts at hdls, Royal Winton, 6⅝x5¼"...315.00
Majestic, plate, Athena, 6" 60.00
Majestic, plate, serving; 5-section, Royal Winton, 12x10¾"........ 255.00
Marguerite, bonbon dish, center hdl, Royal Winton, 5½x9¼" 75.00
Marina, cake plate, Lord Nelson, 10" 175.00
Marina, jug, Lord Nelson, 4⅞" 195.00
Marina, trio, Lord Nelson, c/s+7½" plate 125.00
Morning Glory, cup & saucer, demi; Royal Winton 55.00
Nantwich, creamer, for stacking set, Royal Winton 110.00
Nantwich, mustard jar, Royal Winton, 2⅜" 200.00
Old Cottage, breakfast set, Countess, Royal Winton, 5-pc 450.00

Old Cottage, butter dish, Royal Winton, 6" L, $165.00. (Photo courtesy Du Mouchelles/ LiveAuctioneers.com)

Old Cottage, milk jug, Dutch, Royal Winton, 3¾"...................... 200.00
Old Cottage, mustard jar, Royal Winton, 2¼" 165.00
Old Cottage, plate, Ascot, sq, Royal Winton, 6" 35.00
Old Cottage, trivet, Royal Winton, 8¼x6¾" 65.00
Pansy, candy dish, shell shape, Royal Albert, 5x5¼" 38.00
Primula, cup & saucer, Royal Albert 35.00
Queen Anne, compote, Royal Winton, 2½x7x5¾".......................... 125.00
Queen Anne, jam jar, Ascot, w/lid, Royal Winton......................... 175.00
Queen Anne, plate, Royal Winton, 9".. 40.00
Queen Anne, relish, Royal Winton, 1½x10½x5" 80.00
Rapture, pin dish, James Kent, 3¼x3¼" 25.00
Rapture, sugar bowl, James Kent, mini... 50.00
Rosalynd, toast rack, 4-slice, James Kent, rare............................ 500.00
Royal Anne, tray, 3-lobe, Gem, Royal Winton............................. 125.00
Royal Brocade, cup, jumbo; Lord Nelson, 4x4⅛"........................... 20.00

Royal Brocade, cup & saucer, Royal Nelson, 2¾x3", 5¾" 60.00
Royalty, creamer & sugar bowl, Ascot, Royal Winton.................. 100.00
Royalty, hot water jug, Countess, w/lid, Royal Winton, 7" 775.00
Royalty, milk jug, Globe, Royal Winton, 4"........................... 300.00
Shrewsbury, milk jug, Countess, Royal Winton, 2½"..................... 145.00
Spring Glory, breakfast set, Countess, 5-pc 500.00
Stratford, butter dish, Royal Winton................................ 235.00
Summertime, compote, Royal Winton, 2¼x6¼" 85.00
Summertime, cup & saucer, Royal Winton.............................. 100.00
Summertime, milk jug, Dutch, Royal Winton, 4½"...................... 350.00
Summertime, nut dish, Royal Winton, sm 75.00
Summertime, plate, Royal Winton, 9¾"................................. 95.00
Summertime, teapot, stacking; Royal Winton, 3-pc 725.00
Summertime, tray, Royal Winton, 8x5"................................ 495.00
Sweet Pea, mustard jar, Ascot, Royal Winton, 2⅛" 245.00
Sweet Pea, plate, Ascot, sq, Royal Winton, 6"....................... 90.00
Victoria, creamer, Royal Cauldon, w/lid 20.00
Victorian Rose, nut dish, Ascot, Royal Winton, ind 95.00

Welbeck, biscuit barrel, Royal Winton, $950.00.
(Photo courtesy Mary Jane Hastings)

Welbeck, jam jar, Rosebud, w/lid, Royal Winton 225.00
Welbeck, plate, Ascot, sq, Royal Winton, 6"......................... 150.00

Chocolate Glass

Jacob Rosenthal developed chocolate glass, a rich shaded opaque brown sometimes referred to as caramel slag, in 1900 at the Indiana Tumbler and Goblet Company of Greentown, Indiana. Later, other companies produced similar ware. Only the latter is listed here. See also Greentown. Our advisor for this category is Sandi Garrett; she is listed in the Directory under Indiana. See also Greentown.

Bowl, Aldine, oval, w/lid... 1,650.00
Bowl, Beaded Triangle, 4½"... 350.00
Bowl, Geneva, McKee, oval, 10½".................................... 275.00
Bowl, Shield w/Daisy & Button, 8⅜" 1,300.00
Butter dish, Fleur-de-Lis, Royal 750.00
Butter dish, Water Lily & Cattails, Fenton......................... 1,200.00
Butter dish, White Oak, McKee...................................... 6,000.00
Carafe, Chrysanthemum Leaf... 2,500.00
Celery tray, Jubilee, 10"... 300.00
Comb & brush tray, Venetian, McKee & Bros, 8x10" 375.00
Compote, Chrysanthemum Leaf, 4½" dia 325.00
Compote, Melrose, Royal, 7¾".. 225.00
Cracker jar, Chrysanthemum Leaf, w/lid.............................. 2,500.00
Creamer, Rose Garland... 1,350.00
Creamer, Wild Rose w/Bowknot 225.00
Dish, Honeycomb, rectangular, Royal, 6¾x4"........................ 400.00
Flowerpot, Russell... 750.00
Hatpin holder, Orange Tree, Fenton 700.00
Jewel box, Venetian, McKee... 400.00
Lamp, Cloverleaf... 1,250.00
Mug, Swirl... 600.00
Nappy, Navarre, hdl, McKee... 200.00

Pickle dish, Aurora, violin shape, Royal 175.00
Pitcher, Geneva 750.00
Pitcher, Rose Garland.. 3,000.00
Plate, Serenade, 6¼" 125.00
Salt dip, master; Honeycomb, 3½" dia 650.00
Sauce dish, Waffle 450.00
Shaker, Big Rib 500.00
Shaker, Geneva 375.00
Smoking set, McKee, 3-pc 1,100.00
Spooner, Fleur-de-Lis, Royal....................................... 175.00
Spooner, Touching Squares 1,000.00
Sugar bowl, Water Lily & Cattails, w/lid, Fenton.................... 625.00
Syrup jug, Geneva, metal lid 700.00
Toothpick holder, Chrysanthemum Leaf 800.00
Toothpick holder, Kingfisher 1,000.00

Toothpick holder, picture frame shape, marked R&M, 3½", $1,500.00.
(Photo courtesy Kodner Galleries Inc./ LiveAuctioneers.com)

Tumbler, File, Royal Glass... 600.00
Tumbler, Water Lily & Cattails, Fenton 200.00
Vase, #400, Fenton, 6" 600.00
Vase, Beaded Triangle, 6¼"... 200.00
Vase, Masonic, 6".. 475.00

Christmas Collectibles

Christmas past… lovely mementos from long ago attest to the ostentatious Victorian celebrations of the season.

St. Nicholas, better known as Santa, has changed much since 300 A.D. when the good Bishop Nicholas showered needy children with gifts and kindnesses. During the early eighteenth century, Santa was portrayed as the kind gift-giver to well-behaved children and the stern switch-bearing disciplinarian to those who were bad. In 1822 Clement Clark Moore, a New York poet, wrote his famous *Night Before Christmas*, and the Santa he described was jolly and jovial — a lovable old elf who was stern with no one. Early Santas wore robes of yellow, brown, blue, green, red, white, or even purple. But Thomas Nast, who worked as an illustrator for *Harper's Weekly*, was the first to depict Santa in a red suit instead of the traditional robe and to locate him the entire year at the North Pole headquarters.

Today's collectors prize early Santa figures, especially those in robes of fur or mohair or those dressed in an unusual color. Some early examples of Christmas memorabilia are the pre-1870 ornaments from Dresden, Germany. These cardboard figures — angels, gondolas, umbrellas, dirigibles, and countless others — sparkled with gold and silver trim. Late in the 1870s, blown glass ornaments were imported from Germany. There were over 6,000 recorded designs, all painted inside with silvery colors. From 1890 through 1910, blown glass spheres were often decorated with beads, tassels, and tinsel rope.

Christmas lights, made by Sandwich and some of their contemporaries, were either pressed or mold-blown glass shaped into a form similar to a water tumbler. They were filled with water and then hung from the tree by a wire handle; oil floating on the surface of the water served as fuel for the lighted wick.

Kugels are glass ornaments that were made as early as 1820 and as late as 1890. Ball-shaped examples are more common than the fruit and vegetable forms and have been found in sizes ranging from 1" to 14" in diameter. They were made of thick glass with heavy brass caps, in cobalt, green, gold, silver, red, and occasionally in amethyst.

Although experiments involving the use of electric light bulbs for the Christmas tree occurred before 1900, it was 1903 before the first manufactured socket set was marketed. These were very expensive and often proved a safety hazard. In 1921 safety regulations were established, and products were guaranteed safety approved. The early bulbs were smaller replicas of Edison's household bulb. By 1910 G.E. bulbs were rounded with a pointed end, and until 1919 all bulbs were hand blown. The first figural bulbs were made around 1910 in Austria. Japan soon followed, but their product was never of the high quality of the Austrian wares. American manufacturers produced their first machine-made figurals after 1919. Today figural bulbs (especially character-related examples) are very popular collectibles. Bubble lights were popular from about 1945 to 1960 when miniature lights were introduced. These tiny lamps dampened the public's enthusiasm for the bubblers, and manufacturers stopped providing replacement bulbs.

Feather trees were made from 1850 to 1950. All are collectible. Watch for newly manufactured feather trees that have been reintroduced. For further information concerning Christmas collectibles, we recommend *Pictorial Guide to Christmas Ornaments and Collectibles* by George Johnson, available from Collector Books or your local bookstore.

Note: Values are given for bulbs that are in good paint, with no breaks or cracks, and in working order. When no condition is mentioned in the description, assume that values are for examples in EX/NM condition except paper items; those should be assumed NM/M.

Bulbs

Boy boxer, milk glass, 3", from $100 to 125.00
Cat in an evening gown, milk glass, Japan, ca 1950, 3", from $150 to .. 175.00
Crystal Spire Light, purple glass, ca 1935, Japan, 2½", from $40 to .. 50.00
Dog (frowning) in basket, milk glass, Japan, 2¾", from $30 to 40.00
Elephant sitting on ball, milk glass, 2¾", from $30 to 40.00
Hippo w/raised arms, clear glass, Japan, 2", from $125 to 150.00
Jack-o'-lantern w/leaves, milk glass, ca 1950, 1¾", from $45 to 55.00
Lion reclining, clear glass, Germany, 2¼", from $250 to 275.00
Monkey w/stick, clear glass, 2¼", from $75 to............................... 100.00
Mushroom, tan glass, Austria, ca 1920 .... 25.00
Pineapple, clear glass, Japan, ca 1950, 2", from $70 to 80.00
Rabbit sitting w/paws on hips, milk glass, 2½", from $75 to 85.00
Rooster playing golf, milk glass, ca 1950, 2¾", from $25 to 30.00
Tadpole, clear glass, Japan, ca 1950, 2½", from $90 to 100.00
Turkey by house, milk glass, Germany, 3", from $300 to 375.00

Candy Containers

Santa sitting on stump, Herbach head, bisque face, crepe-paper attire, cardboard base, 8¾", EX, $1,020.00. (Photo courtesy Noel Barrett Antiques & Auctions)

Bedroll, fabric-covered paper, 4", from $225 to 250.00
Bubble lights, Deer Brand #1207, snap-over set, 12-socket, Hong Kong . 300.00
Canteen, paper w/cord trim & hdl, 4¾", from $200 to 225.00
Clock, printed paper, Russian, 4", from $110 to........................... 125.00
Drum, emb silver paper, 3", from $110 to..................................... 135.00
Ear of corn, paper, 4¾", from $100 to 125.00
Globe, printed paper on cb, 3", from $150 to 175.00
Guitar, foil on cb, A&C, 3½", from $75 to 90.00
Hot-air balloon, paper, Dresden, 3", from $450 to 500.00
Liberty shield, fabric covered cb, 3", from $90 to.......................... 110.00
Man's hat box, pnt cb w/leather accents, 2", from $110 to 115.00
Pine cone, pnt paper, w/sm red bow, ca 1948, 7", from $35 to 50.00
Santa on dmn-shaped box, ca 1930, from $60 to 70.00
Slipper, Dresden-like, netting on top holds candy, 7½", from $75 to .. 100.00

Novelty Lighting

Bells, Raylite, plastic, 6-socket, ca 1950.................................... 30.00
Bubble light, mini; Glolite #840, 10-socket replacements, 1957.... 60.00
Bubble light, mini; Noma #421, USA, 10-socket, 1949 .... 55.00
Bubble light, mini; Noma #3108, USA, 8-socket, 1961 .... 175.00
Bubble light, Pifco #1261, 7-tube snap-over set, ca 1950 .... 225.00
Candelabra, Noma #520, 10-socket, ca 1958................................ 60.00
Candelabra, Raylite, #340K, 7-socket, ca 1948............................ 300.00
Candelabra, Royal Electric #782, 8-socket, ca 1954, mini 65.00
Fairy Bubbles, McElroy Mfg, England, ca 1950......................... 300.00
Fairy Tales, Noma of Canada #105, images on 8 plastic bells, 1940 . 10.00
Lantern cover, Santa figure, Dresden, ca 1928, sm 350.00
Socket replacement, mini; Noma #C-151, Mexico, ca 1960.......... 15.00
Socket set, Howdy Doody, Leco, 8 character lights, ca 1955..... 3,000.00
Socket set, Japan #485, 10 pk candles, ca 1960 .... 15.00
Socket set, Lighted Ice, Raylite #556K, Japan, 7-socket, ca 1960 .. 25.00
Socket set, mini; Krystal Snow, Raylite #330K, 1947 .... 450.00
Socket set, mini; Raylite #1330K, 8-socket, ca 1949 .... 125.00
Socket set, Royalite, Royal Electric #8408, ca 1958 .... 60.00
Socket set, St Nick, Hy-G #B68, 8-socket, ca 1960.................... 100.00
Socket set, Twinkling Star, Noma #3148, 8 stars & 48 lights, 1961 .. 85.00
Socket set, Wonder Star, Matchless #2000, 8-socket, ca 1935 ..... 450.00
Table topper, Angel Candelite, Majestic Electric #6720, ca 1950.. 20.00
Tree, Glolite #560, prewired, 9-socket, w/base, 1956, 16" 150.00
Tree, Raylite, prewired, 1-socket, w/base, ca 1950, 9".................... 25.00
Tree, Royal Electric #980, prewired, 11 mini sockets, ca 1949, 22" .. 150.00
Tree topper, Elite Angel, Noma #700, 1941............................... 35.00
Tree topper, Star of Bethlehem, Noma #124, ca 1935 .... 20.00
Tubelites, 8-tube set, ca 1955 .... 400.00
Wall hanger, Santa's Coming to Town, Royal Electric #906, 1955, 15" . 60.00
Wall hanger, wht chenille cross, Raylite #181M, 8-socket, 1936 ... 75.00
Wall sconce, M Propp #300, 8 mini sockets, ca 1927 .... 100.00
Wreath, Noma #1508, 9-socket, 1935.. 75.00
Wreath, Raylite #6A, plastic Santa face in chenille wreath, ca 1950 . 30.00

Ornaments

American flags crossed on ball, emb glass, 1950s, 2½", from $50 to . 75.00
Angel w/decorated tree, paper w/tinsel, 6½", from $50 to 65.00
Basket, glass, pk w/clear hdl, fabric flowers inside, 5", from $100 to . 125.00
Basket, woven wire, 1920-30, 1½", from $15 to 20.00
Bear w/trainer, glass, Dresden, 2x3", from $600 to...................... 625.00
Bell, molded glass, stars around middle, ca 1930-40, from $5 to 10.00
Bust of lady w/flowers, glass, Germany, 1970s, from $150 to 175.00
Carousel w/rnd top, emb glass, 3¼", from $50 to 75.00
Carrot, cotton, 4", from $25 to 30.00
Cello, wire-wrapped glass, 6½", from $50 to 60.00
Champagne bottle, cotton, 3", from $50 to 75.00

Cigar-smoking dog (cigar missing), Bonzo from comic strip by George Studdy, from $150.00 to $175.00. (Photo courtesy George Johnson)

Civil War soldier, flat metal, Dresden, 4", from $90 to 110.00
Duck in egg, glass, Germany, 3¼", from $225 to 250.00
Girl on skis, cotton girl, glass skis, 4½x6", from $400 to.............. 450.00
Girl w/roses, paper & cloth, 1910, 20", from $175 to 200.00
Goat mother, cotton w/pnt face, 6¼", from $250 to 275.00
Horse prancing, glass, Dresden, 2¼", from $160 to 180.00
Knight, flat metal, Dresden, 10¼", from $175 to 225.00
Man in derby hat, glass, 3", from $200 to.................................... 250.00
Nativity scene in wreath, plastic, ca 1940-50s, from $10 to 15.00
Parrot on branch w/leaves, flat glass, Dresden, 7¾", from $110 to. 125.00
Peacock on ball, glass, Germany, 3½", from $65 to....................... 85.00
Sailboat w/sails, glass, D Blumchen, 6½", from $40 to................... 50.00
Santa head on cb star w/tinsel, 7¼", from $15 to.......................... 20.00
Snow angel w/nest of birds, paper, Heymann & Schmidt, 10½" 70.00
Snow children (5) w/toys, paper w/tinsel, 7¾", from $100 to....... 125.00
Stork, fabric, 4½", from $85 to 95.00
4th of July boy, cotton, Cynthia Jones, 5¼", from $60 to 90.00

Miscellaneous

Sleigh, Santa pulled by reindeer, paper on wood, R. Bliss, 1890s, 12", EX, $1,450.00. (Photo courtesy Bertoia Auctions)

Bank, Rudolph, recumbent, battery, ca 1960, 5¼" 35.00
Belsnickle Santa, high collar, 9¼", from $850 to 950.00
Belsnickle Santa, 7", from $300 to 400.00
Chain, glass berry beads, Blumchen & Co, from $35 to 45.00
Fireplace, cb w/bubble light, battery, Japan, ca 1960 .... 40.00
Lantern, snowman, Amico #59861, Japan, ca 1960....................... 35.00
Lapel pin, Santa in chimney, battery, USA, ca 1956...................... 20.00
Plaque, church in snow scene, A Merry Christmas, oval, 1945, 12½" ...40.00
Santa, doll, posable fabric arms & legs, Germany, ca 1925, 10" ... 450.00
Santa, doll, straw-stuffed, ca 1920s-30s, 25½", from $200 to........ 275.00
Santa, roly-poly; Germany, 6", from $300 to................................ 400.00
Santa, waving, papier-maché, ca 1920-30, 9", from $85 to............. 95.00
Santa on nodder donkey, fabric on compo, 8x6½", from $600 to. 700.00
Santa Wind-up Drummer, celluloid/cloth, Japan, 10½", from $310 to . 350.00
Socket clips, gr enamel on metal, Malex Mfg, 20 clips, ca 1920 .... 20.00
Tester, lamp & fuse; Royal Electric #910, ca 1949 .... 45.00

Chrysanthemum Sprig, Blue

This is the blue opaque version of Northwood's popular pattern, Chrysanthemum Sprig. It was made at the turn of the century and is today very rare, as its values indicate. Prices are influenced by the amount of gold remaining on the raised designs. Unless noted otherwise, our values are for examples with excellent to near-mint gold.

Bowl, berry; ind, M gold, 2⅝x5x3¾", from $90 to 125.00
Bowl, master fruit; 8x5x10½" 400.00
Butter dish.. 900.00
Compote, jelly... 250.00

Condiment set, four-piece, from $2,100.00 to $2,200.00. (Photo courtesy Mildred and Ralph Lechner)

Condiment tray, rare, VG gold... 600.00
Creamer, from $300 to 325.00
Cruet, from $750 to 900.00
Pitcher, water; from $800 to 900.00
Shakers, pr.. 300.00
Spooner.. 250.00
Sugar bowl, M gold, w/lid, 7", from $400 to............................... 425.00
Toothpick holder, 2¾" 350.00
Tumbler, 3¾", from $90 to 125.00

Cleminson

A hobby turned to enterprise, Cleminson is one of several California potteries whose clever hand-decorated wares are attracting the attention of today's collectors. The Cleminsons started their business at their El Monte home in 1941 and were so successful that eventually they expanded to a modern plant that employed more than 150 workers. They produced not only dinnerware and kitchen items such as cookie jars, canisters, and accessories, but novelty wall vases, small trays, plaques, etc., as well. Though nearly always marked, Cleminson wares are easy to spot as you become familiar with their distinctive glaze colors. Their grayed-down blue and green, berry red, and dusty pink say 'Cleminson' as clearly as their trademark. Unable to compete with foreign imports, the pottery closed in 1963. For more information we recommend *Collector's Encyclopedia of California Pottery, Second Edition*, by Jack Chipman (Collector Books).

Bowl, Galagray, 4x11x9"... 65.00
Bowl, Gram's on front, roses on brn wreath on lid, 2½" $30.00
Butterdish, Distlefink, bird form.. 35.00
Cookie canister, Galagray.. 90.00
Cookie jar, Carrot Head 165.00
Cookie jar, Potbellied Stove, 9", from $140 to............................ 150.00
Creamer & sugar bowl, PA Dutch decor 17.50
Darning egg, lady w/Darn It on front, 5 .... 50.00
Pitcher, Distlefink, cylindrical, 5".. 30.00

Pitcher, watering can shape, wht w/bl & magenta floral, 5" 35.00
Plate, rooster crowing, yel decor rim, 9½" 22.00
Plaque, Family Tree, child & bunny at bottom, from $60 to 75.00
Shakers, Cherry, 6", pr 40.00
Shakers, Distlefink, 6", pr 40.00
String holder, heart shape w/You'll Always Have a Pull w/Me 45.00
Toothpick holder, butler figural, 4½" 40.00
Wall pocket, mortgage bank 27.50

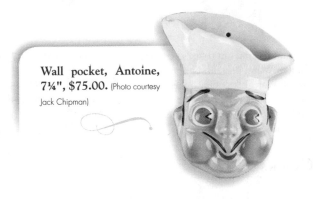

Wall pocket, Antoine, 7¼", $75.00. (Photo courtesy Jack Chipman)

Clewell

Charles Walter Clewell was a metal worker who perfected the technique of plating an entire ceramic vessel with a thin layer of copper or bronze treated with an oxidizing agent to produce a natural deterioration of the surface. Through trial and error, he was able to control the degree of patina achieved. In the early stages, the metal darkened and if allowed to develop further formed a natural turquoise-blue or green corrosion. He worked alone in his small Akron, Ohio, studio from about 1906, buying undecorated pottery from several Ohio firms, among them Weller, Owens, and Cambridge. His work is usually marked. Clewell died in 1965, having never revealed his secret process to others.

Prices for Clewell have advanced rapidly during the past few years along with the Arts and Crafts market in general. Right now, good examples are bringing whatever the traffic will bear.

Our advisors for this category are Suzanne Perrault and David Rago; they are listed in the Directory under New Jersey.

Vase, medium patina, #4098, signed Clewell 1088, 12¼x7", $8,400.00.

(Photo courtesy David Rago)

Bowl, strong patina, #384-2-6, 4x9½", EX 1,080.00
Jar, floral panels, Weller Claywood blank, unmk, 6x5¼" 1,000.00
Pitcher, tankard form, emb Arts & Crafts design, copper patina, 5¾" .. 990.00
Urn, solid bronze, #501-21, filled-in hole on bottom, 9x6" 3,700.00
Vase, brn to bright gr patina, #417-206, 4½" 475.00
Vase, bronze patina, w/hdls, #505-21, 7¼x7" 450.00
Vase, bud; copper patina, #361-2-6, 10x4½" 1,025.00

Vase, copper & brn patina, #255B-215, 17¼x7¼" 5,100.00
Vase, copper clad, #351-2-9, 7x3¾ 1,350.00
Vase, copper patina to strong gr at base, ftd, #424-26, 8" 500.00
Vase, hammered copper look, 4 buttress ft, #4098/#1088-12, 20x7", NM. 8,400.00
Vase, landscape emb, EX orig patina, sm splits to copper, X2, 13½" . 3,900.00
Vase, mythological motif, Weller Burntwood blank, #257-01, 8¼", NM. 1,300.00
Vase, verdigris, few lines/worn spots, #442-29, 9¾x9" 1,600.00

Cliff, Clarice

Between 1928 and 1935 in Burslem, England, as the director and part owner of Wilkinson and Newport Pottery Companies, Clarice Cliff and her 'paintresses' created a body of hand-painted pottery whose influence is felt to the present time.

The name for the oevre was Bizarre Ware, and the predominant sensibility, style, and appearance was Deco. Almost all pieces are signed. There were over 160 patterns and more than 400 shapes, all of which are illustrated in *A Bizarre Affair — The Life and Work of Clarice Cliff*, published by Harry N. Abrams, Inc., written by Len Griffen and Susan and Louis Meisel.

Note: Non-hand-painted work (transfer printed) was produced after World War II and into the 1950s. Some of the most common names are 'Tonquin' and 'Charlotte.' These items, while attractive and enjoyable to own, have little value in the collector market.

Beaker, Pine Grove, blk band at base, 5" 300.00
Bowl, Delecia, 5x11" 360.00
Bowl, Inspiration Fruit, rpr, 5x10" 350.00
Bowl, Inspiration Lily, stepped sides, sq 850.00
Bowl, Inspiration Odilon, conical, ftd, 4⅛" 240.00

Bowl, Latona Trees, 16½", $1,650.00. (Photo courtesy Skinner Inc. Auctioneers & Appraisers of Antiques & Fine Art/ LiveAuctioneers.com)

Clog, Coral Firs, 5½" L 375.00
Cup & saucer, demitasse; Cabbage Flower, 3" 400.00
Cup & saucer, demitasse; Capri, 3" 350.00
Jardiniere, Autumn, scenic, orange bands, 7½x8½" 660.00
Jardiniere, water lily form, 1940s, 5x7" 175.00
Jug, Celtic Harvest, ca 1930, 11x7" 95.00
Jug, Crocus, flared ft, 6" 250.00
Jug, milk; Oranges Cafe-Au-Lait, 3½" 300.00
Jug, milk; Pebbles, squat, 4" 425.00
Jug, My Garden, twig hdls w/leaves at base, 9" 200.00
Planter, Sungold, yel/orange/brn/wht, 6¾x7½" 515.00
Plate, Autumn Pastel, mc bands form border, smooth rim, 10" 725.00
Plate, Gibralter, rainbow-like border, 6" 300.00
Plate, Leaf Tree on speckled orange, gr border, 7½" 480.00
Plate, Pink Pearls, pastel floral, smooth rim, 6" 11.00
Plate, Secrets, tree to left of landscape, 6" 135.00
Plate, Summerhouse, yel border, 10" 550.00

Plate, Sunrise, smooth rim, 8¾" 660.00
Plate, Woodland, Deco style & colors, 9" 395.00
Preserves pot, Forest Glen, beehive form, 4" 395.00
Preserves pot, Moonflower, beehive form, 3½" 300.00
Preserves pot, Trees & House, cylindrical, 3½" 565.00
Sugar sifter, Coral Firs, autumn tones, 5" 660.00
Sugar sifter, Fragrance, mc flowers, Bonjour shape 400.00
Sugar sifter, Hononulu, landscape, conical, 5½" 1,450.00
Teacup & saucer, Green Cowslip, 6-sided 360.00
Teapot, Crocus, gr & wht lid, 5" 200.00
Teapot, early geometric pattern, cream/bl/orange, 4½" 360.00
Toast rack, Crocus, sm 150.00
Vase, Caprice, flared cylinder, 7" 900.00

Vase, Fantasque, 7¾", $1,900.00. (Photo courtesy Skinner Inc. Auctioneers & Appraisers of Antiques & Fine Art/LiveAuctioneers.com)

Vase, Goldstone, jug-like w/hdl 240.00
Vase, Inspiration Odilon, stepped sq sides, ftd, 7½" 725.00
Vase, Liberty, mc bands on wht, 3½" 300.00
Vase, Nasturtium, triangular, 7½" 300.00
Vase, Patina Country, flared cylinder, 8¼" 360.00
Vase, Patina Tree, shaped rim, 6" 600.00
Vase, Patina Tree, slightly bulbous, ring-trn base, 8¼" 600.00
Vase, Poplar, simple floral w/orange & red-orange bands, 12" ... 1,150.00

Clifton

Clifton Art Pottery of Clifton, New Jersey, was organized ca 1903. Until 1911 when they turned to the production of wall and floor tile, they made artware of several varieties. The founders were Fred Tschirner and William A. Long. Long had developed the method for underglaze slip painting that had been used at the Lonhuda Pottery in Steubenville, Ohio, in the 1890s. Crystal Patina, the first artware made by the small company, utilized a fine white body and flowing, blended colors, the earliest a green crystalline. Indian Ware, copied from the pottery of the American Indians, was usually decorated in black geometric designs on red clay. (On the occasions when white was used in addition to the black, the ware was often not as well executed; so even though two-color decoration is very rare, it is normally not as desirable to the collector.) Robin's Egg Blue, pale blue on the white body, and Tirrube, a slip-decorated matt ware, were also produced.

Coffeepot, Crystal Patina, gr, bulbous w/cylinder body, 6½" 125.00
Creamer, Indian Ware, blk on red clay, #274 .... 85.00
Vase, Crystal Patina, celadon w/yel & gr drips, w/hdls, #116, 4½" ..300.00
Vase, Crystal Patina, dk gr, hexagonal, squat, 1905, 4" dia........... 420.00
Vase, Crystal Patina, gr, cylindrical neck, #115, 1906, 5¼" 390.00
Vase, Crystal Patina, gr, deeply cvd fish, #180, 1906, 3½x3½" 500.00
Vase, Crystal Patina, gr, integral rim-to-shoulder hdls, 1906, 7x8" ... 570.00
Vase, Crystal Patina, gr w/tan flambé bottle shape, 1906/148/CAP, 9x5"..400.00

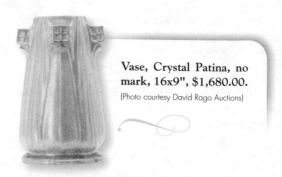

Vase, Crystal Patina, no mark, 16x9", $1,680.00.
(Photo courtesy David Rago Auctions)

Vase, Crystal Patina, tan to gr, sq trumpet neck, 1905, 7¼x5¼" ..275.00
Vase, Indian Ware, blk, tan & gray on red clay, #219, 3¼x6"....... 120.00
Vase, Indian Ware, blk & gray on red clay, gourd shape, #231, 12x9". 480.00
Vase, Indian Ware, blk & tan incised on red clay, #241, 10x13"..480.00
Vase, Indian Ware, blk & tan on red clay, #205, 6½x6¼" 300.00
Vase, Indian Ware, blk on red clay, #218, 1906, 2¾"................... 200.00

Clocks

In the early days of our country's history, clock makers were influenced by styles imported from Europe. They copied the Europeans' cabinets and reconstructed their movements — needed materials were in short supply; modifications had to be made. Of necessity was born mainspring motive power and spring clocks. Wooden movements were made on a mass-production basis as early as 1808. Before the middle of the century, brass movements had been developed.

Today's collectors prefer clocks from the eighteenth and nineteenth centuries with pendulum-regulated movements. Bracket clocks made during this period utilized the shorter pendulum improvised in 1658 by Fromentiel, a prominent English clock maker. These smaller square-face clocks usually were made with a dome top fitted with a handle or a decorative finial. The case was usually walnut or ebony and was sometimes decorated with pierced brass mountings. Brackets were often mounted on the wall to accommodate the clock, hence the name. The banjo clock was patented in 1802 by Simon Willard. It derived its descriptive name from its banjo-like shape. A similar but more elaborate style was called the lyre clock.

The first electric novelty clocks were developed in the 1940s. Lux, who was the major producer, had been in business since 1912, making wind-up novelties during the '20s and '30s. Another company, Mastercrafter Novelty Clocks, first obtained a patent to produce these clocks in the late 1940s. Other manufacturers were Keebler, Westclox, and Columbia Time. The cases were made of china, Syroco, wood, and plastic; most were animated and some had pendulettes. Prices vary according to condition and rarity. Unless noted otherwise, values are given for eight-day time only clocks in excellent condition. Clocks that have been altered, damaged, or have had parts replaced are worth considerably less. Our advisor is Bruce A. Austin; he is listed in the Directory under New York.

Key:
br — brass
dl — dial
esc — escapement
mcr — mercury
mvt — movement
pnd — pendulum

reg — regulator
rswd — rosewood
T — time
S — strike
wt — weight

Calendar Clocks

Atkins, rswd case, spring driven, 10"/6" dls & pnd bob, 1860s, 26"..850.00
E Ingraham Ionic, rswd-grained case, 12" dl, spring driven, 29". 1,200.00

Ithaca, Farmer's #10, walnut, not running, 26" **600.00**
Ithaca #8 library shelf, walnut 6"/8" dls, not running, 25¼" **725.00**
Ithaca Granger, walnut w/Welch mvt, ca 1884, rstr, 26x13" **725.00**
S Thomas, dbl dial in rswd case, 27x14" **725.00**
S Thomas #10, walnut w/2 10" dls, 49", NM **12,000.00**
S Thomas #9 Parlor, spring driven mvt, rpl dls, 30" **4,750.00**
Southern Calendar Clock Co, S Thomas mvt, walnut, 1870s, 32x15" ..**3,250.00**
Southern Calendar Clock Co #2 Fashion, walnut vnr, short pnd, 31" . **1,200.00**
Waterbury, gingerbread oak case, 27¾" **550.00**
Welch, oak kitchen type w/gingerbread case, 23x15" **155.00**
Welch #2 Reg, rswd vnr, 10"/10" dls, weight driven, not running, 36" . **1,200.00**

Novelty Clocks

Dixie Boy, Lux, 9", EX, $350.00. (Photo courtesy Morphy Auctions)

Bird in cage, gilt metal, German?, mk GESCH #204, 19th C, 3¾" .. **395.00**
Knight's helmet, porc dl, Camerden & Forster, 1880s, 11½", VG .. **1,200.00**
Liberty Bell, wood front, Lux, 5½" **200.00**
Lighthouse, revolving lantern top, 2" dl, New Haven, 12½", VG .**1,200.00**
Rotating sphere w/pnd held by 3 br pillars, US Clock Co, 10½"..**240.00**
Sambo w/banjo, blinking eyes, 34-hr, partial rpt, 15½" **1,800.00**
Stacked Arms (named Army), triangular base/gilt flag, Ansonia .**900.00**
Tick Tack, Nouveau lady beside clock, Syrian bronze look, Ansonia, 10".**250.00**
Winged cherub stands beside clock on pillar, gilt bronze, New Haven .**395.00**

Shelf Clocks

Brewster, mahog Gothic beehive case w/cut glass tablet, wooden dl, 19" ..**5,300.00**
Brewster Ives Pat, rswd vnr Venetian case, blk/gold glass, 1860s, 18".. **4,800.00**
Crane's Pat Month Clock, grpt/gilt/etch tablet/gilt dl, 1840s, 23". **11,000.00**
Crane's Pat 12-Month, 4-column ebonized/gilt case w/br mts, 23".**8,200.00**
Crane's Pat 8-Day, mahog, hinged top/etch tablet, pnd, 1840s, 21".**4,700.00**
E Terry, mahog Pillar & Scroll, scroll top, pnt dl, rvpt tablet, 31" .**1,100.00**
E Terry & Son, mahog Fed Pillar & Scroll, rvpt Mt Vernon, pnd, 31".**2,800.00**
S Thomas, mahog Fed Pillar & Scroll, br urns, 30-hr, 1820s, 31"..**1,500.00**
Willard, Boston; mahog w/br mts, kidney dl, 8-day TS, 1790, 34" ..**70,500.00**
Willard, mahog Classical Revival, rvpt tablet, wt-drive mvt, 1820, 33"..**3,400.00**
Wm Cooper, mahog vnr bracket, dbl fusee, br face panel, rfn, 18x11x7".**6,300.00**

Tall Case Clocks

Am, cherry/pine, pierced fretwork/spiral-trn columns, 30-hr mvt, 97". **1,550.00**
Barlow, Stockport; mahog inlay, Britannia figure at crest, 96"...**8,300.00**
Crampton, Dublin; mahog Irish Georgian, cvd hood, 2-train mvt, 85"...**10,600.00**
Dund, Scotland; cvd/inlaid mahog w/swan's neck crest, 1850s, 86" .**3,800.00**
E Warner, Lexington KY; cherry, broken arch mvt, 30-hr, pnd, 94".**3,225.00**
Fessler, Fredericktown; mahog/walnut, pnt dl, pnd, rfn, 97" **13,225.00**
Garty, Dublin; mahog Regency, rnd hood, pnt face, 2-train mvt, 76".**3,050.00**
Geo II, mahog w/inlay, dentiled cornice, br mvt, pnd, rfn, 80" .**2,050.00**
Gibbs, Haverfordwest; mahog w/inlay, gilt metal mts, 19th C, 84" ..**5,300.00**
Hughes, London; walnut QA, br/steel face, rectangular crest, 89" . **3,300.00**

Jennens & Son, Renaissance Revival, oak, 5 gongs/br & steel, 95" .**3,300.00**
Nicholl, mahog, scrolled hood/br rosettes/much cvg, T&S, 1815, 94" ..**35,250.00**
Unsgn, grpt pine, flat top, tombstone door, 30-hr, pnt dl, pnd, 84" ..**4,600.00**
Waltham, mahog, 3 trn finials, swan's nest crest, dentil mold, 98" .**3,000.00**
Willard, pnt birch QA, domed hood, br T&S, moon's age dl, 1760s, 89".**5,400.00**
Young, Liverpool; mahog w/cvg, swan's neck crest, 19th C, 91".**5,000.00**

Wall Clocks

Hilgers, Paris; Louis XVI bronze Cartel, 2-train mvt, 1790s, 30" ...**1,400.00**
L Curtis, mahog banjo, br trim/orig tablets, rfn, 40" **5,000.00**
NE (att), mahog/pine banjo, rvpt marine scene, acorn drop, rprs, 42" . **1,200.00**
NE (att), mahog/pine banjo, rvpt tablets, eagle finial, 31x10" **900.00**

Seth Thomas Jupiter, moon dial, bell strike, oak, refinished and restored, 59", $7,800.00. (Photo courtesy R.O. Schmitt Fine Arts)

S Willard, mahog coffin type, pnd, rfn, 35x11" **15,000.00**
Whiting, mahog banjo, br bezel, pnt dl, wood ornaments, wt-dr mvt, 33" ..**3,000.00**
Willard Jr, mahog banjo, rvpt Aurora scene/scrolls, alarm, 33".**4,700.00**

Cloisonné

    Cloisonné is defined as 'enamel ware in which the surface decoration is formed by different colors of enamel separated by thin strips of metal.' In the early original process, precious and semi-precious stones were crushed and their colors placed into the thin wire cells (cloisons) in selected artistic designs. Though a French word, cloisonné was first made in tenth-century Egypt. To achieve the orginal result, many processes may be used. There are also several styles and variations of this art form. Standard cloisonné involves only one style, using opaque enamel within cloison borders. Besides metal, cloisonné is also worked into and on ceramics, glass, gold, porcelain, silver, and wood. Pliqué a jour is a style in which the transparent enamel is used between cloisons that are not anchored to a base material. In wireless cloisonné, the wires (cloisons) are pulled from the workmanship before the enamel is ever fired. Household items, decorative items, and ceremonial pieces made for royalty have been decorated with cloisonné. It has been made for both export and domestic use.

    General cloisonné varies in workmanship as well as color, depending on the country of origin. In later years some cloisonné was made in molds, almost by assembly line. Examples of Chinese cloisonné made in the past 100 years or so seem to have brighter colors, as does the newer Taiwan cloisonné. In most of the Japanese ware, the maker actually studies his subject in nature before transfering his art into cloisonné form.

    Cloisonné is a medium that demands careful attention to detail; please consult a professional for restoration. Our advisor for this category is Jeffery M. Person. Mr. Person has been a collector and dealer for 40 years. He is a speaker, writer, and appraiser on the subject of cloisonné. He is listed in the Directory under Florida.

Chinese

Basin, horses & waves, int w/foo dogs, Ming period, 18"........... **7,650.00**
Box, foo dogs & qiln circle rim, bat/peach reserve, 4½x9x8" **600.00**
Censor, tripod ft, Buddhist lion finial, 19th C, 8" **900.00**
Figure, seated Quan Yin, bronze face/bib/hands/ft, 23" **820.00**
Plate, foo dog surrounded w/5 red floral-design petals on turq, 12".....**115.00**
Table, rosewood w/floral insert top, 20th C, 24x14" dia **120.00**
Teapot/wine server, foo lions on bl, rpl wire hdl, 1800s, 5½x7"....**135.00**
Vase, floral, mc on iron red, baluster, 1900-30, 9½x4½" **180.00**
Vase, mc patterns, acorn form w/4 lg bronze buttresses, 1900, 14" ..**525.00**
Vase, peonies, bl on geometric wht, tassel rim, stick neck, 15x7" . **960.00**

Japanese

Temple dog, repoussé bronze full figure, 20" long, $350.00. (Photo courtesy Jackson's International Auctioneers & Appraisers of Fine Art & Antiques)

Charger, flying crane on bl, 19th C, 14¼"................................... **350.00**
Vase, allover sm mc flowers w/gold on blk, bulbous, 15"........... **1,600.00**
Vase, birds & wisteria on dk bl, silver wire type, 1900s, 10", pr.**1,295.00**
Vase, birds on flowering tree, silver wire type, 1920s, 12½".......**2,935.00**
Vase, bl reserve w/lg bird & roses, bk: 2nd bird/floral reserve, 18" ..**4,000.00**
Vase, finches & pk blossoms on gr, sm bruise, 12"; pr **500.00**
Vase, flowering tree/bird/rooster/hen on blk, 7½", pr.................**1,560.00**
Vase, lg rooster, bk: hen, ovoid w/long neck, 6", pr **3,000.00**
Vase, orchid flowers on pale apricot, ca 1900, 9" **585.00**
Vase, pheasants/quail/sparrows/etc, gilt silver mts, 19th C, 9", pr..**3,300.00**
Vase, roosters/flowers/banana trees on yel, Meijo period, 27", pr. **2,825.00**

Clothing and Accessories

The field of collectible clothing is highly personalized and often confusing for the novice collector or nonspecialty dealer. Prices vary enormously from marketplace to marketplace. Four basic factors contribute to the valuation of clothing. They are:

1. Size. Larger sizes are more valuable as they can be worn or displayed on full-size mannequins. The rule of thumb here is 'The Bigger, The Better.' Adult clothes in tiny sizes are nearly impossible to sell and must be drastically discounted.

2. Condition. Even the smallest tear, rip, stain, or discoloration devalues a piece by as much as 75%.

3. Quality. High quality in construction, type of fabrics and trims, and design add greatly to the value of the piece. The more elaborate the piece, the higher the price.

4. Age. This is sometimes difficult to determine. Beware of reproductions and/or mismarked pieces. A good pictoral fashion reference book is recommended. A few clues to help in dating clothing are as follows:

If you see:	the date is:
machine stitching	after 1850
snaps	after 1912
zippers	after 1935
elastic	after 1915
boning or metal stays in bodice	before 1905
boning or metal stays, collar only	after 1904
tags on waistband	after 1870
tags on neckline	after 1905

For further information we recommend *Ladies' Vintage Accessories* by LaRea Johnson Bruton; and *Antique & Vintage Clothing: A Guide to Dating and Valuation of Women's Clothing, 1850 – 1940*, by our advisor, Diane Snyder-Haug. (Ms. Snyder-Haug is listed in the Directory under Florida.) Vintage denim values are prices realized at Flying Deuce Auctions, who specialize not only in denims but Hawaiian shirts, souvenir jackets, and various other types of vintage clothing. They are listed in the Directory under Auction Houses. Our values are for items of ladies' clothing unless noted 'man's' or child's.' Assume them to be in excellent condition unless otherwise described.

Key:

cap/s — cap sleeves	ms — machine sewn
embr — embroidery	n/s — no sleeves
hs — hand sewn	plt — pleated
l/s — long sleeves	s/s — short sleeves

Apron, floral cotton, gathered waist, patch pocket, 1940s-50s........ **24.00**
Apron, ivory batiste waist type w/embr pk silk bows, 1920s........... **15.00**
Apron, wht muslin, sq neck w/wide straps, rickrack/embr, 1930s... **28.00**
Bed jacket, pk rayon w/rnd neck, ribbon tie, n/s, 1940s **45.00**
Bed jacket, printed lav satin w/lace trim, sash ties, s/s, 1940s......... **48.00**
Bloomers, brn wool tweed, wide waist yoke, button cuff band, 1920s..**85.00**
Blouse, beige cotton floral lace, V-neck w/ruffled collar, s/s, 1930s...**78.00**
Blouse, blk lace, scoop neck w/satin binding, l/s, flat front, 1920s. **155.00**
Blouse, blk satin knit, Western style w/patch pockets, l/s, 1970s ... **18.00**
Blouse, blk silk sack style w/starburst plts at waist, 1960s............... **45.00**
Blouse, blk/pk stripe cotton, sash tie at neck, cap/s, 1950s............. **58.00**
Blouse, pk batiste, V-neck w/spread collar, ruffle front, s/s, 1930s .. **65.00**
Blouse, printed cotton, boat neck, elbow/s cut from same pc, 1960s..**48.00**
Blouse, printed cotton, notched collar, button front, ¾/s, 1950s.... **32.00**
Blouse, yel cotton band collar w/petal tie, button front, s/s, 1950s...**32.00**
Bodice, blk Chantilly lace w/ivory net over pk silk, l/s, ca 1913 .... **85.00**
Bolero, ivory machine lace, dbl ruffle border, bias/s, ca 1904 .... **125.00**
Boxer shorts, man's, printed cotton, elastic waist, 1950s **28.00**
Bra, ivory lace & pk silk, ribbon straps, 1930s **35.00**
Bra, peach silk w/lace & embr, narrow straps, 1940s....................... **35.00**
Bustle pad, red & bl striped muslin, metal coil, straw stuffing, 1890s .**125.00**
Camisole, wht cotton & knitted lace w/pk rosebuds, button front, 1890s. **65.00**
Cape, blk wool w/brn fur collar, appliqué work, lined, 1890s **165.00**
Cape, fuchsia velvet w/chinchilla collar & cuffs, lined, 1920s **695.00**
Cape, plaid wool w/ivory collar, botton front, lined, 1970s............ **58.00**
Chemise, pk silk w/ivory lace, hook & eye front, 1920s **58.00**
Coat, blk wool brocade w/mink collar/cuffs, 1960s....................... **160.00**
Coat, eggplant silk w/mink collar & trim, ¾/s, Saks 5th Ave, 1950s .**250.00**
Coat, gray knit w/astrakhan collar/cuffs, dbl-breasted, 1960s....... **148.00**
Coat, man's, gray wool, sm collar, raglan/s w/cuffs, 1950s............... **65.00**
Coat, mohair w/stand-up neckline, elbow/s, 1960s....................... **148.00**
Coat, motoring; silk/linen, lg collar, raglan/s, sash belt, 1910s..... **285.00**
Coat, pea; navy wool, dbl-breasted w/gold buttons, lined, 1960s ... **98.00**
Coat, wht & gold jacquard, wide stand collar, raglan/s, 1940s **150.00**
Dickey, embr net w/lace bands, button-bk, drawstring waist, 1910s.**55.00**
Dress, bl cotton, sm collar/button front, dolman/s, full skirt, 1950s .**65.00**
Dress, bl silk taffeta w/silk corsage, bubble skirt, 1950s.................. **85.00**
Dress, bl taffeta, strapless top w/rosette, full skirt w/net, 1960s **215.00**
Dress, blk & wht knit w/tiered/s w/blk cotton edging, 1960s **78.00**
Dress, blk crepe w/blk net inserts in skirt, n/s, 1960s...................... **75.00**
Dress, blk crepe w/notched lapels, flower buttons, l/s, belt, 1940s.. **85.00**
Dress, blk lace & chiffon, bustier-style chemise w/overblouse, 1950s. **95.00**
Dress, blk rayon, platter coller w/beads & ribbonwork, s/s, 1950s .. **50.00**

Dress, blk silk chiffon w/pk ribbon trim, plt l/s, 1960s 145.00
Dress, blk silk jersey top w/l/s & floral brocade skirt 1960s............. 78.00
Dress, blk taffeta w/beading, swagged bodice/draped bk, n/s, 1920s..595.00
Dress, blk/ivory satin w/tulle/crochet, s/s, cummerbund/train, 1910s .395.00
Dress, cotton print, wrap front w/ties at left, red piping, s/s, 1940s...58.00
Dress, dotted silk w/velvet applique, cummerbund w/buckle, l/s, 1910s..425.00
Dress, floral chiffon, cape collar w/ties, bias flounce, 1930s 265.00
Dress, floral chiffon, V-neck w/sm bow, l/s, dropped waist, 1920s. 135.00
Dress, floral cotton w/ribbon trim, A-line, s/s, belt w/buckle, 1930s..75.00
Dress, hostess; emerald gr velvet w/mink collar, ¾/s, 1950s.......... 245.00
Dress, ivory/blk crepe w/lg pk bow, deep V neck, cap/s, 1970s 65.00
Dress, peach taffeta w/tangerine lace, strapless, full skirt, 1950s .. 185.00
Dress, printed chiffon, dbl-ruffle neck, tiered/s, bias skirt, 1930s..198.00
Dress, printed chiffon w/rhinestones, ¾/s, fully lined, 1960s 185.00
Dress, printed cotton w/spread collar, navy piping, l/s, belt, 1930s...85.00
Dress, printed paper, n/s, Arlene Knitwear, 1960s, MIP 78.00
Dress, printed paper, n/s, Waste Basket Boutique, 1960s 95.00
Dress, printed rayon, wrap front, s/s, panel skirt, 1940s 92.00
Dress, printed silk w/rhinestones, s/s, circle skirt 1950s 85.00
Dress, printed wool knit, scoop neck, n/s, plt skirt, maxi, 1970s 68.00
Dress, printed/puckered organdy, sweetheart neck, wide straps, 1940s...98.00
Dress, purple silk w/tatted lace yoke, V-neck, 2-pc l/s, ca 1902 .... 275.00
Dress, silk crepe, V-neck w/wrap bodice, bias skirt, l/s, 1930s....... 125.00
Dress, silk jersey knit, draped bodice, shirred l/s, slim skirt, 1950s . 85.00
Dress, striped cotton, sweetheart neckline, rickrack trim, s/s, 1940s .55.00
Dress, tan linen, scoop neck, raglan s/s, orange embr/ribbons, 1950s . 98.00
Dress, turq silk chiffon w/sequined top, shoulder scarf, 1960s 185.00
Dress, wht batiste, flat-panel front, pin tucks, elbow/s, ca 1900s..248.00
Dress, wht batiste, wrap front, shawl collar, ¾/s, full skirt, 1900s . 195.00
Dress, wht batiste w/lace trim, elbow/s, gathered skirt, ca 1900s..185.00
Dress, wht cotton, V-neck w/sm tie, drop waist, n/s, plt skirt, 1920s .. 85.00
Dress, wht cotton crochet, l/s w/scallops, sash tie, 1970s 98.00
Dress, wht cotton w/bl embr, sq neck, s/s, slim skirt, 1950s 110.00
Dress, wht linen, V-neck, glass buttons, s/s jacket, slim skirt, 1930s..88.00

Dress, white linen with embroidered designs, bell sash, ca 1914, $300.00.
(Photo courtesy Treadway Gallery Inc.)

Dress, yel silk chiffon & lace, scoop neck, s/s, slim skirt, 1950s...... 85.00
Dress, yel silk taffeta, scoop neck, cummerbund/sash, s/s, 1920s ..225.00
Dress coat, rayon crepe, starburst quilted shoulders, belt, 1930s 88.00
Girdle, tan spandex, attached garter straps, Munsingwear, 1950s .. 20.00
Gown, morning; fuchsia silk, V-neck w/gathers, elbow/s, c 1912 .395.00
Halter top, cotton/linen, removable strap, 1950s........................... 35.00
Hat, brn paisley velvet toque w/wired lace trim/gold accents, VG+...95.00
Hat, burgundy satin & velvet turban cloche, pleated w/twist, 1920s . 58.00
Hat, gold bullion toque w/lace crown & grosgrain ribbon, 1920s, M .165.00

Hat, navy woven chip straw with flower cluster and netting, ca. 1940s, $80.00. (Photo courtesy Vintage Martini)

Hat, quilted fur felt w/folded brim, wing at left side, Paris, 1920s .. 95.00
Jacket, bl floral lace w/linen trim, s/s, 1950s................................... 38.00
Jacket, gr silk brocade, shawl collar, button decor, curved hem, 1950s..145.00
Jacket, man's, blk/gold brocade tuxedo, notched collar/1 button, 1950s.125.00
Jacket, man's, ivory linen, shawl collar, 1 button, lined, 1950s 125.00
Jacket, man's, red irid silk, shawl collar, 1 button, l/s, 1950s 165.00
Jacket, man's, windowpane wool, notched lapels, 1 button, 1940s. 95.00
Jacket, navy wool, long collar w/notched lapels, silk lined, ca 1912...145.00
Jacket, yel batiste w/mc needlework, bands at open front, l/s, 1920s .. 70.00
Jumpsuit, red crepe, l/s, long fringe covers pants, 1970s 145.00
Lounger/jumper, printed knit, V-neck w/zipper front, l/s, 1970s..... 58.00
Merry widow, embr nylon organza & spandex, 1950s 45.00
Nightgown, blk silk georgette & lace, V-neck, 1920s 125.00
Nightgown, satin w/ivory lace, sq neck, s/s, bias skirt, 1940s.......... 75.00
Nightgown, silk georgette w/ribbon rosettes, Empire waist, 1920s ..128.00
Pajamas, man's, striped perma press, V-neck w/inset pocket, 1950s .45.00
Pants, blk gabardine, high waist, plts, 1940s 115.00
Pants, man's, blk felt tuxedo, flat front w/silk ribbon sides, 1920s .. 58.00
Pants, man's, blk gabardine, flat front, martingale bk, 1910s.......... 95.00
Pants, man's, brn wool gabardine, plt front, cuffs, 1950s 85.00
Peignoir, yel crinkle batiste w/ivory lace, gown & robe, 1970s....... 80.00
Petticoat, wht batiste w/lace insert, ruffled hem, embr flowers, 1910s..68.00
Petticoat, wht cotton, gored w/front box pleat, crochet trim, 1910s .85.00
Petticoat, wht muslin & organdy, gathered panels, flounce, 1950s...35.00
Playsuit, striped cotton, sq neck, n/s, skirt-all & bloomers, 1950s..68.00
Robe, man's, bl brocade, shawl collar, sash ties, l/s w/cuffs, 1950s..58.00
Robe, printed cotton, wrap front w/2 lg button, s/s, 1940s 68.00
Shawl, wht organdy w/embr floral edge, floral lace trim, 1840s.... 295.00
Shell, tan knit w/copper pearls/beads/sequins/etc, lined, n/s, 1960s .85.00
Shirt, man's, blk wool knit w/vinyl front, pullover, l/s, 1960s.......... 78.00
Shirt, man's, gr nylon, wide spread collar, 2 pockets, s/s, 1950s...... 65.00
Shirt, man's, Hawaiian print cotton, spread collar, s/s, 1960s.......... 78.00
Shirt, man's, Hawaiian print rayon, patch pockets, s/s, 1950s 125.00
Shirt, man's, patterned cotton oxford, patch pocket, l/s, 1970s....... 28.00
Shirt, man's, printed rayon, winged collar, patch pockets, s/s, 1950s.. 78.00
Shirt, man's, striped cotton, sm collar, patch pockets, l/s, 1950s 38.00
Shirt, man's, striped knit polo, s/s, 1970s 85.00
Shirt, man's, wool gabardine, rnd collar, 2 patch pockets, l/s, 1950s .48.00
Shirt, navy wool w/Western embr & wht twill piping, l/s, 1950s ... 98.00
Shirt, plaid cotton blend, spread collar, button front, s/s, 1950s 40.00
Shirt, red gabardine, spread collar, patch pocket, l/s, 1950s 78.00
Shirt, tropical print cotton, notched lapels, n/s, darts, 1950s 65.00
Shirt, yel rayon w/blk bowling pins & embr name, s/s, 1950s......... 60.00
Shirt waist, ivory silk organza w/gingham collar/lace, l/s, ca 1915.. 65.00
Shirt waist, wht batiste w/crochet, stand collar, button bk, l/s, 1908..125.00
Shoes, bl silk faille pumps w/metallic bl leather trim, 1930s 95.00
Shoes, blk & wht leather lace-up boots, 3" Louis XV heel, 1890s. 345.00
Shoes, blk leather lace-up boots, high-tops, 2½" heels, 1900s........ 75.00
Shoes, blk leather platform w/peep toes, sling-bk, 4½" heel, 1940s.225.00
Shoes, blk silk oxfords w/patent leather trim, 3" Fr heel, 1930s 65.00
Shoes, blk silk pumps w/high vamp, rnd toe, 2½" Louis heel, 1910s ..125.00
Shoes, blk silk/wool lace-up ankle boots w/muslin lining, 1840s..395.00
Shoes, blk suede sling-bk w/cutout on sides, 3½" heels, 1930s 145.00
Shoes, blk suede w/open toes, rhinestone trim, 3½" heels, 1950s... 78.00

Shoes, brn crocodile platforms, sling-bk w/side buckle, 4" heel, 1940s.. 345.00
Shoes, brn/clear floral plastic w/3" Lucite heels, 1950s 85.00
Shoes, cotton bathing slippers w/wht grommets, rubber soles, 1920s .. 65.00
Shoes, leather sandals, crisscross straps, sling-bk, 4" heels, 1950s .. 75.00
Shoes, silver glitter pumps, 4½" spike heels, 1950s 95.00
Shoes, spats, blk wool felt, side buttons, bottom strap, high-tops... 45.00
Shorts, ivory linen, side buttons, red appliquè on pocket, 1940s.... 38.00
Shorts, red & wht seersucker, wide waist band, side buttons, 1940s. 38.00
Skirt, bl wool w/Russian-style embr on waistband & near hem, 1930s... 78.00
Skirt, blk knit w/accordion plts w/crochet border, high waist, 1970s.. 48.00
Skirt, felt circle w/appl carousel horse, 1950s............................. 150.00
Slip, pk rayon w/lace trim, bias skirt, 1930s 35.00
Suit, brn suede, sm collar/button front/sash belt/A-line skirt, 1970s .. 45.00
Suit, dk tweed, sm collar, patch pockets, l/s, slim skirt, 1950s 145.00
Suit, dotted navy faille, button front, patch pockets, ¾/s, 1950s .. 145.00
Suit, man's, cotton/wool blend, notched lapel, 3-button, 1960s .. 145.00
Suit, man's, navy gabardine, wide collar, dbl-breasted, 1940s......... 95.00
Suit, navy silk, dbl-breasted l/s jacket w/slip-top skirt, 1960s 145.00
Suit, windowpane knit w/blk sleeves, lg blk buttons, slim skirt, 1950s... 85.00
Sweater, pk cotton ribbed knit, dbl-breasted, elbow/s, collar, 1950s.. 68.00
Sweater, pk sequins, zipper front, l/s, 1960s 65.00
Swim trunks, man's, printed cotton, lace-up front, bk pocket, 1970s... 38.00
Swimsuit, man's, wool knit, top attaches to trunks w/zipper, 1930s.. 85.00
Swimsuit, printed cotton, halter top, trunks w/attached skirt, 1940s . 65.00
Vest, man's, gray flannel wool, 2 chest/2 waist pockets, 1920s........ 48.00
Vest, man's, silk brocade, shawl collar, 3-button, lined, ca 1915 .... 65.00
Wrapper, red wool, stand-up collar w/lace, button front, l/s, 1900s .. 165.00

Vintage Denim

Condition is very important in evaluating vintage denims. Unless otherwise described, assume our values are for items in Number 1 grade. To qualify as a Number 1 grade, there must be no holes larger than a pinhole. A missing belt loop is permissible as long as it has not resulted in a hole. Only a few very light stains and minor fading may be present, the crotch seam must be strong with no holes, and the item must not have been altered. Be sure to access the condition of the garment you are dealing with objectively, then adjust our prices up or down as your assessment dictates. The term 'deadstock' refers to a top-grade item that has never been worn or washed and still has its original tags. 'Hedge' indicates the faded fold lines that develop on the front of denim jeans from sitting.

Bib overalls, Levi, exposed rivets, prof rpr, 1920s 2,250.00
Bib overalls, Osh Kosh Union Made Vestbk, button fly, 1940s 100.00
Jacket, Lee 91B, lg, deadstock 200.00
Jacket, Levi E, dk bl, lg... 50.00
Jacket, Levi 70505e, single-stitch, indigo, 1960s, G sz/condition... 45.00
Jacket, Sledge's, plt front, buckle bk, cuffs, 1940s 115.00
Jeans, Lee 101B, med dk bl, 31x31" 200.00
Jeans, Levi Cargo, 2 patch pockets, snap closures, 1970s.............. 275.00
Jeans, Levi 501, single-stitch red-lines, very dk, 33x32" 285.00
Jeans, Levi 501E, A-patch, G soiled look, slight damage............. 300.00
Jeans, Levi 501E, paper patches, lg 375.00
Jeans, Levi 501E, very dk, 32x31", from $400 to......................... 450.00
Jeans, Levi 501e, single-stitch, good color, slight hege, rpr, $150 to . 180.00
Jeans, Levi 501XX E, button fly/red-lines, #4 top button, good hege, G .. 135.00
Jeans, Levi 502E, very dk, 32x31" 475.00
Jeans, Levi 505E, med bl, good hege, 38x30", EX 120.00
Jeans, Levi 517, single-stitch, med color, good hege, 33x32" 80.00
Jeans, Levi 70505E, dk bl, sz 38, EX 125.00
Jeans, Wrangler Blue Bell, med dk color, 31x33"......................... 210.00
Shirt, Wrangler Blue Bell, wht denim Western style, 1960s, VG. 225.00
Tote bag, Levi E, 13x15", VG... 20.00

Cluthra

The name cluthra is derived from the Scottish word 'clutha,' meaning cloudy. Glassware by this name was first produced by J. Couper and Sons, England. Frederick Carder developed cluthra while at the Steuben Glass Works, and similar types of glassware were also made by Durand and Kimball. It is found in both solid and shaded colors and is characterized by a spotty appearance resulting from small air pockets trapped between its two layers. See also specific manufacturers.

Vase, blk to wht, 6" 240.00
Vase, cream/orange/yel, bulbous w/flared rim, Kimball, 8" 465.00
Vase, gr, bulbous w/flared rim, att Kimball, 4¾" 180.00

Vase, green shading to white, Steuben, 10", $1,000.00. (Photo courtesy John Shuman III)

Vase, orange, spherical, K (Kimball) 1995-6, 5⅛x5" 300.00
Vase, posy; yel, wide flanged rim, att Kimball, 1½x5¼" 100.00
Vase, sky bl w/crystal ft, K (Kimball) 2011-8, 8½" 360.00
Vase, wht, flared rim, K (Kimball) 1710-6, 6½" 165.00
Vase, yel/brn/wht/rust, Kimball, Dec 22, 12" 575.00

Coalport

In 1745 in Caughley, England, Squire Brown began a modest business fashioning crude pots and jugs from clay mined in his own fields. Tom Turner, a young potter who had apprenticed his trade at Worcester, was hired in 1772 to plan and oversee the construction of a 'proper' factory. Three years later he bought the business, which he named Caughley Coalport Porcelain Manufactory. Though the dinnerware he produced was meant to be only everyday china, the hand-painted florals, birds, and landscapes used to decorate the ware were done in exquisite detail and in a wide range of colors. In 1780 Turner introduced the Willow pattern which he produced using a newly perfected method of transfer printing. (Wares from the period between 1775 and 1799 are termed 'Caughley' or 'Salopian.') John Rose purchased the Caughley factory from Thomas Turner in 1799, adding that holding to his own pottery which he had built two years before in Coalport. (It is from this point that the pottery's history that the wares are termed 'Coalport.') The porcelain produced there before 1814 was unmarked with very few exceptions. After 1820 some examples were marked with a '2' with an oversize top loop. The term 'Coalbrookdale' refers to a fine type of porcelain decorated in floral bas relief, similar to the work of Dresden.

After 1835 highly decorated ware with rich ground colors imitated the work of Sevres and Chelsea, even going so far as to copy their marks. From about 1895 until the 1920s, the mark in use was 'Coalport' over a crown with 'England A.D. 1750' indicating the date claimed as the founding, not the date of manufacture. From the 1920s until 1945, 'Made in England' over a crown and 'Coalport' below was used. Later the mark was 'Coalport' over a smaller crown with 'Made in England' in a curve below.

Each of the major English porcelain companies excelled in certain areas of manufacture. Coalport produced the finest 'jeweled' porcelain, made by picking up a heavy mixture of slip and color and dropping it onto the surface of the ware. These 'jewels' are perfectly spaced and are often graduated in size with the smaller 'jewels' at the neck or base of the vase. Some ware was decorated with very large 'jewels' resembling black opals or other polished stones. Such pieces are in demand by the advanced collector.

It is common to find considerable crazing in old Coalport, since the glaze was thinly applied to increase the brilliance of the colors. Many early vases had covers; look for a flat surface that would have supported a lid (just because it is gilded does not mean the vase never had one). Pieces whose lids are missing are worth about 40% less. Most lids had finials which have been broken and restored. You should deduct about 10% for a professional restoration on a finial.

In 1926 the Coalport Company moved to Shelton in Staffordshire and today belongs to a group headed by the Wedgwood Company. See also Indian Tree.

Basket, pk roses w/gold, 4 gold ft, ca 1810-20, 10".....................**3,950.00**
Bowl, dessert; Rock & Tree, oval, ca 1805, 11¼" L...................**1,100.00**
Bowl, flowers & insects, floral finial, hdls, ca 1830, 8½", EX........ **500.00**
Bowl, moth/insects reserve on bl w/gold, shell shape, ca 1810, 8¼" ...**2,000.00**
Goblet, landscape reserves w/gold on cobalt, H Percy, 3-hdl, 1900s, 8"..**1,750.00**
Ice pail, floral on wht w/gr & gold bands, ca 1820, 14¾", pr **4,485.00**
Plaque, mixed flowers in vase, S Lawrance, oval, 1824, 14¾" ...**9,600.00**
Plate, Dragon in Compartment, notched gold border, 19th C, 8". **150.00**
Plate, plain wht center, pk rim w/gold scrolls, 8¾", 8 for.............. **660.00**
Platter, Rock & Tree, Imari colors, oval, ca 1805, 18"................**2,280.00**
Teapot, fluted body w/gold foliage on cobalt bands, 9⅞" **300.00**
Vase, Dragons in Compartments/landscape panel, 1840s, mtd as lamp, 24"..**2,700.00**
Vase, figures in reserves on gr w/gold, w/lid, ca 1851-61, 12", pr.. **2,150.00**
Vase, landscape panel w/gold & jewels, hdls, #V5955, 1900s, 9¼", pr.. **2,200.00**
Vase, pk w/raised gold foliage, 1890s, 6", pr **850.00**

Vase, scenic medallion, parcel gilt and allover jeweling, retailed by Bailey Banks & Biddle, 8", $3,600.00. (Photo courtesy Alex Cooper Auctioneers Inc./ LiveAuctioneers.com)

Coca-Cola

J.S. Pemberton, creator of Coca-Cola, originated his world-famous drink in 1886. From its inception the Coca-Cola Company began an incredible advertising campaign which has proven to be one of the most successful promotions in history. The quantity and diversity of advertising material put out by Coca-Cola in the last 100 years is literally mind-boggling. From the beginning, the company has projected an image of wholesomeness and Americana. Beautiful women in Victorian costumes, teenagers and schoolchildren, blue-and white-collar workers, the men and women of the Armed Forces, even Santa Claus, have appeared in advertisements with a Coke in their hands. Some of the earliest collectibles include trays, syrup dispensers, gum jars, pocket mirrors, and calendars. Many of these items fetch prices in the thousands of dollars. Later examples include radios, signs, lighters, thermometers, playing cards, clocks, and toys — particularly toy trucks.

In 1970 the Coca-Cola Company initialed a multimillion-dollar 'image-refurbishing campaign' which introduced the new 'Dynamic Contour' logo, a twisting white ribbon under the Coca-Cola and Coke trademarks. The new logo often serves as a cut-off point to the purist collector. Newer and very ardent collectors, however, relish the myriad of items marketed since that date, as they often cannot afford the high prices that the vintage pieces command. For more information we recommend *Petretti's Coca-Cola Collectibles Price Guide*; and *B.J. Summers' Guide to Coca-Cola*, *B.J. Summers' Pocket Guide to Coca-Cola*, and *Collectible Soda Pop Memorabilia*, all by B.J. Summers. Our advisor for this category is Craig Stifter; he is listed in the Directory under Oklahoma.

Key.
cb — cardboard　　　　　　　　sf — self-framed
CC — Coca-Cola　　　　　　　tm — trademark
dc — diecut

Reproductions and Fantasies

Beware of reproductions! Warning! The 1924, 1925, and 1935 calendars have been reproduced. They are identical in almost every way; only a professional can tell them apart. These are *very* deceiving! Watch for frauds: genuinely old celluloid items ranging from combs, mirrors, knives, and forks to doorknobs that have been recently etched with a new double-lined trademark. Still another area of concern deals with reproduction and fantasy items. A fantasy item is a novelty made to appear authentic with inscriptions such as 'Tiffany Studios,' 'Trans Pan Expo,' 'World's Fair,' etc. In reality, these items never existed as originals. For instance, don't be fooled by a Coca-Cola cash register; no originals are known to exist! Large mirrors for bars are being reproduced and are often selling for $10.00 to $50.00.

Of the hundreds of reproductions (designated 'R' in the following examples) and fantasies (designated 'F') on the market today, these are the most deceiving.

Belt buckle, no originals thought to exist (F), up to **10.00**
Bottle, dk amber, w/arrows, heavy, narrow spout (R)...................... **10.00**
Bottle carrier, wood, yel w/red logo, holds 6 bottles (R)................. **10.00**
Clock, Gilbert, regulator, battery-op, ¾-sz, NM+ (R) **175.00**
Cooler, Glascock Jr, made by Coca-Cola USA (R) **200.00**
Doorknob, glass etched w/tm (F)..**3.00**
Knife, bottle shape, 1970s, many variations (F), ea **5.00**
Knife, fork or spoon w/celluloid hdl, newly etched tm (F) **5.00**
Letter opener, stamped metal, Coca-Cola for 5¢ (F) **3.00**
Pocket watch, often old watch w/new face (R)............................... **10.00**
Pocketknife, yel & red, 1933 World's Fair (F)................................**2.00**
Sign, cb, lady w/fur, dtd 1911, 9x11" (F)......................................**3.00**
Soda fountain glass holder, word 'Drink' on orig (R)......................**5.00**
Thermometer, bottle form, DONASCO, 17" (R)........................... **10.00**
Trade card, copy of 1905 'Bathtub' foldout, emb 1978 (R)............ **15.00**

The following items have been reproduced and are among the most deceptive of all:
Pocket mirrors from 1905, 1906, 1908, 1909, 1910, 1911, 1916, and 1920
Trays from 1899, 1910, 1913, 1914, 1917, 1920, 1923, 1925, 1926, 1934, and 1937
Tip trays from 1907, 1909, 1910, 1913, 1914, 1917, and 1920
Knives: many versions of the German brass model
Cartons: wood versions, yellow with logo
Calendars: 1924, 1925, and 1935
These items have been marketed:
Brass thermometer, bottle shape, Taiwan, 24"
Cast-iron toys (none ever made)

Cast-iron door pull, bottle shape, made to look old

Poster, Yes Girl (R)

Button sign, has one round hole while original has four slots, most have bottle logo, 12", 16", 20" (R)

Bullet trash receptacles (old cans with decals)

Paperweight, rectangular, with Pepsin Gum insert

1930 Bakelite radio, 24" tall, repro is lighter in weight than the original, of poor quality, and cheaply made

1949 cooler radio (reproduced with tape deck)

Tin bottle sign, 40"

Fishtail die-cut tin sign, 20" long

Straw holders (no originals exist)

Coca-Cola bicycle with cooler, fantasy item: the piece has been totally made-up, no such original exists

1914 calendar top, reproduction, 11¼x23¾", printed on smooth-finish heavy ivory paper

Countless trays — most unauthorized (must read 'American Artworks; Coshocton, OH.')

Centennial Items

The Coca-Cola Company celebrated its 100th birthday in 1986, and amidst all the fanfare came many new collectible items, all sporting the 100th-anniversary logo. These items are destined to become an important part of the total Coca-Cola collectible spectrum. The following pieces are among the most popular centennial items.

Bottle, gold-dipped, in velvet sleeve, 6½-oz 75.00
Bottle, Hutchinson, amber, Root Co, ½-oz, 3 in case 375.00
Bottle, International, set of 9 in plexiglas case 300.00
Bottle, leaded crystal, 100th logo, 6½-oz, MIB 150.00
Medallion, bronze, 3" dia, w/box 100.00
Pin set, wood fr, 101 pins 300.00
Scarf, silk, 30x30" 40.00
Thermometer, glass cover, 14" dia, M 35.00

Coca-Cola Originals

Ashtray, Enjoy Ice Cold Coke on bib, 1941, EX 65.00
Banner, King Size, paper, 1958, 36x20", NM 110.00
Bottle, aqua, block print emb on base, 6½-oz, EX 35.00
Bottle, Hutchinson, emb Birmingham Bottling Co, AL, 7", VG ..2,415.00
Bottle carrier, cb, triangular, 1950s, M 65.00
Bowl, Vernonware, Drink CC emb on gr ceramic, 1930s, 4x10", NM .450.00
Calendar, 1920, lady in yel dress w/golf course in distance, 32x12", G..345.00
Carton insert, Take Home This Handy..., 1936, EX 175.00
Clock, Drink CC in Bottles, red/wht bull's-eye face, rnd, EX 400.00
Clock, Drink CC in Bottles red dot on wht, wood fr, 1939, sq, 16", EX...350.00
Clock, Drink CC red fishtail, metal/glass, 1960s, 15x15", EX 185.00
Clock, Gilbert, oak w/paper dial, girl below, 1910, 37x19", VG. 4,370.00

Clock, light-up, ca. 1930s – 1940s, VG, $4,800.00. (Photo courtesy Gary Metz)

Clock, light-up countertop, Serve Yourself, 1940s-50s, EX 650.00
Clock, regulator, oak, key-wind, 1980s, 23", M............................ 225.00

Cooler, lunchbox; Progress Refrigerator Co., 14x18x9", VG, $90.00. (Photo courtesy James D. Julia Inc.)

Cooler, picnic; metal, bottle-in-hand decal, 1940s-50s, 8x13x12", EX. 375.00
Cooler, Westinghouse Jr, holds 51 bottles, 1935, 34x25", EX....... 800.00
Coupon, Hilda Clark, red/wht, 1901, 1½x3½", EX...................... 475.00
Cuff links, bottle form, gold, mk 1/10, 10k,¾", NM, pr 50.00
Decal, Drink CC Ice Cold, 1960, G 30.00
Dispenser, arched top, red, Drink CC on sides, 1930s, NM+ 1,295.00
Display, cb, Friends for Life, fishing boy, Rockwell, 1935, 36", VG ..2,200.00
Display, window; dc cb, girl drinks CC by cooler, 1939, 42x31", G.395.00
Display, 3-D dc cb, button/soda jerk/patrons at counter, 1955, EX... 550.00
Display bottle, clear glass, no cap, 1923, 20", M 225.00
Doll, Buddy Lee in uniform w/hat, compo, 1950s, EX+.............. 800.00
Door push, metal & plastic, Have a Coke!, 1930, NM................. 155.00
Door push, porc w/CC push plate, bright colors, 1940s-50s, 8x4". 450.00
Drinking glass, flared, frosted 5¢ arrow logo, lg, G...................... 400.00
Fan, Quality Carries On, bottle in hand, 1950, EX 65.00
Festoon, Autumn Girl, 5-pc, 1927, NM.....................................3,250.00
Festoon, Know Your State Tree, 3-pc, 1950s, EX (orig envelope). 700.00
Festoon, Poppies, 5-pc, 1930s, unused, M (orig envelope) 1,000.00
Frisbee, plastic w/wave logo, 1960s, EX....................................... 15.00
Ice bucket, waxed cb, striped swag around top, EX+ 50.00
Ice pick, wood hdl w/bottle-opener finial, 1930, EX 40.00
Jug, clear glass w/diagonal paper label, 1910, 1-gal, EX 250.00
Lamp, Tiffany-style leaded glass, CC, chain hanger, 1920s, 16" dia, VG..4,000.00
Lampshade, ceiling; milk glass shaped globe w/red Drink CC, 18", EX...1,010.00
Lighter, bottle shape, 1950, M.. 30.00
Magazine, Red Barrel, Jackie Cooper cover, 1934, NM................. 65.00
Match holder, metal wall mt, wht w/red trim, CC Bottling Co, 1940s, G...350.00
Matchbook dispenser, metal tabletop, vertical, 1959, EX............ 225.00
Menu board, menu tabs either side of red button, 1950s, 14x60", NM...1,900.00
Menu board, metal, Silhouette Girl in lower corner, 1939, NM ..450.00
Note pad, leather cover, 1905, 4½x2¾", EX................................. 225.00
Opener, metal lion head, 1910-30s, EX.. 160.00
Opener, steel, skate key style, 1910s-20s, EX 25.00
Pencil holder, ceramic 1896 dispenser form, 1960s, 7", EX 150.00
Playing cards, Sign of Good Taste, girl in pool, 1959, EX.............. 80.00
Playing cards, Welcome Friend!, 1958, MIB................................ 175.00

Pocket mirror, cat's face, cardboard backing, 1920s, EX+, $350.00. (Photo courtesy Morphy Auctions/ LiveAuctioneers.com)

Pocket mirror, girl w/bottle, 1916, oval, G.................................. 225.00
Pocket mirror, Wherever You Go You Will Find CC...Fountains 5¢, rnd, G..950.00
Postcard, CC girl, 1910, NM+.. 650.00

Postcard, Weldmech truck, 1930, EX.................................... 25.00
Radio, can w/dynamic wave, 1970s, EX 45.00
Service pin, 15 yrs, EX 90.00
Sign, cb, Autumn Girl, orig wooden fr, 1941, 27x16", EX 800.00
Sign, cb, Betty, 1914, 41x26", VG.................................... 650.00
Sign, cb, Bring Home the..., Santa at bench, 1956, 28x14", EX .. 225.00
Sign, cb, girl seated on diving board w/bottle, 1939, 29x60", EX. 675.00
Sign, cb, Have a Coke, bottle on iceberg, 1944, 20x36", NM...... 125.00
Sign, cb, Planning Hospitality, hand at 6-pack, 16x27", EX 375.00
Sign, cb, Play Refreshed/Have a Coke, girl/cooler, fr, 30x40", VG+ ..275.00
Sign, cb, Refreshed Through 70 Years, 2-sided, 1955, 28x56", EX..300.00
Sign, cb, Santa's Helpers, w/2 bottles, 19660s, 32x66", EX 125.00
Sign, cb, Things Go Better..., skaters, fr, 1960s, 24x40", EX 175.00
Sign, cb, We Sell CC Part of Every Day/Served../bottle, gold sf, 22" L.. 475.00
Sign, cb, Weissmuller & O'Sullivan, 1934, 29½x13½", EX+ 2,700.00
Sign, cb, Welcome Friend/graphics on 'oak,' beveled, 1957, 12x14", EX... 375.00
Sign, cb, Wherever You Go/bottle/travel/button, gold fr, 1950s, EX..325.00
Sign, cb dc, lady w/6-pack, 60", EX 375.00
Sign, cb standup, Santa, Greetings From CC, 1948, 14", NM+... 300.00
Sign, cb standup, Santa w/toy bag at feet, button logo, 1945, 13", EX..250.00
Sign, countertop; clock, Drink CC, Please Pay Cashier, 1950s, 20" L, G.400.00
Sign, crossing; porc 3-D policeman, Slow School Zone, 1950s, 63", VG.1,500.00
Sign, Edgebrite motion light-up, Pause, 1950s, 9x20", EX 750.00
Sign, fiberboard, Please Pay When Served, Kay Displays, 13" dia, VG...525.00
Sign, metal button, CC over bottle on red, 1950s, 48", EX.......... 500.00
Sign, neon, CC Classic..., palm tree, 1980s, 28" dia, NM+ 1,500.00
Sign, neon, Coke w/Ice, 3-color, 1980s, EX 400.00

Sign, one-sided die-cut self-framed porcelain, dated 1925, 46x60", VG, $1,900.00.

Sign, paper, Pause a Minute/Refresh..., girl/bottle, 1928, 20", EX... 1,800.00
Sign, paper, Treat Yourself Right, man w/bottle, 1920s, 20x12", EX ..550.00
Sign, paper, Which?/CC or Goldelle Ginger Ale/lady, 1913, 24x18", EX+...9,500.00
Sign, paper cutout, Home Refreshment/25¢ 6-pack, 1940s, 16x22", NM. 50.00
Sign, porc, Come In! Have a CC, yel & wht, 1940s, 54", NM..1,200.00
Sign, porc, Drink CC, Ingram-Richardson Co, 1915-20, 9x21", VG. 2,750.00
Sign, porc, Fountain Service, dc fr sign, 1930s, 14x27", VG+...... 850.00
Sign, porc button, CC lettered over bottle, red, 24" dia, EX+...... 550.00
Sign, porc 2-sided dc, Fountain Service, 1933, 26x23", +scrolled arm . 4,000.00
Sign, rvpt glass light-up on base, Brunoff, 1930s, 14x12", EX+.5,000.00
Sign, sidewalk; metal, fishtail/bottle, wht/gr stripes, 1960s, 33", EX...400.00
Sign, tin, ...Enjoy That Refreshing, fishtail/bottle, 53x18", VG+.. 300.00
Sign, tin, Cold Drinks, fishtail center, 1960s, 15x24", NM 300.00
Sign, tin, Drink CC above/below bottle, wht/red/gr, 1931, 14x6", EX+...550.00
Sign, tin, Drink CC/D&R, bottle at left, Dasco, 1920s, 11x35", VG.. 235.00
Sign, tin, emb Christmas CC bottle to left, Robertson, 12x36", VG .. 200.00
Sign, tin, Gas Today/Drink CC While You Wait, 1930, 20x28", EX.4,500.00
Sign, tin, Ice Cold CC Sold Here/bottle, 1914, 20x28", EX...... 1,250.00
Sign, tin, str-sided bottle emb, Shonk litho, 1914, 20x27", VG.1,800.00
Sign, tin bottle form, 1930s, 39", G+ 425.00
Sign, tin button, Drink CC/Sign of..., yel/wht letters, 1950s, 16", NM ..550.00
Sign, tin button red w/wht vertical, Serve...Home/6-pack, 44x16", EX..875.00
Sign, tin dc, school-crossing policeman, 1950s, 3X+ 3,000.00
Sign, tin disk, Ice Cold CC Sold Here, red/gr rim, 1932, 20" dia, EX . 1,500.00
Sign, tin flange, Drink CC, bottle on yel dot, 1940s, 20x24", EX+ 500.00

Sign, tin flange, Grocery/fishtail logo/Refreshes You Best, 15x18", EX .275.00
Sign, tin triangle hanger w/filigree top, 2-sided, 1930s, 23", VG.. 700.00
Sign, trolley; cb, Drink CC/D&R, 2 girls/bottle, 1914, 11x21", EX .2,750.00
Sign, trolley; cb, 4 seasons, 1923, 10x20", NM 3,500.00
Sign, wood, Refreshing/red dot, metal scrolled hanger, 8x24", EX ..165.00
Sign, wood, Silhouette Girl, metal hanger, 1940, G.................... 150.00
Sign, wood plaque/metal filigree top, 2 glasses, 1930s, 12x9", NM.. 595.00
Syrup bottle, Drink CC in wreath (frosted), metal cap, 1910, 13", EX.500.00
Syrup bottle, red on wht CC label, fancy pumpkin-shaped cap, 12", EX.775.00
Syrup jug, paper label w/Coke glass, 1950s, EX.......................... 20.00
Thermometer, dc dbl-bottle gold version, 1942, 16", NM............ 525.00
Thermometer, dial, Drink CC in Bottles, red, 1950s, 12" dia, VG... 130.00
Thermometer, Masonite, Thirst Knows No Season, 1940s, 17", NM. 475.00
Thermometer, porc, Silhouette Girl, red & gr, 1939, 18", EX...... 625.00
Thermometer, tin bottle shape, 1950s, 17", EX 100.00
Thermometer, wood, Drink CC/D&R, 1905, 21", EX 395.00
Tip tray, 1903, VG 900.00
Tip tray, 1903, Victorian girl on purple ground, 4" dia, EX........1,440.00
Tip tray, 1906, girl drinks from glass, tin litho, 4½" 250.00
Tip tray, 1907, G+... 300.00
Tip tray, 1907, oval, 6", VG... 315.00

Tip tray, 1909, St. Louis Fair in distance, 6x4", EX+, $875.00.

(Photo courtesy Gary Metz)

Tip tray, 1910, NM+ 1,540.00
Tip tray, 1916, Elaine, VG+.. 115.00
Tip tray, 1916, EX+ 275.00
Toy truck, Lincoln, metal, red pnt, 10 (of 12) cases, tarp, 15", EX ... 850.00
Toy truck, Marx, metal, yel w/red, 6 plastic cases & dolly, 13", NMIB.... 700.00
Toy truck, Metalcraft, metal, red & yel, 10 glass bottles, 11", EX.. 775.00
Toy truck, Smith Miller, metal, 6 cases (24 bottles ea), 13", MIB .. 1,450.00
Wallet, leather, blk w/emb gold lettering, 1907, EX 100.00
Writing tablet, landmarks of the USA, 1960s, EX......................... 10.00

Trays

Trays that have been reproduced are indicated with a (+). The 1934 Weismuller and O'Sullivan tray has been reproduced at least three times. To be original, it will have a black back and must say 'American Artworks, Coshocton, Ohio.' It was not reproduced by Coca-Cola in the 1950s.

All 10½x13½" original serving trays produced from 1910 to 1942 are marked with a date, Made in USA and the American Artworks Inc., Coshocton Ohio. All original trays of this format (1910 – 1940) had REG TM in the tail of the C.

1897, Victorian Lady, 9¼" dia, VG...15,000.00
1901, Hilda Clark, 9¾", VG..4,000.00
1903, Hilda Clark, oval, 18½x15", EX 5,750.00
1905, Lillian Russell, glass or bottle, 10½x13¼", EX 3,000.00
1906, Juanita, glass or bottle, oval, 13¼x10½", EX...................2,000.00
1907, Relieves Fatigue, 10½x13¼", NM 3,250.00

1907, Relieves Fatigue, 13½x16½", EX 3,400.00
1908, Topless, Wherever Ginger Ale..., 12¼" dia, NM 8,500.00
1909, St Louis Fair, 10½x13¼", EX 1,500.00
1909, St Louis Fair, 13½x16½", NM............ 2,900.00
1910, Coca-Cola Girl, Hamilton King, 10½x13¼", EX+ 950.00
1914, Betty, oval, 12¼x15¼", EX+ 375.00
1914, Betty, 10½x13¼", EX+............ 500.00
1916, Elaine, 8½x19", NM 500.00
1920, Garden Girl, oval, 10½x13¼", EX+ 700.00
1921, Autumn Girl, oval, 10½x13¼", EX+ 700.00
1922, Summer Girl, 10½x13¼", NM............ 950.00
1923, Flapper Girl, 10½x13¼", NM............ 500.00
1924, Smiling Girl, brn rim, 10½x13¼", NM 600.00
1924, Smiling Girl, maroon rim, 10½x13¼", EX+............ 950.00
1925, Party, 10½x13¼", NM............ 550.00
1926, Golfers, 10½x13¼", EX+ 700.00
1927, Curbside Service, 10½x13¼", EX 750.00
1928, Bobbed Hair, 10½x13¼", NM 750.00
1929, Girl in Swimsuit w/Glass, 10½x13¼", EX+............ 500.00
1930, Swimmer, 10½x13¼", EX 400.00
1930, Telephone, 10½x13¼", NM............ 550.00
1931, Boy w/Sandwich & Dog, 10½x13¼", NM............ 800.00
1932, Girl in Swimsuit on Beach, Hayden, 10½x13¼", EX+ 600.00
1933, Francis Dee, 10½x13¼", NM............ 800.00

1934, Johnny Weiss-muller and Maureen O'Sullivan, NM, $1,200.00. (Photo courtesy Morphy Auctions/LiveAuctioneers.com)

1935, Madge Evans, 10½x13¼", NM 550.00
1936, Hostess, 10½x13¼", NM............ 650.00
1937, Running Girl, 10½x13¼", NM............ 400.00
1938, Girl in the Afternoon, 10½x13¼", NM 250.00
1939, Springboard Girl, 10½x13¼", NM 350.00
1940, Sailor Girl, 10½x13¼", NM............ 395.00
1941, Ice Skater, 10½x13¼", NM............ 395.00
1942, Roadster, 10½x13¼", NM+ 475.00
1950s, Girl w/Wind in Hair, screen bkground, 10½x13¼", M........ 95.00
1950s, Girl w/Wind in Hair, solid bkground, 10½x13¼", NM 200.00
1955, Menu Girl, 10½x13¼", M............ 45.00
1957, Birdhouse, 10½x13¼", NM............ 110.00
1957, Rooster, 10½x13¼", NM............ 150.00
1957, Umbrella Girl, 10½x13¼", M............ 300.00
1961, Pansy Garden, 10½x13¼", NM 25.00

Vendors

Though interest in Coca-Cola machines of the 1949 – 1959 era rose dramatiacally over the last decade, values currently seem to have leveled off. The major manufacturers of these curved-top, 5¢ and 10¢ machines were Vendo (V), Vendorlator (VMC), Cavalier (C or CS), and Jacobs. Prices are for machines as noted in the description. A mint restored model will bring approximately twice as much as the same model in excellent condition.

Cavalier, model #CS72, M rstr............ 2,850.00
Cavalier, model #C27, EX orig............ 1,000.00

Cavalier, model #C51, EX orig............ 950.00
Jacobs, model #26, EX orig............ 950.00
Vendo, model #23, EX orig............ 750.00
Vendo, model #39, EX orig............ 1,000.00

Vendo, model #44, 1950s, 58x16", EX original, $3,100.00.

Vendo, model #56, EX orig............ 1,200.00
Vendo, model #80, EX orig............ 550.00
Vendo, model #81, EX orig............ 1,250.00
Vendorlator, model #27, EX orig............ 1,150.00
Vendorlator, model #27A, EX orig............ 800.00
Vendorlator, model #33, EX orig............ 1,000.00
Vendorlator, model #44, EX orig............ 1,500.00
Vendorlator, model #72, EX orig............ 1,100.00

Coffee Grinders

These listings represent current values of mills the collector will most likely encouter. Very rare examples have been eliminated, but we will continue to occasionally list mills that have set record prices in order to illustrate the effect condition has on pricing.

Please be aware that many coffee mill parts are being reproduced, and it is possible to restore mills to a very high degree of accuracy in relation to their original appearance. You can find accurate replacement wing nuts, labels, brass hoppers, decals, and iron or tin receiving cups. Note that there are several mills that show up on internet auction sites on a fairly regular basis that are not old. These mills are either made from the old original molds with new names added, or molds have been made from an original mill and altered to include the new maker's name. One you may see will be labeled 'Ye Olde Coffee Mill'; another may be listed as 'Enterprise #2 with a removable, domed iron lid.' (To the knowlege of our advisor, no original Enterprise mill was ever made with such a lid.) Though neither of these mills is very old, they are worth collecting, as long as you know what it is you are buying. We are advised to beware of possible reproduction of some of the glass receiving cups. Among them are the cup for the Kitchen Aid A-9 electric coffee mill originally produced in the 1930s. Due to an abundance of these cups without their mills, they seem highly suspect. Because some original cups sell from $125.00 to $500.00 each, unscrupulous sellers would certainly have a motive to market them as old instead of selling them as a replacement. As always, research is the key. We recommend joining online collector clubs, website chat rooms, and collector organizations to learn more. (See Association of Coffee Mill Enthusiasts listed under Clubs, Newsletters, and Catalogs in the Directory.) Our advisor for this category is Shane Branchcomb; he is listed in the Directory under Virginia.

Arcade #5, iron, wood bk brd, Pat June 94, EX............ 130.00
Arcade #777 IXL, ornate CI hopper, side crank, NM............ 425.00

Arcade Bell, ornate CI front, bell-shaped window, NM 850.00
Arcade Crystal #3, glass hopper, iron body, EX 125.00
Arcade Crystal #3, w/orig mk glass cup, EX 250.00
Arcade Crystal #4, glass hopper, iron body, EX 135.00
Arcade Crystal #9010, Art Deco, orig glass cup 300.00
Arcade Favorite #7, iron, wall mt, on bk brd, EX 95.00
Arcade Favorite #17, lg version of #7, EX 115.00
Arcade Imperial #999, box mill, orig label, NM 145.00
Arcade Jewel, rectangular glass hopper, tin lid, NM 595.00
Arcade Our Baby, toy mill, paper label, NM 135.00
Arcade Royal, CI, wall mt, iron receiving cup, EX 115.00
Arcade Telephone, ornate CI face plate, NM 650.00
Arcade X-Ray, CI grinder, wood box, glass front, EX 145.00
Belmont Hardware Lightning, tin canister, wall mt, EX 200.00
Bronson & Walton Ever-Ready No 2, w/cup, EX 225.00
Bronson & Walton Silver Lake, glass, scarce, NM 900.00
Cavanaugh Bros, wood box, front fill, 1-lb, NM 300.00
Cavanaugh Bros, wood box, ornate CI legs, NM 795.00
Chatillon #11, same as Enterprise #1, side crank, EX 275.00
Coles No 00, CI, wall mt, w/cup, NM 350.00
Crescent #3, Rutland VT, CI, 2 wheels, EX 1,000.00
Crescent #4, Rutland VT, CI, nickel hopper, EX 1,200.00
Crescent #7, iron hopper, 20" wheels, EX 1,300.00
Enterprise #0, CI, clamps to table, EX 95.00
Enterprise #00, CI, w/CI cup, wall mt, NM 175.00
Enterprise #1, CI, counter, side crank, EX 175.00
Enterprise #2, CI, decals, 8¾" wheels, EX 900.00

Enterprise #3, patented 1898, EX, $950.00.

(Photo courtesy Morphy Auctions)

Enterprise #7, CI, counter, 17" wheels, EX 1,100.00
Enterprise #50, single wheel grist mill, NM 125.00
Enterprise #100, glass wall type w/mk cup, NM 250.00
Golden Rule, ornate CI front, wall mill by Arcade, NM 425.00
Grand Union Tea Co (on flip-up lid), CI, Griswold, NM 750.00
Griswold, CI box, same as Grand Union Tea Co, NM 1,200.00
J Fisher, primitive PA box type, hand dvtls, EX 185.00
Landers, Frary & Clark #11, CI side crank, EX 175.00
Landers, Frary & Clark #20, CI, 8¾" wheels, EX 975.00
Landers, Frary & Clark #24, orig mk hopper, NM 180.00
Logan & Strobridge #60 Acme, wall type, w/cup, NM 250.00
Logan & Strobridge Franko American, wood box, EX 115.00
Logan & Strobridge Queen, glass, wall mt, NM 650.00
National Specialty #0, CI w/CI lid, clamps to table, EX 350.00
National Specialty #1, CI, rnd hopper, w/lid, EX 325.00
National Specialty #1, CI, 8-sided hopper, w/lid, EX 425.00
National Specialty #2, CI, 8¾" wheels, EX 1,200.00
National Specialty #7, CI, 16½" wheels, EX 1,400.00
NCRA, rectangular, glass window, wall mt, 1915, EX 125.00
NCRA, rnd glass hopper, ca 1922, EX 115.00
Old 74, CI, parts mk 71, 72, 73, 74, ca 1840, NM 170.00
Parker #50 Eagle, side mill, brass label, EX 95.00
Parker #50 Farm, eagle emb in tin, EX 85.00

Parker #200, CI, mk iron drw front, EX 1,100.00
Parker #260 Columbia, domed iron top, side crank, EX 525.00
Parker #350, ornate CI, CI lid, on wood bk, NM 175.00
Parker #450, CI, side mt, orig rectangular cup 300.00
Parker #555, wood, 1-lb box type, paper label, NM 155.00
Parker #1200, CI, orig pnt, 25½" wheels, EX 3,000.00
Steinfeld, Simplex No 6, on wheels, nickel hopper, EX 1,000.00
Steinfield, glass, wall type, mk lid & hopper, NM 145.00
Sun #25 Success, rnd, wood box type, EX 300.00
Sun #94, stamped tin hopper, side mill, EX 100.00
Sun #1080 1-lb Challenge, fast grinder, label, NM 145.00
Swift, Lane Bros #12, tin receiver, single 9" wheel, EX 550.00
Swift, Lane Bros #14, tin receiver, 15" wheels, EX 850.00
Waddel A-17, CI, sunflower design, wall mt, EX 300.00
Woodruff & Edwards Elgin National, 12" wheels, EX 850.00
Wrightsville Hardware, ca 1968, 6¾" wheels, NM 250.00
Wrightsville Hardware Peerless #200, glass, EX 155.00
WWW Weaver, primitive PA box type, hand dvtls, EX 250.00

Coin-Operated Machines

Coin-operated machines may be the fastest-growing area of collector interest in today's market. Many machines are bought, restored, and used for home entertainment. Older examples from the turn of the twentieth century and those with especially elaborate decoration and innovative features are most desirable.

The www.GameRoomAntiques.com website is an excellent source of information for those interested in coin-operated machines. Another source available is the Coin-Operated Collector's Association (www.coinopclub.org). See the Clubs, Newsletters, and Catalogs section of the Directory for publishing information. Jackie and Ken Durham are our advisors; they are listed in the Directory under the District of Columbia.

Arcade Machines

Baseball, gumball, w/penny return, 1950s, 16x9x8", rstr 495.00
Chicago Coin Goalee, hockey game, 1954, EX 3,450.00

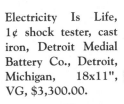

Electricity Is Life, 1¢ shock tester, cast iron, Detroit Medial Battery Co., Detroit, Michigan, 18x11", VG, $3,300.00.

Fortune, penny drop, rpt wood case, 1930s-40s, EX 675.00
Hi-Ball, ball flip, 1940s-50s, rstr 2,250.00
Jr Deputy Sheriff Pistol Range, 1940s-50s, 62", EX 1,250.00
Mercury Strength Tester, works 3 ways, rstr 1,995.00
Mutoscope, w/Babe Ruth Reel, 1930s-40s, rstr 3,650.00
Rollfast Exercise Bike, w/speedometer, 1930s-40s, EX 1,875.00
Seeburg Coon Hunt, Ray-O-Lite shooting game, rstr 3,900.00
Williams Deluxe Batting Champ, pitch & bat, 1961, rstr 4,550.00
Williams Gridiron Football, 1968, rstr 2,995.00

Jukeboxes

The coin-operated phonograph of the early 1900s paved the way for the jukeboxes of the '20s. Seeburg was first on the market with an automatic eight-tune phonograph. By the 1930s Wurlitzer was the top name in the industry with dealerships all over the country. As a result of the growing ranks of competitors, the '40s produced the most beautiful machines made. Wurlitzers from this era are probably the most popularly sought-after models on the market today. The model #1015 of 1946 is considered the all-time classic and even in unrestored condition often brings prices in excess of $8,000.00.

AMI Rowe Tropicana JBM-200, 45 rpm, 1964, EX 1,995.00
Seeburg #147, 78 rpm, EX 2,995.00
Seeburg #161, 1958, rstr 7,295.00
Seeburg #201, 1958, rstr 7,295.00
Seeburg #222, 1959, rstr 6,295.00
Seeburg B, 1951, rstr 5,995.00
Seeburg C, Art Deco case, 1953, rstr 6,295.00
Seeburg DS-160 external speakers, 45 rpm, 1962, VG+ 2,995.00
Seeburg G, 1952, rstr 7,995.00
Seeburg J, rstr, 1955 .... 6,295.00
Seeburg Q 160, ca 1960, EX 1,995.00
Seeburg R, Art Deco, 1954, rstr 7,995.00
Seeburg V 200, 1955, rstr 11,495.00
Seeburg W, 1953, rstr 6,595.00

Wurlitzer #850 Peacock, mahogany with bubble glass inserts, original working condition, 66", $18,000.00. (Photo courtesy Randy Inman Auctions Inc.)

Wurlitzer #1015, 78 rpm, rstr 14,995.00
Wurlitzer #1100, holds 24 78 rpms, late 1940s, rstr 8,450.00

Pinball Machines

Bally Fireball, rstr 4,995.00
Bally Future Spa, 1979, EX 1,995.00
Bally Kiss, rstr 4,995.00
Bally Mr & Mrs Pac-Man, 1982, EX orig 1,950.00
Bally Twilight Zone, rstr 4,995.00
Sega Independence Day, 1996, EX 3,595.00
Standard Jockey Club Horse Race 1¢, 1933, rstr 2,450.00
Williams Allstar Baseball, 6-player, 1956, EX rstr 5,995.00
Williams World Series Baseball, pitch & bat, 1962, EX orig 4,850.00

Slot Machines

Many people enjoy the fun of playing a slot machine in their home. Antique slots have become very collectible. The legality of owning a slot machine is different in each state. Also beware of reproduction or re-manufactured slot machines.

Bally #809 5 Coin Play, fruit reels, 1968, rstr 2,500.00
Bally #831 25¢, 3-line fruit slot, 1968, rstr 2,500.00
Bally #856 25¢, 5-coin multiplier, 1974-75, rstr 2,000.00
Bally #873, criss-cross fruit reels, 5-line, 1970, rstr 2,995.00
Bally #1091 Dollar, 3-coin multiplier, 1973, rstr 1,500.00
Bally #8000, 5-line play, 1980s, rstr 2,795.00
Bally Star Special (742 Money Honey) 25¢, 1964, rstr 2,500.00
Bally Stars & Bars, converted to free play, rstr 1,495.00
Jennings Deluxe Chief Silver Dollar w/Chinese front, 1947-48, rstr .. 7,495.00
Jennings Golden Nugget Standard Chief 25¢, 1945, rstr 6,595.00
Jennings Hunting, hunting scene w/2 Indians, late 1930s, rstr .. 4,495.00
Jennings Little Duke 1¢, w/side vendor, 1933, rstr 4,495.00
Jennings Little Duke 5¢, rare, rstr 4,495.00
Jennings Sportsman Golf Ball, rstr 14,995.00
Jennings Super Chief 25¢, orig pnt, 1937, EX 2,995.00

Mills 5¢ FOK, double mint vendor, 27x16x16", EX, $2,500.00.

Mills Admiral Dewey Upright, ca 1899, rstr 2,750.00
Mills Black Cherry 50¢, fish mouth coin entry, 1948, rstr 6,495.00
Mills Bonus 25¢, working marque, 1949, rstr 4,495.00
Mills Brn Front Bursting Cherry 25¢, chromed castings, 1938-42, rstr. 3,195.00
Mills Castle Front 25¢, dbl jackpot, 1930s, rstr 2,595.00
Mills Castle Front 50¢ w/fish mouse coin entry, ca 1938, rstr.... 6,495.00
Mills Extra Bell 25¢, modern design, red or wht, rstr 2,995.00
Mills Futurity, rstr 5,900.00
MIlls Golden Nugget 25¢, blk or wht, rstr 2,495.00
Mills Golden Nugget 50¢, 1947, rstr 3,195.00
Mills High Top 25¢, authentic-made rpl wood case/bk bonnet, rstr... 2,495.00
Mills Hole-in-One Golf 25¢, EX rstr 2,995.00
Mills Vest Pocket 5¢, hidden reel strips, 8" cube, rstr, minimum . 850.00
Watling Rol-A-Top Checkerboard 5¢, 1947-51, rstr 6,495.00
Watling Rol-A-Top 5¢, ca 1936, rstr 6,995.00
Watling Treasury 5¢, mint vendor front, 1934-35, rstr 8,595.00
Watling Treasury 5¢, 1935, rstr 7,495.00

Trade Stimulators

Buckley Groetchen Cent-A-Pack, cigarette reel strips, 1935, EX rstr... 895.00
Cowber Cracker Jacks, 1898-1911, rstr w/new base 4,750.00
Daval Cent-A-Smoke, cast aluminum case, ca 1936, VG orig 875.00
Daval Penny Pack, cigarette reel strips, 1939, EX rstr 895.00
Drobish Star Advertiser, cigar vendor oak case, ca 1897, rstr.... 2,450.00
Fairest Wheel, nickel drop, pointer shows cigars won, 1890s, rstr .. 1,575.00
Gem 1¢ by Garden City Novelty, lg gumball window, rpt, 1937.. 595.00
Griswald Star Wheel of Fortune, 5¢ drop, cigar vendor, 1902, EX. 1,350.00
Groetchen Ball Gum, fruit reel strips, 1930s, EX rstr 895.00
Hit the Target, gumball vendor, all metal, 1960s, rstr 575.00
Mills Jumbo Success, ca 1900, rstr 7,850.00
Puritan Bell, cash register shape, 1930s, VG orig 1,650.00

Spino, 1¢ drop, winner every time, 1940s-50s, EX rstr 650.00
Try Your Luck, 5¢ drop, 1950-60s, G........................... 275.00

Spitfire, gum ball vendor, WWII theme, repainted, ca. 1940s, 21½x14½x9", $900.00. (Photo courtesy Wm. Morford Auctions)

Vendors

Vending machines sold a product or a service. They were already in common usage by 1900 selling gum, cigars, matches, and a host of other commodities. Peanut and gumball machines are especially popular today. Older machines made of cast iron are especially desirable, while those with plastic globes have little collector value. When buying unrestored peanut machines, beware of salt damage.

Abby, dbl, single attached base, 1940s, rstr, 8½x14½x8" 585.00
Advance Big Mouth 1¢, peanuts/candy, oval glass globe, ca 1920, rstr. 595.00
Advance 1¢, gumball, glass globe, 1920s, 14", rstr 595.00
Atlas Bantam 5¢, peanuts, tray base, 1940s, 11x10x8", rstr.......... 485.00
Baby Grand, all purpose, Project-OpView windows, ca 1951, 12", EX ... 195.00
Baseball 1¢, gumball, penny return feature, 1950s, 16x9x8", rstr . 575.00
Bluebird 1¢, gumball, rare penny return feature, 1920s, EX 875.00
Columbus A 1¢, hourglass shape, glass globe, 1920s, 16½", rstr ... 675.00
Columbus M, glass globe, 1920s, 14½", rstr................................. 550.00
Dietz 5¢, gum packets, 1940s, 14½x9x5", EX............................... 575.00
Ford 1¢, gumball, glass globe, aluminum base, 1930s-60s, 12", rstr... 180.00
Hawkeye 1¢, glass globe, 1940s, rstr 550.00
Lions International 1¢, 2 glass globes, aluminum base w/decal, 1930s, rstr...650.00
Masters 1¢/5¢, emb casting, 15½x8x8", rstr 875.00
Northwestern, gumball, orig decal, porc base, 1930s, 14", EX 650.00
Northwestern #33, gumball, ca 1933, 15x6" dia, rstr 495.00
Northwestern 1¢, peanuts, porc base, Deco style, 1930s, 15", EX . 575.00
Pulver Spearmint, gum, 1-column w/tab, 1950s, 26", rstr............. 475.00
Pulver Yel Kid 1¢, animated tab gum vendor, 1920s-30s, 21", EX.1,475.00
Regal, polished aluminum, 1940s, rstr.. 195.00
Silver King Hot Nut 5¢, red hobnail glass top lights up, 1947, rstr .. 485.00
Silver King 1¢, peanuts/candy, glass globe, 1940s, 11", rstr 295.00
Victor Topper 1¢, glass globe, 1940s-50s, 11", rstr 195.00
Victor V, metal globe, ca 1940, rstr 195.00
William Michaels Nat'l, gumball, 1910, 11", rstr........................... 875.00
Wrigley's Chewing Gum 5¢, packs, Kayem Products, ca 1947, 14x8x4", EX..550.00
4-in-1, peanuts/candy, Deco style, 4-compartment, chrome, 1930s, EX .1,895.00

Cole, A. R.

A second generation North Carolina potter, Arthur Ray Cole opened his own shop in 1926, operating under the name Rainbow Pottery until 1941 when he adopted his own name for the title of his business. He remained active until he died in 1974. He was skilled in modeling the pottery and highly recognized for his fine glazes.

Ashtray, blk drips on brn, ca 1930, 4" dia 50.00
Basket, turq/bl/gr mottle w/sm drips, scalloped rim, twist hdl, 9½" ..75.00
Pitcher, cobalt/violet/gr/aqua/gr/wht splashes, #244, 11¼x5½" 275.00
Teapot, turq satin, late 1950-62, 7" 40.00
Vase, brn mottle, lt bl ring at bottom, barrel shape, 5" 56.00
Vase, rose gloss, neck-to-hip hdls, #276, 12¾" 130.00

Compacts

The use of cosmetics before WWI was looked upon with disdain. After the war women became liberated, entered the work force, and started to use makeup. The compact, a portable container for cosmetics, became a necessity. The basic compact contains a mirror and a powder puff.

Vintage compacts were fashioned in a myriad of shapes, styles, materials, and motifs. They were made of precious metals, fabrics, plastics, and in almost any other conceivable medium. Commemorative, premium, patriotic, figural, Art Deco, plastic, and gadgetry compacts are just a few of the most sought-after types available today. Those that are combined with other accessories (music/compact, watch/compact, cane/compact) are also very much in demand. Vintage compacts are an especially desirable collectible since the workmanship, design, techniques, and materials used in their execution would be very expensive and virtually impossible to duplicate today.

For more information we recommend *Ladies' Compacts of the 19th and 20th Centuries, Vintage Vanity Bags and Purses, Vintage and Contemporary Purse Accessories, Vintage Ladies' Compacts, Vintage & Vogue Ladies' Compacts,* and *The Estée Lauder Solid Perfume Compact Collection,* all by Roselyn Gerson. She is listed in the Directory under New York. Another excellent references is *Mueller's Overview of American Compacts and Vanity Cases* by Laura M. Mueller. See Clubs, Newsletters, and Catalogs for information concerning the compact collectors' club and their periodical publication, *The Powder Puff.*

Princess, purse shaped, gold-tone with engraving, colored stones and enameling, Czechoslovakia, 3½x3", from $150.00 to $200.00. (Photo courtesy Rosely Gerson; Photographer Alvin Gerson)

Agme, gold/silver-tone, dials on sides move center Paris scenes, 2x3" .. 150.00
Antonin of France, blk celluloid, eng/enamel lady's face, rnd, 3".. 150.00
Atomette, brushed gold-tone w/crystal poodle, rnd, 2¾".............. 100.00
DBF Co, bl enamel w/windmill scene, w/finger ring, chain & key, 2x3"..200.00
DF Briggs, silver/gold-tone, gypsy w/crystal ball in center, 2x2¾".. 85.00
Dorothy Gray, silver-tone, eng, center dome forms lady's hat, rnd, 4"...150.00
Dorset, gold-tone, valentine w/I Love You script border, rnd, 2½". 70.00
Eisenberg Original, gold-tone w/mc marquise & rnd stones, sq, 3" .. 150.00
Elgin American, brn on gold-tone, Greek key border, shield shape, 3x2".. 60.00
Elgin American, gold/silver-tone w/3 running deer, rectangle, 2¼x3" ...55.00
Elizabeth Arden, silver w/bl stones, shepherdess/sheep center, rnd, 3"..300.00
Estee Lauder, gold-tone, turq stone in lt & dk bl bull's-eye, 1½" 25.00
Evans, silver-tone & blk enamel panels, pentagonal, w/chain, 2x2"..120.00
Evans, silver-tone starburst design w/rhinestones in center, sq, 3" . 60.00
France, gr irid Lucite w/enamel lady on swing, rnd, 2½" 180.00
Germaine Monteil, gold-tone w/mobe pearl amid turq stones, rnd, 2" ..45.00
KIGU, gold-plate w/mc bouquet on purple enamel, scalloped rim, rnd, 3"..65.00
La Mode, silver-tone w/military wings on gold-tone sq, 1¾x2¾" ... 60.00
Lampl, blk enamel, gold-tone fr, slide-out comb, sq, 3" 160.00
Max Factor, gold-tone, gr cabochon stone amid 4 emb fish, rnd, 2" .60.00
Paul Flato, blk enamel/gold-tone/rhinestones, lipstick tube, 2½x2" .60.00

Roger & Gallet, gold-tone w/sunburst medallion, rnd, 3" 60.00
Stratton, gold-plate w/mc butterfly on lt bl enamel, thin, rnd, 3" .. 50.00
Stratton, gold-tone w/ballerina on wht, musical, rectangle, 2½".... 50.00
Stratton, gold-tone w/mc enamel Zodiac images on wht, rnd, 3"... 65.00
Stratton, portrait of lady in '50s nightclub attire on gold-tone, rnd . 100.00
Unmk, celluloid/Bakelite, ballerina in orange tutu on blk/wht, rnd, 2"..400.00
Unmk, cvd amber Bakelite base w/red lid, rnd, ca 1940-50s, 3"..... 80.00
Unmk, Deco-style chrome w/blk & gold enamel, w/chain, 1920s, 3x1½"..265.00
Unmk, gold-tone w/silver confetti Lucite, 4" snake chain, 3x5x1" ..70.00
Unmk, gold-tone w/wht scalloped guilloche lid, rectangle, 2¾x2"..80.00
Unmk, silver w/guilloche turq enamel, pk roses & bl bows, rnd, 1½" . 250.00
Unmk, silver-tone w/enamel pk & bl flowers on yel, w/chain, sq. 125.00
Volupté, drum major w/2 musicians on wht enamel, horseshoe, 3¼x3" . 90.00
Volupté, gold-tone w/blk geometric Deco enamel, swing hdl, sq, 3" .55.00
Volupté, sterling silver w/raised flowers, vase & swirls, sq, 2½" 100.00

Consolidated Lamp and Glass

The Consolidated Lamp and Glass Company of Coraopolis, Pennsylvania, was incorporated in 1894. For many years their primary business was the manufacture of lighting glass such as oil lamps and shades for both gas and electric lighting. The popular 'Cosmos' line of lamps and tableware was produced from 1894 to 1915. (See also Cosmos.) In 1926 Consolidated introduced their Martele line, a type of 'sculptured' ware closely resembling Lalique glassware of France. (Compare Consolidated's 'Lovebirds' vase with the Lalique 'Perruches' vase.) It is this line of vases, lamps, and tableware which is often mistaken for a very similar type of glassware produced by the Phoenix Glass Company, located nearby in Monaca, Pennsylvania. For example, the so-called Phoenix 'Grasshopper' vases are actually Consolidated's 'Katydid' vases.

Items in the Martele line were produced in blue, pink, green, crystal, white, or custard glass decorated with various fired-on color treatments or a satin finish. For the most part, their colors were distinctively different from those used by Phoenix. Although not foolproof, one of the ways of distinguishing Consolidated's wares from those of Phoenix is that most of the time Consolidated applied color to the raised portion of the design, leaving the background plain, while Phoenix usually applied color to the background, leaving the raised surfaces undecorated. This is particularly true of those pieces in white or custard glass.

In 1928 Consolidated introduced their Ruba Rombic line, which was their Art Deco or Art Moderne line of glassware. It was only produced from 1928 to 1932 and is quite scarce. Today it is highly sought after by both Consolidated and Art Deco collectors.

Consolidated closed its doors for good in 1964. Subsequently a few of the molds passed into the hands of other glass companies that later reproduced certain patterns; one such reissue is the 'Chickadee' vase, found in avocado green, satin-finish custard, or milk glass. For further information we recommend *Phoenix and Consolidated Art Glass, 1926 – 1980*, by Jack D. Wilson. Our advisor for this category is David Sherman; he is listed in the Directory under New York.

Bird of Paradise, fan vase, gr wash, 6"... 125.00
Bird of Paradise, fan vase, pk wash, 10".. 475.00
Bittersweet, milk glass, 9½"... 48.00
Bittersweet, vase, bl-gr & orange on milk glass, 9½" 215.00
Bittersweet, vase, purple cased.. 295.00
Bittersweet, vase, ruby stain on crystal.. 150.00
Blackberry, umbrella vase, russet wash, rare, 18".......................... 700.00
Catalonian, candlestick (Spanish knobs), yel, ea 50.00
Catalonian, vase, amethyst, triangular top, 4" 36.00
Chickadee, vase, bl on milk glass, 6½" 85.00
Chickadee, vase, gr wash on crystal.. 110.00

Chrysanthemum, vase, dk red, 12"... 300.00
Chrysanthemum, vase, gold on milk glass, 12" 125.00
Chrysanthemum, vase, ruby stain on crystal, metal surmount...... 200.00
Chrysanthemum, vase, 3-color on milk glass, 12"........................ 145.00
Con-Cora, cookie jar, violets on milk glass, orig label, 9" 145.00
Dancing Girls, lamp base, dk red, 20½" 725.00
Dancing Girls, vase, bl on satin milk glass, 11½".......................... 350.00

Dancing Girls (Pan or Satyr) vase, tricolor on satin custard, 11½", $450.00. (Photo courtesy Jackson's International Auctioneers & Appraisers of Fine Art & Antiques/ LiveAuctioneers.com)

Dancing Nymph, goblet, frosted... 85.00
Dancing Nymph, palace platter, clear/frosted, 16"....................... 900.00
Dancing Nymph, plate, frosted, 8¼" 110.00
Dancing Nymph, plate, reverse ruby stain, rare, 8¼".................... 250.00
Dogwood, lamp, 3-color on satin milk glass.................................. 125.00
Dogwood, vase, yel cased, 10½".. 300.00
Dragon Fly, vase, gr & brn on satin milk glass, 6" 85.00
Dragon Fly, vase, gr cased, orig Martele label, 6" 175.00
Five Fruits, plate, purple wash, 14".. 150.00
Five Fruits, tumbler, gr wash, ftd.. 30.00
Floral, vase, bl & gr on milk glass, 9½"... 95.00
Foxglove, lamp, wht w/lav-bl flowers & gr leaves, 10".................. 125.00
Hummingbird, powder jar, purple wash, 5" 125.00
Hummingbird, vase, 3-color on satin custard, 5½" 135.00
Iris, jug, sepia wash.. 275.00
Katydid, vase, bl on satin milk glass, ovoid, 7"............................. 165.00
Katydid, vase, gr & brn on milk glass, ovoid, 7"........................... 180.00
Katydid, vase, gr & brn on satin custard, cylindrical, paper label, 8"..180.00
Line 700, bowl, fruit; bl crystal, 10"... 175.00
Line 700, vase, dk red, 10"... 575.00
Line 700, vase, gold on custard, 10" 300.00
Line 700, vase, Reuben Blue reverse highlights on crystal, 6½" ... 300.00
Lovebird, banana boat, Reuben Blue reverse highlights on crystal, 15" ...475.00
Lovebird, puff box, gr wash, 4" 150.00
Lovebird, vase, bl on milk glass, 10½".. 250.00
Olive, bowl, reverse bl highlighting (rare color), 8" 225.00
Olive, vase, purple & gr on satin custard, 4" 125.00
Pine Cone, vase, purple cased, 6½" 295.00
Pine Cone, vase, reverse rose highlights on glossy custard 185.00
Poppy, vase, irid metallic red & gold on glossy custard, rare, 10½"...300.00
Poppy, vase, purple cased 400.00
Poppy, vase, straw opal, ormolu mts 450.00
Regent Line, cookie jar (Florette), ash-rose pk on wht opal......... 195.00
Ruba Rombic, candleholder, lav, ea 265.00
Ruba Rombic, finger bowl, lav... 150.00
Ruba Rombic, plate, salad; jade, 8".. 225.00
Ruba Rombic, vase, Jade Green, 9½".. 2,400.00
Ruba Rombic, vase, smoky topaz, 9½"... 1,600.00
Ruba Rombic, whiskey glass, jungle gr 225.00
Screech Owl, vase, sepia cased, 5¾".. 250.00
Seagull, vase, orange highlights on satin custard, 11"................... 275.00
Tropical Fish, tray, ruby stain reverse highlights on crystal, 10" ... 325.00
Tropical Fish, vase, straw opal, 9"... 350.00

Conta & Boehme

The Conta & Boehme company was in business for 117 years in the quaint town Poessneck, Germany (Thuringer district). Hand-painted dishes and pipe heads were their main products. However, in 1840, when the owner's two young sons took over the company, production changed drastically from dishes to porcelain items of almost every imaginable type.

For their logo, the brothers chose an arm holding a dagger inside a shield. This mark was either impressed or ink stamped onto the porcelain. Another mark they used is called the 'scissor brand' which looks just like it sounds, a pair of scissors in a blue or green ink stamp. Not all pieces were marked, many were simply given a model number or left completely unmarked.

England and the U.S. were the largest buyers, and as a result the porcelain ended up at fairs, gift shops, and department stores throughout both countries. Today their fairings are highly collectible. Fairings are small, brightly colored nineteenth-century hard-paste porcelain objects, largely figural groups and boxes. Most portray amusing if not risqué scenes of courting couples, marital woes, and political satire complete with an appropriate caption on the base. For more information we recommend *Victorian Trinket Boxes* by Janice and Richard Vogel, and their latest book, *Conta & Boehme Porcelain*, published by the authors.

Conta & Boehme often produced their porcelain items in several different sizes (sometimes as many as nine). When ranges are used in our listings, it is to accomodate these different sizes (unless a specific size is given). Values are for items with no chips, cracks, or repairs. Our advisors for this category are Richard and Janice Vogel; they are listed in the Directory under South Carolina.

Fairings, Boxes

Trinket, girl with arms about two cats, uncaptioned 'Anti Vivisectors' box, from **$125.00 to $150.00** (Photo courtesy Janice and richard Vogel)

Bureau, washstand w/wash set on top, #487, from $35 to	55.00
Dresser, boy & girl reading book, #3538	115.00
Dresser, dog & cat playing, #2998	115.00
Dresser, flower atop, #3611	55.00
Dresser, girl & cat in seesaw, #3635	170.00
Dresser, girl w/jack-in-the-box, #3673	150.00
Trinket, angel praying under altar, #2481, from $75 to	75.00
Trinket, boy & girl playing checkers, #3639, lg	415.00
Trinket, boy on mantel w/pitcher & bowl peers into mirror, 4", $75 to	95.00
Trinket, lg cat on mantel, #3520, from $125 to	130.00
Trinket, The Last in Bed To Put Out the Light, from $100 to	115.00
3-spot, Am eagle & flag, from $200 to	225.00
3-spot, Zouave soldiers	225.00

Fairings, Figural

An Awkward Interruption, #2875, from $125 to	150.00
Cat! A Cat!, #2896, from $75 to	95.00
Children's Meeting, #3375	150.00
Fair Play Boys, #2878, from $300 to	300.00
God Save the Queen, #3307	225.00
He Don't Like His Pants, minimum value	300.00
Kiss Me Quick, #2865	150.00

Lovers Disturbed, #2854, minimum value	300.00
O'Do Leave Me a Drop, #3350	150.00
Returning to the Ball, #3308	225.00

Spoils of War, #3357, from **$125.00 to $200.00.** (Photo courtesy Janice and Richard Vogel)

To Epsom, #2884, minimum value	600.00
Tug of War, #3356, from $125 to	150.00
Who Said Rats?, #3359	115.00

Figurines

Boy (girl) w/umbrella, he w/book, she w/purse, #5316, 5¾", pr	95.00
Boy & girl share parasol, #1457, 8"	150.00
Cherub, holds cap in left hand, cradle under right arm, #1246, 6½"	115.00
Five Senses, #7640, 5 in series, ea from $100 to	115.00
Macaw, red/bl bird on gray tree stump w/gr leaves, 6¼"	60.00
Man seated w/violin in left hand w/right hand on side of head, #5305	70.00
Man w/flower basket seated on bench w/openwork bk, #470, 7¼"	130.00
Toasting man (lady), period attire, #8076, 8", pr	95.00

Nodders

Baby, seated, tongue nods, unmk, 2"	190.00
Elephant, #2376, 8½x11"	1,125.00
Gentleman carrying birdcage, bird/head nod, #8630/8587, shield/B, 9"	375.00
Girl w/kitten in bl chair, #5317, 6¾"	225.00
Lady w/fan at table on base, 2-light candleholder, unmk, 8", ea	130.00
Old lady in chair, #7636	115.00
Oriental couple carrying bowl in ea arm, #7670, pr	340.00
Oriental couple seated arm-in-arm, heads nod, unmk	225.00
Spinet player (lady), male singer, heads nod #7578/7577	300.00

Piano Babies

Seated, baby holding cup, #482, 7½"	170.00
Seated, baby holding cup, #482, 14"	600.00
Seated, bow on right shoulder/ball in right hand, unmk, 3¾", $50 to	55.00
Seated, holding sponge, #489, from $175 to	210.00

Miscellaneous

Candleholder, Black man on elephant, 2-light, #8325, shield mk, 9", ea	190.00
Candleholders, Oriental girl & face in flower, bl/wht, unmk, 8", pr	170.00
Cigar holder, chicken stands beside basket & sm bucket, #3063, 7½"	115.00
Cigar holder, man hunting w/dog, #3039, 5"	210.00
Cigar holder, wishing well w/chained bucket, #1621, 3¾"	70.00
Condiment set, group of 3 clowns: 1 tall, 2 sm, from $100 to	115.00
Condiment set, 3 owls, #5775, 3½"	95.00
Doll, Frozen Charlie, imp shield/#00, 13½", from $900 to	900.00
Humidor, man reading New York Times, #2557, 9½", from $200 to	210.00
Inkwell, boy w/drum reclining on lid, #134, sz VI, from $50 to	55.00
Inkwell, dog & cat on pillow, unmk	95.00
Inkwell, mother holds baby while 2 children look on, unmk, 5"	340.00
Jardiniere, girl by wicker/floral-appl basket on cart, #5030, $150 to	150.00
Jardiniere/nodder, man (lady) w/bird, #8587/7589.90 AG, 8½", pr	280.00

Match striker, boy w/watering can, #4200...................................... 75.00
Matchbox, dog in doghouse w/cat atop, #993, 4" 95.00
Matchstriker, boy (girl) by blackboard w/ABCs, ea from $150 to . 150.00
Pincushion, supported by 3 dolphins, unmk, 3", from $75 to 95.00
Shakers, owls, unmk, pr 38.00
Tobacco box, dog on lid, Orphans, unmk, 8", from $300 to 375.00
Toothpick holder, cigar bundle, florals on wht w/pk tie, #800, 2½"..50.00
Trinket dish, upright hand holding shell, #2420, 5½"..................... 70.00

Cookbooks

Cookbooks from the nineteenth century, though often hard to find, are a delight to today's collectors both for their quaint formats and printing methods as well as for their outmoded, often humorous views on nutrition. Recipes required a 'pinch' of salt, butter 'the size of an egg' or a 'walnut,' or a 'handful' of flour. Collectors sometimes specialize in cookbooks issued as advertising premiums. Especially desirable are the figurals that were shaped like a jar, a slice of bread, or some other form relative to the product. Others with unique features such as illustrations by well-known artists or references to famous people or places are priced in accordance. Cookbooks written earlier than 1874 are the most valuable and when found command prices as high as $200.00; figurals usually sell in the $10.00 to $15.00 range.

Our listings are for examples in near-mint condition. As is true with all other books, if the original dust jacket is present and in nice condition, a cookbook's value goes up by at least $5.00. Right now, books on Italian cooking from before circa 1940 are in demand, and bread-baking is important this year. Our advisor for this category is Charlotte Safir; she is listed in the Directory under New York.

Key:
CB — Cookbook	prt — printing
dj — dust jacket	rb — ring binder
hb — hardbound	shb — spiral hardback
pb — paperback	spb — spiral paperback
pm — pamphlet	

Agate Iron Ware CB, L&G Mfg Co, pb, 1880, 36 pgs..................... 80.00
All-Ways Preferable CB, Malleable Steel Range Mfg, pb, 1898, 96 pgs . 75.00
American Frugal Housewife, Mrs Childs, hb, 1836, 130 pgs, G ... 145.00
American Practical Cookery Book, JE Potter Co, hb, 1859, 319 pgs ..200.00
American Pure Food CB, M Hill Co, pb, 1899, 508 pgs, G............ 35.00
Appledore CB, Maria Parloa, Graves Locke & Co, hb, 1872....... 200.00
Baker's Cut-Up Cake Party Book, Dell, 1960, 128 pgs 38.00
Ballet CB, Tanaquil Le Clercq, Stein & Day, hb w/dj, 1966, 416 pgs ... 175.00
Baron's CB, Paroutand & Watson, pb, 1900, 96 pgs..................... 100.00
Better Homes & Garden Heritage CB, Darling & McConnell, pb, 1975 . 37.50
Bettina's Cakes & Cookies, LB Weaver & HC LeCron, hb, 1924 . 90.00
Betty Crocker's CB, Golden Press, hb in red cloth, 1972, 480 pgs . 55.00
Betty Crocker's Picture CB, hb, 1956, 472 pgs................................ 35.00
Buckeye Cookery & Practical Housekeeping, Wilcox, hb, 1877, 462 pgs.150.00
Catering for Special Occasions, Fannie M Farmer, hb, 1911, 249 pgs....60.00
Common Sense in the Household, M Harland, Scribner, hb, 1881, 546 pgs..100.00
Culinary Arts Institute...CB, Berolzheimer, hb, 1950, 974 pgs....... 45.00
Culinary Gems: A Collection of Choice Recipes, E Squire, hb, 1884..100.00
Dessert Lovers' Handbook, Eagle Brand, pb, 1973, 31 pgs.............. 10.00
Dr Price CB, Royal Baking Powder, pb, 1929 .... 15.00
Family & Householder's Guide, EG Storke, Auburn, hb, 1859, 288 pgs..250.00
Good Housekeeping International CB, Official World's Fair..., hb, 1964. 37.50
Home Queen World's Fair Souvenir CB, John F Waite, hb, 1895, 608 pgs.90.00
Joy of Cooking, Irma S Rambauer, hb w/dj, 1936 .... 105.00
Let's Start Cooking, Garel Clark, illustrated by K Elgin, spb, 1951..34.00
Lucky CB for Boys & Girls, Scholastic, oversized pb, 1969, 48 pgs..18.00

McNess Recipes From Around the World CB, Furst-McNess, ca 1930, 64 pgs ... 16.00
New New Can Opener CB, Poppy Cannon, hb, 1968, 314 pgs 14.00
Pyrex Prize Recipes, Corning Glass Works, hb, 1953, 128 pgs 20.00
Ralston Mother Goose Recipe Book, Ralston Purina Co, pb, 1919, 16 pgs.45.00
Reader's Service Bureau CB, R Berolzheimer, hb, 1941, 816 pgs ... 15.00
Recipes From the Old South, Martha L Meade, hb w/dj, 1961 ...... 24.00
Treasury of Great Recipes, Mary & Vincent Price, hb, 1965........ 125.00
Women's Favorite CB, Annie E Gregory, hb, 1902, 610 pgs 55.00

White House Cook Book, F.L. Gillett and Hugo Ziemann, published by Saalfield, 1924, 605 pages, hardback, $60.00.

(Photo courtesy Frank Daniels)

Cookie Cutters

Early hand-fashioned cookie cutters command stiff prices at country auctions, and the ranks of interested collectors are growing steadily. Especially valuable are the figural cutters; and the more complicated the design, the higher the price. A follow-up of the carved wooden cookie boards, the first cutters were probably made by itinerant tinkers from leftover or recycled pieces of tin. Though most of the eighteenth-century examples are now in museums or collections, it is still possible to find some good cutters from the late 1800s when changes in the manufacture of tin resulted in a thinner, less expensive material. The width of the cutting strip is often a good indicator of age; the wider the strip, the older the cutter. While the very early cutters were 1" to 1½" deep, by the '20s and '30s, many were less than ½" deep. Crude, spotty soldering indicates an older cutter, while a thin line of solder usually tends to suggest a much later manufacture. The shape of the backplate is another clue. Later cutters will have oval, round, or rectangular backs, while on the earlier type the back was cut to follow the lines of the design. Cookie cutters usually vary from 2" to 4" in size, but gingerbread men were often made as tall as 12". Birds, fish, hearts, and tulips are common; simple versions can be purchased for as little as $12.00 to $15.00. The larger figurals, especially those with more imaginative details, often bring $75.00 and up. Advertising cutters and product premiums (usually plastic) are collectible as well, so are the aluminum cutters with painted wood handles. Hallmark makes cutters in plastic — many of them character related and often priced in the $15.00 to $35.00 range. The cookie cutters listed here are tin and handmade unless noted otherwise.

Acorn, sq bk w/appl hdl, heavy tin, wide blade, 4¾x4⅛" 120.00
Antlered deer, conforming bk, 5⅞x4¾" 270.00
Bull, oval bk, 3½x5"... 18.00
Chicken w/fan tail, oversz comb & human ft, ca 1820, 2⅞x3¾"..300.00
Chimney sweep, tinned sheet iron, 19th C, wear, 8x6" 660.00
Dog running, 3x6"... 36.00
Dutch girl, simple oval shape, w/appl, wear, 4x2¾" 12.50
Dutch man, oval bk w/appl hdl, late, 5½x3" 24.00
Hatchet, triangular bk, 8½x5"... 85.00
Heart, conforming bk w/appl hdl, ca 1870, 9"............................... 150.00
Horse, primitive style, flat bk, 8" W 95.00
Horse standing, 19th C, 6x7½" 900.00
Horse stands w/1 leg raised, no bk (pattern), orig pnt/patina, 6".... 90.00

Lady w/hat, wide skirt, cut-out arms & legs, 6¾x3" 215.00
Man in the moon, sq bk, spotty solder, 5¼x3⅝" 132.00
Man on horsebk, conforming bk, minor dents, 7½" 360.00
Man on horsebk, EX primitive style, conforming bk, 8½" 660.00
Rabbit leaping, primitive style, 4x6½" 60.00
Rabbit seated, naturalistic, 10½" 215.00
Rocking horse, rectangular bk, some rust, 7x10¼" 60.00

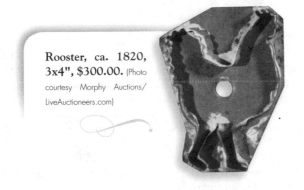

Rooster, ca. 1820, 3x4", $300.00. (Photo courtesy Morphy Auctions/ LiveAuctioneers.com)

Cookie Jars

The appeal of the cookie jar is universal; folks of all ages, both male and female, love to collect 'em! The early '30s' heavy stoneware jars of a rather nondescript nature quickly gave way to figurals of every type imaginable. Those from the mid to late '30s were often decorated over the glaze with 'cold paint,' but by the early '40s underglaze decorating resulted in cheerful, bright, permanent colors and cookie jars that still have a new look 50 years later.

Stimulated by the high prices commanded by desirable cookie jars, a broad spectrum of 'new' cookie jars are flooding the marketplace in three categories: 1) Manufacturers have expanded their lines with exciting new designs specifically geared toward attracting the collector market. 2) Limited editions and artist-designed jars have proliferated. 3) Reproductions, signed and unsigned, have pervaded the market, creating uncertainty among new collectors and inexperienced dealers. One of the most troublesome reproductions is the Little Red Riding Hood jar marked McCoy. Several Brush jars are being reproduced, and because the old molds are being used, these are especially deceptive. In addition to these reproductions, we've also been alerted to watch for cookie jars marked Brush-McCoy made from molds that Brush never used. Remember that none of Brush's cookie jars were marked Brush-McCoy, so any bearing the compound name is fraudulent. For more information on cookie jars and reproductions, we recommend *The Ultimate Collector's Encyclopedia of Cookie Jars* by Fred and Joyce Roerig, our advisors for this category; they are listed in the Directory under South Carolina.

The examples listed below were made by companies other than those found elsewhere in this book; see also specific manufacturers.

Albert Apple, Pitman-Dreitzer & Co, from $90 to 115.00
Alpo Dan the Dog, USA, from $50 to 60.00
Balloon Lady, Pottery Guild, unmk 125.00
Bartender, Pan American Art 175.00
Beaver Fireman, Sigma 250.00
Blue Bonnet Sue, Nabisco, from $60 to 80.00
Bud, Army man, brn, RRPCo, 1942-43, 12", from $425 to 475.00
Calypso Mammy, fruit on apron & turban, Made in Indonesia 50.00
Checkered Taxi Sedan, Canvanagh 300.00
Circus Wagon, Sierra Vista Ceramics Pasadena Cal, from $75 to .. 85.00
Clown, Maurice c Calif USA, from $200 to 250.00
Cookie Bakery, gr roof, CA Originals #863 USA, from $35 to 45.00
Cookie Factory, Fitz & Floyd c FF 1987, FF Japan label, from $80 to... 90.00

Cool Cookie Penguin, Hallmark Cards Inc, from $300 to 350.00
Corn, yel & gr, Terrace Ceramics USA #4299, from $35 to 45.00
Cow on Moon, yel cow, mk J 2 USA, Doranne of California, from $275 to... 325.00
Cowardly Lion, Star Jars, from $250 to 300.00
Doctor, Doranne of California, CJ-130 .... 200.00
Dog on Drum, Sierra Vista California, from $40 to 50.00
Dorothy & Toto, Star Jars, from $325 to 375.00
Dutch Girl, gold trim, RRPCo Roseville Ohio, 1956, 12", from $275 to. 325.00
Edmund, A Little Co c 1992, 19" 125.00
Elsie, unmk Pottery Guild 400.00
Ernie the Keebler Elf, c 1898 Keebler Co, Benjamin Medwin 80.00
Fred Flintstone, Vandor c 1989, from $150 to 175.00
Frog Sitting, bowl/flowers, CA Originals #877 USA, from $40 to . 50.00
Garfield on Cookie, Enesco 325.00
Gnome, Holiday Designs 40.00
Goose, red vest & gr bow tie, Made in Mexico on paper label 40.00
Gulden's Mustard, glass, 12¼" 200.00
Harley-Davidson Gas Tank, Taiwan, from $75 to 125.00

Haunted House, Fitz & Floyd, Taiwan, 1987, from $85.00 to $150.00.

Hen w/Chick, mc, USA (American Bisque), 8⅞x9½", $100 to ... 125.00
Herman Munster, Star Jars/Treasure Craft c 1996, from $250 to.. 300.00
Hippo, brn, CJ 6 USA, from $30 to 40.00
Hobo, Treasure Craft Compton, California Made in USA, from $35 to . 45.00
Horse Mechanic, Japan 45.00
Indian Couple, A Little Co c 1991 .... 150.00
Indian Maiden, Wihoa's Limited...1989 Rick Wisecarver, from $175 to. 200.00
Jack in Box, mk USA (American Bisque), 1958, from $125 to ... 150.00
Jukebox, Vandor 150.00
King, DeForest of California, 1957, minimum value 450.00
Kitten & Beehive, USA (American Bisque), 1958, sm, from $65 to... 80.00
Las Vegas Jackpot Slot Machine, Doranne of California, mk J-64 c USA ... 50.00
Little Red Riding Hood, California Originals, #320 USA 275.00
Mammy (Gone w/the Wind), Enesco, paper label 300.00
Michael Jordan & Bugs Bunny Space Jam, TM & c 1996 WB, from $125 to. 150.00
Mother Goose, gr w/gold, mk CJ-16 USA, Doranne of California, $225 to. 250.00
Mushrooms, Sierra Vista Ceramics...USA c 1957 .... 40.00
Nick at Night Television, Treasure Craft for Nickelodeon 600.00
Oscar the Grouch, California Originals #972 .... 100.00
Owl, Whoo's eating 'owl' cookies?, Enesco E-9227, c 1997 .... 30.00
Panda, Fitz & Floyd 125.00
Peasant Woman, Department 56 .... 125.00
Peter Panda, DCJ-24 c 1985...NAC, from $30 to 50.00
Pickup Truck (4x4), Doranne of California 200.00
Pirate Bust, Treasure Craft c Made in USA, from $225 to 275.00
Polka-Dot Witch, Fitz & Floyd 325.00
Queen, Maddux of CA USA c 210, from $100 to 125.00
Rabbit in Hat, brn w/mc details, DeForest of California c USA, $35 to... 40.00
Rocking Horse, Lane 125.00
Rudolph, American Bisque, c RLM, minimum value 400.00
Snoopy Doghouse, Benjamin & Medwin c '58 '66 UFS, Taiwan, $35 to. 40.00

Soccer Ball, Treasure Craft c Made in USA, from $40 to.............. 45.00
Spaceship, spaceman finial, Napco.. 900.00
Strawberry Shortcake, American Greetings Corp, MCML XXXIII . 450.00
Sylvester Head w/Tweety, Applause 95.00
Tepee, Whihoa's...Rick Wisecarver...No 1 89 .... 250.00
Train, smiling face, Sierra Vista California, from $50 to............... 60.00

Watermelon Sammy, Carol Gifford, 1987, $165.00. (Photo courtesy Pat and Ann Duncan)

Wilma on the Telephone, mk USA (American Bisque), 11½" 950.00
Yellow Cab, California Originals, unmk 175.00

Cooper, Susie

A twentieth-century ceramic designer whose works are now attracting the attention of collectors, Susie Cooper was first affiliated with the A.E. Gray Pottery in Henley, England, in 1922 where she designed in lustres and painted items with her own ideas as well. (Examples of Gray's lustreware is rare and costly.) By 1930 she and her brother-in-law, Jack Beeson, had established a family business. Her pottery soon became a success, and she was subsequently offered space at Crown Works, Burslem. In 1940 she received the honorary title of Royal Designer for Industry, the only such distinction ever awarded by the Royal Society of Arts solely for pottery design. Miss Cooper received the Order of the British Empire in the New Year's Honors List of 1979. She was the chief designer for the Wedgwood group from 1966 until she resigned in 1972. After 1980 she worked on a free-lance basis until her death in July 1995.

Key:
CW — Crown Works   HP — hand painted, painting
GP — Gray's Pottery   hs — hand signed

Bowl, cereal; Patricia Rose, 6½" 22.50
Bowl, serving; White Flute, w/lid, ca 1950, lg.............................. 45.00
Bowl, soup; Autumn Leaf, 8" 35.00
Bowl, vegetable; Endon, 9" 50.00
Bowl, vegetable; Whispering Grass, 9½" 40.00
Coffee/tea set, architectural view w/pillars/arches, 8½" pot+cr/sug... 485.00
Coffeepot, White Flute, unmk, ca 1950, 8½"............................... 50.00
Creamer, White Flute, ca 1950... 20.00
Creamer, Wild Strawberry, 8-oz.. 28.00
Cup, Polka Dot, lt bl on wht, Bone China England, sm................. 40.00
Cup & saucer, Autumn Leaf... 28.00
Cup & saucer, demitasse; fruit (various), 2½", 5½", set of 6 .... 90.00
Cup & saucer, Endon.. 28.00
Cup & saucer, Whispering Grass.. 25.00
Cup & saucer, Wild Strawberry, flat 25.00
Gravy boat, Wild Strawberry.. 65.00
Jug, bird reserve w/silver o/l, bulbous, GP, 5½" 95.00
Jug, Gloria Lustre, HP foliage, GP, 4½" 145.00
Jug, mc bands on wht, GP, 8½"... 40.00
Jug, Moon & Mountains, GP, 4¾"... 400.00

Lamp, geometric Art Deco motif on half-moon base with original Doumergue laced 'parchment' shade, both pieces marked, 15x13", $1,200.00.

(Photo courtesy David Rago Auctions/ LiveAuctioneers.com)

Lamp base, Nosegay, yel trim, CW, 8" 130.00
Mustache cup & saucer, barber theme, CW, 2½x4", 6¼" 235.00
Plate, dinner; Dresden Spray #1005 .... 25.00
Plate, dinner; Patricia Rose, 10"... 35.00
Plate, luncheon; Endon, 9" 20.00
Plate, luncheon; Patricia Rose, 9"....................................... 22.00
Plate, salad; Autumn Leaf, 8" 18.00
Plates, dinner; swirling foliate design, CW, 11½", 15 for 125.00
Sandwich set, flowers & foxglove, red trim, GP, 1928, tray+6 sq plates.. 350.00
Teacup, gray w/pk abstracts, pk rim, CW 65.00
Teapot, Glen Mist... 35.00
Teapot, White Flute, squat, ca 1950, 5" 45.00
Vase, dbl band of grooved decor on cream, ca 1935, 8⅜" 270.00

Coors

The firm that became known as Coors Porcelain Company in 1920 was founded in 1908 by John J. Herold, originally of the Roseville Pottery in Zanesville, Ohio. Though still in business today, they are best known for their artware vases and Rosebud dinnerware produced before 1939.

Coors vases produced before the late '30s were made in a matt finish; by the latter years of the decade, high-gloss glazes were also being used. Nearly 50 shapes were in production, and some of the more common forms were made in three sizes. Typical colors in matt are white, orange, blue, green, yellow, and tan. Yellow, blue, maroon, pink, and green are found in high gloss. All vases are marked with a triangular arrangement of the words 'Coors Colorado Pottery' enclosing the word 'Golden.' You may find vases (usually 6" to 6½") marked with the Colorado State Fair stamp and dated 1939. Please note: Prices for Coors, like many other collectibles, have taken a downward turn. Our prices here reflect those adjustments for today's current market.

Our advisor for this category is Rick Spencer; he is listed in the Directory under Utah.

Rosebud

Apple baker, w/lid.. 45.00
Baker, lg.. 40.00
Baker, tab hdls, 7" 20.00
Bean pot, hdls, lg... 70.00
Bean pot, sm... 65.00
Bowl, batter; lg... 65.00
Bowl, batter; sm... 45.00
Bowl, cream soup; 4"... 22.00
Bowl, fruit; lg.. 45.00
Bowl, mixing; hdls, 1½-pt.. 40.00
Bowl, mixing; 3-pt... 35.00
Bowl, mixing; 6-pt... 50.00
Bowl, oatmeal 22.00
Bowl, pudding; 2-pt.. 40.00
Bowl, pudding; 7-pt.. 75.00
Cake knife... 85.00

Cake plate, 11".. 30.00
Casserole, Dutch; w/lid, 1¾-pt 50.00
Casserole, Dutch; w/lid, 3¾-pt 72.00
Casserole, French; w/lid, 3¾-pt 45.00
Casserole, triple service; w/lid, lg, 7-pt 55.00

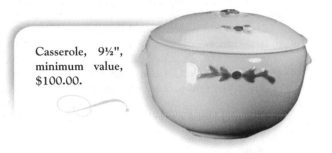

Casserole, 9½", minimum value, $100.00.

Cup & saucer 50.00
Egg cup... 55.00
Honey pot, w/lid, no spoon................................. 80.00
Honey pot, w/lid & spoon 300.00
Loaf pan 40.00
Muffin set, w/lid, rare 25.00
Pitcher, w/lid, lg 150.00
Pitcher, water; w/stopper................................... 120.00
Plate, 7¼" 10.00
Plate, 9¼" 23.00
Platter, 12x9" 38.00
Ramekin 45.00
Saucer, 5½"..5.00
Shakers, either syle, sm or lg, pr 50.00
Shakers, sm, pr 50.00
Shirred egg dish.. 25.00
Sugar bowl, w/lid.. 40.00
Sugar shaker 60.00
Teapot, 2-cup, rare 150.00
Teapot, 6-cup 125.00
Tumbler, ftd... 125.00
Water server, cork stopper, 6-cup 120.00

Copper

Handcrafted copper was made in America from early in the eighteenth century until about 1850, with the center of its production in Pennsylvania. Examples have been found signed by such notable coppersmiths as Kidd, Buchanan, Babb, Bently, and Harbeson. Of the many utilitarian items made, teakettles are the most desirable. Early examples from the eighteenth century were made with a dovetailed joint which was hammered and smoothed to a uniform thickness. Pots from the nineteenth century were seamed. Coffeepots were made in many shapes and sizes and, along with mugs, kettles, warming pans, and measures, are easiest to find. Stills ranging in sizes of up to 50-gallon are popular with collectors today. Mary Frank Gaston has compiled a lovely book, *Antique Brass and Copper*, with many full-color photos which we recommend for more information. Mrs. Gaston is listed in the Directory under Texas. See also Arts and Crafts, Roycroft, Stickley, and other specific categories.

Bathtub, EX patina, full sz 1,950.00
Birdbath, 26x16" dia 72.50
Boiler, 2 hdls, oval, polished, 12x25" 30.00
Bowl, brass hdl, polished, no mk, 4½x8¼" 36.00
Cauldron, EX patina, 19th C, 15x24" 185.00
Firewood bucket, hammered, EX patina, Townshends Ld, 13x16"..480.00

Fish steamer, appl hdls, w/lid, 19th C, 2x9x4" ... 42.50
Jardiniere, appl brass hdls, 19x25" dia 395.00
Kettle, gooseneck spout, appl hdl, polished, lg.... 215.00
Olla, hand formed w/peened finish, swing hdl, EX patina, 1940s, 5x10" .215.00
Pitcher, tin lined, unmk, 17x11" 36.00
Plates, hammered, EX patina, 10", 6 for 65.00
Pot, bulbous, EX patina, 24x27½" dia 120.00
Soup pot, hammered, 2 loop hdls, tinned int, ca 1860, 8x9", G...475.00

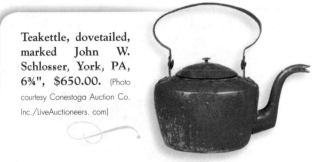

Teakettle, dovetailed, marked John W. Schlosser, York, PA, 6¾", $650.00. (Photo courtesy Conestoga Auction Co. Inc./LiveAuctioneers. com)

Teakettle, dvtl, swing hdl, brass finial, dents, A&I Sheriff, 7" 485.00
Teakettle, handwrought w/dvtl seams, brass lid, swing hdl, 8x13½". 180.00
Tray, geometric silver inlay, 15½" 55.00
Umbrella stand, emb Oriental scenic reserves on basketweave, EX patina..215.00
Washtub, hdls, polished, 20" dia........................ 240.00
Washtub, rectangular, 2 appl hdls, 7x25x16" 215.00
Watering can, emb rings, strap hdl...................... 36.00

Copper Lustre

Copper lustre is a term referring to a type of pottery made in Staffordshire after the turn of the nineteenth century. It is finished in a metallic rusty-brown glaze resembling true copper. Pitchers are found in abundance, ranging from simple styles with dull bands of color to those with fancy handles and bands of embossed, polychromed flowers. Bowls are common; goblets, mugs, teapots, and sugar bowls much less so. It's easy to find, but not in good condition. Pieces with hand-painted decoration and those with historical transfers are the most valuable.

Jug, embossed dancing figures, cobalt trim, 8", $75.00.

Cup, emb floral bands, 2¾" 20.00
Pitcher, bl band, 5¼" 45.00
Pitcher, bl floral band, 5" 55.00
Pitcher, geometric band at neck, pk floral band on body, 19th C, 8"..150.00
Pitcher, Lafayette portrait & Revolutionary war scene on yel band, 4" ..570.00
Pitcher, stags & game dog on wide bl band, dog hdl, 19th C, 5" 60.00
Pitcher, Wm H Harrison/bk: cabin, blk transfer on bl band, 8½" ... 7,200.00
Pitcher, Wm H Harrison/bk: blk transfer on wht reserve, 1840s, 8".4,800.00
Pitcher, 2 wide bl bands, unmk, 7", NM................ 60.00
Teapot, florals on pk band, angle hdl, 5½" 80.00

Coralene Glass

Coralene is a unique type of art glass easily recognized by the tiny grains of glass that form its decoration. Lacy allover patterns of seaweed, geometrics, and florals were used, as well as solid forms such as fish, plants, and single blossoms. (Seaweed is most commonly found and not as valuable as the other types of decoration.) It was made by several glasshouses both here and abroad. Values are based to a considerable extent on the amount of beading that remains. Our readers should know that recent coralene has raised bead decoration that is at least 10 millimeters thick.

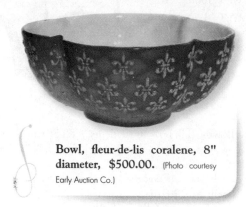

Bowl, fleur-de-lis coralene, 8" diameter, $500.00. (Photo courtesy Early Auction Co.)

Bowl, dk bl w/wht floral & geometric pattern, ca 1900, 6½" 275.00
Cup, pk to wht w/yel seaweed, wht hdl, 3¾x3" 60.00
Vase, bl & wht vertical bands w/yel seaweed, waisted neck, 9" 360.00
Vase, peachblow w/yel seaweed, flared neck, 8¼x4" 235.00
Vase, rose pk to wht w/yel seaweed, sq top, ca 1910, 2¾" 240.00
Vase, shaded pk w/yel seaweed, bulbous base, 9" 250.00
Vase, yel cased w/wildflowers & butterflies, 8¾" 395.00
Vase, yel to wht w/yel seaweed, bulbous w/flared neck, 7" 180.00

Cordey

The Cordey China Company was founded in 1942 in Trenton, New Jersey, by Boleslaw Cybis. The operation was small with less than a dozen workers. They produced figurines, vases, lamps, and similar wares, much of which was marketed through gift shops both nationwide and abroad. Though the earlier wares were made of plaster, Cybis soon developed his own formula for a porcelain composition which he called 'Papka.' Cordey figurines and busts were characterized by old-world charm, Rococo scrolls, delicate floral appliqués, ruffles, and real lace which was dipped in liquefied clay to add dimension to the work.

Although on rare occasions some items were not numbered or signed, the 'basic' figure was cast both with numbers and the Cordey signature. The molded pieces were then individually decorated and each marked with its own impressed identification number as well as a mark to indicate the artist-decorator. Their numbering system began with 200 and in later years progressed into the 8000s. As can best be established, Cordey continued production until sometime in the mid-1950s. Boleslaw Cybis died in 1957, his wife in 1958.

Due to the increased availability of Cordey on the internet over the last year, values of the more common pieces have fallen off. All items in our listings are considered to be in mint condition unless noted otherwise. Our advisor for this category is Sharon A. Payne; she is listed in the Directory under Washington.

#155, lamp, little girl figure 95.00
#303, man, plumed hat, ff, 16" 95.00

#324R, mallard, 1940s, 14" 100.00
#343, pheasant, vibrant mc, very early, scarce, 17" 175.00
#624, cup & saucer, appl pk roses, leaves on cup 35.00
#861, wall sconces w/roses, pr 85.00
#1027, centerpiece planter, lg swan 150.00
#1047, vase, rtcl top w/appl flower band, 12", EX 60.00
#4027, lady w/parasol, 8" 90.00
#4074, gentleman, lace shirt neck & cuffs, 13" 125.00
#4128, lady in lacy gown, curls, dbl bustle, 10½" 140.00
#5014, bust of lady, 6" 40.00
#5028, lady, ff, blond ringlets, Jr Colonial group, 6¾" 60.00
#5036, bust of lady in silver gown, bl hat w/pk roses, 8½" 65.00
#5077, woman praying, 13" 90.00
#5091, man holds coattail wide as if to bow, 10½" 55.00

#6037, box with roses and cherubs, $125.00. (Photo courtesy Sharon A. Payne)

#6046, ashtray 10.00
#7028, wall shelf, Art Nouveau nude w/cornucopia, 8x6½" 85.00
#7032, candlesticks, pk roses, 7½", pr 75.00
#7033, vase, wide mouth, 9" 35.00
Candlesticks, appl flowers at base, 7¼", M, pr 125.00
Dish, Cupid among bed of roses w/lav shawl, gold trim, 8½x6" 110.00
Lamp, lady in kimono, 11¼" figure, 24½" overall 90.00

Corkscrews

The history of the corkscrew dates back to the mid-1600s, when wine makers concluded that the best-aged wine was that stored in smaller containers, either stoneware or glass. Since plugs left unsealed were often damaged by rodents, corks were cut off flush with the bottle top and sealed with wax or a metal cover. Removing the cork cleanly with none left to grasp became a problem. The task was found to be relatively simple using the worm on the end of a flintlock gun rod. So the corkscrew evolved. Endless patents have been issued for mechanized models. Handles range from carved wood, ivory, and bone to porcelain and repoussé silver. Exotic materials such as agate, mother-of-pearl, and gold plate were also used on occasion. Celluloid lady's legs are popular.

For further information, we recommend *The Ultimate Corkscrew Book* and *Bull's Pocket Guide to Corkscrews* by Donald Bull, our advisor for this category. He is listed in the Directory under Virginia. In the following descriptions, values are for examples in excellent condition, unless noted otherwise.

Abyssinian type w/threaded tube, dbl hdls 78.00
Advertising, beer, Nifty, from $10 to 50.00
Barrel, chromed, closed, hdl mk Italy, from $20 to 34.00
Barrel, perpetual type, mk Dico Wakefield Mass Pat Pend, from $250 to .. 400.00
Bow, folding type w/corkscrew & foil cutter, from $75 to 150.00
Can opener combination, mini, 3", from $35 to 50.00
Carter's Ink, folding, Pat 1894 .... 18.00
Clough's 1899 oak hdl, wire terminates in button above worm, $40 to .. 50.00

Codd type, boxwood hdl, J&W Roper of Birmingham, from $100 to .150.00
Columbus, metal hdl mk Langbein Germany, from $75 to...........100.00
Dbl-action, wood, Copex Made in France, from $10 to 20.00
Dbl-lever, 1880 English Pat by Wm Baker of Birmingham England, $800 to...1,200.00
England, ebonized wood hdl, thick disk, 1880s, EX......................50.00
England, polished steel peg & worm, ca 1810, 4½" 130.00
England, 4-finger pull, w/button, ca 1895 ....27.50
Figural, anchor, friction-fit sheath covers worm, HMS Victory, $20 to..30.00
Figural, Mannekin Pis, holding worm w/1 or 2 hands, ea from $10 to .50.00
Figural, monk's head lifts to expose corkscrew, from $30 to...........60.00
Finger pull, 2-finger, direct pull, unmk, from $10 to 20.00
Flynut, brass, Edwin Jay Made in Italy, from $10 to.......................20.00
Flynut fixed to fr, J Perille Depose Paris/Helice JHP Depose, $50 to 80.00
Frame, ivory or bone hdl, unmk, mini, from $100 to 300.00
Frame, Ornate cast metal w/spring & wood hdl, from $200 to.....300.00
Frame, rococo design w/locking roll-over hdl, from $300 to 800.00
Frame, Wulfruna, Stephen Plant's 1884 English Pat, from $150 to..200.00
France, wood hdl, metal ends, dimpled shaft, ca 1875, EX.............30.00
Germany, spring over shaft, ca 1895, VG, from $20 to...................80.00
Happy Face, ca 1935, 10"...75.00
Italy, swivel-collar type, NP brass, VG 15.00
London Rack, rack & pinion actions, unmk English, 1800s, from $150 to .250.00
Mini, folding bow, plain, folded: ¾-1¾", from $20 to 40.00
Mini, fr type w/ivory or bone hdl, from $100 to...........................300.00
Perfume, tiger head, Birmingham 1896, from $400 to 500.00
Picnic, wood sheath, rare, from $200 to.....................................300.00
Pocket, silver w/various hdls, English or Dutch, 19th C, $600 to..1,200.00
Pocket folder, So-Ezy, Made in USA Pat Pend, from $40 to 50.00
Pocket folder, Turkey Foot, cap lifter & sm spoon, from $80 to ...120.00
Prong puller, Magic Cork Extractor, Pats 1879 & 1892, from $700 to . 1,000.00
Rack & pinion, Four Poster, King's Screw, bone-top, hdl, from $800 to .1,200.00
Roundlet, eng NP w/threaded cases, w/ or w/o advertising, from $150 to..250.00
Roundlet, silver threaded case slides apart & forms hdl, from $150 to..350.00
Sardine key, w/folding fork, from $150 to 200.00
Single-lever, Lund & Hipkins, single worm, 1854, from $100 to .250.00
Single-lever, Tucker, Pat 1878, from $1,800 to 3,000.00
Spring, Richard Recknagel's 1899 German Pat, diagonal guide, $250 to ..300.00
Staghorn hdl, mk sterling cap, 7½" 85.00
T-hdl, metal, fancy design w/cork-gripping teeth, from $150 to...250.00
T-hdl w/button, wood, from $75 to 200.00

Two-pillar frame with ivory hand gripping bar, from $6,000.00 to $8,000.00; Handle is turned to lift stem, reverses to extract the cork, from $2,200.00 to $2,500.00; John Coney's 1854 English patent, from $700.00 to $1,000.00. (Photo courtesy Donald Bull)

US, brass band & boar's tooth hdl, 6", EX 85.00
US Hollweg 1891 Pat, Pabst Milwaukee advertising, EX 150.00
US Williamson 1897 Pat Bullet, copper finish, early......................80.00
Waiter's friend, Davis Pat w/knife blade on top of hdl, from $150 to ..200.00
Waiter's friend, Liftmaster, chrome body, from $15 to 25.00
Waiter's friend, Universal, 1906 Am Pat by H Noyes, from $30 to..50.00
Weir's Pat 12804 25, Sept 1884, VG bronze finish 125.00
Williamson's Don't Swear, Catalin sheath, from $25 to 50.00
15 Tools in One, Nathan Jenkins, 1930, from $300 to 400.00
2-finger celluloid ivory hdl, mid sz (3-4½"), from $50 to 60.00
3-finger pull (eyebrow hdl spanning 2¼-3¼"), unmk, from $5 to...25.00

Cosmos

Cosmos, sometimes called Stemless Daisy, is a patterned glass tableware produced from 1894 through 1915 by Consolidated Lamp and Glass Company. Relief-molded flowers on a finely crosscut background were painted in soft colors of pink, blue, and yellow. Though nearly all were made of milk glass, a few items may be found in clear glass with the designs painted on. In addition to the tableware, lamps were also made.

All prices are for pieces in very good condition. Some roughness or 'fleabites' around the edges of most pieces (e.g. lamp globes, top of the covered butter dish) are acceptable, except for the tumblers where they severely reduce their value. Any cracks or significant chips reduce the values considerably. These are average 'selling' prices; some dealers may ask as much as 20% to 30% more but will often come down to close a sale. Our advisors for this category are Michael A. and Valarie Bozarth (info@BeauxArtsUSA.com). They are listed in the Directory under New York.

Bottle, cologne; w/stopper, rare, 4¾" 275.00
Butter dish, underplate only 45.00
Butter dish, 5x8"...180.00
Condiment set, w/orig lids, rare..325.00
Creamer, 5"...90.00
Lamp, base only, 7"...105.00
Lamp, mini; base only, 3½"...65.00

Lamp, miniature; 7½", $290.00. (Photo courtesy John Schuman III)

Lamp, w/globe, 16"...425.00
Pickle castor, fr mk Toronto, rare 690.00
Pitcher, milk; 5"..250.00
Pitcher, water; 9"...190.00
Shakers, w/orig lids, 2½", pr...130.00
Spooner, 4"...95.00
Sugar bowl, open...90.00
Sugar bowl, w/lid..165.00
Sugar shaker, rare..350.00
Syrup pitcher, rare, 6½"..325.00
Tumbler, 3¾"...55.00
Water set, pitcher (9") w/6 tumblers 525.00

Cottageware

You'll find a varied assortment of novelty dinnerware items, all styled as cozy little English cottages or huts with cone-shaped roofs; some may have a waterwheel or a windmill. Marks will vary. English-made Price Brothers or Beswick pieces are valued in the same range as those marked Occupied Japan, while items marked simply Japan are considerably less pricey. All of the following examples are Price Brothers/Kensington unless noted otherwise.

Bank, dbl slot, 4½x3½x5" 80.00
Bell, minimum value 60.00
Bowl, salad 50.00
Butter dish, cottage int (fireplace), Japan, 6¾x5", from $65 to 80.00
Butter dish, from $50 to 65.00
Butter dish, oval, Burlington Ware, 6" 60.00
Butter dish, rnd, Beswick, England, w/lid, 3½x6" 75.00
Butter pat, emb cottage, rectangular, Occupied Japan 20.00
Chocolate pot, 9½", from $85 to 135.00
Condiment set, mustard, 2½" s&p on 5" hdld leaf tray 75.00
Condiment set, mustard pot, s&p, tray, row arrangement, 6" 45.00
Condiment set, mustard pot, s&p, tray, row arrangement, 7¾" 45.00
Condiment set, 3-part cottage on shaped tray w/appl bush, 4½" 75.00
Cookie jar, pk/brn/gr, sq, Japan, 8½x5½" 60.00
Cookie jar, wicker hdl, Maruhon Ware, Occupied Japan, 6½" 80.00
Cookie jar, windmill, wicker hdl, from $145 to 165.00
Cookie jar/canister, cylindrical, 8½x5", from $85 to 125.00
Cookie/biscuit jar, Occupied Japan, 6½" 80.00
Covered dish, Occupied Japan, sm 35.00
Creamer, windmill, Occupied Japan, 2⅝" 25.00
Creamer & sugar bowl, 2½x4½" 40.00
Cup & saucer, chocolate; str-sided cup, 3½x2¾", 5½" 35.00
Cup & saucer, 2½", 4½" 35.00
Demitasse pot, 6x6¼", from $80 to 110.00
Egg cup set, 4 (single) on 6" sq tray 65.00
Gravy boat & tray, rare, from $250 to 275.00
Hot water pot, Westminster, England, 8½x4" 50.00
Marmalade, 4" 45.00
Marmalade & jelly, 2 conjoined houses, 5x7" 75.00
Mug, 3⅞" 55.00
Pin tray, 4" dia 22.00

Pitcher, large flower on handle, $100.00.

Pitcher, tankard; rnd, 7 windows on front, from $80 to 120.00
Pitcher, tankard; 5" 30.00
Platter, oval, 11¾x7½" 60.00
Reamer, windmill, Japan 150.00
Sugar box/butterdish, roof as lid, 6½" L 50.00
Tea set, Japan, child's, serves 4 .... 165.00
Teapot, Keele Street, w/creamer & sugar bowl 65.00
Teapot, Occupied Japan, 6½" 45.00
Teapot, Ye Olde Fireside, Occupied Japan, 9x5", from $70 to 85.00
Teapot, 6½", from $50 to 65.00
Toast rack, 3-slot, 3½" 75.00
Toast rack, 4-slot, 5½" 75.00
Tumbler, Occupied Japan, 3½", set of 6 .... 65.00

Coverlets

The Jacquard attachment for hand looms represented a culmination of weaving developments made in France. Introduced to America by the early 1820s, it gave professional weavers the ability to easily cre-

ate complex patterns with curved lines. Those who could afford the new loom adaptation could now use hole-punched pasteboard cards to weave floral patterns that before could only be achieved with intense labor on a draw-loom.

Before the Jacquard mechanism, most weavers made their coverlets in geometric patterns. Use of indigo-blue and brightly colored wools often livened the twills and overshot patterns available to the small-loom home weaver. Those who had larger multiple-harness looms could produce warm double-woven, twill-block, or summer-and-winter designs.

While the new floral and pictorial patterns' popularity had displaced the geometrics in urban areas, the mid-Atlantic, and the Midwest by the 1840s, even factory production of the Jacquard coverlets was disrupted by cotton and wool shortages during the Civil War. A revived production in the 1870s saw a style change to a center-medallion motif, but a new fad for white 'Marseilles' spreads soon halted sales of Jacquard-woven coverlets. Production of Jacquard carpets continued to the turn of the century.

Even earlier, German weavers in the eighteenth century made double-weave coverlets in a style of weaving called Beiderwand that produced a two-layer fabric from a single set of warp threads with patterns created by selecting threads at specific intervals that tied the layers together. Most are quite colorful, and patterns were often very elaborate.

Rural and frontier weavers continued to make geometric-design coverlets through the nineteenth century, and local craft revivals have continued the tradition through this century. All-cotton overshots were factory produced in Kentucky from the 1940s, and factories and professional weavers made cotton-and-wool overshots during the past decade. Many Beiderwand and Jacquard-woven coverlets have dates and names of places and people (often the intended owner — not the weaver) woven into corners or borders.

Note: In the listings that follow, examples are blue and white and in excellent condition unless noted otherwise. When dates are given, they actually appear on the coverlet itself as part of the woven design.

Key: mdl — medallion

Jacquard

Two-piece double weave: Birds of paradise, Boston Town side borders, attributed to Ohio, EX, 74x86", $490.00; Birds of paradise, floral vine sides, double baskets of fruit end borders, 77x82", $490.00; Twenty-four star blocks, two-story houses across end border, attributed to Gilmour Brothers, Union County, Indiana, with their sailboat corner blocks dated 1839, 72x86", VG, $1,265.00; Peacocks and houses, buildings and flower borders, Cadiz, Ohio, G, $720.00. (Photo courtesy Garth's Auctions Inc.)

Beiderwand, eagle/branches/foliage/roses, red/bl/wht, 2-pc, 90x74" .400.00
Beiderwand, floral mdls w/trees/crowned lions/swords border, 76x86" .. 3,725.00
Beiderwand, floral mdls/grapevine borders, 4-color, 2-pc, 1859, 86x78" .925.00
Beiderwand, floral/dmn mdls/bird/foliage, 4-color, sgn/1854, 71x84" .. 2,350.00
Beiderwand, mdls/grapevines, red/bl/aqua/cream, 2-pc, sgn/1859, 78x86" ...960.00
Beiderwand, roses/baskets/birds, red/bl/tan, 2-pc, OH/1850, 90x76" ..400.00
Beiderwand, roses/rosettes/grapevines, 4-color, 2-pc, 92x76"+fringe..575.00
Beiderwand, roses/stars/fruit baskets, red/gr/gray/natural, 91x86" ..1,300.00
Birds/flowers/triple border, 4-color, single weave/2-pc, 92x89" 175.00
Capital buildings/monuments/foliage, gr/rust, 2-pc, OH, 84x87", VG..200.00
Capital in WA 1846, bl/red/natural, 2-pc, dbl weave, 78x85" 800.00
Eagles/stars/borders, 2-pc, sgn/1849, 88x82"+fringe......................460.00
Floral mdl, floral/foliate borders, 2-pc, dbl-weave, 90x80" 475.00
Floral mdl amid strawberry vines, bl/gr/red, dbl weave, sgn/1850, 75". 1,100.00
Floral mdls (12 lg+6 sm), 2-pc, Delhi 1839, 93x74" 600.00
Floral/birds/chickens/roosters, blk/wht, sgn/1833, 69x92" 3,360.00
Flowers/foliage/leaves, 2-pc/dbl weave, IN/1845, 84x77" 300.00
Geometric floral, eagle & shield corners, dbl weave, sgn/1834, 80x91" ..1,680.00
Geometric floral on stripes, turq/gr/red/bl, sgn/1840, 96x84", VG.. 1,560.00
Geometrics/trees, wool/cotton, 2-pc, early 1800s, 94x76" 300.00

Overshot

Dmns & triangles, red/navy bl/olive-amber/natural, 2-pc, 91x77" ..500.00
Geometric, dk gr/wht, 2-pc, VA, 96x72"...................................425.00
Geometric floral, dk gr/cream, J Brosney/D Ginrich, 1840, 95x73"..450.00
Geometric floral w/Pine Tree border, bl/natural, reversible, 92x68" .360.00
Geometric grid, navy/gold/natural, 2-pc, EX color rstr at top, 92x90" ..425.00
Monk's Belt variant, red/bl/natural, 2-pc, fringe, 92x77"..............435.00
Optical, dk & lt bl, 2-pc, fringe on 3 sides, 86x70" 300.00
Optical, red/blk/natural, 2-pc, lt wear/sm hold, 84x84" 240.00
Stars w/a Table, blk/natural, 2-pc, fringe, 90x68" 180.00
Sunrise, dk bl/cream, 2-pc, lt wear, 92x72" 300.00

Cowan

Guy Cowan opened a small pottery near Cleveland, Ohio, in 1913, where he made tile and artware on a small scale from the natural red clay available there. He developed distinctive glazes — necessary, he felt, to cover the dark red body. After the war and a temporary halt in production, Cowan moved his pottery to Rocky River, where he made a commercial line of artware utilizing a highly fired white porcelain. Although he acquiesced to the necessity of mass production, every effort was made to insure a product of highest quality. Fine artists, among them Waylande Gregory, Thelma Frazier, and Viktor Schreckengost, designed pieces which were often produced in limited editions, some of which sell today for prices in the thousands. Most of the ware was marked 'Cowan,' except for the 1930 mass-produced line called 'Lakeware.' Falling under the crunch of the Great Depression, the pottery closed in 1931.

Bookends, kneeling camels by Alexander Blazys, beige and brown crackle, 1927 – 1931, floral stamp, 8¾x9½", $4,100.00.

(Photo courtesy David Rago Auctions/LiveAuctioneers.com)

Ashtray, boat form w/oars, April Green, #770, 2½" 95.00
Ashtray, Clown, Special Ivory, 3"..48.00
Bookend, Scholar, Antique Green, #522, 6¼", ea 240.00
Bookends, horses kicking, Egyptian Blue, W Gregory, #E1, 8½" ...2,000.00
Bookends, Polar Bear, Primrose, att M Postgate, ca 1929-30, 6⅛".7,200.00
Bookends, Sunbonnet Girl, Verde Green, 7¼" 360.00
Bowl, cream soup; Colonial, Daffodil Yellow, w/underplate 25.00
Bowl, emb floral, Parchment Green, Gregory, 3-ftd, #B16 ....480.00
Bowl, Flamingo, Oriental Red (w/dk mottle), #B4, 15" L 165.00
Bowl, Larkspur, #666, 6" H 20.00
Bowl, Pterodactyl, Flemish Blue, A Blazys, #729, 17" L 180.00
Candlestick, Byzantine, turq, #746, 9", ea.................................300.00
Candlestick, Rowfant, Pine Green, F Wilcocks, 1925, 9¼", ea.1,550.00
Candlesticks, flower form, Lapis, #735, 4¼", pr 85.00
Cigarette holder, Chickadee, April Green, 5"............................110.00
Compote, Larkspur, sea horse base, 4" 48.00
Figurine, Dancer, Russian peasant, terra cotta crackle, A Blazys, 11".775.00
Figurine, elephant w/tucked trunk, sq ft, orange matt, 4¾" 235.00
Figurine, Spanish Dancer (lady), Primrose, E Anderson, 1928, 8¾" ..315.00
Flower frog, Awakening, Special Ivory, RG Cowan, #F 8, 9" 360.00
Flower frog, flamingo, Special Ivory, W Gregory, #D2F9, 12" 275.00
Flower frog, Pavlova, Caramel w/gr overtones, RG Cowan, #698, 6¼"..660.00
Flower frog, Repose, Orig Ivory, RG Cowan, #612, 6¼", NM 275.00
Humidor, emb ribs, Oriental Red w/mottling, TF Winter, 6".......235.00
Lamp base, Deco fountain form, Antique Green, 7¾".................250.00
Lamp base, Woodland Nymph, Special Ivory, W Gregory, 14" .4,500.00
Plate, flower form, Special Ivory w/gr stain, 8".............................25.00
Tea tile, fish, mc, 6½" dia...165.00
Vase, Azure, #609, 4" 30.00

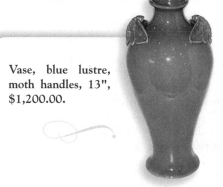

Vase, blue lustre, moth handles, 13", $1,200.00.

Vase, bud; Sea Horse, Delphinium, #725, 7½" 36.00
Vase, copper, #563, 13"...350.00
Vase, Fur Green w/ormolu mts, #545, 7", pr...............................165.00
Vase, Larkspur, #629, 10"...70.00
Vase, Logan, Sunrise, rtcl hdls, #6498, 8", NM...........................110.00
Vase, Marigold, bulbous top, 5¼" 48.00
Vase, Mother-of-Pearl w/slight irid, #822, 9" 250.00
Vase, Peacock, mk Lakeware, #610, 3"..36.00
Vase, Sea Horse, Larkspur, #715-B, 8"...55.00
Vase, Squirrel, Mother-of-Pearl, Gregory, #V19, 1930, 8¼" 1,450.00
Vase, 6-sided, Oriental Red, #546, 6"..95.00

Cracker Jack

Kids have been buying Cracker Jack since it was first introduced in the 1890s. By 1912 it was packaged with a free toy inside. Before the first kernel was crunched, eager fingers had retrieved the surprise from the depth of the box — actually no easy task, considering the care required to keep the contents so swiftly displaced from spilling over the side! Though a little older, perhaps, many of those same kids still are looking — just as eagerly — for the Cracker Jack prizes. Point of sale, company collectibles, and the prizes as well have over the years reflected America's changing culture. Grocer sales and incentives from around the turn of the twentieth century — paper dolls, postcards, and song books — were often marked Rueckheim Brothers (the inventors of Cracker Jack) or Reliable Confections. Over the years the company made some changes, leaving a trail of clues that often helps collectors date their items. The company's name changed in 1922 from Rueckheim Brothers & Eckstein (who had been made a partner for inventing a method for keeping the caramelized kernels from sticking together) to The Cracker Jack Company. Their Brooklyn office was open from 1914 until it closed in 1923. The first time the sailor Jack logo was used on their packaging was in 1919. The sailor image of a Rueckheim child (with red, white, and blue colors) was introduced by these German immigrants in an attempt to show support for America during the time of heightened patriotism after WW I. For packages and 'point of sale' dating, note that the word 'prize' was used from 1912 to 1925, 'novelty' from 1925 to 1932, and 'toy' from 1933 on.

The first loose-packed prizes were toys made of wood, clay, tin, metal, and lithographed paper (the reason some early prizes are stained). Plastic toys were introduced in 1946. Paper wrapped for safety purposes in 1948, subjects echo the 'hype' of the day — yo-yos, tops, whistles, and sports cards in the simple, peaceful days of our country, propaganda and war toys in the '40s, games in the '50s, and space toys in the '60s. Few of the estimated 15 billion prizes were marked. Advertising items from Angelus Marshmallow and Checkers Confections (cousins of the Cracker Jack family) are also collectible. When no condition is indicated, the items listed below are assumed to be in excellent to mint condition. 'CJ' indicates that the item is marked. Note: An often-asked question concerns the tin Toonerville Trolley called 'CJ.' No data has been found in the factory archives to authenticate this item; it is assumed that the 'CJ' merely refers to its small size. For further information see *Cracker Jack Toys, The Complete, Unofficial Guide for Collectors*, by Larry White. Our advisor for this category is Harriet Joyce; she is listed in the Directory under under Florida. Also look for *The Prize Insider* newsletter listed in the Directory under Clubs, Newsletters, and Catalogs.

Dealer Incentives and Premiums

Badge, pin-bk, celluloid, lady w/CJ label on bk, 1905, 1¼" 75.00
Blotter, CJ question mk box, yel, 7¾x3¾" 185.00
Book, pocket; riddle/sailor boy/dog on cover, RWB, CJ, 1919 .... 14.00
Book, Uncle Sam Song Book, CJ, 1911, ea 18.00
Corkscrew/opener, metal plated, CJ/Angelus, 3¾" tube case 22.00
Jigsaw puzzle, CJ or Checkers, 1 of 4, 7x10", in envelope 35.00
Mask, Halloween; paper, CJ, series, 10" or 12", ea 28.00
Mirror, oval, Angelus (redhead or blond) on box 60.00
Pen, ink; w/nib, tin litho bbl, CJ 300.00
Pencil top clip, metal/celluloid, tube shape w/pkg 220.00
Puzzle, metal, CJ/Checkers, 1 of 15, 1934, in envelope, ea 12.00
Tablet, school; CJ, 1929, 8x10" 195.00
Thimble, aluminum, CJ Co/Angelus, red pnt, rare, ea 120.00
Wings, Air Corps type, silver or blk, stud-bk, CJ, 1930s, 3", ea 35.00

Packaging

Box, popcorn; red scroll border, CJ 'Prize,' 1912-25, ea 300.00
Canister, tin, CJ Candy Corn Crisp, 10-oz 65.00
Canister, tin, CJ Coconut Corn Crisp, 10-oz 65.00
CJ Commemorative canister, wht w/red scroll, 1980s 5.00

Prizes, Cast Metal

Badge, 6-point star, mc CJ Police, silver, 1931, 1¼" 45.00

Button, stud bk, Xd bats & ball, CG pitcher/etc series, 1928 .... 130.00
Coins, Presidents, 31 series, CJ, mk cancelled on bk, 1933, ea 18.00
Dollhouse items, lantern, mug, candlestick, etc, no mk, ea 6.50
Pistol, soft lead, inked, CJ on bbl, early, rare, 2⅛" 180.00
Rocking horse, no rider, 3-D, inked, early, 1⅛" 15.00
Spinner, early pkg in center, 'More You Eat...,' CJ, rare 295.00

Prizes, Paper

Book, Animals (or Birds) To Color, Makatoy, unmk, 1949, mini... 35.00
Book, Birds We Know, CJ, 1928, mini 90.00
Book, Chaplin flip book, CJ, 1920s, ea 85.00
Book, Twigg & Sprigg, CJ, 1930, mini 65.00
Decal, cartoon or nursery rhyme figure, 1947-49, CJ 12.00
Disguise, ears, red (still in carrier), CJ, 1950, pr 22.00
Disguise, glasses, hinged, w/eyeballs, unmk, 1933 .... 6.00
Fortune Teller, boy/dog on film in envelope, CJ, 1920s, 1¾x2½" ... 80.00
Game, Midget Auto Race, wheel spins, CJ, 1949, 3⅜" H 15.00
Game spinner, ...baseball at home, unmk, 1946, 1½" dia 60.00
Hat, Indian headdress, CJ, 1910-20, 5⅜" H 275.00
Hat, Me for CJ, early, ea 120.00
Magic game book, erasable slate, CJ, series of 13, 1946, ea 15.00
Movie, pull tab for 2nd picture, yel, early, 3", in envelope 125.00
Movie Goofy Zoo, trn wheel(s) to change animals, unmk, 1939 ... 25.00

Sand toys, tilt picture and sand moves from one area to another, 1960, $45.00 each. (Photo courtesy Harriet Joyce)

Top, string; Rainbow Spinner, 2-pc, cb, different designs, ea 45.00
Transfer, iron-on, sport figure or patriotic, unmk, 1939, ea 6.00
Whistle, Blow for More, CJ/Angelus pkgs, 1928, '31 or '33, ea 45.00
Whistle, Razz Zooka, C Carey Cloud design, CJ, 1949 .... 25.00

Prizes, Plastic

Animals, standup, letter on bk, series of 26, Nosco, 1953, ea 2.00
Baseball players, 3-D, bl or gray team, 1948, 1½", ea 4.00
Disk, emb fish plaque, oval, series of 10, 1956, unmk, ea 14.00
Figure, circus; stands on base, 1 of 12, Nosco, 1951-54 .... 3.00
Fob, alphabet letter w/loop on top, 1 of 26, 1954, 1½" 4.00
Palm puzzle, ball(s) roll into holes, dome or rnd, from 1966, ea 6.00
Palm puzzle, ball(s) roll into holes, sq, CJ, 1920s, ea 45.00
Ships in a bottle, 6 different, unmk, 1960, ea 4.00
Spinner, tops varied colors, 10, designs, from 1948, ea 2.50
Toys, take apart/assemble, variety, from 1962, unassembled, ea 8.00
WWII Cl Cloud punch-out war vehicles, CJ, series of 10, ea 30.00

Prizes, Tin

Badge, boy & dog die-cut, complete w/bend-over tab, CJ 125.00
Bank, 3-D book form, red/gr/or blk, CJ Bank, early, 2" 120.00

Brooch or pin, various designs on card, CJ/logo, early, ea............ 125.00
Clicker, 'Noisy CJ Snapper,' pear shape, aluminum, 1949.............. 12.00
Doll dishes, tin plated, CJ, 1931, 1¾", 1⅞", & 2⅛" dia, ea............. 35.00
Helicopter, yel propeller, wood stick, unmk, 1937, 2⅝".................. 27.00
Horse & wagon, litho die-cut, CJ & Angelus, 2⅛" 45.00
Horse & wagon, litho die-cut, gray/red mks, CJ, 1914-23, 3⅛" 350.00
Pocket watch, silver or gold, CJ as numerals, 1931, 1½" 30.00
Small box shape, electric stove litho, unmk, 1⅛" 80.00
Small box shape, garage litho, unmk, 1⅛" 60.00
Soldier, litho, die-cut standup, officer/private/etc, unmk, ea 17.00
Spinner, wood stick, Fortune Teller Game, red/wht/bl, CJ, 1½".... 90.00
Spinner, wood stick, 2 Toppers, red/wht/bl, Angelus/Jack, 1½"...... 55.00
Standup, oval Am Flag, series of 4, unmk, 1940-49, ea 12.00
Tall box shape, Frozen Foods locker freezer, unmk, 1947, 1¾" 75.00
Tall box shape, grandfather clock, unmk, 1947, 1¾" 65.00
Train, engine & tender, litho, CJ Line/512 .... 95.00
Train, litho engine only, red, unmk, 1941 .... 10.00
Train, Lone Eagle Flyer engine, unmk... 60.00
Truck, litho, RWB, CJ/Angelus, 1931, ea.................................... 45.00
Wagon shape: CJ Shows, yel circus wagon, series of 5, ea 125.00
Wagon shape: Tank Corps No 57, gr & blk, 1941 .... 30.00
Wheelbarrow, tin plated, bk leg in place, CJ, 1931, 2½" L............. 22.00

Miscellaneous

Ad, Saturday Evening Post, mc, CJ, 1919, 11x14" 18.00
Lunch box, tin emb, CJ, 1970s, 4x7x9"...................................... 30.00
Medal, CJ salesman award, brass, 1939, scarce............................ 125.00

Poster, trolley card, early 1910s, 10½x20½", EX, $400.00. (Photo courtesy Harriet Joyce)

Sign, bathing beauty, 5-color cb, CJ, early, 17x22" 250.00
Sign, Santa & prizes, mc cb, Angelus, early, lg 220.00
Sign, Santa & prizes, mc cb, CJ, early, lg 265.00

Crackle Glass

Though this type of glassware was introduced as early as the 1880s (by the New England Glass Co.), it was made primarily from 1930 until about 1980. It was produced by more than 500 companies here (by Benko, Rainbow, and Kanawah, among others) and abroad (by such renown companies as Moser, for example), and its name is descriptive. The surface looks as though the glass has been heated then plunged into cold water, thus producing a network of tight cracks. It was made in a variety of colors; among the more expensive today are ruby red, amberina, cobalt, cranberry, and gray. For more information we recommend *Crackle Glass From Around the World* by Stan and Arlene Weitman, our advisors this category; they are listed in the Directory under New York. See also Moser.

Apple, red w/gr stem & leaf, Blenko, 1950s-60s, from $100 to 125.00

Ashtray, amberina, Viking, 1944-70, 7¼", from $45 to 65.00
Basket, red w/clear twisted hdl, Hamon/Kanawha, 1960s-70s, 5", $75 to.. 100.00
Beaker, clear w/sea gr leaves, Blenko, 1940s-50s, 7", from $110 to...150.00
Bonbon, red heart shape w/yel hdl, 1950s-60s, 3¼", from $85 to . 110.00
Bottle, bl, flat-sided, unkown maker, 8", from $80 to..................... 90.00
Candlesticks, bl, Rainbow, 1940s-50s, 6", pr from $150 to........... 175.00
Candy dish, dk topaz/clear ribbed pan hdl, Hamon, 5½", from $100 to..125.00
Candy dish, ruby, Bischoff, 1940-63, 4½x5" dia, from $85 to....... 115.00
Compote, tangerine, Blenko, 1950s, 6", from $100 to 125.00
Creamer, bl, drop-over hdl, unknown maker & date, 3⅛", from $50 to ... 75.00

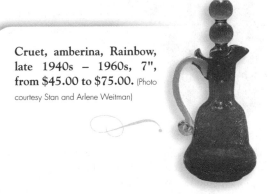

Cruet, amberina, Rainbow, late 1940s – 1960s, 7", from $45.00 to $75.00. (Photo courtesy Stan and Arlene Weitman)

Cruet, bl, pulled-bk hdl, Pilgrim, 1949-69, from $75 to 100.00
Cup, amberina, drop-over hdl, Kanawha, 1957-87, 2½", from $40 to....50.00
Decanter, clear, pointed stopper, Pilgrim, 1949-69, 11", from $100 to ..125.00
Decanter, clear ball/pnt flowers, bl stopper/hdl, Czech, 1920s, 10"...650.00
Decanter, gr pitcher w/ball stopper, Bischoff, 1950s, from $125 to..150.00
Decanter, topaz, lg ball stopper, Rainbow, 1953, 11", from $150 to..175.00
Dish, lt bl w/5 lg scallops (star), Blenko, 1960s, 5½", from $55 to . 65.00
Fish wine bottle, topaz, unknown maker, 1960s, 9x21", from $160 to ..185.00
Hat, amberina, Kanawha, 1957-87, 2", from $50 to 75.00
Hurricane lamp, amber, Kanawha, 1957-87, 8¼", from $100 to... 125.00
Mug, amber, bulbous w/drop-over hdl, 1950s-60s, 6¼", from $30 to .35.00
Pear, pale sea gr, Blenko, 1950s-60s, 5", from $100 to 125.00
Pitcher, bl w/clear pulled-bk hdl, Pilgrim, 1940-69, 7", from $80 to... 90.00
Pitcher, clear w/amber drop-over hdl, Hamon, 1960s, 5¼", $50 to ..55.00
Pitcher, gr, pulled-bk hdl, Pilgrim, 1949-69, 4½", from $45 to 50.00
Pitcher, gr, ribbed drop-over hdl, Pilgrim, 1949-69, 4½", $50 .... 55.00
Pitcher, tangerine w/clear drop-over hdl, Blenko, 1960s, 11", $110 to..150.00
Pitcher, yel, drop-over hdl, Rainbow, 1940s-60s, 9", from $90 to. 100.00
Punch bowl w/lid, clear, Germany, 10x8½" dia, from $350 to...... 450.00
Punch cup, clear, Germany, 2½", from $50 to................................ 75.00
Rose bowl, bl w/inverted fluting, Blenko, 1950s, 8", from $110 to ..135.00
Swan dish, orange w/clear neck & head, Kanawha, 1957-87, 7", $100 to.125.00
Tumbler, pinched, bl-gr, Blenko, 1940s-50s, 6", from $75 to........ 100.00
Vase, clear goblet w/sea gr stem, Blenko, 1940s-50s, 8", from $100 to ..125.00
Vase, lemon-lime tumbler form, Viking, 1944-60, 7¾", from $100 to. 125.00
Vase, sea gr, pinched, Blenko, 1940s-50s, 3¾", from $75 to 95.00
Vase, sea gr jug w/sm neck, Blenko, 1960s, 7½", from $110 to 130.00

Cranberry

Cranberry glass is named for its resemblance to the color of cranberry juice. It was made by many companies both here and abroad, becoming popular in America soon after the Civil War. It was made in free-blown ware as well as mold-blown. Today cranberry glass is being reproduced, and it is sometimes difficult to distinguish the old from the new. Ask a reputable dealer if you are unsure. For further information we recommend *American Art Glass* by John A. Shumann III, available from Collector Books or your local bookstore. See also Cruets; Salts; Sugar Shakers; Syrups.

Bowl, banana, 4 clear ft, clear ruffle, 7½x11" 40.00
Bowl, Hobnail, wht opal fluted rim, 9" 110.00
Cruet, emb ribs, wht & gold lily-of-valley, faceted stopper, 8⅛" ... 240.00
Decanter, Invt T'print, bulbous, clear hdl & stopper, 10" 75.00
Pitcher, appl rigaree at base of neck, clear hdl, 8x6" 60.00
Pitcher, bulbous, clear hdl, 7" 72.50
Pitcher, Dmn Quilt, clear reeded hdl, 7½" 110.00
Pitcher, Invt T'print, scalloped rim, bulbous, clear hdl, 4" 25.00

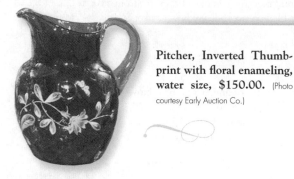

Pitcher, Inverted Thumbprint with floral enameling, water size, $150.00. (Photo courtesy Early Auction Co.)

Pitcher, water birds among reeds, bulbous, clear angle hdl, 5⅝" ... 360.00
Vase, bud; ruffled rim, clear appl trim & ft, 13" 180.00
Vase, emb grapes, bulbous, 1930s, 14" 150.00
Vase, Invt T'print, pleated rim, clear hdl, 9" 85.00
Vase, silver Nouveau floral o/l, trumpet neck, ca 1900, 12" 110.00
Vase, slightly waisted, ruffled/crimped rim, 9¼x6½" 42.50
Vase, swirl, bulbous, cylinder neck, 6x5" 45.00

Creamware

Creamware was a type of earthenware developed by Wedgwood in the 1760s and produced by many other Staffordshire potteries, including Leeds. Since it could be potted cheaply and was light in weight, it became popular abroad as well as in England, due to the lower freight charges involved in its export. It was revived at Leeds in the late nineteenth century, and the type most often reproduced was heavily reticulated or molded in high relief. These later wares are easily distinguished from the originals since they are thicker and tend to craze heavily. See also Leeds; Wedgwood.

Basket, emb floral w/pk feather edge, Herculaneum, 10½"+undertray.... 575.00
Basket, much rtcl, scalloped, hdls, 4x5"+rtcl underplate 660.00
Bowl, potpourri; rtcl form w/rose finial, twist hdls, 13" 1,950.00
Jug, sparrow-beak spout, loop hdl, ca 1770, 3⅛", EX 60.00
Pitcher, syrup; emb dmns/fleur-de-lis/flowers, pewter lid, 1850s, 7".. 55.00
Plate, dinner; pierced rim w/emb swags/scallops, 18th C, 10", 12 for .6,000.00
Plate, rtcl border w/beaded edge, 1780-1800, 9", 4 for 1,450.00
Plate, rtcl border w/swags, sm scallops, 1800s, 11½" L 360.00
Platter, gr scalloped feather edge, Britain, ca 1800, 19" 560.00
Teapot, Aurora in chariot/angels among clouds, globular, 18th C, 5". 1,300.00
Teapot, Prodigal Son blk transfer scenes, Greatbatch, 18th C, 5¾" ... 825.00

Crown Devon, Devon

Devon and Crown Devon were trade names of S. Fielding and Company, Ltd., an English firm founded after 1879. They produced majolica, earthenware mugs, vases, and kitchenware. In the 1930s they manufactured an exceptional line of Art Deco vases that have recently been much in demand.

Basket, floral w/gold on rouge lustre w/gold hdls, Fielding, 3⅜x7" . 60.00

Bowl, butterflies on bl lustre, C Howe, Fielding, 3½" H 132.50
Bowl, floral w/gold, scalloped rim, Fielding, 8" +8½" underplate ... 85.00
Chamber pot, floral transfer w/gold, 6x9½" 75.00
Egg caddy, floral on cream w/gold hdl, w/6 cups, 4x9½x5½" 145.00
Jug, flower garlands w/gold, cylindrical, 6¾" 65.00
Jug, Queen Anne Wye, 6½" 45.00
Jug, Scotsman in tartan, bk: Auld Lang Syne verse, thistle hdl, 7x5" . 185.00
Jug, Widdicombe Fair, musical, Fielding, 7" 100.00
Mug, Daisy Bell, couple on bicycle, missing music box, 5" 50.00
Pitcher, Captain Cook, kangaroo hdl, ca 1930, 9" 65.00
Plate, grapevines on cream, sq, 8½" 25.00
Tray, sailing ship & gulls on bl lustre, 8x4¼" 48.00
Vase, Fairy Castle, ovoid, #2406, 4¼" 375.00
Vase, floral on rouge lustre, hdls, Fielding, #A148-9, 8x6¼" 90.00
Vase, Oriental landscape on bl w/gold o/l, ca 1930, 7½x4" 55.00
Washbowl & pitcher, medallions/swags on cream, ca 1909, 13", 15" .435.00

Vase, wisteria and butterflies on cobalt with gold, lustre interior, 5¾", $150.00. (Photo courtesy Cincinnati Art Gallery)

Crown Ducal

The Crown Ducal mark was first used by the A.G. Richardson & Co. pottery of Tunstall, England, in 1925. The items collectors are taking a particular interest in were decorated by Charlotte Rhead, a contemporary of Suzie Cooper and Clarice Cliff, and a member of the esteemed family of English pottery designers and artists. See also Chintz.

Bowl, floral chintz, rose border on blk int, 8-sided, 1890s, 4x8" 48.00
Charger, Blue Peony, C Rhead, 12½" 425.00
Charger, floral, blk/gold on crackled ivory, C Rhead, 12¾" 425.00
Charger, Manchu (dragon) C Rhead, #4511, 1930s, 14½" 195.00
Compote, Orange Tree, ftd, 3½x8½" 32.50
Pitcher, Deco floral w/lustre, C Rhead, #146, ca 1920, 7" 90.00
Pitcher, geometric linear band on rust speckles, C Rhead, #186, 7⅝".. 55.00
Plate, dragon, mc on gr, geometric border, C Rhead, 13" 60.00
Plate, Florentine, fruit & flowers, 1900s, 9" 110.00
Plate, Monticello commemorative, red transfer 42.50
Vase, butterflies on orange lustre, hexagonal trumpet shape, 7½" .. 95.00
Vase, daffodils on ivory, C Rhead, 8" 60.00
Vase, fish on orange lustre, Deco style, 11" 195.00
Vase, flowers & foliage, mc on cream, #121, 9" 60.00
Vase, fruit band, trumpet form, C Rhead, 6" 110.00
Vase, Hydrangea, sgn B (Violet Barber), #198, 7½" 180.00
Vase, Spectria Flambé, red/blk/gold, shouldered, 3⅞" 85.00
Vase, stylized floral w/lustre, C Rhead, 1920s, 6¾" 90.00

Crown Milano

Crown Milano was a line of decorated milk glass (or opal ware) introduced by the Mt. Washington Glass Co. of New Bedford, Massachusetts, in the early 1890s. It had previously been called Albertine Ware.

Some pieces are marked with a 'CM,' and many had paper labels. This ware is usually highly decorated and will most likely have a significant amount of gold trim. The shiny pieces were recently discovered to have been called 'Colonial Ware'; these were usually marked were a laurel wreath and a crown. This ware was well received in its day, and outstanding pieces bring high prices on today's market.

Atomizer, mums HP on cream to peach, swirled body, 6½".......... 300.00
Biscuit jar, floral, mc on frost to yel, lid mk MF #4404, 7"............ 275.00
Biscuit jar, floral on cream, SP lid, ovoid, 7" 240.00
Biscuit jar, floral w/gold-lined leaves on cream, SP lid, 6½" 480.00

Biscuit jar, Garden of Allah scene, #3910/530, lid marked with 'P in diamond' trademark, 8½", $1,900.00. (Photo courtesy Early Auction Co.)

Biscuit jar, gold thistles on cream, emb lid/butterfly finial, 6½".... 700.00
Biscuit jar, starfish/seaweed on Hobnail sea gr, butterfly finial, 9" ... 1,100.00
Bride's bowl, yel ruffle, int leaf decor, SP fr w/bird hdls, 11x9" 575.00
Creamer, floral & gold netting on melon lid, SP lip/hdl, #313, 4½"...525.00
Creamer & sugar bowl, floral w/gold on cream, reeded hdls, w/lid, 4".600.00
Cup & saucer, Colonial, gold scroll medallions w/floral on opal, 5" W.275.00
Ewer, mums, gold/mauve on opal, loop hdl, paper label, 6½" 395.00
Hatpin holder, floral on mushroom form, 5" W 475.00
Lamp, Colonial, mallards/gold leaves, ball shade, vasiform base, 36".4,500.00
Marmalade, pansies w/gold on Hobnail, squatty, #4417-A, 6" dia...825.00
Mustard, gold flowers/emb medallions, mc on cream, SP lid, 4"... 300.00
Plate, Colonial (shiny), mixed flowers, 7"................................... 550.00
Rose bowl, pansies on cream, #818, 4½" 100.00
Sweetmeat, Dmn Quilt, fall leaves/jewels on cream, w/lid, 6", NM ...400.00
Sweetmeat, floral sprays/emb stars on opal, branch finial, 5"........ 180.00
Sweetmeat, jeweled starfish, chain hdl, emb lid, MW #4417, 6"..600.00
Syrup, chrysanthemums on wht, melon ribs, emb metal lid, 5½".635.00
Syrup, floral/netting on melon ribs, SP spout/hdl, #313, 5½", NM. 1,600.00
Vase, Colonial, floral sprays on opal, 4-point rim, ovoid, 9¼" 750.00
Vase, Colonial, thistles/spider webs, bulbous, prof rpr, 14" 600.00
Vase, fern leaves/scrolls in gold, swirled ribs, pull-down top, 5x4"...575.00
Vase, floral sprays w/gold on cream, ovoid/shouldered, 9" 975.00
Vase, gold beads/mc panels on cream, bulbous, 8½" 240.00
Vase, gold thistles/cream scrolls, pierced top, thorn hdls, 7½"...1,600.00
Vase, goldfish/seaweed on pastel ocean waves, rnd w/can neck, 11"...7,900.00
Vase, tulips w/gold scrolls, melon ribs, stick neck, 13¼"............4,600.00

Cruets

Cruets, containers made to hold oil or vinegar, are usually bulbous with tall, narrow throats, a handle, and a stopper. During the nineteenth century and for several years after, they were produced in abundance in virtually every type of glassware available. Those listed below are assumed to be with stopper and mint unless noted otherwise. See also specific manufacturers; Custard Glass; Opalescent Glass; other types of glass.

Ada #2577, TeePee body w/cut neck, Cambridge, ca 1903, 8-oz.... 60.00
Amazon, Bar-in-Hand stopper, ftd, 8½" 185.00
Amberette 90.00
Amberina, Invt T'print, conical, amber hdl/faceted stopper, Hobbs, 9" .350.00

Amberina, swirled ribs, deep color, Mt. Washington, $475.00.

Apollo, rose, McKee 95.00
Arched Ovals 60.00
Argonaut Shell, wht opal 350.00
Artichoke 65.00
Basketweave, bl 90.00
Beaded Grape/California, gr, 6¾", NM 40.00
Beaded Medallion, gr 250.00
Beaded Ovals in Sand, gr opal 225.00
Bismark Star 50.00
Brittanic 55.00
Broken Column 60.00
Cane Column 45.00
Cathedral 60.00
Chrysanthemum Base Swirl, gr opal... 675.00
Consolidated Criss-Cross, wht opal.. 275.00
Cupid & Venus 175.00
Daisy & Button, bulbous, faceted stopper, 7½" 130.00
Daisy & Fern, wht opal, Northwood 225.00
Dewey.. 65.00
Diamond Quilt, bl satin MOP 210.00
Diamond Quilt, cranberry stain 110.00
Elson Dewdrop #2, wht opal 90.00
Faceted Flower (Swirl)... 65.00
Fandango, 2 szs, from $45 to 60.00
Galloway 55.00
Guttate, glossy pk w/clear hdl & faceted stopper, Consolidated, 5¾".. 125.00
Heisey #300 Colonial, made in 5 szs 85.00
Hildalgo, frosted.. 70.00
Honeycomb w/Star 50.00
Indiana 45.00
Intaglio, vaseline opal 795.00
Invt T'print, Prussian Blue w/HP floral, 5".................................. 80.00
Invt T'print, rubena verde, gr stopper/faceted hdl, 6" 225.00
Invt T'print, rubena verde teepee shape, Hobbs Brockunier, 7" ... 550.00
Jacob's Ladder.. 95.00
King's Block 50.00
Masonic 45.00
Michigan.. 65.00
New Garland #284, amber, tall melon-ribbed stopper, Fostoria, 9" 300.00
New Jersey 50.00
Panelled Forget-Me-Not.. 55.00
Panelled 44... 50.00
Pennsylvania 45.00
Plume 40.00

Polka-Dot #308, rubena verde, Hobbs Brockunier, 7", NM.......... 350.00
Portland.. 65.00
Prize, gr... 225.00
Reverse Cruet, vaseline opal... 175.00
Ribbed Opal Lattice, cranberry opal 500.00
Rose Point, loop hdl, Cambridge, 5-oz................................... 150.00
Scroll w/Acanthus, vaseline opal 325.00
Sextec... 50.00
Spatter, gr w/emb leaves 200.00
Spangle, blk w/gold inclusions, blown stopper, Hobbs Brockunier, 6". 425.00
Spanish Lattice, wht opal 200.00
Starburst, etched florals, notched neck, faceted top, 6½" 70.00
Stripe, wht opal.. 175.00
Teasel... 65.00
Thousand Eye, apple gr.. 65.00
Tiny Optic, amethyst w/decor 125.00
Utopia Optic, gr... 150.00
Wheat Sheaf, dbl hdl, scarce 65.00
Wht opal, royal bl wafer above opal ft, royal bl hdl/stopper, 9½" . 125.00
Z-Ray, gr w/gold 250.00
Zipper 45.00

Cup Plates, Glass

Before the middle 1850s, it was socially acceptable to pour hot tea into a deep saucer to cool. The tea was sipped from the saucer rather than the cup, which frequently was handleless and too hot to hold. The cup plate served as a coaster for the cup. It is generally agreed that the first examples of pressed glass cup plates were made about 1826 at the Boston and Sandwich Glass Co. in Sandwich, Cape Cod, Massachusetts. Other glassworks in three major areas (New England, Philadelphia, and the Midwest, especially Pittsburgh) quickly followed suit.

Antique glass cup plates range in size from 2⅝" up to 4¼" in diameter. The earliest plates had simple designs inspired by cut glass patterns, but by 1829 they had become more complex. The span from then until about 1845 is known as the 'Lacy Period,' when cup plate designs and pressing techniques were at their peak. To cover pressing imperfections, the backgrounds of the plates were often covered with fine stippling which endowed them with a glittering brilliance called 'laciness.' They were made in a multitude of designs — some purely decorative, others commemorative. Subjects include the American eagle, hearts, sunbursts, log cabins, ships, George Washington, the political candidates Clay and Harrison, plows, beehives, etc. Of all the patterns, the round George Washington plate is the rarest and most valuable — only four are known to exist today.

Authenticity is most important. Collectors must be aware that contemporary plates which have no antique counterparts and fakes modeled after antique patterns have had wide distribution. Condition is also important, though it is the exceptional plate that does not have some rim roughness. More important considerations are scarcity of design and color.

The book *American Glass* by George and Helen McKearin has a section on glass cup plates. The definitive book is *American Glass Cup Plates* by Ruth Webb Lee and James H. Rose. Numbers in the listings that follow refer to the latter. When attempting to evaluate a cup plate, remember that minor rim roughness is normal. See also Staffordshire; Pairpoint.

Note: Most of the values listed below are prices realized at auction. The more common varieties generally run between $35.00 to $75.00 in very good condition. Unless noted otherwise, our values are for examples in very good to excellent condition.

R-3, blown molded GII-1, rim folded outward, att Sandwich, 4" 190.00
R-20, cobalt, 15 scallops w/shelves, Sandwich, 3½" 2,525.00
R-38, amethyst, 17 even scallops, Sandwich, 3¼" 2,875.00

R-61, fiery opal, 48 even scallops, thin, Sandwich, 3⅜", NM....... 420.00
R-83, bl opaque, dk bl plain rim, att Sandwich, rare, 4", NM..2,400.00
R-108, octagonal slightly concave plain rim, Eastern, 3⅜", NM.. 120.00
R-127, dk amethyst, plain rope rim, Midwestern, 3", NM.........2,880.00
R-147, 30 bull's-eye scallops, Midwestern, 3", NM 145.00
R-181, 48 even scallops, Midwestern, 3¼", NM 160.00
R-191-A, 48 even bull's-eye scallops, Midwestern, 3⅛", NM....... 515.00
R-222, cloudy, plain rope hdl, Midwestern, 3½", M.................... 510.00
R-227-B, brilliant dk gr, 9 lg scallops w/4 sm scallops between, 3½"..2,280.00
R-242, cloudy amber w/blk impurities, 60 even scallops, 3½", NM..3,360.00
R-265, fiery opal, 53 even scallops, att Sandwich, 3½", NM 180.00
R-284, 24 lg peacock eyes w/point between, 3³⁄₁₆", NM 120.00
R-295, cobalt, 62 even scallops, att Sandwich, 3⅛"................... 170.00
R-425, amethyst, 9 lg scallops w/heart between, Sandwich, 3⅜", NM. 2,520.00
R-439, peacock bl, 57 even scallops, Sandwich, 3½" 195.00
R-439-B, brilliant emerald, 55 even scallops, Sandwich, 3½", NM. 2,400.00
R-465, violet bl, 63 even scallops, att Sandwich, 3⅜", NM 330.00
R-465-B, yel gr, 54 even scallops w/flatter arc variation, 3⁵⁄₁₆" 165.00
R-523-A, yel gr, 62 even scallops, att Sandwich, 3", M............... 190.00
R-535, plain rim, att Curlings Ft Pitt Works, 3¹¹⁄₁₆", NM 170.00
R-562-X-1, Henry Clay, 49 even scallops w/higher arc variant, 3½".. 155.00
R-605, 24 bull's-eye scallops w/point between, att Midwestern, 3½"... 500.00
R-605-A, clambroth, octagonal w/7 scallops between corners, 3½", NM.. 510.00
R-615-A, 25 scallops w/point between, 3⅜" 135.00
R-619, wht opal, Benjamin Franklin, 48 even scallops, Sandwich, 3½".170.00
R-631, emerald, Chancellor Livingston, 63 even scallops, 3½".2,160.00
R-641, canary yel, 76 even scallops, Sandwich, 3½", NM 570.00
R-650, lt bl, plain rope rim, New England, 3¹¹⁄₁₆" 540.00
R-654, cloudy, plain rim, att Midwestern, 3" 220.00
R-655, pebbly allover, 30 even scallops, Midwestern, 3¹⁄₁₆", NM 130.00

R-661, brilliant medium blue with opalescent overcast, attributed to Boston & Sandwich, 3½", $3,900.00. (Photo courtesy Green Valley Auctions/LiveAuctioneers.com)

R-685, cloudy, New Patent Steam Coach, ribbed edge, rare, 3⅝" .3,600.00
R-691-A, 42 even scallops, att Midwestern, 3" 300.00
R-842, sulfide crucifixion of Christ, 15 scallops w/shelves, 3½".... 450.00

Cups and Saucers

The earliest utensils for drinking were small porcelain and stoneware bowls imported from China by the East Indian Company in the early seventeenth century. European and English tea bowls and saucers, imitating Chinese and Japanese originals, were produced from the early eighteenth century and often decorated with Chinese-type motifs. By about 1810, handles were fitted to the bowl to form the now familiar teacup, and this form became almost universal. Coffee in England and on the continent was often served in a can — a straight-sided cylinder with a handle. After 1820 the coffee can gave way to the more fanciful form of the coffee cup.

An infinite variety of cups and saucers are available for both the new and experienced collector, and they can be found in all price ranges. There is probably no better way to thoroughly know and understand the various ceramic manufacturers than to study cups and saucers. Our advisors for this category, Susan and Jim Harran, have written a series entitled *Collectible Cups and Saucers, Identification and Values, Books I, II, III,* and *IV*, published by Collector Books. Book IV contains more than 1,000 full-color photos; it is divided into six collectible eras: cabinet cups, nineteenth- and twentieth-century dinnerware, English tablewares, miniatures, Chinese tea and tea-serving vessels. The Harrans are listed in the Directory under New Jersey.

Breakfast, floral chintz, wht int, loop hdl, Lipper & Mann, 1930s-50s. 65.00
Chocolate, orange/yel flowers on wht, ornate hdl, Limoges, 1882-1890. 60.00
Chocolate, pk flowers on gold, ornate hdls, w/lid, Limoges, 1920-30s .. 350.00
Chocolate, rose transfer on cream, angular hdl, RS Prussia, 1904-38. 85.00
Coffee, gold on cobalt, wht int, high coiled hdl, Limoges, 1950s. 275.00
Coffee, gold w/Greek key border, ribbed can cup, Royal Vienna, 1855 .. 275.00
Coffee, HP flowers on pk & gold, interior band, KPM Berlin, 1837-44 .250.00
Coffee, mc petals w/bows, gold ft, snake hdl, Meissen, 1860, $900 to. 950.00
Coffee, medallion w/lady on bl, wht int, ftd, ring hdl, Sevres, 1900.... 375.00
Coffee, ornate gold flower w/jewels on pk, loop hdl, Germany, 1895.....36.00
Coffee, pk dragons on wht w/gold, flute shape, loop hdl, Meissen, 1900.... 265.00
Coffee, Regency pattern, can cup, Copeland Spode, 1950s-60s, $75 to . 95.00
Coffee, wht leaves on cobalt & gold, loop hdl, Schoenau Bros, 1900-20 .. 135.00
Demi, cobalt w/silver o/l, ftd, Hutschenreuther, 1950-63, $125 to 150.00
Demi, dk pk, gold beading & int, quatrefoil, ring hdl, Coalport, 1900.. 325.00
Demi, HP flowers w/gold, int band, KPM Berlin, 1870-90, $300 to.... 350.00
Demi, HP lady, gold w/beads & paste flowers, Dresden, 1900-40, $300 to...350.00
Demi, Japanese Grove pattern, can cup, loop hdl, Coalport, 1881-90.. 225.00
Demi, medallions of courting scenes on bl, quatrefoil, Dresden, 1890s. 175.00
Demi, wht/turq jewels/gold, raised well, ftd, Prov Saxe, 1902-38 .... 115.00
Mini coffee, castle scenes on gold, can cup, ring hdl, Coalport, 1885 . 475.00
Mini coffee, HP flowers & courting scenes on blk, Dresden, 1843-83 .. 265.00
Mini coffee, HP pk flowers in relief, paneled, sq hdl, unmk, ca 1900 .....85.00
Mini tea, HP appl flowers on wht, loop hdl, Meissen, 1820-60, $600 to.. 700.00

Miniature teacup, Imari pattern #1909, Royal Crown Derby, ca 1905, ¾x1½"; 2¼", from $275.00 to $325.00. (Photo courtesy Susan and Jim Harran)

Mini tea, Indian Tree pattern, loop hdl, Coalport, 1960-70, $75 to.... 100.00
Mini tea, mc floral transfer w/gold, ribbed cup, Hammersley, 1940..60.00
Tea, bl band w/gold flowers, rose in int & well, loop hdl, Leart, 1955.. 35.00
Tea, emb gold flowers on wht, bl & gold band, fluted, Brownfield, 1880 . 135.00
Tea, HP bird w/pearl & gold beading, loop hdl, Royal Worcester, 1876. 425.00
Tea, HP butterflies/gold on porc, quatrefoil, ornate hdl, Kutani, 1885.. 200.00
Tea, HP flowers on blk w/silver, gold int, loop hdl, Russia, 1970s 275.00
Tea, HP flowers w/gold, gold well, loop hdl, Ginori, 1900-20, $150 to . 175.00
Tea, HP mc flowers (int also), gold rim & hdl, Coxon Belleek, 1926-30. 135.00
Tea, mc flower on gold, wht exterior, loop hdl, Embassy Ware, 1950s . 80.00

Currier and Ives by Royal

Royal China was founded in 1934 by three entrepreneurs: Beatrice L. Miller, John 'Bert' Briggs, and William H. Habenstreit. They chose the former E.H. Sebring Building in Sebring, Ohio, as the location of their new company. During the brunt of the Great Depression, the company initially began with only $500.00 in cash, six months of free rent, and employees working without pay. In 1969 the company was sold to the Jeannette Glass Corporation. Jeannette continued to operate Royal from the building until fire destroyed the plant in 1970. After the fire, operations moved to the French Saxon China Company which Royal had

previously purchased in 1964. In 1976 the Coca-Cola Bottling Company of New York bought the company and continued operations until 1981 when the Jeannette Corporation was sold to the 'J' Corporation, a private investment group. Three years later, Nordic Capital Corporation of New York bought the company. It is interesting to note that 1984 was the fiftieth anniversary of the Nordic Group and the slogan they adoped was 'A New Beginning.' Unfortunately, however, Jeannette filed bankruptcy early in 1996, and in March Royal China shut down completely. The building and its contents were sold during a bankruptcy auction in January of 1987. It is currently being used as a warehouse.

The number of shapes and patterns produced by Royal can boggle the mind of even the most advanced collector. The most popular line by far is Currier and Ives. Its familiar scrolled border was designed by Royal's art director, the late Gorden Parker. Our suggested values for this pattern reflect the worth of examples in the blue colorway. The line was also produced in limited quantities in the following colors: pink, brown, black, and green. To evaluate examples in these colors, double the prices for blue.

For further reading on Royal China, we recommend *Royal China Company, Sebring, Ohio*, by David J. Folckemer and Deborah G. Folckemer. Our advisor for this category is Mark J. Skrobis; he is listed in the Directory under Indiana.

Plate, deviled egg; very rare, 10½", $250.00. (Photo courtesy Jack and Treva Jo Hamlin)

Ashtray, 5½"	15.00
Bowl, candy; from Hostess set, 7¾"	65.00
Bowl, cereal; 6¼" or 6⅝", ea	15.00
Bowl, cream soup; tab hdl, 7"	55.00
Bowl, dip; from Hostess set, 4⅜"	125.00
Bowl, fruit nappy; 5½"	6.00
Bowl, lug soup; tab hdl, 7"	55.00
Bowl, soup; 8½"	10.00
Bowl, vegetable; deep, 10¼"	30.00
Bowl, vegetable; 9"	20.00
Butter dish, winter or summer scene, ¼-lb, from $35 to	45.00
Cake plate, flat, 10"	45.00
Cake plate, from Hostess set, flat, 10"	35.00
Cake plate, ftd, 10"	200.00
Candle lamp, w/globe	375.00
Casserole, angle hdls, w/lid	100.00
Casserole, angle hdls, all wht lid	175.00
Casserole, creamer, rnd hdl, tall, rare	50.00
Casserole, tab hdls, w/lid	200.00
Clock, 10" or 12" plate, bl #s, 2 decals, Charles Denning	1,000.00
Coffee mug, Express Train	35.00
Coffee mug, Fashionable Turnouts	25.00
Creamer, angle hdl	8.00
Cup & saucer, angle hdl	6.00
Gravy boat, tab hdls, w/liner (like 7" plate)	150.00
Gravy boat, 2-spout	20.00
Mug, coffee; Express Train	35.00
Mug, coffee; Fashionable Turnouts	25.00
Pie baker, from Hostess set, 11"	60.00
Pie baker, 10", (depending on print) from $25 to	45.00
Plate, bread & butter; 6⅜", from $3 to	5.00

Plate, calendar; 10" 20.00
Plate, chop; Getting Ice, 12½" 30.00
Plate, dinner; 10" 5.00
Plate, luncheon; very rare, 9" 20.00
Platter, oval, 13" 35.00
Shakers, pr from $30 to 35.00
Sugar bowl, no hdls, str sides, w/lid 35.00
Teacup, flared rim 10.00
Teacup, str sides 2.00
Teapot, 8 different decal & shape variations, from $125 to 200.00
Tile & rack, 6x6" 150.00
Tray, deviled egg; from Hostess set 250.00
Tray, sugar bowl, flare top, w/lid 50.00
Tray, tidbit; 3-tier (factory-made only) 75.00

Tray for gravy boat, white tab handles, 7" plate decal, $100.00. (Photo courtesy Jack and Treva Jo Hamlin)

Tumbler, iced tea; glass, 12-oz, 5½" 15.00
Tumbler, juice; glass, 5-oz, 3½" 15.00
Tumbler, water; glass, 8½-oz, 4¾" 15.00
Wall plaque, very scarce 1,000.00

Custard Glass

As early as the 1880s, custard glass was produced in England. Migrating glassmakers brought the formula for the creamy ivory ware to America. One of them was Harry Northwood, who in 1898 founded his company in Indiana, Pennsylvania, and introduced the glassware to the American market. Soon other companies were producing custard, among them Heisey, Tarentum, Fenton, and McKee. Not only dinnerware patterns but souvenir items were made. Today custard is the most expensive of the colored pressed glassware patterns. The formula for producing the luminous glass contains uranium salts which imparts the cream color to the batch and causes it to glow when it is examined under a black light.

Argonaut Shell, bowl, master berry; gold & decor, 10½" L 200.00
Argonaut Shell, bowl, sauce; ftd, gold & decor 60.00
Argonaut Shell, butter dish, gold & decor 175.00
Argonaut Shell, butter dish, no gold 125.00
Argonaut Shell, compote, jelly; gold & decor, scarce 125.00
Argonaut Shell, creamer, gold & decor 95.00
Argonaut Shell, creamer, no gold 50.00
Argonaut Shell, cruet, gold & decor 450.00

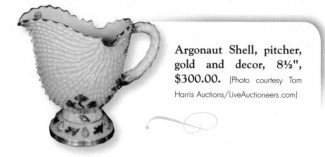

Argonaut Shell, pitcher, gold and decor, 8½", $300.00. (Photo courtesy Tom Harris Auctions/LiveAuctioneers.com)

Argonaut Shell, shakers, gold & decor, pr 250.00
Argonaut Shell, spooner, gold & decor 75.00
Argonaut Shell, sugar bowl, w/lid, gold & decor 150.00
Argonaut Shell, tumbler, gold & decor 60.00
Bead Swag, bowl, sauce; floral & gold 50.00
Bead Swag, goblet, floral & gold 65.00
Bead Swag, tray, pickle; floral & gold, rare 300.00
Bead Swag, wine, floral & gold 60.00
Beaded Circle, bowl, master berry; floral & gold 275.00
Beaded Circle, butter dish, floral & gold 300.00
Beaded Circle, creamer, floral & gold 125.00
Beaded Circle, pitcher, water; floral & gold 450.00
Beaded Circle, shakers, floral & gold, pr 1,000.00
Beaded Circle, spooner, floral & gold 125.00
Beaded Circle, tumbler, floral & gold 75.00
Cane Insert, berry set, 7-pc 250.00
Cane Insert, table set, 4-pc 275.00
Cherry & Scales, bowl, master berry; nutmeg stain ... 145.00
Cherry & Scales, butter dish, nutmeg stain 150.00
Cherry & Scales, creamer, nutmeg stain 95.00
Cherry & Scales, pitcher, water; nutmeg stain, scarce ... 275.00
Cherry & Scales, spooner, nutmeg stain, scarce 95.00
Cherry & Scales, sugar bowl, w/lid, nutmeg stain, scarce 125.00
Cherry & Scales, tumbler, nutmeg stain, scarce 60.00
Chrysanthemum Sprig, bowl, master berry; gold & decor 250.00
Chrysanthemum Sprig, bowl, master berry; no gold ... 125.00
Chrysanthemum Sprig, bowl, sauce; ftd, gold & decor ... 60.00
Chrysanthemum Sprig, butter dish, gold & decor 250.00
Chrysanthemum Sprig, celery vase, gold & decor, rare 750.00
Chrysanthemum Sprig, compote, jelly; gold & decor ... 110.00
Chrysanthemum Sprig, compote, jelly; no decor 75.00
Chrysanthemum Sprig, creamer, gold & decor 75.00
Chrysanthemum Sprig, cruet, gold & decor, 6¾" 495.00
Chrysanthemum Sprig, pitcher, water; gold & decor .. 375.00
Chrysanthemum Sprig, pitcher, water; no decor 250.00
Chrysanthemum Sprig, shakers, gold & decor, pr 250.00
Chrysanthemum Sprig, spooner, gold & decor 110.00
Chrysanthemum Sprig, spooner, no gold 50.00
Chrysanthemum Sprig, sugar bowl, gold & decor 175.00
Chrysanthemum Sprig, toothpick holder, gold & decor 175.00
Chrysanthemum Sprig, toothpick holder, no decor 75.00
Chrysanthemum Sprig, tray, condiment; gold & decor, rare 595.00
Chrysanthemum Sprig, tumbler, gold & decor 65.00
Dandelion, mug, nutmeg stain 175.00
Delaware, bowl, sauce; pk stain 65.00
Delaware, creamer, breakfast; pk stain 75.00
Delaware, tray, pin; gr stain 85.00
Delaware, tumbler, pk stain 65.00
Diamond w/Peg, bowl, master berry; roses & gold 225.00
Diamond w/Peg, bowl, sauce; roses & gold 50.00
Diamond w/Peg, butter dish, roses & gold 175.00
Diamond w/Peg, creamer, ind; no decor 35.00
Diamond w/Peg, creamer, ind; souvenir 50.00
Diamond w/Peg, creamer, roses & gold 85.00
Diamond w/Peg, mug, souvenir 50.00
Diamond w/Peg, napkin ring, roses & gold 75.00
Diamond w/Peg, pitcher, roses & gold, 5½" 175.00
Diamond w/Peg, sugar bowl, w/lid, roses & gold 135.00
Diamond w/Peg, toothpick holder, roses & gold 125.00
Diamond w/Peg, tumbler, roses & gold 60.00
Diamond w/Peg, water set, souvenir, 7-pc 350.00
Diamond w/Peg, wine, roses & gold 65.00
Diamond w/Peg, wine, souvenir 40.00
Everglades, bowl, master berry; gold & decor 295.00

Everglades, bowl, saucer; gold & decor.. 60.00
Everglades, butter dish, gold & decor.. 300.00
Everglades, creamer, gold & decor... 155.00
Everglades, cruet, EX gold & decor, rare 2,250.00
Everglades, shakers, gold & decor, pr 375.00
Everglades, spooner, gold & decor 160.00
Everglades, sugar bowl, w/lid, gold & decor 235.00
Everglades, tumbler, gold & decor.. 100.00
Fan, bowl, master berry; good gold 295.00
Fan, bowl, sauce; good gold 60.00
Fan, butter dish, good gold 225.00
Fan, creamer, good gold 110.00
Fan, ice cream set, good gold, 7-pc 500.00
Fan, pitcher, water; good gold... 300.00
Fan, spooner, good gold 100.00
Fan, sugar bowl, w/lid, good gold 125.00
Fan, tumbler, good gold 65.00
Fan, water set, good gold, 7-pc 500.00
Fine Cut & Roses, rose bowl, fancy int, nutmeg stain 85.00
Fine Cut & Roses, rose bowl, plain int.. 69.00
Geneva, bowl, master berry; floral decor, ftd, oval, 9" L 110.00
Geneva, bowl, master berry; floral decor, rnd, 9" 130.00
Geneva, bowl, sauce; floral decor, oval.. 50.00
Geneva, bowl, sauce; floral decor, rnd... 50.00

Geneva, floral decor: Butter dish, $175.00; Sugar bowl with lid, $150.00; Spooner, $75.00; Creamer, $115.00.

Geneva, butter dish, no decor 145.00
Geneva, compote, jelly; floral decor... 95.00
Geneva, cruet, floral decor.. 475.00
Geneva, pitcher, water; floral decor.. 275.00
Geneva, shakers, floral decor, pr.. 175.00
Geneva, sugar bowl, open, floral decor.. 85.00
Geneva, syrup, floral decor 500.00
Geneva, toothpick holder, floral w/M gold 175.00
Geneva, tumbler, floral decor 60.00
Georgia Gem, bowl, master berry; good gold 135.00
Georgia Gem, bowl, master berry; gr opaque 115.00
Georgia Gem, butter dish, good gold.. 200.00
Georgia Gem, celery vase, good gold.. 145.00
Georgia Gem, creamer, good gold 100.00
Georgia Gem, creamer, no gold 60.00
Georgia Gem, cruet, good gold.. 295.00
Georgia Gem, mug, good gold 45.00
Georgia Gem, powder jar, w/lid, good gold 80.00
Georgia Gem, shakers, good gold, pr.. 140.00
Georgia Gem, spooner, souvenir 55.00
Georgia Gem, sugar bowl, w/lid, no gold... 95.00
Grape (& Cable), bottle, scent; orig stopper, nutmeg stain.......... 495.00
Grape (& Cable), bowl, banana; ftd, nutmeg stain........................ 275.00

Grape (& Cable), bowl, master berry; flat, nutmeg stain.............. 200.00
Grape (& Cable), bowl, orange; ftd, flat top, nutmeg stain.......... 400.00
Grape (& Cable), bowl, orange; ftd, nutmeg stain 500.00
Grape (& Cable), bowl, sauce; ftd, nutmeg stain 50.00
Grape (& Cable), butter dish, nutmeg stain 250.00
Grape (& Cable), compote, jelly; open, nutmeg stain.................... 125.00
Grape (& Cable), cracker jar, nutmeg stain.................................... 850.00
Grape (& Cable), creamer, breakfast; nutmeg stain 80.00
Grape (& Cable), humidor, bl stain, rare 950.00
Grape (& Cable), nappy, nutmeg stain, rare.................................... 60.00
Grape (& Cable), pitcher, water; nutmeg stain 550.00
Grape (& Cable), plate, nutmeg stain, 7" 50.00
Grape (& Cable), plate, nutmeg stain, 8" 65.00
Grape (& Cable), powder jar, nutmeg sain 350.00
Grape (& Cable), punch bowl, w/base, nutmeg stain...............1,900.00
Grape (& Cable), spooner, nutmeg stain 155.00
Grape (& Cable), sugar bowl, breakfast; open, nutmeg stain 85.00
Grape (& Cable), sugar bowl, w/lid, nutmeg stain......................... 225.00
Grape (& Cable), tray, dresser; nutmeg stain, scarce, lg 375.00
Grape (& Cable), tray, pin; nutmeg stain 150.00
Grape (& Cable), tumbler, nutmeg stain 75.00
Grape & Gothic Arches, bowl, master berry; pearl w/gold.......... 200.00
Grape & Gothic Arches, bowl, sauce; pearl w/gold, rare.............. 80.00
Grape & Gothic Arches, butter dish, pearl w/gold........................ 235.00
Grape & Gothic Arches, creamer, pearl w/gold, rare.................... 100.00
Grape & Gothic Arches, favor vase, nutmeg stain 80.00
Grape & Gothic Arches, goblet, pearl w/gold 75.00
Grape & Gothic Arches, pitcher, water; pearl w/gold 300.00
Grape & Gothic Arches, spooner, pearl w/gold.............................. 85.00
Grape & Gothic Arches, sugar bowl, w/lid, pearl w/gold 135.00
Grape & Gothic Arches, tumbler, pearl w/gold............................... 65.00
Grape Arbor, vase, hat form 90.00
Heart w/Thumbprint, creamer.. 90.00
Heart w/Thumbprint, lamp, good pnt, scarce, 8".......................... 450.00
Heart w/Thumbprint, sugar bowl, ind.. 95.00
Honeycomb, wine.. 65.00
Horse Medallion, bowl, gr stain, 7"... 85.00
Intaglio, bowl, master berry; gold & decor, ftd, 9" 250.00
Intaglio, bowl, sauce; gold & decor 50.00
Intaglio, butter dish, gold & decor 225.00
Intaglio, compote, jelly; gold & decor.. 125.00
Intaglio, creamer, gold & decor... 110.00
Intaglio, pitcher, water; gold & decor... 225.00
Intaglio, shakers, gold & decor, pr.. 175.00
Intaglio, spooner, gold & decor 110.00
Intaglio, sugar bowl, w/lid, gold & decor 150.00
Intaglio, tumbler, gold & decor... 65.00
Inverted Fan & Feather, bowl, master berry; gold & decor.......... 275.00
Inverted Fan & Feather, bowl, sauce; gold & decor........................ 75.00
Inverted Fan & Feather, butter dish, gold & decor....................... 275.00
Inverted Fan & Feather, compote, jelly; gold & decor, rare 350.00
Inverted Fan & Feather, cruet, gold & decor, scarce, 6½" 1,100.00
Inverted Fan & Feather, pitcher, water; gold & decor 450.00

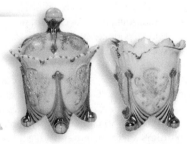

Inverted Fan and Feather, gold and decor: Sugar bowl with lid, $225.00; Creamer, $150.00. (Photo courtesy Early Auction Co.)

Inverted Fan & Feather, punch cup, gold & decor 250.00
Inverted Fan & Feather, shakers, gold & decor, pr 1,250.00
Inverted Fan & Feather, spooner, gold & decor 150.00
Inverted Fan & Feather, tumbler, gold & decor 100.00
Jackson (Alaska Variant), bowl, master berry; ftd, good gold 150.00
Jackson (Alaska Variant), creamer, good gold 85.00
Jackson (Alaska Variant), pitcher, water; good gold 250.00
Jackson (Alaska Variant), pitcher, water; no decor 175.00
Jackson (Alaska Variant), shakers, good gold, pr 195.00
Jackson (Alaska Variant), tumbler, good gold 50.00
Louis XV, bowl, master berry; good gold 250.00
Louis XV, bowl, sauce; ftd, good gold 50.00
Louis XV, butter dish, good gold 175.00
Louis XV, creamer, good gold 85.00
Louis XV, cruet, gold decor, 6¾" 200.00
Louis XV, pitcher, water; good gold 250.00
Louis XV, spooner, good gold 110.00
Louis XV, sugar bowl, w/lid, good gold 165.00
Louis XV, tumbler, good gold 65.00
Maple Leaf, bowl, master berry; gold & decor, scarce 350.00
Maple Leaf, bowl, sauce; gold & decor, scarce 50.00
Maple Leaf, butter dish, gold & decor 350.00
Maple Leaf, compote, jelly; gold & decor, rare 475.00
Maple Leaf, creamer, gold & decor 150.00
Maple Leaf, cruet, gold & decor, rare 3,000.00
Maple Leaf, pitcher, water; gold & decor 400.00
Maple Leaf, shakers, gold & decor, very rare, pr 1,500.00
Maple Leaf, spooner, gold & decor 175.00
Maple Leaf, sugar bowl, w/lid, gold & decor 250.00
Maple Leaf, tumbler, gold & decor 100.00
Panelled Poppy, lamp shade, nutmeg stain, scarce 900.00
Peacock & Urn, bowl, ice cream; nutmeg stain, sm. 80.00
Peacock & Urn, bowl, ice cream; nutmeg stain, 10" 250.00
Punty Band, shakers, pr 125.00
Punty Band, spooner, floral decor 100.00
Punty Band, tumbler, floral decor, souvenir 65.00
Ribbed Drape, bowl, sauce; roses & gold 45.00
Ribbed Drape, butter dish, scalloped, roses & gold 400.00
Ribbed Drape, compote, jelly; roses & gold, rare 200.00
Ribbed Drape, creamer, roses & gold, scarce 180.00
Ribbed Drape, cruet, roses & gold, rare 700.00
Ribbed Drape, pitcher, water; roses & gold, rare 365.00
Ribbed Drape, shakers, roses & gold, rare, pr 400.00
Ribbed Drape, spooner, roses & gold 195.00
Ribbed Drape, sugar bowl, w/lid, roses & gold 250.00
Ribbed Drape, toothpick holder, roses & gold 475.00
Ribbed Drape, tumbler, roses & gold 75.00
Ribbed Thumbprint, wine, floral decor 80.00
Ring Band, bowl, master berry; roses & gold 200.00
Ring Band, bowl, sauce; roses & gold 50.00
Ring Band, butter dish, roses & gold 225.00
Ring Band, compote, jelly; roses & gold, scarce 150.00
Ring Band, creamer, roses & gold 75.00
Ring Band, cruet, roses decor, orig clear Heisey stopper 350.00
Ring Band, pitcher, roses & gold, 7½" 275.00
Ring Band, shakers, roses & gold, pr 155.00
Ring Band, spooner, roses & gold 75.00
Ring Band, syrup, roses & gold, scarce 475.00
Ring Band, table set, 4-pc 450.00
Ring Band, toothpick holder, roses & gold 155.00
Ring Band, tray, condiment; roses & gold 200.00
Singing Birds, mug, nutmeg stain 85.00
Tarentum's Victoria, bowl, master berry; gold & decor 200.00
Tarentum's Victoria, butter dish, gold & decor, rare 350.00

Tarentum's Victoria, celery vase, gold & decor, rare 300.00
Tarentum's Victoria, creamer, gold & decor, scarce 135.00
Tarentum's Victoria, pitcher, water; gold & decor, rare 375.00
Tarentum's Victoria, spooner, gold & decor 135.00
Tarentum's Victoria, sugar bowl, w/lid, gold & decor 175.00
Tarentum's Victoria, tumbler, gold & decor 75.00
Vermont, butter dish, bl decor 150.00
Vermont, toothpick holder, bl decor 95.00

Vermont, tumbler, floral decor, 4", $70.00.

Vermont, vase, floral decor, jeweled 125.00
Wide Band, bell, roses 125.00
Wild Bouquet, bowl, sauce; gold & decor 60.00
Wild Bouquet, butter dish, gold & decor, rare, 11" L 250.00
Wild Bouquet, creamer, no gold 145.00
Wild Bouquet, spooner, gold & decor 250.00
Wild Bouquet, tumbler, no decor 100.00
Winged Scroll, bowl, master berry; gold & decor, 11" L 175.00
Winged Scroll, bowl, sauce; good gold 50.00

Winged Scroll, butter dish, gold and decor, $235.00. (Photo courtesy Neila and Tom Bredehoft)

Winged Scroll, butter dish, good gold 175.00
Winged Scroll, butter dish, no decor 125.00
Winged Scroll, celery vase, good gold, rare 350.00
Winged Scroll, cigarette jar, scarce 195.00
Winged Scroll, compote, ruffled, rare, 6¾x10¾" 495.00
Winged Scroll, cruet, good gold, clear stopper 350.00
Winged Scroll, hair receiver, good gold 135.00
Winged Scroll, pitcher, water; bulbous, good gold 400.00
Winged Scroll, shakers, bulbous, good gold, rare, pr 400.00
Winged Scroll, shakers, str sides, good gold, pr 250.00
Winged Scroll, sugar bowl, w/lid, good gold 175.00
Winged Scroll, syrup, good gold 450.00
Winged Scroll, tumbler, good gold 75.00

Cut Glass

The earliest documented evidence of commercial glass cutting in the United States was in 1810; the producers were Bakewell and Page of Pittsburgh. These first efforts resulted in simple patterns with only a moderate amount of cutting. By the middle of the century, glass cutters began experimenting with a thicker glass which enabled them to use deeper cuttings, though patterns remained much the same. This period is usually referred to as rich cut. Using three types of wheels — a flat edge, a mitered edge, and a convex edge — facets, miters, and depressions were combined to produce various designs. In the late 1870s, a curved miter was developed which greatly expanded design potential. Patterns became more elaborate, often covering the entire surface. The brilliant period of cut glass covered a span from about 1880 until 1915. Because of the pressure necessary to achieve the deeply cut patterns, only glass containing a high grade of metal could withstand the process. For this reason and the amount of handwork involved, cut glass has always been expensive. Bowls cut with pinwheels may be either foreign or of a newer vintage, beware! Identifiable patterns and signed pieces that are well cut and in excellent condition bring the higher prices on today's market. For more information, we recommend *Evers' Standard Cut Glass Value Guide* (Collector Books). See also Dorflinger; Hawkes; Libbey; Tuthill; Val St. Lambert; other specific manufacturers.

Basket, Zesta, Pitkins & Brooks, P&B Grade, 7", from $300 to ...350.00
Bell, Premier, JD Bergen, 6", from $200 to....................................225.00
Bonbon, Diamond, Averbeck, from $60 to 75.00
Bonbon, Saratoga, Averbeck, from $65 to 80.00
Bonbon/olive dish, Bedford, JD Bergen, 7", from $60 to 75.00
Bonbon/olive dish, Walter Scott, Higgins & Seiter, 4x8", from $65 to..75.00
Bottle, cologne; Prism, JD Bergen, 9", from $100 to.....................125.00
Bottle, cologne; Radium, Averbeck, 3½", from $50 to...................60.00
Bottle, cologne; St George, TB Clark & Co, sq, 12-oz, from $125 to . 140.00
Bowl, Arlington, Higgins & Seiter, 8", from $70 to........................80.00
Bowl, Cairo, Averbeck, 9", from $200 to 250.00
Bowl, Desdemona, TB Clark & Co, 9", from $200 to...................225.00
Bowl, Goldenrod, JD Bergen, 10", from $200 to 250.00
Bowl, Manhattan, TB Clark & Co, ftd, 9", from $250 to.............300.00
Bowl, Mars Fancy, Pitkins & Brooks, P&B grade, 9½", from $300 to . 350.00
Bowl, Monarch, 8", from $80 to 100.00
Butter plate, Ashland, Averbeck, from $25 to 30.00
Butter plate, Ruby, JD Bergen, w/hdl, 5", $75 to.........................95.00
Candelabra, 5-light, JB Bergen, ea from $350 to 400.00
Candlestick, Oro, Pitkins & Brooks, P&B grade, 8", ea from $200 to ..250.00
Candlestick, Victoria, JD Bergen, 7", ea from $125 to..................150.00
Carafe, Daisy, Averbeck, qt, from $150 to....................................200.00
Carafe, Diamond Fan, Higgins & Seiter, qt, from $100 to 125.00
Carafe, Jewel, TB Clark, qt, from $125 to....................................150.00
Carafe, Newport, JD Bergen, qt, from $150 to.............................175.00
Carafe, Progress, JD Bergen, qt, from $200 to 250.00
Celery dip, Pitkins & Brooks, 2", from $8 to..................................10.00
Celery dish, Delhi, Higgins & Seiter, 4½x11¾", from $75 to.......100.00
Celery dish, Winola, TB Clark & Co, from $75 to........................100.00
Celery tray, Liberty, Averbeck, 11¼", from $175 to 200.00
Celery tray, Nordica, TB Clark & Co, from $75 to.......................100.00
Celery tray, Rajah Fancy, Pitkins & Brooks, P&B grade, 11½" 250.00
Cheese dish, Glenwood, JD Bergen, 5", from $150 to 175.00
Cigar jar, Majestic, Higgins & Seiter, 6½", from $200 to.............225.00
Compote, Enterprise, JD Bergen, 8", from $150 to.......................200.00
Compote, Manhattan, TB Clark & Co, 6", from $100 to 150.00
Compote, Maud Adams, Averbeck, from $200 to 250.00
Compote, Topaz, Pitkins & Brooks, P&B grade, 9x6", from $300 to .350.00
Creamer, Emblem, JD Bergen, ½-pt, from $50 to...........................70.00
Cruet, Bermuda, Pitkins & Brooks, P&B grade, 8½", from $175 to ...200.00
Cruet, Strawberry Diamond & Fan, Higgins & Seiter, ½-pt, from $75 to . 100.00
Cruet, Viola, JD Bergen, ½-pt, from $175 to................................200.00
Cup, Edna, JD Bergen, from $25 to...30.00
Cup, Electric, JD Bergen, from $25 to..35.00
Cup, Mars, Pitkins & Brooks, P&B grade, from $20 to 25.00
Cup, Occident, Averbeck, ftd, from $40 to....................................45.00
Cup, Wabash, JD Bergen, from $25 to 30.00
Decanter, Ashton, JD Bergen, 1-qt, from $275 to.........................325.00
Decanter, Marie, JD Bergen, 1-qt, from $350 to 400.00
Decanter, Savoy, JD Bergen, 1-pt, from $150 to 200.00

Finger bowl, Winola, TB Clark & Co, from $35 to 40.00
Goblet, Florence, Higgins & Seiter, from $65 to 75.00
Goblet, Venice, Pitkins & Brooks, from $40 to 50.00
Hair Receiver, Larose, Pitkins & Brooks, P&B grade, 5", from $200 to..250.00
Ice cream tray, Adonis, TB Clark & Co, from $400 to.................450.00
Ice tub, The Estelle, Higgins & Seiter, 4¾x4", from $150 to........175.00
Knife rest, Pitkins & Brooks, hexagon, std grade, 4", from $15 to.. 18.00

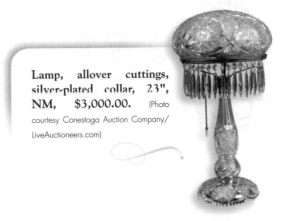

Lamp, allover cuttings, silver-plated collar, 23", NM, $3,000.00. (Photo courtesy Conestoga Auction Company/ LiveAuctioneers.com)

Lamp, electric; Poppy, Pitkins & Brooks, P&B grade w/prisms, 22"..21,000.00
Mayonnaise bowl & plate, Napoleon, Higgins & Seiter, from $200 to ..250.00
Nappy, Corsair Berry, Pitkins & Brooks, std grade, 7", from $100 to... 120.00
Olive dish, Priscilla, Averbeck, 7¾", from $125 to 150.00
Pin tray, Ruby, Averbeck, from $50 to...70.00
Pitcher, Alabama, Averbeck, 1-qt, from $225 to 250.00
Pitcher, Arbutus, TB Clark & Co, wide mouth, 3-pt, from $175 to...250.00
Pitcher, Delta, JD Bergen, 1-qt, from $175 to...............................200.00
Pitcher, Dewey, Higgins & Seiter, 1-qt, from $150 to...................175.00
Pitcher, Electric, JD Bergen, 1-qt, from $200 to 225.00
Plate, Golf, JD Bergen, 5", from $70 to..80.00
Pomade jar, Prism, JD Bergen, from $100 to................................150.00
Salt dip, JD Bergen, rnd, 2¾", from $15 to.....................................18.00
Spooner, Saratoga, Averbeck, from $125 to...................................150.00
Sugar bowl, Golf, JD Bergen, from $50 to......................................60.00
Tumbler, Coral, TB Clark & Co, from $40 to................................45.00
Tumbler, Melba, Averbeck, from $18 to...20.00
Vase, Amanda, Pitkins & Brooks, P&B grade, 10", from $150 to . 200.00
Vase, Halle, Pitkins & Brooks, P&B grade, 14", from $150 to 175.00

Vase, brilliant cuttings with hobstars and feather arches, 16", $440.00. (Photo courtesy Jackson's International Auctioneers & Appraisers of Fine Arts & Antiques)

Cut Overlay Glass

Glassware with one or more overlying colors through which a design has been cut is called 'Cut Overlay.' It was made both here and abroad. Watch for new imitations!

Bottle, scent; wht/clear, t'prints, clear faceted stopper, 7½" 110.00
Bowl, cobalt/clear, floral, serrated rim, 5x9" 55.00
Bowl, red/clear, geometric cuttings, scalloped, clear ft, 10½x11" . 120.00
Bowl, ruby/clear, grapevines at rim, ca 1900, 13" 95.00
Decanter, red/wht, geometric floral, cylindrical, clear hdl, 11½".. 135.00

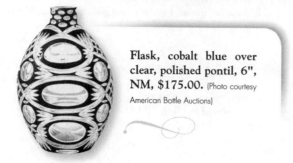

Flask, cobalt blue over clear, polished pontil, 6", NM, $175.00. (Photo courtesy American Bottle Auctions)

Newel-post finial, red/clear, Quatrefoil & Loop, 7½x3½" 1,200.00
Vase, amethyst/clear, starbursts/geometrics, 12¼x7¼", NM 48.00
Vase, cobalt/clear, detailed geometrics, scalloped, 3x8½" 36.00
Vase, ruby/clear, geometric bands, scalloped top, clear ft, 15" 150.00
Wine, gr/clear, 6 windows w/gold tracery, optic stem, rnd ft, 6½" .. 60.00

Cut Velvet

Cut Velvet glassware was made during the late 1800s. It is characterized by the effect achieved through the execution of relief-molded patterns, often ribbing or diamond quilting, which allows its white inner casing to show through the outer layer.

Finger bowl, Dmn Quilt, bl, 2½" 230.00
Pitcher, Dmn Quilt, dk sapphire bl, bl reeded hdl, 8¾x6" 400.00
Pitcher, Dmn Quilt, pk, shouldered ewer form, 7½" 165.00
Pitcher, Dmn Quilt, rose to wht, ewer form, 11" 425.00
Rose bowl, Ribbon (swirled), bl, 4" 235.00
Tumbler, Dmn Quilt, yel w/pk int, 4" 100.00
Vase, Dmn Quilt, dk to lt pk, ruffled 4-lobe top, Mt WA, 4¼x3". 225.00
Vase, Dmn Quilt, lt gold, dbl-gourd w/curved neck, 13½" 650.00
Vase, Dmn Quilt, pk, gold coralene, red jewels, 11½" 300.00

Vase, Diamond Quilted, robin's egg blue over white, 9", $185.00. (Photo courtesy John Schuman III)

Vase, Herringbone, pk, bulbous, 11" 335.00
Vase, vertical ribs, bl, crimped rim, 4¼" 70.00

Cybis

Boleslaw Cybis was a graduate of the Academy of Fine Arts in Warsaw, Poland, and was well recognized as a fine artist by the time he was commissioned by his government to paint murals in the Polish Pavilion's

Hall of Honor at the 1939 World's Fair. Finding themselves stranded in America at the outbreak of WWII, the Cybises founded an artists' studio, first in Astoria, New York, and later in Trenton, New Jersey, where they made fine figurines and plaques with exacting artistry and craftsmanship entailing extensive handwork. The studio still operates today producing exquisite porcelains on a limited edition basis.

Attis (half man/half horse, companion of Cybele), #90, 10x8".... 900.00
Ballerina w/sm crown stands on pointe, 1983, 9"........................ 150.00
Beatrice, half-figure of lady w/flowers in hair, retired, 13" 480.00
Beaverhead Medicine Man, fine details, 1979, 18", NM 1,950.00
Betty Blue standing w/flowing bl ribbon on gown, 8½" 150.00
Big Top, dog w/hat & bl bow tie, 5", NM................................... 110.00
Bison standing, 3¼x5¾", NM 50.00
Bride standing w/bouquet in left hand, 8" 120.00
Calla lily, limited ed, 16x8x7" 350.00
Chantilly, cat w/bl ribbon, 4x8" 85.00
Clara, ballerina from Nutcracker, 9x2" 180.00
Clarion Lily, 12x9" 325.00
Clown boy's head, ruffled collar, 2 bl balls on hat, 9".................. 155.00
Clown juggling, ball in ea hand, 1 resting on hat, 10" 450.00
Cynthia, ballerina, 9x3" 150.00
Deer mouse in clover, 3½" 60.00
Felicity flower basket, blk-eyed susans/peach blossoms, 1976....... 215.00
George Washington bust, wht bsk, 11" on 2" bsk base 265.00
George Washington standing by plinth, bl coat, 14" 515.00
Girl's head, short curls, butterfly in hair, 7"+blk base 265.00
Guinevere, ¾-figure, limited ed, 12"... 360.00
Harlequin standing w/hand on head, artist proof, 1980, 15¼x6" . 780.00

Heron, #105, 17", $1,140.00. (Photo courtesy Brunk Auctions/LiveAuctioneers.com)

Horses (2) running, #837, 8x12" 600.00
Juliet, half-figure of girl w/flower, 12x6" 480.00
Kestrel w/wings up, perched on log before walking stick, 16x9"... 480.00
King Richard the Lionheart, #69, 14⅞" 660.00
Lady Barengaira (King Richard's wife) w/falcon, #404, 15".......... 785.00
Lady Godiva on wht horse, 13x15" 1,200.00
Little Miss Muffet on tuffet w/spider, 1979, 7" 95.00
Madonna w/bird, 12" 100.00
Madonna w/Wreath of Roses bust, 11x4".................................. 360.00
Magnolia flower & bud, 6x11", NM 120.00
Maximillan, dormouse on driftwood eating acorns, 6" 180.00
Mick the Melodious Cat, cat in vest playing concertina, 7"......... 150.00
Mr Fluffy Tail, squirl w/tail up, 7½x3¾" 90.00
Nanook bust, Eskimo child, 10x6" 95.00
Pandora seated w/box, Children's Collection, 4½x4" 110.00
Phineas, circus elephant w/trunk up, 7x6" 425.00
Rabbit seated w/ears bk, wht w/pnt details, 3" 48.00
Raffles, raccoon on base, 7" 240.00
Rapunzel, seated/holds flowers, lilac dress, #218, 1979, rpr, 8" 395.00

Sandpiper, bird on grassy base, limited ed, 5x8".............................150.00
Storyteller, girl seated w/book, Children Series, 9x4"...................215.00
Sugar Plum, carousel horse, on ebonized wooden stand, 13¼x9¼"..300.00
Taffy, Toffy & Tiger; 3 kittens curled up together, 4½x5"............150.00
Thumbelina, girl seated, 4"...150.00
Unicorn's head, #64, on wooden base, 13"...................................360.00
Wendy, girl stands w/doll in left hand, 6½".................................60.00

Czechoslovakian Collectibles

Czechoslovakia came into being as a country in 1918. Located in the heart of Europe, it was a land with the natural resources necessary to support a glass industry that dated back to the mid-fourteenth century. The glass that was produced there has captured the attention of today's collectors, and for good reason. There are beautiful vases — cased, ruffled, applied with rigaree or silver overlay — fine enough to rival those of the best glasshouses. Czechoslovakian art glass baskets are quite as attractive as Victorian America's, and the elegant cut glass perfumes made in colors as well as crystal are unrivaled. There are also pressed glass perfumes, molded in lovely Deco shapes, of various types of art glass. Some are overlaid with gold filigree set with 'jewels.' Jewelry, lamps, porcelains, and fine art pottery are also included in the field.

More than 70 marks have been recorded, including those in the mold, ink stamped, acid etched, or on a small metal nameplate. The newer marks are incised, stamped 'Royal Dux Made in Czechoslovakia' (see Royal Dux), or printed on a paper label which reads 'Bohemian Glass Made in Czechoslovakia.' (Communist controlled from 1948, Czechoslovakia once again was made a free country in December 1989. Today it no longer exists; after 1993 it was divided to form two countries, the Czech Republic and the Slovak Republic.) For a more thorough study of the subject, we recommend *Made in Czechoslovakia* and *Made in Czechoslovakia, Book 2*, by Ruth A. Forsythe. Other fine books are *Czechoslovakian Perfume Bottles and Boudoir Accessories* by Jacquelyne Y. Jones North, and *Czechoslovakian Pottery* by Bowers, Closser, and Ellis. In the listings that follow, when one dimension is given, it refers to height; decoration is enamel unless noted otherwise. See also Amphora; Erphila.

Glass

Basket, mc mottle, twisted thorn hdl, 6½x4"..................................55.00
Bowl, cobalt w/silver o/l lines & bands, wide ft, dome lid, 6x7".....55.00
Candy compote, yel w/blk ft & knobbed stem, w/lid, 10x4½"......150.00
Compote, orange cased, blk rim/ball in stem, 4½x6¼"................235.00
Decanter, angular intaglio-cut panels & stopper, 9¾", +6 wines, EX .180.00
Figurine, musician, Am Cut Crystal Corp, 8".............................125.00
Figurine, stylized fish, sgn Exbor, 9" L......................................180.00
Jar, ribbing between horizontal bands, gr/orange, cylinder w/lid, 8" ...125.00
Vase, bands of wavy lines, yel/brn on clambroth to orange, 9x6", EX .145.00
Vase, bl w/irid oil spots, flaring toward base, sgn pontil, 3½"........250.00
Vase, cased lt gr free-form w/red int, beak-like mouth, Arcadia, 11"......75.00
Vase, cobalt threading on pk fan form, 9½", pr.............................225.00
Vase, cobalt w/silver o/l floral band at shoulder, 12½".................145.00
Vase, dk tones/millefiori canes, bulbous w/flared top, att Kralik, 10"...360.00
Vase, horses running frieze, cased/frosted, spherical, 6"...............150.00
Vase, lt gr w/thorny ribbing, gourd form, ca 1930s, 10¼x4½", EX. 300.00
Vase, parrot on branch pnt on orange-cased yel, blk trim, 6½", NM..70.00
Vase, ruby cornucopia form w/clear stem on sq base, 7x8", pr......145.00
Vase, stylized floral, etched/enameled on cased clear, gourd form, 9" .180.00
Vase, wht w/orange drips & areas of gr/yel spatter, 3-step bulb, 6x5"....80.00

Lamps

Basket, beaded, filled w/glass fruits/nuts, metal ft, nonworking, 9" .1,500.00

Basket, beaded, filled w/lg pcs of glass fruits/nuts, w/hdl, 11".....1,900.00
Basket, beaded, filled w/mc glass flowers, metal ft, 12"................960.00
Basket, beaded, filled w/red berries, metal ft, 10".......................525.00
Boudoir, stone bridge in woods HP on bl frost, Ruckl, 12½"........150.00
Cylinder orange shade w/blk silhouettes jumping rope, bronze ft, 10" ..250.00
Lady (metal) on bk/arms behind head, balances 7" glass ball, 23", EX..360.00
Peacock, figural spelter bird, glass beadwork fanned tail, 13x9" ...425.00
Perfume, wht floral on frosted egg shape, mk on base rim, 5", NM ..85.00
Shade only: all-over mc single grapes, dome: 3x6", EX................150.00
Shade only: spatter glass, bl/gr, globe w/angular protrusions, 7½".. 200.00
Toadstool shape w/acid-etched pastel florals, Bellova #2181, 13x9".2,650.00

Perfume Bottles

Birth of Venus, amber, swirling fish, nude stopper, 7"................2,000.00
Bl, stepped/faceted fan-like base, fan stopper w/intaglio floral, 4".. 95.00
Bl pyramid, jewels/filigree/ball ft, dancer in long skirt stopper, 6" ...3,850.00
Bl stepped form, clear open teardrop stopper w/dauber, 3⅞"........225.00
Blk, faceted sides/lg pk jewel, clear rosebush stopper, Ingrid, 6" .1,800.00
Blk w/geometrics, fan-shaped stopper w/cvd flowers & dauber, 5". 350.00
Blk w/HP boy playing trumpet, orange stopper w/dauber, 5¾"..6,090.00
Clear, dmn emb cylinder, Scotty on lid w/brass filigree, Trice, 2¼".280.00
Clear, shallow/flared, lg stopper: frosted nude w/wings, 8½"......1,550.00

Clear and frosted, nude at each side, marked, 5¼", $650.00. (Photo courtesy Monsen & Baer)

Clear shouldered form w/abstract decor, red crystal stopper, 4¾". 300.00
Clear w/appl mc stones & gold decor, nude intaglio stopper, 5"... 900.00
Dk yel w/faceted sides, 4-ftd, intaglio floral stopper, 6"...............300.00
Gr, pyriform ribbed base, notched disk stopper w/horn of plenty, 5x4" ...45.00
Lav, flat-sided w/undulating sides, Cupid in 4-lobe stopper, 4¾"..120.00
Pk, body resembling sun rays, kneeling nude stopper, 6"...........5,000.00
Pk faceted base w/9 ft, nude holding world stopper, 7½"...........4,500.00
Purple frost, w/jewels in gold-tone metalwork, fan stopper, 7"..1,200.00
Turq opaque, emb maid kneels/bk: deer, frosted roses stopper, Ingrid..2,250.00
Yel w/ornate geometric design, faceted stopper, 6".......................250.00

Pottery

Box, trinket; hand-painted flowers and leaves, 6" long, from $40.00 to $45.00. (Photo courtesy Dale and Diane Barth & Helen M. Rose)

Bowl, mc Dresden-type floral on wht porc w/gold trim, 6", set of 6..35.00
Bowl, orange form w/lid, porc, mk PV, lt wear, 3x4", set of 6.........60.00
Bowl, shallow shell form, 3-D maid w/lyre seated on rim, 9x10"..350.00
Box, bands/dots/etc, orange/brn on ivory, oval, w/lid, 3x6" L........38.00

Cup, fruit in low relief, strong colors on red, cylindrical, 4" 45.00
Ewer, 2 ladies in reserve, gold trim, Nouveau scrolls/hdl, 8" 40.00
Figure vase, heron standing, bill tucked to breast, wht/gr/brn 38.00
Figurine, nude seated on grass, leaning bk, 1 knee up, head trn, 9".120.00
Figurine, nude seated on sphere w/geometric star, P in circle mk, 12". 585.00
Fish set, fish/water plants/ Haas-Czjzek Schlaggenwald, 19th C, 11-pc .. 345.00
Flower frog, bird on arched branch on donut base, Czecho-Slovakia, 4".. 30.00
Flower frog/bud vase, yel bird on tree branch w/3 openings, #13-25, 5". 20.00
Flowerpot, angels in central band, majolica glazes, hdls, ftd, 10" . 360.00
Humidor, head of man, pipe in mouth, yel hat w/blk bill, gr mk.... 95.00
Pitcher, cat, tail hdl, Deco, red/blk on ivory, Ditmar-Urbach, 8". 420.00
Pitcher, figural cat hdl, pearl lustre w/lav rim, #31, 6½" 28.00
Pitcher, floral, mc on ivory, red rim/hdl, tankard form, Urbach, 8"..75.00
Pitcher, floral/fruit, bright colors on med bl, ftd, Urbach, 7½x6".. 85.00
Pitcher, primitive blk rooster on ivory, Czecho-Slovakia, 3¾" 40.00
Pitcher, pussy willow branches/bl leafy twigs on wht, 7"............... 35.00
Pitcher, stylized fruit, strong colors on blk/yel, Ditmar-Urbach, 7"..135.00
Planter, section of tree trunk w/bird on lower end, rnd mk 40.00
Plaque, classical figure scene, oval w/integral gold fr, 8½", pr....... 345.00
Plaque, stylized head/hand of lady w/flower, appl curls, FBS #157, 10" . 120.00
Plate, 3 mc floral stations on blk, Victoria China, 7½".................. 15.00
Platter, Antoinette (roses/gold border), J Hiacken, 11"................. 50.00
Salt box, 3 Deco floral reserves/SALT, bl/blk on wht, wood lid, #123..35.00
Teapot, gr lustre w/yel int, blk trim, 6", +cr/sug & service for 6 ... 135.00
Vase, castle/bridge on yel w/lg bl stars, lg brn/yel hdls/ft, 8" 28.00
Vase, Deco floral sprig, bright colors on lt bl, shouldered, 5x6"...... 80.00
Vase, vertical blk finger-like panels on orange mottle, loop hdls, 10".. 120.00
Vase, wht w/3 lg handmade pastel floral stems appl to side, 6x5", EX ..50.00
Wall pocket, bird by birdhouse on forked branch, #55, 5x5"......... 22.00
Wall pocket, bird w/lg tail feathers, opening in bk, #5952-A, 7" ... 50.00

D'Argental

D'Argental cameo glass was produced in France from the 1870s until about 1920 in the Art Nouveau style. Our advisor for this category is Don Williams; he is listed in the Directory under Missouri.

Cameo

Box, lilies, brn on yel to amber, w/lid, 6¼" dia.............................. 960.00
Vase, berries/leaves, amethyst on yel frost, swollen, ftd, 8"........... 900.00
Vase, cherries/leaves, bl on citron, swollen w/slim neck, 11½"..1,445.00
Vase, floral, purple/brn on lt bl frost, shouldered, slim, 18" 1,200.00
Vase, floral on leafy vine, brn on shaded amber & frost, slim, 11¾" ...1,025.00
Vase, floral/leaves, red on yel frost, shouldered, 4"........................ 275.00
Vase, fronds, amber on gr, ca 1905, 4½" 775.00
Vase, rocky coast w/ships, orange/pk on yel frost, swollen, 3¾x4" ...480.00

Vase, trumpet vines, dark cocoa and amber on citron, 9¾", $1,100.00. (Photo courtesy Cincinnati Art Galleries)

Vase, village landscape, brn/red/pk on yel frost, shouldered, 8"....780.00
Vase, wild roses, amethyst on citron, bulbous w/slim neck, 7"...... 900.00

Daum Nancy

Daum was an important producer of French cameo glass, operating from the late 1800s until after the turn of the century. They used various techniques — acid cutting, wheel engraving, and handwork — to create beautiful scenic designs and nature subjects in the Art Nouveau manner. Virtually all examples are signed. Daum is still in production, producing many figural items. Our advisor for this category is Don Williams; he is listed in the Directory under Missouri.

Key: fp — fire polished

Cameo

Vase, wisteria, ca 1900, 7¼", $3,360.00. (Photo courtesy David Rago Auctions)

Bowl, grapes, purple/burgundy on orange/yel, appl snail, 6" 4,600.00
Bowl, underwater flora, orange/butterscotch/gr/brn on bl, 3x14¼"...3,165.00
Ewer, crocus/branches, cut/pnt, mc on textured frost, 9¾" 4,375.00
Inkwell, berries/leaves, bl/gr/brn on gr to frost, 3¼x5"...............8,000.00
Lamp, leaves, gr on yel to cream, 3-arm matching std, 13½x7" .. 10,350.00
Lamp, winter scenic, cut/pnt on orange to yel, 14¾"...............16,800.00
Rose bowl, columbines, cut/pnt burnt yel to mauve, 2"............. 1,600.00
Rose bowl, trees/lake/sky, dk gr on orange mottle, sq sides, 2½"... 865.00
Tumbler, berries/leaves, cut/pnt on yel mottle, 3¼" 1,265.00
Tumbler, poppies, cut/pnt on yel to orange mottle, gold ft, 5"...2,000.00
Vase, berries/leaves, cut/pnt on orange to dk mauve, sq sides, 3¾" ...1,150.00
Vase, berries/leaves, cut/pnt on orange to mauve, pyramidal, 10"......2,350.00
Vase, berries/leaves, cut/pnt on yel to purple, pillow form, 4¾" ... 2,875.00
Vase, blackbirds in winter, blk on bl & wht mottle, HP details, 6".....7,250.00
Vase, blk-eyed Susans, burnt salmon/olive gr on martelé frost, 8¾" ...9,775.00
Vase, bud; wild orchids, burgundy/gr on yel/orange/mauve, 5"..2,100.00
Vase, crocuses, red on martelé clear/frost, 5½" 3,600.00
Vase, Deco geometrics, yel/amber on brn mottle w/bubbles, 10¾" ...1,150.00
Vase, floral, bl/gr on wht mottle, ftd, ca 1900, 9½" 6,600.00
Vase, floral, cut/pnt on lt bl to peach, slim, 19½" 9,200.00
Vase, floral, gr on martelé lt gr/apricot/frost/gr, 10½"...............10,925.00
Vase, floral, orange/gr on martelé clear, ca 1895, 6½" 5,400.00
Vase, floral, wht & chocolate on wht to bl, shouldered/slim, 7½" .. 8,000.00
Vase, fruit, gr on yel/orange/raspberry mottle, trumpet neck, 19" ... 3,450.00
Vase, fruit, orange/brn on raspberry to gr, slim, ftd, 15½" 8,000.00
Vase, fruit/leaves, orange/gr on raspberry/citron, ftd, 15¼"......11,500.00
Vase, gulls/turtle/sun/waves, cut/pnt on clear to frost, 15½" 10,350.00
Vase, lake scene, cut/pnt en grisaille on lav to frost, 3¼x4¼"....1,150.00
Vase, leaves/cornflowers, cut/pnt on bl to mauve, egg form, 3¾".... 7,000.00
Vase, marguerites, pk/wht w/appl cabochon centers on yel, 15" ...25,300.00
Vase, morning glories, cut/pnt on yel mottle, cylindrical, 13½"....10,350.00
Vase, moth/spider webs/leaves, yel/cerulean to indigo, 11½".....7,765.00

Vase, mushrooms, brn/red/gr on yel/orange/mauve, slim, 16" ..17,250.00
Vase, rose hip berries/leaves, cut/pnt on yel-orange to purple, 3¼" ...1,495.00
Vase, roses, pk on frost to yel, 5 appl cabochons/gold trim, 10¼"... 12,650.00
Vase, sailboats in harbor, purple/gr on mc mottle, ca 1900, 14" ..2,400.00
Vase, spring scenic, cut/pnt on frost to purple to gr, pillow form, 4" ..4,315.00
Vase, sweet peas, cut/pnt, fuchsia/gr on orange, 2¾" 1,600.00
Vase, trees, cut/pnt on yel, bottle form, 2¼" 575.00
Vase, trees/lake/sky, purple/bl on yel mottle, 7½" 1,800.00
Vase, trees/sky, cut/pnt brn/gr on yel to frost, 4¾" 2,875.00
Vase, winter scenic, cut/pnt on butterscotch, sm shoulder/slim, 10" 5,175.00
Vase, wooded landscape, autumn colors on yel mottle, 1910s, 11¾" 5,700.00
Vase, wooded landscape, dk gr on yel/red/purple mottle, ca 1900, 13" .5,000.00

Enameled Glass

Bottle, poppies, mc on yel to ecru, silver cap, 4¾" 1,650.00
Bottle, thistles, mc w/gold on textured frost, metal lid, 4½" 750.00
Vase, berries/leaves, mc on orange mottle, slim, ftd, 12" 785.00
Vase, bleeding hearts on amber mottle, stick neck, ca 1900, 4½" ... 1,800.00
Vase, flowers/foliage, red/gr on bl, slim baluster, 13⅜" 7,800.00
Vase, morning glories, mc on frost to amber mottle, 19½" 7,200.00
Vase, mushrooms/vegetation on orange/yel mottle, ca 1900, 5½" ..7,200.00
Vase, winter landscape on orange/yel mottle, ca 1900, 4" 3,000.00
Vase, wisteria, mauve/gr on frosted orange/brn mottle, 7¼" 3,350.00

Vase, winter scene on gray background, 11¾", $4,250.00. (Photo courtesy Jackson's International Auctioneers & Appraisers of Fine Art & Antiques)

Miscellaneous

Bowl, clear w/cut & etched geometrics, flared, 6¼x11" 780.00
Lamp, purple-bl ribs on gr to raspberry 9" shade; yel to bl std, 17" 13,800.00
Vase, controlled bubbles, lt bl, tapering body, 4½x4½" 180.00
Vase, purple ribs on powdered/shaded orange to gr, cylinder neck, 14" 2,300.00
Vase, ribbed & bubbled, clear bl, shoulderd, slim neck/flared rim, 14" 900.00
Vase, smoky w/cvd geometrics, ovoid, 10" 750.00

De Vez

De Vez was a type of acid-cut French cameo glass produced by Cristallerie de Pantin in Paris around the turn of the century. Our advisor for this category is Don Williams; he is listed in the Directory under Missouri.

Cameo

Bell, floral, red on amber, gilt-metal collar & hanger, 10" 1,950.00
Bowl, trumpet flowers/foliage, brn/salmon on yel, 3⅛x4¾", NM...1,200.00
Box, sunset scene, brn/gray on rose-red, 2⅝x3¼" 360.00
Lamp, fisherman/boats, bl/pk on orange, brass ft, 1900s, 6½" 950.00
Lamp, leaves/rocks/water on base & globe, 2-color, 1920s, 12" 600.00

Vase, alpine scene, bl/yel on wht to pk, shouldered, 10½" 1,550.00
Vase, birch/lake scene, brn/gr on shaded bl, slim, fanned rim, 11" ..850.00
Vase, boats/water/branches, reds on lt gr, shouldered, 8" 850.00
Vase, castle scene, cobalt/terra cotta on lt yel, 7½" 950.00
Vase, eagle/nest/woods, brns on pk, 7½" 850.00
Vase, fishing boats in harbor, purple/blk on rose pk, gourd form, 7x4" ..550.00
Vase, fishing boats/village scene, mauve/gr on yel to orange, 17" ... 1,950.00
Vase, gondola in moonlight, brn/red on shaded yel, slim, 10" ...1,550.00
Vase, lady/castle scene, gr/pk on wht, sm ft, 7" 785.00
Vase, mtn goat/evergreens/mtns, bl/wht on pk sky, 10¼" 1,560.00
Vase, mtn lake/woods, gr/red on yel to wht, flared cylinder, 12¼" .. 1,500.00
Vase, mtn/cabin/stag, 2-color, slim, 9¾" 725.00
Vase, mtn/lake/trees, gr/dk bl on med to lt bl, 8¼" 850.00
Vase, Nouveau flowers, red/gr on yel, bulbous, 7½" 1,000.00
Vase, swans/lake/mtns, bl/gray on yel, bulbous, 9½x10" 2,000.00
Vase, swans/mtns/branches, bl on yel to frost, slim, 7" 660.00
Vase, trees/water/village, gr/yel on frost, ca 1920, 14x4" 1,325.00
Vase, tropical scene, bl/gr/yel on amber opal, 10" 900.00
Vase, wisteria/waterfront, bl/gr on yel to pk, slim, ftd, 15" 2,750.00

De Vilbiss

Perfume bottles, atomizers, and dresser accessories marketed by the De Vilbiss Company are appreciated by collectors today for the various types of lovely glassware used in their manufacture as well as for their pleasing shapes. Various companies provided the glass, while De Vilbiss made only the metal tops. They marketed their merchandise not only here but in Paris, England, Canada, and Havana as well. Their marks were acid stamped, ink stamped, in gold script, molded in, or on paper labels. One is no more significant than another. Our advisor for this category is Randy Monsen; he is listed in the Directory under Virginia.

Key:
A — atomizer   B — bulb

Bottles

Atomizer, orange with exterior in gold abstract design, new ball and tassel, 7½", $350.00. (Photo courtesy Monsen & Baer)

Bl Aurene, brass stopper, Steuben #6136, DeVilbiss mk, slim/ftd, 6" .. 515.00
Bl irid, slender stem w/flared ft, A, rpl gold B w/tassel, 8" 450.00
Clear w/swirled feathers in relief, bulbous, 3¾" 42.50
Clear/frosted floral cylinder, gold cap, orig sticker, 1920s, 5¼" 96.00
Cobalt w/Deco HP floral, Moser type, flared ft, 6½" 110.00
Cranberry w/cut patterns/bright gold, A, non-working B, 10", pr ...415.00
Crystal irid, 6-sided ft, A, rpl bulb, 6" 120.00
Gold to bl Aurene w/cut floral, cylinder w/flared ft, A/no B, 8½" ...600.00
Gr w/bird figural stem, disk ft, A w/orig ball/tassel, 6⅜" 1,200.00
Gr/gold/blk geometrics, purple int, disk ft, A w/rpl B/tassel, 10" ..1,500.00

Jade gr w/gold at lower body & disk ft, long dauber, 7".............. 275.00
Lav, bulbous top w/slim stem, disk ft, A, hard B, 6"................ 80.00
Marigold, shouldered, 6-sided ft, A, no bulb, 7½"................ 110.00
Orange base, gold & blk top, Deco look, A, no bulb, 7"........ 240.00
Orange w/gold enamel, disk ft, gold stopper, 7" 350.00
Pearl lustre w/cameo bird & branches, much gold, A, G- B, 10¼"..415.00
Pk stain w/gold at neck & base, slim w/flared ft, A, orig B, 7½" ...240.00
Purple w/Deco dragonflies, gold stopper w/dauber, disk ft, 5⅞" 135.00

Miscellaneous

Cigarette box, gr w/HP gold bird & foliage, 3⅜x4¾"............ 350.00
Ginger jar, amber w/gold pine needle design, W/A insert, 6½"....250.00
Perfume lamp, fairy silhouettes, sm rpr, 8x2½"................ 475.00
Perfume lamp, monkey among leaves, Deco shape, 1920s, 8½" .1150.00
Powder jar, coral pk w/blk abstract decor lid, 4¾"............ 65.00

Tray, enameled and gilded flowering vines, 7x10½", $365.00. (Photo courtesy Monsen & Baer)

Decanters

Ceramic whiskey decanters were brought into prominence in 1955 by the James Beam Distilling Company. Few other companies besides Beam produced these decanters during the next 10 years or so; however, other companies did eventually follow suit. At its peak in 1975, at least 20 prominent companies and several on a lesser scale made these decanters. Beam stopped making decanters in mid-1992. Now only a couple of companies are still producing these collectibles.

Liquor dealers have told collectors for years that ceramic decanters are not as valuable, and in some cases worthless, if emptied or if the federal tax stamp has been broken. Nothing is further from the truth. Following are but a few of many reasons you should consider emptying ceramic decanters:

1) If the thin glaze on the inside ever cracks (and it does in a small percentage of decanters), the contents will push through to the outside. It is then referred to as a 'leaker' and worth a fraction of its original value.

2) A large number of decanters left full in one area of your house poses a fire hazard.

3) A burglar, after stealing jewelry and electronics, may make off with some of your decanters just to enjoy the contents. If they are empty, chances are they will not be bothered.

4) It is illegal in most states for collectors to sell a full decanter without a liquor license.

Unlike years ago, few collectors now collect all types of decanters. Most now specialize. For example, they may collect trains, cars, owls, Indians, clowns, or any number of different things that have been depicted on or as a decanter. They are finding exceptional quality available at reasonable prices, especially when compared with many other types of collectibles.

We have tried to list those brands that are the most popular with collectors. Likewise, individual decanters listed are the ones (or representative of the ones) most commonly found. The following listing is but a small fraction of the thousands of decanters that have been produced.

These decanters come from all over the world. While Jim Beam owned its own china factory in the U.S., some of the others have been imported from Mexico, Taiwan, Japan, and elsewhere. They vary in size from miniatures (approximately two-ounce) to gallons. Values range from a few dollars to more than $3,000.00 per decanter. Most collectors and dealers define a 'mint' decanter as one with no chips, no cracks, and label intact. A missing federal tax stamp or lack of contents has no bearing on value. All values are given for 'mint' decanters. A 'mini' behind a listing indicates a miniature. All others are fifth or 750 ml unless noted otherwise. Our advisor for this category is Roy Willis; he is listed in the Directory under Kentucky.

Aesthetic Specialties (ASI)

Golf, Bing Crosby 39th............... 50.00
Truck, Ice Cream 69.00
Truck, Telephone 65.00

Beam

Wheel Series, '57 Chevy, turquoise and white, 1991, $75.00.

Casino Series, Harold's Club Slot Machine, bl............... 15.00
Casino Series, Harold's Club Slot Machine, gray............... 10.00
Centennial Series, Antioch............... 4.00
Centennial Series, Chicago Fire............... 16.00
Centennial Series, Dodge City, Boot Hill............... 15.00
Centennial Series, Laramie............... 5.00
Centennial Series, Yellowstone............... 7.00
Executive Series, 1955, Royal Porcelain............... 165.00
Executive Series, 1957, Royal Dimonte............... 39.00
Executive Series, 1960, Blue Cherub............... 60.00
Executive Series, 1968, Presidential............... 12.00
Executive Series, 1972, Regency............... 12.00
Foreign Series, Australia, Queensland............... 16.00
Foreign Series, Australia, Sidney Opera House............... 19.00
Foreign Series, Australia, Tigers............... 16.00
Foreign Series, Germany, Hansel & Gretel............... 10.00
Foreign Series, Germany, Pied Piper............... 10.00
Foreign Series, Germany, Wiesbaden............... 10.00
Organization Series, Ducks Unlimited #1, 1974............... 28.00
Organization Series, Ducks Unlimited #2, 1975............... 32.00
Organization Series, Ducks Unlimited #3, 1977............... 32.00
Organization Series, Ducks Unlimited #4, 1978............... 36.00
Organization Series, Ducks Unlimited #5, 1979............... 36.00
Organization Series, Fleet Reserve............... 5.00
Organization Series, Kentucky Colonel............... 10.00
Organization Series, Marine Corps Emblem............... 45.00
Organization Series, Pearl Harbor, 1972............... 18.00
Organization Series, Shriner Indiana............... 5.00
Organization Series, VFW............... 8.00
People Series, Buffalo Bill............... 20.00
People Series, Captain & Mate............... 12.00
People Series, General Stark............... 12.00

People Series, Hatfield or McCoy, ea 20.00
People Series, Indian Chief 20.00
People Series, Rocky Marciano 35.00
State Series, Arizona 8.00
State Series, Florida Shell 5.00
State Series, Illinois 7.00
State Series, Michigan 10.00
State Series, Nebraska 10.00
Wheel Series, Army Jeep 50.00
Wheel Series, Cadillac Convertible, 1959, pk 65.00
Wheel Series, Casey Jones Caboose, red 20.00
Wheel Series, Casey Jones Tank Car, wht 50.00
Wheel Series, Corvette, 1953, wht 150.00
Wheel Series, Corvette, 1957, blk 80.00
Wheel Series, Corvette, 1984, red 80.00
Wheel Series, Corvette, 1984, wht 75.00
Wheel Series, Duesenberg, 1934, lt bl 100.00
Wheel Series, Ford, 1903 Model A, blk or red 45.00
Wheel Series, Ford, 1928 Model A Coupe, gr 60.00
Wheel Series, Ford, 1929 Phaeton, gr 65.00
Wheel Series, Ford, 1935 Pickup - Clermont Supply 65.00
Wheel Series, Grant Coal Tender 65.00
Wheel Series, Jewel Tea Wagon 60.00
Wheel Series, Train, Baggage Car 50.00
Wheel Series, Train, Casey Jones Box Car, gr 60.00
Wheel Series, Train, Casey Jones Locomotive w/Tender 45.00
Wheel Series, Train, Dining Car 75.00
Wheel Series, Train, Grant Locomotive 60.00
Wheel Series, Train, Observation Car 65.00
Wheel Series, Train, Passenger Car 45.00
Wheel Series, 1928 Model-A Coupe, gr 60.00
Wheel Series, 1957 Bel Air Hardtop, red & wht 80.00

Brooks

Quail, 1970, $12.00.

American Legion, Hawaii, 1973 .... 14.00
Amvets Polish Legion 10.00
Bareknuckle Fighter 28.00
Basketball Player 16.00
Betsy Ross 10.00
Cardinal, Virginia 18.00
Cards - Jack, Queen or King 15.00
Delta Belle, Riverboat 8.00
Duesenberg 25.00
Equestrienne 10.00
Goldpanner 10.00
Grandfather Clock 8.00
Hambletonian 25.00
Harold's Club Dice 15.00
Jayhawk, Kansas 20.00
Kachina #1, Morning Singer 65.00

Kachina #2, Hummingbird 55.00
Kachina #3, Antelope 55.00
Kitten on Pillow 12.00
Lion on Rock 10.00
Owl, Old EZ #1 .... 35.00
Owl, Old EZ #1, mini 18.00
Panda 16.00
Shrine, Sphynx 10.00

Dant, J.W.

Fort Sill 6.00
Mount Rushmore 8.00
Paul Bunyan 5.00

Doubles

Cadillac, 1913 .... 22.00
Pierce Arrow, 1915 .... 30.00
Stutz Bearcat, 1919 .... 25.00

Famous Firsts

Locomotive, DeWitt Clinton 30.00
Racer, Marmon Wasp 65.00
Racer, Marmon Wasp, mini 30.00
Racer, National #8 .... 55.00
Racer, National #8, mini 30.00
Spirit of St Louis, lg 160.00
Spirit of St Louis, midi 85.00
Spirit of St Louis, mini 50.00

Hoffman

Betsy Ross 50.00
College Series, Helmet - Georgia 45.00
College Series, Helmet - LSU 45.00
College Series, Helmet - Nebraska 50.00
College Series, Mascot - Kentucky Football or Basketball 60.00
College Series, Mascot - LSU, Running or Passing 50.00
Mr Lucky Series, Mr Carpenter 40.00
Mr Lucky Series, Mr Carpenter, mini 18.00
Mr Lucky Series, Mr Harpist 30.00
Mr Lucky Series, Mr Harpist, mini 16.00
Mr Lucky Series, Mr Photographer 50.00
Mr Lucky Series, Mr Photographer, mini 22.00
Race Car, Donohue, Sunoco #66 .... 125.00
Race Car, Rutherford #3 .... 110.00
Wildlife Series, Bobcat & Pheasant 45.00
Wildlife Series, Panda 50.00

Kontinental

Editor 30.00
Editor, mini 15.00
Goldsmith 30.00
Goldsmith, mini 15.00
Innkeeper 30.00
Lumberjack 30.00

Lionstone

Annie Oakley 30.00
Bartender 35.00

Bartender, mini 16.00
Baseball Players 50.00
Basketball Players 40.00
Bath, Saturday Night 75.00
Boxers 55.00
Cavalry Scout 20.00
Cavalry Scout, mini 15.00
Chinese Laundryman 22.00
Cowboy 25.00
Cowboy, mini 15.00
Cowgirl 30.00
Custer's Last Stand, set of 4 .... 400.00
Fireman #1, red hat 100.00
Fireman #1, yel hat 125.00
Fireman #2, carrying child 95.00
Goldfinch 22.00
Judge Roy Bean 28.00
Madame 50.00
OK Corral Shootout, mini, set of 3 .... 200.00
OK Corral Shootout, set of 3 .... 375.00
Oriental Workers, 6 different, ea 35.00
Perfessor 50.00
Perfessor, mini 24.00
Telegrapher 28.00
Trapper 30.00

McCormick

Bicentennial Series, Betsy Ross 28.00
Bicentennial Series, Paul Revere 35.00
Bicentennial Series, Spirit of '76 .... 45.00
Charles Lindbergh 50.00
Charles Lindbergh, mini 20.00
Eleanor Roosevelt 28.00
Elvis, Aloha 175.00
Elvis, Aloha, mini 150.00
Elvis, Bust 40.00
Elvis, Gold Tribute, 1979 .... 150.00

Elvis, Karate, 1982, $350.00.

Elvis, Sargeant 195.00
Elvis, 25th Silver Anniversary, 1980 .... 140.00
Henry Ford 30.00
Henry Ford, mini 18.00
King Arthur's Court, Merlin 50.00
King Arthur's Court, Sir Lancelot 40.00
Muhammad Ali 150.00
Shrine, Imperial Council 35.00
Shrine, Noble 30.00
Strowger Telephone 28.00
US Grant 45.00

Will Rogers 35.00
Will Rogers, mini 15.00

Old Commonwealth

Coins of Ireland, 1979 .... 25.00
Dogs of Ireland, 1980 .... 30.00
Fisherman, A Keeper 50.00
Golden Retriever 50.00
Leprechaun, Elusive, 1980 .... 45.00
Leprechaun, Irish Minstrel 1982 .... 45.00
Leprechaun, Lucky, 1983 .... 45.00
Princeton University 29.00
Tennessee Walking Horse 50.00
Western Boot 25.00
Western Boot, mini 12.00

Old Fitzgerald

Irish Charm, 1977 .... 22.00
Irish Counties, 1973 .... 20.00
Irish Patriots, 1971 .... 18.00
Songs of Ireland, 1974 .... 20.00
Sons of Ireland, 1969 .... 18.00

Ski Country

Badger Family 40.00
Badger Family, mini 20.00
Bald Eagle on Water 135.00
Bald Eagle on Water, mini 40.00
Barn Owl 75.00
Barn Owl, mini 25.00
Bluebirds Wall Plaque 75.00
Bull Rider 75.00
Bull Rider, mini 35.00

Cardinals, Holiday, $95.00. (Photo courtesy Roy Willis)

Cedar Waxwings 55.00
Cedar Waxwings, mini 20.00
Duck, King Eider 50.00
Duck, King Eider, mini 28.00
Ducks Unlimited #3, Mallard, 1980 .... 65.00
Ducks Unlimited #3, Mallard, 1980, mini 40.00
Ducks Unlimited #4, Canvasback, 1981 .... 55.00
Ducks Unlimited #4, Canvasback, 1981, mini 24.00
Ducks Unlimited #5, Wood Duck, 1982 .... 100.00
Ducks Unlimited #5, Wood Duck, 1982, mini 40.00
Flycatcher 125.00
Flycatcher, mini 45.00
Fox on Log 70.00
Fox on Log, mini 95.00

Fox on Log, 1¾-liter......................................200.00
Harpy Eagle...110.00
Harpy Eagle, mini...70.00
Indian, End of the Trail.................................195.00
Indian, End of the Trail, mini............................65.00
Indian, Great Spirit...95.00
Indian, Great Spirit, mini..................................20.00
Indian, Lookout...60.00
Indian, Lookout, mini.......................................25.00
Kestrel Wall Plaque..65.00
Lion on Drum..38.00
Lion on Drum, mini..20.00
Mountain Lion...40.00
Mountain Lion, mini...24.00
Peace Dove...55.00
Peace Dove, mini...25.00
PT Barnum...40.00
PT Barnum, mini...24.00
Raccoon Wall Plaque.......................................100.00
Rainbow Trout...60.00
Rainbow Trout, mini...28.00
Salmon - Landlocked...45.00
Salmon - Landlocked, mini.................................25.00
Screech Owl Family..90.00
Screech Owl Family, mini...................................50.00
Screech Owl Family, 1-gal.................................275.00
Sea Gull Wall Plaque...55.00
Squirrel Wall Plaque..150.00
US Ski Team..30.00
US Ski Team, mini..15.00

Wild Turkey

Series I, #1, #2, #3, or #4, mini, ea.......................18.00
Series I, #1, 1971...160.00
Series I, #2..100.00
Series I, #3 or #4..50.00
Series I, #5..20.00
Series I, #5, #6, #7 & #8, mini, set of 5.................175.00
Series I, #6 or #7, ea..22.00
Series I, #8..40.00
Series II, Lore #1..20.00
Series II, Lore #2..35.00
Series II, Lore #3..45.00
Series II, Lore #4..50.00
Series III, #1, In Flight....................................110.00
Series III, #1, In Flight, mini..............................50.00
Series III, #2, Turkey & Bobcat.............................140.00
Series III, #2, Turkey & Bobcat, mini........................60.00
Series III, #3, Fighting Turkeys............................150.00
Series III, #3, Fighting Turkeys, mini.......................60.00
Series III, #4, Turkey & Eagle...............................95.00
Series III, #4, Turkey & Eagle, mini.........................85.00
Series III, #5, Turkey & Raccoon.............................95.00
Series III, #5, Turkey & Raccoon, mini.......................45.00
Series III, #6, Turkey & Poults..............................95.00
Series III, #6, Turkey & Poults, mini........................45.00
Series III, #7, Turkey & Red Fox.............................95.00
Series III, #7, Turkey & Red Fox, mini.......................60.00
Series III, #8, Turkey & Owl................................100.00
Series III, #8, Turkey & Owl, mini...........................60.00
Series III, #9, Turkey & Bear Cubs..........................100.00
Series III, #9, Turkey & Bear Cubs, mini.....................60.00
Series III, #10, Turkey & Coyote.............................95.00

Series III, #10, Turkey & Coyote, mini.......................50.00
Series III, #11, Turkey & Falcon.............................95.00

Series III, #12, Turkey and Skunks, $125.00.

Series III, #12, Turkey & Skunks, mini.......................60.00
Series III, Turkey & Falcon, mini............................60.00

Decoys

American colonists learned the craft of decoy making from the Indians who used them to lure birds out of the sky as an important food source. Early models were carved from wood such as pine, cedar, balsa, etc., and a few were made of canvas or papier-maché. There are two basic types of decoys: water floaters and shorebirds (also called 'stick-ups'). Within each type are many different species, ducks being the most plentiful since they migrated along all four of America's great waterways. Market hunting became big business around 1880, resulting in large-scale commercial production of decoys which continued until about 1910 when such hunting was outlawed by the Migratory Bird Treaty.

Today decoys are one of the most collectible types of American folk art. The most valuable are those carved by such artists as Laing, Crowell, Ward, and Wheeler, to name only a few. Each area, such as Massachusetts, Connecticut, Maine, the Illinois River, and the Delaware River, produces decoys with distinctive regional characteristics. Examples of commercial decoys produced by well-known factories — among them Mason, Stevens, and Dodge — are also prized by collectors. Though mass produced, these nevertheless required a certain amount of hand carving and decorating. Well-carved examples, especially those of rare species, are appreciating rapidly, and those with original paint are more desirable. In the listings that follow, all decoys are solid-bodied unless noted hollow.

Key:
CG — Challenge Grade	OWP — original working paint
DDF — Dodge Decoy Factory	PDF — Peterson Decoy Factory
DG — Detroit Grade	PG — Premier Grade
EDF — Evans Decoy Factory	SG — Standard Grade
MDF — Mason's Decoy Factory	WDF — Wildfowler Decoy Factory
OP — original paint	WOP — worn original paint
ORP — old repaint	

Black duck, Ben Dye, ORP, neck crack/sm dents.........................750.00
Black duck, Ira Hudson, football body w/fluted tail, ORP, minor wear...450.00
Black duck, John Blair, OP/ORP, crack in tail.........................6,250.00
Black duck, PDF, CG, OP, minor to moderate wear.....................5,000.00
Black duck, Sanford Gorsline, hollow, OP, minor wear................8,500.00
Black-Bellied Plover, Harry V Shrouds, OP, minor wear...............1,750.00
Bluebill drake, John Holly, ORP, few cracks/chips.....................600.00
Bluebill hen, JR Wells, hollow, orig comb pnt, cracks/dents/shot marks...2,800.00
Bluebill pr, Charlie Joiner, 1976, pnt eyes, NM.......................900.00
Bluewing Teal drake, EDF, OP, minor to moderate wear................1,200.00
Brant, Hurley Conklin, swimming, earlier style, OP, VG................425.00
Brant, Madison Mitchell, cork body, NM................................350.00

Bufflehead drake, Hurley Conklin, hollow, EX 700.00
Bufflehead hen, Cigar Daisey, detailed feather cvg, EX 650.00
Canada goose, Capt Ed Phillips, orig 'tiger stripe' pnt, moderate wear 2,900.00
Canada goose, Cigar Daisey, 1971, cork body, OP, minor wear 900.00
Canada goose, Jasper Dodge, OP, sm dents 9,500.00
Canada goose, Ward Bros, ca 1930, Bishop Head's Club style, ORP .. 4,500.00

Canada Goose, Wildflowler Factory, glass eyes, slightly turned head, presentation piece, excellent original paint with fine detailing and carving, $550.00. (Photo courtesy Decoys Unlimited Inc.)

Canvasback drake, Leonard Pryor, preening, ORP, cracks/dents .. 800.00
Canvasback drake, Taylor Boyd, high head, OP, few cracks 1,200.00
Canvasback drake, Tom Chambers, short bodied, hollow, G comb pnt...7,000.00
Curlew, Harry V Shrouds, OP, moderate wear 2,550.00
Dowitcher, Massachucetts, laminated 3-pc body, OP, moderate wear.....250.00
Dowitcher, MDF, glass eyes, fall plumage, ca 1900, OP, minor wear...2,200.00
Golden plover, Massachusetts, tack eyes, OP, sm dents 300.00
Goldeneye drake, Jess Urie, OP, sm neck crack, few dents 400.00
Goldeneye hen, Elmer Crowell, fluted tail, OP, minor wear......7,500.00
Goldeneye hen, John R Wells, JA & C brand, OP, sm crack/few dents..1,300.00
Gull, Connecticut, 1940s, hollow, extended wing tips, OP, minor wear.5,000.00
Long-billed curlew, MDF, late 1890s, OP, moderate wear..........3,250.00
Magnum Bluebill drake, EDF, OP, few cracks...........................1,300.00
Mallard drake, Charles Perdew, OP/sm dents/shot marks..........2,500.00
Mallard drake, Charlie Joiner, sleeping, 1975, VG OP..............1,050.00
Mallard drake, Heck Whittington, orig comb pnt......................3,200.00
Mallard hen, Ned Burgess, OP, minor wear, very rare..............21,000.00
Merganser drake, Chincoteague VA, red-breasted, OP, moderate wear..350.00
Merganser drake, Doug Jester, short body style, OP, minor wear . 1,750.00
Merganser hen, WDF, worn OP, some chips 500.00
Owl, Leonard Doren, glass eyes, OP, moderate wear..................2,500.00
Pintail drake, Ed Phillips, lifted head/extended tail sprig, OP, EX . 10,500.00
Pintail drake, Ignatius Staichowiak, OP, sm neck crack/sm dents .. 1,600.00
Pintail drake, Joe Morgan, raised/appl primaries, hollow, ORP 200.00
Pintail hen, Dave Watson, worn OP, numerous dents 400.00
Pintail hen, MDF, glass eyes, OP, 2 bk cracks...........................9,000.00
Pintail hen, Xavier Bourg, relief wing cvg, OP, minor wear.......... 400.00
Pintail pr, Charlie Joiner, flat bottoms w/wooden keels, EX 3,250.00
Redhead drake, Jim Currier, OP, NM.. 500.00
Redhead drake, Ward Bros, 1940s, balsa/slightly trn cedar head, OP.. 2,200.00
Redhead pr, Charlie Joiner, 1985, pnt eyes, NM....................... 950.00
Robin snipe, Harry V Shrouds, spring plumage, OP, EX..........10,750.00
Shoveler drake, Davey W Nichol, unweighted, unused, M.......2,100.00
Shoveler pr, Madison Mitchell, 1979, EX 1,200.00
Surf scoter drake, Gus Wilson, inlet head, cvd eyes/wings, ORP, chips...1,600.00
Swan, Jim Cockey, cvd eyes, ORP, age bk split/sm cracks 30,000.00
Swan, John Vickers, ORP, several cracks 800.00
Turkey, Sherman Jones & Lloyd Tyler, relief wing cvg, ⅔ sz, NM.....2,750.00
White-wing scoter, Gus Wilson, extended head, raised wings, ORP .2,500.00
Widgeon drake, Delbert Hudson, OP pnt by Ira Hudson, moderate wear...1,000.00
Widgeon drake, MDF, glass eyes, EX OP, PG.........................55,000.00
Widgeon hen, DDF, ca 1890, OP, minor wear..............................950.00

Dedham Pottery

Originally founded in Chelsea, Massachusetts, as the Chelsea Keramic Works, the name was changed to Dedham Pottery in 1895 after the firm relocated in Dedham, near Boston, Massachusetts. The ware utilized a gray stoneware body with a crackle glaze and simple cobalt border designs of flowers, birds, and animals. Decorations were brushed on by hand using an ancient Chinese method which suspended the cobalt within the overall glaze. There were 13 standard patterns, among them Magnolia, Iris, Butterfly, Duck, Polar Bear, and Rabbit, the latter of which was chosen to represent the company on their logo. On the very early pieces, the rabbits face left; decorators soon found the reverse position easier to paint, and the rabbits were turned to the right. (Earlier examples are worth from 10% to 20% more than identical pieces manufactured in later years.) In addition to the standard patterns, other designs were produced for special orders. These and artist-signed pieces are highly valued by collectors today.

Though their primary product was the blue-printed, crackle-glazed dinnerware, two types of artware were also produced: crackle glaze and flambé. Their notable volcanic ware was a type of the latter. The mark is incised and often accompanies the cipher of Hugh Robertson. The firm was operated by succeeding generations of the Robertson family until it closed in 1943. Our advisor for this category is Dale MacLean; he is listed in the Directory under Massachusetts. See also Chelsea Keramic Art Works.

Ashtray, Rabbit, stamped/registered, 4"...400.00
Bacon rasher, Magnolia, stamped/registered/imp, 1½x9¾" 475.00
Bacon rasher, Swan, stamped/registered, 1½x9½"......................550.00
Bowl, Double Turtle, stamped, 3x6"..800.00
Bowl, lotus; Lotus Petal, stamped, 2½x5"....................................600.00
Bowl, nappy, Rabbit, stamped, 1½x5¼"......................................395.00
Bowl, Rabbit, stamped, 2½x10½"...450.00
Bowl, Swan, #2, stamped/registered, 3½x8"................................500.00
Candleholders, Rabbit, stamped/registered, 1¾", pr 500.00
Charger, Horse Chestnut, stamped, 12"..490.00
Charger, Rabbit (clockwise), M Davenport, stamped/imp, 12¼" .480.00
Coaster, Rabbit, stamped, 4"..375.00
Coffeepot, Rabbit (clockwise), stamped, 7x9"..............................950.00
Compote, Rabbit, hdls, partial stamp, 3½x6"...............................475.00
Creamer & sugar bowl, Lion Head, w/lid, stamped, 4½", 6½"...2,000.00
Cup & saucer, bouillon; Azalea, stamped/registered, 2x5½", 6" ...250.00
Cup & saucer, chowder; Rabbit, stamped/registered, 7", 6¼" 450.00
Cup & saucer, Grape, stamped, 2¼", 5¾".....................................350.00
Cup & saucer, Rabbit, stamped registered, 3¼x5", 6¾" 275.00
Dish, child's, Cat, stamped/registered, 1⅛x7¾"..........................5,000.00
Egg cup, Elephant & Baby, stamped /registered, 4¼x5" 800.00
Flower holder, rabbit standing on dome, stamped, 6¾x4½"..........975.00
Flower holder, turtle, stamped/registered, 3½" dia 500.00

Humidor, log cabin and farmhouse, incised, #13, 6¾", $3,000.00. (Photo courtesy Smith & Jones Inc.)

Knife rest, rabbit crouching, stamped, rstr, 3x3½" 425.00
Mug, child's, Rabbit, early stamp, 2¾x4" 400.00

Mug & saucer, coffee; Rabbit, stamped, 4½x5½", 6½" 490.00
Oyster dish, Rabbit, 4½" L 600.00
Paperweight, turtle, partial stamp, 1¾x4½" 650.00
Pitcher, Elephant & Baby, tapered, early stamp, 5¼x4¼" 925.00
Pitcher, Rabbit, #2, stamped, 4¾x6" 550.00
Pitcher, Rabbit, floral band, stamped/imp, 8½x8" 600.00
Plate, Azalea, stamped/imp, 7½" 325.00
Plate, Bird in Potted Orange Tree, imp, 10" 500.00
Plate, Clover, CPUS, 8½" 900.00
Plate, Crab, stamped/imp, 8½" 600.00
Plate, Duck, stamped/imp, 9¾" 475.00
Plate, Elephant, stamped, 7¾" 675.00
Plate, Elephant, stamped/imp, 6½" 650.00
Plate, Fish, w/cobalt wave, stamped, 8½" 2,250.00
Plate, Grape, dbl stamped/imp, 8¾" 275.00
Plate, Grape, stamped/registered/imp, 7½" 225.00
Plate, Horse Chestnut, stamped, 6" 225.00
Plate, Landscape & Boat, stamped, 6" 900.00
Plate, Lobster, stamped/imp, 8½" 675.00
Plate, Magnolia, stamped/imp, 8½" 275.00
Plate, Moth, stamped/imp, 6", NM 475.00
Plate, Pineapple, CPUS, 8½" 750.00
Plate, Polar Bear, stamped/imp, 8½" 800.00
Plate, Polar Bear, stamped/imp, 10" 850.00
Plate, Pomegranate, #98/unidentified initials, 8½" 1,500.00
Plate, Pond Lily, registered/imp, 6" 250.00
Plate, poppy amid poppy pods, stamped/imp, rare, 6¼" 700.00
Plate, Rabbit, Single Ear; stamped, 8¼" 350.00
Plate, Scottie Dog Pr, stamped/registered/1931, hairline, 8½" 800.00
Plate, soup; Rabbit, stamped/imp, 1½x8¼" 275.00
Plate, Tufted Duck, imp, 10¼" 400.00
Plate, Turkey, early stamp, 10" 500.00
Plate, Turtle, stamped/imp, 6¼" 650.00
Platter, fish; Rabbit, stamped, 1½x12½" 1,800.00
Salt cellar, Walnut on Leaf, sgn DP in bl, 3" 475.00
Shakers, Rabbit, bulbous, long necks, mk DP, 3½", pr 450.00
Stein, Rabbit, incised/stamped, 5x5¼" 575.00
Tea tile, Elephant & Baby, stamped/registered, rstr kiln pop, 5½" ...800.00
Tea tile, Rabbit, stamped, 6¼", EX 450.00
Teapot, Elephant, stamped, 6¾x8½" 1,500.00
Tureen, Rabbit, dome lid w/knob hdl, stamped, 4x7", NM 700.00

Tureen, Rabbit, incised rabbit mark, with lid, 11" long, rim chip, $1,700.00. (Photo courtesy James D. Julia Inc.)

Miscellaneous

Lamp base, cherubs in relief, wht crackle, mk, 1942, 5¾x5¾" 975.00
Vase, clear gr drips over wht/bl crackle, H Robertson, flaw, 7x4" 1,100.00
Vase, emerald gr opaque drips on wht orange peel, H Robertson, 6¼" . 1,800.00
Vase, forest gr & bl mottle, H Robertson, experimental, 7¼x4¼" .1,000.00
Vase, khaki gr on bl & gr, H Robertson, 7¾x5" 1,200.00
Vase, mahog & oxblood flambé, H Robertson, HCR/DP24A, flaw, 8x6" ...2,750.00
Vase, thick bl-gray & oxblood, H Robertson, experimental, 5x4" .. 1,000.00
Vase, volcanic amber/gr/brn mottle, experimental, HCR, ca 1900, 7¼" ..1,200.00

Vase, thick mottled dripping over volcanic glaze, Dedham Pottery HCR/13/DP17F, 11x5½", $4,000.00. (Photo courtesy David Rago Auctions)

Degenhart

The Crystal Art Glass factory in Cambridge, Ohio, opened in 1947 under the private ownership of John and Elizabeth Degenhart. John had previously worked for the Cambridge Glass Company and was well known for his superior paperweights. After his death in 1964, Elizabeth took over management of the factory, hiring several workers from the defunct Cambridge Company, including Zack Boyd. Boyd was responsible for many unique colors, some of which were named for him. From 1964 to 1974, more than 27 different moulds were created, most of them resulting from Elizabeth Degenhart's work and creativity. Over 145 official colors were also developed. Elizabeth died in 1978, requesting that the 10 moulds she had built while operating the factory were to be turned over to the Degenhart Museum. The remaining moulds were to be held by the Island Mould and Machine Company, who (complying with her request) removed the familiar 'D in heart' trademark. The factory was eventually bought by Zack's son, Bernard Boyd. He also acquired the remaining Degenhart moulds, to which he added his own logo.

In general, slags and opaques should be valued 15% to 20% higher than crystals in color.

Bird Salt, Vaseline 20.00
Bird w/Cherry Salt, Autumn 15.00
Bow Slipper, Crown Tuscan 20.00
Candy Dish w/lid, Tomato 50.00
Child's Stork & Peacock Mug, End of Blizzard 25.00
Creamer & Sugar Bowl, Daisy & Button, Vaseline 60.00
Elizabeth Degenhart Portrait Plate, Amber 20.00
Hand Ashtray/Pin Dish, Amethyst 10.00
Hand Ashtray/Pin Dish, Vaseline 6.00
Heart Box, Bittersweet 10.00
Heart Jewel Box, Antique Blue, from $25 to 45.00
Heart Jewel Box, Opal 25.00
Heart Toothpick Holder, Milk Blue 15.00
Hen Covered Dish, Bloody Mary, 2" 45.00
Hen Covered Dish, Heliotrope, 2" 40.00
Hen Covered Dish, Honey Amber, 2" 20.00
Hen Covered Dish, Opal, 2" 15.00
Hen Covered Dish, Pink Carnival, 2" 35.00
Hen Covered Dish, Ruby, 2" 40.00
Hen Covered Dish, Sapphire Blue, 2" 15.00
Hen Covered Dish, Toffee Slag, 3" 30.00
Kat Slipper, Bloody Mary 40.00
Kat Slipper, Opal 15.00
Owl, Amberina 40.00
Owl, Crown Tuscan 30.00
Owl, Crystal 12.00
Owl, Dark Amethyst 20.00

Owl, Dark Caramel.. 75.00
Owl, Dichromatic.. 50.00
Owl, Light Heliotrope 100.00
Owl, Pea Green Jade (PJ Special) 100.00
Owl, Periwinkle 40.00
Owl, Rose Marie 20.00
Owl, Sapphire Blue.. 10.00
Owl, Vaseline.. 20.00
Owl, Wonder Blue Variant 30.00
Pooch, Caramel Slag, 3" 20.00
Pooch, Gray Tomato.. 30.00
Pooch, Tomato, 3" 35.00
Portrait Plate, Vaseline 30.00
Priscilla Doll, Light Amethyst................................ 80.00
Robin Covered Dish, Dark Amberina, 5" 70.00
Roller Skate, Crown Tuscan.................................... 50.00
Roller Skate, Dark Amethyst 30.00
Toothpick Holder, Daisy & Button, Custard............ 20.00
Toothpick Holder, Forget-Me-Not, Bittersweet........ 20.00
Toothpick Holder, Forget-Me-Not, Lavender Green.... 25.00
Toothpick Holder, Heart, Vaseline.......................... 15.00
Turkey Covered Dish, Amber, 5"............................ 30.00
Turkey Covered Dish, Vaseline, 5".......................... 35.00

Delatte

Delatte was a manufacturer of French cameo glass. Founded in 1921, their style reflected the influence of the Art Deco era with strong color contrasts and bold design. Our advisor for this category is Don Williams; he is listed in the Directory under Missouri.

Key: fp — fire polished

Box, bird on floral branch, red on lt gr, 2½" dia 515.00
Vase, blackberries, reds on yel to wht, bulbous, 5¾" 960.00

Vase, fish in seascape, black and green on pink, flared lip, 6½", $3,000.00. (Photo courtesy Don Williams)

Vase, floral, brn on yel mottle, teardrop, 8".................................... 775.00
Vase, floral, purple on frost, gourd shape, 7¼"............................... 550.00
Vase, floral, reds on pk to wht mottle, fp, gourd shape, 8" 900.00
Vase, fruit on thorny branches, amethyst on wht mottle, bulbous, 6" . 575.00
Vase, landscape, caramel on yel, tapered cylinder, 7¾".................. 480.00
Vase, orchids & leaves, purple/gr on pk, ovoid, 8x5".................. 1,765.00
Vase, trumpet flowers, 4-color, bulbous, ca 1900, 7½" 900.00

Delft

Old Delftware, made as early as the sixteenth century, was originally a low-fired earthenware coated in a thin opaque tin glaze with painted-on blue or polychrome designs. It was not until the last half of the nineteenth century, however, that the ware became commonly referred to as Delft, acquiring the name from the Dutch village that had become the major center of its production. English, German, and French potters also produced Delft, though with noticeable differences both in shape and decorative theme.

In the early part of the eighteenth century, the German potter Bottger, developed a formula for porcelain; in England, Wedgwood began producing creamware — both of which were much more durable. Unable to compete, one by one the Delft potteries failed. Soon only one remained. In 1876 De Porcelyne Fles reintroduced Delftware on a hard white body with blue and white decorative themes reflecting the Dutch countryside, windmills by the sea, and Dutch children. This manufacturer is the most well known of several operating today. Their products are now produced under the Royal Delft label.

For further information we recommend *Discovering Dutch Delftware, Modern Delft and Makkum Pottery*, by Stephen J. Van Hook (Glen Park Press, Alexandria, Virginia). Examples listed here are blue on white unless noted otherwise. See also specific manufacturers. Our advisor is Ralph Jaarsma; he is listed in the Directory under Iowa.

Bowl, England, floral, 18th C, 10⅜" 480.00
Bowl, Holland, flower vase, floral rim, 18th C, 9", NM 260.00
Charger, England, chinoiserie, 18th C, 13⅝", EX...................... 275.00
Charger, England, floral w/yel centers, 18th C, 13½" 900.00
Charger, English, flower basket & flower borders, 18th C, 13"..... 785.00
Charger, Holland, exotic bird, flower & feather borders, rstr, 12" 450.00
Charger, Holland, figures in landscape, scrolled border, 19th C, 16"..725.00
Charger, Holland, figures in sleigh, Maastricht, 18th C, 15½" 90.00
Charger, Holland, floral, 3 reserves in border, 20th C, 14¼" 120.00
Charger, Holland, floral w/much bl, ca 1900, 15½" 240.00
Charger, Holland, flower basket, floral rim, 18th C, 13½" 950.00
Charger, Holland, mixed flowers, vining border, 18th C, 12", NM .660.00

Charger, polychrome landscapes with figures, David Kam, first quarter eighteenth century, 20", $5,600.00. (Photo courtesy Skinner Inc. Auctioneers & Appraisers of Antiques & Fine Art)

Jar, wet drug; Holland, Rosar Sol, w/spout, mid-18th C, rpr, 9" ...925.00
Lamp base, England, rampant lion figural, ca 1880-1890, 17"...1,200.00
Pitcher, Holland, windmill scene, integral hdl, Maastricht, 7x4¼".135.00
Plaque, Holland, Mother & Child, OT Schwartz, 1850s, 17½x11"+fr.780.00
Plate, England, bird & floral, mc, 18th C, 8⅞" 515.00
Plate, England, pagoda & flowers, WCA 1716 on rim, 8⅞" 1,675.00
Plate, England, Sarah Pearson Born 17th Agust (sic) 1734, 9⅛"2,650.00
Plate, England, vase/figure/flag w/floral border, 18th C, 8½" 150.00
Vase, England, scenic reserve, urn form, bird finial, 18th C, 14", pr.1,975.00
Vase, Holland, floral, bulbous body, 8-sided base, ca 1740, 9½" ...900.00
Vase, Holland, teasel, HJ Sanders, shouldered, 5¾".................... 300.00

Denbac

The French pottery was founded in Vierzon in 1909 by René Denert. René Denert became known as Denbac in 1921 when René Louis Balichon became its financial manager (Denbac being a contraction of the partners' names). They became well known for producing not only Art Nouveau-style wares, Art Deco majolica and stoneware, but Arts and Crafts designs as well. Micro-crystalline glazes were their specialty. Operations halted temporarily during WWII but resumed again shorly thereafter. The company closed in 1952.

Pitcher, multi-tone brn crystalline, gourd form, 8½" 150.00
Vase, dragonflies, bl/gr/brn crystalline, 8" W........................ 200.00
Vase, gr/gray crystalline drip, gourd form, 9½" 375.00

Vase, molded leaves under matt brown, marked/#15, 3¾", $210.00. (Photo courtesy Cincinnati Art Galleries/ LiveAuctioneers.com)

Vase, multi-tone brn crystalline, twisted form, 8½" 200.00
Vase, organic design, gr/bl/brn crystalline, 4 rim-to-hip hdls, 9¼"...225.00
Vase, organic design at shoulder, blk & brn crystalline, 11¼" 300.00
Vase, organic designs, gr/brn crystalline, low integral hdls, 8"...... 300.00

Depression Glass

Depression glass is defined by Cathy and Gene Florence, authors of several bestselling books on the subject, as 'the inexpensive glassware made primarily during the Depression era in the colors of amber, green, pink, blue, red, yellow, white, and crystal.' This glass was mass produced, sold through five-and-dime stores and mail-order catalogs, and given away as premiums with gas and food products.

The listings in this book are far from being complete. If you want a more thorough presentation of this fascinating glassware, we recommend *Collector's Encyclopedia of Depression Glass, Pocket Guide to Depression Glass, Elegant Glassware of the Depression Era, Glass Candlesticks of the Depression Era,* and *Florences' Glassware Pattern Identification Guide, I – IV,* all by Cathy and Gene Florence, whose address is listed in the Directory under Kentucky. See also McKee; New Martinsville.

Adam, gr, candy jar, w/lid, 2½" 125.00
Adam, gr, plate, grill; 9".. 22.00
Adam, gr, platter, 11¾".. 25.00
Adam, gr or pik, platter, 11¾"... 25.00
Adam, pk, bowl, 7¾"... 26.00
Adam, pk, cake plate, ftd, 10" 28.00

Adam, pink, plate, salad; 7¾", $18.00. (Photo courtesy Cathy and Gene Florence)

Adam, pk, sugar bowl.. 20.00
Adam's Rib, irid, candlestick, 9", ea... 50.00
Adam's Rib, irid, mug 75.00
Adam's Rib, non-irid, plate, luncheon; 8".................................... 14.00
Adam's Rib, non-irid, shakers, pr 60.00
American Pioneer, crystal or pk, bowl, console; 10¾" 50.00

American Pioneer, crystal or pk, creamer, 3½" 18.00
American Pioneer, crystal or pk, ice bucket, 6" 45.00
American Pioneer, crystal or pk, mayonnaise, 4¼" 45.00
American Pioneer, crystal or pk, plate, 8" 10.00
American Pioneer, crystal or pk, vase, 7" 125.00
American Pioneer, gr, bowl, hdls, 9" 35.00
American Pioneer, gr, mayonnaise, 4½" 60.00
American Pioneer, gr, vase, 4 styles, 7" 150.00
American Pioneer, gr, whiskey, 2-oz, 2¼"....................................... 65.00
American Sweetheart, cobalt, plate, salad; 8".............................. 120.00
American Sweetheart, Monax, bowl, cereal; 6" 16.00
American Sweetheart, Monax, bowl, cream soup; 4½" 90.00
American Sweetheart, Monax, plate, dinner; 10¼" 25.00
American Sweetheart, Monax or pk, tidbit, 2-tier, 8" & 12", ea.... 60.00
American Sweetheart, pk, creamer, ftd 12.00
American Sweetheart, pk, platter, 13" L 50.00
American Sweetheart, pk, shakers, ftd, pr.................................... 550.00
American Sweetheart, pk, tidbit, 2-tier; 8" & 12" 60.00
American Sweetheart, Ruby, cup 100.00
American Sweetheart, Smoke, plate, dinner; 9¾" 80.00

Aunt Polly, blue, sugar bowl, $35.00; blue, sugar bowl lid, $150.00. (Photo courtesy Cathy and Gene Florence)

Aunt Polly, bl or gr, bowl, 1-hdl, 5½" 22.00
Aunt Polly, bl or gr, bowl, 8⅜" L 150.00
Aunt Polly, bl or gr, butter dish 200.00
Aunt Polly, bl or gr, candy dish, hdls, ftd 50.00
Aunt Polly, bl or gr, plate, sherbet; 6" 10.00
Aunt Polly, irid, sherbet..9.00
Aurora, cobalt or pk, bowl, cereal; 5⅜" 11.00
Aurora, cobalt or pk, cup 14.00
Aurora, cobalt or pk, plate, 6½" 9.00
Aurora, cobalt or pk, saucer..3.00
Aurora, gr, cup 8.00
Avocado, crystal, pitcher, 64-oz... 350.00
Avocado, gr, bowl, relish; ftd, 6" 27.00
Avocado, gr, bowl, salad; 7½" 65.00
Avocado, gr, creamer, ftd 25.00
Avocado, gr, pitcher, 64-oz 1,500.00
Avocado, pk, cake plate, hdls, 10¼" 40.00
Avocado, pk, cup, ftd.. 25.00
Beaded Block, crystal, pk or gr, bowl, sq, 5½" 18.00
Beaded Block, crystal, pk or gr, vase, 6" 20.00
Beaded Block, gr, bowl, deep, 6" 22.00
Beaded Block, gr, bowl, flared, 7¼"... 25.00
Beaded Block, opal, bowl, celery; 8¼".. 50.00
Beaded Block, pk, creamer.. 15.00
Block Optic, gr, bowl, berry; lg, 8½" 35.00
Block Optic, gr, candy jar, w/lid, 6¼" 60.00
Block Optic, gr, ice bucket 40.00
Block Optic, gr, pitcher, 54-oz, 8½" 90.00
Block Optic, gr, shakers, ftd, pr 40.00
Block Optic, gr or pk, sandwich plate, center hdl.......................... 60.00
Block Optic, gr or pk, whiskey, 2-oz, 2¼".. 30.00
Block Optic, pk, saucer, w/cup ring, 6⅛"...7.00

Block Optic, pk, tumbler, ftd, 3-oz, 3¼" 30.00
Block Optic, yel, plate, grill; 9" 125.00
Bowknot, gr, bowl, berry; 4½" 20.00
Bowknot, gr, bowl, cereal; 5½" 25.00
Bowknot, gr, tumbler, 10-oz, 5" 22.00
Cameo, crystal w/platinum rim, decanter, 10" 300.00
Cameo, gr, bowl, rimmed soup; 9" 75.00
Cameo, gr, butter dish 200.00
Cameo, gr, goblet, wine; 3½" 750.00
Cameo, gr, pitcher, milk; 20-oz, 5¾" 295.00
Cameo, gr, plate, sandwich; 10" 20.00

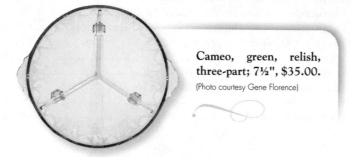

Cameo, green, relish, three-part; 7½", $35.00.

(Photo courtesy Gene Florence)

Cameo, pk, goblet, wine; 3½" 400.00
Cameo, pk, plate, dinner; 9½" 85.00
Cameo, yel, butter dish 1,350.00
Cameo, yel, creamer, 3¼" 16.00
Cameo, yel, pitcher, milk; 20-oz, 5¾" 2,000.00
Cameo, yel, plate, luncheon; 8" 8.00
Cameo, yel, platter, hdls, 12" 40.00
Cherry Blossom, Delphite, plate, sherbet; 6" 8.00
Cherry Blossom, gr, bowl, flat soup; 7¾" 80.00
Cherry Blossom, gr, bowl, vegetable; 9" L 40.00
Cherry Blossom, gr, plate, grill; 9" 28.00
Cherry Blossom, pk, butter dish 75.00
Cherry Blossom, pk, coaster 10.00
Cherry Blossom, pk, platter, 13" 50.00
Cherry Blossom, pk, tumbler, patterned rim, 12-oz, 5" 65.00
Cherryberry, crystal, olive dish, 1-hdl, 5" 9.00
Cherryberry, pk or gr, compote, 5¾" 25.00
Cherryberry, pk or gr, plate, salad; 7½" 12.00
Chinex Classic, Brownstone or ivory, bowl, vegetable; 7" ... 9.00
Chinex Classic, Browntone or ivory, sugar bowl 5.00
Chinex Classic, decal decor, bowl, salad; 6¾" 16.00
Circle, gr, bowl, 8" 35.00
Circle, gr, goblet, water; 8-oz 9.00
Circle, pk, plate, luncheon; 8¼" 10.00
Cloverleaf, blk, cup 10.00
Cloverleaf, gr, candy dish 65.00
Cloverleaf, gr or yel, bowl, dessert; 4" 40.00
Cloverleaf, gr or yel, plate, grill; 10¼" 30.00
Colonial, crystal, tumbler, iced tea; 12-oz 18.00
Colonial, gr, bowl, soup; low, 7" 70.00
Colonial, gr, cheese dish 250.00
Colonial, gr, plate, dinner; 10" 55.00
Colonial, gr, wine, stemmed, 4½-oz or 2½-oz 20.00
Colonial, pk, bowl, berry; lg, 9" 26.00
Colonial, pk, mug, 12-oz, 4½" 600.00
Colonial, pk, pitcher, 68-oz, 7¾" 60.00
Colonial, pk, shakers, pr 130.00
Columbia, crystal, bowl, ruffled edge, 10½" 16.00
Columbia, crystal, bowl, salad; 8½" 16.00
Columbia, crystal, plate, 6" 3.00
Columbia, pk, plate, luncheon; 9½" 30.00

Coronation, pk, bowl, 4¼" 100.00
Coronation, pk, cup 4.00
Coronation, Ruby, bowl, berry; 1-hdl, 8" 18.00
Coronation, Ruby, bowl, nappy; 1-hdl, 6½" 18.00
Cube, gr, bowl, salad; 6½" 12.00
Cube, pk, pitcher, 45-oz, 8¾" 235.00
Cube, pk, powder jar, 3-leg, w/lid 30.00
Diamond Quilted, amber, sandwich server, center hdl 50.00
Diamond Quilted, bl, bowl, crimped rim, 7" 22.00
Diamond Quilted, bl, compote, w/lid, 11½" 125.00
Diamond Quilted, bl or blk, bowl, cream soup; 4¾" 22.00
Diamond Quilted, gr or pk, bowl, cream soup; 4¾" 12.00
Diamond Quilted, gr or pk, pitcher, 64-oz 55.00
Diamond Quilted, gr or pk, plate, luncheon; 8" 8.00
Diamond Quilted, gr or pk, sugar bowl 10.00
Diamond Quilted, gr or pk, wine, 2-oz 14.00
Diana, amber, bowl, scalloped rim, 12" 20.00
Diana, amber, tumbler, 9-oz, 4⅛" 25.00
Diana, crystal, platter, 12" L 12.00
Diana, pk, ashtray, 3½" 3.50
Diana, pk, candy jar, w/lid 30.00
Diana, pk, coaster, 3½" 8.00
Dogwood, gr, bowl, cereal; 5½" 32.00
Dogwood, gr, saucer 6.00
Dogwood, gr, sugar bowl, 2½" 40.00
Dogwood, pk, plate, luncheon; 8" 6.00
Dogwood, pk, plate, salver; 12" 25.00
Doric, gr, bowl, cereal; 5½" 95.00
Doric, gr, creamer, 4" 14.00
Doric, gr, relish tray, 4x8" 18.00
Doric, gr, tumbler, 9-oz, 4½" 100.00
Doric, pk, cake plate, 3-leg, 10" 20.00
Doric, pk, plate, grill; 9" 24.00
Doric, pk, plate, salad; 7" 22.00
Doric & Pansy, pk, bowl, berry; 4½" 12.00
Doric & Pansy, pk, creamer 100.00
Doric & Pansy, Ultramarine, plate, sherbet; 6" 6.00
Doric & Pansy, Ultramarine, tray, hdls, 10" 35.00
English Hobnail, gr or pk, bottle, scent; 5-oz 35.00
English Hobnail, gr or pk, compote, honey; ftd, 6" 30.00
English Hobnail, gr or pk, compote, 5" 25.00
English Hobnail, gr or pk, nut dish, ftd, ind 20.00
English Hobnail, ice bl or turq, candlestick, 9", ea 55.00
English Hobnail, pk or gr, bowl, grapefruit; 6½" 22.00
Fancy Colonial, colors, bonbon, 1-hdl, 5½" 20.00
Fancy Colonial, colors, bowl, lily; cupped rim, 8" 40.00
Fancy Colonial, colors, compote, ftd, 4" 25.00
Fancy Colonial, colors, custard cup, flared rim 15.00
Fancy Colonial, colors, oil cruet, w/stopper, 6¼-oz 60.00
Fancy Colonial, colors, pitcher, 3-pt 150.00
Fancy Colonial, colors, plate, salad; 7½" 15.00
Fancy Colonial, colors, sherbet, low ft, 4¼" 20.00
Fancy Colonial, colors, tumbler, 8-oz 15.00
Fancy Colonial, colors, vase, ruffled rim, beaded base, 10" ... 85.00
Fancy Colonial, colors, wine, 2-oz 25.00
Fire-King Philbe, bl, cup 195.00
Fire-King Philbe, bl, plate, grill 95.00
Fire-King Philbe, bl, platter, hdls, 12" L 195.00
Fire-King Philbe, crystal, plate, luncheon; 8" 20.00
Fire-King Philbe, gr or pk, bowl, cereal; 5½" 50.00
Fire-King Philbe, gr or pk, bowl, vegetable; 10" L 95.00
Floral, gr, butter dish 100.00
Floral, gr, plate, dinner; 9" 18.00
Floral, pk, candlesticks, 4", pr 75.00

Floral, pk, relish dish, 2-part, oval 18.00
Floral & Diamond Band, gr, compote, 5½" 20.00
Floral & Diamond Band, pk, tumbler, 4" 18.00
Florentine No 1, gr, bowl, cream soup; 5" 30.00
Florentine No 1, gr, sugar bowl, ruffled rim 40.00
Florentine No 1, pk or yel, tumbler, iced tea; 12-oz, 5¼", ea 30.00
Florentine No 1, yel, bowl, berry; 5" 16.00
Florentine No 1, yel, pitcher, 48-oz, 7½" 135.00
Florentine No 1, yel, shakers, ftd, pr 50.00
Florentine No 2, gr, bowl, berry; 8" 28.00
Florentine No 2, gr, vase, 6" 35.00
Florentine No 2, yel, bowl, berry; 4½" 20.00
Florentine No 2, yel, gravy boat 50.00
Florentine No 2, yel, plate, grill; 10¼" 18.00
Flower Garden w/Butterflies, bl, compote, 4¾x10¼" ... 85.00
Flower Garden w/Butterflies, bl, plate, 7" 25.00
Flower Garden w/Butterflies, gr or pk, candy dish, 6" ... 130.00
Flower Garden w/Butterflies, gr or pk, vase, 10½" ... 135.00
Flower Garden w/Butterflies, pk, bottle, scent; w/stopper, 7½" 225.00
Flute & Cane, crystal, bowl, sq, 6½" 15.00
Flute & Cane, crystal, butter dish, w/dome lid 55.00
Flute & Cane, crystal, compote, w/ruffled rim 25.00
Flute & Cane, pk, pitcher, 22-oz, 5¼" 40.00
Fortune, pk, bowl, 4½" 8.00
Fortune, pk, candy dish 20.00
Fruits, gr, cup 7.00
Fruits, gr, sherbet 12.00
Fruits, gr or pk, plate, luncheon; 8", ea 10.00
Grape, colors, cup 10.00
Grape, colors, plate, luncheon; 8" 8.00
Hex Optic, gr or pk, bowl, mixing; 8¼" 18.00
Hex Optic, gr or pk, bucket reamer 70.00
Hex Optic, gr or pk, platter, 11" dia 15.00
Hex Optic, gr or pk, refrigerator dish, 4x4" 18.00
Hex Optic, gr or pk, sugar shaker 250.00

Holiday, pink, pitcher, 6¾", $42.00.

Homespun, crystal or pk, creamer, ftd 11.00
Homespun, crystal or pk, platter, hdls, 13" 18.00
Homespun, pk, butter dish 55.00
Homespun, pk, plate, dinner; 9¼" 20.00
Indiana Custard, ivory, bowl, cereal; 6½" 20.00
Indiana Custard, ivory, cup 28.00
Indiana Custard, ivory, plate, bread & butter; 5¾" 5.00
Indiana Custard, ivory, plate, dinner; 9¾" 22.00
Indiana Custard, ivory, platter, 11½" 30.00
Iris, crystal, bowl, cereal; 5" 75.00
Iris, crystal, candlesticks, pr 28.00
Iris, crystal, candy jar, w/lid 100.00
Iris, crystal, sherbet, 4" 18.00
Iris, crystal or irid, pitcher, ftd, 9½" 25.00
Iris, irid, butter dish 30.00
Iris, irid, goblet, wine; 4" 20.00

Iris, irid, pitcher, ftd, 9½" 25.00
Iris, irid, plate, sandwich; 11¾" 32.00
Iris, irid, sherbet, 4" 295.00
Iris, irid, vase, 9" 195.00
Jubilee, pk, bowl, 3-ftd, 11½" 210.00
Jubilee, pk, cup 22.00
Jubilee, pk or yel, cheese & cracker set 175.00
Jubilee, yel, cordial, 1-oz, 4" 250.00
Jubilee, yel, creamer 15.00
Jubilee, yel, tumbler, ftd, 6-oz, 5" 75.00
Jubilee, yel, vase, 12" 210.00
Laced Edge, bl or gr, bowl, divided, oval, 11" 100.00
Laced Edge, bl or gr, bowl, divided oval; 11" 100.00
Laced Edge, bl or gr, bowl, soup; 7" 65.00
Laced Edge, bl or gr, bowl, vegetable; 9" 95.00
Laced Edge, bl or gr, creamer 30.00
Laced Edge, bl or gr, mayonnaise, 3-pc 110.00
Laced Edge, bl or gr, plate, salad; 8" 22.00
Laced Edge, bl or gr, platter, 13" 150.00
Laced Edge, bl or gr, saucer 8.00
Laced Edge, bl or gr, tumbler, 9-oz 30.00
Lake Como, wht w/bl scenes, bowl, flat soup 75.00
Lake Como, wht w/bl scenes, plate, salad; 7¼" 15.00
Lake Como, wht w/bl scenes, shakers, pr 20.00
Laurel, ivory, plate, grill; scalloped rim, 9⅛" 15.00
Laurel, ivory, sugar bowl 11.00
Laurel, ivory, tumbler, 7-oz, 3⅜" 30.00
Laurel, Jade, candlesticks, 4", pr 65.00
Laurel, Jade, shakers, pr 90.00
Laurel, Jade or bl, bowl, berry; 4¾" 15.00
Laurel, Jade or bl, bowl, vegetable; 9¾" 55.00
Lincoln Inn, bl, bowl, crimped rim, 6" 18.00
Lincoln Inn, bl, plate, 12" 60.00
Lincoln Inn, bl or red, bowl, crimped rim, 6" 18.00
Lincoln Inn, bl or red, nut dish, ftd 25.00
Lincoln Inn, red, vase, ftd, 12" 250.00
Lois, crystal, pitcher, milk 55.00
Lois, gr, bowl, cereal; 6" 60.00
Lois, gr or pk, cake plate, ped ft 55.00
Lorain, crystal, plate, dinner; 10¼" 65.00
Lorain, crystal, tray, snack; 35.00
Lorain, crystal or gr, bowl, salad; 7¼" 50.00
Lorain, crystal or gr, creamer, ftd 18.00
Lorain, gr, platter, 11½" L 30.00
Lorain, yel, relish, 4-part, 8" 28.00

Madrid, amber, butter dish: top, from $38.00 to $50.00; bottom, from $30.00 to $40.00.

Madrid, amber, jelly dish, 7" 25.00
Madrid, gr, bowl, salad; 8" 17.50
Madrid, gr, jam dish, 7" 20.00
Madrid, gr, pitcher, 80-oz, 8½" 185.00
Madrid, gr, plate, dinner; 10½" 40.00
Madrid, gr, tumbler, 12-oz, 5½" 22.00
Madrid, gr or pk, plate, salad; 7½" 9.00
Manhattan, crystal, ashtray, sq, 4½" 14.00

Manhattan, crystal, bowl, berry; hdls, 5⅜" 18.00
Manhattan, crystal, bowl, fruit; 1-hdl, 9½" 30.00
Manhattan, crystal, candlesticks, 4½", pr... 18.00
Manhattan, crystal, plate, sandwich; 14" 25.00
Manhattan, pk, shakers, sq, 2", pr 35.00
Manhattan, pk, sherbet... 18.00
Manhattan, pk, sugar bowl, oval 15.00
Manhattan, pk, tumbler, ftd, 10-oz.. 25.00
Mayfair (Federal), crystal, bowl, cream soup; 5" 15.00
Mayfair (Federal), gr, cup... 10.00
Mayfair (Open Rose), bl, cookie jar 250.00

Mayfair/Open Rose, blue, vase, sweet pea; 5½", $145.00.

Mayfair (Open Rose), pk, celery dish, 10" 45.00
Mayfair (Open Rose), pk, cookie jar 48.00
Mayfair (Open Rose), yel, cookie jar.. 895.00
Mayfair Federal, amber, bowl, cream soup; 5" 18.00
Mayfair Federal, amber, creamer, ftd 11.00
Mayfair Federal, gr, plate, grill; 9½" 13.00
Mayfair/Open Rose, bl, cake plate, w/hdls, 12" 60.00
Mayfair/Open Rose, pk, bowl, low flat, 11¾" 55.00
Mayfair/Open Rose, pk, cocktail, 3-oz, 4" 80.00
Mayfair/Open Rose, pk, saucer, w/cup ring 28.00
Mayfair/Open Rose, pk, tumbler, 5-oz, 3½" 40.00
Miss America, amethyst, bowl, soup; 7½" 100.00
Miss America, crystal, compote, 5" 13.00
Miss America, crystal, platter, 12¼" L 12.00
Miss America, crystal, shakers, pr... 30.00
Miss America, crystal, tumbler, 14-oz, 5¾" 22.00
Miss America, gr, plate, 6¾" 14.00
Miss America, pk, platter, 12¼" L 40.00
Miss America, pk, shakers, pr 60.00
Miss America, pk, sugar bowl 20.00
Moderntone, amethyst, plate, dinner; 9" 12.00
Moderntone, amethyst, tumbler, 9-oz... 25.00
Moderntone, amethyst, tumbler, 12-oz.. 80.00
Moderntone, cobalt, bowl, cereal; 6½" 85.00
Moderntone, cobalt, cheese dish, w/metal lid 295.00
Moderntone, cobalt, tumbler, 12-oz... 110.00
Moderntone, cobalt, tumbler, 5-oz... 65.00
Moondrops, bl or red, ashtray.. 25.00
Moondrops, bl or red, bowl, ruffled rim, 3-leg, 9½" 65.00
Moondrops, bl or red, butter dish 425.00
Moondrops, gr or pk, gravy boat.. 80.00
Moondrops, pk or gr, butter dish 250.00
Mt Pleasant, amethyst, blk or cobalt, bowl, fruit; sq, ftd, 4⅞" 22.00
Mt Pleasant, amethyst, blk or cobalt, bowl, turned-up rim, hdls, 10"... 22.00
Mt Pleasant, amethyst, blk or cobalt, candlesticks, dbl; pr 35.00
Mt Pleasant, amethyst or cobalt, candlesticks, pr 25.00
Mt Pleasant, blk, plate, hdls, 8" 20.00
Mt Pleasant, gr or pk, sugar bowl.. 18.00
New Century, crystal, bowl, casserole; w/lid, 9" 75.00
New Century, crystal, decanter, w/stopper 75.00
New Century, crystal, sherbet, 3" 12.00
New Century, crystal, tumbler, 5-oz, 3½" 18.00

New Century, gr, bowl, cream soup; 4¾" 20.00
New Century, gr, cup 12.00
New Century, gr, decanter, w/stopper.. 75.00
New Century, gr, pitcher, 80-oz, 8".. 40.00
Newport, amethyst, creamer... 12.00
Newport, cobalt, plate, luncheon; 8½"... 10.00
Newport, cobalt, shakers, pr.. 40.00
Newport, cobalt, tumbler, 9-oz, 4½".. 40.00
No 610 Pyramid, gr, bowl, 9½" L... 45.00
No 610 Pyramid, pk, creamer 30.00
No 610 Pyramid, pk, ice tub 135.00
No 610 Pyramid, pk, pitcher.. 395.00
No 610 Pyramid, pk, tumbler, ftd, 8-oz... 50.00
No 610 Pyramid, yel, bowl, pickle; 1-hdl, 9½x5¾" 55.00
No 610 Pyramid, yel, pitcher... 550.00
No 610 Pyramid, yel, sugar bowl 35.00
No 612 Horseshoe, gr, bowl, berry; 4½" 26.00
No 612 Horseshoe, gr, bowl, vegetable; 8½" 35.00
No 612 Horseshoe, yel, plate, sandwich; 11½" 25.00
No 612 Horseshoe, yel, platter, oval, 10¾" 35.00
No 612 Horseshoe, yel, sherbet 18.00
No 612 Horseshoe, yel, sugar bowl, open 12.00
No 616 Vernon, crystal, cup 8.00
No 616 Vernon, crystal, sugar bowl 10.00
No 616 Vernon, gr or yel, creamer 25.00
No 618 Pineapple & Floral, amber, compote, dmn-shaped 8.00
No 618 Pineapple & Floral, amber, sherbet, ftd............................. 15.00
No 618 Pineapple & Floral, crystal, plate, sandwich; 11½" 14.00
No 618 Pineapple & Floral, crystal, relish, divided, 11½" 20.00
Old Cafe, crystal, pitcher, 36-oz, 6" 140.00
Old Cafe, pk, bowl, cereal; 5½" 32.00
Old Cafe, pk, bowl, hdls, 5½" 12.00
Old Cafe, red, lamp.. 150.00

Old Colony/Lace Edge, pink, candy jar, $50.00.

Old English, amber, gr or pk, compote, ruffled rim, 3½" 30.00
Old English, amber, gr or pk, vase, ftd, 12" 85.00
Old English, pk, tumbler, ftd, 4½" 22.00
Orchid, bl or red, bowl, hdls, 8½"... 150.00
Orchid, bl or red, mayonnaise, w/plate & ladle 145.00
Parrot, amber, bowl, soup; 7" 35.00
Patrician, gr, cookie jar 675.00
Patrician, pk, bowl, berry; lg, 8½" 30.00
Patrician, pk, tumbler, 14-oz, 5½" 40.00
Patrick, pk, cheese & cracker 110.00
Patrick, yel, cocktail, 4" 75.00
Patrick, yel, tray, center hdl, 11" 75.00
Petalware, pk, cup..6.00
Petalware, pk, platter, 13" L 22.00
Pillar Optic, gr or pk, pitcher, w/ice lip, 80-oz 40.00
Pillar Optic, gr or pk, plate, luncheon; 8" 12.00
Pillar Optic, red, creamer, ftd 100.00
Pillar Optic, red, sugar bowl, ftd.. 100.00
Primo, gr or yel, plate, grill; w/indent, 10" 15.00
Primo, gr or yel, tray, hostess; hdls... 50.00

Princess, gr, cookie jar 55.00
Princess, gr or pk, bowl, berry; 4½" 30.00
Princess, gr or pk, cup 9.00
Queen Mary, pk, plate, sandwich; 12" 20.00
Raindrops, gr, plate, luncheon; 8" 5.00
Raindrops, gr, tumbler, 5-oz, 3⅞" 6.50
Ribbon, gr, bowl, str sides, 8" 85.00
Ribbon, gr, tumbler, 10-oz, 6" 32.00
Ring, crystal, cocktail shaker 20.00
Ring, crystal, pitcher, 60-oz, 8" 17.50
Ring, crystal & gr w/decor, decanter, w/stopper 40.00
Ring, crystal & gr w/decor, sherbet, ftd, 4¾" 11.00
Rock Crystal, crystal, cake plate, ped ft, 11" 30.00
Rock Crystal, crystal, candelabra, 2-light, pr 30.00
Rock Crystal, crystal, egg plate 35.00
Rock Crystal, red, bowl, scalloped edge, 4½" 30.00
Rock Crystal, red, jelly dish, scalloped edge, ftd, 5" 42.50
Rock Crystal, red, sugar bowl, open, 10-oz 40.00
Rock Crystal, red, vase, cornucopia 275.00
Rose Cameo, gr, bowl, cereal; 5" 20.00
Rose Cameo, gr, sherbet 12.00
Rosemary, amber, bowl, cream soup; 5" 10.00
Rosemary, gr, plate, grill 20.00
Rosemary, gr, saucer 5.00
Roulette, crystal, plate, sandwich; 12" 11.00
Roulette, crystal, tumbler, 5-oz, 3¼" 7.00
Roulette, gr, bowl, fruit; 9" 25.00
Roulette, gr or pk, tumbler, 9-oz, 4⅛" 20.00
Round Robin, gr, cup, ftd 6.00
Round Robin, irid, sugar bowl 8.00
Royal Lace, bl, bowl, cream soup; 4¾" 38.00

Royal Lace, cobalt: Creamer or sugar bowl, $50.00 each; Sugar bowl lid, $195.00.

Royal Lace, bl, sherbet, ftd 60.00
Royal Lace, pk, butter dish 225.00
Royal Lace, pk, plate, grill; 9⅞" 25.00
Royal Ruby, red, tray, 6x4½" 12.50
S Pattern, amber, cake plate, heavy, 13" 95.00
S Pattern, amber, plate, dinner; 9¼" 10.00
S Pattern, crystal, pitcher, 80-oz 60.00
S Pattern, crystal, tumbler, 12-oz, 5" 12.00
Sandwich (Indiana), crystal, basket, 10" 30.00
Sandwich (Indiana), crystal, candlesticks, 3½", pr 14.00
Sandwich (Indiana), crystal, plate, dinner; 10½" 7.00
Sandwich (Indiana), pk, decanter, w/stopper 150.00
Sandwich (Indiana), pk, wine, 4-oz, 3" 25.00
Sharon, amber, bowl, vegetable; 9½" L 16.00
Sharon, gr, platter, 12½" L 28.00
Sharon, pk, jelly dish, 7½" 250.00
Ships, bl & wht, cocktail shaker 40.00
Ships, bl & wht, tumbler, roly poly, 6-oz 14.00
Sierra, gr, butter dish 80.00
Sierra, gr, pitcher, 32-oz, 6½" 150.00
Sierra, pk, creamer 20.00
Sierra, pk, platter, 11" L 35.00
Spiral, gr, cake plate 18.00
Spiral, gr, jelly dish, w/lid 18.00
Spiral, gr, shakers, pr 35.00
Springtime, crystal w/24k gold, decanter, w/cut faceted stopper, 26-oz ... 125.00
Springtime, crystal w/24k gold, wine, 2½-oz 25.00
Starlight, crystal, bowl, 2¾x12" 35.00
Starlight, crystal, relish dish 12.00
Strawberry, crystal, sugar bowl, lg 20.00
Strawberry, gr or pk, compote, 5¾" 35.00
Strawberry, gr or pk, pickle dish, 8¼" L 20.00
Sunburst, crystal, bowl, 10¾" 20.00
Sunburst, crystal, plate, dinner; 9¼" 15.00
Sunburst, crystal, tumbler, 9-oz, 4" 32.00
Sunflower, gr, paperweight 150.00
Sunflower, gr, plate, dinner; 9" 22.00
Swirl, pk, bowl, console; ftd, 10½" 20.00
Swirl, pk, candleholders, dbl, pr 60.00
Swirl, pk, plate, dinner; 9¼" 15.00
Swirl, pk, vase, ruffled rim, ftd, 6½" 26.00
Swirl, Ultramarine, candy dish, w/lid 150.00
Swirl, Ultramarine, cup 12.00
Swirl, Ultramarine, tumbler, 9-oz, 4" 40.00
Tea Room, gr, bowl, finger 60.00
Tea Room, gr, ice bucket 75.00
Tea Room, gr, marmalade, w/notched lid 210.00
Tea Room, gr, tumbler, ftd, 6-oz 35.00
Tea Room, pk, celery, 8¼" 32.00
Tea Room, pk, lamp, electric, 9" 140.00
Thistle, gr, cup 25.00
Thistle, gr, plate, grill; 10¼" 35.00
Thistle, pk, bowl, cereal; 5½" 30.00
Thistle, pk, saucer 9.00
Tulip, amethyst or bl, candleholder, 3x5¼", ea 50.00
Tulip, crystal or gr, plate, 10" 28.00
Twisted Optic, bl or yel, powder jar, w/lid 90.00
Twisted Optic, bl or yel, vase, rolled rim, hdls, 7¼" 75.00
Twisted Optic, gr or pk, bowl, crimped rim, 7" 20.00
Twisted Optic, gr or pk, plate, cracker; 9½" 18.00
Twisted Optic, gr or pk, platter 25.00
US Swirl, gr, candy dish, hdls, ftd 27.50
US Swirl, gr, compote 35.00
US Swirl, gr or pk, pickle dish, 8¼" L 30.00
Victory, bl, bonbon, 7" 20.00
Victory, pk, mayonnaise, w/plate & ladle 40.00
Victory, pk, sherbet, ftd 12.00
Waterford, crystal, butter dish 25.00
Waterford, crystal, shakers, pr 8.00
Windsor, pk, coaster 12.00
Windsor, pk, relish, divided; 11½" 250.00

Derby

William Duesbury operated in Derby, England, from about 1755, purchasing a second establishment, The Chelsea Works, in 1769. During this period fine porcelains were produced which so impressed the King that in 1773 he issued the company the Crown Derby patent. In 1810, several years after Duesbury's death, the factory was bought by Robert Bloor. The quality of the ware suffered under the new management, and the main Derby pottery closed in 1848. Within a short time, the work was revived by a dedicated number of former employees who established their own works on King Street in Derby.

The earliest known Derby mark was the crown over a script 'D'; however this mark is rarely found today. Soon after 1782, that mark was augmented with a device of crossed batons and six dots, usually applied in underglaze blue. During the Bloor period, the crown was centered within a ring containing the words 'Bloor' above and 'Derby' below the crown, or with a red printed stamp — the crowned Gothic 'D.' The King Street plant produced figurines that may be distinguished from their earlier counterparts by the presence of an 'S' and 'H' on either side of the crown and crossed batons.

In 1876 a new pottery was constructed in Derby, and the owners revived the earlier company's former standard of excellence. The Queen bestowed the firm the title Royal Crown Derby in 1890; it still operates under that name today. See also Royal Crown Derby.

Vase, three-color swirl, 4¼", $30.00.

Bowl, Imari-like floral, 19th C, 10" 60.00
Figurine, Britannia w/shield, much gold, late 18th C, 10⅜" 500.00
Figurine, Dr Syntax on horsebk, 19th C, 7½" 395.00
Figurine, Fame, draped angel blowing horn, rstr, late 18th C, 11"...240.00
Figurines, musketeer & lady in fine attire, red mk, 9¼", pr........... 350.00
Inkstand, floral w/gr bands, 4-compartment, 1840s, 5½x11½x7" . 480.00
Platter, meat; Japan pattern, red iron mk, ca 1830, 16" L............. 600.00
Soup tureen, Japan pattern, ftd, w/hdls & lid, ca 1810, 13".......... 950.00

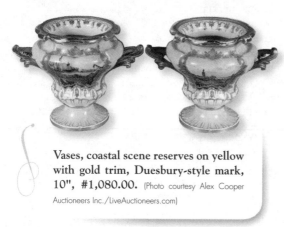

Vases, coastal scene reserves on yellow with gold trim, Duesbury-style mark, 10", #1,080.00. (Photo courtesy Alex Cooper Auctioneers Inc./LiveAuctioneers.com)

Desert Sands

As early as the 1850s, the Evans family living in the Ozark Mountains of Missouri produced domestic clay products. Their small pot shop was passed on from one generation to the next. In the 1920s it was moved to North Las Vegas, Nevada, where the name Desert Sands was adopted. Succeeding generations of the family continued to relocate, taking the business with them. From 1937 to 1962 it operated in Boulder City, Nevada; then it was moved to Barstow, California, where it remained until it closed in the late 1970s.

Desert Sands pottery is similar to Mission Ware by Niloak. Various mineral oxides were blended to mimic the naturally occurring sand formations of the American West. A high-gloss glaze was applied to add intensity to the colorful striations that characterize the ware. Not all examples are marked, making it sometimes difficult to attribute. Marked items carry an ink stamp with the Desert Sands designation. Paper labels were also used.

Bowl, flared rim, 2x4" 25.00
Bowl, nut; T'print pattern, early mk, 1¾x3½" 35.00
Bowl, 3½x9½" 50.00
Compote, flared ft, bell-like bowl, unmk, 4¾x5⅝".......................... 45.00
Compote, flared ft & rim, 7"... 150.00
Compote, ftd, sgn Evans, 7x8½" 100.00
Shakers, slim waisted form, 5", pr.. 30.00
Vase, flared cylinder, 2 paper labels, Hand Made by Ferrel on base, 7".36.00
Vase, 7⅝x3¾" 40.00

Documents

Although the word 'document' is defined in the general sense as 'anything printed or written, etc., relied upon to record or prove something...,' in the collectibles market, the term is more diversified with broadsides, billheads, checks, invoices, letters and letterheads, land grants, receipts, and waybills some of the most sought after. Some documents in demand are those related to a specific subject such as advertising, mining, railroads, military, politics, banking, slavery, nautical, or legal (deeds, mortgages, etc.). Other collectors look for examples representing a specific period of time such as colonial documents, Revolutionary, or Civil War documents, early Western documents, or those from a specific region, state, or city.

Aside from supply and demand, there are five major factors which determine the collector-value of a document. These are:

1) Age — Documents from the eastern half of the country can be found that date back to the 1700s or earlier. Most documents sought by collectors usually date from 1700 to 1900. Those with twentieth-century dates are still abundant and not in demand unless of special significance or beauty.

2) Region of origin — Depending on age, documents from rural and less-populated areas are harder to find than those from major cities and heavily populated states. The colonization of the West and Midwest did not begin until after 1850, so while an 1870s billhead from New York or Chicago is common, one from Albuquerque or Phoenix is not, since most of the Southwest was still unsettled.

3) Attractiveness — Some documents are plain and unadorned, but collectors prefer colorful, profusely illustrated pieces. Additional artwork and engravings add to the value.

4) Historical content — Unusual or interesting content, such as a letter written by a Civil War soldier giving an eye-witness account of the Battle of Gettysburg or a western territorial billhead listing numerous animal hides purchased from a trapper, will sell for more than one with mundane information.

5) Condition — Through neglect or environmental conditions, over many decades paper articles can become stained, torn, or deteriorated. Heavily damaged or stained documents are generally avoided altogether. Those with minor problems are more acceptable, although their value will decrease anywhere from 20% to 50%, depending upon the extent of damage. Avoid attempting to repair tears with Scotch tape — sell 'as is' so that the collector can take proper steps toward restoration.

Foreign documents are plentiful; and though some are very attractive, resale may be difficult. The listings that follow are generalized; prices are variable depending entirely upon the five points noted above. Values here are based upon examples with no major damage. Common grade documents without significant content are found in abundance and generally have little collector value. These usually date from the late 1800s to mid-1900s. It should be noted that the items listed below are examples of those that meet the criteria for having collector value. There is little demand for documents worth less than $5.00. For more information we recommend *Owning Western History* by Warren Anderson. Cheryl Anderson is our advisor; her address may be found in the Directory under Utah.

Key:
illus — illustrated   vgn — vignette
pp — pre-printed

Account of items used by 52nd PA Volunteer, 1885, 10x15" 12.00
Account of Sales, 7th Cavalry, dtd 1878, sgn 15.00
Appointment of Commissioner of Deeds, CA, pp, w/gold seal, 1868 ..55.00
Certificate, Airline Transport Pilot, pp, 1941 .... 12.00
Certificate, steamboat inspection, pp, vgn, 1950, +fr 30.00
Certificate, steamship inspection, pp, eagle vgn, 1844, 8x10" 48.00

Check, Carson, Nevada, Warrant to Senator J. Gallagher, $56.00 for a week's work, dated 1881, mining and railroad illustrations, EX, from $20.00 to $25.00. (Photo courtesy Warren Anderson)

Civil War claims, partially pp, sgn by Paymaster General, 1865, 1-pg .48.00
Civil War discharge, IA, 1864, w/GAR medal, in shadowbox fr.. 132.50
Deed of release, property in PA, 1794, 28½x12" 30.00
Grand jury findings, GA, selling liquor to slave, 1853, 9x12½" pg... 110.00
Indenture, for land in VA, 1795, on vellum, 27x25" 48.00
Land grant, member of TX militia, emb seal, sgn Buchanan, 1859 .. 120.00
Land grant, Montgomery Co VA, sgn by Governor B Randolf, 1789, 13x14".230.00
Land transfer, MA, sgn/witnessed, 1716, 10x15" 270.00
Ledger pg, itemized business receipts, 1830, 12½x8" 18.00
Letter, Civil War soldier, camp activities/etc, 1862, 4-pg 60.00
Letterhead, AG Spalding & Bros, w/logo, sgn/dtd 1929................. 12.00
Letterhead, Findlay Baseball Assoc, ca 1910................................... 48.00
Letterhead, Philadelphia A's, sgn John D Shibe, 1932.................... 18.00
License to trade w/Sioux, partial pp, sgn JQ Smith, 1844, 1-pg ... 425.00
List of quartermaster's stores, Fort Snelling, 1865, 10¼x16"......... 135.00
Promise of payment, $3,000 amount, sgn/sealed/witnessed, 1865, 8x8".. 12.00
Receipt, Army shipment of hay bales via ship, 1864, +envelope ... 18.00
Receipt, bounty paid to serve 3 months in army, 1776, 1-pg........ 110.00
Receipt, for discharge pay/etc, NY Volunteer, 1863, 8x10" 18.00
Receipt, Moline Plow Co, pp, vgn, 1878 .... 36.00
Receipt, sale of 2 slaves, KY, 1817, 10x7½", VG 315.00
Receipt, to Sheriff of Frederick Co, taxes, pp, 1860, 2x6½" 12.00
Register of Revolutionary War warrants, 1928, folio, leather bound 345.00
Slave document, TN, use of freed 8-yr old, 1867, +revenue stamp .215.00
Substance account, Artillery Corps, Fort Constitution, 1813 .... 65.00

Dollhouses

Dollhouses were introduced commercially in this country late in the 1700s by Dutch craftsmen who settled in the east. By the mid-1800s, they had become meticulously detailed, divided into separate rooms, and lavishly furnished to reflect the opulence of the day. Originally intended for the amusement of adults of the household, by the late 1800s their status had changed to that of a child's toy. Though many early dollhouses were lovingly hand fashioned for a special little girl, those made commercially by such companies as Bliss and Schoenhut are highly valued.

Furniture and furnishings in the Biedermeier style featuring stenciled Victorian decorations often sell for several hundred dollars each. Other early pieces made of pewter, porcelain, or papier-maché are also quite valuable. Certainly less expensive but very collectible, nonetheless, is the quality, hallmarked plastic furniture produced during the '40s by Renwal and Acme, and the 1960s Petite Princess line produced by Ideal. For more information and suggested values for dollhouse furniture, see *Schroeder's Collectible Toys, Antique to Modern,* and *Garage Sale and Flea Market Annual,* both published by Collector Books. Our advisor for this category is Barbara Rosen; she is listed in the Directory under New Jersey. See also Miniatures.

Bliss, Adirondack log cabin, 4 rooms, paper litho on wood, 18" H, VG ..520.00
Bliss, fire station No 2, 2-story, paper litho on wood, 13" H, VG ..1,130.00
Bliss, Queen Ann Victorian, 2-story, 4 rooms+attic, pnt wood, 43x33" .1,980.00
Converse, bungalow, pnt wood, arched window, stone porch, 14" L, VG.150.00
Converse, 2-story, stained wood w/simulated brickwork, 18" H, EX ..250.00
Gottschalk, gambrel, 2-story, pnt wood, furnished, 24x31", VG ...1,750.00
Jayline, 2-story, 5 rooms, litho tin, 1949, 14½x18½", VG 50.00
Marx, colonial, 2-story, tin, clapboard over brick, breezeway, NM...75.00
Marx, split-level, tin, patio above garage, red w/gray roof, VG 65.00
McLoughlin Bros, New Folding Dollhouse, 2-story, 2 rooms, cb, GIB....1,100.00
Meritoy, Cape Cod, tin w/plastic window inserts, 1949, 21x14", M.... 150.00

Ohio Art, Midget Manor, 1949, 8x3x5½", furniture included, MIB, $300.00. (Photo courtesy Bob and Marcie Tubbs)

Reed, Gutter House, 2-story, paper litho on wood, 18x9x10", VG...1,050.00
Rich, bungalow, cb, 1930s, 32x21", VG... 200.00
Schoenhut, cottage, 1 room, litho on wood, side opens, 15x19", EX.. 600.00
Schoenhut, 2-story, pnt wood w/brick look, metal furniture, 15", EX. 550.00
Tootsietoy, Spanish-style mansion, 7 rooms, cb, '30s, 20x30x18", EXIB..3,025.00
Vict, 2-story, bay windows/wraparound porches (2), pnt wood, 20x24x12"...1,650.00
Wolverine, colonial mansion, no garage, ½" scale, EX 50.00
Wolverine, country cottage, #800, 1986, ½" scale, EX 50.00

Dolls

To learn to invest your money wisely as you enjoy the hobby of doll collecting, you must become aware of defects which may devaluate a doll. In bisque, watch for eye chips, hairline cracks and chips, or breaks on any part of the head. Composition should be clean, not crazed or cracked. Vinyl and plastic should be clean with no pen or crayon marks. Though a quality replacement wig is acceptable for bisque dolls, composition and hard plastics should have their originals in uncut condition. Original clothing is a must except in bisque dolls, since it is unusual to find one in its original costume.

It is important to remember that prices are based on condition and rarity. When no condition is noted, either in the line listing or the subcategory narrative, dolls are assumed to be in excellent condition. In relation to bisque dolls, excellent means having no cracks, chips, or hairlines, being nicely dressed, shoed, wigged, and ready to to be placed into a collection. Some of our values are for dolls that are 'mint in box' or 'never removed from box.' As a general rule, a mint-in-the-box doll is worth twice as much (or there about) as one mint, no box. The same doll, played with and in only good condition, is worth half as much (or even less) than the mint-condition doll. Never-removed-from-box examples sell at a premium; allow an additional 10% to 20% over MIB prices for a doll in this pristine condition.

For a more thorough study of the subject, refer to *Collector's Guide to Dolls of the 1960s and 1970s* by Cindy Sabulis; *Collector's Encyclopedia of American Composition Dolls, 1900 – 1950, Vols. 1* and *2,* by Ursula R. Mertz; *Doll Values* by Linda Edwards; *Hosman Dolls, The Vinyl Era,* by Don Jensen; *Collectible African American Dolls* by Yvonne H. Ellis; and *Collector's Guide to Horsman Dolls* by Don Jensen. Several other book are referenced throughout this category. All are published by Collector Books.

Key:

bjtd — ball-jointed	OC — original clothes
blb — bent limb body	o/m — open mouth
b/o — battery operated	p/e — pierced ears
c/m — closed mouth	pwt — paperweight
hh — human hair	RpC — replaced clothes
hp — hard plastic	ShHd — shouder head
jtd — jointed	ShPl — shoulder plate
MIG — Made In Germany	SkHd — socket head
NC — no clothes	str — straight
o/c/e — open closed eyes	trn — turned
o/c/m — open closed mouth	

American Character

Unless noted MIB, our values are for dolls in mint condition. For more information we recommend *American Character Dolls* by Judith Izen (Collector Books).

Baby Sue, vinyl, o/c/e, says mama, OC, 1963, 21"	225.00
Betsy McCall, vinyl, rooted hair, chemise, 1958, 14", MIB	600.00
Chuckles, vinyl/cloth, rooted saran hair, OC, 19"	225.00
Hedda Get Bedda, 3-face w/knot on nightcap, OC, 1961, 23"	325.00
Little Girl Toodles, vinyl, Peek-a-Boo eyes, OC, 1960, 25", MIB	550.00
Little Love, compo/cloth, o/m/2 teeth, o/c/e, says mama, OC, 21"	300.00
Petite Baby Doll, compo ShPl, cloth body, crier, OC, 12½", MIB	350.00
Ricky Jr, vinyl, rooted brn hair, o/c/e, drinks/wets, OC, 1954, 21"	300.00
Sally, compo, o/c/e, hh wig, OC, 1930s, 16"	275.00
Sally Joy, compo ShPl, cloth body, crier, cotton dress, 1930s, 20"	250.00
Sweet Sue, hp walker, rooted hair, School Girl outfit, 15", MIB	350.00
Sweet Sue Sophisticate, vinyl walker, bl gown, 1957, 14", MIB	1,000.00
Tiny Tears, hp w/rubber body, christening gown/jacket, 11½", MIB	500.00
Tiny Tears, hp w/rubber body, molded hair, romper, 1950s, 16"	250.00
Tiny Tears, vinyl, platinum hair w/bangs, romper, 1950s, 16"	250.00
Toni, vinyl, rooted hair, o/c/e, c/m, jtd, Country Club oufit, 14"	600.00
Tressy, vinyl, platinum blond, str legs, OC, 1964, 11½", MIB	125.00

Annalee

Barbara Annalee Davis began making her dolls in the 1950s. What began as a hobby, very soon turned into a commercial venture. Her whimsical creations range from tiny angels atop powder puff clouds to funky giant frogs, some 42" in height. In between there are dolls for every occasion (with Christmas being her specialty), all characterized by their unique construction methods (felt over flexible wire framework) and wonderful facial expressions. Naturally, some of the older dolls are the most valuable (though more recent examples are desirable as well, depending on scarcity and demand), and condition, as usual, is very important. To date your doll, look at the tag. If made before 1986, that date is only the copyright date. (Dolls made after 1986 do carry the manufacturing date.) Dolls from the '50s have a long white red-embroidered tag with no date. From 1959 to 1964, that same tag had a date in the upper right-hand corner. From 1965 until 1970, it was folded in half and sewn into the seam. In 1970, a satiny white tag with a date preceded by a copyright symbol in the upper right-hand corner was used. In '75, the tag was a long white cotton strip with a copyright date. This tag was folded over in 1982, making it shorter. Our advisor for Annalees is Jane Holt; she is listed in the Directory under New Hampshire. Values are for dolls in at least excellent condition.

1962, monk, wht beard, blk hooded robe & skullcap, 10"	100.00
1966, beach girl w/towel, 10"	275.00
1970, Country Cousin boy & girl mice, 7", pr	100.00

1971, Bunny Boy, yellow or white with butterfly on his nose, 18", $125.00; Bunny Girl, yellow or white with polka-dot bandanna, missing basket, 18", $125.00. (Photo courtesy Jane Holt)

1972, reindeer w/flat face (36") w/2 18" gnomes in red	375.00
1974, choir girl, 10"	40.00
1974, leprechaun w/sack, 10"	75.00
1975, Mrs Cratchet holding plum pudding, 18"	95.00
1976, elephant, 18"	250.00
1978, pilgrim couple, 18" & 16", pr	75.00
1979, Disco mouse, 7"	35.00
1979, Santa w/card holder mailbag, 18"	50.00
1980, clown, 18"	75.00
1981, Christmas giraffe, w/10" elf, produced 1 yr, 22"	225.00
1981, clown, 42"	350.00
1983, Easter Parade boy & girl bunnies, 29", pr	100.00
1983, snowman w/red & wht hat & broom, 7"	30.00
1985, downhill skier, 10"	35.00
1985, kid w/sled, 12"	50.00
1986, Valentine panda, 10"	75.00
1987, bride & groom cats, 10", pr	100.00
1987, Santa (velour) w/sleigh & reindeer, 10"	50.00
1987, State Trooper, w/glass dome, 10"	200.00
1987-91, Ghost kid, carrying pumpkin, 7"	25.00
1988, bear on sled, 10"	30.00
1988, Mrs Santa w/tray, 30"	100.00
1988, reindeer w/gifts in pouches, 36"+antlers, EX	70.00
1989, toy soldier, 30"	95.00
1990, tree-top angel holding star, 12"	40.00
1990, Victorian Mrs Claus, 30"	75.00
1990, wise man w/camel, from Nativity set	100.00
1991, cat, blk, 12"	40.00
1991, man or woman skater, 10", ea	45.00
1991-92, spider, mobile, 12"	50.00
1992, angel on cloud, 5"	20.00
1993, Indian boy mouse, 12"	50.00
1994, Halloween elf holding holiday cookie cutter, blk, 5"	10.00
1994, naughty angel w/blk eye holding slingshot, 7"	30.00
1994, Thanksgiving turkey, lg, 24"	45.00
1995, girl scarecrow, 12"	45.00
1997, Mrs Santa, Last Minute Wrapping, 30"	125.00
1998, buffalo, 12"	50.00
1998, mailman elf, 10"	30.00
1998, wht reindeer, 18"	50.00
2001, Precious Cargo kid, Doll Society, 7"	45.00

Armand Marseille

#225, character child, bsk SkHd, glass eyes, teeth, jtd, RpC, 14" ..3,600.00
#259, Kiddiejoy, bsk solid-dome or wigged SkHd, glass eyes, RpC, 12" ..350.00
#310, Just Me, bsk SkHd, flirty eyes, wig, compo body, RpC, 8".. 1,500.00
#341, My Dream Baby, bent-limb compo body, RpC, 12" 325.00
#341, My Dream Baby, toddler body, RpC, 28" 1,200.00
#350, glass eyes, c/m, ca 1926, RpC, 16" 2,250.00
#370, bsk ShHd, o/m, glass eyes, kid body, RpC, 12" 135.00
#500, domed ShHd, molded/pnt hair, intaglio eyes, ca 1910, RpC, 10".650.00
#500, intaglio eyes, bent-limb compo, RpC, 15"........................ 600.00
#520, domed head, glass eyes, o/m, kid body, RpC, 16" 900.00
#590, sleep eyes, o/c/m, ca 1926, RpC, 9" 500.00
#800, SkHd, ca 1910, RpC, 18"......................................2,200.00
#1330, skKd, o/m, glass eyes, wig, bent-leg baby, RpC, 21" 600.00
Baby Betty, bent-leg baby body, RpC, 16"............................. 500.00
Baby Betty mold, bsk ShHd, glass eyes, wig, RpC, 16" 450.00
No mold #, child, bsk SkHd, glass eyes, 5-pc body, EX quality, RpC, 7".250.00
No mold #, child, bsk SkHd, glass eyes, 5-pc body, G quality, RpC, 12".135.00
No mold #, child, bsk SkHd, o/m, glass eyes, jtd compo, wig, RpC, 10".275.00
No mold #, child, bsk SkHd, o/m, glass eyes, jtd compo, wig, 16". 300.00
No mold #, child, bsk SkHd, o/m, glass eyes, jtd compo, wig, 36". 900.00
Queen Louise or Rosebud mold, bsk SkHd, glass eyes, wig, RpC, 13"...300.00

Barbie Dolls and Related Dolls

Though the face has changed three times since 1959, Barbie is still as popular today as she was when she was first introduced. Named after the young daughter of the first owner of the Mattel Company, the original Barbie had a white iris but no eye color. These dolls are nearly impossible to find, but there is a myriad of her successors and related collectibles just waiting to be found.

For further information we recommend *Barbie, The First Thirty Years*, by Stefanie Deutsch; *Collector's Encyclopedia of Barbie Doll Exclusives, Collector's Encyclopedia of Barbie Doll Collector's Editions*, and *Barbie Doll Around the World*, all by J. Michael Augustyniak. *Barbie Doll Fashion, Vols. I, II*, and *III*, by Sarah Sink Eames, give a complete history of the wardrobes of Barbie, her friends, and her family. *Schroeder's Toys, Antique to Modern*, is another good source for current market values. All these are published by Collector Books.

Barbie, Japanese Side-part American Girl, from $3,700.00 to $5,000.00 (modeling a rare Japanese kimono, $700.00). (Photo courtesy Stefanie Deutsch)

Allan, 1964, str legs, red-pnt hair, MIB.................................. 100.00
Allan, 1965, bendable legs, MIB.. 300.00
Barbie, 1958-59, #1, blond or brunette, MIB, from $5,000 to 5,250.00
Barbie, 1962, #6, any hair color, MIB, ea from $375 to 425.00
Barbie, American Girl, 1966, Color-Magic, NRFB 3,000.00
Barbie, Antique Rose, 1996, NRFB....................................... 190.00
Barbie, Blossom Beautiful, 1992, NRFB.................................. 225.00

Barbie, Bubble-Cut, 1962, blond or brunette, MIB, from $175 to...200.00
Barbie, Career Girl, 1964, MIB 750.00
Barbie, Celebration, 1986, NRFB... 65.00
Barbie, Day-to-Night, 1985, NRFB....................................... 45.00
Barbie, Dramatic New Living, 1970, MIB................................ 225.00
Barbie, Fabulous Fur, 1986, NRFB.. 65.00
Barbie, Glinda (Wizard of Oz), 2000, NRFB............................ 40.00
Barbie, Holiday, 1991, NRFB 75.00
Barbie, Live Action on Stage, 1970, NRFB.............................. 275.00
Barbie, Pepsi Spirit, 1989, Toys R Us, NRFB........................... 75.00
Barbie, Pink & Pretty, 1982, MIB 50.00
Barbie, Sun Valley, 1973, NRFB.. 125.00
Barbie, Swirl Ponytail, 1964, brunette, MIB............................ 625.00
Barbie, That Girl, 2003, Pop Culture Collection, NRFB 35.00
Barbie, Twist 'n Turn, 1969, flip hairdo, blond or brunette, NRFB...475.00
Brad, 1970, darker skin, bendable legs, NRFB.......................... 200.00
Cara, Free Moving, 1974, MIB.. 115.00
Christie, Kissing, 1979, MIB.. 50.00
Christie, Talking, 1970, MIB.. 250.00
Francie, Growin' Pretty Hair, 1971, MIB................................ 150.00
Francie, Malibu, 1971, NRFB... 50.00
Ginger, Growing Up, 1977, MIB.. 115.00
Kelley, Quick Curl, 1972, NRFB.. 80.00
Ken, 1961, flocked hair, blond or brunette, NRFB 150.00
Ken, Arabian Nights, 1964, NRFB....................................... 400.00
Ken, Free Moving, 1974, MIB 75.00
Ken, Malibu, 1976, NRFB... 30.00
Ken, Mod Hair, 1973, NRFB... 100.00
Ken, Rocker, 1986, MIB 30.00
Ken, Talking, 1970, NRFB 115.00
Ken, Walk Lively, 1972, MIB... 150.00
Midge, 1965, bendable legs, any color hair, MIB....................... 450.00
Midge, Cool Times, 1989, NRFB 15.00
PJ, Fashion Photo, 1978, MIB.. 75.00
Ricky, 1965, MIB.. 130.00
Scott, 1979, MIB.. 55.00
Skipper, 1965, bendable legs, any hair color, MIB...................... 150.00
Skipper, Malibu, 1977, MIB.. 50.00
Stacy, Twist 'n Turn, 1969, any hair color, NRFB...................... 450.00
Teresa, Rappin' Rockin', 1992, NRFB.................................... 30.00
Tutti, 1967, any hair color, MIB... 175.00
Whitney, Style Magic, 1989, NRFB...................................... 15.00

Barbie Accessories and Gift Sets

Case, Barbie, All That Jazz, 1967, NM.................................... 40.00
Case, Barbie Goes Travelin', 1965, EX+ 75.00
Case, Barbie in Party Date/Ken in Sat Night Date on blk, 1963, EX...50.00
Case, Easter Parade, 1961, EX+.. 20.00
Case, Skipper & Scooter, 1965, NM 150.00
Furniture, Barbie & Midge Queen Size Chifferobe (Susy Goose), NM..100.00
Furniture, Barbie Dream House Bedroom, 1981, MIB.....................6.00
Furniture, Barbie Fashion Living Room Set, #7404, 1984, NRFB.. 30.00
Furniture, Go-Together Chaise Lounge, MIB............................. 75.00
Gift Set, Barbie's Wedding Party, 1964, MIB............................ 700.00
Gift Set, Cinderella, 1992, NRFB... 125.00
Gift Set, Dance Sensation Barbie, 1985, MIB............................ 35.00
Gift Set, Pretty Pairs 'n Fran, 1970, NRFB.............................. 250.00
Gift Set, Skipper Party Time, 1964, NRFB............................... 500.00
House, Magical Mansion, 1989, MIB...................................... 125.00
House, Party Garden Playhouse, 1994, MIB.............................. 275.00
House, Surprise House, 1972, MIB.. 100.00
House, Tuttie Playhouse, 1966, M.. 100.00
House, World of Barbie, 1966, MIB....................................... 175.00

Outfit, Barbie, Baby Doll Pinks, #3403, 1971, NRFP 100.00
Outfit, Barbie, Bouncy Flouncy, #1805, 1967, NRFP.................... 300.00
Outfit, Barbie, Fun Fakes, #3412, 1971, NRFP 100.00
Outfit, Barbie, Movie Groovie, #1866, 1969, NRFP.................... 125.00
Outfit, Barbie, Perfectly Pink, #4805, 1984, NRFP...................... 10.00
Outfit, Barbie, Rare Pair, #1462, 1970, NRFP............................ 125.00
Outfit, Barbie, Sugar Plum Fairy, #9326, 1976, NRFP 40.00
Outfit, Francie, Hip Knits, #1265, 1966, NRFP.......................... 225.00
Outfit, Francie & Casey, Cool It! Fashion Pak, 1968, MIP 50.00
Outfit, Ken, Big Business, #1434, 1970, NRFP 75.00
Outfit, Ken, Date Night, #5651, 1983, NRFP.............................. 10.00
Outfit, Ken, Fun on Ice, #791, 1963, NRFP............................... 125.00
Outfit, Ken, Sea Scene, #1449, 1971, NRFP................................ 60.00
Outfit, Skipper, Budding Beauty, #1731, 1970, NRFP 75.00
Outfit, Skipper, Chilly Chums, #1973, 1969, NRFP................... 125.00
Room, Barbie Cookin' Fun Kitchen, MIB.................................. 100.00
Shop, Barbie Beauty Boutique, 1976, MIB.................................. 40.00
Shop, Superstar Barbie Beauty Salon, 1977, MIB........................ 55.00
Vehicle, Barbie & Ken Dune Buggy, Irwin, pk, 1970, MIB 250.00
Vehicle, Snowmobile, Montgomery Ward, 1972, MIB.................. 65.00

Belton Type

Bru-type face, EX bsk, o/c/m, wig, RpC, 12", EX 2,500.00
French-type face, bsk, o/c/m or c/m, wig, RpC, 13" 1,900.00
French-type face, bsk, o/c/m or c/m, wig, RpC, 18" 2,400.00
French-type face, bsk, o/c/m or c/m, wig, RpC, 22" 3,000.00
German-type face, bsk, o/c/m or c/m, wig, RpC, 8" 850.00
German-type face, bsk, o/c/m or c/m, wig, RpC, 15" 1,600.00
German-type face, bsk, o/c/m or c/m, wig, RpC, 20" 2,200.00

Betsy McCall

The dolls listed are with complete, original outfits and have rooted hair unless noted otherwise.

Am Character, hp, sleep eyes, jtd knees, 1957-63, OC, 8" 275.00
Am Character, hp, sleep eyes, jtd knees, 1957-63, undies only, 8" ..250.00
Am Character, Linda McCall (cousin), vinyl, Betsy face, 1959, OC, 34". 900.00

American Character, white ballerina (outfit only), MOC, minimum value, $400.00. (Photo courtesy Marci Van Ausdall)

Companion sz, vinyl, McCall Corp 1959 on head, OC, 34" 900.00
Horsman, vinyl w/hp body, sleep eyes, 1974, OC & accessories, 12½" ... 60.00
Ideal, vinyl, flat ft, slim, rnd sleep eyes, OC, 14" 400.00
Ideal, vinyl, flirty eyes, 1-pc torso, 1959, OC, 20" 350.00
Ideal, vinyl, sleep eyes, fully jtd, 1961, OC, 22"............................ 200.00
Ideal, vinyl head, hp Tony body, saran wig, 1952-53, OC, 14"..... 300.00
Rothschild, hp, sleep eyes, 35th Anniversary, 1986, OC, 8" 35.00
Uneeda, vinyl, sleep eyes, slim, 1964, OC, 11½" 125.00

Boudoir Dolls

Boudoir dolls, often called bed dolls, French dolls, or flapper dolls, were popular from the late teens through the 1940s. The era of the 1920s and 1930s was the golden age of boudoir dolls!

More common boudoir dolls are usually found with composition head, arms, and high-heeled feet. Clothes are nailed on (later ones have stapled-on clothes). Wigs are usually mohair, human hair, or silk floss. Smoking boudoir dolls were made in the late teens and early 1920s. More expensive boudoir dolls were made in France, Italy, and Germany, as well as the U.S. Usually they are all cloth with elaborate sewn or pinned-on costumes and silk, felt, or velvet painted faces. Sizes of boudoir dolls vary, but most are around 30". These dolls were made to adorn a lady's boudoir or sit on a bed. They were not meant as children's playthings! Our advisor for this category is Bonnie Groves; she is listed in the Directory under Texas.

Amelia Earhardt, cloth, silk face, M flight suit, 27" 675.00
Anita, compo & cloth, pk floss hair, 1920s, EX 330.00
Anita, OC, 27", VG 230.00
Anita, smoker, compo, 1925, OC, 27", VG 385.00
Anita, smoker, compo & cloth, 1920s, OC, 30", G 135.00
Anita, trn head, OC, 30", EX, minimum value 475.00
Apache male, cloth, OC, 26", VG, minimum value 500.00
Blossom, cloth, OC, tagged, 30", G... 600.00
Blossom, cloth, 1930s, OC, 30", EX 1,000.00
Blossom, Garbo face, OC, 20", EX, minimum value................... 1,000.00
Blossom, Pierrette, 1930s, OC, 30", VG, minimum value 500.00
Bride, 1940s, OC, 29", VG 165.00
Bucilla kit for making boudoir doll costume, EX, minimum value ..400.00
Cloth, Gerling type, 1920s, OC, 30", VG, minimum value 500.00
Cloth, long-faced egg head, 1920s, RpC, VG 200.00
Cloth, std quality, 1920s, OC, 16", EX, minimum value 265.00
Cloth, std quality, 1920s, OC, 32", EX, minimum value 325.00
Compo, std quality, 1930s-40s, OC, 28", EX, from $125 to.......... 175.00
Compo & cloth, 1930s-40s, OC, 25", NM, minimum value 75.00
Cubeb, smoker, compo, jtd, 1925, OC, 25", EX, minimum value ...900.00
Etta, cloth, OC, 30", G, minimum value 500.00
French, cloth, OC, 29", VG 355.00
French, cloth w/bsk arms & legs, tagged, 18", VG, pr.................. 395.00
French, cloth w/bsk arms & legs, 1920s, OC, 27", VG 455.00
French, topsy-turvy, cloth w/bsk arms, 21", VG, minimum value ...395.00
Gerbs, cloth, FR, 1920s, OC, 25", EX, minimum value................ 375.00
Gerbs, cloth, FR, 1920s, OC, 30", G, minimum value 300.00
German, Pierrot w/compo face, OC, 16", G 330.00
Halloween, std quality, OC, 27", minimum value........................ 500.00
Lenci, Fadette, RpC, 26", VG 2,050.00
Lenci, Fadette, smoker, 25", VG, minimum value 3,000.00
Lenci, Pierrot, OC, 26", VG.. 2,750.00
Lenci, salon lady, OC, 25", EX, minimum value......................... 3,000.00

Patriotic, standard quality, 1940s, 25", G, minimum value $200.00 each. (Photo courtesy Bonnie Groves)

Ring lady, cloth w/floss hair, 1920s, OC, 31", minimum value..... 375.00
Shoes, orig, 3", G 25.00
Shoes, repro, 3" 22.50
Silk face, bsk arms & legs, Fr, 33", VG, from $300 to.................. 600.00
Smoker, cloth, 1920s, OC, 16", EX 500.00
Smoker, cloth, 1920s, OC, 25", EX 525.00
Sterling, Halloween, 1930s, OC, 28", G, minimum value............. 400.00
Sterling, 1930, OC, 27", VG, minimum value............................. 200.00

W-K-S, compo & cloth, 1930s, OC, 25", G.................................... 50.00
W-K-S, compo head & hands, cloth body, nude, 1920s, G 40.00
W-K-S, Gypsy, OC, 25", VG, minimum value............................ 125.00
W-K-S, Remember Pearl Harbor, compo/cloth, 1940s, OC, EX .. 350.00

Bru

Bebe Automate (breathing/talking), torso mechanism, RpC, 24"... 17,000.00
Bebe Baiser (kiss-throwing), string mechanism, 1892, RpC, 15"..4,400.00
Bebe Modele, Brevete face, cvd wood body, 1880+, RpC, 18"..2,250.00
Bru Brevete, bsk SkHd, pwt eyes, c/m, wig, jtd body, RpC, 11".. 17,000.00
Bru Jne, bsk SkHd on ShPl, pwt eyes, c/m, mohair wig, RpC, 10"..21,000.00
Bru Jne R, bsk SkHd on ShPl, pwt eyes, o/m, 1891-99, RpC, 12".1,550.00
Circle dot or crescent mk, bsk swivel head, pwt eyes, hh wig, RpC, 13".15,000.00
Fashion lady, bsk SkHd w/spring, kid body, RpC, 13"................4,200.00
Fashion lady, bsk SkHd w/spring, smiling c/m, kid body/arms, RpC, 11".3,700.00
Fashion lady, bsk SkHd w/spring, wood lower arms, kid body, RpC, 17"..6,000.00
Fashion lady, bsk SkHd w/spring, wooden body, RpC, 18"........8,500.00
Nurser, o/m, screw key at bk of head, RpC, 13" 9,000.00

China

1840 style, center part w/bun or coronet, pk tint, RpC, 13"......2,200.00
1840 style, center part w/sausage curls, pk tint, RpC, 7" 325.00
1840 style, center part w/sausage curls, pk tint, RpC, 14" 650.00
1840 style, KPM, lady, brn hair w/bun, RpC, 16" 6,500.00
1840 style, KPM on ShPl, lady, pk tint, RpC, 15" 2,800.00
1850 style, Alice in Wonderland, snood/headband, RpC, 12" 675.00
1850 style, bald head, hh or mohair wig, RpC, 12"..................... 800.00
1850 style, fashion lady, pnt eyes, kid body, wig, RpC, 12"........2,900.00
1850 style, Greiner type, glass eyes, varied hairdos, RpC, 13"..3,700.00
1850 style, Greiner type, pnt eyes, various hairdos, RpC, 18"...1,800.00
1850 style, high forehead, curls, rnd face, RpC, 13" 300.00
1850 style, high forehead, curls, rnd face, RpC, 15" 500.00
1850 style, lady w/morning glories molded in brn hair, RpC, 21"..8,000.00
1850 style, molded necklace, RpC, 21" 700.00
1850 style, young Queen Victoria, molded braids, RpC, 18".....2,600.00
1860 style, Conta & Boehme, p/e, RpC, 18" 1,400.00
1860 style, Currier & Ives, long hair on shoulders, RpC, 15"....... 700.00
1860 style, Dolly Madison, molded brow, RpC, 20"..................... 750.00
1860 style, flat-top blk hair, center part, swivel neck, RpC, 15".. 1,400.00
1860 style, flat-top blk hair w/center part/curls, RpC, 24"........... 475.00
1860 style, man w/curls, RpC, 17"..1,800.00
1860 style, Mary Todd Lincoln, blk hair, gold snood, RpC, 18".. 1,100.00
1860 style, Mary Todd Lincoln, blond w/snood, RpC, 16" 1,100.00
1870 style, Adelina Patti, center part w/ringlets at bk, RpC, 15". 500.00
1870 style, blk hair w/full bangs, RpC, 14" 400.00
1870 style, blond hair w/full bangs, RpC, 18" 550.00
1870 style, Jenny Lind, blk hair pulled bk into bun, RpC, 15"...1,550.00
1870 style, ShHd, fine pnt, pk tint, blk or blond hair, RpC, 16"..400.00
1880 style, Bawo & Dotter, Pat 1880, RpC, 18" 425.00
1880 style, child, blk or blond curls, RpC, 16"............................. 425.00
1890 style, center-part wavy hairdo, jeweled necklace, RpC, 20". 425.00
1890 style, center-part wavy hairdo, short forehead, RpC, 8" 125.00
1890 style, center-part wavy hairdo, short forehead, RpC, 10" 175.00
1899-1933, Agnes, Bertha, Daisy, etc, German mfg, RpC, 9" 150.00
1910-20, Japan, mk or unmk, blk or blond hair, RpC, 10" 125.00
1950 style, Alice in Wonderland, snood/headband, RpC, 20" ..1,150.00

Cloth Dolls

A cloth doll in very good condition will display light wear and soiling, while one assessed as excellent will be clean and bright. Our values are for dolls in excellent condition.

Arnold Printworks, Brownie, 1892-1907, 7½", from $75 to 100.00
Arnold Printworks, Dolly Dear, Flaked Rice, etc, printed undies, 9".. 95.00
Art Fabric Mills, printed, 16" 125.00
Chad Valley, Grenadier Guard, glass eyes, 1930s, OC, 21" 1,200.00
Dollywood Studios, Miss Catalina, pnt bl eyes, ca 1946, OC, 13" ..100.00
Foxy Grandpa, 18", from $200 to 225.00
Georgene Averill, Dutch girl, mask face, yarn hair, 1930s-40s, 13"..75.00
Gorham, Taffy, Sweet Inspirations, molded face, brn curls, 1985, 19"..50.00
Improved Life Sz Doll, printed undies, 1876+, 16-18", from $125 to.150.00
JB Sheppard & Co, Philadelphia Baby, oil-pnt head, ca 1900, OC, 21"..750.00
Martha Chase baby, oil-pnt stockinette head, 1889+, 27"........... 385.00
Molly, Susette of France, mask face, blk yarn hair, 1940s, OC, 14"...75.00
Peck, Santa Claus, printed, Pat 1886, 14½" 275.00
Saalfield, Golden Locks Girl, litho on cloth, c 1908, 24" 165.00
Tiny Town, thread wrapped, wht wig, pnt features, 1940s, OC, 4½".. 35.00

Effanbee

Bernard Fleischaker and Hugo Baum became business partners in 1910, and after two difficult years of finding toys to buy, they decided to manufacture dolls and toys of their own. The Effanbee trademark is a blending of their names, Eff for Fleischaker and bee for Baum. The company still exists today. For more information we recommend *Collector's Encyclopedia of American Composition Dolls, 1900 – 1950*, by Ursula R. Mertz. Unless noted otewise, values are for early dolls in excellent condition; mint values reflect the worth of later dolls.

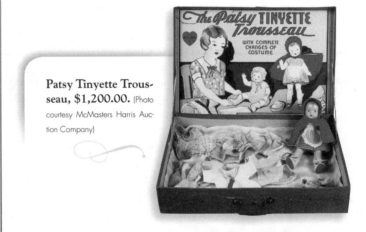

Patsy Tinyette Trousseau, $1,200.00. (Photo courtesy McMasters Harris Auction Company)

Alyssa, vinyl/hp, o/c/e, jtd body, walker, 1960-61, OC, 23", M....225.00
Ann Shirley, all compo, grown-up body style, 1936-40, OC, 15"....275.00
Baby Bud, Black, compo, pnt features, o/c/m, RpC, 1918+, 6".....225.00
Baby Dainty, compo/cloth, 1912+, OC, 12" 240.00
Baby Effanbee, compo/cloth, 1925, OC, 12-13", from $165 to 185.00
Baby Evelyn, compo/cloth, 1925, OC, 17", from $250 to.............275.00
Baby Grumpy Gladys, compo ShHd, cloth body, 1923, OC, 15".325.00
Babyette, compo, eyes molded closed, 1943, OC, 13", from $325 to ..400.00
Betty Bounce, compo w/tousel head, o/c/e, 1932+, OC, 19"........400.00
Bubbles, compo ShHd, o/c/m, pnt eyes, toddler, 1924+, OC, 18"...425.00
Button Nose, vinyl head, cloth body, 1968-71, OC, 18", M...........30.00
Candy Kid, all compo, o/c/e, toddler, 1946+, OC, 13" 425.00
Christina, all vinyl, jtd, rooted hair, 1984, OC, 15", M.................110.00
Flower girl, all vinyl, 1984 only, OC, M..95.00
Fluffy, all vinyl, Girl Scout, 1954+, OC, 10".................................75.00
Grumpykins, compo/cloth, 1927, OC, 12"...................................300.00
Harmonica Joe, cloth body, rubber ball provides air, 1923, OC, 15"..450.00
Historical replica, all compo, jtd body, hh wigs, 1939+, OC, 14"....600.00
Honey Walker, hp, walker, 1952+, OC, 14" 350.00
Ice Queen, compo, o/m, 1937+, orig skater outfit, 17" 850.00
Johnny Tu-face, compo head, crying o/c/m, 1912, OC, 16" 425.00

Lamkin, compo/cloth, o/c/e, o/m, curled fingers, 1930+, OC, 16" ..475.00
Little Lady, compo, o/c/e, wig, 1939+, OC, 18" 450.00
Mae Starr, compo ShHd, cloth body, talker, 1928, OC, 29".........750.00
Miss Chips, vinyl, o/c/e, fully jtd, rooted hair, 1966-81, OC, 17", M . 45.00
Pat-a-Pat, compo/cloth, pnt eyes, claps hands, 1925+, OC, 15" ..200.00
Patrica Joan, compo, o/c/e, slim body, wig, 1935, OC, 16" 650.00
Patsy, compo/cloth, o/m w/teeth, o/c/e, hh wig, 1924, OC, 15" ...350.00
Patsy Ann, vinyl, o/c/e, 1959 ltd ed, OC, 15", M 265.00
Patsy Baby, compo w/molded hair, 1931, OC, 10-11", from $350 to 375.00
Patsy Joan, compo, 1931, OC, 16" 550.00
Patsy Mae, compo ShHd, cloth body, o/c/e, swing legs, 1934, OC, 29" 1,600.00
Patsyette/Ann Shirley, compo, mk Effanbee Patsyette Doll, OC, 9½" 325.00
Polka Dottie, vinyl/cloth, molded pigtails, 1954, OC, 21" 165.00
Sister, compo/cloth, pnt eyes, yarn hair, OC, 12" 275.00
Susie Sunshine, vinyl, o/c/e, jtd, rooted hair, 1961-79, OC, 18", M..60.00
Suzette, compo, pnt eyes, c/m, fully jtd, wig, 1939, OC, 12" 325.00
WC Fields, compo ShHd, hinged mouth, 1929+, OC, 17½" 950.00
Wee Patsy, head molded to body, 1935, OC, 5¾" 450.00

Half Dolls

Half dolls were never meant to be objects of play. Most were modeled after the likenesses of lovely ladies, though children and animals were represented as well. Most of the ladies were firmly sewn onto pincushion bases that were beautifully decorated and served as the skirts of their gowns. Other skirts were actually covers for items on milady's dressing table. Some were used as parasol or brush handles or as tops to candy containers or perfume bottles. Most popular from 1900 to about 1930, they will most often be found marked with the area of their origin, usually Bavaria, Germany, France, and Japan. You may also find some fine quality pieces marked Goebel, Dressel and Kester, KPM, and Heubach.

Arms away, china or bsk, bald head w/wig, 6"................................210.00
Arms away, dome head, wig, Goebel mk, 5" 195.00

Arms away, Dressel & Kister mark, molded hair and hat, M, 3½", $300.00. (Photo courtesy McMasters Harris Auction Company)

Arms away, flamenco dancer, pincushion, 6" 430.00
Arms away, holding item, 4"...185.00
Arms away, mk by maker or mold #, 6" 300.00
Arms away, mk by maker or mold #, 12" 900.00
Arms in, close to figure, bald head w/wig, 6"................................115.00
Arms in, decorated bodice, necklace, fancy hair or holding article, 3" . 125.00
Arms in, hands attached, 5" 45.00
Arms in, mk by maker or mold #, 5" 135.00
Arms in, papier-maché or compo, 6"..80.00
Arms in, w/legs, dressed, fancy decor, 5" 300.00
Jtd shoulders, china or bsk, molded hair, 7" 200.00
Jtd shoulders, solid dome, mohair wig, 6".....................................400.00
Man or child, 6"...160.00
Mk Germany, 6"..400.00
Mk Japan, 3" 25.00
Mk Japan, 6" 50.00

Handwerck, Heinrich

#69, child, bsk SkHd, o/m, o/c/e or set eyes, wig, Rpc, 10"..........500.00
#79, bsk ShHd, o/m, o/c/e or set eyes, kid body, RpC, 18"............575.00
#79, child, bsk SkHd, c/m, o/c/e or set eyes, wig, RpC, 20".......2,400.00
#89, child, bsk ShHd, c/m, o/c/e or set eyes, wig, RpC, 26".........800.00
#99, child, bsk SkHd, o/m, o/c/e or set eyes, wig, RpC, 36".......1,800.00
#119, child, bsk SkHd, o/m, o/c/e or set eyes, wig, RpC, 22"........700.00
#139 or no #, child, bsk ShHd, o/m, glass eyes, kid body, RpC, 12" ...225.00
#139 or no #, child, bsk ShHd, o/m, glass eyes, kid body, RpC, 18" ...350.00
#189, child, bsk SkHd, o/m, o/c/e or set eyes, wig, RpC, 15"........850.00

Hertel, Schwab, and Company

#126, so-called Skippy, toddler body, RpC, 9" 875.00
#127, child, character face, dome w/molded hair, o/c/e, RpC, 15".. 1,450.00
#130, baby, bsk head, o/m or o/c/m w/teeth, sleep eyes, RpC, 12". 475.00
#131, child, character face, solid dome, pnt c/m, ca 1912, RpC, 18"..1,300.00
#134, child, character face, o/c/e, c/m, ca 1915, RpC, 15" 4,000.00
#136, child, character face, Made in Germany, ca 1912, RpC, 24"..600.00
#140, child, character face, glass eyes, laughing, ca 1912, RpC, 12"...3,400.00
#142, bsk head, o/m/teeth, o/c/e or pnt eyes, RpC, 19" 575.00
#150, baby, bsk head w/molded hair, o/c/e, compo body, RpC, 22"..650.00
#152, bsk head, molded hair, o/m, toddler body, RpC, 20"...........800.00

Heubach, Ernst

#250, baby, SkHd, o/m, glass eyes, 5-pc compo body, wig, RpC, 5"..250.00
#250, child, o/m, kid body, RpC, 8" 175.00
#261, character child, bsk ShHd, pnt eyes, cloth body, RpC, 12" . 400.00
#275, child, ShHd, o/m, kid body, RpC, 16" 300.00
#300, baby, SkHd, o/m, glass eyes, 5-pc body, RpC, 14" 400.00
#302, pnt bsk, o/m, kid body, RpC, 16"...............................225.00
#338, newborn baby, solid dome w/pnt hair, c/m, glass eyes, RpC, 12"...425.00

#342, toddler, 10", $800.00. (Photo courtesy McMasters Harris Auction Company)

#1900, child, ShHd, o/m, glass eyes, kid or cloth body, RpC, 12" ...150.00
#1900, ShHd, o/m, glass eyes, kid or cloth body, RpC, 26" 550.00

Heubach, Gebruder

#764, SkHd, o/c/m w/2 teeth, ca 1912, RpC, 14" 6,200.00
#5636, SkHd, glass eyes, laughing o/c/m w/teeth, RpC, 15"......2,300.00
#5730, Santa, SkHd, made for Hamburger & Co, RpC, 16" 1,700.00
#5777, Dolly Dimple, ShHd, RpC, 19" 1,100.00
#5777, Dolly Dimple, SkHd, o/m, for Hamburger & Co, RpC, 16"...2,600.00
#6688, character child, molded hair, intaglio eyes, RpC, 10".......625.00
#6692, character, ShHd, intaglio eyes, c/m pouty, RpC, 20" 900.00
#6736, character child, sq pnt eyes, laughing/m, RpC, 13" 1,100.00
#6811, SkHd, intaglio eyes, laughing o/c/m, ca 1912, RpC, 11" ..600.00

#6894, character baby, SkHd, bent-limb body, RpC, 7" 350.00
#6969, SkHd, glass eyes, c/m, RpC, 9" 1,250.00
#7268, SkHd, glass eyes, c/m, RpC, 12" 5,000.00
#7681, dome head, intaglio eyes, c/m, RpC, 12" 575.00
#7759, character baby, intaglio eyes, c/m, bent-limb body, RpC, 20".. 1,000.00
#7761, character baby, intaglio eyes, crying o/c/m, RpC, 16" 7,200.00
#7852, character child, molded hair in braids, RpC, 16" 2,200.00
#8381, Princess Juliana, molded hair/ribbon, pnt eyes, c/m, RpC, 16"... 13,000.00
#8940, laughing girl, bl hair bow, RpC, 18" 7,200.00
No mold #, adult, o/m, glass eyes, mk Heubach, RpC, 14" 4,500.00
No mold #, o/c/m, dimples, RpC, mk Heubach, 18" 4,450.00

Horsman

Baby Bumps, Black, compo, cloth body, cork stuffing, orig romper, 11"..350.00
Baby Bumps, compo/cloth, cork stuffing, orig romper, 11" 250.00
Baby Butterfly (Oriental), compo head/hands, ca 1913, OC, 15" ...400.00
Baby Twist, compo, jtd waist, OC, 11" 250.00
Billiken, compo/cloth, molded hair, slanted eyes, OC, 12" 400.00
Campbell Kid, all compo, 1930-40s, OC, 13" 475.00
Campbell Kid, compo head/arms, cloth body/ft, 1910+, OC, 11" ...350.00
Can't Break 'Em character, Cotton Joe, Black, OC, 13" 400.00
Can't Break 'Em character boy or girl, 1911+, OC, 11-13", ea $200 to..275.00
Ella Cinders, compo/cloth, o/c/m, pnt hair or wig, OC, 14" 450.00
Gene Carr Kid, Snowball, Black, compo, o/c/m w/teeth, OC, 14"..550.00
Gold Metal Baby, compo head/limbs, 1911+, OC, 12" 300.00

Indian girl, composition flange head with painted eyes, cloth body with composition arms and legs, Campbell Kid mold, original tagged outfit, marked E.I.H. Co. Inc, 13", VG, $225.00.
(McMasters Harris Auction Company)

Peek-a-Boo, all compo, Grace Drayton design, OC, 8" 125.00
Tynie Baby, bsk or compo head, cloth body, 1924-29, OC, 21".... 425.00

Ideal

Two of Ideal's most collectible lines of dolls are Crissy and Toni. For more information, refer to *Collector's Guide to Ideal Dolls, Third Edition*, by Judith Izen (Collector Books).

Baby, compo/cloth, o/c/e or sleep eyes, pnt hair or wig, OC, 16" .. 250.00
Buster Brown, compo/cloth, tin eyes, OC, 17" 375.00
Charlie McCarthy, hand puppet, compo/felt/cloth, Edgar Bergen's, 8"..60.00
Child/toddler, compo/cloth, o/c/e, wig, OC, 15" 250.00
Cracker Jack boy, compo/cloth, sailor suit, 1917, 14" 375.00
Deanna Durbin, all compo, brn o/c/e, o/m/teeth, OC, 15" 550.00
Deanna Durbin, all compo, brn o/c/e, o/m/teeth, wig, OC, 24" ... 1,300.00
Flossie Flirt, compo/cloth, crier, tin flirty eyes, OC, 14" 250.00
Flossie Flirt, compo/cloth, crier, tin flirty eyes, OC, 22" 375.00
Happy Hooligan, compo/cloth, 1910s, OC, 21" 525.00
Naughty Marietta, Coquette type, compo/cloth, 1912, OC, 14" .. 150.00
Princess Beatrix, compo/cloth, flirty o/c/e, OC, 16" 275.00

Snoozie, compo/rubber/cloth, yawning o/m, OC, 14" 200.00
Snow White, cloth mask face, cloth body, blk mohair wig, OC, 16" .550.00
Soozie Smiles, compo head w/2 faces, cloth body, OC, 15" 375.00
Sparkle Plenty, hp, Magic Skin body, yarn hair, all orig, 14" 200.00
Tickletoes, compo/rubber/cloth, flirty o/c/e, o/m, OC, 20" 350.00
Uneeda Kid, compo/cloth, OC w/rain slicker & biscuit box, 16".. 500.00

Toni, hard plastic, sleep eyes with real lashes, five-piece body, tagged dress, ca. 1949, red metal trunk with additional wardrobe, $355.00.
(Photo courtesy McMasters Harris Auction Company)

Jumeau

The Jumeau factory became the best known name for dolls during the 1880s and 1890s. Early dolls were works of art with closed mouths and paperweight eyes. When son Emile Jumeau took over, he patented sleep eyes with eyelids that drooped down over the eyes. This model also had flirty (eyes that move from side to side) eyes and is extremely rare. Over 98% of Jumeau dolls have paperweight eyes. The less-expensive German dolls were the downfall of the French doll manufacturers, and in 1899 the Jumeau company had to combine with several others in an effort to save the French doll industry from German competition.

#230, child, SkHd, glass eyes, o/m, compo body, RpC, 12" 1,100.00
BL Bebe, SkHd, pwt/e, c/m, p/e, wig, jtd body, RpC, 18" 4,200.00
Depose above E # J mk, bsk SkHd, pwt/e, p/e, wig, 16" 7,000.00
Depose Jumeau & sz #, poured bsk head, pwt/e, c/m, p/e, RpC, 20" ...6,400.00
EJ Bebe, # over initals, bsk SkHd, pwt/e, c/m, wig, RpC, 18"..10,250.00
Fashion type, #d swivel head, c/m, pwt/e, p/e, kid body, RpC, 13" ...2,900.00
Fashion type, #d swivel head, c/m, pwt/e, p/e, kid body, RpC, 18" ...3,800.00
Fashion type, #d swivel head, c/m, pwt/e, p/e, wood body, RpC, 14" .. 5,200.00
Fashion type, #d swivel head, portrait face, wood body, RpC, 21"... 12,000.00
Long-face bebe, # only on head, pwt/e, c/m, p/e, mk body, RpC, 23" ...24,000.00
Phonograph in torso, bsk head, o/m, working, RpC, 25" 8,000.00
Portrait child, almond pwt/e, c/m, p/e, wig, 1st series, RpC, 14½".. 1,650.00
RR Bebe, pwt/e, c/m, jtd compo body, wig, RpC, 23" 4,800.00
Tete Jemeau, bsk SkHd w/red stamp, glass eyes, c/m, wig, RpC, 10". 10,000.00
Tete Jumeau, bsk SkHd w/red stamp, glass eyes, p/e, RpC, 24"..10,200.00

Kammer and Reinhardt

#100, character baby, solid dome, intaglio eyes, o/c/m, RpC, 14" 500.00
#101, character, Marie, pnt eyes, c/m, jtd body, RpC, 17" 4,100.00
#101, Peter, pnt eyes, c/m, jtd body, RpC, 10" 2,400.00
#102, character, Elsa, pnt eyes, molded hair, c/m, RpC, 14" 32,000.00
#103, glass eyes, pout c/m, OC, 20" 2,500.00
#107, Karl, pnt intaglio eyes, c/m, RpC, 12" 1,300.00
#109, Elise, pnt eyes, c/m, RpC, 10" 35.00
#115, solid dome, pnt hair, o/c/e, c/m, toddler body, RpC, 12" .2,200.00
#117, Mein Liebling, glass eyes, c/m, RpC, 14" 3,800.00
#117X, SkHd, o/c/e, o/m, RpC, 22" 1,300.00
#118A, o/c/e, o/m, baby body, RpC, 11" 1,200.00
#121, o/c/e, o/m, toddler body, RpC, 10" 1,000.00
#126, Mein Liebling Baby, flirty eyes, bent-leg baby, RpC, 10" 475.00
#128, bsk SkHd, o/c/m, glass eyes, jtd body, OC, 12" 2,000.00

#128, o/c/e, o/m, baby body, RpC, 10" 600.00
#142, child, bsk SkHd, glass eyes, o/m, bjtd body, OC, 8" 575.00
#143, character, SkHd, glass eyes, o/m, jtd body, OC, 8" 950.00
#145, child, ShHd, o/c/e, o/m, plaster pate, kid body, wig, OC, 16" ...350.00
#146, child, bsk SkHd, glass eyes, o/m, bjtd body, OC, 20" 900.00
#155, child, bsk SkHd, glass eyes, o/m, 5-pc body, OC, 32" 900.00
#172, Gibson Girl, ShHd, glass eyes, c/m, kid body, OC, 10" 950.00
#192, bsk SkHd, o/c/e, c/m, jtd compo body, RpC, 7" 700.00
#192, child, bsk SkHd, o/c/e, jtd compo body, RpC, 22" 2,700.00
#192, child, bsk SkHd, o/c/e, o/m, jtd compo body, RpC, 18" 900.00
#210, solid-dome ShHd, o/c/e, o/c/m, OC, 12" 1,000.00
#214, ShHd, pnt eyes, c/m, muslin body, RpC, 15" 2,600.00
#237, Hilda, bald solid dome, o/c/e, o/m, OC, 11" 1,900.00
#239, SkHd, o/c/e, o/m, toddler, OC, 15" 3,600.00
#241, SkHd, o/c/e, o/m, OC, 18" 5,100.00
#246, SkHd, o/c/e, o/m, OC, 16" 1,900.00
JDK, solid dome bsk SkHd, glass o/c/e, bent-leg, RpC, 12" 550.00
Lady, bsk SkHd, glass eyes, o/m, compo body, OC, 16" 1,300.00
No mold #, child, dolly face, jtd compo body, RpC, 12" 475.00
No mold #, child, ShHd, kid body, RpC, 22" 475.00
No mold #, sq face, c/m, OC, 16" 2,200.00
No mold # or mold #191/#401/#402/#403, dolly face, 5-pc body, RpC, 7" ..475.00
Sz # only, child, bsk ShHd, glass eyes, plaster pate, c/m, wig, 14" .. 550.00
Sz # only, child, ShHd, glass eyes, plaster pate, o/m, wig, OC, 22" ..500.00
Sz # only, trn ShHd, c/m, OC, 22" 850.00

Lenci

Characteristics of Lenci dolls include seamless, steam-molded felt heads, quality clothing, childishly plump bodies, and painted eyes that glance to the side. Fine mohair wigs were used, and the middle and fourth fingers were sewn together. Look for the factory stamp on the foot, though paper labels were also used. The Lenci factory continues today, producing dolls of the same high quality. Values are for dolls in excellent condition — no moth holes, very little fading. Dolls from the 1940s, 1950s, and beyond generally bring the lower prices; add for tags, boxes, and accessories. Mint dolls and rare examples bring higher prices. Dolls in only good condition are worth approximately 25% of one rated excellent.

Spanish lady, glass eyes, five-piece body, tagged outfit, 19", $1,500.00. (Photo courtesy McMasters Harris Auction Company)

Benedetta, 18", from $1,000 to 1,100.00
Child, hard face, less ornate costume, 1940s-50s, 13" 400.00
Child, softer face, ornate costume, 1920s-30s, 13", from $1,300 to 1,500.00
Child, softer scowling face (model #1500), ornate costume, 1920s, 17" .2,200.00
Cupid, 17" 5,200.00
Eugenia, regional costume, 25" 1,100.00
Flirty glass eyes, 15" 2,200.00
Flower girl, ca 1930, 20" 1,400.00
Golfer, ca 1930, 17", VG+ 2,700.00
Madame Butterfly, ca 1926, 25" 4,800.00

Mascotte, regional costume, 9", from $350 to 375.00
Modern, 1979+, 13", from $95 to 125.00
Modern, 1979+, 21", from $150 to 200.00
Pan, hoofed ft, 8" 1,000.00
Spanish girl, ca 1930, 17" 1,000.00
Tom Mix, 18" 3,500.00

Madame Alexander

Beatrice Alexander founded the Alexander Doll Company in 1923 by making an all-cloth, oil-painted face, Alice in Wonderland doll. With the help of her three sisters, the company prospered; and by the late 1950s there were over 600 employees making Madame Alexander dolls. The company still produces these lovely dolls today. For more information, refer to *Collector's Encyclopedia of Madame Alexander Dolls* and *Madame Alexander Collector's Doll Price Guide* by Linda Crowsey. Both are published by Collector Books. In the listings that follow, values represent dolls in mint condition; those made after 1972 must have their original boxes to qualify for these prices.

American Indian, compo, Little Betty, 1938-39, 9" 375.00
Anna Ballerina, compo, Pavlova (Wendy Ann), 1940, 18", minimum value..950.00
Baby Betty, compo, 1933-36, 10-12" 300.00
Baby Brother or Sister, cloth/vinyl, Mary Mine, 1977-79, 20", ea ...125.00
Baby Lynn, compo/vinyl, 1973-76, 20" 125.00
Blue Boy, cloth, 1930s, 16" 650.00
Bobby Q, cloth, 1940-42 .... 750.00
Bridesman, compo, Little Betty, 1937-39, 9" 350.00
Bonnie Walker, hp, skater, 1955, 15", minimum value 700.00
Caroline, vinyl, riding habit, 1961-62, 15" 375.00
Carrot Top, cloth, 1967, 21" 125.00
Chatterbox, plastic/vinyl talker, 1961, 24" 250.00
Country Cousins, cloth, 1940s, 26" 650.00
Danish, compo, Tiny Betty, 1937-41, 7" 325.00
Dilly Dally Sally, compo, Tiny Betty, 1937-42 .... 325.00
Dude Ranch, hp, Wendy Ann, 1955, #449, 8", minimum value .. 750.00
Easter Sunday, hp, American Series, 1993, #340 or #340-1, 8", ea....65.00
Edith the Lonely Doll, plastic/vinyl, Mary-Bel, 1958-59, 16" 325.00
Emily, cloth/felt, 1930s 600.00
Fairy Princess, compo, Wendy Ann, 1939, 11" 425.00
Flower Child, Maggie, 1999, #17790, 8" 60.00
Flower Girl, compo, Princess Elizabeth, 1939, 1944-47, 16-18" ... 650.00
Flower Girl, hp, Margaret, 1954, 15", minimum value 800.00
Get Well, hp, red striped outfit/vase of flowers, 1998-99, #21090, 8". 65.00

Glamour Girl, hard plastic, sleep eyes, all original, 1953, 18", NM, $,1900.00. (Photo courtesy McMasters Harris Auction Company)

Gold Rush, hp, Cissette, 1963, 10" 1,400.00
Grandma Jane, plastic/vinyl, Mary Ann, 1970-72, #1420, 14" 225.00
Happy, cloth/vinyl, 1970, 20" 200.00
Heidi, compo, Tiny Betty, 1938-39, 7" 325.00

Hiawatha, hp, Wendy Ann (Americana Series), 1967-69, #720, 8"..375.00
Japanese Bride, in kimono, #28590, 10".......................................125.00
Karen Ballerina, compo, Margaret, 1946-49, 15", minimum value ..950.00
Kelly, hp, Lissy, 1959, 12" 500.00
Lady Lee, Storybook Series, 1988, #442, 8" 60.00
Laura Ingalls, Mary Ann (Classic Series), 1989-91, #1531, 14"..... 85.00
Little Bo Peep, compo, Little Betty/Wendy Ann, 1936-40, 9-11"...350.00
Melinda, plastic/vinyl, party dress, 22" 475.00
Mimi, hp, jtd, in formal, 1961, 30"...950.00
Mistress Mary, compo, Tiny Betty, 1937-41, 7" 375.00
Natasha, Jacqueline, 1989-90, brn & paisley brocade, #2255, 21"..325.00
Nina Ballerina, compo, Little Betty, 1939-41, 9"........................375.00
Oliver Twist, compo, Tiny Betty, 1935-36, 7"..............................300.00
Patty, plastic/vinyl, 1965, 18"...275.00
Persia, compo, Tiny Betty, 1936-38, 7"......................................300.00
Pitty Pat, cloth, 1950s, 16" 475.00
Red Riding Hood, compo, Tiny Betty, 7".....................................375.00
Rodeo, hp, Wendy Ann, 1955, #483, 8", minimum value...........850.00
Ruffles the Clown, 1954, 21"...425.00
Scarlett O'Hara, compo, Wendy Ann, 1941-43, 14-15"...............800.00
So Lite Baby or Toddler, cloth, 1930s-40s, 20", ea minimum value.. 375.00
South American, compo, Little Betty, 1939-41, 9"......................325.00
Tommy, hp, Lissy, 1962, 12" 800.00
Victoria, hp, Margaret, 1950-51, 14"...900.00
Virginia Dare, compo, Little Betty, 1940-41, 9" 450.00
Wendy Ann, compo, pnt eyes, 1936-40, 9"..................................375.00

Papier-Maché

Clown, pnt face, c/m, wig, cloth body, RpC, 14" 485.00
French child, brighter coloring, wig, ethnic costume, 13" 125.00
French type (Germany), ShHd, glass eyes, pnt hair, o/m, RpC, 14"...1,700.00
French type (Germany), ShHd, pnt eyes, pnt blk hair, RpC, 12"..800.00
Milliner's type, 'Apollo' topknot, sm waist, kid body, RpC, 16" .1,900.00
Milliner's type, braided bun, sm waist, kid body, 11" 1,100.00
Milliner's type, coiled braids over ears, braided bun, RpC, 11" .1,100.00
Milliner's type, molded bonnet, kid body, wooden limbs, RpC, 15".1,700.00
Patent Washable, ShHd w/mohair wig, glass eyes, G quality, RpC, 12".175.00
Patent Washable, ShHd w/mohair wig, o/m or c/m, EX quality, RpC, 18" 700.00
Pre-Grenier type, ShHd, molded/pnt blk hair, glass eyes, RpC, 22".1,900.00
ShHd, molded pnt hair, pnt eyes, wood limbs, RpC, 12"..............675.00
ShHd, molded/pnt hair, glass eyes, wood limbs, RpC, 24".........2,400.00
ShHd, molded/pnt hair w/long curls, pnt eyes, wood limbs, RpC, 16" 1,550.00

Parian

Alice in Wonderland, molded headband or comb, RpC, 10" 1,300.00
Countess Dagmar, headband, curls on forehead, unmk, RpC, 21" ...1,300.00
Empress Eugenie, headpc snood, RpC, 25" 1,300.00
Lady, common hairdo, molded bodice, fancy trim, RpC, 17" 800.00
Lady, common hairdo, no decor, cloth body, RpC, 1850-90+, 15"..325.00
Lady, fancy hairdo, glass eyes, p/e, RpC, 20" 2,700.00
Lady, fancy hairdo, pnt eyes, p/e, RpC, 16"..............................900.00
Lady, fancy hairdo, swivel neck, glass eyes, RpC, 15" 2,700.00
Lady w/molded hat, blond or blk pnt hair, pnt eyes, RpC, 19"..2,900.00
Man or boy, glass eyes, RpC, 16" 2,800.00
Man or boy, pnt eyes, decor shirt & tie, RpC, 13" 775.00

Schoenhut

Albert Schoenhut left Germany in 1866 to go to Pennsylvania to work as a repairman for toy pianos. He eventually applied his skills to wooden toys and later designed an all-wood doll which he patented on January 17, 1911. These uniquely jointed dolls were painted with enam-els and came with a metal stand. Some of the later dolls had stuffed bodies, voice boxes, and hollow heads. Due to the changing economy and fierce competition, the company closed in the mid-1930s.

Baby Boy, wig, pnt eyes, RpC, 12", EX..200.00
Baby Girl, pnt hair & eyes, bent arms & legs, RpC, 13", EX........300.00
Character Boy, #309, wig, intaglio eyes, smiling, 16", VG 3,025.00
Character Girl, #16/306, wig, intaglio eyes, c/m, OC, 16" 4,125.00
Girl, cvd bobbed hair w/headband, intaglio eyes, OC, 17", EX.1,550.00
Girl, wig, intaglio eyes, OC, 14", VG 700.00
Girl, wig, intaglio eyes, RpC, 16", VG 600.00

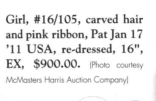

Girl, #16/105, carved hair and pink ribbon, Pat Jan 17 '11 USA, re-dressed, 16", EX, $900.00. (Photo courtesy McMasters Harris Auction Company)

Griziana Boy, cvd hair combed forward, intaglio eyes, OC, 16½", VG1,980.00
Griziana Girl, human hair wig/middle part, intaglio eyes, OC, 16", EX3,575.00
Miss Dolly, wig, pnt eyes, OC, 19½", VG 250.00
Nature Boy, pnt hair, spring-jtd, RpC, 12½", G 110.00
Toddler Boy, wig, pnt eyes, OC, 11", G+......................................200.00
Toddler Girl, wig, intaglio eyes, RpC, 16", VG.............................400.00
Walker Boy, wig, intaglio eyes, closed mouth, RpC, EX 350.00
Walker Girl, wig, intaglio eyes, OC, 16", VG................................300.00

SFBJ

By 1895 Germany was producing dolls at much lower prices than the French dollmakers could, so to save the doll industry, several leading French manufacturers united to form one large company. Bru, Raberry and Delphieu, Pintel and Godshaux, Fleischman and Bodel, Jumeau, and many others united to form the company Society Francaise de Fabrication de Bebes et Jouets (SFBJ).

#60, child, bsk head, glass eyes, o/m, p/e, RpC, 18" 550.00
#226, character face, glass eyes, c/m, rpC, 20" 2,200.00
#227, bsk SkHd, glass eyes, o/m/teeth, RpC, 17" 2,200.00
#230, character face, glass eyes, o/m/teeth, RpC, 22" 1,200.00
#233, character face, glass eyes, crying/m, RpC, 16" 4,000.00
#247, character face, glass eyes, o/c/m, RpC, 13" 2,100.00
#250, character face, o/m/teeth, RpC, 18" 3,400.00
#252, baby, glass eyes, pouty c/m, RpC, 15" 4,000.00
#301, child, bsk head, 5-pc body, RpC, 8"....................................200.00
Jumeau type, no mold #, o/m, glass eyes, RpC, 28" 2,300.00
Jumeau type, no mold #, o/m, RpC, 15" 1,000.00
Kiss thrower, child, bsk head, glass eyes, o/m, p/e, RpC, 24" 1,750.00

Shirley Temple

Prices are suggested for dolls in excellent condition, in complete original outfits, and made by the Ideal Toy Company unless noted otherwise.

Baby Shirley, compo, gr o/c/e, o/m/teeth, mohair wig, 1934-40s, 18"..1,100.00
Bsk, unlicensed Japanese, 6"..225.00

Celluloid, unlicensed Japanese, Dutch girl, 1937+, 13".............. 320.00
Celluloid, unlicensed Japanese, 5".. 175.00
Compo, gr o/c eys, o/m/teeth, mohair wig, 1934-40s, 22"......... 1,150.00
Compo, gr o/c/e, o/m/teeth, mohair wig, 1934-40s, 16".............. 775.00
Compo, Hawaiian Marama, blk yarn hair, Ideal, 18".................. 950.00
Compo, unlicensed Japanese, molded brn curls pnt eyes, 7½"...... 275.00

Composition, 27", wig, original clothing, VG+, $600.00. (Photo courtesy McMasters Harris Auction Company)

Vinyl, o/c/e, rooted wig, o/c/m/teeth, mk ST//12 on head, 12"..... 375.00
Vinyl, 1960, jtd wrists, mk ST-35-38-2, 36-36".........................2,100.00

Simon and Halbig

Simon and Halbig was one of the finest German makers to operate during the 1870s into the 1930s. Due to the high quality of the makers, their dolls still command large prices today. During the 1890s a few Simon & Halbig heads were used by a French maker, but these are extremely rare and well marked S&H.

#151, character face, bsk SkHd, pnt eyes, laughing c/m, RpC, 15" ..5,000.00
#530, child, SkHd, glass eyes, compo body, RpC, 22".................... 575.00
#600, child, o/c/e, o/m, RpC, 17" 900.00
#719, child, SkHd, glass eyes, c/m, p/e, RpC, 22" 6,000.00
#720, child, dome ShHd, glass eyes, kid body, RpC, 10" 600.00
#749, child, SkHd, glass eyes, wig, RpC, 13" 1,100.00
#749, SkHd, glass eyes, wig, p/e, wood body, RpC, 21"..............3,400.00
#886, child, swivel neck, all bsk, peg jtd, glass eys, wig, RpC, 8"... 800.00
#939, child, SkHd, glass eyes, p/e, compo body, RpC, 16".........3,500.00
#949, child, SkHd, glass eyes, o/m, wig, RpC, 24" 1,700.00
#1039, child, ShHd, kid body, RpC, 19" 525.00
#1160, lady, ShHd, glass eyes, c/m, fancy wig, RpC, 14" 675.00

#1249, open mouth with teeth, repaired, 27", $450.00. (Photo courtesy McMasters Harris Auction Company)

#1294, character face, pnt eyes, o/c/m, bent-leg baby, RpC, 16" .. 750.00
#1303, lady face, glass eyes, c/m, RpC, 14" 5,815.00
#1488, baby, glass eyes, o/c/m, bent-leg body, RpC, 20" 4,500.00
Fashion type, bsk SkHd, kid over wood body, c/m, RpC, 18"....2,700.00
S&H w/no mold #, child, ShHd, molded hair, c/m, RpC, 17"... 1,375.00
S&H w/no mold #, child, ShHd, swivel neck, RpC, 12" 1,500.00

Steiner

Jules Nicholas Steiner established one of the earliest French manufacturing companies (making dishes and clocks) in 1855. He began with mechanical dolls with bisque heads and open mouths with two rows of bamboo teeth; his patents grew to include walking and talking dolls. In 1880 he registered a patent for a doll with sleep eyes. This doll could be put to sleep by turning a rod that operated a wire attached to its eyes.

Baby w/rnd face, bsk SkHd, c/m, dimples, rpC, 18" 11,500.00
Baby w/rnd face, bsk SkHd, pwt/e, o/m/teeth, p/e, wig, Rpc, 18"...6,800.00
Bebe, Series A or C, bsk SkHd, cb pate, pwt/e, p/e, wig, RpC, 10"..8,000.00
Bebe, Series E, bsk SkHd, cb pate, pwt/e, c/m, p/e, RpC, 24"..22,000.00
Bebe w/figure mks, bsk SkHd, glass eyes, c/m, p/e, RpC, 14" 4,400.00
Crying/kicking child, key-wind, solid dome/glass eyes, teeth, RpC, 20"..2,200.00
Motchman-type baby, dome head, glass eyes, c/m, wig, RpC, 20" .. 5,000.00

Vogue

This is the company that made the Ginny doll. Composition was used during most of the 1940s, but by 1948, hard plastic dolls were being produced. Dolls of the late 1950s often had vinyl heads and hard plastic bodies, but the preferred material throughout the decade of the '60s was vinyl. An original mint-condition composition Ginny would be worth a minimum of $450.00 on the market today (played-with, about $90.00). The last Ginny came out in 1969. Another Vogue doll that is becoming very collectible is Jill, whose values are steadily climbing. For more information, we recommend *Collector's Encyclopedia of Vogue Dolls* by Judith Izen and Carol Stover. Our advisor for Jill dolls is Bonnie Groves; she is listed in the Directory under Texas.

Baby Dear, vinyl/cloth, 1959-64, 18", from $275 to...................... 325.00
Baby Too Dear, vinyl toddler, o/m w/2 teeth, 1963-65, 17", $200 to..250.00
Dora Lee, compo, o/c/e, c/m, 11", from $375 to........................... 425.00
Ginnette, vinyl, sleep eyes, o/m, 1956-79, 8", from $200 to......... 250.00
Ginny, Black, hp walker, sleep eyes, dynel wig, 1953-54, 8"......... 600.00
Ginny, hp, bent-knee walker, sleep eyes, saran wig, 1957-62, 8".. 150.00
Ginny, hp, pnt eyes, strung joints, mohair wig, 1948-50, 8", $375 to.. 425.00
Ginny, hp, sleep eyes, strung joints, 1953, 8", from $450 to 550.00
Ginny, hp, sleep eyes, 7-pc body, saran wig, 1954-56, 8", from $195 to ..225.00
Ginny, hp walker, o/c/e, dynel wig, common dress, 1950-54, 8", $250 to .. 300.00
Ginny, soft vinyl & hp, sleep eyes, rooted hair, 1963-65, 8", $35 to... 50.00
Ginny, vinyl, resembles 1963-71 Ginny, Hong Kong, 1984-86, 8", $35 to...55.00
Ginny, vinyl, sleep eyes, non-walker, Hong Kong, 1977-82, 8", $25 to .35.00
Ginny, vinyl, sleep eyes, non-walker, rooted hair, 1965-72, 8", $35 to.50.00
Ginny baby, vinyl, sleep eyes, jtd body, drinks/wets, 1959-82, 12". 40.00
Ginny Crib Crowd, baby w/curved legs, o/c/e, caracul wig, 1950, 8"..600.00
Ginny outfit, 1948-53, from $65 to 95.00
Ginny outfit, 1954-62, minimum value... 40.00
Jan, vinyl head, 6-pc rigid vinyl body, 10½", from $125 to........... 150.00
Jeff, vinyl head, 5-pc body, molded/pnt hair, 11", from $85 to 100.00
Jill, 7-pc teenage body, bend-knee walker/high-heels, 10½", $175 to.. 225.00
Little Miss Ginny, vinyl, 1-pc hp body, 1965-71, 12", from $30 to...40.00
Littlest Angel, vinyl head, o/c/e, rooted hair, 1961-63, 10½" 175.00
Miss Ginny, soft vinyl head, jtd arms/swivel waist, 1960s, 15-16".. 40.00
Toodles, compo, 1937-48, 8", from $450 to 625.00
Wee Imp, hp, orange saran wig, 1960, 8", from $250 to 350.00

Wax, Poured Wax

Bride, rose wax ShHd, bl glass eyes, c/m, wig, kid body, RpC, 15".. 1,650.00
Child, ShHd, inserted hair, glass eyes, wax limbs, RpC, 15" 1,100.00
Infant nurser, trn ShHd, glass eyes, o/m, wig, cloth body, RpC, 26"...1,325.00
Over compo or reinforced ShHd, child, glass eyes, cloth body, RpC, 12"..425.00

Over compo ShHd, child, glass eyes, o/m or c/m, later, RpC, 12" ...250.00
Over compo ShHd, glass eyes, molded hair, cloth body, RpC, 15"...375.00
Over compo ShHd, glass eyes, RpC, 18"....1,100.00
Over papier-maché, mechanical baby, glass eyes, bellows, RpC, 18"..2,000.00
Over SkHd, child, glass eyes, RpC, 18"....1,500.00
Poured ShHd, pnt features, glass eyes, c/m, cloth body, wig, RpC, 18". 1,400.00
Poured ShHd, pnt features, glass eyes, c/m, cloth body, wig, RpC, 25". 2,150.00
2-faced (laughing/crying), 1880-90s, RpC, 15"....900.00

Door Knockers

Door knockers, those charming precursors of the doorbell, come in an intriguing array of shapes and styles. The very rare ones come from England. Cast-iron examples made in this country were often produced in forms similar to the more familiar doorstop figures. Beware: Many of the brass door knockers being offered on internet auctions are of recent vintage! Our values represent examples in excellent original condition unless otherwise noted. Those with mint paint will bring premium prices.

Basket of daffodils, bow at top, pnt CI, 4¼x2½"....300.00
Bat w/wings open on top, pnt CI, JM 75 mk, 1-lb 12-oz, 9⅜" L....75.00
Birdhouse, cream w/mc, pnt CI, Hubley #629, 3¾x8x2⅝"....525.00
Boy on fence, dog as knocker, pnt CI, 1930s, 3½x2", VG....300.00
Bulldog, brass, unmk, 3" dog on 5" bkplate....75.00

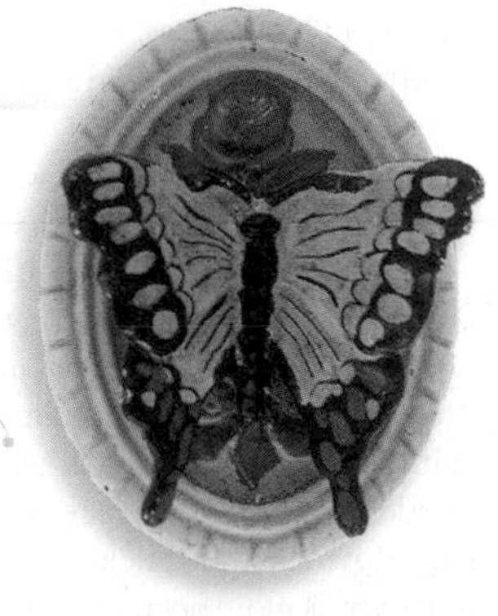

Butterfly and rose, painted cast iron, Waverly Studios, 3½", $275.00. (Photo courtesy Morphy Auctions/LiveAuctioneers.com)

Cardinal on twigs, pnt CI, rare, 5x3", M....350.00
Centurion on figurative base, blk CI, Iron Art JM 79, 4½x2"....155.00
Cherub faces amid ornate scrolls, pnt CI, 10x7"....90.00
Dartmoor Pixie on mushroom base, pnt brass, ca 1900, 3¼"....100.00
Dog at door of doghouse, pnt CI, 3-color, 4x3"....785.00
Dragon, tooled wrought iron, w/strike, 6½"....115.00
Eagle, talons holding ball, detailed, gold on bronze, ca 1900, 8½"...275.00
Flower basket, pnt CI, Hubley #287, 4x1⅞"....75.00
Flower on ornate knocker, Kenrick & Sons #423, brass, ca 1880, 9"..200.00
Gargoyle, pnt CI, ca 1900, 4½"....100.00
Hand holding ball (detailed) on shield, wood, ca 1900, 11x6½", NM..985.00
Hand of Fatima, bronzed patina, #609, 6"....185.00
Hand w/hammer (knocker) on figural coin amid leaves, bronze, 7½x5"..165.00
Heart in hands, arms form ring, brass, 6¼"....60.00
Highlander w/bagpipes, brass, mk Made in Great Britain, 6"....85.00
Ivy pot, pnt CI, Hubley #123....250.00
Kewpie, brass, ca 1920, 4¾"....80.00
Liberty Bell, pnt CI, ca 1920, 3¼"....175.00
Lion head w/beaded ring knocker, brass, England, 1920s, 9½x6x3½". 460.00
Lions & shields, Tudor style, w/peep hole, cast bronze, ca 1920, 9x6". 300.00
Monks on Sherborne Abby base, bronze, 1911-12, 4x3"....120.00
Morning glory (knocker) on leaves, pnt CI, 1890-1910, 3½x3x1¼"..250.00
Parrot on leafy branch on oval, pnt CI, Hubley, ca 1900, 4¼x3"...65.00
Pear, pnt CI, flower bkplate, rare, 4¼x3", M....300.00
Rooster, pnt CI, wht variation, 4½x3"....275.00
Rose & 2 buds on oval base w/leaf & scrolls, pnt CI, 3x4"....75.00
Russian eagle, dbl-headed, brass, 12¾x12¼"....105.00
Spaniels (2), shell shape at top of base, brass, ca 1930, 3½x2¼"..100.00
Spider w/captured fly, pnt CI, rare, 3½x1¾"....450.00
Tulip, wide fr, aluminum, 8x5¼"....165.00
Zinnias, pnt CI, mk Pat Pend LVL, rare, 3¾x2½"....550.00

Doorstops

Although introduced in England in the mid-1800s, cast-iron doorstops were not made to any great extent in this country until after the Civil War. Once called 'door porters,' their function was to keep doors open to provide better ventilation. They have been produced in many shapes and sizes, both dimensional and flat-backed. Doorstops retained their usefulness and appeal well into the 1930s. In some areas of the country, it may be necessary to adjust prices down about 25%. Most of our listings describe examples in excellent original condition; all are made of cast iron. To evaluate a doorstop in only very good paint, deduct at least 35%. Values for examples in near-mint or better conditon sell at a premium, while prices for examples in poor to good paint drop dramatically. See also Bradley and Hubbard.

Airplane 'flying' over mountains, gold pnt, Pat Appld For LVL, 10"..920.00
Apple blossoms in woven basket, Hubley #329, 7⅝x5⅜", $100 to..150.00
Basket of kittens (3), M Rosenstein, 1932, 10x7"....425.00
Bellhop, bl uniform, #1244, 8⅞x4⅝", from $275 to....350.00
Boston terrier begging, 8¾x5", from $300 to....375.00
Budda, 8⅞x8⅛"....200.00
Buster Brown in sailor suit, on base, 7¾x5¼", from $425 to....475.00
Castle on mountain w/road, 8x5¼", from $350 to....425.00
Cat sleeping, 4½x13½x10¼", NM....925.00
Cat w/bell on braided rug, c Sarah W Symonds..., rare, 13x10", VG..2,300.00
Cavalier King Charles spaniel, 9¼x6⅞"....1,380.00
Clipper ship, National Foundry #3, 9½x12"....520.00
Clown, Hubley, 10½x4½"....975.00
Cockatoo (wht) on branch w/red blossoms, 11¼x9½"....5,175.00
Concertina player (Black man), on base, mc pnt, 7"....1,380.00
Cosmos flower basket, National Foundry #42, 8⅜x7", G....115.00
Cottage, Albany Foundry, 5¾x8¾"....290.00
Cottage, Hiram Powers, rare, 5½x11¾"....4,025.00
Cottage doorway w/flowers, Leave Grouch Behind..., S Symonds, 6", NM...2,590.00
Duck in bl bonnet, 6¼x4⅜", VG....345.00
Elephant, 10¾x9¾", VG....180.00

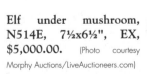

Elf under mushroom, N514E, 7½x6½", EX, $5,000.00. (Photo courtesy Morphy Auctions/LiveAuctioneers.com)

Engish bulldog standing, Hubley #220, 7x9"....520.00
English bulldog, sitting, Hubley, 4⅞x4", G....800.00
Fence w/urn & shrubs, c Sarah W Symonds, 8x4⅞", VG....1,265.00
German shepherd, Littco, 9x10¾"....200.00
Gladiolas in vase, Hubley #489, 10x8", VG....200.00
Goldenrod flowers, Hubley #268, 7⅛x5½"....575.00

Hessian soldier, 21x11¾", NM 700.00
Indian brave w/spear on rearing horse, oblong base, mc pnt, 9½" ...430.00
Jungle boy kneeling, oblong base, leopard pelt around waist, mc, 13". 1,150.00
Milkmaid lady in apron, CJO #1242, 9x4¾" 200.00
Mill w/bridge & road, c 1926 Greenblatt...#3, 9¾x7¼" 2,070.00
Monkey & organ grinder, 10x6", NM 2,600.00
Mouse on wedge of cheese, mc pnt, 2¼" 2,000.00
Olive picker, Hubley #507, 7¾x7½", NM 800.00
Owl facing forward, 6¼x3½" 145.00
Peacock, tail closed, National Foundry #56, 15¼x7⅛", VG 173.00
Peacock, tail spread, 6¼x6½" 230.00
Pelican on dock, Albany Foundry, 8x7¼" 690.00
Pheasant, Hubley #458, c Fred Everett, 8½x7½", NM 630.00
Pirate girl w/sword, 13½x7" 200.00
Pirate w/pack on bk, 12x9¾", NM 2,875.00
Popeye, Hubley, c 1929 King Features Syn Made in USA, 9x4½" ...6,900.00
Puppy w/Duck, c 1922 by AM Greenblatt Boston Mass, 9¾x8⅝" .. 1,035.00
Rabbit in top hat & tails, National Foundry, 10x4¾", NM 1,725.00
Rabbit sitting, life-sz, 11x5/8x12", VG......................... 275.00
Red Riding Hood w/Wolf, Nuydea #860, Pat Pending..., 7⅜x9⅝", NM..2,900.00
Roses w/flowers in ftd basket, 8x7" 230.00
Scotty, Hubley #412, 11¾x16" 16.00
Sealyham, natural pnt, Hubley #382, rare, 9½x14" 4,025.00
Sheep, folky sheep facing left, mk Julia, 7¼x10"........................ 1,380.00
Snooper detective, mk The Snooper, 13¼x4½", NM 1,265.00
Spanish dancer w/fan, hand on hip, skirt flared up, Trade WS Mark, 10". 350.00
Squirrel w/nut, Emig #1382, 8x5½" 345.00
St Bernard, natural lifelike pnt, scarce, 6⅝x10" 3,450.00
Sunbonnet Girl w/lg bow, 9x5¾" 400.00
Wine Man, multiple bottles in ea hand, 9¾x7" 1,100.00

Dorchester Pottery

Taking its name from the town in Massachusetts where it was organized in 1895, the Dorchester Pottery Company made primarily utilitarian wares, though other types of items were made as well. By 1940 a line of decorative pottery was introduced, some of which was painted by hand with scrollwork or themes from nature. The buildings were destroyed by fire in the late 1970s, and the pottery was never rebuilt. In the listings that follow, the decorations described are all in cobalt unless otherwise noted. Our advisor for this category is Dale MacLean; he is listed in the Directory under Massachusetts.

Key:
CAH — Charles A. Hill (noted artist)   IM — in memory of
EHH — Ethel Hill Henderson

Basket, wht gloss, flared rim, paper label, 11¾x9¼ 150.00
Bedwarmer, stoneware, no decor, stamped, 5x11" 75.00
Bowl, cereal; scrollwork, CAH/IMEHH, 2x5¾" 75.00
Bowl, clown; CAH/N Ricci, 1⅛x4" 110.00
Candleholder, cobalt scrollwork, CAH/Ricci/IMEHH, 6" dia, ea. 125.00
Casserole, Pine Cone, CAH, w/lid, 2¼x4½"................................ 225.00
Charger, Fruit, stamped, 12½" 400.00
Creamer, Strawberry, CH.. 100.00
Cup & saucer, Pine Cone, CAH, stamped, 3", 6¼" 100.00
Dish, Tear Drop, CAH, 4½x7½" 150.00
Mug, Anchor, stylized anchor & rope on ivory, stamped, 4½" 100.00
Mug, Apple, CAH, 3", set of 4 .... 250.00
Mug, Pine Cone & Blizzard, ...Blizzard of 1978, stamped, 4⅛" 225.00
Pitcher, Daffodil, CAH/Ricci, 5x5½" 250.00
Pitcher, Pilgrim, sgn RT (Robert Trotter), stamped, 7½", EX....... 300.00
Pitcher, Pussy Willow, CAH/N Ricci, stamped, 5½x4¼".............. 225.00

Plate, Blueberry, CAH/N Ricci, 10"............................... 225.00
Plate, Lily of the Valley, CAH/Ricci, 7½" 200.00

Star dish, Eagle, painted with incised feather detail, signed CAH/EHH, Centennial 1776 – 1976, 8", $200.00.

(Photo courtesy Smith & Jones Inc.)

Sugar bowl, Blueberry, w/lid 150.00
Sugar bowl, Sacred Cod, CAH, stamped, w/lid, 4x4½" 150.00
Syrup, flowers, CAH/N Ricci, w/lid, 5" 175.00
Syrup, Half Scroll, striped hdl, sgn, stamped, w/lid, 4¾" 175.00
Vase, 2-tone bl, 4-sided, crimped mouth, bulbous, stamped, 4½x5". 125.00

Dorflinger

C. Dorflinger was born in Alsace, France, and came to this country when he was 10 years old. When still very young, he obtained a job in a glass factory in New Jersey. As a young man, he started his own glassworks in Brooklyn, New York, opening new factories as profits permitted. During that time he made cut glass articles for many famous people including President and Mrs. Lincoln, for whom he produced a complete service of tableware with the United States Coat of Arms. In 1863 he sold the New York factories because of ill health and moved to his farm near White Mills, Pennsylvania. His health returned, and he started a plant near his home. It was there that he did much of his best work, making use of only the very finest materials. Christian died in 1915, and the plant was closed in 1921 by consent of the family. Dorflinger glass is rare and often hard to identify. Very few pieces were marked. Many only carried a small paper label which was quickly discarded; these are seldom found today. Identification is more accurately made through a study of the patterns, as colors may vary.

Bottle, cologne; Button & Cane, ruby to clear, 6x3¾" 780.00
Loving cup, floral & star cuttings, silver collar, 5½x8¾x6¾"........ 275.00
Pitcher, milk; geometric cuttings, scalloped rim, bulbous, 5" 132.50
Pitcher, notched miters & punties, serrated rim, star-cut base, 8", NM ..165.00

Pitcher, Triple diamond, light wear, 12", $360.00.

(Photo courtesy SUSANIN'S Auctions/ LiveAuctioneers.com)

Vase, etched floral w/gold trim, goblet form, 7" 60.00
Vase, Kalana Poppy, tinted (rare) trumpet form, 10" 780.00
Vase, Strawberry, Dmn & Fan, gr to clear, trumpet form, 10¼".... 550.00
Vase, Strawberry, Dmn & Fan, slim trumpet form, 14"................. 215.00

Dragon Ware

Dragon Ware has always been fairly easy to find. Today, internet auctions have made it even more so. It is still being produced and is often marketed in areas with a strong Asian influence and in souvenir shops in major cities around the United States and abroad.

As the name suggests, this china features a slip-painted dragon. Behind and around the moriage dragon (often done in a whitish color) are swirling clouds (rain), lines of color (water), fire, and in the dragon's clutch, a pearl — the dragon's most prized possession. (Although most Dragon Ware is ceramic, on rare occasion, you may find some beautiful examples of Dragon Ware executed in slip on glassware as well.) Gray (varying tones of gray and black) is the most common background color, however, it may also be done in shades of green, blue, orange, yellow, pink, white, pearl, and red. Sometimes the slip decoration will be applied in a flatter, slicker manner, rather than in the more traditional raised moriage style. On these pieces the dragon may be any color, and often the colors will be brighter and crisper. This style of painting is newer, seen on pieces from the 1940s and later.

Sometimes a three-dimensional dragon may act as the spout of a teapot or may seem to 'fly off' a vase; items with this type of modeling are a form of (but not actually considered true) Dragon Ware.

A lithophane is made by varying the density of the china in order to create an image when viewed with light behind it. They are often found in the bottom of coffee, demitasse, and sake cups and in this ware typically represet a geisha girl portrayed from the shoulders up. On rare occasions you may find nude ladies, usually only one, though groups of two and three may be found as well. Some cups have actual pictures in the bottom instead of lithophanes; these are newer.

Dragon Ware is divided into three categories. Nippon or Nippon quality pieces are the most desirable. The dragon and its background are typically done in vibrant, bold colors, and the slip work is well defined. Translucent jewels are often used for the dragon's eyes instead of the blue slip found on the more commonplace items. These pieces are usually executed in the gray tones; however, other colors have also been used. Many pieces have a lustre interior. Nippon or Nippon-quality pieces with a recognizable Nippon mark command the highest prices.

Mid-century Dragon Ware was mass produced in the late 1930s, 1940s, and 1950s. Tea sets could be found in the local drug store. These sets would serve up to six people and became popular in the days of bridge club and tea parties. Colors vary in this era of Dragon Ware, and interiors are sometimes painted in a goldish peach lustre. The slip work is not as detailed as it is on the earlier ware, and the onset of mass-production techniques are evident. Many of these sets do not carry a mark, signature, or paper label, as they were brought to the states by servicemen who had been stationed in Japan. Other sets may have had only one or two marked pieces. Mid-century Dragon Ware falls in the mid-price range, although many of the pieces most popular with collectors were made during this era.

Turn-of-the-century pieces made from the 1970s up to the present time are obviously mass produced; the dragon often falls flat, without detail or personality. Background colors are no longer vibrant but lack-lustre with a shiny appearance. Pastel pink, teal, orange, and green are commonly seen. These pieces are usually marked; however, some carried a paper label which may have been lost or removed. Dealers sometimes mistake unmarked pieces for the older ware and often sell them as such. Typically these pieces, if identified and priced correctly, would represent the lower end of the price spectrum.

These three styles are in addition to the typical gray pattern seen and positively recognized as Dragon Ware. Swirl: All the colors, including the background are actually slipped on, giving the effect of color having been 'drizzled' onto the surface. These pieces are usually made with white china, though on the occasion when the china body is more nearly a shade lighter than the drizzled paint, a 'squiggled' design is achieved. Cloud: These pieces have backgrounds that have been airbrushed on, achieving a flowing, soft, unified cloud effect. Solid: This type is first painted in a solid color before the dragon is applied. There may be slip painting (to represent the clouds, water, and fire) or airbrushing. Pearlized painting as well as lustre painting would fall under this category, as both techniques are, in effect, one overall color.

At the present time, the older pieces in colors other than gray are commanding the higher prices; so are the more unusual items. As always, condition is a major price-assessing issue, so be sure to check for damage before buying or selling. Overall, prices have increased. Our advisor for this category is Suzi Hibbard; she is listed in the Directory under California. In the following listing, all pieces listed are in the typical Dragon Ware style and from the mid century period unless noted otherwise.

Key:
HP — hand painted
lth — lithophane
MIJ — Made in Japan
MIOJ — Made in Occupied Japan
NQ — Nippon Quality

Ashtray, blk, jewel eyes, HP Nippon, 3¾x5", from $125 to.......... 200.00
Bell, pk, souvenir of Niagara Falls, 5¾x3", from $10 to 25.00
Console bowl, gray w/gold lustre, HP Japan, NQ, +pr sticks, $175 to... 250.00
Cookie jar, blk swirl, glass eyes, Noritake, 8x5", from $350 to 750.00
Creamer & sugar bowl, orange & wht, 3½", from $25 to................ 45.00
Cup & saucer, coffee; bl, Dianan, no lth, from $25 to 45.00
Cup & saucer, coffee; blk cloud, HP Betsons, from $25 to 45.00
Cup & saucer, demitasse; bl swirl, MIJ, from $25 to 30.00
Cup & saucer, demitasse; dbl nude lth, Niknoiko China, from $75 to . 125.00
Cup & saucer, demitasse; goggly eyes, orange solid, from $25 to.... 60.00
Cup & saucer, demitasse; gr w/blk rim, HP, Shafford, from $30 to. 45.00
Cup & saucer, demitasse; nude lth, gray, from $45 to 75.00
Cup & saucer, demitasse; orange cloud, MIOJ, from $20 to 50.00
Cup & saucer, gr solid, child sz, from $10 to 20.00
Dutch shoe, gray, from $20 to.. 30.00
Incense burner, gray, HP MIJ, 3½", from $15 to.......................... 25.00
Lamp, gray, jewel eyes, 7¾", from $150 to................................. 225.00
Nappy, brn, HP MIJ, sq, 5½", from $25 to................................. 45.00
Pitcher, yel cloud, MIJ, mini, 2⅞", from $15 to 25.00
Planter, orange solid, w/frog, MIJ, 5½", from $35 to 75.00
Plate, bl cloud, 7¼", from $25 to 40.00
Saki cups, red cloud, whistling, set of 6, from $50 to 125.00
Saki set, bl cloud, geisha lth, Kutani, w/plate, 8-pc, from $75 to . 175.00
Saki set, bl cloud, whistling, kitten on decanter/plate, 8-pc, $125 to .. 225.00
Saki set, wht & gold, Orient China Japan, 7-pc, from $50 to 100.00
Saki set, wht pearlized, whistling, HP Japan, 5-pc, from $50 to ... 125.00
Shakers, bl cloud, unmk, pr from $10 to 30.00
Shakers, orange solid, pagoda style, Japan, 4", pr from $15 to........ 40.00
Snack set, brn cloud, gold dragon, RS MIJ, 2-pc, from $35 to........ 75.00
Table lighter, blk solid, from $50 to... 100.00
Tea set, demitasse; gray, Nippon bl circle mk, NQ, 17-pc, $225 to..350.00
Tea set, demitasse; wht pearl, Japan, newer, 17-pc, $50 to 100.00
Tea set, gray, MIOJ, 7½" pot+cr/sug+4 c/s, from $75 to................ 175.00
Tea set, gray w/gold, 7½", pot+cr/sug, from $45 to 70.00
Tea set, stacking, blk, MIJ, 5½x6½", from $45 to......................... 75.00
Tea set, yel, child's, pot+c/s, 4-pc, from $45 to 65.00
Tea/coffee set, gr cloud, lth, dragon spout, 23-pc, $175 to............ 275.00
Teapot, gr cloud, 8x3", from $35 to.. 75.00
Teapot, gray, 6-sided, 7¼x4¾", from $45 to................................. 60.00
Tidbit tray, gray, Nippon, 9x6½", from $100 to............................ 225.00
Vase, aqua solid, Deco style, MIJ, 10¼", from $100 to................. 175.00
Vase, bl cloud, wide mouth, 5", from $30 to 50.00
Vase, blk solid, MIJ, 6", from $25 to.. 50.00
Vase, gr swirl, unmk, 3¾", from $10 to... 25.00

Vase, gray, glass eyes/ftd, HP Nippon w/wreath, NQ, 4⅜", $125 to.. 275.00
Vase, gray, jewel eyes, gr HP Nippon M in wreath, 9¾", $500 to ..1,500.00
Vase, orange, MIJ, 7½", from $30 to... 75.00
Vase, orange, 4", from $20 to.. 50.00
Vase, orange/yel w/cloud, HP MIJ/MIOJ, 5", from $15 to 25.00
Vase, yel solid, MIJ, 5", from $10 to 25.00
Vase, yel swirl, MIJ, 5", from $15 to 50.00

Vases and pitcher, 5½", each: from $20.00 to $28.00. (Photo courtesy Jackson's International Auctioneers & Appraisers of Fine Art & Antiques/LiveAuctioneers.com)

Wall pocket, bl/orange lustre, Japan flower mk, 7", from $35 to..... 75.00
Wall pocket, orange solid, MIJ, 9", from $50 to............................. 75.00
Watering can, gr solid, MIJ, 2½", from $7.50 to............................. 15.00

Dresden

The city of Dresden was a leading cultural center in the seventeenth century and in the eighteenth century became known as the Florence on the Elbe because of its magnificent baroque architecture and its outstanding museums. Artists, poets, musicians, philosophers, and porcelain artists took up residence in Dresden. In the late nineteenth century, there was a considerable demand among the middle classes for porcelain. This demand was met by Dresden porcelain painters. Between 1855 and 1944, more than 200 painting studios existed in the city. The studios bought porcelain white ware from manufacturers such as Meissen and Rosenthal for decorating, marketing, and reselling throughout the world. The largest of these studios include Donath & Co., Franziska Hirsch, Richard Klemm, Ambrosius Lamm, Carl Thieme, and Helena Wolfsohn.

Most of the Dresden studios produced work in imitation of Meissen and Royal Vienna. Flower painting enhanced with burnished gold, courting couples, landscapes, and cherubs were used as decorative motifs. As with other hand-painted porcelains, value is dependent upon the quality of the decoration. Sometimes the artwork equaled or even surpassed that of the Meissen factory.

Some of the most loved and eagerly collected of all Dresden porcelains are the beautiful and graceful lace figures. Many of the figures found in the maketplace today were not made in Dresden but in other area of Germany. For more information, we recommend *Dresden Porcelain Studios* by Jim and Susan Harran, our advisors for this category. They are listed in the Directory under New Jersey.

Basket, HP floral w/gold & X-hatching, 3 hdls, F Hirsch, 1901-30 ..225.00
Basket, mini; appl rose & forget-me-nots, ftd, Thieme, 1920s, 2½" ..75.00
Bowl, HP appl flowers w/gold, rtcl, 4 ft, hdls, ca 1920-50s 150.00
Bowl, HP floral center, scalloped gold rim, sq, Lamm, 1887-1914, 9" ...175.00
Bowl, HP floral w/rtcl rim, F Hirsch, 1901-1930, 9¼" 150.00
Box, HP garlands & vases w/gold, egg-shaped w/lid, F Hirsch, 1901-30.175.00
Cake plate, HP flowers w/rtcl rim, ped ft, Donath & Co, 9½" dia...400.00
Candelabra, HP appl flowers, 2-light, 2-pc, Thieme, 1950s, 9½x7" ...400.00

Candlesticks, four figures sit on each base, 13", $650.00 for the pair. (Photo courtesy Du Mouchelles/LiveAuctioneers.com)

Charger, HP floral/courting scene w/gold, scalloped, Klemm, 1900, 14"..375.00
Coffeepot, gold over & under HP floral, ftd, F Hirsch, 1901-30...275.00
Compote, courting scene w/gold, rtcl rim/ft, Thieme, 1888-1901, 6x8".375.00
Cup & saucer, bouillon; gr band w/gold garlands, 2 hdls, Klemm, 1900.100.00
Cup & saucer, coffee; floral w/gold, Donath & Co, 1893-1916 .... 115.00
Cup & saucer, demi; courting scenes/pk panels, quatrefoil, Wolfsohn.. 150.00
Cup & saucer, demi; floral/courting scenes, quatrefoil, Donath, 1900... 150.00
Egg plate, floral w/gold, 10 wells, F Hirsch, 1901-14..................... 375.00
Ewer, HP floral garlands w/gold, ftd, Thieme, ca 1900, 16" 500.00
Figurine, bird on branch, Thieme, ca 1950s-60s, 1¾".................... 60.00
Hair receiver, garlands w/gold, can form, F Hirsch, 1901-30........ 150.00
Hors d'oeuvres dish, floral w/gold, 4-part w/bowl, F Hirsch, 1901-30.. 450.00
Pitcher, water; HP floral w/gold, Donath & Co, 1893-1916, 5x5½".... 150.00
Plate, HP couple on bench, scalloped rim, Klemm, 1888-1916, 6¼" .. 125.00
Plate, HP couples/floral on yel panels, Klemm, 1888-1916, 8¼" 75.00
Plate, HP floral/rtcl rim, F Hirsch, 1901-1930, 10¼" 275.00
Plate, HP Marie Antoinette theme, pk fish scale, Thieme, 1900s, 8" ...200.00
Plate, service; raised gold flowers & beads, Lamm, 1931-45, 10¾"..200.00
Plate, show; HP Leda & the Swan, gold border, Lamm, 1887-1914, 10".500.00
Ramekin, HP floral w/scalloped gold rim, F Hirsch, 1901-30......... 35.00
Relish, HP courting scenes, thick gold trim, 2-part, Lamm, 12½x9"... 300.00
Tea strainer, HP floral w/gold, Wolfsohn, 1880s, 5½x4"+underplate .. 225.00
Teacup & saucer, courting scenes & floral panels, F Hirsch, 1901-30. 115.00
Teacup & saucer, mini; scenes/floral panels, feather hdl, Klemm, 1900..250.00
Teapot, HP sailboat scene, gold seashell finial, 1887-1914, sm 400.00
Tray, HP floral w/gold, scalloped rim, F Hirsch, 1901-1930, 12x8½"..300.00
Urn, HP fishing scene, Wolfsohn, 1886-1890, 13" 1,500.00
Vase, HP lg flowers, tapered, Klemm, 1891-1914, 8" 250.00
Vase, HP monk w/wine, E von Grutzner style, Donath & Co, ca 1900, 9"..900.00
Vase, mini; HP courting scene, sea horse hdls, Klemm, 1893-1916, 3".250.00

Dryden

World War II veteran, Jim Dryden founded Dryden Pottery in Ellsworth, Kansas, in 1946. Starting in a Quonset hut, Dryden created molded products which he sold at his father's hardware store in town. Using Kansas clay from the area and volcanic ash as a component, durable glossy glazes were created. Soon Dryden was selling pottery to Macy's of New York and the Fred Harvy Restaurants on the Santa Fe Railroad.

After 10 years, 600 stores stocked Dryden Pottery. However direct sales to the public from the pottery studio offered the most profit because of increasing competition from Japan and Europe. Using dental tools to make inscriptions, Dryden began to offer pottery with personalized messages and logos. This specialized work was appreciated by customers and is admired by collectors today.

In 1956 the interstate bypassed the pottery and Dryden decided to move to Hot Springs National Park to find a broader and larger tourist base. Again, local clays and quartz for the glazes were used. Later, in order to improve consistency, commercial clay (that fired bone white) and controlled glazes were used. Sometimes overlooked by collectors who favor the famous potteries of the past, Jim Dryden's son Kimbo, and grandsons

Zach, Cheyenne, and Arrow, continue to develop new glazes and shapes in the studio in Hot Springs, Arkansas. Glazes comparable to those created by Fulper, Grueby, and Rookwood can be found on pottery for sale there. Dryden was the first to use two different glazes successfully at the same time.

In 2001 The Book Stops Here published the first catalog and history of Dryden pottery. The book shows the evolution of Dryden art pottery from molded ware to unique hand-thrown pieces; the studio illustrations show the durable and colorful glazes that make Dryden special. Visitors are always welcome at the Dryden Pottery, Hot Springs, Arkansas, studio where they can watch pottery being made by the talented Dryden family.

Kansas pieces have a golden tan clay base and were made between 1946 and 1956. Arkansas pieces made after 1956 were made from bone white clay. Dryden pottery has a wide range of values. Many collectors are interested in the early pieces while a fast-growing number search for wheel-thrown and hand-decorated pieces made within the past 20 years. One-of-a-kind specialty pieces can exceed $500.00. Our advisor for this category is Ralph Winslow; he is listed in the Directory under Missouri.

Kansas Dryden (1946 – 1956)

Ashtray, fish	29.00
Ashtray, Lamer Hotel, 5½"	25.00
Berry set, 7-pc	38.00
Boot, #90, souvenir	30.00
Bowl, ruffled, #7F, 8½"	16.00
Candleholders, #42, 4", pr	22.00
Creamer & sugar bowl, #108	12.00

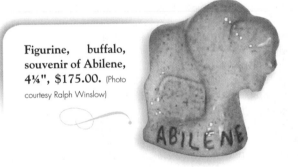

Figurine, buffalo, souvenir of Abilene, 4¼", $175.00. (Photo courtesy Ralph Winslow)

Figurine, elephant, #10, 11"	50.00
Jug, #H1, 3½"	10.00
Leaf dish, souvenir, #110, 4½"	18.00
Mug, #41, 6"	8.00
Mug, coffee; #3	10.00
Pitcher, #7, 5½"	15.00
Pitcher, #49, +6 #4 tumblers	45.00
Pitcher, #50, 6⅛"	15.00
Pitcher, souvenir, #180, 4"	15.00
Pitcher, syrup; Greensburg, Kans, #94	28.00
Planter, #X, 10"	22.00
Planter, elephant, #313, 3½"	20.00
Planter, lion, 8"	175.00
Planter, Madonna, #87, 4¾"	22.00
Planter, rooster, #Y	20.00
Shakers, jugs, souvenir, 4", pr	20.00
Vase, cactus, #B1	25.00
Vase, cornucopia; souvenir, #7K, 4½"	18.00
Vase, fish form, 8¼"	35.00
Vase, pillow form, #100	31.00
Vase, rose, souvenir, 4"	22.00
Wall pocket, #87, 6¼"	22.00

Arkansas Dryden (1956 to Present)

Bowls, 5", 5 for	32.00
Cookie jar, 50th Anniversary, 1997	65.00
Dealer sign	42.00
Dish, butterfly, 9½"	9.00
Figurine, lioness smiling, 4½"	18.00
Pitcher, Maij Lis, 10¼"	32.00
Spoon rest, bird	12.00
Vase, powder horn, 9"	23.00
Vase, rnd, LOI, 6"	28.00
Vase, ruffled, JK, 15¾"	125.00
Vase, wheel thrown, #DD77, 10"	23.00
Vase, wheel thrown, JK, 15½"	43.00
Vase, 5-neck, 5½"	25.00

Vase, gloss and matt finish, J.K. Dryden Original, 50th Anniversary, #96, 7¾", $95.00. (Photo courtesy Ralph Winslow)

Duncan and Miller

The firm that became known as the Duncan and Miller Glass Company in 1900 was organized in 1874 in Pittsburgh, Pennsylvania, a partnership between George Duncan, his sons Harry and James, and his son-in-law Augustus Heisey. John Ernest Miller was hired as their designer. He is credited with creating the most famous of all Duncan's glassware lines, Three Face. (See Pattern Glass.) The George Duncan and Sons Glass Company, as it was titled, was only one of 18 companies that merged in 1891 with U.S. Glass. Soon after the Pittsburgh factory burned in 1892, the association was dissolved, and Heisey left the firm to set up his own factory in Newark, Ohio. Duncan built his new plant in Washington, Pennsylvania, where he continued to make pressed glassware in such notable patterns as Bagware, Amberette, Duncan Flute, Button Arches, and Zippered Slash. The firm was eventually sold to U.S. Glass in Tiffin, Ohio, and unofficially closed in August 1955.

In addition to the early pressed dinnerware patterns, today's Duncan and Miller collectors enjoy searching for opalescent vases in many patterns and colors, frosted 'Satin Tone' glassware, acid-etched designs, and lovely stemware such as the Rock Crystal cuttings. Milk glass was made in limited quantity and is considered a good investment. Ruby glass, Ebony (a lovely opaque black glass popular during the '20s and '30s), and, of course, the glass animal and bird figurines are all highly valued examples of the art of Duncan and Miller.

Add approximately 40% to 50% to listed prices for opalescent items. Etchings, cuttings, and other decorations will increase values by about 50%. For further study we recommend *The Encyclopedia of Duncan Glass* by Gail Krause; she is listed in the Directory under Pennsylvania. Several Duncan and Miller lines are shown in *Elegant Glassware of the Depression Era* by Cathy and Gene Florence. Our advisor for this category is Roselle Shleifman; she is listed in the Directory under New York. See also Glass Animals and Figurines.

Canterbury, crystal, ashtray, 3"	5.00
Canterbury, crystal, basket, crimped, 3½"	35.00

Canterbury, crystal, bowl, sweetmeat; star shape, hdls, 6x2" 15.00
Canterbury, crystal, bowl, 1-hdl, 5½x1¾" 7.00
Canterbury, crystal, celery dish, hdls, 9x4x1¼" 22.50
Canterbury, crystal, cocktail, 3½-oz, 4¼" 12.00
Canterbury, crystal, compote, high stem, 6x5½" 20.00
Canterbury, crystal, finger bowl, 4½x2" 12.00
Canterbury, crystal, lamp, hurricane; w/prisms, 15" 135.00
Canterbury, crystal, mayonnaise, 6x3¼" 24.00
Canterbury, crystal, pitcher, martini; 32-oz, 9¼" 80.00
Canterbury, crystal, plate, 11¼" 25.00
Canterbury, crystal, relish, 5-part, 11x2" 33.00
Canterbury, crystal, saucer 3.00
Canterbury, crystal, top hat, 3" 20.00
Canterbury, crystal, tumbler, ice tea; 13-oz, 6¼" 18.00
Canterbury, crystal, tumbler, str sides, 9-oz, 4½" 14.00
Canterbury, crystal, tumbler, whiskey; 1½-oz, 2½" 12.50
Canterbury, crystal, urn, 4½x4½" 15.00
Canterbury, crystal, vase, cloverleaf, 4" 17.50
Canterbury, crystal, vase, cloverleaf, 5" 25.00
Canterbury, crystal, vase, crimped, 3½" 15.00
Canterbury, crystal, vase, crimped, 7" 35.00
Caribbean, bl, bowl, punch; 6¼-qt, 10" 495.00
Caribbean, bl, creamer 22.00
Caribbean, bl, finger bowl, 4½" 30.00
Caribbean, bl, ice bucket, hdl, 6½" 210.00
Caribbean, bl, pitcher, water; w/ice lip, 72-oz, 9" 595.00
Caribbean, bl, plate, 8½" 30.00
Caribbean, bl, salt cellar, 2½" 25.00
Caribbean, bl, tumbler, ftd, 8½-oz, 5½" 55.00
Caribbean, crystal, bowl, vegetable; 9¼" 40.00
Caribbean, crystal, cocktail shaker, 33-oz, 9" 100.00
Caribbean, crystal, mustard, w/slotted lid, 4" 35.00
Caribbean, crystal, punch ladle 35.00
Caribbean, crystal, relish, oblong, 9½" 25.00
Caribbean, crystal, server, center hdl, 5¾" 13.00
Caribbean, crystal, vase, ruffled rim, ftd, 5¾" 22.00
First Love, crystal, ashtray, #30, 5x3¼" 20.00
First Love, crystal, bottle, oil; w/stopper, #5200, 8" 50.00
First Love, crystal, bowl, #6, 12x3½" 70.00
First Love, crystal, bowl, 3-part, ftd, #117, 7½x3" 35.00
First Love, crystal, candleholder, #115, low, 3", ea 25.00
First Love, crystal, carafe, water; #5200, w/stopper 195.00
First Love, crystal, cocktail, #115, 3-oz, 4¼" 16.00
First Love, crystal, compote, #111, 3½x4¾" 30.00
First Love, crystal, cornucopia, #117, 8x4¾" 65.00
First Love, crystal, cup, #115 .... 12.50
First Love, crystal, hat, #30, 5½x8½x6¼" 350.00
First Love, crystal, mayonnaise, #111, w/hdld tray, 5¾x3" ... 35.00
First Love, crystal, nappy, #115, hdl, 5x1¾" 18.00
First Love, crystal, plate, #111, sq, 6" 14.00
First Love, crystal, plate, #115, 11¼" 55.00
First Love, crystal, plate, torte; #111, 13¼" 60.00

First Love, crystal, shakers, #30, pr............................... 25.00
First Love, crystal, urn, #111, 4½x4½" 25.00
First Love, crystal, vase, #126, 10½" 175.00
First Love, crystal, vase, flared rim, #115, 4" 25.00
First Love, crystal, wine, #5111 1/2, 3-oz, 5¼" 25.00
Lily of the Valley, crystal, ashtray, 3" 25.00
Lily of the Valley, crystal, candy dish, w/lid 95.00
Lily of the Valley, crystal, cheese & cracker 75.00
Lily of the Valley, crystal, plate, 9" 45.00
Lily of the Valley, crystal, sherbet, high stem 25.00
Nautical, bl, ashtray, 6" 40.00
Nautical, bl, cake plate, hdls, 6½" 35.00
Nautical, bl, cigarette jar 75.00
Nautical, bl, relish, 7-part, 12" 75.00
Nautical, bl, sugar bowl 45.00
Nautical, bl, tumbler, highball...................................... 33.00
Nautical, crystal, bowl, 10" L 60.00
Nautical, crystal, cigarette holder................................. 15.00
Nautical, crystal, ice bucket.. 95.00
Nautical, crystal, plate, 8" 10.00
Nautical, crystal, shakers, pr, w/tray 65.00
Nautical, crystal, tumbler, juice; ftd 15.00
Nautical, crystal, tumbler, water; ftd, 9-oz 15.00
Nautical, opal, compote, 7"... 595.00
Plaza, amber or crystal, bowl, cereal; 6¼" 8.00
Plaza, amber or crystal, cocktail................................... 10.00
Plaza, amber or crystal, mustard, w/slotted lid................ 17.50
Plaza, amber or crystal, parfait..................................... 12.00
Plaza, amber or crystal, plate, 6½" 3.00
Plaza, amber or crystal, tumbler, juice............................6.00
Plaza, amber or crystal, vase, 8" 30.00
Plaza, amber or crystal, wine 14.00
Plaza, gr or pk, bottle, oil 60.00
Plaza, gr or pk, bowl, vegetable; deep, 10"..................... 50.00
Plaza, gr or pk, bowl, vegetable; 9" L 55.00
Plaza, gr or pk, candlestick, 2-light, 4¾x7", ea................ 45.00
Plaza, gr or pk, candy dish, rnd, w/lid, 4½"..................... 35.00
Plaza, gr or pk, plate, hdls, 10½" 35.00
Plaza, gr or pk, saucer..4.00
Plaza, gr or pk, sherbet, 3¾" 12.00
Plaza, gr or pk, tumbler, tea... 20.00
Plaza, gr or pk, tumbler, whiskey................................... 15.00
Puritan, all colors, bowl, cream soup; hdls 20.00
Puritan, all colors, bowl, 9¼"....................................... 55.00
Puritan, all colors, cup, demi 15.00
Puritan, all colors, goblet.. 20.00
Puritan, all colors, plate, 7½".......................................8.00
Puritan, all colors, saucer.. 2.00
Puritan, all colors, server, center hdl 35.00
Puritan, colors, tumbler, tea... 20.00
Sandwich, crystal, ashtray, sq, 2¼" 7.00
Sandwich, crystal, basket, oval, w/loop hdl, 10" 250.00
Sandwich, crystal, bonbon, ftd, w/lid, 7½"..................... 45.00
Sandwich, crystal, bowl, hdls, 5½"................................ 12.50
Sandwich, crystal, bowl, ice cream; ped ft, 5-oz, 4¼".......8.00
Sandwich, crystal, bowl, nut; cupped, 11"...................... 50.00
Sandwich, crystal, bowl, salad; shallow, 12" 35.00
Sandwich, crystal, butter dish, w/lid, ¼-lb 50.00
Sandwich, crystal, canape, 6" 10.00
Sandwich, crystal, candelabra, 3-light, w/bobeche & prisms, 16", ea .. 225.00
Sandwich, crystal, candlestick, 3-light, 5", ea................. 40.00
Sandwich, crystal, candy jar, ftd, w/lid, 8½".................... 75.00
Sandwich, crystal, coaster, 5".......................................9.00
Sandwich, crystal, compote, low ft, 5" 25.00

First Love, crystal, relish, five-part; 12", $55.00. (Photo courtesy Cathy and Gene Florence)

Sandwich, crystal, nappy, 2-part, 6" 14.00
Sandwich, crystal, pitcher, w/ice lip, 64-oz, 8½" 100.00
Sandwich, crystal, plate, cake; plain ped ft, 13" 75.00
Sandwich, crystal, plate, deviled egg; 12" 65.00
Sandwich, crystal, plate, service; hdls, 11½" 35.00
Sandwich, crystal, relish, 2-part, rnd, ring hdl, 6" 20.00
Sandwich, crystal, shakers, w/glass tops, 2½", pr 20.00
Sandwich, crystal, sugar bowl, 5-oz 8.00
Sandwich, crystal, teacup, 6-oz 9.00
Sandwich, crystal, tray, mint; rolled edge, w/ring hdl, 7" 22.00
Spiral Flutes, amber, gr or pk, bowl, mayonnaise; 4" 17.50
Spiral Flutes, amber, gr or pk, candlestick, 9½", ea 90.00
Spiral Flutes, amber, gr or pk, celery dish, 10¾x4¾" 17.50
Spiral Flutes, amber, gr or pk, chocolate jar, w/lid 195.00
Spiral Flutes, amber, gr or pk, compote, 6⅝" 17.50
Spiral Flutes, amber, gr or pk, finger bowl, 4⅜" 7.00
Spiral Flutes, amber, gr or pk, nappy, hdls, 6" 20.00
Spiral Flutes, amber, gr or pk, nappy, 9" 27.50
Spiral Flutes, amber, gr or pk, plate, pie; 6" 3.00
Spiral Flutes, amber, gr or pk, plate, torte; 13⅝" 27.50
Spiral Flutes, amber, gr or pk, platter, 13" 55.00
Spiral Flutes, amber, gr or pk, sherbet, low, 5-oz, 3¾" 7.00
Spiral Flutes, amber, gr or pk, vase, 10½" 38.00
Spiral Flutes, amber, gr or pk, wine, 3½-oz, 3¾" 15.00
Tear Drop, crystal, basket, candy; oval, hdls, 5½x7½" 85.00
Tear Drop, crystal, bottle, oil; 3-oz 18.00
Tear Drop, crystal, bowl, flower; flared, 11½" 32.50
Tear Drop, crystal, bowl, salad; 9" 30.00
Tear Drop, crystal, bowl, sq, 4-hdl, 12" 40.00
Tear Drop, crystal, canape set, 6" plate w/ring, 4-oz ftd, cocktail ... 30.00
Tear Drop, crystal, celery dish, hdls, 11" 20.00
Tear Drop, crystal, compote, low ft, hdl, 6" 15.00
Tear Drop, crystal, creamer, 3-oz 8.00
Tear Drop, crystal, finger bowl, 4¼" 7.00
Tear Drop, crystal, marmalade, w/lid, 4" 40.00
Tear Drop, crystal, olive dish, 2-part, 6" 15.00
Tear Drop, crystal, plate, hdls, 11" 27.50
Tear Drop, crystal, relish, 3-part, hdls, 11" 32.50
Tear Drop, crystal, shakers, 5", pr 25.00
Tear Drop, crystal, sugar bowl, 8-oz 8.00
Tear Drop, crystal, teacup, 6-oz 6.00
Tear Drop, crystal, tumbler, iced tea; ftd, 14-oz, 6" 18.00
Terrace, amber or crystal, ashtray, sq, 4¾" 20.00
Terrace, amber or crystal, bowl, ftd, 9x4½" 42.00
Terrace, amber or crystal, candy urn, w/lid 135.00
Terrace, amber or crystal, claret, #5111½, 4½-oz, 6" 45.00
Terrace, amber or crystal, cup 15.00
Terrace, amber or crystal, plate, lemon; hdls, 6" 12.00
Terrace, amber or crystal, plate, torte; rolled edge, 13" 37.50
Terrace, amber or crystal, plate, 6" 10.00
Terrace, cobalt or red, cheese stand, 3x5¼" 40.00
Terrace, cobalt or red, creamer, 10-oz, 3" 35.00
Terrace, cobalt or red, finger bowl, #5111½", 4¼" 65.00
Terrace, cobalt or red, pitcher 995.00
Terrace, cobalt or red, plate, cracker; w/ring, hdls, 11" 100.00
Terrace, cobalt or red, saucer champagne, #5111½", 5-oz, 5" ... 50.00
Terrace, cobalt or red, urn, 10½x4½" 350.00

Durand

Durand art glass was made by the Vineland Flint Glass Works of Vineland, New Jersey. Victor Durand Jr. was its proprietor. Hand-blown art glass in the style of Tiffany and Quezal was produced from 1924 to 1931 through a division called the 'Fancy Shop.' Durand hired owner Martin Bach Jr. along with his team of artisans from the failed Quezal Art Glass and Decorating Co. in Brooklyn, New York, to run this division. Much Durand art glass went unsigned; when it was, it was generally signed Durand in silver script within the polished pontil or across the top of a large letter V. The numbers that sometimes appear along with the signature indicate the shape and height of the object. Decorative names such as King Tut, Heart and Vine, Peacock Feather, and Egyptian Crackle became the company's trademarks. In 1926 Durand art glass was awarded a gold medal of honor at the Sesquicentennial International Exposition in Philadelphia. Durand had by this time taken its place alongside other famous art glass manufacturers such as Tiffany, Stueben, and Quezal, and was regarded as the epitome of American art glass. Our advisor for this category is Edward J. Meschi, author of *Durand — The Man and His Glass* (Antique Publications); he is listed in the Directory under New Jersey.

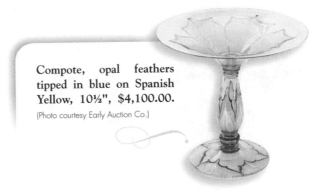

Compote, opal feathers tipped in blue on Spanish Yellow, 10½", $4,100.00.

(Photo courtesy Early Auction Co.)

Compote, King Tut, silver & gold on bl, oil lustre ft/finial, 10¼" ..3,000.00
Ginger jar, King Tut, wht & gold on bl, #1964-6, 7½x5¾" 4,600.00
Shade, Moorish Crackle, gold/wht/bl, scalloped rim, 8x6" 780.00
Vase, bl irid, flared cylinder w/incurvate rim, #1970, 6" 780.00
Vase, coil pattern, wht on gold, stick neck, bulbous, #1974-15, 14" ...2,525.00
Vase, gold, bulbous w/trumpet neck, #20167, 14" 840.00
Vase, gold w/opal coils, #1868-6, 6x4¼" 1,150.00
Vase, gold w/raised ribs, slightly bulbous, 1920s, 11" 780.00
Vase, gr/wht/gold crackle, bulbous, 10", NM 1,200.00
Vase, Heart & Vine, gr on marigold irid, #1968, 6" 1,800.00
Vase, Heart & Vine, wht on ambergris, cylindrical, 12¼" 565.00
Vase, Heart & Vine, wht on bl, gold ft, 9" 3,600.00
Vase, Heart & Vine, wht on bl irid, shouldered, flared rim, 7¾".. 1,200.00
Vase, King Tut, gold on bl-gr, #1968-6V, 6" 900.00
Vase, King Tut, opal on bl irid, #1970, 8x8¼" 1,800.00
Vase, King Tut, opal on gold, 6x4¼" 1,150.00
Vase, King Tut, silver on bl irid, flared cylinder, wide rim, 6" 850.00
Vase, Lady Gay Rose, pk w/opal-tipped gold feathers, gold int, 10½" . 8,000.00
Vase, Lady Gay Rose, red optic ribs, gold int, 1977-10, 8x11" ..6,000.00
Vase, Peacock Feather, red & wht (at base) on cranberry, #1907, 9¾". 1,150.00
Vase, threading, bl on bl irid, #1968, 8x5¼" 1,200.00
Vase, threading on bl irid, #2028, 8½" 1,325.00

Durant Kilns

The Durant Pottery Company operated in Bedford Village, New York, in the early 1900s. Its founder was Mrs. Clarence Rice; she was aided by L. Volkmar to whom she assigned the task of technical direction. (See also Volkmar.) The art and table wares they produced were simple in form and decoration. The creative aspects of the ware were carried on almost entirely by Volkmar himself, with only a minimal crew to help with production. After Mrs. Rice's death in 1919, the property was purchased by Volkmar, who chose to drop the Durant name by 1930. Prior to 1919 the ware was marked simply Durant and dated. After that time a stylized 'V' was added.

Bowl, aubergine flambé, geometrics, ftd, 1929, 3x9"................390.00
Bowl, center; Persian Blue, flared rim, ftd, 1918, 3¾x10"............360.00
Bowl, volcanic Persian Blue, flared rim, ca 1915, 6x15½", EX.....600.00
Chamberstick, dolphin figural, wht crackle, 1916, 7½", EX, pr....425.00
Jar, Sang de Boeuf, bulbous w/lid, Leon, 1923, 4½"..................1,100.00
Vase, Apple Green, bulbous, collared rim, flared ft, 1930, 7¾"..1,200.00
Vase, Apple Green, Oriental form, ca 1930, 7¾"......................1,200.00
Vase, aubergine flambé, bulbous, flared rim, ftd, 1924, 5¼x7"......570.00
Vase, brn/tan mottle on stoneware, #26A, 1934, 5½x4¾"............350.00
Vase, cobalt w/hammered look, bulbous vasiform, Leon, 1920s, 12"..2,400.00
Vase, geometrics, bl on clear, bulbous, 6"................................240.00
Vase, gray mottle w/brn speckles, slightly bulbous, 1936, 10½", NM..660.00
Vase, indigo matt, sgn, 3-hdl, 7x6"..960.00
Vase, iron spot, bulbous, recessed ft, 1919, 12".....................1,200.00
Vase, Persian Blue, morning-glory form, 1914, 3¼x5½".............110.00
Vase, Persian Blue, vasiform, ca 1920, 8¼"................................850.00
Vase, Persian Blue, vasiform body, lipped rim, 1920, 8¼".............840.00

Vase, thick curdled white volcanic glaze on sheer amber, 1923, 4x5½", $625.00. (Photo courtesy David Rago Auctions)

Easter

In the early 1900s to the 1930s, Germany made the first composition candy containers in the shapes of Easter rabbits, ducks, and chicks. A few were also made of molded cardboard. In the 1940s West Germany made candy containers out of molded cardboard. Many of these had spring necks to give a nodding effect. From the 1930s and into the 1950s, United States manufacturers made Easter candy containers out of egg-carton material (pulp) or pressed cardboard. Ducks and chicks are not as high in demand as rabbits. Rabbits with painted-on clothes or attached fabric clothes bring more than the plain brown or white rabbits. When no condition mentioned in the description, assume that values reflect excellent to near mint condition for all but paper items; those assume to be in near mint to mint condition. Our advisor for this category is Jenny Tarrant; she is listed in the Directory under Missouri.

Note: In the candy container section, measurements given for the rabbit and cart or rabbit and wagon containers indicate the distance to the tip of the rabbits' ears.

Candy Containers

German, begging rabbit, brn w/glass eyes, compo, 1900-30s, 5".....88.00
German, begging rabbit, brn w/glass eyes, compo, 1900-30s, 7"...105.00
German, begging rabbit, brn w/glass eyes, compo, 1900-30s, 9"...130.00
German, begging rabbit, mohair covered, compo, 1900-30s, 4"...135.00
German, begging rabbit, mohair covered, compo, 1900-30s, 6"...195.00
German, duck, yel w/glass eyes, compo, 1900-30s, 3"..................75.00
German, duck, yel w/glass eyes, compo, 1900-30s, 5"..................130.00
German, duck or chick, pnt-on clothes, compo, 1900-30s, 3-4"..125.00
German, duck or chick, pnt-on clothes, compo, 1900-30s, 6"......185.00
German, duck or chick, pnt-on clothes, compo, 1900-30s, 7"......200.00
German, egg, molded cb, 1900-30, 3-7", from $65 to....................45.00
German, egg, molded cb, 1900-30, 8".......................................65.00

German, egg, tin, 1900-10, EX, 2-3".......................................55.00
German, rabbit (dressed) in shoe, compo, 1900-30s, from $250 to..275.00
German, rabbit (dressed) on egg, compo, 1900-30s, from $250 to..250.00
German, rabbit pulling fancy wood/moss wagon, brn compo, 1900-30s, 7"..300.00
German, rabbit pulling wood cart, mohair covered, 1900-30s, 4"...175.00
German, rabbit pulling wood cart, mohair covered, 1900-30s, 6"...250.00
German, rabbit pulling wood wagon, brn compo, 1900-30s, 4"....150.00
German, rabbit pulling wood wagon, brn compo, 1900-30s, 6"....195.00
German, rabbit w/fabric clothes, compo, 1900-30s, 4"................250.00
German, rabbit w/fabric clothes, compo, 1900-30s, 6"................325.00
German, rabbit w/fabric clothes, compo, 1900-30s, 7", minimum value..350.00
German, rabbit w/glass beading, compo, 1900-30s, 6"................150.00
German, rabbit w/pnt-on clothes, compo, 1900-30s, 5"..............200.00
German, rabbit w/pnt-on clothes, compo, 1900-30s, 7"..............250.00
German, sitting rabbit, brn w/glass eyes, compo, 1900-30s, 6".....110.00
German, sitting rabbit, mohair covered, compo, 1900-30s, 4".....140.00
German, sitting rabbit, mohair covered, compo, 1900-30s, 5".....160.00
German, sitting rabbit, mohair covered, compo, 1900-30s, 6".....175.00
German, standing rabbit (Ma or Pa), pnt-on clothes, molded cb, 10½"..250.00
German, walking rabbit, brn w/glass eyes, compo, 1900-30s, 6"...110.00
German, walking rabbit, brn w/glass eyes, compo, 1900-30s, 8"...150.00
German, walking rabbit, mohair covered, compo, 1900-30s, 4"...150.00
German, walking rabbit, mohair covered, compo, 1900-30s, 6"...225.00
German, walking rabbit, mohair covered, compo, 1900-30s, 7"...245.00
US, begging rabbit, pulp, 1940-50, w/base....................................55.00
US, sitting rabbit, pulp, brn w/glass eyes, Burk Co, 1930..............85.00
US, sitting rabbit next to lg basket, pulp, 1930-50......................75.00

U.S., sitting rabbit with basket on back, pulp, 1940 – 1950, $75.00. (Photo courtesy Jenny Tarrant)

W German/US Zone, dressed duck or chick, cb, spring neck, 1940-50..60.00
W German/US Zone, dressed rabbit, cb, spring neck, 1940-50......80.00
W German/US Zone, egg, molded cb, 1940-60, 3-8", from $25 to 40.00
W German/US Zone, plain rabbit, cb, spring neck, 1940-50.........60.00

Miscellaneous

Celluloid chick or duck, dressed, 3-5", M................................45.00
Celluloid chick or duck, dressed, 6-8", M................................75.00
Celluloid chicken pulling wagon w/rabbit, M............................125.00
Celluloid rabbit, dressed, 3-5", M..65.00
Celluloid rabbit, dressed, 6-8", M..75.00
Celluloid rabbit, plain, 3-5", M..20.00
Celluloid rabbit, plain, 6-7", M..30.00
Celluloid rabbit & chick in swan boat, M.................................150.00
Celluloid rabbit driving car, M...150.00
Celluloid rabbit pulling wagon, M...125.00
Celluloid rabbit pushing or pulling cart, lg, M...........................125.00
Celluloid rabbit pushing or pulling cart, sm, M..........................75.00
Celluloid windup toy, Japan or Occupied Japan, M.....................150.00
Cotton batten chick, Japan, 3"..22.00
Cotton batten rabbit w/paper ears, Japan, 1930-50, 2-5", $30 to...30.00
Cotton batten rabbit w/paper ears, Japan, 1930-50, 6"................45.00

Egg Cups

Egg cups, one of the fastest growing collectibles, have been traced back to the ruins of Pompeii. They have been made in almost every country and in almost every conceivable material (ceramics, glass, metal, papier maché, plastic, wood, ivory, even rubber, and straw). Popular categories include Art Deco, Black memorabilia, chintz, personalities, figurals, golliwoggs, railroadiana, steamship, souvenir ware, etc.

Still being produced today, egg cups appeal to collectors on many levels. Prices range from the inexpensive to thousands of dollars. Those made prior to 1840 are scarce and sought after, as are the character/personality egg cups of the 1930s. For a more thorough study of egg cups we recommend *Egg Cups: An Illustrated History and Price Guide* (Antique Publications) by Brenda Blake, our advisor. You will find her address listed in the Directory under Maine.

Key:
bkt — bucket, a single cup without a foot
dbl — two-sided with small end for eating egg in shell, large end for mixing egg with toast and butter
fig — figural, an egg cup actually molded into the shape of an animal, bird, car, person, etc.
hoop — hoop, a single open cup with waistline
inst. dbl — large custard cup shape
set — tray or cruet (stand, frame, or basket) with two to eight cups
sgl — with a foot; goblet shaped

American

Bkt, mustard, Paul Revere Pottery	90.00
Dbl, Autumn, mc fruit basket, Lenox	35.00
Dbl, Ballerina, khaki-gr, Universal	15.00
Dbl, Bride, Cleminson, 1940s	35.00
Dbl, Brittany, Homer Laughlin	19.00
Dbl, Festival, Stangl	24.00
Dbl, Homespun, plaid, Vernon Kilns, 1950s	32.00
Dbl, Magnolia, Stangl, 1950s	25.00
Dbl, Rooster, Pennsbury	28.00
Dbl, woman in apron, Cleminson, 1940s	30.00
Sgl, Apple, Franciscan	32.00
Sgl, Valencia, Louise Bauer, Shawnee, 1937	22.00
Sgl, yellow ware, no decor, ca 1880	325.00

Characters/Personalities

Bucket, Beatles, Keele St. Pottery, 1¾", $275.00 for the set of four. (Photo courtesy Brenda Blake)

Bkt, Katzenjammer Kids, color illus, early	100.00
Bkt, Marilyn Monroe, transfer, 1993, rare	65.00
Bkt, Tonto, molded face against stump, Keele St Pottery, 1961	60.00
Fig, ET	22.00

Fig, Humpty Dumpty on brick ball, Mansell	85.00
Fig, Prince Charles, Spitting Image, 1982	70.00
Fig, Snow White, standing by egg cup, WD Enterprises, 1937	220.00
Set, Beatles (4 bkts), blk & wht bust portraits w/names, KSP mk	275.00
Sgl, Donald Duck, Good Morning Series	16.00
Sgl, Prince Ranier/Princess Grace of Monaco, wedding, Limoges, 1950s	100.00
Sgl, Tom & Jerry decals on wht ceramic cup, England, 1967, 2"	20.00

English/Staffordshire

Bkt, Burleigh ware, red print, Stonewall kitchen, MIE, recent	6.00
Bkt, Crocus, Clarice Cliff	125.00
Bkt, Orange Tree, Art Deco, Crown Ducal	38.00
Bkt, Primavera, Midwinter	25.00
Dbl, Cornishware, bl bands, TC Green, 1930s	45.00
Dbl, Madras, flow bl, Royal Doulton, ca 1900	110.00
Dbl, Old Mill Stream, Johnson Bros	20.00
Dbl, Rose Chintz, Johnson Bros	20.00
Set, Amherst Japan, 6 scalloped-rim cups w/stand & base, Minton	12,000.00
Set, 6 tulip cups in chrome stand, English	70.00
Sgl, Blue Dragon, Royal Worcester	30.00

Single, Clarice Cliff, Moderne, $100.00.

Sgl, integral saucer, bl, Nigella Lawson, recent	11.00
Sgl, silver, attached saucer w/rooster, Royal Doulton	72.00
Sgl, Tea Rose, yel, Royal Albert	22.00

Figurals

Bellhop, pillbox hat, smoking cigarette, Art Deco, Made in France	75.00
Black male face, Germany, ca 1912	80.00
Boat, orange, Honiton	25.00
Duck, bl, Fanny Farmer, 1930s	25.00
Duck pulling egg cart, unmk Japan, 2"	15.00
Hen, Keele St Pottery	16.00
Legs walking, gr shoes, Carlton	40.00
Miss Priss, Lefton	30.00
Rabbit pushing wheelbarrow cup, plastic	20.00
Sergeant Chimp, plastic, w/lid	28.00
Swan, lustre, Japan, 1930s	15.00
Whistler, bear, lustre, Foreign	100.00

Foreign

Bkt, Cardinal Tuck, red robe, Goebel, 1960s	175.00
Dbl, Peasant, yel & gr, floral panels, HB Quimper	45.00
Dbl, rooster & hen, yel base, T&V Limoges	60.00
Set, cup+salt shaker+tray, Limoges	28.00
Set, majolica basket w/6 egg cups, leaf pattern, 1880s	500.00
Sgl, Blue Flower, Royal Copenhagen, ca 1940	25.00
Sgl, Devon Motto Ware, Torquay	28.00
Sgl, fruit & flowers w/Greek key border, China	12.00
Sgl, Oriole, Goebel, 1989	20.00
Sgl, Saladon, Bavarian style, Hutchenreuther	22.00
Sgl, Seagull, Bing & Grondahl	45.00

Glass

Dbl, English Hobnail, amber, Westmoreland, 1930s-40s	30.00
Dbl, Hobnail, milk glass, Fenton	55.00
Fig, chicken, bl, Portieux	25.00
Fig, chicken, milk glass, John E Kemple	15.00
Fig, rooster, vaseline, Boyd	14.00
Sgl, Argus, flint, ca 1850-70	28.00
Sgl, bottle glass, gr, 2-part mold, ca 1910	32.00
Sgl, Hobnail, ruby flashed	55.00
Sgl, lacy glass, leaf pattern, ca 1925-40	90.00
Sgl, Smocking, amethyst, Sandwich, 1840s	275.00

Railroad/Steamship

Dbl, Luckenbach Lines	40.00
Dbl, Meridale, Wabash RR	35.00
Dbl, Presidential Lines, gr band, maroon bird	48.00
Hoop, Atlantic Transport Line, Wedgwood	135.00
Sgl, Bows & Leaves, Canadian Pacific	45.00
Sgl, Denver & Rio Grand, recent	15.00

Single, Maybrook pattern by Syracuse, date code for 1939, from $24.00 to $30.00. (Photo courtesy Barbara Conroy)

Sgl, Minbreno, ATSF	500.00
Sgl, Traveler, CMStP&P	125.00

Souvenir

Bkt, British Airways, bl border, silver stripes, Royal Doulton	16.00
Dbl, US Coast & Geodetic Survey	100.00
Sgl, Channel Tunnel, 1988-94, 1994	16.00
Sgl, Graceland, Japan, 1970s	20.00
Sgl, World's Fair, St Louis 1904, transfer scene, 1904	100.00

Elfinware

Made in Germany from about 1920 until the 1940s, these miniature vases, boxes, salt cellars, and miscellaneous novelty items are characterized by the tiny applied flowers that often cover their entire surface. Pieces with animals and birds are the most valuable, followed by the more interesting examples such as diminutive grand pianos, candleholders, etc. Items covered in 'spinach' (applied green moss) can be valued at 75% to 100% higher than pieces that are not decorated in this manner. See also Salts, Open.

Boot, appl flowers, fan-shaped lid, sm	25.00
Box, appl flowers, basketweave & rope design, 1¼x2½x1¾"	35.00
Box, piano form w/appl flowers & spinach, 3-leg, 2x2¾"	40.00
Box, trinket; HP floral on fan-shaped lid, Germany, sm	25.00
Poodle, standing on base w/gr grass, 4½"	125.00
Salt cellar, appl roses & spinach, simple hdls, 2½x2½x1¾"	30.00
Shoe, curled toe, appl flowers, 2¼x5¼"	100.00
Vase, rose w/spinach & forget-me-nots on top, Germany, 1⅝"	70.00

Epergnes

Popular during the Victorian era, epergnes were fancy centerpieces often consisting of several tiers of vases (called lilies), candleholders, dishes, or a combination of components. They were made in all types of art glass, and some were set in ornate plated frames.

It is important to examine each component for authenticity. Make sure the glassware is original to the base, as more modern bowls and vases (Fenton, for example) are often used to replace the broken Victorian pieces. Our advisor for this category is Barbara Aaronson; she is listed in the Directory under California.

Bl opal, 4 ruffled lilies, Lg Wright, 1930s	425.00
Cranberry lilies (3) w/clear ruffles+3 baskets on bowl base, 21"	1,650.00
Crystal lily on crystal & bronze base, w/crystal tray, Fr, 17x12"	1,100.00
Cut bowl top on Rococo Revival SP fr, 3 candle arms, ea w/sm bowl, 29"	3,250.00
Cut crystal bowls (1 lg/4 sm) on 4-arm SP fr, 1800s, 13x22½" dia	2,150.00
Cut trumpet vase atop SP fr w/2 cut tray tiers, ca 1899, 36x9½" dia	2,400.00
Etched crystal bowls (3) on gilt metal figures, 1875, rpr, 23x21x13"	2,650.00
Gr, 1 lg+3 sm flutes, 3 spiral arms w/baskets, ruffled base, 21"	600.00
Gr opal lily w/3 baskets on ruffled bowl base w/bronze mts, 18¾"	800.00

Green opalescent, three baskets around center lily over ruffled bowl, 21", $750.00. (Photo courtesy Early Auction Co.)

Lime gr opal, 1 lg+4 sm lilies w/crystal serpentine, scallop base, 18"	950.00
Pk opal & cranberry cased, 1 ruffled/crimped lily, brass base, 13"	495.00
Pk-to-wht lily/bowl w/gr ruffles on SP Cupid/Venus fr w/2 bowls, 24"	3,500.00
Teal gr jack-in-pulpit vases (3) w/appl ribbons, ca 1900, 23x11"	1,100.00
Vaseline, 7 screw-in flower forms, SP curving Nouveau fr, 22½" W	500.00
Vaseline & cranberry, 1 lg+3 sm lilies, ruffled base, 21x12", NM	675.00
Wht opal lilies (2) w/bl rim/appl rigaree, bowl base w/bronze mts, 24"	850.00
Yel cased lilies (3)+2 baskets on bowl base w/bronze mts, 22x21"	1,100.00

Erickson

Carl Erickson of Bremen, Ohio, produced hand-formed glassware from 1943 until 1960 in artistic shapes, no two of which were identical. One of the characteristics of his work was the air bubbles that were captured within the glass. Both clear and colored glass was produced. Rather than to risk compromising his high standards by selling the factory, when Erickson retired, the plant was dismantled and sold.

Ashtray, bl w/controlled bubbles, 3 rests, 5"	60.00
Ashtray, smoke w/controlled bubbles, 4-fold top, 3x7x6"	40.00
Bottle, scent; orange sphere w/controlled bubbles, 3½x4½"	135.00
Bowl, bl free-form w/fold at rim, 2 layers of bubbles, shallow, 7½"	70.00
Bowl, emerald gr w/controlled bubbles, sq rim, 3x5¼x5¼"	45.00
Bowl, smoke on clear ped w/controlled bubbles, 7½x11⅛"	115.00

Bowl, smoke on crystal ped w/controlled bubbles, 6x7½" 36.00
Decanter, crystal w/gr flame base & controlled bubbles, ball top, 11" . 115.00
Decanter, gr w/controlled bubbles, pinched, clear stopper, 15½" ... 55.00

Martini pitcher, emerald green with clear bubbled paperweight base, 13", with stirrer, $125.00.
(Photo courtesy Apple Tree Auction Center/ LiveAuctioneers.com)

Punch cup, smoke w/crystal hdl & rosettes, 2¾x3" 90.00
Shot glass, crystal w/gr 5-point flame base, 3" 32.00
Vase, bud; ruby w/crystal base w/controlled bubbles, 11x2¾" 30.00
Vase, crystal on paperweight base w/controlled bubbles, att, 13x4" .. 72.50
Vase, fan; emerald gr on crystal ped w/controlled bubbles, 9½x10".. 85.00
Vase, gr w/controlled bubbles, clear sq base, 15x6" 42.50
Vase, smoke w/paperweight base & controlled bubbles, 5¼x5x3½" .. 48.00

Erphila

The Erphila trademark was used by Ebeling and Ruess Co. of Philadelphia between 1886 and the 1950s. The company imported quality porcelain and pottery from Germany, Czechoslovakia, Italy, and France. Pieces more readily found are from Germany and Czechoslovakia. A variety of items can be found and pieces such as figural teapots and larger figurines are moving up in value. There is a variety of marks, but all contain the name Erphila. One of the earlier marks is a green rectangle containing the name Erphila Germany. In general, Erphila pieces are scarce, not easily found.

Ashtray, Black boy stacking 2 lg dice, mc on blk base, 4x4" 24.00
Bust, Geo washington, pnt facial details, blk coat, 5" 30.00
Dresser doll/powder box, Madame Pompador, 1920s-30s, 5¼" 225.00
Dresser doll/powder box, Nancy Pert, lady in pk, 7½x6" 120.00
Figurine, dachshund, brn to blk, 7" 60.00
Figurine, Deco lady in blk gown, hands away from body, 1920s, 12".. 88.00
Flower frog, sailing ship, wht gloss, 12" 72.50
Flower holder, draped nude before 3 joined stumps, wht, 6½x6⅜" ... 30.00
Pitcher, Deco bird figural, blk/red/cream, #881, 9x7½" 200.00
Pitcher, Deco ram figural, red/blk/yel, #1042, 8¾" 150.00

Powder jar, lady figural, 7¾", $100.00.

Vase, calla lilies, wht/gr/yel on cobalt, 7½x5" 42.50
Vase, geometrics, earth tones, cylindrical neck, 4x3½" 42.50

Eskimo Artifacts

While ivory carvings made from walrus tusks or whale teeth have been the most emphasized articles of Eskimo art, basketry and woodworking are other areas in which these Alaskan Indians excel. Their designs are effected through the application of simple yet dramatic lines and almost stark decorative devices. Though not pursued to the extent of American Indian art, the unique work of these northern tribes is beginning to attract the serious attention of today's collectors.

Basket, coiled, bulbous, w/lid, late 1800s, 10" dia 300.00
Boots, sealskin, heavy formed soles, sinew sewn, 1890s, 9½x10½" .. 350.00
Bowl, cvd wood w/stylized avian figure/red pigment, 1800s, 18" L ... 1,175.00
Cribbage board, walrus ivory w/inked scrimshaw, ca 1900, 13x1½" . 200.00
Cvg, bust of man w/animal-head headdress, stone/metal eyes, 1900s, 7".. 2,650.00
Cvg, hawk on prey, illegible mk, dk stone, Eskimo art label, 10x6x9" .. 800.00
Cvg, Inuit mother nursing child, dk stone, 11¼x14x14" 2,300.00
Cvg, native lady, cvd walrus ivory w/red/blk stain, ca 1920s, 2½" .. 1,325.00
Cvg, polar bear effigy, fossilized walrus ivory, 4¼" L 1,325.00
Cvg, walrus, argillite w/ivory tusks, articulated flippers, Kavik, 8" ... 575.00
Cvg, walrus sailing vessel w/full sails, ivory, 1950s, 10" 1,850.00
Cvg, whale, driftwood, 4½" 100.00
Fleshing tool, patinated stone w/blunt working edge, 5¼" 195.00
Goggles, cvd wood w/bk side pnt blk, thread bridging nose, 5½" 1,325.00
Hammer head, whale bone, side notches, hafted head, 3" 100.00
Harpoon tip, stained bone, opposing barbs & cord holes, AK, 2½" .. 85.00
Knife, mineralized bone, drilled hdl hole, prehistoric, 6⅝" 225.00
Lip plug, walrus ivory, 1x3/4" 50.00
Mask, cvd wood, oversz features, pierced eyes/nose/mouth, 1900s, 9x6" .2,150.00
Pipe-cleaning tool, walrus ivory, pre-1895, 4" 50.00
Scraper, blk flint blade, bone hdl, ca 1850s, 4" 250.00
Spirit mask, cvd/pnt alder & cedar, 5 appendages, 1940s, 19x21" 800.00
Spoon, cvd bone, Old Bering Sea culture, ca 1000 AD, 6" 100.00
Spoon, simple form w/chevron tip, late 1800s, 10x3½" 350.00
Swivel/toggle, cvd ivory, 1¾" 50.00
Ulu (blubber knife), wide radiating blade, scrimshaw hdl, recent, 4x6".60.00

Eyewear

Collectors of Americana are beginning to appreciate the charm of antique optical items, and those involved in the related trade find them particularly fascinating. Anyone, however, can appreciate the evolution of technology apparent when viewing a collection of vintage eyewear, and at the same time admire the ingenuity involved in the design and construction of these glasses.

In the early 1900s the choice of an eyeglass frame was generally left to the optician, much as the choice of medication was left to the family doctor. By the 1930s, however, eyeglasses had emerged as fashion accessories. In 1939 Altina Sanders' 'Harlequin' frame (a forerunner of the 1950s 'cat-eyes'), won an American Design award. By the 1950s manufacturers were working overtime to enhance the allure of eyewear, hosting annual competitions for 'Miss Beauty in Glasses' and 'Miss Specs Appeal.'

Particularly sought after today are the flamboyant and colorful designs of the '50s and '60s. These include 'cat-eyes' with their distinctively upswept brow edges; 'highbrows,' often heavily jeweled or formed in the shape of butterfly or bird wings; and frames with decorative temples ranging from floral wreaths to musical notes. Many of today's collectors have such novel eyeglass frames fitted with their own prescription lenses for daily wear.

For further information on eyewear of this era, we recommend *Specs Appeal: Extravagant 1950s & 1960s Eyewear* (Schiffer) by Leslie Piña and Donald-Brian Johnson (our advisor for this category). Mr Johnson is listed in the Directory under Nebraska.

Eyeglass stand, Lucite, bk-cvd red rose, from $15 to 20.00
Eyeglasses, aluminum combos, blk w/bl steel brow decor, Kono, $55 to . 65.00
Eyeglasses, Batwing, gray, from $375 to.. 400.00
Eyeglasses, Bird Wing, nesting bird, from $600 to 650.00
Eyeglasses, blk/gold mesh, pearl/bl rhinestone brow clusters, $120 to . 140.00
Eyeglasses, Cat-Eye, blk w/silver aluminum inlay, Hudson, $175 to...200.00
Eyeglasses, Cat-Eye, lt bl w/clear cutaways, rhinestone trim, $70 to... 80.00
Eyeglasses, Cat-Eye, pk & rhinestones, folding, from $100 to 120.00
Eyeglasses, Cat-Eye shape w/rhinestones, Hong Kong, 1950s, $70 to ..80.00
Eyeglasses, child's, clear, wht laminate brow, stem accents, Shuron ..35.00
Eyeglasses, child's, Graceline, pk w/gold strip laminate, from $30 to.. 40.00
Eyeglasses, Dbl-Flare Cat-Eye, yel lenses, rhinestones, 1950s, $140 to..160.00
Eyeglasses, Dbl-Pointed Cat-Eye, aurora rhinestones, Frame Fr, $200 to .225.00
Eyeglasses, Dior granny style/bl cloisonné rhinestones/pearls, $150 to..200.00
Eyeglasses, Dr Scholl's Health Glasses, from $25 to........................ 35.00
Eyeglasses, Earring Chains, yel or check fr, 1960s, from $120 to..160.00
Eyeglasses, elaborate highbrow fr, from $1,000 to 1,200.00
Eyeglasses, floral temple wreath trim, Tura, from $275 to............ 325.00
Eyeglasses, folding, bl & silver-gray, from $175 to 200.00
Eyeglasses, gold metal w/gr lenses, Tura, from $70 to..................... 80.00
Eyeglasses, Granny style, faceted rosy pk lenses, 1960s, from $60 to . 75.00
Eyeglasses, Headband style, butterscotch, from $250 to 275.00
Eyeglasses, highbrows, taupe w/rhinestone decor, from $300 to ... 325.00
Eyeglasses, irregular fr w/rhinestone trim, France, from $45 to....... 55.00
Eyeglasses, Octette oversz 8-sided fr, Selecta, 1970s, from $50 to .. 60.00
Eyeglasses, oversz rnd blk fr w/rhinestones, Oleg Cassini, $100 to...125.00
Eyeglasses, Ram Horn highbrows, brn w/rhinestones, Qualite Fr, $550 to...600.00
Eyeglasses, silver-gray fr w/rhinestone swags, J Hasday, from $70 to ..80.00
Eyeglasses, swan highbrows, wht pearlized, from $450 to 550.00
Eyeglasses, Triple-Flare Cat-Eye w/rhinestones, Fr, from $140 to. 160.00
Eyeglasses, Trucco Shallow Make Up Frames, demi-amber, Selecta, $50 to..60.00
Eyeglasses, twist Cat-Eye fr in blk & clear, TWE, from $90 to 100.00
Eyeglasses, yel pearlized plastic, gold floral appliqué, Fr, $120 to.. 135.00
Lorgnette, silver w/yel & gr stones, 1900s, closed: 3½", $275 to .. 300.00
Lorgnette, 14k yel gold folding type w/monogram, 1900s, EX, $325 to..360.00
Opera glasses, floral HP on brass, Salon & Co, London, 1900s, $400 to..425.00

Opera glasses, handle and eyepiece both decorated with lounging cherubs, 6" long, from $375.00 to $400.00. (Photo courtesy Early Auction Co.)

Opera glasses, MOP & gold plate, lenses adjust, Lemaire, from $375 to ..395.00
Opera glasses, MOP w/brass fittings, ca 1900, EX in case, $160 to..180.00
Opera glasses, tortoiseshell, lenses adjust/hinged hdl, 1900s, $375 to.. 395.00
Reading glasses, Selecta, 'Scala Shiny Gold,' from $55 to.............. 65.00
Sunglasses, bug-eye, Playboy Austria, from $90 to........................... 95.00
Sunglasses, highbrows w/musical note shapes, from $375 to 400.00
Sunglasses, novelty, eyelash finge trim, from $350 to 375.00
Sunglasses, Red Wings, Ray-Ban, from $60 to 70.00
Sunglasses, Schiaparelli design, yel-gold w/fruit clusters, $230 to . 250.00
Sunglasses, Selecta 4000 White Pearl, from $55 to 65.00
Sunglasses, Suntimer, pk/blk/wht laminate, 1960s, from $110 to.. 125.00
Sunglasses, wraparounds, Polaroid, from $60 to............................. 70.00
Sunglasses, zebra-pattern fr w/blk temples, from $60 to................. 70.00

Face Jugs

The most recognizable form of Southern folk pottery is the face jug. Rich alkaline glazes (lustrous greens and browns) are typical, and occasionally shards of glass are applied to the surface of the ware which during firing melts to produce opalescent 'glass runs' over the alkaline. In some locations clay deposits contain elements that result in areas of fluorescent blue or rutile; another variation is swirled or striped ware, reminiscent of eighteenth-century agateware from Staffordshire. Face vessels came in several forms as well. In America, from New England to the Carolinas, they were made as early as the 1840s. Collector demand for these unique one-of-a-kind jugs is at an all-time high and is still escalating. Choice examples made by Burlon B. Craig and Lanier Meaders range from $1,000.00 to over $5,000.00 on the secondary market. If you're interested in learning more about this type of folk pottery, contact the Southern Folk Pottery Collectors Society; their address is in the Directory under Clubs, Newsletters, and Catalogs. Our advisor for this category is Billy Ray Hussey; he is listed in the Directory under North Carolina.

Abee, Steve; brn/tan/bl swirls, clay teeth in open mouth, 12" 180.00
Crocker, Dwayne L; brn & cream swirls, 7" 180.00
Crocker, Michael; rock teeth, bl pupils, dimple in chin, 8½" 240.00
Fleming, Walter; dk brn w/clay teeth & dripping eyes, 10½" 150.00
Freeman, Henry; bl w/clay teeth, bl pupils, Ivory Bluff, 1990, 8" ... 90.00
Hewell, Matthew; wht clay teeth, wht eyes w/bl pupils, 11" 120.00
Hussey, Billy Ray; bearded man, nude woman hdl, 2-color, 8" 600.00
Lisk, Chas; swirlware, wht clay teeth/eyes w/pupils, unibrow, 14" ...515.00
Lisk, Chas; 4-color swirl, clay teeth/raised brows, now a lamp, 11" ..215.00
Meaders, David; Centennial Celebration, streaky brn, 9" 215.00
Meaders, Edwin; cobalt bl w/dripping eyes, 11" 1,325.00

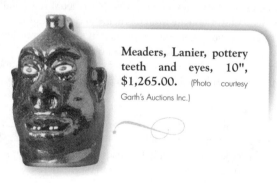

Meaders, Lanier, pottery teeth and eyes, 10", $1,265.00. (Photo courtesy Garth's Auctions Inc.)

Meaders, L; dk brn w/rock teeth & dripping eyes, 10"...............3,300.00
Teague, A; 5 clay teeth, wht eyes w/dk pupils, yel clay, 7"............ 350.00

Fans

The Japanese are said to have invented the fan. From there it went to China, and Portuguese traders took the idea to Europe. Though usually considered milady's accessory, even the gentlemen in seventeenth-century England carried fans! More fashionable than practical, some were of feathers and lovely hand-painted silks with carved ivory or tortoise sticks. Some French fans had peepholes. There are mourning fans, calendar fans, and those with advertising. Fine antique fans (pre-1900) of ivory or mother-of-pearl are highly desirable. Those from before 1800 often sell for upwards of $1,000.00. Fans are being viewed as works of art, and some are actually signed by known artists. Values are given for examples in good, as-found condition, except for those rated excellent.

Blk lacquer sticks (22) w/gold Oriental decor strung w/ribbon 500.00
Celluloid w/HP florals, strung w/ribbon 120.00

Feathers, ostrich; wht, known as Sally Rand, ca 1920, 30x50" 250.00
Gauze, HP emb peacock on bl w/sequins, wooden sticks, 1900s .. 275.00
Gauze w/embr sequins, cvd/rtcl ivory sticks, 1790s, 10", EX...... 1,540.00
Ivory, floral cvgs, cord tied, Continental, late 1700s, 7¾" 550.00
Ivory, HP 1700s figures/ducks in outdoors scene, 1900s, 11x14" .. 765.00
Kidskin, HP adults & children on lawn, ca 1800, EX 1,200.00
Lace, Brussels, on cream silk, MOP sticks, 1870s, 10", EX 500.00
Lace, rosepoint, cvd/gilt MOP sticks, Continental, 1900, 12", EX.. 800.00
Lace flowers appl to blk net, tortoiseshell sticks, 1870s, 11", EX.. 350.00
Paper, HP classical figures, cvd MOP sticks 725.00
Paper, HP court scenes w/gold, MOP guards on rtcl sticks, 1800s, 26".. 300.00
Paper, HP courting scenes/sewn sequins, cvd ivory fr, 17x27" 350.00
Paper, HP religious scenes/flowers, ivory sticks, ca 1900, 14x24" . 240.00
Paper, HP ships scene, rtcl/ivory sticks, China trade, 1850s, 25", EX. 5,000.00
Paper litho w/HP details & gold, bone sticks, worn varnish, 14", +box.. 215.00
Parchment, HP French lady scene, MOP rtcl/gilt/silvered sticks, 1700s. 1,075.00
Silk, HP bird on branch, cvd bone sticks, 22" 100.00
Silk, HP classical reserves & flowers, ivory sticks, 12x19½", EX .. 120.00
Silk, HP farm scene, cvd ivory sticks, ca 1830 .... 500.00
Silk, HP Renaissance courtiers, cvd geometric sticks, 1700s, 20" 625.00
Silk, HP violets & butterflies, cvd wooden sticks, 1910s, 14" 125.00
Tortoiseshell brise w/3 HP scenes & gold lacquer, 1860s, 12", EX... 475.00

Farm Collectibles

Country living in the nineteenth century entailed plowing, planting, and harvesting; gathering eggs and milking; making soap from lard rendered on butchering day; and numerous other tasks performed with primitive tools of which we in the twenty-first century have had little first-hand knowledge. Values listed below are for items in excellent original condition unless noted otherwise. See also Cast Iron; Lamps, Lanterns; Woodenware; Wrought Iron.

Auger, hand; Millers Falls No 2, wood hdl w/2 interchangable bits, EX... 50.00
Bee fogger, metal w/wood, working patina, 6½x9" 30.00
Booklet, Plans for Making Farm Tools & Equipment, 1950, 32 pgs, EX... 10.00
Bucksaw, No 2 Yorktown..., 31", VG... 35.00
Bull-nose lead tongs, CI w/rope, VG... 20.00
Castrator/Bander, mk Burdizzo Made in Italy, 3½x16", VG............ 20.00
Chain detacher, Herschel No 111, CI, 8", VG 18.00
Corn cutter, 9½" scythe blade w/22" wooden hdl, VG 25.00
Corn seed planter, metal w/wooden hdl, 33½" overall, VG............ 35.00
Corn sheller, Black Hawk 808, EX 65.00
Cow bell, hand forged, 5¾x3¼" 28.00
Cranberry picker, wood w/hdl & tines, 10x8x4", G....................... 35.00
Cream separator, Am Wonder...NY, stacked cones, Indian decal, EX .. 500.00
Dolly, Fairbanks, oak, 45x19", VG... 55.00
Draw knife, mk USA, #8, metal w/wooden hdls, EX 32.00
Feed sack, Alfalfa, Fagley Seed Co, Archbold OH, NM................. 27.00
Funnel, amethyst glass, 12½x10¾" dia, NM................................. 48.00
Grain carrier, gr-pnt wood w/cvd star, dvtl, sq nails, EX................ 45.00
Grain shovel, softwood, str front edge, arched hdl, 37x12", VG 45.00
Hames, metal & glass w/leather collar, 30x18", EX 95.00
Hatchet, Keen Kutter, 3½x6½" single blade w/hammer end, 12" hdl. 25.00

Hay harpoon, cast iron, 33" long, $90.00.

(Photo courtesy Lang's Auctions/LiveAuctioneers.com)

Hay hook, 5¼" wooden hdl 15.00
Horse collar, EX leather, rpl straps.. 75.00
Implement seat, HP Deuscher, CI, old pnt, 17x13", EX 325.00
Implement seat, South Bend Chilled Plow, CI, no pnt, 17x15" ... 200.00
Lantern, pine w/glass panels, pegged, rprs, 10"........................... 430.00
Lantern, tin, ring hdl, pierced air vent, 2 glass panels, 15".......... 265.00
Leather riveter, Rex, PAT MAR27 OCT9..., EX........................... 25.00
Milk can, aluminum, bail hdl, 9½" 20.00
Nail keg, wooden barrel w/metal bands, 17x12", VG 30.00
Plane, PATD 2-17-20, 18" 50.00
Potato grader, Duplex, conveyor type, 10" iron wheels, EX.......... 100.00
Poultry waterer, clear glass dish w/qt-sz Ball jar, EX 18.00
Pulley, #H126, CI & wood, VG 28.00
Pulley, Meyers 108, CI, EX 50.00
Rope maker, Ideal, Pat 1907, EX 225.00
Saw, crosscut; 5⅛x71⅛" blade, 2 wooden hdls, VG 65.00
Saw, dehorning; Keen Kutter, wooden hdl, 10", VG 28.00
Scoop, metal w/iron & wood hdl, 10x6", VG 24.00
Scythe, label mk Scythe Snaths, 30" blade w/60" hdl, VG............ 85.00
Scythe, 18" blade w/48" wooden hdl, EX 35.00
Sifter, garden; 12x22" tin sifting tray w/wooden hdl, 1800s, VG ... 45.00

Sign, John Deere Farm Implements, 24x72", EX, $2,240.00. (Photo courtesy Don and R. C. Raycraft)

Tobacco knife, 2¾x4¼" metal blade w/about a 24" wooden hdl, VG. 25.00
Wagon seat, mixed woods, slat bk/trn arms/rush seat, seats 2, 29" H 145.00
Wheelbarrow, gr-pnt wood, chamfered slats w/chip-cvd ends, EX 100.00
Wire fence stretcher, Page, metal, 25½", EX 40.00
Wrench, Allis Chalmers 800755, ⅞" hexagonal end & 1⅛" sq end, VG 30.00
Wrench, plow; H-46, 6½" 15.00
Wrench, plow; Rock-Island, 7", EX.. 15.00
Yoke, wood w/sm center metal ring, 37x18x5", EX...................... 50.00

Fenton

The Fenton Art Glass Company was founded in 1905 by Brothers Frank L. and John W. Fenton. In the beginning they were strictly a decorating company, but when glassware blanks supplied by other manufacturers became difficult to obtain, the brothers started their own glass manufactory. This factory remains in operation today; it is located in Williamstown, West Virginia.

Early Fenton consisted of pattern glass, custard glass, and carnival glass. During the 1920s and 1930s, Fenton introduced several Depression-era glass patterns, including a popular line called Lincoln Inn, along with stretch glass and glassware in several popular opaque colors — Chinese Yellow, Mandarin Red, and Mongolian Green among them.

In 1939 Fenton introduced a line of Hobnail glassware after the surprising success of a Hobnail cologne bottle made for Wrisley Cologne. Since that time Hobnail has remained a staple in Fenton's glassware line. In addition to Hobnail, other lines such as Coin Spot, the crested lines, and Thumbprint have been mainstays of the company, as have their popular opalescent colors such as cranberry, blue, topaz, and plum. Their milk glass has been very successful as well. Glass baskets in these lines and colors are widely sought after by collectors and can be found in a variety of different sizes and shapes.

Today the company is being managed by third- and fourth-generation family members. Fenton glass continues to be sold in gift shops and retail stores. Additionally, exclusive pieces are offered on the television shopping network, QVC. Desirable items for collectors include limited edition pieces, hand-painted pieces, and family signature pieces. With the deaths of Bill Fenton (second generation) and Don Fenton (third generation) in 2003, family signature pieces are expected to become more desirable to collectors. Watch for special exclusive pieces commemorating the company's 100th anniversary!

For further information we recommend *Fenton Art Glass Hobnail Patterns*, *Fenton Art Glass Patterns, 1939 – 1980*, and *Fenton Art Glass Colors and Hand-decorated Patterns, 1959 – 1980*, by Margaret and Kenn Whitmyer; *Fenton Glass, The Third Twenty-Five Years*, by William Heacock (with 1998 value guide); and *Fenton Glass: The 1980s Decade* by Robert E. Eaton, Jr. (1997 values). Additionally, two national collector clubs, the National Fenton Glass Society (NFGS) and the Fenton Art Glass Collectors of America (FAGCA) promote the study of Fenton Art through their respective newsletters, *The Fenton Flyer* and *The Butterfly Net* (See Clubs, Catalogs, and Newsletters in the Directory). Our advisors for this category are Laurie and Richard Karman; they are listed in the Directory under Illinois. See also Carnival Glass; Custard Glass; Stretch Glass.

Aqua Crest, basket, #1923, 1941-43, 6", from $90 to 110.00
Aqua Crest, vase, #36, 1942-43, 6¼", from $28 to 32.00
Asters & Butterflies, basket, opal satin, #2777 Cracker Barrel, 8".. 55.00
Basket Weave, bowl, bl satin, #8222-BA, 1974-80, from $22 to 27.00
Basket Weave, bowl, lav satin, #8222LN, 1977-79, from $40 to 45.00
Black Crest, bowl, #7321, Gift Shop, 1960s, 12", from $85 to 115.00
Black Crest, compote, #7228BC, ca 1970, from $70 to 75.00
Black Crest, relish, heart shape, #7333BC, from $80 to 100.00
Black Rose, bowl, #7227BR, 1953-55, 7", from $90 to 110.00
Blue Overlay, bottle, scent; #192A, 1943-48, from $50 to 60.00
Blue Overlay, top hat, #1924-5, 1949-51, from $22 to 27.00
Blue Ridge Crest, hat, #1923, 1939, 6", from $100 to 120.00
Burmese, vase, #7253BR, 1971-72, 7", from $70 to 80.00
Butterfly & Berry, basket, Shell Pink, House Warmings #9766PE, 6½".40.00
Butterfly & Berry, bowl, amethyst carnival, #8428CN, 1974-77, $35 to.. 45.00
Butterfly & Berry, spittoon, aqua opal carnival, Levay #8240/4, 4" .95.00
Cactus, compote, bl opal, Levay #3429BO, from $40 to 50.00
Cactus, cracker jar, chocolate, Levay #3480CK, from $200 to..... 225.00
Cactus, cruet, aqua opal carnival, Levay #3463IO, from $150 to. 165.00
Cactus, cruet, red Sunset Carnival, Levay #3463RN, $125 to 150.00
Cactus, goblet, Colonial Pink, #3445CP, 1962-63, from $10 to..... 12.00
Cactus, shakers, custard satin, 3406CU, 1974-75, from $18 to 20.00
Carnival, mug, Beaded Shell; amber, 1971, from $45 to................ 55.00
Carnival, plate, cake; Lions Plunger, Emerald Green, ped ft, $75 to.. 85.00
Coin Dot, basket, cranberry opal, Levay #1446CR, 7", from $125 to . 150.00
Coin Dot, hat, Persian Blue opal, Gift Shop #1492XC, from $45 to . 55.00
Coin Dot, lamp, honey amber, 1977-78, 21", from $225 to.......... 250.00
Colonial, candy box, Wisteria, #8488WT, 1977-79, from $30 to... 35.00
Crystal Crest, basket, #1523, 1942, 13", from $300 to.................. 350.00

Diamond Optic, pitcher, purple carnival, Levay #1764, 10½", $200 to..225.00
Dot Optic, decanter, ruby overlay, #2478RO, 1960-65, from $250 to. 300.00
Dotted Swiss, vase, Rose Magnolia, Cracker Barrel #3214, from $65 to. 75.00
Emerald Crest, plate, cake; low ft, #5813EC, 1954-56, from $90 to. 125.00
Empress, goblet, Colonial Blue, #9245CB, 1962-67, from $14 to .. 16.00
Empress, vase, orange, #8252OR, Jan 1968-July 1968, from $90 to . 100.00
Empress, vase, orange satin, #8252OE, Jan 1968-July 1968, from $100 to...125.00
Fern, ewer, opaline w/Rosalene crest, #4026, Gift Shop, from $150 to.175.00
Fine Cut & Grape, basket, Persian Blue opal, basket, 3-toed, #9638XC..115.00
Georgian, tumbler, crystal, #6550CY, 1952-54, 9-oz, from $3 to.......5.00
Georgian, tumbler, gr transparent, #6545DG, 1953-54, 5-oz, from $5 to ..7.00
Gold Crest, bowl, #682, 1943-44, 9½", from $35 to........................ 40.00
Gold Overlay, jug, #711, Jan-Oct 1949, 6", from $35 to................ 45.00
Grape & Cable, bowl, peach opal, ruffled, Coyne's & Co, 10", $100 to.125.00
Grape & Cable, spittoon, deep cranberry opal carnival, Levay, 7½" ..315.00
Green Overlay, bottle, #711, 1949-51, 5½", from $80 to................ 95.00
Green Overlay, vase, tulip; #711, 1949-50, 9", from $55 to........... 65.00
Heart & Vine, bowl, amethyst carnival, #8237CN, 1973-74, from $37 to...42.00
Hobnail, apothecary jar, Colonial Green, #3689, 1964-70, from $55 to .. 65.00
Hobnail, basket, cranberry, deep, #3637, 1963-65, 7x7", from $300 to....350.00
Hobnail, basket, Peach Blow, #3835, 1952-56, from $75 to 85.00
Hobnail, basket, Wisteria opal, #3834, 1942-44, 4½", from $90 to .110.00
Hobnail, bell, plum opal, crimped, Levay #3645PO, from $65 to .. 85.00
Hobnail, bonbon, Peach Blow, 6-point star shape, #3921, 1953-57, 3" .50.00
Hobnail, bottle, oil; topaz opal, #3869, 1942-44, 4¾" w/stopper ..100.00
Hobnail, bowl, dessert; bl opal, #3828, 1951-54, 2x3½", from $35 to...45.00
Hobnail, bowl, hanging; milk glass, brass chains, #3705, 1959-68, 11".150.00
Hobnail, bowl, plum opal, Carolyn's Collectibles, 10", from $65 to...85.00
Hobnail, bowl, punch; pk opal, 14-pc, Gift Shop #A3712UO, from $350 to....400.00
Hobnail, butter dish, bl opal, #3977, 1954-55, ¼-lb, from $300 to.....350.00
Hobnail, candleholder, Decorated Holly, #3974DH, 1971-72, ea, $15 to.. 20.00
Hobnail, candleholder, turq, #3974, 1955, ea from $20 to............. 22.00
Hobnail, candy jar, pk chiffon opal, ftd, #3688, 2001-03, 7", $25 to.. 30.00
Hobnail, compote, plum opal, #3727, 1960-64, 3¾x8", from $100 to ..125.00
Hobnail, compote, topaz opal, ruffled, Douglas Parks, from $65 to ..75.00
Hobnail, cookie jar, bl opal, hdls, 1941-43, 7¼x7", from $500 to.. 600.00
Hobnail, decanter, red Sunset carnival, Levay, 1 of 120 made, $200 to..225.00
Hobnail, egg cup, ruby, Collector's Club, ftd, from $25 to.............. 35.00
Hobnail, epergene, amber, 4-pc, #3701, 1959, from $60 to............ 75.00
Hobnail, fairy light, bl satin, #3608BA, 1978-81, from $30 to....... 35.00
Hobnail, hat, milk glass, #3991, 1950-69, from $14 to.................. 16.00
Hobnail, jug, topaz opal, #3964, 1941-44, from $90 to................. 110.00
Hobnail, lamp, pillar; bl opal, #3907, 1978-81, 26", from $360 to ..400.00
Hobnail, lamp, student; cranberry, #3307, 1984-89, 15", from $175 to ..200.00

Hobnail, lamp, student; milk glass with decoration, 21", 1974 – 1976, from $200.00 to $250.00.

(Photo courtesy Margaret and Kenn Whitmyer)

Diamond Lace, epergne, French opal with aqua crest, #1948, $315.00.

(Photo courtesy Margaret and Kenn Whitmyer)

Hobnail, nut dish, milk glass, ftd, #3629, 1962-78, 5x5½", $14 to. 16.00
Hobnail, pitcher, Peaches 'n Cream, w/ice lip, Gracious Touch #3664.135.00
Hobnail, relish, topaz opal, heart shape w/ring hdl, #3733, 1959, 8" L...90.00

Hobnail, shakers, glossy vaseline opal, ftd, Levay #3609TO, pr, $75 to .95.00
Hobnail, toothpick, bl opal, Levay #3795BO, 2¾", from $20 to 30.00
Hobnail, tray, sandwich; topaz opal, chrome hdl, #3791, 1959-74, 13"..85.00
Hobnail, tumbler, bl opal, #3946, 1940-55, 16-oz, 6", from $65 to...85.00
Hobnail, tumbler, crystal, 1940-41, 4", from $6 to..........................7.00
Hobnail, vase, bud; Decorated Holly, 1974-75, 10", from $30 to 35.00
Hobnail, vase, swung; topaz opal, #3759, 1959-60, 16", from $190 to ..220.00
Hobnail, vase, Wild Rose, #3656, 1961-63, 5½", from $45 to 55.00
Hobnail, wine, French opal, sq, #3844, 1951-54, from $35 to........ 45.00
Inverted Strawberry, basket, aqua opal carnival, Levay #400C, 7" L..140.00
Ivory Crest, plate, #682, 1940-42, 12", from $50 to......................60.00
Ivy Overlay, vase, mini; #711, 1949-51, from $40 to 45.00
Lacy Edge, compote, rose pastel, #9028RP, 1954-57, from $40 to.. 50.00
Lacy Edge, plate, milk glass, #9011MI, 1953-60, 11", from $14 to. 16.00
Lacy Edge, plate, milk glass, ftd, #9017MI, 1954-59, from $40 to .. 50.00
Lacy Edge, plate, rose pastel, #9012RP, 1955-57, 12", $25 to 30.00
Lacy Edge, shell, turq, #9030TU, 1955-56, from $12 to 15.00
Lily of the Valley, bell, amethyst carnival, #8265CN, 1979-80, $28 to..32.00
Lily of the Valley, candy box, bl opal, #8489BO, 1979-80, from $35 to.. 40.00
Lily of the Valley, plate, cake; cameo opal, #8411CO, 1979-80, $70 to..80.00
Lily of the Valley, vase, bud; topaz opal, #8458TO, 1980, from $30 to ..35.00
Love Bird, vase, Lime Sherbet, #8258LS, 1974-76, from $37 to 42.00
Medallion, bell, Cardinals in Winter, #8267CW, 1977-80, from $30 to .. 35.00
Medallion, candy box, Holly on ruby, #8288-RH, 1976-80, from $85 to.. 95.00
Paneled Daisy, toothpick, Lime Sherbet, #8294LS, 1973-76, from $16 to. 18.00

Paneled Sprig, peach blow with Moss Rose decoration, from $120.00 to $140.00.
(Photo courtesy Carrie and Gerald Domitz)

Peach Crest, basket, #1523, 1940-52, 13", from $240 to 250.00
Peach Crest, candy jar, #711, 1949-50, from $100 to 125.00
Persian Medallion, chalice, custard satin, #8241CU, 1972-74, $25 to.30.00
Persian Medallion, fairy light, Colonial Amber, #8408CA, 1974-76. 30.00
Persian Medallion, plate, Wisteria carnival, Levay #8219, 9½"...... 90.00
Pink Blossom, egg, custard satin, #5143PY, 1972-75, from $32 to . 35.00
Pink Blossom, swan, custard satin, #5161PY, 1978-80, from $25 to.30.00
Pinwheel, compote, Independence Blue Carnival, 1976-77, $27 to .. 32.00
Pinwheel, compote, ruby irid, #8227RN, 1976-78, from $30 to..... 35.00
Polka Dot, decanter, bl transparent, #2478BU, 1960-62, from $200 to..250.00
Regency, butter dish, ruby marble, rnd, Levay #8680RX, from $150 to..165.00
Rib Optic New World, shakers, topaz opal, Collector's Club, pr, $30 to... 35.00
Rose, compote, Lime Sherbet, #9222LS, 1974-77, from $20 to 22.00
Rose Crest, candlestick, #1523, 1946-48, ea from $40 to 45.00
Rose Overlay, basket, #203, hdl, 1943-49, 7", from $40 to............. 45.00
Rose Overlay, jug, #192, 1943-49, 8", from $50 to........................ 55.00
Sables Arch, bell, lt amethyst carnival, Gift Shop #9065DT, 6", $50 to. 65.00
Sheffield, bowl, Petal Pink, crimped, Hallmark #6626PN, from $30 to.35.00
Silver Crest, basket, cone shape, #36, 1943-47, from $35 to 40.00
Silver Crest, basket, mini fan; #37, 1943-48, 2½", from $100 to .. 125.00
Silver Crest, basket, 2-hdl, #711, 1949-52, 7", from $80 to............ 90.00
Silver Crest, bonbon, #36, 1943-80, 5½", from $10 to.................... 12.00
Silver Crest, bottle, #193, 1943-49, 5½", from $50 to 60.00
Silver Crest, bowl, #205, 1943-48, 8½", from $40 to 45.00

Silver Crest, bowl, soup; #680, 1949-56, 5½", from $30 to............. 35.00
Silver Crest, candleholder, #680, 1949-52, ea from $35 to............. 45.00
Silver Crest, chip & dip, #7402SC, 1975-76, from $70 to 85.00
Silver Crest, creamer, hdld, #711, 1949-50, 4", from $30 to........... 35.00
Silver Crest, jug, squat, #711, 1949-50, from $85 to..................... 95.00
Silver Crest, planter, 3-tier, #680, 1950-52, from $55 to 65.00
Silver Crest, plate, #681, 1943-49, 9", from $25 to........................ 30.00
Silver Crest, plate, cake; low ft, #5813SC, 1954-80, from $35 to .. 40.00
Silver Crest, vase, #186, 1943-67, 8", from $25 to........................ 30.00
Silver Crest, vase, tulip; #711, 1949-58, 6", from $28 to 35.00
Silver Crest w/Spanish Lace, bell, #3567SC, 1973-80, from $40 to..45.00
Silver Jamestown, vase, #7350SJ, 1957-59, 5", from $45 to 55.00
Spiral Optic, candy box, bl opal, #3180-BO, 1979-80, from $110 to .125.00
Swirl, ashtray, Springtime Green, #7076GT, 1970s, 7½", from $12 to . 14.00
Swirl, ashtray, Wisteria, #7076WT, 1977-78, 7½", from $18 to...... 22.00
Sydenham, bell, gr opal w/cobalt rim, Gift Shop #9063GK, from $75 to. 85.00
Thumbprint, lamp, student; Colonial Green, #1410CG, 1960s, 20", $60 to 70.00
Tree of Life, compote, Colonial Amber, #9322CA, 1977-78, from $9 to 11.00
Tree of Life, compote, Springtime Green, #9322GT, 1977-79, from $11 to 13.00
Water Lily, jardiniere, wht satin, #8498WS, 1975-77, $25 to 30.00
Wave Crest, candy jar, opaque bl o/l, #6080OB, 1962-63, $100 to .110.00
Wave Crest, shakers, ruby o/l, #6006RO, 1956-63, pr from $50 to 60.00
Wild Rose & Bowknot, rose bowl, Celestial Blue satin, Levay, 5" . 80.00
Yellow Overlay, vase, #3001, 1950-51, 5", from $45 to................... 55.00

Fiesta

Fiesta is a line of dinnerware that was originally produced by the Homer Laughlin China Company of Newell, West Virginia, from 1936 until 1973. It was made in 11 different solid colors with over 50 pieces in the assortment. The pattern was developed by Frederick Rhead, an English Stoke-on-Trent potter who was an important contributor to the art-pottery movement in this country during the early part of the century. The design was carried out through the use of a simple band-of-rings device near the rim. Fiesta Red, a strong red-orange glaze color, was made with depleted uranium oxide. It was more expensive to produce than the other colors and sold at higher prices. During the '50s the color assortment was gray, rose, chartreuse, and dark green. These colors are relatively harder to find and along with medium green (new in 1959) command the highest prices.

Fiesta Kitchen Kraft was introduced in 1939; it consisted of 17 pieces of kitchenware such as pie plates, refrigerator sets, mixing bowls, and covered jars in four popular Fiesta colors. As a final attempt to adapt production to modern-day techniques and methods, Fiesta was restyled in 1969. Of the original colors, only Fiesta Red remained. This line, called Fiesta Ironstone, was discontinued in 1973.

Two types of marks were used: an ink stamp on machine-jiggered pieces and an indented mark molded into the hollow ware pieces.

In 1986 HLC reintroduced a line of Fiesta dinnerware in five colors: black, white, pink, apricot, and cobalt (darker and denser than the original shade). Since then yellow, turquoise, seafoam green, 'country' blue, lilac, persimmon, sapphire blue, chartreuse, gray, juniper, cinnabar, plum, sunflower yellow, shamrock, tangerine, scarlet, peacock, and the newest color, heather, have been added. For more information we recommend *The Collector's Encyclopedia of Fiesta, Harlequin, and Riviera, Tenth Edition*, by Sharon and Bob Huxford and Mike Nickel. (For information on Harlequin and Riviera, see Garage Sale and Flea Market Annual.)

Note: More than ever before, condition is a major price-assessing factor. Unless an item is free from signs of wear, smoothly glazed, and has no distracting manufacturing flaws, it will not bring 'book' price.

Dinnerware

Ashtray, '50s colors, from $55 to 65.00

Ashtray, red, cobalt or ivory, from $40 to.................................. 50.00
Ashtray, yel, lt gr or turq, from $30 to... 40.00
Bowl, covered onion soup; cobalt or ivory, from $600 to............. 675.00
Bowl, covered onion soup; red, from $625 to............................. 700.00
Bowl, covered onion soup; yel or lt gr, from $525 to.................. 625.00
Bowl, cream soup; '50s colors, from $50 to................................. 65.00
Bowl, cream soup; red, cobalt or ivory, from $55 to.................... 70.00
Bowl, cream soup; yel, lt gr or turq, from $30 to........................ 45.00
Bowl, dessert; 6", '50s colors, from $35 to.................................. 45.00
Bowl, dessert; 6", red, cobalt or ivory, from $30 to..................... 40.00
Bowl, dessert; 6", yel, lt gr or turq, from $20 to......................... 30.00
Bowl, fruit; 4¾", '50s colors, from $20 to................................... 30.00
Bowl, fruit; 4¾", red, cobalt or ivory, from $25 to...................... 30.00
Bowl, fruit; 4¾", yel, lt gr or turq, from $20 to.......................... 25.00
Bowl, fruit; 5½", '50s colors, from $25 to................................... 30.00
Bowl, fruit; 5½", med gr, from $65 to... 70.00
Bowl, fruit; 5½", red, cobalt or ivory, from $25 to...................... 30.00
Bowl, fruit; 5½", yel, lt gr or turq, from $20 to.......................... 25.00
Bowl, fruit; 11¾", red, cobalt, ivory or turq, minimum value........ 200.00
Bowl, fruit; 11¾", yel or lt gr, minimum value............................ 175.00
Bowl, ftd salad; red, cobalt, ivory or turq, minimum value........... 300.00
Bowl, ftd salad; yel or lt gr, minimum value................................ 250.00
Bowl, ind salad; 7½", med gr, from $100 to................................. 120.00
Bowl, ind salad; 7½", red, turq or yel, from $80 to....................... 90.00
Bowl, nappy; 8½", '50s colors, from $35 to................................. 50.00
Bowl, nappy; 8½", med gr... 150.00
Bowl, nappy; 8½", red, cobalt, ivory or turq, from $40 to.............. 50.00
Bowl, nappy; 8½", yel or lt gr, from $25 to................................. 30.00
Bowl, nappy; 9½", red, cobalt, ivory or turq, from $50 to.............. 60.00
Bowl, nappy; 9½", yel or lt gr, from $45 to................................. 55.00
Bowl, Tom & Jerry; ivory w/gold letters, minimum value............. 200.00
Bowl, unlisted salad; red, cobalt, or ivory, minimum value........2,000.00
Bowl, unlisted salad; yel, from $80 to... 100.00
Candleholders, bulb; red, cobalt, ivory or turq, pr from $80 to.... 100.00
Candleholders, bulb; yel or lt gr, pr from $80 to.......................... 110.00
Candleholders, tripod; red, cobalt, ivory or turq, pr, minimum value.. 500.00
Candleholders, tripod; yel or lt gr, pr, minimum value 400.00
Carafe, red, cobalt, ivory or turq, from $225 to........................... 250.00
Carafe, yel or lt gr, from $180 to.. 220.00
Casserole, French; standard colors other than yel, no established value
Casserole, French; yel, from $250 to 300.00
Casserole, w/lid, '50s colors, from $195 to.................................. 225.00
Casserole, w/lid, med gr, minimum value.................................1,000.00
Casserole, w/lid, red, cobalt or ivory, from $150 to...................... 175.00
Casserole, w/lid, yel, lt gr or turq, from $125 to.......................... 150.00
Coffeepot, demi; red, cobalt, ivory or turq, minimum value......... 500.00

Coffeepot, demitasse; yellow or light green, from $350.00 to $400.00.

Coffeepot, regular, '50s colors, from $250 to................................ 300.00
Coffeepot, regular, red, cobalt or ivory, from $200 to................... 250.00
Coffeepot, regular, yel, lt gr or turq, from $150 to....................... 180.00
Compote, sweets; red, cobalt, ivory or turq, from $100 to............ 120.00
Compote, sweets; yel or lt gr, from $70 to................................... 90.00
Compote, 12", red, cobalt, ivory or turq, from $180 to.................. 220.00

Compote, 12", yel or lt gr, from $160 to..................................... 175.00
Creamer, ind; red, minimum value.. 325.00
Creamer, ind; yel, from $60 to.. 80.00
Creamer, regular, '50s colors, from $25 to................................... 30.00
Creamer, regular, med gr, from $90 to... 120.00
Creamer, regular, red, cobalt or ivory, from $25 to...................... 30.00
Creamer, regular, yel, lt gr or turq, from $20 to.......................... 25.00
Creamer, stick hdld, red, cobalt, ivory or turq, from $55 to........... 65.00
Creamer, stick hdld, yel or turq, from $45 to............................... 60.00
Cup & saucer, demitasse; '50s colors, minimum value.................. 325.00
Cup & saucer, demitasse; red, cobalt or ivory, from $65 to........... 80.00
Cup & saucer, demitasse; yel, lt gr or turq, from $60 to............... 75.00
Egg cup, '50s colors, from $100 to.. 135.00
Egg cup, red, cobalt, or ivory, from $60 to................................... 70.00
Egg cup, yel, lt gr or turq, from $50 to....................................... 60.00
Lid, for mixing bowl #1-#3, any color, minimum value 500.00
Lid, for mixing bowl #4, any color, minimum value 800.00

Marmalade, red, cobalt, ivory, or turquoise, from $365.00 to $400.00.

Marmalade, yel or lt gr, from $350 to.. 375.00
Mixing bowl, #1, red, cobalt, ivory or turq, from $225 to............. 250.00
Mixing bowl, #1, yel or lt gr, from $175 to.................................. 200.00
Mixing bowl, #2, red, cobalt, ivory or turq, from $100 to............. 135.00
Mixing bowl, #2, yel or lt gr, from $90 to................................... 115.00
Mixing bowl, #3, red, cobalt, ivory or turq, from $100 to............. 135.00
Mixing bowl, #3, yel or lt gr, from $90 to................................... 125.00
Mixing bowl, #4, red, cobalt, ivory or turq, from $130 to............. 165.00
Mixing bowl, #4, yel or lt gr, from $90 to................................... 125.00
Mixing bowl, #5, red, cobalt, ivory or turq, from $165 to............. 200.00
Mixing bowl, #5, yel or lt gr, from $160 to.................................. 180.00
Mixing bowl, #6, red, cobalt, ivory or turq, from $230 to............. 275.00
Mixing bowl, #6, yel or lt gr, from $200 to.................................. 245.00
Mixing bowl, #7, red, cobalt, ivory or turq, minimum value 400.00
Mixing bowl, #7, yel or lt gr, minimum value 300.00
Mug, Tom & Jerry; '50s colors, from $60 to................................. 80.00
Mug, Tom & Jerry; ivory w/gold letters, from $45 to.................... 60.00
Mug, Tom & Jerry; red, cobalt or ivory, from $50 to..................... 70.00
Mug, Tom & Jerry; yel, lt gr or turq, from $35 to......................... 50.00
Mustard, red, cobalt, ivory or turq, from $250 to......................... 300.00
Mustard, yel or lt gr, from $240 to.. 275.00
Pitcher, disk juice; gray, minimum value..................................2,000.00
Pitcher, disk juice; Harlequin Yellow, from $50 to....................... 65.00
Pitcher, disk juice; red, minimum value 450.00
Pitcher, disk juice; yel, from $30 to.. 40.00
Pitcher, disk water; '50s colors, minimum value 200.00
Pitcher, disk water; red, cobalt or ivory, from $90 to 135.00
Pitcher, disk water; yel, lt gr or turq, from $65 to........................ 90.00
Pitcher, ice; red, cobalt, ivory or turq, from $100 to 125.00
Pitcher, ice; yel or lt gr, from $100 to 125.00
Pitcher, jug, 2-pt; '50s colors, from $100 to................................. 120.00
Pitcher, jug, 2-pt; red, cobalt or ivory, from $95 to...................... 105.00
Pitcher, jug, 2-pt; yel, lt gr or turq, from $60 to 75.00
Plate, cake; red, cobalt, ivory or turq...................................... 1,200.00
Plate, cake; yel or lt gr 1,000.00

Plate, calendar; 1954 or 1955, 10", from $45 to.............................. 55.00
Plate, calendar; 1955, 9", from $45 to 55.00
Plate, chop; 13", '50s colors, from $70 to 95.00
Plate, chop; 13", med gr... 500.00
Plate, chop; 13", red, cobalt or ivory, from $45 to 55.00
Plate, chop; 13", yel, lt gr or turq, from $40 to 50.00
Plate, chop; 15", '50s colors, from $100 to 135.00
Plate, chop; 15", red, cobalt or ivory, from $90 to 100.00
Plate, chop; 15", yel, lt gr or turq, from $65 to 75.00
Plate, compartment; 10½", '50s colors, from $60 to 70.00
Plate, compartment; 10½", red, cobalt or ivory, from $40 to 45.00
Plate, compartment; 10½", yel, lt gr or turq, from $35 to 40.00
Plate, compartment; 12", red, cobalt or ivory, from $55 to............. 60.00
Plate, compartment; 12", yel or lt gr, from $40 to 50.00
Plate, deep; '50s colors, from $40 to 50.00
Plate, deep; med gr, from $130 to 145.00
Plate, deep; red, cobalt or ivory, from $50 to 60.00
Plate, deep; yel, lt gr or turq, from $35 to 40.00
Plate, 6", '50s colors, from $7 to 10.00
Plate, 6", med gr, from $30 to 45.00
Plate, 6", red, cobalt or ivory, from $5 to......................................7.00
Plate, 6", yel, lt gr or turq, from $4 to...6.00
Plate, 7", '50s colors, from $10 to 12.00
Plate, 7", med gr, from $30 to 45.00
Plate, 7", red, cobalt or ivory, from $8 to 10.00
Plate, 7", yel, lt gr or turq, from $7 to...9.00
Plate, 9", '50s colors, from $20 to 25.00
Plate, 9", med gr, from $60 to 75.00
Plate, 9", red, cobalt or ivory, from $15 to 20.00
Plate, 9", yel, lt gr or turq, from $10 to 15.00
Plate, 10", '50s colors, from $30 to 50.00
Plate, 10", med gr, minimum value 125.00
Plate, 10", red, cobalt or ivory, from $30 to 35.00
Plate, 10", yel, lt gr or turq, from $25 to 32.00
Platter, '50s colors, from $40 to 50.00
Platter, med gr, from $165 to 200.00
Platter, red, cobalt or ivory, from $40 to....................................... 50.00
Platter, yel, lt gr or turq, from $35 to 40.00
Relish tray, 6 colors represented, 6-pc, minimum value............... 350.00
Sauceboat, '50s colors, from $50 to 60.00
Sauceboat, med gr, from $200 to 225.00
Sauceboat, red, cobalt or ivory, from $50 to.................................. 60.00
Sauceboat, yel, lt gr or turq, from $30 to 35.00
Shakers, '50s colors, pr from $50 to 60.00
Shakers, med gr, pr from $175 to 225.00
Shakers, red, cobalt or ivory, pr, from $25 to................................. 30.00
Shakers, yel, lt gr or turq, pr from $22 to 25.00
Sugar bowl, ind; turq, from $400 to 500.00
Sugar bowl, ind; yel, from $125 to 175.00
Sugar bowl, w/lid, '50s colors, from $60 to 70.00
Sugar bowl, w/lid, med gr, minimum value 200.00
Sugar bowl, w/lid, red, cobalt or ivory, from $60 to 80.00
Sugar bowl, w/lid, yel, lt gr or turq, from $50 to 65.00
Syrup, red, cobalt, ivory or turq, from $400 to 425.00
Syrup, yel or lt gr, from $375 to 400.00
Teacup & saucer, '50s colors, from $35 to 40.00
Teacup & saucer, med gr, from $50 to 65.00
Teacup & saucer, red, cobalt or ivory, from $25 to......................... 40.00
Teacup & saucer, yel, lt gr or turq, from $15 to............................. 20.00
Teapot, lg; red, cobalt, ivory or turq, from $300 to 350.00
Teapot, lg; yel or lt gr, from $250 to 300.00
Teapot, med; '50s colors, from $200 to... 250.00
Teapot, med; red, cobalt or ivory, from $150 to 200.00
Teapot, med; yel, lt gr or turq, from $110 to 145.00

Tray, figure-8; cobalt, from $90 to.. 100.00
Tray, figure-8; turq, from $350 to..400.00
Tray, figure-8; yel, from $500 to 600.00
Tray, utility; red, cobalt, ivory or turq, from $45 to...................... 50.00
Tray, utility; yel or lt gr, from $40 to 45.00
Tumbler, juice; chartreuse, or dk gr, minimum value 750.00
Tumbler, juice; red, cobalt or ivory, from $45 to 50.00
Tumbler, juice; rose, from $55 to 60.00
Tumbler, juice; yel, lt gr or turq, from $25 to 35.00
Tumbler, water; red, cobalt, ivory or turq, from $70 to 80.00
Tumbler, water; yel or lt gr, from $60 to 70.00
Vase, bud; red, cobalt, ivory or turq, from $60 to 75.00
Vase, bud; yel or lt gr, from $50 to 60.00
Vase, 8", red, cobalt, ivory or turq, from $650 to 800.00
Vase, 8", yel or lt gr, from $600 to 700.00
Vase, 10", red, cobalt or ivory or turq, from $800 to 1,100.00
Vase, 10", yel or lt gr, from $800 to 1,000.00
Vase, 12", red, cobalt, ivory or turq, from $1,400 to 1,900.00
Vase, 12", yel or lt gr, from $1,100 to 1,500.00

Kitchen Kraft

Bowl, mixing; 6"... 50.00
Bowl, mixing; 8"... 65.00
Bowl, mixing; 10"... 95.00
Cake plate 35.00
Cake server, from $90 to 125.00
Casserole, ind; from $150 to.. 145.00
Casserole, 7½" 75.00
Casserole, 8½" 70.00

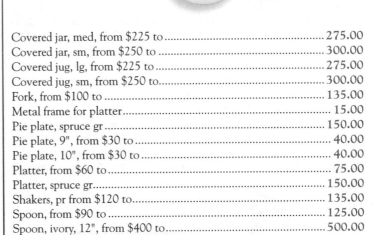

Covered jar, large, from $350.00 to $375.00.

Covered jar, med, from $225 to 275.00
Covered jar, sm, from $250 to 300.00
Covered jug, lg, from $225 to 275.00
Covered jug, sm, from $250 to.. 300.00
Fork, from $100 to 135.00
Metal frame for platter.. 15.00
Pie plate, spruce gr 150.00
Pie plate, 9", from $30 to 40.00
Pie plate, 10", from $30 to 40.00
Platter, from $60 to 75.00
Platter, spruce gr.. 150.00
Shakers, pr from $120 to 135.00
Spoon, from $90 to 125.00
Spoon, ivory, 12", from $400 to.. 500.00
Stacking refrigerator lid, from $100 to 150.00
Stacking refrigerator lid, ivory, from $200 to 225.00
Stacking refrigerator unit, from $50 to.. 60.00
Stacking refrigerator unit, ivory, from $200 to............................ 210.00

Fifties Modern

Postwar furniture design is marked by organic shapes and lighter woods and forms. New materials from war research such as molded plywood and fiberglass were used extensively. For the first time, design was extended to the masses, and the baby-boomer generation grew up surrounded by modern shape and color, the perfect expression of postwar optimism. The top designers in America worked for Herman Miller and Knoll Furniture Company. These include Charles and Ray Eames, George Nelson, and Eero Saarinen.

Unless noted otherwise, values are given for furnishings in excellent condition; glassware and ceramic items are assumed to be in mint condition. This information was provided to us by Richard Wright. See also Italian Glass.

Key:

alum — aluminum	plwd — plywood
cntl — cantilevered	rswd — rosewood
fbrg — fiberglass	ss — stainless steel
lcq — lacquered	uphl — upholstered
lm — laminated	vnr — neneer

Armchair, Eames, Alum Group, swivel base, wool sling seat, 33", pr.950.00
Armchair, Pollock/Knoll, leather sling, tubular fr, alum rests, pr 1,500.00
Armchair, Wegner/Getama, teak fr w/caned bk, cushion, 27", pr... 1,500.00
Bench, Probber, mahog fr, drw, loose cushion on half, 15x72x18" ..800.00
Cabinet, Juhl/Baker, birch/walnut, 2 doors/4 drws, metal pulls, 30x72" ..3,000.00
Cabinet, Juhl/Baker, birch/walnut, 2-door, blk pulls, 30x36x18" ...1,400.00
Cabinet, McCobb/Calvin, mahog, 2 sliding doors, brass trim, 41x49x14"...600.00
Cabinet, Nelson/Miller, birch, 4 drw/1 door, M-shaped pulls, 30x56x19".500.00
Cabinet, Nelson/Miller, Thin Edge, rswd/4-drw/hourglass pulls, 30x34"..1,500.00
Cabinet, Probber, bleached mahog, 2 caned doors, 4-drw, 23x78x18"..700.00
Cabinet, Probber, lm top, bleached mahog, 9-drw, 30x21x18"..1,000.00
Cabinet, Probber, mahog, 4-drw, cut-out pulls, 33x36x18" 450.00
Cabinet, stereo; Nelson/Miller, walnut, drop-down door, 35x82x23" . 700.00
Cart, Mategot, metal top/shelf, enameled steel fr, castors, 29x29x23" .700.00
Cart, serving; McCobb/Calvin, marble top, pull-out shelf, drws, 36" L .700.00
Chair, Bellman/Horgen-Glanus; birch plwd w/cutout, birch legs, 33" .. 200.00
Chair, Bertoia/Knoll, Diamond, fabric seat, steel rod base, 3 for .. 350.00
Chair, club; flared form w/tapered wood legs, reuphl, 28" 425.00
Chair, Eames/Miller, DCW, birch plwd seat/bk/fr, rfn, 29", 6 for . 2,500.00
Chair, Eames/Miller, Eiffel Tower, blk fabric, 32", 4 for 850.00
Chair, Eames/Miller, Eiffel Tower, fbrg on blk wire base, 31", 4 for ..600.00
Chair, Eames/Miller, LCM, red plwd, chromed steel fr, 26".......1,000.00
Chair, high-bk w/flared arms, reuphl, steel fr, 32x32x36", +ottoman .700.00
Chair, lounge; Eames/Miller, rswd plwd & blk leather, 35", +ottoman. 2,800.00
Chair, lounge; Frankl, tufted seat, floating bk, att, 26", G, pr....1,500.00
Chair, lounge; McCobb/Calbin, wht uphl, mahog-stain birch legs, 31".650.00
Chair, lounge; Noreil/Sweden, leather uphl, ca 1970, 30", pr+ottoman.5,500.00
Chair, lounge; Wormley/Dunbar, even-arm, mohair uphl, 27x37x34" . 375.00
Chair, lounge; Wormley/Dunbar, uphl seat w/bk cushion, walnut base..650.00
Chair, Mathsson/Mathsson, Eva, beech fr w/orig webbing, 33", VG..475.00
Chair, Nakashima/Knoll, walnut, curved bk w/dowels/slab seat, 30"..275.00
Chair, Nelson/Miller, Coconut, steel shell w/uphl seat, 32", +ottoman ..3,250.00

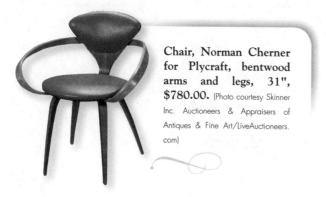

Chair, Norman Cherner for Plycraft, bentwood arms and legs, 31", $780.00. (Photo courtesy Skinner Inc. Auctioneers & Appraisers of Antiques & Fine Art/LiveAuctioneers. com)

Chair, Probber, mahog fr w/curved caned bk, rnd cushion, 24", pr. 2,200.00
Chair, side; Conover/Conover, redwood w/wrought-iron rod fr, 30" ... 950.00
Chair, side; Juhl/Baker #402½, uphl vinyl, walnut fr, 32", 6 for.....4,750.00
Chair, side; Rojle/Denmark, teak, sculptural bks, 33", 4 for 600.00
Chair, slipper; Kroehler, channeled uphl bks, fringed cushion 31" 1,200.00
Chair, slipper; Probber, orig wool uphl, mahog X-base fr, 34"...1,000.00
Chaise, vander Rohe/Knoll, ss fr w/channeled leather cushion, 39" ..1,600.00
Chaise, Woodard, wire mesh, bk adjusts, 2 wheels, 37x60x25" 250.00
Chaise, Wormley/Dunbar, tulip uphl/4 loose cushions/mahog legs, 71".2,200.00
Chest, Wormley/Drexel, 5 drw amid 2 doors, worn, 33x67x20"... 400.00

Clock, mantle; Gilbert Rohde/Herman Miller, rosewood, 17" long, $6,000.00.
(Photo courtesy David Rago Auctions)

Clock, Nelson/Miller, Petal, wht paddles/brass center, 18" dia..1,500.00
Clock, Nelson/Miller, Sunburst, blk spikes/brass center, #2202, 19" ..300.00
Day bed, Gibbings/Widdicomb, tufted cushion/walnut fr/brass legs, 77"..4,250.00
Desk, McCobb/Calvin, Irwin Collection, wht glass top, mahog fr, 60"...1,400.00
Desk, Probber, lm top, bleached mahog, 4-drw, 29x48x27".......... 650.00
Dresser, Rohde/Miller, Deco birch/mahog, 4-drw, 35x43", pr...1,100.00
Dresser, WormleyTrexel, beech/elm, 10-drw, platform base, 33x62x19"..900.00
Fire dogs, Nelson/Miller, iron, 5½x15¾x2½", pr......................1,000.00
Fire tools, Nelson/Miller, wrought-iron stand, 3 tools, 34"........1,800.00
Globe, Wormley/Dunbar, internal lighted globe in mahog fr, 34x21" dia..2,000.00
Headbrd, Frankl/Johnson, latticework, orig finish, 38x80"........... 450.00
Headbrd, Wormley/Dunbar, mahog w/uphl panels w/drop-down arms, 81" W..2,500.00
Lamp, floor; McCobb/Calvin, wht paper shade, brass std, 3-ftd base..700.00
Lamp, table; McCobb/Calvin, leather-covered hourglass form, 29" . 400.00
Log holder/magazine rack, Bel Geddes/Revere, chrome/copper, 16x18x15" .1,000.00
Magazine rack, Probber, dk stain mahog X form, 21x20x15"........ 600.00
Mirror, Frankl/Johnson, cork w/wood bking, 30¼x26¼x2½".....2,500.00
Modular seating, Chadwick/Miller, 6 wedge-shaped pcs, orig uphl .. 300.00
Screen, Eames/Miller, FSW-8, 8 birch panels, 68x57"............... 4,000.00
Sculpture, Weinberg, reclining nude, pnt plaster, 3¼x10½x6"..... 300.00
Shelf, style of Knoll, walnut w/3 hidden drw, 4x21x14" 400.00
Sidebrd, Frankl/Johnson, 2 center doors/8 drw, brass pulls, 32x73"...1,200.00
Sofa, Compact, Eames/Miller, bl vinyl uphl, chromed steel fr, folds...1,300.00
Sofa, Jacobsen/Hansen, Series 330, wool uphl, ss fr, 71", +28" chair..2,100.00
Sofa, Kjaerholm PK 31/3, blk leather cushions, chromed fr, 78" ..4,250.00
Sofa, Knoll, harlequin chenille reuphl, birch legs, 30x90x33" ..1,300.00
Sofa, Probber, uphl, ebonized wood/brass fr w/repeating Xs, 109"..5,500.00
Sofa, Risom, uphl slab seat & tufted bk, walnut fr, 1960s, 79" ..1,000.00
Sofa, Robsjohn-Gibbings, uphl seat w/loose cushion, walnut fr, 76" ..6,000.00
Sofa, Wormley/Dunbar, reuphl 3-cushion seat/bk, walnut fr, 82" ..1,000.00
Stand, telephone; Noyes/IBM, lam/pnt steel, tripod base, 16x14" ..800.00
Stool, bar; Bertoia/Knoll, blk wire w/vinyl seat cushion, 42½", pr...750.00
Stool, Eames/Miller Time-Life, trn walnut, 15x13" 1,000.00
Table, coffee; Eames/Miller, lm top, birch plwd legs, 16x35x24"..750.00
Table, coffee; Frankl/Johnson, cork top w/apron, mahog base, 48" dia. 3,750.00
Table, coffee; Juhl/Baker, walnut fr w/birch top, #521, 22x64x31"..850.00
Table, coffee; Laverne, Italian marble, chromed steel legs, 16x60x22" .950.00
Table, coffee; Probber, oval compo pebble top, walnut base, 14x67x20"..450.00
Table, coffee; Wormley/Dunbar, glass/mahog platform basc, 46" dia..1,200.00
Table, coffee; Wormley/Dunbar, mahog w/brass stretchers, shelf, 48" L ..1,300.00

Table, conference; Eames/Miller, rswd, alum/blk metal base, 72". 700.00
Table, console/dining; Wormley/Dunbar, walnut, flip-top, 29x72x34" .650.00
Table, dining; Juhl/Baker, walnut bookmatched top, 2 20" leaves, 68". 1,200.00
Table, dining; McCobb/Winchendron, Planner, maple, 2 leaves, 29x30x28" 300.00
Table, dining; Probber, mahog w/apron, mahog/brass bases, 66x41" 2,100.00
Table, dining; Robsjohn-Gibbings, walnut, plinth bases, rfn, 70" L .1,300.00
Table, dining; Saarinen/Knoll, marble top, enameled ped base, 50" dia .950.00
Table, dining; Saarinen/Knoll, wht lm top, wht enamel metal base, 54"..400.00
Table, dining; Vignelli/Knoll, Paperclip, blk laminate, ss rods, 48" .900.00
Table, occasional; Bellman/Knoll, Popsicle, plwd, fold-up, 22" dia .700.00
Table, occasional; Probber, compo hexagon top w/brass trim, 3-leg, 22".1,100.00
Table, Singer & Sons, walnut, rectangle top, shelf, drw, 23x26x23" ..350.00
Table, Wormley/Drexel, elm, 2-tier w/leather inset top, 26x24x16"...275.00
Table, Wormley/Drexel, elm sq top over recessed sq base, 17x30x20"..400.00
Table, Wormley/Dunbar, walnut top, steel/walnut base, 29x79x42" ..1,000.00
Table/nightstand, Nakashima, sap walnut case/drw/splayed legs . 3,750.00
Vanity/desk, Frankl/Johnson, 3-drw/2 doors, brass pulls, +swivel chair ...2,700.00

Finch, Kay

Kay Finch and her husband, Braden, operated a small pottery in Corona Del Mar, California, from 1939 to 1963. The company remained small, employing from 20 to 60 local residents who Kay trained in all but the most requiring tasks, which she herself performed. The company produced animal and bird figurines, most notably dogs, Kay's favorites. Figures of 'Godey' type couples were also made, as were tableware (consisting of breakfast sets) and other artware. Most pieces were marked, but ink stamps often came off during cleaning.

After Kay's husband, Braden, died in 1962, she closed the business. Some of her molds were sold to Freeman-McFarlin of El Monte, California, who soon contracted with Kay for new designs. Though the realism that is so evident in her original works is still strikingly apparent in these later pieces, none of the vibrant pastels or signature curliques are there. Kay Finch died on June 21, 1993.

For further information we recommend *Kay Finch Ceramics, Her Enchanted World* (Schiffer), written by our advisors for this category, Mike Nickel and Cynthia Horvath; they are listed in the Directory under Michigan.

Note: Original model numbers are included in the following descriptions — three-digit numbers indicate pre-1946 models. After 1946 they were assigned four-digit numbers, the first two digits representing the year of initial production. Unless otherwise described, our prices are for figurines decorated in multiple colors, not solid glazes.

Box, heart; #B5051, bird on lid, 2½" 50.00
Canister, emb raspberry vines, purple/gr on wht, 9½" 75.00
Cookie jar, Cookie Puss, #4614, 11¾", $1,250 to 1,500.00
Figurine, Afghan angel standing, bl-tipped wings, 2½x2¼" 450.00
Figurine, Airedale dog standing, caramel & blk, #4832, 5x5" 180.00
Figurine, Ambrosia, cat, #155, 10½", minimum value 300.00
Figurine, Bride & Groom, #204, 6½", 6", pr 250.00
Figurine, Canister, Santa, 10½" 100.00
Figurine, Choir Boy, kneeling, #211, 5½" 40.00
Figurine, Cockatoo, #5401, 15" 400.00
Figurine, Colt, #4806, 11" 250.00
Figurine, Dog Show Boxer, #5025, 5x5" 500.00
Figurine, Dog Show Yorkie, #4851 .... 300.00
Figurine, Godey couple, pk w/bl accents, 9¾", 9½", pr 75.00
Figurine, Grumpy, pig, #165, 6x7½" 125.00
Figurine, Guppy, fish, #173, 2½" 50.00
Figurine, Happy Monkey, #4903, 11" 600.00
Figurine, Jezebel, cat, 6x7" 100.00
Figurine, Kneeling Madonna, #4900, 6" 50.00
Figurine, Littlest Angel, #4803, 2½" 95.00

Figurine, Mermaid, #161, 6½" 300.00
Figurine, Peasant Boy & Girl, #113, #117, 6¾", pr 70.00
Figurine, Pekingese, #154, 14" L 250.00
Figurine, Perky, poodle, #5419, 16" 2,500.00

Figurine, Petey the Donkey, #4776, 30", $2,000.00.
(Photo courtesy Cincinnati Art Galleries/ LiveAuctioneers.com)

Figurine, Scandi boy & girl, #126/#127, 5¼", pr 50.00
Moon bottle, #5502, 13" 75.00
Planter, Animal Book series, #B5145, 6½", ea 50.00
Plaque, Baby Fish, 2¼x3" 45.00
Plate, Santa face, 6½" 50.00
Shakers, stallion heads, 5", pr 75.00
Tea tile, Yorkshire Terrier emb, 5½" sq 75.00
Tumbler, Afghan design (emb), mk Kay & Brayden, 6" 250.00
Tureen, Turkey, platinum/gray, #5361, 9", w/ladle 150.00
Vase, Elephant, #B5155, 6" 75.00
Wall pocket, Girl & Boy, #5501, 10", ea 250.00

Findlay Onyx and Floradine

Findlay, Ohio, was the location of the Dalzell, Gilmore, and Leighton Glass Company, one of at least 16 companies that flourished there between 1886 and 1901. Their most famous ware, Onyx, is very rare. It was produced for only a short time beginning in 1889 due to the heavy losses incurred in the manufacturing process.

Onyx is layered glass, usually found in creamy white with a dainty floral pattern accented with metallic lustre that has been trapped between the two layers. Other colors found on rare occasions include a light amber (with either no lustre or with gilt flowers), light amethyst (or lavender), and rose. Although old tradepaper articles indicate the company originally intended to produce the line in three distinct colors, long-time Onyx collectors report that aside from the white, production was very limited. Other colors of Onyx are very rare, and the few examples that are found tend to support the theory that production of colored Onyx ware remained for the most part in the experimental stage. Even three-layered items have been found (they are extremely rare) decorated with three-color flowers. As a rule of thumb, using white Onyx prices as a basis for evaluation, expect to pay five to ten times more for colored examples.

Floradine is a separate line that was made with the Onyx molds. A single-layer rose satin glassware with white opal flowers, it is usually valued at twice the price of colored Onyx.

Chipping around the rims is very common, and price is determined to a great extent by condition. Unless noted otherwise, our prices are for examples in near-mint condition.

Floradine

Bowl, fluted, squat bulbous base, 4" 750.00
Bowl, low, 5¾" 1,000.00
Celery vase, fluted cylinder neck, bulbous body, 6½" 1,000.00
Creamer, bulbous, 4⅝" 900.00
Mustard pot 1,250.00

Spooner, 4¾" 900.00
Sugar bowl, bulbous, w/lid, 5½" 1,100.00
Sugar shaker 1,500.00

Onyx

Bowl, wht w/raspberry decor, fluted top, 2½x4½" 2,000.00
Bowl, wht w/silver decor, 2¾x8", from $400 to 500.00
Butter dish, wht w/silver decor, 3x6" 1,250.00
Celery vase, wht w/silver decor, 6¾" 485.00
Covered dish, wht w/silver decor, 5½" 1,000.00

Creamer, white with silver decoration, 4½", from $435.00 to $485.00. (Photo courtesy Jackson's International Auctioneers & Appraisers of Fine Art & Antiques/LiveAuctioneers.com)

Mustard, wht w/raspberry decor, hinged metal lid, 3¼" 2,900.00
Mustard, wht w/silver decor, 3½" 600.00
Pitcher, apricot w/orange decor, 4½" 4,200.00
Pitcher, water; wht w/silver decor, 8" 1,300.00
Shaker, wht w/silver decor, Pat 2/23/1889, 2⅝" 800.00
Spooner, raisin w/wht decor, 4" 2,250.00
Spooner, wht w/orange decor, 4" 1,500.00
Spooner, wht w/silver decor, 4½x4", from $450 to 500.00
Sugar bowl, wht w/silver decor, w/lid, 5½" 650.00
Sugar shaker, wht w/silver decor, brass mts, 5½" 335.00
Sugar shaker, wht w/silver decor, sterling cap, 6¼", from $600 to .. 700.00
Syrup, gr (unusual color) w/silver decor 3,000.00
Syrup, wht w/silver decor, 7¾", from $850 to 950.00
Toothpick holder, wht w/silver decor, rare 1,300.00
Tumbler, wht w/apricot decor, lt line unseen from w/in, bbl 2,300.00
Tumbler, wht w/silver decor, bbl shape, 3½" 250.00
Tumbler, wht w/silver decor, thin str sides (rare), 3¾" 1,250.00
Vase, wht w/silver decor, 9", VG 800.00

Firefighting Collectibles

Firefighting collectibles have always been a good investment in terms of value appreciation. Many times the market will be temporarily affected by wild price swings caused by the 'supply and demand principle' as related to a small group of aggressive collectors. These collectors will occasionally pay well over market value for a particular item they need or want. Once their desires are satisfied, prices seem to return to their normal range. It has been noticed that during these periods of high prices, many items enter the marketplace that otherwise would remain in collections. This may (it has in the past) cause a price depression (due again to the 'supply and demand principle' of market behavior).

The recent phenomena of internet buying and selling of firefighting collectibles and antiques has caused wild swings in prices for some fire collectibles. The cause of this is the ability to reach into vast international markets. It appears that this has resulted in a significant escalation in prices paid for select items. The bottom-line items still languish price wise but at least continue to change hands. This marketplace continues to be active, and many outstanding items have appeared recently in the fire antiques and collectibles field. But when all is said and done, the careful purchase of quality, well-documented firefighting items will continue to be an enjoyable hobby and an excellent investment opportunity.

The earliest American fire marks date back to 1752 when 'The Philadelphia Contributionship for the Insurance of Houses From Loss By Fire' (the official name of this company, who is still in business) used a plaque to identify property they insured. Early fire marks were made of cast iron, sheet brass, lead, copper, tin, and zinc. The insignia of the insurance company appeared on each mark, and they would normally reward the volunteer fire department who managed to be the first on the scene to battle the fire. First used in Great Britain about 1780, English examples were more elaborate than U.S. marks, and usually were made of lead. Most copper and brass fire marks are of European origin. By the latter half of the nineteenth century, they became nearly obsolete, though some companies continued to issue them for advertising purposes. Many of these old fire marks are being reproduced today in cast iron and aluminum.

Fire grenades preceded the pressurized metal fire extinguishers used today. They were filled with a mixture of chemicals and water and made of glass thin enough to shatter easily when thrown into the flames. Many varieties of colors and shapes were used. Not all grenades contain salt-brine solution, some, such as the Red Comet, contain carbon tetrachloride, a powerful solvent that is also a health hazard and an environmental threat. (It attacks the ozone layer.) It is best to leave any contents inside the glass balls. The source of grenade prices are mainly auction results; current retail values will fluctuate.

Today there is a large, active group of collectors for fire department antiques (items over 100 years old) and an even larger group seeking related collectibles (those less than 100 years old). Our advisors for this category (except grenades) are H. Thomas and Patricia Laun; they are listed in the Directory under New York. They will be glad to return your phone call as soon as possible. Our fire grenades advisor is Willy Young; he is listed in the Directory under Nevada. In the following listings, values are for items in excellent to near-mint condition unless otherwise noted.

Alarm, Belcher & Loomis...RT, 4-needle, brass bell, oak case, 8x13" ... 400.00
Alarm box, Gamewell, Fire Alarm Station #112, w/inner box & key .. 110.00

Alarm key for Gamewell box, 5" long, $1,000.00. (Photo courtesy Skinner Inc. Auctioneers & Appraisers of Antiques & Fine Art/LiveAuctioneers.com)

Axe, CI w/Comp Weldon Fire Co & advertising, 9½" L 90.00
Axe, hand; steel w/wood hdl, sm 35.00
Axe head, curved blade w/dmn points, wood hdl & spike tip 125.00
Badge, Asst Foreman Hook & Ladder..., steel w/helmet/trumpets at top . 45.00
Badge, Chief Fire Dept, bl emblem on 10k gold w/eagle 60.00
Badge, Pequot Engine Co-6-LFD 30 Yrs, Sterling, sm 40.00
Badge, West Park/Stowe Twp, SP brass, 1930s, 1¾" 35.00
Bell, apparatus; Mack-W B model bracket, 3-leg 975.00
Bell, apparatus; NP, 10" dia, w/stand 675.00
Bell, captain's tapper; electromechanical, brass acorn 750.00
Bell, Mack B Model, chrome plate, 12" dia, w/bracket 1,000.00
Bell, muffin; trn wood hdl, 3-3½" 250.00
Bell, muffin; trn wood hdl, 5" 435.00
Bell, rocking cradle type, nickel, 10" dia 1,250.00
Belt, parade; Asst Engineer, VG 45.00
Belt, parade; Washington on wht leather, w/keeper 85.00
Bookends, Hartford Fire Ins Co 1810-1935, brass, 5½", pr 80.00

Box, alarm; Holtzer Cobot, CI/brass, institutional style 75.00
Box, ballot; 2-compartment, hinged lid, blk & wht marbles 65.00
Bracket, apparatus; for Deitz Queen lantern (or similar) 125.00
Bucket, gr pnt leather w/mustard & blk banner, 13¼", G 660.00
Bucket, leather, Cairns, 1960s 80.00
Bucket, leather, old blk w/faded gold letters: B&A, 12" 465.00
Bucket, overhaul; rubberized canvas 95.00
Bucket, pnt leather, Gabrielle blowing horn, name/Active 1806, 12½" .3,450.00
Bucket, pnt leather, gr/blk over orig red w/name & 1843, wear, 20" ..825.00
Bucket, pnt leather, Warren Fire Club...1829, broken hdl, 12" ..2,415.00
Can, Minimax Refill, tin, graphics on front, G 40.00
Catalog, Motor Fire Apparatus, Am LaFrance, 1916 .... 140.00
Catalog, 148 pgs of equipment, Silsby Mfg Co, 1888, VG 245.00
Decanter, Mack 1911 rotary fire pumper on wht ceramic, dog stopper ..45.00
Engine seat, metal w/red pnt & gold-leaf trim, VG 425.00
Extinguisher, Boyce, empty w/paper labels, mounting bracket, 12" 180.00
Extinguisher, Childs (Utica), riveted copper, common, 2½-gal, G 25.00
Extinguisher, DC Ranger, complete 35.00
Extinguisher, Fire Dust, tin tube, dry powder, 3x13¼", G 65.00
Extinguisher, Phomene, Pyrene Mfg Co, chrome, 25" 25.00
Extinguisher, Rex, soda & acid, early, 2½-gal 30.00
Extinguisher, Stop Fire, w/gauge & shut-off, VG 15.00
Fire mark, FA, CI, 11¼x7¼" 80.00
Fire mark, JT Jones Hose Co, CI axe form, 1890s, 12x5", G 130.00
Fire mark, tree/#105 in relief on CI oval w/red enamel, 3x2⅓" 110.00
Frontispc, leather, C Volunteer Assn (some letters missing), 8"... 125.00
Frontispc, leather, high front, blk & wht raised letters: Engine 1 OFD...225.00
Gauge, sprinkler; Am Fire Extinguisher, NP brass, 6" 30.00
Gong, Gamewell, mahog feather-top case, 18" bell 4,350.00
Gong, house; Gamewell, 6" bell, Excelsior oak case 1,250.00
Gong, turtle; Gamewell, polished well, orig key for winding, 10" ...165.00
Gong/indicator combination, house; Gamewell, 15", fancy cvd case ... 12,500.00
Grenade, Barnum, amber 750.00
Grenade, C&N-W Ry, clear w/cobalt contents 350.00
Grenade, Flagg, amber, str line date 850.00
Grenade, Harden's Improved...Oct 7th 1884, cobalt/clear, 2-pc, 4¾" .. 1,600.00
Grenade, Harden's...Aug 14 1883, smoke gr w/bl striations, 6¼" . 900.00
Grenade, Harkness, teal bl 550.00
Grenade, Harkness Fire Destroyer, cobalt, ribbed, label, 6¼" 400.00
Grenade, Hazelton's Fire Keg, amber 350.00
Grenade, Magic Fire Extinguisher, yel w/amber tone, crude, 6¼" 850.00
Grenade, Nutting HSN, dk amber 450.00

Grenade, Royal, medium cobalt, embossed circular panels and hobnails, Patent Applied for June 1884, rare, 5", $3,500.00. (Photo courtesy Glass-Works Auctions)

Grenade, Sinclair & Co...London label, cobalt, Toot on base, 7¼" .. 450.00
Grenade, UNIC, amber, FR 650.00
Helmet, aluminum, leather front: Engine 2 HFD, w/liner 125.00
Helmet, leather, high eagle, fancy frontispc, 4-comb, 1840s, EX . 500.00
Helmet, leather, high eagle, jockey style, VG 450.00
Helmet, leather, high eagle, metal frontispc: Montgomery 1, 1847.. 750.00
Helmet, leather, high eagle, Wilson of NY, 1870s, VG 425.00
Hose, riveted leather section, VG 70.00
Hose rack, interior; #5, 9x19" 30.00
Hydrant, Chapman Valve Mfg Boston, pnt CI, ca 1888-90, 33½" ..150.00

Indicator, Gamewell, w/vibrating 8" bell 4,500.00
Key, alarm system; brass, Gamewell, VG 50.00
Lamp, motion; Insure Before the Fire, burning building, 18x24" . 550.00
Lantern, Dietz Fire King Dept, tin, VG 150.00
Lantern, Dietz Queen Fire Dept, NP brass, hand sz 710.00
Lantern, Dietz Tubular, tin, slide-over cage/clear globe, 1881-93. 200.00
Lantern, hand; Am LaFrance, battery 85.00
Lantern, hand; Seagrave 'Grether,' battery 175.00
Lantern globe, for Deitz, 2-color, gr over clear (globe only) 1,100.00
Lantern globe, for Dietz King, cobalt bl 100.00
Log, Amoskeag Steam Fire Engine Co #2, NJ, 1897-98 .... 225.00
Mug, Defiance #5 1908 in bl on wht ceramic 75.00
Nozzle, brass w/chrome Am LaFrance tip, complete 135.00
Nozzle, copper & brass, 3-part, 67" 500.00
Nozzle, copper & brass w/string wrap, Underwriter's Test 45.00
Paperweight, Monarch Fire Insurance...Cleveland, pewter-like, 5½" .. 100.00
Pipe, cord covered, 2-hdl play pipe, Powhattan, Underwriter's, 15" ..60.00
Pole, pike, trn hdl, 46½", VG 40.00
Portrait, fireman, FD 281 Phila, oval 21x16" fr 165.00
Rattle, single reed, golden oak w/trn hdl, working 80.00
Rattle, watchman's, brass ends, eng NO 6 SG 100.00
Ribbon, Houtzpale PA convention, 1897 .... 15.00
Sign, Boston Fire Insurance Co Boston MA, rvpt, 17½x23½" 350.00
Siren, Federal Q2B Fire Siren 950.00
Siren, Sterling Model H, hand crank 750.00
Siren, Sterling Model 30, 12-volt 325.00
Spanner wrench, Civil Defense, CI, mk CD in circle 7.50
Strainer, NP brass, 17x5" dia 45.00
Torch, apparatus, NP/brass, to mt on bk of horse-drawn pc 125.00
Torch, NP brass w/wood hdl, VG 675.00
Torch, parade; nickel/brass, 3" 45.00
Transmitter, Gamewell, w/50 brass code wheels, oak case 2,500.00
Trophy, 2nd Prize Hose Coupling Contest...1913, silver 50.00
Trumpet, presentation; SP w/eng steamer, 1892, 21" 1,300.00
Trumpet, speaking; brass w/gold tassel, dvtl seam, 16" 500.00
Trumpet, speaking; presentation, Alert No 2...NJ, silver, 18" 625.00
Trumpet, working; NP brass, vintage 320.00
Uniform overcoat, wool w/nickel buttons, 1960s 28.00
Wrench, spanner; American LaFrance Foamite Corp, 11½" L 20.00

Fireglow

Fireglow is a type of art glass that first appears to be an opaque cafe au lait, but glows with rich red 'fire' when held to a strong source of light.

Bottle, floral panels, atomizer, 6" 72.50
Pitcher, morning glories/butterfly, 7x4x4" 90.00
Vase, autumn flowers, trumpet form, 18" 315.00
Vase, bird & flowers, ovoid, ftd, 11" 135.00

Vase, brown and white floral decor, Sandwich, 9", $165.00. (Photo courtesy John A. Shumann III)

Vase, courting scene & flowers, cylindrical neck, 12" 145.00
Vase, flowers & leaves, stick neck, ca 1890, 12", pr 315.00
Vase, thistles, autumn colors, shouldered, ftd, 13½" 150.00

Fireplace Implements

In the colonial days of our country, fireplaces provided heat in the winter and were used year round to cook food in the kitchen. The implements that were a necessary part of these functions were varied and have become treasured collectibles, many put to new use in modern homes as decorative accessories. Gypsy pots may hold magazines; copper and brass kettles, newly polished and gleaming, contain dried flowers or green plants. Firebacks, highly ornamental iron panels that once reflected heat and protected masonry walls, are now sometimes used as wall decorations. By Victorian times the cook stove had replaced the kitchen fireplace, and many of these early utensils were already obsolete; but as a source of heat and comfort, the fireplace continued to be used for several more decades. See also Wrought Iron.

Andirons, brass, Baroque Revival w/gadrooning/emb foliage/mask, 14". 265.00
Andirons, brass & CI w/eng, urn finial, Philadelphia, 1780s, 27" ... 2,400.00
Andirons, bronzed finish on CI, dragon detail, 19x27x12" 600.00
Andirons, CI, Gothic, att Savery & Co, 1850s, 17" 2,000.00
Andirons, iron, pheasant figural, EX patina, 20x24x22" 850.00

Bellows, carved North Wind faces, W. R. Pries 433 Canal of N. Y., wear, 30", $7,800.00. (Photo courtesy Skinner Inc. Auctioneers & Appraisers of Antiques & Fine Art/ LiveAuctioneers.com)

Bellows, floral HP on wood, brass tacks, EX leather, rprs, 21" 175.00
Bellows, turtle-bk, pnt pear/apples on mustard yel, new leather, 17".. 300.00
Bucket, brass, Edwardian style, w/lid 215.00
Coal basket, CI, Gothic Revival style 48.00
Coal basket, pnt wrought iron, Victorian 60.00
Coffee roaster, CI, hinged door, trn wooden hdl, 52" L 260.00
Fender, brass rail, vertical wires w/swag border, 19th C, 10x35x11". 475.00
Fender, brass rail over vertical wirework & wire swags, 1800s, 24x39" . 2,700.00
Fender, brass rails held by balusters, wirework, ball ft, 18x34x12" . 1,000.00
Fender, pierced brass U shape w/scrolling ivy, 19th C, 46" L 450.00
Fender, urn-form finials, brass rail over wires/wire scrolls, 21x59" . 2,800.00
Firescreen, maple pole w/needlework shield in fr, rfn, 53" 200.00
Insert, cast brass, ornate, 16x26x15" 475.00
Mantle, Eastlake style w/mirror bk, fire box: 42x36", VG............. 965.00
Scoop, pnt wood & metal, primitive 72.50
Screen, brass segmented fan shape, opens to 38" 60.00
Screen, dk wood w/neoclassical tapestry panel 360.00
Scuttle, brass helmet form 48.00
Scuttle, copper, footed scoop form 240.00
Scuttle, floral pnt on metal, slant lid, ftd 240.00
Surround, CI, Classical Revival style, 36x37" 600.00
Surround, hammered copper w/repoussé hood, 41x43" 2,100.00
Surround, wht marble, Louis XVI style w/ormolu bronze mts 900.00

Tongs, ember; wrought iron, spring loaded, curlique hdl, 16" 375.00
Trammel, CI w/Maltese cross & acorn finials, winch operated, 49" . 285.00

Fischer

Ignaz and Emil Fisher were art pottery designers and producers from Hungary. Ignaz Fisher founded a workshop in Budapest, Hungary, in 1866. He had previously worked for M.F. Fisher, owner of the famous Herend factory, also in Hungary. His first products included domestic items that utilized a cream-colored clay; styles were copied from the Herend factory. His ware is recognized by the pale yellow, soft-lead glaze, usually decorated with painted ethnic Hungarian designs.

Emil Fischer took the business over from his father around 1890. The workshop was closed in 1908 and reopened for only a short time. Production from this period was influenced by the high-style designs of the Zsolnay factory in Pecs, Hungary. Unable to compete, they turned to the manufacture of building materials. Marks (incised and painted): Fisher J. Budapest; initials: F.E. under a crown.

Bowl, bird figural, floral & gold, heavy rctl, ftd, 1867, 11½x13"... 390.00
Charger, floral & intricate rtcl overall, scalloped, 14" 265.00
Compote, mc w/gold, navette form in rococo taste, 13x16½" 450.00
Jug, geometric circles, gold/bl/wht, 9" 170.00
Vase, moon; floral, ftd, 1900, 8½" 360.00

Vase, dragon handles, reticulated applications, 17", VG, $335.00. (Photo courtesy William J. Jenack Auctioneers/ LiveAuctioneers.com)

Fisher, Harrison

Harrison Fisher (1875 – 1934), noted illustrator and creator of the Fisher Girl, was the son of landscape artist, Hugh Antoine Fisher. His career began in his teens in San Francisco where he did artwork for the Hearst papers. Later in New York his drawings of beautiful American women attracted much attention and graced the covers of the most popular magazines of the day such as *Puck, Ladies' Home Journal, Saturday Evening Post,* and *Cosmopolitan.* He also illustrated novels, and his art books are treasured. His drawings appeared on thousands of postcards and posters. His creation of the Fisher Girl and his panel of six scenes of the *Greatest Moments in a Woman's Life* made him the most sought-after and well-paid illustrator of his day.

Book, Hiawatha, 16 color plates, hardcover, Bobbs-Merrill, 1906, VG .70.00
Book, Love Finds the Way, blk/wht prints, Dodd-Meade, 1904, 6x9", VG.. 60.00
Book, Lovely Woman, Bobbs-Merrill, c 1910, 11¼x10⅛", G 80.00
Magazine, Cosmopolitan, stylish lady cover, April 1931, VG+ 35.00
Postcard, A Love Score, tennis couple, Reinthal Newman #839, EX .. 35.00
Postcard, An Old Song, lady singing, Reinthal Newman, 1909, VG. 20.00
Postcard, Dumb Luck, lady w/horse, Reinthal Newman, unused, EX. 45.00
Postcard, Her Future, lady & crystal ball, EX 35.00
Postcard, Sweethearts Asleep, Reinthal Newman, 1913, EX 35.00

Postcard, The Rose, Reinthal & Newman, #181, VG 22.50
Print, Am Girl in Ireland, Scribners, 1908, 17x12", EX 70.00
Print, Best Gift, lady w/ring, 1909, oval in 17x11" gesso fr, EX.... 125.00
Print, blond in feathered hat, Curtis, 1911, 11¾x8", EX 85.00
Print, equestrienne & horse, Curtis, 1911, 11¾x8", EX 100.00
Print, lady in lilac gown, Gray Litho, 1903, 16x13", VG 125.00
Print, lady w/3 dogs, Crowell, sgn, 1911, 11¾x8", VG+ 75.00
Print, Luxury, lady in bed w/book, Scribners, 1912, 17x12", VG+.. 75.00
Print, Minnehaha or Laughing Water, from 1908 book, 10½x9", VG .38.00
Print, The Kiss, romantic couple, Scribners, 1910, 17x12", EX .. 225.00
Print, The Proposal, couple, Scribners, 16x12", EX, +mat & fr ... 125.00
Print, Waiting, lady w/tennis racket, Scribners, sgn/1911, 12x17", EX...225.00

Print, You Will Marry a Dark Man, sight: 20x16", matted under glass and framed, $120.00. (Photo courtesy Du Mouchelles)

Fishing Collectibles

Collecting old fishing tackle is becoming more popular every year. Though at first most interest was geared toward old lures and some reels, rods, advertising, and miscellaneous items are quickly gaining ground. Values are given for examples in excellent or better condition and should be used only as a guide. For more information we recommend *The Fred Arbogast Story* by Scott Heston; *The Pflueger Heritage* by Wayne Ruby; *Spring-loaded Fish Hooks, Traps, and Lures* by William Blauser and Timothy Mierzwa; *Fishing Lure Collectibles, An Encyclopedia of the Early Years, 1840 to 1940*, by Dudley Murphy and Rick Edmisten; *Fishing Lure Collectibles, An Encyclopedia of the Modern Era, 1940 to Present*, by Dudley Murphy and Deanie Murphy; *Captain John's Fishing Tackle Price Guide* by John Kolbeck; and *Modern Fishing Lure Collectibles, Vols. 1 – 5*, by Russell Lewis. These books are all published by Collector Books. Our advisor for this category is Dave Hoover; he is listed in the Directory under Indiana.

Catalog, Allcocks Fishing Tackle, 1932, hardcover, 163 pgs, EX . 130.00
Catalog, Bristol Fishing Rods, Reels & Lines, ca 1914, 28 pgs, EX ..50.00
Catalog, Bronson-Made JA Cox.../Bronson Fishing Reels, 1952, EX... 75.00
Catalog, Fox Reels for Finer Fishing, 1930s, 8 pgs, VG 165.00
Catalog, Ideal Fishing Float Co...No ID-102, 1920-30, 12 pgs, EX .. 165.00
Catalog, L Allcock & Co Ltd Fishing Tackle #36, 1947, 16 pgs, VG+.100.00
Catalog, Penn Reels Catalog No 9, 1941, 28 pgs, G 95.00
Catalog, Storm Lures 30th Anniversary, 1964-94, unused, NM+ .. 55.00
Creel, Meier & Frank, tightly woven wicker w/leather 100.00
Decoy, cvd, gold foil on wood fish w/5 metal fins, pnt eyes, 6⅜" 90.00
Decoy, cvd/pnt fish w/6 metal fins, tack eyes, HL Way, 1950s, $50 to....75.00
Decoy, Paw Paw, cvd/pnt wood fish, 3 wooden fins, 1930s, 7½", MIB. 150.00
Hook, Kingfisher #668658, steel & lead, 1901, 3", from $100 to . 150.00
Hook, Lathrop #426027, brass & japanned steel, 1890, 6" closed...750.00
Hook, lever; Greer #641857, blued steel, 1900-08, 3½" 70.00
Hook, lever; Stevenson #1608631, NP steel, 1926, 7", minimum....1,000.00
Hook, Mack Automatic #9, brass spinner blade, ca 1890, 5" 80.00
Hook, Monarch Automatic #1507344, steel, 1924, 4½", from $20 to..40.00

Hook, Red's Sure-Catch #2213624, brass/lead/steel, 1940, 4", $15 to..20.00
Hook, spring-loaded; Aspelin #1417482, steel, 1922, 4½", $500 to....750.00
Hook, Surestrike, spring-loaded, #2642694, steel, 1953, 3½" L.... 175.00
Hook, trolling spoon, Harlow #378678, brass, 1888, 3", minimum.. 150.00
Ice tester, wood, FLO-PAC BRUSHES..., ca 1950s, 29" L, from $15 to. 25.00
Jigging stick, Bay De Noc Lure Co, wood, from $10 to.................. 15.00
Lure, Bauer, Mike's Creeper, wood w/pnt eyes, 2 trebles, 1970s, 4½".. 25.00
Lure, Creek Chub, Baby Wiggler #200, 1917-54, 2¾", from $20 to ..30.00
Lure, Creek Chub, Injured Minnow #1500P, plastic, 1961-78, from $15 to..40.00
Lure, Creek Chub, Jointed Pikie #2600, 3 trebles, 1950s, minimum.. 25.00
Lure, Creek Chub, Skipper #4600, weighted tail, 1936-51, 3", $15 to.20.00
Lure, Creek Chub, Tiny Tim #6400, deep diving lip, 1950-54, 1¾".45.00

Lure, Elman 'Bud' Stewart, One-Eyed Minnow, 1968, 2¾", from $45.00 to $60.00.
(Photo courtesy Dudley Murphy & Deanie Murphy)

Lure, Gaddis, Gaddis Dilly, gold plated, 1950s-60s, 3¼", from $5 to . 10.00
Lure, Heddon, Broomstick Frog, 4 single hooks, 1890, 2¾".......4,000.00
Lure, Heddon, Harden's Waltz, 3 trebles/2 propellers, 1930, 4¼". 300.00
Lure, Heddon, Old Zaragoss #6500, pnt eye, 2 trebles, 1920-55, 4¼". 45.00
Lure, Heddon, Saltwater Torpedo #30, 3 trebles, 1949, 4⅛", $15 to... 20.00
Lure, Heddon, Tiger Cub #1010, 2 trebles, 1967, 2⅖", from $20 to 30.00
Lure, Heddon, Tiny Chugger Spooks #335, 2 trebles, 1961, minimum .. 15.00
Lure, Herter's, Big Eye, from top Herter's fly line bag, minimum.... 20.00
Lure, Jack's Tackle Mfg, Skip Jack, 1 treble, minimum................... 10.00
Lure, Jamison, Chicago Wobbler, 3 trebles, 1917, 4", from $75 to ..125.00
Lure, Jamison, smacker, 1 single dressed hook, 1934, 6", from $25 to ..40.00
Lure, Moonlight, Feather Minnow #1500, 1 single hook, 1926, 1½" ...85.00
Lure, Paw Paw, Croaker #71, frog skin, 2 trebles, 1940s, from $275 to.. 325.00
Lure, Paw Paw, Dreadnought #5100J, jtd, 3 trebles, 1940s, 7"...... 120.00
Lure, Pflueger, Kent Floater, 3 trebles, 1910, 2¼", from $300 to... 400.00
Lure, Pflueger, Musky Mustang, 3 trebles, 1940s, 7¼", from $200 to ..225.00
Lure, Shakespeare, Egyptian Wobbler #6636, glass eyes, 1930, 5".. 70.00
Lure, Shakespeare, Evolution, 3 trebles/propeller, 1902, 3⅝"....... 150.00
Lure, Shakespeare, Wood Revolution, 3 trebles 1900, 3½", $600 to ..800.00
Lure, South Bend, Be Bop #903, 2 trebles, ca 1950, 4½", $15 to.... 20.00
Lure, South Bend, Underwater Minnow #905, 5 trebles, 1935, 3⅝".85.00
Lure, Thompson Doll Top Secret Model TS 21-SF, 2 trebles, 1969 ..50.00
Reel, BF Meek & Sons, #3, 1890-1916, w/leather case 700.00
Reel, fly; Shakespeare Model 1837 Tru-Art, Model GD, 1947, minimum...25.00
Reel, fly; St George, Hardy Bros, ribbed reel arms, 2⁹⁄₁₆" 515.00
Reel, fly; St John, Hardy Bros, 1965, w/padded case, NM 310.00
Reel, South Bend Model No 50, 1960s, from $35 to 50.00
Rod, casting; Fenwick Feralite FC 61, 3-pc, 6' 300.00
Rod, fly; Heddon Bluewater #10, bamboo, 5-pc, w/bag, VG 200.00
Rod, fly; Wright & McGill Granger Special, bamboo, 4-pc, w/case, NM . 710.00

Florence Ceramics

Figurines marked 'Florence Ceramics' were produced in the '40s and '50s in Pasadena, California. The quality of the ware and the attention given to detail has prompted a growing interest among today's collectors. The names of these lovely ladies, gents, and figural groups are nearly always incised into their bases. The company name is ink stamped.

Examples are evaluated by size, rarity, and intricacy of design. For more information we recommend *Collector's Encyclopedia of California Pottery, Second Edition*, by Jack Chipman; *The Florence Collectibles* by Doug Foland; and *The Complete Book of Florence Ceramics: A Labor of Love* by Sue and Jerry Kline and Margaret Wehrspaun. Our advisor for this category is Jerry Kline; he is listed in the Directory under Tennessee.

Abigail, 8", from $125 to 140.00
Adeline, fancy, 8¼", from $225 to 250.00
Amber, 9¼", from $600 to 675.00
Angel, 7¾", from $60 to... 80.00
Anita, brocade, rare, 15", from $2,750 to................................3,000.00
Annette, 8¼", from $400 to 450.00
Baby, flower holder, 10½", from $50 to... 70.00
Barbara, child, 8½", from $115 to 130.00
Birthday Girl, 9", from $2,600 to..2,800.00
Blue Boy, 11¾", from $275 to 325.00
Bride, rare, 8¾", from $1,800 to...2,000.00
Butch, 5½", from $125 to.. 140.00
Camille, hands, 8½", from $325 to 360.00
Camille, plain, 8½", from $160 to 180.00
Catherine, 7¾", from $700 to 775.00
Charmaine, hands away, 8½", from $180 to 225.00
Chinese Couple, blk & wht w/yel flowers, 8½", pr from $80 to.... 120.00
Cinderella & Prince Charming, pr from $1,800 to 2,100.00
Cindy, 8", from $325 to 375.00
David, 7½", from $90 to 110.00
Dear Ruth, lamp, from $900 to 925.00

Dot and Bud, each: from $900.00 to $1,100.00.

(Photo courtesy Doug Foland)

Douglas, 8¼", from $100 to.. 120.00
Edward, 7", from $325 to 400.00
Elizabeth, 8½x7", from $300 to 350.00
Gary, 8½", from $115 to 130.00
Gesille, from $1,000 to 1,250.00
Irene, pk dress, 6", from $40 to 60.00
Jim, child, 6¼", from $40 to 60.00
Josephine, 9", from $250 to 300.00
Joyce, 9", from $450 to... 500.00
Lady Diana, lav dress w/lace at neck, 10", from $1,000 to.........1,250.00
Louise, 7½", from $110 to 125.00
Marilyn, carring hat box, violet, 8", from $400 to 475.00
Masquarade, rare, 8¼", from $700 to.. 800.00
Melanie, gray dress w/Royal Red trim, from $100 to 125.00
Mermaid, from $125 to 150.00
Our Lady of Grace, wht w/gold trim, 9½", from $200 to............... 225.00
Pamela, 7¼", from $275 to.. 325.00
Patrice, pk & wht, flower holder, 6", from $160 to 180.00
Peter, rare, 9¼", from $450 to 500.00
Rhett, violet, 9", from $225 to.. 275.00
Shirley, 8", from $200 to 300.00
Sue Ellen, holding flowers, pk dress, 8¼", from $160 to............... 180.00
Summer, 6¼", from $325 to 375.00

Suzette, 6", from $100 to 120.00
Violet, wall pocket, w/gold, 7", from $100 to............................... 120.00
Vivian, coral dress, hat & parasol, 10", from $225 to.................... 275.00
Yvonne, plain, 8¾", from $400 to.. 450.00

Flow Blue

Flow Blue ware was produced by many Staffordshire potters; among the most familiar were Meigh, Podmore and Walker, Samuel Alcock, Ridgway, John Wedge Wood (who often signed his work Wedgewood), and Davenport. It was popular from about 1825 through 1860 and again from 1880 until the turn of the century. The name describes the blurred or flowing effect of the cobalt decoration, achieved through the introduction of a chemical vapor into the kiln. The body of the ware is ironstone, and Oriental motifs were favored. Later issues were on a lighter body and often decorated with gilt. For further information we recommend *Gaston's Flow Blue China, The Comprehensive Guide*, by Mary Frank Gaston (Collector Books); she is listed in the Directory under Texas.

Abbey, bowl, footed, Maastricht, Holland, 4½x8", $250.00.

Abbey, plate, Geo Jones, 10" 45.00
Abbey, plate, Maastricht, 9" 55.00
Alaska, bowl, serving; Grindley, 1891-1914, 9¾" 200.00
Alaska, toothbrush holder, gold accents, C&H Tunstall, 5¾"........ 75.00
Albany, bowl, vegetable; scalloped ft, hdls, Johnson Bros, 7x11½"... 135.00
Albany, plate, Johnson Bros, ca 1900, 10" 100.00
Albany, platter, emb beaded scalloped rim, hdls, Johnson Bros, 12" L.. 185.00
Albany, shaving mug, Grindley, 3⅝x3¼" 160.00
Alexis, plate, soup; Adderleys, 8½" 35.00
Alton, plate, Grimwades Staffordshire Pottery, ca 1930, 10" 60.00
Anemone, butter pat, gold accents, 3" 60.00
Arabia, platter, 11x8"... 40.00
Asiatic Pheasants, plate, T Hughes, 9".. 55.00
Baltic, plate, beaded scalloped rim, Grindley, 9"............................ 45.00
Bamboo, platter, Bates & Walker, ca 1876, 18½x14¾"................. 335.00
Belmont, platter, emb scalloped rim, JHW & Sons, ca 1892, 14x10" ... 160.00
Bermuda, bowl, William A Adderley Co, ca 1890, 16" 300.00
Blue Willow, plate, scalloped rim, Deans Ltd, ca 1910-1919, 7" 50.00
Cambridge, bowl, dessert; scalloped rim, England, ca 1890, 5" 85.00
Cattle Scenery, gravy boat, scalloped ft, beaded rim, Adams, ca 1870.40.00
Cattle Scenery, plate, pie crust rim, Adams, ca 1940s, 10".......... 140.00
Chatsworth, platter, gold rim, Keeling & Co, 1886-1890, 16x12½"...185.00
Circassia, bowl, ped ft, w/lid, J&G Alcock, ca 1839.................1,000.00
Clarence, platter, England, ca 1900, 16x12" 435.00
Columbia, sugar bowl, w/lid, Clementson & Young, ca 1845-47... 900.00
Conway, platter, New Wharf, ca 1890, 10½" L 75.00
Coral, butter pat, unevenly scalloped rim, Johnson Bros, ca 1900, 3" ..65.00
Cows, plate, Wedgwood, ca 1906, 10"... 150.00
Cyprus, plate, Ridgway Bates & Co, ca 1857, 9½"....................... 100.00
Davenport, bowl, 8-sided, ftd, w/lid & hdls, Amoy, 9" 455.00
Delamere, platter, scalloped rim w/gold, H Alcock, ca 1900, 14½" L.. 460.00
Delph, platter, Blair & Co, 1912-23, 12x9½".................................. 45.00
Douglas, platter, scalloped rim, Ford & Sons, 9x12" L................. 160.00
Eastern Plants, platter, Wood & Brownsfield, ca 1838-50, 19" L...1,100.00
English Scenery, platter, scalloped rim, Wood & Sons, ca 1917, 12" L. 140.00

Excelsior, teapot, Thomas Fell..1,100.00
Fairy Villa, bowl, soup; W Adams & Co, 9"....................... 50.00
Flora, cracker jar, gold accents, Cumberlidge..., ca 1890, 6¾x5".. 210.00
Floral, platter, unevenly scalloped rim, ca 1900, 15½x11½".........120.00
Floral & Scroll, platter, Doulton, 1891-1902, 14" L 140.00
Florida, butter pat, beaded rim, Grindley, 3⅛"...................... 85.00
Florida, plate, beaded scalloped rim w/gold, Grindley, 8" 65.00
Gainsborough, cheese dish, w/lid, Ridgways 550.00
Glenwood, plate, soup; emb rim, Johnson Bros, 10" 70.00
Glorie De Dijon, footbath, scalloped rim.................................2,230.00
Grace, butter pat, emb scalloped rim w/gold, Grindley, 3½"....40.00
Grecian, platter, thin gold rim, Ford & Sons, ca 1908, 18¾x13½"...160.00
Grecian Statue, berry strainer, Brownfields Pottery, ca 1891-1900...250.00
Haarlem, trivet, rnd, Burgess & Leigh, 6¾"............................... 90.00
Holland, cup & saucer, Johnson Bros, 6" saucer, 2x4½" cup.......... 85.00
Holland, plate, Johnson Bros, ca 1895, 10".......................... 85.00
Holland, sugar bowl, scalloped ft, w/lid & hdls.......................... 225.00
Indian Plant, bowl, emb rim, Kaolin Ware, ca 1828-59, 10" 70.00
Indiana, plate, Wedgwood, 7½".. 40.00
Jacobean, pitcher, tankard form, Ye Old Crown & Sceptre, Doulton, 9".900.00
Janette, washbowl & pitcher, Grindley 2,300.00
Jewel, plate, w/gold trim, Adams, 9"...................................... 45.00
Keele, platter, gold accents, Grindley, ca 1890-1915, 14" L 400.00
Kensington, bowl, soup; gold accents & rim, Doulton, ca 1880, 10".. 75.00
Kyber, plate, scalloped rim, W Adams & Co, 9"........................... 85.00
Kyber, plate, 12-sided, W Adams & Co, 1891-1910, 9" 65.00
La Belle, biscuit jar 450.00
LaBelle, chocolate pot 900.00
Lakewood, plate, scalloped rim w/gold, Wood & Sons, 9"............... 75.00
Landscape, plate, Wedgwood, 10½"...................................... 70.00
Libertas Prussia, plate, emb scalloped rim, ca 1920, 9".............. 45.00
Lily & Rose, wall plate, lg scalloped rim w/gold, D-L Co, ca 1950...60.00
Lonsdale, platter, Ridgways, ca 1880, 11½" L 335.00
Lorne, bowl, fruit; beaded scalloped rim, Grindley, ca 1900, 5¼"... 50.00
Lorne, plate, scalloped rim, Grindley, ca 1900, 9" 85.00
Lorraine, gravy boat & underplate, Clementson Bros, 1910, 4x8½"..140.00
Madras, pitcher, Doulton, 1902, 6x6" 165.00
Madras, plate, soup; Wood & Son, ca 1891-1907 .... 75.00
Mandarin, tureen, sauce; w/lid/tray/ladle, Pultney, 1910, 5x8½x7"..400.00
Manilla, plate, Podmore Walker & Co, ca 1834-59, 9½" 110.00
Meissen, butter pat, bl rim band, 3½".................................... 30.00
Meissen, cake plate, lipped, ped ft, BWM & Co, ca 1865, 3x10½"..135.00
Meissen, canister, Sugar on front, Hornberg Baden, 7" 40.00
Melrose, bowl, scalloped rim, Doulton, ca 1800, 10½"................. 70.00
Monarch, platter, emb scalloped rim, Montreal Crockery Co, 1920, 14" L...250.00
Montrose, washbowl & pitcher, H Alcock, ca 1910 ....1,500.00
Morning Glory, cake plate, raised hdls, ca 1880, 13"...................300.00
Napier, plate, Keeling & Co, ca 1886-1936, 9"......................... 30.00
Newport Rhode Island, plate, souvenir, 9".............................. 75.00
Niagara Falls, plate, souvenir, various scenes, ca 1893-1938, 9"...140.00
Ning Po, plate, Ralph Hall, ca 1845, 6"................................. 75.00
Non Pareil, butter pat, Burgess & Leigh, ca 1891, 3"................. 70.00
Non Pareil, platter, Burgess & Leigh, ca 1891-1919, 12" L 500.00
Norfolk, cake plate, 8-sided, hdls, Doulton, ca 1920, 9"................ 85.00
Norfolk, creamer, Doulton, ca 1928-32, 2" 55.00
Normandy, plate, ruffled rim, Johnson Bros, ca 1900, 8" 110.00
Normandy, plate, soup; emb scalloped rim w/gold, Johnson Bros, 10"..115.00
Onion, saucer, Allertons, ca 1900, 5¾"................................. 30.00
Ornithology, plate, Brown Westhead & Moore, ca 1870, 7" 90.00
Oxford, platter, scalloped rim, Johnson Bros, ca 1900, 14" L 400.00
Paris, plate, emb scalloped rim, New Wharf, ca 1891, 9" 85.00
Pekin, plate, AEJ & Co, Staffordshire, 1905-20, 7", VG.............. 30.00
Philadelphia, plate, Independence Hall 1776, scalloped rim, 9" 85.00
Plymouth, tureen, soup; ftd, w/lid, New Wharf Pottery, 1880, 6x11½"...120.00

Pompadour, plate, Kneeling & Co, ca 1912, 9½"........................... 45.00
Poppy, casserole, gold trim, hdls, Grindley, 1891-1914, 7x11½"... 120.00
Portman, plate, beaded scalloped rim, Grindley, ca 1891-1914, 8"....85.00
Portman, platter, beaded scalloped rim, Grindley, ca 1891, 18½" L..535.00
Princess, bowl, vegetable; scalloped, w/lid & hdls, Beech, 1877, 9"....160.00
Princeton, plate, Johnson Bros, 7".. 80.00
Prisilla, pitcher, J Maddock & Sons, ca 1900, 7½"......................110.00
Quebec, creamer, Ridgways, 4¼" 75.00
Rex, platter, scalloped rim, Adderley's, ca 1900, 13½" L 75.00
Rose, bowl, Grindley, 1891-1914, 8½" L 50.00
Rural England, plate, Midwinter Ltd, ca 1910, 8"......................115.00
Rustic, tureen, vegetable; w/lid & hdls, Grindley, 1860, 10¾" L..100.00
Savoy, plate, soup; scalloped rim w/gold, Johnson Bros, ca 1900, 10"..115.00
Savoy, platter, emb scalloped rim w/gold, Johnson Bros, ca 1900, 16" L...335.00

Scinde, serving dish, Alcock, 7x13x9", EX, $1,380.00. (Photo courtesy James D. Julia Inc.)

Shanghai, plate, beaded rim, Grindley, ca 1875, 10" 120.00
Shanghai, plate, soup; Grindley, 1891-1914, 10"........................160.00
Temple, plate, Wood & Brownfield, 1845, 7" 140.00
Tonquin, platter, late 1800s, 13½x17"....................................360.00
Touraine, plate, H Alcock, 1891-1910, 8".................................. 40.00
Trilby, cake plate, Wood & Sons, ca 1891, 10½".......................... 90.00
Triumphal Car, trivet, gold rim, rnd, Warwick Ware, 7½".............. 65.00
Tulip, platter, Gibson & Son, 1912, 12½" L...............................120.00
Turin, saucer, Johnson & Bros, 5¾".. 30.00
Tyrene, pitcher, England, 5"..150.00
Venice, plate, ca 1908, 9½"... 85.00
Venice, tureen, sauce; w/plate, lid & ladle, 1880-1890................ 400.00
Verona, plate, scalloped rim w/gold, Meakin, ca 1900, 7" 85.00
Violette, waste bowl, ftd, Keller & Guerin, ca 1900, 3x6"............110.00
Virginia, butter pat, emb rim, Maddock's, 3".............................. 60.00
Waldorf, platter, 10¾x9"..120.00
Wildrose, creamer, Royal Bonn, ca 1900, 3½" 40.00

Flue Covers

When spring housecleaning started and the heating stove was taken down for the warm weather season, the unsightly hole where the stovepipe joined the chimney was hidden with an attractive flue cover. They were made with a colorful litho print behind glass with a chain for hanging. In a 1929 catalog, they were advertised at 16¢ each or six for 80¢. Although scarce today, some scenes were actually reverse painted on the glass itself. The most popular motifs were florals, children, animals, and lovely ladies. Occasionally flue covers were made in sets of three — one served a functional purpose, while the others were added to provide a more attractive wall arrangement. They range in size from 7" to 14", but 9" is the average.

Apples spilling from basket, beaded metal fr, Germany, 9½" 50.00
Basket of violets, beaded brass fr, Germany, 9¾"........................ 80.00
Boys (2) on fence teasing dogs, w/chain, 9½"............................. 70.00
Children (1 boy & 1 girl) by water w/angel watching, 11¾" 135.00
Children (1 boy & 1 girl) riding ponies, 1800s, 6"......................125.00
Girl in bright bl dress holding blk cat, gold border, 7¾" 45.00
Girl in lg hat holding violets, metal chain, 9"...........................160.00

Girl in pk standing in egg, Easter Greetings above flowers, 10x7½"..40.00
Girl in winter coat & hat holding 1 glove, late 1800s, 8"............... 60.00
Girls (2) w/5 rabbits, ornate brass fr & chain, 6" 50.00
Girls (4) holding hands & dancing in meadow, 9½"..................... 260.00
Indian w/rifle on horse looking down valley, Tabots Clothing, 12x9". 160.00
Kittens (3) watching fly on wall, metal beaded rim, Germany, 9¾"...215.00
Ladies (1 in pk & 1 in gr) holding flower garland high, 1800s, 9½"..80.00
Lady fairy w/flowing blk hair w/nest of swallows, metal chain, 8" .. 90.00
Lady gypsy profile portrait, gold pnt border, 1800s, 8" 60.00
Lady w/bare shoulders & flowers in hair, oval, metal fr, Germany, 9". 70.00

Lovely lady in fur wrap, 9¾", $135.00.
(Photo courtesy Tom Harris Auctions)

Mother & daughter in wht dresses under parasol, 1800s, 9½" 105.00
Waterfall scene in center, floral/girl panel border, 9½" 60.00

Folk Art

That the creative energies of the mind ever spark innovations in functional utilitarian channels as well as toward playful frivolity is well documented in the study of American folk art. While the average early settler rarely had free time to pursue art for its own sake, his creativity exemplified itself in fashioning useful objects carved or otherwise ornamented beyond the scope of pure practicality. After the advent of the Industrial Revolution, the pace of everyday living became more leisurely, and country folk found they had extra time. Not accustomed to sitting idle, many turned to carving, painting, or weaving. Whirligigs, imaginative toys for the children, and whimsies of all types resulted. Though often rather crude, this type of early art represents a segment of our heritage and as such has become valued by collectors.

Values given for drawings, paintings, and theorems are 'in frame' unless noted otherwise. See also Baskets; Decoys; Frakturs; Samplers; Trade Signs; Weather Vanes; Wood Carvings.

Articulated figure, dancing man w/bottle-cap hat, mc pnt, 17", VG..175.00
Bank, pnt tin house w/stenciling, Chartered Christmas 1871, 5⅝"..2,350.00
Birdhouse, Victorian church w/tall steeple, mc pnt, 27x14x15", VG+ ...2,645.00
Cutwork, Temperance Is Wisdom/eagle/foliage, HP details, mtd/fr, 8x12" ..9,400.00
Cvg, Am Indian chief w/headdress/tomahawk, sandstone, E Reed, 50" .7,000.00
Cvg, horned owl w/lg eyes, sandstone, E Reed, 15" 800.00
Cvg, mermaid w/merbaby, sandstone, E Reed, 16" L 3,600.00
Drawing, equestrian couple, pen & ink on paper, unsgn, 9x12"+fr..260.00
Family record, HP/ink/paper, hearts/statistics, 1824, fr, 15x11"... 1,650.00
Painting on board, puppies w/pan of milk, 6x12" in gilt 12x18" fr ..925.00
Painting on canvas, cat on chair at window eyes prey, 25x18"..... 700.00
Pen wipe, hen w/chicks, cotton/beads/wood, 1800s, 2¼x5" 385.00
Pen wipe, pig figural, tan velvet/bead eyes/felt base, 1800s, 3½" ..500.00
Pen wipe, rabbit form, cotton/wool/bead eyes, on yarn mat, 2x8" dia...470.00
Spencerian drawing, eagle w/rabbit/eaglets in nest, 14x18"+fr..... 575.00
Spencerian drawing, lion, brn & blk ink, lt foxing, in 26x32" gilt fr..575.00
Theorem on paper, fruit basket, in 10x10½" pine cone-on-cb fr ..375.00
Theorem on paper, fruit basket, slight foxing, ca 1825, 14x17"+gilt fr.1,950.00
Theorem on paper, pieces of fruit, watercolor, in 7x8½" gilt fr..... 350.00
Theorem on velvet, flower urn, watercolor, stains, in grpt 17x13" fr..375.00

Whirligig, Am Indian w/rotating hatched panels, pnt wood, 55" on stand .650.00
Whirligig, gardener hoeing, shrubs nearby, mc pnt wood, 21x19"...600.00
Whirligig, man, baluster-trn figure, glass bead eyes, mc pnt, 16x13" ..175.00

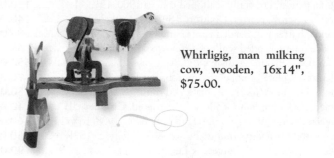

Whirligig, man milking cow, wooden, 16x14", $75.00.

Whirligig, Roman centurion, pnt wood, rpr, on stand, 17" 800.00
Whirligig, sailor w/paddle arms, cvd/pnt wood, Nantucket, 1900s, 19" ..2,500.00
Whirligig, soldier, red hat & coat, rpl arm paddles, 1800s, 20"... 2,350.00

Fostoria

The Fostoria Glass Company was built in 1887 at Fostoria, Ohio, but by 1891 it had moved to Moundsville, West Virginia. During the next two decades, they produced many lines of pressed patterned tableware and lamps. Their most famous pattern, American, was introduced in 1915 and was produced continuously until 1986 in well over 200 different pieces. From 1920 to 1925, top artists designed tablewares in colored glass — canary (vaseline), amber, blue, orchid, green, and ebony — in pressed patterns as well as etched designs. By the late '30s, Fostoria was recognized as the largest producer of handmade glassware in the world. The company ceased operations in Moundsville in 1986.

Many items from both the American and Coin Glass lines have been reproduced by Lancaster Colony. In some cases the new glass is superior in quality to the old. Since the 1950s, Indiana Glass has produced a pattern called 'Whitehall' that looks very much like Fostoria's American, though with slight variations. Because Indiana's is not handmade glass, the lines of the 'cube' pattern and the edges of the items are sharp and untapered in comparison to the fire-polished originals. Three-footed pieces lack the 'toe' and instead have a peg-like foot, and the rays on the bottoms of the American examples are narrower than on the Whitehall counterparts. The Home Interiors Company offers several pieces of American look-alikes which were not even produced in the United States. Be sure of your dealer and study the books suggested below to become more familiar with the original line.

Coin Glass reproductions flood the market. Among items you may encounter are an 8" round bowl, 9" oval bowl, 8¼" wedding bowl, 4½" candlesticks, urn with lid, 6¼" candy jar with lid, footed comport, sugar and creamer; there could possibly be others. Colors in production are crystal, green, blue, and red. The red color is very good, but the blue is not the original color, nor is the emerald green. Buyer beware! For further information see *Elegant Glassware of the Depression Era* by Cathy and Gene Florence, and *Fostoria Stemware* and *The Fostoria Value Guide*, both by Milbra Long and Emily Seate. See also Glass Animals and Figurines.

Alexis, crystal, bottle, catsup... 65.00
Alexis, crystal, bottle, oil; 4-oz.. 35.00
Alexis, crystal, cocktail, 3-oz.. 12.50
Alexis, crystal, cup, custard; hdls... 10.00
Alexis, crystal, decanter, w/stopper 110.00
Alexis, crystal, egg cup, ped ft 12.50
Alexis, crystal, nappy, 7".. 20.00
Alexis, crystal, pitcher, 16-oz.. 45.00
Alexis, crystal, shakers, pr.. 35.00

Alexis, crystal, sugar shaker 65.00
Alexis, crystal, tray, olive 20.00
Alexis, crystal, vase, ftd, 7" 50.00
Alexis, crystal, wine, 2½-oz 14.00
American, bl, candelabrum, 2-light, 16-lustre, 8" 200.00
American, crystal, bottle, bitters; w/tube, 4½-oz, 5¼" 70.00
American, crystal, bowl, rolled edge, 11½" 50.00
American, crystal, butter dish, ¼-lb 22.00
American, crystal, candlestick, octagon ft, 6" 25.00
American, crystal, candlestick, 2-light, 4½", ea 20.00
American, crystal, coaster, 3¾" 8.00
American, crystal, hat, Western style 295.00
American, crystal, mayonnaise, ped ft, w/ladle 55.00
American, crystal, napkin ring 15.00
American, crystal, nappy, 4½" 12.00
American, crystal, pitcher, w/ice lip, ½-gal, 8¼" 85.00
American, crystal, plate, torte; 24" 225.00
American, crystal, plate, 6" 10.00
American, crystal, ring holder 200.00
American, crystal, sauceboat w/liner 50.00
American, crystal, soap dish 995.00
American, crystal, sugar bowl, open 10.00
American, crystal, syrup, w/drip-proof top 35.00
American, crystal, tray, muffin; 2 upturned sides, 10" 32.50
American, crystal, tray, oval, 10½x5" 45.00
American, crystal, tumbler, #2056½, str side, 8-oz, 4" 12.00
American, crystal, tumbler, whiskey; #2056, 2½" 10.00
American, crystal, vase, sq ped ft, 9" 45.00
American, crystal, vase, str sides, 12" 250.00
American, crystal, vase, 4½" 80.00
American, crystal, wine, #2056, hexagonal ft, 2½-oz, 4½" 9.00
Baroque, bl, bowl, cream soup 85.00
Baroque, bl, bowl, pickle; 8" 32.50
Baroque, bl, candy dish, 3-part, w/lid 140.00
Baroque, bl, mustard, w/lid 110.00
Baroque, bl, vase, 7" 160.00
Baroque, crystal, ashtray 10.00
Baroque, crystal, bottle, oil; w/stopper, 5½" 85.00
Baroque, crystal, bowl, relish; 3-part, 10" 22.00
Baroque, crystal, tumbler, ftd, 9-oz, 5½" 12.00
Baroque, yel, bowl, celery; 11" 35.00
Baroque, yel, bowl, fruit; 5" 30.00
Baroque, yel, candlestick, 8-lustre, 8", ea 80.00
Baroque, yel, cup 24.00
Baroque, yel, pitcher, w/ice lip, 7" 550.00
Baroque, yel, platter, 12" L 52.50
Brocade, Grape, bl, candlestick, #2324, 4", ea 35.00
Brocade, Grape, bl, rose bowl, #2339, cupped rim, 7½" ... 85.00
Brocade, Grape, gr, candy box, #2331, 3-part, w/lid 145.00
Brocade, Grape, gr, ice bucket, #2378 .... 90.00
Brocade, Oakleaf, bl, mayonnaise, #2315 .... 70.00
Brocade, Oakleaf, crystal, bonbon, #2375 .... 30.00
Brocade, Oakleaf, crystal, bowl, #2398, cornucopia hdls, 11" ... 100.00
Brocade, Oakleaf, crystal, cake plate, #2375, 10" 65.00
Brocade, Oakleaf, crystal, candlestick, #2394, 3-toed, 2", ea 40.00
Brocade, Oakleaf, ebony, cigarette box, #2391, w/lid 125.00
Brocade, Oakleaf, ebony, vase, #2292, ftd, 8" 125.00
Brocade, Oakleaf, gr or rose, candlestick, #2375, 3", ea ... 60.00
Brocade, Oakleaf, gr or rose, cheese & cracker, #2368 ... 75.00
Brocade, Oakwood, azure or orchid, bonbon, #2375 .... 50.00
Brocade, Oakwood, azure or orchid, compote, #2400, pulled stem, 8" .. 115.00
Brocade, Oakwood, azure or orchid, plate, cake; #2375, 10" ... 90.00
Brocade, Oakwood, azure or orchid, tray, #2342, 8-sided, center hdl 150.00
Brocade, Oakwood, azure or orchid, wine, #877, 2¾-oz ... 95.00

Brocade, Palm Leaf, gr or rose, bowl, #2375, hdls, 10" ... 165.00
Brocade, Palm Leaf, gr or rose, bowl, #2394, flared rim, 3-toed, 12" ... 150.00
Brocade, Palm Leaf, gr or rose, compote, #2400, 6" 125.00
Brocade, Paradise, gr or orchid, bowl, centerpc; #2329, 11" ... 100.00
Brocade, Paradise, gr or orchid, candlestick, #2324, 4", ea ... 35.00
Brocade, Paradise, gr or orchid, compote, #2327, tall twist stem, 7" ... 75.00
Coin, amber, cruet, #1372/531, w/stopper, 7-oz 65.00
Coin, amber, pitcher, 32-oz 38.00
Coin, amber, sugar bowl, #1372/673 .... 35.00
Coin, amber, sugar bowl, w/lid 35.00
Coin, bl, ashtray, #1372/123, 5" 25.00
Coin, bl, bowl, ftd, 8½" 90.00

Coin, blue, candy jar, $80.00; Wedding bowl, $90.00.

Coin, bl, urn, #1372/829, ftd, w/lid, 12¾" 140.00
Coin, bl, vase, bud; 8" 30.00
Coin, crystal, bowl, 8" 25.00
Coin, crystal, cup, punch; #1372/615 .... 30.00
Coin, crystal, decanter, w/stopper, 1-pt 95.00
Coin, crystal, punch bowl, #1372/600, 1½-gal, 14" 150.00
Coin, gr, bowl, nappy, w/hdl, 5⅜" 38.00
Coin, gr, candleholders, 4½", pr 50.00
Coin, gr, creamer, #1372/680 .... 30.00
Coin, gr, decanter, #1372/400, w/stopper, 1-pt, 10¼" 325.00
Coin, olive, ashtray, 7½" dia 25.00
Coin, olive, candy box, 4⅛" 33.00
Coin, olive, pitcher, 32-oz 45.00
Coin, olive, wine, ftd, 4" 35.00
Coin, ruby, bowl, ftd, 8½" 75.00
Coin, ruby, creamer 20.00
Coin, ruby, plate, 8" 40.00
Coin, ruby, tumbler, #1372/58, 14-oz, 5¼" 75.00
Coin, ruby, vase, bud; 8" 45.00
Colony, crystal, bonbon, 3-ftd, 7" 12.00
Colony, crystal, bowl, 4½" 10.00
Colony, crystal, cheese & cracker 50.00
Colony, crystal, cocktail, 3½-oz 8.00
Colony, crystal, lamp, electric 195.00
Colony, crystal, pitcher, w/ice lip, 2-qt 100.00
Colony, crystal, plate, torte; 13" 28.00
Colony, crystal, vase, cornucopia; 9" 80.00
Fairfax #2375, amber, baker, oval, 9" 16.00
Fairfax #2375, amber, bowl, lemon; hdls, 9" 10.00
Fairfax #2375, amber, bowl, nut; blown 12.00
Fairfax #2375, amber, plate, grill; 10" 15.00
Fairfax #2375, bl, orchid or rose, bowl, fruit; 5" 18.00
Fairfax #2375, bl, orchid or rose, butter dish 150.00
Fairfax #2375, bl, orchid or rose, compote, 7" 40.00
Fairfax #2375, bl, orchid or rose, plate, canape 20.00
Fairfax #2375, bl, orchid or rose, shakers, ftd, pr 60.00
Fairfax #2375, gr or topaz, candlestick, 3", ea 16.00
Fairfax #2375, gr or topaz, plate, dinner; 10" 28.00
Fairfax #2375, gr or topaz, sugar pail 45.00

Fairfax #2375, gr or topaz, tumbler, ftd, 9-oz, 5"............................ 13.00
Fuchsia, crystal, bowl, #2395, 10".. 95.00
Fuchsia, crystal, cocktail, #6004, 3-oz.. 22.00
Fuchsia, crystal, compote, #2470, low ped, 6"............................... 35.00
Fuchsia, crystal, cordial, #6004, ¾-oz.. 65.00
Fuchsia, crystal, cup, #2440.. 20.00
Fuchsia, crystal, plate, #2440, 6"...8.00
Fuchsia, crystal, plate, cake; 10".. 60.00
Fuchsia, crystal, saucer champagne, #6004, 5½-oz, 5½"............... 22.00
Fuchsia, crystal, tumbler, #833, 2-oz... 25.00
Fuchsia, Wisteria, bowl, #2470, 12"... 150.00
Fuchsia, Wisteria, candlestick, #2470, 5½", ea............................ 175.00
Fuchsia, Wisteria, parfait, #6004, 5½-oz, 6"................................. 75.00
Glacier, crystal, bowl, onion soup; w/lid.. 50.00
Glacier, crystal, shakers, pr 37.50

Heather, crystal, three-part relish tray, 11", $35.00.

Hermitage, amber, gr or topaz, bottle, oil; #2449, 3-oz 40.00
Hermitage, amber, gr or topaz, mustard, #2449, w/lid & ladle........ 35.00
Hermitage, amber, gr or topaz, plate, #2449½, 9"........................... 20.00
Hermitage, amber, gr or topaz, tumbler, #2449, ftd, 9-oz, 4".......... 10.00
Hermitage, azure, ashtray, #2449...8.00
Hermitage, azure, relish, #2449, 3-part, 7".................................... 17.50
Hermitage, azure, sugar bowl, #2449, ftd....................................... 10.00
Hermitage, crystal, bowl, cereal; #2449½, 6"....................................6.00
Hermitage, crystal, pitcher, #2449, 3-pt... 60.00
Hermitage, crystal, sherbet, #2449, low ft, 7-oz, 3".........................2.00
Hermitage, Wisteria, compote, #2449, 6"....................................... 35.00
Hermitage, Wisteria, plate, #2449½, 8"... 20.00
Hermitage, Wisteria, saucer, #2449...6.00
June, bl or rose, bowl, whipped cream.. 30.00
June, bl or rose, decanter 2,000.00
June, bl or rose, platter, #2375, 12"... 125.00
June, crystal, bowl, mint; 3-ftd, 4½"... 15.00
June, crystal, creamer, ftd, #2375½".. 15.00
June, crystal, plate, chop; 13".. 25.00
June, topaz, bowl, 10"... 85.00
June, topaz, oyster cocktail, 5½-oz.. 25.00
June, topaz, plate, 9½".. 30.00
Kashmir, bl, bowl, cereal; 6".. 38.00
Kashmir, bl, candy dish, #2430, w/lid.. 195.00
Kashmir, bl, whiskey, ftd, 2-oz... 28.00
Kashmir, gr or yel, bottle, oil; ftd.. 295.00
Kashmir, gr or yel, shakers, pr... 100.00
Kashmir, gr or yel, tumbler, 11-oz... 20.00
Lafayette, amber or crystal, nappy, 8".. 30.00
Lafayette, amber or crystal, platter, 15" L...................................... 50.00
Lafayette, burgundy, cup.. 35.00
Lafayette, Empire Green, bowl, sweetmeat; 4½".......................... 33.00
Lafayette, Empire Green, plate, torte; 13".................................... 110.00
Lafayette, Empire Green, sugar bowl, ftd, 3½".............................. 40.00
Lafayette, gr, rose or topaz, plate, 10" 45.00
Lafayette, gr, rose or topaz, vase, ftd, 7"....................................... 60.00
Lafayette, Wisteria, celery, 11½".. 90.00

Narcissus, crystal, candlestick, #134, 2-light, ea 35.00
Narcissus, crystal, cup, #1519.. 30.00
Narcissus, crystal, relish, #1519, 3-part, 8"................................... 35.00
Narcissus, crystal, tumbler, #3408, ftd, 5-oz................................. 24.00
Navarre, crystal, bell, dinner.. 75.00
Navarre, crystal, bottle, dressing; #2083, 6½".............................. 495.00
Navarre, crystal, bowl, #2496, 3-corners, 4½"............................... 20.00
Navarre, crystal, bowl, nut; #2496, 3-ftd, 6".................................. 23.00
Navarre, crystal, bowl, pickle; #2440, 8½"..................................... 30.00
Navarre, crystal, cake plate, #2496, hdls, 10"................................ 50.00
Navarre, crystal, claret, #6106, 4½-oz, 6½".................................... 35.00
Navarre, crystal, mayonnaise, #2496½, 3-pc.................................. 60.00
Navarre, crystal, plate, #2440, 9½".. 45.00
Navarre, crystal, plate, torte; #2464, 16"...................................... 120.00
Navarre, crystal, relish, #2496, 4-part, 10".................................... 55.00
Navarre, crystal, sauce dish, #2496, 6½x5".................................. 100.00
Navarre, crystal, vase, #4121, 5".. 120.00
New Garland, amber or topaz, bowl, soup; 7" 30.00
New Garland, amber or topaz, candlestick, 9½", ea....................... 30.00
New Garland, amber or topaz, decanter.. 145.00
New Garland, amber or topaz, platter, 15"..................................... 50.00
New Garland, amber or topaz, sherbet, #6002, high stem 18.00
New Garland, amber or topaz, vase, 8"... 75.00
New Garland, rose, bonbon, hdls.. 20.00
New Garland, rose, compote, 6".. 28.00
New Garland, rose, ice bucket, #2375.. 120.00
New Garland, rose, tumbler, #6002, ftd, 10-oz.............................. 20.00
New Garland, rose, wine, #6002.. 28.00
Pioneer, amber, crystal or gr, bouillon, #2350½, ftd...................... 10.00
Pioneer, amber, crystal or gr, bowl, baker, oval, 10" 40.00
Pioneer, amber, crystal or gr, cup, #2350½, ftd............................. 10.00
Pioneer, amber, crystal or gr, sauceboat.. 22.50
Pioneer, azure or orchid, relish, 3-part... 20.00
Pioneer, azure or orchid, 3¾".. 18.00
Pioneer, bl, butter dish.. 100.00
Pioneer, bl, nappy, 8".. 25.00
Pioneer, bl, platter, 10½" L... 30.00
Pioneer, ebony, creamer, #2350½, ftd.. 10.00
Pioneer, ebony, plate, 6"...8.00
Pioneer, ebony, plate, 10"... 20.00
Pioneer, ebony, sugar bowl, #2350½, ftd....................................... 10.00
Pioneer, rose or topaz, ashtray, 3¾"... 16.00
Pioneer, rose or topaz, compote, 8".. 30.00
Pioneer, rose or topaz, sugar bowl, #2350½, ftd............................ 12.00
Priscilla, amber or gr, bowl, cream soup.. 15.00
Priscilla, amber or gr, tumbler, ftd, hdls.. 12.00
Priscilla, bl, bowl, custard; ftd, hdls.. 15.00
Priscilla, bl, plate, 8".. 15.00
Rogene, crystal, jelly, #825... 22.50
Rogene, crystal, jug, #2270, w/lid.. 250.00
Rogene, crystal, plate, w/cut star, 11".. 27.50
Rogene, crystal, tumbler, #4095, ftd, 5-oz.................................... 12.50
Royal, amber or gr, #2327, 7"... 25.00
Royal, amber or gr, ashtray, #2350, 3½".. 20.00
Royal, amber or gr, bowl, console; #2329, 13".............................. 30.00
Royal, amber or gr, bowl, pickle; #2350, 8".................................. 20.00
Royal, amber or gr, candlestick, #2324, 9" 65.00
Royal, amber or gr, cocktail, #869, 3-oz.. 15.00
Royal, amber or gr, cup, #2350..9.00
Royal, amber or gr, ice bucket, #2378.. 65.00
Royal, amber or gr, nappy, #2350, 8".. 30.00
Royal, amber or gr, plate, canapé; #2321, 8¾"............................... 30.00
Royal, amber or gr, platter, #2350, 10½"....................................... 25.00
Royal, amber or gr, tray, #2287, center hdl, 11"............................ 25.00

Royal, amber or gr, tumbler, #859, 12-oz.. **25.00**
Royal, amber or gr, urn, #2324, ftd.. **100.00**
Seville, amber, bouillon, #2350 .... **13.50**
Seville, amber, bowl, ftd, 10" **35.00**
Seville, amber, bowl, soup; #2350, 7¾" **20.00**
Seville, amber, plate, #2350, 10½"... **30.00**
Seville, gr, bowl, cereal; #2350, 6½"... **25.00**
Seville, gr, celery, #2350, 11" **17.50**
Seville, gr, tumbler, #5084, ftd, 2-oz **30.00**
Sun Ray, crystal, bottle, oil; w/stopper, 3-oz **35.00**
Sun Ray, crystal, coaster, 4" **8.00**
Sun Ray, crystal, crimped, 6" **40.00**
Sun Ray, crystal, plate, sandwich; 12" **32.00**
Sun Ray, crystal, sugar bowl, ftd **10.00**
Sunray, crystal, bonbon, hdld, 6½"... **16.00**

Trojan, rose, bowl, scroll; #2395, 10" long, $110.00. (Photo courtesy Cathy and Gene Florence)

Trojan, rose, candy dish, #2394, w/lid, ½-lb................................. **200.00**
Trojan, rose, oyster cocktail, #5099, ftd.. **28.00**
Trojan, topaz, cheese & cracker, #2375, #2368............................... **60.00**
Trojan, topaz, plate, cake; #2375, hdld, 10" **45.00**
Trojan, topaz, platter, #2375, 15".. **110.00**
Versailles, bl, compote, #5098, 3"... **45.00**
Versailles, bl, decanter, #2439, 9"..**2,000.00**
Versailles, bl, pitcher, #5000 .... **595.00**
Versailles, gr, bowl, cereal; #2375, 6½".. **45.00**
Versailles, gr, cocktail, #5098, 3-oz, 5" **32.00**
Versailles, gr, shakers, #2375, ftd, pr **140.00**
Versailles, pk or yel, bowl, centerpc; #2375, flared, 12" **70.00**
Versailles, pk or yel, plate, #2375, 8"... **15.00**
Versailles, pk or yel, sweetmeat, #2375 .... **20.00**
Woodland, crystal, cocktail, 3-oz... **12.50**
Woodland, crystal, creamer, #1851.. **15.00**
Woodland, crystal, nappy, ftd, 6"... **20.00**
Woodland, crystal, pitcher, #300, 65-oz **175.00**
Woodland, crystal, plate, torte; #2238, 11"..................................... **14.00**
Woodland, crystal, syrup, #2194, w/cut-off top, 8-oz **95.00**

Frackelton, Susan

Born in Milwaukee, Wisconsin, in 1848, Susan worked at her family's pottery import business where as a young adult she began experimenting with china painting, potting, and glazing, and gradually became well known for her efforts in creating a unique type of art pottery, most of which was salt-glaze stoneware with underglaze blue designs taken from nature (such as those listed below). More often than not, these pieces combined dimensional applications in combination with the hand painting. Some of her pieces were painted on the inside as well. She was awarded a gold medal at the 1893 Columbian Exposition for her stoneware creations and was greatly admired by her contemporaries.

Though salt-glazed stoneware had for many decades been a mainstay of Wisconsin pottery production, Susan was recognized as the first to apply these principals to the manufacture of art pottery.

In addition to her artistic accomplishments, Susan also developed a gas-fired kiln specifically for use in the home.

She retired and moved to Chicago in 1904, where she died in 1932.

Key: stw — stoneware

Jar, stoneware with applied wreath on floral-carved base, incised SF 1898, 5x4½", $9,450.00. (Photo courtesy David Rago Auctions)

Bowl, appl indigo poppy in center, bl floral on gray stw, 3x5" ... **1,800.00**
Vase, bl acorns & leaves, stw gourd shape, 3¼".......................... **7,140.00**
Vase, cvd foliate & heraldic devices in gr & indigo stw, 7"....... **18,000.00**
Vase, cvd stylized leaves, bl on wht stw, bulbous, 2⅛".................. **660.00**
Vase, indigo roses/stylized cross, stw, #108, 3¾" **720.00**
Vase, oak-leaf branches/acorns in indigo stw, #109, 3¼" **8,400.00**

Frakturs

Fraktur is a German style of black letter text type. To collectors the fraktur is a type of hand-lettered document used by the people of German descent who settled in the areas of Pennsylvania, New Jersey, Maryland, Virginia, North and South Carolina, Ohio, Kentucky, and Ontario. These documents recorded births and baptisms and were used as bookplates and as certificates of honor. They were elaborately decorated with colorful folk-art borders of hearts, birds, angels, and flowers. Examples by recognized artists and those with an unusual decorative motif bring prices well into the thousands of dollars; in fact, some have sold at major auction houses well in excess of $100,000.00. Frakturs made in the late 1700s after the invention of the printing press provided the writer with a prepared text that he needed only to fill in at his own discretion. The next step in the evolution of machine-printed frakturs combined woodblock-printed decorations along with the text which the 'artist' sometimes enhanced with color. By the mid-1800s, even the coloring was done by machine. The vorschrift was a handwritten example prepared by a fraktur teacher to demonstrate his skill in lettering and decorating. These are often considered to be the finest of frakturs. Those dated before 1820 are most valuable.

The practice of fraktur art began to diminish after 1830 but hung on even to the early years of the twentieth century among the Pennsylvania Germans ingrained with such customs. Our advisor for this category is Frederick S. Weiser; he is listed in the Directory under Pennsylvania. (Mr. Weiser has provided our text, but being unable to physically examine the frakturs listed below can not vouch for their authenticity, age, or condition. When requesting information, please include a self-addressed stamped evelope.) These prices were realized at various reputable auction galleries in the East and Midwest and should be regarded as minimum values. Buyers should be aware that there are many fakes on the market, a real problem for beginning collectors. Know your dealer. Unless otherwise noted, values are for examples in excellent condition. Note: Be careful not to confuse frakturs with prints, calligraphy, English-language marriage certificates, Lord's Prayers, etc.

Key:
lp — laid paper   wc — watercolored
pr — printed   wp — wove paper
p/i — pen and ink

Birth Record

Cutwork flowers/birds, mc, Jac Botz, 1792, 6¾x5¼"+sponged fr.. 4,800.00
P/i/wc, birds/flowers/mermaid, att H Otto, PA, 1761, 12½x15"+fr..2,150.00
P/i/wc/lp, birds/vines/text, JH Otto, PA, 1770, +grpt 13x16" fr.. 3,600.00

Ink and watercolor, daisy and tulips below German text, dated 1852, minor damage, 11x8", in 14½x11½" painted frame, $6,670.00. (Photo courtesy Garth's Auctions Inc.)

P/i/wc/lp, flower baskets/vines, PA, 1754, 7¼x6¼"+later fr 900.00
P/i/wc/lp, flowers/tulips/script, Schuylkill, 1833, 12x14¼"+fr..4,200.00
P/i/wc/lp, heart/columns/angels, Continental, 1834, 12x9".......1,100.00
P/i/wc/lp, hearts/vines/verses, M Brechall, PA, ca 1826, 13x16"+fr..1,550.00
P/i/wc/lp, ladies/parrots/tulip vines, D Peterman, PA, 1861, 14x12" ..3,600.00
P/i/wc/lp, parrots/mermaids/flowers, H Otto, 1793, 13x16"+fr..2,900.00
P/i/wc/lp, shields/tulips/pinwheels/text, PA, 1807, 13x16¼"+fr..3,600.00
P/i/wc/lp, tulips/geometrics/text, D Otto, PA, 1814, in 15x19" fr..4,000.00
P/i/wc/lp, vining flowers/birds/text, PA, 1800s, 12x8"+fr.............. 700.00
P/i/wc/lp w/pinpricks, flowers/birds, 1816, 7x5½"+fr, VG............. 600.00
P/i/wc/wp, couple/stars/flowers, att H Young, 1828, 12x7½"+fr..5,500.00
P/i/wc/wp, hearts/eagles/verse in lg heart, PA, 1821, 12x12½"+fr..2,350.00
P/i/wc/wp, tulips/hearts/3-panel text, att B Mission, 1821, 13x8"+fr..2,150.00
P/i/wc/wp, tulips/thistle/bird, att B Mission, PA, 1826, 8x13"+far..2,650.00
Pr/wc, flowers in circle, VA, 1817, 8x10"+fr.............................2,500.00
Pr/wc, flowers/hearts, S Bauman, PA, 1811, 12½x15"+fr.............. 850.00
Pr/wc/lp, angels/birds/etc, TF Scheffer, PA, 1859, 17x13"+fr....1,500.00
Pr/wc/lp, flower basket/parrots/tulips, Krebs, 1813, 16x18½"+fr... 800.00

Miscellaneous

Bookplate, i/wc, birds/tulip/checked border, PA, 1808, 6½" L+fr.... 3,400.00
Family record, p/i/wc/lp, PA, ca 1803, creases/toning, 15x13"+fr. 725.00
Marriage blessing, p/i/lp, Spencerian style, Dutch, 1721, 15x12"+fr..1,800.00
Marriage certificate, p/i/wc, flowers/etc, Brechall/1837, 11x16"+fr. 1,550.00
P/i/wc, fish, detailed, PA, 1800s, 3¼x6½"+fr.............................1,100.00
P/i/wc, flowering tree w/birds, PA, 1800s, 5x3¼"+chip-cvd fr...3,600.00
P/i/wc/lp, flower basket, reverse: prayer, 5¼x3¼"+fr..................... 800.00
P/i/wc/lp, lover's knot, 1833, 6½x6½"+fr..................................2,400.00
Religious text, p/i/wc, flowers/angel/birds/figures, 1800, 4x7"+fr.. 900.00
Vorschrift, ABCs in blocks/decanters/bird, Gottschall, 1835, 8x13"...19,500.00
Wc, Adam & Eve in Eden, PA, early 1800s, 8¾x16"+fr............1,650.00

Frames

Styles in picture frames have changed with the fashion of the day, but those that especially interest today's collectors are the deep shadow boxes made of fine woods such as walnut or cherry, those with Art Nouveau influence, and the oak frames decorated with molded gesso and gilt from the Victorian era. The last few years have seen the middle- to late-Victorian molded composition-on-wood frames finally being recognized as individual works of art. While once regulated to the trash heap, they are now being rescued and appreciated.

As is true in general in the antiques and collectibles fields, the influence of online trading is greatly affecting prices. Many items once considered difficult to locate are now readily available in the .com world; as a result, values have declined. Our advisor for this category is Michael Hinton; he is listed in the Directory under Pennsylvania.

Note: Unless another date is given, frames described in the following listings are from the nineteenth century.

Ash burl, 7-sided w/trn concentric circles around opening, 8x6".. 260.00
Blk walnut & gold leaf, Pat 1871, 35x31", EX 1,150.00
Brass & pietra dura, pierced birds/lilies, in wood surround, 10" H...700.00
Brass-plated CI, pierced foliage, Vict, 13x10" 85.00
Chip cvd, old red pnt & natural, easel bk, 7x6"...........................250.00
CI w/gilt, rtcl leaves, metal bk, desk type, 11½x8¼"......................65.00
Curly maple, nut brn stain, 17⅜x15" 230.00
Cut brass, filigree, Italian, 1700s, 9x7" 595.00
Ebonized, Vict Eastlake styling, 13", w/feather-art bird, pr...........150.00
Gesso, gold leaf, inner/outer liners w/emb foliage, 30x25" 200.00
Gesso w/cvg, old gold pnt, 1800s, 50x44" 1,150.00
Giltwood & gesso w/foliate scrolls, shell corners, 1850s, 55x45"...635.00
Gnarled/entwined tree roots appl to wooden fr, ca 1900, 39x47"..4,800.00
Mahog, beveled w/flame grpt, opening: 10½x13½", 14x17¼".......200.00
Mahog vnr, 2⅛" W, 16x18"..50.00
Plaster over wood, oval shadow box, Vict, 20x17x4"....................150.00
Pnt wood, appl half trns, blk & gold, 11¾x9¾".............................200.00
Poplar w/half-trn stiles, corner blocks, porc buttons, 17x13" 200.00
Tortoiseshell vnr on wood, 1800s, 7½x6½", 5x4", pr 400.00
Walnut, beveled, 2" molding, 17x14"..100.00
Walnut, oval liner, incised decor, dtd 1871, 20x30" 950.00

Franciscan

Franciscan is a trade name used by Gladding McBean and Co., founded in northern California in 1875. In 1923 they purchased the Tropico plant in Glendale where they produced sewer pipe, gardenware, and tile. By 1934 the first of their dinnerware lines, El Patio, was produced. It was a plain design made in bright, attractive colors. El Patio Nouveau followed in 1935, glazed in two colors — one tone on the inside, a contrasting hue on the outside. Coronado, a favorite of today's collectors, was introduced in 1936. It was styled with a wide, swirled border and was made in pastels, both satin and glossy. Before 1940, 15 patterns had been produced. The first hand-decorated lines were introduced in 1937, the ever-popular Apple pattern in 1940, Desert Rose in 1941, and Ivy in 1948. Many other hand-decorated and decaled patterns were produced there from 1934 to 1984.

Dinnerware marks before 1940 include 'GMcB' in an oval, 'F' within a square, or 'Franciscan' with 'Pottery' underneath (which was later changed to 'Ware.') A circular arrangement of 'Franciscan' with 'Made in California USA' in the center was used from 1940 until 1949. At least 40 marks were used before 1975; several more were introduced after that. At one time, paper labels were used.

The company merged with Lock Joint Pipe Company in 1963, becoming part of the Interpace Corporation. In July of 1979 Franciscan was purchased by Wedgwood Limited of England, and the Glendale plant closed in October 1984.

Note: Due to limited space, we have used a pricing formula, meant to be only a general guide, not a mechanical ratio on each piece. Rarity varies with pattern, and not all pieces occur in all patterns. Our advisor for this category is Shirley Moore; she is listed in the Directory under Oklahoma. See also Gladding McBean.

Coronado, 1936 – 1956

Both satin (matt) and glossy colors were made including turquoise, coral, celadon, light yellow, ivory, and gray (in satin); and turquoise, coral, apple green, light yellow, white, maroon, and redwood in glossy glazes. High-end values are for maroon, yellow, redwood, and gray. Add 10 – 15% for gloss.

Bowl, casserole; w/lid, from $45 to	90.00
Bowl, cereal; from $10 to	15.00
Bowl, cream soup; w/underplate, from $25 to	40.00
Bowl, fruit; from $6 to	12.00
Bowl, nut cup; from $8 to	12.00
Bowl, onion soup; w/lid, from $25 to	40.00
Bowl, rim soup; from $14 to	25.00
Bowl, salad; lg, from $20 to	35.00
Bowl, serving; oval, 10½", from $20 to	33.00
Bowl, serving; 7½" dia, from $12 to	18.00
Bowl, serving; 8½" dia, from $10 to	17.00
Bowl, sherbet/egg cup; from $10 to	15.00
Butter dish, from $25 to	35.00
Cigarette box, w/lid, from $40 to	75.00
Creamer, from $8 to	12.00
Cup & saucer, demitasse; from $20 to	32.00
Cup & saucer, jumbo	32.00
Demitasse pot, from $100 to	150.00
Fast-stand gravy, from $25 to	35.00
Jam jar, w/lid, from $45 to	60.00
Pitcher, 1½-qt, from $25 to	45.00
Plate, chop; 12½" dia, from $18 to	32.00
Plate, chop; 14" dia, from $20 to	30.00
Plate, crescent hostess; w/cup well, no established value	
Plate, crescent salad; lg, no established value	
Plate, ind crescent salad; from $22 to	32.00
Plate, 6½", from $5 to	8.00
Plate, 7½", from $7 to	10.00
Plate, 8½", from $8 to	11.00
Plate, 9½", from $10 to	15.00
Plate, 10½", from $12 to	18.00
Platter, oval, 10", from $12 to	20.00
Platter, oval, 13", from $24 to	36.00
Platter, oval, 15½", from $25 to	45.00
Relish dish, oval, from $12 to	25.00
Shakers, pr, from $15 to	30.00
Sugar bowl, w/lid, from $10 to	20.00
Teacup & saucer, from $8 to	12.00

Teapot, from $75.00 to $95.00. (Photo courtesy The Auction House/LiveAuctioneers.com)

Tumbler, water; no established value	
Vase, 5¼"	65.00
Vase, 6¾", no established value	
Vase, 8½", no established value	
Vase, 9½", no established value	

Desert Rose

For other hand-painted patterns, we recommend the following general guide for comparable pieces (based on current values):

Daisy	-20%
October	-20%
Cafe Royal	Same as Desert Rose
Forget-Me-Not	Same as Desert Rose
Meadow Rose	Same as Desert Rose
Strawberry Fair	Same as Desert Rose
Strawberry Time	Same as Desert Rose
Fresh Fruit	Same as Desert Rose
Bountiful	Same as Desert Rose
Desert Rose	Base Line Values
Apple	+10%
Ivy	+10%
Poppy	+50%
Original (small) Fruit	+50%
Wild Flower	200% or more!

There is not an active market in Bouquet, Rosette, or Twilight Rose, as these are scarce, having been produced only a short time. Our estimate would place Bouquet and Rosette in the October range (-20%) and Twilight Rose in the Ivy range (+20%).

There are several Apple items that are so scarce they command higher prices than fit the above formula. The Apple ginger jar is valued at $600.00+, the 4" jug at $195.00+, and any covered box in Apple is at least 50% more than Desert Rose.

Ashtray, ind.	15.00
Ashtray, oval	95.00
Ashtray, sq.	150.00
Bell, Danbury Mint	95.00
Bell, dinner	95.00
Bowl, bouillon; w/lid, from $195 to	295.00
Bowl, cereal; 6"	15.00
Bowl, divided vegetable	45.00
Bowl, fruit	10.00
Bowl, mixing; lg	175.00
Bowl, mixing; med	165.00
Bowl, mixing; sm	155.00
Bowl, porringer	175.00
Bowl, rimmed soup	25.00
Bowl, salad; 10"	95.00
Bowl, soup; ftd	25.00
Bowl, vegetable; 8"	32.00
Bowl, vegetable; 9"	40.00
Box, cigarette	95.00
Box, egg	145.00
Box, heart shape	145.00
Box, rnd	165.00
Butter dish	45.00
Candleholders, pr	95.00
Candy dish, oval, from $150 to	225.00
Casserole, 1½-qt	75.00
Casserole, 2½-qt, minimum value	295.00
Coffeepot	125.00
Coffeepot, ind, from $300 to	395.00
Compote, lg	75.00
Compote, low	125.00
Cookie jar	295.00
Creamer, ind	40.00
Creamer, regular	20.00
Cup & saucer, demitasse	35.00
Cup & saucer, jumbo	30.00
Cup & saucer, tall	35.00
Cup & saucer, tea	10.00
Egg cup	35.00

Ginger jar 225.00
Goblet, ftd 225.00
Gravy boat 38.00
Hurricane lamp, from $250 to 325.00
Jam jar 125.00
Long 'n narrow, 15½x7¾" 495.00
Microwave dish, oblong, 1½-qt 195.00
Microwave dish, sq, 1-qt 150.00
Microwave dish, sq, 8" 95.00
Mug, bbl, 12-oz 45.00
Mug, cocoa; 10-oz 95.00
Mug, 7-oz 35.00
Napkin ring 50.00
Piggy bank, from $195 to 295.00
Pitcher, milk 65.00
Pitcher, syrup 75.00
Pitcher, water; 2½-qt 125.00
Plate, chop; 12" 50.00
Plate, chop; 14" 95.00
Plate, coupe dessert 65.00
Plate, coupe party 125.00
Plate, coupe steak 145.00
Plate, divided; child's, from $125 to 195.00

Plate, grill; 11", from $80.00 to $100.00.

Plate, side salad 35.00
Plate, TV; from $95 to 125.00
Plate, 6½" 7.00
Plate, 8½" 12.00
Plate, 9½" 20.00
Plate, 10½" 18.00
Platter, turkey; 19" 295.00
Platter, 12¾" 35.00
Platter, 14" 45.00
Relish, 3-section 65.00
Relish/pickle dish, oval, 10" 28.00
Shaker & pepper mill, pr, from $195 to 295.00
Shakers, rose bud, pr 22.50
Shakers, tall, pr, from $75 to 95.00
Sherbet 20.00
Soup ladle 75.00
Sugar bowl, open, ind 45.00
Sugar bowl, regular 25.00
Tea canister 295.00
Teapot 125.00
Thimble 75.00
Tidbit tray, 2-tier 95.00
Tile, in fr 50.00
Tile, sq 50.00
Toast cover 195.00
Trivet, rnd, from $150 to 195.00
Tumbler, juice; 6-oz 45.00
Tumbler, 10-oz 30.00
Tureen, soup; flat bottom 595.00

Tureen, soup; ftd, either style 695.00
Vase, bud 95.00

Apple Pieces Not Available in Desert Rose

Bowl, batter; from $450 to 650.00
Bowl, str sides, lg 55.00
Bowl, str sides, med 45.00
Casserole, stick hdl & lid, ind 65.00
Coaster, from $25 to 35.00
Jam jar, redesigned 425.00
Shaker & pepper mill, wooden top, pr from $295 to 395.00
½-apple baker, from $150 to 195.00

El Patio, 1934 – 1954

This line includes a few pieces not offered in Coronado, and the colors differ; but per piece, these two patterns are valued about the same.

Franciscan Fine China

The main line of fine china was called Masterpiece. There were at least four marks used during its production from 1941 to 1977. Almost every piece is clearly marked. This china is true porcelain, the body having been fired at a very high temperature. Many years of research and experimentation went into this china before it was marketed. Production was temporarily suspended during the war years. More than 170 patterns and many varying shapes were produced. All are valued about the same with the exception of the Renaissance group, which is 25% higher.

Bowl, vegetable; serving, oval 50.00
Cup 20.00
Plate, bread & butter 18.00
Plate, dinner 30.00
Plate, salad 25.00
Saucer 12.00

Starburst

Gravy boat with attached undertray, from $35.00 to $40.00.

Ashtray, ind 20.00
Ashtray, oval, lg, from $95 to 120.00
Bowl, divided, 8", from $25 to 35.00
Bowl, fruit; ind, 5", from $15 to 20.00
Bowl, oval, 8", from $50 to 60.00
Bowl, salad; ind, from $20 to 25.00
Bowl, salad; 12" 135.00
Bowl, soup/cereal; 7", from $25 to 35.00
Bowl, vegetable; 8½", from $35 to 45.00
Butter dish, from $80 to 90.00
Candlesticks, pr from $175 to 200.00
Canister/jar, w/lid, depending on sz, from $250 to 350.00
Casserole, 8½", from $100 to 120.00
Coffeepot, from $175 to 225.00
Creamer, from $25 to 35.00

Cruet, vinegar or oil; ea from $80 to 110.00
Cup & saucer, from $15 to.. 18.00
Dish, w/ring hdl 1 side, 8", from $40 to... 50.00
Dish, 3-part, triangular, 6½x6½"... 125.00
Gravy ladle, from $35 to... 45.00
Mug, sm, 2¾"... 60.00
Mug, tall, 5", from $65 to... 80.00
Mustard jar, spoon slot in lid, 3½"... 65.00
Pepper mill, chrome top, 7¼", from $200 to 250.00
Pitcher, water; 10".. 135.00
Pitcher, 7½", from $80 to... 95.00
Plate, chop; from $55 to... 65.00
Plate, crescent salad; 9½" L, from $65 to... 80.00
Plate, dinner; 10½", from $20 to... 35.00
Plate, luncheon; hard to find, 9½", from $50 to 60.00
Plate, 6", from $10 to.. 15.00
Plate, 8", from $15 to.. 20.00
Platter, 13" 62.00
Platter, 15" 65.00
Relish tray, 3-part, oval, 9", from $45 to 65.00
Salt grinder, chrome top, 6¼", from $200 to 250.00
Shakers, bullet shape, sm, 2½", pr, from $25 to.............................. 35.00
Shakers, bullet shape, 3½", pr from $35 to 50.00
Shakers, bullet shape, 6", pr from $30 to 40.00
Snack/TV tray w/cup rest, 12½", from $75 to 85.00
Sugar bowl, from $35 to.. 50.00
Teapot, 5½x8½", from $175 to.. 225.00
Tumbler, 6-oz, 3½", from $75 to.. 90.00

Frankart

During the 1920s Frankart, Inc., of New York City, produced a line of accessories that included figural nude lamps, bookends, ashtrays, etc. These white metal composition items were offered in several finishes including verde green, jap black, and gunmetal gray. The company also produced a line of caricatured animals, but the stylized nude figurals have proven to be the most collectible today. With few exceptions, all pieces were marked 'Frankart, Inc.' with a patent number or 'pat. appl. for.' All pieces listed are in very good original condition unless otherwise indicated. Our advisor for this category is Walter Glenn; he is listed in the Directory under Georgia.

Aquarium, nude seated on wrought-iron fr w/sq fishbowl, 14" ..1,150.00
Aquarium, nude sits atop wrought-iron stand, sq aqua glass, 14"...1,200.00
Ashtray, dancing nude holds tray on side, box on base, 10" 850.00
Ashtray, nude on horseshoe base holds tray aloft, 23" 1,200.00
Ashtray, nude on pointe, 3 trays form ballerina's tutu, 10"........... 750.00
Ashtray, nude on toptoe arches bk, holds 4" tray......................... 750.00
Ashtray, nude stands, 3" ash ball on geometric base, 10".............. 750.00
Ashtray, stylized dachshund spans 4½" sq tray, 5" 350.00
Bookends, nude sits atop human skull, 8" 1,050.00
Bookends, nude sits atop metal book, 10".................................... 600.00
Bookends, nude sits atop mushrooms, 8"...................................... 650.00
Bookends, Roman-inspired masks, 7½"... 650.00
Bookends, standing nude 'peek-a-boos' around books, 8"............. 600.00
Bookends, stylized parrot on arched perch, 7"............................. 300.00
Clock, nude stands ea side rectangular frosted glass clock, 10½" . 2,650.00
Lamp, nude stands ea side of 8" crackle globe, 9" 1,500.00
Lamp, 2 bk-to-bk dancing nudes hold sq glass cylinder, 13"......1,850.00
Lamp, 2 bk-to-bk nudes kneel, 8" crackle globe between, 9" 1,500.00
Lamp, 2 bk-to-bk nudes stand/hold skyscraper globe, 21" 1,450.00
Plaque, Diana the Huntress, sq, 8".. 600.00
Sconce, seated nude on floral framework, 6"................................. 700.00

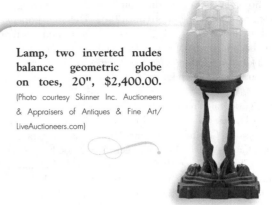

Lamp, two inverted nudes balance geometric globe on toes, 20", $2,400.00.
(Photo courtesy Skinner Inc. Auctioneers & Appraisers of Antiques & Fine Art/LiveAuctioneers.com)

Frankoma

John Frank opened a studio pottery in Norman, Oklahoma, in 1933, creating bowls, vases, etc., which bore the ink-stamped marks 'Frank Pottery' or 'Frank Potteries.' At this time, only a few hundred pieces were produced. Within a year, Mr. Frank had incorporated. Though not everything was marked, he continued to use these marks for two years. Items thus marked are not easy to find and command high prices. In 1935 the pot and leopard mark was introduced.

The Frank family moved to Sapulpa, Oklahoma, in 1938. In November of that year, a fire destroyed everything. The pot and leopard mark was never re-created, and today collectors avidly search for items with this mark. The rarest of all Frankoma marks is 'First Kiln a Sapulpa 6-7-38' which was applied to only about 100 pieces fired on that date.

Grace Lee Frank worked beside her husband, creating many limited edition Madonna plates, Christmas cards, advertising items, birds, etc. She died in 1996.

Clay is important in determining when a piece was made. Ada clay, used through 1954, is a creamy beige color. In 1955 they changed over to a red brick shale from Sapulpa. Today most clay has a pinkish-red cast, though the pinkish cast is sometimes so muted that a novice might mistake it for Ada clay.

Rutile glazes were created early in the pottery's history; these give the ware a two-tone color treatment. However the US government closed the rutile mines in 1970 and Frank found it necessary to buy this material from Australia. The newer rutile produced different results, especially noticeable with their Woodland Moss glaze.

Upon John Frank's death in 1973, their daughter Joniece became president. Though the pottery burned again in 1983, the building was quickly rebuilt. Due to so many setbacks, however, the company found it necessary to file chapter 11 in order to remain in control and stay in business.

Mr. Richard Bernstein purchased Frankoma in 1991. Sometime in 2001, Mr. Bernstein began to put the word out that Frankoma Pottery Company was for sale. It did not sell and because of declining sales, he closed the doors on December 23, 2004. The company sold July 1, 2005, to another pottery company owned by Det and Crystal Merryman of Las Vegas, Nevada. They took possession the next day and began bringing life back into the Frankoma Pottery once more. Today they are producing pottery from the Frankoma molds as well as their own pottery molds, which goes by the name of 'Merrymac Collection,' a collection of whimsical dogs.

Frank purchased Synar Ceramics of Muskogee, Oklahoma, in 1958; in late '59, the name was changed to Gracetone Pottery in honor of Grace Lee Frank. Until supplies were exhausted, they continued to produce Synar's white clay line in glazes such as Alligator, Woodpine, White Satin, Ebony, Wintergreen, and a black and white straw combination. At the Frankoma pottery, an 'F' was added to the stock number on items made at both locations. New glazes were Aqua, Pink Champagne, Cinnamon Toast, and Black, known as Gunmetal. Gracetone was sold in 1962 to Mr.

Taylor, who had been a long-time family friend and manager of the pottery. Taylor continued operations until 1967. The only dinnerware pattern produced there was Orbit, which today is hard to find. Other Gracetone pieces are becoming scarce as well. If you'd like to learn more, we recommend *Frankoma and Other Oklahoma Potteries* by Phyllis Boone (Bess), our advisor; you will find her address in the Directory under Oklahoma.

Ashtray, cigar; Draft Proof, Prairie Green, #455 .... 50.00
Ashtray, Fish, Desert Gold, Sapulpa clay, #T7 .... 15.00
Ashtray, Tulsa Oil Capital..., OK state shape, brn satin, Sapulpa clay.. 15.00
Bean pot, Wagon Wheel, Prairie Green, horseshoe hdls, #94W 55.00
Bookends, Charger Horse, Prairie Green, #420, 7" 225.00
Bookends, Collie Head, White Sand, Sapulpa clay, #122 .... 200.00
Bowl, cereal; Desert Gold, Sapulpa clay, 5" 8.00
Bowl, Clamshell, dk Coffee w/Flame int, Sapulpa clay, #T1 .... 30.00
Bowl, console; Dogwood, Prairie Green, Sapulpa clay, #200.......... 35.00
Bowl, Crescent, Turquoise, Ada clay, #211, 1942-51, 5x12½x4½"...45.00
Bowl, Dogwood, Prairie Green, shallow, 13x8½", from $25 to 30.00
Bowl, Plainsman, Prairie Green, 10⅝x18¾"................................... 75.00
Bowl, vegetable; Plainsman, Desert Gold, sq, from $17.50 to 20.00
Candleholder, Aladdin Lamp, Brown Satin, Sapulpa clay, #309, ea . 25.00
Candleholders, Dogwood, Prairie Green, pr from $25 to................ 30.00
Casserole, Wagon Wheel, Prairie Green, Ada clay, w/lid, from $60 to..75.00
Christmas card, 1944, from $500 to 600.00
Christmas card, 1947-48, from $95 to 115.00
Christmas card, 1949, from $85 to 95.00
Christmas card, 1950-51, from $125 to 150.00
Christmas card, 1952, Donna Frank, from $150 to 200.00
Christmas card, 1952, from $125 to 140.00
Christmas card, 1953, from $90 to 110.00
Christmas card, 1954 .... 110.00
Christmas card, 1957 .... 70.00
Christmas card, 1958-60 .... 65.00
Christmas card, 1969-71 .... 40.00
Christmas card, 1972 .... 35.00
Christmas card, 1973-75 .... 30.00
Christmas card, 1976-82 .... 25.00
Christmas plate, Flight Into Egypt, Della Robia White, J Frank, 1968 ..60.00
Dealer sign, Frankoma Pottery, brn & tan, 6½" L, from $35 to 40.00
Decanter, Prairie Green, #7JH, w/lid, 10¼" 55.00
Flower holder, Duck, Prairie Green, Ada clay, #184, 1942, 3¾"... 240.00
Jug, mini; Uncle Slug, Prairie Green, #561, 2¼"............................ 145.00
Leaf dish, dk brn satin, #226, med, from $10 to............................. 12.50
Mug, Aztec, Woodland Moss, from $5 to.. 8.00
Mug, Donkey, Plum, 1983 .... 45.00
Mug, Elephant, blk, 1997 .... 50.00
Mug, Elephant, Nat'l Republican Women's Club, gray, 1968......... 60.00
Mug, Elephant, Reagan/Bush, Celery Green w/wht int, 1981, from $30 to .35.00
Mug, Elephant or Donkey, 1973-76, from $30 to............................ 40.00
Mug, US Mail, National Maintenace Training Center, wht, from $10 to . 15.00
Napkin rings, Butterfly, Sapulpa clay, #263, 4 for 20.00
Pitcher, mini; Spiral, Ivory, Ada clay, 2", from $75 to 85.00
Pitcher, White Sand, #26D, 1-qt, from $20 to................................ 30.00
Planter, Cactus, Prairie Green, orig label, 7x5x3".......................... 70.00
Plate, Christmas, Flight Into Egypt, Della Robia White, J Frank, 1968.. 60.00
Plate, Christmas, Good Will Toward Men, 1965 .... 62.50
Plate, Christmas; No Room at the Inn, White Sand, 1971 .... 20.00
Plate, Oklahoma State, Desert Gold 25.00
Plate, Teenagers of Bible, Martha the Homemaker, 1982, 6½", $20 to ..25.00
Ramekin (bbl w/lid), Desert Gold, Sapulpa clay, 1950-61, #97U, $40 to .. 45.00
Sculpture, Greyhound, Autumn Yellow, 1983 limited ed, #827, $200 to..225.00
Sculpture, Puma, Dusty Rose, Ada clay, 7", from $85 to 125.00
Sculpture, Turtle, Prairie Green, Ada Clay, 1¼x4½x3" 45.00
Shakers, Bull, blk gloss, Ada clay, 2x3", pr from $165 to.............. 175.00

Shakers, milk can, Desert Gold, Sapulpa clay, 4¾x2½", pr............. 45.00
Spoon rest, fish form, yel/gr/brn, Christmas pc made in 1960s, 4".. 55.00
Teacup, Plainsman, Prairie Green, 5-oz, from $10 to..................... 12.00
Tray, Palm Leaf, Desert Gold, Sapulpa clay, #226 .... 85.00
Trivet, Horseshoe, Desert Sand, 3-ftd, #5TR, 6", from $22 to........ 25.00
Vase, bottle form, royal med bl, Ada clay, rnd O mk, 9¾", $275 to .. 300.00
Vase, bud; Snail, Flame, Sapulpa clay, #31, from $30 to 40.00
Vase, collector; V-1, from $125 to 150.00
Vase, collector; V-2, 12", from $80 to... 90.00
Vase, collector; V-3, V-4 and V-5, ea... 85.00
Vase, collector; V-6, from $80 to 90.00
Vase, collector; V-7, 13" 80.00
Vase, collector; V-8, w/stopper, 13" 75.00
Vase, collector; V-9, w/stopper, 13" 65.00
Vase, collector; V-10 & V-11, ea from $40 to 50.00
Vase, collector; V-12 & V-13, ea 65.00
Vase, collector; V-14, from $75 to 80.00
Vase, Flower Girl, mc, Sapulpa clay, #700, 1942-52, 5½", $100 to ..150.00
Vase, Pansy/Wedding Ring, turq, Sapulpa clay, #200 .... 50.00
Vase, Ram's Head, Verde Bronze, Ada clay, #38, 5⅝x5⅛", $65 to .. 85.00
Wall pocket, Billiken, Prairie Green, Jesters Day..., 6½", $85 to .. 100.00

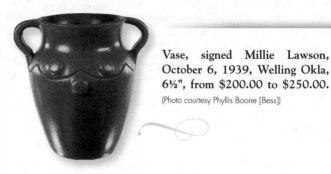

Vase, signed Millie Lawson, October 6, 1939, Welling Okla, 6½", from $200.00 to $250.00.
(Photo courtesy Phyllis Boone [Bess])

Fraternal

Fraternal memorabilia is a vast and varied field. Emblems representing the various organizations have been used to decorate cups, shaving mugs, plates, and glassware. Medals, swords, documents, and other ceremonial paraphernalia from the 1800s and early 1900s are especially prized. Our advisor for Odd Fellows is Greg Spiess; he is listed in the Directory under Illinois. Information on Masonic and Shrine memorabilia has been provided by David Smies, who is listed under Kansas. Assistance concerning Elks collectibles was provided by David Wendel; he is listed in the Directory under Missouri.

Eagles

Brooch, gold-tone bow w/FOE emblem button, Ladies' Auxilary, 1½" ..15.00
Pendant charm, gold-tone metal w/enamel, 2-sided 22.50
Ring, eagle & FOE, 10k gold, red & bl enameling............................ 40.00
Sauceboat, Eagle on wht restaurantware body, 3½x9" 15.00
Watch fob, emb eagle & FOE above enameled shield, Whitehead & Hoag...90.00

Elks

Decanter, star in relief on brn tones, Jim Beam, 1968 .... 20.00
Lapel pin, elk & clock in relief, bl & gold enamel, screw-type bk.. 15.00
Match case, 11th Hour emblem on 14k yel gold........................... 250.00
Ring, Elks Club & blk onyx stone on 18k yel gold, MIB............... 45.00
Statue, elk bust, CI, on marble base, 9x5".................................... 42.50
Token, copper-colored aluminum, Good for 1 Drink..................... 15.00
Watch fob, elk's tooth, 1⅛", w/orig chain...................................... 65.00

Knights Templar

Cuff links, mc enamel & gilt in clear dome glass, crusader seal...... 22.00
Cuff links, sword & star symbols on gold, 1950s, ⅞"................. 220.00
Medal, 50th Annual Conclave, Philadelphia...1903, dangling disk .. 10.00
Ring, sterling, seal, XPISTI SIGILLUM MILITUM 158.00
Sword, ivory hdl, many symbols, 1900s, +scabbard 325.00

Masons

Apron, bl silk & wht leather, 3 bl silk circles, snake fastener....... 200.00
Ashtray, sq & compass, in bl & gold on wht ceramic, 1954, 6¼x6¼"..20.00
Book, Freemasonry & Concordant Orders..., leather bound, 1915, NM...315.00
Bookends, sq & compass, bronze finish, 5⅜" 130.00
Centerpc, w/2 hanging baskets, Walker & Hall Sheffield, ca 1915 ..800.00
Chart/hieroglyphic monitor, emblems/degrees/etc, hardcover, 1856..135.00
Collar, burgundy velvet w/silver embr/fringe/tassels 120.00
Decanter, symbols & open book, ceramic, much gold, 1971 .... 75.00
Fan, silk w/HP emblems in collage, wooden sticks, VG 55.00
Fez, blk wool, red tassel, handmade, M 55.00
Florists form, wireware, hammer & axe.. 395.00
Hat, dbl-headed eagle, Prince of Royal Secret, 32nd degree, 1915...50.00
Locket, 14k wht gold, etched sq & compass/scrollwork, lady's portrait...245.00
Medal, eye & compass, 14k yel gold, ca 1917, 2⅜" 285.00
Medal, 18k yel gold w/bl enamel, 3-part, Spencer London, ca 1906 ..325.00
Pendant/charm, 9k yel gold w/symbols & rnd carnelian stone, 1¼"...275.00
Ring, .25ct total weight dmns in 10k wht gold 415.00
Ring, skull & X-bones, 14k yel gold, Memento Mori, 3rd degree....725.00
Ring, 32nd degree, .20ct VS-2/GH dmn+6 sm dmns in 14k yel gold...735.00
Ring, 5 .48ct total weight emeralds in wht gold mts, 18k yel gold band.315.00
Robe, king's; purple velvet & spun metallic silk, brass chains, 1890s .135.00
Robe, priest's; purple/blk/gold silk w/jeweled ephod, 1880s.......... 135.00
Sash, red & bl silk w/triangular symbol, gold thread, fringe 70.00
Sword, etch blade w/gold, MC Lilley & Co...OH, 36¼", +leather case..300.00
Wristwatch, triangular porc dl, gold-plated bezel, Waltham, 17-jewel..985.00

Odd Fellows

Staff, heart in hand motif, carved and painted, $1,100.00. (Photo courtesy Aston Macek Auctions)

Banner, cream cloth w/gold trim & tassels, embr dove, 29x19" 35.00
Banner, parade; pnt silk, seeing eyes/symbols, gold fringe, 1900s . 155.00
Book, Constitution, Rules & Regulations, cloth spine, 1904, 4x5"...10.00
Chip, crest & seal, yel, US Playing Card, 1924 .... 22.50
Cornucopia, pnt wood, cvd to mt on wall, 1800s, 20" 2,250.00
Coverlet, fraternal symbols, red/yel, 1-pc, Beiderwand, 94x83" 450.00
Cupboard, grained pine w/IOOF on 2-panel do, fitted int, 32x25x14"...635.00
Hat, red velvet w/gold embr & brass piping, ca 1900 .... 40.00
Hourglass, pnt wood, representing life/flight of time, 1800s, 10" ...1,060.00
Magic lantern slides, mc, MC Lilley...OH, 1915, 40 in wooden box..100.00
Mask, Goliath face, papier-maché, ca 1900, 14x14x12", G 50.00

Ribbon, IOOF Amity Encampment, purple w/gold fringe, 1890s .. 50.00
Ring, eye/skull/X-bones, 10k wht gold w/enamel, 1920s 345.00
Robe, blk velvet w/cream accents, Ward-Stilson Co, ca 1940s 45.00
Scepter, cvd/pnt wood, gilt finial & rings, 1800s, 36¼" 1,000.00
Shelf, cvd walnut, crest/X mallets/hourglass/scrolls, 1800s, 24x17x7". 165.00
Staff, cvd pnt shaft w/heart-in-hand finial, ca 1900, 63" 3,750.00
Staff, cvd pnt shaft w/serpent figure, OH, 1800s, 65¼"................. 880.00
Staff, cvd walnut, 11" heart-in-hand finial, IN, 59"...................2,750.00
Stick pins, 3 oval interlocked rings, gold plated,¾" 15.00
Sword, ornate etched blade, W Clauberg Sollingen, 35½", +scabbard . 375.00

Shrine

Book rack, brass-plated CI, camels, folds flat, 1920s 195.00
Brooch, heart w/dangling symbols in center, rhinestones, ORA, 1½"..25.00
Brooch, rhinestone-encrusted crown w/gold-tone sword, ⅞".......... 15.00
Brooch, yel enamel moon crescent/gold-tone star/saber in wreath...18.00
Humidor, glass w/wht metal lid, symbol finial, 1914..................... 125.00
Plate, Potentate's Ball 1950, gold trim, H&K Tunstall, 9¾".......... 20.00
Tumbler, donkey transfer on milk glass, dtd 1917, 3⅞"................. 60.00
Tumbler, emb/HP Indian chief, temple emblem, Pittsburgh 1903, 3¼".. 65.00

Miscellaneous

Am Legion, token, 20th Anniversary Armistice Day, 1918-1938.. 10.00
Daughters of Am Revolution, yearbook, heavy paper cover, 1932-33 . 15.00
Knights of Columbus, matchbook cover, 2 shields, brass, 1919...... 75.00
Knights of Pythias, sword, eng 26" blade, Pettibone Bros, +scabbard.. 110.00
Knights of Pythias, watch fob, gold-filled w/mc enamel, 1⅜x⅞" 55.00
Order of Moose, bookends, bronze-color moose, 1920-30s............. 55.00
Order of Moose, lapel pin, 10k gold w/4 stones, CLUB at bottom. 48.00
Order of Moose, ring, 10k gold, PAP & LOOM on sides................ 65.00
Order of Moose, watch fob, ca 1900, no chain, 1½x1⅝" 32.00
Order of Sons of Am, badge, cello w/bronze holder, 1906, +mc ribbon.. 50.00
Patrons of Husbandry, ribbon w/cello pin, fringe, 1890s................. 32.50
Rotary, songbook, glossy cover, WWII era...5.00
Royal Order of Buffalos, badge, brass 6-point star w/bl enamel 50.00
Shepherds of Bethlehem, brooch, gold-tone w/bl & wht enamel... 10.00
Tie tack, mc enamel on gold-tone, Have Done My Bit, LOOM 24.00

Fruit Jars

As early as 1829, canning jars were being manufactured for use in the home preservation of foodstuffs. For the past 25 years, they have been sought as popular collectibles. At the last estimate, over 4,000 fruit jars and variations were known to exist. Some are very rare, perhaps one-of-a-kind examples known to have survived to the present day. Among the most valuable are the black glass jars, the amber Van Vliet, and the cobalt Millville. These often bring prices in excess of $20,000.00 when they can be found. Aside from condition, values are based on age, rarity, color, and special features. Unless noted otherwise, values are given for clear glass jars. Our advisor for this category is John Hathaway; he is listed in the Directory under Maine.

Atlas E-Z Seal, aqua, qt 1.50
Atlas E-Z Seal, gr, qt 10.00
Atlas Good Luck, ½-pt 18.00
Atlas Mason (Mini), strong shoulder, 2-pc lid, pt............................25.00
Ball (dropped 'a' script) Sure Seal, tall, bl, 22-oz 150.00
Ball (script) Perfect Mason, gr base, clear jar, pt..............................5.00
Ball Eclipse Wide Mouth, pt...1.00
Ball Ideal, rnd, ½-gal...3.00
Ball Sure Seal, base: Patent July 14, 1908, bl, ½-gal 25.00

Ball Sure Seal, bl, ½-pt 135.00
Black-eyed Susan, Morning Glory, pt................................3.00
Canton Manufacturing Co Boston (base), amber, ½-pt 20.00
Crown, JC Baker's Pat Aug 14 1860, aqua, qt.................... 250.00
Crown Crown (bulged crown), aqua, midget..................... 85.00
Crown Mason, pt 2.00
Cunningham & Ihmsen Pittsburgh PA, lt bl, ½-gal 50.00
Drey Perfect Mason (on 2 lines), ½-pt 35.00
Eclipse, lt gr, w/lid, qt.. 600.00
F&J Bodine Philadelphia, aqua, 52-oz........................... 400.00
Fahnestock Albree Co, open pontil, bl, w/o stopper, qt............ 250.00
Gem, aqua, midget.. 50.00
Gilberds Improved (Star), aqua, qt............................. 325.00
Imperial, Patent April 20th 1886 on base, w/lid, pt.......... 150.00
JW Beardsley's Sons New York USA Patent Feb 10 1903, ½-pt..... 10.00
Kerr Self Sealing Mason, 65th Anniversary 1903-63, gold, qt 60.00
La Lorraine (arch above thistle blossom), w/lid, 1-liter................. 80.00
Leotric, sm mouth, sun-colored amethyst, qt 45.00
Magic Star, aqua, w/reproduced clamp, qt................... 300.00
Magic Star, gr, w/orig clamp, qt................................ 575.00
Magic TM Mason Jar, qt..1.00
Mason, Patent Nov 30th 1858, amber, ½-gal................. 450.00
Mason (arched) Ball, bl, qt....................................... 15.00
Mason Jar of 1858 (in circle & sq), aqua, qt 125.00
Mason's (cross) Patent Nov 30th 1858, lt emb, ½-gal 190.00
Mason's Improved (hourglass), Patent May 10th 1870, aqua, qt.... 25.00
Mason's Patent Nov 30th 1858, aqua, qt 4.00
Mason's Patent Nov 30th 1858, base: ES Co, aqua, midget 120.00
Mason's Patent Nov 30th 1858, base: Hero 5 in 1858, aqua, midget ...50.00
Mason's Patent Nov 30th 1858, base: S&R, aqua, ½-gal.............. 35.00
Mason's Patent Nov 30th 1858, emb in circle, aqua, midget........ 600.00
Mason's 32 Patent Nov 30th 1858, bl, qt...................... 200.00
Mason Star Jar, qt..1.00
Model, Patent Aug 27 1867, aqua, ½-gal 300.00
Newman's Patent Dec 20th 1859, w/lid, aqua, qt 1,500.00
Port Mason's Patent Nov 30th 1858, Port arched on base, aqua, qt. 200.00
Presto, ½-pt.. 35.00
Putnam (on base), aqua, 7⅜"....................................... 75.00
Royal (in crown), full measure, ½-gal 25.00
Saleman's Sample, base: Putnam, aqua, ½-pt................ 200.00
Sealtight, base: PA G Co, qt....................................... 18.00
Smalley's Royal (on neck), ½-pt.................................. 25.00
Stark (K in star) Patent, w/lid, qt.............................. 100.00
Trademark Lightning, Registered US Patent Office, apple gr, qt.. 100.00
Victory Circle, Patent Feb 9th 1864...June 22 1867, aqua, qt 100.00
Wears (in circle), pt...9.00
WW Lyman 43, Patent Feb 9th 1984, aqua, qt.................. 40.00

Fry

Henry Fry established his glassworks in 1901 in Rochester, Pennsylvania. There, until 1933 when it was sold to the Libbey Company, he produced glassware of the finest quality. In the early years they produced beautiful cut glass; and when it began to wane in popularity, Fry turned to the manufacture of occasional pieces and oven glassware. He is perhaps most famous for the opalescent pearl art glass called 'Foval.' It was sometimes made with Delft Blue or Jade Green trim in combination. Because it was in production for only a short time in 1926 and 1927, it is hard to find. See also Kitchen Collectibles, Glassware.

Ashtray, Rose Pink, 4 buttress ft, 4 rests.......................... 50.00
Bean pot, mk Fry Ovenware #1924-1, w/lid, 1-qt 85.00
Bonbon, cut, dmns & fans, sgn, 5¾".............................. 60.00

Bottle, scent; Foval, eng, intaglio to Delft Blue top, bell form, 4" ...600.00
Bowl, center; Foval, Delft Blue rim & flat ft, 5¼x9¼" 475.00
Bowl, console; Jade Green, silver o/l to everted rim/disk ft, 5x10" ..500.00
Bowl, cut, Pinwheel, 8".. 150.00
Cake plate, pearl ovenware, sq, #1947 .... 25.00
Candleholder, blk, wide flat ft, 3", ea 18.00
Candlesticks, Jade Green w/sterling o/l to rim, cup & disk ft, 10", pr.. 800.00
Casserole, gr, w/lid, #1938, 7"................................... 110.00
Compote, Foval, Delft Blue stem, opal body & disk ft, 7x6" 250.00
Compote, Foval, Jade Green stem, silver o/l, #2502, 7"............ 350.00
Compote, Grape etching (bowl only), ftd...................... 50.00
Creamer & sugar bowl, Foval, Delft Blue hdls/bases, #2001, 3", 2½" .150.00
Cup, custard; eng, 6-oz, from $10 to............................ 12.00
Dish, cut, heart shape, mk, 5¾".................................. 160.00
Percolator, plain opal, cylindrical, w/glass basket, stem & lid, 9". 225.00
Plate, grill; amber, 3-part 45.00
Plate, grill; pk, 3-part, 8½" 50.00
Plate, pie; pearl ovenware w/orange trim, #1916, 9" 35.00
Ramekin, pearl ovenware, 3", from $15 to...................... 18.00
Sherbet, Rose Pink w/etched panels, ftd, 4¾x3½" 18.00
Snack set, pearl ovenware, #1968, from $45 to................. 50.00
Teapot, Foval w/Delft Blue spout/finial/hdl, silver trim, 7", +6c/s..1,000.00
Tray, biscuit; pearl ovenware, #1934........................... 20.00
Trivet, pearl ovenware, #1959, 8"................................ 30.00
Tumbler, lemonade; Foval, Jade Green hdl, #9416, 5½"................ 50.00
Vase, bud; Azure Blue, ruffled rim 200.00
Vase, Foval, Delft Blue knop/ft, tall U-form w/slight flare, 9x5" .. 325.00
Vase, Foval, Delft Blue rim/3 ball ft, triple gourd w/flared top, 5".. 350.00
Wine, Foval, Jade Green disk base, silver o/l, 4½" 110.00

Vase, Foval, 7x6½", $250.00. (Photo courtesy De Fina Auctions)

Fulper

Throughout the nineteenth century the Fulper Pottery in Flemington, New Jersey, produced utilitarian and commercial wares. But it was during the span from 1902 to 1935, the Arts and Crafts period in particular, that the company became prominent producers of beautifully glazed art pottery. Although most pieces were cast rather than hand decorated, the graceful and classical shapes used together with wonderful experimental glaze combinations made each piece a true work of art.

The company also made dolls' heads, Kewpies, figural perfume lamps, and powder boxes. Their lamps with the colored glass inserts are extremely rare and avidly sought by collectors. Examples prized most highly by collectors today are those produced before the devastating fire in 1929 and subsequent takeover by Martin Stangl (see Stangl Pottery).

Several marks were used: a vertical in-line 'Fulper' being the most common in ink or incised, an impressed block horizontal mark, Flemington, Rafco, Prang, and paper labels. Unmarked examples often surface and can be identified by shape and glaze characteristics. Values are determined by size, desirability of glaze, and rarity of form. Our advisor for this category is Douglass White; he is listed in the Directory under Florida.

Bowl, Café-au-Lait over mustard, grinding chips/fleck, 6½x14½"..2,000.00
Bowl, effigy; mustard on Café-au-Lait, Cat's-Eye flambé int, 7x11"..725.00
Bowl, 3 figural supports, brn & bl crystalline, 7x10½" 300.00
Candlesticks, Cucumber Gr/Cat's-Eye flambé, firing lines, 16", pr..1,560.00
Lamp, Café-au-Lait matt, ldgl glass inserts on 10" shade, #804, 17"...6,600.00
Lamp, Cat's Eye & Flemington Gr flambé shade & std, Pat Pend, 21x16".17,000.00
Lamp, Chinese Blue flambé, ldgl glass inserts on shade, 17x9¼", NM..4,800.00
Lamp, Flemington Green flambé, mushroom form w/ldgl inserts, rstr, 17"..9,600.00

Lamp, green flambé with caramel slag leaded glass shade (restored), 17x14", $11,000.00. (Photo courtesy David Rago Auctions)

Lamp, Leopard Skin crystalline, mushroom form, ldgl insets, 17x17", NM..36,000.00
Pitcher, gray & bl drip, flared cylinder, 10", +4 3½" mugs 275.00
Urn, Leopard Skin crystalline w/hammered texture, hdls, 12x11½"..1,000.00
Urn, multi-tone bl matt, rim-to-hip hdls, drilled, 10½"................. 100.00
Vase, amber crystalline, 4 buttresses, 10¼x8"...........................2,700.00
Vase, bl & gr flambé, shouldered, 11½" 300.00
Vase, bl/brn/tan streaks w/bl crystalline, incurvate rim, 8¼" 400.00
Vase, brn crystalline over mustard matt, 8x10", EX...................2,200.00
Vase, caramel flambé, bullet form, 6½x4¾" 400.00
Vase, Cat's-Eye crystalline, teardrop shape, 13x7½"...................1,675.00
Vase, Cat's-Eye flambé, melon shape, 7x5½" 480.00
Vase, Chinese Blue crystalline flambé, hdls, 9½x7" 500.00

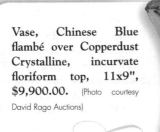

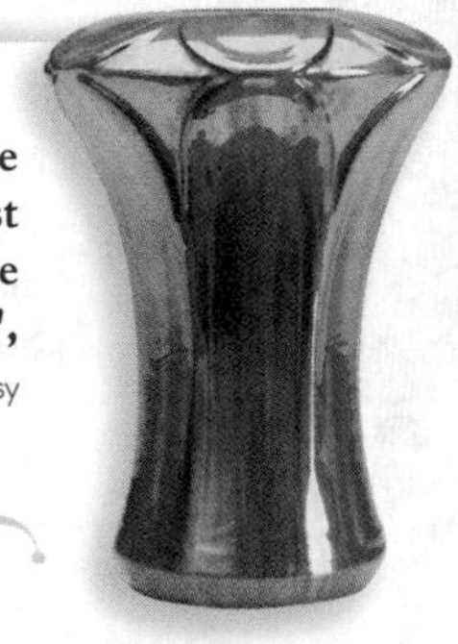

Vase, Chinese Blue flambé over Copperdust Crystalline, incurvate floriform top, 11x9", $9,900.00. (Photo courtesy David Rago Auctions)

Vase, Chinese Blue flambé, 10½x10½".......................................1,000.00
Vase, Chinese Blue flambé, 17½x7", NM...................................1,440.00
Vase, Flemington Green flambé, baluster, 17x8½".....................1,680.00
Vase, frothy cucumber matt, baluster, 12x4¾" 1,000.00
Vase, frothy cucumber over buff, scalloped rim, hdls, 9¼x11"...... 660.00
Vase, frothy gunmetal, spherical, 5¾x7" 1,000.00
Vase, frothy turq on Famille Rose flambé, bbl form, 17x16", EX..720.00
Vase, khaki gr/cobalt/Cat's-Eye flambé, faceted, 9¾x5½" 515.00
Vase, Mirror Black to Chinese Blue flambé, shouldered, 12x11½"..3,000.00
Vase, Mirror Black/cobalt/Famille Rose flambé, shouldered, 7½x7"..660.00
Vase, Mushroom Ikebana, Elephant's-Breath flambé, 10x4½"...1,025.00
Vase, tan/bl/brn crystalline, hdls, label, 12" 475.00

Furniture

Throughout history a person's wealth and status could quickly be determined by the type of furniture he possessed. Throughout each period of time, there have been distinct changes in styles, choice of woods, and techniques — all clues the expert can use to determine just when an item was made. Regional differences as well as secondary wood choices give us clues as to country of origin. The end of the Civil War brought with it the Industrial Revolution and the capability of mass producing machine-made furniture.

Important to the collector (and dealer) is the ability to recognize furniture on a 'good, better, best' approach. Age alone does not equal value. During this recessionary market, the 'best' of forms have continued to sell and appreciate, while the 'better' middle market has shown a slight decline both at auction and at retail. Many of the values given this year emphasize the ups and downs apparent in today's marketplace.

Pre-sale estimates by auction houses appear to be less speculative this year and are closer to the actual selling price. Top collectors are paying more attention to the details of quality items. Good vintage reproductions from the first half of the twentieth century are gaining in popularity. Both American and English furniture are good choices for buyers. On the upswing from previous years are original painted pieces that fall under the best of form in the primitive category. Prices for 'floor ready' upholstered pieces in classical styles show that they are still in demand.

Since there are many items that have sold at auction for at least 25% lower than their normal market value, we will not note them this year with the usual (*). Items marked with (**) are pieces in the best of form and of museum quality.

Please note: If a piece actually dates to the period of time during which its style originated, we will use the name of the style only. For example: 'Hepplewhite' will indicate an American piece from roughly the late 1700s to 1815. The term 'style' will describe a piece that is far removed from the original time frame. 'Hepplewhite style' refers to examples from the turn of the century. When the term 'repro' is used it will mean that the item in question is less than 30 years old and is being sold on a secondary market. When only one dimension is given, for blanket chests, dry sinks, settees, sideboards, sofas, and tables, it is length, unless otherwise noted.

Condition is the most important factor to consider in determining value. It is also important to remember that *where* a piece sells has a definite bearing on the price it will realize, due simply to regional preference. To learn more about furniture, we recommend *Heywood-Wakefield Modern Furniture* by Steve and Roger Rouland; *The Market Place Guide to Oak Furniture* by Peter S. Blumdell; and *Early American Furniture* by John Obbard. In the listings that follow, items are in good condition unless noted otherwise. See also Art Deco, Art Nouveau; Arts and Crafts; Fifties Modern; Limbert; Nutting, Wallace; Shaker; Stickley; Wright.

Our advisor for this category is Suzy McLennan Anderson, CAPP of Bachelorhill Antiques and Appraisals of Walterboro, South Carolina. Her mailing address is listed in the Directory under South Carolina. Requests that do not include a SASE regretfully can no longer be answered.

Key:

* — auction price but 25% under the norm	Geo — Georgian
	grpt — grainpainted
** — museum quality	hdbd — headboard
: — over (example, 1 do:2 drw)	hdw — hardware
bj — bootjack	Hplwht — Hepplewhite
brd — board	mar — marriage
Co — country	mahog — mahogany
cvd, cvg — carved, carving	NE — New England
c&b — claw and ball	QA — Queen Anne
do — door	R/R — Renaissance Revival
drw — drawer	rswd — rosewood
Emp — Empire	trn — turning, turned
Fed — Federal	uphl — upholstered/upholstery

Fr — French
ftbd — footboard
G — good

Vict — Victorian
vnr — veneer
W/M — William and Mary

Armoires, See also Wardrobes

Cypress, cornice:panel do:tapered legs, pegged, old bl pnt, 1850s, 66".. 1,200.00
Cypress Acadian, 2 panel do:scalloped apron:cabriole legs, 55x38x19"..5,650.00
Mahog Fed, cornice:frieze:dbl panel do, Ionic capitals, 78x26".. 8,225.00
Mahog Fed, stepped/breakfronted cornice:Gothic panel do, 94x72x33"..9,695.00
Rswd Am Rococo, arched cornice:mirrored do:cvd drw, Meeks, 93x51x29"..7,635.00
Rswd Rococo, scroll crest:mirrored do:sq base:castors, 108x46" . 10,575.00
Walnut, flat top:panel do:scalloped skirt, ca 1800, 57x45x20" ..21,150.00

Beds

Poster, curly maple w/bold trns, 2-panel hdbd, OH Valley, 49x76x51"...500.00
Rope, cherry 4-post w/cannonballs, spindled hd/ftbrds, 61x83x52" ...200.00
Rope, red/blk grpt, trn posts, shaped hdbd, trn blanket roll, 53x71"...315.00
Rope, walnut 4-poster, shaped hdbd, fine trns, 53x76x53" 230.00
Rope trundle, maple, cannonball posts, mortised/pegged, red pnt, 66"...575.00
Rope trundle, maple, mushroom finials, casters, 19x70x44"........ 150.00
Tall post, curly maple, 1-brd hdbd w/scrolled ends, 76" 2,750.00
Tall post, mahog, cvd crests & posts, paw ft, 64x73x43" 700.00
Tall post, maple/pine/figured vnr, scalloped hdbd, rpr, 78x76x58"...750.00
Tester, mahog Am Rococo, arched/paneled hdbd, shaped rails, 107x79x60". 11,750.00
Tester, mahog Fed w/much cvg, brass molding, paneled rails, 103x73x57". 11,200.00
Tester, mahog NE Sheraton, canopy:trn posts:shaped hdbd, 85x80x55"..2,100.00
Tester, walnut Dutch Renaissance style w/much cvg, 80x79x46"..2,350.00

Benches

Bucket, chestnut, 1-brd, sloped bksplash/bj ends, yel over red, 34x44". 1,500.00
Bucket, pine Co, curved top, gray pnt, NE, 21x73x23" 2,500.00
Bucket, pine Co, 2-shelf, ends w/arched tops, old pnt, NE, 24x50x10"..880.00
Bucket, pnt poplar, appl edge, demilune bj ends, 30x62x15" 1,200.00

Church bench, oak, ca. 1920s, 50", from $200.00 to $250.00. (Photo courtesy Robert and Harriet Swedberg)

Cypress, beaded skirt:shaped legs, 1800s, 18x69x11" 795.00
Fireside, walnut W/M, brocade cushion:4 block & trn legs, 22x44x19". 500.00
Pew, walnut Continental Renaissance, paneled bkrest/scroll ends, 88".. 150.00
Pine, mortised, bj ends, bk braces, appl molding, old pnt, 20x70x14". 400.00
Pine Co, bj ends, old red pnt, age crack, 19x58x12"..................... 300.00
Pine Co, cut-out ft, weathered bl pnt, 19x70x13" 90.00
Pine Co, plank seat w/scalloped arch supports, red stain, 17x89x12".825.00
Walnut Spanish Baroque, hinged bkrest, wrought-iron stretcher, 79" L.325.00

Blanket Chests, Coffers, Trunks, and Mule Chests

Dome top, patterned pnt w/blk borders, dvtl, hinged lid, 1800s, 23" L. 2,200.00
Dome top, pine w/grpt on yel, dvtl, sq nails, rprs, 20x24x12" 345.00
Dower, poplar, lift top:3 short drw, floral pnt, OH/1800s, 32x42x21" . 17,625.00
Maple/chestnut, 2 false:2 drw, rosehead nails, modern pnt, 40x38x19"..485.00
Oak Jacobean w/demilune palmette moldings, EX cvg, block ft, 27x56x21"..950.00

Patterned mustard/brn putty pnt, 6-brd, hinged top, 1830s, 22x39x16" .2,200.00
Pine, old red rpt, strap hinges, dvtl, rprs, 17x34x21" 400.00
Pine, 6-brd w/bj ends, chalky bl pnt, 26x44x19"........................... 500.00
Pine, 6-brd w/long drw, bj ends, brn pnt, rprs, NE, 36x43x19"..... 800.00
Pine Co, hinged lid w/cotterpin hinges:drw:bracket ft, old rpt, 32x47" ..500.00
Poplar, orig red pnt w/stenciled name/1852 & flowers, rpr, 44x23x21"..2,100.00
Poplar, 3 false drw fronts:2 drw, brn pnt:red, rpl brass, 41x44x19"...865.00
Walnut/poplar w/inlay initials, w/till/bear-trap lock, dvtl, 24x44x21". 435.00

Bookcases

Breakfront, mahog Geo III, cornice:4 glazed do:4 drw & 2 do, 100x94"..17,000.00
Secretaire, mahog Regency w/gilt-bronze foliate mts, 94x47x23" 10,000.00
Walnut Am Gothic, cornice w/acorn pendants:3 do:lg sq ft, 99x87x25"..16,450.00
Walnut Fed in Gothic style, dentils:sliding do:molded base, 104x80".. 6,175.00
Walnut/walnut burl Vict breakfront, 4 lg glass do:4 drw, much cvg, 86" .2,100.00

Bureaus

Cherry Chpndl w/cvg, serpentine front:4 drw:c&b ft, 33x34x21"**..11,160.00
Mahog, swell front:4 grad drw:bracket ft, rfn, 35x38x22"..........4,125.00
Mahog Fed w/inlay, bowfront:4-drw:bracket ft, rpl, 36x40x25".. 3,800.00
Mahog Louis XVI style w/cvg & leather top, center drw+2 side, 64".. 1,500.00
Maple/bird's-eye maple/mahog Fed, elliptical front, 4-drw, rfn, 43x42"...6,400.00

Cabinets

Breakfront, mahog Geo III style, 4 glazed do:4 panel do, 1900s, 82x88"...2,500.00
Bucket, walnut/chestnut, tray top w/drain:2 panel do:skirt, 20x40x21"....2,525.00
Butler's pantry, red cyprus, 5 etched glass panel do:shelf:3 drw:5 do .6,100.00
China, quartersawn oak Rococo, satyrs cvgs, dbl do, 66x56x20".... 4,600.00
Corner, fruitwood Fr Provincial, triangular top:frieze drw:do, 37x26" ... 650.00

Corner, paint decorated to simulate tiger and figured maple, Pennsylvania, probably Strausburg, interior fitted with shelves, 82x45x27", from $6,000.00 to $8,000.00. (Photo courtesy James D. Julia Inc.)

Linen, mahog Geo III style, molded top:2 oval-panel do:3 drw, 84x52" .3,525.00
Mahog/pietra dura Louis XVI style w/gilt bronze mts, 50x23" 2,695.00
Vitrine, Louis XV style, glass top/ebonized vnr/ormolu trim, 29x24x17" ... 300.00
Vitrine, mahog Louis XV style, glass top, dmn shape, 29x21x19" 300.00
Vitrine, pnt Vernis Martin Louis XV style w/gilt-metal mts, 57x24"..3,000.00
Vitrine, tulipwood Louis XVI style w/cast mts, glass sides, 66x31x15".. 3,650.00

Candlestands

Apple gr pnt, sq tray:trn shaft:tripod cabriole legs, 26x17x16"... 1,525.00
Cherry/curly maple tilt-top Fed, shaped top:baluster:splayed legs, rfn... 485.00
Chestnut/burled chestnut, trn shaft, scroll-cut legs, OH, 30x22x19".. 800.00
Curly maple/cherry Co Chpndl, baluster-trn shaft:snake ft, rfn, 25x15".175.00
Mahog Fed w/inlaid edge, trn shaft:snake ft, rfn, 29x18x18"........ 635.00
Maple Chpndl, rnd top:urn & column shaft:snake ft, wrought spider, rfn. 550.00

Pnt Fed w/checkerbrd top, pnt decor post:tripod, 28x17x17" ...6,000.00
Poplar Co, rnd top:urn & baluster shaft:scrolled ft, dry pnt, 22" dia...700.00
Tilt-top, birch Fed, trn column:slender legs, red stain, 30x24x15". 1,150.00
Tilt-top, birch Fed w/red stain, 8-sided top:tripod, 30x21x14"**..18,800.00
Tilt-top, cherry Fed, 1-brd:trn column:tripod base, old rfn, 38x23x16" ..300.00
Tilt-top, cherry Fed w/inlay, urn & baluster shaft, rfn/rpr, 29x20x16" ...375.00
Tilt-top, papier-maché top w/abalone inlay/pnt scene, tripod base...635.00
Walnut rotating top:birdcage:trn post:tripod, NC, 1830s, 27x18" dia . 4,100.00
Walnut/cherry Fed, sq top:trn shaft:tripod, alligatored finish, 20x19". 260.00

Chairs

Arm, hickory Adirondack, basketweave bk & seat, dbl box stretcher, 34" ..750.00
Arm, long horns form bk/arms/legs, cowhide uphl, ca 1900, 42" 575.00
Arm, mahog George III, vasiform splat, open arms, slip seat, 18"..... 265.00
Arm, maple QA Co, crown crest:shaped splat:rush seat, CT, 44½"..1,095.00

Armchair, Old Hickory, re-caned seat, brand and metal tag, 44x29", with footstool, $1,450.00. (Photo courtesy David Rago Auctions)

Chamber, walnut Chpndl w/pierced/cvd splat, slip seat, 40" 3,200.00
Corner, mahog Geo III, open splats:slip seat:molded stretchers........ 850.00
Corner, walnut/maple Chpndl style, circular arm rail, splint seat, rfn . 385.00
Lolling, mahog Chpndl, arched crest, open arms, fine reuphl........1,725.00
Lounge, walnut Fr Art Deco, curved open arms, reuphl mohair, 32", pr ..3,500.00
Rocker, platform; bentwood, reuphl seat/bk, att Thonet, 33" 225.00
Side, blk-pnt QA, yoke bk w/vasiform slat, trn stiles/front legs, 42"...1,000.00
Side, cherry Chpndl, scrolled crest:pierced slat:slip seat, rprs, 37" 230.00
Side, cherry Chpndl, serpentine crest:compass slip seat:b&c ft, 38"...1,765.00
Side, Italian Art Nouveau, cvd ladies' heads/frog/flowers, silk uphl..2,000.00
Side, mahog Chpndl, pierced/cvd splat:needlework seat:b&c ft, 42" .775.00
Side, maple QA Co, vasiform splat:block & trn legs, rush seat, 40". 175.00
Side, oak Dutch-style marquetry inlay, shell-cvd crest, b&c ft, 45" ..460.00
Side, red japanned W/M w/gold chinoiserie, scrolled crest, caned seat...1,200.00
Side, walnut Chpndl w/pierced/cvd vasiform splat, slip seat, 43" .8,225.00
Windsor arm, 7-spindle bk & tablet crest, bamboo trns, 34" 175.00
Windsor brace-bk arm, mixed woods, 7-spindle, old gr pnt, 37"...1,150.00
Windsor brace-bk arm, shaped crest:7-spindle, blk & gilt pnt, PA, 40"..13,800.00
Windsor brace-bk continuous arm, bowed crest:saddle seat, 38" ...2,585.00
Windsor brace-bk side, old gr:salmon pnt, CT, 1780s, 35", pr 3,000.00
Windsor comb-bk continuous arm, bamboo-trn/worn pnt, NE, 1810s, 43"..1,300.00
Windsor fan-bk side, 7-spindle, old red pnt, seat rpr, 40" 1,150.00
Windsor high-bk arm, maple/hickory, concave crest:scroll arms, RI, 45". 3,800.00
Windsor sack-bk arm, bowed crest rail:7-spindle, NE, 40" 2,500.00
Windsor step-down rod bk w/bamboo trns, old brn pnt, youth sz, 33" ..460.00
Windsor writing, mixed woods, trn spindles/legs, old rpt, 46"........... 600.00
Windsor-style comb-bk writing, 2-drw, dk gr pnt over red, 46".........350.00
Wing, mahog Chpndl style, arched crest:scroll arms, Kittinger, 46". 350.00
Wing, mahog Chpndl style, curving arms & bk, reuphl, 42" 635.00
Wing, mahog Geo III, molded Marlborough legs, damask uphl, 48"..2,450.00
Wing, mahog QA w/serpentine crest, reuphl, Am, 50x33x18" .. 33,000.00

Chair Sets

Dining, elm English, 5 arched slats:woven seats, 42", 4 side+2 arm . 575.00
Dining, oak w/cvd North Wind masks, reuphl seat, 43", 6 for...... 700.00
Side, bird's-eye maple Fed, 2-slat bk:slip seat:saber legs, 6 for ...3,525.00
Side, mahog Fed, figured crest:cvd splat:slip seat:reeded legs, 6 for ..2,000.00
Side, mahog Geo III Hplwht, shield bk w/Prince of Wales plumes, 8 for .4,500.00
Side, rswd English, curved crest:cvd splat:silk seat, 1840s, 6 for .. 1,765.00
Windsor birdcage side, 7-spindle bk, bamboo trns, rfn, 33", 6 for....750.00
Windsor side, stepped crest:raked bks:bamboo trns, rfn, 8 for 450.00

Chests (Antique), See also Dressers

Birch Chpndl, 4 grad cockbeaded drw, red pnt, NE, rstr/rpl, 36x38"..2,350.00
Birch Chpndl oxbow, molded top:4 grad drw:fan cvg:c&b ft, 34x39" .. 2,500.00
Bird's-eye maple/cherry Fed, 4 grad drw, rpl brasses/rfn, VT, 37x38" ..3,400.00
Bonnet, cherry/poplar, 4 drw:3 grad drw, OH, rfn, 45x41" 1,380.00
Butler's, mahog Hplwht w/inlay, fold-down top:3 drw, rfn, 41x41x20"..2,200.00
Campaign, blk lcq w/chinoiserie, brass bound, 1800s, 37x20x16"..2,950.00
Cherry Chpndl w/inlay, serpentine front, 4 grad drw, 33x39x19".. 11,500.00
Cherry Sheraton bowfront, 4 grad drw, panel sides, rprs, 46x43x24" .. 2,100.00
Cherry/poplar Hplwht w/inlay, 3 grad dvtl drw, eagle brasses, 38x38". 865.00
Cherry/poplar/walnut Sheraton, 2-brd:3 short:3 long drw, 45x43x21" . 1,375.00
Curly maple/cherry Fed, bowfront top:4 dvtl drw, rfn, 38x39x20"....1,500.00
Curly maple/cherry/walnut Emp, 2 glove drw:5 drw, rfn, 52x36x18" .1,600.00
Louis XV Provincial, fruitwood, serpentine top:3 bombé drw, 33x51" . 8,800.00
Mahog Geo III, pull-out slide:4 grad drw, dust brds, 32x34x18" .2,400.00
Mahog Geo III, serpentine front, dressing slide:4 drw, rprs, 34x37x23"...4,300.00
Mahog Geo III, serpentine top:2 molded drw:scalloped apron, 28x32x16".2,800.00
Mahog/cherry Chpndl, 4 grad drw, full dust brds, sm rprs, PA, 33x37". 10,350.00
Mahog/oak English Chpndl, overhang:2 drw:3:bracket base, rstr, 37x39". 1,000.00
Maple Chpndl, cornice:6 grad drw:bracket ft, old rfn, 57x36x19".. 7,650.00

Maple inlaid Federal bowfront, brass beading, mahogany and tiger maple panels, replaced brasses, refinished, 43x42x23", $6,750.00. (Photo courtesy Skinner Inc. Auctioneers & Appraisers of Antiques & Fine Art)

On chest, curly maple Chpndl, cvd pediment:3:4 drw:4 grad drw, 92x42" .17,250.00
On chest, mahog Geo III, dentil cornice:2 short:3 grad drw:3, 75x47" ...4,700.00
On chest, mahog Geo III, 2-pc, 2 short:3 drw:slide:3 grad drw, 73x43"...2,750.00
On fr, mahog QA style, dry surface, all orig, 74x39x18"............1,000.00
Pine Chpndl, 5 grad drw, old red pnt, rpl brasses, NE, 43x39" .2,645.00
Sugar, butternut Sheraton, lift top:drw:tapered legs, 37x32x16"....7,000.00
Sugar, cherry/poplar/walnut, dvtl drws, old rfn, rprs, 39x37x20" .3,500.00
Tall, cherry Fed cornice:3:2:4 drw, reeded columns, fr ft, 62x40"..6,325.00
Tall, maple Chpndl, molded top:4 thumb-molded grad drw:cut-out base.. 5,600.00
Tall, maple/chestnut Chpndl, 2 short:4 grad drw, grpt, NE, 47x38" .6,325.00
Tiger maple/maple Fed, overhanging top:4 grad drw, rfn, MA, 34x41"...4,400.00
Walnut Chpndl, 2 short:3 grad dvtl drw, full dust brds, 36x37x20"..2,415.00
Walnut/pine Chpndl, 1-brd top:4 grad drw, 1-brd sides, PA, rpr, 41x39"..4,000.00
Walnut/poplar Fed w/inlay, 4 dvtl bead drw, rpl brasses, OH, 43x40x19" .. 1,150.00

Cupboards, See also Pie Safes

Cherry Co, crown mold:2 6-pane do:shelf:3 drw:2 do, 2-pc, 83x60"..**5,750.00**
Cherry/pine, crown molding:panel do, pnt traces, rprs, PA, 31x25x13"..**1,380.00**
Chestnut Co, 2 panel do:shelf:2 panel do, old bl pnt, 2-pc, 79x48".**3,750.00**
Chimney, curly maple, 1-do w/5 shelves, DT Smith repro, 72x24x23"..**500.00**
Chimney, pine Co, 3 panel do, mustard pnt, PA, 81x25"..........**2,645.00**
Corner, cherry OH, crown molding:dbl 2-panel do:dbl panel do, 78x44".**1,495.00**
Corner, cherry w/flame/burled vnr, 1-pc bowfront, much cvg, 103x55"..**7,000.00**
Corner, cherry/poplar Co, cornice:4 panel do:skirt, rfn/rpl, 88x54"....**1,380.00**
Corner, cherry/walnut 1-pc step-bk, 2 8-pane do:shelf:2 drw:2 do, 92"..**2,415.00**
Corner, cherrywood Co, cornice:dbl 6-pane do:2 panel do, 81x46"..**4,400.00**
Corner, pine/poplar, dbl 10-pane do form arch:drw:dbl do, 93x54"..**3,800.00**
Corner, pnt Co, cornice:3 arch do:drw/2 faux drw:dbl do, PA, 86x40"**..**28,200.00**
Corner, pnt pine Co, cornice:arched panel do, rosehead nails, 35x29"..**1,035.00**
Corner, poplar Co, 2-pc, 4 panel do, old pnt/rpl latches, OH, 82x55"..**1,840.00**
Corner, walnut/chestnut, stepped cornice:2 panel do:2 panel do, 86x43"..**3,000.00**
Corner, walnut/pine, cornice:cvd do w/tulips:bracket ft, OH, 62x36"..**3,335.00**
Corner, walnut/poplar, 2 panel do:2, old bl pnt, cut nails, 81x32x22"..**4,300.00**
Linen, cherry Fed, cornice:dbl panel do:base w/3 drw:trn legs, 82x44".**5,900.00**
Linen, mahog/oak Chpndl, dentil molding:2 panel do:2 drw, 84x54"..**4,500.00**
Pine, scalloped bksplash, wainscot fr do & sides, 19th C, 78x19x12"..**595.00**
Pine Co, cornice:dbl 6-pane do, old red pnt, ca 1800, 38x38x16"..**3,800.00**
Pine Co, cornice:3-shelf open case:shelf:2 panel do, old rpt, 84x56"..**4,400.00**
Pine Co, dbl do w/brass knobs, 3-shelf, red pnt, 1800s, 14x11x4"..**825.00**
Pine Fed, cornice:2 6-pane do:long drw/candle drws:dbl do, 87x53x19"..**17,625.00**
Step-bk, curly maple/walnut/poplar, 2 6-pane do:shelf:3 drw:2 do, 87"..**4,000.00**
Step-bk, maple Chpndl-style, 21-pane top:shelf:5 drw:2 do, 89x70x21"..**12,650.00**
Walnut, lift lid compartment:plank do:bracket ft, PA, 32x28x13"..**725.00**
Walnut Co, cornice:do w/2 flat panels, 2-shelf, rprs, 47x28x15"..**550.00**
Walnut Co step-bk, 2 panel do:shelf:2 panel do, rfn, ft damage, 77x40"..**500.00**
Walnut/pine Italian Renaissance-style, 1 do, overall cvg, rprs, 81x45".**4,000.00**
Walnut/poplar Co, dvtl case, drw:2-panel do, OH, 64x47x20"..**1,000.00**

Desks

Cherry Chippendale slant-lid desk, Connecticut, ca. 1790, 44x40", $3,175.00.

(Photo courtesy Skinner Inc. Auctioneers & Appraisers of Antiques & Fine Art)

Cherry Hplwht w/inlay, dbl tambour do:fold-out top:4 drw, 42x39"..**3,450.00**
Cherry/butternut Fed, slant lid:4 grad drw, rprs/rpl, 45x38x22"..**865.00**
Cherry/curly maple Chpndl style, slant lid:3 drw:ogee ft, 1850, 41x36"..**1,100.00**
Mahog Dutch Rococo-style, slant lid, bombé case, 45x38x21"..**700.00**
Mahog NE Chpndl, block front w/4 grad drws:bracket ft, rfn, 44x41"..**11,500.00**
Mahog/vnr/pine kneehole w/checkered inlay, 9 dvtl drw, 31x54x24"..**575.00**
Partners', walnut/burl walnut Geo III style, leather top, 9-drw, 58"..**2,000.00**
Plantation, walnut, scallop:pigeonholes:shelves:slant lid:drws, 66"..**950.00**
Poplar Chpndl Co, slant front:3 grad drw:bracket ft, rstr, 42x41"..**485.00**
Rswd/bird's-eye vnr davenport, leather-covered slant lid:panel do, 35"..**1,725.00**
Table-top, dvtl pine w/pnt decor, hinged lid, att NE, 10x22x21"..**1,095.00**
Tiger maple, gallery:shelf:lift lid w/beading:trn legs, rfn, 37x24"..**235.00**
Tiger maple Chpndl, slant lid:4 grad drw:bracket base, rfn, 38x35x19"..**6,400.00**

Tiger maple Fed, slant lid:4 grad drw:bracket ft, rpl/rfn, 39x34x18"..**4,600.00**
Walnut/poplar Chpndl, slant lid:3 grad drws, dvtl, rpl brasses, 41x38"..**2,875.00**
Writing, Wm IV, leather top:reeded edge:2 drw:trn legs, 37"..**1,400.00**
Writing table, mahog Louis XVI style, leather top:3 frieze drw..**1,880.00**

Dry Sinks

High-bk, pine Co, 3-shelf top:dvtl case:panel do, old pnt, 72x36x23"..**3,000.00**
Pine Co, bksplash, bead-brd base w/cut-out ft, NE, 35x36x19"..**1,000.00**
Pine/poplar, 3 drw:2 panel do, dvtl/thru-tenons, old gray pnt, 44x49"..**4,300.00**
Poplar w/comb grpt, scalloped bksplash, dbl do, rprs, 35x36x19"..**1,600.00**
Walnut, 2 panel do, shaped ft/ends, yel pnt over gray, OH, 43" W..**1,400.00**

Hall Pieces

Bench, mahog Vict style, dolphin arms, claw ft, 1890s, 46x55x21"..**1,600.00**
Chair, oak Gothic w/floral needlepoint uphl, 1870s..**400.00**
Chair, oak w/Italian cvg, dk stain, 1800s, 50x18"..**300.00**
Chair, walnut, R/R w/uphl demilune lift-top seat, 18702, 39", pr..**725.00**

Pier table, stenciled rosewood, American Federal, white marble top, barley twist supports, 40x55x21", $12,700.00. (Photo courtesy Neal Auction Company Auctioneers & Appraisers of Fine Art)

Stand, fruitwood/ivory marquetry German, grotesque cvgs, 96x51x10".**4,000.00**
Table, console; mixed wood Deco style, U-shaped supports, 34x48x17"..**395.00**
Table, console; walnut Vict, wht marble:drw:shelf, 1870s, 37x43x15"..**375.00**
Table, mahog Geo III w/foliate/shell cvgs, paw ft, 29x50x25"..**3,500.00**
Table, mahog Louis Philippe, marble top:2 drw:2 shelves, 1850s, 38x45"..**1,950.00**
Table, oak Emp style w/stretcher shelf:c&b ft, Baker, 39x39x24"..**2,500.00**
Tree, faux bamboo, tripod base, att RJ Horner of NY, 74½"..**465.00**
Tree, oak Eastlake, mirror bk w/cvg, armchair base..**240.00**
Tree, oak post (simple) w/4 hooks, 4 curved legs, 67"..**50.00**
Tree, oak Vict, cvd bk w/mirror, table base w/drw:shelf, 83x48"..**660.00**
Tree/chair, ash Vict, mirror/4 hooks, lift-top seat..**350.00**

Highboys

Cherry QA style, 2-pc, alligatored finish, DT Smith repro, 75x43"..**2,000.00**
Cherry/pine QA, cornice drw:2:3 drw:base w/3 drw & shell cvg, NE, 72"..**6,325.00**
Cherry/pine QA, flat top:2:4 grad drw:1:3 short drw:skirt, NE, 73x39"..**8,625.00**
Mahog QA, 2:3 drw:3 sm drw:cabriole legs:pad ft, rstr marriage, 65x40".**1,600.00**
Mahog/poplar Chpndl style, arch:3:2:3 drw:1:3 drw:c&b ft, 94x44"..**7,000.00**
Maple/pine QA, crown mold:4 grad drw:case w/3 drw, marriage, 70".**6,900.00**
Oak/chestnut/pine Chpndl, broken arch pediment/rosettes, 2-pc, 93x42"..**8,625.00**
Poplar QA-style, 2 short:4 grad drw: base w/4 drw, old pnt, 76x42"..**3,750.00**

Pie Safes

Oak w/center do, screened all sides, 3 oval shelves, 27x26"..**300.00**
Oak w/2 drw:2 do, ea do w/2 pierced tin panels, 45¼"..**360.00**
Pine Co, brn pnt/punched mansions on orig tin panels, 1800s, 54x42x18"..**10,000.00**
Poplar, dbl do w/6 punched tin panels, old bl pnt, VA, 1800s, 56x42"..**1,750.00**
Poplar, drw:dbl do w/6 punched tin panels, splits/rust, 1880s, 51x43"..**1,000.00**
Poplar, 12 punched tins w/sunflowers/geometrics, rfn, 62x41x19"..**1,375.00**
Walnut/pine, peaked pediment, 8 punched tin panels, OH or IN, 67x40"..**1,600.00**

Secretaries

Cherry/birch Chpndl, C-scroll cornice:slant lid:4 drw, CT, 88x40" . 8,625.00
Cherry/figured cherry/mahog Sheraton, 3 drw:shaped skirt, rfn, 53x43" .. 925.00
Mahog Fed, bookcase top:fall-front:3 grad drw:trn legs, 82x42x21" . 4,900.00
Mahog Fed, 3 drw:2 do:slant lid:4 grad drw:skirt, 62x42x19" 4,000.00
Mahog Fed, 3 inlaid do:slant lid:4 grad drw, eagle brasses, 55x43x20" .. 1,850.00
Mahog Geo III, glazed dbl do:slant lid:2 short:3 drw, marriage, 83x37" . 3,000.00
Mahog Hplwht w/inlay, bookcase:2 do:writing top:4 drw, rprs, 85x40" . 1,500.00
Mahog Sheraton, astragal glazed dbl do:step-bk:hinged lid:3 drw, 87" . 5,175.00
Mahog/pine/walnut Hplwht w/inlay, bookcase:slant lid:4 drw, 84x36x22" . 6,600.00
Walnut/burl walnut QA style, dbl-dome do top:slant lid:4 drw, 92x41" . 4,995.00

Settees

Camelbk, Irish, eagle w/snake-cvd arms, paw ft, reuphl, 1740s, 38x62" .. 5,000.00
Mahog Chpndl, triple chair-bk w/ribbon cvgs, c&b ft, 1880s, 41x54" 4,350.00
Mahog Fed w/inlay, arched bk:cvd arms:trn legs, rfn/reuphl, 71" .. 10,600.00
Mahog Regency, paneled crest/scrolled arms, caned, brass cuffs, 89" . 5,875.00
Rswd Am Rococo w/much cvg, reuphl, att Meeks, 1850s, 48½x61" . 9,600.00
Walnut Venetian Rococo w/scalloped crest, rolled arms, reuphl, 88" . 6,000.00
Windsor, 8-spindle bk:1-brd seat:trn legs, old gr pnt, rprs, 73" L . 1,380.00

Settles, See Benches

Shelves

Etagere, mahog Fed, urn finials:3 tiers:drw, 51½x18x15" 1,175.00
Pine, 3-tier, scroll-cut ends, old gr pnt, 39x44x6" 260.00
Pine, 4-tier, shoe ft, old red-brn pnt, 64x38x9" 460.00
Pine Co, appl molding:paneled/molded bracket, old bl pnt, 6x26x6" . 350.00
Pine Co, 3-tier, shaped sides, brn pnt, rprs, Am, 19th C, 27x21x6" 530.00
Pine Co, 3-tier, shoe ft, old red pnt, att NE, 61x30x8" 1,035.00
Pine Co, 4-tier, scrolled ends, dk brn pnt, 1850s, 38x40x8½" ... 1,650.00
Pine Co w/old grpt on red, CT, 17x14x10" 635.00
Teak Anglo-Indian w/much cvg, 3-tier, trestle base, 55x40x26", pr ... 6,600.00
Whatnot, mahog Wm IV, 3-tier w/full gallery, 44x53x21" 3,400.00

Sideboards

Cherry/mahog/rswd Fed w/stencil, 2 drw:candle+bottle drw:2 do, 60x44" .. 3,500.00
Credenza, pnt Venetian style, drw:4 sm drw & 2 do, 43x82x20" 2,825.00

Inlaid mahogany bowfront Sheraton, Massachusetts North Shore, figured oval birch panels, 70" long, $5,500.00. (Photo courtesy James D. Julia Inc.)

Mahog Fed w/gilt bronze, stepped drws:2 ped cupboards w/paw ft, 52x85" .. 5,575.00
Mahog Geo III w/inlay, brass gallery:2 drw & 2 do, cvd fans, 51x66x22" . 2,350.00
Mahog Hplwht, ovolo front w/central drw:2 do amid 2 do, rfn, 48x72" ... 3,750.00
Mahog Hplwht style, serpentine front, A Chapin, CT, 39x78x26" . 2,000.00

Mahog Hplwht style bowfront w/inlay, 2 drw amid 2 do w/faux drw fronts . 2,300.00
Mahog Late Fed, splash rail:molded drws:bowed center do, much cvg, 74" . 3,525.00
Pine/poplar/figured vnr Sheraton, 2 short:long drw:shelf, 36x36x19" ... 800.00
Server, red pnt on pine, 2-brd:dvtl drws:dbl panel do, 43x52x18" 2,500.00
Teak Danish, 5 drw, 2 sliding do, fitted int, 1960s, 32x57x19" 400.00

Sofas

Cherry Chpndl style, Marlboro front legs, damask uphl, 36x72" .. 975.00
Chesterfield, brn tufted leather Edwardian classic form, 1900s, 78" . 2,350.00
Chesterfield, dk gr leather, 2-cushion, 29x64x29" 1,925.00
Chpndl-style camelbk, molded sq legs, new uphl, 1890s, 79" 635.00
Lodge, faux leather w/antlers forming crest/arms/legs, 45x71x25" ... 350.00

Mahogany American Federal, scrolled acanthus carved terminals, hairy paw feet, 89" long, $4,500.00. (Photo courtesy James D. Julia Inc.)

Mahog Chpndl camelbk, rolled arms, fine uphl, 35½x70" 1,725.00
Mahog Emp style, paneled crest:scrolled arms, rfn/reuphl, 32x62" ... 250.00
Mahog Fed, bbl crest rail w/cvg, curved arms, reuphl, 89" 3,750.00
Mahog Fed, crest rail w/acanthus ears, rnded arms, reuphl, 35x73" ... 3,525.00
Mahog Fed w/inlay, serpentine bk, scrolling arms, reuphl, 36x85" .. 17,625.00
Mahog Hplwht style, arched bk:bowed seat:4 prs legs, Kittinger, 78" . 1,150.00
QA style w/bold curves, cabriole legs:pad ft, new uphl, 1900s, 48x63" . 800.00
Recamier, mahog Fed w/rosette cvgs, paw ft, horsehair uphl, 35x68" ... 2,500.00
Walnut Fed, cornucopia on crest:scrolled arms, old uphl, rprs, 75" L 275.00

Stands

Bedside, mahog Fed, molded drw:rope-twist legs, 32x20x16" 1,880.00
Bird's-eye maple Fed, overhang:drw:skirt:sq legs, rfn/rpl, 29x20x17" ... 900.00
Book, mahog, bk adjusts, trn support, rnd base, 13x10x6½" 500.00
Chamber/corner, mahog Fed, bksplash:quarter-rnd shelf, rfn, 41x22x16" . 765.00
Cherry Co, 2-brd grpt top:sq apron:thin trn legs, 28x18x17" 515.00
Cherry Fed, deep drw, str skirt, orig red pnt, 32x16x15" 2,600.00
Cherry Sheraton, dvtl/scratch-beaded drw, att OH Valley, 27x17x18" . 400.00
Cherry/curly maple Sheraton, drw, trn legs:ball ft, rfn/rpl, 29x20x18" . 350.00
Cherry/curly maple Sheraton, 2-drw, rope-trn legs, rfn, 28x21x21" ... 1,000.00
Cherry/pine Sheraton, 1-brd:dvtl drw:rope-twist legs, rfn, 29x20x18" .. 635.00
Dressing, pine, trn legs, floral stencil, blk/red grpt, NE, 33x32x14" 460.00
Kettle, mahog Geo, dished top:trn stem:spiral base:tripod, 28x11" dia ... 2,400.00
Work, cherry/figured vnr Emp, hinged top:curved drw, 29x23x19" .. 285.00

Stools

Footstool, chestnut/poplar, scroll-cut skirt w/appl dmns, 9x18x10" 200.00
Footstool, fruitwood Louis XVI, cvd rosettes, reuphl, 19x26x23" ... 1,880.00
Footstool, japanned decor on cabriole legs, reuphl, 12x16x13", VG .. 115.00
Footstool, mahog Fed, ogee molded fr:c&b ft, 16x20x19" 500.00
Footstool, mahog Fed, period ticking, splayed trn legs, pr 1,765.00
Footstool, pine w/dk red stain, openwork compass star top, 8x12x6" .. 285.00
Footstool, pnt pine, scroll-cut skirt, bj ends, 12x17x10" 115.00
Footstool, walnut, vase-trn legs w/Spanish ft, reuphl, 17x18x15" 230.00

Footstool, walnut Co, alligatored varnish, 4 flared ft, OH............315.00
Footstool, Windsor, 1-brd top:trn legs, 21x18x18" 460.00
Piano, rswd Fed, sq uphl seat w/serpentine edges, ped base, 20x15x15"..345.00

Tables

Banquet, mahog Geo III, 3-part, sq tapered legs w/spade ft, 103x45".. 2,235.00
Banquet, mahog Geo IV, 2 D-end tops/sq center, 3-ped, 30x117x59"..7,000.00
Bureau plat, mahog Louis XVI-style, leather:drw, bronze mts, Sormani..7,635.00
Center, gilt-bronze mtd ebonized & marquetry inlay R/R, 4-leg, 31x23"....900.00
Center, rswd Wm IV, oval beaded/molded top:twist support:cvd legs, 56"..2,585.00
Coffee, Art Deco, birch checkerbrd vnr, ebonized legs, 14x48x24"....450.00
Coffee, Kittinger drop-leaf, oval w/molded sq legs, 19x54x16" 115.00
Commode, mahog Fed, gallery:marble top:drw:do:cvd/lobed ft, 36x25x20" .3,525.00
Console, Continental Rococo pnt/parcel-gilt, marble top, 34x44x12"..2,000.00
Console, Louis XV style, faux marble:serpentine skirt, 51" 2,400.00
Console, mahog Fed w/brass inlay/bronze mts, marble top/pilasters, 71"..15,275.00
Console, pine Fed, demilune top:triangle skirt, blk rpt, 29x39x20" .800.00
Dining, mahog Emp style, beaded apron:ped:scroll ft, 60" dia+3 leaves .925.00
Dining, rswd Danish Modern, oval top:ped, Mobler, 1960s, 39x59x40"..425.00
Dressing, cherry Am QA, molded edge:long drw:3 short, fan cvg, 35x20"..3,165.00
Dressing, mahog/oak Chpndl, 2 drw:scroll-cut skirt, rfn, 37x32x19" .. 2,185.00
Dressing, mahog/oak Geo III, drw:shaped skirt:pad ft, rfn, 28x27x19"....860.00
Dressing, pine/chestnut/walnut Co, grpt w/yel pinstripe, 32x28" 1,850.00
Drop-leaf, mahog QA, cabriole legs:shaped knees, old finish, 41x40" .. 9,400.00
Drop-leaf, mahog/oak Co QA, 1-brd top, rprs, 31x33"+2 10" leaves .. 800.00
Drop-leaf, maple Chpndl, overhang top:str apron, NE, 28x41x42"..1,400.00
Drop-leaf, maple QA w/arched skirt:cabriole legs:pad ft, rprs, 43x43" ..550.00
Drop-leaf, tiger maple/maple QA, apron:cabriole legs:pad ft, 48x43"**...11,165.00
Drop-leaf, walnut QA, arched skirt, rosehead nails, rfn, 28x33x31" .2,400.00
Drop-leaf banquet, mahog/cherry Sheraton, swing legs, 3-pc, 86x45" .. 3,450.00
Drop-leaf/gate-leg, cherry/pine Sheraton, rfn, 29x62x21" 400.00
Farm, poplar, 2-brd top:trn legs, worn gr pnt, OH, 30x71x36"..1,500.00
Game, mahog Fed, shaped top:apron:acanthus cvd legs, rfn, 30x38x18" .. 3,000.00
Game, mahog Fed style, 1 leaf, rope-twist legs, rfn/rpr, 30x35x17"... 345.00
Game, mahog/pine Hplwht w/string inlay, rfn/rprs, 30x35x34".. 1,725.00
Game, walnut, 2 gate legs support top leaf, 2 candle shelves, 36x24"....575.00
Game/demilune, mahog George III w/string inlay, 1700s, 28x36x18" ..700.00
Library, elmwood R/R w/grpt, drw, faceted legs:spade ft, 120x30" 1,765.00
Library, mahog English, shaped top:massive c&b ft, 32x74x42".. 2,185.00
Lodge, oak top w/legs/supports made from entwined antlers, 30x45x31"..1,265.00
Pembroke, burled wood Hplwht style, 2 rnded leaves, drw, open: 45x23"....345.00
Pembroke, cherry Chpndl, 28x18"+hinged leaves w/serpentine edges. 1,725.00
Pembroke, maple/pine Hplwht w/red wash, 29x39x36"+2 leaves ...865.00
Pembroke, maple/tiger maple W/M gate-leg, old rfn, 42"**....23,500.00
Pier, ebonized/gilt Fed, marble top:Ionic capitals:cvd ft, 39x41x21"...3,750.00
Pier, marble top:skirt:2 marble columns:mirror:platform:cvd ft, 42" W..2,750.00
Pier, rswd Fed w/stencil, marble top:bead molding:barley twist, 40x55". 10,575.00
Refectory, elmwood British Renaissance style, trestle ft, 91x35" 4,100.00
Sawbuck, breadbrd top:red-brn grpt base, keyed dowel stretcher, 61". 1,800.00
Sawbuck, pine Co, 2-brd top, mortise & tenon, dry pnt, 27x37x26".. 4,000.00
Sawbuck, pine Co, 8-brd top w/breadbrd ends:brn pnt base, 28x46x24" .1,650.00
Sawbuck, scrubbed pine, 1-brd top: red pnt base, cracks, 24x34x21".550.00
Serving, mahog Geo III, rectangular top:fretwork frieze, 36x78x32" .. 4,000.00
Sewing, mahog Sheraton w/inlay, 2 drw (2nd w/cloth bag), 29x22x16"**.9,250.00
Sewing, mahog Vict w/inlay, satinwood/ebony int, lyre supports, 21x15"..725.00
Side, padoukwood SE Asian Export, frieze cvg, beast-form legs, 35x52".1,650.00
Side, rswd/faux marble Rococo Revival, drw, mc cvg, 29x38x18" .. 2,800.00
Tavern, maple QA Co, old red wash, scrubbed top, 26x36x27" ... 460.00
Tavern, maple/pine, breadbrd ends:str apron:sq stretchers, rfn, 55"..... 4,000.00
Tavern, maple/pine QA, breadbrd ends:str skirt:drw, NE, 28x46x28" .. 3,300.00
Tavern, pine Co, stretcher base w/trn legs, pegged, red pnt, 24x25x18".575.00
Tavern, pine/maple, 2-brd:str apron, pnt traces, NE, rpr, 27x36x28" .. 2,875.00
Tea, mahog Chpndl tilt-top, birdcage:trn post:tripod, 29x23" dia**.43,500.00

Tea, QA-style tray top w/C-scroll cabriole legs, 2-shelf, Kittinger...600.00
Tilt-top, mahog Geo III, twist-trn baluster stem:tripod, 29x33x29" 700.00
Tilt-top, mahog/maple QA, urn & column shaft, old rfn, 27 x34" dia.. 350.00
Tilt-top, walnut Chpndl, 1-brd:birdcage:tripod base, rfn/rpt, 28" dia .. 750.00
Tilt-top breakfast, mahog, 2-brd:trn ped:saber legs:brass ft, 49x36" 800.00
Tilt-top breakfast, mahog Regency, 3-sided plinth, 50" dia 1,200.00
Vitrine, mahog inlay & glass, canted corners, box stretcher, 27x24x17"..15,000.00

Work, inlaid mahogany Sheraton, raised glove box with figured mahogany splash guard, spiral-twist bobbin and onion turned legs, 37x20x20", $2,500.00. (Photo courtesy James D. Julia Inc.)

Work, mahog Fed, top w/ovolu corners:2 drw:trn legs, 30x22x17"**.23,500.00
Work, mahog/oak Geo III lady's, swivel/folding top, drw, rstr, 19x14" . 700.00
Work, tiger/bird's-eye maple, 2 banded drw:skirt:trn legs, rfn, 22x18". 1,400.00

Wardrobes

Kas, pine Am, cornice w/crest:panel do:drw:apron, ca 1870, 77x45".. 2,585.00
Mahog Chpndl style, cornice:3 drw:bombé base w/3 drw, 82x72x20".. 2,115.00
Pnt pine/poplar, crest:crown molding:2 panel do:drw, rpl lock, 78x45"..2,415.00
Poplar Co, single panel do w/appl devices, mustard pnt, OH, 81x48x22". 1,500.00
Walnut/poplar Am Gothic, knock-down type, 2 arch-panel do, 85x66x22"..2,200.00

Washstands

Cherry/pine Am Hplwht, apron:shelf:drw, old finish, 29x17x17" ...350.00
Curly maple/poplar Hplwht style, arched bk:drw:panel do, 33x22x18"..375.00
Mahog Fed, scrolled/arched top:drw:shaped shelf:trn legs, 38x21x15" . 1,295.00
Mahog/pine Sheraton, high bksplash:shelf:drw:trn legs, rfn, 41x24x17"..315.00

Mahogany Sheraton, three-quarter shaped and scalloped splash guard fitted with corner candle cups fitted for wash basin, 41x22x18", from $1,000.00 to $1,400.00. (Photo courtesy James D. Julia Inc.)

Tiger maple/cherry Fed, gallery:drw:apron, 35x20x15½" 1,000.00
Walnut/pine Sheraton, gallery:shelf:drw:trn legs, split, 37x22x19" ..375.00

Miscellaneous

Bed step, mahog, cut-out hdl, arched sides, 1800s, 18x17x12".....735.00

Coat rack, pine w/ornate cvg, brass & horn hooks, 1800s, 12x42x9".. 250.00
Cooler, wine; mahog Irish Geo III, brass mts, 20x32x22".......... 7,600.00
Pedestal, poplar w/red stain, pentagonal top, 1900s, 25x20x18" .. 400.00
Towel rack, cvd/pnt fans/tulips, pendant acorns conceal rod, 1942, 20" .1,200.00
Trolley, mahog English, gallery:2 tiers, castors, 1850s, 45x42x20" .1,400.00

Galena

Potteries located in the Galena, Illinois, area generally produced plain utility wares with lead glaze, often found in a pumpkin color with some slip decoration or splashes of other colors. These potteries thrived from the early 1830s until sometime around 1860. In the listings that follow, all items are made of red clay unless noted otherwise.

Flowerpot, redware, mottled earth tones, drain hole, 8", NM 110.00
Jar, canning; redware, splotchy oranges, 8⅛x4¾".......................... 235.00
Jar, canning; redware w/orange & gr splotches, 8x4¾" 440.00

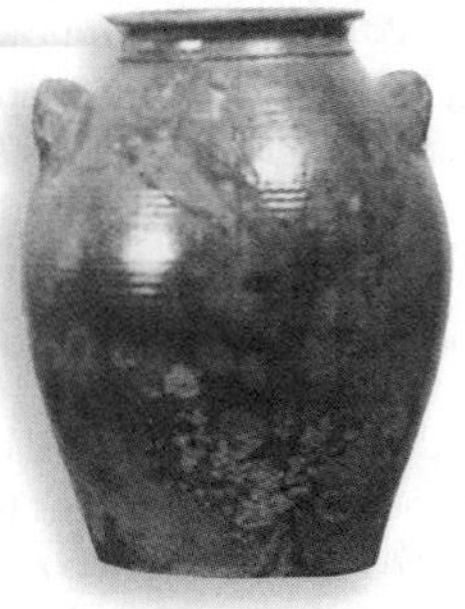

Jar, orange and brown dots on green, incised lines around body, 18", EX, $800.00. (Photo courtesy Garth's Auctions Inc.)

Jar, redware, gr w/orange & brn dots, ovoid, flared rim, hdls, 18", NM....1,250.00
Jug, pumpkin w/3 yel balloon-like splotches, strap hdl, 10".......6,300.00
Jug, redware, dk gr w/burnt orange spots, ribbed/strap hdl, 8¼", NM ...95.00

Galle

Emile Galle was one of the most important producers of cameo glass in France. His firm, founded in Nancy in 1874, produced beautiful cameo in the Art Nouveau style during the 1890s, using a variety of techniques. He also produced glassware with enameled decoration, as well as some fine pottery — animal figurines, table services, vases, and other objets d' art. In the mid-1880s he became interested in the various colors and textures of natural woods and as a result began to create furniture which he used as yet another medium for expression of his artistic talent. Marquetry was the primary method Galle used in decorating his furniture, preferring landscapes, Nouveau floral and fruit arrangements, butterflies, squirrels, and other forms from nature. It is for his cameo glass that he is best known today. All Galle is signed. Our advisor for this category is Don Williams; he is listed in the Directory under Missouri.

Key: fp – fire polished

Cameo

Atomizer, trees/mtns/lake, purple/bl/gr on frost, metal mts, 5½" ..800.00
Biscuit jar, floral, tangerine on clambroth, SP mts, Nouveau hdl, 10" .. 1,600.00
Bowl, clematis, lav & bl gray on lt bl, 4-lobe mouth, 3¼x6¼" ..1,035.00
Lamp, butterflies, earthen tones on pk/frost, 7" dome shade, 15½"...17,825.00
Lamp, butterflies/floral, 3-arm wrought base, 2¼" dome shade, 4"...975.00
Vase, bees/honeycombs, honey yel on clear, Cristallerie, 6¼"...10,925.00
Vase, bleeding hearts, red on amber/gr, red disk ft, 16½".........11,500.00
Vase, butterflies/foliage, gr/frost on mint gr, slim/waisted, 22½"... 4,000.00
Vase, cherries (mold blown), red-brn/gr/brn on peach frost, 10¼"... 12,650.00

Vase, cyclamen, red on gr to amber, windowpane technique, 6¼"....3,250.00
Vase, dragonflies/water lilies, caramel on med to lt bl, slim, 18" 14,950.00
Vase, dragonfly/pond, caramel on bl/frost/lt bl, stick neck, 22"..14,375.00
Vase, dragonfly/water lilies, tangerine on frost to bl, hdls, 8" 6,325.00
Vase, floral, mauve-brn on yel w/bl tinges, stick neck, 9" 1,560.00
Vase, floral, purples on frost, partly fp, flared rim, 12½"............. 3,600.00
Vase, floral branches, orange/red on lemon frost, cylindrical, 6½" .. 1,200.00
Vase, fruit, orange/sienna on med & dk brn to amber, sm neck, 15" .5,750.00
Vase, irises, lav/brn on amber to frost to gr-amber, 14½" 7,765.00
Vase, irises, purple on frost, 10" 4,000.00
Vase, morning glories, purple/gr/wht on martele, ca 1900, 11"..9,600.00
Vase, peonies, burgundy/pk on frost, flared cylinder, ca 1900, 18" .. 3,600.00
Vase, plums on branches, brn & gr on amber/wht frost, bl opal rim, 13"..12,075.00
Vase, raspberries (mold blown), red on yel, windowpane technique, 10"..6,325.00
Vase, roses, red on amber, windowpane technique, 12½" 7,250.00
Vase, trees/rocks/mtns, purple/bl on frost, 10¼"........................5,400.00
Vase, wisteria, gr & wht on lt olive frost, ca 1900, 23¼" 2,750.00

Vase, trumpet vine, red to cinnamon on bright yellow, 13½", $6,325.00. (Photo courtesy James D. Julia Inc.)

Enameled Glass

Pitcher, floral, mc w/gold, clear hdl, 7½" 3,000.00
Pitcher, floral/fruit, mc on smoky yel, geometric pnt amber hdl, 8" ..2,750.00
Plate, floral w/appl cabochons, ruffled rim, 6¼" 865.00

Vase, ferns, flowers, and butterfly on light amber with optic ribs, 7½", $5,500.00. (Photo courtesy Early Auction Co.)

Vase, floral, appl cabochon centers on opal amber, ftd, 4".........1,850.00
Vase, nymphs on 2 (of 4) prints, gold trim, ca 1890, 6½x9" 3,000.00
Vase, poppies on pale gr frost, 1890s, 7⅛" 3,125.00

Marquetry, Wood

Tray, lilies of the valley, ca 1890, 2½x11¼x14½" 1,025.00
Cabinet, display, clematis, glass door, side shelves, 60x32x18"..9,600.00
Table, dragonflies, ornate cvgs/scrolls, shelf, ca 1910s, sm 450.00
Table, nesting; floral studies, set or 4, lg: 28½x21¾x16".............8,000.00
Tray, cat sitting, ca 1890, 3¼x24½x6¼" 1,200.00

Pottery

Dish, asparagus; man w/harp beside lady, bl/yel leaves on wht, 11" ..315.00

Figurine, dog, sitting, bl/wht spots on yel, glass eyes, 13" 1,560.00
Pitcher, shepherd/flock/lake scene, bulbous, angle hdl, 6x5" 1,325.00
Tureen, yel rope/bl border/bud finial, 9x14", +18" underplate ... 1,000.00

Gambling Memorabilia

Gambling memorabilia from the infamous casinos of the West and items that were once used on the 'Floating Palace' riverboats are especially sought after by today's collectors.

Cage, chuck-a-luck; chromed cast metal w/5 Bakelite dice, 11½" ... 130.00
Cage, chuck-a-luck; iron base w/red & butterscotch Bakelite, 11x7" .. 250.00
Cage, chuck-a-luck; metal on wood base, 19x9½" sq, +felt layout .. 180.00
Card shuffler, metal w/wooden crank hdl, Nestor Johnson, NMIB ... 35.00

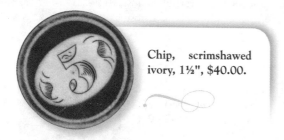

Chip, scrimshawed ivory, 1½", $40.00.

Coin changer, 4-column, NP steel w/push-down levers, 1940s 55.00
Dice, Flamingo Hotel, red w/wht dots, set of 6, MIB (clear w/logo) .. 70.00
Dice, gr (2nd amber), w/wht dots, ⅝", pr 15.00
Dice, ivory, bbl shape, late 1800s, EX, pr 65.00
Dice, orange mottled Bakelite, 2x2", pr 40.00
Dice cup, ribbed leather w/stitching, +5 blk/wht dice 60.00
Dice tray, pnt wood, felt lined, early 1900s, 16½x19½" 150.00
Game, Dmn Game-Fair Play, walnut w/glass face/marbles, Jones, 1890s ... 475.00
Game, Monte Carlo Craps, metal & glass, Mason & Co, Chicago, 2x24" .. 275.00
Game, pnt wheel w/star center, CI base, Mason & Co, 93x57" ... 2,470.00
Keno goose, mahog, trn oviform, late 1800s, 22x12½" 785.00
Keno goose, walnut, complete w/#d balls, ca 1910, 23x12½" 725.00
Penny toy, gaming wheel spinner, pnt tin, Germany, 3¾", NM 395.00
Poker chip, Dunes $1, sheik/harem girl/camel, bl border 80.00
Poker chip, ivory w/4 cvd leaves w/in detailed star border, 1880s .. 55.00
Poker chips, cvd flower center, red & gold borders, 1½", 9 for 180.00
Poker chips, red/bl/yel/wht plastic in sq wooden case w/hinged lid ... 50.00
Poker chips, red/blk/butterscotch Bakelite in rnd wooden holder ... 135.00
Poker chips, red/gr/butterscotch Bakelite, in red Bakelite holder 225.00
Poker chips, Royal Flush, 1870s, 180 metal chips in 10½x5" case ... 785.00
Poker table, 6 solid wood inserts for chips, felt top, base folds 120.00
Punch board, Slip Off Shore, pinup girl, 1940s, 9¼x5", NM 100.00

Wheel, gaming; wooden, ca. 1950s, 30", $480.00.

(Photo courtesy Morphy Auctions)

Wheel, pnt wood, dbl-sided, spoked center, 25" dia 165.00
Wheel, pnt wood, dice pnt on red w/gold, iron center hub, 26" dia ... 480.00

Wheel, pnt wood, red & blk, some nails missing, wall mt bracket, 24" .. 250.00
Wheel, tin litho, playing cards on gr, 11" dia 150.00
Wheel, traveling roulette; w/layout & chips, EX in 11x13" case .. 180.00

Gameboards

Gameboards, the handmade ones from the eighteenth and nineteenth centuries are collected more for their folk art quality than their relation to games. Excellent examples of these handcrafted 'playthings' sell well into the thousands of dollars; even the simple designs are often expensive. If you are interested in this field, you must study it carefully. The market is always full of 'new' examples. Well-established dealers are often your best sources; they are essential if you do not have the expertise to judge the age of the boards yourself. Our advisor for this category is Louis Picek; he is listed in the Directory under Iowa.

Carom, red/mustard pnt on pine, recessed pockets, 1800s, 31x31" ... 6,000.00
Checkers, blk/bl pnt, sq w/appl molding, bk: pnt figure, 18x18" .. 4,400.00
Checkers, blk/wht/red/salmon/bl pnt, 1-brd, 1800s, 16x15" 2,700.00
Checkers, blk/yel pnt, 1-brd w/appl molding, 15x12" 825.00
Checkers, pnt/stripes/geometrics (dbl-sided), ca 1900, 20x10" ... 2,500.00
Checkers, red/wht pnt w/stars/shields/etc at border, 1890s, 19x18" ... 18,800.00
Checkers, red/yel/blk pnt, 1-brd, w/appl molding, 1890s, 15x15" .. 1,880.00
Checkers, salmon/blk olive pnt, 1800s, 16½x16" 2,000.00
Checkers, yel/blk checks, mc pnt borders, 1-brd, 19th C, 17x14" .. 4,700.00
Checkers (dbl-sided), blk/mustard/dk bl pnt, wear, 1800s, 25x15" .. 1,300.00
Checkers/backgammon, mc pnt on canvas, crackling, 22x30" .. 1,500.00
Checkers/backgammon, mc pnt on panel, appl molding, splits, 18x16" .. 2,600.00

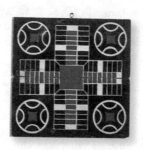

Checkers/parcheesi, folding, American, late 1800s, 21x21", $1,840.00. (Photo courtesy Skinner Inc. Auctioneers & Appraisers of Antiques & Fine Art)

Checkers/parcheesi, mc pnt, molding (losses), 1800s, 19x17" ... 4,000.00
Parcheesi, mc on creamy wht pnt, mitered fr, ca 1900, 17x17" . 4,400.00
Parcheesi, muted mc pnt on brd, appl molding, ca 1900, 13x13" .. 6,500.00
Parcheesi, scenic corners, mc pnt, sgn LC, 18x18" 660.00
Parcheesi, 4-color on wht sq panel, losses/age cracks, ca 1900, 10x20" ... 5,900.00
Snakes & Ladders, mc pnt, breadbrd ends, age crack, ca 1900, 24x18" 64,625.00

Games

Collectors of antique games are finding it more difficult to find their treasures at shows and flea markets. Most of the action these days seems to be through specialty dealers and auctions. The appreciation of the art on the boards and boxes continues to grow. You see many of the early games proudly displayed as art, and they should be. The period from the 1850s to 1910 continues to draw the most interest. Many of the games of that period were executed by well-known artists and illustrators. The quality of their lithography cannot be matched today. The historical value of games made before 1850 has caused interest in this period to increase. While they may not have the graphic quality of the later period, their insights into the social and moral character of the early nineteenth century are interesting.

Twentieth-century games invoke a nostalgic feeling among collectors who recall looking forward to a game under the Christmas tree each year. They search for examples that bring back those Christmas-morning memories. While the quality of their lithography is certainly less than the early games, the introduction of personalities from the comic strips, radio, and later TV created new interest. Every child wanted a game that featured their favorite character. Monopoly, probably the most famous game ever produced, was introduced during the Great Depression. For further information, we recommend *Schroeder's Collectible Toys, Antique to Modern*, available from Collector Books.

ABC Card Game, Parker Bros, 1900s, VGIB 15.00
Across the Continent, Parker Bros, 1960s, EXIB 25.00
Air Mail, Archer Toy, 1930s, EX+IB 80.00
Alee-Oop, Royal Toy, 1937, EXIB 20.00
America's Yacht Race, McLoughlin Bros, 1904, EXIB 475.00
Baseball Challenge, Tri-Valley, 1980s, NM+IB 40.00
Batter Up, M Hopper, 1940s, EX+IB 35.00
Battle Checkers, Pen Man, 1920s, EX+IB 25.00
Beat the 8 Ball, Ideal, 1975, NM+IB 20.00
Bible Baseball, Standard, 1950s, NM+IB 100.00
Boy Scouts, McLoughlin Bros, 1910s, EXIB 115.00
Camelot, Parker Bros, 1950s, EX+IB 25.00
Clean Sweep, Schaper, 1960s, NM+IB 25.00

Conflict, Parker Bros., first edition with Tootsie-toy game pieces, ca. 1940 – WWII, EX, $225.00.

(Photo courtesy Paul Fink)

Country Fair Card Game, Parker Bros, 1890s, EXIB 50.00
Derby Day, Parker Bros, 1930, EXIB 50.00
Doctors & the Quack Card Game, Parker Bros, 1890s, VGIB 40.00
Dog Race, Transogram, 1930s, EX+IB 25.00
Dogfight, Milton Bradley, 1960s, NMIB 50.00
Easy Money, Milton Bradley, 1936, VGIB 25.00
Ella Cinders, Milton Bradley, 1944, EXIB 25.00
Fast Mail Game, Milton Bradley, 1910s, VGIB 75.00
Fortune Teller, Milton Bradley, Whitman, 1934, VGIB 35.00
Game of Advance & Retreat, Milton Bradley, 1900s, EXIB 100.00
Game of Friendly Fun, Milton Bradley, 1939, EX+IB 75.00
Game of the Wild West, Bliss, 1880s, VGIB 600.00
Games You Like To Play, Parker Bros, 1920s, EXIB 50.00
Graphic Baseball, Northwestern Prod, 1930s, VGIB 125.00
Green Ghost Game, Transogram, 1960s, NMIB 100.00
Hit That Line, LaRue Sales, 1930s, VGIB 50.00
Home Court Basketball, 1950s, EXIB 150.00
Intercollegiate Football, Hustler, 1920s, EX+IB 200.00
Journey to Bethlehem, Parker Bros, 1920s, EXIB 100.00
Kentucky Derby Racing, Whitman, 1930s, EXIB 25.00
Lame Duck, Parker Bros, 1920s, EX+IB 75.00
Leslie's Ballgame, Perfection, 1910s, EXIB 150.00
Let's Play Polo, American Toy, 1940s, EXIB 50.00
Little Boy Blue, Milton Bradley, 1910s, NMIB 75.00
Lost in the Woods, McLoughlin Bros, 1895, VGIB 500.00
Mail Run, Quality Games, 1960s, EX+IB 50.00
Man Hunt, Parker Bros, 1930s, VGIB 125.00
Merry Hunt, Singer, VGIB 150.00
Merry Milkman, Hasbro, 1950s, NMIB 75.00
Movie Millions, Transogram, 1930s, EX+IB 150.00
Neck & Neck, Wolverine, 1930s, EX+IB 75.00
New Game of Piggies, Selchow & Righter, 1894, VGIB 225.00

Owl & the Pussy Cat, Clark, 1900s, EXIB 200.00
Race for the Cup, Milton Bradley, 1910s, VGIB 150.00
Rat Patrol, Transogram, 1966, EX+IB 50.00
Rin-Tin-Tin, Transogram, 1950s, NMIB 50.00
Runaway Sheep, Bliss, 1890s, EXIB 150.00
Sandlot Slugger, Milton Bradley, 1960s, EX+IB 40.00
Skirmish, Milton Bradley, 1970s, NMIB 50.00
SOS, Durable Toy & Novelty, 1940s, EXIB 75.00
Stratego, Milton Bradley, 1960s, wooden parts, VGIB 35.00
Superboy Game, Hasbro, 1960s, EXIB 50.00
Sweepstakes, Haras, 1930s, EXIB 50.00
Ten Pins, Mason & Parker, 1920s, EX+IB 50.00
Thorobred, Lowe, 1940s, EXIB 50.00
Tourist, A Railroad Game, Milton Bradley, 1900s, VGIB 75.00
Varsity Race, Parker Bros, 1899, EXIB 450.00
West Point, Ottoman, 1900s, EX+IB 150.00
Winko Baseball, Milton Bradley, 1940s, EXIB 50.00
Winnie-the-Pooh Game, Parker Bros, 1933, EX+IB 100.00
Yacht Race, Pressman, 1930s, VGIB 50.00
Zippy Zepps, All-Fair, 1930s, VGIB 300.00

Personalities, Movies, and TV Shows

Adventures of Popeye, Transogram, 1950s, EX+IB 50.00
Alice in Wonderland, Parker Bros, 1930s, VGIB 50.00
Babes in Toyland, Whitman, 1960s, NMIB 30.00
Bat Masterson, Lowell, 1950s, EX+IB 25.00
Buck Rogers Siege of Gigantica Game, Lutz & Scheinkman, 1930s, VGIB... 500.00
Captain Gallant Desert Fort Game, Transogram, 1950s, EXIB 25.00
Charlie McCarthy's Flying Hats, Whitman, 1930s, EX+IB 30.00
Crusader Rabbit TV Game, Tryne, 1960s, EX+IB 75.00
Dick Tracy Detective Game, Einson-Freeman, 1930s, VGIB 50.00
Dick Tracy Playing Card Game, Whitman, 1930s, NMIB 50.00
Donald Duck's Own Party Game, Parker Bros, 1930s, EXIB 50.00
Dracula Mystery Game, Hasbro, 1960s, NMIB 150.00
Elsie the Cow Game, Selchow & Righter, 1940s, EXIB 35.00
Farmer Jone's Pigs, McLoughlin Bros, 1890s, VGIB 100.00
Fugitive, Ideal, 1960s, EX+IB 40.00
Game of Red Riding Hood, Chaffee & Selchow, 1890s, EX+IB .. 250.00
Game of Skippy, Milton Bradley, 1930s, VGIB 50.00
Get Smart, Ideal, 1960s, EXIB 25.00
Gilligan's Island, Game Gems, 1960s, EX+IB 150.00
Godzilla, Mattel, 1970s, EX+IB 40.00
Good Old Game of Oliver Twist, Parker Bros, 1880s, VGIB 100.00
Green Acres, Standard Toykraft, 1960s, EXIB 75.00
Gunsmoke, Lowell, 1950s, EX+IB 50.00
Hogan's Heroes, Transogram, 1960s, EXIB 50.00
Howdy Doody's TV Game, Milton Bradley, 1950s, EXIB 25.00
Jack & Jill, Milton Bradley, 1900s, EXIB 50.00
Jack & the Beanstalk Adventure Game, Transogram, 1950s, NMIB... 35.00
James Bond Message From M, Ideal, 1960s, EXIB 150.00
James Bond 007 Goldfinger Game, Milton Bradley, 1960s, EX+IB... 45.00
Jonny Quest Game, Transogram, 1960s, EX+IB 250.00
Justice League of America, Hasbro, 1960s, EXIB 75.00
Kate Smith's Own Game America, Toy Creations, 1940s, EXIB ... 35.00
Little Black Sambo, Einson-Freeman, 1930s, EX+IB 100.00
Little Jack Horner, Milton Bradley, 1910s, EXIB 50.00
Little Orphan Annie Game, Milton Bradley, 1920s, EX+IB 150.00
Lone Ranger Game, Parker Bros, 1930s, EXIB 50.00
Mickey Mouse Basketball, Gardner, 1950s, EXIB 50.00
Mickey Mouse Circus Game, Marks Bros, 1930s, EX+IB 200.00
Mickey Mouse Old Maid Game, Whitman, 1930s, EX+IB 50.00
Mighty Hercules Game, Hasbro, 1960s, EX+IB 175.00
Miss Muffet Game, 1910s, EX+IB 75.00

Monkees Game, Transogram, 1960s, EX+IB............ 75.00
Mother Goose Bowling Game, Crandall, 1880s, EXIB................. 500.00
Munsters Picnic Game, Hasbro, 1965, VG+IB.............. 150.00
Murder on the Orient Express, Ideal, 1960s, EXIB 25.00
My Favorite Martian, Transogram, 1960s, VGIB............. 30.00
My First Game (Walt Disney Character), Gabriel, 1960s, EXIB.... 25.00
Nancy Drew Mystery Game, Parker Bros, 1950s, NMIB 100.00
National Velvet Game, Transogram, 1950s, EXIB.................. 20.00
Nebbs on the Air, A Radio Game, Milton Bradley, 1930s, EX+IB .. 100.00
Petticoat Junction, Toykraft, 1960s, NMIB.................. 60.00
Pinocchio the Merry Puppet Game, Milton Bradley, EXIB............ 50.00
Planet of the Apes, Milton Bradley, 1970s, EXIB 25.00

Popeye Shipwreck Game (board only), King Features, heavy cardboard, 1933, matted and framed, 21x27", $150.00. (Photo courtesy Bertoia Auctions)

Rebel, Ideal, 1960s, EXIB 50.00
Red Riding Hood & The Wolf, McLoughlin Bros, 1880s, VGIB... 50.00
Red Ryder 'Whirli-Crow' Target Game, Daisy, 1940s, EX+IB...... 175.00
Ricochet Rabbit, Ideal, 1960s, EXIB...................... 50.00
Shazam, Captain Marvel's Own Game, Reed & Associated, 1950s, EXIB..35.00
Smokey The Forest Fire Prevention Bear, Ideal, 1960s, EX+IB 40.00
Snagglepuss Fun at the Picnic, Transogram, 1960s, NMIB............ 45.00
Three Stooges Fun House Game, Lowell, 1950s, EXIB 150.00
Time Tunnel Game, Ideal, 1966, EXIB 100.00
Toonerville Trolley Game, Milton Bradley, 1920s, EX+IB 150.00
Twilight Zone, Ideal, 1960s, VGIB........................... 50.00
Uncle Sam's Mail, McLoughlin Bros, 1890s, VGIB..................... 125.00
Uncle Wiggily's New Airplane Game, Milton Bradley, 1920s, EX+IB... 100.00
Walt Disney's Sleeping Beauty Game, Whitman, 1950s, EXIB...... 35.00
Wanted Dead or Alive, Lowell, 1950s, NMIB.................. 75.00

Garden City Pottery

Founded in 1902 in San Jose, California, by the end of the 1920s this pottery had grown to become the largest in Northern California. During that period production focused on stoneware, sewer pipe, and red clay flowerpots. In the late '30s and '40s, the company produced dinnerware in bright solid colors of yellow, green, blue, orange, cobalt, turquoise, white, and black. Royal Arden Hickman, who would later gain fame for the innovative artware he modeled for the Haeger company, designed not only dinnerware but a line of Art Deco vases and bowls as well. The company endured hard times by adapting to the changing needs of the market and during the '50s concentrated on production of garden products. Foreign imports, however, proved to be too competitive, and the company's pottery production ceased in 1979.

Because none of the colored-glazed products were ever marked, to learn to identify the products of this company, you'll need to refer to *Sanford's Guide to Garden City Pottery* by Jim Pasquali. Values apply to items in all colors (except black) and all patterns, unless noted otherwise. Due to relative rarity, 20% should be added for any item found in black.

Bean pot, Deco, w/lid, lg.......................... 85.00
Bean pot, plain, 1-qt........................ 25.00

Bowl, Bulb, 10" 45.00
Bowl, mixing; Wide-Ring, solid color, #3 (mid sz)..................... 30.00
Bowl, nappy, #4................................. 25.00
Bowl, soup; plain, solid color 35.00
Bowl, Succulent, 11"........................ 60.00
Candleholders, flared ft, solid color, 3", pr 45.00

Carafe, flaring panels, 10", $450.00. (Photo courtesy Jack Chipman)

Casserole, narrow or wide rings, solid color, 7", ea........................ 35.00
Cookie jar, Deco style, solid color, 7½" 75.00
Crock, 2-gal.................................. 45.00
Cup, punch 15.00
Frog, sm.................................. 15.00
Jardiniere, ribbed solid color, 10"................... 45.00
Mug, chowder; solid color, w/lid..................... 45.00
Oil jar, hand thrown, mini................... 150.00
Pitcher, 2-qt 55.00
Plate, artichoke; solid color 40.00
Plate, dinner; solid color, 9"................ 20.00
Ramekin, solid color, 3".................... 20.00
Teapot, Deco style, solid color, 4-cup 75.00
Vase, Deco, 4½x10" 65.00
Vase, Ribbed Cylinder, 8" 35.00
Water cooler, crockery........................ 75.00

Gardner Porcelain

Models of wonderfully complicated and detailed subjects illustrating people of many nations absorbed in day-to-day activities were made by this company from the turn of the nineteenth cuentury until well past the 1850s. The factory was founded in 1765 near Moscow, Russia, by an Englishman by the name of Francis Gardner. They are still in business today.

Bowl, floral reserves on burgundy w/gold, late 19th C, 7⅛".......... 475.00
Figurine, coachman, long bl coat, hands on hips, ca 1845, 7⅜"... 4,800.00
Figurine, grain seller stands w/coins before grain mound, 19th C, 8" .. 2,150.00
Figurine, man in hat/long coat, stands w/watch in hand, 1810s, 7⅛" ... 19,500.00
Figurine, nude lady w/pk bonnet & fur muff, ca 1845, 7¾" 11,750.00
Figurine, peasant girl w/flower basket, early 19th C, 5¼" 3,850.00
Figurine, peasant lady dancing, wht apron, 19th C, 8" 1,200.00
Figurine, peasant lady on bench feeds baby, child beside, 5½" ..1,200.00
Figurine, peasant man dancing, long fur-lined coat, 10½".........1,800.00
Figurine, peasant man seated & sprinkling salt on bread, 19th C, 6"..2,100.00
Figurine, Spaniard w/short coat over his shoulders, 1820s, 7¾".. 8,400.00
Figurine, vagabond seated, boots/ bag beside him, late 19th C, 6x4" ..660.00
Figurine, woodsman w/load of kindling in wheelbarrow, 8½"....1,950.00
Figurine, youthful man stands & holds tree branch, mid-19th C, 4"..2,850.00
Pen holder, dog seated by tree trunk, rococo base, 19th C, 2½" .. 1,325.00
Plate, Napoleon entering Moscow, gr & gold rim, 19th C, 10"....960.00

Gas Globes and Panels

Gas globes and panels, once a common sight, have vanished from the countryside but are being sought by collectors as a unique form of advertising memorabilia. Early globes from the 1920s (some date back to as early as 1912), now referred to as 'one-piece' (Type 4) globes, were made of molded milk glass and were globular in shape. The gas company name was etched or painted on the glass. Few of these were ever produced, and this type is valued very highly by collectors today.

A new type of pump was introduced in the early 1930s; the old 'visible' pumps were replaced by 'electric' models. Globes were changing at the same time. By the mid-teens a three-piece (Type 3) globe consisting of a pair of inserts and a metal body was being produced in both 15" and 16½" sizes. Collectors prefer to call globes that are not one-piece or metal frame 'three-piece glass' (Type 2). Though metal-framed globes with glass inserts (Type 3) were most popular in the 1920s and 1930s, some were actually made as early as 1914. Though rare in numbers, their use spans many years. In the 1930s Type 2 globes became the replacements of the one-piece globe and Type 3 globes. The most recently manufactured gas globes are made with a plastic body that contains two 13½" glass lenses. These were common in the '50s but were actually used as early as 1932. This style is referred to as Type 1 in our listings. Values here are for examples with both sides in excellent condition: no chips, wear, or other damage. Our advisor for this category is Scott Benjamin; he is listed in the Directory under Ohio. For more information we recommend *Value Guide to Gas Station Memorabilia* by B.J Summers and Wayne Priddy.

Note: Standard Crowns with raised letters are one-piece globes that were made in the 1920s; those made in the 1950s (no raised letters), though one-piece, are not regarded as such by today's collectors.

Type 1, Plastic Body, Glass Inserts (Inserts 13½") — 1931 – 1950s

Aro Flight, dk bl/wht/orange-red, EX	1,500.00
D-X Marine, rare	1,800.00
Dino Supreme, sm dinosaur, red/wht/gr	250.00
Dixie, plastic band	250.00
Fleet-Wing	400.00
Frontier Gas, Rarin' To Go, w/horse	1,000.00
Hercules Ethyl Gasoline, red/wht/gr, new Capco gr fr	375.00
Kendal Deluxe, Capco body w/red pnt, 13½"	350.00
Malco, orig bl-gr Capco fr	2,000.00
Marathon, no runner	250.00
New State 88	750.00
Phillips 66	350.00
Phillips 66 Flite-Fuel	450.00
Pride Ethyl, red/wht/bl, oval, new Capco fr, scarce	450.00
Pure, blk on milk glass, orig Capco fr, 1960s	375.00
Road King, knight on horse, red on wht, Capco fr, 1950s	1,250.00
Sinclair Dino	300.00
Sinclair H-C Gasoline, red & gr on wht	250.00
Skelly Keotane	250.00
Speedway 79, red/wht/bl, Capco fr, ca 1955	550.00
Spur, oval body	350.00
Stone's Ethyl, yel/bl/wht, Capco fr	400.00
Sunray Ethyl Corp	1,600.00
Super Flash, red lighting flash, Capco fr, 1960s	650.00
Texaco Diesel Chief, Capco body, 13½"	1,000.00
Viking, pictures Viking ship	2,500.00

Type 2, Glass Frame, Glass Inserts (Inserts 13½") — 1926 – 1940s

Aerio, w/airplane	15,000.00
Aladdin Gasoline, 2-lens w/side body	850.00

Amoco, Gill body, 13½"	500.00
Atlantic, red/wht/bl, ca 1966	500.00
Atlantic (new logo), Gill body, ca 1966	650.00
Atlantic Hi-Arc, red/wht/bl, Gill fr, ca 1936	650.00
Barnsdall Be Square Gasoline, 2 lenses in wide body	600.00
Bay Ethyl, Gill glass	750.00
Capitol Gasoline Ethyl Corp	500.00
Capitol Kerosene Oil Co	600.00
Col-Tex Service Gasoline, 5-color	1,250.00
Derby, Gill body	750.00
Derby's Flexgas Ethyl, threaded base, Gill fr, 1940s	850.00
Esso	325.00
Frontier Gas, Double Refined	400.00
Gladiator Gasoline, w/swords, 3 pc glass, 1930s	1,500.00
Globe Gasoline, metal base ring	2,000.00
Guyler Brand, milk glass	1,400.00
Hustol, yel & blk on milk glass, wide fr	450.00
Kan O Tex, Gill body, metal base ring	1,250.00
Lion, Knix Knox, metal base	3,000.00
Marine Gasoline, sea horse, red/turq/wht, 1940s	2,500.00
Martin Purple Martin Ethyl	850.00
Never Nox Ethyl	750.00
Pitman Streamlined, Gill body, 13½"	15,000.00
Pure	500.00
Safeway Perfecto Regular Oil Co, single lens, 1930s-40s	1,000.00
Sinclair H-C Gasoline, red/wht/gr	500.00
Sinclair Pennant	1,000.00
Sky Chief, Gill body, 13½"	650.00
Sohio Diesel Supreme, orig wide fr	350.00
Standard Crown, bl	800.00
Standard Crown, gr crown, tractor fuel, rare	2,000.00
Standard Crown, gray	2,000.00
Standard Crown, red or gold, ea	400.00
Standard Crown, wht	350.00
Texaco Ethyl	2,000.00
Tydol A Ethyl, red/blk on milk glass, Gill fr, ca 1946	1,250.00
United Hi-Test Gasoline, red/wht/bl	450.00
White Flash, Gill body	650.00
WNAX, w/radio station pictured	5,000.00

Aetna Motor Gasoline, 13½", $1,000.00. (Photo courtesy B. J. Summers and Wayne Priddy)

Type 3, Metal Frame, Glass Inserts (Inserts 15" or 16½") — 1915 – 1930s

Aero Mobilgas, new metal body, rare, 15"	3,000.00
Atlantic Ethyl, 16½"	950.00
Atlantic White Flash, 16½"	850.00
Blue Anti-Knock Gasoline, Interstate Oil Gas	1,200.00
Blue Flash (Richfield Oil), ca 1925, 15"	750.00
Bluebird Anti-Knock Gasoline, bl on milk glass, 1930s, 15"	2,750.00
Conoco Gasoline, silhouette figure on yel, 1913-29	6,000.00
Farmer's Union High Octane, red/wht/bl, high-profile metal body, 15"	850.00
General Ethyl, 15" fr, complete	4,000.00
General Motor Fuel, red/yel/blk on wht, early, 15"	2,000.00

Humble Oils, red/bl/wht, orig red fr, NM....2,500.00
Marathon, low-profile metal body, 15"....1,500.00
Mobilgas, red Pegasus, blk letters, 16½"....850.00
Mobilgas Ethyl, no horse, 16½", EX....600.00
Mohawk Gasoline, Indian's portrait, red version, 1930s....12,000.00
Peerless Gasoline, red & bl on milk glass, 15"....850.00
Phillips Benzo, low-profile metal body, 15"....6,000.00
Purol Gasoline, w/arrow, porc body....900.00
Purol the Pure Oil, bl & wht, 15"....750.00
Red Star Gasoline, blk w/red star on wht, new fr, 1920s, 15"....850.00
Richfield Ethyl, blk & yel eagle, red lettering, ca 1939....1,250.00
Rocor Gasoline, eagle, blk & yel on milk glass, ca 1939....1,250.00
Royal Gasoline w/Maine pictured, high-profile metal body, 15"....2,500.00
Signal, old stoplight, 15"....8,000.00
Stonolined Aviation, rare, 16½"....20,000.00

Super Speed, complete, $2,850.00; Mobilgas, complete, $750.00. (Photo courtesy Collector's Auction Service)

Texaco Leaded, glass globe....4,000.00
White Star, 15" fr, complete....2,000.00

Type 4, One-Piece Glass Globes, No Inserts, Co. Name Etched, Raised or Enameled — 1912 – 1931

Atlantic, chimney cap....6,000.00
Imperial Premier Gasoline, red & yel on milk glass, rpt....1,000.00
Mobil Gargoyle, gargoyle pictured, oval....2,500.00
Newport Gasoline Oils, orange & gr on milk glass, VG....2,500.00
Pierce Pennant, etched....4,500.00
Shell, rnd, etched....750.00
Sinclair Gasoline, etched, orig pnt, 1920s, VG+....2,000.00
Sinclair Gasoline baked on milk glass, ca 1926-29....1,750.00
Sinclair HC Gasoline, red/wht/blk on milk glass, 1927-29....1,750.00
Sinclair Oils, etched, 1920s, G- pnt....2,000.00
Standard Crown, red or gold, ea....400.00
Standard Crown, wht....350.00
Super Shell, clam shape....1,800.00
Super Shell, clam shape, rnd version....3,500.00
Texaco, etched letters, wide body....2,500.00
Texaco Ethyl....2,500.00
That Good Gulf..., emb, orange & blk letters....1,500.00
White Eagle, blunt nose, 20¾"....1,800.00
White Eagle, detailed eagle, 20¾"....2,500.00
White Rose, boy pictured, pnt....5,000.00

Gaudy Dutch

Inspired by Oriental Imari wares, Gaudy Dutch was made in England from 1800 to 1820. It was hand decorated on a soft-paste body with rich underglaze blues accented in orange, red, pink, green, and yellow. It differs from Gaudy Welsh in that there is no lustre (except on Water Lily). There are seventeen patterns, some of which are War Bonnet, Grape, Dahlia, Oyster, Urn, Butterfly, Carnation, Single Rose, Double Rose, and Water Lily.

Values hinge on condition, strength of color, detail, and variations to standard designs. Unless otherwise noted, our values are based on near-mint to mint condition items, with only minimal wear or scratches. Even a piece rated excellent may bring from 60% to 75% less than these prices. We have used the term 'chain' to refer to a border device less detailed than one with distinguishable hearts or leaves, as the latter will bring higher prices. When ranges are used, the higher side will represent an item with better than average color and execution.

Butterfly, plate, bl band w/wavy line+inner leaf border, 8"....2,200.00
Butterfly, plate, yel chain in bl band+wavy line border, 6½"....3,100.00
Butterfly, plate, yel ovals in bl band+inner leaf border, 8", $2,200 to .3,100.00
Butterfly, teapot, bl band w/wavy lines on body/lid, rprs, 5½", VG..725.00
Carnation, cup plate, yel chain in bl band border, 3¾", VG....1,550.00
Carnation, plate, yel chain in bl band+waves border, 5½"....480.00
Carnation, plate, yel chain in bl band+waves border, 6¾"....960.00
Carnation, plate, yel ovals in bl band+inner leaf border, 8"....1,550.00

Carnation, plate, yellow ovals in blue band, yellow leaf inner border, strong colors, 9", EX, $600.00. (Photo courtesy Garth's Auctions Inc./LiveAuctioneers.com)

Carnation, soup plate, yel ovals in bl band+inner leaf border, 8½"....700.00
Carnation, soup bowl, yel ovals in bl band+inner leaf border, 10"....1,080.00
Carnation, sugar bowl, yel chain in bl band border, w/lid, 5x6", VG..780.00
Carnation, teapot, yel chain in bl band, strong colors, 6¼x10½"..2,880.00
Carnation, waste bowl, yel chain in bl band border, 3x6½", VG..480.00
Dahlia, plate, bl band, red hearts & wavy line border, 8"....6,600.00
Dahlia, tea bowl & saucer, bl band, red hearts border, sm flakes to ft..4,500.00
Dahlia, waste bowl, bl band, red heart border, 3x5½"....8,600.00
Double Rose, creamer, helmet shape, shaped hdl, 5"....1,375.00
Double Rose, creamer, mask under spout, octagonal, 6", EX....9,000.00
Double Rose, cup plate, 3⅝"....1,350.00
Double Rose, plate, 7½", from $420 to....540.00
Double Rose, plate, 10"....1,560.00
Double Rose, platter, 10" L....7,200.00
Double Rose, soup plate, 9"....540.00
Double Rose, soup plate, 10"....900.00
Double Rose, sugar bowl, w/lid, 5", EX....2,400.00
Double Rose, tea bowl & saucer, from $400 to....535.00
Double Rose, teapot, rectangular, 6¼", from $2,400 to....3,200.00
Double Rose, waste bowl, 2⅝x5½"....350.00
Dove, plate, bl band w/wavy lines+inner leaf border, 9¾"....880.00
Dove, plate, narrow bl rim band, 7½"....475.00
Dove, tea bowl & saucer, bl band w/wavy lines border, VG+....1,020.00
Dove, waste bowl, inside rim w/band of stripes & flowers, 2¾x5½"..1,200.00
Grape, cup plate, yel chain on bl band, 3½"....990.00
Grape, pitcher, yel chain on bl band border, 4¾"....2,000.00
Grape, pitcher, yel hearts on bl band border, flaring ft, 9½", VG+..9,600.00
Grape, plate, yel chain on bl band border, 9⅞"....1,100.00
Grape, soup plate, yel chain on bl band border, sm mfg flaw, 7"....495.00
Grape, tea bowl & saucer, flared sides, yel chain on bl band border....780.00
Grape, teapot, 7"; creamer, 4½"; sugar bowl, w/lid, 5½", all EX.2,400.00
Grape, toddy plate, yel heart chain on bl band border, 4½"....1,500.00
Leaf, bowl, yel heart chain in bl band border, 1⅝x8⅜", EX....4,200.00
Oyster, bowl, deep, 10"....750.00

Oyster, plate, 6⅜", from $400 to 510.00
Oyster, tea bowl & saucer, from $500 to 650.00
Oyster, tea bowl & saucer, w/King's Rose, pk band w/hearts & swags, EX . 400.00
Oyster, teapot, w/King's Rose, pk trim, 5¼"........................2,530.00
Oyster, teapot, 6⅛", from $2,500 to 2,650.00
Primrose, tea bowl & saucer, yel heart chain in bl band border, EX ...3,200.00

Single Rose, coffeepot, acanthus spout and handle, repair, 11", from $2,800.00 to $3,000.00. (Photo courtesy Garth's Auctions Inc./ LiveAuctioneers.com)

Single Rose, coffeepot, domed lid, scroll hdl, acanthus spout, EX, 12" 2,300.00
Single Rose, creamer, yel chain in bl band border, EX, 4¼" 720.00
Single Rose, plate, exceptional detail, pale pk flowers, 8⅜".......1,800.00
Single Rose, plate, yel chain in lt bl band border, 8⅛"..................535.00
Single Rose, soup bowl, yel ovals in bl band border, 9⅞".............840.00
Single Rose, tea bowl & saucer, variant 2,640.00
Single Rose, teapot, yel chain in bl band border, VG 780.00
Single Rose, toddy plate, imp flower mk, 4" 840.00
Sunflower, plate, bl band w/waves+inner leaf border, 9¾".........1,000.00
Sunflower, plate, deep; 9¾"...1,800.00
Sunflower, tea bowl & saucer, bl band w/waves, from $500 to 660.00
Sunflower, teapot, bl/dk brn band w/waves border, prof rstr, 10" ...5,700.00
Urn, plate, paneled floral border, 10", EX 480.00
Urn, plate, yel chain on bl band+waves border, 7½" 1,020.00
Urn, tea bowl & saucer, EX+, from $300 to 450.00
War Bonnet, bowl, shallow, 8⅛"......................................960.00
War Bonnet, creamer, line border, 4⅜", EX 850.00
War Bonnet, cup plate, 4⅝"...1,450.00
War Bonnet, plate, 9¾", from $1,300 to...............................1,450.00
War Bonnet, soup plate, 8½"..825.00
War Bonnet, tea bowl & saucer..800.00
Zinnia, plate, dk brn-lined bl band w/leaf chain, Riley, 8¼"......3,000.00

Gaudy Welsh

Gaudy Welsh was an inexpensive hand-decorated ware made in both England and Wales from 1820 until 1860. It is characterized by its colors — principally blue, orange-rust, and copper lustre — and by its uninhibited patterns. Accent colors may be yellow and green. (Pink lustre may be present, since lustre applied to the white areas appears pink. A copper tone develops from painting lustre onto the dark colors.) The body of the ware may be heavy ironstone (also called Gaudy Ironstone), creamware, earthenware, or porcelain; even styles and shapes vary considerably. Patterns, while usually floral, are also sometimes geometric and may have trees and birds. Beware! The Wagon Wheel pattern has been reproduced. Our advisor for this category is Cheryl Nelson; she is listed in the Directory under Texas.

Note: Prices are rising. Each day more collectors enter the field. For the first time British auction houses are picturing and promoting Gaudy Welsh. Demand for Columbine, Grape, Tulip, Oyster, and Wagon Wheel is slow. We should also mention that the Bethedsa pattern is very similar to a Davenport jug pattern. No porcelain Gaudy Welsh was made in Wales.

Aster, plate, 9" 265.00
Beanstock, jug, 5¼".. 650.00
Betws-y-coed, jug, 7".. 525.00
Billingsley Rose, cup & saucer 300.00
Brecon, jug, 6".. 550.00
Cardiff, jug, 7"... 600.00
Castle, cup & saucer 135.00
Columbine, cup & saucer 55.00
Dotted Circle, cup & saucer 135.00
Fence, plate, 7⅞"... 160.00
Fruit, teapot, 8"... 700.00
Grape, jug, 7".. 250.00
Grape & Lily, mug, 7".. 575.00
Gwyrrd, jug, 7".. 545.00
Herald, jug, 5".. 325.00
Honeysuckle, cup & saucer... 85.00
Horton, jug, 5½".. 225.00
Leaf, mug, 2½".. 235.00
Llanrug, jug, 6".. 595.00
Marigold, cup & saucer.. 75.00
Melyn & Glas, mug, 2½" 235.00
Morning Glory, plate, 7" 265.00
Oyster, cup & saucer 35.00
Poppy, jug, 8"... 445.00
Rainbow, plate, 8".. 275.00
Sahara, plate, 9".. 285.00
Scollop, mug, 2".. 135.00
Strawberry, jug, 7¼"... 595.00
Tulip, creamer, 5".. 100.00
Village, plate, 9".. 215.00

Geisha Girl

Geisha Girl porcelain was one of several key Japanese china production efforts aimed at the booming export markets of the U.S., Canada, England, and other parts of Europe. The wares feature colorful, kimono-clad Japanese ladies in scenes of everyday Japanese life surrounded by exquisite flora, fauna, and mountain ranges. Nonetheless, the forms in which the wares were produced reflected the late nineteenth- and early twentieth-century Western dining and decorating preferences: tea and coffee services, vases, dresser sets, children's items, planters, etc.

Over 100 manufacturers were involved in Geisha Girl production. This accounts for the several hundred different patterns, well over a dozen border colors and styles, and several methods of design execution. Geisha Girl porcelain was produced in wholly hand-painted versions, but most were hand painted over stenciled outlines. Be wary of Geisha ware executed with decals. Very few decaled examples came out of Japan. Rather, most were Czechoslovakian attempts to hone in on the market. Czech pieces have stamped marks in broad, pseudo-Oriental characters. Items with portraits of Oriental ladies in the bottom of tea or sake cups are *not* Geisha Girl porcelain, unless the outside surface of the wares are decorated as described above. These lovely faces, formed by varying the thickness of the porcelain body, are called lithophanes and are collectible in their own right.

The height of Geisha Girl production was between 1910 and the mid-1930s. Some post-World War II production has been found marked Occupied Japan. The ware continued in minimal production during the 1960s, but the point of origin of the later pieces was not only Japan but Hong Kong as well. These productions are discerned by the pure whiteness of the porcelain; even, unemotional borders; lack of background washes and gold enameling; and overall sparseness of detail. A new wave of Nippon-marked reproduction Geisha emerged in 1996. If the Geisha Girl productions of the 1960s – 1980s were overly plain, the mid-1990s repros are overly ornate. Original Geisha Girl porcelain was enhanced by brush strokes of color over a stenciled design; it was never the 'color perfectly within the lines' type of decoration found on current reproductions. Original Geisha Girl porcelain was decorated with color washes; the reproductions are in heavy enamels. The backdrop decoration of the current reproductions feature solid, thick colors, and the patterns feature too much color; period Geisha ware had a high ratio of white space to color. The new pieces also have bright shiny gold in proportions greater than most period Geisha ware. The Nippon marks on the reproductions are wrong. Some of the Geisha ware created during the Nippon era bore the small precise decaled green M-in-Wreath mark, a Noritake registered trademark. The reproduced items feature an irregular facsimile of this mark. Stamped onto the reproductions is an unrealistically large M-in-Wreath mark in shades of green ranging from an almost neon to pine green with a wreath that looks like it has seen better days, as it does not have the perfect roundness of the original mark. Other marks have also been reproduced. Reproductions of mid-sized trays, chunky hatpin holders, an ornate vase, a covered bottle, and a powder jar are among the current reproductions popping up at flea and antique markets.

Many of our descriptions contain references to border colors and treatments. This information is given immediately preceding the mark and/or size. Our advisor for this category is Elyce Litts; she is listed in the Directory under New Jersey.

Basket vase, Bamboo Trellis, gr hdl & brn ft w/gold, 8½" 150.00
Biscuit jar, Court Lady, cobalt w/blk-outlined reserves, J #1 .... 75.00
Bowl, Boat Festival, bl border w/gold lacing, Japan mk, 7½" 25.00
Bowl, carp, red w/gold, 6" 15.00
Bowl, Parasol Modern, incurvate rim, Japan, 2x6" 15.00
Bowl, salad; Garden Bench A, 9-lobed, red, 9" 35.00
Butter pat, Flower Gathering B, red-orange, 3¼" 8.00

Chocolate pot, apple green with gold border, 8", $55.00. (Photo courtesy Elyce Litts)

Compote, Boat Festival, river scene, ftd, #4, 6" 55.00
Cup & saucer, bouillon; mc, Rendevous, J#88, w/lid 45.00
Dresser tray, Blind Man's Bluff on cobalt, scalloped, 11½x8½" 85.00
Egg cup, dbl, Child Reaching for Butterfly, red w/gold 13.00
Hair receiver, Footbridge A, red w/gold 25.00
Jelly dish, Parasol C, red border/gold buds, triangular, Japan, 5x5" .. 16.00
Jug, Battledore, apple gr, fluted edge & base, ribbed, 5" 40.00
Luncheon set, Garden Bench D, mc border, teapot+6 c/s+6 plates .. 225.00
Match holder, Parasol C, red border, Japan, 3¼x2¼" 26.00
Napkin ring, Temple, oval, #15A 30.00
Plate, Lady in Rickshaw B, red/gold border, Mikado, 5" 14.00
Plate, lemon; Child Reaching for Butterfly, 2-hdl, Japan, 6¼x5¾" . 16.00
Plate, River's Edge, red & gold border, Japan mk, 7¼" 12.00
Plate, Wait for Me, floriate shape, red-orange w/gold buds, 8¾" 26.00
Platter, Parasol C, red border, pierced hdls 27.00
Relish, Fan Dance D, red border w/gold, pierced hdls, 8¾x4¾" 25.00
Shakers, Parasol H, HP, red & gold border, w/pk flowers, pr 16.00
Spoon warmer, oyster-shaped, red, Parasol K, 4¾" L 24.00
Teacup & saucer, child's, Mother & Son A, diapered border, unmk .. 12.00

Teacup & saucer, Garden Bench N, floral surround, Japan............ 14.00
Teapot, Garden Bench Q, mc/gold border, Cherry Blossom mk, 4½"...32.00
Toothpick holder, In a Hurry, bl scalloped border w/gold, 2¼"....... 22.00
Tray, dresser; Garden Bench D, HP gr & red w/gold...................... 55.00

Georgia Art Pottery

In Cartersville, Georgia, in August 1935, W.J. Gordy first fired pottery turned from regional clays. By 1936 he was marking his wares 'Georgia Pottery' (GP) or 'Georgia Art Pottery' (GAP) and continued to do so until 1950 when he used a 'Hand Made by WJ Gordy' stamp (HM). There are different configurations of the GAP mark, one being a three-line arrangement, another that is circular and thought to be the earlier of the two. After 1970 his pottery was signed. Known throughout the world for his fine glazes, he won the Georgia Governor's Award in 1983. Examples of his wares are on display in the Smithsonian. His father W.T.B. and brother D.X. are also well-known potters.

Creamer, bl-gr, Gordy's Pottery, ca 1935-55, 3¾".......................... 95.00
Flower frog, Mountain Gold, 1950s mk, ball form, 5½".............. 130.00
Jug, Georgia Corn, JW Gordy, mini, 3x2½" 55.00
Pitcher, bl-gr on red clay, 1935-55, 6½x5" 170.00
Pitcher, mottled brn, Handmade WJ Gordy, 8" 145.00

Strawberry pot, 7", $180.00. (Photo courtesy Ken's Antiques & Auction/LiveAuctioneers.com)

German Porcelain

Unless otherwise noted, the porcelain listed in this section is marked simply 'Germany.' Products of other German manufactures are listed in specific categories. See also Bisque; Pink Paw Bears; Pink Pigs; Elfinware.

Plaque, nude sits among rocks, Berlin, 4x5½", in brass frame crowned with basket of flowers, $1,000.00. (Photo courtesy Early Auction Co.)

Figurine, lady w/breasts exposed, ½-figure, #648, 3½" 125.00
Figurine, 18th-C lady w/pug dog on hip, ca 1900, 8¾" 250.00
Plaque, girl w/lute in snowstorm, Sachs, late 19th C, 8½x5¾"..4,000.00

Plaque, gypsy girl w/coin-accented headdress, in ebonized fr, 7⅜".. 2,100.00
Plate, gypsy reads tea leaves for girl, cobalt & gold, SPM, 9¼"..... 325.00

Gladding McBean and Company

This company was established in 1875 in Lincoln, California. They first produced only clay drainage pipes, but in 1883 architectural terra cotta was introduced, which has been used extensively in the United States as well as abroad. Sometime later a line of garden pottery was added. They soon became the leading producers of tile in the country. In 1923 they purchased the Tropico Pottery in Glendale, California, where in addition to tile they also produced huge garden vases. Their line was expanded in 1934 to included artware and dinnerware.

At least 15 lines of art pottery were developed between 1934 and 1942. For a short time they stamped their wares with the Tropico Pottery mark; but the majority was signed 'GMcB' in an oval. Later the mark was changed to 'Franciscan' with several variations. After 1937 'Catalina Pottery' was used on some lines. (All items marked 'Catalina Pottery' were made in Glendale.) For further information we recommend *Collector's Encyclopedia of California Pottery, Second Edition,* by Jack Chipman (Collector Books). See also Franciscan Ware.

Ashtray, Nautical Artware, coral shell form, ca 1939, 4x3⅜"......... 30.00
Bowl, batter; Cocinero line, gr, 5x9" 35.00
Bowl, console; turq, Catalina Pottery, #C204, 3⅞x17¾x11".......... 40.00
Bowl, gr, scalloped/ribbed, Sunkist, 3½x10"............................... 60.00
Bowl, mixing; Cocinero line, bl, 5½x12" 120.00
Bowl, seashell form, Terra Cotta Specialties, turq int, 15" L, $55 to .. 75.00
Bowl, shell form, wht w/coral int, USA, 15" L 75.00
Carafe, syrup; turq, w/stopper, wood hdl, 6½" 55.00
Creamer & sugar bowl, turq, lg tab hdls, open, GMcB, 2½x5" dia. 25.00
Cup & saucer, demi; assorted solid colors, GMcB, set of 6 .... 75.00
Head vase, ivory gloss w/HP decor, Door Bothwell, #C801, 5¾x7" ...185.00
Pitcher, water; pk-tan, Catalina Pottery, 8" 125.00
Platter, bl, Catalina Pottery, 12½" 30.00
Quiche, yel w/gr ext, scalloped sides, 2¼x12" 25.00
Vase, Cielito, ruby w/wht int, GMcB #114, 8¾"........................... 200.00

Vase, Coronado, ivory satin, #8, 10", $150.00. (Photo courtesy Jack Chipman)

Vase, Oxblood, flared neck, bulbous body, Catalina Pottery, 6" ... 150.00
Vase, Ruby Art Ware, bulbous bottom w/flared rim, 4¾".............. 100.00
Vase, shell form, wht w/turq int, Catalina Pottery, 7¼"................. 45.00
Vase, sunfish form, wht w/bl int, Catalina Pottery #C-362 USA, 8x9" ..235.00
Vase, yel w/wht int, Ming shape, GMcB, 8½"................................ 95.00
Wall pocket, tropical leaf, lt bl, Catalina Pottery, 8x6" 60.00

Glass Animals and Figurines

These beautiful glass sculptures have been produced by many major companies in America — in fact, some are still being made today. Heisey, Fostoria, Duncan and Miller, Imperial, Paden City, Tiffin, and Cambridge made the vast majority, but there were many other companies involved on a lesser scale. Very few marked their animals.

As many of the glass companies went out of business, their molds were bought by companies still active, who have used them to produce their own line of animals. While some are easy to recognize, others can be very confusing. For example, Summit Art Glass now owns Cambridge's 6½", 8½", and 10" swan molds. We recommend *Glass Animals, Second Edition,* by Dick and Pat Spencer, if you are thinking of starting a collection or wanting to identify and evaluate the glass animals and figural-related items that you already have. The authors are our advisors for this category and are listed in the Directory under Illinois.

Cambridge

Bashful Charlotte, flower frog, Dianthus, 6½"................................ 200.00
Bashful Charlotte, flower frog, Moonlight Blue satin, 11½", minimum..950.00
Bird, crystal satin, 2¾" L 20.00
Bird on stump, flower frog, gr, 5¼", minimum value 350.00
Bridge hound, ebony, 1¼"... 35.00
Buddha, amber, 5½".. 325.00
Draped Lady, flower frog, crystal frost, 13¼".............................. 125.00
Draped Lady, flower frog, Gold Krystol, 8½" 150.00
Draped Lady, flower frog, ivory, oval base, 8½", minimum value 1,000.00
Draped Lady, flower frog, Moonlight Blue, 13¼", minimum value . 1,000.00
Eagle, bookend, crystal, 5½x4x4", ea... 75.00
Frog, crystal satin 30.00
Mandolin Lady, flower frog, crystal.. 200.00
Mandolin Lady, flower frog, lt emerald.. 350.00
Owl, lamp, ivory w/brn enamel, ebony base, 13½", minimum value..1,250.00
Rose Lady, flower frog, dk amber, tall base, 9¾" 250.00
Scottie, bookends, crystal, hollow 200.00

Seagull, flower block, crystal, 9¾", $50.00. (Photo courtesy Dargate Auctions Galleries/LiveAuctioneers.com)

Swan, Carmen, #3 style, 8½"... 325.00
Swan, Carmen, 6½"... 250.00
Swan, Crown Tuscan, 8½".. 125.00
Swan, crystal, #1 style, 10½"... 100.00
Swan, ebony, 8½"... 250.00
Swan, ebony, 10½".. 300.00
Swan, emerald, 3" 45.00
Swan, milk glass, 6½".. 100.00
Swan, milk glass, 8½".. 150.00
Swan, punch bowl (15") & base, crystal, +12 cups.........................3,000.00
Swan, yel, 8½".. 225.00
Turkey, gr, w/lid.. 500.00
Two Kids, flower frog, amber satin, 9¼"....................................... 325.00

Duncan and Miller

Bird of Paradise, crystal.. 600.00

Dove, crystal, head down, w/o base, 11½" L 100.00
Duck, ashtray, red, 7" 375.00
Goose, crystal, fat, 6x6" 200.00
Heron, crystal satin, 7" 100.00
Swan, milk glass w/red neck, 10½" 400.00
Swordfish, bl opal, rare 500.00
Tropical fish, ashtray, pk opal, 3½" 50.00

Fenton

Airedale, Rosalene, 1992 issue for Heisey 60.00
Bunny, lt bl, #5162, 3" 20.00
Butterfly on stand, ruby carnival, 1989 souvenir, 7½" 30.00
Filly, Rosalene, head front, 1992 issue for Heisey 60.00
Fish, paperweight, red carnival, lt ed, 4½" 55.00
Peacock, bookends, crystal satin, 5¾" 350.00
Turtle, flower block, amethyst, 4" L 65.00

Fostoria

Bird, candleholder, crystal, 1½", ea 15.00
Chanticleer, blk, 10¾" 500.00

Chanticleer, crystal, 1950 – 1958, 10¾", $250.00.

Deer, milk glass, sitting or standing, ea 25.00
Eagle, bookend, crystal, 7½", ea 125.00
Goldfish, crystal, vertical 150.00
Pelican, amber, 1987 commemorative 50.00
Seal, topaz, 3⅞" 55.00

Heisey

Airedale, crystal 1,400.00
Colt, amber, kicking 600.00
Dolphin, candlesticks, crystal, #110, pr 400.00
Duck, ashtray, Moongleam 250.00
Duck, flower block, Flamingo 150.00
Elephant, amber, lg or med, ea 2,400.00
Elephant, crystal, lg or med, ea 350.00
Filly, crystal, head bkwards 1,200.00
Fish, bowl, crystal, 9½" 400.00

Flying Mare, crystal, from $4,000.00 to $4,500.00.

Gazelle, crystal, 10¾" 1,200.00
Giraffe, crystal, head bk 175.00
Giraffe, crystal, head to side 175.00
Goose, crystal, wings up 75.00
Hen, crystal, 4½" 400.00
Horse head, bookend, crystal, ea 125.00
Irish setter, ashtray, crystal 20.00
Irish setter, ashtray, Flamingo 40.00
Kingfisher, flower block, Flamingo 200.00
Mallard, crystal, wings down 250.00
Mallard, crystal, wings up 175.00
Plug horse, cobalt 1,400.00
Rabbit, paperweight, crystal, 2¾x3¾" 125.00
Ram head, stopper, crystal, 3½" 300.00
Rooster, amber, 5⅝" 2,500.00
Rooster, crystal, 5½x5" 450.00
Rooster, vase, crystal, 6½" 125.00
Rooster head, cocktail, crystal 45.00
Rooster head, cocktail shaker, 1-qt 85.00
Scottie, crystal 115.00
Show horse, crystal 1,200.00
Sparrow, crystal 80.00
Swan, ind nut, crystal, #1503 .... 20.00
Swan, pitcher, crystal 650.00
Tropical fish, crystal, 12" 2,000.00
Wood duck, crystal, mother 600.00
Wood duck, crystal, standing 200.00

Imperial

Chick, milk glass, head down 15.00
Clydesdale, Salmon 175.00
Colt, caramel slag, balking 90.00
Colt, Sunshine Yellow, standing 15.00
Donkey, caramel slag 40.00

Dragon, candleholder, frosted crystal, 1949, $150.00 each.

Elephant, caramel slag, sm 60.00
Filly, satin, head forward 75.00
Fish, candlestick, Sunshine Yellow, 5", ea 20.00
Flying mare, amber, NI mk, extremely rare 1,250.00
Giraffe, amber, ALIG mk, extremely rare 200.00
Mallard, caramel slag, wings up 30.00
Owl, Hootless; caramel slag 35.00
Owl, jar, caramel slag, 16½" 65.00
Owl, milk glass 50.00
Piglet, ruby, standing 15.00
Rooster, amber 200.00
Scolding bird, Cathay Crystal 150.00
Scottie, milk glass, 3½" 35.00
Tiger, paperweight, Jade Green, 8" L 75.00
Wood duckling, Sunshine Yellow satin, floating 15.00
Wood duckling, Ultra Blue, standing 30.00

L.E. Smith

Camel, crystal 45.00

Goose Girl, crystal, orig, 6".. 20.00
Horse, bookend, amber, rearing, ea 35.00
Rooster, butterscotch slag, ltd ed, #208................... 80.00
Swan, milk glass w/decor, 8½"................................... 35.00
Swan, soap dish, crystal 25.00

New Martinsville

Chick, frosted, 1"... 25.00
Pig, mama, crystal 275.00
Porpoise on wave, orig 300.00
Rabbit, mama, crystal 300.00
Seal, baby w/ball, crystal... 40.00
Seal, candleholders, crystal, lg, pr.......................... 120.00
Seal w/ball, bookends, crystal, 7"........................... 100.00
Swan, sweetheart candy dish, red, 5"........................ 30.00
Woodsman, crystal, sq base, 7⅜".............................. 80.00

Paden City

Bunny, cotton-ball dispenser, bl frost, ears bk 295.00
Bunny, cotton-ball dispenser, milk glass, ears bk........... 325.00
Dragon swan, crystal, 9¾" L..................................... 200.00
Horse, crystal, rearing 275.00
Pelican, crystal 650.00
Pheasant, Chinese; crystal, 13¾"............................... 90.00

Pheasant, Chinese; medium blue, 13¾" long, $175.00.
(Photo courtesy Lee Garmon and Dick Spencer)

Pheasant, crystal, head bk, 12" 90.00
Pony, blk, 12"... 350.00
Pony, crystal, 12".. 110.00
Rooster, Barnyard; bl, 8¾" 250.00
Rooster, Barnyard; crystal, 8¾" 110.00
Rooster, Elegant; lt bl, 11" 325.00
Starfish, bookends, crystal... 225.00

Tiffin

Cat, blk satin, raised bumps, #9445, 6¼", minimum value 400.00
Cat, Sassy Suzie, milk glass, minimum value................... 450.00
Fawn, flower floater, Citron Green 200.00
Fish, crystal, solid, 8¾x9" 300.00
Owl, lamp, cobalt, 1934-39, minimum value............1,000.00
Pheasants, Copen Blue, paperweight bases, male & female pr 450.00

Viking

Angelfish, blk, 6½"... 200.00
Angelfish, milk glass, pr... 400.00
Bird, candy dish, med gr, w/lid, 12" 50.00
Bird, orange, #1311, 10"... 40.00
Bird, Orchid, 9½".. 100.00
Bird, ruby, #1310, 12" 50.00
Duck, crystal, fighting, head up or down, Viking's Epic Line, ea 40.00
Duck, dk teal, Viking's Epic Line, 9" 55.00
Duck, orange, rnd, ftd, 5"... 30.00

Duck, vaseline, 5" 60.00
Egret, orange, 12".. 45.00
Horse, aqua bl, 11½".. 125.00
Penguin, crystal, 7" 20.00
Rabbit, amber, 6½".. 35.00
Rabbit (Thumper), crystal, 6½"................................. 25.00
Seal, Persimmon, 9¾" L 35.00
Swan, bowl, amber, 6".. 15.00
Swan, orange, fluted, 6½x2x4"................................... 20.00

Westmoreland

Butterfly, Blue Mist, 2½".. 25.00
Butterfly, Green Mist, 2½".. 25.00
Cardinal, Green Mist... 20.00
Porky Pig, milk glass, hollow, 3" L............................ 15.00
Robin, crystal, 5⅛".. 15.00
Robin, red, 5⅛".. 26.00
Starfish, candleholders, milk glass, 5", pr 40.00
Turtle, cigarette box, crystal 25.00
Turtle, flower block, gr, 7 holes, 4" L........................ 45.00
Wren, Crystal Mist, 2½".. 20.00
Wren, red, 2½"... 25.00
Wren, smoke, 3½"... 25.00
Wren on perch, lt bl on wht, 2-pc.............................. 35.00

Miscellaneous

American Glass Co., ringneck pheasant, crystal, 11½" long, from $40.00 to $50.00. (Photo courtesy Lee Garmon and Dick Spencer)

Blenko, owl, paperweight, amber 30.00
Co-Operative Flint, elephant, crystal, 13" 350.00
Federal, Mopey dog, crystal, 3½" 10.00
Haley, horse, crystal, jumping, 9½" L 35.00
Haley, thrush, crystal 40.00
Indiana, panther, bl, walking................................... 400.00
Indiana, pouter pigeon, bookend, crystal frost, ea.... 35.00
Kemple, horse, milk glass, jumping 50.00
LG Wright, turtle, amber.. 70.00
Viking for Mirror Images, baby bear, ruby 75.00
Viking for Mirror Images, mama bear, ruby............ 100.00
Viking for Mirror Images, wolfhound, ruby carnival.... 100.00

Glidden

    Genius designer Glidden Parker established Glidden Pottery in 1940 in Alfred, New York, having been schooled at the unrivaled New York State College of Ceramics at Alfred University. Glidden pottery is characterized by a fine stoneware body, innovative forms, outstanding hand-milled glazes, and hand decoration which make the pieces individual works of art. Production consisted of casual dinnerware, artware, and accessories that were distributed internationally.

    In 1949 Glidden Pottery became the second ceramic plant in the country to utilize the revolutionary Ram pressing machine. This allowed for increased production and for the most part eliminated the previously used slip-casting method. However, Glidden stoneware continued to reflect the same superb quality of craftsmanship until the factory closed in 1957. Although the majority of form and decorative patterns were Mr. Parker's personal designs, Fong Chow and Sergio Dello Strologo also designed award-winning lines.

Glidden will be found marked on the unglazed underside with a signature that is hand incised, mold impressed, or ink stamped. Interest in this unique stoneware is growing as collectors discover that it embodies the very finest of mid-century high style. Our advisor is David Pierce; he is listed in the Directory under Ohio.

Boat, Gulfstream Blue, #4034.. 85.00
Bowl, cobalt, #15 .... 37.00
Bowl, Gulfstream Blue, #4012 .... 130.00
Bowl, lug soup; High Tide, #467... 21.00
Bowl, lug soup; Viridian, #467.. 17.00
Bowl, Sage & Sand, #15 .... 26.00
Bowl, Turquoise Matrix, #21 .... 16.00
Casserole, Chi-Chi Poodle, #167 .... 24.00
Casserole, Clover Pink, #163 .... 30.00
Casserole, Mexican Cock, #167 .... 10.00
Charger, leaf pattern, #68.. 150.00
Cup & saucer, Glidden Blue, #441-A & #442 .... 31.00
Planter, Bird Ivy, yel/gr/bl, #4008 .... 115.00
Plate, Amiable Cats (Gourmet), #35 .... 40.00
Plate, Cat (Fern Mays), #35 .... 18.00
Plate, Dog, Boxer, #35 .... 29.00
Plate, Dog, Chi-Chi Poodle, #31.. 32.00
Plate, Dog, Dalmatian, #35... 48.00

Plate, dog, Pekingese, #35, $50.00. (Photo courtesy David Pierce)

Plate, Dog, Terrier, #35 .... 22.00
Plate, Donkey, #35 .... 54.00
Plate, Goldfish, #35.. 15.00
Plate, grill; Chi-Chi Poodle, #300 .... 32.00
Plate, grill; Chicken, #300 .... 24.00
Plate, Handsome Fish, Viridian, #410 .... 22.00
Plate, Horse, #35 .... 27.00
Plate, Menagerie, Antelope, #35 .... 17.00
Plate, Menagerie, Hippo, #35 .... 30.00
Plate, Menagerie, Tiger, #35 .... 13.00
Plate, Viridian, #465 .... 22.00
Server, deviled relish; Menagerie, #280.................................. 33.00
Server, shirred egg; Menagerie, Tiger, #027........................... 27.00
Server, shirred egg; Mexican Cock, #025 .... 32.00
Sugar bowl, Feather, #144, w/lid... 27.00
Tray, Candynut, Leaf (Fred Press), w/o stand, #200 .... 400.00
Vase, Cobalt, #6.. 23.00
Vase, Early Pink, #4 .... 20.00
Vase, Feather, #6... 27.00
Vase, Gulfstream Blue, Candelabrum, #4046......................... 210.00
Vase, Turquoise Matrix, #128-P.. 15.00
Vase, Yellowstone, #6... 17.00
Vase, Yellowstone, #47... 30.00
Vase, Yellowstone, #62... 25.00

Goebel

F.W. Goebel founded the F&W Goebel Company in 1871, located in Rodental, West Germany. They manufactured thousands of different decorative and useful items over the years, the most famous of which are the Hummel figurines first produced in 1935 based on the artwork of a Franciscan nun, Sister Maria Innocentia Hummel.

The Goebel trademarks have long been a source of confusion because all Goebel products, including Hummels, of any particular time period bear the same trademark, thus leading many to believe all Goebels are Hummels. Always look for the Hummel signature on actual Hummel figurines (these are listed in a separate section).

There are many other series — some of which are based on artwork of particular artists such as Disney, Charlot Byj, Janet Robson, Harry Holt, Norman Rockwell, M. Spotl, Lore, Huldah, and Schaubach. Miscellaneous useful items include ashtrays, bookends, salt and pepper shakers, banks, pitchers, inkwells, perfume bottles, etc. Figurines include birds, animals, Art Deco pieces, etc. The Friar Tuck monks and the Co-Boy elves are especially popular.

The date of manufacture is determined by the trademark. The incised date found underneath the base on many items is the mold copyright date. Actual date of manufacture may vary as much as 20 years or more from the copyright date. Our advisors for this category are Gale and Wayne Bailey; they are listed in the Directory under Georgia.

Most Common Goebel Trademarks and Approximate Dates Used
1.) Crown mark (may be incised or stamped, or both): 1923 – 1950
2.) Full bee (complete bumble bee inside the letter 'V'): 1950 – 1957
3.) Stylized bee (dot with wings inside the letter 'V'): 1957 – 1964
4.) Three-line (stylized bee with three lines of copyright info to the right of the trademark): 1964 – 1972
5.) Goebel bee (word Goebel with stylized bee mark over the last letter 'e'): 1972 – 1979
6.) Goebel (word Goebel only): 1979 – present

Cardinal Tuck (Red Monk)

Ashtray, #ZF43/0, TMK-4, 2½x3" 70.00
Ashtray, flat, #RF142, TMK-4.. 160.00
Bottle topper 125.00
Christmas ornament, 3".. 75.00

Creamer, #S141/1, TMK-3, $40.00. (Photo courtesy William J. Jenack Auctioneers/ LiveAuctioneers.com)

Creamer, #S1512/0, mini, 3" 55.00
Egg cup, #E95A, 2" 95.00
Egg cups, set of 4 on wht #E95B tray...................................... 315.00
Flask, friar in bas relief, #KL97, TMK-3 .... 250.00
Mug, #T74/0, TMK-3, 4½" 100.00
Mug, #T74/1, TMK-3, ½-liter 125.00
Stuber, #RX107, TMK-3, 2⅛" 78.00

Charlot Byj Redheads and Blonds

Wagtime tune, #685-R, TMK-6, $65.00.

At Work, BYJ-74	125.00
Atta Boy, BYJ-7, TMK-3, from $40 to	65.00
Baby Sitter, BYJ-66, TMK-6	85.00
Dating & Skating, BYJ-52, TMK-3, 4½"	85.00
Dealer's sign, BYJ-47, TMK-4, 4x6"	60.00
Dropping In, BYJ-45, TMK-4	55.00
Eeeek, BYJ-9, TMK-4, from $50 to	70.00
Forbidden Fruit, BYJ-20, TMK-4	55.00
Kibitzer, BYJ-23, TMK-4	45.00
Little Miss Coy, BYJ-4, TMK-3	45.00
Nurse, BYJ-63, TMK-4, 5¼"	67.50
Nurse, BYJ-63, TMK-5	60.00
Oops, BYJ-3, TMK-3, from $65 to	80.00
Prayer Girl, BYJ-17, TMK-4, 5¼"	45.00
Roving Eye, boy & dog, BYJ-2, TMK-3	60.00
Salon Shabby O'Hair (aka Shear Nonsense), BYJ-5, TMK-3	110.00
Say Aaah, BYJ-58, TMK-4, 5½"	72.00
Skating 'n Dating, BYJ-52, TMK-4, 5"	55.00
Sleepyhead, BYJ-11, TMK-3	48.00
Stolen Kiss, boy & girl, BYJ-18, TMK-4	60.00
Strike, BYJ-1, TMK-6	55.00
Trim Lass, BYJ-49, TMK-4, 4½"	85.00
Young Man's Fancy, BYJ-6, TMK-5, 4½"	77.00

Co-Boy Figurines

Rick the Fireman, signed EP, 7", $125.00. (Photo courtesy Affiliated Auctions & Realty LLC/LiveAuctioneers.com)

Ben the Blacksmith, 1980, 8"	85.00
Bob the Bookworm, Well #510, TMK-4	75.00
Brad the Clock	165.00
Candy the Confectioner, w/cake, TMK-5, 8½"	42.50
Chuck riding pig, 1986	195.00
Conny the Nightwatchman, #5200, TMK-4	65.00
Dealer plaque, Wells #516, 8x6"	75.00
Doc, gnome, TMK-6	75.00

Flips the Fisherman, TMK-5, 7½x5½"	60.00
Gilda, girl w/doll, TMK-6, 4", MIB	50.00
Jack the Pharmacist, Well #517, 1972	50.00
Jim the Bowler, #1752617, TMK-3	55.00
Marthe the Nurse, TMK-6	150.00
Nick the Nightclub Singer, TMK-6	70.00
Plum the Pastry Chef, Well #506, 1970	60.00
Robby the Vegetarian, Well #520, TMK-4	65.00
Ted the Tennis Player, #5782, TMK-6	30.00
Walter the Jogger, TMK-6	60.00
William the Butcher, Well #507, TMK-4	30.00

Cookie Jars

Cat, TMK-5, from $100 to	125.00
Chimney Sweep, from $150 to	175.00
Dog, TMK-5, from $100 to	125.00
Friar Tuck, K-29, TMK-5	250.00
Owl, #607/36, 15"	125.00
Panda Bear, TMK-5, from $70 to	125.00
Pig, TMK-5, from $100 to	125.00

Friar Tuck (Brown Monk)

Ashtray, flat, #RF142, TMK-3	70.00
Bank, 3 monks surround bbl, mk West Germany, 1957, 2¾"	265.00
Condiment set, jar & shakers on tray, #P153/1, #P153/0 & #M42A, TMK-2	125.00
Cruets, vinegar & oil; bl robes, #M80/B & #M80/C, TMK-6, MIB, pr	195.00
Humidor, #RX106, TMK-3, 7⅝"	250.00
Mug, mini, #RX704/b, TMK-2, 2"	62.50
Perpetual calendar, TMK-5, 3½x4¼"	85.00
Plaque, #WZ2, TMK-4	155.00
Razor blade bank, toes showing, #X103, TMK-3, 4½"	100.00
Shot glasses, #KL94, 2", set of 4	85.00
Stein, w/lid, #T74/3, TMK-3	140.00
Thermometer, #KF56, TMK-6	80.00

Shakers

Bunny, orange-red body, silver-clad face/ears, Germany, 2¾", pr	55.00
Cats, 1 blk/1 wht, gr eyes, nylon whiskers, #P179A & B, pr	35.00
Chinese couple, #P71/A & #P71/B, TMK-2, pr	35.00
Dickens men (aka Pickwick Duo), #M64B, TMK-3, pr	38.00
Dutch boy & girl, bl & wht, pr	42.00
Flower the Skunk, TMK-2, 2¾", pr	62.50
Fox in wht jacket w/S or P on front, TMK-4, pr	28.00
Girls, 1 w/heart & flowers, 2nd w/rutabaga & beer stein, TMK-3, pr	35.00
Owl on book, brn tones, #P84, TMK-2, 2¾", pr	48.00
Thumper, TMK-2, pr	70.00

Miscellaneous

Bust, JS Bach, wht, #18010-19, 7½x4¼"	95.00
Figurine, Cairn terrier, 1¾x3"	25.00
Figurine, camel (nativity), #4682111, TMK-6, 8" L	125.00
Figurine, eagle, wht head, wings wide, #CV104, TMK-5, 9½"	95.00
Figurine, Flower Madonna, open halo, #10/1, TMK-2, 9½"	130.00
Figurine, Goofy playing fiddle, Disney, #17328, TMK-6, 4"	55.00

Goldscheider

The Goldscheider family operated a pottery in Vienna for many generations before seeking refuge in the United States following Hitler's invasion of their country. They settled in Trenton, New Jersey, in the early 1940s where they established a new corporation and began producing objects of art and tableware items. (No mention was made of the company in the Trenton City Directory after 1950, and it is assumed that by this time the influx of foreign imports had taken its toll.) In 1946 Marcel Goldscheider established a pottery in Staffordshire where he manufactured bone china figures, earthenware, etc., marked with a stamp of his signature. Larger artist-signed examples are the most valuable with the Austrian pieces bringing the higher prices. Also buyers should know that the 1920s era terra cotta items, masks, busts, and figures are really costly now, while religious items have fallen in value.

A wide variety of marks has been found: 1.) Goldscheider USA Fine China; 2.) Original Goldscheider Fine China; 3.) Goldscheider USA; 4.) Goldscheider-Everlast Corp.; 5.) Goldscheider Everlast Corp. in circle; 6.) Goldscheider Inc. in circle; 7.) Goldcrest Ceramics Corp. in circle; 8.) Goldcrest Fine China; 9.) Goldcrest Fine China USA; 10.) A Goldcrest Creation; and 11.) Created by Goldscheider USA. Our co-advisors are Randy and Debbie Coe (listed in the Directory under Oregon) and Darrell Thomas (listed under Wisconsin).

Key: tc — terra cotta

American

Juliet & the Doves, ¾-figure, 1940s, 11½"	350.00
Lady dancing, holds skirt, Helen Liedloff, Ovington, 15⅛", $350 to	500.00
Lady in long gr gown holds skirt wide, 15½x10"	1,250.00
Madonna, tan robe w/gold, bl collar, 12¾"	85.00

Madonna and Child, USA, Everlast, ca. 1940, 17¾", $200.00. (Photo courtesy O'Gallerie/LiveAuctioneers.com)

Penguin, Made in USA, 6", NM	125.00
Temple dancer man & lady, traditional attire, H Linduff, 8¼", pr	500.00
Victorian lady in bl gown, object in left hand, USA, 7"	250.00

Austrian

Black boy in ragged clothes, tc, #1460-30-34, 33"	3,250.00
Black boy in top hat, Suis-je assez beau on base, tc, #1521-84-70, 33"	5,700.00
Black boy w/monacle seated on bamboo chair, tc, #168-299-65, 21"	7,800.00
Black man w/cigar seated in rocking chair, tc, #8334-1365-52, 18"	3,500.00
Boy holds bl flowers, gr base, Wein, 5⅝"	360.00
Bust, Arabian man, tc, #925-68, 19"	2,500.00
Bust, lady praying, bl floral scarf, Lorenzl, #751-23-14, 7x6½"	1,600.00
Bust, lady's head, lt gr face w/dk gr hair, tc, #0177, 1920s, 12½"	2,800.00
Bust, lady's head, wht face, gilt/pnt curls, Wein, 12x7"	3,000.00
Deco dancer w/flowing skirt, Lindner, #4690-333-16, 12½", $2,400 to	2,600.00
Deco lady dancer holds skirt wide, Wein, 15½", from $1,800 to	1,300.00
Deco lady dancing, pk & floral print gown, 22"	1,250.00
Deco lady dancing w/clown, ca 1930, 16"	2,500.00
Lady dressed in blk lace reclines on wht base, Lorenzl, 5¾x9", NM	2,000.00
Lady in gr w/wolfhound, ca 1940, 12"	2,600.00
Mercury, seated on oak pedestal, tc, 48"	9,500.00
Nude w/butterfly wings, Lorenzl, #7640/83/4, 11x12½x4"	2,600.00
Russian wolfhound, blk & wht, #569-77, rare, 6x13"	1,500.00
St George Slaying the Dragon, tc, #8596, Wein, 12"	1,950.00
Tennis player boy & girl, simple wht bases, 12", pr	1,700.00
Wall mask, lady w/bl scarf, Wein, 11"	1,900.00
Wall mask, lady w/brn wavy hair, bl cap & beads, 1920s, 12"	2,400.00
Wall mask, lady w/orange curls holds blk mask, Wein, 13¾"	3,000.00

Gonder

Lawton Gonder grew up with clay in his hands and fire in his eyes. Gonder's interest in ceramics was greatly influenced by his parents who worked for Weller and a close family friend and noted ceramic authority, John Herold. In his early teens Gonder launched his ceramic career at the Ohio Pottery Company while working for Herold. He later gained valuable experience at American Encaustic Tile Company, Cherry Art Tile, and the Florence Pottery. Gonder was plant manager at the Florence Pottery until fire destroyed the facility in late 1941.

After years of solid production and management experience, Lawton Gonder established the Gonder Ceramic Art Company, formerly the Peters and Reed plant, in South Zanesville, Ohio. Gonder Ceramic Arts produced quality art pottery with beautiful contemporary designs which included human and animal figures and a complete line of Oriental pottery. Accentuating the beautiful shapes were unique and innovative glazes developed by Gonder such as flambé (flame red with streaks of yellow), 24k gold crackle, antique gold, and Chinese crackle. (These glazes bring premium prices.)

All Gonder is marked with the company name and mold number. They include 'Gonder U.S.A' in block letters, 'Gonder' in script, 'Gonder Original' in script, and 'Gonder Ceramic Art' in block letters. Paper labels were also used. Some of the early Gonder molds closely resemble RumRill designs that had been manufactured at the Florence Pottery; and because some RumRill pieces are found with similar (if not identical) shapes, matching mold numbers, and Gonder glazes, it is speculated that some RumRill was produced at the Gonder plant. In 1946 Gonder started another company which he named Elgee (chosen for his initials LG) where he manufactured lamp bases until a fire in 1954 resulted in his shifting lamp production to the main plant. Operations ceased in 1957.

Vase, modeled leaves, #H-77, 8½", $30.00.

Cookie jar, brn drips on gr, #P-24, 8x8"	27.00
Ewer, burgundy purple, #H-73, 8½"	40.00
Figurine, cat, streaky brn over dk gold, 1957, 11"	190.00
Figurine, hula girl water carrier, chartreuse, 1950, 13x10"	35.00
Figurine, panther, yel w/brn accents, #210, 19" L	50.00
Lamp, panther, wht, ca 1950, 5x21"	92.00
Planter, gondola-like w/scrolling base, seafoam gr, #557, 7x16"	60.00
Relish dish, streaky brn on yel, 6-part, 10x14"	35.00
Vase, Deco style, yel, ftd, #598, 15"	47.00

Vase, flamingo figural, teal w/brn undertones, 8¼x4" 60.00
Vase, hat shape, lt gr w/dk pk int, #H-36, 6x9"................. 52.00
Vase, long neck, shouldered, w/high twisted hdls, gr, #H-5, 9x5" .. 25.00
Vase, ribbon candy, yel w/brn & wht undertones, 11" 75.00
Vase, scalloped shell, streaky lav, #J-60, 8x11"................. 60.00
Vase, shell w/3 fish at base, pk w/bl/gray undertones, #H-85, 9"..... 34.00
Vase, swans (2) at base, flared scalloped rim, wht w/pk int, 8x6½"....38.00

Goofus Glass

Goofus glass is American-made pressed glass with designs that are either embossed (blown out) or intaglio (cut in). The decorated colors were aerographed or hand applied and not fired on the pieces. The various patterns exemplify the artistry of the turn-of-the-century glass crafters. The primary production dates were ca 1908 to 1918. Goofus was produced by many well-known manufacturers such as Northwood, Indiana, and Dugan.

When no condition is given, our values are for examples in mint original paint. Our advisor for this category is Steven Gillespie of the *Goofus Glass Gazette;* he is listed in the Directory under Missouri. See also Clubs, Newsletters, and Catalogs.

Basket, Diamond & Daisy, 6½", EX.................................... 55.00
Bowl, Butterfly, red & gold, ruffled, 2½x10½", EX+ 65.00
Bowl, Carnation, La Belle & Roses in Snow, sq, 5½" 12.00
Bowl, Cherry, red & gold, Dugan, 2¼x10⅛" 65.00
Bowl, Cherry, ruffled rim, 3¼x10", NM 75.00
Bowl, Hearts, 7" 45.00
Bowl, Jeweled Heart, 2x9", NM 45.00
Bowl, Poppy, red & gold, ftd, 4x9", EX 60.00
Bowl, Poppy, Two Fruits & Olympic Torch, pattern decor, rare, 9" .. 130.00
Bowl, Rose, 5-sided (hard to find) 110.00

Bowl, roses, 9", $35.00.
(Photo courtesy Moorland Auction Services/LiveAuctioneers.com)

Bread tray, The Last Supper.. 35.00
Cake plate, Acorn & Leaf, 12" 30.00
Cake plate, Wild Flower, crackle glass border, 12" 25.00
Compote, Butterfly, 6⅞x10¼", EX 70.00
Dish, Hearts, rolled rim, 10" 50.00
Lamp, Cabbage Rose, matching chimney, 12" 150.00
Lamp, oil; Grape & Leaves, minor flaking, 13¼" 275.00
Lamp, oil; Nosegay, #2, EX 250.00
Lamp, oil; Wild Rose, Riverside, finger loop, 15" overall 250.00
Plate, Butterfly, Dugan, rare, 11" 125.00
Plate, Chrysanthemum, frosted ground, 6¼", EX 45.00
Plate, Hearts, 10" 45.00
Plate, Little Bo Peep, minor gold flaking, 6½".................. 80.00
Plate, rose in base amid 8 long-stemmed roses, red/gold, 10¾", EX ... 55.00
Plate, Temple of Music, Pan Am Expo Buffalo NY, 7¼", EX.......... 60.00
Relish plate, Rose, glass hdls, 7"................................... 50.00
Shakers, Vintage, dk gr & gold on milk glass, G orig lids, 3¾", pr.. 55.00
Tray, Fruit, sq, 8½" 50.00

Tray, The Lord's Supper, 7x11".. 65.00
Vase, Cabbage Rose, 15".. 95.00
Vase, Magnolia Blossoms, filigree top & bottom, 9½"............ 75.00
Vase, Peacock, red & gold, 15¼"..................................... 100.00
Vase, Poppy, red flower w/gold leaves, 10"......................... 15.00
Vase, Poppy, 5"... 15.00
Vase, Tree Flowers (uncommon), 14½"............................... 95.00
Vase, Victorian Vase & Rose Buds, 14½"............................. 85.00

Goss and Crested China

William Henry Goss received his early education at the Government School of Design at Somerset House, London, and as a result of his merit was introduced to Alderman William Copeland, who owned the Copeland Spode Pottery. Under the influence of Copeland from 1852 to 1858, Goss quickly learned the trade and soon became their chief designer. Little is known about this brief association, and in 1858 Goss left to begin his own business. After a short-lived partnership with a Mr. Peake, Goss opened a pottery on John Street, Stoke-on-Trent, but by 1870 he had moved his business to a location near London Road. This pottery became the famous Falcon Works. Their mark was a spread-wing falcon (goss-hawk) centering a narrow, horizontal bar with 'W.H. Goss' printed below.

Many of the early pieces made by Goss were left unmarked and are difficult to discern from products made by the Copeland factory, but after he had been in business for about 15 years, all of his wares were marked. Today, unmarked items do not command the prices of the later marked wares.

Adolphus William Henry Goss (Goss's eldest son) joined his father's firm in the 1880s. He introduced cheaper lines, though the more expensive lines continued in production. Shortly after his father's death in 1906, Adolphus retired and left the business to his two younger brothers. The business suffered from problems created by a war economy, and in 1936 Goss assets were held by Cauldon Potteries Ltd. These were eventually taken over by the Coalport Group, who retained the right to use the Goss trademark. Messrs. Ridgeway Potteries bought all the assets in 1954 as well as the right to use the Goss trademark and name. In 1964 the group was known as Allied English Potteries Ltd. (A.E.P.), and in 1971 A.E.P. merged with the Doulton Group.

Bowl, Abbey & Town Hall Hexham, 2x4"........................... 80.00
Cathedral Church Norwich... 85.00
Cup & saucer, Warren House Inn 70.00
Goblet, 60th Yr of Reign of Our Beloved Queen, 1896-97 ...... 85.00
HMS Donner Blitzen tank, Whitehaven Crest, ca 1900-1919..... 125.00
Lewes Urn, Weston Super Mare, transfer print..................... 130.00
Model of Roman Jug, Great Yarmouth (Norfolk) 110.00
Pincushion, 2 butterflies 165.00

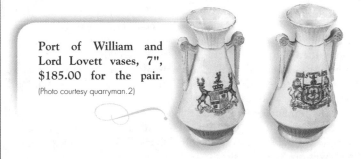

Port of William and Lord Lovett vases, 7", $185.00 for the pair.
(Photo courtesy quarryman.2)

Posy basket, fluted sides, twisted hdl, ca 1858-87.......................... 325.00
Punch & Judy Show, Good Morning Mr Punch 48.00
Robert Burns' Cottage 90.00
Shakespeare's House 70.00
Toby jug, dk bl coat, 3⅜".. 150.00

Miscellaneous

Arcadian, banjo, Botreaux Arms......................... 36.00
Arcadian, Black boy & spider, Hastings crest 160.00
Arcadian, blk cats in basket, Bognor Regis (West Sussex) crest... 280.00
Arcadian, bride & chest, Margate crest........................... 120.00
Arcadian, castle, Westgate 36.00

Arcadian, dispatch rider, crest of Borough of Reading, 1920, 4½x3½", $375.00.
(Photo courtesy quarryman.2)

Arcadian, model of blk cat in well, Stowmarket crest, 2⅜" 80.00
Arcadian, model of 2 blk cats on seesaw, Cheltenham crest 415.00
Arcadian, petrol pump attendant, Bridport crest......................... 330.00
Arcadian, tour bus, City of London.. 48.00
Arcadian, WWI sailor, Sevenoaks (Kent) crest, 5⅜" 78.00
Carlton, puppy w/ear raised, Redcar crest, 3" 10.00
Carlton, upright piano, St Leonard's crest................................ 32.00
Carlton, vase, Northallerton crest, 2¼"................................. 15.00
Carlton, WWI floating mine, Nottingham crest........................ 70.00
Foley, model of bronze bowl, Glastonbury crest, 1½" 90.00
Shelley, cow bell, Wallasey crest, 2½" 35.00
Shelley, Lincoln Imp, Lincoln crest, 4¾" 60.00
Shelley, pig, Dunblane crest, 1½" 85.00
Shelley, water bottle, Scarborough crest, 1¾" 42.50
Willow Art, sun, Windmere crest.................................... 25.00

Gouda

Gouda is an old Dutch market town in the province of South Holland, famous for producing Gouda cheese. Gouda's ceramics industry had its beginnings in the early sixteenth century and was fueled by the growth in the popularity of smoking tobacco. Initially learning their craft from immigrant potters from England who had settled in the area, the clay pipe makers of Gouda were soon regarded as the best. While some authorities give 1898 (the date the Zuid-Holland factory began operations) as the initial date for the manufacturing of decorative pottery in Gouda, C.W. Moody, author of *Gouda Ceramics* (out of print), indicates the date was ca 1885. Gouda was not the only town in the Netherlands making pottery; Arnhem, Schoonhoven, and Amsterdam also had earthenware factories, but technically the term 'Gouda pottery' refers only to pieces made within the town of Gouda. Today, no Gouda-style factories are active within the city's limits, but in the first quarter of the twentieth century there were several firms producing decorative pottery there — the best known being Zuid, Regina, Zenith, Ivora, and Goedewaagen. At present Royal Goedewagen is making three patterns of limited editions. They are well marked as such.

This information was provided to us by Adela Meadows; she is listed in the Directory under California. For further information we recommend *The World of Gouda Pottery* by Phyllis T. Ritvo (Front & Center Press, Weston, Massachussets).

Bowl, Ivora, pansies, incurvate rim, #358, 1920, 3x13½" 115.00
Candlestick, Holland, geometrics, G Veerman, PZH, 15½", ea.... 250.00
Candlesticks, Holland, abstract flowers, van den Akker, PZH, 1927, 9"..250.00
Candy dish, Holland, Laila, tulips, Royal Goedewaagen, 1980s, 6½"... 30.00

Compote, Holland, hdls, PZH, #1196, 4¾x9" 150.00
Ewer, Holland, Fruto, stylized leaves, Goedewaagen, ca 1930, 8x5"...100.00

Jar, stylized flowers, high glaze, logo containing DW/ Holland/#777 P, possible restoration, 5¼", $500.00.
(Photo courtesy Cincinnati Art Galleries)

Jardiniere, England, Docoro, pansies, 1930s-40s, 7x8" 275.00
Jardiniere, Holland, Distel, stylized wolves, blk/wht/gr, ca 1930, 8" . 350.00
Jug, historic building/sailboats/fruit, sgn J, PZH, 5¾".................... 500.00
Jug, Holland, lg wht blossom on gray w/bl swirls, #616, 5½" 125.00
Jug, Holland, magenta flowers, bulbous base, PZH, 8x6½" 275.00
Lantern holder, Holland, Costa, floral, sgn R, PZH, 19½x9¼"..1,100.00
Planter, Holland, Henley, circles in bands, #484, 4x12" 200.00
Plaque, Holland, abstracts, Breetvelt, PZH, #1164/26, 1925, 10¾".. 200.00
Plaque, Holland, chrysanthems, Gidding, PZH, 1925-26, 16½"... 150.00
Plaque, Holland, pastoral scene, P Poerlee, PZH, ca 1904-10, 8½" .. 250.00
Pot, Holland, Ivora pansies, 3-ftd, ca 1920, 4x6" 175.00
Vase, Candia, abstracts, flared lip, PZH, #104/3, 8¼x6", NM....... 175.00
Vase, Holland, Arnhem Rooster, sgn BI, stick neck, 10½x5" 600.00
Vase, Holland, Blanca, floral, Lanooij, #187, ca 1900-06, 19½x9"..1,100.00
Vase, Holland, chrysanthemums, sgn MBL & VV, #679, ca 1910-15, 10x5"....350.00
Vase, Holland, Ciara, floral on bl, hdls, 1922, 5¾x6" 230.00
Vase, Holland, Cobo, floral w/abstracts, #426, 1921, 4¾" 150.00
Vase, Holland, geometrics, J van Schaick, PZH, 5¾x5½" 325.00
Vase, Holland, Kelat, flower & foliage, PZH, 11x5" 200.00
Vase, Holland, Nouveau abstracts, J Hartgring, PZH, 11x4½" 400.00
Vase, Holland, Polo, geometrics, #252, 1918, 7x5½" 200.00
Vase, Holland, Tessel, #1203, 1919, sm bruise, 8x5" 150.00

Grand Feu

The Grand Feu Art Pottery existed from 1912 until about 1918 in Los Angeles, California. It was owned and operated by Cornelius Brauckman, who developed a method of producing remarkably artistic glaze effects achieved through extremely high temperatures during the firing process. The body of the ware, as a result of the intense heat (2,500 degrees), was vitrified as the glaze matured. Brauckman signed his ware either with his name or 'Grand Feu Pottery, L.A. California.' His work is regarded today as being among the finest art pottery ever produced in the United States. Examples are rare and command high prices on today's market.

Vase, forest green crystalline exceptional glaze, #70, 10½x3¾", minimum value, $9,000.00. (Photo courtesy David Rago Auctions)

Bowl vase, yel-speckled indigo/dk brn on red clay, 4½x7½" 5,400.00
Vase, brn, 3-color flambé, shouldered, BR #1730, 7½x5" 5,400.00
Vase, brn/tan mottled crystalline, shouldered, wide neck, 7x3½" ..7,200.00
Vase, bud; indigo mottle, bulbous bottom, slim neck, 4¾x2½" ...1,320.00

Graniteware

Graniteware, made of a variety of metals with enamel coatings, derives its name from its appearance. The speckled, swirled, or mottled effect of the vari-colored enamels may look like granite — but there the resemblance stops. It wasn't especially durable! Expect at least minor chipping if you plan to collect.

Graniteware was featured in 1876 at Phily's Expo. It was mass produced in quantity, and enough of it has survived to make at least the common items easily affordable. Condition, color, shape, and size are important considerations in evaluating an item; cobalt blue and white, green and white, brown and white, and old red and white swirled items are unusual, thus more expensive. Pieces of heavier weight, seam constructed, riveted, and those with wooden handles and tin or matching graniteware lids are usually older. Pieces with matching granite lids demand higher prices than ones with tin lids.

For further study we recommend *The Collector's Encyclopedia of Graniteware, Book II*, by our advisor, Helen Greguire. It is available from the author. For information on how to order, see her listing in the Directory under South Carolina. For the address of the National Graniteware Society, see the section on Clubs, Newsletters, and Catalogs.

Baking pan, lg cobalt & wht swirl, wht int, blk trim, hdls, 17", NM..295.00
Biscuit sheet, bl & wht swirl, wht int, makes 12, rare, M 5,500.00
Bowl, cereal; solid yel w/wht int, blk trim, 6", NM.........................35.00
Bowl, lg bl & wht swirl, wht int, blk trim, rare color, 2x6", VG...175.00
Bread raiser, solid lt bl, dk bl trim/hdls, ftd, tin lid, 11x18", VG..145.00
Bucket, brn & wht swirl, blk trim, bail hdl, w/lid, rare, 4x4½", NM...2,600.00
Canister, lg cobalt & wht mottle, wht int & dk bl trim, seamless, VG...325.00
Casserole, lg bl & wht swirl, blk lid knob, trim & hdls, 5x9", NM...485.00
Chamber pail, lg cobalt & wht swirl, wht int, wooden bail hdl, NM..425.00
Coaster, bl shading to lt bl, advertising, Norvell-Shapleigh, 4", VG..200.00
Coffee biggin, lg cobalt & wht swirl, wht int, bl trim, 3-pc, 10", VG.. 1,025.00
Coffee biggin, lg red & wht mottle, red trim & hdl, 4-pc, 9½", NM ..625.00
Coffee boiler, lg bl & wht swirl, bl trim, seamed, 11½x8½", VG..365.00
Coffee boiler, lt bl & wht wavy mottle, blk trim, strap hdl, 11", NM..475.00
Coffeepot, gr & wht relish pattern, bl trim, metal lid, 6½x4", VG..235.00
Coffeepot, lg bl & wht swirl, wht int, blk trim & hdl, rare, 9x6", VG...340.00
Coffeepot, lg red & wht swirl, blk trim, seamed, ca 1950, 9½x5", VG..245.00
Colander, solid wht, lg hdls, 2½x7½" dia, VG 45.00
Cream can, dk sea gr shading to moss gr, wire bail, 7½x4", NM...495.00
Cream can, med cobalt & wht swirl, wht int & blk trim, bail hdl, M...675.00
Creamer, solid red, wht int, blk trim, ca 1970, 3½x3½", VG..........45.00
Creamer, solid wht, bl trim, squatty, 3¾x4", M.............................125.00
Cup, aqua gr & wht swirl, bl trim, flared, strap hdl, 2½x3¾", VG..95.00
Cup, custard; bl shading to lt bl shading to bl, 2x3½", VG...........125.00
Cuspidor, solid bl inside & out, blk trim, 4x7½" dia, VG 85.00
Dipper, Windsor; lg bl & wht mottle, blk tubular hdl, 3½x6½", VG...165.00
Dishpan, bl & wht splash-type mottle, blk-trim hdls, 14½" dia, VG..210.00
Double boiler, blk & wht swirl, chrome-plated lid, Ebony Ware, 8", NM...325.00
Drainer pan, brn & wht marble inside & out, 3x11" dia, NM.........55.00
Dustpan, solid red, rare, 13½x10½", NM 265.00
Egg cup, solid lt bl, wht int, ped ft, 2¾x2" dia, VG 85.00
Egg pan, lg gray mottle, holds 5 eggs, w/hdl, 12" dia, NM 295.00
Foot tub, dk gray med mottle, seamed, hdls, oval, 9x19x13", VG...215.00
Fry pan, gr shading to ivory, blk hdl, Old Ivory Ware, 2x11½", NM..180.00
Fry pan, red & wht swirl inside & out, blk trim & hdl, 1x8", M ..185.00
Funnel, lav bl & wht swirl, wht int, blk hdl, squatty, 5½x6", NM...195.00

Funnel, old red & wht swirl inside & out, blk hdl, rare, 6x6", NM ..5,000.00
Grater, solid dk gray, ftd, w/hdl, 11¾", VG 675.00
Gravy boat, lg bl & wht swirl, wht int, bl trim & hdl, 8½x4", NM ..2,950.00
Kettle, solid dk gr, wht int, bl trim, emb 16 on lid, 6½x6½", NM .. 45.00
Ladle, soup; sm gray mottle, riveted hdl, 8x3" dia, VG..................75.00
Measure, lg cobalt & wht mottle, wht int, blk trim & hdl, 3½x3", VG..450.00
Measuring cup, fine brn & wht mottle inside & out, 1-C grad, VG .110.00
Melon mold, solid cobalt w/wht int, w/hdld tin lid, 4x7x5½", M..115.00
Muffin cup, ind; lg gray mottle, 3" dia, NM 85.00
Muffin cup, ind; med bl & wht relish pattern, bl trim, 1x3", M 85.00
Muffin pan, lg bl & wht swirl, wht int, blk trim, 7½x14", VG ..1,950.00
Mug, lg bl & wht mottle, wht int, blk trim & hdl, 3x3½", NM......65.00
Mug, mush; old red & wht swirl, wht int, bl trim & hdl, rare, 5x6", VG..2,395.00
Pie plate, cream w/gr trim, 1½x10", VG..45.00
Pie plate, dk sea gr shading to moss gr, wht int, ¾x9", M...............65.00
Pie plate, lg bl & wht swirl, wht int, blk trim, Columbian, 11"....110.00
Pitcher, milk; brn & wht mottle, blk hdl, Onyx Ware, 5½x4½", VG..155.00
Pitcher, water; dk bl shading to lt bl, blk trim & hdl, 10x6½", M....575.00
Pitcher, water; lt bl & wht wavy mottle, blk trim & hdl, 9x5", M...850.00
Pitcher, water; red & wht mottle, wht int, Snow on the Mountain, 9", G...600.00
Pitcher & bowl, solid wht w/blk trim & hdl, 2-pc, 8x8½", VG 125.00
Platter, lg bl & wht swirl, bl trim, Blue Diamond Ware, 18x14", NM...465.00
Preserving kettle, lg bl & wht swirl, bail hdl, lipped, 3x7" dia, M ...175.00
Pudding pan, lg bl & wht swirl, wht int, blk trim, 3x9½" dia, VG ..195.00
Refrigerator dish, cream w/gr trim, US Certified..., 2¾x8x4", VG 45.00
Rice boiler, lg bl & wht swirl, blk trim/ears/hdl, 3-pc, 6½x6", NM...485.00
Roaster, bl & wht swirl, wht int, hdls, w/flat lid, 7½x17½", VG...425.00
Roaster, cream & gr inside & out, emb Savory, w/hdls, 8x17x10½", VG ..125.00
Saucepan, blk & wht swirl, seamed, blk hdl & lid, 5½x7", NM ...310.00
Saucepan, solid cobalt w/wht int, hdl, 3x5" dia, VG 65.00
Scoop, lg gray mottle, rolled seamed edges, 2½x8½x4½", VG......465.00
Scoop, spice; solid red w/gold bands & trim, deep, 1¾x4"(+hdl), NM...185.00
Scoop, thumb; bl/wht/gray mottle, riveted hdl, rare, 6x3", NM ...675.00

Scoop, thumb; blue and white medium swirl, VG, $425.00; Pie plate, blue and white medium swirl, NM, $65.00. (Photo courtesy Helen Greguire)

Shell mold, brn shading to tan, wht int, ring for hanging, 3x3", M..175.00
Shoehorn, lg bl & wht swirl on front & bk, rare, 7x2", NM.......2,450.00
Skillet, blk w/lt gray med mottle, CI base, 1x5", NM 45.00
Skimmer, dk gray, Extra Agate Nickel... label, 12x3½" dia, NM 70.00
Soap dish, solid red, hanging, w/wire sponge/toothbrush holder, 7", VG...135.00
Spoon, lg brn & wht swirl, spoon bowl w/wht int, 13½x2", NM...225.00
Spoon, slotted; solid wht, 12x2", NM 75.00
Stove pot, brn relish pattern, bl trim, wire bail, w/lid, 8½x8", VG..200.00
Sugar bowl, lg bl & wht mottle, wht int, w/matching lid, 4½x5", VG..435.00
Sugar bowl, lg gray mottle, metal mts, lid & hdls, squatty, 6", M .. 600.00
Sugar bowl, lg red & wht mottle, ped ft, open, bl trim, 2½x4", NM...65.00
Syrup, aqua gr & wht swirl, wht int, rolled hdl, metal top, 9x5", NM .. 1,550.00
Syrup, gray lg mottle base w/eng metal top, 4½x3½", NM 225.00
Tart pan, lg gray mottle, 6" dia, VG 55.00
Tea steeper, med bl & wht swirl, wht int, blk trim, 4½x4½", M ...310.00
Teakettle, cobalt & wht mottle, wht int, blk trim/ears/bail, 7", VG...425.00
Teapot, dk sea gr shading to lt moss gr, riveted hdl, squatty, 7", VG...295.00
Teapot, lg brn & wht swirl, wht int, blk trim, seamed spout, 11x7", NM...750.00
Teapot, lg gray mottle, scalloped rim, metal spout, lid & hdls, 11", M ..325.00

Teapot, solid wht w/bl trim, hdl & knob, squatty, 4½x3¾", VG... 115.00
Trivet, orange, turtle-shape, cut-out center, ca 1960, 6" dia, VG... 75.00
Tube cake pan, lt bl & wht swirl, wht int, 3½x10½", VG............. 395.00
Tumbler, lg yel & wht swirl inside & out, blk trim, ca 1950, 4", M .. 110.00
Urinal, lg gray mottle, seamed, riveted hdl, 4½x10x6", NM 95.00
Vegetable dish, lg yel & wht swirl inside & out, blk trim, 8x11", M...165.00
Vegetable dish, re-dipped lav bl & wht swirl, blk trim, 8x10", NM....235.00
Washbasin, lg pk & wht mottle, wht int, bl trim, child's, 2x8", VG...425.00
Washboard, solid cobalt/wood/metal, advertising, Wayne Mfg, 24x12", VG..200.00
Washbowl, lg old red & wht swirl, bl trim, eyelet for hanging, 12", NM..950.00
Water carrier, med gray mottle, covered spout & ears, 16x10", NM ..1,395.00

Green Opaque

Introduced in 1887 by the New England Glass Works, this ware is very scarce due to the fact that it was produced for less than one year. It is characterized by its soft green color and a wavy band of gold reserving a mottled blue metallic stain. It is usually found in satin; examples with a shiny finish are extremely rare. Values depend to a large extent on the amount of the gold and stain remaining.

Bowl, w/lid, EX stain, 6" dia, from $900 to 1,000.00
Bowl, w/lid, M stain & gold, appl finial, 6" dia 3,500.00

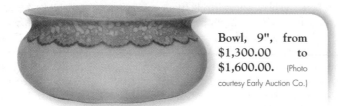

Bowl, 9", from $1,300.00 to $1,600.00. (Photo courtesy Early Auction Co.)

Celery vase, blk mottling, VG gold, 6¼".. 750.00
Creamer, EX stain & gold... 950.00
Cruet, M stain & gold, orig stopper.. 1,950.00
Mug, M stain & gold, 2½"... 700.00
Punch cup, worn stain & gold, 2½".. 225.00
Shaker, M stain & gold, 2½"... 400.00
Spooner, EX stain & gold, 4".. 925.00
Sugar bowl, EX stain & gold, 5½" W... 920.00
Toothpick holder, EX stain, 2⅜", from $325 to........................ 375.00
Toothpick holder, M stain & gold 1,150.00
Tumbler, EX gold & stain, 3¾"... 400.00
Tumbler, lemonade; w/hdl, M stain & gold, 5"........................... 950.00
Tumbler, M stain & gold, 3¾".. 600.00

Greenaway, Kate

Kate Greenaway was an English artist who lived from 1846 to 1901. She gained worldwide fame as an illustrator of children's books, drawing children clothed in the styles worn by proper English and American boys and girls of the very early 1800s. Her book, *Under the Willow Tree,* published in 1878, was the first of many. Her sketches appeared in leading magazines, and her greeting cards were in great demand. Manufacturers of china, pottery, and metal products copied her characters to decorate children's dishes, tiles, and salt and pepper shakers as well as many other items.

What some collectors/dealers call Kate Greenaway items are not actual Kate Greenaway designs but merely look-alikes. Genuine Kate Greenaway items (metal, paper, cloth, etc.) must bear close resemblance to her drawings in books, magazines, and special collections. Our advisor

for this category is James Lewis Lowe; he is listed in the Directory under Pennsylvania. See also Napkin Rings.

Ink and watercolor, 5½x4", $950.00. (Photo courtesy Gorringes, Lewes, England/ LiveAuctioneers.com)

Almanac, 1883, Geo Routledge & Sons, EX 50.00
Biscuit jar, ceramic, boy w/tinted features, w/lid.......................... 165.00
Book, A Apple Pie, cloth, Saalfield, 1907, EX+ 85.00
Book, A Apple Pie, Warne, 1940, w/dust jacket, VG.................... 30.00
Book, Almanack for 1884, printed by Edmund Evans, EX 135.00
Book, Good-Night Stories for Little Folks, NY & London, no date, EX+. 65.00
Book, Greenway's Babies, cloth, Saalfield, 1907, EX+.................... 85.00
Book, Kate Greenaway Pictures, London, Warne, 1st ed, 1921, VG .300.00
Book, Kate Greenaway's Alphabet, London, 1880, EX 190.00
Book, Kate Greenaway's Book of Games, Routledge, 1st ed, 1889, NM..475.00
Book, Little Ann & Other Poems, by Taylor, VG 50.00
Book, Marigold Garden, London, 1888, VG................................. 60.00
Book, Mother Goose, London, later print of 1st ed, VG 150.00
Book, Pictures & Rhymes for Children..., paperbk, McLoughlin, ca 1900...65.00
Book, Pied Piper of Hamlin, NM 100.00
Book, Ring-Round-a-Rosy, red cover, cloth, Saalfield, 1907, EX+ ..100.00
Book, Ring-Round-a-Rosy, wht cover, cloth, Saalfield, 1907, EX+ ...85.00
Book, Sunshine for Little Children, 1884, EX 80.00
Book, Under the Window, ca 1900 (no date), mini, 4x5", VG...... 85.00
Book, Under the Window, Routledge, 1st ed, orig cloth 165.00
Bowl, Daisy & Button, amber; Reed & Barton SP fr w/girl & dog ..525.00
Butter pat, children playing (transfer), pre-1910 .... 40.00
Button, Autumn from Almanack, metal silhouette, ½".................. 40.00
Button, Christening, metal silhouette, 1" 60.00
Button, Johnny at Fence Post, metal, ¾"....................................... 30.00
Button, Johnny's Friend, metal, 2" 50.00
Button, Little Bo Peep, flat or cupped metal, ⅝-¾", from $20 to ... 25.00
Button, Little Bo Peep, metal silhouette, scalloped, ¾-1", $20 to.. 30.00
Button, Miss Pelicoes, metal silhouette, rear or front view, 1¼"..... 40.00
Button, Pretty Patty & Trumpeter, cupped metal, ⅝" 30.00
Button, Pretty Patty Sitting on Fence, cupped metal silhouette, ¾"..20.00
Button, Pretty Patty Sitting on Fence, metal, ¾"........................... 20.00
Button, Pretty Patty Sitting on Fence, thin metal, felt bk, 1½"...... 30.00
Button, Ring the Bells Ring, 4 girls in queue, gold on glass, ⅝" 30.00
Button, Ring the Bells Ring, 4 girls in queue, gold on glass, ⅞" 40.00
Button, Ring the Bells Ring, 4 girls in queue, silver on glass, ⅞".... 40.00
Button, See-Saw from Mother Goose, gold & wht metal, fancy, 1½" ..80.00
Button, Spring from Almanack, glass, 1" 40.00
Button, Spring from Almanack, metal silhouette, ⅝"..................... 30.00
Button, Spring from Almanack, wht metal on brass, ¾"................. 40.00
Button, Summer from Almanack, brass on bl metal, ¾-⅞", from $20 to......25.00
Button, Summer from Almanack, glass, ¾"................................... 20.00
Button, Summer from Almanack, metal, sq, ¾"............................. 25.00
Button, Summer from Almanack, metal silhouette, 1".................. 25.00
Button, Winter from Almanack, metal silhouette, ¾x⅞", from $20 to 30.00
Button, 2 Girls Sitting on Rail, metal, ¾"..................................... 50.00
Button, 2 Lazy Loons, wht metal on MOP, ⅝" 50.00

Calendar, chromolithograph, Routledge, 1884, 7⅜x9½", EX 60.00
Card, Christmas; girl in wht w/roses, Tuck, metal stand, 7x8¾"... 100.00
Cup & saucer, children transfer, pk lustre trim, pre-1910............. 125.00
Engraving, Harper's Bazaar, Jan 1879, full-pg.............................. 25.00
Figurine, girl (seated) tugs on lg hat, bsk, pre-1910, sm............... 75.00
Hatpin holder, SP, girl figural, Meriden, 4"............................... 125.00
Inkwell, bronze, boy & girl 215.00
Match holder, ornate SP, girl in fancy clothes, Tufts 195.00
Paperweight, CI, Victorian girl in lg bonnet, pre-1910, 3x2¾" 110.00
Pencil holder, pnt porc, pre-1910... 100.00
Pickle castor, bl; SP fr w/2 girls, blown-out florals......................... 455.00
Plate, ABC, girl in lg hat, Staffordshire, 7".............................. 120.00
Scarf, children on silk, early, EX... 65.00
Tea set, semi-porc, floral motif, pre-1910, child sz, 3-pc 95.00
Toothpick holder, SP, girl holds amberina cup, ornate base, 5".... 785.00
Toothpick holder, SP, girl stands by Sandwich glass holder w/crane...750.00
Wall pocket, ceramic, 6 girls on open book form, 6x9x3" 137.00
1883, Almanac, Geo Routledge & Sons, EX 50.00

Greentown Glass

Greentown glass is a term referring to the product of the Indiana Tumbler and Goblet Company of Greentown, Indiana, ca 1894 to 1903. Their earlier pressed glass patterns were #75 (originally known as #11), a pseudo-cut glass design; #137, Pleat Band; and #200, Austrian. Another line, Dewey, was designed in 1898. Many lovely colors were produced in addition to crystal. Jacob Rosenthal, who was later affiliated with Fenton, developed his famous chocolate glass in 1900. The rich, shaded opaque brown glass was an overnight success. Two new patterns, Leaf Bracket and Cactus, were designed to display the glass to its best advantage, but previously existing molds were also used. In only three years Rosenthal developed yet another important color formula, Golden Agate. The Holly pattern was designed especially for its production. The dolphin covered dish with a fish finial is perhaps the most common and easily recognized piece ever produced. Other animal dishes were also made; all are highly collectible. There have been many repros — not all are marked! The symbol (+) at the end of some of the following lines was used to indicate items that have been reproduced. Our advisor for this category is Sandi Garrett; she is listed in the Directory under Indiana. See the Pattern Glass section for clear pressed glass; only colored items are listed here.

Animal dish, bird w/berry, amber (+).................................... 325.00
Animal dish, bird w/berry, emerald gr (+)............................... 350.00
Animal dish, cat on hamper, canary, tall (+) 800.00
Animal dish, cat on hamper, Nile Green, tall (+) 1,500.00
Animal dish, dolphin, beaded, cobalt 1,500.00
Animal dish, dolphin, clear, beaded edge............................... 600.00
Animal dish, dolphin, wht opaque, sawtooth edge (+) 925.00

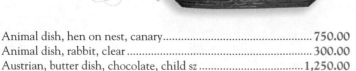

Animal dish, fighting cocks, chocolate glass, rare, 5½" long, $2,500.00. (Photo courtesy Cowan's Auctions Inc./ LiveAuctioneers.com)

Animal dish, hen on nest, canary... 750.00
Animal dish, rabbit, clear.. 300.00
Austrian, butter dish, chocolate, child sz................................. 1,250.00

Austrian, cordial, emerald gr 275.00
Austrian, sugar bowl, chocolate, w/lid, 2½" 150.00
Austrian, vase, Nile Green, 6"... 475.00
Brazen Shield, butter dish, bl.. 275.00
Brazen Shield, sugar bowl, bl, w/lid.. 200.00
Cactus, bowl, chocolate, 7¼"... 140.00
Cactus, compote, chocolate, 5¼" dia.. 110.00

Cactus, cracker jar, chocolate, 7¾", $200.00. (Photo courtesy John Shuman III)

Cactus, cruet, chocolate, w/stopper... 135.00
Cactus, mug, chocolate.. 60.00
Cactus, syrup, chocolate, metal thumb-lift lid, 6"........................... 200.00
Cactus, tumbler, bl-wht opal rim.. 700.00
Cactus, tumbler, chocolate, 5".. 35.00
Cord Drapery, mug, amber, ftd.. 200.00
Cord Drapery, sauce bowl, amber, ftd, 3⅞"..................................... 95.00
Cord Drapery, syrup, chocolate, 6½" 175.00
Cupid, butter dish, chocolate 700.00
Cupid, spooner, chocolate 350.00
Cupid, spooner, Nile Green.. 425.00
Dewey, bowl, emerald gr, 8".. 75.00
Dewey, cruet, amber, w/stopper 125.00
Dewey, sugar bowl, amber, w/lid, 2¼"... 45.00
Diamond Prisms, tumbler, chocolate... 675.00
Early Diamond, dish, amber, rectangular, 8x5" 225.00
Early Diamond, tumbler, canary 300.00
Early Diamond, tumbler, chocolate 225.00
Herringbone Buttress, bowl, amber, 5¼"... 350.00
Herringbone Buttress, bowl, emerald gr, 9¼" 300.00
Herringbone Buttress, nappy, emerald gr.. 225.00
Holly, sugar bowl, White Agate, no lid... 650.00
Holly Amber, bowl, oval, ped ft.. 1,750.00
Holly Amber, bowl, 8½".. 700.00
Holly Amber, compote, jelly; w/lid, 4½" 1,350.00
Holly Amber, creamer 850.00
Holly Amber, syrup pitcher, metal lid 2,250.00
Holly Amber, toothpick holder (+).. 450.00
Holly Amber, vase, 6" 850.00
Leaf Bracket, butter dish, cobalt.. 1,400.00
Leaf Bracket, celery tray, chocolate, 11" 90.00
Leaf Bracket, pitcher, chocolate 300.00
Leaf Bracket, toothpick holder, chocolate 350.00
Leaf Bracket, tumbler, chocolate 45.00
Mug, dog & child, Nile Green.. 1,000.00
Mug, indoor drinking scene, chocolate, handleless 350.00
Mug, Serenade, amber 95.00
Novelty, buffalo, wht opaque, dtd 1901.. 1,250.00
Novelty, corn vase, amber, 4⅝"... 850.00
Novelty, Dewey bust, teal bl, w/base 325.00
Novelty, hairbrush, Nile Green 1,250.00
Novelty, mitted hand, chocolate 1,600.00

Novelty, wheelbarrow, teal bl 250.00
Paneled, pitcher, water; chocolate 600.00
Pattern No 75, bowl, emerald gr, rectangular, 8x6½" 80.00
Pattern No 75, relish tray, cobalt, 6" 175.00
Pattern No 75, toothpick holder, emerald gr 75.00
Pleat Band, cordial, canary 350.00
Pleat Band, wine, canary 275.00
Sawtooth, tumbler, chocolate 85.00
Scalloped Flange, tumbler, chocolate 125.00
Shuttle, champagne, chocolate 2,000.00
Shuttle, mug, cobalt 425.00
Shuttle, tumbler, chocolate 110.00

Squirrel, water pitcher, chocolate, $550.00.

Teardrop & Tassel, bowl, cobalt, 7¼" 175.00
Teardrop & Tassel, compote, Nile Green, open, 7½" dia ... 400.00
Teardrop & Tassel, sugar bowl, wht opaque, w/lid 185.00
Teardrop & Tassel, wine, emerald gr 350.00
Toothpick holder, dog head, amber frost 375.00
Toothpick holder, picture frame, teal bl 400.00
Toothpick holder, witch head, Nile Green (+) 350.00

Grueby

William Henry Grueby joined the firm of the Low Art Tile Works at the age of 15 in 1894. After several years of experience in the production of architectural tiles, he founded his own plant, the Grueby Faience Company, in Boston, Massachusetts. Grueby began experimenting with the idea of producing art pottery and had soon perfected a fine glaze (soft and without gloss) in shades of blue, gray, yellow, brown, and his most successful, cucumber green. In 1900 his exhibit at the Paris Exposition Universelle won three gold medals.

Grueby pottery was hand thrown and hand decorated in the Arts and Crafts style. Vertically thrust tooled and applied leaves and flower buds were the most common decorative devices. Tiles continued to be an important product, unique (due to the matt glaze decoration) as well as durable. Grueby tiles were often a full inch thick. Many of them were decorated in cuenca, others were impressed and filled with glaze, and some were embossed. Later, when purchased by Pardee, they were decorated in cuerda seca.

Incompatible with the Art Nouveau style, the artware production ceased in 1907, but tile production continued for another decade. The ware is marked in one of several ways: 'Grueby Pottery, Boston, USA'; 'Grueby, Boston, Mass.'; or 'Grueby Faience.' The artware is often artist signed. Our advisors for this category are Suzanne Perrault and David Rago; they are is listed in the Directory under New Jersey.

Bowl, gr, leaves (2 rows), 4-sided, nicks, 3½x10" 4,500.00
Jar, brn, 3 sm hdls, w/lid, stilt pull, 7¼x5¾" 2,000.00
Jar, gr, bulbous, sterling collar, w/lid, 4¾x6" 1,675.00
Paperweight, scarab, dk gr, 1½x4x2¾" 540.00
Tile, cherub & cymbals, cream on gr, 6x6" 360.00

Tile, Cheshire Cat (Alice in Wonderland series), cuerda seca, 4" .. 1,920.00
Tile, dragon & lion, gr/bl, #d, 6" 3,120.00
Tile, evergreens landscape, 4-color, #39, 6x6" 3,000.00
Tile, Frog Footman (Alice in Wonderland series), cuerda seca, 4" ... 1,080.00
Tile, Grueby Tile & candlestick, 6x4½" 3,600.00
Tile, houses/hill/seashore, 6-color, 4x4" 2,880.00
Tile, Pines, 4-color, sm chips/abrasion, unmk, 6x6" 2,500.00
Tile, polar bear, 5½x7" 11,400.00
Tile, rabbit, cuenca, in trivet mt, 6" 3,000.00
Tile, St George slaying dragon, cuerda seca, 8" 10,800.00
Tile, stag & tree, 5-color, sm fleck, 4x4" 3,360.00
Tile, tall ship, cuenca, yel/mustard/brn/gr, burst bubble, 6x6" ... 1,800.00
Tile, tulip, brn on gr, chip, 6x6" 1,925.00
Tile, winged Pegasus, brn on gr, copper-ftd mt, sm rstr, 6x6" 4,000.00
Tiles, geometric/floral, dk clay/curdled brn, 8", set of 9 .... 1,325.00
Vase, brn, leaves w/wht buds, sm chips, 3½x5" 4,500.00
Vase, brn froth, leaves, R Erickson, experimental, 4¼x5¼" 3,360.00
Vase, gr, curled leaves in 3 rows, fine rstr, #41N, 6x8" 6,000.00

Vase, green, leaves, minor restoration, 9¼x8½", $84,000.00. (Photo courtesy David Rago Auctions)

Vase, gr, leaves, shouldered, thick lipped rim, 5½x4" 1,440.00
Vase, gr, leaves, squat, sgn WP, rstr chips, 5½" W 800.00
Vase, gr, leaves (full height), #WP104, prof rstr chip, 8x5½" 3,300.00
Vase, gr, leaves (2 rows), gourd shape, #33, 12x8", NM 24,000.00
Vase, gr, leaves & buds, A Lingley, sm rpr, 9" 2,400.00
Vase, gr, leaves & buds, Faience stamp, 7½x4½" 2,650.00
Vase, gr, leaves & yel buds, prof rstr chip, 12x6 5½" ... 9,600.00
Vase, gr, leaves & yel buds, tapered bottom, slim neck, 12½" H ... 11,400.00
Vase, gr, ribbed, slim cylinder, irregular rim, 7" 570.00
Vase, indigo, leaves, ovoid, #180, kiln kiss, rstr rim, 8x4" 1,140.00
Vase, lt gr, leaves on bulbous bottom, cylindrical neck, 12½" H .. 4,800.00
Vase, mustard, leaves & ivory buds, prof rstr, 11x8½" 12,000.00

Gustavsberg

Gustavsberg Pottery, founded near Stockholm, Sweden, in the late 1700s, manufactured faience, creamware, and porcelain in the English taste until the end of the nineteenth century. During the twentieth the factory produced some inventive modernistic designs, often signed by their artists. Wilhelm Kage (1889 – 1960) is best remembered for Argenta, a stoneware body decorated in silver overlay, introduced in the 1930s. Usually a mottled turquoise, Argenta can also be found in cobalt blue and white. Other lines included Cintra (an exceptionally translucent porcelain), Farsta (copper-glazed ware), and Farstarust (iron oxide geometric overlay). Designer Stig Lindberg's work, which dates from the 1940s through the early 1970s, includes slab-built figures and a full range of tableware. Some pieces of Gustavsberg are dated. Our advisors for this category are Suzanne Perrault and David Rago; they are listed in the Directory under New Jersey.

Bowl, Argenta, fish on turq, 7" 195.00
Bowl, Argenta, mermaid on turq, emb horizontal ribs, 9" 600.00
Bowl, geometrics, bl & yel irid, 8-sided, 5x10" 600.00

Charger, Argenta, 3 fish on turq, 12" 455.00
Cigarette holder, Argenta, concentric rings on turq, Kage, 3½".....85.00
Figurine, bull, stylized, brn tones, paper label, 4½" 135.00
Figurine, cat, blk & wht stripes, yel eyes, L Larsen, 4½" 195.00
Figurine, Jonah & whale, cobalt & wht, 5¼" 335.00
Figurine, kangaroo w/removable joey, brn, Lisa Larson, 9" 270.00
Jug, Argenta, lappet-patterned body, 12" 335.00
Plaque, bird figural (stylized), bl & gr, Lisa Larson, 7x10" 225.00
Statue, boy & frog, wht parian, dtd '04, 20" 240.00
Vase, Argenta, geese on turq, W Kage, 7" 600.00
Vase, Argenta, linear design, W Kage, 5½x5¾" 235.00
Vase, Argenta, mermaid on turq, slim cylinder, 9" 660.00
Vase, Argenta, sm leaves on turq, Kage, cylindrical, 7⅜", NM.....425.00
Vase, emb ribs, wht porc, anchor mk, 6" 60.00
Vase, red irid, slim neck, 18x7" 240.00
Vase, sgraffito floral, bl on cream, Ekberg, 11" 360.00

Wall plaque, modeled fish, original label, 11", $360.00. (Photo courtesy David Rago Auctions)

Hadley, M. A.

Founded by artist-turned-potter Mary Alice Hadley, this Louisville, Kentucky, company has been producing handmade dinnerware and decorative items since 1940. Their work is painted freehand in a folk-art style with barnyard animals, whales, sailing ships, and several other patterns. The palette is predominately blue and green. Each piece is signed with Hadley's first two initials and her last name, and her artwork continues to be the inspiration for modern designs. Among collectors, horses and other farm animals are a popular subject matter. Older pieces are generally heavier and, along with the more unusual items, command the higher prices. Our advisor for this category is Lisa Sanders; she is listed in the Directory under Indiana.

Bowl, cereal; bouquet, 5⅝", 4 for......................................40.00
Butter dish, cow, rectangular, 7¾" L 25.00
Butter dish, cow, rnd, w/dome lid, 6½" 25.00
Cake plate, birthday cake center, A Very Happy Birthday..., 1½x13" ..35.00
Canister, Flour & scroll work...30.00
Casserole, pig & cow, w/lid, 7x8", from $30 to 40.00
Creamer & sugar bowl, horse, all bl, w/lid, 3¾", 4"...............40.00
Egg cup, dbl; sheep, 4½" 15.00
Fountain, oval face & bowl, wall mt 1,200.00
Hor d'oeuvres, house in center of 7" attached bowl, 15" dia 65.00
Ladle, punch bowl..30.00
Mug, cow, tall..15.00
Mustard jar, Mustard & scroll work 30.00
Piggy bank, flowers all over, 4½x9x5"...................................40.00
Pitcher, bird on branch, 7½"...40.00
Pitcher, pig, 2-qt 40.00
Plate, house, 8¾", 4 for 48.00
Plate, sailing ship, 11"..18.00
Platter, bouquet, 15" dia 30.00

Platter, farmer & wife, 17x11¼" 40.00
Punch bowl, farmer & wife, 6½x15", w/stand, no ladle 125.00
Sculpture, bird, mottled brn, 4¼x7", pr...................................30.00
Sculpture, chicken, 4"...12.00
Teapot, bouquet, 6-cup 26.50
Tray, berries, oval, 1¼x9x5¼" 25.00
Tumbler, water; farmer, wife, pig & sheep, 9-oz, 5", 4 for...............50.00

Water cooler, basket of flowers, 16x9", $135.00. (Photo courtesy Michael Sessman)

Hagen-Renaker

Hagen-Renaker Potteries was founded in a garage in Culver City, California, in 1945. By 1946 they had moved to a Quonset hut in Monrovia, California, where they produced hand-painted dishes decorated with fruits and vegetables or animal designs. These dishes were usually signed 'HR Calif' in paint on the back. In 1948 the company began producing miniature animal figurines, which quickly became their bestselling line. Remarkably, this is still true, and some of the old miniatures from the '50s are still being produced today.

In 1952 Hagen-Renaker introduced a new larger line of animal figurines called Designer's Workshop. These pieces were designed by many remarkable artists. Their design, mold detail, and painting were amazing. They made hundreds of different Designer's Workshop pieces — birds, cats, dogs, farm animals, horses, insects, and wildlife — that actually looked more like real animals than pottery renditions. Their horses are particularly prized by collectors.

When Disneyland opened in 1955, Hagen-Renaker made many Disney pieces and continued producing them until 1960. Walt Disney was particularly impressed, saying that Hagen-Renaker made the finest three-dimensional figurines he had ever seen. Hagen-Renaker made these groups of figurines: Alice in Wonderland, Bambi, Cinderella, Dumbo, Fantasia, Mickey Mouse & Friends, Peter Pan, Sleeping Beauty, a few miscellaneous pieces, and two sizes of Snow White and the Seven Dwarfs. Most of the Disney pieces were minis, but they also produced larger items, including banks and cookie jars. A chamber pot was also produced that Walt Disney gave to employees with new babies, pink for girls and blue for boys. A second larger set of Fantasia pieces was made in 1982.

The late 1950s and early 1960s was a very difficult time for all US potteries. Most were forced to close due to cheap Japanese imports. Many of these imports were unauthorized copies of US-made pieces. The company initiated new products and cost-cutting measures, trying to compete with these imports. They introduced many new lines including Little Horribles, Rock Wall plaques and trays (glazed with brightly colored primitive animals similar to cave drawings), Zany Zoo pieces, and Black Bisque animals. They also tried Aurasperse, a cold paint that didn't have to be fired in a kiln, thus saving time and money. The problem with this paint was that it washed off very easily. Because these pieces weren't long in production, they are treasured today due to their scarcity. Even with these new lines, paints, and many other cost-saving efforts,

Hagen-Renaker was still forced to shut down; however, the shutdown lasted only a few months. Shortly after reopening, the company moved to San Dimas, California, where they still operate today.

In 1980 Hagen-Renaker bought the Freeman-McFarlin factory in San Marcos, California, and operated that factory for six years. They specialized in making large Designer's Workshop pieces. Some were new designs while others were Freeman-McFarlin's, but the majority were re-issued Designer's Workshop pieces. Most of these old molds had to be re-worked, so many of the pieces from the San Marcos era vary slightly from the earlier products. Hagen-Renaker continued to produce Freeman-Mc-Farlin pieces using the glazes and colors that company originally favored, usually white or gold leaf. They also made some items in new colors. In many cases, it is impossible to make a distinction between products of the two companies.

In the late '80s, Hagen-Renaker started Stoneware and Specialty lines which are larger than the minis and smaller than the Designer's Workshop pieces. The Stoneware line was short lived, but they still make the Specialty pieces. Recently, Hagen Renaker issued a line of dogs called the Pedigree line, which are mostly redesigns of Designer's Work-shop pieces. The current Hagen-Renaker line consists of 45 Specialty pieces, 13 Pedigree dogs, and 202 miniatures. The company is currently releasing some large Designer's Workshop-sized horses as well. Some are new designs, but most are new versions of the old Designer's Workshop horses. Currently, 17 of these larger horses are available in various colors with more to come. Our advisors for this category are Ed and Sheri Alcorn; they are listed in the Directory under Florida. Feel free to visit their Hagen-Renaker Online Museum where you will find over 2,500 Hagen-Renakers pictured.

Black Bisque, Crown-tailed Bird, blk bsk & wht, #22, 1959, 3½" .. 50.00
Black Bisque, Pelican, bl-gr enamel on blk bsk, #10, 1959, 3½" 60.00
Designer's Workshop, Bingo, duckling, #746, 1961-86, 1½" 35.00
Designer's Workshop, Borzoi, caramel & wht, #1003, 1972, 3¾" ... 75.00
Designer's Workshop, chick w/wings up, #524, 1952, 3" 45.00
Designer's Workshop, Choo Choo, Pekingese pup, #1534, 1956-61, 2". 30.00

Designer's Workshop, Clydesdale, #50, matt and glossy, 1983 – 1986, 7½", $400.00 each. (Photo courtesy Ed and Sheri Alcorn)

Designer's Workshop, Crusader, Percheron, wht, #706, 1959-67, 6¼".. 600.00
Designer's Workshop, Daniel, Bongo Rat, w/bongo, #678, 1957, 5½" ..200.00
Designer's Workshop, Dick, Siamese cat sitting, #728, 1960, 6½"....60.00
Designer's Workshop, Fuzzy, calico cat, rare color, #758, 1966, 3"...175.00
Designer's Workshop, Girl Gosling, bl hat, #48, 1983-86, 3¼" 30.00
Designer's Workshop, Golden Lady, collie, #1515, 1955-56, 6" ... 100.00
Designer's Workshop, Heidi's Goat, #79, 1984-86, 4½"................. 75.00
Designer's Workshop, Man O' War, famous racehorse, #742, 1961-74, 7"...250.00
Designer's Workshop, Maverick, buckskin quarter horse, #688, 1958+, 6"..450.00
Designer's Workshop, quail standing, #534, 1950s, 5" 80.00
Designer's Workshop, ram's head, gold, #61, 1981-82, 7½" 150.00
Designer's Workshop, Starlite, Persian cat, #683, 1963-78, 6½" 30.00

Designer's Workshop, Toulouse, goose, #636, 1956, 7"................. 200.00
Designer's Workshop, Tria, Morgan horse, palomino, #104, 1995-96, 4" ..150.00
Designer's Workshop, Zara, Arabian mare, blk, #708, currrent, 6½" ..200.00
Designer's Workshop, Zara, sm Arabian mare, gray, #708, 1970s, 6½".. 250.00
Disney miniature, Dumbo, 1956, 4"... 200.00
Disney miniature, Faun, right leg up, 1957, 1¼" 150.00

Disney miniature, Figaro, 2¼", Jiminy Cricket, 3½", 1956 only, $300.00 each.
(Photo courtesy Ed and Sheri Alcorn)

Disney miniature, Goofy, 1956, 2¼"... 85.00
Disney miniature, Hop Lo, mushroom, 1956-57,¾"........................ 50.00
Disney miniature, Madame Upanova, ostrich, 1982, 3¼" 300.00
Disney miniature, Pedro, chihuahua, 1955-59, 1⅜"...................... 60.00
Disney miniature, Si & Am, Siamese cats, 1955-59, 1¼", ea 100.00
Little Horribles miniature, Dark Eyes, #404, 1958, 1" 50.00
Little Horribles miniature, FHA, #434, 1959, scarce, 1⅜" 150.00
Little Horribles miniature, Hole in the Head, #422, 1959, 2¼" 85.00
Little Horribles miniature, Hula Hooper, #432, 1959, 2¼" 65.00
Miniature, aerobic pig, holds leg/pk outfit, A-3246, 1997-2003, 1⅛"...12.00
Miniature, anteater, wire tongue, rare, A-069, 1966, 1¾".......... 250.00
Miniature, Anvil (horse), silver & brn, A-394, 1959.................. 100.00
Miniature, Arabian mare, wht, A-046, 1959-70, 3"...................... 75.00
Miniature, Banty rooster, stretching neck, brn, A-94, 1970s, 2⅛" ...20.00
Miniature, beaver w/stump, A-399/400, 1960-90, 1"..................... 15.00
Miniature, Bichon Frise, A-3272, 1998-current, 1⅜" 6.00
Miniature, blk cat lying, A-326, 1990s, 1¼" 20.00
Miniature, Clydesdale foal, A-3156, 1994-2000, 2¾"................... 12.00
Miniature, dancing cats, romantic, #A-2002, 1988-2007, 2½" 15.00
Miniature, elephant on circus drum, A-881, 1987-97, 2".............. 15.00
Miniature, fantail goldfish, orange, A-426, 1960-76, 1" 20.00
Miniature, frisky colt, palomino, A-147R/147L, 1951-54, 2" 40.00
Miniature, goat mama, wht, A-848, 1984-current, 1⅜".....................7.00
Miniature, hammerhead shark, A-3187, 1995-97, 3¾" 15.00
Miniature, kitten climbing, Siamese, A-377, 1958-92, 1⅜" 10.00
Miniature, kitten in armchair, A-997-998, 1976-79, 1½" 35.00
Miniature, llama baby, A-873, 1986-87, 1⅛" 46.00
Miniature, Mr Dove, A-895, 1987-88, 1"................................... 12.00
Miniature, octopus, orange, A-3198, 1966-2001,¾".................... 12.00
Miniature, Pekingese facing left, A-2076, 1966-67, 1¾" 30.00
Miniature, Puffin, A-894, 1987-current, 1½".............................. 10.00
Miniature, pup playing (early), A-16, 1949,¾"............................. 40.00
Miniature, raccoon baby, brn, A-164, 1972-81, 1" 10.00
Miniature, St Bernard, A-3064, 1992-2006, 2"............................ 10.00
Miniature, Swaps, famous racehorse, A-030, 1991-93, 2¾"............ 35.00
Miniature, zebra mama, A-173, 1983-86, 1½" 45.00
Plaque, doe, red, 1959, 14x8½" 150.00
Plaque, geisha mosaic, 1959, 22x10½" 125.00
Plaque, Iris, sgn HR Calif, oval, #651, 1946-49, 5" 40.00
Plate, dinner; turkey/duck/rooster, #652, 1946-49, 8¾" 75.00
Shakers, duck design, rare, 1946-49, 2½", pr................................ 150.00
Specialty, Henny Penny, #3132, 2½"... 30.00
Specialty, Mother Goose, #3293, 1999-2001, 3½"........................ 25.00
Specialty, Nativity angel, blond, #3023, 1991-92, 2"...................... 45.00
Specialty, sea horse, orange, #2089, 1990-91, 2½"....................... 30.00

Specialty, seagulls, #3050, 1992-95, 4½" 45.00
Specialty, Sizzle, Appaloosa foal, #3268, 1998-2000, 2½" 40.00
Specialty, unicorn lying, #3040, 1991-current, 2⅜" 20.00
Tray, butterfly, Arizona Flagstone, 1960, sm, 10½x5½" 100.00
Zany Zoo, mouse, purple Aurasperse, 1960 only, 2¼" 250.00

Hagenauer

Carl Hagenauer founded his metal workshops in Vienna in 1898. He was joined by his son Karl in 1919. They produced a wide range of stylized sculptural designs in both metal and wood.

Bust of a woman in profile, chrome finish, applied and incised features, #1289W, 22x18x6", $12,000.00.

(Photo courtesy David Rago Auctions)

Candlesticks, brass, trumpet shape w/flat rim, 4-ftd, 1950, 6½", pr... 335.00
Figurine, abstract; Christ w/arms outstretched, bronze, ca 1930, 5"..205.00
Figurine, African women (4) paddling boat, wood/bronze/brass, 20" L ..900.00
Figurine, bear cup, modernist, bronze, 2x3" 170.00
Figurine, Black boy w/hands behind bk, bronze, w/brass necklace, 2"... 170.00
Figurine, female dancer, Deco style, bronze, ca 1925, 12¾" 70.00
Figurine, fowl, stylized, wood, 7½" 110.00
Figurine, hedgehog, bronze, 6 stacking parts, 2¾x4¼" 105.00
Figurine, horse head, curved neck, hollow metal on oval base, 5¼x5"..240.00
Figurine, Indian drawing bow, Deco style, bronze, 6½x3½" 195.00
Figurine, knight on horse jousting w/lance letter opener, bronze, 3x6".125.00
Figurine, mouse w/tail curved over head, bronze, ca 1930, 2" 75.00
Figurine, stag leaping, bronze, 4½x7¼" 115.00

Hair Weaving

A rather unusual craft became popular during the mid-1800s. Human hair was used to make jewelry (rings, bracelets, lockets, etc.) by braiding and interlacing fine strands into hollow forms with pearls and beads added for effect. Wreaths were also made, often using hair from deceased family members as well as the living. They were displayed in deep satin-lined frames along with mementoes of the weaver or her departed kin. The fad was abandoned before the turn of the century. The values suggested below are for mint condition examples. Any fraying of the hair greatly lowers value.

See also Mourning Collectibles.

Key:
p-w — palette work   t-w — table work

Bracelet, open t-w, p-w clasp, sewn-on hair flowers, ca 1850s 675.00
Bracelet, plaited w/gold-plated box clasp, 1840-70, VG 100.00
Bracelet, t-w (7) in 2 weaves, locket clasp w/daguerrotype, 1840s ..500.00
Bracelet, t-w braided tubes w/mini man's portrait in gold case, 1790s... 1,645.00
Bracelet, t-w in 3 weaves, gold mts, 1¼x6¾", VG+ 395.00

Bracelet, t-w weave w/box clasp & yel stone, 1850-80s................ 325.00
Bracelet, 3 braided t-w rows w/gold locket clasp, 1850-70s 525.00
Brooch, braided, under beveled glass amid pearls, 1830s, 1½"...... 375.00
Brooch, gold over brass, reverses w/hair ea side, 1860-80s, 1½" ... 350.00
Brooch, p-w basketweave, jet mt, 1850-60s, 2x1¼" 225.00
Brooch, p-w curl/flowers on gold-filled mt, 1½x1" 300.00
Brooch, p-w curls/flowers under glass in hollow gold fr, 1840s, 1⅞"..450.00
Brooch, p-w flowers/seed pearls, 1790-1830s, 1¼" 750.00
Brooch, swirl under glass in dmn-shaped jet fr, 1860-80s, 1"........ 150.00
Brooch, t-w balls & gold acorns, 1860-70s, 1x2⅝" 425.00
Brooch, t-w tubular bow w/gold mts, acorn drops, 1850-70s, 2½x2" ..475.00
Brooch, 18k yel gold eagle w/braids, early 1800s.....................1,000.00
Brooch/pendant, t-w on hard core w/gold mts, 1860-80s, 2x1⅜". 350.00
Earrings, open-weave t-w w/gold mts, 1850-70s, 1⅜", pr.............. 445.00
Earrings, t-w bell form w/gutta-percha details, 1850-70s, 1⅝", pr. 475.00
Earrings, t-w teardrop form w/gold mts, 1840-70s, 3¾", pr 425.00
Earrings, t-w w/openweave dangles, gold mts, 1850s-70s, 2½x1" . 550.00

Flower bouquet in shadow-box frame, dated 1878, 25x21", $900.00. (Photo courtesy Du Mouchelles/LiveAuctioneers.com)

Medallion, Prince of Wales feathers p-w on milk glass, 1840s, 1" 250.00
Necklace, t-w chain w/gold heart drop, 1850-80s, 14" 595.00
Necklace, t-w elongated caged balls in gold frs, 1850-80s, 18"..... 625.00
Necklace, t-w rows (3) in 2 weaves, gold mts, 1840-60s, 14" 450.00
Necklace, t-w 2-tone in X weave, gold balls & mts, 1840-80s 325.00
Ring, hollow gold band w/t-w insert, cutouts reveal hair, 1840-80..375.00
Ring, weaving under crystal, gold mt w/pearls, head: ½x¼" 425.00
Stickpin, t-w horseshoe w/gold mts, 1840-80s 125.00
Watch chain, t-w 2-color horsehair, ca 1860-90s, 13" 155.00
Watch chain, 2 rows t-w in 2 weaves, gold fob w/amethyst, 1850s... 225.00

Hall

The Hall China Company of East Liverpool, Ohio, was established in 1903. Their earliest products were whiteware toilet seats, mugs, jugs, etc. By 1920 their restaurant-type dinnerware and cookingware had become so successful that Hall was assured of a solid future. They continue today to be one of the country's largest manufacturers of this type of product.

Hall introduced the first of their famous teapots in 1920; new shapes and colors were added each year until about 1948, making them the largest teapot manufacturer in the world. These and the dinnerware lines of the '30s through the '50s have become popular collectibles. For more thorough study of the subject, we recommend *Collector's Encyclopedia of Hall China, Third Edition*, by Margaret and Kenn Whitmyer; their address may be found in the Directory under Ohio.

Blue Bouquet, bowl, cereal; D-style, 6" 22.00
Blue Bouquet, bowl, salad; 9" 20.00
Blue Bouquet, creamer, modern... 30.00
Blue Bouquet, plate, D-style, 8¼" 11.00
Blue Bouquet, spoon 135.00

Blue Bouquet, tureen, soup 320.00
Cameo Rose, butter dish, ¼-lb. 500.00
Cameo Rose, gravy boat, w/underplate 35.00
Cameo Rose, platter, 11¼" L 18.00
Cameo Rose, tidbit tray, 3-tier 75.00
Century Fern, creamer 12.00
Century Fern, ladle 22.00
Century Fern, saucer 1.50
Century Fern, shakers, pr 30.00
Century Garden of Eden, casserole 60.00
Century Garden of Eden, gravy boat 32.00
Century Sunglow, ashtray 9.00
Century Sunglow, plate, 8" 9.50
Century Sunglow, teapot, 6-cup 195.00
Christmas Tree & Holly, bowl, oval 60.00
Christmas Tree & Holly, cookie jar, Zeisel 350.00
Christmas Tree & Holly, plate, 10" 45.00
Christmas Tree & Holly, sugar bowl, open 45.00
Crocus, bowl, flat soup; 8½" 35.00
Crocus, cake plate 50.00

Crocus, coffeepot, Terrace shape, 8", from $50.00 to $65.00.

Crocus, jug, Simplicity 350.00
Crocus, leftover, sq. 120.00
Crocus, plate, D-style, 6" 8.00
Crocus, platter, D-style, 13¼" L 35.00
Crocus, pretzel jar 200.00
Gaillardia, baker, French; fluted 30.00
Gaillardia, bowl, D-style, Radiance, 9" 30.00
Gaillardia, cup, D-style 12.00
Gaillardia, drip jar, Radiance 35.00
Gaillardia, sugar bowl, Art Deco, w/lid 35.00
Game Bird, bowl, oval 65.00
Game Bird, bowl, thick rim, 8½" 45.00
Game Bird, creamer, New York 40.00
Game Bird, mug, Irish coffee 75.00
Game Bird, sugar bowl, New York, w/lid 55.00
Golden Oak, coffeepot, Kadota 85.00
Golden Oak, cup 6.00
Golden Oak, gravy boat 20.00
Golden Oak, plate, D-style, 9" 10.00
Golden Oak, shakers, hdld, pr 18.00
Heather Rose, bowl, cereal; 6¼" 10.00
Heather Rose, coffeepot, Terrace 45.00
Heather Rose, pickle dish, 9" 11.00
Heather Rose, plate, 6½" 3.50
Heather Rose, plate, 10" 12.50
Heather Rose, teapot, London 30.00
Homewood, coffeepot, Terrace 75.00
Homewood, cup, D-style 8.00
Homewood, saucer, D-style 1.50
Homewood, teapot, New York 175.00
Mums, bowl, D-style, 9¼" 45.00
Mums, bowl, Radiance, 7½" 27.00

Mums, creamer, New York 27.00
Mums, plate, D-style, 6" 5.50
Mums, pretzel jar 250.00
Mums, teapot, Boston 300.00
No 488, bowl, flat soup; 8½" 35.00
No 488, casserole, Five Band 75.00
No 488, cookie jar, Five Band 300.00
No 488, drip coffeepot, #691 .... 500.00
No 488, jug, Rayed 75.00
No 488, platter, D-style, 13¼" L 55.00
No 488, sugar bowl, Meltdown, w/lid 50.00
Orange Poppy, bowl, fruit; C-style, 5½" 8.50
Orange Poppy, cake plate 45.00
Orange Poppy, casserole, #76, rnd 40.00
Orange Poppy, match safe 110.00
Orange Poppy, mustard w/liner 145.00
Orange Poppy, pie baker 55.00
Orange Poppy, plate, C-style, 9" 30.00
Orange Poppy, teapot, Melody 360.00
Orange Poppy, teapot, Streamline 350.00
Pastel Morning Glory, bowl, D-style, 9¼" 45.00
Pastel Morning Glory, canister, Radiance 450.00
Pastel Morning Glory, drip jar, #1188, open 47.00
Pastel Morning Glory, gravy boat, D-style 35.00
Pastel Morning Glory, pie baker 50.00
Pastel Morning Glory, tea tile 120.00
Prairie Grass, bowl, oval, 9¼" 25.00
Prairie Grass, creamer 13.00
Prairie Grass, plate, 10" 14.00
Prairie Grass, tidbit, 3-tier 75.00
Primrose, ashtray 10.00
Primrose, bowl, salad; 9" 18.00
Primrose, jug, Rayed 22.00
Primrose, plate, 7¼" 6.50
Primrose, platter, 13¼" L 25.00
Red Poppy, cup, D-style 14.00
Red Poppy, custard 25.00
Red Poppy, jug, #5, Radiance 45.00
Red Poppy, plate, D-style, 8¼" 10.50

Red Poppy, pretzel jar, from $600.00 to $800.00. (Photo courtesy Margaret and Kenn Whitmyer)

Red Poppy, shakers, hdld, pr 50.00
Red Poppy, teapot, Aladdin 155.00
Sears' Arlington, bowl, flat soup; 8" 10.00
Sears' Arlington, bowl, vegetable; w/lid 40.00
Sears' Arlington, platter, 13¼" L 22.00
Sears' Fairfax, creamer 9.00
Sears' Fairfax, plate, 6½" 3.50
Sears' Fairfax, sugar bowl 17.00
Sears' Monticello, bowl, fruit; 5¼" 5.00
Sears' Monticello, plate, 10" 11.00
Sears' Monticello, platter, 15½" L 30.00
Sears' Mount Vernon, bowl, cereal; 6¼" 10.00

Sears' Mount Vernon, coffeepot 225.00
Sears' Mount Vernon, platter, 11¼" L 22.00
Serenade, bowl, flat soup; 8½" 14.00
Serenade, creamer, Art Deco 27.00
Serenade, drip jar, Radiance, w/lid 37.00
Serenade, pie baker 45.00
Serenade, platter, 13¼" L 27.00
Serenade, pretzel jar 160.00
Serenade, sugar bowl, Modern 30.00
Silhouette, bowl, vegetable; D-style, 9¼" 35.00
Silhouette, casserole, Medallion 45.00
Silhouette, custard, Medallion 30.00
Silhouette, gravy boat, D-style 35.00
Silhouette, leftover, sq 75.00
Silhouette, plate, 9" 18.00
Silhouette, shakers, Teardrop, pr 50.00
Silhouette, teapot, New York 250.00
Silhouette, teapot, Streamline 285.00
Springtime, cake plate 18.00
Springtime, pie baker 25.00
Springtime, plate, D-style, 7¼" 6.00
Springtime, saucer, D-style 2.50
Springtime, teapot, French 90.00
Tulip, bowl, D-style, 9¼" 35.00
Tulip, casserole, tab-hdld 125.00
Tulip, coffeepot, Perk 65.00
Tulip, platter, D-style, 11¼" L 30.00
Wildfire, bowl, 9" 32.00
Wildfire, creamer, Sani-Grid 30.00
Wildfire, cup, D-style 14.00
Wildfire, jug, Sani-Grid, 6" 75.00
Wildfire, plate, D-style, 10" 70.00
Wildfire, sugar bowl, Modern 35.00
Wildfire, teapot, Streamline 600.00
Yellow Rose, bowl, salad; 9" 27.00
Yellow Rose, custard 18.00
Yellow Rose, gravy boat, D-style 35.00
Yellow Rose, teapot, New York 200.00

Zeisel Designs, Hallcraft

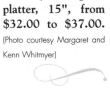

Century Sunglow, platter, 15", from $32.00 to $37.00.
(Photo courtesy Margaret and Kenn Whitmyer)

Tomorrow's Classic Arizona, butter dish 175.00
Tomorrow's Classic Arizona, onion soup, w/lid 37.00
Tomorrow's Classic Arizona, teapot, 6-cup 195.00
Tomorrow's Classic Bouquet, bottle, vinegar 95.00
Tomorrow's Classic Bouquet, bowl, celery; oval 30.00
Tomorrow's Classic Bouquet, candlestick, 8", ea 55.00
Tomorrow's Classic Bouquet, creamer 15.00
Tomorrow's Classic Bouquet, ladle 25.00
Tomorrow's Classic Bouquet, plate, 11" 16.00
Tomorrow's Classic Bouquet, platter, 15" L 35.00
Tomorrow's Classic Bouquet, saucer, AD 3.00

Tomorrow's Classic Buckingham, bowl, fruit; 5¾" 9.00
Tomorrow's Classic Buckingham, egg cup 55.00
Tomorrow's Classic Buckingham, platter, 17" L 40.00
Tomorrow's Classic Caprice, baker, open, 11-oz 22.00
Tomorrow's Classic Caprice, candlestick, 8", ea 45.00
Tomorrow's Classic Caprice, cup 10.00
Tomorrow's Classic Caprice, gravy boat 40.00
Tomorrow's Classic Caprice, plate, 11" 13.00
Tomorrow's Classic Caprice, sugar bowl 22.00
Tomorrow's Classic Caprice, teapot, 6-cup 195.00
Tomorrow's Classic Dawn, bowl, coupe soup; 9" 13.00
Tomorrow's Classic Dawn, butter dish 190.00
Tomorrow's Classic Dawn, platter, 15" L 37.00
Tomorrow's Classic Dawn, vase 95.00
Tomorrow's Classic Fantasy, bowl, vegetable; sq, 8¾" 25.00
Tomorrow's Classic Fantasy, casserole, 2-qt 55.00
Tomorrow's Classic Fantasy, marmite w/lid 40.00
Tomorrow's Classic Fantasy, plate, 8" 8.50
Tomorrow's Classic Flair, ashtray 10.00
Tomorrow's Classic Flair, bowl, salad; 14½" 45.00
Tomorrow's Classic Flair, casserole, 1¼-qt 40.00
Tomorrow's Classic Flair, jug, 3-qt 47.00
Tomorrow's Classic Flair, shakers, pr 36.00
Tomorrow's Classic Frost Flowers, baker, 11-oz 22.00
Tomorrow's Classic Frost Flowers, bowl, cereal; 6" 12.00
Tomorrow's Classic Frost Flowers, egg cup 50.00
Tomorrow's Classic Frost Flowers, plate, 6" 5.50
Tomorrow's Classic Harlequin, casserole, 2-qt 65.00
Tomorrow's Classic Harlequin, cookie jar, Zeisel-style . 300.00
Tomorrow's Classic Harlequin, platter, 17" 40.00
Tomorrow's Classic Lyric, candlestick, 4½", ea 32.00
Tomorrow's Classic Lyric, coffeepot, 6-cup 110.00
Tomorrow's Classic Lyric, cup 10.00
Tomorrow's Classic Lyric, onion soup, w/lid 37.00
Tomorrow's Classic Lyric, vase 80.00
Tomorrow's Classic Mulberry, bowl, celery; oval 24.00
Tomorrow's Classic Mulberry, candlestick, 8", ea 45.00
Tomorrow's Classic Mulberry, gravy boat 40.00
Tomorrow's Classic Mulberry, saucer, AD 4.50
Tomorrow's Classic Peach Blossom, bowl, fruit; ftd, lg .. 40.00
Tomorrow's Classic Peach Blossom, jug, 1¼" 28.00
Tomorrow's Classic Peach Blossom, platter, 17" 38.00
Tomorrow's Classic Peach Blossom, sugar bowl, AD, open .. 13.00
Tomorrow's Classic Pine Cone, bowl, coupe soup; 9" 16.00
Tomorrow's Classic Pine Cone, candlestick, 4½", ea 30.00
Tomorrow's Classic Pine Cone, coffeepot, 6-cup 105.00
Tomorrow's Classic Pine Cone, cup 7.00
Tomorrow's Classic Pine Cone, marmite w/lid 37.00
Tomorrow's Classic Pine Cone, plate, 8" 9.50
Tomorrow's Classic Pine Cone, saucer 2.00
Tomorrow's Classic Pine Cone, vase 80.00
Tomorrow's Classic Spring/Studio 10, bowl, salad; lg, 14½" . 35.00
Tomorrow's Classic Spring/Studio 10, casserole, 1¼-qt ... 35.00
Tomorrow's Classic Spring/Studio 10, egg cup 45.00
Tomorrow's Classic Spring/Studio 10, plate, 11" 13.00
Tomorrow's Classic Spring/Studio 10, platter, 17" L 38.00
Tomorrow's Classic Spring/Studio 10, shakers, pr 38.00

Teapots

Airflow, Canary, gold special, from $125 to 150.00
Airflow, Indian Red, from $125 to 150.00
Airflow, rose, standard gold, from $75 to 100.00
Aladdin, Cadet, gold label, from $200 to 225.00

Aladdin, maroon, solid color, from $75 to 85.00
Aladdin, turq, standard gold, from $90 to 110.00
Albany, blk, standard gold, from $50 to 60.00
Albany, emerald, solid color, from $50 to 60.00
Albany, Marine, standard gold, from $85 to............................. 90.00
Albany, pk, gold label, from $150 to 175.00
Art Deco, bl, Adele, from $200 to.. 250.00
Art Deco, gr, Damascus, from $190 to.................................. 210.00
Art Deco, yel, Danielle, from $170 to................................... 190.00
Baltimore, Cadet, standard gold, from $75 to 85.00
Baltimore, ivory w/pk rose decal, from $200 to..................... 225.00
Bellevue, orchid, 2-cup, from $200 to.................................. 250.00
Boston, blk, solid color, 1- to 3-up, from $20 to...................... 25.00
Boston, cobalt, old gold design, 1- to 3-cup, from $100 to 125.00
Boston, cobalt, standard gold, 1- to 3-cup, from $57 to.............. 65.00
Boston, ivory, gold label, 1- to 3-cup, from $55 to 60.00
Cleveland, Chinese Red, solid color, from $300 to 340.00
Cleveland, turq, standard gold, from $75 to............................. 85.00
French, Dresden, solid color, 1- to 3-cup, from $35 to 45.00
French, gray, gold label, 1- to 3-cup, from $65 to 70.00
French, rose, solid color, 4- to 8-cup, from $40 to.................... 50.00
Globe, Camellia, standard gold, from $70 to 80.00
Globe, emerald, solid color, from $100 to 150.00
Hollywood, blk, standard gold, from $50 to 55.00
Hollywood, Marine, gold label, from $100 to 125.00
Hook Cover, Canary, standard gold, from $50 to....................... 60.00
Hook Cover, Silver Luster, solid color, from $100 to.................. 125.00
Illinois, Chinese Red, solid color, from $450 to 500.00
Illinois, Stock Brown, standard gold, from $140 to................... 160.00
Indiana, ivory, standard gold, from $250 to........................... 275.00
Indiana, Warm Yellow, solid color, from $300 to 400.00
Kansas, maroon, solid color, from $300 to............................. 350.00
Kansas, maroon, standard gold, from $400 to 500.00
Los Angeles, Dresden, standard gold, from $50 to 55.00
Los Angeles, pk, gold label, from $75 to 85.00
Melody, blk, standard gold, from $125 to 155.00
Melody, turq, solid color, from $190 to 210.00
Moderne, Canary, solid color, from $45 to 55.00
Moderne, Chinese Red, solid color, from $125 to...................... 160.00
Musical, Canary, from $155 to.. 170.00
Nautilus, ivory, solid color, from $100 to 125.00
Nautilus, turq, standard gold, from $240 to 260.00
New York, Dresden, standard gold, 1- to 4-cup, from $40 to.......... 50.00
Newport, Warm Yellow, solid color, from $50 to 60.00
Ohio, cobalt, standard gold, from $350 to.............................. 400.00
Ohio, pk, gold dot, from $250 to 300.00
Philadelphia, Indian Red, solid color, from $165 to.................. 190.00
Sundial, blk, solid color, from $50 to.................................... 60.00
Sundial, emerald, standard gold, from $85 to........................... 95.00

Tea for Two, Cadet with gold Illinois decoration, from $120.00 to $140.00. (Photo courtesy Margaret and Kenn Whitmyer)

Halloween

Though the origin of Halloween is steeped in pagan rites and su-perstitions, today Halloween is strictly a fun time, and Halloween items are fun to collect. Pumpkin-head candy containers of papier-maché or pressed cardboard, noisemakers, postcards with black cats and witches, costumes, and decorations are only a sampling of the variety available.

Here's how you can determine the origin of your jack-o'-lantern:

American 1940 – 1950s	German 1900 – 1930s

items are larger	items are generally small
made of egg-carton material	made of cardboard or composition
bottom and body are one piece	always has a cut-out triangular nose; simple, crisscross lines in mouth; blue rings in eyes
	have attached cardboard bottoms

For further information we recommend *More Halloween Collectibles, Anthropomorphic Vegetables and Fruits of Halloween*, by Pamela E. Apkarian-Russell (Schiffer). Other good reference books are *Halloween in America* by Stuart Schneider and *Halloween Collectables* by Dan and Pauline Campanelli.

Our advisor for this category is Jenny Tarrant; she is listed in the Directory under Missouri. See Clubs, Newsletters, and Catalogs for information concerning the *Trick or Treat Trader,* a quarterly newsletter. Unless noted otherwise, values are for examples in excellent to near mint condition except for paper items, in which case assume the condition to be near mint to mint.

American

Most American items were made during the 1940s and 1950s, though a few date from the 1930s as well. Lanterns are constructed either of flat cardboard or the pressed cardboard pulp used to make the jack-o'-lantern shown on the left above.

Pirate's Auto, 1950s, 5" long, $450.00. (Photo courtesy Morphy Auctions/LiveAuctioneers.com)

Jack-o'-lantern, pressed cb pulp w/orig face, 4-4½", from $95 to.. 110.00
Jack-o'-lantern, pressed cb pulp w/orig face, 5-5½", from $115 to ...125.00
Jack-o'-lantern, pressed cb pulp w/orig face, 6-6½", from $130 to ...135.00
Jack-o'-lantern, pressed cb pulp w/orig face, 7" 150.00

Jack-o'-lantern, pressed cb pulp w/orig face, 8", minimum value.. 175.00
Lantern, cat, pressed cb pulp w/orig face................................. 175.00
Lantern, cat (full body), pressed cb pulp, 7x6½"...................... 350.00
Lantern, cb w/tab sides, any... 75.00
Lantern, pumpkin man (full body), pressed cb pulp 350.00
Plastic Halloween car 450.00
Plastic pumpkin stagecoach, witch & cat.............................. 550.00
Plastic witch holding blk cat w/wobbling head, on wheels, 7" 300.00
Plastic witch on rocket, horizontal, on wheels, 7" 300.00
Plastic witch on rocket, on wheels, 4" 95.00
Plastic witch on rocket, vertical, on wheels, 7"...................... 300.00
Tin noisemaker, bell style 35.00
Tin noisemaker, can shaker 35.00
Tin noisemaker, clicker 35.00
Tin noisemaker, frying-pan style 35.00
Tin noisemaker, horn 35.00
Tin noisemaker, sq spinner 35.00
Tin noisemaker, tambourine, Chein..................................... 75.00
Tin noisemaker, tambourine, Kirkoff 95.00
Tin noisemaker, tambourine, Ohio Art, 1930s, 6" dia 75.00

Celluloid (German, Japanese, or American)

Blk cat, plain, celluloid, M 150.00
Egg-shape house, celluloid, M 400.00
Long-leg veggie rattle, celluloid, M.................................... 300.00
Owl, plain, celluloid, M... 85.00
Owl on pumpkin, celluloid, M 125.00
Owl on tree, celluloid, M.. 200.00
Pumpkin-face man, celluloid, M 350.00
Pumpkin-face pirate, celluloid, M 400.00
Scarecrow, celluloid, M.. 200.00
Witch, plain, celluloid, M 200.00
Witch in auto, celluloid, M 450.00
Witch in corncob car, celluloid, M..................................... 450.00
Witch pulling cart w/ghost, celluloid, M.............................. 400.00
Witch pulling pumpkin cart w/cat, celluloid, M 400.00
Witch sitting on pumpkin, celluloid, M................................ 350.00

German

As a general rule, German Halloween collectibles date from 1900 through the early 1930s. They were made either of composition or molded cardboard, and their values are higher than American-made items. In the listings that follow, all candy containers are made of composition unless noted otherwise.

Candy container, blk cat walking, glass eyes, head removes, 3-4" ...225.00
Candy container, blk cat walking, glass eyes, head removes, 5-6" ...350.00
Candy container, cat sitting, glass eyes, 4-6".......................... 200.00
Candy container, cat sitting, 3-5"...................................... 175.00
Candy container, cat walking, w/mohair, 5" 350.00
Candy container, compo, witch or pumpkin man, head removes, 4".225.00
Candy container, compo pumpkin-head man (or any vegetable), on box, 3"...175.00
Candy container, compo pumpkin-head man (or any vegetable), on box, 4"...185.00
Candy container, compo pumpkin-head man (or any vegetable), on box, 5"...225.00
Candy container, compo pumpkin-head man (or any vegetable), on box, 6"...275.00
Candy container, compo witch, pumpkin people, devil, ghost, etc, 3" .225.00
Candy container, compo witch or pumpkin man, head removes, 5" .350.00
Candy container, compo witch or pumpkin man, head removes, 6" ..400.00
Candy container, compo witch or pumpkin man, head removes, 7" ..450.00
Candy container, lemon-head man, pnt compo, 7" 575.00
Candy container, witch, pumpkin people, devil, etc, solid figure, 4"..150.00
Candy container, witch, pumpkin people, devil, etc, solid figure, 5"..175.00

Candy container, nodder girl pulls pumpkin on wheels, composition, 4", $420.00. (Photo courtesy Morphy Auctions/LiveAuctioneers.com)

Candy container, witch, pumpkin people, devil, etc, solid figure, 6"..200.00
Die-cut, bat, emb cb, M, from $95 to.................................. 125.00
Die-cut, cat, emb cb, from $55 to...................................... 95.00
Die-cut, cat (dressed), emb cb 150.00
Die-cut, devil, emb cb, from $95 to 150.00
Die-cut, jack-o'-lantern, emb cb.. 65.00
Die-cut, pumpkin man or lady, emb cb, 7½" 125.00
Jack-o'-lantern, compo w/orig insert, 3"............................... 225.00
Jack-o'-lantern, compo w/orig insert, 4"............................... 250.00
Jack-o'-lantern, compo w/orig insert, 5"............................... 350.00
Jack-o'-lantern, molded cb w/orig insert, 3".......................... 95.00

Jack 'o lantern, molded cardboard w/paper face insert, ca 1920, 4", minimum value, $300.00. (Photo courtesy Morphy Auctions/ LiveAuctioneers.com)

Jack-o'-lantern, molded cb w/orig insert, 4"........................... 125.00
Jack-o'-lantern, molded cb w/orig insert, 5"........................... 155.00
Jack-o'-lantern, molded cb w/orig insert, 6"........................... 185.00
Lantern, cat, cb, molded nose, bow under chin, 3".................... 250.00
Lantern, cat, cb, molded nose, bow under chin, 4".................... 300.00
Lantern, cat, cb, molded nose, bow under chin, 5".................... 450.00
Lantern, cat, cb, simple rnd style...................................... 225.00
Lantern (ghost, skull, devil, witch, etc), molded cb, 3-4", minimum .300.00
Lantern (ghost, skull, devil, witch, etc), molded cb, 5"+, minimum ..350.00
Lantern (skull, devil, witch, etc), compo, 3", minimum value 300.00
Lantern (skull, devil, witch, etc), compo, 4", minimum value 400.00
Lantern (skull, devil, witch, etc), compo, 5", minimum value 450.00
Noisemaker, cat (3-D) on wood rachet................................. 95.00
Noisemaker, cb figure (flat) on rachet................................. 95.00
Noisemaker, cb paddle w/die-cut face 95.00
Noisemaker, devil (3-D) on wood rachet............................... 95.00
Noisemaker, pumpkin head (rnd, 3-D) on wood rachet 95.00
Noisemaker, tin frying-pan paddle, Germany, no rust or dents, 5" L.. 75.00
Noisemaker, tin horn, Germany, 3"..................................... 75.00
Noisemaker, veggie (3-D) horn (w/pnt face) 125.00
Noisemaker, veggie or fruit (3-D) horn (no face), ea.................. 55.00
Noisemaker, witch (3-D) on wood rachet............................... 115.00
Noisemaker, wood & paper tambourine w/pumpkin face 150.00

Hampshire

The Hampshire Pottery Company was established in 1871 in Keene,

New Hampshire, by James Scollay Taft. Their earliest products were red-ware and stoneware utility items such as jugs, churns, crocks, and flower-pots. In 1878 they produced majolica ware which met with such success that they began to experiment with the idea of manufacturing art pottery. By 1883 they had developed a Royal Worcester type of finish which they applied to vases, tea sets, powder boxes, and cookie jars. It was also utilized for souvenir items that were decorated with transfer designs prepared from photographic plates.

Cadmon Robertson, brother-in-law of Taft, joined the company in 1904 and was responsible for developing their famous matt glazes. Colors included shades of green, brown, red, and blue. Early examples were of earthenware, but eventually the body was changed to semiporcelain. Some of his designs were marked with an M in a circle as a tribute to his wife, Emoretta. Robertson died in 1914, leaving a void impossible to fill. Taft sold the business in 1916 to George Morton, who continued to use the matt glazes that Robertson had developed. After a temporary halt in production during WWI, Morton returned to Keene and re-equipped the factory with the machinery needed to manufacture hotel china and floor tile. Because of the expense involved in transporting coal to fire the kilns, Morton found he could not compete with potteries of Ohio and New Jersey who were able to utilize locally available natural gas. He was forced to close the plant in 1923.

Interest is highest in examples with the curdled, two-tone matt glazes, and it is the glaze, not the size or form, that dictates value. The souvenir pieces are not particularly of high quality and tend to be passed over by today's collectors. Our advisors for this category are Suzanne Perrault and David Rago; they are listed in the Directory under New Jersey.

Bowl, gr, emb water lily buds & pads, 3¼x10" 480.00
Ewer, gr, stylized hdl, ftd, 8" 110.00
Lamp, fairy; gr, squat, loop hdl, w/ribbed frosted shade, #140, 3", EX.400.00
Lamp base, gr, emb tulips, squat, 6x11½" 1,200.00
Pitcher, gr, emb leaves/vines, leafy top, vine hdl, #8P/M, 8½x5"... 575.00
Pitcher, lt gr matt, flared bottom, emb rim, 12" 570.00
Vase, bl, bulbous, 5" 180.00

Vase, bl, dandelions embossed on feathered cobalt, #464, 6x5¼", $1,140.00. (Photo courtesy David Rago Auctions)

Vase, bl, emb gr feathers, trumpet neck, #124, 9¼x6½" 1,400.00
Vase, bl, 2 rows emb leaves, #127/M, 8¼" 840.00
Vase, bl & gr leather-like matt, bulbous, 8¾x9¾" 3,500.00
Vase, bl & gr mottle, emb buds at shoulder, bulbous, #130, 7¾x7".. 1,320.00
Vase, bl mottle, shouldered, thick lipped rim, #110/M, 4½" 230.00
Vase, bl mottle (volcanic), shouldered, #90, 9" 1,100.00
Vase, bl/gr, organic form w/leafy top, #24, 2¾" 660.00
Vase, bl/gr (frothy), shouldered, #66, 12¼x5" 900.00
Vase, bl/gr (frothy) w/cobalt/apricot shoulder, emb leaves, #98, 7x5" . 990.00
Vase, bl/gr crystalline, emb acanthus leaves, #98, 7" 1,140.00
Vase, bl/gr mottle, bulbous, flared rim, #118, 5¼" 725.00
Vase, bl/gray matt w/glossy int, geometrics at neck, #103, 12" 775.00
Vase, curdled bl over gr, emb panels, shouldered, #129, 5½x6½".... 1,200.00
Vase, gr, emb Greek key, cylindrical neck, buttressed hdls, 14¾"... 1,550.00
Vase, gr, emb leaves, ovoid, #46/H, 3½x3½" 450.00

Vase, gr, emb lilies, trumpet form, disk ft, 15" 845.00
Vase, gr, lg emb leaves, shouldered, tapered bottom, 15x9".......2,500.00
Vase, gr (flowing), emb panels, shouldered, #68/M, 8½" 780.00
Vase, gr (flowing), emb panels on melon form, #119, 5" 740.00
Vase, gr orange peel, 7" 360.00

Handel

Philip Handel was best known for the art glass lamps he produced at the turn of the century. His work is similar to the Tiffany lamps of the same era. Handel made gas and electric lamps with both leaded glass and reverse-painted shades. Chipped ice shades with a texture similar to overshot glass were also produced. Shades signed by artists such as Bailey, Palme, and Parlow are highly valued.

Teroma lamp shades were created from clear blown glass blanks that were painted on the interior (reverse painted), while Teroma art glass (the decorative vases, humidors, etc. in the Handel Ware line) is painted on the exterior. This type of glassware has a 'chipped ice' effect achieved by sand blasting and coating the surface with fish glue. The piece is kiln fired at 800 degrees F. The contraction of the glue during the cooling process gives the glass a frosted, textured effect. Some shades are sand finished, adding texture and depth. Both the glassware and chinaware decorated by Handel are rare and command high prices on today's market. Many of Handel's chinaware blanks were supplied by Limoges.

Key:
chp — chipped/lightly sanded   h/cp — hammered copper

Handel Ware

Unless noted china, all items in the following listing are glass.

Charger, birds of paradise, chipped ice finish on opal glass, 20", $2,000.00. (Photo courtesy Cincinnati Art Galleries)

Candlestick, Teroma, widmill scene, invt trumpet form, 8½", ea 750.00
Humidor, bronzed matt, china, #4091/AC, 7" 960.00
Humidor, cigars & horse's head, china, #4091H, pnt losses, 6x3.. 475.00
Humidor, Indian portrait, china, bronze-mtd hinged lid, #89/130, 8"... 1,200.00
Mug, monk reading, red-brn tones on wht china......................... 350.00
Pitcher, man on horse in landscape, earth tones, china, 6x9" 515.00
Vase, cameo floral, amber to clear, #4258, 11x4½" 1,325.00
Vase, Teroma, landscape w/trees & birds, sgn Bragg, #4217, 11½" ...2,150.00
Vase, Teroma, trees/foliage, flared cylinder, #4219, 10¾x6¾" 1,800.00

Lamps

Base, bronze maiden holding jug, 3-socket, 24¾x7" 7,800.00
Boudoir, egg form w/HP lady wht crackle #7267-62 shade; wood base, 8"...400.00
Boudoir, rvpt floral 7" #6649 shade; basketweave-style std, 14"..1,265.00
Boudoir, rvpt 6½" foliage #5512 shade; bronzed std, 14" 6,000.00
Boudoir, rvpt 7" cranes/bamboo #7061 shade; mk bronzed std, 16"..2,800.00
Boudoir, rvpt 7" desert scenic #6557 shade; mk bronzed std, 16"...4,315.00
Candlestick, 15½" roses panel #7792 shade; 2-candle base, 20" .. 2,400.00

Chandelier, 5 drops w/gold Aurene shades; hammered metal mts, 22x42" .6,000.00
Floor, chp 13½" hemispherical shade w/stenciled band; harp fr, 59" ..4,500.00
Floor, gr Steuben 6x7½" shade; bronze std w/verdigris, 55½" 7,200.00
Floor, o/l 23" panel shade w/leaf decor; re-patinated bronzed std, 64" ... 6,500.00
Floor, o/l 24" 8-panel Arts & Crafts shade; bronzed std, 65" 5,175.00
Floor, o/l 24½" 8-panel pine trees/needles shade; ribbed std, 65" ...9,200.00
Floor, rvpt 10" floral shade; bronzed harp std, 57" 2,200.00
Globe, pnt trees/birds on acid-etched lustre, #6885, 18x9" dia ..4,200.00
Piano, ldgl 7" shade; bronze base adjusts, 9x18" 4,200.00
Piano, Mosserine 8" brn shade; lily-pad base w/curved arm, 13" .. 800.00
Sconces, yel slag & opal 4" petal shade; bronze mts, 8" from wall, pr.. 1,495.00
Student, dbl; o/l 7" Hawaiian sunset shades w/palms; bronzed std, 25"....3,100.00
Student, Mosserine 12½" #6028 shade; fluted bronze std, 15" ...1,450.00
Table, HP/etched 18" peacock dome shade; classical bronze std, 24"..22,800.00
Table, ldgl 9" cylindrical shade; arched bronzed base, 15" 960.00
Table, ldgl 19" geometric shade; 4-socket bronze std, 27" 600.00

Table, metal overlay palm trees, 24x20", $6,900.00. (Photo courtesy James D. Julia Inc.)

Table, o/l 11½" sq shade w/ivy/berry border, simple std, 19½" ... 1,035.00
Table, o/l 16" grapevine shade; mk leaf-design std, 20½"...........2,875.00
Table, o/l 16" 7-panel floral shade; 3-socket stick std, 22" 4,025.00
Table, o/l 16½" caramel slag bent-panel shade; bronzed std, 22"....3,675.00
Table, o/l 18" fishscale on 8-panel shade; mk bronzed std, 22", NM...2,525.00
Table, o/l 20" floral pattern on gr slag shade; 4-socket h/cp std, 28". 18,000.00
Table, o/l 20" shade w/bellflower border; unmk bronzed std, 23" ...4,600.00
Table, o/l 20" 8-panel cattail #924457 shade; Nouveau std, 23" ... 11,500.00
Table, obverse/rvpt 16" scenic #5641 shade; rpt 6-sided std, 24" ...2,875.00
Table, rvpt 11" leafy-decor mushroom #5468 shade; bronze std, 20" ..7,200.00
Table, rvpt 14" roses #6175 shade; unmk bronze std, 20¼"........3,000.00
Table, rvpt 14" roses on yel #6396 shade; bronzed base (crack), 20" ..1,880.00
Table, rvpt 18" cranes/bamboo shade; Oriental bronzed std, 24" .. 18,000.00
Table, rvpt 18" flowers/leaves #5564 shade; bronzed std, 23¾" .16,800.00
Table, rvpt 18" moonlit landscape #6324 shade; bronze std, 23½".. 7,200.00
Table, rvpt 18" parrots/floral #7128 shade; mk bronze std, 25" .. 13,200.00
Table, rvpt 18" Persian #6747 shade; bronzed metal std, 24".....4,000.00
Table, rvpt 18" roses/butterfly #6688 shade; bronzed std, 23¼".12,000.00
Table, rvpt 18" Venetian harbor #5935 shade; bronzed unmk std, 25" . 9,600.00
Table, rvpt/chp 18" parrot/tropics #6874P shade; bronze std, 23" . 12,000.00
Table, rvpt/chp 18" river scenic shade; ribbed bronze std, 25½" . 10,800.00
Table, 18" rvpt Bedigie landscape #7118 shade; bronzed std, 23½" ..9,000.00
Table, 18" rvpt daffodil #7122 shade; bronzed Pat # std, 24¼" .13,200.00
Tulip, gr & wht bent-panel shade; lily pad base, 12", EX............. 480.00

Harker

The Harker Pottery was established in East Liverpool, Ohio, in 1840. Their earliest products were yellow ware and Rockingham produced from local clay. After 1900 whiteware was made from imported materials. The plant eventually grew to be a large manufacturer of dinnerware and kitchenware, employing as many as 300 people. It closed in 1972 after it was purchased by the Jeannette Glass Company. Perhaps their best-known lines were their Cameo wares, decorated with white silhouettes in a cameo effect on contrasting solid colors. Floral silhouettes are standard, but other designs were also used. Blue and pink are the most often found background hues; a few pieces are found in yellow. For further information we recommend *The Best of Collectible Dinnerware* by Jo Cunningham (Schiffer). Our advisor for this category is Ted Haun; he is listed in the Directory under Indiana.

Springtime, tray, 11½", from $9.00 to $12.00.

Amy, bean pot, ind, 2¼" 7.00
Amy, rolling pin, 13" 100.00
Apple/Pear, bowl, cereal; red rim, 5⅜" 25.00
Apple/Pear, bowl, swirled, 9" 37.50
Apple/Pear, cheese plate, 11" 50.00
Apple/Pear, coffee/teacup 12.50
Apple/Pear, cookie jar, from $75 to 95.00
Bridal Rose, creamer 15.00
Bridal Rose, cup & saucer, 2⅝" 15.00
Bridal Rose, plate, luncheon; 9½" 8.00
Bridal Rose, platter, 12¼" L 35.00
Bridal Rose, platter, 16" L.. 50.00
Brown-Eyed Susan, plate, bread & butter 6.00
Brown-Eyed Susan, plate, dinner; 10" 9.00
Brown-Eyed Susan, platter, 13½" L 45.00
Brown-Eyed Susan, saucer 6.00
Cameo Dainty Flower, ashtray, bl, Virginia shape, 5" 10.00
Cameo Dainty Flower, bowl, vegetable; bl, swirl, 9" 20.00
Cameo Dainty Flower, bowl, yel (rare), 2½x5¾" 45.00
Cameo Dainty Flower, casserole, bl, Zephyr shape, w/lid, 1-qt, 8½" ...100.00
Cameo Dainty Flower, casserole, pk, w/lid & underplate, 5x6⅝" ... 40.00
Cameo Dainty Flower, plate, bl, Virgina shape, 9"......................... 12.00
Cameo Dainty Flower, platter, bl, swirl, 12x9"............................ 20.00
Cameo Dainty Flower, platter, tan, 11½x9⅞" 15.00
Cameo Dainty Flower, saucer, bl 5.00
Cameo Dainty Flower, sugar bowl, pk, Virgina shape, open 17.00
Cameo Dainty Flower, teapot, bl, Zephyr shape, 4-cup 90.00
Chesterton, bowl, vegetable; oval, 2⅝x8¾" 35.00
Chesterton, cake lifter, 9¾" 12.00
Chesterton, coffee cup 7.00
Chesterton, platter, 11¾" L 40.00
Chesterton, sauceboat.. 25.00
Chesterton, snack plate & cup, 9½" 12.00
Modern Tulip, bowl, cereal; 6" 10.00
Modern Tulip, cake plate, metal fr 20.00
Modern Tulip, casserole, w/lid, 3¾x7⅜"..................................... 75.00
Modern Tulip, creamer 20.00
Modern Tulip, cup & saucer 20.00
Modern Tulip, pie serving plate, 9" 45.00
Modern Tulip, rolling pin, 13"... 85.00
Pate Sur Pate, bowl, fruit; 5½" 7.00
Pate Sur Pate, bowl, vegetable; oval, 9½" 20.00
Pate Sur Pate, cup & saucer...5.00

Pate Sur Pate, plate, salad; 7⅜"	6.00
Pate Sur Pate, sugar bowl, w/lid	24.00
Petit Point, bowl, mixing; 9"	35.00
Petit Point, bowl, swirl, 9¼"	25.00
Petit Point, casserole, w/lid, 8½"	50.00
Petit Point, egg cups, dbl, 3¼", set of 4 in metal fr	85.00
Petit Point, plate, dinner; 9¼"	10.00
Petit Point, salad fork & spoon	30.00
Petit Point, teapot	35.00

Hatpin Holders

Most hatpin holders were made from 1860 to 1920 to coincide with the period during which hatpins were popularly in vogue. The taller types were required to house the long hatpins necessary to secure the large hats that were in style from 1890 to 1914. They were usually porcelain, either decorated by hand or by transfer with florals or scenics, although some were clever figurals. Glass examples are rare, and those of slag or carnival glass are especially valuable.

For information concerning the American Hatpin Society, see the Clubs, Newsletters, and Catalogs section of the Directory. Our advisor for this category is Virginia Woodbury; she is listed in the Directory under California (SASE required).

Schafer and Vater, figural poppy, from $575.00 to $650.00. (Photo courtesy Robert Larsen)

Austria, HP floral w/gold, ca 1899-1918, 4¼"	145.00
Austria, Nouveau gold leaves w/emb swirls, 4x3"	65.00
Goss, City of York crest, solid base, 3½"	110.00
Limoges, classical lady & peacock w/gold, 7-hole, LP, 3⅝"	250.00
Nippon, cottage & meadow, gold beading, 5"	95.00
Nippon, violets reserves w/gold, tapered sq, pre-1921, 4¾"	125.00
Royal Bayreuth, clover form, 13-hole, bl mk, 4½x2¼", $425 to	500.00
Royal Bayreuth, crocus form, 16-hole, bl mk, 1¾", from $475 to	550.00
Royal Bayreuth, lady's portrait, 15-hole, bl mk, 4½"	450.00
Royal Doulton, Ophelia on dk cream, gr trim, 7-hole, 5x3½"	285.00
Schafer & Vader, basket w/roses, hangs/11-hole, 1910s, 6½", $225 to	275.00
Schafer & Vader, lady cameo, Jasper, hangs, 6-hole, 6¾"	350.00
SP w/thistle-cut faux amethyst, plush cushion, ca 1900, 4½"	185.00
Unmk wht bsk, HP pastel figures/gold trim, triangular, 4½"	250.00
Willow Art China, transfer, souvenir of Jerusalem, 5½"	110.00

Hatpins

A hatpin was used to securely fasten a hat to the hair and head of the wearer. Hatpins, measuring from 7" to 12" in length, were worn from approximately 1850 to 1920. During the Art Deco period, hatpins became ornaments rather than the decorative functional jewels that they had been. The hatpin period reached its zenith in 1913 just prior to World War I, which brought about a radical change in women's headdress and fashion. About that time, women began to scorn the bonnet and adopt 'the hat' as a symbol of their equality. The hatpin was made of every natural and manufactured element in a myriad of designs that challenge the imagination. They were contrived to serve every fashion need and complement the milliner's art. Collectors often concentrate on a specific type: hand-painted porcelains, sterling silver, commemoratives, sporting activities, carnival glass, Art Nouveau and/or Art Deco designs, Victorian gothics with mounted stones, exquisite rhinestones, engraved and brass-mounted escutcheon heads, gold and gems, or simply primitive types made in the Victorian parlor. Some collectors prefer the long pin-shanks while others select only those on tremblants or nodder-type pin-shanks.

If you are interested in collecting or dealing in hatpins, see the information in the Hatpin Holders introduction concerning a national collectors' club. Our advisor for this category is Virginia Woodbury; she is listed in the Directory under California (SASE required).

Aquamarine set in enameled Greek key surround, inner band of gilded metal rope, ⅜x1" head, 6" pin, $260.00. (Photo courtesy neatstuffdave)

Antiqued brass w/4 faux topaz, 2¾" on brass pin, 1910, $135 to	250.00
Baroque MOP w/gold-strap mt, faceted red glass accents, 1½", $85 to	100.00
Cabachon garnet tops 1" head, 5½" gilt pin, from $110 to	135.00
Ceramic, HP Deco design, button-sleeve mt, 1½", from $95 to	125.00
Gr faceted stone amid 15 brilliants, 1x1", brass pin, up to	165.00
Ivory hollow-cvd floral 1" head, steel pin, finding unscrews, $185 to	250.00
Jet glass faceted stones in wire fr, japanned shank, from $155 to	225.00
Oxodized brass Nouveau triangle w/purple stone, 1900s, 1¼", $75 to	95.00
Peacock Eye glass, ⅞" oval head, 7½" steel pin, ca 1905, $45 to	95.00
Porc, ball w/transfer & HP details, gold o/l, 1895, 1¼", $185 to	300.00
Satsuma, HP birds & leaves, 1½", 10½" steel pin, from $180 to	295.00
Sterling, Billiken figural, Trade Mark Billiken, 1x1½", brass pin	180.00
Sterling, lady's head in suffragette cap, repoussé, 1900s, 1", $100 to	150.00
Sterling, Nouveau stylized lady w/repoussé work, Am, ca 1905, $85 to	100.00

Haviland

The Haviland China Company was organized in 1840 by David Haviland, a New York china importer. His search for a pure white, nonporous porcelain led him to Limoges, France, where natural deposits of suitable clay had already attracted numerous china manufacturers. The fine china he produced there was translucent and meticulously decorated, with each piece fired in an individual sagger.

It has been estimated that as many as 60,000 chinaware patterns were designed, each piece marked with one of several company backstamps. 'H. & Co.' was used until 1890 when a law was enacted making it necessary to include the country of origin. Various marks have been used since that time including 'Haviland, France'; 'Haviland & Co. Limoges'; and 'Decorated by Haviland & Co.' Various associations with family members over the years have resulted in changes in management as well as company name. In 1892 Theodore Haviland left the firm to start his own business. Some of his ware was marked 'Mont Mery.' Later logos included a horseshoe, a shield, and various uses of his initials and name. In 1941 this branch moved to the United States. Wares produced here are marked 'Theodore Haviland, N.Y.' or 'Made In America.'

Though it is their dinnerware lines for which they are most famous, during the 1880s and 1890s they also made exquisite art pottery using a technique of underglaze slip decoration called Barbotine, which had been invented by Ernest Chaplet. In 1885 Haviland bought the formula and hired Chaplet to oversee its production. The technique involved mixing heavy white clay slip with pigments to produce a compound of the same consistency as oil paints. The finished product actually resembled oil paintings of the period, the texture achieved through the application of the heavy medium to the clay body in much the same manner as an artist would apply paint to his canvas. Primarily the body used with this method was a low-fired faience, though they also produced stoneware. Numbers in the listings below refer to pattern books by Arlene Schleiger. For further information we recommend Mary Frank Gaston's *Collector's Encyclopedia of Limoges Porcelain, Third Edition* (the first two editions are out of print), which offers examples and marks of the Haviland Company. Mrs. Gaston is listed in the Directory under Texas.

Bowl, dk bl bands on wht w/gold, nut finial on lid, H&Co, 12"...475.00
Bowl, lg bl floral w/brn leaves on cream, sq, H&Co, 10"................75.00
Cake plate, Moss Rose center, pk border, H&Co, 9½"..................150.00

Game service, Theo Haviland, 19" platter and eight 9" plates, $3,500.00.

(Photo courtesy O'Gallerie/LiveAuctioneers.com)

Plate, shellfish; gr floral border w/gold trim, H&Co.....................225.00
Plate, Silver Anniversary pattern, H&Co, 10"..............................55.00
Sugar bowl, Moss Rose w/bl accents, emb ropes, w/lid, H&Co, 7½"..185.00

Hawkes

Thomas Hawkes established his factory in Corning, New York, in 1880. He developed many beautiful patterns of cut glass, two of which were awarded the Grand Prize at the Paris Exposition in 1889. By the end of the century, his company was renowned for the finest in cut glass production. The company logo was a trefoil form enclosing a hawk in each of the two bottom lobes with a fleur-de-lis in the center. With the exception of some of the very early designs, all Hawkes was signed. (Our values are for signed pieces.)

Bowl, brilliant cuttings, scalloped rim, 9½"...................................330.00
Bowl, brilliant cuttings, ftd, ca 1890-1910, sm chip, 8x8¾".........660.00

Bowl, Cetus (extremely rare and desirable cutting), 4x9", $2,600.00.

Bowl, hobstar cuttings, scalloped rim, oval, 15"............................480.00
Cocktail shaker, etched, sterling top, 12"....................................480.00
Decanter, brilliant cuttings, cruet shape, 12"...............................600.00
Goblets, Clarendon cuttings, 8½", set of 12.................................960.00
Goblets, sherry; Clarendon cuttings, 7½", set of 10.....................600.00
Mayonaise, brilliant cuttings, 2-pc, 7"..600.00
Platter, star, fan & wheel cuttings, scalloped rim, 12" dia............660.00
Platter, wheel & star cuttings, notched/scalloped rim, 15½x10½"...720.00
Punch bowl, hobstar & fan cuttings, on stand, chips, 1900, 14x14"..2,700.00
Tantalus, dmn cuttings, w/padlock, 9¾x9".................................840.00
Vase, gravic cuttings, bulbous, ruffled rim, ftd, 12".....................600.00
Vase, Navarre cuttings, flared scalloped rim, flared bottom, 11½".960.00
Vase, Queen's cuttings, flared scalloped rim, ftd, chips, 12"..........480.00
Vase, spider mum cuttings, bubble stem, flared rim, sterling ft, 14".400.00
Vase, zippered panels w/fan border, bulbous bottom, flared rim, 9½"..325.00

Head Vases

Vases modeled as heads of lovely ladies, delightful children, clowns, famous people — even some animals — were once popular as flower containers. Most of them were imported from Japan, although some American potteries produced a few as well. For more information, we recommend *Head Vases, Identification and Values*, by Kathleen Cole; and *The World of Head Vase Planters* by Mike Posgay and Ian Warner. Our advisor for this category is Larry G. Pogue (L&J Antiques and Collectibles); he is listed in the Directory under Texas.

Young lady, blond hair, three pink flowers, pearl earring, black bodice, Rubens Original, Japan, 6", $275.00.

(Photo courtesy Larry Pogue, L&J Antiques and Collectibles)

Baby against pillow, lustre, #92-USA, 5¾"..................................65.00
Baby in bonnet, head trn, gold trim, Artmark, 6"..........................95.00
Girl child w/bow in ponytail, lg eyes/hands to high pleated collar, 6"..85.00
Girl in headscarf tied at chin, Velco #6686, 5½"..........................175.00
Girl w/flowers in updo, Wales/Made in Japan, 6"..........................95.00
Girl w/gr leaf on head, cheek to shoulder, eyes shut, Velco #6690, 5"..175.00
Girl w/umbrella, head cocked, eyes closed, #52/271, 5" (8" overall)..195.00
Girl w/umbrella, head cocked, upturned collar, 5½" overall.........195.00
Girl w/umbrella, pigtails, bl & wht, lg scalloped collar, 7" overall...195.00
Girl w/umbrella, pigtails, blk & wht plaid w/yel brim hat, 8" overall..145.00
Girl w/umbrella, pigtails, glancing eyes, plaid, 8" overall.............145.00
Girl w/umbrella, pigtails, looking ahead, lg collar/pearls, 7" overall...195.00
Girl w/umbrella, pigtails, puffy sleeves/Peter Pan collar, 8" overall...145.00
Girl w/umbrella, pigtails, purple plaid, 5" (8" overall)..................145.00
Girl w/umbrella, pigtails, purple/gr/yel, right hand, 5" (8" overall)...185.00
Jackie Kennedy, blk & wht, Inarco #E-1852, 1964, 6"................895.00
Lady, flat-brim hat, hands clasped, pearls, gold trim, #434, 4½"..155.00
Lady, flat-brim hat, head trn, upturned collar, Relpo #K1009B, 6"..175.00
Lady, flat-brim hat, updo, hands to cheek & chest, #2703, 6½"..215.00
Lady, flat-brim hat (blk) w/perforations, #S673B, 4½"..................97.50
Lady, flat-brim hat w/feathers, ruffled neckline, Lefton #2359, 7½"....255.00
Lady, flat-brim hat/ruffled edge, stern brows, pursed lips, pearls, 7"...225.00

Lady, flowery hat, updo, hand to cheek, pearls, Relpo #K1402, 7" ..275.00
Lady, frosted flip/middle part, bl hand to face, 3 daisies at neck, 8" ..245.00
Lady, frosted hair, gr hat & bodice, pearls, Napco #C7498, 10½" 795.00
Lady, pillbox hat, blond flip, blk gloved hand to chin, 5½" 175.00
Lady, updo w/gold-trim hair ornament, neck bow, blk-gloved hand, 6" . 195.00
Lady, updo w/3 curls & rose, hand to cheek, pearls, Inarco #E-779, 6" . 195.00
Young lady, flip hairdo, scalloped neckline w/bow, Napco #C5675, 6" ...175.00
Young lady, frosted hair, head trn, pearls, Napco #C7472, 6" 195.00
Young lady, frosted hair, head trn, pearls, Napco #C7474, 8½" 325.00
Young lady, frosted hair, leaf brooch/pearls, Napco #C7474, 8" ...345.00
Young lady, frosted hair, plain neckline, pearls, Ardco #C-1615, 6" . 225.00
Young lady, frosted hair, 2 flowers at neckline, Ardco (unmk) 6" . 195.00
Young lady, frosted updo, neckline tied at shoulder, Napco #C7293, 6" . 165.00
Young lady, lg hair bow, ruffled V neckline, pearls, #T-1576, 6" ...185.00
Young lady, side flip, 2-tiered neck ruffles, Napco #CE6060, 3½" ... 95.00
Young lady, side flip, 2-tiered neck ruffles, Napco #C5939, 6" 165.00

Heino, Otto and Vivika

Born in East Hampton, Connecticut, in 1915, Heino served in the Air Force during WWII. He had always been interested in various crafts, and through the Air Force, he was able to take classes in England, where he learned the basics of silversmithing, painting, and ceramics. He had the oportunity to visit Bernard Leach's studio, where he was fascinated to see the inert clay come to life under the absolute and total control of the potter. Returning to America he met Vivika, the woman who was to become his wife. She was already well advanced in the trade, and Otto became her student. They eventually moved to California and until her passing in 1995 worked together to become a team well known for producing large bowls, vases, bottles, and jars glazed in fantastic textures and rich colors, often decorated with organic forms or calligraphic images.

Otto is still working at his studio in Ojai, California.

Our advisors for this category are Suzanne Perrault and David Rago; they are listed in the Directory under New Jersey. In the listings that follow, all pieces are signed by both Otto and Vivika unless otherwise noted.

Bowl vase, cvd rings, gold splotches on wht, ftd, 5x6" 615.00
Bowl vase, dk gr splotches on brn & wht, 8¾x11½" 1,560.00
Charger, brn on rust, rnd, 3x12½", EX 300.00
Vase, cvd rings, bl splotches on wht, bulbous, 4½x6" 400.00
Vase, cvd rings, oxblood on gray, bulbous, sm neck, 4" 375.00
Vase, cvd rings, volcanic ivory/yel/brn speckle, 7x9" 960.00

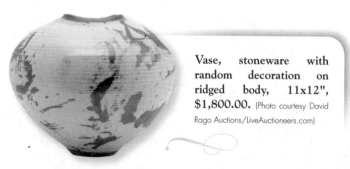

Vase, stoneware with random decoration on ridged body, 11x12", $1,800.00. (Photo courtesy David Rago Auctions/LiveAuctioneers.com)

Heintz Art Metal Shop

Founded by Otto L. Heintz in Buffalo, New York, ca 1909, the Heintz Art Metal Shop (HAMS) succeeded the Art Crafts Shop (begun in 1903) and featured a new aesthetic. Whereas the Art Craft Shop offered products of hammered copper with applied color enamel and with an altogether somewhat cruder or more primitive and medieval-looking appearance, HAMS presented a refined appearance of applied sterling silver on bronze. Most pieces are stamped with the manufacturer's mark — the letters HAMS conjoined within a diamond, often accompanied by a Aug. 27, 1912 patent date — although paper labels were pasted on the bottom of lamp bases. Original patinas for Heintz pieces include a mottled brown or green (the two most desirable), as well as silver and gold (less desirable). Desk sets and smoking accessories are common; lamps appear less frequently. The firm, like many others, closed in 1930, a victim of the Depression. Silvercrest, also located in Buffalo, produced products similar though not nearly as valuable as Heintz. Please note: Cleaning or scrubbing original patinas will diminish value. Our advisor for this and related Arts & Crafts subjects is Bruce A. Austin; he is listed in the Directory under New York.

Vase, tree applied on cylindrical bronze form, 8x3", $2,400.00. (Photo courtesy Treadway Gallery Inc./ LiveAuctioneers.com)

Candlestick, landscape, 4x3¾" 1,150.00
Desk set: ink blotter, letter holder, blotter corners & clip 650.00
Inkwell, berries, orig insert, 6¾" 275.00
Lamp, boudoir; poppies, mica-lined shade, 10x9" 1,200.00
Vase, Art Nouveau floral, shouldered, flared rim, #8791, 12½" .1,025.00
Vase, evergreen tree, flared bottom, tall cylindrical neck, 7¼" 600.00
Vase, floral, cylindrical, #3724, 4½" 180.00
Vase, French Gray Silver patina, Art Nouveau iris, flared neck, 6½" .330.00
Vase, leaves, #5796B, 8x4" 500.00
Vase, stick neck, disk ft, #3683, 12" 110.00

Heisey

A.H. Heisey began his long career at the King Glass Company of Pittsburgh. He later joined the Ripley Glass Company which soon became Geo. Duncan and Sons. After Duncan's death Heisey became half-owner in partnership with his brother-in-law, James Duncan. In 1895 he built his own factory in Newark, Ohio, initiating production in 1896 and continuing until Christmas of 1957. At that time Imperial Glass Corporation bought some of the molds. After 1968 they removed the old 'Diamond H' from any they put into use. In 1985 HCA purchased all of Imperial's Heisey molds with the exception of the Old Williamsburg line.

During their highly successful period of production, Heisey made fine handcrafted tableware with simple, yet graceful designs. Early pieces were not marked. After November 1901 the glassware was marked either with the 'Diamond H' or a paper label. Blown ware is often marked on the stem, never on the bowl or foot. For more information we recommend *Heisey Glass, 1896 – 1957*, by Neila and Tom Bredehoft. For information concerning Heisey Collectors of America, see the Clubs, Newsletters, and Catalogs section of the Directory. See also Glass Animals and Figurines.

Charter Oak, crystal, candleholder, 1-light, #130 Acorn, ea 150.00
Charter Oak, crystal, plate, #1246 Acorn & Leaves, 10½" 30.00
Charter Oak, Flamingo, compote, frd, #3362, 7" 65.00
Charter Oak, Flamingo, tumbler, #3362, 12-oz 20.00

Charter Oak, Hawthorne, bowl, flower; #116 Oak Leaf, 11" 85.00
Charter Oak, Hawthorne, cocktail, #3362, 3-oz 45.00
Charter Oak, Marigold, compote, low ft, #3362, 6" 100.00
Charter Oak, Marigold, sherbet, low ft, #3362, 6-oz 40.00
Charter Oak, Moongleam, candlestick, #116 Oak Leaf, 3", ea 45.00
Charter Oak, Moongleam, plate, #1246 Acorn & Leaves, 6" 12.50
Chintz, crystal, bowl, cream soup 18.00
Chintz, crystal, bowl, pickle & olive; 2-part, 13" 15.00
Chintz, crystal, ice bucket, ftd 85.00
Chintz, crystal, plate, hdls, 12" 25.00
Chintz, crystal, shakers, pr 40.00
Chintz, crystal, tray, celery; 10" 15.00
Chintz, crystal, wine, #3389, 2½-oz 18.00
Chintz, Sahara, bowl, mint; ftd, 6" 32.00
Chintz, Sahara, bowl, vegetable; oval, 10" 35.00
Chintz, Sahara, cup 25.00
Chintz, Sahara, oyster cocktail, #3389, 4-oz 22.00
Chintz, Sahara, plate, sq or rnd, 6" 15.00
Chintz, Sahara, platter, 14" L 90.00
Chintz, Sahara, tumbler, ftd, #3389, 10-oz 22.00
Crystolite, crystal, basket, 6" 450.00
Crystolite, crystal, bottle, oil; w/stopper, 2-oz 35.00
Crystolite, crystal, bowl, dessert; 5½" 14.00
Crystolite, crystal, bowl, punch; 7½-qt 120.00
Crystolite, crystal, cheese dish, ftd, 5½" 27.00
Crystolite, crystal, cocktail shaker, w/#1 strainer, #86 stopper, 1-qt. 350.00
Crystolite, crystal, jam jar, w/lid 60.00
Crystolite, crystal, mustard, w/lid 45.00
Crystolite, crystal, plate, coupe; 7½" 40.00
Crystolite, crystal, plate, sandwich; 14" 55.00
Crystolite, crystal, puff box, w/lid, 4¾" 75.00
Crystolite, crystal, shakers, pr 40.00
Crystolite, crystal, syrup, Drip-Cup 135.00
Crystolite, crystal, tray, relish; 3-part, oval, 12" 35.00
Crystolite, crystal, tumbler, blown, 8-oz 25.00
Crystolite, crystal, vase, 12" 225.00
Empress, Alexandrite, bowl, ind nut; dolphin ft 170.00
Empress, Alexandrite, bowl, relish; 3-part, 7" 200.00
Empress, Alexandrite, saucer 25.00
Empress, cobalt, mayonnaise, ftd, w/ladle, 5½" 400.00
Empress, cobalt, plate, sq, 7" 60.00
Empress, Flamingo, bowl, cream soup 30.00
Empress, Flamingo, cup, bouillon; hdls 35.00
Empress, Flamingo, tray, sandwich; sq, center hdl, 12" 52.00
Empress, Moongleam, bonbon, 6" 30.00

Empress, Moongleam, bowl, mint; footed, $60.00. (Photo courtesy Neila and Tom Bredehoft)

Empress, Moongleam, plate, 7" 17.00
Empress, Moongleam, tray, hors d'oeuvres; 7-part, 10" 20.00
Empress, Sahara, candy dish, dolphin ft, 6" 150.00
Empress, Sahara, saucer champagne, 4-oz 40.00
Empress, Sahara, vase, flared, 8" 150.00
Greek Key, crystal, bowl, banana split; 9" 45.00
Greek Key, crystal, butter dish, hdls 200.00
Greek Key, crystal, claret, 4½-oz 150.00

Greek Key, crystal, compote, 5" 75.00
Greek Key, crystal, hair receiver 170.00
Greek Key, crystal, jar, pickle; w/knob lid 160.00
Greek Key, crystal, jug, 1-qt 180.00
Greek Key, crystal, nappy, 4½" 25.00
Greek Key, crystal, plate, 5" 18.00
Greek Key, crystal, plate, 6" 30.00
Greek Key, crystal, shakers, pr 135.00
Greek Key, crystal, sherbet, shallow, ftd, 4½-oz 25.00
Greek Key, crystal, spooner, lg 110.00
Greek Key, crystal, sugar bowl 50.00
Greek Key, crystal, toothpick holder 900.00
Greek Key, crystal, tray, celery; 9" L 50.00
Greek Key, crystal, tumbler, flared rim, 7-oz 60.00
Greek Key, crystal, tumbler, str sides, 10-oz 90.00
Greek Key, crystal, water bottle 220.00
Greek Key, crystal, wine, 2-oz 100.00
Ipswich, cobalt, bowl, flower; ftd, 11" 450.00
Ipswich, crystal, cocktail shaker, w/strainer & #86 stopper, 1-qt .. 225.00
Ipswich, crystal, plate, sq, 8" 35.00
Ipswich, crystal, tumbler, ftd, 8-oz 30.00
Ipswich, Flamingo, creamer 70.00
Ipswich, Flamingo, oyster cocktail, ftd, 4-oz 60.00
Ipswich, Flamingo, sugar bowl 70.00
Ipswich, Moongleam, candy jar, w/lid, ½-lb 500.00
Ipswich, Moongleam, finger bowl, w/underplate 100.00
Ipswich, Moongleam, goblet, knob in stem, 10-oz 140.00
Ipswich, Moongleam, pitcher, ½-gal 950.00
Ipswich, Moongleam, tumbler, ftd, 5-oz 85.00
Ipswich, Sahara, bottle, oil; ftd, w/#86 stopper, 2-oz 275.00
Ipswich, Sahara, creamer 90.00
Ipswich, Sahara, tumbler, cupped rim, 10-oz 100.00
Kalonyal, crystal, bottle, oil; 4-oz 120.00
Kalonyal, crystal, bowl, deep, 5" 35.00
Kalonyal, crystal, bowl, punch; w/stand, 12" 325.00
Kalonyal, crystal, bowl, shallow, 9" 65.00
Kalonyal, crystal, burgundy, 3-oz 60.00
Kalonyal, crystal, claret, 5-oz 100.00
Kalonyal, crystal, compote, 8" 225.00
Kalonyal, crystal, cup, punch; 3½-oz 26.00
Kalonyal, crystal, mug, 8-oz 175.00
Kalonyal, crystal, plate, 6" 35.00
Kalonyal, crystal, sherbet, ped ft, 6-oz 40.00
Kalonyal, crystal, sugar bowl, tall 95.00
Kalonyal, crystal, toothpick 375.00
Kalonyal, crystal, tray, celery; 12" 55.00
Lariat, crystal, basket, ftd, 10" 185.00
Lariat, crystal, bowl, cream soup; hdls 50.00
Lariat, crystal, bowl, salad; 10½" 35.00
Lariat, crystal, candlestick, 3-light, ea 35.00
Lariat, crystal, cigarette box 45.00

Lariat, crystal, cologne bottle, $75.00. (Photo courtesy Apple Tree Auction Center/LiveAuctioneers.com)

Lariat, crystal, creamer.. 18.00
Lariat, crystal, ice tub.. 75.00
Lariat, crystal, oyster cocktail, 4¼-oz.................. 12.00
Lariat, crystal, plate, buffet; 21"........................ 70.00
Lariat, crystal, plate, cookie; 11"........................ 35.00
Lariat, crystal, plate, sandwich; hdls, 14"............ 50.00
Lariat, crystal, plate, 7".................................... 14.00
Lariat, crystal, platter, 15" L............................. 60.00
Lariat, crystal, sherbet, low, 6-oz.........................7.00
Lariat, crystal, tumbler, blown, 5-oz................... 20.00
Lariat, crystal, urn, w/lid, 12".......................... 150.00
Lariat, crystal, vase, swung.............................. 135.00
Lariat, crystal, wine, blown, 2½-oz.................... 20.00
Lariat, crytal, sugar bowl................................. 18.00
Minuet, crystal, bowl, sauce; ftd, 7½".................. 70.00
Minuet, crystal, candelabrum, 1-light, w/prisms, ea.... 110.00
Minuet, crystal, compote, #5010, 5½".................. 40.00
Minuet, crystal, cup.. 25.00
Minuet, crystal, dinner bell, #3408 .... 75.00
Minuet, crystal, mayonnaise, dolphin ft, 5½".......... 50.00
Minuet, crystal, plate, service; 10½"................. 120.00
Minuet, crystal, plate, snack; w/#1477 center, 16".... 80.00
Minuet, crystal, shakers, #10, pr........................ 75.00
Minuet, crystal, sherbet, ftd, #5010, 6-oz............ 25.00
Minuet, crystal, sugar bowl, ind; #1509 Queen Ann 37.50
Minuet, crystal, tray, 15".................................. 65.00
Minuet, crystal, vase, #4192, 10"....................... 110.00
Minuet, crystal, vase, centerpc, #1511 Toujours, w/prisms 200.00
New Era, crystal, ashtray.................................. 40.00
New Era, crystal, candelabra, 2-light, w/#4044 bobeche & prisms, ea .. 140.00
New Era, crystal, claret, 4-oz 18.00
New Era, crystal, pilsner, 8-oz 40.00
New Era, crystal, plate, 9x7"............................. 25.00
New Era, crystal, sherbet, ftd, 6-oz 10.00
New Era, crystal, sugar bowl............................. 37.50
New Era, crystal, tumbler, ftd, 8-oz.................... 14.00
New Era, crystal, wine, 3-oz 22.00
Octagon, crystal, bowl, vegetable; 9"................... 15.00
Octagon, crystal, cup, AD 10.00
Octagon, crystal, plate, muffin; #1229, 12".......... 20.00
Octagon, crystal, plate, 6"..................................4.00
Octagon, crystal, sugar bowl, #500 .... 10.00
Octagon, Flamingo, basket, #500, 5"................. 300.00
Octagon, Flamingo, bowl, #1203, 12"................. 55.00
Octagon, Flamingo, cup, #1231 .... 15.00
Octagon, Flamingo, mayonnaise, ftd, #1229, 5½"..... 25.00
Octagon, Flamingo, platter, 12" L....................... 25.00
Octagon, Hawthorne, bonbon, upturned sides, #1229, 6".... 40.00
Octagon, Hawthorne, cheese dish, #1229, hdls, 6"..... 15.00
Octagon, Hawthorne, ice tub, #500 .... 129.00
Octagon, Hawthorne, plate, 14".......................... 50.00
Octagon, Marigold, bowl, ice cream..................... 30.00
Octagon, Marigold, bowl, mint; #1229, 6"............ 30.00
Octagon, Moongleam, bowl, cream soup; hdls......... 30.00
Octagon, Moongleam, candlestick, 1-light, 3", ea..... 40.00
Octagon, Moongleam, plate, 8"........................... 15.00
Octagon, Moongleam, saucer, AD 10.00
Octagon, Moongleam, tray, 4-part, #500 variety, 12"..... 120.00
Octagon, Sahara, bowl, cream soup; hdls.............. 25.00
Octagon, Sahara, compote, #1229, 8".................. 35.00
Octagon, Sahara, ice tub, #500 .... 80.00
Octagon, Sahara, plate, hors d'oeuvres, #1229, 13"..... 35.00
Old Sandwich, cobalt, candlestick, 6", ea.............. 250.00
Old Sandwich, cobalt, tumbler, ftd, 12-oz............. 45.00

Old Sandwich, crystal, bottle, condiment; w/#3 stopper 70.00
Old Sandwich, crystal, creamer, 12-oz................... 32.00
Old Sandwich, crystal, parfait, 4½-oz.................. 15.00
Old Sandwich, crystal, shakers, pr...................... 40.00
Old Sandwich, Flamingo, bottle, oil; w/#85 stopper, 2½-oz......... 250.00
Old Sandwich, Flamingo, bowl, flower; ftd, oval, 12"..... 80.00
Old Sandwich, Flamingo, cup 65.00
Old Sandwich, Flamingo, wine, 2½-oz.................. 45.00
Old Sandwich, Moongleam, beer mug, 12-oz........... 300.00
Old Sandwich, Moongleam, cigarette holder............ 65.00
Old Sandwich, Moongleam, pilsner, 10-oz.............. 42.00
Old Sandwich, Moongleam, plate, sq, 8"............... 32.00
Old Sandwich, Sahara, bowl, popcorn; cupped, ftd..... 110.00
Old Sandwich, Sahara, decanter, w/#98 stopper, 1-pt..... 200.00
Old Sandwich, Sahara, pitcher, w/ice lip, ½-gal....... 165.00
Old Sandwich, Sahara, sundae, 6-oz 30.00

Orchid, crystal, mayonnaise, 5½", $55.00; Plate, $20.00.
(Photo courtesy Cathy and Gene Florence)

Pleat & Panel, crystal, bowl, bouillon; hdls, 5"...................................7.00
Pleat & Panel, crystal, creamer, hotel 10.00
Pleat & Panel, crystal, plate, 7"...........................4.00
Pleat & Panel, crystal, sherbet, ftd, 5-oz................4.00
Pleat & Panel, Flamingo, cheese & cracker, 10½"......... 75.00
Pleat & Panel, Flamingo, marmalade, 4¾"............. 30.00
Pleat & Panel, Flamingo, nappy, 4½".................... 11.00
Pleat & Panel, Flamingo, plate, 10¾".................. 48.00
Pleat & Panel, Flamingo, tumbler, 8-oz................ 17.50
Pleat & Panel, Moongleam, bowl, chow chow; 4"...... 14.00
Pleat & Panel, Moongleam, pitcher, w/ice lip, 3-pt..... 165.00
Pleat & Panel, Moongleam, plate, 7".................... 10.00
Pleat & Panel, Moongleam, saucer..........................5.00
Pleat & Panel, Moongleam, vase, 8".................... 120.00
Provincial/Whirlpool, creamer, ftd....................... 95.00
Provincial/Whirlpool, crystal, bowl, punch; 5-qt...... 100.00
Provincial/Whirlpool, crystal, butter dish.............. 80.00
Provincial/Whirlpool, crystal, nappy, 5½".............. 20.00
Provincial/Whirlpool, crystal, plate, torte; 14"....... 35.00
Provincial/Whirlpool, Limelight Green, mayonnaise, 3-pc, 7" 150.00
Provincial/Whirlpool, Limelight Green, plate, buffet; 18".......... 250.00
Provincial/Whirlpool, Limelight Green, tumbler, ftd, 9-oz 80.00
Ridgeleigh, crystal, ashtray, 4" 22.00
Ridgeleigh, crystal, bottle, cologne; 4-oz.............. 100.00
Ridgeleigh, crystal, bowl, centerpc; 11"............... 50.00
Ridgeleigh, crystal, bowl, fruit; flared, 12"........... 50.00
Ridgeleigh, crystal, bowl, jelly; hdls, 6"............... 30.00
Ridgeleigh, crystal, bowl, lemon; w/lid, 5"............ 65.00
Ridgeleigh, crystal, candlestick, 1-light, 2", ea....... 35.00
Ridgeleigh, crystal, cocktail, pressed.................... 25.00
Ridgeleigh, crystal, cordial, blown, 1-oz.............. 160.00
Ridgeleigh, crystal, creamer.............................. 30.00
Ridgeleigh, crystal, goblet, pressed, 9-oz............. 35.00
Ridgeleigh, crystal, oyster cocktail, pressed.......... 30.00
Ridgeleigh, crystal, plate, hors d'oeuvres; oval...... 850.00
Ridgeleigh, crystal, plate, salver; 14".................. 50.00
Ridgeleigh, crystal, plate, sq, 8"........................ 32.00
Ridgeleigh, crystal, plate, 8" 20.00

Ridgeleigh, crystal, saucer champagne, blown, 5-oz.................. 25.00
Ridgeleigh, crystal, shakers, pr.. 45.00
Ridgeleigh, crystal, tumbler, pressed, ftd, 12-oz..................... 50.00
Ridgeleigh, crystal, vase, 8".. 75.00
Saturn, crystal, bowl, flower; 13".................................... 37.00
Saturn, crystal, bowl, pickle; 7"..................................... 35.00
Saturn, crystal, cup 10.00
Saturn, crystal, pitcher, blown, w/ice lip, 70-oz.................... 65.00
Saturn, crystal, plate, 8".. 10.00
Saturn, Zircon Limelight, bottle, oil; 3-oz.......................... 650.00
Saturn, Zircon Limelight, marmalade, w/lid 500.00
Saturn, Zircon Limelight, nappy, 5".................................. 90.00
Saturn, Zircon Limelight, vase, 10½"................................. 260.00
Stanhope, crystal, bowl, mint, hdls, 6".............................. 35.00
Stanhope, crystal, creamer, hdl...................................... 45.00
Stanhope, crystal, nappy, hdl, 4½"................................... 30.00
Stanhope, crystal, relish, 4-part, hdls, 12"......................... 55.00
Stanhope, crystal, vase, ball form, 7".............................. 100.00
Sunburst, crystal, bowl, punch; w/stand, 15"........................ 275.00
Sunburst, crystal, bowl, scalloped rim, 4½".......................... 22.00
Sunburst, crystal, bowl, 10"... 50.00
Sunburst, crystal, bowl, 7" L.. 35.00
Sunburst, crystal, compote, 6"....................................... 45.00
Sunburst, crystal, creamer, ind...................................... 45.00
Sunburst, crystal, goblet... 150.00
Sunburst, crystal, pitcher, bulbous, 3-pt........................... 150.00
Sunburst, crystal, sugar bowl, lg.................................... 45.00
Sunburst, crystal, vase, orchid; 6"................................. 125.00
Twist, Alexandrite, bowl, flower; 4-ftd, oval, 12"................. 550.00
Twist, crystal, bowl, flower; 9"..................................... 25.00
Twist, crystal, ice bucket, w/metal hdl.............................. 50.00
Twist, crystal, mustard, w/lid & spoon............................... 40.00
Twist, crystal, oyster cocktail, ftd, 3-oz........................... 10.00
Twist, crystal, plate, 10½".. 40.00
Twist, Flamingo, bowl, hdls, 6"...................................... 20.00
Twist, Flamingo, cup, zigzag hdls.................................... 25.00
Twist, Flamingo, platter, 12" L...................................... 50.00
Twist, Marigold, plate, 8"... 30.00
Twist, Marigold, tray, celery; 13"................................... 50.00
Twist, Marigold, wine, 2-block stem, 2½-oz.......................... 125.00
Twist, Moongleam, cocktail shaker, metal top........................ 900.00
Twist, Moongleam, relish, 3-part, 13"................................ 22.00
Twist, Moongleam, tumbler, ftd, 12-oz................................ 50.00
Twist, Sahara, bowl, cream soup..................................... 100.00
Twist, Sahara, tray, celery; 10".................................... 40.00
Victorian, crystal, bowl, rose....................................... 90.00
Victorian, crystal, decanter w/stopper, 32-oz....................... 70.00
Victorian, crystal, plate, 8".. 35.00
Victorian, crystal, shakers, pr...................................... 65.00
Victorian, crystal, vase, 4"... 50.00
Waverly, crystal, bowl, fruit; 9".................................... 30.00
Waverly, crystal, box, chocolate; w/lid, 5".......................... 80.00
Waverly, crystal, candleholder, 3-light, ea.......................... 70.00
Waverly, crystal, cheese dish, ftd, 5½".............................. 20.00
Waverly, crystal, vase, ftd, 7"...................................... 30.00
Yeoman, crystal, bottle, cologne; w/stopper 100.00
Yeoman, crystal, finger bowl 5.00
Yeoman, Flamingo, creamer.. 25.00
Yeoman, Flamingo, marmalade.. 35.00
Yeoman, Hawthorne, plate, 6"... 13.00
Yeoman, Hawthorne, saucer, AD 10.00
Yeoman, Marigold, gravy boat, w/underplate.......................... 45.00
Yeoman, Marigold, pitcher, 1-qt..................................... 180.00
Yeoman, Moongleam, bowl, vegetable; 6"............................... 16.00

Yeoman, Moongleam, cruet, oil; 4-oz.................................. 85.00
Yeoman, Sahara, champagne, 6-oz...................................... 18.00
Yeoman, Sahara, cup.. 20.00

Herend

Herend, Hungary, was the center of a thriving pottery industry as early as the mid-1800s. Decorative items as well as tablewares were made in keeping with the styles of the times. One of the factories located in this area was founded by Moritz Fisher, who often marked his wares with a cojoined MF. Items described in the following listings may be marked simply Herend, indicating the city, or with a manufacturer's backstamp.

Dinnerware

Chanticleer, dish, shell-shaped, 8¾" 180.00
Chanticleer, plate, salad; 7½"....................................... 75.00
Chanticleer, plate, serving; w/bamboo hdls........................... 65.00
Chinese Bouquet, bowl, vegetable; 8"................................. 80.00
Chinese Bouquet, creamer, 6-oz....................................... 60.00
Chinese Bouquet, plate, dinner; 10½"................................. 70.00
Chinese Bouquet, plate, salad; 7½"................................... 40.00
Coronation, saucer.. 25.00

Floral pattern, hand painted with gilt trim, #7369, ca. 1950s, 10", set of four, $425.00. (Photo courtesy Dallas Auction Gallery/ LiveAuctioneers.com)

Fortuna, cup, 2"... 45.00
Fortuna, tureen, w/lid 785.00
Indian Basket, cake plate, 13" 195.00
Indian Basket, cup & saucer, 2"..................................... 105.00
Kimberly, plate, bread & butter; 6".................................. 25.00
Kimberly, plate, dinner; 10½".. 60.00
Queen Victoria, bowl, dessert; 6".................................... 55.00
Queen Victoria, creamer, 8-oz.. 90.00
Queen Victoria, cup, 2".. 75.00
Queen Victoria, plate, chop; 12".................................... 195.00
Queen Victoria, platter, 17" L...................................... 300.00
Queen Victoria, teapot.. 300.00
Red Dynasty, tureen, ornate leaf finial, w/hdls & underplate, 11" L...830.00
Rothschild Bird, bowl, cranberry; 5" 98.00
Rothschild Bird, bowl, cream soup; 2½".............................. 112.00
Rothschild Bird, bowl, rimmed soup; 8"............................... 82.00
Rothschild Bird, bowl, salad; 10½".................................. 200.00
Rothschild Bird, cake plate, 10½".................................. 180.00
Rothschild Bird, egg cup, dbl, 4".................................... 60.00
Rothschild Bird, plate, salad; 7½"................................... 60.00
Rothschild Bird, plate, serving; 11"................................ 115.00
Rothschild Bird, tureen, bird finial on lid, ftd, w/hdls, 9x13"....1,125.00
Rothschild Bird, tureen, ftd, w/hdls & lid, 15" L, +18" underplate... 900.00

Miscellaneous

Figurine, ducks (2) conjoined, mc w/gilt beaks, 10x15" 935.00
Figurine, flamingo, rust, #VH-15881, 10" 900.00

Figurine, giraffe, hand painted, 15", $1,800.00. (Photo courtesy Leland Little Auction & Estate Sales Ltd.)

Figurine, lion & lioness, rust fishnet on wht, 7x9" 700.00
Figurine, nude female astride horse, wht, 15x17" 685.00
Figurine, nude kneeling w/gr robe at side, #5707, 13¼" 285.00
Figurine, rabbit, rust fishnet on wht, w/gold nose & ft, 12¼" 750.00
Figurine, rooster, aqua tones & fishnet, w/gold, #5030, 16x13½" .. 700.00
Figurine, toucan on branch, #MCD-15858, 8½x7" 835.00
Lamp, Rothschild Bird, electric, rtcl base, w/gold, 15" 800.00
Stein, rtcl pk & wht design, serpent hdl & finial, ftd, 12" 940.00
Vase, HP butterfly & floral on wht, w/gold trim, slim neck, 19" ... 625.00

Heubach

Gebruder Heubach is a German company that has been in operation since the 1800s, producing quality bisque figurines and novelty items. They are perhaps most famous for their doll heads and piano babies, most of which are marked with the circular rising sun device containing an 'H' superimposed over a 'C.' Items with arms and hands positioned away from the body are more valuable, and color of hair and intaglio eyes affect price as well. Our advisor for this category is Grace Ochsner; she is listed in the Directory under Illinois. See also Dolls, Heubach.

Baby, chewing on toes, #4862, 7x8", EX 800.00
Baby girl seated in red-orange bonnet pulling off socks, 6" 325.00
Baby in gr tub w/1 ft in mouth, 4½x5½" 500.00
Baby playing w/toes, 7½x13" 900.00
Baby seated w/ft crossed, intaglio eyes, 11", from $500 to 650.00

Baby sitting in wicker chair, pulling off his sock, 6½", NM (firing line), 6½", $450.00. (Photo courtesy McMasters Harris Auction Company)

Box, boy wrapped in lettered banner atop book w/alphabet design, 7".315.00
Boy (bust) leaning on tree branch w/hands cupping face, 7" 315.00
Boy in suit & hat seated, 5" 425.00
Bulldog seated on basket (bed) w/blanket, head tilted, 7" 150.00
Cat sleeping, wht w/mc circles on turq collar, 6" L 140.00
Dog in baby's 'knitted' bonnet w/turq ribbons, 2½x3½" 65.00

Dutch boy & girl seated, intaglio eyes, 7", pr 400.00
Girl seated in bonnet w/arms crossed at wrists & head tilted, 4" .. 315.00
Santa sitting on log (candy container), bl intaglio eyes, 8x6" 850.00

Higgins

Acclaimed contemporary glass artists Frances and Michael Higgins founded their Chicago-area studio in 1948. The Higgins are credited with rediscovering and refining the ancient craft of glass fusing, resulting in 'modern miracles with everyday glass.'

Essentially, fusing can be described as the creation of a 'glass sandwich.' On one piece of enamel-coated glass, a design is either drawn with colored enamels or pieced with glass segments. Over this, another piece of enameled glass is laid. Placed on a mold, the object is then heated. Under heat the glass 'slumps' into the shape of the mold. The design is fused between the outer glass pieces with additional layers often adding to the texture and color complexity.

The Higgins applied their fusing technique to everything from tableware such as bowls, plates, and candleholders, to ashtrays, jewelry, vases, mobiles, sculptures, lamps, clocks, and even 'rondelay' room dividers. Higgins buyers in the 1950s were immediately attracted to the novelty of fused glass, the colorful 'modern' designs, and the variety of items available. Today collectors can also appreciate the artistry and skill involved in the creation of Higgins glass and the imaginative genius of its makers.

In 1957, Michael and Frances Higgins became associated with Dearborn Glass Company of Chicago. Dearborn marketed Higgins designs to a mass audience, greatly increasing the couple's 'brand-name' recognition. Following a brief association in 1965 with Haeger Potteries, the Higgins opened their own studio in Riverside, Illinois. Michael Higgins died in 1999, Frances Higgins in 2004. The studio continues today under the direction of their longtime associates and designated successors, Louise and Jonathan Wimmer, still creating glass objects in the distinctive Higgins style.

Higgins pieces are readily identifiable by an almost-always-present lower-case signature. From 1948 until 1957, pieces were engraved on the reverse with the name 'higgins,' or the complete artist name. In 1951, a raised 'dancing man' logo was also added. Dearborn and Haeger pieces (1957 – 1965) are denoted either by a gold 'higgins' signature on the surface or by a signature in the colorway. Since 1966 the marking has been an engraved 'higgins' on the reverse, sometimes accompanied by the artist's name. Following the death of Frances Higgins, pieces have been signed 'higgins studio.'

The Higgins Glass Studio is located at 33 East Quincy Street, Riverside, IL 60546 (708-447-2787, www.higginsglass.com). For more information we recommend *Higgins: Adventures in Glass,* and *Higgins: Poetry in Glass* (Schiffer), both by our advisor Donald-Brian Johnson and Leslie Piña. Mr. Johnson is listed in the Directory under Nebraska.

Ashtray, Clocks (Watches), rectangular, 10x14", from $150 to ... 175.00
Ashtray, Gemspread, 7¼" longest sides, from $275 to 325.00
Ashtray, Roman Stripe, rectangular, 5x7", from $75 to 100.00
Ashtray, She Loves Me, 10x14", from $150 to 175.00
Bowl, Castilian, olive/tangerine/salmon/wht/clear/gold, 8", $175 to ..200.00
Bowl, Chrysanthemums, octagonal, 8", from $225 to 250.00
Bowl, Filigree, lav-bl or aqua-gray, squarish, 10", from $300 to 325.00
Bowl, Greenray, 12¼", from $300 to 350.00
Butter dish, Clocks, 7½x3¾", from $95 to 125.00
Cake stand, common, squarish, production pc, 10", from $175 to ..300.00
Candy dish, Mandarin, slim stem, ftd, 6½" dia, from $250 to 275.00
Cigarette box, Midnight, walnut base, 7x4", from $250 to 275.00
Dish, White Peacock, sq, 9", from $175 to 200.00
Jewelry, choker w/amber stones/wire connectors/blot imprints, $700 to ..750.00
Lamp, Rondelantern, 2-tier, 16", from $1,500 to 1,750.00
Mobile, 15" L, from $300 to 350.00

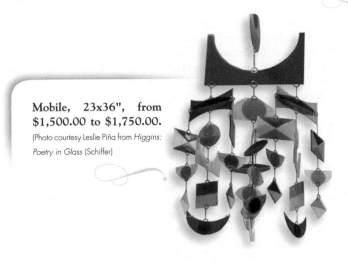

Mobile, 23x36", from $1,500.00 to $1,750.00. (Photo courtesy Leslie Piña from *Higgins: Poetry in Glass* (Schiffer))

Ornament, Butterfly, from $50 to	75.00
Plate, Carousel, red/gray/blk, 16¾", from $400 to	450.00
Plate, Crossroads (Jonathan Wimmer), 15", from $900 to	1,000.00
Plate, Four Seasons trees (Frances Higgins), 7½", ea set, $900 to	1,000.00
Plate, King (Michael Higgins), 11", from $1,500 to	1,750.00
Plate, Thistledown, mauve/purple/chartreuse, 12¼", from $200 to	225.00
Sculpture, Bubbles (F Higgins), circles/foam, brass stand, 13", $1,500	1,700.00
Sculpture, Summer Tree (F Higgins), copper edging, 10x10", $1,500 to	1,750.00
Sculpture, Walkpast Eye (Michael Higgins), 10x11", from $2,500 to	2,750.00
Server, 6-pocket, Delphinium Blue, 18" dia, from $400 to	600.00
Spoon rest, bl & yel, 10½" L, from $200 to	250.00
Vase, Posy Pocket, flip pattern, 32" L, from $400 to	450.00
Wall sconces, Stardust, 6" dia, pr from $200 to	225.00

Hilton Pottery

The Hilton family was involved in pottery making in the Catawaba Valley of North Carolina as early as the end of the Civil War. The branch responsible for items marked 'Hilton' was established in 1935 by Ernest Hilton in Marion. The wares they produced were of the typical 'Jugtown' variety, high glazed and hand thrown. Ernest died in 1948, and the pottery closed in 1953.

Ashtray, squirrel eating nut by branch in bowl, gr/cream, 2x4¾"	400.00
Figurine, lady w/vessel & shawl, brn tones, 7¾"	1,325.00
Flower frog, cobalt, 5½x4½"	120.00
Leaf dish, appl acorn & & twig hdl, speckled gr, Mrs FW Hilton, 6½"	660.00
Pitcher, lamb on speckled brn, att Maude Hilton, 3", EX	230.00
Vase, cabin scenic, Clara M Hilton, rpr, 10"	480.00
Vase, mtn scenic, earth tones & bl, Ernest & Clara Hilton, 7¼"	450.00
Wall pocket, yel buff w/emb Y symbols at rim, 7x3"	390.00

Vase, church and grove of trees, signed Clara Maude Brunk, 4½", $660.00. (Photo courtesy Brunk Auctions/LiveAuctioneers.com)

Historical Glass

Glassware commemorating particularly significant historical events became popular in the late 1800s. Bread trays were the most common form, but plates, mugs, pitchers, and other items were also pressed in clear as well as colored glass. It was sold in vast amounts at the 1876 Philadelphia Centennial Exposition by various manufacturers who exhibited their wares on the grounds. It remained popular well into the twentieth century.

In the listings that follow, L numbers refer to a book by Lindsey, a standard guide used by many collectors. Our advisor for this category is Darlene Yohe; she is listed in the Directory under Arkansas. See also Bread Plates; Pattern Glass.

Ale glass, Mephistopheles	95.00
Bank, Liberty Bell	38.00
Bottle, Granger, L-266	110.00
Bowl, berry; Lindbergh, sm	15.00
Butter dish, American Shield	195.00
Butter dish, Garfield Drape	90.00
Butter dish, Log Cabin	325.00
Celery vase, Lincoln Drape	80.00
Cup, Harrison & Morton, bl	235.00
Egg cup, Lincoln Drape	50.00
Goblet, GAR Encampment	165.00
Goblet, Knights of Labor	175.00
Goblet, Pittsburgh Centennial	95.00
Hat, Uncle Sam, no pnt, L-110	35.00
Lamp, Emblem, L-62	195.00
Match safe, Jenny Lind	250.00
Mug, beer; Philadelphia Centennial	65.00
Mug, Columbus Landing	65.00
Mug, Garfield & Lincoln	75.00
Mug, McKinley	30.00
Mug, Protection & Plenty	50.00
Mug, shaving; Garfield & Lucretia Randolf Garfield, milk glass, 6"	250.00
Mustard dish, Dewey bust, Xd flags on lid, milk glass, 4¼"	55.00
Pickle dish, E Pluribus Unum	45.00
Pitcher, Admiral Dewey, Gridly You May Fire..., 9¼"	140.00
Pitcher, Garfield Drape, scarce	145.00
Pitcher, President McKinley Assassination	275.00
Pitcher, Washington Centennial	155.00
Plate, Battleship Maine, openwork border, 5½"	16.00
Plate, Columbus, milk glass, L-7	65.00
Plate, Dewey, clear/frosted, sm	15.00
Plate, Egyptian Pyramids	125.00
Plate, For President Winfield D Hancock, 8"	110.00
Plate, Garfield Alphabet, 7"	75.00
Plate, Grant, Patriot & Soldier, amber, sq, 9½"	50.00
Plate, Louisiana Purchase Expedition, 7½"	90.00
Plate, Protection & Plenty, 8½"	65.00
Plate, Texas Campaign, lt bl, 9½"	200.00

Plate, U. S. Grant — Patriot and Soldier, Bryce Higbee, 1885, 11", $85.00. (Photo courtesy Bill Edwards and Mike Carwile)

Plate, Yankee Doodle, Egg & Dart border, 5¼" 35.00
Platter, Centennial Hall 65.00
Shaker, Centennial, boot 27.00
Shot glass, Bryan & McKinney, 1896, NM 130.00
Spooner, Log Cabin, L-184 .... 115.00
Statuette, Ruth the Gleaner, frosted, 1876 Phila Expo, Gillinder ... 175.00
Sugar shaker, Proclaim Liberty Throughout the Land 195.00
Tumbler, Admiral Dewey 60.00
Tumbler, America, L-48 .... 25.00
Tumbler, Union Forever...Bumper to the Flag, 3⅛" 120.00
Wine, Washington Centennial 65.00

Hobbs, Brockunier, and Company

Hobbs and Brockunier's South Wheeling Glass Works was in operation during the last quarter of the nineteenth century. They are most famous for their peachblow, amberina, Daisy and Button, and Hobnail pattern glass. The mainstay of their operation, however, was druggist items and plain glassware — bowls, mugs, and simple footed pitchers with shell handles.

Berry set, Daisy and Button, amberina, 10" master berry and six boat-shaped individual bowls, $465.00. (Photo courtesy Jackson's International Auctioneers & Appraisers of Fine Art & Antiques)

Bowl, berry; Dew Drop, frosted w/amber band, sq, 4" 15.00
Bowl, finger; Greeley, sapphire alabaster 65.00
Bowl, finger; Venetian, wht loopings w/bl threading, minimum .. 700.00
Bowl, Hobnail, frosted w/amber band, ftd, berry pontil, 6x10" 150.00
Bowl, Hobnail, frosted w/amber band, 10" 90.00
Bowl, Quartered Block w/Stars, frosted w/amber band, oval, 10" ... 65.00
Butter dish, Hobnail, frosted w/amber band, from $80 to 120.00
Butter dish, Sawtooth, opal 50.00
Butter dish, Swirl, frosted w/amber band 95.00
Chandelier, Hobnail, amber font, brass fr, 14" dia 950.00
Compote, Tree of Life, canary, 6" 65.00
Creamer, Daisy & Button, amberina, cylindrical, 5¼" 135.00
Cup, lemonade; Polka Dot, crystal w/sapphire hdl, 2¾" 20.00
Cup, lemonade; Polka Dot, vaseline w/amber hdl, 3⅔" 28.00
Goblet, Blackberry, crystal 75.00
Goblet, Quartered Block w/Stars, frosted w/amber band 140.00
Jug, Tree of Life, marine gr, ½-gal 225.00
Lamp shade, Dew Drop, bl opal, 23x7½" 90.00
Molasses can, Hobnail, frosted w/amber band 375.00
Mustard jar, Swirl, frosted w/amber band, from $90 to 125.00
Pickle dish, Paneled Wheat, opal, 8" 45.00
Pitcher, Dew Drop, cranberry opal, clear hdl, 8" 175.00
Pitcher, Viking, crystal, face below spout & on hdl, ½-gal 160.00
Pitcher, Viking, crystal, plain under spout & hdl, ½-gal 220.00
Plate, Swirl, frosted w/amber band, 6" 30.00

Spooner, Hobnail, vaseline opal, 4" 50.00
Sugar bowl, Hobnail, frosted w/amber band, w/lid, from $65 to 80.00
Sugar bowl, Swirl, frosted w/amber band, w/lid 80.00
Tumbler, Dew Drop, clear w/amber band, 4" 30.00
Tumbler, medicine; pressed glass, ftd, 16-oz, 8" 30.00
Vase, Hobnail, opal, ruffled rim, ftd, 6½" 20.00

Holt Howard

Novelty ceramics marked Holt Howard were produced in Japan from the 1950s into the 1970s, and these have become quite collectible. They're not only marked, but most are dated as well. There are several lines to reassemble — the rooster, the white cat, figural banks, Christmas angels and Santas, to name only a few — but the one that most Holt Howard collectors seem to gravitate toward is the Pixie Ware. For more information see *Garage Sale and Flea Market Annual* (Collector Books).

Key: KK — Kozy Kitten

Bank, Dandy-Lion, nodder, 6", from $165.00 to $200.00. (Photo courtesy Jim and Bev Mangus)

Air freshener, girl w/Christmas tree, 1959, 6½" 32.00
Bottle topper, Pixie Ware, 300 Proof 300.00
Butter dish, KK, 2 kittens peek from under lid, 7", from $90 to ... 100.00
Candleholder, angel, 4", ea from $25 to 30.00
Candleholder, Santa in open car, 1959, 3½", ea from $18 to 22.00
Candleholders, mouse among Christmas greenery, 1958, 2¼", pr .. 12.00
Candleholders, Rooster, figural, 1960, pr from $20 to 25.00
Cheese crock, Stinky Cheese, mouse & cheese finial 35.00
Cherries jar, Pixie Ware, blk-haired/Xd-eyed spoon finial, $550 to .. 600.00
Coffeepot, Rooster, wht w/rooster decor, electric, 1960, from $50 to ... 65.00
Cookie jar, KK, head form 40.00
Cutting board, Rooster, 5x8½", from $85 to 95.00
Grease jar, KK, Keeper of the Grease, figural kitten, 4½" 375.00
Ketchup jar, Pixie Ware, from $60 to 75.00
Lamp, oil; Holly Girl, unused wick, 7" 40.00
Mug, KK, cat on side, w/squeaker, 8-oz, from $35 to 45.00
Mug, Rooster, emb decor, 3 szs, ea from $6 to 9.00

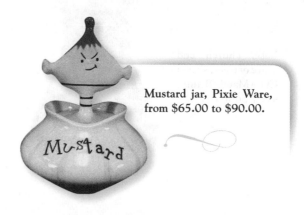

Mustard jar, Pixie Ware, from $65.00 to $90.00.

Napkin holder, Rooster, 6", from $30 to.. 35.00
Oil cruet, Pixie Ware, blond pixie girl w/cork stopper................... 62.50
Pitcher, Santa head, 1960, 4¼".. 30.00

Onions jar, butler (Jeeves), $45.00; Cherries jar, $90.00; Olives jar, $45.00.

Shakers, cowboy, 6¼", pr 20.00
Shakers, fit together to form apple, 2½", pr............................... 22.00
Shakers, KK, head only, male in cap, pr from $35 to 55.00
Shakers, KK, 1 w/pk bow tie, 2nd w/bl, noisemaker, 1958, pr 30.00
Shakers, Santa, Happy New Year on beard, pr............................ 22.00
Shakers, tomato, 1962, 3x3", pr.. 15.00
String holder, KK, kitten's face, from $40 to.............................. 50.00
Sugar bowl, Rooster, wht w/red bottom, rooster finial, 1960s, $25 to... 35.00
Tea bag holders, teapot shapes, set of 4 in metal caddy 40.00
Vase, Rooster, figural, 6¼", from $25 to.................................... 35.00
Wall pocket, KK, full-bodied cat w/hook tail, 7x3", from $45 to ... 60.00

Homer Laughlin

The Homer Laughlin China Company of Newell, West Virginia, was founded in 1871. The superior dinnerware they displayed at the Centennial Exposition in Philadelphia in 1876 won the highest award of excellence. From that time to the present, they have continued to produce quality dinnerware and kitchenware, many lines of which are very popular collectibles. Most of the dinnerware is marked with the name of the pattern and occasionally with the shape name as well. The 'HLC' trademark is usually followed by a number series, the first two digits of which indicate the year of its manufacture. For further information we recommend *Collector's Encyclopedia of Fiesta, 10th Edition*, by Sharon and Bob Huxford (available from Collector Books). Another fine source of information is *Homer Laughlin, A Giant Among Dishes*, by Jo Cunningham (Schiffer). Our advisors for Virginia Rose are Jack and Treva Hamlin; they are listed in the Directory under Ohio.

Our values are base prices, and apply to decaled lines only — not solid-color dinnerware. Very desirable patterns on the shapes named in our listings may increase values by as much as 75%. See also Blue Willow; Fiesta; Harlequin; Riviera.

Century

Except for some of the harder-to-find service pieces (which can be pricey no matter what pattern they're in), items in English Garden, Sun Porch, and the Mexican lines are often double the values listed below. Some items from these lines are rare (for instance the teapot in Sun Porch), and no market value has been established for them.

Hacienda butter dish, from $135.00 to $150.00; Teapot, from $145.00 to $165.00; Cream soup bowl, rare, from $60.00 to $80.00.

Bowl, fruit; from $8 to.. 10.00
Bowl, onion soup; from $22 to.. 30.00
Bowl, oyster; 1-pt, from $23 to... 32.00
Bowl, 9", from $26 to.. 30.00
Cake plate, 11½", from $40 to... 45.00
Casserole, w/lid, from $90 to.. 130.00
Creamer, from $20 to.. 28.00
Egg cup, dbl, from $28 to... 34.00
Plate, 6", from $7 to...9.00
Plate, 10", from $18 to.. 21.00
Platter, sq well, 11", from $20 to.. 25.00
Teacup, from $11 to.. 16.00
Teapot, from $100 to... 150.00

Debutante

For Suntone, add 20%; add 25% for Karol China gold-decorated items.

Bowl, onion soup, from $8 to.. 10.00
Bowl, 7", from $10 to.. 12.00
Bowl, 10", from $16 to.. 18.00
Coffeepot, from $50 to.. 60.00
Plate, chop; 15", from $16 to.. 20.00
Plate, 10", from $8 to...9.00
Platter, 13", from $16 to.. 20.00
Shakers, pr from $20 to... 30.00

Eggshell Georgian

Baker, 9", from $22 to... 28.00
Bowl, cream soup; from $22 to.. 28.00
Bowl, 9", from $20 to.. 28.00
Egg cup, dbl, from $30 to... 40.00
Plate, sq, 8", from $16 to... 22.00
Sauceboat, from $30 to.. 35.00
Shakers, pr from $35 to... 60.00
Sugar bowl, from $25 to... 35.00

Eggshell Nautilus

Floral pattern teapot, ca. 1950s, 6½", $250.00. (Photo courtesy Suellen Blasdell, Canfield OH)

Baker, 10", from $24 to	32.00
Bowl, deep, 5", from $14 to	20.00
Bowl, 10", from $22 to	32.00
Casserole, w/lid, from $55 to	85.00
Creamer, from $15 to	25.00
Cup, AD; from $18 to	22.00
Plate, chop; 14", from $35 to	50.00
Plate, 7", from $8 to	10.00
Plate, 10", from $15 to	20.00
Platter, 13", from $24 to	32.00

Empress

Add 25% for solid colors. See also Bluebird China.

Baker, 11", from $24 to	26.00
Cake plate, 10", from $15 to	20.00
Creamer, ind; 4-oz, from $10 to	12.00
Cup, bouillon; 6-oz, from $10 to	14.00
Cup, coffee; rare, from $8 to	10.00
Jug, 36s, 11-oz, from $25 to	30.00
Plate, deep, 7", from $8 to	10.00
Plate, 9", from $8 to	10.00
Platter, 11", from $18 to	22.00
Platter, 17", from $30 to	35.00
Sauceboat, 2 hdls, from $40 to	50.00

Marigold

Bowl, cream soup; w/underplate, from $28 to	36.00
Bowl, oatmeal; from $12 to	17.00
Butter dish, from $60 to	70.00
Pitcher, milk; from $30 to	40.00
Plate, deep, from $12 to	18.00
Plate, 7", from $8 to	10.00
Saucer, from $5 to	6.00

Nautilus

Bowl, onion soup; from $14 to	16.00
Bowl, 10", from $22 to	28.00
Casserole, from $47 to	62.00
Creamer, from $14 to	20.00
Mug, Baltimore coffee; from $20 to	27.00
Plate, 6", from $7 to	9.00
Teapot, from $67 to	87.00

Rhythm

Add 25% for American Provincial.

American Provincial: spoon rest, from $100.00 to $125.00; Shakers, $18.00; Sugar bowl with lid, $16.00; Pitcher, $30.00; Gravy boat, $18.00.

Bowl, cereal; 5½", from $7 to	10.00
Cup, coffee; from $16 to	20.00
Jug, 2-qt, from $30 to	40.00
Plate, 8", from $10 to	12.00
Platter, 11½", from $20 to	22.00
Tidbit, from $25 to	45.00

Swing

Add 30% for Oriental patterns and Mexicali.

Bowl, cream soup; from $23 to	28.00
Creamer, from $20 to	30.00
Plate, 8", from $10 to	14.00
Plate, 10", from $16 to	20.00
Platter, 11", from $22 to	30.00
Platter, 15", from $40 to	50.00
Sauceboat, from $25 to	35.00
Saucer, from $5 to	7.00
Sugar bowl, from $25 to	35.00
Tray, utility; from $20 to	30.00

Virginia Rose

Use the high end of the price range to evaluate popular patterns such as JJ59, VR128, Spring Wreath, and Wild Rose.

Baker, 10", from $24 to	32.00
Bowl, fruit; from $7 to	10.00
Bowl, onion soup; from $20 to	25.00
Bowl, 9", from $22 to	30.00
Butter dish (Jade), from $95 to	125.00
Cake plate, rare, from $40 to	50.00
Jug, w/lid, rare, 7½", from $145 to	195.00
Jug, 7½", from $115 to	155.00
Plate, 7", from $8 to	11.00
Platter, 15½", from $35 to	55.00

Wells

Add 25% for solid colors Sienna Brown, French Rose, or Leaf Green.

Baker, 8", from $18 to	20.00
Bowl, bouillon; from $15 to	20.00
Bowl, cream soup; w/underplate, from $32 to	40.00
Creamer, from $18 to	25.00
Jug, 42s, w/lid, from $40 to	50.00
Plate, sq, 8", from $18 to	20.00
Plate, 6", from $7 to	9.00
Plate, 8", from $10 to	12.00
Plate, 10", from $15 to	18.00
Platter, 11½", from $24 to	30.00
Sugar bowl, ind; open, from $14 to	16.00

Hoya Crystal Inc.

Hoya Cristal Inc. originated in 1946 in the town of Hoya, Japan. They were manufacturers of fine crystal. Upon learning that General McArthur partook of a glass or two of scotch every evening, Hoya designed a double old-fashioned glass especially for him and presented it to him for his enjoyment during the evening cocktail hour. Today, Hoya Crystal is one of the world's largest and most respected crystal companies.

Bowl, Samurai, crystal, 9½" H 3,000.00
Bowl, Trio, crystal, globular, 4 points at rim, w/box 900.00
Sculpture, obelisk, crystal, 15" 1,300.00
Sculpture, panther, crystal, 6" 110.00
Sculpture, rocking sailboat, crystal, 7⅜" 550.00
Vase, crystal, flared ft & rim, 9" 30.00

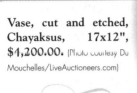

Hull

The A.E. Hull Pottery was formed in 1905 in Zanesville, Ohio, and in the early years produced stoneware specialities. They expanded in 1907, adding a second plant and employing over 200 workers. By 1920 they were manufacturing a full line of stoneware, art pottery with both airbrushed and blended glazes, florist pots, and gardenware. They also produced toilet ware and kitchen items with a white semiporcelain body. Although these continued to be staple products, after the stock market crash of 1929, emphasis was shifted to tile production. By the mid-'30 interest in art pottery production was growing, and over the next 15 years, several lines of matt pastel floral-decorated patterns were designed, consisting of vases, planters, baskets, ewers, and bowls in various sizes.

The Red Riding Hood cookie jar, patented in 1943, proved so successful that a whole line of figural kitchenware and novelty items was added. They continued to be produced well into the '50s. (See also Little Red Riding Hood.) Through the '40s their floral artware lines flooded the market, due to the restriction of foreign imports. Although best known for their pastel matt-glazed ware, some of the lines were high gloss. Rosella, glossy coral on a pink clay body, was produced for a short time only; and Magnolia, although offered in a matt glaze, was produced in gloss as well.

The plant was destroyed in 1950 by a flood which resulted in a devastating fire when the floodwater caused the kilns to explode. The company rebuilt and equipped their new factory with the most modern machinery. It was soon apparent that more modern equipment and processing was necessary and the new plant concentrated on high-gloss artware lines such as Parchment and Pine and Ebb Tide. Figural planters and novelties, piggy banks, and dinnerware were produced in abundance in the late '50s and '60s. By the mid-'70s dinnerware and florist ware were the mainstay of their business. The firm discontinued operations in 1985.

Our advisor, Brenda Roberts, has compiled two lovely books, *The Collector's Encyclopedia of Hull Pottery* and *The Collector's Ultimate Encyclopedia of Hull Pottery*, both with full-color photos and current values, available from Collector Books.

Special note to Hull collectors: Reproductions are on the market in all categories of Hull pottery — matt florals, Red Riding Hood, and later lines including House 'n Garden dinnerware.

Blossom Flite, basket, #T-2, 6", 1955-56, from $65 to 105.00
Blossom Flite, honey pot, #T-1, 6", from $65 to.......................... 105.00
Bow-Knot, basket, #B-12, 1949-50, 10½", from $800 to 1,100.00

Bow-Knot, candleholder, #B-17, 4", ea from $140 to 175.00
Bow-Knot, jardiniere, #B-19, 1949-50, 9⅜", from $800 to 1,000.00
Bow-Knot, vase, #B-14, 1949-50, 12½", from $900 to 1,100.00
Butterfly, ashtray, #B-3, 1956, 7", from $40 to 60.00
Butterfly, bonbon, #B-4, 1956, 6½", from $20 to 25.00
Butterfly, bowl, #B-16, 1956, 10½", from $70 to 100.00
Calla Lily, console bowl, #590/32, 1938-40, 13", from $175 to 225.00
Calla Lily, ewer, #506, 1938-40, 10", from $380 to 480.00
Camellia, basket, #107, 1943-44, from $350 to 425.00
Camellia, candleholder, #117, 1943-44, 6½", ea from $180 to 225.00
Camellia, console bowl, #116, 12", from $300 to.......................... 375.00
Camellia, ewer, #126, 4¾", from $95 to 140.00
Camellia, teapot, #110, 1943-44, 8½", from $350 to 425.00
Capri, candy dish, w/lid, unmk, 8½", from $50 to 75.00
Capri, leaf basket, 12¼", from $50 to 75.00
Capri, vase, #58, 13¾", from $55 to 75.00
Continental, basket, #55, 1959-60, 12¾", from $145 to 215.00
Continental, bud vase, #66, 1959-60, 9½", from $35 to 50.00
Continental, flower bowl, #69, 9¼", from $40 to 60.00
Continental, vase, #64, 10", from $50 to 80.00
Dogwood, console bowl, #511, 11½", from $285 to 395.00
Dogwood, ewer, #520, 1942-43, 4¾", from $135 to 160.00
Dogwood, vase, #502, 1942-43, 6½", from $240 to 300.00
Dogwood, vase, #516, 4¾", from $75 to 95.00
Dogwood, window box, #508, 1942-43, 10½", from $195 to 275.00
Ebb Tide, ashtray, #E-8, 1955, 5", from $170 to 225.00
Ebb Tide, console bowl, #E-12, 15¾", from $215 to 260.00
Ebb Tide, creamer, #E-15, 1955, 4", from $95 to.......................... 125.00
Ebb Tide, vase, #E-6, 1955, 9¼", from $150 to 200.00
Imperial, basket, unmk, 1985, 8", from $40 to 60.00
Imperial, ewer, #F-480, 1965, 10½", from $45 to 75.00
Imperial, planter, #405 USA, 1958, 8¼", from $8 to 10.00
Iris, basket, #408, 1940-42, 7", from $265 to................................. 310.00
Iris, candleholder, #411, 5", ea from $125 to................................. 155.00
Iris, jardiniere, #413, 5½", from $175 to.. 205.00
Iris, rose bowl, #412, 1940-42, 7", from $220 to............................ 275.00
Iris, vase, #402, 1940-42, 7", from $150 to.................................... 200.00
Lusterware, bulb bowl, unmk, 7½", from $60 to............................ 75.00
Lusterware, candleholder, unmk, 1927-30, 3", ea from $30 to........ 40.00
Lusterware, flower frog, unmk, 4½", from $20 to 30.00
Lusterware, vase, unmk, 1927-30, 10", from $60 to 80.00
Lusterware, wall pocket, unmk, 1927-30, 8½", from $75 to.......... 100.00
Magnolia, gloss; basket, #H-14, 1947-48, 10½", from $400 to 450.00
Magnolia, gloss; candleholder, #H24, 1947-48, 4", ea from $40 to...55.00
Magnolia, gloss; console bowl, #H-23, 13", from $125 to.............. 165.00
Magnolia, gloss; ewer, #H-3, 5½", from $60 to............................... 85.00
Magnolia, gloss; vase, #H-1, 1947-48, 5½", from $40 to................. 60.00
Magnolia, matt; candleholder, #27, 1946-47, 4", ea from $65 to.... 95.00
Magnolia, matt; cornucopia, #19, 1946-47, 8½", from $155 to 210.00
Magnolia, matt; vase, #17, 12¼", from $300 to............................. 385.00

Magnolia, matt; vase, #21, 12½", from $400.00 to $500.00. (Photo courtesy Bean & Bean Auctions Inc./LiveAuctioneers.com)

Magnolia, matt; vase, #22, 1946-47, 12½", from $300 to 365.00
Marcrest, mug, 1958, 3¼", from $6 to 8.00
Marcrest, pitcher, 1958, 7½", from $40 to...................................... 60.00
Mardi Gras/Granada, bulb bowl, #532, 2¾", from $40 to 60.00
Mardi Gras/Granada, cornucopia, #210, 5½", from $30 to 40.00
Mardi Gras/Granada, teapot, #33, 5½", from $195 to................... 295.00
Mardi Gras/Granada, vase, #214-9, from $50 to 80.00
Medley, bulb bowl, #107, 1952, 7", from $30 to............................ 40.00
Novelty, dachshund figure, 1952, 14", from $175 to 225.00
Novelty, kitten planter, #61, 7½", from $40 to 55.00
Novelty, peacock vase, #73, 1951, 10½", from $35 to..................... 50.00
Novelty, rooster planter, #53, 1953, 5¾", from $100 to 135.00
Novelty, twin geese planter, #95, 1951, 6½", from $50 to 80.00
Orchid, basket, #305, 7", from $600 to 800.00
Orchid, bud vase, #306, 6¾", from $175 to 225.00
Orchid, bulb bowl, #312, 1939-41, 7", from $150 to 200.00
Orchid, candleholder, #315, 1939-41, 4", ea from $135 to............ 160.00
Orchid, jardiniere, #310, 1939-41, 4¾", from $155 to.................. 180.00
Pagoda, vase, #P-5, 1960, 12½", from $30 to 40.00
Parchment & Pine, basket, #S-8, 1951-54, 16½", from $195 to... 235.00
Parchment & Pine, candleholder, #S-10, 1951-54, 5", ea from $25 to ..35.00
Parchment & Pine, sugar bowl, #S-13, 3¾", from $20 to 35.00
Parchment & Pine, teapot, #S-11, 1951-54, 6", from $100 to...... 140.00
Poppy, basket, #601, 9", from $600 to 700.00
Poppy, bowl, #602, low, 1943-44, 6½", from $225 to 260.00
Poppy, ewer, #610, 1943-44, 4¾", from $165 to............................ 200.00

Poppy, ewer, #610, 13½", from $800.00 to $1,000.00. (Photo courtesy Belhorn Auction Services LLC/LiveAuctioneers.com)

Poppy, vase, #607, 1943-44, 8½", from $235 to 275.00
Poppy, wall pocket, #609, 9", from $310 to................................... 410.00
Regal, bowl, unmk, 1960, 6½", from $10 to 15.00
Regal, Flying Duck vase, #310, 1960, 10½", from $40 to................. 65.00
Regal, planter, #301, 1960, 3½", from $10 to................................. 15.00
Rosella, cornucopia, #R-13, 1946, 8½", from $125 to................... 165.00
Rosella, creamer, #R-3, 1946, 5½", from $45 to............................. 65.00
Rosella, ewer, #R-7, 9½", from $1,200 to 1,500.00

Rosella, lamp, unmk, 1946, 6¾", from $200 to 310.00
Rosella, wall pocket, #R-10, 6½", from $150 to 175.00
Sunglow, basket, #84, 6¼", from $95 to 130.00
Sunglow, grease jar, #53, 1948-49, 5¼", from $45 to..................... 65.00
Sunglow, pitcher, w/ice lip, 1942-45, 7½", from $155 to 200.00
Sunglow, tea bell, matt, unmk, 1949, 6¾", from $300 to 375.00
Sunglow, wall pocket, unmk, 1948-49, 6", from $165 to 210.00
Tulip, vase, #100-33, 1938-40, 6½", from $130 to 150.00
Tulip, vase, #101-33, 1938-40, 9", from $295 to 360.00
Tulip, vase, #105-33, 1938-41, 8", from $265 to 310.00
Water Lily, cornucopia, #L-7, 1948-49, 6½", from $115 to........... 160.00
Water Lily, teapot, #L-18, 1948-49, 6", from $245 to 300.00
Water Lily, vase, #L-2, 1948-49, 5½", from $60 to......................... 85.00
Wildflower, console bowl, #W21, 1946-47, 12", from $225 to 265.00
Wildflower, vase, #W-17, 1946-47, 12½", from $275 to 350.00
Wildflower, vase, #W-3, 1946-47, 5½", from $55 to 80.00
Wildflower (# series), basket, #66, 1942-43, 10¼", from $800 to....1,000.00
Wildflower (# series), candleholder, 2-light, #69, 4", ea from $165 to... 200.00

Wildflower (number series), ewer, #55, 13½", from $900.00 to $1,200.00. (Photo courtesy Burchard Galleries/LiveAuctioneers.com)

Wildflower (# series), ewer, #57, 1942-43, 4½", from $100 to 145.00
Woodland, gloss; ewer, #W-3, 1949-50, 5½", from $80 to 120.00
Woodland, matt; planter, #W-19, 1949-50, 10½", from $175 to .. 235.00
Woodland, matt; sugar bowl, #W-28, 1949-50, 3½", from $155 to... 200.00
Woodland, matt; wall pocket, #W-13, 1949-50, 7½", from $250 to ...300.00

Dinnerware and Kitchenware Items

Avocado, bowl, soup/salad; 1968-71, 6½", from $4 to 6.00
Avocado, coffee server, 1968-71, 11", from $35 to.......................... 55.00
Avocado, Leaf chip 'n dip, 1968-71, 15x10½", from $45 to 75.00
Avocado, shakers, 1968-71, 3¾", pr from $20 to............................. 30.00
Avocado, sugar bowl, 1968-71, from $15 to 22.00
Blue Star & Lattice Cereal Ware, spice jar, Pepper, 5", from $40 to..... 55.00
Cinderella Kitchenware (Blossom), creamer, #28, 1948, 4", from $45 to .. 60.00
Cinderella Kitchenware (Blossom), shakers, #25, 3½", pr from $40 to.... 60.00
Cinderella Kitchenware (Blossom), teapot, #26, 42-oz, from $140 to... 180.00
Cinderella Kitchenware (Bouquet), pitcher, #29, 32-oz, from $25 to ..35.00
Conventional Rose Cereal Ware, canister, Coffee, 8½", from $55 to...85.00
Country Belle, baker, rectangular, 1985, 14", from $40 to.............. 60.00
Country Belle, cheese shaker, 1985, 6½", from $20 to.................... 30.00
Country Belle, pie plate, 1985, 11", from $25 to............................ 35.00
Country Belle, plate, 1985, 10", from $10 to 12.00
Country Belle, platter, 1985, 12" L, from $15 to 20.00
Crab Apple, jardiniere, 1925-35, 6½", from $60 to 90.00
Crescent Kitchenware, bowl, #B-1, 1952-54, 9½", from $30 to 40.00
Crescent Kitchenware, creamer, #B-15, 1952-54, 4½", from $16 to... 22.00
Crescent Kitchenware, mug, #B-16, 1952-54, 4¼", from $15 to 20.00
Crestone, butter dish, 1965-67, ¼-lb, from $25 to......................... 35.00

Crestone, gravy boat w/underplate, 1965-67, 10-oz, from $15 to ... 22.00
Crestone, plate, 1965-67, 10½", from $8 to 10.00
Crestone, teapot, 1965-67, 7", from $45 to 65.00
Debonair Kitchenware, casserole, #O-2, ca 1954, 8½", from $45 to... 65.00
Debonair Kitchenware, teapot, #O-13, ca 1954, 8", from $75 to . 100.00
Diamond Quilt, batter jug, #B-7, 1937-40, 5", from $40 to............ 55.00
Diamond Quilt, bean pot, #B-19, 1937-40, 5½", from $45 to 65.00
Diamond Quilt, custard, #B-14, 1937-40, 2¾", from $12 to........... 15.00
Drape & Panel, bowl, mixing; #D-1, 1937-40, 9½", $35 to 45.00
Drape & Panel, cookie jar, #D-20, 1937-40, 2-qt, 8", from $125 to ...150.00
Floral, casserole, ind; #47, open, 5", from $15 to 20.00
Floral, grease jar, #43, 1951-54, 5¾", from $40 to........................ 55.00
Floral, pitcher, #46, 1951-54, 1-qt, from $40 to 55.00
Floral, shakers, #44, 1951-54, 3½", pr from $30 to........................ 40.00
Flying Blue Bird Cereal Ware, canister, Rice, 8½", from $65 to..... 95.00
Flying Blue Bird Cereal Ware, spice jar, Nutmeg, 5", from $50 to.. 70.00

Gingerbread Man, cookie jar, Flint, 9", from $250.00 to $350.00. (Photo courtesy Fred and Joyce Roerig)

Gold Grecian Cereal Ware, canister, Cereal, 8½", from $50 to...... 80.00
Heartland, bowl, fruit; 1982-85, from $8 to 10.00
Heartland, creamer, 4¾", from $25 to 35.00
Heartland, mug, 5", from $10 to.. 14.00
Heartland, pitcher, 4", from $25 to 35.00
Heartland, plate, 7¼", from $8 to.. 10.00
Heritageware, cruet, oil or vinegar; 6¼", ea from $25 to 35.00
Heritageware, pitcher, #A-7, 4½", from $18 to.............................. 22.00
Mirror Almond, bowl, 5¼", from $3 to 4.00
Mirror Almond, plate, steak; oval, 11¾", from $15 to.................... 20.00
Mirror Almond, plate, 10¼", from $8 to 10.00
Mirror Almond, stein, 5", from $8 to 12.00
Mirror Brown, baker, oval, 10", from $20 to 30.00
Mirror Brown, bowl, divided vegetable; 10¾", from $4 to.................6.00
Mirror Brown, bowl, 6½", from $4 to 6.00
Mirror Brown, butter dish, 7½", from $20 to.................................. 25.00
Mirror Brown, canister, Flour, 1978-81, 9", from $150 to............. 200.00
Mirror Brown, casserole, w/figural duck lid, 9", 1972-85, $135 to . 170.00
Mirror Brown, cheese shaker, 6½", from $30 to 40.00
Mirror Brown, Gingerbread Boy, spoon rest, 5", from $20 to 30.00
Mirror Brown, Gingerbread Man, cookie jar, 1984, 12", from $150 to...250.00
Mirror Brown, leaf dish, 7½", from $15 to..................................... 20.00
Mirror Brown, mug, 3½", from $4 to 6.00
Mirror Brown, stein, university logo in gold, 1976, from $20 to 30.00
Mirror Brown, vase, cylindrical, 9", from $35 to............................ 45.00
Mirror Brown Ringed Ware, pitcher, 9", from $95 to 135.00
Mirror Brown Ringed Ware, shakers, 3¼", pr from $30 to.............. 40.00
Orange Tree, pitcher, batter; w/lid, 1925-35, 7", from $275 to..... 375.00
Rainbow, bud vase, #F-90, 6½", from $15 to 20.00
Rainbow, pitcher, 9", from $40 to.. 60.00
Serenade, casserole, #S-20, w/lid, 9", from $120 to....................... 165.00
Stoneware, batter bowl, #25-3, 9", from $95 to 135.00
Tangerine, ashtray, 8", from $25 to.. 35.00

Tangerine, bean pot w/warmer, 9", from $60 to 80.00
Tangerine, butter dish, 7½", from $20 to....................................... 30.00
Tangerine, teapot, 6½", from $20 to... 35.00
Tangerine, tidbit, 2-tier, 10", from $50 to 75.00
Wheat, canister, Coffee, H in diamond mk, 6½", from $130 to ... 165.00
Wheat, salt box, emb Salt, 5¾", from $80 to 110.00

Hummel

Hummel figurines were created through the artistry of Berta Hummel, a Franciscan nun called Sister M. Innocentia. The first figures were made about 1935 by Franz Goebel of Goebel Art Inc., Rodental, West Germany. Plates, plaques, and candy dishes were also produced, and the older, discontinued editions are highly sought collectibles. Generally speaking, an issue can be dated by the trademark. The first Hummels, from 1935 to 1949, were either incised or stamped with the 'Crown WG' mark (TMK-1). The 'Full Bee in V' mark (TMK-2) was employed with minor variations until 1957. At that time the bee was stylized and represented by a solid disk with angled symetrical wings completely contained within the confines of the 'V' (TMK-3, the 'Stylized Bee'). The 'Three-Line mark,' 1964 – 1972 (TMK-4), utilized the stylized bee and included a three-line arrangement: 'c by W. Goebel, W. Germany.' Another change in 1972 saw the 'Stylized Bee in V' suspended between the vertical bars of the 'b' and 'l' of a printed 'Goebel, West Germany.' Collectors refer to this mark as the 'Last Bee' or 'Goebel Bee' (TMK-5). The mark in use from 1979 to 1990 omits the 'bee in V' and is thus called the 'missing bee mark' (TMK-6). The New Crown (NC or TMK-7) mark, in use from 1991 to 1999, is a small crown with 'WG' initials, a large 'Goebel,' and a small 'Germany,' signifying a united Germany. The current Millennium Mark came into use in the year 2000 and features a large bee between the letters 'b' and 'l' in Goebel (TMK-8). For further study we recommend *Hummel, An Illustrated Handbook and Price Guide*, by Ken Armke; *Hummel Figurines and Plates, A Collector's Identification and Value Guide*, by Carl Luckey; *The No. 1 Price Guide to M.I. Hummel* by Robert L. Miller; and *The Fascinating World of M.I. Hummel* by Goebel. These books are available through your local book dealer. See also Limited Edition Plates.

Key:

CM — Crown Mark	NC — New Crown Mark
cn — closed number	oe — open edition
FB — Full Bee	SB — Stylized Bee
LB — Last Bee	tw — temporarily withdrawn
MB — Missing Bee	3L — Three-Line Mark

#304, The Artist, TMK-5 (Last Bee), 1970, 5½", $210.00. (Photo courtesy Dargate Auction Galleries/LiveAuctioneers.com)

#III/110, Let's Sing, box, CM, 6¼" 540.00
#1, Puppy Love, CM, 5-5¼" 575.00
#5, Strolling Along, FB, 4¾-5¾" 360.00
#6 2/0, Sensitive Hunter, MB, 4" 125.00
#9, Begging His Share, FB, 5¼-6" 360.00
#13 2/0, Meditation, SB, 4¼" 160.00
#21/I, Heavenly Angel, CM, 6¾-7¼" 575.00
#26/0, Child Jesus, font, CM, 2¾x5¼" 165.00
#27/3, Joyous News, FB, 4¼x4¾" 720.00
#28/II, Wayside Devotion, FB, 7¼" 580.00
#33, Joyful, ashtray, CM, 3¾x6" 290.00
#44A, Culprits, table lamp, CM, 9" 470.00
#47/0, Goose Girl, FB, 4¾x5¼" 360.00
#48/0, Madonna, plaque, CM, 3¼x4¼" 235.00
#53, Joyful, CM, 3½-4¼" 250.00
#57/0, Chick Girl, CM, 3½" 395.00
#63, Singing Lessons, CM, 2¾-3" 325.00
#64, Shepherd's Boy, FB, 6" 325.00
#66, Farm Boy, CM, 5½" 540.00
#69, Happy Pastime, CM, 3¼-3½" 360.00
#73, Little Helper, CM, 4¼-4½" 325.00
#79, Globe Trotter, SB, 5-5¼" 215.00
#84, Worship, CM, 5¼" 380.00
#85/0, Serenade, CM, 4¾-5¼" 290.00
#88, Heavenly Protection, FB, 9¼" 940.00
#89/I, Little Cellist, FB, 5¼-6¼" 325.00
#89/II, Cellist, FB, tw, 7½-7¾" 575.00
#92, Merry Wanderer, plaque, CM, 4½x5" 325.00
#100, Shrine, lamp, CM, 7½" 5,600.00
#102, Volunteers, table lamp, CM, 7½" 5,760.00
#103, Farewell, table lamp, CM, 7½" 5,760.00
#111/I, Wayside Harmony, FB, tw, 5-5½" 325.00
#114, Let's Sing, ashtray, CM, 3½x6¼" 615.00
#119, Postman, LB, 5-5½" 190.00
#130, Duet, CM, 5¼" 580.00
#136/I, Friends, FB, 5¼" 325.00
#137A, Child in Bed (looking left), plaque, CM, 3x3" 3,500.00
#141/V, Apple Tree Girl, 3L, 10¼" 1,190.00
#142/X, Apple Tree Boy, 3L, 30" 11,200.00
#144, Angelic Song, CM, 4" 325.00
#151, Madonna Holding Child, bl, CM, 12½" 1,400.00
#152B, Umbrella Girl, CM, 8" 2,800.00
#164, Worship, font, FB, 3¼x5" 110.00
#165, Swaying Lullaby, wall plaque, CM, tw, 4½x5¼" 575.00
#17/0, Congratulations, FB, 5¾" 255.00
#177, School Girls, FB, 9½" 2,100.00
#177/I, School Girls, LB, 7½" 1,150.00
#184, Latest News, LB, 5" 270.00
#192, Candlelight, candleholder, CM, 7", ea...................975.00
#197, Be Patient, FB, 6¼" 395.00
#198, Home to Market, FB, 4½" 270.00
#199/0, Feeding Time, SB, 4¼-4½" 235.00
#202, Old Man Reading Newspaper, table lamp, cn, 8¼".......10,800.00
#223, To Market, table lamp, FB, 9½" 505.00
#226, The Mail Is Here, FB, 4½x6¼" 830.00
#230, Apple Tree Boy, table lamp, LB, 7½" 290.00
#237, Star Gazer, wall plaque, FB, cn, 4¾-5" 7,200.00
#240, Little Drummer, FB, 4" 235.00
#241, Angel Joyous News w/Lute, FB, cn, 3x4½" 1,080.00
#256, Knitting Lessons, SB, 7½"..630.00
#257, For Mother, LB, 5-5¼" 190.00
#262, Heavenly Lullaby, 3L, 3½x5" 540.00
#263, Merry Wanderer, wall plaque, 3L, cn, 4x5⅜" 7,200.00
#305, The Builder, FB, tw, early sample, 5½" 2,880.00

#312/1, Honey Lover, MB, 3¾" 290.00
#322, Little Pharmacist, SB, 6"..580.00
#328, Carnival, SB, 6" 580.00
#338, Birthday Cake, candleholder, SB, 3¾", ea...................2,160.00
#344, Feathered Friends, 3L, 4¾" 540.00

#600, We Wish You the Best (sixth figure in the Century Collection), TMK-7 (New Crown), $1,100.00. (Photo courtesy Dargate Auction Galleries/LiveAuctioneers.com)

Hutschenreuther

The Porcelain Factory C.M. Hutschenreuther operated in Bavaria from 1814 to 1969. After the death of the elder Hutschenreuther in 1845, his son Lorenz took over operations, continuing there until 1857 when he left to establish his own company in the nearby city of Selb. The original manufactory became a joint stock company in 1904, absorbing several other potteries. In 1969 both Hutschenreuther firms merged, and that company still operates in Selb. They have distributing centers in both France and the United States.

Figurine, bird pair, K. Tutter, 8¾", $95.00. (Photo courtesy Tom Harris Auctions/ LiveAuctioneers.com)

Candelabra, putti playing flute at base, 3-arm, pastels, 17", ea.....250.00
Figurine, bl heron pr on nest w/eggs, G Granget, 19½"+later base.3,150.00
Figurine, cat, yel & brn tabby, gr mk on paw, paper label, 11" L ..960.00
Figurine, donkey w/dog, cat & rooster stacked on bk, 7½" 175.00
Figurine, draped dancer w/leg extended, arm raised, 1950s, 10¾" 215.00
Figurine, eagle in flight, Granget, 19x13½x10"....................1,250.00
Figurine, eagle w/wings up, K Tutter, 15" 215.00
Figurine, horses galloping (2), wht porc, 17x21" 1,800.00
Figurine, hummingbird, gr mk, 5x5"....................................180.00

Figurine, man in tights w/cape & sword, red/blk/brn, 10" 250.00
Figurine, mother tossing child in air, K Tutter, 11x7" 170.00
Figurine, nude lady dancer w/gold sphere balanced on ankle, 8½" ..635.00
Figurine, nude w/gold ball, wht gloss, C Werner, 9½x7½" 450.00
Figurine, nude woman & 2 leopards running, #118716, 10¾"...... 385.00
Figurine, rabbit w/carrot, realistic, mc, 4x3½" 110.00
Figurine, Safe at Home, pintail ducks, G Granget, ca 1990, 15x13" ..900.00
Figurine, Sea Frolic, 3 seals, wht porc, on hardwood stand, 14x25"....960.00
Plaque, Echo, lady in red w/hand to ear, Wagner, #311, 7x5" ...3,450.00
Plaque, Marguerite, lady in red w/flowers in hair, Wagner, 7¼x5".2,700.00
Plate, Lisctinische Madonna, gold/cobalt border, 1814-1914, 8¾"..215.00

Imari

Imari is a generic term which covers a broad family of wares. It was made in more than a dozen Japanese villages, but the name is that of the port from whence it was shipped to Europe. There are several types of Imari. The most common features a design with panels of birds, florals, or people surrounding a central basket of flowers. The colors used in this type are underglaze blue with overglaze red, gold, and green enamels. The Chinese also made Imari wares which differ from the Japanese type in several ways — the absence of spur marks, a thinner-type body, and a more consistent control of the blue. Imari-type wares were copied on the Continent by Meissen and by English potters, among them Worcester, Derby, and Bow. Unless noted otherwise, our values are for Japanese ware.

Bowl, landscape scene, floral/reserves in border, 8-sided, 19th C, 12" ... 480.00
Bowl, landscape scene, triangular pattern border, 19th C, 7½" 50.00
Bowl, scalloped rim, ftd, 1870s, 4¼x10"... 300.00
Bowl, 3 figures in reserves, floral medallions, 19th C, 4x11" 265.00
Charger, central floral bouquet, gold trim, late 19th C, 14" 1,450.00
Charger, storks & flowers in panels, ca 1860-90, 18½" 515.00
Dish, floral landscape/pagoda, ca 1960, 6x6½"+stand................... 180.00

**Floor vase, pastoral and floral panels, Meiji Period, 30",
$3,500.00.** (Photo courtesy Jackson's International Auctioneers & Appraisers of Fine Art & Antiques)

Jar, cylindrical, 19th C, 9x7" dia 215.00
Jar, floral reserves, domed lid, ca 1920, 13¼" 100.00
Platter, scalloped rim, ca 1840, 13x10" 85.00
Punch bowl, Oriental decor/flowers, 19th C, 6x13½"+teakwood base ...1,200.00
Tureen, floral, flower-form hdls, w/lid, 19th C, sm rpr, 11x17x10" . 1,035.00
Umbrella jar, floral urns, cylindrical, early 20th C, 23½x8¾"....... 480.00
Urn, bird & floral reserves, mtd as lamp, late 19th C, 14½" 360.00
Vase, landscape panels/floral/geometrics, Meiji period, 31x16"..2,875.00

Imperial Glass

The Imperial Glass Company was organized in 1901 in Bellaire, Ohio, and started manufacturing glassware in 1904. Their early products were jelly glasses, hotel tumblers, etc., but by 1910 they were making a name for themselves by pressing quantities of carnival glass, the iridescent glassware that was popular during that time. In 1914 NuCut was introduced to imitate cut glass. The line was so popular that it was made in crystal and colors and was reintroduced as Collector's Crystal in the 1950s. From 1916 to 1924, they used the lustre process to make a line called Art Glass, which today some collectors call Imperial Jewels. Free-Hand ware, art glass made entirely by hand using no molds, was made from 1923 to 1924. From 1925 to 1926, they made a less expensive line of art glass called Lead Lustre. These pieces were mold blown and have similar colors and decorations to Free-Hand ware.

The company entered bankruptcy in 1931 but was able to continue operations and reorganize as the Imperial Glass Corporation. In 1936 Imperial introduced the Candlewick line, for which it is best known. In the late '30s the Vintage Grape Milk Glass line was added, and in 1951 a major ad campaign was launched, making Imperial one of the leading milk glass manufacturers.

In 1940 Imperial bought the molds and assets of the Central Glass Works of Wheeling, West Virginia; in 1958 they acquired the molds of the Heisey Company and in 1960 the molds of the Cambridge Glass Company of Cambridge, Ohio. Imperial used these molds, and after 1951 they marked their glassware with an 'I' superimposed over the 'G' trademark. The company was bought by Lenox in 1973; subsequently an 'L' was added to the 'IG' mark. In 1981 Lenox sold Imperial to Arthur Lorch, a private investor (who modified the L by adding a line at the top angled to the left, giving rise to the 'ALIG' mark). He in turn sold the company to Robert F. Stahl, Jr., in 1982. Mr. Stahl filed for Chapter 11 to reorganize, but in mid-1984 liquidation was ordered, and all assets were sold. A few items that had been made in '84 were marked with an 'N' superimposed over the 'I' for 'New Imperial.' For more information, we recommend *Imperial Glass Encyclopedia, Vols I, II,* and *III,* edited by James Measell. See also Candlewick; Carnival Glass; Glass Animals and Figurines; Slag Glass; Stretch Glass.

Amelia/Line 671, clambroth, bowl, sq, 5½" 25.00
Amelia/Line 671, clambroth, compote, crimped rim...................... 30.00
Amelia/Line 671, clambroth, pitcher, milk or hotel...................... 33.00
Amelia/Line 671, clambroth, plate, luncheon; 9½"....................... 30.00
Amelia/Line 671, rubigold, bowl, nut; ftd, 5½" 35.00
Amelia/Line 671, rubigold, plate, dessert; 6½"............................. 35.00
Amelia/Line 671, smoke, bowl, nappy, 6" 40.00
Amelia/Line 671, smoke, goblet, wine 75.00
Cape Cod, crystal, ashtray, #160/150, 5½" 17.50
Cape Cod, crystal, bottle, condiment; #160/224, 6-oz.................... 65.00
Cape Cod, crystal, bowl, #160/7F, 7½" 22.00
Cape Cod, crystal, bowl, mint; w/hdls, #160/183, 3" 20.00
Cape Cod, crystal, bowl, oval, #160/131B, 12" 95.00
Cape Cod, crystal, bowl, soup; tab hdls, #160/198, 5½" 22.50
Cape Cod, crystal, candy jar, w/wicker hdl, #160/194, 5"............. 125.00
Cape Cod, crystal, coaster, #160/1R, 4½"...................................... 10.00
Cape Cod, crystal, coaster, sq, #160/78, 4".................................... 15.00
Cape Cod, crystal, compote, #160F, 5¼" 27.50
Cape Cod, crystal, compote, oval, #1602, 11" 200.00
Cape Cod, crystal, creamer, #160/30..8.00
Cape Cod, crystal, cruet, w/stopper, #160/241, 6-oz 40.00
Cape Cod, crystal, cup, coffee; #160/37 ....6.00
Cape Cod, crystal, decanter, #160/244, 26-oz 110.00
Cape Cod, crystal, egg cup, #160/225.. 28.00
Cape Cod, crystal, finger bowl, #1604 1/2A, 4½" 15.00

Cape Cod, crystal, fork, #160/701 .... 12.00
Cape Cod, crystal, gravy boat, #160/202, 18-oz 85.00
Cape Cod, crystal, mayonnaise, 3-pc, #160/52H 37.50
Cape Cod, crystal, mug, #160/188, 12-oz................................ 60.00
Cape Cod, crystal, oyster cocktail, #1602 ....8.00
Cape Cod, crystal, pitcher, #160/24, 2-qt 85.00
Cape Cod, crystal, plate, #160/3D, 7" 8.00
Cape Cod, crystal, punch ladle 25.00
Cape Cod, crystal, relish, 5-part, #160/102, 11" 55.00
Cape Cod, crystal, salt cellar, #160/61 .... 20.00
Cape Cod, crystal, shakers, #160/96, pr.................................. 16.00

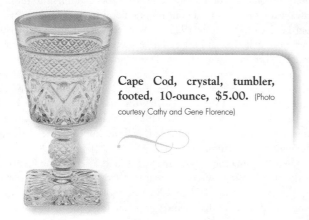

Cape Cod, crystal, tumbler, footed, 10-ounce, $5.00. (Photo courtesy Cathy and Gene Florence)

Cape Cod, crystal, vase, ftd, #160/87F, 8" 215.00
Cape Cod, crystal, wine, #1600, 3-oz 30.00
Crocheted Crystal, crystal, basket, 6" 30.00
Crocheted Crystal, crystal, bowl, console; 12" 35.00
Crocheted Crystal, crystal, candleholder, bowl shape, ea 45.00
Crocheted Crystal, crystal, cheese & cracker, ftd, 12" 40.00
Crocheted Crystal, crystal, cup, punch; closed hdl 3.00

Crocheted Crystal, crystal, hors d'oeuvres dish, four-part, 10½", $25.00. (Photo courtesy Cathy and Gene Florence)

Crocheted Crystal, crystal, ladle, mayonnaise.................................5.00
Crocheted Crystal, crystal, lamp, hurricane; 11" 75.00
Crocheted Crystal, crystal, mayonnaise, 5" 12.50
Crocheted Crystal, crystal, plate, 17" 40.00
Crocheted Crystal, crystal, sherbet, 6-oz, 5" 20.00
Crocheted Crystal, crystal, sugar bowl, ftd............................... 20.00
Crocheted Crystal, crystal, tumbler, 6-oz, 6" 25.00
Fancy Colonial, any color, bonbon, w/hdl, 5½" 20.00
Fancy Colonial, any color, bowl, nappy, 5" 12.00
Fancy Colonial, any color, cake plate, 10½" 35.00
Fancy Colonial, any color, compote, 4"..................................... 25.00
Fancy Colonial, any color, creamer, ftd.................................... 20.00
Fancy Colonial, any color, plate, 5¾"...8.00
Fancy Colonial, any color, sugar bowl...................................... 30.00
Fancy Colonial, any color, vase, flared, ftd, 8" 65.00
Free-Hand, vase, cream w/cobalt hdls/lip/ft, orig label, 6¾x7" 635.00
Free-Hand, vase, drapery, gr on wht, orange int, 3-ftd, 6½x6" ..1,100.00
Free-Hand, vase, gr & wht marbleized swirl, trumpet neck, 10"... 400.00

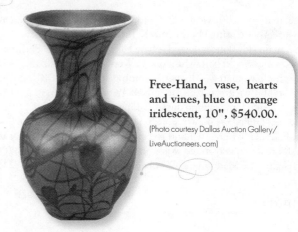

Free-Hand, vase, hearts and vines, blue on orange iridescent, 10", $540.00. (Photo courtesy Dallas Auction Gallery/ LiveAuctioneers.com)

Free-Hand, vase, hearts & vines, pk & gr on wht, 11" 1,800.00
Free-Hand, vase, hearts & vines, wht on cobalt, 11½x5" 1,325.00
Monticello, crystal, basket, 5½".. 20.00
Monticello, crystal, bowl, 6".. 10.00
Monticello, crystal, celery, oval, 9" 20.00
Monticello, crystal, cupsidor.. 65.00
Monticello, crystal, goblet, water 15.00
Monticello, crystal, lily bowl, 5".. 20.00
Monticello, crystal, pitcher, w/ice lip, 52-oz 65.00
Monticello, crystal, plate, 9".. 20.00
Monticello, crystal, shakers, w/glass tops, pr 20.00
Monticello, crystal, tidbit, 2-tier 40.00
Monticello, crystal, vase, 6"... 20.00
Mt Vernon, crystal, candlestick, 9", ea..................................... 22.00
Mt Vernon, crystal, finger bowl, 5"... 12.00
Mt Vernon, crystal, pickle jar... 35.00
Mt Vernon, crystal, plate, torte; 13¼" 25.00
Mt Vernon, crystal, punch bowl 30.00
Mt Vernon, crystal, tumbler, iced tea; 12-oz 12.50
Mt Vernon, crystal, vase/orange bowl, 10" 50.00
Olive, bl or red, bowl, flared, ftd, 6½" 20.00
Olive, bl or red, candy jar 40.00
Olive, bl or red, creamer.. 15.00
Olive, bl or red, plate, 8"...8.00
Olive, emerald or pk, bowl, salad; 10¼" 30.00
Olive, emerald or pk, compote, 6".. 11.00
Olive, emerald or pk, cup...8.00
Olive, emerald or pk, plate, 12" 15.00
Square, cobalt or ruby, bowl, soup/salad; 7"............................. 25.00
Square, cobalt or ruby, cup.. 25.00
Square, cobalt or ruby, server, center hdl, 10½" 50.00
Square, cobalt or ruby, shakers, sq, ftd, pr 70.00
Square, crystal, gr or pk, bowl, nappy, 4½" 12.00
Square, crystal, gr or pk, plate, dessert; 6" 6.00
Square, crystal, gr or pk, saucer...4.00
Square, crystal, gr or pk, shakers, sq, ftd, pr............................ 40.00

Imperial Porcelain

The Blue Ridge Mountain Boys were created by cartoonist Paul Webb and translated into three-dimension by the Imperial Porcelain Corporation of Zanesville, Ohio, in 1947. These figurines decorated ashtrays, vases, mugs, bowls, pitchers, planters, and other items. The Mountain Boys series were numbered 92 through 108, each with a different and amusing portrayal of mountain life. Imperial also produced American Folklore miniatures, 23 tiny animals one inch or less in size, and the Al Capp Dogpatch series. Because of financial difficulties, the company closed in 1960.

Ashtray, #92, 2 men by tree stump, for pipes, from $35 to.............. 50.00
Ashtray, #101, man w/jug & snake, from $30 to............................ 45.00
Ashtray, #103, hillbilly & skunk, from $35 to................................ 50.00
Ashtray, #105, baby, hound dog & frog, from $35 to 40.00
Ashtray, #106, Barrel of Wishes, w/hound, from $25 to 40.00
Box, cigarette; #98, dog atop, baby at door, sq, from $50 to 75.00
Dealer's sign, Handcrafted Paul Webb Mtn Boys, rare, 9", minimum value.. 150.00
Decanter, #100, outhouse, man & bird, from $30 to 45.00
Decanter, #104, Ma leaning over stump, w/baby & skunk, from $50 to . 65.00
Figurine, #101, man leans against tree trunk, 5", from $30 to 45.00
Figurine, man on hands & knees, 3", from $30 to........................... 45.00
Figurine, man sitting, 3½", from $30 to...................................... 45.00
Figurine, man sitting w/chicken on knee, 3", from $30 to............. 45.00
Jug, #101, Willie & snake, from $25 to.. 40.00

Mug, Mt. Rug cutting, $45.00.

Mug, #94, Bearing Down, 6", from $20 to.................................... 25.00
Mug, #94, dbl baby hdl, 4¼", from $20 to................................... 25.00
Mug, #94, ma hdl, 4¼", from $20 to... 25.00
Mug, #94, man hdl, 4¼", from $15 to.. 20.00
Mug, #99, Target Practice, boy on goat, farmer, 5¾", from $20 to.. 25.00
Pitcher, lemonade; from $65 to 85.00
Planter, #81, man drinking from jug, sitting by washtub, from $30 to....40.00
Planter, #100, outhouse, man & bird, from $35 to......................... 50.00
Planter, #105, man w/chicken on knee, washtub, from $35 to 50.00
Planter, #110, man, w/jug & snake, 4½", from $30 to.................... 40.00
Shakers, Ma & Old Doc, pr from $28 to 40.00

Indian Tree

Indian Tree is a popular dinnerware pattern produced by various potteries since the early 1800s to recent times. Although backgrounds and borders vary, the Oriental theme is carried out with the gnarled, brown branch of a pink-blossomed tree. Among the manufacturers' marks, you may find represented such notable firms as Coalport, S. Hancock and Sons, Soho Pottery, and John Maddock and Sons. See also Johnson Brothers.

Basket, #581/4, HJ Woods, 8x4x6"... 60.00
Bowl, cereal; fluted rim, Coalport, 1½x6x5" 25.00
Bowl, cream soup; 6½", w/7" underplate, Copeland....................... 45.00
Bowl, rimmed soup; Coalport, 8".. 45.00
Bowl, serving; Coalport, 3¾x11"... 75.00
Bowl, serving; hdls, Coalport, w/lid, 9" 325.00
Bowl, serving; scalloped, oval, Coalport, 2x10x8" 115.00
Bowl, serving; sq, Spode, 9".. 105.00
Cake plate, ped ft, Coalport, 3x9½" 150.00
Cake plate, tab hdls, Coalport, 9x10" 55.00
Casserole, Maddock, w/lid, 12x7", from $65 to............................ 80.00
Coffeepot, scalloped edges, ribbed body, Spode, 9"...................... 275.00
Creamer, Coalport, 4"... 45.00
Cup & saucer, bouillon; scalloped rim, flat, Coalport 40.00

Cup & saucer, chocolate; Coalport, 2½x3½", 5¼" 22.50
Egg cup, unmk England, 1930s-40s 18.00
Gravy boat, attached tray, Maddock, 9" L 20.00
Loving cup, hdls, Coalport, 5½" 55.00
Plate, bread & butter; ribbed, Spode, 6½" 15.00
Plate, dinner; Coalport, 10½" 55.00
Plate, dinner; ribbed, Spode, 10½", from $25 to 35.00
Plate, luncheon; 9" 45.00
Platter, Copeland Spode, 15" L, from $95 to 110.00
Platter, scalloped rim, Spode, 11x6½" 110.00

Teacup and saucer, Coalport, 1891, from $45.00 to $60.00. (Photo courtesy Jim and Susan Harran)

Teapot, gold trim, Aynsley, 6"... 60.00
Teapot, Maddock, 4-cup, from $40 to 60.00
Teapot, ribbed, Spode, 6", from $145 to..................................... 165.00
Tray, hors d'oeuvres, 3-part, Maddock, 10" 50.00
Urn/vase, hdls, w/lid, Coalport, 7", NM...................................... 75.00

Inkwells and Inkstands

Receptacles for various writing fluids have been used since ancient times. Through the years they have been made from countless materials — glass, metal, porcelain, pottery, wood, and even papier-mache. During the eighteenth century, gold or silver inkstands were presented to royalty; the well-known silver inkstand by Philip Syng, Jr., was used for the signing of the Declaration of Independence; and they were proud possessions of men of letters. When literacy vastly increased in the nineteenth century, the dip pen replaced the quill pen. Inkwells and inkstands were produced in a broad range of sizes in functional and decorative forms from ornate Victorian to flowing Art Nouveau and stylized Art Deco designs. However, the acceptance of the ballpoint pen literally put inkstands and inkwells 'out of business.' But their historical significance and intriguing diversity of form and styling fascinate today's collectors. It should be noted here that many cast white-metal inkwells have lost much of their value. Collectors and antique dealers are leaning toward more valuable materials such as brilliant cut glass, silver, and copper. See also Bottles, Ink.

Bronze with gilt patina, dolphin supporting clamshell, 4¾", $525.00. (Photo courtesy Alderfer Auction Company/LiveAuctioneers.com)

Aluminum, elk head, Detroit Mich on forehead, glass bottle, 6½", EX..115.00
Black Forest, kitten's head in shoe, brass well, ca 1900 .... 800.00
Brass, camel w/howdah, recumbent, 3½x6½"................................... 300.00
Brass, court jesters, 1 balancing/1 atop lid, glass insert, 7", EX..... 100.00
Brass, rtcl bell form w/porc well in center, European, 19th C....... 110.00
Bronze, eagle w/wings wide grasps 2 flags, 2 wells, marble base, 1890s ..180.00
Bronze, Nouveau lady w/flowing hair on leaf form, glass insert, 11" L .. 1,560.00
Bronze, 3 winged figures support well, putti finial, 1930s, 9x8" ... 215.00
Cast iron, fox head, head opens to glass insert, 5½" W, EX 285.00
Cast iron, horseshoe on ftd base, glass bottle/pen tip tray, 6", EX....115.00
Cast iron, owl figural, hinged head forms lid, 4x9¼" 300.00

Cast iron, owl with wings spread, attributed to Bradley and Hubbard, 9" wide, $140.00. (Photo courtesy Bertoia Auctions/LiveAuctioneers.com)

Cranberry glass & metal, bee figural, 3½x6¼"................................. 60.00
Gilt bronze, Egyptian Revival, Egyptian figural, 1880s................. 450.00
Glass, Daisy & Button, gr, minor chips on lid............................. 120.00
Glass, gr cased, sq, late Victorian, 5x3¼" 235.00
Porc, floral w/gold, Fr, 6-sided, 2" 85.00
Spelter, camel figural, recumbent, 1930s, 5x5"............................. 60.00
Tortoiseshell vnr w/silver mts, ivory ball ft, 2 cut bottles, 4x12x6" ... 1,750.00

Insulators

The telegraph was invented in 1844. The devices developed to hold the electrical transmission wires to the poles were called insulators. The telephone, invented in 1876, intensified their usefulness; and by the turn of the century, thousands of varieties were being produced in pottery, wood, and glass of various colors. Even though it has been rumored that red glass insulators exist, none have ever been authenticated. There are amber-colored insulators that appear to have a red tint to the amber, and those are called red-amber. Many insulators are embossed with patent dates. Of the more than 3,000 types known to exist, today's collectors evaluate their worth by age, rarity, color and, of course, condition. Aqua and green are the most common colors in glass, dark brown the most common in porcelain. Threadless insulators (for example, CD #701.1), made between 1850 and 1865, bring prices well into the hundreds, sometimes even the thousands, if in mint condition.

In the listings that follow, the CD numbers are from an identification system developed in the late 1960s by N.R. Woodward. Those seeking additional information about insulators are encouraged to contact Line Jewels NIA #1380 (whose address may be found in the Directory under Clubs, Newsletters, and Catalogs) or attend a club-endorsed show. (For information see Directory under Florida for Jacqueline Linscott Barnes.) In the listings that follow those stating 'no name' have no company identification but do have embossed numbers, dots, etc. Those stating 'no embossing' are without raised letters, dots, or any other markings. Please note: Our values are for threaded pin type insulators unless 'threadless' is included in the description; assume them to be in mint condition unless noted otherwise.

Key:
* (asterisk) — Canadian
BE — base embossed
CB — corrugated base
CD — Consolidated Design
FDP — flat drip points
RB — rough base
RDP — round drip points
SB — smooth base
SDP — sharp drip points

CD 102, NEGMCo, SB, bl aqua.. 15.00
CD 1038, Cutter Pat April 26, 04, SB, threadless, aqua.............. 300.00
CD 109, Chicago Insulating Co/Pat Oct 16, 1883, aqua...........2,500.00
CD 112, California, SB, purple 45.00
CD 113, No Name - Canada, SB, royal purple 200.00
CD 121, Am Tel & Tel Co, SB, lt gr aqua 5.00
CD 122, Armstrong No 2/Made in USA, SB, clear....................2.00
CD 122*, Dominion-16, RDP, lt peach.....................................2.00
CD 125, Hemingray/No 15, SDP, gr.. 100.00
CD 129, Kerr TS, SB, off-clear...5.00
CD 132.2, ST Paisley/Maker/Beaver Falls, PA, SB, aqua 2,000.00
CD 133, California, SB, lt purple 150.00
CD 133, OVGCo, SB, aqua 75.00
CD 133.3, no emb, SB, dk aqua 50.00
CD 134, KCGW, SB, ice bl 75.00
CD 134, T-HECo, SB, olive gr 1,250.00
CD 135, Chicago Insulating Co, BE, milky bl 600.00
CD 136, B&O, SB, gr 400.00
CD 136.5, Boston Bottle Works - Pat Oct 15 72, SB, aqua.......3,500.00
CD 140, Jumbo, SB, dk aqua 400.00
CD 141.7, WR Twiggs, SB, clear...20,000.00
CD 141.8, JF Buzby/Pat'd May 6/1890, SB, aqua 20,000.00
CD 141.9, Emminger's, BE, lt aqua 20,000.00
CD 143, Dwight, SB, purple.. 500.00
CD 143.5, T-HECo, SB, aqua 125.00
CD 145, BGMCo, SB, lt purple 250.00
CD 149, no emb, CD, dk aqua 40.00
CD 150, Barclay, SDP, aqua..7,500.00

CD 150, Brookfield, Pat. Oct. 8, 1907, $190.00. (Photo courtesy Hassinger & Courtney Auctioneering/LiveAuctioneers.com)

CD 154, Hemingray-42, RDP, aqua.......................................1.00
CD 154, Hemingray-42, SB, Hemingray Blue 30.00
CD 154, Maydwell-42/USA, RDP, straw 2.00
CD 155, Kerr DP 1, SB, clear...2.00
CD 158, Boston Bottle Works/Patent Applied For, SB, aqua....... 700.00
CD 160, Brookfield/New York, SB, olive amber 75.00
CD 160, emb star, SB, lt yel olive gr 75.00
CD 161, California, SB, purple 30.00
CD 162, BGMCo, SB, purple... 300.00
CD 162, California, SB, sage gr..5.00
CD 162, Hamilton Glass Co, RB, lt aqua 30.00

CD 162, WFGCo, SB, lt purple 40.00
CD 190 & CD 191, 2-pc/Transposition, SB, milky aqua 400.00
CD 197, Hemingray-53, CB, clear 2.00
CD 208, California, sB, lt purple 125.00
CD 214, Armstrong's No 10, SB, clear.................................2.00
CD 228, Brookfield, RB, dk aqua 600.00
CD 238, Hemingray-514, cb, honey amber....................... 325.00
CD 251, NEGMCo, RB, aqua 30.00
CD 254, No 3 Cable, RB, aqua 40.00
CD 262, NO2 Columbia, SB, lt bl aqua............................ 175.00
CD 267.5, NEGMCo, SB, emerald gr 200.00
CD 269, Jumbo, SB, aqua 500.00
CD 288, By RD Mershon, SB, aqua 100.00
CD 292.5, Boston/'Knowles 6,' SB, aqua........................ 300.00
CD 308, No 100, SB, dk aqua 175.00
CD 317, Chambers/Pat Aug 14 1877, SB, lt aqua 500.00
CD 701.1, no emb, SB, threadless, citrine 3,000.00
CD 724, Chester, NY, BE, threadless, cobalt 5,000.00
CD 735, Chester/NY, SB, threadless, aqua 600.00
CD 736, NY&ERR, SB, threadless, lt gr aqua.............3,500.00
CD 742.3, MTCo, BE, threadless, lt teal bl 1,500.00

Irons

History, geography, art, and cultural diversity are all represented in the collecting of antique pressing irons. The progress of fashion and invention can be traced through the evolution of the pressing iron. Over 700 years ago, implements constructed of stone, bone, wood, glass, and wrought iron were used for pressing fabrics. Early ironing devices were quite primitive in form, and heating techniques included inserting a hot metal slug into a cavity of the iron, adding hot burning coals into a chamber or pan, and placing the iron directly on hot coals or a hot surface.

To the pleasure of today's collectors, some of these early irons, mainly from the period of 1700 to 1850, were decorated by artisans who carved and painted them with regional motifs typical of their natural surroundings and spiritual cultures. Beginning in the mid-1800s, new cultural demands for fancy wearing apparel initiated a revolution in technology for types of irons and methods to heat them. Typical of this period is the fluter which was essential for producing the ruffles demanded by the nineteenth-century ladies. Hat irons, polishers, and numerous unusual iron forms were also used during this time, and provided a means to produce crimps, curves, curls, and special fabric textures. Irons from this era are characterized by their unique shapes, odd handles, latches, decorations, and even revolving mechanisms.

Also during this time, irons began to be heated by burning liquid and gaseous fuels. Gradually the new technology of the electrically heated iron replaced all other heating methods, except in the more rural areas and undeveloped countries. Even today the Amish communities utilize gasoline fuel irons.

In the listings that follow, prices are given for examples in best possible as-found condition. Damage, repairs, plating, excessive wear, rust, and missing parts can dramatically reduce value. For further information we recommend *Irons by Irons*, *More Irons by Irons*, and *Even More Irons by Irons* by our advisor Dave Irons; his address and information for ordering these books are given in the Directory under Pennsylvania.

Alcohol, Manning-Bowman...USA, tank missing, ca 1900, 7", $100 to . 125.00
Billard table, beveled edge, Geo Wright...London, 1890s, 10", $100 to ... 150.00
Box, English, brass w/wigglework decor, mid-1800s, 5½", $200 to 300.00
Box, Laundry Queen #2, top lifts off, late 1800s, 6¼", $200 to 300.00
Buttonhole, Pat June 1904..., removable hdl, button slot, $200 to..300.00
Charcoal, box, brass, openwork top, Dutch, mid-1800s, 8½", $150 to..200.00
Charcoal, box, Eclipse...1983 w/star, 6¾", from $50 to 70.00

Combination/revolving, Majestic, Pat by HP Carver, 1899, 6¼", up to...750.00
Dragon, Pomeroy Peckover...1854, figural chimney, 11", over 750.00
Flatiron, cast swan, late 1800s, 5", from $500 to.......................... 750.00
Flatiron, cold hdl, coiled upright, 6⅛", from $200 to 300.00

Flatiron for holding coals, figural head lifter, 8x8", $40.00. (Photo courtesy Auction Gallery of the Palm Beaches./LiveAuctioneers.com)

Flower, J Alente NY, brass top/iron base, late 1800s, 9½", $100 to... 125.00
Fluter, HB Adams Pat Pending, clamp-on, ca 1875, from $200 to ..300.00
Fluter machine, Dudley...1876, red pinstripes/decals, from $300 to.. 500.00
Gasoline, Diamond...Made in USA, early 1900s, 7½", from $50 to..70.00
Gasoline, Sunshine...USA Pat Pending, 1900s, 7½", from $70 to...100.00
Goffering, dbl; brass on marble base, English, 1850s, 10¼", over . 750.00
Goffering, dbl; brass w/wood base, English, late 1800s, 8x3½", over ..750.00
Hat, Schadler No 5471 Pat, curved base, ca 1900, 4½", from $200 to..300.00
Hat, shackle, iron, flat bottom, late 1800s, 5⅛", from $100 to 125.00
Ox tongue, acorn details, Europe, early 1800s, 8½", from $200 to ..250.00
Ox tongue, slug or gas jet heat, cast dragon, open bk, 1890s, 7¾" ...500.00
Pan, Greek, rnd w/high ridges in bottom, ca 1900, 18", $100 to.. 150.00
Poking stick, English, all iron, early 1800s, 12½", from $200 to... 300.00
Rocker, Geneva Hand Fluter...1866, brass top/plates, 5¾", $200 to...300.00
Rocker fluter, late 1800s, 1⅞", from $200 to 300.00
Sadiron, steel w/silver inlay, European, late 1800s, mini, 2", over. 750.00
Slug, Pat Apd For, Daniel Barns NY...1877, swan latch, 7", over .. 750.00
Sm, removable cold hdl, PET, ca 1900, 3¾", from $200 to........... 300.00
Sm, Wrought, mid-1800s, 3½", from $100 to.............................. 150.00
Smoothing brd, European, horse hdl, mid-1800s, 25", from $300 to..500.00
Tailor, Sensible...Sept 6 '87, removable cold hdl, 9½", $200 to.... 300.00
Tailor's, #8, removable cold hdl, late 1800s, 8⅛", from $100 to ... 150.00
Tall chimney, E Bless R Drake...1852, vulcan face damper, 6½"... 150.00
Wire hdl, FR, thin base, early 1900s, 3⅜", from $70 to 100.00

Ironstone

During the last quarter of the eighteenth century, English potters began experimenting with a new type of body that contained calcinated flint and a higher china clay content, intent on producing a fine durable whiteware — heavy, yet with a texture that would resemble porcelain. To remove the last trace of yellow, a minute amount of cobalt was added, often resulting in a bluish-white tone. Wm and John Turner of Caughley and Josiah Spode II were the first to manufacture the ware successfully. Others, such as Davenport, Hicks and Meigh, and Ralph and Josiah Wedgwood, followed with their own versions. The latter coined the name 'Pearl' to refer to his product and incorporated the term into his trademark. In 1813 a 14-year patent was issued to Charles James Mason, who called his ware Patented Ironstone. Francis Morley, G.L. Asworth, T.J. Mayer, and other Staffordshire potters continued to produce ironstone until the end of the century. While some of these patterns are simple to the extreme, many are decorated with in-mold designs of fruit, grain, and foliage on ribbed or scalloped shapes. In the 1830s transfer-printed designs in blue, mulberry, pink, green, black, and some two-tone became popular; and polychrome versions of Oriental wares were manufactured to compete with the Chinese trade. See also Mason's Ironstone.

Tureen, vegetable; J&G Meakin, 11" long, $150.00. (Photo courtesy Du Mouchelles/LiveAuctioneers.com)

Bowl, Double Sydenham, ped ft, H&G Harvey, 7⅞x10⅝" 375.00
Bowl, fruit; radiating ribs/scalloped rim, ftd, Powell & Bishop, 4x19" ... 275.00
Butter tub, staved barrel w/tab hdls, blk 'Butter,' Staffordshire, rpr . 125.00
Cake stand, flared ped ft, notched apron, Turner & Goddard, 4x8½" ... 585.00
Hot toddy bowl/tureen, Cable & Ring, ftd, w/ladle, Onondaga, 8¾x12". 235.00
Pitcher, Berlin Swirl, Mayer & Elliot, 6½" 180.00
Pitcher, Canada, poppies/wheat stems, waisted, Clementson, 8½" .. 395.00
Pitcher, Corn & Oats, scalloped rim, Davenport, 6½x4¾x4" 75.00
Pitcher, Double Leaf, paneled body, James Edwards, 13" 95.00
Pitcher, emb ribbed borders, rectangular, Wood & Son, 1870s, 9" ... 95.00
Pitcher, Forget-Me-Not, Wood Rathbone & Co, 1800s, 12" 435.00
Pitcher, Fuchsia, George Jones, 9¾" 395.00
Pitcher, Medallion Sprig, Powell & Bishop, 12¼x7½" 190.00
Pitcher, Mother & Child, bark & berries, Cork & Edge, 8½", EX ... 150.00
Pitcher, Paris, Walley, 11½" 350.00
Pitcher, Prairie, Clementson, 9½", NM 175.00
Platter, emb floral, faint mk, 17½" L 145.00
Platter, emb scalloped thin border, Meakin, 20x14", NM 100.00
Platter, Fig, emb border, 8-sided, Wedgwood, 1850s, 20½x16" 250.00
Syrup pitcher, all-over netting, pewter lid, ca 1860, 6" 225.00
Teapot, Calla Lily, gold trim, 10½" 200.00
Teapot, Dallas shape, Clementson, ca 1839, 9½" 285.00
Teapot, emb ribs, leafy finial, Furnival, ca 1895, rprs, 9½" 85.00
Teapot, Gothic, emb grapes etc, Venables, 9" 150.00
Teapot, Heirloom, Red Cliff, 10½" 65.00
Teapot, shaped paneled sides, Meakin, 10" 120.00
Tureen, Double Leaf, James Edwards, ca 1851, 7½x10¾" 200.00
Tureen, sauce; emb grapes/paneled, w/ladle & hdld undertray, Red Cliff . 135.00
Tureen, scrolled hdls, fig finial, Hughes & Bennett, 7x12x7" 125.00
Tureen, Sydenham, w/lid, T&R Boote, 8x11½x9" 200.00
Tureen, uptrn hdls, w/lid, Gelson Bros Hanley England, 6x7x5" ... 95.00
Tureen, vegetable; Corn, w/lid, 6½x12x8" 215.00

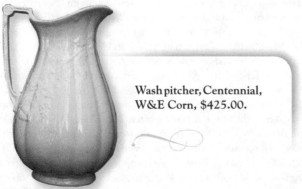

Wash pitcher, Centennial, W&E Corn, $425.00.

Washbowl & pitcher, Ceres, Elsmore & Forster, 13¼", 14" 550.00
Washbowl & pitcher, Sydenham, 14" dia, 11" 135.00

Italian Glass

Throughout the twentieth century, one of the major glassmaking centers of the world was the island of Murano. From the Stile Liberte work of Artisi Barovier (1890 – 1920s) to the early work of Ettore Sottsass in the 1970s, they excelled in creativity and craftsmanship. The 1920s to 1940s featured the work of glass designers like Ercole Barovier for Barovier and Toso and Vittorio Zecchin, Napoleone Martinuzzi, and Carlo Scarpa for Venini. Many of these pieces are highly prized by collectors.

The 1950s saw a revival of Italy as a world-reknown design center for all of the arts. Glass led the charge with the brightly colored work of Fulvio Bianconi for Venini, Dino Martens for Aureliano Toso, and Ercole Barovier for Barovier and Toso. The best of these pieces are extremely desirable. The '60s and '70s have also seen many innovative designs with work by the Finn Tapio Wirkkala, the American Thomas Stearns, and many other designers. Unfortunately, among the great glass, there was a plethora of commercial ashtrays, vases, and figurines produced that, though having some value, do not compare in quality and design to the great glass of Murano.

Venini: The Venini company was founded in 1921 by Paolo Venini, and he led the company until his death in 1959. Major Italian designers worked for the firm, including Vittorio Zecchin, Napoleone Martinuzzi, Carlo Scarpa, and Fulvio Bianconi. After his death, his son-in-law, Ludovico de Santillana, ran the factory and employed designers like Toni Zucchieri, Tapio Wirkkala, and Thomas Stearns. The company is known for creative designs and techniques including Inciso (finely etched lines), Battuto (carved facets), Sommerso (controlled bubbles), Pezzato (patches of fused glass), and Fascie (horizontal colored lines in clear glass). Until the mid-'60s, most pieces were signed with acid-etched 'Venini Murano ITALIA.' In the '60s they started engraving the signatures. The factory still exists.

Barovier: In the late 1920s, Ercole Barovier took over the Artisti Barovier and started designing many different vases. In the 1930s he merged with Ferro Toso and became Barovier and Toso. He designed many different series of glass including the Barbarico (rough, acid-treated brown or deep blue glass), Eugenio (free-blown vases), Efeso, Rotallato, Dorico, Egeo (vases incorporating murrine designs), and Primavera (white etched glass with black bands). He designed until 1974. The company is still in existence. Most pieces were unsigned.

Aureliano Toso: The great glass designer Dino Martens was involved with the company from about 1938 to 1965. It was his work that produced the very desirable Oriente vases. This technique consisted of free-formed patches of green, yellow, blue, purple, black, and white stars and pieces of zanfirico canes fused into brilliantly colored vases and bowls. His El Dorado series was based on the same technique but was not opaque. He also designed pieces with alternating groups of black and white filigrana lines. Pieces are unsigned.

Seguso: Flavio Poli became the artistic director of Seguso in the late 1930s and remained until 1963. He is known for his Corroso (acid-etched glass) and his Valve series (elegant forms of two to three layers of colored glass with a clear glass casing).

Archimede Seguso: In 1946 Archimede Seguso left the Seguso Vetri D'Arte to open a new company and designed many innovative pieces. His Merlatto (thin white filigrana suspended three dimensionally) series is his most famous. The epitome of his work is where a colored glass (yellow or purple) is windowed in the merlotti. His Macchia Ambra Verde is yellow and spots on a gold base encased in clear glass. The A Piume series contained feathers and leaves suspended in glass. Pieces are unsigned.

Alfredo Barbini: Barbini was a designer known for his sculptures of sea subjects and his amorphic-shaped vases with an inner core of red or blue glass with a heavy layer of finely incised outer glass. He worked in the 1950s to the 1960s, and some pieces are signed.

Vistosi: Although this glassworks was started in the 1940s, fame came in the 1960s and 1970s with the birds designed by Allesandro Pianon and the early work of the Memphis school designer, Ettore Sottsass. Pieces may be signed.

AVEM: This company is known for its work in the 1950s and 1960s. The designer, Ansolo Fuga, did work using a solid white glass with inclusions of multicolored murrines.

Cenedese: This is a postwar company led by Gino Cenedese with Alfredo Barbini as designer. When Barbini left, Cenedese took over the design work and also used the free-lanced designs of Fulvio Bianconi. They are known for their figurines and vases with suspended murrines.

Cappellin: Venini's original partner (1921 – 1925), Giacomo Cappellin, opened a short-lived company (1925 – 1932) that was to become extremely important. His chief designer was the young Carlo Scarpa who was to create many masterpieces in glass both for Cappellin and then Venini.

Ettore Sottsass: Sottass founded the Memphis School of Design in the 1970s. He is an extremely famous modern designer who designed several series of glass for the Vistosi Glass Company. The pieces were created in limited editions, signed and numbered, and each piece was given a name.

Basket, bl opalino w/gr highlights, Venini, 1950-60, 11½x6¾" **240.00**
Basket, red/bl sommerso in clear, att Salviati, 13x9½" **250.00**
Bottle, bl cased in clear, textured surface, ball stopper, Seguso, 8"..**240.00**
Bottle, cobalt/gold/pk spiral stripes, w/stopper, att Toso, 9x4" **725.00**
Bottle, gray-blk w/wht ribbon around body & stopper, Murano, 12x4½" ..**600.00**
Bottle, red/bl/clear sommerso, elongated stopper, Seguso, 17" **335.00**
Bottle, scent; bullicani clear w/blk sommerso, bulbous, 1950s, 5x4" ..**180.00**
Bowl, blk w/gold aventurine, contoured rim, Seguso, 3x8" **240.00**
Bowl, leaf form, clear w/wht threads between layers, Venini, 3⅜x8"..**425.00**
Bowl, 3 tropical fish/plants cased in clear, Cenedese, 6x7½x2½" .. **780.00**
Candlestick, gold mica on beige w/clear stem & base, Cenedese, 19", ea..**850.00**
Chandelier, 9 gr stem-like arms, dbl-bloom flowers, 1895, 72x34" ...**4,700.00**
Decanter, gr & bl incalmo, bulbous body, att Gio Ponti, 1989, 13"..**950.00**
Pitcher, alternating bl & gr stripes, bulbous, Venini, 10¼"........... **360.00**
Sculpture, bird, clear, hollow w/appl purple eyes/blk ft, Murano, 12"..**240.00**
Sculpture, bird, pk to amber, lg curling tail, ped ft, Venini, 15", NM **175.00**
Sculpture, fish, purple/bl cased in clear, tail up, Alvin, 1950s, 18" ..**240.00**

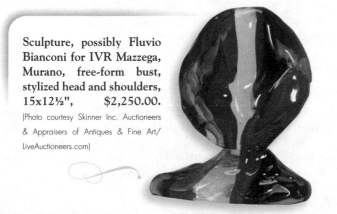

Sculpture, possibly Fluvio Bianconi for IVR Mazzega, Murano, free-form bust, stylized head and shoulders, 15x12½", $2,250.00. (Photo courtesy Skinner Inc. Auctioneers & Appraisers of Antiques & Fine Art/ LiveAuctioneers.com)

Sculpture, head, wht w/appl blk, minimalist style, Murano, 12" .. **950.00**
Sculpture, lady w/flowing cape/skirt, blk & wht latticinio, 11½"... **725.00**
Sculpture, man w/fish, mc w/aventurine, 1950s, 12¼"................. **150.00**
Sculpture, rooster, aventurine/gold foil/red ribbons in clear, 12"..**240.00**
Sculpture, rooster, cranberry w/bubbles, aventurine details, 11" ..**240.00**
Sculpture, swan, bl to clear sommerso, Murano, 1950s, 14x7x5" .. **120.00**
Sculptures, man & lady, pk/yel/clear, Murano, 14¾", pr.............. **200.00**

Vase, bl twisted form w/internal fish/plants, att Barbini, 1950s, 12" ...**660.00**
Vase, bl w/wht pulled feathers, stick neck, Murano, 17x5½"........ **780.00**
Vase, bl w/2 openings in body, att Fulvio, Murano, 1965-66, 16½"..**1,200.00**
Vase, bl/gr/wht/red swirls, narrow rim, bulbous, 9x5½"................. **180.00**
Vase, cornucopia, yel cased in clear, Murano, 10x7" **240.00**
Vase, flower form, orange cased/gold mica, Barovier & Toso, 18½"..**275.00**
Vase, Intarsa, amber/smoky triangular patchwork, Barovier & Toso, 12"...**3,250.00**

Vase, Lino Tagleapietra, Mugambo, 14x10", $8,500.00. (Photo courtesy Early Auction Co.)

Vase, lt violet soffiati, urn form, att V Zecchin, 11"...................... **480.00**
Vase, mc a fasce bands on red, Cenedese, 11x8¾" **400.00**
Vase, mc herringbone pattern, Barovier & Toso, 1958, 11½"....**7,000.00**
Vase, mc swirls w/gold aventurine, Murano, 15x6¾" **480.00**
Vase, pk & clear filigree, ftd, trumpet neck, Cenedese, 10x3½" ... **850.00**
Vase, powder bl opaque handkerchief form, Fazzoletto, 6¼x8¾".. **120.00**
Vase, red & wht spirals, slim neck, ruffle, Toso, 8¼x3" **180.00**
Vase, red & wht stripes, clear ruffle/hdls, canes inside, Toso, 5¼" . **150.00**
Vase, red to clear to lt bl, ribs & pinched waist, Toso, 1950, 10x7" .. **120.00**
Vase, red to clear w/bullicani & pulled top sommerso, Murano, 12x6".**240.00**
Vase, somersso bullicanti, lav & clear w/pulled design, Seguso, 7x7" .**1,500.00**
Vase, Zanfirico, filigrana in rows of brn & cream threading, 7x12" .**900.00**
Vase, 5-color swirled stripes, wht int, teardrop, Barovier & Toso, 14" ... **180.00**

Ivory

Ivory has been used and appreciated since Neolithic times. It has been a product of every culture and continent. It is the second most valuable organic material after pearls. Ivory is defined as the dentine portion of mammalian teeth. Commercially the most important ivory comes from elephant and mammoth tusks, walrus tusks, hippo teeth, and sperm whale teeth. The smaller tusks of boar and warthog are often used whole.

Ivory has been used for artistic purposes as a palette for oil paints, as inlay on furniture, and especially as a medium for sculptures. Some are in the round, others in the form of plaques. Ivory also has numerous utilitarian uses such as cups and tankards; combs; handles for knives and medical tools; salt and pepper shakers; chess, domino, and checker pieces; billiard balls; jewelry; shoehorns; snuff boxes; brush pots; and fans.

There are a number of laws domestically and internationally to protect endangered animals including the elephant, walrus, and whale. However ivory taken and used before the various enactment dates is legal within the country in which it is located, and can be shipped internationally with a permit. Ivory from mammoths, hippopotamus, warthogs, and boar is excepted from all bans. Prices have risen slightly over the previous several years for the majority of ivory items with the exception of jewelry, which has fallen in price, and better European and Japanese ivory carvings which have increased substantially over the last 18 months. Prices are lowest for African and Indian ivories. As with all collectibles, the very best pieces will appreciate most in the years to come. Small, poorly carved pieces will not appreciate to any extent. Our advisor for this category is Robert Weisblut; he is listed in the Directory under Florida.

Apple w/pierced village scene, removable stem, 5" 400.00
Bust of Voltaire on marble plinth, Fr, 1800s, 10" 9,500.00
Candle screen, angels, irregular floral rim, European, 1800s, 20x6"..8,500.00
Chalice, silver mts, high relief stags, European, 1800s, 10½x2".. 1,500.00
Children, Communist Chinese era, 9½" 1,250.00
Clock, 5 musical nymphs, Dieppe, Fr, late 1800s, 8½x6" 8,000.00
Fisherman in boat bringing in nets, 3x14½"+base 510.00

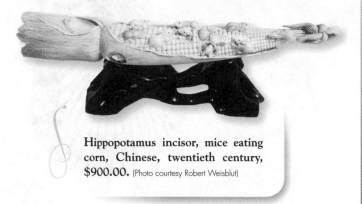

Hippopotamus incisor, mice eating corn, Chinese, twentieth century, $900.00. (Photo courtesy Robert Weisblut)

Lady holding flowers (Kwan Yin?), sm age split, 14" on stand 625.00
Lady in flowing robes holds lotus blossom, crane at ft, 7¾" on base . 200.00
Lady w/parasol, European, late 1800s, 7x3" 1,400.00
Lady w/weaving implements, Chinese, early 1900s, 9" 675.00
Narwhal tusk shakers, scrimshawed, 2½", pr 350.00
People (6) along sides of covered bridge, detailed, 25¼" L 925.00
Plaque, openwork w/phoenix/dragon/twining roses, 4x11"+stand...725.00
Plate, sectioned floral rim/goddess center, Japanese, 1900s, 8" ..2,200.00
Snuff bottle, deep relief, China, 1800s, 5" 1,250.00
Study of rose branch, Japan, early 1900s, 13" 1,750.00
Temple jar, dragon cvgs, 3 mask ft, foo dog finial, ring hdls, 12".. 1,500.00
Triptych, Marie Antoinette, scenes w/in skirt, Fr, late 1800s, 9x5" ..2,500.00
Village scene, Japanese, ca 1900, 5½" 2,000.00

Jervis

W.P. Jervis began his career as a potter in 1898. By 1908 he had his own pottery in Oyster Bay, New York. His shapes were graceful; often he decorated his wares with sgraffito designs over which he applied a matt glaze. Many pieces were incised 'Jervis' in a vertical arrangement. The pottery closed around 1912. Our advisors for this category are Suzanne Perrault and David Rago; they are listed in the Directory under New Jersey.

Jar, northern landscape silhouette, acorn finial, 6-sided, 7", NM...2,400.00
Mug, There Is Nothing Like a Good..., gr & dk bl, 4½" 400.00
Pitcher, stylized irises, indigo on blk, 4¼x5¼" 800.00
Vase, dk aventurine, squat, 3x5¼" 1,200.00

Vase, goose in flight, white on indigo, incised Jervis, 4x4", $1,850.00.
(Photo courtesy David Rago Auctions)

Vase, irises on brn, spherical, 3½x4" 1,560.00
Vase, stylized trees, brn/gr/ochre, much cvg, 5x3" 1,080.00

Jewelry

Jewelry as objects of adornment has always been regarded with special affection. Today prices for gems and gemstones crafted into antique and collectible jewelry are based on artistic merit, personal appeal, pure sentimentality, and intrinsic value. Note: In general, Diamond prices vary greatly depending on cut, color, clarity, etc., and to assess the value of any diamond of more than a carat in weight, you will need to have information about all of these factors. Values given here are for jewelry with a standard commercial grade of diamonds that are most likely to be encountered.

Our advisor for fine jewelry is Rebecca Dodds-Metts; her address may be found in the Directory under Florida. Marcia 'Sparkles' Brown is our advisor for costume jewelry and the author of *Rhinestone Jewelry*; *Unsigned Beauties of Costume Jewelry*; *Signed Beauties of Costume Jewelry*, Books 1 and 2; *Coro Jewelry* (Collector Books); she is also the host of the videos *Hidden Treasures*. Mrs. Brown is listed in the Directory under Oregon. Other good references are *Collecting Costume Jewelry 101* and *Collecting Costume Jewelry 202* by Julia C. Carroll; *Inside the Jewelry Box: 20th Century Costume Jewelry* by Katie Joe Aikens; *Collectible Costume Jewelry* by Cherri Simonds; *Costume Jewelry* by Fred Rezadeh; *100 Years of Collectible Jewelry*, and *Fifty Years of Collectible Fashion Jewelry* by Lillian Baker; *Inside the Jewelry Box* by Ann Mitchell Pitman; and *Pictorial Guide to Costume Jewelry* by Ariel Bloom (all available from Collector Books). See also American Painted Porcelain; Hair Weaving.

Key:
ab — aurora borealis	gw — gold washed
B — Bakelite	k — karat
C — Catalin	L — Lucite
ca — cellulose acetate	lm — laminate
cab — cabachon	pl — plastic
clu — celluloid	plat — platinum
ct — carat	r — resin
dmn — diamond	r'stn — rhinestone
dwt — penny weight	st — silver-tone
Euro — European cut	stn — stone
fct — faceted	t — thermoset
fl — filigree	tw — total weight
gf — gold filled	wg — white gold
gp — gold plated	yg — yellow gold
grad — graduated	ygf — yellow gold filled
gt — gold-tone	

Bracelet, 18k wg, rubies (13.4ct tw) & rnd dmns (2.23ct tw), 7x½" ..3,850.00
Bracelet, cuff; Sadia, silver dragons/8-ruby sunburst, yg trim, 1 W ...2,525.00
Bracelet, 14k wg w/35 dmn links: 490 w/tw of 7.0cts, 7x½" 4,150.00
Brooch, 10k yg fl w/5mm garnet, 10¼" 230.00

Brooch, 14k white gold filigree set with a 55ct. blue topaz and approximately 100 white diamonds total weight 1.0ct., 1½" wide, $865.00. (Photo courtesy Jackson's International Auctioneers & Appraisers of Fine Art & Antiques/LiveAuctioneers.com)

Brooch, 14k wg dragonfly w/pavé .20ct tw dmns, 1¼x1⅛" 635.00
Brooch, 14k yg, nesting birds (4), ruby eyes, sm dmn in beak, 11.8 dwt. 435.00
Brooch, 14k yg dragonfly w/pk 2.0ct tw sapphires & tiny dmns, 1¾" W.. 1,380.00
Brooch, 14k yg fr w/onyx panel w/4 seed pearls, 1¾x1½" 315.00
Brooch, 14k yg free-form bow w/5mm dmn, 2¾" 400.00
Brooch, 18k wg dragonfly w/4.13ct amethyst & tiny dmns/sapphires, 2x3".. 1,725.00
Brooch, 18k yg dragonfly w/bl detail to gr enamel wings, 1⅝x1⅛" .. 575.00
Brooch, 18k yg holly leaves w/8 cultured pearls, 2" W 465.00
Earrings, 14k yg fr w/14.5mm maube pearl............................... 145.00
Earrings, 18k wg w/3.93ct teardrop emerald w/sm .29 tw dmns.. 1,600.00
Earrings, 22k yg drop w/7 turq beads, cut-out center, 2¾" 460.00
Earrings, 8 6.87ct tw rubies+15 .89ct tw dmns,¾" dia 1,875.00
Necklace, Kalo, silver blossom/leaf links, #953, 17" 2,050.00
Necklace, pearls, 5-strand, 6mm-7mm, 16-20" w/14k yg clasp..... 425.00
Necklace, 14k yg, aquamarine 1¼" teardrop in yg fr w/7 sm dmns.. 865.00

Parure, 14k yellow gold opal and emerald melee, bracelet, brooch, and earrings, 20dwt, $1,000.00. (Photo courtesy James D. Julia Inc.)

Pendant, shell cameo in 14k yg fr w/stylized leaf clip bail, 1¾" 150.00
Pendant, 14k yg fl cross w/pearl in center, sm dmn ea tip, 2½" 125.00
Pendant, 14k yg Nouveau lady w/plique-a-jour HP fan ea side, 1¼" .. 800.00
Ring, man's, 14k yg w/4.3ct dmn (G/H/I/SI1) 28,750.00
Ring, plat, .70ct Euro dmn (SI/KL), prong set 775.00
Ring, plat, oval 1.50ct bl sapphire w/2.50ct tw dmns 1,100.00
Ring, plat, 2.76ct cab ruby amid 36 sm .79ct tw dmns.............. 2,250.00
Ring, plat, 3.56ct fiery opal w/17.50ct tw dmns 1,750.00
Ring, plat, 4.50ct pavilion-cut alexandrite+2 .50ct triangular dmns. 14,950.00
Ring, plat, 6.03ct 8-sided pavilion-cut sapphire+2 1.25 tw dmns.. 15,525.00
Ring, 14k yg, .41ct dmn (G/VS1-VS2) on wg prongs................... 900.00
Ring, 14k yg, .57ct dmn (SI/KL), w/wedding band....................... 750.00
Ring, 14k yg, .78ct dmn cluster (G-H/VS2-S11) in wg oval 350.00
Ring, 14k yg, .78ct emerald amid pavé .65ct tw dmns forming petals.. 525.00
Ring, 14k yg, 1.40ct full-cut dmn (VS/HI) w/16 .50ct tw dmns.. 2,000.00
Ring, 14k yg, 11mm bezel-set maube pearl................................ 60.00
Ring, 14k yg, 6.5mmx16.8mm jadeite gr saddle w/wht edges 300.00
Ring, 14k yg crown w/2 pear-shaped 7.7x5.7mm sapphires+41 sm dms... 300.00
Ring, 18k wg, 1.90ct Euro dmn (VS/IJ), prong set..................... 4,000.00
Ring, 18k yg, 5 quadrillion-cut dmn 1ct tw (VS/GH) 500.00
Ring, 18k yg dome wire mesh w/13x9.1mm cab turq in yg bezel.. 500.00
Ring, 18k yg w/2 4.4mm/5mm sapphires+14 1.9mm dmns........... 400.00

Costume Jewelry

Rhinestone jewelry has become a very popular collectible. Rhinestones are foil-backed, leaded crystal, faceted stones with a sparkle outshining diamonds. Copyrighting jewelry came into effect in 1955. Pieces bearing a copyright mark (post-1955) are considered 'collectibles,' while pieces (with no copyright) made before then are regarded as 'antiques.' Fur clips are two-pronged, used to anchor fur stoles. Dress clips have a spring clasp and are used at the dress neckline. Look for signed and well-made, unmarked pieces for your collections and preserve this American art form. Our advisor for costume jewelry is Marcia Brown (see introductory paragraphs for information on her books and videos).

Bracelet, Coro, 4 amber stns on scrolled gt links, 1942, 7½x1" 125.00
Bracelet, Marvella, red r'stns/pearl on gt flower on pearl strand, 7".. 50.00
Bracelet, Schiaparelli, ab r'stns & purple cabs 225.00
Bracelet, Schiaparelli, pk r'stn flowerets on gt 105.00
Bracelet, Weiss, 3 lg bl prong-set cabs amid bl & gr r'stns 150.00
Bracelet, West Germany, bangle, abtract, sterling silver, FS mk, 1960.. 125.00
Bracelet & earrings, Coro, creamy moonstones w/sm r'stns, 7", ¾" .. 65.00
Brooch, Art, butterfly, mc cabs & pearls on scalloped wings, 2x1½" 50.00
Brooch, Boucher, wheelbarrow, bl & clear r'stns, wheel spins, 1x2".. 150.00
Brooch, Cadoro, turtle, yel B shell on gt body, gr stn eyes, 1½x2".. 80.00
Brooch, Cadoro, 4 lg sq mc crystals form sq 350.00
Brooch, Christmas wreath, Art, mc stones w/red bow on gt, 1½x1¾".. 25.00
Brooch, Coro, moonstone, pk & ab r'stn cluster 95.00
Brooch, Coro, peacock, bl ab r'stns on gt 35.00
Brooch, Coro, snowflake, blk & crystal r'stns................................. 48.00
Brooch, Coro, 4 gt flowers w/bl cab center 70.00
Brooch, Dodds, bell, bl ab r'stns w/swinging clapper, 2x1½" 35.00
Brooch, Dodds, Maltese cross, olive gr stns on ornate gt, 2½" 35.00
Brooch, Hattie Carnegie, zebra, blk pnt & r'stns on gt, 2½x1½" 90.00
Brooch, sea horse, pearl belly, gt... 55.00

Brooch, Staret, fuchsia blossom pavé set with clear stones and blue crystals, $325.00. (Photo courtesy Marcia Brown)

Brooch, Trifari, figural gt pea pod w/pearl peas 195.00
Brooch, Trifari, floral clusters, clear centers w/red stn petals, 3x3"..200.00
Brooch, Weiss, hand-blown pk flowers amid pk r'stns.................... 290.00
Brooch, Weiss, lt pk prong-set stns form 3-D leaf, 2½x1½" 85.00
Brooch & earrings, Coro, flower w/bl crystals w/dk tips form petals.. 80.00
Brooch & earrings, Kramer, bl r'stns w/linked bl beads, 2¾", 1½" ... 100.00
Earrings, Coro, amber r'stns on blk enamel cut-out disks 10.00
Earrings, Hobe, gold, amber & blk glass beads w/blk enamel caps, 1" .. 40.00
Earrings, Hobe, r'stn baguettes on gt mesh dangle, 2¾" 45.00
Earrings, Lisner, flowers, frosted 2-tone glass w/red centers, 1½" 40.00
Earrings, Vendome, lg bl r'stn drops under sm r'stns, 2½" clips....... 40.00
Earrings, Weiss, lav glass flowers... 60.00
Necklace, Ciner, oval pavé r'stn & blk enamel links, hidden clasp, 16"..200.00
Necklace, Coro, topaz r'stn on gp links 38.00
Necklace, De Mario, peach/tan pearls, amber/gt beads, sq beads, 17". 110.00
Necklace, Goldette, pillbox pendant (2") w/turq & red stns, 8 chains ..40.00
Necklace, Hattie Carnegie, crystal seed beads, 10-strand............. 125.00
Necklace, Hobe, bl & clear r'stn locket, hammered gt link chain ... 195.00
Necklace, Hollycraft, gr r'stns & tiny pearls on gt 120.00
Necklace, Kramer, red navette r'stns on gt, 17" 65.00
Necklace, M Haskell, bl-gr marble-like beads, ornate clasp, 3-strand ...180.00
Necklace, M Haskell, grad gr marble glass beads, 28" 115.00
Necklace, Schreiner, red, pk & diamanté r'stns on gunmetal........ 310.00
Necklace, Trifari, bl & gr crackle-glass beads, 15" 30.00
Necklace, Trifari, dk bl & bl topaz r'stns on gt braid, 1963............. 95.00
Necklace, Vendome, orange/yel/amber glass beads w/spacers, 17"...75.00
Necklace, Weiss, diamanté r'stn bib, plat-tone 280.00
Necklace & earrings, Coro, pk marble & pearl beads, 2-strand...... 60.00
Necklace & earrings, Florenza, bl ab/red cab grapes, 16", 1½" 100.00
Necklace & earrings, Leo Glass, clear r'stns, choker, screw bks...... 65.00
Necklace & earrings, M Haskell, red glass beads & disks, 2-strand ..800.00

Necklace & earrings, Schiaparelli, lg pk rose crystals & sm ab r'stns..340.00
Necklace & earrings, Trifari, grad gr beads & crystals, 6-strand 80.00
Ring, E Kauppi, rotating mc agate in silver mt 175.00

Parure, Crown Trifari, gold plated with clear rhinestones, $350.00. (Photo courtesy Marcia Brown)

Plastic Jewelry

Bracelet, B, butterscotch beads in gr casings, 1935, from $150 to ...175.00
Bracelet, B, red, brass spacers, expandable elastic, 1950, from $85 to.. 100.00

Bracelet, Bakelite and metal, probably European, $2,200.00. (Photo courtesy Skinner Inc. Auctioneers & Appraisers of Antiques & Fine Art/LiveAuctioneers.com)

Bracelet, bangle; B, butterscotch w/cvg, 1935, from $75 to.......... 100.00
Bracelet, bangle; B, translucent red, fct, 1935, from $150 to........ 175.00
Bracelet, bangle; L, pearlized gr, 1950, 1" wide, from $35 to 45.00
Bracelet, bangle; L, wht w/r'stns, 1935, from $75 to 85.00
Bracelet, bangle; Lea Stein, ca snake, 1960-80, from $85 to 125.00
Bracelet, bangle; wood & pl, brn w/Indian design, 1935, from $75 to .. 100.00
Bracelet, Ciner, B & gilt brass links, 1950, from $135 to.............. 150.00
Bracelet, clamper; KJ Lane, L, blk w/diagonal pattern in clear r'stns..150.00
Bracelet, cuff; KJ Lane, B & wood on gilded brass, $150 to.......... 195.00
Bracelet, L, wht w/clear r'stns, 1935, from $75 to 85.00
Bracelet, t-pl, translucent gr links, 1935, from $75 to 95.00
Bracelet & earrings, t-pl lemon-color links, 1950, from $45 to...... 55.00
Brooch, B, African princess w/r'stns, blk over butterscotch, 3¼" .. 350.00
Brooch, B, blk cameo in cvd blk fr, oval, 1930, lg, from $85 to.... 110.00
Brooch, B, cvd scarab, ca 1925, lg, from $125 to 150.00

Brooch, Bakelite, fish, carved and painted, 3" long, $660.00. (Photo courtesy Skinner Inc. Auctioneers & Appraisers of Antiques & Fine Art/LiveAuctioneers.com)

Brooch, B & metal, sword, blk w/chrome accent, 1935, from $90 to.100.00
Brooch, DiNicola, moon/star/scales, enamel & turq accents, 1970....100.00
Brooch, Joseff, Tenite flower w/gold center, 1950s, from $175 to .. 275.00
Brooch, Missoni, r, abstract mc mask, 1980, from $95 to 105.00
Brooch, pl, scratch-cvd purple bird w/r'stn eye, 1935, from $55 to...65.00
Brooch, Sarah Coventry, t-pl, turq w/gr glass stones, metal bk, 1960 ...60.00
Brooch, wood, cvd L & brass beading, bird, 1930s, from $95 to... 125.00
Buckle, France, clu, side-by-side disks, mc floral, 1930, from $85 to .. 95.00
Buckle, pl, brn elephants (2) w/trunks together, 1935, lg, from $65 to ..75.00
Clip, B, cvd butterscotch leaves, 2½", from $60 to 70.00
Clip, B, cvd red flower, 1930, from $35 to...................................... 55.00
Comb, clu, amber w/r'stns, 1950, from $10 to 15.00
Earrings, B, blk buttons studded w/r'stns, 1935-40, from $65 to 85.00
Earrings, B, cvd red cherries, 1930, from $175 to.......................... 200.00
Earrings, B, yel triangular drops, flat-cut, 1935, from $55 to 75.00
Earrings, Lisner, t-pl, leaves, translucent autumn tones, 1935........ 45.00
Earrings, t-pl, yel w/metal bks, 1950, from $15 to.......................... 20.00
Earrings, t-pl set in rhodium, ca 1950, from $10 to........................ 15.00
Earrings, Trifari, pl, dk amber drops w/cut-out center, 1970 .... 50.00
Necklace, B, blk ridged segments, 1935, from $95 to 125.00
Necklace, Christie Romero, B, glass pharaoh images, metal chain, 1935..175.00
Necklace, clu link chain w/B mc fruit, 1935, from $750 to 795.00
Necklace, Encore, L, clear rnd & sq beads, 1970, from $65 to 85.00
Necklace, England, C, mc swirl links on tan chain, 1920, from $125 to..150.00
Necklace, France, B, cvd red pendant on coiled chrome chain, 1930 ..400.00
Necklace, Ginger Moro, clu, pk floral drops on pk chain, 1950 ..... 65.00
Necklace, KJ Lane, t-pl, mc beads, 5-strand, 1975, from $225 to.. 275.00
Necklace, KJL, angel-skin floral design, 1960-90, from $275 to... 325.00
Necklace, pl, mc flower basket drops on gr chain, 1925, from $135 to ...150.00
Pedant, lm clu w/appl brass Egyptian design, 1925, from $75 to 85.00
Ring, B, cvd flower dome, brn marbled, 1935, from $85 to 100.00
Ring, L, blk w/clear r'stns, from $45 to.. 55.00
Ring, L, embedded w/insect or sea creature, 1960-80, from $35 to....50.00

Johnson Brothers

A Staffordshire-based company operating since well before the turn of the century, Johnson Brothers has produced many familiar lines of dinnerware, several of which are becoming very collectible. Some of their patterns were made in both blue and pink transfer as well as in polychrome, and many of their older patterns are still being produced. Among them are Old Britain Castles, Friendly Village, His Majesty, and Rose Chintz. However, the lines are less extensive than they once were.

Values below range from a low base price for patterns that are still in production or less collectible to a high that would apply to very desirable patterns such as Tally Ho, English Chippendale, Wild Turkeys, Strawberry Fair, Historic America, Harvest Fruit, etc. Mid-range lines include Coaching Scenes, Millsteam, Old English Countryside, Rose Bouquet (and there are others). These prices apply only to pieces made before 1990. Lines currently in production are being sold in many retail and outlet stores today at prices that are quite different from the ones we suggest. While a complete place setting of Old Britain Castles is normally about $50.00, in some outlets you can purchase it for as little as half price. For more information on marks, patterns, and pricing, we recommend *Johnson Brothers Dinnerware Pattern Directory and Price Guide* by Mary J. Finegan, who is listed in the Directory under North Carolina.

Bowl, cereal/soup; rnd, sq or lug, ea from $10 to............................. 20.00
Bowl, soup; rnd or sq, 7", from $12 to 25.00
Bowl, vegetable; oval, from $30 to upwards of................................ 50.00
Butter dish, from $50 to.. 80.00
Chop/cake plate, from $50 to 80.00
Coffee mug, from $20 to upwards of... 25.00

Coffeepot, from $90 to upwards of	100.00
Demitasse set, 2-pc, from $20 to	30.00
Egg cup, from $15 to	30.00
Pitcher/jug, from $45 to upwards of	55.00
Plate, dinner; from $14 to	30.00
Plate, salad; sq or rnd, from $10 to upwards of	18.00
Platter, med, 12-14", ea from $45 to upwards of	55.00
Sauceboat/gravy, from $40 to upwards of	48.00
Shakers, pr, from $40 to upwards of	48.00
Sugar bowl, open, from $30 to	40.00
Teacup & saucer, from $15 to upwards of	30.00
Turkey platter, 20½", from $200 to upwards of	300.00

Teapot, Rose Chintz, $90.00.

Josef Originals

Figurines of lovely ladies, charming girls, and whimsical animals marked Josef Originals were designed by Muriel Joseph George of Arcadia, California, from 1945 to 1985. Until 1960 they were produced in California, but costs were high and copies of her work were being made in Japan. To remain competitive, she and her partner, George Good, found a company in Japan to build a factory and produce her designs to her specifications. Muriel retired in 1982; however, Mr. Good continued production of her work and made some design changes on some figurines. The company was sold in late 1985; the name is currently owned by Dakin/Applause, and a limited amount of figurines with the Josef Originals name are being made. Those made during the ownership of Muriel are the most collectible. They can be recognized by these characteristics: The girls have a high-gloss finish, black eyes, and most are signed on the bottom. As of the late 1970s, bisque finish was making its way into the lineup, and by 1980 glossy girls were fairly scarce in the product line. Brown-eyed figurines date from 1982 through 1985. Applause uses a red-brown eye, although they are starting to release 'copies' of early pieces that are signed Josef Originals by Applause or by Dakin. The animals were nearly always done in a matt finish and bore paper labels only. In the mid-1970s they introduced a line of fuzzy flocked-coat animals with glass eyes. Our advisors, Jim and Kaye Whitaker (see the Directory under Washington, no appraisal requests please) have written three books: *Josef Originals, Charming Figurines, Revised Edition; Josef Originals, A Second Look;* and *Josef Originals, Figurines of Muriel Joseph George.* These are all currently available, and each has no repeats of items shown in the other books. Please note: All figurines listed here have black eyes unless specified otherwise. As with many collectibles, values have been negatively impacted to a measurable extent since the advent of the internet.

Angels playing various sports, Sports Angels series, Japan, 2¾", ea	35.00
Birthday Girls, Angels, #1-16, Japan, ea	30.00
Buggy Bugs series, various poses, wire antenna, Japan, 3¼", ea	12.00
Character Cat series, Cleo/Honey/Tiger/Sweetheart/etc, Japan, 4", ea	30.00
Chipmunk family, set of 3, mini, Japan, 1¼-1½"	35.00
Christmas angel praying by decorated tree nightlight, 7"	50.00

Christmas mouse, various poses, Japan, 2¼", ea	10.00
Cow creamer, bl flowers on wht, orig label	25.00
Dalmatian, Kennel Club series, Japan, 3½"	20.00
Days of the Week, 7 in series, California, 3½", ea	55.00
England, brn eyes, holds umbrella, Small World series, Japan, 4½"	35.00
Farmer's Daughter, girl w/hen & basket of eggs, Japan, 5"	45.00
Flower Girls series, girl w/flower hat, 6 in series, Japan, 4", ea	45.00
Four Seasons series, Spring/Summer/etc, Japan, 9", ea	95.00
Girl cutting cake, Japan, 6", from $45 to	50.00
Happy Home, dove greeting angel, Japan, 3¾"	35.00
Horoscope Angel, 12 in series, Japan, 3¾"	35.00
International series, various countries, 4¾", ea	45.00
Italian Aristocrats, lady & escort, Japan, 7", ea	75.00
Johnny, w/marbles, Joseph's Children, California, 4¾"	85.00

Joseph II, 5½", $40.00; Marie Antoinette, 5½", $40.00. (Photo courtesy Jim and Kaye Whitaker)

Lipstick, First Time series, Japan, 4½", from $35 to	45.00
Little Gourmet, girl w/recipe, 6 in series, Japan, 3½", ea	35.00
Love Story series, courtship to wedding, 6 in series, Japan, 8", ea	95.00
Lullaby & Good Night, 2 in series, California, 3¾", ea	55.00
Make Believe series, Japan, 4½", ea	40.00
Melody, lady by Victrola, Sweet Memories series, Japan, 6½"	85.00
Miss Mary, Nursery Rhymes series, Japan, 4"	45.00
Missy, girl in bonnet, several colors, California, 4"	45.00
Monogram Girls series, girl w/alphabet letter, brn eyes, Japan, 4", ea	25.00
Nanette, half-doll w/jewels, several colors, California, 5½"	55.00
New Home, girl w/key, Special Occasions series, Japan, 4½"	35.00
Ostrich Babies, 3 poses, Japan, ½", ea	25.00
Pixie, Christmas Helper, painting toy, Japan, 4¾"	25.00
Poodle family, Japan, set of 3, mini, 1½-2½"	18.00
Rose, girl w/flower hat, Flower Girl series, Japan, 4¼"	35.00
Ruby, girl w/'ruby' in crown, Little Jewels series, Japan, 3½"	35.00
Secret Pal, girl w/fan, various colors, California, 3½"	35.00
Skunk w/wht hair tuft on head, Japan, 2½"	18.00

The Trousseau, lady holding gown, wearing engagement ring, 9½", from $90.00 to $125.00. (Photo courtesy Jim and Kaye Whitaker)

Village Mouse, many poses, Japan, 2¼", ea	10.00
Wee Folk, various poses, Japan, 4½", ea	20.00
Yorkshire & various other breeds, Kennel Club series, Japan, 3", ea	20.00
Zodiac Girls series, Japan, 4¾", ea	45.00

Judaica

The items listed below are representative of objects used in both the secular and religious life of the Jewish people. They are evident of a culture where silversmiths, painters, engravers, writers, and metal workers were highly gifted and skilled in their art. Most of the treasures shown in recently displayed exhibits of Judaica were confiscated by the Germans during the late 1930s up to 1945; by then eight Jewish synagogues and 50 warehouses had been filled with Hitler's plunder. Judaica is currently available through dealers, from private collections, and annual auctions held in Israel, New York City, and Boston.

Our advisor for this category is Arthur M. Feldman, executive director of the Sherwin Miller Museum of Jewish Art (Tulsa); he is listed in the Directory under Oklahoma.

Astrolabe, brass, horse pointer, eng symbols, 19th C, 3⅝" dia...... 360.00
Bowl, silver, eng temple/forest, ftd, Russia, #84, 13x13½" 4,750.00
Bowl, silver, Jerusalem scenes, rtcl, 1950s, 9" W............................. 65.00
Bowl, silver w/gold int, chased Moses scenes, ftd, ca 1900, 12½" ..2,100.00
Candelabra, silver, 5-light, Austria, 23-oz, 20" 180.00
Candlesticks, silver, rtcl/chased grapes & vines, 32 troy ozs, 10", pr...600.00
Candlesticks, SP, foliage/lion heads, 13x5½", pr 600.00
Cup, hand washing; copper w/lead-lined int, 2-hdl, 1860-909, 5½".36.00
Cup, silver o/l on brass, 7-branch candelabra/star, 19th C, 4⅛" .1,325.00
Etrog container, silver melon form, Nuremberg, 19th C, 5⅛" L.5,200.00
Ewer, copper & brass, Arts & Crafts style, Russia, ca 1900, 6½x6" .110.00
Gavel, Zionist, wooden, w/Yiddish inscr/plaque, 1930s, 10x3½".. 300.00
Goblet, HP religious portrait on clear w/gilt, Moser style, 7¾" 300.00

Hanukkah menorah, silver with Art Nouveau foliage and crowned urn, 9" high, 17-ounce, $2,250.00. (Photo courtesy Freeman's/LiveAuctioneers.com)

Kiddush cup, silver w/turq in star centers, Israeli, 7½"................... 240.00
Menorah, brass, lions & crown, 19th C, 9½x11x2½" 1,050.00
Menorah/wall sconce, Deco silver, Star of David & grapes, 14x9" .2,150.00
Oil on canvas, rabbi at prayer, Wm Wichter, 24x29"+fr 435.00
Plate, pewter, Adam & eve etching, Germany, ca 1900, 1x9¼"... 480.00
Scroll, book of Esther, ca 1850, mini, 120x35" 450.00
Sculpture, Man Dancing, bronze, Boobis-Chanin, 16¼" 515.00
Seder plate, pewter, eng star/animals/text, English, 18th C, rprs, 15".4,350.00
Spice box, silver wirework, ca 1900, mini, 1½x1½" 120.00
Spice container, gilt silver, eng fruit form, Poland, 19th C, 8⅝". 11,000.00
Spice holder, silver, man w/covered basket figural, 2".................... 170.00
Spice tower, Havdalah, repoussé silver, Continental, 7½"............ 350.00
Sukkoth Kiddush cup, silver, eng scenes/symbols, Germany, 18th C, 4" ...16,000.00
Tora pointer, silver filigree, London, 1899, 12¾" 3,600.00
Torah weight, SP & MOP, 13½" L 150.00

Jugtown

The Jugtown Pottery was started about 1920 by Juliana and Jacques Busbee, in Moore County, North Carolina. Ben Owen, a young descen-

dant of a Staffordshire potter, was hired in 1923. He was the master potter, while the Busbees experimented with perfecting glazes and supervising design and modeling. Preferred shapes were those reminiscent of traditional country wares and classic Oriental forms. Glazes were various: natural-clay oranges, buffs, Tobacco-spit Brown, Mirror Black, white, Frog Skin Green, a lovely turquoise called Chinese Blue, and the traditional cobalt-decorated salt glaze. The pottery gained national recognition, and as a result of their success, several other local potteries were established. The pottery closed for a time in the late 1950s due to the ill health of Mrs. Busbee (who had directed the business after her husband died in 1947) but reopened in 1960. Jugtown is still in operation; however, they no longer use their original glaze colors which are now so collectible and the circular mark is slightly smaller than the original.

Bowl, Chinese Blue, small restoration, 4x8", $540.00. (Photo courtesy David Rago Auctions/LiveAuctioneers.com)

Bowl, Chinese Blue w/much red, 4½x7¾"...................................1,000.00
Bowl, cobalt flowers on salt glaze, cobalt int, Ben Owen, 6" 45.00
Crock, floral, tan on redware, w/lid, 11½"....................................... 60.00
Vase, Chinese Blue & red w/crystalline, bulbous, hdls, 9½" 1,200.00
Vase, Chinese Blue, shouldered, squat, 6x6½" 350.00
Vase, Chinese Blue, shouldered, 15¾"...6,600.00
Vase, Chinese Blue, 5½x7" 400.00
Vase, Chinese Blue w/Frog Skin int, 1930s, 8" 3,200.00
Vase, Chinese Blue w/red splotches, incurvate rim, 4" 600.00
Vase, Frog Skin, slightly bulbous, incurvate rim, 6¼" 155.00
Vase, glossy Frog Skin, 4 sm hdls, 8" 300.00

Vase, Chinese Blue, EX, 5½", $480.00. (Photo courtesy Cincinnati Art Galleries/LiveAuctioneers.com)

Kayserzinn Pewter

J. P. Kayser Sohn produced pewter decorated with relief-molded Art Nouveau motifs in Germany during the late 1800s and into the twentieth century. Examples are marked with 'Kayserzinn' and the mold number within an elongated oval reserve. Items with three-dimensional animals, insects, birds, etc., are valued much higher than bowls, plates, and trays with simple embossed florals, which are usually priced at $100.00 to about $200.00, depending on size. Copper items are rarely found. Assume that all other items are made of pewter.

Basket, emb flower w/inchworm on hdl, 4 ball ft, #4320, 6x9¼".. 110.00
Bowl/pot, figures at hip, emb flowers, 11¾x11½" 365.00
Decanter, duck figural, head stopper, #4358, ca 1900, 7¾" 525.00
Drinking set, bird-form 14½" pot+5 organic cups+tray, all w/mk ... 1,150.00

Nut dish, emb squirrel, #4430, ca 1900, 3½x7½" 185.00
Platter, pheasants w/wheat medallion & carrots on border, oval, 10x16". 75.00
Tankard, razor-bill duck figural, hinged lid, H Leven, 1901, 11½"...435.00

Tray, embossed foliage, detailed dragonfly handles, #4188, 19" long, $1,000.00. (Photo courtesy Showplace Antique Center/LiveAuctioneers.com)

Vase, emb orchids, slim, #4079, ca 1885-1915, 9" 200.00
Vase, emb organic decor, 3-hdl waisted form, #4474, 10" 325.00

Keeler, Brad

Keeler studied art for a time in the 1930s; later he became a modeler for a Los Angeles firm. By 1939 he was working in his own studio where he created naturalistic studies of birds and animals which were marketed through giftware stores. They were decorated by means of an airbrush and enhanced with hand-painted details. His flamingo figures were particularly popular. In the mid-'40s, he developed a successful line of Chinese Modern housewares glazed in Ming Dragon Blood, a red color he personally developed. Keeler died of a heart attack in 1952, and the pottery closed soon thereafter. For more information, we recommend *Collector's Encyclopedia of California Pottery, Second Edition*, by Jack Chipman (Collector Books).

Figurine, cockatoo, signed, 8½x3", $75.00.
(Photo courtesy Clars Auction Gallery/LiveAuctioneers.com)

Bone dish, fish figure, teal gr to tan, #151, 8" 35.00
Bowl, lettuce leaf bowl w/lobster on dome lid, #825, 11" L 85.00
Box, duck figure, brn & gr w/wht band at neck, 4½x5½", $25 to ... 35.00
Butter dish, lobster finial, ladle for melted butter, 6" L 38.00
Dish, 2 red radishes on gr leaf, #863, 7x6½", from $15 to.............. 20.00
Figurine, Asian peafowl standing on 1 ft, #22, 7" 75.00
Figurine, bird on stump, brn & gray, #40, 6½" 50.00

Figurine, bird on stump, rose on wht, #17, 6" 50.00
Figurine, bird on stump, rose on wht, #18, 8¼" 50.00
Figurine, bluebird on stump, #718, 5¼".. 35.00
Figurine, bunny scratching, #981, 3" 30.00
Figurine, canary, yel & blk on brn stump, 6", from $15 to 20.00
Figurine, chipmunk holding acorn, brn & gr tones, mk BBK, #629, 3" .. 35.00
Figurine, cockatoo, yel & gr tones, #34, 6x7½", from $35 to.......... 50.00
Figurine, cocker spaniel puppy, blk & gray, #748, 4½".................. 50.00
Figurine, deer, recumbent, #876, 4½x5½" 65.00
Figurine, flamingo w/head down in tall grass, #3, 7½", from $70 to... 90.00
Figurine, flamingo w/wings up & head down, #47, 10¼" 140.00
Figurine, hen w/head up, mc, #936, 4½x4¾" 40.00
Figurine, pheasant, #9-38A, 7x11", from $75 to 100.00
Figurine, rooster w/head down & tail up, blk w/gr accents, 8x9½"...45.00
Figurine, Siamese cat on red pillow, #944, 2½x3" 45.00
Figurine, Siamese cat standing w/head turned, 12", from $125 to ...140.00
Figurine, squirrel, brn tones, #627, 2¼x3½" 15.00
Figurine, swan w/wings spread, wht w/blk detail, #705, 15", $175 to .225.00
Planter, Santa waving from sled, #909, 7½x8½x4½" 30.00
Plate, lobed leaf shape, gr, to use w/Lobster Ware, 13" 30.00
Shelf sitters, Siamese cats, #798/#760, 7" & 10", pr, from $80 to... 95.00
Tray, lobster between 2 gr leaves, 12x7", from $45 to 55.00
Tureen, lobster-on-lettuce-leaf lid, w/tray & ladle, #871, 4x8"....... 90.00

Keen Kutter

Keen Kutter was the brand name chosen in 1870 by the Simmons Firm for a line of high-grade tools and cutlery. The trademark was first applied to high-grade axes. A corporation was formed in 1874 called Simmons Hardware Company. In 1922 Winchester merged with Simmons and continued to carry a full line of hardware plus the Winchester brand. The merger terminated in March of 1929 and converted back to the original status of Simmons Hardware Co. It wasn't until July 1, 1940, that Simmons Hardware Co. was purchased by Shapleigh Hardware Company. All Simmons Hardware Co. trademark lines were continued, and the business operated successfully until its closing in 1962. Today the Keen Kutter logo is owned by the Val-Test Company of Chicago, Illinois. For further study we recommend *Collector's Guide to E. C. Simmons Keen Kutter Cutlery Tools*, an illustrated price guide by our advisors for this category, Jerry and Elaine Heuring, available at your favorite bookstore or public library. The Heurings are listed in the Directory under Missouri. See also Knives. Unless otherwise noted, values are for examples in at least excellent condition.

Apple parer or peeler, from $65 to.. 100.00
Axe, broad; mk Keen Kutter, 12" cutting edge, from $100 to....... 150.00
Axe, fireman's; lg logo, 12½" 475.00
Axe box, dovetailed, for #12 K2 Dayton pattern axes, from $25 to ..30.00
Bearing scraper, from $25 to 35.00
Bit, countersink; from $15 to... 20.00
Bit, gimlet; single cut, size 5, from $7 to.......................................9.00
Bit, screwdriver; from K106 brace, dbl-ended, 5", from $35 to....... 45.00
Bits, electrician's or bell hangers; sz 16, 12, 10, 8 or 6, ea............... 12.00
Calendar, Silver Splendor Scene, 1955, from $50 to 75.00
Chisel, butt; tanged beveled edge w/rosewood hdls, 3 szs, ea.......... 50.00
Chisel, mortising; wood hdl, ⅜", from $10 to................................ 25.00
Chisel, socket firmer; beveled edge, 1½", from $10 to 25.00
Clippers, horse; K940, 10½", from $25 to 30.00
Clock, red enamel w/wht dial, KKEC, w/stand, 18¾" dia.........2,000.00
Coffee mill, Koffee Krusher, SH Co, sliding lid & drw, 12½x5" ... 450.00
Dandelion weeder, from $20 to 25.00
Fan, hand; fold-out, logo on front, bk: floral, from $250 to 350.00
Fan, hand; sm girl w/dog, bk: name of hardware store, $75 to 100.00

File, taper; mk Keen Kutter, from $3 to................................8.00
Grindstone, sit-down style, from $100 to 150.00
Hammer, ball-pein; EC Simmons, 32-oz 45.00
Hammer, claw; hexagon head, 16-oz, from $40 to 55.00
Hammer, jeweler's; from $125 to 175.00
Hatchet, flooring; w/nail slot, EC Simmons, from $45 to............. 55.00
Hatchet, Keen Kutter & Boy Scout logos 100.00
Hatchet, 3½x6½" single blade w/hammer end, 12" wooden hdl, VG ..25.00
Hatchet sheath, from $40 to.. 60.00
Ice shaver, K33, from $50 to 75.00
Knife, farrier's; bone hdl, from $35 to 45.00
Knife, ham slicer; K52, 10" blade 15.00
Knife, hunting; Simmons Hardware..., 5" blade, stag hdl, w/sheath ...300.00
Knife, paring; 3" blade, from $10 to 20.00
Level, KK30, adjustable, brass tip, Pat 12/20/04, 30", from $50 to . 70.00
Level, KK40, adjustable, brass tip/top plate/binding, 30", $125 to ..175.00
Level, pocket; F3764GKm, wood, 9", from $50 to 75.00
Nippers, reversible & interchangeable jaws, 8", from $30 to.......... 45.00

Padlock, 3¾", from $100.00 to $125.00.

Plane, carriage maker's rabbet; KK10, from $200 to 250.00
Plane, jointer; K8, iron, from $75 to 100.00
Plane, KK No 5, corrugated.. 60.00
Plane, K31, wood bottom, 24", from $65 to 85.00
Pliers, K45, 5", from $20 to... 30.00
Pliers, pistol grip, KK7, Pat Applied For Shapleigh..., from $125 to...175.00
Pliers, rnd nose, K66-6, from $30 to 40.00
Pliers, slip joint; K160, from $10 to.............................. 20.00
Pocketknife, #0214TK, 2-blade, from $100 to 150.00
Pocketknife, office; K02220, 2 lg blades, etched wht hdl, 3¾", M ...150.00
Rasp, horse; tanged, 14", from $5 to 10.00
Razor, safety; metal hdl, from $5 to 10.00
Razor, straight; K746, gold etch on blade, celluloid hdl, from $30 to ... 45.00
Reamer, wood; sq blade, K115, from $25 to 35.00
Sander, electric, KK250B, from $40 to.......................... 50.00
Saw, coping; K50, heavy pattern w/logo, from $10 to..................... 15.00
Saw, dehorning; wooden hdl, 10", VG........................... 35.00
Saw, hack; K188A, adjustable for 8" to 12" blades, from $25 to..... 35.00
Saw, hand; K24, logo & lettering on 26" blade, from $50 to 75.00
Saw, meat; K2, 12" blade, from $35 to 50.00
Saw, 2-man; from $125 to.. 175.00
Scissors, medical; Germany, 5½", from $20 to 25.00
Screwdriver, brass ferrule, 8", from $20 to..................... 30.00
Screwdriver, offset; K7, 6¾", from $30 to..................... 40.00
Screwdriver, wht #s on red plastic hdl, from $8 to 15.00
Sign, advertising store & location, tin, 9¾x27¾", from $85 to 125.00
Square, KC3, copper finish, from $25 to 35.00
Square, sliding T-bevel, wood hdl, 6", from $20 to 30.00
Table cutlery set, SP, 6 knives+6 forks, in orig wood box 50.00
Thermometer, Bakelite bk, 9x2½", from $90 to............... 125.00
Tinner snips, K9... 15.00

Tri-square, wooden hdl, logo on blade, 4½", from $20 to 35.00
Vise, pipe; KP200,⅛" to 2" capacity, 9¼", from $50 to.................... 75.00
Waffle iron, CI, 4-part, Simmons, 6¼", from $75 to 125.00

Scissors, S128AK, EX in original cardboard box, from $25.00 to $45.00.
(Photo courtesy Jerry and Elaine Heuring)

Kelva

Kelva was a trademark of the C.F. Monroe Company of Meriden, Connecticut; it was produced for only a few years after the turn of the century. It is distinguished from the Wave Crest and Nakara lines by its unique Batik-like background, probably achieved through the use of a cloth or sponge to apply the color. Large florals are hand painted on the opaque milk glass; and ormolu and brass mounts were used for the boxes, vases, and trays. Most pieces are signed. Our advisors for this category are Dolli and Wilfred Cohen; they are listed in the Directory under California.

Box, Bishop's Hat, wild roses on gr, w/grayed border, 3x4" 500.00
Box, floral, pk on bl, 3x4"... 500.00
Box, floral bouquets, pk on gray, 3x6" 595.00
Box, lilies on pk, 8-sided, 4x6" 650.00
Box, parrot tulips, pk/wht on gr, 8-sided, 4x6" 600.00
Box, roses on bl & cream w/gold, sq, 8"........................ 950.00
Ferner, floral on pk, ogee sides, 7½" dia....................... 795.00
Humidor, Cigars/flowers on bl, metal mts/lid/hdl, 4½x8¾"........... 995.00

Humidor, pink flower on green, 5", $795.00.
(Photo courtesy John Coker Ltd./ LiveAuctioneers.com)

Match holder/ash receiver, floral on gr w/beading, ftd 500.00
Shakers, floral on gr, gr enamel top, 3", pr.................... 600.00
Tray, daisies on maroon, rnd w/emb metal rim, rope hdl, 3½" 195.00
Vase, floral on gray, gold metal mts & ft, 17¼x10" 3,500.00
Vase, floral spray on fuchsia, cone shape w/ormolu, 6x2" 650.00
Vase, lg floral bouquet on gr/pk (shiny), 8x3" 950.00
Vase, lg rose on gr, ornate ormolu hdls & 4-ftd base, 16" 2,500.00
Whiskbroom holder, floral on bl, ornate ormolu backplate 750.00
Whiskbroom holder, floral on red, ornate ormolu backplate 850.00

Vase, silver-plated foot and rim, 13", $425.00.
(Photo courtesy Skinner Inc. Auctioneers & Appraisers of Antiques & Fine Art/LiveAuctioneers.com)

Kenton Hills

Kenton Hills Porcelain was established in 1940 in Erlanger, Kentucky, by Harold Bopp, former Rookwood superintendent, and David Seyler, noted artist and sculptor. Native clay was used; glazes were very similar to Rookwood's of the same period. The work was of high quality, but because of the restrictions imposed on needed material due to the onset of the war, the operation failed in 1942. Much of the ware is artist signed and marked with the Kenton Hills name or cipher and shape number.

Bookend, Devil Horse, Spanish Red w/Goldstone, Hentschel, 6½", ea ... 625.00
Bowl, stylized leaves, brn & bl, hemispherical, Hentschel #186, 5x6" .. 590.00
Figurine, female head w/floral scarf over brn hair, D Seyler, 10".. 3,875.00
Figurine, Mammy w/infant, metallic brn glaze, #161, 6½" 750.00
Figurine, mother & child, brn glaze, D Seyler, 13½" 935.00

Lamp/Vase, flowers and leaves, signed Wm. Hentschel, #178, factory drilled, 12½", $1,000.00.
(Photo courtesy Treadway Gallery Inc.)

Paperweight, Suzanne, head of sleeping baby, Goldstone, D Seyler, 4"...375.00
Vase, abstract, brn on yel, experimental, Hentschel, drilled, 8" ... 345.00
Vase, calla lilies on indigo butterfat, #153, 11½" 750.00
Vase, deer, brn w/bl leaves on wht mottle, Haupt, ca 1940, 9".....560.00
Vase, designs eng on gr, bulbous, Seyler, 4x4" 215.00
Vase, floral, brn on wht, A Stratton Unica, 8".............................. 375.00
Vase, floral emb on milky wht, flared rim, ftd, #125, 6½" 280.00
Vase, geometric designs emb on Brazilian Catseye, #153, 11½x5" ..625.00
Vase, gr rings on Green Tiger Eye, Hentschel, #153, drilled, 11½"...365.00

Vase, leaves, muted bl & pk tones on wht, Deco style, Hentschel, 13" ..875.00
Vase, leopards on Spanish Red, ftd, #174, sq, 7x6¼" 1,000.00
Vase, linear designs, brn & wht on pk, Hentschel, #174, sq, 7x6½"...555.00
Vase, lotus blooms w/uneven bl over pk, waisted, Hentschel, #114, 13"..530.00
Vase, lotus flower on stippled gray over blk, #153, drilled, 11½"..465.00
Vase, magnolias, red on gray, bl rim, ftd, Hentschel, 7¼x6½" ...1,060.00
Vase, Moresque design, Aventurine, Conant, #103, w/hdls, 6" 185.00
Vase, rings, brn on yel matt, shouldered, #109, 8½" 500.00
Vase, stylized floral on wht, Hentschel, #176, 12⅛x5 ½ 685.00
Vase, stylized leaves, earth tones on lt bl, #87, 9¾" 200.00

Kentucky Derby Glasses

Kentucky Derby glasses are the official souvenir glasses sold at Churchill Downs filled with mint juleps on Derby Day. Many folks from all over the country who attend the Derby take home the souvenir glass, and thus the collecting begins. The first glass (1938) is said to have either been given away as a souvenir or used for drinks among the elite at the Downs. This one, the 1939 glass, two glasses from 1940, the 1940 – 1941 aluminum tumbler, the 'Beetleware' tumblers from 1941 to 1944, and the 1945 short, tall, and jigger glasses are the rarest, most sought-after glasses, and they command the highest prices. Some 1974 glasses incorrectly listed the 1971 winner Canonero II as just Canonero; as a result, it became the 'mistake' glass for that year. Also, glasses made by the Federal Glass Company (whose logo, found on the bottom of the glass, is a small shield containing an F) were used for extra glasses for the 100th running in 1974. There is also a 'mistake' and a correct Federal glass, making four to collect for that year. Two glasses were produced in 1986 as the mistake glass has an incorrect 1985 copyright printed on it. Another mistake glass was produced in 2003 as some were made with the 1932 winner Burgoo King listed incorrectly as a Triple Crown winner instead of the 1937 winner of the Triple Crown, War Admiral.

The 1956 glass has four variations. On some 1956 glasses the star which was meant to separate the words 'Kentucky Derby' is missing making only one star instead of two stars. Also, all three horses on the glass were meant to have tails, but on some of the glasses only two have tails making two tails instead of three. To identify which 1956 glass you have, just count the number of stars and tails.

In order to identify the year of a pre-1969 glass, since it did not appear on the front of the glass prior to then, simply add one year to the last date listed on the back of the glass. This may seem to be a confusing practice, but the current year's glass is produced long before the Derby winner is determined.

The prices on older glasses remain high. These are in high demand, and collectors are finding them extremely hard to locate. Values listed here are for absolutely perfect glasses with bright colors, all printing and gold complete, no flaws of any kind, chipping or any other damage. Any problem reduces the price by at least one-half. Our advisor for this category is Betty Hornback; she is listed in the Directory under Kentucky.

1938..4,000.00
1939..6,500.00
1940, aluminum 1,000.00
1940, French Lick, aluminum...1,000.00
1940, glass tumbler, 2 styles, ea, minimum value 10,000.00
1941-44, plastic, Beetleware, ea from $2,500 to.........................4,000.00
1945, jigger, gr horse head, I Have Seen Them All 1,000.00
1945, regular, gr horse head facing right, horseshoe...................1,600.00
1945, tall, gr horse head facing right, horseshoe 450.00
1946-47, clear frosted w/frosted bottom, L in circle, ea 100.00
1948, clear bottom, gr horsehead in horseshoe & horse on reverse..225.00
1948, frosted bottom, gr horse head in horseshoe & horse on reverse...250.00
1949, He Has Seen Them All, Matt Winn, gr on frosted.............225.00

1950, gr horses running on track, Churchill Downs behind......... 450.00
1951, gr winner's circle, Where Turf Champions Are Crowned... 650.00

1952, Gold Derby Trophy, Kentucky Derby Gold Cup, $225.00. (Photo courtesy Betty Hornback/Photographer Dean Langdon)

1953, blk horse facing left, rose garland 200.00
1954, gr twin spires.. 225.00
1955, gr & yel horses, The Fastest Runners, scarce...................... 200.00
1956, 1 star, 2 tails, brn horses, twin spires............................... 275.00
1956, 1 star, 3 tails, brn horses, twin spires............................... 400.00
1956, 2 stars, 2 tails, brn horses twin spires............................... 200.00
1956, 2 stars, 3 tails, brn horses, twin spires............................. 250.00
1957, gold & blk on frosted, horse & jockey facing right 150.00
1958, Gold Bar, solid gold insignia w/horse, jockey & 1 spire 175.00
1958, Iron Leige, same as 1957 w/'Iron Leige' added 225.00

1960, black and gold, $100.00.

1961, blk horses on track, jockey in red, gold winners.................. 110.00
1962, Churchill Downs, red, gold & blk on clear 80.00
1963, brn horse, jockey #7, gold lettering 70.00
1964, brn horse head, gold lettering... 25.00
1965, brn twin spires & horses, red lettering................................. 85.00
1966-68, blk, blk & bl respectively, ea 65.00
1969, gr jockey in horseshoe, red lettering..................................... 65.00
1970, gr shield, gold lettering 70.00
1971, gr twin spires, horses at bottom, red lettering 60.00
1972, 2 blk horses, orange & gr print 60.00
1973, wht, blk twin spires, red & gr lettering................................. 60.00
1974, Federal, regular or mistake, brn & gold, ea........................... 200.00
1974, Libbey, mistake, Canonero in 1971 listing on bk................. 18.00
1974, regular, Canonero II in 1971 listing on bk 16.00
1975.. 16.00
1976, plastic tumbler or regular glass, ea....................................... 16.00
1977... 14.00
1978-79, ea.. 16.00
1980.. 22.00
1981-82, ea.. 15.00
1983-85, ea.. 12.00
1986.. 14.00
1986 (1985 copy).. 20.00
1987-89, ea.. 12.00
1990-92, ea.. 10.00

1993-95, ea..9.00
1996-98 ....8.00
1999-2000, ea..7.00
2001-05, ea..6.00
2003, mistake, 1932 incorrectly listed as Derby Triple Crown Winner.. 7.50
2006-2008, ea..4.00

Keramos

Keramos (Austria) produced a line of decorative items including vases, bowls, masks, and figurines that were imported primarily by the Ebeling & Ruess Co. of Philadelphia from the late 1920s to the 1950s. The figurines they manufactured were of high quality and very detailed, similar to those made by other Austrian firms. Their glazes were very smooth, though today some crazing is present on older pieces. Most items were marked and numbered, and some bear the name or initials of the artist who designed them. In addition to Ebeling & Ruess (whose trademark includes a crown), other importers' stamps and labels may be found as well. Knight Ceramics employed a shield mark, and many of the vases produced through the 1940s are marked with a swastika; these pieces are turning up with increasing frequency at shops as well as internet auction sites. Although the workmanship they exhibit is somewhat inferior, the glazes used during this period are excellent and are now attracting much attention among collectors. Masks from the 1930s are bringing high prices as well. Beware of reproduction masks online.

Detail is a very important worth-assessing factor. The more detailed the art figures are, the more valuable. Artist-signed pieces are quite scarce. Many artists were employed by both Keramos and Goldscheider. The molds of these two companies are sometimes very similar as well, and unmarked items are often difficult to identify with certainty. Items listed below are considered to be in excellent, undamaged condition unless otherwise stated. Our advisor for this category is Darrell Thomas; he is listed in the Directory under Wisconsin.

Figurine, Boston Terrier sitting, Vienna Austria, 6"..................... 120.00
Figurine, boy walking w/hands at hips, Austria, 12x6" 250.00
Figurine, buck & doe white-tail deer, on wht base....................... 650.00

Figurine, child rests on coral branches, Weiner Kunst Keramaik, 1982, 10", $540.00. (Photo courtesy Skinner Inc. Auctioneers & Appraisers of Antiques & Fine Art/ LiveAuctioneers. com)

Figurine, English Setters (2) pointing, Vienna Austria, 12" L........ 75.00
Figurine, moose, #9-1897, Wein, 15½x16" 155.00
Figurine, Octavian w/rose in hand, hat in other, Austria, 11"...... 185.00
Figurine, penguin, on wht base w/silver band, Austria, 5" 95.00
Powder jar, Vict lady figural, floral gown, 3-ftd, #342, 9¼x6¼" 300.00
Wall plaque, lady's face, turq hair w/gold, eyes shut, #942, 9x7½" .. 1,650.00
Wall plaque, lady's head, eyes half closed, WK mk, 10x5", $1,700 to ... 1,900.00

Kew Blas

The Union Glass Company was founded in 1854, in Somerville, Massachusetts, an offshoot of the New England Glass Co. in East Cambridge. They made only flint glass — tablewares, lamps, globes, and shades. Kew Blas was a trade name they used for their iridescent, lustered art glass produced there from 1893 until about 1920. The glass was made in imitation of Tiffany and achieved notable success. Some items were decorated with pulled leaf and feather designs, while others had a monochrome lustre surface. The mark was an engraved 'Kew Blas' in an arching arrangement.

Bowl, bl, wide flared rim, 2x11½" 450.00
Candleholders, gold waves on cream w/gold irid int, 5¾", pr 460.00
Tumbler, gold, 4 dimples near base, 4" 375.00
Vase, drag loops, lt bl on bl, bulbous, 6" 400.00

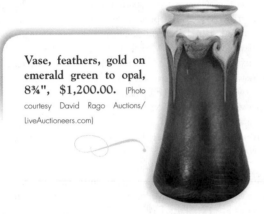

Vase, feathers, gold on emerald green to opal, 8¾", $1,200.00. (Photo courtesy David Rago Auctions/ LiveAuctioneers.com)

Vase, feathers, gold on opal, gold int, 5" 500.00
Vase, feathers, gr on gold irid, cylinder w/bulbous base, 7¾x3¾" . 425.00
Vase, feathers, gr on gold on opal, scalloped rim, 1920s, 8" 585.00
Vase, gold, poppy bud form, 10¼" 240.00
Vase, pulled zigzags, gr on gold irid, shouldered, flared rim, 8¼" ... 950.00
Vase, swirls, gold on lt orange, spherical, 4" 350.00

Kindell, Dorothy

Yet another California artist that worked during the prolific years of the 1940s and 1950s, Dorothy Kindell produced a variety of household items and giftware, but today she is best known for her nudes. One of her most popular lines consisted of mugs, a pitcher, salt and pepper shakers, a wall pocket, bowls, a creamer and sugar set, and champagne glasses, featuring a lady in various stages of undress, modeled as handles or stems (on the champagnes). In the set of six mugs, she progresses from wearing her glamorous strapless evening gown to ultimately climbing nude, head-first into the last mug. These are relatively common but always marketable. Except for these and the salt and pepper shakers, the other items from the nude line are scarce and rather pricey. Collectors also vie for her island girls, generally seminude and very sensuous.

Ashtray, Beachcombers, 2 sets of legs under lg sombrero, 6x4½" ... 65.00
Ashtray, Hawaiian hula girl in 7" dia blk tray, 4½" 530.00
Box, turq, kneeling Hawaiian hula girl on lid, 5¾x6½x4½" 425.00
Champagne glass, blk glass goblet w/gold nude on side, 6" 235.00
Dresser box, turtle lying on bk, 7x5" 80.00
Figurine, Airedale, seated, marbled glaze, 6" 45.00
Figurine, Carmen, nude, flowers in hair, legs raised, 9x9", $160 to..175.00
Figurine, horse, Registered California sticker, 6½" 45.00

Head vase, Black native girl, red lips & necklace, 5", from $65 to. 75.00
Head vase, Black native girl, red lips/blk hair, separate necklace, 6".95.00
Head vase, Oriental lady w/gr tricorner hat, high-button collar, 7" .70.00
Lamp base, Polynesian man on knees, gr headpc, 13½x9¼" 275.00
Mug, 'Pop,' staved barrel form w/rope border, nude hdl, 4¼" 85.00
Mug, nude figural hdl, series of 6, common, ea from $35 to 40.00
Toby mug, sailor's face, wht beard, bl hat, 4", NM 75.00
Wall pocket, lady removing her gown as cup hdl, from mug series, rare .200.00

Bookend, horses' heads, 7x6½", $100.00. (Photo courtesy Jack Chipman)

King's Rose

King's Rose was made in Staffordshire, England, from about 1820 to 1830. It is closely related to Gaudy Dutch in body type as well as the colors used in its decoration. The pattern consists of a full-blown, orange-red rose with green, pink, and yellow leaves and accents. When the rose is in pink, the ware is often referred to as Queen's Rose.

Coffeepot, molded foliate and reeded decoration on spout and handle, #5 impressed on base, $3,600.00. (Photo courtesy Alderfer Auction & Appraisal/LiveAuctioneers.com)

Bowl, pk int band, deep, 5½" 175.00
Coffeepot, vine border, pearlware, dome lid, 11½" 2,500.00
Creamer, pk molded rim band w/scalloped edge, roses reserve, 4½". 145.00
Creamer, roses in molded/scrolled reserves, Queen's border, 4", EX .230.00
Creamer, vine border, red rim band, helmet shape, 4", EX 100.00
Cup & saucer, Queen's, pearlware 130.00
Pitcher, dk red rose, bl/yel flowers w/gr leaves, wear, 5⅜" 220.00
Plate, cup; solid border, 3½" 450.00
Plate, orange/red roses & yel flowers, Queen's border, lt wear, 7½"..150.00
Plate, pk border w/emb dmns, 8" 220.00
Plate, pk border w/X-hatching & floral reserves, creamware, 9½" . 100.00
Plate, pk lustre rim bands, 6¾" 90.00
Plate, solid border, bright colors, minor decor loss, 10" 240.00
Plate, toddy; Queen's, scalloped, 5½" 110.00
Plate, vine border, 7⅜" 100.00
Tea bowl & saucer, vine border 245.00
Teapot, sectional border, lt wear, 6" 350.00

Kitchen Collectibles

During the last half of the 1850s, mass-produced kitchen gadgets were patented at an astonishing rate. Most were ingeniously efficient. Apple peelers, egg beaters, cherry pitters, food choppers, and such were only the most common of hundreds of kitchen tools well designed to perform only specific tasks. Today all are very collectible. Unless noted otherwise, our values are for items in excellent condition.

For further information we recommend *Kitchen Glassware of the Depression Years* and *Anchor Hocking's Fire-King & More, Second Edition,* both by Cathy and Gene Florence; and *Hot Kitchen & Home Collectibles of the 30s, 40s, and 50s* by C. Dianne Zweig. See also Appliances; Butter Molds and Stamps; Cast Iron; Cookbooks; Copper; Glass Knives; Molds; Pie Birds; Primitives; Reamers; String Holders; Tinware; Trivets; Wooden Ware; Wrought Iron.

Cast-Iron Bakers and Kettles

Be aware that cast-iron counterfeit production is on the increase. Items with phony production numbers, finishes, etc., are being made at this time. Many of these new pieces are the popular miniature cornstick pans. To command the values given below, examples must be free from damage of any kind or excessive wear. Waffle irons must be complete with all three pieces and the handle. The term 'EPU' in the description lines refers to the **Erie PA, USA** mark. The term 'Block TM' refers to the lettering in the large logo that was used ca 1920 until 1940; 'Slant TM' refers to the lettering in the large logo ca 1900 to 1920. 'PIN' indicates 'Product Identification Numbers,' and 'FW' refers to 'full writing.' Victor was Griswold's first low-budget line (ca 1875). Skillets #5 and #6 are uncommon, while #7, #8, and #9 are easy to find. See also Keen Kutter; Clubs, Newsletters, and Catalogs.

Aebleskiver pan, unmk, makes 7, 7x9"+hdl............... 75.00
Ashtray, Griswold #770, sq, from $20 to 30.00
Baster, Wagner #9, drip-drop, lg.................................. 75.00
Bundt cake pan, Wagner Ware B, from $100 to............ 150.00
Cake mold, Lamb, Griswold, PIN 866, from $75 to..... 100.00

Cake mold, rabbit, Griswold, $165.00. (Photo courtesy sandcea/Sharon and Charly Harvey)

Chicken fryer, Wagner, sq, w/lid, 3x10x10"+hdl 155.00
Cornbread pan, Wagner, tea sz 60.00
Display rack, Griswold skillet/Griswold plate, brn wood rails, $300 to.. 350.00
Dutch oven, Favorite Piqua Ware #8, TM, from $30 to 50.00
Dutch oven, Griswold #8, Tite-Top Baster, Slant TM, from $50 to .. 75.00
Dutch oven, Griswold #9, Late Tite-Top, Block TMs, w/trivet, $50 to..80.00
Dutch oven lid, Griswold #8, hinged, from $25 to 30.00
Gem pan, GF Filley #8, makes 11 rectangles, 1¼x13x6" 255.00
Gem pan, Griswold #11, Fr roll pan, mk NES oN (sic), 11, $40 to...60.00
Gem pan, Griswold #18, popover, wide hdl, 6 cups, from $50 to ... 70.00
Gem pan, Griswold #88, Fr roll pan, mk NES NO 11, from $30 to ..50.00
Golf ball pan, Griswold #9, FW...................................... 150.00

Griddle, Griswold #8, Slant TM, X-bar support, hdl, from $20 to 40.00
Griddle, Griswold #14, Bailed, Block TM, from $50 to................. 75.00
Griddle, Wapak #8, oval, early TM, from $50 to 75.00
Heat regulator, Griswold #300, dbl-sided 325.00
Hot plate, Griswold #33, 3-burner, w/gas valves, 4-leg............... 215.00
Kettle, Griswold #8, Maslin shape, 6-qt.................................. 75.00
Kettle, Wagner, deep fat fryer, w/basket, C #1265, from $50 to 75.00
Kettle, Wagner, rimmed pot, mk Wagner, from $75 to................ 100.00
Loaf pan, Griswold #877, w/lid, #859, from $800 to..................... 900.00
Muffin pan, Filley #6, 11 cups, from $150 to............................. 200.00
Muffin pan, Griswold #3, mk #3 & #943 only, 11 cups, from $150 to ..175.00
Muffin pan, Griswold #18, popover, wide hdl, 6 cups, from $1,000 to.. 1,500.00
Muffin pan, Griswold #50, heart & star, 6 cups, from $1,000 to.. 1,500.00
Roaster, Oval; Griswold #3, Block TMs, w/lid, from $475 to 525.00
Roaster, Oval; Griswold #5, Block TMs, FW lid, from $200 to....350.00
Roaster, Oval; Griswold #7, FW lid, w/trivet............................. 600.00
Roaster, Oval; Griswold #9, Blocks TMs, FW lid, from $425 to....475.00
Roaster, Oval; Wagner #7, TM, incised writing lid, from $175 to...225.00
Sandwich toaster, Wagner, w/low bailed base, sq, from $125 to ... 150.00
Saucepan, Griswold #737, 2-spout, PIN 737, 2-qt 200.00
Skillet, Griswold, 5-in-1 Breakfast 150.00
Skillet, Griswold #0, Block TM, Erie PA/562, ca 1950................. 315.00
Skillet, Griswold #2, Slant TM, Rau Brothers, from $500 to 600.00
Skillet, Griswold #4, Slant/Erie TM, NP, from $40 to 60.00
Skillet, Griswold #6, Victor (FW)... 325.00
Skillet, Griswold #6A, Erie TM 255.00
Skillet, Griswold #7, Erie TM, inset heat ring, from $25 to 50.00
Skillet, Griswold #8, extra deep, Block TM, no heat ring, $50 to.. 75.00
Skillet, Griswold #8, Spider TM, from $1,100 to....................... 1,400.00
Skillet, Griswold #9, Victor/EPU TM, Pin 723........................... 45.00
Skillet, Griswold #10, Block TM, no heat ring, from $40 to 60.00
Skillet, Griswold #11, Erie TM, inset heat ring, from $125 to 175.00
Skillet, Griswold #12, Slant TM, from $125 to 175.00
Skillet, Griswold #13, Block TM, from $1,400 to.......................1,600.00
Skillet, Griswold #13, Slant TM, from $800 to........................1,000.00
Skillet, Griswold #14, Block TM, from $125 to......................... 175.00
Skillet, Griswold #15, oval, from $250 to 300.00
Skillet, Piqua Ware #14, 2-spout, 14¾" dia............................. 250.00
Skillet, Wagner, Sizzle Server, C #1095, from $15 to..................... 25.00
Skillet, Wagner #2, Stylized TM, from $50 to 75.00
Skillet, Wagner #11, pie logo 475.00
Skillet, Wagner #14, PIN 1064, 15" dia.................................. 225.00
Skillet, Wapak #8, Indian TM.. 70.00
Skillet lid, Griswold, sq glass, Block TM knob, 9½x9½", $50 to .. 100.00
Skillet lid, Griswold #8, high dome top logo, Block TM, from $30 to ...40.00
Teakettle, Griswold #8, Spider TM top, from $400 to................. 500.00
Trivet, Griswold, Family Tree, PIN 1726, lg/decorative, from $10 to ...20.00
Trivet, Old Lace (coffeepot), PIN 1739, lg, from $75 to.............. 125.00

Turk head pan, Griswold #2, PIN 953, 10½" long, $300.00. (Photo courtesy sandcea/Sharon and Charly Harvey)

Waffle iron, Griswold #7, finger hinge, low hdl base, from $100 to 125.00
Waffle iron, Griswold #19, Heart & Star, low bailed base, $250 to .. 300.00
Wall clock, frying pan w/windup works, Griswold/Erie, 14½", up to .. 4,400.00

Egg Beaters

Egg beaters are unbeatable. Ranging from hand-helds, rotary-crank and squeeze power to Archimedes up-and-down models, egg beaters are America's favorite kitchen gadget. A mainstay of any kitchenware collection, over time egg beaters have come into their own — nutmeg graters, spatulas, and can openers will have to scramble to catch up! At the turn of the century, everyone in America owned an egg beater. Every household did its own mixing and baking — there were no pre-processed foods — and every inventor thought he/she could make a better beater. Thus American ingenuity produced more than 1,000 egg beater patents, dating back to 1856, with several hundred different models being manufactured dating back to the nineteenth century. As true examples of Americana, egg beaters have enjoyed a solid increase in value for quite sometime, though they have leveled off and even decreased in the past few years, due to a proliferation of internet sales. Some very rare beaters will bring more than $1,000.00, including the cast-iron, rotary crank 'Dodge Race Course egg beater.' But the vast majority stay under $50.00. Just when you think you've seen them all, new ones always turn up, usually at flea markets or garage sales. For further information, we recommend our advisor (author of the definitive book on egg beaters) Don Thornton, who is listed in the Directory under California (SASE required).

AJ, crank type, Pat Oct 9 1923, on 4-cup gr glass measure, 12¼x5" .. 35.00
AJ, crank type, Pat...1923...in USA, on 2-cup vaseline glass measure ... 50.00
Androck, crank type, Made in USA, on orange bowl w/wht int, 5½x4" .. 25.00
Ashley, Archimedes type, Pat May 1, 1860, 11½" 625.00
Dover, crank type, Dover Pattern Improved...Taplins, Made in USA, 11" .. 17.00
EKCO, crank type, stainless steel, wooden hdl & knob, 1950s, 11" .. 18.00
Flint, crank type, #676, 1950s, 12", MIB 25.00
KC, crank type, red hdl, gr knob, bubble-blower beaters 20.00
Keystone, fits on clear glass Westmoreland base, 11" 45.00
Lyon, propeller, mk USA 100.00

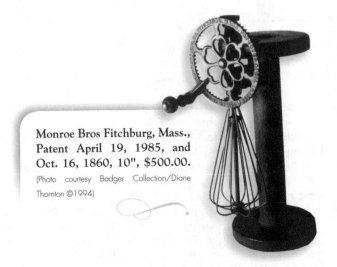

Monroe Bros Fitchburg, Mass., Patent April 19, 1985, and Oct. 16, 1860, 10", $500.00.
(Photo courtesy Badger Collection/Diane Thornton ©1994)

Nutbrown Foodmixer, CI, table mt, ...#863902 Made in England ... 50.00
Standard, fold-flat type, Pat June 29 '80 on gear wheel 125.00
Unmarked, crank type w/green wooden hdl on Jadite bowl, 11x5" ... 50.00

Egg Timers

Black chef, seated w/timer in right hand, ceramic, mc, Germany, 4½" ... 50.00
Dog holding timer w/front paws, ceramic, wht w/mc, Japan, #59462 ... 35.00

Duck w/hat & umbrella, ceramic, mc, Germany, #11564, 4½" 35.00
George Washington, Kitchen Independence, ceramic, mc, Enesco, 5½" .. 27.50
Kitchen Prayer Lady, ceramic, pk, Enesco, 5¾", from $50 to 70.00
Lady talking on phone, ceramic, mc, Germany, 1930s, 4" 45.00
Little Black Sambo, ceramic, mc, Japan, 1950s, 4½" 50.00
Mammy, pnt chalkware, frying pan in right hand, timer in left, 5⅞" .. 265.00
Mickey Mouse, timer at end of nose, porc, mc, Germany, #1417, 3" .. 50.00
Santa stands by tall package, ceramic, mc, Sonsco Japan, 4¼" 70.00
Welsh lady & spinning wheel, ceramic, mc, mk Foreign, 4" 42.50

Glass

Bowl, batter; Fruits, Anchor Hocking, w/spout & hdl, from $200 to .. 225.00
Bowl, batter; gr, Tufglass, w/spout & tab hdl, from $60 to 65.00
Bowl, Delphite, LE Smith, 7", from $65 to 75.00
Bowl, drippings; Jadite, McKee, blk lettering, 4x5", from $125 to ... 145.00
Bowl, opaque yel, McKee, 4½", from $10 to 12.00
Bowl, soup; Delphite, Pyrex, 7¾" 9.50
Butter dish, Chalaine Blue, ribbed, tab hdls, from $425 to 475.00
Butter dish, pk, open hdl on lid, from $65 to 75.00
Cake plate, pk, emb center snowflake, from $30 to 35.00
Canister, opaque yel, Hocking, blk lettering, 40-oz, from $175 to ... 225.00
Canister, Peacock Blue, 5-lb, from $325 to 350.00
Casserole, crystal, emb grapes, Fry, w/lid, 7", from $55 to 65.00
Cocktail shaker, amber, Cambridge, from $135 to 150.00
Cruet, Emerald-Glo, Rubel, from $30 to 40.00
Cruet, oil/vinegar; yel, Fostoria, ea from $100 to 110.00
Cup, Jadite, Hocking, str sides, 6-oz, from $12 to 14.00
Decanter, gr, Hocking, pinched-in, from $75 to 85.00
Dispenser, soda; pk w/blk base, Orange Crush, from $225 to 300.00
Drip jar, gr, Hocking, from $50 to 55.00
Egg cup, amber, Paden City, from $15 to 18.00
Fork, Cobalt Blue, Hazel-Atlas, from $40 to 45.00
Funnel, crystal, Radnt, from $45 to 50.00
Gravy boat, pk, Imperial, from $55 to 65.00
Ice bucket, blk, Fostoria #2543, from $60 to 65.00
Ice bucket, yel, Paden City, from $145 to 155.00
Knife, Aer-Flo, amber, 7½", from $300 to 350.00
Knife, crystal, plain hdl, 8½", from $12 to 15.00
Knife, Dur-X, 5-leaf, bl, 8½", from $38 to 45.00
Knife, rose spray, amber, 8½", from $275 to 295.00
Knife, Steel-ite, crystal, from $35 to 40.00
Knife, Stonex, amber, 8¼", from $275 to 300.00
Knife, 3 Star, pk, 8½", from $32 to 35.00
Ladle, crystal, Fostoria, from $18 to 20.00
Measuring cup, crystal, Glasbake, McKee, 2-cup, from $40 to 45.00

Mixing bowls, Delphite Blue: 7½", from $75.00 to $85.00; 9¾", from $115.00 to $125.00. (Photo courtesy Cathy and Gene Florence)

Mold, gelatin; crystal, Glasbake, from $15 to 18.00
Mold, gelatin; pk, Tufglas, from $55 to 65.00
Mug, cobalt, Cambridge, from $75 to 80.00

Napkin holder, gr clambroth, Serve-All emb on front, from $200 to.. 225.00
Pitcher, custard, 2-cup, from $35 to 40.00
Platter, crystal, Fry, 13" L, from $40 to 45.00
Reamer, amber, Federal, tab hdl, from $300 to 325.00
Reamer, amber, Federal, 6-sided cone, vertical hdl, from $325 to ...350.00
Refrigerator dish, gr, Hocking, paneled, 8x8", from $50 to............. 55.00
Relish, Emerald-Glo, Rubel, from $55 to 65.00
Rolling pin, clambroth, wooden hdls, from $125 to 135.00
Rolling pin, opaque yel, McKee, w/screw-on metal lid, from $350 to ...450.00
Shakers, crystal, Jeannette, ftd, pr from $26 to 40.00
Sherbet, gr clambroth, from $12 to 15.00
Soap dish, yel, from $20 to 25.00
Spoon, yel, lg, from $60 to.. 70.00
Spoon holder, crystal, Pat Feb 11, 1913, from $20 to 25.00
Straw holder, red, w/metal lid, tall, from $200 to........................ 225.00
Sugar bowl, gr, Hazel-Atlas, open, from $75 to............................ 80.00
Syrup, pk, Paden City #11, from $75 to 85.00
Teakettle, crystal, Silex, from $25 to 30.00
Toothpick holder, gr, Hocking, from $25 to 30.00
Tray, clambroth, 10½" sq, from $25 to.. 30.00
Tumbler, gr, Paden City, ftd, from $18 to 20.00
Tumbler, Jadite, from $25 to 30.00
Vase, bud; Jadite, Jeannette #519, from $20 to 25.00

Miscellaneous

**Apple peeler, Goodell,
Pat. 1884, 12", $270.00.**

(Photo courtesy Rich Penn Auctions/
LiveAuctioneers.com)

Apple peeler, Reading, CI, clamps to table, Pat May 5, 1868......... 80.00
Apple peeler, Reading, CI, crank hdl, clamps to table, 1872........ 115.00
Apple peeler, RP Scott & Co...Mar 1860, ornate hearts on outer gear ..30.00
Apple peeler, Sinclair Scott, CI, crank hdl, clamps to table........... 45.00
Baster, Pyrex, ArtBek, 1946, 8", M in orig tube 25.00
Bowl, mixing; Diana, plastic, bl w/wht polka dots, wht int, 7½" 75.00
Bowl, mixing; red Melmac w/mc confetti, Brookpark, 5x11½" 27.50
Bowl, mixing; Texasware, gray-gr Melmac w/mc confetti, #118, 10" ...30.00
Bowl, mixing; Texasware, mc Melmac (confetti), #125, 11½" 50.00
Bowl, mixing; Texasware, pk Melmac w/fine confetti, #125, 5x11" ... 85.00
Bowl, serving; Boonton, wht Melmac, divided, w/lid, 8½" 18.00
Bread box, gr enamel w/wht int, vents in hinged lid, 9x19x6" 100.00
Butter dish, Boonton, aqua Melmac.. 12.00
Can opener, CI, 1 finger ring, European, ca 1900, 3½" 75.00
Can opener, Daisy Universal, CI, hand crank, wall mt, 6x6" 40.00
Carrier, cake; Regal Ware, red aluminum, blk Bakelite hdl, 7x13".... 65.00
Carrier, cake/pie; Regal, aluminum, holds 5 cakes/pies, strap hdl... 60.00
Cheese slicer, wire cutter w/brn swirl Bakelite hdl......................... 12.00
Chopper, dbl curved blades, wooden hdl, 5x6" 35.00
Chopper, single curved blade, wood hdl, 8x6" 35.00
Churn, ...Mixer & Whipper & Handy Kitchen Aid on label, 4-qt, 14x6"...70.00
Churn, Dazey #4, red 'football' on lid, tulip-shaped base, 1956.... 175.00

Churn, Dazey #10, glass embossed with circular logo, 11½", $700.00. (Photo courtesy Rich Penn Auctions/LiveAuctioneers.com)

Churn, Dazey #20, from $100 to 150.00
Churn, Dazey #30, Pat 1922, from $175 to 200.00
Churn, Dazey #30, Pat 1922, M 250.00
Churn, Dazey #40, 4-qt.. 125.00
Churn, Dazey #60, from $120 to 150.00
Churn, Dazey #80, from $175 to 225.00
Churn, SMP Triumph Trade, General Steels, metal, 1920s, 14", EX ...60.00
Colander, Wear-Ever, aluminum, w/stand & mallet, 8¼" dia 20.00
Crimper, aluminum, spoon-like shape, Seller, 5" 15.00
Cutter/slicer, Ekco Miracle French Fry, 2 blades, red hdl, MIB...... 15.00
Drawer organizer, Plas-Tex Corp, turq, 1950s, 14¾x11¼" 14.00
Food mill, Foley, 2 bottom clips, metal w/red wood hdl, 7½" dia ... 30.00
French fry cutter, Made in USA, wires in metal fr, loop hdl, 12½x5" ..25.00
Garlic press, Simplex III, aluminum, Switzerland, 6" 15.00
Ice pick, red wood hdl w/metal end, 8¼" 16.00
Jar lifter, Earthgrown, tong-like, gr coating on clasp, blk hdls, 8" .. 12.50
Juicer/press, Universal...Pat Dec 89942, aluminum, squeeze type, 9x11".. 25.00
Juicer/strainer, Wear-Ever, aluminum, lever action, 3-ftd.............. 40.00
Knife, chef's; Sabatier, steel blade, elephant & 4 stars on hdl, 17" ...120.00
Knife sharpener, Cutco Professional Honing Stone, w/instructions, MIB.. 20.00
Knife sharpener, Ekco Cherrywood Series, steel w/wood hdl, 1970s .. 20.00
Measuring cups, copper can shape, brass hdls, ea w/emb sz, set of 4 ..60.00
Meat grinder, Landers Frary Clark...#71, complete in box............. 50.00
Meat tenderizer, CI, 3" rnd grid w/hdl, 7" 10.00
Melon baller, gr wooden hdl, EX 10.00
Noodle cutter, metal rotary blades, red Bakelite hdl...................... 13.00
Nutcracker, Ideal, NP CI, ca 1915, 5" 22.00
Nutmeg grater, Edgar type, spring-loaded grip, 1890s, 5x5"........... 30.00
Nutmeg grater, tin, cylindrical, emb NUTMEG at top, 7½x2" 20.00
Nutmeg grater, tin, w/snap-up lid for storage, 5½" 38.00
Pastry blender, Androck, arched wires held by yel Bakelite hdl..... 12.50
Platter, Boonton, yel Melmac, 14½x10¼"..................................... 20.00
Platter, Brookpark, strawberries & flowers on wht Melmac, #1521, 21"... 20.00
Potato masher, primitive, solid wood, 2½" dia bottom, 11" w/hdl.. 20.00
Ricer/press, Co Mt Joy PA USA, CI, removable basket, 1800s, 4x10" ..20.00
Scoop, sugar; Wagner #2, aluminum, 5x12½" 15.00
Sifter, Androck, red & wht checkerboard/baked goods, tin litho, 1950s.. 35.00
Sifter, Androck Handi-Sift, lady baking, tin litho, 3-screen, $40 to.. 55.00
Sifter, Androck Handi-Sift, starbursts, tin litho, 3-screen, NM 25.00
Sifter, red morning glories on white, red crank hdl, 4½x5¾".......... 32.00
Spatula, A&J, stainless steel w/gr Bakelite hdl, 12" 25.00
Spoon, serving; Androck, metal w/ribbed bullet Bakelite hdl, 9½" ...20.00
Spoon rest, Japan, owl figural w/daisies, gr/yel/wht, ceramic, 8¼" ... 25.00
Spoon rest, Napco, chef holds over-sz spoon, ceramic, 8" L 50.00
Spoon rest, Royal Albert, roses on wht w/gold, 8½" L.................... 25.00
Spoon rest, Western Stoneware, bl spatter, 2¾x7½" 20.00
Strawberry huller, Boston Huller...Oct 30 94, pincher type............ 18.00
Tomato slicer, Ekco, metal, red pnt hdl, EX.................................. 12.00
Tray, serving; Texasware, red Melmac, 15½x10½" 25.00

Knife Rests

Recording the history of knife rests has to begin in Europe. There is a tin-glazed earthenware knife rest at the Henry Francis Dupont Winterthur Museum. It's dated 1720 – 1760 and is possibly Dutch. Many types have been made in Europe — porcelain, Delft, majolica, and pottery. European companies made knife rests to match their dinnerware patterns, a practice not pursued by American manufacturers. Research has found only one American company, Mackenzie-Childs of New York, who made a pottery knife rest. This company no longer exists.

Several scholars feel that porcelain knife rests originated in Germany and France; from there, their usage spread to England. Though there were glasshouses in Europe making pressed and cut glass, often blanks were purchased from American companies, cut by European craftsmen, and shipped back to the states. American consumers regarded the European cut glass as superior. When economic woes forced the Europeans to come to the U.S., many brought their motifs and patterns with them. American manufacturers patented many of the designs for their exclusive use, but in some cases as the cutters moved from one company to another, they took their patterns with them.

Knife rests of pressed glass, cut crystal, porcelain, sterling silver, plated silver, wood, ivory, and bone have been collected for many years. Signed knife rests are especially desirable. It was not until the Centennial Exhibition in Philadelphia in 1876 that the brilliant new cut glass rests, deeply faceted and shining like diamonds, appeared in shops by the hundreds. There were sets of twelve, eight, or six that came in presentation boxes. Sizes vary from 1¼" to 3¼" for individual knives and from 5" to 6" for carving knives. Glass knife rests were made in many colors such as purple, blue, green, vaseline, pink, and cranberry. These colors have been attributed to European manufacturers.

There are many items of glass and pottery that resemble knife rests but are actually muddlers, toothpick holders (sanitary types that allow you to pick the toothpicks up by the centers), and paperweights. Collectors should be familiar with these and able to recognize them for what they are. It is important to note that prices may vary from one area of the country to another and from dealer to dealer. EBay sales are closing with steadily declining winning bids; good and unusual knife rests are not being offered. For further information we recommend our advisor, Beverly Schell Ales; she is listed in the Directory under California.

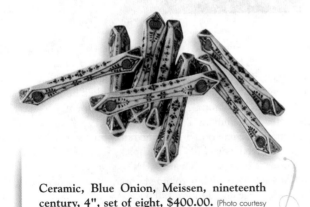

Ceramic, Blue Onion, Meissen, nineteenth century, 4", set of eight, $400.00. (Photo courtesy Cowan's Auction Inc./LiveAuctioneers.com)

Ceramic, duck & ladybug on wht log shape, 1930, 3½"	45.00
Glass, cut, Hawkes, catalog 1889, 4x3", from $100 to	200.00
Glass, cut; dmn-cut bar w/ends cut into 4-pointed star, 1880, 3½"	110.00
Glass, cut; Eggington, Creswick, 2x5", from $200 to	300.00
Glass, cut; Hoare, Monarch, catalog 1897-1911, lapidary, 4x1", $100 to	200.00
Glass, cut; Libbey, lapidary ends, 3¾", from $50 to	100.00
Glass, cut; Mt WA, oval & notched, catalog 1892, 2x5", from $100 to	200.00
Glass, cut; squash form	75.00
Glass, cut; 7-point stars on dumbbell shape, 5¼"	75.00
Glass, cut; 8-sided bar, w/dmn-cut ball end, 5½"	60.00

Glass, Dorflinger, strawberry diamond with fan and crosshatching, catalog 1886, 2x4½", from $100.00 to $200.00. (Photo courtesy Beverly Schell Ales)

Glass, pressed; Heisey, dmn & H mk IG, from $35 to	50.00
Glass, Sabino, bl w/duck ends	50.00
Porc, Konigliche Por Mfg (KPM) Germany, 1x4", from $200 to	300.00
Porc, Limoges, dolphin fish vase, 1x4", from $25 to	50.00
Pottery, Henriot Quimper, bl, HB, #797, ca 1883	75.00
Silver, lg dog figures (walking & looking at ea other) bar ends, 4"	230.00
Silver, pheasant figure on end of bar, detailed, 1¼x4"	140.00
SP, Meriden, cherubs on ends, 1x3", from $35 to	50.00
Sterling, Kerr, bar w/thistle & leaves on ends, ca 1900, 2x4"	90.00
Waterford, mk, lg, from $50 to	75.00

Knives

Knife collecting as a hobby began in earnest during the 1960s when government regulations required for the first time that knife companies mark their products with the country of origin. The few collectors and dealers aware of this change at once began stockpiling the older knives made before this law was enacted. Another impetus to the growing interest in this area came with the Gun Control Act of 1968, which severely restricted gun trading. Frustrated gun dealers transferred their attention to knives. Today there are collectors' clubs in many of the states.

The most sought-after pocketknives are those made before WWII. However, as time goes on knives no older than 20 years are collectible if in mint condition. Most collectors prefer knives in 'as found' condition. Do *not* attempt to clean, sharpen, or in any way 'improve' on an old knife.

Please note: Length is measured with blades *closed*. Our values are for knives in used/excellent condition (unless specified 'mint'). Most old knives are usually not encountered in mint condition. Therefore to give a mint price could mislead the novice collector. If a knife has been used, sharpened, or blemished in any way, its value decreases. It is common to find knives made in the 1960s and later in mint condition. Knives made in the 1970s and 1980s may be collectible in mint condition, but not in used condition. Therefore a used knife 30 years old may be be worth no more than a knife for use. For further information refer to *The Standard Knife Collectors Guide, Big Book of Pocket Knives*, and *Remington Knives* by Ron Stewart and Roy Ritchie; and *The Case Cutlery Dynasty: Tested XX* by Brad Lockwood (all are published by Collector Books). *Sargent's American Premium Guide to Knives and Razors, Identification and Values*, 6th Edition, by Jim Sargent is another good reference. Our advisor for this category is Bill Wright, author of *Theatre-Made Military Knives of World War II* (Schiffer). Mr. Wright is listed in the Directory under Indiana.

Key:

alum — aluminum	jack — jackknife
bd — blade	lb — lockback
gen — genuine	pat — pattern
imi — imitation	wb — winterbottom

A Davy & Sons (Sheffield England), 2-bd, Liberty & Union bolster ... 700.00
Aerial Cutlery Co, 2-bd jack, bone hdl, 3⅜" 60.00
Anheuser-Busch, red & gold emb hdl, w/peephole & picture 375.00
Barnett Tool Co, bone hdl, bd+punch+pliers 175.00
Boker, Henrich (German), 1-bd, bone hdl, 4½" 65.00
Boker (German), 4-bd congress, bone hdl, 4" 125.00
Boker (USA), 3-bd stockman, imi pearl hdl, 4" 40.00
Boker (USA), 4-bd congress, bone hdl, 3¾" 65.00
Bulldog Brand (Germany), 3-bd whittler, gen abalone hdl, 5⅛", M ... 150.00
Case, Tested XX, 5202½, 2-bd, gen stag hdl, 3⅜" 100.00
Case, Tested XX, 6220, 2-bd, rough blk hdl, peanut pat, 2⅜" 100.00
Case, Tested XX, 6392, 3-bd, gr bone hdl, stockman pat, 4" 175.00

Case, Tested XX, 6592, green bone handle, 4" closed, used, rare, $2,500.00. (Photo courtesy Wright Collection)

Case, Tested XX, 8383, 2-bd, gen pearl hdl, whittler pat, 3½" 500.00
Case, Tested XX, 61093, 1-bd, gr bone hdl, toothpick pat, 5" 200.00
Case, Tested XX, 62031½, 2-bd, gr bone hdl, 3¾" 150.00
Case, Tested XX, 62100, 2-bd, gr bone hdl, saddlehorn pat, 4⅜" .. 500.00
Case, XX, 2-bd, bone hdl, muskrat pat, 3⅜" 150.00
Case, XX, 3347hp, 3-bd, yel compo hdl, stockman pat, 3⅜" 85.00
Case, XX, 5254, 2-bd, gen stag hdl, trapper pat, 4⅛" 300.00
Case, XX, 5375, 3-bd, gen red stag hdl, long pull, stockman, 4¼" ... 600.00
Case, XX, 6185, 1-bd, bone hdl, doctor's pat, 3¾" 125.00
Case, XX, 6231½, 2-bd, bone hdl, 3¾" 75.00
Case, XX, 6250, 2-bd, bone hdl, sunfish pat, 4½" 200.00
Case, XX, 6294, 2-bd, bone hdl, cigar pat, 4¼" 250.00
Case, XX, 6308, 3-bd, bone hdl, whittler pat, 3¼" 100.00
Case, XX, 6488, 4-bd, bone hdl, congress pat, 4⅛" 500.00
Case, XX, 6565sab, 2-bd, bone hdl, folding hunter pat, 5¼" 125.00
Case, XX, 62009, 1-bd, bone hdl, barlow pat, 3⅜" 40.00
Case, XX USA, 10 dots, 6111½, 1-bd, bone hdl, lb, 4⅜", M 325.00
Case, XX USA, 52131, 2-bd, gen stag hdl, canoe pat, 3⅜", M 350.00
Case Bros, Little Valley NY, 2-bd, wood hdl, 3¼" 125.00
Case Bros, Springville NY, 8250, 2-bd, pearl hdl, sunfish pat 3,000.00
Cattaraugus, D2589, 4-bd, bone hdl, Official Scout Emblem, 3½" ... 200.00
Cattaraugus, 3-bd+nail file, gen pearl hdl, lobster gun stock, 3" 150.00
Cattaraugus, 12839, 1-bd, bone hdl, King of the Woods, 5⅜" 500.00
Cattaraugus, 22346, 2-bd, wood hdl, jack pat, 3⅜" 85.00
Cattaraugus, 22919, 2-bd, bone hdl, cigar pat, 4¼" 300.00
Cattaraugus, 32145, 3-bd, bone hdl, stockman pat, 3⅜" 200.00
Challenge Cutlery, 1-bd, bone hdl, lb pat, 4¾" 200.00
Challenge Cutlery, 3-bd, bone hdl, cattle pat, 3⅜" 125.00
Diamond Edge, 2-bd, bone hdl, jack, 3⅜" 75.00
Diamond Edge, 2-bd, pearl celluloid hdl, gun stock, 3" 100.00
Frost Cutlery Co (Japan), 3-bd, bone hdl, lb whittler pat, 4" 15.00
H&B Mfg Co, 3-bd, buffalo horn hdl, whittler pat, 3⅜" 150.00
Hammer Brand, NY Knife Co, 2-bd, bone hdl, 3⅜" 85.00
Hammer Brand, 1-bd, bone hdl, NYK on bolster, lb, 5¼" 375.00
Hammer Brand, 1-bd, tin shell hdl, powder-horn pat, 4¾" 25.00
Hammer Brand, 2-bd, bone hdl, dog-leg pat, 3¾" 225.00
Hammer Brand, 2-bd, wood hdl, jack, 3¾" 85.00
Henckels, JA; 3-bd, bone hdl, whittler pat, 3¼" 65.00
Henckels, JA; 4-bd, bone hdl, congress pat, 4" 150.00
Hibbard, Spencer, Bartlett & Co, 2-bd, bone hdl, barlow, 3⅜" 85.00
Hibbard, Spencer, Bartlett & Co, 2-bd, bone hdl, dog-leg pat, 3⅜" ... 110.00
Holley Mfg Co, 1-bd, wood hdl, 5" 140.00
Holley Mfg Co, 3-bd, pearl hdl, whittler pat, 3¼" 225.00
Holley Mfg Co, 4-bd, bone hdl, congress pat, 3½" 375.00
Honk Falls Knife Co, 1-bd, bone hdl, 3" 125.00
I*XL (Sheffield England), 4-bd, gen stag hdl, congress, 4" 350.00
I*XL (Sheffield), 2-bd, wood hdl, heavy jack, 4" 125.00
Imperial Knife Co, 2-bd, bone hdl, dog-leg pat, 3⅜" 50.00
Imperial Knife Co, 2-bd, mc hdl, 3¼" 35.00
John Primble, Belknap Hdw Co, 3-bd, bone hdl, 4" 75.00
John Primble, Belknap Hdw Co, 4-bd, bone hdl, 3¾" 85.00
John Primble, India Steel Works, 2-bd, gen stag hdl, 4¼" 500.00
John Primble, India Steel Works on bolster, celluloid hdl, 3" 125.00
Ka-Bar, Union Cutlery, knife & fork, bone hdl, 5¼" 350.00
Ka-Bar, Union Cutlery, 2-bd, gen stag hdl, dog head, 5¼" 300.00
Ka-Bar, Union Cutlery, 3-bd, bone hdl, whittler pat, 3¾" 150.00
Ka-Bar, 2-bd, gen stag hdl, Old Time Trapper, 4⅛" 85.00
Ka-Bar, 3-bd, bone hdl, cattle pat, 3⅜" 100.00

Keen Kutter, Centennial, MIB, $85.00. (Photo courtesy Burley Auction Group/LiveAuctioneers.com)

Keen Kutter, EC Simmons, 1-bd, bone hdl, lb, 4¼" 200.00
Keen Kutter, EC Simmons, 1-bd, bone hdl, 3¼" 50.00
Keen Kutter, EC Simmons, 2-bd, bone hdl, trapper, 3⅞" 250.00
Keen Kutter, EC Simmons, 2-bd, colorful celluloid hdl, 3⅜" 70.00
Keen Kutter, EC Simmons, 2-bd, pearl hdl, doctor pat, 3⅜" 250.00
Keen Kutter, EC Simmons, 2-bd, wood hdl, jack, 3¼" 75.00
Keen Kutter, EC Simmons, 3-bd, bone hdl, whittler pat, 3⅜" 75.00
Keen Kutter, 1-bd, bone hdl, TX toothpick, 5" 125.00
Keen Kutter, 2-bd, bone hdl, barlow, 3⅜" 75.00
Keen Kutter, 2-bd, bone hdl, folding hunter, 5¼" 125.00
LF&C, 2-bd, jigged hard rubber hdl, jack, 3⅜" 75.00
LF&C, 3-bd, gen pearl hdl, whittler pat, 3½" 125.00
Maher & Grosh, 2-bd, bone hdl, jack, 3⅜" 150.00
Marbles, 1-bd, gen stag hdl, Safety Folding Hunter, lg 700.00
Marbles, 1-bd, gen stag hdl, Safety Folding Hunter, sm 500.00
Miller Bros, 2-bd, bone hdl, jack, 3½" 100.00
Miller Bros, 2-bd, screws in bone hdl, 4¼" 500.00
Miller Bros, 3-bd, gen stag hdl, stockman, 4" 350.00
Miller Bros, 3-bd, screws in gen pearl hdl, 3⅜" 250.00
Morley, WH & Sons; 3-bd, bone hdl, whittler pat, 3¼" 65.00
MSA Co, Marbles, 2-bd, pearl hdl, sunfish pat, rare, 4" 3,500.00

Napanoch Knife Co, X100X, 1-bd, bone hdl, very rare, 5⅜" 2,500.00
Napanoch Knife Co, 2 lg bd, bone hdl, 3⅜" 250.00
Napanoch Knife Co, 4-bd, bone hdl, 3¼" 150.00
Northfield Knife Co, 2-bd, bone hdl, dog-leg pat, 3¾" 500.00
Northfield Knife Co, 2-bd, bone hdl, jack, 3⅜" 165.00
Pal, 2-bd, bone hdl, easy-open, 3¾" 85.00
Pal, 3-bd, bone hdl, jack, 3⅜" 60.00
Parker, Eagle (Japan), 1-bd, bone hdl, lb, 4½", M 25.00
Parker, Eagle (Japan), 4-bd, gen abalone hdl, congress, 3⅜", M ... 100.00

**Queen, carbon steel blades, winterbottom
bone handle, ca 1945, 3¹⁵⁄₁₆", M, $100.00.**
(Photo courtesy Wright Collection)

Queen, #18, 2-bd, wb bone hdl, jack, 3¹¹⁄₁₆" 50.00
Queen, #19, 2-bd, wb bone hdl, trapper, 4⅛" 150.00
Remington, RB43, 2-bd, bone hdl, barlow, 3⅜" 75.00
Remington, RS3333, 4-bd, bone hdl, scout shield, 3¾" 125.00
Remington, R173, 2-bd, bone hdl, teardrop jack, 3¾" 150.00
Remington, R555, 2-bd, candy stripe celluloid hdl, 3¼" 125.00
Remington, R775, 2-bd, red/wht/bl hdl, 3½" 185.00
Remington, R1123, (old) 2-bd, silver bullet on bone hdl, 4½" 750.00
Remington, R1153, 2-bd, bone hdl, jack, 4½" 250.00
Remington, R1225, 2-bd, wht compo hdl, 4¼" 125.00
Remington, R1306, (old) gen stag hdl, lb, silver bullet, 4⅝" 600.00
Remington, R3054, 3-bd, gen pearl hdl, stockman, 4" 300.00
Robeson, Shuredge, 2-bd, gen pearl hdl, jack, 3½" 150.00
Robeson, Shuredge, 2-bd, strawberry bone hdl, jack, 3¾" 100.00
Robeson, Shuredge, 3-bd, bone hdl, stockman, 3⅜" 125.00
Rodgers, Jos & Sons, multi-bd, stag hdl, sportsman's 350.00
Rodgers, Jos & Sons, 2-bd, gen stag hdl, jack, 3⅜" 125.00
Rodgers, Jos & Sons, 3-bd, bone hdl, stockman, 4" 150.00
Russell, 2-bd, bone hdl, barlow, 3⅜" 175.00
Russell, 2-bd, bone hdl, barlow, 5" 250.00
Schatt & Morgan (current), 1-bd, w/bone hdl, lb, 5¼", M 100.00
Schatt & Morgan (old), 2-bd, bone hdl, jack, 3⅜" 150.00
Schrade Walden, 2-bd, peach seed bone hdl, 4¼" 250.00
Schrade Walden, 3-bd, peach seed bone hdl, 3⅜" 75.00
Ulster Knife Co, 1-bd, bone hdl, barlow, 5", M 200.00
Ulster Knife Co, 4-bd, imi bone hdl, scout/campers 30.00
Wade & Butcher (Germany), 3-bd, gen stag hdl, whittler pat 125.00
Wade & Butcher (Sheffield England), 4-bd, gen stag hdl, 4" 500.00
Walden Knife Co, 1-bd, bone hdl, toothpick pat, 5" 150.00
Wards, 4-bd, bone hdl, cattle pat, 3⅝" 85.00
Winchester, 1920, (old) 1-bd, bone hdl, 5¼" 650.00
Winchester, 2046, (old) 2-bd), celluloid hdl, jack, 3¾" 85.00
Winchester, 2904, (old) 2-bd, bone hdl, trapper, 3⅞" 350.00
Winchester, 2974, (old) 2-bd, bone hdl, dog-leg jack, 3½" 125.00
Winchester, 3350, (old) 3-bd, gen pearl hdl, whittler pat, 3¼" 125.00
Winchester, 3960, (old) 3-bd, bone hdl, stockman, 4" 275.00
Winchester, 3971, dtd 89 (1989), 3-bd, bone hdl, whittler pat, M....75.00

Sheath Knives

Over the past several years knife collectors have noticed that the avail-

ability of quality old pocketknives has steadily decreased. Many collectors have now started looking for sheath knives as an addition to their hobby. In many cases, makers of pocketknives also made quality hunting and sheath knives. Listed below is a small sampling of collectible sheath knives available. Length is given for overall knife measurement; price includes original sheath and reflects the value of knives in excellent used condition.

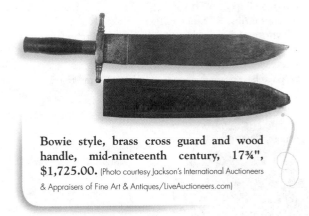

**Bowie style, brass cross guard and wood
handle, mid-nineteenth century, 17¾",
$1,725.00.** (Photo courtesy Jackson's International Auctioneers
& Appraisers of Fine Art & Antiques/LiveAuctioneers.com)

Case, (XX) 515-5, stacked leather hdl, 9" 35.00
Case, (XX) 523-5, gen stag hdl, 9¼" 85.00
Case (Bradford PA), bk of tang: Case's Tested XX, 8¼" 150.00
Case (WR & Sons), bone hdl, Bowie knife, 11" 400.00
Case (XX USA), gen stag hdl, Kodiak hunter, 10¾" 125.00
Case (XX), V-44, blk Bakelite hdl, WWII, 14½" 350.00
Cattaraugus, gen stag hdl, alum pommel, 10¼" 85.00
Cattaraugus, 225Q, stacked leather hdl, WWII, 10⅜" 45.00
I*XL (Sheffield), Bowie knife, ca 1845, 14" 2,000.00
I*XL (Sheffield), leather hdl w/stag, ca 1935, 10" 100.00
Ka-Bar, Union Cutlery Co, jigged bone hdl, 9¾" 150.00
Ka-Bar, Union Cutlery Co, leather hdl w/stag, 8½" 125.00
Ka-Bar, USMC, stacked leather hdl, WWII, 12¼" 100.00
Keen Kutter, EC Simmons, K1050-6, Bowie knife, 10" 500.00
Marbles, Ideal, all gen stag hdl, 10" 275.00
Marbles, Ideal, stacked leather hdl w/alum, 9" 100.00
Marbles, Ideal, stacked leather hdl w/stag, 11⅜" 500.00
Marbles, Woodcraft, stacked leather hdl w/alum, 8¼" 125.00
Randall, Springfield MA, leather hdl, WWII, 13" 1,750.00
Remington, RH36, stacked leather hdl w/alum, 10½" 200.00
Remington, RH40, stacked leather hdl w/alum, rare, 14½" 1,500.00
Remington, RH73, gen stag hdl, 8" 75.00
Ruana, alum w/elk horn hdl, skinner, current, 7½" 100.00
Ruana, RH; alum w/elk horn hdl, ca 1980, 6½" 200.00
Ruana, RH; M stamp, alum w/elk horn hdl, skinner, 9¼" 275.00
Winchester, W1050, jigged bone hdl, Bowie knife, 10" 750.00
Wragg, SC (Sheffield); stag hdl, Bowie knife, 13½" 1,500.00
WWII, theater knife, mc Bakelite hdl, 12" 200.00
WWII, theater knife, mc hdl, Bowie knife, 12¾" 125.00
WWII, theater knife, mc hdl, dagger, 11" 100.00
WWII, theater knife, Plexiglass hdl w/picture, 12" 175.00

Kosta

Kosta glassware has been made in Sweden since 1742. Today they are one of that country's leading producers of quality art glass. Two of their most important designers were Elis Bergh (1929 – 1950) and Vicke Lindstrand, artistic director from 1950 to 1973. Lindstrand brought to the company knowledge of important techniques such as Graal, fine figural engraving, Ariel, etc. He influenced new artists to experiment with these techniques and inspired them to create new and innovative designs. In

1976 the company merged with two neighboring glasshouses, and the name was changed to Kosta Boda. Today's collectors are most interested in pieces made during the 1950s and 1960s.

Bottle, scent; rnd cuts on sides, amber oval int, Manolos, #95120, 3"... 120.00
Bowl, brn ribs on gr, oval, gr ft, Lindstrand, #146, 2⅞x5⅜" 600.00
Bowl, fluted, scalloped, A Ehnyr, 6x10" 425.00
Bowl, horizontal ribs, A Ehmes, #79332, 3¼x14" 300.00
Bowl, yel/wht/brn horizontal lines, ruffled handkerchief, 5½" H.. 110.00
Pitcher, orange w/bl hdl, low ribs, A Wahlstrom, #8953, 9½" 215.00
Sculpture, eagle, World Wildlife Fund, 1976, 5" 30.00
Sculpture, polar bear swimming inside gr iceberg, V Lindstrand, 8x10". 480.00

Sculpture, raspberry pink, signed G. Warff Unik, 7½", $900.00.
(Photo courtesy Cincinnati Art Galleries/LiveAuctioneers.com)

Vase, bl/gr yel spiral stripes, cylindrical, A Ehrner, 1948, 14½".... 425.00
Vase, bl/sea gr spirals in clear, Linstrand, ca 1958-59, 8¼" 480.00
Vase, brn spirals on lt brn to wht, stick neck, Vallien, #40132, 11"....350.00
Vase, face HP on clear, Coll/48746/Ulinca HV, 10x4½" 360.00
Vase, face HP on mottled gray, UHV/KT, #48962, 14x9" 215.00
Vase, ovoid, etched w/linear design w/in, LS, #612, 5½x4¾" 300.00
Vase, ship etched on teardrop form, Lindstrand, #42290, 1955-63, 12½".. 180.00
Vase, tree w/mc spatter leaves, V Lindstrand, 6½" 2,400.00
Vase, wht loops on pillow form, B Vallien, #98972, 6" 120.00

Vase, white festoons over ruby core, V. Lindstrand, LH 1115, 1950 – 1952, 6", $385.00. (Photo courtesy Cincinnati Art Galleries/LiveAuctioneers.com)

KPM Porcelain

The original KPM wares were produced from 1823 until 1847 by the Konigliche Porzellan Manfaktur, located in Berlin, Germany. Meissen used the same letters on some of their porcelains, as did several others in the area. The mark contains the initials KPM. Watch for items currently being imported from China; they are marked KPM with the eagle but the scepter is not present. Our advisor for this category is Don Williams; he is listed in the Directory under Missouri.

Bowl, center; courting scene/landscape, w/gold, ftd, w/hdls, 11x15" ..3,125.00

Box, busts/shells/cornucopias/putti, lid w/ornate hdl, 14x15"....8,440.00
Candle lamp, 3 animal faces (cat/bulldog/owl), ca 1900, 4x3¾" .. 395.00
Figurine, faun w/parrot, porc base, Puchegger, 1910, 12½"........5,870.00
Figurine, lady in ball gown on bench holding flowers, 9½" 1,180.00
Figurine, nobleman, gold on sword/belt/harp/cape chain, rnd base, 15".685.00
Hot water jug, floral spray w/gold, 6¼" 215.00
Jar, floral w/gold, pierced, appl rose finial, leaf hdls, 11½" 2,000.00
Jardiniere, floral w/gold on wht, ram's head hdls, 10" 850.00

Plaque, Bussende Magdalena, incised septer mark, 21x23", in double wood gilt and blue matt frame, $9,600.00.
(Photo courtesy Early Auction Co.)

Plaque, Christ w/crown of thorns, after Guido Reni, 10½x5½"+fr ...3,250.00
Plaque, classical maid in rose garden, ca 1900, 9¾x7" 8,200.00
Plaque, Cupid sharpening arrow, 10¼x8¼"+gilt fr 3,500.00
Plaque, Entflohen (2 beauties), ornate gilt border, #8129, 13" dia+fr ...24,000.00
Plaque, Epanouissement, oval, after Asti, 13x11", +hand-cvd gilt fr ..22,500.00
Plaque, Helena Fourment & son Peter Paul, after Rubens, 15x12"+gilt fr ..33,750.00
Plaque, lady watching urn painter, after Thumann, 10¾x7"+gilt fr ..8,750.00
Plaque, maid illuminated by candlestick, oval, 6¼x5" 875.00
Plaque, maid standing by cherry tree, 12½x6¼"+gilt fr 12,000.00
Plaque, maid w/cherub leaning on shoulder, ca 1900, 9¾x7"+gilt fr....11,020.00
Plaque, maid w/long tresses in robe, Wagner, 13x8"+gilt fr 13,210.00
Plaque, maids w/puppet in Oriental scene, 9¼x6½" 11,250.00
Plaque, Napoleon Bonaparte, after Francois Gerard, Wagner, 9½x6" .. 9,375.00
Plaque, nudes (2) on river bank w/bulrushes, Wagner, 8¼x11" 11,875.00
Plaque, Princess Louise on staircase, 12¾x7½"+gilt fr 6,600.00
Plaque, Queen Louise (bust), oval, 9x6¾" 815.00
Plaque, Repentant Magdalene, 1800s, 7¼x12½"+fr 3,600.00
Plaque, Vestal Virgin, after Angelica Kaufmann, 20¾x14½"...18,750.00
Platter, butterflies w/floral on wht, w/basketweave rim, 19½" L... 1,200.00
Teapot, HP armorial crest on wht w/gold, bird spout, 1720s, 5¼".. 47,800.00
Urn, flowers/game bird/fruit, octagon ped ft, ornate dragon hdls, 36"...11,250.00
Vase, classical figures on burgundy, gilt bronze swags & ft, 10"..1,500.00

Kutani

Kutani, named for the Japanese village where it originated, was first produced in the seventeenth century. The early ware, Ko Kutani, was made for only about 30 years. Several types were produced before 1800, but these are rarely encountered. In the nineteenth century, kilns located in several different villages began to copy the old Kutani wares. This later, more familiar type has large areas of red with gold designs on a white ground decorated with warriors, birds, and flowers in controlled colors of red, gold, and black.

Bowl, children playing, 19th C, 12" 395.00
Charger, bird/dragons/foliage on mc geometrics w/gilt, ca 1900, 27"... 3,250.00
Charger, figures in landscape w/gold & iron red, 12" 145.00
Charger, horsemen (2) in winter scene, gold geometric trim, 24" .. 1,250.00
Cup, wedding; floral on wht w/iron red & gold, ftd, 1880s, 6¼"..... 85.00
Cup & saucer, floral w/iron red & gold, scalloped rim 30.00
Figurine, cat sleeping, mc geometrics/roundels on blk w/gold, 4x10".. 1,125.00
Figurine, cat w/bat ears waving paw, wide floral collar, Meiji, 9x5" ..1,935.00
Figurine, duck w/head down, mc w/gold, detailed feathers, 7½x12".1,000.00
Figurine, geisha in full costume, 20th C, 12" 515.00
Figurine, lady in kimono holds lantern, 19th C, 12½"............... 2,500.00
Plate, Mt Fuji on lt bl w/silver & gilt clouds, 4 red ft, sq, 7½"...9,000.00
Platter, mixed floral on wht w/iron red & gold border, 15½" L..... 60.00
Sake bottle, coiled dragon figural, detailed, donut-shape, 7½" 815.00
Sake bottle, landscape reserves on brocade, kinrande palette, 7½" ..215.00
Sake cup washer, floral reserves, geometrics, 19th C, 4½x6" 120.00
Vase, bamboo stalks, silver on red-brn, globular, 20th C, 5"........... 42.50
Vase, figure in lg oval reserve, shouldered, slim, 12" 160.00
Vase, figures among birds & floral on red, cvd lid & base, 27"..2,000.00
Vase, fish/riverscape/brocade w/gold, 3 conjoined balusters, 9½" .. 515.00
Vase, flowers & birds, baluster, 19th C, 14" 300.00
Vase, flowers & leaves on iron red, classic form, 14"..................... 120.00
Vase, lg hydrangeas w/leaves on yel roundels, shouldered, 13x6"..1,375.00
Vase, seated nobleman/landscape on rust, trumpet form, 19th C, 20" ..750.00

Vase, panels depicting women in garden, 1970, 19", $240.00. (Photo courtesy Du Mouchelles/LiveAuctioneers.com)

Labels

Before the advent of the cardboard box, wooden crates were used for transporting products. Paper labels were attached to the crates to identify the contents and the packer. These labels often had colorful lithographed illustrations covering a broad range of subjects. Eventually the cardboard box replaced the crate, and the artwork was imprinted directly onto the carton. Today these paper labels are becoming collectible — not only for the art, but also for their advertising appeal. Our advisor for this category is Cerebro; their address is listed in the Directory under Pennsylvania. While common labels are worth very little, some sell for several hundred dollars. We have tried to list some of the better examples below.

Can, Alko Brand Spices, White Pepper, Egyptian scene, M 10.00
Can, Carroco June Peas, butterflies & flowers, EX.......................... 30.00
Can, Cobcut, hand cutting corn from ear onto plate, 1930, M...... 10.00
Can, Eastern Estate Brand Sweet Corn, red, EX............................ 15.00
Can, Eastern Estate Tea Co Coffee, red, wht & bl, G.................... 12.00
Can, Flag Brand Peaches, peaches & flag, EX................................ 30.00
Can, Guilford Tomato Juice/Sachems Head, mc, M........................8.00
Can, Heinz Strained Apricots & Applesauce, shield logo/baby, gr, EX..10.00
Can, Helen Refugee Beans, girl w/vegetable basket/bowl of gr beans, M . 20.00
Can, Holly Bartlett Pears, pear/sprig of holly, EX 10.00
Can, Homestead, mushrooms, country home, M........................... 18.00
Can, Homestead Mushroom Gravy, country home in reserve, M .. 15.00

Can, Maid O' Honey, sm girl w/bouquet in meadow, VG............... 15.00
Can, Norwood Sorghum & Corn Syrup, gr, EX 12.00
Can, Pride of Fairfield, sailboat on river/country home/corn, M 15.00
Can, Robin Hood Hawaiian Pineapples, man kneeling w/bow & arrow, EX..40.00
Can, Shield Label Fig Preserves, gold reserve w/bl flowers, M...........8.00
Cigar box, inner; Abe Lincoln, profile portrait & branches, EX .. 100.00
Cigar box, inner; Admiral Gherardi, portrait, M 65.00
Cigar box, inner; Bandera Cubana, lg flag over beach scene, EX ... 50.00
Cigar box, inner; Chapman House, Arabian lady in profile in oval .. 10.00
Cigar box, inner; Empire State, NY skyscraper, M......................... 12.00
Cigar box, inner; King Carlos, king w/many military metals, M 10.00
Cigar box, inner; Lord Russell, seated at desk, VG 75.00
Cigar box, inner; Miss Primroses, lady w/lg hat in reserve, M 12.00
Cigar box, inner; Selectos, woman/eagle/much gilt, EX 15.00
Cigar box, outer; Cuban-Americans, shields/coins over sunrays, EX ...50.00
Cigar box, outer; Gisela, long-haired lady, Art Nouveau, M 20.00
Cigar box, outer; King V, king behind shield/weapons, M.................6.00
Cigar box, outer; Knickerbocker Club, colonial man/NY landmarks, M ... 20.00
Cigar box, outer; La Composa, Lady Justice w/scales, VG.............. 12.00
Cigar box, outer; Liberty Bond, document promoting Am bonds, M ..15.00
Cigar box, outer; Mi Idolatria, lady's portrait, canted corners, M...40.00
Cigar box, outer; Mi-Lu, lady's portrait in profile, M 35.00
Cigar box, outer; Patrick Browne, clover below portrait, M..............8.00
Cigar box, outer; Roman bowing to empress, M 12.00
Cigar box, outer; Rosa de Rica, lady & flowers, M......................... 12.00
Crate, apple; Jackie Boy, sm boy in naval attire w/apple, 1925, M ...12.00
Crate, cranberry; Pilgrim Brand, pilgrims in reserve, M 10.00
Crate, fruit; Anchor Brand New York State Grapes, grapes/anchor, EX..6.00
Crate, fruit; Appleton Brand Apples, lady w/roses/orchard, 1915, M..7.00
Crate, onions; Flavon, chef w/baking tray of onions, G................. 30.00
Crate, orange, Leslie, orange w/facial features looking at man, VG ..50.00
Crate, orange; Marc Anthony, Roman portrait, CA, 1930, M....... 12.00
Crate, orange; Orbit, orange as comet, CA, M 20.00
Crate, orange/lemon; Cepaval, smiling beach girl, M..................... 60.00

Crate, tobacco; Good Luck, Four Leaf Clover, 11x11", $100.00. (Photo courtesy Philip Weiss Auctions/ LiveAuctioneers.com)

Crate, vegetable; Beverly, girl on bench, sample, EX...................... 75.00
Firecracker, Alligator, alligator scene, penny pack, 1¼x1", EX 40.00
Firecracker, Corsair, pirate scene, box label, M............................. 55.00
Firecracker, King Kong...Flashlight, gorilla w/wings, 1940s, 1½", M...145.00
Firecracker, Kwong Man Lung, Oriental figures/dragons, 11x6¼", M ..75.00
Firecracker, Nightraider, figure w/skeleton face, brick sz, M........... 35.00
Firecracker, Peony Brand, figures w/parade dragons, 3x2⅞", NM... 58.00
Firecracker, Rocket Brand, conical missile in blk sky, 3x1¾", EX .. 30.00

Jar, Heinz's Sweet Mixed Pickles, 14" long, $275.00. (Photo courtesy Morphy Auctions)

Soap, Poudre de Riz a la Violete...Paris, violets, 1930s, 3¼", NM 6.00
Soap, Savon Pur Royal Yedo, Oriental man reserve, 1930s, 6½x3", EX...6.00
Soap, 20 Mule Team Borax, mule washing clothes, 9½x6½", VG.....3.00
Tobacco, Black Bird, bird on branch, c 1886, 13½x7", EX 30.00
Tobacco, Derby, horse race scene, 1880s, 6¾x13", G.....................35.00
Tobacco, High Admiral of Navies, King of Seas, 7x13", NM.......210.00
Tobacco, Jockey, 2 Black jockeys on saddles, Calvert, 2¾" dia, VG.100.00
Tobacco, Melodia, Virginia USA, 2 girls w/instruments, 14x7", EX ..55.00

Labino

Dominick Labino was a glassblower who until mid-1985 worked in his studio in Ohio, blowing and sculpting various items which he signed and dated. A ceramic engineer by trade, he was instrumental in developing the heat-resistant tiles used in space flights. His glassmaking shows his versatility in the art. While some of his designs are free-form and futuristic, others are reminiscent of the products of older glasshouses. Because of problems with his health, Mr. Labino became unable to blow glass himself; he died January 10, 1987. Work coming from his studio since mid-1985 has been signed 'Labino Studios, Baker,' indicating ware made by his protegee, E. Baker O'Brien. In addition to her own compositions, she continues to use many of the colors developed by Labino.

Bowl, red/mauve/swirled ochre, 1982, 5" 235.00
Bowl, shaded pk transparent, 1969, 2x7" 350.00
Paperweight, pinwheel/floral, yel on red cushion, 1974, 2½" 275.00
Paperweight, yel/blk/cinnamon flower in clear, 1978, 3" 350.00
Pitcher, dk red, integral hdl, blown in 1 pc, 1969, 6¾"..................350.00
Sculpture, Emergence, pk/yel/pk in clear dome, 1980, 6½" 3,000.00

Sculpture, green with internal air trap section and red agate glass, 1975, 8¼", $1,800.00. (Photo courtesy Jackson's International Auctioneers & Appraisers of Fine Art & Antiques)

Vase, amber in clear w/trapped air decor, 1975, 4x5"....................600.00
Vase, amber w/yel pull-up designs, incurvate rim, 1980, 5" 600.00
Vase, bands, orange/wht on dk red, Chelsea Collection label, 1972, 4"..465.00
Vase, cobalt & yel w/pulled decor encased in clear, 1981, 5½"..1,175.00
Vase, orange/wht/bl nailsea loops, spherical, 1973, 4" 475.00
Vase, plumes, mc on wht, incurvate rim, paperweight base, 1982, 5" 480.00
Vase, plumes, orange & wht on amethyst, ovoid, flared rim, 1977, 6" 515.00

Vase, robin's egg blue with ribbing, 1971, 9", $425.00. (Photo courtesy Early Auction Co.)

Vase, yel/wht/rust/orange abstract pattern, incurvate rim, 1983, 6"....900.00
Vase, 3 orange intarsia fish in purple, spherical, 1977, 6" 480.00

Lace, Linens, and Needlework

Two distinct audiences vie for old lace and linens. Collectors seek out exceptional stitchery like philatelists and numismatists seek stamps or coins — simply to marvel at its beauty, rarity, and ties to history. Collectors judge lace and linens like figure skaters and gymnasts are judged: artist impression is half the score, technical merit the other. How complex and difficult are the stitches and how well are they done? The 'users' see lace and linens as recyclables. They seek pretty wearables or decorative materials. They want fashionable things in mint condition, and have little or no interest in technique. Both groups influence price.

Undiscovered and underpriced are the eighteenth-century masterpieces of lace and needle art in techniques which will never be duplicated. Their beauty is subtle. Amazing stitches often are invisible without magnification. To get the best value in any lace, linen, or textile item, learn to look closely at individual stitches, and study the design and technique. The finest pieces are wonderfully constructed. The stitches are beautiful to look at, and they do a good job of holding the item together. Unless noted otherwise, values are for examples in at last excellent condition.

Key: embr — embroidered

Baby bonnet, wht cotton w/pk ribbon inserts, 3 frills at edge, 6" dia..85.00
Bedcover, wht Marcella w/heavy all-over embr, ca 1900, 95x90"....200.00
Bow, wht voile, embr w/lace edge, 2 layers, 1920s, 7x10"..............50.00
Cape, blk French Chantilly lace, diamanté clasp, ca 1885, 52x226"..525.00
Chairback, wht linen w/much openwork/embr flower basket, 1900s, 45x20"..45.00
Chairbacks, wht linen w/3 openwork & embr grape clusters, 46x24", pr.65.00
Christening cape, wht cotton w/Broderie Anglaise inserts, ribbons, 32"..25.50
Christening gown, wht cotton, pintucks, embr bottom, 1890s, 40" L.225.00
Collar, ivory, Irish Carrickmacross lace, 49" L from inside neck ..190.00
Collar, ivory lace w/leaves & vines, ca 1880, 36" L from inside neck..145.00
Collar, wht Brussels lace w/scalloped edge, ca 1890, 42x4" 175.00
Collar, wht Irish crochet lace, ca 1920, 18" around neck, 4½" W..60.00
Collar, wht Point de Colbert lace, ca 1880, 31" L from inside neck..95.00
Collar, wht Sweet Irish crochet lace, ca 1900, 17½x2½"................50.00
Cuffs, ivory Irish Carrickmacross lace, 1920s, 9x12", pr................65.00
Cuffs, wht lace w/draw thread at top, 3" W.....................................55.00
Curtain, ivory linen, mc embr lady in pk & birds in hearts, 66x35"...100.00
Curtains, sheer ivory cotton w/lace detail 35" from bottom, 72x36", pr.290.00
Doily, ivory silk w/embr center & lace border, 1930s, 8½" 45.00
Doily, wht crochet lace, ca 1920, 13" 35.00
Doily, wht dotted linen w/wide lace edge, ca 1920, 10x12"............50.00
Doily, wht linen center w/handmade lace 'petals', ca 1900s, 12" dia..55.00
Doily, wht linen w/cutwork & lt bl embr edge, oval, 1920s, 11x5", pr...50.00
Doily, wht linen w/handmade bobbin lace, ca 1900, 7" dia............50.00
Doily, wht linen w/scalloped edge & fine embr, 1920s, 6x12" 35.00
Doily, wht linen w/1½" Duchesse lace trim, ca 1900, 6x10"...........65.00
Glove holder, ivory linen w/yel embr letters & scalloped edge, 18x10"..35.00
Handkerchief, wht cotton w/Brussels lace edges, 12x12" 40.00
Handkerchief, wht lawn w/dainty bl embr scalloped corners, 14x14"..30.00
Handkerchief, wht linen w/lace flower bowl insert & cutwork, 12x12" .30.00
Handkerchief, wht linen w/Princess lace at 1 corner, 12" sq 30.00
Lappets, ivory bobbin lace, ca 1890, 60x4½", pr............................65.00
Memorial, embr silk panel w/lady by plaque w/attached label, 17x23"+fr.435.00
Modest front, ivory Princess lace, high neck, ca 1890, 12" L 65.00
Napkins, aqua linen w/wht embr corner & edge, 1930s, 14" sq, 4 for ..30.00
Napkins, wht linen w/embr & lace inserts, 1930s, 7x7", 8 for........85.00
Napkins, WHT linen w/organdy floral insert, 1930s, 7½x5", 10 for..85.00
Napkins, wht linen w/woven floral, drawn edge, 1920s, 19x17", 12 for..125.00

Needlework, bird on fruit tree, silk embr/X-stitch on wool, 14x14"+fr. 4,000.00
Needlework, flower basket, silk/chenille on silk, 1816, 19x22" ..1,400.00
Needlework, lady at harp/mother/child, silk/HP, 19th C, 18x20"..1,800.00
Needlework, silk embr religious scene w/2 figures at well, 14x17"+fr.115.00
Pillow shams, wht linen w/lace inserts/trim/edge frill, 1920s, 27" sq ..250.00
Pillowcases, wht cotton w/cutwork & embr on scalloped edge, 33x20", pr..60.00
Runner, ivory French Alencon lace, ca 1920, 37x14½" 130.00
Runner, wht linen w/all-over floral punch work, 1920s, 56x22" 65.00
Runner, wht linen w/embr butterflies, scalloped, ca 1900, 53x18"..70.00
Shawl, blk French Chantilly lace, triangular, ca 1885, 108x50".... 200.00

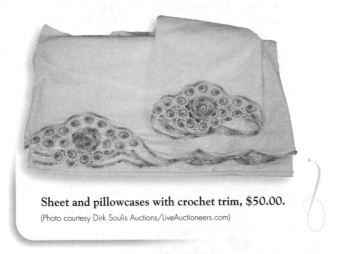

Sheet and pillowcases with crochet trim, $50.00.

(Photo courtesy Dirk Soulis Auctions/LiveAuctioneers.com)

Sheet, bed; wht linen w/embr & applied swans & ships, 1930s, 58x34"... 70.00
Sofa-bk, wht linen, embr flower baskets on bottom edge, 1900s, 39x23" . 45.00
Table mats, orandy & linen w/embr floral edge, ca 1930, set of 10, 6" ...75.00
Table runner, ivory linen, Madeira embr, scalloped edge, 1930s, 44x15"..65.00
Table runner, wht linen w/embr, lace inserts, lace trim, 1900s, 50x19"...100.00
Table topper, wht linen w/lace inserts & 5½" border, 1920s, 33" dia..115.00
Table topper, wht linen w/2 rows of lace inserts, lace edge, 23" sq. 65.00

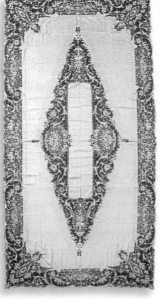

Tablecloth, hand-worked lace, 135x65", $1,000.00.

(Photo courtesy Brunk Auctions/LiveAuctioneers.com)

Tablecloth, ivory Irish dbl damask linen, 1910s, 65x50", +6 lg napkins . 85.00
Tablecloth, wht cotton w/hand embr, oval, 1930s, 100x68"........ 185.00
Tablecloth, wht Irish linen dbl damask, no decor, 1930s, 90x72" .. 75.00
Tablecloth, wht linen w/embr dmn & floral sprigs, 1900s, 52x52" ..125.00
Tablecloth, wht linen w/14" heavy lace border, ca 1900, 56x56". 175.00
Tablecloth, wht linen w/4-embr birds/cutwork/lace edge, 1900s, 42" dia.100.00

Tablecloth, wht linen w/5½" lace inserts, 1920s, 90x70" 250.00
Tablecloth, wht organdy w/appl pastel flowers, 106x62", +12 napkins . 290.00
Tapestry, muted mc village scene w/dancer & musicians, 1925, 26x35". 100.00
Tea cozy, wht lace w/pk silk padded lining, ca 1900, 7½x24x6" ... 160.00
Towel, lt yel linen w/embr organdy insert, scalloped edge, 17x11", pr....55.00
Towel, wht Irish linen w/embr & appliquéd flowers, 1930s, 11x17", pr .80.00
Towel, wht linen w/embr stork, castellated edges, 1920s, 22½x15" ..50.00
Towel, wht linen w/lace insert & lace edge on 1 end, 1930s, 17x10" ...45.00
Towel, wht linen w/Madeira embr berries & lace trim, 1930s, 18x12".50.00
Towel, yel linen w/mc embr angel playing fiddle, 1920s, 21x14", pr..60.00
Tray cloth, wht cotton w/cutwork & embr corner baskets, 1920s, 18x13". 60.00
Tray cloth, wht linen w/embr cutwork butterflies, oval, 1900s, 21x12"..70.00

Lalique

Having recognized her son's talent at an early age, René Lalique's mother apprenticed him at the age of 21 to a famous Parisian jeweler. In 1885 he opened his own workshop, and his unique style earned him great notoriety because of his use of natural elements in his designs — horn, ivory, semiprecious stone, pearls, coral, enamel, even plastic or glass.

In 1900 at the Paris Universal Exposition at the age of 40, he achieved the pinnacle of success in the jewelry field. Already having experimented with glass, he decided to focus his artistic talent on that medium. In 1907 after completing seven years of laborious work, Lalique became a master glassmaker and designer of perfume bottles for Francois Coty, a chemist and perfumer, who was also his neighbor in the Place Vendome area in Paris. All in all he created over 250 perfume bottles for Roger et Gallet, Coty, Worth, Forvil, Guerlain, D'Orsay, Molinard, and many others. In the commercial perfume bottle collecting field, René Lalique's are those most desired. Some of his one-of-a-kind experimental models have gone for over $100,000.00 at auction in the last few years. At the height of production his factories employed over 600 workers.

Seeking to bring art into every day life, he designed clocks, tableware, stemware, chandeliers, inkwells, bowls, statues, dressing table items, and, of course, vases. Lalique's unique creativity is evident in his designs through his polishing, frosting, and glazing techniques. He became famous for his use of colored glass in shades of blue, red, black, gray, yellow, green, and opalescence. His glass, so popular in the 1920s and 1930s, is still coveted today.

Lalique's son Marc assumed leadership of the company in 1948, after his father's death. His designs are made from full lead crystal, not the demi-crystal Rene worked with. Designs from 1948 on were signed only Lalique, France. The company was later taken over by Marc's daughter, Marie-Claude, and her designs were modern, clear crystal accented with color motifs. The Lalique company was sold in 1995, and Marie-Claude Lalique retired shortly thereafter.

Condition is of extreme importance to a collector. Grinding, polished out chips, and missing perfume bottle stoppers can reduce the value significantly, sometimes by as much as 80%.

Czechoslovakian glassware bearing fradulent Lalique signatures is appearing on all levels of the market. Study and become familiar with the various Lalique designs before paying a high price for a fraudulent piece. Over the past five years Lalique-designed glass has been showing up in a deep purple-gray color. These are clear glass items that have been 'irradiated' to change their appearance. Buyer beware. Our advisor for this category is John Danis; he is listed in the Directory under Illinois.

Key:
cl/fr — clear and frosted
L — signed Lalique
LF — signed Lalique France

RL — signed R. Lalique
RLF — signed R. Lalique, France

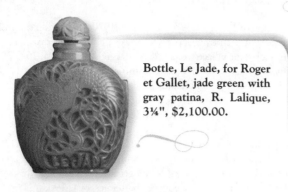

Bottle, Le Jade, for Roger et Gallet, jade green with gray patina, R. Lalique, 3¼", $2,100.00.

Bottle, Bouquet de Faunes, sepia wash, urn shape, 4" 1,100.00
Bottle, Nenuphar, cl/fr w/gr wash, RLF #492, 1911, 4½" 3,950.00
Bottle, Semis de Fleurs, cl w/blk enamel, 2¾" 1,550.00
Bottle, Sirene, cl w/bl wash, 1927, 5" 57,000.00
Bowl, Dauphins, dolphins swimming, cl/opal, RLF, 9¼" 925.00
Bowl, Nemours, floral, brn wash w/blk enamel, RLF, 10" 1,000.00
Bowl, Phalenes, butterflies/flowers, wht opal, RLF, 15⅛" 6,000.00
Box, children, cl w/brn wash, fr stopper, RLF, 4x3½" dia, NM ..1,375.00
Box, powder; Vaucluse, birds/leaves, cl/fr w/sepia wash, 2¾" dia ...1,200.00
Carafe, Masque, cl w/amber-brn wash to masks, RL, 10" 2,300.00
Chandelier, Trevise, cl/fr, brass fleur-de-lis hanger, RLF, 12x16" dia .2,875.00
Clock, Moineaux, birds, cl/fr w/sepia wash, orig face, 6½x8½" ..2,400.00

Clock, Roitelets, clear and frosted with black enamel numerals, 7½", $4,300.00. (Photo courtesy David Rago Auctions)

Clock, Sirenes, cl/fr, RLF, ca 1928, 10¼x10¾" 14,200.00
Inkwell, Serpents, dk amber opal, RL, ca 1920, 6¼" dia............4,250.00
Inkwell, Syrenes, nudes, bl wash, 2x6" 2,585.00
Jar, Cariatides, stylized nudes, cl/smoky gray fr, RLF #924, 8" ...2,875.00
Lamp base, nudes, fr w/gold, RL, 18¾" 1,150.00
Mascot, Archer, cl/fr, RL, ca 1926, 4¾" 2,500.00
Mascot, Coq Nain, rooster, cl/fr, RLF, ca 1928, 8" 900.00
Mascot, Longchamp, horse head, cl/fr, blk base, RL/RLF, 1929, 6" L..10,800.00
Mascot, Petite Libellule, insect, cl/fr, ca 1928, 6¼" L 10,800.00
Mascot, St Christophe, cl/fr, RL, ca 1928, 4½" 1,200.00
Menu holder, Faune, cl/fr w/sepia wash, RLF, ca 1928, 5½" 840.00
Menu plaque, Raisin Muscat, cl/fr, ca 1924, RL, 6" L 270.00
Mirror, Deux Chevres, cl/fr w/sepia wash, orig fr, ca 1919, L, 6" dia ...1,000.00
Plaffonier, floral & foliage on fr, drilled, Lalique, 12" dia 925.00
Rose bowl, Houpes, pompoms, lt amber on fr, RL, 5x7½" 1,300.00
Statuette, Chat Couche, cat, cl/fr, 4½x9¼" 3,600.00
Statuette, nude kneeling w/grapes, brn wash, RLF, 8" 1,725.00
Statuette, Sirene, opal, RL/RLF, ca 1920, 4" 3,350.00
Statuette, stag, cl/fr, LF, 10¼x8¼" 800.00
Statuette, Vierge a L'Enfant, cl/fr, RLF, wooden base, 15" 1,200.00
Vase, Ajaccio, gazelles & stars, cl/fr, LF, 7⅞" 1,025.00
Vase, Archer, cl/fr w/olive gr wash, RL, 10½" 12,000.00
Vase, Avallon, birds & berries, cobalt wash, RLF, 5¾x6¼" 2,525.00
Vase, Avallon, birds & berries, opal w/gr wash, RL, ca 1927, 6" ...3,500.00
Vase, Bacchus, centaur among ivy, gray wash, RLF, 7" 2,300.00

Vase, Bacchus, cl/fr w/gray wash, RLF, 7" 2,300.00
Vase, Bagatelle, birds/vines, cl/fr w/gray wash, RLF, 6¾" 1,450.00
Vase, Bordure Epines, cl/fr w/sepia wash, RL, 8" 3,000.00
Vase, Borneo, birds, cl/fr w/gr enamel, ca 1930, RLF, 9¼" 3,400.00
Vase, Bresse, turq opal, spherical, RLF, ca 1931, 3½" 3,900.00
Vase, Canards, cased butterscotch opal w/wht wash, RLF, 5½" .4,200.00
Vase, Ceylon, parakeets, cl opal/fr w/brn wash, RL, 9½" 9,000.00
Vase, Chamarande, thistles, floral hdls, dk smoky brn, RL, 7½", EX ..480.00
Vase, Coqs et Plumes, roosters, cl/fr w/bl-gr patina, cylindrical, 6" .2,100.00
Vase, Courges, electric bl, bulbous, RL, ca 1914, 7" 12,000.00
Vase, Courlis, birds, dk gr w/wht wash, RLF, ca 1931, 6½" 8,400.00
Vase, Domremy, flower heads, emerald gr, RLF, ca 1926, 8" 7,200.00
Vase, Druides, berries & stems, dbl-cased jade gr opal, bulbous, 7" ...5,150.00
Vase, Dursin, cl/fr w/bl wash, RLF, 7¼" 1,700.00
Vase, Emilion, birds, fr w/lt gr wash, RLF, 10", NM 4,000.00
Vase, Epis, ribbed panels, cl w/bl wash, RLF, 6½" 1,150.00
Vase, Fougeres, floral, cl w/bl wash, bulbous, RL, 6" 3,600.00
Vase, Gui, berries & vines, gr, bulbous, RL, 6½" 4,800.00
Vase, Malines, vertical bands, fr w/bl wash, RLF #957, 4¾" 1,325.00

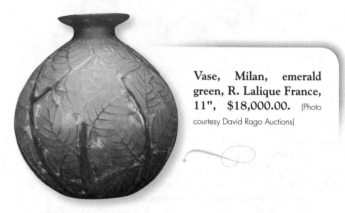

Vase, Milan, emerald green, R. Lalique France, 11", $18,000.00. (Photo courtesy David Rago Auctions)

Vase, Milan, leafy branches, cl/fr dk amber, RL, 11x9½" 11,500.00
Vase, Monnaie du Pape, leaves, dk amber w/orange overtones, RL, 9" ...8,400.00
Vase, Nefliers, leaves/flowers, cl w/bl wash, RLF #940, 5½" 1,400.00
Vase, Ormeaux, leaves, smoky gray, bottle neck, RLF #984, 6½" ..1,140.00
Vase, Ornis, birds, cl w/opal birds & ft, RL, 7¼" 4,600.00
Vase, Penthievre, fish, gray, bulbous, RLF, ca 1926, 10" 16,700.00
Vase, Perruches, parakeets, bl-gray wash, bulbous, 10", NM 7,000.00
Vase, Pinsons, birds & berries, cl/fr, RL, 7½x9" 575.00
Vase, Rampillon, leaves, opal, RLF, ca 1927, 4½" 3,150.00
Vase, Rennes, animals w/curled horns, cl w/med gr wash, 4⅞" ..1,380.00
Vase, Roses, cl/fr, RLF, 9", NM 4,200.00
Vase, Sauterelles, grasshoppers, cl/fr w/bl-gr wash, RL, 10¾" 9,000.00
Vase, Sirenes Avec Bouchon Figurine, nude stopper, cl/fr, RLF, 14" ..13,200.00
Vase, Soudan, gazelles, fr w/brn wash, bulbous, RLF, 6¾" 2,875.00
Vase, Spirals, zipper edge, cl w/peach wash, RLF, 6½", NM.......4,800.00
Vase, St Francois, birds on branches, fr & opal w/lt bl wash, RLF, 7" ..3,165.00
Vase, St Francois, birds/branches, lt bl wash, RLF, 7" 2,875.00
Vase, St Tropez, stems & berries, opal, RLF, 7⅜" 2,300.00
Vase, Tournesols, electric bl, RLF, ca 1926, 4½", NM................3,150.00

Lamps

The earliest lamps were simple dish containers with a wick that hung over the edge or was supported by a channel or tube. Grease and oil from animal or vegetable sources were the first fuels used. Ancient pottery lamps, crusie, and Betty lamps are examples of these early types. In 1784 Swiss inventor Ami Argand introduced the first major improvement in lamps. His lamp featured a tubular wick and a glass chimney. During the first half of the nineteenth century, whale oil, burning fluid (a highly explosive mixture of turpentine and alcohol) and lard were the most common fuels used in North America. Many lamps were patented for specific use with these fuels.

Kerosene was the first major breakthrough in lighting fuels. It was demonstrated by Canadian geologist Dr. Abraham Gesner in 1846. The discovery and drilling of petroleum in the late 1850s provided an abundant and inexpensive supply of kerosene. It became the main source of light for homes during the balance of the nineteenth century and for remote locations until the 1950s.

Although Thomas A. Edison invented the electric lamp in 1879, it was not until two or three decades later that electric lamps replaced kerosene household lamps. Millions of kerosene lamps were made for every purpose and pocketbook. They ranged in size from tiny night or miniature lamps to tall stand or piano lamps. Hanging varieties for homes commonly had one or two fonts (oil containers), but chandeliers for churches and public buildings often had six or more. Wall or bracket lamps usually had silvered reflectors. Student lamps, parlor lamps (now called Gone-With-the-Wind lamps), and patterned glass lamps were designed to complement the popular furnishing trends of the day. Gaslight, introduced in the early nineteenth century, was used mainly in homes of the wealthy and public places until the early twentieth century. Most fixtures were wall or ceiling mounted, although some table models were also used.

Few of the ordinary early electric lamps have survived. Many lamp manufacturers made the same or similar styles for either kerosene or electricity, sometimes for gas. Top-of-the-line lamps were made by Pairpoint, Tiffany, Bradley and Hubbard, and Handel. See also these specific sections.

When buying lamps that have been converted to electricity, inspect them very carefully for any damage that may have resulted from the alterations; such damage is very common, and when it does occur, the lamp's value may be lessened by as much as 50%. Lamps seem to bring much higher prices in some areas than others, especially the larger cities. Conversely, in rural areas they may bring only half as much as our listed values. One of our advisors for lamps is Carl Heck; he is listed in the Directory under Colorado. Jeff Bradfield (in Virginia) is our advisor for pattern glass lamps. See also Stained Glass.

Note: When only one color is given in a two-layer cut overlay lamp description, the second layer is generally clear; in three-layer examples, the second will ususally be white, the third clear. Exceptions will be noted.

Key: col — cut overlay

Aladdin Lamps, Electric

From 1908 Aladdin lamps with a mantle became the mainstay of rural America, providing light that compared favorably with the electric light bulb. They were produced by the Mantle Lamp Company of America in over 18 models and more than 100 styles. During the 1930s to the 1950s, this company was the leading manufacturer of electric lamps as well. Still in operation today, the company is now known as Aladdin Mantle Lamp Co., located in Clarksville, Tennessee. For those seeking additional information on Aladdin Lamps, we recommend *Aladdin — The Magic Name in Lamps, Aladdin Electric Lamps Collector's Manual & Price Guide #5,* and *Aladdin Collector's Manual and Price Guide #22,* all written by our advisor for Aladdins, J. W. Courter; he is listed in the Directory under Kentucky. Mr. Courter has also written *Angle Lamps, Collector's Manual and Price Guide* and *Center-draft Kerosene Lamps.*

Bedroom, P-51, ceramic	25.00
Boudoir, G-40, Alacite, 1952	40.00
Boudoir, M-123, metal figurine	175.00
Figurine, G-16, lady, crystal, etched	700.00
Figurine, G-234, pheasant	275.00
Pin-up, G-352, Panel & Scroll, Alacite	100.00

Pin-up, P-057, Gun-n-Holster, ceramic, EX	125.00
Ranch House, G-378C, Bullet, Alacite, lit/decaled urn, EX, $350 to	400.00
Table, E-200, Vogue Ped, gr	375.00
Table, G-2, marble-like glass, from $300 to	350.00
Table, G-223, Alacite, from $75 to	100.00
Table, G-309, Alacite, illuminated base, tall harp, from $70 to	90.00
Table, P-408, planter lamp, ceramic, from $40 to	50.00
TV, M-384, shell, ceramic, from $40 to	60.00
TV, MT-520, cherry & brass base, NM, from $400 to	500.00

Aladdin Lamps, Kerosene

Values are for kerosene lamps with correct burners.

Crystal Vase Model #12, variegated tan, 12"	175.00
Floor Model B, #1254, bronze & gold, 1933-35	175.00
Floor Model B-293, Antique Ivory lacquer, 1939-42, from $175 to	225.00
Foreign Table Model #8, London, NM	275.00
Hanging Model #2, w/#203 shade	450.00
Hanging Model #11 w/#516 shade, EX, from $250 to	300.00
Table Model #12 Florentine Vase, Rose Moonstone, EX, from $2,500 to	3,000.00
Table Model #21C, B-139, aluminum font, from $35 to	50.00
Table Model A Venetian, rose, EX, from $100 to	200.00
Table Model B-49 Washington Drape, amber crystal, bell stem, $275 to	350.00
Table Model B-80, Beehive, clear, from $80 to	100.00
Table Vertique, B-87, Pink Moonstone	450.00

Table, #1230-A, emerald green, $350.00. (Photo courtesy Tom Harris Auctions/LiveAuctioneers.com)

Wall bracket Model #2, from $400 to	450.00
Wall bracket Model #12, from $125 to	175.00

Angle Lamps

The Angle Lamp Company of New York City developed a unique type of kerosene lamp that was a vast improvement over those already on the market; they were sold from about 1896 until 1929 and were expensive for their time. Nearly all Angle lamps are hanging lamps and wall lamps. Table models are uncommon. Our Angle lamp advisor is J.W. Courter; he is listed in the Directory under Kentucky. See the narrative for Aladdin Lamps for information concerning popular books Mr. Courter has authored. Old glass pieces for Angle lamps are scarce to rare; unless noted otherwise, the lamp values that follow are for examples with no glass.

Gas adaptor, polished brass, old glass, EX	850.00
Glass, chimney top, wht, petal-top, EX	85.00

Glass, chimney top, wht, ribbed, EX 75.00
Glass, elbow globe, clear w/floral bouquet hand, EX 250.00
Hanging, #254, rose floral, 2-burner, polished brass, lamp only, EX....1,000.00
Hanging, #263, polished brass, old glass, EX 475.00
Hanging, #352, Fleur-de-Lis, polished brass, 3 milk glass chimneys....850.00
Hanging, Classic, antique gold, cast tank, 2-burner, NM 2,250.00
Hanging, Leaf & Vine, 2-burner, nickel, EX 400.00

Brass ring tiers w/cut prisms & ball drop, top 2 tiers w/openwork, 36" .. 400.00
Bronze patina, 5 arms w/pendant shades+5 w/bowl shades, 55x32" ...3,500.00
Bronzed metal w/grapevines/cornucopias/etc, 6-light, gasolier, 60x36" ...2,235.00
Cast fr w/swags, 5-socket, concentric prism tiers, 19x19" 500.00
Copper/iron, 4 caramel slag lined lanterns, unmk, 38x17" 1,025.00
Frosted etched globes (4), copper patina scrolls/foliage, 34x19" .. 200.00
Wht satin quatrefoil shades w/HP birds, 5-arm, 35x32" 575.00

Hanging, with two milk glass chimneys, $250.00. (Photo courtesy Tom Harris Auctions/LiveAuctioneers.com)

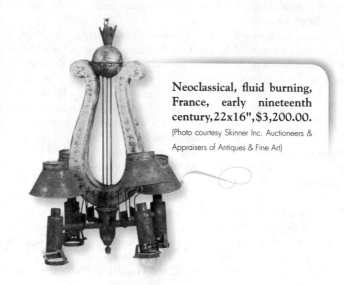

Neoclassical, fluid burning, France, early nineteenth century, 22x16", $3,200.00. (Photo courtesy Skinner Inc. Auctioneers & Appraisers of Antiques & Fine Art)

Hanging, 4-burner, emb brass font, milk glass shades, 18x18" ...1,450.00
Wall, #103, plain can, nickel, EX 150.00
Wall, #185, pinwheel, antique brass, EX 400.00
Wall, Classic #3, antique gold, cast tank, no glass, EX 1,200.00
Wall, MW 966-NF, Leaf & Vine, nickel, 2-burner, EX 350.00
Wall cone, #101, tin, blk pnt, no glass, EX 150.00

Banquet

Col (2-layer), bl, Moorish Windows/Quatrefoil & Punty, Sandwich, 20". 7,975.00
Col (2-layer), gr, cut/frosted 5" shade, #2 Jones burner, 30¾" .11,000.00
Col (2-layer), opal to cranberry, floral cut globe, ormolu base, 20"..425.00

Decorated Kerosene Lamps

Cut overlay, red to white, 12½", $500.00. (Photo courtesy Jackson's International Auctioneers & Appraisers of Fine Art & Antiques/ LiveAuctioneers.com)

Cranberry with cut overlay standard, 25", $1,450.00. (Photo courtesy Cordier Antiques & Fine Art/ LiveAuctioneers.com)

Col (2-layer), cobalt to clear, Punty, stepped marble base, 8¼".... 720.00
Col (2-layer), ruby to clear, floral, marble base, 9" 780.00
Col (2-layer), wht to clear, cobalt Baroque base, 9¾" 350.00
Col (2-layer), wht to clear, gr glass std, marble base, Sandwich, 14" ..480.00
Col (2-layer), wht to ruby, Moorish Windows, 9¾" 350.00
Col (2-layer), wht to ruby, Oval & Punty w/gold, Sandwich, 13½" ...720.00
Col (2-layer), wht to ruby, Punty & Oval, wht base, 12x4¼" 660.00

Poppies emb on red satin, brass fittings, CI base/claw ft, 1890s, 26" .1,250.00
Violet-bl opaque base, clambroth font, scalloped ft, 15" 300.00

Fairy Lamps

Chandeliers

Bl to wht frost w/deep ruffles, matching low base, 6½" 345.00
Burmese, petticoat skirt on matching base, missing cup, 6¼" 345.00
Burmese, prunus decor, S Clarke Pat Trademk on cup, 5¼" ...1,150.00
Cameo, citron/wht/red floral, Irish Pat No 23195, 5¼" 3,000.00
Brass, 10 candle lights above 5 pendants w/frosted shades, 44x32" .. 500.00
Dmn-cut dome w/pressed tiered & ribbed base, Clarke, 5½x6¼", EX...145.00
Nailsea, bl/wht, upright ribbon-rim base, missing cup, 6x8¼", EX ..115.00

Nailsea, citron, insert marked S. Clarke Trademark Fairy, 5", $600.00. (Photo courtesy Early Auction Co.)

Cranberry, diamond quilted pattern, 14", $300.00. (Photo courtesy Early Auction Co.)

Nailsea, citron/wht, ruffled base, missing cup, 6½" 500.00
Nailsea, cranberry/wht, ruffled base, 5½x9" 700.00
Nailsea, wht/clear, upright ribbon-rim base, missing cup, 5x5½"... 550.00
Pk satin w/4 jewels, fluted base, 5¾", EX........................ 115.00
Raspberry satin, Dmn Quilt, ribbon-edge base, missing cup, 5½".. 145.00
Rose Tiente Pinwheel, Baccarat Depose, 4¼", EX 230.00

Gone-With-the-Wind Lamps

Floral on wht to pk ball shade & base, rpl mts, electrified, 32" 165.00
Gilt chinoiserie on gr to yel ball shade & base, gilt-metal mts, 24".. 350.00
Gr satin w/emb octagons on ball shade & base, 23" 900.00
Milk glass w/HP floral on ball shade & base, ca 1875, 19"........... 110.00

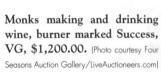

Monks making and drinking wine, burner marked Success, VG, $1,200.00. (Photo courtesy Four Seasons Auction Gallery/LiveAuctioneers.com)

Peonies HP on wht to pk ball shade & base, gilt metal mts, 1880s, 27"...240.00
Red opaque w/HP floral on ball shade & base, 21" 120.00
Roses on gr shaded to yel on ball shade & base, gilt metal mts, 27" ...600.00

Hanging Lamps

Brass w/lighted jewels, electrified, 15" dia 480.00
Cranberry hobnail, clear font, prisms, 36x14"........................ 150.00
Cranberry hobnail shade, brass font, 46x14" 800.00
Floral on milk glass, gilt mts, prisms, electrified 200.00
Gr shade w/HP floral, emb brass font, 43x14" 450.00
Library, HP floral on milk glass, prisms, 1870s-80s, 38" 110.00
Library, pk cased, gilt mts, prisms, 1870-80, 41" 480.00
Wht opaque shade w/HP floral, aqua glass font, urns on fr, 41x14".. 325.00
Wht opaque shade w/HP lilies, aqua glass font, 39x14"............... 285.00
Wht opaque w/yel blush, couple transfer, brass font, 39x14"........ 465.00
Yel shade w/leaves transfer, pressed glass font, 38x14" 450.00

Lanterns

Brass bell shape w/blown & etched globe, 1800s, 18x9¾" 900.00
CI & tin, Kinnear's Pat Feb 4 1851, 8½x6"........................ 66.00
Clear bulbous globe w/wrought-iron fr, hangs from 3 chains, 20".. 180.00
Skater's, bl glass, brass mts, bail hdl, 6" 215.00
Tin, 4 glass panes, peaked top w/vents, ring hdl, 9" 250.00
Tin base/top w/punched stars, glass globe, tin font w/burner, 12".. 175.00
Tin w/glass onion globe, pierced top, 9"+hdl 385.00
Wooden post fr, staple hinges, punched tin, 13" 650.00

Lard Oil/Grease Lamps

Betty, dbl; iron, removable pan, Am, ca 1760, 6x4¼" 395.00
Betty, iron, shield crest w/2 Xd hammers, twisted hanger, 5", G .. 285.00
Betty, wrought iron, w/hanger, 3¾", +trn tidy w/gallery rim, 5⅜".. 635.00
Bronze, lions/bearded male masks, dolphin arms, hanger, 11x12x12"...215.00
Earthenware, brn slip, saucer base, appl ear hdl, 8" 250.00
Iron, fluted pan, 5" spout, w/hook for hanging, 1770s, 6½" 300.00
Iron, spike w/pear-shaped pan, Am, ca 1750, 11" H 215.00
Iron, 4-spout, eyelet for hanging, Am, 1750s, 6x3½"..................... 180.00
Pewter, saucer base, appl hdl, dents, 10½x6½"................................ 85.00
Stoneware, gr w/strap hdl & saucer base, 3½", EX 850.00
Stoneware, 2-spout, strap hdl, saucer base, att Rouston, chip, 5½"...2,100.00
Tin, conical base, hollow stem, scroll finial, wick pick, 7"............ 300.00
Wrought iron, 2nd tier w/removable basin, minor pitting, 13" 400.0

Miniature Lamps, Kerosene

Miniature oil lamps were originally called 'night lamps' by their manufacturers. Early examples were very utilitarian in design — some holding only enough oil to burn through the night. When kerosene replaced whale oil in the second half of the nineteenth century, 'mini' lamps became more decorative and started serving other purposes. While mini lamps continue to be produced today, collectors place special value on the lamps of the kerosene era, roughly 1855 to 1910. Four reference books are especially valuable to collectors as they try to identify and value their collections: *Miniature Lamps* by Frank and Ruth Smith, Schiffer Publishing, 1968 (referred to as SI); *Miniature Lamps II* by Ruth Smith, Schiffer Publishing, 1982 (SII); *Miniature Victorian Lamps* by Marjorie Hulsebus (source of the H numbers below), Schiffer Publishing, 1996; and *Price Guide for Miniature Lamps* by Marjorie Hulsebus, Schiffer Publishing. References in the following listings correlate with each lamp's plate number in these books.

Amethyst w/wht floral & gold, Hornet burner, S1-262 variant, 8¾"..350.00
Bl, snowflake silver filigree, Nutmeg burner, S1-474, 7", VG 1,035.00
Bl Hobnail, Nutmeg burner, S1-477, 7½" 635.00
Bl opal swirl, clear ft, Nutmeg burner, S1-513, 8"....................2,100.00
Bl opaque w/mc floral, Foreign burner, S1-350, 7½" 635.00
Bl satin MOP, Raindrop, frosted ft, Nutmeg burner, S1-602, 7¾" ...925.00
Bl shoe w/appl hdl, Hornet burner, S1-51, 3" to top of collar, EX ..3,185.00
Chartreuse satin w/emb decor, Nutmeg burner, S1-570, 8¾" 925.00
Cobalt col, berries & leaves, Hornet burner, S2-413, 9¼"............230.00
Columbus, milk glass, Nutmeg burner, S1-491, 10"...................8,625.00
Cosmos, pk cased w/emb flowers, Nutmeg burner, S1-286, 7½"...300.00
Cranberry Snowflake, Nutmeg burner, S1-473, 7"....................1,265.00
Cranberry w/optic ribs/silver filigree, Nutmeg burner, S2-253, 7"..1,725.00
Custard w/emb panels, Dutch scenes, Hornet burner, S1-215, 7¾"..285.00

Eagle, SI-275, $425.00.

Elephant figural, porc w/mc pnt, mk RD 10261, S1-329, 5¼" 700.00
Gold to clear overshot, Tulip, Nutmeg burner, S1-287, 8¼" 520.00
Gr w/mc & gold decor, Foreign burner, S1-584, 9¾" 1,725.00
Lady Fox base, porc, brn glass eyes, S2-321, 7" 700.00
Log cabin, bl opaline, Hornet burner, S1-50, 3½" to top of collar ..1,380.00
Lt gr textured w/rose & flowers, Foreign burner, S2-480, 7¼" 725.00
Mc spatter, cased/beaded swirl, Hornet burner, S1-369, 8½", VG ...150.00
Milk glass, pnt owl on ball shade, Acorn burner, S1-348, 9"........635.00
Milk glass w/fired-on decor, Harrison 1892, S2-252, 9½" 575.00
Milk glass w/fired-on pk & brn, Hornet burner, S1-218, 9½" 300.00
Milk glass w/mc floral, Hornet burner, S1-218, 9¼" 345.00
Peachblow conical shade, SP base, Foreign burner, S2-429, 9" 350.00
Pk cased w/emb design, Hornet burner, S1-374, 8½"..................1,150.00
Pk opaline, 5 crystal ft, Nutmeg burner, S1-536, 8½", NM 1,150.00
Red satin, Artichoke, S1-figure III, 8"...175.00
Red satin w/emb panels/flowers, Nutmeg burner, S1-399, 8"........250.00
Salmon cased, Hobnail, leaf ft, Foreign burner, S1-566, 11", VG ...575.00
Santa Claus, milk glass w/red & gray pnt, Acorn burner, S2-349, 9¼".5,465.00
Shoe, amber, Pat emb on sole, Hornet burner, S1-51, 3" to collar..1,035.00
Shoe, bl, Atterbury, Hornet burner, S1-51, 3" to top of collar ..2,185.00
Spatter, beaded ribs, Hornet burner, S1-378, 9", NM 345.00
Wht satin MOP, Raindrop, Nutmeg burner, S1-600, 7¾" 1,150.00
Yel cased pansy ball shade & melon-rib base, Nutmeg burner, S1-389, 7".460.00
Yel cased w/emb ribs & basket, Nutmeg burner, S1-279, 6¾" 360.00
Yel custard w/emb beads/boats/windmill/etc, Hornet burner, S1-215, VG...300.00

Moss Lamps

Moss lamps, a unique blend of Plexiglas and whimsical design, enjoyed their heyday during the 1940s and 1950s. Created by Moss Mfg. Co. of San Francisco, the lamps were the brainchild of company co-owner Thelma Moss and principal designers Duke Smith and John Disney. Plexiglas was initially used to offset World War II metal rationing, but its

adaptability and translucence made it an ideal material for the imaginative and angular Moss designs. Adding to the novelty of Moss lamps were oversize 'spun glass' shades and revolving platforms which held figurines by many top ceramic firms of the day, including Hedi Schoop, Ceramic Arts Studio, Lefton, and Dorothy Kindell. Later additions to the Moss lamp line incorporated everything from clocks and music boxes to waterwheels and operating fountains. The 'Moss Fish Tank Bar' even combined the functions of lamp, aquarium, and bar, all in one unit!

Moss ceased production in 1968, but the company's lamps remain in great demand today, as eye-catching accent pieces for retro decorating schemes. Moss lamps are also cross-collectibles, for those interested in figural ceramics. For further information we recommend *Moss Lamps: Lighting the '50s* (Schiffer) by Donald-Brian Johnson and Leslie Piña. Mr. Johnson is our advisor for this category; he is listed in the Directory under Nebraska.

#T 476, Siamese Dancer (deLee), 33", from $200 to 225.00
#T 544, Bell Girl corner table lamp, 3 pod shades, 34", from $300 to. 325.00
#T 569, hanging lantern 'birdcage' style, 28", from $225 to 250.00
#T 617, Rhumba Dancer on base, 34", from $200 to...................225.00
#T 688, Leaf lamp, late 1940s, 27", from $75 to 100.00
#T 690, Woman w/2 Lanterns (att J Manley) table lamp, 31½", $175 to..200.00
#T 731, Prom Girl (Decoramic) table lamp, 43½", from $300 to. 325.00
#T 744, lady figurine revolves, spun glass shade, 34", from $175 to..200.00
#XT 801, Mambo, Oriental lady on base, 34", from $175 to........200.00
#XT 806, Poodle Girl (H Schoop), revolving platform, 31½", $275 to..300.00
#XT 808, Lantern Man (Hedi Schoop) table lamp, 32", from $250 to ..275.00
#XT 809, Water Man (Ceramic Arts Studio), 28", from $350 to. 375.00

#XT 815, Siamese Dancer (deLee) clock lamp, 35", from $200.00 to $225.00. (Photo by Leslie Piña from *Moss Lamps: Lighting the '50s*, Schiffer)

#XT 821, Egyptian lady on base, 32", from $200 to.......................225.00
#XT 826, turbaned man w/scimitar on base, fringed shade, 31", $125 to.150.00
#XT 827, Marilyn figure on base, stary Plexi, 32", from $375 to ..400.00
#XT 838, Mambo, lady on 2-tier base, 42½", from $325 to..........350.00
#XT 848, pk & blk Plexi, lady on base, music box, 33", from $250 to ..275.00
#XT 855, Temple Dancer, wht & gold, music box, 27", from $275 to ..300.00
#1, aquarium/cocktail table/lamp, 16x50", from $700 to..............800.00
#55 A, Tami, Oriental scene, 46", from $50 to 75.00
#2272, room divider w/spun glass gong, 64", from $750 to........1,000.00
#2295, Comedy/Tragedy floor lamp, 60½", from $250 to..............275.00
#2306, floor lamp, 2 angled stems w/fluorescent tubes, 60", $225 to ...250.00
#2334, suspended cone shade & angled gold lace Plexi, 68", $500 to. 525.00
#2355, room divider w/hanging birdcage center, from $1,000 to......1,200.00
#2369, floor-to-ceiling lamp w/2 spun glass balls, 8-9' ext, $425 to......450.00
#3016, clock combo w/pendulum on triangular bk, 8-day, from $325 to..350.00

Motion Lamps

Animated motion lamps were made as early as 1920 and as late as the 1980s. They reached their peak during the 1950s when plastic became widely used. They are characterized by action created by the heat of a light bulb which causes the cylinder to revolve and create the illusion of an animated scene. Some of the better-known manufacturers were Econolite Corp., Scene in Action Corp., and LA Goodman Mfg. Co. As with many collectible items, prices are guided by condition, availability, and collector demand. Collectors should be aware that reproductions of lamps featuring cars, trains, sailing ships, fish, and mill scenes are being made. Values are given for original lamps in mint condition. Any damage or flaws seriously reduce the price. As has been true in many areas of collecting, internet auctions have affected the prices of motion lamps. Erratic ups and downs in prices realized have resulted in a market that is often unpredictible. Our advisors for motion lamps are Kaye and Jim Whitaker; they are listed in the Directory under Washington.

Advertising, Beer, Black Shell, various, 13", ea 50.00
Advertising, 7-Up, 13".. 75.00
Bar Is Open, various designs, 13", ea.. 50.00
Econolite, child's lamp, various carousel styles, 10", ea 85.00
Econolite, Fireplace, Potbelly Stove, blk or silver, 1958, 11" 145.00
Econolite, Fish (Salt Water), #752, 11" 110.00
Econolite, Fountain of Youth, #861, 11" 95.00
Econolite, Fountains of Versailles, #758, 11" 200.00
Econolite, Hawaiian Scene, #701, 11" 175.00
Econolite, Jet Planes, #774, 11"... 250.00
Econolite, Oriental Garden, #703, 11".. 165.00
Econolite, Picture Frame style, various scenes, ea.......................... 95.00
Econolite, Seattle World's Fair, 1962, 11" 170.00
Econolite, Train, #763, 11"... 110.00
Econolite, Waterski, #771, 11" 275.00
LA Goodman, Davy Crockett 150.00
LA Goodman, fish, flowers, butterflies or geese in bowl, bl, w/top, ea. 125.00
LA Goodman, Forest Fire, #2003, 11" 65.00
LA Goodman, Ship/Lighthouse, 11"... 110.00
LA Goodman, Trains, 1950s, 11" 95.00
National Co, Winter Scene, 13" 195.00
Roto-Vue Jr, Econolite, Fountain of Youth, 10"............................. 95.00

Roto-Vue Jr, Econolite, Niagara Falls, $55.00. (Photo courtesy Tom Harris Auctions/ LiveAuctioneers.com)

Roto-Vue Jr, Merry Go Round, red, yel or bl, 1949, 10"................. 90.00
Scene in Action, Forest Fire, 10" 125.00
Scene in Action, Japanese Twilight, 13" 150.00
Scene in Action, Niagara Falls, 10" 100.00
Scene in Action, Ship/Lighthouse, 1931, 10"................................ 135.00

Pattern Glass Lamps

The letter/number codes in the following descriptions refer to *Oil Lamps, Books I, II,* and *III,* by Catherine Thuro (book, page, item number or letter). Our advisor for this section is Jeff Bradfield who is listed in the Directory under Virginia.

Acorn, fine-rib bkground, 1860s, T2-67g, 9" 300.00
Aquarius, lt bl, US Glass, T1-315e, 8⅛" 175.00
Atterbury Buckle, iron base, T1-136a, 7⅞".................................... 150.00
Birch Leaf, iron stem base, T1-173g, 8⅝".................................... 175.00
Blackberry, bl alabaster/clambroth, wht 1-step glass ft, T1-116A, 8"..660.00
Butterfly & Anchor, T2-102a 325.00
Clarissa, 3-pc straw-holder style, P&A Victor burner, T1-pg 285, 17"..360.00
Coin Dot, wht opal, flat hand lamp, T1-152a, 2⅞"....................... 400.00
Diamond Band & Shield, T1-102b, 3¼", minimum value 150.00
Essex, broad rib font, leaded glass base, T1-90c, 6¼" 75.00
Eye Winker T'print w/Oval Window font, T1-250e, 10¼".............. 75.00
Fleur-de-Lis & Tassel, US Glass, T1-315g, 8½", minimum value ... 70.00
Gothic, marble base, 1850s, 7½" 300.00
Harmony w/Round font, after 1800, T1-262a, 8", minimum value ..40.00
Heart & Thumbprint, gr opaque, stand lamp, T2-103o, 9½" 300.00
Hearts & Stars, color, T1-145g, 10¼" 950.00
Herringbone Band, pre-1880, T1-96d, 9", minimum value 75.00
Inverted Teardrop Band, Bridges, T1-188a, 12" 150.00
Loop & Dart & Heart, T2-36f, 10⅝".. 275.00
Paneled Fern, pre-1880, T1-100a, 8⅞".. 75.00
Princess Feather, cobalt, T1-279i, 9½" (+) 475.00
Princess Feather, wht opaque, 1880-1900, T1-279i, 9½".............. 400.00
Queen Heart, gr, Pat 1877, finger lamp, 1890s, T1-252b, 3¾" 215.00
Ribbed Loop, gem base, T1-139j, 10⅞".. 125.00
Ring Punty, leaded glass base, T1-85a, 8⅝" 160.00
Riverside Ring & Rib, T2-111j, 8¼" 125.00
Roulette, T2-114a, 8½" 125.00
Scalloped Rib Band, pre-1880, T1-94a, 10¾"................................ 350.00
Scalloped Ribbon Band, 1880-1900, T1-290a, 7¼" 85.00
Semi-circle Rib & Jewel, T1-143d, 8½"... 100.00
Sheldon Swirl, blk stem, 1880-1900, T1-287, 8¾" 250.00
Shield w/Diagonal Bars, T2-98b... 300.00
Stippled Fishscale & Rib, 1880-1900, T1-278d, 9¼"....................... 70.00
Thousand Eye, amber, T1-214, 13¼" 250.00
Triple Flute & Bar, marble base, T1-160c, 11"............................. 200.00
Triple Scallop & Rib, iron stem base, T1-170a, 9⅞"..................... 125.00
Wave, amber Beaded Bar base, Atterbury, T1-140e, 9¼" 110.00
Wild Rose, carnival base, T2-120g..1,400.00

Peg Lamps

Bl Dmn Quilt MOP, 3-leg bird holder, Foreign burner, 13" 600.00
Col (2-layer), raspberry to wht, Oval & Punty, electrified, 26" ..1,080.00
Col (2-layer), wht to bl, Oval & Punty, electrified, 26¾".........1,200.00
Col (2-layer), wht to ruby, Oval/Punty/Vesica cuts, marble base, 26". 1,450.00
Pk cased, matching font, brass-plated ft, Foreign burner, 14½" 120.00
Pk Dmn Quilt MOP, SP holder w/3 winged dragons, Foreign burner, 12" ...700.00
Yel to cream satin w/emb swirls, marble ft, Foreign burner, 14½".. 285.00

Perfume Lamps

One catalog from the 1950s states that a perfume lamp 'precipitates and absorbs unpleasant tobacco smoke in closed rooms; freshens air in rooms, and is decorative in every home — can be used as a night lamp or television lamp.' An earlier advertisement reads 'an electric lamp that breathes delightful, delicate fragrance as it burns.' Perfume-burner lamps can be traced back to the earliest times of man. There has always been a desire to change, sweeten, or freshen air. Through the centuries the evolution of the perfume-burner lamp has had many changes in outer form, but very little change in function. Many designs of incense burners were used not only for the reasons mentioned here, but also in various ceremonies — as they still are to this day. Later, very fine perfume burners were designed and produced by the best glasshouses in Europe. Other media such as porcelain and metal also were used. It was not until the early part of the twentieth century that electric perfume lamps came into existence. Many lamps made by both American and European firms during the '20s and '30s are eagerly sought by collectors.

From the mid-1930s to the 1970s, there seems to have been an explosion in both the number of designs and manufacturers. This is especially true in Europe. Nearly every conceivable figure has been seen as a perfume lamp. Animals, buildings, fish, houses, jars, Oriental themes, people, and statuary are just a few examples. American import firms have purchased many different designs from Japan. These lamps range from replicas of earlier European pieces to original works. Except for an occasional article or section in reference books, very little has been written on this subject. The information contained in each of these articles generally covers only a specific designer, manufacturer, or country. To date, no formal group or association exists for this area of collecting.

Cat on pillow, brn & wht, porc, Germany, #12077, unwired, 6½" ..150.00
Deco children/butterflies, bronze & porc, 8" 480.00
Fulper, lady squatting, ruffled skirt, peach to wht, 6" 250.00
Fulper, masked lady in hoop skirt, #331, 13" 1,000.00
Lustre, pulled designs/threads, bronzed angels on finial/base, 15" ..1,000.00
Threaded/pulled feathers, att Durand, Pat Aug 28 23 USA, 10½" ... 425.00

Monkey, porcelain, crown over N mark, 7½", $440.00. (Photo courtesy Monsen & Baer)

Reverse-Painted Lamps

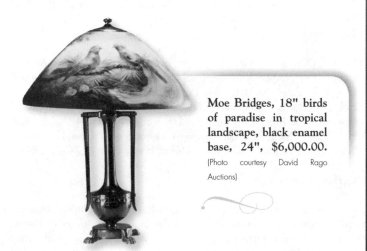

Moe Bridges, 18" birds of paradise in tropical landscape, black enamel base, 24", $6,000.00. (Photo courtesy David Rago Auctions)

Jefferson, rvpt landscape #2384OC shade; mk std w/verdigris, 22"...1,900.00
Jefferson, 14" house/trees/road #2909 shade; bronze std 900.00

Jefferson, 16" autumn scenic shade; bronze std, 21"...................1,325.00
Jefferson, 18" shade only, poppies/dragonflies/bees, #2614 ....5,400.00
Moe Bridges, 8" harbor scenic shade; bronzed std, 13" 780.00
Moe Bridges, 16" river scenic mk shade; mk bronzed std, 21"...1,675.00
Moe Bridges, 18" autumn scenic shade; mk bronzed std, 24" 960.00
Moe Bridges, 18" duck scenic mk shade; bronzed metal std, 23"..3,575.00
Moe Bridges, 18" landscape shade; bronzed metal std, 23" 2,900.00
Phoenix, 18" cabin scenic shade; mk 2-socket base, 24", EX.....1,725.00
Pittsburgh, piano, 9" moon/ocean waves shade; emb floral std, 12", EX..1,375.00
Unmk, 18" daisies & bees shade; bronzed metal std, 23" 3,600.00
Unmk, 18" sunset scenic shade; bronzed Nouveau std w/gr enamel, 22"..1,375.00

Student Lamps, Kerosene

Brass with pink cased melon-ribbed shade with crystal drops, 22x10", $720.00.

(Photo courtesy Early Auction Co.)

Brass w/gr swirl shade, oil burner, 20½".. 240.00
Dbl, brass w/wht Hobnail shades, 23x26x10"................................ 275.00
Dbl, bronze, emerald gr shades, Harvard, 1800s, 15x17" 1,800.00
Dbl, tin scrolled arms, pierced shades, saucer base, rpt, 19".......... 460.00
NP brass, clear shade, w/burner, Bridgeport Lamp Co, 1800s, 17". 240.00
SP brass, bl opaque shade, electrified, 19" 480.00
Tin candle socket & shade on wrought post w/brass ring, 20"...... 500.00
Tin socket, pierced shade, saucer base, blk rpt, rprs, 22"............... 375.00

TV Lamps

When TV viewing became a popular pastime during the 1940s, TV lamps were developed to provide just the right amount of light — not bright enough to compromise the sharpness of the picture, but just enough to prevent the eyestrain it was feared might result from watching TV in a darkened room. Most were made of ceramic, and many were figurals such as cats, owls, ducks and the like, or made in the shape of Conestoga wagons, sailing ships, seashells, etc. Some had shades and others were made as planters. Few were marked well enough to identify the maker without some study. *TV Lamps to Light the World* by John A. Shuman III (Collector Books) provides many photos and suggested value ranges for those who want more information. All lamps listed below are ceramic unless otherwise described. See also Maddux; Morton Pottery; Rosemeade; other specific manufacturers.

Bulldog w/flock coating, eyes glow, from $60 to.............................. 80.00
Cityscape, Deco style, 13x12", NM... 90.00
Deco horse head on front of planter, brn/gr wash, from $60 to 75.00
Donkey w/planter, wood base, Royal Haeger label, from $95 to... 105.00
Dove pr, bl w/gold speckles, orig plastic flowers, from $75 to 95.00
Duck flying, brn & turq, wooden base, from $82 to 97.00

Exotic bird w/planter, mc, from $85 to 100.00
Fanned feather-like form, wht marble Lucite, Roucier, 20x17" 55.00

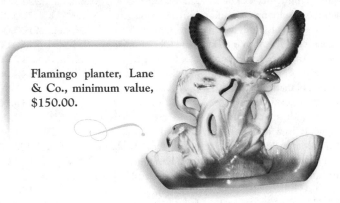

Flamingo planter, Lane & Co., minimum value, $150.00.

Gazelle leaping on grassy planter base, dk gr, from $70 to 90.00
Hawaiian girl's head & shoulders, vase at side, Lane, 9x9½" 850.00
Horse & colt, brn, from $85 to 90.00
Leaf, airbrushed plaster, from $35 to 55.00
Madonna & Child, plaster, bulb lights up faces, from $150 to 175.00
Male ballet dancer, plaster w/Fiberglas shade, Am Statuary, $85 to ..95.00
Matador, all wht, Lane of California 65.00
Owl, light-up eyes, Kron, from $75 to 100.00
Panther crouching, planter on bk, 22k gold decor, Royal China.. 150.00
Panther on rocks, blk, from $65 to 75.00
Rooster, gr, att Haeger, 14½", NM 75.00
Rooster w/rising sun, bl-gr, from $95 to 125.00
Sailboat, ftd brass base, Made in Calif, from 465 to 85.00
Sailfish on wave, mc pastels, Lane #8525, 12x11x5", NM 185.00
Siamese cats (2), rhinestone eyes, Lane, 13" 95.00
Siamese mother & 2 kittens, pnt eyes, Lane, 13" 180.00
Swan, gr, holes in wings light up, from $55 to 80.00
Swordfish leaping, blk & wht against pk, brass base holder, $75 to ..90.00

Whale Oil/Burning Fluid Lamps

Bristol glass, original oil font, 22", $300.00. (Photo courtesy Jackson's International Auctioneers & Appraisers of Fine Art & Antiques)

Aqua blown bulbous font, hollow shaft, dome base, 10¼" 360.00
Clear blown ball font w/pressed baluster/ft, 1850s, 11x4¾" 215.00
Clear blown bulb font, swollen shaft, tin drop burner, 10¼" 350.00
Clear blown bulbous font, ornate brass cap, 4-ftd glass base, 19" ... 150.00

Clear blown bulbous front w/everted rim, hollow shaft, tin burner, 7" .. 400.00
Clear blown font w/etch foliage, stepped sq base, 9¾x3½", EX 180.00
Clear blown ovoid font, patterned base, hand lamp, 6¾" 1,650.00
Clear blown pear-shaped font, lacy sq base, w/burner, 8½" 300.00
Cobalt blown font w/appl loop hdl, drop-in tin wick, att Sandwich, 4" ..5,400.00
Cobalt lobed font, brass column/marble plinth, missing burner, 11", pr..1,950.00
Col (2-layer), ruby, punty & oval, opal Baroque base, w/burner, 12" 1,400.00
Wht opaque blown ball font, conical stem, monument base, 1830s, 14" .259.99

Miscellaneous

Argand, brass, 2-arm, frosted shades, electrified, 1800s, 16x16" ... 480.00
Argand, polished brass, etched satin glass shade, bobeches, 22x12" ...575.00
Astral, brass fluted shaft, marble base, cut shade, electrified, 32" 2,400.00
Astral, Dbl Ring shade, prisms, porc base, 1860s, 28" 3,150.00
Astral Sinumbra, brass w/marble base, prisms, 19" 1,800.00

Metal overlay 18" shade; similar base, 25", $1,150.00.
(Photo courtesy Early Auction Co.)

Lang, Anton

    Anton Lang (1875 – 1938) was a German studio potter and an actor in the Oberammergau Passion Plays early in the twentieth century. Because he played the role of Christ three times, tourists brought his pottery back to the U.S. in suitcases, which accounts for the prevalence of smaller examples today. As the only son in the family, he took up his father's and grandfather's trade. Following the successful completion of an apprenticeship in his father's workshop in 1891, Lang worked for master potters in Wolfratshausen, Munich, and Stuttgart to better learn his craft. Returning to Oberammergau in 1898, Lang resumed working with his father. The next year the village elders surprised everyone by selecting Lang to play the role of Christ in the 1900 Passion Play. He proved to be a popular choice with the audience and became an international celebrity.

    In 1902 Lang married Mathilde Rutz. In that same year, with the help of an assistant and an apprentice, he built his own workshop and a kiln. In the early days of the pottery Mathilde helped in the pottery as a decorator until Lang could afford to employ girls from the local art school.

    During 1923 – 1924 Anton Lang and the other 'Passion Players' toured the U.S. selling their crafts. Lang would occasionally throw pottery when the cast passed through a pottery center such as Cincinnati, where Rookwood was located. The pots thrown at Rookwood are easy to identify as Lang hand signed the side of each piece and they have a 1924 Rookwood mark on the bottom. Lang visited the U.S. only once, and contrary to popular belief, he was never employed by Rookwood. His pottery, marked with his name in script, is fairly scarce and highly valued for its artistic quality.

His son Karl (1903 – 1990) was also a gifted potter. Karl apprenticed with his father and then completed his training at the national ceramic school in Landshut. He took over the day-to-day operations of the pottery while his father was touring America. Over time Karl became the chief designer and was responsible for creating most of the modern pieces and inventing many new glazes. Only pieces bearing a hand-written signature (not a facsimile) are certain to be Anton Lang originals instead of the work of Karl or the Langs' assistants. Anton and Karl also made pieces together; Karl might design a piece and Anton decorate it. One piece has been found with a handwritten 'Anton Lang' signature and a hand incised 'KL' (Karl Lang) mark. Very few pieces have been found with a 'Karl Lang' mark.

In 1925 Karl went to Dresden to study with sculptor Arthur Lange. Under the influence of the famous artist Ernst Barlach, Karl designed his greatest work, the 'Wanderer in the Storm.' This large figure depicts a man dressed in a long coat and hat resisting a violent wind. Between 1925 and 1930, four or five examples of the 'Wanderer' were made in the Lang workshop in Oberammeragau. One of the three known examples has only a 'KL' (Karl Lang) mark. The other two are unmarked or the mark is obscured by the glaze. At least two additional 'Wanderers' were produced at a later date, probably after WWII. They are marked with the 'Anton Lang' shop mark, a facsimile of Anton's signature, and are much cruder in appearance than the originals. Underneath they have two horizontal supports carrying the weight of the figure; the originals have only one horizontal support. The later versions appear to have been made from a mold taken from one of the originals.

In 1936 Karl Lang was put in charge of the complete operation of the pottery and enlarged and modernized the enterprise. He continued to operate the workshop as the Anton Lang pottery after his father's death in 1938. The pottery is now owned and operated by Karl's daughter, Barbara Lampe, who took over for her father in 1975. The facsimile 'Anton Lang' signature was used until 1995 when the name was changed to Barbara Lampe Pottery. Her mark is an interlocked 'BL' in a circle. Pieces with a facsimile signature and an interlocked 'UL' in a circle were made by Lampe's former husband, Uli Lampe, and date from 1975 to 1982. The 'Anton Lang' mark is not sharp on pieces made in 1975 and later. The brick red clay used in their manufacture can be seen on the bottoms as well as three lighter circular tripod marks. The later pieces are considerably heavier than the earlier work. Our advisor for this category is Clark Miller; he is listed in the Directory under Minnesota.

Bowl, brn & olive gr, linear decor inside, flared sides, 1¾" H 75.00
Bowl, burgundy w/bl accents, 3-hdl, 4¾x7" 175.00
Bowl, floral, red & bl on gr, hand sgn, 2x4½" 65.00
Bowl, flower band, mc, hand sgn, 3½x6" 110.00
Bowl, frog-skin, 2½x10" 60.00
Candleholder, turq, 6¼x5", ea 30.00

Egg cup, floral (simple), mc on bl, 2⅝" 45.00
Ewer, gray-bl w/stars in relief, firing chip, 7¾" 120.00
Figurine, bird, mc, 4x4x4" 225.00
Figurine, Madonna & Child w/earth/moon/stars, bl & yel, 11¾" .. 200.00
Holy water font, lamb w/flag & cross, gr, 7½" 100.00
Jug, mustard; yel w/brn int, Bought in Oberammergau...1963 label, 5" ..80.00
Photo, Anton & Karl Lang, 1922, 6½x8½" 17.00
Pitcher, bl & gr on red overflow, twisted body, pewter lid, 9¾" 140.00
Pitcher, bl matt, mini, 2" 36.00
Pitcher, frog-skin, 3x4½" 36.00
Pitcher, indistinct horizontal stripes, cream/bl/brn/yel, 4¼x3" 50.00
Plaque, Jesus w/cross in relief, mc, 5" dia 32.50
Plaque, Mary w/Jesus & angel, mc, hand sgn, KL mk, 1927, 11x7¾x2" .150.00
Plate, floral/calligraphy, mc/wht/bl, hand sgn, ca 1930, 8½" 110.00
Time magazine, Anton Lang on cover, Dec 17, 1923 .... 20.00
Vase, bsk, hdls, 6x4½" 100.00
Vase, floral panels (2) w/butterfly/birds on bl w/blk squiggles, 10" ...500.00
Vase, maroon & bl flambé, 6x3¾" 50.00
Vase, Nubian Black, sgn at shoulder, Rookwood mk, 1924, 3⅝" ..660.00
Vase, peacock & floral, mc on tan, hand sgn, nicks, 3¾" 40.00
Vase, streaky gr/brn/tan on bl, Oberammergau, hairline, 6⅞" 60.00
Vase, stylized design in bl & aqua, flared form, 7" 250.00
Vase, turq matt, 3 rim-to-hip hdls, 9½" 200.00
Wall pocket, girl in pinafore & winged cherub, mc, 6¼x3½" 90.00

Le Verre Francais

Le Verre Francais was produced during the 1920s by Schneider at Epinay-sur-Seine in France. It was a commercial art glass in the cameo style composed of layered glass with the designs engraved by acid. Favored motifs were stylized leaves and flowers or geometric patterns. It was marked with the name in script or with an inlaid filigrane. Our advisor for this category is Don Williams; he is listed in the Directory under Missouri.

Bowl, berries/leaves, dk bl over frost, Charder, 4¼" 230.00
Bowl, Deco fruit, amethyst on yel/orange mottle, 10" 865.00
Lamp, Escargot (snails), orange/brn on yel 8½" dia shade/base, 13" ..51,620.00
Lamp, hanging; floral, orange/bl on yel mottle bullet-nose shade ..3,100.00
Vase, Algues (algae), orange/gr on wht, trumpet neck, Charder, 7" .1,550.00
Vase, cherries, orange/violet on mauve, shouldered, 17" 4,150.00
Vase, chestnuts, raisin on orange, Nouveau form w/hdls, slim, 14" ..1,495.00
Vase, dahlia, lav on lt lav to pk mottle, ftd, Ovington, 13" 2,750.00
Vase, dahlia, lav to purple on pk/mauve mottle, bulb w/long neck, 31" ..5,000.00
Vase, floral, bl to fuchsia mottle on bl/yel, compote form, 16" ..6,325.00
Vase, flowering trees, orange/red on peach/yel, spherical, 11" ...3,360.00

Candleholder, two boys riding fish, ca. 1925 – 1938, 7x9x3", $500.00.

(Photo courtesy Clark Miller)

Vase, flowers, ruby on tan and orange mottle, 16", $1,900.00.

(Photo courtesy Early Auction Co.)

Vase, foxglove, orange to red on pk mottle, pear form, Ovington, 10".. 1,265.00
Vase, freesia/leaves, orange/raisin on yel/orange mottle, Charder, 19".. 3,795.00
Vase, fuchsia, orange to indigo on maize to bl, appl hdls, 12x9".. 3,960.00
Vase, geese/cattails, amethyst/bl on yel mottle, amethyst hdls/ft, 14".. 2,530.00
Vase, hollyhocks, flower heads at central width, bl/yel on lt yel, 14"..2,645.00
Vase, iris, red/raisin on yel, slim w/bun ft, 22"............................3,335.00
Vase, leaves/fruit, brn on lightly mottled orange, slim w/bun ft, 20".1,950.00
Vase, lg beetle, purple on yel-orange, slim, sm neck hdls, 12"..4,200.00
Vase, morning glory vines, red/mauve on red mottle, bun ft, 16"..2,160.00
Vase, palm trees, yel/orange on frosted mottle, spherical, 7½"..3,100.00
Vase, peacock/floral, orange/bl on peach mottle, bun ft, 16".....3,120.00
Vase, roses, lav on mottled lav w/amber mottle, Charder, 16¼"..2,750.00
Vase, wisteria, purple on frost, Charder, 12¼"............................1,925.00
Vase, wisteria, purple on shaded bl, str sides narrow at bun ft, 6"...1,440.00

Leach, Bernard

An English artist, Bernard Leach studied traditional pottery in China and Japan from 1909 until 1920. He returned home a superior potter, one who would revolutionize the craft through his technique and materials. His ceramics are marked with a 'BL' seal and a 'S' seal for St. Ives, where his pottery was located in England. Our advisors for this category are Suzanne Perrault and David Rago; they are listed in the Directory under New Jersey.

Bottle, fish, brn on wht, stoneware, chop mk, BL, 12x5½", NM ..11,900.00
Bottle, scratch decor on blk, ftd flat form, 7½"..........................2,700.00
Charger, zodiac, brn & Ochre HP on stoneware, ca 1927, BL, 15" ..960.00
Pilgrim bottle, spiral eng on dk red, stoneware, ftd flat form, 13"...27,000.00
Pilgrim bowl, tenmoku on stoneware, ca 1950s, BL, 3x14".......3,400.00
Vase, gr/brn mottle, hexagonal form, BL, St Ives, 7½"................. 140.00

Rice bowl, dogwood pattern, chop mark + BL, 3¼x6", $1,140.00.
(Photo courtesy David Rago Auctions/LiveAuctioneers.com)

Leeds, Leeds Type

The Leeds Pottery was established in 1758 in Yorkshire and under varied management produced fine creamware, often highly reticulated and transfer printed, shiny black-glazed Jackfield wares, polychromed pearlware, and figurines similar to those made in the Staffordshire area. Little of the early ware was marked; after 1775 the impressed 'Leeds Pottery' mark was used. From 1781 to 1820, the name 'Hartley Greens & Co.' was added. The pottery closed in 1898. Today the term 'Leeds' has become generic and is used to encompass all polychromed pearlware and creamware, wherever its origin. Thus similar wares of other potters (Wood for instance) is often incorrectly called 'Leeds.' Unless a piece is marked or can be definitely attributed to Leeds by confirming the pattern to be authentic, 'Leeds-Type' would be a more accurate nomenclature.

Bowl, floral, sprig & leaf border, hairline, 4⅛x9⅜" 1,000.00
Bowl, floral & Push the Bowl Round Boys, early 1800s, 3¾x9½", EX.. 1,200.00
Bowl, heraldic eagle, red transfer, bl feather edge, ca 1810, 8", NM...... 1,550.00
Bowl, peafowl & spatter trees, 5-color, hairlines/flakes, 3½x7¼" ...1,950.00
Brandy keg, floral/concentric rings, 5-color, 4⅜x3½", EX+ 1,000.00

Charger, flowers in urn, 5-color, bl feather edge, 14⅜" 3,250.00
Charger, peafowl in tree, 4-color, bl feather edge, 13¼", NM..2,150.00
Charger, peafowl on branch, 3-color, bl feather edge, 13¼" 1,800.00
Pitcher, milk; floral & foliage, leaf-form spout, bulbous, 5¾", EX..1,550.00
Plate, cottage w/tree & flower, 4-color, bl feather edge, 9⅞", EX .950.00
Plate, cup; heraldic eagle, mc, bl feather edge, ca 1810, 3¾", EX ..1,950.00
Plate, dahlia & acorn, 4-color, scalloped gr feather edge, 7¾"...... 635.00
Plate, flower basket, 4-color, gr feather edge, 8⅛", EX 1,800.00
Plate, heraldic eagle w/shield, 3-color, bl feather edge, 1800s, 8" ..1,650.00
Plate, heraldic eagle w/shield/etc, 4-color, early 1800s, 6½" 1,650.00
Plate, peafowl on branch, 4-color, gr feather edge, 8", VG........... 285.00
Plate, peafowl on leafy branch, 5-color, smooth rim, 9¾"..........1,325.00
Plate, pomegranate & foliage, bl feather edge w/emb floral, 10¼"..9,600.00
Plate, toddy; peafowl & vines, bud & vine border, 4¾", EX 1,550.00
Platter, bl chinoiserie, bl feathered edge, 1810s, 16x12"............... 945.00
Platter, 3 flowers, bl tones, bl feather edge, early 1800s, 17x12½"...2,400.00

Tea bowl and saucer, five-color peacock, professional restoration, $600.00. (Photo courtesy Garth's Auctions Inc./ LiveAuctioneers.com)

Tea bowl & saucer, floral, 4-color, bl chain border, 2½", 5¾", VG...850.00
Tea bowl & saucer, flowers & leaves, 3-color, sm rim, 2½", 5⅝"...850.00
Tea bowl & saucer, peafowl among foliage, 5-color, bl rim, child's, EX. 2,750.00
Teapot, floral emb/HP, globular, crabstock hdl/spout, 18th C, 4¼"...1,200.00
Teapot, flowers/Mary Neck Ilsington/verse, 1809, 6½x8¾", VG ...3,250.00

Lefton

The Lefton China Company was the creation of Mr. George Zoltan Lefton who migrated to the United States from Hungary in 1939. In 1941 he embarked on a new career and began shaping a business that sprang from his passion for collecting fine china and porcelains. Though his funds were very limited, his vision was to develop a source from which to obtain fine porcelains by reviving the postwar Japanese ceramic industry, which dated back to antiquity. As a trailblazer, George Zoltan Lefton soon earned the reputation as 'The China King.'

Counted among the most desirable and sought-after collectibles of today, Lefton items such as Bluebirds, Miss Priss, Angels, all types of dinnerware and tea-related items are eagerly acquired by collectors. As is true with any antique or collectible, prices may vary, dependent on location, condition, and availability.

Bank, Herbert the Lion, 8" 40.00
Bank, owl figural, bsk, #479, 6½" 26.00
Bank, pk elephant w/bl rhinestone eyes, #2429, 7"......................... 35.00
Basket, Green Holly, #5175, 5½".. 25.00
Bell, Green Holly, #787, 3½"... 18.00

Bell, pk w/Forget-Me-Nots, w/sponged gold, #8293, 3" 30.00
Butter dish, Bessie the Cow, #6514, 7¾" 28.00
Candleholder, pk w/appl forget-me-nots & gold, saucer base, #771, pr..50.00
Candleholders, White Holly, #6052, 5", pr 40.00
Candy box, Pear 'n Apple, ftd, #3766 .... 18.00
Candy box, red heart shape w/cherub on lid, #2210, 6½" 30.00
Candy dish, Minty Rose, leaf shape, #5517 .... 20.00
Cheese dish, Miss Priss, #1505, 5½" 175.00
Child's set, Miss Priss, mug & plate, #3553 .... 100.00
Coffeepot, Poinsettia, #4383, 8½" 90.00
Compote, Heavenly Rose, rtcl, #109, 7" 38.00
Compote, Mardi Gras, #20438, 5½" 105.00
Compote, wheat design on wht w/gold, lattice rim, #112, 7" 32.00
Cookie jar, Chef Girl, #2360, 9¾" 165.00
Cookie jar, Fruits of Italy, #621 .... 45.00
Cookie jar, Green Holly, #1359 .... 90.00
Cookie jar, Green Orchard, #3762, 10" 60.00
Cookie jar, Honey Bee, #1279 .... 100.00
Cookie jar, Little Helper, girl's head, lg bow on lid 200.00

Cookie jar, Miss Priss, from $90.00 to $120.00. (Photo courtesy Loretta DeLozier)

Cookie jar, Regal Rose, PY6971 .... 60.00
Cookie jar, Sweet Violets, #2853, 7½" 75.00
Cookie jar, White Holly, #6054 .... 85.00
Creamer, Brown Heritage, 3" 20.00
Creamer & sugar bowl, Green Holly, #1355, 3-pc 25.00
Creamer & sugar bowl, Miss Priss 85.00
Cup & saucer, demi; Blue Rose, #2120 .... 30.00
Cup & saucer, Jumbo Dad, #3400 .... 35.00
Dish, bone; Poinsettia, #4398, 6" 18.00
Dish, Miss Priss, 2-part, #1507, 9" 100.00
Egg cup, Bluebird, #286 .... 60.00
Egg cup, Golden Wheat, #20121, 3" 20.00
Figurine, angel in gr w/holly wreath in hair playing flute, #1259 ... 30.00
Figurine, Bobwhite, #2002, 4" 25.00
Figurine, boy leaning on tree, #5051, 6" 40.00
Figurine, eagle w/head down & wings up, #802, 11" 75.00
Figurine, Fifi, #5742, 7½" 150.00
Figurine, lady w/2 pk poodles, #692, 5¼" 42.00
Figurine, Madonna w/Child, #2583, 6½" 42.00
Figurine, old man w/boy fishing, #2807, 6¾" 80.00
Figurine, raccoon by branch, #4752, bsk, #4752, 5" 25.00
Figurine, red fox on woodland base, #5058, 5½x8" 30.00
Figurines/shelf sitters, Mr & Mrs Claus, #1996, 5½", pr 40.00
Jam jar, Thumbelina, w/spoon & underplate, #1697 .... 45.00
Lamp, kerosene; Green Holly, #4863, 5¾" 35.00
Mug, Holly Garland, #2041, 3" 15.00
Pin box, baby figure sleeping on lid, #2710, 3" 12.00
Pitcher, Brown Heritage, Floral, #3114, 8-cup, from $80 to 90.00
Pitcher & bowl, White Holly, #6075, 5½" bowl, pr 23.00
Planter, Bluebird, #288 .... 65.00

Planter, Calico donkey, #5897, 5½" 30.00
Plate, Holly Garland, #1804, 9" 20.00
Plate, luncheon; Brown Heritage 16.00
Plate, Rose Chintz, #658, 7½" 23.00
Platter, Green Holly, #2369, 18" L 75.00

Platter, turkey, #50758, $65.00.
(Photo courtesy Morphy Auctions/LiveAuctioneers.com)

Ring holder, hand figural, #1444, 3¾" 25.00
Shakers, Poinsettia, #4390, 2½", pr 18.00
Shakers, White Holly, #6061 .... 20.00
Snack set, Brown Heritage, #1864 .... 30.00
Snack set, Green Holly, #1363, 2-pc 20.00
Teabag holder, Miss Priss, #1506 .... 55.00
Teapot, Bluebird, musical, #734, minimum value 200.00
Teapot, Cabbage Cutie, #2123, 6-cup 75.00

Teapot, Green Holly, $45.00; Creamer and sugar bowl with lid, $20.00. (Photo courtesy Loretta DeLozier)

Teapot, Miss Priss, #1516 .... 85.00
Tidbit, 2-tier, White Holly, #6065 .... 60.00
Wall plaque, Colonial couple, #3438, oval 110.00
Wall plaque, fish figural, blk & wht w/sponged gold, #60114, 6", pr..38.00
Wall pocket, angels (2) w/dove on oval, bsk, #1697, 6" 30.00

Legras

Legras and Cie was founded in St. Denis, France, in 1864. Production continued until the 1930s. In addition to their enameled wares, they made cameo art glass decorated with outdoor scenes and florals executed by acid cuttings through two to six layers of glass. Their work is signed 'Legras' in relief and in enamel. Our advisor for this category is Don Williams; he is listed in the Directory under Missouri.

Cameo

Bowl, flowers, carved and enameled red leaves on crystal with star-shaped texturing, 14", $480.00. (Photo courtesy Early Auction Co.)

Bowl, leaves & vines, maroon on frost, low, 8¼" 535.00
Vase, berries & leaves, maroon on peach, waisted cylinder, 10¾" ...660.00
Vase, bud; floral, 3-color on beige, ca 1920, 5" 360.00
Vase, Deco band, brn on mottled brn/opal, ovoid, ca 1925, 15" .. 840.00
Vase, Deco daisies, maroon on textured pk, bulbous, 8¼" 660.00
Vase, Deco geometrics, cobalt on textured frost, gourd shape, 9" .. 400.00
Vase, floral, 2-color, stick neck, 1910s, 15" 1,950.00
Vase, pods on leafy branches, gr on apricot to gr, flattened, 8¼" .. 960.00
Vase, river scenic, cut/HP, flared 4-scallop rim, squat, 3¼" 475.00
Vase, riverscape, mahog/brn/olive on brick red, waisted, 5¼" 395.00
Vase, sailboats in harbor, 3-color, flared ft, 7¼" 900.00
Vase, spring landscape, cut/HP, ovoid, 6" 600.00
Vase, stylized flowers, fuchsia on pk, ovoid, 14" 395.00
Vase, trees/lake/sailboat, gr/wht on lemon/orange, 7⅝" 1,550.00
Vase, winter scene w/mtns, brn/wht on orange opal, 5¼" 1,175.00
Vase, wisteria, fuchsia/gr on opal, slim, 18¾" 1,950.00
Vase, woodland scene, gr on salmon, pulled rim, slim, 23¾" 2,150.00

Enameled Glass

Rose bowl, enameled winter scene, touched-up rim, 7", $225.00. (Photo courtesy Early Auction Co.)

Bowl, winter landscape at sunset, ovoid, 10¼" L 360.00
Rose bowl, winter landscape at sunset, scalloped rim, 5½" 300.00
Vase, Chinese pheasant in foliage, mc on frost, 12" 260.00
Vase, floral roundel on mottled orange/yel/opal, baluster, 18⅛" . 1,950.00
Vase, lady in winter scene, waisted cylinder, 5½" 245.00
Vase, peacock/floral spray, mc on frost, 12¾" 345.00

Lenox

Walter Scott Lenox, former art director at Ott and Brewer, and Jonathan Coxon founded The Ceramic Art Company of Trenton, New Jersey, in 1889. By 1906 Cox had left the company, and to reflect the change in ownership, the name was changed to Lenox Inc. Until 1930 when the production of American-made Belleek came to an end, they continued to produce the same type of high-quality ornamental wares that Lenox and Coxon had learned to master while in the employ of Ott and Brewer. Their superior dinnerware made the company famous, and since 1917 Lenox has been chosen the official White House china. The dinnerware they produced is listed here; see Ceramic Art Company for examples of their belleek.

Dinnerware

Abigail, bowl, vegetable; 9" 65.00
Abigail, creamer 25.00
Abigail, plate, dinner; 10½", from $30 to 35.00
Abigail, platter, 16" L 145.00
Autumn, bowl, cream soup; w/hdls & undertray 150.00
Autumn, bowl, rimmed soup; 8¼" 60.00
Autumn, bowl, vegetable; w/lid, 5½x10¾" 275.00
Autumn, bowl, 2x9⅝x7¼" 90.00
Autumn, cake stand 175.00
Autumn, coffeepot, 9¼" 150.00
Autumn, gravy boat, w/underplate, from $150 to 175.00
Autumn, mug, coffee/tea 45.00

Autumn, plate, 10½", $45.00. (Photo courtesy Dirk Soulis Auctions/ LiveAuctioneers.com)

Autumn, platter, 16" dia 175.00
Autumn, platter, 16x11" 145.00
Autumn, platter, 8-sided, 12⅜" 100.00
Autumn, shakers, pr 85.00
Autumn, soup tureen, w/lid, 5½x11½" 395.00
Ballad, cup & saucer, 2" 15.00
Ballad, plate, bread & butter; 6½" 10.00
Ballad, plate, luncheon; 8½" 14.00
Jewel, bowl, rimmed soup; 9" 25.00
Jewel, bowl, 2x6" 27.50
Jewel, mug, coffee/tea 12.00
Jewel, plate, bread & butter; 6¼" 12.00
Jewel, sugar bowl, w/lid, from $60 to 80.00
Ming, bowl, vegetable; oval, w/lid, 5¼x10¾x7⅛" 65.00
Ming, creamer & sugar bowl, w/lid 100.00
Ming, gravy boat, w/attached underplate 85.00
Ming, pitcher, cylindrical, 8" 90.00
Ming, plate, dinner; 10½" 28.00
Ming, platter, 16¾" L 90.00
Ming, tumbler, 10-oz, 4¾" 30.00
Princess, bowl, vegetable; w/lid, 2½x11" 125.00
Princess, creamer & sugar bowl, w/lid 50.00
Princess, cup & saucer 15.00
Princess, plate, salad/dessert; 7⅞" 10.00
Princess, teapot, 7", from $150 to 165.00

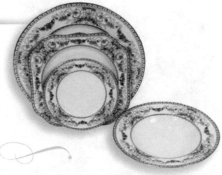

Renaissance: Plate, 10½", $60.00; Plate, salad; square, $48.00; Bowl, dessert; $22.00; Bowl, rim soup; $45.00. (Photo courtesy Du Mouchelles/LiveAuctioneers.com)

Westbury, bowl, dessert; 5½" 35.00
Westbury, cup, 2" 25.00
Westbury, gravy boat, w/underplate.................. 40.00
Westbury, plate, bread & butter; 6" 8.00
Westwind, bowl, vegetable; 9⅝" L 60.00
Westwind, chop plate, 12" 45.00
Westwind, coffeepot 90.00
Westwind, creamer & sugar bowl, w/lid 65.00
Westwind, gravy boat, attached underplate 40.00
Westwind, plate, bread & butter; 6¼" 7.50
Westwind, plate, dinner; 10⅜" 22.00
Westwind, platter, med, 16x11" 55.00

Miscellaneous

Bowl, swan figural, wht w/much gold, gr 1920s mk, 4x4½" 350.00
Figurine, German shepherd dog, wht, recumbent, 1930-53, 4½x7¾" ... 150.00
Figurine, jaybird, lt pk, gr wreath on bottom, 4" 70.00
Figurine, llama, yel, Deco style, post 1930 mk, 9x6" 495.00
Figurine, penguin, wht gloss & blk matt, 1930-53, 6¼x3½" 65.00
Loving cup, oxblood w/3 hdls, sterling collar, Bigelow & Kennard, 6" ... 180.00
Luminaire, Leda (nude) & Swan figural, 19x5", NM................. 315.00
Pendant, rose etched in crystal, w/pouch, 2½x1¼" 45.00
Pitcher, flower bud form, wht, leaf forms hdl, gr mk, 6x4½" 110.00
Planter, lt gr w/gold rim, #3477-X-561, 5½x6½" 20.00
Plate, birds in center, gold border, ...Boehm Birds..., 1976, 11" ... 35.00
Vase, creamy wht w/swan hdls, gr mk, 8½x4¼", pr 145.00

Libbey

The New England Glass Company was established in 1818 in Boston, Massachusetts. In 1892 it became known as the Libbey Glass Company. At Chicago's Columbian Expo in 1893, Libbey set up a ten-pot furnace and made glass souvenirs. The display brought them worldwide fame. Between 1878 and 1918, Libbey made exquisite cut and faceted glass, considered today to be the best from the brilliant period. The company is credited for several innovations — the Owens bottle machine that made mass production possible and the Westlake machine which turned out both electric light bulbs and tumblers automatically. They developed a machine to polish the rims of their tumblers in such a way that chipping was unlikely to occur. Their glassware carried the patented Safedge guarantee. Libbey also made glassware in numerous colors, among them cobalt, ruby, pink, green, and amber. Our advisors for this category are Don and Anne Kier; they are listed in the Directory under Ohio. See also Amberina.

Bowl, cut, fluted, Kimberly, 10" 425.00
Bowl, Maize, gr husks on oyster wht, 4x8¾" 235.00

Bowl, Señora, cut, 9¾", $600.00. (Photo courtesy Du Mouchelles/ LiveAuctioneers.com)

Butter dish, Maize, bl husks on irid 650.00
Butter dish, Maize, gr husks on custard 225.00
Candlesticks, camel stem, wht opal & clear, 5¼", pr ... 780.00
Celery vase, Maize, gr husks on custard........... 140.00
Celery vase, Maize, lg gold irid on clear, 6¾" ... 150.00
Compote, giraffe stem, wht opal & clear, 7" ..1,050.00
Creamer & sugar bowl, cut, strawberry dmn & hobstars, w/lid 330.00
Decanter, intaglio floral, slim neck, faceted stopper, 12¼" 775.00
Goblet, cut, Cornucopia, 7¼" 65.00
Pickle castor, Maize, amber stain, SP fr 595.00
Plate, cut, Sultana, 11¾" 950.00
Punch bowl, cut, hobstars/fans, no base, 14¼" ... 900.00
Rose bowl, cut, leaves & floral, flared ruffled top, 4¼" ... 230.00
Shakers, Maize, bl husks w/gold edge on custard, pr ... 495.00
Stem, claret, bear, blk, 5½" 175.00
Stem, cordial, crystal, flat ribbed stem, Embassy #4900, 6½", EX ..1,750.00
Stem, cordial, monkey, wht opal, 5" 145.00

Stems: Goblet, cat, black stem, $250.00; Cocktail, kangaroo, amberina stem, $895.00. (Photo courtesy Du Mouchelles/LiveAuctioneers.com)

Stem, goblet, cat, wht opal 200.00
Stem, wine, monkey, frosted, 5" 150.00

Sugar shaker, Maize, gold husks on oyster white, $350.00. (Photo courtesy Jackson's International Auctioneers & Appraisers of Fine Art & Antiques/ LiveAuctioneers.com)

Sugar Shaker, Maize, pearlized lustre, yel husks, 5½" ... 270.00
Toothpick holder, Maize, gr husks w/gold edge on custard ... 500.00
Tray, cut, hobstars w/cane, star center, scalloped rim, ca 1890, 12"...2,500.00
Tray, cut, Wisteria & Lovebirds, 11½x4½" 1,900.00
Tray, ice cream; cut, stars on waffle center/serrated rim, 10¾", NM....400.00
Tray, ice cream; Empress variation, ca 1880-1915, 17½x10" ...1,250.00
Tumbler, juice; cut, Corinthian variant........................ 70.00
Tumbler, Maize, gr husks on irid........................ 110.00
Vase, amberina, flanged rim, ftd, 13½" 920.00
Vase, brilliant cut, waisted, 12" 780.00
Vase, crystal, eng Johnny Appleseed, flared rim, ftd, 11" ... 545.00
Vase, Maize, yel/gold husks on custard, 6½" 210.00
Vase, peacock feather texture, pk/amethyst on clear, cylinder, 7"....140.00

Lightning Rod Balls

Used as ornaments on lightning rods, the vast majority of these balls were made of glass, but ceramic examples can be found as well. Their average diameter is 4½", but it can vary from 3½" up to 5½". Only a few of the 400 pattern-and-color combinations are listed here. The most common are round and found in sun-colored amethyst or milk glass. Lightning rod balls are considered mint if they have no cracks or holes and if any collar damage can be covered with a standard cap. Some patterns are being reproduced without being marked as such, and new patterns are being made as well. Collectors are cautioned to look for signs of age (stains) and learn more before investing in a 'rare' lightning rod ball. Our advisor is Rod Krupka, author of a book (out of print) on this subject. He is listed in the Directory under Michigan.

Blood red, Chestnut, 4", $420.00. (Photo courtesy Rich Penn Auctions/ LiveAuctioneers.com)

Amber, D&S, 10-panel	80.00
Bl opaque, med to dk swirls, rnd, 3½x3½"	30.00
Bl opaque, Moon & Star, 4½"	50.00
Clear, Chestnut, 3½x3¼"	75.00
Cobalt, ceramic, plain rnd, 5¼x4½"	125.00
Cobalt, Pleat Round, 4¼"	110.00
Cobalt, Shinn-System, 4½"	140.00
Gr, rnd, 4½"	175.00
Lt bl opaque, D&S, 10-panel, 5x3¾"	40.00
Lt bl opaque, WC Shinn, emb ribs, 4½"	35.00
Lt gr opaque, rnd, 5x4½"	85.00
Mercury glass, National, rnd, correct tube/caps, 5x4½"	350.00
Milk glass, Electra, 4¼"	35.00
Milk glass, Horizontal Ribbed, 4x3½"	30.00
Milk glass, Pleat Round, 4½x5"	30.00
Ruby, rnd, 4½"	80.00
Sun-colored amethyst, Moon & Star, 4½x5"	90.00
Sun-colored amethyst, Swirl	115.00
Wht, ceramic, staircase, 4x4"	50.00

Limbert

Charles P. Limbert formed his firm in 1894 in America's furniture capital, Grand Rapids, Michigan, and from 1902 until 1918, produced a line of Arts & Crafts furniture. While his wide-ranging line of furniture is not as uniformly successful as Gustav Stickley, the Limbert pieces that do exhibit design excellence stand among the best of American Arts & Crafts examples. Pieces featuring cutouts, exposed construction elements (e.g., key and tenon), metal and ebonized wood inlays, and asymmetric forms are among the most desirable. Less desirable are the firm's Outdoor Designs that show exposed metal screws and straight grain, as opposed to quartersawn oak boards. His most aesthetically successful forms mimic those of Charles Rennie Mackintosh (Scotland) and, to a lesser extent, Joseph Hoffmann (Austria). Usually signed with a rectangular mark (a paper label, branded in the wood, or a metal tag) showing a man planing wood, and the words Limbert's Arts Craft Furniture Made in Grand Rapids and Holland. The firm continued to produce furniture until 1944. Currently, only his Arts & Crafts-style furniture holds any interest among collectors.

Please note: Furniture that has been cleaned or refinished is worth less than if its original finish has been retained. Our values are for pieces in excellent original condition unless noted otherwise. Our advisor for this and related Arts & Crafts categories is Bruce A. Austin; he is listed in the Directory under New York.

Key:
b — brand   l — label
h/cp — hammered copper

Armchair, #643, 4-slat bk/1-slat arms, rfn, b, 41x29x28"	700.00
Bookcase, #334½, 2 ldgl doors, 8-shelf, castors, ca 1905, 56x42"	12,000.00
Bookcase, #355, 1-door, 3-shelf, cut-out panels, l, 48x33x12"	8,400.00
Bookcase, #359, 3-door, 3 adjustable shelves per section, 57x67x14"	10,000.00

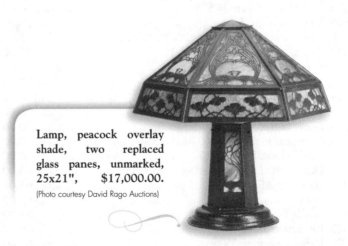

Chair, Morris; recovered, light overcoat to finish, paper label, 38x35x43", $14,400.00. (Photo courtesy David Rago Auctions)

China cabinet, 1 door+3 fixed, stains, 57x47x15"	3,000.00
Desk, #105, 1-drw, slatted shelves, b, 29½x42x28"	1,500.00

Lamp, peacock overlay shade, two replaced glass panes, unmarked, 25x21", $17,000.00. (Photo courtesy David Rago Auctions)

Magazine stand, #300, 4-shelf, slab sides w/cutout, 37x20x14"	950.00
Magazine stand, ebon-oak w/caned side panels, arched bk, b, 30x20x11"	1,925.00
Magazine stand, oak, 4-shelf, arched bottom, 2-slat sides, 43x16x13"	1,200.00
Mirror, #22, 4 hammered dbl hooks & 3 single hooks, 25x37½"	2,160.00
Pedestal, #246, rnd top on corbelled base, b, 32x14" dia	1,700.00
Rocker, cut-out crest rail, rush seat, 33x26x21"	1,675.00
Settle, even-arm, broad vertical slats, leather seat, l, 73"	4,200.00
Sideboard, mirrored gallery, cutouts, l, 57x60x22"	6,600.00

Table, #146, oval top, slab sides w/cutouts, shelf, b, 29x45x30" . 2,300.00
Table, conference; arched aprons, canted legs, rfn/rstr, 29x108x48".6,300.00
Table, lamp; broad X-stretchers, canted legs, sq cutouts, 30" dia . 1,500.00
Table, library, turtle-shaped top, long corbels, b, 30x48x30" 3,000.00
Table, library; #146, cutouts, b, 29½x45x29½" 1,900.00
Table, library; #158, dbl oval, b, 29½x47¾x36" 9,600.00
Table, library; #1141, 2-drw, b, 29x48x32" 2,525.00
Table, library; chalet style, 12-drw, appl dmn decor, shelf, rfn, 48"..500.00
Table, library; 8-sided top, wide legs w/cutouts, b, 29x52x52" ... 8,400.00
Window seat, #243½, 4 cutouts ea side, b, 24x25x18" 4,800.00

Limited Edition Plates

Current values of some limited edition plates remained steady, while many others have fallen. Prices charged by plate dealers in the secondary market vary greatly; we have tried to suggest an average. Since Goebel Hummel plates have been discontinued, values have started to decline. While those who are trying to complete the series continue to buy them, few seem interested in starting a collection. As for the Danish plates, Royal Copenhagen and Bing and Grondahl, more purchases are for plates that commemorate the birth year of a child or a wedding anniversary than to add to a collection.

Bing and Grondahl

1895, Behind the Frozen Window, from $5,500 to 6,000.00
1896, New Moon, from $2,000 to 2,200.00
1897, Christmas Meal of Sparrows, from $1,250 to 1,400.00
1898, Roses & Star, from $700 to 750.00
1899, Crows Enjoying Christmas, from $1,000 to..................... 1,250.00
1900, Church Bells Chiming, from $800 to 850.00
1901, 3 Wise Men, from $300 to 325.00
1902, Gothic Church Interior, from $275 to 300.00
1903, Expectant Children, from $225 to..................................... 275.00
1904, View of Copenhagen From Fredericksberg Hill, from $75 to.. 100.00
1905, Anxiety of the Coming Christmas Night, from $90 to....... 120.00
1906, Sleighing to Church, from $65 to 85.00
1907, Little Match Girl, from $85 to 100.00
1908, St Petri Church, from $75 to 90.00
1909, Yule Tree, from $75 to 80.00
1910, Old Organist, from $60 to 75.00
1911, Angels & Shepherds, from $60 to 75.00
1912, Going to Church, from $60 to... 75.00
1913, Bringing Home the Tree, from $60 to 75.00
1914, Amalienborg Castle, scarce, from $100 to 150.00
1915, Dog on Chain Outside Window, from $100 to 120.00
1916, Prayer of the Sparrows, from $60 to 70.00
1917, Christmas Boat, from $60 to... 70.00
1918, Fishing Boat, from $60 to 70.00
1919, Outside the Lighted Window, from $55 to 65.00
1920, Hare in the Snow, from $50 to 65.00
1921, Pigeons, from $50 to 65.00
1922, Star of Bethlehem, from $50 to 65.00
1923, Hermitage, from $50 to... 65.00
1924, Lighthouse, from $50 to 65.00
1925, Child's Christmas, from $45 to 55.00
1926, Churchgoers, from $45 to 55.00
1927, Skating Couple, from $45 to 55.00
1928, Eskimos, from $45 to... 55.00
1929, Fox Outside Farm, from $60 to... 80.00
1930, Tree in Town Hall Square, from $60 to.............................. 80.00
1931, Christmas Train, from $60 to... 80.00
1932, Lifeboat at Work, from $55 to 75.00

1933, Korsor-Nyborg Ferry, from $45 to.................................... 55.00
1934, Church Bell in Tower, from $45 to.................................... 55.00
1935, Lillebelt Bridge, from $45 to 55.00
1936, Royal Guard, from $60 to 80.00
1937, Arrival of Christmas Guests, from $60 to 80.00
1938, Lighting the Candles, from $100 to 115.00
1939, Old Lock-Eye, The Sandman, from $125 to 145.00
1940, Delivering Christmas Letters, from $160 to 175.00
1941, Horses Enjoying Meal, from $160 to 175.00
1942, Danish Farm on Christmas Night, from $150 to................ 175.00
1943, Ribe Cathedral, from $165 to 180.00
1944, Sorgenfri Castle, from $100 to.. 110.00
1945, Old Water Mill, from $110 to 115.00
1946, Commemoration Cross, from $75 to 85.00
1947, Dybbol Mill, from $75 to 85.00
1948, Watchman, from $70 to 80.00
1949, Landsoldaten, from $60 to 80.00
1950, Kronborg Castle at Elsinore, from $100 to 120.00
1951, Jens Bang, from $60 to 75.00
1952, Old Copenhagen Canals & Thorsvaldsen Museum, from $80 to. 90.00
1953, Royal Boat, from $80 to.. 100.00
1954, Snowman, from $80 to 90.00
1955, Kaulundborg Church, from $80 to 90.00
1956, Christmas in Copenhagen, from $85 to 110.00
1957, Christmas Candles, from $85 to... 110.00
1958, Santa Claus, from $80 to 95.00
1959, Christmas Eve, from $75 to 85.00
1960, Village Church, from $90 to.. 110.00
1961, Winter Harmony, from $70 to 85.00
1962, Winter Night, from $65 to 75.00
1963, Christmas Elf, from $65 to 75.00
1964, Fir Tree & Hare, from $30 to... 40.00

1965, Bringing Home the Tree, from $25.00 to $35.00.

1966, Home for Christmas, from $25 to....................................... 35.00
1967, Sharing the Joy, from $25 to 35.00
1968, Christmas in Church, from $25 to 35.00
1969, Arrival of Guests, from $20 to... 25.00
1970, Pheasants in Snow, from $15 to... 20.00
1971, Christmas at Home, from $15 to 20.00
1972, Christmas in Greenland, from $15 to................................. 20.00
1973, Country Christmas, from $15 to... 20.00
1974, Christmas in the Village, from $15 to 20.00
1975, The Old Water Mill, from $15 to 20.00
1976, Christmas Welcome, from $15 to 20.00
1977, Copenhagen Christmas, from $15 to 20.00
1978, A Christmas Tale, from $15 to 20.00
1979, White Christmas, from $15 to 20.00
1980, Christmas in the Woods, from $15 to 20.00
1981, Christmas Peace, from $15 to 20.00
1982, The Christmas Tree, from $15 to 20.00
1983, Christmas in Old Town, from $15 to.................................. 20.00

1984, Christmas Letter, from $15 to.................................. 20.00
1985, Christmas Eve, Farm, from $15 to............................ 20.00
1986, Silent Night, from $20 to 30.00
1987, Snowman's Christmas, from $20 to.......................... 30.00
1988, In King's Garden, from $20 to.................................. 30.00
1989, Christmas Anchorage, from $20 to........................... 30.00
1990, Changing Guards, from $20 to................................. 30.00
1991, Copenhagen Stock Exchange, from $35 to......................... 45.00
1992, Pastor's Christmas, from $35 to................................. 45.00
1993, Father Christmas in Copenhagen, from $45 to.................... 50.00
1994, Day in Deer Park, from $45 to.................................. 55.00
1995, Towers of Copenhagen, from $45 to........................... 55.00
1996, Winter at the Old Mill, from $45 to 55.00
1997, Country Christmas, from $45 to............................... 55.00
1998, Santa the Storyteller, from $45 to............................. 55.00
1999, Dancing on Christmas Eve, from $45 to 55.00
2000, Christmas at Bell Tower, from $45 to......................... 55.00

M. I. Hummel

1971, Heavenly Angel, from $200 to 250.00
1972, Hear Ye, Hear Ye, from $60 to 75.00
1973, Globe Trotter, from $60 to....................................... 75.00
1974, Goose Girl, from $55 to.. 65.00
1975, Ride Into Christmas, from $40 to.............................. 55.00
1976, Apple Tree Girl, from $40 to.................................... 55.00
1977, Apple Tree Boy, from $35 to.................................... 50.00
1978, Happy Pastime, from $35 to 50.00
1979, Singing Lesson, from $30 to 40.00
1980, School Girl, from $25 to 40.00
1981, Umbrella Boy, from $25 to 40.00

1982, Umbrella Girl, from $30.00 to $50.00.

1983, The Postman, from $40 to.. 65.00
1984, Little Helper, from $30 to.. 50.00
1985, Chick Girl, from $35 to... 50.00
1986, Playmates, from $45 to... 60.00
1987, Feeding Time, from $45 to....................................... 60.00
1988, Little Goat Herder, from $45 to................................ 60.00
1989, Farm Boy, from $45 to.. 60.00
1990, Shepherd's Boy, from $45 to 60.00
1991, Just Resting, from $45 to 60.00
1992, Meditation, from $45 to 60.00
1993, Doll Bath, from $45 to.. 60.00
1994, Doctor, from $45 to.. 60.00
1995, Come Back Soon, from $35 to 45.00

Royal Copenhagen

1908, Madonna & Child, from $3,750 to 4,000.00
1909, Danish Landscape, from $225 to 250.00
1910, Magi, from $175 to 195.00

1911, Danish Landscape, from $175 to 195.00
1912, Christmas Tree, from $175 to 195.00
1913, Frederik Church Spire, from $150 to 175.00
1914, Holy Spirit Church, from $125 to 150.00
1915, Danish Landscape, from $125 to 150.00
1916, Shepherd at Christmas, from $100 to 125.00
1917, Our Savior Church, from $100 to 125.00
1918, Sheep & Shepherds, from $80 to 100.00
1919, In the Park, from $80 to 100.00
1920, Mary & Child Jesus, from $80 to 100.00
1921, Aabenraa Marketplace, from $80 to 100.00
1922, 3 Singing Angels, from $80 to 100.00
1923, Danish Landscape, from $80 to 100.00
1924, Sailing Ship, from $80 to 100.00
1925, Christianshavn Street Scene, from $70 to 90.00
1926, Christianshavn Canal, from $70 to......................... 90.00
1927, Ship's Boy at Tiller, from $90 to 115.00
1928, Vicar's Family, from $80 to 100.00
1929, Grundtvig Church, from $80 to 100.00
1930, Fishing Boats, from $80 to 100.00
1931, Mother & Child, from $80 to.................................. 100.00
1932, Frederiksberg Gardens, from $80 to........................ 100.00
1933, Ferry & Great Belt, from $100 to 150.00
1934, Hermitage Castle, from $150 to 175.00
1935, Kronborg Castle, from $175 to 225.00
1936, Roskilde Cathedral, from $175 to 225.00
1937, Main Street of Copenhagen, from $250 to 275.00
1938, Round Church of Osterlars, from $275 to................ 350.00
1939, Greenland Pack Ice, from $450 to.......................... 500.00
1940, Good Shepherd, from $450 to 500.00
1941, Danish Village Church, from $400 to 450.00
1942, Bell Tower, from $425 to 450.00
1943, Flight Into Egypt, from $500 to 550.00
1944, Danish Village Scene, from $275 to 325.00
1945, Peaceful Scene, from $400 to 500.00
1946, Zealand Village Church, from $200 to 225.00
1947, Good Shepherd, from $225 to 265.00
1948, Nodebo Church, from $150 to 175.00
1949, Our Lady's Cathedral, from $150 to 175.00
1950, Boeslunde Church, from $200 to............................ 225.00
1951, Christmas Angel, from $275 to 350.00
1952, Christmas in Forest, from $50 to 60.00
1953, Frederiksberg Castle, from $80 to 100.00
1954, Amalienborg Palace, from $80 to 100.00
1955, Fano Girl, from $120 to 140.00
1956, Rosenborg Castle, from $100 to 120.00
1957, Good Shepherd, from $75 to 90.00
1958, Sunshine Over Greenland, from $75 to 90.00
1959, Christmas Night, from $100 to............................... 125.00
1960, Stag, from $70 to.. 90.00
1961, Training Ship, from $70 to 90.00
1962, Little Mermaid, from $125 to................................ 150.00
1963, Hojsager Mill, from $40 to.................................... 50.00
1964, Fetching the Tree, from $40 to............................... 50.00
1965, Little Skaters, from $30 to..................................... 45.00
1966, Blackbird, from $30 to 45.00
1967, Royal Oak, from $25 to 30.00
1968, Last Umiak, from $25 to 30.00
1969, Old Farmyard, from $25 to..................................... 30.00
1970, Christmas Rose & Cat, from $20 to 25.00
1971, Hare in Winter, from $20 to................................... 25.00
1972, In the Desert, from $15 to 20.00
1973, Train Home Bound, from $15 to 20.00
1974, Winter Twilight, from $15 to................................. 20.00

1975, Queen's Palace, from $15 to 20.00
1976, Danish Watermill, from $15 to... 20.00
1977, Immervad Bridge, from $15 to... 20.00
1978, Greenland Scenery, from $15 to.. 20.00
1979, Choosing the Tree, from $20 to.. 30.00
1980, Bringing Home the Tree, from $20 to 30.00
1981, Admiring the Tree, from $20 to 30.00
1982, Waiting for Christmas, from $30 to.. 40.00
1983, Merry Christmas, from $30 to 40.00
1984, Jingle Bells, from $30 to.. 40.00
1985, Snowman, from $35 to 40.00
1986, Wait for Me, from $35 to 40.00
1987, Winter Birds, from $35 to 40.00
1988, Christmas Eve Copenhagen, from $45 to 55.00
1989, Old Skating Pond, from $45 to.. 55.00
1990, Christmas in Tivoli, from $50 to 70.00
1991, St Lucia Basilica, from $50 to... 70.00
1992, Royal Coach, from $40 to... 50.00
1993, Arrival Guests by Train, from $65 to...................................... 75.00
1994, Christmas Shopping, from $40 to 50.00
1995, Christmas at Manorhouse, from $200 to 250.00
1996, Lighting the Street Lamps, from $40 to 60.00
1997, Roskilde Cathedral, from $40 to 60.00
1998, Welcome Home, from $100... 125.00
1999, Sleigh Ride, from $40 to... 60.00
2000, Trimming the Tree, from $40 to 60.00

Limoges

From the mid-eighteenth century, Limoges was the center of the porcelain industry of France, where at one time more than 40 companies utilized the local kaolin to make a superior quality china, much of which was exported to the United States. Various marks were used; some included the name of the American export company (rather than the manufacturer) and 'Limoges.' After 1891 'France' was added. Pieces signed by factory artists are more valuable than those decorated outside the factory by amateurs. The listings below are hand-painted pieces unless noted otherwise.

For a more thorough study of the subject, we recommend you refer to *Collector's Encyclopedia of Limoges Porcelain, Third Edition* (with beautiful illustrations and current market values), by our advisor, Mary Frank Gaston; she is listed in the Directory under Texas. Limoges porcelain is totally French in origin, but one American china manufacturer, The Limoges China Company, marked its earthenware 'Limoges' to reflect its name.

Cachepot, hand-painted scene each side, William Guerin Co., 13x10", $835.00. (Photo courtesy Buchard Galleries/LiveAuctioneers.com)

Biscuit jar, cherubs w/dove, sponged gold trim, Bawo & Dotter, 7½".. 425.00
Biscuit jar, pk roses on wht w/gold, ftd, sq, Latrille Freres, 7" 375.00
Bowl, bl-gray floral w/gold trim, ftd, Bawo & Dotter, w/lid, 10" ... 250.00
Bowl, grapes on gr w/gold trim, Blakeman & Henderson, oval, 11x8"..275.00
Cachepot, pk & wht floral w/gold trim, hdls, & ft, Guerin, 9"..1,000.00
Celery dish, pk & gr floral w/gold trim, Luc, Flambeau, 5½x12½"...400.00
Charger, autumn leaves & berries, gold trim, Duval, Borgfeldt, 12". 500.00
Charger, mc floral w/gold, Pouyat, 14½x18", from $450 to.......... 500.00
Chocolate fan, roses, pk w/bray leaves & gold, Coiffe, 10"........... 475.00
Compote, gold abstract border, Rucheler, 1914, 7½", from $200 to ...250.00
Compote, red floral, gr fleur-de-lis w/gold, Blakeman & Henderson ..160.00
Cup & saucer, red berries on lt gr w/gold, Duval, Lanternier, $150 to.... 175.00
Ferner, pk & wht mums w/gold, ftd, MEK 1898, Klingenberg & Dwenger, 9".550.00
Hair reciever, pk roses w/gold, Klingenberg & Dwenger, 2¾x4" .. 225.00
Jardiniere, daisies on bl-gr w/gold rim, Bawo & Dotter, 6x8" 600.00
Leaf dish, floral on rust, heavy gold trim, Mullidy, Bawo & Dotter, 6"..165.00
Pitcher, cider; red & pk roses on gr w/gold, T&V, 8" dia, from $425 to ..475.00
Pitcher, syrup; gold vines on wht, gold spout & hdl, Klingenberg, 5".... 185.00
Plaque, bird flying, gold trim, Dubois, Flambeau, 9¾", from $250 to.....275.00
Plaque, lady standing w/basket, Le Pic, Borgfeldt, 10", from $275 to 325.00
Plaque, 2 turkeys, L Coudert, Borgfeldt, 9½", from $175 to 200.00
Plate, daisies on lt gr, T&V, 8¼", from $70 to............................... 85.00
Plate, fish w/pk floral on wht, Levy, Flambeau, 8¾", from $60 to ... 75.00
Plate, sm courting scene on wht, w/gold enamel, Coiffe, 10" 350.00
Plate, violets HP on wht w/gold rim, Guérin, 9"........................... 100.00
Potpourri jar, lady by river on cream & gr, CJ Doyle, Guérin, 15"..2,000.00
Sandwich set, floral on cream, sponged gold trim, D&Co, from $175 to.225.00
Tankard, floral, mc on lav & cream w/gold, Blackeman & Henderson, 14"..1,235.00
Tankard, HP nude w/water jug, w/much gold, Pouyat, 13", from $3,000 to...3,500.00
Tankard, pk roses on lt gr, dragon-shaped hdl, Pouyat, 14½".....2,000.00
Tea caddy, lilies, pk & wht w/gold scrolls, Guérin, from $225 to.. 250.00
Tea tile, Moss Rose, CFH, 6½" dia, from $125 to 150.00
Tray, church scene w/gold floral, rim & hdls, E Garber, H&Co, 17"..800.00
Vase, abstract red/gr/yel, appl metal ft, Fauré (att), 3" 100.00
Vase, geometrics, gr/blk/wht, swollen tapered form, Fauré, 11"..5,500.00
Vase, geometrics, 5-color, gourd form, Fauré, 5" 1,500.00
Vase, lady's portrait on pk floral, K Ruybix, Pouyat, 14 ", $2,200 to.2,500.00
Vase, poppies, lav & orange on gr, B&Co, 10", from $550 to....... 650.00
Vase, roses, pk & wht w/gr leaves, 3 ornate gold ft, Guérin, 14½"..1,200.00
Vase, roses, pk & yel w/gr leaves, A Bronssillon, Borgfeldt, 15"..1,800.00
Vase, 3-D design, 4-color, incurvate rim, Fauré, 3½" 1,900.00

Lithophanes

Lithophanes are porcelain panels with relief designs of varying degrees of thickness and density. Transmitted light brings out the pattern in graduated shading, lighter where the porcelain is thin and darker in the heavy areas. They were cast from wax models prepared by artists and depict views of life from the 1800s, religious themes, or scenes of historical significance. First made in Berlin about 1803, they were used as lamp shade panels, window plaques, and candle shields. Later steins, mugs, and cups were made with lithophanes in their bases. Japanese wares were sometimes made with dragons or geisha lithophanes. See also Dragon Ware; Steins.

Candle stand, couple in castle hall; bronze cherub stem, 19" 2,375.00
Lamp, shade w/4 mc panels; brass putti stem, 1900, 18" 500.00
Lamp, shade w/5 genre panels; onyx base, 17" 565.00
Lamp, shade w/5 landscape panels; brass w/sq wht marble base ... 815.00
Lamp, shade w/6 panels mk PPM; 11½" NP base (married), 17½"..750.00
Panel, girl seated in garden, 7½x6½"+fr fitted for candleholder... 175.00
Panel, monk/boy on beach, att KPM, 12½x9½", +bklit gilt fr....... 345.00
Panel, 2 children among flowers, 6⅝x6⅜"+bklit wood fr............. 125.00

Candle lamp, castle scene, marked KPM, figural stem, 7x6", $780.00. (Photo courtesy Skinner Inc. Auctioneers & Appraisers of Antiques & Fine Art/LiveAuctioneers.com)

Little Red Riding Hood

Though usually thought of as a product of the Hull Pottery Company, research has shown that a major part of this line was actually made by Regal China. The idea for this popular line of novelties and kitchenware items was developed and patented by Hull, but records show that to a large extent Hull sent their whiteware to Regal to be decorated. Little Red Riding Hood was produced from 1943 until 1957. Buyers need to be aware that it has been reproduced. These reproductions are characterized by inferior detail and decoration; many reproduction molds carry the original patent number. Unless you're confident in your ability to recognize a reproduction when you see one, we would suggest that you buy only from reputable dealers. For further information we recommend *The Collector's Ultimate Encyclopedia of Hull Pottery* by our advisor Brenda Roberts, and *The Ultimate Collector's Encyclopedia of Cookie Jars* by Joyce and Fred Roerig. Both are published by Collector Books.

Bank, standing, 7", from $600 to	900.00
Butter dish, from $350 to	400.00
Canister, cereal	1,375.00
Canister, coffee, sugar or flour; ea from $600 to	700.00
Canister, salt	1,100.00
Canister, tea	700.00
Casserole, red w/emb wolf, RRH, Grandma & axe man, 11¾", $1,800 to	2,300.00

Child's feeding dish, 4¾x8", $1,750.00. (Photo courtesy Belhorn Auction Services LLC/LiveAuctioneers.com)

Cookie jar, closed basket, from $400 to	500.00
Cookie jar, full skirt, from $600 to	700.00
Cookie jar, open basket, from $300 to	400.00
Cracker jar, unmk, from $600 to	750.00
Creamer, side pour, from $150 to	225.00
Creamer, top pour, no tab hdl, from $275 to	325.00
Creamer, top pour, tab hdl, from $250 to	300.00
Dresser jar, 8¾", from $450 to	575.00
Lamp, from $1,500 to	2,000.00

Match holder, wall hanging, from $400 to	600.00
Mustard jar, w/orig spoon, from $375 to	460.00
Pitcher, 7", from $450 to	600.00
Pitcher, 8", from $550 to	750.00
Planter, wall hanging, from $325 to	475.00
Shakers, Pat design 135889, med sz, pr (+) from $800 to	900.00
Shakers, 3¼", pr from $95 to	140.00
Shakers, 5½", pr from $180 to	235.00
Spice jar, sq base, ea from $450 to	600.00
String holder, from $1,800 to	2,300.00
Sugar bowl, crawling, no lid, from $200 to	300.00
Sugar bowl, standing, no lid, from $175 to	225.00
Sugar bowl, w/lid, from $275 to	325.00
Sugar bowl lid, minimum value	110.00
Teapot, from $270 to	325.00
Wolf jar, red base, from $750 to	900.00
Wolf jar, yel base, from $650 to	800.00

Liverpool

In the late 1700s Liverpool potters produced a creamy ivory ware, sometimes called Queen's Ware, which they decorated by means of the newly perfected transfer print. Made specifically for the American market, patriotic inscriptions, political portraits, or other States themes were applied in black with colors sometimes added by hand. (Obviously their loyalty to the crown did not inhibit the progress of business!) Before it lost favor in about 1825, other English potters made a similar product. Today Liverpool is a generic term used to refer to all ware of this type.

Jug, Apotheosis/Geo WA rising to heaven, blk transfer, 8¼"	3,000.00
Jug, Apotheosis/3-mast ship, blk transfer w/gold, 13"	2,250.00
Jug, Arms of Johnston/eagle/florals, blk transfer w/mc, 11¾"	3,500.00
Jug, Boston Fusilier/eagle & 13 stars, mc transfer, ca 1790, 12"	15,000.00
Jug, British ship/Susan's Farewell, blk transfer, 10", EX	1,100.00
Jug, Country Alehouse Door/mill house scene, blk transfer, rpr hdl, 7"	125.00
Jug, Defeat of England/eagle w/wings spread, ca 1800, 8"	1,875.00
Jug, Emblem of Am/Independence, blk transfer, 7"	690.00
Jug, Farmer's Arms/village scene, blk transfer, silver rim, 10"	565.00
Jug, Geo WA bust/names of 15 states, bk: ship w/Am flag, mc, 10"	9,600.00
Jug, Geo WA/poem on Washington's victories, blk transfer, 11"	2,400.00
Jug, Newburyport Harbor chart/ships, mc transfer, 19th C, 12"	10,625.00
Jug, Peace & Commerce/masted ship, mc transfer, Herculaneum, 1804, 10"	2,400.00

Jug, ship with three-color enamel, reverse: When the first sea struck her..., 10½", G, $1,670.00. (Photo courtesy James D. Julia Inc.)

Jug, young couple/Cupid/flowers, blk transfer, ca 1780-90, 9½"	725.00
Jug, Zebulon Pike/Jacob Jones, blk transfer, ca 1820, 6½"	1,950.00
Mug, Am Declared Independence July 4 1776, blk transfer, 4⅞"	5,000.00
Mug, names 16 states/verse, ribbon border, blk transfer, 6¼"	1,650.00
Mug, Peace, Commerce & Honest...w/eagle, blk transfer, 4¾"	2,460.00

Lladro

Lladro porcelains are currently being produced in Labernes Blanques, Spain. Their retired and limited edition figurines are popular collectibles on the secondary market.

Aesthetic Pose, mid 1800s girl, #4850, 1973-85, 15½" 185.00
Afternoon Promenade, girl w/parasol, #07636, 1995, 9½" 245.00
Appreciation, lady holding flowers, #1396, retired, 10½" 575.00
At the Circus, clown w/girl, #5052, retired 1985, 13" 540.00
Autumn Sheperdess, girl holding wheat, retired 1985, w/base, 18"..480.00
Baby Outing, lady & baby carriage, #01014838, 1976-1992, 13" .. 465.00
Bashful, girl holding lg hat in front, #5008, 1978-97, 10" 130.00
Big Sister, boy & girl on couch, #5735, retired, 7" 450.00
Blessed Lady, lady w/cherubs, #01001579, retired 1989, 20", MIB . 1,250.00

Boy and girl on elephant, 9x8", $480.00. (Photo courtesy Du Mouchelle's/LiveAuctioneers.com)

Boy on Carousel Horse, #1470, retired, MIB 420.00
Circus Sam, clown holding violin at side, #5472, 1987, 9" 135.00
Close to My Heart, Black girl holding cat, #5603, 1989-97, 8½" . 135.00
Clown Playing Violin, half-figure, #5600, 6" 175.00
Clown w/Concertina, #1027, ca 1963-1993, 18", MIB................. 375.00
Clown w/Violin, #1126, retired 1978, 13¾" 630.00
Dancer, girl arching bk holds up hem of dress, #01005050, 1979, 12" ..240.00
Day's Work, boy on tractor, #6563, retired, 8", MIB................... 500.00
Dog in Basket, #1128, retired 1985, 7½" 175.00
Dog's Best Friend, girl & dog, #5688, 1990-2005, 6" 210.00
Don Quixote, #D29A, 1980, 16".. 255.00
Dream Come True, couple dancing, #6364, 2000 .... 350.00
Dutch Couple w/Tulips, #5124, 1982-85, 11" 825.00
Embroiderer, lady in chair, #4865, retired, 11"............................. 460.00
Evita, girl w/parasol, #5212, retired 1998, 7"............................... 160.00
Flamenco Dancers, man w/lady at ft, ca 1975, retired, 19¾x12¾" ..625.00
Flor Maria, Spanish girl w/flowerpot, #05490, 1988-2006, 10"..... 310.00
Florinda, girl seated w/flower basket, 1974-85, 6" 265.00
Flower Song, girl kneeling w/flower basket, #7607, retired 1988, 7". 190.00
For You, boy gives flower to lady, #5453, retired 330.00
Geisha Girl, kneeling at table w/flower urn, #4840, 1973-90s, 7½".. 260.00
Girl w/Parasol, #5221, retired 2002, 8½"................................... 160.00
Great Chef, boy w/lg pot, #6234, retired 1998, 7½", MIB............ 300.00
Holy Mary, #1394, ca 1982, retired, w/fr certificate, 15" 825.00
In the Gondola, #1350, ca 1978, 17¼x30½", MIB 1,440.00
In Touch w/Nature, Oriental lady w/birds, #6572, retired, 15½", MIB . 520.00
Jazz Band Bass Player, Black man, #5834, 1990, 10" 175.00
Juggler Sitting, boy playing mandolin, #01001382, 1978-85, 12"....275.00
Kitty Confrontation, cat stalking, #1442, 5"................................. 135.00
Kneeling Thai Dancer, #2069, retired, 16½"............................... 330.00
Lady at Dressing Table, #1242, retired 1978, 2-pc, dresser 12"..1,640.00
Lady w/Shawl, holds umbrella/walks dog, #4914, retired, 17", MIB.... 580.00

Little Pals, clown w/lamb in pocket, #7600, retired 1986, 9", MIB ..1,025.00
Little Traveler, boy clown w/sack, #7602, retired, 8½" 465.00
Love & Marriage, bride & groom in carriage, #1802, retired, NMIB.. 760.00
Lovers From Verona (Romeo & Juliet), #1343, ca 1975, retired, 15x8".845.00
Melancholy, clown bust w/hands by face, #5542, ca 1989, retired...375.00
Mirage, mermaid, #1415, 1983, 6".. 225.00
Morning Chores, nun w/broom & pail, #5552, retired, 10", MIB ...550.00
My Hungry Brood, girl seated feeding ducks, #5074, 1980-97, 6½"..245.00
My Wedding Day, #1492, ca 1986, retired, 15½", MIB................. 830.00
New Horizons, Inspiration Millennium #6570, retired, 15", MIB ...425.00

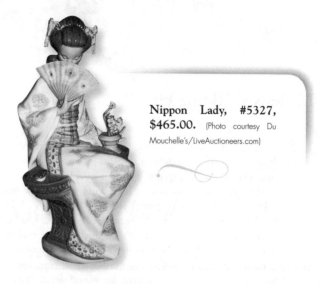

Nippon Lady, #5327, $465.00. (Photo courtesy Du Mouchelle's/LiveAuctioneers.com)

Old Dog, #1067, retired 1978, 2¾x12"... 500.00
Pensive Clown Bowler, head of sad clown, #5130, 1982-2000, 10"..215.00
Playful Dogs, 2 poodles & lg ball, 1974-1981............................... 450.00
Pocket Full of Wishes, boy w/flowers in pockets, #7650, 1997, 10" .. 195.00
Poodle w/Pups, mama nursing 5 babies, ca 1974-81, 6" 360.00
Preening Crane, #1612, retired, 7", MIB...................................... 520.00
Princess & the Unicorn, #1755G, 1991-1993, 11" 1,250.00
Princess of Peace, holding up flower urn, #6324, 1995-2000, 17"....350.00
Puppet Painter, #5396, retired, 9½x8¾" 700.00
Puppy Love, boy & girl, #1127, retired, 10" 150.00
Purr-fect, 3 cats in flower basket, #1444, 5½"............................. 230.00
Rebirth, lady in floral archway, #6571, retired, 16½x11", MIB..... 715.00
Roving Photographer, camera/tripod over shoulder, #01005194, 1984-85 ..500.00
Shepherdess, half-figure w/shock of wheat, #01012133, 1983-85, 18"..475.00
Sport Billy, boy on skis, 1978, 8"... 130.00
Spring Bouquet, girl holding 2 bouquets, #7603, retired 1997, 8½"....250.00
Summer Breeze, girl w/flowers, #6543, retired............................ 175.00
Sweet Girl, girl w/closed umbrella, #4987, retired, 10½" 200.00
Take Your Medicine, girl w/bandage dog, #5921, retired, 7½x7" ... 330.00
Tea Time, lady standing w/cup & saucer, #5470, retired, 14", MIB..415.00
Ten & Growing, pre-teen couple, #7635, retired 1995, 8" 250.00
Two Women w/Flagons, ladies w/jugs on heads, #1014, retired 1985, 19"...485.00
Unlikely Friends, dog & cat sleeping together, #6417, retired, 6½".. 135.00
Wedding, vintage bride & groom, #K-28, 1982-1997, 12½" 210.00
Wheelbarrow w/Flowers, boy pushing wheelbarrow, #1283, 1974-91, 9"..215.00

Lobmeyer

J. and L. Lobmeyer, contemporaries of Moser, worked in Vienna, Austria, during the last quarter of the 1800s. Most of the work attributed to them is decorated with distinctive enameling; a favored motif is people in eighteenth-century garb. Our advisor for this category is Don Williams; he is listed in the Directory under Missouri.

Decanter, romantic scene, jeweling and gilt, 10½", $1,680.00. (Photo courtesy Kodner Galleries Inc./LiveAuctioneers.com)

Pitcher, courting scene/florals, gilt trim, ftd, sgn, 9¼"	850.00
Plate, courting scene/florals/gilt, sgn, 1800s, 10½"	190.00
Tray, amber-yel w/Islamic-style mc decor w/gold, 12¾"	7,000.00
Tumblers, floral w/HP pictorial medallions, pr	875.00

Locke Art

By the time he came to America, Joseph Locke had already proven himself many times over as a master glassmaker, having worked in leading English glasshouses for more than 17 years. Here he joined the New England Glass Company where he invented processes for the manufacture of several types of art glass — amberina, peachblow, pomona, and agata among them. In 1898 he established the Locke Art Glassware Co. in Mt. Oliver, a borough of Pittsburgh, Pennsylvania. Locke Art Glass was produced using an acid-etching process by which the most delicate designs were executed on crystal blanks. All examples are signed simply 'Locke Art,' often placed unobtrusively near a leaf or a stem. Some pieces are signed 'Jo Locke,' and some are dated. Most of the work was done by hand. The business continued into the 1920s. For further study we recommend *Locke Art Glass, Guide for Collectors*, by Joseph and Janet Locke, available at your local bookstore.

Our advisor for this category is Richard Haigh; he is listed in the Directory under Virginia.

Cup, punch; Poppy	95.00
Goblet, Ivy	125.00
Goblet, 3 flowers/buds on random stems, 4¼"	125.00
Pitcher, Vintage Grape, corseted, etch hdl, 8½", +6 tumblers	995.00
Plate, Poinsettia, 7"	125.00
Sherbet, fruits	125.00
Tankard, poppies/fern fronds/grasses, waisted, 8"	495.00
Tumbler, Grape & Vine	110.00
Tumbler, sheaves of wheat, 2¾"	95.00
Vase, birds & poppies, flared rim, 5"	395.00
Vase, Poppy, 6x3"	350.00
Vase, Rose, flared rim, 6¼"	350.00
Wine, floral, dbl-knob stem, rnd ft, 5¾"	125.00

Locks

The earliest type of lock in recorded history was the wooden cross bar used by ancient Egyptians and their contemporaries. The early Romans are credited with making the first key-operated mechanical lock. The ward lock was invented during the Middle Ages by the Etruscans of Northern Italy; the lever tumbler and combination locks followed at various stages of history with varying degrees of effectiveness. In the eighteenth century the first precision lock was constructed. It was a device that utilized a lever-tumbler mechanism. Two of the best-known of the early nineteenth-century American lock manufacturers are Yale and Sargent, and today's collectors value Winchester and Keen Kutter locks very highly. Factors to consider are rarity, condition, and construction. Brass and bronze locks are generally priced higher than those of steel or iron. Our advisor for this section is Joe Tanner; he is listed in the Directory under California. See also Railroadiana.

Key:	
bbl — barrel	st — stamped

Brass Lever Tumbler

Ames Sword Co, Perfection st on shackle, 2¾"	75.00
Bingham's Best Brand, BBB emb on front, 3¼"	150.00
Chubbs, Patent London, st, 6⅛"	350.00
Cleveland, emb on front, 4-way, 3⅛"	55.00
Crusader, shield, swords emb on boy, 2¾"	45.00
Fagoma, Fagoma emb in shield on front, 3"	125.00
Good Luck, emb, 2¾"	45.00
JWM, emb, bbl key, 2⅝"	25.00
Motor, Motor emb on body, 3¼"	35.00
Roeyonoc, Roeyonoc st on body, 3¼"	60.00
Ruby, Ruby emb in scroll on front, 2¾"	30.00

Slaymaker, T.C. Co., 3½", $195.00. (Photo courtesy Hassinger & Courtney/LiveAuctioneers.com)

Sphinx, sphinx & pharaoh head emb on front, 2¾"	35.00
W Bohannan & Co, SW emb in scroll on front, 2⅜"	40.00
Watch, emb, flat key, 3"	30.00
1898, emb, 2¾"	40.00

Combinations

Chicago Combination Lock Co, st on front, brass, 2¾"	60.00
Iowa Lock & Mfg emb on lock, 3½"	100.00
Junkunc Bros Mfrs, all st on bk, brass, 1⅞"	35.00
Miller Keyless, st, iron, 3¼"	70.00
Number or letter disk, st, 4-disk, brass, 3½"	200.00
Number or letter disk, st, 4-disk, iron, 4½"	325.00
Permutation Lock Den Co, emb, brass, 3⅝"	900.00
Sorel Limited Canada, st, brass, 3¼"	450.00
Sutton Lock Co st on body, 3"	400.00
Your Own st on body, 3⅞"	400.00

Eight-Lever Type

Blue Chief, st, steel, 4½"	40.00
Excelsior, st, steel, 4¾"	30.00

Mastadon, st, brass, 4½" 30.00
Reese, st, steel, 4¾" 15.00

Iron Lever Tumbler

Bear, emb, 2⅝" 25.00
Caesar, emb, 2¾" 15.00
Eagle, 4 dice emb on front, 2¾" 40.00
Jupiter, Word Jupiter/star & moon emb on front, 3¼" 18.00
Mars, emb, 2¼" 20.00
Red Chief, words Red Chief emb on body, 3¾" 400.00
Star Lock Works, st, 3⅛" 90.00
W Bohannon, Brook NY WB, st, 3¼" 35.00

Lever Push Key

California, emb, brass, 2½" 500.00
Cherokee, emb, 6-Lever, iron, 2½" 200.00
Columbia, emb Columbia 6-Lever, brass push-key type, 2¼" 35.00
Crescent, 4-Lever, emb, iron, 2" 40.00
Duke, emb 6-Lever, 2⅛" 65.00
Empire, emb, 6-Lever, brass, 2½" 20.00
HS&Co, 6-Lever, emb, brass, 2¼" 150.00
Jewett Buffalo, emb, brass, 2¼" 275.00
National Lock Co, emb, brass, 2½" 200.00
Smith & Egge Mfg Co, Smith & Egge st on front, 3" 75.00

Logo — Special Made

City of Boston Dept of Schools, st, brass, 2⅞" 110.00
Delco Products, st, brass 20.00
Heart-shape brass lever type st Board Education, bbl key, 3½" 65.00
Ordinance Dept, st, brass, 2⅞" 75.00
Sq Yale-type brass pin tumbler, st Shell Oil Co on body, 3⅛" 25.00
Texaco, emb, brass, 2¾" 150.00
USBIR, st, brass, 3¾" 80.00
Zoo, st, iron, 2½" 25.00

Pin-Tumbler Type

Fulton, emb Fulton on body, 2⅝" 30.00
Il-A-Noy, emb Il-A-Noy on body, 2½" 40.00
Rich-Con, emb, iron, 2⅞" 50.00
Segal, iron, emb Segal on shackle, 3¾" 30.00
Simmons, emb, iron, 2⅝" 30.00
99 Miller, emb 99, brass, 1¾" 80.00

Scandinavian (Jail House) Type

Backalaphknck (Russian), st, iron, 5" 600.00
R&E Co, emb, iron, 3¼" 40.00
Star, emb line on bottom, iron, 3¾" 200.00

Six-Lever Type

Eagle, brass, Eagle Six-Lever st on body 18.00
Miller, Six-Lever, st, brass, 3⅞" 20.00
Olympiad Six-Lever, st, iron, 3¾" 25.00
SHCo Simmons Six-Lever, emb, iron, 3⅝" 200.00

Story and Commemorative

CI, emb skull/X-bones w/florals, NH Co on bk, 3¼" 300.00
Mail Pouch emb on lock, lock in shape of mail pouch, 3⅛" 275.00

National Hardware Co (NHCo), emb SK, iron, 3½" 900.00
NY to Paris Lindbergh's Flight, brass, warded, 2⅝" 600.00
Russell & Erwin (R&E), emb Aztec figure, iron, 2¼" 650.00
Russell & Erwin (R&E), emb mailbox, iron, 3⅛" 850.00
1901 Pan Am Expo, brass, emb w/buffalo, 2⅝" 650.00

Warded Type

Cruso Chicken, emb, brass, 2¾" 35.00
G&B, st, brass, 3" 15.00
Kirby, emb, brass, 2¼" 75.00
Navy, iron pancake ward key, bk: scrolled emb letters, 2½" 40.00
Rex, steel case, emb letters, 2⅝" 18.00
Safe, brass sq case, emb letters, 1⅞" 8.00
Sampson, emb, iron, 2½" 20.00
Texas, emb, brass, 2½" 175.00
Van Guard, emb, iron, 2⅞" 18.00

Wrought Iron Lever Type (Smokehouse Type)

DM&Co, bbl key, 4¼" 20.00
R&E, 4½" 40.00
WT Patent, 3¼" 20.00

Loetz

The Loetz Glassworks was established in Klostermule, Austria, in 1840. After Loetz's death the firm was purchased by his grandson, Johann Loetz Witwe. Until WWII the operation continued to produce fine artware, some of which made in the early 1900s bears a striking resemblance to Tiffany's. In addition to the iridescent Tiffany-style glass, he also produced threaded glass and some cameo. The majority of Loetz pieces will have a polished pontil. Our advisor for this category is Don Williams; he is listed in the Directory under Missouri.

Bowl, Creta Papillon, bl irid, ruffled, 9" 115.00
Bowl, earthen gr w/Nouveau platinum swirls, cvd, 2¾x9" 1,000.00
Bowl, Phanomen Gre, platinum decor on vaseline w/silver o/l, 9½" .. 2,300.00
Lamp, amber irid 7" dome shade; Nouveau base w/serpent ft, 16½" ... 2,300.00

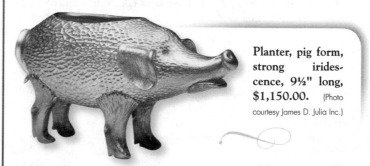

Planter, pig form, strong iridescence, 9½" long, $1,150.00. (Photo courtesy James D. Julia Inc.)

Vase, bl free-form sqs & oil spots on amber, 9" 8,000.00
Vase, bl irid w/wavy lines & oil spots, cobalt trim, 8x12" 4,800.00
Vase, Candia Silveriris, elongated neck, 6¼" 275.00
Vase, cobalt w/Phanomen Gre decor on lower body, ruffled rim, 6½" .. 1,000.00
Vase, Creta Papillon, med gr w/platinum decor, shouldered, 6", NM .. 235.00
Vase, Cystisus, yel w/gr decor & platinum oil spots, 4½" 1,600.00
Vase, gold irid w/gold oil spots & bl irid, conch shell form, 8x6½" ... 1,150.00
Vase, gold irid w/raised loops on cylinder, faux Tiffany mk, 14" ... 500.00
Vase, irid waves on violet, 4-crimp rim, ca 1900, 5¼" 2,400.00
Vase, King Tut, cobalt w/gold irid, gourd form, 4¼" 925.00
Vase, Medici, bronze hue w/purple irid, platinum decor, 6½" 750.00

Vase, Medici, dk earthen hue w/platinum & silver floral o/l, 6" .. 3,750.00
Vase, Medici, rose pk w/platinum decor, swirled body, 6" 1,950.00
Vase, Phanomen Gre, platinum feathers on peach irid, 6" 4,500.00
Vase, platinum/bl feathers on amber, cylinder neck, 8¾" 2,125.00
Vase, red w/papillon decor, ruffled rim, metal ft, 8x9" 300.00
Vase, silver o/l vines on rust to yel, incurvate rim, 3¾" 2,875.00
Vase, Titania, gr & orange decor w/floral silver o/l shoulder, 4½" .. 3,600.00
Vase, yel w/waves/oil spots, floral silver o/l, 7" 4,315.00

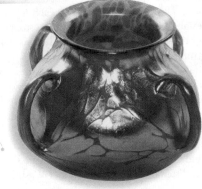

Vase, Candia reddish-brown with blue Phanomen iridescent finish, four pulled handles, 7½" wide, $4,900.00. (Photo courtesy Early Auction Co.)

Lomonosov Porcelain

Founded in Leningrad in 1744, the Lomonosov porcelain factory produced exquisite porcelain miniatures for the Czar and other Russian nobility. One of the first factories of its kind, Lomonosov produced mainly vases and delicate sculptures. In the 1800s Lomonosov became closely involved with the Russian Academy of Fine Arts, a connection which has continued to this day as the company continues to supply the world with these fine artistic treasures. In 1992 the backstamp was changed to read 'Made in Russia,' instead of 'Made in USSR.'

Bathing beauty fastening bathing cap, rnd base, 6½" 130.00
Bear sitting w/front paws down looking ahead, 3½" 25.00
Colt resting w/head up, 5½" 32.00
Fawn resting in curled-up position, 6½" 30.00
Fox resting w/head on front paws, 8½" 30.00
Fox sitting upright w/head turned, 5" 30.00
Fox terrier in wide stance, 6¾x7½" 40.00
Giraffe resting w/head straight up, 12x7½" 35.00

Hound, red USSR mark, 7¾" long, $120.00. (Photo courtesy The Cleveland Auction Co./ LiveAuctioneers.com)

Leopard sitting upright, looking bk, 4½" 25.00
Moose resting, looking back, 5x6" 65.00
Peasant girl dancing, gold trim at hem, 3¼" 25.00

Poodle resting w/head up, wht w/gray face, 4½" 25.00
Spitz Eskimo dog seated looking forward, wht w/blk detail, 3" 25.00

Longwy

The Longwy workshops were founded in 1798 and continue today to produce pottery in the north of France near the Luxembourg-Belgian border under the name 'Société des Faienceries de Longwy et Senelle.' The ware for which they are best known was produced during the Art Deco period, decorated in bold colors and designs. Earlier wares made during the first quarter of the nineteenth century reflected the popularity of Oriental art, cloisonné enamels in particular. Examples are marked 'Longwy,' either impressed or painted under glaze. Our advisors for this category are Suzanne Perrault and David Rago; they are listed in the Directory under New Jersey.

Bowl, floral, mc on turq, oval, 11" 155.00
Bowl, floral border, mc on wht crackle, #3021, 10½" 240.00
Cake stand, Deco leaves & berries in center & along rim, 11" 145.00
Charger, nude among fruit trees, flakes, 15" 900.00
Charger, water birds reserve w/wide floral border, 14⅜" 360.00
Cigarette holder, floral on turq w/cobalt trim, ftd, 3" 50.00
Dutch shoes, floral on turq w/geometric trim, 6" L, pr 165.00
Figurines, Primavera, hound seated, burgundy, 8½x7", pr 360.00
Jar, floral on wht, acorn finial, flared ft, #1320, 6" 380.00
Jardiniere, floral, mc on yel-gr, geometric decor rim, 8x14", pr ... 4,200.00
Lamp base, winged dragon & flowers on cobalt, brass mts, 12" 480.00
Plate, dragon (detailed), mc on wht crackle, D-32, 8¾" 350.00
Plate, floral, mc on cobalt, #3301, decor #5996, 10" 135.00
Plate, floral, mc on turq, 9", pr 300.00
Plate, floral, rtcl bl rim, 7¾" 150.00
Plate, winged dragon & flowers on wht to bl, 9½", pr 900.00

Table, floral tilework in Bradley and Hubbard brass mounts, $3,000.00. (Photo courtesy David Rago Auctions/LiveAuctioneers.com)

Teapot, floral, mc on turq w/cobalt trim, 6½", NM 235.00
Tile, birds & palms, mc on wht, in Tiffany brass 3-light fr, 16½" H.. 515.00
Tile, Mt Fuji coastal scene reserve/floral, mc on turq, 7⅞x7⅞" 235.00
Tray, birds & water scene reserve on floral w/cobalt trim, 12x10½" 395.00
Trivet, stork/floral reserve on floral, mc on turq, 8-sided, 9¾" 235.00
Vase, birds/flowers reserves on mc floral, #3221, 9⅛", pr 850.00
Vase, bud; floral, mc on turq, waisted, 9", pr 360.00
Vase, Deco dmns in French Blue & cobalt, slim, 10" 660.00
Vase, Deco florals at shoulder, tapered/octagonal, 9½" 750.00
Vase, floral, mc on pk, cylindrical, 9½", pr 725.00
Vase, floral, mc on turq w/cobalt rim, cylindrical, 6½" 135.00
Vase, floral on turq, sq sides, lion's-head hdls, 9" 215.00

Vase, nude woman picking fruit/full moon, 1937 Commemorative, 10¼".. **1,200.00**
Vase, Primavera, blk linear decor on bl, bulbous, #17, 11½x10" .. **785.00**
Vase, Primavera, stylized birds & plants on bl, cylindrical, 4¾" ... **250.00**
Wall pocket, 5-deer border, R Chevalier, 8½x17½" **2,150.00**

Lonhuda

William Long was a druggist by trade who combined his knowledge of chemistry with his artistic ability in an attempt to produce a type of brown-glazed slip-decorated artware similar to that made by the Rookwood Pottery. He achieved his goal in 1889 after years of long and dedicated study. Three years later he founded his firm, the Lonhuda Pottery Company. The name was coined from the first few letters of the last name of each of his partners, W.H. Hunter and Alfred Day. Laura Fry, formerly of the Rookwood company, joined the firm in 1892, bringing with her a license for Long to use her patented airbrush-blending process. Other artists of note, Sarah McLaughlin, Helen Harper, and Jessie Spaulding, joined the firm and decorated the ware with nature studies, animals, and portraits, often signing their work with their initials. Three types of marks were used on the Steubenville Lonhuda ware. The first was a linear composite of the letters 'LPCO' with the name 'Lonhuda' impressed above it. The second, adopted in 1893, was a die-stamp representing the solid profile of an Indian, used on ware patterned after pottery made by the American Indians. This mark was later replaced with an impressed outline of the Indian head with 'Lonhuda' arching above it. Although the ware was successful, the business floundered due to poor management. In 1895 Long became a partner of Sam Weller and moved to Zanesville where the manufacture of the Lonhuda line continued. Less than a year later, Long left the Weller company. He was associated with J.B. Owens until 1899, at which time he moved to Denver, Colorado, where he established the Denver China and Pottery Company in 1901. His efforts to produce Lonhuda utilizing local clay were highly successful. Examples of Denver Lonhuda are sometimes marked with the LF (Lonhuda Faience) cipher contained within a canted diamond form.

Creamer & sugar bowl, yel & gr floral, w/lid, ca 1892, 2½" & 3½"... **500.00**
Ewer, poppies, slim neck, #218, Weller shield mk, sgn EA, 9" **875.00**
Pitcher, floral, orange/yel/gr/brn, #79, shield mk, JRS, 1893, 7", EX... **250.00**
Powder box, nasturtiums, #209 & Weller shield mk, 2½" **530.00**

Vase, cowboys by a stream and Native Americans on nearby hill, shield mark, 9", $5,400.00. (Photo courtesy David Rago Auctions/LiveAuctioneers.com)

Vase, floral, yel & gr on brn, #265 Faience, sgn JRS, 11" **250.00**
Vase, floral on dk brn, bulbous bottom, integral hdls, mk, 5" **185.00**
Vase, leaves & vines, orange & gr on brn, Denver shield mk, 8", EX.. **375.00**
Vase, lotus & leaves on celadon & brn, gourd form, 10" **350.00**
Vase, nautilus shells & cattails, squat, 3-ftd, #205, ca 1895, 6" **280.00**

Lotton

Charles Lotton is a contemporary glass artist who began blowing glass full time in January 1973. He developed his own glass formulas and original designs, becoming famous for his multi-flora design and his unique lamps. He has work on display in many major museums and collections, among them the Smithsonian, the Art Institute of Chicago, the Museum of Glass at Corning, and the Chrysler Museum. Every piece is made free-hand, decorated with hot glass, and has a polished pontil. Charles' three sons, David, Daniel, and John each learned the art from their father and established their own studios. John stopped blowing glass in 2002, and his work is becoming scarce. David's sons, Jeremiah and Joshua are now beginning their careers in glass. Daniel's son, Tim, is also venturing into his initial designs. Scott Bayless, not a relative, and Charles' nephew, Jerry Heer, each produce unique designs signed with their names, the year, and Lotton Studios. All of the artists produce distinctive work. They sell their work at craft shows and at their showrooms in Crete, Illinois, as well as in their gallery on Michigan Avenue in Chicago, and in art galleries across the US. For further information read *Lotton Art Glass* by Charles Lotton and Tom O'Conner. Our advisors are Gerald and Sharon Peterson; they are listed in the Directory under Washington.

Key:
CL — Charles Lotton   JL — John Lotton
DL — David Lotton   JoL — Joshua Lotton
DnL — Daniel Lotton   pwt — paperweight
fct — faceted   SB — Scott Bayless
JH — Jerry Heer   td — teardrop stopper
JhL — Jeremiah Lotton   TL — Tim Lotton

Bowl, Anthuriums, pink on Neodymium Crystal, rolled collar, Daniel Lotton, 1996, 6¾x7¾", $1,400.00.
(Photo courtesy Gerald and Sharon Peterson)

Bottle, Wisteria, bl/gold ruby, Oriental form, CL, 2004, 9x6¼"... **2,200.00**
Bowl, Asters, wht on blk, DnL, 2004, 5¼x7½" **1,400.00**
Bowl, leaves, pk/Selenium Red irid, rolled rim, JH, 2004, 4x5½" **350.00**
Bowl, magnum; Egyptian symbols, blk/verre-de-soie, JL, 2001, 7½x9". **3,200.00**
Bowl, magnum; floral branches, pk/bl/opal, lt bl int, JL, 2000, 9x12" ... **4,600.00**
Bowl, magnum; long-stem flowers, wht on crystal, JL, 2000, 17x5½" ... **2,600.00**
Bowl, Multi-flora, lav/Opal Cypriot w/2-color crush, CL, 2006, 7x9" .. **2,800.00**
Bowl, Multi-flora, pk/Mandarin Yel/blk, tall neck, CL, 2006, 8x10½" . **5,000.00**
Bowl, Multi-flora, pk/Sunset Cypriot, trn collar, CL, 2007, 8x9½"... **3,800.00**
Bowl, pulled leaves, gr on Sunset, DL, 2005, 3¾x6⅜" **350.00**
Bowl, Tulipticus, lav on crystal w/Sunset int, DnL, 2005, 6x6½" .. **1,100.00**
Bowl, Tulipticus, pk/crystal w/Sunset int, DnL, 2005, 5x8" **1,100.00**
Bowl, vines, blk/silver/crystal w/pk crush, free-form, JL, '01, 8x17" .. **2,250.00**
Bowl, vines, pk on cobalt irid, JH, 2007, 3¼x4¾" **300.00**
Bowl, vines, pk/aurene/opal, cobalt int, rolled rim, JH, 2004, 3x5".. **350.00**
Bowl, vines/leaves, pk/gold on cobalt irid, JL, 1994, 4½x6" **400.00**
Candlestick, morning glories, purple on Sunset, JhL, '02, 3¾x2¼" .. **150.00**
Jack-in-pulpit, verre-de-soie Cypriot, no decor, DL, 2002, 10x3½" .. **350.00**
Jack-in-pulpit, Wisteria, aurene/cobalt irid, CL, 1994, 13¾x8".. **2,200.00**
Jack-in-pulpit, yel, no decor, DL, 2002, 9¼x2⅞" **275.00**

Jardiniere & ped, Multi-flora, pk/irid gold Ruby Cypriot, CL, '06, 25"... 10,000.00
Lamp, floor; Multi-flora, cased pk/fuchsia, CL, 2004, 71x21½" .. 14,000.00
Lamp, mushroom; floral, pk on Selenium Red, DnL, 2002, 12½x7½" 1,600.00
Lamp, table; Anthuriums, pk on gr, DnL, 2003, mini, 13¼x12".. 3,400.00
Lamp, table; Anthuriums, pk on opal w/red int, DnL, 1998, 27x14½" ...4,500.00
Lamp, table; Fern, pk on Selenium Red, ruffled, DnL, 1992, 20x13".. 3,000.00
Ornament, Pulled Loop, Gold Ruby & cobalt, DnL, 2007, 3¼"... 200.00
Paperweight, calla lilies, wht/verre-de-soie, facets, SB, '05, 4¼" .. 350.00
Paperweight, calla lilies, 6-color/crystal, SB, 2004, 4x4" 350.00
Paperweight, flowers, pk/wht/crystal w/irid veil, JL, 2000, 8½"... 5,400.00
Paperweight, Max Erlacher eng, gold irid to cobalt, DL, 1993, 2¼" ...600.00
Paperweight, orchids, purple & yel, DL, 1998, 3¼x3¾" 200.00
Paperweight, orchids, purple w/appl leaf & vine, JoL, 2007, 2¾x4" ...300.00
Paperweight, orchids, rose/crystal, SB, 2007, 4"........................... 210.00
Paperweight, orchids/hollyhocks, pk/purple/ruby crush, DL, '01, 5¾"...900.00
Pendant, flower, lav/verre-de-soie, DL, 1998, 1½x1⅛" 125.00
Pendant, scarab, blk border w/irid center, DL, 2002, 2½x2"......... 125.00
Perfume, Cynthia Flowers, orange/crystal, teardrop top, DnL, '03, 12"...600.00
Perfume, leaves, pk/verre-de-soie, teardrop stopper, JH, 2005, 5½" .. 275.00
Perfume, vine, pk/aurene/opal irid w/Gold Ruby int, JH, 2004, 3¼"..195.00
Perfume, vines, pk/aurene/opal/gold ruby crush, JH, 2000, 4½" ... 325.00
Sculpture, Bridal Veil, crystal w/3 irid veils, DL, 1998, 11¼x7" ... 850.00
Sculpture, Cypriot w/silver lava draping, TL, 2006, 6½x5¼" 250.00
Sculpture, leaves/vines, purple/gr/crystal w/Sunset irid, DL, '98, 11"... 800.00
Sculpture, orchids/reeds, yel/gr/purple in clear, DL, 2005, 10½".. 2,200.00
Sculpture, threading, copper bl & crystal, TL, 2005, 6½x11½".... 250.00
Sculpture, threading, pk & gr on crystal, TL, 2006, 8¼x20" 350.00
Slipper, King Tut, opal w/aventurine/Mandarin Red, CL, 2007, 4½" L..400.00
Vase, blk & yel threading on opal, lt gr int, DL, 2000, 4¼x5½" ... 250.00
Vase, Cactus Flowers, opal, Oriental shape, DnL, 2007, 8¼x5¾"..1,800.00
Vase, Clematis, purple on crystal, DL, 2003, 7¼x4¼".................. 500.00

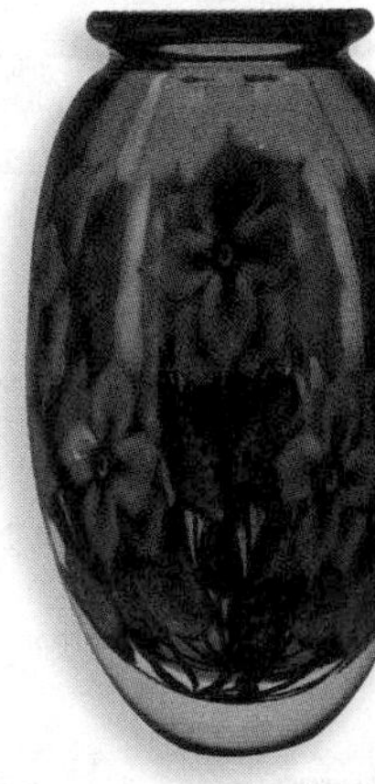

Vase, Cynthia flowers, two-layer, Neodymium Crystal on lavender, Daniel Lotton, 2007, 11x6", $3,400.00. (Photo courtesy Gerald and Sharon Peterson)

Vase, flowers, wht/opal w/pk crush, globular, JhL & JL, 2006, 3¼" ... 225.00
Vase, Lava Drape, bl/irid Gold Ruby Cypriot, cut/curled, CL, 1995, 8" ..1,600.00
Vase, long-stem flowers, pk/crystal free-form, JL, 2001, 18x16" ... 2,700.00
Vase, paperweight; calla lilies, varied colors, SB, 2006, 9¼"......1,200.00
Vase, paperweight; flowers, purple/gr/crystal w/yel veil, DL, '03, 8" 650.00
Vase, paperweight; orchids, purple/fuchsia/crystal, DL, 1997, 6x3½" .. 450.00
Vase, Peacock, orange irid w/aurene rim, trn collar, CL, 2005, 10x7"... 2,400.00
Vase, Pulled Loop/Drop Leaf, coral irid w/gr/aurene, DnL, 1992, 3½" ..600.00
Vase, pulled loops/feathers, cobalt/opal, JhL, 2002, 7¾x3¼" 325.00
Vase, reverse pulls, yel/purple/opal, JhL, 2002, 6⅜x2¾" 275.00
Vase, threaded ext, dk gr w/lt gr wide collar, DL, 2005, 3¼x4¼".. 275.00
Vase, vines, gr/blk w/gr crush, JhL & JL, 2006, mini, 4¼x3¼" 200.00

Lotus Ware

Isaac Knowles and Issac Harvey operated a pottery in East Liverpool, Ohio, in 1853 where they produced both yellow ware and Rockingham. In 1870 Knowles brought Harvey's interests and took as partners John Taylor and Homer Knowles. Their principal product was ironstone china, but Knowles was confident that American potters could produce as fine a ware as the Europeans. To prove his point, he hired Joshua Poole, an artist from the Belleek Works in Ireland. Poole quickly perfected a Belleek-type china, but fire destroyed this portion of the company. Before it could function again, their hotel china business had grown to the point that it required their full attention in order to meet market demands. By 1891 they were able to try again. They developed a bone china, as fine and thin as before, which they called Lotus. Henry Schmidt from the Meissen factory in Germany decorated the ware, often with lacy filigree applications or hand-formed leaves and flowers to which he added further decoration with liquid slip applied by means of a squeeze bag. Due to high production costs resulting from so much of the fragile ware being damaged in firing and because of changes in tastes and styles of decoration, the Lotus Ware line was dropped in 1896. Some of the early ware was marked 'KT&K China'; later marks have a star and a crescent with 'Lotus Ware' added. Non-factory decorated pieces are usually lower in value. Our advisor for this category is Mary Frank Gaston; she is listed in the Directory under Texas.

Bowl, pk floral on bl, ruffled/beaded gilt rim, rtcl hdls, oval, 4x7" ...250.00
Chocolate jug, gold-paste florals, Quincy design, ca 1890-1905, 4x5" ..600.00
Ewer, appl wht floral on lt gr, ornate hdl, 6"................................. 285.00
Ewer, heavily filigreed, undecorated wht, 9½"..........................1,065.00
Jar, Luxor, rtcl raised medallions/tassels & cords, 4-ftd, 7", EX..... 800.00

Jardiniere, flowers and jewels with gold trim, reticulated bosses each side, losses and repair, 4x6½", $840.00. (Photo courtesy David Rago Auctions/ LiveAuctioneers.com)

Rose jar, wht, beaded rim, heavily filigreed band under lid, 4½" .. 200.00
Tray, shell w/ruffled edge & gilt highlights, HP floral, 8½" L........ 185.00
Vase, HP boat w/appl gold fishnet, ruffled rim, ftd, rpr, 4x5", EX .. 250.00
Vase, HP pastel floral & wht fishnet panels, 4 gold ball ft, 8x5"... 200.00
Vase, Roman, wht ware, integral hdls, bulbous base, 10"...........1,000.00
Vase, wht w/appl gr floral, slim neck, scalloped rim, w/hdl, 10", EX...250.00

Lu Ray Pastels

Lu Ray Pastels dinnerware was introduced in the early 1940s by Taylor, Smith, and Taylor of East Liverpool, Ohio. It was offered in assorted colors of Persian Cream, Sharon Pink, Surf Green, Windsor Blue, and Chatham Gray in complete place settings as well as many service pieces. It was a successful line in its day and is once again finding favor with collectors of American dinnerware. Our advisor for this category is Shirley Moore; she is listed in the Directory under Oklahoma.

Bowl, coupe soup; flat 18.00
Bowl, cream soup 70.00
Bowl, fruit; Chatham Gray, 5" 16.00
Bowl, fruit; 5" 6.00
Bowl, lug soup; tab hdls 24.00
Bowl, mixing; 5½" 125.00

Bowl, mixing; 7".. 125.00
Bowl, mixing; 8¾"... 125.00
Bowl, mixing; 10¼"... 150.00
Bowl, salad; any color other than yel 65.00
Bowl, salad; yel... 55.00
Bowl, vegetable; oval, 9½"... 25.00
Bowl, 36s oatmeal 60.00
Bud vase 400.00
Butter dish, any color other than Chatham Gray, w/lid 60.00
Butter dish, Chatham Gray, rare color, w/lid 90.00
Calendar plates, 8", 9" & 10", ea 40.00
Casserole 140.00
Chocolate cup, AD; str sides 80.00
Chocolate pot, AD; str sides 400.00
Coaster/nut dish.. 65.00
Coffee cup, AD 22.50

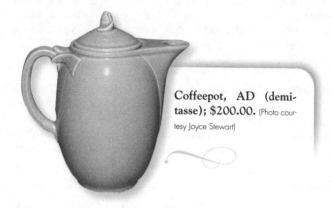

Coffeepot, AD (demitasse); $200.00. (Photo courtesy Joyce Stewart)

Creamer.. 10.00
Creamer, AD, ind 40.00
Creamer, AD, str sides, ind, from chocolate set 92.00
Egg cup, dbl 30.00
Epergne 125.00
Jug, water; ftd 150.00
Muffin cover.. 140.00
Muffin cover, w/8" underplate 165.00
Nappy, vegetable; rnd, 8½".. 25.00
Pickle tray 28.00
Pitcher, bulbous w/flat bottom, any color other than yel 125.00
Pitcher, bulbous w/flat bottom, yel 95.00
Pitcher, juice 200.00
Plate, cake 70.00
Plate, Chatham Gray, rare color, 7"................................. 16.00
Plate, chop; 15" 38.00
Plate, grill; 3-compartment... 35.00
Plate, 6".. 3.00
Plate, 7".. 12.00
Plate, 8".. 25.00
Plate, 9".. 10.00
Plate, 10".. 25.00
Platter, oval, 11½"... 20.00
Platter, oval, 13"... 24.00
Relish dish, 4-part 125.00
Sauceboat.. 28.00
Sauceboat, fixed stand, any color other than yel............. 35.00
Sauceboat, fixed stand, yel.. 27.50
Saucer, coffee; AD 12.50
Saucer, coffee/chocolate 30.00
Saucer, cream soup... 28.00
Saucer, tea 2.00
Shakers, pr.. 18.00

Sugar bowl, AD; str sides, w/lid, from chocolate set 92.00
Sugar bowl, AD; w/lid, ind 40.00
Sugar bowl, w/lid... 15.00
Teacup.. 8.00
Teapot, curved spout, w/lid.. 125.00
Teapot, flat spout, w/lid.. 160.00
Tumbler, juice 50.00
Tumbler, water 80.00

Lunch Boxes

Early twentieth-century tobacco companies such as Union Leader, Tiger, and Dixie sold their products in square, steel containers with flat, metal carrying handles. These were specifically engineered to be used as lunch boxes when they became empty. (See Advertising, specific companies.) By 1930 oval lunch pails with colorful lithographed decorations on tin were being manufactured to appeal directly to children. These were made by Ohio Art, Decoware, and a few other companies. In 1950 Aladdin Industries produced the first 'real' character lunch box — a Hopalong Cassidy decal-decorated steel container now considered the beginning of the kids' lunch box industry. The other big lunch box manufacturer, American Thermos (later King Seely Thermos Company) brought out its 'blockbuster' Roy Rogers box in 1953, the first fully lithographed steel lunch box and matching bottle. Other companies (ADCO Liberty; Landers, Frary & Clark; Ardee Industries; Okay Industries; Universal; Tindco; Cheinco) also produced character pails. Today's collectors often tend to specialize in those boxes dealing with a particular subject. Western, space, TV series, Disney movies, and cartoon characters are the most popular. There are well over 500 different lunch boxes available to the astute collector. For further information we recommend *The Illustrated Encyclopedia of Metal Lunch Boxes* by Allen Woodall and Sean Brickell. In the following listings, unless specific information to the contrary is included in the description, assume the lunch boxes to be made of metal and values to reflect the worth of boxes that are complete with their original vaccum bottles. The low side of our range represents examples in excellent condition; the high side represents mint.

A-Team, 1980s, from $30 to.. 50.00
Action Jackson, 1970s, from $650 to 900.00
Annie, 1980s, vinyl, from $50 to..................................... 75.00
Barbarino, 1970s, vinyl, from $125 to 150.00
Batman & Robin, 1960s, from $65 to 95.00
Beverly Hillbillies, 1960s, from $150 to 225.00

Bozo, dome-top, 1960s, from $175.00 to $225.00; Metal Thermos bottle, from $25.00 to $50.00. (Photo courtesy Morphy Auctions/LiveAuctioneers.com)

Brady Bunch, 1970s, from $175 to 250.00
Casey Jones, 1960s, dome top, from $500 to................ 700.00

Charlie's Angels, 1970s, from $60 to............................120.00
Close Encounters of the Third Kind, 1970s, from $60 to 120.00
Davy Crockett/Kit Carson, 1955, no bottle, from $150 to 225.00
Disney School Bus, 1990s, plastic, from $20 to........................30.00
Doctor Doolittle, 1960s, from $95 to 165.00
Dudley Do-Right, 1960s, from $775 to 1,125.00
Emergency!, 1973, from $70 to..............................115.00
ET, 1980s, from $30 to 60.00
Family Affair, 1960s, from $65 to 130.00
Fire Station Engine Co #1, 1970s, vinyl, from $115 to.................135.00
Flipper, 1960s, from $120 to 190.00
Gene Autry Melody Ranch, 1950s, from $225 to 375.00
Green Hornet, 1960s, from $250 to 400.00
Happy Days, 1970s, 2 versions, ea from $60 to 95.00
Hopalong Cassidy, 1954, from $350 to...........................500.00
Incredible Hulk, 1970s, from $35 to 95.00
Indiana Jones, 1980s, from $25 to 55.00

Jetsons, dome-top, 1960s, from $1,000.00 to $1,800.00. (Photo courtesy Morphy Auctions/LiveAuctioneers.com)

Johnny Lightning, 1970s, from $55 to...........................105.00
Julia, 1960s, from $65 to....................................140.00
Jungle Book, 1960s, from $60 to.............................120.00
Krofft Supershow, 1970s, from $65 to.........................125.00
Kung Fu, 1970s, from $45 to..................................95.00
Land of the Giants, 1960s, from $120 to.....................200.00
Li'l Jodie, 1980s, vinyl, from $50 to.........................75.00
Little Dutch Miss, 1959, from $70 to.........................140.00
Lone Ranger, 1950s, no bottle, from $300 to..................450.00
Looney Tunes, 1959, from $200 to 300.00
Magic Lassie, 1970s, from $60 to.............................110.00
Man From UNCLE, 1960s, from $120 to.........................190.00
Mary Poppins, 1960s, from $65 to.............................130.00
Mary Poppins, 1970s, vinyl, from $75 to......................100.00
Mickey Mouse, 1980s, plastic head form, from $30 to...........40.00

Munsters, 1960s, from $450.00 to $650.00.

(Photo courtesy Morphy Auctions/LiveAuctioneers.com)

Paladin, 1960s, from $190 to................................275.00
Partridge Family, 1970s, from $55 to.........................100.00
Peanuts, 1960, from $40 to...................................80.00
Peter Pan, 1960s, from $70 to................................140.00
Pink Panther, 1980s, vinyl, from $75 to......................100.00
Popeye, 1962, from $525 to...................................850.00
Popeye, 1980s, from $50 to...................................100.00
Psychedelic Blue, 1970s, vinyl, from $40 to...................60.00

Psychedelic, 1970s, from $75.00 to $150.00.

(Photo courtesy Morphy Auctions/LiveAuctioneers.com)

Rat Patrol, 1960s, from $95 to...............................165.00
Rifleman, 1960s, from $325 to................................150.00
Robot Man, 1980s, from $20 to................................30.00
Rough Rider, 1970s, from $65 to..............................100.00
Roy Rogers & Dale Evans, 1950s, many versions, ea from $200 to .325.00
Scooby-Doo, 1970s, various, any, ea from $70 to...............140.00
Six Million Dollar Man, 1970s, various, ea from $50 to........75.00
Spider-Man & the Hulk, 1980, from 1980s, from $40 to..........80.00
Strawberry Shortcake, 1980, vinyl, from $75 to 135.00
Super Friends, 1970s, from $50 to............................100.00
Super Heroes, 1970s, from $45 to.............................90.00
Superman, 1980s, plastic, phone booth scene, from $30 to.......40.00
Tarzan, 1960s, from $125 to..................................200.00
The Sophisticate, 1970s, vinyl drawstring bag, from $50 to....75.00
Tic-Tac-Toe, 1970s, vinyl, from $50 to.......................75.00
Tom Corbett Space Cadet, 1952, from $130 to..................250.00
UFO, 1970s, from $65 to......................................115.00
V, 1980s, from $95 to..165.00
Welcome Back Kotter, 1970s, from $60 to......................100.00
Wild Bill Hickok & Jingles, 1950S, from $190 to...............280.00
Wild Wild West, 1960s, from $200 to..........................300.00
Woody Woodpecker, 1970s, from $125 to 200.00
World of Barbie, vinyl, 1971, from $50 to.....................75.00
Yogi Bear, 1990s, plastic, from $15 to.......................25.00
Zorro, 1950s or 1960s, ea from $150 to 250.00

Lundberg Studios

This small studio has operated in Davenport, California, since 1970, when founder James Lundberg (now deceased) began making quality handcrafted glassware using a variety of techniques — some reminiscent of Tiffany. Their production includes vases, lamps, paperweights, perfume bottles, and marbles. Each piece they make is signed with the studio's name, the artist's name, a registration number, and the date.

Lamp, Starry Nights, yel stars on bl swirls, ftd, sgn, 15"............1,050.00

Paperweight, intaglio angels/doves/floral on bl, #042854, 1989, 3" 1,000.00
Paperweight, Pond Reflection Extra, Steven, #031729, 1989, 2½" 1,300.00

Perfume bottle, daffodils in clear glass, signed Steven, 1991, 6", $325.00. (Photo courtesy Monsen & Baer)

Shade, lt gr/dk gr/ivory swirls, 2½" top opening, sgn, 10" 1,250.00
Shade, red, ivory & gold swirls, ruffled bottom edge, sgn, 9" 625.00
Vase, feathers, red/purple/bl on gold, trumpet form, 2000, 11" 225.00
Vase, Oriental women in ornate attire, bl tones, Hawke, #90312, 10" 1,500.00
Vase, paperweight; Daffodil Garden, clear, #013102, sgn, 2001, 6½" 1,000.00
Vase, paperweight; floral on bl tones in clear, #071117, sgn, 1996, 6". 120.00
Vase, paperweight; undersea life on amber in gr swirled clear, 4½". 1,500.00
Vase, pulled leaves, dk gr on gr, James, #032207, 1988, 8½" 525.00
Vase, pulled silver & purple on yel, bulbous at top, unmk, 7x3½".1,200.00
Vase, woven yel & bl in opal, bulbous, 1981, 9" 325.00

Maddux of California

One of the California-made ceramics now so popular with collectors, Maddux was founded in the late 1930s and during the years that followed produced novelty items, TV lamps, figurines, planters, and tableware accessories.

Ashtray, gunmetal gray, triangular, #731, 10½" 15.00
Ashtray, hippopotamus w/wide mouth open, #1152?, 4x4" 25.00
Clock, Zodiac, #7118R, 12" dia... 45.00
Cookie jar, Beatrix Potter Rabbit, from $75 to 85.00
Cookie jar, Grapes Cylinder, #8412, from $25 to........................... 35.00
Cookie jar, Humpty Dumpty, #2113, 11" 40.00
Cookie jar, Squirrel Hiker, #2110, from $175 to........................... 200.00
Dish, serving; gr leaves, #3051, 10x15" 28.50
Figurine, blk horse rearing, #925, 13x4".. 25.00
Figurine, rooster, gold & wht brushed finish, #934, 11" 30.00
Nightlight, chihuahua figural, #E-21855-M, 8x5½"........................ 90.00
Planter, blk swan, #150, 11" 25.00
Planter, flamingo in flight, #515, 10½x6½" 90.00
Planter, leaf design w/rose center, 2 ped ft, 4x10" 18.00
Planter, Oriental girl holding bird, planter in bk, 6¼" 50.00
Planter, 3-D stag on side, #526, 11x7x5".. 20.00
Plaque, Aquarius emb on yel, 1967, 3⅜".. 25.00
Snack server, gr w/emb ribs, 2-compartment, #3151, 1½x11x6¼". 15.00
TV lamp, bull, brn, #859, 10x10".. 45.00
TV lamp, horse trotting, 12½x10½".. 30.00
TV lamp, pk flower on ea side of gold ½-cylinder shade w/Xs, 6x10"... 40.00
Vase, gazelle in relief on either side, brn, 1959, 12½x3½" 35.00
Vase, pk flamingo (2) figural, wings form body of dbl vase, 5x6½". 25.00
Vase, spittoon shape, wht, #676, 6x8" 12.00
Wall sconce, yel w/fine brn lines, #107W, 4½x4½", +metal hanger ..20.00

Majolica

Majolica is a type of heavy earthenware, design-molded and decorated in vivid colors with either a lead or tin type of glaze. It reached its height of popularity in the Victorian era; examples from this period are found in only the lead glazes. Nearly every potter of note, both here and abroad, produced large majolica jardinieres, umbrella stands, pitchers with animal themes, leaf shapes, vegetable forms, and nearly any other design from nature that came to mind. Not all, however, marked their ware. Among those who sometimes did were Minton, Wedgwood, Holdcroft, and George Jones in England; Griffin, Smith and Hill (Etruscan) in Phoenixville, Pennsylvania; and Chesapeake Pottery (Avalon and Clifton) in Baltimore.

Color and condition are both very important worth-assessing factors. Pieces with cobalt, lavender, and turquoise glazes command the highest prices. For further information we recommend *The Collector's Encyclopedia of Majolica* by Mariann Katz-Marks (see Directory, Pennsylvania). Unless another condition is given, the values that follow are for pieces in mint condition. Our advisor for this category is Hardy Hudson; he is listed in the Directory under Florida.

Basket, creamy tan basketweave w/gray cat at rim, Brownfield, 12" L.. 1,200.00
Bough pot, goats in meadow, Minton, 6½" dia..........................2,185.00
Bowl, center; daisy & leaf rim, rtcl center, 3 pigeons, Minton, 13" .3,650.00
Bowl, centerpc; satyrs eating grapes, Copeland, 17" 1,750.00
Box, lizard atop basketweave, rectangular, Palissy Ware, 6" L..1,450.00
Butter dish, Blackberry on turq, G Jones................................. 1,550.00
Butter tub, swan, butterflies & dragonflies on cobalt, prof rstr 545.00
Cake stand, Shell & Seaweed, Etruscan, 4¾x9" 900.00
Charger, nude woman on serpent, flower border, Wedgwood, 15¼" ... 650.00
Cheese keeper, apple blossoms on picket fence, turq, G Jones, 10" ..2,150.00
Cheese keeper, Blackberry on turq tree bark, cow finial, 9½", NM 950.00
Cheese keeper, parrot on branch w/palm leaves, 12" 1,550.00
Compote, fox looking into hole w/rabbit under tree, G Jones, 8".. 9,600.00
Compote, playing cane on turq pebble ground, low, Holdcroft, 9¾"..200.00
Compote, Pond Lily, G Jones, 9".. 865.00
Compote, scalloped bowl, cherub on aquatic base, Wedgwood, 1870s, 9"...700.00
Creamer, ear of corn, Etruscan, 4" 95.00
Flower holder, 2 putti hold bbl w/pierced top, Holdcroft, 10", NM..1,450.00

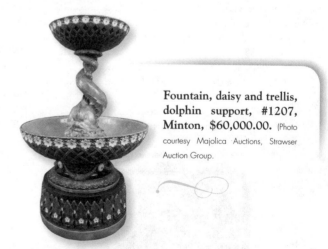

Fountain, daisy and trellis, dolphin support, #1207, Minton, $60,000.00. (Photo courtesy Majolica Auctions, Strawser Auction Group.)

Game dish, fox atop ferns finial, dead game on turq, G Jones, rpr, 11". 4,485.00
Game dish, game emb on brn, chick finial, w/liner, Wedgwood, 9" L .. 2,200.00
Game dish, game emb on brn, rabbit finial, Wedgwood, Argenta, 9½" L....825.00
Humidor, Isle of Man on coil of rope, Holdcroft, 9½" 1,665.00
Jar, Swan & Cattails on cobalt, Holdcroft, prof rpr, 15x16" 750.00
Jardiniere, berries & blossoms on bark, Wedgwood, Argenta, 9"... 400.00

Jardiniere, dragonfly/bulrush/water lily on turq, G Jones, 10x11", NM ...1,375.00
Jardiniere, ram's head w/floral drape on turq, Minton, 14" 2,875.00
Jardiniere, wild rose on tree bark, blossom hdls, G Jones, 9", NM .. 1,100.00
Jug, Bird & Fan on cobalt, Wedgwood, ca 1884, 7 1 /4" 325.00
Jug, cobalt w/foliate bands, pewter lid, Wedgwood, ca 1871, 8¾" ...650.00
Muffin dish, Apple Blossom on cobalt, branch hdl, prof rpr, 10"... 850.00
Oyster plate, Shell (mc) & Seaweed on turq, Fielding, 9".........1,950.00
Oyster plate, Shell (6) & Seaweed, cobalt, Holdcroft, 10", NM ...1,175.00

Oyster plate, Water Lily, 9", $2,000.00. (Photo courtesy Majolica Auctions, Strawser Auction Group)

Oyster plate, 4 turq shells on basketweave, ca 1882, 8¾x7½" ...3,500.00
Pitcher, Asparagus, Fr, 8", NM 1,035.00
Pitcher, chestnut & floral, G Jones, prof rpr hdl, 12½".............9,450.00
Pitcher, Diana, bearded man below spout, Minton, 11½" 400.00
Pitcher, fish figural, curled tail forms hdl, 10" 155.00
Pitcher, fish w/serpent hdl, waves at base, Palissy style, 11", NM .. 900.00
Pitcher, monkey figural w/bamboo hdl, prof rpr, 10".................2,400.00
Pitcher, Orchid & Tree Bark, leaf hdl, prof rpr, G Jones, 5½" ...1,265.00
Pitcher, Water Lily & Iris on cobalt, G Jones, 8"......................3,150.00
Plate, Asparagus & Artichoke, Luneville, 9" 300.00
Plate, Bamboo, Etruscan, 8"..120.00
Plate, lobster on cobalt w/vegetable border, Wedgwood, 8½"....... 800.00
Platter, fish & bulrushes on turq, Holdcroft, 25" L....................2,650.00
Punch bowl, morning glory, wheat, ribbon & bow, Fielding, 6½x14" ... 265.00

Punch bowl, Punch as support, 11" diameter, $25,000.00. (Photo courtesy Majolica Auctions, Strawser Auction Group)

Sardine box, Barrel in Ocean w/Seaweed, Wedgwood Argenta, 7½"... 1,785.00
Sardine box, Crate in Ocean, rope hdl, Wedgwood Argenta 1,250.00
Shelf, eagle bracket support, G Jones, 9½x9½" 1,800.00
Sweetmeat dish, conch shell supported by 2 dolphins, Minton, 9¼" .. 2,300.00
Sweetmeat dish, putti w/hooved ft holds turq shell, G Jones, 9" .. 925.00
Table center, man w/wheelbarrow, #413, ca 1869, prof rpr, 13x13" ..2,400.00
Table center, mermaid supporting shell, Minton, #852, 15"......2,200.00
Teapot, Fish Swallowing Fish, gr/brn/yel, 6½"............................. 785.00
Teapot, Isle of Man, Union Jack w/flag, Brownfield, prof rpr, 7¾" .. 1,200.00
Teapot, Monkey & Coconut, Minton, prof rpr, 8½".................4,600.00
Teapot, Spikey Fish, Minton, 1878, prof rpr, 7¼" 8,625.00
Tray, Bulrush & Lotus, lotus center hdl, Minton, #1041, 15½", NM .3,200.00
Tray, Butterfly, Dragonfly & Wheat, bamboo border, G Jones, 13" 3,225.00
Tray, fishnet amid fish & shells w/in bamboo fr, Longchamp, 15x15". 1,200.00
Tray, kingfisher on bulrush & pond lilies, G Jones.....................6,000.00
Tray, Lotus & Bulrush, Minton, EX color/detail, 15½" 3,100.00
Tray, napkin on yel, bamboo hdls, Wedgwood, 13" L 1,200.00
Tray, 3 leaf-form dishes attach to center hdl, Wedgwood, 1866, 16" L ...350.00
Tureen, boar & hunting dogs, boar's head finial & hdls, 12½" L, NM.. 7,200.00
Tureen, lobster; lobster finial, shells & seaweed, Minton, 14" L ...11,215.00
Umbrella stand, fan/scroll/butterfly, bamboo rim, Fielding, 23", EX...515.00
Umbrella stand, herons on marshy shore on lt bl, 22¼", NM ...1,265.00
Umbrella stand, lg grizzly bear beside tree, chip, 26" 4,350.00
Umbrella stand, Pond Lily & Fern, Holdcroft, 22", NM 1,175.00
Umbrella stand, Stork & Cattail, turq, Holdcroft, prof rpr, 22"... 2,000.00
Umbrella stand, tobacco leaf & floral on turq, Holdcroft, 20½", NM .. 1,675.00
Vase, marine life on cobalt, 3 mermen at base, Minton, prof rpr, 17" ... 2,500.00

Malachite Glass

Malachite is a type of art glass that exhibits strata-like layerings in shades of green, similar to the mineral in its natural form. Some examples have an acid-etched mark of Moser/Carlsbad, usually on the base. However, it should be noted that in the past 30 years there have been reproductions from Czechoslovakia with a paper label. These are most often encountered.

Basket, allegorical scenes in relief, 5½" 50.00
Box, nudes in relief, 4" dia.. 95.00
Box, reclining nude in relief on lid, rectangular, 2x5x4" 150.00
Dish, nude reclines at edge of pool, 3x8x5" 120.00
Figurne, stylized woman, 9" 60.00
Vase, classical woman in relief, 10" 215.00

Vases, nudes and vintage, from the Ingrid Series, Schlevogt, 8½", $325.00 for the pair. (Photo courtesy Early Auction Co.)

Maps and Atlases

Maps are highly collectible, not only for historical value but also for their sometimes elaborate artwork, legendary information, or data that since they were printed has been proven erroneous. There are many types of maps including geographical, military, celestial, road, and railroad. Nineteenth-century maps, particularly of U.S. areas, are increasing in popularity and price. Rarity, area depicted (i.e. Texas is more sought after than North Dakota), and condition are major price factors. World globes as a form of round maps are increasingly sought after, especially lighted and black ocean globes. Any tape other than archival tape hurts the value of maps — better still torn than badly mended. Our advisor for this category is Murray Hudson; he is listed in the Directory under Tennessee. Unless otherwise noted, our values are for maps in excellent condition.

Key: hc — hand colored

Atlases

Beacon's Handy...World, Hammond, US territories, NY, 1910, 114-pg, G-..40.00

Brown County OH, Grigging & Stevenson, 1876, folio............... 330.00
Butler County...& Pictorial Review, Republican Publishing, OH, 1914....270.00
Centennial...Warren County OH, Centennial Atlas Assoc, 1903, folio...230.00
Cincinnati & Hamilton County OH, Titus, rebound in leather, 1869.480.00
Clermont County OH, Titus, rebound in leather, 1870 .... 750.00
Cram's Unrivaled...World, Chicago, 560 color maps, 1911, NM.475.00
Harmsworth...& Gazetteer, Philip & Son, London, 500 maps/etc, 1910.500.00
New Encyclopedic...& Gazetteer..., Reynolds, Special 1912 ed, 256-pg.185.00
New Reference...World, Hammond, NY, special chapters, 1910 .225.00
People's Handy...World, Geographical Publishing, Chicago, 1911, 123-pg..95.00
Rand McNally...Unrivaled...World, Chicago/NY, color, 1910, 357-pg.175.00
Scarborough's New Std...World, Hammond, 100+ maps, sm folio, 1910.225.00

Maps

Africa, JH Colton, NY, hc/litho, Slave Coast noted, 1860, 12x14" 75.00
Americae Retectio, T De Bry, Frankfurt, silver eng, 1594, 6x8", matted......500.00
Asia, J Gibson, London, full hc/copper eng, Cupid vignette, 1762, 6x8" 225.00
Canada, Feville, outline hc/copper eng, Paris, 1765, 11½x17", EX+ 450.00
Chart of World on Mercator's Projection, Doolittle, Boston, 1796, 7x9" ..200.00
L'Asie (Asia), Buffier, Paris, copper eng, 1744, 5½x7" 125.00
N Am, Arrowsmith, Boston, partial hc/copper eng, tribes, 1795, 7x10" 200.00
N Am, J Yeager, M Carey & Son, Philadelphia, hc/copper eng, 1827, 6x4" 85.00
Nova et Accuratissima...Terrarum..., Blaeu, hc/eng, 1662, 16x22"+fr.....7,000.00

Nuove Scoperte de Russi...Sinell Asia, shows western half of America, parts of Mexico and Canada, and the northeast tip of Russia, 1776, hand colored, 15x20", with linen mat and oak frame, $400.00. (Photo courtesy Garth's Auction Co.)

Oceana, SG Goodrich, Boston, outline hc/copper eng, 1826, 6x8", G- 125.00
OH, RT Anderson, J Tumbull, 1828, hc w/orig leather cover, 15x13"+fr..3,000.00
Pictorial...US, paper on linen, mc, Ensign & Thayer, 31x43½"+rods 1,095.00
Poli Arctici..., Hondy, hc/eng, scenic spandrels, in 22x25" fr 865.00
Road From Ft Smith Ark to Santa Fe NM, Indian locations, 1847, 17x31" 650.00
Territory of NM, Rio Del Norte/Santa Fe/etc, hc, ca 1847, 26x20¼" ...325.00
US/Canada/New Brunswick/Nova Scotia/Mexico, Monk, 1853, mc, 60x62" 300.00
Washington County OH, Titus, Simmons & Titus, mc, 1874, 16x26+fr 150.00
World, Bowen, Gentleman's Magazine/London, hc/copper eng, 1779, 11x18" 900.00

Marblehead

What began as therapy for patients in a sanitarium in Marblehead, Massachusetts, has become recognized as an important part of the Arts and Crafts movement in America. Results of the early experiments under the guidance of Arthur E. Baggs in 1904 met with such success that by 1908 the pottery had been converted to a solely commercial venture.

Simple vase shapes were sometimes incised with stylized animal and floral motifs or sailing ships. Some were decorated in low relief; many were plain. Matt glazes in soft yellow, gray, wisteria, rose, tobacco brown, and their most popular, Marblehead blue, were used alone or in combination. They also produced fine tiles decorated with ships, stylized floral or tree motifs, and landscapes. Early examples were lightly incised and matt painted (these are the most valuable) on 1"-thick bodies. Others, 4" square and thinner, were matt painted with landscapes in indigoes in the style of Arthur Wesley Dow.

The Marblehead logo is distinctive — a ship with full sail and the letters 'M' and 'P.' The pottery closed in 1936. Our advisors for this category are Suzanne Perrault and David Rago; they are listed in the Directory under New Jersey. Unless noted otherwise, all items listed below are marked and in the matt glaze.

Bowl, berry band, three colors on navy blue, 3x5¾", $1,850.00. (Photo courtesy David Rago Auctions)

Bowl, fruit band, gr/russet on brn to mustard, A Baggs, 1½x4½" ...3,600.00
Bowl, gr, incurvate rim, paper label, 6" 450.00
Tile, fish, pnt/cvd, sgn, collection of Arthur Baggs, 6"............12,000.00
Tile, house, pnt/cvd, sgn, collection of Arthur Baggs, 6".........10,800.00

Tile, incised landscape, signed, from the collection of Arthur Baggs, $114,000.00. (Photo courtesy David Rago Auctions/LiveAuctioneers.com)

Tile, landscape, HP indigo/yel, unsgn, collection of Arthur Baggs, 8" ..14,400.00
Tile, oak tree, gr, pnt/cvd, sgn, collection of Arthur Baggs, 6" ..4,500.00

Vase, band of crouching panthers, three-color, Hannah Tutt, 7x5", $33,600.00. (Photo courtesy David Rago Auctions)

Vase, berries & leaves, bl/gr/brn on brn, H Tutt, 4½" 3,600.00
Vase, berries & leaves, brn & gr on mustard, pear shape, 4½" ...1,325.00
Vase, bl, swollen cylinder, 9" 550.00
Vase, butterfly/floral band, cvd/mc on mustard, hairline, 4¼x4" .. 5,000.00
Vase, deep lav, swollen cylinder, label, 5¼" 360.00

Vase, dk bl, ovoid w/flared rim, 7¾" 480.00
Vase, floral, charcoal on dk gr speckled, A Baggs, 9½", NM...... 3,100.00
Vase, floral band, mc on gray speckled, 4¼x5" 2,400.00
Vase, floral panels, brn/indigo on gr, H Tutt, rstr, 5¼x6½" 3,900.00
Vase, fruit branches, yel/gr/gray, H Tutt, 6¾x5" 7,800.00
Vase, geometric band, indigo on gr, bulbous, 4x4¼" 2,650.00
Vase, geometric band, mc on gr stippled, H Tutt/A Baggs, 1912, 4"...5,750.00
Vase, geometrics (simple), dk gr on indigo, H Tutt, 6x3" 4,200.00
Vase, geometrics & lines, brn/indigo/gr, paper label, rstr, 8¼x4"....7,250.00
Vase, gr, swollen cylinder, 5½" 470.00
Vase, gr-brn, tapered, 5¼" 480.00
Vase, grapevines, bl/brn/gray, A Baggs, glaze bursts, 9½x6½" 6,000.00
Vase, grapevines, mc on gray, bulbous, H Tutt, 1912, hairline, 4"... 3,100.00
Vase, indigo speckled, dk gr decor band, spherical, 3½" 2,250.00
Vase, lav, swollen cylinder, 8x6", NM 480.00
Vase, mustard speckled, cylindrical, 9x5" 2,040.00
Vase, Persian crackleware glaze test, 3¾x5½" 1,200.00
Vase, purple, slightly waisted, 7¼" 300.00
Vase, sqs/crouching panthers at top, gray/yel/gr/bl, 6½x5", NM ...25,200.00
Vase, trees, 3-color, swollen cylinder, H Tutt, 1912, 7".............7,200.00
Vase, trees, 3-color on caramel, H Tutt/A Baggs, 4¼" 4,200.00
Vase, turq, flared rim, 4" 300.00
Wall pocket, bl, flared rim, ca 1906-36, 5¼" 180.00

Marbles

Marbles have been popular with children since the mid-1800s. They've been made in many types from a variety of materials. Among some of the first glass items to be produced, the earliest marbles were made from a solid glass rod broken into sections of the proper length which were placed in a tray of sand and charcoal and returned to the fire. As they were reheated, the trays were constantly agitated until the marbles were completely round. Other marbles were made of china, pottery, steel, and natural stones. Below is a listing of the various types, along with a brief description of each.

Agates: stone marbles of many different colors — bands of color alternating with white usually encircle the marble; most are translucent.

Ballot Box: handmade (with pontils), opaque white or black, used in lodge elections.

Bloodstone: green chalcedony with red spots, a type of quartz.

China: with or without glaze, in a variety of hand-painted designs — parallel bands or bull's-eye designs most common.

Clambroth: opaque glass with outer evenly spaced swirls of one or alternating colors.

Clay: one of the most common older types; some are painted while others are not.

Comic Strip: a series of 12 machine-made marbles with faces of comic strip characters, Peltier Glass Factory, Illinois.

Crockery: sometimes referred to as Benningtons; most are either blue or brown, although some are speckled. The clay is shaped into a sphere, then coated with glaze and fired.

End of the Day: single-pontil glass marbles — the colored part often appears as a multicolored blob or mushroom cloud.

Goldstone: clear glass completely filled with copper flakes that have turned gold-colored from the heat of the manufacturing process.

Indian Swirls: usually black glass with a colored swirl appearing on the outside next to the surface, often irregular.

Latticinio Core Swirls: double-pontil marble with an inner area with net-like effects of swirls coming up around the center.

Lutz Type: glass with colored or clear bands alternating with bands which contain copper flecks.

Micas: clear or colored glass with mica flecks which reflect as silver dots when marble is turned. Red is rare.

Onionskin: spiral type which are solidly colored instead of having individual ribbons or threads, multicolored.

Peppermint Swirls: made of white opaque glass with alternating blue and red outer swirls.

Ribbon Core Swirls: double-pontil marble — center shaped like a ribbon with swirls that come up around the middle.

Rose Quartz: stone marble, usually pink in color, often with fractures inside and on outer surface.

Solid Core Swirls: double-pontil marble — middle is solid with swirls coming up around the core.

Steelies: hollow steel spheres marked with a cross where the steel was bent together to form the ball.

Sulfides: generally made of clear glass with figures inside. Rarer types have colored figures or colored glass.

Tiger Eye: stone marble of golden quartz with inclusions of asbestos, dark brown with gold highlights.

Vaseline: machine-made of yellowish-green glass with small bubbles.

Prices listed below are for marbles in near-mint condition unless noted otherwise. Polished marbles have greatly reduced values. We do not list tinted marbles because there is no way of knowing how much color the tinting has, and intensity of color is an important worth-assessing factor. For a more thorough study of the subject, we recommend *Everett Grist's Big Book of Marbles* (published by Collector Books); you will find his address in the Directory under Tennessee.

Akro Agate, bl slag, ½-1" 1.00
Akro Agate, corkscrew, ½-1" 2.00
Akro Agate, Popeye corkscrew, bl/lt purple/yel, shooter, ¾" 345.00

Akro Agate, tri-color corkscrew, MIB, $900.00.
(Photo courtesy Everett Grist/Gray and Sally Dolly)

Akro Agate, wht semi-opaque w/oxblood spiral, corkscrew style, 25/32" ...300.00
Akro Agate, 3-colored corkscrew, from $10 to 35.00
Banded Opaque, gr w/red bands, wht & bl streaks, 1¾", EX......... 160.00
China, decorated, HP over glaze for 2nd firing, ⅝" 100.00
China, Pennsylvania Dutch, bl/gr/blk flower & turq leaves, 1¾" . 700.00
China, sailing ship/ornate leaf spray, 1860-1900, 23/32" 960.00
Christensen Agate, clear base w/orange bands, 2-seam, 1920s, 21/32" ... 300.00
Christensen Agate Exotic, lt & dk bl/wht/brn swirl, 2-seam, 19/32"...250.00
Christensen Agate Flame Swirl, 4-color w/lt bl base, flame tips, ¾" 575.00
Christensen Agate Guinea Cobra, clear w/mc stretched flecks, 19/32" .. 600.00
Christensen Agate Submarine, dk bl w/orange & wht swirls, 21/32"...... 850.00
Clambroth, lt bl opaque w/wht strands, 1870-1915, 19/32" 550.00
Clambroth, wht opaque w/9 pk/5 gr/4 bl bands, 1870-1915, 13/16"..480.00
Clay, common, ⅝" 50
Clay, common, 1¾" 5.00
Clear w/red & gr core, wht & gold flake outer bands, ⅝" 180.00
Cloud, clear w/bl/pk spots in 2 panels, 1870-1915, 1¾"............... 720.00
Cloud, clear w/yel subsurface & pk clouds, 16 shallow lobes, 2⅛"...480.00
Clown, wht core w/clear base, 4-color stretched bands, 13/16" 435.00
Comic, Betty (Boop), mustard base, red patch, 1930s, 11/16" 300.00
Comic, Cote's Master Loaf, 1930s, 1 11/16" 875.00
Comic, Kayo, 1930-35, 21/32" 300.00

Comic, Little Orphan Annie, 11/16", M 100.00
Confetti, clear w/pk/yel/gr/red/wht, 1920s-30s, 17/16", EX 915.00
Indian Swirl, bl/yel/red, sm air blow-out, 13/16" 275.00
Joseph Coat, clear base, partial bands/flecks in 7 colors, 19/16" 915.00
Joseph Swirl, bright bl w/red strands, 5/8" 300.00
Lutz, blk opaque core w/heavy bands, clear outer layer, 25/32" 250.00
Lutz, butterscotch w/lt bl bands, 3/4" 360.00
Lutz, dbl orange ribbon w/wht-edge bands, 1870-1915, 7/8" 785.00
Lutz, 2 wide wht-edge Lutz bands/4 yel bands on gr opaque, 25/32" ... 1,375.00
Lutz Indian, blk opaque w/3 bands (wht/bl/lt bl), 23/32" 800.00
Lutz Onionskin, clear w/wht core, pk & bl skin, 1870-1915, 7/8" .. 700.00

Lutz type, blue banded, 2", $540.00. (Photo courtesy Morphy Auctions/LiveAuctioneers.com)

Lutz type, clear w/gold swirls, bl & wht borders, 5/8" 125.00
Lutz type, orange banded, 7/8" 265.00
Lutz type, red ribbon core, single gold swirl w/wht border, 5/8" 300.00
Lutz type, yel bands, 15/32" 420.00
Marble King, mc rainbow 4.00
Marble King Watermelon, gr & red patch & ribbon, 1960-75, 5/8" ... 575.00
Millefiori flowers, tight pattern, pontil mk, 1½", EX 575.00
Onionskin, clear base/wht core, speckled 4-color w/mica, 13/16" 600.00
Onionskin, pk w/silver mica, bl & yel spots, 1¾", EX 360.00

Onionskin, pink, 11 13/16", $335.00. (Photo courtesy Morphy Auctions/LiveAuctioneers.com)

Onionskin, 2 wht panels w/bl streaks & 2 yel w/red streaks, 2¼" .. 1,125.00
Onionskin, 8-lobe, clear w/wht subsurface, pk skin, 1870-1915, 2⅛" .. 600.00
Peltier Golden Rebel, 6-ribbon (4 red/2 fiery aventurine), 9/16" 600.00
Peltier Superboy, 3-color/8-ribbon on lt bl opaque base, 29/32" 585.00
Peltier Superman, 3-color, 7-ribbon on lt bl opaque base, 21/32" 515.00
Peltier Superman, 3-color 6-ribbon on lt bl opaque base, 23/32" 335.00
Ribbon Onionskin, clear w/wht opaque ribbon w/overall pk skin, 21/32" .. 475.00
Submarine, clear blizzard mica core w/2 onionskin panels, 1¼", NM . 1,325.00
Sulfide, #9, well centered, 1870-1915, 1⅝" 475.00
Sulfide, angel (full body) w/wreath, 1870-1915, 2⅜" 700.00
Sulfide, boy on hobbyhorse blowing horn, 1870-1915, 19/16" 650.00
Sulfide, boy w/pond racer, air bubbles, 1870-1915, 1 13/16", NM..... 250.00
Sulfide, cat, blk details, well centered, 1870-1915, 17/16" 1,325.00
Sulfide, cherub, air bubbles, well centered, 1870-1915, 1⅝" 815.00
Sulfide, dog, transparent caramel brn, 1870-1915, 15/16" 900.00
Sulfide, James Garfield/Chester Arthur in clear, 1881-85, 17/16" ... 900.00
Sulfide, Jenny Lind, well centered, 1870-1915, 15/16" 325.00
Sulfide, lady w/basket in left arm, dog at right, 1870-1915, 1⅜" .. 1,050.00
Sulfide, lovebirds kissing on log, off-center, 1870-1915, 1⅞" 600.00
Sulfide, monkey seated, sm bubbles, well centered, 1870-1915, 21/16" ... 250.00

Sulfide, nude child holding sm ball, 1870-1915, 1¾" 700.00
Sulfide, sheep grazing in dk purple, lt wear, 1870-1915, 1⅞" 800.00
Sulfide, squirrel w/EX detail, 1 11/16", VG..................................... 325.00
Sulfide, turtle, sm air bubbles, well centered, 1870-1915, 17/16" 285.00
Sulfide, wild turkey, no air bubbles, 1870-1915, 17/16" 475.00
Swirl, gr/bl/wht/yel strands, solid core, wht/yel bands, 1⅜" 180.00
Swirl, lt bl w/wht core, 4 bands (2 pk/gr/wht & 2 pk/bl/wht), 17/16".. 480.00
Swirl, orange solid core, red & wht outer swirls, 13/16" 120.00
Swirl, yel/gr/bl/pk, solid wht core, wht outer bands, 1½" 180.00
Swirl/Dbl-Ribbon, pk/bl/wht & pk/yel/gr, yel & wht outer bands, 1¾".210.00
Transitional, oxblood w/wht & clear, hand-gathered, late 1800s, ¾" .650.00
Vitro Agate Parrot, wht w/aventurine gr/red/bl/yel, 1945-55, 29/32"...250.00

Sulfide, hawk in green glass, 1½", $840.00. (Photo courtesy Morphy Auctions/LiveAuctioneers.com)

Marine Collectibles

Vintage tools used on sea-going vessels, lanterns, clocks, and memorabilia of all types are sought out by those who are interested in preserving the romantic genre that revolves around the life of the sea captains, their boats and their crews; ports of call; and the lure of far-away islands. See also Steamship Collectibles; Telescopes; Scrimshaw; Tools.

Binnacle, ATMC Master Unit, brass w/mtd head, all orig, 14x12" dia.360.00
Binnacle, brass, in drum case w/in gimbals, wood ped/iron spheres, 52".900.00
Binnacle, Deviastat, John Hands, Philadelphia, brass, 13"........... 435.00
Binnacle, Dirigo, Seattle WA, brass gig type, red/gr balls............. 550.00
Binnacle, Kelvin White Boston, freestanding, 52x34" dia 1,450.00
Binnacle, lifeboat; Coubro & Scrutton London, w/mtd compass & lamp, 9".335.00

Binnacle and compass, Kelvin & Hughes Marine Ltd. London, oak and brass, 50", $2,150.00. (Photo courtesy Du Mouchelles/LiveAuctioneers.com)

Certificate of membership, Boston Marine Society, vignettes, 1886 .. 30.00
Chest, captain's liquor; oak w/fitted int, 3 bottles, 12x17x12" 480.00
Chest, pine w/cvd pnt clipper ship/Am flag/etc, becket hdls, 16x38x17".1,725.00
Chest, pnt dvtl/canted wood, rope hdls, iron strap hinges, 19th C, 44"..575.00
Chronometer, Bliss & Creighton NY #858, 56-hr, VG in case .3,350.00
Chronometer, Hamilton #22, in orig case & outer storage case .1,800.00
Chronometer, Hamilton #8176, in 7½x7½" mahog case, +log book .2,150.00
Chronometer, Ulysse Nardin #5673, in brass-bound mahog 7½" case . 2,500.00

Chronometer, Widenham #1668, rosewood/brass, 1820s, 4" dia, in case.2,535.00
Clock, ship's bell; Chelsea, brass w/silver dial/blk numbers, 7¼".. 715.00
Compass, Merril NY, brass, 8¼" dia+gimbal ring, in dvtl box 315.00
Compass, S Thaxter & Son, Boston, gimballed mt, in 10" pine case.300.00
Compass, W Davenport-Maker Phila, brass, 19th C, 15x6" dia, +cover, G..850.00
Desk, captain's davenport; mahog w/inlay, ivory escutcheons, 36x21x17"...1,200.00
Desk, captain's lap, vnr wood, trifold w/fitted int, 1800s 1,000.00
Desk, captain's lap; exotic wood, dvtl, 5½x16x10" 150.00
Desk, captain's writing; mahog w/felt top, 19th C, 31x37x53" 850.00
Diorama, whaler/tugboat/schooner/lighthouse, in 12x22x12" glass case..575.00
Harpoon, dbl-flue Arctic style, 27½" 360.00
Harpoon, pnt wood shaft w/wrought-iron point & swivel barb, 92" ..1,150.00
Harpoon, slot at side of pocket, CI, mk Peters, ca 1900 .... 780.00
Harpoon, toggle; triangular head, single flue, 30" 480.00
Harpoon, toggle; 2-flue head, CI, 19th C, 39" 1,450.00
Harpoon, wrought iron, 30".. 60.00
Lance, killing; oval flat head, rope-bound hdl, mk UAB, 49" 660.00
Lance, killing; w/bronze harpoon tip, 63" 240.00
Log book, engineer's; worn cover, late 1800s, VG 180.00
Log book, MA schooner, entries from 1914, 14x9", VG............... 480.00
Model, Corsair (Am steam yacht) owned by JP Morgan, 20x49x8", +case...8,000.00
Model, schooner ½-hull w/extended fantail, planks, on brd, 10x44" .1,950.00
Octant, A Johnson Liverpool, ebony/ivory/brass, 14", EX in case ...660.00
Octant, E&GW Blunt, all orig, NM in case 1,000.00
Octant, English, ebony dbl T fr w/brass arm, 1830s-50s, 9⅝" radius.... 850.00
Octant, F Primavessi & Son, Swansea, ebony/ivory/brass, EX in case ..960.00
Octant, Spencer, Brown & Rust, London, ca 1800, 15x4", EXIB 1,100.00
Oil on canvas, City of Paris ship's portrait, WH York, 22x38"+fr.....9,485.00
Pastel on canvas, Captain W Hathorn of SS Algier, Sarony, 27x22"+fr..800.00
Quadrant, FB Roberts, Boston, ivory inlay, ca 1800, 12", EXIB ... 725.00
Quadrant, Gowland, Liverpool, ebony/bone/brass, 19th C 660.00
Quadrant, Spencer Browning, London, ebony w/ivory inlay, EX in 14" box ..720.00
Sextant, Adams, London, brass, 10x10", EXIB............................. 900.00
Sextant, compact; Stanley-London, brass, early 20th C, 3" dia.... 120.00

Sextant, in box marked John Bruce & Son Liverpool, ca. 1918, $500.00. (Photo courtesy Neal Auction Company Auctioneers & Appraisers of Fine Art/ LiveAuctioneers.com)

Stern board, eagle cvg, pine w/old dry red wash/gilt, 17x72".....4,600.00
Trunk, cvd teakwood, 6-brd, dvtl, 1850s, 18x37x17" 900.00
Trunk, pnt pine, rope hdls, 1850s, 17x34x16"............................... 180.00
Wheel, ship's throttle; brass, Durkee Marine Products Corp, NY.. 240.00
Wheel, ship's; maple & brass, iron bound, 8-spoke, old red pnt, 41"..250.00
Wheel, ship's; mixed woods, 8 trn spokes & hdls, 42" 240.00
Wheel, ship's; teak & mahog, weathered bl-gr pnt, 67"............... 700.00
Wheel, ship's; wood w/8 trn spokes & hdls, iron bands ea side, 40" dia..475.00

Martin Bros.

The Martin Bros. were studio potters who worked from 1873 until 1914, first at Fulham and later at London and Southall. There were four brothers, each of whom excelled in their particular area. Robert, known as Wallace, was an experienced stonecarver. He modeled a series of grotesque bird and animal figural caricatures. Walter was the potter, responsible for throwing the larger vases on the wheel, firing the kiln, and mixing the clay. Edwin, an artist of stature, preferred more naturalistic forms of decoration. His work was often incised or had relief designs of seaweed, florals, fish, and birds. The fourth brother, Charles, was their business manager. Their work was incised with their names, place of production, and letters and numbers indicating month and year.

Though figural jars continue to command the higher prices, decorated vases and bowls have increased a great deal in value. Our advisors for this category are Suzanne Perrault and David Rago; they are listed in the Directory under New Jersey.

Grotesque jar and lid, signed RW Martin & Bros. London & Southall, 1893, 15x9", $54,000.00. (Photo courtesy David Rago Auctions/LiveAuctioneers.com)

Jar, grotesque creature, rstr to head lid, 1888, 8" 15,600.00
Jar, smiling bird, hooded eyes, standing on base, 1893, 15x9" ..56,250.00
Jardiniere, irises on wht, ped stand w/foliage & flamingo, 61x22" ... 25,000.00
Jug, 2-faced, matt brn tones, 1911, 9x7½"...............................12,500.00
Match holder, woman's head on disk, w/bonnet, unglazed red clay, 6". 1,000.00
Pencil holder, Scotsman's head w/tam, 3½x3" 900.00
Pitcher, fish & vegetation band, bl/gr on tan w/brn lines,ftd, 10".. 20,000.00
Pitcher, grotesque sea creatures, sm rstr/varnish, 1895, 7¼x6" ..3,480.00
Pitcher, yel quatrafoils w/brn leaves on gray, w/brn drips, 9¾" 600.00
Spoon warmer, grotesque creature, cobalt/teal matt, 8¾x9" 6,600.00
Urn, mc crabs on amber, bulbous & flat, 1903, rstr line, 7½x6" ...800.00
Vase, crabs & anemones, mc on bl, 4-sided, 1903, 8¾" 6,250.00
Vase, dragons, brn/blk on cream, 1901, 11½x3¾".......................3,600.00
Vase, floral, gold/purple/gr lustre, 4 hdls at base, 14" 19,350.00
Vase, floral, yel/bl/gr on brn & ivory, neck to waist hdls, 1882, 9"...875.00
Vase, grotesque face on overlapping fans, bulbous w/flat bk, 8x4½" .4,685.00
Vase, grotesque sea creatures, brn/bl/gr on tan, 4-sided, 1913, 6x3"..4,700.00

Vase, incised crabs on amber, incised: 6-1903, Martin Bros London & Southall, restored line, 8", $800.00. (Photo courtesy David Rago Auctions)

Vase, lg fish amid sea life, earth tones w/bl, 1891, 8½x5½"........7,500.00
Vase, Renaissance floral, 1888, rstr rim/neck, ftd, 7¾x3"...........1,185.00

Vase, thistles HP on amber, #11, 1905, 10¼x5" 3,000.00
Vase, 4-faced, dimpled & cvd, earth tones, 7x6½" 18,750.00
Wall pocket, dragonfly figural, mc lustre, ca 1900, 15½" 12,000.00
Wall pocket, fish head & acanthus leaves, earth tones, rstr chip, 8x7". 1,190.00

Mary Gregory

Mary Gregory glass, for reasons that remain obscure, is the namesake of a Boston and Sandwich Glass Company employee who worked for the company for only two years in the mid-1800s. Although no evidence actually exists to indicate that glass of this type was even produced there, the fine colored or crystal ware decorated with figures of children in white enamel is commonly referred to as Mary Gregory. The glass, in fact, originated in Europe and was imported into this country where it was copied by several eastern glasshouses. It was popular from the mid-1800s until the turn of the century. It is generally accepted that examples with all-white figures were made in the U.S.A., while gold-trimmed items and those with children having tinted faces or a small amount of color on their clothing are European. Though amethyst is rare, examples in cranberry command the higher prices. Blue ranks next; and green, amber, and clear items are worth the least. Watch for new glass decorated with screen-printed children and a minimum of hand painting. The screen effect is easily detected with a magnifying glass.

Barber bottle, blk, boy/foliage, w/stopper 265.00
Barber bottle, cobalt, girl playing tennis, stopper, 8¼" 420.00
Barber bottle, ruby, boy/foliage, rolled lip, 7½" 175.00
Barber's vase, amber, boy w/hoop, rare, 7" 385.00
Biscuit barrel, cranberry, boy/gold scrolls, metal lid/bail, 8x5" 390.00
Bottle, scent; blk, girl/floral, cylinder, int crystal stopper, 2½"......420.00
Bowl, amber, boy w/stick & hoop, honeycomb sides, sq, 3¼x9½".. 85.00
Box, amber, boy/foliage, hinged, 1¾" dia 165.00
Box, cranberry, 2 children on dome lid, metal mts, 5" H..............265.00
Box, gr, wht/mc/coralene boy, 4" dia 575.00
Box, jewelry; amber, fence/yel birds, sq, metal mts, 6x5x5" 550.00
Box, jewelry; cobalt, girl/wood fence, bulbous base, metal mts, 4" H ..265.00
Candleholders, cranberry to clear ft, child at play, gold trim, 4", pr .175.00
Charger, cranberry, 2 maids in wooded landscape, 12" 325.00
Cruet, cranberry w/clear stopper/hdl, child, 6½", pr 90.00
Jar, cranberry, girl on lid, floral on side, gold bands, 4¾" 300.00
Lamp, cranberry, boy w/butterfly net, 9¾" base..............................375.00
Lustres, ruby, children swinging, w/prisms, 11", pr.......................225.00
Mug, lime gr, child, 2¾", pr 95.00
Pitcher, clear, 3 scenes w/child, lt wear, 10" 75.00
Pitcher, gr, boy picking flowers, gold trim, bi-cone tankard, 10½".. 95.00
Pitcher, med gr, boy/flowering trees, int lobes, str sides, 8" 435.00
Shot glasses, various colors, children, w/hdl, 1½", set of 4............185.00
Tankard, lt gr, child, pewter lid, 15",+ 4 6½" ftd glasses...............480.00
Tankard, sapphire, girl/bird, rows of t'prints, 11½"........................265.00
Toothpick holder, lt gr, girl/flower, spherical w/short collar, 2".....300.00
Tumbler, ruby, girl/foliage, gold trim, 3¾" 135.00

Vase, black, boy with toy cow tied to stick, 1850s, 13", $385.00. (Photo courtesy John A. Shuman III)

Vase, blk w/girl & foliage, cylinder w/arch top, bk: mc floral, 8", pr .300.00
Vase, bright gr satin, lovely lady w/cornucopia, bun ft, 14", pr, EX .175.00
Vase, clear, boy/foliage, flared top, ped ft, 8½" 135.00
Vase, cobalt, maid/tree, shouldered/bun ft, 10¾" 265.00
Vase, cranberry, children, flared top/bun base/ftd, 6", pr...............140.00
Vase, cranberry, girl at water trough, gilt, att Muhlhaus, 8x5", pr..540.00
Vase, cranberry, lady profile portrait in gold scroll reserve, 13", pr ..540.00
Vase, med gr, child in leaf reserve, ruffled/scalloped, 13", pr.........360.00
Vase, med gr, girl at water's edge, tapered cylinder, 16", pr...........385.00
Vase, med gr, hunter w/flesh-tone face, rigaree down ea side, 10½"....195.00
Vase, ruby, lady w/bird, ftd teardrop form, 11", pr 300.00

Mason's Ironstone

In 1813 Charles J. Mason was granted a patent for a process said to 'improve the quality of English porcelain.' The new type of ware was in fact ironstone which Mason decorated with colorful florals and scenics, some of which reflected the Oriental taste. Although his business failed for a short time in the late 1840s, Mason re-established himself and continued to produce dinnerware, tea services, and ornamental pieces until about 1852, at which time the pottery was sold to Francis Morley. Ten years later, Geo. L. and Taylor Ashworth became owners. Both Morley and the Ashworths not only used Mason's molds and patterns but often his mark as well. Because the quality and the workmanship of the later wares do not compare with Mason's earlier product, collectors should take care to distinguish one from the other. Consult a good book on marks to be sure. The Wedgwood Company now owns the rights to the Mason patterns.

American Marine, creamer, red, scalloped rim, 1890-1900, 3½x4", EX.125.00
Bandana, cup & saucer, demi; blk & wht on burnt-orange, 1860s ..150.00
Bandana, jug, mc, ca 1840, 4¾x3½", NM 250.00
Colored Blue Pheasants, jug, mc, ca 1830, 4½x4" 250.00
Colored Pheasants, bowl, octagonal, 1840s, 4¼x8½"+underplate...250.00
Double Landscape, compote, mc, ca 1862, 5¾x10½x4" 325.00
Double Landscape, jug, mc, hexagonal, ca 1840, 4¾"...................450.00
English scene, cup plate, red, ca 1813, 4¾" 100.00
Floral, bowl, soup; mc, ca 1873-90, 10"...70.00
Floral, plate, mc, ca 1913-1825, 9½" 125.00

Floral reserves, pitcher, serpent handle, 7", from $375.00 to $425.00. (Photo courtesy Mary Frank Gaston)

Flowering Bush, plate, mc, ca 1830, 8¾"..80.00
Flowering Bush, plate, mc, scalloped, ca 1840, 8¾" 125.00
Flying Bird, bowl, mc on wht w/blk transfer, 1890, 10¼" 175.00
Fruit Basket, plate, mc on wht, 1890-1900, 7¾", 3 for...................70.00
Gay Japan/House, jug, mc, dragon hdl, much gold, att, ca 1840s, 4½"..650.00
Mongol, plate, mc, ca 1818, pnt wear, 10½x9¼" 200.00
Orange Leaf, plate, mc, ca 1813-25, 8½"......................................175.00
Oriental, washbowl & pitcher, 11½", 16" dia................................300.00
Oriental Pheasants, dish, mc, ca 1818, 9½x8", EX 250.00
Persiana, washbowl & pitcher, mc, child sz, 3¾", 4¼" dia 500.00

Red Scale, pitcher, ca 1890 – 1900, 5¼x6¼", $325.00; Tea caddy, 6¾x6¼", $500.00. (Photo courtesy A&B Auctions)

Rich Ruby, plate, mc, scalloped, ca 1840, 10¼"	150.00
Table & Flowerpot, platter, mc, 1813-25, 9x6¼"	325.00
Vase Japanned, bowl, serving; mc, scalloped, ca 1840, 9½", pr	150.00
Vase Japanned, compote, mc, scalloped, ped ft, ca 1840, 9½x13½"	400.00
Vase Japanned, dish, mc, scalloped hdls, ca 1840, 9½" W	100.00
Vase Japanned, platter, mc, ca 1840, 18x14", NM	550.00
Vase Japanned, platter, mc, scalloped, ca 1840, 21x16½"	800.00
Vista, plate, dinner; red, 1925-50 mk, 10¾", 3 for	100.00
Vista, trivet, red, 1925-30 mk, 6x6"	150.00
Water Lily, dish, mc, ca 1813-25, 10¾x7½"	600.00
Water Lily, plate, mc, panelled, faint scallops, ca 1813-25, 8½"	200.00
Willow, bowl, soup; flow bl, ca 1862, 10½"	80.00
Willow, teapot, bl, 1890-1900, 7¼"	300.00

Massier, Clément

The Massier family's work in ceramics goes back in France to the middle eighteenth century. Clément, his brother Delphin, and their cousin Jerome, brought about a renaissance of the ceramics industry in Vallauris, in the south of France. Clément apprenticed and worked under his father until his father's death, after which Clément set up his own pottery in nearby Golfe-Juan. Artistic director Lucien Lévey-Dhurmer introduced Massier to Spanish iridescent glazes in 1887; and through the use of bronze, brass, and gold salts, Massier developed his own. He won the pottery an award at the Paris Exposition Universelle in 1889.

Jacques Sicard, one of his artists, took the glaze formula with him to the Weller Pottery in Zanesville, Ohio, closely replicating the overall floral patterns he had learned in France. This particular type of glaze proved difficult to fire on both continents, seldom yielding the perfectly crisp decoration and smooth lustre desired. Perfectly fired pieces sell quickly and for a premium.

Vase, iridescent with applied silver peapod, 6", $1,100.00. (Photo courtesy David Rago Auctions/LiveAuctioneers.com)

Fountain, putti w/garland under urn-form body, turq, 4-ftd, 36x28"	3,300.00
Jardiniere, nude woman on rock, metallic, Golfe Juan CM, 8", EX	3,600.00
Vase, bud; butterflies on lustre, pierced wing-like hdls, ca 1900, 12"	4,500.00
Vase, bud; silver peapod o/l on lustre, twisted body, 6x2¼", NM	1,100.00
Vase, dragonfly & cattails, tan mottle, gr & gold, pinched, 7½", EX	1,800.00
Vase, floral irid, trumpet form, 2" rim to 6" base, paper label, 18"	2,880.00
Vase, irises, metallic, 4 appl twist hdls, Golfe Juan AM, 6"	660.00
Vase, mice in field, swollen base, Golfe Juan AM, 14½"	2,500.00

Match Holders

John Walker, an English chemist, invented the match more than 100 years ago, quite by accident. Walker was working with a mixture of potash and antimony, hoping to make a combustible that could be used to fire guns. The mixture adhered to the end of the wooden stick he had used for stirring. As he tried to remove it by scraping the stick on the stone floor, it burst into flames. The invention of the match was only a step away! From that time to the present, match holders have been made in amusing figural forms as well as simple utilitarian styles and in a wide range of materials. Both table-top and wall-hanging models were made — all designed to keep matches conveniently at hand. The prices in this category are very volatile due to increased interest in this field and the fact that so many can be classified as a cross or dual collectible. Caution: As prices for originals continue to climb, so do the number of reproductions. Know your dealer.

Advertising, Cerasota Flour, child on bbl, die-cut body, 5½"	300.00
Advertising, Ceresota Flour, boy (flat figure)/bbl, tin litho, 5½"	175.00
Advertising, Gabby Shoes, cb w/metal kettle holder, camp scene, 10x6"	160.00
Advertising, Juicy Fruit, Wrigley's portrait, tin, 3½x4½"	200.00
Advertising, turtle, figural CI, Insure in the Old..., 5¼", EX	230.00
Black Forest, dog peering into bucket, ca 1900	255.00
Brass, ribbed cup atop bell w/ring lever on rnd tray base, 6½", EX	140.00
Bronze, shield shape w/relief bust of bearded Civil War officer, 6"	265.00
Bsk, peasant boy w/fish, mc, striker on bk, unmk, 1900s, 5"	80.00
China, chamberstick w/matchbox holder, Dresden	110.00
CI, acorn on 6-pointed leafy stand, mechanical, dtd 1862, 4½", EX	115.00
CI, bbl on bench, striker on side, wall mt, 6¾", VG	85.00
CI, bust of WF Cody (Buffalo Bill), Teals London, dtd 1887, 5½", EX	525.00
CI, devil portrayed in medieval stocks, smiling/legs Xd, 1900, 6½"	475.00
CI, whimsical head w/removable hat, 4¼", G	200.00
Majolica, frog playing banjo, unmk, 5x6"	310.00
Metal w/marble base, boy straddles 'wooden' bucket w/bail hdl, 6", VG	100.00
Porc, violets on wht, wall mt, unmk, ca 1900s	65.00
Silver, cherub/floral emb motif, .925 fine silver mk, 1½", EX	100.00
Silver, Deco-dragon w/holder on bk, Moller Trondhj, 1915-30	650.00
Souvenir, Nat'l Restaurant Assoc Convention, Shenango China, 4x3x2"	120.00
Wht metal, man w/basket on bk straddles chair, 5½", VG	115.00

Wood, Indian chief, early twentieth century, 8½", $350.00. (Photo courtesy Jackson's International Auctioneers & Appraisers of Fine Art & Antiques)

Match Safes

Before the invention of the safety match in 1855, matches were carried in small pocket-sized containers because they ignited so easily. Aptly called match safes, these containers were used extensively until about 1920, when cigarette lighters became widely available. Some incorporated added features (hidden compartments, cigar cutters, etc.), some were figural, and others were used by retail companies as advertising giveaways. They were made from every type of material, but silver-plated styles abound. Both the advertising and common silver-plated cases generally fall in the $50.00 to $100.00 price range.

Beware of reproductions and fakes; there are many currently on the market. Know your dealer.

Advertising, Advance Thresher Co...Traction Engine, cello, 2¾" ..300.00
Advertising, Cameron Pump Works, cello & NP, Whitehead & Hoag...500.00
Advertising, Molassine Horse & Cattle Food, nude lady, 2¾" 265.00
Brass, emb Gothic design of St George & dragon, EX..................185.00

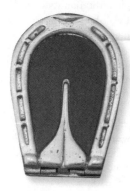

Brass, horseshoe with leather push-button lid release, $85.00 – 110.00.
(Photo courtesy George Sparacio)

Brass, lobster & claw w/cultured pearl..315.00
Brass, man's boot, creased leather look, lid snaps shut..................170.00
Brass, owl figural, detailed feathers, carnelian agate eyes..............200.00
Bronze, dragon figural, EX patina, 1880s, 2½"..............................500.00
Egyptian Sarcophagus, brass w/emb detail, interior striker, 4", EX+...175.00
Enamel portrait of Woodrow Wilson & White House, Capitol on bk, 2⅜".210.00
Gilt brass, Nouveau floral, cylindrical, mid-1800s, 2½".................145.00
Silver, Am Indian chief in relief, monogram, Sterling, 3¼x1¾" ..700.00
Silver, Cupid w/raised floral & scrolls/monogram, Sterling, B1305..465.00
Silver, emb ferns, ca 1895, 2⅜x1¼"..235.00
Silver, heart shape w/floral scrolls, monogram, English hallmk....150.00
Silver, horse-head figural, 2⅝x1⅛" 460.00
Silver, Leda & Swan emb/monogram, Sterling, 2½x2".................345.00
Silver, man at steering wheel wearing hat/coat/gloves emb, Sterling ..485.00
Silver, man smoking & drinking, dtd 1911, Paye & Baker, 2½"...675.00
Silver, Nouveau grapes, monogram, 2½".......................................195.00
Silver, Vicorian lady on skis, Sterling, late 19th C, 2½x1½" 895.00
Silver, 4-leaf clover (Nouveau style) emb, hinged lid, 1¾" 165.00
SP, lady's torso, corseted waist, bare breasts, unmk, 1¾" 865.00

Sterling with enameled Masonic emblem, F. S. Gilbert, press emblem to release lid, 2½x1½", from $250.00 to $300.00. (Photo courtesy George Sparacio)

Tortoisehell & MOP, book form, ca 1900, EX...............................150.00
18k gold, risqué enameling, Fr, 1800s, 2x1⅜" 1,150.00

Mauchline Ware

Mauchline ware is the generic name for small, well-made, and useful wooden souvenirs and giftware from Mauchline, Scotland, and nearby locations. It was made from the early nineteenth century into the 1930s. Snuff boxes were among the earliest items, and tea caddies soon followed. From the 1830s on, needlework, stationery, domestic, and cosmetic items were made by the thousands. Today, needlework items are the most plentiful and range from boxes of all sizes made to hold supplies to tiny bodkins and buttons. Napkin rings, egg cups, vases, and bowls are just a few of the domestic items available.

The wood most commonly used in the production of Mauchline ware was sycamore. Finishes vary. Early items were hand decorated with colored paints or pen and ink. By the 1850s, perhaps even earlier, transfer ware was produced, decorated with views associated with the place of purchase. These souvenir items were avidly bought by travelers for themselves as well as for gifts. Major exhibitions and royal occasions were also represented on transferware. An alternative decorating process was initiated during the mid-1860s whereby actual photos replaced the transfers. Because they were finished with multiple layers of varnish, many examples found today are still in excellent condition.

Tartan ware's distinctive decoration was originally hand painted directly on the wood with inks, but in the 1840s machine-made paper in authentic Tartan designs became available. Except for the smallest items, each piece was stamped with the Tartan name. The Tartan decoration was applied to virtually the entire range of Mauchline ware, and because it was favored by Queen Victoria, it became widely popular. Collectors still value Tartan ware above other types of decoration, with transferware being their second choice. Other types of Mauchline decorations include Fern ware and Black Lacquer with floral or transfer decorations.

When cleaning any Mauchline item, extreme care should be used to avoid damaging the finish! Mauchline ware has been reproduced for at least 25 years, especially some of the more popular pieces and finishes. Collectors should study the older items for comparison and to learn about the decorating and manufacturing processes.

Book, Fernware (early, not pre-printed), Scott's poems, tilt edge. 120.00
Book cover, Tartan w/ferns in oval, Burns' poems, Gall Inglis, book: G ...225.00
Bookmark, Hairpin Bend Mohawk Trail, w/ca 1920s autos, 6½" L ..95.00
Box, Ledge in Front of Mtn House Catskills NY, ¾x1⅞" dia.........145.00
Box, Severn Bridge Near Chepstow, brass clasp, 1¾x2¾x4"..........115.00
Box, Tartan: McBeth, hinged lid, 1½x3½x6¾", VG.....................135.00
Dice holder, Oldmachar Cathedral, 2¾x2"....................................85.00
Etui, Palace Place Paicnton, egg shape, holds thimble/needles/etc...110.00
Frame, Mossoiel, arched top, 5¼x6½" 115.00

Match holder, Black babies, St. Petersburg, Florida, souvenir, with striker, 2½", $300.00.
(Photo courtesy neatstuffdave)

Money box (model of clock), Bournemouth, 4¼x3x2½", VG..........80.00
Photo album, Balmoral From the NW/Linn of Dee, leather spine, +photos...120.00
Pipe rack, Les Fables d' Olonne le Remblai, 3-arch top, 8¾x5¼".....75.00
Shot glass holder, Langholm Library, sycamore, w/glass, 2¾" 100.00
Tea caddy, Tartan, gr/navy w/strong red lines, dome lid, 4x7½" 495.00
Thimble case, Calais - Dover ferry, bbl form, NM................ 135.00
Thread holder, Edinburgh From Castle+3 scenes, 6 eyelets, sycamore...85.00
Thread holder, mc bird on lid of bucket shape, Chadwick label, 3" ... 75.00
Watch stand, Burns' Cottage, made from wood from site, 4"........ 125.00
Whistle, St Cuthbert's Church, 2½" L, NM................................. 125.00

McCoy

The third generation McCoy potter in the Roseville, Ohio, area was Nelson, who with the aid of his father, J.W., established the Nelson McCoy Sanitary Stoneware Company in 1910. They manufactured churns, jars, jugs, poultry fountains, and foot warmers. By 1925 they had expanded their wares to include majolica jardinieres and pedestals, umbrella stands, and cuspidors, and an embossed line of vases and small jardinieres in a blended brown and green matt glaze. From the late '20s through the mid-'40s, a utilitarian stoneware was produced, some of which was glazed in the soft blue and white so popular with collectors today. They also used a dark brown mahogany color and a medium to dark green, both in a high gloss. In 1933 the firm became known as the Nelson McCoy Pottery Company. They expanded their facilities in 1940 and began to make the novelty artware, cookie jars, and dinnerware that today are synonymous with 'McCoy.' More than 200 cookie jars of every theme and description were produced.

More than a dozen different marks have been used by the company; nearly all incorporate the name 'McCoy,' although some of the older items were marked 'NM USA.' For further information consult *The Collector's Encyclopedia of McCoy Pottery* by Sharon and Bob Huxford; or *McCoy Pottery Collector's Reference & Value Guide, Vol. I, II, and III*, by Margaret Hanson, Craig Nissen, and Bob Hanson (all published by Collector Books). Also available is *Sanfords Guide to McCoy Pottery* by Martha and Steve Sanford (Mr. Sanford is listed in the Directory under California.)

Alert! Stimulated by the high prices commanded by desirable cookie jars, a broad spectrum of 'new' cookie jars have flooded the marketplace in three categories: 1) Manufacturers have expanded their lines with exciting new designs to attract the collector market. 2) Limited editions and artist-designed jars have proliferated. 3) Reproductions, signed and unsigned, have pervaded the market, creating uncertainty among new collectors and inexperienced dealers. After McCoy closed its doors in the late 1980s, an entrepreneur in Tennessee tried (and succeeded for nearly a decade) to adopt the McCoy Pottery name and mark. This company reproduced old McCoy designs as well as some classic designs of other defunct American potteries, signing their wares 'McCoy' with a mark which very closely approximated the old McCoy mark. Legal action finally put a stop to this practice, though since then they have used other fraudulent marks as well: Brush-McCoy (the compound name was never used on Brush cookie jars) and B.J. Hull.

Still under pressure from internet exposure and the effects of a slow economy, the cookie jar market remains soft. High-end cookie jars are often slow to sell. Our advisor for McCoy cookie jars is Judy Posner; she is listed in the Directory under Florida.

Cookie Jars

Animal Crackers.. 100.00
Apollo Age... 400.00
Apple, 1950-64.. 50.00

Apples on Basketweave 70.00
Asparagus 50.00
Astronauts... 400.00
Bananas 95.00
Barnum's Animals... 150.00
Barrel, Cookies sign on lid.. 75.00
Baseball Boy... 95.00
Basket of Eggs.. 40.00
Basket of Potatoes.. 40.00
Bear, cookie in vest, no 'Cookies'... 85.00
Betsy Baker (+)... 95.00
Black Kettle, w/immovable bail, HP flowers 40.00
Black Lantern... 65.00
Blue Willow Pitcher.. 55.00
Bobby Baker.. 65.00
Bugs Bunny 95.00
Burlap Bag, red bird on lid... 50.00
Caboose.. 95.00
Cat on Coal Scuttle 125.00
Chairman of the Board (+)... 550.00
Chef Head 95.00
Chilly Willy 65.00
Chipmunk.. 125.00
Christmas Tree... 350.00
Churn, 2 bands.. 35.00
Circus Horse, blk... 125.00
Clown Bust (+).. 75.00
Clown in Barrel, yel, bl or gr 85.00
Clyde Dog.. 95.00
Coalby Cat... 150.00
Coca-Cola Can.. 75.00
Coca-Cola Jug... 55.00
Coffee Grinder 45.00
Coffee Mug.. 45.00
Colonial Fireplace... 85.00
Cookie Bank, 1961.. 95.00
Cookie Barrel, from $35 to 45.00
Cookie Boy.. 225.00
Cookie Cabin... 80.00
Cookie Jug, dbl loop 35.00
Cookie Jug, single loop, 2-tone gr rope 35.00
Cookie Jug, w/cork stopper, brn & wht 40.00
Cookie Log, squirrel finial.. 45.00
Cookie Mug 45.00
Cookie Pot, 1964.. 40.00
Cookie Safe 45.00
Cookstove, blk or wht.. 35.00
Corn, row of standing ears, yel or wht, 1977.......................... 85.00
Corn, single ear.. 150.00
Covered Wagon 95.00
Cylinder, w/red flowers... 45.00
Dalmatians in Rocking Chair (+) 150.00
Davy Crockett (+).. 300.00
Dog in Doghouse.. 95.00
Dog on Basketweave 75.00
Drum, red.. 90.00
Duck on Basketweave 75.00
Dutch Boy.. 65.00
Dutch Girl, boy on reverse, rare 250.00
Dutch Treat Barn 50.00
Eagle on Basket, from $35 to 50.00
Early American Chest (Chiffoniere).. 65.00
Elephant.. 125.00
Elephant w/Split Trunk, rare, minimum value.................... 200.00

Engine, black, $125.00.

Flowerpot, plastic flower on top	350.00
Football Boy (+)	125.00
Forbidden Fruit	90.00
Fortune Cookies	50.00

Freddy Gleep, minimum value $350.00. (Photo courtesy Ermagene Westfall)

Friendship 7	125.00
Frog on Stump	75.00
Frontier Family	55.00
Fruit in Bushel Basket	65.00
Gingerbread Boy	75.00
Globe	195.00
Grandfather Clock	75.00
Granny	95.00
Hamm's Bear (+)	125.00
Happy Face	80.00
Hen on Nest	95.00
Hillbilly Bear, rare, minimum value (+)	900.00
Hobby Horse, brn underglaze (+)	150.00
Hocus Rabbit	45.00
Honey Bear, rustic glaze	80.00
Hot Air Balloon	40.00
Ice Cream Cone	45.00
Indian, brn (+)	250.00
Indian, majolica	350.00
Jack-O'-Lantern	400.00
Kangaroo, bl	250.00
Keebler Tree House	70.00
Kettle, bronze, 1961	40.00
Kissing Penguins	75.00
Kitten on Basketweave	90.00
Kittens (2) on Low Basket	600.00
Kittens on Ball of Yarn	85.00
Koala Bear	85.00
Kookie Kettle, blk	35.00
Lamb on Basketweave	90.00
Lemon	75.00

Leprechaun, minimum value (+)	1,800.00
Liberty Bell	75.00
Little Clown	75.00
Lollipops	80.00
Mac Dog	95.00
Mammy, Cookies on base, wht w/cold pnt (+)	150.00
Mammy w/Cauliflower, G pnt, minimum value (+)	900.00
Milk Can, Spirit of '76	45.00
Modern	65.00
Monk	50.00
Mother Goose	95.00
Mouse on Clock	40.00
Mr & Mrs Owl	90.00
Mushroom on Stump	55.00
Nursery, decal of Humpty Dumpty, from $70 to	80.00
Oaken Bucket, from $25 to	45.00
Orange	55.00
Owl, brn	70.00
Pear, 1952	85.00
Pears on Basketweave	70.00
Penguin, yel or aqua	95.00
Pepper, yel	40.00
Picnic Basket	75.00
Pig, winking	250.00
Pine Cones on Basketweave	70.00
Pineapple	80.00
Pineapple, Modern	90.00
Pirate's Chest	95.00
Popeye, cylinder	125.00
Potbelly Stove, blk	30.00
Puppy, w/sign	85.00
Quaker Oats, rare, minimum value	400.00
Raggedy Ann	110.00
Red Barn, cow in door, rare, minimum value	150.00
Rooster, wht, 1970-1974	60.00
Rooster, 1955-57	95.00
Round w/HP Leaves	40.00
Sad Clown	85.00
Snoopy on Doghouse (+), mk United Features Syndicate	125.00
Snow Bear	75.00
Spaniel in Doghouse, bird finial	125.00
Stagecoach, minimum value	650.00
Strawberry, 1955-57	65.00
Strawberry, 1971-75	45.00
Teapot, 1972	60.00
Tepee, slant top	250.00
Tepee, str top (+)	200.00
Thinking Puppy, #0272	40.00
Tilt Pitcher, blk w/roses	50.00
Timmy Tortoise	45.00
Tomato	60.00
Touring Car	75.00
Traffic Light	50.00
Tudor Cookie House	95.00
Tulip on Flowerpot	100.00
Turkey, gr, rare color	150.00
Turkey, natural colors	150.00
Upside Down Bear, panda	50.00
WC Fields	125.00
Wedding Jar	90.00
Windmill	85.00
Wishing Well	40.00
Woodsy Owl	150.00
Wren House, side lid	95.00

Yellow Mouse (head) 45.00
Yosemite Sam, cylinder 95.00

Miscellaneous

Basket, hanging; basketweave, bright bl, unmk, 1940s, 7½" 50.00
Bookends, horse rearing, bl, USA mk, 1940s, 8", from $100 to ... 120.00
Candy boat, gondola, Sunburst Gold, 3½x11½", from $40 to 50.00
Ferner, Butterfly, pastel, braided rim, 3½x9", from $250 to 300.00
Ferner, Hobnail, pastel matt, NM mk, 1940s, 5½", from $25 to 35.00
Ferner, Hobnail, pastel matt, 1940s, 5½", from $25 to 35.00
Flower bowl ornament, peacock, ivory, unmk, 4¾", from $100 to 125.00
Flower holder, angelfish, wht or gr, unmk, 1940s, 6", from $300 to .. 400.00
Flower holder, fish, yel or rose, NM mk, 3¼x4¼", from $125 to ... 200.00
Flower holder, pigeon, gr, NM mk, 3½x4", from $40 to 65.00
Flowerpot, Hobnail, pastel matt, 1940s, 5", from $40 to 50.00
Hand vase, gr, NM mk, 1940s, 8¼", from $30 to 50.00
Jar, oil; blended red & wht, rim-to-shoulder hdls, 18", from $300 to ... 400.00
Jar, oil; coral, NM mk, ca 1938, 4", from $125 to 200.00
Jar, sand; emb bl leaves on hdls, brn matt, 1930s, 18", from $1,200 to .. 1,500.00
Jar, sand; Sphinx, lt bl matt, ca 1930s, 16", from $1,500 to 2,500.00
Jardiniere, basketweave, bl, NM mk, 1940s, 4½" 50.00
Jardiniere, basketweave, blended brn & gr, 7½", from $65 to 80.00
Jardiniere, Fish, brn spray, 1958, 7½", from $300 to 400.00
Jardiniere, Swallows, Onyx, brn, 4", from $45 to 65.00
Jardiniere, Swallows, Onyx, yel, 7", from $90 to 125.00
Lamp, Model-A pick-up truck, Sunburst Gold, 1956, from $85 to .. 100.00
Pet dish, Man's Best Friend, His Dog, brn, 1930s, 7½", $70 to 90.00
Pitcher, ball jug, yel or wht, 1940s, 7", from $35 to 50.00
Pitcher, elephant, bl, NM mk, 7x5", from $350 to 400.00
Pitcher, Hobnail, yel, unmk, 48-oz, 6", from $100 to 150.00
Planter, clown & pig, wht w/mc details, 1951, 8½", from $80 to ... 100.00
Planter, cornucopia, bl, NM mk, 1940s, 5", from $35 to 50.00
Planter, football, antiqued finish, 1957, 4½x7", from $75 to 100.00

Planter, hunting dog, 1954, 12½" long, from $200.00 to $250.00. (Photo courtesy Bill and Betty Newbound)

Planter, kitten beside basket w/ball of yarn, pk, NM mk, 1940s, 6" ... 60.00
Planter, lt gr, 4-scallop rim, 4-ftd, globular, NM mk, 1940s, 3½" 45.00
Planter, Mary Ann shoe, pastel, NM mk, 1940s, 5" L, from $25 to ... 40.00
Planter, shell, spiky, pastel matt, 1940s, 7½x5½", from $50 to 60.00
Planter, zebra, blk & wht, 1956, 6½x8½", from $650 to 800.00
Strawberry jar, maroon, brn or gr, w/3 chains, 1953, 6x7", $40 to .. 45.00
Stretch animal, dachshund, pastel matt, unmk, 1940s, 5x8¼" 225.00
Stretch animal, lion, unmk, pastel matt, 1940s, 5½x7½" 250.00
Teapot, Daisy, shaded brn/gr/wht, 1940s, from $40 to 50.00
Vase, Butterfly, bl, hdls, USA mk, 10", from $150 to 200.00
Vase, Butterfly, bl, USA mk, 5½x7½", from $90 to 110.00
Vase, Contrasting Leaf, chartreuse, 1955, 9", from $175 to 225.00
Vase, cornucopia, Sunburst Gold, 3¼x4", from $35 to 50.00

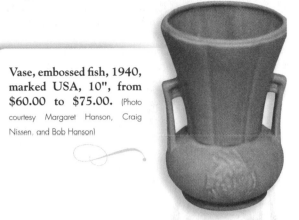

Vase, embossed fish, 1940, marked USA, 10", from $60.00 to $75.00. (Photo courtesy Margaret Hanson, Craig Nissen, and Bob Hanson)

Vase, emb floral & leaves, wht matt, integral hdls, ftd, 8", $80 to ... 100.00
Vase, emb leaves & berries, wht matt, flared top & bottom, 1930s, 6". 75.00
Vase, Hand of Friendship (Prayer Hands), gr, NM mk, 3x4", from $75 to ... 100.00
Vase, heart shape, pk, unmk, 1940s, 6" 60.00
Vase, swan form, gr, unmk, 1940s, 6" 35.00
Wall pocket, bananas w/gr leaves, unmk, early 1950s, 7x6", $125 to . 150.00
Wall pocket, berries & leaves, bl, unmk, 1940s, 7", from $200 to . 300.00
Wall pocket, pear w/gr leaves, unmk, 1950s, 7x6", from $60 to 80.00

Wall pocket, three owls, from $65.00 to $85.00. (Photo courtesy Morphy Auctions/LiveAuctioneers.com)

Wall pocket, umbrella, gr gloss, mk, 1950s, 8¾x6", from $60 to 80.00
Wall pocket, violin, brn or aqua, mk, 1950s, 10¼", from $100 to . 130.00

McCoy, J. W.

The J.W. McCoy Pottery Company was incorporated in 1899. It operated under that name in Roseville, Ohio, until 1911 when McCoy entered into a partnership with George Brush, forming the Brush-McCoy Company. During the early years, McCoy produced kitchenware, majolica jardinieres and pedestals, umbrella stands, and cuspidors. By 1903 they had begun to experiment in the field of art pottery and, though never involved to the extent of some of their contemporaries, nevertheless produced several art lines of merit.

The company rebuilt in 1904 after being destroyed by fire, and other artware was designed. Loy-Nel-Art and Renaissance were standard brown lines, hand decorated under the glaze with colored slip. Shapes and artwork were usually simple but effective. Olympia and Rosewood were relief-molded brown-glaze lines decorated in natural colors with wreaths of leaves and berries or simple floral sprays. Although much of this ware was not marked, you will find examples with the die-stamped 'Loy-Nel-Art, McCoy,' or an incised line identification.

Corn Line, salt box, #56, 5½x5⅞" 215.00
Loy-Nel-Art, bowl, floral, ftd, 5" 120.00
Loy-Nel-Art, jardiniere, floral, 4-ftd, 7½" 195.00
Loy-Nel-Art, jardiniere, tulips, 6½" 180.00
Loy-Nel-Art, jardiniere & ped, floral, 27x12½", NM 400.00
Loy-Nel-Art, pitcher, open roses, #117, sm rstr, 8¼" 50.00
Loy-Nel-Art, spittoon, floral, 6¾x8", NM 165.00
Loy-Nel-Art, tankard, floral, 11⅞" 175.00
Loy-Nel-Art, vase, berries, sm hdls, #5, 6⅛" 115.00
Loy-Nel-Art, vase, floral, 10x5½" 225.00

Loy-Nel-Art, vase, pansies, with handles, 10½", $250.00.

Loy-Nel-Art, vase, pillow; floral, 5x5½", NM 75.00
Olympia, bowl, ftd, 11½x14½", NM... 325.00
Olympia, jardiniere, #70, 7½", from $95 to................................. 120.00
Sylvan (Avenue of Trees), vase, #06, crazing, 6" 110.00

McKee

McKee Glass was founded in 1853 in Pittsburgh, Pennsylvania. Among their early products were tableware of both the flint and non-flint varieties. In 1888 the company relocated to avail themselves of a source of natural gas, thereby founding the town of Jeannette, Pennsylvania. One of their most famous colored dinnerware lines, Rock Crystal, was manufactured in the 1920s. Production during the '30s and '40s included colored opaque dinnerware, Sunkist reamers, and 'bottoms up' cocktail tumblers as well as a line of black glass vases, bowls, and novelty items. All are popular items with today's collectors, but watch for reproductions. The mark of an authentic 'bottoms up' tumbler is the patent number 77725 embossed beneath the feet. The company was purchased in 1916 by Jeannette Glass, under which name it continues to operate. See also Animal Dishes with Covers; Carnival Glass; Depression Glass; Kitchen Collectibles; Reamers.

Covered dish, Moses in the Bulrushes, milk glass, $465.00. (Photo courtesy Cowan's Auctions Inc./LiveAuctioneers.com)

Ashtray, custard w/blk ring at opening, ball shaped, 3¼" 90.00
Baking set, Betty Jane, child sz, 9-pc, MIB................................... 70.00
Bottoms Up, tumbler, lt butterscotch opal, 3¼", +matching coaster.. 85.00
Compote, Innovation #407, stars & flowers, high std, 8½x6½"...... 55.00
Decanter, Seville Yellow, pinched body, w/stopper, 8¾" 65.00
Jardiniere, Skokie Green, Chevron design, 3-ftd, 5⅛" H................ 35.00
Lamp, Danse de Lumiere, gr, from $550 to.................................. 650.00
Mug, Jade-ite w/Tom & Jerry in blk, 3½" 35.00
Punch set, Concord, ftd bowl, 9x12", +10 cups & glass ladle......... 65.00
Rose bowl, Hickman, sm ft, 5½x4½" 60.00
Vase, nude in relief ea side (3), blk, ftd, 8½", NM 75.00
Water bottle, red/orange, pinched sides, tumbler fits over neck, 5"...40.00
Wren hut, wht w/red roof, metal bottom, 5" 80.00

Medical Collectibles

The field of medical-related items encompasses a wide area from the primitive bleeding bowl to the X-ray machines of the early 1900s. Other closely related collectibles include apothecary and dental items. Many tools that were originally intended for the pharmacist found their way to the doctor's office, and dentists often used surgical tools when no suitable dental instrument was available. A trend in the late 1800s toward self-medication brought a whole new wave of home-care manuals and 'patent' medical machines for home use. Commonly referred to as 'quack' medical gimmicks, these machines were usually ineffective and occasionally dangerous.

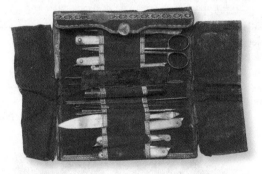

Kit, surgeon's; 14 instruments including folding scalpels with horn handles, in embossed leather folding case with fitted red velvet lining, 7" long when folded, VG, $460.00. (Photo courtesy Garth's Auctions Inc.)

Bag, brn leather, Emdee by Schell, 11x15x7", +assorted sm tools ...135.00
Bag, brn leather w/emb decor, NP fittings, 1890s, 8" H, G........... 180.00
Bleeder, brass, Wiegland & Snowden, 4½", in fitted case 80.00
Book, Derangements of Liver...Nervous System, J Johnson, 1832...120.00
Book, Physiology of Common Life, GH Lewes, cloth cover, 1872. 42.50
Cabinet, dental; oak/stainless, Deco style, 4 drws/2 doors, 1940s. 240.00
Cabinet, pnt steel, dbl doors over 3 drws over 2 doors, 67x30x16"... 600.00
Cabinet, sterilizer; oak & glass w/wire, Erie City Mfg, 13" W 240.00
Case, apothecary; bold grpt, dvtl case w/13 drws, 21x39x10½" ..2,415.00
Chart, anatomy & physiology, W&AK Johnson, rolls down, 45x50", VG..85.00
Chest, apothecary; 20 grad drw, dvtl beaded case, rprs, 1900s, 30x25" 2,600.00
Chest, apothecary; 9 drw, blk pnt w/yel lettering, ca 1800, 24x35x14" ...3,175.00
Cupboard, apothecary; pine w/old pnt, 27 drws, Weeks & Gilson, 76x36".3,225.00
Fleam, 2 steel blades in 3½" brass sleeve, ca 1812.......................... 165.00
Fleam, 3-blade, brass hdl, folding type, 1800s 120.00
Instrument, B-D Venous Pressure Apparatus, L Cohen, EX in 2x13" case...60.00
Instrument, lens cystoscope, Am Cystoscope Makers, NY, in 2x13" case.. 265.00
Instrument, Thompson Resectoscope, V Vueller Chicago, EX in 2x14" case.36.00
Machine, electro-cardiograph, Sanborn, MA, paper readout, oak case ..180.00

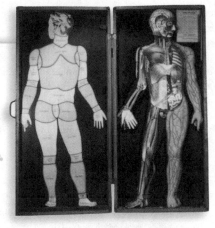

Model, heart, comes apart & shows chambers/valves/veins, mc, 17", EX. 30.00
Model, human skull, plaster, in sections, NY Scientific, 1900s, 8" ..300.00
Model, lady's torso, cast resin, 20" 900.00
Model, skull (real/human), hinged jaw, 8x6" 180.00
Postcard, photo of med students/dr/cadaver, blk & wht 240.00
Quack device, Dr Macaura's blood circulator, NMIB 110.00
Quack device, Fischer, electrical shock, 11x22x15" 850.00
Quack device, ozone generator, oak case, 6x22x12" 48.00
Report, Observations on Cow-Pox, Wm Woodville, London, 1800s, 43-pg...80.00
Scalpel, bone hdl, Mappin & Webb, 15cm L, in sheath................. 10.00
Skeleton, papier-maché, held w/wire & tin strips, pnt details, 59" ... 700.00
Stethoscope, monaural, trn wood, 7" 615.00
Stethoscope, trn fruitwood w/bell-shaped crest pc, 7" 150.00
Tongue depresser, NP brass, ebony hdl, Shepard & Dudley............ 60.00
Tooth key, dbl claw w/steel shaft & ebony hdl, 6" 240.00
Tooth key, single claw w/locking pin & trn wood hdl, 6" 225.00
Wheelchair, wicker seat, wooden footrest, 3 metal wheels, 1800s...480.00
X-ray tube, purple glass, 22" L 110.00

Meissen

The Royal Saxon Porcelain Works was established in 1710 in Meissen, Saxony. Under the direction of Johann Frederick Bottger, who in 1708 had developed the formula for the first true porcelain body, fine ceramic figurines with exquisite detail and tableware of the highest quality were produced. Although every effort was made to insure the secrecy of Bottger's discovery, others soon began to copy his ware; and in 1731 Meissen adopted the famous crossed swords trademark to identify their own work. The term 'Dresden ware' is often used to refer to Meissen porcelain, since Bottger's discovery and first potting efforts were in nearby Dresden. See also Onion Pattern.

Group, Cupid reading a book as others look on, 12", $6,500.00. (Photo courtesy Skinner Inc. Auctioneers & Appraisers of Antiques & Fine Art)

Figurine, boy seated, dabbing eyes/holding book, 19th C, 5¾", EX ..850.00
Figurine, Chinaman sits/threads needle, blanc de chine, 1930s, 8" ..660.00
Figurine, Cupid hammering a heart on anvil, gold details, 7¼" ...865.00
Figurine, goat kid w/forelegs on overturned bowl, 20th C, 5¾"....425.00
Figurine, lady dancing, purple skirt, short blk cape, 20th C, 5¼".470.00
Figurine, lady in regional costume dancing, early 1900s, 5¼" 480.00
Figurine, man w/hoop & dog on hind legs, #B94, 19th C, 5"....1,650.00
Figurine, shepherd stands & knits, 3 sheep follow, modern, 14x18".1,100.00
Figurine, 2 women & cherubs, #F65, late 1800s, 9½" 2,150.00
Nodders, Asian man & lady seated, head/hands nod, 5¾", pr...8,625.00
Plate, floral w/rtcl basketweave at rim, 9½".....................................75.00
Plate, 2 hunters in landscape, flower/insect rim, 1880s, 9½" 125.00

Platter, allegorical scene, 21" long, $7,500.00. (Photo courtesy Robert Doyle)

Vase, bud; wht paste cherub reserve on mauve w/gold, 19th C, 5½"..3,500.00
Vase, floral reserve on cobalt, urn form w/snake hdls, ca 1900, 11" ..600.00

Urn, cobalt blue with coiled snake handles on embossed gilt pedestals, crossed sword marks, 20", $3,300.00 for the pair. (Photo courtesy Jackson's International Auctioneers & Appraisers of Fine Art & Antiques)

Mercury Glass

Silvered glass, commonly called mercury glass, was a major scientific achievement of the nineteenth century. It was developed by the glass industry, who was searching for an inexpensive substitute for silver. Though very fragile, it was lightweight and would not tarnish. Mercury glass was made with two thin layers, either blown with a double wall or joined in sections, with the space between the walls of the vessel filled with a silvering compound, the perfecting of which involved much experimentation. Colored glass was also silvered. Green, blue, and amber were favored. Occasionally, colors were achieved using clear glass by adding certain chemicals to the compound. Besides hollow ware items, flat surfaces were silvered as well, through a process whereby small facets were cut on the underneath side, then treated with the silvering compound. Sometimes mercury glass was decorated by engraving; it was also hand painted. Besides decorative items such as vases and candlesticks, for instance, utilitarian items — doorknobs, curtain tiebacks, and reflectors for lamps — were also popular. Silvered Christmas ornaments were produced in large quantities.

Condition is an issue, though opinions are divided. While some prefer their acquisitions to be in mint condition, others accept items with flaked silvering. Watch for reproductions marked Made in China. In the listings that follow, all examples are silver unless noted another color.

For further information we recommend *Pictorial Guide to Silvered Mercury Glass* by Diane Lytwyn (Collector Books).

Bowl, bl geometric decoration, ftd, w/lid, 6"	120.00
Candlestick, bl, bulbous, ftd, 3", pr	70.00
Candlestick, scrolling geometric foliage & fauna, ftd, 12½", pr	145.00
Compote, mc glass jewels & bright etching, gold int, 7x7"	250.00
Doorknobs, 2" dia, pr	95.00
Gazing ball, Dithridge, ca 1867-75, 7" dia, +matching stand	800.00
Jar, HP floral (worn), Czech mks on lid & base, 8½"	285.00
Lamp, table; urn form, chrome-plated metal base, 21"	420.00
Plate, thick w/raised lip, 11"	120.00
Sugar bowl, tulip & leaf etching, 1890s, 8½"	215.00
Tie-backs, eng floral on rnd knob, 3¼", pr	125.00
Vase, ball form, ca 1880, 7x7"	85.00
Vase, HP floral, baluster, 10½", pr	130.00
Vase, HP flowers w/jewel centers, ftd, 28¾"	3,500.00
Vase, HP wht cattails & ferns, ftd, 11"	135.00
Vase, turq, long trumpet neck, ftd, 9¾"	120.00

Vases, floral decor, 14", $200.00 for the pair.

Merrimac

Founded in 1897 in Newburyport, Massachusetts, the Merrimac Pottery Company primarily produced gardenware. In 1901 they introduced a line of artware, covered mostly in semi-matt green glaze, somewhat in the style of Grueby's, but glossier and with the appearance of a second tier below the top, feathered one. Marked examples carry an impressed die-stamp or a paper label, each with the firm name and the outline of a sturgeon, the meaning of the Native American word, Merrimac. Our advisors for this category are Suzanne Perrault and David Rago; they are listed in the Directory under New Jersey.

Cachepot, gr (feathered) matt, 4x5"	2,250.00
Humidor, frothy gr mottle, 3 sm hdls, w/lid, unmk, 6½x5½"	1,000.00

Jardiniere, cvd & emb lotus leaves, gr feathered matt, sgn EB, 5x9"	3,125.00
Jardiniere, frothy gr/gunmetal, bulbous, paper label, 5½x9"	1,600.00
Vase, appl leaves, gr feathered matt, bulbous, sgn EQ, 1903, 3x4"	2,000.00
Vase, appl leaves, gr matt, bulbous, fish mk, 4½x6"	1,750.00
Vase, frothy gr, hdls, illegible mk, 4x4¼"	850.00
Vase, frothy yel matt, ovoid, nicks, 9¼x4¾"	3,475.00
Vase, gr curdled matt, bulbous, sm neck, flared rim, hdls, 4½x8"	2,250.00
Vase, gr/brn mottle, ovoid, paper label, 10x4½"	2,400.00
Vase, gr/gunmetal feathered matt, bulbous, fish mk, 6x5"	2,100.00

Vase, gunmetal and green mottle, three small handles, 15", $22,000.00. (Photo courtesy David Rago Auctions)

Vase, speckled indigo matt, high shoulder, wide rim, fish mk, 5x3½"	1,125.00
Vase, yel mottle matt, ovoid, fish mk, 9½"	3,600.00

Metlox

Metlox Potteries was founded in 1927 in Manhattan Beach, California. Before 1934 when they began producing the ceramic housewares for which they have become famous, they made ceramic and neon outdoor advertising signs. The company went out of business in 1989. Well-known sculptor Carl Romanelli designed artware in the late 1930s and early 1940s (and again briefly in the 1950s). His work is especially sought after today.

Some Provincial dinnerware lines can be confusing. There are two 'rooster' lines, Red Rooster (red, orange, and brown) and California Provincial (dark green and burgundy), and there are three 'homestead' lines, Colonial Heritage (red, orange, and brown like the Red Rooster pieces), Homestead Provincial (dark green and burgundy like California Provincial), and Provincial Blue (blue and white). For further information we recommend *Collector's Encyclopedia of Metlox Potteries, Second Edition*, by our advisor Carl Gibbs, Jr.; he is listed in the Directory under Texas.

Cookie Jars

Ali Cat, from $125 to	150.00
Ballerina Bear, from $75 to	100.00
Basket, apple on lid, from $35 to	45.00
Basket, squirrel & nuts on lid, natural, from $65 to	90.00
Blue Bird on Stump, glaze decor, from $120 to	140.00
Brownie Scout, minimum value	395.00
Bucky Beaver, from $65 to	90.00
Clown, wht w/blk accents, from $125 to	140.00
Clown, yel, from $65 to	90.00
Cookie Bandit (raccoon), from $65 to	90.00
Daisy Cookie Canister, from $35 to	45.00
Debutante, bl or pk dress, minimum value	350.00
Dina-Stegsaurus, aqua or French Blue, from $100 to	150.00
Dutch Boy, minimum value	300.00
Easter Bunny Rabbit, color glazed, from $250 to	280.00

Flamingo, minimum value 300.00
Gingham Dog, bl, from $125 to 150.00
Granada Green, from $25 to 30.00
Grapefruit, from $100 to 150.00
Happy the Clown, minimum value 295.00
Hen & Chick, minimum value 295.00
Humpty Dumpty, no ft, minimum value 400.00
Jolly Chef, bl or blk eyes, from $285 to 325.00
Koala Bear, from $80 to 100.00
Lamb Head, wht, from $100 to 125.00
Lighthouse, from $190 to 235.00
Little Piggy Pig, decor, from $75 to 90.00
Lucy Goose, from $65 to 90.00
Mac's Barn, from $175 to 200.00
Mammy Cook, bl/wht, from $150 to 180.00
Merry-Go-Round, from $175 to 200.00
Miller's Sack, from $35 to 45.00
Pear, gr or yel, from $60 to 75.00
Pumpkin, boy on lid, minimum value 400.00
Rabbit on Cabbage, from $65 to 90.00
Rag Doll, boy, from $125 to 145.00
Red Apple, 9½", from $45 to 50.00
Rooster, bl, from $275 to 300.00

Rose, from $375.00 to $400.00. (Photo courtesy Carl Gibbs, Jr.)

Salty Pelican, from $145 to 170.00
Santa Head, from $275 to 325.00
Scottie Dog, wht, from $100 to 125.00
Sir Francis Drake Duck, from $35 to 50.00
Slenderella Pig, from $85 to 125.00
Sun, from $90 to 125.00
Wells Fargo, from $500 to 550.00
Woodpecker on Acorn, from $250 to 300.00

Dinnerware

Aztec, bowl, coupe soup.. 12.50
Aztec, creamer & sugar bowl, w/lid 40.00
Aztec, platter, 11" L 35.00
California Apple, bowl, vegetable; 11½" 40.00
California Apple, plate, dinner; 10" 20.00
California Apple, plate, luncheon; 9" 7.00
California Apple, platter, 13" L, from $25 to 35.00
California Freeform, bowl, divided, 14x14" 200.00
California Freeform, cup & saucer 14.00
California Freeform, sugar bowl 24.00
California Ivy, bowl, coupe soup 18.00
California Ivy, bowl, divided vegetable; 11" 25.00
California Ivy, cup & saucer 8.00
California Ivy, mug 45.00
California Ivy, plate, dinner 15.00

California Provincial, bowl, fruit/dessert 7.50
California Provincial, bowl, vegetable; 8" 30.00

California Provincial, casserole with chicken lid, one-quart, 10-ounce, from $185.00 to $200.00.

California Provincial, chop plate, 12" 27.50
California Provincial, creamer 12.50
California Provincial, mug, 3½" 42.00
California Provincial, plate, dinner; 10" 15.00
Camellia, chop plate, 13" 20.00
Camellia, cup & saucer 12.50
Camellia, plate, luncheon; 9" 7.00
Camellia, sugar bowl, w/lid 20.00
Colonial Heritage, bowl, vegetable; 10" 32.00
Colonial Heritage, butter dish 22.00
Colonial Heritage, coffeepot 75.00
Colonial Heritage, gravy boat 40.00
Colonial Heritage, plate, dinner; 10" 7.50
Colonial Heritage, platter, 16" L 35.00
Delphinium, bowl, fruit/dessert; 6" 6.00
Delphinium, plate, bread & butter 5.00
Delphinium, plate, dinner; 10" 12.50
Delphinium, shakers, pr 20.00
Golden Fruit, bowl, rimmed soup 6.50
Golden Fruit, bowl, vegetable; 8¼" 14.00
Golden Fruit, cup & saucer, from $6 .... 8.00
Golden Fruit, platter, 16" L 35.00
Grape Arbor, bowl, cereal 7.00
Grape Arbor, coffeepot 35.00
Grape Arbor, creamer 12.50
Grape Arbor, plate, bread & butter 4.00
Happy Time, chop plate, 12" 30.00
Happy Time, gravy boat 35.00
Happy Time, plate, dinner; 10" 16.00
Happy Time, shakers, pr 22.00
Happy Time, sugar bowl, w/lid 20.00
Happy Time, teapot 115.00
Homestead Provincial, bowl, cereal; 7" 16.00

Homestead Provincial, creamer, $12.00; Sugar bowl with lid, $15.00.

Homestead Provincial, kettle casserole, w/lid 90.00
Homestead Provincial, mug, w/lid 55.00
Homestead Provincial, plate, luncheon; 9" 20.00
Iris, plate, dinner; 10" 10.00
Iris, platter, 13" L 28.00
Iris, shakers, pr 16.00
Navajo, bowl, cereal; 7" 8.00
Navajo, bowl, vegetable; 9" 14.00
Navajo, cup & saucer 75.09
Navajo, sugar bowl, w/lid 17.00
Provincial Blue, creamer 8.00
Provincial Blue, mug, w/spout, lg 80.00
Provincial Blue, plate, dinner; 10" 12.00
Provincial Blue, soup server, ind, 6" 18.00
Provincial Flower, bowl, divided vetetable; rectangular 38.00
Provincial Flower, coffeepot 48.00
Provincial Flower, platter, 13½" L 28.00
Provincial Flower, shakers, pr 20.00
Provincial Fruit, bowl, soup server; ind 12.50
Provincial Fruit, creamer 7.50
Provincial Fruit, cup & saucer 7.50
Provincial Fruit, plate, dinner; 10½" 7.50
Provincial Fruit, sugar bowl, w/lid 14.00
Provincial Rose, bowl, vegetable; 10" 15.00
Provincial Rose, creamer 15.00
Provincial Rose, plate, dinner 12.50
Provincial Rose, platter, 15" L 28.00
Red Rooster, bowl, vegetable; 10" 9.00
Red Rooster, chop plate, 12" 22.50
Red Rooster, covered dish, hen on nest 60.00
Red Rooster, plate, bread & butter 5.00
Red Rooster, plate, dinner; 10" 12.50
Red Rooster, platter, 13" L 16.00
Rooster Bleu, bowl, cereal; 7¼" 7.50
Rooster Bleu, butter dish 35.00
Rooster Bleu, gravy boat 25.00
Rooster Bleu, plate, salad; 7½" 7.00

Sculptured Grape, teapot, from $65.00 to $90.00.

Sculptured Zinnia, bowl, cereal; 7½" 7.50
Sculptured Zinnia, bowl, divided vegetable; 8½" 27.50
Sculptured Zinnia, platter, 14" L 20.00
Sculptured Zinnia, sugar bowl, w/lid 14.00
Woodland Gold, bowl, vegetable; w/lid, sm 20.00
Woodland Gold, bowl, vegetable; 11" L 28.00
Woodland Gold, mug 15.00
Woodland Gold, plate, dinner; 10½" 8.00
Woodland Gold, platter, 13" L 16.00
Woodland Gold, teapot 30.00

Disney

Bambi, jumbo, from $1,000 to 1,500.00

Bambi w/butterfly, #203, from $225 to 250.00
Cinderella, in gown, #278, from $400 to 450.00
Donald Duck w/guitar, #267, from $275 to 300.00
Dumbo seated w/bonnet, front legs up, from $200 to 225.00
Dwarf (Snow White), any, from $200 to 250.00
Faline (Bambi's girlfriend), #204, from $140 to 165.00
Figaro standing, #239, from $175 to 225.00
Hippo (Fantasia), from $325 to 400.00
Jiminy Cricket, #248, mini, 1¼", from $175 to 225.00
Jose of 3 Caballeros, #210, from $325 to 350.00
Mamma Mouse (Cinderella), #285, from $175 to 200.00
Pinocchio, from $400 to 450.00
Pluto sniffing, #264, from $225 to 250.00
Sprite (Fantasia), from $175 to 250.00
Three Little Pigs, 1¼", ea from $150 to 200.00
Timothy Mouse (aka Dumbo Mouse), mini, 1¼", from $200 to ... 250.00
Tinker Bell, #243, from $450 to 500.00
Tweedle Dum or Tweedle Dee (Alice in Wonderland), from $225 to .. 250.00

Miniatures

Ardvark, from $75 to 175.00
Banjo Boy, 6", from $80 to 125.00
Bird, wings up, sm, from $60 to 80.00
Camel resting, minimum value 350.00
Circus Horse, front legs raised, 6", from $225 to 275.00
Elephant, trunk raised, 6¼", from $60 to 85.00
Goose, 3¾", from $30 to 40.00
Turtle standing, from $140 to 160.00

Nostalgia Line

Reminiscent of the late nineteenth and early twentieth centuries, the Nostalgia line contained models of locomotives, gramophones, early autos, stage coaches, and baby carriages. There were also wagons and carts pulled by horses or donkeys, sometimes with separate drivers and passengers. The line was produced from the late 1940s through the 1960s.

Chevrolet, Antique Automobiles, #619, from $75 to 85.00
Clydsdale, American Royal Horses, minimum value 175.00
Drum table, #613, from $35 to 40.00
Fire Wagon, #659, from $60 to 85.00
Piano & lid, #603, from $50 to 65.00
Stagecoach, from $80 to 100.00
Trolley car, from $70 to 90.00

Poppets

From the mid-'60s through the mid-'70s, Metlox produced a line of 'Poppets,' 88 in all, representing characters ranging from royalty and professionals to a Salvation Army group. They came with a name tag; some had paper labels, others backstamps.

Kitty, little girl, from $50.00 to $60.00.

Casey, policeman, from $45 to.. 55.00
Chester, saxophone man, 8", from $80 to 90.00
Chimney Sweep, 7¾", from $55 to.................................... 65.00
Colleen, 7¼", from $45 to 55.00
Dutch Girl, 5", from $40 to 50.00
Elliot, boy tennis player, 6½", from $40 to 50.00
Emma the Cook, 8", from $45 to 55.00
Minnie, mermaid, from $55 to 65.00
Mother Goose w/4" bowl, from $70 to 80.00
Nick, organ grinder, from $55 to 65.00
Sally w/4" bowl, from $50 to... 60.00

Romanelli Artware

Figurine, Cowboy on Bucking Bronco, minimum value 750.00
Figurine, Great Dane, 17", minimum value 500.00
Flower holder, Cornucopia Maid, 8¾", from $250 to.................... 275.00
Flower holder, modern head, 11", from $325 to............................ 350.00
Incense burner, Confucius, 6", from $275 to 325.00
Mug, Pearl Harbor, from, $100 to 125.00
Vase, Zodiac, 12 different, 8", ea from $175 to............................. 200.00

Mettlach

In 1836 Nicholas Villeroy and Eugene Francis Boch, both of whom were already involved in the potting industry, formed a partnership and established a stoneware factory in an old restored abbey in Mettlach, Germany. Decorative stoneware with in-mold relief was their specialty, steins in particular. Through constant experimentation, they developed innovative methods of decoration. One process, called chromolith, involved inlaying colorful mosaic designs into the body of the ware. Later underglaze printing from copper plates was used. Their stoneware was of high quality, and their steins won many medals at the St. Louis Expo and early world's fairs. Most examples are marked with an incised castle and the name 'Mettlach.' The numbering system indicates size, date, stock number, and decorator. Production was halted by a fire in 1921; the factory was not rebuilt.

Key:
L — liter   PUG — print under glaze
tl — thumb lift

#144-528, plaque, PUG: Tellskapelle, 12" 280.00
#171, stein, relief: people around body, inlaid lid, .25L.................. 120.00
#202, stein, relief: choir, detailed pewter lid, #202, 1L, NM.......... 200.00
#228, stein, relief; 4 scenes of people, pewter lid, .5L, NM..............80.00
#485, stein, relief: musicians, inlaid lid, .5L.................................. 200.00
#675, stein, character: Barrel, inlaid lid, .5L....................................95.00
#1005, stein, relief: people drinking, inlaid lid, rpr, .5L 80.00
#1036, stein, threading/glazed: repeating design, inlaid lid, .3L..... 300.00
#1044, plaque, PUG: Hamburg, Deichthorfleeth, 12" 365.00
#1044, plaque, PUG: Hamburg, Jungfernstieg, 12" 280.00
#1044-512, plaque, PUG: Bratwurst Glocklein Nurnberg, 12" 360.00
#1044-9027, plaque, PUG: fox, worn gold, 14", NM 665.00
#1133, stein, threading/glazed: repeating design, inlaid lid, .4L, EX 180.00
#1327-1287, beaker, PUG: donkey barmaid feeds fox gentleman, .25L..... 215.00
#1370, stein, relief: verse, rpl pewter lid, .5L..................................70.00
#1436, vase, etch/glazed: repeating pattern, 4½" 240.00
#1467, stein, relief: 4 scenes of people, inlaid lid, .5L 130.00
#1526, stein, relief: Yale University, pewter lid, .5L 185.00
#1526, stein, transfer/HP: European beer map pewter lid, .5L....... 445.00
#1526, stein, transfer/HP: Salzburger...1900, pewter lid, .5 L...........95.00
#1526, stein, transfer/HP: Student Society, 1923, hairline, .5L..... 240.00
#1527, stein, etch: cavaliers drinking, Warth, horn tl/pewter lid, 1L 375.00

#1532, stein, etch: crest w/lion, inlaid lid, .5L................................ 345.00
#1662, stein, etch: tapestry/workman drinking, pewter 1889 lid, .5L....240.00
#1695, stein, etch: hunters, inlaid lid, .5L 675.00

#1741, stein, etched, signed C. Warth Tubingen, replaced pewter lid, .5L, $475.00; #2780, stein, etched, inlaid lid, top rim break and inlay repair, 1L, $310.00.
(Photo courtesy Andre Ammelounx)

#1803, stein, etch/glazed: repeating design, inlaid lid, .25L........... 265.00
#1909-1008, stein, PUG: man playing harp, Schlitt, rpr pewter lid, .5L ..275.00
#1909-1179, stein, PUG: Gesang, pewter lid, .5L........................... 475.00
#1909-1180, stein, PUG: Tanz, pewter lid, .5L 385.00
#1909-1288, stein, PUG: fox drinking beer, pewter lid, .5L 485.00
#2074, stein, etch: bird in cage, pewter lid, .5L 1,595.00
#2092, stein, etch: dwarf adjusting clock, Schlitt, inlaid lid, .5L ...1,000.00
#2097, stein, etch: musical design, inlaid lid w/hairline, .5L........ 215.00
#2140, stein, transfer/HP: 4F Turner, pewter lid, .5L.................... 310.00
#2192, stein, etch: Etruscan, Schlitt, inlaid lid, .5L...................... 725.00
#2231, stein, etch: cavaliers, inlaid lid, silent music box base, .5L ..380.00
#2327-1273, beaker, PUG: drunken man, .25L 195.00
#2373, stein, etch: St Augustine FL, alligator hdl, inlaid lid, .5L. 725.00
#2388, stein, character: Pretzels, inlaid lid, .5L............................. 325.00
#2440, stein, relief: Capo-di-Monte style, rpl pewter lid, .5L 175.00
#2443, plaque, cameo: ladies, Stahl, firing flaw, 18"..................... 395.00
#2542, charger, etched & glazed: maiden at pond, 15¾" 3,900.00

#2547, charger, Nouveau maid picking irises in forest, R. Thevenin, 16", $3,360.00. (Photo courtesy David Rago Auctions)

#2583, stein, etch: Blk Whale of Ascolon, Quidenus, pewter lid, 1L, NM..315.00
#2690, stein, etch: drinking scene, Quidenus, inlaid lid, 1.4L...1,450.00
#2715, stein, cameo/etch: 3 scenes of couples, inlaid lid, .5L....... 725.00
#2719, stein, etch/glazed: baker occupation, inlaid lid, .5L 1,950.00
#2721, stein, etch/glazed: carpenter occupation, inlaid lid, .5L.2,300.00
#2724, stein, etch/glazed: mason occupation, inlaid lid, .5L......2,415.00
#2727, stein, etch/glazed: printer occupation, inlaid lid, .5L.....2,645.00
#2729, stein, etch/glazed: blacksmith occupation, inlaid lid, .5L. 4,600.00
#2730, stein, etch/glazed: butcher occupation, inlaid lid, .5L....4,600.00
#2917, stein, etch/relief: Minchin, rpl inlaid lid, 1L 925.00
#2917, stein, etch/relief: Munchen, inlaid lion/shield lid, .5L.2,550.00
#3340, bowl, etch: floral, 6½x6" 345.00

#5241, plaque, etch: Delft, 15¼" 235.00
#7042, plaque, Phanolith: people at table, Stahl, 12x15½"+fr .. 1,840.00

#2568, vase, carved and painted birds in landscape, signed Chevrolon, 14", $800.00. (Photo courtesy Treadway Gallery Inc.)

Microscopes

The microscope has taken on many forms during its 250-year evolutionary period. The current collectors' market primarily includes examples from England, surplus items from institutions, and continental beginner and intermediate forms which sold through Sears Roebuck & Company and other retailers of technical instruments. Earlier examples have brass main tubes which are unpainted. Later, more common examples are all black with brass or silver knobs and horseshoe-shaped bases. Early and more complex forms are the most valuable; these always had hardwood cases to house the delicate instruments and their accessories. Instruments were never polished during use, and those that have been polished to use as decorator pieces are of little interest to most avid collectors. Unless otherwise described, all examples in the following listing are in excellent condition and retain their original cases.

Acme, brass & iron, +14" case, EX 350.00
Bausch & Lomb, brass w/gutta percha, 13½" closed, EX in case .. 700.00
Bausch & Lomb, NP Continental type, triple nosepc, VG 400.00
Bausch & Lomb, triple nosepc, brass tube, Y-ft, 10½", EX in case ... 950.00
Beck, brass, binoculars, 1890s, w/many accessories, EX in case 650.00
C Reichert, brass folding compound, extended: 10", EX in case .. 1,115.00
Culpeper type, brass tube, circular ft, rack-work focus, 10" 1,525.00
Ernest Leitz, 3 brass objectives, rpl mirror, 1910, VG+ 650.00
French, student's compound, brass, rack-work, swivel magnifier, 9½" ... 165.00
Gwo Wales, compound w/brass tube, CI U-form limb, Y-ft, 11" .. 650.00
J Swift & Son #286, folding compound, dbl nosepc, folded: 9", +case .. 765.00
JW Queen & Co Philada 1637, ca 1886, 13½x10", EX 425.00
Moritz Pillischer #470, brass, rack-work+fine screw adjustments, 16" ... 885.00
Newton, brass compound, nosepc, adjusts w/screw, 4-stop aperture, 14" .. 885.00
Queen, brass & iron, Y-base, 14", G in case 325.00

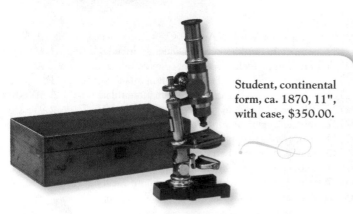

Student, continental form, ca. 1870, 11", with case, $350.00.

Watson & Sons, 2 lenses, revolving turret, 1931, EX 675.00
Watson & Sons Kima, 1940, 14", MIB w/booklet 215.00
Zentmeyer, brass, complex, dbl pillar, tripod base, 18", G 1,250.00

Militaria

Because of the wide and varied scope of items available to collectors of militaria, most tend to concentrate mainly on the area or areas that interest them most or that they can afford to buy. Some items represent a major investment and because of their value have been reproduced. Extreme caution should be used when purchasing Nazi items. Every badge, medal, cap, uniform, dagger, and sword that Nazi Germany issued is being reproduced today. Some repros are crude and easily identified as fakes, while others are very well done and difficult to recognize as reproductions. Purchases from WWII veterans are usually your safest buys. Reputable dealers or collectors will normally offer a money-back guarantee on Nazi items purchased from them. There are a number of excellent Third Reich reference books available in bookstores at very reasonable prices. Study them to avoid losing a much larger sum spent on a reproduction. Our advisor for this category is Ron L. Willis; he is listed in the Directory under Washington.

Key: insg — insignia

Imperial German

Badge, silver airship w/in wreath, CE Juncker Berlin, 2½" W 575.00
Box, cartridge; eagle & cross on leather flap, brass lion-head ends. 85.00
Buckle, Gott Mitt Uns, brass, WWI era, w/brn leather belt 85.00
Coat, artillery officer's, bl wool w/red trim, gold braid, ca 1909, EX ... 300.00
Helmet, Imperial Saxon, 17th Uhlan, w/brass chin strap, late 1800s ... 1,100.00
Helmet, spike; Fusilier battalion officer's, silver death head 3,950.00
Helmet, spike; officer's, brass hdw, w/chin strap, WWI 385.00
Medal, Crown Order Cross, 2nd class, enamel/metal, 1861, rpl ribbon .. 400.00
Medal, Iron Cross, 1st class, enamel on silver, dtd 1914 .... 85.00
Medal, Iron Cross, 2nd class, 1813-70, w/combatant's ribbon 240.00
Medal, Order of Griffin, breast cross w/red enamel inlay, pin-bk . 900.00
Medal, Pour Le Merite Blue Max, J Godet & Sohn, ¾" dia, w/ribbon . 1,100.00
Medal, Prince Regent Jubilee, dtd 1905, w/red & gr ribon 25.00

Third Reich

Badge, Luftwaffe Sea Battle, metal, J Godet Sohn Berlin, WWII era ... 360.00
Badge, NSFK, winged figure & swastika, bl enameling, 1938 .... 80.00
Badge, Sniper, 3rd grade, eagle head/oak leaves on gr cloth 235.00
Badge, Tank Battle, eagle/swastika/tank, zinc, late issue 45.00
Barometer, U-boat, silvered dial w/Third Reicht insignia, 6" dia. 150.00
Book, Brown Book of Hitler Terror, Alfred A Knopf, NY, 1933 .... 25.00
Book, Rise & Fall of 3rd Reich, WL Shirer, Easton Press, Vols 1 & 2 .. 85.00
Book, With Hitler in West, photo book, soft cover, 1940, 130-pg .. 175.00
Card, Horrors of War, Hitler making speech, #283, 1938, G 200.00
Flag, Hitler reserve/swastikas, blk/wht/red stripes, 1940s, 10x15" .. 180.00
Hatpin, copper head w/silver swastika, 6⅞" L 60.00
Helmet, M35, steel body w/brn/blk camo, orig liner & chin strap .. 280.00
Magazine, Adolph Hitler, His Life & Work, Dutch, 1940s, 30-pg .. 150.00
Medal, Auschwitz Cross, concentration camp survivor, silver, 1939-45. 250.00
Medal, Knight's Cross of Iron Cross, silver & blk enamel, MIB ... 325.00
Medal, Mother's Cross, gold (mothers w/8 in military), 1940s, EXIB .. 425.00
Money box, book form w/facing cover pnt w/Party Drape 80.00
Poster, Hitler portrait, Hitler the Liberator (Ukranian), 1938, 47x33". 1,450.00
Shorts, Sandfarbe, lt khaki cotton, button-closure pockets 70.00
Trench coat, Luftwaffe officer's, blk leather, EX 425.00

Japanese

Cap, Navy officer, $275.00. (Photo courtesy Jackson's International Auctioneers & Appraisers of Fine Art & Antiques)

Cap, Army IJA, yel star on khaki cloth, cloth bill, WWII era 200.00
Currency, Japan Allied, 1,000 Yen, ca 1951 .... 480.00
Flag, red sun on wht silk, hemmed 3 sides, WWII era, 8¼x12½" ... 55.00
Flight suit, Army IJA, olive gr gabardine, WWII era, VG 150.00
Medal, Russo-Japanese War Military Service, bronze, 1904-05, w/bar ... 70.00
Tunic, Army enlisted, gr w/Manchurian issue stampings 60.00

United States

Book, Life of Major Gen Zachary Taylor, J Frost, NY, 1947, 1st edition . 240.00
Buckle, Civil War, CS on brass w/rope border, on leather belt .. 6,325.00
Bullet mold, Enfield 577, brass scissors type, VG 460.00
Bullet mold, 64 caliber rnd ball, single cavity, iron scissors type .. 750.00
Canteen, Civil War, Confederate, cedar wood, 7", EX 3,165.00
Canteen, Indian Wars, canvas cover, w/stopper & chain, ca 1872 ... 195.00
Cap box, Civil War Confederate, leather w/single strap, VG 700.00

Cartridge box, Condict & Co., Newark, New Jersey, small oval 'US' plate old but not original, old restoration and splits to strap, $230.00. (Photo courtesy Garth's Auctions Inc.)

Cup, Army, tin, mk hdl, ca 1894 .... 132.50
Drum, Mexican War/Civil War, maple w/brass tacks, orig heads . 550.00
Hat, Navy, brn & blk beaver w/gold tassel, fore & aft style, 1860s ... 180.00
Hat, visor; Army Senior officer, blk wool crown, gold eagle, 1930s . 150.00
Helmet, M 1917, pnt metal w/sand finish, w/strap & liner 135.00
Holster, Civil War era, open-top Slim Jim style, brn leather 260.00
Holster, revolver; brn leather, Milwaukee Saddlery Co, dtd 1944 ... 180.00
Insignia, E Pluribus Unum/eagle/stars, brass, 1800s, 1⅝x2½" 135.00
Jacket, artillery shell; Civil War, bl wool w/red, brass buttons, VG .. 1,725.00
Jacket, Navy Academy, blk wool w/24 buttons, ca 1880, EX 120.00
Medal, Civil War Confederate Southern Cross of Honor, EX 800.00
Medal, gold cross, 12k gold, 1941-45, 3.53 grams 435.00
Mess kit, Army, 27 enamelware pcs in wooden 14x18x14" case, 1940s . 235.00
Photograph, officers row (houses) at Ft Hays KS, blk/wht, 1889, 5x10" . 240.00
Shako, 1858 Pattern, NY Militia brass plate, beaver skin/wool plume .. 350.00

Spurs, cavalry; Buermann US, metal w/leather straps, 5½x4", pr . 132.50
Uniform, West Point Cadet, coat+pants, brass buttons, 1943, NM ... 300.00

Milk Glass

Milk glass is today's name for milk-white opaque glass. The early glass-maker's term was Opal Ware. Originally attempted in England in the eighteenth century with the intention of imitating china, milk glass was not commercially successful until the mid-1800s. Pieces produced in the U.S.A., England, and France during the 1870 – 1900 period are highly prized for their intricate detail and fiery, opalescent edges. For further information we recommend *Collector's Encyclopedia of Milk Glass, An Identification & Value Guide*, by Betty and Bill Newbound. (CE numbers in our listings refer to this publication.) Other highly recommended books are *The Milk Glass Book* by Frank Chiarenza and James Slater; Ferson's *Yesterday's Milk Glass Today*, and Belknap's *Milk Glass*. The newest reference, published in 2001, is *Milk Glass Imperial Glass Corporation* by Myrna and Bob Garrison. Our advisor for this category is Rod Dockery; he is listed in the Directory under Texas. See also Animal Dishes with Covers; Bread Plates; Historical Glass; Westmoreland.

Key:
B — Belknap   G — Garrison
CE — Newbound   MGB — Milk Glass Book
F — Ferson

Pitcher, owl, Challinor Taylor, ca. 1891, F-587, 7½", from $135.00 to $150.00. (Photo courtesy Bill and Betty Newbound)

Bottle, Deco shape, w/finger ring, CE-17, 8" 20.00
Bottle, scent; sculpted, CE-11a, 4½", from $25 to 30.00
Bowl, cereal; HP red geometric border, Hazel-Atlas, 1940s, from $15 to .. 20.00
Bowl, Daisy Ray, ftd, w/hdls, CE-26, 4¾x8", from $18 to 22.00
Bowl, Gothic cut-out border, att Canton Glass, B-132c, 7½" 25.00
Box, dresser; emb girl & doll on lid, CE-37a, 4", from $35 to 40.00
Box, glove; scrolls & floral decals, CE-35a, 4x10½", from $55 to ... 65.00
Cake stand, HP floral/bbands, Challinor Taylor, ca 1890, CE-107, 6x9" .. 35.00
Candlestick, satin finish w/emb roses, CE-66a, 4", ea from $25 to . 30.00
Candlesticks, Dutch Boudoir, att US Glass, CE-76, 1910, 3", pr . 125.00
Candlesticks, Georgian style, HP bl leaves, octagonal, CE-69, pr .. 30.00
Compote, Swirled Split Rib, bl, Porteiux-Vallerysthal, CE-185a ... 70.00
Cookie jar, tufted pillow/HP leaves, Con-Cora/Consolidated, CE-186, 9" .. 75.00
Covered dish, boar's head, Atterbury, May...1888, F-332, 9½" L .. 2,000.00
Covered dish, deer on tree base, opal antlers/tail, F-34, 5x6½" 240.00
Covered dish, horse on split-rib base, McKee, F-60, from $250 to .. 265.00
Creamer, child's; Tappan, ftd, CE-84a, 2¾", from $25 to 30.00
Figure, swan, open, LE Smith, CE-204a, ca 1930, 9" L, from $35 to .. 40.00
Goblet, Jewel & Dewdrop, Kemple, CE-218b, 6", from $20 to 22.00
Hair receiver, Beaded Shell, ca 1910, 3¾x3¾", from $30 to 35.00
Jar, candy; Parakeet, ring finial, Imperial Glass, ca 1958, G-Pg 127 .. 85.00
Jar, ginger; HP floral, Regent line, Consolidated, 7½", from $40 to ... 45.00
Lamp, emb decor, lg ftd shape, w/shade, CE-235, from $90 to 125.00

Lamp, Fleur-de-Lis, gold trim, Eagle Glass, CE-242b, 1901, 7", (+) ...220.00
Mug, Bird & Wheat, gold trim, ftd, Atterbury, ca 1881, F-486, 3"...55.00
Pitcher, Birds on Branch, gold trim, CE-320, 7" 95.00
Plate, HP blackberry, beaded edge, Westmoreland, 7½", from $15 to .. 18.00
Punch bowl, child's, emb nursery rhyme, US Glass, CE-80, 3½x4½".110.00
Punch cup, child's, emb nursery rhyme, US Glass, CE-80, 1½x1⅝".. 25.00
Salt dip, Daisy, ftd, CE-291d, 2", from $10 to 12.00
Shakers, Tassel, metal top, CE-282a, 3¼", pr from $25 to 30.00
Sugar bowl, Flute & Crown, 4-ftd, CE-302d............................... 25.00
Sugar bowl, Rib, 3-ftd, w/lid, Vallerysthal, CE-185b, 6½x4½" 35.00
Toothpick holder, owl w/spread wings, open, Westmoreland, CE-325c, 3"..22.00
Vase, Grille & Scroll, gold trim, Butler Bros, 1912, CE-376, 8½" .. 35.00
Wall pocket, Whiskbroom, Imperial Glass, G-Pg 145 .... 35.00

Millefiori

Millefiori was a type of art glass first produced during the 1800s. Literally the term means 'thousand flowers,' an accurate description of its appearance. Canes, fused bundles of multicolored glass threads such as are often used in paperweights were cut into small cross sections, arranged in the desired pattern, refired, and shaped into articles such as cruets, lamps, and novelty items. It is still being produced, and many examples found on the market today are fairly recent in manufacture. See also Paperweights.

Inkwell & stopper, pk/bl/lt bl/wht in clear, mallet form, 6½" 280.00
Lamp, bronze & porc circus performer w/mc ball shade atop ft, 25½" .. 1,875.00
Lamp, bronze bird beside mc ball shade, wht marble base, 7½".... 300.00
Lamp, mc flowers, matching mushroom form shade & shaft, 21x10½"...530.00
Lamp, mini; gr/wht/lav floral on gr, ball shade, 9".........................345.00
Lamp, wht floral in mc shapes, crystal prisms on mushroom shade, 18" .800.00
Lamp, yel & pk floral in gr ovals on amethyst, w/o shade, 14x6½"...65.00
Vase, bulbous body, lg appl ornate rim to waist hdls, 2½x2" 70.00
Vase, bulbous body, swollen neck, flared rim, 6x4¼" 215.00
Vase, bulbous body, wide flat rim, appl hdls, 6½x6¾" 115.00
Vase, jug form, gr/purple/burgundy/wht, w/hlds, 6"........................ 275.00
Vase, trees (3) w/burgundy & wht flowers on clear, w/gold, 12½"... 1,000.00

Miniature Paintings

Miniature works of art vary considerably in value depending on many criteria: as with any art form, those that are signed by or can be attributed to a well-known artist may command prices well into the thousands of dollars. Collectors find paintings of identifiable subjects especially interesting, as are those with props, such as a child with a vintage toy or a teddy bear or a soldier in uniform with his weapon at his side. Even if none of these factors come to bear, an example exhibiting fine details and skillful workmanship may bring an exceptional price. Of course, condition is important, and ornate or unusual frames also add value. When no medium is described, assume the work to be watercolor on ivory; if no signature is mentioned, assume them to be unsigned. When frame or case information follows the size, the size will pertain only to the painting itself; otherwise assume that the width of the frame is minimal and adds only nominally to the size.

Key: wc — watercolor

Baby in red dress, gold case w/chased bezel, ca 1835, 2⅛x1⅝" ..2,115.00
Black man in bl & red jacket, wc on paper, 1800s, 1¼", +brass fr..2,700.00
Boy in red jacket, brn curls, 1810s, gold pendant fr, 2⅝"...........2,800.00
Child in wht w/coral necklace, gold pendant fr/hair lock, 2" 2,115.00
Child in wht w/rattle, att C Peters, 1840s, 3x2", velvet-covered fr.... 11,750.00

Garden of Love, lovers/cherubs, Beetz, 5⅜x4⅝", +ornate fr 850.00
Girl holding doll, coral necklace, 2¼", repro blk fr w/brass bezel...1,115.00
Girl holds red book, dk bl dress, G- leather case, 3¼" 645.00
Girl in pk dress w/wht ruffle, 1810s, brass fr, easel bk, 2¾" 440.00
Girl w/flowers in hair, hand to face, wc on paper, pendant fr, 2¾"...230.00
Hope, lady leaning on anchor, copper pendant case, 19th C, 1¼" . 1,000.00
Lady, child & servant, DJ Watkins/1842, 3⅜x2⅝", +mahog fr..7,000.00
Lady in bl, gold necklace, identified, 1800s, lined case, 3½" 235.00
Lady in bl dress holds bouquet, wc on laid paper, +8x6" fr 400.00
Lady in bl Empire dress (identified), on paperbrd, gilt fr, 2⅞" 765.00
Lady in blk coat & bonnet, sgn Caligalieri, on paper, in fr, 4¼x3"..150.00
Lady in courtyard, bl sash/coral necklace, gilt fr, 3⅝" 645.00
Lady in fine bonnet, bl dress/jewelry, rnd brass fr, 3¼" dia............ 400.00
Lady in red, flowers in dk hair, 1830s, gilt pendant fr, 1⅞" 880.00
Lady in wht before red drapery, 1810s, 3", +arched brass mt/fr..3,400.00
Lady in wht dress w/bl sash, ca 1795, brass pendant fr, 2⅜".......... 880.00
Lady w/curls, lacy bodice, att Verstille, ca 1800, pendant fr, 2¼"...3,400.00
Lady w/gauzy drape over head & shoulders, on porc, brass fr, 5x4"... 525.00
Lady w/long curls, flowing scarf, oil on paper, Richter, ivory fr 100.00
Lady w/lovely curls (identified), 3⅛x2¼", +gold pendant case..1,525.00
Lady w/wavy hair, striped bodice, orig foliate fr, 4¾" 235.00
Madame de Pompadour after Boucher, 19th C, 4½", +gilt metal fr...1,000.00
Man in bl jacket/brass buttons, Prigart, 1799, gold fr, 2" dia 1,050.00
Man in bl jacket/wht cravat, ca 1805, copper pendant fr, 2¾" 825.00
Man in blk formal wear w/gold pin, Boston, in lined case, 4¼x3¾"...575.00
Man in blk jacket, att EG Malbone, ca 1800, brass pendant fr, 2¾"..5,580.00
Man in blk jacket, wht shirt/cravat, 1790s, pendant fr, 2¾"......1,000.00
Man in blk jacket, wht shirt/tie, bust length, ca 1815, 2x1⅞", +fr ..945.00
Man in blk jacket & cravat, ca 1830, 2¼x1¾", +copper fr........... 265.00
Man in blk jacket/yel vest, hairwork border, 1810s, leather case, 3"..4,115.00
Man in gr coat, lt gray hair, 3¼x3", +oval copper fr in fitted case ...375.00
Man w/beard, floral vest, blk jacket, brass case, 2¼x1⅞" 880.00
Man w/curls in blk jacket/wht cravat, ca 1805, gilt pendant fr, 2⅜"...1,050.00
Man w/dog in landscape, 1820s, 2¾", +molded wooden fr w/brass liner ..2,115.00
Navy officer w/gold epaulets, gilt-lined wood fr, 2¾x2⅝" 765.00

Portrait of Moses Waterhouse Esquire, dated 1839, 4½x4", in painted period frame, $8,225.00. (Photo courtesy Skinner Inc. Auctioneers & Appraisers of Antiques & Fine Art)

Scholarly-looking man in blk, wht shirt, on paper, 8", +wide fr... 235.00
Theresa Queen of Prussia, well dressed lady w/gray hair, in case, 5" ...230.00

Miniatures

There is some confusion as to what should be included in a listing of miniature collectibles. Some feel the only true miniature is the salesman's sample; other collectors consider certain small-scale children's toys to be appropriately referred to as miniatures, while yet others believe a miniature to be any small-scale item that gives evidence to the craftsmanship of its creator. For salesman's samples, see specific category; other types are listed below. See also Dollhouses and Furnishings; Children's Things.

Bandbox, wood w/wallpaper covering, oblong, 2¼x4x3½" 355.00
Box, document; pine w/wire staple hinges, floral decor, drw, 5x7x4"..700.00
Box, floral wallpaper covering, Am, 19th C, 2x2½x1⅞" 3,000.00
Bucket bench, bl pnt pine, bootjack ft, 19th C, 2⅜x9x5/8x1½" .. 295.00
Cabinet, mahog Sheraton w/inlay, crest/dbl doors/4 drw/Fr ft, 19x11". 2,100.00

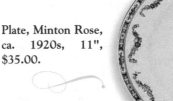

Chest, grain-painted Empire form, wooden knobs, nineteenth century, 8½x9½", $350.00.

(Photo courtesy James D. Julia Inc.)

Chest, mahog, molded top, 2 short drw over 3 grad drw, 1900s, 10x10" ..550.00
Chest, mahog Chpndl style, 4 grad drw, bracket ft, 8x7x5" 1,300.00
Chest, pine Fed w/cvg & inlay, 2 short/2 long drw, rfn, 1830s, 14x14"....1,650.00
Chest, walnut/curly walnut Emp, 1 lg drw:3 grad drw, 26x22x12".. 1,900.00
Chest, 6-brd, old gr pnt, leather hinges, 1816, 4x4¾x2½" 600.00
Chest over drw w/geometric inlay, hinged lid, glass pulls, 8x12x6" ..1,300.00
Compote, wirework w/stone fruit (13 pcs), 4⅞x3½" dia 645.00
Cupboard, cornice, 2 doors, pnt shelves, NE, 19th C, 18x17x5".. 475.00
Firkin, pine staves, maple lapped hoops, MA, 19th C, 2½" 440.00
Footstool, pnt pine, shaped skirt/legs, stenciling, 19th C, 3x6x3"..... 1,060.00
Hutch, walnut/poplar, cornice/5 drw/shelf/3 short drw/2 doors, 23". 1,100.00
Jug, stoneware, cobalt flower on salt glaze, 19th C, 3⅛" 880.00
Stand, dressing; mahog, shaped bkbrd, 2 short drw/long drw, 10x16x8".1,500.00

Minton

Thomas Minton established his firm in 1793 at Stoke on Trent and within a few years began producing earthenware with blue-printed patterns similar to the ware he had learned to decorate while employed by the Caughley Porcelain Factory. The Willow pattern was one of his most popular. Neither this nor the porcelain made from 1798 to 1805 was marked (except for an occasional number series), making identification often impossible.

After 1805 until about 1816, fine tea services, beehive-shaped honey pots, trays, etc., were hand decorated with florals, landscapes, Imari-type designs, and neoclassic devices. These were often marked with crossed 'Ls.' It was Minton that invented the acid gold process of decorating (1863), which is now used by a number of different companies. From 1816 until 1823, no porcelain was made. Through the 1920s and 1930s, the ornamental wares with colorful decoration of applied fruits and florals and figurines in both bisque and enamel were usually left unmarked. As a result, they have been erroneously attributed to other potters. Some of the ware that was marked bears a deliberate imitation of Meissen's crossed swords. From the late '20s through the '40s, Minton made a molded stoneware line (mugs, jugs, teapots, etc.) with florals or figures in high relief. These were marked with an embossed scroll with an 'M' in the bottom curve. Fine parian ware was made in the late 1840s, and in the 1850s Minton experimented with and perfected a line of quality majolica which they produced from 1860 until it was discontinued in 1908. Their slogan was 'Majolica for the Millions,' and for it they gained widespread recognition. Leadership of the firm was assumed by Minton's son Herbert sometime around the middle of the nineteenth century. Working hand in hand with Leon Arnoux, who was both a chemist and an artist, he managed to secure the company's

financial future through constant, successful experimentation with both materials and decorating methods. During the Victorian era, M. L. Solon decorated pieces in the pate-sur-pate style, often signing his work; these examples are considered to be the finest of their type. After 1862 all wares were marked 'Minton' or 'Mintons,' with an impressed year cipher.

Many collectors today reassemble the lovely dinnerware patterns that have been made by Minton. Perhaps one of their most popular lines was Minton Rose, introduced in 1854. The company itself once counted 47 versions of this pattern being made by other potteries around the world. In addition to less expensive copies, elaborate hand-enameled pieces were also made by Aynsley, Crown Staffordshire, and Paragon China. Solando Ware (1937) and Byzantine Range (1938) were designed by John Wadsworth. Minton ceased all earthenware production in 1939.

See also Majolica; Parian.

Bowl, centerpiece; gr w/latticework rim, radiant design center, 9x11" ..400.00
Bowl, rim soup; Minton Rose, 7⅞" 35.00
Charger, cows in stream & horses in field, 1875, 17" 270.00
Charger, Minton Rose, 12" 70.00
Charger, Oriental bird & flowers on blk w/gold, 1872, 16½" 860.00
Cup & saucer, Minton Rose, 2⅛", 3½" 30.00
Ewer, lady's portrait reserve on cobalt w/gold, Sutton, rpr, 9¼" 100.00
Figurine, child carrying basket (bolted to tray), gr & wht, 7½" 360.00
Figurine, parrot on tree stump, gr & yel, 14½" 720.00
Garden seat, stylized flowers & foliage transfers, #2038, 19th C, 19".. 2,500.00
Gravy boat, Minton Rose, attached underplate, 5x8½", from $90 to.. 100.00
Jug, village view/foliage, gr transfer, 1890s, 8½x8½", NM 120.00
Pedestal, floral transfer on earthenware, ca 1884, 18¼" 360.00
Plaque, deer in forest scene, earth tones, sgn C Henk, 16" 270.00
Plaque, rooster in pasture scene, sgn JE Dean, 1926, 9" 1,850.00
Plate, HP girl w/flowers in hair & lap, earthenware, 1875, 23" .2,280.00
Plate, lady w/draped hair covering, ca 1890, 11¾" 360.00

Plate, Minton Rose, ca. 1920s, 11", $35.00.

Platter, Minton Rose, 16⅞" L 80.00
Vase, bluebird & grapes on orange, 4-ftd canteen form, #1303, 6", NM ..350.00
Vase, bright yel, bulbous, shouldered, 14" 75.00
Vase, bud; underglazed birds on bl, geometrics on neck, #508, 13" ..70.00
Vase, malachite slip on brn w/yel band, waisted, 10" 215.00
Vase, nautilus shell on rockwork base, #1539, 10½", pr............. 1,200.00
Vase, Nouveau flowers & leaves, brns on bl, waisted, 1920s, 11" . 110.00
Vase, turq runs on bl on tan mottle w/gilt foil underglaze, 1880s, 7" ..475.00

Mirrors

The first mirrors were made in England in the thirteenth century of very thin glass backed with lead. Reverse-painted glass mirrors were made in this country as early as the late 1700s and remained popular throughout the next century. The simple hand-painted panel was separated from the mirrored section by a narrow slat, and the frame was either the dark-finished Federal style or the more elegant, often-gilded Sheraton.

Mirrors changed with the style of other furnishings; but whatever type you purchase, as long as the glass sections remain solid, even broken or flaking mirrors are more valued than replaced glass. Careful resilvering is acceptable if excessive deterioration has taken place. In the listings that follow, items are from the nineteenth century unless noted otherwise. The term 'style' (example: Federal style) is used to indicate a mirror reminiscent of but made well after the period indicated. Obviously these retro styles will be valued much lower than their original counterparts. As with most other items in antiques and collectibles, the influence of online trading is greatly affecting prices. Many items once considered difficult to locate are now readily available on the internet. Our advisor for this category is Michael Hinton; he is listed in the Directory under Pennsylvania.

Key:

Chpndl — Chippendale	QA — Queen Anne
Emp — Empire	Vict — Victorian
Fed — Federal	vnr — veneer

Bull's-eye, reeded fr w/close spherules, blk pnt liner, convex, 22"....585.00
Cheval, mahog Fed, ogee fr, tapered uprights, trestle legs, 73x34x24".. 2,950.00
Courting, molded fr w/rvpt floral panels, rpl, 15½x10½"..............315.00
Courting, pine w/mc crest, pnt on gesso, pendant at bottom, 19x10"....485.00
Gilt Baroque style, pomegranates crest, acanthus leaves, 45x33x7"....3,525.00
Gilt Chpndl, much cvg, 2 brass swing-arm candleholders, 54x26"....5,500.00
Gilt Fed w/cove-molded cornice, rvpt panels, rpl mirror, 40x22".. 865.00
Gilt gesso w/eagle & cornucopia crest, rstr gilt, 24x27"................600.00
Giltwood, tongue pattern, floral stops, foliage/dragons/urns, 25x42"... 1,115.00
Giltwood Fed, broken pediment/acorn drops/sunflower, 46x31x3"..2,950.00
Giltwood Fed, molded cornice, rvpt lady & child, columns, 44"....1,700.00
Giltwood Fed, ropework w/fruit/nuts/leaves crest, bow below, 36x20". 1,175.00
Giltwood Fed, rvpt Lady Liberty at Washington's tomb, 42x24"......2,100.00
Giltwood Fed, rvpt landscape reserve, rstr/rpl, 45x27" 1,725.00
Giltwood Fed, rvpt portrait of DeWitt Clinton, 31x17"............3,450.00
Giltwood Fed, split baluster w/foliate/reeded elements, 48x34"... 4,400.00
Giltwood Fed, split baluster w/tulips/fleur-de-lis spandrels, 57x30" ..2,300.00

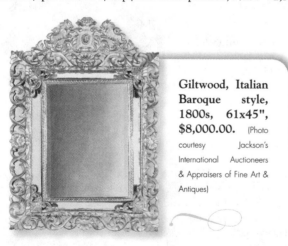

Giltwood, Italian Baroque style, 1800s, 61x45", $8,000.00. (Photo courtesy Jackson's International Auctioneers & Appraisers of Fine Art & Antiques)

Giltwood Rococo, pierced crest w/flower basket, 41x21" 650.00
Mahog Chpndl, rtcl acanthus crest, gold rpt liner, rpl mirror, 32x18"... 500.00
Mahog Fed, inlaid conch shell on crest, string inlay liner, 46x23"......5,000.00
Mahog Fr Neo-Classical, cornice/2 doors, sphinx busts/paw ft, 105"..3,815.00
Mahog QA w/openwork crest, appl gesso ornaments, old finish, 27x13" ..430.00
Mahog/giltwood Chpndl, bird crest/gilt liner, 41x24" 1,525.00
Mahog/giltwood Chpndl, scroll fr w/pierced crest, NE, 40x18"..1,525.00
Overmantel, giltwood Fed, cornice/baluster fr w/rosettes/etc, 29x68"...600.00
Overmantel, giltwood Fed, rosette blocks, split columns, 36x65"...1,585.00
Overmantel, giltwood Neo-Greco, anthemia/rosettes/etc, 1870s, 75x56". 2,700.00

Overmantel, giltwood/pnt Rococo style, courting scene in arch, 40x38".400.00
Pier, Empire-style mahog, cast metal mts, 65x34½" 450.00
Pier, giltwood Fed, molded fr, divided mirror plate, 72x36x3"...3,950.00
Pnt Fr-style fr w/center oval romantic medallion w/gold, 61x36"..1,400.00
Pnt QA, shaped crest above molded fr, early surface, 12x11"....1,500.00
Scroll, mahog Chpndl w/gilt, floral scrolled crest, 1770s, 52x24"..3,300.00
Walnut Blk Forest, stag head/scrolled sides w/game, rnd mirror, 28x20"...2,115.00

Mocha

Mochaware is utilitarian pottery made principally in England (and to a lesser extent in France) between 1780 and 1840 on the then prevalent creamware and pearlware bodies. Initially, only those pieces decorated in the seaweed pattern were called 'Mocha,' while geometrically decorated pieces were referred to as 'Banded Creamware.' Other types of decorations were called 'Dipped Ware.' During the last 40 to 50 years the term 'Mocha' has been applied to the entire realm of 'industrialized slipware' — pottery decorated by the turner on his lathe using coggle wheels and slip cups. It was made in numerous patterns — Tree, Seaweed (or Dandelion), Rope (also called Earthworm or Loop), Cat's-eye, Tobacco Leaf, Lollypop or Balloon, Marbled, Marbled and Combed, Twig, Geometric or Checkered, Banded, and slip decorations of rings, dots, flags, tulips, wavy lines, etc. It came into its own as a collectible in the latter half of the 1940s and has become increasingly popular as more and more people are exposed to the rich colorings and artistic appeal of its varied forms of abstract decoration. (Please note: Values hinge to a great extent on vivid coloration, intricacy of patterns, and unusual features.)

The collector should take care not to confuse the early pearlware and creamware Mocha with the later kitchen yellow ware, graniteware, and ironstone sporting Mocha-type decoration that was produced in America by such potters as J. Vodrey, George S. Harker, Edwin Bennett, and John Bell. This type was also produced in Scotland and Wales and was marketed well into the twentieth century.

Our values are prices realized at auction, where nearly every example was in exceptional condition. Unless a repair, damage, or another rating is included in the description, assume the item to be in NM condition.

Bowl, cat's eyes, 3-color on yel band w/blk stripes, 4x8½", EX.....435.00
Canister, seawead, dk brn on tan w/brn stripes, conical, 4½"....2,350.00
Creamer, cat's eyes (2 rows) on dk brn band, gr band, leaf hdl, 3½"...475.00
Creamer, earthworm (dbl), pale bl bands, leaf hdl, 5", EX 500.00
Goblet, tobacco leaf, dk/med brn/wht, striped ft, 3⅞" 6,000.00
Jug, cat's eyes in 2 rows on brn, tooled gr band, leaf hdl, 4", EX...480.00
Jug, cat's eyes on brn band, bl & blk stripes, chip/flaw, 5" 425.00
Jug, earthworm & cat's eye, 3-color on tan w/bl/blk stripes, 6", EX..480.00
Jug, feathered marbleing in brn/tan/wht, gr tooled rim, 5⅝"...3,500.00
Jug, horizontal bl/blk/brn bands on wht, ear hdl, ovoid, 9" 1,200.00
Jug, marbleized gray & wht, wht hdl/spout, flakes, 4¾" 275.00
Jug, seaweed, blk on gr w/tooled gr band, cream sz, 4½" 875.00

Jugs: branches bracketed by earthworm banding, G, 8", $3,500.00; Trailed and marbled slip, EX, 9¾", $6,500.00; Cat's eye bands bracketing earthworm and slip-trailed diamond bands, repaired handle, 8½", $5,525.00. (Photo courtesy Skinner Inc. Auctioneers & Appraisers of Antiques & Fine Art/ LiveAuctioneers.com)

Mug, bl bands, gr & blk stripes, tooled blk bands, leaf hdl, 4" 400.00
Mug, blk/wht scallops, gr tooled bands, tan stripes, leaf hdl, 4", EX . 1,650.00
Mug, cat's eye, bl/wht/brn on brn, bl stripes, tooled rim, 5½", EX... 1,325.00
Mug, earthworm, 3-color on lt bl, brn/bl/tan stripes, leaf hdl, 5", EX.525.00
Mug, marbleized tan/brn/wht/gold, dk brn edges, leaf hdl, 4⅞", EX .2,650.00
Mug, seaweed, blk on brn, brn & bl stripes, prof rstr, 3¾" 850.00

Mug, wavy lines and stripes, 3¾", EX, $2,350.00; Mustard pot, diamonds and stripes, 3½", EX, $2,585.00. (Photo courtesy Skinner Inc. Auctioneers & Appraisers of Antiques and Fine Arts)

Mustard, cat's eyes & stripes, wht/pumpkin/brn, lid chips, 3½".4,250.00
Pepper pot, blk circles on wht, tan band, blk stripes, 4½" 1,175.00
Pepper pot, earthworm, 3-color on gray, tooled gr band, 4¾", EX .2,400.00
Pepper pot, feathers, wht/umber/blk on tan, umber/gr stripes, 4", EX . 3,000.00
Pepper pot, gr tooled band/brn stripes/blk checks, stain/flakes, 4" .1,450.00
Salt cellar, seaweed, blk on brn band, wht ft, 1¾x2¾", EX........... 500.00
Sugar bowl, seaweed on brn band, lt bl stripes, w/lid, 4¼" 480.00

Molds

Food molds have become popular as collectibles — not only for their value as antiques, but because they also revive childhood memories of elaborate ice cream Santas with candy trim or barley-sugar figurals adorning a Christmas tree. Ice cream molds were made of pewter and came in a variety of shapes and styles with most of the detail on the inside of the mold. Chocolate molds were made in a wider variety of shapes, showing more detail on the outside of the mold, making it more decorative to look at. They were usually made of tin or copper, then nickel-plated to keep them from tarnishing or rusting as well as for sanitary reasons. (Many chocolate molds have been recently reproduced. These include Christmas trees and Santa Claus figures as well as some forms of rabbits. They are imported from Europe and may affect the market.) Hard candy molds were usually metal, although primitive maple sugar molds (usually simple hearts, rabbits, and other animals) were carved from wood. Cake molds were made of cast iron or cast aluminum and were most common in the shape of a lamb, a rabbit, or Santa Claus.

Chocolate Molds

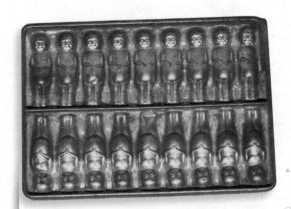

Babies, two rows of nine, 8¾x6", $150.00.

(Photo courtesy Du Mouchelle's/LiveAuctioneers.com)

Angel emptying a cornucopia, hinged, 4x2¾" 50.00
Baby, nude, hands on tummy, w/clips, #5983, 6x3" 55.00
Bellboy (chubby), #13/#6, 2 clips, 6¾" 25.00
Boy (newsboy look) w/hands in pockets, Germany, #17503, 1930s, 6¼" . 55.00
Boy w/hands on pockets, Germany, #17503, 1930s, 6¼" 65.00
Bride & Groom, hinged, 5¼x5" 150.00
Buck deer standing, 3-pc, #790, 7x7x5" 210.00
Bulldog sitting, Herman Walter, #8388, 5x5" 120.00

Car, Kenton Sedan style, pressed steel, 7½" long, $120.00. (Photo courtesy Bertoia Auctions)

Cat heads (5), Leilong/Paris #2112, 2¼x9x½" 75.00
Child on bicycle (3), #790, 2½x7" (2x1½" ea) 32.00
Christmas tree, Weygandt, 4x3" 180.00
Cross w/emb floral motif, w/clips, 8½x5½" 25.00
English Bobby, F Cluydts Antwerpen, #16324, 1960s, 5⅛" 55.00
Girl in pointed (elf-like) hat, 4½" 30.00
Handgun, 2-pc, w/2 metal clamps, 5" 20.00
Heart w/roses, France, #15880, 8x7" 45.00
Kewpie doll, clips, 7½x2¾" 125.00
Keystone cop, Anton Reiche, #17541, 6½" 90.00
Lamb lying down, 8½x11x4" 130.00
Lambs (4), hinged, 4½x15½" 40.00
Lion (full figure), 3x4¾" 25.00
Mr Peanut (2) in hinged fr, detailed, Planters Peanuts, rare, 7"... 1,140.00
Peacock w/tail closed, Sommet, 1920-50, 11x11x3½" 270.00
Popeye, Made in Germany #9034 stamp, 7½x3" 180.00
Rabbit (mother) doing laundry, 6" 165.00
Rabbit (mother) pushing baby carriage, 6¼x5x1¾" 365.00
Rabbit (3) in hinged fr, 5¾x10½" 75.00
Rabbit sitting, 9x6¼" 45.00
Rabbit standing over basket, Made in USA, #248/6218, 12x10" ... 70.00
Rabbit standing upright, Anton/Dresden, #6322/4203, 5x3½" 65.00
Rabbit w/basket on back, Eppelsheimer & Co, #8231, 1935, 9x3¾" .. 85.00
Rabbit w/chick, TC Weygandt...Made in USA, #8219, 10x6½" .. 110.00
Rabbits (2) on motorcycle, Ges Gesch, #979, 5x5¾x2¼" 150.00
Rabbits (4) in a row, 3½x12" L 50.00
Rooster, Ges Gesch, 8" 50.00
Sailboats (3), #114, 2x10" (ea boat measures 2½x1½") 45.00
Sailor w/beer mug, France, 6½x4" 120.00
Santa (4) w/tree on shoulder, Made in Germany, #4964, ca 1910, 4x7" ..130.00
Santa standing, #8003, 5x3¼" 45.00
Scottie dog, #15556, 4" 160.00
Truck (stake bed), France or Holland, 3x8" 85.00
Turkey standing, Eppelsheimer & Co, Pat #1948146, 1937, 4½x4" ...300.00
Turkey w/removable tail, Eppelsheimer, #4922, lg 120.00
Violin, Anton Reiche, 4x1¾x10½" 95.00
Watering cans (3), heavy CI or steel, #239, 1⅝x7" 40.00
Witch on broom, Weygandt, 5x3" 260.00
Witch on broomstick, detailed, hinged, 6x3¾" 70.00

Ice Cream Molds

Castle on hillside, 2-pc, 11"..............................2,300.00
Castle tower, 2-pc, 12¾" 1,100.00
Cornucopia & cherub, 6-part, 8 hinges, #128, 9x10" 835.00
Fleur-de-lis, hinged, E&Co NY, 4¾x4" 125.00
Frog on mushroom, S&Co, #180, 4x3½" 125.00

Heart, S&Co., three-pint, $300.00. (Photo courtesy Bunte Auction Services Inc./LiveAuctioneers.com)

Hen sitting, S&Co, 4-pt, 9"............................300.00
Log w/ax, 3¼x1½x5½"...................................150.00
Owl, detailed, hinged, #175..............................38.00
Pansy, hinged, Schall & Co, #269, 3¾x4½"............130.00
Pumpkin, hinged, orig pin, E&Co, #309, open: 6½" W 60.00
Rabbits on either side of lg egg, w/metal brackets, 10x7½" 140.00
Santa blowing Merry Christmas in Gothic script, #646, 2¾x4" 85.00
Ship sailing on waves, CC & Marque de Fabrique..., 12½x10½" ..780.00
Squirrel standing, E&Co, #676, 5½x3½" 200.00
Turtle, hinged, S&Co, ca 1900, 4½x3½"...............80.00
Walnut, hinged lid, #27, 2½".............................35.00
Watermelon w/slice removed, S&Co, 4-pt, 9½" L 420.00

Miscellaneous

Cast iron, hen sitting, #4103, 2-pc, 7x6½"..............50.00
Cast iron, lamb, recumbent, head trn right, 2-pc, 8x3", from $50 to.. 60.00
Cast iron, 6 joined hearts form center star, w/cast hanger 20.00
Copper, heart shape, hammered look, EX patina, ca 1950, 6½x6" . 60.00
Copper, ribbed log shape, Christian Wagner, Germany, 2¾x11x4⅝"...85.00
Copper, 10 'posts' joined in circle, mid-1800s, 2¼x5½" dia..........295.00
Copper/tin, flower form w/heart-shaped leaves, heavy, 4½x9" 125.00
Copper/tin, flower form w/spade leaves along rim, 4½x8" 55.00
Copper/tin, nautilus shell, 3½x5x3½" 50.00
Copper/tin, swirled flower form, 19th C, 4x7½" 75.00
Tin, artichokes form ring, ca 1900, 3½x7" 60.00

Indian on horseback, $40.00.

Monmouth

The Monmouth Pottery Company was established in 1892 in Mon-

mouth, Illinois. It was touted as the largest pottery in the world. Their primary products were utilitarian: stoneware crocks, churns, jugs, water coolers, etc. — in salt glaze, Bristol, spongeware, and Albany brown. In 1906 they were absorbed by a conglomerate called the Western Stoneware Company. Monmouth Pottery Co. became their #1 plant and until 1930 continued to produce stoneware marked with the Western Stoneware Company's maple leaf logo. Items marked 'Monmouth Pottery Co.' were made before 1906. Western Stoneware Co. introduced a line of artware in 1926. The name chosen for the artware was Monmouth Pottery. Some stamps and paper labels add ILL to the name. All the ware in this category was produced from 1892 through 1906 when the Monmouth Pottery Co. became part of the Western Stoneware Company and ceased to exist as the original entity.

Bowl, salt glazed, brn int, mk, 2-gal.............................200.00
Churn, #3, cobalt on salt glaze, 3-gal, 13".....................250.00
Churn, #4, cobalt on salt glaze, 16½".............................250.00
Churn, #5, cobalt on salt glaze, 5-gal............................325.00
Churn, Bristol, Maple Leaf mk, 2-gal.............................250.00
Churn, cobalt on salt glaze, 6-gal.................................400.00
Churn, salt glaze, mini, 4"..1,200.00
Churn, 2 Men in a Crock stencil, 5-gal..........................1,000.00
Cooler, ice water; bl & wht spongeware, mini 1,500.00

Cooler, ice water, blue and white spongeware, with lid and spigot, eight-gallon, $2,000.00.

(Photo courtesy Jim Martin)

Cow & calf, brn, Monmouth Pottery Co, mk 5,000.00
Crock, Bristol, mini, 2½" 600.00
Crock, Bristol, 10-gal...100.00
Crock, Bristol, 20-gal...200.00
Crock, Bristol, 60-gal..2,000.00
Crock, Bristol Monmouth Pottery Co, bl stencil, 1-qt 250.00
Crock, Bristol w/Albany slip int, 4-gal...........................85.00
Crock, Bristol w/Maple Leaf mk, 2½x3¼"........................40.00
Crock, Bristol w/Maple Leaf mk, 2-gal............................75.00
Crock, early dull Bristol w/cobalt stencil 300.00
Crock, salt glaze, Albany slip int, 3-gal.........................95.00
Crock, salt glaze, hand decor, mk, 2-gal......................250.00
Crock, salt glaze, unmk, 2-gal....................................60.00
Crock, stencil, bl on dk brn Albany slip, 3-gal 400.00
Crock, stencil, bl on dk brn Albany slip, 6-gal 600.00
Crock, 2 Men in a Crock stencil, 10-gal 700.00
Dog, Monmouth Pottery Co, mk, Albany slip 8,000.00
Hen on nest, bl & wht spongeware 1,200.00
Jug, Bristol, bl stencil (early rectangle), 5-gal 250.00
Jug, Bristol, Maple Leaf mk, 5-gal.............................200.00
Jug, Bristol w/Albany slip top, mini, 2½" 500.00
Letterhead, 1898 letter 45.00
Pig, Bristol, Monmouth Pottery Co, mk..................1,500.00
Snuff or preserve jar, wax seal..................................350.00
Tobacco jar, monk, brn Albany slip........................3,000.00

Pig, marked Monmouth Pottery Co., $1,000.00. (Photo courtesy Jim Martin)

Mont Joye

Mont Joye was a type of acid-cut French cameo glass produced by Cristallerie de Pantin in Paris around the turn of the century. It is accented by enamels. Our advisor for this category is Don Williams; he is listed in the Directory under Missouri.

Ewer, foliage, gr on gr flash, enameled scrolls, ornate metal rim, 13"..400.00
Vase, acorns & leaves, gold & silver on dk gr, goblet form, 20" ... 2,500.00

Vase, enameled flowers on optic ribbed amethyst body, 4", $350.00.
(Photo courtesy Early Auction Co./ LiveAuctioneers.com)

Vase, floral, gold on gr, gilt rim, 13" 880.00
Vase, floral/leaves, gold/gr on raisin, stick neck, 8" 660.00
Vase, hydrangeas, enamel w/gilt stems & leaves, scalloped rim, 6x3".. 685.00
Vase, irises, gold on textured frost, off-set hdls, 11" 800.00
Vase, mistletoe, gold on gr, bulbous w/slim neck, gilt rim, 6" 465.00
Vase, peonies, pk/wht/gold stems on gr, 4-sided, appl gold rim, 12"..1,400.00
Vase, thistles, enamel & gold on cranberry, quadrefoil, 12½"....... 940.00
Vase, thistles, gold/bronze/pk on celery, stick neck, 26" 3,500.00

Moorcroft

William Moorcroft began to work for MacIntyre Potteries in 1897. At first he was the chief designer but very soon took over their newly created art pottery department. His first important design was the Aurelian Ware, part transfer and part hand painted. Very shortly thereafter, around the turn of the century, he developed his famous Florian Ware, with heavy slip, done in mostly blue and white. Since the early 1900s there has been a succession of designs, most of them very characteristic of the company. Moorcroft left MacIntyre in 1913 and went out on his own. He had already well established his name, having won prizes and gold medals at the St. Louis World's Fair as well as in Paris. In 1929 Queen Mary, who had been collecting his pottery, made him 'Potter to the Queen,' and the pottery was so stamped up until 1949. William Moorcroft died in 1945, and his son Walter ran the company until recent years. The factory is still in existence. They now produce different designs but continue to use the characteristic slipwork. Moorcroft pottery was sold abroad in Canada, the

United States, Australia, and Europe as well as in specialty areas such as the island of Bermuda.

Moorcroft went through a 'Japanese' stage in the early teens with his lovely lustre glazes, Oriental shapes, and decorations. During the mid-teens he began to produce his most popular Pomegranate Ware and Wisteria (often called 'Fruit'). Around that time he also designed the popular Pansy line as well as Leaves and Grapes. Soon he introduced a beautiful landscape series called variously Hazeldine, Moonlit Blue, Eventide, and Dawn. These wonderful designs along with Claremont (Mushrooms) seem to be the most sought after by collectors today. It would be possible to add many other designs to this list. During the 1920s and 1930s, Moorcroft became very interested in highly fired flambé (red) glazes. These could only be achieved through a very difficult procedure which he himself perfected in secret. He later passed the knowledge on to his son.

Dating of this pottery is done by knowledge of the designs, shapes, signatures, and marks on the bottom of each piece; an experienced person can usually narrow it down to a short time frame. Auction prices, eBay LiveAuctioneers.com in particular, are rising sharply, especially for the pre-1935 designs of William Moorcroft, as it is items from that era that attract the most collector interest. Prices in the listings below are for pieces in mint condition unless noted otherwise; no reproductions are listed here.

Ashtray, Dawn, landscape, silver mts, Sheffield, 1927, 3⅞" dia.... 525.00
Bowl, Anemone on gr to cobalt, ftd, ca 1950, 3½x4¼" 180.00
Bowl, Blackberry & Leaf, sm ft, 7½".. 600.00
Bowl, Claremont, mushrooms, Cobridge factory mk, ca 1914+, 3x8½" .1,950.00
Bowl, Clematis, shallow, MIE, 3" 50.00
Bowl, Eventide, landscape, incurvate rim, 1½x4¼" 120.00
Bowl, Freesia, floral, shallow, 1935, 12"... 785.00
Bowl, Moonlight Blue, landscape, SP rim, ca 1925, 8⅜" 1,200.00
Bowl, Pomegranate, sm ft, 5", NM 700.00

Bowl, Pomegranate, three angle supports, ca. 1918, 3½x6", $600.00. (Photo courtesy Cincinnati Art Galleries/ LiveAuctioneers.com)

Bowl, Pomegranate, w/gr hdls, ca 1916, 4¼x11"........................1,300.00
Box, Dawn, bl/gr/wht/rose, domed lid, 4x6¼" dia 2,350.00
Candlestick, Claremont, flattened gourd shape, ca 1905, 7¼" 950.00
Compote, Clematis on cobalt, 14½" 200.00
Compote, Hibiscus on cobalt, slim stem, 4½x8½" 250.00
Compote, Moonlit Blue, landscape, cobalt ft, 5½x7" 2,650.00
Egg cup, Florian, cobalt & wht, 2" 900.00
Ginger jar, Hibiscus on gr, MIE, 6¼x5" 240.00
Humidor, Poppy, Liberty's Tudric pewter mts & lid, 6x5x5"......2,000.00
Jardiniere, Pomegranate on cobalt, 9x7", NM 845.00
Jug, Claremont, mushrooms, 2¾x4½" 2,100.00
Lamp base, Leaf & Berry on flambé, 10½x5½"...........................1,000.00
Lamp base, Orchid, bronze mt, 15½".. 450.00
Tazza, Pomegranate, Liberty's Tudric pewter base, 5¾x8½" 800.00
Trio, Orchid, 2½" cup+5½" saucer+6½" plate 550.00
Vase, Anemone on cobalt, shouldered, MIE, 8¼".......................... 395.00
Vase, Claremont, Made for Liberty & Co/#180/#1300, ca 1905, 5½"...850.00
Vase, Clematis on cobalt, baluster, 9¼"... 850.00
Vase, Clematis on cobalt, shouldered, sm burst bubble, 4x2½" 360.00
Vase, Dawn, landscape, baluster, 1926-30, 4" 1,325.00

Vase, Eventide, landscape, shouldered, 6" 2,150.00
Vase, Florian, gr & gold, Nouveau shape, Macintyre, early 1900s, 9" ... 1,600.00
Vase, Florian, peacock feathers, cobalt & wht, ftd, 6" 1,200.00
Vase, Florian, rose garland on wht, Macintyre, 7¾x6½" 800.00

Vase, Florian-style decoration, 12", $1,380.00. (Photo courtesy Treadway Gallery Inc.)

Vase, Hibiscus on gr, slightly bulbous, MIE, 3½" 175.00
Vase, Moonlight Blue, landscape, ovoid, MIE, 3½x2" 2,600.00
Vase, Moonlit Blue, landscape, cylindrical, MIE, 11x6" 3,900.00
Vase, Orchid on cobalt, bulbous, ca 1930s, 11" 950.00
Vase, Pansy on cobalt, flared rim, slim, 15" 7,350.00
Vase, Peacock Feather, gourd shape, 10½" 2,800.00
Vase, Pomegranate, bulbous, MIE, 9½x5¼" 900.00
Vase, Poppy, baluster, #65, 9½x5¼", pr 6,600.00
Vase, Poppy on cobalt, trumpet neck, 6¼x4½" 785.00
Vase, Poppy on flambé, #200, ca 1915, 8x5¼" 985.00
Vase, White Wisteria, baluster, M45, 3¾" 575.00

Moravian Pottery and Tile Works

The Moravian Pottery and Tile Works, Doylestown, Pennsylvania, was founded by Dr. Henry Chapman Mercer in 1898. He discovered the art and science of tile making on his own, without training from the existing American or European tile industry. This, along with his diverse talents as an author, anthropologist, historian, and artist, led Dr. Mercer to create something unique. He approached tile design with an historic point of view, and he created totally new production methods that ultimately became widely accepted by manufacturers of handcrafted tile. The subject matter for the designs he preferred included nature and the arts, colonial tools and artifacts, storytelling, and medieval themes. Both of these 'new' approaches (to design and production) allowed Dr. Mercer to become extremely influential in the development of pottery and tile in the Arts & Crafts Movement in America.

After Mercer's death in 1930, the Tile Works was managed by Frank Swain until 1954. In 1967 it was purchased by the Bucks County Dept. of Parks & Recreation. Tiles are being produced there today in the handmade tradition of Mercer; they are marked with a conjoined MOR and dated. Collectors look for the early tiles (mostly pre-1940), the preponderance of which bear no backstamps. These tiles were made using both red and white clays and are also referred to as 'Mercer' tiles. Our advisor for this category is Suzanne Perrault; she is listed in the Directory under New Jersey.

Box, Swan & Tower, bl & ivory w/red clay showing, open, 3¾", EX .1,100.00
Fish flask, gr on cream, 2-sided, detailed, 1800s, 2½x4½" 21,250.00
Medallion, Silva Vocat, red bird on branch, 17½", EX 6,000.00
Plaque, Socrates, gr & ivory, 15½x10¼", EX 3,650.00
Tile, Persian Anetlope, ivory & bl w/red clay showing, 7x6" 600.00
Tile, The City of God, bl & ivory, unmk, 5½", EX 540.00
Vase, pond lilies, gr/brn/gold on amethyst, bulbous w/stick neck, 13". 1,065.00
Wall sconces, birds & fleur-de-lis, gr/ivory on red clay, 11", EX, pr .280.00

Wall sconces, 2 rnd reserves on ea w/bird, gr/ivory, unmk, 11x4", pr..770.00
Wall sconces, 2 sq reserves ea w/ship, ivory/bl, unmk, 11x4", NM, pr...725.00

Medallion, Autumn, MR, 16¾", from $3,000.00 to $4,000.00. (Photo courtesy David Rago Auctions)

Morgan, Matt

From 1883 to 1885, the Matt Morgan Art Pottery of Cincinnati, Ohio, produced fine artware, some of which resembled the pottery of the Moors with intense colors and gold accents. Some of the later wares were very similar to those of Rookwood, due to the fact that several Rookwood artists were also associated with the Morgan pottery. Some examples were marked with a paper label, others were either a two- or three-line impression: 'Matt Morgan Art Pottery Co.,' with 'Cin. O.' sometimes added.

Bowl, sparrows & bamboo, blk on pumpkin w/gold, globular, ball ft, 6".375.00
Charger, yel finch on branch, Limoges style, wide gold rim, 16"....1,000.00
Plaque, cherubs (5) in relief on terra cotta, 6x11½" 200.00

Urn, painted in Barbotine with birds on dogwood branch, embossed brown and gold band, repaired drill hole, 15½x10½", $1,200.00.

Vase, bees & pk floral on aqua, gold accents & rim, pillow form, 15" ... 1,750.00
Vase, bird & leaves, brn on mustard w/sponged gold, 2½x5" 175.00
Vase, butterfly & floral, pk & gr on yel, gold accents, hdls, 5¼" ... 315.00
Vase, marsh bird in underbrush, gr on rust, scrolled hdls, #281, 10" .1,250.00

Morgantown Glass

Incorporated in 1899, the Morgantown Glass Works experienced many name changes over the years. Today 'Morgantown Glass' is a generic term used to identify all glass produced there. Purchased by Fostoria in 1965, the factory was permanently closed in 1971.

Golf Ball is the most recognized design with crosshatched bumps equally distributed along the stem (very similar to Cambridge #1066, identified with alternating lines of dimples between rows of crosshatching). Color identification is difficult and much information is provided by Cathy and Gene Florence in their book *Stemware Identification*. Prices for Golf Ball with ranges begin with lower values referring to colors other than Steigel Green, Spanish Red, or Ritz Blue with the high range reflecting values for those colors. For further information we also recommend *Elegant Glassware of the Depression Era* by Cathy and Gene Florence (both of the Florences' books are published by Collector Books).

American Beauty, crystal, custard, #8851, hdld 75.00
American Beauty, crystal, goblet, water; 9-oz, 7" 32.50
American Beauty, crystal, plate, 7" 12.50
American Beauty, crystal, sherry, #7695 trumpet, 3-oz, 6" 50.00
American Beauty, crystal, tumbler, bar; #8107 Sherman, 3-oz, 2¼" ..38.00
American Beauty, crystal, vase, #25 Olympic, 12" 200.00

Golden Iris, light amber, #23 Margaret guest set, $250.00.

Golf Ball, India Black, creamer 175.00
Golf Ball, India Black, vase, ivy ball, ruffled rim, 4" 150.00
Golf Ball, Old Amethyst, oyster cocktail, 4½-oz, 4½" 25.00
Golf Ball, Old Amethyst, tumbler, tea; ftd, 12-oz, 6¾" 24.00
Golf Ball, Spanish Red, champagne, 5-oz, 5" 25.00
Golf Ball, Spanish Red, oyster cocktail, 4½-oz, 4½" 40.00
Queen Louise, crystal w/Anna Rose, plate (finger bowl liner), 6" ...110.00
Sunrise Medallion, bl, cordial, 1½-oz 295.00
Sunrise Medallion, bl, cup 100.00
Sunrise Medallion, bl, sugar bowl 295.00
Sunrise Medallion, crystal, tumbler, ftd, 5-oz, 4" 35.00
Sunrise Medallion, crystal, tumbler, 5½" 25.00
Sunrise Medallion, crystal, vase, bud; 10" 75.00
Sunrise Medallion, crystal, wine, 2½-oz 30.00
Sunrise Medallion, gr or pk, creamer 275.00
Sunrise Medallion, gr or pk, plate, 8½" 20.00
Sunrise Medallion, gr or pk, tumbler, ftd, 4-oz, 3½" 35.00
Sunrise Medallion, gr or pk, vase, bulbous, 10" 425.00

Tinkerbell, Azure or green, vase, 10", $350.00. (Photo courtesy Cathy and Gene Florence)

Tinkerbell, Azure or gr, cocktail, 3½-oz 110.00
Tinkerbell, Azure or gr, cordial, 1½-oz 225.00
Tinkerbell, Azure or gr, goblet, water; 9-oz 175.00
Tinkerbell, Azure or gr, tumbler, ftd, 9-oz 90.00
Tinkerbell, Azure or gr, vase, #36 Uranus, ftd, 10" 395.00

Top Hat 'Mr Boston,' cocktail glass, from $75.00 to $90.00. (Photo courtesy Cathy and Gene Florence)

Mortens Studios

Oscar Mortens was already established as a fine sculptural artist when he left his native Sweden to take up residency in Arizona. During the 1940s he developed a line of detailed animal figures which were distributed through the Mortens Studios, a firm he co-founded with Gunnar Thelin. Thelin hired and trained artists to produce Mortens' line, which he called Royal Designs. More than 200 dogs were modeled and over 100 horses. Cats and wild animals such as elephants, panthers, deer, and elk were made, but on a much smaller scale. Bookends with sculptured dog heads were shown in their catalogs, and collectors report finding wall plaques on rare occasions. The material they used was a plaster-type composition with wires embedded to support the weight. Examples were marked 'Copyright by the Mortens Studio,' either in ink or decal. Watch for flaking, cracks, and separations. Crazing seems to be present in some degree in many examples. When no condition is indicated, the items listed below are assumed to be in near-mint condition, allowing for minor crazing.

Airedale terrier standing w/tail up, tan, brn & blk, 5½x6" 44.00
Borzoi standing, dk brn & wht, 6½x7" 80.00
Boxer female standing, brn & wht, 5½x6" 90.00
Boxer scratching, brn/wht/blk, 3x4" 50.00
Bulldog standing, brn & tan, chip on face, 4½x6" 42.00
Chihuahua seated, 3½" 65.00
Collie pup sitting, 3¼x3½" 35.00

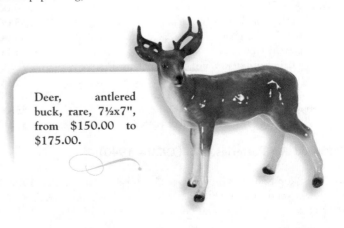

Deer, antlered buck, rare, 7½x7", from $150.00 to $175.00.

Doberman, recumbent, blk & tan, 4½x7½" 32.00
Doberman, standing, blk & tan, 7¼x8½" 50.00
German shepherd rolling, 2x3¾" 80.00

Horse, #705, 8¼" long, from $80.00 to $90.00.

Jack Russell terrier begging, brn & tan, 4x3" 37.00
Labrador standing, blk, 5x6" 45.00
Pekingese standing, lt brn, 3x4½" 65.00
Pointer puppy, recumbent, 4¾" L 50.00
Poodle standing, tan, 5x6" 22.00
Springer spaniel, recumbent, brn & wht, 2¼x5¼", from $45 to 60.00
St Bernard standing, tan & wht, tongue out, 7x8", from $70 to 95.00

Morton Pottery

Six potteries operated in Morton, Illinois, at various times from 1877 to 1976. Each traced its origin to six brothers who immigrated to America to avoid military service in Germany. The Rapp brothers established their first pottery near clay deposits on the south side of town where they made field tile and bricks. Within a few years, they branched out to include utility wares such as jugs, bowls, jars, pitchers, etc. During the 90 years of pottery operations in Morton, the original factory was expanded by some of the sons and nephews of the Rapps. Other family members started their own potteries where artware, gift-store items, and special-order goods were produced. The Cliftwood Art Pottery and the Morton Pottery Company had showrooms in Chicago and New York City during the 1930s. All of Morton's potteries were relatively short-lived operations with the Morton Pottery Company being the last to shut down on September 8, 1976. For a more thorough study of the subject, we recommend *Morton's Potteries: 99 Years* and *Morton Potteries: 99 Years, Vol. II*, by Doris and Burdell Hall; their address can be found in the Directory under Illinois.

Morton Pottery Works — Morton Earthenware Co. (1877 – 1917)

Bowl, mixing; brn, Rockingham, 4½" 25.00
Chamber pot, yel ware, mini 70.00
Cuspidor, brn, 7" 50.00
Marble, brn, Rockingham, 4¼" 35.00
Milk jug, brn, Rockingham, 1-pt 55.00
Milk jug, cobalt, 1-pt 75.00
Miniature, coffee dripolator, brn, Rockingham, 3" 70.00
Pie baker, yel ware, 7" 75.00
Pie baker, yel ware, 9 .... 100.00
Rice nappy, plain, yel ware, 13" 85.00
Stein, yel ware, 2 bl slip stripes top & bottom 50.00

Cliftwood Art Potteries, Inc. (1920 – 1940)

Bookends, lion & lioness on Heritage Green bases, 4¼x6¼" 150.00
Bowl, sq, gr/yel drip over wht, w/lid, 6" 50.00
Creamer, cow figural, tail forms hdl, chocolate drip, 3¼x6½" 125.00

Dresser set, apple gr, tray+jar+powder box+2 candleholders 65.00
Figurine, mini lion, gold/brn, 1¾x4" 50.00
Figurine, police dog, chocolate drip, 5x8½" 80.00
Flower frog, Lorelei, bl/Mulberry drip, 6½" 75.00
Lamp, pillar base, star-emb globe, wht, Art Deco #23, 8½" 50.00
Reamer, Herbage Green, rare 55.00
Vase, rectangular, w/simulated palm fronds, turq matt, 14" 45.00
Vase, tree-trunk shape, Heritage Green, 8x3" 70.00
Wall pocket, tree trunk w/3 openings, chocolate drip, 8½" 80.00

Batter, 7¼", Umpire, 6½", Pitcher, 6¾", $300.00 each. (Photo courtesy Doris and Burdell Hall)

Midwest Potteries, Inc. (1940 – 1944)

Candleholder, Jack-Be-Nimble type, handle, lime gr, 7", ea 24.00
Creamer, cow figural, brn drip w/yel hdl, 5" 30.00
Figurine, cockatoo, yel w/gr drip, on ped, 6" 24.00
Figurine, deer, wht w/gold decor, 8-point antlers, 12" 50.00
Miniature, camel, brn, 2½" 18.00
Pitcher, cow, tail hdl, wht w/gold, 4½" 25.00
Planter, deer, recumbent, brn spray, 6½x5½" 24.00
Wall mask, man's head caricature, short hair, winking, yel, 5x3¼" ... 35.00

Morton Pottery Company (1922 – 1976)

Ashtray, teardrop, Rival Crock Pot, 6" 40.00
Bank, church, brn, 3½x4x2" 30.00
Bank, pig, wall hanger, bl 40.00
Cookie jar, circus animals, cylindrical, yel/orange 45.00
Cookie jar, Panda, head is lid 95.00
Easter planter, hen w/bonnet, yel/bl, 4¾" 20.00
Figurine, political; donkey, gray, mk Kennedy, 2¼x2¼" 100.00
Grass grower, Christmas tree 25.00
Lamp, teddy bear 50.00
Water fountain figure, fish, pk 40.00

TV lamp, horse, #327, $38.00. (Photo courtesy Doris and Burdell Hall)

American Art Potteries (1947 – 1963)

Bowl, flat leaf shape, gr, #351, 1½x7" 15.00
Doll parts, head, arm & legs, HP, 3½", 6" dia 72.00

Ewers (one with Norwood label), large: $25.00, small: $20.00. (Photo courtesy Doris and Burdell Hall)

Figurine, Poland China hog, wht w/gray spots, gr base, 5½x7½" 50.00
Flower bowl, S shape, yel/wht, 2x10" 20.00
Nightlight, wall mt, brn/wht spray, rare, 6x3x3¼" 50.00
Planter, pig, blk w/wht stripe 30.00
TV lamp, conch shell, tan w/gr spray, 6½" 40.00
Vase, ewer form, pk, 14" 20.00

Mosaic Tile

The Mosaic Tile Company was organized in 1894 in Zanesville, Ohio, by Herman Mueller and Karl Langenbeck, both of whom had years of previous experience in the industry. They developed a faster, less costly method of potting decorative tile, utilizing paper patterns rather than copper molds. By 1901 the company had grown and expanded with offices in many major cities. Faience tile was introduced in 1918, greatly increasing their volume of sales. They also made novelty ashtrays, figural boxes, bookends, etc., though not to any large extent. Until they closed during the 1960s, Mosaic used various marks that included the company name or their initials — 'MT' superimposed over 'Co.' in a circle.

Figurine, bear on base, blk, 6x9½" 300.00
Figurine, bear on base, wht, 6x9½" 235.00
Figurine, German shepherd sitting, tan, 9¼x8", from $125 to 150.00
Paperweight, Abraham Lincoln, wht cameo profile on bl, hexagon, 3".. 50.00
Pin tray, wirehair terrier, blk & wht, 5½" 115.00

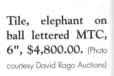

Tile, elephant on ball lettered MTC, 6", $4,800.00. (Photo courtesy David Rago Auctions)

Tile, ship sailing on waves, mc pastels, sq, 6" 815.00
Tile, woodland landscape, mc pastels outlined in dk bl, sq, 6" 625.00

Moser

Ludwig Moser began his career as a struggling glass artist, catering to the rich who visited the famous Austrian health spas. His talent and popularity grew and in 1857 the first of his three studios opened in Karlsbad, Czechoslovakia. The styles developed there were entirely his own; no copies of other artists have ever been found. Some of his original designs include grapes with trailing vines, acorns and oak leaves, and richly enameled, deeply cut or carved floral pieces. Sometimes jewels were applied to the glass as well. Moser's animal scenes reflect his careful attention to detail. Famed for his birds in flight, he also designed stalking tigers and large, detailed elephants, all created in fine enameling.

Moser died in 1916, but the business was continued by his two sons who had been personally and carefully trained by their father. The Moser company bought the Meyr's Neffe Glassworks in 1922 and continued to produce quality glassware.

When identifying Moser, look for great clarity in the glass; deeply carved, continuous engravings; perfect coloration; finely applied enameling (often covered with thin gold leaf); and well-polished pontils. Our advisor for this category is Don Williams; he is listed in the Directory under Missouri. Items described below are enameled unless noted otherwise. If no color is mentioned in the line, the glass is clear.

Basket, cranberry w/tavern scene, ribbed, pinched rim, clear hdl, 8x5"..125.00
Bowl, alexandrite, facted, flared to rim, 5x16" 1,400.00
Bowl, amber, mc floral & vines, appl rigaree at neck, 3½x3½" 65.00
Bowl, pk w/butterfly & bee, gold rigaree rim, partial label, 5¼" ... 800.00
Box, cranberry, heavy mc floral w/gold leaves, rnd, 2" H 280.00
Compote, cranberry cabochon panels (12) w/gold, scalloped rim/ft, 5x5". 250.00
Cracker jar, wht, earth-tone leaves & jewel acorns, gold lid & hdl, 8" . 400.00
Decanter, clear, emb gold band on body, gold rim, 11" 280.00
Ewer, bl, bird among mc leaves & branches, amber hdl, disk ft, 17" .10,500.00
Ewer, bl w/allover scrolls/butterflies/bee, acanthus ft, 6½" 800.00
Goblet, bowl w/floral heart medallions, flowers, wht beading, 7¾" ..935.00
Goblet, optic dmn rainbow w/gold overall scrolling, baluster stem, 9"..750.00
Jar, gold w/pastel leaves & insects overall, ftd, 4" 940.00
Pitcher, amber, bl collar/appl drips/ hdl, floral branches, 9" 750.00
Pitcher, aqua, mc bugs/leaves/appl acorns, w/gold, clear hdl, 8½" ... 1,625.00
Pitcher, bl w/leaves/birds/insects, bl opal rim/spout, amber hdl, 7" . 2,245.00
Pitcher, cranberry, heavy appl insect/foliage, clear hdl, cylinder, 6"....750.00

Pitcher, green with allover enameled leaves and berries, much gold, 10½", $1,200.00. (Photo courtesy Early Auction Co.)

Plate, floral cabachons (6) in clear, bl/gr/gold, gold rim, 12½" ..2,700.00
Punch set, amethyst w/silver floral overlay, 10 cups/liner/bowl (12") .. 940.00
Shell dish, cranberry, bl/pk/gold overall floral, gold rim, 10½" 815.00
Tumbler, clear w/mc grape leaves/insects, appl grapes/stems, 4¾"....275.00

Vase, African Safari, mc on lt gr, red & gold rings, slim neck, 12"..6,000.00
Vase, amber, eng mare & foal in woodland scene, spherical, 9½x10" . 2,500.00
Vase, amber, pheasant/floral, 4 bl hdls, wht beads/gilt trim, 12"... 190.00
Vase, amber w/floral, bl drips/rim/ft (3), tree trunk form, 13", pr..1,060.00
Vase, bl w/mc overall floral, saw-tooth rim, amber ft, egg shape, 8"..1,200.00
Vase, clear gray w/jeweled fish (3) & floral, shouldered, 8½"........ 750.00
Vase, clear to orange, enameled yel/gold leaves & scrolls, slim, 10" ...125.00
Vase, clear to purple, eng floral, sq, 10"...................................... 450.00
Vase, clear to violet, HP irises, cylindrical, ribbed int, 10"........... 600.00
Vase, clear w/eng birds & gold, quartrefoil, bulbous bottom, 11"...1,000.00
Vase, dk amethyst, gold elephants & palm trees, gold bands, ovoid, 7"...1,200.00
Vase, floral, clear w/mc, shouldered, 10¼".............................. 125.00
Vase, floral & appl serpent, clear brn w/gold, 7½x4½".................. 940.00
Vase, gr, pk & wht floral & scrolls w/gilt, slim neck, disk ft, 9" 90.00

Vase, intaglio cutting and marquetry flowers, 13", $4,250.00. (Photo courtesy Early Auction Co.)

Vase, peach cased, cloisonné-like floral, gold hdls, 5½" 1,375.00
Vase, rust, eng fish & sea foliage, globular, ca 1930, 7" 1,750.00
Wine, clear frost, w/gold leaves border & trim on rim & ft, 9".....250.00

Moss Rose

Moss Rose was a favorite dinnerware pattern of many Staffordshire and American potters of the mid-1800s. In America the Wheeling Pottery of West Virginia produced the ware in large quantities, and it became one of their bestsellers, remaining popular well into the '90s. The pattern was colored by hand; this type is designated 'old' in our listings to distinguish it from the more modern Moss Rose design of the twentieth century, which we've also included. It's not hard to distinguish between the two. The later ware you'll recognize immediately, since the pattern is applied by decalcomania on stark white backgrounds. It has been made in Japan to a large extent, but companies in Germany and Bavaria have produced it as well. Today, there is more interest in the twentieth century items than in the older ware. In the listings that follow, when no manufacturer is given, assume that item to have been made in twentieth-century Japan.

Coffeepot, Limoges, 10", from $325.00 to $375.00. (Photo courtesy Mary Frank Gaston)

Bowl, shell shaped, gold rim, Royal Albert, 5"............................. 35.00
Bowl, soup; flat, bl trim, H&Co, 1880, 9"................................. 35.00
Bowl, soup; scalloped rim, Haviland, 1950s, 7½", from $12 to....... 15.00
Bowl, vegetable; ftd/hdld, w/lid, Haviland, 1950s, 7x11x8½", $60 to ..85.00
Butter pat, 4 rtcl segments on rim, Rosenthal, 4"........................8.00
Cake plate, emb scroll & gold rim, hdld, Rosenthal, 11x12½"....... 60.00
Coffeepot, emb rope decor, gold accents, Haviland, 1860s, 9" 240.00
Cup & saucer, gold trim, Japan, 2", 4½".................................. 30.00
Cuspidor, bl banded neck & rim, Haviland, ca 1877, 6x7" 360.00
Egg cup 9.00
Ginger jar, gold trim, Royal Albert 60.00
Gravy boat, gold trim, w/underplate, Royal Albert.................... 45.00
Nut dish w/4 nut cups 35.00
Plate, dinner; scalloped rim, gold trim, Rosenthal, 10"................ 32.00
Plate, sandwich; tab hdls, fluted edge, 10"............................ 50.00
Platter, gold trim, hdld, Japan, 8½x12"................................ 30.00
Platter, scalloped rim, gold trim, Royal Albert, 12x15".............. 90.00
Sauce dish, scalloped rim, gold trim, Haviland, 1950s, 5" 12.00
Saucer, sm scalloped rim, gold trim, Japan, 5½" 10.00
Shakers, bublous bottom w/slim neck, sterling tops, Rosenthal, 5", pr...60.00
Shaving mug 35.00
Sugar shaker, unmk Japan, 6x3" 45.00
Tea set, child sz, 15-pc 275.00
Teapot, Rosenthal, 7½"... 70.00
Tidbit, 2-tiered, Haviland, 1950s, 7½" & 5½"......................... 45.00
Tray, gold trim, Royal Albert, 6½x6".................................... 30.00
Tray, sandwich; tab hdld, sq, 6¾x11½"................................. 45.00
Tray, tiered 32.00
Tureen, w/lid, Pompadour, Rosenthal, 7¼x12" 110.00
Vase, bud; 3½".. 15.00

Mother-of-Pearl Glass

Mother-of-Pearl glass was a type of mold-blown satin art glass popular during the last half of the nineteenth century. A patent for its manufacture was issued in 1886 to Frederick S. Shirley, and one of the companies who produced it was the Mt. Washington Glass Company of New Bedford, Massachusetts. Another was the English firm of Stevens and Williams. Its delicate patterns were developed by blowing the gather into a mold with inside projections that left an intaglio design on the surface of the glass, then sealing the first layer with a second, trapping air in the recesses. Most common are the Diamond Quilted, Raindrop, and Herringbone patterns. It was made in several soft colors, the most rare and valuable is rainbow — a blend of rose, light blue, yellow, and white. Occasionally it may be decorated with coralene, enameling, or gilt. Watch for twentieth-century reproductions, especially in the Diamond Quilted pattern. See also Coralene; Stevens and Williams.

Bowl, Flower & Acorn, wht w/cranberry int, smooth rim, 2¾x9¾" ...725.00
Bowl, Raindrop, canary yel w/bl int, pinched, ruffled, ftd, 4¾" 475.00
Bowl, Raindrop, cranberry to wht, 3 twig ft, 4½x6½" 500.00
Bowl, reeded wht w/bl int, ruffled rim w/clear edge, 4¼x11x8" 375.00
Canister, Herringbone, bl, frosted ball finial, 8"...........................475.00

Creamer and sugar bowl, Coinspot, peach to caramel with camphor handles, 4½", $700.00. (Photo courtesy Early Auction Co.)

Cruet, Dmn Quilt, cranberry, clear glass hdl, patterned stopper, 7"...90.00
Decanter, Swirl, bl, 6-lobe, pinched neck, 8¾" 525.00
Ewer, Dmn Quilt, yel w/frosted thorn hdl, 13¼" 300.00
Ewer, Herringbone, rainbow, frosted thorn hdl, 12" 1,150.00
Lamp, Dmn Quilt, rainbow, crimped shade, w/burner, 10", NM . 3,000.00
Pitcher, Dmn Quilt, bl, clear twig hdl, Patent, 8½" 1,800.00
Pitcher, Dmn Quilt, rainbow, cylindrical, frosted hdl, 5" 2,500.00
Pitcher, Herringbone, yel to wht, frosted hdl, 5¾".......................480.00
Pitcher, Raindrop, rainbow, triangular mouth, 10½".....................575.00
Rose bowl, Dmn Quilt, bl w/wht int, 2¾" 25.00
Rose bowl, Peacock Eye, bl to gr over yel, HP floral, 5⅛"..........4,800.00
Vase, bud; Dmn Quilt, rainbow neck, wht bulbous base, 6" 725.00

Vase, Diamond Quilt, azure blue to pearl with gold prunus, attributed to Thomas Webb and Sons, 6½", $925.00. (Photo courtesy Early Auction Co.)

Vase, Dmn Quilt, rainbow, appl yel rim & ft, Patent, 4" 780.00
Vase, Dmn Quilt, rainbow, ovoid w/scalloped rim, 3-ftd, Patent, 7" ..1,200.00
Vase, Dmn Quilt, rainbow, slightly waisted, 5" 700.00
Vase, Dmn Quilt, red to peach, stick neck, 11½"...........................400.00
Vase, Dmn Quilt, scalloped/ruffled/pleated rim, 9½" 300.00
Vase, Fern, cranberry, crimped rim, 5⅜".......................................785.00
Vase, Flower & Acorn, canary yel, waisted, pinched top, 6½" 850.00
Vase, Herringbone, bl, stick neck w/emb ribs, 7½" 300.00
Vase, Herringbone, pk w/amber thorn hdls & rim, 10", NM.....1,450.00
Vase, Raindrop, bl, folded rim, 5¾" 395.00
Vase, Raindrop, faint rainbow, ovoid, 12½" 350.00
Vase, Raindrop, gr, vertical indents, ruffled/crimped rim, 8¾"......425.00
Vase, Rays, pk & lav w/appl frosted rose & briar, ruffled rim, 13", NM...785.00
Vase, Swirl, cranberry, bulbous w/shaped neck, 7¼" 360.00
Vase, Teardrop, pk on dk bl, wht int, ruffled/crimped rim, ovoid, 10"... 2,650.00
Vase, Zipper, bl w/HP bird, frosted hdls, can neck, 7"...................150.00
Vase, Zipper w/swirls, apricot w/pk int, bulbous, 5¾" 1,000.00

Movie Memorabilia

Movie memorabilia covers a broad range of collectibles, from books and magazines dealing with the industry in general to the various promotional materials which were distributed to arouse interest in a particular film. Many collectors specialize in a specific area — posters, pressbooks, stills, lobby cards, or souvenir programs (also referred to as premiere booklets). In the listings below, a one-sheet poster measures approximately 27" x 41", three-sheet: 41" x 81", and six-sheet: 81" x 81". Window cards measure 14" x 22". Lobby and title cards measure 11" x 14", while an insert poster is 36" x 14". Values are for examples in excellent condition unless noted otherwise. Our advisor for this category is Robert Doyle; he is listed in the Directory under New York. See also Autographs; Cartoon Art; Magazines; Paper Dolls; Personalities; Rock 'n Roll Memorabilia; Sheet Music.

Insert, Country Girl, G Kelly/W Holden/B Crosby, 1954, VG+ 50.00
Insert, Harvey, J Stewart/J Hull, 1950, 36x14", EX........................ 80.00

Insert, I Can Get It for You Wholesale, S Hayward, 36x14", EX .250.00
Insert, Our Man in Havana, A Guiness/N Coward, 1960, EX 35.00
Insert, Pennies From Heaven, S Martin, 1981 .... 30.00
Insert, Thirteen Ghosts, C Herbert/J Morrow, 1960, 36x14", NM .300.00
Lobby card, Adam's Rib, S Tracy/K Hepburn, 1949, NM............225.00
Lobby card, Ali Baba Goes to Town, E Cantor, 1937, NM 150.00
Lobby card, All About Eve, #2, B Davis, 1950, NM.....................160.00
Lobby card, American Graffiti, R Howard, 1973, 1-sheet, NM....450.00
Lobby card, Brother Orchid, H Bogart/EG Robinson, 1940, EX..600.00
Lobby card, Bus Stop, M Monroe/D Murray, 1956, EX................ 125.00
Lobby card, From Russia With Love, S Connery, 1970 reissue, NM .. 30.00
Lobby card, Hell in the Heavens, W Baxter, 1934, NM................. 90.00
Lobby card, High School Confidential, M Van Doren, 1958, NM. 70.00
Lobby card, Hound of the Baskervilles, B Rathbone, 1959 ....325.00
Lobby card, Jumping Jacks, J Lewis, VG 35.00
Lobby card, Lolita, J Mason/S Lyon, 1962, EX+ 250.00
Lobby card, Reach for the Sky, K More, 1956, VG........................ 60.00
Lobby card, Test Pilot, C Gable, 1938, NM..................................225.00
Lobby card, The Horse Soldiers, J Wayne, 1959, EX 75.00
Lobby card set, Black Sunday, B Steel, 1961, EX..........................100.00
Poster, Abbott & Costello Meet the Mummy, 1955, 1-sheet, NM...1,250.00
Poster, Airport, D Martin/H Hayes/G Kennedy, 1970, 1-sheet, NM .. 125.00
Poster, Alamo (The), J Wayne/R Widmark, 1960, 1-sheet, NM..600.00
Poster, Alias Jesse James, B Hope, 1959, 1-sheet, VG 175.00
Poster, Alias Jesse James, B Hope, 1959, 3-sheet, VG 275.00
Poster, Amazing Colossal Man, G Langan/C Downs, 1957, ½-sheet, EX+...900.00
Poster, American Graffiti, R Howard, 1973, 1-sheet, NM............ 450.00
Poster, Apartment (The), J Lemmon/S McLain, 1960, ½-sheet, NM. 600.00
Poster, Apartment (The), J Lemmon/S McLain, 1960, 3-sheet, NM . 900.00
Poster, Bad News Bears, W Matthau/T O'Neal, 1976, 1-sheet, VG.... 125.00
Poster, Beach Blanket Bingo, F Avalon/A Funicello, 1965, 60x40", VG . 300.00
Poster, Beatles Come to Town, 1963, 1-sheet (linenbk), NM ...1,500.00

Poster, Between Men, Wm. S. Hart, Ritchey stone lithograph, re-release ca. 1919, 41x27", G, $330.00. (Photo courtesy Randy Inman Auctions Inc.)

Poster, Blonde Bait, B Michaels, 1956, 40x30", NM 750.00
Poster, Blue Max (The), G Peppard/J Mason/U Andress, 1966, 1-sheet, NM..250.00
Poster, Bombs Over London, C Farrell, 1939, 1-sheet, NM 450.00
Poster, Butch Cassidy & Sundance Kid, 1969, 1-sheet (linen-bk), NM ..850.00
Poster, Call Northside 777, J Stewart, 1948, 1-sheet, EX 300.00
Poster, Casino Royale, D Craig as Bond, 2006, 1-sheet (dbl-sided), NM+ ..100.00
Poster, Casino Royale, P Sellers/U Andress, 1967, 1-sheet, EX ...300.00
Poster, Cat on a Hot Tin Roof, 1958, 1-sheet (linen-bk), NM..1,350.00
Poster, Charade, A Hepburn/C Grant, 1963, EX+ 750.00
Poster, Chitty Chitty Bang Bang, D Van Dyke, 1969, 1-sheet, NM.225.00
Poster, Cool & Crazy, S Marlowe/G Perreau, 1958, ½-sheet, NM.350.00
Poster, Fargo, F McDormand/S Buscemi, 1996, 1-sheet, NM.......150.00
Poster, Flight to Tangier, J Fontaine/J Palance, 1953, 1-sheet, NM..125.00

Poster, Flight to Tangier, J Fontaine/J Palance, 1953, 3-sheet, NM .. 175.00
Poster, Fool's Gold, W Boyd, 1946, 1-sheet, VG 175.00
Poster, For a Few Dollars More, C Eastwood, 1967, 1-sheet, NM........ 900.00
Poster, Frankenstein, B Karloff, 1962 reissue, 1-sheet, NM 1,200.00
Poster, Giant, R Hudson/E Taylor, 1956, 1-sheet 510.00
Poster, Gimme Shelter, Rolling Stones, etc, 1971, 3-sheet, NM .. 900.00
Poster, Girl Crazy, J Garland/M Rooney, 1943, 1-sheet, EX 1,200.00
Poster, Goldfinger, S Connery, 1964, 1-sheet, EX 650.00
Poster, Goldfinger, S Connery, 1964, 1-sheet (linen-bk), NM+ .. 1,200.00
Poster, Great Waldo Pepper, R Redford, 1975, 1-sheet, NM 75.00
Poster, Hawaii, J Andrews/M Von Sydow, 1966, 1-sheet, NM 35.00
Poster, High & the Mighty, J Wayne/C Trevor, 1954, 1-sheet, NM ... 750.00
Poster, High School Confidential, M Van Doren, 1958, 1-sheet, G... 175.00
Poster, Hollywood Cowboy, G Parker/C Parker, 1937, 1-sheet, NM .. 750.00
Poster, Hot Rod Rumble, L Snowden/B Halsey, 1958, 1-sheet, NM .. 900.00
Poster, I Married a Witch, V Lake/F March, 1948 reissue, 3-sheet, VG . 750.00
Poster, Jaws, R Schieder/R Shaw/R Dreyfuss, 1975, 1-sheet, NM.... 475.00
Poster, Kelly's Heroes, C Eastwood/T Savalas, 1970, 1-sheet, EX+ .250.00
Poster, Kid Galahad, Elvis, 1962, 3-sheet, VG 350.00
Poster, King Solomon's Mines, Kerr/Granger, 1962 reissue, 1-sheet, EX .. 50.00
Poster, Konga, M Johns/C Gordon, 1961, 3-sheet, NM+ 750.00
Poster, Live & Let Die, R Moore, 1973, 1-sheet (linen-bk, NM .. 450.00
Poster, Long Long Trailer, L Ball/D Arnez, 1954, 3-sheet, NM+ .. 600.00
Poster, Lost Boys, J Patrick/K Sutherland, 1987, 1-sheet, EX+ 150.00
Poster, Love Me Tender, Elvis, 1956, 1-sheet (linen-bk), NM .. 1,200.00
Poster, Major Dundee, C Heston/R Harris, 1965, 1-sheet, EX+ ... 175.00
Poster, Mame, L Ball, 1974, 1-sheet, NM 35.00
Poster, Melody of the Plains, F Scott, 1937, 6-sheet, NM 2,500.00
Poster, Miracle Worker, P Duke/A Bancroft, 1962, ½-sheet, VG.... 100.00
Poster, Murder on the Orient Express, Amsel artwork, 1974, 1-sheet, EX.... 50.00
Poster, National Lampoon's Animal House, J Belushi, 1978, 1-sheet, NM .350.00
Poster, Night of Dark Shadows, D Selby/L Parker, 1971, 1-sheet, NM. 150.00
Poster, North by Northwest, C Grant, 1966 reissue, 1-sheet, NM ... 1,750.00
Poster, Not of This Earth, B Garland/P Birch, 1957, 3-sheet, NM... 1,750.00
Poster, On Her Majesty's Secret Service, 1970, 1-sheet, EX......... 250.00

Poster, On Top of Old Smoky, Gene Autry, 1953, 27x41", EX, $360.00.
(Photo courtesy Morphy Auctions/ LiveAuctioneers.com)

Poster, Pearl Harbor, B Afflack, 2001, 1-sheet, M......................... 200.00
Poster, Planet Outlaws, B Crabbe, 1953, 1-sheet, EX 360.00
Poster, Reach for the Sky, K More, 1956, 1-sheet, NM 500.00
Poster, Return of the Ape Man, B Lugosi/J Carradine, 1944, 1-sheet, NM.. 900.00
Poster, Shootist, J Wayne, 1976, 1-sheet, NM+ 275.00
Poster, Stardust on the Sage, Autry, 1942, 1-sheet (linen-bk), EX+ .. 375.00
Poster, Suddenly Last Summer, Taylor/Hepburn/Clift, 1960, 3-sheet, EX . 200.00
Poster, Take a Letter Darling, Russell/MacMurray, 1942, 3-sheet, NM .. 275.00
Poster, The Noose Hangs High, Abbott & Costello, 1948, 1-sheet ... 340.00
Poster, Thunderball, S Connery, 1965, 1-sheet (linen-bk), NM 1,250.00
Poster, Thunderball, S Connery, 1965, 6-sheet, NM 2,100.00

Poster, Tora! Tora! Tora!, M Balsam, 1970, 10-sheet, VG 75.00
Poster, Torn Curtain, P Newman/J Andrews, 1966, 3-sheet, EX+... 150.00
Poster, Twelve O'Clock High, G Peck, 1949, 1-sheet, VG........ 1,250.00
Poster, Twilight on Rio Grande, G Autry, 1947, 1-sheet (linen-bk), NM. 400.00
Poster, Two Mules for...Sarah, C Eastwood/S McLaine, 1970, 1-sheet, M. 175.00
Poster, Viva Cisco Kid, C Romero, 1940, 1-sheet, EX+ 250.00
Poster, Wagon Train, T Holt, 1940, 1-sheet (linen-bk), NM 350.00
Poster, War Wagon, J Wayne/K Douglas, 1967, 1-sheet, (linen-bk), NM. 350.00
Poster, Where the Boys Are, C Francis/G Hamilton, 1961, 1-sheet, EX... 150.00
Poster, Who Done It?, Abbott & Costello, 3-sheet, EX 1,250.00
Poster, Winchester 73, J Stewart, 1950, 1-sheet (linen-bk), NM .2,250.00
Poster, World at War, War Dept documentary, 1942, 1-sheet, VG .. 350.00
Poster, Wyatt Earp, K Costner, 1994, 1-sheet, NM+ 175.00
Poster, You Only Live Twice, S Connery, 1967, 45x60", NM.... 1,200.00
Poster, Young Frankenstein, G Wilder/P Boyle, 1964, 1-sheet, NM ..350.00
Pressbook, Konga, M Johns/C Gordon, 1961, 8-pg, EX+ 125.00
Title card, Peyton Place, L Turner, 1958 .... 45.00
Window card, Ali Baba Goes to Town, E Cantor, 1937, 14x8", VG... 175.00
Window card, Gone w/the Wind, C Gable/V Leigh, 1986 reissue, M.. 100.00
Window card, Shane, A Ladd, 1953, NM................................. 600.00

Mt. Washington

The Mt. Washington Glass Works was founded in 1837 in South Boston, Massachusetts, but moved to New Bedford in 1869 after purchasing the facilities of the New Bedford Glass Company. Frederick S. Shirley became associated with the firm in 1874. Two years later the company reorganized and became known as the Mt. Washington Glass Company. In 1894 it merged with the Pairpoint Manufacturing Company, a small Brittania works nearby, but continued to conduct business under its own title until after the turn of the century. The combined plants were equipped with the most modern and varied machinery available and boasted a work force with experience and expertise rival to none in the art of blowing and cutting glass. In addition to their fine cut glass, they are recognized as the first American company to make cameo glass, an effect they achieved through acid-cutting methods. In 1885 Shirley was issued a patent to make Burmese, pale yellow glassware tinged with a delicate pink blush. Another patent issued in 1886 allowed them the rights to produce Rose Amber, or amberina, a transparent ware shading from ruby to amber. Pearl Satin Ware and Peachblow, so named for its resemblance to a rosy peach skin, were patented the same year. One of their most famous lines, Crown Milano, was introduced in 1893. It was an opal glass either free-blown or pattern-molded, tinted a delicate color and decorated with enameling and gilt. Royal Flemish was patented in 1894 and is considered the rarest of the Mt. Washington art glass lines. It was decorated with raised, gold-enameled lines dividing the surface of the ware in much the same way as lead lines divide a stained glass window. The sections were filled in with one or several transparent colors and further decorated in gold enamel with florals, foliage, beading, and medallions. For more information, see *Mt. Washington Art Glass* by Betty B. Sisk (Collector Books). See also Amberina; Cranberry; Salt Shakers; Burmese; Crown Milano; Mother-of-Pearl; Royal Flemish; etc.

Biscuit jar, daisies, gold on bl, melon ribs, SP lid & hdl 575.00
Biscuit jar, fern etch on amberina, SP lid & hdl mk MW, 7½x5".. 475.00
Biscuit jar, floral on wht opal w/melon ribs, SP #4415 lid, 9" 175.00
Biscuit jar, pansies on wht satin, melon ribs, SP lid, 7¼" dia........ 400.00
Biscuit jar, Queen's, dotted floral, SP lid & hdl mk MW #4402, 7".. 475.00
Biscuit jar, spider mums reserve on gr, SP lid & hdl mk MW....... 250.00
Box, floral reserve on lid, wht honeycomb pattern, 8" dia" L 850.00
Celery vase, wht swirled satin, ruffled, in #1303 Pairpoint fr, 11".. 425.00
Condiment set, Ribbed Pillar floral shakers+mustard, Pairpoint fr, 8" ..300.00
Cruet, Dmn Quilt, cranberry satin, 7¼" 120.00

Lamp, cameo griffins, pk on wht, etched pendant, brass mts........ 900.00
Pitcher, Dmn Quilt, pk to wht satin, frosted hdl, 9x6" 120.00
Shaker, Lying Egg, floral on bl to wht, 1¾", ea........................ 60.00
Shakers, Egg, floral sprays, pr.. 135.00
Shakers, Fig, floral, wht on bark-textured cranberry, pr............. 1,075.00
Shakers, Tomato, floral, 2½" dia, pr.................................. 180.00
Sugar shaker, Egg, forget-me-nots on bl to wht, 4¼" 120.00
Sugar shaker, Egg, oak leaves & acorns on yel to wht, 4½" 400.00
Sugar shaker, floral panels, bulbous, 3"............................... 60.00
Sugar shaker, melon form, HP floral on wht, roughness on lid..... 125.00
Toothpick holder, Fig, floral, 1¾" 360.00
Toothpick holder, floral on ribbed satin custard, 2" 120.00
Toothpick holder, mums on wht lobed body, 1¾", NM 360.00
Tumbler, Lava, rare raspberry w/mc inclusions, gold outlines, 3". 6,000.00
Vase, Lava, blk w/mc inclusions & gold, bulbous, 3¾" 5,175.00
Vase, Napoli, spider mums/gold webbing, slim/ftd, #841, 18¼", EX ...300.00

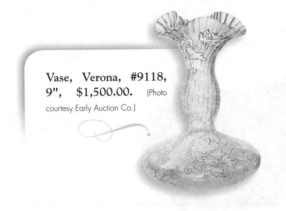

Vase, Verona, #9118, 9", $1,500.00. (Photo courtesy Early Auction Co.)

Mulberry China

Mulberry china was made by many of the Staffordshire area potters from about 1830 until the 1850s. It is a transfer-printed earthenware or ironstone named for the color of its decorations, a purplish-brown resembling the juice of the mulberry. Some pieces may have faded out over the years and today look almost gray with only a hint of purple. (Transfer printing was done in many colors; technically only those in the mauve tones are 'mulberry'; color variations have little effect on value.) Some of the patterns (Corean, Jeddo, Pelew, and Formosa, for instance) were also produced in Flow Blue ware. Others seem to have been used exclusively with the mulberry color. Our advisor for this category is Mary Frank Gaston; she is listed in the Directory under Texas.

Abbey, creamer 195.00
Abbey, pitcher, 8-sided, 7¼" 75.00
Athens, cup.. 45.00
Athens, pitcher, 6½" 85.00
Athens, plate, Adams & Sons, 7⅝"................................... 70.00
Athens, sugar bowl, Adams, w/lid, EX 225.00
Beauties of China, bowl, Mellor Venables, 1x5⅛" 55.00
Bochara, bowl, vegetable; w/lid 375.00
Bochara, platter; Edwards, 14"...................................... 200.00
Calcutta, teapot 275.00
Castle Scenery, pitcher, 8"... 425.00
Corean, bowl, shallow, wide flange, Podmore Walker, 5¼" 75.00
Corean, bowl & pitcher, NM 1,100.00
Corean, pitcher, 1½-qt, 8¾" 475.00
Corean, plate, Podmore Walker, 7⅝" 65.00
Corean, plate, Podmore Walker, 10" 75.00
Corean, sugar bowl, Clementson..................................... 375.00
Cyprus, platter, Davenport, 16"..................................... 300.00

Cyprus, teapot, Davenport, 8½"..................................... 225.00
Foliage, bowl, serving; Edwards & Walley, w/lid, 7½x9"........... 425.00
Foliage, plate, 9"... 75.00
Foliage, platter, 11".. 190.00
Game, pitcher, 9", VG... 185.00

Gondola, plate, Enoch Woods & Sons, 10", from $150.00 to $175.00. (Photo courtesy Mary Frank Gaston)

Heath's Flower, platter, 14".. 335.00
Jeddo, pitcher, Adams, 2-qt.. 435.00
Jeddo, plate, 14-panel, W Adams, 9¼".............................. 140.00
Marble, creamer, 5½"... 75.00
Medina, sugar bowl, Furnival....................................... 195.00
Panama, creamer, Challinor 245.00
Pelew, cup & saucer, handleless; Challinor 75.00
Pelew, plate, Challinor, 8½" 90.00
Pendant Flower, pitcher, Kaolin Ware, 12⅛"........................ 265.00
Peruvian, cup & saucer, handleless................................. 70.00
Pomerania, cup plate, Ridgway, 4".................................. 110.00
Regina, platter, 8-sided, Challinor, 15½x12"....................... 300.00
Rhone Scenery, coffeepot, Podmore Walker.......................... 400.00
Rhone Scenery, platter, Mayer, 18x14¼" 425.00
Rhone Scenery, sauce tureen, w/underplate.......................... 250.00
Rose, platter, Challinor, 14x11".................................... 185.00
Shapoo, cup plate... 65.00
Sydenham, creamer.. 130.00
Tavoy, platter, 15"... 175.00
Temple, plate, Podmore Walker, 9¾"................................. 90.00
Tivoli, teapot.. 325.00
Tuscan Rose, plate, Ridgway, 10½".................................. 160.00
Venus, plate, Wedgwood, 8¾".. 70.00
Vincennes, pitcher, water; John Alcock, 8½"........................ 325.00
Vincennes, relish... 195.00
Washington Vase, creamer, Podmore Walker 250.00
Washington Vase, sugar pot, lion's head hdls....................... 240.00
Wreath, bowl, vegetable; w/lid, 11"................................ 425.00

Muller Freres

Henri Muller established a factory in 1900 at Croismare, France. He produced fine cameo art glass decorated with florals, birds, and insects in the Art Nouveau style. The work was accomplished by acid engraving and hand finishing. Usual marks were 'Muller,' 'Muller Croismare,' or 'Croismare, Nancy.' In 1910 Henri and his brother Deseri formed a glassworks at Luneville. The cameo art glass made there was nearly all produced by acid cuttings of up to four layers with motifs similar to those favored at Croismare. A good range of colors was used, and some later pieces were gold flecked. Handles and decorative devices were sometimes applied by hand. In addition to the cameo glass, they also produced an acid-finished glass of bold mottled colors in the Deco style. Examples were signed 'Muller Freres' or 'Luneville.' Our advisor for this category is Don Williams; he is listed in the Directory under Missouri.

Cameo

Vase, butterflies perched on pine branch, 9½", $3,250.00. (Photo courtesy Early Auction Co.)

Ewer, sailboat night scene, blk/bl on mottled orange/bl/cream, 17"..3,000.00
Vase, carnations, red & yel on polished mottled ground, 1900s, 17"..3,125.00
Vase, floral, maroon/gr on frost, flared rim, 18" 3,500.00
Vase, floral, red/gr/yel on frost, ovoid, 7½" 1,200.00
Vase, lake scene, bl on frost, ca 1900, 2¼" 425.00
Vase, lake scene w/storks, bl/gray/pk on frost, incurvate rim, 5½"..1,200.00
Vase, leaves, purple on gray-wht, shouldered, 2¾" 395.00
Vase, men raking field/sheep, red-brn/orange on yel, flared rim, 5" ..850.00
Vase, panthers/geometrics, bl on frost w/silver flecks, 9½".........4,200.00
Vase, trees & leaves, purple/gr on gray-bl, stick neck, 2½" 275.00
Vase, wisteria, gr/bl/cobalt on gray, ovoid, ca 1900, 14" 4,800.00

Miscellaneous

Atomizer, wisteria, etched/HP on clear, gold metal mts, 1920s, 6¾" ..850.00
Bowl, French Blue/silver/yel mottle, 4-petal rim, 4x12½" 360.00
Chandelier, orange/bl mottled bowl & shades (3), wrought fr, 37x24". 3,300.00
Chandelier, purple mottled bowl & shades (3), 4-light, ca 1900, 35" H.800.00
Vase, autumn leaves, etched/HP, stick neck, 28½" 3,350.00
Vase, hunters/dogs/boar, clear/frosted, ftd, 9x10¼" 2,000.00
Vase, lake scene/dragonflies, HP flattened form, 6½x3½", NM .2,100.00

Muncie

The Muncie Pottery was established in Muncie, Indiana, by Charles O. Grafton; it operated there from 1922 until about 1935. The pottery they produced is made of a heavier clay than most of its contemporaries; the styles are sturdy and simple. Early glazes were bright and colorful. In fact, Muncie was advertised as the 'rainbow pottery.' Later most of the ware was finished in a matt glaze. The more collectible examples are those modeled after Consolidated Glass vases — sculptured with lovebirds, grasshoppers, and goldfish. Their line of Art Deco-style vases bear a remarkable resemblance to the Consolidated Glass Company's Ruba Rombic line. Vases, candlesticks, bookends, ashtrays, bowls, lamp bases, and luncheon sets were made. A line of garden pottery was manufactured for a short time. Items were frequently impressed with MUNCIE in block letters. Letters such as A, K, E, or D and the numbers 1, 2, 3, 4, or 5 often found scratched into the base are finishers' marks. In our listings the first number in the description is the shape number, taken from old company catalogs or found on examples of the company's pottery. (These numbers are preceded by a number sign.)

Bowl, console; gr on rose, #187, 4x12" L...65.00
Bowl, Rombic, gr on rose, #306, 3x8¾"...240.00

Candleholder, Spanish, Orange Peel, R Haley, #277, 2½x4", ea.... 80.00
Candlesticks, Peachskin, #149, 6", pr..175.00
Lamp base, nude panels, gr on pk, #U33, hammered metal base, 23"..500.00
Lamp base, rose matt, Deco shape, #222, 8½x6¼" 145.00
Vase, blk gunmetal, squat, #113, 3½x4½" 150.00
Vase, gr matt, rim-to-hip hdls, #143, 6⅞x6⅜"..................................165.00
Vase, gr on lilac, #442, 6¼x4¼" 80.00
Vase, gr on lilac, horizontal ribs, #460, 12x6" 250.00
Vase, gr on lilac, rim-to-hip hdls, #143, 6⅜x6".................................80.00
Vase, gr on lilac, sm hdls at center of body, #463, 10⅛x5⅞".........215.00
Vase, gr on pumpkin, lobed body, #191, 8½x7¾" 120.00
Vase, gr on rose, corseted cylinder, 11"...275.00
Vase, gr on rose, ring hdls, #192, 9x9"...120.00
Vase, gr on rose, sm angular hdls, #182, 5½x8" 100.00
Vase, gr shading to lilac w/crystalline, #191, 6x4½" 60.00
Vase, gunmetal blk, ring hdls, #192, 6⅜x6⅛"...................................90.00
Vase, Katydid, wht matt on bl, #194, sm rpr, 6x5" 100.00
Vase, Peachskin, integral hdls, #143, 6½x6" 135.00
Vase, Rombic, gr on rose, #310, 4½" 475.00
Vase, Rombic, gr on rose, #312, 5" 550.00

Vase, Rombic, gunmetal, 4x6", $660.00. (Photo courtesy Treadway Galleries/Live Auctioneers.com)

Vase, Rombic, Peachskin, #302, 4" 600.00
Vase, Spanish 'Aorta,' gr on pumpkin, R Haley design, 4½" 325.00
Vase, Spanish, Orange Peel, 4-hdl, 6¾" 350.00
Vase, wht drip on pk, 4-fold rim, #2H, 3¾"......................................50.00
Vase, wht on bl, flared 4-scallop rim, #U8, 7⅜x6⅜" 110.00
Vase, wht on pk, wide shoulder, 7x7"...90.00

Musical Instruments

The field of automatic musical instruments covers many different categories ranging from watches and tiny seals concealing fine early musical movements to huge organs and orchestrions which weigh many hundreds of pounds and are equivalent to small orchestras. Music boxes, first made in the early nineteenth century by Swiss watchmakers, were produced in both disc and cylinder models. The latter type employs a cylinder with tiny pins that lift the teeth in the comb of the music box (producing a sound much like many individual tuning forks), and music results. The value of a cylinder music box depends on the length and diameter of the cylinder, the date of its manufacture, the number of tunes it plays (four or six is usually better than 10 or 12), whether it has multiple cylinders, if it has extra instruments (like bells, an organ, or drum), and its manufacturer. Nicole Freres, Henri Capt, LeCoultre, and Bremond are among the the most highly regarded, and the larger boxes made by Mermod Freres are also popular. Examples with multiple cylinders, extra instruments (such as bells or an organ section), and those in particularly ornate cabinets or with matching tables bring significantly higher prices. Early cylinder boxes were wound with a separate key which was inserted on the left side of the case. These early examples are known as 'key-wind' boxes and bring a premium. While smaller cylinder boxes are still being made, the larger ones (over 10" cylinders) typically date from before 1900. Disc music boxes were introduced about 1890 but were replaced by the phonograph only 25 years later. However, during that time hundreds of thousands were made. Their great advantage was in playing inexpensive interchangeable discs, a factor that remains an attraction for today's collector as well. Among the most popular disc boxes are those made by Regina (USA), Polyphon, Mira, Stella, and Symphonion. Relative values are determined by the size of the discs they play, whether they have single or double combs, if they are upright or table models, and how ornate their cases are. Especially valuable are those that play multiple discs at the same time or are incorporated into tall case clocks.

Player pianos were made in a wide variety of styles. Early varieties consisted of a mechanism which pushed up to a piano and played on the keyboard by means of felt-tipped fingers. These use 65-note rolls. Later models have the playing mechanism built in, and most use 88-note rolls. Upright pump player pianos have little value in unrestored condition because the cost of restoration is so high. 'Reproducing' pianos, especially the 'grand' format, can be quite valuable, depending on the make, the size, the condition, and the ornateness of the case; however the market for 'reproducing' grand pianos has been very weak in recent years. 'Reproducing' grand pianos have very sophisticated mechanisms and are much more realistic in the reproduction of piano music. They were made in relatively limited quantities. Better manufacturers include Steinway and Mason & Hamlin. Popular roll mechanism makers include AMPICO, Duo-Art, and Welte.

Coin-operated pianos (Orchestrions) were used commercially and typically incorporate extra instruments in addition to the piano action. These can be very large and complex, incorporating drums, cymbals, xylophones, bells, and dozens of pipes. Both American and European coin pianos are very popular, especially the larger and more complex models made by Wurlitzer, Seeburg, Cremona, Weber, Welte, Hupfeld, and many others. These companies also made automatically playing violins (Mills Violin Virtuoso, Hupfeld), banjos (Encore), and harps (Whitlock); these are quite valuable.

Collecting player organettes is a fun endeavor. Roller organs, organettes, player organs, grind organs, hand organs — whatever the name — are a fascinating group of music makers. Some used wooden barrels or cobs to operate the valves, or metal and cardboard discs or paper strips, paper rolls, metal donuts, or metal strips. They usually played from 14 to 20 keys or notes. Some were pressure operated or vacuum type. Their heyday lasted from the 1870s to the turn of the century. Most were reed organs, but a few had pipes. Many were made in either America or Germany. They lost favor with the advent of the phonograph, as did the music box. Some music boxes were built with little player organs in them. Any player organette in good working condition with rolls will be worth from $200.00 to $600.00, depending on the model. Generally the more keying it has and the larger and fancier the case, the more desirable it is. Rarity plays a part too. There are a handfull of individuals who make new music rolls for these player organs. Some machines are very rare, and music for them is nearly impossible to find. For further information on player organs we recommend *Encyclopedia of Automatic Musical Instruments* by Bowers.

Unless noted, prices given are for instruments in fine (NM) condition, playing properly, with cabinets or cases in well-preserved or refinished condition. In all instances, unrestored instruments sell for much less, as do those with broken or missing parts, damaged cases, and the like. On the other hand, particularly superb examples in especially ornate case designs and those that have been particularly well kept will often command more. Our advisor for mechanical instruments is Martin Roenigk; he is listed in the Directory under Arkansas.

Key:
c — cylinder   d — disc

Mechanical

Automata, bird in box, Griesebaum, 1900s...............................1,200.00
Automata, birds (2) in cage, Fr, 21", EX.....................................2,800.00
Box, Bremond, 13" c, exposed bells, 10-tune, rosewood case, EX...2,115.00

Box, Bremond #15416, 17" cylinder, two-piece comb, burr-walnut veneered case, boxwood stringing, tulipwood banding, 29" wide, $12,925.00. (Photo courtesy Skinner Inc. Auctioneers & Appraisers of Antiques & Fine Art)

Box, Criterion, 10⅝" d, cherry case, dbl comb, EX....................1,450.00
Box, Ducommun-Girod, 7¾" c, 3-tune, 110 teeth, key-wind, EX ..1,800.00
Box, Imperator #27, 5½" d, single comb, 1904 fair decal, 5x8x7"..500.00
Box, Junod, 9¼" c, 12-tune, 5 bells w/ball strikers, 22", EX.......1,400.00
Box, Lecoultre, 11" c, key-wind, 4-tune, walnut case w/inlay, EX ..1,650.00
Box, Mermod Freres Sublime Harmony Piccolo, 16" c/3 combs/8-tune, rprs..2,000.00
Box, Nicole Freres, 11" c, key-wind, 6-tune, grpt case, 18" W ..1,850.00
Box, Paillard Sublime Harmonie Tremolo Zither, dbl spring, 17" c, EX..3,200.00
Box, Piano, Melodica, 30-key, EX, +6 books of music...............3,700.00
Box, Regina, 15½" d, dbl combs, Gothic Revival case, 1897, 21" W.3,750.00
Box, Regina, 8¼" d, 1 comb, Pat 1899, 12½" W, +20 d.............1,100.00
Box, Regina #33 (late), 27" changer, cvd dragons, EX, +12 d.22,500.00
Box, Stella, 17¼" d, dbl combs, mahog table model, EX 4,500.00
Box, Symphonion, 14½" d, dbl combs, walnut case, EX, +7 d ..2,800.00
Box, Thornward, 15½" d, 1 comb, 12½x25x19", EX 2,500.00
Nickelodeon, Englehardt, w/pipes, art glass, Mission-style case, EX...9,800.00
Nickelodeon, Peerless #44, rfn oak case, M rstr, +20 rolls.........8,500.00
Orchestrelle, Aeolian V, oak, EX 2,000.00
Orchestrelle, Wilcox & White Angelus push-up player, rstr, +12 rolls...1,000.00
Orchestrion, Coinola X, older rstr..14,000.00

Orchestrion, Velte Briscovia A, 100-note roll-operated movement, quarter-veneered golden oak case with inlay, pillars, and Titania figure, beveled glass mirrors, 96x66x29", $70,500.00. (Photo courtesy Skinner Inc. Auctioneers & Appraisers of Antiques & Fine Art)

Organ, band; Wurlitzer #146-B, single roll fr, rstr...................18,000.00
Organ, fairground; Gavioli, 65-key, EX....................................26,000.00

Organ, monkey; Bacigalupo, 43-key, 96 pipes, rstr.....................9,300.00
Organ, paper roll; Organette Co...350.00
Organette, Ariston, 13" d, EX 550.00
Piano, Chickering Ampico upright, EX 1,200.00
Piano, grand; Marshall & Wendall Ampico, 60", EX 1,600.00
Pianolin, N Tonwanda, 2 ranks of pipes/art glass, oak cabinet, EX..12,500.00
Volcano, Mills Virtuoso, single violin & piano, oak, G...........26,000.00

Non-Mechanical

Accordion, Arpeggio, MOP inlay, 19" W, +case.......................1,950.00
Accordion, Silvio Soprani, faux MOP case, 41 keys/5 music keys, +case..240.00
Accordion, Wurlitzer Professional #1030, blk finish, 41 keys, +case..395.00
Banjo, Bacon & Day NE Plus Ultra #6, gold-plating, 1927.......8,800.00
Banjo, Lange Paramount, 4-string, rosewood laminate resonator, 1920s..275.00
Banjo, tenor; Bacon & Day, 25-bracket, 13¹⁄₁₆" pot dia 360.00
Banjo, tenor; Bacon & Day Silver Bell #3, rpl tuners, 1925-30..2,500.00
Banjo, tenor; Weymann & Son Keystone State, gold decal, 1925, 11" ring..2,585.00
Banjo-mandolin, Fairbanks Vega Little Wonder, 1921.................360.00
Clarinet, Alto in F, C Mahilon Brussels, 19 keys, ca 1875, 36½"...650.00
Clarinet, B Flat, Selmer Paris 10 G, grenadilla w/silver keys, +case ...1,200.00
Cornet, F Besson London Silver Pocket, ca 1885, +case...........2,700.00
Drum set, Pearl Strata-Blk EXR, bass+3 toms+snare+high hats+cymbals...475.00
Drum set, Remo snares (3) w/blk finish, silver-tone mts, 12", 13", 16".300.00
Flute, Firth Hall & Pond, wooden w/4 brass spoon keys, ivory mts..265.00
Flute, VQ Powell Boston, silver w/eng, ca 1956, +case 4,700.00
Flute, WS Haynes Boston, grenadilla w/silver keys, 1900, +case...825.00
Guitar, CF Martin EMP-1, pearl inlay, 1998, 19⅜" bk, +case ...1,880.00
Guitar, Epiphone Zephyr Emperor Varitone, 21⅝" bk, +case....4,700.00
Guitar, Fender Electric Stratocaster, contoured body, 1955, 15⅝" bk.32,900.00

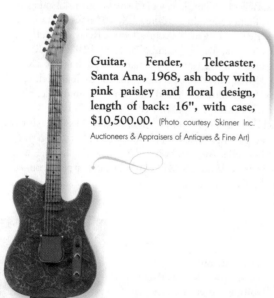

Guitar, Fender, Telecaster, Santa Ana, 1968, ash body with pink paisley and floral design, length of back: 16", with case, $10,500.00. (Photo courtesy Skinner Inc. Auctioneers & Appraisers of Antiques & Fine Art)

Guitar, Gibson Advanced Jumbo, pearl inlay, 1938, 20¼" bk, +case..45,825.00
Guitar, Gibson Byrdland, electric, 1968, 21" bk, +case 4,350.00
Guitar, Gibson L-75, pearl inlay at headstock, ca 1935, 20¼" bk..1,525.00
Guitar, Gretsch Syncromatic Sierra 6007, 1947, 20¾" bk, +case..415.00
Harmonica, Hohner Chord, silver-tone, 23", +case 180.00
Harmonica, Hohner Tremelo, 4-part, 4 keys made as 1 unit, 9½", NMIB...120.00
Harp, Lyon & Healy Prelude, gilt & gold pnt soundboard, 63x34"..5,150.00
Harp, mahog case, simple cvg, 58x28" 500.00
Harp, mahog w/floral cvg, unmk, 40" 180.00
Harp, mahog w/inlay, unmk, 66x27" 600.00
Mandolin-guitar, Gibson Style A-3, pearl inlay, ca 1918, 14", +case..2,000.00
Piano, baby grand; Chickering, mahog, 65"...............................4,800.00

Piano, baby grand; Hardman, mahog w/cvd legs, 1925-30, 68" L..2,300.00
Piano, grand; Erard Louis XV style, mahog vnr/gilt paw ft, 1800s, 77"...25,000.00
Piano, grand; Steinway & Sons Model B, mahog, ca 1987, 82½".36,000.00
Piano, grand; Steinway & Sons Parlor Model B, ebony, 1890s, 80" L..12,000.00
Piano, spinet; T Christensen Denmark, rosewood, 85-key, 50½" L..1,450.00
Pianoforte, Aster & Norwood, rosewood/mahog Regency, 1800s, 34x68x24".1,680.00
Pianoforte, grand; Mayer & Haitzmann, Vienna, ca 1835, 91½"...6,000.00
Pianoforte, M Cleminti & Co, English Regency, sq, 73-note, 1800s, 71"..2,150.00
Saxophone, B Flat, Selmer Paris, laquered/eng, 1951, +case.....9,000.00
Saxophone, Buescher Low Pitch, MOP finger pads, ca 1928, +case..360.00
Saxophone, Conn Alto, floral eng, ca 1914, VG 300.00
Saxophone, Martin Elto Elkhard, floral eng/pearl inlay, 1923, +case.265.00
Trombone, Conn 88HT-O Symphony Tenor, w/Lundberg mouthpc, +case....850.00
Trombone, King #1407 Liberty 2B, brass w/M-31 mouthpc, 1960, M....6,000.00
Trumpet, Conn New Wonder, rotary valve, eng bell, 1917, +case..240.00
Trumpet, Martin Committee Model DeLuxe, ca 1950, +case ...1,295.00
Ukelele, CF Martin, 1947, 9⅜" bk, +soft cover 445.00
Ukelele, CF Martin Style #3, mk peghead, 1935, 9⅜" bk, +case..2,350.00
Violin, Melegari...Torino, 1879, 13⅞" bk................................10,575.00
Violin, Wm E Hill & Sons, 1899, 13¹⁵⁄₁₆" bk 7,000.00
Violin bow, rnd stick mk Lupot at butt, ebony frog w/pearl eye, 1840..7,000.00
Violin bow, rnd stick w/silver mts, ebony frog w/Parisian eye, Knopf.1,400.00
Violoncello, Carletti, Fece in Pieve di Cento, 1948, 29" bk....18,800.00

Harp, J. Erat Maker, Wardour Street, Soho London, single action, ca. 1805 – 1807, regilded and restored, 66", in wooden case, $5,175.00. (Photo courtesy Garth's Auctions Inc.)

Mustache Cups

Mustache cups were popular items during the late Victorian period, designed specifically for the man with the mustache! They were made in silver plate as well as china and ironstone. Decorations ranged from simple transfers to elaborately applied and gilded florals. To properly position the 'mustache bar,' special cups were designed for the 'lefties.' These are the rare ones! Our advisor for this category is Robert Doyle; he is listed in the Directory under New York.

Anglo Japanese style, brn tones w/gold, ca 1880s, 2½", +6" saucer ..160.00
Deer & hunter snow scene HP on wht, flared rim, ca 1910, 3½" ...55.00
Father in cobalt & heavy gold on wht, gothic script, 3½" 80.00
Floral & bl tassel HP on wht, emb swirl body, twist hdl, 1940s, 3½"..30.00
Floral etched on silver, Barbour Bros Co Silver Quadruple #30, +saucer...65.00
Floral HP inside & out on wht, gold trim, RC Germany #2338, 1905, 2".90.00
Floral HP on wht w/gold ornate gold border, KPM mark, 3", +6" saucer.135.00
Floral transfer on wht, lt gr emb beads w/gold, Weimar, 1900, +saucer....180.00

Floral w/gold HP on wht, sgn AJ Surely, May 25, 1900, +saucer.. 120.00
Pk roses & mc leaves HP on wht, gold trim, Charles Ford, 1880, +saucer ...170.00

Native American decal, $100.00. (Photo courtesy Tom Harris Auctions/LiveAuctioneers.com)

Nailsea

Nailsea is a term referring to clear or colored glass decorated in contrasting spatters, swirls, or loops. These are usually white but may also be pink, red, or blue. It was first produced in Nailsea, England, during the late 1700s but was made in other parts of Britain and Scotland as well. During the mid-1800s a similar type of glass was produced in this country. Originally used for decorative novelties only, by that time tumblers and other practical items were being made from Nailsea-type glass. See also Lamps, Fairy.

Bell, clear w/wht loops, clear hdl, 19th C, 12" 180.00
Flask, amber w/wht swirls, faint pontil mk, 1 pt, 7⅝" 475.00
Flask, pk w/wht loopings, pontil mk, 8⅝"................................ 155.00
Flask, red w/wht loopings, bottle neck, flat rim, 1840s, 10½" 155.00
Flask, red w/wht loopings, ca 1790, 7".................................. 265.00
Jug, claret; red w/wht loopings, tapered cylinder, SP mts.............. 200.00

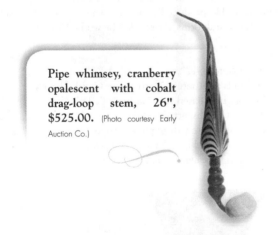

Pipe whimsey, cranberry opalescent with cobalt drag-loop stem, 26", $525.00. (Photo courtesy Early Auction Co.)

Pitcher, wht w/bl loopings, cobalt hdl, 4½" 85.00
Sugar bowl, brn & aqua over wht, wht ft/3-knop finial, 9¾" 2,400.00
Vase, cranberry w/wht loopings, ruffled/crimped rim, 5"............... 120.00
Whimsey, pipe w/long curved hdl, wht w/pk combed decor, 19½" ..250.00

Nakara

Nakara was a line of decorated opaque milk glass produced by the C. F. Monroe Company of Meriden, Connecticut, for a few years after the turn of the century. It differs from their Wave Crest line in several ways. The shapes were simpler; pastel colors were deeper and covered more of the surface; more beading was present; flowers were larger; and large transfer prints of figures, Victorian ladies, cherubs, etc., were used as

well. Ormolu and brass collars and mounts complemented these opulent pieces. Most items were signed; however, this is not important since the ware was never reproduced.

Ashtray, flowers on gr hexagonal bowl, ormolu mts, sm 150.00
Box, Bishop's Hat, floral, wht/pk on yel, ormolu ft, 5x5½" 495.00

Box, blown-out flower on lid, 2¾x3¾", $365.00. (Photo courtesy neatstuffdave/David Elyea)

Box, blown-out rose on bl, hexagonal, 3¾" dia............................. 700.00
Box, Collars & Cuffs, Gibson girl transfer 2,500.00
Box, Collars & Cuffs & pk azaleas on bright bl, 8½x8½" 795.00
Box, lady's portrait on gr, 2¾x4½" 495.00
Box, Princess Louise on pk/yel, ftd, sqd, 4x4½" 750.00
Box, ring; man & lady on yel & pk, 2½x2¾" 1,200.00
Box, roses, pk/wht on gr, crown mold, rpl lining, 8½" dia 995.00
Box, roses, red/wht, on pk to gr w/wht beadwork, 6" dia 595.00
Box, 3 Greenway girls at tea, lace decor, 3x6" 795.00
Cracker jar, floral on rose w/gold, gold metal hdl & lid 750.00
Hair receiver, children at tea on bl w/wht beading, dmn shape.... 450.00
Humidor, Old Sport, bulldog transfer on brn, ovoid, 7" 695.00
Jardiniere, pk floral on gr, gold trim...................................... 625.00
Photo receiver, Indian chief on yel/olive, 2½x4" L...................1,250.00
Pin tray, floral, pk/wht on pk/gr, ormolu rim w/pointed hdls, 6" L...225.00
Toothpick holder, beaded ovals & pk flowers on gr, ormolu mts .. 495.00
Toothpick holder, flowers & scrolls on mauve, 8-sided, 2" 425.00
Tray, wht beadwork/floral on pk to yel, mirror in ormolu frwork..750.00
Vase, wild roses & scrolls on beige, 4-ftd, ormolu base, 9".......... 795.00

Napkin Rings

Napkin rings became popular during the late 1800s. They were made from various materials. Among the most popular and collectible today are the large group of varied silver-plated figurals made by American manufacturers. Recently the larger figurals in excellent condition have appreciated considerably. Only those with a blackened finish, corrosion, or broken and/or missing parts have maintained their earlier price levels. When no condition is indicated, the items listed below are assumed to be all original and in very good to excellent condition. Check very carefully for missing parts, solder repairs, marriages, and reproductions.

A timely warning: Inexperienced buyers should be aware of excellent reproductions on the market, especially the wheeled pieces and cherubs. However, these do not have the fine detail and patina of the originals and tend to have a more consistent, soft pewter-like finish. There may also be pitting on the surface. These are appearing at the large, quality shows at top prices, being shown along with authentic antique merchandise. Our advisor for this category is Barbara Aaronson; she is listed in the Directory under California.

Key:
gw — gold washed
R&B — Reed & Barton

SH&M — Simpson, Hall, & Miller

Angel sitting w/legs crossed, ring behind, Pairpoint #7, 3½".....1,450.00
Antelope stands w/ring on bk, Meriden Britannia #204............... 725.00
Bear on base beside scrolled ring, Hamilton #127, from $200 to.. 350.00
Boy crawling behind ring to snare bunny, Meriden SP #0232, minimum. 500.00
Buffalo standing beside ring, unmk, rare 840.00
Bull by hexagon holder, Knickerbocker #1248, from $200 to 350.00
Cat on oval base by sheet music on stand, ringless, Tufts #1609.. 1,200.00
Cat on sq pillow-shaped base, Meriden #293, $750 to................. 950.00
Cherries & leaves on side of fluted holder, Meriden #626, from $200 to . 350.00
Cherub reaching for eggs in bird's nest on holder, Meriden #0226... 350.00
Chick popping through cracked-shell holder, Derby #371 .... 200.00
Child & dachshund on ring, rnd base, Van Berg #19 .... 660.00
Civil War soldier w/rifle by holder, Meriden #0260, from $900 to.. 1,200.00
Crane standing on 1 ft, rnd woodland base, Meriden #163, from $500 to ...750.00
Cupid reaching for arrow, hearts & bow atop ring, R&B #1315.. 1,175.00

Dachshund with ring on back, unmarked, $750.00. (Photo courtesy Morphy Auctions/LiveAuctioneers.com)

Dog & goat on base ea side of ring on ped, Webster #148, from $200 to... 350.00
Dog stands facing frog on ring, #224, from $600 to 750.00
Donkey wearing saddle by plain holder, from $200 to 350.00
Eagle w/ring atop wings, Meriden #203, from $500 to 750.00
Flatiron form w/opening sides, Tufts #1636 .... 350.00
Giraffe eating leaves, Rogers & Bros #239 ....1,450.00
Girl carrying flower in left hand & basket in right, Middleton #107..350.00
Girl seated on snail reading book beside ring, #0262, from $500 to ...600.00
Girl skipping rope before ring, Meriden #330 ....1,175.00
Grapes & leaves support ring, Standard #730, rstr...................... 375.00
Greenaway girl w/dog before ring, unmk, from $350 to............... 500.00
Greenaway infant in chair, Middleton #98 ....2,500.00
Greenaway lady on toboggan, ring on lap, Wilcox #4342 ....2,400.00
Greenaway lady w/umbrella & boy w/hoop, Tufts #1597...........1,550.00
Greyhound on oval base, raised border w/palmette motif, floral design..500.00
Greyhound w/ring on bk, oval vase, unmk.................................. 660.00
Horse rearing atop holder, base has acorn-shaped ft, unmk, $200 to... 350.00
Lady tennis player (long skirt), Meriden Britannia #283, $1,500 to.2,000.00
Lamb stands beside ring, Barbour #13 .... 750.00

Lizard with ring on back, Meriden Silver Plate Co. #0202, $520.00. (Photo courtesy Morphy Auctions/LiveAuctioneers.com)

Nude holding metal bud vase & ring, Rockford #178, from $400 to..550.00
Owl on branch beside ring, no base, Middleton #112 .... 325.00
Parakeet on hdl of wheeled base supporting ring, unmk............. 725.00
Pitcher-shaped vase, scroll hdl w/flower, R&B #1337, $200 to 350.00

Rabbit beside log (ring), SH&M #210, from $600 to 850.00
Rabbit on haunches w/ring at side, Rogers Smith & Co #233, $1,000 to.. 1,200.00
Rabbit rests front paw on ring, unmk 850.00
Rabbits (2) beside ring, #68, from $500 to 750.00
Red Riding Hood stands w/basket beside ring, R&B #1492 .....1,100.00
Reindeer pulling child atop ring on base, SH&M #18, from $500 to.750.00

Sailor boy, hands in pockets, Simpson, Hall & Miller #07, $550.00. (Photo courtesy Morphy Auctions/LiveAuctioneers.com)

Sailor holding rope to anchor, w/pitcher bud vase, R&B #1357 .. 700.00
Sphinx w/ring on bk, Meriden Britannia #165 .... 600.00
Strawberry on 3 leaves, emb w/fortresses, tree & mountain, $200 to .350.00
Tom Sawyer-type boy w/hands in pockets before holder, unmk, $350 to.500.00
Turtle w/ring on bk, Pairpoint #51 .... 550.00
Winged cherub on ring resting on bird's tail, Rockford #151, $750 to..950.00

Nash

A. Douglas Nash founded the Corona Art Glass Company in Long Island, New York. He produced tableware, vases, flasks, etc. using delicate artistic shapes and forms. After 1933 he worked for the Libbey Glass Company.

Bowl, Chintz, gr & rose, 12" 300.00
Bowl, orange bands alternate w/feathered gold, ftd, 2¼x4¼" 125.00
Candlesticks, gold irid, flared rim, Nash #650, 3¾X4", pr 400.00
Compote, irid, melon ribs, att, 7" 250.00
Goblet, bl bands alternate w/lt gr pulled stripes, #77 081, 6½" 225.00
Lamp, 8" Dmn Quilt gold irid shade; bronze #708 std, 16", EX. 3,250.00
Plate, Chintz, orange & clear radiating design, unmk, 6½" 115.00

Vase, blue with enameled design, unsigned, 8", $325.00. (Photo courtesy Treadway Gallery Inc.)

Vase, vertical zippers on bl-gr irid mottle, GD78, 8" 900.00
Wine, Chintz, bl & gr stripes, ca 1930, 5¼", pr........................... 400.00

Natzler, Gertrude and Otto

The Natzlers came to the United States from Vienna in the late 1930s. They settled in Los Angeles where they continued their work in ceramics, for which they were already internationally recognized. Gertrude created the forms; Otto formulated a variety of interesting glazes, among them volcanic, crystalline, and lustre. Our advisors for this category are Suzanne Perrault and David Rago; they are listed in the Dirctory under New Jersey.

Bottle, lt turq on mauve, 8¾" 3,375.00
Bowl, bl & brn hare's fur, hemispherical, 3x4½" 3,400.00
Bowl, brn & grn flambé, hemispherical, 2¾x5½" 750.00
Bowl, chartreuse dead-matt, 3-folded sides, sm rim chip, 2x7" 565.00
Bowl, olive gr/turq/brn mottled semi-matt, ftd, hemispherical, 6x9"..1,750.00
Bowl, orange & brn glaze, label: L029, 2x5½" 1,200.00
Bowl, runny red glaze (pooled in center & ft ring), w/case, 2x4½" ...2,750.00
Bowl, turq on brn clay, slightly folded, label: J230, 1½x5".........1,875.00
Bowl, volcanic gr & yel on red clay, 1x4⅝"..............................1,065.00
Bowl, yel, conical on narrow ft, label: N379, 3x8"....................2,375.00
Bowl, yel mottle, flared to rim, label: N909, 3½x5½" 3,600.00

Chalice, mottled sky blue and amber, signed, paper label: L712, 10x3½", $23,600.00. (Photo courtesy David Rago Auctions/LiveAuctioneers.com)

Vase, copper microcrystalline on dk brn, ftd, cylindrical, 11x5" ...13,750.00
Vase, gunmetal volcanic, conical, 10½x7½" 10,000.00
Vase, sulfur yel volcanic, barrel shaped, 7¾x5" 11,250.00

Naughties and Bathing Beauties

These daring all-bisque figurines were made in various poses, usually in one piece, in German and American factories during the 1920s. Admired for their fine details, these figures were often nude but were also made with molded-on clothing or dressed in bathing costumes. Items below are all in excellent undamaged condition. Our advisors for this category are Don and Anne Kier; they are listed in the Directory under Ohio.

Action figure, Germany, 5".. 350.00
Action figure, Germany, 7½" 600.00
Action figure, w/wig, Germany, 7" 650.00
Elderly woman in suit w/legs crossed, rare, 5¼" 1,400.00
Glass eyes, 5"... 400.00
Glass eyes, 6"... 650.00
Japan mk, 3".. 40.00
Japan mk, 5-6", ea.. 65.00
Japan mk, 9" 95.00

Lady in woven suit and cap, molded slippers, mohair wig, Gallubat and Hoffman, 2¾", $960.00. (Photo courtesy Bertoia Auctions/ LiveAuctioneers.com)

Painted eyes, 3" 165.00
Painted eyes, 6" 325.00
Swivel neck, 5" 700.00
Swivel neck, 6" 750.00
With animal, 5½"...1,200.00
2 molded together, 4½-5½", ea 1,600.00

New Geneva

In the early years of the nineteenth century, several potteries flourished in the Greensboro, Pennsylvania, area. They produced utilitarian stoneware items as well as tile and novelties for many decades. All failed well before the turn of the century.

Bank, applied letters with dots, stripes, and vining floral, repair and minor loss, 9½", $5,750.00. (Photo courtesy Garth's Auctions Inc.)

Churn, eagle surrounded by foliage, HP lines at shoulder & hdls, 15" ..375.00
Creamer, reddish brn floral on redware, 3½" 2,250.00
Crock, bl stenciled letters & HP squiggles, w/hdls, 16-gal, 23½x13"... 1,500.00
Crock, HP bl stripes & flourishes w/'02,' flakes, 12"...................... 470.00
Crock, stenciled bl letters, A Condon/New Geneva/PA, 9¾" 125.00

New Martinsville

The New Martinsville Glass Company took its name from the town in West Virginia where it began operations in 1901. In the beginning years pressed tablewares were made in crystal as well as colored and opalescent glass. Considered an innovator, the company was known for their imaginative applications of the medium in creating lamps made entirely of glass, vanity sets, figural decanters, and models of animals and birds. In 1944 the company was purchased by Viking Glass, who continued to use many of the old molds, the animals molds included. They marked their wares 'Viking' or 'Rainbow Art.' Viking recently ceased operations and has been purchased by Kenneth Dalzell, president of the Fostoria Company. They, too, are making the bird and animal models. Although at first they were not marked, future productions will be marked with an acid stamp. Dalzell/Viking animals are in the $50.00 to $60.00 range. Values for cobalt and red items are two to three times higher than for the same item in clear. See also Depression Glass; Glass Animals and Figurines.

Addie, blk, cobalt, jade or red, candlestick, 3½", ea 30.00
Addie, blk, cobalt, jade or red, sugar bowl, open, ftd...................... 17.50
Addie, blk, cobalt, jade or red, tumbler, ftd, 9-oz........................... 22.50
Addie, crystal or pk, creamer, ftd... 10.00
Addie, crystal or pk, tray, sandwich; hdld 25.00
Addie, crystal or pk, tumbler, ftd, 9-oz 15.00

Circlet #24, amethyst with platinum trim, decanter, 24 ounces, with six three-ounce footed bar tumblers, minimum value, $1,200.00. (Photo courtesy Jerry Gallagher)

Janice, bl or red, bonbon, hdld, 4x6"... 30.00
Janice, bl or red, bowl, flared, 3-toed, #4511, 10½"........................ 85.00
Janice, bl or red, bowl, fruit; ruffled rim, 12" 110.00
Janice, bl or red, creamer, 6-oz.. 20.00
Janice, bl or red, ice pail, hdld, #4589, 10"................................... 595.00
Janice, bl or red, plate, cheese; swan hdls, #4528-25J, 11".............. 40.00
Janice, bl or red, shakers, pr... 85.00
Janice, bl or red, vase, ball form, 9" 135.00
Janice, crystal, basket, #4552, 11" 75.00
Janice, crystal, bowl, 10".. 37.50
Janice, crystal, candy box, 5½" 65.00
Janice, crystal, cordial.. 100.00
Janice, crystal, jam jar, #4577, 6".. 20.00
Janice, crystal, plate, salad; #4579, 8½" 10.00
Janice, crystal, shakers, pr.. 40.00

Janice, red, plate, salad; #4579, 8½", $17.50. (Photo courtesy Cathy and Gene Florence)

Lions, amber or crystal, candleholder, #37, ea 25.00
Lions, amber or crystal, creamer, #37 .... 15.00
Lions, blk, candy dish, w/lid 110.00
Lions, blk, cup, #34... 35.00

Lions, blk, plate, cracker; 12" 40.00
Lions, blk, sugar bowl, open, #34... 35.00
Lions, gr or pk, compote, cheese.. 25.00
Lions, gr or pk, plate, 8"... 20.00
Meadow Wreath, crystal, bowl, crimped, ftd, #4266/26, 11" 45.00
Meadow Wreath, crystal, bowl, punch; #4221/26, 5-qt 140.00
Meadow Wreath, crystal, compote, #4218/26, 10" 35.00
Meadow Wreath, crystal, creamer, ftd, tab hdl, #42/26 .... 12.00
Meadow Wreath, crystal, mayonnaise, w/liner & ladle, #42/26 ..... 40.00
Meadow Wreath, crystal, plate, #42/26, 14" 40.00
Meadow Wreath, crystal, relish, 3-part, #4228/26, 8" 30.00
Meadow Wreath, crystal, vase, flared, #42/26, 10" 50.00
Moondrops, bl or red, bowl, console; 3-ftd, 12" 75.00
Moondrops, bl or red, bowl, cream soup; 4¼" 100.00
Moondrops, bl or red, bowl, ruffled, 3-ftd, 9½" 70.00
Moondrops, bl or red, candleholders, ruffled, 2", pr...................... 25.00
Moondrops, bl or red, decanter, 7¾" 67.50
Moondrops, bl or red, goblet, 8-oz, 5¾"....................................... 40.00
Moondrops, bl or red, pickle dish, 7½" 35.00
Moondrops, colors other than bl or red, cocktail shaker, metal lid...35.00
Moondrops, colors other than bl or red, decanter, 11¼".................. 50.00
Moondrops, colors other than bl or red, pitcher, 32-oz, 8" 115.00
Moondrops, colors other than bl or red, sherbet, 4½"..................... 16.00
Moondrops, colors other than bl or red, tumbler, 7-oz, 4½" 10.00
Radiance, amber, punch bowl, 9" 125.00
Radiance, amber, punch cup...7.00
Radiance, amber, punch ladle... 100.00
Radiance, bl or red, butter dish 465.00
Radiance, bl or red, relish dish, 2-part, 7" 35.00
Radiance, bl or red, vase, flared or crimped, 12" 175.00

Newcomb

The Newcomb College of New Orleans, Louisiana, established a pottery in 1895 to provide the students with first-hand experience in the fields of art and ceramics. Using locally dug clays — red and buff in the early years, white-burning by the turn of the century — potters were employed to throw the ware which the ladies of the college decorated. From 1897 until about 1910, the ware they produced was finished in a high glaze and was usually surface painted. After 1905 some carving was done as well. The letter 'Q' that is sometimes found in the mark indicates a pre-1906 production (high glaze). After 1912 a matt glaze was favored; these pieces are always carved. Soft blues and greens were used almost exclusively, and decorative themes were chosen to reflect the beauty of the South. The end of the matt-glaze period and the art-pottery era was 1930.

Various marks used by the pottery include an 'N' within a 'C,' sometimes with 'HB' added to indicate a 'hand-built' piece. The potter often incised his initials into the ware, and the artists were encouraged to sign their work. Among the most well-known artists were Sadie Irvine, Henrietta Bailey, and Fannie Simpson.

Newcomb pottery is evaluated to a large extent by era (early, transitional, or matt), decoration, size, and condition. In the following descriptions, unless noted otherwise, all decoration is carved and painted on matt glaze. The term 'transitional' defines a period of a few years, between 1910 and 1916, when matt glazes were introduced as waxy, with green finishes. One can tell a 'transitional' piece by the use of ink marks with matt glazes. Our advisors for this category are Suzanne Perrault and David Rago; they are listed in the Directory under New Jersey.

Biscuit jar, landscape, Somewhere Above Us..., L Jordan, 7x5", NM ... 9,600.00
Bowl, daffodils, bl & yel on bl, S Irvine, 1926, 3x9"....................1,325.00

Bowl, jonquils on bl, AF Simpson, #MJ73, 8¾"..........................2,700.00
Charger, fish (3), S Wells, #TT73, 1904, 9¼", NM 6,000.00
Charger, magnolias, S Wells, 1903, #LL74, X, 1903, 9¼"..........9,600.00

Charger, painted in the Delft style with Old Newcomb Chappel, S. E. Bres, 8¾", $5,400.00. (Photo courtesy Davis Rago Auctions)

Jar, peacock feathers, A Roman, w/lid, 1898, 3¼x5½"...............4,800.00
Jardiniere, irises, H Joor, #H48X, 1902, rstr hairline, 10x12"..18,000.00
Pitcher, flower band at rim on bl, #NU87/196, 4" 1,600.00
Pitcher, freesia, AF Simpson, transitional, 1917, 4x5"...............3,000.00
Tile, oaks, grs & bls, S Irvine, #NC SI7, 7½x10"+orig wood fr... 16,800.00
Tile, White Rabbit, w/pocket watch & umbrella, L Nicholson, 4¾" sq....1,700.00
Vase, bl & purple streaks, organic decor, MGB, #TF75, 6"........2,100.00
Vase, cottage in bayou, S Irvine, #250/J07, 1918, 8x4" 4,500.00
Vase, crocus on ivory, AF Simpson, #R075, 6" 4,000.00
Vase, daffodils, AF Simpson, 1908, 9x3½" 7,800.00
Vase, daffodils on bl, A Mason, #HD7, 4½x7"............................2,200.00
Vase, Espanol pattern, bl-gr, AF Simpson, 1929, paper label, 4½x2" .. 1,440.00
Vase, Espanol pattern, H Bailey, tear-shaped, 1926, 5¼x4".......3,250.00
Vase, floral, bl on bl, S Irvine, 1929, 7½x4" 2,000.00
Vase, floral band, A Mason, bulbous bottle form, #HC93, 5"....3,250.00
Vase, fruit on branches, S Irvine, 1923, 8¼x7" 3,500.00
Vase, gardenias on cobalt band, A Lonnegan, #XX63, 1904, 7x7"..12,000.00
Vase, grape clusters, S Irvine, #253, 1917, 4¼x7¼" 2,400.00

Vase, high glaze, clusters of white flowers on green stems on light blue and indigo ground, Harriet Joor, 13½", $36,000.00. (Photo courtesy David Rago Auctions)

Vase, irises on bl, S Irvine, 1924, bruise/chips, 10¾x6½"...........5,100.00
Vase, moon/moss/oaks, AF Simpson, baluster, 1919, 7¼x4¼" ...4,500.00
Vase, moon/moss/oaks, AF Simpson, bulbous, 1930, 6x6".........9,000.00
Vase, moon/moss/oaks, AF Simpson, 1928, 10½x5" 15,000.00
Vase, moon/moss/oaks, S Irvine, #209/KU68, 1920, 7x3¾" 5,700.00
Vase, moon/moss/oaks, S Irvine, cylindrical, 1928, 5½x4" 3,250.00
Vase, moon/moss/oaks, S Irvine, 1932, 3½x4½"...........................2,650.00

Vase, nicotina leaves & blossoms, S Irvine, 1922, 7½x4"..........3,600.00
Vase, paperwhites, AF Simpson, #R020/77, 1929, 6¾x4"..........4,000.00
Vase, paperwhites, AF Simpson, shouldered, 1914, 8¼x4"........7,200.00
Vase, paperwhites, S Irvine, bulbous, 1918, 4¼x5" 1,900.00
Vase, pine cones/needles on bl, H Bailey, #UL61, 4¼"............2,150.00
Vase, pine trees, AF Simpson, bulbous base, 1913, 9x5" 8,400.00
Vase, pine trees, S Irvine, #224/IB94, 5¾" 3,000.00
Vase, pine trees, S Irvine, transitional, 1911, 12x5" 13,200.00
Vase, pine trees/full moon, AF Simpson, 1916, #367/238, 4x2½" ..3,250.00
Vase, pine trees/full moon/river, S Irvine, flakes, 1917, 9¾"....10,800.00
Vase, pines/full moon, AF Simpson, 1919, 8¼x3¾".................9,000.00
Vase, pitcher plants in gr & bl, H Bailey, #UP8, label, 4" 2,500.00
Vase, ribbed, indigo & gr crystalline, 5¼x3¾".......................... 850.00
Vase, rose branches on bl, S Irvine, #RG82, 1928, 8¼x4¾" 2,400.00
Vase, trefoils, S Irvine, #KW82/179, 1920, 8¾x4½" 4,800.00
Vase, trumpet vine, wht on bl, AF Simpson, 1922, 3½x2¾" 1,150.00

Newspapers

People do not collect newspapers simply because they are old. Age has absolutely nothing to do with value — it does not hold true that the older the newspaper, the higher the value. Instead, most of the value is determined by the historic event content. In most cases, the more important to American history the event is, the higher the value. In over 200 years of American history, perhaps as many as 98% of all newspapers ever published do not contain news of a significant historic event. Newspapers not having news of major events in history are called 'atmosphere.' Atmosphere papers have little collector value. (See price guide below.) To learn more about the hobby of collecting old and historic newspapers, visit this internet website: www.historybuff.com/. The e-mail address for the NCSA is help@historybuff.com/. See Newspaper Collector's Society of America in Clubs, Newsletters, and Catalogs for more information.

1803, Columbian Centinel & Massachusetts Federalist, printed text of the Louisianna Purchase Treaty on front page, Boston, four-page, 21x13½", VG, $575.00. (Photo courtesy Early American History Auctions)

1836, Texas declares independence, from $60 to 85.00
1845, Annexation of Texas, from $35 to.. 45.00
1846, Start of Mexican War, from $25 to...................................... 35.00
1846-1847, Major battles of Mexican War, from $25 to................. 30.00
1850, Death of Zachary Taylor, from $45 to................................... 65.00
1859, John Brown executed, from $40 to.. 85.00
1860, Lincoln elected 1st term, from $115 to 225.00
1861, Lincoln's inaugural address, from $140 to 275.00
1861-1865, Atmosphere editions: Confederate titles, from $110 to...165.00
1861-1865, Atmosphere editions: Union titles, from $7 to............ 12.00
1861-1865, Civil War major battle, Confederate report, $225 to.. 390.00

1861-1865, Civil War major battle, Union first report, $60 to..... 120.00
1862, Emancipation Proclamation, from $85 to 225.00
1863, Gettysburg Address, from $165 to 380.00
1865, April 29 edition of Frank Leslie's, from $225 to.................. 325.00
1865, April 29 edition of Harper's Weekly, from $200 to 300.00
1865, Capture & Death of J Wilkes Booth, from $85 to.............. 165.00
1865, Fall of Richmond, from $85 to 275.00
1865, NY Herald, April 15 (Beware: reprints abound), from $700 to... 1,200.00
1865, Titles other than NY Herald, Apr 15, from $300 to 500.00
1866-1900, Atmosphere editions, from $3 to 5.00
1876, Custer's Last Stand, first reports, from $100 to 250.00
1876, Custer's Last Stand, later reports, from $30 to 80.00
1880, Garfield elected, from $30 to 40.00
1881, Gunfight at OK Corral, from $175 to.............................. 400.00
1882, Jesse James killed, first report, from $165 to...................... 385.00
1882, Jesse James killed, later report, from $60 to....................... 120.00
1889, Johnstown flood, from $25 to 40.00
1892, Lizzie Borden crime & trial, from $40 to............................. 85.00
1900, James Jeffries defeats Jack Corbett, from $20 to.................. 35.00
1900-1936, Atmosphere editions, from $2 to 3.00
1901, McKinley assassinated, from $45 to.............................. 100.00
1903, Wright Brother's flight, from $200 to 500.00
1904, Teddy Roosevelt elected, from $25 to 35.00
1906, San Francisco earthquake, other titles, from $25 to 50.00
1906, San Francisco earthquake, San Francisco title, from $300 to ...500.00
1912, Sinking of Titanic, first reports, from $150 to 350.00
1912, Sinking of Titanic, later reports, from $45 to...................... 115.00
1918, Armistice, from $25 to.. 85.00
1924, Coolidge elected, from $20 to 30.00
1927, Babe Ruth hits 60th home run, from $50 to 125.00
1927, Lindbergh arrives in Paris, first reports, from $65 to 125.00

1927, Welcome Lindy, New York Journal, excellent graphics, from $75.00 to $100.00. (Photo courtesy Rick Brown)

1929, St Valentine's Day Massacre, from $100 to 225.00
1929, Stock market crash, from $75 to...................................... 180.00
1931, Al Capone found guilty, from $40 to.................................. 80.00
1931, Jack 'Legs' Diamond killed, from $30 to............................. 45.00
1932, FDR elected first term, from $20 to.................................. 30.00
1933, Hitler becomes Chancellor, from $20 to 55.00
1934, Dillinger killed, from $100 to 250.00
1937, Amelia Earhart vanishes, from $30 to................................. 85.00
1937, Hindenburg explodes, from $75 to 150.00
1939-45, WWII major battles, from $20 to.................................. 50.00
1940, FDR elected 3rd term, from $20 to................................... 30.00
1941, Dec 8 editions w/first reports, from $30 to 50.00
1941, Honolulu Star-Bulletin, Dec 7, first extra (+), from $300 to .. 600.00
1944, D Day, from $25 to... 60.00
1945, FDR dies, from $20 to.. 55.00
1948, Chicago Daily Tribune, Nov 3, Dewey Defeats Truman, from $500 to 800.00
1952, Eisenhower elected first term, from $20 to.......................... 25.00
1957, Soviets launch Sputnik, from $5 to.................................... 15.00

1958, Alaska joins union, from $15 to 25.00
1960, JFK elected, from $30 to.. 45.00
1963, JFK assassination, Nov 22, Dallas title, from $45 to 65.00
1963, JFK assassination, Nov 22, titles other than Dallas, from $3 to. 7.00
1967, Super Bowl I, from $15 to.. 30.00
1968, Assassination of Martin Luther King, from $20 to............... 35.00
1968, Assassination of Robert Kennedy, from $3 to 5.00
1969, Moon landing, from $5 to.. 12.00
1974, Nixon resigns, from $15 to.. 20.00

Nicodemus

Chester R. Nicodemus was born near Barberton, Ohio, August, 17, 1901. He started Pennsylvania State University in 1920, where he studied engineering. Chester got a share of a large paper route, a job that enabled him to attend Cleveland Art School where he studied under Herman Matzen, sculptor, and Frank Wilcox, anatomy illustrator, graduating in 1925. That fall Chester was hired to begin a sculpture department at the Dayton Art Institute.

Nicodemus moved from Dayton to Columbus, Ohio, in 1930 and started teaching at the Columbus Art School. During this time he made vases and commissioned sculptures, water fountains, and limestone and wood carvings. In 1941 Chester left the field of teaching to pursue pottery making full time, using local red clay containing a large amount of iron. Known for its durability, he called the ware Ferro-Stone. He made teapots and other utility wares, but these goods lost favor, so he started producing animal and bird sculptures, nativity sets, and Christmas ornaments, some bearing Chester's and Florine's names as personalized cards for his customers and friends. His glaze colors were turquoise or aqua, ivory, green mottle, pussy willow (pink), and golden yellow. The glaze was applied so that the color of the warm red clay would show through, adding an extra dimension to each piece. His name is usually incised in the clay in an arch, but paper labels were also used. Chester Nicodemus died in 1990. For more information we recommend *Sanfords Guide to Nicodemus, His Pottery and His Art*, by James Riebel.

Bank, figural squirrel, turq, 4½" 125.00
Box, molded as a carton of strawberries, ivory & brn, 4" 190.00
Figurine, cardinal, red w/crystal glaze, 8" L 750.00
Figurine, cat sleeping, gray, 7½" L 1,000.00
Figurine, duckling, brn, 3" 145.00
Figurine, horse, ivory, 12x8" 4,800.00
Figurine, Joseph, tan & brn, 8" 130.00
Figurine, lion cub, brn, 3" 175.00
Figurine, mini; bear sitting, brn over bl,¾" 660.00
Figurine, mini; duck, yel, 1¼" 360.00
Figurine, penguin, Optimist, 3" 175.00
Figurine, robin, 4½" 150.00
Figurine, rooster, blk, 6" 775.00
Figurine, rooster, gray & brn, 6" 1,000.00
Figurine, rooster crowing, gr, 8" 780.00

Figurine, spaniel, medium green gloss, #18, Ferro-Stone label, 5", $335.00.
(Photo courtesy Cincinnati Art Galleries/ LiveAuctioneers.com)

Figurine/vase, flower girl, turq, 6" 135.00
Flower frog, figural Madonna, w/bowl, gr & brn, 11½x10⅜" 300.00
Jardiniere, turq & brn, 4½" 250.00
Mug, Ohio State emb on side, ivory & brn, bulbous, ftd, 5½" 200.00
Paperweight, abstract Madonna & Child, tan, St Ann's Hospital, 4½"..120.00
Pitcher, brn mottle w/brn rim, 3-pt 420.00
Planter, figural swan, brn, 6½" L 900.00
Vase, brn mottle w/brn rim, 3-hdl, 6" 960.00
Vase, turq w/brn rim, rim-to-hip rope hdls, 8½" 165.00
Vase, yel, diagonal ribbing, rectangular, 7½" 600.00

Wall pocket, Rope, double cornucopia, $600.00. (Photo courtesy Pottery Peregrinators)

Niloak

During the latter part of the 1800s, there were many small utilitarian potteries in Benton, Arkansas. By 1900 only the Hyten Brothers Pottery remained. Charles Hyten, a second generation potter, took control of the family business around 1902. Shortly thereafter he renamed it the Eagle Pottery Company. In 1909 Hyten and former Rookwood potter Arthur Dovey began experimentation on a new swirl pottery. Dovey had previously worked for the Ouachita Pottery Company of Hot Springs and produced a swirl pottery there as early as 1906. In March 1910, the Eagle Pottery Company introduced Niloak — kaolin spelled backwards.

In 1911 Benton businessmen formed the Niloak Pottery corporation. Niloak, connected to the Arts and Crafts Movement and known as Mission Ware, had a national representative in New York by 1913. Niloak's production centered on art pottery characterized by accidental, swirling patterns of natural and artificially colored clays. Many companies through the years have produced swirl pottery, yet none achieved the technical and aesthetic qualities of Niloak. Hyten received a patent in 1928 for the swirl technique. Although most examples have an interior glaze, some early Mission Ware pieces have an exterior glaze as well; these are extremely rare.

In 1934 Hyten's company found itself facing bankruptcy. Hardy L. Winburn, Jr., along with other Little Rock businessmen, raised the necessary capital and were able to provide the kind of leadership needed to make the business profitable once again. Both lines (Eagle and Hywood) were renamed 'Niloak' in 1937 to capitalize on this well-known name. The pottery continued in production until 1947 when it was converted to the Winburn Tile Company.

Of late, poor copies of Niloak Mission Ware swirl and Hywood pieces have been seen at flea markets and on the internet. These pieces even bear a Niloak mark, but this is a 'fantasy' mark. To the experienced eye, the pieces are blatantly bogus. Buyer beware!

Virtually all of Niloak Misson Ware/swirl pottery is marked with die stamps. The exceptions are generally vases, wall pockets, lamp bases, and whiskey jugs. The terms 'first' and 'second art marks' used in the listings refer to specific die-stamped trademarks. The earlier mark was used from

1910 to 1925, followed by the second, very similar mark used from then until the end of Mission Ware production. Letters with curving raised outlines were characteristic of both; the most obvious difference between the two was that on the first, the final upright line of the 'N' was thin with a solid club-like terminal.

Be careful not to confuse the swirl production of the Evans Pottery of Missouri with Niloak. The significant difference is the dark brown matt interior glaze of Evans pottery. Our advisor for this category is Lila Shrader; she is listed in the Directory under California.

Key:
FHN — 1st Hywood mark   NB — Niloak (block letters)
  (black circular stamp)   NI — Niloak (impressed)
IH — incised Hywood   NL — Niloak (in low relief)

Mission Ware

Ashtray, str sides, no rests, 5½" dia.. 80.00
Bowl, flared ft, dome lid w/acorn-like finial, 2nd art mk, 5¾" ...2,685.00
Bowl, incurvate rim, 1st art mk, 2x10½" 300.00
Candlestick, drip rim, cupped base, 1st art mk, 3¾", ea............... 190.00
Candlesticks, drip rim, flared base, 2nd art mk, 8½", pr............... 300.00
Chamberstick, drip rim, flared base, hdl, 1st art mk, 4x4¾" 280.00

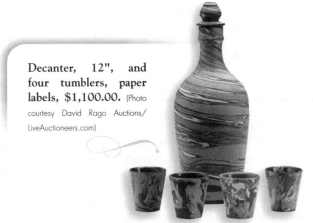

Decanter, 12", and four tumblers, paper labels, $1,100.00. (Photo courtesy David Rago Auctions/ liveAuctioneers.com)

Flower frog, layer-cake style, unmk, 1½x3¼" 80.00
Humidor, cup-like lid w/recess for sponge, 2nd art mk, 4½" 550.00
Humidor, str sides, lid w/recess for sponge, 2nd art mk, 6¼".........695.00
Jar, flared rim, bulbous, w/knobbed lid, 3¾x5" 365.00
Jug, Pensacola Goldencorn emb on side, no hdl, 2nd art mk, 3¼" ...65.00
Jug, Pensacola Goldencorn impressed on side, 2nd art mk, 3" 155.00
Match holder, str sides, flared base, 1st art mk, 2¼x2¾" dia 100.00
Mug, slightly bbl shaped, 1st art mk, 4¼"..................................... 250.00
Pencil holder, cylindrical, slight flare at base, 1st art mk, 2¾"...... 100.00
Plate, flat bowl form w/no rim, dk colors, 1st art mk, 9" 620.00
Powder dish, fancy finial, 1st art mk, 3x4½" dia........................... 750.00
Tankard, elongated hdl, 2nd art mk, 10½" 1,350.00
Tumbler, flared rim, Pat Pending, 5¼" 155.00
Vase, classic form, rolled collar, brick red dominates, 2nd art mk, 7" .185.00
Vase, cylindrical, flared base, 1st art mk, 8¾x3¼" 145.00
Vase, cylindrical, sm flare at top, tan/cream, 1910, 8½x4¼" 880.00
Vase, cylindrical w/str sides, vine pattern, 2nd art mk, 9" 190.00
Vase, high shoulders, cupped rim, brn/tan/cream, 1st art mk, 10¾"....625.00
Vase, high shoulders, rolled rim, bl/brn/tan, 1st art mk, 16¼", NM..1,525.00
Vase, pear form w/elongated cylindrical neck, 1st art mk, 9½".....400.00
Vase, planter-like w/rolled rim, 2nd art mk, 8x9½"....................... 365.00
Vase, squat w/rolled rim, 2nd art mk, 3x5½" 255.00
Vase, teardrop shape w/narrow neck, 1st art mk, 10½" 525.00
Wall pocket, flat bk, elongated w/'ring' at base, unmk, 8½" L 500.00

Miscellaneous

Ashtray, frog w/lg open mouth, gr mottle, 3½" 100.00
Bathtub, Hot Springs Arkansas emb on side, NI, 1½x3¾" 45.00
Bowl, Peter Pan seated at rim, gr gloss, NB, 7¾" H 55.00
Bowl, swan w/open body fitted for glass bowl, S-shape neck, 2nd art mk .. 125.00
Cornucopia on ocean wave-like ped, wht matt, NI, 6x9" 40.00
Cup & saucer, Bouquet, matt, NI, 5" dia... 27.00
Ewer, crown design, Ozark Dawn II, 16½" 215.00
Figure, Razorback Hog, emb Arkansas on side of base, NB, 3½x5½" .. 200.00
Figure, Razorback Hog, unmk, NB, 3½x5¾" 180.00

Figurine, recumbent fox, Ozark Dawn, 7" long, $60.00. (Photo courtesy Belhorn Auction Services LLC/LiveAuctioneers.com)

Letter on mc letterhead re distribution woes, 1934, 11x8½" 75.00
Mug, Bouquet, matt, NI, 3½" 16.00
Pitcher, Deco ball form w/orig cork/ceramic stopper, Hywood, 7½" ...190.00
Pitcher, Deco streamline design, gr gloss, inset hdl/lid, 6" 245.00
Pitcher, minimally defined spout, gr gloss, appl hdl, no lid, 6½" 65.00
Pitcher, tulips emb, matt, slim, 10¾"... 16.00
Planter, bird w/wings wide, yel gloss, NB, 5½" 28.00
Planter, bunny resting w/ears up, dk gr matt, NB, 4½" L 26.00
Planter, camel resting, attached basketweave container, NB, 3½" . 22.00
Planter, Scottie dog, NL, 3½x4¼" 20.00
Shakers, bluebird, bl matt, unmk, 2½x3", pr.................................. 30.00
Shakers, tanks, WWI, open turret, NI, 3x4¼", pr............................ 75.00
Teapot, Aladdin style w/intricate hdl, glossy, sticker, 6½" 135.00
Vase, flamingo & palm tree, ornate hdls, wht matt, NI, 7¼" 65.00
Vase, Ozark Dawn, 3 curved hdls, Hywood, Stoin, 6¼"................ 600.00
Vase, tulip, 6 openings, Ozark Dawn, 7½"..................................... 32.00
Vase, tulip; 5 openings, glossy, N, 7" 10.00
Vase, tulip; 5 openings, matt, N, 7"... 25.00

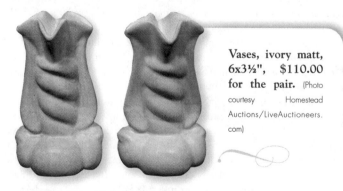

Vases, ivory matt, 6x3½", $110.00 for the pair. (Photo courtesy Homestead Auctions/LiveAuctioneers. com)

Nippon

Nippon generally refers to Japanese wares made during the period from 1891 to 1921, although the Nippon mark was also used to a limited extent on later wares (accompanied by 'Japan'). Nippon, meaning Japan, identified the country of origin to comply with American impor-

tation restrictions. After 1921 'Japan' was the acceptable alternative. The term does not imply a specific type of product and may be found on items other than porcelains. For further information we recommend *Van Patten's ABC's of Collecting Nippon* by Joan Van Patten. In the following listings, items are assumed hand painted unless noted otherwise. Numbers included in the descriptions refer to these specific marks:

Key:
#1 — Patent
#2 — M in Wreath
#3 — Cherry Blossom
#4 — Double T Diamond in Circle
#5 — Rising Sun
#6 — Royal Kinran
#7 — Maple Leaf
#8 — Royal Nippon, Nishiki
#9 — Royal Moriye Nippon

Ashtray, Mexican cowboy, 3 rests, Imperial mk, 6½", from $275 to ...350.00
Bowl, floral, golden eagle on cobalt border, #2, 8½", from $175 to...225.00
Bowl, floral w/cobalt, scalloped rim, #6, 11½", from $500 to........ 650.00
Bowl, roses on shaded yel w/ornate gold border, unmk, 11¼"....... 425.00
Box, cigarette; river scenic, bl #2, 4½" W, from $400 to............... 475.00
Box, trinket; gold o/l on wht, 6-sided, HP mk, 3½", from $75 to .. 120.00
Cake plate, roses, HP/jeweled butterfly, hdls, #7, 10½", $650 to ..750.00
Chocolate pot, floral w/gold beading, waisted, #6, 9½", $700 to ..900.00
Chocolate pot, lace/floral foliage, wht on gr, cylindrical, unmk, 9" ..800.00
Cigarette box, Howo bird on lid, #2, from $300 to....................... 375.00
Creamer, mc roses on yel w/much gold, #7, 3", from $125 to 160.00
Demitasse pot, gulls on gr w/much gold, mk, 6¾", +cr/sug 350.00

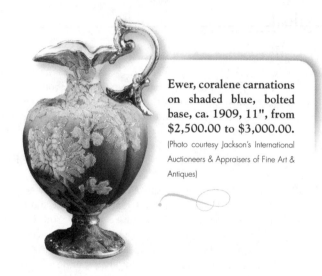

Ewer, coralene carnations on shaded blue, bolted base, ca. 1909, 11", from $2,500.00 to $3,000.00. (Photo courtesy Jackson's International Auctioneers & Appraisers of Fine Art & Antiques)

Ewer, irises w/coralene, slim neck/ruffled rim, #1, 10½", $2,400 to...2,800.00
Ewer, moriage floral (ornate) w/much gold, bulbous, unmk, 7½" .. 750.00
Ferner, Gouda-like Deco-style floral, ftd, gr hdls, #2, 6", $400 to. 500.00
Ginger jar, bl cloud, Lego MIJ, 5", from $45 to 75.00
Hatpin holder, red-breasted bird on wht, #5, 4¾", from $90 to 130.00
Hatpin/ring holder w/attached tray, floral, #3, 4½", from $150 to ...200.00
Humidor, Black man w/banjo HP on cream, gr #2, 5¼", from $800 to...1,000.00
Humidor, floral w/moriage details on gr, squirrel finial, 7", $900 to ..1,100.00
Lemon dish, birds, bl on wht, pierced hdls, #5, 5½", from $20 to... 30.00
Loving cup, airplane scene, brn angle hdls, gr #2, 4", from $600 to..700.00
Mug, horse portrait reserve on wht, gr #2, 5", from $300 to 400.00
Pen tray, floral on cobalt w/gold, HP mk, 7¾", from $250 to........ 300.00
Pin box, monoplane scene, gr #2, 3¼" dia, from $600 to.............. 700.00
Plaque, buffalo scene in relief, gr #2, 10½", from $800 to............. 950.00
Plaque, cows at water's edge, rectangular, #2, 10¼", from $2,400 to...2,800.00
Plaque, Deco-style floral, Royal Kinjo, 10", from $1,000 to.......1,200.00
Plaque, hunting scene, red-decor border, bl #7, 9½", from $700 to ..850.00
Plaque, roses (3) in full bloom, gold rim, #7, 9½", from $300 to .. 400.00

Plaque, portrait of a lion molded in relief, green M in wreath mark, 10¾", from $1,600.00 to $2,000.00. (Photo courtesy Joan Van Patten)

Plate, rose, gold & jewels on cobalt rim, #7, 10¼", from $700 to . 900.00
Stein, Am Indian's chief's portrait (incised), brn tones, #2, 7" 850.00
Stein, monk surrounded by grapevines, #2, 7", from $1,000 to . 1,200.00
Tankard, palms w/moriage, angle hdl, #2, 11", +6 mugs, from $1,800 to..2,100.00
Tea strainer, floral on cobalt w/gold, #2, from $325 to 375.00
Urn, daffodils reserve, ornate gold hdls, bolted, #2, 8½" 750.00
Vase, American Indian on horse, angle hdls, Imperial Nippon, 12"...750.00
Vase, bird among grapes, moriage trim, bl #7, 7", from $825 to ... 950.00
Vase, Cleopatra's barge scenic band on bl w/gold, #2, 12", $900 to 1,200.00
Vase, coaching scene, bulbous, integral hdls, #2, 6", from $850 to 1,000.00
Vase, coralene landscape, earth tones, ornate hdls, mk, 12", $1,400 to...1,800.00
Vase, coralene lilies on shaded gr w/gold, #1, 1909, 9x5", $1,100 to ..1,300.00
Vase, country road scenic band on bl w/gold, hdls, #7, 9", $1,200 to..1,400.00
Vase, figure on path beside lake in fall, gold hdls, #2, 8½" 350.00
Vase, floral band on cobalt w/gold, cylindrical, #2, 6", from $350 to..425.00
Vase, floral emb, mc w/gold, hdls, #7, 9½", from $1,200 to........1,400.00

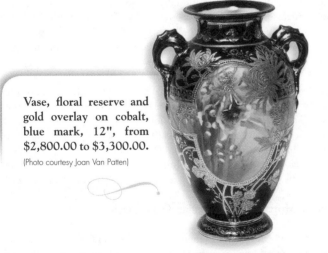

Vase, floral reserve and gold overlay on cobalt, blue mark, 12", from $2,800.00 to $3,300.00.

(Photo courtesy Joan Van Patten)

Vase, floral reserves, moriage trim, hdls, unmk, 7", from $600 to . 700.00
Vase, gleaners scenic reserve, 3-hdl, #2, 12", from $2,400 to.....2,900.00
Vase, golden forest reserve on cobalt, slim, #2, 18", from $5,000 to .6,500.00
Vase, grapevines on wht, gold angle hdls, bulbous, #2, 8", $300 to .375.00
Vase, lady's portrait reserve on cobalt w/gold, bulbous, #7, 4¾" ... 675.00
Vase, moriage bird on branch, cylindrical, #7, 13", from $1,400 to ..1,600.00
Vase, moriage flying swans on brn shaded to cream, #7, 14", $3,000 to ..3,500.00
Vase, moriage gulls over water, sm hdls, #7, 9½", from $1,200 to ..1,350.00
Vase, mtn scenic band on cobalt w/gold, angle hdls, #7, 8", $1,200 to . 1,500.00
Vase, mums, mc w/much gold, bottle neck, #7, 24", from $6,000 to ..8,000.00
Vase, pansies reserve on gr w/much gold, ftd, gold hdls, mk, 5" ... 350.00
Vase, poppies on wht, brn hdls & ft, bulbous, #2, from $350 to ... 425.00
Vase, river scenic in earth tones, sm hdls, 4 sm ft, #2, 8", $165 to...235.00
Vase, roses in spiral twist w/gold beading, hdls, #7, 12", $1,000 to.. 1,200.00
Vase, roses w/much gold, ornate organic-shaped gold hdls, unmk, 7¼" ..650.00

Vase, swans reserve on wht w/gold, hdls, #2, 15½", from $1,800 to..2,200.00
Vase, sweet peas w/coralene, gold angle hdls, #1, 6½", $850 to.1,000.00
Vase, wide lotus band on cobalt w/gold, sq sides, #7, 8¾", $400 to..500.00
Vase, wide winter scene band, ornate gold hdls, #2, 6½", $225 to...300.00
Vase/lamp base, Wedgwood, cream on bl, can neck, sm hdls, #7, 10". 800.00
Whiskey jug, Rodney Stone (bulldog), gr #2, 6¾", from $1,200 to ..1,400.00

Nodders

So called because of the nodding action of their heads and hands, nodders originated in China where they were used in temple rituals to represent deity. At first they were made of brass and were actually a type of bell; when these bells were rung, the heads of the figures would nod. In the eighteenth century, the idea was adopted by Meissen and by French manufacturers who produced not only china nodders but bisque as well. Most nodders are individual; couples are unusual. The idea remained popular until the end of the nineteenth century and was used during the Victorian era by toy manufacturers. See also Conta and Boehme.

Buddha laughing, pnt porc, head/tongue/hands nod, Meissen, 13x14"....10,200.00
Cat, chalkware w/blk, red & yellow accents, 19th C, 4x8" 400.00
Clown, pnt papier maché, bl nose, glass eyes, Labarre Livres on base... 1,320.00
Donald Duck, pnt celluloid, long bill, tin base, Japan, 6" 780.00
Felix the Cat on motorcycle, spring in tail, Germany, 7½" 600.00
Geisha in kimono seated, Banko Ware, 4x3½" 135.00
Goose on wheeled platform, pnt tin, 2x3½" 600.00
Happy Hooligan, pnt compo figure on wood base, DRGM, ca 1915, 9", EX.300.00
Old woman in chair w/cats at feet, pnt compo, wood base, 4½"... 240.00

Oriental 'Pagoda Nodders,' male and female, Meissen, #153 and #154, 5¾", $5,000.00 for the pair. (Photo courtesy James D. Julia Inc.)

Pluto, celluloid, tan w/blk & red details, orig tag, 8" L 450.00
Queen of Hearts, Alice in Wonderland, Goebel, 1950s, 5½", EX ...720.00
Santa on donkey w/metal wheels, donkey head nods, German, ca 1900, 12"...725.00

Nordic Art Glass

Finnish and Swedish glass has recently started to develop a following, probably stemming from the revitalization of interest in forms from the 1950s. (The name Nordic is used here because of the inclusion of Finnish glass — the term Scandinavian does not refer to this country.) Included here are Flygsfors, Hadeland, Holmegaard, Iittala, Maleras, Motzfeldt, Nuutajarvi, Pukeberg, Reijmyre, and Stromberg-shyttan. Our suggested prices are fair market values, developed after researching the Nordic secondary markets, the current retail prices on items still being produced, and American auction houses and antique stores.

Flygsfors Glass Works, Sweden

Flygsfors Glass Works was established in 1888 and continued in production until 1979 when the Orrefors Glass Group, which had acquired this entity, ceased operations. The company is well known for art glass designed by Paul Kedelv, who joined the firm in 1949 with a contract to design light fittings, a specialty of the company. Their 'Coquille' series, which utilizes a unique overlay technique combining opaque, bright colors, and 'Flamingo' have become very desirable on today's secondary market. Other internationally known artists/designers include Prince Sigvard Bernadotte and the Finnish designer Helene Tynell.

Basket, Coquille, 1959, 18½", $300.00. (Photo courtesy Rose Hill Auction Gallery/LiveAuctioneers.com)

Bowl, bl & red in clear, Alexandrite-style free-form, 1957, 15" L ...155.00
Bowl, blk & wht in clear, free-form w/flared ends, 1950s, 14¼" L ...120.00
Bowl, red cased in clear, Coquille, 8x13" 75.00
Vase, pk & wht in clear, 2 pulled ends, Coquille, 1961, 9¼" 60.00

Hadeland Glassverk, Norway

Glass has been produced at this glass works since 1765. From the beginning, their main product was bottles. Since the 1850s they have made small items — drinking glasses, vases, bowls, jugs, etc. — and for the last 40 years, figurines, souvenirs, and objects of art. Important designers include Willy Johansson, Arne John Jutrem, Inger Magnus, Severin Brorby, and Gro Sommerfelt.

Bowl, Bergslien, horizontal bands, red foot, 1960s, 5¾x7", $180.00. (Photo courtesy Treadway Gallery/LiveAuctioneers.com)

Bowl, Dmn Quilt, olive gr w/bl rolled rim, AJJ, #4115, 3⅜x5¾".... 75.00
Vase, bl, shouldered w/short neck/flared rim, WJ, #2132, 1960s, 6½" ...120.00
Vase, bl cased in gr, Severin Brorby, #70/8, 6¾x3½" 270.00
Vase, bl gray w/scattered plum splotches & bubbles, WJ, #2132, 6⅝"... 165.00
Vase, brn in clear w/gr accents, WJ, #59, 9¼x4" 110.00
Vase, brn spirals w/coral red base, Gro Sommerfeldt, 5½x8¾" 200.00
Vase, lt brn in clear, dmn shape, WF, #2128, 7" 350.00
Vase, moss gr w/coral & cream thread/mc splashes, AJJ, #60, 4⅞" ..120.00
Vase, raspberry red, long slim neck, AJJ, #54, foil label, 9" 85.00
Vase, smoky gray w/suspended mocha core, JW, #2129, 2⅝" 550.00

Vase, spaced ruby stripes, controlled bubbles, WJ, #54, 4⅝".........425.00
Vase, wht opal w/vertical bubbles, WJ, #55, 3¾" 550.00

Holmegaard Glassvaerk, Denmark

This company was founded in 1825. Because of a shortage of wood in Denmark, it became necessary for them to use peat, the only material available for fuel. Their first full-time designers were hired after 1923. Orla Juul Nielson was the first. He was followed in 1925 by Jacob Band, an architect. Per Lukin became the chief designer in 1941. His production and art glass incorporates a simple yet complex series of designs. They continue to be popular among collectors of Scandinavian glass. During 1965 the company merged with Kastrup and became Kastrup Holmegaard AS; a merger with Royal Copenhagen followed in 1975.

Bowl, bl, incurvate rim, 3½x7½" 60.00
Bowl, clear w/curved lip, Per Lukin, 4½x16¼" 100.00
Bowl, pale smoky gray, incurvate rim, 5⅛x16½" 195.00
Candleholders, bl, Danish Modern style, low, 6¾" dia, pr 60.00
Ceiling light fixture, gray cased, 16x10", pr 575.00
Decanter, bl, Kluk Kluk, wht stopper, #L60, 15¼x5" 100.00
Sculpture, stylized rooster, smoke to clear, 7¼x7" 30.00
Vase, bl, stacking cylinders (2) w/flat rim, #L60, 15¼x5" 180.00
Vase, clear w/frosted nude intaglio, FW, #A3, 1957, 8" 395.00

Iittala Glass Works, Finland

This glassworks was founded in 1881; it was originally staffed by Swedish workers who produced glassware of very high quality. In 1917 Ahiststrom OY bought and merged Iittala with Karhula Glass Works. After 1945 Karhula's production was limited to container glass. In 1946 Tapio Wirkkala, the internationally known artist/designer, became Iittala's chief designer. Timo Sarpeneva joined him in 1950. Jointly they successfully spearheaded the promotion of Finnish glass in the international markets, winning many international awards for their designs. Today, Oiva Toikka leads the design team.

Candlesticks, Festivo, icy clear, Sarpaneva, 1967, 12⅜", pr.......... 360.00
Vase, amethyst & bl in clear, hollow base, Tapio Wirkkala, #3892, 11"..1,950.00
Vase, Bamboo, clear w/controlled bubbles, K Franck, 6x4½" 1,100.00
Vase, clear w/icicle appearance, #3429, 1954, 9¾" 950.00
Vase, cobalt in clear, spherical, Timo Sarpeneva, 7¾" 240.00
Vase, jack-in-pulpit; clear w/cut lines, T Wirkkala, #55, 4¾x5"... 235.00
Vase, smoky gray w/folded lip, Sarpaneva, 1957, 5¾x8½" 240.00

Benny Motzfeldt, Norwegian Glass Artist

Benny Motzfeldt, a graduate of the Arts and Crafts School of Oslo, Norway, started her career in glass in 1954 by responding to an ad for a designer of engraving and decoration at Christiania Glassmagasin and Hadeland Glassverk. After several years at Hadeland, she joined the Plus organization and managed their glass studio in Frederikstad. She is acknowledged as one of the leading exponents of Norwegian art glass and is recognized internationally. She challenged the rather sober Norwegian glass designs with a strong desire to try new ways, using vigorous forms and opaque colors embedded with silver nitrate patterns.

Bowl, cranberry/mocha/wht spatter in amber, 2⅜x4⅝" 75.00
Vase, bl opaque w/3 abstract butterflies, BM, #89, 7x6½" 300.00
Vase, blk w/silvery metallic inclusions/random bubbles, BM, #70, 8" ... 360.00
Vase, clear w/blk & teal swirls & boiling bubbles, bottle form, 8⅝" ...195.00
Vase, clear w/random bubbles, dk fibers/cobalt patches, BM, #91, 7"..350.00
Vase, coral w/blk oxide patches, globular, 3½" 155.00
Vase, crystal w/mc mesh patches, random bubbles, BM, #77, 4⅜"...180.00

Vase, dk bl w/open-weave fabrics/metallic inclusions, BM, #72, 4⅜".. 240.00
Vase, lav w/abstract bl & wht flowers, BM, #84, 5⅜".................... 240.00
Vase, pistachio w/dk fabric/bubbles/indigo pigments, BM, #78, 6x6½". 360.00
Vase, toffee w/bl & lav granules, short neck, sq sides, 3⅝" 265.00

Nuutajarvi Glass Works, Finland

Sculpture, bird, Oiva Toikka, 1992, 6¼x11x5" 180.00
Vase, blown, clear w/bottle neck, JAJ Franck, 10" 155.00
Vase, clear w/forest gr drops & air bubbles, S Hopea, #55, 8¾".1,200.00
Vase, clear w/purple drops & air bubbles, S Hopea, #55, 6½x4" .. 1,325.00
Vase, orange opaque w/blk inclusions, H Orvola, A Wartisila, 12" 395.00
Vase, plum in clear w/trapped bubbles, Gunnel Nyman, 1930s, 12" ..435.00
Vase, wht opaque spiral in clear, Gunnel Nyman, ca 1948, 17"... 1,950.00

Noritake

The Noritake Company was first registered in 1904 as Nippon Gomei Kaisha. In 1917 the name became Nippon Toki Kabushiki Toki. The 'M in wreath' mark is that of the Morimura Brothers, distributors with offices in New York. It was used until 1941. The 'tree crest' mark is the crest of the Morimura family. The company has produced fine porcelain dinnerware sets and occasional pieces decorated in the delicate manner for which the Japanese are noted. (Two dinnerware patterns are featured below, and a general range is suggested for others.)

Authority Joan Van Patten has compiled a lovely book, *The Collector's Encyclopedia of Noritake*, with many full-color photos; you will find her address in the Directory under New York. In the following listings, examples are hand painted unless noted otherwise. Numbers refer to these specific marks:

Key:
#1 — Komaru   #2 — M in Wreath

Azalea

The Azalea pattern was produced exclusively for the Larkin Company, who gave the lovely ware away as premiums to club members and their home agents. From 1916 through the 1930s, Larkin distributed fine china which was decorated in pink azaleas on white with gold tracing along edges and handles. Early in the '30s, six pieces of crystal hand painted with the same design were offered: candleholders, a compote, a tray with handles, a scalloped fruit bowl, a cheese and cracker set, and a cake plate. All in all, 70 different pieces of Azalea were produced. Some, such as the 15-piece child's set, bulbous vase, china ashtray, and the pancake jug, are quite rare. One of the earliest marks was the Noritake 'M in wreath' with variations. Later the ware was marked 'Noritake, Azalea, Hand Painted, Japan.' Our advisor for Azalea is Linda Williams; she is listed in the Directory under Massachusetts.

Basket, mint; Dolly Varden, #193.. 185.00
Bonbon, #184, 6¼" 60.00
Bowl, #12, 10" 38.00
Bowl, candy/grapefruit; #185 .... 285.00
Bowl, cream soup; #363 .... 120.00
Bowl, deep, #310 .... 60.00
Bowl, fruit; #9, 5¼" 8.00
Bowl, fruit; scalloped, glass 95.00
Bowl, fruit; shell form, #188, 7¾" 325.00
Bowl, oatmeal; #55, 5½" 25.00
Bowl, soup; #19, 7⅛" 28.00
Bowl, vegetable; divided, #439, 9½".. 250.00
Bowl, vegetable; oval, #101, 10½" 48.00

Bowl, vegetable; oval, #172, 9¼"... 38.00
Butter chip, #312, 3¼" 80.00
Butter tub, w/insert, #54 .... 30.00
Cake plate, #10, 9¾" 35.00
Candleholders, glass, 3½", pr 120.00
Candy jar, w/lid, #313, from $525 to.. 625.00
Casserole, gold finial, w/lid, #372 .... 275.00
Casserole, w/lid, #16 .... 70.00
Celery tray, #444, closed hdls, 10" 275.00
Celery/roll tray, #99, 12" 35.00
Cheese/butter dish, #314 .... 110.00
Cheese/cracker, glass 75.00
Child's set, #253, 15-pc...2,500.00
Coffeepot, demitasse; #182 .... 575.00
Compote, #170 .... 90.00
Compote, glass 80.00
Condiment set, #14, 5-pc 42.00
Creamer & sugar bowl, #7 .... 38.00
Creamer & sugar bowl, demitasse; open, #123......................... 110.00
Creamer & sugar bowl, gold finial, #401 .... 85.00
Creamer & sugar bowl, scalloped, ind, #449 .... 475.00
Creamer & sugar shaker, berry; #122....................................... 150.00
Cruet, #190 .... 180.00
Cup & saucer, #2... 15.00
Cup & saucer, bouillon; #124, 3½".. 25.00
Cup & saucer, demitasse; #183 .... 125.00
Egg cup, #120 .... 35.00
Gravy boat, #40 .... 40.00
Jam jar set, #125, 4-pc 125.00
Mayonnaise set, scalloped, #453, 3-pc.................................... 500.00
Mustard jar, #191, 3-pc 60.00
Olive dish, #194 .... 25.00
Pickle/lemon set, #121 .... 24.50
Pitcher, milk jug; #100, 1-qt.. 180.00
Plate, #4, 7½" 10.00
Plate, bread & butter; #8, 6½" 8.00
Plate, breakfast/luncheon; #98 .... 15.00
Plate, dinner; #13, 9¾" 18.00
Plate, grill; 3-compartment, #38, 10¼" 210.00
Plate, salad; 7⅝" sq 65.00
Plate, scalloped sq, salesman's sample, from $875 to................ 950.00
Plate, tea; #4, 7½" 10.00
Platter, #17, 14", from $55 to 60.00
Platter, #56, 12", from $45 to 50.00
Platter, cold meat/bacon; #311, 10¼" 175.00
Platter, turkey; #186, 16" 450.00
Refreshment set, #39, 2-pc 38.00
Relish, #194, 7⅛" 52.00
Relish, oval, #18, 8½" 15.00
Relish, 2-part, #171 .... 45.00
Relish, 2-part, loop hdl, #450 .... 280.00
Relish, 4-section, #119, rare, 10" 145.00
Saucer, fruit; #9, 5¼" 10.00
Shakers, bell form, #11, pr 40.00
Shakers, bulbous, #89 .... 40.00
Shakers, ind, #126, pr 28.00
Spoon holder, #189, 8" 95.00
Syrup, #97, w/underplate & lid... 98.00
Tea tile 65.00
Teapot, #15 .... 125.00
Teapot, gold finial, #400, from $350 to 380.00
Toothpick holder, #192... 80.00
Vase, bulbous, #452...1,100.00
Whipped cream/mayonnaise set, #3, 3-pc 35.00

Vase, fan form, footed, #187, $225.00. (Photo courtesy Linda Williams)

Tree in the Meadow

Another of their dinnerware lines has become a favorite of many collectors. Tree in the Meadow is a scenic hand-painted pattern which features a thatched cottage in a meadow with a lake in the foreground. The version accepted by most collectors will have a tree behind the cottage and will not have a swan or a bridge. The colors resemble a golden sunset on a fall day with shades of orange, gold, and rust. This line was made during the 1920s and 1930s and seems today to be in good supply. A fairly large dinnerware set with several unusual serving pieces can be readily assembled. Our advisor for Tree in the Meadow is Linda Williams; she is listed in the Directory under Massachusetts.

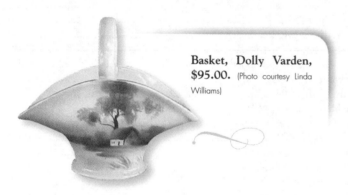

Basket, Dolly Varden, $95.00. (Photo courtesy Linda Williams)

Bowl, cream soup; 2-hdl	75.00
Bowl, fruit; shell form, #210	195.00
Bowl, oatmeal	25.00
Bowl, oval, 9½"	48.00
Bowl, oval, 10½"	45.00
Bowl, soup	38.00
Bowl, vegetable; 9"	35.00
Butter pat	25.00
Butter tub, open, w/drainer	35.00
Cake plate, open hdl	35.00
Candy dish, octagonal, w/lid, 5½"	250.00
Celery dish	25.00
Cheese dish	75.00
Coffeepot, demitasse	175.00
Compote	75.00
Condiment set, 5-pc	45.00
Creamer & sugar bowl, berry	110.00
Creamer & sugar bowl, demitasse	125.00
Cruets, vinegar & oil; cojoined, #319, from $210 to	275.00
Cup & saucer, breakfast	18.00
Cup & saucer, demitasse	45.00
Egg cup	30.00
Gravy boat	40.00
Jam jar/dish, cherries on lid, 4-pc	98.00
Lemon dish	15.00

Mayonnaise set, 3-pc	48.00
Plate, dessert; 6½"	8.00
Plate, dinner; 9¾"	60.00
Plate, rare, 7⅝" sq	75.00
Plate, salad; 8"	12.00
Platter, 10"	75.00
Platter, 11¾x9"	58.00
Platter, 13¾x10¼"	65.00
Relish, divided	30.00
Snack set (cup & tray), 2-pc	48.00
Tea tile	60.00
Teapot	75.00
Vase, fan form	95.00

Miscellaneous

Ashtray, cat perched at side, gold & bl lustre, gr mk, 3x4¾"	155.00
Ashtray, cigarette & matches HP on brn, 3 rests, gr mk, 2x4½"	140.00
Ashtray, fox hunter on horse leaping fence, Deco shape, red mk, 4"	40.00
Bowl, river scenic on yel, gold hdls, #2, 7"	60.00
Bowl, sailboat scene, 3-lobe w/rtcl rim, #2, mk, 1½x7⅛"	12.00
Cake plate, floral medallion/swags, gr rim, MIJ mk, 9¾"+hdls	27.50
Candy dish, floral w/tan lustre rim, pierced hdls, 1½x8⅜" L	20.00
Chocolate pot, exotic bird w/gold, #2, 8¾", +6 c/s	350.00
Compote, floral w/orange lustre rim, gr mk, 5x11x8"	25.00
Egg cup, flower blossom at rim, leaves on side, mc w/orange lustre	12.50
Humidor, lion killing python in relief on red, #2, 6¾"	850.00
Humidor, owl on branch w/acorns in relief, 6¾"	635.00

Inkwell, two-part harlequin bust, red M-in-wreath mark, $3,200.00. (Photo courtesy Jackson's International Auctioneers & Appraisers of Fine Art & Antiques/LiveAuctioneers.com)

Plate, lady in voluminus gown w/bouquet, mc/lustre, Morimuma, 7¾"	700.00
Plate, lady w/petticoat showing/bird/flowers, mc lustre, wear, 6½"	160.00
Shaving mug, river scenic, earth tones w/gold, #2, 3¾"	120.00
Toast rack, bl lustre w/bird finial, #2, 5½" L	125.00
Vase, castle ruins, ornate hdls, much gold, gr mk, 1890s-1920s, 12"	300.00
Vase, Deco fans/flowers, mc on emerald gr, 6-sided, 9⅞"	155.00
Vase, Deco floral, mc on blk, gr mk, 11½"	285.00
Vase, Deco poppies on bl w/orange lustre, 6-sided, red mk, 11¼"	135.00
Vase, desert scene band on cobalt w/gold, classic form, 10½"	135.00
Vase, floral on bl at top & shoulder, curtain-like body, gr mk, 8"	115.00
Vase, flowers w/gold, 3 dolphins at base, mc lustre, 5½x3"	95.00
Vase, geometrics, mc on gr, irregular rim, Deco, 6½x5½"	135.00
Vase, swan figural, mc lustre, red mk, 4½"	95.00
Wall pocket, musician w/wide ruffled collar on lustre, #2, 6"	300.00

Various Dinnerware Patterns, ca. 1933 to Present

So many lines of dinnerware have been produced by the Noritake company that to list them all would require a volume in itself. And while many patterns had specific names, others did not, and it is virtually impossible to identify them all. Outlined below is a general guide for the more common pieces and patterns. The high side of the range will represent lines from about 1933 until the mid-1960s (including those marked 'Occupied Japan'), while the lower side should be used to evaluate lines made after that period.

Bowl, berry; ind, from $8 to.. 12.00
Bowl, soup; 7½", from $12 to... 16.00
Bowl, vegetable; rnd or oval, ca 1945 to present, from $35 to........ 60.00
Butter dish, 3-pc, ca 1933-64, from $40 to...................... 50.00
Creamer, from $18 to.. 28.00
Cup & saucer, demitasse; from $12 to 17.50
Gravy boat, from $35 to.. 60.00
Pickle or relish dish, from $18 to...................................... 28.00
Plate, bread & butter, from $8 to 12.00
Plate, dinner; from $15 to... 30.00
Plate, luncheon; from $14 .... 18.00
Plate, salad; from $10 to 15.00
Platter, 14", from $50 to.. 80.00
Shakers, pr, from $25 to... 45.00

Sheridan, shakers, 3", $25.00 for the pair.

Sugar bowl, w/lid, from $18 to.. 30.00
Teapot, demitasse pot, chocolate pot or coffeepot, ea from $75 to ... 150.00

Norse

The Norse Pottery was established in 1903 in Edgerton, Wisconsin, by Thorwald Sampson and Louis Ipson. A year later it was purchased by A.W. Wheelock and moved to Rockford, Illinois. The ware they produced was inspired by ancient bronze vessels of the Norsemen. Designs were often incised into the red clay body. Dragon handles and feet were favored decorative devices, and they achieved a semblance of patina through the application of metallic glazes. The ware was marked with model numbers and a stylized 'N' containing a vertical arrangement of the remaining letters of the name. Production ceased after 1913. Our advisor for this category is John Danis; he is listed in the Directory under Illinois.

Bowl, band of owls, #30, 3¾", $395.00.
(Photo courtesy Cincinnati Art Galleries/LiveAuctioneers.com)

Candlesticks, snakes, verdrigris on bl, slim, #54, 11½", pr............ 300.00
Humidor, verdigris on bronze, Egyptian-revival snakes, animal ft, 8" ... 1,800.00

Mug, geometrics, patinated copper look, #51, ca 1909, 5x4¾"..... 165.00
Pedestal, women (hammered/tooled) on bronze, #98, 19x12", NM ..1,440.00
Urn, blk bronzed w/emb foliate branches, 4-hdl, #24, 9"...........1,325.00
Vase, Aztec birds & faces, verdigris on blk, 3-ftd, #62, 6½"..........780.00
Vase, Egyptian warrior & foe, verdigris on bronze, hdls, #10, 13"..1,200.00
Vase, snake heads/lions, verdigris on bronze, 3-ftd, #31, 5½".......515.00
Vase, tepees & water incised, verdigris on bronze, baluster, 9½x8"...780.00
Vase, verdigris on blk, 2 dragon hdls/3 dragon-head ft, 14" W..1,080.00
Vase, verdigris on bronze, appl salamander, trumpet neck, 11½x7"..1,200.00

North Dakota School of Mines

The School of Mines of the University of North Dakota was established in 1890, but due to a lack of funding it was not until 1898 that Earle J. Babcock was appointed as director, and efforts were made to produce ware from the native clay he had discovered several years earlier. The first pieces were made by firms in the east from the clay Babcock sent them. Some of the ware was decorated by the manufacturer; some was shipped back to North Dakota to be decorated by native artists. By 1909 students at the University of North Dakota were producing utilitarian items such as tile, brick, shingles, etc. in conjunction with a ceramic course offered through the chemistry department. By 1910 a ceramic department had been established, supervised by Margaret Kelly Cable. Under her leadership, fine artware was produced. Native flowers, grains, buffalo, cowboys, and other subjects indigenous to the state were incorporated into the decorations. Some pieces have an Art Nouveau – Art Deco style easily attributed to her association with Frederick H. Rhead, with whom she studied in 1911. During the '20s the pottery was marketed on a limited scale through gift and jewelry stores in the state. From 1927 until 1949 when Miss Cable announced her retirement, a more widespread distribution was maintained with sales branching out into other states. The ware was marked in cobalt with the official seal — 'Made at School of Mines, N.D. Clay, University of North Dakota, Grand Forks, N.D.' in a circle. Very early ware was sometimes marked 'U.N.D.' in cobalt by hand. Our advisor for this category is William M. Bilsland III; he is listed in the Directory under Iowa.

Bowl, band of tepees on a river front, Margaret Cable, 3½x7", $7,800.00.
(Photo courtesy David Rago Auctions)

Plate, man in sombrero on donkey, mc on gr, MEA/4/14/51, 9½"...840.00
Vase, band of figures holding hands, brn matt, D Nasset, 4½x4¾" ...1,300.00
Vase, daffodils, gr, J Mattson/M Cable, 5x5"...............................2,300.00
Vase, forest landscape, Thorne & Flora Huckfield, rstr chip, 10½"...8,400.00
Vase, irises (cvd), wht on indigo, S Mason, 1935, 8x5".............4,500.00
Vase, prairie rose, F Huckfield/student, #207, 5¾x5¼" 850.00
Vase, prairie rose, gr matt, M Cable, #44, 8½x5¾" 1,300.00
Vase, stylized flowers, yel on celadon, F Huckfield, 9¼x5¼"....10,250.00
Vase, stylized trees, brn on amber, ME Collins, 7¾x4¾"............4,500.00
Vase, tepees on geometric band, J Mattson, Elgin, 4¾x6" 800.00
Vase, Viking ships, bls/grs, J Mattson, #236, 3¾x4¼" 1,800.00

North State

In 1924 the North State Pottery of Sanford, North Carolina, began small-scale production, the result of the extreme fondness Mrs. Rebecca

Copper had for potting. With the help of her husband Henry and the abundance of suitable local clay, the pottery flourished and became well known for lovely shapes and beautiful glazes. They shared the knowledge they gained from their glaze experiments with the ceramic engineering department of North Carolina University, and during summer vacation they often employed some of the university students. Salt-glazed stoneware was produced in the early years but was quickly abandoned in favor of Henry's vibrant glazes. Colors of copper red, Chinese Red, moss green, and turquoise blue were used alone and in combination, producing bands of blending colors. Some swirl ware was made as well. The pottery was in business for 35 years; most of its ware was sold in gift and craft shops throughout North Carolina. Items in the following descriptions are earthenware unless noted salt glazed (stoneware) within the line.

Bowl, dbl-dip bl, flat loop hdls, 2nd mk, 4½x6" 120.00
Bowl, gr to crimson, free-form, 8" 36.00
Pitcher, bl-gr runs on bl, 2nd stamp, 6½" 155.00
Pitcher, refrigerator; Chinese Blue, high arched hdl, 8½" 360.00
Pitcher, turq bl, horizontal ribs, 5½" 72.50
Teapot, yel, w/lid, glaze chip, 6¾x7½x5" 300.00
Vase, Chinese Blue, att Walter Owen, 8⅜" 155.00
Vase, chrome red, sm loop hdls, 7" 395.00
Vase, dbl-dip bl on bl, rim-to-hip hdls, unmk, 8" 85.00
Vase, dbl-dip bl over dk gr, 2nd stamp, 6¾" 235.00
Vase, dk gr, loop hdls, 4¼" 72.50

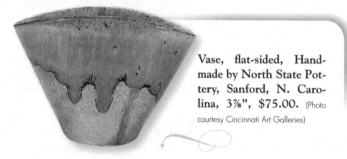

Vase, flat-sided, Handmade by North State Pottery, Sanford, N. Carolina, 3⅞", $75.00. (Photo courtesy Cincinnati Art Galleries)

Vase, salt glaze over cobalt, bulbous w/ruffled rim, 2nd mk, 8¼" .. 475.00
Vase, salt glaze w/dk brn drips, squat w/rolled rim, 5¼x6" 480.00
Vase, tan w/dk/red/bl/lt bl drips, 8⅜" 360.00
Vase, turq & gray matt, ovoid, att, 6½x5" 150.00

Northwood

The Northwood Company was founded in 1896 in Indiana, Pennsylvania, by Harry Northwood, whose father, John, was the art director for Stevens and Williams, an English glassworks. Northwood joined the National Glass Company in 1899 but in 1901 again became an independent contractor and formed the Harry Northwood Glass Company of Wheeling, West Virginia. He marketed his first carnival glass in 1908, and it became his most popular product. His company was also famous for its custard, goofus, and pressed glass. Northwood died in 1923, and the company closed. See also Carnival, Custard, Goofus, Opalescent, Pattern Glass.

Basket, mc pull-ups w/pk lining, ruffled rim, clear hdl/ft, 12x11¾"...1,150.00
Bowl, berry; Invt Fan & Feather, pk, 6½" 1,000.00
Bowl, Zipper, cranberry w/robin's-egg bl int, crimped rim, 3½" H ..1,450.00
Compote, Invt Fan & Feather, pk slag, ped ft w/4 toes, 5" 650.00
Cracker jar, Leaf Umbrella, cranberry to clear finial, 8¾" 2,350.00
Cruet, Invt Fan & Feather, pk slag, all orig................................... 900.00
Jug, claret, intaglio flowers/vines/thorns on clear, 10¼".............1,325.00
Pickle castor, Royal Ivy, rubena; Eastlake-style SP fr, 10½" 480.00

Pitcher, Royal Ivy, cranberry, 8½"..155.00
Sauce dish, Invt Fan & Feather, pk slag, scalloped, 4-ftd, 2½x4" ..200.00
Shaker, Nestor, amethyst, ca 1902-06, 3⅛", ea 95.00
Shaker, Quilted Phlox, lav, 3", ea from $165 to.......................... 180.00
Shaker, Wild Bouquet, lt bl w/slight opal, ca 1898-99, 3⅜", ea....250.00
Shakers, Leaf Umbrella, cranberry, 3", pr...................................... 300.00
Shakers, Parian Swirl, bl opaque, ca 1894-1896, 2¾", pr.............. 235.00
Sugar shaker, Leaf Umbrella, bl cased in wht, 4½" 240.00
Sugar shaker, Leaf Umbrella, pk & wht spatter, 4½" 550.00
Sugar shaker, Royal Ivy, rubena, 4⅜".. 155.00
Syrup pitcher, Leaf Mould, cranberry spatter, 6½" 265.00
Toothpick holder, Invt Fan & Feather, pk slag, flat 500.00
Toothpick holder, Invt Fan & Feather, pk slag, ftd...................1,500.00
Toothpick holder, Leaf Holder, Rose DuBarry, 2¼" 85.00
Toothpick holder, Leaf Mould, yel/red/wht spatter, 1⅞" 135.00
Toothpick holder, Leaf Umbrella, bl cased in wht, 2½" 215.00
Toothpick holder, Leaf Umbrella, cranberry, 2⅜x2¼" 265.00
Toothpick holder, Leaf Umbrella, cranberry frost, 2¼" 360.00
Tumbler, Invt Fan & Feather, pk slag 235.00
Tumbler, Leaf Umbrella, cranberry, 3¾".. 120.00
Vase, Zipper, salmon/apricot/peach hues, 10-rib baluster, 6¼" 900.00

Compote, Ribbon and Star, cobalt with gold trim, $75.00. (Photo courtesy Bill Edwards and Mike Carwile)

Norweta

Norweta pottery was produced by the Northwestern Terra Cotta Company of Chicago, Illinois. Both matt and crystalline glazes were employed, and terra cotta vases were also produced. It was made for approximately 10 years, beginning sometime before 1907. Not all were marked.

Doorstop, seated elf, 9x5", $400.00. (Photo courtesy David Rago Auctions)

Lamp base, stylized tulip, brn/gr/bl matt, 12¼x8"+mts..............2,150.00
Vase, bl & tan crystalline, flat shoulder, firing line, 8⅜" 1,200.00
Vase, bl & wht crystalline, shouldered, sm blisters, 4" 360.00
Vase, cobalt & beige crystalline, baluster, 8x5"...........................1,325.00
Vase, full-height leaves on turq matt w/brn clay showing, 8¼x5"....725.00

Nutcrackers

The nutcracker, though a strictly functional tool, is a good example of one to which man has applied ingenuity, imagination, and engineering skills. Though all were designed to accomplish the same end, hundreds of types exist in almost every material sturdy enough to withstand sufficient pressure to crack the nut. Figurals are popular collectibles, as are those with unusual design and construction. Patented examples are also desirable. For more information, we recommend *Nutcrackers* by Robert Mills.

Bear head, Black Forest cvg, glass eyes, ca 1900, 7½x3¾" 150.00
Dog, cast brass, tail activates jaws, Weiser Hdwe Mfg, 6½x11" 40.00
Dog, CI, flat blk pnt, tail activates jaw, 4x8", VG 50.00
Dog, CI, Harper Supply Co, late 19th C 50.00
Eagle head, CI w/pnt chips & losses, 7x7½x3" 75.00
Elephant, CI, orange-red pnt w/blk & wht details, twine tail, 10" ..100.00
Fox head, CI w/NP traces, walnut base, Pat June 1920, 6x10" 50.00
Koi fish, wood w/gouge-cvd eyes/scales/etc, articulated body, 8½" L ..110.00
Man in the moon, wood cvg, EX detail, hinged jaws, 5x5½x2" ...215.00
Man w/beard & cap, cvd walnut, articulated jaw & hdl, 8" L 110.00
Monkey seated, pnt wood, glass eyes, articulated jaw & hdl, 8½" ...200.00

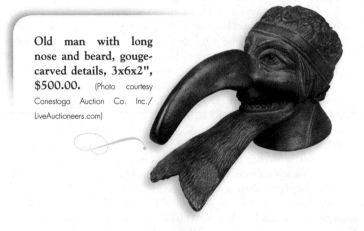

Old man with long nose and beard, gouge-carved details, 3x6x2", $500.00. (Photo courtesy Conestoga Auction Co. Inc./ LiveAuctioneers.com)

Parrot, pnt CI, tall hdl works beak, 5¼x10", NM 100.00
Prussian military man's head w/helmut & mustache, cvd wood, 9"..550.00
Rabbit head, Black Forest cvg, glass eyes, pnt mouth, 1900s, 7" ..275.00
Rabbit's head, glass eyes, pyro decor, folk art, 9" 275.00
Squirrel, CI, full figure w/tail hdl, 10x9x4" on wooden base 395.00
Squirrel, CI w/spring-loaded tail up, glass eyes 165.00
Squirrel w/nuts perched atop pliers style, cvd wood, 9½" 225.00
Woman's head, elderly w/head covering, cvd wood, European, 8" L ..145.00

Nutting, Wallace

Wallace Nutting (1861 – 1941) was America's most famous photographer of the early twentieth century. A retired minister, Nutting took more than 50,000 pictures, keeping 10,000 of his best and destroying the rest. His popular and bestselling scenes included exterior scenes (apple blossoms, country lanes, orchards, calm streams, and rural American countrysides), interior scenes (usually featuring a colonial woman working near a hearth), and foreign scenes (typically thatch-roofed cottages). His poorest selling pictures, which have become today's rarest and most highly collectible, are classified as miscellaneous unusual scenes and include categories not mentioned above: animals, architecturals, children, florals, men, seascapes, and snow scenes. Process prints are 1930s machine-produced reprints of 12 of Nutting's most popular pictures. These have minimal value and can be detected by using a magnifying glass.

Nutting sold literally millions of his hand-colored platinotype pictures between 1900 and his death in 1941. He started in Southbury, Connecticut, and later moved his business to Framingham, Massachusetts. The peak of Wallace Nutting picture production was 1915 – 1925. During this period Nutting employed nearly 200 people, including colorists, darkroom staff, salesmen, and assorted office personnel. Wallace Nutting pictures proved to be a huge commercial success and scarcely an American household was without one by 1925.

While attempting to seek out the finest and best early American furniture as props for his colonial interior scenes, Nutting became an expert in early American antiques. He published nearly 20 books in his lifetime, including his 10-volume *State Beautiful* series and various other books on furniture, photography, clocks, stools, chairs, settles, settees, tables, stands, desks, mirrors, beds, chests of drawers, cabinet pieces, and treenware. He made furniture as well, which he clearly marked with a distinctive paper label that was glued directly onto the piece, or a block or script signature brand which was literally branded into the furniture.

The overall synergy of the Wallace Nutting name — on pictures, books, and furniture — has made anything 'Wallace Nutting' quite collectible. Our advisor for this category is Michael Ivankovich, author of many books on Nutting: *The Collector's Guide to Wallace Nutting Pictures* and corresponding *Price Guide*, *The Alphabetical and Numerical Index to Wallace Nutting Pictures*, *Collector's Guide to Wallace Nutting Furniture*, *The Guide to Wallace Nutting Furniture*, *Collector's Value Guide to Early 20th Century Prints*, *The Guide to Wallace Nutting-Like Photographers of the Early 20th Century*, and *The Hand-Painted Pictures of Charles Henry Sawyer*. Mr. Ivankovich is also expert in Bessie Pease Gutmann, Maxfield Parrish, and R. Atkinson Fox and has written *Guide to Popular Early 20th Century Prints*, containing a wealth of information on their work. Mr. Ivankovich is listed in the Directory under Pennsylvania. Prices below are for pictures in good to excellent condition. Mat stains or blemishes, poor picture color or frame damage can decrease value significantly.

Books

England Beautiful, 2nd ed 45.00
Furniture of the Pilgrim Century 100.00
Ireland Beautiful 50.00
Maine Beautiful, 2nd ed 40.00
New Hampshire Beautiful, 2nd ed 40.00
Vermont Beautiful, 2nd ed 40.00
Wallace Nutting Biography 100.00

Furniture

Bed, mahog, #823-B 2,600.00
Butterfly table, #625 .... 2,200.00

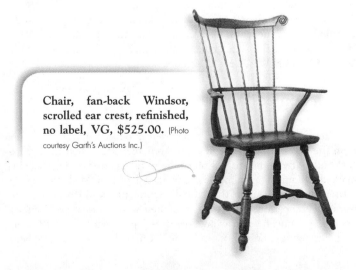

Chair, fan-back Windsor, scrolled ear crest, refinished, no label, VG, $525.00. (Photo courtesy Garth's Auctions Inc.)

Chaise lounge, adjustable bk, 43x75x23"	965.00
Country Dutch chair, #461	400.00
Hutch table, pine	825.00
Ladder-bk side chair, 4-rung, #392, block brand	475.00
Mirror, gold, 3-feather, #761, impressed brand	575.00
Table, Pembroke; #628	1,600.00
Table, refractory; oak, #601, block brand	935.00
Windsor armchair, 6-spindle fan-bk, bentwood arms, rfn, 41"	515.00
Windsor candlestand, tripod, #17, block brand	525.00
Windsor side chair, #301	525.00
Windsor side chair, maple, 9-spindle bk, orig label, #38X311, 45"	575.00
Windsor tenon arm chair, #422	1,500.00
Windsor writing-arm chair, #730	5,100.00
Winsor side chair, fan-bk, #310	750.00

Pictures

As It Was in 1700, 10x12"	360.00
Chair for John, 11x14"	180.00
Christmas Jelly, 7x13	500.00
Coming Out of Rosa, 13x16"	300.00
In Tenderleaf, 11x17"	150.00
Patti's Favorite Walk, 10x12"	275.00
Quilting Party, 11x14"	325.00

Ready for Callers, 13 x 16", in mat and frame, $150.00. (Photo courtesy Michael Ivankovich)

Stepping Heavenward, 29x19"	1,080.00
Sturdy Beauty, 29x19"	275.00
Summer Wind, 11x14"	185.00
Trimming the Pie, 7½x9"	240.00
Untitled river scene, 3x6¼"	120.00
Water Tracery	95.00
Where Grandma Was Wed	190.00

Occupied Japan

Items marked 'Occupied Japan' were produced during the period from the end of World War II until April 18, 1952, when the occupation ended. By no means was all of the ware exported during that time marked 'Occupied Japan'; some was marked 'Japan' or 'Made In Japan.' It is thought that because of the natural resentment felt by the Japanese toward the occupation, only a fraction of these wares carried the 'Occupied' mark. Even though you may find identical 'Japan'-marked items, because of its limited use, only those with the 'Occupied Japan' mark are being collected to any great extent. Values vary considerably, based on the quality of workmanship. Generally, bisque figures command much higher prices than porcelain, since on the whole they are of a finer quality.

Our advisor for this category is Florence Archambault; she is listed in the Directory under Rhode Island. She represents the Occupied Japan Club, whose mailing address may be found in the Directory under Clubs, Newsletters, and Catalogs. All items described in the following listings are common ceramic pieces unless noted otherwise.

Ashtray, dragon decor w/gold accents, from $3 to	5.00
Ashtray, floral on gr, from $2 to	3.00
Basket, figural bird hdl, from $10 to	12.00
Biscuit/cracker jar, tomato figural, Maruhonware, w/hdl, from $85 to	100.00
Bookends, girl seated w/watering can, 3½", from $25 to	30.00
Bookends, ship, emb wood, from $65 to	75.00
Bowl, cereal; Blue Willow, MIOJ, 5¾", from $13 to	16.00
Box, cigarette; Moss & Rose on wht, HP Andrea, from $8 to	10.00
Box, cigarette; wht w/pk rose & gold, from $10 to	13.00
Box, piano form, emb world w/wings on lid, metal, from $15 to	20.00
Cornucopia, w/seated angel, pastels, from $60 to	70.00
Creamer, bl floral band on wht, Aichi China, from $8 to	10.00
Cup & saucer, demi; floral medallion on rust, H Kato, from $13 to	16.00
Cup & saucer, ladies, red rim, Ardalt Lenwile China #6521, from $20 to	22.00
Doll, baby in red snowsuit, celluloid, from $40 to	50.00
Figurine, ballerina, Orion Pat #7672, 4¾", from $45 to	50.00
Figurine, boy seated playing guitar, from $4 to	5.00
Figurine, bulldog standing, from $18 to	20.00
Figurine, Cinderella & Prince Charming, Maruyama, 8", from $150 to	175.00
Figurine, cowgirl, from $8 to	10.00
Figurine, dog w/hat & pipe, 3½", from $8 to	10.00
Figurine, Dolly Dimples w/rabbit, from $10 to	13.00
Figurine, elf w/log, from $10 to	13.00
Figurine, frog w/accordion, sm, from $10 to	12.50
Figurine, girl w/feather in hair, bsk, 4½", from $10 to	12.00
Figurine, girl w/songbook, Ucagco, 5¾", from $35 to	40.00
Figurine, lady & man w/mandolin, 5", from $35 to	40.00
Figurine, lady in crinoline dress, #526, 5½", from $20 to	30.00
Figurine, lady w/fan & man w/hat, HP, 6½", from $50 to	60.00
Figurine, ladybug w/broom, #92796, from $10 to	13.00
Figurine, old lady gnome, 3¾", from $6 to	8.00
Figurine, Oriental lady w/basket on head, 8", from $25 to	28.00
Figurine, peacock w/head up & tail around feet, 5", from $18 to	20.00
Figurine, Spanish lady w/wide brim hat & basket, Ucagco, 7", from $35 to	40.00
Lamp, colonial couple seated, pastels, bsk, Maruyama, from $65 to	75.00
Pitcher, figural rooster, beak spout, tail hdl, from $23 to	26.00
Planter, dog w/blk spots, rainbow-like mk, 4½", from $6 to	8.00

Planter, duck, from $15.00 to $17.00. (Photo courtesy Cathy and Gene Florence)

Planter, shepherd boy & lamb beside well, from $8 to	10.00
Plate, cabin scene w/chickens, from $18 to	20.00
Plate, geisha girls at river's edge, #6078 Ardalt HP, from $25 to	30.00
Plate, lg yel flower on wht, gold rim, Ucagco, from $13 to	16.00
Plate, serving; floral on blk, papier-maché, Isco, from $8 to	12.00
Plate, yel floral on wht, sq w/hdls, JA in HP shield, from $8 to	10.00

Platter, Blue Willow, 12", from $30 to............................. 35.00
Platter, sm apple design on wht, Ucagco China, 15", from $20 to ...25.00
Saucer, alternating bl & floral on wht panels, Aiyo China, from $2 to.. 3.00
Saucer, orange flower on blk, from $2 to.............................3.00
Shakers, clown on drum, pr from $80 to 90.00
Shakers, strawberry, pr from $10 to 12.00
Stein, emb couple w/dog, twisted vine-like hdl, 8½", from $35 to . 40.00
Sugar bowl, sm apple design, Ucagco China in gold, from $10 to.. 13.00

Teapot, mustached man, 4½", from $35.00 to $40.00. (Photo courtesy Cathy and Gene Florence)

Teapot, pnt emb floral on brn, ornate hdl, from $35 to 40.00
Toy phone, floral decor, mini, from $5 to.........................8.00
Tray, floral, papier-maché, rectangular, from $15 to...................... 18.00
Vase, angel boy supports flower-form vase, pastels, 3½" 15.00
Vase, pnt emb dragon on blk w/gold, from 15 to................... 18.00
Wall pockets, colonial couple on lt gr bsk, 3½", pr from $20 to 25.00

Toy, baseball catcher, celluloid clockwork, 5¼", $65.00. (Photo courtesy Noel Barrett/LiveAuctioneers.com)

Ohr, George

Finding his vocation late in life, George Ohr set off in a two-year learning journey around 1880, visiting as many potteries as he could find in the 16 states he traveled through, including the Kirkpatrick brothers' Anna Pottery and Susan Frackelton's studio. Upon his return George built his Pot-Ohr-y, took a wife, made babies — some flesh, some clay. After a devestating fire destroyed a large section of the town in 1893, George rebuilt his homestead and studio and seemed to gain inspiration from new surroundings. His 'Mud Babies' became paper-thin, full of movement, wild ear-shaped handles, impish snakes, suggestive shapes, and inventive glazes. Ohr threw out the rules of folk pottery's sponge-glazing, covering only a section of a vessel with a particular color or pattern, mixing dead-matt greens or purples with bright yellow flambés, and topping it all in brown gunmetal drips. This was accomplished among the derisive smiles and lack of understanding he encountered from a society accustomed to the propriety of neo-Japanese wares such as Rookwood and Trenton Belleek or the plainness of salt-glazed stoneware.

About the time he decided to move away from branding his pots with one version or another of 'GEORGE E OHR, Biloxi, Miss.' and start signing them 'as if it were a check,' Ohr also came to the realization that he did not care to glaze them anymore. He appreciated the qualities of unadorned fired clays and enjoyed mixing different types, which he often dug from the neighboring Tchoutacabouffa river. His shapes became increasingly more abstract and modern, probably ostracizing him even more from a potential clientel, to whom he would relent to sell only his entire output of thousands of pieces at once.

Today George Ohr's legacy shines as the unequaled, unrivaled product of the preeminent art potter — iconaclast, inventive, multi-faceted, the first American abstract artist. Our advisors for this category are Suzanne Perrault and David Rago; they are listed in the Directory under New Jersey.

Bank, bsk, shaped as pouch, slot in side, 3x3"........................... 1,450.00
Beaker, Oriental flower branch, possibly meant to have hdl, 3x3" ...2,400.00
Bowl, marbleized bsk, pinched/folded, crenelated rim, rstr, 4x7½" ...2,760.00
Cup & saucer, demitasse; brushed yel leaves on gunmetal, w/price tag ...1,020.00
Hat novelty, speckled gunmetal on amber, 3¼x3¼" 2,000.00

Inkwell, bayou home with picket fence, fine amber and green glaze, 3½x6x4½", $72,00.00. (Photo courtesy David Rago Auctions)

Loving cup, amber/indigo/raspberry/gr/gunmetal, 3-hdl, rstr, 4x6½" ..7,800.00
Pitcher, bsk, 2 deep in-body twists, ribbon hdl, 5¼" 6,600.00
Puzzle mug, gr & gunmetal mottle, floral hdl, 3½x5" 900.00
Token, terra cotta, emb message, 1¼" dia, 5 for 1,200.00
Vase, blk & brn sponging on gr speckled, stovepipe neck, 4½" ..4,500.00
Vase, blk gloss w/swirling gr/wht highlights, swollen, 3¾".........1,200.00
Vase, brn & gr sponging, squat w/flared rim, 2¾x4¼" 1,440.00
Vase, brn-speckled khaki gr & orange, sm chip, 5x3½" 1,200.00
Vase, bsk, deep in-body twist/folded rim, str walls, 4¼x3" 2,000.00
Vase, cobalt & brn sponging on wht clay, incurvate rim, 2½x3½" ...2,650.00
Vase, cobalt w/gr mottle, dimpled shoulder, lobed neck, 3½x5¼" . 13,200.00
Vase, copper gunmetal w/orange int, pinched/notched/folded, 4¼", NM . 7,200.00
Vase, dk bl-gray, in-body twist, floriform folds, 3x4¼", NM 7,800.00

Vase, exhibiting several test glazes, deep in-body twist, 3½x4½", $15,600.00. (Photo courtesy David Rago Auctions)

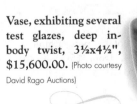

Vase, gr & amber mottle, re-glazed rim, 6¼x3½" 1,200.00
Vase, gr & indigo gunmetal, milk-can shape w/snake, curled hdl, 6" .. 15,600.00
Vase, gunmetal, pinched corners at rim, ftd, 3x5½"................... 2,280.00
Vase, gunmetal & brn speckles on gr, squat, 3x4½" 2,150.00
Vase, gunmetal & gr, folded rim, 4¾x2¾" 4,800.00

Vase, gunmetal & gr speckles, in-body twist, spherical, 3½x3¾" ...6,000.00
Vase, gunmetal brn, deep dimples, bottle form, 4x2½" 1,550.00
Vase, gunmetal brn speckled, 2 ribbon hdls, 4½x4" 5,400.00
Vase, gunmetal to mottled gr on beige, pie-crust rim, 3¼x6" 5,400.00
Vase, gunmetal w/tortoise-shell int, dimpled, closed-in rim, 3x5¼" ...3,350.00
Vase, indigo, baluster, 3¾x2¼" 1,550.00
Vase, marbleized forest gr, 2½x3" 1,560.00
Vase, mc drips on mottled leathery matt, folded rim, 4¾x5" ...36,000.00
Vase, mirrored cobalt w/gunmetal base, pinched rim, 4½x4½"..5,000.00
Vase, mottled gunmetal brn, closed-in rim, 3½x5" 1,450.00
Vase, orange/raspberry/gr/cobalt sponging, twist at rim, 3x4"....6,000.00
Vase, red & gr matt, bulbous, 1905, 4x3½" 600.00
Vase, volcanic raspberry w/gr int, low, 2¼x4" 5,400.00
Vessel, multi-tone brn, single hdl, pierced sides, 3½" 1,600.00

Old Ivory

Old Ivory dinnerware was produced from 1882 to 1920 by Herman Ohme, of Lower Salzbrunn in Silesia. The patterns are referred to by the numbers stamped on the bottom of most pieces. There are some early patterns with no number, but these seem to be stamped with a blank name. The factory mark most often seen is a small fleur-de-lis sometimes having either Silesia, Germany, or Prussia under it. The handwritten numbers are artist identification or manufacturing numbers, not the pattern number. Patterns #16 and #84, being the easiest to find, have seen a decline in value with the popularity of internet sales. The patterns with flowers in pink, lavender, yellow, and some pieces with fruit decor bring higher prices at this time. These are still on the soft ivory background, Worn gold and any damage will certainly reduce the value of any item unless it is extremely rare. Holly patterns remain very desirable and command 70% to 200% more than the more common patterns, Beware of copy-cat pieces produced by other manufacturers. They are not included in this listing. Also note that portrait vases have retained their high prices, even with the finding of more and different shapes.

The clear glazed hotel ware by Ohme is steadily climbing in popularity and price. We have included some pieces in this finish for comparison. There are many more shapes and patterns of the clear glaze than the Old Ivory. Even a few experimental pieces have shown up. One such piece is a tapestry (similar to Royal Bayreuth tapestry) pickle dish.

For more information, we recommend *Collector's Encyclopedia of Old Ivory China, The Mystery Explored,* by Alma Hillman (our advisor), David Goldschmitt, and Adam Szynkiewicz. Ms. Hillman is listed in the Directory under Maine.

Chocolate pot, Empire, #134, from $500.00 to $700.00. (Photo courtesy Alma Hillman)

Basket, #134, oblong, 8", from $300 to 425.00
Bowl, berry; #7, 5", from $25 to.. 45.00

Bowl, ftd, #28, 6", from $200 to.. 300.00
Bowl, vegetable; #15, oval, 9½", from $125 to............................. 185.00
Butter dish, w/insert, #16, 7½", from $700 to.............................. 800.00
Cake plate, #122, open hdls, 10" or 11", ea from $175 to............ 275.00
Celery dish, #10, 11¼", from $100 to 195.00
Coffeepot, #84, Deco variant, from $1,200 to............................1,500.00
Compote, #U2, 9", from $500 to 700.00
Compote, #U3, 9", from $600 to 1,000.00
Cup & saucer, chocolate; #16, 2¼", from $95 to......................... 125.00
Cup & saucer, demitasse; #84, 2½", from $100 to........................ 150.00
Cup & saucer, tea; #7, 3¼", from $65 to 85.00
Dish, #200, 3-lobed, 6", from $50 to... 95.00
Egg cup, #16, 2½", from $450 to.. 700.00
Jam jar, #200, 3½", from $200 to 400.00
Plate, coupe; #75, 6¼", from $50 to 75.00
Plate, dinner; #11, 9½" or 10", from $200 to................................ 275.00
Porringer, #32, 6¼", from $75 to 150.00
Shakers, #75, 2¾", pr from $100 to 150.00
Sugar bowl, #22, 5½", from $100 to 200.00

Clear-Glazed Hotelware by Hermann Ohme, Various Floral Patterns

Because of climbing values for Old Ivory, interest is growing for the clear-glazed pieces by Ohme, which are still reasonable, though escalating in price. It was produced between 1882 and 1928 in Niedersalzbrunn, Selesia, Germany (now western Poland). The body of the ware was white, and many of the Old Ivory patterns and shapes were utilized. It is often marked with the blue fleur-de-lis stamp. In comparison, while an Old Ivory open-handled cake plate might sell for $125.00 to $145.00, a comparable clear-glazed example might go for $45.00 to $55.00 with the same mark.

Chocolate pot, Worcester blank, from $65 to.............................. 150.00
Creamer & sugar bowl, Eglantine blank, from $35 to.................... 75.00
Cup & saucer, mustache; Eglantine blank, from $100 to.............. 250.00
Gravy boat, Deco blank, from $35 to 50.00
Plate, dinner; Alice blank, 9¾", from $25 to 45.00
Spittoon, Worchester blank, from $150 to.................................... 300.00
Teapot, Dresden decor, sm, from $250 to 350.00

Teapot, Dresden Swirl, decorated, from $350.00 to $450.00. (Photo courtesy Alma Hillman)

Teapot, Mignon blank, from $75 to.. 150.00
Vase, Elysee blank, 12", from $100 to.. 200.00
Vase, Eylsee blank, 14", from $200 to.. 300.00

Old Paris

Old Paris porcelains were made from the mid-eighteenth century until about 1900. Seldom marked, the term refers to the area of manufacture rather than a specific company. In general, the ware was of high quality, characterized by classic shapes, colorful decoration, and gold application.

Biscuit jar, floral on wht, SP mts & lid (worn), 7½x6" 45.00
Bonbonnier, flower sprays on wht w/gold, ped ft, w/lid, 7¼x6x6".. 300.00
Bottle, scent; floral reserves & gold on wht, ped ft, 5" 135.00
Bottle, wht cylinder w/gold at rim, ball stopper, 8" 72.50
Bowl, center; florals & gold on gr, ornate hdls/ft, 10½x16" 425.00
Bowl, center; rtcl border & base, gold & wht, 12x15" 425.00
Bowl, Neoclassical decor, boat style, 1810s, 2¾x12x8¾".............. 575.00
Box, gr w/bronze mts, rectangular, early 20th C, 6" L.................. 360.00
Box, wht w/metal mts, hinged lid, 4x5x3" 425.00
Charger, floral sprays & reserves w/gold, ca 1840, 16" 300.00
Crocus pot, floral reserves w/gold, 1890s, missing liner, 6x9x4" ... 375.00
Dessert set, gilt floral bouquet, 1870s, 2 9" tazzas+11 plates 415.00
Dish, shell form w/gold lobster dividing center, 1890s, 5x14x10"....300.00
Figurine, parrot on base, EX detail/color, 19th C, rprs, 14x8", pr. 660.00

Garniture vases, figural cartouche, ca 1860s, 21", $1,265.00. (Photo courtesy Neal Auction Company Auctioneers & Appraisers of Fine Art)

Inkstand, scrolled shell on ped, no inserts, 1850s, 6½x9x7½" 360.00
Lantern, yel w/dolphin stem, 20th C, 16", pr.................................. 425.00
Salt cellar, bl w/glass liner, Nouveau rtcl metal fr, 1¾x3" 110.00
Sauceboat, floral reserves on bl, grapes finial, 19th C, 7x10", NM ..350.00
Teapot, seaside village scene w/gold borders & finial, 19th C, 10½" ..575.00
Tray, roses form wreath on wht, pierced scroll hdls, 19th C, 15" dia ..300.00
Tureen, wht w/gold borders & scroll hdls, shell finial, 19th C, 10" L .660.00
Urn, floral resseves on gold, ornate gold griffin hdls, 1820s, 13", pr....600.00
Urn, lady's portrait reserve, low hdls, wht ped base, 19th C, 11", pr....660.00
Urn, scenic reserves w/gold, low uptrn hdls, 1820s, 19x12" 725.00
Urns, landscape scenic w/gold, low hdls, 1880s, rprs, 9x7", pr...... 600.00
Vase, figures in reserves w/much gold, ornate rtcl hdls, 19th C, 18x8"..425.00
Vase, floral reserves on wht w/much gold, 19th C, 14", pr............ 600.00
Vase, gr, baluster, 19½" 425.00
Vase, musicians/lovers w/much gold on wht, low hdls, 11", pr 660.00
Vase, pastoral scenes/flowers/vines/fruit, much gold, 19th C, 22", pr..550.00
Vase, pk, baluster, 4½" 48.00
Vase, scenic reserve w/gold on pk, ornate hdls, 19th C, 13½", pr. 360.00

Old Sleepy Eye

Old Sleepy Eye was a Sioux Indian chief who was born in Minnesota in 1780. His name was used for the name of a town as well as a flour mill. In 1903 the Sleepy Eye Milling Company of Sleepy Eye, Minnesota, contracted the Weir Pottery Company of Monmouth, Illinois, to make steins, vases, salt crocks, and butter tubs which the company gave away to their customers. A bust profile of the old Indian and his name decorated each piece of the blue and gray stoneware. In addition to these four items, the Minnesota Stoneware Company of Red Wing made a mug with a verse which is very scarce today.

In 1906 Weir Pottery merged with six others to form the Western Stoneware Company in Monmouth. They produced a line of blue and white ware using a lighter body, but these pieces were never given as flour premiums. This line consisted of pitchers (five sizes), steins, mugs, sugar

bowls, vases, trivets, and mustache cups. These pieces turn up only rarely in other colors and are highly prized by advanced collectors. Advertising items such as trade cards, pillow tops, thermometers, paperweights, letter openers, postcards, cookbooks, and thimbles are considered very valuable. The original ware was made sporadically until 1937. Brown steins and mugs were produced in 1952. Our advisor for this category is Jim Martin; he is listed in the Directory under Illinois.

Barrel, flour; orig paper label, 1920s 1,000.00
Barrel, grapevine-effect banding..2,500.00
Barrel, oak w/brass bands 3,000.00
Barrel label, mk Chief/Strong Bakers, image in center, 16", NM .. 175.00
Barrel label, mk Cream, red circle, many repros 170.00
Blanket, horse, w/logo, EX...1,000.00
Butter crock, Flemish bl & gray, from $400 to 600.00
Cabinet, bread display; Old Sleepy Eye etched in glass 950.00
Calendar, 1904, NM 375.00
Cookbook, Indian on cover, Sleepy Eye Milling Co, 4¾x4" 200.00
Cookbook, loaf-of-bread shape, NM 120.00
Coupon, for ordering cookbook.. 200.00
Dough scraper, tin/wood, To Be Sure, EX 300.00
Fan, die-cut image of Old Sleepy Eye, EX+.................................. 200.00
Flour sack, cloth, mc Indian, red letters 345.00
Flour sack, paper, Indian in blk, blk lettering, NM....................... 125.00
Hot plate/trivet, bl & wht 2,000.00
Ink blotter 125.00
Letter opener, bronze 500.00
Match holder, pnt 800.00
Match holder, wht 850.00
Mug, bl & gray, 4¼" 300.00
Mug, bl & wht, 4¼" 150.00
Mug, verse, Red Wing, EX...1,200.00
Mustache cup, bl & wht, very rare 3,000.00
Paperweight, bronzed company trademk.. 300.00
Pillow cover, Sleepy Eye & tribe meet President Monroe 500.00
Pillow cover, trademk center w/various scenes, 22", NM 800.00
Pin-bk button, Indian, rnd face.. 250.00
Pitcher, bl & gray, 5" 300.00
Pitcher, bl & wht, #1, ½-pt... 150.00
Pitcher, bl & wht, #2, 1-pt.. 200.00
Pitcher, bl & wht, #3, w/bl rim, 1-qt 800.00
Pitcher, bl & wht, #3, 1-qt.. 275.00
Pitcher, bl & wht, #4, ½-gal.. 300.00
Pitcher, bl & wht, #5, 1-gal 350.00

Pitchers, from #1 to #5 (3½" to 9"), blue and white, see line listings for values.

Pitcher, bl on cream, 8", M.................................220.00
Pitcher, brn on yel, Sesquicentennial, 1981, from $100 to...........125.00
Pitcher, standing Indian, good color..................1,000.00
Postcard, colorful trademk, 1904 Expo Winner........185.00
Ruler, wooden, 15".......................................700.00
Salt crock, Flemish bl & gray, 4x6½"...............500.00
Sheet music, in fr......................................200.00
Sign, litho on paper, Indian in center, 'chief' below, 1910s, oak fr, 21" dia..1,200.00
Sign, self-fr tin, portrait w/multiple scenes on border, 24x20", G ..4,000.00
Sign, tin litho die-cut Indian, ...Flour & Cereals, 13½"............1,650.00
Spoon, demitasse; emb roses in bowl, Unity SP..........60.00
Spoon, Indian-head hdl....................................70.00
Stein, bl & wht, 7¾".....................................500.00
Stein, Board of Directors, all yrs, 40-oz.............265.00
Stein, Board of Directors, 1969, 22-oz...............350.00
Stein, brn, 1952, 22-oz...................................150.00
Stein, brn & wht.......................................1,000.00
Stein, brn & yel, Western Stoneware mk..............1,000.00
Stein, chestnut, 40-oz, 1952.............................200.00
Stein, cobalt..800.00
Stein, Flemish bl on gray...............................500.00
Stein, ltd edition, 1979-84, ea..........................125.00
Sugar bowl, bl & wht, 3"................................500.00
Thermometer, front rpl..................................600.00
Vase, cattails, all cobalt..............................700.00
Vase, cattails, bl & wht, good color, 9"..............500.00
Vase, cattails, brn on yel, rare color...............1,000.00
Vase, cattails, gr & wht, rare........................1,500.00
Vase, Indian & cattails, Flemish bl & gray, 8½"......250.00

Vase, Indian and cattails, Flemish, 10½", $250.00.

(Photo courtesy Tom Harris Auctions)

O'Neill, Rose

Rose O'Neill's Kewpies were introduced in 1909 when they were used to conclude a story in the December issue of *Ladies' Home Journal*. They were an immediate success, and soon Kewpie dolls were being produced worldwide. German manufacturers were among the earliest and also used the Kewpie motif to decorate chinaware as well as other items. The Kewpie is still popular today and can be found on products ranging from Christmas cards and cake ornaments to fabrics, wallpaper, and metal items. In the following listings, 'sgn' indicates that the item is signed Rose O'Neill. The copyright symbol is also a good mark. Unsigned items can sometimes be of interest to collectors as well, Many are authentic and collectible; some are just too small to sign. Unless noted othewise, our values are for examples in at least near mint condition with no chips or repairs. Our advisors for this category are Don and Anne Kier; they are listed in the Directory under Ohio.

Bowl, Kewpies in meadow, Royal Rudolstadt, 6¼"...........75.00

Card, Klever Kard, bride & groom w/verse, ca 1915, EX...............75.00
Cup & saucer, Kewpies in meadow on bl, Royal Rudolstadt........135.00
Cup & saucer, Kewpies on wht w/pk-tint edges, Germany............65.00
Dresser box, bsk, Kewpie on lid, 4½", EX...............165.00
Feeding dish, 8 action kewpies, Royal Rudolstadt, 1⅝x7¾".........180.00

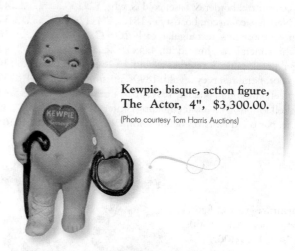

Kewpie, bisque, action figure, The Actor, 4", $3,300.00.

(Photo courtesy Tom Harris Auctions)

Kewpie, bsk, action figure, Black Hottentot, Germany, rare, 5"...575.00
Kewpie, bsk, action figure, Carpenter, tool apron, Germany, 8½"..1,100.00
Kewpie, bsk, action figure, crawler, eye shut/ft up, #487SJ/76, 2½"..130.00
Kewpie, bsk, action figure, German Soldier, movable arms, Germany, 4"..2,765.00
Kewpie, bsk, action figure, held by bear, Germany, 3½"..............275.00
Kewpie, bsk, action figure, Jester in wht hat, 4½", minimum value..850.00
Kewpie, bsk, action figure, kneeling, Germany, 4".......................600.00
Kewpie, bsk, action figure, nude holding drawstring bag, #4882, 4½"...1,105.00
Kewpie, bsk, action figure, Red Cross w/dog, Germany, 4"...........300.00
Kewpie, bsk, action figure, Roughrider, jtd arms, Germany, 5½"...2,750.00
Kewpie, bsk, action figure, Sailor, USN on hat, 4½"...................300.00
Kewpie, bsk, action figure, Santa hat/hands on hips, Jesco, 4", MIB..60.00
Kewpie, bsk, action figure, seated in gr chair holding book, 5½"..3,900.00
Kewpie, bsk, action figure, seated w/chick, Germany, 2".............530.00
Kewpie, bsk, action figure, seated w/turkey at ft, 2½"..................425.00
Kewpie, bsk, action figure, Traveler w/umbrella & bag, Germany, 5"..475.00
Kewpie, bsk, action figure, w/baby & bottle, Germany, 3½"......5,400.00
Kewpie, bsk, action figure, Writer, pen in hand, Germany...........550.00
Kewpie, bsk, action figure in striped bathing suit, w/pail, 4½", EX..2,050.00
Kewpie, bsk, immobile, bl wings, pnt hair, Germany, 6"..............250.00
Kewpie, bsk, jtd hips & shoulders, Germany, 7"........................750.00
Kewpie, bsk, jtd shoulders, Germany, 2"................................85.00
Kewpie, bsk, jtd shoulders, molded clothing article, Germany, 6"..295.00
Kewpie, bsk, nude seated on log w/mandolin & dog, #7709, 2x3½"..1,700.00
Kewpie, cast steel on sq base, 5½"....................................55.00
Kewpie, celluloid, bride & groom, 4"..................................40.00
Kewpie, cloth, Krueger Cuddle Kewpie, silk-screened face, 13"...600.00

Kewpie, composition, Cameo, 24", M, $500.00 for the pair.

(Photo courtesy Dunbar Galleries)

Kewpie, compo, jtd shoulders, Hottentot, heart decal, ca 1946, 11" ... 595.00
Kewpie, compo, jtd shoulders, rnd bl base, 13" 325.00
Kewpie, soft rubber, Cameo, 9½" 45.00
Kewpie, vinyl, molded in 1 pc, 9" 25.00
Kewpie Doodle Dog, blk & wht w/bl wings, 3" 2,200.00
Napkin ring, Kewpie beside ring, sterling, P&B, 2½x1½" dia 210.00
Newspaper clipping, Kewpie Korner, 1 Black & 1 wht Kewpie w/verse, EX. 40.00
Newspaper comic, Tom, Dick & Harry Meet the Kewpies, full pg, 1918. 40.00
Paper dolls, Kewpie Kutouts, Little Assunta w/doll, 1913 magazine pg.. 20.00
Pin box, bsk, Kewpie in bed, 2¾x3" 550.00
Pitcher, jasperware, Kewpies playing, Germany, 4¼" 245.00
Plate, bl jasperware, 5 Kewpies, 3 groups of flowers, heart shape, 7".185.00
Plate, Kewpies playing in meadow, Royal Rudolstadt, 7¾" 85.00
Saucer, Kewpies playing in meadow, Royal Rudolstadt, 5" 60.00
Tea set, child's; Kewpies on bl w/brn shading, Germany, 23-pc, MIB . 3,125.00

Tea tile, Royal Rudolstadt, copyright Rose O'Neill, 5¾", 125.00; Pitcher, 4½", 135.00.

(Photo courtesy Tom Harris Auctions/ LiveAuctioneers.com)

Tray, Leaning Tree, 6 action Kewpies, Royal Rudolstadt, 10" dia.. 180.00
Trinket box, jasperware w/3 Kewpies on ea side, 4 on lid, 3¼" 130.00
Trinket box, Kewpie stands on sm boat, Royal Rudolstadt, 1⅝x2¼" ... 360.00

Onion Pattern

The familiar pattern known to collectors as Onion acquired its name through a case of mistaken identity. Designed in the early 1700s by Johann Haroldt of the Meissen factory in Germany, the pattern was a mixture of earlier Oriental designs. One of its components was a stylized peach, which was mistaken for an onion; as a result, the pattern became known by that name. Usually found in blue, an occasional piece may also be found in pink and red. The pattern is commonly associated with Meissen, but it has been reproduced by many others including Villeroy and Boch, Hutchenreuther, and Royal Copenhagen (whose pattern is a variation of the standard design).

Many marks have been used, some of them fraudulent Meissen marks. Study a marks book to become more familiar with them. In our listings, 'Xd swords' indicates first-quality old Meissen ware. Meissen in an oval over a star was a mark of C. Teichert Stove and Porcelain Factory of Meissen; it was used from 1882 until about 1930. Items marked simply Meissen were produced by the State's Porcelain Manufactory VEB after 1972. The crossed swords indication was sometimes added. Today's market abounds with quality reproductions.

Blue Danube is a modern line of Onion-patterned dinnerware produced in Japan and distributed by Lipper International of Wallingford, Connecticut. At least 100 items are available in porcelain; it is sold in most large stores with china departments.

Bottle, scent; rose finial, Xd swords, 4½", pr 210.00
Bowl, basketweave rim w/4 cartouches, Xd swords, 2x12x9"........ 175.00

Bowl, cereal; Blue Danube, banner mk, 6" 20.00
Bowl, Japan, 7" 12.00
Bowl, rice; Blue Danube, 2½x4½", from $25 to 30.00
Bowl, rimmed soup; Blue Danube, banner mk, 8¼", from $15 to... 20.00
Bowl, sq w/scalloped edge, Xd swords, 10½" 235.00
Bowl, vegetable; Blue Danube, divided, rectangular mk, 10¾" L . 40.00
Butter dish, Blue Danube, rectangular mk, 8½" dia, from $55 to ... 65.00
Cake plate, pierced hdls, Xd swords, 10¾" 145.00
Candy dish, Blue Danube, 5-sided, open lattice border, 2x7½" 22.00
Canister, Prunes on central wht band, Germany, 5¾" 300.00
Casserole, Blue Danube, banner mk, w/lid, 8" dia 70.00
Chocolate pot, Vienna Woods, 9¾" 45.00
Coaster, Blue Danube, 3½", from $5 to 7.00
Compote, rtcl border, Xd swords, 6x7" 85.00
Creamer, German clover mk, 3¾" 30.00
Creamer, 3-ftd, gold at rim, Xd swords, 5", from $115 to 130.00
Creamer & sugar bowl, Blue Danube, 'Y' hdls, 4¾", 3½", $28 to .. 42.00
Cup, bouillon; 2-hdl, Xd swords, 2½x3¼", +underplate 125.00
Cup & saucer, demi; Xd swords, 1¾", from $100 to 125.00
Cup & saucer, Royal Copenhagen, ribbed 35.00
Cup & saucer, Xd swords, 2", 5¾" 75.00

Dessert stand, three-tier with gentleman as finial, under-glaze Meissen marks, 22x11", $2,650.00. (Photo courtesy Neal Auction Company Auctioneers & Appraisers of Fine Art/ LiveAuctioneers.com)

Dish, Hutschenreuther, sq, 2x9" 35.00
Dish, triangular, Xd swords, 10" 375.00
Funnel, unmk, 5½x3¾" 35.00
Gravy boat, Blue Danube, fancy hdl, banner mk, 6½x9¾" 45.00
Mug, Coffee on wht band, Xd arrows (Japan) 15.00
Pie server, Blue Danube, pistol-grip hdl, 10½" 25.00
Pitcher, milk; 3-ftd, Xd swords, 6½" 125.00
Plate, Hutschenreuther, sq, 8⅜" 25.00
Plate, rtcl basketweave rim, Xd swords, 8" 85.00
Plate, Xd swords, 9½" 110.00
Platter, Blue Danube, banner mk, 16x11", from $75 to 90.00
Platter, oval, Huschenreuther, 15x10" 75.00

Platter, upturned handles, #22, blue under-glaze crossed swords mark, 13", $125.00. (Photo courtesy DuMouchelles/ LiveAuctioneers.com)

Platter, w/SP warmer/ft/hdls, bird mk/#51, 16" 285.00
Potato masher, ball end w/long trn wood hdl, 13" 80.00
Relish, 2-part, joined shells w/center hdl, Xd swords, 2x10¾x9"... 300.00
Relish, 4-part, center hdl, Xd swords, 15" dia 450.00
Smoker's set, cigarette jar, w/lid, Japan, 5¾", +2 3¼" ashtrays........ 70.00
Spoon, serving; Xd swords, 8½" 90.00
Spoon rest, hourglass shape, Xd arrows, 5½x9½" 30.00
Steak knives, Blue Danube, Sheffield, set of 6, MIB 95.00
Teapot, bulbous, rose finial, Xd swords, 5¼x9¼", from $165 to.... 185.00
Teapot, German clover mk, 5½" 85.00
Tray, hdls, oval mk w/star, Meissen #25, 14x9" 200.00
Tray, shaped rim w/pierced hdls, sq, Germany, 10¼" 125.00
Tureen, Meissen in oval, w/lid & attached tray, 5¾x9x5⅜"........... 70.00
Tureen, vegetable; Cauldon, w/lid, 8x11" 125.00

Opalescent Glass

First made in England in 1870, opalescent glass became popular in America around the turn of the century. Its name comes from the milky-white opalescent trim that defines the lines of the pattern. It was produced in table sets, novelties, toothpick holders, vases, and lamps. Note that American-made sugar bowls have lids; sugar bowls of British origin are considered to be complete without lids. For further information we recommend *Standard Encyclopedia of Opalescent Glass* by Bill Edwards and Mike Carwile (Collector Books). See also Sugar Shakers; Syrup Pitchers; etc.

Abalone, bowl, gr... 35.00
Abalone, bowl, wht... 25.00
Acorn Burrs (& Bark), bowl, sauce; bl.. 60.00
Acorn Burrs (& Bark), bowl, sauce; wht.. 30.00
Ala-Bock, candy dish, vaseline or canary 100.00
Ala-Bock, rose bowl, bl.. 130.00
Ala-Bock, tumbler, vaseline 35.00
Alaska, bowl, master; bl.. 145.00
Alaska, bowl, master; wht... 75.00
Alaska, shakers, wht, pr... 90.00
Albany Reverse Swirl, sugar shaker, canary 135.00
Albany Reverse Swirl, water bottle, wht...................................... 115.00
Arabian Nights, pitcher, wht... 285.00
Arabian Nights, syrup, wht... 185.00
Argonaut Shell (Nautilus), bowl, sauce; bl.................................. 45.00
Argonaut Shell (Nautilus), compote, jelly; vaseline or canary, mk .. 125.00

Argonaut Shell, sauce dish, blue, $45.00. (Photo courtesy Bill Edwards and Mike Carwile)

Argonaut Shell (Nautilus), spooner, bl.. 200.00
Argus (Thumbprint), compote, gr.. 95.00
Ascot, biscuit jar, bl.. 175.00
Ascot, biscuit jar, vaseline or canary 160.00
Autumn Leaves, nappy, wht.. 125.00
Band & Rib (Threaded Optic), rose bowl, wht.............................. 30.00
Banded Hobnail, bottle, dresser; bl... 75.00
Barbells, bowl, gr.. 40.00
Barbells, vase, gr.. 50.00
Basketweave (Open Edge), nappy, bl... 35.00
Basketweave (Open Edge), plate, vaseline.................................... 100.00

Beaded Block, celery vase, gr.. 75.00
Beaded Block, sugar bowl, wht.. 75.00
Beaded Cable, rose bowl, gr, ftd.. 60.00
Beaded Fleur de Lis, compote, bl or gr.. 50.00
Beaded Fleur de Lis, compote, wht.. 45.00
Beaded Ovals in Sand, cruet, gr... 225.00
Beaded Ovals in Sand, toothpick holder, wht.............................. 125.00
Beaded Stars & Swag, plate, advertising; bl................................ 450.00
Beaded Stars & Swag, rose bowl, gr.. 60.00
Beatty Honeycomb, celery vase, bl.. 80.00
Beatty Honeycomb, creamer, wht.. 50.00
Beatty Honeycomb, mustard pot, wht.. 75.00
Beatty Honeycomb, tumbler, bl.. 50.00
Beatty Rib, bowl, master; bl... 55.00
Beatty Rib, cracker jar, bl.. 125.00
Beatty Rib, salt cellar, wht.. 45.00
Beatty Rib, tumbler, wht.. 30.00
Beatty Swirl, bowl, sauce; wht... 20.00
Beatty Swirl, butter dish, wht... 150.00
Beatty Swirl, celery vase, bl... 75.00
Beatty Swirl, mug, canary.. 85.00
Beaumont Stripe, pitcher, vaseline or canary.............................. 350.00
Belmont Swirl, tumbler, gr... 70.00
Blackberry Spray, hat, amethyst... 85.00
Blooms & Blossoms, nappy, gr, hdl... 50.00
Blown Drapery, sugar shaker, wht... 300.00
Blown Drapery, vase, gr... 85.00
Blown Twist, pitcher, cranberry... 900.00
Blown Twist, syrup, cranberry... 400.00
Blown Twist, tumbler, cranberry.. 125.00
Brideshead, butter dish, bl... 100.00
Brideshead, tray, oval, bl.. 125.00
Brideshead, tray, vaseline, oval.. 120.00
Broken Pillar (& Reed), compote, bl... 160.00
Bubble Lattice, finger bowl, canary.. 45.00
Bubble Lattice, toothpick holder, wht.. 150.00
Bulbous Base Coinspot, syrup, wht.. 110.00
Bull's Eye, bowl, bl... 50.00
Bull's Eye, lamp shade, wht... 40.00
Butterfly & Lily, epergne, bl or gr... 150.00
Button Panels, bowl, wht.. 35.00
Buttons & Braids, bowl, cranberry.. 110.00
Buttons & Braids, pitcher, bl.. 200.00
Cabash, bowl... 120.00
Cane & Diamond Swirl, tray, vaseline or canary, stemmed........... 70.00
Cane Rings, bowl, bl, 8½"... 75.00
Cane Rings, creamer, vaseline.. 65.00
Casbah, compote, wht.. 45.00
Cherry, wine, bl... 80.00
Chippendale, basket, canary.. 80.00
Chippendale, basket, vaseline or canary 80.00
Chippendale, plate, vaseline or canary, 6¼".................................. 95.00
Christmas Pearls, cruet, gr.. 280.00

Christmas Snowflake, pitcher, cranberry, 9", $2,400.00. (Photo courtesy Green Valley Auctions Inc.)

Chrysanthemum Base Swirl, cruet, wht 200.00
Chrysanthemum Base Swirl, mustard pot, wht 120.00
Circled Scroll, bowl, sauce; gr 50.00
Circled Scroll, butter dish, bl 475.00
Circled Scroll, creamer, gr 95.00
Circled Scroll, sugar bowl, gr 150.00
Circled Scroll, tumbler, wht 75.00
Coinspot, pickle castor, wht 225.00
Colonial Stairsteps, creamer, bl 100.00
Colonial Stairsteps, toothpick holder, bl 200.00
Compass, rose bowl, wht 90.00
Concave Columns, vase, bl, canary or vaseline 100.00
Conch & Twig, wall pocket, bl, vaseline or canary ... 110.00
Consolidated Criss-Cross, shakers, gr or cranberry, ea 135.00
Consolidated Criss-Cross, sugar shaker, cranberry 550.00
Contessa, basket, amber, hdl 250.00
Contessa, basket, bl 60.00
Coral Reef, bottle, barber; bl 200.00
Coral Reef, bottle, bitters; bl 200.00
Coral Reef, bottle, bitters; wht 125.00
Coral Reef, lamp, finger; wht, ftd 325.00
Corolla, vase, canary 200.00
Coronation, pitcher, bl, vaseline or canary 200.00
Coronation, tumbler, bl, canary or vaseline 40.00
Crown Jewels, pitcher, bl 250.00
Crown Jewels, plate, bl 100.00
Crown Jewels, platter, bl 110.00
Daffodils, lamp, hanging; gr 300.00
Daffodils, lamp, oil; cranberry 425.00
Daffodils, vase, canary 265.00
Daisy & Button, tray, bun; bl 150.00
Daisy & Fern, butter dish, cranberry 300.00
Daisy & Fern, butter dish, wht 175.00
Daisy & Fern, cruet, bl, faceted stopper, 7½" 250.00
Daisy & Fern, tumbler, bl or gr 50.00
Daisy & Fern, vase, wht 100.00
Daisy & Fern, wht, bulbous w/clear hdl & faceted stopper, 7" 100.00
Daisy & Plume, basket, wht, rare 85.00
Daisy & Plume, rose bowl, bl, ftd 60.00
Daisy & Plume, rose bowl, wht, ftd 35.00
Daisy in Criss-Cross, pitcher, bl 450.00
Daisy in Criss-Cross, syrup, cranberry 475.00
Daisy May (Leaf Rays), nappy/bonbon, gr 45.00
Davidson Drape, vase, bl, canary or vaseline, squat 150.00
Decorated English Swirl, rose bowl, cranberry 250.00
Diamond & Daisy (Caroline), basket, bl 100.00
Diamond Maple Leaf, bowl, gr, hdls 70.00
Diamond Maple Leaf, bowl, wht, hdl 45.00
Diamond Optic, compote, bl 50.00
Diamond Point & Fleur-de-Lis, nut bowl, gr 65.00
Diamond Spearhead, butter dish, gr 275.00
Diamond Spearhead, butter dish, wht 175.00
Diamond Spearhead, carafe, water; vaseline or canary 350.00
Diamond Spearhead, mug, gr 200.00
Diamond Spearhead, shakers, bl, pr 150.00
Diamond Wave, pitcher, cranberry, w/lid 175.00
Diamond Wave, vase, cranberry, 5" 85.00
Diamonds, cruet, rubena 250.00
Diamonds, cruet, wht 75.00
Diamonds, tumbler, cranberry 70.00
Dolly Madison, bowl, gr, ruffled rim, 8" 40.00
Dolly Madison, creamer, bl 90.00
Dolphin & Herons, tray, novelty; wht, ftd 100.00
Dorset (English), sugar bowl, bl, open 50.00

Double Greek Key, celery vase, wht 125.00
Double Greek Key, spooner, bl 110.00
Double Greek Key, tray, pickle; bl 200.00
Dragon Lady (Dugan's Diamond Compass), rose bowl, wht 90.00
Drapery (Northwood), pitcher, bl 250.00
Drapery (Northwood), spooner, wht 55.00
Drapery (Northwood), vase, bl 140.00
Duchess, butter dish, vaseline or canary 175.00
Duchess, creamer, bl, canary or vaseline 65.00
Dugan Intaglio Peach, compote, wht 100.00
Dugan Intaglio Strawberry, bowl, fruit; wht, stemmed 85.00
Dugan's Honeycomb, bowl, bl, various shapes, rare, ea 85.00
Dugan's Intaglio Acorn, bowl, bl, 10" 115.00
Dugan's Intaglio Grape, compote, wht 85.00
Dugan's Intaglio Pear & Plum, bowl, wht, 10" 135.00
Dugan's Plain Panel, vase, bl or gr 55.00
Elipse & Diamond, tumbler, cranberry 115.00
Elson Dewdrop, bowl, berry; lg 45.00
Elson Dewdrop, mug, wht 65.00
Elson Dewdrop #2, bowl, sauce; wht 15.00
Elson Dewdrop #2, cruet, wht 90.00
Elson Dewdrop #2, punch cup, wht 35.00
Embossed Spanish Lace, vase, canary, 4¼" 100.00
English Drape, vase, bl 65.00
English Oak Leaf, bowl, bl 200.00
English Ripple, tumbler, bl, vaseline or canary 80.00
English Wide Stripe, pitcher, cranberry 350.00
Everglades, creamer, wht 45.00
Everglades, shakers, bl, pr 220.00
Everglades, tumbler, wht 60.00
Fan, bowl, sauce; bl or gr 30.00
Fan, creamer, gr 60.00
Fan, gravy boat, bl or gr 50.00
Fan, tumbler, gr 75.00
Fancy Fantails, bowl, vaseline 40.00
Feathers, vase, bl 35.00
Fenton's #220 (Stripe), tumbler, gr, w/hdl 35.00
Fenton's #370, bonbon, amber 50.00
Fenton's #370, nappy, amber 55.00
Fern, bottle, barber; wht 100.00
Fern, cruet, bl 225.00
Fern, cruet, wht 150.00
Fern, shakers, cranberry, pr 165.00
Fern, toothpick holder, cranberry, rare 475.00
Field Flowers, compote, vaseline or canary, 2 szs ... 250.00
File & Fan, bowl, wht 95.00
Fish-in-the-Sea, vase, wht, scarce 150.00
Flora, bowl, master; bl, canary or vaseline 100.00
Flora, bowl, master; wht 80.00
Flora, butter dish, bl 425.00
Flora, pitcher, bl 500.00
Flora Eyelet, tumbler, bl or wht 100.00
Fluted Scrolls (Klondyke), butter dish, canary 70.00
Fluted Scrolls (Klondyke), epergne, bl, sm 125.00
Fluted Scrolls (Klondyke), rose bowl, wht 100.00
Fluted Scrolls (Klondyke), spooner, bl 55.00
Four Pillars, vase, gr 70.00
Frosted Leaf & Basketweave, creamer, vaseline or canary 135.00
Frosted Leaf & Basketweave, sugar bowl, canary or vaseline 165.00
Galaxy, rose bowl, wht 130.00
Gonterman (Adonis) Hob, cruet, amber 425.00
Gonterman (Adonis) Swirl, celery vase, amber 200.00
Gonterman (Adonis) Swirl, pitcher, bl 110.00
Gonterman (Adonis) Swirl, spooner, amber 125.00

Gonterman (Adonis) Swirl, syrup, bl 400.00
Gonterman (Adonis) Swirl, toothpick holder, amber 200.00
Grape & Cable, bowl, centerpiece; bl or gr 300.00
Grape & Cable w/Thumbprints, bowl, gr 175.00
Greely (Hobbs), finger bowl, bl 225.00
Greener Diamond Column, epergne, amber 350.00
Harlequin, rose bowl, bl 250.00
Harrow, cordial, bl, vaseline or canary, stemmed 35.00
Harrow, creamer, vaseline or canary 70.00
Harrow, wine, bl, canary or vaseline 40.00
Hearts & Flowers, bowl, wht 150.00
Hearts & Flowers, compote, wht 85.00
Heron & Peacock, mug, bl 75.00
Herringbone, tumbler, bl 100.00
Herringbone, tumbler, cranberry 150.00
Herringbone, tumbler, wht 65.00
Hobb's Polka Dot, cheese dish, gr/sapphire, w/lid 235.00
Hobnail (Hobbs), bottle, bitters; bl 150.00
Hobnail (Hobbs), bride's basket, canary 425.00
Hobnail & Paneled Thumbprint, cordial, bl, canary or vaseline 35.00
Hobnail & Paneled Thumbprint, pitcher, bl, canary or vaseline . 300.00
Hobnail 4-Footed, spooner, cobalt 60.00
Hobnail-in-Square (Vesta), bowl, w/stand, wht 150.00
Hobnail-in-Square (Vesta), butter dish, wht 200.00
Honeycomb, vase, wht 45.00
Honeycomb (Blown), bowl, bl 75.00
Honeycomb (Blown), cracker jar, wht 250.00
Honeycomb & Clover, bowl, master; gr 75.00
Honeycomb & Clover, bowl, master; gr, Fenton 60.00
Idyll, butter dish, wht 300.00
Idyll, sugar bowl, gr, scarce 250.00
Idyll, toothpick holder, gr 325.00
Inside Ribbing, celery vase, vaseline or cranberry 60.00
Inside Ribbing, creamer, canary or vaseline 80.00
Inside Ribbing, tray, bl 55.00
Inside Ribbing, tray, wht 30.00
Intaglio, compote, jelly; bl 50.00
Intaglio, shakers, wht, pr 90.00
Intaglio (Dugan), nappy, wht, 6-9" 45.00
Interior Panel, vase, fan; bl, canary or vaseline 55.00
Interior Poinsettia, tumbler, gr 65.00
Interior Swirl, rose bowl, bl 100.00
Inverted Fan & Feather, bowl, master; bl 300.00
Inverted Fan & Feather, bowl, sauce; bl or gr 100.00
Inverted Fan & Feather, creamer, wht 175.00
Inverted Fan & Feather, spooner, wht 150.00
Inverted Fan & Feather, sugar bowl, wht 225.00
Iris w/Meander, pickle dish, canary, gr or vaseline 75.00
Jackson, epergne, bl, sm 175.00
Jackson, pitcher, bl 300.00
Jackson, powder jar, gr 80.00
Jackson, tumbler, wht 65.00
Jefferson #270, bowl, sauce; bl or gr 45.00
Jefferson Spool, vase, wht 45.00
Jefferson Wheel, bowl, gr 45.00
Jewel & Fan, bowl, banana; bl 125.00
Jewel & Fan, bowl, gr 55.00
Jewel & Flower, creamer, vaseline or canary 95.00
Jewel & Flower, pitcher, wht 250.00
Jeweled Heart, tumbler, bl 100.00
Jeweled Heart, tumbler, gr 65.00
Jewelled Heart, bowl, sauce; bl 45.00
Jewelled Heart, compote, bl or gr 150.00
Jewelled Heart, toothpick holder, wht 300.00

Jewels & Drapery, vase, aqua 75.00
Jewels & Drapery & Variant, vase, aqua 75.00
Keyhole, rose bowl, bl or gr 175.00
King's Panel, creamer, bl 35.00
Lady Caroline, creamer, bl, canary or vaseline 60.00
Lady Chippendale, basket, cobalt 80.00
Lady Chippendale, compote, cobalt, tall 100.00
Lady Chippendale, sugar bowl, canary 90.00
Late Coinspot, pitcher, gr 150.00
Late Coinspot, tumbler, gr 35.00
Lattice Medallions, rose bowl, bl 75.00
Lattice Medallions, rose bowl, wht 50.00
Leaf & Beads, bowl, bl, ftd or dome 60.00
Leaf & Beads, bowl, whimsey, wht 45.00
Leaf Mold, bowl, master; cranberry 140.00
Leaf Mold, sugar bowl, cranberry 300.00
Leaf Mold, sugar shaker, cranberry 350.00
Leaf Mold, tumbler, cranberry 100.00
Leaf Mold, celery vase, cranberry 325.00
Linking Rings, pitcher, bl, canary or vaseline 125.00
Lords & Ladies, butter dish, bl 100.00
Lords & Ladies, celery boat (in wire basket), bl 200.00
Lords & Ladies, plate, bl, 7½" 100.00
Lords & Ladies, plate, vaseline or canary, 7½" 125.00
Lustre Flute, butter dish, wht 200.00
Many Loops, bowl, gr, ruffled rim 45.00
Maple Leaf, compote, jelly; bl 75.00
Maple Leaf, compote, jelly; gr 65.00
Mavis Swirl, bottle, bitters; bl 100.00
Mavis Swirl, bottle, bitters; wht 85.00
Mavis Swirl, tumbler, canary 75.00
Mavis Swirl, tumbler, wht 50.00
Meander, bowl, nut; bl 70.00
Melon Swirl, pitcher, bl 375.00
Murano Floral, vase, wht, decor, speckled 390.00
National Swirl, pitcher, bl or gr 275.00
Nesting Robin, bowl, wht 300.00
Netted Cherry, plate, wht 65.00
Northern Star, banana bowl, gr 70.00
Northern Star, banana bowl, vaseline 50.00
Old Man Winter, basket, bl, lg ft 150.00
Old Man Winter, basket, canary, ftd, lg 275.00
Old Man Winter, basket, gr, sm 85.00
Opal Loops, decanter, wht 160.00
Opal Loops, flask, wht 195.00
Opal Loops, glass pipe, wht 180.00
Opal Loops, vase, wht 110.00
Opalberry, plate, bl 200.00
Open O's, spittoon, whimsey, canary, gr or vaseline 100.00
Over-All Hobnail, bowl, sauce; bl 40.00
Over-All Hobnail, spooner, bl 100.00
Over-All Hobnail, tumbler, wht 25.00
Overlapping Leaves (Leaf Tiers), plate, wht, ftd 195.00
Palm Beach, bowl, master; bl, canary or vaseline 85.00
Palm Beach, compote, jelly; wht 150.00
Palm Beach, creamer, vaseline or canary 140.00
Palm Beach, spooner, bl, canary or vaseline 150.00
Paneled Cornflower, vase, wht 135.00
Paneled Flowers, nut cup, bl, ftd 60.00
Paneled Holly, bowl, wht 135.00
Paneled Holly, butter dish, bl 400.00
Paneled Holly, butter dish, wht 250.00
Paneled Holly, creamer, bl 125.00
Paneled Holly, shakers, bl, pr 250.00

Paneled Holly, shakers, wht, pr............150.00
Paneled Sprig, toothpick holder, wht............100.00
Pearl Flowers, rose bowl, bl............70.00
Pearl Flowers, rose bowl, gr, ftd............60.00
Pearls & Scales, compote, emerald............80.00
Piasa Bird, bowl, wht............45.00
Piasa Bird, plate, wht, ftd............60.00
Piccadilly, basket, bl, sm............100.00
Piccadilly, basket, wht, sm............70.00
Picket, planter, bl............75.00
Pine Cone, plate, wht............75.00
Pinwheel, cake plate, canary, ped ft, 12"............135.00
Poinsettia, bowl, fruit; cranberry............175.00
Poinsettia, bowl, fruit; gr............110.00
Poinsettia, bowl, fruit; gr, 2 szs............110.00
Poinsettia, sugar shaker, bl or gr............300.00
Poinsettia, sugar shaker, cranberry............450.00
Polka Dot, syrup, cranberry............725.00
Polka Dot, tumbler, bl............70.00
Popsicle Sticks, bowl, gr, ftd............50.00
Popsicle Sticks, shade, wht............35.00
Pressed Buttons & Braids, tumbler, canary or vaseline............100.00
Prince William, creamer, bl............100.00
Prince William, toothpick holder, bl............65.00
Princess Diana, compote, bl, metal base............150.00
Princess Diana, plate, vaseline, crimped rim............60.00
Princess Diana, sugar bowl, bl, open............70.00
Pussy Willow, vase, vaseline or canary, 4½"............60.00
Queen's Spill, candlesticks, canary or vaseline, pr............350.00
Queen's Spill, vase, spill; bl, 4"............90.00
Quilted Daisy, lamp, fairy; wht............375.00
Quilted Rose, pitcher, wht............100.00
Quilted Wide Stripe, finger bowl, cranberry............70.00
Ray, vase, bl............55.00
Rayed Jane, nappy, bl............50.00
Regal (Northwood), bowl, sauce; gr............45.00
Regal (Northwood), bowl, sauce; wht............20.00
Regal (Northwood), butter dish, gr............175.00
Regal (Northwood), celery vase, gr............175.00
Regal (Northwood), celery vase, wht............100.00
Regal (Northwood), cruet, bl or gr............750.00
Regal (Northwood), pitcher, wht............150.00
Reverse Drapery, bowl, bl or gr............45.00
Reverse Drapery, plate, bl............90.00
Reverse Drapery, vase, amethyst............100.00
Reverse Swirl, bottle, water; wht............100.00
Reverse Swirl, custard cup, cranberry............150.00
Reverse Swirl, finger bowl, cranberry............100.00
Reverse Swirl, syrup, bl............175.00
Reverse Swirl, syrup, wht............100.00
Ribbed (Opal) Lattice, bowl, master; bl............70.00
Ribbed (Opal) Lattice, creamer, bl............75.00
Ribbed (Opal) Lattice, toothpick holder, wht............175.00
Ribbed (Opal) Lattice, tumbler, cranberry............150.00
Ribbed Coinspot, butter dish, wht............295.00
Ribbed Coinspot, tumbler, cranberry............200.00
Ribbed Pillar, bowl, berry; cranberry, lg............95.00
Ribbed Pillar, shakers, cranberry, pr............135.00
Ribbed Spiral, bowl, bl, ruffled rim............55.00
Ribbed Spiral, bowl, wht, ruffled rim............40.00
Ribbed Spiral, pitcher, bl............525.00
Ribbed Spiral, pitcher, wht............385.00
Ribbed Spiral, vase, canary or vaseline, squat, 4-7"............75.00
Ribbed Spiral, vase, wht, squat, 4-7"............35.00

Ribbon Swirl, spittoon, gr............175.00
Richelieu, compote, jelly; bl............75.00
Richelieu, cracker jar, bl............200.00
Richelieu, tray, bl............50.00
Richelieu, tray, canary or vaseline............55.00
Richelieu, tray, wht............40.00
Ring Handle, ring tray, gr............150.00
Ring Handle, shakers, bl, pr............100.00
Rose & Ruffles, bottle, scent; bl, canary or vaseline............250.00
Rose & Ruffles, bowl, bl, canary or vaseline, lg............150.00
Rose & Ruffles, bowl, bl, canary or vaseline, sm............100.00
Roulette, bowl, novelty; bl............50.00
Roulette, bowl, novelty; wht............30.00
Roulette, plate, bl or gr............60.00
Royal Scandal, wall vase, bl, canary or vaseline............250.00
Royal Scandal, wall vase, wht............200.00

Ruffles and Rings, novelty bowl, green, $45.00. (Photo courtesy Bill Edwards and Mike Carwile)

Ruffles & Rings, nut bowl, gr............40.00
Ruffles & Rings w/Daisy Band, bowl, wht, ftd............60.00
S-Repeat, tumbler, bl............65.00
Scottish Moor, celery vase, bl............65.00
Scottish Moor, cracker jar, bl............350.00
Scottish Moor, cracker jar, wht............225.00
Scroll w/Acanthus, creamer, bl............100.00
Scroll w/Acanthus, creamer, wht............65.00
Scroll w/Acanthus, cruet, vaseline or canary............350.00
Scroll w/Acanthus, shakers, wht, pr............195.00
Scroll w/Acanthus, spooner, bl............85.00
Seaweed, bowl, master; wht............40.00
Seaweed, creamer, cranberry............225.00
Seaweed, pickle caster, cranberry, complete............650.00
Seaweed, sugar bowl, cranberry............225.00
Seaweed, sugar bowl, wht............145.00
Serpent Threads, epergne, canary or vaseline............300.00
Shell (Beaded Shell), bowl, sauce; gr............65.00
Shell & Dots, nut bowl, bl............45.00
Shell & Dots, rose bowl, wht............35.00
Shell Beaded, bowl, sauce; gr............65.00
Shell Beaded, bowl, sauce; wht............35.00
Shell Beaded, tumbler, bl............100.00
Shell Beaded, tumbler, wht............75.00
Sir Lancelot, bowl, bl, ftd............65.00
Sir Lancelot, bowl, wht, ftd............40.00
Smooth Rib, bowl, wht, on metal stand............100.00
Snowflake, oil lamp, cranberry............550.00
Somerset, dish, bl, oval, 9"............40.00
Somerset, pitcher, juice; vaseline or canary, 5½"............90.00
Spanish Lace, bottle, water; canary or vaseline............325.00
Spanish Lace, bottle, water; cranberry............425.00
Spanish Lace, butter dish, bl............425.00
Spanish Lace, cruet, cranberry............750.00

Spanish Lace, cruet, wht...200.00
Spanish Lace, jam jar, bl..300.00
Spanish Lace, water bottle, vaseline or canary.............325.00
Spatter, vase, bl, 9"...95.00
Speckled Stripe, shakers, wht, pr...............................100.00
Speckled Stripe, sugar bowl, canary.............................50.00
Spool, compote, bl or gr..50.00
Squirrel & Acorn, bowl, wht..175.00
Squirrel & Acorn, compote, bl.....................................190.00
Stars & Stripes, bottle, bitters; cranberry.....................350.00
Stars & Stripes, bottle, bitters; wht.............................100.00
Stippled Scroll & Prism, goblet, gr, 5"...........................30.00
Stripe, bowl, wht...60.00
Stripe, rose bowl, bl...100.00
Stripe (Wide), cruet, wht..175.00
Sunburst-on-Shield, butter dish, canary or vaseline.......400.00
Sunburst-on-Shield, butter dish, wht............................275.00
Sunburst-on-Shield (Diadem), creamer, bl.....................100.00
Swag w/Brackets, bowl, canary, bl or vaseline.................45.00
Swag w/Brackets, bowl, master; bl.................................85.00
Swag w/Brackets, spooner, gr.......................................80.00
Swirl, cheese dish, wht...250.00
Swirl, cruet, red, tri-fold rim, camphor hdl, clear stopper, Hobbs, 7"..225.00
Swirl, custard cup, cranberry...75.00
Swirl, finger bowl, bl...65.00
Swirl, finger lamp, wht...350.00
Swirl, shot glass, wht...65.00
Swirl, spittoon, cranberry..150.00
Swirl, spittoon, wht...70.00
Swirling Maze, bowl, salad; gr.......................................90.00
Target Swirl, tumbler, cranberry....................................95.00
Thin & Wide Rib, vase, bl or gr.....................................60.00
Thin & Wide Rib, vase, canary......................................75.00
Thorne Lily, epergne, canary or vaseline.......................300.00
Thousand Eye, celery vase, wht....................................100.00
Thousand Eye, sugar bowl, wht....................................100.00
Three Fruits w/Meander, bowl, bl, ftd...........................165.00
Tokyo, compote, jelly; wht..30.00
Tokyo, creamer, gr...65.00

Tokyo, plate, footed, blue, $55.00. (Photo courtesy Bill Edwards and Mike Carwile)

Tokyo, plate, wht...35.00
Tokyo, vase, bl..55.00
Tree of Life, shakers, bl, pr...200.00
Tree of Life, shakers, wht, pr......................................100.00
Tree of Love, plate, wht, 2 szs, rare.............................135.00
Tree Stump, mug, gr...95.00
Tree Stump, mug, wht...60.00
Triangle, match holder, bl...75.00
Triangle, match holder, wht..55.00
Tut, vase, whimsey; bl or gr..125.00

Tut, vase, whimsey; canary or vaseline.........................165.00
Tut, vase, whimsey; wht..100.00
Twigs, vase, bl, sm, 5½"...65.00
Twigs, vase, vaseline or cranberry, panelled, 7"..............85.00
Twist (Miniatures), sugar bowl, vaseline or canary.........150.00
Twister, bowl, bl...50.00
Twister, plate, bl...100.00
Victoria & Albert, butter dish, wht..............................110.00
Victoria & Albert, creamer, bl.......................................80.00
Victoria & Albert, creamer, wht....................................50.00
Vulcan, sugar bowl, bl..85.00
Vulcan, sugar bowl, wht..70.00
War of Roses, compote, bl, w/metal stand.....................150.00
Water Lily & Cattails, bonbon, amethyst........................45.00
Water Lily & Cattails, bonbon, bl...................................45.00
Water Lily & Cattails, gravy boat, gr..............................55.00
Water Lily & Cattails, gravy boat, wht..........................410.00
Water Lily & Cattails, relish, gr, hdls.............................60.00

Water Lily and Cattails (Northwood), tumbler, blue, $75.00. (Photo courtesy Bill Edwards and Mike Carwile)

Waves, plate, novelty; gr..100.00
Wild Bouquet, compote, jelly; bl..................................175.00
Wild Bouquet, compote, jelly; gr..................................135.00
Wild Bouquet, spooner, gr...150.00
Wild Grapes, bowl, wht...40.00
Wild Rose, bowl, banana; amethyst................................80.00
William & Mary, cake plate, bl, stemmed......................150.00
Willow Reed, basket, bl...175.00
Windows (Plain), bottle, bitters; cranberry....................325.00
Windows (Plain), lamp shade, wht.................................35.00
Windows (Swirled), cruet, cranberry, clear hdl/faceted stopper, 7"..325.00
Windows (Swirled), mustard jar, bl.................................75.00
Windows (Swirled), mustard jar, cranberry....................150.00
Windows (Swirled), mustard jar, wht..............................55.00
Windows (Swirled), sugar shaker, wht............................175.00
Windows (Swirled), tumbler, bl......................................85.00
Wishbone & Drapery, plate, gr.......................................60.00
Wreath & Shell, celery vase, bl....................................225.00
Wreath & Shell, salt cellar, bl.....................................140.00
Wreath & Shell, salt cellar, wht....................................85.00
Wreath & Shell, spooner, bl...130.00
Zipper & Loops, vase, bl, ftd...65.00

Opaline

A type of semiopaque opal glass, opaline was made in white as well as pastel shades and is often enameled. It is similar in appearance to English Bristol glass, though its enamel or gilt decorative devices tend to exhibit a French influence.

Atomizer, gr w/gilt metal mts & orig bulb, 5¾".............60.00

Bottle, wht, w/bronze mts, shouldered cylinder, ball stopper, 8"..... 75.00
Bowl, wht w/Deco HP on lid, ca 1926, 4½x7", from $350 to 425.00
Box, wht w/brass trim, hinged lid, rectangular, 3½x5½x3¼" 250.00
Box, wht w/bronze mts & key escutcheon, oval, 5x4x3½" 660.00
Ewer, wht, HP butterfly, frosted hdl, crimped mouth, 9¼" 75.00
Mugs, wht w/bl opaque hdls, 3¼", 4 for.................................... 145.00
Tumbler, bl, HP bird on floral branch w/coralene leaves 85.00
Vase, apple gr w/gold banding, bulbous w/slim neck flared rim, 13x7" . 75.00
Vase, bl, HP classical lady among flowers, shouldered, 1880s, 18"...180.00
Vase, pk w/jeweled HP rim & ft, bulbous, 8" 350.00
Vase, wht, shouldered/ftd form, 8¾", NM 60.00

Orient & Flume

A Victorian home built in the late 1890s between Orient and Flume streets in Chico, California, was purchased by Douglas Boyd in 1972 and converted into a glass studio. Due to his on-going success in producing fine, contemporary art glass reminiscent of masters such as Tiffany, Loetz, and Steuben, the business flourished and about a year later had become so successful that larger quarters were required nearby. Today, examples of their workmanship are found in museums and galleries all over the world. In addition to the items listed here, they also produced beautiful paperweights. See also Paperweights.

Vase, feathers, dk burgundy on gold irid, 1977, 4" 145.00
Vase, jack-in-pulpit; pulled festoons on gr, gold top, 1979, 8½" ... 465.00
Vase, lilies, pk on bl w/oil spots, Smallhouse, ftd, 12".................... 350.00
Vase, millefiori flowers w/brn stems on bl irid, shouldered, 8" 300.00
Vase, paperweight; fish & sea grasses in clear, Beyers, 6" 180.00
Vase, paperweight; frog on lily pad, Hudin, 1984, 4¼" 95.00

Vase, pulled feathers, mc on gr to bl, Hansen, 1975, 10¼" 135.00
Vase, pulled feathers, mc on lav, ovoid, 6" 195.00

Orientalia

The art of the Orient is an area of collecting currently enjoying strong collector interest, not only in those examples that are truly 'antique' but in the twentieth-century items as well. Because of the many aspects involved in a study of Orientalia, we can only try through brief comments to acquaint the reader with some of the more readily available examples. We suggest you refer to specialized reference sources for more detailed information. See also specific categories.

Key:
Ch — Chinese	hdwd — hardwood
cvg — carving	Jp — Japan
drw — drawer	Ko — Korean
Dy — Dynasty	lcq — lacquer
E — export	mdl — medallion
FR — Famille Rose	rswd — rosewood
FV — Famille Verte	tkwd — teakwood
gb — guard border	

Blanc de Chine

Figurine, Buddha stands w/smiling face, 20th C, 12" 480.00
Figurine, Kuan Yan on throne w/servant, Te Hua, 18th C, 8½" .. 2,150.00
Figurine, lady w/vase & monkey w/peach, Ch'ien Lung, 18th C, 7¼"..850.00
Figurine, monk seated w/arms folded, ca 1920, 12", +teak base ... 900.00
Figurine, Quan Yan standing on wave sphere, 19th C, 19x6" 950.00

Blue and White Porcelain

Beaker, warrior above lotus band, cylindrical, 17th C, 14"........7,200.00
Cachepot, lotus & vines, Ch, 18th C, 9" dia 3,300.00
Charger, birds/peonies/chrysanthemums, scalloped, 1572-1620, 14¼"....3,300.00
Figurine, riders on elephants, Ch, late Qing Dy, 9¼", pr 1,950.00
Jar, precious objects, w/lid, Kangxi Dy, 6", pr.........................3,300.00
Jar, prunus blossoms, baluster, domed lid, Ch, Kangxi Dy, 17½".. 2,750.00
Jardiniere, flowers & foliage, E, 18th C, 15¼x18".....................4,350.00
Kendi, elephant form, Ch, Wanli Dy, ca 1600, rstr, 8¾"............8,400.00
Vase, dragon & foliage, cylindrical, Ch, ca 1650, 15"...............5,250.00
Vase, dragon among clouds, baluster, Ko, Yi/Choson Dy, 11½".2,350.00
Vase, dragon pursues flaming pearl/flowers/etc, Ch, Yuan/Ming Dy, 7"..6,600.00
Vase, riverscape baluster, w/lid, Ch, Kangxi Dy, 16".................8,400.00

Bronze

Figure, elephant w/trunk raised, pnt details, blk patina, 13x13"..... 85.00
Figure, foo dog w/pierced sphere, 14¼x19" 1,265.00
Figure, peasant man w/yoke & 2 baskets, marble base, 12x11"....... 90.00
Figure, warrior on horsebk, much detail, 40" 1,080.00
Incense burner, birds/flowers in relief, dragon hdls, ftd, 8" 180.00
Incense burner, cast designs on base w/4 mask legs, rtcl lid, 17x15"...750.00
Incense burner, foo dog, hinged lid & open mouth 1,100.00
Urn, mtn scene, gold hdls & trim, 12" 120.00
Vase, dragon in relief, cylindrical neck, 9" 150.00
Vase, elephant heads & tusks in relief, old rpr, 12½x8½" 1,550.00

Celadon

Bowl, petal rim, Ming Dy, 5" 450.00
Charger, emb ribs, Ming Dy, 12" 950.00

Ewer, carved floral scrolling, eleventh century, Yuch ware, lacking lid, 5", $2,250.00. (Photo courtesy Skinner Inc. Auctioneers & Appraisers of Antiques & Fine Art)

Vase, crackle glaze, domed lid w/foo dog finial, Ch, 21", pr.......... 465.00
Vase, crackle glaze on ribbed body, sq, 10" 135.00
Vase, incised floral, bottle neck, Ch, 8".. 145.00

Furniture

Cabinet, lacquered and brass bound, gilt and polychrome prunus blossoms, peonies and birds, 33x31x17", $2,500.00. (Photo courtesy Neal Auction Company Auctioneers & Appraisers of Fine Art)

Cabinet, blk lcq, gold/appl figures, 3 glass doors on base w/drws, 84" .. 700.00
Cabinet, red lcq, mortised, 2 blind doors, shelved int, 2 drws, 73x45" .. 180.00
Cabinet, sliding panels & drws, bentwood shelf, glass doors, 38x30x11" ... 975.00
Cabinet on fr, blk lcq w/HP landscape, 2 doors/3 drws, 31x32x21"..... 300.00
Chest, apothecary; 37-drw, brass ring pulls, mortised, Ch, 47x27x19"....315.00
Plant stand, tkwd, pk marble top, pierced/cvd legs & shelf, 19x14x14"..725.00
Press, red lcq w/gold decor, dbl doors, Shan Xi province, 70x52x24".. 1,150.00
Screen, coromandel; blk lcq w/MOP inlay, appl stones, 6-panel, 72" H 600.00
Screen, cvd wood fr, silk panel w/embr shrimp, 40x38"................ 235.00
Screen, semiprecious stones/lcq landscape, wood fr in base, 36x40"...1,500.00
Server, elm, scalloped returns/apron, 3-drw, 30x83x10" 525.00
Stand, hdwd, 2-tier, pierced aprons, mid-1800s, 31x20x12"........ 315.00
Table, alter; teak w/pierced/cvd cloud-band frieze, 1950s, 33x45x17"... 600.00

Hardstones

Amethyst, bottle, cvd lotus plants, 2" 300.00
Amethyst, cvg, Quan Yin, Ch, 7"... 90.00
Jade, belt cuckle, wht, dragons cvg, 1¾x4¼"............................... 4,250.00
Jade, brush holder, celadon w/russet areas, birds/trees cvgs, 5" ..7,800.00
Jade, cigarette holder, gr, silver mts mk Lebkuecher & Co, ca 1900...2,650.00
Jade, cvg, celadon, Shoulao w/staff & peach, ca 1900, 13"........7,800.00
Jade, cvg, gr & brn, animals & fruit, rectangular, early 20th C, 6" . 2,500.00
Jade, cvg, wht, carp leaping, lg age crack, 15x10½" 5,100.00
Jade, cvg, wht, sheep (3) in huddle, 1½"+stand......................... 4,450.00
Jade, rouge box, wht, cvd Ju'i knots/dragon, K'ang Hsi, 3½" dia .. 13,250.00
Jade, scholar's paperweight, wht, foliate cvg, wire inlay stand, 2" ... 5,250.00
Nephrite jade, cvg, Buddha holding Chinese scepter, 8⅛" 115.00
Rose quartz, cvgs, phoenix bird, Ch, 13x19"+stand, pr 3,000.00
Rose quartz, table lamp, cvd florals, brass mts, 16" urn form, 38"... 4,800.00
Rose quartz, vase, shield form w/foliage, foo lion finial, 10"+stand... 2,750.00

Jade, jar, carved with scholars at various activities, lid with dragons and clouds, jump ring handles, Ch'ien Lung mark, 15", $36,425.00. (Photo courtesy Skinner Inc. Auctioneers & Appraisers of Antiques & Fine Art)

Inro

Gold lacquer, Bishamond in gold takazogan against temple veranda setting, five-case, signed Hanryusai, 1800s, 4", $6,325.00; Two fighting cocks on brown togidashi, interior in chu nashiji and lacquer, four-case, 2⅞", $1,495.00.

Bone, finely cvd figure of man in boat/Senin, 19th C, 2¼" 425.00
Gold lcq w/emb flowering trees, 4-part, Sagemono, 19th C, w/netsuke .780.00
Gold lcq w/emb tigers by waterfall, 19th C.................................. 840.00
Gold lcq w/maki-e of sparrows/bamboo, 4-compartment, 19th C, 3¼" ..1,200.00
Ivory w/lcq & ryusa, Sagemono, late 19th C, w/katydid netsuke . 400.00
Lcq w/pearl/coral/MOP inlay insects & flowers, 5-compartment, 19th C....600.00

Lacquer

Lacquerware is found in several colors, but the one most likely to be encountered is cinnabar. It is often intricately carved, sometimes involving hundreds of layers built one at a time on a metal or wooden base. Later pieces remain red, while older examples tend to darken.

Box, immortals scene, blk w/yel bkground, 3x4".......................... 180.00
Box, lady seated in garden, red cinnabar, hinged lid, 6x4" 120.00
Box, landscapes & flowers, blk & gold, brass swing hdls, 19th C, 14" L.. 425.00
Cabinet, jewelry; exotic birds & flowers w/MOP inlay, 16x12x6" ...240.00
Cigar case, dk cinnabar, little cvg, Jp, ca 1833, 4¾" 60.00
Vase, cinnabar w/ornately cvd florals, 10", pr, EX........................ 200.00
Vase, red cinnabar w/ornately cvd florals, classic form, 15½" 150.00

Netsukes

A netsuke is a miniature Japanese carving made with two holes called the Himitoshi, either channeled or within the carved design. As kimonos (the outer garment of the time) had no pockets, the Japanese man hung his pipe, tobacco pouch, or other daily necessities from his waist sash. The most highly valued accessory was a nest of little drawers called an Inro, in which they carried snuff or sometimes opium. The netsuke was the toggle that secured them. Although most are of ivory, others were made of bone, wood, metal, porcelain, or semiprecious stones. Some were inlaid or lacquered. They are found in many forms — figurals the most common, mythological beasts the most desirable. They range in size from 1" up to 3", which was the maximum size allowed by law. Many netsukes represented the owner's profession, religion, or hobbies. Scenes from the daily life of Japan at that time were often depicted in the tiny carvings. The more detailed the carving, the greater the value.

Careful study is required to recognize the quality of the netsuke. Many have been made in Hong Kong in recent years; and even though some are very well carved, these are considered copies and avoided by the serious collector. There are many books that will help you learn to recognize quality netsukes, and most reputable dealers are glad to assist you. Use your magnifying glass to check for repairs. In the listings that follow, netsukes are ivory unless noted otherwise; 'stain' indicates a color wash.

Badger hiding under lotus, boxwood, ca 1800, 1¾" 500.00
Dog w/2 puppies, boxwood, EX patina, 19th C, 2" 4,250.00
Figure w/silver clapper in hands, mc stain, 1½" 1,150.00
Fisherman w/oversz pufferfish, inlaid eyes, 19th C, 2" 660.00
Foreigner w/trumpet, inlaid eyes, Issan, ca 1800, 1½" 950.00
Horse w/inlaid eyes, att Tanatoshi, 20th C, 2" 1,325.00
Hotei sleeping w/bag of wealth, boxwood w/ivory inlay, Tokasai, 1800s.1,800.00
Hotei standing on bag of wealth, 18th C, 2" 475.00
Man holding mask, mc stain, 1¼" 480.00

Manjushri on the back of a lion, boxwood, signed Kyokusai, 1½", $5,500.00. (Photo courtesy Skinner Inc. Auctioneers & Appraisers of Antiques & Fine Art)

Marine life surrounds clamshell, Iwami school, late 1700s, 2¾".8,400.00
Mogyoko clapper w/oni, Shomin w/kakihan, 19th C, 2x1½" 3,350.00
Quail w/millet plant, rich brn stain, Okatomo, 1½" 1,150.00
Rabbit w/red inset eyes, Gyokuzan, 19th C, 1¼x2" 1,200.00
Sage holding loquat over shoulder, late 18th C, 2¾" 850.00
Toad on worn-out sandal, boxwood, EX patina, Masanao, 18th C...5,000.00

Porcelain

Chinese export ware was designed to appeal to Western tastes and was often made to order. During the eighteenth century, vast amounts were shipped to Europe and on westward. Much of this fine porcelain consisted of dinnerware lines that were given specific pattern names. Rose Mandarin, Fitzhugh, Armorial, Rose Medallion, and Canton are but a few of the more familiar.

Bowl, vegetable; Orange Fitzhugh with American eagle, banner, and shield, gilt monogram, fruit finial, 8x9¾", $1,100.00. (Photo courtesy Garth's Auctions Inc.)

Bowl, vegetable; Rose Canton, mc w/gold, w/lid, Ch, 1890s, 6½x10x8"..3,325.00
Food warmer, E, Fitzhugh, bl, domed lid w/fruit finial, 1850s, 13" L. 750.00
Jar, E, FV, figures w/horse, w/lid, mtd as lamp, 22x6¾" 480.00
Mug, E, FR, maritime scene w/Am ship, 19th C, 5½", NM.......... 925.00
Platter, FR, E, central medallion, quilted border, 17¼x14"........... 285.00
Punch bowl, E, FR, sm banded/diapered decor w/in & w/o, 1800s, 4x10". 925.00
Spittoon, E, FR, birds/butterflies/bugs/flowers, 1850s, 7¼x8" 700.00
Tray, warming; E, Fitzhugh, bl, mid-1800s, 2¾x15¾x11" 575.00
Tureen, Rose Canton, mc w/gold, w/lid, Ch, 1890s, 11x13½", EX..450.00
Vase, E, children at play, appl children figures, 12½", pr.............. 575.00
Vase, E, FR, floral, foo dog hdls, flared rim, 18", NM................... 300.00
Vase, E, FR, floral sprays, gilt dragons/butterflies, 24", pr..........1,150.00
Vase, E, Mandarin, lion & ring gilt hdls, prof rstr, 1850s, 24x8½" ..2,300.00

Rugs

The 'Oriental' or Eastern rug market has enjoyed a renewal of interest as collectors have become aware of the fact that some of the semi-antique rugs (those 60 to 100 years old) may be had at a price within the range of the average buyer. Unless noted otherwise, values are for rugs in excellent or better condition.

Afshar, dk bl abrash grd, burgundy/dk bl borders, 96x63"..........1,150.00
Afshar, ornate floral, fringe, 1920s, 89x58" 700.00
Afshar, red spandrels on bl, flat woven ends, 105x59" 750.00
Armenian Shirvan, bright mdls on salmon, ivory/bl borders, 111x46".635.00
Bahktiari, dk bl w/wide ivory border, 246x81" 2,415.00
Caucasian, geometrics, monochromatic, 1910s, 69x48" 400.00
Caucasian Kazak, indigo & madder red, ca 1930, 103x68"........1,700.00
Ferahan Sarouk, floral on tan, 1920s, 76x49"................................ 650.00
Hamadan, floral, bl border on brick red, lt wear/losses, 70x60".1,400.00
Heriz, floral, wide bl borders/ivory spandrels on red, 151x113".1,850.00
Indo-Serape, camel spandrels/bl border on salmon, 114x96" 500.00
Kars Karaba, dk bl w/red & ivory borders, 67x50" 700.00

Kazak, dark borders and red ground, 94x63", $600.00. (Photo courtesy Garth's Auctions Inc.)

NW Persia, geometric dmns, ca 1925, 61x32" 850.00
NW Persia, stylized floral, 1930s, 118x37" 700.00
Persian Heriz, center mdl, red tones, ca 1970, 146x99" 900.00
Persian Kashan, floral, rose tones, ca 1910, lt wear, 82x51".......... 950.00
Peshawar Serapi, geometric floral, rust colors, 120x98" 1,600.00
S Persia, stylized flowers on red & bl, ca 1920, 84x60" 850.00
Sarouk, burgundy border on dk bl, lt wear, fringe, 78x49"........... 550.00
Sarouk, burgundy w/wide bl border, 256x118" 1,150.00
Sarouk, stylized floral on red, ca 1910s, 75x50"........................... 600.00
Serapi, bl mdl w/ivory spandrels on red w/red border, 144x115"...18,400.00
Shiraz, dk bl spandrels/mc borders on brn, 84x74"....................... 500.00

Shirvan prayer, dk bl w/geometric borders, bright mc, 76x46" 575.00
Tabriz, dk bl w/wide pale pk border, 154x110" 1,150.00
Turkish, geometrics on red, ca 1925, 69x45" 400.00

Snuff Bottles

The Chinese were introduced to snuff in the seventeenth century, and their carved and painted snuff bottles typify their exquisite taste and workmanship. These small bottles, seldom measuring over 2½", were made of amber, jade, ivory, and cinnabar; tiny spoons were often attached to their stoppers. By the eighteenth century, some were being made of porcelain, others were of glass with delicate interior designs tediously reverse painted with minuscule brushes sometimes containing a single hair. Copper and brass were used but to no great extent.

Amber, well hollowed, Ch, 19th C, 2½" 2,400.00
Amethyst, vasiform w/cvd flowers, w/stopper, Ch, 3" 250.00
Bronze, cicada clutches cvd jade floret, coral stopper, 19th C, 2¾" .600.00
Ceramic, cabbage shape, gr to wht, coral stopper, Ch, ca 1900, 2⅜" 725.00
Cloisonné lotus blossoms on turq, gilt metal rims, 2½" 1,450.00
Fluorite, dull gr, cvd masks/ram's head hdls, Ch, 1⅞" 660.00
Fossiliferous limestone, carnelian stopper w/ivory collar, 20th C, 2" ..550.00

Ivory, deep relief, 1800s, 5", $1,250.00. (Photo courtesy Robert Weisblut)

Jade, dk yel w/lotus branch cvg, ovoid, Qing Dy 1,100.00
Jade, pebble form, lav w/gr streaks, 2" 1,325.00
Jade, spinach nephrite, lobed melon, 1890s, 2⅜" 2,400.00
Jade, wht, 2 cvd figures, coral stopper, 19th C, 2¼" 6,000.00
MOP, gourd form w/pod, coral stopper, Ch, late 19th C, 2½" 660.00
Nephrite, gray to wht, globular, late 19th C, 2" 780.00
Opal, robed man w/flower bundle figural, coral stopper, 1890s, 2" ...950.00
Porc, dragon chasing pearl, bl/wht, cylinder, red stopper, 19th C, 5"..550.00
Porc, HP landscapes, Ch, early 20th C, 2¾" 1,950.00
Ruby glass, 8 Horses cvg, coral stopper, Ch, Qing Dy, 3¾" 1,650.00

Textiles

Kimono, vertical stripes on silk, Jp, ca 1900 .... 120.00
Kimono, wedding; embr gold/wht flowers on wht silk, Jp, mid-1900s. 300.00
Obi, brocade silk w/flowering prunus blossoms, Jp, 1940s............. 200.00
Panel, river landscape & immortals woven in silk, Ch, 19th C, 81x40" .5,500.00
Panel, warriors on horsebk, woven silk, gold threads, Quing Dy, 90x61"..6,500.00
Robe, bl silk kesi w/floral embr, Ch, 18th C............................... 5,700.00
Robe, dragon/Buddhist emblems in gold & bl embr on silk, Ch.. 5,150.00
Robe, dragons & gold threads embr on bl silk, Ch, 19th C, 59" L.3,150.00
Robe, dragons chasing pearl w/gold, lishui stripes, Qing Dy...... 7,200.00
Robe, dragons/bats/etc embr on bl silk, Ch, 19th C 5,500.00
Robe, Imperial court, silk w/embr symbols of authority, ca 1900 ..12,000.00
Skirt, wht w/much embr & quilted padding, Ch, 19th C.......... 2,750.00
Tapestry, cranes in marsh, silk on linen, late 19th C, 67x45" 850.0

Woodblock Prints

Framed prints are of less value than those not framed, since it is impossible to inspect their condition or determined whether or not they have borders or have been trimmed.

Goyo, Hashiguchi; Woman Holding Towel, 1920, 17¼x11".....2,400.00
Harunobu, Suzuki; Girl in Bathhouse, 18th C, 7½x10¼"..........2,400.00
Hashiguchi, Goyo; Woman Holding Tray, 1920, 15⅛x10"........6,000.00
Hoshi, Joichi; Red Tree, 1973, 16½x22" 4,750.00
Kiyoshi, Kobayakawa; Dance (Odori), 1931, 16⅝x11⅞"..........2,150.00
Kogan, Tobari; Profile of School Girl, 1920s, 15x9¾" 3,450.00
Kotondo, Torii; Snow (Yuki), seated geisha, 1929, 16⅛x10⅜"..3,600.00
Lum, Bertha; Theatre Street Scene, 1905, 8⅞x4⅜" 6,000.00
Nakayama, I Wish To Fly Too, 1971, 29½x21½" 4,350.00

Samurai with Geisha, Tutgawa Toyokuni (1769 – 1825), with seal, 13x9½", $235.00. (Photo courtesy Leslie Hindman)

Yoshida, Hiroshi, Moraine Lake, 1925, 14½x9¾" 3,600.00
Yoshida, Hiroshi; Night in Kyoto, 1933, 14¾x9⅝" 2,700.00

Orrefors

Orrefors Glassworks was founded in 1898 in the Swedish province of Smaaland. Utilizing the expertise of designers such as Simon Gate, Edward Hald, Vicke Lindstrand, and Edwin Ohrstrom, it produced art glass of the highest quality. Various techniques were used in achieving the decoration. Some were wheel engraved; others were blown through a unique process that formed controlled bubbles or air pockets resulting in unusual patterns and shapes. (Remember: When no color is noted, the glass is clear.)

Bowl, Ribbon, mc in clear w/bubbles, I Lundin/Expo 2647, 4¼x6½".. 725.00
Chalice, Graal, nudes/animals, bl cased/amber cased ft, Cyren, '78, 6" ...1,800.00
Vase, apple, gr, I Lundin, Orrefors Expo DU 32-57, 16½x14" ...5,500.00
Vase, Ariel, cased blk/bl, geometrics, I Lundin, Nr 476-63, 5¾".. 1,100.00
Vase, Ariel, cobalt cased, I Lundin, #424.E5, 8½x4¼"...............1,150.00
Vase, Ariel, girl & dove, cobalt cased w/amber shaded int, #292-E3, 7" .1,950.00
Vase, Ariel, girl's face, E Ohrstrom, #99, 1939, 7½x6⅛"..........15,600.00
Vase, Ariel, girl's face, maroon cased, E Ohrstrom, 1968, 7" 9,600.00
Vase, Graal, Engagement, mauve/cobalt/gr, Englund, #968430, 1987, 14"..9,000.00
Vase, Graal, fish, gr in clear, E Hald, #859L, 4½" 780.00
Vase, Graal, fish/plants, gr/blk/clear, E Hald, #2770D, 5¼x4½"... 1,150.00
Vase, Javanese Dancer, etched clear, S Gate, ca 1950, 9½" 1,450.00
Vase, Kraka, bl cased w/internal bubbles, S Palmqvist, #322, 12"....950.00
Vase, Ravenna, ruby on clear, S Palmqvist, #796, 2x4½" 1,450.00
Vase, Thunderstorm, cobalt, flared, E Hald, 1920, label, 4⅜"....1,550.00

Vase, Graal, fish, Edward Hald, ca. 1937, exhibited in Paris in 1937, Graal nr 31 Hald Orrefors 1937 Sweden, 7", $4,750.00. (Photo courtesy Treadway Gallery Inc.)

Ott and Brewer

The partnership of Ott and Brewer began in 1865 in Trenton, New Jersey. By 1876 they were making decorated graniteware, parian, and 'ivory porcelain' — similar to Irish Belleek though not as fine and of different composition. In 1883, however, experiments toward that end had reached a successful conclusion, and a true Belleek body was introduced. It came to be regarded as the finest china ever produced by an American firm. The ware was decorated by various means such as hand painting, transfer printing, gilding, and lustre glazing. The company closed in 1893, one of many that failed during that depression. In the listings below, the ware is Belleek unless noted otherwise. Our advisor for this category is Mary Frank Gaston; she is listed in the Directory under Texas. See also Parian.

Bowl, recumbent female nude, wht, shell shape, 3 snail shell ft, 3x11" ...2,625.00
Ewer, cranes & cattails, emb gold enamel & gilt, crabstock hdl, 13"..155.00
Pitcher, daisies, gilt on ivory, branch hdl, squat w/dimpled sides, 8"..850.00
Pitcher, orchid, bl on wht w/gold, rtcl hdl, crown/sword mk, 17¼" ..2,350.00
Vase, bird mc w/gold on gr, bottle form, early red moon stamp, 10".7,200.00
Vase, floral/gilt, appl rose w/wraparound stem & leaf, globular, 7"...315.00
Vase, herons & bamboo, gold tones on wht, bulbous, slim sq neck, 10x7" ..2,940.00

Vase, multicolored bird with gilt details, early crescent moon red stamp, 10", $7,200.00. (Photo courtesy Dave Rago Auctions)

Vase, posy; leaves & butterflies, gold on wht, Belleek O&B, 5½"....150.00
Vase, tea roses on wht w/gold, dolphin hdls, crown mk, sm rstr, 18x10" ..900.00

Overbeck

Four genteel ladies set up the Overbeck pottery around 1911 in the unlikely area of Cambridge City, Indiana. Margaret, Hannah, Elizabeth, and Mary would produce high-quality hand-thrown vases featuring vertical panels excised with floral, landscape, or figural decoration, at first with an Arts & Crafts stylization, then moving on to a more modern, Art Deco geometry. Mary, holding up the fort starting in 1937, increasingly turned to the production of hand-sized figurines in period dress, which she would often give to children visiting the pottery. The operation closed in 1955. Most vases and figurines are stamped OBK, sometimes with the addition of a first-name initial. In the last couple of years, some convincing copies have been appearing on the market. Collectors should buy with a guarantee of authenticity or otherwise take their chances. Our advisors for this category are Suzanne Perrault and David Rago; they are listed in the Directory under New Jersey. In the listings that follow, unless otherwise noted, assume that each example has been decorated by Overbeck's typical carved and painted method.

Bowl, floral, caramel mottled matt, flat bottom, OBK/F, 2x6" ...2,375.00
Bowl, HP housing landscape, pk/gr/lt bl/brn on bl, ftd, OBK, 5". 1,250.00
Brooch, floral cluster, tan/gr/yel/bl/pk, 1¾" 375.00
Candlestick, floral panels on tan, saucer ft, paper label, EF, 5"..3,375.00
Figurine, cello player w/pk leaf hat, rustic bow, OBK, 3½" 425.00
Figurine, rooster, overly lg ft, 4".. 560.00
Figurine, squirrel eating nut, flowers on base, OBK, 2⅜" 515.00
Figurine, turtle w/4 spindley legs, pastels, OBK, 1⅝" 550.00
Figurine, Victorian lady in hoop dress, mc pastels, 4¼" 395.00
Figurine, 3 ducks squawking, grassy base, 2"................................. 550.00
Ink & watercolor study, marigolds, HO, 7¾x5" 6,000.00
Ink & watercolor study, milkweed, HO, 10x8" 10,625.00
Pitcher, trees w/blossoms, bl/gray on brn matt, OBK/F, 5x10" ...3,750.00
Vase, birds, gr gloss, E/H, 6½" 1,200.00
Vase, birds in panels, gr & brn, OBK/EF, 4¾x5¼" 5,750.00
Vase, birds/flowers, mustard on brn, bbl shape, OBK/EF, 9¼x6" ...15,600.00
Vase, elephants & birds, russet on orange, OBK/EF, 3½x5½" 9,250.00
Vase, fawns, wht on turq, OBK, E/MF, 5½", NM 3,000.00
Vase, fawns & accents, wht band on turq, wide neck, OBK, 6"... 3,125.00
Vase, floral, red/yel/wht on blk, flared rim, OBK, 1920, 9" 3,150.00
Vase, floral (deeply cvd), tan & lt rust, OBK/EMF, 11½".........16,250.00
Vase, frothy pk & wht glass, ovoid, OBK, 8¼x6½" 1,250.00
Vase, HP bird/pine trees/floral, mc on wht, OBK/EF, 9" 6,875.00
Vase, pine cones (cvd/pnt), forest gr/mustard, OBK E/H, 8¾x4¾".. 16,800.00
Vase, Queen Anne's Lace, brn/red/turq mottle on brn/mauve, OBK, 8½"..25,000.00

Vase, stylized figures of children and hollyhocks on mustard ground, 10½", $60,000.00. (Photo courtesy David Rago Auctions/ LiveAuctioneers.com)

Overshot

Overshot glass originated in sixteenth century Venice, and the ability to make this ware eventually spread to Bohemia, Spain, and elsewhere in Europe. Sometime prior to 1800, the production of this glass seems to have stopped. The Englishman Apsley Pellatt, owner of the Falcon Glass Works, is credited with reviving this decorative technique around 1845 – 1850. He acknowledged the origin of this technique by calling his product 'Venetian Frosted Glass' or 'Anglo-Venetian Glass.' Later it would be called by other names, such as Frosted Glassware, Ice Glass, or Craquelle Glass.

It is important to understand the difference between crackle glass and overshot glass. All crackle is not overshot, and all overshot is not crackle. However, most overshot is also crackle glass. Two different processes or steps were involved in making this glassware.

Crackle glass was produced by dipping a partially blown gob of hot glass in cold water. The sudden temperature change caused fissures or cracks in the glass surface. The gob was then lightly reheated and blown into its full shape. The blowing process enlarged the spaces between fissures to create a labyrinth of channels in varying widths. When cooled in the annealing lehr, the surface of the finished object had a crackled or cracked-ice effect.

Overshot glass was made by rolling a partially inflated gob of hot glass on finely ground shards of glass that had been placed on a steel plate called a marver. The gob was then lightly reheated to remove the sharp edges of the ground glass and blown to its final shape. Most overshot pieces were immersed in cold water before application of the ground glass, and such glassware can be considered both crackle and overshot. Sometimes an object was blown to full size before being rolled over the glass shards. As Barlow and Kaiser explained on page 104 in *The Glass Industry in Sandwich, Vol. 4*, 'The ground particles adhered uniformly over the entire surface of the piece, showing no roadways, because the glass was not stretched after the particles had been applied. Overshot glass produced by this second method is much sharper to the touch.' Overshot glass produced by the first method — with the 'roadways' — has been mistaken for the Tree of Life Pattern. However, this pattern is pressed glass, whereas overshot is either free-blown or mold-blown. Overshot pieces could be further embellished, requiring a third decorative technique at the furnace, such as the application of vaseline glass designs or fine threads of glass that were picked up and fused to the object. The latter decorative style, called Peloton, was patented in 1880 by Wilhelm Kralik in Bohemia.

Boston & Sandwich, Reading Artistic Glass Works, and Hobbs Brockunier were among the companies that manufactured overshot in the United States. Such products were quite utilitarian — vases, decanters, cruets, bowls, water pitchers with ice bladders, lights, lamps, and other shapes. Colored overshot was produced at Sandwich, but research has shown that the applied ground glass was always crystal. Czechoslovakia is known to have made overshot with colored ground glass. Many such pieces are acid stamped 'Czechoslovakia.' Undamaged, mint-condition overshot is extremely hard to find and expensive. Our advisors for this category are Stan and Arlene Weitman; they are listed in the Directory under New York.

Pitcher, blue with amber handle, 7½", $200.00.
(Photo courtesy Dirk Soulis Auctions/ LiveAuctioneers.com)

Basket, appl rope hdls, 6½x10½" L 425.00
Basket, cranberry to crystal, thorn hdl, rectangular, 10x7½" 750.00
Bowl, bl, appl mc glass fruit on lid, 4x6" 140.00
Compote, tall ped, 7½x6¾" 475.00
Creamer, crystal, appl hdl, long & wide spout, 1880s, 4¼" 95.00
Fairy lamp, clear w/melon ribs, S Clarke, 3-pc, 7" 175.00
Mustard jar, crystal w/metal lid, 5" 85.00
Pitcher, champagne; cranberry, clear hdl & rigaree, ice bladder, 12"..1,250.00
Pitcher, cranberry to clear, cylindrical, low hdl, 7" 750.00
Pitcher, tankard; cranberry, clear reeded hdl, 9⅜x4½" 995.00
Pitcher, water; bl, reeded hdl, ca 1870-87, 7¼" 525.00
Rose bowl, crystal, branches form ft, 4½x4½" 95.00
Rose bowl, rubena, 6x5" 275.00
Tumbler, gr to clear, 3¾x2¾" 100.00
Vase, clear w/appl vaseline flower, sq sides, vaseline ft, 12"..........1,000.00
Vase, cranberry to clear w/appl vaseline decor, slim neck, 7¼" 850.00
Vase, metallic gold, indented sides, slight twist to 6" neck, 10" 60.00

Owen, Ben; Master Potter

Ben Owen worked at the Jugtown Pottery of North Carolina from 1923 until it temporarily closed in 1959. He continued in the business in his own Plank Road Pottery, stamping his ware 'Ben Owen, Master Potter,' with many forms made by Lester Fanell Craven in the late 1960s. His pottery closed in 1972. He died in 1983 at the age of 81. The pottery was reopened in 1981 under the supervision of Benjamin Wade Owen II. One of the principal potters was David Garner who worked there until about 1985. This pottery is still in operation today with Ben II as the main potter.

Candlesticks, lead glaze, Ben Owen Master Potter, 1960s, 17½", pr...550.00
Candlesticks, lead glaze, Ben Owen Master Potter, 1960s, 9¼", pr...345.00
Candlesticks, wht gloss, Ben Owen Master Potter, 12½", pr 385.00
Cookie jar, Tobacco Spit Brown, Ben Owen Master Potter, 10½"...240.00

Han Dynasty style, Chinese Blue and turquoise over red, incised rings, Ben Owen Master Potter, 10½", $5,100.00. (Photo courtesy Leland Little Auction & Estate Sales Ltd./ LiveAuctioneers.com)

Jar, foamy wht, ear hdls, w/lid, Ben Owen Master Potter, 8¼", NM...600.00
Jug, stoneware w/multi-lined incised rings, ovoid, 1960s, 12" 385.00
Lamp base, Frogskin Green w/vertical linear decor, bulbous, 12"..225.00
Pie dish, chick (yel) on brn gloss, Ben...Potter, 3½x12¾" 345.00
Vase, Dogwood, wht, Ben Owen Master Potter, 1960s, 13½x6"...480.00
Vase, foamy wht, incurvate rim, Master Ben Owens, 1950s, 7".... 180.00
Vase, olive gr, shouldered, Ben Owen Master Potter, 4¼" 100.00
Vase, Oriental Translation, Chinese White, incurvate rim, 7¼"..135.00
Vase, stoneware w/vertical lines/wide center band, Ben Owen III, 8"...130.00
Vase, wht ovoid w/brn scallop near base, Ben Owen III, 1985, 12"..180.00
Vase, wht w/2 appl bosses at shoulder, Ben...Master Potter, 8".....450.00

Owens Pottery

J.B. Owens founded his company in Zanesville, Ohio, in 1891, and until 1907, when the company decided to exert most of its energies in the area of tile production, made several quality lines of art pottery. His first line, Utopian, was a standard brown ware with underglaze slip decoration of nature studies, animals, and portraits. A similar line, Lotus, utilized lighter background colors. Henri Deux, introduced in 1900, featured incised Art Nouveau forms inlaid with color. In time, the Brush McCoy Pottery acquired many of Owens' molds and reproduced a line similar to Henri Deux, which they called Navarre. (Owens pieces were usually marked Henri Deux and have a heavier body and coarser feel to the glaze than similar McCoy pieces.) Other important lines were Opalesce, Rustic, Feroza, Cyrano, and Mission, examples of which are rare today. The factory burned in 1928, and the company closed shortly thereafter. Values vary according to the quality of the artwork and subject matter. Examples signed by the artist bring higher prices than those that are not signed. For further information we recommend *Owens Pottery Unearthed* by Kristy and Rick McKibben and Jeanette and Marvin Stofft. Mrs. Stofft is listed in the Directory under Indiana.

Aborigine, vase, geometrics, slightly bulbous, 4¾x3¾" 95.00
Alpine (rare line), vase, floral, slim neck, #119, 14", NM 350.00
Cyrano, jardiniere, raised filigree & bl sponging, 8⅛" 300.00
Delft, jardiniere, Dutch lady & daughter at pier, 8x9½" 650.00
Henri Deux, jardiniere, Nouveau figure in landscape, 7½" 550.00
Henri Deux, jardiniere, Nouveau lady & leaves, 8¼x10", EX 650.00
Henri Deux, vase, Nouveau floral on brn, 8½" 500.00
High Glaze, vase, squeeze-bag Nouveau decor, #1178, 12¾" 550.00
Lotus, vase, floral & squeeze-bag borders, #1175, 5¾" 600.00
Lotus, vase, lotus blossoms/bud/leaves, cylindrical, #1249, 16⅝" ... 1,600.00
Lotus, vase, stylized leafless tree, slim, shouldered, 9⅜" 360.00
Majolica, jardiniere, emb decor, gr/cream/brn, 6x7" 200.00
Matt Green, vase, cvd geometrics, rtcl windows at neck, 7x8¼" ... 1,100.00
Matt Green, vase, dragonflies, 4⅛" 1,325.00
Matt Green, vase, stenciled bird, ftd, 8¾", NM 350.00
Matt Lotus, vase, Nouveau stylized wht poppies, #1146, 13" 800.00
Matt Utopian, pansies on bl & biscuit, #1010, 10" 360.00
Opalesce, vase, Nouveau floral, shouldered, 13" 1,100.00
Sunburst (scarce line), vase, roses, J Herold, #787, 13⅝" 500.00
Tile, butterfly, 4-color, 6x6" 275.00
Tile, goose by pond, 5-color cuenca, sm chip, 11¾x8¾" 1,800.00

Tile, landscape with house, 11½x17½", $4,200.00. (Photo courtesy David Rago Auctions/ LiveAuctioneers.com)

Utopian, humidor, smoking cigar & matches, #1017, 7⅛" 550.00
Utopian, jardiniere, chrysanthemums, ruffled rim, 7½" 195.00
Utopian, jug, cherry branch, #790, 5x6½" 95.00
Utopian, jug, corn on ear, 7x5" 200.00
Utopian, jug, flower, high curled hdl, 6" 150.00
Utopian, loving cup, floral, 3-hdl, #826, 7" 235.00
Utopian, mug, currants, sgn MT, 4½" 125.00
Utopian, mug, grapes, #1035, 5¼" 125.00
Utopian, mug, leaves & berries, #1035, 5" 80.00
Utopian, tankard, floral, cylindrical, 1915, 11" 345.00
Utopian, vase, daisies, ovoid w/short neck, #1030, 9½" 250.00
Utopian, vase, daisies, 4 tapered ft, #821, 5¼" 180.00
Utopian, vase, floral, bottle form, 13" 200.00
Utopian, vase, floral, sgn C Fouts, stick neck, 13" 225.00
Utopian, vase, floral, shouldered, tapered neck, 7" 235.00
Utopian, vase, floral, slim neck, wide shoulder, #107/8, 3½" 85.00
Utopian, vase, floral, stick neck, #1076, 13" 215.00
Utopian, vase, floral, swollen cylinder, 14" 325.00
Utopian, vase, floral, twisted body, ftd, 4¾" 85.00
Utopian, vase, irises, slim, 13½" 275.00
Utopian, vase, leaves, flared cylinder, #792, 7½", NM 240.00
Utopian, vase, roses, bulbous, blemish, 12" 400.00
Utopian, vase, roses, integral hdls, 4" 135.00

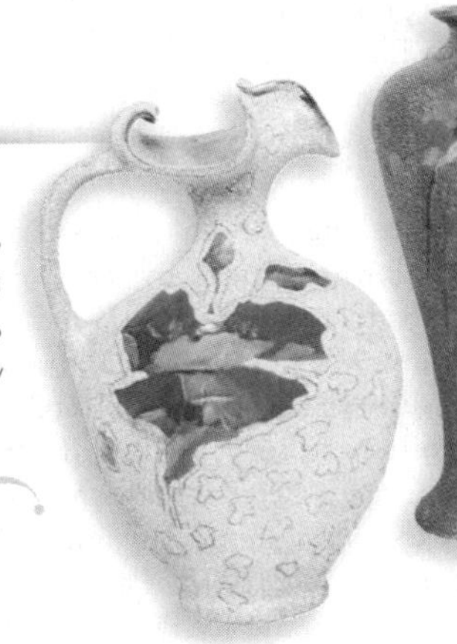

Opalescent, ewer, floral, 10", $875.00; Vase, floral, 11", $875.00. (Photo courtesy David Rago Auctions)

Paden City Glass

Paden City Glass Mfg. Co. was founded in 1916 in Paden City, West Virginia. It made both mold-blown and pressed wares and is most remembered today for its handmade lines in bright colors with fanciful etchings. A great deal of Paden City's business was in supplying decorating companies and fitters with glass; therefore, Paden City never identified their glass with a trademark of any kind, and the company's advertisements were limited to trade publications, rather than retail. In 1948 the management of the company opened a second plant to make utilitarian, machine-made wares such as tumblers and ashtrays, but the move was ill-advised due to a glut of similar merchandise already on the market. The company remained in operation until 1951 when it permanently closed the doors of both factories as a result of the losses incurred by Plant No. 2. (To clear up an often-repeated misunderstanding, dealers and collectors alike should keep in mind that The Paden City Glass Mfg Co. had absolutely no connection with the Paden City Pottery Company, other than their identical locale.)

Today Paden City is best known for its numerous acid-etched wares that featured birds, but many other ornate etchings were produced. Fortunately several new books on the subject have been published, which have provided names for and increased awareness of previously undocumented etchings. Currently, collectors especially seek out examples of Paden City's most detailed etching, Orchid, and its most appealing etching, Cupid. Pieces in the company's plainer pressed dinnerware lines, however, have remained affordable, even though some patterns are quite scarce. After several years of rising prices, internet auction sites have increased the supply of pieces with more commonly found etchings such as Peacock & Rose, causing a dip in prices. However, pieces bearing documented etchings on shapes and/or colors not previously seen combined continue to fetch high prices from advanced collectors.

Following is a list of Paden City's colors. Names in capital letters indicate original factory color names where known, followed by a description of the color.

Amber — several shades

Blue — early 1920s color, medium shade, not cobalt

Cheriglo — pink

Copen, Neptune, Ceylon — various shades of light blue

Crystal — clear

Ebony — black

Emeraldglo — thinner dark green, not as deep as Forest Green

Forest Green — dark green

Green — various shades, from yellowish to electric green

Mulberry — amethyst

Opal — white (milk glass)

Primrose — amber with reddish tint (rare)

Rose — dark pink (rare)

Royal or Ritz Blue — cobalt

Ruby — red

Topaz — yellow

Collectors seeking more information on Paden City would do well to consult the following: *Paden City, The Color Company*, by Jerry Barnett (out of print, privately published, 1979); *Colored Glassware of the Depression Era 2* by Hazel Marie Weatherman (Glassbooks, 1974); *Price Trends to Colored Glassware of the Depression Era 2* by Hazel Marie Weatherman (Glassbooks, editions in 1977, 1979, and 1981). Also available are *Paden City Company Catalog Reprints from the 1920s* (Antique Publications, 2000); *Paden City Glassware* by Paul and Debora Torsiello and Tom and Arlene Stillman (Schiffer, 2002); *Paden City Glass Company* by Walker, Bratkovich & Walker (Antique Publications, 2003); and *Encyclopedia of Paden City Glass* by Carrie and Gerald Domitz (Collector Books, 2004). There is also a quarterly newsletter currently being published by the Paden City Glass Collectors Guild; this group is listed the Directory under Clubs, Newsletters, and Catalogs. Our advisor for this category is Michael Krumme; he is listed in the Directory under California.

Ardith, amber, tumbler, ice tea; blown, 12-oz, from $75 to 125.00

Ardith, blk, candlestick, ea from $35 to 45.00

Ardith, blk, compote, 7½", from $45 to 55.00

Ardith, cobalt or red, saucer, from $25 to 35.00

Ardith, cobalt or red, tray, center hdl, 10½", from $225 to 275.00

Ardith, gr or pk, plate, cracker; 10", from $75 to 125.00

Ardith, gr or pk, vase, 6½", from $75 to 95.00

Ardith, yel, pitcher, plain, 7¾", from $375 to 450.00

Black Forest (etched), amber, batter jug, 8", from $175 to 200.00

Black Forest (etched), amber, bottle, scent; from $150 to 175.00

Black Forest (etched), blk, bottle, scent; from $200 to 225.00

Black Forest (etched), blk, cake plate, 2x11", from $125 to 150.00

Black Forest (etched), crystal, cup, from $65 to 75.00

Black Forest (etched), gr or pk, decanter, w/stopper, 10" 450.00

Black Forest (etched), gr or pk, egg cup, from $150 to 175.00

Black Forest (etched), gr or pk, pitcher, 72-oz, 10½", from $550 to.. 750.00

Black Forest (etched), gr or pk, vase, 10", from $175 to 225.00

Black Forest (etched), red, cup, from $150 to 200.00

Crow's Foot, amber, tumbler, 4", from $50 to 65.00

Crow's Foot, amethyst, creamer, from $25 to 35.00

Crow's Foot, blk, bowl, ftd, 7", from $75 to 85.00

Crow's Foot, cobalt, cake plate, 2½x12", from $250 to 275.00

Crow's Foot, cobalt, cracker plate, 11", from $100 to 120.00

Crow's Foot, cobalt, punch bowl, 8¾", from $700 to 900.00

Crow's Foot, crystal, bowl, nasturtium; 6x8", from $75 to 95.00

Crow's Foot, crystal, compote, tall stem, 7x6¾", from $40 to 50.00

Crow's Foot, crystal, plate, w/hdls, 11½x13", from $25 to 35.00

Crow's Foot, gr or pk, candy dish, w/lid, 5¾x5¾", from $125 to... 175.00

Crow's Foot, gr or pk, sugar bowl, from $22 to 30.00

Crow's Foot, red, candlestick, 2-light, ea from $100 to 125.00

Crow's Foot, red, plate, luncheon; 8", from $40 to 45.00

Crow's Foot, red, plate, w/hdls, 11½x13", from $100 to 120.00

Crow's Foot, red, punch cup, roly poly, from $15 to 20.00

Crow's Foot, red, sugar bowl, from $40 to 60.00

Cupid (etched), gr or pk, bowl, center loop hdl, 11", from $250 to.. 300.00

Cupid (etched), gr or pk, bowl, salad; 9", from $125 to 150.00

Cupid (etched), gr or pk, cheese & cracker, 10", from $350 to 400.00

Cupid (etched), gr or pk, mayonniase set, 3-pc, from $350 to...... 450.00

Cupid (etched), gr or pk, plate, oval, 7½x10½", from $250 to 300.00

Cupid (etched), gr or pk, sugar bowl, ribbed, from $65 to 75.00

Cupid (etched), gr or pk, vase, fan form; 8½", from $750 to 900.00

Cupid (etched), gr or pk, 5", from $750 to 950.00

Delilah Bird, amber, yel or Primrose, bowl, sq, 10", from $150 to.... 200.00

Delilah Bird, amber, yel or Primrose, cracker jar, 5½" 450.00

Delilah Bird, bl or red, candlestick, keyhole, 5", ea from $100 to.... 125.00

Delilah Bird, bl or red, compote, low, 3¾x7", from $150 to 200.00

Delilah Bird, crystal, bowl, ftd, 4½x11", from $150 to 250.00

Delilah Bird, crystal, creamer, 2¾", from $20 to 25.00

Delilah Bird, ebony, plate w/hdls, 10", from $100 to 125.00

Delilah Bird, gr or pk, gravy boat, ftd, 5x7½", from $200 to 250.00

Delilah Bird, gr or pk, vase, 6", from $300 to 400.00

Emerald Glo, Emerald Green, cheese & cracker, metal lid, 12" 65.00

Emerald Glo, Emerald Green, cocktail shaker, 11", from $75 to.. 100.00

Emerald Glo, Emerald Green, epergne, from $200 to 250.00

Emerald Glo, Emerald Green, nappy, divided, w/hdls, from $20 to...24.00

Emerald Glo, Emerald Green, platter, 14½", from $24 to 30.00

Emerald Glo, Emerald Green, relish, 5-part, 12", from $45 to 55.00

Emerald Glo, Emerald Green, shakers, 3", pr from $22 to 25.00

Emerald Glo, Emerald Green, tidbit, 2-tier; 7" & 14", from $30 to...40.00

Gazebo (etched), bl, candy dish, ftd, 10½", from $95 to 125.00

Gazebo (etched), bl, compote, flared, 10x7½", from $125 to 150.00

Gazebo (etched), bl, creamer, from $35 to 45.00

Gazebo (etched), bl, mayonnaise set, 2½x4½", from $75 to 100.00

Gazebo (etched), bl, relish, 2-part, 5x6¾", from $40 to 50.00

Gazebo, blue, server with center handle, 11", $85.00. (Photo courtesy Cripple Creek Auctions/LiveAuctioneers.com)

Gazebo (etched), crystal, bowl, 12", from $65 to 75.00

Gazebo (etched), crystal, candlestick, 6", ea from $20 to 25.00

Gazebo (etched), crystal, candy dish, ftd, 10½", from $50 to 65.00

Gazebo (etched), crystal, compote, flared, 10x7½", from $45 to 50.00

Gazebo (etched), crystal, plate, 11", from $45 to 55.00

Gazebo (etched), crystal, punch bowl liner, from $45 to 55.00

Gazebo (etched), crystal, punch cup, from $8 to 10.00

Gazebo (etched), crystal, tray, center hdl, 11", from $50 to 65.00

Gazebo (etched), crystal, tray, w/hdls, 13", from $55 to 75.00

Gazebo (etched), punch bowl, from $200 to 250.00

Gothic Garden (etched), amber or blk, candlestick, keyhole, ea... 45.00

Gothic Garden (etched), amber or blk, plate, 7", from $18 to 20.00

Gothic Garden (etched), blk or yel, vase, 8", from $125 to 175.00

Gothic Garden (etched), gr or pk, creamer, 3", from $45 to 50.00

Gothic Garden (etched), gr or pk, vase, 8", from $175 to 200.00

Gothic Garden (etched), yel, bowl, w/hdls, 10", from $65 to......... 85.00

Gothic Garden (etched), yel, snack set, 10" plate/6" bowl, from $75 to ..125.00

Gothic Garden, yellow, candlestick, #411, 5", from $45.00 to $55.00. (Photo courtesy Carrie and Gerald Domitz)

Peacock and Rose/Nora Bird, green, fan vase, #300, 8½", from $550.00 to $750.00. (Photo courtesy Carrie and Jerry Domitz)

Peacock & Rose/Nora Bird, amber, creamer, from $45 to	55.00
Peacock & Rose/Nora Bird, bl, ice bucket, 6x4½", from $500 to	600.00
Peacock & Rose/Nora Bird, bl, tray, loop hdl, 10½", from $450 to	500.00
Peacock & Rose/Nora Bird, bl, vase, elliptical, 8", from $400 to	450.00
Peacock & Rose/Nora Bird, blk, ice bucket, 6x4½", from $125 to	150.00

Largo, amber or crystal, bowl, center hdl, 10½", from $50 to	75.00
Largo, amber or crystal, box, cigarette; from $60 to	75.00
Largo, amber or crystal, candlestick, 2-light, 5", ea from $20 to	30.00
Largo, amber or crystal, cup, from $18 to	22.00
Largo, amber or crystal, plate, 9", from $18 to	20.00
Largo, amber or crystal, platter, 11½x9½", from $30 to	50.00
Largo, amber or crystal, vase, from $65 to	85.00
Largo, bl or red, bowl, crimped, w/hdls, 7¾x12¾", from $85 to	95.00
Largo, bl or red, candy dish, ftd, 7", from $100 to	125.00
Largo, bl or red, plate, 9", from $25 to	30.00
Largo, bl or red, relish, 5-part, oval, from $75 to	100.00
Largo, bl or red, vase, from $150 to	175.00
Maya, bl, plate, ftd, from $65 to	80.00
Maya, crystal, bowl, w/hdls, 10½", from $50 to	65.00
Maya, crystal, compote, 10x6", from $35 to	50.00
Maya, crystal, server, center hdl, 11", from $50 to	75.00
Maya, crystal, sugar bowl, from $12 to	15.00
Maya, lt bl, candy dish, 7", from $125 to	150.00
Maya, lt bl, cheese & cracker, w/lid, 12½", from $140 to	165.00
Maya, red, bowl, center hdl, from $100 to	125.00
Maya, red, candlestick, 5", ea from $50 to	75.00
Maya, red, compote, 10x6", from $75 to	100.00
Maya, red, plate, ftd, 14", from $75 to	100.00
Nerva, crystal, bowl, console; 13", from $45 to	65.00
Nerva, crystal, candy dish, w/lid, 7", from $50 to	65.00
Nerva, crystal, compote, tall stem, 8x6", from $75 to	95.00
Nerva, crystal, relish, 3-part, 6½x11", from $45 to	65.00
Nerva, red, bowl, cereal; 6½", from $25 to	35.00
Nerva, red, cake plate, 12", from $150 to	175.00
Nerva, red, compote, 9½", from $100 to	120.00
Nerva, red, relish, 3-part, 6½x11", from $65 to	85.00
Orchid (etched), bl or red, compote, low, 3½x6½"	175.00
Orchid (etched), bl or red, plate, w/hdls, 12x14", from $150 to	200.00
Orchid (etched), bl or red, vase, collared, 7½", from $500 to	575.00
Orchid (etched), gr or pk, candy jar, 8", from $250 to	300.00
Orchid (etched), gr or pk, tray, plain, 4½x11", from $30 to	45.00
Orchid (etched), yel, bowl, ftd, 4½x9½", from $225 to	300.00
Party Line, amber or crystal, bowl, flared, 9" H, from $25 to	30.00
Party Line, amber or crystal, bowl, mixing; 9", from $35 to	45.00
Party Line, amber or crystal, candy dish, blown, w/lid, ½-lb	50.00
Party Line, bl, cheese dish, w/lid, 3½x4½", from $40 to	45.00
Party Line, bl, refrigerator box, 5½", from $65 to	80.00
Party Line, blk, cocktail shaker, 18-oz, from $275 to	325.00
Party Line, blk, water bottle, 48-oz, 9½", from $200 to	225.00
Party Line, gr or pk, bowl, berry; ind, 4½", from $10 to	15.00
Party Line, gr or pk, cheese & cracker, w/lid, 10½", from $100 to	125.00
Party Line, gr or pk, refrigerator box, 5½", from $45 to	55.00
Party Line, gr or pk, shakers, 3", pr from $50 to	65.00
Peacock & Rose/Nora Bird, amber, cheese & cracker, 11", from $175 to	200.00

Peacock & Rose/Nora Bird, gr or pk, bowl, oval, 8½", from $125 to	175.00
Peacock & Rose/Nora Bird, gr or pk, syrup, from $150 to	175.00
Peacock & Rose/Nora Bird, plate, luncheon; 8½", from $45 to	65.00
Penny Line, amber or crystal, cocktail shaker, 40-oz, from $75 to	100.00
Penny Line, amber or crystal, cordial, 1¼-oz, from $12 to	18.00
Penny Line, amber or crystal, wine, 3-oz, from $12 to	16.00
Penny Line, bl or red, plate, 8", from $30 to	45.00
Penny Line, bl or red, sugar bowl, from $20 to	25.00
Penny Line, bl or red, tumbler, 9-oz, from $28 to	33.00

Pairpoint

The Pairpoint Manufacturing Company was built in 1880 in New Bedford, Massachusetts. It was primarily a metalworks whose chief product was coffin fittings. Next door, the Mt. Washington Glassworks made quality glasswares of many varieties. (See Mt. Washington for more information concerning their artware lines.) By 1894 it became apparent to both companies that a merger would be to their best interest.

From the late 1890s until the 1930s, lamps and lamp accessories were an important part of Pairpoint's production. There were three main types of shades, all of which were blown: puffy — blown-out reverse-painted shades (usually floral designs); ribbed — also reverse painted; and scenic — reverse painted with scenes of land or seascapes (usually executed on smooth surfaces, although ribbed scenics may be found occasionally). Cut glass lamps and those with metal overlay panels were also made. Scenic shades were sometimes artist signed. Every shade was stamped on the lower inside or outside edge with 1) The Pairpoint Corp., 2) Patent Pending, 3) Patented July 9, 1907, or 4) Patent Applied For. Bases were made of bronze, copper, brass, silver, or wood and are always signed. (In our listings all information before the semicolon pertains specifically to the shade.)

Because they produced only fancy, handmade artware, the company's sales lagged seriously during the Depression, and as time and tastes changed, their style of product was less in demand. As a result, they never fully recovered; consequently part of the buildings and equipment was sold in 1938. The company reorganized in 1939 under the direction of Robert Gundersen and again specialized in quality hand-blown glassware. Isaac Babbit regained possession of the silver departments, and together they established Gundersen Glassworks, Inc. After WWII, because of a sharp decline in sales, it again became necessary to reorganize. The Gundersen-Pairpoint Glassworks was formed, and the old line of cut, engraved artware was reintroduced. The company moved to East Wareham, Massachusetts, in 1957. But business continued to suffer, and the firm closed only one year later. In 1970, however, new facilities were constructed in Sagamore under the direction of Robert Bryden, sales manager for the company since the 1950s. In 1974 the company began to produce lead glass cup plates which were made on commission as fund-raisers for various churches and organizations. These are signed with a 'P' in diamond and are becoming quite collectible. See also Burmese; Napkin Rings.

Glass

Bowl, butterfly & floral intaglio, shallow, 13" 120.00
Bowl, daisies & leaves, cut, ca 1910, 8" 48.00
Bowl, fruit, Colias, cut flowers & butterfly in spider web, 8" 165.00
Bowl, Mistletoe, cut, scalloped sawtooth rim, 9" 360.00
Box, butterfly & floral cuttings, SP hinge, 6½" dia 250.00
Butter dish, Nevada, cut, 4 hobstar panesl, faceted knob, 6x8".... 425.00
Candlestick, HP floral on yel (8½") on walnut stem, 15¾" 425.00
Candlesticks, gr w/clear spherical std w/diffused bubbles, 9", pr... 335.00
Centerpc, cut bowl on SP stem w/3 SP baskets, 1930s, 21x12x12" .. 300.00
Compote, amber w/clear ball stem, flared rim, blown, 6x12" 395.00
Compote, amethyst, conical, disk ft, 5¾x10" 48.00

Dresser box, opal glass with portrait reserve and gold trim, 7½" long, $900.00. (Photo courtesy JK Galleries Inc./LiveAuctioneers.com)

Vase, Adelaide, cut, controlled bubble ped base, 11½" 215.00
Vase, Anona, cut, waisted, 12" 180.00
Vase, floral etch, flared cylinder, 14" 180.00
Vase, floral etch, ruffled scalloped rim, ball stem, 8" 90.00
Vase, floral etch, trumpet form, 6" 50.00
Vase, floral HP on wht, scalloped rim, SP rtcl sleeve, 1900s, 6¾".... 120.00

Vases, cranberry with bubble ball connectors, 12", $720.00 for the pair. (Photo courtesy Kaminski Auctions/LiveAuctioneers.com)

Lamps

Boudoir, candle form w/gr cut stem, 6 crystal prisms, 13¼", pr..... 300.00
Puffy 12" Am Beauty rose shade; 4-arm rpt wht #C3003 std, 20".. 3,735.00
Puffy 12" butterflies/roses shade; bronze std w/sq base, VG........ 4,750.00
Puffy 12" pansy shade; 4-arm ornate Nouveau std, 19", NM ... 21,275.00
Puffy 14" Venice shade w/roses; 4-arm silver & gilt std, 22"...... 5,750.00

Puffy 6¾" rose bouquet shade; gilt tree-trunk base, #3079, 11½"...3,360.00
Puffy/rvpt 16" floral #D3070 shade; mk bronze std w/triangular ft, 20" .. 13,250.00
Radio, rvpt poppies on panel held in SP base, #E3035, 11", NM ..1,600.00
Rvpt Olympic Torch & Laurel Wreath mk shade; #C3069 std, 24"...2,150.00
Rvpt 13½" Italian garden shade sgn Morley; slim std, 19".........4,250.00
Rvpt 17" farm scene shade sgn H Fisher; bronzed std, VG 1,950.00
Rvpt 17¾" peacock & fauna frieze shade; #D3063 3-socket std, 22"..2,625.00
Rvpt 18" exotic birds/flowers shade; 3-ftd SP #3070 std, 23".....4,000.00
Rvpt 18" floral shade w/rprs; bronze 2-hdld std, 22½"...................600.00
Rvpt 20" sea gull scenic shade; matching glass std, 24" 6,600.00
Shade only, puffy, roses, mk, 7x13", VG.................................1,950.00

Obverse painted 12" Palm Tree lamp; signed base, 23", $6,625.00. (Photo courtesy James D. Julia Inc./LiveAuctioneers.com)

Paper Dolls

No one knows quite how or when paper dolls originated. One belief is that they began in Europe as 'pantins' (jumping jacks). During the nineteenth century, most paper dolls portrayed famous dancers and opera stars such as Fanny Elssler and Jenny Lind. In the late 1800s, the Raphael Tuck Publishers of England produced many series of beautiful paper dolls. Retail companies used paper dolls as advertisements to further the sale of their products. Around the turn of the century, many popular women's magazines began featuring a page of paper dolls.

Most familiar to today's collectors are the books with dolls on cardboard covers and clothes on the inside pages. These made their appearance in the late 1920s and early 1930s. The most collectible (and the most valuable) are those representing celebrities, movie stars, and comic-strip characters of the '30s and '40s. When no condition is indicated, the dolls listed below are assumed to be in mint, uncut, original condition. Cut sets will be worth about half price if all dolls and outfits are included and pieces are in very good condition. If dolls were produced in die-cut form, these prices reflect such a set in mint condition with all costumes and accessories. For further information we recommend *20th Century Paper Dolls Identification and Values* (Collector Books), *Tomart's Price Guide to Lowe and Whitman Paper Dolls*, and *Tomart's Price Guide to Saalfield and Merrill Paper Dolls*, all by Mary Young, our advisor for this category; she is listed in the Directory under Ohio. We also recommend *Schroeder's Collectible Toys, Antique to Modern*; and *Paper Dolls of the 1960s, 1970s, and 1980s* by Carol Nichols (both from Collector Books).

Around the World w/Bob & Barbara, Children's Press #3000, 1946.. 30.00
Betsy McCall's Fashion Shop, Avalon/Standard Toykraft #402, 1959 ...50.00
Brother Jack, Kaufmann & Strauss #13, 1915.............................. 75.00
Class Mates, Gabriel #D91 .... 35.00
Cloth Dresses To Sew for Polly Pet, Gabriel #D104 .... 50.00
Cuddly Dolls, Charles E Graham #0225, 1900s 75.00

Darling Dick, Gabriel #10, ca 1911 .... 100.00
Dennison TV Playhouse, Dennison #522, ca 1950 .... 30.00
Doll Cut Out Book, MA Donohue #756, ca 1913 .... 35.00
Dolly Dingle at Play, John H Eggers, 1927 .... 65.00

Dolly Dingle's Travels, Series 2, from a four-page set, John H. Eggars Co., 1921, $75.00. (Photo courtesy Mary Young)

Dolly's Kut-Out Klothes, American Toy Works #3081, 1930s 35.00
Dutton's Dolls for Dressing, Dolly Dear, EP Dutton & Co #1129 .. 90.00
Fairy Folk, George W Jacobs & Co 100.00
Fashion Parade Dolls Book, Child Art, 1977 .... 15.00
Felt-O-Gram Doll & Her Wardrobe, Poster Products #10, 1932 .... 50.00
Five Round About Wood Dolls, Milton Bradley #4552 .... 60.00
Foreign Friends, Gabriel #D172 .... 50.00
Froggie Went A Courting, DeJournette Mfg #35 .... 25.00
Gidget, Avalon/Standard Toycraft #601, 1965 .... 50.00
Heidi, DeJournette Mfg #200 .... 18.00
Honey Bun, DeJournette Mfg #R-50 .... 18.00
Just From College, Gabriel #D125 .... 60.00
Lacey Daisy, Kits Inc #1050, 1949 .... 20.00
Little Miss Muffet, DeJournette Mfg #902 .... 22.00
Little Sister, Blaise Publishing #1003, 1963 .... 12.00
Little Sister, Dandyline Co, 1919 .... 25.00
Magic Doll, Parker Brothers, ca 1948 .... 45.00
Magic Mary Jane, Milton Bradley #4010-3, 1972 .... 25.00
Make-It Book, Rand McNally & Co #RM 103, 1928 .... 10.00
Mary Lou & Her Friends, Platt & Munk Co #235B, 1950s 60.00
Mary Ware Doll Book, hardbk, LC Page & Co, 1914 .... 200.00
Mayflower Sewing Set, Concord Toy #235 .... 30.00
Moderne Sewing for Little Girls, American Toy Works #417, 1930s ... 35.00
Mods, The; Milton Bradley #4727, 1967 .... 15.00
Mother & Daughter, Jaymar Specialty/Great Lakes Press #974 ...... 30.00

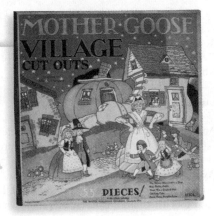

Mother Goose Village, Harter Publishing Co. #H-164, 1935, $40.00. (Photo courtesy Mary Young)

Movieland, Reuben H Lilja #906, 1947 .... 35.00
My Pet Dressing Dolls, Am Colortype Co, box set w/4 dolls, 1910s .. 65.00
Neddy Neverstill, American Colortype Co #735, 1920s 85.00
Nursery Rhyme Party Dolls in Costume, McLoughlin Bros #544, 1920s... 75.00
Outdoor Fun, Reuben H Lilja #924, ca 1942 .... 12.00
Paper Dolls of the World, George W Jacobs & Co, 1909 .... 80.00

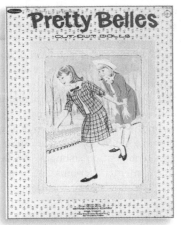

Pretty Belles, Whitman/Western #1966, two die-cut dolls and 35 outfits, from $15.00 to $25.00.

(Photo courtesy Carol Nichols)

Pretty Polly, Goldsmith #2005, 1930 .... 30.00
Sandra the Bride, Avalon/Standard Toycraft #801-3, 1969 .... 15.00
Snow White Cut-Out Doll, Pressman Toy Corp #1212 .... 40.00
Suzie Sweet, Gabriel #D94 .... 35.00
Sweet Sue, Magic Wand #108, ca 1960 .... 25.00
Ten Round About Dolls, McLoughlin Bros #555, 1936 .... 60.00
Wardrobe Dolls, Miss Teens Chris, C&M Publishing, 1950s 15.00
Wedding Belles, Dot & Peg Productions, 1945 .... 50.00
Winnie Winkle & Her Paris Costumes, Gabriel #D115, ca 1933 .... 200.00
Young Designer, DeJournette Mfg, 1940 .... 20.00

Paperweights

Glass paperweight collecting has grown in intensity over the past 25 years. Perhaps it is because there are many glass artists who today are creating beautiful examples that generally sell for less than $100.00. Hundreds of glass artisans and factories in the United States, China, Mexico, Italy, and Scotland produce these 'gift range' paperweights. Collectors have the option of choosing strictly from that price range, or they can choose to buy more costly pieces that sometimes range into the thousands of dollars. Additionally, astute collectors are beginning to piece together collections of old Chinese paperweights first imported into this country during the 1930s — unrefined imitations of the lovely French weights of the mid-1800s. When viewed more than 70 years later, their beauty and craftsmanship is very evident. Of particular note are the weights containing an opaque white glass disk hand painted with charming and sometimes quite intricate designs. Other weights gaining in popularity (and still relatively inexpensive) are motto weights (No Place Like Home, Remember Me, Happy Birthday, etc.) and those made of English bottle glass — especially examples with sulfide inclusions. Plaque weights, such as those created by Degenhart, and Liverpool-process weights made by Mosser are disappearing from the marketplace into the hands of collectors. With the demise of Perthshire Paperweights (Scotland), collectors are seeking out high-end, very limited edition 'Collection' and Christmas paperweights. There is strong interest in advertising paperweights because they are abundant and relatively inexpensive. Collectors who have a larger budget for these exquisite 'glass balls' may choose to purchase only antique French paperweights from the classic period (1845 – 1860), the wonderful English or American weights from the 1840s, or examples of the high quality contemporary workmanship of today's master glass artists.

Baccarat, St. Louis, Clichy, Pantin, and St. Mande (names synonymous with classic French paperweights) as well as some American factories discontinued production between the 1880s and 1910 when paperweights fell out of favor. In the 1950s Baccarat and St. Louis revived paperweight production, creating very high quality, limited-production weights. St. Louis discontinued paperweights several years ago. In the 1960s many American glass studios began to spring up due to the development of smaller glass furnaces that allowed the individual glassmaker more freedom in design and fabrication from the fire to the annealing kiln. Such success stories are evident in the creative glass produced by Lundberg Studios, Orient & Flume, and Lotton Studios, to name only a few.

Many factors determine value, particularly of antique weights, and auction-realized prices of contemporary weights usually differ from issue price. Be cautious when comparing weights that may seem very similar in appearance; their values may vary considerably. Size, faceting, fancy cuts on the base, the inclusion of a seemingly innocuous piece of frit, or a tear in a lampworked leaf are some conditions that can affect cost. Of course, competition among new collectors has greatly influenced prices, as have internet auction sales. Some paperweights heretofore purported to be 'rare' now appear with some frequency on internet auctions, driving down their prices. However, as the number of collectors multiply, the supply of antique weights decrease, forcing prices upwards. Fine antique paperweights have steadily increased in value as has the work of many now-deceased contemporary pioneer glass artists (i.e., Paul Ysart, Joe St. Clair, Charles Kazian, Del Tarsitano, and Ray Banford).

The dimension given at the end of the description is diameter. Prices are for weights in perfect or near-perfect condition unless otherwise noted. Our advisors for this category are Betty and Larry Schwab, The Paperweight Shoppe; they are listed in the Directory under Illinois. See Clubs, Newsletters, and Catalogs in the Directory for the Paperweight Collector's Associations, Inc., with chapters in many states. They offer assistance to collectors at all levels. The values for cast-iron weights are prices realized at auction.

Key:
con — concentric
(d) — deceased
fct — facets, faceted
gar — garland
grd — ground
jsp — jasper
latt — latticinio
mill — millefiori
o/l — overlay
sil — silhouette

Ayotte, Rick

Ballerina Rose, upright/multi-tiered, pk on cobalt, 5½x9¾"......4,400.00
Ducks (3) on pond, mossy shore, 1992 ltd ed, 4", from $1,800 to... 2,500.00
Red poinsettia w/dk gr leaves on clear grd, 1996, 2¼", $350 to.... 450.00
Salamander/mushrooms/rocks/flowers on sandy grd, 1989, 3⅝"... 1,500.00
Scarlet-chested parrot on flowers on clear, 1986, 3½", $1,300 to...1,900.00

Baccarat, Antique

Animal sil (8) on wht star grd, B1848 cane, 3⅛", from $15,000 to......... 17,000.00
Bl clematis buds (5) w/leaves, clear star-cut grd, 2⅞" 800.00
Complex close-packed mill canes w/B1847 sil canes, 3⅞", $12,000 to.. 16,000.00

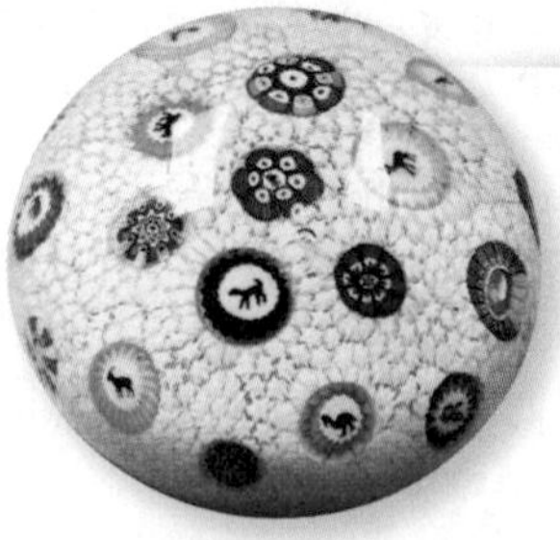

Eight canes with black silhouettes of animals, one marked B1824, on white star background, 3", $16,000.00. (Photo courtesy Brunk Auctions/LiveAuctioneers.com)

Mc flowers on latt grd w/animal sils, B1848 cane, 2⅞", $3,000 to .. 3,500.00
Mill stars/flowers closely packed, B1847 cane, 3⅛", $3,500 to...4,500.00
Paneled honeycomb on aqua carpet, 2¾", from $10,000 to.....15,000.00
Rose/bud/dbl clematis/pansy & leaves, 1/6 fct, 3¼", $11,000 to 18,000.00
Scattered mill/Gridel sil canes, wht upset muslin, 3¹⁄₁₆", $3,000 to...4,000.00
5-petal flower/2 buds w/in mill gar, star-cut grd/fcts, 3⅛" 4,500.00
6 shamrock/complex/13 butterfly canes, wht upset muslin, 3⅛" ... 12,500.00

Baccarat, Modern

Cherry blossoms/wht buds/blk branch, amethyst grd, 1987, 3", $600 to...800.00
Coppered Snake (coiled), 1979, 2½", MIB, from $450 to 650.00
Fruit in brn woven basket on wht grd, 1/6 fct, 1976, 3¹⁄₁₆" 400.00
Pears (3) & gr leaves on wht grd, 1974, 3¹⁄₁₆" 400.00
Rose & bud w/gr leaves on clear, star-cut grd, 1976, 3", from $450 to... 600.00
Snail & 3 flowers/gr leaves/silver pebbles, 1977, 3¹⁄₁₆", $450 to.... 700.00

Banford, Bob and Ray

Cabbage rose bouquet w/leaves, cobalt grd, 1/10 fct, 2⅜x2", $800 to . 1,000.00
Cabbage roses on clear grd, top fct/rows of flutes, 3", from $800 to .. 1,000.00
Christmas tree/stars in dk bl sky, 3", from $300 to 400.00
Clematis/buds/gr leaves, wht star-cut grd, 1/5 fct, 2⅝", $700 to 1,000.00
Pk primrose/gr leaves, pk/bl torsade on upset muslin, 3", from $300 to...400.00
Snowman & leafless tree on snowy grd w/bl sky, 3", from $300 to ..400.00

Caithness

Butterfly & mc flowers w/gr stems, ltd ed, 3", from $200 to.......... 400.00
Christmas tree amid gar, ruby grd, 1/6 fct, 1982, 3¹⁄₁₆", $300 to.... 400.00
Mixed flowers among grasses w/butterfly, 3", from $250 to 350.00
Partridge in a Pear Tree, fcts, ltd ed, 2¾", from $150 to............... 250.00

Clichy, Antique

Bull's-eye cane amid complex mill flower panels on cobalt, 3⅜" ...4,250.00
C-scroll mill gar w/pk roses on clear, 2¾".................................4,000.00
Complex mill canes on sodden snow, 3⅛", from $4,000 to........6,000.00

Patterened Millefiori trefoil on deep pink ground, internal crack/repolished, 3¼", $1,265.00. (Photo courtesy Garth's Auctions Inc./LiveAuctioneers.com)

Pk/bl/wht pinwheel w/center mc cane, 3", from $2,500 to 3,000.00
Rose amid complex mc canes on bl & wht latt, 3", from $7,000 to..9,000.00
Rose/mill gar/mc cog canes, star-cut grd, 1/5 fct, 2⅞", $1,800 to . 2,300.00
Trefoil mill gar in 3 loops, stardust canes on bl, 3¹⁄₁₆", $1,800 to.. 2,200.00
5-flower bouquet w/pk ribbon on clear grd, 3¹⁄₁₆", from $10,000 to.. 12,000.00

Lundberg Studios

Angelic youths/flowers/doves, bl aurene, Richter/'89, 2⅞", $900 to .1,100.00
Daffodil w/gr leaves, Steven, 1987, 3x2¼", from $1,500 to 1,800.00
Flowers (2) w/gr leaves on blk, 2½", from $250 to 350.00
Pond Reflection, lilies/cattails on bl, Steven/'89, 2½", MIB......1,300.00
Purple dragonfly & 5 purple flowers, Salazar/'89, 1¾", from $300 to......... 400.00
Toadstool Trio, mushrooms/etc on pebbled grd, Steven/'89, 2½" .. 950.00

New England Glass, Antique

Apples & pears on dbl-swirl wht latt basket, 2⅝", from $800 to.. 1,000.00
Complex canes amid gr/wht/red star-cane border on wht latt, 2⅝" 700.00
Fruit bouquet on wht dbl-swirl latt basket, 2¹¹⁄₁₆", from $800 to.. 1,200.00

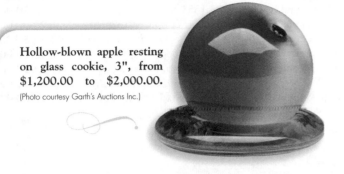

Hollow-blown apple resting on glass cookie, 3", from $1,200.00 to $2,000.00.
(Photo courtesy Garth's Auctions Inc.)

Mill nosegay w/4 leaves & 2 mill gar on clear grd, 2⅝" 650.00
Mushroom, mc w/tapered stem, star-cut grd, 1/4 fct, 3¼", $100 to ... 150.00
Pear, 3-D, chartreuse/russet on clear rnd cookie base, 2⅝" dia 900.00
Pears (2) & gr stem w/leaves on clear, 2⅞" 900.00
4 eagle sil canes/wht star w/complex canes, wht latt cushion, 2¾" ...1,000.00

Orient & Flume

Apple, golden irid w/appl striped leaf & stem, 2½" 50.00
Feather & heart design, mc on teal, 3" 250.00
Flowers & butterfly on bl irid, 1978, 3" 250.00
Frog appl to top of lily pad on bl sphere 300.00
Mill, 1985, 2¾", from $300 to... 600.00
Peach w/gr leaf & brn stem, 2¾" 50.00
Spirals, mc irid, 3", from $100 to.. 150.00

Perthshire

Butterfly center & 2 flower rings on blk grd, 2¾".....................2,875.00
Flowers (2 & 1 bud) on stems on purple grd, 3"............................ 500.00
Mc flowers (4) w/gr leaves on dk grd, 3"...................................... 575.00
Mill flowers in close-packed pattern, 3" 350.00
Poinsettia w/gr leaves amid gr & wht gar, 3"................................ 400.00
Swan (sm) among greenery, multi-faceted, 3"............................... 500.00
5-petal mc flower w/gr leaves on wht latt base, 2¾"...................... 200.00

Rosenfeld, Ken

CA Discovery, mc flowers/gr leaves/rocks on dk earth grd, 2002, 3¼".. 1,100.00
Candy canes/holly/berries/pine branches on clear, '92, 3¼", $350 to .. 500.00
Mixed berries/wht blossom/bud/gr leaves on wht grd, 2001, 2½" .. 250.00
Pears (3)/holly swags w/pk bow on clear, 1992, 3⁵⁄₁₆", from $500 to ...700.00
Pk wild roses (3) w/closed bud on bl grd, 2004, 3¼" 500.00
6-flower bouquet w/gr leaves on wht grd, 1988, 3½", from $700 to 900.00

Sandwich Glass

Pansy (pk & bl) w/2 gr leaves on pebbled grd, 2⅞", from $750 to 900.00
Plums (2) on gr leafy branch on clear grd, 2⅝", from $800 to ...1,000.00
Poinsettia (bl) w/Lutz wht rose cane center, gr leaves, 2¹³⁄₁₆" 650.00
Striped flower/bud/leaves/thick stem on clear grd, 3¹⁄₁₆", $1,000 to...1,200.00
Wheatflower w/leaves on wht dbl-swirl latt cushion, 3⅛", $2,000 to.. 2,500.00

St. Louis, Antique

Con mill mushroom & cobalt torsade, SL 1848, 3³⁄₁₆", from $4,000 to...600.00

Louis Napoleon Bonaparte sulfide amid mill gar, 3¼".................. 600.00
Mc bouquet on clear, fct, 3½x4⅛", from $8,000 to 12,000.00
Mushroom-shaped bouquet, wht latt basket, ca 1848, 3", from $4,000 to... 12,000.00

Stankard, Paul

Bellflower & 3 buds w/gr leaves on wht grd, 1974, 2½", $700 to.. 900.00
Desert flowers on pebbly grd, undtd, 3" 12,000.00
Paphiopedilum orchid w/leaves & roots in clear, 1989, 2¼"......1,000.00
Prickly pear, dk gr w/2 yel buds, red grd, 1985, 3¹⁄₁₆".................1,800.00
Thistles & bee on clear grd, 3¼" 2,500.00
Wild flowers/berries/bumblebee, 1994, 3" 2,500.00
Yel flowers (4) & leaves on red grd, undtd, early, 3" 800.00

Tarsitano, Debbie

Bouquet & mill gar w/ladybugs/bl latt snake on pk grd, 3" 2,500.00
Lampwork flowers (28) scattered on clear grd, 3¼" 4,500.00
Mc bouquet/buds/berries/leaves, clear grd, 1/7 fct, 3⁷⁄₁₆" 2,500.00

Tarsitano, Delmo

Lizard among desert flowers on pebbled grd, 3¾" 1,800.00
Snaked coiled among desert flowers on pebbled grd, 3½" 1,560.00
Spider on webs bordered by mc flowers w/gr leaves, sandy grd, 3½" ...2,000.00
Strawberries (2) & buds among leaves, 3"..................................... 800.00

Trabucco, Victor

Floral bouquet w/leaves on clear, magnum, 5" 1,200.00
Pk & red flowers (3) w/gr leaves & stems on clear, 3"................... 425.00
Red rose/bud/purple berries/gr leaves, wht upset muslin, 2001, 3⅛" 800.00
Snake coiled near lav flower/2 rocks on earth grd, 1999, 3⅞" ...1,000.00
Violets w/gr leaves & stems on clear, 1984, 3" 350.00

Whitefriars

Christmas, manger scene 650.00
Christmas, 3 Kings.. 800.00
Telephone amid mc tiny flowers, intricate design, 3".................... 800.00

Whittemore, Francis D.

Berries (3) & stem w/gr leaves on pk grd, 1¾" 350.00
Bleeding hearts on stem w/gr leaves on gr grd, ltd ed, 2⅜" 350.00
Daffodil w/bud & leaves on purple, 1970s, 2¼" 360.00
Partridge in pear tree w/gr leaves on ruby grd, 2⁷⁄₁₆"..................... 375.00
Pk rose w/gr leaves on ped, 3"... 375.00

Ysart, Paul

Clematis w/gr leaves on radiating wht latt on red grd, 2¹³⁄₁₆" 900.00
Clematis w/gr leaves/complex cane border on red/wht jsp grd, 2⅞" ...900.00
Flower basket sulfide, red/wht latt torsade on blk grd, 2¹⁵⁄₁₆" 2,500.00
Flower bouquet floating on pk jsp grd, 1974, MIB 650.00
Flower bouquet on wht latt basket, 2¹⁵⁄₁₆"................................... 650.00
Flower spray w/gr leaves on wht latt grd, 3" 900.00
Red/wht/bl flowers (3) on wht latt, 2½" 800.00

Miscellaneous

Buzzini, Chris; Bittersweet Nightshade Bouquet, 1990, 3⅛" 1,000.00
Buzzini, Chris; Pastel Bouquet on clear grd, 1990, 3⅛".............. 1,200.00
Ebelhare, D; con mill rings, gr grd, mc stave basket, 1993, 2⁵⁄₁₆" ..350.00

Ebelhare, D; con mill rings w/in staved 2-color basket, 1995, 2⅛" 300.00
Kaziun, C Jr; horse/jockey sil in oval on turq grd w/torsade, 2⁵⁄₁₆"... 4,000.00
Kaziun, C Jr; 6-petal yel flower/leaves, gold speckled grd, 2¼"+ped ...360.00
Millville, morning glory, teal & wht, top fct, ftd base, 3⅜x3⅛".... 750.00
Parabelle, con mill w/lg red/wht twist torsade, 1985, 3⅛" 800.00
Parabelle, scattered mill on moss grd, 1996 ltd ed, 3⅝" 2,500.00
Smith, G; orchids & buds w/gr leaves on clear grd, 1987, 3¹⁄₁₆" ...600.00
Smith, G; strawberries on spiraling vine on clear grd, 1985, 3¹⁄₁₆"...600.00
Val St Lambert, Jesus sulfide/cross canes on bl, ruby o/l, fcts, 4" .. 1,200.00

Czechoslovakian upright flower, multi-faceted, ca 1920 – 1930, 3¼", from $175.00 to $250.00 (based on interior design). (Photo courtesy Betty and Larry Schwab)

Papier-Maché

The art of papier-maché was mainly European. It originated in Paris around the middle' of the eighteenth century and became popular in America during Victorian times. Small items such as boxes, trays, inkwells, frames, etc., as well as extensive ceiling moldings and larger articles of furniture were made. The process involved building layer upon layer of paper soaked in glue, then coaxed into shape over a wood or wire form. When dry it was painted or decorated with gilt or inlays. Inexpensive twentieth-century 'notions' were machine processed and mold pressed. See also Christmas; Candy Containers.

Box, chinoiserie scenes on lid, England, ca 1870, 12x3¾" 230.00
Display pc for Bronx Zoo, tiger, string stripes, orig pnt, 16" 1,850.00
Mask, tiger's face, realistic, fits over head, VG.............................. 215.00
Table, chinoiserie on blk, w/later Georgian-style stand, 18x24x19"...850.00
Table, floral on blk w/gold trim, oval, on blk stand, 20x30x24"... 2,150.00
Tray, blk w/gold molded rim, Jennens & Bettridge, 1890s, 31x23"...850.00
Tray, chinoiserie landscape/floral borders, 19th C, 30x23" 1,765.00
Tray, floral/butterflies/moths/gold trim, 19th C, 2x24x128" 1,400.00
Tray, grapevines on brn, scalloped rim, rpr seam, wear, 31" L....... 265.00
Tray, MOP inlay on blk, serpentine rim, Jennens & Bettridge, 28x15" ..850.00
Tray, sailing ships at sunset reserve on blk, scalloped rim, 27x22" ...360.00

Tray, peacock by fountain, Jennens & Bettridge, late nineteenth century, 32" long, $2,235.00. (Photo courtesy Skinner's Inc. Auctioneers & Appraisers of Antiques & Fine Art)

Parian Ware

Parian is hard-paste unglazed porcelain made to resemble marble.

First made in the mid-1800s by Staffordshire potters, it was soon after produced in the United States by the U.S. Pottery at Bennington, Vermont. Busts and statuary were favored, but plaques, vases, mugs, and pitchers were also made.

Bust, Abraham Lincoln, low socle, English, ca 1900, 12"............ 700.00
Bust, Admiral Nelson, J Pitt, 1853, 9¼".. 550.00
Bust, B Franklin, mk Broome, Ott & Brewer, 1876, 8½x6".......2,600.00
Bust, child w/head slightly trn, Broome, Ott & Brewer, 6¾x5".1,550.00
Bust, Clytie, C Delpech, 1855, att Copeland, 13¼" 400.00
Bust, Love, classical maiden, R Monti, 1874, Copeland, 13¼" 950.00
Bust, Mother, holding child, R Monti, Copeland, 1876, 15".....1,050.00
Bust, US Grant, Isaac Broome, Lenox Pottery, 1914, 9¾x7".....1,900.00

Diana, Minton, 183, 13½", $1,300.00. (Photo courtesy Skinner Inc. Auctioneers & Appraisers of Antiques & Fine Art/ LiveAuctioneers.com)

Figure, Chastity, classical lady, Durham, 1865, 25" 600.00
Figure, girl w/plate & dishcloth, bucket at ft, late 19th C, 22"..... 250.00
Figure, Greek Slave, nude female, H Powers, Minton & Co, 1851, 14".765.00
Figure, Sabrina, draped nude, WC Marshall, Copeland, 1850s, 11¾" ..650.00

Parrish, Maxfield

Maxfield Parrish (1870 – 1966), with his unique abilities in architecture, illustrations, and landscapes, was the most prolific artist during 'The Golden Years of Illustrators.' He produced art for more than 100 magazines, painted girls on rocks for the Edison-Mazda division of General Electric, and landscapes for Brown & Bigelow. His most recognized work was 'Daybreak' that was published in 1923 by House of Art and sold nearly two million prints. Parrish began early training with his father who was a recognized artist, studied architecture at Dartmouth, and became an active participant in the Cornish artist colony in New Hampshire where he resided. Due to his increasing popularity, reproductions are now being marketed. In our listings, values for prints apply to those that are in their original frames (or very nice and appropriate replacement frames) unless noted otherwise. Bobby Babcock, our advisor for this category, is listed in the Directory under Colorado.

Book, Golden Age, 1904, Bodley Press 200.00
Book pg, Autumn, from A Golden Treasury, 1911, 9¼x7" overall. 20.00
Bookplate, City of Brass, 11x8½" overall, +dbl matt 30.00
Bookplate, End, 1925, from Knave of Hearts, 10x12" 130.00
Bookplate, Villa Bella, Italian Villas & Their Gardens, new matt & fr 25.00
Calendar, Christmas Eve, 1946, Brown & Bigelow, cropped, 8½x10¾".146.00
Calendar, Daybreak, 1951, Brown & Bigelow, cropped, 18x22"... 180.00
Calendar, Early Autumn, 1939, Brown & Bigelow, cropped, 11¾x15¾".200.00
Calendar, Egypt, 1922, Edison-Mazda, complete, lg 3,500.00
Calendar, Evening Shadows, 1953, Brown & Bigelow, cropped, 12x15".400.00

Calendar, Of Friendship, 1925, desk sz................................. 150.00
Calendar, Spirit of the Night, 1919, Edison-Mazda, full pad, 19x9½". 4,500.00
Calendar, Sunlit Valley, 1950, Brown & Bigelow, complete, 11½x17"...350.00
Calendar, Under Summer Skies, 1959, Brown & Bigelow, cropped, 9x12".125.00
Calendar top, Lampseller of Bagdad, Edison-Mazda, 1923, 18x14".. 250.00
Calendar top, Primitive Man, 1921, Edison-Mazda, cropped, sm. 650.00
Chocolate box, Crane, textured cb w/Rubaiyat image insert, 11x7x1", EX ..950.00
Display, Get Together, GE light bulbs, 1920s, 26½x16x3" 3,500.00
Magazine cover, Boar's Head, Collier's, Dec 16, 1905.................... 125.00
Magazine cover, Christmas Issue, 1920 .... 125.00
Painting, Morning, artist sgn, 15x19½"...............................70,000.00
Playing cards, Ecstasy, Edison-Mazda, 1930, M in wrapper........... 275.00
Postcard, Pied Piper, 7x7" foldout, 1915 .... 175.00

Poster, for Scribner's 1897 Christmas magazine featuring a butler carrying a Christmas pudding, 28x19", EX, $825.00.

(Photo courtesy Wm. Morford Auctions)

Print, Air Castles, 1904, 16x12"... 275.00
Print, Aladdin, 1907, unfr, 9x11" 125.00
Print, Bellerophon Watching by the Fountain, 1910, 8x10" 125.00
Print, Canyon, 1924, 6x10"... 225.00
Print, Cassim, 1906, 9x11" 175.00
Print, Centaur, 1914, 12x6"... 195.00
Print, Checkerboard Chefs, 1925, 6x11".................................. 195.00
Print, Cleopatra, Reinthal Newman House of Art, 1917, 15x27⅝"...625.00
Print, Dreaming, Reinthal Newman House of Art, 1928, 11¾x15"...325.00
Print, Early Autumn, Brown & Bigelow, 22x18" overall (cropped) ...200.00
Print, Errant Pan, 11x9" 350.00
Print, Fisherman & Genie, 1906, orig label, 9x11", NM.............. 250.00
Print, Florentine Fete, 1920, 7x10" 225.00
Print, Garden of Allah, 1918, 15x30", from $295 to 550.00
Print, Jason & the Talking Oak, 1910, 7x9" 150.00
Print, Lights of Home, Brown & Bigelow, 1945, 17x15" 350.00
Print, Love's Pilgrimage, 1912, 6¼x15" 165.00
Print, Lute Players, 1924, 10x18" 350.00

Print, Old King Cole, 1906, 6½x24" 850.00
Print, Peaceful Valley, Brown & Bigelow, 1936, 16x11" 300.00
Print, Queen Gulnare, 1907, 9x11"....................................... 250.00
Print, Reveries, Edison-Mazda, 14½x22" (cropped)..................... 600.00
Print, Stars, House of Art, 1927, 10x6" 350.00
Print, Villa Chigi, 1904, 7x10" 100.00
Print, Wild Geese, 1924, 12x15", from $325 to 395.00
Print, Winken Blinken & Nod, Scribner's, 1905, 17x12½".......... 495.00
Stamp, Brill Brothers, 1915, 1½x2½", +dbl matt............................ 75.00

Pate-De-Verre

Simply translated, pate-de-verre means paste of glass. In the manufacturing process, lead glass is first ground, then mixed with sodium silicate solution to form a paste which can be molded and refired. Some of the most prominent artisans to use this procedure were Almaric Walter, Daum, Argy-Rouseau, and Decorchemont. See also specific manufacturers.

Bowl, bl w/internal latticework, scalloped rim, Decorchemont, 8¾" .3,600.00
Bowl, gr w/purple mottle, lobed w/lappet rim, Decorchemont, 5⅜"...1,375.00
Bust, woman, orange mottle, Despret, 5".. 960.00
Mask, Napoleon, orange mottle, Despret, 5".................................... 720.00
Panel, bull & foliage, mauve & gr on bl & wht mottle, Despret, 10" L ..600.00

Plaque, Ave Maria profile, signed J.D., framed, 4½", $550.00.

(Photo courtesy Treadway Gallery Inc.)

Vase, gr w/emb waves, fish-form hdls, Decorchemont, 6" 5,500.00
Vase, gray w/mc streaks, stylized waves, fish hdls, Decorchemont, 5" ...11,500.00

Pate-Sur-Pate

Pate-sur-pate, literally paste-on paste, is a technique whereby relief decorations are built up on a ceramic body by layering several applications of slip, one on the other, until the desired result is achieved. Usually only two colors are used, and the value of a piece is greatly enhanced as more color is added.

Print, Morning, 1926, 16x13", $200.00. (Photo courtesy Wm. Morford Auctions)

Vase, seated nymph holding Cupid as four cherubs look on, white on olive, pilgrim's flask form, 10½", $22,000.00.

(Photo courtesy Freemans/ LiveAuctioneers.com)

Charger, 2 lady bathers by water, G Jones, 1924-51, 12" dia 2,150.00
Condensed milk container, classical figures, unmk Continental, 6"... 65.00
Plaque, nymph at monument on dk bl, att Solon, 6¼" dia+mat+fr, pr ...5,750.00
Plaques, nymph at cauldron w/cherubs, L Solon, 9x4"+fr, pr ..13,250.00
Vase, classical figure & flowers, gold uptrn hdls, w/lid, 15", pr 275.00
Vase, portrait reserve, rtcl rim, cornucopia hdls, L Solon, 8½"..... 725.00

Pattern Glass

Pattern glass was the first mass-produced fancy tableware in America and was much prized by our ancestors. From the 1840s to the Civil War, it contained a high lead content and is known as 'flint glass.' It is exceptionally clear and resonant. Later glass was made with soda lime and is known as non-flint. By the 1890s pattern glass was produced in great volume in thousands of patterns, and colored glass came into vogue. Today the highest prices are often paid for these later patterns flashed with rose, amber, canary, and vaseline; stained ruby; or made in colors of cobalt, green, yellow, amethyst, etc. Demand for pattern glass declined by 1915, and glass fanciers were collecting it by 1930. No other field of antiques offers more diversity in patterns, prices, or pieces than this unique and historical glass that represents the Victorian era in America.

Our advisor for this category is Darlene Yohe; she is listed in the Directory under Arkansas. For a more thorough study on the subject, we recommend *Standard Encyclopedia of Pressed Glass, 1860 – 1930, Identification & Values*, by Bill Edwards and Mike Carwile, and *American Pattern Glass Table Sets* by Cathy and Gene Florence, coordinated by Danny Cornelius and Don Jones, available from Collector Books. See also Bread Plates; Cruets; Historical Glass; Salt and Pepper Shakers; Salts, Open; Sugar Shakers; Syrups; specific manufacturers such as Northwood.

Note: Values are given for open sugar bowls and compotes unless noted 'w/lid.'

Acorn, compote, open 40.00
Acorn, compote, w/lid 60.00
Acorn, pitcher 95.00
Acorn Band, egg cup 20.00
Acorn Band, tumbler 25.00
Actress, butter dish 135.00
Actress, candlestick, ea 110.00
Ada, bowl, berry; lg 45.00
Ada, creamer 25.00
Ada, pickle dish 15.00
Adam's Plume, cake stand 45.00
Adam's Plume, goblet 30.00
Adam's Plume, sugar bowl 30.00
Adonis, bowl, berry; sm 10.00
Adonis, butter dish 50.00
Adonis, celery vase 20.00
Adonis, plate, 10-11" 25.00
Alabama, bowl, 8" 50.00
Alabama, nappy 30.00
Alabama, syrup 70.00
Alaska, butter dish 75.00
Alaska, pitcher 125.00
Alaska, tumbler 30.00
Almond Thumbprint, celery vase 25.00
Almond Thumbprint, cruet 60.00
Almond Thumbprint, salt cellar, lg 20.00
Almond Thumbprint, wine 15.00
Amazon, bowl, oval, w/lid, 5-7" 40.00
Amazon, butter dish 55.00
Amazon, compote, open, 4-6" 25.00
Amazon, tumbler 15.00

Amberette, bowl, 7" 40.00
Amberette, celery tray 50.00
Amberette, creamer 75.00
Amberette, olive dish 30.00
Amberette, sugar bowl 110.00
Amboy, bowl, berry; lg 40.00
Amboy, goblet 35.00
American Beauty, pitcher 75.00
American Beauty, spooner 20.00
Arcadia Lace, nappy 30.00
Arcadia Lace, rose bowl 30.00
Arch & Forget-Me-Not Bands, sugar bowl 30.00
Arched Fleur-De-Lis, butter dish 65.00
Arched Fleur-De-Lis, shaker, ea 20.00
Arched Ovals, cake stand 40.00
Arched Ovals, cruet 45.00
Arrowhead, celery dish 20.00
Arrowhead, spooner 25.00
Art, biscuit jar 120.00
Art, relish dish 20.00
Art, wine 20.00
Ashburn, wine, amber 20.00
Ashburton, butter dish, amethyst 85.00
Ashburton, claret, amber 25.00
Ashburton, decanter, bl or gr 75.00
Ashman, butter dish 60.00
Ashman, pickle jar 35.00
Atlanta, celery vase 30.00
Atlanta, syrup 45.00
Baby Face, champagne 115.00
Baby Face, compote, w/lid, 8" 250.00
Baby Face, pitcher 350.00
Ball & Swirl, butter dish 55.00
Ball & Swirl, mug 20.00
Ball & Swirl, spooner 20.00
Baltimore Pear, honey dish 30.00
Baltimore Pear, plate, bread 35.00
Banded Buckle, egg plate 30.00
Banded Fleur-De-Lis, pitcher 85.00
Banded Raindrops, cup & saucer 45.00
Banded Raindrops, relish dish, sq 15.00
Banded Star, pitcher 90.00
Banded Star, tumbler 20.00
Bar & Diamond, creamer 30.00
Bar & Diamond, sugar shaker 50.00
Barberry, honey dish 20.00
Barberry, plate 25.00
Barley, jam jar 35.00
Barred Forget-Me-Not, butter dish 60.00
Barred Forget-Me-Not, sugar bowl, amber 35.00
Basketweave, pitcher 90.00
Bead Swag, cake stand, ruby stain 80.00
Bead Swag, rose bowl, bl or gr 40.00
Bead Swag, syrup, milk glass 95.00
Bead Swag, wine, vaseline 20.00
Beaded Arch Panels, goblet 45.00
Beaded Band, cordial 25.00
Beaded Band, spooner 20.00
Beaded Tulip, champagne 25.00
Beaded Tulip, plate 20.00
Beaumont's Columbia, cruet 60.00
Beaumont's Columbia, toothpick holder, bl or gr 55.00
Bellflower, egg cup 40.00
Bellflower, relish dish 30.00

Birch Leaf, butter dish 80.00
Bird & Strawberry, rose bowl, ftd, lg.. 175.00
Bird & Strawberry, wine 75.00
Birds at Fountain, sugar bowl.. 90.00

Blackberry, tumbler, (aka Dewberry), clear with gold trim, $20.00. (Photo courtesy Cathy and Gene Florence)

Bleeding Heart, relish tray 25.00
Bleeding Heart, waste bowl 20.00
Blockade, celery vase 20.00
Blockade, sugar bowl.. 25.00
Box Pleat, compote.. 30.00
Brazilian, butter dish 65.00
Brazilian, cruet 60.00
Brittanic, carafe... 50.00
Brittanic, cracker jar 35.00
Broken Column, cake stand 40.00
Broken Column, plate, 7½" 25.00
Bryce Hobnail, celery vase.. 25.00
Bryce Hobnail, sugar bowl.. 40.00
Bryce Ribbon Candy, cup & saucer.. 30.00
Bryce Ribbon Candy, pickle dish... 20.00
Bull's Eye & Fan, bowl, berry; bl or gr 15.00
Bull's Eye & Fan, toothpick holder... 30.00
Bull's Eye & Fan, wine, bl or gr 40.00
Butterfly, compote, w/lid.. 65.00
Butterfly, mustard jar... 60.00
Butterfly, relish dish 25.00
Button Arches, pitcher, milk 35.00
Button Arches, sauce dish 15.00
Cabbage Rose, champagne 15.00
Cabbage Rose, tumbler 20.00
Cambridge #2351, punch bowl.. 125.00
Cambridge #2351, punch cup.. 10.00
Cane, celery vase, amber 25.00
Cane, cordial, vaseline... 30.00
Cane, goblet, bl or gr 40.00
Cardinal, bowl, berry; lg 55.00
Cardinal, honey dish, open.. 35.00
Cathedral, bowl, amethyst, 7-8" 85.00
Chain w/Star, bread plate 25.00
Chain w/Star, shaker, ea 20.00
Chandelier, pitcher... 165.00
Chandelier, tumbler.. 50.00
Checkerboard, creamer.. 25.00
Checkerboard, wine 20.00
Chippendale, butter dish 75.00
Chippendale, sugar bowl... 35.00
Circular Saw, cracker jar.. 30.00
Classic, bowl, w/lid, 7" 150.00
Classic, pitcher, milk; ftd 475.00

Clover, bowl, berry; sm 15.00
Clover, sauce dish 10.00
Colorado, cup, eng... 20.00
Comet, goblet 40.00
Comet, sugar bowl 25.00
Compact, See Snail
Connecticut, dish, oblong or rnd 20.00
Cord Drapery, cruet.. 85.00
Cord Drapery, toothpick holder, amber.. 450.00
Cord Drapery, toothpick holder, bl or gr 500.00
Cottage, compote, w/lid, 6-8" 45.00
Cottage, plate, 9-10" 30.00
Country Kitchen, plate, 7" 95.00
Croesus, condiment set, amethyst 225.00
Croesus, tray 25.00
Crow's Foot, See Yale
Crystal Wedding, banana bowl, scarce 110.00
Cupid & Venus, jam jar 60.00
Currier & Ives, decanter 40.00
Cut Log, nappy... 30.00
Dahlia, egg cup, dbl 25.00
Dahlia, egg cup, dbl, amber 85.00
Daisy & Bluebell, goblet.. 50.00
Daisy & Button (Hobbs), parfait, amber 25.00
Dakota, plate.. 65.00
Deer & Dog, cheese dish 160.00
Delaware, cup, bl or gr 30.00
Delaware, puff box 150.00
Diamond Cut w/Leaf, sugar bowl... 35.00
Diamond Cut w/Leaf, vaseline 50.00
Diamond Swag, cracker jar 40.00
Doric, see Feather
Dot, creamer 20.00
Double Pinwheel, butter dish 60.00
Double Pinwheel, pitcher 75.00
Double Ribbon, egg cup... 20.00
Double Ribbon, sauce dish, ftd 25.00
Doyle's Shell, mug, ruby stain 50.00
Doyle's Shell, waste bowl 30.00
Duncan #40, finger bowl... 20.00
Duncan Homestead (#63), cruet 50.00
Duncan Homestead (#63), toothpick holder 30.00
Early Excelsior, jelly glass.. 60.00
Early Excelsior, water bottle 100.00
Egg in Sand, dish, swan center 35.00
Egyptian, plate, pyramids.. 125.00
Elephant, see Jumbo
Empress, punch bowl 75.00
Empress, punch cup 10.00
Esther, cracker jar... 80.00
Esther, cracker jar, bl or gr 200.00
Evangeline, cake plate, ftd 45.00
Eyewinker, oil lamp.. 125.00
Falling Leaves, pitcher, ftd, 1-qt 55.00

Fancy Arch, cup, from $14.00 to $17.00. (Photo courtesy Cathy and Gene Florence)

Fancy Loop, bonbon 35.00
Fancy Loop, salt cellar, ind 10.00
Fandango, ice bowl w/plate 50.00
Fashion, custard cup.. 10.00
Fashion, nappy 25.00
Feather, plate, bl or gr, 10" 80.00
Feather, plate, 7-8" 35.00
Federal #1910, cup 15.00
Federal #1910, vase, 3 szs, from $20 to 40.00
Finecut & Block, compote, amber...................... 50.00
Finecut & Block, egg cup, amber....................... 50.00
Finecut & Panel, platter 25.00
Finecut & Panel, platter, bl or gr 45.00
Fishscale, celery vase 25.00
Fishscale, plate, 9-10" 35.00
Fleur de Lis & Drape, pitcher 65.00
Flora, compote 30.00
Florida, mustard pot 35.00
Florida, sauce dish, bl or gr 25.00
Flower & Pleat, spooner 30.00
Flute & Cane, cordial 20.00
Flute & Cane, pitcher... 65.00
Framed Jewel, butter dish 50.00
Framed Jewel, butter dish, ruby stain 70.00
Frosted Lion, syrup 275.00
Frosted Stork, platter, 8 ¼-12" 95.00
Fuchsia, plate 25.00
Garden of Eden, mug 25.00
Garden of Eden, tumbler 25.00
Garfield Drape, compote, high or low stem, w/lid ... 70.00
Garfield Drape, plate, star center 65.00
Gem, decanter... 65.00
Gem, decanter, ruby stain 100.00
Gem, see Nailhead
Gonterman Swirl, finger bowl, bl or gr 45.00
Gooseberry, goblet 25.00
Gooseberry, wine, milk glass 30.00
Grand, dish, oval, 7-9" 25.00
Grand, sherbet 15.00
Grape & Festoon, relish tray 20.00
Grape Bunch, pitcher 80.00
Grape w/Thumbprint, toothpick holder............. 25.00
Grated Ribbon, butter dish 55.00
Hamilton (Cape Cod), creamer 30.00
Hamilton (Cape Cod), salt cellar 20.00
Hand, syrup.. 65.00
Hanover, bowl, amber, 7-10", from $25 to 45.00
Hanover, plate, 4", bl or gr................................ 40.00
Hanover, puff box 55.00
Hartley, celery vase 25.00
Harvard Yard, egg cup 20.00
Harvard Yard, spooner, vaseline 30.00
Heart Band, sugar bowl, ruby stain 65.00
Heart w/Thumbprint, ice bucket 55.00
Heavy Finecut, cheese plate, w/lid 70.00
Heavy Finecut, molasses can, amber 50.00
Heavy Jewel, compote 40.00
Hickman, bonbon, sq.. 20.00
Hickman, nappy... 15.00
Hickman, plate 20.00
Hidalgo, cruet 55.00
Hinto, sugar bowl, vaseline................................ 45.00
Hobbs Polka Dot, custard cup 20.00
Hobbs Polka Dot, custard cup, sapphire............. 90.00

Hobnail w/fan, tray, bl or gn............................. 35.00
Hobnail w/fan, dish, oblong, amber................... 25.00
Hobstar & Tassels, nut bowl, 5" 35.00
Hobstar & Tassels, plate, 7½" 55.00
Holly, cake stand 140.00
Horn of Plenty, plate, bl or gr 110.00
Hummingbird, pickle dish 30.00
Hummingbird, sugar bowl, bl or gr 100.00
Hummingbird, tumbler, vaseline 50.00
Illinois, basket 40.00
Illinois, pickle jar 30.00
Illinois, water jug, squatty 55.00
Indiana, berry bowl, bl or gr, lg 35.00
Indiana, compote 30.00
Indiana, vase 20.00

Innovation, vase, $30.00.
(Photo courtesy Bill Edwards and Mike Carwile)

Inside Ribbing, butter dish 50.00
Iverna, biscuit jar 35.00
Iverna, punch bowl 75.00
Jacob's Ladder, castor set, complete 125.00
Jacob's Ladder, marmalade jar 90.00
Jersey Swirl, cake stand, vaseline 95.00
Jersey Swirl, jam jar... 45.00
Jeweled Heart, rose bowl, bl or gr 55.00
Jubilee, wine... 15.00
Jumbo, creamer 275.00
Jumbo, sauce dish... 75.00
King's Crown, punch bowl............................... 250.00
King's Crown, toothpick holder, ruby stain........ 45.00
Klondike, champagne 110.00
Knobby Bull's-Eye, bowl, 10" 35.00
Kokomo, casserole, w/lid 55.00
Kokomo, tray, ruby stain 100.00
Lacy Dewdrop, mug 20.00
Lacy Dewdrop, pitcher....................................... 85.00
Leaf & Dart, compote 35.00
Leaf & Dart, compote, w/lid 70.00
Leaf & Dart, sugar bowl 50.00
Leaf & Rib, butter dish, amber 80.00
Leaf & Rib, vase, vaseline................................... 35.00

Leaf and Star/#711, goblet, New Martinsville Glass Co., 1916, $30.00. (Photo courtesy Cathy and Gene Florence)

Leaf Mould, perfume bottle, vaseline 375.00
Lily of the Valley, cake stand 45.00
Lily of the Valley, egg cup 30.00
Loop, carafe 45.00
Loop, plate 30.00
Loop w/Dewdrop, pitcher 80.00
Loop w/Dewdrop, tumbler 10.00
Lozenges, compote 40.00
Magna, butter dish 65.00
Maize, decanter 40.00
Maltese, tray, 9x15" 60.00
Manhattan, biscuit jar 55.00
Manhattan, plate, 5" 20.00
Maple Leaf, dish, sq, vaseline 75.00
Maple Leaf, dish, sq, 10" 30.00
Maple Leaf, tumbler, bl or gr 50.00
Mardi Gras, cocktail 25.00
Mardi Gras, epergne 165.00
Mardi Gras, wine, ruby stain 70.00
Medallion, relish tray, bl, gr or vaseline 30.00
Medallion, waste bowl, bl or gr 40.00
Melrose, goblet 25.00

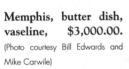

Memphis, butter dish, vaseline, $3,000.00.
(Photo courtesy Bill Edwards and Mike Carwile)

Memphis, nappy 65.00
Memphis, toothpick holder 95.00
Millard, compote, ruby stain 45.00
Millard, sauce dish 10.00
Minnesota, carafe 40.00
Minnesota, cup 20.00
Minnesota, plate 25.00
Missouri, pitcher, bl or gr 150.00
Monkey, berry bowl, sm 90.00
Monkey, spooner 135.00
Moon & Star, water bottle 45.00
Morning Glory, salt cellar 100.00
Nail, mustard pot 30.00
Nail, sugar shaker 75.00
Nailhead, goblet 50.00
New Hampshire, jug, 3-pt 125.00
New Hampshire, plate, ruby stain, 8" 75.00
New Jersey, butter dish 85.00
New Jersey, butter dish, ruby stain 200.00
Northwood's Intaglio, cruet, bl or gr 85.00
O'Hara Diamond, honey dish 20.00
O'Hara Diamond, lamp 70.00
Open Plaid, pitcher 75.00
Open Plaid, tumbler 15.00
Oregon, bowl, w/lid, 6-8", from $20 to 50.00
Oregon, carafe 45.00
Oregon, vase 25.00
Overshot, goblet 50.00
Palm Beach, butter dish 85.00
Palm Beach, jelly compote 35.00

Panel & Rib, creamer 25.00
Panel & Rib, sugar bowl, vaseline 60.00
Panelled Cane, ice tub 40.00
Panelled Cane, wine 15.00
Panelled Forget-Me-Not, bl or gr 70.00
Panelled Forget-Me-Not, shaker, ea 55.00
Pavonia, cake plate 25.00
Pavonia, plate 15.00
Pennsylvania, oil bottle 45.00
Pennsylvania, pickle jar w/lid 100.00
Persian, carafe 45.00
Persian, salt cellar 15.00
Pert, tumbler 15.00
Pert, tumbler, amethyst or vaseline 35.00
Petal & Loop, champagne 20.00
Petal & Loop, cordial, vaseline 30.00
Pilgrim Bottle, butter dish, vaseline 125.00
Plutec, compote 40.00
Plutec, nut bowl 25.00
Polar Bear, sauce dish 85.00
Polar Bear, waste bowl 125.00
Popcorn, goblet 40.00
Popcorn, wine 25.00
Potpourri, cake stand 450.00
Pressed Diamond, cake plate, ftd, vaseline 80.00
Pressed Diamond, plate, bl or gr, 11" 40.00
Primrose, bowl, milk glass 25.00
Primrose, goblet, bl, gr or milk glass 55.00
Primrose, relish tray, milk glass or vaseline 25.00
Priscilla, toothpick holder 30.00
Prism, decanter 40.00
Prism, wine 10.00
Queen, celery vase, amber or vaseline 40.00
Queen, pitcher, bl or gr 125.00
Queen Anne, syrup 40.00
Quintec, cracker jar 40.00
Rainbow, bowl, berry; sm 20.00
Rainbow, salt cellar 30.00
Raindrop, butter dish 45.00
Raindrop, butter dish, vaseline 95.00
Rayed Heart, pitcher 75.00
Red Block, cup, ruby stain 35.00
Reverse Torpedo, plate 25.00
Rexford, honey jar 45.00
Rexford, spooner 25.00
Ribbon, milk pitcher 75.00
Ribbon, platter 70.00
Rising Sun, custard cup 10.00
Rising Sun, pickle dish 15.00
Robin Hood, goblet, bl or gr 45.00
Robin Hood, tumbler 20.00
Roman Key, castor set 110.00
Roman Key, decanter 55.00
Roman Key, wine 15.00
Rose, dresser tray 40.00
Rose Sprig, nappy, bl or gr 40.00
Rose Sprig, punch bowl, ftd, amber 175.00
Rosette Band, creamer 20.00
Rosette Band, creamer, ruby stain 45.00
Royal Crystal, compote 50.00
Royal Crystal, syrup, ruby stain 85.00
Saint Bernard, cruet 45.00
Saint Bernard, jam jar 25.00
Sandwich Star, champagne, amethyst 325.00

Sandwich Star, spill holder, ftd.................................225.00
Sawtooth, bowl, w/lid, 6"...50.00
Sawtooth, egg cup...50.00
Sawtooth Band see Amazon
Scalloped Skirt, jelly compote...................................35.00
Scalloped Skirt, spooner...25.00
Scalloped Swirl, plate..25.00
Scalloped Swirl, plate, bl or gr..................................40.00
Sedan, pitcher...85.00
Sequoia, butter pat...10.00
Sequoia, pickle jar..35.00
Sheaf & Block, sugar bowl..30.00
Shell & Jewel, banana stand.......................................60.00
Sheraton, bread plate, amber, bl or gr, oval.............40.00
Sheraton, goblet...40.00
Singing Birds, bowl, berry; lg....................................55.00
Slewed Horseshoe, goblet...35.00
Snail, celery vase, ruby stain......................................90.00
Snail, finger bowl...55.00
Snail, sugar shaker, ruby stain.................................175.00
Spangled, creamer..90.00
Spirea Band, platter, bl or gr......................................60.00
Spirea Band, sugar shaker, amber.............................60.00
Star & Crescent, shaker, ea..15.00
Star & File, relish dish, w/hdls..................................25.00
Sterling, creamer..20.00
Sterling, wine...15.00
Strawberry & Cable, goblet...25.00
Strawberry & Cable, sugar bowl.................................30.00
Sunbeam, toothpick holder...20.00
Sunflower, pitcher..85.00
Sunflower, tumbler, milk glass...................................50.00
Sunk Honeycomb, decanter..45.00
Sunk Honeycomb, wine, ruby stain...........................35.00
Swan on Pond, butter dish..60.00
Swan on Pond, creamer, amber..................................35.00
Sydney, compote, w/lid..50.00
Tacoma, goblet, ruby stain..70.00
Tacoma, plate..20.00
Teardrop, bowl, rectangular, from $15 to..................40.00
Teardrop, pickle dish...15.00
Teasel, celery vase..30.00
Teasel, cruet...65.00
Texas, horseradish, w/lid...100.00
Texas, olive dish, ruby stain.......................................40.00
Theatrical, See Actress
Thousand Eye, cake plate, ftd.....................................40.00
Thousand Eye, cake plate, ftd, vaseline....................125.00
Thousand Eye, dish, bl or gr, sq, 10".........................60.00

Three Panel, goblet..35.00
Three Panel, spooner, vaseline...................................50.00
Three Panel, tumbler, amber......................................30.00
Three-in-One, biscuit jar...60.00
Three-in-One, nappy..25.00
Three-in-One, shot glass..25.00
Tidy, sugar bowl...35.00
Tile, decanter..40.00
Tile, olive dish..15.00
Tile, wine..15.00
Togo, cruet, ruby stain...85.00
Togo, olive dish, leaf shape..20.00
Tree of Love, compote..40.00
Tree of Love, cup..20.00
Truncated Cube, decanter...70.00
Tucoma, plate...20.00
Tulip, sugar bowl...25.00
US Coin, celery tray, amber..45.00
US Coin, pickle dish, ruby stain.................................40.00
US Comet, goblet..45.00
US Comet, goblet, vaseline..70.00
US Sheraton, sundae dish..20.00
V-in-Heart, compote...75.00
Venice, pickle jar, amber...30.00
Victor, claret...25.00
Victor, ice tub, ruby stain..80.00
Waffle & Finecut, pitcher..95.00
Waffle & Finecut, tumbler...15.00
Washington Centennial, egg cup................................30.00
Washington Centennial, shaker, ea............................55.00
Wedding Ring, creamer..20.00
Wedding Ring, sugar bowl...100.00
Wheat & Barley, spooner, bl or gr..............................50.00
Wheat & Barley, syrup...90.00
Wheat & Barley, tumbler, vaseline.............................30.00
Wild Flower, champagne, vaseline..............................50.00
Wild Flower, platter, amber...40.00

Winged Scroll, sugar bowl, green with gold trim, $50.00. (Photo courtesy Bill Edwards and Mike Carwile)

Wooden Pail, butter dish, amethyst..........................250.00
Wooden Pail, jelly bucket, amber or vaseline............60.00
Wyoming, creamer..25.00
Wyoming, wine..40.00
X-Logs, mug..25.00
X-Ray, shaker, ea..25.00
X-Ray, toothpick holder, bl or gr...............................75.00
Yale, bowl, berry; sm..15.00
Yale, syrup...65.00
Yutec, sugar bowl...25.00
Zipper, goblet...50.00
Zipper, vase, ftd...30.00
Zipper Slash, banana dish...30.00

Three Face/Shell and Tassel, compote, rare combination of patterns, 9x7", $5,200.00. (Photo courtesy Green Valley Auctions Inc.)

Paul Revere Pottery

The Saturday Evening Girls was a group of young immigrant girls headed by philanthropist Mrs. James Storrow who started meeting with them in the Boston library in 1899 for lectures, music, and dancing. Mrs. Storrow provided them with a kiln in 1906. Finding the facilities too small, they soon relocated near the Old North Church and chose the name Paul Revere Pottery. Under the supervision of Ms. Edith Brown, the girls produced simple ware. Until 1915 the pottery operated at a deficit, then a new building with four kilns was constructed on Nottingham Road. Vases, miniature jugs, children's tea sets, tiles, dinnerware, and lamps were produced, usually in soft matt glazes often decorated with wax-resist (cuerda seca) or a black-outlined stylized pattern of flowers, landscapes, or animals. Examples in black high gloss may also be found on occasion. Several marks were used: 'P.R.P.'; 'S.E.G.'; or the circular device, 'Boston, Paul Revere Pottery,' with the horse and rider. The pottery continued to operate; and even though it sold well, the high production costs of the handmade ware caused the pottery to fail in 1946. Our advisors for this category are Suzanne Perrault and David Rago; they are listed in the Directory under New Jersey.

Mug, three fishing boats, green, brown, blue, and ivory, $2,300.00. (Photo courtesy David Rago Auctions)

Bowl, daffodils, 2-tone on tan/yel/wht, SEG/6-14/FL, 2½x8½", NM.. 1,925.00
Bowl, geometric rim, brn on gray mottle, blk trim, SEG/4-15, 3"....310.00
Bowl, gr, flared rim, ftd, circular PRP mk, 3x7½" 175.00
Bowl, groups of 3 rabbits in band, SEG/345.2.10, 2¼x5½" 1,685.00
Bowl, iris band wht on yel, 4-compartment, 2½x8½", NM 300.00
Bowl, landscape, CBT Compliments..., SEG/5-17, 6½" 1,080.00
Bowl, purple w/int band: Eat Thy Bread in Joy..., house center, 10".2,125.00
Bowl, red, PRP/SEG/#s/initials, 2½x8¼" 65.00
Bowl, sailboats, brn/gr on bl & wht, SEG/8-15/AM, 5x6".........2,160.00
Bowl, ships on sea int band, bl/yel/gr/brn on lt bl, flared rim, 9"....1,500.00
Bowl, wht camelia, SEG/10-16/AM, hairlines, 2½x8½" 1,500.00
Cup, Greek key, bl & gr on turq w/wht int, SEG, ca 1910, 2x4½" ..235.00
Inkwell, sailing ships, SEG, 4" 2,000.00
Plate, lotus blossoms border, wht on bl, sgn AM, rim chips, 10" .. 315.00
Plate, ships (2) in sea scene, mc on bl, SEG/4-14/AM, 12½"..17,500.00
Plate, swan medallion on bl, SEG/8-19, 8" 600.00
Pot, tree band on mustard, w/lid & holes for lamp, globular, 6"... 3,500.00
Tile, fox, mustard on celadon, SEG/388.5'10/FR, label remnant, 5¼".. 2,880.00

Tile, Hull Street Galloupe House, marked, 3¾", $10,200.00. (Photo courtesy David Rago Auctions/LiveAuctioneers.com)

Tile, Paul Revere's House, North Square, mc, 3¾" 3,000.00
Tile, stylized house & trees in center, mc on turq matt, V2-25/FL, 6". 470.00
Tile, tulip center, gr/bl/wht/yel/blk on yel, EM/6.25, 4½" 375.00
Vase, lt bl, shouldered, 1929, 13½"... 750.00
Vase, ochre semi-matt, shouldered, 9¼" 280.00
Vase, olive gr, shouldered/ftd, circular PRP mk & F/8/23, 6½x4½" ..500.00
Vase, trees in landscape, mustard on sand, incurvate rim, 1917, 6" 1,550.00
Vase, trees in landscape on indigo, SEG/12-20/JMD, 1920, 3¾" ...1,440.00
Vase, trees in landscape on yel, SEG/4-19, 7¾x3½" 3,600.00

Vase, village seen through tall trees, signed 2?8.11.11. SEG IG, restored rim chip, 6¾", $65,000.00. (Photo courtesy David Rago Auctions/LiveAuctioneers.com)

Pauline Pottery

Pauline Pottery was made form 1883 to 1888 in Chicago, Illinois, from clay imported from the Ohio area. The company's founder was Mrs. Pauline Jacobus, who had learned the trade at the Rookwood Pottery. Mrs. Jacobus moved to Edgerton, Wisconsin, to be near a source of suitable clay, thus eliminating shipping expenses. Until 1905 she produced high-quality wares, able to imitate with ease designs and styles of such masters as Wedgwood and Meissen. Her products were sold through leading department stores, and the names of some of these firms may appear on the ware. Not all are marked; unless signed by a noted local artist, positive identification is often impossible. Marked examples carry a variety of stamps and signatures: 'Trade Mark' with a crown, 'Pauline Pottery,' and 'Edgerton Art Pottery' are but a few.

Bowl, Art Nouveau poppies, crown mark, 6x10", $540.00. (Photo courtesy Cincinnati Art Galleries/ LiveAuctioneers.com)

Jardiniere, Nouveau poppies on gr, #94, 6x10", NM..................... 550.00
Pitcher, bearded man drinking/smoking reserve, leaves surround, 10".. 2,875.00
Vase, bird & flowers on brn, flared neck, rpr/hairlines, 22" 3,150.00
Vase, cobalt w/beige int, bulbous w/cylindrical neck, 5¾x4", NM ..275.00

Peachblow

Peachblow, made to imitate the colors of the Chinese Peachbloom porcelain, was made by several glasshouses in the late 1800s. Among them were New England Glass, Mt. Washington, Webb, and

Hobbs, Brockunier and Company (Wheeling). Its pink shading was achieved through the action of the heat on the gold content of the glass. While New England's peachblow shades from deep crimson to white, Mt. Washington's tends to shade from pink to blue-gray. Many pieces were enameled and gilded. While by far the majority of the pieces made by New England had a satin (acid) finish, they made shiny peachblow as well. Wheeling glass, on the other hand, is rarely found in satin. In the 1950s Gundersen-Pairpoint Glassworks initiated the reproduction of Mt. Washington peachblow, using an exact duplication of the original formula. Though of recent manufacture, this glass is very collectible.

Apple, NE Glass, from 1893 World's Fair, 4½" 85.00
Bottle, scent; Webb, sq w/gold foliage, silver emb lid, 6" 800.00
Bowl, Gundersen, rim-to-hip hdls, 6" W 215.00
Bowl, Mt WA, 3 tapered/reeded ft, scalloped rim, 5½x7½" 3,500.00
Bowl, NE Glass, smooth str rim, 2⅝x4¼" 240.00
Bowl, Wheeling, sm ft, 2¾x4" 360.00
Creamer, Mt WA, sq top, reeded hdl, 4½" 725.00
Creamer & sugar bowl, Mt WA, crimped rims, 5¼", 3" 2,350.00
Creamer & sugar bowl, NE Glass, ribbed, lg wht hdls 180.00
Cup, Webb, crystal hdl, shiny, 2⅜" 85.00
Decanter, Wheeling, bulbous, amber hdl & stopper, shiny, 9½"... 850.00
Ewer, NE Glass, slim neck, wht hdl, 9" 185.00
Goblet, NE Glass, pk int, shiny, 7¼" 315.00
Jug, claret; Wheeling, reeded amber hdl & neck decor, 9½" 3,250.00

Pitcher, New England, 7", $1,150.00. (Photo courtesy Early Auction Co.)

Pitcher, Wheeling, amber draped pattern, shiny, reeded hdl, 8⅛" .. 1,550.00
Pitcher, Wheeling, bulbous, sq mouth, amber hdl, shiny, 7" 900.00
Pitcher, Wheeling, bulbous, sq mouth, amber hdl, 4" 660.00
Pitcher, Wheeling, bulbous, sq mouth, amber hdl, 8½" 1,950.00
Shakers, NE Glass, shiny, pewter lids, 3¾", pr 600.00
Toothpick holder, Mt WA, tricorner, 2¼" 475.00
Toothpick holder, Webb, mc floral, bulbous, 2½" 515.00
Toothpick holder, Wheeling, 2¼x2" 950.00
Tumbler, Wheeling, 3⅝" 125.00
Vase, lily; Mt WA, crimped rim, 12¾" 2,750.00
Vase, lily; NE Glass, 3-fold rim, gold flowers/vines, 10¼" 1,950.00
Vase, lily; NE Glass, 3-fold rim, 14½" 800.00
Vase, Morgan; Wheeling, amber griffin holder, sm base chips, 10⅞"..2,350.00
Vase, Mt WA, alternating pk & bl panels, 4¼" 2,350.00
Vase, Mt WA, floral, dbl gourd, 8" 3,100.00
Vase, Mt WA, floral beading/enameling, stick neck, 7⅞" 4,800.00
Vase, Mt WA, ovoid w/tapered neck, 8" 850.00
Vase, Mt WA, Queen's pattern, dbl gourd, 8" 3,450.00
Vase, Mt WA, scalloped rim, low waist, 6⅞" 2,400.00
Vase, NE Glass, cylindrical, 4-sided scalloped rim, 6½" 400.00
Vase, NE Glass, dimpled sides, pinched neck, 11¼" 1,325.00
Vase, NE Glass, stick neck, 8½" 575.00
Vase, Stevens & Wms, appl Oriental-style wht/amber flowers, 8¼"...350.00
Vase, Webb, birds & flowers w/gold, bulbous, 10"........................ 425.00

Vase, Webb, gold & platinum floral vine, shiny, 5" 180.00
Vase, Webb, gold floral, shiny, 9½"... 475.00
Vase, Webb, ovoid, 6⅛".. 180.00
Vase, Wheeling, amber draped pattern, ruffled/pleated rim, shiny, 10".550.00
Vase, Wheeling, gourd shape, shiny, 7".. 950.00
Vase, Wheeling, shouldered, shiny, 8½".. 900.00
Vase, Wheeling, stick neck, 8¾".. 725.00

Vase, Mt. Washington, Queen's design, 9", $20,000.00. (Photo courtesy Early Auction Co.)

Peking Cameo Glass

The first glasshouse was established in Peking in 1680. It produced glassware made in imitation of porcelain, a more desirable medium to the Chinese. By 1725 multilayered carving that resulted in a cameo effect lead to the manufacture of a wider range of shapes and colors. The factory was closed from 1736 to 1795, but glass made in Po-shan and shipped to Peking for finishing continued to be called Peking glass. Similar glassware was made through the first half of the twentieth century such as is listed below. Our advisor for this category is Jeff Person; he is listed in the Directory under Florida.

Bottle, scent; lotus & other flowers, red on clear, dauber, 6¼" 480.00
Bowl, ducks & foliage, red on wht, 8¼" 120.00
Bowl, wildlife & foliage, yel on wht, 3x6¾", pr............................. 300.00
Vase, birds & trees, gr on wht, 8" 110.00
Vase, fish, bl on wht, dbl-gourd shape, 9¾"................................... 180.00
Vase, flowering trees, citrine to pale amber, baluster, 8½" 480.00
Vase, flowers & foliage, gr on wht, shouldered, 12", pr 715.00
Vase, pheasant & foliage, red on wht, 8"... 90.00
Vase, vining floral, cobalt on wht, baluster, 11" 180.00
Vase, vining floral, gr on wht, slim neck w/flared rim, 9½" 90.00

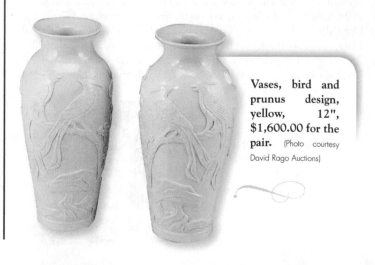

Vases, bird and prunus design, yellow, 12", $1,600.00 for the pair. (Photo courtesy David Rago Auctions)

Peloton

Peloton glass was first made by Wilhelm Kralik in Bohemia in 1880. This unusual art glass was produced by rolling colored threads onto the transparent or opaque glass gather as it was removed from the furnace. Usually more than one color of threading was used, and some items were further decorated with enameling. It was made with both shiny and acid finishes.

Basket, cranberry w/wht strings, clear rope hdl, 7½" 280.00
Card holder, mint gr w/mc strings, jewel & gilt ft, 4½" 215.00
Pitcher, clear w/mc strings, clear hdl, 4½" 185.00
Tumbler, clear w/gr strings, 3¼x2⅝" 175.00
Vase, bl w/wht strings, scalloped & ruffled rim, 6½" 400.00

Vase, clear with multicolor strings, 4½", $165.00; Vase, cased rose with multicolor strings, clear handles, 5½", $260.00. (Photo courtesy Dallas Auction Gallery/ LiveAuctioneers.com)

Vase, cranberry w/mc strings, scalloped & ruffled rim, 4½" 150.00
Vase, cranberry w/yel strings, ruffled rim, 4½" 140.00
Vase, pk w/red, bl & wht strings, 4-scalloped rim, 5½" 290.00

Pennsbury

Established in the 1950s in Morrisville, Pennsylvania, by Henry Below, the Pennsbury Pottery produced dinnerware and novelty items, much of which was sold in gift shops along the Pennsylvania Turnpike. Henry and his wife, Lee, worked for years at the Stangl Pottery before striking out on their own. Lee and her daughter were the artists responsible for many of the early pieces, the bird figures among them. Pennsbury pottery was hand painted, some in blue on white, some in multicolor on caramel. Pennsylvania Dutch motifs, Amish couples, and barbershop singers were among their most popular decorative themes. Sgraffito (hand incising), was used extensively. The company marked their wares 'Pennsbury Pottery' or 'Pennsbury Pottery, Morrisville, PA.'

In October of 1969 the company closed. Contents of the pottery were sold in December of the following year, and in April of 1971, the buildings burned to the ground. Items marked Pennsbury Glenview or Stumar Pottery (or these marks in combination) were made by Glenview after 1969. Pieces manufactured after 1976 were made by the Pennington Pottery. Several of the old molds still exist, and the original Pennsbury Caramel process is still being used on novelty items, some of which are produced by Lewis Brothers, New Jersey. Production of Pennsbury dinnerware was not resumed after the closing. Our advisor for this category is Shirley Graff; she is listed in the Directory under Ohio. Note: Prices may be higher in some areas of the country — particularly on the East Coast, the southern states, and Texas. Values for examples in the Rooster patterns apply to both black and red variations.

Ashtray, Amish, 5" dia 25.00

Ashtray, Rooster, 4" 20.00
Bank, jug, pig decor, cork top, 7" 55.00

Bookends, eagle, 8½x6½", $340.00. (Photo courtesy Belhorn Auction Services LLC/LiveAuctioneers.com)

Bowl, divided vegetable; Rooster, 9½x6¼" 50.00
Bowl, pretzel; Amish Couple 85.00
Bowl, Rooster, 9" 45.00
Butter dish, Rooster, ¼-lb, from $45 to 50.00
Cake stand, Harvest or Hex, 4½x11½" 80.00
Candlesticks, hummingbird, wht, #117/#117L, 5", pr 120.00
Candlesticks, Rooster, 4", pr 85.00
Candy dish, Hex, heart shaped, 6x6" 35.00
Canister, Hex, Flour, 7½" 110.00
Chip 'n dip, Folkart 80.00
Coaster, Gay Ninety, 5" dia 35.00
Coffeepot, Folkart, 2-cup, 6½" 25.00
Compote, holly decor, 5" 25.00
Creamer & sugar bowl, Amish 30.00
Cruets, oil & vinegar; Rooster, pr 150.00
Desk basket, National Exchange Club, 5" 40.00
Egg cup, Folkart 16.00
Figurine, Audubon's Warbler, #122, 4" 160.00
Figurine, barn swallow, #123, 6¼" 165.00
Figurine, blue jay, #108, 10½" 400.00
Figurine, bluebird, #103, 3½" 235.00
Figurine, crested chickadee, #101, 4" 195.00
Figurine, duckling pr, 6½" 295.00
Figurine, goldfinch, #102, 3" 195.00
Figurine, nuthatch, #110, 3⅝" 145.00
Figurine, rooster, #127, 11½" 165.00
Figurine, Slick-Chick, 5½" 50.00

Figurine, Western Tanager, #104, 5½x5", from $180.00 to $210.00. (Photo courtesy Belhorn Auction Service LLC/ LiveAuctioneers.com)

Figurine, wren, #106, 6½" 315.00
Figurine, wren, #109, 3¼" 165.00
Mug, beer; Barber Shop Quartet 25.00

Mug, Beer; Fisherman... 45.00
Mug, coffee; Gay Ninety, 3¼"... 35.00

Pie plate, Hex, 9", from $40.00 to $45.00. (Photo courtesy Lucille Henzke)

Pitcher, Delft Toleware, bl, 5"... 55.00
Pitcher, Hex, 6¼"... 65.00
Pitcher, Yellow Daisy, ca 1959, 4"....................................... 32.00
Planter, bird on gourd w/opening, #301, 5", pr................... 110.00
Plaque, Amish Reading Bible, no primary colors, 9"............... 75.00
Plaque, Amish Sayings, 7x5"... 25.00
Plaque, Charles W Morgan, ship decor, 11x8"...................... 110.00
Plaque, Fisherman, 5" dia 28.00
Plaque, horse & carriage, 6"... 50.00
Plaque, It Is Whole Empty, 4" dia 35.00
Plaque, Mercury Dime, 8" dia 65.00
Plaque, Pennsylvania Railroad 1856, Tiger Locomotive, 8x5⅝" 48.00
Plaque, Swallow the Insult, 6" dia 25.00
Plaque, United States Steel, 1954, 8"................................... 40.00
Plaque, Washington Crossing the Delaware, 5" dia 25.00
Plate, bread; Give Us This Day Our Daily Bread, 9x6" 40.00
Plate, Neshaminy Woods, 11½" 120.00
Plate, Rooster, 10".. 35.00
Platter, Rooster, 11" L... 48.00
Snack tray & cup, Folkart or Hex 20.00
Tea tile, skunk, Why Be Disagreeable, 6"............................ 40.00
Tray, cigarette; Eagle, 7½x5" 40.00
Tray, Laurel Ridge, famous old landmark, 8½x5¼" 40.00
Tray, tulip, 7½x5"... 40.00
Wall pocket, bellows shape w/eagle in high relief, 10" 50.00
Wall pocket, cowboy, from $75 to 90.00
Wall pocket, ship w/brn border, 6½" sq............................... 50.00

Pens and Pencils

The first metallic writing pen was patented in 1809, and soon machine-produced pens with steel nibs gradually began replacing the quill. The first fountain pen was invented in 1830, but due to the fact that the ink flow was not consistent (though leakage was), they were not manufactured commercially until the 1880s. The first successful commercial producers were Waterman in 1884 and Parker with the Lucky Curve in 1888. The self-filling pen of the early 1900s featured the soft, interior sack which filled with ink as the metal bar on the outside of the pen was raised and lowered. Variations of the filling mechanisms were tried until 1932 when Parker introduced the Vacumatic, a sackless pen with an internal pump. Unless otherwise noted, prices below are for pens in near mint or better condition which have been professionally restored to full operating capacity. For unrestored as-found pens, approximately one third should be deducted from the values below. For more information we recommend *Fountain Pens, Past & Present*, by Paul Erano (Collector Books). Our advisor for this category is Gary Lehrer; he is listed in the Directory under Connecticut. For those interested in purchasing pens through catalogs, our advisor, Mr. Lehrer publishes extensive catalogs.

Key:
AF — aeromatic filler
BF — button filler
CF — capillary filler
CPT — chrome-plated trim
ED — eyedropper filler
GF — gold-filled
GFT — gold-filled trim
HR — hard rubber
LF — lever filler
NP — nickel plated
NPT — nickel-plated trim
PF — plunger filler
PIF — piston filler

Fountain Pens

Carter's Pearltex, blue plastic with gold-filled trim, lever fill, ca. 1931, 5", from $200.00 to $250.00. (Photo courtesy Paul Erano)

Aiken Lambert, 1900, #2, ED, GF Gopheresque (rare), med, NM .. 600.00
C Stewart, 1938, #15, LF, gr pearl, NPT, NM 75.00
C Stewart, 1950, #74, twist filler, red herringbone, fretwork band, NM. 200.00
C Stewart, 1951, #27, LF, silver candy-stripe, GFT, NM 175.00
C Stewart, 1951, #55, LF, gr marble, GFT, NM 150.00
C Stewart, 1952, #27, LF, Tiger's Eye, GFT, NM 250.00
C Stewart, 1955, #55, LF, bl marble, GFT, NM 200.00
C Stewart, 1955, #58, LF, gr pearl web, GFT, NM 200.00
C Stewart, 1956, #76, gr herringbone, GFT, NM 200.00
C Stewart, 1956, #85, LF, bl pearl w/gold veins, GFT, NM 150.00
Carters, 1928, #6 sz INX, LF, coral, GFT, NM 825.00
Carters, 1928, #6 sz INX, LF, Ivory Pearltex, GFT, NM............. 600.00
Carters, 1928, #7 sz INX, bl pearl, GFT, NM........................... 600.00
Chilton, 1924, #6 sleeve filler, blk, GFT, NM 400.00
Conklin, 1918, #20, CF, blk chased HR, GFT, NM 175.00
Conklin, 1918, #40, crescent filler, blk chased HR, GFT, NM..... 250.00
Conklin, 1927, #2, LF, wht w/blk veins (rare), GFT, NM 300.00
Conklin, 1927, Endura Lg, LF, blk, GFT, NM 450.00
Conklin, 1927, Endura Lg, LF, sapphire bl, GFT, NM 650.00
Conklin, 1927, Endura Oversz, blk, HR, long cap/section, GFT, NM.. 1,200.00
Conklin, 1927, Endura Standard, LF, Cardinal, GFT, NM........... 250.00
Conklin, 1930, Endura Symetric Oversz, LF, blk/bronze, GFT, NM...350.00
Conklin, 1932, Nozac, PF, gr pearl w/blk stripe, GFT, NM 300.00
Crocker, 1910, #2, blow filler, blk chased HR, NM 200.00
Crocker, 1932, #2, hatchet filler, blk chased HR, GFT, NM 175.00
Dunn, 1921, #2, pump filler, blk HR, GFT, NM 200.00
Eclipse, 1931, #2, LF, Mandarin Yellow w/jade ends, GFT, NM... 150.00
Esterbrook, 1949, LJ Pen, LF, red, NM................................... 35.00
Esterbrook, 1949, SJ Pen, LF, red, NM................................... 30.00
Esterbrook, 1950, Pastel Pen, LF, wht, NM............................. 75.00
Esterbrook, 1950, Relief #12, Tiger's Eye web, GFT, NM 275.00
Leboeuf, 1928, #4, sleeve filler, Green Pearltex, GFT, NM 450.00
Leboeuf, 1932, #8, sleeve filler, Green Pearltex, GFT, NM 1,500.00
Mabie Todd, 1925, #44 Eternal, LF, blk, NM 150.00
Mabie Todd, 1925, #44 Eternal, LF, jade, NM 225.00
Mabie Todd, 1938, Blackbird, bulb filler, gr & gold spiral, GFT, NM ... 175.00
Mabie Todd, 1939, #4, LF, silver pearl snakeskin, NM 275.00
Mabie Todd, 1947, Swan #3240, LF, dk gr, GFT, NM................ 125.00
Montblanc, 1927, #1266, PIF, chrome plate flute, NM............... 200.00
Montblanc, 1935, #20, blk, GFT, NM 600.00
Montblanc, 1935, #20, Coral Red, GFT, NM............................ 750.00

Montblanc, 1935, #25, blk, GFT, NM 750.00
Montblanc, 1935, #25, Coral Red, GFT, NM 900.00
Montblanc, 1935, #30, blk, GFT, NM 850.00
Montblanc, 1935, #30, Coral Red, GFT, NM 1,100.00
Montblanc, 1937, #134, blk w/long window, NM 650.00
Montblanc, 1937, #333½, PIF, blk, GFT, NM........................... 450.00
Montblanc, 1939, #139, PIF, blk, GFT & silver trim, NM 3,000.00
Montblanc, 1941, #25 Masterpiece, PIF, 12-sided marble, GFT, NM 1,500.00
Montblanc, 1947, #136, PIF, blk, GFT, NM 900.00
Montblanc, 1950, #146, PIF, gr stripe, GFT, NM....................1,250.00
Montblanc, 1950, #246, PIF, blk, GFT, short window, NM.......... 450.00
Montblanc, 1950, #642N, silver striped, brushed chrome cap w/GFT, NM .600.00
Montblanc, 1952, #142, PIF, blk GFT, NM 350.00
Montblanc, 1955, #82, PIF, GF pinstripe 275.00
Montblanc, 1955, #124, PF, GF, fluted, M 250.00
Moore, 1925, L-96, dk bl, GFT, NM 400.00
Moore, 1925, L-96, LF, maroon/burgundy, GFT, NM 500.00
Moore, 1946, #2, LF, gr pearl web, GFT, NM 125.00
Parker, 1918, Black Giant, ED, blk HR, NP clip, NM.............1,500.00
Parker, 1921, Duofold Jr, BF, red HR, bandless cap, NM 300.00
Parker, 1921, Duofold Sr, BF, red HR, bandless cap, MIB.........1,500.00
Parker, 1928, Duofold Sr, BF, Mandarin Yellow, GFT, NM 1,750.00
Parker, 1930, Duofold Special, BF, red, GFT, EX 250.00
Parker, 1932, BF, blk, bandless, NM 75.00
Parker, 1932, Thrift Time, BF, gray marble, GFT, NM................. 200.00
Parker, 1935, Victory, BF, bl marble, GFT, NM 300.00
Parker, 1937, Vacumatic Oversz, blk, GFT, NM 400.00
Parker, 1937, Vacumatic Oversz, brn banded, GFT, NM 450.00
Parker, 1937, Vacumatic Oversz, gr banded, NPT, NM 450.00
Parker, 1937, Vacumatic Oversz, red banded, GFT, NM 650.00
Parker, 1937, Vacumatic Oversz, silver banded, GFT, NM 400.00
Parker, 1939, Duofold Jr, BF, silver geometric, NPT, NM 125.00
Parker, 1939, Vacumatic Slender, red laminated, GFT, NM 150.00
Parker, 1945, Vacumatic Major, silver laminated, NPT, dbl jeweled, EX .175.00
Parker, 1946, #51, AF, forest gr, brushed lustraloy cap, M 125.00
Parker, 1946, NS (New Style) Duofold, gray, NPT, NM 300.00
Parker, 1948, #51, AF, Buckskin, GF cap w/pinstripe & plain panels, NM..200.00
Parker, 1948, #51, AF, plum, GF cap, NM 175.00
Parker, 1950, #51, Mark II, AF, rare later version, NM 150.00
Parker, 1951, #51, plum, brushed lustraloy cap, NM 175.00
Parker, 1957, #61, wick filler, blk, 2-tone lustraloy cap, NM........ 100.00
Parker, 1960, #45, cartridge/converter, bronzed/anodized, M 100.00
Parker, 1965, #75, sterling silver crosshatch (flat ends), NM 175.00
Parker, 1965, #75 Spanish Treasure LE, sterling silver crosshatch, MIB..1,600.00
Parker, 1970, #T-1 (Titanium), M 750.00
Parker, 1970, #T-1 Titanium Ball (ballpoint) Pen, M................... 300.00
Parker, 1970, #75 Titanium, M... 800.00
Parker, 1975, #75, sterling silver crosshatch (dimpled ends), NM...150.00
Parker (Valentine), 1935, #32, BF, burgundy pearl web, GFT, rare, NM..150.00
Pelikan, 1937, #100N, gr pearl, GFT, NM 350.00
Pelikan, 1937, #101N, tortoise w/matching cap/derby, NM 1,250.00
Pelikan, 1938, #100N, gr pearl, chased GF band/clip, NM 325.00
Pelikan, 1938, #100N, tortoise w/red cap, NM 1,250.00
Pelikan, 1938, IBIS, PIF, blk, GFT, NM 175.00
Pelikan, 1950, #400, PIF, brn stripe, GFT, NM 200.00
Pelikan, 1950, #400, PIF, gr stripe, GFT, NM 175.00
Pelikan, 1950, #400, PIF, gr V stripe, gr cap/tuning knob/section, NM ..450.00
Salz, 1920, Peter Pan, LF, dk red w/blk veins, GFT, NM 75.00
Salz, 1925, Peter Pan, LF, blk, HR, GFT, rare longer length, NM.. 60.00
Salz, 1925, Peter Pan, LF, tan/brn Bakelite, GFT, NM 60.00
Sheaffer, 1930, Lifetime Balance Lg, LF, brn stripe, GFT, NM..... 325.00
Sheaffer, 1930, Lifetime Balance Lg, LF, Carmine Red stripe, GFT, NM.600.00
Sheaffer, 1930, Lifetime Balance Lg, LF, ebonized pearl, GFT, NM ...500.00
Sheaffer, 1930, Lifetime Balance Lg, LF, gr stripe, GFT, NM 350.00

Sheaffer, 1930, Lifetime Balance Lg, LF, Roseglow stripe, GFT, NM.. 1,400.00
Sheaffer, 1936, Feather Touch #8 Lg Balance, gray marble, NM.. 750.00
Sheaffer, 1937, Standard Sz Lifetime Balance, LF, blk, GFT, NM ...150.00
Sheaffer, 1942, Lifetime Triumph, PF, silver laminated, NPT, EX ...125.00
Sheaffer, 1950, Triumph Snorkle, GF, NM 150.00
Sheaffer, 1952, Clipper Snorkle, sage gr, chrome cap w/GFT, MIB.. 150.00
Sheaffer, 1954, Valiant Snorkle, burgundy, NM 75.00
Sheaffer, 1954, Valiant Snorkle, pk, NM 125.00
Sheaffer, 1958, Lady Skripsert, gold-plated, jeweled ring, EX 50.00
Sheaffer, 1959, PFM I, blk, blk cap, CPT, NM 200.00
Sheaffer, 1959, PFM II, blk, stainless steel cap, NM 250.00
Sheaffer, 1959, PFM II, burgundy, stainless steel cap, GFT, NM.. 200.00
Sheaffer, 1959, PFM III, blk, blk cap, GFT, NM......................... 200.00
Sheaffer, 1959, PFM III, gray (rare), GFT, NM 375.00
Sheaffer, 1959, PFM III Demonstrator, transparent, GFT, blk shell, NM .. 1,000.00
Sheaffer, 1959, PFM IV, blk, GF cap, GFT, NM 400.00
Sheaffer, 1959, PFM V, blk polished chrome cap, GFT, NM........ 350.00
Soennecken, 1952, 111 Extra, PIF, gr herringbone, NM 1,250.00
Soennecken, 1952, 111 Superior, PIF, golden weave, NM 600.00
Soennecken, 1952, 222 Extra, PIF, blk................................... 450.00
Soennecken, 1952, 222 Superior, PIF, silver lizard, NM 375.00
Wahl Eversharp, 1920, #0, LF, GF pinstripe, NM 55.00
Wahl Eversharp, 1927, Gold Seal, LF, rosewood, NM 200.00
Wahl Eversharp, 1929, #2, LF, rosewood, GFT, NM 175.00
Wahl Eversharp, 1929, Equipoised, LF, blk & pearl, GFT, NM.... 350.00
Wahl Eversharp, 1929, Oversz Deco Band, LF, blk, GFT, NM 450.00
Wahl Eversharp, 1929, Oversz Deco Band, LF, Lapis, GFT, NM.. 900.00
Wahl Eversharp, 1929, Oversz Deco Band, woodgrain, GFT, NM ..650.00
Wahl Eversharp, 1934, #2 Doric, LF, blk & pearl, NPT, NM 300.00
Wahl Eversharp, 1942, Skyline Jr, LF, bl Moderne stripe, GFT, NM..125.00
Wahl Eversharp, 1951, Symphony, LF, blk, GFT, M w/orig label . 100.00
Waterman, 1910, #18S Safety ED, blk, HR, rare, M 2,600.00
Waterman, 1915, #52, LF, blk chased HR, NPT, NM.................. 150.00
Waterman, 1920, #52½ V, LF, Cardinal HR, GFT, NM............... 200.00
Waterman, 1920, #554½ LEC, LF, GF Gothic eng, NM 400.00
Waterman, 1924, #54, LF, blk HR, GFT, NM 175.00
Waterman, 1924, #452, LF, sterling Gothic, NM........................ 400.00
Waterman, 1925, #58, blk HR, GFT, NM 800.00
Waterman, 1925, #552½, ED, Secretary in GF filigree, NM 400.00
Waterman, 1926, #7, LF, red ripple w/red band, GFT, NM+........ 400.00
Waterman, 1927, #7, LF, red ripple, pk band, 1st yr model, NM.. 500.00
Waterman, 1929, Patrician, LF, moss agate................................1,250.00
Waterman, 1929, Patrician, LF, Nacre (blk & pearl), GFT, M color..2,250.00
Waterman, 1929, Patrician, LF, Onyx (red cream), GFT, M color...2,500.00
Waterman, 1930, #94, LF, bl & cream, NPT, NM 225.00
Waterman, 1930, #94, LF, brn & cream (mahog), GFT, NM 250.00
Waterman, 1930, #94, LF, red ripple HR, GFT, NM 400.00
Waterman, 1940, #2 Model 513, LF (England), GFT, NM 125.00
Waterman, 1940, 100 yr, blk, smooth cap/bbl, GFT, NM............. 400.00

Mechanical Pencils

Anonymous, rifle shape, cocking mechanism, eng Rin Tin Tin, NM ..75.00
Autopoint, 1945, 2-color (blk & bl), w/clip, M.............................. 15.00
Conklin, 1929, Symetric, gr marble, GFT, EX 50.00
Cross/Tiffany 1990, sterling silver pinstripe, clip: Tiffany, MIB.... 100.00
Eversharp, 1940, blk snakeskin-pattern leather cover, GFT, NM.. 100.00
Montblanc, 1924, #6, octagonal, blk HR, rare, lg, NM 1,350.00
Montblanc, 1930, #92 Repeater, blk HR, NPT, NM 125.00
Montblanc, 1939, #392 Repeater, blk HR, NM.......................... 80.00
Parker, 1929, Duofold Jr, jade, GFT, NM 50.00
Parker, 1929, Duofold Jr, Mandarin Yellow, GFT, NM 250.00
Parker, 1930, Duofold Vest Pocket, burgundy, GFT, w/opener taper, NM ...250.00
Parker, 1948, Duofold Repeater, gray, GFT, NM......................... 150.00

Sheaffer, 1925, Balance, deep jade, GFT, NM+ 50.00
Sheaffer, 1925, Balance, gr marble, GFT, NM+ 40.00
Sheaffer, 1959, PRM III, blk, GFT, M w/orig decal 175.00
Wahl Eversharp, 1929, Oversz Deco Band, blk & pearl, GFT, NM ... 175.00
Wahl Eversharp, 1939, Coronet, blk w/smooth GF cap, NM 100.00
Waterman, 1925, blk HR, GFT, M 100.00
Waterman, 1928, #52½ V, olive ripple, GFT, NM 85.00

Sets

Eversharp Skyline, blue striped cap and barrel, lever filler, ca. 1942, set: from $150.00 to $200.00. Pen alone: from $100.00 to $150.00. (Photo courtesy Paul Erano)

Parker, 1940, Vacuum Jr, gr/bronze/blk stripes, GFT, NM 175.00
Parker, 1957, GF, alternating pinstripes & panels, M 200.00
Sheaffer, 1925, #3-25 Tall, blk plastic, GFT, NM 100.00
Sheaffer, 1936, Junior, LF, gray marble, NPT, NM 100.00
Sheaffer, 1952, Clipper Triumph Snorkle, bright red, chrome caps, MIB.. 200.00
Sheaffer, 1958, Lady Skripsert, GF filigree & bl, MIB 45.00
Sheaffer, 1959, PFM III, blk, GFT, MIB 325.00
Wahl Eversharp, #4, GF w/chased wave pattern, NM 175.00
Waterman, 1925, #52, LF, red ripple, GFT, NM 250.00

Personalities, Fact and Fiction

One of the largest and most popular areas of collecting today is character-related memorabilia. Everyone has favorites, whether they be comic-strip personalities or true-life heroes. The earliest comic strip dealt with the adventures of the Yellow Kid, the smiling, bald-headed Oriental boy always in a nightshirt. He was introduced in 1895, a product of the imagination of Richard Fenton Outcault. Today, though very hard to come by, items relating to the Yellow Kid bring premium prices.

Though her 1923 introduction was unobtrusively made through only one newspaper, New York's *Daily News*, Little Orphan Annie, the vacant-eyed redhead in the inevitable red dress, was quickly adopted by hordes of readers nationwide, and before the demise of her creator, Harold Gray, in 1968, she had starred in her own radio show. She made two feature films, and in 1977 'Annie' was launched on Broadway.

Other early comic figures were Moon Mullins, created in 1923 by Frank Willard; Buck Rogers by Philip Nowlan in 1928; and Betty Boop, the round-faced, innocent-eyed, chubby-cheeked Boop-Boop-a-Doop girl of the early 1930s. Bimbo was her dog and KoKo her clown friend.

Popeye made his debut in 1929 as the spinach-eating sailor with the spindly-limbed girlfriend, Olive Oyl, in the comic strip *Thimble Theatre*, created by Elzie Segar. He became a film star in 1933 and had his own radio show that during 1936 played three times a week on CBS. He obligingly modeled for scores of toys, dolls, and figurines, and especially those from the '30s are very collectible.

Tarzan, created around 1930 by Edgar Rice Burroughs, and Captain Midnight, by Robert Burtt and Willfred G. Moore, are popular heroes with today's collectors. During the days of radio, Sky King of the Flying Crown Ranch (also created by Burtt and Moore) thrilled boys and girls of the mid-1940s. Hopalong Cassidy, Red Rider, Tom Mix, and the Lone Ranger were only a few of the other 'good guys' always on the side of law and order.

But of all the fictional heroes and comic characters collected today, probably the best loved and most well known is Mickey Mouse. Created in the late 1920s by Walt Disney, Micky (as his name was first spelled) became an instant success with his film debut, 'Steamboat Willie'. His popularity was parlayed through windup toys, watches, figurines, cookie jars, puppets, clothing, and numerous other products. Items from the 1930s are usually copyrighted 'Walt Disney Enterprises'; thereafter, 'Walt Disney Productions' was used.

For more information we recommend *Schroeder's Collectible Toys, Antique to Modern*, by Sharon and Bob Huxford. For those interested in Disneyana, we recommend *Collecting Disneyana* by David Longest. Both are available from Collector Books. See also Autographs; Banks; Big Little Books; Children's Books; Comic Books; Cookie Jars; Dolls; Games; Lunch Boxes; Movie Memorabilia; Paper Dolls; Pin-Back Buttons; Posters; Puzzles; Rock 'n Roll Memorabilia; Toys.

Betty Boop, figure, celluloid on tin base, prewar, Made in Japan, VG, $575.00. (Photo courtesy Morphy Auctions)

Alf, hand puppet, plush w/Born to Rock shirt, Alien Prod, NM.... 20.00
Alice in Wonderland, figurine, ceramic, standing, WDP, 1960s, 6", M .45.00
Alvin & the Chipmunks, bank, Alvin w/harmonica, vinyl, CBS Toys, NM..20.00
Alvin & the Chipmunks, jack-in-the-box, Alvin pop-up, CBS Toys, 9", NM .. 35.00
Andy Panda, Writing Paper, Whitman, 1949, complete, EXIB 50.00
Annie Oakley, belt, tooled leather, AO & Tagg on buckle, 1950s, MOC. 75.00
Archies, hand puppet, Archie, vinyl, Ideal, 1973, MIP (TV Favorites) .125.00
Aristocats, pitcher, characters on wht ceramic, Bareuther, 8", M .. 25.00
Augie Doggie, coloring book, Whitman #1186, 1960, some use, EX . 35.00
Baby Huey, drinking glass, Big Baby Huey, Pepsi, 1970s, 5" Brockway, M . 15.00
Bambi, planter, airbrushed ceramic, Leeds, 1950s, 4½", NM+ 60.00
Bambi, wristwatch, Birthday Series, Ingersoll-US Time/WDP, 1949, MIB..275.00
Bambi & Thumper, wall pocket, w/tree stump, ceramic, Leeds, 1950s, NM.75.00
Banana Splits, club membership kit, 1968, NM (w/mailer) 100.00
Barney, nightlight, Barney in hot-air balloon, plastic, 1990s, MIP....18.00
Barney Google & Spark Plug, drum, litho tin/paper, 1920s, 10" dia, G..275.00
Barney Google & Spark Plug, figure set, wood/cloth, Schoenhut, VG...600.00
Barney Google & Spark Plug, pull toy, wheeled base, tin, Nifty, EX..2,100.00
Bashful (Snow White), figurine, ceramic, Enesco, 1960s, 5", M 80.00
Bat Masterson, cane, 1958, EX+ 35.00
Batman, coloring book, Adventures of..., Whitman, 1966, some use, EX+ .25.00
Batman, flowerpot, wht ceramic w/Super Plants & image, 3", M ... 20.00
Batman, fork & spoon, name & emb images on hdls, Imperial, 1966, NM .30.00
Batman, hand puppet, cloth w/vinyl head, Ideal, 1966, NM+ 75.00
Batman, Helmet & Cape Set, Ideal, 1966, NM 75.00
Batman, lamp, Vanity Fair Industries, 7½", NM 175.00
Batman, mug, milk glass w/blk images front/bk, Westfield, 1966, EX.....45.00
Batman, Press-Out Book, Whitman, 1966, unused, M 80.00
Batman, Utility Belt, complete w/accessories, Remco, MIB......... 950.00
Batman & Robin, bubble bath containers, Colgate, 1960s, NM, ea .. 30.00

Batman & Robin, Talking Alarm Clock, Robin in car, Janex, 1970s, EXIB...125.00

Beaky (Buzzard), pencil holder, name on base, Moss Metal, 1940s, EX..100.00

Belder (Coneheads), figure, vinyl, rnd base, Presents, 1991, 12", EX+.25.00

Belle (Peanuts), doll, cheerleader, vinyl, Knickerbocker, '80s, 8", M ...25.00

Ben Casey MD, Play Hospital Set, Transogram, 1962, NMIB......550.00

Ben Casey MD, Sweater Guard, chain w/charms, Bing Crosby Prod, MIB..45.00

Betty Boop, bank, pnt chalkware figure, 1950s-60s, 14", VG 125.00

Betty Boop, doll quilt, Fleischer Studios, 1930s, 18x13", EX........ 100.00

Betty Boop, figure, pnt wood bead type w/jtd limbs, 1930s, 4½", EX.. 75.00

Big Bird, jack-in-the-box, Playskool, 1986, 10", NM+ 25.00

Bimbo, figure, celluloid, Japan, prewar, 6½", NM 850.00

Bimbo, figure, cloth, blk/wht, name on chest, French Novelty, 12", EX...2,500.00

Blondie, Paint Book, 1940, some use, VG 45.00

Bonzo, figure, compo w/jtd arms & head, lg bl eyes, 1920s, 13", G..775.00

Bonzo, figure, velvet, jtd, Chad Valley, 1920s, 22", EX.............. 1,000.00

Bonzo, mustard jar, 4", EX, $100.00.
(Photo courtesy Morphy Auctions/LiveAuctioneers.com)

Bonzo, pull toy, Bonzo on scooter, tin, Chein, 7", EX+ 625.00

Boob McNutt, marionette, Schoenhut, 10½", EX 550.00

Bozo the Clown, bank, bust figure w/big smile, vinyl, 1987, 5", NM.. 20.00

Bozo the Clown, doll, pull-string talker, Mattel, 1962, 21", EX 35.00

Bozo the Clown, hand puppet, cloth/vinyl, Knickerbocker, 1962, EX+.. 55.00

Broom Hilda, bubble bath container, Lander, 1977, EX 20.00

Buck Rogers, pocket knife, Camillus Cutlery/Cream of Wheat, 1935, EX ..975.00

Buck Rogers, Solar Scouts ring, rare, NM 3,150.00

Buck Rogers, Space Ranger Kit, Sylvania TV, 1952, unused, NM+IP.. 150.00

Bugs Bunny, alarm clock, Bugs resting, Ingraham, 1940s, 4" sq, EX 175.00

Bugs Bunny, bank, chalk figure seated w/carrot, 1940s-50s, 16", VG 70.00

Bugs Bunny, figure, litho tin, w/carrots, Talking Toy Co, 1949, 9", EX..75.00

Bugs Bunny, glow-in-the-dark picture, landscape, fr, 1940s, 11x9", NM+ . 30.00

Bugs Bunny, planter, ceramic, sad Bugs, fence planter, Am Pottery, NM+...75.00

Bullwinkle, bank, rnd clock form w/Bullwinkle, Larami, 1969, MOC..75.00

Bullwinkle, Brain Twisters dexterity puzzles, Larami, 1969, MOC. 20.00

Bullwinkle, jewelry holder, SP figure, 1960s, 5½", EX+ 30.00

Buttercup & Spare-Ribs, pull toy, wheeled base, Nifty/Chein, 4", VG.725.00

Captain America, badge, Sentinels of Liberty, enamel inlay, EX+ ..700.00

Captain America, Official Utility Belt, Remco, 1979, MIB 75.00

Captain America, Scooter, friction, Marx, 1968, MIP 1,075.00

Captain Gallant, coloring book, Lowe #2505, 1956, unused, NM. 85.00

Captain Hook, marionette, Peter Puppet Playthings, 1950s, NM ...275.00

Captain Kangaroo, fr-tray puzzle, Whitman #4446, 1960, EX........ 38.00

Captain Kangaroo, hand puppet, cloth & vinyl, Rushton, 1950s, NM+. 75.00

Captain Kangaroo, table cover, birthday graphics, CA Reed, 1950s, MIP. 50.00

Captain Marvel, compass ring, 1946, EX 350.00

Captain Marvel, Flying Captain Marvel punch-out toy, Reed, 1944, MIP ..45.00

Captain Marvel, Fun Book, Fawcett, 1944, unused, EX 95.00

Captain Marvel, pocket watch, full-figure image, Fawcett, 1948, EXIB.850.00

Captain Midnight, playsuit, US Flight Commander, Collegeville, EX...175.00

Casper, doll, terry cloth & plastic, talker, Mattel, 1960s, 15", EX+ .. 100.00

Cat in the Hat, doll, plush, Eden, 1979, 24", NM 50.00

Charlie Brown, comb & brush set, Avon, 1971, NM+IB 25.00

Charlie Brown, doll, terry pillow type, Determined, '70s, 9", MIP. 35.00

Charlie Brown, marionette, Pelham, 1970s, 8", EX+..................... 50.00

Charlie McCarthy, doll, Eddie Bergen's CM, Effanbee, 19", VGIB.. 450.00

Charlie McCarthy, pencil sharpener, Bakelite 2-D bust, 1930s, 2", EX..65.00

Chilly Willy, paint book, Whitman #2946, 1960, some use, EX+.. 35.00

Cinderella, wristwatch, full figure on face, Timex, 1950s, MIB 300.00

Cindy Bear, doll, stuffed felt, Knickerbocker, 1973, 8", MIB.......... 50.00

Cisco Kid & Pancho, cereal bowl, milk glass w/blk graphics, NM+ ..45.00

Clarabelle (Howdy Doody), marionette, Peter Puppet, 1952, 15", NMIB...150.00

Curious George, jack-in-the-box, metal, Schylling, 1995, EX 25.00

Dale Evans, lamp, plaster figure on horse, printed shade, 8", EX.. 150.00

Dale Evans, Western Dress-Up Kit, Colorforms/Roy Rogers, 1959, EXIB....50.00

Daniel Boone, coonskin cap, Arlington/Am Tradition, 1964, EX . 50.00

Davy Crockett, Auto Magic Picture Gun, 1950s, complete, EX+IB... 175.00

Davy Crockett, guitar, plastic, w/up musical, Mattel, EX 50.00

Davy Crockett, pencil case, brn vinyl holster w/gun form, 8", VG....50.00

Davy Crockett, Punch-Out Book, Whitman #1943, 1955, M......... 75.00

Dennis the Menace, doll, walking pose, vinyl, Hall Syndicate, 8", NM ... 40.00

Dennis the Menace, whistle, locomotive w/mouth pc, Fortune, MIP.. 15.00

Dick Dastardly, Flying Propeller, Larami, 1973, MOC 35.00

Dick Tracy, badge, Inspector Gen/DT/Secret Service Patrol, 1938, EX..250.00

Dick Tracy, Comiccooky Baking Set, Pillsbury, 1930s, MIB......... 200.00

Dick Tracy, Detective Set, Pressman, 1930s, NMIB 200.00

Dick Tracy, Wrist Radio, Da-Maco Prod, 1940s, EXIB 300.00

Dishonest John (Beanie & Cecil), hand puppet, Mattel, 1962, NM .. 175.00

Don Winslow, pocket watch, New Haven, 1938-39, EX 1,600.00

Donald Duck, coloring book, Whitman #1183, 1960, unused, EX...30.00

Donald Duck, handkerchief, Donald sets sail w/nephews, 50s, 8" sq, EX . 25.00

Donald Duck, jack-in-the-box, compo head/cloth body, Spear, 1940s, NM...200.00

Donald Duck, pull toy, Ice Cream Wagon, paper on wood, Marx, 9", EXIB...200.00

Donald Duck, tea set, wht china/red trim, 10-pc, Occupied Japan, EXIB.200.00

Donald Duck, wristwatch, little Donalds on band, Ingersoll, 1936, EXIB.2,750.00

Dr Dolittle, Colorforms Kit, 1967, NMIB.................................... 30.00

Dukes of Hazzard, paint set, Craft Master #N38001, 1980, NRFB. 75.00

Emmet Kelly, hand puppet, Willie the Clown, Baby Berry, 1950s, NM+.. 100.00

ET, charm bracelet, enameled metal, Aviva, 1982, MOC.................6.00

Fantastic Four, flicker ring, silver-tone plastic, 1960s, M............... 65.00

Fat Albert, doll, cloth & vinyl, Hey Hey Hey..., Remco, 1985, 22", MIB.. 90.00

Felix the Cat, candy dish, Will You Walk With Felix, gold trim, early, 5", EX+, $90.00. (Photo courtesy Morphy Auctions/LiveAuctioneers.com)

Felix the Cat, figure, orange cloth, papier-maché face, 1930s, 24", EX. 1,550.00

Felix the Cat, figure, squeeze legs & arms move, 8", EX 1,450.00

Felix the Cat, figure, wht, Yes/No head movement, 1920s, 13", VG..550.00

Felix the Cat, sparkler, tin, name on tie, Chein, 5½", EXIB......1,230.00

Felix the Cat, tea set, tan lustre, 14-pc, 1930s, EX 400.00

Flintstones, doll, Bamm-Bamm, cloth/felt, Knickerbocker, 70s, 8", MIB. 50.00

Flintstones, doll, Barney, furry outfit, Knickerbocker, 12", EX 75.00

Flintstones, fr-tray puzzle, Whitman #4428, 1960, NM 40.00

Flintstones, Fred Flintstone Camera, Hong Kong, 1960s, MIB 35.00

Flintstones, hand puppet, Barney, Knickerbocker, 1960s, NM 50.00

Flintstones, mug, molded plastic heads, F&F Mold Co, 3", NM, ea .. 12.00

Flintstones, Nite Lite, plastic Barney, Cable Electric, 1974, MOC ... 15.00

Flintstones, pencil topper, any character, mk Hong Kong, 1½", M, ea ... 12.00

Flintstones, push-button puppet, any character, Kohner, 1960s, NM, ea . 50.00

Flintstones, squeeze toy, Wilma talking on phone, Lanco, 1960s, 6", NM. 50.00

Flip the Frog, doll, stuffed velvet, Dean's Rag Book Co, 6", EX ... 400.00

G-Men, Fingerprint Set, NY Toy & Game Co, EX (in 12x15" hinged case) .300.00

G-Men, pencil box, blk & wht on red, 1930s, 5x8½", EX 85.00

Gabby Hayes, doll, stuffed cloth w/fur beard & felt hat, 1960s, 13", M .. 40.00

Garfield, bank, as hobo w/tooth missing & holding hat, vinyl, 8", NM .. 20.00

Garfield, doll, plush, User Friendly, Dakin, 1980s, 9", NM+ 12.00

Garfield, yo-yo, plastic, Avon, 1990s, 3½", MOC 8.00

Gene Autry, Cowboy Paint Book, Merrill, 1940, unused, NM+ 50.00

Gene Autry, fr-tray puzzle, Whitman #2962, 1950, VG+ 65.00

Gene Autry, wallet, leather w/zipper closure, Aristocrat, 1950s, VGIB .. 75.00

Gene Autry, wristwatch, Six Shooter, New Haven, 1950s, MIB .. 650.00

Gene Autry, writing tablet, Gene playing guitar, 1940s, 8x10", NM .. 45.00

Gomer Pyle, gum cards, blk & wht, 1960s, set of 66, all M 80.00

Gomez (Addams Family), doll, stuffed, Ace Novelty, 1992, 13", NM+ . 15.00

Green Hornet, coloring book, Whitman, 1966, unused, NM+ 55.00

Green Hornet, fr-tray puzzles, boxed set of 4, Whitman, 1966, NMIB. 125.00

Green Hornet, Print Putty, Colorforms, 1966, MIP 80.00

Green Hornet, spoon, enamel oval inlayed on ornate hdl, 1966, M .. 25.00

Green Lantern, comic book, Fall Issue #1, 1941, EX 11,500.00

Grinch (Dr Seuss), doll, plush, Macy's, 1997, 30", EX+ 35.00

Gulliver's Travels, top, litho tin, Chein, 1930s, 8" dia, EX 85.00

Gumby & Pokey, paint set, watercolors, Henry Gordy Int'l, 1988, MOC. 13.00

Gumby & Pokey, windup figures, vinyl, Lakeside, 1966, 4", EX, ea .. 45.00

Hansel (Hansel & Gretel), marionette, working mouth, Hazelle, 14", NM+ ..115.00

Heckle & Jeckle, hand puppet, plush, Rushton Creations, 1950s, ea .. 75.00

Herman (Munsters), doll, talker, Mattel, 1965, 21", NM 150.00

Hopalong Cassidy, alarm clock, Hoppy/Topper, name on base, US Time, EX .650.00

Hopalong Cassidy, Coloring Outfit, Transogram, 1950s, NM+IB .. 85.00

Hopalong Cassidy, comic book, Fawcett #3, 1946, NM, from $350 to . 550.00

Hopalong Cassidy, Figure & Paint Set, Laurel Ann, complete, used, EXIB .. 250.00

Hopalong Cassidy, nightlight, glass gun & holster, Aladdin, 1950s, NM .. 350.00

Hopalong Cassidy, sweater, never worn, $150.00.

Howdy Doody, bank, Howdy in wide stance, plastic, Straco, 1976, 9", EX 35.00

Howdy Doody, bath mitt, terry cloth w/image & name, 1950s-60s, 8", EX ... 15.00

Howdy Doody, doll, compo w/pnt hair, cloth outfit, Effanbee, 23", EXIB 350.00

Howdy Doody, hand puppet, full figure, working eyes/mouth, Pride, MIB ... 125.00

Howdy Doody, jigsaw puzzle, It's Howdy Doody Time, Kagran, 9x12", NM ... 100.00

Howdy Doody, marionette, Peter Puppet Playthings, 1952, NMIB .. 225.00

Howdy Doody, plate, ceramic, Howdy w/lasso, Smith-Taylor, 8½", EX+ . 50.00

Howdy Doody, push-button puppet, Kohner, 1950s, NMIB 175.00

Howdy Doody, Sun-Ray Camera Outfit, Silver Rich Corp, NMIB . 125.00

Huckleberry Hound, doll, vinyl, Knickerbocker Knixies, 6", NM .. 40.00

Huckleberry Hound, Fan Club Kit, Better Breakfast, 1960s, complete, EX .. 35.00

Jack Armstrong, Dragon's Eye ring, glow-in-the-dark plastic, 1940, G . 350.00

Jackie Coogan, stickpin doll, pipe-cleaner style, 1920s, 4", EX+ 40.00

James Bond 007, Electric Drawing Set, Lakeside, 1960s, MIB 200.00

Joker, bank, bust figure w/emb name, plastic, Mego, 1970s, 8", NM .. 75.00

Josie & the Pussycats, wristwatch, Bradley, 1971, w/3 bands, MIB .. 350.00

King Little (Gulliver's Travels), figure, bead type, Ideal, 1930s, EX+ .1,375.00

Kit Carson, 3-Powered Binoculars, 1950s, EXIB 125.00

Krazy Kat, figure, pnt wood bead type, Chein, 1920s, 7", NM ... 1,250.00

Laurel & Hardy, bank, Stan, vinyl figure, Play Pal, 1972, 14", NM ... 50.00

Laurel & Hardy, doll, Oliver or Stan, vinyl, Dakin, 1970s, 8", MIP .. 60.00

Stan Laurel, plastic figure, 1972, 14", $28.00.

Laurel & Hardy, roly poly, Oliver, plastic, chimes, 70s, 11", VG 32.00

Li'l Abner, doll, vinyl/cloth outfit, Baby Barry Toys, 1950s, 14", NM . 100.00

Little Orphan Annie, clothespins, 1930s, MIB, $125.00. (Photo courtesy Dunbar Galleries)

Little Orphan Annie, Colorforms, 1968, NMIB 30.00

Little Orphan Annie, doll set, Annie/Sandy, compo, 12" & 7", EXIB .. 450.00

Little Red Riding Hood, hand puppet, MPI Toys, 1960, NM 85.00

Little Red Riding Hood, marionette, Hazelle, 15", NM 150.00

Little Red Riding Hood, tea set, tin, Ohio Art, 1920s-30s, 9-pc, EX+ .. 350.00

Little Red Riding Hood, tea set, tin, Ohio Art, 1960s, 11-pc, NM+ .. 100.00

Lone Ranger, comic book, Dell #1, 1948, EX+, from $550 to 650.00

Lone Ranger, Picture Puzzles, set of 2, Whitman #3902, NMIB 125.00

Lone Ranger, push puppet, w/Silver, Press-Action Toys, 1939, NMIB ... 150.00

Lone Ranger, record player, wood case, Decca/Lone Ranger Inc, EX . 350.00

Lone Ranger, Ring Toss, Rosebud Art #160, 1946, unused, NMIB 350.00

Lucy (Peanuts), doll, stuffed cloth/printed features, Ideal, 8", MIP 40.00

Mad Hatter, marionette, talker, Peter Puppet Playthings, EX 100.00

Margaret (Dennis the Menace), hand puppet, Hall Syndicate, 1959, NM .100.00

Mary Poppins, doll, plastic w/synthetic hair, Gund, 1960s, 12", NM ...75.00

Maverick, Eras-O-Picture Book, Hasbro, 1958, complete, EX.............40.00

Melvin Pervis, ring, Jr G-Men Corps, EX 85.00

Mickey Mouse, Circus Train Set #1536, Lionel, 1935, EXIB.........7,475.00

Mickey Mouse, comic book, Dell #27, 1943, VG, from $165 to.......175.00

Mickey Mouse, doll, compo/parade attire, Knickerbocker/Cossack, 9", EX...1,350.00

Mickey Mouse, drum, cb/tin, parade graphics, Happy Hak #601, 6", EX .150.00

Mickey Mouse, figure, Fun-E-Flex wooden bead type, 1930s, 7", MIB ...3,100.00

Mickey Mouse, lamp, tin ball-shaped base w/Mickey decal, 1935, 11", EX .275.00

Mickey Mouse, Movie Projector, Keystone, 1934-35, NMIB 1,050.00

Mickey Mouse, pillow cover, Vogue Needlecraft, 1930s, 17x15", EX...50.00

Mickey Mouse, wristwatch, metal bracelet band, Ingersoll, 1930s, VGIB. 1,500.00

Mighty Mouse, Merry Pack Punchouts, Post Cereal/CBS, unused, 1956, EX .75.00

Minnie Mouse, doll, stuffed, toothy grin, Dean Rag/Borgfeldt, 8", EX..525.00

Mister Magoo, doll, UPA Pictures, 1962, EX 150.00

Mork, doll, stuffed printed cloth, talker, Mattel, 1979, 16", EX.........35.00

Morocco Mole, bubble bath container, Purex, 1966, rare, NM+..........65.00

Munsters, coloring book, Whitman, 1965, some use, G.....................32.00

Mutt & Jeff, drum, litho tin, Converse, 13" dia, EX 300.00

Olive Oyl, doll, cloth & vinyl, Presents/Hamilton Gifts, 1985, 12", NM..25.00

Olive Oyl, doll, vinyl, Dakin, 1970s, 7", MIB (Cartoon Theater)........40.00

Olive Oyl, marionette, Gund, 1950s, 12", complete, NM....................90.00

Oswald the Rabbit, doll, squeeze rubber, Sun Rubber, 1940s, 8", VG+..65.00

Oswald the Rabbit, doll, stuffed/molded face, Ideal, early, 21", EX+ .250.00

Oswald the Rabbit, planter, ceramic, Napco, 1958, 6", EX+ 55.00

Partridge Family, wristwatch, family image on face, 1970s, NM 175.00

Patrolman Francis Muldoon (Car 54 Where Are You?), hand puppet, NM ..175.00

Peter Pan, Animated Coloring Book, Derby Foods, 1950s, some use, NM..30.00

Peter Pan, pencil case, cb w/snap closure, drw, 1950s, 5x9", EX 25.00

Pinocchio, doll, compo w/cloth outfit & hat, Ideal, 1940s, 20", EX+.. 450.00

Pixie & Dixie, bop bag, Pixie/Dixie reversible images, Kestral, 18", M... 50.00

Popeye, coloring book, Lowe #2834, 1962, unused, EX+ 55.00

Popeye, pipe, Official../It Lites It Toots, Micro-Lite Prod, 1958, MOC.. 90.00

Popeye, pocket watch, New Haven, 1936, 1¾" dia, NM+, from $550 to.. 1,000.00

Popeye, Popeye Music Box (jack-in-the-box), Mattel, 11", NM..650.00

Popeye, push-button puppet, Kohner, 1960s, NM+ 75.00

Popeye, Thimble Theatre Mystery Playhouse, Harding, 1959, EXIB.. 990.00

Popeye, wristwatch, different Popeyes on face, New Haven, 1935, NMIB..4,000.00

Porky Pig, bank, standing w/arms behind bk, bsk, 1940s, 5", G+ ... 75.00

Porky Pig, wristwatch, Ingraham/Warner Bros, 149, MIB 875.00

Porky Pig & Petunia, pull toy, on horses, paper/wood, Brice #920, EX .110.00

Prince Valiant, coloring book, Saalfield #4611, 1957, unused, EX. 50.00

Raggedy Andy, bank, vinyl/cloth Spirit of '76 outfit, Royalty, '74, NM .35.00

Raggedy Andy, doll, Knickerbocker, 1976, 13", MIB.....................75.00

Raggedy Andy, pencil sharpener, 'Keep Sharp w/..,' Janex, 1974, NM.25.00

Raggedy Ann, bank, standing, ceramic, Lefton, 1970s, 8", NM..... 25.00

Raggedy Ann, doll, Knickerbocker, 1979, 12", MIB.......................75.00

Raggedy Ann, doll, squeeze vinyl, Regent Baby Products, 1970s, 6", MIP ...22.00

Red Ryder, postcard, Victory Patrol application, unused, M 100.00

Robin Hood, comic book, Dell #1, 1963, NM, from $85 to 95.00

Rocky (Rocky & Bullwinkle), doll, vinyl, Dakin, 1970s, 6½", MIB..75.00

Rootie Kazootie, handkerchief, RK Inc, 1950s, 9x9", EX 25.00

Roy Rogers, Double-R-Bar Ranch Coloring Book, Whitman, '55, unused, EX.25.00

Roy Rogers, Fix-It Chuck Wagon & Jeep Set, Ideal, 1950s, 24", NMIB..350.00

Roy Rogers, fountain pen, name on blk plastic, gold trim, 1950s, VG.50.00

Roy Rogers, fr-tray puzzle, Whitman #4427, VG+................................40.00

Roy Rogers, Lucky Horseshoe game, Ohio Art, 1950s, complete, EX..50.00

Roy Rogers, saddle ring, silver, EX..350.00

Roy Rogers, Western Dinner Set, Ideal, complete, NM+IB.................150.00

Schroeder, bubble bath container, seated, Avon, 1970s, M (piano box) ..30.00

Schroeder, ornament, seated at piano, ceramic, 1970s, 3", M 30.00

Scooby Doo, figure, vinyl, jtd, Dakin, 1980, 7x6" L, NM+ 95.00

Secret Squirrel, coloring book, Watkins-Strathmore #1850-E, unused, EX .50.00

Sgt Preston of the Yukon, coloring book, Whitman #2946, 1953, unused, M.35.00

Sgt Preston of the Yukon, Ore Detector, NM (w/orig mailer box) 200.00

Sgt Snorkel (Beetle Bailey), doll, cloth/vinyl, Presents, 15", NM 30.00

Sgt Snorkel (Beetle Bailey), nodder figure, compo, Lego, 1960s, 8", M ...115.00

Shadow, Blue Coal ring, plastic, 1941, EX+ 200.00

Shaggy Dog, figure, squeeze vinyl, Dell, 1960s, 5½", NM+ 45.00

Shaggy Dog, figurine, at steering wheel, ceramic, Enesco, 1960s, 5", M ... 60.00

Shmoo, ashtray, yel ceramic figure, 1940s-50s, 5", NM+ 100.00

Shmoo, deodorizer, ceramic figure, wht w/cold-pnt features, 1940s, EX+.. 100.00

Shmoo, doll, plump & plush w/vinyl head, 1940s-50s, 12", EX+ 115.00

Skeezix, pull toy, die-cut wood, Skeezix on Pal, Trixie Toy, 1930s, G ..65.00

Sky King, Aztec ring, EX..800.00

Sleeping Beauty, tumbler, 6 different, 1950s, ea from $8 to...............15.00

Sleepy (Snow White), doll, hard-stuffed, beard, 1960s-70s, 8", NM....25.00

Smokey Bear, coloring book, Abbott #320, 1950s, unused, M.............75.00

Smokey Bear, Jr Forest Ranger Kit, USDA, 1956-57, complete, EX+IP..65.00

Smurfs, Chatter Chum, seated, plastic, Mattel talker, 1983, 7", EX 20.00

Smurfs, top, litho tin w/suction cup, Ohio Art, 1982, 9" dia, EX+.......28.00

Smurfs, trinket box, porc, Smurf w/ice-cream cone on lid, 1982, 3", M ...22.00

Snagglepuss, squeeze doll, vinyl, Bucky, 9", EX 75.00

Sneezy (Snow White), figure, squeeze vinyl, 1950s, 8½", VG...............22.00

Snidley Whiplash, bop bag, inflatable vinyl, 1982, 15", M 25.00

Sniffles (Looney Tunes), bank, w/barrel, pot metal, Moss Metal, 1940s... 120.00

Snoopy, Action Toy, Snoopy as hockey player, Aviva, 1970s, 5", MIP ..45.00

Snoopy, alarm clock, Snoopy w/tennis racket, Equity, 1970s, 5", NM ...45.00

Snoopy, bank, on watermelon slice, ceramic, 1970s, MIB....................60.00

Snoopy, bank, seated, clear glass, Anchor Hocking, 1980s, 6", M........20.00

Snoopy, carryall, canvas, Flying Ace, Aviva, 1970s-80s, 14x19", M.....20.00

Snoopy, doll, jtd vinyl w/blk plush ears, Determined, 1970s-80s, 8", M.... 25.00

Snoopy, magic slate, Child Art Productions, 1970s, MIP (sealed) 15.00

Snoopy, pencil holder, Everybody Loves a Winner, ceramic, 2½", MIB... 30.00

Snoopy, plate, Christmas 1981, porc, Schmid, MIB 25.00

Snoopy, Pound-A-Ball game, Child Guidance, 1978, EXIB.................65.00

Snoopy, Roly Poly Penholder/Cool Writer, plastic, Butterfly Orig, MIB.. 18.00

Snoopy, squeeze toy, Flying Ace in airplane, vinyl, Danara, 1970s, NM .. 30.00

Snow White, handkerchief set, 4 different prints, WDE, 1930s, MIB..175.00

Snow White, picture cubes, paper on wood, 20 cubes, VG+IB (wood box)...125.00

Sparkle Plenty (Dick Tracy), bank, in highchair, ceramic, 13", EX.. 100.00

Sparkle Plenty (Dick Tracy), doll, compo, yarn hair, Ideal, 13", NMIB..350.00

Spider-Man, bank, plastic half-figure, Street Kids, 1991, 7", MIP.. 16.00

Spider-Man, doll, stuffed cloth, Knickerbocker, 1978, 19", NM ..25.00

Superman, DC Comics #3, 1943, EX, from $2,000 to 2,250.00

Superman, figure, squeeze vinyl, boy features, waving, 1978, 7", EX+..35.00

Superman, horseshoe set, Super Swim Inc, 1950s, EXIB..............100.00

Superman, Movie Viewer, Chemtoy, 1965, unused, MOC..............30.00

Superman, Paint-By-Numbers Watercolor Set, Transogram, 1954, EXIB. 80.00

Superman, scrapbook, Saalfield #178, 1940, some use, EX...........100.00

Superman, Secret Chamber ring, Defense Milk Club Program, 1941, VG.3,500.00

Superman, tumbler, plastic, comic/Christopher Reeve graphics, 1978, 6". 16.00

Swee' Pea (Popeye), doll, cloth, vinyl head & hands, Uneeda, 1979, MIB..40.00

Sylvester the Cat, bank, tubby figure, vinyl, Dakin, 1976, 7", NM ..20.00

Sylvester the Cat, figurine, on tree stump, bsk, Price, 1979, 5", M...30.00

Sylvester the Cat, Plast-O-Plak (Cast & Paint Kit), Ableman, 1962, MIP .35.00

Tarzan, comic book, Dell Vol 1 #52, Lex Barker cover, EX, from $55 to.. 65.00

Tasmanian Devil, alarm clock, vinyl, open mouth/boulder, 1995, 6", NM+ .25.00

Three Little Pigs, alarm clock, Who's Afraid..., rnd case, EX 825.00

Three Little Pigs, bsk figures w/instruments, Borgfeldt, 3½", NMIB...250.00

Thumper, bank, ceramic figure, Leeds, 1950s, 7", NM+ 75.00

Thumper, planter, Thumper/dbl bowls, ceramic, Leeds, 1950s, 6", NM+.. 75.00

Tigger, doll, lt brn ribbed cloth, Sears, 1960s, 6" L, NM.................35.00

Tigger, figurine, seated upright, ceramic, Enesco, 1964, 5½", NM.....60.00

Tinkerbell, doll, jtd plastic, costume/wings, Duchess, 1950s, 8", EX+ .75.00

Tom & Jerry, bank, Tom atop hamburger, ceramic, Gorham, 1981, 5", M...50.00

Tom & Jerry, kaleidoscope, metal w/graphics, Green Monk, 1973, EX+..35.00

Tom & Jerry, nightlight, T&J in laundry basket, ceramic, Presents, MIB ..35.00

Tom & Jerry, soap figures, Fine Quality Toilet Soap, England, MIB, ea .25.00
Tom Corbett Space Cadett, face ring, EX 125.00
Tom Corbett Space Cadett, wristwatch, Ingraham, 1950s, NM+IB ..2,600.00
Tom Mix, comic book, Ralston Straight Shooters #3, EX 50.00
Tom Mix, Draw & Paint Book, Whitman, 1935, unused, G 20.00
Tom Mix, periscope, Straight Shooters, Ralston, 1939, EX............ 50.00
Tom Mix, Shooting Gallery, Parker Bros, c 1930, complete, EXIB ..230.00
Tonto, doll, stuffed body w/compo head, cloth outfit, EX............. 500.00
Top Cat, figure, inflatable vinyl, Flintstones Inflatables, 1960s, MIP.. 30.00
Tubby (Little Lulu), figure, squeeze vinyl, 1980s, 7½", EX+ 25.00
Tweety Bird, bank, atop birdhouse, compo, Holiday Fair, 1971, 9", NM+.45.00
Tweety Bird, finger puppet, vinyl half-figure, Dakin, 60s-70s, 3", MIP.... 22.00
Tweety Bird, liquor decanter, ceramic figure, Alpa (Italy), 1970s, NM+.. 65.00
Tweety Bird, planter, next to cage, compo, Holiday Fair, 1977, 6", EX ... 55.00
Uncle Fester (Addams Family), doll, vinyl, Remco, 1965, 5", EX+ 125.00
Uncle Scrooge, squeeze toy, US/nephews around safe, Dell, 1960s, 7", M....75.00
Underdog, costume, Collegeville, 1974, MIB 40.00
Wally Walrus, coloring book, Saalfield #4547, 1962, unused, NM+ 55.00
WC Fields, bank, figural, vinyl, Play Pal Plastics, 1970s, 7½", EX+ ..18.00
Wendy the Witch, doll, plush w/vinyl face, Gundikins, 1950s, 10", NM. 65.00
Wild Bill Hickok, Treasure Map & Secret Treasure Guide, 1950s, MIP.125.00
Wild Bill Hickok, wallet, fastens w/Western buckle, NM+ 75.00
Wile E Coyote, finger puppet, vinyl half-figure, Dakin, 1970s, MOC..20.00
Wile E Coyote, mug, ceramic head figure, Applause, 1989, 4x8", M ...15.00
Wimpy (Popeye), ornament, Wimpy in wreath, ceramic, 1980s, 3" dia, NM+..18.00
Winnie the Pooh, magic slate, Western Publishing, 1950s, unused, NM+ ..50.00
Wonder Woman, Flashmite, Jane X, 1976, MOC................................25.00
Wonder Woman, iron-on transfers, several different, 1970s, MIP, ea...15.00
Woody (Toy Story), wristwatch, w/Woody plaque, Fossil, 1996, MIB ...75.00
Woody Woodpecker, doll, plush, Ace Novelty, 1989, 19", NM 18.00
Woody Woodpecker, Sticker Fun Book, Whitman #2180, 1964, EX+ .. 25.00
Wyatt Earp, comic book, Dell #860, EX+, from $75 to 85.00
Yogi Bear, bank, Yogi leaning on shed, vinyl, Homecraft, 1973, 11", NM....65.00
Yogi Bear, hit-&-spin Yogi rattle, plastic, Sanitoy, 1980, EX+ 18.00
Yogi Bear, Play Doh Play Set, Kenner, 1980, unused, MIB 35.00
Yogi Bear, Sticker Fun Book, Whitman #2190, 1964, unused, NM+ ...65.00
Yogi Bear, Super Magnet, bl plastic horseshoe form, Laurie, 1976, MOC.. 18.00
Yosemite Sam, bank, w/treasure chest, ceramic, Applause, 1988, 6", MIB...40.00
Yosemite Sam, bell, figure on top, bsk, Price, 1979, 4", M....................25.00
Yosemite Sam, doll, vinyl w/cloth outfit, fuzzy beard, Dakin, 8", EX+..20.00
Ziggy, bank, pottery figure looking up, WWA Inc, 1981, 4", NM.........25.00
Ziggy, tile, ceramic, Plants Are Some of My Favorite..., WWA, 4", NM+ ...12.00
Zorro, accessory set w/mask, whip, lariat & ring, Shimmel, MOC..150.00
Zorro, bolo tie, metal medallion w/plastic insert featuring Zorro, NM ...50.00
Zorro, fr-tray puzzle, Whitman, 1957, EX+ 50.00

Zorro, playset, Marx #3754, MIB (sealed), $9,200.00. (Photo courtesy Morphy Auctions)

Peters and Reed

John Peters and Adam Reed founded their pottery in Zanesville, Ohio, just before the turn of the century, using the local red clay to produce a variety of wares. Moss Aztec, introduced about 1912, has an unglazed exterior with designs molded in high relief and the recesses highlighted with a green wash. Only the interior is glazed to hold water. Pereco (named for Peters, Reed and Company) is glazed in semi-matt blue, maroon, cream, and other colors. Orange was also used very early, but such examples are rare. Shapes are simple with in-mold decoration sometimes borrowed from the Moss Aztec line. Wilse Blue is a line of high-gloss medium blue with dark specks on simple shapes. Landsun, characterized by its soft matt multicolor or blue and gray combinations, is decorated either by dripping or by hand brushing in an effect sometimes called Flame or Herringbone. Chromal, in much the same colors as Landsun, may be decorated with a realistic scenic, or the swirling application of colors may merely suggest one. Vivid, realistic Chromal scenics command much higher prices than weak, poorly drawn examples. (Brush-McCoy made a very similar line called Chromart. Neither will be marked; and due to the lack of documented background material available, it may be impossible make a positive identification. Collectors nearly always attribute this type of decoration to Peters and Reed.) Shadow Ware is usually a glossy, multicolor drip over a harmonious base color but occasionally is seen in an overall matt glaze. When the base is black, the effect is often iridescent.

Several other lines were produced, including Mirror Black, Persian, Egyptian, Florentine, Marbleized, etc., and an unidentified line which collectors call Mottled-Marbleized Colors. In this high-gloss line, the red clay body often shows through the splashed-on multicolors. At one time, the brown high-glaze artware line with 'sprigged' decoration was attributed to Peters and Reed, though this line has recently been re-attributed to Weller pottery by the Sanfords in their latest book on Peters and Reed pottery. This conclusion was drawn from the overwhelming number of shapes proven to be Weller molds. Since the decoration was cut out and applied, however, it is possible that Peters and Reed or yet another Zanesville company simply contracted for the Weller greenware and added their own decoration and finishes. A few pieces from this line are included in the listings that follow. In 1922 the company became known as the Zane Pottery. Peters and Reed retired, and Harry McClelland became president. Charles Chilcote designed new lines, and production of many of the old lines continued. The body of the ware after 1922 was light in color. Marks include the impressed logo or ink stamp 'Zaneware' in a rectangle.

Bowl, Chromal, bl, low, 3x9¼" 200.00
Candleholder, Marbleized, brn/blk/olive, 1½x5½"........................... 75.00

Jar, Shadow Ware, multicolor on black, with lid, 7½", NM, $285.00. (Photo courtesy David Rago Auctions)

Jardiniere, Moss Aztec, grapes border, 8x10"................................. 250.00
Jug, lions/grapes appl on dk brn, spherical, 4" 65.00

Mug, grapes & leaves appl on dk brn, 5½" 60.00
Planter, Moss Aztec, roses emb, tight line, 6x6½" 75.00

Umbrella stand, Moss Azetc, no mark, 24", NM, $575.00. (Photo courtesy Davis Rago Auctions/LiveAuctioneers.com)

Vase, bud; Marbleized, blk/yel/brn/gr, 6" 80.00
Vase, cherub & floral appl to dk brn, angle hdls, 13½" 175.00
Vase, Chromal, landscape in swirled brns, incurvate rim, flaw, 10" ..450.00
Vase, Chromal, night scene: castle/mtns, 5½x4½" 750.00
Vase, floral appl on dk brn, pillow form, integral hdls, 5" 95.00
Vase, Landsun, bl/gr/tan, 8" 115.00
Vase, Landsun, bl/tan/pk, incurvate rim, 3" 80.00
Vase, Landsun, tan/gr/brn/bl, slim, ftd, 12" 175.00
Vase, Marbleized, agate drips at rim, ovoid, 12" 195.00
Vase, Marbleized, gr/yel/blk, flared rim, 10" 150.00
Vase, Marbleized, mustard/cobalt/blk, 6-sided, 9" 125.00
Vase, Moss Aztec, floral emb, 10x4" 175.00
Vase, Moss Aztec, roses emb, stain, 17" 295.00
Vase, Moss Aztec, 8" 150.00
Vase, Shadow Ware, blk/bl/gr/yel, glaze skips, 7⅞" 200.00
Vase, Shadow Ware, caramel runs on dk brn, hdls, 21", NM 750.00
Vase, Shadow Ware, mc drips on caramel, bulbous, 5x5" 150.00
Vase, Wilse Blue, dragonfly emb, 2x5⅛" 60.00
Vase, wisteria emb on bl matt, waisted, 12" 155.00
Wall pocket, Moss Aztec, sgn Ferrell, 8" 200.00

Pewabic

The Pewabic Pottery was formally established in Detroit, Michigan, in 1907 by Mary Chase Perry Stratton and Horace James Caulkins. The two had worked together following Ms. Perry's china painting efforts, firing wares in a small kiln Caulkins had designed especially for use by the dental trade. Always a small operation which relied upon basic equipment and the skill of the workers, they took pride in being commissioned for several important architectural tile installations. Some of the early artware was glazed a simple matt green; occasionally other colors were added, sometimes in combination, one over the other in a drip effect. Later Stratton developed a lustrous crystalline glaze. (Today's values are determined to a great extent by the artistic merit of the glaze.) The body of the ware was highly fired and extremely hard. Shapes were basic, and decorative modeling, if used at all, was in low relief. Mary Stratton kept the pottery open until her death in 1961. In 1968 it was purchased and reopened by Michigan State University; it is still producing today. Several marks were used over the years: a triangle with 'Revelation Pottery' (for a short time only); 'Pewabic' with five maple leaves; and the impressed circle mark. Our advisors for this category are Suzanne Perrault and David Rago; they are listed in the Directory under New Jersey.

Box, figures & animals emb on turq & fuchsia irid, w/lid, 3½" dia ..345.00
Plate, rabbit border (Dedham style), navy on tan, 9¼" 345.00
Plate, rooks, blk on gold lustre, 10" 4,800.00
Tile, bird in high relief on gr, sq, 6" 50.00
Vase, amber (thick/dripping), shouldered, 10½x6¾" 1,900.00
Vase, bl all-over high lustre, ribbed, ftd, circle mk, 7⅛x6½".....1,000.00
Vase, bl irid over dk bl mottle, ftd, imp circle mk, 4½x5".........2,250.00
Vase, bl irid w/silver patches, faint ribbing, slightly bulbous, 7" ...625.00
Vase, bl lustre, shouldered, w/matching stand, 2-pc, 14x9" 8,125.00

Vase, blue lustre, stamped mark, 11½x11", $24,000.00. (Photo courtesy David Rago Auctions/LiveAuctioneers.com)

Vase, brn metallic lustre, shouldered, rstr ft, 10x6" 1,065.00
Vase, celadon w/turq drips, bulbous at top, 6" 595.00
Vase, copper red over mauve, slightly bulbous, faint ribbing, 10½" ..3,500.00
Vase, dk gr & oxblood (leathery), bottle form, 7x4¾" 725.00
Vase, geometrics emb on matt flambé, cylinder neck, 14½x11" .. 4,500.00
Vase, gr w/lustre drips, 6¼x4½" 1,000.00
Vase, leaves cvd on gray crystalline on gr matt, tapers toward ft, 4" ...315.00
Vase, lustred flambé, baluster, rstr chip, 20x9" 7,200.00
Vase, olive gr over bl, slightly bulbous, 8x6" 1,065.00
Vase, ultramarine w/lustre drips, grinding chip, early, 8x8" 5,400.00
Vase, volcanic blk/bl/purple, bulbous body, rstr rim chip, 15½" ... 5,000.00

Pewter

Pewter is a metal alloy of tin, copper, very small parts of bismuth and/or antimony, and sometimes lead. Very little American pewter contained lead, however, because much of the ware was designed to be used as tableware, and makers were aware that the use of lead could result in poisoning. (Pieces that do contain lead are usually darker in color and heavier than those that have no lead.) Most of the fine examples of American pewter date from 1700 to the 1840s. Many pieces were melted down and recast into bullets during the American Revolution in 1775; this accounts to some extent why examples from this period are quite difficult to find. The pieces that did survive may include buttons, buckles, and writing equipment as well as the tableware we generally think of. After the Revolution makers began using antimony as the major alloy with the tin in an effort to regain the popularity of pewter, which glassware and china was beginning to replace in the home. The resulting product, known as britannia, had a lustrous silver-like appearance and was far more durable. While closely related, britannia is a collectible in its own right and should not be confused with pewter.

Key: tm — touch mark

Basin, Love & London tms, ca 1800, 2⅞x11½" 1,000.00
Basin, Samuel Pierce eagle tm, ca 1792-1830, 2¼x8" 750.00
Basin, Thomas Melville II tm, polished, lt wear, 2x8" 575.00
Basin, W&S Yale partial tm, ca 1813-20, 1⅝x6⅝" 575.00
Charger, unmk, minor wear, 11½" 90.00
Coffeepot, Ashbil Griswold tm, polished, rpt hdl & finial, 10½" .. 375.00

Coffeepot, Boardman & Hart tm, bulbous, ivory finial, rpt hdl, 11½" ..515.00
Flagon, communion; unmk form used by Sheldon & Feltman (NY), 10½".375.00
Jug, cider; Sellew & Co tm, scrolled hdl, rpr, 10" 635.00
Lamp, oil; att Roswell Gleason, removable glass lens, 8½" 375.00
Lamp, Smith & Co tm, lozenge font, whale-oil burner, polished, 6"..285.00
Pitcher, R Dunham tm, sm dent, ca 1837-61, 6½"......................300.00
Plate, N Austin tm, single reeded trim, 18th C, 8"......................600.00
Plate, S Danforth tm, single reed trim, 7⅞" 385.00
Plate, W Billings tm, polished, lt scratches, 8¼"........................865.00
Porringer, F Bassett tm, Old English hdl, ca 1761-1800, 4⅜" 220.00
Porringer, Hamlin eagle tm on flowered hdl, ca 1767-1801, 5½" .800.00
Porringer, IG tm on crown hdl, ca 1800, polished, 4⅝" 315.00
Porringer, Richard Lee tm, sm dents, 3¾" 500.00
Porringer, SG tm on crown hdl, 5½" 200.00
Porringer, TD & SB tm on crown hdl, polished, lt wear, 5" 515.00
Tall pot, Boardman & Co NY, ogee sides, domed lid, dents, 11¾"..460.00
Tall pot, F Porter tm, lighthouse form, ca 1835-60, 10¾"............200.00
Tall pot, G Richardson tm, lighthouse form, polished, sm rpt, 11".....635.00
Tankard, English griffin tm, scroll hdl, heart on thumbpc, 7".......750.00
Teapot, Boardman & Hall Philada tm, wooden finial, blk pnt hdl, 7½".375.00

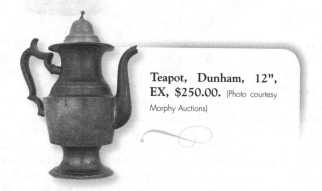

Teapot, Dunham, 12", EX, $250.00. (Photo courtesy Morphy Auctions)

Teapot, Putnam tm, minor wear/pinpoints, ca 1830-35, 8½" 200.00
Teapot, R Gleason tm, wooden wafer finial, blk pnt hdl, 8¾" 400.00
Teapot, Smith & Co tm, scroll hdl, petal wafer finial, G blk pnt, 7"...200.00
Teapot, unmk, scrolled hdl, wafer finial, sm dings, 6½" 145.00

Pfaltzgraff

Pfaltzgraff has operated in Pennsylvania since the early 1800s making redware at first, then stoneware crocks and jugs, yellow ware and sponge-ware in the 1920s, artware and kitchenware in the 1930s, and stoneware kitchen items through the 1940s. To collectors, they're best known for their Gourmet Royal (circa 1950s), a high-gloss dinnerware line of solid brown with frothy white drip glaze around the rims, and their giftware line called Muggsy, comic-character mugs, ashtrays, bottle stoppers, children's dishes, pretzel jars, cookie jars, etc. It was designed in the late 1940s and continued in production until 1960. The older versions have protruding features, while the features of later examples were simply painted on.

Their popular Village line, an almond-glazed pattern with a brown-stenciled folk-art tulip design, was produced for years, many items targeted for collectors. Today, only basic pieces are shown on the company's web-site. Yorktowne and Folk Art, two similar lines that are also readily identi-fied as Pfaltzgraff are available as well, but both lines are very limited. (In general, use Village prices to help you evaluate those two lines.)

Though scheduled to close several years ago, Pfaltzgraff was bought out by Lifetime Brands Inc. in 2005. For more information on their dinnerware, we recommend *The Flea Market Trader* and *Garage Sale and Flea Market Annual*, both by Collector Books. Keep in mind that our values are for mint examples. Crazing and/or scratches affect values drastically. Our advisor for the Muggsy line is Judy Posner; she is listed in the Directory under Florida.

Christmas Heritage, bowl, vegetable; 12-sided oval, 11x8¼" 18.00
Christmas Heritage, cake plate, ped ft, 12" 25.00
Christmas Heritage, cheese tray, #533, 10½"x7½" 9.00
Christmas Heritage, coffee cup, 4" 5.00
Christmas Heritage, gravy boat & undertray 20.00
Christmas Heritage, ornament, angel, 1987, MIB, from $22 to 30.00
Christmas Heritage, pitcher, tankard, 7½" 25.00
Christmas Heritage, shakers, lighthouse form, pr.....................15.00
Christmas Heritage, tumbler, glass, 5½", set of 10 ....35.00
Christmas Heritage, 2-tier dish, 10" & 8" plate, MIB 20.00

Folk Art, child's dish, bear form, from $16.00 to $20.00.

Gourmet Royale, ashtray, #69, 10" 15.00
Gourmet Royale, ashtray, #618, 10" 25.00

Gourmet Royale, au gratin, #7633, 11" long, $14.00.

Gourmet Royale, baker, #323, 9½", from $12 to 15.00
Gourmet Royale, bean pot, #11-1, 1-qt, from $10 to 12.00
Gourmet Royale, bean pot, #11-4, 4-qt...............................35.00
Gourmet Royale, bean pot warming stand 10.00
Gourmet Royale, bowl, cereal; #934SR, 5½" 5.00
Gourmet Royale, bowl, mixing; 8", from $10 to 15.00
Gourmet Royale, bowl, mixing; 14" 70.00
Gourmet Royale, bowl, soup; 2¼x7¼", from $6 to....................9.00
Gourmet Royale, bowl, vegetable; divided, #341......................14.00
Gourmet Royale, cheese shaker, bulbous, 5¾", from $12 to 15.00
Gourmet Royale, egg plate, center hdl, 8x12" 20.00
Gourmet Royale, gravy boat, 2-spout, #426, lg, +underplate, from $9 to.14.00
Gourmet Royale, ladle, sm, from $12 to...............................15.00
Gourmet Royale, mug, #392, 16-oz 12.00
Gourmet Royale, platter, #20, 14" 25.00
Gourmet Royale, roaster, oval, #326, 16", from $25 to.................32.00
Gourmet Royale, tidbit, 2-tier, from $10 to 14.00
Heritage, butter dish, #002-028......................................6.00
Heritage, cake plate, pedestal, 6½x12½" 75.00
Heritage, canisters, set of 4, from $55 to.............................60.00
Heritage, coffee/teapot, 13½" 40.00
Heritage, honey pot, w/lid & drizzler.................................40.00

Heritage, pitcher, 5" 17.50
Heritage, plate, dinner; 10" 8.00
Heritage, punch bowl, 6 cups & ladle 75.00
Heritage, salt crock jar, #560 .... 35.00
Muggsy, ashtray 125.00
Muggsy, bottle stopper, head, ball shape.............. 85.00
Muggsy, canape holder, Carrie, pierced head holds toothpicks, $125 to...150.00
Muggsy, cigarette server 95.00
Muggsy, clothes sprinkler bottle, Myrtle, Black, from $275 to 375.00
Muggsy, clothes sprinkler bottle, Myrtle, wht, from $250 to 295.00
Muggsy, cookie jar, character face, minimum value 250.00

Muggsy, mug, action figure (Rodney Reel), from $65.00 to $85.00.

Muggsy, mug, Black action figure.................................... 125.00
Muggsy, mug, character face 38.00
Muggsy, shot mug, character face, from $40 to 50.00
Muggsy, tumbler... 60.00
Muggsy, utility jar, Handy Harry, hat w/short bill as flat lid.......... 150.00
Village, bowl, vegetable; 2-part, 13x8½" 25.00
Village, bowl, w/hdls, oval, 12" 26.00
Village, chip & dip set, 2-pc, from $20 to 30.00

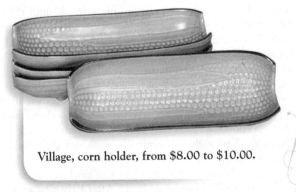

Village, corn holder, from $8.00 to $10.00.

Village, cruets, vinegar & oil; pr from $30 to................ 40.00
Village, ice bucket, metal liner.................................... 55.00
Village, pitcher, #416, 2-qt, from $20 to 25.00
Village, seafood baker, fish shape, 10½"....................... 45.00
Village, soup tureen, #160, w/lid & ladle, 3½-qt, from $40 to........ 45.00
Village, teakettle, 3-qt 35.00
Village, welcome plaque, oval, 4¾x6¾" 30.00

Phoenix Bird

Blue and white Phoenix Bird china has been produced by various Japanese potteries from the early 1900s. With slight variations the design features the Japanese bird of paradise and scroll-like vines of Kara-Kusa, or Chinese grass. Although some of their earlier ware is unmarked, the majority is marked in some fashion. More than 125 different stamps have been cataloged, with 'Made in Japan' the one most often found. Coming

in second is Morimura's wreath and/or crossed stems (both having the letter 'M' within). The cloverleaf with 'Japan' below very often indicates an item having a high-quality transfer-printed design. Among the many categories in the Phoenix Bird pattern are several shapes; therefore (for identification purposes), each has been given a number, i.e. #1, #2, etc. Post-1970 items, if marked at all, carry a paper label. Compared to the older ware, the coloring of the 1970s items is whiter and the blue more harsh. The design is sparse with more ground area showing. Although collectors buy later pieces, the older is, of course, more highly prized and valued.

The Flying Turkey is a pattern similar to Phoenix Bird, but with several differences: the phoenix bird's head is facing back or to the right, while the turkey faces forward and has a heart-like border design. Values are given for this line as well.

Because of the current over-supply of Phoenix Bird's 'everyday' pieces on eBay in the last year or two, versus today's 'demand' for the latter, most collector's 'wants' are not as great as they used to be, and the market shows it! As in the past, it's the very 'hard-to-find' shapes that still bring the higher prices today! However, for the new collector, today's 'over-supply' is a great opportunity to build an inexpensive, useable collection. Therefore, the advanced collector must persevere, keeping tuned-in to various internet sites for unique shapes and/or titles that sellers use, to find rare shapes to add to their collection. For further information we recommend *Phoenix Bird Chinaware, Books I – V*, written and privately published by our advisor, Joan Oates; her address is in the Directory under Michigan. Information regarding Phoenix Bird Collectors of America (PBCA) is included in the Clubs, Newsletters, and Catalogs section of the Directory.

Bowl, fruit; scalloped, 9¼" 65.00
Bowl, sauce; #2, 5¾" 45.00
Butter dish, #1 .... 150.00
Candy dish, #1, phoenix inside only 75.00
Chamberstick, #2, on attached saucer...................... 125.00
Cheese & cracker, 2-tier.. 125.00
Chocolate pot, #1 .... 135.00
Coffeepot, #1 .... 65.00
Coffeepot, #7 .... 75.00
Coffeepot, #9 .... 175.00
Creamer & sugar bowl, #20-B, 3-pc 25.00
Flowerpot, ftd, post-1970... 35.00
Jar, Bath Salts, 5" 50.00
Ladle, gravy; #3 .... 125.00
Pin dish, w/lid, 1½x2½" 25.00
Pitcher, buttermilk; 6" 75.00
Plate, cheese & cracker; 2 tiers................................ 125.00
Plate, chop; EX quality, 11½" 175.00

Plate, grill; Phoenix Bird in center, Blue Willow border, $65.00.

(Photo courtesy Joan Oates)

Reamer & strainer, #1 .... 75.00
Sweetmeat dish, #6, centered phoenix....................... 30.00

Tea strainer, #3... 65.00
Teapot, #19, Myott & Son.. 155.00
Tray, relish; #10... 55.00
Tumbler, flared top, 3¾"... 30.00
Tureen, child's, #1-B.. 55.00
Tureen, rice; #3-A... 130.00

Phoenix Glass

Founded in 1880 in Monaca, Pennsylvania, the Phoenix Glass Company became one of the country's foremost manufacturers of lighting glass by the early 1900s. They also produced a wide variety of utilitarian and decorative glassware, including art glass by Joseph Webb, colored cut glass, Gone-With-the-Wind style oil lamps, hotel and barware, and pharmaceutical glassware. Today, however, collectors are primarily interested in the 'Sculptured Artware' produced in the 1930s and 1940s. These beautiful pressed and mold-blown pieces are most often found in white milk glass or crystal with various color treatments or a satin finish. Phoenix did not mark their 'Sculptured Artware' line on the glass; instead, a silver and black (earliest) or gold and black (later) foil label in the shape of the mythical phoenix bird was used.

Quite often glassware made by the Consolidated Lamp and Glass Company of nearby Coraopolis, Pennsylvania, is mistaken for Phoenix's 'Sculptured Artware.' Though the style of the glass is very similar, one distinguishing characteristic is that perhaps 80% of the time Phoenix applied color to the background leaving the raised design plain in contrast, while Consolidated generally applied color to the raised design and left the background plain. Also, for the most part, the patterns and colors used by Phoenix were distinctively different from those used by Consolidated. In 1970 Phoenix Glass became a division of Anchor Hocking which in turn was acquired by the Newell Group in 1987. Phoenix has the distinction of being one of the oldest continuously operating glass factories in the United States. For more information refer to *Phoenix and Consolidated Art Glass, 1926 – 1980*, written by Jack D. Wilson. Our advisor, David Sherman, is listed in the Directory under New York. See also Consolidated Glass.

Figured, vase, frost on yellow, 6", $80.00.

Blackberry, wine glass, milk glass irid.............................. 125.00
Bluebell, vase, lt pk w/pearlized design, 7"...................... 125.00
Bluebell, vase, rose w/pearlized design, 7"...................... 125.00
Cosmos, vase, bl on milk glass, 7½"................................ 145.00
Cosmos, vase, brn shadow, 7½".................................... 145.00
Cosmos, vase, purple pearlized, 7½".............................. 185.00
Daisy, vase, bl on frosted, 9x9".................................... 350.00
Daisy, vase, bl w/frosted flowers, 9"............................. 350.00
Dancing Girl, vase, lav-bl on wht, 12"............................ 515.00
Dancing Girl, vase, red pearlized, 12"............................ 625.00
Dancing Girl, vase, tan shadow on wht, 12", NM 450.00
Dancing Girl, wht on powder bl, 12".............................. 450.00
Diving Girl, banana boat, bl on gr w/pearlized design 475.00

Fern, vase, bl pearlized, 7"... 145.00
Fern, vase, reverse decor: bl & gr on satin milk glass, 7" 225.00
Fern, vase, tan on milk glass, 7".................................... 145.00
Lace & Dewdrop, compote, bl on milk glass, 6⅛x6¼" 100.00
Lily, vase, aqua wash, 3-crimp, 9".................................. 450.00
Madonna, vase, lt bl on milk glass, 10"........................... 195.00
Madonna, vase, med gr on milk glass, 10"....................... 195.00
Moon & Stars, fruit holder, heavy caramel irid.................. 250.00
Philodendron, vase, wht on bl, 11½"............................... 195.00
Phlox, ashtray, slate bl pearlized, 5½"............................ 225.00
Phlox, cigarette box, deep burgundy pearlized, w/lid 180.00
Star Flower, vase, aqua w/frosted design, 7"................... 200.00
Star Flower, vase, bl & milk glass, 7"............................. 145.00
Thistle, vase, lav-pk on wht, 18"................................... 650.00
Thistle, vase, lime gr pearlized, 18".............................. 650.00
Thistle, vase, med gr pearlized, 18".............................. 650.00
Tiger Lily, bowl, wht frosted, 11½"................................ 325.00
Wild Geese, vase, lime gr pearlized, 9x12"..................... 275.00
Zodiac, vase, slate bl over milk glass, 10½" 850.00

Phonographs

The phonograph, invented by Thomas Edison in 1877, was the first practical instrument for recording and reproducing sound. Sound wave vibrations were recorded on a tinfoil-covered cylinder and played back with a needle that ran along the grooves made from the recording, thus reproducing the sound. Very little changed to this art of record making until 1885, when the first replayable and removable wax cylinders were developed by the American Graphophone Company. These records were made from 1885 until 1894 and are rare today. Edison began to offer musically recorded wax cylinders in 1889. They continued to be made until 1902. Today they are known as brown wax records. Black wax cylinders were offered in 1902, and the earlier brown wax cylinders were discontinued. These wax two-minute records were sold until 1912. From then until 1929, only four-minute celluloid blue amberol record cylinders were made. The first disc records and disc machines were offered by the inventor Berliner in 1894. They were sold in America until 1900, when the Victor company took over. In the 1890s all machines played 7" diameter disc records; the 10" size was developed in 1901. By the early 1900s there existed many disc and cylinder phonograph companies, all offering their improvements. Among them were Berliner, Columbia, Zonophone, United States Phono, Wizard, Vitaphone, Amet, and others.

All Victor I's through VI's originally came with a choice of either brass bell, morning-glory, or wooden horns. Wood horns are the most valuable, adding $1,000.00 (or more) to the machine. Spring models were produced until 1929 (and even later). After 1929 most were electric (though some electric-motor models were produced as early as 1910). Unless another condition is noted, prices are for complete, original phonographs in at least fine to excellent condition. Note: Edison coin-operated cylinder players start at $7,000.00 and may go up to $20,000.00 each. All outside-horn Victor phonographs are worth at least $1,000.00 or more, if in excellent original condition. Machines that are complete, still retaining all their original parts, and with the original finish still in good condition are the most sought after, but those that have been carefully restored with their original finishes, decals, etc., are bringing high prices as well.

Key:
cyl — cylinder   NP — nickel plated
mg — morning glory   rpd — reproducer

Aretino, disc, orig gr mg horn, 3" center spindle 750.00
Berliner Trade Mark, disc, Clark-Johnson rpd, brass horn......... 5,000.00

Bush & Lane, triple rpd, mahog floor model 200.00
Busy Bee Grand, disc, orig rpd, red mg horn, w/decal 700.00
Chevy, mahog floor model 200.00
Columbia AA, cyl, eagle rpd, blk horn, oak 1,000.00
Columbia AB (McDonald), cyl, eagle rpd, brass horn, 2 mandrels .. 1,400.00
Columbia AK, disc, orig rpd, brass bell horn, 7¼" turntable 800.00
Columbia AU, disc, from $450 to 600.00
Columbia AZ, cyl, Lyric rpd, repro blk/brass horn 500.00
Columbia BI Sterling, disc, Columbia rpd, oak horn 2,250.00
Columbia BK Jewel, cyl, Lyric rpd, orig horn, striping 450.00
Columbia Grafonola, disc, orig rpd, inside horn, mahog upright ... 200.00
Columbia Graphophone Q, cyl, repro horn, oak case 350.00
Columbia P Premium, disc, orig rpd, red horn 625.00
Columbia Q, cyl, 2-min, rstr rpd, EX japanning/label, rpl horn ... 675.00
Columbia Regent Desk, disc, Columbia rpd, inside horn, mahog ... 400.00
Edison A-250, floor model 600.00
Edison Amberola VIII, cyl, Dmn B rpd, inside horn, oak table model .. 400.00
Edison Business C, table model 175.00
Edison Concert, cyl, D rpd, brass horn/stand, 5" mandrel 2,500.00
Edison Concert C, cyl, R rpd, 30" brass bell, floor stand 2,500.00
Edison Dmn Disc A-110, DD rpd, inside horn, Moderne golden oak ... 350.00
Edison Dmn Disc C-19, floor model 250.00
Edison Fireside A, cyl, Dmn B rpd, oak Music Master horn 2,250.00

Edison Fireside, 20" red horn, EX, $425.00.

(Photo courtesy Morphy Auctions/ LiveAuctioneers.com)

Edison Gem Black, cyl 400.00
Edison Gem D Maroon, cyl, K rpd, maroon Fireside horn, w/crane ... 1,800.00
Edison Home, cyl, C rpd, bl mg horn w/bracket 725.00
Edison Home A, no rpd, all brass horn (poor solder), mahog case .. 750.00
Edison Opera, mahog case & Music Master horn 6,750.00
Edison Standard, cyl, 2-4 min, C rpd, mg horn 650.00
Edison Standard Flat Top, cyl, VG 600.00
Edison Triumph, cyl, 2-4 min repeater, O rpd, wood cygnet horn .. 2,800.00
Edison Triumph D, cyl, 2-4 min, H rpd, 23" bell horn 1,000.00
Kalamazoo Duplex, disc, Kalamazoo rpd, 2 blk/brass horns, rare ... 4,300.00
Melodograph, disc, CI, G 175.00
Nirona box type, disc, Norona rpd, sound reflector, red metal case, sm .. 550.00
Pathe Coq, cyl, ebonite rpd, aluminum horn, walnut cover 425.00
Pathephone B, disc, low-set mg horn, minor pnt rstr, walnut case ... 1,350.00
Regina Hexaphone #103, cyl, Hexaphone rpd, oak horn, rstr ... 7,500.00
Standard A, disc, red mg horn, orig decal 995.00
Standard Talking Machine X2, bl horn, 1906, VG 450.00
United Symphony, disc, United rpd, inside horn, table model 250.00
Victor, VV-VI, disc, Exhibition rpd, inside horn, table model 200.00
Victor II, disc, Exhibition rpd, brass bell horn 1,200.00
Victor II, disc, Exhibition rpd, oak horn & case 2,500.00
Victor IV, disc, mahog w/mahog horn & case 4,000.00
Victor IV, disc, no horn, tiger oak case 425.00

Victor IV, complete, all original, $1,950.00.

(Photo courtesy Morphy Auctions)

Victor P, disc, brass bell horn 1,200.00
Victor R Royal, disc, Exhibition rpd, 9½" brass bell, oak 1,000.00
Victor Type Z, disc, Exhibition rpd, brass bell horn 1,400.00
Victor VI, Exhibition rpd, quartersawn oak case, M rstr 465.00
Victor VV-216, disc, console 200.00
Victor VV-50, disc, #2 rpd, inside horn, oak portable 150.00
Victor XXV, Schoolhouse, disc, oak schoolhouse horn, oak upright .. 4,500.00
Victrola Orthophonic, mahog floor model 200.00
Victrola VIA, disc, rstr rpd, Exhibition sound box, post-1918 style ... 495.00
Zonophone, disc, rear mt, oak, red petal horn 1,050.00
Zonophone A, disc, Concert rpd, brass horn, glass sides 2,500.00
Zonophone Parlor, disc, brass bell horn, rear crank 1,100.00

Photographica

Photographic collectibles include not only the cameras and equipment used to 'freeze' special moments in time but also the photographic images produced by a great variety of processes that have evolved since the daguerrean era of the mid-1800s. For the most part, good quality images have either maintained or increased in value. Poor quality examples (regardless of rarity) are not selling well. Interest in cameras and stereo equipment is down, and dealers report that average-priced items that were moving well are often completely overlooked. Though rare items always have a market, collectors seem to be buying only if they are bargain priced. Our advisor for this category is John Hess; he is listed in the Directory under Massachusetts. Unless noted otherwise, values are for examples in at least near-mint condition.

Albumens

These prints were very common during the nineteenth century. The term comes from the emulsion of silver salts and albumen that was used to coat the paper they were printed on.

Battleship Maine as it lays in bottom of Havana harbor, Hoy, 10x7" ... 35.00
Chinatown (San Francisco) street scene, rich tones, 5½x8" 335.00
Civil War Ft Darling (Drewry's Bluff) interior scene, 1860s, 2½x3" ... 120.00
Logging scene in winter w/steam locomotive, sight: 5x7"+fr 90.00
Negresse, African lady (lovely), JP Sebah (Egypt), 10½x8¼" 300.00
Slopes of Mt Vesuvius, sight: 10x14"+fr 240.00
Sumo wrestlers (2) in wrestling pose, 1880s, 11⅛x8¾" 240.00
Surveyers (9) w/various surveying tools, 7x9"+fr 120.00

Ambrotypes

An ambrotype is a type of photograph produced by an early wet-plate process whereby a faint negative image on glass is seen as positive when held against a dark background.

Niagara Falls, three couples look on, in brass matt and brown leather case, 3¼x4½", $35.00.

(Photo courtesy Skinner Inc. Auctioneers & Appraisers of Antiques and Fine Art)

Half plate, lady seated w/sm child standing beside, +case 65.00
Whole plate, man w/wht hair & beard, wide collar, Moulton, +fr ..150.00
Whole plate, 4 men stand by Niagara Falls, +gold-tone fr 385.00
4th plate, lady in fine dress, tinted cheeks, +case 150.00
4th plate, 2 men in top hats & open shotguns, tinted cheeks, +case... 240.00
6th plate, Black man in finery seated, +gilt mat & case 85.00
6th plate, boy dressed as assistant teacher, 1860s, +fr 120.00
6th plate, brother & sister, ages 3 to 5 in studio pose, +case 65.00
6th plate, Confederate soldier seated, +split case 245.00
6th plate, wounded Union soldier seated w/wife, 1860s, +fr & case...155.00
9th plate, adolescent girl seated, +wooden fr 95.00
9th plate, fireman w/badge on collar, bow tie, PA, 1860s, +fr 110.00
9th plate, 2 unidentified Civil War soldiers seated, +case 150.00

Cabinet Photos

When the popularity of carte de visites began to wane in the 1880s, a new fascination developed for the cabinet card, a larger version measuring about 4½x6½". These photos were produced by a variety of methods. They remained popular until the turn of the century.

Acapulco village scene, 1800s, 11x14".................................... 48.00
Auto radiator shop interior, early 1900s.................................. 55.00
Barn raising scene w/workers on ground & on roof framing, 1880s?.....55.00
CA landscapes w/mules & wagon crossing water, sgn Fassold, 1890s.110.00
Carpathia (ship) docked, 8x12".. 150.00
Chief Running Antelope, DF Barry, 1880s 450.00
James Garfield, half-length, Ryder, 6¼x4¼" 100.00
Man stands at base of huge redwood tree, 1890s, 14x11" 65.00
OK car dealership w/salesmen standing before lot of cars, 8x11" ... 24.00
Shrewsbury Baseball Club, outdoor group shot, ca 1910, 12x10"... 65.00
Sitting Bull seated, Bailey, Dix & Mead, c 1882 .... 900.00
Wuh-To-Val (Old Man Left Hand), Indian w/horse, I Chikasha.. 360.00

Cameras

Collectible high-quality cameras are not easy to find. Most of the pre-1900 examples will be found in the large format view cameras or studio camera types. There are quite a few of these that can be found in well-worn condition, but there is a large difference in value between an average-wear item and an excellent or mint-condition camera. It is rare indeed to find one of these early cameras in mint condition.

The types of cameras are generally classified as follows: large format, medium format, early folding and box types, 35 mm single-lens-reflex (SLR), 35mm rangefinders, twin-lens reflex (TLR), miniature or subminiature, novelty, and even a few others. Collectors may specialize in a type, a style, a time period, or even in high-quality examples of the same camera.

In the 1900 to 1940 period, large quantities of various makes of box cameras and folding bellows type cameras were produced by many manufacturers, and the popular 35mm camera was introduced in the 1930s. Most have low values because they were made in vast numbers, but mint-condition cameras are prized by collectors. In the 1930 to 1955 period, the 35mm rangefinders and the SLR's and TLR's became the cameras

of choice. The most prized of these are the early German or Japanese rangefinders such as the Leica, Canon, or Nikon. Earlier, German optics were favored, but after WWII, Japanese cameras and optics rivaled and/ or even exceeded the quality of many German optics.

Now there are thousands of different cameras to choose from, and collectors have many options when selecting categories. Quality is the major factor; values vary widely between an average-wear working camera and one in mint condition, or one still in the original box and unused. This brief list suggests average prices for good working cameras with average wear. The same camera in mint condition will be valued much higher, while one with excessive wear (scratches, dents, corrosion, poor optics, nonworking meters or rangefinders) may have little value.

Buying, selling, and trading of old and late vintage cameras on the internet, both in direct transactions and via e-mail auctions, have tremendously affected the number of cameras that are available to collectors today. As a result, values have fluctuated as well. Large numbers of old, mass-produced box cameras and folding cameras have been offered; many are in poor condition and have been put up for sale by persons who know nothing about quality. So in general, prices have dropped, and it is an excellent buyer's market at the present, except for the mint quality offerings. Many common models in poor to average condition can be bought for $1.00 to $10.00. The collector is advised to purchase only quality cameras that will enhance his collection. To date, no appreciable collector's market has developed for most old movie cameras or projectors. The Polaroid type of camera has little value, although a few models are gaining in popularity among collectors, and values are expected to increase. Today's new camera market is dominated by digital cameras. The initial effect on yesterday's film cameras has been dramatic, reducing both demand and prices of regular film-type cameras. There is no immediate collector's market for digital cameras. Many fakes and copies have been made of several of the classic cameras such as the German Leica, and caution is advised in purchasing one of these cameras at a price too good to be true. Consult a specialist on high-priced classics if good reference material is not available. Our advisor for this category is Gene Cataldo; he is listed in the Directory under Alabama (e-mail: genecams@aol.com). SASE required for information by mail.

Agfa, Isolette... 20.00
Agfa, Optima, 1960s, from $15 to 35.00
Alpa, Standard, 1946-52, Swiss, from $700 to.........................1,500.00
Ansco, Folding, Nr1 to Nr 10, ea from $5 to 30.00
Ansco, Memo, 1927 type, from $60 to...................................... 80.00
Argoflex, Seventy-five, TLR, 1949-58 ....7.00
Argus A, early model, 35mm Bakelite, 1936-41, from $20 to 30.00
Argus C3, blk brick type, 1940-50..8.00
Asahi Pentax, Original, 1957 .... 200.00
Baldi, by Balda-Werk, 1930s... 30.00
Bell & Howell Foton, 1948, from $500 to................................. 700.00
Braun Paxette I, 1952, from $15 to 30.00
Canon A-1, from $60 to 130.00
Canon IIB, 1949-53 .... 225.00
Canon IV SB, rangefinder w/50/fl.8 lens, 1952-55, from $200 to.. 350.00
Canon J, 1939-44, from $3,000 to...5,000.00
Canon Rangefinder IIF, ca 1954, from $200 to 300.00
Canon S-II, Seiki-Kogaku, 1946-47, from $500 to 800.00
Canon 7, 1961-64, from $200 to 400.00
Conley, 4x5 Folding Plate, 1905, from $70 to............................ 120.00
Eastman Folding Brownie Six-20 .... 12.00
Eastman Kodak Bantam, Art Deco, 1935-38 .... 30.00
Eastman Kodak Retina II, from $40 to..................................... 60.00
Eastman Kodak Retina IIIC, from $250 to................................ 350.00
Eastman Kodak Retinette, various models, ea from $15 to............ 50.00
Eastman Kodak Signet 80.. 40.00
Eastman Premo, many models exist, ea from $30 to 200.00

Edinex by Wirgen 25.00
Fed 1, USSR, prewar, from $70 to.......................... 100.00
Fujica AX-5.. 90.00
Graflex Speed Graphic, various szs, ea from $60 to 200.00
Kodak Jiffy Vest Pocket, 1935-41, from $20 to 35.00

Kodak Signet 35, Ektar lens, ca. 1951 – 1958, from $15.00 to $30.00.
(Photo courtesy C.E. Cataldo)

Konica FS-1 .... 50.00
Leica II, 1963-67, from $200 to.............................. 400.00

Leica M3, ca. 1954 – 1966, from $500.00 to $1,100.00. (Photo courtesy C.E. Cataldo)

Mamiyaflex TLR, 1951, from $70 to 100.00
Minolta HiMatic Series, various models, ea from $10 to 25.00
Minolta SR-7 .... 40.00
Minolta SRT-202, from $40 to 80.00
Minolta X-700, from $60 to...................................... 125.00
Minolta XD-11, 1977, from $75 to............................ 125.00
Minolta 35, early Rangefinder models, 1947-50, ea from $250 to ...400.00
Minolta-16, mini, various models, ea from $15 to 30.00
Minox B, spy camera.. 125.00
Miranda Automex II, 1963....................................... 70.00
Nikkormat (Nikon), various models, ea from $60 to 150.00
Nikon FG 85.00
Nikon FM.. 125.00
Nikon S Rangefinder, 1951-54, from $450 to 800.00
Nikon SP Rangefinder, 1958-60, from $1,500 to......... 2,000.00
Nikon S2 Rangefinder, 1954-58, from $700 to 1,000.00
Olympus OM-1, from $75 to..................................... 120.00
Olympus OM-10, from $40 to 60.00
Olympus Pen F, compact half-fr SLR, from $100 to..... 200.00
Pax M3, 1957... 30.00
Pentax ME, from $50 to... 75.00
Pentax Spotmatic, many models, ea from $40 to 100.00
Petri FT, FT-1000, FT-EE & similar models, ea from $35 to 70.00
Petri-7, 1961 .... 20.00
Plaubel-Makina II, 1933-39...................................... 200.00
Polaroid, most models, ea from $5 to 10.00
Polaroid SX-70, from $20 to...................................... 35.00
Polaroid 110, 110A, 110B, ea from $20 to 40.00
Polaroid 180, 185, 190, 195, ea from $100 to............ 250.00
Praktica FX, 1952-57 .... 30.00
Praktica Super TL 40.00
Realist Stereo, 3.5 lens... 80.00

Regula, King, interchangable lens, various models, ea from $40 to ...60.00
Ricoh Diacord 1, TLR, built-in meter, 1958 .... 65.00
Ricoh Singlex, 1965, from $40 to 70.00
Rollei 35, mini, Germany, 1966-70, from $125 to 225.00
Rollei 35, mini, Singapore, from $80 to 150.00
Rolleicord II, 1936-50, from $70 to 90.00
Rolleiflex Automat, 1937 model 125.00
Rolleiflex SL35M, 1978, from $75 to 100.00
Samoca 35, 1950s... 25.00
Seroco 4x5, Folding Plate, Sears, 1901, from $90 to 135.00
Spartus Press Flash, 1939-50...................................... 10.00
Tessina, mini, from $300 to 500.00
Topcon Super D, 1963-74... 125.00
Tower 45, Sears, w/Nikkor lens 200.00
Tower 50, Sears, w/Cassar lens 20.00
Univex-A, Univ Camera Co, 1933............................... 25.00
Voightlander Bessa, w/rangefinder, 1936................... 140.00
Voightlander Vitessa L, 1954, from $125 to 200.00
Voightlander Vito II, 1950... 40.00
Voigtlander Vitessa T, 1957, from $110 to 175.00
Yashica A, TLR... 35.00
Yashica Electro-35, 1966.. 25.00
Yashica FX-70 .... 60.00
Yashicamat 124G, TLR, from $100 to......................... 175.00
Zeiss Baldur Box Tengor, Frontar lens, 1935, from $35 to 125.00
Zeiss Contax III, 1936-42, from $175 to 350.00
Zeiss Ikon Juwell, 1927-39... 500.00
Zeiss Ikon Nettar, Folding Roll Film, various szs, ea from $25 to ... 35.00
Zenit A, USSR, from $20 to... 35.00
Zorki USSR, 1950-56, from $20 to 40.00
Zorki-4, USSR, Rangefinder, 1956-73, from $35 to....... 50.00

Mercury II CX, 65 exposures on standard 35mm film, 35/f 2.7 lens, ca. 1945, from $25.00 to $35.00.
(Photo courtesy C.E. Cataldo)

Cartes De Visites

Among the many types of images collectible today are carte de visites, known as CDVs, which are 2¼" x 4" portraits printed on paper and produced in quantity. The CDV fad of the 1800s enticed the famous and the unknown alike to pose for these cards, which were circulated among the public to the extent that they became known as 'publics.' Note: A common portrait CDV is worth only about 50¢ unless it carries a revenue stamp on the back; those that do are valued at about $2.00 each.

Black Civil War soldier seated by table, PA, ca 1863-65 .... 900.00
Buffalo Bill, waist up, long hair, wide jacket lapels & overcoat.... 300.00
Civil War Confederate man standing by podium, hat in hand, 4" ..240.00
Declaration of Independence signatures, overall fading 240.00
Edwin M Stanton, chest-up portrait, Brady 110.00
General US Grant stands w/blk armband (mourning Lincoln), 4x2½" ...340.00
Giuseppi Garibaldi standing, C Bernieri 70.00
Jefferson Davis bust portrait, Brady 120.00
Jesse James death portrait, c RG Smith, rare, 4⅛x2½" 1,685.00
Lady circus performer w/ornate hairdo, hand-colored, NY 25.00
Man's head & shoulders, high collar & bow tie, 3x2".................. 15.00

Man seated by sm girl standing at side, holding hands, 4x2½" 12.50
Mary Lincoln seated w/hand resting on sm table, Brady.............. 265.00
Postmortem of young boy, 2½x4" 36.00
Sojourner Truth, seated, wearing cap, shawl & apron, rare 600.00

Daguerreotypes

Among the many processes used to produce photographic images are the daguerreotypes (made on a plate of chemically treated silver-plated copper) — the most-valued examples being the 'whole' plate which measures 6½" x 8½". Other sizes include the 'half' plate, measuring 4½" x 5½", the 'quarter' plate at 3¼" x 4¼", the 'sixth' plate at 2¾" x 3¼", the 'ninth' at 2" x 2½", and the 'sixteenth' at 1⅜" x 1⅝". (Sizes may vary slightly, and some may have been altered by the photographer.)

Half plate, lady in elegant clothes w/elbow resting on table, 1839-55... 360.00
Half plate, 7 young ladies in finery, tarnished mat, no case 500.00
Whole plate, family of 8, 7 adults & 1 sm child in finery, 1840s.. 3,000.00

Whole plate, gentleman in top hat, scratches, 8½x6½", $1,500.00.
(Photo courtesy Garth's Auctions Inc.)

4th plate, boy in plaid finery stands beside lg dog on chair, +fr 900.00
4th plate, lady in lace cap, facing left, ca 1839-55 .... 250.00
4th plate, lovely young mother holding deceased baby, ca 1846, +case.. 660.00
4th plate, sm child (2 or younger) seated, +gutta percha case...... 215.00
4th plate, young couple w/2 sm children & dog, ca 1845 .... 350.00
6th plate, French lady seated in chair, 1839-55, +wood & plaster fr ..120.00
6th plate, lady in blk mourning clothes, somber expression, ca 1855.120.00
6th plate, lady seated w/striped cat (rare subject), 1839-55, +fr . 1,650.00
6th plate, ship's captain in ocean-side studio setting, 1840s, +case .. 360.00
9th plate, baby in mother's arms, +mat & fr 80.00
9th plate, sleeping baby, ca 1845, +ornate mat & case 240.00

Photos

Photogravure, couple by fireplace, James Arthur, 1904, in 26x22" fr ... 85.00
Photogravure, Departure From...Lodge - Cheyenne, E Curtis, 6x8"+fr.. 200.00
Photogravure, Indian basketmaker, ES Curtis, #310, 1912, 12x15"+mat/fr...1,495.00
Photogravure, John Ruskin portrait, Hollyer/Collis, 1890s, 5x4" ... 35.00
Photogravure, Native American portrait, sepia tone, Curtis, 15x12".. 700.00
Photogravure, Portrait of Lady, bobbed hair, finery, 22x15"+fr....... 36.00
Photogravure, Qahatika Water Girl, E Curtis, +matt/18x12" fr..... 85.00
Photogravure, Shatila - Pomo, brn tone, ES Curtis, ca 1924, 18x13"+fr..275.00
Photogravure, Summer Camp - Lake Pomo, ES Curtis, 1924, 17½x12"...350.00
Platinum print, Black Bear, Sioux chief, Rinehart, 1899, 9¼x7¼"...1,100.00
Platinum print, Jason Reed Chairmaker, D Ulmann, 7⅞x6"+mat & fr..925.00
Platinum print, Last Horse, Sioux chief, FA Rineheart, 1899, 20x16"+fr.. 1,000.00
Platinum print, Musk Mallow, flowers, EH Lincoln, 1906, 9¼x7¼"...425.00
Platinum print, 3 Chiefs Piegan, ES Curtis, 11x14"+orig batwing fr..9,000.00
Sepia tone, Plains Indian warrior/wife, 1910s, 10x8"+Victorian fr.....125.00
Sepia tone, Pueblo Indian in traditional dress, R Price, 1920s, 13x9" ... 120.00

Silver gelatin print, Marilyn Monroe in Korea w/troops, 11x14". 120.00
Silver gelatin print, Nude w/Brush, G Hurrell, 1958, 12x9½"...... 660.00
Silver gelatin print, sailing vessel, WE Worden, early 1900s, 24x18"...90.00
Silver gelatin print, Wounded Man w/5th Army, M Bourke-White, 10x8" .240.00

Stereoscopic Views

Stereo cards are photos made to be viewed through a device called a stereoscope. The glass stereo plates of the mid-1800s and photo prints produced in the darkroom are among the most valuable. In evaluating stereo views, the subject, date, and condition are all-important. Some views were printed over a 30- to 40-year period; 'first generation' prices are far higher than later copies, made on cheap card stock with reprints or lithographs, rather than actual original photographs. It is relatively easy to date an American stereo view by the color of the mount that was used, the style of the corners, etc. From about 1854 until the early 1860s, cards were either white, cream-colored, or glossy gray; shades of yellow and a dull gray followed. While the dull gray was used for a very short time, the yellow tones continued in use until the late 1860s. Red, green, violet, or blue cards are from the period between 1865 until about 1870. Until the late 1870s, corners were square; after that they were rounded off to prevent damage. Right now, quality stereo views are at a premium.

A Cake Walk - Walking the Line, Black Americana, ca 1900 .... 30.00
Abraham Lincoln close-up portrait, Keystone, late copy (ca 1905) ...660.00
Devil's Den, Gettysburg Battlefield, ca 1875 .... 60.00
Field Marshall Marquis Oyama w/4 unknown figures, 1903 ....7.50
General Sumner in field w/battle flag beside him, Brady 325.00

Group of 16 (two shown), Native American scenes of various cultures and tribes, Illingsworth, from $500.00 to $800.00.
(Photo courtesy Jackson's International Auctioneers & Appraisers of Fine Art & Antiques)

Libby Prison Richmond VA, outside view, Anthony.................... 240.00
Lindbergh w/Spirit of St Louis, Keystone, common....................... 30.00
Mice River disaster scene, pr 30.00
Native American weaver, hand colored... 60.00
Neue Synagogue in Berlin, interior view, ca 1880, 3¼x5¾" 60.00
Palestine, Keystone, set of 100, EXIB.. 155.00
Unidentified Indian chief, Seaver, on Smithsonian mt, dtd 1873 ...275.00
Union Avenue in Kansas City flooded w/rushing water, 1903 .... 12.00
WWI military scenes, incomplete set of 93, EXIB........................ 145.00

Tintypes

Tintypes, contemporaries of ambrotypes, were produced on japanned iron and were not as easily damaged.

Full plate, Civil War soldier w/rifle & revolver............................ 900.00
Full plate, cowboy w/gun in belt, knife showing, EX color, scarce...925.00
Full plate, outdoor scene of farm family & buildings, dk spots 36.00
Full plate, Parker's Drugstore, Bainbridge OH, street scene.......... 450.00
Full plate, Prairie Flower, Iroquois Indian lady w/baby & gun...... 900.00
Half plate, boy on horsebk, wht canvas bkdrop, +leatherette case. 60.00

4th plate, carpenter w/tools on lap, saw at side, +foil mat & fr 550.00
4th plate, Civil War Union soldier in 9-button frock coat, w/saber ...145.00
4th plate, man in buckskins, wide-brim hat & rifle, scarce, +brass mat ..850.00
6th plate, drummer in full uniform, NY militia, 1870s 215.00
6th plate, trapper w/pelts & Winchester rifle, +half case............. 480.00
9th plate, soldier w/musket, ¾-length image, +mat & fr 275.00

6th plate, U.S. Civil War Union soldier holding a MK 1860 sword, $375.00. (Photo courtesy Jackson's International Auctioneers & Appraisers of Fine Art & Antiques)

Union Cases

From the mid-1850s until about 1880, cases designed to house these early images were produced from a material known as thermoplastic, a man-made material with an appearance much like gutta percha. Its innovator was Samuel Peck, who used shellac and wood fibers to create a composition he called Union. Peck was part owner of the Scoville Company, makers of both papier-maché and molded leather cases, and he used the company's existing dies to create his new line. Other companies (among them A.P. Critchlow & Company; Littlefield, Parsons & Company; and Holmes, Booth & Hayden) soon duplicated his material and produced their own designs. Today's collectors may refer to cases made of this material as 'thermoplastic,' 'composition,' or 'hard cases,' but the term most often used is 'Union.' It is incorrect to refer to them as gutta percha cases.

Sizes may vary somewhat, but generally a 'whole' plate case measures 7" x 9⅛" to the outside edges, a 'half' plate 4⅞" x 6", a 'quarter' plate 3¾" x 4¾", a 'sixth' 3⅛" x 3⅝", a 'ninth' 2⅜" x 2⅞", and a 'sixteenth' 1¾" x 2". Clifford and Michele Krainik and Carl Walvoord have written a book, *Union Cases*, which we recommend for further study. Another source of information is *Nineteenth Century Photographic Cases and Wall Frames* by Paul Berg. Values are for examples in excellent condition unless noted otherwise.

Half plate, Geometrics, K-16, NM 210.00
4th plate, Chasse Au Faucon, +tintype of boy by corner chair 200.00
4th plate, Fireman Saving Child, K-118 .... 150.00
4th plate, Parting of Hafed & Hinda, K-35, VG...................... 200.00
4th plate, Roger deCoverly & Gypsies Fortune, K-30, EX 175.00
6th plate, Faithful Hound, +2 daguerreotypes....................... 225.00
6th plate, Geometrics, K-270, VG 85.00
6th plate, Mixed Flower Bouquet, +daguerreotype of bearded man ..85.00
6th plate, Rebecca at the Well, +ambrotype bust of man............ 125.00
6th plate, Ten Dollar Piece w/floral border, +ambrotype of lady ..225.00
6th plate, Union & Constitution, K-373, EX 125.00
9th plate, American Gothic, K-374 .... 95.00
9th plate, Chess Players, R-41 variant............................. 100.00
9th plate, Geometrics/Scrolls, Patent American, K-502 .... 50.00
9th plate (dbl), Children w/Toys, R-29 .... 135.00

Miscellaneous

Stanhope, monocular, ivory, ⅝" 50.00
Stanhope, pen w/letter-opener blade, mosque pictured 50.00

Stereoscope, Alex Beckers, rosewood vnr, Pat 1859, 49¼" H........ 950.00
Stereoscope, beech wood w/magnifying glass, Victorian............... 80.00
Stereoscope, Brewster type, silver w/chased florals, 1860s 1,500.00
Stereoscope, Gaumont, wood table type, rack & pinion movement, 1920 .765.00
Stereoscope, J Wood, acromatic lenses, rack/pinion focus, rare, NM.. 9,000.00
Stereoscope, walnut w/fret-cvd rack, Victorian....................... 350.00

Piano Babies

A familiar sight in Victorian parlors, piano babies languished atop shawl-covered pianos in a variety of poses: crawling, sitting, on their tummies, or on their backs playing with their toes. Some babies were nude, and some wore gowns. Sizes ranged from about 3" up to 12". The most famous manufacturer of these bisque darlings was the Heubach Brothers of Germany, who nearly always marked their product; see Heubach for listings. Watch for reproductions. These guidelines are excerpted from one of a series of informative doll books by Patsy Moyer, published by Collector Books. Values are for examples in near-mint condition. See also Conta and Boehm.

Bisque, intaglio eyes, open/closed mouth with teeth, seated with plate, kitten at side, 7", $275.00. (Photo courtesy McMaster Harris Auction Company)

Blk, bsk, 4", EX quality 600.00
Blk, bsk, 4", med quality, unmk 500.00
Blk, bsk, 5", EX quality 600.00
Blk, bsk, 8", EX quality 600.00
Blk, bsk, 8", med quality 550.00
Blk, bsk, 9", EX quality 675.00
Blk, bsk, 12", EX quality 675.00
Blk, bsk, 12", med quality 600.00
Blk, bsk, 14", EX quality 900.00
Blk, bsk, 16", EX quality 1,000.00
Blk, bsk, 16", med quality 900.00
Bsk, may not have pnt finish on bk, unmk, 4", med quality 410.00
Bsk, may not have pnt finish on bk, unmk, 8", med quality 375.00
Bsk, may not have pnt finish on bk, unmk, 12", med quality 500.00
Bsk, molded hair, unjtd, molded-on clothes, 4", EX quality 500.00
Bsk, molded hair, unjtd, molded-on clothes, 4", med quality 525.00
Bsk, molded hair, unjtd, molded-on clothes, 6", EX quality 675.00
Bsk, molded hair, unjtd, molded-on clothes, 8", EX quality 825.00
Bsk, molded hair, unjtd, molded-on clothes, 8", med quality 500.00
Bsk, molded hair, unjtd, molded-on clothes, 9", EX quality 800.00
Bsk, molded hair, unjtd, molded-on clothes, 12", EX quality 900.00
Bsk, molded hair, unjtd, molded-on clothes, 16", EX quality 1,095.00
Bsk, w/animal/pot/flowers/etc, 4", EX quality..................... 500.00
Bsk, w/animal/pot/flowers/etc, 5", EX quality..................... 500.00
Bsk, w/animal/pot/flowers/etc, 8", EX quality..................... 600.00
Bsk, w/animal/pot/flowers/etc, 10", EX quality................... 700.00
Bsk, w/animal/pot/flowers/etc, 12", EX quality................... 800.00
Bsk, w/animal/pot/flowers/etc, 16", EX quality, minimum value... 950.00

Pickard

Founded in 1895 in Chicago, Illinois, the Pickard China Company was originally a decorating studio, importing china blanks from European manufacturers. Some of these early pieces bear the name of those companies as well as Pickard's. Trained artists decorated the wares with hand-painted studies of fruit, florals, birds, and scenics and often signed their work. In 1915 Pickard introduced a line of 24k gold over a dainty floral-etched ground design. In the 1930s they began to experiment with the idea of making their own ware and by 1938 had succeeded in developing a formula for fine translucent china. Since 1976 they have issued an annual limited edition Christmas plate. They are now located in Antioch, Illinois.

The company has used various marks. The earliest (1893 – 1894) was a double-circle mark, 'Edgerton Hand Painted' with 'Pickard' in the center. Variations of the double-circle mark (with 'Hand Painted China' replacing the Edgerton designation) were employed until 1915, each differing enough that collectors can usually pinpoint the date of manufacture within five years. Later marks included the crown mark, 'Pickard' on a gold maple leaf, and the current mark, the lion and shield. Work signed by Challinor, Marker, and Yeschek is especially valued by today's collectors.

Bonbon, shell shape, yel w/gold, Pickard blank, 1938-present, 5" L... 50.00
Bonbon, violets w/gold, scalloped, Mark, JPL blank, 1898-1903, 5½"..150.00
Cake plate, vellum Enchanted Forest, Marker, Japan blank, 1918-19, 10"..395.00
Charger, Golden Pheasant, Challinor, 1919-22, 12½"................. 600.00
Charger, Twin Lilies, Walters, JHR Bavaria Favorite blank, 1910s, 11"..275.00
Chocolate pot, Challinor Nasturtiums, J&C Louise blank, 1903-05, 6"....595.00

Cider pitcher, flower garden scene, vellum glaze, signed E. Challinor, ca. 1895 – 1898, 8x8x6", $395.00. (Photo courtesy Brunk Auctions/LiveAuctioneers.com)

Creamer & sugar bowl, Carnation & Platinum, w/lid, 1905-10...350.00
Cup & saucer, roses, mc on yel w/gold, Blaha, JPL blank, 1898-1903...200.00
Jug, Venice; Carnation Garden, Yeschek, T&V blank, 1903-05, 10½"..1,300.00
Lemonade jug, peaches on gr, Heap, CAC blank, 1903-05, 8"..... 500.00
Mug, Falstaff, Gasper, gold hdl, 1905-10, 7", from $575 to........... 650.00
Pitcher, strawberry clusters, Michel, JPL blank, 1898-1903, 5" 600.00
Pitcher, White Poppy & Daisy, Gasper, Bavaria blank, 1910-12, 6"...565.00
Plate, Cornflower Conventional, CA France blank, 1903-05, 8½"....300.00
Plate, floral w/gold rim, McCorkle, RC Bavaria blank, 1905-10, 8¾".. 75.00
Plate, tiger lilies on brn border, JPL blank, 1898-1903, 8½".........225.00
Plate, Triple Tulip, Heschek, Favorite Bavaria blank, 1912-18, 8½"..275.00
Plate, Tulip Conventional, wishbone hdls, T&B blank, 1903-05, 7½"..325.00
Plate, Tulip Moderne, C Hahn, T&V blank, 1898-1903, 8" 200.00
Shakers, lily pads on gold border, Schoner, 1905-10, 3¼", pr....... 100.00
Syrup & underplate, Violet Nouveau, Coufall, D&Co blank, 1905-10, 6"...295.00
Vase, narcissus on gr, Post, #3660 blank, 1903-05, 8" 450.00
Vase, nude in woods, Grane, slim w/ornate gold hdls, 1898-1903, 20". 8,000.00
Vase, Praying Mohammedan, Farrington, RC Bavaria blank, 1903-05, 14"..3,000.00
Vase, vellum Classic Ruins, F Bobor, T&V blank, 1912-18, 13"..950.00
Vase, vellum woodland scene, Challinor, rectangular, 1912-18, 6"..400.00

Pickle Castors

Affluent Victorian homes seemed to have something for every purpose, and a pickle castor was not only an item of beauty but of practicality. American Victorian pickle castors can be found in old catalogs dating from the 1860s through the early 1900s. (Those featured in catalogs after 1900 were made by silver manufacturers that were not part of the International Silver Company which was formed in 1898 — for instance, Reed and Barton, Tufts, Pairpoint, and Benedict.) Catalogs featured large selections to choose from, ranging from simple to ornate. Inserts could be clear or colored, pattern glass or art glass, molded or blown. Many of these molds and design were made by more than one company as they merged or as personnel took their designs with them from employer to employer. It is common to see the same insert in a variety of different frames and with different lids as viewed in these old catalogs.

Pickle castors are being reproduced today. Frames are being imported from Taiwan and sold by L.G. Wright. New enameling is being applied to old jars; and new or old tumblers, vases, or spooners are sometimes used as jars in old original frames. Beware of new mother-of-pearl jars. The biggest giveaway in this latter scenario is that old glass is not perfect glass. In the listings below, the description prior to the semicolon refers to the jar (insert), and the remainder of the line describes the frame. Unless noted 'rstr' (restored), the silver plate is assumed to be in very good original condition. When tongs are present, they will be will be indicated. Glass jars are assumed to be in at least near-mint condition. Our advisor for this category is Barbara Aaronson; she is listed in the Directory under California. For additional photographs and values, visit her website: thevictorianlady.com.

Bl Coinspot w/floral; Roger Bros stand, squatty, 4-ftd, 9" 725.00
Bl Cone, dog finial; rstr Rockford #630 fr, 13" 795.00
Bl Daisy & Button, cylinder; Roger Smith fr, 11", +fork & tongs....600.00
Bl ribbed w/pk & gr floral; Forbes fr w/leafy scrolling, 10"........... 450.00
Clear w/emb birds; Reed & Barton floral-emb fr, 14", +tongs 540.00
Clear w/intaglio floral; Pairpoint fr, +tongs................................ 420.00
Clear 12-sided etched insert; Barbour Bros fr, 14", +fork............. 780.00
Cranberry & wht swirl; fr mk #32, 11", +fork 475.00
Cranberry T'print w/daisies; ornate Eagle fr, 12", +tongs 510.00

Cranberry Thumbprint with enameled floral; Weeton frame, 10½", with tongs, $500.00. (Photo courtesy Jackson's International Auctioneers & Appraisers of Fine Art & Antiques)

Cranberry T'print; ornate Meriden #195 fr, 4-ftd, 11" 750.00
Cranberry w/floral; Derby leaf-shaped fr w/bird on lid.................. 775.00
Leaf Mold, spatter; Rogers #452 fr w/flowers at hdl, 10½" 950.00
Pk w/emb leaves; Wilcox fr w/cucumber vines.............................. 600.00
Purple slag; Rogers SP fr, 9½", +tongs 400.00
Rubina w/yel daisies; ornate Wilcox gold-washed holder, 4 ball ft, 12"...500.00
Wht rectangular insert; Reed & Barton fr w/cucumber finial, 9", +fork.720.00

Pie Birds

A pie bird or pie funnel (pie vent) is generally made of pottery, glazed inside and out. Most are 3" to 5" in height with arches at the base to allow steam to enter. The steam is then released through a single exit hole at the top. The English pie funnel was as tall as the special baking dish was deep and held the crust even with the dish's rim, thereby lifting the crust above the filling so it would stay crisp and firm. These dishes came in several different sizes, which accounts for the variances in the heights of the pie birds.

The first deviations from the basic funnels were produced in the mid-1930s to late 1940s: the Clarice Cliff (signed Midwinter or Newport) pie bird (reg. no. on white base) and the signed Nutbrown elephant. Shortly thereafter (1940s – 1960s), figures of bakers and colorful birds were created for additional visual baking fun. From the 1980s to present, many novelty pie vents have been added to the market for the enjoyment of both the baker and collector. These have been made by commercial (including Far East importers) and local enterprises in Canada, England, and the United States. A new category for the 1990s includes an array of holiday-related pie vents. Basic tip: Older pie vents were air-brushed, not hand painted.

Incense burners (i.e., elephants and Oriental people), one-hole pepper shakers, dated brass toy bird whistles, egg timers (missing glass timer), and ring holders (i.e., elephant with clover on his tummy) should not be mistaken for pie vents. Our advisor for this category is Linda Fields; she is listed in the Directory under Tennessee.

Baker, wht w/red on hat, cuffs & lips, blk hair & brows, 5½" 55.00
Bird, bl & wht on base, Royal Worchester, 2-pc, MIB.................... 90.00
Bird, bl & wht w/yel chest, head up, on base, 4½"........................... 20.00
Bird, bl w/pk eyes & wingtips, Shawnee for Pillsbury, 5½" 50.00
Bird, blk w/yel head bk, Midwinter England, 4½"........................... 45.00
Bird, pk w/gr eyes & wingtips, Shawnee.. 50.00
Bird, wht w/gr wings & eyes, pk beak & base, Morton, 5½" 50.00
Bird, yel w/pk beak & blk eyes, Josef Originals, 3"......................... 65.00
Blk cat, red bow & collar, Halloween style, 4¾"............................. 40.00
Boy, gr sombrero, mk Pie Boy 400.00
Canary w/puffed chest, teal or pk 450.00
Chef w/bl coat, wht hat, 1930-40s... 160.00
Donald Duck, Walt Disney, yel & wht w/dk bl details, 4¾" 1,100.00
Duck, pk w/blk emb wings, yel beak & ft, 5".................................. 70.00
Elephant on drum, solid pk base, CCC... 150.00
Funnel, pagoda, Gourmet Pie Cup, Reg No 369793 .... 75.00
Funnel, wht, unmk Nutbrown Pie Funnel Co, 1940s, 3".............. 25.00
Golliwog kneeling, bl shirt, wht & yel striped pants, England, 4".. 60.00
Mammy, pk scarf, bl apron, unmk, 1940s, 4¾".............................. 75.00
Mammy, red dress/wht apron, yel dots on bandana, Taiwan Import, 4¾" .. 15.00
Rabbit (Wilford), brn & wht w/tall ears, bl eyes, England, 4¼" ... 120.00
Rooster, bl w/pk, Morton, 5¼", from $2,500 to..........................3,000.00
Rooster, mc, mk Cleminson or Cb 50.00
Rooster, wht w/blk/red/yel details, Marion Drake, 5".................... 125.00
Teddy bear, pk & blk highlights, 4"... 40.00
Train engine, blk, mk Boyd Special, Boyd Glass, 3½x3¾".............. 25.00
Welsh lady, Cymru, from $75 to... 95.00
Yankee Blackbird, Made in England, 1950-60s, 4¼"....................... 40.00

Pierce, Howard

William Manker, a well-known ceramist, hired Howard Pierce to work for him in 1938. After three years, Pierce opened a small studio of his own in LaVerne, California. Not wanting to compete with Manker, Pierce began designing miniature animal figures, some of which he made into jewelry. Today, his pewter brooches, depending on the type of animal portrayed, sell for as much as $275.00. Howard married, and he and his wife Ellen (Van Voorhis) opened a small studio in Claremont, California. In the early years, he used polyurethane to create animal figures — mostly roadrunners on bases, either standing or running; or birds on small, flat bases. Pierce quickly discovered that he was allergic to the material, so a very limited number of polyurethane pieces were ever produced; today these are highly collectible.

The materials used by Pierce during his long career were varied, probably to satisfy his curiosity and showcase his many talents. He experimented with a Jasperware-type body, bronze, concrete, gold leaf, porcelain, Mt. St. Helens ash, and others. By November 1992, Pierce's health had continued to worsen, and he and Ellen destroyed all the molds they had created over the years. After that they produced smaller versions of earlier porcelain wares, and they developed a few new items as well. Pierce died on February 28, 1994. Much of his work quickly appreciated in value, and items not seen before began to appear on the market.

Bowl, bl on blk, mk Pierce 1991, 4x6¼" 125.00
Figurine, angel singing, creamy wht, 6".. 30.00
Figurine, bear cub, brn/gr, blk stamp, 4¾x5¼".............................. 50.00
Figurine, bird on stump, tail up, brn tones, 1991, 5x2½" 30.00
Figurine, birds (3) on branch, bl, brn stamp, 4x7"........................ 100.00
Figurine, bison, wht glossy, blk stamp, 2½x3½"............................. 75.00
Figurine, cat, bl/blk tones, 14x6".. 275.00
Figurine, chipmunk, brn tones, 5"... 30.00
Figurine, coyote howling, brn tones, 7⅛x3½" 40.00
Figurine, dachshund, brn, blk stamp, 3¼x10".............................. 100.00
Figurine, elephant, trunk up, pk on gray, blk stamp, 4½x4", minimum ..200.00
Figurine, girl holding bird, brn & bl, blk stamp, 7¼" 85.00
Figurine, girl holding basket, gray tones, 9½"................................. 45.00
Figurine, girl playing mandolin, gr/blk, blk stamp, 8x4", minimum....150.00
Figurine, girl w/bowl standing by jugs, brn speckled, blk stamp, 9".....100.00
Figurine, koala bear, brn speckled, brn stamp, 4¼x4½" 85.00
Figurine, Madonna, stylized form, shaded bls, 7¾x2¾".................. 65.00
Figurine, native female, blk w/blk & wht speckled skirt, blk stamp, 7" ... 75.00
Figurine, owl, brn tones, 5"... 25.00
Figurine, panther stalking, blk glossy, brn stamp, 2x12", minimum..200.00
Figurine, pelican, brn speckled, blk stamp, 7½x4½" 85.00
Figurine, penguin, brn tones, 6" 50.00
Figurine, pigeon, blk w/blk & wht speckled breast, blk stamp, 7x5½"....65.00
Figurine, polar bear, wht glossy, blk stamp, 4½x8½"...................... 35.00
Figurine, rabbit, ears up, gray, 3¼x3½".. 35.00
Figurine, roadrunner, brn tones, detailed, 4½x12"......................... 65.00
Figurine, robin, blk w/orange breast, blk stamp, 4½x3½" 65.00
Figurine, Siamese cat, creamy brn tones, seated, 11".................... 150.00
Figurine, Siamese cat, gray, recumbent, 4½x6" 60.00
Figurine, Siamese cat, gray, seated, 11x3½".................................... 90.00
Figurine, skunk, tail up, blk & wht, 5x6" 100.00
Figurine, squirrel, brn/wht mottle, blk stamp, 5½x4¾".................. 65.00
Figurine, toad, warty bk, brn speckled, blk stamp, 3x3¾".............. 50.00
Figurines, bear mother & cub, gr-blk gloss, 3½", 2½", pr 55.00
Figurines, birds, brn tones, detailed, from 4-5", set of 3 .... 45.00

Figurines, fish, 4¾" and 3¼", $150.00 for the pair. (Photo courtesy Susan Cox)

Figurines, kittens (nesting), gray, 2¾", 3", pr 75.00
Flower holder, girl w/basket, 2 vessels at ft, 3 openings, 9½" 45.00
Flower holder, 2 birds on tree stump, gray, 9x3x3" 45.00
Magnet, coyote, brn/gray speckled, 5½" 75.00
Planter, wht leaves on gr, ribbed mint gr body, mk Howard...82P, 7x10" .. 75.00
Vase, deer (2) on bl w/lt bl border, mk Howard...70F, 6x6" 125.00
Vase, gr w/wht appl giraffe, #250P, 8x5x3" 50.00
Vase, gr w/wht deer & tree insert, sq, 11½x6½" 120.00
Vase, owls (2) on branches, burnt amber highlights, mk Pierce, 5½" ... 75.00
Vase, owls in tree, brn tones, 5" 45.00
Wall plaque, raccoons (2) on branch, rare, 26x17", minimum..... 500.00

Pierrefonds

Pierrefonds is a small village in France, best known today as the place to see a castle once owned and inhabited by Napoleon III. Pottery collectors, however, know it better as the location of The Societe Faienciere Heraldique de Pierrefonds studio, which became famous for stoneware art pottery often finished in flambé or crystalline glazes. The pottery was founded in 1903 by Comte Hallez d'Arros, who was also an innovative contributor to the advancement of photography. The ware they produced was marked with a helmet between the letters P (for Pierrefonds) and H (for Hallez).

Vase, bl & brn crystalline, bulbous w/rnded buttresses, 6½x10½"....550.00
Vase, bl & brn crystalline, integral hdls, 13½x9½" 850.00
Vase, bl & brn crystalline, twisted dbl-gourd shape, 11¾x7½" 950.00
Vase, bl crystalline running on yel, integral hdls, #447, 10¼" ... 1,000.00
Vase, lt bl crystalline on mustard, bulbous/shouldered, 9¾" 480.00

Pigeon Blood

Pigeon blood glass, produced in the late 1800s, may be distinguished from other dark red glass by its distinctive orange tint.

Biscuit jar, HP floral on ribbed body, SP lid, ca 1900, 7½" 60.00
Ewer, ornate gold w/floral, bird & butterfly, att Webb, 8" 225.00
Lamp, oil; conical shade w/gold floral, repeated on front, 2-part, 8"...650.00
Water set, Bulging Loops, 9" pitcher w/clear hdl+6 tumblers....... 600.00

Vases, enameled Moser-type flowers, ca. 1880, 10½", $320.00 for the pair. (Photo courtesy Du Mouchelles)

Pigeon Forge

Douglas J. Ferguson and Ernest Wilson started their small pottery in Pigeon Forge, Tennessee, in 1946. Using red-brown and gray locally dug clay and glazes which they themselves formulated, bowls, vases, and sculptures were produced there. Their primary target was the tourist trade. Since Ferguson's death in 2000, the pottery is no longer in operation. Note: 'PFP' in the listings indicates a 'Pigeon Forge Pottery' mark.

Bowl, brn to cream, hand thrown, D Ferguson, 2¼x6½" 20.00
Candlestick, bl crystalline, saucer base, w/hdl, 2½" 75.00
Figurine, chipmunk, brn tones, 5½" L 25.00
Figurine, frog, brn w/cream wash, 2¼x3½" 55.00
Figurine, owl, textured brn & cream, 4¼" 15.00
Figurine, owl, textured brn & cream, 7¼" 42.50
Jug, brn over gr crystalline, 6½" 20.00
Mug, Christmas tree, brn on gr 20.00
Vase, bl crystalline on gray-brn, bulbous, 5⅛" 78.00
Vase, brn & wht speckled, cylindrical, 10" 42.50
Vase, brn over gr crystalline, waisted neck, 7x5¼" 90.00
Vase, wht textured over brn, stick neck, 6" 25.00

Pilkington

Founded in 1892 in Manchester, England, the Pilkington pottery experimented in wonderful lustre glazes that were so successful that when they were displayed at exhibition in 1904, they were met with critical acclaim. They soon attracted some of the best ceramic technicians and designers of the day who decorated the lustre ground with flowers, animals, and trees; some pieces were more elaborate with scenes of sailing ships and knights on horseback. Each artist signed his work with his personal monogram. Most pieces were dated and carried the company mark as well. After 1913 the company became known as Royal Lancastrian. Their Lapis Ware line was introduced in the late 1920s, featuring intermingling tones of color under a matt glaze. Some pieces were very simply decorated while others were painted with designs of stylized leafage, scrolls, swirls, and stripes. The line continued into the '30s. Other pieces of this period were molded and carved with animals, leaves, etc., some of which were reminiscent of their earlier wares. The company closed in 1938 but reopened in 1948. During this period their mark was a simple P within the outline of a petaled flower shape.

Bottle, chevrons & spades, bl on purple irid, long neck, #2906, 6¼" .765.00
Charger, horseman, brn & cobalt, 1980s, 15" 1,200.00
Vase, arches in brn & cream, Mycock, Royal Lancastrian, #193, 8½" .. 350.00
Vase, geometric bands divide bl neck & orange body, #3185, 6", pr. 360.00
Vase, heraldic beasts band & floral in gold lustre, 10½" 850.00

Vase, jaguars and flowers on lustre glaze, PXII England, missing lid, 9x6½", $1,000.00. (Photo courtesy David Rago Auctions/LiveAuctioneers.com)

Vase, mottled orange, Royal Lancastrian, #2085, 9¾" 100.00
Vase, vining leaves, bl on Kingfisher Blue, #6063, 8⅝" 265.00

Pillin

Polia Pillin was born in Poland in 1909. She came to the U.S. as a teenager and showed an interest and talent for art, which she studied in Chicago. She married William Pillin, who was a poet and potter. They ultimately combined their talents and produced her very distinctive pottery from the 1950s to the mid-1980s. She died in 1993. Polia Pillin won many prizes for her work, which is always signed Pillin with the loop of the 'P' over the full name. Some undecorated pieces are signed W&P, to indicate her husband's collaboration. Her work is prized for its art, not for the shape of her pots, which for the most part are simple vases, dishes, bowl, and boxes. Wall plaques are rare. She pictured women with hair reminiscent of halos, girls, an occasional boy, horses, birds, and fish. After viewing a few of her pieces, her style is unmistakable. Some of her early work is very much like that of Picasso. Her pieces are somwhat difficult to find, as all the work was done without outside help, and therefore limited in quantity. In the last few years, more and more people have become interested in her work, resulting in escalating prices.

Bowl, lady w/2 cats on wht, irregular shape, 2¾x8" 1,500.00
Bowl, 2 ladies on brn, 6½x7½" 1,100.00

Box, dancers on blue, internal firing lines, 2x8" diameter, $3,100.00. (Photo courtesy David Rago Auctions/LiveAuctioneers.com)

Box, lady w/bird, mc on gr & brn, 2x4" dia.................................. 375.00
Bust, lady w/2 stylized birds, mc.. 425.00
Compote, freize of lady's face on lt marigold w/turq wash, 5x6" ... 650.00
Cordial pitcher, birds on antique wht, slim, rstr, 13", +2 cups...... 840.00
Covered dish, lady w/mandolin, mc on shaded bl, 2x4" dia 375.00
Decanter, abstract design, flared cylinder, cork top, 10", +6 tumblers ... 725.00
Dish, 2 dancing harlequins on brn, 6" dia 350.00
Dish, 2 full-length women, elliptical form, 17½" 2,400.00
Goblet, bust portrait of lady, bl/gr/tan on brn, 9" 750.00
Jug, blistered yel/brn gloss, 7¾x5½" 275.00
Lighter, lady & man, Evans, 4x2¾" 285.00
Pendant, female portrait on marigold, 3¼x2½"............................ 500.00
Plaque, 2 ladies by tree w/bird, rectangular, 11" L..................... 2,000.00
Plaque, 5 dancers against gr wall, 15½" L 3,150.00
Plate, horses, 5 wht/1 blk on streaky teal, 7¾" 1,000.00
Plate, lady & bird, 7¾".. 850.00
Plate, lady w/chicken & birds, mc on bl, 8½" 1,650.00
Tray, ballerinas, 3 in leotards/1 center front in wht tutu on bl, 9x9"...950.00
Tray, bird on brn, 5" dia 350.00
Tray, lady's portrait (lg/detailed), sm nick, 8¼x6" 1,325.00
Tray, 2 women & bird, oval, 8½" L.. 925.00
Tray, 4 aliens, 6½x2x6", NM 425.00
Vase, abstract figure on all 4 sides, 11½x3¾"............................ 975.00
Vase, avocado gr over lt seaweed gr, onion base, can neck, 6½" ... 250.00
Vase, birds frolicking (9) on bl, flat rim, 4x3½" 700.00
Vase, blended lav, red/yel/purple, W+P Pillin, 6⅛"...................... 360.00
Vase, cat/rooster, trees/female dancers on marigold, 4½x3¾" 1,000.00
Vase, complex geometrics, mc w/blk, bulbous, 6½x6" 600.00
Vase, dk gr/bl crystalline, 1950s, 9¾" 250.00
Vase, fish (9) on pastel sea, 6½x6"... 495.00
Vase, gr mottle, shouldered, 12x5" 675.00
Vase, horse & 2 ladies, wht on peacock & rust, 9x7".................... 850.00
Vase, horses, lady w/balloons, mc on bl, can form, 4½" 495.00
Vase, horses (3) galloping, stick neck, 6x5½" 400.00

Vase, horses (4) prancing on gr to pk, spherical, 4¾" 585.00
Vase, ladies, 1 w/birds, 2nd w/horse, bottle shape, 6½x2½" 650.00
Vase, ladies (2, 1 w/bird on hand) & lg rooster, 4⅛x4½" 425.00
Vase, ladies (2), ea w/mc fish on line, conical, 3¾"...................... 585.00
Vase, ladies (2) holding fish-laden nets, cylindrical, 14" 2,400.00
Vase, ladies (2) seining for fish, bulbous, 4¼"............................ 475.00
Vase, ladies (2) w/fish, slim bottle form, 22" 3,300.00
Vase, ladies (3) standing, cylindrical, bk metal base, 14⅛"........ 1,750.00
Vase, lady, chicken & deer, cylindrical, 4½" 450.00
Vase, lady (full-length), cylindrical, 14¾x3", NM 1,895.00
Vase, leathery turq & bl-gr mottle w/cobalt melt fissures, 14½x5".. 1,175.00
Vase, lt to dk gr gloss, bulbous w/sm opening, 6½"...................... 200.00
Vase, roosters (3), pastel colors on streaky yel, bottle form, 6" 530.00
Vase, scarlet flambé gloss, spherical w/short neck, 9½x7"............ 425.00
Vase, sea gr gloss w/bl & umber shadings, spherical, 8x13" 1,525.00
Wine cup, rooster, gr w/mc, 2½" 325.00

Pin-Back Buttons

Buttons produced up to the early 1920s were made of a celluloid covering held in place by a ring (or collet) to the back of which a pin was secured. Manufacturers used these 'cellos' to advertise their products. Many were of exceptional quality in both color and design. Many buttons were produced in sets featuring a variety of subjects. These were given away by tobacco, chewing gum, and candy manufacturers, who often packed them with their product as premiums. Usually the name of the button maker or the product manufacturer was printed on a paper placed in the back of the button. Often these 'back papers' are still in place today. Much of the time the button maker's name was printed on the button's perimeter, and sometimes the copyright was added. Beginning in the 1920s, a large number of buttons were lithographed on tin; these are referred to as tin 'lithos.' Nearly all pin-back buttons are collected today for their advertising appeal or graphic design. There are countless categories to base a collection on.

The following listing contains non-political buttons representative of the many varieties you may find. Values are for pin-backs in near-mint condition, unless noted otherwise. Our advisor for this category is Michael J. McQuillen; he is listed in the Directory under Indiana.

American, early automobile, ca. 1905, no back paper, NM, $325.00. (Photo courtesy Morphy Auctions/LiveAuctioneers.com)

Atlanta Federation...Labor Day 1907, eagle & clasped hands, 2½"...65.00
Beatles, All You Need Is Love, blk & wht photo, 2¼".................... 23.00
Boston Sunday Herald, What Did the Woggle Bug Say? on wht, 1¼", EX..60.00
Brooklyn Dodgers, dk red lettering & bats on wht, 1¼", VG 24.00
Cloverine Salve, lady in center, mc on yel, Whitehead & Hoag, 1½" ...60.00
Ducks Unlimited, duck flying on bl, Rochester series, 1973, 2¼" .. 20.00
Dupont Smokeless, dogs in hunting scene, Lewis Swift, 1920s, 1". 90.00
Horlick's Malted Milk, ...Meat & Drink to Me, lady & cow, 1896, 1¼". 35.00
Ice Follies Skating School, red, wht & bl, oval, 1940s 23.00
Los Angeles DONS, red, wht & bl w/ribbon, AAFC, 1940s, 1¾".. 85.00
Meet Me at Macy's w/Santa portrait, Philadelphia Badge Co, 1¼" ...45.00
Member Roy Rogers Camera Club, blk & wht portrait on yel, 1950, 1¼"...160.00
Muhammad Ali blk & wht head shot, Flies Like a..., 1971, 2¼", EX ..20.00
Port Huron, The Only General Purpose, tractor on wht, 1890s, 1½" ...240.00

Railroad Day, Pan American, train on yel, Sept 14, 1901, 1"....... 195.00
Range Rider Brand, blk & wht photo on red, 1950s, 1¼" 26.50
Santa's Visitor, North Pole NY, Santa & reindeer on wht, 1½", EX... 20.00
Shirley Temple Little Princess Contest, blk & wht portrait, 1¼", EX .. 35.00
Shoot Peters Shells on wht, shotgun shell in center, 1900s, 1", EX... 60.00
Sportman's League, yel w/Laurentide fishing fly in wht center 32.00
Stag Beer Expert, dart-throwing award, brass, 1¼" 32.00
Tennessee State-Wide Hunting..., bl & wht, metal, 1941, 2½ "L...200.00
Think Act Work for V Wright Employees, red, wht & bl, Bastian Bros, 2".25.00
Wisconsin, wht lettering on red, 1920s, 1¾".................................. 60.00

Pine Ridge

In the mid-1930s, the Indian Bureau of Affairs and the Work Progress Administration offered the Native Americans living on the Pine Ridge Indian Reservation in South Dakota a class in pottery making. Originally, Margaret Cable (director of the University of North Dakota ceramics department) was the instructor and Bruce Doyle was director. By the early 1950s, pottery production at the school was abandoned. In 1955 the equipment was purchased by Ella Irving, a student who had been highly involved with the class since the late 1930s. From then until it closed in the 1980s, Ella virtually ran the pot shop by herself. The clay used in Pine Ridge pottery was red and the decoration reminiscent of early Native American pottery and beadwork designs. A variety of marks and labels were used. For more information we recommend *Collector's Encyclopedia of the Dakota Potteries* by Darlene Hurst Dommel; she is listed in the Directory under Minnesota.

Mug, geometric border, tan on red-brn, Cottier, 3⅝"...................... 48.00
Pitcher, incised geometrics, tan on brn, Sioux E Irving, 7½x3"...... 72.50
Plate, geometrics, cream & red-brn, E Carter, 11" 275.00
Vase, turq w/horizontal ridges, bulbous, M Cable, 1937, rstr, 5½" ...360.00

Vase, incised by Olive Cottier, 2½x4¾", minimum value, $250.00. (Photo courtesy Darlene Dommel)

Pink Lustre Ware

Pink lustre was produced by nearly every potter in the Staffordshire district in the late eighteenth and first half of the nineteenth centuries. The application of gold lustre on white or light-colored backgrounds produced pinks, while the same over dark colors developed copper. The wares ranged from hand-painted plaques to transfer-printed dinnerware.

Cup & saucer, floral band, 3x5".. 30.00
Jug, cottage & ribbed decor, 7"... 265.00
Jug, Gardner's Arms motto, blk transfer w/lustre trim, 8¼", EX ... 360.00
Jug, North Umberland 74 (clipper ship), blk transfer w/lustre trim, 9". 575.00
Spooner, bird & floral transfer, ftd, 4½", EX............................ 50.00
Teapot, flowers & leaves, Staffordshire, 1820s, 6x10".................. 265.00

Pink-Paw Bears

These charming figural pieces are very similar to the Pink Pigs described in the following category. They were made in Germany during the same time frame. The cabbage green is identical; the bears themselves are whitish-gray with pink foot pads. You'll find some that are unmarked while others are marked 'Germany' or 'Made in Germany.' In theory, the unmarked bears are the oldest, made prior to 1890 when the McKinley Tariff Act required imports to be marked with the country of origin. Those marked 'Made In' were probably produced after the revision of the Act in 1914. Our advisor for this category is Mary 'Tootsie' Hamburg; she is listed in the Directory under Illinois.

1 by bean pot.. 135.00
1 by graphophone 150.00
1 by honey pot.. 145.00
1 by top hat.. 125.00
1 in front of basket... 135.00
1 in roadster (car identical to pk pig car)................................ 225.00
1 on binoculars.. 175.00
1 peaking out of basket.. 135.00
1 sitting in wicker chair.. 150.00
2 in hot air balloon 175.00
2 in purse... 165.00
2 in roadster 225.00
2 on pin dish 175.00
2 on pin dish w/bag of coins 160.00
2 peering in floor mirror.. 150.00
2 sitting by mushroom 160.00
2 standing in washtub 150.00
3 in roadster 250.00
3 on pin dish 160.00

Pink Pigs

Pink Pigs on cabbage green were made in Germany around the turn of the century. They were sold as souvenirs in train depots, amusement parks, and gift shops. 'Action pigs' (those involved in some amusing activity) are the most valuable, and prices increase with the number of pigs. Though a similar type of figurine was made in white bisque, most serious collectors prefer only the pink ones. They are marked in two ways: 'Germany' in incised letters, and a black ink stamp 'Made in Germany' in a circle. The unmarked pigs are the oldest, made prior to 1890 when the McKinley Tariff Act required imports to be marked with the country of origin. Those marked 'Made In' were probably produced after the revision of the Act in 1914. Pink Pigs may be in the form of a match holder, salt cellar, a vase, stickpin holder, and (the hardest to find) a bank.

At this time three reproduction pieces have been found: a pig by an outhouse, one playing the piano, and one poking out of a large purse. These not difficult to spot because they are found in a rough, poor quality porcelain in a darker green. Our advisor for this category is Mary 'Tootsie' Hamburg; she is listed in the Directory under Illinois.

1 as chef w/shamrocks, 2 salt cellars aside, 4¼" 200.00
1 at trough, gold trim, 4½".. 110.00
1 at water trough among side tree, 3½" 110.00
1 beside gr drum, wall-mt match holder.................................... 95.00
1 beside lg basket, 3".. 125.00
1 beside lg purse 115.00
1 beside shoe 115.00
1 coming out of suitcase.. 95.00
1 coming through gr fence, post at sides, open for flowers............... 125.00
1 going through purse 110.00
1 holding cup by fence.. 140.00
1 on binoculars, gold trim.. 175.00
1 on haunches, bottle, blk wood cork top, 2½" 110.00
1 on horseshoe-shaped dish w/raised 4-leaf clover 110.00
1 reclining on horseshoe ashtray 85.00

One seated on binoculars, $175.00. (Photo courtesy Tom Harris Auctions/LiveAuctioneers.com)

1 riding train 235.00
1 sitting in oval bathtub, gold trim, 4½" W 200.00
1 sitting on log, mk Germany 175.00
1 standing in oversz opera-house box, gold trim, 3½" ... 250.00
1 w/basketweave cradle, gold trim, 3½" W 140.00
1 w/binoculars, brn/gr coat & hat, lg money bag, 5" ... 160.00
1 w/devil pulling on hose 225.00
1 w/flag, 2 Black children in skiff, match holder w/striker ... 500.00
1 w/front ft in 3-part dish containing 3 dice, 1 ft on dice ... 175.00
1 w/grandfather clock, 7" 250.00
1 w/lg umbrella, picnic basket & water bucket, 5¼" ... 150.00
1 w/red lobster pulling leg 185.00
1 w/tennis racket stands beside vase, Lawn Tennis, 3¾" ... 180.00
1 w/typewriter, Gentlemen 165.00
1 wearing chef's costume, holds frypan, w/basket 275.00
2, fat couple sitting, A Fine Looking Couple 200.00
2, mother & baby in bl blanket in tub, rabbit on board atop ... 175.00
2, mother & baby in cradle, Hush a Bye..., gold trim, 3¼x3¼" ... 225.00
2, mother in tub gives baby a bottle, lamb looks on, 4x3½" ... 175.00
2, 1 cutting hair of 2nd, A Little Bit Off the Top, 3x3½" ... 250.00
2, 1 lg (Scratch My Back) & 1 sm (Me Too), match holder, 5" ... 155.00
2 at confession, 4½" 145.00
2 at pump, bank, Good Old Annual, 3¾" 170.00
2 at pump & trough, 3¼" W 170.00
2 at telephone, unmk, 4" 165.00
2 at wishing well 165.00
2 by eggshell 110.00
2 by washtub, toothpick holder, souvenir of White City, 3¾" W ... 135.00
2 coming out of woven basket, 3" W 115.00
2 courting in touring car, trinket holder, 4½" W 225.00
2 dancing, in top hat, tux & cane 175.00
2 in carriage 175.00
2 in front of oval washtub w/hdls, 3" W 135.00
2 in open trunk, 3¾" 125.00
2 in purse 115.00
2 looking in phonograph horn, tray, 4½" W 200.00
2 on cotton bale, 1 peers from hole, 1 over top 175.00
2 on seesaw on top of pouch bank 175.00
2 on top hat 125.00
2 on tray hugging 125.00
2 singing, receptacle behind, gold trim, 4½" 265.00
2 sitting at table playing card game 'Hearts' 225.00
2 sitting by heart-shaped opening, trinket holder, 4" W ... 110.00
2 teeter-tottering over log bank, 3½" L 125.00
2 w/accordion camera, tray, 4½" W 150.00
3, mother w/2 babies, The Dinner Bell, planter, 3¾" W ... 145.00
3, 1 on lg slipper playing banjo, 2 dancing on side 195.00
3, 2 sit in front of coal bucket, 3rd inside 175.00
3 (center pig w/accordion) on tray, gold trim, 6½" L ... 275.00
3 dressed up on edge of dish 150.00
3 in trolley car, conductor at front, 4¼x3¼" 175.00

3 piglets behind oval trough, mk, 2¾x2½x1¾" 135.00
3 piglets in egg-shaped basin, Triplets of Fancy, mk Germany ... 150.00
3 sitting at trough, 4½" 100.00
3 w/baby carriage, father & 2 babies, Wheeling His Own ... 225.00
3 w/carriage, mother & 2 babies, Germany 195.00
4, mother pushing cart w/3 babies, clovers on wheels, vase, 3½" ... 195.00
4, 3 piglets in cart, 1 wheeling, More the Merrier 150.00

Pisgah Forest

The Pisgah Forest Pottery was established in 1920 near Mount Pisgah in Arden, North Carolina, by Walter B. Stephen, who had worked in previous years at other locations in the state — Nonconnah and Skyland (the latter from 1913 until 1916). Stephen, who was born in the mountain region near Asheville, was known for his work in the Southern tradition. He produced skillfully executed wares exhibiting an amazing variety of techniques. He operated his business with only two helpers. Recognized today as his most outstanding accomplishment, his Cameo line was decorated by hand in the pate-sur-pate style (similar to Wedgwood Jasper) in such designs as Fiddler and Dog, Spinning Wheel, Covered Wagon, Buffalo Hunt, Mountain Cabin, Square Dancers, Indian Campfire, and Plowman. Stephen is known for other types of wares as well. His crystalline glaze is highly regarded by today's collectors.

At least nine different stamps mark his wares, several of which contain the outline of the potter at the wheel and 'Pisgah Forest.' Cameo is sometimes marked with a circle containing the line name and 'Long Pine, Arden, NC.' Two other marks may be more difficult to recognize: 1) a circle containing the outline of a pine tree, 'N.C.' to the left of the trunk and 'Pine Tree' on the other side; and 2) the letter 'P' with short uprights in the middle of the top and lower curves. Stephen died in 1961, but the work was continued by his associates. Our advisor for this category is R. J. Sayers; he is listed in the Directory under North Carolina.

Bowl, cobalt w/unglazed int, illegible date, 3x5" 60.00
Bowl, cvd heart & floral, turq (thin), 1951, 6½" 48.00
Bowl, gr w/yel int, 2⅝x7½" 42.50
Jar, gr w/rose int, w/lid, 1951, 4x3¾" 42.50
Jar, plum w/wht int, w/lid, 1953, 4x3¾" 55.00
Jar, turq w/pk int, 1953, w/lid, 4x3¾", NM 55.00
Jug, purple crackle, glaze bursts, 1934, 10x6½" 265.00
Pitcher, plum w/wht int, illegible date, 3⅝x4¼" 25.00
Planter, gr w/horizontal ribs, peach int 36.00
Vase, bl crackle w/dk red accents, shouldered, 1930s, 11¾x6¼" ... 800.00

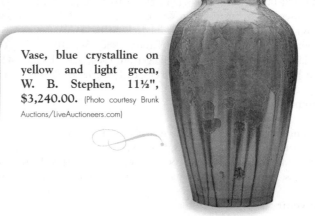

Vase, blue crystalline on yellow and light green, W. B. Stephen, 11½", $3,240.00. (Photo courtesy Brunk Auctions/LiveAuctioneers.com)

Vase, bl to rose crystalline, bulbous, 6" 120.00
Vase, Cameo, figures, wht on gr, Stephen, 1959, 13½x8" ... 1,350.00

Vase, Cameo, wagon train, dk gr w/seafoam base, 1953, 4½" 350.00
Vase, gr & tan crystalline, spherical, 4x5" 275.00
Vase, gr & yel crystalline, 7½x4" 330.00
Vase, gr w/pk int, baluster, 1951, 6½" 60.00
Vase, ivory & bl crystalline on celadon, baluster, 1946, 9x5" 1,100.00
Vase, ivory crystalline w/pk int, flared rim, 4½x4" 315.00
Vase, lt turq crackle w/pk int, 4" 50.00
Vase, maroon & gray speckled, flared rim, 3¼" 75.00
Vase, plum, squat, 1941, 3x4⅛" 42.50
Vase, turq w/pk int, squat, 1950, 3⅝x4⅜" 72.50
Vase, wht/bl/amber crystalline, baluster, 1939, 6¼x4", NM 490.00

Playing Cards

Playing cards can be an enjoyable way to trace the course of history. Knowledge of the art, literature, and politics of an era can be gleaned from a study of its playing cards. When royalty lost favor with the people, kings and queens were replaced by common people. During the periods of war, generals, officers, and soldiers were favored. In the United States, early examples had portraits of Washington and Adams as opposed to kings, Indian chiefs instead of jacks, and goddesses for queens. Tarot cards were used in Europe during the 1300s as a game of chance, but in the eighteenth century they were used to predict the future and were regarded with great reverence.

The backs of cards were of no particular consequence until the 1890s. The marble design used by the French during the late 1800s and the colored wood-cut patterns of the Italians in the nineteenth century are among the first attempts at decoration. Later the English used cards printed with portraits of royalty. Eventually cards were decorated with a broad range of subjects from reproductions of fine art to advertising.

Although playing cards are now popular collectibles, prices are still relatively low. Complete decks of cards printed earlier than the first postage stamp can still be purchased for less than $100.00. In the listings that follow, decks are without boxes unless the box is specifically mentioned.

For more information we recommend *Collecting Playing Cards* by Mark Pickvet (Collector Books). Information concerning the American Antique Deck Collectors Club, 52 Plus Joker, may be found in the Directory under Clubs, Newsletters, and Catalogs.

Key: J — joker

Advertising

Alcoa Steamship, dbl deck w/red/blk bks, 1960s, MIB 15.00
Anheuser-Busch, Army-Navy, gilt edges, early 1900s, 52, NMIB ... 950.00
Anheuser-Busch, Spanish-Am War, early 1900s, 52, NMIB 1,080.00
Cooks Products, boy painter bks, dbl deck, MIB 50.00
Dupont Hotel, Fournier Heraclid Vitoria, 1980s, 54, MIB 60.00
President Suspenders, gr bks, CA Edgerton, 1904, 52+J, EXIB 425.00
Wht Star Cruise Line, sailing ship bks, ca 1940, 52, EX/VG box. 360.00

Pinups

MacPherson brunette, 1944, 52+special card, EX in special box ... 15.00
Quick on the Draw, cowgirl bks, 1946, 52+J, EXIB 15.00
Vargas cowgirls on bks, Brown & Bigelow, 1947, dbl deck, EXIB .. 30.00
Wolf bks, varied nudes on fronts, 1950s, 52+J, EXIB 30.00

Souvenir

Columbian World's Fair, fair buildings bks, GW Clark, 1893, 52+J, EXIB...72.50
Jeffries Championship, boxer photos, ca 1910, 62+J, VGIB 195.00

Jim Jefferies Championship, heavyweight boxer, 1909, 52 plus joker, extra card and booklet, NMIB, $600.00.

Lyndon Johnson Air Force One, dbl decks, MIB 60.00
NASA Fireproof Bicycle Brand, ca 1960s, 52+J, EXIB 95.00
Ronald Reagan Air Force One, dbl deck, sealed, MIB 265.00

Miscellaneous

Blk character photos & illustrations, Baldwin, 1896, 52, EX 240.00
Commander in Chief, Abraham Lincoln, Union figures, 1860s, 44, EX.. 30.00
Eagle/stars/laurel wreath bks, Samuel Hart & Co, 1880s, 52, EXIB.. 135.00
Game of Fireside Authors, Cincinnati, 1897, EXIB 72.50
Knuckle Down, marble players bks, 1906, 2 complete decks, ea EXIB .850.00
Lafayette Ace of Spades, J Ford, MA, 1824, single 3½x2½", NM..1,200.00
Native Am photos on front, geometric bks, 1920s, 52+J, EX 360.00
No 916 Squared Faro, A Ball & Bro, 52, EXIB 900.00
Stevens Am Royalty, Pat Sept 21 1869, 52+J, NMIB, from $850 to .. 1,325.00
Tiffany Harlequin Transformation, CE Carryl, ca 1879, 52C, NM ..1,450.00
Transparent Playing Cards, 1860s, 52+J+Bazique Register, EX+ 1,450.00

Political

Many of the most valuable political items are those from any period which relate to a political figure whose term was especially significant or marked by an important event or one whose personality was particularly colorful. Posters, ribbons, badges, photographs, and pin-back buttons are but a few examples of the items popular with collectors of political memorabilia. Political campaign pin-back buttons were first mass produced and widely distributed in 1896 for the president-to-be William McKinley and for the first of three unsuccessful attempts by William Jennings Bryan. Pin-back buttons have been used during each presidential campaign ever since and are collected by many people. Some of the scarcest are those used in the presidential campaigns of John W. Davis in 1924 and James Cox in 1920.

Contributions to this category were made by Michael J. McQuillen, monthly columnist of *Political Parade*, which appears in *AntiqueWeek* newspapers; he is listed in the Directory under Indiana. Our advisor for this category is Paul J. Longo; he is listed under Massachusetts. See also Autographs; Historical Glass; Watch Fobs.

Badge, police; emb Inauguration...Eisenhower...Nixon, 1953, 3¼x3" . 600.00
Cane, Abe Lincoln bust on front, walnut & rosewood, 1900, 35"...875.00
Cartoon, GOP elephant in tails dancing, OH BOY!, CL Mortison, '56, 11" ..70.00
Cartoon, Hoover as lg elephant w/$300 billion 'Economy Bills,' 13x10" . 175.00
Coin, commemorative; Jimmy Carter portrait on gold, Jan 20, 1971. 40.00
Coin, commemorative; Nixon/Agnew, Franklin Mint, Jan 20 1973, 2¾". 35.00
Cuff links, Ronald Reagan Presidential seal, mc, 1981,¾", MIB ..250.00
Doll, Ronald Reagan wearing suit, Special Edition, 1987, 19x8", MIB..30.00
Drum, Grover Cleveland Our Next President, HP portrait, 36½" dia.. 1,150.00
Lapel pin, Abe Lincoln portrait, celluloid, 1909 issue, 1¼" 20.00
Lapel pin, Cleveland & Thurman, emb metal, clip-on, 1888, ½" .. 45.00
License plate, Roosevelt for President, red letters on wht 85.00
License plate topper, Win With Landon, wht letters on red, 1930s, 6" L.....125.00

Matchbook cover, JFK photo, Kennedy for President, Vote Democratic... 12.00
Pennant, Barry Goldwater portrait, red VOTE Goldwater on wht, 1964.. 35.00
Pennant, Truman Inauguration, wht letters on maroon, Jan 20, 1949 ..... 180.00
Photo (CDV), Andrew Jackson, E&HT Anthony Manufacturers..., 4x2½".175.00
Plate, Aboard Air Force One & Jimmy Carter sgn emb on clear glass, 8"....170.00

Plate, from Dwight D. Eisenhower administration, inscribed 'The White House November 1955,' marked Castleton Studios, bone china, 11½", $6,500.00. (Photo courtesy Skinner Inc. Auctioneers & Appraisers of Antiques & Fine Art)

Poster, Democratic Convention Nominees, blk & red on wht, 1960, 30x45"..175.00
Poster, FDR & Uncle Sam portraits, I Want You...Job!, 1939, 21x16½"..300.00
Poster, Kennedy/Healey portraits, Vote Democratic..., 1960, 21x13½"..70.00
Poster, Robert Kennedy portrait, Kennedy in red & bl letters, 19x12" ..60.00
Poster, Uncle Sam w/thumb down, No Third Term!, ...Willkie, 4x8" ...60.00
Print, Harry Truman sitting at desk, wht fr, 1949, 27x22" 60.00
Ribbon, Abraham Lincoln portrait, blk letters on bl, 1864, 6x2½" ..2,300.00
Ribbon, Benjamin Harrison portrait, Delaware Co Delegation, 1888, 7".. 75.00
Ribbon, McKinley/Hobart portraits on red/wht/bl, 1896, 7x2" 65.00
Stick pin, William H Taft's emb face & For President, NJ Aluminum.40.00
Ticket, Democratic National Convention; Convention Floor Staff, 1924...35.00
Tie clasp, Kennedy on boat emb on front, JFK PT109, brass, 1960, 2" ..35.00
Token, Bryan's Money w/4 stars & head emb on metal, 1900 .... 70.00
Tray, Roosevelt/McKinley portraits, oval, Kobacker's, 1900s, 13x16" . 600.00
Tray, William Jennings Bryan portrait, floral rim, oval, tin, 16x13"..... 200.00
Watch fob, cello Woodrow Wilson button on leather, w/buckle, 1916 .70.00

Pin-back Buttons

Alton Parker/HG Davis portraits w/flag, 1904, 1¼"..................... 110.00
Bryan/Stevenson portraits on red/wht/bl shield, 1900s, 1¼" 75.00
Herbert Hoover blk & wht portait, For President, metal rim, 1".... 40.00
Hoover/Curtis jugate, blk & wht portraits, Greenduck Co, 1928, 1", VG. 75.00
Joseph W Savage portrait, For Leader (Tammany Hall), 1905, 1", G ..28.00
Kennedy/Johnson, Leaders of Our Country...World, red/wht/bl, 3" ..52.00
Mamie Eisenhower/Pat Nixon portraits, 1952, 3½"........................ 25.00
McKinley & Harris Ohio, disk hangs from clasped hands, tin, 1891, 3"... 65.00
McKinley portrait, Count Us for McKinley, Buffalo Express, 1896, 1" ..52.00
Our President Harry S Truman, blk & wht portrait center, 1½"... 155.00
Parker & Davis portraits in heart, lady w/flag at bottom, 1904, ⅞" .125.00
Theodore Roosevelt, blk & wht portrait & red/wht/bl flag, 1¼" ..125.00
Theodore Roosevelt, First Voters Club, sepia portrait, 1904, 1"..... 90.00
Truman & Forrest Smith, bl letters on wht, 2" 1,900.00
Vote Republican/All the Way, flasher, Pictorial..., 1952, 2½" 38.00
We Want Harold Stassen, crossed guns, red/wht/bl, 1948, 1¾"...... 35.00
Who? Who? Hoover, owl shape, enameled metal............................ 40.00
William Howard Taft portrait, Whitehead & Hoag, 1" 45.00
Wilson/Marshall, blk & wht portraits, 1", VG................................ 30.00

Pomona

Pomona glass was patented in 1885 by the New England Glass Works. Its characteristics are an etched background of crystal lead glass often decorated with simple designs painted with metallic stains of amber or blue. The etching was first achieved by hand cutting through an acid resist. This method, called first ground, resulted in an uneven feather-like frost effect. Later, to cut production costs, the hand-cut process was discontinued in favor of an acid bath which effected an even frosting. This method is called second ground.

Bowl, fruit; 2nd ground, cornflowers, ruffled, 8½" 300.00
Bowl, 1st ground, cornflowers, petaled base, 3½x8" 500.00
Card holder, 1st ground, ruffled amber rim, 2¼x4" 350.00
Celery vase, 2nd ground, crimped top, appl ft, 6½" 200.00
Creamer & sugar bowl, 2nd ground, ruffled rim, amber hdls, 2¾" ...185.00
Creamer & sugar bowl, 2nd ground, ruffled rim, ftd, 5½" W; 3½" W .225.00
Pickle castor, 2nd ground, cornflowers; rstr Meriden #228 fr, 11¾" ..1,800.00

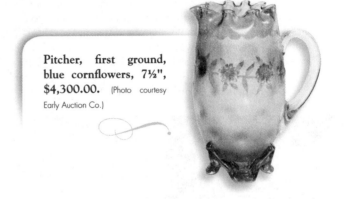

Pitcher, first ground, blue cornflowers, 7½", $4,300.00. (Photo courtesy Early Auction Co.)

Salt cellar, bl cornflowers, cylindrical, 3½" 425.00
Tumbler, lemonade; 1st ground, cornflowers, 5¾"........................ 350.00
Wine, 1st ground, 5⅜" 550.00

Postcards

Postcards are often very difficult to evaluate, since so many factors must be considered — for instance the subject matter or the field of interest they represent. For example: A 1905 postcard of the White House in Washington D.C. may seem like a desirable card, but thousands were produced and sold to tourists who visited there, thus the market is saturated with this card, and there are few collectors to buy it. Value: less than $1.00. However, a particular view of small town of which only 500 were printed could sell for far more, provided you find someone interested in the subject matter pictured on that card. Take as an example a view of the courthouse in Hillsville, Virginia. This card would appeal to those focusing on that locality or county as well as courthouse collectors. Value: $5.00.

The ability of the subject to withstand time is also a key factor when evaluating postcards. Again using the courthouse as an example, one built in 1900 and still standing in the 1950s has been photographed for 50 years, from possibly 100 different angles. Compare that with one built in 1900 and replaced in 1908 due to a fire, and you can see how much more desirable a view of the latter would be. But only a specialist would be aware of the differences between these two examples.

Postcard dealers can very easily build up stocks numbering in the hundred thousands. Greeting and holiday cards are common and represent another area of collecting that appeals to an entirely different following than the view card. These types of cards range from heavily embossed designs to floral greetings and, of course, include the ever popular Santa Claus card. These were very popular from about 1900 until the 1920s, when postcard communication was the equivalent of today's quick phone call or e-mail. Because of the vast number of them printed, many have little if any value to a collector. For instance, a 1909 Easter card with tiny images or a common floral card of the same vintage, though almost

100 years old, is virtually worthless. It's the cards with appeal and zest that command the higher prices. One with a beautiful Victorian woman in period clothing, her image filling up the entire card, could easily be worth $3.00 and up. Holiday cards designed for Easter, Valentine's Day, Thanksgiving, and Christmas are much more common than those for New Year's, St. Patrick's Day, the 4th of July, and Halloween. Generally, then, they can be worth much less; but depending on the artist, graphics, desirability, and eye appeal, this may not always be true. The signature of a famous artist will add significant value — conversely, an unknown artist's signature adds none.

In summary, the best way to evaluate your cards is to have a knowledgeable dealer look at them. For a list of dealers, send an SASE to the International Federation of Postcard Dealers, c/o Juanita Clemens, 462 Freeman Rd., Greensburg, PA 15601. Do not expect a dealer to price cards from a list or written description as this is not possible. For individual questions or evaluation by photocopy (front and back), you may contact our advisor, Jeff Bradfield, 90 Main St., Dayton, VA 22821. You **must** include an SASE for a reply. For more information we recommend *The Collector's Guide to Postcards* by Jane Wood, *Vintage Postcards for the Holidays* by Robert and Claudette Reed, and *The Golden Age of Postcards, Early 1900s*, by Benjamin H. Penniston (Collector Books).

Real photo, baseball team, silver print, light wear at corners, VG, $15.00. (Photo courtesy Cowan's Auctions Inc/LiveAuctioneers.com)

Posters

Advertising posters by such French artists as Cheret and Toulouse-Lautrec were used as early as the mid-1800s. Color lithography spurred their popularity. Circus posters by the Strobridge Lithograph Co. are considered to be the finest in their field, though Gibson and Co. Litho, Erie Litho, and Enquirer Job Printing Co. printed fine examples as well. Posters by noted artists such as Mucha, Parrish, and Hohlwein bring high prices. Other considerations are good color, interesting subject matter and, of course, condition. The WWII posters listed below are among the more expensive examples; 70% of those on the market bring less than $65.00. Values are for examples in excellent condition to near mint unless noted otherwise. See also Movie Memorabilia; Rock 'n Roll.

Advertising

Chocolate Menier, girl writing on wall, Camis, Paris, 1896, 15x11"..450.00
Hercules Powder, Game Bird of Future - Chinese Pheasants, 18x21"............525.00
Monster Beery Exhibitions, Wild West images, OH, 1918, 36x24"...........475.00
Overland, July, blk bird's silhouette on bl, 18½x13" 1,100.00
Placards, Zurich Art Business Museum, Pfister, 1953, 50x36" 250.00
Prof EB Carver's Horse Training Exhibition, Courier, 28x21".........725.00
Ragan-Malone Dry Goods & Notions, lady w/flower, ca 1900, 29x20".........725.00
Remington UMC, man & dog hunt birds, Watson, 26x18" 1,550.00
Schweizerische Radio & Fernseh-Ausstellung..., 1950s, 60x36" ..325.00
Shell Cracker, 2 Shots in 1, man shooting on yel, 1950s, 27x19"...........50.00
Shoot DuPont Powders, various scenes, Bogue-Hunt, 1920, 30x20" 160.00
Stetson, Last Drop From His Stetson, man & horse, 30x24" 200.00
Stickney & Poor's Mustards, Yours for..., child in red, 20x15" 300.00
We Sell Peters Shells, mallards in flight, Ketterlinus, 9x12" 1,050.00
Western Ammunition, Warning, moose scene, Edwards, 1921, 30x17"...........2,000.00

Circus

Key:
   B&B — Barnum & Bailey   RB — Ringling Brothers

Al G Barnes & Sells - Floto, lion on elephant's bk, 41x28" 950.00
B&B, LaRoche et la Boule Mysteriuse, in 41x31" 1,650.00
B&B, Greatest Show..., 4 trains w/70 railroad cars, 1839, 42x33"...850.00

Cole Bros. Circus, The Great Florenzo, Erie Litho Mfg. Co., EX, $700.00. (Photo courtesy Morphy Auctions/LiveAuctioneers.com)

RB/B&B, Berta Beeson trapeze artist, 41x28" 600.00
RB/B&B, chariot, 1934, 28x22", VG+..160.00
RB/B&B, Clown head, See You At..., 1950s, 63x50" 600.00
RB/B&B, Gargantua the Great, 1936, 24x42+bottom date sheet....................1,100.00
RB/B&B, Greatest Show..., elephant balancing, 1944, 44x61"....................950.00

Theatrical

Daly's Theatre, Artist's Model, Paris, P Dupont, 1895, 14x11"+fr...325.00
Folly or Saintliness, Jose Echegaray, Boston, 1895, 20¾x15"+fr...600.00
Jane Marnac, Casino de Paris, lady w/feathers, Kiffer/1928, 62x46"..........4,800.00
Madison Sq, Young Mrs Winthrop, portrait/12 scenes, Morgan, 30x23"...........480.00
Marsyas of de Betooverde Bron, Nouveau lady, Roland-Holst, 40x29"............2,650.00
My 'Soldier' Boy, Criterion Theatre, D Allen & Sons, 29x19"............240.00
Palais de Glase, lady in red, J Cheret, 1894, 22¼x15" 950.00
Stormbeaten, Ships Afire, Union Theater, Strobridge, 29x19"..........825.00
Terry's Theatre, White Night, Allen &B Sons, Harrow, 28x18" 240.00
Theatre Cluny, Le Fance de Thilda, Paris, 1900, 32x22", VG 250.00
Theatre Natl de L'Opera Bal Gavarni, lady in blk/wht, 1923, 62x47"..........2,300.00

Travel

Budapest, Cathedral of St Matthias, 1930s, 37½x25" 900.00
Cheverny, Chateaux de la Loire, E Paul Champseix, 1930s, 39x24"..525.00
CO Rockies, Black Hills & UT, Veentstra, ca 1935, 41x27".....2,150.00
Holland, sailboat scene, Wilmink, linen bk, 1930s, 39x25" 850.00
Lights of Adelaide from Mount Lofty Ranges, Letterpress, 1935, 40x24".. 1,550.00
Mexico, trains/cars/planes in cityscape, 1940s, 36½x27"..............850.00
N Wales for Holiday, Snowdon Summit, Broders, 1929, 40x25"...3,200.00
San Francisco, old bridge, H Koslow, ca 1964, 38x25" 1,325.00
Ski Stowe Vermont, snowy mountain scene, Maurer, 40x23½" ...675.00
Switzerland, Territet-Mont-Fleur, mountain scene, 1904, 39x37"...780.00
Visit Palestine, tree w/cityscape beyond, ca 1930, 39x27".........2,150.00

War

WWI, Civilians When We Go..., soldiers, Jewish Welfare Board, 33x21"..900.00
WWI, Keep These Off USA, bloody boots, Norton, 1918, 40½x30½"..400.00
WWI, Sure We'll Finish the Job, farmer w/hand in pocket, 1918, 38x26" ..480.00
WWI, You Can Help, Red Cross, lady knitting, Benda, 1918, 40x20".425.00
WWII, Even a Little Can Help a Lot, mother & daughter, Parker, 20x14"..235.00
WWII, My Daddy Bought Me a...Bond, blond girl, prof rpr, 30x20"... 240.00
WWII, This Is Enemy, cobra w/swastika on raised head, 1943, 34x26" ..1,200.00
WWII, We Made a Monkey..., satire of Hitler & Uncle Sam, King, 19x15"..175.00

Pot Lids

Pot lids were pottery covers for containers that were used for hair dressing, potted meats, etc. The most common were decorated with colorful transfer prints under the glaze in a variety of themes, animal and scenic. The first and probably the largest company to manufacture these lids was F. & R. Pratt of Fenton, Staffordshire, established in the early 1800s. The name or initials of Jesse Austin, their designer, may sometimes be found on exceptional designs. Although few pot lids were made after the 1880s, the firm continued into the twentieth century. American pot lids are very rare. Most have been dug up by collectors searching through sites of early gold rush mining towns in California. In the following listings, all lids are transfer printed. Minor rim chips are expected and normally do not detract from listed values. When no condition is given, assume that the value is based on an example in such condition.

Alas Poor Bruin, mc transfer, Pratt, sm, VG, +base 110.00
Begging Dog, mc transfer, Pratt, 3" 80.00
Blue Boy, mc transfer, Pratt, 4¾" dia 125.00
Boots Cash Chemists Tooth Paste, blk transfer, ca 1900, 2¾" 75.00
Bryan of Gravesend Hair Restorer, blk transfer, 1870-80, 3" 160.00
Celetrated Heal All Ointment, Mrs Ellen Hales..., blk transfer ... 125.00
Creme Laferriere Secret de Jeunesse, blk transfer, 3½" 90.00
Crosse Blackwell Anchovy Paste, brn transfer, EX, +base 160.00
Dr Ziemer's Alexandra Tooth Paste, blk & wht w/gold border, 3¾". 250.00
James Atkinson's Bears Grease, blk transfer, 2½", +base 110.00
Paris Exhibition 1878, Crystal Palace, mc transfer, +base 165.00
Peasant Boys, mc transfer w/gold flecks, 4¾", EX, +base 165.00
Shooting Bears, mc transfer, Pratt, 3" 180.00
Thornton's Celebrated Toilet Cream, blk transfer 125.00
Victor Emmanuel Meeting Garibaldi, mc transfer, EX 125.00
Village Wakes, mc transfer, Pratt, 3", EX, +base 195.00

William's Swiss Violet Shaving Cream prepared by the J. B. Williams Co., ca. 1870 – 1890, multicolored transfer, 3¾", with original pot, $345.00. (Photo courtesy Glass-Works Auctions)

Powder Horns and Flasks

Though powder horns had already been in use for hundreds of years, collectors usually focus on those made after the expansion of the United States westward in the very early 1800s. While some are basic and very simple, others were scrimshawed and highly polished. Especially nice carvings can quickly escalate the value of a horn that has survived intact to as high as $1,000.00 or more. Those with detailed maps, historical scenes, etc., bring even higher prices. Metal flasks were introduced in the 1830s; by the middle of the century they were produced in quantity and at prices low enough that they became a viable alternative to the powder horn. Today's collector regards the smaller flasks as the more desirable and valuable, and those made for specific companies bring premium prices.

Flask, brass, Ames, US insignia, clasped hands, dtd 1946, EX 400.00
Flask, brass, Batty, shield/flags/trumpet/cannon/etc, dtd 1849, X 395.00

Flask, brass, Batty, shield/stars/coat of arms/eagle, 1853, 9¼", VG.... 350.00
Horn, cvd landscape w/birds/flags/banners/etc, 19th C, 8¾" 1,200.00
Horn, cvg at spout, brass tacks at base & neck, 1850s, 14x3"....... 750.00

Horn, Civil War-era warships, motto: Don't Give Up the Ship, two large fish, stacking hearts, and original wood base cap partially encircled with brass tacks, 14½", $1,450.00. (Photo courtesy Jackson's International Auctioneers & Appraisers of Fine Art & Antiques)

Horn, scratch-cvd sailing ships/fort/lighthouse/flags, 15½".......... 575.00
Horn, scratched-cvd name/1771, wooden cap, splits at plug, 12"..1,150.00

Pratt

Prattware has become a generic reference for a type of relief-molded earthenware with polychrome decoration. Scenic motifs with figures were popular; sometimes captions were added. Jugs are most common, but teapots, tableware, even figurines were made. The term 'Pratt' refers to Wm. Pratt of Lane Delph, who is credited with making the first examples of this type, though similar wares were made later by other Staffordshire potters. Pot lids and other transfer wares marked Pratt were made in Fenton, Staffordshire, by F. & R. Pratt & Co. See also Pot Lids.

Creamer, cow figural/boy at side, tail hdl, mc, 1890s, 5½" 230.00
Figurine, lioness, ochre & brn, 1790-1810, 3x4" 450.00
Figurine, Netherfish, sheep head/fish body, mc, rstr, 1810s, 7¾".. 2,400.00
Flask, Frolicking Cherubs, mc, vertical ribs at top & base, 5¾" ... 600.00
Jug, Mischievous Children, mc scenes, acanthus border, 1790s, 7" .. 350.00
Jug, tavern scenes, feather motif at spout/hdl, 9", VG 2,750.00
Mug, man on donkey among cattle & sheep, mc reserve on red, 3"... 150.00
Plate, 4 boys w/birds in nest, blk transfer, mc rim, 1830s, 7½" 150.00
Vase, man by tree stump, duck & dog at ft, mc, 1780-1830, rstr, 6" . 475.00

Primitives

Like the mouse that ate the grindstone, so has collectible interest in primitives increased, a little bit at a time, until demand is taking bites instead of nibbles into their availability. Although the term 'primitives' once referred to those survival essentials contrived by our American settlers, it has recently been expanded to include objects needed or desired by succeeding generations — items representing the cabin-'n-corn-patch existence as well as examples of life on larger farms and in towns. Through popular usage, it also respectfully covers what are actually 'country collectibles.' From the 1600s into the latter 1800s, factories employed carvers, blacksmiths, and other artisans whose handwork contributed to turning out quality items. When buying, 'touchmarks,' a company's name and/or location and maker's or owner's initials, are exciting discoveries.

Primitives are uniquely individual. Following identical forms, results more often than not show typically personal ideas. Using this as a guide (combined with circumstances of age, condition, desire to own, etc.) should lead to a reasonably accurate evaluation. For items not listed, consult comparable examples. For more information refer to *Antique Tools, Our American Heritage,* by Katheryn McNerney (Collector Books). See also Butter Molds and Stamps; Boxes; Copper; Farm Collectibles; Fireplace Implements; Kitchen Collectibles; Molds; Tinware; Weaving; Woodenware; Wrought Iron.

Bedwarmer, copper w/tooled bird/flowers, wood hdl, 42" L 315.00
Bucket, stave & hoop, mc pnt sqs/speckles, MA, 19th C, 3½x4⅜"....300.00
Bucket, staved/interlocking hoops, cvd/pegged/pin hdls, red pnt, 8"..260.00
Butter paddle, maple w/central pinwheel w/geometric cvgs, 9".... 285.00
Churn, staved wood, old red pnt, inset lid & dasher, OH, 22x14"..545.00
Drying rack, cypress, folding/3-part, CI mts, 50x30" (ea section)....950.00
Firkin, bentwood bands w/copper & iron tacks, old gr rpt, 14x15".....575.00

Firkin, green-painted pine, marked C. Wilder & Sons, So. Hingman, Massachusetts, 12", VG, $735.00. (Photo courtesy Skinner Inc. Auctioneers & Appraisers of Antiques & Fine Art/LiveAuctioneers.com)

Firkin, staved w/stapled bentwood bands, yel stain, w/lid, OH, 10" ...145.00
Firkin, staved wood, metal/wood bands, copper tacks, old pnt, 6½"...450.00
Firkin, staved wood w/2-finger bentwood bands, gr pnt, 9¼" 250.00
Firkin, 3-finger w/1 finger lid, old gr pnt, 10x9½" 865.00
Loom, tape; thick pine w/sq nails, 2 ratchet posts, 16x18x10" 230.00
Mortar, curly maple, 9⅛x6", +trn pestle... 315.00
Mortar, trn burl w/old rfn & good color, 7x5½", +trn pestle 260.00
Slaw cutter, curly maple w/EX color, att OH, 14½x5¾" 200.00
Tub, staved wood, iron bands, pierced hdls, pnt, 19th C, 20x23" dia.880.00
Yarn winder, 3-leg, old pnt w/HP foliage, clicking mechanism, 42" ...285.00

Prints

The term 'print' may be defined today as almost any image printed on paper by any available method. Examples of collectible old 'prints' are Norman Rockwell magazine covers and Maxfield Parrish posters and calendars. 'Original print' refers to one achieved through the efforts of the artist or under his direct supervision. A 'reproduction' is a print produced by an accomplished print maker who reproduces another artist's print or original work. Thorough study is required on the part of the collector to recognize and appreciate the many variable factors to be considered in evaluating a print. Prices vary from one area of the country to another and are dependent upon new findings regarding the scarcity or abundance of prints as such information may arise. Although each collector of old prints may have their own varying criteria by which to judge condition, for those who deal only rarely in this area or newer collectors, a few guidelines may prove helpful. Staining, though unquestionably detrimental, is nearly always present in some degree and should be weighed against the rarity of the print. Professional cleaning should improve its appearance and at the same time help preserve it. Avoid tears that affect the image; minor margin tears are another matter, especially if the print is a rare one. Moderate 'foxing' (brown spots caused by mold or the fermentation of the rag content of old paper) and light stains from the old frames are not serious unless present in excess. Margin trimming was a common practice; but look for at least ½" to 1½" margins, depending on print size.

When no condition is indicated, the items listed below are assumed to be in very good to excellent condition. See also Nutting, Wallace; Parrish, Maxfield. For more information we recommend *Beaux Arts Pocket Guide to American Art Prints* by Michael Bozarth and *Collector's Value Guide to Early 20th Century American Prints* by Michael Ivankovich.

Audubon, John J.

Audubon is the best known of American and European wildlife artists. His first series of prints, 'Birds of America,' was produced by Robert Havell of London. They were printed on Whitman watermarked paper bearing dates of 1826 to 1838. The Octavo Edition of the same series was printed in seven editions, the first by J.T. Bowen under Audubon's direction. There were seven volumes of text and prints, each 10" x 7", the first five bearing the J.J. Audubon and J.B. Chevalier mark, the last two, J.J. Audubon. They were produced from 1840 through 1844. The second and other editions were printed up to 1871. The Bien Edition prints were full size, made under the direction of Audubon's sons in the late 1850s. Due to the onset of the Civil War, only 105 plates were finished. These are considered to be the most valuable of the reprints of the 'Birds of America Series.' In 1971 the complete set was reprinted by Johnson Reprint Corp. of New York and Theaturm Orbis Terrarum of Amsterdam. Examples of the latter bear the watermark G. Schut and Zonen. In 1985 a second reprint was done by Abbeville Press for the National Audubon Society. Although Audubon is best known for his portrayal of birds, one of his less-familiar series, 'Vivaparous Quadrupeds of North America,' portrayed various species of animals. Assembled in corroboration with John Bachman from 1839 until 1851, these prints are 28" x 22" in size. Several Octavo Editions were published in the 1850s. In the listings that follow, prints are unframed unless noted otherwise. Note: These prints have long been reproduced; with a magnifying glass or a jeweler's loop, check for the tiny dots that comprise an image made by photolithography. None are present on authentic Havell and Bien prints, since these were made from printing plates; brushstrokes will all so be apparent as these were hand tinted. Only prints from the Amsterdam Edition will have the dots; however, these must also bear the 'G Schut and Zonen Audubon' watermark to be authentic.

Our suggested values are actual current prices realized at auction. Our advisor for this category is Michael Bozarth; he is listed in the Directory under New York.

American Flamingo, Bien/375, 1960, sm losses, 38x25¾" 9,600.00
American Sparrow Hawk, Havell/142, 1832, fr: 32½x25½" 2,650.00
Azure Warbler, Havell/48, 1831, full sheet, 20x12½" 2,450.00
Black Warrior, J Whitman 1830, 29x25¼"+fr...........................5,750.00
Canada Jay, Havell/107, 1831, approximately 38x25", +fr........6,600.00
Canada Porcupine, JT Bowen/36, 1844, sight: 30x25", +fr 2,350.00
Chestnut-Backed Titmouse..., Havell/353, 1837, 38⅛x25⅜" 4,250.00
Common or Virginian Deer...Female, JT Bowen/136, 1848, 21⅝x27¼" .6,600.00
Fishhawk, Havell/81, 1830, 38½x25⅝" 16,800.00
Grizzly Bear, JT Bowen/131, Imperial folio, 1848, 21¼x27"...7,800.00
House Wren, Havell/83, 1831, sm rstr, 38x25¼", +fr 6,600.00
Ivory-Billed Woodpecker, Havell/66, 1829, 39x25⅝".............16,800.00
Jaguar, Female, JT Bowen/CL, 1846, 25x30", +fr......................1,175.00
Little Screech Owl, Havell/97, 1934, 38¼x25⅜", +mat & fr.........7,800.00
Mocking Bird, Bien #32/plate 138, 1860, old rstr, sight: 35½x23".1,880.00
Mocking Bird, Havell/21, London, 1827, 25¼x36¾", +fr........13,200.00
Nine-Banded Armadillo, JT Bowen/146, 1848, 21⅝x27¼".......7,800.00
Olive Sided Flycatcher, #174, Havell, 1833, elephant folio 3,950.00
Painted Finch, Havell/53, ca 1827-34, 19½x12¼", +mat & fr ..7,250.00
Red Breasted Merganser, Havell/CCCCI, 1837, 25x38" 12,000.00
Red Tailed Hawk, Havell/51, 1891, 38¼x25¼", +fr..................6,600.00
Ruffed Grouse, Havell/41, 1828, 25¹¹⁄₁₆x39" 11,400.00
Sandwich Tern, Florida Cray Fish; Havell, 1829, 25x37¼".......4,115.00
Stanley Hawk, Havell & Son, 1818, 29x25⅝", +fr...................5,575.00

Stanley Hawk, R Havell & Son, London 1828, 29x25⅜", +fr...**5,500.00**
Swift Fox - Male, JT Bowen/52, Philadelphia, 1844, full sheet .**6,000.00**
Texan Lynx, JT Bowen/92, 1846, full sheet, fr: 21¾x27½" **3,250.00**
Three-Toed Woodpecker, Havell/132, 1932, elephant folio, +fr ...**6,600.00**
Yellow Bird or American Goldfinch, Havell/33, 1828, 38x24¾" ...**7,800.00**
Yellow-Crowned Heron, Bien, 1960, 40x27" **5,150.00**

Currier and Ives

Nathaniel Currier was in business by himself until the late 1850s when he formed a partnership with James Merrit Ives. Currier is given credit for being the first to use the medium to portray newsworthy subjects, and the Currier and Ives views of nineteenth-century American culture are familiar to us all. In the following listings, 'C' numbers correspond with a standard reference book by Conningham. Values are given for prints in very good condition; all are colored unless indicated black and white. Unless noted 'NC' (Nathaniel Currier), all prints are published by Currier and Ives. Our advisor for this category is Michael Bozarth; he is listed in the Directory under New York.

American Country Life — Pleasures of Winter, large folio, $3,225.00. (Photo courtesy Garth's Auctions Inc.)

Accommodation Train, 1876, C-32, sm folio................................**400.00**
American Game, 1866, C-163, lg folio **750.00**
American Prize Fruit, C-183, lg folio, 30x38" **1,150.00**
Arguing the Point, NC, 1855, C-265, lg folio..........................**5,200.00**
Autumn in Adirondacks (Lake Harrison), undtd, C-323, sm folio ..**350.00**
Beautiful Brunette, undtd, C-453, sm folio **75.00**
Beauty of New England, undtd, C-462, sm folio...........................**65.00**
Between Two Fires, 1879, C-511, sm folio **300.00**
Bombardment of Fort Pulaski...April, 1862, C-595, sm folio **350.00**
Burning of Clipper...Golden Light, NC, undtd, C-740, sm folio..**450.00**
Catherine, NC, 1845, C-849, sm folio **90.00**
Champion Stallion Directum, 1893, C-975, sm folio **300.00**
Chicky's Dinner, undtd, C-1029, sm folio...................................**175.00**
City of New York, NC, 1855, C-1102, lg folio...........................**3,000.00**
Cottage Dooryard, Evening; NC, 1855, C-1265, med folio.........**400.00**
Custer's Last Charge, 1876, C-1333, sm folio **350.00**
Day of Marriage, 1847, NC, C-1459, sm folio............................**100.00**
Disputed Heat, Claiming Foul; 1878, C-1587, lg folio **1,800.00**
Drive Through the Highlands, undtd, C-1627, med folio **700.00**
Dutchman & Hiram Woodruff, 1871, C-1640, sm folio **700.00**
Elizabeth, NC, 1846, C-1698, sm folio..**95.00**
English Winter Scene, undtd, C-1745, sm folio...........................**525.00**
Flora Temple, NC, 1853, C-2015, lg folio................................**1,900.00**
Fruit & Flowers Piece, 1863, C-2160, med folio **400.00**
Gem of the Atlantic, NC, 1849, C-2228, sm folio **750.00**

General Lewis Cass, NC, 1846, C-2288, sm folio **95.00**
God Bless Our Home, undtd, C-2392, sm folio **250.00**
Got the Drop on Him, 1881, C-2455, sm folio **275.00**
Grand Pacer Richball, 1890, C-2519, sm folio **300.00**
Great Conflagration at Pittsburgh, NC, undtd, C-2581, sm folio....**650.00**
Last War Whoop, NC, 1856, C-3457, lg folio **2,800.00**
Life of a Hunter, Tight Fix; 1861, C-3522, lg folio.....................**4,400.00**
Lincoln Family, 1867, C-3546, sm folio **100.00**
Maiden's Rock, Mississippi River; C-3891, sm folio **500.00**
New England Winter Scene, 1861, C-4420, lg folio.................**6,450.00**
Peytona & Fashion in Their Great Match..., NC, undtd, C-4763, lg folio..**4,700.00**
President of the United States, C-4903, sm folio **175.00**
Ready for Trot, Bring Up Your Horses; 1877, C-5085, lg folio ..**2,000.00**
Road - Winter, NC, 1853, C-5171, lg folio...............................**25,850.00**
Snow Storm, undtd, C-5580, med folio **2,350.00**
Splendid Naval Triumph on Mississippi...1862, 1862, C-5659, lg folio...**1,050.00**
Steamer Penobscot, 19th C, C-5736, 26¼x38½" **6,325.00**
Summer Ramble, undtd, C-5874, med folio **400.00**
Surrender of General Burgoyne...1777, NC, 1852, C-5907, lg folio.**5,000.00**
Taking Back Track, Dangerous Neighborhood; 1866, C-5961, lg folio..**10,575.00**
Through to the Pacific, 1870, C-6051, sm folio **525.00**
Trolling for Blue Fish, 1866, C-6158, lg folio...........................**11,750.00**
Whale Fishery Laying On, NC, 1852, C-6626, sm folio.............**1,650.00**
Winter Evening, 1854, C-6734, med folio **1,300.00**
Winter Morning, 1861, C-6740, med folio **2,250.00**
Zachary Taylor, Nation's...; NC, 1847, C-6874, sm folio **175.00**

Erte (Romain de Tirtoff)

Dancer, 21¼x16"+fr..**575.00**
Deco nude, Print #4, sight: 22x17", +fr....................................**780.00**
Diva I, Diva II; from Diva Suite, sight: 35x26", +fr, pr **2,750.00**
Enchanted Melody, sight: 37x26", +fr......................................**1,650.00**
Glutton, serigraph, 19½x14", +silver metal fr **300.00**
Kiss of Fire, Love & Passion Suite, sight: 33x28", +fr.................**1,680.00**
Letter O, from Alphabet Suite, 15½x10½", +metal fr **300.00**
Marriage Dance, Love & Passion Suite, sight: 28x33", +fr........**2,400.00**
Portrait of a Woman, 20½x15¼" **575.00**
Pride, 19½x14¾", +silver metal fr **300.00**
Queen of Sheba, serigraph, 1980, sight: 25x18", +mat & fr **780.00**
Three Graces, 1985, sight: 26x18½", +mat & fr **1,800.00**
Vamps Suite, sight: 20x16", +fr, 6 for **2,400.00**
Winter Resorts, 1982, sight: 23x27", +mat & fr **600.00**
Woman in Cape, sight: 30½x20", +fr...**1,650.00**
3, from Numerals Suite, sight: 17¼x12⅜", +fr **395.00**

Fox, R. Atkinson

A Canadian who worked as an artist in the 1880s, R. Atkinson Fox moved to New York about 10 years later, where his original oils were widely sold at auction and through exhibitions. Today he is best known, however, for his prints, published by as many as 20 print makers. More than 30 examples of his work appeared on Brown and Bigelow calendars, and it was used in many other forms of advertising as well. Though he was an accomplished artist able to interpret any subject well, he is today best known for his landscapes. Fox died in 1935. Our advisor for Fox prints is Pat Gibson whose address is listed in the Directory under California.

Blooming Time, #37, 15x19" **250.00**
Canadian Landscape, #140, 1930s, 14x20"+orig bl & gold fr.......**185.00**
Colorful Rockies, The; #9, 8x10" **110.00**
Day's Work Done, The; #626, unfr, 8x11".................................**185.00**
Dreamland, #41, 1920-30s, 12x8"+orig ornate fr........................**65.00**
Fountain of Love, #3, 10x16" **100.00**

Moonlight & Roses, #39, 14x18" 125.00
Promenade, #10, 8x12"+Deco fr 75.00
Shower of Daisies, unsgn, #77, 6x14" 185.00
Spirit of Youth, #4, 1926, 9x15"+orig simple fr 100.00
Where Nature Beats in Perfect Tune, unsgn, #155, 10x18" 190.00

Gutmann, Bessie Pease (1876 – 1960)

Delicately tinted prints of appealing children sometimes accompanied by their pets, sometimes asleep, often captured at some childhood activity are typical of the work of this artist; she painted lovely ladies as well and was a successful illustrator of children's books. Her career spanned the five decades of the 1900s, and she recorded over 800 published artworks. Our advisor for this cagegory is Dr. Victor J.W. Christie; he is listed in the Directory under Pennsylvania.

Aeroplane, The; #266/#695, 14x21" 900.00
Always, #744, 14x21" 2,600.00
American Girl, The; #220, 13x18" 500.00
An Anxious Moment, #714, 14x21" 650.00
Annunciation, #705, 14x21" 1,200.00
Awakening, #664, 14x21" 125.00
Baby's First Birthday, #618, 14x21" 750.00
Baby's First Christmas, #158 .... 500.00

The Bedtime Story, #712, 14x21", $750.00.
(Photo courtesy Dr. J.W. Christie)

Betty, #787, 14x21" 250.00
Billy, #790, 14x21" 270.00
Blossom Time, #654, 14x21" 800.00
Blue Bird, The; #265/#666, 14x21" 650.00
Bobby, #789, 14x21" 225.00
Brown Study, A; #611, 14x20" 1,500.00
Bubbles, #779, 14x21" 350.00
Butterfly, The; #632, 14x18" 210.00
Call to Arms, A; #806, 14x21" 850.00
Caught Napping, #153, 9x12" 2,000.00
Chip of the Old Block, #728, 14x21" 600.00
Chuckles, #799, 11x14" 150.00
Chums, #665, 14x21" 350.00
Contentment, #781 .... 90.00
CQD, #149, 9x12" 450.00
Cupid, After All My Trouble; #608, 16x20" 800.00
Cupid's Reflection, #602, 14x21" 800.00
Daddy's Coming, #644, 14x21" 495.00
Divine Fire, #722, 14x21" 700.00
Double Blessing, A; #643, 14x21" 500.00
Fairest of the Flowers, The; #659, 14x21" 700.00
Feeling, #19, 6x9" 250.00
First Dancing Lesson, The; #713, 14x21" 825.00
Friendly Enemies, #215, 11x14" 155.00
Going to Town, #797, 14x21" 650.00
Goldilocks, #771, 14x21" 1,100.00

Good Morning, #801, 14x21" 250.00
Guest's Candle, The; #651, 14x21" 500.00
Hearing, #22, 6x9" 250.00
His Majesty, #793, 14x21" 320.00
His Queen, #212, 14x20" 700.00
Home Builders, #233/#655, 14x21" 235.00
How Miss Tabitha Taught School, Dodge Publishing Co, 11x16" ..900.00
In Arcady, #701, 14x21" 700.00
In Disgrace, #792, 14x21" 200.00
In Slumberland, #786, 14x21" 120.00
Kitty's Breakfast, #805, 14x21" 350.00
Knit Two - Purl Two, #657, 14x21" 850.00
Little Bit of Heaven, A; #650, 14x21" 125.00
Little Bo Peep, #200, 11x14" 150.00
Little Mother, #803, 14x21" 450.00
Lorelei, #645, 14x21" 1,700.00
Love's Blossom, #223, 11x14" 100.00
Love's Harmony, #791, 14x21" 400.00
Lullaby, The; #819, 14x21" 2,100.00
Madonna, The; #674, 14x21" 2,100.00
May We Come In, #808, 14x21" 385.00
Merely a Man, #218, 13x18" 800.00
Message of the Roses, The; #641, 14x21" 400.00
Mighty Like a Rose, #642, 14x21" 200.00
Mine, #798, 14x21" 225.00
Mischief Brewing, #152, 9x12" 2,000.00
Mothering Heart, The; #351, 14x21" 700.00
My Honey, #765, 14x21" 1,200.00
New Pet, The; #709, 14x21" 950.00
Nitey Nite, #826, 14x21" 175.00
Now I Lay Me, #620, 14x21" 1,800.00
Off to School, #631, 14x21" 1,200.00
On Dreamland's Border, #692, 14x21" 155.00
On the Up & Up, #796, 14x21" 295.00
Our Alarm Clock, #150, 9x12" 250.00
Perfect Peace, #809, 14x21" 500.00
Popularity (Has Its Disadvantages), #825, 14x21" 150.00
Poverty & Riches, #640, 14x21" 700.00
Priceless Necklace, A; #744, 14x21" 1,600.00
Rosebud, A; #780, 14x21" 320.00
Seeing, #122, 11x14" 250.00
Smile Worth While, A; #180, 9x12" 800.00
Snowbird, #777, 14x21" 650.00
Springtime, #775, 14x21" 750.00
Star From the Sky, A; #817, 14x21" 175.00
Sunbeam in a Dark Corner, A; #638, 14x21" ...2,200.00
Sunkissed, #818, 14x21" 125.00
Sweet Innocence, #806, 11x14" 150.00
Symphony, #702, 14x21" 650.00
Tabby, #172, 9x12" 600.00
Taps, #815, 14x21" 550.00
Television, #821, 14x21" 110.00
Thank You, God, #822, 14x21" 175.00
To Have & To Hold, #625, 14x21" 800.00
To Love & To Cherish, #615, 14x21" 265.00
Tom, Tom the Piper's Son, #219, 11x14" 175.00
Tommy, #788, 14x21" 175.00
Touching, #210, 11x14" 150.00
Vanquished, The; #119, 9x12" 750.00
Verdict: Love for Life, The; #113, 9x12" 550.00
When Daddy Comes Marching Home, #668, 14x21" 3,800.00
Who's Sleepy, #816, 14x21" 260.00
Winged Aureole, The; #700, 14x21" 500.00
Wood Magic, #703, 14x21" 750.00

Icart, Lewis

Louis Icart (1888 – 1950) was a Parisian artist best known for his boudoir etchings in the '20s and '30s. In the '80s prices soared, primarily due to Japanese buying. The market began to readjust in 1990, and most etchings now sell at retail between $1,400.00 and $2,500.00. Value is determined by popularity and condition, more than by rarity. Original frames and matting are not important, as most collectors want the etchings restored to their original condition and protected with acid-free mats.

Beware of the following repro and knock-off items: 1. Pseudo engravings on white plastic with the Icart 'signature.' 2. Any bronzes with the Icart signature. 3. Most watercolors, especially if they look similar in subject matter to a popular etching. 4. Lithographs where the dot-matrix printing is visible under magnification. Some even have phony embossed seals or rubber stamp markings. Items listed below are in excellent condition unless noted otherwise. Our advisor is William Holland, author of *Louis Icart: The Complete Etchings* and *The Collectible Maxfield Parrish*; he is listed in the Directory under Pennsylvania.

Autumn Storm, 9x7" 1,650.00
Coursing II, 16x25" 2,750.00
Departure, 1941, 21x17" 1,495.00
Elegance, 18x15" 1,750.00
Finale, 1931, 19x15" 2,125.00
Gust of Wind, 1925, 21x18" 2,600.00
He Loves Me, He Loves Me Not, 1926, 19x16", VG 1,265.00

Il Pleut Bergere, 1927, sight: 21x14", $1,950.00. (Photo courtesy Skinner Inc. Auctioneers & Appraisers of Antiques & Fine Art)

La Chechette (Hiding Place), Les Graveurs, sight: 26x21" 1,650.00
Le Lis, lady & lilies, 1934, 27¾x18¾" 3,250.00
Look, oval, 24x18" 1,500.00
Madame Bovary, lady at window, oval, 1929 .... 1,400.00
Martini, 13½x17½" 5,500.00
Miss America, 1927, sheet: 26x20" 4,000.00
Peacock, 24x19" 4,750.00
Peonies, 1935, 14x17", VG 1,600.00
Pink Alcove, 1929, 10½x13" 1,250.00
Southern Charm, 1940, 20x14" 1,675.00
Speed, 1933, 22x31" 3,950.00
Sweet Mystery, oval, 19x24" 3,650.00
Venus, open edition, oval, unfr, 18x25" 25.00
View of Paris, 1948, 5x8" 1,900.00
Zest, 1928, 10x15", sheet: 25x19⅜" 2,800.00

Kurz and Allison

Louis Kurz founded the Chicago Lithograph Company in 1833. Among his most notable works were a series of 36 Civil War scenes and 100 illustrations of Chicago architecture. His company was destroyed in the Great Fire of 1871, and in 1880 Kurz formed a partnership with Alexander Allison, an engraver. Until both retired in 1903, they produced hundreds of lithographs in color as well as black and white. Unless noted otherwise, values are for prints in excellent condition.

Battle Between the Monitor & Merrimac, c 1889, 22x28", +mat ... 725.00
Battle of Antietam Army of the Potomac...1862, c 1888, 22x28", +fr. 1,100.00
Battle of Big Horn, image; 22x28", +mat & fr 9,600.00
Battle of Cold Harbor...1864, 1888, 20x26", +mat 1,800.00
Battle of Gettysburg, 1884, 22x28", +mat & gilt fr 900.00
Battle of Missionary Ridge, 1886, 22x28⅛", +mat 2,350.00
Battle of New Orleans January 8 1815, 22x28" 850.00
Battle of Spotsylvania...Laurel Hill...1864, c 1888, 22x28", +mat. 2,150.00
Battle of the Wilderness...Plank Road...1864, c 1887, 22x28", +mat. 2,150.00
Great Conemaugh Valley Disaster, 22x36", +Black Forest, fr 1,950.00

Max, Peter

Born in Germany in 1937, Peter Max came to the United States in 1953 where he later studied art in New York City. His work is colorful and his genre psychedelic. He is a prolific artist, best known for his designs from the '60s and '70s that typified the 'hippie' movement.

Anger, 1971, 29½x21½", fr 480.00
Goofy, 4 prints in single fr, 1996, ea: 16x14" 1,175.00
Great Genie, 1976, sheet: 14¼x15½" 475.00
Image for Rainforest Foundation, embellished, 22x16½" 900.00
JFK - Four Kennedy's, enhanced w/pnt, 1989, 40x32" 1,550.00
Lady in a Flower Hat, enhanced w/pnt, 20x15" 850.00
Men Running to Maiden, litho between glass, 3¾x10" 850.00
Moonscape I, 1971, 18¾x23⅜" 425.00
Rama, serigraph, artist proof, ca 1971, 29x21" 3,000.00
Toulouse Lautrec, pk bkground, 42x30" 1,325.00
Untitled: vase of flowers, edition of 300, 21x15½" 480.00

Toulouse Lautrec, 1967, 36x24", $1,320.00. (Photo courtesy Swann Galleries Inc./ LiveAuctioneers.com)

McKenney and Hall

Aseola, Seminole Leader, 20x14" 3,850.00
John Ridge, A Cherokee, Greenough, 1838, sight: 16½x12" 1,200.00
Keokuk, Chief of Sacs & Fox, 19½x14¼" 1,550.00
Ki-On-Twog-Ky, EC Biddle, 20⅜x15¼" 950.00
Kish-Ke-Kosh, A Fox Brave, Greenough, Bowen, 1838, 20¼x14", +mat. 1,200.00
Ma-Has-kah, Ioway Chief, sight: 16¾x12¾", +mat & fr 2,150.00
McIntosh, Philadelphia, 1937-44, 18½x12½" 1,325.00
Ne-Sou-a-Quoit, A Fox Chief, Bowen, 1838, sm tear, 20¼x14⅝" ... 1,550.00
Not-Chi-Mi-Ne, An Ioway Chief, Greenough, sight: 16¾x12¾", +fr. 1,175.00
Okee-Makee-Ouid, A Chippeway Chief, 16x11¾" 1,650.00
Red Jacket, w/Washington Peace Medal, 1837, 11¾x8¼" 1,500.00
Se-Quo-Yah, 20x14" 1,550.00

Tah-Col-O-Quoit, Rice & Clark, 1842, sight: 16½x10¾", +fr 960.00
Wa-Na-Ta, EC Biddle, 1837, 20¼x14½" 1,550.00
War Dance of Sauks & Foxes, Bowen, 1938, 14½x20¼" 1,175.00

Yard-Longs

Values for yard-long prints are given for examples in near mint condition, full length, nicely framed, and with the original glass. To learn more about this popular area of collector interest, we recommend *Those Wonderful Yard-Long Prints and More*, *More Wonderful Yard-Long Prints, Book 2*, and *Yard-Long Prints, Book 3*, by our advisors Bill Keagy, and Charles and Joan Rhoden. They are listed in the Directory under Indiana and Illinois respectively. A word of caution: Watch for reproductions; know your dealer.

At the North Pole, Jos Hoover & Son, c 1904 .... 425.00
Battle of the Chicks, Ben Austrian, c 1920.................................. 325.00
Carnation Symphony, Violin & Birds 275.00
Chrysanthemums, Paul DeLongpre, c 1895 .... 300.00
Hula Girl, girl on surfboard, sgn Gene Pressler 600.00
ISNS, The College Lad & Lassie series, Frank J March, c 1911 ... 500.00
ISTC, College Lad & Lassie series, Alice Luella Fidler, c 1908.... 500.00
Our Feathered Pets, 12 birds sitting on fence, Paul DeLongpre ... 400.00

Pabst brunette in white hat and dress, with pink flower at her bosom, dated 1910 with information on back, $550.00. (Photo courtesy Bill Keagy and Charles and Joan Rhoden)

Pabst Extract American Girl on horse, c 1912............................ 500.00
Pabst Malt Extract 'Jewel' calendar, 1908 .... 500.00
Pompeian Art Panel 'Irresistible,' c 1930................................... 500.00
Pompeian Mary Pickford, Forbes, c 1916 or '17 .... 475.00
Pompeian Mary Pickford, Forbes, c 1918 .... 500.00
Schlitz Malt Extract 'Indian Girl,' c 1908 .... 500.00
Selz Good Shoes, Earl Christy, c 1928 .... 500.00
Spring's Message, Paul DeLongpre 325.00
Walk-Over Shoe Co, girl dressed in cowgirl outfit....................... 500.00
Walk-Over Shoe Co, lady seated in boat, c 1912 .... 400.00
Yard of Dogs, 8 different breeds, c 1903 .... 325.00
Yard of Kittens, sgn Guy Radford 425.00
Yard of Pansies, sgn ME Hart.. 325.00
Yard of Roses, Newton A Wells, c 1898 .... 275.00
Yard of Tulips, Paul DeLongpre 325.00

Purinton

With its bold colors and unusual shapes, Purinton Pottery is much admired by today's dinnerware collectors. In 1939 Bernard Purinton purchased the East Liverpool Pottery in Wellsville, Ohio, and re-named it the Purinton Pottery Company. One of its earliest lines was Peasant Ware, featuring simple shapes and bold, colorful patterns. It was designed by William H. Blair, who also designed what have become the company's most recognized lines, Apple and Intaglio. The company was extremely successful, and by 1941 it became necessary to build a new plant, which they located in Shippenville, Pennsylvania. Blair left Purinton to open his own pottery (Blair Ceramics), leaving his sister Dorothy Purinton (Bernard's wife) to assume the role of designer. Though never a paid employee, Dorothy painted many one-of-a-kind special-occasion items that are highly sought after by today's collectors who are willing to pay premium prices to get them. These usually carry Dorothy's signature.

Apple was Purinton's signature pattern; it was produced throughout the entire life of the pottery. Another top-selling pattern designed by Dorothy Purinton was Pennsylvania Dutch, featuring hearts and tulips. Other long-term patterns include the Plaids and the Intaglios. While several other patterns were developed, they were short-lived. One of the most elusive patterns, Palm Tree, was sold only through a souvenir store in Florida owned by one of the Purinton's sons. In addition to dinnerware, Purinton also produced a line of floral ware, including planters for NAPCO. They did contract work for Esmond Industries and RUBEL, who were both distributors in New York. They made the Howdy Doody cookie jar and bank for Taylor Smith & Taylor; both items are highly collectible.

The pottery was sold to Taylor, Smith & Taylor in 1958 and closed in 1959 due to heavy competition from foreign imports. Most items are not marked, but collectors find their unusual shapes easy to identify. A small number of items were ink stamped 'Purinton Slip-ware.' Some of the early Wellsville pieces were hand signed 'Purinton Pottery,' and several have emerged carrying the signature 'Wm. H. Blair' or simply 'Blair.' Blair's pieces command a premium price. See Clubs, Newsletters, and Catalogs in the Directory for information concerning *Purinton News and Views*.

Cookie jar, Howdy Doody, unmarked, minimum value, $500.00. (Photo courtesy Susan Morris-Snyder)

Apple, cup, 2½" 11.00
Apple, pickle dish, 6"... 95.00
Apple, plate, chop; 12" 50.00
Apple, plate, dinner; 10" 30.00
Apple, snack set, plate & cup... 110.00
Apple, sugar bowl, 3¼" 21.00
Apple, teapot, 3½-cup 75.00
Apple, tumbler, 12-oz 20.00
Brown Intaglio, bowl, cereal; 5½"...6.50
Brown Intaglio, chop plate, 12".. 20.00
Brown Intaglio, oil cruet, w/cork stopper 27.00
Brown Intaglio, pickle dish, 6" 20.00
Brown Intaglio, shakers, mini mug, pr.. 12.00
Chartreuse, lap plate & cup.. 35.00
Chartreuse, wall pocket, 3½" 50.00
Crescent, teapot, 2-cup 50.00
Daisy, canister, cobalt trim, 9" 75.00
Fruit, creamer, 3".. 20.00
Fruit, Dorothy Purinton sgn plate, 12", minimum value.............. 650.00
Fruit, jug, Oasis; rare, minimum value... 750.00

Fruit, sugar bowl, 3" 32.00
Fruit, tumbler, 12-oz, from $16 to.. 20.00
Grapes, bowl, range; w/lid, 5½" 45.00
Heather Plaid, grease jar, 5½" 60.00
Intaglio, cookie jar, oval, 9½" 75.00
Intaglio, tea & toast set (cup & lap plate), 2½" & 8½" 25.00
Intaglio, tray, roll; 11" 35.00
Ivy-Red, honey jug, 6¼" 15.00
Ivy-Yellow, jug, Dutch; 2-pt 20.00
Maywood, plate, dinner; 9½" 30.00
Ming Tree, chop plate, 12" 125.00
Mountain Rose, cookie jar, oval, 9" 125.00
Mountain Rose, decanter, 5" 45.00
Mountain Rose, wall pocket, 3½" 65.00
Normandy Plaid, beer mug, 16-oz, 4¾" 40.00
Normandy Plaid, grease jar, w/lid, 5½" 60.00
Palm Tree, basket planter, 6¼" 100.00
Palm Tree, shakers, Pour & Shake, pr 75.00
Peasant Garden, pitcher, Rubel mold, 5" 125.00
Peasant Garden, shakers, jug style, mini, 2½", pr................ 65.00
Pennsylvania Dutch, cookie jar, sq, w/pottery lid, 9½" 125.00
Pennsylvania Dutch, platter, meat; 12" 50.00
Pennsylvania Dutch, shakers, pour & shake, pr.................... 75.00
Petals, honey jug, 6¼" 15.00

Petals, teapot, two-cup, 4", $45.00.
(Photo courtesy Susan Morris-Snyder)

Petals, teapot, 8-cup, 8" 75.00
Provincial Fruit, grease jar, 5" 30.00
Saraband, beer mug.. 45.00
Saraband, cookie jar, oval, w/lid, 9½" 100.00
Saraband, platter, 12"... 30.00
Saraband, shakers, mini jug, pr.. 45.00
Tea Rose, creamer & sugar bowl, w/lid................................ 95.00
Turquoise (Intaglio), plate, dinner; 9¾" 35.00
Turquoise (Intaglio), shakers, mini jug, pr 40.00
Woodflowers, relish tray, 8" 45.00

Purses

Purses from the early 1800s are often decorated with small, brightly colored glass beads. Cut steel beads were popular in the 1840s and remained stylish until about 1930. Purses made of woven mesh date back to the 1820s. Chain-link mesh came into usage in the 1890s, followed by the enamel mesh bags carried by the flappers in the 1920s. Purses are divided into several categories by (a) construction techniques — whether beaded, embroidered, or a type of needlework; (b) material — fabric or metal; and (c) design and style. Condition is very important. Watch for dry, brittle leather or fragile material. For those interested in learning more, we recommend *More Beautiful Purses* and *Combs and Purses* by Evelyn Haertigi of Carmel, California; *Purse Masterpieces* by Lynell Schwartz; and *100 Years of Purses, 1880s to 1980*, by Ronna Lee Aikins. Unless otherwise noted, our values are for examples in 'like-new' condition, showing very little if any wear.

Wood, Enid Collins, Texas, Love in green stain on wood with bead accents, 8¾" long, EX, from $145.00 to $160.00.

Alligator, bl-gr Kelley style, snap closure, w/hdl, 1950s, 8x11x2"....215.00
Alligator, brn w/gold fr, Lesco/Saks Fifth Ave, 7½x11x3½", EX..... 85.00
Alligator, dk brn w/drawstring top, w/hdl, 1940s, 8x11", EX.......... 95.00
Beaded, blk & wht, cloth-lined beaded strap, 1950s, 8x12", from $60 to. 85.00
Beaded, blk & wht dog on bl, blk fr, mini, 3x3", from $135 to..... 165.00
Beaded, blk satin w/heavy beads on flap, Brand TKK, 1965, 6x8½"..35.00
Beaded, bold mc Deco design, Bakelite fr, bl satin lining, 1920, 8x6" .420.00
Beaded, brn striped front w/blk bk, UKK, Hong Kong, 1960s, 12x14" ..60.00
Beaded, mc earth tones, clutch, Sears catalog, 1937, from $28 to.. 38.00
Beaded, mc geometric pattern on blk, bottom fringe, 1940s, 11½x9"..25.00
Beaded, orange & blk check pattern, drawstring, fringe, 1925, 6½x3"..150.00
Beaded, pastels on cream, clutch, 1940s, 6x9", from $40 to 60.00
Beaded, sm bl beads, gold-tone fr/chain, bottom tassel, 1910, 8x6", VG..175.00
Beaded, tiny cream beads on wht, Lemured Petite, 1950s, 9x12", $80 to..100.00
Beaded, wht, gr, bl & yel on red, red Bakelite fr, Poppy Bag, 1945, 7"..55.00
Beaded, wht & pastels, chain drawstring, 1950s, 9½x9", from $50 to ..80.00
Beaded pearls, blk & wht seed pearl floral, 1935, 5x6", $23 to....... 33.00
Beaded pearls, floral, clutch, R Gorwood, 1940s, 4x7", $20 to....... 30.00
Beaded pearls, wht, gold-tone fr & chain, Carolyne Barlon, 1940s, 6x8"... 35.00
Beaded pearls, wht w/blk diamondesque front, 1940s, 3¾x7", $20 to ..40.00
Crochet, wht, ornate cherub on wide silver-tone fr, 6x7", from $600 to.800.00
Fabric, blk floral, clutch, Majestic in gold, 1972, 5x8", from $30 to.45.00
Fabric, circular silver glitter design, 5" chain, 1970s, 5x9", $50 to. 70.00
Fabric, cream w/pk floral, hinged, 12" chain, 1950, 7x10", from $35 to.50.00
Fabric, Flower Basket, Enid Collins, 8¼x11x3½", EX.................. 175.00
Fabric, It Grows on Trees, Enid Collins, 1963, 11x13x4", EX...... 115.00
Fabric, Mira Flores, Enid Collins, 1966, EX 110.00
Fabric, Sea Garden, Enid Collins, jeweled seahorse/fish/plants, 1965 . 260.00
Fabric, mc paisley, wide straw hdl, 1940s, 12x10", from $40 to...... 65.00
Felt, rhinestones & metal in starburst design, clutch, 1950s, 3x5" ..155.00
Leather, ostrich, gold-tone fr & clasp, Town & Country Shoes, 8½x8".65.00
Leather, tooled butterflies/etc on brn, Bakelite clasp, strap, Meeker.... 135.00
Leather, tooled floral/basketweave on brn, wrapped hdl, '60s, 12" W . 125.00
Leather, tooled leaves, bucket style w/whipstitch border, 14x13x5".... 110.00
Leather, tooled satchel style w/strap hdl, 1960s-70s, 16x13x8" 90.00
Lucite, blk cylinder w/gold-tone clasps, curved hdls, Miles Orig, 11".330.00
Lucite, clear w/cvgs, rhinestones & gold on sides, 1950s, 3x8x4".. 400.00
Lucite, clear w/rhinestones & pearl tiles, Wiesner, 3⅝x9x3½"+hdl.. 395.00
Lucite, gr w/gold threads & rhinestones, Patricia of Miami, 8", +hdl.. 500.00
Lucite, mc feathering w/gold, circle hdl, Myles Orig, 1950s, 10¾" L..275.00
Lucite, silver & gray w/clear eng floral top, ftd, Rialt of NY, 1950s 120.00
Mesh, Alumesh flamingo pk, cream celluloid fr & hdl, 1930s, 5x8" ...85.00
Mesh, gold-tone, gold-tone fr borders flap, #1519246, 1970s, 4½x8" ...65.00
Mesh, shiny gold-tone, 19½" chain, BEE mk, 1970s, 6½x9", $70 to..80.00
Mesh, shiny silver, 19" rope chain, AE, Made in China, 1970s, 5x9" ..60.00
Mesh, silver-tone, emb floral fr, w/chain, 1900-10, from $85 to ... 100.00
Mesh, silver-tone w/bobcat design, chain, Whiting & Davis, 1910, 7x5"..175.00
Mesh, wht, wht pnt metal fr & chain, gold trim, 1970s, 6x9", $50 to..65.00
Mesh, 14k yel gold w/hinged closure w/3 sm dmns, 20.2dwt, 2¾" L....750.00
Mesh, 14k yel gold w/hinged closure w/3 sm dmns, 20.2dwt, 2¾" L....750.00

Satin, blk, gold-tone fr, chain & clasp, 1960s, 5¾x10½", $20 to.... 40.00
Satin, dk gr, rhinestones gold-tone fr, Mel-Ton, 1950s, 8x9", $70 to....90.00
Sequined, gold bead design on gr, silver-tone fr w/rhinestone, 5x11"...85.00
Sequined, gold w/blk trim & hdl, Delill Made in China, 1970s, 7x8"..50.00
Sequined, gold-tone, bead trim, drawstring, 1940s, 7x5", from $30 to.40.00
Snakeskin, blk, brn & copper, 4 sm ft, gold-tone fr, 1950s, 8x11"..55.00
Snakeskin, copper-tone, 15" chain, Varon, 1970s, 6x10", $120 to..140.00
Straw, cream, gold-tone hdls & buckle clasp, Fashion Imports, 7x8½".100.00
Straw, red w/yel & bl stripe, clutch, Anton Made in Italy, 1980, 13" L..70.00
Straw, tortoiseshell Lucite hdls, Hand Made British Hong Kong, 9x12"...100.00
Straw, tortoiseshell Lucite hdls, Simon...Mister Ernest, 1945, 7x11"......65.00
Tapestry, floral, brass fr & clasp, vinyl hdl, Empress, 1940s, $60 to.........80.00
Tapestry, floral, Lucite hdl, Dover Made in USA, 1945, 11x14", $70 to....90.00
Tapestry, floral on cream w/blk border, gold-tone fr & hdl, 1955, 6x9"..80.00
Tapestry, floral w/village scene center, blk fr, 7x9", from $450 to.550.00
Tapestry, geometric floral on shield shape, braid hdl, 7x5", $450 to.550.00
Tapestry, gr, red & bl floral on blk fabric, vinyl fr & hdl, 1940s......85.00
Tapestry, lady in pastoral scene, jeweled enamel fr, 8x9", $950 to .1,200.00
Tapestry, mc birds on cream, filigree jeweled fr, 9½x7", $750.......850.00
Vinyl, blk, scalloped tortoiseshell fr & hdl, 1940s, 7x9", $50 to.....75.00
Vinyl, pk, gold-tone clasp, 5" hdl, Bobbi Jermone, 1950s, 10x10".55.00
Vinyl, silver-tone, crown clasp, w/chain, 1960s, 4¾x8", from $30 to...40.00
Vinyl, yel, gold-tone fr & clasp, yel hdl, 1962, 5½x12½", $40 to...60.00
Vinyl, 3-toned brn, gold-tone fr, dbl hdls, Kismet Creations, 6x13"..65.00
Wood, Sophistikit II, Enid Collins, 1965, 8½x11x3", EX............275.00
Wood, pea gr, floral design, wht Lucite hdl, 1960s, 9x4¾".........110.00

Pyrography

Pyrography, also known as wood burning, Flemish art, or poker work, is the art of burning designs into wood or leather and has been practiced over the centuries in many countries.

In the late 1800s pyrography became the hot new hobby for thousands of Americans who burned designs inspired by the popular artists of the day including Mucha, Gibson, Fisher, and Corbett. Thousands of wooden boxes, wall plaques, novelties, and pieces of furniture that they purchased from local general stores or from mail-order catalogs were burned and painted. These pieces were manufactured by companies such as The Flemish Art Company of New York and Thayer & Chandler of Chicago, who printed the designs on wood for the pyrographers to burn. This Victorian fad developed into a new form of artistic expression as the individually burned and painted pieces reflected the personality of the pyrographers. The more adventurous started to burn between the lines and developed a style of 'allover burning' that today is known as Pyromania. Others not only created their own designs but even made the pieces to be decorated. Both these developments are particularly valued today as true examples of American folk art. By the 1930s its popularity had declined. Like Mission furniture, it was neglected by generations of collectors and dealers. The recent appreciation of Victoriana, the Arts and Crafts Movement, the American West, and the popularity of turn-of-the-century graphic art has rekindled interest in pyrography which embraces all these styles.

Key: hb — hand burned

Bedroom set, hb/pnt, Wm Rogers/Forusville PA, 1904-07, 3-pc.4,000.00
Box, flatware; factory burned/pnt poinsettias, Rogers, 9x11x5"....195.00
Box, hb/pnt lady petting horse amid flowers, 1920s, 1⅛x13x4½"...70.00
Box, lady w/flowing hair, Flemish Art Co, 1909, 11¼x4¼".........120.00
Box, Miller Bros Steel Pens, 1900, stamped to look hb, 7" L, +contents..45.00
Catalog, Thayer-Chandler, Chicago, 1904, 92 pgs, 12 in full color..27.00
Checker/backgammon brd, red & gr decor/glass bead insets, 30x15".1,550.00
Chest, blanket; hb/pnt swans/lady's head/flower/etc, ca 1890.......850.00

Cue holder, hb pool-hall scene, folk art, unique..........................650.00
Etching set, Snow White, Disney/Marks, 1938, electric pen, complete.175.00
Frame, hb/pnt cherries, standing type, 7½x6", EX.........................85.00
Frame, owls in tree, 2 Is Company, 2 oval cutouts.....................145.00
Humidor, trees & landscape on lid, gold & bl pnt on pine, 3x9x6"..295.00
Knife rack, hb Lizzie Borden w/axe, 5 hooks below, rare..............550.00
Mirror, hand; grapes, 1920s, 8½x4½"..65.00
Mirror, hand; hb/pnt lady's head w/flowing hair, 13¼x6¾"..........180.00
Panel, basswood, burned/pnt orange, Thayer-Chandler, 16x30"..465.00
Pedestal, hb/pnt Nouveau flowers & vines, 45".........................400.00
Ping-Pong paddle, Gibson girl, ca 1905, 11¼x5½".....................160.00
Plaque, cvd/burned/pnt strawberry basket, 3-ply, 12" dia..............70.00
Plaque, girl bathing puppies, #854, 14½"..................................125.00
Plaque, Native American chief, etched/tinted, JP Graham, 30" dia...840.00
Plaque, Nouveau lady w/cherries, 19½"....................................150.00
Plaque, Oddfellows, hb IOOF in center, early 1900s, 16x10".........87.00
Ribbon holder, hb/pnt Sunbonnet babies (3), 5x12"....................160.00
Screen, birds & foliage, mc pnt, 3-part, 63x73"..........................400.00
Table, hb/pnt daisies & scrolls, lower shelf, 16½x11x11".............315.00
Tie rack, factory stamp, HP soldier/nurse/sailor, WWI motto......125.00

Quezal

The Quezal Art Glass and Decorating Company of Brooklyn, New York, was founded in 1901 by Martin Bach. A former Tiffany employee, Bach's glass closely resembled that of his former employer. Most pieces were signed 'Quezal,' a name taken from a Central American bird. After Bach's death in 1920, his son-in-law, Conrad Vohlsing, continued to produce a Quezal-type glass in Elmhurst, New York, which he marked 'Lustre Art Glass.' Examples listed here are signed unless noted otherwise.

Vase, pink and gold lapets; green, gold, and pink hooked designs, #C270, 10½", $6,400.00. (Photo courtesy Early Auction Co.)

Bowl, gold w/scalloped rim, tapering sides, D663, 2x4¼"............275.00
Charger, gold w/2" W stretched rim, 10¼"................................175.00
Compote, gold w/wht int, flared ft, 4⅜x9⅞"..............................240.00
Compote, leafy sprigs, gr on wht, gold int (scratches), 3½x12"....400.00
Cup & saucer, gold, curled hdl, curved rims................................425.00
Lamp, candle; Dmn Quilt gold corseted shade; ornate std, 18", pr..1,375.00
Lamp, feather 16" shade: gr & gold on wht; bronze hoofed-ft std, 22"..3,600.00
Lamp base, feathers, silver & gold on rouge, bronze ft, 28" overall...6,600.00
Lamp base, feathers, wht on gold & wht w/bl, 2-socket, 22".....1,100.00
Salt cellar, gold w/ribs, 2½" dia..300.00
Shade, feathers, bl & wht on gold, ruffled, 5¼"..........................575.00
Shade, feathers, gr & ivory on gold, 4"....................................725.00
Shade, feathers, wht & gold on clambroth, 5x5".........................230.00
Shade, gold w/emb ribs, flared rim, 6".....................................180.00

Shade, hearts & vines, gold on wht, 5x3½" 395.00
Shade, King Tut, gold on wht, 4½" w/2½" fitter 275.00
Shade, wht w/emb ribs, gold int, flared edge, 3⅛" 135.00
Shades, feathers, bl w/gold on wht, gold int, ruffled, 7", 4 for 780.00
Vase, bud; gold on amber disk ft, slim cylinder, 11⅝" 300.00
Vase, feathers, gold & gr on gold w/wht center, 3½x4" 3,150.00
Vase, feathers, gold on opal to gr striped, #E286, 7¼" 6,600.00
Vase, feathers, gr & gold on wht & gold, hourglass form, 9" 4,100.00
Vase, feathers, gr on wht, gold int, ftd, #K312, 8¾" 1,650.00
Vase, floriform; feathers, gr & gold on cream w/gold int, #431, 5½" ... 2,000.00
Vase, floriform; feathers, gr on opal, zippered gold/gr ft, #466, 7" ... 2,875.00
Vase, floriform; gold, 9" 1,250.00
Vase, floriform; gr & wht pulled design, gold int, ftd, #S760, 5x6" ... 2,100.00
Vase, gold, cylindrical, flared rim & ft, 12x4½" 350.00
Vase, gold, 3-scallop rim, ftd, 5½" 425.00
Vase, gold w/bl-purple irid, silver floral o/l, #D1196, 7½" 2,650.00
Vase, gold w/bl/purple irid, flared rim, slightly waisted, 8" 300.00
Vase, gold w/purple irid, trumpet w/fold-down top, #R487, 4½" .. 350.00
Vase, jack-in-pulpit; feathers, gr on gold, #A483, 8½" 4,200.00
Vase, jack-in-pulpit; stretched gold top to purple bulbous base, 13" ... 6,000.00
Vase, King Tut, ivory on gold, waisted neck, 9¼" 1,100.00
Vase, leaves & vines, gr & gold on wht, 8" 1,800.00
Vase, Lincoln Drape, gold on opal, flared rim, ftd, 15" 5,600.00
Vase, spiral loops, wht on gold to gr to bl, 6" 4,550.00

Quilts

Quilts, though a very practical product, nevertheless represent an art form which expresses the character and the personality of the designer. During the seventeenth and eighteenth centuries, quilts were considered a necessary part of a bride's hope chest; the traditional number required to be properly endowed for marriage was a 'baker's dozen'! American colonial quilts reflect the English and French taste of our ancestors. They would include the classifications known as Lindsey-Woolsey and the central medallion appliqué quilts fashioned from imported copper-plate printed fabrics.

By 1829 spare time was slightly more available, so women gathered in quilting bees. This not only was a way of sharing the work but also gave them the opportunity to show off their best handiwork. The hand-dyed and pieced quilts emerged, and they are now known as sampler, album, and friendship quilts. By 1845 American printed fabric was available.

In 1793 Eli Whitney developed the cotton gin; as a result, textile production in America became industrialized. Soon inexpensive fabrics were readily available, and ladies were able to choose from colorful prints and solids to add contrast to their work. Both pieced and appliquéd work became popular. Pieced quilts were considered utilitarian, while appliquéd quilts were shown with pride of accomplishment at the fair or used when itinerant preachers traveled through and stayed for a visit. Today many collectors prize pieced quilts and their intricate geometric patterns above all other types. Many of these designs were given names: Daisy and Oak Leaf, Grandmother's Flower Garden, Log Cabin, and Ocean Wave are only a few. Appliquéd quilts involved stitching one piece — carefully cut into a specific form such as a leaf, a flower, or a stylized device — onto either a large one-piece ground fabric or an individual block. Often the background fabric was quilted in a decorative pattern such as a wreath or medallions. Amish women scorned printed calicos as 'worldly' and instead used colorful blocks set with black fabrics to produce a stunning pieced effect. To show their reverence for God, the Amish would often include a 'superstition' block which represented the 'imperfection' of Man!

One of the most valuable quilts in existence is the Baltimore album quilt. Made between 1840 and 1860 only 300 or so still exist today. They have been known to fetch over $100,000.00 at prominent auction houses in New York City. Usually each block features elaborate appliqué work such as a basket of flowers, patriotic flags and eagles, the Oddfellow's heart in hand, etc. The border can be sawtooth, meandering, or swags and tassels.

During the Victorian period the crazy quilt emerged. This style became the most popular quilt ever in terms of sheer numbers produced. The crazy quilt was formed by random pieces put together following no organized lines and was usually embellished by elaborate embroidery stitches. Fabrics of choice were brocades, silks, and velvets.

Another type of quilting, highly prized and rare today, is trapunto. These quilts were made by first stitching the outline of the design onto a solid sheet of fabric which was backed with a second having a much looser weave. White was often favored, but color was sometimes used for accent. The design (grapes, flowers, leaves, etc.) was padded through openings made by separating the loose weave of the underneath fabric; a backing was added and the three layers quilted as one.

Besides condition, value is judged on intricacy of pattern, color effect, and craftsmanship. Examine the stitching. Quality quilts have from 10 to 12 stitches to the inch. A stitch is defined as any time a needle pierces through the fabric. So you may see five threads but 10 (stitches) have been used. In the listings that follow, examples rated excellent have minor defects, otherwise assume them to be free of any damage, soil, or wear. Also assume that all the stitching is hand done; any machine work will be noted. Values given here are auction results; retail may be somewhat higher.

Key:
ms — machine sewn   qlt — quilted, quilting

Amish

Block w/Sawtooth & blk borders, crib sz, 38x36" 6,000.00
Dmns & sqs, gr/purple/brn, 1950s, full sz 1,950.00
Hole in the Barn Door, bl/purple/blk/brn/tan, hired man's, 68x35" ... 3,600.00
Pierced stars/blocks/bars, mc wool, crib sz, 44½x34" 13,250.00
Spider Web Star, mc on bl w/blk borders, rose bking, stains, 33x62" .. 260.00
Sunshine & Shadows, red/bl/purple, printed floral bk, 88x85" .. 1,100.00

Appliquéd

California Rose, appliqué and trapunto, late nineteenth century, ink signature on back, 101x94", $1,200.00. (Photo courtesy Skinner Inc. Auctioneers & Appraisers of Antiques & Fine Art)

Dresden Plate, mc on wht w/unusual snake border, Deco look, 90x74" .. 850.00
Eagles & flowers, brn/yel/red on wht, late 19th C, full sz 850.00
Floral, red & gr on wht, fine qlt, PA, ca 1920, 83x81" 900.00

Floral wreaths, red & gr on wht, sawtooth border, 19th C, 92x92" ..1,800.00
Flowers/dots cats/hands, red/gr/yel on wht, trapunto, 80x80" 3,500.00
Flowers/tree/peafowl, mc on wht w/gr border, ca 1840, 106x93" ..2,300.00
Grapes on vines, mc on wht, sgn/dtd 1851, full sz 950.00
Poinsettias, red & gr on wht w/red border, 1930s, 94x88" 425.00
Poinsettias & vines, gr/red/wht cottons, OH, 1850s, 90x88" 635.00
Pomegranite, mc on cream, 1870s, 72x82" 1,550.00
Rose of Sharon, mc cottons, close qlt, unwashed, att KY, 81x81" ..2,400.00
Sq in Dmn w/stars/swags/peacock/etc, mc on wht, 1820s, full sz ..2,350.00
Tulip medallions/vines/wreaths, mc on wht, 19th C, 87x84" 3,600.00
Tulips w/vine border, yel & gr on wht, appl name, 1851, 82x82" ..1,325.00
Vining flowers & spirals, mc calicos on wht cotton, fading, 81x81" .350.00
Wild Poppies, red/gr/yel on natural, red binding, 98x98" 9,750.00
16 blocks w/birds/monuments/flowers/etc, sgn/dtd 1850, 107x106" ..32,000.00
4 Pots of Flowers, red/gr/wht, ca 1880s, 76x75" 8,400.00

Mennonite

Bar, dk gr print & orange stripes, att PA, 88x77" 515.00
Basket, red/gr/yel on wht w/gr grid, yel/gr borders, PA, full sz.......600.00
Hexagon Ring, calicos, 1¼" blocks/2½" hexagons, 91x79" 480.00
Shoo-Fly, wools/cottons, 2-pc flannel bk, ca 1900, 80x67" 780.00
Straight Furrows Log Cabin, cotton w/red wool border, 1890s, 77x76" ..480.00
X pattern, mc w/pk & bl sashing, sawtooth border, 94x83" 1,025.00

Pieced

Star of Bethlehem, calico prints, Pennsylvania, ca. 1890s, 80x90", $1,250.00. (Photo courtesy Skinner Inc. Auctioneers & Appraisers of Antiques & Fine Art)

Block & Star, bl/wht/lav/yel, PA, 19th C, 78x84" 4,575.00
California Rose, 9 trapunto roses, mc on wht, 19th C, 101x94" ..1,200.00
Carpenter's Wheel, cotton, 3-color, PA, ca 1885, 86x85" 7,200.00
Christmas Tree, red & gr on wht, leaf qlt, ca 1910, 92x91 ....1,200.00
Crazy, silks/brocades/velvets/ribbons, embr & gold stitches, 60x60"...5,300.00
Crazy, silks/brocades/velvets/ribbons, feather qlt, KY, 1880s, 60x60" .4,500.00
Dmn-in-Sq, gr/red/bl, cotton bk, patterned hq, late 19th C, 80x80" .6,000.00
Dmn-Pattern Star w/birds & hearts, bl/wht/yel, PA, 19th C, 85x75" .4,350.00
Drunkard's Path, red & wht, sawtooth border, dtd 1891, 78x78" ..1,325.00
Feather Star Variant, yel-orange & gr, wreath/chain qlt, MD, 84x84" 2,400.00
Floral chintz pcs in bands, PA, 1850s, 106x92" 2,650.00
Flying Geese, chintz border, PA, 19th C, 100x106" 3,150.00
Friendship, floral sqs, gr/red/yel/wht, stains, 100x95" 3,000.00
Geometric Album Block, pk & wht gingham, ca 1900, full sz ..3,600.00

Geometric patchwork, printed cotton/chintz, dtd 1853, 90x93" ...2,650.00
Goose in Flight, mc on cream, hs, 81x82" 1,350.00
Honey Bee, vegetal dyes on wht, feather/stipple qlt, 1870s, 76x77" ..1,200.00
Irish Chain, pk & wht, wht border, 1930, full sz 3,600.00
Joseph's Coat of Many Colors, rainbow colors, patterned qlt, 82x82". 1,950.00
LeMoyne Star, bl & wht w/Birds in Air border, patterned qlt, 96x93" ...635.00
Log Cabin, mc w/piano key border, homespun red checked bk, 78x66" ..3,000.00
Log Cabin w/sawtooth edge, bls & lavs, early 20th C, 86x86" ..1,950.00
Log Cabin w/Windmill Blades, tan & red on wht, 1880s, 88x77". 900.00
Log Cabin w/Windmill Blades, wool challis, 1870s, 83x77" 2,350.00
Odd Fellows pattern, dress prints, sawtooth border, plume qlt, 90x78".635.00
Star & satellites w/lightning bolt border, mc on gr, 86x88" 3,600.00
Star w/in Star, mc cotton prints, dmn qlt, 102x102" 1,265.00
Sunburst, calicos on wht, sgn ABD, ca 1840, 94x92" 1,200.00
Tree of Life, yel & gr on red, wreaths/rising sun qlt, 78x75" 2,150.00
Trip Around the World, calicos, 9-patch corners, 1880s, 82x84" .10,200.00
Variable Star, printed/solid calicos, patterned qlt, 1880s, 84x82" ..1,325.00
8-Pointed Star (9), mc on red, fine qlt, 84x84" 2,750.00

Quimper

Quimper pottery bears the name of the Breton town in northwestern France where it has been made for over 300 years. Production began in 1690 when Jean-Baptiste Bousquet settled into a small workshop in the suburbs of Quimper, at Locmaria. There he began to make the hand-painted, tin enamel-glazed earthenware which we know today as faience. By the last quarter of the nineteenth century, there were three factories working concurrently: Porquier, de la Hubaudiere (the Grand Maison), and Henriot. All three houses produced similar wares which were decorated with scenes from the everyday life of the peasant folk of the region. Their respective marks are an AP or a P with an intersecting B (similar to a clover), an HB, and an HR (which became HenRiot after litigation in 1922). The most desirable pieces were produced during the last quarter of the nineteenth century through the first quarter of the twentieth century. These are considered to be artistically superior to the examples made after World War I and II with the exception of the Odetta line, which is now experiencing a renaissance among collectors here and abroad.

Most of what was made was faience, but there was also a history of utilitarian gres ware (stoneware) having been produced there. In 1922 the Grande Maison HB revitalized this ware and introduced the line called Odetta, examples of which seemed to embody the bold spirit of the Art Deco style. The companion faience pieces of this period and genre are classified as Modern Movement examples and frequently bear the name of the artist who designed the mold. These artist-signed examples are dramatically increasing in value.

Currently there are two factories still producing Quimper pottery. La Societe Nouvelle des Faienceries de Quimper is owned by Sarah and Paul Jenessens along with a group of American investors. Their mark is a stamped HB-Henriot logo. The other, La Faiencerie d'art Breton, is operated by the direct descendents of the HB and Henriot families. Their pieces are marked with an interlocked F and A conjoined with an inverted B. Other marks include HQF which is the Henriot Quimper France mark and HBQ, the HB Quimper mark. If you care to learn more about Quimper, we recommend *Quimper Pottery: A French Folk Art Faience* by Sandra V. Bondhus, our advisor for this category, whose address can be found in the Directory under Connecticut.

Bannette, wedding scene w/decor riche, HBQ, 10¼x8" 350.00
Bell, bagpipe shape, peasant man/floral spray, HQF, 3½" 160.00
Bowl, courting peasant couple, scalloped, HRQ, 12" 150.00
Bowl, red petals/bl dots in garland, geometric center, HBQ, 1½x4" ..20.00
Bowl, rooster strutting, a la touche garland, att AP, 4x11¼" 150.00
Box, lady & flower garland, 8-pointed star-shaped lid, HBQ 8, 4" ..200.00

Cake plate, Botanique, floral spray/insect, PB, 4½x8" 1,200.00
Charger, Breton musician, decor riche, HBQ, 13½" 375.00
Charger, dancing couple, nosegays border, HBQ, 14" 220.00
Compote, Mistletoe, couple in meadow, hdls, HRQ, 11½x7" 400.00
Coupe, bride & groom in meadow, yel trim, HB, 6¾", NM 350.00
Figurine, Colaik, man w/walking stick, HQF 197, 3¼" 85.00
Figurine, Marik, lady w/folded umbrella, HA 156, 3¼", NM 85.00
Figurine, Ste Anne in ermine robe, child Mary beside, HQF 127, 5¾" .85.00
Figurine, Village Breton couple, HenRiot...JES (Sevellec), 3" 200.00
Inkewll, dbl, stamp tray, Breton couple/ermines, HBQ, 4x8½x4½".. 250.00
Inkwell, lady w/basket/bl lattice, demi-fantasie, HQF, 3½x3½".... 120.00
Inkwell, man playing bagpipes, decor riche, HRQ, 4" 240.00

Jardiniere, bagpipe form, HB Quimper France mark, 7x12", $750.00. (Photo courtesy Sandra A. Bondhus)

Jardiniere, piqué fleurs chest w/false drws, HRQ, sm rpr 1,350.00
Lamp base, Modern Movement, lady w/basket on shoulder, HenRiot, 9½" .500.00
Match holder, Breton man, bk: lady, flowers/dots, HRQ, 2¼" 120.00
Mustard pot, peasant man & plants, gr sponged hdl, w/lid, HR, 3¾" .130.00
Pitcher, Breton couple/flowers, faience populaire, HB, 19th C, 10", NM.. 100.00
Pitcher, geometric Modern Movement, Breton man hdl, Fouillen, 5½"..325.00
Pitcher, Grecian ewer form, dancing couple, decor riche, HQ 103, 17"...750.00
Pitcher, tennis ball pattern, geometrics, HQF, 7¼" 185.00
Plate, crab among branches, cobalt border, HRQ, 8¾" 850.00
Plate, lady knitting, purple coif, Avergne, HB, 9", NM 180.00
Plate, lady w/fish basket, floral sprays, HB, 19th C, 9¾" 175.00
Plate, Roscoff, 2 men look out to sea, 1st Period PB, 8¾" 1,250.00
Platter, Breton man & lady, fish form, HBQ, 11¾x24" 200.00
Platter, Seashell & Seaweed on blk, HenRiot, 10½" L 100.00
Relish, Petit Breton, goose finial, 3-part, HQ, 2x12½" 225.00
Salt shaker, Bigoudienne lady's head form, Gallard, HQ, 3", ea ... 110.00
Snuff bottle, Breton man/fleur-de-lis, book form 250.00
Sugar bowl, Normandie, Modern Movement, Fouillen, rpl lid, 8" ..230.00
Tray, man playing flute, demi-fantasie, HQ 74, 9¼" 100.00
Vase, Broderie Breton, lady & Celtic patterns, hdls, HBQ, 8½" .. 200.00
Vase, couple dancing/musicians/Crest of Brittany, hdls, HRQ, 13½" .500.00
Vase, lady spins/man w/bagpipes, horseshoe form, HB 5, 19th C, 5½" ...450.00
Vase, lady w/distaff/man w/flute, demi-fantasie, HRQ, 7x5½x2¼" ..225.00
Vase, quintal; ivoire corbelle, peasant lady, HQ 90, 3½", NM........ 70.00
Wall pocket, lady & fleur-de-lis, conical, 1st Period PB, 5½" 650.00
Wall pocket, man w/horn & flower, conical, 19th C, 10½" 180.00
Wall pocket, peasant couple on shoe form w/curled toe, HB, flaw, 10".200.00

Radford, Alfred

Pottery associated with Albert Radford can be categorized by three periods of production. Pottery produced in Tiffin, Ohio (1896 – 1899), consists of bone china (no marked examples known) and high-quality jasperware with applied Wedgwood-like cameos. Tiffin jasperware is often impressed 'Radford Jasper' in small block letters. At Zanesville, Ohio,

Radford jasperware was marked only with an incised, two-digit shape number, and the cameos were not applied but rather formed within the mold and filled with a white slip. Zanesville Radford ware was produced for only a few months before the Radford pottery was acquired by the Arc-en-Ciel company in 1903. Production in Zanesville was handled by Radford's father, Edward (1840 – 1910), who remained in Zanesville after Albert moved to Clarksburg, West Virginia, where the Radford Pottery Co. was completed shortly before Albert's death in 1904. Jasperware was not produced in Clarksburg, and the molds appear to have been left in Zanesville, where some were subsequently used by the Arc-en-Ciel pottery. The Clarksburg, West Virginia, pottery produced a standard glaze, slip-decorated ware, Ruko; Thera and Velvety, matt glazed ware often signed by Albert Haubrich, Alice Bloomer, and other artists; and Radura, a semimatt green glaze developed by Albert Radford's son, Edward. The Clarksburg plant closed in 1912.

Jardiniere & ped, Majolica, birds & flowers, 3 strap hdls, 41½", NM.. 1,175.00
Jardiniere & ped, Ruko, poppies on brn, rpr, 29⅞" 725.00
Vase, Jasper, angels, bk: eagles, #23, 9⅜", NM 220.00

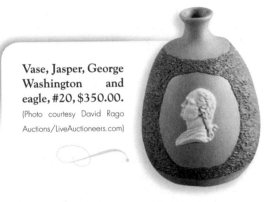

Vase, Jasper, George Washington and eagle, #20, $350.00. (Photo courtesy David Rago Auctions/LiveAuctioneers.com)

Vase, Jasper, Lincoln profile, bk: eagle w/shield, #12, 7" 325.00
Vase, Jasper, Lincoln profile, unusual 1-color glaze, #12, 7" 275.00
Vase, Thera, flower on gr, slim, 12" 215.00
Vase, Velvety, blackberries on gr, sgn AH, bottle form, 11x4" 540.00
Vase, Velvety, heron by stream, wht on bl, slim, 19½" 4,250.00

Radios

Vintage radios are very collectible. There were thousands of styles and types produced, the most popular of which today are the breadboard and the cathedral. Consoles are usually considered less marketable, since their size makes them hard to display and store. For those wishing to learn more about the subject, we recommend *Collector's Guide to Antique Radios* by John Slusser and the staff of Radio Daze, available through Collector Books.

Unless otherwise noted in the descriptions, values are given for working radios in near mint to mint condition. Our advisor for this category is Dr. E. E. Taylor; he is listed in the Directory under Indiana. See also Plastics.

Key:
BC — broadcast
b/o — battery-operated
LW — long wave
pb — push button

R/P — radio-phonograph
s/r — slide rule
SW — short wave
tbl/m — table model

A-C Dayton, AC-9980 Navigator, console, wood, BC, 1929, from $110 to ..145.00
A-C Dayton, XL-10, tbl/m, plate glass, BC, b/o, 1925, from $530 to.. 580.00
Addison, B2B, tbl/m, plastic Deco style, BC, 1940, minimum value .. 850.00

Adler, 325, console, wood, BC, highboy, inner dial, 1930, from $140 to . 180.00
Admiral, 4D11, portable, plastic, BC, b/o, 1948, from $40 to 50.00
Admiral, 4L26, tbl/m, yel plastic, BC, 1958, from $20 to.............. 25.00
Admiral, 5Z, tbl/m, plastic & chrome, BC, 1937, from $90 to..... 105.00
Admiral, 6P32, portable, faux alligator, BC, palm tree grille, b/o... 80.00
Advance Electric, 88, cathedral, wood, BC, 1930, from $220 to... 250.00
Air Castle, G-722, console-R/P, wood, BC, pb, 1948, $60 to......... 80.00
Air King, A-410, portable/camera, faux alligator, b/o, 1948, $110 to.. 145.00
Airline, 14BR-736A, tbl/m, wood, BC, SW, 1941, from $50 to..... 75.00
Airline, 62-211, tombstone, wood, BC, b/o, 1936, from $80 to ... 105.00
Amrad, AC-5-C, console, mahog, lowboy, BC, 1926, from $240 to ..300.00
Amrad, 70 Sonata, console, walnut, highboy, BC, 1928, from $140 to..195.00
Arvin, 255T, tbl/m, ivory plastic, BC, 1949, from $40 to 50.00
Arvin, 617 Rhythm Maid, tombstone, wood, BC, SW, 1936, from $200 to...225.00
Atwater Kent, 33, console, wood, BC, b/o, 1927, from $220 to 295.00
Atwater Kent, 112S, console, wood, BC, SW, 1934, from $290 to .. 390.00
Belmont, 1170, console, wood, BC, SW, 1936, from $140 to....... 180.00
Bendix, 114, tbl/m, brn plastic, BC, 1948, from $270 to 320.00
Browning-Drake, 5-R, wood, BC, lift top, b/o, 1926, from $140 to.. 180.00
Chelsea, Super Six, tbl/m, wood, BC, b/o, 1925, from $130 to 170.00
Clarion, AC-70, cathedral, wood, convex-concave top, BC, 1931, $325 to...350.00
Coronado, 43-8160, tbl/m, plastic, BC, 1947, from $100 to......... 135.00
Crosley, D10BE, tbl/m, bl plastic, BC, 1951, from $140 to........... 180.00
Crosley, 10-139, tbl/m, aqua plastic, BC, 1950, from $100 to 135.00
Crosley, 48 Johnny Smoker, console, wood, sm, BC, 1931, from $370 to.. 495.00
Day-Fan, OEM-5, tbl/m, wood, BC, b/o, ca 1920s, from $140 to .. 180.00
Dewald, 524, tombstone, wood, BC, 1931, from $120 to 160.00
Echophone, S-3, cathedral, wood, BC, 1930, from $220 to.......... 290.00
Emerson, 517 Moderne, plastic, BC, 1947, from $50 to 70.00
Eveready, 32, console, wood, BC, 1929, from $160 to 220.00
Farnsworth, AT-21, tbl/m, onyx 'beetle' plastic, BC, SW, 1939, $220 to...290.00
Federal, 141, tbl/m, mahog, BC, b/o, 1925, from $480 to............. 600.00
Firestone, 4-A-115, tbl/m, wood, BC, 1953, from $30 to 45.00
French, Junior, cathedral, wood, ornate trim, BC, 1931, from $360 to...450.00
Garod, EC, console, wood, highboy, BC, 1926, from $180 to 240.00
Garod, 5A2, tbl/m, plastic, BC, 1946, from $50 to......................... 70.00

General Electric, A-64 tombstone, broadcast, short wave, from $90.00 to $110.00. (Photo courtesy John Slusser and the staff of Radio Daze)

General Electric, A-125, console, wood, BC, SW, LW, 1935, from $170 to..230.00
General Electric, tbl/m, wood, BC, SW, 1946, from $40 to............ 50.00
General Electric, 328, console-R/P, blond wood, BC, FM, 1949, $60 to .. 80.00
Gilfillan, 119, console, wood, lowboy, BC, 1940, from $270 to.... 360.00
Gilfillan, 8-T, tombstone, wood, BC, SW, 1934, from $270 to..... 360.00
Grantline, 605, tbl/m, plastic, BC, 1946, from $140 to 195.00
Grunow, 1181, console, wood, BC, SW, 1937, from $270 to........ 360.00
Howard, 400, console, wood, BC, SW, from $140 to.................... 180.00
Kadette, 649X, chair-side, wood, BC, SW, 1937, from $110 to... 145.00
Knight, 2117, tombstone, wood, BC, SW, ca 1950s, from $110 to.. 145.00
Lafayette, D-140, tbl/m, ivory plastic, BC, 1940, from $100 to.... 135.00
Lafayette, FE-143, tbl/m, walnut plastic, Deco, BC, 1940, from $140 to..180.00
Majestic, tbl/m, walnut, BC, SW, 1939, from $70 to...................... 90.00

Majestic, 15A, tombstone, wood, BC, 1932, from $110 to........... 145.00
Majestic, 3BC90-B, console, walnut, Deco, BC, SW, 1939, from $160 to...220.00
Mantola, R-76262, chair-side, wood, BC, 1948, from $80 to 105.00
Michigan, MRC-4, tbl/m, mahog, BC, b/o, 1923, from $280 to... 350.00
Motorola, 41S Sporter, portable, leatherette, BC, b/o, 1939, $40 to .. 55.00
Motorola, 6-T, tbl/m, BC, SW, 1937, from $80 to 105.00
Philco, 17L, console, wood, lowboy, BC, SW, 1933, from $120 to... 160.00
Philco, 38-89K, console, wood, BC, SW, 1938, from $100 to 135.00
RCA, R-4 Superette, cathedral, wood, BC, 1932, $290 to........... 350.00
RCA, Radiola 20, tbl/m, wood, BC, b/o, 1925, from $140 to....... 195.00
RCA, 6BK6, console, wood, BC, SW, 1936, from $100 to 135.00
RCA, 8QBK, console, wood, BC, SW, 1940, from $110 to 145.00

RCA, #568, polished chrome case, Raymond Loewy design, ca 1933, 7x12x6½", EX, $950.00.
(Photo courtesy Treadway Gallery Inc.)

Remler, MP5-5-3 Scottie, tbl/m, plastic, BC, 1946, from $140 to...180.00
Sentinel, 3291, tbl/m, ivory plastic, BC, 1948, from $40 to 50.00
Setchell-Carlson, 570, tbl/m, cylindrical, BC, 1950, from $80 to....105.00
Silvertone, 4487, console, wood, BC, SW, 1937, from $110 to.... 145.00
Sonora, P-99 Teeny-Weeny, tbl/m, wood, midget, BC, 1938, from $60 to...80.00
Westinghouse, H-354C7, console-R/P, wood, BC, FM, 1952, from $70 to..90.00
Westinghouse, WR-5, console, walnut, BC, 1930, from $110 to .. 145.00

Catalin/Bakelite

Garod Model 6AU1, red with butterscotch grille and knobs, 11½" high, EX, $2,400.00. (Photo courtesy Randy Inman Auctions Inc./LiveAuctioneers.com)

Addison, B-2E, mahog & ivory, 10½", EX 500.00
Addison, brn & butterscotch, vertical grille, 6x10½x4½" 1,100.00
Addison, Model 5, 1940, 8¾x12"...2,250.00
Admiral, 4L28, BC, 1958, from $20 to.. 50.00
Air King, 66, tombstone, BC, 1935...3,000.00
Airline, 14BR-514B, pnt, BC, 1941, from $85 to 105.00
Arvin, 432, maroon & butterscotch, vertical grille, 6x8½", VG .. 480.00
Bendix, 526C, gr marbleized & blk, 1946, 7x11"...................... 660.00
Colonial, New World Globe 700, blk w/gold pnt, ca 1933, 16" .. 1,450.00
Crosley, V, wood/Bakelite, BC, 1922, from $240 to 300.00
Detrola, 218 PeeWee, blk & ivory, 1930s, 4x6" 900.00
Dewald, A-301, harp-style case, brn, 6½x9½", VG.................... 480.00
Dewald, A-301, harp-style case, butterscotch, 6½x9½" 1,100.00
Dewald, A-502, butterscotch, 6½x10x6½"................................. 660.00
Emerson, AX-235, butterscotch w/blk trim, 5½x8½", VG 360.00
Emerson, Patriot, red/wht/bl, rstr, 1940s, 7x11" 1,550.00
Fada, L-56, gr & butterscotch, 9", EX 1,200.00
Fada, 44, orange, ribbed tuning/volume knobs, sq dial, 5½x9x4" 3,150.00
Fada, 115, butterscotch & red, bullet form, 10½", EX 1,200.00
Fada, 252 Temple, blk & butterscotch, sm cracks/stains, 10" W......600.00
Fada, 605, cream, rnd knobs, w/instructions, MIB...................... 425.00

Radios

Fada, 700, maroon & ivory, 1946, 6x10½" 1,500.00
Fada, 1000, bullet, maroon & butterscotch, 10½", EX 1,100.00
Fada, 1000 Bullet, brn & butterscotch (slight stains), 10" W....1,325.00
Fada, 1000 Bullet, butterscotch, 7¼x10¼x5¾", VG 780.00
Jewel, 300, butterscotch w/maroon dials, nonworking, 5¾x8" 150.00
Majestic, 7T11, brn, curved horizontal grille, 1939, 8x12"...........275.00
RCA, 66X, red w/brn knobs, 1946, 8½x15" 1,050.00

Novelty Radios

Beer Keg, Magic-Tone 900, 'spigot' is dial, BC, 1948, from $240 to...325.00
Coca Cola cooler, red plastic, BC, 1949, from $590 to.................780.00
Colonial New World, globe on stand, plastic, BC, 1933, from $800 to..950.00
Horse (saddled) standing on radio base, Abbotwares Z477, BC, $270 to...360.00
Liquor Bottle, Magic-Tone 504, dial on neck, BC, 1947, from $340 to..460.00
Log Cabin, wood, knobs in windows, BC, ca 1935, from $180 to ...240.00
Marlboro cigarette pack, plastic w/metal foil, CDI, BC, from $620 to..830.00
Sailing Ship, Majestic Melody Cruiser, wood & chrome, BC, '46, $320 to...420.00
Stack of books, Sentinel 238-V, leatherette, BC, 1941, from $150 to...205.00
Teakettle, Guild T/K 1577, wood, china & brass, ca 1959, from $110 to..145.00
Treasure Chest, Majestic 381, wood, BC, 1933, from $220 to......290.00

Transistor Radios

Post-World War II baby boomers, now in their fifties, are rediscovering prized possessions of youth, their pocket radios. The transistor
wonders, born with rock 'n roll, were at the vanguard of miniaturization
and futuristic design in the decade which followed their introduction to
Christmas shoppers in 1954. The tiny receiving sets launched the growth
of Texas Instruments and shortly to follow abroad, Sony and other Japanese giants.

The most desirable sets include the 1954 four-transistor Regency
TR-1 and colorful early Sony and Toshiba models. Certain pre-1960
models by Hoffman and Admiral represented the earliest practical use
of solar technology and are also highly valued. To avoid high tariffs,
scores of two-transistor sets, boys' radios, were imported from Japan with
names like Pet and Charmy. Many early inexpensive transistor sets could
be heard only with an earphone. The smallest sets are known as shirt-
pocket models while those slightly larger are called coat-pockets. Early
collectible transistor radios all have civil defense triangle markings at
640 and 1240 on the frequency dial and nine or fewer transistors. Very
few desirable sets were made after 1963. Model numbers are most commonly found inside.

Admiral, Y701R, vertical, AM, ca 1960 .... 15.00
Admiral, 221, horizontal, 6 transistors, AM, 1958 .... 35.00
Airline, GEN-1202A, horizontal, 6 transistors, AM, 1962 .... 30.00
Arvin, 61R69, vertical, 6 transistors, AM, 1963............................. 25.00
Channel Master, 6528, horizontal, 6 transistors, AM, 1960.......... 20.00
Columbia, C-605, horizonal, 5 transistors, AM, 1962 .... 15.00
Crown, TR-680, vertical, 6 transistors, AM, ca 1960 .... 25.00
Delmonico, 7YR707, sq, 7 transistors, AM, 1965 .... 55.00
Emerson, 888 Vanguard, vertical, 8 transistors, AM, 1958............. 75.00
Everplay, 2836A, vertical, 8 transistors, AM, 1963 .... 35.00
General Electric, P745B, horizontal, 5 transistors, AM, 1958........ 25.00
General Electric, P1818B, horizontal, 10 transistors, AM/FM, 1965 ...10.00
Hilton, TR108, vertical, 10 transistors, AM, ca 1964 .... 25.00
Hitachi, WH-761M, vertical, 7 transistors, AM, 1961................... 25.00
ITT, 6509, vertical, 9 transistors, AM/FM, 1963 .... 15.00
Jefferson-Travis, JT-D210, vertical, 4 transistors, AM, 1961 .... 30.00
Lafayette, FS-238, horizontal/desk set, 7 transistors, AM, 1964..... 25.00
Magnavox, 2AM-70, vertical, 7 transistors, AM, 1964 .... 30.00
MMA, F100, horizontal, 11 transistors, AM, 1963........................ 20.00
Motorola, X40S, vertical, 8 transistors, AM, 1962 .... 25.00

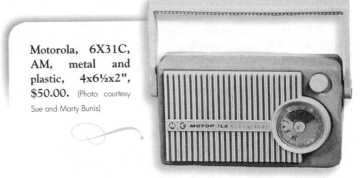

Motorola, 6X31C, AM, metal and plastic, 4x6½x2", $50.00. (Photo courtesy Sue and Marty Bunis)

Olympic, 447, horizontal, 4 transistors, AM, 1957 ....135.00
Philco, T-64, horizontal, 6 transistors, AM, 1963 .... 15.00
RCA, 1-TP-2E, vertical, 6 transistors, AM, 1961........................... 25.00
Regency, vertical, 4 transistors, AM, 1959..................................... 65.00
Sharp, FX-404, horizontal, 9 transistors, AM/FM, ca 1964 .... 25.00
Sony, TFM-951, horizontal, 9 transistors, AM, 1964...................... 30.00
Sony, TR-650, vertical, 6 transistors, AM, 1963............................. 40.00
Toshiba, 6TP-31A, vertical, 6 transistors, AM, 1963 .... 75.00

Toshiba, 7TP-303, metal, with speaker box, AM, 4½x2¾x1½", $125.00. (Photo courtesy Sue and Marty Bunis)

Truetone, DC3306, horizontal, 6 transistors, AM, 1963................. 20.00
Victoria, TR-650, vertical, 6 transistors, AM, 1961 .... 20.00
Westinghouse, H-730P7, horizontal, 7 transistors, AM, 1960........ 15.00
Zenith, Royal 150, vertical, 6 transistors, AM, 1962...................... 30.00

Railroadiana

Collecting railroad-related memorabilia has become one of America's most popular hobbies. The range of collectible items available is
almost endless; not surprising, considering the fact that more than 185
different railroad lines are represented. Some collectors prefer to specialize in only one railroad, while others attempt to collect at least one item
from every railway line known to have existed. For the advanced collector, there is the challenge of locating rarities from short-lived railroads;
for the novice, there are abundant keys, buttons, and passes. Among the
most popular specializations are dining-car collectibles — flatware, glassware, dinnerware, etc., in a wide variety of patterns and styles. Railroad
blankets are also collectible. Most common are Pullman blankets. The
early ones had a cross-stitch pattern; these were followed by one in a
solid cinnamon color; both are marked clearly with the Pullman name.
In the 1920s, Pullman put out a blue blanket marked Pullman, specifically for the use of Black porters. There is one in the Sacramento railroad
museum. Other railroads had their own 'marked' blankets that are even
more desirable, such as the Soo line, the Chessie, and one marked Pheasant (which was a private car on the Milwaukee Line that was reserved to
carry special parties for hunting trips).

Another name among railroad dining collectors is Fred Harvey. (See below for information about a new book on this subject.) From 1893 until after WWII, Fred Harvey masterminded all the dining halls and dining cars on the Santa Fe Railroad System from Chicago to the West Coast. (A little known fact, he also had dining facilities on the Frisco railroad.) He had his famous Harvey girls, as portrayed by Judy Garland, and a lot of personal dining china, silver, and linens marked with his 'FH.' Fred Harvey's operations, not heretofore known, extended well beyond WWII and into the 1960s, having dining facilities in California, Death Valley, and the East.

Berth keys have become scarce and expensive as more and more collectors purchase private rail cars. This is also true of 'window lifters,' specially designed pry bars made of wood used to ram the windows open in the old wood coaches. Most recently Otto Mears (of Silverton Colorado railroad fame) 1893 silver filigree railroad passes have surfaced. They are very scarce; made to the individual with possibly only 100 issued. These are appraised at $12,000.00 and have recently sold for near $11,000.00.

As is true in most collecting fields, scarcity and condition determine value. There is more interest in some railway lines than in others; generally speaking, it is greater in the region serviced by the particular railroad. American collectors prefer American-made products and items with ties to American railroads. For example, English switch lanterns, though of superior quality, usually sell at lower prices, as does memorabilia from Canadian railways such as Canadian Pacific or Canadian National.

Reproductions abound in railroadiana collectibles — from dinnerware and glassware to lanterns, keys, badges, belt buckles, timetables, and much more. Railroad police badges replicas have glutted the market. They are professionally made and only the expert is able to differentiate the replica from the original. Beware of 'fantasy' shot glasses. Repro handexecuted, reverse-painted glass signs have been abundant throughout the country, most of them read 'Santa Fe,' but some say 'Whites Only.' Lately, markets in the East have been inundated with Baltimore & Ohio reproductions: menus, glass water carafes, demitasse sets in the George Washington theme, and more. Watch for a Union Pacific brass spittoon, tall, somewhat weighted, and with a Union Pacific medallion on the front. The Union Pacific never had one like this. Railroad drumheads are coming out of collections. A drumhead is a large (approximately 24" diameter) glass sign in a metal case. They were used on the back end of all railroad observation cars to advertise a special train or a presidential foray, etc. They're now beginning to surface, and a good one like the Flying Crow from the Kansas City Southern Railroad will go for $2,500.00, as will many others. When items of this value come out, the counterfeiters are right there. It is important to 'Know Thy Dealer.' For a more thorough study, we recommend *Fred Harvey: Behind the Scenes at Newton, Florence and Hutchinson* by John 'Grandpa' White. (See the Directory for ordering information.) The values noted for most of our dinnerware, glassware, linen, silverplate, and timetables are actual selling prices. However, because prices are so volatile, the best pricing sources are often monthly or quarterly 'For Sale' lists. Our advisor for this category is Lila Shrader (see Directory, California). See also Badges.

Key:

BL — bottom logo	R&B — Reed & Barton
BS — bottom stamped	SM — side marked
FBS — full back stamp	TL — top logo
NBS — no back stamp	TM — top mark

Dinnerware

Many railroads designed their own china for use in their dining cars or company-owned hotels or stations. Some railroads chose to use stock patterns to which they added their name or logo; others used the same stock patterns without the added identification. A momentary warning: The railroad dinnerware market has fallen considerably; only the rare and scarce items are saleable — otherwise don't speculate in dining china.

Bowl, flat soup; UP, Columbine, BS w/Columbine, 5½" 185.00
Bowl, oatmeal; SP, Prairie Mtn Wildflowers, BS, 6" dia............... 180.00
Bowl, sauce; CRI&P, Sage Green, RI TL, FBS, Buffalo, Albert Pick, 5"..650.00
Bowl, serving; WA & ORRR, Harriman Blue, SL, Maddock's, 6½"..1,325.00
Butter pat, ACL, Flora of the South, BS, Buffalo, 3½" 70.00
Butter pat, ATSF, Bleeding Blue, TL, Albert Pick, 3x3" 350.00

Butter pat, Baltimore and Ohio, blue transfer, Scammell Lamberton, from $40.00 to $60.00. (Photo courtesy Grand View Antiques & Auction/LiveAuctioneers.com)

Butter pat, B&O, Capitol, rich gold, TL, 3½"............................. 178.00
Butter pat, Chicago, N Shore & Milwaukee Elec, Fontenelle, NBS.... 90.00
Butter pat, DE & Hudson, Canberbury, NBS, no TL 10.00
Butter pat, Pullman, Indian Tree (w/flower but no tree), TM, 3¼" ... 45.00
Butter pat, Southern RR, Peach Blossom, TL, Lamberton, 3¼"... 225.00
Butter pat, UP, Portland Rose, BS, 3½"..................................... 388.00
Child's mug, GN, Rocky, SL, 3" 155.00
Compote, CMStP&P, Peacock, ped ft, NBS, 2⅛x6½".................. 155.00
Creamer, IL Central, Louisiane, solid hdl, SL, ind, 2¼" 35.00
Creamer, MKT, Blue Bonnet, BS, Buffalo, 4" 335.00
Cup, bouillon; ATSF, CA Poppy, hdls, Made Expressly For..., BS ...210.00
Cup & saucer, ACL, Flora of the South, FBS, Buffalo................ 110.00
Cup & saucer, CMStP&P, Dulany, gr Deco border, Buffalo, ea w/BS ... 865.00
Cup & saucer, demitasse; SP, Prairie Mtn Wildflowers, Syracuse .. 230.00
Cup & saucer, demitasse; Wabash, Banner, SL, Syracuse 470.00
Cup & saucer, NP, Monad, SL & TL, NBS................................. 330.00
Egg cup, dbl, UP, Desert Wildflower, custard cup-like, BS, 2¾x3"....36.00
Gravy/sauceboat, Pullman, Calumet, w/hdl, SL, Bauscher, 5"...... 155.00
Hot food cover, B&O, Centenary, Thos Viaduct 1835, NBS, 5¾"... 630.00
Hot water/chocolate pot, ATSF, Mimbreno, BS, 5½".................. 360.00
Hot water/chocolate pot, B&O, Centenary, Scammell Lamberton, 6"..360.00
Ice cream shell, ATSF, Mimbreno, oval w/tab hdl, FBS, 5x5¼" ... 168.00
Ice cream shell, UP, Winged Streamliner, tab hdl, NBS, 4⅛" 30.00
Pitcher, ATSF, Bleeding Blue, SL, Lamberton, Albert Pick, 9"...... 45.00
Pitcher, B&O, Centenary, bl int line, FBS, Scammell Lamberton, 7".. 960.00
Plate, Central of NJ, Seagull w/Sandy Hook TL, NBS, 9"........... 795.00
Plate, CP, cobalt floral, BS, Spode, 1915, 10½"......................... 150.00
Plate, grill; B&O, Centenary, 3-compartment, Lamberton, 10¼"...200.00
Plate, IL Central, Coral, Syracuse, 1948, 7¼" 30.00
Plate, service; ATSF, Turquoise Room, TM, bl BS, 1950, 10⅛"... 2,175.00
Plate, service; C&O, Homestead Hotel Nature Study, Poppy, HP, BS, 11" .. 160.00
Plate, service; CB&Q, Aksarben, TL, Bauscher, 1931, 10½" 4,225.00
Plate, Wabash, Banner, Follow the Flag TL, Syracuse, 1962, 9½" ...160.00
Plate, Wabash, Banner, TM, Syracuse, 7¼" 480.00
Platter, B&O, Centenary, Cumberland Narrows, Pat...For, BS, 11½" L..300.00

Platter, Great Northern Railway, Glory of the West exclusive pattern, ca. 1940 – 1957, Onondaga Pottery, railroad stamp, 9", from $125.00 to $160.00. (Photo courtesy Barbara J. Conroy)

Teapot, CB&Q, cobalt, SL, Hall China, 9-oz 165.00
Teapot, KCS, Roxbury, NBS, ind, 4".. 35.00
Teapot, SF, Mimbreno, BS, spout to hdl: 7½" 555.00

Glass

Ashtray, ATSF, Santa Fe pyro in cursive in bottom, 4½x3¼" 42.00
Ashtray, B&O, bl SL & Capitol dome, 4½" 27.00
Ashtray, NYC emb in bottom, extended rests, 5½" 10.00
Bottle, beverage; Fred Harvey, Newton KS, side emb, aqua, 8".... 260.00
Bottle, club soda; SFRR Fred Harvey Service, paper label, gr, 7¼" ...95.00
Bottle, milk; MOPAC Lines emb w/in circle, Ben Bush Farms, ⅓-pt 28.00
Brandy snifter, B&O, Capitol Dome SL+5 encircling lines, ftd, 4½" 85.00
Carafe, PRR, wheel-cut SL, unmk hinged SP ltd/hdl, Internat'l, 9¼". 415.00
Champagne, CMStP&P, etched box SL, hollow stem, 5" 145.00
Cordial, ATSF, etched Santa Fe (script) w/5 horizontal lines, 3¼"... 120.00
Decanter/carafe, Grand Trunk Pacific, etched Fort Garry SL, 8½"... 220.00
Goblet, Gulf, Mobile & OH, silkscreen winged SL, ftd pilsner, 6"...36.00
Pitcher, Wabash, Follow the Flag etched SL, silver fr, 10".........1,135.00
Shot glass, DL&W, etched Phoebe Snow SL, ftd, 3¼", from $40 to... 75.00
Swizzle stick, B&O, Capitol Dome, bl, 4¾" 44.00
Swizzle stick, PRR keystone logo, Washington 7502, w/spoon feature, 6"....16.00
Tumbler, C&O in bl silkscreen, thick base, flared rim, 4½" 65.00
Tumbler, D&RG, optic inside, etched Curecanti SL, heavy base, 4" .. 145.00
Tumbler, GN, etched Rocky SL, 5" 65.00
Tumbler, WP, concave horizontal ridge, Feather River pyro, SL, 3½" ..26.00
Wine stem, IL Central, etched dmn SL, 4½" 88.00

Lamps

Adlake nonsweating, marker, WP, 4 lenses+font+burner+bracket+bail.. 500.00
Adlake nonsweating, 2 red/2 gr Kopp lenses, all orig, 16¼", NM.. 265.00
CNRy, P&A Mfg Waterbury Conn, kerosene burner, 2-pc, wall mt, 4½" H...85.00
Coach car, Patentee Hicks & Smith, wall mt, ca 1871-75, 17¼x10" .. 575.00

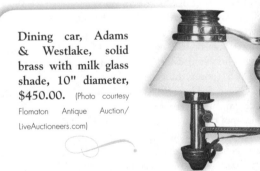

Dining car, Adams & Westlake, solid brass with milk glass shade, 10" diameter, $450.00. (Photo courtesy Flomaton Antique Auction/ LiveAuctioneers.com)

Finger, Boston, FO Dewey & Co, tin w/glass font, orig burner, 1871, NM ..100.00
Oiler's/mechanic's, MOPAC, Eagle, short spout w/wick, long hdl...100.00

Lanterns

Before 1920 kerosene brakemen's lanterns were made with tall globes, usually 5⅜" high. These are most desirable to collectors and are usually found at the top of the price scale. Short globes from 1921 through 1940 normally measure 3½" in height, except for those manufactured by Dietz, which are 4" tall. (Soon thereafter, battery brakemen's lanterns came into widespread usage; these are not highly regarded by collectors and are generally not railroad marked.) All lanterns should be marked with the name or initials of the railroad — look on the top, the top apron, or the bell base (if it has one). Globes may be found in these colors (listed in order of popularity): clear, red, amber, aqua, cobalt, and two-color. Any lantern's value is enhanced if it has a colored globe.

Adlake Reliable, LA&SL, clear 5⅜" globe, wire ring base, Pat 1909 .735.00
B&M, FO Dewey, emb TM, SM gr globe, brass top, bell bottom base . 2,185.00
Brakeman's, Adlake Kero, Hiram L Piper, red globe, complete, 15".....70.00
Brakeman's, Dressel, str fr, fuel pot/burner, bl-gr 3½" globe 100.00
Brakeman's, New Haven RR, Dietz Vesta, amber globe w/K logo ...125.00
Brakeman's, Oxweld #2155, carbide burner, flip cap, worn finish .. 55.00
Caboose, NP, 1 red/3 gr lenses 575.00
CN Rys, Adlake Kero, clear globe, gr pnt, 9x7" 40.00
CNR, Adlake Kero, Hiram L Piper, tin & wire fr, red globe, 9¾"....120.00
CNX, Adams & Westlake, clear Adlake globe, gr pnt, 1857, 10"+hdl..95.00
Contractor's, Dietz No 2 Blizzard, red pnt, rpl shade, 1930s 35.00
Switch, St Louis, Handlan w/Adlake burner & wick, 16x10x10" ...175.00

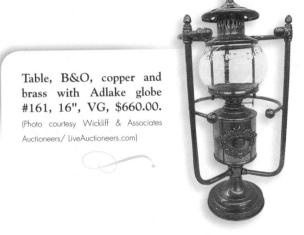

Table, B&O, copper and brass with Adlake globe #161, 16", VG, $660.00. (Photo courtesy Wickliff & Associates Auctioneers/ LiveAuctioneers.com)

Linens and Uniforms

Over the years the many railroad companies took great pride in their dining car table presentation. In the very early years of railroad dining car service, the linens used at the tables were of the finest quality white damask. Most railroads would add their company's logo, name, initials, or even a spectacular scene that would be woven into the cloth (white on white). These patterns were not evident unless the fabric was held at a particular angle to the light. The dining car staff's attire generally consisted of heavily starched blinding white jackets with shiny buttons.

In later years, post-World War II, color began to be used for table linens. Florida railroads created some delightfully colorful items for the table as well as for headrests. The passenger train crew, the conductor, and the brakemen, were generally attired in black suits, white shirts, and black ties. Their head gear generally bore a badge denoting their position. These items have all become quite collectible. Sadly, however, replicas of badges and pins have been produced as well as 'fantasy' items (items that do not replicate an older item but are meant to mislead or deceive).

Key:
RBH — reinforced button holes   w/w — white on white damask

Apron, CA Zephyr, woven over Pullman logo, wht cotton............. 22.00
Bath mat, GN in red script on wht heavy toweling, 33x21".......... 36.00
Blanket, CP woven on edge, Native Indian design, wool, 43x76" ..200.00
Blanket, DM&NRR, includes embr Northland, wool, 80x68"..... 170.00
Blanket/lap robe, Wabash stitched in center, cotton, 36x44"......... 32.00
Cap, Union News, blk embr on wht cotton.................................. 18.00
Hat, ATSF Conductor, blk wool, bl & wht enamel & brass hat badge. 180.00
Hat, CP Gateman, all woven into hat, buttons, braid.................. 565.00
Hat, GN Conductor, wool, GN Rocky enamel-on-brass pin........ 380.00
Hat, Seaboard Porter, gr wool, gold cording, brass badge.............. 140.00
Headrest, ATSF, wht huck w/bl Santa Fe logo on bl stripe, RBH, 15x18"....26.00
Headrest cover, CMStP&P Domeliners woven on edge, tan, RBH, 13x18"...18.00

Headrest cover, GM&O, red script on wht huck, brass grommets 7.00
Jacket, club car; IC Porter, IC logo & piping in orange on wht cotton..34.00
Napkin, El Paso & Southwestern, bow-tied ribbon logo, w/w, 23x23"...78.00
Napkin, SF center script logo w/scattered oak leaves, w/w, 23x23".... 23.00
Napkin, SP, Daylight, coastal scenes, mc, 19x19" 26.00
Pillowcase, SL&SF, The Frisco Line woven in bl on bl, 27x19"........5.00
Shop cloth, CMStP&P, safety slogans, 14x14", package of 10, M w/tag... 10.00
Tablecloth, CP, orange center CP Dining Cars logo, w/w/, 63x52" ..114.00
Tablecloth, PRR, keystone logo woven all corners, w/w, 62x48" ... 85.00
Tablecloth, SOO, ornate boxed center logo, w/w, Simtex, 64x54" ...70.00
Towel, bath; Seaboard woven in gr ea end, Dundee, 45x25" 36.00
Towel, hand; CP woven on bl stripe, wht huck, 19x12" 5.00
Towel, hand; NP, mc Monad logo on wht huck, 17x13" 12.50
Towel, hand; PRR woven in script on red stripe, wht huck, 18x12" .17.00
Uniform, NYC, cap w/no badge, coat & vest w/buttons & woven insignia..135.00

Locks

Brass switch locks (pre-1920) were made in two styles: heart-shaped and Keen Kutter style. Values for the heart-shaped locks are determined to a great extent by the railroad they represent and just how its name appears on the lock. Most in demand are locks with large embossed letters; if the letters are small and incised, demand for that lock is minimal. For instance, one from the Union Pacific line (even with heavily embossed letters) may go for only $45.00, while the same from the D&RG railroad could go easily sell for $250.00. Old Keen Kutter styles (brass with a 'pointy' base) from Colorado & Southern and Denver & Rio Grande could range from $600.00 to $1,200.00. Steel switch locks (circa 1920 on) with the initials of the railroad incised in small letters — for example BN, L&H, and PRR — are usually valued at $20.00 to $28.00.

Car, UP Ry, CAR, brass, 4", w/chain & key.................................. 100.00
Signal, B&MRR, Corbin on dust cover, steel 24.00
Signal, L&N, 1966, w/chain.. 25.00
Signal, NYCS, steel, 3½", w/key & chain 28.00
Signal, SL&SF, steel, 3½", w/key 48.00
Signal, Wabash, Yale, w/key 90.00
Signal, Yale & Town, brass 70.00
Switch, B&LE, Bohannan, brass, heart shape, 3¼", w/chain & key 100.00
Switch, N&WRY CO on hasp, Slaymaker, w/chain & key............ 80.00
Switch, P&LE, Adlake, w/chain & brass key................................. 130.00

Silver-Plated Flatware

Corn holders, NC&STL, SM, R&B, pr 140.00
Crumber, ATSF, Albany, BS, Harrison & Hawson, 12"................ 160.00
Fork, dinner; PRR, Broadway, TL, Internat'l, 7⅛" 15.00
Fork, dinner; PRR keystone TL, Kings, Internat'l, 7" 32.00
Fork, dinner; SP, Broadway, BM, Internat'l, 7⅛".......................... 23.00
Fork, seafood; GN, Astoria, TM, Wallace, 6" 42.00
Fork, seafood; PRR, Broadway, TM, Internat'l, 6" 44.00

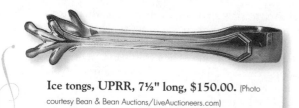

Ice tongs, UPRR, 7½" long, $150.00. (Photo courtesy Bean & Bean Auctions/LiveAuctioneers.com)

Iced teaspoon, Erie RR, Grecian, TM, Internat'l, 7½" 28.00
Knife, dinner; Lehigh Valley, hammered, TM, Heinrichs, 9½" 70.00
Knife, luncheon; ACL, Zephyr, TM, Internat'l, 7" 14.00

Ladle, condiment; UP, Windsor, BM, Internat'l, 6" 30.00
Ladle, sauce; DE & Hudson, Roal, D&H TM, R&B, 7" 55.00
Ladle, sauce; NYC, Century, BM, Internat'l, 4¾" 30.00
Spoon, cream soup; IL RR, Cromwell, Internat'l, BM, 6" 32.00
Spoon, cream soup; Lehigh Valley RR, Rex, TL, R&B, 5½".......... 130.00
Spoon, cream soup; NYC, Century, BM, Internat'l, 5¾" 32.00
Spoon, cream soup; SP, Modern w/Flying Wheel TL, BM, R&B ..200.00
Spoon, demi; NYC & Hudson River, Vendome, BM, R&B, 4½".....34.00
Spoon, grapefruit; SP, Broadway, serrated edge, TL, Internat'l, 6½"..23.00
Spoon, soup; Fred Harvey, Fiddle, TM, Rogers, 7¾".................... 38.00
Spoon, soup; Fred Harvey, Manhattan, BM, Internat'l, 7¼" 26.00
Sugar tongs, B&O, Clovelly, TL, R&B, 4¼" 82.50
Sugar tongs, Lehigh Valley RR, Rex, TL (flag), R&B, 4½" 175.00
Sugar tongs, PA RR, Kings, keystone TL, R&B, 4½" 75.00
Sugar tongs, SP, Grecian, BS, Internat'l, 4½" 58.00
Teaspoon, ATSF, TM, Cromwell, 6" 19.00
Teaspoon, D&RG, Navarre, TM, Rogers, 6"................................ 148.00
Teaspoon, New Haven, Modern, BS, Internat'l, 6" 13.00
Teaspoon, PRR, Cromwell, BS, Internat'l, 6" 28.00

Silver-Plated Hollow Ware

The value of silver plate, hollow ware, or flatware is influenced by the location of the logo or railroad name and, of course, by condition. A side- or top-marked piece is preferable to one with a bottom mark. Examine a prospective purchase carefully. Some unmarked flatware has been 'enhanced' with a rather crude stamping of the railroad's name. Authentic railway markings were done at the time of manufacture and were generally executed in a flawless manner.

Bar jigger, UP, Overland shield SL, Meridian, 4½" 455.00
Bowl, B&M, Arrow logo TM, Internat'l, 4½"................................ 230.00
Butter pat, D&RG, Curecanti TM, R&B, sq, 2¾" 215.00
Butter pat, L&N, old boxed TL, Internat'l, 3⅜" 55.00
Butter pat, UP, oval w/sm tab hdls, BM, R&B, 3x4¼" 25.00
Champagne bucket, LA & SL, hdls, SL, R&B, 9½" 635.00
Cocktail shaker, FEC, Royal Poinciana, TL, Rogers Meriden, 5¾".. 285.00
Coffeepot, TX & Pacific, eagle SL, hinged lid, BM, Internat'l, 10"..395.00
Condiment set, SP, winged finial on bail, sugar+4 s&p, TM & BS, R&B.365.00
Creamer, ATSF, hinged lid w/tab, Santa Fe BM, Internat'l, 4½".... 80.00
Creamer, NYC, Art Deco Century, hinged lid, TM, Internat'l, 4¼".. 95.00
Creamer, Southern, Queen & Crescent Route SL, hdl, 2¼" 85.00
Finger bowl, WP, rtcl rim, BL, Internat'l, 4¾" 150.00
Ice bucket, NYC, SL, appl band at top edge, Internat'l, 4½"........240.00
Menu holder, NYC SL, w/pencil holder, Deco ft, Internat'l, 4¾"....250.00
Menu holder, PRR, w/pencil holder, raised keystone SL, 4½" 165.00
Pitcher, Nickel Plate Road, glass insert in SM fr, hinged lid, 10" .. 515.00
Pitcher, NYC, glass insert in TM fr, hinged lid, Internat'l, 9¼" ... 540.00
Sauceboat & liner, MP, both BM, Internat'l, 2½", 6x3½"............ 78.00
Seafood icer, PRR, appl keystone logo, glass insert, Internat'l...... 250.00
Shakers, B&O, both BM in script, 3", pr 155.00
Sugar bowl, ATSF, hinged lid, hdls, Santa Fe SL, Internat'l, 6¼" W... 168.00
Sugar bowl, CB&Q, w/lid & hdls, Burlington Rte boxed SL, R&B. 130.00
Sugar bowl, DL&W, Lackawana Route SL, w/lid, Internat'l, 5"..... 50.00
Syrup, ACL, attached tray & hinged lid, SL, Internat'l, 6" 370.00
Syrup, PRR, hinged lid, raised keystone SL & BS, Internat'l, 6"..370.00
Syrup, UP Overland Rte, attached tray/lid, SL, R&B, 4½"............ 265.00
Tray, pastry; New Haven, 4-leg, rectangular, BS, R&B, 9x6".................. 158.00

Switch Keys

Switch keys are brass with hollow barrels and round heads with holes for attaching to a key ring. They were used to unlock the padlocks on track-side switches when the course of the tracks had to be changed.

(Switches were padlocked to prevent them from being thrown by accident or vandals, a situation that could result in a train wreck). A car key used to open padlocks on freight cars and the like is very similar to the switch key, except the bit is straighter instead of being specifically curved for a particular railroad and its accompanying switch locks. A second type of 'car' key was used for door locks on passenger cars, Pullmans, etc.; this type was usually of brass, but instead of having a hollow barrel, they were shaped like an old-fashioned hotel door key. In order for a key to be collectible, the head must be marked with a name, initials, or a railroad identification, with 'switch' generally designated by 'S' and 'car' by 'C' markings. Railroad, patina 'not polished,' and the presence of a manufacturer's mark other than Adlake all have a positive effect on pricing and collectibility.

CC&StL, brass, hollow bbl, 2⅛"	35.00
CPRR, brass bbl, 2"	20.00
MOPAC, brass, hollow bbl, 2¼"	26.00
NP, brass bbl, 2¼"	20.00
NYCS, brass, 2"	20.00
PRR, brass, 2"	45.00
SOO Line, brass, 2"	35.00

Miscellaneous

Timetables and railroad travel brochures continue to gain in popularity and offer the collector vast information about the glory days of railroading. Annual passes continue to be favored over trip and one-time passes. Their value is contingent upon the specific railroad, its length of run, and the appearance of the pass itself. Many were tiny works of art enhanced with fancy calligraphy and decorated with unique vignettes. Pocket calendars are popular as well as railroad playing cards. Pins, badges, and uniform buttons bearing the name or logo of a railroad are also sought after. The novice needs to be cautious about signs (metal as well as cardboard) and belt buckles. Reproductions flourish in these areas.

Accident report #3991 by ICC re ATSF, Lomax, IL, 1963, 9-pg,	230.00
Advertising ruler, ATSF, wooden, 3-sided, metal SF logo, 12"	25.00
Ashtray, GN, Snuf-A-Rette, cobalt, TL, 4¼"	170.00
Ashtray, Monon TM, alligator's open mouth receives ashes, detailed, 9"	60.00
Ashtray/match holder, C&O, G Washington silhouette, Buffalo, 4½x7"	100.00
Ashtray/matchbook holder, B&O, Snuf-A-Rette, TM, B&O bio on bottom	148.00
Badge, breast; SP, Police/AZ, 6-point silver star, Irvine & Jachiens	4,495.00
Badge, breast; UP, Waiter Instructor, blk Bakelite, 2⅛" dia	125.00
Badge, hat; D&RG Conductor, brass, 1⅛x4⅛"	360.00
Badge, hat; L&N, Train Caller, gold-tone metal, 2¾x4"	700.00
Blotter, ATSF, Chico holding SF logo, unused, 16x20"	38.00
Blotter, CRI&P, IA NE Ltd to Chicago, unused, 3½x8"	30.00
Bond, NP, $100, payable in gold, sgn J Cooke, uncancelled, 1870	2,365.00
Book, Cab Forward - SP Articulated Locomotives, Church, 1968, 1st ed.	175.00
Book, Signal Directory, hardbound leather, 1908, 600+ pgs, 8x12", G	695.00
Book, UP System Official Ry Guide, hardbk, 1,500-pg, 1922	155.00
Booklet, ATSF, All Private Room Streamliner, 9-pg, 1930s, 5x7"	70.00
Booklet, GN Secrets (Oriental Ltd recipes), 1930s, 32-pg, 7¼x5¼"	85.00
Booklet, PRR, Division of Maps, Office Chief Engineer, 14 maps, 1964	55.00
Builder's plate, C&O, Am Loco Corp, brass, A H4...2-6-6-2, 1913, 8x14"	945.00
Builder's plate, PRR, M1 Baldwin Locomotive Works, brass, 1926	1,300.00
Bulletin board, MKT, for chalk notations, dated 190_, 36x25"	1,950.00
Button, Central VT (CV), gilt or brass tone, Scovill Mfg, ⅝"	46.00
Button, OR Electric Ry, OE, silver-tone metal, Scovill Mfg, ⅝"	10.00
Calendar, ATSF, celluloid, 1936 or 37, pocket sz, ea	395.00
Calendar, ATSF, celluloid, 1939, pocket sz, G	22.00
Calendar, GN, Weinold Reiss Evening Star lady, 13 sheets, 1954, 33x16"	58.00
Calendar, NPYPL logo, CS, 1949, pocket sz	98.00
Calendar, PRR, Grif Teller mining operation, 1941, complete, 28½"	170.00

Calendar postcard, GN, September 1914, opens to 9x12"	385.00
Catalog, Baldwin Steam Locomotive parts, hardbk, 1924, 9½x11"	698.00
Cigarette lighter, NYC&StL, Nickel Plate Road, Zippo-like	23.00
Decal, Authorized Watch Inspector, SP, mc, 9x6½"	135.00
Doorknob, ICRR CO, emb brass	188.00
Fan, MKT, Bouquet Bluebonnets, Compliments of Katy Line, CS, 11"	27.00
Fire alarm box, PRR, Gamewell, TM, red CI, 10x16x5"	900.00
Fire grenade, MPRR emb oval SM, Harden, glass w/vertical ribs, 8"	1,525.00

Handkerchief, Chessie, made for Chesapeake & Ohio Railway, 8x8", $25.00.

Handkerchief, NYC, red bandana w/logos, 22x22"	25.00
Jack, Duff Barrett RR type used by gandy dancers, 22"	60.00
Jug, GN, Property of...Ry Co, stoneware, 13", 1-gal	200.00
Key, caboose; Adlake, brass, solid bbl, 4½"	30.00
Key, caboose; B&O, brass, solid bbl, 3½"	35.00
Lapel pin, Wabash, Follow the Flag Banner logo, red/bl enamel, ⅞"	10.00
Light fixture, ceiling; Pullman, brass/curved glass panels, 13" dia	600.00
Luggage sticker, CMStP&P, Olympian/Milwaukee Rd, 3½"	9.00
Luggage tag, ME Central, leather strap, brass	66.00
Magazine, employee; B&O, November, 1941	11.00
Magazine, employee; Kansas City Southern, July, 1928	52.00
Magazine, employee; MP Lines, January, 1955	26.00
Magazines, Trains, 12 issues, hardbk, 11/1942 to 10/1943	145.00
Manual, LA Ry, Car House Organization & Oper, hardbk, 70-pg, 1926	130.00
Manual, UP, Rotary Snow Plow...Instructions, spiral bound, illus	160.00
Map, 1862 Southern states, Duval & Son, provenance, 54x31"	6,750.00
Matchbook, Central of GA, Serving the Southeast, 1950s, unused	13.00
Matchbox, ATSF logo, Turquoise Room, no matches, 1x2¼"	22.50
Matches, UP, 4 unused books in boxcar-like box, EX graphics, 4" L	5.00
Menu, B&O Capital Ltd, 1925-26, opens to 11x17"	55.00
Menu, IL Central, Club Lounge, 1948, 4½x6¼"	10.00
Menu, New Haven, Yankee Clipper, CS, 1930, folds to 9½x5¾"	180.00
Menu, PRR, train to 1931 World Series, photo cover, 9x6"	90.00
Menu, UP, die-cut squirrel, colorful, child's	30.00
Napkin, C&O, Chessie logo in corner, mc, paper, unused, from $4 to	8.00
Napkins, cocktail; C&NW, pics of name trains on paper, pkg of 100	20.00
Number plate, PRR 5370 locomotive, keystone shape, red pnt CI, 20"	3,350.00
Pamphlet, Lehigh Valley, Summer Tours...Resorts, 1900, 63-pg, 6½x9"	140.00
Pamphlet, N Shore Line/Milwaukee to Chicago, 1920s, 24-pg	360.00
Pamphlet, SOO Line, Pacific Coast Tours, Canadian Rockies, 1923	28.00
Paperweight, NYC, Hudson locomotive on tiered base, metal, 9½"	155.00
Pass, annual; CRI&P, Rock Island, 1925	10.00
Pass, annual; Galena & Chicago Union RR, paper, 1857, 2¼x3½"	190.00
Pass, annual; Marietta & Cincinnati RR & Branches, 1880, 2¼x3½"	160.00
Pass, annual; SP Sunset Route, 1895, 2¼x3½"	135.00

Pass, employee; Northern Pacific Railway, July 22, 1910, VG, $15.00. (Photo courtesy gasolinealleyantiques.com)

Pass, lifetime; IL Central, 40 Years of Service, 1959, w/case........... 24.00
Pass, trip; C&O, paper, issued & expired in 1938, 3x7" 10.00
Pencils, various RRs, unsharpened, w/erasers, lot of 26 .... 14.00
Photo, D&RG, Rocky Mtn scenery, hand tinted, plaque on oak fr, 29x24" .300.00
Pin-bk, GN, ND Development Tour, space for name, 1890s, 4" .. 145.00
Playing cards, Burlington Rte, Nat'l Park Line, dbl deck, +case .. 275.00
Playing cards, DRGW, Rio Grande Main Line..., unopened, M in slipcase .75.00
Postcard, Albany/Springfield, OR, McKeen Motor Car RR, RP, 1910-20...55.00
Postcard, construction of railway station, Freeville NY, photo, 1900s... 100.00
Postcard, depot, Windsor CA, wagon/workers/freight photo, 1910....160.00
Postcard, IL Central, Million Dollar Subway, blk/wht photo, 1914 .. 50.00
Postcard, NY roundhouse, rail yards/switch engines photo, 1909 .. 65.00
Poster, ATSF, Land of Pueblos/Santa Fe, 1960s, 18x24" 600.00
Print, annual; AKRR, Denali Park Station, 1988, 21x23" 30.00
Ring, retirement; UP, birthstone & shield logo, silver-tone, 1992 ...70.00
Semiphore assembly, UP, 48" blade, lenses, CI counterweight, 72".. 790.00
Sign, MP buzz-saw logo/Eagle, Post Cereal, tin, 1950s, 2½x3½" 7.00
Sign, PRR depot; Ravena OH, elongated keystone, pnt CI, 25x50"..5,550.00
Sign, WP, Feather River logo, porc on steel, 8 grommets, 24x24" ...415.00
Swizzle stick, PRR on keystone logo, Resume Speed, plastic, set of 10 ..10.00
Test gauge, steam train, Yosemite Valley RR, in 7x9" leather case ..900.00
Ticket puncher, PRR, SM, spring action, 5¼" L 160.00
Timetable, employee; Susquehanna & NY, #48, 1936, 14-pg....... 120.00
Water can, KCS SM, galvanized, spigot, strap hdl & bail hdl, 18½" .. 45.00
Wax sealer, DE & Hudson, Whitehall NY, wood hdl, brass seal .. 270.00
Wax sealer, NYC & Hudson RR, Terrytown NY, brass w/wood hdl, 3½"....430.00
Whistle, PRR, 3-chime, brass, side-mt, 21x6", 32" overall........2,656.00

Razors

As straight razors gain in popularity, prices of those razors also increase. This carries with it a lure of investment possibilities which can encourage the novice or speculator to make purchases that may later prove to be unwise. We recommend that before investing serious money in razors, you become familiar with the elements which make a razor valuable. As with other collectibles, there are specific traits which are desirable and which have a major impact on price.

The following information is based on the third edition of *Standard Guide to Razors* by Roy Ritchie and Ron Stewart (available from R&C Books, Box 2421, Hazard KY 41702, $12.95 +$4.00 S&H). It describes the elements most likely to influence a razor's collector value and their system of calculating that value. This is the most used collector's guide for straight razors currently available.

There are five major factors to be considered in determining a razor's value. These are the brand and country of origin, the age of the razor, the handle material, the artistic enhancements found on the handles and/ or blade and the condition of the razor. Ritchie and Stewart freely admit that there are other factors that may come into play with some collectors, but these are the major components in determining value. They have devised a system of evaluation which utilized some components that are thoroughly described in this book.

The most important factor (Chart A) is the value placed on the brand and country of origin. This is the price of a common razor made by (or for) a particular company. It has plain handles, probably made of plastic, no artwork, and is in collectible condition. It is the beginning value. Hundreds of these values are provided in the 'Listings of Companies and Base Values' chapter in the book.

Next (Chart B), because age plays such an important role, you must determine the age of your razor. There are four age categories or divisions in this appraisal system. Determine your razor's age and multiply 'brand value' times the number in parenthesis (). Take this value to the next step.

The Chart C category is that of handle material. This covers a wide range of materials, from fiber on the low end to ivory on the high end.

Because celluloid and plastics were used to mimic a wide variety of other handle materials, the collector needs to be able to identify the different handle materials when he sees them. This is especially true with ivory and mother-of-pearl.

The artistic category (Chart D) is without doubt the most subjective. Nevertheless, it is extremely important in determining the value of a straight razor. Artwork can include everything from logo art to carving and sculpture. It may range from highly ornate to tastefully correct. Blade etching as well as handle artistry are to be considered. Perhaps what some call the 'gotta have it' or the 'neatness' factors properly fall into this category. You must accurately determine the artistic merits of your razor when you evaluate it relative to this factor.

Finally (Chart E), the condition is factored in. The book's scales run from 'parts' (10% +/-) to 'Good' (150% +/-). Average (100% +/-) is classified as 'Collectible.'

Samplings from charts:

Chart A, Companies and Base Values:

Abercrombie & Finch, NY	15.00
Aerial, USA	26.00
Boker, Henri & Co, Germany	15.00
Brick, F; England	10.00
Case Mfg Co, Spring Valley NY	40.00
Chores, James; England	11.00
Dahlqres, CW; Sweden	16.00
Diane, Japan	10.00
Electric Co, NY	17.00
Faultless, Germany	13.00
Fox Cutlery, Germany	12.00
Fredericks (Celebrated Cutlery), England	14.00
Gilbert Bros, England	12.00
Griffon XX, Germany	12.00
Henckels, Germany	15.00
Holley Mfg Co, CT	30.00
International Cutlery Co NY/Germany	13.00
IXL, England	16.00
Jay, John; NY	12.00
KaBar, Union Cut Co, USA	30.00
Kanner, J; Germany	12.00
Kern, R&W; Canada/England	12.00
LeCocltre, Jacque; Switzerland	12.00
Levering Razor Co, NY/Germany	18.00
McIntosh & Heather, OH	14.00
Merit Import Co, Germany	11.00
Monkhouse, Carl NY	14.00
National Cut Co, OH	13.00
Oxford Razor Co, Germany	11.00
Palmer Brothers, Savannah, GA	22.00
Primble, John; Indian Steel Works, Louisville KY	25.00
Queen City NY	14.00
Querelle, A; Paris France	14.00
Quigley, Germany	10.00
Radford, Joseph & Sons; England	13.00
Rattler Razor Co, Germany	12.00
Robeson Cut Co, USA	30.00
Salamander Works, Germany	12.00
Soderein, Ekilstuna Sweden	13.00
Taylor, LM; Cincinnati OH	16.00
Tower Brand, Germany	18.00
Ulmer, Germany	12.00
US Barber Supply, TX	13.00
Vinnegut Hdw Co, IN	13.00
Vogel, Ed; PA	11.00

Chart B, Age Factor:

You must determine the approximate age of your razor. The book goes into much detail about how to do this. We have determined four general categories for purposes of factoring age into your appraisal.

1740 – 1820 (Chart A values x 2 = B value)

1820 – 1870 (Chart A value x 1.5 = B value)

1870 – 1930 (Chart A value x 1 = B value)

1930 – 1950 (Chart A value x .75 = B value)

Chart C, Handle Materials:

The following is an abbreviated version of the handle materials list in *Standard Guide to Razors*. It is an essential category in the use of the appraisal system developed by the authors.

Genuine Ivory	600%
Tortoise Shell	500%
Pearl	400%
Stag	400%
Jigged Bone	350%
Smooth Bone	300%
Celluloid	250%
Composition	150%
Plastic	100%

Chart D, Artistic Value:

As poined out earlier, this is a very subjective area. It takes study to determine what is good and what is not. Taste can also play a significant role in determining the value placed on the artistic merit of a razor. The range is from exceptional to nonexistent. Categories generally are divided as follows:

Unique (off the charts)

'Unique' has a feature that makes the razor uncommonly special. The feature, whether design, inlay, or ownership by a 'famous' historical figure (etc.), makes the razor beyond exceptional and distinctive.

Exceptional	650%
Superior	550%
Good	400%
Average	300%
Minimal	200%
Plain	100%
Nonexistant	0%

Chart E, Condition:

Condition is also very subjective. This chart will help you determine the condition of the razor. You must judge accurately if the appraisal system is to work for you.

Good   150%

Does not have to be factory mint to fall within this category. However, there can be no visible flaws if it is to be calculated at 150%.

Collectible   100%

May have some flaws that do not greatly detract from the artwork or finish.

Parts   10%

Unrepairable, valuable as salvageable parts.

Razors may fall between any of these categories, i.e. collectible to 112%.

Now to determine the value of your razor: Find the code value from the brand chart (A) and multiply it times the age factor (B) to determine the 'B' value. Multiply B times C and multiply B times D. Add your two answers togethers and multiply this sum times E. The answer you get is your collector value (F). See the example below:

(A) Brand & Origin Base Value	(B) Age Factor % Value	(C) Handle Material % Value	(D) Artwork % Value	(E) Condition % Value	(F) Collector Value
John Primble Belknap; Louisville KY $25.00	1870 – 1930 x1= $25.00	Celluloid colorful 25 x 300%= $75.00	Escutcheon inlay 25 x 200%= $50.00	Collectible 100%	$75+$50= $125 $125 x 100%= $125.00

Reamers

The largest producer of glass reamers was McKee, who pressed their products from many types of glass — custard; Delphite and Chalaine Blue; opaque white; Skokie Green; black; caramel and white opalescent; Seville Yellow; and transparent pink, green, and clear. Among these, the black and the caramel opalescents are the most valuable. Prices vary greatly according to color and rarity. The same reamer in crystal may be worth three times as much in a more desirable color.

Among the most valuable ceramic reamers are those made by American potteries, for example the Spongeband reamer by Red Wing, Coorsite reamers, and figural reamers. China one- and two-piece reamers are also very desirable and command very respectable prices.

A word about reproductions: A series of limited edition reamers is being made by Edna Barnes of Uniontown, Ohio. These are all marked with a 'B' in a circle. Other reproductions have been made from old molds. The most important of these are Anchor Hocking two-piece two-cup measure and top, Gillespie one-cup measure with reamer top, Westmoreland with flattened handle, Westmoreland four-cup measure embossed with orange and lemons, Duboe (hand-held darning egg), and Easley's Diamonds one-piece.

For more information concerning reamers and reproductions, contact or the National Reamer Collectors Association (see Clubs, Newsletters, and Catalogs). Be sure to include an SASE when requesting information.

Ceramic

Clown, Made in Japan, ca. 1940s, 9x8", $150.00. (Photo courtesy House in the Woods Auction Gallery Inc./LiveAuctioneers.com)

Camel kneeling, beige lustre w/lt gr top, 4¼", from $200 to......... 250.00
Clown, wht w/gr hat (reamer), ruffle & socks, blk details, Japan ... 75.00
Duck, orange & gr on wht pearlized body 110.00
Floral w/gold, Nippon, 2-pc.. 195.00
Pitcher, blk w/gold wheat, 2-pc, 8".. 45.00
Plaid design, gr & wht, Japan, 2-pc, 6¼"..................................... 250.00
Puddinhead, 2-pc, 6¼"... 250.00
Rose, pk w/gr leaves, Germany, 1¾".. 225.00
Sailboat, yel or red, 3", ea.. 125.00
Toucan, mc on wht pearlescent lustre, unmk Japan, 2¾x5¾"....... 165.00

Glass

Cambridge, cobalt, ribbed, from $2,750 to................................3,000.00
Cambridge, crystal, ribbed, from $25 to 28.00
Federal, gr, pointed cone, tab hdl, from $25 to............................. 28.00
Federal, pk, ribbed, loop hdl, from $45 to..................................... 50.00
Fry, gr, str sides, ribbed, tab hdl, from $40 to................................ 45.00
Fry, Pearl, fluted, from $75 to... 85.00
Hazel-Atlas, bl dots on wht, ftd, 2-pc, from $65 to........................ 70.00
Hazel-Atlas, cobalt, lg tab hdl, from $325 to 335.00
Hazel-Atlas, crystal, emb crisscross, tab hdl, from $20 to 22.00
Hazel-Atlas, gr, emb crisscross, from $35 to................................... 40.00
Hazel-Atlas, gr, 4-cup stippled pitcher & reamer set, from $45 to . 50.00
Hazel-Atlas, pk, emb crisscross, tab hdl, from $325 to.................. 335.00
Hazel-Atlas, wht, lg tab hdl, from $30 to 38.00
Hocking, gr, ribbed, ftd, loop hdl, from $30 to............................... 35.00

Hocking, Mayfair Blue, two-cup measuring cup with reamer top, from $1,600.00 to $1,800.00. (Photo courtesy Cathy and Gene Florence)

Indiana Glass, crystal, tab hdl, from $25 to................................... 28.00
Indiana Glass, pk, 6-sided cone, vertical hdl, from $175 to.......... 195.00
Jennyware, pk, ribbed, ftd, from $110 to...................................... 125.00
Lindsay (emb), gr, vertical hdl, from $450 to................................ 500.00
MacBeth-Evans Glass, clambroth, vertical hdl, from $185 to...... 200.00
McKee, grapefruit, blk, vertical hdl, from $1,000 to..................1,200.00
Saunders (emb), Jadeite, cone top, from $1,600 to....................1,700.00
Sunkist, butterscotch, from $375 to 395.00
Sunkist, custard, emb McKee, ring hdl, from $35 to........................ 45.00
Sunkist (emb), Crown Tuscan, from $375 to................................. 395.00
Sunkist (emb), Jadeite, from $75 to 85.00
Sunkist (emb), lt caramel, from $375 to 395.00
US Glass, amber, 2-cup pitcher set, ftd, 2-pc, from $325 to 375.00
US Glass, crystal w/orange decor, 2-cup pitcher set, ftd, 2-pc 60.00
US Glass, gr, 4-cup pitcher set, ftd, from $140 to 150.00
US Glass, wht, 2-cup pitcher set, ftd, 2-pc, from $110 to............. 125.00
Valencia, gr, vertical hdl, from $100 to... 125.00
Valencia, mustard slag, emb fleur-de-lis, from $375 to.................. 400.00
Valencia, pk/amber, vertical hdl, from $325 to 350.00
Valencia (emb), gr, vertical hdl, from $250 to............................... 275.00
Valencia (emb), wht, vertical hdl, from $135 to............................. 150.00

Westmoreland, crystal w/decor, 2-pc, from $75 to 95.00
Westmoreland, pk frosted, 2-pc, from $185 to 195.00

Records

Records of interest to collectors are often not the million-selling hits by 'superstars.' Very few records by Bing Crosby, for example, are of any more than nominal value, and those that are valuable usually don't even have his name on the label! Collectors today are most interested in records that were made in limited quantities, early works of a performer who later became famous, and those issued in special series or aimed at a limited market. Vintage records are judged desirable by their recorded content as well; those that lack the quality of music that makes a record collectible will always be 'junk' records in spite of their age, scarcity, or the obsolescence of their technology.

Records are usually graded visually rather than aurally, since it is seldom if ever possible to first play the records you buy at shows, by mail, at flea markets, etc. Condition is one of the most important determinants of value. For example, a nearly mint-condition Elvis Presley 45 of 'Milk Cow Blues' (Sun 215) has a potential value of over $1,500.00. A small sticker on the label could cut its value in half; noticeable wear could reduce its value by 80%. A mint record must show no evidence of use (record jackets, in the case of EPs and LPs, must be equally choice). Excellent condition denotes a record showing only slight signs of use with no audible defects. A very good record has noticeable wear but still plays well. Records of lesser grades may be unsaleable, unless very scarce and/or highly sought-after.

While the value of most 78s does not depend upon their being in appropriate sleeves (although a sleeveless existence certainly contributes to damage and deterioration!), this is not the case with most EPs (extended play 45s) and LPs (long-playing 33⅓ rpm albums), which must have their jackets (cardboard sleeves), in nice condition, free of disfiguring damage, such as writing, stickers, or tape. Often, common and minimally valued 45s might be collectible if they are in appropriate 'picture sleeves' (special sleeves that depict the artist/group or other fanciful or symbolic graphic and identify the song titles, record label, and number), e.g. many common records by Elvis Presley, the Beatles, and the Beach Boys.

Promotional copies (DJ copies) supplied to radio stations often have labels different in designs and/or colors from their commercially issued counterparts. Labels usually bear a designation 'Not for Sale,' 'Audition Copy,' 'Sample Copy,' or the like. Records may be pressed of translucent vinyl; while most promos are not particularly collectible, those by certain 'hot' artists, such as Elvis Presley, the Beach Boys, and the Beatles are usually premium disks.

Many of the most desirable and valuable 45s have been bootlegged (counterfeited). For example, there are probably more fake Elvis Presley *Sun* records in circulation than authentic copies — certainly in higher grades! Collectors should be alert for these often deceptive counterfeits.

Our advisor for this category is L.R. Docks, author of *American Premium Record Guide,* which lists 60,000 records by over 7,000 artists in its sixth edition. He is listed in the Directory under Texas. In the listings that follow, prices are suggested for records that are in excellent condition; worn or abused records may be worth only a small fraction of the values quoted and may not be saleable at all. EPs and LPs are priced 'with jacket.'

Blues, Rhythm and Blues, Rock 'n Roll, Rockabilly

Adams, Jo Jo; Didn't I Tell You, Chance 1127, 45 rpm 30.00
Ames, Tessie; High Yellow Blues, Silvertone 3576, 78 rpm.......... 150.00
Anderson, Jelly Roll; Good Time Blues, Gennett 6181, 78 rpm .. 300.00
Andy & the Live Wires, Maggie, Applause 1249, 45 rpm.............. 15.00
Avons, Baby, Hull 722, 45 rpm.. 20.00
Baker, Willie; Crooked Woman Blues, Gennett 6846, 78 rpm..... 300.00
Barton, Tippy; High Brown Cheater, Vocalion 1742, 78 rpm....... 100.00

Beach Boys, Surfin', Candix 301, 45 rpm 75.00
Belmonts, Summertime, Sabina 521, 45 rpm 20.00
Berry, Chuck; One Dozen Berrys, Chess 1432, LP, 45 rpm 50.00
Bilbro, DH; Chester Blues, Victor 23831, 78 rpm........................... 75.00
Blake, Tommy; Cool It (Baby), Buddy 107, 45 rpm...................... 150.00
Blue Belle, Ghost Creepin' Blues, Okeh 8588, 78 rpm................... 40.00
Blue Dots, Hold Me Tight, De Luxe 6067, 45 rpm 30.00
Brim, Grace; Hospitality Blues, JOB 117, 78 rpm, from $100 to.. 150.00
Brown, Charles; Moonrise, Aladdin 3163, 45 rpm 15.00
Browne, Doris; My Cherie, Gotham 298, 45 rpm 15.00
Bumble Bee Slim & His 3 Sharks, Deep Bass Blues, Decca 7053, 78 rpm....15.00
Campbell, Louis; Natural Facts, Excello 2035, 45 rpm 30.00
Capris, God Only Knows, Gotham 7304, 45 rpm 40.00
Carolina Slim, Worry You Off My Mind, Acorn 323, 78 rpm 10.00
Carter, Bo; & Walter Jacobs, Shake 'Em On Down, Bluebird 7927, 78 rpm ...30.00
Channels, Gleam in Your Eyes, Whirlin 102, 45 rpm 20.00
Clefs, We Three, Chess 1521, 78 rpm 50.00
Collins, Sam; Dark Cloudy Blues, Gennett 6260, 78 rpm 400.00
Continentals, It Doesn't Matter, Hunter 3502, 45 rpm 30.00
Curry, Elder; Hard Times, Okeh 8879, 78 rpm 80.00
Davis, Link; Don't Big Shot Me, Starday 255, 45 rpm 20.00
Davis, Walter; Worried Man Blues, Bluebird 5129, 78 rpm........... 80.00
Denson, Lee; Heart of a Fool, Vik 0251, 45 rpm.......................... 30.00
Douglas, Davey; Shivers, Ditto 110, 45 rpm 20.00
Downing, 'Big' Al; Miss Lucy, White Rock 1113, 45 rpm.............. 60.00
Dranes, Arizona; Don't You Want To Go?, Okeh 8646, 78 rpm..... 60.00
Earls, My Heart's Desire, Rome 5117, 45 rpm 10.00
Enchanters, True Love Gone, Mercer 992, 45 rpm 150.00
Fiestas, All That's Good, #1166, 45 rpm 10.00
Five Spots, Get With It, Future 2201, 45 rpm 30.00
Four Lovers, Joy Ride, RCA 1317, LP.. 200.00
Gay Notes, For Only a Moment, Drexel 905, 45 rpm 80.00
Gibson, Cifford; Stop Your Rambling, Paramount 12923, 78 rpm ..300.00
Green, Rudy; Teeny Weeny Baby, Excello 2090, 45 rpm 30.00
Hadley, Jim; Midnight Train, Buddy 117, 45 rpm 30.00
Hamner, Curley; Piano Turner, Fling 720, 45 rpm 30.00
Harris, Wynonie; Night Train, King 4565, 45 rpm 15.00
Heartbreakers, My Love, Vik 0299, 45 rpm 30.00
Henderson, Rosa; Get It Fixed, Vocalion 15044, 78 rpm 40.00
Heralds, Eternal Love, Herald 435, 45 rpm 40.00
Irby, Jerry; Clickety Clack, Daffan 108, 45 rpm 20.00
Jenkins, Bo Bo; Democrat Blues, Chess 1565, 45 rpm 60.00
Johnson, Louise; On the Wall, Paramount 13008, 78 rpm 250.00
Jones, Grandpa; Greatest Hits, King 554, LP............................... 20.00
Kearney, Ramsey; Rock the Bop, Jaxon 501, 45 rpm 50.00
Lee, Harry; Rockin' on a Reindeer, Igloo 101, 45 rpm 60.00
Lightfoot, Papa; PL Blues, Aladdin 3171, 45 rpm 50.00
Liston, Virginia; Rolls-Royce Papa, Vocalion 1032, 78 rpm 100.00
Magnificents, Don't Leave Me, Vee Jay 281, 45 rpm 20.00
Morris, Gene; Lovin' Honey, Edmoral 1012, 45 rpm 40.00
Paul, Jerry; Step Out, Holiday 1001, 45 rpm............................... 15.00
Preston, Johnny; Running Bear, Mercury 20592, LP 40.00
Ravens, Don't Mention My Name, Mercury 70060, 45 rpm 30.00

Redd, Johnny; Rockin' With Ruby, Corallen, 45 rpm 30.00
Robbins, Marty; Pretty Mama, Columbia 21461, 45 rpm 12.00
Robin Hood Brians, Dis a Itty Bit, Fraternity 803, 45 rpm 50.00
Robinson, Elzadie; Tick-Tock Blues, Paramount 12544, 78 rpm .. 120.00
Robinson, James 'Bat'; Humming Blues, Champion 16745, 78 rpm ..400.00
Serenaders, I Want To Love You Baby, Red Robin 115, 45 rpm ... 100.00
Smith, Bessie; Back Water Blues, Columbia 14195-D, 78 rpm 50.00
Sunny Boy & His Pals, Don't You Leave Me Here, Champion 15283, 78 rpm....300.00
Tate, Rose; Money Woman Blues, Champion 15417, 78 rpm 175.00
Tucker, Bessie; Old Black Mary, Victor V38538, 78 rpm.............. 200.00
Vincent, Walter; Mississippi Yodelin' Blues, Brunswick 7190, 78 rpm....150.00
Wallace, Sippie; Jealous Woman Like Me, Okeh 8301, 78 rpm ... 200.00
Williamson, Sonny Boy; Blue Bird Blues, Bluebird 7098, 78 rpm .. 30.00
Young, Billie; You Done Played Out Blues, Victor 23339, 78 rpm ..350.00

Country and Western

Allen Brothers, Ain't That Skippin?, Columbia 15270-D, 78 rpm .. 100.00
Ashley & Foster, My North Carolina Home, Vocalion 02900, 78 rpm .. 50.00

Gene Autry, That's Why I Left the Mountains, QRS Q-1048-A, very rare, from $3,000.00 to $5,000.00. (Photo courtesy Les Docks)

Baldwin, Luke; It Won't Happen Again, Champion 16142, 78 rpm.. 20.00
Blake, Charley; Alabama Blues, Supertone 9600, 78 rpm 15.00
Blue Boys, Memphis Stomp, Okeh 45314, 78 rpm 100.00
Bowers, Contented Hobo, Superior 2607, 78 rpm 25.00
Butcher, Dwight; Your Voice Is Calling, Victor 23810, 78 rpm 150.00
Carolina Twins, Mr Brown Here I Come, Victor V40098, 78 rpm...30.00
Chesnut, Ted; Bring Back My Boy, Gennett 6603, 78 rpm 20.00
Coon, Walter; & His Joy Boys, Polly Wolly Doodle, Gennett 7079, 78 rpm ..30.00
Cross, Ballard; Wabash Cannon Ball, Vocalion 5377, 78 rpm 15.00
Delmore Brothers, Frozen Girl, Bluebird 5338, 78 rpm 15.00
Ferguson, John; Railroad Daddy, Challenge 159, 78 rpm 15.00
Georgia Crackers, Diamond Joe, Okeh 45098, 78 rpm 30.00
Green's String Band, Rickett's Hornpipe, Champion 16489, 78 rpm...30.00
Hart Brothers, Prodigal Son, Paramount 3265, 78 rpm 15.00
Hess, Bennie & His Nation's Play Boys, Texas Stars, Opera 1019, 78 rpm .8.00
Hopkins, Andy; Prison Warden's Secret, Supertone 9713, 78 rpm ..12.00
Hughey, Dan; Sweet Kitty Wells, Champion 15502, 78 rpm 10.00
Johnson, Paul & Charles; Wild Cat Hollow, Gennett 7313, 78 rpm ...75.00
Justice, Dick; Henry Lee, Brunswick 367, 78 rpm........................ 20.00
La Dieu, Pierce; Shanty-Man's Life, Columbia 15278-D, 78 rpm .. 30.00
Leake County Revelers, Beautiful Bells, Columbia 15501-D, 78 rpm..20.00
Lonesome Cowboy, Memphis Gal, Champion 16767, 78 rpm 75.00
Lullaby Larkers, Chicken Roost Blues, Champion 16364, 78 rpm . 40.00
Major, Jack; Tennessee Mountain Girl, Brunswick 252, 78 rpm 20.00
Martin, John; Railroad Blues, Superior 2626, 78 rpm................... 30.00
Martin Brothers, Whistling Rufus, Paramount 3217 .... 50.00
Massey Family, Sweet Mama Tree Top Tall, Vocalion 02993, 78 rpm..12.00
Mattox, Jimmie; Good Bye Mama, Gennett 7227, 78 rpm 50.00
Maynard, Ken; Cowboy's Lament, Columbia 2310-D, 78 rpm 100.00
McKinney Brothers, Old Uncle Joe, Champion 16830, 78 rpm..... 15.00
McPherson, Whitney; Brakeman Blues, Vocalion 03937, 78 rpm.. 10.00
Nabell, Charles; After the War Is Over, Okeh 45021, 78 rpm 15.00
Newton County Hillbillies, Happy Hour Breakdown, Okeh 45520, 78 rpm ..50.00

Reb's Legion Club 45's, Steppin' High, Hollywood Record, from $300.00 to $500.00. (Photo courtesy Les Docks)

Oaks, Charlie; Poor Little Joe, Vocalion 15103, 78 rpm.............. 10.00
Pavey, Phil; Utah Mormon Blues, Okeh 45355, 78 rpm.............. 12.00
Pine Mountain Boys, Apron String Blues, Victor 23605, 78 rpm 100.00
Puckett, Holland; He Lives on High, Gennett 6206, 78 rpm........ 15.00
Red Headed Fiddlers, Cheat 'Em, Brunswick 470, 78 rpm 20.00
Red Heads, Wild & Foolish, Pathe-Actuelle 36492, 78 rpm.......... 30.00
Renfro Valley Boys, Loreena, Paramount 3321, 78 rpm 40.00
Roane County Ramblers, Roane County Rag, Columbia 15398-D, 78 rpm. 50.00
Rodgers, Jessie; Headin' Home, Bluebird 5853, 78 rpm............... 10.00
Rodgers, Jimmie; My Good Gal's Gone, Bluebird 5942, 78 rpm 40.00
Stanton, Frank; Poor Old Dad, Superior 2544, 78 rpm 50.00
Thompson, Bud; Lie He Wrote Home, Crown 3489, 78 rpm......... 12.00
Turner, Cal; Only a Tramp, Champion 15587, 78 rpm................. 18.00
Virginia Dandies, God's Getting Worried, Crown 3145, 78 rpm.... 20.00
Williams, Marc; Jesse James, Brunswick 269, 78 rpm 12.00

Jazz, Dance Bands, Personalities

Arcadian Serenaders, Fidgety Feet, Okeh 40272, 78 rpm.............. 40.00
Astaire, Fred; Pick Yourself Up, Brunswick 7717, 78 rpm 10.00
Auburn, Frank & His Orchestra; Little Girl, Clarion 11001-C, 78 rpm .. 20.00
Austin, Gene; Without That Gal!, Victor 22739, 78 rpm.............. 12.00
Banta, Frank; Wild Cherry Rag, Gennett 4735, 78 rpm................. 20.00
Bernard, Al; Stavin' Change, Brunswick 2448, 78 rpm.....................8.00
Blue Jay Boys, My Baby, Decca 7240, 78 rpm 15.00
Blythe's Blue Boys, My Baby, Champion 15528, 78 rpm 200.00
Bobby's Revelers, Heebie Jeebies, Silvertone 3551, 78 rpm........... 75.00
Brown, Henry; Blues Stomp, Paramount 12934, 78 rpm 200.00
Campbell, Buddy & His Orchestra; Last Dollar, Okeh 41532, 78 rpm ..12.00
Carlson, Russ & His Orchestra; Me!, Crown 3177, 78 rpm 8.00
Charleston Chasers, You're Lucky to Me, Columbia 2309-D, 78 rpm.. 20.00
Chocolate Dandies, That's My Stuff, Vocalion 1617, 78 rpm 150.00
Cotton Pickers, What'll You Do?, Gennett 6380, 78 rpm 75.00
Crosby, Bing; Some of These Days, Brunswick 6351, 78 rpm 12.00
Detroiters, Spanish Mamma, Romeo 625, 78 rpm 10.00
Dixie Jazz Band, West End Blues, Jewel 5412, 78 rpm 15.00
Dixie Stompers, Goose Pimples, Harmony 545-H, 78 rpm 15.00
Dixieland Jug Blowers, Carpet Alley, Victor 20480, 78 rpm 60.00
Dubin's Dandies, Gettin' Along, Cameo 0105, 78 rpm 8.00
English, Sharlie; Broke Woman Blues, Paramount 12644, 78 rpm..100.00
Fuller, Bob; Growin' Old Blues, Ajax 17117, 78 rpm 40.00
Gene & His Glorians, Jig Time, Timely Tunes 1582, 78 rpm 30.00
Gold, Lou & His Orchestra; Roll 'em Girls, Perfect 14530, 78 rpm .. 10.00
Goody's Good Timers, Diga Diga Doo, Perfect 15083, 78 rpm....... 15.00
Gulf Coast Seven, Santa Claus Blues, Columbia 14107-D, 78 rpm ..75.00
Halstead, Henry; His Orchestra, Panama, Victor 19514, 78 rpm... 25.00
Harmonians, I Wanna Be Loved by You, Harmony 762-H, 78 rpm..8.00
Hill, Sam; & His Orchestra, ... Loves My Baby, Oriole 303, 78 rpm.. 30.00
Jazz Masters, Bees Knees, Black Swan 2109, 78 rpm...................... 20.00
Jungle Band, Maori, Brunswick 4776, 78 rpm............................... 20.00
Kentucky Grasshoppers, Icky Blues, Banner 6323, 78 rpm 12.00
Lewis, Ted; & His Band, Bugle Call Rag, Columbia 826-D, 78 rpm .. 10.00
Lumberjacks, Spanish Dream, Cameo 8356, 78 rpm 10.00
Melody Sheiks, Mighty Blue, Okeh 40484, 78 rpm 20.00
Memphis Melody Men, New Moten Stomp, Superior 2737, 78 rpm.. 150.00
Missourians, Vine Street Drag, Victor V 38103, 78 rpm................ 100.00
Moonlight Revelers, Alabama Shuffle, Grey Gull 1775, 78 rpm.... 50.00
Morland, Peg; You're Gonna Miss Me, Victor V40137, 78 rpm..... 15.00
Mound City Blue Blowers, Hello Lola, Victor V38100, 78 rpm..... 25.00
New Orleans Jazz Band, My Sweet Louise, Domino 3524, 78 rpm. 15.00
Original Memphis Five, 31st Street Blues, Emerson 10741, 78 rpm..30.00
Preer, Evelyn; Sunday, Banner 1895, 78 rpm 12.00
Sepia Serenaders, Breakin' the Ice, Bluebird 5782, 78 rpm 20.00
Shreveport Sizzlers, Zonky, Okeh 8918, 78 rpm............................ 75.00

Smith, Kate; Morning, Noon & Night, Clarion 5124-C, 78 rpm .. 15.00
State Street Ramblers, Careless Love, Champion 16464, 78 rpm ...250.00
Sullivan, Joe; Onyx Bringdown, Columbia 2925-D, 78 rpm 40.00

State Street Ramblers, Cootie Stomp, Gennett 6232, $400.00 for EX condition (shown in lesser grade). (Photo courtesy Les Docks)

Tin Pan Paraders, Puttin' on the Ritz, Gennett 7148, 78 rpm........ 20.00
We Three, Trumpet Sobs, Perfect 14645, 78 rpm 25.00
Whoopee Makers, Misty Mornin', Pathe-Actuelle 36923, 78 rpm...16.00

Red Wing

The Red Wing Stoneware Company, founded in 1878, took its name from its location in Red Wing, Minnesota. In 1906 the name was changed to the Red Wing Union Stoneware Company after a merger with several of the other local potteries. For the most part they produced utilitarian wares such as flowerpots, crocks, and jugs. Their early 1930s catalogs offered a line of art pottery vases in colored glazes, some of which featured handles modeled after swan's necks, snakes, or female nudes. Other examples were quite simple, often with classic styling. After the addition of their dinnerware lines in 1935, 'Stoneware' was dropped from the name, and the company became known as Red Wing Potteries, Inc. They closed in 1967. For more information we recommend, *Red Wing Collectibles* and *Red Wing Stoneware* by Dan DePasquale, Gail Peck, and Larry Peterson (Collector Books).

Artware

Bowl, Greek design w/orange/gr/bl/gold, 1920s-30s, 6"................... 25.00
Canoe, Birch Bark line, #735, 12"... 175.00

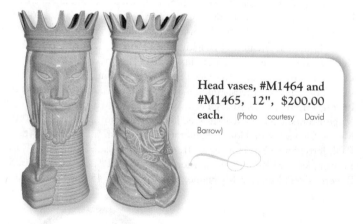

Head vases, #M1464 and #M1465, 12", $200.00 each. (Photo courtesy David Barrow)

Pitcher, Deco style, gr, #1580, 5"... 85.00
Pitcher, pk gloss, #909, 3⅝"... 60.00
Vase, bronze gloss, urn form w/sq base, #850, 7½" 37.50
Vase, cactus emb on pk, curled hdls, #764, 8½x8¼" 25.00
Vase, gladiola; cinnamon w/lt gr int, #416, 12" 55.00
Vase, ivory w/gr int, gladiolus shape w/2 openings, #B1427, 8"...... 30.00
Vase, maroon w/gray int, 6 lobes, #887, 7½" 35.00
Vase, med bl w/pk int, fan form, #892, w/sticker, 7" 38.00

Vase, Modernist style w/sq ft, blk-bl to wht, #2336, 9¾" 90.00
Vase, Neoclassic, lt gr w/pk int, #674, 15" 315.00
Vase, pk speckled w/geometric pattern, ftd, #M1440, 8¼" 30.00
Vase, pk speckled w/swirled bulbous body, #B1431, 8x4½" 34.00
Vase, pk twisted cylinder, #733, 12" 25.00
Vase, Shell Ginger from Tropicana line, chartreuse, #B2100, 8x6x3¼".. 32.00
Vase, turq gloss, low hdls, #505, 7¼" 30.00
Vase, vines, purple-brn on gray-wht, #1162, 9"........................ 35.00

Cookie Jars

Be aware that there is a very good reproduction of the King of Tarts. Except for the fact that the new jars are slightly smaller, they are sometimes difficult to distinguish from the old.

Apple, turq, from $75 to.................................. 90.00
Barrel, yel, hdld, unmk, from $65 to............................ 90.00
Bob White, brn & bl quail scene on flecked wht, from $90 to 110.00
Cabbage, bl, rare, from $480 to 520.00
Cabbage, other colors, from $435 to 465.00
Carousel, mc w/pk & wht stripes, mk, from $300 to 345.00
Chef, yel w/brown, mk & stamp, from $75 to.................... 95.00

Dutch Girl (Katrina), from $125.00 to $150.00.
(Photo courtesy Jackson's International Auctioneers & Appraisers of Fine Art & Antiques/LiveAuctioneers.com)

Friar Tuck, yel w/brn trim, unmk, from $90 to 110.00
Happy, tan fleck, emb Happy the children..., pk floral trim.......... 150.00
Jack Frost, figure w/paints on lid, short, from $550 to................ 600.00
King of Tarts, mc, from $850 to........................... 950.00
Round Up, cowboy scene on wht, from $285 to 315.00

Dinnerware

Dinnerware lines were added in 1935, and today collectors scramble to rebuild extensive table services. Although interest is obvious, right now the market is so volatile, it is often difficult to establish a price scale with any degree of accuracy. Asking prices may vary from $50.00 to $200.00 on some items, which indicates instability and a collector market trying to find its way. Sellers seem to be unfamiliar with pattern names and proper identification of the various pieces that each line consists of. There were many hand-decorated lines; among the most popular are Bob White, Tropicana, and Round-up. But there are other patterns that are just as attractive and deserving of attention. Ray Reiss has published a book called *Red Wing Dinnerware, Price and Identification Guide*, which shows nearly 100 patterns on its back cover alone.

Town and Country, designed by Eva Zeisel, was made for only one year in the late 1940s. Today many collectors regard Zeisel as one of the most gifted designers of that era and actively seek examples of her work. Town and Country was a versatile line, adaptable to both informal and semiformal use. It is characterized by irregular, often eccentric shapes, and handles of pitchers and serving pieces are usually extensions of the rim. Bowls and platters are free-form comma shapes or appear tilted, with one side slightly higher than the other. Although the ware is unmarked, it is recognizable by its distinctive shapes and glazes. White (often used to complement interiors of bowls and cups), though an original color, is actually more rare than Bronze (metallic brown, also called gunmetal), which enjoys favored status; gray is unusual. Other colors include Rust, Dusk Blue, Sand, Chartreuse, Peach and Forest Green. Pieces have also shown up in Mulberry and Ming Green and are considered quite rare. (These are Red Wing Quartette colors!) In our listings, use the higher side to evaluate white, Bronze, Mulberry, and Ming Green, mid-range for gray, and the lower values for the more common colors. Eva Zeisel gave her permission to reissue a few select pieces of Town and Country; these were made by World of Ceramics. In 1996 salt and pepper shakers were reproduced in new colors not resembling Red Wing colors. In 1997 the mixing bowl and syrup were reissued. All new pieces are stamped EZ96 or EZ97 and are visibly different from the old, as far as glaze, pottery base, and weight. Charles Alexander (who is listed in the Directory under Indiana) advises us on the Town and Country market.

Key:
c/s — cobalt on stoneware   RW — Red Wing
MN — Minnesota   RWUS — Red Wing Union
NS — North Star   Stoneware

Blossom Time, plate, egg; w/lid................. 73.00
Blossom Time, shakers, pr...................... 12.00
Bob White, bowl, rimmed soup 18.00
Bob White, plate, dinner; 10"................... 12.00
Bob White, relish, 3-part 53.00
Bob White, sauce dish 10.00
Bob White, tray, 24" 72.00
Brittany, jug, water; from $60 to................. 75.00
Brittany, nappy, 9".......................... 30.00
Brittany, plate, chop; 12"..................... 52.00
Capistrano, casserole, w/lid, 7x9" 32.00

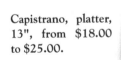
Capistrano, platter, 13", from $18.00 to $25.00.

Capistrano, platter, 15", from $28 to................. 35.00
Capistrano, soup tureen, w/lid.................... 26.00
Country Garden, coffeepot....................... 48.00
Country Garden, teacup & saucer.................. 18.00
Country Garden, teapot, 4-cup................... 72.00
Desert Sun, butter dish 32.00
Desert Sun, shakers, pr........................ 20.00
Granada, gravy boat.......................... 34.00
Granada, shakers, pr......................... 22.00
Granada, vegetable dish, divided................. 23.00
Iris, bowl, cereal 10.00
Iris, plate, salad; 7"......................... 15.00
Lexington, nappy............................ 12.50
Lexington, spoon rest........................ 12.00
Lotus, creamer.............................. 10.00

Lotus, creamer & sugar bowl, w/lid, from $20 to............................ 25.00
Lotus, cup & saucer.. 10.00
Lotus, gravy boat w/attached underplate, from $30 to................. 35.00
Lotus, pitcher, 56-oz, from $35 to.. 45.00
Lotus, plate, 10½".. 12.00
Lotus, sugar bowl, hdld.. 14.00
Lute Song, bowl, salad; lg... 26.00
Lute Song, butter dish, from $20 to.. 25.00
Lute Song, casserole, ftd, w/lid.. 42.00
Lute Song, gravy boat, stick hdl, w/lid, from $35 to.................... 40.00
Lute Song, sugar bowl, w/lid.. 22.50
Lute Song, teapot, 4-cup, from $125 to...................................... 150.00
Lute Song, vegetable dish... 22.00
Normandy, gravy boat.. 42.00
Normandy, jug, water... 60.00
Normandy, plate, dinner; 10", from $12 to.................................. 15.00

Orleans, plate, dinner; 10", $22.00. (Photo courtesy B.L. and R.L. Dollen)

Orleans, shakers, pr.. 30.00
Orleans, teapot, 4-cup.. 100.00
Pepe, bean pot, 1½-qt.. 32.00
Pepe, celery dish.. 16.00

Pepe, cup and saucer, from $10.00 to $12.00.

Pepe, sauce dish 8.00
Round-Up, bowl, salad; 5".. 42.00
Round-Up, bowl, salad; 12".. 100.00
Round-Up, platter, 13"... 80.00
Smart Set, butter dish.. 70.00
Smart Set, cruets, pr... 95.00
Smart Set, jug, water.. 80.00
Town & Country, casserole, wht int, w/lid, 13½" L, from $65 to ... 95.00
Town & Country, condiment/mustard jar, from $195 to.............. 225.00
Town & Country, creamer & sugar bowl, 4½", 4", from $65 to...... 95.00
Town & Country, cruet, from $75 to... 95.00
Town & Country, jug, syrup; from $85 to.................................... 100.00
Town & Country, pitcher, 3-pt, from $150 to.............................. 195.00
Town & Country, platter, comma shape, 15x12", from $45 to....... 65.00
Town & Country, shaker, Shmoo form, pr from $75 to 115.00
Town & Country, teapot, from $250 to.. 350.00
Town & County, casserole, w/lid... 64.00
Two Step, butter dish... 30.00
Two Step, plate, salad; 8"... 12.00
Two Step, vegetable dish 22.00

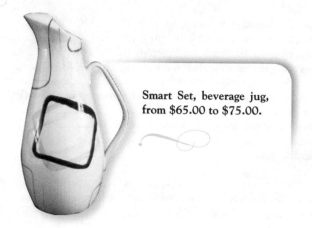

Smart Set, beverage jug, from $65.00 to $75.00.

Stoneware

Bowl, beater; Albany slip, RW, from $50 to 60.00
Bowl, Greek Key, bl & wht, 10".. 175.00
Butter jar, Albany slip, low, MN, 10-lb 100.00
Chamber pot, Albany slip, MN.. 300.00
Churn, #5/leaf, c/s, unmk, 5-gal 600.00
Churn, #5/red wing on wht, Union oval, 5-gal............................ 300.00
Churn, #10/2 birch leaves, c/s, RWUS, 10-gal.......................... 1,600.00
Cooler, #6/Ice Water/flower, c/s, RW, 6-gal.............................10,000.00
Crock, #8/elephant ear leaves, cobalt on wht, MN, 8-gal 150.00
Crock, #20/elephant ear leaves, cobalt on wht, MN, 20-gal 300.00
Cuspidor, bl & wht sponging, unmk... 650.00
Cuspidor, bl bands on salt glaze, German style, unmk 650.00
Jar, packing; #3/red wing on wht, bail hdl, 3-gal....................... 400.00
Jar, wax sealer, Albany slip, MN, ½-gal..................................... 60.00
Jug, bl bands on wht, cone top, MN, 1-gal................................. 400.00
Jug, common, wht, MN, ½-gal.. 75.00
Jug, molded seam, Albany slip, bail hdl, MN, 1-gal................... 300.00
Jug, shoulder; #3/birch leaves, cobalt on wht, MN, 3-gal 175.00
Jug, shoulder; advertising, RWUS, 5-gal 700.00
Jug, shoulder; brn & salt glaze, std top, RW, 1-gal...................... 150.00

Mason Fruit Jar, one-gallon, zinc lid, $400.00. (Photo courtesy Buffalo Bay Auction Co.)

Milk pan, Albany slip, MN, any sz 125.00
Pitcher, mustard; Albany slip, NS 350.00
Spittoon, German style, incised decor/bl bands on salt glaze, unmk ..700.00
Spittoon, salt glaze, RW.. 800.00
Umbrella stand, bl sponging, unmk... 1,400.00
Washbowl & pitcher, lt bl on wht, emb lily decor, RW 875.00

Redware

The term redware refers to a type of simple earthenware produced by the Colonists as early as the 1600s. The red clay used in its production was abundant throughout the country, and during the eighteenth and nineteenth centuries redware was made in great quantities. Intended for utilitarian purposes such as everyday tableware or use in the dairy, redware was simple in design and decoration. Glazes of various colors were used, and a liquid clay referred to as 'slip' was sometimes applied in patterns such as zigzag lines, daisies, or stars. Plates often have a 'coggled' edge, similar to the way a pie is crimped or jagged, which is done with a special tool. In the following listings, EX (excellent condition) indicates only minor damage. Our advisor for this category is Barbara Rosen; she is listed in the Directory under New Jersey.

Ink bottle, brn streaks/splotches/incised lines, 19th C, 6" 1,800.00
Jar, brn manganese splotches, incised lines, 19th C, 9¾" 1,300.00
Jar, brn manganese splotches, lug hdls, ovoid, chips/lines, 9⅝" 355.00
Jar, canning; manganese daubs w/gr traces, 11x7", EX 145.00
Jar, gr spit glaze w/running streaks, 2 sm hdls, 8¾x6½", EX 230.00
Jar, gr/golden brn w/streaky brn splotches, incised lines, 19th C, 8" ... 475.00
Jar, speckled olive gr w/brn brushstrokes, rim collar, 19th C, 4" ... 265.00
Jardiniere, burnt orange w/brn splotches, att CT area, 1830s, 9". 1,595.00
Jug, brn manganese splotches, incised line at shoulder, MA, 19th C, 9".1,880.00
Jug, brn manganese splotches, strap hdl, MA, 19th C, 5½" 265.00
Jug, brn speckles w/gr touches, att J Corliss, 19th C, 5⅜" 300.00

Jug, green glaze with orange highlights, 6¼", VG, $1,265.00. (Photo courtesy James D. Julia Inc.)

Jug, mottled olive gr w/brn halos, ovoid, strap hdl, NE, 7⅞" 1,000.00
Jug, olive gr w/mc halos, ovoid w/strap hdl, NH, 19th C, 5½" 765.00
Jug, vinegar; olive gr & brn w/brn splashes, strap hdl, ME, 4¾" ... 350.00
Jug bank, brn manganese/brn copper splotches, reeded hdl, PA, rpr, 4".. 200.00

Pie plate, yellow slip wavy lines and dots, coggled rim, 10½", NM, $850.00. (Photo courtesy Garth's Auctions Inc.)

Pie plate, 3 yel slip lines, coggled rim, 9½", EX 260.00
Plate, bands of yel slip wavy lines, coggled rim, 11" 1,110.00
Plate, stylized yel slip, coggled rim, sm chips, 8¾" 400.00
Plate, sunflower in mc slip, 1825 in blk slip, ca 1825, 12" 1,375.00
Plate, yel slip loops, coggled rim, flakes, 12¼" 545.00
Plate, yel slip squiggles, coggled rim, att PA, 1830s, 10¾" 900.00

Regal China

Located in Antioch, Illinois, the Regal China Company opened for business in 1938. Products of interest to collectors are Jim Beam decanters, cookie jars, salt and pepper shakers, and similar novelty items. The company closed its doors sometime in 1993. The Old MacDonald Farm series listed below is especially collectible, so are the salt and pepper shakers.

Note: Where applicable, prices are based on excellent gold trim. (Gold trim must be 90% intact or deductions should be made for wear.) Our advisor for this category is Judy Posner; she is listed in the Directory under Florida. See also Decanters.

Cookie Jars

Alice in Wonderland, $3,200.00. (Photo courtesy Joyce and Fred Roerig)

Cat, from $425 to 375.00
Churn Boy 175.00
Clown, gr collar 450.00
Davy Crockett 300.00
Diaper Pin Pig 250.00
Dutch Girl 450.00
Dutch Girl, peach trim 550.00
FiFi Poodle, minimum value 500.00
Fisherman, from $650 to 720.00
French Chef, from $475 to 525.00
Goldilocks (+), from $150 to 200.00
Harpo Marx 1,080.00

Hubert Lion, minimum value, $800.00. (Photo courtesy Joyce and Fred Roerig)

Humpty Dumpty, red 125.00
Little Miss Muffet, from $200 to 275.00

Majorette 250.00
Oriental Lady w/Baskets, from $725 to 775.00
Peek-a-Boo (+), from $925 to 975.00
Quaker Oats 95.00
Rocking Horse 250.00
Three Bears 175.00
Toby Cookies, unmk, from $675 to 725.00
Tulip 150.00
Uncle Mistletoe 765.00

Old McDonald's Farm

Butter dish, cow's head 95.00
Canister, flour, cereal, coffee; med, ea 150.00
Canister, pretzels, peanuts, popcorn, chips, tidbits; lg, ea, $150 to ..200.00
Canister, salt, sugar, tea; med, ea from $75 to ... 85.00

Canister, soap, from $200.00 to $250.00.

Cookie barn 95.00
Creamer, rooster 60.00
Grease jar, pig 95.00
Pitcher, milk 125.00
Shakers, boy & girl, pr 75.00
Shakers, churn, gold trim, pr 75.00
Shakers, feed sacks w/sheep, pr from $80 to 110.00
Spice jar, assorted lids, sm, ea from $75 to 95.00
Sugar bowl, hen 85.00
Teapot, duck's head 125.00

Shakers

A Nod to Abe, 3-pc nodder, from $200 to 250.00
Bendel, bears, wht w/pk & brn trim, pr 75.00
Bendel, bunnies, wht w/blk & pk trim, pr 75.00
Bendel, kissing pigs, gray w/pk trim, lg, pr from $250 to 275.00
Bendel, love bugs, burgundy, lg, pr 125.00
Bendel, love bugs, gr, sm, pr 65.00
Cat, sitting w/eyes closed, wht w/hat & gold bow, pr 225.00
Clown, pr 250.00
Dutch Girl, pr from $200 to 225.00
FiFi, pr 250.00
Fish, mk C Miller, 1-pc 55.00
French Chef, wht w/gold trim, pr 250.00
Humpty Dumpty, pr 75.00
Peek-a-boo, red dots, lg, pr (+) from $350 to 400.00
Peek-a-boo, red dots, sm, pr from $125 to 150.00
Peek-a-boo, wht solid, sm, pr 175.00
Pig, pk, mk C Miller, 1-pc 75.00

Tulip, pr 35.00
Van Tellingen, bears, brn, pr from $25 to 28.00
Van Tellingen, boy & dog, wht, pr 45.00
Van Tellingen, bunnies, solid colors, pr from $28 .. 32.00
Van Tellingen, ducks, pr 25.00
Van Tellingen, Dutch boy & girl, from $45 to 50.00
Van Tellingen, Mary & lamb, pr from $40 to 50.00
Van Tellingen, sailor & mermaid, from $100 to ... 125.00

Van Tellingen, Black boy and dog, $55.00. (Photo courtesy Mary Jo Swingle)

Relief-Molded Jugs

For the first three quarters of the nineteenth century, molded relief decoration provided a popular option for the English potter. Produced by a large number of makers in both stoneware (opaque) and parian (translucent), the jugs reflect the changing styles of the period as well as Victorian interests in mythology and literature, history, and natural sciences. Beginning collectors are urged to utilize the publication of retired dealer Kathy Hughes whose research and enthusiasm did much to promote collecting interest in jugs in the country. Collectors should heed Hughes's warning as printed in previous editions of this guide: 'Watch for recent reproductions; these have been made by the slip-casting method. Unlike relief-molded ware which is relatively smooth inside, slip-cast pitchers will have interior indentations that follow the irregularities of the relief decoration.' Values below are for pieces in excellent condition. Our advisor for this category is Tim Sublette; he is listed in the Directory under Ohio.

Key: Reg — Registered

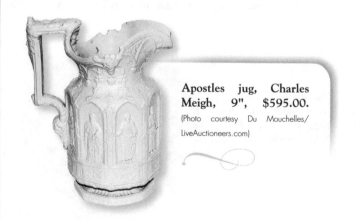

Apostles jug, Charles Meigh, 9", $595.00. (Photo courtesy Du Mouchelles/ LiveAuctioneers.com)

Arabic, lav & wht, Samuel Alcock, 10" 550.00
Babes in the Woods, bl & wht, ca 1850, mini, 3¾", NM 175.00
Babes in the Woods, mc, ca 1855, 8½" 350.00
Bacchanalian Boys, smear glazed, Spode, 1800-10, 5⅞x5" 495.00
Bacchanalian Dance, wht, Charles Meigh, 7" 425.00
Bird & Ivy, brn & wht, Reg Nov 17, 1849, 6¼" 300.00

Bird Nesting, mc on yel, ca 1870, 7½" 200.00
Botanic, bl & wht, Cork & Edge, ca 1855, 8" 295.00
Bulrushes, brn, unmk Ridgway & Abington, 6⅝" 295.00
Charles Dickens figural, wht, ca 1880, 5½" 135.00
Cottage, mc on wht, ca 1830, 5¼" 200.00
Cup Tosser, wht porc, ca 1855, 3¾" 195.00
Eglington, bl, Wm Ridgway, 5¾" 195.00
Fern & Rope, brn & bl on wht, Staffordshire, ca 1868, 9" 250.00
Floral, bl & wht parian, unmk Staffordshire, ca 1865, 7½" 70.00
Gipsey, brn, Jones & Walley, 5½" 325.00
Grinning Bacchus, bl & wht parian, ca 1855, 4¾" 130.00
Hanging Game, mc on wht w/stippled bkground, ca 1870, 9¾" 250.00
Idle Apprentices, wht stoneware, ca 1840, 6¾" 145.00
Miser & Spendthrift, wht parian, ca 1850, 5" 125.00
Music pattern, wht, Dudson, ca 1870, 7¾" 185.00
Oak, gold on wht, tankard form, ca 1845, 11" 295.00
Paul & Virginia, wht w/bl bkground, Mayer, Reg Dec 2, 1851, 8⅝" 450.00
Pk prunus, Staffordshire, mini, 2½" 195.00
Putti & Goat, wht parian, unmk, ca 1850, 6½" 125.00
Shakespeare's Bust, lt bl, ca 1870, 4" 200.00
Shell, wht w/gr accents, ca 1860, 6¼" 250.00
Sleeping Beauty, bl, Dudson, ca 1860, 8¼" 125.00
Society of Arts Prize Jug, bl & wht, Minton, 6½" 375.00
Stylized leaves, wht w/bl trim, Staffordshire, ca 1870, 7½" 295.00
Twining Flowers, wht parian, Minton, Reg May 14, 1855, 6" 300.00
Wainright's Two Children, bl & wht, 1870s, 7½" 250.00
Wheat, wht, ca 1870, 6¼" 80.00
Willie, wht, Ridgway, ca 1851, 6½" 225.00

Restraints

Since the beginning of time, many things from animals to treasures have been held in bondage by hemp, bamboo, chests, chains, shackles, and other constructed devices. Many of these devices were used to hold captives who awaited further torture, as if the restraint wasn't torturous enough. The study and collecting of restraints enables one to learn much about the advancement of civilization in the country or region from which they originated. Such devices at various times in history were made of very heavy metals — so heavy that the wearer could scarcely move about. It has only been in the last 60 years that vast improvements have been made in design and construction that afford the captive some degree of comfort. Our advisor for this category is Joseph Tanner; he is listed in the Directory under California.

Key:

bbl — barrel	lc — lock case
d-lb — double lock button	NST — non-swing through
K — key	ST — swing through
Kd — keyed	stp — stamped

Foreign Handcuffs

Deutshce Polizei, ST, middle hinge, folds, takes bbl-bit K.......... 80.00
East German, heavy steel, NP single lg hinge, NST, bbl K.......... 120.00
English, Chubb Escort, steel multi-bit lever.......... 300.00
Flexibles, steel segmented bows, NST Darby type, screw K.......... 300.00
French Revolved, oval, ST, takes 2 Ks: bbl & pin tumbler.......... 190.00
German, 3-lb steel set, 2⅝" thick, center chain, bbl K.......... 175.00
German Darby, adjusts, well finished, NST, sm.......... 120.00
Hiatt English, figure-8 (w/chain), steel, screw K.......... 85.00
Hiatt English Darby, like US CW Darby, stp Hiatt & #d.......... 75.00
Hiatt English non-adjust screw K Darby style, uses screw K.......... 120.00
Russian modern ST, blued bbl K, unmk, crude.......... 100.00

Foreign Leg Shackles

East German, aluminum, lg hinge, cable amid 4 cuffs, bbl key.......... 150.00
Hiatt English combo manacles, handcuff/leg irons w/chain.......... 325.00
Hiatt Plug leg irons, same K-ing as Plug-8 cuffs, w/chain.......... 600.00

U.S. Handcuffs

Adams, teardrop lc, bbl Kd, NST, usually not stp.......... 350.00
Bean Cobb, mk Pat 1899, 1 link between cuffs.......... 180.00
Bean Giant, sideways figure-8, solid center lc, dbl-bit K.......... 800.00
Civil War padlocking type, various designs w/loop for lock.......... 225.00
Elias Rickert (ER), screw K, 1878.......... 900.00
H&R Super, ST, shaft-hinge connector takes hollow titted K.......... 150.00
Judd, NST, used rnd/internally triangular K, stp Mattatuck.......... 250.00
Kimbel, screw K at top side, 1964.......... 3,000.00

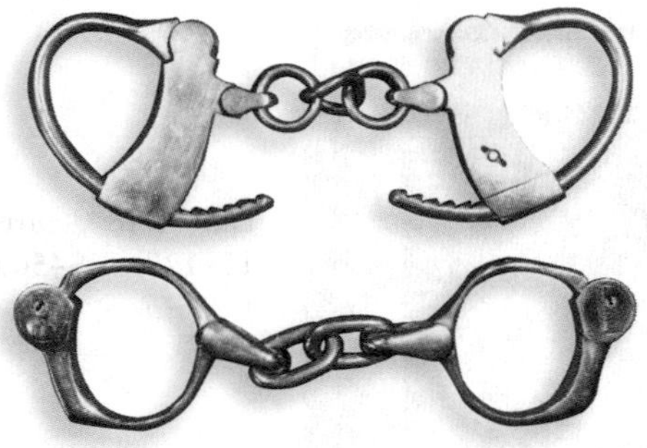

Mattatuk, marked, propeller-type key, $150.00; H&R Bean, marked H&R Arms Company, steel, small flattish key, $250.00. (Photo courtesy Joseph and Pamela Tanner)

Peerless, ST, takes sm bbl K, stp Mfg'ered by S&W Co.......... 75.00
Providence Tool Co, stp, NST, Darby screw K style.......... 350.00
Romer, NST, takes flat K, resembles padlock, stp Romer Co.......... 600.00
Strauss, ST, takes lg solid bitted K, stp Strauss Eng Co.......... 120.00
Tower bar cuffs, cuffs separate by 10-12" steel bar.......... 300.00
Tower-Bean, NST, sm rnd lc, takes tiny bbl-bitted K, stp.......... 175.00

U.S. Leg Shackles

Bean Cobb, mk Patented 1899, steel.......... 375.00
FR, screw K.......... 950.00
H&R Bean, mk H&R Hdw Co, steel, takes sm flattish K.......... 400.00
Judd, as handcuffs.......... 300.00
Oregon boot, break-apart shackle on above ankle support.......... 3,000.00
Strauss, as handcuffs.......... 200.00
Tower ball & chain, leg iron w/chain & 6-lb to 50-lb ball.......... 700.00

Various Other Restraining Devices

African slave Darby-style cuffs, heavy iron/chain, handmade.......... 200.00
African slave padlocking or riveted forged iron shackles.......... 170.00
English figure-8 nipper, claws open by lifting top lock tab.......... 120.00
Gale finger cuff, knuckle duster, non-K, mk GFC.......... 300.00
Hiatt High Security, hinged bbl K & pin-tumbler K (2 Ks).......... 150.00
Jay Pee, thumb cuffs, mk solid body, bbl K.......... 20.00
Korean, hand chain model, blk, bbl K.......... 60.00
Mighty-Mite, thumb cuffs, solid body, ST, mk, bbl K.......... 225.00
New Model Russian, chain bbl K, blued.......... 125.00
New Model Russian, hinged, bbl key, blued.......... 140.00
Thomas Nipper, claw, push button on top to open.......... 150.00

Reverse Painting on Glass

Verre eglomise is the technique of painting on the underside of glass. Dating back to the early 1700s, this art became popular in the nineteenth century when German immigrants chose historical figures and beautiful women as subjects for their reverse glass paintings. Advertising mirrors of this type came into vogue at the turn of the century. Our values are for examples in at least excellent condition.

Andrew Jackson, military portrait, border flakes, 12x9¼", +orig fr. 1,500.00
Castle scene w/sailboats & cottage, 21¼x29¼", +birdseye maple fr .. 65.00
Cowboy on wht horse roping cow, Ginger Briggs, 23½x29½", +fr...155.00
Duc de Bordeaux, young boy, military dress w/sword, 12x10", +fr, VG. 340.00
European castle on coast scene, 1900s, 18x38", +gilt fr................. 65.00
European market scene, 1800s, 46½x23", +fr, VG........................ 625.00

Lady in turban, 15x12", $450.00.

(Photo courtesy Garth's Auctions Inc./LiveAuctioneers.com)

Napoleon, military portrait, 1831, 11¼x10", +orig fr, VG 345.00
Oriental beauty w/fan & flowers, Qing dynasty, 19th C, 23x17", +fr.. 875.00
Oriental boy w/flower basket, dbl fr w/gold liner, 29x35" overall . 315.00
Oriental lady in brocade robe w/scroll, late Qing dynasty, 16x12" ..690.00
Oriental lady sitting at sm table, 1800s, 19½x13½", +rosewood fr ..280.00
Oriental noblewoman seated at table, in pnt 19x16" fr............... 750.00
Qianlong Emperor, portrait on throne, 20th C, in cvd wood stand, 35" ..140.00

Rhead

Frederick Hurten Rhead was born in 1880 in Hanely, Staffordshire, England, into a family of prominent ceramists. He went on to became one of the most productive artisans in the history of the industry.

His career began in England at the Wardel Pottery. At only 19 years of age, he was named art director there. He left England in 1902 at the age of 22, and came to America.

He was associated with many companies during his career in America — Weller, Vance/Avon Faience, Arequipa, A.E. Tile, and lastly Homer Laughlin China. He organized his own pottery in Santa Barbara, California, ca 1913. Admittedly more of a designer than a potter, Rhead hired help to turn the pieces on the wheel but did most of the decorating himself. The process he favored most involved sgraffito designs inlaid with enameling. Egyptian and Art Nouveau influences were evidenced in much of his work. The ware he produced in California was often marked with a logo incorporating the potter at the wheel and 'Santa Barbara.' Our advisors for this category are Suzanne Perrault and David Rago; they are listed in the Directory under New Jersey. See also Roseville; Weller; Vance/Avon Faience.

Key:
s-b — squeezebag   w-r — wax-resist

Bowl, band of carp in wax resist, Rhead Sta. Barbara, 3½x9½", $15,600.00. (Photo courtesy David Rago Auctions)

Bowl, cvd camellia & leaves on brn & blk, turq int, Santa Barbara, 10" ..6,600.00
Bowl, cvd stylized squirrel, UC/#5148, att, 2x4¾" 4,600.00
Bowl, s-b stylized trees, mtns & clouds, #269, 2¼x6¼"...........20,400.00
Bowl, w-r carp band at rim, blk, ftd, Santa Barbara, 3½x9½" ..15,600.00
Chargers, s-b man/lady in traditional garb, Foley/1899, rstr, 14", pr ...2,400.00
Jardiniere & ped, stylized lotus blossoms & leaves, flakes, 33x16" .. 9,600.00
Vase, cvd pnt ornate flowers/pods, chips, 6¼x4" 25,000.00
Vase, cvd stylized trees, gr matt, University City, 1911, #5045, 9x5"..5,100.00

Richard

Richard, who at one time worked for Galle, made cameo art glass in France during the 1920s. His work was often multilayered and acid cut with florals and scenics in lovely colors. The ware was marked with his name in relief. Our advisor for this category is Don Williams; he is listed in the Directory under Missouri.

Atomizer, floral, burgundy on bl, flared foot, rpl bulb, 6¼" 480.00
Atomizer, Russian church/water/trees, pk on ivory, 20th C, 12".. 1,200.00
Box, holly & berries, cobalt on pumpkin/red mottle, ftd, 1910s, 5x6" ..660.00

Vase, Alpine village along river's edge, 8", $460.00.

(Photo courtesy Cincinnati Art Galleries)

Vase, chateau/trees/lake, red to bl, ovoid w/ped ft, ca 1910, 8" 800.00
Vase, country village, navy-blk on bright orange, slim ovoid, 15" .. 1,000.00
Vase, flamingos/lake/tree, gr/raspberry/yel, 5" 480.00
Vase, floral, brn on yel frost, slim, 8½" 600.00
Vase, floral, magenta on lt bl, wide shoulders, ca 1900, 4¼"......... 550.00
Vase, floral, magenta on pk, stick neck, 7¼" 400.00
Vase, house/mtn/lake/trees, brn on amber, flared ft, ca 1910, 7¾" . 600.00
Vase, landscape, red-brn on orange, invt baluster form, 1920s, 8½" . 600.00
Vase, Nouveau poppies & vines, lav on pk, slim neck, 19th C, 8¾" ..900.00
Vase, orchids, raspberry on cream, slim w/flared ft, 11⅝"............. 660.00
Vase, petunia & foliage, brn on lt yel, flared ft, 1910s, 10¼" 550.00
Vase, scenic, bl on burnt orange, slim tapered form, ca 1920, 13". 950.00
Vase, trees/mtns/lakes/castle, gr/brn on yel, ovoid, 15".............2,150.00

Rie, Lucie

Lucie Rie was born in 1902. She moved to London in 1938 and shared her studio with Hans Coper from 1946 to 1958. Her ceramics look modern; however they are based on shapes from many world cultures dating back to Roman times. Lucie Rie is best known for the use of metallic oxides in her clay and glazes. She specializes in the hand throwing of thin porcelain bowls, which is a very difficult process. Her works are in the world's best museums. All of her ceramics are impressed with a seal mark on the bottom, a cojoined 'L & R' within a rectangular reserve. Recently, when her work is offered at auction, it has been bringing prices that are sometimes double the presale estimates.

Vase, blue crystals on celadon, artist's initials carved on side, #526, 4½", NM, $13,200.00. (Photo courtesy David Rago Auctions)

Robj

Robj was the name of a retail store that operated in Paris for only a few years, from about 1925 to 1931. Robj solicited designs from the best French artisans of the period to produce decorative objects for the home. These were executed mostly in porcelain but there were glass and earthenware pieces as well. The most well known are the figural bottles which were particularly popular in the United States. However, Robj also promoted tea sets, perfume lamps, chess sets, ashtrays, bookends, humidors, powder jars, cigarette boxes, figurines, lamps, and milk pitchers. Robj objects tend to be whimsical, and all embody the Art Deco style. Items listed below are ceramic unless noted otherwise. Our advisors for this category are Randall Monsen and Rod Baer; their address is listed in the Directory under Virginia.

Vase, matt gazes of green, charcoal, ivory, and pink, 10", $9,150.00. (Photo courtesy Treadway Gallery Inc.)

Bowl, brn w/blk splash rim, stemmed, ca 1955, 4¾" 2,200.00
Bowl, radiating sgraffito lines on pk & bronze matt, 4¾x9", NM .. 10,750.00
Vase, running wht/pk brn, LRG Wein, 5¾" 5,400.00

Bottle, Cusenier, 10½" 2,125.00
Bottle, Joueur De Cornemuse, 10¼" 500.00
Bottle, Kummel Cursky De Cointreau, bl & wht, 10½" 2,500.00
Bottle, L'Ecuyere, gr military-style jacket, wht bottom, w/purse, 12" ..4,050.00
Bottle, La Cantinere, 12½" 2,750.00
Bottle, Le Muscadin Ou L'Incroyable, 12½" 4,685.00
Bottle, Les Trois Matelots, 3 bk-to-bk sailors in bl, 11" 4,700.00
Bottle, male figure, Scots piper in regimental wht, 10½" 480.00
Bottle, mammy in yel & gr, 10¾" 810.00
Bottle, Maquette de Le Seyeux, 11¾" 1,250.00
Bottle, Paysanne Revolutionnaire, 10½" 3,500.00
Bottle, scent; blk sultan, wht & gold, 6¼x5" 1,065.00
Jar, pointed hat as lid, bottom w/facial features, gold crackle, 9".. 280.00
Vase, Deco floral on bl, Luneville, 4½" 95.00

Robineau

After short-term training in ceramics in 1903, Adelaide Robineau (with the help of her husband Samuel) built a small pottery studio at her home in Syracuse, New York. She was adept in mixing the clay and throwing the ware, which she often decorated by incising designs into the unfired clay. Samuel developed many of the glazes and took charge of the firing process. In 1910 she joined the staff of the American Women's League Pottery at St. Louis, where she designed the famous Scarab Vase. After this pottery failed, she served on the faculty of Syracuse University. In the 1920s she worked under the name of Threshold Pottery. She was also the founder and publisher of *Keramic Studio* magazine. Her work was and is today highly acclaimed for the standards of excellence to which she aspired. Our advisors for this category are Suzanne Perrault and David Rago; they are listed in the Directory under New Jersey.

Perfume lamp, pair of birds, ca. 1920, marked, 7½", $1,380.00. (Photo courtesy David Rago Auctions)

Bowl, kylix; lt brn w/bl crystals, blk hdls, rose-to brn int, 3½x8" ...1,650.00
Doorknobs, various glazes on porc, 1x2¼", 4 for 2,280.00
Vase, brn & bl crystalline, ink scribble, 2¼x2" 1,200.00
Vase, bud; amber crystalline; AR w/rnd mk, rstr chip, 7x2" 11,000.00
Vase, celadon crystalline, shouldered, Y AR, 2¾x2¼" 2,400.00
Vase, cobalt crystalline, squat, RP'5/481, 4¼x6" 4,200.00
Vase, turq & purple mottle, bulbous, #2, 1922, 6x7½" 10,800.00
Vase, turq crystalline, squat, narrow rim, #956 05/label, 2¾x5"... 4,800.00
Vase, wht & ivory crystalline, #26, 2¼x2" 1,200.00

Roblin

The intimate and short-lived Roblin pottery was founded at the turn of the last century in San Francisco by descendants of the Robertson family, Scottish ceramicists for generations, and California potter Linna Irelan. Its name came from the contraction of Robertson and Linna, and its product from their joined experience and tastes. The two shared a fondness for local clays, which Alexander Robertson threw along classical shapes. Mrs. Irelan embellished them with painted and applied decoration, often minimal beading, sometimes with applied lizards or mushrooms. Most were stamped Roblin along with a bear drawing. The company was forced to close after the great earthquake of 1906. Our advisors for this category are Suzanne Perrault and David Rago; they are listed in the Directory under New Jersey.

Vase, brn drips on celadon flambé, squat, AWR, 2¼x3¼" 1,950.00
Vase, bsk, cylinder w/tooling at top, cvd & stepped ft, 2½x1½" ...215.00
Vase, bsk, swollen cylinder w/tooled banded lines, 2¼x1¾" 350.00

Vase, cinquefoils, white on brown, Linna Irelan, glaze bubbles, 5x4", $3,600.00.

Vase, gunmetal, cylindrical w/prunt, L Irelan, 4" 650.00
Vase, multi-tone tan & brn on bsk, sm ft, 2" 550.00

Rock 'n Roll Memorabilia

Memorabilia from the early days of rock 'n roll recalls an era that many of us experienced firsthand; these listings are offered to demonstrate the many and various aspects of this area of collecting. Beware of reproductions! Many are so well done even a knowledgeable collector will sometimes be fooled. Unless otherwise noted, our values are for examples in near-mint to mint condition. Our advisor for this category is Bob Gottuso, author of Beatles, KISS, and Monkees sections in *Garage Sale Gold II* by Tomart. He is listed in the Directory under Pennsylvania. See also Decanters.

Beatles, phonograph, NEMS, 1960s, $2,500.00. (From the collection of Dick Clark) (Photo courtesy Gurnsey's/LiveAuctioneers.com)

Aerosmith, jacket, brn leather, Robert Comstock, 1993 ....100.00
Aerosmith, tour book, emb gold on bl cover, 1977, EX..................75.00
Alice Cooper, pin, half face/half skull on ALICE, metal, 2x1", 1980s ...35.00

Alice Cooper, sweatshirt, mc on blk, Trash tour, 1989 ....45.00
Beatles, beach hat, blk images/signatures on wht w/red trim........175.00
Beatles, binder, group photo on wht, EX......................................100.00
Beatles, cake topper, 4 3-D head shots on plastic pc, 4½" L 120.00
Beatles, coin purse, John figural, mc vinyl, w/zipper 50.00
Beatles, coin purse, 4 headshots, wht on red rubber, squeeze, 2x3"....80.00
Beatles, hair comb, blk & wht headshots/signatures on lt gr plastic ...330.00
Beatles, lobby card, Yellow Submarine, #1, EX.............................280.00
Beatles, model kit, Ringo w/drum, MIB.......................................300.00
Beatles, Paint-by-Number, Ringo, unused, EXIB.........................825.00
Beatles, plate, bl, blk & gray decal on wht ceramic 120.00
Beatles, program, Christmas, Odeon Theatre, UK 190.00
Beatles, purse, group image on tan vinyl, brass hdl, 10x9¾".........430.00
Beatles, record player, group photo in lid.................................2,500.00
Beatles, tumbler, group w/instruments photo on yel coating, glass, 5"...180.00
Bee Gees, belt buckle, gold letters on bl, 1977 ....20.00
Bee Gees, lunchbox, Barry Gibb on front/concert photo bk, 1979, EX..45.00
Bee Gees, poster, wearing wht & gold, One Stop Posters, 1979, 60x40"..35.00
Bill Haley, poster, holding guitar in front of moon, mc, 1974, 35x22" 25.00
Black Sabbath, security T-shirt, blk letters on yel, Chicago, 1974 . 70.00
Bobby Darin, photo, blk & wht portrait, 1962, 8x10" 25.00
Bon Jovi, T-shirt, Shot Thru the Heart on blk, Slippery When Wet, 1987 .40.00
Bon Jovi, tour jacket, denim, Slippery When Wet, Lee, 1987......210.00
Bruce Springsteen, T-shirt, World tour, 1980-81 ....100.00
Creedence Clearwater Revival, group photo, blk & wht, 1969, 8x10" ... 30.00
Creedence Clearwater Revival, poster, group on stage, 1971, 25x37", EX. 35.00
Dave Clark 5, sheet music, Reelin' & Rockin', group on cover, 1960s ..15.00
David Bowie, jersey, mc on blk w/red sleeves, Serious Moonlight, 1983 .. 30.00
David Bowie, poster, Young Americans, RCA, 1975, 30x24½", EX..50.00
David Bowie, promo photo, holding guitar, Greg Gorman, blk & wht, 1986 .25.00
David Bowie, T-shirt, blk & wht on bl, 1970s...............................30.00
David Bowie, tour book, Diamond Dogs, 1974, 20-pg, 9x12" 45.00
David Bowie, wall mural, photo, SOLD OUT on blk in corner, 16x20', EX...45.00
David Cassidy, 3-ring binder, Westab, 1972, from $40 to 50.00
Def Leppard, book, Animal Instinct, David Frincke, 1987, 144-pg...60.00
Def Leppard, jersey, mc on blk w/red sleeves, Pyromania tour, 1983 .. 45.00
Def Leppard, tour book, Hysteria, 1987, 47-pg, 8½x5¼" 45.00
Donnie & Marie, dolls, pk/purple outfits, Mattel, w/microphones, 1977 . 25.00
Donnie & Marie, record player, photo image inside & on lid, ca 1970s ...40.00
Doobie Brothers, poster, group photo, Dargis Associates, 1978, 34x22" ...25.00
Doors, handbill, Strange Nights Are Coming, info on bk, 1967, 8½x6"....770.00
Doors, poster, Folk-Rock Festival, Jim Morrison photo, 1968, 34x22" ...300.00
Doors, tour program, Strange Days, Jim Morrison in repose (blk), 1968..275.00
Elton John, bobble head, bl jacket, red shoes & glasses, resin, 6½" ...80.00
Elton John, poster, Caribou, in tiger-stripe shirt, MCA, 1974, 35x22"...100.00
Elton John, promo sign, wht album artworks (6) on blk, 1970.......45.00
Elton John, T-shirt, Goodbye Yellow Brick Road, wht, 1976 ....25.00
Elton John, tour book, Yellow Brick Road, 20-pg, 1973 ....100.00
Elton John, tour program, pk & wht cover, photos, Mar 14, 1974 ...50.00
Elvis, book, Bring Him Back!, Joe Tunzi, concert photos, 1970 ... 100.00
Elvis, book, Life of Elvis Presley, S Shaver & H Noland, hardbk, 1979 ..100.00
Elvis, concert program, Grand Ole Opry, 20-pg, 1950s, EX..........155.00
Elvis, diary, blk-line Elvis drawing on pk leatherette, 1956, VG..570.00
Elvis, film transparency, w/Julie Parish, Paradise Hawaiian Style, '68.. 150.00
Elvis, guitar pick, EP in wht on blk, NBC TV Special, 1968 ....410.00
Elvis, hat, mc images & letters on wht band, blk, Magnet, 1956, w/tag ...160.00
Elvis, hound dog, stuffed figure, Elvis Summer Festival on ears, 10"....260.00
Elvis, jacket, mc badges on blk nylon, Elvis in Concert, Auburn, 1970 ...130.00
Elvis, magazine, Official Elvis Presley Album, Elvis info & ads, 1956. 100.00
Elvis, menu, Las Vegas Hilton Hotel, photo cover, 1975..............290.00
Elvis, portrait on velvet, Elvis & Lisa Marie, D Rouen, 1978, 20x16" 210.00
Elvis, program book, Rock & Roll Hall of Fame, 24-pg, 1986, 12x8½" ..130.00
Elvis, record case, blk-line drawing on pk leatherette, 1950s, VG+ 200.00
Elvis, scarf, images in ea corner, Summer Festival, gr, 1970, 27x26"....370.00

Elvis, sheet music, Hound Dog, photo cover, 1956......................... 95.00
Elvis, sheet music, Santa Bring My Baby Back, photo cover, 1957... 100.00

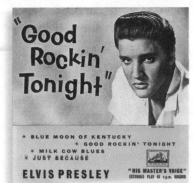

Elvis, vinyl EP, first release, laminated sleeve, NM, $500.00. (Photo courtesy Nate D. Sanders/LiveAuctioneers.com)

Grateful Dead, concert poster, wht letters on bl w/photo, 1972, 22x17".. 575.00
Jackson 5, tour book, Destiny, 1979, 16-pg, 11½x11½" 28.00
Jimi Hendrix, concert poster, Blue Cheer, 1968, 28x20" 395.00
Jimi Hendrix, concert poster, 2 elephants on orange, 1967, 20x15"... 2,850.00

KISS, costume, Gene Simmons, Collegeville, 1978, MIB, $150.00.

KISS, costume, Paul Stanley, outfit, hair & mask, 1978, M (EX box) .. 150.00
KISS, poster, Gene Simmons, Phantom of the Park, Italy, 33x13½" 110.00
KISS, poster, group in costume, Destroyer, Germany concert, 34x34".. 565.00
KISS, record player, photo on inside & on lid, red & wht, Tiger, EX.... 390.00
KISS, ring, group's image enameled on gold-tone metal, 1970s, EX 85.00
KISS, sleeping bag, mc on red & bl, 1978..................................... 165.00
KISS, trash can, mc pnt on metal, concert scene, cylindrical, 1978. 235.00
Little Richard, promo photo, sepia, 1955, 8x10" 45.00
Lynyrd Skynyrd, poster, group photo, Street Survivors, 1977, 22x14" ... 40.00
Pink Floyd, concert poster, Fillmore Auditorium, CA, 1967, 21x14" . 500.00
Pink Floyd, T-shirt, red/gr/wht pig on blk, Animals tour, 1977 .... 100.00
Prince, promo poster, Prince w/guitar, Controversy, 1981, 36x36", EX.. 50.00
Ricky Nelson, paper dolls, Whitman, 1959 .... 65.00
Ricky Nelson, promo photo, blk & wht, 1980s, 8x10" 24.00
Rolling Stones, concert poster, Oakland Coliseum, Nov 9, 1969, 22x14"... 200.00
Rolling Stones, novelty telephone, red tongue & lips, 1983, MIB.. 280.00
Rolling Stones, promo poster, Exile on Main Street on orange, 28x20"... 350.00
Rolling Stones, snapshot photo, group backstage, blk & wht, 1966, 4".... 210.00
Rolling Stones, T-shirt, mc/wht, Steel Wheels tour, Shea Stadium, 1989. 90.00
Rolling Stones, tour book, Mick & lips on blk cover, 66-pg, 1972. 75.00

Rockingham

In the early part of the nineteenth century, American potters began to prefer brown- and buff-burning clays over red because of their durabil-

ity. The glaze favored by many was Rockingham, which varied from a dark brown mottle to a sponged effect sometimes called tortoiseshell. It consisted in part of manganese and various metallic salts and was used by many potters until well into the twentieth century. Over the past two years, demand and prices have risen sharply, especially in the East. See also Bennington.

Book flask, amber glaze, 5⅝" 390.00
Book flask, dk glaze, att OH, sm flakes, 6" 240.00
Bowl, columns & dots, ca 1860, 3½x10½" 75.00
Figurine, sheep standing on base, ca 1900, 5¼x4⅞x3½" 130.00
Figurine, spaniel seated, free-standing front legs, molded base, 10".. 480.00

Flask, fish form, England, ca 1875, 9" long, minimum value, $1,450.00.

(Photo courtesy Lisa S. McAllister)

Flask, mermaid w/curled tail, 8".. 175.00
Frame, oval, ca 1850s, 10x8¼" 800.00
Pitcher, bow-tied wheat stalks & tavern scenes, w/ice lip & lid, 12".. 240.00
Pitcher, dog begging figural, tricornered hat forms lid, 1850, 11", EX ... 215.00
Pitcher, leaves, baluster w/hexagonal ft, 19th C, 7½" 240.00
Plate, pleated corners w/scroll designs, sq, 1½x8½", NM.............. 325.00
Teapot, Rebecca at the Well, ca 1850, sm..................................... 90.00

Pitcher, embossed game, eagle spout, dog handle, 10", $540.00.

(Photo courtesy Pook & Pook Inc./ LiveAuctioneers.com)

Rockwell, Norman

Norman Rockwell began his career in 1911 at the age of 17 doing illustrations for a children's book entitled *Tell Me Why Stories*. Within a few years he had produced the *Saturday Evening Post* cover that made him one of America's most beloved artists. Though not well accepted by the professional critics of his day who did not consider his work to be art but 'merely' commercial illustration, Rockwell's popularity grew to the extent that today there is an overwhelming abundance of examples of his work or those related to the theme of one of his illustrations.

The figurines described below were issued by Rockwell Museum and Museum Collections Inc.; for Rockwell listings by Gorham see last year's edition of *Schroeder's Antiques Price Guide*. Our advisor for this category is Barb Putratz; she is listed in the Directory under Minnesota.

A Walkin' & a Whistlin', 1986 .... 70.00
Adventures Between Adventures, 1986.................................... 100.00
All Wrapped Up, 1984 .... 100.00
Almost Grown Up, 1982 .... 175.00
America's Artist, ltd ed 5,000, 1985 .... 210.00
Another Masterpiece by Norman Rockwell, ltd ed of 5,000, 1985 .. 210.00
Apple for the Teacher, Museum Collections Inc, 1986 .... 70.00
Artist, The; Museum Collections Inc, ltd ed 2,500, 1986 .... 95.00
At the Circus, 1982 .... 190.00
Baby's First Step, 1979 .... 175.00
Barefoot Boy, Museum Collections Inc, ltd ed 5,000, 1986 ...... 110.00
Bedtime, LCF series, ltd ed 1,000, 1982 .... 225.00
Bicycle Boys, 1981 .... 120.00
Birthday Party, The; 1980.. 150.00
Bored of Education, 1984 .... 95.00
Bottom of the Sixth, Museum Collections Inc, ltd ed 5,000, 1986 .. 200.00
Boy Meets His Dog, A; 1986 .... 100.00
Bride & Groom, 1981 .... 140.00
Bringing Home the Christmas Tree, 1982............................... 125.00
Celebration, 1982 .... 190.00
Checking His List, 1980 .... 90.00

The Circus Comes to Town, Rockwell Museum, $125.00.

Cobbler, LCF Series, ltd ed 1,000, 1982................................. 225.00
Cobbler, The; 1979... 80.00
Collect Fine Porcelain figures (ad stand), 1984 .... 140.00
Couragous Hero, 1982 .... 185.00
Dollhouse for Sis, A; 1979 .... 80.00
Dreams in the Antique Shop, Museum Collections Inc, 1986....... 80.00
Drummer's Friend, The; 1982.. 125.00
First Car in Town, The; ltd ed 2,500, 1985 .... 235.00
First Haircut, The; 1979 .... 150.00
First Prom, The; 1979 .... 125.00
Freedom of Fear, ltd ed 5,000, 1982....................................... 350.00
Freedom of Speech, ltd ed 5,000, 1982 .... 350.00
Freedom of Worship, ltd ed 5,000, 1982 .... 350.00
Giving Thanks, 1982 .... 200.00
Goin' Fishin', 1984 .... 95.00
Good Food Good Friends, 1982 .... 225.00
Happy Birthday, Dear Mother, 1979 .... 140.00
Helping Mother, 1982 .... 120.00
High Stepping, 1982.. 110.00
Home for Fido, A; Museum Collections Inc, 1986 .... 75.00
Homerun Slugger, 1982 .... 145.00
Late Night Dining, Museum Collections Inc, 1986...................... 80.00
Letterman, The; Museum Collections Inc, ltd ed 2,500, 1986 ..... 165.00
Lighthouse Keeper's Daughter, The; LCF series, ltd ed 1,000, 1982 ...225.00
Little Mother, 1980... 135.00
Little Patient, 1981 .... 120.00
Little Salesman, 1982 .... 185.00
Lovely in Lipstick, Museum Collections Inc, 1988...................... 75.00

Memories, LCF Series, ltd ed 1,000, 1983............................... 225.00
Memories, 1980... 90.00
Mom's Helper, ltd ed 15,000, 1986.. 120.00
Music Master, The; 1980 .... 90.00
Mysterious Malady, Museum Collections Inc, 1986.................. 100.00
New Arrival, Museum Collections Inc, 1981 .... 160.00
Off to School, LCF series, ltd ed 1,000, 1981.......................... 115.00
Out Fishin', Museum Collections Inc, ltd ed 25,000, 1985 .... 100.00
Outward Bound, ltd ed 5,000, 1984 .... 200.00
Partygoers, Museum Collections Inc, ltd 2,500, 1984............... 235.00
Pest, The; 1982 .... 125.00
Playing Pirates, ltd ed 2,500, 1984 .... 235.00
Practice Makes Perfect, Museum Collections Inc, ltd ed 2,500, 1987... 170.00
Pride of Parenthood, 1986 .... 100.00
Puppy Love, 1983... 95.00
Report Card, Museum Collections Inc, 1986............................. 80.00
Rosie the Riveter, Museum Collections Inc, ltd ed 2,500, 1987... 165.00
Santa Takes a Break, Museum Collections Inc, ltd ed 3,500, 1987 .. 110.00
Saturday's Hero, 1984 .... 105.00
Sneezing Spy, Museum Collections Inc, ltd ed 2,500, 1986 .... 160.00
Soda Jerk, The; ltd ed 5,000, 1986 .... 205.00
Space Age Santa, 1984 .... 115.00
Space Pioneers, 1982 .... 185.00
Special Treat, A; 1982 .... 100.00
Spirit of America, The; ltd ed 5,000, 1982 .... 185.00
Spring Fever, 1981 .... 100.00
Student, The; 1980... 165.00
Summer Fun, 1982 .... 120.00
Sunday Morning, Museum Collections Inc, ltd ed 2,500, 1986 ... 225.00
Sweet Dreams, 1981... 190.00
Sweet Sixteen, 1979 .... 125.00
Tattoo Artist, Museum Collections Inc, ltd ed 2,500, 1987 .... 170.00
Toymaker, The; LCF series, ltd ed 1,000, 1982 .... 225.00
Toymaker, The; 1979 .... 95.00
Trumpeter, The; Museum Collections Inc, ltd ed 2,500, 1986 ..2,000.00
Vacation's Over, 1981 .... 120.00
Visiting the Vet, Museum Collections Inc, 1988 .... 85.00
Waiting for Santa, 1982 .... 135.00
We Missed You Daddy, 1981 .... 190.00
Weighty Matters, ltd ed 5,000, 1986 .... 180.00
Wet Behind the Ears, Museum Collections Inc, 1986 .... 80.00
Winter Fun, 1982.. 95.00
Words of Wisdom, 1982... 130.00
Wrapping Christmas Presents, 1980....................................... 130.00

Rogers, John

John Rogers (1829 – 1904) was a machinist from Manchester, New Hampshire, who turned his hobby of sculpting into a financially successful venture. From the originals he meticulously fashioned of red clay, he had bronze master molds made from which plaster copies were cast. He specialized in five different categories: theatrical, Shakespeare, Civil War, everyday life, and horses. His large detailed groupings portrayed the life and times of the period between 1859 and 1892. In the following listings, examples are assumed to be plaster castings in excellent condition unless noted bronze or parian. Many plaster examples will be in poor condition, be sure to adjust prices accordingly.

Bath...2,000.00
Bubbles...2,000.00
Bushwacker 2,000.00
Charity Patient, VG 700.00
Chess..1,200.00

Coming to the Parson, VG 660.00
Council of War, Pat Mar 31 1868, pnt flakes, 24" 635.00
Council of War, 24x14x12" 2,645.00
Country Post Office, VG 750.00
Courtship in Sleepy Hollow, VG- 550.00
Elder's Daughter 475.00
Faust & Marguerite, Leaving the Garden...................................1,200.00
Favored Scholar, miniature, 1941, 4x2½" 165.00
Favored Scholar, VG- 780.00
Fighting Bob, 1889...1,100.00
First Ride, VG 725.00
Foundling 900.00
Frolic at the Old Homestead, 18x16" 900.00
Home Guard 800.00
It Is So Nominated in the Bond, mc pnt, 23x19x11" 1,500.00
Mail Day..2,000.00
Matter of Opinion, VG... 600.00
Mounted to the Rear - One More Shot, parian, 20½" 3,800.00
One More Shot.. 550.00
Parting Promise, 22x10x9", VG 635.00
Parting Promise (older man), VG 475.00
Peddler at the Fair, VG 700.00
Photographer, 1878..4,000.00
Picket Guard, VG 750.00
Polo, bronze, 2 horsemen, 21" 45,000.00
Referee 800.00
Rip Van Winkle - At Home, VG- 500.00
Rip Van Winkle on the Mountain, VG- 575.00
Ruth Gleaning, wht marble, missing 2 fingers, 47" 24,000.00
School Days, 22x12x8".. 800.00
Shaughraun & Tatters, bronze w/gr-brn patina, 20"...............19,000.00
Slave Auction 2,000.00
Speak for Yourself John, VG- 500.00
Taking the Oath & Drawing Rations, 23", VG............................. 850.00
Tap on the Window 525.00

Uncle Ned's School, EX, $2,100.00. (Photo courtesy Early American History Auctions/LiveAuctioneers.com)

Village Schoolmaster, VG 850.00
Watch on the Santa Maria 1,000.00
Weighing the Baby, 21x15", VG 675.00
Wounded Scout, brn pnt, 23x11x9", VG...................................1,100.00
Wounded to the Rear - One More Shot, parian, 19" 4,800.00

Rookwood

The Rookwood Pottery Company was established in 1879 in Cincinnati, Ohio, by Maria Longworth Nichols. From a wealthy family, Ms. Nichols was provided with sufficient financial backing to make such an enterprise possible. She hired competent ceramic artisans and artists of note, who through constant experimentation developed many lines of superior art pottery. While in her employ, Laura Fry invented the airbrush-blending process for which she was issued a patent in 1884. From this, several lines were designed that utilized blended backgrounds. One of their earlier lines, Standard, was a brown ware decorated with underglaze slip-painted nature studies, animals, portraits, etc. Iris and Sea Green were introduced in 1894 and Vellum, a transparent mat-glaze line, in 1904. Other lines followed: Ombroso in 1910 and Soft Porcelain in 1915. Many of the early artware lines were signed by the artist. Soon after the turn of the twentieth century, Rookwood manufactured 'production' pieces that relied mainly on molded designs and forms rather than freehand decoration for their esthetic appeal. The Depression brought on financial difficulties from which the pottery never recovered. Though it continued to operate, the quality of the ware deteriorated, and the pottery was forced to close in 1967.

Unmarked Rookwood is only rarely encountered. Many marks may be found, but the most familiar is the reverse 'RP' monogram. First used in 1886, a flame point was added above it for each succeeding year until 1900. After that a Roman numeral added below indicated the year of manufacture. Impressed letters that related to the type of clay utilized for the body were also used — G for ginger, O for olive, R for red, S for sage green, W for white, and Y for yellow. Artware must be judged on an individual basis. Quality of the artwork is a prime factor to consider. Portraits, animals, and birds are worth more than florals; and pieces signed by a particularly renowned artist are highly prized. Our advisors for this category are Suzanne Perrault and David Rago; they are listed in the Directory under New Jersey.

Black Opal

Bowl, floral, L Epply, #2287, 1926, X, 3½x8", NM 270.00
Vase, cascading flowers, H Wilcox, #2977, 1926, 7½" 1,550.00
Vase, dogwood blossoms, H Wilcox, #2101, 1926, 7" 1,175.00
Vase, edelweiss at shoulder, H Wilcox, #2918E, 1929, 6⅝" 3,550.00
Vase, floral (very dk), H Wilcox, #2065, 1924, 8" 1,450.00

Cameo

Candlestick, floral, E Abel, #508, 1891, 6", ea........................ 360.00
Candlestick, flower (sm), unknown artist, #508, W, 1891, 5¼", ea .. 145.00
Ewer, floral, H Wilcox, #101C, Y, 1887, 9x5" 550.00
Ewer, wht rose, unidentified artist, #40W, S/R, 1888, 6¼x4"........ 360.00
Plate, coupe; chrysanthemums, S Toohey, #205C, W/W, 1½x8".. 155.00
Potpourri jar, bird on branch, AR Valentien, #27, Y, 1886, 7½x6" ..850.00

Potpourri jar, bird on branch, Matt Daly, 1886/237/MAD, $1,950.00. (Photo courtesy David Rago Auctions/LiveAuctioneers.com)

French Red

Bowl vase, floral band, S Sax, #955, 1922, 2¾x4½" 3,750.00

Vase, floral band at collar, cream body, S Sax, #2259, 1917, 4x5⅜" ...2,500.00
Vase, fuchsias, S Sax, #2191, 1922, 5⅛" 13,200.00

Glaze Effect

Vase, bl & tan, baluster, S, 1932, 8" 390.00
Vase, bl/fuchsia/brn, #6307, 1932, 3" 450.00
Vase, bl/lt/bl/gray, #6307F, 1932, 2⅞" 390.00
Vase, chartreuse/bl/dk bl, #6514E, 1957, 3½" 155.00
Vase, red/gray/bl on Coromandel, #6307F, 1932, 3" 600.00

Vase, lobster and foliage, Shirayamadani, #670-C, 9¾", $19,200.00. (Photo courtesy Cincinnati Art Galleries/LiveAuctioneers.com)

Iris

Ewer, pansies, C Baker, #495C, 1895, 4¾" 3,200.00
Vase, apple blossoms, S Coyne, #938C, 1907, 7⅝" 1,175.00
Vase, camellias, S Sax, #925C, W, 1903, 9½" 2,500.00
Vase, clematis, E Diers, #886D, 1904, 8½" 1,950.00
Vase, clovers, F Rothenbusch, #614F, W, 1902, 6" 1,200.00
Vase, crocuses, F Rothenbusch, #801D, W, 1902, 7⅜" 1,800.00
Vase, cyclamen, L Asbury, #907E, W, 1910, 8⅝" 2,550.00
Vase, daisies, L Asbury, #917B, W, 1907, 9⅛" 6,000.00
Vase, hollyhock branches, L Asbury, #1278C, X, 1910, 12x6"..7,800.00
Vase, hollyhocks, L Asbury, #1278C, 1910, 11⅞" 10,800.00
Vase, hyacinths, S Sax, #950C, 1905, 10⅛" 3,250.00
Vase, irises, L Asbury, #951C, 1905, 10¼" 3,000.00
Vase, Japanese irises, K Shirayamadani, #589F, W, 1894, 7"......2,000.00
Vase, magnolias, C Schmidt, #952C, W, 1906, 10¼" 6,150.00
Vase, mushrooms, C Schmidt, #901D, W, 1902, 7¼" 2,600.00
Vase, peacock feather, C Schmidt, #9026, 1904, 9⅜" 44,400.00
Vase, poppies, silver o/l, S Sax, #80B, W, 1900, 6⅝" 3,150.00
Vase, rose (lg), C Schmidt, #901C, W, 1901, 9" 2,350.00
Vase, roses, F Rothenbusch, #1598D, 1909, 9¼"........................3,000.00
Vase, swan scenic, C Schmidt, #951C, 1906, 9½" 4,800.00
Vase, trees & shoreline, S Lawrence, #932B, W, 1902, 14¾" 6,000.00
Vase, trumpet flowers, R Fechheimer, #30F, 1901, 6" 660.00
Vase, Venetian harbor, C Schmidt, #932, W, 1900, 5¼" 3,600.00
Vase, violets, E Wildman, #1120, W, 1911, 4½" 1,050.00
Vase, wild roses at top, M Mitchell, #932E, 1904, 7½" 725.00
Vase, winter landscape, F Rothenbusch, #1357D, X, 1909, 8½".. 3,000.00

Limoges

Basket, butterflies, lion's head ft, AR Valentien, 1882, 9¾x20" L ...550.00
Dish, bird among reeds, WP McDonald, w/hdl, 1883, 6¾" W 150.00
Ewer, butterflies & flowers, unknown artist, 1882, 12x7", NM.....250.00
Jug, owls & bats under moon on dk gr, N Hirschfeld, 1880, 3x2"....660.00
Jug, perfume; birds/clouds/grasses, AR Valentien, 1882, 4¾", NM ..350.00
Pilgrim flask, dogwood, L Johnston, 1883, 6½" 725.00
Pitcher, bats/owls/moon, AR Valentien, 1882, 7½x7½" 400.00
Pitcher, dragonfly/grasses, N Hirschfeld, horn shape, G, 1883, 6½" ..780.00

Pitcher, floral, AR Valentien, bulbous, 1881, 9" 960.00
Vase, butterfly among reeds, M Rettig, #205, 1885, 9" 240.00
Vase, floral branches in barbotine, 1885, 13½x8" 725.00

Matt

Note: Both incised mat and painted mat are listed here. Incised mat descriptions are indicated by the term 'cvd' within the line; all others are hand-painted mat ware.

Tankard, cvd apple branches, Todd, 1912, X (2 sm glaze misses), 12"...900.00
Vase, autumnal leaves, S Toohey, #193GZ, 1901, flaw, 9x3½" ..2,650.00
Vase, cattails, W Hentschel, #581E, 1910, X, 12¾x6½" 1,800.00
Vase, cvd Arts & Crafts border, W Hentschel, #915, 1914, 8"..1,800.00
Vase, cvd fish, A Pons, slightly bulbous, 1907, 6½" 1,650.00
Vase, cvd floral/geometric band, C Todd, #886C, 1915, 11⅛x8½"...2,100.00
Vase, cvd gingko leaves & nuts, E Lincoln, #9191, 1908, 4¼x4½"...1,025.00

Vase, carved stylized floral, Wm. Hentschel, #946, 1913, 11", $2,280.00. (Photo courtesy David Rago Auctions)

Vase, cvd swirling lines, W Hentschel, #1016C, 1913, 8¼" 1,175.00
Vase, cvd triangular flowers w/stems, W Hentschel, #2039D, 1913, 10"..1,800.00
Vase, exotic birds on trees, butterfat, L Epply, #2914, 1927, 8¼"...2,750.00
Vase, floral, L Lincoln, #807, 1921, 13¼x5"...............................1,550.00
Vase, floral, M McDonald, #6602, 6½x5½" 1,075.00
Vase, floral, S Coyne, cylindrical, 1924, 8⅞"...............................1,075.00
Vase, floral, squeezebag, E Barrett, #2918E, 1929, 6¾x5¼" 835.00
Vase, geometric panels, J Harris, #2254D, 1930, 5¼" 900.00
Vase, hydrangea branches on butterfat, L Epply, #2246C, 1928, 14½"....5,600.00
Vase, irises, K Shirayamadani, #9075, 1945, 7¾" 1,800.00
Vase, landscape (mottled), M McDonald, #6743, 1939, 7½" 960.00
Vase, lilies, K Shirayamadani, bulbous, 1926, 6½x6" 3,600.00
Vase, Moderne, horses & rider, W Rhem, 1934, 5x4¼"...............1,200.00
Vase, Moderne, leafy sprigs, F Barrett, #2368, 1927, 17x7" 2,200.00
Vase, Moderne, leafy sprigs, W Hentschel, #977, 1927, 10¼x5".. 480.00
Vase, peacock feathers, L Lincoln, #837, 1921, 10½x6" 1,650.00
Vase, poppies, K Shirayamadani, #6006, 1929, grinding chips, 11½".. 3,000.00
Vase, stylized floral, V Tischler, ovoid, 1924, 15x6½" 1,450.00

Porcelain

Bowl, exotic birds/foliage, ET Hurley, #2254D, 1929, 5⅜" 1,800.00
Charger, deer/flowers, bl/wht, E Barrett, #6937, 1946, 12⅞" 1,150.00
Ginger jar, mixed flowers, K Shirayamadani, #2451, 1923, 10".6,300.00
Plate, Jewel, chinoiserie, bl & wht, W Hentschel, #K2A, 1924, 10¼". 1,325.00
Plate, 12 apposles under sheer ivory, trial pc, KB, 12½" 330.00
Temple jars, cascading flowers, L Asbury, #2463, 1923, 9⅝", pr.. 2,400.00
Vase, antelopes, squeezebag/crystalline, W Rehm, S, 1934, 5½"...2,400.00
Vase, birds & flowers, S Sax, #112, 1919, 6¾" 1,800.00
Vase, birds & foliage, E Barrett, #2187, 1944, 8¾" 1,650.00

Vase, clematis vines, K Shirayamadani, #1664D, 1922, 11" 6,600.00
Vase, daisies, S Coyne, #546C, 1924, 9½"..............................3,500.00
Vase, dmns, Nacreous glaze, S Sax, #2182, P, 1915, 4¾" 1,800.00
Vase, elephants & flowers, E Barrett, #6315, 1944, 6½x5½" 2,750.00
Vase, exotic flowers/birds, ET Hurley, 1924, 11⅜" 2,400.00
Vase, fish, L Epply, #6203C, XXX, 1930, 8x6¼" 4,750.00
Vase, fish & vegetation, ET Hurley, #6877, 1944, 7½x8", NM.....15,500.00
Vase, floral, J Jensen, Anniversary glaze int, #2996, 1931, 8⅜"....2,450.00
Vase, floral & birds, A Conant, #2370, 1919, 20¾".................32,500.00
Vase, floral collar, S Sax, #975D, 1919, 6⅝".............................1,950.00
Vase, floral garland, L Epply, #1122B, 1919, 8¾".....................2,400.00
Vase, floral shoulder, A Conant, #2306, 1917, 7"......................1,100.00
Vase, geometric floral, S Sax, #2969, 1929, 7½x6½"................3,150.00
Vase, irises, ET Hurley, #30E, 1949, 8½".................................1,800.00
Vase, Jewel, bird among peonies, A Conant, #2544, X, 1921, 8x4" ...2,280.00
Vase, Jewel, birds of paradise/blossoms, ET Hurley, 1924, 11½x6"...5,400.00
Vase, Jewel, cherry blossoms, K Shirayamadani, #589F, 1922, 7½x3" ...4,200.00
Vase, Jewel, chrysanthemums, A Conant, #999C, 1918, 8¾x6¾" ..10,800.00
Vase, Jewel, floral, A Conant, #2347, 1921, 7x4½" 3,150.00
Vase, Jewel, floral on ivory butterfat, L Epply, #2983, 1928, 15½"..3,950.00
Vase, Jewel, floral sprigs, W Hentschel, #2499C, 1920, 14x5" ..8,000.00
Vase, Jewel, flower sprays, L Epply, #2077, 1927, 6¼x5" 1,000.00
Vase, Jewel, lotus blossoms, K Shirayamadani, #1358C, 1924, 10½" ..2,050.00

Vase, Jewel, Persian floral, Lorinda Epply, #784-C, 1923, 10¾", $2,650.00. (Photo courtesy David Rago Auctions)

Vase, lake scene w/trees, A Conant, #2306, 1919, 7" 2,450.00
Vase, magnolias, S Sax, #2640C, 1930, 13¼" 9,600.00
Vase, magnolias, W Hentchel, 8-sided, 1923, 11½"...................2,400.00
Vase, magnolias/birds, H Wilcox, #2033D, 1920, 10".................7,200.00
Vase, orchids, C McLaughlin, #951D, 1918, 8⅞" 3,250.00
Vase, Oriental birds/flowers/mtns, A Conant, shouldered, 1920, 10" . 3,850.00
Vase, Oriental scenic, A Conant, #0551, 1920, 6⅝" 4,800.00
Vase, peacock feathers, E Diers, squat, 3x6½"...........................1,325.00
Vase, Venetian harbor, C Schmidt, #904C, 1923, 12¼".............9,600.00
Vase, Venetian harbor, C Schmidt, #2721, 1924, 6⅛" 3,600.00
Vase, wisteria cascades, E Diers, #2545F, 1924, 6¾"...................2,350.00

Sea Green

Loving cup, hop leaves/vines/fruit, Demarest, silver mts, #656C, 1900...7,200.00
Mug, clovers, ET Hurley, Commercial Club of Cincinnati, 1905, 5¼"...1,100.00
Vase, fish, cylindrical, E Hurley, #951C, 1905, 10¼x4" 1,325.00
Vase, fruit blossoms, A Van Briggle, #589E, G, 1898, 8½" 5,250.00
Vase, Imperial cranes, C Schmidt, cylindrical, #589D, G, 1898, 11⅛"..20,000.00
Vase, irises, A Sprague, #604C, G, 1900, 9½"...........................3,500.00
Vase, pansies, C Baker, #536E, X, 1904, 3¼x5" 600.00

Standard

Coffeepot, floral, M Perkins, #613, 1893, 9½x7" 1,000.00
Ewer, palm frond & flower w/silver o/l, A Valentien, #723, 1895, 7".. 3,850.00
Humidor, Geronimo, E Felton, #672, 1903, 5½" 4,800.00
Jug, ear of corn (detailed) w/silver o/l, E Abel, #S975, 1892, 8x6" ...4,800.00
Loving cup, Conquering Bear (Sioux), A Sehon, #659C, 1915, 6" .4,800.00
Mug, chimpanzee dressed & carrying bag, M Daly, #587, W, 1891, 4½"..2,750.00

Pitcher, yellow roses, silver overlay with pomegranates, K. Shirayamadani, #437-A, hairlines, $4,800.00. (Photo courtesy David Rago Auctions/LiveAuctioneers.com)

Puzzle mug, man w/pipe, B Horsfall, #711, 1894, 5x5" 1,325.00
Stein, ear of corn (detailed), K Shirayamadani, #T970, W, 1894, 7"..5,200.00
Vase, autumn leaves, M Nourse, #903B, L, 1899, 10"................1,325.00
Vase, cherries & leaves w/silver o/l, E Lincoln, #880, 1900, 6"...3,900.00
Vase, clovers w/silver o/l, H Stuntz, #706, 1893, 4½x5" 3,350.00
Vase, daffodils, L Lindeman, #30E, 1902, 7¾" 1,325.00
Vase, floral w/silver o/l, J Zettel, #798B, 1894, 9½x5"................3,600.00
Vase, Geo Shakespeare (Arapahoe), G Young, #30E, 1901, 7⅝" .. 13,200.00
Vase, hummingbird & bittersweet, C Lindeman, #907E, 1906, 8⅝"..1,550.00
Vase, Indian lady & baby, G Young, #604C, 1900, 9"...............31,500.00
Vase, lilies of the valley, K Matchette, #612C, W, 1893, 5⅝".......785.00
Vase, man's portrait, J Wareham, #625, 1893, 5½" 1,175.00
Vase, monkeys, B Horsfall, #690C, X, 1893, 8¾"......................7,150.00
Vase, pansies w/silver o/l, J Zettel, #607C, 1893, 5x4"...............3,575.00
Vase, poppies, K Shirayamadani, #664B, X, 1897, 10⅜"............1,325.00
Vase, red-hot pokers (floral) in relief, J Wareham, #732B, 1900, 10"..6,000.00
Vase, roses w/silver o/l, M Daly, #932C, 1902, 11½"..................6,500.00
Vase, thistles, A Sprague, #488, W, 1894, 6½" 1,100.00
Vase, tulip vines, AR Valentien, #139A, 1893, rstr drill hole, 18x9".. 3,250.00
Vase, violets, AR Valentien, basketweave silver o/l, 1893, 11¾", NM....1,450.00
Vase, water lilies, AM Valentien, #5688, X (but mint), 1900, 9x5"...500.00

Tiger Eye

Ewer, cherry blossoms, A Valentien, #441, 1889, 12x5" 600.00
Jug, incised Rookwood symbol, dtd Dec 21 '86, sgn SLS, 8¾" 300.00
Vase, apple branches, AR Valentien, #589C, 12½x3¾" 1,500.00
Vase, dragons w/goldstone, K Shirayamadani, #644, R, 1893, 18½" ..9,000.00
Vase, McIntosh Arts & Crafts design, AR Valentien, #270, R, 1886, 11"...1,550.00

Vellum

Plaque, Along the River, L Asbury, 1917, 9x12½"+orig fr.........6,000.00
Plaque, autumnal landscape, unidentified artist, 1912, 8¼x10½" ...4,800.00
Plaque, Birches, E Hurley, 14x9"+fr 13,000.00
Plaque, birds on bough, S Sax, 1900, sight: 7¼x5½"+fr...........10,800.00
Plaque, CA coastline scene, L Epply, 1912, 7½x5½"+orig fr 4,200.00
Plaque, Close of Day - Venice, C Schmidt, 9¼x14½"+fr.........12,000.00
Plaque, El Nan Set Southern Arapaho, S Laurence, 1898, 17x13"+fr ..14,500.00
Plaque, lake/mtn/trees, ET Hurley, 1946, 10x12"+fr 19,500.00

Plaque, Morning in Lagoon - Venice, C Schmidt, flame mk, 12x9"+fr. 16,800.00
Plaque, Mt Ranier, S Sax, 1920, 9x11¼" fr 7,550.00
Plaque, mtn lake scene in pks, ET Hurley, 1946, 14½x12½"+fr 14,400.00
Plaque, pines & snow, ET Hurley, V, 1912, 10⅜x8¼" 5,000.00
Plaque, trees & water (EX art), E Diers, 1914, 11x8½"+ebonized fr 14,000.00
Plaque, Venetian Sunset, E Diers, 9½x7½" fr 16,800.00
Vase, autumnal scenic, E Diers, #1358D, 1925, 8¾x4¾" 3,600.00
Vase, birds in gnarled branches, K Curry, #2118, V, 1917, 7⅝" 3,750.00
Vase, butterflies border, S Sax, #703, V, 1917 5½" 5,250.00
Vase, cows at stream, E Diers, #581D, V, 1917, 12⅛" 37,500.00
Vase, crocuses, C Schmidt, #2745, V, 1924, 9⅝" 4,250.00
Vase, Deco floral band, L Asbury, #614C, V, 1926, 13⅛" 4,350.00
Vase, dogwood blossoms, K Shirayamadani, #S2136, 1944, 13¼" 4,750.00
Vase, dragonflies, C Schmidt, #915D, X (peppering), 1904, 7x5½" 9,000.00
Vase, evening scenic, ET Hurley, #614D, V, 1926, 10¾" 8,000.00
Vase, fish on turq-gr, ET Hurley, #952E, V, 1905, 7x3" 6,600.00
Vase, floral w/geometric border, L Asbury, #2368, P, 16¼" 10,800.00
Vase, irises, C Schmidt, #987C, V, 1913, area of slight discolor, 10" 6,000.00
Vase, jasmine blossoms, ET Hurley, #951D, 1917, 9½x3½" 660.00
Vase, lake & trees, C Schmidt, #1358B, V, 13⅞" 9,350.00
Vase, lake at sunrise, C Schmidt, #907C, XX, V, 14" 13,750.00
Vase, lakeshore landscape, ET Hurley, #940D, 1921, 10x5" 4,250.00
Vase, landscape w/yel sky, E Diers, #922B, V, 1914, 11x5½" 5,150.00
Vase, lily pads & flowers, K Shirayamadani, #950D, 1907, 11" 5,875.00
Vase, mushrooms, C Schmidt, ovoid, 1906, 7x5½" 10,250.00
Vase, nasturtiums, F Rothenbusch, #2726, 1928, 6¼x4½" 850.00
Vase, ocean waves, ET Hurley, #907B, 1909, 17¼" 7,250.00
Vase, Oriental floral, Kate Van Horne, #30E, 1915, 9x3¾" 3,000.00
Vase, pine & lake band on gr, S Sax, V, GV, 1911, 7¾" 7,250.00
Vase, pines & mtn, S Sax, #1654D, 1909, 9½x4½" 9,000.00

Vase, poppies, Ed Diers, #1369-D/V, 9", $7,200.00. (Photo courtesy David Rago Auctions)

Vase, poppies on red, S Sax, #932D, 1917, 9⅞" 7,250.00
Vase, river scenic, ET Hurley, 1948, S, 8½x4¼" 3,500.00
Vase, sailboats on lake (EX art), E Hurley, #922D, 1943, 7¾" 13,750.00
Vase, sailboats w/city beyond, C Schmidt, ovoid, 1916, 12¾x7½" 11,750.00
Vase, sheep & apple trees, ET Hurley, 1914, 9x12¼" 27,000.00
Vase, squirrels on branches, E Diers, 1901, 11½x4½" 10,800.00
Vase, sunflowers, H Wilcox, #2819, 1926, 17⅞" 9,850.00
Vase, swallows (9) & trees (EX art), K Shirayamadani, #952B, 1906, 12" 14,500.00
Vase, swallows border, E Hurley, #938C, 1907, 8¼" 3,000.00
Vase, swans, C Schmidt, cylindrical #907C, V, 1915, 14¾" 18,750.00
Vase, swans (stylized) on pond, E Diers, #1858, 1907, 8¾x4¾" 1,550.00
Vase, trees & hills, Arts & Crafts style, L Epply, #999C, 1911, 9⅜" 12,000.00
Vase, trees & hills, L Epply, #139B, V, 17¾x9" 12,000.00
Vase, trees in winter, S Sax, V, GV, 1912, 8⅛" 5,000.00
Vase, trees scenic, E Diers, bulbous, #295C, 1924, 11x5" 8,400.00
Vase, trees scenic, F Rothenbusch, #926B, 1924, 11" 6,600.00
Vase, trees scenic, F Rothenbusch, #944A, V, 1920, 17¾" 12,500.00
Vase, tropical landscape, ET Hurley, #2038C, 1913, 12½x5½" 4,200.00
Vase, Venetian harbor scene, C Schmidt, #2032D, V, 1920, 9⅞" 10,250.00
Vase, wisteria, E Diers, #900A, V, 1926, 13¼" 12,000.00

Wax Matt

Bowl, leafy wreath, S Coyne, #2632, 3-ftd, 1922, 5¼x11" 780.00
Vase, birds & sunflower, E Lincoln, #324, 1925, 17¼x8" 5,400.00
Vase, blossoms, J Pullman, #6193C, 1930, 8¼x6" 850.00
Vase, camelias, K Jones, #614E, 1924, 8¾x4¾" 1,675.00
Vase, fish & seaweed, W Hentschel, #2918E, 1931, 6½" 5,200.00

Vase, floral wreath at shoulder, Louise Abel, 1923, $1,500.00. (Photo courtesy David Rago Auctions)

Vase, flower clusters, L Abel, #1848, 1925, 5½x7" 900.00
Vase, grapes on vine, C Todd, #668, 1912, 6¼" 600.00
Vase, maple leaves, J Harris, #2969, 1929, peppering, 7½x6½" 660.00
Vase, peacock feathers, W Hentschel, #4948, 1912, 4½x7¾" 1,900.00
Vase, rabbits, W Rehm, #6197F, 1943, 4¾" 2,550.00
Vase, roses, J Jensen, #2932, 1929, 14x5½" 2,000.00
Vase, roses on bl, unidentified artist, #614C, 1925, 13x6¼" 3,900.00
Vase, tulips on gr, J Jensen, #951D, 1929, 9x3¾" 1,000.00
Vase, wild roses, unidentified artist, #614C, 1935, 13x6¼" 4,000.00
Vase, woman on horse in squeezebag, W Rehm, S, 1934, 5⅛" 3,350.00

Miscellaneous

Basket, #1641, 1918, bl matt, P, 4¾" 85.00
Bookend, #2446, 1927, girl on bench, lt bl, ea 55.00
Bookends, #2444D, 1921, elephant, gr matt, 4¾x6", pr 400.00
Bookends, #2502, 1921, boys (2) w/book, gr matt w/brn, 6½", pr 1,900.00
Bookends, #2659, 1927, penguins (2), wht matt, rstr beaks, pr 1,300.00
Bookends, #6384, 1933, hippopotamus, ivory matt, 4x6½", pr 3,500.00
Bookends, #6883, 1945, St Francis, brn, gray & fleshtone, pr 425.00
Bowl, #1745, 1921, bl matt, 2¾x5" 120.00
Bowl, #2152, 1921, floral emb on yel matt, 2x4½" 85.00
Bowl, #2161, 1920, pk, 1¾" H 36.00
Bowl, #2384, 1919, ducks emb on bl matt, 2x5" 132.50
Candleholder, #6059, 1929, elephant seated w/holder on head, 4", ea 180.00
Candleholders, #2932, 1946, water lily forms, 3", pr 80.00
Inkwell, #1677, 1920, gr matt w/brn highlights, 3-pc, 2½" 575.00
Inkwell, Z-Line, #407Z, 1903, swirling maiden on gr, A Valentien, 4x5" 4,000.00
Paperweight, #1233, 1906, frog, dk gr matt, 3¼x4½" 1,325.00
Paperweight, #1623, 1920, rook, bl matt, 3x4" 280.00
Paperweight, #1623, 1930, rook, gr & brn matt, 3x4" 500.00
Paperweight, #1855, 1912, geese (2), brn matt, 4" 515.00
Paperweight, #1855, 1933, geese (2), ivory matt, 4" 240.00
Paperweight, #2677, 1929, monkey on book, gray-gr matt, 3½" 335.00
Paperweight, #2747, 1924, foo dog, dk bl, 4" 660.00
Paperweight, #2747, 1924, foo dog, gr w/brn, 3¾" 480.00
Paperweight, #2756, 1929, frog, pk & gr mottle, 2x5" 465.00
Paperweight, #2777, 1927, dog, bl over brn matt, 5x3½" 375.00
Paperweight, #2797, 1928, elephant on base, wht matt, 3¼" 390.00
Paperweight, #2868, 1929, nude seated, ivory matt, 4" 360.00
Paperweight, #2921, 1927, rook, mottled brn matt, 4x5" 950.00
Paperweight, #6025, 1925, squirrel w/nut, chestnut brn matt, 4" 480.00

Paperweight, #6070, 1928, fish, Aventurine, 2½x5" 660.00
Paperweight, #6084, 1965, monkey, Mustard Seed, 3¾".............. 360.00
Paperweight, #6160, 1930, rabbit, wht matt, 3⅛" 360.00
Paperweight, #6182, 1946, cat, chartreuse, 6¾" 360.00
Paperweight, #6241, 1931, burro, caramel-gray matt, 5⅞x4¾" 360.00
Paperweight, #6277, 1931, woodpecker, med bl, 4½" 900.00
Paperweight, #6441, 1934, Easter lily, ivory matt 1,200.00
Paperweight, #6528, 1935, gazelle, Oxblood, 4¾" 360.00
Pitcher, #2974, 1926, gr glass, dragon-like hdl, 9" 480.00
Planter, #6269, 1931, pk gloss, 2⅞x6" 110.00

**Tile, advertising, original frame, 4½x9",
$26,400.00.** (Photo courtesy David Rago Auctions)

Tile, scrub oak tree medallion, 6"+dk wood fr............................ 1,800.00
Trivet, #2349, 1929, bird on branches, brn & ivory, 6" dia 215.00
Trivet, #3069, 1930, lady w/umbrella, mc pastels, 5½x5½" 275.00
Trivet, #3124, 1928, dove, mc, 5½x5½" 275.00
Vase, #356F, 1919, mottled indigo gloss w/raspberry int, 6¼" 275.00
Vase, #357F, 19??, Wine Madder (brn gloss), 6⅛" 65.00
Vase, #390Z, 1902, swirls on gr matt, 6¾" 360.00
Vase, #516, 1914, swirling floral on cobalt, nick, 11x12" 2,200.00
Vase, #720C, 1911, panels on maroon mottle w/gr, 3¾x6" 275.00
Vase, #915C, 1906, Am Indian design on gr matt, 7½" 360.00
Vase, #918E, 1913, panels on gr over pk, 6" 165.00
Vase, #1370, 1914, floral on dk red w/gr, 6⅞" 780.00
Vase, #1660E, 1912, organic band on gr matt, 7¼" 550.00
Vase, #1660F, 1912, linear decor on red-brn, 6" 300.00
Vase, #1712, 1919, jonquils & foliage on caramel, 8⅞" 475.00
Vase, #1808, 1923, floral on blk, bl int, 3½" 385.00
Vase, #1905, 1930, peacock feathers on pk, 7¾" 180.00
Vase, #2088, 1934, pk, 5" 135.00
Vase, #2097, 1921, swans on gr, 3⅜" 195.00
Vase, #2111, 1928, bellflowers on yel matt, 6" 155.00
Vase, #2135, 1926, Greek key design on gr matt, 6" 180.00
Vase, #2167, 1920, floral on pk & gr, XX, 8½" 235.00
Vase, #2179, 1921, vining flowers on pk w/gr highlights, 3¾" 110.00
Vase, #2204, 1915, birds on branches on gr to brn, 9⅜" 900.00
Vase, #2207, 1927, floral on rose matt, 5⅜" 180.00
Vase, #2210, 1930, fruit garlands on pk w/gr, 7" 240.00
Vase, #2218, 1927, Moresque design on bl crystalline, 5"............. 215.00
Vase, #2375, 1929, peacock feathers on lav, 9" 660.00
Vase, #2378, 1923, stylized flowers on brn crystalline, 6⅞" 480.00
Vase, #2379, 1919, calla lilies on dk bl, 10" 425.00
Vase, #2380, 1928, stylized daisies on dk bl, 6¼" 300.00
Vase, #2382, 1929, stylized flowers on pk matt, 6" 240.00
Vase, #2393, 1928, lav, 8⅞" 575.00
Vase, #2407, 1925, chocolate brn crystalline, 7"......................... 480.00
Vase, #2412, 1921, geometrics on yel matt, 7" 155.00
Vase, #2417, 1929, peacock feathers on pk w/gr, 9" 425.00

Vase, #2421, 1917, panels on purple matt, 9½"........................... 425.00
Vase, #2421, 1921, panels on streaky turq, 10" 385.00
Vase, #2424, 1929, tulips on pk matt, 8" 215.00
Vase, #2433, 1931, molded band on tan matt w/bl crystalline, 10" .. 270.00
Vase, #2543, 1921, dancers on cobalt, yel int, 13" 515.00
Vase, #2693, 1923, leaves on bl & tan, 4¼" 425.00
Vase, #2780, 1925, lappet flowers on pk w/gr, 6" 145.00
Vase, #2891, 1927, geometrics on stippled bl on gr, 9" 275.00
Vase, #2917E, 1926, bl crystalline, 6⅜" 480.00
Vase, #2972, 1928, bl matt, 5½" 150.00
Vase, #2988, 1928, pk, 7" 240.00
Vase, #2990, 1928, floral band on gr crystalline, 6⅜".................. 120.00
Vase, #6006, 1929, poppies on pk, 11⅜" 395.00
Vase, #6229, 1931, turq matt, 5" 125.00
Vase, #6444, 1941, seed pods on bl matt, 5" 200.00
Vase, #6462, 1935, Deco leaves on Coromandel brn, 5" 850.00
Vase, #6469, 1934, bl crystalline, 8½" 200.00

**Vase, #6476, 1935, four
panels with nature studies,
green crystalline, designed
by Shirayamadani, 8",
$635.00.** (Photo courtesy Cincinnati
Art Galleries)

Vase, #6561, 1936, gr cube, 5½x5½" 60.00
Vase, #6625, 1942, Aventurine, 5" 480.00
Vase, #6777, 1944, floral on tan gloss, 11⅝" 240.00
Vase, #7057, 1957, floral on ivory matt, 5¾"............................. 65.00
Vase, bud; #2308, 1922, purple gloss, 7".................................. 135.00
Vase, Z-line, #661, 1901, draped maiden at rim, flambé matt, 4¼". 3,000.00
Vase, Z-Line, reclining nude, ivory, AM Valentien, 2½x3¼" 1,700.00
Vase, Z-Line, 1901, reclining nude, red, AM Valentien, 3½", NM .. 2,400.00
Wall pocket, #1395, 1919, peacock feathers on pk, 11¼"............. 425.00

Rorstrand

The Rorstrand Pottery was established in Sweden in 1726 and is today Sweden's oldest existing pottery. The earliest ware, now mostly displayed in Swedish museums, was much like old Delft. Later types were hard-paste porcelains that were enameled and decorated in a peasant style. Contemporary pieces are often described as Swedish Modern. Rorstrand is also famous for their Christmas plates.

Bowl, dogwood at at incurvate rtcl rim, 2⅞x5" 850.00
Pedestal, Neo-Renaissance style, 3 joined majolica pcs w/gold, 46" .. 3,600.00
Vase, berries & branches, pate-sur-pate, red/gray/wht, NL, #23, 8" .. 950.00
Vase, Diatreta, rtcl twigs/leaves, 2 frogs climb sides, mc, 6¾" 1,100.00
Vase, fish cvd/HP w/tails covering hdls on wht, 10¾x5" 2,400.00
Vase, floral, lav/gr on wht, CM, 3⅜"....................................... 780.00
Vase, floral, WL, #6718, 20½x9", NM...................................... 900.00
Vase, Nouveau pansies w/raised petals, NL, #20613, 1910s, 10½" .. 2,150.00
Vase, roses w/raised petals, gr stems/leaves, KI, 10⅜"................ 1,450.00
Vase, snow scene at twilight, sgn L NL, shouldered, 18" 5,250.00
Vase, stamped sqs, bl-gray w/orange crystals, Nyland, 28x12" ... 3,900.00

Vase, storks in flight emb on lt bl at shoulder, ca 1900, 32¼"....9,000.00
Vase, tulips w/raised petals & swirling stems, #40443, 16½x8", NM..2,150.00
Vase, vining floral, mc on wht, shouldered, 8½" 850.00

Figurine, hippopotamus, brown and gunmetal, Nylunt, 7" long, $265.00. (Photo courtesy Cincinnati Art Galleries/LiveAuctioneers.com)

Rose Mandarin

Similar in design to Rose Medallion, this Chinese Export porcelain features the pattern of a robed mandarin, often separated by florals, ladies, genre scenes, or butterflies in polychrome enamels. It is sometimes trimmed in gold. Elaborate in decoration, this pattern was popular from the late 1700s until the early 1840s.

Bowl, cut corners, 19th C, 9¾" 950.00
Bowl, oval, lt wear, 11" 465.00
Chamber set, foo dogs/birds/flowers/geometrics, 8" pot+6x17" bowl... 460.00
Charger, central genre scene, gilt, 14"... 800.00
Dish, retcl borders, 19th C, 8x9½", NM 400.00
Garden seat, hexagonal, 4 scenes/pierced medallions, 19" H 700.00
Jug, milk; 19th C, 5" 185.00

Pitcher, 7½", $780.00. (Photo courtesy Skinner Inc. Auctioneers & Appraisers of Antiques & Fine Art/ LiveAuctioneers.com)

Plate, genre scene in center, ca 1830, 6", 4 for.............................. 300.00
Punch bowl, continuous genre scene, gilt/red rim int, 5x12" 2,150.00
Punch bowl, 19th C, 16", cvd hardwood stand..........................2,700.00
Sauceboat, intertwined hdl, 19th C, 8¼" 325.00
Shrimp dish, 19th C, 10½" 415.00
Tray, mtd on bronze doré stand, 6¾x12" 1,600.00
Tray, serving; w/pierced liner, 19th C, 16" 950.00
Tureen, continuous genre, gilt, w/lid, 15" L, +undertray 650.00
Vase, bottle form, 19th C, 15" 785.00
Vase, foliate mouth, pear shape, appl gold dragons, 19th C, 9½" . 355.00
Vase, paneled genre scenes, shaped reserves, gilt, w/lid, 10", pr... 1,175.00

Rose Medallion

Rose Medallion is one of the patterns of Chinese export porcelain

produced from before 1850 until the second decade of the twentieth century. It is decorated in rose colors with panels of florals, birds, and butterflies that form reserves containing Chinese figures. Pre-1850 ware is unmarked and is characterized by quality workmanship and gold trim. From about 1850 until circa 1860, the kilns in Canton did not operate, and no Rose Medallion was made. Post-1860 examples (still unmarked) can often be recognized by the poor quality of the gold trim or its absence. In the 1890s the ware was often marked 'China'; 'Made in China' was used from 1910 through the 1930s.

Basin, butterflies/birds/flowers/bats, ca 1860, 4¾x16⅛" 1,100.00
Basin, everted rim w/butterflies/birds/flowers/bats, 1860s, 5x16" ...1,000.00
Bottle, water; stick neck, 19th C, lt wear, 13"............................... 480.00

Bowl, domestic scenes, 16" diameter, on 6½" stand, from $2,500.00 to $3,000.00. (Photo courtesy Jackson's International Auctioneers & Appraisers of Fine Art & Antiques)

Bowl, exotic bird in center, scalloped rim, early 20th C, 13¼"..... 180.00
Bowl, punch; floral band, modern, 6¾x14" 150.00
Bowl, scalloped rim, 19th C, 1½x8⅛" 275.00
Chamber pot, domestic scenes/flowers, w/lid, rpr, 6¼x11½"......... 700.00
Charger, ladies in reserves/flowers, gold trim, 19th C, 13½"......... 600.00
Lamp, scenic reserves, lion-head ring hdls, 1850s, mtd as lamp, 17" ..850.00
Plate, orange & blk koi in center, rtcl rim, 19th C, 8½", pr 240.00
Platter, well & tree; late 19th C, rprs, 19¼x15¼" 180.00
Shrimp dish, rstr hdl, 10"... 120.00
Teapot, figures/birds/flowers, domed lid, 1850s, 8¾" 465.00
Vase, gilt lion-head ring hdls, bronze base, 1850s, mtd as lamp, 17"...825.00
Vase, scenic reserves, foo dog hdls, 19th C, mtd as lamp, 14", pr...1,200.00
Vase, scenic reserves, Ku form, late 19th C, 13¼" 575.00
Vase, temple; scenic reserves, 19th C, rpr, 25¼" 1,325.00
Vases, garniture; garden scenes, sq, 19th C, 16½", pr..................2,875.00
Water bottle & basin, kilt ball knop, 16½", 5¾x18½" 1,500.00

Rosemeade

Rosemeade was the name chosen by the Wahpeton Pottery Company of Wahpeton, North Dakota, to represent their product. The founders of the company were Laura A. Taylor and R.J. Hughes, who organized the firm in 1940. It is most noted for small bird and animal figurals, either in high gloss or a Van Briggle-like matt glaze. The ware was marked 'Rosemeade' with an ink stamp or carried a 'Prairie Rose' sticker. The pottery closed in 1961. Our advisor for this category is Bryce L. Farnsworth; he is listed in the Directory under North Dakota.

Ashtray, Fin and Feather, ca. 1940s, 7" long, $1,700.00 at auction. (Photo courtesy Jackson's International Auctioneers & Appraisers of Fine Art & Antiques)

Ashtray, mallard hen, 3½x6½", from $325 to.................................. 350.00
Bank, panda bear, rare, 3½x5", minimum value........................1,000.00
Bowl, swirl cloverleaf, 1½x3½", minimum value 200.00
Candleholder, bird w/flower base, 3¼x3¼", ea from $25 to 35.00
Cotton dispenser, rabbit, 4¾x2½", from $150 to.......................... 200.00
Creamer & sugar bowl, Prairie Rose, from $75 to......................... 100.00
Figurine, alligator, rare, 7¾" L, minimum value........................1,000.00
Figurine, cock pheasant, 9¼x14", from $250 to 300.00
Figurine, deer standing in grass, 7¾x7¾", from $100 to.............. 125.00
Figurine, hen pheasant, 4x11½", from $350 to 400.00
Figurine, mallard drake, 6¼x6", from $250 to.............................. 300.00
Figurine, parakeet on tall base, 7x2¾", from $150 to.................... 200.00
Figurine, puppy begging, bl, solid, 3x3", from $75 to...................... 85.00
Hen on basket, 5½x5½", from $350 to... 400.00
Mug, pheasant decal, Hausauer Beverages mk, 4¼", from $150 to ..175.00
Paperweight, teddy bear, Teddy Roosevelt Memorial Park, 3½" ...325.00
Pin, fish, bl, 2½", minimum value...1,000.00
Pin, mallard drake, 4", minimum value.......................................1,000.00
Pin, Prairie Rose, 2½", minimum value.......................................1,000.00
Pin holder, cock strutting, 3¾x2¾", from $100 to 125.00
Planter, cock pheasant, 3¾x9¼", minimum value 500.00
Planter, swan, 4¾x5", from $35 to... 65.00
Planter, wooden shoes, 2¾x¾", from $45 to.................................. 65.00
Plaque, Dakota Centennial decal, 6", from $75 to......................... 100.00
Plate, National Memorial Park, gr, 8½", from $350 to.................. 375.00
Shakers, blk ducklings, 2½", 2¼", pr from $75 to.......................... 100.00
Shakers, bobwhite quail, 2¼", 1½", pr from $50 to........................ 75.00
Shakers, Chief Sitting Bull heads, 2⅝", pr from $250 to 300.00
Shakers, crappie, 2¼x4", pr, minimum value 500.00
Shakers, pelicans, pk, 3¼", pr from $85 to.................................... 100.00

Shakers, pig, 3¾", from $125.00 to $150.00 for the pair. (Photo courtesy Darlene Hurst Dommel)

Shakers, red fox, pr, from $350 to.. 400.00
Shakers, swans, 2", pr from $75 to... 100.00
Shakers, wheat shock, brn, 3¾", pr from $125 to 150.00
Tea bell, peacock, 5½", from $250 to 300.00
Toothpick holder, bear standing by tree stump, 2¼", minimum value.. 2,000.00
Vase, bl/tan, glossy, 4¾", minimum value..................................... 250.00
Vase, peacock figural, 7¾", from $250 to..................................... 300.00
Vase, swirl, crumpled rim, Badlands mk, 2½x2¾", minimum value....500.00
Wall pocket, lovebirds in crescent moon, 6¼x6¼", minimum value..500.00
Wall pocket, wht kitten in bl stocking, rare, 6½", minimum value 850.00

Rosenthal

In 1879 Phillip Rosenthal established the Rosenthal Porcelain Factory in Selb, Bavaria. Its earliest products were figurines and fine tablewares. The company has continued to operate to the present decade, manufacturing limited edition plates.

Bust, youth in Renaissance costume, wht porc, 15½x9½" 475.00

Figurine, Asian lady w/lantern, 1930s, 13½" 1,450.00
Figurine, carousel horse, HP details, ca 1940, 8¼x10x3½" 480.00
Figurine, falconer, bronze & cold pnt, G Jaeger, 9½" 2,150.00
Figurine, female nude kneeling, Klimsch, mid-20th C, 16x8¼" ... 480.00
Figurine, foal reclining, AH Hussman, 1941, 6¼x12½x4½" 1,200.00
Figurine, goldfish (2) among sea grasses, wht, Heidenreich, 16x9"... 480.00
Figurine, goldfish among sea grasses, blk & wht w/gold, 10x8"..... 425.00
Figurine, Harlequin seated w/guitar, D Charol, 1920s, 6" 925.00
Figurine, heron, mc w/silver, HM Fritz, #5282, 20th C, 13" 600.00
Figurine, lady holding staff w/putto finial, 14½" 850.00
Figurine, lady running w/leaping dog at side, Deco style, 12x13" .. 660.00
Figurine, moose on rocky base, F Heidenreich, 18x18½" 515.00
Figurine, Olympic shot-put thrower, wht porc, rpr, 11x6" 395.00

Figurine, panther with ball, Schliepstein, ca. 1933, 9" long, $210.00. (Photo courtesy Du Mouchelles)

Figurine, Pierrot reclining w/legs crossed, sgn May, 13" 725.00
Figurine, Victorian lady w/arms extended for dive, att, 15", NM .. 175.00
Figurine, Young Love, 2 kissing nude children, Lunburg, 1923, 5x10".. 515.00
Figurines, Musicians, Blackamoors, H Meisel, #1056/#1057, 8½", pr ... 425.00
Plaque, girl reading letter, red gown, 12x9¾"+fr 480.00
Plate, draped nude seated on rock, floral rim w/gold, 19th C, 10" ...850.00

Roseville

The Roseville Pottery Company was established in 1892 by George F. Young in Roseville, Ohio. Finding their facilities inadequate, the company moved to Zanesville in 1898, erected a new building, and installed the most modern equipment available. By 1900 Young felt ready to enter into the stiffly competitive art pottery market. Roseville's first art line was called Rozane. Similar to Rookwood's Standard, Rozane featured dark blended backgrounds with slip-painted underglaze artwork of nature studies, portraits, birds, and animals. Azurean, developed in 1902, was a blue and white underglaze art line on a blue blended background. Egypto (1904) featured a matt glaze in a soft shade of old green and was modeled in low relief after examples of ancient Egyptian pottery. Mongol (1904) was a high-gloss oxblood red line after the fashion of the Chinese Sang de Boeuf. Mara (1904), an iridescent lustre line of magenta and rose with intricate patterns developed on the surface or in low relief, successfully duplicated Sicardo's work. These early lines were followed by many others of highest quality: Fudjiyama and Woodland (1905 – 1906) reflected an Oriental theme; Crystalis (1906) was covered with beautiful frost-like crystals. Della Robbia, their most famous line (introduced in 1905), was decorated with carved designs ranging from florals, animals, and birds to scenes of Viking warriors and Roman gladiators. These designs were worked in sgraffito with slip-painted details. Very limited but of great importance to collectors today, Rozane Olympic (1905) was decorated with scenes of Greek mythology on a red ground. Pauleo (1914) was the last of the artware lines. It was varied — over 200 glazes were recorded — and some pieces were decorated by hand, usually with florals.

During the second decade of the century until the plant closed 40 years later, new lines were continually added. Some of the more popular of the middle-period lines were Donatello, 1918; Futura, 1928; Pine Cone, 1936; and Blackberry, 1933. The floral lines of the later years have become highly collectible. Pottery from every era of Roseville production — even its utility ware — attest to an unwavering dedication to quality and artistic merit.

Examples of the fine art pottery lines present the greatest challenge to evaluate. Scarcity is a prime consideration. The quality of artwork varied from one artist to another. Some pieces show fine detail and good color, and naturally this influences their values. Studies of animals and portraits bring higher prices than the floral designs. An artist's signature often increases the value of any item, especially if the artist is one who is well recognized.

The market is literally flooded with imposter Roseville that is coming into the country from China. An experienced eye can easily detect these fakes, but to a novice collector, they may pass for old Roseville. Study the marks. If the 'USA' is missing or appears only faintly, the piece is most definitely a reproduction. Also watch for lines with a mark that is not correct for its time frame; for example, Luffa with the script mark, and Woodland with the round Rozane stamp from the 1917 line.

For further information consult *Collector's Encyclopedia of Roseville Pottery, First* and *Second Series*, by Sharon and Bob Huxford and Mike Nickel (Collector Books). Other books on the subject include *Collector's Compendium of Roseville Pottery, Volumes I, II*, and *III*, by R.B. Monsen (see Directory, Virginia); and *Roseville in All Its Splendor With Price Guide* by Jack and Nancy Bomm (self-published). Our advisor for this category is Mike Nickel; he is listed in the Directory under Michigan.

Apple Blossom, basket, #309, gr or pk, 8", from $275 to 325.00
Apple Blossom, bowl, #326-6, gr or pk, 2½x6½", from $100 to.... 125.00
Apple Blossom, ewer, #318, gr or pk, 15", from $600 to 700.00

Apple Blossom, jardiniere (#303-10) and pedestal (#306-10), blue, from $1,500.00 to $1,750.00.

(Photo courtesy David Rago Auctions)

Apple Blossom, vase, #388, bl, gr or pk, 10", from $250 to 300.00
Apple Blossom, vase, #392-15, bl, hdls, 15½", from $800 to 900.00
Apple Blossom, window box, #368-8, gr or pk, from $150 to 175.00
Artcraft, jardiniere, tan, 4", from $150 to 200.00
Artwood, planter, #1054, 6½x8½", from $85 to 95.00
Artwood, planter, #1055-9, 7x9½", from $85 to 95.00
Artwood, 3-pc planter set, 2 #1050/1 #1051, 4" & 6", from $90 to....110.00
Aztec, vase, waisted, floral, 9", from $350 to 400.00
Azurean, mug, #4, floral, from $350 to 400.00
Baneda, candleholders, #1088, gr, 4½", pr from $600 to............... 650.00
Baneda, center bowl, #233, gr, hdls, 3½x10", from $400 to 500.00
Baneda, center bowl, #237, pk, 13" W, from $650 to................... 750.00

Baneda, vase, #597-10, green, 10", from $1,700.00 to $1,800.00.

(Photo courtesy David Rago Auctions)

Baneda, vase, #603, pk, 4½", from $350 to 400.00
Bittersweet, basket, #809-8, 8½", from $150 to 200.00
Bittersweet, candlesticks, #851-3, 3", pr from $80 to.................... 100.00
Bittersweet, cornucopia, #857-4, 4½", from $75 to 85.00
Bittersweet, ewer, #816, 8", from $85 to....................................... 95.00
Bittersweet, planter, #827-8, 11½", from $90 to 110.00
Blackberry, basket, from $900 to 1,000.00
Blackberry, jardiniere & ped, 9¼x12" & 19½x12", from $2,500 to ..3,000.00
Blackberry, wall pocket, #1267, from $1,250 to 1,500.00
Bleeding Heart, candlesticks, #1139-4 ½, bl, 5", pr from $150 to....200.00
Bleeding Heart, ewer, #927, gr or pk, 10", from $350 to 400.00
Bleeding Heart, plate, #381-10, bl, 10½", from $150 to 200.00
Bushberry, dbl bud vase, #158-4½, orange, 4½", from $100 to 125.00
Bushberry, hanging basket, gr, 7", from $250 to 300.00
Bushberry, hanging basket, orange, 7", from $200 to 250.00
Bushberry, jardiniere, #657, orange, 3", from $80 to 90.00
Cameo II, flowerpot, 5½", from $250 to....................................... 350.00
Cameo II, jardiniere, 8", from $300 to 350.00
Cameo II, jardiniere, 9", from $350 to 400.00
Capri, ashtray, #598-9, 9", from $40 to 50.00
Capri, leaf dish, #532-16, 16", from $35 to 45.00
Capri, planter, #558, 7", from $60 to 70.00
Capri, shell dish, from $40 to 50.00
Carnelian I, center bowl, 5x12½", from $100 to........................... 125.00
Carnelian I, ewer, 15", from $300 to 350.00
Carnelian I, loving cup, 5", from $90 to...................................... 100.00
Carnelian I, pillow vase, 5", from $80 to 90.00
Carnelian I, wall pocket, 8", from $150 to 200.00
Carnelian II, basket, 4x10", from $225 to 275.00
Carnelian II, planter, hdls, 3x8", from $125 to 150.00
Carnelian II, vase, squatty/trumpet neck, hdls, 10", from $225 to...275.00

Carnelian II, vase, 6" high, from $450.00 to $500.00. (Photo courtesy Treadway Gallery Inc.)

Cherry Blossom, hanging basket, #350, pk/bl, 8", from $1,250 to .. 1,500.00
Cherry Blossom, vase, #621, brn, from $300 to............................ 350.00
Clemana, bowl, #281, bl, 4½x6½", from $250 to 275.00
Clemana, bowl, #281, gr, 4½x6½", from $225 to 250.00
Clemana, vase, #123, bl, 7", from $350 to.................................... 400.00
Clemana, vase, #758, tan, hdls, 8½", from $450 to....................... 500.00
Clematis, candleholders, #1159, bl, 4½", pr from $100 to............. 125.00
Clematis, cookie jar, #3, brn or gr, 10", from $300 to 350.00

Clematis, flowerpot/saucer, #668-5, brn or gr, 5½", from $125 to . 150.00
Columbine, bookend planters, #8, bl or tan, 5", pr from $300 to . 350.00
Columbine, cornucopia, #149-6, bl or tan, 5½", from $100 to 125.00
Columbine, cornucopia, #149-6, pk, 5½", from $150 to 175.00
Columbine, hanging basket, pk, 8½", from $300 to 350.00
Corinthian, ashtray, 2", from $100 to.................................... 125.00
Corinthian, candleholders, 8", pr from $100 to 125.00
Corinthian, compote, 5x10" dia, from $125 to 150.00
Corinthian, wall pocket, 8", from $200 to 225.00
Cosmos, basket, #358, gr, 12", from $375 to 425.00
Cosmos, flower frog #39, bl, 3½", from $125 to 150.00
Cosmos, flower frog, #39, tan, 3½", from $100 to 125.00
Cosmos, hanging basket, #361, bl, 7", from $300 to 350.00
Cosmos, hanging basket, #361, tan, 7", from $225 to 250.00
Cosmos, vase, #956-12, tan, hdls, 12½", from $375 to 425.00
Cremona, bowl, sq, 9" W, from $100 to 125.00
Cremona, fan vase, 5", from $100 to 125.00
Cremona, urn, 4", from $100 to.. 125.00
Dahlrose, center bowl, oval, 10", from $125 to 150.00
Dahlrose, pillow vase, #419, 5x7", from $175 to..................... 225.00
Dahlrose, vase, #364, 6", from $150 to 200.00
Dahlrose, window box, #377, 6x12½", from $350 to 400.00
Dawn, ewer, #834-16, gr, 16", from $400 to 450.00
Dawn, ewer, #834-16, pk or yel, 16", from $500 to 550.00
Dawn, vase, #826, gr or pk, 6", from $150 to 175.00

Della Robbia, vase, Arts and Crafts design, 11", $8,000.00 – 9,000.00.
(Photo courtesy Treadway Gallery Inc.)

Della Robbia, vase, floral, 5-color, bottle form, Rozane seal, 12" ..4,500.00
Della Robbia, vase, penguins & trees, 2-color, Rozane seal, 8½" ...3,750.00
Della Robbia, vase, stylized floral on celadon, trumpet neck, 14" ..5,500.00
Dogwood I, bowl, 2", from $75 to...................................... 100.00
Dogwood I, tub, hdls, 4x7", from $150 to 175.00
Dogwood II, bowl, 2½" H, from $125 to 150.00

Dogwood II, vase, 9½", $350.00. (Photo courtesy Treadway Gallery Inc.)

Dogwood II, wall pocket, from $300 to 350.00

Donatello, bowl, 3", from $75 to 95.00
Donatello, dbl bud vase, gate type, 5", from $100 to 125.00
Donatello, pitcher, 6½", from $275 to.................................. 325.00
Donatello, plate, 8", from $300 to...................................... 350.00
Donatello, powder jar, 2x5", from $400 to 450.00
Dutch, pin tray, 4", from $65 to 75.00
Dutch, pitcher, 7½", from $150 to 200.00
Dutch, plate, incurvate rim, 11", from $100 to 125.00
Dutch, toothbrush holder, 4", from $100 to 125.00
Earlam, bowl, #218, hdls, 3x11½", from $350 to..................... 400.00
Earlam, planter, #89, 5½x10½", from $350 to 400.00
Earlam, vase, #522, 9", from $650 to 750.00
Egypto, pitcher vase, 11", from $1,750 to..........................2,000.00
Falline, candlesticks, #1092, bl, 4", pr from $800 to................. 900.00
Falline, center bowl, #244, bl, hdls, 11", from $400 to 500.00

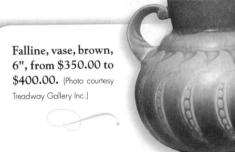

Falline, vase, brown, 6", from $350.00 to $400.00. (Photo courtesy Treadway Gallery Inc.)

Falline, vase, #647, bl, hdls, 7½", from $1,000 to.....................1,250.00
Falline, vase, #647, tan, 7½", from $600 to 700.00
Ferella, bowl/frog, #211, red, 5", from $800 to 900.00
Ferella, bowl/frog, #211, tan, 5", from $550 to 650.00
Ferella, candlesticks, #1078, red, pr from $800 to.................... 900.00
Ferella, candlesticks, #1078, tan, 4½", pr from $550 to 650.00
Florane, basket, 8½", from $200 to..................................... 250.00
Florane, bud vase, 7", from $30 to 35.00
Florane, planter, 10", from $45 to 50.00
Florentine, bowl, 9", from $75 to...................................... 100.00
Florentine, compote, 10" dia, from $125 to 150.00
Florentine, jardinere, 8" H, from $150 to 175.00
Foxglove, basket, #373, bl, 8", from $200 to 250.00
Foxglove, cornucopia, #166-6, gr/pk, 6", from $150 to............. 175.00
Foxglove, hanging basket, #466, pk, 6½", from $225 to 400.00
Foxglove, vase, #53-14, bl, 14", from $350 to 400.00
Freesia, center bowl, #464-6, bl, 8½", from $75 to................... 100.00
Freesia, window box, #1392-8, gr, 10½", from $150 to 175.00
Fuchsia, candlesticks, #1132, brn/tan, 2", pr from $100 to 125.00
Fuchsia, frog, #37, gr, from $175 to 200.00
Fuchsia, vase, #897-8, brn/tan, 8", from $175 to...................... 225.00

Fuchsia, vase, #903-12, brown, 12¼", $450.00 – 500.00.

Futura, fan vase, #82, 6", from $550 to..650.00
Futura, frog, #187, from $100 to...125.00
Futura, pillow vase, #81, 5x6", from $350 to......................450.00
Futura, planter, #191, 7", from $600 to..............................650.00
Gardenia, basket, #610-12, 12", from $300 to...................350.00
Gardenia, bowl, #641-5, 5", from $100 to..........................125.00
Gardenia, hanging basket, #661, 6", from $225 to.............250.00
Gardenia, vase, #689-14, hdls, 14", from $275 to..............325.00
Gardenia, window box, #658-8, 3x8½", from $100 to..........125.00
Holland, powder jar, w/lid, 3", from $150 to......................175.00
Holland, tankard, #2, 9½", from $200 to............................250.00
Imperial I, basket, #7, 9", from $175 to.............................225.00
Imperial I, basket, 13", from $250 to.................................300.00
Imperial I, compote, 6½", from $150 to..............................175.00
Imperial II, bowl, 4½", from $250 to.................................300.00
Iris, basket, #335-10, bl, 9½", from $350 to.......................400.00
Iris, basket, #335-10, pk or tan, 9½", from $300 to............350.00
Iris, pillow vase, #922-8, bl, 8½", from $250 to.................275.00
Ivory II, bowl vase, #259, Russco shape, 6", from $75 to........95.00
Ivory II, ewer, #941-10, 10½", from $75 to..........................95.00
Ixia, basket, #346, 10", from $250 to.................................300.00
Ixia, center bowl, #330-7, 3½x10½", from $125 to..............150.00
Ixia, hanging basket, 7", from $225 to...............................250.00
Ixia, vase, #853, 6", from $125 to.....................................150.00
Jonquil, bowl, #523, 3", from $125 to................................150.00
Jonquil, jardiniere, #621, 4" H, from $125 to.....................150.00
Jonquil, jardiniere, #621, 6" H, from $200 to.....................250.00
Jonquil, vase, #529, hdls, 8", from $350 to........................400.00
Juvenile, cake plate, chicks, 9½", from $500 to..................600.00
Juvenile, cup & saucer, rabbit, 2" & 5", from $175 to.........200.00
Juvenile, custard, goose, 2½", from $400 to.......................450.00
Juvenile, mug, bear, 3½", from $450 to..............................500.00
Juvenile, mug, fancy cat, 3", from $1,000 to...................1,250.00
Juvenile, mug, fat puppy, 3½", from $375 to.......................425.00
Juvenile, pudding dish, chicks, 3½", from $200 to..............225.00
Juvenile, teapot, goose, 4", from $1,000 to.....................1,250.00
La Rose, wall pocket, 9", from $225 to...............................250.00
Laurel, bowl, #251, russet, 7", from $225 to.......................250.00
Laurel, bowl, #252, gold, 3½", from $200 to.......................250.00
Laurel, bowl, #252, gr, 3½", from $300 to..........................325.00
Laurel, bowl, #252, russet, 3½", from $250 to....................275.00
Lotus, vase, #L3, 10", from $225 to...................................250.00
Luffa, lamp, bl/rose or bl/gr, 9½", from $750 to.................850.00
Luffa, vase, #683, hdls, 6", from $225 to...........................250.00
Luffa, vase, #685, 7", from $300 to...................................350.00
Lustre, basket, 10", from $150 to......................................200.00
Lustre, vase, 12", from $200 to...250.00
Magnolia, ashtray, #28, brn or gr, 7", from $100 to............125.00
Magnolia, basket, #385, bl, 10", from $250 to....................275.00
Magnolia, pitcher, #1327, 7", from $300 to.........................350.00
Magnolia, planter, #388-6, brn or gr, 8½", from $85 to..........95.00
Magnolia, vase, #91-8, brn or gr, hdls, 8", from $125 to......150.00
Mara, vase, #13, average glaze, 5½", from $2,500 to........3,000.00
Mayfair, bowl, #1119-9, 10", from $60 to.............................70.00
Mayfair, planter, #113-8, 3½x8½", from $70 to.....................85.00
Ming Tree, ashtray, #599, 6", from $75 to.............................85.00
Ming Tree, bookends, #559, 5½", pr from $200 to...............235.00
Ming Tree, bowl, #526-9, 4x11½", from $95 to....................110.00
Ming Tree, center bowl, #528, 10", from $125 to.................150.00
Mock Orange, basket, #909, 8", from $200 to......................225.00
Mock Orange, pillow vase, #930-8, 7", from $125 to............150.00
Mock Orange, planter, #931-8, 3½x9", from $100 to.............125.00
Mock Orange, planter, #981, 7", from $125 to.....................150.00
Mock Orange, vase, #973-8, hdls, 8½", from $125 to............150.00

Moderne, compote, #295, 5", from $200 to..........................225.00
Moderne, triple candlestick, #1112, 6", ea from $225 to......250.00
Moderne, vase, #796-8, 8½", from $200 to...........................225.00
Mongol, bowl vase, flared rim, 2½" H, from $300 to............400.00
Mongol, vase, bowl shaped w/flared rim, 2½", from $300 to........400.00

Mongol, vase, 14", from $1,500.00 to $2,000.00.
(Photo courtesy Treadway Gallery Inc.)

Montacello, basket, #333, bl or tan, 6½", from $650 to...............750.00
Morning Glory, basket, #340, gr, 10½", from $800 to.................900.00
Morning Glory, basket, #340, ivory, 10½", from $600 to.............750.00
Morning Glory, candlesticks, #1102, ivory, 5", pr from $300 to...400.00
Morning Glory, center bowl, #270, gr, 4½x11½", from $475 to...500.00
Morning Glory, vase, #730, ivory, 10", from $450 to.................500.00
Moss, bowl vase, #290, bl, from $300 to..............................350.00
Moss, bowl vase, #290, pk/gr or orange/gr, 6", from $350 to....400.00
Moss, pillow vase, #781, bl, 8", from $300 to........................350.00
Moss, pillow vase, #781, orange/gr or pk/gr, 8", from $350 to.......400.00
Mostique, compote, 7", from $250 to..................................275.00
Mostique, hanging basket, 7", from $275 to.........................350.00
Orian, bowl vase, #274, tan, 6", from $300 to......................350.00
Orian, candleholders, #1108, tan, 4½", pr from $200 to.........250.00
Orian, candleholders, #1108, yel, 4½", pr from $250 to..........300.00
Orian, compote, #272, red, 4½x10½", from $250 to..............300.00
Orian, vase, #733, turq, hdls, from $150 to.........................175.00
Orian, vase, #742, yel, 12", from $450 to...........................500.00
Pauleo, vase, #340, 19", from $1,000 to...........................1,200.00
Pauleo, vase, broken glaze, #340, 19", from $1,250 to.........1,500.00
Pauleo, vase, long trumpet neck w/squatty base, 19", from $1,500 to..2,000.00
Peony, basket, #379-12, 11", from $250 to..........................275.00
Peony, conch shell, #436, 9½", from $110 to........................135.00
Peony, mug, #2-3½, 3½", from $100 to...............................125.00
Peony, wall pocket, #1293, 8", from $200 to........................225.00
Persian, hanging basket, geometric floral/leaves, 9", from $350 to ..400.00
Pine Cone, basket, #353-11, brn, from $400 to.....................450.00
Pine Cone, dbl tray, #462, bl, 13", from $550 to..................600.00
Pine Cone, fan vase, #472, gr, 6", from $175 to...................225.00
Pine Cone, pitcher, #485-10, bl, 10½", from $750 to.............850.00
Pine Cone, planter, #124, bl, 5", from $175 to....................225.00
Pine Cone, planter, #124, gr, 5", from $125 to....................150.00

Pine Cone, vase, #912-15, blue, from $1,800.00 to $2,000.00.
(Photo courtesy David Rago Auctions)

Poppy, bowl, #336-10, gray/gr, 12", from $150 to........................175.00
Poppy, ewer, #876, gray/gr, 10", from $250 to 275.00
Poppy, ewer, #880-18, gray/gr, 18½", from $600 to 650.00
Poppy, ewer, #880-18, pk, 18½", from $700 to 750.00
Poppy, vase, #872-9, pk, hdls, 9", from $300 to..........................350.00
Primrose, vase, #760-6, bl or pk, hdls, 7", from $150 to.................175.00
Primrose, vase, #767, bl or pk, 8", from $250 to.........................300.00
Raymor, casserole, #183, med, 11", from $75 to............................85.00
Raymor, divided vegetable bowl, #164, 13", from $55 to...................65.00
Raymor, gravy boat, #190, 9½", from $30 to................................35.00
Raymor, water pitcher, #180, 10", from $100 to...........................150.00
Rosecraft Blended, vase, #35, 10", from $90 to...........................100.00
Rosecraft Blended, vase, 12½", from $100 to..............................125.00
Rosecraft Hexagon, bowl, brn, hdls, 7½", from $150 to...............175.00
Rosecraft Hexagon, bowl vase, gr, 4", from $300 to.....................350.00
Rosecraft Hexagon, vase, glossy bl, rare, 5", from $350 to...........400.00
Rosecraft Panel, candlestick, gr, 8", ea from $250 to 300.00
Rosecraft Panel, covered jar, brn, 10", from $450 to......................500.00
Rosecraft Panel, covered jar, gr, 10", from $550.........................650.00
Rosecraft Panel, pillow vase, brn, 8", from $200 to......................225.00

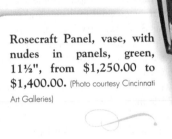

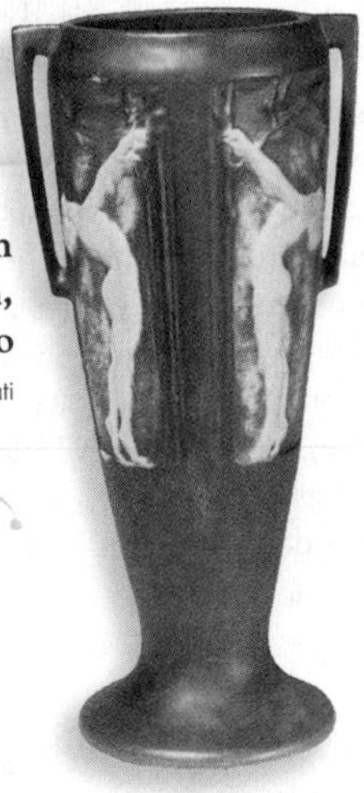

Rosecraft Panel, vase, with nudes in panels, green, 11½", from $1,250.00 to $1,400.00. (Photo courtesy Cincinnati Art Galleries)

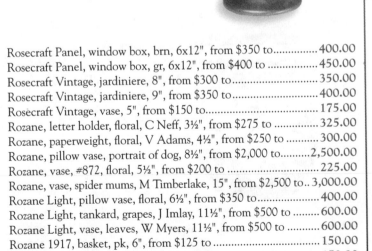

Rosecraft Panel, window box, brn, 6x12", from $350 to...............400.00
Rosecraft Panel, window box, gr, 6x12", from $400 to 450.00
Rosecraft Vintage, jardiniere, 8", from $300 to...........................350.00
Rosecraft Vintage, jardiniere, 9", from $350 to...........................400.00
Rosecraft Vintage, vase, 5", from $150 to.................................175.00
Rozane, letter holder, floral, C Neff, 3½", from $275 to 325.00
Rozane, paperweight, floral, V Adams, 4½", from $250 to...............300.00
Rozane, pillow vase, portrait of dog, 8½", from $2,000 to............2,500.00
Rozane, vase, #872, floral, 5½", from $200 to 225.00
Rozane, vase, spider mums, M Timberlake, 15", from $2,500 to.. 3,000.00
Rozane Light, pillow vase, floral, 6½", from $350 to....................400.00
Rozane Light, tankard, grapes, J Imlay, 11½", from $500 to 600.00
Rozane Light, vase, leaves, W Myers, 11½", from $500 to.............600.00
Rozane 1917, basket, pk, 6", from $125 to 150.00
Rozane 1917, bowl, ftd, hdls, 5", from $125 to............................150.00
Rozane 1917, compote, 8", from $100 to 125.00
Russco, triple cornucopia, 8x12½", from $200 to........................250.00
Silhouette, ewer, #717, 10", from $125 to..................................150.00
Silhouette, vase, #780-6, 6", from $75 to...................................85.00
Silhouette, vase, #789-14, 14", from $250 to..............................275.00
Snowberry, ashtray, #1AT, bl or pk, from $100 to........................125.00
Snowberry, basket, #1BK-12, gr, 12½", from $275 to....................325.00
Snowberry, pillow vase, #1FH-6, bl or pk, 6½", from $150 to.......175.00
Sunflower, candlesticks, 4", pr from $800 to 900.00
Sunflower, center bowl, hdls, 3x12½", from $800 to....................900.00

Sunflower, vase, 10", from $1,500.00 to $1,600.00. (Photo courtesy Smith & Jones Inc.)

Sunflower, vase, #619, 6", from $1,250 to 1,500.00
Sunflower, window box, 3½x11", from $1,250 to..........................1,500.00
Teasel, vase, #644, dk bl or rust, 5", from $125 to 150.00
Teasel, vase, #887-10, dk bl or rust, 10", from $250 to..................275.00
Thorn Apple, bowl vase, #305-6, 6½", from $150 to...................175.00
Thorn Apple, dbl bud vase, #119, 5½", from $125 to.....................150.00
Thorn Apple, vase, #808, 4", from $100 to.................................125.00
Thorn Apple, vase, #816-8, hdls, 8½", from $225 to....................250.00
Thorn Apple, vase, #820-9, hdls, 9½", from $275 to....................325.00
Topeo, dbl candlesticks, bl, 5", pr from $375 to.........................425.00
Topeo, dbl candlesticks, red, 5", pr from $250 to.......................275.00
Topeo, vase, red, 9", from $275 to...325.00
Tourmaline, bowl, shallow, 8", from $75 to..................................90.00
Tourmaline, cornucopia, 7", from $75 to......................................90.00
Tourmaline, pillow vase, 6", from $90 to....................................100.00
Tuscany, console bowl, gray/lt bl, 11", from $125 to....................150.00
Tuscany, console bowl, pk, 11", from $150 to 175.00
Tuscany, vase, gray/lt bl, 4", from $75 to...................................100.00
Tuscany, vase, pk, 12", from $250 to...275.00
Velmoss, bowl, #266, gr, 3x11", from $150 to.............................175.00
Velmoss, dbl bud vase, #116, bl, from $250 to 300.00
Velmoss, vase, #721, bl, hdls, 12½", from $400 to 450.00
Velmoss Scroll, compote, 9x4" dia, from $150 to 175.00
Velmoss Scroll, vase, 5", from $100 to 125.00
Vista, basket, 9½", from $700 to...800.00
Vista, vase, #121-15, 15", from $1,000 to....................................1,200.00
Vista, vase, #134-18, 18", from $1,500 to....................................1,750.00
Water Lily, candlesticks, #1155-4½", bl, 5", pr from $150 to........200.00
Water Lily, frog, #48, brn w/gr, 4½", from $100 to 125.00
Water Lily, hanging basket, #468, bl, 9", from $250 to.................275.00
Water Lily, hanging basket, #468, rose w/gr, 9", from $275 to......300.00
Water Lily, jardiniere, #663, rose w/gr, 3", from $80 to..................90.00
White Rose, console bowl/frog, #393-12/#41, hdls, from $125 to ...150.00
White Rose, dbl bud vase, #148, 4½", from $85 to 95.00
White Rose, pitcher, #1324, from $200 to 225.00
White Rose, vase, #991-12, hdls, 12½", from $250 to....................275.00
Wincraft, cornucopia, #221-8, 9x5", from $100 to.......................125.00
Wincraft, ewer, #218-18, 19", from $400 to................................450.00
Windsor, center bowl, rust, 3½x10½", from $300 to....................325.00

Windsor, vase, geometrics on blue neck band, paper label, 6x6¾", $350.00 – 450.00.

(Photo courtesy David Rago Auctions)

Wisteria, hanging basket, #351, tan, 7½", from $500 to 550.00
Wisteria, vase, #682, bl, 10", from $1250 to............................ 1,500.00
Wisteria, vase, #682, tan, 10", from $650 to 700.00
Woodland, bud vase, floral, 4-sided, 7", from $700 to.................. 800.00
Zephyr Lily, ewer, #24, bl, 15", from $475 to 550.00
Zephyr Lily, hanging basket, bl, 7½", from $250 to..................... 300.00
Zephyr Lily, pillow vase, #206-7, bl, 7", from $175 to.................. 200.00
Zephyr Lily, tray, brn, 14½", from $200 to............................. 225.00

Rowland and Marsellus

Though the impressive back stamp seems to suggest otherwise, Rowland and Marsellus were not Staffordshire potters but American importers who commissioned various English companies to supply them with the transfer-printed crockery and historical ware that had been a popular import commodity since the early 1800s. Plates (both flat and with a rolled edge), cups and saucers, pitchers, and platters were sold as souvenirs from 1890 through the 1930s. Though other importers — Bawo & Dotter and A. C. Bosselman & Co., both of New York City — commissioned the manufacture of similar souvenir items, by far the largest volume carries the R. & M. mark, and Rowland and Marsellus has become a generic term that covers all twentieth-century souvenir china of this type. Their mark may be in full or 'R. & M.' in a diamond. We have suggested values for examples with transfers in blue, though other colors may occasionally be found as well. Our advisors for this category are Angi and David Ringering; they are listed in the Directory under Oregon.

Key:
r/e — rolled edge   v/o — view of
s/o — souvenir of

Creamer, Plymouth, mk as Burbank 45.00
Cup, Philadephia, s/o.. 65.00
Cup & saucer, farmer's.. 45.00
Pitcher, American Pilgrims, #527014, 6¼".................................... 285.00
Plate, American Authors, 9½"... 55.00
Plate, Asbury Park, r/e, s/o, 10" 75.00
Plate, Bunker Hill Monument, Ye Old Historical Pottery, 9"......... 35.00
Plate, Cape Cod, fisherman's portrait, 9" 65.00
Plate, Charles Dickens, London scenes, r/e, 10" 55.00
Plate, Cincinnati OH, v/o, 9".. 45.00
Plate, Denver, coupe, v/o, 10" 55.00
Plate, East Hampton, r/e, v/o, 10" 65.00
Plate, Hermitage, fruit & flower border, 9¾".................................. 50.00
Plate, Historical Philadelphia, 6 scenes, r/e, 10" 55.00
Plate, Hudson River, r/e, s/o, 10".. 55.00
Plate, Longfellow's Early Home, r/e, 10" 55.00
Plate, Lookout Mountain TN, s/o, r/e, 10"...................................... 70.00
Plate, Mayflower Coat of Arms, 1909, gold edge, 6"...................... 30.00

Plate, New Bedford, Mass., souvenir of, 10", $70.00. (Photo courtesy Mary Frank Gaston)

Plate, New York, Statue of Liberty, r/e, v/o, 10"............................. 55.00
Plate, New York & Brooklyn Bridge, r/e, s/o, 10" 70.00
Plate, Niagara Falls NY, s/o, 9".. 45.00
Plate, Portland OR, s/o, coupe, 10".. 50.00
Plate, Priscilla & John Adams, fruit & flower border, 10" 50.00
Plate, Seattle WA, r/e, s/o, 10"... 70.00
Plate, Sherbrooke, s/o, 10"... 85.00
Plate, Teddy Roosevelt, r/e, 10"... 75.00
Plate, Vassar College, 6 scenes at border, r/e, 10" 85.00
Plate, Waterbury CT, r/e, s/o, 10" 75.00
Tumbler, Ashville, s/o... 95.00
Tumbler, Fall River MA, v/o.. 85.00
Tumbler, Ottawa Canada, v/o.. 85.00

Royal Bayreuth

Founded in 1794 in Tettau, Bavaria, the Royal Bayreuth firm originally manufactured fine dinnerware of superior quality. Their figural items, produced from before the turn of the century until the onset of WWI, are highly sought after by today's collectors. Perhaps the most abundantly produced and easily recognized of these are the tomato and lobster pieces. Fruits, flowers, people, animals, birds, and vegetables shapes were also made. Aside from figural items, pitchers, toothpick holders, cups and saucers, humidors, and the like were decorated in florals and scenic motifs. Some, such as the very popular Rose Tapestry line, utilized a cloth-like tapestry background. Transfer prints were used as well. Two of the most popular are Sunbonnet Babies and Nursery Rhymes (in particular, those decorated with the complete verse).

Caution: Many pieces were not marked; some were marked 'Deponiert' or 'Registered' only. While marked pieces are the most valued, unmarked items are still very worthwhile. Our advisor for this category is Harold Brandenburg; he is listed in the Directory under Kansas.

Figurals

Jar, Santa Claus, Depose, 5", $2,000.00. (Photo courtesy Hassinger & Courtney Auctioneering/ LiveAuctioneers.com)

Ashtray, Art Nouveau lady, Deponiert, 4" 750.00
Ashtray, Devil & Cards (2 cards), bl mk, 2½x4½"........................... 225.00
Berry set, tomato, bl mk, 9" master+8 5" bowls.............................. 350.00
Boot, man's 8-eyelet work type, blk, bl mk, 3⅜x4⅞" 135.00
Bowl, Nouveau lady, bl mk, 5¾".. 800.00
Bowl, tomato, bl mk, 4x8"... 95.00
Bowl, tomato, bl mk, 11¾" L... 200.00
Box, stamp; Queen of Hearts & Devil, bl mk, 2¼x3¾x1¾"........ 1,000.00
Cake plate, murex shell, bl mk, 10"... 150.00
Cake plate, poppy, lav MOP, bl mk, 10".. 200.00
Candy dish, Devil & Cards, bl mk, 7" 365.00
Celery dish, seashell w/shell hdl, gr mk, 13x5¼"............................. 115.00
Chocolate pot, poppy, bl mk, 8½"... 650.00

Clock, wall; devil, red on gray, unmk, 4½" 1,550.00
Compote, tomato, unmk, 3¾" 210.00
Cracker jar, lobster, bl mk, NM 350.00
Cup, stirrup; fox, unmk 2,800.00
Cup & saucer, demi; cabbage leaf w/lobster hdl, bl mk 195.00
Cup & saucer, rose, pk, bl mk, 2", 4" 200.00
Dish, pear, w/lid, 4x3" 550.00
Hatpin holder, owl, bl mk, 4" 475.00
Humidor, Devil & Cards, bl mk, 7½" 950.00
Incense burner, Buddha, bl mk, 4x2½" 3,500.00
Inkwell, elk, w/lid, gr mk 400.00
Jar, pineapple, bl mk, 7" 380.00
Match holder, clown, wall hanging, bl mk, 5¼" 400.00
Mustard, Santa (missing spoon), w/lid, Depose bl mk, NM....5,000.00
Mustard jar, lobster, bl mk, w/spoon, 4¼", NM 150.00
Nappy, strawberry blossoms & leaves, bl mk, 4¾" 125.00
Pitcher, alligator, bl mk, cream sz, 3½" 275.00
Pitcher, alligator, bl mk, milk sz, 5" 300.00
Pitcher, apple, yel, bl mk, cream sz, 3¾" 125.00
Pitcher, apple, yel, bl mk, lemonade sz, 7½x10" 550.00
Pitcher, blk cat, tail hdl, bl mk, milk sz, 5½" 375.00
Pitcher, bull's head, brn & gray, bl mk, cream sz, 3¾" 150.00
Pitcher, butterfly, bl mk, 4½" 250.00
Pitcher, butterfly, wings closed, unmk, 6½" 2,200.00
Pitcher, cat, blk w/red mouth & inner ears, bl mk, cream sz....200.00
Pitcher, cat hdl, yel on bl, bl mk, 4" 275.00
Pitcher, chimpanzee, gray-blk, Deponiert, cream sz, 4¼" 350.00
Pitcher, chrysanthemum, bl mk, 3½" 300.00
Pitcher, coachman, bl mk, water sz, 7" 360.00
Pitcher, cow, unmk, cream sz, 3" 150.00
Pitcher, crow, blk, Deponiert, cream sz, 4½" 175.00
Pitcher, Devil, red, bl mk, cream sz 375.00
Pitcher, Devil & Cards, gr mk, water sz, 7½" 475.00
Pitcher, duck, bl mk, 3¾x4" 175.00
Pitcher, eagle, bl mk, 4" 150.00
Pitcher, eagle, unmk, 6½" 500.00
Pitcher, elk, bl mk, water sz, 7" 300.00
Pitcher, elk, bl mk, 3½" 450.00
Pitcher, fish head, bl mk, cream sz, 4¼" 150.00
Pitcher, flounder, bl mk, 3½" 450.00
Pitcher, gazelle head, #5330/2, unmk, 3¼" 475.00
Pitcher, girl w/basket, bl mk, 3½" 300.00
Pitcher, girl w/jug, Deponiert, 3½" 300.00
Pitcher, happy hound, emb Germany on hip, cream sz, 3¾" ...50.00
Pitcher, lobster, bl mk, water sz, 6¾" 375.00
Pitcher, lobster, bl mk, 5" 200.00
Pitcher, maple leaf, Deponiert, 4" 225.00
Pitcher, melon, gr stripes, bl mk, 4¾" 250.00
Pitcher, milkmaid, gr dress, bl mk, 4½" 300.00
Pitcher, monk, brn & tan, bl mk, 4" 300.00
Pitcher, monk, unmk, milk sz, 5" 500.00
Pitcher, monkey, gr, unmk, milk sz, 5" 325.00
Pitcher, mtn goat's head, bl mk, cream sz, 3½" 200.00
Pitcher, Nouveau lady, Deponiert, 7" 900.00
Pitcher, Nouveau lady, pastel bsk (rare finish), bl mk, 4" 450.00
Pitcher, orange, leaf spout, stem hdl, bl mk, milk sz, 4½" 185.00
Pitcher, pansy, purple & yel, bl mk, cream sz, 4" 185.00
Pitcher, parakeet, mc, unmk, 4" 195.00
Pitcher, parrot/parakeet, mc, unmk, med sz, 6½" 565.00
Pitcher, poodle, blk, bl mk, milk sz, 5¼" 325.00
Pitcher, poodle, wht, bl mk, 4½" 225.00
Pitcher, rabbit sitting up, mk Registered, milk sz, 5¼" 3,950.00
Pitcher, rooster, bl mk, 4" 200.00
Pitcher, rooster, blk w/red comb, bl mk, 7½x10" 1,350.00

Pitcher, rooster, mc, bl mk, cream sz, 4⅜" 250.00
Pitcher, rose, pk, bl mk & Deponiert, milk sz, 4¼" 350.00
Pitcher, Santa, Deponiert, milk sz, 5¼" 2,300.00
Pitcher, Santa, flat strap hdl, Deponiert, 4" 1,700.00
Pitcher, snake, bl mk, 4" 750.00
Pitcher, squirrel, bl mk (rarely mk), cream sz, 4¾" 1,500.00
Pitcher, squirrel, bl mk (rarely mk), water sz, 8" 3,500.00
Pitcher, strawberry, unmk, water sz, 6½" 500.00
Pitcher, tangerine, bl mk, 5" 225.00
Pitcher, tomato, Deponiert, cream sz 55.00
Pitcher, trout, unmk, ca 1910, cream sz, 4¼" 400.00

Pitcher, turtle, bl mk, cream sz, 2" 795.00
Pitcher, turtle, bl mk, lemonade sz, 4½" 9,500.00
Pitcher, turtle, bl mk, water sz, 3½" 1,000.00
Pitcher, turtle, bl mk, 3" 450.00
Plate, leaf, gr, bl mk, 6x4¾" 40.00
Plate, tomato & vine w/2 sm buds, bl mk, 7½" 50.00
Relish, holly w/red berries, bl mk, 8½" 325.00
Shakers, radish, bl mk, 3¼", pr 250.00
Shaving mug, elk head, glossy, bl mk 450.00
String holder, rooster, mc, bl mk, 6" 250.00
Sugar bowl, alligator, w/lid, unmk, 4½" L 1,550.00
Sugar bowl, pansy, bl mk, w/spoon, 3" 180.00
Sugar bowl, perch, bl mk 1,075.00
Sugar bowl, tomato, Deponiert, w/lid, 4" 65.00
Toothpick holder, spikey shell, pearl lustre, 3-ftd, 3", from $150 to..160.00
Tray, Devil & Cards, bl mk, 10x7", NM 650.00
Whipped cream set, poppy, bl mk, 6" bowl+7" plate+ladle 300.00

Nursery Rhymes

Note: Items with a printed verse bring a premium.

Bell, Jack & Beanstalk, w/rhyme, w/clapper, bl mk...................... 350.00
Bowl, child's feeding; Jack & Jill, bl mk, w/lid, 7".................. 150.00
Box, pin; Jack & the Beanstalk, bl mk, 5½" L........................ 225.00
Candlestick, Little Bo Peep, bl mk, 4¼"............................. 180.00
Chamberstick, Little Jack Horner, bl mk 180.00
Cruet, Jack & Beanstalk, bl mk, no stopper, 6½"..................... 200.00
Match holder, Little Jack Horner, bl mk, 3½"........................ 250.00
Mug, Jack & Beanstalk, w/verse, bl mk, lg.......................... 250.00
Mug, Ring Around the Rosies, bl mk, 6"............................. 200.00
Pitcher, Jack & the Beanstalk, bl mk, water sz..................... 350.00

Pitcher, Little Boy Blue, 4", $80.00. (Photo courtesy Hassinger & Courtney Auctioneering/ LiveAuctioneers.com)

Pitcher, Ring Around the Rosies, bl mk, cream sz 100.00
Pitcher, Ring Around the Rosies, unmk, 2¾" 75.00
Plate, Jack & Jill w/verse, bl mk, 6".............................. 125.00
Sugar bowl, Little Boy Blue, bl mk................................. 225.00
Vase, Babes in the Woods, bl mk, 4"................................ 200.00

Scenics and Action Portraits

Bowl, sheep in landscape, bl mk, 10½"................................ 195.00
Box, Dutch woman, shell shape, bl mk, 1½x3x2¾" 115.00
Candleholder, Brittany woman, bl mk, 4¼x2¼", ea..................... 70.00
Charger, Arab on wht horse, gold trim, bl mk, 13"................... 150.00
Charger, 3 nudes w/castle bkground, gold scroll rim, bl mk, 11½"...350.00
Chocolate pot, Arab on horsebk, gr mk, 8", +2 c/s w/gr mks........ 395.00
Coal scuttle, man w/2 harnessed horses, w/hdl, bulbous, unmk, 3" ..125.00
Covered dish, man fishing from boat, bl mk, 5".................... 125.00

Cracker jar, exotic parrots, metal bail, no mark, 6½", $800.00.
(Photo courtesy Harold Brandenburg)

Creamer & sugar bowl, penguins, ftd 295.00
Cruet, bears (brn) in landscape, bl mk, 5"........................ 300.00
Dish, dogs after moose in rover, buckle & strap at side, bl mk, 5½".. 195.00
Dresser set, girl & chickens, bl mk, 7½x4½" tray +3 sm dishes 295.00
Hair receiver, 2 equestrians w/3 dogs on lid, 3 gold ft, bl mk, 4" .. 125.00

Hairpin holder, fisherman in boat, rectangular, bl mk, 5½" L....... 125.00
Hatpin holder, peacock in landscape, bl mk, 4¾" 395.00
Jug, dogs chase moose into river, bl mk, 6¼", from $130 to......... 150.00
Mug, cavaliers at table, bl mk, 5" 100.00
Mug, cows in pasture, 3-hdl, bl mk, 3⅜" 95.00
Pitcher, cattle in pastoral scene, bl mk, cream sz 75.00
Pitcher, children on beach, bl mk, milk sz, 4½" 85.00
Pitcher, girl w/dog, bl mk, milk sz, 4⅝" 120.00
Pitcher, jester, Penny in Pocket..., Noke, unmk, lemonade sz 700.00
Pitcher, polar bears in Arctic scene, bl mk, 4" 425.00
Pitcher, poodle dog, gray, bl mk, 4½" 95.00
Pitcher, poppy, Deponiert, 3½" 95.00
Pitcher, sailboat scene, bl mk, milk sz, 5" 75.00
Plaque, cavaliers, bl mk, 11½" 125.00
Plate, bull & cow elk in grassy landscape, bl mk, 9½" 140.00
Plate, sunset, 4-hdl, bl mk, 3½" 50.00
Tankard, 2 mules/boy/farmhouse, cylindrical, bl mk, 13⅝".......... 500.00
Teapot, hunting scene, bl mk, 4¼x7" 135.00
Teapot, rooster & hen, bl mk, 6½" W 165.00
Tray, Goose Girl, bl mk, 12x9" 150.00
Vase, Dutch ice skaters, bl mk, 4¼" 125.00
Vase, frogs & bees, bl mk, sq, 4x3¼" 225.00
Vase, goats in woods, 2 gold hdls, bl mk, 7" 125.00
Vase, horses (4) in pasture, unmk, 5¼" 125.00
Vase, hummingbirds, unmk, 6½" 300.00
Vase, lady in garden, hdls, bl mk, 5" 225.00
Vase, lady's w/purple shawl, bl mk, 7" 250.00
Vase, lady w/shawl, cobalt & gold at top, bl mk, 5¾" 125.00
Vase, nude fairy, pierced neck, vine hdls, 4" 150.00
Vase, nudes bathing, bl mk, 3½" 95.00
Vase, nymph on gr, bl mk, 7½" 200.00
Vase, pheasant scene, ruffled rim, bl mk, 3¾" 125.00
Vase, roses on wht, bl mk, 7" 95.00
Vase, The Chase, hounds & stag, integral hdls, bl mk, 3", NM...... 75.00
Vase, waterfalls & mtn, bl mk, ornate ring hdls, rtcl rim, 7" 295.00
Vase, 3 hounds after moose in river, bl mk, 9⅝".................... 275.00
Wall plaque, cavaliers at table, scalloped rim, bl mk, 11½" 125.00

Sunbonnet Babies

Basket, 1 sweeping, 2nd washing, unmk............................. 350.00
Bowl, cereal; sweeping, bl mk, 5¼"................................ 150.00
Bowl, hanging clothes, bl mk, 7½".................................. 175.00
Candlesticks, sweeping, bl mk, 4¼", pr 425.00
Candlesticks, washing, bl mk, 4¼", pr 425.00
Chamberstick, cleaning, bl mk, 5½x4½"............................. 275.00
Cup & saucer, fishing, bl mk...................................... 225.00
Nappy, washing, w/hdl, bl mk, 6" L................................ 225.00
Pitcher, cleaning, tankard form, bl mk, 5"........................ 225.00
Pitcher, ironing, bl mk, cream sz, 3⅛" 175.00
Pitcher, mending, tankard shape, bl mk, 5¼"....................... 175.00
Pitcher, sweeping, bl mk, milk sz, 4½"............................ 175.00
Pitcher, washing, ruffled spout on ewer form, bl mk, 4¼" 225.00
Planter, fishing, low gold hdls, bsk insert, bl mk, 2¾x3½" 250.00
Plate, fishing, bl mk, 6"... 125.00
Plate, washing, bl mk, 6"... 125.00
Sugar bowl, cleaning, bl mk, 3¼".................................. 250.00
Tumbler, cleaning, bulbous, 3½"................................... 225.00

Tapestries

Bowl, pansy, bl mk, 2¼x5½" 200.00
Box, dancing couple, oval, bl mk, 4½" L........................... 210.00
Box, Rose Tapestry, clover shape w/gold, bl mk, 5¾"............... 175.00

Royal Bayreuth

Box, Silver Tapestry, bl mk, 5" L 1,000.00
Clock, Rose Tapestry, bl mk, 4¾" 395.00
Cracker jar, Rose Tapestry, appl hdls, gold trim, 5½" 700.00

Creamer, turkey hunting scene, 3½", $150.00. (Photo courtesy Jackson's International Auctioneers & Appraisers of Fine Art & Antiques)

Hair receiver, Rose Tapestry, 3 gold ft, bl mk, 2½x4" 150.00
Humidor, goat scene, bl mk, 5½", NM 750.00
Jar, Rose Tapestry, gold hdls, ped ft, bl mk, 5¼x6¼" 295.00
Leaf dish, Rose Tapestry, 3-color, bl mk, 4¼x5" 295.00
Pitcher, perch, bl mk, cream sz, 4" 295.00
Pitcher, polar bear, bl mk, 8" 1,950.00
Pitcher, Rose Tapestry, bl mk, water sz, 6½" 450.00
Pitcher, Rose Tapestry, corseted, bl mk, milk sz, 4¾" 225.00
Pitcher, Rose Tapestry, unmk, cream sz, 3¼" 125.00
Pitcher, stag in stream/gazebo on hill, bl mk, milk sz, 5¼" 250.00
Pitcher, takard; Rose Tapestry, gold hdl/pinched spout, bl mk, 3¼".. 195.00
Plaque, temple scene w/river & deer, bl mk, 11¼" 210.00
Plate, Rose Tapestry, bl mk, 7½" 175.00
Plate, Rose Tapestry, 3-color, bl mk, 9½" 195.00
Set, Rose Tapestry, bl mk, hatpin holder+box+hair receiver+tray ..750.00
Tray, tavern scene on wht, branching gold hdl, bl mk, 5" L 125.00
Vase, castle scene w/gold, bulbous, bl mk, 3½" 150.00
Vase, polar bears, 2 in Arctic scene, bl mk, 8x4½" 1,800.00
Vase, Rose Tapestry, ftd, gold hdls, bl mk, 4" 225.00
Vase, Rose Tapestry, low gold hdls, scalloped rim, bl mk, 2¾" 125.00
Vase, Rose Tapestry, ornate gold hdls, bl mk, 9½" 475.00
Vase, Rose Tapestry, slightly bulbous, bl mk, 4½" 110.00
Vase, Rose Tapestry, unmk, 7x4" 125.00
Vase, tavern scene, 2 gold hdls at shoulder, bl mk, 4⅝" 125.00
Watering can, wildlife in landscape, unmk, 3" 650.00

Royal Bonn

Royal Bonn is a fine-paste porcelain, ornately decorated with scenes, portraits, or florals. The factory was established in the mid-1800s in Bonn, Germany; however, most pieces found today are from the latter part of the century.

Candleholders, floral w/gold, Ovington, 1888-1920, 14x6¼", pr... 550.00
Clock, La Lomme, pansies w/gold, time & strike, 4" dial, 11¼x12" ...700.00
Clock, La Nord, floral on bl, pendulum, 1870s, 11½x14" 660.00
Clock, La Roca, floral, open escapement, 8-day, gong, 11½" 850.00
Clock, La Vera, floral w/bl, 8-day, ½-hr gong, 12½" 975.00
Clock, La Verden, floral on red, 5" open escapement, 14" 950.00
Plaque, Queen Louise portrait, E Volk, ca 1900, in oval gilt bronze fr. 575.00
Umbrella stand, wht floral, mc majolica glazes, #6076, 21¾x10" . 575.00
Urn, floral on cream w/gold, #D3149/670, 12", pr 1,800.00
Urn, grapes, artist sgn, old rprs to lid, 47" 2,350.00
Urn, putti in clouds w/instruments, gold hdls, 1880-1920, 18½". 1,325.00
Vase, cavalier courting scene, lion mask ft, 48", +23" stand...... 1,325.00
Vase, East Indian lady, sgn Bauar, 21" 575.00
Vase, lady in flower garden tapestry, putti hdls, 1890s, 13¾" 1,950.00
Vase, lady in landscape, Sticher, gold hdls, w/lid, ca 1900, 14x7"....600.00
Vase, lady's portrait, blown-out berries, Sticher, hdls, 1900s, 16"...1,325.00
Vase, roses, Dirkmann, gold hdls, #1755, 18½" 850.00

Vase, stylized floral, #1456, 6", $520.00. (Photo courtesy Treadway Gallery Inc.)

Royal Copenhagen

The Royal Copenhagen Manufactory was established in Denmark in about 1775 by Frantz Henrich Muller. When bankruptcy threatened in 1779, the Crown took charge. The fine dinnerware and objects of art produced after that time carry the familiar logo, the crown over three wavy lines. For further information we recommend *Royal Copenhagen Porcelain, Animals and Figurines,* by Robert J. Heritage (Schiffer). See also Limited Edition Plates.

Bust of woman in bl cap, stoneware, Hedegaard, #21616, 1948+, 18"..240.00
Figurine, Amagar woman knitting, #1317, 9" 110.00
Figurine, bird w/red topknot, #1050, Dahl Jensen, 15" 100.00
Figurine, boy wrapped in bl stands w/dog, #782, 7½" 120.00
Figurine, children w/dog, C Thomsen design, #707, 6" 350.00
Figurine, courting couple about to kiss, #3049, 17¼" 550.00

Figurine, dachshund, printed marks, 13" long, $235.00. (Photo courtesy Jackson's International Auctioneers & Appraisers of Fine Art & Antiques)

Figurine, dog w/slipper, #3476, 3½" 85.00
Figurine, Fano, girls kneels w/floral garland, #12413, 1964, 5¾" .. 480.00
Figurine, farmer stands beside hog, #848, 7½x8" 275.00
Figurine, fisherman, #12214, 13½" 725.00
Figurine, girl seated holds golden horn aloft, #12242, 1958, 8⅜" .. 425.00
Figurine, hunter seated w/gun, dog at ft, #1087, 9x6" 360.00
Figurine, ladies (2/elderly) gossiping, #1319, 12" 480.00
Figurine, maiden w/goats, #694, 9x7½" 215.00
Figurine, medieval boy & girl on base, #3171, 19x9" 600.00
Figurine, mother stands w/baby in arm & daughter beside, #12159, 6" ..515.00
Figurine, native girl w/beads, Dahl Jensen, #1353, 5" 275.00
Figurine, Oriental dancer, #12238, 11½" 900.00
Figurine, owls (2 conjoined), #283, 12½" 660.00
Figurine, Pan, #1713, 3x4" 200.00
Figurine, Pan w/panpipes, #1736, 5½" 250.00
Figurine, Pan w/parrot, C Thomsen design, 7" 300.00
Figurine, penguins (2), #2918, 8" 300.00
Figurine, Sjaelland, girl in native costume, #12418, 1964, 4" 550.00
Figurine, soldier speaking to witch, #1112, 8" 475.00
Figurine, spaniel, Dahl Jensen, #1304, 5" 225.00

Figurine, terrier standing w/tail up, #1452/2967, 6½x8½" 110.00
Figurine, Wave & Rock, #1132, 18¼" 1,200.00
Figurine, wolf & cubs, #1788, 4x5½" 215.00
Figurine Scottie dog, Dahl Jensen, #1078, 7" 215.00
Plate, narcissus, artist monogram, #29/1125, 10" 60.00
Tea caddy, songbird reserve on wht, Paaske, 1918 .... 60.00
Vase, colonial couple reserve, waisted, Jul 1895, 11¼" 300.00
Vase, daffodil & leaves on bl, #2640/137, 12½" 240.00
Vase, Frisk Kuling Udfor Kobenhavn, sailing ships, 1927, 19½" .. 850.00
Vase, grotesque decor w/bl borders, gold dolphin hdls, 19th C, 22" ..9,000.00
Vase, herringbone incising, brn orange peel, Salto/#20737 29?, 10¼" .. 1,200.00
Vase, honeycomb-like pattern, gray/olive matt, Salto, #20708, 7x5½" ..3,600.00
Vase, honeycomb-like pattern, turq matt, Salto, #20685, 6x2¾" 3,000.00
Vase, organic form w/vertical ribs, gray/brn/bl mottle, Salto, 5" ... 600.00
Vase, sailboats in harbor, #MCX 2609-1049, 9x5" 215.00
Vase, sculpted rim, bl & mustard mottle, Salto, #21439, 5¼x3½" .. 3,150.00
Vase, stylized poppies, A Krog, #231, pre-1923, 10¾" 425.00
Vase, swans among waves, VT Fischer, 1896, 14¾" 960.00
Vase, swans on lake, St Ussing, #8897, 13½" 850.00
Vase, tree pattern emb, blk & mahog, spherical, Salto, #1243, 7¾" ..3,600.00
Vase, wisteria on wht, #184, 11", EX 75.00

Royal Copley

Royal Copley is a decorative type of pottery made by the Spaulding China Company in Sebring, Ohio, from 1942 to 1957. They also produced two other major lines — Royal Windsor and Spaulding. Royal Copley was primarily marketed through five-and-ten cent stores; Royal Windsor and Spaulding were sold through department stores, gift shops, and jobbers. Items trimmed in gold are worth 25% to 50% more than the same item with no gold trim. For more information we recommend *Collecting Royal Copley Plus Royal Windsor & Spaulding* by our advisor for this category, Joe Devine; he is listed in the Directory under Iowa.

Ashtray, deer leaping, pk, mk USA, from $35 to 40.00
Ashtray, rooster & hen emb, Spaulding, mk USA, 7x7", from $50 to .60.00
Bank, pig w/striped shirt, paper label, 4½", from $55 to 60.00
Candleholders, Strange Tracks, gray w/pk int, 3", pr from $20 to .. 25.00
Coaster, hunting dog, chrome rim, unmk, from $35 to 40.00
Creamer, yel w/brn leaf hdl, emb mk, 3", from $35 to 40.00
Figurine, bantam rooster, paper label, 6½", from $60 to 75.00
Figurine, hen, brn breast, 7¾", from $100 to 125.00
Figurine, mallard, bending head, Royal Windsor, paper label, 8¾" ..60.00
Figurine, mallard, Royal Windsor, 6", from $20 to 25.00
Figurine, rooster, feet not showing, paper label, 8", from $50 to 60.00
Figurine, sparrow, yel, paper label, 5", from $15 to 20.00
Hot pad holder, rooster, wall mt, AD Priolo, USA, from $50 to 60.00
Lamp, figural lady dancing, red & wht, rare, from $150 to 200.00
Lamp, sm pk floral decals on wht, ftd, w/hdls, Spaulding, 8" 50.00
Pitcher, Pome Fruit, orange on bl, gr stamp, 8", from $65 to 75.00
Pitcher, Pome Fruit, yel on cobalt, gr stamp, scarce, 8", from $90 to..100.00
Planter, angel praying, red, paper label, 6½", from $35 to 40.00
Planter, dog by mailbox, blk & wht, 8½", from $125 to 150.00
Planter, farm boy w/fishing pole, bl & yel, emb mk, 6½" 35.00
Planter, lady w/bare shoulders, red, paper label, 6", from $70 to 75.00
Planter, Linley decal, ftd, sm hdls, gold stamp, 4", from $12 to 15.00
Planter, Madonna, bl & wht, Royal Windsor, emb mk, 8½", from $40 to . 45.00
Planter, Oriental girl w/lg basket at ft, emb mk, 8", from $20 to 25.00
Planter, poodle, recumbent, Royal Windsor, 8½" L, from $75 to ... 80.00
Planter, red finch on apple, paper label, 6½", from $40 to 45.00
Planter, red hummingbird on yel flower, paper label, 5", from $55 to... 60.00
Planter, ribbed, emb mk, 4", from $12 to 15.00
Planter, rooster, blk & wht, high tail, emb mk, 7¾", from $150 to ... 175.00

Planter, rooster & wheelbarrow, paper label, 8", from $150 to 175.00
Planter, sectioned, brn w/lt gr int, emb mk, 2½x6", from $8 to 10.00
Planter, teddy bear w/mandolin, paper label, rare, 7", from $65 to...75.00
Planter, wht cockatiel on blk kidney shape, paper label, 8½" 70.00
Sugar bowl, pk & yel w/gr leaf hdls, emb mk, scarce, 3", from $35 to...40.00
Tray, emb apple & pear in bottom, pk, w/hdls, Spaulding, 6x10", $40 to.45.00
Vase, bud; warbler on branch, emb mk, 5", from, $20 to 25.00
Vase, Floral Elegance, pk on cobalt, gr stamp, 8", from $28 to 32.00
Vase, horse, brn & yel, paper label, 8", from $35 to 40.00
Vase, Pink Beauty, gold trim, ftd, w/hdls, gold stamp, 6", from $12 to..14.00
Vase, Virginia decal, ftd, w/hdls, paper label, 7", from $12 to 15.00
Wall plaque, fruit, blk rim, emb mk, 6¾", from $35 to 40.00

Wall pocket, Blackamoor prince, 8", from $40.00 to $45.00. (Photo courtesy Malter Galleries Inc./LiveAuctioneers.com)

Wall pocket, cocker spaniel head figural, emb mk, 5", from $35 to ...40.00
Wall pocket, Constable Valley Farm Amsterdam Holland, paper label, 8"..65.00
Wall pocket, decal on plaque shape, paper label, 8", from $65 to .. 75.00
Wall pocket, Island Lady, Royal Windsor, 8", from $100 to 125.00

Royal Crown Derby

The Royal Crown Derby company can trace its origin back to 1848. It first operated under the name of Locker & Co. but by 1859 had became Stevenson, Sharp & Co. Several changes in ownership occurred until 1866 when it became known as the Sampson Hancock Co. The Derby Crown Porcelain Co. Ltd. was formed in 1876, and these companies soon merged. In 1890 they were appointed as a manufacturer for the Queen and began using the name Royal Crown Derby.

In the early years, considerable 'Japan ware' decorated in Imari style, using red, blue, and gold in Oriental patterns was popular. The company excelled in their ability to use gold in the decoration, and some of the best flower painters of all time were employed. Nice vases or plaques signed by any of these artists will bring thousands of dollars: Gregory, Mosley, Rouse, Gresley, and D'esiré Leroy. We have observed porcelain plaques decorated with flowers signed by Gregory selling at auction for as much as $12,000.00. If you find a signed piece and are not sure of its value, if at all possible, it would be best to have it appraised by someone very knowledgeable regarding current market values.

As is usual among most other English factories, nearly all of the vases produced by Royal Crown Derby came with covers. If they are missing, deduct 40% to 45%. There are several well illustrated books available from antique booksellers to help you learn to identify this ware. The back stamps used after 1891 will date every piece except dinnerware. The company is still in business, producing outstanding dinnerware and Imari-decorated figures and serving pieces. They also produce custom (one only) sets of table service for the wealthy of the world.

Beaker, Old Imari, w/hdl, #1128, 3¾" 110.00
Bowl, Imari, #2451, 3x6" 145.00

Bowl, Imari, #2451, 10½" L 250.00
Bowl, Imari, pierced gold oak leaf hdls, #2451, 8¼x11¾".......... 475.00
Bowl, Imari, 8-sided, #2451, 4½x10¾" 480.00
Bowl, Old Imari, #1128, 10½" L 250.00
Bowl, Old Imari, 8-sided, gold trim, #1128, 3½x8¾" 315.00
Bowl, Red Aves, 4½x10¾" 300.00
Bowl, soup; Old Imari, #1128, 8½", set of 6 .... 550.00
Candlesticks, floral w/cobalt & gold, sq base, bone china, 10½", pr ...900.00
Candlesticks, Red Aves, birds & flowers, 10½", pr.......... 325.00

Centerpiece bowl, pheasant and flowers, XXXIII, $335.00.
(Photo courtesy Du Mouchelles/ LiveAuctioneers.com)

Coffeepot, Imari, ovoid, #2451, 8" 425.00
Compote, Old Imari, ftd, #1128, 5x9½" 360.00
Compote, Old Imari, ftd, #1128, 5x11" 550.00
Cup & saucer, Imari, #2451 .... 60.00
Cup & saucer, Old Imari, #1128 .... 100.00
Dinnerware, Vine, 12 lg plates+12 c/s 425.00
Dish, floral sprays, bl starbursts & gold at rim, 1850s, 7½" L 240.00
Figurine, Bengal tiger on base, Imari colors, artist sgn, 5" 215.00
Figurine, bull on base, Imari colors, artist sgn, 5x7½" 275.00
Figurine, John Milton, arm rests on books on column, prof rpr, 7"... 175.00
Figurine, Lion (male) on base, Imari colors, artist sgn, 6½"......... 315.00
Figurine, pheasant on naturalistic base, realistic HP, 6¼x7¼" 215.00
Figurine, zebra on base, Imari colors, artist sgn, 5½" 275.00
Ginger jar, Old Imari, gold trim, #1128, 14x8" 950.00
Pitcher, Imari, incurvate throat, #2451, 4½".................... 125.00
Pitcher, milk; Old Imari, #1128, 3¼" 135.00
Plate, dessert; Imari, #2451, 7" 40.00
Plate, dessert; Old Imari, #1128, 8½" 55.00
Plate, dinner; Gold Aves, 1930s, 10", 12 for 480.00
Plate, dinner; Lombardy, 10⅝", 10 for........................... 550.00
Plate, dinner; Old Imari, #1128, 10" 135.00
Plate, luncheon; Imari, #2451, 9" 60.00
Plate, salad; Old Imari, #1128, 8½" 65.00
Platter, Imari, oval, #2451, 14½" 850.00
Sugar bowl, Imari, w/lid, #2451, 5½" W 225.00
Tray/dish, Imari, sq w/hdls, #2451, 9¾x10¾" 225.00
Tureen, bittersweet floral w/cobalt & gold, w/lid & tray, 1920s, 16" L..900.00
Urns, floral reserves w/cobalt & gold, early 19th C, 6½x5½", pr..600.00
Vase, Aesthetic Movement, much decor, rtcl hdls, Picotee, 10¼".. 1,200.00
Vase, bud; Imari, #2451, 4½" 165.00
Vase, floral, gold on pk, bulbous, 1890s, 9½" 515.00
Vase, floral sprays, pastel w/gold, slim neck, bulbous, 19th C, 7"... 240.00
Vase, Persian decor w/gold, bottle shape, rtcl hdls, 1880s, 11¼" ..425.00
Vase, putti reserve on bleu celeste, teal socle w/gold, 14" 600.00

Royal Doulton

The range of wares produced by the Doulton Company since its inception in 1815 has been vast and varied. The earliest wares produced in the tiny pottery in Lambeth, England, were salt-glazed pitchers, plain and fancy figural bottles, etc. — all utility-type stoneware geared to the practical needs of everyday living. The original partners, John Doulton and John Watts, saw the potential for success in the manufacture of drain and sewage pipes and during the 1840s concentrated on these highly lucrative types of commercial wares. Watts retired from the company in 1854, and Doulton began experimenting with a more decorative product line. As time went by, many glazes and decorative effects were developed, among them Faience, Impasto, Silicon, Carrara, Marqueterie, Chine, and Rouge Flambe. Tiles and architectural terra cotta were an important part of their manufacture. Late in the nineteenth century at the original Lambeth location, fine artware was decorated by such notable artists as Hannah and Arthur Barlow, George Tinworth, and J.H. McLennan. Stoneware vases with incised animal drawings, gracefully shaped urns with painted scenes, and cleverly modeled figurines rivaled the best of any competitor.

In 1882 a second factory was built in Burslem which continues even yet to produce the famous figurines, character jugs, series ware, and table services so popular with collectors today. Their Kingsware line, made from 1899 to 1946, featured flasks and flagons with drinking scenes, usually on a brown-glazed ground. Some were limited editions, while others were commemorative and advertising items. The Gibson Girl series, 24 plates in all, was introduced in 1901. It was drawn by Charles Dana Gibson and is recognized by its blue and white borders and central illustrations, each scene depicting a humorous or poignant episode in the life of 'The Widow and Her Friends.' Dickensware, produced from 1911 through the early 1940s, featured illustrations by Charles Dickens, with many of his famous characters. The Robin Hood series was introduced in 1914; the Shakespeare series #1, portraying scenes from the Bard's plays, was made from 1914 until World War II. The Shakespeare series #2 ran from 1906 until 1974 and was decorated with featured characters. Nursery Rhymes was a series that was first produced in earthenware in 1930 and later in bone china. In 1933 a line of decorated children's ware, the Bunnykin series, was introduced; it continues to be made to the present day. About 150 'bunny' scenes have been devised, the earliest and most desirable being those signed by the artist Barbara Vernon. Most pieces range in value from $60.00 to $120.00.

Factors contributing to the value of a figurine are age, demand, color, and detail. Those with a limited production run and those signed by the artist or marked 'Potted' (indicating a pre-1939 origin) are also more valuable. After 1920 wares were marked with a lion — with or without a crown — over a circular 'Royal Doulton.'

Animals and Birds

Alsatian dog, seated, K13, from $120 to 140.00
Ashtead Applause, collie dog, glossy, #779A, 5", from $75 to...... 100.00
Cardinal bird, K28, 2¾" 215.00

Cat, tabby, HN2583, 2¾" long, $60.00. (Photo courtesy neatstuffdave)

Dachshund seated, K17, from $95 to... 125.00
Dalmatian puppy, HN1113, from $450 to................................... 475.00
Drake, mc w/wht chest, HN807, 1923-77, 2½", from $80 to........ 120.00
Elephant trumpeting, realistic, HN2640, 11x23"......................... 550.00
King Penguin, HN1189, from $800 to 850.00
Penguin w/chick under wing, K20, from $275 to........................... 300.00

Persian cat, wht, HN2539, 1930s, 3x5x3", from $225 to 300.00
Sealyham fox terrier, recumbent, K4, 3¼" L, from $125 to 165.00
Sealyham fox terrier begging, K3, 2½", from $90 to 120.00
Tarryall Maestro, Morgan horse, blk, DA28, 11½" 275.00
Tiger on Rock, Prestige Cats, #2639, 12x16", from $650 to 700.00
Welsh mountain pony, DA164, 1991-97, 6½", from $175 to 200.00

Bunnykins

Artist, DB13, 1975, 3½", from $150 to 225.00
Autumn Days, DB5, 4½", from $!25 to 150.00
Beefeater, DB163, 1996, from $175 to 200.00
Billie, #8302, 1939-45, 4½" 950.00
Collector, DB54, 1987 club pc, 4¼", from $225 to 265.00
Cooling Off (Billie), DB3, from $80 to 110.00
Farmer #8304, 1939-45, 7¼" 1,075.00
Freefall, DB41, 1984, from $100 to 150.00
Grandpa's Story, DB14, 1975, from $150 to 195.00
Happy Birthday, DB21, 1982, MIB, from $25 to 40.00
Helping Mother, DB2, 3¼", from $25 to 35.00
Little John, DB243, 5", from $50 to 65.00

Mary Bunnykin, #8303, 1939 – 1945, 5½", $1,200.00. (Photo courtesy Richard Opfer Auctioneering Inc./ LiveAuctioneers.com)

Mother, #8305, 1939-45, 7½" 725.00
Queen Sophie, DB46, 1984, 4½", from $90 to 125.00
Rise & Shine, DB11, 1974, 3¾", from $95 to 120.00
Rock & Roll, DB124, 4½", 1991, 4½", MIB 350.00
Rocket Man, DB20, from $150 to 175.00
Storytime, DB9, 1974, 2½x3", from $60 to 85.00
Tom, DB72, 1988-93, 3" 75.00
Uncle Sam, DB175, 2nd version, 1977, MIB 225.00

Character Jugs

'Arriet, D6250, mini, from $45 to 65.00
Anne Boleyn, D6644, lg, from $100 to 125.00
Anne of Cleves, D6754, mini, from $115 to 135.00
Bacchus, D6521, 1960-91, mini, from $40 to 50.00
Buffalo Bill, D6735, med, from $125 to 150.00
Capt Ahab, D6500, lg, from $100 to 125.00
Capt Henry Morgan, D6510, 1960-82, mini, from $40 to 50.00
Cardinal, D5614, lg, from $100 to 120.00
Don Quixote, D6460, sm, from $50 to 65.00
Falconer, D6547, 1960-91, mini, from $35 to 50.00
Falstaff, D6287, 1968-71, lg, from $85 to 110.00
Fat Boy, D5840, sm, from $100 to 120.00
Fortune Teller, D6497, lg, from $325 to 375.00
Gaoler, D6584, 1963-83, mini, from $40 to 55.00
George Harrison, D6727, med, from $325 to 345.00
Groucho Marx, D6710, lg, from $180 to 195.00

Gulliver, D6563, sm, from $315 to 345.00
Henry VIII, D6647, sm, from $65 to 75.00
Jarge, D6288, lg, from $200 to 250.00
John Peel, D5612, 1936-60, lg, from $100 to 125.00
London Bobby, D6744, lg, from $185 to 225.00

Lord Nelson, D6335, large, $385.00.

Lumberjack, D6613, 1967-82, sm, from $40 to 60.00
Mad Hatter, D6606, mini, from $70 to 90.00
Merlin, D6529, lg, from $85 to 95.00
Merry Christmas, Santa Claus, wreath hdl, D6794, lg 350.00
Mr McCawber, D6138, mini, from $40 to 50.00
Mr Pickwick, D6254, mini 60.00
North American Indian, D6611, lg 95.00
Old Salt, china, D6551, lg, from $75 to 100.00
Rip Van Winkle, D6517, mini, from $50 to 75.00
Robin Hood, D6234, 1947-60, sm, from $40 to 50.00
Sairey Gamp, D6045, mini, from $40 to 45.00
Sam Johnson, D6289, 1950-60, lg, from $190 to 135.00
Sancho Panza, D6456, lg, from $85 to 95.00
Sleuth, D6635, sm, from $40 to 50.00
Snake Charmer, D6912, lg, from $275 to 300.00
St George, D6618, 1968-75, lg, from $295 to 325.00
Veteran Motorist, D6641, mini, from $90 to 115.00
Yachtsman, D6626, 1971-80, lg, from $120 to 150.00

Figurines

Affection, HN2236 .... 180.00
Afternoon Tea, HN1747, 5¾", from $325 to 550.00
And One for You, HN2970 .... 200.00
Antoinette, HN2326, 2nd version 200.00
As Good As New, HN2971, from $135 to 150.00
Ballerina, HN2116, lg, from $320 to 350.00
Balloon Man, HN1954, from $275 to 325.00
Bedtime Story, HN2059, 1st version, from $135 to 175.00
Belle o' the Ball, HN1997, from $235 to 275.00
Bess, HN2002, from $325 to 345.00
Blithe Morning, HN2021, from $200 to 225.00
Blue Beard, HN2105, from $410 to 435.00
Bridesmaid, HN2874, 5th version, from $45 to 60.00
Captain Cuttle, M77, from $90 to 115.00
Carmen, HN2545, from $275 to 295.00
Celeste, HN2237, from $140 to 170.00
Child From Williamsburg, HN2154, from $175 to 200.00
Christine, HN2792, from $160 to 195.00
Christmas Day, HN4214, from $450 to 485.00
Cissie, HN1809, from $100 to 130.00
Clockmaker, HN2279, from $275 to 325.00
Coralie, HN2307, from $175 to 195.00
Daydreams, HN1731, from $200 to 235.00
Dinky Do, IIN1678, from $100 to 135.00
Doctor, HN2858, from $250 to 300.00

Easter Day, HN2039, from $225 to 275.00
Elaine, HN3214, from $60 to 85.00
Elyse, HN2429, from $175 to 200.00
Enchantment, HN2178 .... 195.00
Entranced, HN3186, from $175 to 200.00
Europa & the Bull, HN2828, from $1,800 to 2,000.00
Fair Lady, HN3336 .... 235.00
Falstaff, HN3236, 3rd version 100.00
Felicity, HN3986, from $525 to 575.00
Flower of Love, HN2460, from $125 to 150.00
Fortune Teller, HN2159, from $565 to 625.00
Fragrance, HN2334, 1st version, from $130 to 165.00
Fragrance, HN3220, from $100 to 125.00
Friar Tuck, HN2143, from $575 to 625.00
Gay Morning, HN2135, from $275 to 300.00
Goody Two Shoes, HN2037, from $100 to 125.00
Gossips, HN2025, from $325 to 350.00
Graduate, HN3017, from $175 to 195.00
Grand Manner, HN2723, from $200 to 225.00
Hannah, HN3369, from $150 to 175.00
Harriet, HN3794 .... 200.00
Hello Daddy, HN3651, from $70 to 90.00
Her Ladyship, HN1977, from $325 to 365.00
In the Stocks, HN2163, from $650 to 750.00
Irish Charm, HN4580, from $285 to 315.00
Jacqueline, HN2333, from $185 to 215.00
Jean, HN3032, from $350 to 385.00
Jennifer, HN3447, from $335 to 375.00
Joanna, HN4711, from $175 to 195.00
Jovial Monk, HN2144, from $265 to 300.00
Joy, HN3875, from $75 to 95.00
Judge, HN2433 .... 165.00
Julia, HN2705, 1974, 7", from $175 to 220.00
Karen, HN2388, from $375 to 400.00
Katie, HN4460, from $285 to 315.00
Kirsty, HN2381, from $180 to 200.00
Lady Betty, HN1967, from $225 to 300.00
Lavinia, HN1955, from $90 to 120.00
Lobster Man, HN2317, from $125 to 175.00
Lunchtime, HN2485, from $165 to 185.00
Lydia, HN1908, 1st version, from $125 to 150.00
Make Believe, HN2224, from $100 to 120.00
Margaret, HN1989, 7½", from $275 to 300.00
Marguerite, HN1946, pk gown, 8¼" 500.00
Marie, HN1370, from $60 to 80.00
May Time, HN2113, 1952, 7½" 300.00
Medicant, HN1365, from $250 to 300.00
Melody, HN2202, from $275 to 295.00
Minuet, HN2019, from $220 to 245.00
Miranda, HN3037, from $135 to 180.00
Miss Muffet, HN1936, from $110 to 140.00
Monica, HN1467, 1st version, from $110 to 125.00
Nanny, HN2221, from $265 to 295.00
Newsvendor, HN2891, from $180 to 200.00
Nicola, HN28804, from $165 to 185.00
October, HN2693, 1st version, from $170 to 200.00
Omar Khayyam, HN2247 .... 200.00
Pantalettes, HN1362, 7½" 150.00
Penelope, HN1901, from $250 to 325.00
Pensive Moments, HN2704, from $175 to 225.00
Pride & Joy, HN2945, from $275 to 300.00
Primrose, HN3710 .... 250.00
Professor, HN2281, from $275 to 300.00
Punch & Judy Man, HN2765 .... 325.00

Rebecca, HN3414, from $125 to 145.00
Repose, HN2272, from $250 to 300.00
Reverie, HN2306, from $200 to 250.00
Rosie, HN4094, from $125 to 150.00
Royal Governor's Cook, HN2233, from $500 to 600.00
Sara, HN3249, from $100 to 130.00
Schoolmarm, HN2223, from $200 to 250.00
Shoreleave, HN2254, from $250 to 285.00
Sir Walter Raleigh, HN1751, 12" 480.00
Skater, HN2117, from $275 to 350.00
Slapdash, HN2277 .... 295.00
Soiree, HN2312, from $120 to 170.00
Song of the Sea, HN2729, from $200 to 250.00
Southern Belle, HN3244 .... 245.00
Spring, HN2085, from $275 to 350.00
Springtime, HN3033, 2nd version, from $165 to 190.00
Sunday Best, HN2698, from $180 to 225.00
Sweet & Twenty, HN1298, from $425 to 450.00
Tall Story, HN2248, from $325 to 400.00
Time for Bed, HN3762, from $70 to 80.00
Tony Weller, M47, from $60 to 75.00

Top o' the Hill, HN1834, 8", $235.00. (Photo courtesy Du Mouchelles/LiveAuctioneers.com)

Town Crier, HN2119, from $200 to 250.00
Uncle Ned, HN2094, from $225 to 300.00
Wedding Vows, HN2750, from $180 to 225.00
Wee Willie Winkie, HN2050, from $250 to 300.00
Young Master, HN2872, from $225 to 300.00

Flambé

Unless another color is noted, all flambé in the listing that follows is red.

Vase, gourd form, Noke/Flambé/FM, 7½", $780.00. (Photo courtesy David Rago Auctions)

Bowl, Sung, Asiatic pheasant on orange, Noke, hdls, early 20th C, 11" ... 3,900.00
Ducklings resting, HN239, from $675 to 700.00

Figurine, elephant standing w/trunk down, 13x18" 3,300.00
Figurine, Genie, HN2999, from $425 to 475.00
Figurine, Lamp Seller, HN3278 .... 435.00
Figurine, tiger stalking, 9" L 525.00
Vase, cottage scene, Noke, bulbous, 6" 450.00
Vase, deer silhouettes in landscape, woodcut, 1920-40, 8" 325.00
Vase, ovoid, Nouveau silver o/l (Gorham), D1460, late 19th C, 6¼" ... 950.00
Vase, Sung, lobed globular shape, #925, ca 1925, 7" 600.00
Vase, Sung, much bl, classic shape, Noke/Freed Moore, 10½" 660.00
Vases, Sung, bottle form, 1930, 10¾", pr 950.00

Lambeth

Humidor, embossed scrolls, 7", $275.00.
(Photo courtesy Jackson's International Auctioneers & Appraisers of Fine Art & Antiques/LiveAuctioneers.com)

Jardiniere, autumn leaves, 7x9" 395.00
Jug, Native Americans, K Kemeys for Burley & Co, 1898, 5½x10" ...515.00
Jug, Royal Jubilee, brn tones, 1887, 6" 150.00
Jug, willow pattern, brn & tan, 1¼" 75.00
Jug, 1893 Columbian Exposition, #8386, 7¼" 275.00
Pitcher, remedy quotes/vignettes, #4738, 9½" 100.00
Toby ashpot, man seated w/mug, HP decor, 4½" 500.00
Vase, floral, mc faience, rprs, 1879, 20¼" 950.00
Vase, floral & scrolls, cobalt/bl/wht, att W Rowe, #1818, 10¾" ... 660.00
Vase, frieze of donkeys, H Barlow, ca 1882, #119/#579, 11¼" ... 1,100.00
Vase, fruit on cobalt, E Beard, #8580, 1920s, 9¾" 395.00
Vase, gray & sage gr w/raised dots, slim, 19th C, mini, 2" 60.00
Vase, Nouveau decor, slim w/flared rim, brn int, 7" 110.00

Nursery Rhymes

Beaker, Polly Put the Kettle On, 3¾" 110.00
Bowl, cereal; Piper w/pig 45.00
Child's dish, Mary Quite Contrary, 7½", EX- 120.00
Pitcher, Little Tommy Tucker, ca 1910, cream sz, 3" 55.00
Plate, Pretty Maid, 8" 40.00
Plate, Simple Simon, ca 1907-39, 8", from $30 to 40.00

Series Ware

Bowl, depicts 'Deaf' and 'Room for One' scenes, crazing, 9", $900.00.

Bowl, Coaching Days, highwaymen chase coach, D2716, 4x8" ... 575.00
Jardiniere, Babes in Woods, girl w/doll, worn gold/crazing, 9x10" ...600.00
Jardiniere, Shakespeare, D2220 .... 275.00
Jug, Dickens, Regency Coach, #287/500, 11x10" 660.00

Jug, Dickens Dream, characters listed, figural hdl, Noke, 10½" .. 1,550.00
Jug, Hunting, John Peel, earthenware, D2716, 9" 450.00
Pastry dish, Landscapes, D2846 .... 110.00
Pitcher, Eglington Tournament, 7" 195.00
Plaque, Jackdaw of Rheims, 15¼" 250.00
Plate, Gibson Girl, She Finds That Exercise...Spirits, 10½" 75.00
Plate, Gibson Girl, Widow & Her Friends, 10½" 85.00
Plates, Coaching Days, ca 1905-55, 10¼", 12 for 450.00
Platter, Hunting, John Peel, oval, D2716, 13x11" 275.00
Punch bowl, Coachman, ftd, 6¾x12", NM 250.00
Punch bowl, Hunting, John Peel, D2716, 8x12" 660.00
Punch set, Dickens, D3020, 8¼x14¼" bowl+9 cups 1,200.00
Sandwich tray, Hunting, John Peel, D2716, 18" W 275.00
Teapot, Hunting, John Peel, low, E3804, 10" W 360.00
Tureen, vegetable; Coaching Days, w/lid, D2716, 1905-55, 6x12½" ..315.00
Vase, Babes in woods, girl w/guitar, gold trim/hdls, unmk, 6¾x6" ...600.00
Vase, Jackdaw of Rheims, 3 monks observe raven, 8¾" 180.00
Washbowl & pitcher, Watchman, ca 1901-02, 4¾x14½", 10½" ... 300.00
Whiskey flask, Kingsware, Scotsman w/bagpipes, 8½" 450.00

Stoneware

Humidor, autumn tree branches, #X8531/5761, early 20th C, 3¾" .. 150.00
Jug, cat reserves/foliage, F Barlow, late 19th C, 7⅜" 4,500.00
Pitcher, stylized plants, funny verse, ca 1910, 7½" 120.00
Pitcher, Twins, Hassall, #6628, 1910, 8" 360.00
Trump indicator, gnome figural, gr, L Harradiane, 1910s, 3⅝" 900.00
Vase, floral emb rim, cobalt & gold, 3-hdl, dtd 1904, 6¾x8" 100.00
Vase, floral tapestry w/gr & bl, sgn EG, flared ft & rim, 8" 100.00
Vase, floral w/gold, bulbous, cobalt neck, Slater's Pat, 15⅝", pr ... 180.00

Vase, freize with mountain goats, Hannah Barlow, 15½", $3,100.00. (Photo courtesy Cincinnati Art Galleries/ LiveAuctioneers.com)

Vase, Naughty Boy at No Fishing Hole, Hassall, X6634, 1910, 5" ..395.00
Vases, lilies on stippled ground, Slater's Pat, ca 1900, 12¾", pr 660.00
Vases, stylized floral band, mc on bl, slim neck, ca 1900, 13⅝", pr ..850.00

Toby Jugs

Falstaff, D6062, lg, from $90 to 120.00
Falstaff, D6063, sm 45.00
Father Christmas, D6940, 5½" 90.00
Happy John, D6031, lg, from $75 to 95.00
Happy John, D6070, sm, from $80 to 100.00
Huntsman, D6320, lg, from $90 to 120.00
Jester, D6910, sm, from $185 to 225.00
Jolly Toby, D6109, from $75 to 100.00
Mr Furrow the Farmer, D6701, from $100 to 120.00
Mr Mcawber, D6202, A mk 150.00
Old Charley, D6069, from $200 to 250.00

Sir Francis Drake, D6660, lg, from $100 to 125.00
Town Crier, D6920, 5" 75.00
Winston Churchill, D6175, sm, from $60 to 75.00

Miscellaneous

Bowl, Chang, lotus blossom shape, Noke/Nixon, 3x6¾" 1,200.00
Loving cup, King Geo/Queen Mary commemorative, Noke/Fenton, 1953, 10".950.00
Planter, Mirrisiar pattern, maidens w/instruments, bl & wht, 10x12" .600.00

Syrup pitcher, Chine, pewter lid, Slater's, 7", $120.00. (Photo courtesy Cincinnati Art Galleries/LiveAuctioneers.com)

Vase, Chang, cylindrical w/flared rim, Noke, 6¾" 2,000.00
Vase, Chang, shouldered w/sm collar, Noke/Nixon, 1920s, 9" ..2,100.00
Vase, farmer w/horses/sunset, Ferneyhough, Holbeinware, Burslem, 11" .600.00
Vase, Santa w/reindeer/Santa hitchhiking, #1046, 1904-14, 3½"....450.00
Vase, Titanium Ware, Herring Gulls, sgn H Allen, ca 1925, 7¾"..1,650.00

Royal Dux

The Duxer Porzellan Manufactur was established by E. Eichler in 1860. Located in what is now Duchcov, Czechoslovakia, the area was known as Dux, Bohemia, until WWI. The war brought about changes in both the style of the ware as well as the mark. Prewar pieces were modeled in the Art Nouveau or Greek Classical manner and marked with 'Bohemia' and a pink triangle containing the letter 'E.' They were usually matt glazed in green, brown, and gold. Better pieces were made of porcelain, while the larger items were of pottery. After the war the ware was marked with the small pink triangle but without the Bohemia designation; 'Made in Czechoslovakia' was added. The style became Art Deco, with cobalt blue a dominant color.

Bowl, center; couple amid waves, Hampel, #1119, 13x12", NM ...1,100.00
Bust, springtime maiden w/apple blossoms, earthenware, ca 1900, 21"...1,650.00
Card Tray, figural maid holds lg shallo bowl, wht, 6¾" 210.00
Centerpiece, couple amidst waves, Hampel, #1119, 13x12", NM..1,100.00
Centerpiece, maiden seated on shell, ca 1890, 19" 900.00
Centerpiece, Nouveau figure w/instrument at side of rim, 17½x14" ..1,550.00
Figurine, angelfish (2) on wht foliate base, #383, 9½" 135.00
Figurine, doe deer w/head down, 7½x11" 75.00
Figurine, elephant w/trunk up, brn-gray tones, 8" L 120.00
Figurine, girl feeding sheep, ca 1910, 30" 1,450.00
Figurine, water nymph rising from pool, early 20th C, 21⅜" 2,750.00
Group, Arab man on camel, servant at ft, 23½x19x18¼", NM..1,450.00
Group, Return from the Hunt, couple embrace, 27¾x15½", NM..2,100.00
Vase, draped nude stands at side, #652, 17½x9x8" 1,325.00
Vase, lady w/mandolin on front, gold & sepia tone, #17707, 23" . 900.00
Vase, leaves & berries, rtcl hdls, wht matt, 310574/BIS, 18½x8" .950.00
Vase, Nouveau lady picking grapes in relief, ca 1900, 25" 1,000.00
Vases, shepherd w/lute & dog/lady w/basket & lamb, ca 1900, 20½", pr.1,650.00

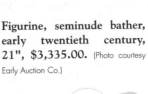

Figurine, seminude bather, early twentieth century, 21", $3,335.00. (Photo courtesy Early Auction Co.)

Royal Flemish

Royal Flemish was introduced in the late 1880s and was patented in 1894 by the Mt. Washington Glass Company. Transparent glass was enameled with one or several colors and the surface divided by a network of raised lines suggesting leaded glasswork. Some pieces were further decorated with enameled florals, birds, or Roman coins.

Biscuit jar, frosted panels w/mc foliage, rpl lid, 1890s, 7" 1,450.00
Biscuit jar, lg Roman coins, SP lid, ovoid, 6½" 1,800.00
Ewer, shields of armor/flowers, bulbous, 1890s, 8¾" 4,550.00
Jug, coats of arms/rampant lions, earth tones w/gold, 1890s, 11¾" . 4,500.00
Lamp, cherub figural, clear glass globe, oil font base 425.00
Toothpick holder, mums, wht/yel on amber, paneled/beaded rim, 1½"...865.00
Vase, dragon/dragon's head w/gold on bittersweet & frost, 7½"..2,350.00
Vase, fish & underwater plants, slim ovoid, ca 1890, 13¾", NM ...9,000.00

Vase, Garden of Allah, 14", $6,000.00. (Photo courtesy Early Auction Co.)

Vase, gold medallions/floral scrolls, spherical, 1890s, 7½" 2,000.00
Vase, griffin medallions, scrollwork stick neck, 1890s, 11¾" 2,500.00
Vase, mythological bird, gold/tans/brns, ruffled rim, 1890s, 14½" ..3,000.00

Royal Haeger, Haeger

In 1871 David Henry Haeger, a young son of German immigrants, purchased a brick factory at Dundee, Illinois. David's bricks rebuilt Chicago after their great fire in 1871. Many generations of the Haeger family have been associated with the ceramic industry, that his descendants have pursued to the present time. Haeger progressed to include artware in its production as early as 1914. That was only the beginning. In the '30s it began to make a line of commercial dinnerware that was marketed through Marshall Fields. Not long after, Haeger's artware was successful enough that a second plant in Macomb, Illinois, was built.

Royal Haeger was its premium line beginning in 1938 and continuing into modern-day production. The chief designer in the '40s was Royal Arden Hickman, a talented artist and sculptor who also worked in mediums other than pottery. For Haeger he designed a line of wonderfully stylized animals, birds, high-style vases, and human figures, all with extremely fine details. His designs are highly regarded by collectors today.

Paper labels have been used throughout Haeger's production. Some items from the teens, '20s, and '30s will be found with 'Haeger' in a diamond shape in-mold script mark. Items with 'RG' (Royal Garden) are part of its Flower-Ware line (also called Regular Haeger or Genuine Haeger). Haeger has produced a premium line (Royal Haeger) as well as a regular line for many years, it just has changed names over the years.

Collectors need to be aware that a certain glaze can bring two to three times more than others. Items that have Royal Hickman in the mold mark or on the label are usually higher valued than without his mark. The current collector trend has leaned more towards the mid-century modern styled pieces of artware. The most desired items are ones done by glaze designers Helmut Bruchman and Alrun Osterberg Guest. These items are from the late '60s into the very early '80s. For those wanting to learn more about this pottery, we recommend *Haeger Potteries Through the Years* by our advisor for this category, David Dilley (L-W Books); he is listed in the Directory under Indiana.

#7, cockatoo, pk, unmk, 1933, 3x4", from $15 to 20.00
#60, bowl planter, Green Agate, ca 1936, 3½x6", from $20 to 30.00
#109-S, Square ashtray, Gold Tweed, 2¼x7", from $8 to 10.00
#134, Palm Leaf ashtray, Green Agate, 2¼x19x4¼", from $10 to .. 15.00
#345-S, bowl, scalloped & indented, Lilac, 5x4¼", from $15 to 20.00
#500-H, planter, Earth Graphic Wrap, Marigold Agate, 8x12", $100 to......125.00
#725, wall pocket, gr, ca 1953, 5¼x6½x2¾", from $20 to................ 25.00
#837, Girl Head, Gold Tweed, 8½x6", from $60 to 75.00
#2058-X, ashtray, Earth Graphic Wrap, brn, 6¾", from $10 to 15.00
#3068, Triple candleholder dish, brn w/wht accents, 12" dia, $30 to ... 45.00
#3928, goblet, gold, 9½x4½", from $10 to....................................... 15.00
#4233-X, vase, Earth Graphic Wrap, brn, 11", from $20 to............. 30.00
#6343, matador, Haeger Red, gold foil crown label, 11⅜", $40 to .. 50.00
#8172, bowl planter, Roman Bronze, 6½x8¾", from $50 to............. 75.00
#8296, Toe Tapper, Bennington Brown Foam, 9¼", from $35 to.... 50.00
R-132, ram bookends, bl-gr w/brn & bl spots, 8x8½", from $125 to.... 150.00
R-158, Inebriated Duck, fallen, 10", from $35 to............................. 50.00
R-185, Flower & Leaf candleholders, lt bl w/gr, 2½", pr, $60 to 75.00
R-188, cookie jar, emb shells, rose & bl, 10½", from $15 to 250.00
R-224, daisy bowl, 12", from $30 to 40.00
R-297, shell dish, chartreuse & Silver Spray, 14" L, from $20 to......30.00
R-303, Laurel Wreath Bow vase, Mauve Agate, 12x7¾", from $50 to 75.00
R-312, Cornucopia candleholders, Green Briar, ca 1949, 5", pr, $25 to ... 35.00
R-320, Elm Leaf vase, Mauve Agate, 12", from $20 to 30.00
R-359, 2 Birds flower frog, Cloudy Blue, 1940s, 8¾x5", from $10 to..... 150.00

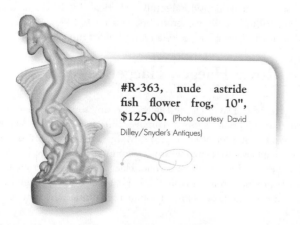

#R-363, nude astride fish flower frog, 10", $125.00. (Photo courtesy David Dilley/Snyder's Antiques)

R-370, Dutch Cup bowl, Green Agate, 18½" L, from $30 to 40.00
R-421, bowl w/clusters, Green Agate, 7x14½x8", from $40 to....... 50.00
R-455, Bow lamp base, Mauve Agate, unmk, 13½x5", from $60 to..... 75.00
R-476, beaded bowl, chartreuse & Silver Spray, 15" L, from $20 to.....25.00
R-508, dolphin vase, 18", from $65 to.. 90.00
R-538, panther planter/bookends, Ebony, 1950s, from $10 to...... 150.00
R-575, Rose of Sharon basket, chartreuse/red flowers, 7" dia, $50 to ... 75.00
R-641, stallion planter/bookends, chartreuse, unmk, 8¾", $40 to 50.00
R-713, swan vase, 8", from $20 to 25.00
R-752, fish planter, 8½", from $18 to 24.00
R-776, cocker spaniel, sleeping, 6", from $30 to 45.00
R-777, cocker spaniel, brn w/blk tail, unmk, 1950s, 3x5½", $35 to.... 40.00
R-831, resting stag planter, 15", from $50 to.................................. 75.00
R-875, colt planter, 14", from $135 to... 150.00
R-1114, open leaf vase, 9", from $30 to.. 40.00
R-1121, vase, Green Agate, foil crown label, 5¾x5¾x3", $15 to ... 20.00
R-1161, window box, 13½", from $20 to.. 25.00
R-1204, leaf bowl, single, 9", from $12 to 18.00
R-1239, bronco TV planter, 12", from $100 to 125.00
R-1262, Prancing Horse TV lamp, chartreuse & Honey, 10¼", $45 to .. 50.00
R-1316, dbl-leaf wall pocket, 11½", from $35 to............................ 45.00
R-1360, shell bowl, 15", from $20 to.. 30.00
R-1416, planter, oblong, w/stand, 14", from $30 to 40.00
R-1730, candy jar, Mandarin Orange, 10x7", from $10 to.............. 15.00
R-1782, lamb w/silk ribbon & bell, White Stone Lace, 15x17", $80 to...100.00

Royal Rudolstadt

The hard-paste porcelain that has come to be known as Royal Rudolstadt was produced in Thuringia, Germany, in the early eighteenth century. Various names and marks have been associated with this pottery. One of the earliest was a hay-fork symbol associated with Johann Frederich von Schwarzburg-Rudolstadt, one of the first founders. Variations, some that included an 'R,' were also used. In 1854 Earnst Bohne produced wares that were marked with an anchor and the letters 'EB.' Examples commonly found today were made during the late 1800s and early 1900s. These are usually marked with an 'RW' within a shield under a crown and the words 'Crown Rudolstadt.' Items marked 'Germany' were made after 1890.

Bust of boy, hand-painted bisque, ca. 1900, bolted pedestal, $200.00. (Photo courtesy Du Mouchelles/LiveAuctioneers.com)

Centerpc, bird perched on cornucopia, 10x15" 360.00
Ewer, violets on wht w/gold, pierced hdl, 14½".............................. 215.00
Figurine, cherubs (2) on basket of flowers, 19th C, 6" 300.00
Figurine, draped nude w/shell stands on raised base, 17½", EX 250.00
Figurine, maiden speaking to cherub on plinth, 19th C, 12x7".....480.00
Figurine, Rebecca at the Well, sm rstr, 27" 900.00
Figurines, man w/feathered hat, girl w/instrument, 19", 18", pr ...550.00

Potpourri jar, floral on ivory, pierced lid, 19th C, 9" 155.00
Urn, floral w/classical busts at hdls, gold trim, 19¼" 360.00
Vase, floral w/gold, Nouveau pierced hdls & rim, #6992, 12½" 155.00

Royal Vienna

In 1719 Claude Innocentius de Paquier established a hard-paste porcelain factory in Vienna where he made highly ornamental wares similar to the type produced at Meissen. Early wares were usually unmarked; but after 1744, when the factory was purchased by the Empress, the Austrian shield (often called 'beehive') was stamped on under the glaze. In the following listings, values are for hand-painted items unless noted otherwise. Decal-decorated items would be considerably lower.

Note: There is a new resurgence of interest in this fine porcelain, but an influx of Japanese reproductions on the market has affected values on genuine old Royal Vienna. Buyer beware! On new items the beehive mark is over the glaze, the weight of the porcelain is heavier, and the decoration is obviously decaled. Our advisor for this category is Madeleine France; she is listed in the Directory under Florida.

Bowl, centerpc; scenic bands, ornate gold, 1860s, 12¼x18½x9½" ... 12,000.00
Box, Psyche after W Kray, cobalt w/gold, #3692, 3¾x6" dia 3,250.00
Charger, Achilles w/centaur hunting, sgn Beers, 16", in 21½" fr .. 4,500.00
Charger, allegorical scene w/gold border, ca 1850, 17½" 5,250.00
Charger, child's portrait, red cap/gr outfit, sgn Calbach, 14" 6,300.00
Charger, classical figures in scene, 19th C, 15" 3,000.00
Charger, figures on raft, red & gold border, 19¾" 3,850.00
Charger, lady w/floral wreath, cobalt & gold, 19th C 7,500.00
Charger, Samson scene, sgn Forster, 1890s, 17⅞" 3,600.00
Group, man w/mask by lady at dressing table, rprs, 18th C, 3¼" ... 1,325.00
Group, 2 girls hold basket planter between them, pastels, 26x16" .. 3,000.00
Humidor, monk smoking cigar on brn w/gold, 8" 1,325.00
Plaque, ladies encircle Cupid, sgn Johner, ornate border, 18x23" ... 3,500.00

Plaque, religious scholars in debate, #859, repaired, 18½x13", in gold frame, 27x22", $1,380.00. (Photo courtesy Early Auction Co.)

Plate, brunette w/low-cut gown, Pilr, floral turq/cobalt/gold rim, 10" .. 1,650.00
Plate, couple at table, sgn Gorner, gold rim, 9⅝", NM 1,800.00
Plate, Flower Seller portrait on cobalt w/gold, 9⅝" 1,200.00
Plate, lady's portrait, sgn Gorner, jeweled rim, 19th C, 9½" 1,800.00
Plate, lady's portrait, sgn Wagner, 9½", in gilt 21x17" fr 3,600.00
Plate, Louise portrait, sgn Wagner, floral rim w/gold, 9¾" 2,650.00
Stein, courting scene on gr w/gold flowers & scrolls, mini, 3¾" ... 1,325.00
Stein, Pan & Venus, gold trim, hinged lid, ca 1900, 6¼" 2,100.00
Tea caddy, Venus & Psyche (in front panel), sgn Knoallez, gold lid, 6" ... 1,950.00

Teapot, children band on cobalt w/gold, bronze doré hdl, rpl lid, 6" .. 1,200.00
Tray, glove; Hector Taking Leave of Andromache, 19th C, 11½x8½" . 1,950.00
Urn, classical panels/cherubs, turq & gold, 3-paw ft, 19th C, 18", pr .6,000.00
Urn, figures in reserves/florals, drum base, gold hdls, 1880s, 22", pr ..8,000.00
Urn, ladies & Cupid on bl, gold hdls & lid, stepped ft, 19th C, 22" .6,600.00
Urn, Wagnerian opera scene, sgn Wagner, 4 ogee ft, w/lid, 1870-90, 21" .. 5,500.00
Urn, 3 ladies in reserve on bl w/gold, pine cone finial, 1890, 33½" ..7,500.00
Vase, Anemone, lady's portrait reserve on copper w/gold, 19th C, 11". 3,250.00
Vase, classical lady seated in gilt fr, sgn Wagner, #38070, 1900, 10" .2,400.00
Vase, draped nude in landscape w/gold, 19th C, 13" 4,000.00
Vase, lady's portrait, Wagner, w/gold, w/flared cylinder, 12" 3,600.00
Vase, man w/pipe/lady at side in reserve on gr w/gold, #3642, 20½" .2,500.00
Vase, nymphs in garden, sgn Zwierzina, gold neck/ft, rpr, 19th C, 26" .. 3,600.00
Vase, putti & goddess, snakes entwine hdls, 19th C, 20½" 4,250.00
Vase, Queen Louise of Prussia, simple gold hdls, ca 1900, 9¾" .. 1,325.00
Vase, Ruth w/wheat in reserve, jewels & gold, socle base, 1870s, 18" ... 3,000.00
Vase, seminude in reserve, gold bands/foliage, late 19th C, 12½" ... 3,500.00
Vase, Spring & Summer, sgn Wagner, coral & ivory w/gold, 20" 4,250.00
Vase, Supplication, prayerful lady, sgn Donath, ca 1900, 32½" ..6,000.00

Roycroft

Near the turn of the twentieth century, Elbert Hubbard established the Roycroft Printing Shop in East Aurora, New York. Named in honor of two seventeenth-century printer-bookbinders, the print shop was just the beginning of a community called Roycroft, which came to be known worldwide. Hubbard became a popular personality of the early 1900s, known for his talents in a variety of areas from writing and lecturing to manufacturing. The Roycroft community became a meeting place for people of various capabilities and included shops for the production of furniture, copper, leather items, and a multitude of other wares which were marked with the Roycroft symbol, an 'R' within a circle below a double-barred cross. Hubbard lost his life on the Lusitania in 1915; production at the community continued until the Depression.

Interest is strong in the field of Arts and Crafts in general and in Roycroft items in particular. Copper items are evaluated to a large extent by the condition and type of the original patina. The most desirable patina is either the dark or medium brown; brass-wash, gunmetal, and silver-wash patinas follow in desirability. The acid-etched patina and the smooth (unhammered) surfaced Roycroft pieces are later (after 1925) developments and tend not to be attractive to collectors. Furniture was manufactured in oak, mahogany, bird's-eye maple, and occasionally walnut or ash; collectors prefer oak. Books with Levant binding, tooled leather covers, Japanese vellum, or hand illumining are especially collectible; suede cover and parchment paper books are of less interest to collectors as they are fairly common. In the listings that follow, values reflect the worth of items in excellent to near-mint original condition unless noted to the contrary. Our advisor for this category is Bruce Austin; he is listed in the Directory under New York.

Key: h/cp — hammered copper

Andirons, blk enameled curled elements w/twisted rings, 1901, 21", pr .6,600.00
Armchair rocker, mahog w/tacked-on vinyl seat, 35½" 1,325.00
Ash stand, h/cp, oak base, cleaned patina, sm split, 32x10" 500.00
Ash stand, h/cp, 4 riveted legs, 28½x7½" 850.00
Bench, Ali Baba #046, plank seat, bark to underside, keyed tenons, 42" ..9,000.00
Bench, piano; keyed-thru tenons, shelf, rfn, 20x36x16" 4,200.00
Bookcase, 3 1-pane doors, 3 adjustable shelves, 61½x79x16" ..9,600.00
Bookends, h/cp, poppies, 5½x5", pr 550.00
Bookends, leather-wrapped w/ornate tooling, 5¼x6", pr 500.00
Bookstand, Little Journeys, top over 2 shelves, tag, 26x26x14" ... 600.00
Bookstand, sq top, 5 fixed shelves, rfn, 64x18x17¾" 6,000.00

Bowl, h/cp, 3-ftd, 4x10½" 1,100.00
Candlesticks, h/cp, flared ft & cup, sm dents, 6½x3¼", pr........... 780.00

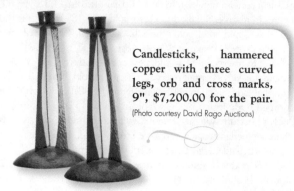

Candlesticks, hammered copper with three curved legs, orb and cross marks, 9", $7,200.00 for the pair.
(Photo courtesy David Rago Auctions)

Candlesticks, Secessionist, sm sqs in rnd base, D Hunter, 8¼x5", pr..8,500.00
Ceiling fixture, ldgl drops w/chains & 20¼" ceiling cap, 22" L..30,000.00
Chairs, dining; vertical slat bks, leather seats, 1 arm+4 sides 4,500.00
Chandelier, h/cp, 3-socket, orig chains/cap, from Roycroft Inn, 31x17"...7,200.00
Chest, bride's; planks w/keyed-thru tenons, iron strap hinges, 21x39".. 12,000.00
Desk, typewriter-concealing flip-top lid, 2 banks of drws, 30x56x30"... 4,200.00
Firestarter, h/cp & brass w/spill tray, cleaned, +19½" hdld stick .. 1,300.00
Footstool, burgundy leather top tacked on, 11x16x9" 1,100.00
Frame, 6-section, mullioned, w/period mottos, 18¼x21"...........2,500.00
Frame w/sgn photo of Elbert Hubbard, rfn, 1914, 21½x17½" 900.00
Lamp, brass-washed 3-socket base; Steuben glass shade, rpl finial, 18"....9,000.00
Lamp, h/cp, amber lustre Steuben shade; 3-socket std, 16x10"...6,000.00
Lamp, h/cp helmet shade w/mica panels, woodgrain std, 13¾x6" .. 3,250.00
Lamp, h/cp helmet shade w/mica panels; orig patina, 14½x7¼".. 4,200.00
Lamp, h/cp sq shade lined w/gr glass; oak base, D Hunter, 23x16x16".. 12,000.00
Lamp, h/cp w/helmet shade, fine patina, 14x6" 2,500.00
Lamp, h/cp w/helmet shade, old cleaned patina, 18½x7½" 2,200.00
Lamp, ldgl conical shade; h/cp baluster std w/2 ring hdls, 19x15" . 20,000.00
Luggage rack, slatted top, 25¾x30x18" 1,200.00
Mat, leather w/tooled flowers & leaves, att, 20x39¼"................2,950.00
Sconce, ldgl cylindrical shade; wall cap, D Hunter, 8½x5x6¼" .. 9,600.00
Sconce, Secessionist, copper/silver w/gr/purple ldgl cylinder, 15x6x6" .36,000.00
Sconces, h/cp, curled hdl, heart-shaped cutout, 10¼x5", pr 660.00
Sign, h/cp, Twildo (It will do), dk patina, unmk, 4x20" 7,800.00
Stand, magazine; #078, 3-shelf, arched top rail, recoated, 38x18x16". 4,800.00
Stand, magazine; #080, trapezoidal, cvd orb & X, 64x17¾x17¾". 14,000.00
Table, library; arrow-shaped stretchers, old rfn, 30x42x30" 1,325.00
Table, library; shelf w/cutouts, keyed-thru tenons, 31x50x33" ..2,525.00
Table, occasional; slat top, trestle ft, 26x30x18" 1,000.00
Table, vanity; #110, 1-drw, w/mirror bk, 56x39x17½" 3,950.00
Tray, h/cp, tooled florals, 10" dia 700.00
Trays, h/cp, hdls, old polish, 15" dia... 950.00
Vase, bud; h/cp in woodgrain pattern, orig glass liner, 8½x3¾" 660.00

Vase, Dard Hunter design, orb and cross mark, 7½", $7,800.00.
(Photo courtesy David Rago Auctions)

Vase, h/cp, Am Beauty, from Grove Park Inn, 21x8"...............6,000.00
Vase, h/cp, Am Beauty, riveted base, cylinder neck, new patina, 12x6"..1,800.00
Vase, h/cp, floriform rim, 9x4" 575.00
Vase, h/cp, floriform/spherical, 3x4" 400.00
Vase, h/cp, ruffled rim, flared ft, 5½" 275.00
Vase, h/cp, sm flared rim, 8¼x4", pr 2,050.00
Vase, h/cp, 4 riveted buttress hdls, 4 sm silver sqs, 7½x4½".......6,000.00
Vase, h/cp w/brass wash & silver o/l, cylindrical, 6x3"............. 950.00
Vase, h/cp w/brass wash full-height buttresses, 7x3½" 3,400.00
Vase, h/cp w/etched dogwood, cylindrical, med patina, unmk, 7x2½"....2,050.00
Vase, h/cp w/silver o/l band, cylindrical, 6¼x3" 1,440.00
Wastebasket, #023, vertical slats, touched up/coated, 16x14x14" . 1,025.00

Rozenburg

Some of the most innovative and original Art Nouveau ceramics were created by the Rozenburg factory at the Hague in the Netherlands between 1883 and 1914, when production ceased. (Several of their better painters continued to work in Gouda, which accounts for some pieces being similar to Gouda.) Rozenburg also made highly prized eggshell ware, so called because of its very thin walls; this is eagerly sought after by collectors. T.A.C. Colenbrander was their artistic leader, with Samuel Schellink and J. Kok designing many of the eggshell pieces. The company liquidated in 1917. Most pieces carry a date code. Our advisor for this category is Ralph Jaarsma; he is listed in the Directory under Iowa.

Charger, rooster, #1293, ca. 1900, 17½", $6,465.00.
(Photo courtesy Skinner Inc. Auctioneers & Appraisers of Antiques & Fine Art)

Cup & saucer, demi; flowers & bird, eggshell ware, 8-sided, 2¼", 4" ..1,800.00
Panel, Dutch cityscape after Springer, 12-tile, 18x24"...............3,575.00
Panel, mother & children at table after Artz, 12-tile, 24x18" ...2,050.00
Plaque, dikes & windmills after Gabriel, sepia tones, 5½x17¼"+fr .. 900.00
Plaque, Gothic cathedral int after Bosboom, ca 1895, 19½x12½".1,080.00
Plaque, man smoking, Eerllman, sepia tones, 1889, sight: 11x8½"+fr.. 1,000.00
Plaque, mother feeds baby after Blommers, sepia tones, 11½x9"+fr.660.00
Plaque, young lady drinking after Terborch, 1895, 20¼x16¾" ..1,325.00
Vase, birds & exotic flowers, integral hdls, 8½", NM................... 550.00
Vase, floral, Schellink, basket form, arched hdl, ftd, 1902, 5¾"..5,750.00
Vase, Nouveau birds & flowers, #W249V, ca 1904, 19½" 5,000.00
Vase, Nouveau floral, brn integral hdls, crown mk, ca 1900, 8" ...480.00

Rubena

Rubena glass was made by several firms in the late 1800s. It is a blown art glass that shades from clear to red. See also Art Glass Baskets; Cruets; Sugar Shakers; Salts; specific manufacturers.

Bottle, scent; cut body, faceted stopper, 5⅜" 150.00
Celery vase, Invt T'print, 6" 85.00
Creamer, Coinspot w/enameled flowers, 4" 150.00
Ewer, claret; birds in garden enamel, bronze mts, 16x4¼" 650.00
Pitcher, Dmn Quilt, 9½x6½" 525.00

Pitcher, Hobnail, sq rim, camphor hdl, 7"......................285.00
Pitcher, Invt T'print, rope twist hdl, 7½" 200.00
Rose bowl, 4"...250.00
Vase, bud; bulbous fuchsia top/ft, slim amber stem, 4"..........950.00
Vase, butterflies, sm neck, 8" 75.00
Vase, gilt spider mums, cylindrical, 9¾" 145.00
Vase, Invt T'print w/HP flowers/birds, Aurora SP fr, 8", NM.......335.00

Rugs

Hooked rugs are treasured today for their folk-art appeal. Rug making was a craft that was introduced to this country in about 1830 and flourished its best in the New England states. The prime consideration when evaluating one of these rugs is not age but artistic appeal. Scenes with animals, buildings, and people; patriotic designs; or whimsical themes are preferred. Those with finely conceived designs, great imagination, interesting color use, etc., demand higher prices. Condition is, of course, also a factor. Our values reflect the worth of hooked rugs in at least excellent condition, unless otherwise noted. Other types of rugs may be listed as well. This information will be given within the lines. Marked examples bearing the stamps of 'Frost and Co.,' 'Abenakee,' 'C.R.,' and 'Ouia' are highly prized. See also Orientalia, Rugs.

Barnyard scene w/animals/birds, wool/cotton on burlap, 31x37" .725.00
Bluebirds & poinsettias, cotton/wool on burlap, 40x25" 230.00
Boy stands w/hat, short pants, high boots, floral border, 40x19" ..800.00
Cat on oval rug, denim & knit stockings on burlap, 41x31" 925.00
Couple silhouettes in landscape, floral border, 46x24" 145.00
Dog w/collar, tan/blk/gr, wool on burlap, 32x53" 780.00
Elephant on striped ground, earth tones, wools, 32x38"...........575.00
Floral designs on stripes, wool on burlap, 30x56"................200.00
Flower wreath, mc on gray & blk squiggles, on hinged stretcher, 57x56".460.00
Flowers in scalloped oval, stylized leaves, wool on canvas, 68x34"..175.00
Flowers in vase/strawberries/hummingbird, wool on burlap, 36x49" ..500.00
German shepherd & Labrador retriever on striations, sm rpr, 24x36". 115.00
Grapevine surrounds mustard center, gray border, wool, 43x25", VG...100.00

Grenfell, Canada Geese, cloth label, $4,560.00. (Photo courtesy Jackson's International Auctioneers & Appraisers of Fine Art & Antiques)

Grid filled w/mc wavy lines, wool/cotton, ca 1900, 70x70" 1,300.00
Horse portrait in medallion, cotton/wool on burlap, 29x43"........250.00
Horse trotting, velvet/wool/sateen on burlap, rprs, 27x39" 300.00
Houses & Christmas trees, mc on beige, wool, ca 1900, 24x40".. 1,400.00
Lion reclines in oval reserve, foliage border, 24x38"....................175.00
Penny, concentric mc disks, wool on cotton bk, 90x26" 3,000.00
Roses bouquet among buds/stems, wool on burlap, 29x56" 345.00

Spaniel reclining, mc border, wool/cotton/rayon on burlap, 21x36" ...240.00
Swan swimming amid foliage & stripes, wool on burlap, rprs, 33x45" ..900.00

RumRill

George Rumrill designed and marketed his pottery designs from 1933 until his death in 1942. During this period of time, four different companies produced his works. Today the most popular designs are those made by the Red Wing Stoneware Company from 1933 until 1936 and Red Wing Potteries from 1936 until early 1938. Some of these lines include Trumpet Flower, Classic, Manhattan, and Athena, the Nudes.

For a period of months in 1938, Shawnee took over the production of RumRill pottery. This relationship ended abruptly, and the Florence Pottery took over and produced his wares until the plant burned down. The final producer was Gonder. Pieces from each individual pottery are easily recognized by their designs, glazes, and/or signatures. It is interesting to note that the same designs were produced by all three companies. They may be marked RumRill or with the name of the specific company that made them. For more information we recommend *RumRill Pottery, The Ohio Years*, by Francesca Fisher (Collector Books). Our advisors for this category are Leo and Wendy Frese; they are listed in the Directory under Texas.

Ball jug, orange, w/orig cork, #50, 7"................................55.00
Centerpiece, dbl-shell cornucopia, cream to brn, 5x19"..............115.00
Figurine, cowgirl, hands in pockets, mc, 10¾" 145.00
Party platter, 3-tier, brn to gr w/emb rockwork, from $35 to 50.00
Planter, pk basket form, #H360, 5¾x9½x6½" 20.00
Planter, wht semigloss, lg arch hdl over 2-lobe leafy base, #H39....50.00

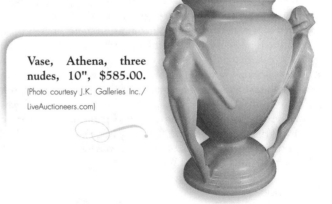

Vase, Athena, three nudes, 10", $585.00. (Photo courtesy J.K. Galleries Inc./ LiveAuctioneers.com)

Vase, bl mottle, emb ribs, w/hdls, #299, 6½x7½" 42.50
Vase, celadon gr, ovoid, 24"..165.00
Vase, Classical Greek form, bl speckles, 5".............................36.00
Vase, cream to gr, hdls, #299, 6½x7½" 42.50
Vase, Dutch Blue, swan hdls, #279, 4½".................................60.00
Vase, gr matt, hexagonal, #297, 5¼x3¾"................................52.50
Vase, gr to orange, elephant-head hdls, #215, sm stain, 6x7" 125.00
Vase, head of woman, bl gloss, #1001, 11" 500.00
Vase, Scarlet/Bay Purple, bulbous w/hdls, #302, 1938, 5½x3" 60.00

Ruskin

This English pottery operated near Birmingham from 1889 until 1935. Its founder was W. Howson Taylor, and it was named in honor of the renowned author and critic, John Ruskin. The earliest marks were 'Taylor' in block letters and the initials 'WHT,' the smaller W and H superimposed over the larger T. Later marks included the Ruskin name.

Vase, bl & wht drips, ovoid, ca 1932, 8¾x5" 100.00
Vase, cream & gr crystalline, 6-sided, 4⅝" 395.00
Vase, flower band at shoulder, gr & rose on teal over purple, 5¼" ...395.00
Vase, gray to cobalt, ovoid, 3¼x2½" 60.00
Vase, lt gr irid, shouldered, 1914, 7⅞x4¼" 85.00
Vase, pk w/almond mottling & MOP lustre, shouldered, 1923, 9¾" ..660.00

Vase, purple, green, and red crystalline, stamped Ruskin 1910 Pottery, 9½", $1,600.00.
(Photo courtesy David Rago Auctions)

Vase, yel drip, trumpet neck, 1924, 8⅞x4" 100.00
Vase, yel lustre, shouldered, 9½x5" 100.00

Russel Wright Dinnerware

Russel Wright, one of America's foremost industrial designers, also designed several lines of ceramic dinnerware, glassware, and aluminum ware that are now highly sought-after collectibles. His most popular dinnerware then and with today's collectors, American Modern, was manufactured by the Steubenville Pottery Company from 1939 until 1959. It was produced in a variety of solid colors in assortments chosen to stay attune with the times. Casual (his first line sturdy enough to be guaranteed against breakage for 10 years from date of purchase) is relatively easy to find today — simply because it has held up so well. During the years of its production, the Casual line was constantly being restyled, some items as many as five times. Early examples were heavily mottled, while later pieces were smoothly glazed and sometimes patterned. The ware was marked with Wright's signature and 'China by Iroquois.' It was marketed in fine department stores throughout the country. After 1950 the line was marked 'Iroquois China by Russel Wright.'

American Modern

To calculate values for American Modern, at the least, double the low values listed for these colors: Canteloupe, Glacier Blue, Bean Brown, and White. Chartreuse is represented by the low end of our range; Cedar, Black Chutney, and Seafoam by the high end; and Coral and Gray near the middle.

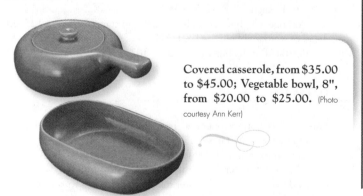

Covered casserole, from $35.00 to $45.00; Vegetable bowl, 8", from $20.00 to $25.00. (Photo courtesy Ann Kerr)

Bowl, salad; 6x11", from $40 to 50.00
Butter dish, orig style, from $150 to 200.00
Casserole, 2-qt, from $50 to 75.00
Coffeepot, 6½", from $175 to 225.00
Creamer, from $15 to 20.00
Plate, chop; 13½", from $35 to 50.00
Plate, dinner; from $20 to 25.00
Plate, salad; 6", from $12 to 18.00
Plate, 8", from $15 to 25.00
Sugar bowl, from $20 to 25.00
Vegetable dish, w/lid, from $50 to 75.00

Glass

Morgantown Modern is most popular in Seafoam, Coral, and Chartreuse. In the Flair line, colors other than crystal and pink are rare and expensive. Seafoam is hard to find in Pinch; Canteloupe is scarce, so double the prices for that color, and Ruby Flair is very rare.

Bartlett-Collins Eclipse, ice tub, from $45 to 50.00
Bartlett-Collins Eclipse, shot glass, 2", from $25 to 28.00
Bartlett-Collins Eclipse, tumbler, iced tea; 7", from $20 to 25.00
Imperial Flare, tumbler, iced tea; 14-oz, from $50 to 60.00
Imperial Pinch, tumbler, water; 11-oz, from $25 to 35.00
Imperial Twist, tumbler, juice; from $35 to 50.00
Old Morgantown/Modern, cordial, 2", from $20 to 25.00

Old Morgantown/Modern, dessert dish, from $35.00 to $45.00. (Photo courtesy Ann Kerr)

Old Morgantown/Modern, goblet, iced tea; 5¼", from $25 to 30.00
Old Morgantown/Modern, sherbet, 2¾", from $25 to 30.00
Snow Glass, bowl, fruit; 5", from $100 to 125.00
Snow Glass, bowl, salad; from $175 to 200.00
Snow Glass, saucer, from $65 to 75.00

Highlight

Creamer, from $40 to 55.00
Cup, from $40 to 55.00
Plate, bread & butter; from $12 to 15.00
Platter, lg, from $55 to 75.00
Vegetable dish, from $100 to 150.00

Iroquois Casual

To price Sugar White, Charcoal, and Oyster, use the high end of the pricing range. Canteloupe commands premium prices, and even more valuable are Brick Red and Aqua.

Bowl, salad, 10", from $35 to 45.00
Carafe, from $200 to 225.00
Casserole, dome lid, 2-qt, 8", from $35 to 45.00
Casserole, wht, domed lid, 6-qt 200.00
Mug, orig, 13-oz, from $80 to 120.00
Plate, chop; 14", from $50 to 60.00

Plate, luncheon; 9½", from $10 to.. 12.00
Platter, 14½", from $55 to... 65.00
Shakers, stacking, pr 200.00

Spun Aluminum

Russel Wright's aluminum ware may not have been especially well accepted in its day — it tended to damage easily and seems to have had only limited market appeal — but today's collectors feel quite differently about it, as is apparent in the suggested values noted in the following listings.

Candelabra, from $225 to... 350.00
Cheese server, domed lid, wooden insert, 16¼" 180.00
Ice bucket, wicker hdl, from Informal line, 7x4x6½"............... 850.00
Ice fork, from $75 to 100.00
Pitcher, sherry; from $250 to 275.00

Spaghetti service, 9" bowl with holder for cheese and sauce pitcher, tray with wooden surface, tongs, $1,700.00. (Photo courtesy David Rago Auctions)

Tidbit, 2-tier, arched wicker hdl, 3½", from $150 to 200.00
Vase, ball form, lg, from $300 to.. 400.00
Vase, ball form, sm, from $150 to... 200.00

Sterling

Celery dish, 11", from $28 to... 36.00
Creamer, 1-oz, from $12 to 15.00
Cup, 7-oz, from $13 to 15.00
Plate, dinner; 10", from $10 to... 15.00
Sauceboat, 9-oz, from $25 to 27.00
Sugar bowl, 10-oz, from $22 to 25.00

Miscellaneous

Country Garden, bowl, serving; from $175 to............................ 250.00
Everlast Gold Aluminite, pitcher, from $200 to 250.00
Everlast Gold Aluminite, tumbler, from $65 to 75.00
Fabric, tablecloth, 63x89", from $150 to................................ 175.00
Flair, bowl, lug soup 12.00
Flair, plate, salad 10.00
Home Decorator, plate, dinner; from $8 to.............................. 10.00
Knowles Esquire, centerpiece server, from $150 to 200.00
Knowles Esquire, platter, 13", from $45 to 55.00
Meladur, cup, from $8 to... 10.00
Meladur, plate, dessert; 6¼", from $6 to................................. 8.00
Oceana, relish dish, starfish, from $450 to 500.00
Pinch cutlery, knife, from $125 to... 150.00
Pinch cutlery, soup spoon, from $100 to 120.00
Pinch stainless flatware, Hull/Japan, set of 13 pcs, VG............... 300.00
Residential, bowl, onion soup; w/lid, from $36 to..................... 40.00
Residential, creamer, from $10 to... 12.00
Theme Formal, bowl, from $100 to 125.00

Theme Informal, platter, from $150 to.................................... 175.00
White Clover, ashtray, from $40 to 50.00
White Clover, shakers, either sz, pr from $30 to....................... 35.00
Wood accessory, chest, 3-drw, from $350 to............................. 500.00

Russian Art

Since 1991, which marked the fall of communism in the Soviet Union, a burgeoning upper middle class lead by the nouveau riche has dramatically and continually pushed up prices for pre-revolutionary (1917) Russian art. In certain areas, particularly in the realm of higher-end objects such as Fabergé, important paintings, bronzes, and icons, prices have skyrocketed in recent years. Unfortunately, such meteoric increases in market values have also spawned a rapidly expanding underworld industry of fakes, forgeries, and altered pieces. Subsequently, buyers should be extremely cautious when considering Russian works and are best advised to purchase from well established dealers and firms who offer guarantees. Sadly, as for authentic unaltered pre-1917 Russian items offered on eBay, the pickings are slim with the vast majority of items being outright fakes, generally over-the-top concoctions emblazoned with Imperial Eagles or monograms, profusely hallmarked, and often with 'original' cases. Nowhere is this more true than in the area of Fabergé — so much so that the term 'Fauxberge' was coined to address the endless stream of fake objects marked Fabergé that entered the market on a daily basis. Furthermore, it is important to note that there are many well documented examples of fake Fabergé pieces being produced as far back as 75 years ago!

Beginning in the nineteenth century and up until the Revolution, there was a Renaissance of sorts in Russian arts, which gave birth to some of the most beautiful and stunning objects ever produced. Every field of art flourished at this time, including jewelry, porcelain, glass, ceramics, sculpture, lacquer ware, paintings, and iconography. However, it was the fields of gold- and silver-smithing that perhaps best reflected the Slavic style distinct to the pre-Revolutionary world of Russian art. The firms of Fabergé, Ruckert, Ovchinnikov, Sazilov, and Kurlykov are quite well known. Yet there are many other lesser makers whose works are no less exquisite. At the present the market is extremely strong for enameled items of any type, the more enameling the better. The market is also strong for fine examples of porcelain, paintings, and bronzes. Icons of exceptional quality are very desirable, but it is, of course, Fabergé that is most highly sought after.

The interest in all things Russian just prior to WWI did not go unnoticed by European or American firms. Subsequently, firms outside of Russia often purchased items to be retailed through their own outlets. Therefore, it is not uncommon, for example, to find articles marked Tiffany while displaying the mark of the original Russian manufacturer as well

Our advisors for this category are James and Tatiana Jackson; they are listed in the Directory under Iowa.

Basket, silver trompe l'oeil, ca 1890, 11" L 8,400.00
Bronze, Evgeny Naps, mtd Cossack, ca 1890, 10⅜" 11,800.00

Card case, eleventh Artel, c. 1908, 3½", $13,440.00. (Photo courtesy Jackson's International Auctioneers & Appraisers of Fine Art & Antiques)

Case, guilloche enameling, Fabergé, ca 1908, 4½" L 70,800.00
Cigarette case, cloisonné, ca 1900, 4½" 2,000.00
Cigarette case, silver w/Troika scene, ca 1890, 4⅜" 1,180.00
Cross, bronze & enamel, ca 1850, 7"..400.00
Cup, Tsar Nicholas II 'Blood Cup,' 1896, 4" 750.00
Dagger (Kindjal), silver & niello, ca 1890, 20"........................900.00
Egg, porc, XB, ca 1900, 5"...1,300.00
Icon, Christ, silver & enamel riza, ca 1900, 12x10".............10,000.00
Icon, Christ, 19th C, 10x12" 500.00
Icon, selected saints, 19th C, 3" 200.00
Icon, the Trinity, ca 1700, 32x26" 64,000.00
Icon, Vladimir Virgin, 19th C, 10x12" 750.00
Kovsh, shaded enamel, 11th Artel, ca 1908, 4½" 7,000.00
Lampada, silver & enamel, Sazikov, 1892.............................2,800.00
Plate, Imperial, from Raphael Service, ca 1905, 9½" 22,000.00
Samovar, brass, ca 1890, 20"..500.00
Shot glass, enameled, ca 1890, 2½" 1,000.00
Spoons, shaded enamel, 6th Artel, ca 1890, 6", set of 6 ....1,400.00
Tea caddy, lacquer, Vishnyakov, ca 1880, 7" L 880.00
Tea glass holder, silver, Moscow, ca 1890, 3½" 1,200.00

Sabino

Sabino art glass was produced by Marius-Ernest Sabino in France during the 1920s and 1930s. It was made in opalescent, frosted, and colored glass and was designed to reflect the Art Deco style of that era. In 1960, using molds he modeled by hand, Sabino once again began to produce art glass using a special formula he himself developed that was characterized by a golden opalescence. Although the family continued to produce glassware for export after his death in 1971, they were never able to duplicate Sabino's formula.

Bonbon, mermaids (3), opal, 6" dia..550.00
Bottle, cologne; flowers emb, opal, bulbous, triangular top, 7½" .. 300.00
Bottle, scent; nudes in low relief, opal, cylindrical, 6" 300.00
Bowl, ballerinas (3), opal, ca 1920-35, 13¾"................................780.00
Bowl, Les Poissons, koi & bubbles, opal, ca 1930, 15"..............1,325.00
Bowl, lotus blossoms, opal, 3-ftd, 3½x10¼"..................................275.00

Box, three mermaids, signed in the mold, 6½" diameter, $400.00. (Photo courtesy Monsen & Baer)

Bust, Praying Madonna, opal, 4" 60.00
Ceiling fixture, frosted glass 3-tier invt water fountain shade, 11x8"..2,700.00
Ceiling fixture, molded/frosted glass, SP mt, 8x9½" dia, pr 2,700.00
Charger, nudes, smoke, ca 1923, 2¼x15", NM..............................240.00
Clock, bust of maiden ea side of dial, opal, 6x8⅜x3½" 1,450.00
Clock, 2 maidens hold dial, opal on blk marble base, ca 1930, 8" .. 1,800.00
Clock, 2 songbirds on floral prunus tree, paw ft, opal, 10x9x5" 725.00
Figurine, Idole, lady seated on cushion, opal, ca 1925, 6⅛".......1,150.00
Figurine, Nouveau nude w/long flowing hair, opal, 7½" 360.00
Figurine, nude in translucent robe, arms outstretched, opal, 9¾" .. 575.00
Figurine, nude lady holding bird, opal, 6¼x3½x3".........................265.00
Group, chickadees (3) on limb w/4th on base, dk opal, 8x7½" 780.00

Group, stylized leopards (2) on base, opal, 5⅞x7¾"......................950.00
Hood ornament, dove w/fanned tail feathers, opal, ca 1930.........725.00
Hood ornament, dove w/head down, clear satin, ca 1930 ....600.00
Lamp, 4½" 6-sided/tiered #4788 shade; triangular blk base, 16" .. 1,200.00
Mask, Triton (son of Poseidon & Aphrodite), opal, 15x10½"+stand... 4,800.00
Sconce, lady's head, opal, 10x8½x5½" 3,600.00
Vase, birds border above 5 nudes, opal flared/ftd cylinder, 9" 950.00
Vase, blooming trees, frosty amber, 7¾" 660.00
Vase, chevron design, bl, ovoid, 12½"..1,100.00
Vase, cockatoos, fiery opal, 10x11"...2,400.00
Vase, flowers (blown-out), amber, ftd, ca 1923, 6x5½" 480.00
Vase, geometric shapes, flat rim, amber, 8½" 850.00
Vase, leaf-patterned stripes, clear & frosted, ovoid, ca 1900, 9" .. 480.00
Vase, nude dancers, opal, ovoid w/everted rim, 14" 2,400.00
Vase, pineapple form, opal, ca 1930, 10".....................................395.00
Vase, rows of lappets, ea w/3-line petals, sepia wash, bulbous, 6" .. 395.00
Vase, water nymphs, gray-gr frost, cylindrical, 9"..........................425.00

Salesman's Samples and Patent Models

Salesman's samples and patent models are often mistaken for toys or homemade folk art pieces. They are instead actual working models made by very skilled craftsmen who worked as model-makers. Patent models were made until the early 1900s. After that, the patent office no longer required a model to grant a patent. The name of the inventor or the model-maker and the date it was built is sometimes noted on the patent model. Salesman's samples were occasionally made by model-makers, but often they were assembled by an employee of the company. These usually carried advertising messages to boost the sale of the product. Though they are still in use today, the most desirable examples date from the 1800s to about 1945. Many small stoves are incorrectly termed a 'salesman's sample'; remember that no matter how detailed one may be, it must be considered a toy unless accompanied by a carrying case, the indisputable mark of a salesman's sample.

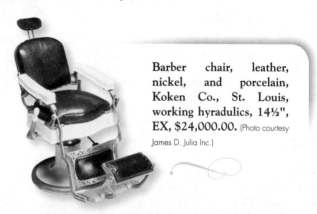

Barber chair, leather, nickel, and porcelain, Koken Co., St. Louis, working hyradulics, 14½", EX, $24,000.00. (Photo courtesy James D. Julia Inc.)

Barber chair, brn leather, ornate silver-tone, Koken Co, 10x16" ... 26,200.00
Bed, Murphy; cherry, w/orig fabric & mattress, ca 1800, 17x11" ...4,375.00
Book, Hershey Chocolate Co, leather cover, ca 1920-24...............2,625.00
Book, 6 children's book titles, sample text & illustrations, 1905, EX .. 185.00
Canoe, ribbed, gr pnt, cane seats, 2 mahog paddles, Old Town, 18" ..7,500.00
Chest, Empire; mahog, 6-drw, 19th C, 18¾x13¾".........................875.00
Furnace, Room Heater, metal, 17", +carrying case, VG 95.00
Ice cream freezer, wood w/metal mechanism & crank, White Mtn Jr, 8x5"..265.00
Icebox, oak cabinet, 4 panel doors, cream enamel int, 6 shelves, 16" .. 3,965.00
Lumber mill, cvd wood, Barlow's, Pat 1868, 19½x13"....................2,125.00
Lures, fishing; 59 assorted, color code on bait, Heddon, +cb case.....595.00
Lures, fishing; 72 assorted Toni lures tied in case, Heddon, 17x21" ..470.00
Optometrist lenses, Nachet & Fils, #3037, in orig case, 12x19½" 190.00
Organ, walnut w/much burl, detailed, Fort Wayne, ca 1885, 28x18x9"...25,000.00

Plow, pnt wood & iron, Township Plow #15/Revolving..., 6¼x15½"...10,625.00
Pool table, Brunswick 1845 American, hardwood/felt/leather, 28" L, EX..2,000.00
Radial arm saw, Rockwell Delta, ca 1960, +box, 17x11x11" 1,875.00
Saddle, Texas Half-Seat Slick Fork, WE Fulps, w/display stand, 7" seat...18,750.00
Safe, Meilink Mfg Co, Fire & Water Proof, 14x8¼"......................1,065.00
Stove, bl speckled porc w/nickel plate, Karr Qualified Range, 21x13" .4,875.00
Toilet system, holding tank, vent pipe & china toilet, +case, 25", EX.. 1,000.00
Washing machine, pnt cast metal, wringer, Maytag, 7½", EX...........500.00
Washing machine, wood & iron w/metal tub, hand-powered, 1900, 17x10".1,375.00
Water heater, pnt pressed steel, iron/copper fittings, Humphrey, 16" .. 375.00

Salt Shakers

John Mason invented the screw-top salt shaker in 1858. Today's Victorian salt shaker collectors have a wide range of interests, and their collections usually reflect their preference. There are many possible variables on which to base a collection. You may prefer shakers made of clear pattern glass, art glass, specific types of glass (custard, ruby stain, Burmese, opaque, chocolate), or glass of a particular color (cranberry, green, blue, or amber, for instance). Some collectors search for examples made by only one maker (in particular Mt. Washington, Dithridge, Northwood, Hobbs Brockunier, and C. F. Monroe). Others may stick to decorated shakers, undecorated examples, or any combination thereof that captures their fancy. If you would like to learn more about Victorian glass salt shakers, we recommend *Early American Pattern Glass* by Reilly and Jenks. Unless noted otherwise, values are for examples in at least near-mint condition with near-mint decorations (when applicable). Unless 'pr' is specified, the value is for a single shaker. See also specific companies.

Victorian Glass

Amberette, amber satin, Duncan, 1885, 2¾" 80.00
Aster & Leaf, emerald gr, bulbous, Beaumont #217, 1895, 3" 100.00
Babe Ruth figural, red & gold pnt, 1924-32, 5"............................ 790.00
Barrel, Footed Optic; cranberry w/HP floral, Mt WA/Pairpoint, 3½".. 190.00
Barrel, Invt Honeycomb; amber w/HP floral, NE Glass, 1884-87, 3¼" ..125.00
Barrel, 21-Rib Rainbow, cranberry w/gr-flashed stripe, 1884-92, 2⅝".. 700.00
Beaded Dahlia, pk cased, Consolidated, 2¾", pr.......................... 130.00
Beaded Scroll, wht w/HP flowers, Helmschmied, 1904, 3¼", pr... 150.00
Blocked Thumbprint Band, ruby stain, Duncan & Miller, 1904-13..45.00
Box-in-Box (aka Riverside's #420), ruby stain, ca 1894, 2⅞" 70.00
Broken Column w/Red Dots, ruby stain, Columbia, 1893, 2⅞" ... 150.00
Bulging Lobes, Footed; wht opal w/HP floral, 1900-10, 3⅞"........... 15.00
Challinor/Taylor #14, opaque bbl w/banded design, 1888-91, 2⅜"....45.00
Champion (aka Fan w/Cross Bars), ruby stain, McKee, 1894, 2⅞" ...75.00
Chrysanthemum Leaf, chocolate opaque, Indiana, 1901-03, 2⅝" ...325.00
Co-Op's #1901, Invt Vs, clear, Co-Operative Flint Glass, ca 1901, 3" ...20.00
Concave Panel, wht opal w/HP floral, Challinor & Taylor, 1¾x2½" ...35.00
Creased Neck, Tapered; opal w/HP scene, Mt WA/Pairpoint, 3½" ..50.00
Curved Body, Atterbury's; wht opaque opal, 2-pc mold, 1877-82, 5¼". 100.00
Dainty Swirl, clear reverse rubena, 2-pc top, 1889-94, 3⅜".......... 210.00
Diamond (pressed), vaseline, cylinder, Central, 1885-91, 2¾"....... 65.00
Double Leaf, purple variegated opaque, ca 1895-1901, 3⅝" 110.00
Douglas, ruby stain w/etch fleur-de-lis, Cooperative Flint, 2⅞"...... 40.00
Fancy Arch, gr w/gold, ca 1891-1903.. 35.00
Fence, 18 vertical ribs, bl, 1891-1901, 2⅞" 35.00
Fleur-de-Lis, Skirted; bl opaque, Dithridge & Co, 1894-1900, 2¾"...45.00
Fleur-de-Lis Spike, aqua, 4" 70.00
Fostoria's #956, fire-polished, ca 1901, 3¼"................................... 20.00
Four Ring, Tubular; amethyst w/HP child & butterfly, 1880s+, 3⅝"...180.00
Georgia Gem, opaque custard w/HP floral, Tarentum, 1900-40, 2½"...75.00
Hexagon, Leaf Base; opal w/HP florals, Fostoria, 1901-07, 3¼"...... 25.00
Idyll (Jefferson #251), bl w/gold scrolls/dots, Jefferson, ca 1907, 3" .. 150.00

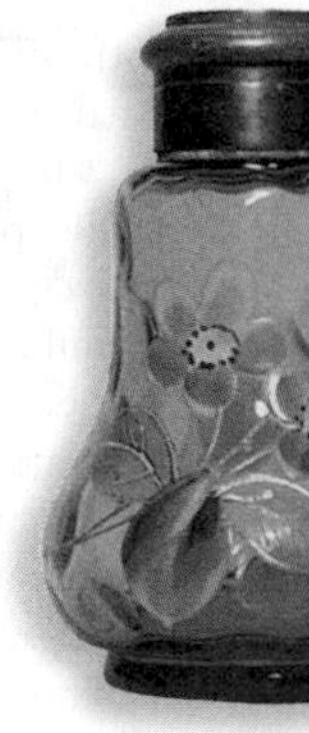

Inverted Thumbprint, Bell Based; electric blue, interior thumbprints, hand-painted florals on smooth outer surface, ca 1886 – 1891, 3", from $60.00 to $70.00. (Photo courtesy Mildred and Ralph Lechner)

Invt T'print, Sphere Variant; cobalt w/HP floral, Mt WA/Pairpoint, 2". 80.00
Leaf & Flower, amber stain, Hobbs Brockunier, 1888-92, 2⅝"..... 100.00
Lobed Elegance, pk to wht opal, HP floral, ca 1893...................... 175.00
Long Buttress, ruby stain, Fostoria, ca 1904-10, 2¾" 70.00
Maryland (Invt Loops & Fans), ruby stain, US Glass, ca 1897, 2½" .. 80.00
Melon, 9-Rib; cranberry, ca 1895-1900, 1⅞"................................. 220.00
National's #1004, wht opal, 15 slanted panels at base, ca 1901, 2½". 15.00
Octagon, Saloon, bl satin opaque, ca 1900-08, 4¼"........................ 55.00
Owl's Head, lime gr opaque, 1890-1891, 2½"................................ 300.00
Paneled Cane, Heisey's #315; 1900-08, 2⅞" 22.00
Pillar Optic Rib, bl w/HP floral, NE Glass, 1883-87, 4⅛"............ 160.00
Piller, Sixteen (Ribbed Lattice); cranberry opal, H&B, 2⅞" 125.00
Plate Band (aka Panel, Ten), chocolate, Jefferson, ca 1898, 3⅛" . 900.00
Pleated Medallion, New Martinsville, ca 1910, 3⅜"...................... 30.00
Reverse Swirl, cranberry opal, Buckeye orig screw-on lid, 2¼" 125.00
Ribbed Drape, custard opaque/HP rose w/gold, Jefferson, 1904, 3¼"..175.00
Ring Neck Variant, bl opal swirls, Hobbs & Brockunier, 1887+, 3"..90.00
Scroll, Gaudy; gr opaque, Gillinder & Sons, 2½" 35.00
Seaweed, cranberry opal, Hobbs & Brockunier, ca 1890s, 3½"..... 195.00
Seaweed, vaseline opal, Beaumont, 1890s, 3½", from $75 to 90.00
Sunset, pk opaque, Dithridge & Co, 1894-97, 2⅞"......................... 75.00
Texas, clear w/gold, US Glass, ca 1900, 2¾" 125.00
Thousand Eye, Ringed Center; canary, ca 1878-88, 3⅛" 80.00
Tripod w/Diamond Band, vaseline, 1904-10, 3½".......................... 85.00
Venetian Diamond, cranberry, Hobbs & Brockunier, 1887, 3"..... 160.00
Washington (aka Beaded Base), ruby stain, ca 1901, 3¾" 25.00
Wellington (aka Staple), ruby stain, Westmoreland, 1903-12, 2⅜" .. 75.00
Wheeling Peachblow, Hobbs & Brockunier, 1886, 2⅜" 420.00
Wild Bouquet, lt bl (slight opalescence), Northwood, 1900s, 3⅜"... 250.00
Zipper, aqua, patterned corners, Belmont #104, 1888-90, 3⅞"....... 75.00

Novelty Advertising

Those interested in novelty shakers will enjoy *Florences' Big Book of Salt and Pepper Shakers* by Gene Florence. It is available at your local library or from Collector Books. Note: 'Mini' shakers are no taller than 2". Instead of having a cork, the user was directed to 'use tape to cover hole.' Only when both shakers are identically molded will we use the term 'pr.' Otherwise we will describe them as '2-pc' or '3-pc' (when a mutual base or a third piece is involved). Our advisor for novelty salt shakers is Judy Posner; she is listed in the Directory under Florida. See also Regal; Rosemeade; Occupied Japan; Shawnee; other specific manufacturers.

Ball Perfect Mason, jar, glass w/emb letters, metal lid, 2⅞", pr....... 24.00
Big Boy, boy & hamburger, Special 1995 Edition, 4½", 2-pc.......... 49.00
Canadian Flame Genie, pottery, red Japan stamp, 1950s, 4", pr... 195.00
Conoco, gas pump, plastic w/decal, 2¾", pr, MIB 55.00
Dr Brown Soda, bottle, glass w/fired-on label, 4¼", pr.................... 45.00
Drewery's Beer, bottle, paper label on brn glass, 1950s, 3½", pr...... 45.00
Grain Belt Beer, bottle, paper label on brn glass, 4", pr.................. 55.00
Heinz Ketchup, bottle, plastic, c JS NY/Made in Hong Kong, 4¼", pr ..19.00

Humble Esso, gas pump, plastic w/decal label, 2¾", pr 39.00
IH logo, TH Johnson & Son, red bl pyro on milk glass, metal lids, pr ...70.00
KFC Colonel Sanders, plastic, wht, 1 w/blk base, Starling, 4⅜", pr....65.00
Kool Cigarettes, Willie & Millie, plastic penguins, pr 25.00
Lennox Furnaces, Lennie Lennox, pottery, front decals, 1950, 5", pr.. 125.00
Magic Chef, chef (in blk) on milk glass, plastic lid, 3½", pr........... 55.00
Magic Chef, plastic w/orig pnt & corks, 1940-50s, 5", pr 65.00
McWilliams Wine, monk, ceramic, Japan, 3½", pr...................... 95.00
Mobilgas, gas pump, plastic, Made in USA, 2¾", pr.................... 165.00
Old Koppitz Beer, bottle, amber glass w/decal, 3⅜", pr 45.00
Peerless Beer, gnome-like character, Hartland Plastic, 1950s, 5", pr...95.00
Pure Oil, gas pump, plastic, ad on bk, 2¾", pr............................. 125.00
Quaker State Motor Oil, can, heavy cb, 1940s-50s, giveaway, 1½", pr...39.00
Schlitz Beer, bottle, amber glass w/metal lid, 4", pr..................... 25.00
South of the Border, Mexican man, plastic, 1960s, 4½", pr............ 20.00
Spiller's Homepride Flour, Flour Fred, plastic, Airfix, 3⅛", pr 55.00
Sunkist, lemon, ceramic, 1950s, 2½", pr 62.50
Sympathetic Ear Restaurant, anthropomorphic ear, 1965, 4", pr ... 75.00
Texaco/Burgey & Gehman Fuel Oil, milk glass, 3¼", pr................ 55.00
VW Volkswagen van, studio pottery, ca 1990, 1¼x3¾", pr 55.00
White Satin Gin, bottle, gr glass w/metal lid, paper label, 4¾", pr. 24.00

Novelty Animals, Fish, and Birds

Alligator, redware, brn tones, EX details, Mexico, 1x5", pr............ 38.00
Anthropomorphic lady bug, pottery, Japan, 1950s, 2½", pr............ 22.00
Anthropomorphic lion w/monocle, ceramic, Japan, 1950s, 4⅝", pr...39.00
Bass fish, ceramic, Made in Japan label, 2x5½", pr 35.00
Beaver, pottery w/appl fur, Enesco foil label, 1950s, 3", pr........... 22.00
Bird & birdhouse, ceramic, Japan, 1950s, 3", 2-pc........................... 19.00
Bluegill fish, ceramic, realistic, Enesco, 2x4", pr........................... 35.00
Cat, Longfellow; ceramic, Norcrest/Japan, H483, 2x9½", pr 35.00
Cat, lustreware, unmk (possibly German), 1930s, 3⅜", pr.............. 85.00
Dinosaur w/tail up, pottery, plastic stopper, unmk, 1970s, 3", pr 28.00
Donkey w/hat laughing, ceramic, Japan, 1950s, 3⅜", pr 22.00
Farmer pig, ceramic, Enesco label, 5", pr...................................... 24.00
Frog w/umbrella, pottery, stacking, 1950s, 4¾", 2-pc 24.00
Hen on nest, gold & bl lustre, Noritake...Japan, 2¼", pr 60.00
Lions on base, nodder heads are shakers, ceramic, 3-pc................. 110.00
Mouse baseball player, mc ceramic, Japan, ca 1950s, 3¼", pr 50.00
Mr & Mrs Pig, nodder heads remove, bodies joined, ceramic, Japan, 3-pc...58.00
Pheasant, ceramic, 1 tail up/2nd tail down, Napco, 1950s, 2-pc 22.00

Rhinoceros, ceramic, German, one-piece, 9" long, $45.00.

Rooster & hen, blk & wht stripes, ceramic, 3½", 3", 2-pc 40.00
Scottie dog, porc, orig corks, Germany mk, 1930s-40s, 2½", pr...... 28.00
Snails (snuggling), ceramic, Crown Art...Japan, tallest: 4½", 2-pc...40.00
Turkey tom & hen, ceramic, Ucagco...Japan label, 1950s, 3", 2-pc..19.00

Novelty Character and Disney

Alice in Wonderland White Rabbit, ceramic, stacking, vintage, 4", 2-pc . 85.00

Bahama Police, ceramic, 1960s, 4⅜", pr.. 28.00
Bambi (base) w/Flower & Thumper (shakers), ceramic, Disney, 3-pc, MIB..55.00
Betty Boop, stacking head & body, ceramic, Benjamin Medwin 1955, 5". 34.00
Billy Sykes & Capt Cuttle, ceramic, Artone, 2½", 2-pc 39.00
Bonzo (dog), ceramic, solid cobalt, unmk flat bottom, 1930s, 3", pr .. 38.00
Charlie Chaplin shoes & hat, ceramic, unmk, 1940+, 1¼", 4", 2-pc.. 29.00
Chip & Dale chipmunks, ceramic, NE Disney China, 3⅜", 2-pc.... 39.00
Daisy Duck & grocery bag, ceramic, Applause/Disney, 3¼", 2-pc . 39.00
Dandy & Preacher Crow from Dumbo, ceramic, 3", 4", 2-pc 80.00
Dumbo, ceramic, Leeds/WD USA, 1940s, 4⅜", pr 95.00
Felix the Cat, bl on wht porc, Germany, 1920s, 2½", pr............... 365.00
Goofy & cake, ceramic, NE Disney Taiwan, 4¾", 2-pc.................. 45.00
Goose & golden egg, ceramic, c Vallona Star, 5½", 2-pc 55.00
Humpty Dumpty on wall, ceramic, unmk, 1940s, 5½", 2-pc 89.00
Jack Spratt & wife, ceramic, he: 3½", 2-pc................................... 52.50
Jock & Tramp (dogs), ceramic, att Japan, 1950s, Jock: 3x3", 2-pc ...55.00
Jonah & whale, ceramic, unmk, 2", 2-pc....................................... 65.00
Kate Greenaway boy (& girl), heavy pottery, HP, FF 77 mk, 4⅜", 2-pc.95.00
Little Mermaid on rock, stacking, ceramic, Disney China, 5¼", 2-pc...30.00
Ludwig & Donald, ceramic, Dan Brechner/WDP 1961/Japan, 5¼", 2-pc.95.00
Mammy & Pappy Yokum on sadiron shape, ceramic, Al Capp, 1968, 2-pc..59.00
Marvin the Martian & spaceship, ceramic, Warner Bros, 1996, 2-pc, MIB.55.00
Mickey & Minnie, ceramic, cold pnt, Leeds China, 1940s, 3¼", 2-pc.45.00
Miss Muffet & spider, mc ceramic, Poinsettia Studio, she: 2½", 2-pc. 60.00
Moon Mullins, glass w/plastic hat, cold pnt, Japan, 1930s, 3", pr... 55.00
Oswald & Homer, ceramic, Walter Lantz/Napco, 1958, 4", 2-pc .. 135.00

Pinocchio, 4¾", $85.00.
(Photo courtesy Morphy Auctions/
LiveAuctioneers.com)

Pixie & Dixie (mice), ceramic, Japan label, 3¼", 2-pc 55.00
Robin Hood on rock, ceramic, Made in Japan, 1950s, 4⅝", 2-pc ... 30.00
Santa & reindeer, ceramic, musical (nonworking), Napco, 2-pc, NMIB. 55.00
Shmoo, Al Capp comic character, chalk-like, 1940s, 3½", pr 225.00
Sylvester the Cat, ceramic, Warner Bros, 1970s, 4¼", pr............... 90.00
Tinkerbell bells, porc, Tinkerbell/castle, gold trim, 50s-60s, 3", pr. 35.00
Wizard of Oz, ceramic, Clay Art, ca 1990s, 3½", pr 29.00
Yoda, ceramic, Sigma, 1983, 4", pr... 195.00

Novelty People

Baby in diaper, pk clay, att CA, 1940s-50s, 2½", pr 45.00
Bare-breasted lady & naughty man, ceramic, Empress Japan, 4½", 2-pc... 59.00
Bellhop w/2 suitcases (shakers), ceramic, Japan, 1950s, 4", 3-pc..... 55.00
Black lady sitting w/lg melon slice, ceramic, Japan, 3½", 2-pc 165.00
Bride & groom, ceramic w/gold, red Japan mk, 1950s, 4⅜", 2-pc ... 25.00
Choir boy (1 in red/1 in blk), ceramic, Japan, 1950s, 4¾", pr 22.00
Clown w/instrument, ceramic, Japan, 1930s, 3½", pr 29.00
Deco girl (slim), ceramic, red Japan mk, 1930s, 4", pr................... 95.00
Drunk & lamppost, ceramic, Maruri...Japan, 1950s, 3-pc............... 22.50
Dutch boy & girl, ceramic, Delft China, 2⅞", 2-pc 24.00
Flower girl, ceramic, pk dress, Japan, 1950s, 4⅜", pr..................... 24.00
Goldilocks w/book & flowers, ceramic, Relco Japan label, 1950s, pr ...36.00
Goodbye Cruel World, man about to flush himself, Japan, 1950s, 2-pc.. 40.00
Happy (& Sad) Baby, ceramic, Clay Art, ca 1990, 3½", 2-pc......... 25.00

Hunter & rabbit, ceramic, unmk, 1950s, 3½", 2-pc 18.00
Indian & teepee, ceramic, Vallona Star 102..., 3¾", 2-pc.............. 59.00
Japanese boy & girl kissing, ceramic, Napco, 3¾", 2-pc 50.00
Lady w/broom sitting on basket (2nd shaker), ceramic, Japan, 2-pc... 85.00
Maid w/2 eggs (shakers) on tray, ceramic, Foreign, 1930s, 3-pc ... 125.00
Mammy & Chef, brn skin tones, ceramic, Japan, 4¾", 2-pc.......... 55.00
Mammy w/mixing bowl, bsk, LAG NO 1977 Taiwan, pr 32.00
Man in doghouse & lady w/rolling pin, ceramic, Vallona Star, 2-pc .. 75.00
Matador & bull, ceramic, Japan, 1950s, 4¼", 2-pc......................... 24.00
Native, wooden head/wire body, drum shakers, Japan, 1950s, 3-pc...60.00
Nude reclining, ceramic, detailed features, 5" L, pr, MIB 55.00
Old-fashioned baseball player w/bat, ceramic, Japan, 1950s, 3⅞", pr.. 35.00
Oriental person, cvd stone, souvenir, Korea 67-68, 4⅜", pr.......... 49.00
Stan Laurel & Oliver Hardy faces on tray, ceramic, Dresden, 3-pc .. 200.00

Miscellaneous Novelties

Alamo replica, bronze-colored metal, Japan, 1¾x2½", pr.............. 39.00
Anthropomorphic, dustpan girl holding broom, ceramic, 1950s, pr...165.00
Anthropomorphic, lemon-head boy (head only), Py, 1950s, pr 65.00
Anthropomorphic, pea-pod person, ceramic, Japan, 1950s, 3", pr ...24.00
Anthropomorphic, plum couple, ceramic, Py, 2-pc, NM............... 35.00
Anthropomorphic, toothpaste girl, ceramic, PY, 1950s, pr.......... 150.00
Bride's Cook Book/Way to His Heart, ceramic, Poinsettia Studios, pr...35.00
Bugle & drum, ceramic, Arcadia, mini, 2-pc 35.00
Coffee mill & graniteware coffeepot, ceramic, Arcadia, mini, 2-pc ..35.00
Eisenhower Lock & ship, St Lawrence Seaway, souvenir, Japan, 2-pc .29.00
Flying saucer spaceship, pottery, red windows, 1950s, pr 49.00
McGuffy's Reader & school bell, ceramic, 1950s, bell: 2⅜", 2-pc... 22.00
Pike's Peak or Bust, chromolitho on metal tray, Japan, 1950s, 3-pc...35.00
Pixie head, ceramic, PY type, #6981 Japan, 3¼", pr...................... 29.00
Singing Tower, silver-tone, metal, FL souvenir, 3½", pr................. 45.00
SS Love Boat, ceramic, c 1979 Enesco, 1⅝x3", pr 29.00
Tokyo, ceramic, Parkcraft Famous Cities series, 2¾", pr 39.00
Worm in apple, ceramic, unmk, 1950s, 2½", 2-pc.......................... 19.00

Salts, Open

Before salt became refined, processed, and free-flowing as we know it today, it was necessary to serve it in a salt cellar. An innovation of the early 1800s, the master salt was placed by the host and passed from person to person. Smaller individual salts were a part of each place setting. A small silver spoon was used to sprinkle it onto the food.

If you would like to learn more about the subject of salts, we recommend *The Open Salt Compendium* by Sandra Jzyk and Nina Robertson; *5,000 Open Salts,* written by William Heacock and Patricia Johnson, with many full-color illustrations and current values; *Pressed Glass Salt Dishes* by L. W. and D. B. Neal; and *The Glass Industry in Sandwich* by Raymond Barlow and Jon Kaiser. See also Blown Glass; Blown Three-Mold Glass.

Key: cl — cobalt liner

Glass

Amber, Cambridge, 6 sides, ea w/intaglio star, lg star in base, +spoon ...30.00
Amber, Czech, intaglio angel/cherub w/flute, hexagonal, 2½" L 35.00
Amber, Portieux, scalloped swirling panels, ca 1900, ped ft, 1½" H..25.00
Amberina, Degenhart, Daisy & Button, str sides, D in heart mk ... 10.00
Bl, Bryce, English Hobnail, sawtooth rim, unmk, 4½" L, EX.......... 15.00
Bl, Czech, Cupid & Venus intaglio, beveled sides, 1920s, 2¼" dia. 18.00
Bl, Depression era, molded notches/facets, 3 sm ft, 2¾" L 8.00
Bright bl, Depression era, thick w/faceted sides, star in base, 2" dia ..25.00
Cameo, Daum Nancy, sailboat/windmills, blk on clambroth opal, 2x2¼" ...385.00
Clear, Heisey, plain rim band over wide ribbing, ftd, 1½x2¾"........ 15.00
Clear w/gold flowers, Czech (?), 3 sm curled ft, 1⅛x2⅞" 22.00
Gr, Cambridge, Stratford, toothed rim, lg hdls, 2⅜x4¾" L............ 32.00
Milk glass, Atterbury/Pat June 30th..., basketweave w/rope/hdls/stem...35.00
Pk, Depression era, dbl w/faceted sides/ft/hdl, 3¼x2x2½"............ 135.00
Pk w/amber int, att Monot Stumpf, petal rim, 1¼x2" L, pr 85.00
Purple slag, Sowerby, Reg Mar 1877, oval tub shape w/hdl ea end, 3" L... 75.00
Vaseline, seashell form, 3 sm ft, 1x2¾' 25.00

Lacy Glass

When no condition is indicated, the items below are assumed to be without obvious damage; minor roughness is normal.

BF-1B, Basket of Flowers, violet-bl, 4-ftd, Sandwich, 2" 155.00
BH-1, Beehive, NE Glass, sm chip, 2"... 135.00
BT-8, Lafayet (sic), med bl fiery opal.. 260.00
BT-9, boat, plain rim & base, Sandwich, 1⅝x4x2" 165.00
CN-1A, Crown, fiery opal, 4 scroll ft, Sandwich, 2⅛"................... 180.00
D1-18, divided, sm chip, 1⅝" 155.00
EE-3B, scrolled eagle, Sandwich, chip, 2x3¼" 135.00
EE-6, known as coffin eagle, Sandwich, chips, 1½" 135.00

EE-8, Cadmus, ships and eagles, 1¾x3", $525.00.
(Photo courtesy Conestoga Auction Co. Inc./LiveAuctioneers.com)

GA-4, Gothic Arch, rectangular, nicks, 1¾" 180.00
LE-2, Lyre, flaw, Sandwich, 1¾" 265.00
MV-1, aqua, Mt Vernon Glass, chip, 1¾" 155.00
NE-1A, wht opaque, NE Glass, 2"... 215.00
OG-10, oblong, Providence Flint Glass, 1¾", NM 145.00
OL-12, cornucopia, oval, Sandwich, 1⅜", EX................................ 120.00
OL-16A, oval, Sandwich, 1¾".. 215.00
OL-27, oval, NE Glass, 1½"... 195.00
OO-RA, oblong octagon, Sandwich, sm chip, 1⅝" 155.00
OP-20, shaped rim, 4-ftd, Philadelphia area, 2¼" 225.00
PO-4, Peacock Eye, oval, 1⅜"... 132.00
PO-6, Peacock Eye, electric bl, oval, Sandwich, 1½x3¾".........1,550.00
PP-1, Peacock Eye, ped ft, Pittsburgh area, sm chip, 2¾" 475.00
PR-10, Peacock Eye, rnd, Sandwich, 1½", NM.............................. 120.00
RP-3, floral, powder bl opaque, 12-scallop, Sandwich, 2".........1,075.00
RP-18, rnd ped, Sandwich, 1¾", NM 120.00
RP-32 (similar), scalloped rim, rnd ped, Pittsburgh area, 2½" 235.00
SN-1, Stag Horn, med amber, Sandwich, 1¾" 165.00

Pottery

Delft, foliate motif, bl/wht, 8-sided base, Holland, 1700s, 1¾", VG ...960.00
Delft, lion figural behind 2 cups, floral decor, 3x4", VG 450.00
Delft, mc floral, 6-side rim/ft, sgn Gerritsz, 1700s, 2½", EX.......1,800.00
Doulton Lambeth, rnd w/sq foliate-cvd base, bl/brns, 1885, 3½" .. 240.00
French faience, lady holds 2 cups aloft, Quimper style, 7", pr 240.00
Geo Jones, majolica, floral on lt bl, pk int.................................... 540.00
Herend, dbl, floral sprig bands, bl/gilt on wht, shield mk, 2x2" 50.00
Herend Rothschild, dbl, bird on bk of rococo 3-ftd base w/gilt.... 325.00
KPM, elegant lady stands on rococo base, cup beside.................... 80.00
Mason's ironstone, Canton (bl/wht transfer), 4 paw ft to base, 6x6" ..100.00

Meissen, Blue Onion, dbl w/center loop hdl 50.00
Meissen, dandy seated between 2 baskets on base, bl/wht, #3024/59, 5" .. 585.00
Moorcroft, floral on gr, 3" dia 120.00
Wedgwood, cobalt w/yel-beaded band top/base, brn rim/ft, 3" dia, pr .. 180.00
Wedgwood, ftd bowl w/ram's head & drapery supports, blended bl/amber ... 180.00

Sterling, Continental Silver, and Enamel

Ball Black & Co, putti & garlands on oval, 1850s, 2½x4¼", pr ... 780.00
Bateman, H; rtcl oval, 4-ftd, cl, 1779, 2x3", pr 1,050.00
Christofle, putti (1 boy w/fowl/girl w/jug & cup), 19th C, 5¼" .. 1,250.00
English, decagonal, 1716-17, 1⅜x2¾", 4.8 troy-oz, pr 1,325.00
English, Geo III, scroll hdls, stepped base, cl, att Abdy, 1799, 3x5" ... 660.00
Hennell, D; Geo III, oval gadrooned rim, hoof ft, cl, 1762, 3½", pr ... 660.00
Liberty & Co, boat shape, #2282, ¾x5¾x2¼", pr 1,800.00
Russian, neoclassical ftd cylinder, Fabergé, 2⅛" dia 7,800.00
Russian, silver-gilt/champlevé foliage, cl, Alder, 1877, 1¼x1⅞" .. 725.00
Scofield, Geo III w/eng floral, 4-leg, ca 1797, 2¼", pr 1,050.00
Wilkinson & Co, Gothic tracery/oak leaves, glass inserts, 2½", pr . 1,175.00

Sheffield, bead and shell suppports, 7⅞x2¾x2¼", $195.00. (Photo courtesy Neal Auction Company Auctioneers & Appraisers of Fine Art/LiveAuctioneers.com)

Samplers

American samplers were made as early as the colonial days; even earlier examples from seventeenth-century England still exist today. Changes in style and design are evident down through the years. Verses were not added until the late seventeenth century. By the eighteenth century, samplers were used not only for sewing experience but also as an educational tool. Young ladies, who often signed and dated their work, embroidered numbers and letters of the alphabet and practiced fancy stitches as well. Fruits and flowers were added for borders; birds, animals, and Adam and Eve became popular subjects. Later houses and other buildings were included. By the nineteenth century, the American eagle and the little red schoolhouse had made their appearances. Many factors bear on value: design and workmanship, strength of color, the presence of a signature and/or a date (both being preferred over only one or the other, and earlier is better), and, of course, condition.

Unless otherwise noted, our values are for examples in good average condition.

ABCs (2 sets)/flowers/berries, silk on linen, sgn/1829, 6x17" 365.00
ABCs/#s, wool & silk on linen, sgn/1777, minor losses, 12x8" 375.00
ABCs/#s/bluebirds, on linen, sgn/1839, in modern 21x11" fr.... 1,150.00
ABCs/#s/flowers/house/verse, silk on linen, sgn/1857, in 17x19" fr.. 575.00
ABCs/#s/long pious verse/vines, silk on linen, sgn/1834, 18x9"+fr .. 575.00
ABCs/#s/trees/birds, silk on linen, 11x9" 315.00
ABCs/#s/verse, silk on linen, sgn/1805, hole/stain, 15x13"+old fr ..925.00
ABCs/#s/verse, silk on linen, sgn/1832, old reeded 19x15" fr....... 400.00
ABCs/bird/flowers/verse, silk on linen, sgn/ca 1780s, 21x19", VG ... 635.00
ABCs/family statistics/flowers, silk on linen, 1827, 17x17"+fr ..3,525.00
ABCs/fruited fines/verse, silk on linen, sgn, Boston, 25x19"+fr .. 1,000.00
ABCs/hearts/lions, silk on linen, sgn/1788, sm losses, 11x10" 315.00
ABCs/house/birds/flowers/etc, silk on linen, sgn/1820, 21x18"+fr ..865.00
ABCs/house/trees/vines/verse, silk on linen, sgn/1840, 17x17"+fr ... 1,400.00

ABCs/long verse/flowers, silk on linen, sgn/dtd 1818, 17x16"...2,000.00
ABCs/ornate stitches/verse, silk on linen, sgn/1828, 19x15"+fr... 975.00

Adam and Eve, silk on linen, name and 1835, 21x18", $1,300.00. (Photo courtesy Skinner Inc. Auctioneers & Appraisers of Antiques & Fine Art)

Caged bird/men w/grapes/crowns/hearts/etc, silk on linen, 1822, 17x15"..575.00
Cherubs/animals/flowering urns/verse, silk on linen, 1836, 18x17"+fr...1,150.00
Draped figures/stars/flowers, silk on linen, sgn/1836, in 16x17" fr....345.00
Flowers/8-point stars/vines, silk on linen, sgn/1843, 16x8"+fr...... 525.00
Map of England & Wales, silk on linen, sgn/1796, stains, 21x18"+fr.. 1,150.00
Peacocks/potted flowers/pious verse, silk on linen, 1817, 17x13"+fr ..600.00
Pious verse/butterflies/flowers, silk on linen, 1798, 16x17"+G- fr...865.00
Snails/deer/hound/hare/flowers, silk on linen, sgn/1805, in 18x18" fr ... 375.00

Sandwich Glass

The Boston and Sandwich Glass Company was founded in 1825 by Deming Jarves in Sandwich, Massachusetts. Their first products were blown and molded, but eventually they perfected a method for pressing glass that led to the manufacture of the 'lacy' glass which they made until about 1840. Up until the closing of the factory in 1888, they made a wide variety of not only flint pattern glass, but also beautiful fancy glass such as cut, overlay, overshot, opalescent, and etched. Today colored Sandwich commands the highest prices, but it all is becoming increasingly rare and expensive. Invaluable reference books are George and Helen McKearin's *American Glass* and Ruth Webb Lee publications. The best book for identifying Sandwich candlesticks and their later wares is *The Glass Industry in Sandwich* by Raymond Barlow and Joan Kaiser. Our advisor for this category is Elizabeth Simpson; she is listed in the Directory under Maine. See also Cup Plates; Salts, Open; Trevaise; other specific types of glass.

Bottle, scent; Star & Punty, dk amethyst, 7x5¼" 4,500.00
Candlestick, clambroth/cornflower bl, Acanthus Leaf hexagon, 9", ea ..315.00
Candlestick, med bl, columnar w/petal socket, 9⅛", ea 345.00
Candlesticks, dolphin base, canary, 1845-70, 10½", pr 1,000.00
Compote, Hairpin, 5¼x10½", NM 1,500.00
Compote, Peacock Eye, hexagonal base, sm chips, 10¾x6½"....2,750.00

Dish, Princess Feather Medallion and Basket of Flowers, canary, 1840 – 1845, 6x10½", G, $20,700.00. (Photo courtesy Skinner Inc. Auctioneers & Appraisers of Antiques & Fine Art)

Jar, pomade; bear figural, starchy bl, J Jauel & Co on base, 4½"... 3,150.00
Sugar bowl, Gothic Arch, vaseline, w/lid, 5½", EX 1,175.00
Sugar bowl, Gothic Arch, wht opal, w/lid, sm chips, 6¼" 4,800.00
Toy candlestick, bottle gr, 1850-70, 1⅝x1¼", ea....................... 1,950.00

Toy flat iron, bl, ca 1850-70, 1x1⅜"	1,375.00
Vase, amethyst, tulip form, 8-sided base, 10¼"	2,700.00
Vase, Gothic Arch, wht opal, 10¼", NM	1,200.00
Vase, tulip; amethyst, octagonal ft, 10"	2,750.00
Vase, tulip; vaseline, 10", pr	1,200.00
Vase, 3-Printie Block, amethyst w/faint wht wisps, att, 10"	1,800.00

Santa Barbara Ceramic Design

Established in 1976 by current director Raymond Markow (after three years of refining his decorative process), Santa Barbara Ceramic Design arose less auspiciously than the 'Ohio' potteries — no financial backing and no machinery beyond that available to ancient potters: wheel, kiln, brushes, and paint. The company produced intricate, colorful, hand-painted flora and fauna designs on traditional pottery forms, primarily vases and table lamps. Although artistically aligned with turn-of-the-century art potteries, the techniques used were unique and developed within the studio. Vibrant glaze stains with wax emulsion were applied by brush over a graduated multicolor background, then enanced by elaborate sgraffito detailing on petals and leaves. In the early 1980s, a white stoneware body was incorporated to further brighten the color palette, and during the last few years sgraffito was replaced by detailing with a fine brush.

Early pieces were thrown. Mid-1980 saw a transition to casting, except for experimental or custom pieces. Artists were encouraged to be creative and often given individual gallery exhibitions. Custom orders were welcomed, and experimentation occurred regularly; the resulting pieces are the most rare and seldom appear today. Limited production lines evolved, including the Collector Series that featured an elaborate ornamental border designed to enhance the primary design. The Artist's Collection was a numbered series of pieces by senior artists, usually combining flora and fauna.

The company's approach to bold colors and surface decoration influenced many contemporary potters and inspired imitation in both pottery and glass during the craft renaissance of the 1970s and 1980s. Several artists successfully made use of the studio's designs and techniques after leaving. Authentic pieces bear the artist's initials, date, and 'SBCD' marked in black stain and, if thrown, the potter's inscription.

At the height of the studio's art pottery period, Markow employed as many as three potters and 12 decorators at any given time. The ware was marketed through craft festivals and wholesale distribution to art and craft galleries nationwide. An estimated 100,000 art pottery pieces were made before a transition in the late 1980s to silk-screened household and garden items. Some of these remain in production today, however the company has expanded into many other media — so much that *Ceramic* has been dropped from the new company name: *Santa Barbara Design Studio*. One interesting foray was a 2005 series of coffee cups featuring black and white stills from 1930s to 1950s and film noir movies in conjunction with *Turner Classic Movies*.

Now 32 years old, the secondary market for Santa Barbara Ceramic Designs' art pottery has seen about 2,000 pieces change hands. These are often viewed as bargains compared to their Rookwood and Weller Hudson counterparts. For images of artist/potter marks visit johnguthrie.com. When borrowing information from this article for publication or sales, please credit johnguthrie.com and *Schroeder's Antiques Price Guide*. Our advisor is John Guthrie; he is listed in the Directory under South Carolina.

Bud vase, beaded iris, Margie Gilson, 1983, 6"	200.00
Candlestick, #5116, morning glory, Laurie Linn, 1982, 7", ea	106.00
Goblet, #C, poppy, Shannon Sargent, 1979, 7½"	77.00
Jar, dutch iris, Dorie Knight, w/lid, 1978, 8"	130.00
Lamp, #5117, iris, Itoko Takeuchi, 1983, 9"	325.00
Lamp, #5119, bouquet, Itoko Takeuchi, 1984, 15½"	592.00
Lamp, #5130, poppy, Laurie Linn-Ball, 1986 (2), 7"	166.00
Lamp, #7105, iris, Dorie Knight-Hutchinson, 1984, 17"	335.00
Lamp, #7115, poppy, Laurie Linn-Ball, 1986, 16"	395.00
Lamp, #7115, tulip, Itoko Takeuchi, 1986, 16"	585.00
Mug, #5121, eucalyptus, Gary Ba-Han, 1983, 5"	39.00
Oil lamp, #1102, swan, Barbara Rose, ca 1978, 6½"	72.00
Pitcher, #5106, carnation, Laurie Linn, 1982, 9"	128.00
Plate, #5114, Pegasus, Shannon Sargent, 1980, 7"	80.00
Platter, #4118, bearded iris, Margie Gilson, 1983, 14½"	343.00
Quiche plate, #1110, geranium, Laurie Cosca, 1980, 1½x10"	176.00
Vase, #5101, bird, Laurie Cosca, 1980, 6-7"	343.00
Vase, #5101, iris, Christine Adcock, 1980, 6½"	152.00
Vase, #5101, iris, Mary Favero, 1980, 7"	91.00
Vase, #5101, morning glory, Michelle Foster, 1982, 6-7"	125.00
Vase, #5101, night blossom, Itoko Takeuchi, 1984, 6"	130.00
Vase, #5101, pansy, Shannon Sargent, 1982, 6-7"	112.00
Vase, #5101cs, tulip, Anne Collinson, 1980, 5"	118.00
Vase, #5102, bearded iris, Laurie Cosca, 1979, 9"	240.00
Vase, #5102, daffodil, Dorie Knight, 1980, 10"	173.00
Vase, #5102, daffodil, Laurie Cosca, 1982, 9"	125.00

Sarreguemines

Sarreguemines, France, is the location of Utzschneider and Company, founded about 1800, producers of majolica, transfer-printed dinnerware, figurines, and novelties which are usually marked 'Sarreguemines.' In 1836, under the management of Alexandre de Geiger, son-in-law of Utzschneider, the company became affiliated with Villeroy and Boch. During the 1850s and 1860s, two new facilities with modern steam-fired machinery were erected. Alexandre's son Paul was the next to guide the company, and under his leadership two more factories were built — one at Digoin and the other at Vitry le Francois. After his death in 1931, the company split but was consolidated again after the war under the name of Sarreguemines - Digoin - Vitry le Francois. Items marked St. Clement were made during the period from 1979 to 1982, indicating the group who owned the company for that span of time. Today the company is known as Sarreguemines - Batiment.

Bowl, basketweave, pk strawberries on lid, w/undertray, 5" H	215.00
Bowl, leafy branch on basketweave, 1⅞x9½"	215.00
Butter pat, pansy form, prof rim rpr	145.00
Center bowl, boat shape w/masks on cobalt, turq int, #1972, 14½" L	240.00
Character jug, Black man w/red bow tie, #3884, 7"	1,080.00
Character jug, dbl face, frowning/smiling, 8½", EX	145.00

Character jug, face of man with closed eyes, 7", $135.00.

Character jug, John Bull, brn hair, pk cheeks, #3257, 6½"	300.00
Character jug, lady w/bonnet, pk & brn tones, #3319, 7", NM	515.00
Character jug, man seated & holding money bags, red coat, 12¾"	345.00
Character jug, man w/receeding hairline, smiling face, #3320, 7⅛"	90.00
Character jug, Puck, dk & lt gr turban, 7"	265.00
Character jug, Scotsman w/smiling face, 7¾"	90.00

Ewer, brn & gold crystalline, shouldered, 12x4" 480.00
Humidor, rabbit seated w/egg between his legs, minor hairline, 5½"..900.00
Oyster plate, turq w/6 shells & center well, 9½" 120.00
Pitcher, cat, blk & wht w/yel eyes, pk tongue, #3675Z, 8½" 240.00
Pitcher, dog begging, blk & wht w/pk tongue, 9" 325.00
Pitcher, parrot on perch, vivid colors, 9" 480.00
Pitcher, pelican w/huge open beak, 8" 650.00
Pitcher, ram's head figural, lt bl int, 9", NM 650.00
Pitcher, toby; tophat/bow tie/vest/jacket, 13", NM 325.00
Plaque, quail (3)/wheat/foliage on cobalt, prof rpr, 23" W 1,500.00
Plate, asparagus on wht, 9½", pr 195.00
Plate, grapes & leaves, pk/gr/ivory, 8" 110.00
Stein, fish/sausages/radish, cat figural hdl, pewter lid, 1-liter 1,325.00
Stein, pottery, transfer: people drinking, pewter lid, .5 liter 240.00
Vase, cobalt & gold w/gr appl flowers, rpr hdl, 24x15" 2,150.00
Vase, water lily on brn & cobalt, cylindrical neck, 9", pr 300.00

Satsuma

Satsuma is a type of fine cream crackle-glaze pottery or earthenware made in Japan as early as the seventeenth century. The earliest wares, made at the original kiln in the Satsuma province, were enameled with only simple florals. By the late eighteenth century, a floral brocade (or nishikide design) was favored, and similar wares were being made at other kilns under the direction of the Lord of Satsuma. In the early part of the nineteenth century, a diaper pattern was added to the florals. Gold and silver enamels were used for accents by the latter years of the century. During the 1850s, as the quality of goods made for export to the Western world increased and the style of decoration began to evolve toward becoming more appealing to the Westerners, human forms such as Arhats, Kannon, geisha girls, and samurai warriors were added. Today the most valuable pieces are those marked 'Kinkozan,' 'Shuzan,' 'Ryuzan,' and 'Kozan.' The genuine Satsuma 'mon' or mark is a cross within a circle — usually in gold on the body or lid, or in red on the base of the ware. Character marks may be included.

Caution: Much of what is termed 'Satsuma' comes from the Showa Period (1926 to the present); it is not true Satsuma but a simulated type, a cheaper pottery with heavy enamel. Collectors need to be aware that much of the 'Satsuma' today is really Satsuma style and should not carry the values of true Satsuma. Our advisor for this category is Clarence Bodine; he is listed in the Directory under Pennsylvania.

Bowl, courtiers, cobalt borders, Japan, early 20thC, 5½" 265.00
Bowl, figures before Mt Juji, 19th C, 10" 475.00
Bowl, samurai w/gold, foliate edge, Japan, ca 1900, 6" 325.00
Cup, sake; ancient Egyptian boat, early 20th C, 5½" 120.00
Figure, Kannon seated on rock throne holding lotus, rprs, 19th C, 12"..765.00
Moon flask, 7 Gods of Luck & Hundred Poets, Japan, late 1800s, 9½"..525.00
Plate, Hundred Rakans, foliate form, Japan, 19th C, 9½" 300.00
Plate, One Hundred Birds, early 20th C, 9¼" 645.00
Tureen, parrots & chrysanthemums, urn form w/dome lid, 19th C, 12x13"....700.00
Vase, birds/flowers/butterflies in panels, sq, Meiji period, 12".......650.00
Vase, dragons & brocade, sgn Senzan, integral hdls, 7x6" 1,400.00
Vase, emb/pnt peonies, Makuzu Kozan, Meiji period, 8½" 3,250.00
Vase, figures in fan-shaped reserves, Japan, early 20th C, 5"......... 150.00
Vase, floral, trumpet mouth, dragon hdls, Meiji period, 25" 450.00
Vase, flowering branch, oviform, Japan, 19th C, 13" 700.00
Vase, men's face/geishas w/dragon, elephant-head hdls, 9½", pr... 525.00
Vase, moriage butterflies & flowers, Japan, late 19th C, 14" 385.00
Vase, tied money bag/chrysanthemums, Meiji period, 5¾" 175.00
Vase, women & brocade, trumpet mouth/shishi hdls, Japan, ca 1900, 29"..400.00
Vase, 6 Orientals, mc w/extensive gold, bk: 3 warriors, 24x12"6"....510.00
Wine pot, women in garden scenes, early 20th C, 4¾" 265.00

Scales

In today's world of pre-measured and pre-packaged goods, it is difficult to imagine the days when such products as sugar, flour, soap, and candy first had to be weighed by the grocer. The variety of scales used at the turn of the century was highly diverse; at the Philadelphia Exposition in 1876, one company alone displayed over 300 different weighing devices. Among those found today, brass, cast-iron, and plastic models are the most common. Fancy postal scales in decorative wood, silver, marble, bronze, and mosaic are also to be found.

A word of caution on the values listed: These values range from a low for those items in fair to good condition to the upper values for items in excellent condition. Naturally, items in mint condition could command even higher prices, and they often do. Also, these are retail prices that suggest what a collector will pay for the object. When you sell to a dealer, expect to get much less. The values noted are averages taken from various auction and other catalogs in the possession of the society members. Among these, but not limited to, are the following: Malter & Co., Inc., Encino, CA; *Auktion Alt Technic*, Auction Team, Koln, Germany.

For those seeking additional information concerning antique scales we recommend *Scales, A Collector's Guide*, by Bill and Jan Berning (Schiffer). You are also encouraged to contact the International Society of Antique Scale Collectors, whose address can be found in the Directory under Clubs, Newsletters, and Catalogs. Visit the society website at www.isasc.org. Our advisor for this category is Jerome R. Katz; he is listed in the Directory under Pennsylvania.

Key:

ap — arrow pointer	h — hanging
bal — balance	hcp — hanging counterpoise
bm — base metal	hh — hand held
br — brass	l+ — label with foreign coin values
Brit — British	lb w/i — labeled box with instructions
Can — Canadian	lph — letter plate or holder
Col — Colonial	pend — pendulum
CW — Civil War	PP — Patent Pending
cwt — counterweight	st — sterling
Engl — English	tt — torsion type
eq — equal arm	ua — unequal arm
Euro — European	wt — weight
FIS — Fairbanks Infallible Scale Co.	

Angldile shop scale, ca. 1900s, restored and complete with mirror, 21", **$2,500.00.** (Photo courtesy Morphy Auction)

Analytical (Scientific)

Am, eq, mahog w/br & ivory, late 1800s, 14x16x8", $200 to 400.00

Assay

Am, eq, mahog box w/br & ivory, plaque/drw, 1890s, $400 to .. 1,000.00

Coin: Equal Arm Balance, American

Blk japanned metal, eagle on lid, late 19th C, $300 to 400.00

Col, oak 6-part box, Col moneys, Boston, 1720-75, $800 to.....**1,800.00**
Post Col to CW, oak 6-part box, 1+, 1843, $400 to...................**1,000.00**

Coin: Equal Arm Balance, English

Charles I, wooden box w/11 Brit wts, 1640s, $900 to................**1,500.00**
1-pc wood box, rnd wts, label, Freeman, 1760s, $250 to **450.00**
6-pc oak box, coin wts label, Thos Harrison, 1750s, $200 to **450.00**

Coin: Equal Arm Balance, French

Solid wood box, 12 sq wts, J Reyne, Bourdeau, 1694, $400 to...**1,000.00**
Solid wood box w/recesses, 5 sq wts, A Gardes, 1800s, $250 to ...**800.00**
1-pc oval box, nested/fractional wts, label, 18th C, $250 to.........**400.00**
1-pc oval box, no wts, label of Fr/Euro coins, 18th C, $150 to.....**250.00**
1-pc walnut box, nested wts, Charpentier label, 1810, $275 to....**675.00**

Coin: Equal Arm Balance, Miscellaneous

Amsterdam, 1-pc box, 32 sq wts, label, late 1600s, $850 to......**2,500.00**
Cologne, full set of wts & full label, late 1600s, $1,200 to........**2,800.00**
German, wood box, 13+ wts beneath main wts, label, 1795, $650 to.**900.00**

Counterfeit Coin Detectors, American

Allender Pat, lb w/i, cwt, Nov 22, 1855, 8½", $350 to **650.00**
Allender PP, rocker, labeled box, cwt, 1850s, 8½", $450 to..........**750.00**
Allender PP, rocker, no box or cwt, 1850s, 8½", $250 to.............**375.00**
Allender PP, space for $3 gold pc, lb w/i, cwt, 1855, $350 to **750.00**
Allender PP, space for $3 gold pc, no box or cwt, 1855, $275 to..**375.00**
Allender Warranted, rocker, no box or cwt, 1850s, 8½", $350 to....**475.00**
FIS, steelyard, combination detector & postal scale, from $900 to...**1,200.00**
Maranville Pat Coin Detector by CE Staples, Mass, from $600 to...**800.00**
McNally-Harrison Pat 1882, rocker, cwt, JT McNally, $275 to ...**500.00**
McNally-Harrison Pat 1882, rocker, cwt & box, FIS, $400 to **750.00**
McNally-Harrison...1882, rocker, CI base, no cwt/box, $250 to..**400.00**
Thompson, Z-formed rocker, Berrian Mfg, 1877 Pat, $175 to......**350.00**
Troemner, rocker, for 25¢ & 50¢ silver coins, from $300 to **500.00**

Counterfeit Coin Detectors, Dutch

Rocker, Ellinckhuysen, brass, +copy of 1829 Patent, $700 to ...**1,000.00**

Counterfeit Coin Detectors, English

Folding, Guinea, self-rising, labeled box, 1850s, $175 to.............**225.00**
Folding, Guinea, self-rising, wood box/label, ca 1890s, $125 to...**175.00**
Folding, Guinea, self-rising, wooden box, pre-1800, $175 to.......**275.00**
Rocker, simple, no maker's name or cb, end-cap box, $85 to **125.00**
Rocker, w/maker's name & cb, end-cap box, $120 to **150.00**

Egg Scales/Graders, 1930s – 1940s

Acme Egg Grade, Specialty Mfg St Paul MN, aluminum, from $30 to..**50.00**
Brower Mfg Save All, sheet steel (cheaply made), Steelyard bal, $50 to..**75.00**
Jiffy Way, Minneapolis MN, steel w/mc bands, pend bal, common, $30 to..**50.00**
Oakes Mft Tipton IN, pend bal, sheet steel, adjustable stop, $30 to..**50.00**
Reliable, rocker bal, all brass, wooden base, 2½x13¾", $75 to **100.00**
Unique..., Specialty Mfg, sheet steel/aluminum, pend bal, $30 to....**50.00**
Zenith, CI, aluminum, brass pointer, pend bal, from $50 to...........**75.00**

Postal Scales

In the listings below an asterisk (*) was used to indicate that any

one of several manufacturers' or brand names might be found on that particular set of scales. Some of the American-made pieces could be marked Pelouze, Lorraine, Hanson, Kingsbury, Fairbanks, Troemner, IDL, Newman, Accurate, Ideal, B-T, Marvel, Reliance, Howe, Landers-Frary-Clark, Chatillon, Triner, American Bank Service, or Weiss. European/U.S.-made scales marked with an asterisk (*) could be marked Salter, Peerless, Pelouze, Sturgis, L.F.&C., Alderman, G. Little, or S&D. English-made scales with the asterisk (*) could be marked Josh. & Edmd. Ratcliff, R.W. Winfield, S. Mordan, STS (Samuel Turner, Sr.), W.&T. Avery, Parnall & Sons, S&P, or H.B. Wright. There may be other manufacturers as well.

Brit/Can Bal, eq, br or CI on base, *, 4"-15", $100 to...................**750.00**
Engl Bal, eq/Roberval, gilt or st, on stand, *, 3"-8", $500 to **2,500.00**
Engl Bal, eq/Roberval, plain to ornate, *, 3"-8", $100 to...........**2,500.00**
Engl Spring, candlestick, br or st, *, 3½"-15", $100 to................**500.00**
Engl Spring, CI, br or NP fr, Salter, ozs/lbs, 7"-10", $25 to...........**200.00**
Engl Steelyard, ua, 1- or 2-beam, h lph, *, 4"-15", $100 to **1,500.00**
Euro pend, gravity, br, CI or NP fr on base, oz/grams, $75 to........**350.00**
Euro pend, gravity, 2-arm, bm, br or NP, *, 6"-9", $50 to **300.00**
Euro/US Spring, br or NP, pence/etc, h or hh, *, 4"-17", $10 to ..**100.00**
US pend, gravity, metal, pnt face, ap, hcp, sm, $20 to..................**100.00**
US Spring, pnt base metal, *, 2½"-8", $10 to...............................**80.00**
US Spring, pnt bm, *, mtd on inkstand, 2½"-8", $200 to.............**400.00**
US Spring, pnt bm, rnd glass-covered face, *, 8"-10", $25 to.......**100.00**
US Spring, SP, oblong base, *, 2½"-8", $100 to **200.00**
US Spring, st, oblong base, *, 2½"-8", $200 to **500.00**
US Steelyard, ua, CI, *, 5"-13" beam, 4½"-12" base, $25 to.........**100.00**

Schafer and Vater

Established in 1890 by Gustav Schafer and Gunther Vater in the Thuringia region of southwest Germany, by 1913 this firm employed over 200 workers. The original factory burned in 1918 but was restarted and production continued until WWII. In 1972 the East German government took possession of the building and destroyed all of the molds and the records that were left.

You will find pieces with the impressed mark of a nine-point star with a script 'R' inside the star. On rare occasions you will find this mark in blue ink under glaze. The items are sometimes marked with a four-digit design number and a two-digit artist mark. In addition or instead, pieces may have 'Made in Germany' or in the case of the Kewpies, 'Rose O'Neill copyright.' The company also manufactured items for sale under store names, and those would not have the impressed mark.

Schafer and Vater used various types of clays. Items made of hard-paste porcelain, soft-paste porcelain, Jasper, bisque, and majolica can be found. The glazed bisque pieces may be multicolored or have an applied colored slip wash that highlights the intricate details of the modeling. Gold accents were used as well as spots of high-gloss color called jewels. Metallic glazes are coveted. You can find the Jasper in green, blue, pink, lavender, and white. New collectors gravitate toward the pink and lavender shades.

Since Schafer and Vater made such a multitude of items, collectors have to compete with many cross-over collections. These include shaving mugs, hatpin holders, match holders, figurines, figural pitchers, Kewpies, tea sets, bottles, naughties, etc.

Reproduction alert: In addition to the crudely made Japanese copies, some English firms are beginning to make figural reproductions. These seem to be well marked and easy to spot. Our advisor for this category is Joanne M. Koehn; she is listed in the Directory under Texas.

Ashtray, lady w/flowing hair smokes cigarette, lav Jasper **155.00**
Bowl, roses in rectangular reserve, 2 birds perched at rim **90.00**
Condiment set, 3 Dutch heads form jar & 2 shakers (all bl), on tray..**210.00**
Creamer, clown w/mandolin figural, mc, 5½" **185.00**

Creamer, lady, looking left, holds sm pitcher way from her, 5½" 85.00
Creamer, maid wearing apron holding pot, pot is spout, 5½" 150.00
Creamer, screaming clown kneels/holds fan, #6323, 4x5" 120.00

Decanter, bearded man on barrel, 6½", $335.00. (Photo courtesy Myers Fine Art/ LiveAuctioneers.com)

Figurine, Black child holding leaf, Guess What I Am!, 5" 230.00
Figurine, Black man in early tennis outfit, Lawn Tennis on base, 7" ..550.00
Figurine, draped skeleton, Poison & 3 crosses on front, ca 1920, 7"...125.00
Figurine, old lady in bed, Att Hyra, 1½x4" 83.00
Hair receiver, wht cherubs & scrolling on bl Jasper, 3x4" 65.00
Humidor, Egyptian head w/bird on hat, Jasper, #5409, 5½" 100.00
Matchholder, full moon figural, smiling face, stick legs, 4½" 125.00
Matchholder, male bust in top hat & tie, wide open mouth, 4" ... 190.00
Nodder, man in coat smoking cigar, What a Night on base, mc .. 125.00
Pin dish, stylized rooster, bl & wht Jasper, unmk 125.00
Tea set, lady w/mandolin, Cupid & flowers, pk Jasper, pot+cr/sug...475.00
Toothpick holder, frog in gown w/mandolin stands by basket, mc ..175.00
Toothpick holder, sailor holding rotund bathing beauty, mc, 3" 60.00
Vase, Art Nouveau lady, wht on gr Jasper, w/hdls, 6" 75.00
Vase, Japanese lady w/fan & goose at sides of egg form................. 145.00

Scheier

The Scheiers began their ceramics careers in the late 1930s and soon thereafter began to teach their craft at the University of New Hampshire. After WWII they cooperated with the Puerto Rican government in establishing a native ceramic industry, an involvement which would continue to influence their designs. The Scheiers now reside in Arizona.

Bowl, parents & children on boat, bl & yel matt, 7½x13½"....12,000.00
Bowl vase, figures on brn stoneware, sm ft, 6¼x8¾" 2,150.00
Charger, Adam & Eve, manganese on celadon, 1945, 2x15" 4,800.00
Charger, fertility scene, brn & beige, 16", NM 1,450.00
Lamp base, faces (4) on bl, 14¼" 1,000.00
Mug, stylized zebras on red clay, 5½" 120.00
Sculpture, man/woman/child w/in mushroom-shaped pod, lt brn, 11x12"..2,100.00
Sculpture, wrapped figure in ftd pod-like structure, brn/cream, 19x14"...1,450.00
Vase, bl matt bowl form, sm ft, 3½x5¼" 300.00
Vase, bl stippled on wht clay, vasiform, 5" 180.00
Vase, faces incised, olive gr mottle, sm ft, 6¼x4½" 1,200.00
Vase, fish & head frieze, brn teardrop shape, 5¼x4" 850.00
Vase, frothy chocolate brn w/zigzag band, 8½x8½" 600.00
Vase, people holding lg fish, gunmetal brn, coupe shape, 13¼x9" ..4,800.00

Schlegelmilch Porcelain

For information about Schlegelmilch Porcelain, see Mary Frank Gaston's book, *R. S. Prussia Popular Lines*, which addresses R. S. Prussia molds and decorations and contains full-color illustrations and current values. Mold numbers appearing in some of the listings refer to this book.

Assume that all items described below are marked unless noted otherwise. Our advisor for this category is Mary Frank Gaston; she is listed in the Directory under Texas.

E.S. Germany

Fine chinaware marked 'E.S. Germany' or 'E.S. Prov. Saxe' was produced by the E.S. Schlegelmilch factory in Suhl in the Thuringia region of Prussia from sometime after 1861 until about 1925.

Bowl, flowers & ferns, shell mold, mk, 4¾x8½" 115.00
Cake plate, cherub in cart pulled by 3 maidens, gold rim, mk...... 250.00
Candy dish, 4 portrait medallions, Récamier center, 7" 195.00
Chamberstick, bl flowers, cobalt inner border, 2x6" 135.00
Chocolate pot, Napoleon portrait 375.00
Lobster dish, tail forms hdl, florals/gilt, bl mk, 10" 85.00
Plate, lady's portrait, scalloped gold rim, hdls, 9½" 195.00
Vase, maidens (4), cobalt & gold trim, 13½", minimum value..3,500.00

R.S. Germany

In 1869 Reinhold Schlegelmilch began to manufacture porcelain in Suhl in the German province of Thuringia. In 1894 he established another factory in Tillowitz in upper Silesia. Both areas were rich in resources necessary for the production of hard-paste porcelain. Wares marked with the name 'Tillowitz' and the accompanying 'R.S. Germany' phrase are attributed to Reinhold. The most common mark is a wreath and star in a solid color under the glaze. Items marked 'R.S. Germany' are usually more simply decorated than R.S. Prussia. Some reflect the Art Deco trend of the 1920s. Certain hand-painted floral decorations and themes such as 'Sheepherder,' 'Man With Horses,' and 'Cottage' are especially valued by collectors — those with a high-gloss finish or on Art Deco shapes in particular. Not all hand-painted items were painted at the factory. Those with an artist's signature but no 'Hand Painted' mark indicate that the blank was decorated outside the factory.

Ashtray, orange poppies, 3¾".. 75.00
Basket, sm pk roses, gold trim, 4" 140.00
Bowl, courting scene, red & gold border, RSP mold #468, 10"..... 160.00
Bowl, Dogwood & Pine on brn, ftd, 6¼".. 55.00

Bowl, roses with red inner border and gilt, steeple mold, 10½", from $400.00 to $500.00. (Photo courtesy Mary Frank Gaston)

Bowl, Summer portrait, wht satin, oval, hdls, RSP mold #25, 8½x13" ...2,000.00
Box, w/lid, Magnolias, leaf shape, RSP mold #834, 4½x3" 200.00
Cake plate, Dogwood & Pine, dk border, 10" 70.00
Cake plate, pk orchids on gr, gold trim, 10" 80.00
Charger, lg wht roses w/yel tint, gold tapestry at top, 12½" 85.00
Chocolate pot, poppies on shaded tan, glossy, ind, 7¼" 140.00
Chocolate pot, wht lilies w/pk, gold trim, w/lid, 9½" 300.00
Creamer & sugar bowl, sm pk roses w/gr leaves, gold trim, w/lid.. 125.00
Jam jar, roses w/shadow flowers, w/lid & underplate 120.00
Plate, dogwood w/enameled gold stems, RSP mold #256, 8½" 60.00
Plate, Lily of the Valley, w/lg gold leaves, smooth rim, 6⅜"........... 35.00

Relish, wht chrysanthemums, 10¼x4½"............................ 70.00
Toothpick holder, wht floral w/gr leaves, gold trim, 3 hdls 175.00
Tray, gold stenciled flowers & leaves, gold hdls, 8½x4¼".............. 150.00
Vase, Windmill scene, RSP mold #909, 4"................................... 500.00

R.S. Poland

'R.S. Poland' is a mark attributed to Reinhold Schlegelmilch's factory in Tillowitz, Silesia. It was in use for a few years after 1945.

Bowl, Rembrandt's Night Watch on gray-gr, 1½x5⅜" 155.00
Coffee set, gold spatter & marbling, pot+6 c/s+cr/sug w/lid 400.00
Ewer, Rembrandt's Night Watch, RSP mold #900, 6¼" 600.00
Tray, bird on branch, floral/geometric border, 14"........................ 135.00
Vase, Chinese peasants, slim neck, RS Suhl mold #15, 9"........... 900.00
Vase, pastoral scene w/gold & cobalt, hdls, RS Suhl mold #3, 8½" ..1,600.00
Vase, roses on shaded brn, Nouveau hdls, mold #956, 12" 550.00
Vase, Sheepherder, ornate gold hdls, 6" 500.00

R.S. Prussia

Art porcelain bearing the mark 'R.S. Prussia' was manufactured by Reinhold Schlegelmilch in the early 1900s in a Germanic area known until the end of WWI as Prussia. The vast array of mold shapes in combination with a wide variety of decorations is the basis for R.S. Prussia's appeal. Themes can be categorized as figural (usually based on a famous artist's work), birds, florals, portraits, scenics, and animals.

Bowl, center; pk roses w/in & w/out, mold #278, 10" 400.00
Bowl, irises on cobalt w/gold, mold #25b, 4x9½x7½" 550.00

Bowl, Madame Lebrun portrait, Tiffany finish, Lily mold, 10½", $2,400.00. (Photo courtesy Forsythe's Auctions LLC/LiveAuctioneers.com)

Bowl, Mill scene, gold scrolls, red mk, 7½" L................................ 225.00
Bowl, Pheasant w/pines, lav highlights, oval, Medallion mold, 14x7".. 1,000.00
Bowl, Récamier w/Tiffany bronze & gold-stencil border, mold #29, 10"..1,400.00
Bowl, Snowbird on satin, pearlized dome shapes, mold #113, 10¾"...300.00
Bowl, Swans on Lake, Icicle mold, 11".. 650.00
Cake plate, lush flower spray, open hdls, Carnation mold, RM, 9½"..300.00
Cake plate, mc roses, bl dome shapes, mold #78, 11" 300.00
Cake plate, Potocka/gold floral on wht, mold #29, unmk, 9½"... 1,600.00
Celery dish, clematis on watered silk finish, Lily mold, 12x5"...... 275.00
Chocolate pot, Swans & Evergreens, Icicle mold, 10".............. 1,400.00
Cracker jar, pk roses, gold emb carnations, mold #526, 5x9"........ 400.00
Creamer, floral w/gold trim, mold #605, 4" 175.00
Ferner, Swans on Lake, gold trim, mold #882, 4x9".................... 650.00
Leaf dish, floral on gr to wht, Leaf mold variant, mold #10g, mk . 165.00
Pitcher, cider; Lilies w/Dogwood, mold #554, 6¼"...................... 400.00
Pitcher, mc floral on gr, gold trim, mold #456, 9½" 600.00
Plate, lady's portrait in wht gown w/leaves & gold, mk, 8½".... 1,250.00
Plate, Snowbird scene, gold stenciled trim, Popcorn mold, 8½" .. 1,400.00
Relish, German court figures portraits (4) & roses, RM, 9¾" 650.00
Relish, Winter portrait on satin w/gold, Iris mold, 9½x4½" 1,400.00

Shaving mug, Castle scene, mold #644, 3½"............................... 400.00
Shell dish, mc flowers w/gold, mold #20, 7¼" 225.00
Tankard, roses on cream w/dk gr on top, gold trim, Lily mold, 15¼"..800.00
Tankard, Swallows, wht water lilies at base, #584, 13" 850.00
Tea set, roses w/gold, RM, 3-pc.. 1,000.00
Tray, Swans (3) w/gazebo, mold #327, 12x9" 700.00
Urn, Cottage scene, ornate gold hdls, w/lid, mold #903, 12½"..2,000.00

R.S. Suhl

Porcelains marked with this designation are attributed to Reinhold Schlegelmilch's Suhl factory.

Bowl, lav & wht flowers w/gold, hdls, 8⅛" 150.00
Bowl, Mill scene, RSP mold #93, 5½" 275.00
Coffee set, Angelica Kauffmann scene, 9" pot+cr/sug+6 c/s...... 1,700.00
Cup & saucer, pk roses, gold stencilling, cup: 1⅞x2".................. 115.00
Cup & saucer, wht, floral int 100.00
Ewer, Victorian lady watering flowers, emb gold, mold #900, 6¼"..1,100.00
Vase, dk pk roses on blk, gold trim, mold #2, 7⅛"...................... 450.00
Vase, floral, pk & wht on blk, bulbous, RSP mold #907, 5"......... 200.00
Vase, Melon Eaters, red w/gold beaded ft, gold hdls, mold #3, 8"..1,400.00
Vase, roses, wht on gray to ivory, mold #10, salesman sample, 3⅛" ..250.00

R.S. Tillowitz

R.S. Tillowitz-marked porcelains are attributed to Reinhold Schlegelmilch's factory in Tillowitz, Silesia.

Bowl, berry; exotic birds & flowers, 3" 18.00
Cake plate, Fruit V decor, pears & grapes, 10⅞" 100.00
Cake plate, red poinsettias, 10" 80.00
Egg cups, wht w/gold, ribbed body, 2¼", 4 on matching tray 175.00
Gravy boat, pk roses on int, 6½" 40.00
Relish, Lily of the Valley, tan border, gold trim, 8x3¾" 45.00
Vase, lg pk tinted flowers w/sm orange flowers on brn, unmk, 6¼"..100.00

Schneider

The Schneider Glass Company was founded in 1914 at Epinay-sur-seine, France. They made many types of art glass, some of which sandwiched designs between layers. Other decorative devices were appliqué and carved work. These were marked 'Charder' or 'Schneider.' During the '20s commercial artware was produced with Deco motifs cut by acid through two or three layers and signed 'LeVerre Francais' in script or with a section of inlaid filigrane. Our advisor for this category is Don Williams; he is listed in the Directory under Missouri. See also Le Verre Francais.

Compote, indigo to orange, purple ft, 4¾x8¼" 800.00
Lamp, bullet form ivory shade w/orange border, Deco std, 16"..2,350.00
Pitcher, orange & rust mottle, blk hdl, ped base, Ovington, 15¾" ..900.00
Pitcher, red to cream mottle, dk red hdl, upright rim, bulbous, 7", NM..600.00
Vase, brn/orange/apricot mottle, waisted neck, ftd, 12"............. 1,450.00
Vase, burnt orange/orange mottle, charcoal stem/ft, 15½" 1,550.00
Vase, clear & frosted to purple at base, ftd, 9¼" 790.00
Vase, cranberry/wht/orange mottle, in wrought-iron fr, 5½x4¾" ...1,100.00
Vase, gr mottle to clear on orange base, 3½" 450.00
Vase, mc mottle on pk, goblet-like, ca 1926-28, 8" 1,450.00
Vase, orange/rust mottle, ovoid, 8".. 450.00
Vase, pk/bl/purple/wht mottle, pinched base, flat rim, 14" 1,450.00
Vase, smoky topaz to dk purple w/2 vertical cvd bands, ftd, 8"..1,200.00
Vase, yel & wht mottle, bulbous rim, ftd, 11½x9" 1,200.00
Vase, yel/orange/purple mottle, waisted rim, ftd, slim, 11¾" 975.00

Cameo

Bottle, scent; Bijoux, yel/wht tea roses w/blk frwork, 4¾" 4,025.00
Lamp, fish & seaweed, brn on bl, mushroom shape, 11" 400.00
Rose bowl, floral, orange & brn on yel mottle, bulbous, 3½" H.... 570.00
Vase, floral, cobalt on frosted Chinese Yellow, 22x6" 4,550.00
Vase, floral, orange & gr on wht mottle, ped ft, flared rim, 10x6"..1,320.00
Vase, floral, orange on wht mottle, shouldered, 10" 1,150.00
Vase, floral, purple on lav/wht mottle, flared bottom, ftd, 7¼" 725.00
Vase, leaves, dk orange & brn on orange mottle, waist-to-hip hdls, 10"..2,400.00
Vase, stylized fruit branches, cinnabar on amber, 16½" 2,500.00
Vase, swans under leafage, purple on orange & yel, ftd, 11" 3,500.00

Schoolhouse Collectibles

Schoolhouse collectibles bring to mind memories of a bygone era when the teacher rang her bell to call the youngsters to class in a one-room schoolhouse where often both the 'hickory stick' and an apple occupied a prominent position on her desk. Our advisor for this category is Kenn Norris; he is listed in the Directory under Texas.

Bell, bronze w/iron yoke, 15" 300.00
Bell, CI, w/clapper, 9x14" 50.00
Book, Mitchell's School Geography, 1845, G 15.00
Book, Sanders School Reader, 4th book, leather cover, 1854, VG...30.00
Desk, master's, cherry Fed w/slanted lift top................................. 275.00
Desk, master's, curly maple/walnut, dvtl gallery, cvd front, 40x38x30" ... 400.00
Desk, master's, oak kneehole w/6 drws, 1920s............................. 150.00
Desk, master's, pine, slant lid, tapered legs, old rpt, 32x26x21".... 150.00
Desk, master's, tiger oak kneehole w/6 drw, 1920s, EX 180.00
Desk, master's, walnut/poplar/pine, slant lid, cvd front, 27x38x25"....700.00
Desk, wooden seat (swivels) & desk on metal base, 22x30x30" 75.00
Desk, wooden seat w/desktop behind, CI base, 1900-20, from $35 to..60.00
Desk chair, wide arm for writing surface, oak, EX finish 75.00
Pencil sharpener, Bakelite, US Army Tank decal on gr tank shape...60.00
Pencil sharpener, Bakelite w/Charlie McCarthy decal 45.00
Pencil sharpener, Bakelite w/Dopey decal on butterscotch figural....75.00
Pencil sharpener, Bakelite w/Popeye decal, figural, King Features.. 75.00
Pencil sharpener, celluloid, Donald Duck figural, Japan, 1930s, 3", VG...225.00
Pencil sharpener, celluloid, elephant on base, wht, Japan 165.00
Pencil sharpener, celluloid, penguin on metal base, Japan 135.00
Pencil sharpener, CI, AB Dick Co Chicago, crank hdl, 6½" L..... 300.00
Pencil sharpener, CI, Favor Ruhl Co NY, crank hdl, 5x14" 300.00
Pencil sharpener, CI, FS Webster Co, blk pnt, Pat June 21 92, 7"...425.00
Pencil sharpener, CI, Indian chief head, worn mc pnt, Japan 20.00
Pencil sharpener, CI, US Automatic Pencil...1908, 5x4½x3½" ... 300.00
Pencil sharpener, CI, wheel w/6 blades, crank hdl, desk mt, 5½" .. 345.00
Pencil sharpener, CI/brass/wood, Jupiter Pencil Pointer, 6x13" ... 360.00
Pencil sharpener, metal, enameled, Great Dane's head, 1¾" 55.00
Pencil sharpener, metal, race car, worn gold pnt, Unis France, 2" .. 1,100.00
Pencil sharpener, pnt cast metal, Black man's head form, 2", VG.. 60.00
Pencil sharpener, pot metal clown w/purple hat, mc pnt, VG........ 30.00

Pencil Boxes

Among the most common of school-related collectibles are the many classes of pencil boxes. Generally from the period of the 1870s to the 1940s, these boxes were made in hundreds of different styles. Materials included tin, wood (thin frame and solid hardwood) and leather; fabric and plastics were later used. Most pencil boxes were in a basic, rectangular configuration, though rare examples were made to resemble other objects such as rolling pins, ball bats, nightsticks, etc. They may still be found at reasonable prices, even though collectors have recently taken a keen in-

terest in them. All boxes listed below are in very good to near mint condition. For further information we recommend *School Collectibles of the Past* by Lar and Sue Hothem. Sue is listed in the Directory under Ohio.

Wooden sled, German, EX, $95.00.

(Photo courtesy Tom Harris Auctions/LiveAuctioneers.com)

Cb litho, Gunsmoke Pencil Case, Matt Dillon on lid, EX 95.00
Litho on wood, Mother Goose scene on lid, 1930s, 8", EX...................65.00
Papier maché, bl chintz w/gold metallic leaves, 1x7¾" 95.00
Papier maché, decoupage scene, push-button latch, 9" L 100.00
Pyrography, pressed/pnt bluebirds/poinsettias, 9" L......................... 65.00

Schoop, Hedi

In the 1940s and 1950s one of the most talented artists working in California was Hedi Schoop. Her business ended in 1958 when a fire destroyed her operation. It was at that time that she decided to do freelance work for other companies such as Cleminson Clay. Schoop was probably the most imitated artist of the time and she answered some of those imitators by successfully suing them. Some imitators were Kim Ward, Ynez, and Yona. Schoop was diversified in her creations, making items such as shapely women, bulky-looking women and children with fat arms and legs, TV lamps, and animals as well as planters and bowls. Schoop used many different marks including the stamped or incised Schoop signature and also a hard-to-find sticker. 'Hollywood, Cal.' or 'California' were occasionally used in conjunction with the Hedi Schoop name. For further information we recommend *Collector's Encyclopedia of California Pottery, Second Edition*, by Jack Chipman; he is listed in the Directory under California.

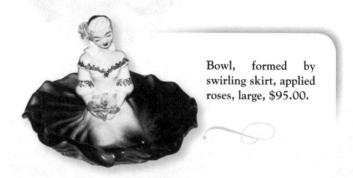

Bowl, formed by swirling skirt, applied roses, large, $95.00.

Figurine, girl in short jumper, poodle on leash, 9" 325.00
Figurine, girl w/basket walks w/poodle beside, 10", from $150 to.175.00
Figurine, lady in exotic outfit, gr w/much gold, open basket, 12½"... 150.00
Figurines, Oriental boy (& girl) w/instrument, pk/wht/blk, 11", pr..135.00
Figurines, Oriental man (& lady) w/bucket, 11½", pr from $100 to...135.00
Planter, bird form, 7½x10", pr, from $50 to................................... 60.00
Planter, horse w/gr saddle, 7½" 50.00
Planter, rooster, gr to brn, 14x11".. 75.00
Plaque, fish, pk to gray, 8¼" L.. 40.00
Tray, seated lady's skirt forms bowl, 6¾x13" 95.00
Vase, girl dancing w/fan, open basket at side, 13x8", pr................. 135.00
Vase, leafless tree in relief, sq, 10¼x7¼".. 55.00

Schramberg

The Schramberg factory was founded in the early nineteenth century in Schramberg Wurttemberg, Germany. The pieces most commonly seen are those made by Schramberger Majolika Fabrik (SMF) dating from 1912 until 1989. Some pieces are stamped with the pattern name (i.e. Gobelin) and the number of the painter who executed it. The imprinted number identifies the shape. Marks may also include these names: Wheelock, Black Forest, and Mepoco.

Perhaps the most popular examples with collectors are those from the Gobelin line. Such pieces have a gray background with as many as 10 other colors used to create that design. For example, Gobelin 3 pieces will be painted with green and orange leaves and yellow eyes along with other colors specific to that design.

Little is known of the designers who worked for Schramberg; however, Eva Zeisel was employed at the factory for nearly two years starting in the fall of 1928. Her duties included design, production, and merchandising. Because of Zeisel's popularity with collectors, designs are being attributed to her. Since she left Schramberg within two years, it is difficult for collectors to know which designs were actually hers and which were designs of other employees.

Basket, Gobelin #4, 4" 115.00
Cup & saucer, Gobelin, Zeisel.. 30.00

Planter, Gobelin 6, 10" long, $52.00. (Photo courtesy Ralph Winslow)

Plate, chalet, 7¾" 20.00
Plate, geometrics, Zeisel, 6½" 44.00
Plate, Gobelin, 8⅜" 38.00
Tray, egg cup; geometric... 95.00
Urn, Gobelin #4, w/lid, 9" 138.00
Vase, chalet, 7"... 44.00
Vase, chalet, 12".. 58.00
Vase, Gobelin, 8½" 60.00

Scouting Collectibles

Boy Scouts

Scouting was founded in England in 1907 by retired Major General Lord Robert Baden-Powell. Its purpose is the same today as it was then — to help develop physically strong, mentally alert boys and to teach them basic fundamentals of survival and leadership. The movement soon spread to the United States, and in 1910 a Chicago publisher, William Boyce, set out to establish scouting in America. The first World Scout Jamboree was held in 1920 in England. Baden-Powell was honored as the Chief Scout of the World. In 1926 he was awarded the Silver Buffalo Award in the United States. He was knighted in 1929 for distinguished military service and for his scouting efforts. Baden-Powell died in 1941.

Unless noted otherwise, values are for items in at least near mint condition. For more information you may contact our advisor, R.J. Sayers, author of *Guide to Scouting Collectibles*, whose address (and ordering information regarding his book) may be found in the Directory under North Carolina. (Correspondence other than book orders requires SASE please.)

Backpack, Official Everest Scout Pak, w/fr, Model 1384, w/tag, 22x12" . 40.00
Bank, can; tin, red/wht/bl graphics, key lock on bottom, 1955, 3" ... 105.00
Belt buckle, Philmont Scout Ranch, gold-tone metal, 3" L, VG.... 42.00
Boy Scout Diary 1923, w/writing (shoveled snow/snow fight w/girls), G ... 30.00
Bugle, brass, Rexcraft, ca 1970, NMIB............................. 120.00
Coo Beads, Kecoghtan Lodge 463, metal acorn in center, red & wht beads . 65.00
Handbook, Manual of Leadership, red cover, 11th ed, 1927, VG .. 55.00
Hat, campaign; olive brn, emb logos on headband, w/logo hat pin, EX.. 52.00
Hat, olive brn, w/mc embr logo on side, sz XL, folded 12" L 40.00
Hatchet, Vaughan, Official Boy Scout Axe on shank, rubber on hdl, EX....50.00
Jacket, tan fabric, insignia on metal buttons, high collar, ca 1915...160.00
Knife, Marbles, leathered hdl, logo on leather sheath, ca 1935...... 95.00
Knife, Western, leathered hdl, 4" blade, Woodcraft, ca 1920, 7½"..120.00
Neckerchief, New York World's Fair..., orange/wht/bl, 1940, 30" sq..65.00
Patch, BSA Camp Hume Lake, 1959, 3", M.................................. 85.00
Patch, Camp Sequoyah, maroon on wht felt, 1948, 3", EX 75.00
Patch, Region 13 Far East Council, Serving Scouting...World, 1962.. 110.00
Pin, Be Prepared suspends red/wht/bl ribbon w/sterling eagle, 3½"..60.00
Pin, metal, God & Country at top of bl ribbon w/red enamel cross, 4"..55.00

Pocket watch, Ingersoll, 1937, $250.00. (Photo courtesy Morphy Auctions/LiveAuctioneers.com)

Ring, sterling, Be Prepared w/Boy Scout insignia, Eagle, sz 12 ..... 110.00
Shirt, red wool, button-down front, emblem on pocket, sz 40........ 55.00
Utencil kit, eating; Shrade, log stamped on leather case, 1942, EX .. 54.00
Watch, National...New York City on face, metal w/leather strap, G.. 55.00

Girl Scouts

Collecting Girl Scout memorabilia is a hobby that is growing nationwide. When Sir Baden-Powell founded the Boy Scout Movement in England, it proved to be too attractive and too well adapted to youth to limit its great opportunities to boys alone. The sister organization, known in England as the Girl Guides, quickly followed and was equally successful. Mrs. Juliette Low, an American visitor to England and a personal friend of the father of scouting, realized the tremendous future of the movement for her own country, and with the active and friendly cooperation of the Baden-Powells, she founded the Girl Guides in America, enrolling the first patrols in Savannah, Georgia, in March 1912. In 1915 National Headquarters were established in Washington, D.C., and the name was changed to Girl Scouts. The first national convention was held in 1914. Each succeeding year has shown growth and increased enthusiasm in this steadily growing army of girls and young women who are learning in the happiest ways to combine patriotism, outdoor activities of every kind, skill in every branch of domestic science, and high standards of community service. Today there are over 400,000 Girl Scouts and more than 22,000 leaders. Mr. Sayers is also our Girl Scout advisor.

Award, girl figure, Appreciation of Leadership, copper plated, '59, 8"..25.00
Bag, leader; bl vinyl, sm emblem on side, w/zipper, hdls, 11x14" ... 33.00
Book, Campward Ho!, Manual for Girl Scout Camps, gr hardbk, 1920, EX. 55.00
Book, Girl Scouts Vacation Adventure, Lavell, hardbk w/jacket, '27, EX. 30.00
Camera, Official...Brownie Scouts, w/flash, bulb & film, 1967, MIB.. 32.00
Catalog, Accessories; 39 pgs, 1934, EX 20.00
Catalog, It's a Girl Scout Christmas, 1941, 16 pgs, EX 22.00
Charm, girl figural, gr enamel on sterling, detailed, 1960s, 1", M... 35.00
Coin, Commemorative, 1912-62, Honor the Past - Serve the Future.. 15.00
Cookbook, Girl Scouts USA Beginner's Cookbook, Cameron, paperbk, 1972. 24.00
Diary, Glimpses..., illustrated, paperbk, unused, 1934, G.............. 24.00
Doll, Brownie, Effanbee, 1965, 8½", EXIB..................................... 50.00
Doll, hard plastic, sleep eyes, head/legs move, Terri Lee, 7½", EX...110.00
Hat, beret; gr & wht GS emblem, gr felt, sz sm, 1950s 15.00
Hat, wide brim w/GS emblem & ribbon bow, gr, 1950s, EX........... 46.00
Knife, Ulster, 5 tools, bone hdl, Divine & Sons, 1925, 3½", EX 50.00
Lunch pail, tin litho w/Scout scenes, hinged lid, ca 1920, VG 85.00
Pin, membership; trefoil w/wht GS, Bakelite, 1⅛x1", EX.............. 50.00
Pin-bk, pk/yel, girl/GS embr in oval center, 1950s, 1¾x1¼", EX ... 25.00
Print, Our America, Learning About the Forest, camp scene, 2x32", EX.. 40.00
Ring, Girls Scouts USA surrounds lg gr faceted stone, gold filled, NM .. 42.00
Scarf, red w/embr gr emblem in corner, triangular, 1950s.............. 32.00
Tie, scarf; silver-tone w/gold accents, emb eagle & GS, 1¼x1", EX .40.00
Watch, Brownie emblem on wht face, red leather strap, Timex, 1962...35.00

Scrimshaw

The most desirable examples of the art of scrimshaw can be traced back to the first half of the nineteenth century to the heyday of the whaling industry. Some voyages lasted for several years, and conditions on board were often dismal. Sailors filled the long hours by using the tools of their trade to engrave whale teeth and make boxes, pie crimpers (jagging wheels), etc., from the bone and teeth of captured whales. Eskimos also made scrimshaw, sometimes borrowing designs from the sailors who traded with them.

Beware of fraudulent pieces; fakery is prevalent in this field. Many carved teeth are of recent synthetic manufacture (examples engraved with information such as ship's or captain's names, dates, places, etc., should be treated with extreme caution) and have no antique or collectible value. A listing of most of these plastic items has been published by the Kendall Institute at the New Bedford Whaling Museum in New Bedford, Massachusetts. If you're in doubt or a novice collector, it's best to deal with reputable people who guarantee the items they sell. Our advisor for this category is John Rinaldi; he is listed in the Directory under Maine. See also Powder Horns.

Busk, baleen w/buildings/ships/flags/eagle, 14½x1¾" 4,750.00
Busk, bone w/hearts/sunbursts/flowers/symbols, NE, 19th C, 14".. 350.00
Busk, pinwheels/hearts/stars/etc, 19th C, 14½x1¾" 1,100.00
Busk, whalebone, scenes, age crack, old patina, 1850s, 14".......... 600.00
Busk, 17 panels w/mc stain, primitive cvgs ea side, 19th C, 12x1½" ..1,950.00
Fid, bone, incised lines, 9" 300.00
Fid, bone w/cvd decor, 11¼" 300.00
Jagging wheel, pierced heart, losses, 19th C, 6¾" 385.00
Jagging wheel, whale ivory, serpent hdl, leaf-form fork, 19th C, 5" ..1,295.00
Knife, ivory hdl w/copper rivets, metal guard, 9½" overall 475.00
Marking gage, cvd whalebone, 8"...2,465.00
Measuring stick, bone, inscr AB (AE Barker), early 19th C, 35⅝" ..1,200.00
Needle holder, love symbols, piercings, cvd needle sheath, 2x1⅝"... 660.00
Pipe tamp, lady's leg form w/patterned cvgs, 19th C, 2¾x1¼"...... 275.00
Rolling pin, rosewood w/ivory ends, 14½" 1,200.00
Snuff bottle, whale tooth w/wht metal lid & end cap, 19th C, 4" ...515.00
Tooth, eagles sparring/fish/palisade/soldiers/tents, 19th C, 5⅞".2,235.00

Tooth, fine lady w/veil/Liberty/flag/shield, cracks, 19th C, 5" ...1,765.00
Tooth, Hornet's Escape...British 74/naval scene, 19th C, 5¾"...4,700.00
Tooth, lady on bench in bower/vessel/eagle/flags, 19th C, 6"...11,165.00
Tooth, Liberty/anchor/shield/banner/vessel, cracks, 19th C, 5⅝"..2,350.00
Tusk, walrus; maidens (1 on horsebk), drilled near tip, 19th C, 20"...1,100.00

Sebastians

Prescott W. Baston first produced Sebastian Miniatures in 1938 in his home in Arlington, Massachusetts. In 1946 Baston bought a small shoe factory in Marblehead, Massachusetts, and produced his figurines there for the next 30 years. Over the years Baston sculpted and produced more than 750 different pieces, many of which have been sold nationwide through gift shops. Baston and The Lance Corporation of Hudson, Massachusetts, consolidated the line in 1976 and actively promoted Sebastians nationally. Many of Baston's commercial designs, private commissions, and even some open line pieces have become very collectible. Aftermarket price is determined by three factors: 1) current or out of production status, 2) labels, and 3) condition. Copyright dates are of no particular significance with regard to value.

Mr. Baston died in 1984, and his son Prescott 'Woody' Baston, Jr. continued the tradition by taking over the designing. To date Woody has sculpted over 250 pieces of his own. After numerous changes in the company that held manufacturing and distribution rights for Sebastions, Woody and his wife Margery are now sculpting and painting the Sebastian Miniatures out of their home in Massachusetts. By personally producing the pieces, Sebastions are the only collectible line that is produced from design to finished product by the artist. Sebastian Miniatures have come full cycle.

America Remembers the Family Picnic, Christmas Series, 1979, 3½". 25.00
Andrew Jackson, 3½" 25.00
Aubry, 50th Anniversary Collection, Marblehead label, 3¼", MIB .. 17.50
Boy & Pelican, 3½" 30.00
Bringing Home the Tree, red label, 3¼" 25.00
Building Days, #407, bl label, 1975, 3¼" 25.00
Call From the Candy Man, 1949, 3x3x1¼" 100.00

Chiquita Bananas, 1951, 4", NM, $500.00.

Christmas Morning, Blair's ed #574, Hudson label, 1984............... 18.00
Colonial Blacksmith, 1970, 3½"... 18.00
Colonial Carriage, yel label, MIB... 35.00
Concord Minuteman, bronzed, 1975.. 110.00
Dicken's Marley, 1997, 2¾" 30.00
Faneuil Hall - Quincy Market, sgn Woody Baston 7/21/84, 2x5"... 20.00
Fiorello de Guardia, pk label, 4" 95.00
Fireside Chat (President Roosevelt), 1989, 2½" 32.00
First Kite, red label, 1981, 3¼" 25.00
Franklin D Roosevelt, MIB.. 22.00
Hanging the Stocking, MIB 20.00
Holy Family, nativity scene, 5½x7".. 55.00

Horse-drawn stagecoach, pen stand, Everett National Bank, 1959, 3x5" .. 42.00
John Alden, sitting on barrel.. 30.00
John Hancock, 1983.. 38.00
Lobster Boat, #522... 45.00
Manger, nativity pc, Hudson MA, sgn Preston W Baston 12/2/80 ...26.00
Mark Twain, lt bl label, 2¼".. 60.00
Midnight Snacks, Mrs Claus, pewter.. 20.00
Midwest Snowman, 1998, MIB 42.50
Paul Bunyan, 1949, 3¼".. 30.00
Peter Stuyvesant, red label, 5" 25.00
Pilgrim Santa, red HP on pewter... 35.00
Rx Obocell, 1950, MIB... 55.00
Sampling the Stew, blk label 25.00
Santa in Dory 27.50
Scale of Justice 25.00
Sebastian Studio Original Works of Art, plaque, 4½" 25.00
Shepherds, nativity pc, Marblehead label................................. 32.00
Snowdays Boy, yel tags.. 25.00
State House, comissioned by MA Masonic Lodge, MIB.............. 125.00
Stuffing the Stockings, 1992.. 18.00
Swan Boat Boston Public Garden, Marblehead label, 1950, 2"...... 17.00
Thanksgiving Couple, Marblehead label 30.00
Williamsburg Capital, Colonial.. 25.00

Sevres

Fine-quality porcelains have been made in Sevres, France, since the early 1700s. Rich ground colors were often hand painted with portraits, scenics, and florals. Some pieces were decorated with transfer prints and decalcomania; many were embellished with heavy gold. These wares are the most respected of all French porcelains. Their style and designs have been widely copied, and some of the items listed below are Sevres-type wares.

Bowl, centerpc; cobalt w/ornate gilt bronze base & hdls, 19th C, 22" W. 12,000.00
Bowl, centerpc; figures on bl, gilt-bronze mts, 19th C, 14x19x10" . 6,600.00
Bowl, centerpc; florals/tropies, gilt ram's heads/loop hdls, 10x14x10" . 2,400.00
Bowl, centerpc; scenic panels, rtcl gilt bronze hdls, 19th C, 14x25" L. 15,500.00
Bowl, centerpc; scenic w/gilt-bronze children w/hooves at base, 22" W... 12,000.00
Box, scenic lid, sgn B Tehau, cobalt w/gold, 4x9x7" 2,400.00
Box, 2 maidens/youth in reserve on cobalt w/gold, 4½x11x8" . 3,950.00
Bust, Marie Antoinette, wht, Lecomte, #1056, ca 1890, 20" 3,200.00
Cache pot, cherubs cartouche amid gilt serpents on turq, 7"....... 900.00
Cache pot, floral, gilt goat head hdls, 19th C, 10x12¾" 4,150.00
Cache pot on stand, rose garlands & gilt swags, Sevres mk, 5x5¾" .. 240.00
Clock, floor; HP w/ormolu bronze mts, marble base, 55x11½" ..5,500.00
Clock, mantel; floral swags/ram's heads, bronze trim, 26½" 5,300.00
Clock, Mother Mary & 2 holy children panel, bronze mts, Paris, 19x12" . 4,750.00
Compote, monogram w/in floral wreath, turq border w/gold, 5½x10" ..575.00
Cup & saucer, Marie Antoinette portrait, cobalt/gold/jewels, 1778. 2,400.00
Ewer, romantic scene on bl, gilt bronze mts & hdl, 19th C, 34". 5,000.00
Group, Le Basier du Faune, after Dalou, terra cotta, 1922, 15" .3,000.00
Lamp, Venus & Cupid scene, Gauthier, brass mts, electrified, 25" ...1,300.00
Plaque, Palais des Tuileries Paris, Guerard, 1822, 5½x8⅜" 4,800.00
Plate, cavalier on horse battling, cobalt/gold border, 19th C, 10" ...350.00
Plate, equestrian battle scene, cobalt & gold rim, 1890s, 9⅜" 395.00
Plate, 2 drunken youths, cobalt & gold scalloped border, 9½" 145.00
Punch bowl, Napoleonic scenic panels on gr w/gold, 7x16", +10 c/s. 2,400.00
Sugar bowl, floral sprays, Celeste Blue w/gold, w/lid, 1780s, 4¼" 3,300.00
Urn, bl molded lappets/gilt bronze mts, campana-style, 19th C, 27"...1,450.00
Urn, courting couple reserve, cobalt & gold, trumpet ft, 19th C, 9" . 360.00
Urn, courting couple w/gold, gilt metal satyr mask hdls, 1900s, 20"...725.00
Urn, draped nude/cupid w/gold & jewels, missing lid, 43½" 1,650.00
Urn, figures in landscape, Porlevin, gilt-bronze mts, w/lid, 1757, 42". 7,800.00

Urn, nurse/mother/child, gilt bronze mts, Sevres mk, w/lid, 50", VG ... 6,500.00
Urn, romantic scenes/gold, Grisard, gilt bronze mts, 19th C, rpr, 49" . 16,500.00

Urns, Napoleon at Austerlitz (after Francois Gerard), signed H. Desprez, gilt bronze eagle handles, 27", $10,300.00 for the pair. (Photo courtesy Neal Auction Company Auctioneers & Appraisers of Fine Art)

Vase, cobalt baluster w/gilt snowflakes, silver mts, 1920s, 19", pr ... 5,250.00
Vase, figures in landscape, cobalt w/gold, ovoid, 19th C, 20x10".... 3,250.00
Vase, wisteria on gold-leaf ground, Milet, #432, 8".................3,000.00

Sewer Tile

Whimsies, advertising novelties, and other ornamental items were sometimes made in potteries where the primary product was simply tile.

Boston terrier, sgn L Staley 1944, OH, 8¾" 575.00
Chimney cap, fluted column on sq base, scalloped rim, 29x12x12" ...260.00
Dog seated, flat head, tooled eyelashes, 9¼"...............................1,000.00
Dog seated, incised fur, att OH, 11" 925.00
Dog seated w/free-standing front legs, att G Bagnell, 10¼" 2,900.00
Eagle plaque, sgn EJE, 5"..115.00
Horned owl on branch, EX detail, 14½" 300.00
Lion reclining on oval base, molded/hand tooled, flakes, 9½x15" ...700.00
Lion reclining on platform, dk brn, OH, 19th C, 6¼" 600.00
Piggy bank, seated, long eyelashes, sgn DRM, OH, 9" 460.00
Pitcher, Liberty & 13 stars (molded/appl) ea side, scroll hdl, 7", EX ..350.00
Planter, stump w/textured surface, appl branches, pnt, 10" 200.00
Spaniel seated, brn w/contrasting eyes/tag, Roy Blind, OH, 8¾" .. 175.00
Spaniel seated w/paw raised, brn lustre, OH, 19th C, 8⅞" 1,200.00
Tree stump container, seated dog finial (glued), 7" 115.00
Umbrella stand, tree stump w/appl vines, tooled bark, 20x8".......200.00

Sewing Items

Sewing collectibles continue to intrigue collectors, and fine nineteenth-century and earlier pieces are commanding higher prices due to increased demand and scarcity. Complete needlework boxes and chatelaines in original condition are rare, but even incomplete examples can be considered prime additions to any collection, as long as they meet certain criteria: boxes should contain fittings of the period; the chains of the chatelaine should be intact and contemporary with the style; and the individual holders should be original and match the brooch. As nineteenth-century items become harder to find, new trends in collecting develop. Needle books, many of which were decorated with horses, children, beautiful ladies, etc., have become very popular. Some were giveaways printed with advertisements of products and businesses. Even early pins are collectible; the first ones were made in two parts with the round head attached separately. Pin disks, pin cubes, and other pin holders also make interesting additions to a sewing collection.

Tape measures are very popular — especially Victorian figurals. These command premium prices. Early wooden examples of transferware and Tunbridge ware have gained in popularity, as have figurals of vegetable ivory, celluloid, and other early plastics. From the twentieth century, tatting shuttles made of plastics, bone, brass, sterling, and wood decorated with Art Nouveau, Art Deco, and more modern designs are in demand — so are darning eggs, stilettos, and thimbles. Because of the decline in the popularity of needlework after the 1920s (due to increased production of machine-made items), novelty items were made in an attempt to regain consumer interest, and many collectors today also find these appealing.

Watch for reproductions. Sterling thimbles are being made in Holland and the U.S. and are available in many Victorian-era designs. But the originals are usually plainly marked, either in the inside apex or outside on the band. Avoid testing gold and silver thimbles for content; this often destroys the inside marks. Instead, research the manufacturer's mark; this will often denote the material as well. Even though the reproductions are well finished, they do not have manufacturers' marks. Many thimbles are being made specifically for the collectible market; reproductions of porcelain thimbles are also found. Prices should reflect the age and availability of these thimbles. For more information we recommend *Sewing Tools & Trinkets* by Helen Lester Thompson and *Antique & Collectible Buttons, Volumes I and II*, by Debra Wisniewski.

Bodkin, bone, ca 1900 .... 15.00
Bodkin, sterling, Webster Co, ca 1915 .... 50.00
Book, Clothing for Women, Baldt, dressmaking, hardbk, 549 pgs, 1920s....140.00
Box, pin; cube, gold & marbleized paper cover, USA, 2¼" 22.00
Box, wicker, HP gr dmns, hinged lid, on stand, 1910, hdl up: 35x12"...100.00
Box, wood, accordion style, 4 legs, hdl, Strommen Bruk Hamar, 21x23"...100.00
Box, wood w/plastic gromets, lg pk knob on lid, 1 drw, 1905, 6x7" 110.00
Button, brass, emb rabbit head & floral, raised rim, loop shank, 1"..105.00
Button, copper, cats (2) on cut-out floral oval, 1½x2" 110.00
Button, glass, Moonglow leaf, med 10.00
Button, MOP, cvd harbor scene & flowers, brass loop, 1" 200.00
Button, red glass w/foil-bk glass inlay, 1950s, lg 25.00
Button, silvered brass, Cupid, lg, 1⅝" 55.00
Buttonhook, steel, bone hdl, ca 1910 .... 3.00
Caddy, Peaseware, 3-part w/metal rods, lt wear/chips, 5¾" 300.00
Caddy, poplar w/mc pnt, bowl-shaped base, mushroom finial, 12x5" ..865.00
Chatelaine, sterling stylized butterfly, 4 chains w/5 tools, ca 1900 ..550.00
Chest, mahog bowfront w/inlay, tray, 3-drw, 1800s, 11x13x7" ..2,350.00
Clamp, CI, dolphin, angle thumbscrew, England, ca 1870, 6x5½"...1,250.00
Darner, faux pk marble egg shape on tan & yel swirl plastic hdl, 7"..55.00
Darner, glass, Amster-Stocking Pat Ap For, cobalt, orig label, 5¼"..130.00
Darner, glass, mc splotches in clear, 6" 100.00
Darner, wood, HP pansy on removable hdl, Germany, ca 1920, 4½"...70.00
Darner, wood, lady figural, mc pnt, 2-pc, 1900, 4½" 30.00
Dress form, adjustable, sz B, w/iron claw-ft base, Acme, 60" 150.00
Gauge, sterling w/plated steel scale, ornate heart shape on end..... 60.00
Handbook, Singer Employees; prices/trade values/parts/rules, 1940, VG...155.00
Hat block/form, lg brim, wood, grooved rim, 30 degree taper, 52"...200.00
Kit, pk & wht enamel on brass bullet shape, thimble/needle/thread, 2". 46.00

Measure, brass, shoe, emb Three Feet in One Shoe, 1910, 1½x2¼"..95.00
Measure, celluloid, basket of fruit, Germany, 1x1½" 170.00
Measure, celluloid, Black boy w/yel scarf on head, Germany, 1¾"...260.00
Measure, celluloid, ship, Germany, ca 1900 .... 75.00
Measure, tin, raised brass horsehead, plastic eye, Germany, 1½" dia .. 50.00
Measure, vegetable ivory acorn w/cvd palm leaves, 1880, 2" 65.00
Needle book, Victorian children, ca 1875 .... 18.00
Needle case, brass, Eclectic Needle..., Milward & Sons Redditch, 3x1". 50.00
Needle case, ivory, cvd Oriental men/pagoda/flowers/trees, 2¾" 90.00
Needle case, MOP, cvd urn & flowers w/cutout, 4½" 300.00
Needle guard, sterling key w/2 silver chains, France, ca 1870, 6".. 170.00
Needle holder, brass, Sheaf of Wheat, Avery & Son, dtd 9/14/1873..300.00
Pincushion, Black Forest, bear holding bl cushion, ca 1890, 3x3"...225.00
Pincushion, pillow form w/needlework top, velvet-covered ft, 5x6x6"...115.00
Pincushion, redware pottery, bulldog, USA, 6" 200.00
Pincushion, strawberry on red blown glass base, worn, 6" 490.00
Pincushion, wood, Victorian boot w/HP roses & butterflies, ca 1900 ..75.00
Scissors, buttonhole; Singer #304, Germany, 4½" 152.00
Scissors, emb Cascade scene, 1904 St Louis World's Fair, Germany, 6" .. 60.00
Scissors, embr; sterling, decorative short blade, USA, ca 1900 ...... 70.00
Scissors, stork figural, unmk 22.00
Sewing bird, CI, heart on thumbscrew, 1880s, 3½" L 130.00
Sewing bird, wrought steel w/spring clamp, disk thumbscrew, 6⅜"..230.00
Spool chest, walnut, brass pulls, rfn 350.00
Stand, walnut/cherry/poplar, pnt decor, att OH, 11x13x6" 2,900.00
Tatting shuttle, celluloid, lt pk, 2½" 12.00
Tatting shuttle, metal, Boy Improved 10.00
Thimble, child's, sterling, eng image & Cow Jumped Over the Moon ..80.00
Thimble, MOP, Palais Royal, pansy medallion w/gold band, 1800-25..650.00
Thimble, sterling, floral on bl enamel band, Simmons Brothers #9..... 100.00
Thimble, sterling, mc floral on gold enamel band, domed bl top, #7, 1"..110.00
Thimble, 14k gold, etched monogram in heart, wht plastic top... 110.00
Thimble, 14k gold, etched scrolls & floral, Ketcham & McDougall, ¾"..120.00
Thimble case, gilt brass, etched scrolls, bullet shape, Germany, 2" 25.00
Thimble holder, basket, clear gr onyx w/brass trim, Mexico, 2x2½"... 95.00
Thimble holder, shoe w/flowers, 10k gold on wht bsk, England, 1890s..90.00
Thread holder, sterling, La Pierre, ca 1900, 1¼" 95.00
Tracing wheel, oak hdl, 6" L 10.00

Sewing Machines

The fact that Thomas Saint, an English cabinetmaker, invented the first sewing machine in 1790 was unknown until 1874 when Newton Wilson, an English sewing machine manufacturer and patentee, chanced upon the drawings included in a patent specification describing methods of making boots and shoes. By the middle of the nineteenth century, several patents were granted to American inventors, among them Isaac M. Singer, whose machine used a treadle. These machines were ruggedly built, usually of cast iron. By the 1860s and 1870s, the sewing machine had become a popular commodity, and the ironwork became more detailed and ornate. Though rare machines are costly, many of the old oak treadle machines (especially these brands: Davis, Home, Household, National, New Home, Singer, Weed, Wheeler & Wilson, and Willcox & Gibbs) have only nominal value. Machines manufactured after 1875 are generally very common, as most were mass produced. Values for these later sewing machines range from $50.00 to $100.00. For more information see *The Encyclopedia of Early American Sewing Machines* by Carter Bays. Our advisor for this category is Peter Frei; he is listed in the Directory under Massachusetts. In the listings that follow, unless noted otherwise, values are suggested for machines in excellent working order.

Bradbury #1, hand-crank, late 1800s, EX in case 425.00
Child's, Betsy Ross, Electric, 1950s, EX in red snakeskin case........ 80.00

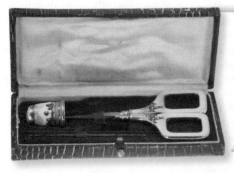

Kit, scissors, thimble, and needle, Delft-style enamel on sterling, in velvet-lined original box, $350.00. (Photo courtesy Fern Kao)

Child's, Eldregette, gr enameling, hand-crank, NMIB...................40.00
Child's, Fischer, tin litho, hand-crank, sliding drw, 1920s, 3".......165.00
Child's, Gateway, red-pnt lightweight steel.....................................50.00
Child's, Ideal, treadle type w/oak top & CI base, 31x18x10" 1,350.00
Child's, Junior Miss, metal body, aluminum handwheel, Artcraft, EX...75.00
Child's, KAYanEE, pressed steel, pk enamel, 6", NMIB.................60.00
Child's, KAYanEE Sew Master, bl pnt, hand-crank, US Zone, 5x8", $30 to..50.00
Child's, Little Mary Mix Up, sheet metal, 1930s, EX 75.00
Child's, Little Modiste, red-pnt metal, battery-op, Japan 75.00
Child's, Made in Germany, pnt metal w/red & gold stencil, 7x6½"+box..300.00
Child's, Montgomery Wards, lock stitch, plastic base, battery-op, EX...35.00
Child's, Sew-O-Matic Junior, cream & red pnt, hand-crank, 5½x6½"...35.00
Child's, Singer #20, blk pnt w/gilt, hand-crank, 7", NMIB 395.00
Child's, Singer Touch & Sew, 1967, NM w/instructions & box.....66.00

Child's, Singer, 6", VG, $110.00. (Photo courtesy Morphy Auctions/LiveAuctioneers.com)

Child's, Stitchwell by National, stencil on blk japanning, 6x9"+case...300.00
Child's, Victor, CI on wooden base, circular design, hand-crank, 8"..1,650.00
Child's, Yankee, HP wood, hand-crank, circular design, 7½" 480.00
Essex, highly chromed, wood base, 1940s-50s, 8" L 130.00
Frister & Rossman, Egyptian sphinx decor, hand-crank, 1927, NM...250.00
Garanteret Fra Johan Hammer..., CI, hand-crank, 13x14x10", VG...220.00
Guhl & Haarbeck, full-sz tabletop, Germany, 1890-1920, VG 175.00
Howe, treadle type, wood top w/CI base, ca 1871, 39x28" 125.00
Max Gristner, hand-crank, high-arm, pre-1900, EX 300.00
Minnesota Model D, hand-crank, tabletop, EX in wood case 350.00
New Home, treadle type, oak cabinet w/4 drw, CI base, 1915........65.00
Singer, treadle type w/oak cabinet, 6 side drw, 36x21x18" 120.00
Singer Featherweight #221, several attachments, +booklet & case..315.00
Singer Featherweight #221-1, 1941, +case & pedal......................475.00
Singer Model #15, blk w/gold decal, ca 1954, EX in case.............50.00
Singer Portable #3, hand-crank, dome case, 1898, NM................150.00
Union, ornate CI, hand-crank, 10x13¾"......................................600.00
Wheeler & Wilson, treadle w/fold-out tabletop, ca 1856-76, VG...125.00
White & Co, treadle type, CI base w/wooden stand & cover, ca 1896..50.00
Wilcox & Gibbs, CI w/walnut base, hand-crank, Pat 1871, 11x13x8½".250.00
Wilcox & Gibbs, treadle type, wood cabinet/CI base, Pat 1857/1870, 39"..300.00
Wilcox & Gibbs, wooden top, CI treadle base, electrified, 31x33x18".300.00

Shaker Items

The Shaker community was founded in America in 1776 at Niskeyuna, New York, by a small group of English 'Shaking Quakers.' The name referred to a group dance which was part of their religious rites. Their leader was Mother Ann Lee. By 1815 their membership had grown to more than 1,000 in 18 communities as far west as Indiana and Kentucky. But in less than a decade, their numbers began to decline until today only a handful remain. Their furniture is prized for its originality, simplicity, workmanship, and practicality. Few pieces were signed. Some were carefully finished to enhance the natural wood; a few were painted. Other methods were used earlier, but most Shaker boxes were of oval construction with overlapping 'fingers' at the seams to prevent buckling as the

wood aged. Boxes with original paint fetch triple the price of an unpainted box; number of fingers and overall size should also be considered.

Although the Shakers were responsible for weaving a great number of baskets, their methods are not easily distinguished from those of their outside neighbors, and it is nearly impossible without first-hand knowledge to positively attribute a specific example to their manufacture. They were involved in various commercial efforts other than woodworking — among them sheep and dairy farming, sawmilling, and pipe and brick making. They were the first to raise crops specifically for seed and to market their product commercially. They perfected a method to recycle paper and were able to produce wrinkle-free fabrics. Our advisor for this category is Nancy Winston; she is listed in the Directory under New Hampshire. Standard two-letter state abbreviations have been used throughout the following listings. Painted pieces are assumed to be in excellent original paint unless another condition code is present or the description contains information to the contrary.

Key:
bj — bootjack	NE — New England
CB — Canterbury	NL — New Lebanon
EF — Enfield	SDL — Sabbathday Lake
ML — Mt. Lebanon	WV — Watervliet

Basket, flat form w/2 hdls, minor breaks, 4x23x22" 360.00
Basket, picnic; pine/ash w/red stain, hinged lid, hdl, NY, 11" L...465.00
Basket, sewing; bentwood, 3 swallowtail fingers, copper tacks, 3x7" ..235.00
Basket, slightly domed base, cvd hdls, att NY, 8x14", EX..........2,600.00
Basket, sq base w/4 runners, cvd hdls, MA, 16x21" dia 800.00
Basket, tight weave, natural, cone-shaped bottom, att SDL, 13x24" ..2,650.00
Box, document; dvtl cherry, butt hinges, sm lock, old finish, 5x11x5"..400.00
Box, Harvard-type single opposing fingers, gr pnt, copper tacks, 3x6"..375.00
Box, spit; maple/pine, copper tacks, lapped sides, yel pnt, NY, 14" L..950.00
Box, 2-finger, red pnt, copper tacks, S Sprague, 2¼x5½"..............975.00
Box, 2-finger, red pnt, copper tacks, 19th C, 2¼x5½"..................725.00
Box, 3-finger, dk gr pnt/varnish, copper tacks, late 19th C, 2x5½"...935.00
Box, 3-finger, maple, gray pnt, copper tacks, NE, sm losses, 2½x8"..380.00
Box, 3-finger, maple, VG gr pnt, copper tacks, NE, 2⅞x7⅞"........600.00
Box, 3-finger, pine/maple, dk stain, copper tacks, NE, 1⅝x3 3¾"..880.00
Box, 3-finger, pine/maple, red pnt, iron tacks, 19th C, 2x5x3", NM..3,650.00
Box, 3-finger, varnish, copper tacks, late 19th C, 2½x6¼x4" 775.00
Box, 4-finger, bl-gr pnt, copper tacks, NE, sm losses, 3⅜x8⅞"....2,000.00
Box, 4-finger, copper tacks, lt rfn/wear, ca 1900, 5⅜x14x10" 600.00
Box, 4-finger, maple, gr pnt, copper tacks, NE, 4⅝x11⅜"..........2,200.00
Box, 4-finger, maple/pine, red pnt, NE, late 1800s, 2x5x3".......2,800.00
Box, 4-finger, natural, copper tacks, NE appl label, 5½x13⅜"...2,100.00
Box, 4-finger, natural w/stained lid, copper tacks, 4x10" 435.00
Box, 4-finger, pine, natural, copper tacks, NL, old rpr, 5x12x8"...800.00
Box, 4-finger, red-brn stain, copper tacks, 4x10⅜".......................700.00
Box, 4-finger, scrubbed salmon to cream pnt, brass tacks, 5x12x9"..950.00
Box, 5-finger, maple, brn stain, copper tacks, NE, crack, 6x15" ...950.00
Box, 5-finger, maple, varnish, copper tacks, 4¾x12¼"..................600.00
Box, 5-finger, maple/pine, yel pnt, copper tacks, 5⅝x13½" 6,600.00
Box, 5-finger, red pnt, copper tacks, 5¾x13⅜x5¾".................6,600.00
Bucket, berry; wood staves w/iron bands, ML, 4½x6" 480.00
Bucket, sap; wood staves w/iron bands, mustard pnt, EF, 11½x12"...515.00
Bucket, sponging on yel, pine staves, 2 iron hoops, wire hdl, EF, 10" ..725.00
Bucket, wood staves w/iron bands, gr pnt/bail hdl, 1800s, att, 10"..575.00
Bucket, wood staves w/metal bands, tapered sides/bail hdl, w/lid, 10"...480.00
Carrier, herb; 3-finger, fixed hdl, orig patina, 9x9½".................1,450.00
Carrier, maple/hickory/pine, red stain, fixed hdl, 1850s, 10½x12"...660.00
Carrier, pine, rectangular/nailed, ash swing hdl w/tacks, NY, 8x10x7" ...325.00
Carrier, 3-finger, maple, old varnish, copper tacks, 1850s, 9¼" H..1,200.00
Chair, arm; #1, 3-slat bk, rpl tape seat, old varnish, 28" 440.00
Chair, arm; #1, 3-slat bk, tape seat, old varnish, NY decal, 28" 2,000.00

Chair, arm; #1, rpl cloth tape seat & bk, ML, ca 1900, 28" 465.00
Chair, arm; #7, 5 arched slats, acorn finials, tape seat, ML 1,800.00
Chair, side; 3 arched slats, red/gr tape seat, rpl tilters, EF, 41" 965.00
Chair, side; 3 arched slats, rpl cane seat, 39½" 850.00
Chair, side; 3 arched slats, wool twill tape seat, Enfield tilter, 41" ...925.00
Chair, side; 3-slat bk, tiger maple/maple, tape seat, 1840s, 39½" ...1,000.00
Churn, bl pnt, bbl form, missing hdl & door, 24x21" dia 850.00

Churn, iron hoop and pine staves with blue paint, Alfred, Maine, nineteenth century, 46", $400.00. (Photo courtesy Skinner Inc. Auctioneers & Appraisers of Antiques & Fine Art)

Churn, red pnt, crank hdl, att, 30x20x20" 600.00
Cloak, dk red wool w/shoulder cape, late 19th C, 47" 650.00
Cupboard, pine w/bl buttermilk pnt, flat door, 19th C, 72x42x18" ..6,000.00
Desk, writing; cherry, old rfn, 33½x35x22½" 1,325.00
Desk, writing; pine, pigeonhole int, rfn, att SDL, 36x32x22" ...1,200.00
Grain bin, pine, long lift lid, bj ends, old dry finish, 36x96x18" .. 4,500.00
Hall tree, grad pegs on pine 8-sided post, shoe-ft base, old pnt, att ..635.00
Highchair, oak/maple w/splint seat, 2-slat ladder-bk, NY, 32" 360.00
Kneeler, dvtl cherry, NH, 25x15½" 360.00
Nightstand, walnut, trn legs, Hancock Community, 27x18x17" .. 950.00
Rack, herb drying; wht pnt traces, 25x25" 600.00
Rocker, arm; #1, 3-slat bk, tape seat, old varnish, ML, 28" 575.00
Rocker, arm; #6, shawl bar/4-slat bk, blk pnt/gilt decal, ML, 35" .. 940.00
Rocker, arm; #6, 4 arched slats, rpl seat, orig finish, NY 850.00
Rocker, arm; #7, shawl bar, tape seat & bk, NY, late 1800s, 40" .. 465.00
Rocker, arm; #7, shawl bar, 4-slat bk, tape seat, ML, ca 1900, 41½" ...515.00
Rocker, arm; #7, 3 arched slats, rattan seat, ML, 42½" 775.00
Rocker, armless; #4, 3 arched slats, paper rush seat, 34½" 230.00
Settee, woven seat & bk, dk varnish, ML, ca 1890, 34x41" 12,000.00
Spinning wheel, att Elder Alban Bates, 60x74" w/45" wheel 480.00
Stand, cherry, drw, trn legs, OH, 1860, rprs, 29x21x18" 360.00
Stand, cherry, rnd top/birdcage/tapered post/tripod, ML, 1830s, 23x22"..22,325.00
Stand, oak, 1-drw, tapered legs, brass knob, rfn, 29x21x15" 1,175.00
Stand, work; birch/pine, drw over shelf, NE, 19th C, 28x27" ... 1,200.00
Table, maple/cherry, 3 arched ft, 38x23" dia 850.00
Table, tailoring; maple/pine, 8 long drw, sq ft, 1850s, 31x95x40" ..5,250.00
Table, work; butternut, drw, old pnt on base, rfn top, 29x30x20" ..1,175.00

Shaving Mugs

Between 1865 and 1920, owning a personalized shaving mug was the order of the day, and the 'occupationals' were the most prestigious. The majority of men having occupational mugs would often frequent the barber shop several times a week, where their mugs were clearly visible for all to see in the barber's rack. As a matter of fact, this display was in many ways the index of the individual town or neighborhood.

During the first 20 years, blank mugs were almost entirely imported from France, Germany, and Austria and were hand painted in this country. Later on, some china was produced by local companies. It is noteworthy that American vitreous china is inferior to the imported Limoges and

is subject to extreme crazing. Artists employed by the American barber supply companies were for the most part extremely talented and capable of executing any design the owner required, depicting his occupation, fraternal affiliation, or preferred sport. When the mug was completed, the name and the gold trim were always added in varying degrees, depending on the price paid by the customer. This price was determined by the barber who added his markup to that of the barber-supply company. As mentioned above, the popularity of the occupational shaving mug diminished with the advent of World War I and the introduction by Gillette of the safety razor. Later followed the blue laws forcing barber shops to close on Sundays, thereby eliminating the political and social discussions for which they were so well noted.

Occupational shaving mugs are the most sought after of the group which would also include those with sport affiliations. Fraternal mugs, although desirable, do not command the same price as the occupationals. Occasionally, you will find the owner's occupation together with his fraternal affiliation. This combination could add anywhere between 25% to 50% to the price, which is dependent on the execution of the painting, rarity of the subject, and detail. Some subjects can be done very simply; others can be done in extreme detail, commanding substantially higher prices. It is fair to say, however, that the rarity of the occupation will dictate the price. Mugs with heavily worn gold lose between 20% and 30% of their value immediately. This would not apply to the gold trim around the rim, but to the loss of the name itself. Our advisor for this category is Burton Handelsman; he is listed in the Directory under New York.

Advertising, Wild Root, Buffalo China 1927 on chrome hdl, 3⅜"... 150.00
Comic, girls (wht/Black) seated w/dress bks open, Koken 230.00

Decorative, frog smoking pipe while fishing, gold trim, $1,100.00. (Photo courtesy Morphy Auctions/LiveAuctioneers.com)

Decorative, photographic man's portrait transfer, gold trim 1,100.00
Fraternal, Indian in headdress/Jr Order of United Am Mechanics... 215.00
Fraternal, Knights of Pythis & Odd Fellows w/flowers, Vienna 850.00
Fraternal, Masonic symbols/flowers/foliage, name on banner, worn gold.. 60.00
Fraternal, Odd Fellows, skull & crossbones, 4" 120.00
Fraternal, Order of Owls (3 owls on limb), T&V Limoges 725.00
Fraternal, 4 clubs/organizations, much gold, T&V Limoges 1,000.00
Fraternal, 7 varied symbols from Masons/Knights Templar, Germany ..600.00
Occupational, boxer w/arms extended, gold borders/pk wrap, KT&K 1,950.00
Occupational, cigars, gold name, 4½", EX 170.00
Occupational, cotton gin operator w/gold, Made in Germany ..2,350.00
Occupational, dare devil, man falling w/parachute, much gold .. 45,000.00
Occupational, dentist, pr of dentures, name, CFM/GDM 500.00
Occupational, doctor attending patient, gold trim, Austria, 1897..2,100.00
Occupational, early motorized moving van, much gold, unmk .3,600.00
Occupational, fire chief monitoring 2 fireman, 1927, Germany .. 1,450.00
Occupational, grocery store scene, ...St Louis on base, 4" 400.00
Occupational, horse-drawn ambulance w/driver & attendant.30,000.00
Occupational, horse-drawn confectionery wagon, bl wrap/gold, Austria .600.00
Occupational, horse-drawn moving-company wagon, lt wear to gold.. 1,000.00
Occupational, house painters working on brick home, Limoges.. 1,200.00
Occupational, man driving horse-drawn hay wagon, T&V Limoges, 3⅜" ..550.00
Occupational, man operating telegraph in office, much gold 750.00
Occupational, man working at bottle-capper, gold borders, 1913...2,400.00

Occupational, man working w/hose at plow, EX art, 4" 1,000.00
Occupational, milk man driving horse-drawn wagon, T&V Limoges ..800.00
Occupational, minister, Bible & 2 Xd swords, much gold, T&V... 500.00
Occupational, Naval Master at arms, blk wrap, T&V Limoges ..1,950.00
Occupational, pig & steer's head, Heckel Bros K-C Mo, 4" 110.00
Occupational, plumber, lady in bathtub, 4" 1,800.00
Occupational, policeman standing w/billy club, Vienna 950.00
Occupational, railroad locomotive engine w/gold, Koken............ 450.00
Occupational, railroad signal pole & name, T&V Limoges 2,400.00
Occupational, sign painter at work, Koken Barber Supply 1,950.00
Occupational, stable hand, boy w/bucket in stable, D&C France ...480.00
Occupational, steamboat in choppy waters, T&V Limoges.......1,650.00
Occupational, tailor shop scene w/6 people, T&V France, 3½" .. 375.00
Occupational, tuba player, gold trim 1,200.00
Rebus, detailed sheep & word Bros (for Sheep Bros), MR France, 3⅝"..170.00

Shawnee

The Shawnee Pottery Company operated in Zanesville, Ohio, from 1937 to 1961. They produced inexpensive novelty ware (vases, flowerpots, and figurines) as well as a very successful line of figural cookie jars, creamers, and salt and pepper shakers. They also produced three dinnerware lines, the first of which, Valencia, was designed by Louise Bauer in 1937 for Sears & Roebuck. A starter set was given away with the purchase of one of their refrigerators. Second and most popular was the Corn line. The original design was called White Corn. In 1946 the line was expanded and the color changed to a more natural yellow hue. It was marketed under the name Corn King, and it was produced from 1946 to 1954. Then the colors were changed again. Kernels became a lighter yellow and shucks a darker green. This variation was called Corn Queen. Their third dinnerware line, produced after 1954, was called Lobsterware. It was made in either black, brown, or gray; lobsters were usually applied to serving pieces and accessory items.

For further study we recommend these books: *The Collector's Guide to Shawnee Pottery* by Janice and Duane Vanderbilt, who are listed in the Directory under Indiana; and *Shawnee Pottery, An Identification and Value Guide*, by our advisors for this category, Jim and Bev Mangus; they are listed in Ohio.

Cookie Jars

Smiley the Pig, with chrysanthemums, USA, from $375.00 to $400.00.

Basketweave, bl w/decal, USA, 7½", from $110 to 125.00
Fruit basket, Shawnee 84, 8", from $125 to....................................150.00
Great Northern Girl, dk gr, Great Northern USA 1026, from $400 to..450.00
Jack, bl pants, USA, from $80 to...100.00
Jack, w/gold & decals, USA, from $400 to..450.00
Jack Tar, blk hair, w/gold, USA, 12", from $1,150 to.................1,200.00
Jack Tar, cold pnt, USA, from $150 to...250.00
Jill, tulip, gold & decals, USA, from $400 to..................................450.00

Jill, yel skirt, USA, from $100 to...125.00
Jumbo Elephant, red or bl tie, cold pnt, USA, from $150 to........200.00
Muggsy, gold & decals, Patented Muggsy USA, 11¾", from $1,000 to...1,100.00
Puss in Boots, maroon bow, gold & decals, long tail, from $500 to.....550.00
Puss in Boots, maroon bow, w/long tail, Puss 'n Boots, from $195 to..225.00
Smiley the Pig, clover bud, USA, from $550 to...........................575.00
Winnie the Pig, shamrocks, red collar w/gold, USA, from $900 to..950.00
Winnie the Pig, w/bl collar, USA, from $325 to...........................400.00

Corn Line

Bowl, cereal/soup; King, Shawnee 94, from $42 to........................45.00
Bowl, mixing; Queen, Shawnee 5, from $20 to..............................22.00
Butter dish, King, Shawnee 72, from $50 to..................................55.00
Corn Roast set, Queen, unmk, from $165 to................................175.00
Cup, Queen, Shawnee 90, from $25 to..30.00
Jug, Queen, Shawnee 71, 40-oz, from $60 to................................65.00
Plate, Queen, Shawnee 68, 10", from $30 to.................................35.00
Platter, King, Shawnee 96, 12", from $50 to.................................55.00
Shakers, pr, 3¼", from $25 to..28.00
Shakers, Queen, unmk, 5¼", from $30 to......................................35.00

Kitchenware

Batter bowl, Snowflake, USA, from $20 to.....................................25.00
Bowl, mixing; medallion on lid, Kenwood 940, from $40 to..........45.00
Canister, Dutch decal, USA, 2-qt, from $45 to..............................50.00
Canister, Snowflake, USA, 2-qt, from $45 to.................................55.00
Canister, yel, USA, 1-qt, from $50 to..55.00
Coffeepot, Pennsylvania Dutch, USA 52, from $240 to..............270.00
Creamer, Flower & Fern, USA, from $18 to....................................20.00
Creamer, Sunflower, USA, from $65 to..70.00
Grease jar, Flower & Fern, w/lid, USA, from $38 to......................40.00
Jug, Bo Peep, USA Pat Bo Peep, 40-oz, from $85 to......................90.00
Jug, Fern, USA, 2-qt, from $45 to..50.00
Jug, Sunflower, ball form, USA, 48-oz, from $75 to.......................80.00
Jug, yel, bulbous, USA, from $95 to...100.00
Pie bird, from $60 to..75.00
Pitcher, Charlie Chicken, decals w/gold, mk Chanticleer, from $330 to..360.00
Pitcher, Laurel Wreath, USA, from $22 to......................................24.00
Pitcher, Smiley, red neckerchief, apple, mk Pat Smiley USA, $230 to...240.00
Pitcher, Stars & Stripes, USA, from $16 to....................................18.00
Pitcher, utility; Snowflake, USA, 24-oz, 5⅛", from $40 to.............45.00
Salt box, Fern, w/lid, USA, from $120 to.....................................125.00
Salt box, Flower & Fern, w/lid, USA, from $95 to........................100.00
Shakers, Chanticleer, decorated w/gold, pr from $150 to.............165.00
Shakers, Dutch Kids, bl w/gold, pr from $55 to.............................55.00
Shakers, Fern, USA, 7-oz, pr from $30 to.......................................35.00
Shakers, Wave Pattern, yel, bl or gr, pr from $30 to......................35.00
Spoon rest, wht, USA, from $18 to...20.00
Sugar bowl, Fern, hdls, open, USA, 9-oz, from $30 to...................35.00
Teapot, Flower & Fern, USA, 2-cup, from $30 to...........................35.00
Teapot, Snowflake, USA, 2-cup, from $50 to.................................55.00
Tumbler, Stars & Stripes, USA, 3", from $12 to.............................14.00

Lobsterware

Bowl, batter; w/hdl, 928, from $50 to..55.00
Casserole, Fr; 904, 2-qt, from $25 to...30.00
Creamer & sugar bowl, 910, set from $85 to..................................90.00
Hors d'oeuvres holder, USA, 7¼", from $250 to...........................275.00
Plate, compartment; gr & blk, Kenwood USA 912, from $55 to ...65.00
Salad set, mk 924, 9-pc, from $130 to..135.00
Utility jar, 907, from $24 to...26.00

Valencia

Bowl, onion soup; w/lid, from $22 to... 24.00
Compote, 12", from $26 to.. 28.00
Egg cup, unmk, from, $18 to... 20.00
Nappy, unmk, 8½", from $18 to.. 20.00
Plate, dinner; 10¾", from $12 to 14.00
Shakers, unmk, pr from $22 to.. 24.00
Spoon, from $38 to.. 40.00
Teapot, unmk, from $45 to.. 55.00
Tray, utility; from $18 to.. 20.00
Vase, 8", from $18 to... 20.00

Miscellaneous

Bank, bear tumbling, from $210 to... 240.00
Carafe, blk, on metal stand, from $55 to....................................... 60.00
Cigarette box, emb trademk, USA, from $240 to.......................... 270.00
Clock, medallion, pk & gold, from $180 to.................................. 195.00
Clock, trellis, from $115 to... 120.00
Figurine, bear tumbling, decals w/gold, from $230 to 240.00
Figurine, rabbit, decals w/gold, from $230 to 240.00
Figurine, raccoon, from $90 to... 95.00
Lamp, Champ the Dog, from $20 to... 25.00
Lamp, native w/drum, from $190 to... 200.00
Planter, fish, USA 717, from $35 to.. 40.00
Planter, gazelle, glossy, Shawnee 840, from $50 to....................... 70.00
Sugar bowl, bucket, Great Northern USA 1042, from $65 to........ 75.00
Wall pocket, birds at birdhouse, w/gold, USA 830, from $25 to 30.00

Shearwater

Since 1928 generations of the Peter, Walter, and James McConnell Anderson families have been producing figurines and artwares in their studio at Ocean Springs, Mississippi. Their work is difficult to date. Figures from the '20s and '30s won critical acclaim and have continued to be made to the present time. Early marks include a die-stamped 'Shearwater' in a dime-sized circle, a similar ink stamp, and a half-circle mark. Any older item may still be ordered in the same glazes as it was originally produced, so many pieces on the market today may be relatively new. However, the older marks are not currently in use. Currently produced Black and pirate figurines are marked with a hand-incised 'Shearwater' and/or a cipher formed with an 'S' whose bottom curve doubles as the top loop of a 'P' formed by the addition of an upright placed below and to the left of the S. Many are dated, '93, for example. These figures are generally valued at $35.00 to $50.00 and are available at the pottery or by mail order. New decorated and carved pieces are very expensive, starting at $400.00 to $500.00 for a six inch pot.

Bean pot, textured/mottled gr, att P Anderson, 1960, 9½" W...... 360.00
Bowl, bl alkaline, incurvate rim, hairline crack, 1950s, 3⅜x8" 150.00
Bowl, bl mottle, P Anderson, 1950s, 3½x9".................................. 660.00
Bowl, blk, P Anderson, 1930s, 3⅞x9¼"...................................... 480.00
Bowl, blk & wht scrolls, 3½x9".. 3,525.00
Bowl, ducks, earth tones, 3¼x10".. 9,600.00
Bowl, fruit/flowers/vines cvd on gr w/brn wash, W Anderson, 5x7"...4,250.00
Bowl, gr mottle, invt cone form w/ft, late 20th C, 3x8" 180.00
Bowl, scarabs, brn & tan, sgn JA, 1992, 2⅛x5½".......................... 550.00
Bowl, striated gr/beige, horizontal bands, 1970s, 6¼x9¾" 215.00
Candleholder, antique gr, flared ft, J Anderson, ca 1878, 4", ea 30.00
Figurine, Bathing Beauty, Oldfield series, WI Anderson, 1970s, 6"...72.50
Figurine, bird (stylized), wht, 5x9¼" 235.00
Figurine, duck w/head forward, bl gloss, JM Anderson, 1930s, 1½"...48.00

Figurine, lion, alkaline bl & deep marine bl, 5½x13½x4" 2,750.00
Figurine, man w/plow, mc, 1989 Christmas M Griffen, 5⅜x7".....195.00
Lamp base, Mr Aspirin, man w/instrument, turq, W Anderson, 8½", NM .785.00
Pitcher, bl alkaline, att P Anderson, 1930-40, 5½"....................... 240.00
Teapot, turq mottle, bulbous, 5½x9½", NM............................... 550.00
Vase, alkaline bl to antique gr w/mottling, flared cylinder, 6" 600.00
Vase, cobalt mottle, ovoid, 6¾".. 240.00
Vase, creamy runs over brn, bulbous, P Anderson, ca 1940, 6⅜" . 300.00
Vase, dk gr w/ornate overall floral o/l, slim, 13⅞"...................... 600.00
Vase, Earth, Sea & Sky, gr & tan, mid-20th C, 12x7¼".........11,750.00
Vase, gr, ovoid, P Anderson, ca 1940, 8".................................... 395.00
Vase, gr & brn matt, ftd, 6½".. 200.00
Vase, gr mottle, bulbous base, 5¾x3¼"....................................... 115.00
Vase, lappet design, brn & cream, bulbous, 6½x7½"..................4,800.00
Vase, pelicans, bl & turq mottle, 2 tight lines, 7x6" 6,600.00
Vase, turq & gunmetal, gourd form, 3¼x2"................................. 275.00
Vase, Wistera (bl-gr), ovoid w/flared rim, 1960s, 6¾".................. 120.00
Vase, Wisteria (pk-bl), rim-to-hip hdls, 1928-30, drilled, 11½" ...850.00

Sheet Music

Sheet music is often collected more for its colorful lithographed covers, rather than for the music itself. Transportation songs (which have pictures or illustrations of trains, ships, and planes), ragtime and blues, comic characters (especially Disney), sports, political, and expositions are eagerly sought after. Much of the sheet music on the market today is valued at under $5.00; some of the better examples are listed here. For more information refer to *Sheet Music Reference and Price Guide*, by Anna Marie Guiheen and Marie-Reine A. Pafik. Values are given for examples in at least near-mint condition.

Anywhere in USA Is Home to Me, SE Clark, patriotic cover, 1910.... 15.00
Babes on Broadway, Freed & Lane, Judy Garland photo cover, 1942...10.00
Battle in the Sky, J Luxton, WWI cover, 1916 .... 15.00
Because, Horwitz & Bowers, Irving Berlin, Leff & Berlin cover, 1926...10.00

Bill Bailey, Won't You Please Come Home, Hughie Cannon, photo: Wilbur Mack, cover artist: Dewey & Black, 1902, $35.00. (Photo courtesy Anna Marie Guiheen and Marie-Reine A. Pafik)

Billiken March, Gideon, Pfeiffer & March cover, 1908................. 15.00
Blue Christmas, B Hayes & J Johnson, Morgan photo cover, 1948...13.00
Brazil, Bob Russell, Saludos Amigos (Disney) cover, 1939............. 25.00
California Here I Come, Jolson/DeSylva/Meyer, Al Jolson cover, 1924...10.00
Carolina Cake Walk, G Mears, Black cover, 1898.......................... 22.00
Close, Cole porter, from movie: Rosalie, 1937................................6.00
Davy Jones' Locker, HW Petrie, 1901 .... 15.00
Dixie Rag, Giblin, Pfeiffer cover, 1913.. 15.00
Don't Let me Down, Lennon & McCartney, photo cover, 1969.... 30.00
Down by the Erie Canal, Geo M Cohan, Cohan cover................... 15.00
Elevator Man, Irving Berlin, Pfeiffer & Berlin cover...................... 15.00
Everybody's Happy When the Moon Shines, Kerry Mills, 1909..... 10.00
Fare Thee Well Molly Darling, WD Cobb & K Mills, 1902........... 10.00
Flapper Blues, Bob Alterman & Claude Johnson, Deco cover, 1922 ...10.00

Go Down Moses, HT Burleigh, Black face cover, 1917 .... 10.00
Golliwog's Cake Walk, Claude Debussy, Black face cover, 1908 .... 16.00
Happy Times, Silvia Fine, Danny Kaye photo cover, 1949 .... 12.00
Hesitation D'Amour, Barrie, Pfeiffer Art Deco cover, 1914 .... 15.00
I Ain't Gwin Ter Work No Mo, Black face cover, 1900 .... 20.00
I Didn't Raise My Ford To Be a Jitney, Jack Frost, 1915 .... 25.00
I'll Be a Soldier, James Thatcher, WWI cover, 1915 .... 12.00
I'm Done w/Rag-Time, Fred Stein & Clas Robinson, 1900 .... 10.00
I Wake Up Smiling, Edgar Leslie & Fred E Ahlert, 1933 .... 7.00
I Wuv a Wabbit, M Berle/E Drake/P Martell, Barbelle cover, 1945 .10.00
Indiana Moon, Benny Davis & Isham Jones, Perret cover, 1923 .... 10.00
It's Not What You Were It's What You Are Today, D Marion, 1898 .. 15.00
Jubilee, S Adams & H Carmichael, Mae West caricature cover, 1937 ..10.00
La Cucaracha, Washington, Wallace Beery & Fay Wray cover, 1934 ....10.00
Letter to Heaven, Lizzie Paine, 1888 .... 15.00
Log Cabin Song, Alexander Kile, 1840 .... 100.00
Love's Sweet Dream, Drumheller, Pfeiffer cover, 1912 .... 10.00
Make That Engine Stop at Louisville, Lewis/Meyer/Richmond, 1914 .20.00
Matrimony Rag, Edgar Leslie & Lews F Muir 10.00
Motor March, Geo Rosey, 1906 .... 30.00
My Gal Sal, Paul Dresser, R Haworth & V Mature photo cover, 1932 ..30.00
Oh Mamma Buy Me That, Al Hillman, 1890 .... 10.00
Paddy Duffy's Cart, E Harrigan & D Braham, 1881 .... 15.00
Road that Leads to Love, Irving Berlin, Berlin cover, 1917 .... 10.00
Since Home Rule Came to Ireland, Kelly & Mullane, artist cover, 1914 .. 15.00
Song of South, Coslow & Johnston, Disney movie cover, 1946 ..... 12.00
Take Me on a Buick Honeymoon, Black, transportation cover, 1922 ..25.00
Throw Him Down McCloskey, JW Kelly, 1890 .... 15.00
War Babies, Al Jolson, Jolson & WWI cover, 1916 .... 15.00

Shelley

In 1872 Joseph Shelley became partners with James Wileman, owner of Foley China Works, thus creating Wileman & Co. in Stoke-on-Trent. Twelve years later James Wileman withdrew from the company, though the firm continued to use his name until 1925 when it became known as Shelley Potteries, Ltd. Like many successful nineteenth-century English potteries, this firm continued to produce useful household wares as well as dinnerware of considerable note. In 1896 the beautiful Dainty White shape was introduced, and it is regarded by many as synonymous with the name Shelley. In addition to the original Dainty (six-flute) design, other lovely shapes were produced: Ludlow (14-flute), Oleander (petal shape), Stratford (12-flute), Queen Anne (with eight angular panels), Ripon (with its distinctive pedestal), and the 1930s shapes of Vogue, Eve, and Regent. Though often overlooked, striking earthenware was produced under the direction of Frederick Rhead and later Walter Slater and his son Eric. Many notable artists contributed their talents in designing unusual, attractive wares: Rowland Morris, Mabel Lucie Attwell, and Hilda Cowham, to name but a few.

In 1966 Allied English Potteries acquired control of the Shelley Company, and by 1967 the last of the exquisite Shelley China had been produced to honor remaining overseas orders. In 1971 Allied English Potteries merged with the Doulton group.

It had to happen: Shelley forgeries! Chris Davenport, author of *Shelley Pottery, The Later Years*, reports seeing Mocha-shape cups and saucers with the Shelley mark. However, on close examination it is evident that the mark has been applied to previously unmarked wares too poorly done to have ever left the Shelley Pottery. This Shelley mark can actually be 'felt,' as the refiring is not done at the correct temperature to allow it to be fully incorporated into the glaze. (Beware! These items are often seen on internet auction sites.)

Some Shelley patterns (Dainty Blue, Bridal Rose, Blue Rock) have been seen on Royal Albert and Queensware pieces. These companies are part of the Royal Doulton Group.

Note: Objects with lids are measured to the top of the finial unless stated otherwise. Be aware that Rose Spray and Bridal Rose are the same pattern. Our advisor for this category is Lila Shrader; she is listed in the Directory under California.

Key:
FMN — Forget-Me-Not   MLA — Mabel Lucie Attwell
LF — Late Foley   W — Wileman, pre-1910

Advertising figure, Shelley Lady seated on ped holding c/s, 11½" .. 7,465.00
Ashtray, Ocean Racht Race, Bermuda, 1960 commemorative, 5½" dia .. 20.00
Ashtray, Summer Glory (pk), 3 rests, #1338?, 3½" dia 22.00
Bell, Morning Glory, Ludlow shape, 5½" 365.00
Bowl, cream soup; Dainty Blue, w/hdls, #051, w/6½" liner 60.00
Bowl, fruit; Intarsio, Nouveau w/silver-banded rim, #3604, W, 9¾" ..600.00
Bowl, fruit; Melody Chintz, horizontal ribs, #8809, 3x8½" 95.00
Butter dish, Rose & Red Daisy, Dainty shape, #13425, 6¼" 80.00
Butter dish, Stocks, Dainty shape, #13428, 7¼" 125.00
Butter pat, Blue Rock, #13591, 3" 55.00
Butter pat, Campanula, Dainty shape, #13886, 3¾" 120.00
Butter pat, Dainty Mauve, Dainty shape, #051/M, 3¾" 198.00
Butter pat, HP mc flowers (vivid), #13092, 3" 67.00
Butter pat, Lily of the Valley, Dainty shape, #13822, 3¾" 82.00
Butter pat, Rambler Rose, Dainty shape, #13671, 3½" 75.00
Cake plate, Drifting Leaves, Richmond shape, tab hdls, #13848, 10" .. 45.00
Cake plate, English Lakes, Cambridge shape, angular tab hdls, #13788 ... 45.00
Cake plate, Heavenly Blue, Dainty shape, #14165, 8x10½" 155.00
Cake plate, Wildflowers, Dainty shape, angular tab hdls, #13668 ...120.00
Cake stand, Blue Rock, Dainty shape, ped ft, #13591, from $125 to .. 165.00
Candy/sweet meat dish, Shamrocks, Dainty shape, #14114, 5¾" ... 65.00
Children's ware, feeding dish, children w/wood train & cart, HC, 8" ... 100.00
Children's ware, MLA creamer, Boo-Boo, sgn, 6" 158.00
Children's ware, MLA tea set, Boo-Boo, mushroom teapot+cr/sug, sgn ...555.00
Children's ware, mug, Little Boy Blue w/verse, 2⅞" 55.00
Children's ware, trio, mc train, Puff Puff Puff, 5¾" plate, 3-pc 98.00
Cigarette holder, Rambler Rose, Dainty shape, #13671, 2⅛" 37.50
Coffee set, Jungle, Daisy shape, #6088, pot+cr/sug+2 c/s 395.00
Coffeepot, Deco decor in yel & blk (bold), Vogue shape, #11776, 7¼" .. 575.00
Coffeepot, Sheraton, Gainsborough w/gooseneck spout, #13291, 7½" ...200.00
Coffeepot, Wildflowers, Dainty shape, #2295, 6½" 395.00
Coffeepot, Wine Grape, Gainsborough w/gooseneck spout, #13698, 7½" ...300.00
Coffeepot, Woodland, Perth shape w/rich gold, #13348, 7" 155.00
Compote, Melody Chintz, ped ft, #8809, 3x7¾", from $95 to 185.00
Condiment set, Begonia, Dainty shape, #13427, s&p+horseradish+stand ..450.00
Creamer, Imari, rich cobalt, red & gold, Alexander shape, W, 4" .. 60.00
Creamer & sugar bowl, Dainty Brown, #051/B 78.00
Creamer & sugar bowl, Dainty White w/yel polka dots 110.00
Crested ware, coach, Charabanc, Monach, Doncaster, #352 .... 70.00
Crested ware, comical cat, Long Eaton, 5½" 55.00
Crested ware, elephant w/trunk down, Crest of Dawlish, #363, 2½" ..100.00
Crested ware, pot, Shrewsbury crest, LF, 2" dia 6.00
Cup & saucer, Bailey's Sweet Pea, Dainty shape, gr hdl, #2445 ... 425.00
Cup & saucer, Black Chintz, gold hdl & ped ft, Ripon shape, #14196 ...665.00
Cup & saucer, Blue Pansy Chintz, Henley shape, #13165 .... 100.00
Cup & saucer, Bramble, Dainty shape, pk hdl, gold trim, #2353 .. 290.00
Cup & saucer, Dainty Blue, Dainty shape, #051/25, mini, 1½" 650.00
Cup & saucer, Dainty Blue, Westminster (not Dainty shape),1½" ... 255.00
Cup & saucer, Dainty Brown, Ludlow shape 135.00
Cup & saucer, demitasse; Bubbles, Bute shape, #11182 .... 42.00
Cup & saucer, demitasse; Dainty Brown 145.00
Cup & saucer, Duchess, coffee-can shape, #13401 .... 16.00
Cup & saucer, Georgian litho, Royal Blue exterior/saucer, Athol shape .. 42.50
Cup & saucer, gr stripes on wht, Hyderbad shape, recessed hdl ... 415.00
Cup & saucer, Melody w/in, solid exterior/saucer, Oleander, #13412 . 130.00

Cup & saucer, Moss Rose, gr hdl, gold trim, Dainty shape, #2427 ..315.00
Cup & saucer, Paisley, bl, Canturbury shape, mini, 1½", 2⅞"....1,350.00
Cup & saucer, Pansy (lg), Dainty shape, #13823 .... 100.00
Cup & saucer, Pyrethrum, Dainty shape, #14189 .... 80.00
Cup & saucer, Rose, Pansy FMN, Canburbury shape, #13424, mini, $90 to ..125.00
Cup & saucer, Summer Glory, lav exterior, ftd Oleander w/gold, #13413 ....65.00
Cup & saucer, Wildflowers, Stratford shape, #13678 .... 50.00
Egg cup, Dainty Blue, ped ft, #051/28, 2½" 80.00
Egg cup, Rosebud, ped ft, Dainty shape, #13426, 2½" 50.00
Figure, Golfer, in knickers, w/bag over shoulder, MLA, 6¼" 1,045.00
Food mold, Crayfish, W, 5¼" 52.00
Gravy/sauceboat, Sheraton, rnd, #13289 .... 32.00
Hot water/chocolate pot, Dainty Blue, #051/28, 7", from $240 to ..275.00
Jam pot, Maytime, apple shape w/slotted lid, #8484, 4" 100.00
Jewelry casket, Geo & Mary 1911 Coronation, sq, LF, 4x5½" 290.00
Jewelry casket, roses & FMN, domed lid, LF, #8295, 1½x2x1½" .. 82.50
Loving cup, Geo & Mary 1911 Coronation commemorative, hdls, 4½" ... 70.00
Mug, Rose Pansy FMN, Dainty shape, #13424, 4" 100.00
Napkin ring, Campanula, self-supports, mk Shelley inside............. 95.00
Napkin ring, Rose Pansy FMN, self-supports, mk Shelley inside ... 55.00
Pin dish, life buoy shape, HP, sgn Hilda Cowham, 3½" dia 170.00

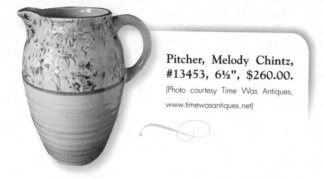

Pitcher, Melody Chintz, #13453, 6½", $260.00.

(Photo courtesy Time Was Antiques, www.timewasantiques.net)

Place setting, Black Trees, Queen Anne shape, #11476, 5-pc 235.00
Place setting, Blue Rock, Dainty shape, #13591, 5-pc 125.00
Place setting, Dainty Mauve, brilliant coloring, #051, 5-pc 400.00
Place setting, Forget-Me-Not, Dainty shape, #2394, 5-pc 150.00
Place setting, Glorious Devon, Richmond shape, #12734 .... 235.00
Place setting, Honeysuckle, Carlisle shape, #14311, 5-pc 225.00
Plate, American Brookline, Dainty shape, #14060, 10½"............. 100.00
Plate, Chippendale, appl enamel, Gainsborough shape, #13228, 10⅞".. 55.00
Plate, Dainty Blue, #051, 10½".. 65.00
Plate, Dainty Orange, #051, 10½" 135.00
Plate, Harebell, Oleander shape, #13590, 10¼" 38.00
Plate, Old Sevres, w/silver fr, #10678, 7"..................................... 42.00
Plate, Rambler Rose, Dainty shape, #13671, 10¾" 100.00
Platter, Dainty Blue, #051/28, 16⅞x13¾" 425.00
Posy ring (pansy ring), Pansy Chintz, mushroom shape, 1½x7½"...150.00
Shaker set, Regency, Dainty, pepper pot+2 shakers+stand w/finger ring..355.00
Shaving mug, Deco fruit, space for soap & brush, 5¼" 55.00
Shaving mug, Primrose Chintz, space for soap & brush, #13586, 4¾" .. 150.00
Sign, Shelly, 10th Anniversery...Club, 2½x3½" 112.00
Smoke set, Dainty Pink, #051/p, ashtray & cigarette holder.......... 65.00
Tea & toast set, Meissenette, Dainty shape w/indent & cup, 8¼" ...130.00
Teapot, Blue Rock, Dainty shape, graceful spout, 313591, 6½" 300.00
Teapot, Ferndown, Windsor shape, #14131, mini, 3½" 120.00
Teapot, Miessenette, Dainty shape, graceful spout, #14260, 5¼" .. 255.00
Teapot, Stocks, Dainty shape w/graceful spout, #13626, 6" 240.00
Tray, sandwich; Begonial, Dainty shape, w/hdls, #13427, 12½x5¾"..35.00
Tray for cr/sug, Dainty Blue, tab hdls, #051/28, 9½x5" 135.00
Trio, Bananas, Queen Anne shape, mc enamel, #1562, 6½" plate ... 160.00
Trio, Duchess, Gainsborough shape w/bl colorway, #13403, 6" plate 62.00
Trio, Fuchsia, Dainty shape, #2421 .... 285.00

Trio, Meissenette, Dainty shape, #14260 .... 178.00
Trio, Rock Garden, Ripon shape, gold trim, #13385, 7" plate........ 90.00
Trio, Sprays of Poppies, Fairy Shape, #9138, W, 7" plate............. 100.00
Tureen, Harebell, Oleander shape, domed lid, w/hdls, #13590, 10¾" ... 145.00
Vase, birds in tree/flowers HP on bl, yel int, 4" 185.00
Vase, Blue Dragon, slim w/rolled collar, #8315, W, 9" 175.00
Vase, floral cartouche w/rich gold, ewer form w/hdls, W, mini, 2" ...255.00
Vase, From Lorne Point, squat, souvenir, 5¼" 78.00
Wash set, earthenware, pitcher+bowl+soap dish+toothbrush holder, W.. 500.00

Silhouettes

Silhouette portraits were made by positioning the subject between a bright light and a sheet of white drawing paper. The resulting shadow was then traced and cut out, the paper mounted over a contrasting color and framed. The hollow-cut process was simplified by an invention called the Physiognotrace, a device that allowed tracing and cutting to be done in one operation. Experienced silhouette artists could do full-length figures, scenics, ships, or trains freehand. Some of the most famous of these artists were Charles Peale Polk, Charles Wilson Peale, William Bache, Doyle, Edouart, Chamberlain, Brown, and William King. Though not often seen, some silhouettes were completely painted or executed in wax. Examples listed here are hollow-cut unless another type is described and assumed to be in excellent condition unless noted otherwise.

Key:
c/p — cut and pasted   l — laid paper
fl — full length   p — profile
hc — hand colored   wc — water color

British officer, half-length p, wc on paperbrd, 4x3"+gilt emb tin fr ..415.00
Couple & child at table, fl, c/p, ink, Edouart, 1834, 12x18" fr ..4,115.00
Lady (identified) in hat & finery, fl rvpt ink on glass, 1800, 4x3"+fr ... 385.00
Lady & man, p, ink/wc on fabric, stains, 1830s, 4½x6¼"+wood fr ...2,585.00
Lady & man (identified), p, ink/hc details, 1830s, 4¼"+fr, pr ...2,465.00
Man, p, c/p, gold ink details, Hubbard Gallery label, 7x6"+maple fr..350.00
Man in frock coat, stands & holds hat, fl, Edouart, 12x8"+maple fr...975.00
Man w/high collar & ruffled shirt, p, sepia pnt/ink/gilt, 4x3"+fr ..235.00
Mother w/fan & son holding hat, fl, c/p, Edouart, 1840, 8½x5"+fr ..1,525.00
Portly man w/hat & cane, fl, ink on paper, bronze details, 9x5"+fr 700.00
Wm Gibson MD, p, fabric bk, CW Peale, 6x4"+bird's-eye maple fr ... 235.00

Silver

Coin Silver

During colonial times in America, the average household could not afford items made of silver, but those fortunate enough to have accumulations of silver coins (900 parts silver/100 parts alloy) took them to the local silversmith who melted them down and made the desired household article as requested. These pieces bore the owner's monogram and often the maker's mark, but the words 'Coin Silver' did not come into use until 1830. By 1860 the standard was raised to 925 parts silver/75 parts alloy and the word 'Sterling' was added. Coin silver came to an end about 1900.

Key:
gw — gold washed   t-oz — troy ounce

Am, porringer, openwork hdl, flared rim, dings, 5¼", 6.6-t-oz...... 515.00
Am, salt cellars, Oriental scenes/figures, glass liners, pr.............. 200.00
B Gardiner, NY; tea set, lobed bodies, pot+cr/sug w/lid, 81.4-t-oz ..3,450.00
G Stephens, NY; punch ladle, Old English pattern, 1790s, 13½" .. 750.00

Hyde & Goodrich, cup, repoussé chased floral, 3-t-oz 1,765.00
Hyde & Goodrich, ladle, fiddle thread/monogram, 14¼", 5½-t-oz...1,085.00
Hyde & Goodrich, tablespoons, fiddle type, 8½", 7 for.................560.00
Hyde & Goodrich, tongs, Bead pattern, 6¾", 7½-t-oz 210.00
IBV (Am?), ink pot & sander, eng monogram, squat, 3-t-oz 575.00
J Conning Co, Mobile; creamer, helmet form, foliate bands, 11-t-oz..3,500.00
J David, Philadelphia; waste bowl, sq ft/beading, 5x6", 14-t-oz.3,000.00
J Musgrave, Philadelphia; coffeepot, fluted, ped ft, 42.75-t-oz...8,225.00

James Reed, Murphreesboro, Tennessee; sugar bowl, acorn finial, leaf bands, 9¾", 21 troy ounces, $4,500.00.
(Photo courtesy Neal Auction Co. Auctioneers & Appraisers of Fine Art)

J Richardson Jr, Philadelphia; soup ladle, curved oval hdl, 13" ..1,175.00
JS Curtis, Memphis; creamer, C-scroll hdl, foliage, 6¼", 11-t-oz ...4,700.00
L Megede, Lexington MO; julep cup, beaded rim/ft, 3¾", 4.9-t-oz...515.00
London, castor set, Geo II, 7 castors in stand, 1743, 34.4-t-oz..2,585.00
Prolifet, Natchez; waste bowl, scrolls at rim, 6x6½", 18-t-oz 6,250.00
Rasch, Philadelphia; soup ladle, fiddle/shell hdl, 13", 4-t-oz.........725.00
Wm L Adams, NY; tureen, emb foliage, 4 claw ft, domed lid, 11x16x9"..9,750.00
Young & Co, New Orleans; soup spoon, fiddle type, 9" 115.00

Flatware

Silver flatware is being collected today either to replace missing pieces of heirloom sets or in lieu of buying new patterns, by those who admire and appreciate the style and quality of the older ware. Prices vary from dealer to dealer; some pieces are harder to find and are therefore more expensive. Items such as olive spoons, cream ladles, lemon forks, etc., once thought a necessary part of a silver service, may today be slow to sell; as a result, dealers may price them low and make up the difference on items that sell more readily. Many factors enter into evaluation. Popular patterns may be high due to demand though easily found, while scarce patterns may be passed over by collectors who find them difficult to reassemble. If pieces are monogrammed, deduct 20% (for rare, ornate patterns) to 30% (for common, plain pieces). Place settings generally come in three sizes: dinner, place, and luncheon, with the dinner size generally more expensive. In general, dinner knives are 9½" long, place knives, 9" to 9⅛", and luncheon knives, 8¾" to 8⅞". Dinner forks measure 7⅜" to 7½", place forks, 7¼" to 7⅜", and luncheon forks, 6⅞" to 7⅛". Our advisor for this category is Rick Spencer; he is listed in the Directory under Utah.

Acorn, Geo Jensen, soup spoon...124.00
Afterglow, Oneida, butter spreader, flat hdl 16.00
Afterglow, Oneida, sugar spoon...19.50
Alexandra, Lunt, teaspoon 28.00
American Classic, Easterling, cold meat fork.....................................52.00
American Classic, Easterling, cream soup spoon 21.00
Ashmont, Reed & Barton, salad fork 40.00
Barocco, Wallace, dinner fork..65.50
Barocco, Wallace, place soup spoon..61.00
Bead, Gorham, salad fork..55.00
Belle Rose, Oneida, butter spreader, hollow hdl 15.00
Belle Rose, Oneida, olive fork 14.00
Blossomtime, Int'l, cream soup spoon 17.00

Blossomtime, Int'l, pie/cake serving knife..24.00
Burgundy, Reed & Barton, luncheon fork...41.00
Burgundy, Reed & Barton, teaspoon 21.00
Candlelight, Towle, gravy ladle..51.00
Candlelight, Towle, ramekin fork...24.00
Celeste, Gorham, mint jelly serving spoon 23.00
Celeste, Gorham, sugar tongs 24.00
Chateau Rose, Alvin, butter spreader, flat hdl 16.00
Chateau Rose, Alvin, iced beverage tea spoon 21.00
Chippendale, Towle, salad fork 34.50
Danish Baroque, Towle, serving fork 75.00
Danish Baroque, Towle, sugar spoon 33.50
Dawn Mist, Wallace, olive fork 15.00
Dawn Mist, Wallace, place fork..25.00
Fontana, Towle, cheese scoop...29.00
Fontana, Towle, cocktail fork...21.00
Forget Me Not, Stieff, fruit spoon 22.00
Forget Me Not, Stieff, teaspoon...22.00
Georgian Rose, Reed & Barton, cream soup spoon 25.00
Georgian Rose, Reed & Barton, salad fork..31.00
Grand Baroque, Wallace, dinner fork...60.00
Grand Baroque, Wallace, ice tongs 242.00
Grand Duchess, Towle, rice server, hollow hdl 24.00
Grand Duchess, Towle, wedding cake knife 46.00
Homewood, Stieff, berry serving spoon...67.00
Hyperion, Whiting, teaspoon..38.00
Imperial Queen, butter spreader, flat hdl..29.00
Impero, Wallace, dinner fork..55.00
Impero, Wallace, place soup spoon..51.00
Irving, Wallace, cocktail fork 18.50
John & Priscilla, Westmoreland, tomato/flat server.........................41.00
King Edward, Gorham, steak carving fork...40.00
King Edward, Whiting, cocktail fork 11.50
King Edward, Whiting, sugar tongs 21.00
Melrose, Gorham, fruit spoon..29.00
Melrose, Gorham, gravy ladle..88.00
Melrose, Gorham, luncheon fork 36.00
Melrose, Gorham, serving fork 88.50
Milburn Rose, Westmoreland, gumbo soup spoon 24.00
Milburn Rose, Westmoreland, table serving spoon, pierced...........36.00
Old Colonial, Towle, dinner fork..41.00
Romantique, Alvin, luncheon fork 24.00
Romantique, Alvin, salad fork..17.00
Royal Rose, Wallace, gravy ladle..92.00
Royal Rose, Wallace, sugar spoon..33.00
Stieff Rose, Stieff, roast carving knife 55.00
Stieff Rose, Stieff, cake fork...37.00
Stieff Rose, Stieff, lemon serving fork 22.00
Vivant, Oneida, olive fork 16.00
Vivant, Oneida, table serving spoon 42.00
William & Mary, Lunt, bouillon soup spoon......................................19.00
William & Mary, Lunt, butter pick 26.00
William & Mary, Lunt, table serving spoon, pierced 65.50

Hollow Ware

Until the middle of the nineteenth century, the silverware produced in America was custom made on order of the buyer directly from the silversmith. With the rise of industrialization, factories sprung up that manufactured silverware for retailers who often added their trademark to the ware. Silver ore was mined in abundance, and demand spurred production. Changes in style occurred at the whim of fashion. Repoussé decoration (relief work) became popular about 1885, reflecting the ostentatious preference of the Victorian era. Later in the century, Greek,

Etruscan, and several classic styles found favor. Today the Art Deco styles of this century are very popular with collectors.

In the listings that follow, manufacturer's name or trademark is noted first; in lieu of that information, listings are by country or item. See also Tiffany, Silver.

Steiff, punch bowl, tray, and ladle, repoussé florals, date letters for 1948 and 1952: Bowl, 9" diameter; Tray, 10½" diameter; Ladle, 14½" long, 97 troy ounces, 13 dwt., $4,115.00. (Photo courtesy Neal Auction Company Auctioneers & Appraisers of Fine Art)

B Webb, Boston; tankard, stepped lid, scroll hdl, 7½", 21.4-t-oz ...6,900.00
Ball, Blk & Co, NY; butter dish, repoussé floral, dome lid, 19-t-oz... 650.00
Bangs, OH; beaker/julep cup, appl rim/ft, 3¼", 5.6-t-oz............... 625.00
Chas Aldridge, London; teapot & stand, swag eng, 1780s, 16.3-t-oz.. 1,300.00
Dublin, cup, Geo III, 2-hdl trophy form, high ft, 7¾", 15.2-t-oz .. 750.00
Duhme, OH; bowl, appl decor, trifid ft, gilt int, 6½", 12.5-t-oz.... 330.00
Duhme, OH; goblet, Presented to Knights Templar Band..., 1870, 7¾".460.00
Emes & Barnard, London; mug, grapevines/snakes, 1810s, 8.7-t-oz . 725.00
FW Smith, MA; tea/coffee set, rococo cartouches, 5-pc, 78-t-oz...1,750.00
G Giles, London; wine funnel, std form w/bowl clip, 4¾", 2-t-oz. 345.00
G Ibbot, London; teapot, hinged domed lid, repoussé floral, 9¾", EX .. 2,285.00
Geo Jensen, Denmark; sauceboat, scroll hdl, ftd, 5¼x8½", 13-t-oz...1,800.00
Geo Jensen, USA; bowl, petaled form, 2 sm scroll ft, 3½x10"...... 300.00
Glasgow, goblet, Geo III, initials in reserve, 1823-24, 13.1-t-oz... 660.00
Gurney & Co, cup, Geo III, 2-hdl, ftd, eng initials, 13.8-t-oz 600.00
Gurney & Cooke, London; sugar bowl, Geo II, stepped ft, 5.5-t-oz ...1,265.00
H Bateman, London; coffeepot, Geo III, domed lid, swan's neck, 27-t-oz.5,175.00
J Tuite, London; salver, Geo II, scalloped rim/eng, 6½", 7.8-t-oz . 460.00
JF, Birmingham; snuff box, Geo V, hinged lid, inset agate, 1922 .. 260.00
JF Hewes, Boston; tazza, hammered, w/curls, 9¼x7"..................3,900.00
JM, Dublin; bowl, repoussé/chased decor, ftd, 3¾x7¼", 14.1-t-oz.. 515.00
Kinsey, beaker/julep cup, die-rolled rim/ft, 1856, 2.9-t-oz 330.00
Kinsey, ewer, chased/repoussé decor, C-scroll hdl, ca 1840s, 23.4-t-oz .. 1,000.00
Kinsey, hot water urn, chased/repoussé decor, 1840s, 17", 77.1-t-oz.3,450.00
LeSage, London; meat dish, Geo III, gadrooning/eng armorial, 22-t-oz..1,560.00
London, bell, Geo II, eng decor w/scrollwork, 1734, 4¾", 5.8-t-oz..1,725.00
London, christening cup, Geo III, scroll hdl, 1762, 3½", 5.3-t-oz....460.00
London, coffeepot, Geo II, baluster, dbl-scroll hdl, 11", 11.3-t-oz.. 1,150.00
London, coffeepot, Geo II, dbl scroll hdl, domed lid, 1740s, 18.5-t-oz.. 1,600.00
London, cream pitcher, Geo III, dbl-bellied form, 1780s, 2.6-t-oz...175.00
London, mustard pot, Geo III, scroll hdl/thumbpc, cobalt liner, 6-t-oz. 575.00
London, sauceboat, Geo II, dbl-scroll hdl, shell ft, 1751-52, 3.3-t-oz.... 550.00
London, sauceboat, Geo III, oval, scroll hdl, 10.2-t-oz................ 800.00
London, sauceboat, Geo III, urn finial, armorial crest, 5x8½", pr..3,600.00
London, sauceboat, Geo IV, rococo style, 1827-28, 3", 3-t-oz...... 180.00
London, tea set, Geo III, floral finials, 1801-02, 6-pc, 116.5-t-oz...5,000.00
M West, Dublin; cup, dbl-bellied, 3 scroll hdls, 1788, 14.5-t-oz.. 1,380.00
P Rundell, London; bowl, scalloped rim, shells/scrolls, 10", 24.9-t-oz . 975.00
P&A Bateman, London; loving cup, S-scroll hdls, 1791, 6", 10-t-oz.. 635.00
P&A Bateman, London; sugar bowl, gw int, reeded hdls, 4x8x5½"....460.00
PAT, Paris; bowl, vegetable; squash blossoms, w/lid, pr: 70.35-t-oz.. 3,300.00
Puiforcat, coffeepot, bulbous w/long slim spout, 11½", 20-t-oz..2,400.00
R Smith, Dublin; coffeepot, repoussé/chased decor, 1844, 82.7-t-oz..1,265.00
RM, England; mustard pot, rtcl, shell thumbpc, cobalt liner, 2.5-t-oz... 175.00
Shaw & Priest, London; cup, Geo III, 2-hdl, ftd, splits, 15.8-t-oz....800.00
Shepheard & Co, chalice, chased Latin motto, 4¼x4½" 2,280.00

SM, London; sauceboat, Geo II, scalloped rim, 1749, 4.5-t-oz..... 515.00
Smith & Sharp, London; saucepan, Geo III, 3¼" dia, 6.3-t-oz..... 460.00
T Bradbury, London; trophy cup, high ft, 1908, 5¾", 20.3-t-oz.... 485.00
T Whipham, London; coffeepot, Geo II, repoussé, 9", 13.8-t-oz ...1,500.00
Wm Grundy, kettle on stand, Geo II, bulbous, domed lid, 1750s, 52-t-oz.3,125.00
Wm Homes Sr, Boston; cann, spurred hdl, 5¼", 10.8-t-oz.........3,750.00
Wm Kersill, London; creamer, repoussé birds/etc, 1750, 2.5-t-oz.430.00

Silver Overlay

The silver overlay glass made since the 1880s was decorated with a cut-out pattern of sterling silver applied to the surface of the ware.

Bottle, dk gr w/floral o/l, matching stopper, 9" 1,000.00
Bottle, emerald gr, Nouveau floral o/l w/monogram, bulbous, 4¼" ..200.00
Bottle, scent; clear canteen, Gorham o/l w/eng monogram, 3¼" . 120.00
Creamer & sugar bowl, clear w/etch floral, floral o/l, o/l hdls, 3".... 35.00
Decanter, clear w/etched floral & floral o/l, glass stopper 20.00
Decanter, clear w/scrolling vines o/l, Alvin, ca 1873, 10¾" 975.00
Decanter, cobalt w/floral o/l, teardrop stopper, 9" 350.00
Pitcher, clear molded Heisey pattern w/floral o/l, bulbous, lg....... 150.00
Pitcher, clear tankard w/Nouveau o/l at rim, water sz..................... 80.00
Shaker, clear w/Nouveau o/l, 6-sided, metal top, ea 25.00
Vase, bl cased w/geometric o/l resembling pineapple, 10" 55.00
Vase, bl w/Nouveau floral o/l, 2¾x3¼" 275.00
Vase, bud; emerald gr w/Nouveau floral o/l, disk ft, 6"................. 360.00
Vase, cobalt bl w/floral & leaf o/l, #999 near base, 6¼" 1,200.00
Vase, cobalt w/vining o/l, baluster, 6".. 240.00

Silverplate

Silverplated flatware is becoming the focus of attention for many of today's collectors. Demand is strong for early, ornate patterns, and prices have continued to rise steadily over the past five years. Our values are based on pieces in excellent or restored/resilvered condition. Serving pieces are priced to reflect the values of examples in complete original condition, with knives retaining their original blades. If pieces are monogrammed, deduct from 20% (for rare, ornate patterns) to 30% (for common, plain pieces). Our advisor for this category is Rick Spencer; he is listed in the Directory under Utah. For more information we recommend *Silverplated Flatware, Revised Fourth Edition*, by Tere Hagan. See also Railroadiana; Silverplate.

Flatware

Adam, Community, dinner fork, 7½" 4.00
Adam, Community, sugar spoon...3.00
Ancestrial 1847, Rogers, master butter knife, flat hdl.......................3.00
Ancestrial 1847, Rogers, tablespoon 7.50
Avon 1847, Rogers, meat fork 21.00
Ballad, Oneida, baby fork 5.50
Berkshire 1847, Rogers, cocktail fork.. 11.25
Berkshire 1847, Rogers, pickle fork... 27.50
Berwick, Rogers, jam spoon.. 22.00
Berwick, Rogers, luncheon fork, 7" 11.00
Caprice, Nobility, iced tea spoon..3.50
Classic Plume, Towle, meat fork, 7½".. 12.00
Classic Plume, Towle, tablespoon, pierced.................................... 11.00
Columbia 1847, Rogers, gravy ladle 26.00
Coronation, Community, grill fork..3.75
Daybreak, Rogers, salad fork, 6" 6.50
Daybreak, Rogers, teaspoon...2.75

Deauville, Comminity, oval soup spoon, 7½"........................6.75
Deauville, Community, sugar spoon 3.25
First Love 1847, Rogers, chipped beef fork........................ 10.50
Floral, Wallace, jam spoon... 45.00
Grenoble, Prestige, cream soup spoon, 6" 5.50
Grenoble, Prestige, tomato server 10.00
Grenoble/Glodia, Rogers, dinner fork.............................. 12.00
Grenodle/Gloria, Rogers, meat fork 40.00
Heraldic 1847, Rogers, salad fork 8.00
Invitation, Gorham, pie/cake server, hollow hdl 17.00
Invitation, Gorham, teaspoon 3.00
Lady Empire, Nobility, coffee spoon 3.25
Longchamps, Prestige, cream soup spoon, 6¼" 6.50
Longchamps, Prestige, grill fork......................................6.75
Longchamps, Prestige, tomato server 21.50
Marquise 1847, Rogers, master butter knife 4.75
May Queen, Holmes & Edwards, tablespoon 10.00
May Queen, Holmes & Edwards, teaspoon 2.25
Milady, Community, oval soup spoon 4.00
Milady, Community, salad fork...6.75
Mystic, Rogers, berry spoon 33.50
Napleon, Holmes & Edwards, grill fork............................5.00
Nobless, Community, tablespoon 11.50
Old Colony 1847, luncheon fork, 7" 5.50
Old Colony 1847, Rogers, grapefruit spoon 11.25
Old Colony 1847, Rogers, sugar spoon..............................5.50
Orange Blossom, Rogers, meat fork................................. 26.00
Patrician, Community, cocktail fork 8.00
Patrician, Community, curved baby spoon..........................8.25
Paul Revere, Community, dinner fork, 7½" 6.75
Queen Bess 1946, Oneida, gravy ladle 13.50
Remembrance 1847, Rogers, iced tea spoon 7.75
Remembrance 1847, Rogers, roast carving set, 2-pc 86.00
Reverie, Nobility, butter spreader.....................................5.00
Reverie, Nobility, seafood fork 5.00
Royal Lace, Nobility, seafood fork 5.75
Sharon 1847, Rogers, meat fork 16.00
Sheraton, Community, gravy ladle 15.00
South Seas, Community, master butter knife......................2.50
South Seas, Community, nut spoon, pierced.......................7.75
Tiger Lily, Reed & Barton, luncheon fork, 7" 9.00
Tiger Lily, Reed & Barton, tablespoon 11.00
Vesta 1847, Rogers, seafood fork 9.25
Vintage 1847, Rogers, butter spreader, flat hdl................ 18.00
Vintage 1847, Rogers, fish fork 35.00
Violet, SG Rogers, meat fork... 21.75
Violet, SG Rogers, pie server, flat hdl.............................. 21.75
White Orchid, Community, dinner fork 9.50
White Orchid, Community, sugar spoon.............................5.00
Windsong, Nobility, gravy ladle 18.00
Windsong, Nobility, iced tea spoon 9.00
Windsong, Nobility, meat fork 18.50
Winsome 1959, Community, oval soup spoon 7.00
Winsome 1959, tablespoon, pierced................................ 15.00
Youth, Holmes & Edwards, grill fork................................3.50
Youth, Holmes & Edwards, tablespoon 6.50

Hollow Ware

Barker & Ellis, punch set, floral 17" bowl+12 cups+21⅜" tray ..4,800.00
Elkington, vase, scenes in relief, w/hdls & liner, 1857 Expo, 18"..2,650.00
English, champagne bucket, eng crest, w/liner, 19th C, 9x10½", pr..3,250.00
Joseph Rogers & Co, venison warming dish, emb rococo, w/lid, 26" L...2,100.00
M Bolton, wine coaster, Geo III, gilt int, 1810s, 3¼x4½" 850.00

M Hall & Co, pitcher, floral repoussé, gilt int, hinged lid, 11"..... 850.00
Middleton, caviar boat w/cherubs, raised on plinth w/waves, 12x12". 1,325.00
Stugart (att), ewer, invt pear form w/eng eagle head, 1800s, 18", pr. 850.00
Tufts, vase, cattails extend to hold sm trumpet vase, #1021, 4½". 285.00
Unknown, biscuit bbl, horse finial, scenic reserves, 1890s, 8x7¾" ..900.00
Unknown, hot water kettle, floral, Regency style, 1850s, 17x10" ...850.00
Unknown, hot water warming dish, Regency style, domed lid, 15x25"..2,000.00
Unknown, supper set, tureen w/lid+4 oval dishes+2 salts, 1900s ..1,175.00
Unknown, wine cooler, classical figures, urn form, gilt int, 13" ..1,175.00
Unknown, wine cooler, Regency style w/lion mask/drop ring hdls, 8x9" ... 1,500.00
WMF, bowl, centerpc; Egyptian Revival, w/glass liner, 19th C, 9x29" 3,850.00

Sheffield

Cake basket, Geo III, navette form, swing hdl, gadrooning, 10x14x10" ..425.00
Candlesticks, Edward VII Classical Revival, 1904, 12", pr........1,550.00
Chafing dish, M Boulton, oval w/rocaille hdls, w/liner/lid, 14", pr..2,650.00
Hot water urn, gadrooned rim, mask hdls, 19th C, 17½".............. 250.00
Meat dome, Walker & Hall, oval w/beaded edge, hdl detaches, 11x18"..175.00
Tankard, Boulton & Fothergill, domed lid, stepped ft, 7½" 700.00
Tea tray, chased borders, eng shield, hdls, 4 scroll ft, 3x33x22".... 650.00
Tray, M Boulton, gadrooned rim/hdls, eng coat of arms, 1790s, 28" L... 785.00
Tureen, navette form w/ped base, domed lid, 8x10x4", pr 800.00
Vase, trumpet-shaped wire fr w/cobalt liner, 16¼x7", pr.............. 700.00

Sinclaire

In 1904 H.P. Sinclaire and Company was founded in Corning, New York. For the first 16 years of production, Sinclaire used blanks from other glassworks for his cut and engraved designs. In 1920 he established his own glassblowing factory in Bath, New York. His most popular designs utilize fruits, flowers, and other forms from nature. Most of Sinclaire's glass is unmarked; items that are carry his logo: an 'S' within a wreath with two shields.

Bowl, floral eng, scalloped rim, 10" 200.00
Bowl, Fuchsia cuttings, 6".. 48.00
Bowl, Queen's pattern, oblong, 9½x7", NM.................................... 625.00
Bowl, 13 hobstars in vessica panels, scalloped/sawtooth rim, 3½x8" ..120.00
Candlesticks, gr, baluster form, 12", pr... 300.00
Candlesticks, gr, baluster form, 16", pr... 575.00
Compote, amber, flared bowl on stem w/ring knob, 4½x12½"...... 180.00

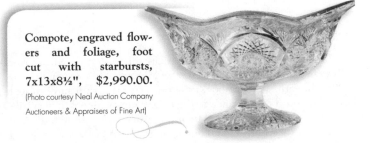

Compote, floral cutting, tall stem, shallow bowl, 6½x6¾"............ 135.00
Compote, intaglio leaf & frosted cherry, ftd, 4x8" 50.00
Goblet, gr w/geometric cuttings, clear stem & ft, 8¾x2¾" 240.00
Pitcher, cut/eng Bull's Eye variation, cylindrical, ca 1905, 14".....240.00
Relish tray, brilliant cuttings, scalloped/sawtooth rim, 2x8x4"....... 48.00
Teapot, Greek key & fluted pattern, 1880s+, 4½", +matching 8" plate..480.00
Vase, Dahlia, intaglio cuttings, 12" 120.00
Vase, floral eng w/bl threading, baluster, 10"................................ 275.00
Vase, floral garland eng, slim w/ruffled rim, 31" 400.00

Sitzendorf

The Sitzendorf factory began operations in what became East Germany in the mid-1800s, adopting the name of the city as the name of their company. They produced fine porcelain groups, figurines, etc., in much the same style and quality as Meissen and the Dresden factories. Much of their ware was marked with a crown over the letter 'S' and a horizontal line with two slash marks.

Candlesticks, seated nymph on floral base w/bronze bobeche, 11x7", pr..235.00
Clock, putti & appl flowers on rococo base, 1890-1900, 12½" 850.00
Clock, 4 seasons allegoricals, brass Roman dial, flakes, 23x14x9"...3,600.00
Compote, tall ped w/figures & appl flowers, 15¼x11".................... 350.00
Figurine, dancer holds lace skirt wide, appl flowers, 8x5x3½" 180.00
Figurine, Exelmans, standing Napoleonic soldier, 9½" 345.00
Figurine, General Bessieres on horsebk, 11x8"............................... 225.00
Figurine, Guarde Imperiale, drummer on horsebk, 11" 275.00
Figurine, Guarde Imperiale, soldier on horse, 11"......................... 480.00
Figurine, lady w/fan, plumed hat, Voght Bros, 19th C, 14" 275.00
Figurine, LaFayette, standing Napoleonic soldier, 9½" 345.00
Figurine, Le Prince Eugene, soldier on horsebk, 11" 360.00
Figurine, Napoleon stands w/hand in shirt, 9½" 275.00
Figurine, semi-nude boy riding bucking goat, 8" 250.00

Figurines, children with baskets on their shoulders, 10", $200.00 for the pair. (Photo courtesy Jackson's International Auctioneers & Appraisers of Fine Art & Antiques)

Figurines, colonial man & lady, she w/locket, he w/hat & rose, 15", pr..275.00
Figurines, man (& lady) w/apples, traditional garb, post-1954, 20", pr ...275.00
Mirror, appl cherubs/flowers, 2 candleholders, ca 1870, 28x17" ... 765.00
Vase, scenic tapestry, cylindrical w/4 gold ft, ca 1890s, 13½" 1,200.00

Skookum Dolls

Representing real Indians of various tribes, stern-faced Skookum dolls were designed by Mary McAboy of Missoula, Montana, in the early 1900s. The earliest of McAboy's creations were made with air-dried apple faces that bore a resemblance to the neighboring Chinook Indian tribe. The name Skookum is derived from the Chinook/Siwash term for large or excellent (aka Bully Good) and appears as part of the oval paper la-

bels often attached to the feet of the dolls. In 1913 McAboy applied for a patent that described her dolls in three styles: a female doll, a female doll with a baby, and a male doll. In 1916 George Borgman and Co. partnered with McAboy, registered the Skookum trademark, and manufactured these dolls which were distributed by the Arrow Novelty Co. of New York and the HH Tammen Co. of Denver. The Skookum (Apple) Packers Association of Washington state produced similar 'friendly faced' dolls as did Louis Ambery for the National Fruit exchange. The dried apple faces of the first dolls were replaced by those made of a composition material. Plastic faces were introduced in the 1940s, and these continued to be used until production ended in 1959. Skookum dolls were produced in a variety of styles, with the most collectible having stern, lined faces with small painted eyes glancing to the right, colorful Indian blankets pulled tightly across the straw- or paper-filled body to form hidden arms, felt pants or skirts over wooden legs, and wooden feet covered with decorated felt suede or masking tape. Skookums were produced in sizes ranging from a 2" souvenir mailer with a cardboard address tag to 36" novelty and advertising dolls. Collectors highly prize 21" to 26" dolls as well as dolls that glance to their left. Felt or suede feet predate the less desirable brown plastic feet of the late 1940s and 1950s. Unless noted otherwise, our values are for skookums in excellent condition. Our advisor for this category is Glen Rairigh; he is listed in the Directory under Michigan.

Baby, looks left, cradle brd, beaded body/head covering, 10½"..1,100.00
Baby, mc blanket, leather headband w/pnt decor, 4" 30.00
Baby/child in loop basket, blanket wrap, necklace, 14"................. 200.00
Boy, brn ft w/pnt decor, Bully Good label, 6½" 100.00
Boy, brn suede ft w/decor, headband, 10" 150.00
Boy, mc blanket, felt pants, leather shoes, 6½", VG 50.00
Chief w/headdress, paper tape shoes w/decor, 12½"....................... 250.00
Family, chief & female w/baby, clothes match, 15", 14" 600.00
Female, w/baby, w/blanket, purple felt/ft/skirt, necklace, 11½" 200.00
Female, w/baby, w/blanket, worn paper tape ft, 12½", VG 150.00
Girl, cotton-wrapped legs, beaded ft decor, headband, 9½" 150.00
Girl, cotton-wrapped legs, pnt suede ft covers, Bully Good, 6½"... 100.00
Mailer, baby in bl & yel cotton, Grand Canyon, 10-1-52 .... 25.00
Mailer, baby in patterned cotton yel cb... 25.00
Mailer, baby in red bandana on yel cb.. 55.00
Mailer, baby w/1 ½¢ postcard attached, feather/ribbon binding, 4"..100.00

Slag Glass

Slag glass is a marbleized opaque glassware made by several companies from about 1870 until the turn of the century. It is usually found in purple or caramel (see Chocolate Glass), though other colors were also made. Pink is rare and very expensive. It was revived in recent years by several American glassmakers, L.E. Smith, Westmoreland, and Imperial among them. The listings below reflect values for items with excellent color.

Caramel, bell, Dresden Girl, Imperial, 8x4"................................... 25.00
Caramel, car epergne, 5".. 120.00
Caramel, elephant, trunk out, Imperial, 3⅞x6½"........................... 40.00
Caramel, jar, beehive w/bees, Imperial, 5x4½"............................... 35.00
Caramel, Log Cabin, creamer & sugar bowl, w/lid, Mosser, 1970s ...50.00
Caramel, Open Rose, bowl, ruffled rim, 3-ftd, 3x8" 20.00
Green, box, emb nudes, Ingrid, 2½x3¾" 60.00
Pk, Invt Fan & Feather, bowl, master berry; 5½x9¼", from $400 to...600.00
Pk, Invt Fan & Feather, butter dish, 8" dia 1,200.00
Pk, Invt Fan & Feather, pitcher, 8", from $1,650 to 1,850.00
Pk, Invt Fan & Feather, punch cup, 2¼", from $200 to................ 250.00
Pk, Invt Fan & Feather, shakers, pr..2,200.00
Pk, Invt Fan &'Feather, tumbler, 3⅞", from $150 to 175.00
Purple, bowl, emb leaves, 4½x9½"... 30.00

Purple, bowl, swan form, Imperial, 3¾" 24.00
Purple, box, 2-compartment, Imperial, 3x8½x4½" 100.00
Purple, butter dish, cow on domed lid, Greener, 7⅞" L 600.00
Purple, butter dish, rectangular, 4x8x6" 100.00
Purple, candy dish, eagle finial, Imperial, 9x6¼" 75.00
Purple, Cherry, butter dish, Imperial, 6x8" 60.00
Purple, compote, eagle finial, Imperial, 5x6" 95.00
Purple, creamer, owl figural, glass eyes, 3¼" 45.00
Purple, cup, birds in relief, Imperial, 3½" 27.50
Purple, fruit bowl, latticed, Imperial, 8½x9" 200.00
Purple, Hobnail, bowl, fan border, 3x7½" 60.00
Purple, Open Rose, bowl, ftd, 3x7½" 35.00
Purple, Open Rose, bowl, Imperial, 9¼", from $100 to 150.00
Purple, Windmill, pitcher, 6½" 60.00
Ruby, basket, milk glass hdl, Imperial, 5x5¼x4½" 20.00
Ruby, Windmill, pitcher, Imperial, 6⅜" 60.00

Smith Bros.

Alfred and Harry Smith founded their glassmaking firm in New Bedford, Massachusetts. They had been formerly associated with the Mt. Washington Glass Works, working there from 1871 to 1875 to aid in establishing a decorating department. Smith glass is valued for its excellent enameled decoration on satin or opalescent glass. Pieces were often marked with a lion in a red shield.

Atomizer, wisteria on swirled opal body, missing bulb, 6½" 550.00
Biscuit jar, pansies on cream, melon ribs, SP lid, 7½x6¼" 215.00
Biscuit jar, roses on wht, melon ribs, SP lid, 7" dia 240.00
Bowl, floral on wht w/gold, squat, 2¾x5¼" 60.00
Bowl, pussy willows/Easter Greetings, melon ribs, 2½x5⅜" 85.00
Box, carnations on wht, emb ribs, 3½x5½" 275.00
Box, pansies on cream, melon ribs, 5½" dia 225.00
Creamer & sugar bowl, floral on custard, SP lids/mts, 3½" 155.00
Humidor, pansies on cream, SP lid, ovoid, 6¾x4½" 300.00
Muffineer, floral on wht, melon ribs, SP lid, ca 1878, 3½" 180.00
Muffineer, floral on wht/beaded band/emb ribs, SP lid, 5½" 395.00
Syrup, floral, gold on custard, melon ribs, ornate SP lid & hdl, 5" .. 785.00
Syrup, violets on wht, plain hinged lid, 5" 275.00
Vase, herons & grasses on bl opal, 3¾"+SP base & stem, pr 240.00
Vase, pansies on yel, bulbous, 6" dia 150.00
Vase, wisteria on cream opal, shouldered, 1870s, 9" 725.00

Snow Babies

During the last quarter of the nineteenth century, snow babies — little figures in pebbly white snowsuits — originated in Germany. They were originally made of sugar candy and were often used as decorations for Christmas cakes. Later on they were made of marzipan, a confection of crushed almonds, sugar, and egg whites. Eventually porcelain manufacturers began making them in bisque. They were popular until WWII. These tiny bisque figures range in size from 1" up to 7" tall. Quality German pieces bring very respectable prices on the market today. Beware of reproductions. Our advisor for this category is Linda Vines; she is listed in the Directory under California.

Babies (2) on hollow globe base, holding Am flag, Germany, 3¼" .. 375.00
Baby hides in ice cave below polar bear, #378, Germany, 2" 360.00
Baby in sled pulled by huskies, Germany, 2" 275.00
Baby inside igloo, Santa on top, Germany, 2" 225.00
Baby on skates, snow hat & sweater, pastel pants, Germany, 2" ... 145.00
Baby standing on lg snowball, Japan, 2½" 50.00

Baby with bear cub inside ice cave, Germany, 1930s, 2", $250.00. (Photo courtesy Linda Vines)

Baby w/seal & red ball, Germany, 2" 225.00
Bear playing w/colorful ball, Germany, 1" 75.00
Boy on tummy atop yel sled, Germany, 3" 50.00
Child, no-snow boy or girl pushing lg snowball, Germany, 2" 140.00
Kewpie standing, 2" 200.00
Penguins (3) walking down brick wall, Germany, 2½" 175.00
Pixies (2) sitting on hobbyhorse, wood stick legs, Germany, 2" ... 145.00
Santa in yel sailboat, Germany, 2" 145.00
Santa riding yel train, pixie in bk, Germany, 3" 225.00
Santa sitting on wht swing, Germany, 3" 165.00
Snow dog, rabbit or cat, Germany, 1", ea 65.00
Snow man sitting, blk top hat, Germany, 2" 80.00
Snow mother pushing twins in red carriage-sled, Germany, 2½" .. 375.00

Snuff Boxes

As early as the seventeenth century, the Chinese began using snuff. By the early nineteenth century, the practice had spread to Europe and America. It was used by both the gentlemen and the ladies alike, and expensive snuff boxes and bottles were the earmark of the genteel. Some were of silver or gold set with precious stones or pearls, while others contained music boxes. See also Orientalia, Snuff Bottles.

Bone book form w/eng/pnt decor, dtd 1828, 2⅛x2⅞" 660.00
Bone book form w/eng/pnt tulips/couple/farm tools, 1828, 2x3" .. 650.00
Brass, Lord Nelson on lid, England Expects Every Man..., 2¾" dia ... 360.00
Brass, tooled designs/MOP inlay & dk red enamel, 1x2½" dia 600.00
Bropnze, gilt w/tourmaline-set border, lady's portrait, 2⅜" dia 550.00
Circassian walnut w/B Franklin medallion & gold leaf, 1¾" dia .. 725.00
Horn, Washington portrait on lid under convex glass, Fr, 3¼" dia ... 1,550.00
Ivory, HP country home scene, English, 1830s, 3½" dia 360.00
Papier-maché w/titled lady's portrait on lid, 1850s, 4" dia 550.00
Shell w/silver inlay & lady's portrait on ivory, 1¼x3⅜" L 500.00
Silver, eng whaling scene, mk C Parker, ¾x3¼x2¼" 1,100.00
Silver, lion figural, hinged lid, 18th C, 3⅛" L 660.00
Silver eng over guilloche enamel, lady's portrait, Fr, 1¼x3x2¼" .. 780.00
Silver gilt w/chased bands, engine trn, Fr, 19th C, 3" dia 600.00
Silver w/eng Cupid & borders, gold-washed int, Fr, ca 1900, 2⅝" L ... 395.00
Silver w/gold putti & monogram, gilt int, mid-19th C, 3" L 425.00
Silver w/Napoleon family portrait/swags/wreath, Fr, 3" dia 550.00
Silver w/3 lg oval amethysts/sm rose-cut dmns/sapphires, 3¼" L ... 1,450.00
Tortoiseshell, 3-comb music player, ca 1815-20, 3½" L 1,000.00
14k yel gold w/cobalt enameling, hand chasing, oval, 2⅞x2" 2,750.00

Soap Hollow Furniture

In the Mennonite community of Soap Hollow, Pennsylvania, the women made and sold soap; the men made handcrafted furniture. Rare today, this furniture was stenciled, grain painted, and beautifully decorated with inlaid escutcheons. These pieces are becoming very sought after. When well kept, they are very distinctive and beautiful. The items described in these listings are in excellent condition unless otherwise described. Assume that all painted decoration is original to the piece unless 'rpt' (repainted) is noted. Our advisor for this category is Anita Levi; she is listed in the Directory under Pennsylvania.

Blanket chest, grpt w/silver/gilt stencil, poplar, ET/1859, 23x44x19" . 7,185.00
Blanket chest, red & blk, gold stencil, CW/1874, 25x45x18" ...6,700.00
Blanket chest, red & blk, gold stencil, decals, JC/1874, 10x17x9" . 5,060.00
Blanket chest, red/gr pnt w/yel stripes/stencil, SH/1868, 24x49"..19,250.00
Chest, 6-drw, cherry w/red stain/ebonized trim, 45x37" 2,750.00
Chest, 6-drw, cherry/poplar w/blk & red pnt, stencil, 1861, 55x39x21"..7,475.00
Chest, 6-drw, dk red w/silver stencil, 56x42x21" 9,500.00
Chest, 6-drw, mc pnt/stencil, dtd 1859, 47x37x20" 14,000.00
Chest, 7-drw, grpt w/blk, gold stencil, MH/1887, 47½x39½" ..18,000.00
Cradle, maroon grpt, gilt stencil, mustard trim 1,100.00
Cupboard, corner; maroon w/blk, stencil, 1856 ....15,500.00
Cupboard, Dutch; 4 doors/2 drws, stencil/old rpt, 1875, 84x65".. 8,000.00
Cupboard, red & gr pnt/striping/stencil, poplar, 2-pc, 87x64".35,200.00
Desk, 5-drw base, red/yel/blk, pine/poplar, 1870, 33x21x15"...33,350.00
Dresser, Emp style, columns on 3 drws, HF/1874 ....2,200.00
Frame, cross pcs, gr/yel striping, 15½x19¾" 1,000.00
Rope bed, red & brn finish on cherry, rare 2,300.00
Sewing chest, 1-drw, red pnt w/floral, 1875, rare, 12x8" 10,300.00
Sewing stand, pnt poplar, dvtl drw/porc knob, 876/LAY, 15x9x7" ...4,600.00

Soapstone

Soapstone is a soft talc in rock form with a smooth, greasy feel from whence comes its name. (It is also called Soo Chow Jade.) It is composed basically of talc, chlorite, and magnetite. In colonial times it was extracted from out-croppings in large sections with hand saws, carted by oxen to mills, and fashioned into useful domestic articles such as footwarmers, cooking utensils, inkwells, etc. During the early 1800s, it was used to make heating stoves and kitchen sinks. Most familiar today are the carved vases, bookends, and boxes made in China during the Victorian era. Our advisor for this category is Clarence Bodine; he is listed in the Directory under Pennsylvania.

Figurine, Buddha seated, EX details, China, 8x5x4" 780.00
Figurine, Buddha seated in dhyanasana, loose robes, 20th C, 7⅝" ..450.00
Figurine, immortal seated in long robes, beaded necklace, China, 12" 725.00
Figurine, morphic creature (walrus/eagle/bird), Inuit, 7½x9½" 780.00
Seal, dragon form w/Chinese characters on front, 20th C, 4⅝x3x3"..950.00
Seal, ox, recumbent, 20th C, 5x2½x2⅜".....................................385.00

Soda Fountain Collectibles

The first soda water sales in the United States occurred in the very late 1790s in New York and New Haven, Connecticut. By the 1830s soda water was being sold in drug stores as a medicinal item, especially the effervescent mineral waters from various springs around the country. By this time the first flavored soda water appeared at an apothecary shop in Philadelphia.

The 1830s also saw the first manufacturer (John Matthews) of devices to make soda water. The first marble soda fountain made its appearance in 1857 as a combination ice shaver and flavor-dispensing apparatus. By the 1870s the soda fountain was an established feature of the neighborhood drug store. The fountains of this period were large, elaborate marble devices with druggists competing with each other for business by having fountains decorated with choice marbles, statues, mirrors, water fountains, and gas lamps.

In 1903 the fountain completed its last major evolution with the introduction of the 'front' counter service we know today. (The soda clerk faced the customer when drawing soda.) By this time ice cream was a standard feature being served as sundaes, ice cream sodas, and milk shakes. Syrup dispensers were just being introduced as 'point-of-sale' devices to sell various flavorings from many different companies. Straws were commonplace, especially those made from paper. Fancy and unusual ice cream dippers were in daily use, and they continued to evolve, reaching their pinnacle with the introduction of the heart-shaped dipper in 1927.

This American business has provided collectors today with an almost endless supply of interesting and different articles of commerce. One can collect dippers, syrup dispensers, glassware, straw dispensers, milk shakers, advertising, and trade catalogs. Assume that our prices are for examples with the correct pump, unless otherwise noted. (Note: The presence of a 'correct' pump enhances the value of a syrup dispenser by 25%.) When no condition is given, values are for items in excellent condition.

Collectors need to be made aware of decorating pieces that are actually fantasy items: copper ice cream cones, a large copper ice cream dipper, and a copper ice cream soda glass. These items have no resale value. Our advisors for this category are Joyce and Harold Screen; they are listed in the Directory under Maryland. See also Advertising: Dr. Pepper, Hires, Moxie, Pepsi, 7-Up; Coca-Cola.

Bottle, syrup; Emerson's Ginger Mint Julep, clear w/label under glass...600.00
Bottle, syrup; Fowler's Cherry Smash, label under glass, 12½" ..1,450.00
Bottle, syrup; Grape Cola, clear w/label under glass, metal cap, 12"...360.00
Bottle, syrup; Moxie, clear w/appl color label, metal cap, 12½" ...575.00
Bottle, syrup; Pepsinola, clear w/label under glass, 1910s, 12".....215.00
Bottle, syrup; Vin Fiz, clear w/label under glass, 1910s, 12" 725.00
Bottle, syrup; 4-section w/appl bands/glass tubes, Fr, 1900s, 11" ..550.00
Canister, Bowey's Hot Chocolate, porc w/spun metal lid, 9x9"....775.00
Canister, malt; Carnation, aluminum w/red & wht advertising ... 100.00
Canister, malt; Thompson's, plastic, red & wht advertising, 1950s ..250.00
Canister, Malted Grape Nuts, clear glass w/Vitrolite label, metal lid .725.00
Canister, Thompson's Malted Milk, porc over steel, orig lid, 10".725.00
Carrier, bottle; Cherry Blossom, tin litho, center hdl, 12x13" dia, G..345.00
Carrier, Dr Pepper, stencil on wood, holds 12-pack, 1920s, 15" L ...550.00
Chairs, ice cream; copper-flashed bent wire w/wood seat, 34", 4 for...200.00
Cone holder, 5 yel plastic tubes, revolves, 39" 775.00
Cooler, Ma's Root Beer on yel, 41x33x19½" 395.00
Dipper, Benedict, #3, sz 20 rnd bowl w/wooden hdl, pre-1928, 10⅜"...55.00
Dipper, Dover, manual lever, sz 24 rnd bowl w/wooden hdl, 1920s, 10".200.00
Dipper, Erie Specialty Co, conical, wood hdl, ca 1909 ....500.00
Dipper, Fisher/Orilla Ont Canada, sz 20 rnd bowl w/wooden hdl, 10½". 75.00
Dipper, FS Co, sz 16 rnd bowl w/wooden hdl................................250.00
Dipper, Gem Spoon Co, sz 6 rnd bowl w/wooden hdl, Pat 1895, 11½"..325.00
Dipper, Gilchrist #22, sz 20 conical bowl w/wooden hdl 325.00
Dipper, Gilchrist #31, oval bowl, NP wooden hdl, 1915, 11½"....550.00
Dipper, Gilchrist #31, sz 12 rnd bowl w/wooden hdl, 11¾", EXIB...175.00
Dipper, Gilchrist #33, conical, NP brass w/wood hdl, ca 1914, 10½".. 180.00
Dipper, HS Geer, sz 10 rnd bowl w/wooden hdl, VG....................225.00
Dipper, Indestructo #4, brass & wood 30.00
Dipper, Kinger Mfg, conical w/4 blades, 8" 60.00
Dipper, Mosteller #79, conical, 2½" dia 85.00
Dipper, sandwich; ICYPI Automatic Cone Co, sq bowl, wood hdl, 10"..120.00
Dipper, sandwich; Jiffy Dispenser Co, German silver w/wood hdl, 1920s..180.00
Dipper, sandwich; Mayer Mfg, German silver w/wood hdl, 12"....120.00
Dipper, unmk, cylinder bowl, German silver w/wooden hdl, 1920s, 9½".575.00
Dispenser, Buckeye Root Beer, ceramic, gnome-like characters .. 5,200.00
Dispenser, copper cone w/jeweled dome, brass dispenser, ICS Co, 21".4,200.00
Dispenser, Crawford's Cherry-Fizz, bulbous, 15".......................7,250.00
Dispenser, Fan Taz, porc baseball form, 16"............................52,000.00
Dispenser, Fowler's Cherry Smash, ruby glass & chrome, 12½".8,500.00
Dispenser, Fowler's Cherry Smash 5¢, wht ceramic, 15½".........4,250.00

Dispenser, Green River, ceramic, 16", GT, $695.00. (Photo courtesy James D. Julia Inc.)

Dispenser, Horlick's Malted Milk, clear cylinder/gr porc base, 19x8" .. 550.00
Dispenser, hot drink; copper & brass, eagle finial, ca 1900, 30x12" .. 395.00
Dispenser, Lime Crush, stoneware lime, w/ball pump, 14" 10,250.00
Dispenser, malted milk; gr porc/glass cylinder, Hamilton Beach, 19x8" .. 725.00
Dispenser, marble base w/stained glass tulip shade, 1890s, 26x7½" .. 950.00
Dispenser, Mission Real Fruit Juice, pk glass w/brass, 13" 550.00
Dispenser, Nesbitt's Hot Fudge, chrome/maroon Bakelite/crockery, 13" .. 850.00
Dispenser, Nesbitt's Orange, amber glass w/brass spigot, 19" 300.00
Dispenser, Orange Crush, amber glass w/chrome dispenser top, 13" .. 1,450.00
Dispenser, Rochester Root Beer, clear/aluminum upright bbl w/hdl, 14" .. 875.00
Dispenser, Root Beer, clear cut/etch glass, 1900s, 21" 550.00
Dispenser, Stern's Root Beer, wooden keg w/metal bands, 13x9" .. 360.00
Dispenser, Ward's Lemon Crush, ceramic lemon w/pump, crack, 14" .. 2,650.00
Dispenser, Ward's Orange crush, ceramic orange w/pump, 1920s, 13" .. 3,000.00
Dispenser, Wine Dip Cola, glass/metal, Cordley NY, 15¾x8" 215.00
Extractor, Sunkist Fruit Juice, gr metal/wht porc, electric, 16" 360.00
Flavor board, Noll's Ice Cream, celluloid w/metal fr, 20x10" 150.00
Fountain dish, clear, rnd paneled bowl w/short ft, 2x5" 45.00
Fountain dish, clear heart shape w/emb scrolled leaves, 1920, 3x4¾" ... 480.00
Fountain dish, clear paneled boat style, 3x3⅝x8" 15.00
Fountain glass, clear ftd malt/shake, fluted w/banded rim, 1950s, 7" ... 10.00
Fountain glass, clear ftd soda, fluted w/banded rim, 1930s, 6" 12.00
Fountain glass, Jr Awful Awful.., clear w/red-pnt label at rim, 5" ... 45.00
Fountain glass, Kist Beverages, clear w/red-pnt label, 1950s, 4⅜" ... 25.00
Fountain glass, Tru Treat Grapefruit Drink, clear w/pnt label, 5⅛" .. 20.00
Fountain glasses, ftd, gr, Paden City, set of 4, 7" 100.00
Fountain glasses, smoked rims, metal hdld holders, set of 4, 1950s .. 25.00
Fountain spoons, SP w/twisted hdls, mk Berlin, set of 4, 6" 30.00
Ice cream cone holder, clear glass w/NP lid & insert, 1910s, 15" .. 600.00
Ice shaver, ornate CI, Zeppelin & floral front, Occupied Japan, 34x19" .. 480.00
Jar, Borden's Malted Milk, clear w/label under glass, w/lid, 9" 950.00
Jar, fruit; clear glass, 10-sided, Near Cut - Pat Apld For, 10" 360.00
Juicer, Sunkist Juicit, chrome & milk glass, 1950s, 9" 150.00
Menu, Tellings Ice Cream, celluloid cover, 1920s 325.00
Mixer, Nesbit It's Frosted, chrome cup, Bakelite lid, 1940s, 15" 150.00
Mug, Richardson Root Beer Rich, etched glass w/band top/bottom, 6½" .. 85.00
Straw dispenser, Hires Root Beer, metal & tin, 4¾x9½", VG.... 3,200.00
Straw holder, amber glass w/appl jewels, w/top, 1880s, 14" 7,250.00
Straw holder, clear/ribbed, metal top/insert, Benedict, 1920s-30s, 14" .. 225.00
Straw holder, cranberry w/emb T'prints, ca 1910, 13" 2,850.00
Straw holder, gr glass w/metal base & lid, ca 1910, 12" 850.00
Table, glass display case top, 4 swing-out CI/mahog seats, 26" sq .. 1,650.00
Tray, girl w/tray of sundaes, blk w/silver moon/gold trim, 13x13" .. 250.00

Spatter Glass

Spatter glass, characterized by its multicolor 'spatters,' has been made from the late nineteenth century to the present by American glass houses as well as those abroad. Although it was once thought to have been made entirely by workers at the 'end of the day' from bits and pieces of leftover scrap, it is now known that it was a standard line of production. See also Art Glass Baskets.

Basket, mc on wht, crimped rim, crystal irregular-shaped hdl, 6" ... **75.00**
Cruet, ruby & wht, clear hdl, faceted stopper, 6¾", NM **60.00**
Pitcher, cranberry/wht/clear, bulbous, clear hdl, 8½" **165.00**
Vase, pk & bl w/swirled body, ruffled rim, 9" **30.00**
Vase, pk & wht w/clear, bulbous, short flared rim, 7x7" **75.00**
Vase, red w/wht pulled pattern, slim, 10¾" **50.00**

Spatterware

Spatterware is a general term referring to a type of decoration used by English potters as early as the late 1700s. Using a brush or a stick, brightly colored paint was dabbed onto the soft-paste earthenware items, achieving a spattered effect which was often used as a border. Because much of this type of ware was made for export to the United States, some of the subjects in the central design — the schoolhouse and the eagle patterns, for instance — reflect American tastes. Yellow, green, and black spatterware is scarce and highly valued by collectors. In the descriptions that follow, the color listed after the item indicates the color of the spatter. The central design is identified next, and the color description that follows that refers to the design. When no condition code is present, assume that the item is undamaged and has only very light wear.

Creamer, bl, peafowl, 3-color, bulbous/paneled, 6" 390.00
Creamer, blk/brn bands, rose, 2-color, flakes, 3¾" 480.00
Creamer, gr, peafowl, 3-color, 3⅜" 250.00
Creamer, red, peafowl, 3-color, bulbous, 2½" 1,800.00
Creamer, red (top half), peafowl on branch, 3-color, leaf hdl, 4" .. 575.00
Creamer, red w/blk bands, tulip, 2-color, rpr chip/hdl, 4" 1,650.00
Cup, gr/brn rainbow, cylinder w/hdl, 2¾" 1,550.00
Pitcher, bl, fort/trees, 3-color, ornate hdl, shouldered/ftd, 10" ... 1,150.00
Pitcher, bl, 6-sided, ornate hdl, 6" 275.00
Pitcher, gr Vs, Christmas Balls, red/yel, str/paneled sides, 6", VG .. 3,600.00
Pitcher, mauve/blk stripes, 6-panel, 6⅜" 1,450.00
Pitcher, purple, tulip, 3-color, bulbous/paneled, 5½" 600.00
Pitcher, purple (full spatter), Lily of the Valley, gr/bl, paneled, 6" .. 2,400.00
Pitcher, purple/bl/blk stripes on wht, 8¾" 1,100.00
Pitcher, red (full spatter), primrose, 3-color, flared/paneled, 6" .. 2,800.00
Plate, bl, dahlia, red/bl, 9⅛" 480.00
Plate, bl, fort, yel/red/blk, 12-panel, early 19th C, 7" 300.00
Plate, bl, peafowl, red/gr, 10-panel, 1820s, 8⅛" 360.00
Plate, bl, tulip, red/gr, 9½" 120.00
Plate, bl (on crimped border only), peafowl, red/bl/gr, 8½" 395.00
Plate, cup; red, peafowl on branch, red/gr/bl, feather-emb rim, mk, 4" .. 510.00
Plate, gr (as tree tops/at rim), peafowl, yel/blk w/imp heart, 10", VG .. 960.00
Plate, red, peafowl, bl/yel/gr, feather-emb rim, 1820s, 8⅛" ...:...... 295.00
Plate, red/gr rainbow, 9½" 550.00
Plate, vivid bl (in rings around paneled edge), peafowl, 3-color, 10" .. 1,550.00
Soup plate, gr, peafowl, bl/yel/red, hairline, 10" 660.00
Sugar bowl, bl, fort, 3-color, prof rstr, w/lid, 4½" 275.00
Sugar bowl, bl, peafowl, 3-color, bulbous/octagonal w/hdls, 7½", VG .. 480.00
Sugar bowl, bl, peafowl, 3-color, simple shape, w/lid, 5" 350.00
Sugar bowl, bl, peafowl, 4-color, ring/shell-emb hdls, w/lid, lg .. 1,550.00
Sugar bowl, blk/pk rainbow, flower, 2-color, prof rstr, w/lid, 6" .. 1,325.00
Sugar bowl, red, rooster, 4-color, w/lid, 4½x5⅛" 600.00
Sugar bowl, yel, thistle, red/gr, w/lid, 7½" 2,650.00
Tea bowl, gr, swags w/red & yel dots, 2½x3⅞" 550.00
Tea bowl & saucer, bl, schoolhouse, 3-color, ca 1840 .... 2,350.00
Tea bowl & saucer, gr, peafowl, 3-color, 2¾x3¾", 6" 425.00

Tea bowl & saucer, pk w/red dots in center, 4" 135.00
Tea bowl & saucer, purple/blk rainbow, peafowl, 3-color, 2", 5" .. 1,950.00
Teapot, bl, tulips, red/bl/gr, sm rprs, 8½" 360.00
Teapot, bl, 4-bud cluster, red/gr, paneled, final reattached, 8", VG.. 1,200.00
Teapot, bl/yel rainbow, rose, 3-color, str sides, gooseneck spout, 10" .. 4,500.00
Teapot, gr, peafowl, 3-color, flakes, 5" 660.00
Teapot, rainbow: 3-color horizontal bands, simple form, much rpr, 7" .. 950.00
Washbowl, red/bl stripes w/crisscross center, rpr, 13¾" 240.00
Washbowl & pitcher, bl, peafowl, 4-color, 1830-50, 10", 12¼", VG ..550.00
Washbowl & pitcher, purple/blk bands on wht, 4¼x12¼", 10" .. 2,750.00
Washbowl & pitcher, rainbow: red/gr stripes, scalloped ft, 12", 14" ..3,600.00

Spelter

Spelter items are cast from commercial zinc and coated with a metallic patina. The result is a product very similar to bronze in appearance, yet much less expensive.

Bank, King Charles spaniel, blk & wht pnt, Germany, 1920s-30s 480.00
Bookends, Deco nude stands in peering position, bronze rpt, 8", EX .. 350.00
Bust, Odette, bronze finish, A Foretay, ca 1900, 19" 435.00
Candleholders, American Indian holds torch, 1900s, 16", EX, pr ..275.00
Centerpc, cherubs along rim, silver patina, metal insert, rpr, 22" L.. 375.00
Chandelier, cherub holds 2 lamp fixtures in hands, worn gilt, 10x6".. 385.00
Figurine, Arum, Nouveau lady w/flowers, after Nanteuil, rprs, 19".. 500.00
Figurine, Deco lady kneels forward, celluloid face & hands, 6x14".. 240.00
Figurine, Distress, lady waves goodbye, Mestais, on socle, 20th C, 21" .. 185.00
Figurine, Don Juan, old gold pnt, Ansonial, 20" 150.00
Figurine, Industry, allegorical man, Wagner, 24" 480.00
Figurine, Perseus & Pegasus, after Picalt, worn patina, 20th C, 22" .725.00
Incense burner, seated flapper holds urn (burner), bronze pnt, 10" ... 120.00
Lamp, Deco jester w/instrument, amber globe shade, bronze pnt, 6x6x4" 160.00
Lamp, Deco lady sits on wht onyx base holds amethyst globe, 20x9".. 350.00
Lamp, Deco nude stands ea side of gr frosted flower shade, 9x10" ...375.00
Lamp, draped Nouveau lady w/raised arm, 2-socket, brass finish, 16x9" ...135.00

Spode/Copeland

The following is a short chronological history of the Spode company:

1733: Josiah Spode I is born on the 23 of March at Lane Delph, Staffordshire.

1740: Spode is put to work in a pottery factory.

1754: Spode, now a fully proficient journeyman/potter, works for Turner and Banks in Stoke-on-Trent.

1755: Josiah Spode II is born.

1761: Spode I acquires a factory in Shelton where he makes cream-colored and blue-painted earthenware.

1770: This is the year adopted as the date Spode I founded the business.

1784: Spode I masters the art and techniques of transfer printing in blue under the glaze on earthenware.

1796: The marks the earliest known record of Spode selling porcelain dinnerware.

1800: Spode II produces the first bone china.

1806: Spode is appointed potter to the royal Family; this continues past 1983.

1813: Spode produces the first stone china.

1821: Spode introduces Feldspar Porcelain, a variety of bone china.

1833: William Taylor Copeland acquires the Spode factory from the Spode family and becomes partners with Garrett until 1847.

1870: System of impressing date marks on the backs of the dinnerware begins.

1925: Robert Copeland is born. (He presently resides in England.)

1976: The company merges with Worcester Royal Porcelain Company and forms Royal Worcester Spode Limited.

1986: The Spode Society is established.

1989: The holding company for Spode becomes the Porcelain and Fine China Companies Limited.

The price quotes listed in these three categories of Spode are for twentieth-century pre-1965 dinnerware in pristine condition — no cracks, chips, crazing, or stains. Minor knife cuts do not constitute damage unless extreme.

The patterns in the first group are the most common and popular earthenware lines. The second group contains the rarer and higher priced patterns; they are both earthenware and stoneware. Bone china patterns comprise the third group.

Our advisor for this category is Don Haase; he is listed in the Directory under Washington.

Dinner plate made especially for Madam Butchart of Butchart Gardens in Victoria, British Columbia, Canada, in 1930s (each type of piece has a different array of flowers), $75.00.

(Photo courtesy Don Haase)

First Group (Earthenware/Imperialware):

Ann Hathaway, Billingsley Rose, Buttercup, Byron, Camilla Pink, Chelsea Wicker, Chinese Rose, Christmas Tree (green), Cowslip, Fairy Dell, Fleur de Lis (blue/brown), Florence, Gadroon, Gainsborough, Hazel Dell, Indian Tree, Jewel, Moss Rose, Old Salem, Raeburn, Reynolds, Romney, Rosalie, Rose Briar, Valencia, Wickerdale, Wickerdell, Wickerlane.

Bowl, cereal; 6½" 25.00
Bowl, fruit; 5¼" 22.00
Coffeepot, 8-cup 195.00
Creamer, lg 55.00
Creamer, sm 45.00
Cup & saucer, demitasse 29.00
Cup & saucer, low/tall 29.00
Plate, bread & butter; 6¼" 16.00
Plate, butter pat 18.00
Plate, dinner 25.00
Plate, luncheon; rnd, 8-9" 22.00
Plate, salad; 7½" 20.00
Platter, oval, 13" 115.00
Platter, oval, 15" 135.00
Platter, oval, 17" 165.00
Sauceboat, w/liner 125.00
Soup, cream; w/liner 32.00
Soup, rim, 7½" 27.00
Soup, rim, 8½" 32.00
Sugar bowl, w/lid, lg 55.00
Sugar bowl, w/lid, sm 45.00
Teapot, 8-cup 195.00
Vegetable, oval, 9-10" 115.00
Vegetable, oval, 10-11" 135.00
Vegetable, sq, 8" 125.00
Vegetable, sq, 9" 145.00
Vegetable, w/lid 275.00
Waste bowl, 6" 29.00

Second Group (Earthenware/Imperialware)

Aster, Butchart, Camilla Blue, Christmas Tree (magenta), Italian, Mayflower, Herring Hunt (green/magenta), Patricia, Tower Blue and Pink, Wildflower (blue/red), Fitzhugh (blue/red/green), Gloucester (blue/red), Rosebud Chintz, Tradewinds (blue/red).

Bowl, cereal; 6¼"	32.00
Bowl, fruit; 5½"	28.00
Coffeepot, 8-cup	345.00
Creamer, lg	75.00
Creamer, sm	65.00
Cup & saucer, demitasse	35.00
Cup & saucer, low/high	39.00
Plate, bread & butter; 6¼"	29.00
Plate, butter pat	27.00
Plate, chop; rnd, 13"	225.00
Plate, dinner; 10½"	55.00
Plate, luncheon; rnd, 8-9"	45.00
Plate, luncheon; sq, 8½"	47.00
Plate, salad; 7½"	35.00
Platter, oval, 13"	145.00
Platter, oval, 15"	165.00
Platter, oval, 17"	210.00
Sauceboat, w/liner	165.00
Soup, rim, 7½"	35.00
Soup, rim, 8½"	45.00
Sugar bowl, w/lid, lg	75.00
Sugar bowl, w/lid, sm	65.00
Teapot, 8-cup	315.00
Vegetable, oval, 9-10"	135.00
Vegetable, oval, 10-11"	155.00
Vegetable, sq, 8"	145.00
Vegetable, sq, 9"	165.00
Vegetable, w/lid	325.00
Waste bowl, 6"	33.00

Third Group (Bone China)

Billingsley Rose Savoy, Bridal Rose, Carolyn, Chelsea Garden, Christine, Claudia, Colonel, Dimity, Dresden Rose Savoy, Fleur de Lis (gray/red/blue), Geisha (blue/pink/white), Irene, Maritime Rose, Primrose (pink), Shanghi, Savoy.

Bowl, cereal; 6¼"	42.00
Bowl, fruit; 5½"	37.00
Coffeepot, 8-cup	425.00
Creamer, lg	110.00
Creamer, sm	110.00
Cup & saucer, demitasse	55.00
Cup & saucer, low/tall	65.00
Plate, bread & butter; 6¼"	39.00
Plate, butter pat	35.00
Plate, chop; rnd, 13"	295.00
Plate, dessert; 8"	45.00
Plate, dinner; 10½"	59.00
Plate, luncheon; rnd, 9"	45.00
Plate, luncheon; sq, 8½"	55.00
Plate, salad; 7½"	49.00
Platter, oval, 13"	195.00
Platter, oval, 15"	225.00
Platter, oval, 17"	265.00
Sauceboat, w/liner	145.00
Soup, cream; w/liner	145.00

Soup, rim, 7½"	55.00
Soup, rim, 8½"	65.00
Sugar bowl, w/lid, lg	120.00
Sugar bowl, w/lid, sm	115.00
Teapot, 8-cup	425.00
Vegetable, oval, 9-10"	215.00
Vegetable, oval, 10-11"	235.00
Vegetable, sq, 8"	245.00
Vegetable, sq, 9"	265.00
Vegetable, w/lid	385.00
Waste bowl, 6"	47.00

Spongeware

Spongeware is a type of factory-made earthenware that was popular during the last quarter of the nineteenth century and into the first quarter of the twentieth century. It was decorated by dabbing color onto the drying ware with a sponge, leaving a splotched design at random or in simple patterns. Sometimes a solid band of color was added. The vessel was then covered with a clear glaze and fired at a high temperature. Blue on white is the most preferred combination, but green on ivory, orange on white, or those colors in combination may also occasionally be found. As with most pottery, rare forms and condition are major factors in establishing value. Spongeware is still being made today, so beware of newer examples. Our values are for undamaged examples, unless a specific condition code is given within the description.

Bowl, mixing; bl/wht, lt patterned sponging in scallops, 13"	275.00
Bowl, mixing; bl/wht, patterned sponging, fluted, str sides, 11"	215.00
Bowl, mixing; bl/wht, patterned sponging w/bl & wht band, 6x11"	150.00
Creamer, bl/wht, dk patterned sponging, tankard form, 4½"	550.00
Jar, bl/wht, Prunes, mk 7 Pat Ap For, 8"	960.00
Jar, preserve; ochre/cream patterned sponging, ca 1870s, 6½", EX	125.00
Piggy bank, red/bl patterned sponging on wht, 3¾" L	195.00
Pitcher, bl/wht, all-allover sponging w/wht bands, bbl shape, 8¾"	325.00
Pitcher, bl/wht, dk all-over sponging, emb scallop shells, 7¼"	480.00
Pitcher, bl/wht, lt all-over sponging, Rhonesboro TX, 1900s, 9½"	780.00
Pitcher, bl/wht, sponged band, Rhonesboro TX, 1900s, 9½"	600.00
Pitcher, bl/wht all-over sponging, emb triangles, bulbous base, 9"	480.00
Pitcher, bl/wht patterned sponging, EX contrast, cylindrical, 9", EX	300.00
Spittoon, bl/wht, patterned sponging & bl band, 6½" dia	180.00
Sugar bowl, red/cream, patterned sponging, w/lid, 7¾x5½"	125.00
Umbrella stand, bl/wht, Nouveau shape, copper-lustre trim, 21"	235.00
Umbrella stand, bl/wht, patterned sponging & bands, cylinder, VG	235.00
Washboard, bl & wht	400.00
Washbowl & pitcher, bl/wht, sponging & bands, 12", 13½"	360.00

Spoons

Souvenir spoons have been popular remembrances since the 1890s. The early hand-wrought examples of the silversmith's art are especially sought and appreciated for their fine craftsmanship. Commemorative, personality-related, advertising, and those with Indian busts or floral designs are only a few of the many types of collectible spoons. In the following listings, spoons are sorted by city, character, or occasion.

Key:
B — bowl	gw — gold washed
emb — embossed	H — handle
eng — engraved	HR — handle reverse
ff — full figure	

Alaska, transfer print enamel finial, sterling, demi, from $5 to 15.00

Atlanta Cotton Expo 1895, crown finial; rose in B; Maier & Berkele .. 110.00
Australia, gum leaf/gum nut finial, handmade, J Harris, from $25 to ... 50.00

Black boys' heads, souvenirs from southern states, from $85.00 to $110.00 each. (Photo courtesy Jackson's International Auctioneers & Appraisers of Fine Art & Antiques)

Black man carrying stick w/dead o'possom, from $100 to 150.00
Boston scenes in B; skyline H; Paye & Baker, ca 1905, 5½" 62.50
Bronco, rider finial, Hirsch & Oppenheimer, from $30 to 50.00
California on H; bear finial; plain B; Shiebler, from $75 to 125.00
Colorado emb on H; Gateway to Garden on Gods in B; from $40 to .. 75.00
Columbus on globe H; MOP B; from $50 to 90.00
Fairbanks AK skyline ff H; JB Erd, from $125 to 175.00
Fort Sumter Charleston SC eng in gw B; Towle, from $25 to 50.00
Gulfport MS & Black boy eating watermelon in B; crown finial, 5¼" ...85.00
House of 7 Gables, Salem MA on H; witch finial; unmk, from $20 to ..50.00
Jacksonville FL/Sunny South in B; Black boy finial; Greenleaf & Crosby. 82.50
Jerusalem Wailing Wall transfer in B; twist H; from $25 to 60.00
Jeweled & faceted ruby inset, unmk Burma, from $20 to 45.00
Liechtenstein castle pnt in B; flower finial; from $20 to 50.00
Louisville KY in B; figural American Indian H; Schiebler, ca 1895 ..90.00
Main St Jackson MI eng in B; various Hs; ea from $25 to 50.00
Mardi Gras woman (mk), HP in B; state H; from $100 to 200.00
Metropolitan Building in New York emb in B; hidden swastika 30.00
Morman Tabernacle Salt Lake City in B; elk's tooth finial, $50 to ..150.00
Muscatine in B; enameled corn on H; from $40 to 75.00
New York skyline H; emb Brooklyn Bridge in B; from $25 to 45.00
Nouveau lady picking grapes on H; plain B; 925 Sterling, 5¾" 90.00
Passaic Falls Paterson NJ eng in B, Chantilly pattern, Gorham 45.00
Pikes Peak CO eng in B; wavy H; Shepard, from $30 to 50.00
Rome, St Peter's Basilica & Vatican, printed scenes in B, from $25 to ..65.00
San Diego Mission ruins in B; SP, from $10 to 15.00
Sidney coat-of-arms, enameled finial; plain B; from $15 to 30.00
Spain, dancing senorita on finial; plain B; demi, from $10 to 20.00
Sphinx cast finial; plain B; from $20 to 30.00
Thomas Jefferson HP in B, from $300 to 500.00
WBA (Woman's Benefit Assoc) on H; plain B; Gorham, Wood & Hughes..50.00
Willet's School Monmouth IL eng in B; Melrose H; Gorham, from $15 to.....40.00
3 Wise Men ff H; plain B; lg (server), from $50 to 90.00

Sporting Goods

Vintage ammunition boxes, duck and goose calls, knives, and fishing gear are just a few of the items that collectors of this type of memorabilia look for today. Also favored are posters, catalogs, and envelopes from well known companies such as Winchester, Remington, Peters, Ithaca, and Dupont. Duck stamps have been widely collectible in recent years. See also Fishing Collectibles.

Book, score; US Cartridge rifle shooting, 50 targets, 1905, 7x4", EX . 50.00
Catalog, Bear Archery 1968, Kodiak/Bearcat bows, etc, 31 pgs, EX... 36.00
Catalog, Dominion Ammunition No 20, 1935, 52 pgs, 5x7½", EX..70.00

Catalog, Marbles Arms No 18, 1920s-30s, 58 pgs, VG+ 75.00
Catalog, Marlin Guns, 1948, 8 pgs w/color photos, 7x9½", VG+ .. 20.00
Catalog, Weatherby's - Tomorrow's Rifles Today, 1950s, 100 pgs, VG+ . 95.00
Cover, Dupont, moose, hunter behind canoe, Goodwin, 1920, EX+ ... 450.00
Cover, J Stevens Arms & Tool Co, man taking aim, ca 1902, EX.. 50.00
Cover, Peters Ammunition, lion w/killed zebra, 3½x6½", EX+ . 1,050.00
Cover, Peters Cartridges, bear, 1932, 3½x6½", EX+ 375.00
Cover, Remington Guns & Rifles, My Favorite..., lady w/gun, 1901, EX.. 110.00
Cover, Remington UMC Gib Game Rifles, man facing bear, 1910, EX ... 160.00
Cover, Stevens Arms & Tool Co, boy w/new rifle, 1909, 3¾x6½", EX...1,050.00
Cover, Winchester, bear & cabin scene, Goodwin, 1928, 3½x6½", EX 525.00
Cover, Winchester, hunting scene, PR Goodwin, 3½x6½", NM.. 110.00
Cover, Winchester, lady on horse holding up rifle, 1934, 5x6", EX+ .700.00
Cover, Winchester Model 1912, man w/gun & dog, 3½x6½", EX...100.00
Cover, Winchester Rifles & Shotguns, camp scene, 3½x6½", NM .. 650.00
Cover, Winchester Rifles & Shotguns, hunter, Pr Goodwin, 1911, EX.. 190.00
Dummy shells, Remington UMC, 6 cutaway 5" shells, NMIB..... 450.00
License, hunting; CA/man w/dog, Mysell/Collings Bank Note Co, 1915, EX. 50.00
Pennant, Mickey Mantle's Holiday Inn, Joplin MO, yel felt, EX. 210.00
Poster, Remington Arms - Union Metallic Cartridges, turkey, 26x17", EX.160.00
Poster, Winchester Ranger...Powder, shell & birds, 1928, 23x17", EX+...170.00
Tin, Rem Oil, DuPont, ca 1930s-40s, 5x2¼x1", EX+ 30.00
Tin, Savage Brand Smokeless Powder, metal jacketed bullets, 6" L, EX+.. 725.00
Tin, Snap Shot Powder, paper labels, 1-lb, 5½x3½x1½", EX......... 230.00
Tin, Winchester Gun Oil, lettering on gr, 4½x2¼x1¼", EX+ 140.00
Tin container, Nobel's Empire Smokeless...Powder, 1-lb, EX 140.00
Tin flask, Hercules Powder, w/belt loop, L Rand paper label, 1-lb, EX..215.00

Sports Collectibles

When sports cards became so widely collectible several years ago, other types of related memorabilia started to interest sports fans. Now they search for baseball uniforms, autographed baseballs, game-used bats and gloves, and all sorts of ephemera. Although baseball is America's all-time favorite, other sports have their own following of interested collectors. Our advice for this category comes from Paul Longo Americana. Mr. Longo is listed in the Directory under Massachusetts. To learn more about old golf clubs, we recommend *The Vintage Era of Golf Club Collectibles* by Ronald O. John (Collector Books).

Baseball

Baseball, Official Am League Ball, cork center, 1925, NM in G box.. 400.00
Baseball, Spalding Official League Leader, cork & rubber center, MIB...150.00
Bat, Babe Ruth #49BR, gold letters, 1933, 36", EX 250.00
Bat, Winchester #2409, wrapped hdl, 1920s, 33", EX.................. 355.00
Catcher's mask, Wilson, wire w/orig leather pads, 1910s, 9x7½", M ..100.00
Glove, Denkert Model #F8, Joe Vosmik Buckleback, leather, ca 1940, NM.60.00
Glove, Rawlings Model MMF, Mickey Mantle, brn leather, 12", NM.. 125.00
Jersey, bat boy; KC Blues, bl letters on wht, yel & blk trim, EX..... 65.00
Magazine, Maris/Mantle, JKW Sports 1962, 60 pgs of photos/text, EX .95.00
Pennant, Kansas City Royals, wht on bl felt, 1960s, NM 35.00
Pennant, New York Giants, yel on blk felt, 1940s-50s, 12x30", NM..120.00
Pennant, SWC Baseball Champions, silver on red felt, 1931, VG ..85.00
Pin-back, Indianapolis Al Lopez Day, w/red & wht ribbon, 1951, 2" dia .250.00
Uniform, gray pinstripes on wht wool, short sleeves, 1920s, EX..... 60.00

Football

Bobblehead, Detroit Lions player on base, 1962, NM 125.00
Boots, brn leather, Henry's Paris, 1900s, sz 11, EX...................... 130.00
Boots, cleats, Steel Plates #8878, sz 11, 1950s, MIB 40.00
Football, All Pro Wilson, Dick Butkus #51, leather, EX................ 30.00

Football, MacGregor, Model #COS 01, leather, EX 25.00
Helmet, Hutch #H-18, silver leather, wht lined, 1930s, NM 150.00
Helmet, Rawlings #A11X, leather w/chin strap, rubber lining, 1945, EX.. 125.00
Helmet, Wilson #F2154, brn & blk leather, 8 panels, 1930s, NM...190.00
Media guide, Oregon Ducks Football, Coach Warren photo cover, 1942, EX.. 35.00
Media guide, UCLA Bruins, 1958, EX 55.00
Megaphone, Michigan University, blk & yel, 1940s, 9½x6", VG .. 85.00
Pennant, Miami w/Indian mascot, wht on red felt, 1940s, NM 60.00
Pennant, Penn State Nittany Lions/player on blk felt, 1930s-40s, NM.. 110.00
Pennant, Wisconsin Badgers, wht on red felt, 1950s, EX 75.00
Poster, Tournament of Roses, Brown vs WA State, 1916, 26x18"+fr.. 1,500.00
Program, Alabama vs Boston, 1946, NM 45.00
Program, Iowa State vs Nebraska, Nov 12, 1949, EX 60.00
Program, Kansas State vs Indiana, Sept 23, 1961, EX 35.00
Program, Nebraska vs Notre Dame, Oct 18, 1947, EX 50.00
Shoulder pads, leather, rubber & canvas, 1950s, EX...................... 35.00
Ticket stub, Southern California vs Notre Dame, Nov 25, 1938, NM...40.00
Trash can, Players of the Philadelphia Eagles, 1971, 16", EX 35.00
Uniform, red & yel jersey w/#22, yel canvas pants, 1920s, VG.... 140.00
Yearbook, Carnegie Tech, The Thistle 1927, hardbk, NM............. 70.00

Tennis Rackets

Most collectible tennis rackets date between 1880 and 1950. The year 1880 is a somewhat arbitrary beginning of the 'modern' tennis era, since the first official Wimbledon tournament was held in 1877, and the US National Lawn Tennis Association was formed in 1881. Many types of tennis rackets were produced well before 1880, but generally these were designed for games far different than the lawn tennis we know today.

Rackets produced between the 1880s and 1950s were generally made of wood, although some like those made by the Dayton Steel Company (1920s) or the Birmingham Aluminum Company (1920s) were made of metal. The most common head shape is oval, but some were flat on top, some flat transitional, and some even lopsided. Handles were generally larger than those seen today, and most were unfinished wood with vertical ribs called 'combing,' rarer models featured cork handles or 'checkered' wood. The leather-wrapped handle common today was not introduced widely until the mid-1930s. Unusual enlargements to the butt end of the handle are generally desirable and might be called fishtail, fantail, bulbous, tall tail, or flared. The 'wedge,' a triangular section of wood located at the junction of the handle and the head, might be solid or laminated and can be a good indication of age, since most solid wedges date to before 1905. Like most collectibles, racket values depend on rarity, age, and condition. Prices for well preserved rackets in this period may range from $50.00 to well over $1,000.00. Tennis ball cans are also very collectible and may be worth hundreds of dollars for rare unopened examples. Our advisor for this category is Donald Jones; he is listed in the Directory under Georgia.

Key:
cx-lam — convex laminated   tran — transitional
cx-s — convex solid

AJ Reach, Driver, concave wedge, combed hdl, oval head, 1920.. 125.00
Dayton, steel w/wooden hdl, 1924 .... 250.00
E Kent, Duchess, concave wedge, bulbous hdl, oval head, 1930.. 200.00
Hazel's Streamline, branched wedge, leather hdl, oval head, 1935... 1,000.00
Horseman, Elberton, concave wedge, smooth hdl, flat-top head, 1885..600.00
Iver Johnson, Special, cx-s wedge, bulbous hdl, tran head, 1900 . 250.00
Magnon, Superior, concave wedge, combed hdl, oval head, 1928. 100.00
Slazinger, Demon, cx-lam wedge, fishtail hdl, oval head, 1910 .... 400.00
Spaulding, Park, cx-s wedge, combed hdl, flat-top head, 1895..... 800.00
Wright-Ditson, Hub, cx-s wedge, checkered hdl, oval head, 1890... 175.00

Miscellaneous

Basketball, laced brn leather, 1915, VG.. 110.00
Basketball, pennant, Boston Celtics/mascot on gr, 1969, EX 35.00
Basketball, pennant, Buffalo Braves, blk & orange on wht, 1969, EX.. 35.00
Boxing, poster, Tuolumne County Youth Boxing Club, 1979, 22x14", EX...25.00
Golf, bag, Geo Lawrance Co, leather, 1857, 34", NM 340.00
Golf, caddie badge, Norwood Hills Country Club, ca 1920, NM... 55.00
Golf, club, Niblick, wood shaft, ca 1900, 38½", EX 55.00
Hockey, pennant, Montreal Canadians, The Flying Frenchman, 1960s, EX...80.00
Hockey, puck, Atlanta Flames, Official Art Ross Tyer, 1973 logo, NM .50.00
Racing, banner, Welcome to the Motor City, yel on bl, 1955, 42x32", M....40.00
Racing, pennant, Indianapolis Motor Speedway, mc on gr, ca 1920, NM. 265.00
Racing, program, Indy 500 Official Racing Program, 1939, NM.. 150.00
Soccer, ball, brn leather panels, rubber int, ca 1950s, EX.............. 50.00
Softball, book, Softball w/Offical Rules, A Noren, hardbk, 1959, EX..15.00
Softball, Louisville Slugger, Minuteman 1776, wrapped hdl, 1970, M...30.00
Track & field, program, Official; USA vs USSR, 1958, EX............ 45.00
Track & field, shoes, Adidas, red/bl stripes on wht leather, 1960s, EX ...40.00

St. Clair

The St. Clair Glass Company began as a small family-oriented operation in Elwood, Indiana, in 1941. Most famous for their lamps, the family made numerous small items of carnival, pink and caramel slag, and custard glass as well. Later, paperweights became popular production pieces. Many command relatively high prices on today's market. Sulfide paperweights are especially popular. Some of the most expensive weights are those made by Bill McElfresh, who signed his pieces Wm Mc in a round reserve; his work is sarce due to the fact that he only worked in the glass during his breaks. Weights are stamped and usually dated, while small production pieces are often unmarked.

Lamps are in big demand with today's collectors, as are items signed by Paul or Ed St. Clair; their work is scarce, since these brothers made glass only during their breaks. Pieces made and signed by Mike Mitchell are also scarce, and always sell well. Prices depend on size and whether or not they have been signed. For further information we recommend *St. Clair Glass Collector's Book*, Vol. II, by our advisor Ted Pruitt. He is listed in the Directory under Indiana.

Paperweight, rose with leaves in clear, signed Joe St. Clair, 3½", $720.00.
(Photo courtesy James D. Julia Inc.)

Animal dish, dolphin, bl, Joe St Clair.. 175.00
Apple, from $100 to.. 125.00
Basket, sm, from $100 to... 125.00
Bell, Holly Carillon, cobalt carnival 35.00
Bottle, Grape & Gable, bl or red carnival, w/stopper, ea from $125 to. 135.00
Bowl, pk slag, ped ft, from $150 to 175.00
Compote, pk slag, ruffled rim, low ped base, from $150 to 175.00
Covered dish, robin on nest, from $125 to...................................... 150.00
Doll, from $35 to 40.00
Doorstop, rooster, from $600 to... 625.00
Figurine, Southern Belle, various colors, from $50 to..................... 75.00

Insulator, from $100 to 125.00
Ivy bowls, pr from $175 to 200.00
Lamp, blown ball shape, unsgn, from $275 to 300.00
Lamp, TV; unsgn, from $975 to 1,000.00
Lamp, 3-ball, sgn Joe & Bob St Clair 1,500.00
Lemonade glass, from $75 to 100.00
Paperweight, pear, bl carnival 100.00
Paperweight, sulfide, Betsy Ross, Joe St Clair 350.00
Paperweight, sulfide, Geo Washington or A Lincoln 200.00
Paperweight, sulfide, president series 100.00
Paperweight, sulfide, president series, w/windows or etched, $125 to.. 150.00
Pen holder, from $65 to 75.00
Pitcher, Holly Band, caramel slag, from $90 to 95.00
Ring holder, clear w/yel flower 50.00
Salt cellar, swan, wht or red, ea from $125 to 150.00
Sauce dish, Paneled Grape, from $35 to 40.00
Statue, buffalo, red, sgn Joe St Clair, from $250 to 300.00
Statue, Scottie dog, blk, sgn R&M (Bob & Maude), minimum value.. 500.00
Toothpick holder, Indian, bl, from $25 to 30.00
Toothpick holder, weighted base, from $55 to 65.00
Tumbler, Fleur-de-Lis, from $40 to 50.00
Tumbler, Grape & Cable, from $40 to 50.00
Vase, blown, waisted, from $175 to 200.00
Vase, clear w/bl floral in base, ruffled rim, from $80 to 85.00

Staffordshire

Scores of potteries sprang up in England's Staffordshire district in the early eighteenth century; several remain to the present time. (See also specific companies.) Figurines and groups were made in great numbers; dogs were favorite subjects. Often they were made in pairs, each a mirror image of the other. They varied in heights from 3" or 4" to the largest, measuring 16" to 18". From 1840 until about 1900, portrait figures were produced to represent specific characters, both real and fictional. As a rule these were never marked.

Historical transferware was made throughout the district; some collectors refer to it as Staffordshire Blue. It was produced as early as 1780, and because much was exported to America, it was very often decorated with transfers depicting scenic views of well-known American landmarks. Early examples were printed in a deep cobalt. By 1830 a softer blue was favored, and within the next decade black, brown, pink, red, and green prints were used. Although sometimes careless about adding their trademark, many companies used their own border designs that were as individual as their names. This ware should not be confused with the vast amounts of modern china (mostly plates) made from early in the twentieth century to the present. These souvenir or commemorative items are usually marketed through gift stores and the like. (See Rowland and Marsellus.) Our advisor for this category is Jeanne Dunay; she is listed in the Directory under South Carolina. See also specific manufacturers.

Key:

blk — black	l/b — light blue
gr — green	m/b — medium blue
d/b — dark blue	m-d/b — medium dark blue

Figures and Groups

Androclese & lion, 19th C, 7⅛", EX 600.00
Arab man on camel, 1850s, 8x5½" 1,200.00
Caernarvon Castle, 3 turret-form spills, 1850s, 7" 200.00
Cottage, bank, HP w/lattice windows, coleslaw trim, 5" 225.00
Cottage, potpourri jar, red & gr details, 19th C, 5½" 85.00
Cow by tree stump, spill vase, 1850s, 11x7½x3½" 2,150.00
Dog on grassy mound, scent bottle, head removes, glass eyes, 2½" ... 1,000.00
Dog on mottled base, pin holder, early, rprs, 5x5¼" 800.00
Dog resting on rectangular platform w/2 inkwells, 19th C, 4x7x4" .. 215.00
Elephant w/howdah by tree stump, spill vase, 1850s, 7" 950.00
Fox head, stirrup cup, 19th C, 5¼" L 360.00
Geo WA, bust, early 19th C, 8" 725.00
Giuseppe Garibaldi, title on base, Sampson Smith, 1864, 14½" .. 765.00
Horse, Pratt-type palette, ca 1800, 5¼" 2,600.00
House w/2 chimneys, figures in relief, bank, late 19th C, 6⅝", EX .. 500.00
Lady w/dog, red cloak, flakes, 9½x5½" 95.00
Lion on base, burnt orange w/gold on wht, glass eyes, 19th C, 10", pr .. 480.00
Men (2) in plumed hats & spaniel by spill vase, 19th C 550.00
Monkey holding animal, 2 tree stumps as pen holder & inkwell, 5x4" ... 145.00
Peacock on tall base w/tail down, spill vase, 1850s, 8", pr 1,325.00
Royal couple seated w/dogs in laps, man w/horn/she w/violin, 7", pr .800.00
Sailor stands w/ship model on shoulder, boy at side, 1850s, 16¼" ... 1,075.00
Scottish hunter w/gun & dead game, dog at side, 19th C, 15" 500.00
Setter dog, red & wht, free-standing front legs, 11¼" 485.00
Shakespeare, fine HP & gilt, 1850s, 10" 200.00
Sir James Whitley Deans Dundas, standing admiral, 1850s, 15½", EX 850.00
Spaniel, recumbent, sweetmeat box w/MOP base/gilt mts, 18th C, 2". 1,325.00
Spaniel seated, blk spots, yel eyes, red collar, 12", pr 175.00
Spaniel standing on free-form oval base, early 19th C, 5", pr 500.00
Spaniels, orange/blk/gold lustre, 1850s, 12¼", pr 750.00
Uncle Tom & Eva, 1850s, 11" 450.00
Uncle Tom w/child on lap, crazing/some discoloration, 9" 725.00
War, military man on horse w/flag & shield, 19th C, 12" NM 850.00
Whippet w/rabbit on base, mc, 1850s, 10½", pr 1,800.00

Transferware

Basket & underplate, castle in landscape, d/b, Adams, 4x10" 650.00
Bowl, Landing of Lafayette at Castle Garden NY, d/b, rprs, 12" ... 475.00
Bowl, Upper Ferry Bridge...Schuylkill, m/b, Stubbs, 12½", EX 500.00
Bowl, vegetable; Arms of VA w/floral border, d/b, Mayer, 12½" L, NM.. 1,650.00
Bowl, vegetable; Hanover Regents Terrace, d/b, 8x6½", +10" platter ... 360.00
Bowl, vegetable; unknown manor house, d/b, w/lid, 7¾x10¼" .. 1,175.00
Coffeepot, Franklin Memorial, d/b, rstr, 10¾" 795.00
Coffeepot, Lafayette at Franklin's Tomb, d/b, 19th C, 11½", NM .. 1,200.00
Creamer, Mt Vernon Seat of Late Gen'l Washington, d/b, 4½" ... 950.00
Creamer, Sower, gr & red, Adams, 19th C, 4¾" 480.00
Cup plate, Brahma bull, red, foliate border, mid-19th C, 3⅞" 395.00
Pitcher, Canova, red & gr, Mayer, 19th C, 7¼" 450.00
Pitcher, Cyprus, blk, 8-sided, Davenport, 1840-80, hairline, 10" .. 360.00
Pitcher, Lake Scene, red & brn, Wood, 19th C, 8¾" 725.00
Pitcher, monument to heroes of War of 1812, d/b, prof rstr, 10" .. 725.00
Pitcher, Views of Erie Canal, d/b, floral border, Wood, rpr, 10" 525.00
Plate, Arms for NC, d/b, 7¼" 480.00
Plate, B&O (on level), d/b, shell border, Wood, 1830s, 10" 1,175.00
Plate, B&O Railroad (incline), d/b, shell border, Wood, 9" 850.00
Plate, Boston State House, m/b, floral border, unmk Wood, 10" .. 200.00
Plate, Caledonia, gr & red, Adams, mid-19th C, 10⅝" 480.00
Plate, Commodore MacDonnough's Victory, d/b, shell border, Wood, 9" . 600.00
Plate, Commodore MacDonnough's Victory, d/b, shell border, Wood, 10" . 550.00
Plate, Dam & Water Works Philadelphia, d/b, Henshall, 10" 725.00
Plate, Library Philadelphia, m/b, floral border, Ridgway, 8¼" 250.00
Plate, Mitchell & Freeman...Boston, d/b, Adams, 10", EX 230.00
Plate, State Arms for NC, d/b, eagle mk, 7¼" 460.00
Plate, Texian Campaigne, brn, 9¼" 575.00
Plate, Water Works Philadelpha, d/b, 19th C, Wood, 10" 660.00
Plate, Winter View of Pittsfield MA, d/b, scalloped, Clews, 8¾" ... 315.00
Platter, Baronial Halls, l/b, octagonal, Mayer, 18x14" 220.00
Platter, Bejapore, d/b, octagonal, 16" L 220.00

Platter, Canova, d/b w/blk border, Mayer, 19th C, 20¼x16¾" 900.00
Platter, Canova, m/b, Mayer, 15½" 360.00
Platter, Castle Prison St Albans, d/b, Hall, 10½x9" 425.00
Platter, Clyde Scenery, blk w/red border, Jackson, 19th C, 15¼".. 900.00
Platter, Festoon Border, purple & gr, Wood, 19th C, 10½x8½".... 660.00

Platter, Hermitage en Dauphine, dark blue, Wood & Sons, 15x11¾", $500.00.

(Photo courtesy Skinner Inc. Auctioneers & Appraisers of Antiques & Fine Art)

Platter, Lady of the Lake, m/b, 21x16¼" 575.00
Platter, Landing of LaFayette...1824, d/b, Clews, 19x14½" 1,880.00
Platter, leopard & gazelle, m/b, unmk, 18½x14" 1,550.00
Platter, Niagara Falls, d/b, rstr, 14⅞" 1,200.00
Platter, Quadrupeds, d/b, prof rstr, 19" L 1,025.00
Platter, Texian Campaigne, blk, Shaw, 1850s, 17½x14" 2,650.00
Platter, Wild Rose, m-d/b, anchor/Middlesborough, 15", NM...... 220.00
Platter, Windsor Castle, d/b, foliage & scroll border, Clews, 17".. 950.00
Platter, 2 soldiers (1 on horsebk) & people, m/b, Granada, 15½"....360.00
Platter, 3 horses/3 cows, d/b, vining border, Adams, 1805-29, 14" ..600.00
Soup, America & Independence, d/b, Clews, 8¾", NM 450.00
Soup, Caledonia, red/gr, Adams, 10½" 480.00
Soup, Landing of General LaFayette, d/b, floral border, 8¾", NM...575.00
Soup, Octagon Church Boston, m/b, floral border, Ridgway, 9¾" ...420.00
Soup, Table Rock Niagara, d/b, shell border, Wood, 10", NM 480.00
Sugar bowl, bald eagle, d/b, closely mismatched lid, 7½" 175.00
Tea bowl, cranes/castle, d/b, floral border 235.00
Tea bowl & saucer, chinoiserie bridge/palm tree, d/b, VG............ 150.00
Tea bowl & saucer, Columbia Star...1840, l/b, Ridgway, flakes..... 315.00
Tea bowl & saucer, Corinthian Ornament, d/b, Clews 235.00
Teapot, Indian Wharf & Broad Street Stores, m/b, Wood, 1819-46 ..850.00
Teapot, Landing of General Lafayette...NY, d/b, 19th C, 7¼" 600.00
Teapot, MacDonnough's Victory, d/b, Wood, 7½", EX 1,400.00
Teapot, spread-wing eagle/acanthus leaves, d/b, flakes, 10" 1,500.00
Trivet, general & officers on horsebk, m/b, 12¼x9", VG 550.00
Tureen, flowers/fretwork, mc, bombé shape w/lid, 19th C, 9½x13" .. 725.00
Tureen, Quadrupeds, d/b, rose finial, Hall, ca 1925, 6⅝" H 480.00
Tureen, Sirius, brn, w/lid & 14½" platter 600.00
Tureen, View of Oxford, m/b, w/lid/ladle/undertray, 11x17" 1,025.00
Washbowl, Lake Scenery, blk & red, Wood, 4¾x13¾" 500.00
Washbowl & pitcher, flower-filled urn, d/b, Stubbs & Kent, 13", 10"... 1,175.00
Washbowl & pitcher, Palestine, m/b, 11¾" 395.00

Miscellaneous

Coffeepot, lead-glazed creamware, bird/flowers, rprs, 18th C, 9½" ..480.00
Jug, lead-glazed creamware, mc mottle, pear-shape, chips, 18th C, 7" ..660.00
Jug, salt glazed, scratch bl floral, 1755-60, 9¼" 9,600.00
Jug, salt glazed w/HP bird/flowers, ca 1760, rstr, 8¾" 6,600.00
Plaque, lead-glazed creamware, Topers, men drinking at tab, 8½x7"..2,750.00
Plate, lead-glazed creamware, leaves emb, 3-color, 18th C, 9½", pr....5,400.00
Plate, lead-glazed creamware, leaves emb, 3-color, 9½" 2,850.00
Plate, salt glazed, Wm Pitt portraits, lobed/barbed rim, 1750s, 9"..5,400.00
Plate, salt glazed w/HP couple in park, floral rim, 1760s, 9⅜", NM ..3,600.00
Platter, lead glazed, mottled brn w/bl & gr splashes, 18th C, 15"...1,100.00
Sauceboat, salt glazed, birds & animals, lamprey hdl, rprs, 1750s, 8"..1,440.00

Stirrup cup, lead-glazed creamware, stag's head, rstr, 4 /34".......1,000.00
Sugar bowl, lead-glazed creamware, floral band, w/lid, 1850s, 5, EX...150.00
Teapot, lead-glazed creamware, berries, bird finial, rstr, 1760s, 4"....425.00
Teapot, lead-glazed creamware, cabbage form, pineapple lid, 1760s, 5"....660.00
Teapot, lead-glazed creamware, flowers & vines, rstr, 18th C, 4"...1,200.00
Teapot, lead-glazed creamware, grapevines, paw ft, rstr, 18th C, 4"..2,400.00
Teapot, lead-glazed creamware, HP floral band, 1850s, 8x12x5", VG... 150.00
Teapot, lead-glazed creamware, HP grapevines/crabstock hdl, 18th C, 4". 2,400.00
Teapot, salt glazed, camel w/howdah, ca 1755, 6¼" 11,400.00
Teapot, salt glazed, floral on turq, ca 1765, 4¾" 7,200.00
Teapot, salt glazed, King of Prussia on ermine ground, 4½", EX .. 4,200.00
Teapot, salt glazed, paneled lozenge shape, serpent spout, 6", EX ... 1,200.00
Teapot, salt glazed w/HP floral & honeycomb-like pattern, 1765, 5".. 7,200.00
Tureen, salt glazed, grotesque ft, w/lid, 1750-60s, 17¼" L..........7,800.00
Tureen, salt glazed, shells & foliage, dog mask hdls, w/lid, 14" L ...2,150.00

Stained Glass

There are many factors to consider in evaluating a window or panel of stained glass art. Besides the obvious factor of condition, quality of leadwork, intricacy, jeweling, beveling, and the amount of selenium (red, orange, and yellow) present should all be taken into account. Remember, repair work is itself an art and can be very expensive. Our advisor for this category is Carl Heck; he is listed in the Directory under Colorado. See also Tiffany.

Ceiling Lights

19" lappet dome, geometric rim, 4 chains, 30" H.......................1,800.00
22" gr slag dome shade w/salmon & gr daffodils, heavy mts, unmk ..2,000.00
24" caramel slag dome w/overall red/gr vining roses, Williamson hdw....5,400.00
24" cone shade w/wide apron, caramel w/red & gr roses, Chicago Mosaic... 1,500.00
24" deep/shaped dome, vivid red/gr wide floral border, Handel crown . 4,800.00
24" floral-border brickwork shade, EX patina, Duffner/Kimberly.. 12,000.00
26" caramel shade, jeweled grapes/gr leaves, Morgan, bronze vine crown.. 6,000.00
28" intricate floral/foliage gr shade, unmk Duffner/Kimberly, 15"..8,500.00
28" 6-panel shade w/6-panel scalloped apron, orange/yel, Suess, 1910. 2,700.00
30", narrow pie-shape scalloped panels, bl to gr to yel, Williamson..3,200.00
30" deep/dome fishscale shade, gr cat's paw w/caramel edge, Handel mts.. 3,600.00

Lamps

16", narrow panels+2 simple horizontal bands; unmk Bigelow/Kennard..4,500.00
16" leaf-band dome shade; bronze std, Bigelow/Kennard, 22" ...4,500.00
18" wide str apron w/rising suns & lotus; bronze std, Suess, 24", EX..4,500.00
18" floral shade w/scalloped rim; bronzed baluster std, 23¼" 1,450.00
18" wisteria shade; bronze std, JH Whaley, 21" 9,600.00
19" cherries in mosaic-pattern shade; bronzed std, 23" 1,200.00
19" floral shade; Grueby organic 12x8" base, Duffner/Kimberly, 23"... 24,000.00
19" paneled open-top shade; 4-socket gold std, Duffner/Kimberly, 24". 2,875.00
19" pond lilies shade; 3-socket std, Duffner/Kimberly, 24½", EX ...5,750.00
20" floral-border umbrella shade; bronze std, ca 1900, 26" 750.00
21" dome shade w/mc over-all floral; bronze std #527, Wilkinson, EX .. 10,800.00
21" tulip/geometric shade; 3-socket library std, Wilkinson, 28"... 3,000.00
22" water lily/cattail dome; metal std, Wilkinson, 26".................8,500.00
23" dome w/over-all red & wht floral/gr leaves; tree trunk std, Suess.. 16,500.00
24" all-over floral shaped dome; bronze std, Chicago Mosaic, EX 3,350.00

Windows and Doors

Beethoven in oval on ribbon-like bkground, 1908, 32x35".......3,400.00
Bible w/bookmark/flower/mc bands, arched top, 35x70½" 1,850.00
Central medallion, vining/scrolls/jewels/borders, 19th C, 78x51" .. 3,750.00
Floral center w/scrolls/rosettes/pyramid jewels, 19th C, 44x36"+fr.. 7,250.00

Floral w/jewels, ca 1890, 23x40½" 2,250.00
Geometrics, In Memory Of on drop-down portion, 79x31", pr.3,500.00
Indian chief portrait, jeweled border, OH, rare, 37¼x34", pr ..22,500.00
Mary w/halo above lady in prayer, ca 1910, 156x63" 3,450.00
Medieval knight w/sword, ca 1880, 59x23" 2,400.00
Medieval knight w/sword, geometric borders, 19th C, 80x30" ..4,750.00
Micro-mosaic floral, Belcher, 28x16", VG 2,750.00
Mosaic w/leafy branch on earth-to-sky ground, Belcher, 53x32" ...3,500.00
Scrolls & foliage w/geometric borders, ca 1900, 87x36", 6 for...4,800.00
St Joan of Ark between capitals/many details, early 20th C, 112x36" .. 2,350.00
Star center, geometric borders, arched transom, 1870s, 36x48"... 4,750.00
Starburst w/Star of David below, 1920s, 69x18", 4 for 3,400.00
Sword & crown among scrolling florals, 76x36" 1,750.00

Stangl

Stangl Pottery was one of the longest-existing potteries in the United States, having its beginning in 1814 as the Sam Hill Pottery, becoming the Fulper Pottery which gained eminence in the field of art pottery (ca 1860), and then coming under the aegis of Johann Martin Stangl. The German-born Stangl joined Fulper in 1910 as a chemical engineer, left for a brief stint at Haeger in Dundee, Illinois, and rejoined Fulper as general manager in 1920. He became president of the firm in 1928. Although Stangl's name was on much of the ware from the late '20s onward, the company's name was not changed officially until 1955. J.M. Stangl died in 1972; the pottery continued under the ownership of Wheaton Industries until 1978, then closed. Stangl is best known for its extensive Birds of America line, styled after Audubon; its brightly colored, hand-carved, hand-painted dinnerware; and its great variety of giftware, including its dry-brushed gold lines. For more information we recommend *Collector's Encyclopedia of Stangl Artware, Lamps, and Birds, Second Edition*, by Robert Runge Jr. (Collector Books). Another good reference is *Stangl Pottery* by Harvey Duke; for ordering information refer to the listing for Nancy and Robert Perzel, Popkorn Antiques (our advisors for this category), in the Directory under New Jersey.

Dinnerware

Blueberry, bowl, 12¼", from $85 to 100.00
Blueberry, casserole, w/lid, ind................................ 25.00
Blueberry, chop plate, 14".................................... 85.00
Blueberry, coffeepot, 8-cup, 9¼" 75.00
Colonial, casserole, w/lid, #1388, 8" dia, from $40 to.......... 50.00
Colonial, relish tray, 2-compartment, 7½x7½", from $20 to 25.00
Colonial, teapot, #1388, 6"................................... 65.00
Country Garden, bowl, coupe soup; 7½"......................... 20.00
Country Garden, bowl, divided vegetable; 2¼x10¾x7¼"............... 25.00
Country Garden, bowl, 8"...................................... 30.00
Country Garden, chop plate, 14" 65.00
Fruit, bowl, divided vegetable; oval, 3x10¼" 32.00
Fruit, chop plate, 12", from $40 to 50.00
Fruit, creamer & sugar bowl, w/lid............................. 35.00
Fruit, plate, dinner; 10".................................... 20.00
Fruit, plate, luncheon; 8¼".................................. 15.00
Fruit, shakers, pr.. 15.00
Fruit, sherbet, 8-oz, 5¾".................................... 25.00
Fruit & Flowers, bowl, dessert; 5½ 9.00
Fruit & Flowers, bowl, soup; 7½" 20.00
Fruit & Flowers, coffeepot, 8-cup, 8½" 95.00
Fruit & Flowers, mug, coffee/tea; 1-cup, 4" 28.00
Fruit & Flowers, pitcher, 1-pt, 6"............................. 35.00
Fruit & Flowers, plate, dinner; 10"........................... 20.00
Garden Flower, bowl, fruit/dessert; 5¾"........................ 10.00

Garden Flower, bowl, vegetable; 10" 45.00
Garden Flower, chop plate, Terra Rose, 12" 45.00
Garden Flower, plate, dinner; 10", from $15 to 20.00
Garden Flower, plate, luncheon; 8¼" 12.00
Kiddieware, cup, Humpty Dumpty, 1-pt........................... 100.00
Kiddieware, cup, Indian Campfire, from $50 to 75.00
Kiddieware, cup, Playful Pup, from $30 to 40.00
Kiddieware, divided dish, Kitten Capers 80.00
Kiddieware, mug, Jack & Jill, musical, from $200 to 250.00
Kiddieware, plate, circus clown, 9¼", from $125 to 150.00
Kiddieware, plate, Little Bo Peep, 9¼"........................... 65.00
Lyric, casual coffee server, 11" 110.00
Lyric, cup & saucer 20.00
Lyric, plate, dinner; 10" 35.00
Magnolia, bowl, lug soup; 1½x6"............................... 10.00
Magnolia, bowl, vegetable.................................... 20.00
Magnolia, gravy boat & underplate............................. 20.00
Magnolia, plate, bread & butter; 6¼"...........................6.00
Magnolia, plate, dinner; 10".................................. 15.00
Magnolia, plate, salad; 8".................................... 10.00
Orchard Song, cake stand, 10¾" 15.00
Orchard Song, chop plate, 12½"................................ 25.00
Orchard Song, cup & saucer.................................... 10.00
Orchard Song, gravy boat & underplate 20.00
Orchard Song, platter, oval 35.00
Star Flower, chop plate, 14" 40.00
Star Flower, teapot, 6¾"...................................... 50.00
Thistle, cigarette box.. 45.00
Thistle, coffeepot, 8-cup..................................... 75.00
Thistle, relish tray.. 20.00
Town & Country, bowl, cereal; bl, 5½"........................ 22.50
Town & Country, bowl, mixing; bl, 7¾"........................ 40.00
Town & Country, candlesticks, yel, 7½", pr from $45 to 50.00
Town & Country, chop plate, gr, 12", from $25 to................ 30.00
Town & Country, pitcher, water; bl, 2½-qt..................... 75.00
Town & Country, plate, dinner; brn, 10" 15.00
Town & Country, shakers, yel, pr.............................. 20.00
Town & Country, soap dish, gr, rectangular, 5⅝"............... 25.00
Yellow Tulip, casserole, w/lid................................ 75.00
Yellow Tulip, chop plate, 14" 60.00
Yellow Tulip, flowerpot, 4"................................... 20.00
Yellow Tulip, plate, dinner; 10", from $15 to 20.00
Yellow Tulip, sherbet, ftd.................................... 25.00
Yellow Tulip, skillet casserole, 6"........................... 22.50

Miscellaneous

Air freshener, terrier pup, Colonial Blue, #3108, 1937, 6", $350 to....400.00
Ashtray, monkey, Persian Yellow, #1324, 1930-31, 5", from $150 to..175.00
Ashtray, Multi-Color Dark, #1337, 1930-31, 4", from $25 to 35.00
Basket, orchids, #3621, 1974, 5½", from $35 to............................. 45.00
Basket, Sunburst, #1456, 1931-1934, 7", from $150 to................ 175.00
Bowl, Orchid, #945S, 6¾", from $60 to 75.00
Bowl, Satin Yellow, scalloped rim, #2064, 1936-38, 9x5", from $10 to..... 15.00
Bowl, Silver Green, oblong/6-sided/ftd, #1202, 1929-34, 12" L, $75 to.. 100.00
Candleholder, Scroll Leaf, Tangerine, #3025, 5½", pr from $40 to....50.00
Candleholders, butterfly, Colonial Blue, #964, pr from $30 to 40.00
Candlesticks, nude sitting, Silver Green, #1087, 5", pr from $200 to.. 300.00
Candy dish, Colonial Blue, #1388, 1932-38, 5x5", from $60 to 75.00
Flower holder, gazelle, Colonial Blue, #1169, 11½", from $125 to ..150.00
Flowerpot, camel, Satin White, #1773, 1933-35, 14", from $150 to ..200.00
Flowerpot, Silver Green, pleated, #1213S, 1929-32, 4", from $20 to ...30.00
Flowerpot, swan, Sunburst w/Persian Yellow, #1771, 10x13", $250 to..350.00
Honey jar, Apple Green, #1005-S, 1925-31, 3½", from $25 to 35.00

Jam jar, Silver Green, #956, oval, 1924-28, 3½x6", from $35 to 45.00
Jar, ginger; Town & Country Brown, 1974-78, from $45 to 60.00
Jar, ribbed, mold-cast, 3-hdl, #1237, 1933-37, 7½", from $50 to 65.00
Jardiniere, Pink Matte, mold-cast, #1261, 1930-37, 8", from $20 to .. 30.00
Planter, rolling pin, Town & Country Yellow, 1976, 13", from $50 to ...65.00
Tray, hors d'oeuvres; Silver Green, #1978, 1935-40, 7", from $8 to... 12.00
Vase, Apple Green, urn form w/hdls, #1328, 1933-38, 15", from $100 to....120.00
Vase, Colonial Blue, #941, 1924-27, 6", from $35 to 45.00
Vase, Ivory, swirled ball form, #1818, 1934-35, 5½", from $45 to... 60.00
Vase, mini; turq, #1903, 1935, 3½", from $50 to........................... 75.00
Vase, rust, rim-to-hip hdls, #1712, 1934-39, 6", from $40 to 50.00

Vase, Sunburst, #1328, 1933 – 1934, from $200.00 to $250.00. (Photo courtesy Robert C. Runge Jr./Chris McGeehan)

Vase, Tangerine, #1329, 1930-33, 18", from $150 to 200.00
Vase, urn form, Apple Green, w/hdls, #1328, 1933-38, 15", from $100 to...120.00
Vase, wide, Tangerine, #1329, 1930-33, 18", from $150 to........... 200.00
Wall pocket, bird figural, Silver Green, #961, 1925-31, 9", $125 to...150.00
Wall pocket, Grapes, Ivory, #989, 1925-28, 8", from $125 to....... 150.00

Stangl Birds and Animals

The Stangl company introduced their line of ceramic birds in 1940, taking advantage of a import market crippled by the onset of WWII. The figures were an immediate success. Additional employees were hired, and eventually 60 decorators worked at the plant itself, with the overflow contracted out to individuals in private homes. After the war when import trade once again saturated the market, Stangl curtailed their own production but continued to make the birds and animals on a limited basis as late as 1978. Nearly all the birds were marked. A four-digit number was used to identify the species, and most pieces were signed by the decorator. An 'F' indicates a bird that was decorated at the Flemington plant. Our advisors for this category are Nancy and Robert Perzel, Popkorn Antiques. (See the Directory under New Jersey.) Recommended reference books are listed in the Stangl category.

Animals

#1076, Piggy bank, sponged wht, not cvd, Early Am Tulip, from $60 to.. 75.00
#1076, Piggy bank, Terra Rose, cvd, Early Am Tulip, from $75 to ..100.00
#3178A, Elkhound, wht w/blk overglaze, 3½", from $40 to 65.00
#3178F, Percheron, wht w/blk overglaze, 3½", from $50 to 60.00
#3178G, Elephant, wht w/blk overglaze, 2½", from $40 to............. 50.00
#3178H, Squirrel, wht w/blk overglaze, 3½", from $50 to 65.00
#3178J, Gazelle, wht w/blk overglaze, 3½" 50.00
#3243, Wire-Haired Terrier, 3¼", from $200 to 225.00
#3244, Draft Horse, 3", from $75 to 100.00
#3245, Rabbit, 2", from $200 to 255.00
#3246, Buffalo, 2½", from $200 .... 250.00
#3247, Gazelle, 3¾", from $200 to 225.00
#3248, Giraffe, 2½", from $400 to.. 500.00

#3249, Elephant, Antique Gold, 5", from $75 to......................... 100.00
#3249, Elephant, 3", from $175 to 200.00
#3277, Colt, 5", from $1,200 to...1,500.00
#3278, Goat, 5", from $1,300 to 1,500.00
#3279, Calf, 3½", from $700 to 800.00
#3280, Dog sitting, 5¼", from $200 to 250.00
#3430, Duck, 22", from $8,000 to..10,000.00
Burro, blk w/wht overglaze, 3¼", from $60 to 70.00
Cat, Siamese, Seal Point sitting, decor, 8½", from $300 to........... 500.00
Cat sitting, Granada Gold, 8½", from $150 to 200.00

Birds

#3250B, Duck preening, 3¼" 60.00
#3250E, Duck drinking, Terra Rose finish, 1941 only, 2¼"............. 50.00
#3273, Rooster, solid bottom, 5¾", from $400 to 500.00
#3275, Turkey, 3½" 350.00
#3276D, Bluebirds (pr), 8½"... 100.00
#3286, Hen, late, 3¼" 50.00
#3400, Lovebird, revised, 4" 50.00
#3402, Oriole, beak down, old style, 3½" 100.00
#3405, Cockatoo, 6" 40.00
#3444, Cardinal, female.. 100.00
#3446, Hen, yellow, 7" 120.00
#3452, Painted Bunting, 5".. 60.00
#3490D, Redstarts (pr), 9" 125.00
#3580, Cockatoo, med, 9" 100.00
#3584, Cockatoo, sgn Jacob, lg, 11⅜" 200.00
#3586, Pheasant (Della Ware), natural colors 1,000.00
#3586, Pheasant (Della Ware), Terra Rose, gr, from $400 to 500.00
#3589, Indigo Bunting, 3½".. 40.00
#3590, Carolina Wren, 4½" 125.00
#3591, Brewer's Blackbird, 3½" 125.00
#3592, Titmouse, 3" 45.00
#3593, Nuthatch, 2½" 35.00
#3595, Bobolink, 4¾" 150.00
#3596, Gray Cardinal, 5" 50.00
#3598, Kentucky Warbler, 3".. 40.00
#3627, Rivoli Hummingbird, pk flower, 6".................................... 120.00
#3629, Broadbill Hummingbird, 4½" 125.00
#3715, Blue Jay, w/peanut, 10¼" 400.00
#3749, Scarlet Tanager, pk gloss, 4¾".. 225.00
#3749, Western Tanager, yel & blk w/red overglaze, tan flower, 4¾"..250.00
#3750D, Western Tangagers (pr), red matt, 8"............................... 300.00
#3751, Red-Headed Woodpecker, red matt, 6¼" 225.00
#3754D, White-Wing Crossbills (pr), pk gloss, 9x8" 300.00
#3757, Scissor-Tailed Flycatcher, 11" 600.00
#3810, Black-Throated Warbler, 3½" 125.00
#3815, Western Bluebird, 7"... 250.00
#3848, Golden-Crowned Kinglet, 4¼" 75.00
#3852, Cliff Swallow, 3½".. 120.00
#3868, Summer Tanager, 4" 600.00
#3924, Yellow Throat, 6" 350.00
Stangl Bird dealer sign 1,200.00

Statue of Liberty

Long before she began greeting immigrants in 1886, the Statue of Liberty was being honored by craftsmen both here and abroad. Her likeness was etched on blades of the finest straight razors from England, captured in finely detailed busts sold as souvenirs to Paris fairgoers in 1878, and presented on colorfully lithographed trade cards, usually satirical, to American shoppers. Perhaps no other object has been represented in more forms or with such frequency as the universal symbol of America. Liberty's keepsakes are also universally accessible. Delightful souvenir models created in 1885 to raise funds for Liberty's pedestal are frequently found at flea markets, while earlier French bronze and terra cotta Liberties have been auctioned for over $100,000.00. Some collectors hunt for the countless forms of nineteenth-century Liberty memorabilia, while many collections were begun in anticipation of the 1986 Centennial with concentration on modern depictions.

Albumen print, John S Johnston, sign/titled/dated 1894, 8¾x6¾" .. 240.00
Bank, copper-colored metal, 8¼" 25.00
Bank, figural, pnt CI, AC Williams, 1910-30, 6", EX 175.00
Belt buckle, cut-out Liberty half dollar w/gold & silver trim 62.50
Book, Photographic Views including NY Harbor, 1889, VG 70.00
Bookmark, Bartholdi souvenir & calendar, fabric, 1887 .... 50.00
Cigar box label, Victory Day, WWII 6.00
Clock, kitchen shelf; rvp Liberty scene, rpl dial, Ingraham, 24x14" ...350.00
Clock/lamp, CI figural, bulb inserts at top of torch, 14½x5" 75.00
Container, Yourex Silver Saver, rnd, cb, ca 1930............................. 27.00
Flyer, Statue of Liberty steamboat excursions, 1890s 25.00
Invitation to statue's unveiling, 1886, G- 200.00
Lighter, exposed flint, Fr, WWI era 125.00
Napkin holder, sterling 15.00
Novelty, sailboat w/image on sails, Japan, 3⅝x2¾" 35.00
Pin, enamel, 77th Div, WWI.. 12.00
Pipe, glazed clay, 1880s 90.00
Plate, emb scene of statue & NY skyline & QE II, Bossons, 10" dia...325.00
Plate, HP scene, Vernon Kilns, 10½" 20.00
Pocketknife, bl image on MOP, 2 blades, Imperial, 3", MIB.......... 35.00
Postcard, Uncle Sam pulling bk US flag to see statue, ca 1907, EX .. 17.50
Scarf, head of Liberty, red/wht/bl, Hermes, 35" sq, NM............... 150.00
Scissors, emb metal, Liberty 1 side/Woolworth building on reverse, 6"... 55.00

Sheet music, The Statue of Liberty Is Smiling, 1918, $20.00. (Photo courtesy Anna Marie Guiheen and Marie-Reine A. Pafic)

Smoke stand/lamp, Liberty at base, torch lights up, 1940s, 27", EX ...150.00
Spoon, Liberty in bowl, St Paul's church on handle, Tiffany.......... 55.00
Statue, bronze-pnt pot metal, 2-pc, American Committee Model, 7"....175.00
Statue, bronzed metal, 19", EX 30.00
Statue, bronzed spelter, 9½" 25.00
Statue, hand-cvd wood, Mexico, 15" 20.00
Statue, pnt resin, 1980s, 18" 100.00
Ticket, souvenir of Gauthier et Cie (Liberty foundry), 1883, lg... 105.00
Tintype, Spanish Am War soldier seated before statue, 6th plate, +case.. 85.00

Steamship Collectibles

For centuries, ocean-going vessels with their venturesome officers and crews were the catalyst that changed the unknown aspects of our world to the known. Changing economic conditions, unfortunately, have now placed the North American shipping industry in the same jeopardy as the American passenger train. They are becoming a memory. The surge of interest in railroad collectibles and the railroad-related steamship lines has lead collectors to examine the whole spectrum of steamship collectibles.

Reproduction (sometimes called 'replica') and fantasy dinnerware has been creeping into the steamship dinnerware collecting field. Some of the 'replica' ware is quite well done so one should practice caution and... 'know thy dealer.' Our advisor for this category is Lila Shrader; she is listed in the Directory under California.

Key:
BM — bottom mark	SM — side mark
BS — back stamped	SP — silver plate
hf — house flag	TL — top logo
Int'l — International Silver	TM — top mark
NBS — no back stamp	w/w — woven design on
R&B — Reed & Barton	white damask
SL — side logo	

Dining Salon

Bowl, fruit; White Star Line, SP, SL, Dickenson hdls, 15" 900.00
Bowl, Mississippi & Dominion SS, belt TL w/flags surround, 2x9¼" .. 820.00
Bowl, Ocean SS Co, Savannah, TL hf, 9" 70.00
Butter pat, Canadian National SS, Bonaventure, TL, Grindley, 3¼" ..128.00
Butter pat, Stella Polaris, SP, ship's image, .830, 3½" 30.00
Champagne stem, United States Line, Eagle SL, 4½" 55.00
Coffeepot, Great Northern, SP, hinged lid, BM, R&B, 5¾" 170.00
Cordial, SS Normandy, CGT TL on ft, R Lalique BS, 3½" 565.00
Cover for platter, American Mail Line, SP, recessed hdl, SL.......... 26.00
Creamer, Canadian Pacific SS Lines, BM, w/hdl, ind, 2½" 22.50
Creamer, Matson, Matsonia, SL, BS SS Wilhelmina, ind, 3½" 70.00
Creamer, Matson SS, SP, SL, Int'l, 3¼".. 68.00
Cup & saucer, Andrea Doria, Italia SM & TM, 2nd class, C of A ..595.00
Cup & saucer, demitasse; Cosulich SS Line, SL, Ginori 132.00
Cup & saucer, Mobil Oil Corp, Mobil Chicago Pegasus SL, Shenango ... 75.00
Egg cup, dbl, Alcoa SS Co, Alcoa Cavaliere, SL, 3x3".................... 55.00
Fork, dinner; American Hawaii SS, SP, TL....................................... 12.50
Ice bucket & stand, Canadian Pacific SS, SP, SL, Mappin & Webb..355.00
Mustard pot, Hudson Nav Co, hinged lid/glass liner, TL/BM, Meridian .100.00
Napkin ring, White Star, SP, hf SL, Elkington 110.00
Pitcher, US Steel, TM MVCF Hood, Mayer China, 5"................. 125.00
Plate, American Mail Line, TL, Buffalo, 7¼" 30.00
Plate, Champlain Ferry Service/D&HRR, Vermont pattern, TL, 5¼" ..55.00
Plate, Cunard, 1st class, image of Lusitania underway, Minton, TM, 9"...1,500.00
Plate, Detroit-Windsor Ferry, DWFCo TL, 8½" 150.00
Plate, Matson, Mariposa pattern w/bird in center, Mayer, BS, 5½" ..55.00
Plate, rimmed soup; United Fruit Line, Columbia Div (bl), TL, 8½"...48.00
Plate, soup; Algoma Central Marine, Polar Bear Marine TL, 8¾" ..100.00
Plate, Std Fruit & SS/Vaccaro Line, Atlanta, hf TL, 9½"................. 55.00
Platter, Bay Line, Old Bay Line, hf TM, NBS, 14x9" 200.00
Platter, Hudson River Day Line, pennant TL, Bauscher, 14x9" 98.00
Pot, Matson, SP, hinged lid, SL, Internat'l, 16-oz, 5½" 55.00
Relish dish, USSB, Granite State, TL, Buffalo, 1925, 9½x4¾" 42.50
Relish tray, Admiral Line Oriental, hf logo w/life ring, TL/BS, 10" L ..75.00
Salt spoon, Cunard, SP, Elkington, 2½" 40.00
Shakers, Grace Line, SP, SL/BM, R&B, 2¾", pr 36.00
Sugar bowl, Alaska SS Co, SP, Yukon SL, Wallace, 2¾" 55.00
Teapot, Baltimore Mail, SP, hinged lid, SL hf, Wallace, 5" 34.00
Teapot, Cunard SS, Cube style, ivory w/stripes, BS, 3½" sq 145.00
Teapot, Pickands-Mather Co, mc hf ea side, Walker China, ind .260.00
Teaspoon, Eastern SS Line, Sierra, SP, TM, R&B, 5⅞" 12.50
Vase, bud; Canadian Pacific SS, SP, Art Deco, SM, Elkington, 6½"...125.00
Wine stem, Indo-China Steam Nav Co, SL full garter crest w/hf, 4½"... 92.00

Miscellaneous

Advertising paperweight, Milwaukee Clipper profile, copper-tone ... 14.00

Ashtray, SS Normandie, French Line, cast CGT TL, frosted, Deco, 5" dia ..255.00
Blanket, Great Northern Pacific SS Co, TL, wool, self-bound, 55x80"..350.00
Book, American Ephemeris & Nautical Almanac, 1911, 2nd edition.52.00
Book, Ocean's Story, Ark to Steamships, 1st ed, 1873, 712-pg....... 50.00
Booklet, CPSS, Empress of Britain, 1932, ports of call/graphics, 64-pg..14.00
Booklet, Pacific Steam...Co, Reina Del Pacifico, 1932, open: 18x32". 100.00
Brochure, Alaska SS+Copper River, 1915, 38-pg, unfolds to 8x9"....75.00
Brochure, Andrea Doria, deck plans & int photos, 1950s, 210-pg ..160.00
Brochure, Inland Steel Fleet/SS Wilford Sykes, history/map, 14-pg, 6x9". 22.00
Brochure, Pacific Coast SS Co, CA/OR/WA/BC/AK, 1887, folds down: 4x6".50.00
Builder's plate, MV Pres Washington, APL, Avondale Shipyards, 1982..785.00
Button, pin-bk; Lusitania, mc on cello, Griffin & Rowland, ⅞"..... 40.00
Button, United Fruit Co, gold-tone, Scoville, dome shape, ⅞".........6.00
Cigarette lighter, Am Export Lines, SS Independence, Zippo, 1956, MIB..100.00
Cigarette lighter, Grace Lines, Zippo, 1964, MIB........................... 55.00
Cigarette lighter, QE II, commemorating maiden voyage, Zippo, MIB..42.00
Compact, RMS Samaria, gold-tone, Stratton, 3", M in cloth bag...100.00
Compass, ship's; John Hand, brass, metal 10" binnacle w/hex glass top..325.00
Figurehead, Fiberglas copy of 1800s Lady Anne, 1980s, 36"........295.00
Horn, ship's air; Kockum's Tyfon T-125, Sweden, brass w/bronze, 19" ...275.00
Jewelry, US Navy WWII sweetheart locket & earrings 100.00
Lighter, Zippo, Moore-McCormack Lines SL, 1950s, MIB...........285.00
Luggage sticker, Alaska SS, SS Aleutian, mc totem pole, 3½" dia 9.00
Luggage sticker, United States Lines, paper, 4x4".............................6.00
Medallion, 1936 Official Queen Mary, bronze, 2½", M in case 325.00
Menu, Cuba Mail Line, Oriente, luncheon, emb cardstock, 1940, 7x9".. 14.00
Menu, dinner; Holland America, MS Noordam, 1947 .... 15.00
Menu, dinner; Matson Nav Co, E Savage cover, 1956, 12x8½"..... 44.00
Pass, annual; Natchez & Vicksburg Packet Co, cardstock, 1897.. 155.00
Passenger list, Cunard, Queen Mary, Southampton to NY, 1936... 70.00
Pencil, mechanical; Royal Mail, RMS Andes floats in bbl, 5¼"..... 20.00
Picture, Cash's, canal boats, woven silk, ca 1900, in fr, 8x11"........ 50.00
Playing cards, GNPSS, 52 views+Joker+info card+booklet, +case ..435.00
Postcard, cargo ship Pontiac w/autos stored on deck, real photo, 1930s..5.00
Postcard, Carpathia, Stevens woven silk, Hands Across Sea, no postmk.1,135.00
Postcard, shipwreck of Galena off Gearhart, OR, blk/wht photo, 1906.. 27.00
Postcard, Titanic, woven silk, Hands Across Sea, Stevengraph... 5,300.00

Sign, Queen Mary, Cunard's White Star Cruise Ship Line, paper lithograph with original advertising mat board and frame, 14x28", from $350.00 to $450.00. (Photo courtesy Wm. Morford Auctions)

Snuff box, Hamburg-Amerika Line emb image, SP, hinged lid, 2x3".. 200.00
Souvenir spoon, SS Leviathan HP in bowl, crest, 4¾" 520.00
Souvenir spoon, Washington Irving side-wheeler, SS, cut-out silhouette.. 18.00
Spittoon, US Shipping Board, stoneware, SL, 10½" 130.00
Stock certificate, Dollar SS Line, Class A, 1929........................... 325.00
Token, Staten Island Ferry, aluminum, pre-1990, ⅞" dia............... 12.00
Towel, hand; Quebec & Ontario Trans Co woven on bl stripe, wht huck...20.00
Whistle/fog horn, salvaged USS Mississinewa, 32" aluminum Kahlenberg...1,200.00

Steins

Steins have been made from pottery, pewter, glass, stoneware, and porcelain, from very small up to the four-liter size. They may be decorated by etching, in-mold relief, decals, and occasionally they may be hand painted. Some porcelain steins have lithophane bases. Collectors often specialize in a particular type — faience, regimental, or figural, for example — while others limit themselves to the products of only one manufacturer. See also Mettlach.

Key:
L — liter   tl — thumb lift
lith — lithophane

Character, alligator, porc, porc lid, E Bohne & Sohne, .5L 550.00
Character, barmaid, porc, Schierholz, rpr lid, .5L 4,225.00
Character, Black student, pottery, inlaid lid, flakes, .5L 275.00
Character, Bock, porc, porc inlaid lid, broken hinge, Schierholz, .5L ...325.00
Character, clown, pottery, Diesinger, #750, rpl lid/hairlines, .5L .455.00
Character, devil, pottery, inlaid lid, .5L, NM............................... 360.00
Character, dog, porc, pipe finial (rpr), Schierholz, .5L 1,085.00
Character, Dutch girl, porc, rare bl color, Schierholz, .5L 1,325.00
Character, elephant, porc w/porc lid, Schierholz, .5L 1,795.00
Character, frog, porc, porc lid, Schierholz, .5L 1,325.00
Character, gentleman, pottery, inlaid lid, Thewalt, .5L 550.00
Character, Happy Radish, porc, inlaid lid, Schierholz, .5L........... 525.00
Character, mountain, pottery, rpl lid, pnt wear, 1L...................... 285.00
Character, Munich Child (relief), pottery, inlaid lid, 4½", EX 275.00
Character, Sad Radish, porc, inlaid lid, rpr chip, .5L.................... 195.00
Character, skull, porc, E Bohne & Sohne, flake, .5L 285.00
Character, skull on book, porc, inlaid lid, E Bohne & Sohne, .5L, NM.525.00
Character, Wilhelm I, porc, porc lid, Schierholz, .5L, NM 900.00
Character, Wilhelm II, porc, porc lid, Schierholz, .5L, NM 725.00
Faience, bl glaze/cold pnt: deer scene, pewter 1793 lid, 1L, G 400.00
Faience, relief: deer hunt/bears in tree, pewter lid, 1900s, 1.5L.... 460.00
Faience, woman & trees, pewter 1806 lid, Dresden, 1L...............1,225.00
Glass, blown, amber w/gr glass prunts, HP designs, pewter lid, .5L... 195.00
Glass, blown, amber w/prunts/HP floral, inlaid lid, dwarf tl, .5L..175.00
Glass, blown, bl, Mary Gregory girl, ribs, pk inlaid lid, 4¼" 215.00
Glass, blown, clear, Germania Sei's Panier, pewter lid, 1909, .5L....845.00
Glass, blown, clear, Mary Gregory girl, bl inlaid lid, 1850s, 4¼" .. 160.00
Glass, blown, clear w/bl stain, eng floral, inlaid lid, 1850s, 3½" ... 150.00
Glass, blown, clear w/gr o/l, all-over cuttings, bl o/l lid, .5L.......1,450.00
Glass, blown, clear w/red stain, Steinbad in Teplitz, inlaid lid, 4" ...170.00
Glass, blown, clear w/wht & pk o/l, eng leaves/berries, .4L.....5,175.00
Glass, blown, peach w/HP floral, clear inlaid lid, 1850s, 3½" 95.00
Glass, pressed, clear, cut design, pewter lid, scuffs, .5L 57.50
Occupation, porc: Metzger (butcher), lith, pewter lid, .5L, NM ..230.00
Porc, HP: couple & flowers, gilt silver lid, 1850s, 8½", NM 1,150.00
Porc, HP: crocodile/3 babies/3 eggs, pewter lid, .5L...................... 600.00
Porc, HP: onion, inlaid lid, Rauenstein Kanne, 1L, 10" 635.00
Porc, transfer/HP: bowling, rpl lid, Hauber & Reuther type body, .5L.. 120.00
Porc, transfer/HP: Munster in Freiburg..., lith, pewter lid, .5L 195.00
Pottery, etch: night watchman, pewter lid, Hauber & Reuther, #420, .5L...415.00
Pottery, etch: Trumpeter of Sackingen, Hauber & Reuther, #203, .5L...360.00
Pottery, HP: ATV Arminia Sei's Panier, Berlin 1896-97, pewter lid, .5L...435.00
Pottery, relief: dwarfs, pewter lid, Diesinger, #728, .5L 195.00
Pottery, relief: Falstaff, pewter lid, Dumler & Breiden, #571, 1L..240.00
Pottery, relief: Fraternal Order of Eagles, rpl pewter lid, .5L 140.00
Pottery, relief: German's meet Romans, pewter lid, #1268, .5L 135.00
Pottery, relief: jockeys jumping ea side, pewter lid, #1542, .5L..... 240.00
Pottery, transfer/HP: Geneve et T Le Mont-Blanc, monument lid, .5L...150.00
Pottery, transfer/HP: Gruss Aus Munchen, Munich Child lid, 3¼" ...200.00

Pottery, transfer/HP: Seminar Zeit 1898-1901, roster, pewter lid, .5L ...**275.00**
Pottery, transfer: rabbits in lid, pewter lid, 3¾" **80.00**
Regimental, porc, Infantry Regt...Hanau 1898-00, eagle tl, .5L...**465.00**
Regimental, porc, 12 Feld Artillerei...1911-13, lion tl, .5L, 13" ...**945.00**
Regimental, porc, 3 Battr...Karlsruhe 1984-96, griffin tl, .5L........ **300.00**
Regimental, porc, 6 Comp...Frankfurt 1906-08, eagle tl, .5L **315.00**
Regimental, pottery, Kgl Bayrisches..., evolution of uniforms, 1L ...**600.00**
Regimental, pottery, transfer/HP: KBI...Munchen 1917, pewter lid, .5L...**175.00**
Regimental, pottery, 1 Esk Kurassier...1906-09, eagle tl, rpr, .5L..**865.00**
Regimental, pottery, 4 Esk...Braunschewig 1907-10, eagle tl, .5L....**865.00**
Regimental, stoneware, 4 Field...1907-09, 4 scenes/lion tl, .5L....**635.00**
Regimental, 5 Komp Kgl...1912-13, porc, 6 scenes/stanhope, .5L ..**2,575.00**
Stoneware, eng: horse, pewter 1797 lid, Westerwald, .5L, VG.....**575.00**
Stoneware, etch/relief: Art Nouveau, inscribed/dtd 1905, #0709, .3L ..**140.00**
Stoneware, etch: cavalier, pewter lid, Marzi & Remy, #1765, .5L ...**320.00**
Stoneware, transfer/HP: man in yel jacket, Ringer, pewter lid, .5L ..**275.00**
Wood burl, naturalistic form, Germany, 1930s, 12" **365.00**

Steuben

Carder Steuben glass was made by the Steuben Glass Works in Corning, New York, while under the direction of Frederick Carder from 1903 to 1932. Perhaps the most popular types of Carder Steuben glass are Gold Aurene which was introduced in 1904 and Blue Aurene, introduced in 1905. Gold and Blue Aurene objects shimmer with the lustrous beauty of their metallic iridescence. Carder also produced other types of 'Aurenes' including red, green, yellow, brown, and decorated, all of which are very rare. Aurene also was cased with calcite glass. Some pieces had paper labels. Other types of Carder Steuben include Cluthra, Cintra, Florentia, Rosaline, Ivory, Ivrene, Jades, Verre de Soie; there are many more.

Frederick Carder's leadership of Steuben ended in 1932, and the production of colored glassware soon ceased. Since 1932 the tradition of fine Steuben art glass has been continued in crystal. In the following listings, examples are signed unless noted otherwise. When no color is mentioned, assume the glass is clear.

Key: ACB — acid cut back

Bottle, scent; Blue Aurene, #2701, paper label, 5", $2,250.00. (Photo courtesy Early Auctions Inc.)

Basket, Gold Aurene, ruffled, berry prunts, #455, 10x6½" **925.00**
Bowl, Blue Aurene, faint ribs, rolled rim, 12½" **1,150.00**
Bowl, Blue Aurene, ftd, incurvate rim, #0806, 4x8" **1,600.00**
Bowl, Gold Aurene, rolled rim, #2687, 4¼x8" **515.00**
Bowl, Gold Aurene, stretched flat rim, 11¼" **635.00**
Bowl, Gold Aurene, 2 Gold Aurene ft, #2586, 8" **515.00**
Bowl, Gold Aurene/Calcite, flattened/rolled rim, 10" **175.00**
Bowl, Grotesque, gr to clear, 5x8" **635.00**
Bowl, Verre de Soie w/mc irid, flared rim, sm ft, 11½" **230.00**
Candlesticks, Amber w/vertical ribs, ped ft, 4½", pr **230.00**
Candlesticks, Pomona Green w/Amber bobeches/ft, 12", pr **700.00**

Chandelier, Brown Aurene w/Intarsia shades (3) on brass fixture, 28" ...**3,000.00**
Console set, Celeste Blue swirl/Amber, 8x8" bowl+2 12" candlesticks...**1,725.00**
Cup, Gold Aurene, bbl shape, #3360, 2x2½" **230.00**
Finger bowl & underplate, Citron Yellow w/emb ribs, 5", 6¼" **175.00**
Goblet, Gold Aurene, twisted stem, #2361, 6" **400.00**
Goblet, Gold Aurene, 4¾" **285.00**
Sherbets, Verre de Soie irid, appl stem & ft, 3¾x3¾", 6 for.......... **300.00**
Urn, Blue Aurene, 3 hdls at shoulder, Marshall Field's sticker, 6½x7" ..**4,140.00**
Urn, Gold Aurene, 3 appl hdls at shoulder, ftd, 6x7" **3,795.00**
Vase, ACB Deco floral, Seafoam Green on frost, incurvate rim, 7" ...**1,450.00**
Vase, Blue Aurene, flower form, #2698, 6"................................**1,150.00**
Vase, Blue Aurene shading to platinum at top, shouldered, 10".. **1,600.00**
Vase, Blue Aurene w/dk bl ft, #2705, 11¾"...............................**1,925.00**
Vase, Blue Aurene w/wht hearts & vines, fan form, #6287, 8¾" ...**4,600.00**
Vase, Cluthra, gr, dispersed bubbles, shouldered, 10"................**1,950.00**
Vase, Cluthra, gr, wht hdls, 10" **1,495.00**
Vase, Cluthra, gr, 8½x7½" **1,200.00**
Vase, Gold Aurene, can neck, #237, 4"......................................**400.00**
Vase, Gold Aurene, ftd teardrop, mini, 2½"...............................**480.00**
Vase, Gold Aurene, shouldered, 8x7".....................................**1,100.00**
Vase, Gold Aurene w/gr hearts & vines, flower form, #576, 10¾". **20,125.00**
Vase, Gold Aurene w/gr peacock eyes/feathers, baluster, #219, 8¾"..**10,350.00**
Vase, Gold Aurene w/hearts/vines/millefiori decor, #578, 11".**17,825.00**
Vase, Gold Aurene w/leaves & vines, fan form, #6297, 8 12"...**5,750.00**
Vase, Gold Aurene w/pulled feathers, slender stem, #2196, 8½". **3,675.00**
Vase, Green Jade, classic form w/M-shaped alabaster hdls, 12x7½"..**1,725.00**
Vase, jack-in-pulpit; Gold Aurene, #2699, 6½" **1,150.00**
Vase, Rosaline w/Alabaster hdls & ft, flared rim, 10x5¾".............**660.00**
Vase, Verre de Soie, 3-stem tree trunk w/saucer ft, hairline, 6" **200.00**

Stevengraphs

A Stevengraph is a small picture made of woven silk resembling an elaborate ribbon, created by Thomas Stevens in England in the latter half of the 1800s. They were matted and framed by Stevens, usually with his name appearing on the mat or often with the trade announcement on the back of the mat. He also produced silk postcards and bookmarks, all of which have 'Stevens' woven in silk on one of the mitered corners. Anyone wishing to learn more about Stevengraphs is encouraged to contact the Stevengraph Collectors' Association, whose address can be found in the Directory under Clubs, Newsletters, and Catalogs. Unless noted otherwise, assume our values are for examples in very good original condition and the pictures matted and framed.

Are You Ready? bk label, unfr, 5x8", EX **510.00**
Bath of Psyche, image: 3¼x10¼", G.. **180.00**
Burns, portrait & verse, 8½x6½", G **500.00**
Clifton Suspension Bridge, story bk label, 6x9" **660.00**
Crystal Palace (inside), unfr, EX+ **1,140.00**
Death, 6x8½", G **70.00**
Declaration of Independence, woven at Columbian Exhibition, 6x10"...**350.00**
Ecce Homo, Christ w/crown of thorns, 9½x6¼" **85.00**
First Innings, Stevengraph ad on bk, NM **3,780.00**
First Over, bk label... **540.00**
First Set, tennis match, bk label, 6x9"... **900.00**
First Train, bk label, 6x9"... **210.00**
For Life or Death Heroism on Land, bl coats, 4 horses, bk label, 6x9" ..**145.00**
For Life or Death Heroism on Land, 2 horses, 5¼x8" **360.00**
Fourth Bridge, bk label, 7½x10½" **300.00**
George Stephenson Pioneer of Railways, portrait, rpl mat, 8x6¾", G...**145.00**
God Speed the Plough (no birds in foreground), bk label, 8x11", EX. **420.00**
Grace Darling, from $100 to.. **150.00**
HM Queen Alexandra, label, 8x6", G... **75.00**

HM Queen Victoria, 5 images, G-..325.00
HM Stanley, portrait, bk label, 7½x4⅝"..............................275.00
HRH Duchess of Cornwall & York, gold crown, red flowers, G-....95.00
Iroquois & Fred Archer, Winner 1881 Derby, Lorillard Co mt, 12x16", EX..7,200.00
Iroquois & Fred Archer, Winner 1881 Derby, on brd, 4x8½"...2,240.00
Kitchener of Kartoum, bk label, 8x6"................................85.00
Landing of Columbus...300.00
Late Fred Archer, jockey, 8x6½".....................................180.00
Leda, she w/swan, bk label 30+32 titles, rare, 8x11", EX.............950.00
Life or Death Heroism on Land, bk label, 6x9".......................450.00
Maj Gen Wauchope CB (Killed in Action), bk label, 6x8", G....120.00
Mater Dolorosa, bk label, inner/outer mats, 9¼x6¼"................950.00
Mersy Tunnel Railway..650.00
Palace in Rome (ceiling painting)...................................210.00
Present Time, 60 Miles an Hour, 7¼x10"..............................150.00
Queen Victoria & Her Premiers, bk label, 11x8½", EX.................420.00
Souvenir of the Wild West, 8 Indians, Buffalo Bill in red shirt..5,500.00
Stephenson's Triumph (train)..90.00
Struggle, 4 horses, no bkground or other horses, unfr...............250.00
Tom Cannon, portrait, yel cap, yel/bl shirt, label, 7½x6½", G.......85.00
Water Jump, 6x9"..180.00
William Prince of Orange, 7¼x10"....................................540.00

Miscellaneous

Bookmark, By Special Appointment to Her Majesty the Queen..., 6"...550.00
Bookmark, Thy Will Be Done in Earth As It Is in Heaven.............85.00
Broadside, Phila Internat'l/Geo WA, Champromy/Larcher, fringed, 7x10"..300.00
Memorial ribbon, Stratford Church/Shakespeare in wreaths, 10½"..85.00
Souvenir, Centennial 1776-1876, Washington portrait, 8⅜".......120.00
Souvenir, Phila Centennial 1876/Geo Washington, 6-color, 6½" L...360.00
Souvenir, Signing Declaration of Independence, Columbian World's Fair..180.00
Souvenir ribbon, Geo Washington American Centennial, 18x3", NM..210.00

Stevens and Williams

Stevens and Williams glass was produced at the Brierly Hill Glassworks in Stourbridge, England, for nearly a century, beginning in the 1830s. They were credited with being among the first to develop a method of manufacturing a more affordable type of cameo glass. Other lines were also made — silver deposit, alexandrite, and engraved rock crystal, to name but a few. Our advisor for this category is Don Williams; he is listed in the Directory under Missouri.

Cameo

Beaker, prunus blossoms, leafy borders, pk/bl on ivory, 1880s, 4⅜"...4,800.00
Bottle, scent; floral, red on wht frost, globular, 1890s, 4½".......1,100.00
Bottle, scent; floral, wht on red, lay-down, ca 1884, 4⅛"...........1,200.00
Vase, apple blossoms/branches, wht on citron, dbl-gourd form, 12"...3,500.00
Vase, floral, wht on citron, elongated gourd form, att, 1885, 12"..480.00
Vase, floral, wht on citron, elongated gourd form, 1880s, 12½"..2,750.00
Vase, floral/insect, pk/wht on citron, baluster, 5⅝", pr.............6,000.00
Vase, flowers/butterflies, wht on apricot, bulbous, 12¼"............6,000.00
Vase, flowers/grasses, wht on red cased to clear, shouldered, 8"..4,800.00
Vase, flowers/leaves, red on wht, gourd shape, 8½"..................3,000.00
Vase, flowers/scrolls (elaborate) wht on champagne, urn form, 1885, 3"..5,150.00
Vase, nasturtiums/beetle, wht on amethyst, ovoid, 1885, 6".......4,800.00

Miscellaneous

Bottle, scent; Pompeian Swirl, red to yel, silver foliage, 3¾".....1,200.00
Ewer, Pompeian Swirl, red to yel, frosted hdl, stick neck, 12½".2,400.00

Vase, amber w/appl bl frog & serpentine, clear fly, 9"..................550.00
Vase, emerald gr w/appl gold & silver acorn & leaves, 4¼x5½".1,325.00
Vase, peachblow w/appl wht flower/amber branch, handkerchief rim, 5"..120.00
Vase, pk cased w/appl amber leaves w/crimped edge, amber rim, 7¼".180.00
Vase, pk cased w/appl wht rose blossoms & vines, folded rim, 9", NM.600.00
Vase, pk opal w/appl red strawberry/gr leaves/amber thorn ft, 6x8x4".480.00
Vase, Pompeian Swirl, chartreuse to bl over wht, dbl-gourd form, 9"..1,450.00
Vase, Pompeian Swirl, gold birds/branches, dbl-gourd form, 7".1,450.00
Vase, Pompeian Swirl, ivory to golden amber, baluster/folded rim, 8".475.00
Vase, Pompeian Swirl, pk MOP, dbl-gourd form, 6⅞"..................550.00
Vase, Pompeian Swirl, purple on bl, gourd shape, everted rim, 8".1,325.00
Vase, Pompeian Swirl, tangerine to peach, stick neck, 12⅜".....1,200.00
Vase, Prussian Blue cut to lt rose in dmn pattern, fluted rim, 9"..700.00
Vase, trumpet blossoms/foliage, mc on crystal w/gold, shouldered, 12".2,750.00

Stickley

Among the leading proponents of the Arts and Crafts Movement, the Stickley brothers — Gustav, Leopold, Charles, Albert, and John George — were at various times and locations separately involved in designing and producing furniture as well as decorative items for the home. (See Arts and Crafts for further information.) The oldest of the five Stickley brothers was Gustav; his work is the most highly regarded of all. He developed the style of furniture referred to as Mission. It was strongly influenced by the type of furnishings found in the Spanish missions of California — utilitarian, squarely built, and simple. It was made most often of oak, and decoration was very limited or non-existent. The work of his brothers display adaptations of many of Gustav's ideas and designs. His factory, the Craftsman Workshop, operated in Eastwood, New York, from the late 1890s until 1915, when he was forced out of business by larger companies who copied his work and sold it at much lower prices. Among his shop marks are the early red decal containing a joiner's compass and the words 'Als Ik Kan,' the branded mark with similar components, and paper labels.

The firm known as Stickley Brothers was located first in Binghamton, New York, and then Grand Rapids, Michigan. Albert and John George made the move to Michigan, leaving Charles in Binghamton (where he and an uncle continued the operation under a different name). After several years John George left the company to rejoin Leopold in New York. (These two later formed their own firm called L. & J.G. Stickley.) The Stickley Brothers Company's early work produced furniture featuring fine inlay work, decorative cutouts, and leaned strongly toward a style of Arts and Crafts with an English influence. It was tagged with a paper label 'Made by Stickley Brothers, Grand Rapids,' or with a brass plate or decal with the words 'Quaint Furniture,' an English term chosen to refer to their product. In addition to furniture, they made metal accessories as well.

The workshops of the L. & J.G. Stickley Company first operated under the name 'Onondaga Shops.' Located in Fayetteville, New York, their designs were often all but copies of Gustav's work. Their products were well made and marketed, and their business was very successful. Their decal labels contained all or a combination of the words 'Handcraft' or 'Onondaga Shops,' along with the brothers' initials and last name. The firm continues in business today. Our advisor for this category is Bruce Austin; he is listed in the Directory under New York.

Note: When only one dimension is given, it is length. Our values are from cataloged auctions and include the buyer's premium. Unless a condition code is present in the line, our values reflect the worth of items that are complete, in original condition, and retaining their original finishes. A rating of excellent (EX) may denote cleaning, small repairs, or touchups. Codes lower than that describe wear, losses, repairs, or damage in degrees relative to the condition given. Cleaning and/or refinishing can lower values as much as 15% to 30%. Replaced hardware or wood will also have a dramatic negative effect.

Key:
b — brand   p — paper label
d — red decal   t — Quaint metal tag
h/cp — hammered copper

Charles Stickley

Chairs, dining; slat bk, reuphl bk & seats, 5 side+1 arm............ 1,200.00
Loveseat, orig drop-in seat reuphl in leather, att, 36x47½x22"... 1,450.00
Rocker, arm; rectangular cutouts to bk, reuphl seat, rfn, rpt, 34" .. 800.00
Rocker, arm; tall bk w/vertical slats, uphl seat, rfn, att, 48".......... 750.00
Rocker, arm; 4 vertical slats, reuphl spring cushion, att, 34" 750.00
Server, plate rail, 2 drws, copper pulls, att, 39x42x20" 1,200.00
Settle, drop-arm; slat bk, 3-seat, reuphl brn vinyl, att, 42x67x27".. 1,800.00
Settle, even-arm; 6-slat bk, wide posts, thru tenons, 34x73" 3,000.00
Sideboard, quartersawn oak, 4 drws amid 2 doors over 2 drws... 4,800.00
Table, lamp; lower shelf, X-stretcher, p, rfn top, 29x30" dia......... 800.00
Table, quartersawn oak on ped w/4 leaves, att 2,400.00

Gustav Stickley

Bed, #923, 4 vertical slats ea end, tapered posts, 47x79x47" 3,500.00
Bookcase, #525, 2-door, mitered mullions, 3 fixed shelves, d, 56x45".. 18,000.00
Bookcase, gallery, 3 fixed shelves, thru tenons, p, d, 56x35x13" .. 8,500.00
Bookcase, open w/3 fixed shelves per side, p, d, 57x43x13"..... 10,200.00
Cabinet, 1-pane door & sides, 1 wood/8 glass shelves, d, 72x24x18".. 11,000.00
Chafing dish, h/cp woodgrain pattern, wood base, terra cotta dish, 15" ..3,100.00
Chair, arm; #2616, U-bk, rush seat, ca 1901, d, 38½" 2,500.00
Chair, arm; ladder-bk arm w/drop-in seat, unmk, oversz, 38½".... 2,500.00
Chair, bungalow arm; #2576, modified seat fr, unmk, 38¼"....... 1,700.00
Chair, cube; even arms, spindled bk & sides, rpl leather, d, 29x26x28"...7,200.00
Chair, Morris; #2340, bow-arm, loose cushion on ropes, unmk, 39".. 11,400.00
Chair, Morris; #2341, rpl leather pillows, unmk, 1901, 38" 10,200.00
Chair, Morris; brn leather cushions, sling base, d, 38x29x34" 5,400.00
Chair, side; H Ellis design, maple, rush seat, varied inlays, 39"... 5,500.00
Chairs, bungalow dining; #1289, rush seats, ca 1901, 38", 6 for.. 11,000.00
Chandelier, 5 h/cp drops, yel glass liners, oak mt, 37x21" 20,400.00
Chest, #626, 2 short drws over 3, hammered iron pulls, d, 43x36x20"....5,000.00
China cabinet, H Ellis design #803, 3-shelf, p, l, 60x36x15¼" ..6,000.00
Costumer, dbl; #53 h/cp straps for umbrellas or canes, 72x14x18" ..2,000.00
Desk, #706, drop front, full gallery int, key, d, 44x30x13" 4,500.00
Desk, chalet; paneled drop front, lower shelf, shoe ft, d, 46x24x16" ..3,125.00
Desk, drop-front; H Ellis design w/inlays, glass inkwells, d, 44" .. 21,600.00
Fire screen, #104, w/period oilcloth, unmk, ca 1901, 35x31x10¾".. 1,700.00
Fire screen, w/Navajo textile, unmk, 35x32½" 4,500.00
Magazine stand, #46, slatted sides, d, 42x21x12" 3,000.00
Magazine stand, #72, arched sides, p, 42x21½x12¾" 2,150.00
Magazine stand, #79, cut-out hdls, b, 40x13¾x10" 1,200.00
Magazine stand, #548, panel sides, 4-shelf, 1902, d, 44x15½x15¼" ..6,000.00
Magazine stand, chalet; #500, unmk, 43x12¾x12¾" 3,500.00
Mirror, hall; 21½x28"... 900.00
Music stand, #780, 4-shelf, partial p, 39¼x22x15" 3,250.00
Plant stand, #44, 10" Grueby indigo tile insert, unmk, 39¾x12½".. 9,600.00
Plate rail, #902, arched top brd, chamfered bk, rfn, d, 26x46x5" .. 1,900.00
Plate rail, custom made, unmk, 1901, 31x96x6" 10,000.00
Rack, wall; slatted sides, d, 26x30x7¾" 5,400.00
Rocker, #323, leather drop-in spring seat, d, 37x29x30" 3,000.00
Server, #955, bksplash, 2 drws, shelf, long drw, ca 1902, 45x59x24" .. 18,000.00
Settee, #214, even-arm, broad vertical slats, loose cushion, d, 31x50".. 7,200.00
Settee, cube; #305, reuphl drop-in spring seat, unmk, 30x56x22" .. 4,500.00
Settle, #212, V-bk w/12 vertical slats at bk, leather seat, d, 48"... 4,750.00
Settle, #222, even-arm, leather drop-in seat, d, 36x79x33".....10,000.00
Settle, #225, even-arm, horizontal brd at bk, reuphl, 29x78x31".. 9,000.00
Settle, cube; #208, leather drop-in seat, 3-cushion bk, 29x76x32" ...8,000.00

Settle, ¾-arm, drop-in foam seat, b, 29¾x80x31½" 4,500.00
Sideboard, #817, w/chamfered plate rack, b, 50x70x25" 14,400.00
Sideboard, butterfly joints, custom made, unmk, 1901, 45¼x100x25" .. 72,000.00
Table, #46, hexagon inset Grueby indigo tile, ca 1901, 21x19" .. 21,600.00
Table, bungalow library; #401, ca 1901, 28x49x29¾" 5,000.00
Table, hall; oilcloth-covered top, ca 1901, 42x54½x20¾"......... 5,000.00
Table, lamp; #240, cutouts, shelf, unmk, 29½x20x20" 3,100.00
Table, lamp; #440, unmk, 1901, 27¾x30" dia 8,400.00
Table, lamp; thru tenons, X-stretchers, 29x36" dia 1,800.00
Table, library; #659, 3-drw, d, 29x54x32"................................ 7,200.00
Table, library; d, ca 1902, 29½x39" dia 6,600.00

Table, Poppy, floriform top and shelf, color added to top, partial label, 20x23", $15,600.00. (Photo courtesy David Rago Auctions)

Table, tea; floriform top, shelf, shaped legs, unmk, 23¼x19", VG+ ..8,400.00
Umbrella stand, #54, copper drip pan, d, 33½x11½x11½" 900.00
Umbrella stand, #254, cutouts, b, 37x12x12" 2,300.00
Wardrobe, child's, 2 paneled doors, h/cp V-pulls, fitted int, 60x34" ..21,600.00
Window seat, #177, thru tenons, ca 1901, 26½x25x19" 3,500.00

L. & J.G. Stickley

Bookcase, #331½, 3 12-pane do, recoated finish, 57x73x12", G....4,500.00
Chair, arm; #816, 6 vertical slats, open arms, reuphl seat, 39", VG.. 475.00
Chair, arm; #838 (similar), leather bk & seat, orig tacks, 39", G... 100.00
Chair, Morris; #406, slatted bow-arm, reuphl seat & bk, d, 38x34x41"...4,200.00
China cabinet, 2 12-pane doors, h/cp strap hinges, d, 70x50x17" . 14,400.00
Desk, drop front w/int gallery 2 drws, bookcase sides, b, 41x38x21"...1,200.00
Magazine rack, #46, Handcraft d, 42x21x12" 2,750.00
Magazine stand, slatted sides, 4-shelf, d, 42x21x12" 2,200.00
Magazine stand, solid trapezoidal sides, 4-shelf, d, 42x20x15"... 4,800.00
Night stand, #550, drw shelf, unmk, 29x20x18" 2,150.00
Pedestal, #27, 4 shoe ft, unmk, 36x18½x18½" 1,300.00
Rocker, #460, slatted bk & arms, loose seat on ropes, d, 38" 1,900.00
Settle, #0738, uneven-arm, loose cushions/pillows, 39x76x30"... 5,000.00
Settle, #281, even-arm, drop-in spring seat, d, 34x76x31" 5,000.00
Sideboard, #745, plate rail, strap hinges, 48½x54x24" 4,800.00
Sideboard, paneled plate rail, wooden knobs, flared ft, d, 44x60x22" ... 3,500.00
Table, dining; #544, X-stretcher base, 29x48" dia....................... 900.00
Table, dining; #716, 5-post ped, d, 29x48" dia, +4 leaves.......... 4,200.00
Table, trestle; #593, dbl key & tenons, shoe-ft base, rfn top, 48x29"...1,500.00
Table, trestle; keyed-thru lg shelf, rfn, unmk, 30x72x45" 3,600.00
Table, trestle; keyed-thru stretcher, mouse-hole cutouts, 60x31"... 3,480.00
Table, trestle; keyed-thru tenons, shelf, overcoat, 29x60x34" ... 2,525.00
Table, trestle; overhanging top, wide lower shelf, d, 29x48x30" .. 1,325.00

Stickley Bros.

Armchair, #357½, 4 vertical slats at top over horizontal rail, 44"....275.00
Bed, paneled, pewter/ebonized wood inlay, unmk, 60½x77¼x57" .. 15,600.00
Bookstand, maple, rectangular top, V-trough supports, 25x24x15" .. 475.00
Cache pot, h/cp, appl hdls, 3-ftd, #82, 9½x10" 350.00

Chair, Morris; #631½, 3-slat bk, rolled arms, worn cushion, 37" ...3,500.00
Chair, side; floriform inlay of various woods, trapezoidal seat, 42"...965.00
Chair, side; 3 vertical trumpeted slats, saddle seat, rfn, 37" 100.00
Chairs, #268 (similar), 5-spindle bk/reuphl seats, 4 side+1 arm ... 700.00
China cabinet, #8447, 2 8-pane do, 4-pane sides, 3-shelf, 60x49x16".. 2,200.00
China cabinet, 2 1-pane doors, partial-mirror bk, b, d, 59½x46x14" .. 2,150.00
Clock, tall case; paneled sides, appl tenons/keys, glass door, 83"...3,250.00
Daybed, 2 new loose cushions, rfn, t, 25x76x29" 800.00
Lamp, h/cp 20" fr w/mica inserts; 3-socket/2-hdl bulbous std, 22" .. 3,600.00
Loveseat, #3887, slat bk, open arms, loose reuphl vinyl cushion, 49" ... 2,760.00
Luggage rack, 5-slat top, t, 16x28½x16½" 375.00
Magazine stand, #4600, notched gallery, 3-shelf, slat sides, 31x16x13"...1,100.00
Magazine stand, circular cutouts, unmk, 49½x14x12" 1,100.00
Magazine stand, 3-shelf, slatted sides, t, 44x24x14".................. 1,150.00
Pedestal, #133, sq top, reverse tapered column, sq base, t, 34x13x13" ..850.00
Pitcher, h/cp, forged riveted hdl, new patina, 14¼" 600.00
Rocker, 4-slot bk w/cutouts, open arms, leather seat, att, 35"....... 325.00
Settle, broad slats, drop arms, loose cushion, t, 37x74x31" 1,700.00
Settle, even-arm, vertical slats, reuphl brn leather cushion, t, 50"...2,775.00
Settle, even-arm, vertical slats, reuphl wht canvas cushion, d, 50"...2,525.00
Sideboard, paneled plate rail/2 sm drws/linen drw/2 doors, b, 46x50"... 3,125.00
Table, dining; ped, p, 29x54" dia, +4 leaves...............................4,000.00
Table, lamp; #130, X-stretcher, thru tenons, t, 30x40½" 1,600.00
Table, lamp; dbl oval, t, 30x36x28¼" 2,400.00
Table, library; #2601, bookshelf sides, rfn top, p, 30x40x26"........ 750.00
Table, library; blind drw, 2 slats ea side, rpr to top, t, 30x36x24"... 850.00
Table, library; drw, oak pulls, lower stretchers, shelf, t, 30x44x29" ... 725.00

Stiegel

Baron Henry Stiegel produced glassware in Pennsylvania as early as 1760, very similar to glass being made concurrently in Germany and England. Without substantiating evidence, it is impossible to positively attribute a specific article to his manufacture. Although he made other types of glass, today the term Stiegel generally refers to any very early ware made in shapes and colors similar to those he is known to have produced — especially that with etched or enameled decoration. It is generally conceded, however, that most glass of this type is of European origin. Our advisor for this category is Mark Vuono; he is listed in the Directory under Connecticut. Unless a color is mentioned in the description, assume the glass to be clear.

Bottle, floral/squiggles in mc enamel, missing cap, 6½" 360.00
Decanter, roses/flowers/shield in mc enamel, att, 10¼x4½"......... 425.00
Pitcher, cobalt w/Dmn Quilt, 3½", 4", pr..................................... 660.00
Pitcher, dk sapphire bl, Dmn T'print, 4x3½" 360.00
Salt cellar, cobalt, expanded dmns, ftd, 3" 465.00
Salt cellar, expanded dmns, petal ft, pontil, 3"............................ 350.00
Tumbler, bird/hearts/flowers in mc enamel on clear, att, 3¼" 395.00

Stocks and Bonds

Scripophily (scrip-awfully), the collecting of 'worthless' old stocks and bonds, gained recognition as an area of serious interest around the mid-1970s. Collectors who come from numerous business fields mainly enjoy its hobby aspect, though there are those who consider scripophily an investment. Some collectors like the historical significance that certain certificates have. Others prefer the beauty of older stocks and bonds that were printed in various colors with fancy artwork and ornate engravings. Autograph collectors are found in this field, on the lookout for signed certificates; others collect specific industries.

Many factors help determine the collector value: autograph value, age of the certificate, the industry represented, whether it is issued or not,

its attractiveness, condition, and collector demand. Certificates from the mining, energy, and railroad industries are the most popular with collectors. Other industries or special collecting fields include banking, automobiles, aircraft, and territorials. Serious collectors usually prefer only issued certificates that date from before 1930. Unissued certificates are usually worth one-fourth to one-tenth the value of one that has been issued. Inexpensive issued common stocks and bonds dated between the 1940s and 1990s usually retail between $1.00 to $10.00. Those dating between 1890 and 1930 usually sell for $10.00 to $50.00. Those over 100 years old retail between $25.00 and $100.00 or more, depending on the quantity found and the industry represented. Some stocks are one of a kind while others are found by the hundreds or even thousands, especially railroad certificates. Autographed stocks normally sell anywhere from $50.00 to $1,000.00 or more. A formal collecting organization for scripophilists is known as The Bond and Share Society with an American chapter located in New York City. As is true in any field, potential collectors should take the time to learn the hobby. Prices vary greatly at websites selling old stocks and bonds, sometimes by hundreds of dollars.

Collectors should avoid buying modern certificates being offered for sale at scripophily websites in the $20.00 to $60.00 range as they have little collector value despite the sales hype. One uncancelled share of some of the modern 'famous name' stocks of the Fortune 500 companies are being offered at two or four times what the stock is currently trading for. These should be avoided, and new collectors who want to buy certificates in modern companies will be better off buying 'one share' stocks in their own name and not someone else's. Take the time to study the market, ask questions, and be patient as a collector. Your collection will be better off. Generally, eBay serves as a good source for information regarding current values — search under 'Coins.' Our advisor for this category is Cheryl Anderson; she is listed in the Directory under Utah. In many of the following listings, two-letter state abbreviations precede the date. Unless noted otherwise, values are for examples in fine condition.

Key:
U — unissued	I/U — issued/uncancelled
I/C — issued/cancelled	vgn — vignette

Am Motor Transportation, bus & passengers vgn, bl ink, DE, 1930, U.. 72.50
Athens, Mfg, GA state arms vgn, GA, 1892, I/C 48.00
Bald Mtn Mining, view of Fryerhill, CO, 1880, I/C 48.00
Baltimore Athenian Society, on laid paper, MD, 1812, I/C 110.00
Bank of Gettysburg, man's portrait/Liberty/Justice, 1857, I/C 110.00
Boyette Electric Car, eagle w/shield vgn, gr seal, FL, 1934, I/C...... 85.00
Brooklyn Academy of Music, lady w/doves vgn, gr, NY, 1921, I/U ...60.00
Chesapeake & OH Ry, man/train vgn, 10 shares common stock, purple, U.72.50
Chicago Aerial Industries, eagle vgn, brn ink, ABN, DE, 1964, I/C.. 24.00
Climber Motor, eagle w/shield vgn, gr print/seal, AR, 1919, I/C... 135.00
Consolidated Alaskan Co, brn/gr print, red seal, 1915, I/C............ 24.00
Consolidated Business College, capitol bldg vgn, DC, 1869, IC.... 60.00
Denver & Santa Fe Ry, train at station vgn, brn, CO, 1893......... 350.00
Doble Steam Motors, olive gr, ornate border, DE, 1922, I/C.......... 95.00
Dundee, Perth & London Shipping, ornate borders, bl, 1914, I/C...30.00
Dupont RY & Land, participation certificate, brn, FL, 1912.......... 36.00
Eclipse Gold Mining, 6,000 shares, ornate border, CA, 1877, I/C ...75.00
Fulton Motor Truck, gold seal/under print, eagle vgn, DE, 1919, I/C...36.00
Gearless Motor, touring car under print, DE, 1921, I/C................. 195.00
Goldfield Consolidated Mines, eagle vgn, gr seal, WY, 1906, I/C.. 36.00
Gray Goose Airways, goose vgn, gold seal, NV, 1932, I/C............. 72.50
Greyhound Corp, 100 common shares, greyhound vgn, gr, ABN, 1970, I/C..24.00
Gyro Air Lines, eagle w/logo, blk w/red border, AZ, 1934, I/C 36.00
Hannibal & St Joseph RR, 7% Preferred Stock, train vgn, 18__, U.. 18.00
Henry Clews & Co, sale of 25 shares of GM stock, 1925 .... 12.50
Iditarod Telephone, ornate border, blk, NV, 1910, I/C.................. 60.00
Interborough-Metropolitan, Preferred Stock, bl, 1911, I/C............ 24.00

Ivanhoe Mfg, factory view vgn, 6% bond/$1,000, NJ, 1884, I/C.... 48.00
Junction RR Co, train vgn, OH, 18__, U 12.50
KY Petroleum & Mining, orange border, KY, 1865, I/C 48.00
Lampazos Silver Mines, miner vgn, gr, DE, 1918, I/C.................... 36.00
London Improved Cab, 168 shares, ornate border, bl, 1896, I/C.... 12.50
MA Cremation Society, ornate border/seal, gr, MA, 1897, I/C.... 110.00
Madison Safe Deposit, dog guards vgn, bl, NY, ABN Co, 19__, U .. 135.00
Middleburgh Bridge, steamshop vgn, NY, 1866, I/C...................... 72.50
Minneapolis Industrial Expo, building vgn, orange/gold seal, 1893, I/C... 72.50
Mt Shasta Gold Mines, miners vgn, gr ink, ABN Co, SD, 1930, I/C ..48.00
North Horn Silver Mining, mining vgn, UT, 1881, I/C 36.00
OH Canal, farm scene/barge/train vgn, $2,500, 1886, I/C 72.50
Owego & Ithaca Turnpike, ornate border, laid paper, 1810, I/C 36.00
Rome Turnpike, decorative panel, stub at left, NY, 18__, U 24.00
Society Paris Carlton Hotel, pk, sm crown, ornate border, 1920, I/C... 12.50
Standard Motor Holding, orange border, DE, 1933 .... 12.50
Stock Security Bank, 2 vgns, proof on India paper, IL, 1850s 900.00
Union Bank of Rochester, Prosperity/Liberty/shield, NY, 18__, U ... 190.00
Upper Potomac Steamboat, sidewheeler vgn, $100, VA, 1875, I/C..95.00
Waterford, Dungarvan & Lismore Railway, purple ink, Ireland, 1888, I/C ..48.00
Waterford & Limerick Rwy, bl paper/pk seal, coat of arms, 1845, I/C ..96.00
Yellow Cab of Atlantic City, eagle vgn, yel seal, NJ, 1923, I/C...... 36.00
Zephyr Mining, bronze w/eagle & mine shaft vgn, CO, 1882, I/C...96.00

Stoneware

There are three broad periods of time that collectors of American pottery can look to in evaluating and dating the stoneware and earthenware in their collections. Among the first permanent settlers in America were English and German potters who found a great demand for their individually turned wares. The early pottery was produced from red and yellow clays scraped from the ground at surface levels. The earthenware made in these potteries was fragile and coated with lead glazes that periodically created health problems for the people who ate or drank from it. There was little stoneware available for sale until the early 1800s, because the clays used in its production were not readily available in many areas and transportation was prohibitively expensive. The opening of the Erie Canal and improved roads brought about a dramatic increase in the accessibility of stoneware clay, and many new potteries began to open in New York and New England.

Collectors have difficulty today locating earthenware and stoneware jugs produced prior to 1840, because few have survived intact. These ovoid or pear-shaped jugs were designed to be used on a daily basis. When cracked or severely chipped, they were quickly discarded. The value of handcrafted pottery is often determined by the cobalt decoration it carries. Pieces with elaborate scenes (a chicken pecking corn, a bluebird on a branch, a stag standing near a pine tree, a sailing ship, or people) may easily bring $1,000.00 to $12,000.00 at auction.

After the Civil War there was a need and a national demand for stoneware jugs, crocks, canning jars, churns, spittoons, and a wide variety of other pottery items. The competition among the many potteries reached the point where only the largest could survive. To cut costs, most potteries did away with all but the simplest kinds of decoration on their wares. Time-consuming brush-painted birds or flowers quickly gave way to more quickly executed swirls or numbers and stenciled designs. The coming of home refrigeration and Prohibition in 1919 effectively destroyed the American stoneware industry.

Investment possibilities: 1) Early nineteenth-century stoneware with elaborate decorations and a potter's mark is expensive and will continue to rise in price. 2) Late nineteenth-century hand-thrown stoneware with simple cobalt swirls or numbers is still reasonably priced and a good investment. 3) Mass-produced stoneware (ca. 1890 – 1920) is available in large quantities, inexpensive, and slowly increases in price over the

years. Generally speaking, prices will be stronger in the areas where the stoneware pottery originates. Skillfully repaired pieces often surface; their prices should reflect their condition. Look for a slight change in color and texture. The use of a black light is also useful in exposing some repairs. Buyer beware! Hint: Buy only from reputable dealers who will guarantee their merchandise. Assume that values are for examples in near mint condition with only minimal damage unless another condition code is given in the description. See also Bennington, Stoneware.

Bank, hen on nest, ochre, 1880s, 3¼" 575.00
Batter pail, dk brn alkaline, orig bail hdl, tin lids, 1870s, 10"....... 275.00
Chicken feeder, wht Bristol 1880s, 5" 65.00
Churn, #3/flower (triple), OA Gifford Watertown NY, 1860s, 14", EX...525.00
Churn, #4/flowering vine, Whites Utica, ca 1865, lime stain, 17" ..745.00
Churn, #6/flower, C Hart Sherburne, bulbous, 1858, hairline, 19"..650.00
Cooler, accents, C Crolius NY, relief bbl staves, 3-gal, 13" 795.00
Crock, #1½/bird on branch, Belmont Ave Pottery, 1880s, 8"....... 330.00
Crock, #1/chicken pecks corn, att Poughkeepsie NY, 1870s, 10½", EX...600.00
Crock, #1/house on hill w/trees & grasses, West Troy, 1880s, rstr, 7" .. 5,175.00
Crock, #2/bird on branch, West Troy, 1880s, 9" 440.00
Crock, #2/bird w/polka-dot wing, S Hart Fulton, 10x8" 750.00
Crock, #2/eagle on stump (lg), att Albany NY, ca 1865, 9½", EX...700.00
Crock, #2/lovebirds, S Hart Fulton, ca 1875, ping, 9" 770.00
Crock, #2/tulips/dmns/stars, FH Cowden Harrisburg, chips, 10" ..400.00
Crock, #3/dbl plume, Mason & Russel Cortland, ca 1835, rare, 9" ..1,430.00
Crock, #3/foliage, J Swank & Co Johnstown PA, rpr, 12x11½" ... 315.00
Crock, #4/flower, Ballard & Brothers Burlington VT, 13⅛" 500.00
Crock, #4/flower, Thomas D Chollar Cortland, crack, ca 1845, 13½"..300.00
Crock, #4/house among palms, AO Whittemore...NY, 1860s-80s, 10", EX..2,350.00
Crock, #4/3 bluebirds on branches, West Troy NY, 12½", EX ...1,400.00
Crock, #5/birds (3), West Troy NY, 1880s, 12½", EX 2,750.00
Crock, #5/folky lion, Hubbell & Chesebro Geddes NY, 1870s, 12½", NM..17,000.00
Crock, #6/flower (drooping), J Fisher & Co Lyons NY, 1880s, 14", EX..330.00
Crock, flower/accents, P Cross Hartford, spider line, ca 1805, 12½"..2,035.00
Crock, flowers, AE Smith & Sons...NY, flakes, 12" 85.00
Crock, parrot, emb label; FB Norton & Co...MA, flake, 7¾"....... 635.00
Crock, Philbrick & Spaulding...Haverhill/feathers, crack, 1870s, 12"...120.00
Crock, Whites Utica NY/eagle, thick rim, minor flakes, 7¼x9" ... 315.00
Flowerpot, bud & flower, att Fort Edward, 1870s, hairline, 7"...... 685.00
Jar, #1/flower (brushed), J Sager Co Homer, misshapen rim, 1830s, 10".770.00
Jar, #2/plume, N Clark & Co Mt Morris, prof rpr, ca 1835, 11" ... 300.00
Jar, #3/bird on stump, JA & CW Underwood...NY, ca 1865, ping, 13" ..2,425.00
Jar, preserve; #1½/butterfly, WA MacQuoid...12th St, 1870s, 11", EX....850.00
Jar, preserve; church/trees, att M Woodruff Cortland NY, w/lid, 7¼" ... 7,700.00
Jar, storage; #2/flower (2), C McArthur & Co Hudson NY, 1850s, 9½"..635.00
Jug, #1/flower & stem, P Mugler & Co Buffalo NY, ping, 1850s, 11".. 1,700.00
Jug, #1/plume (simple), IH Wands Olean NY, ca 1855, stain, 12" ..275.00
Jug, #2/bluebird on branch, PJ Fitzgerald & Bro Troy NY 485.00
Jug, #2/dragonfly, J Fisher Lyons NY, short hairline, 13½"........... 315.00
Jug, #2/floral spray, Lewis & Cady...VT, ca 1860, chip, 15" 380.00
Jug, #2/flower, F Stetzenmeyer...Rochester NY, 1857, 15", NM .. 2,860.00
Jug, #2/flower, G Apley & Co Ithaca NY, 1860s, sm stain, 11½" .. 415.00
Jug, #2/parrot on stump, Whites Utica, ca 1865, 13" 550.00
Jug, #2/snowflake, Albany NY, ca 1865, 13½" 660.00
Jug, #2/tulip, S Johnston & Son Beaver PA, 14½"..................... 1,265.00
Jug, #2/tulip & leaf/spatters, Brewer & Halm Havana, 1852, 13½", EX....440.00
Jug, #2/tulips, Lyons, chip, 13¼"... 145.00
Jug, #3/bird on flowering branch, Whites Utica, 15¼" 450.00
Jug, #3/flower, C Hart & Son Sherburne NY, 1858, chip/stain, 15".250.00
Jug, #3/flower, Jackson & Hallett Wines & Liquors Guelph, EX..375.00
Jug, #3/flower, T Harrington Lyons, 1850s, sm chips, 16½" 495.00
Jug, #3/peacock/foliage, L Seymour Troy, rim crack, 14½" 3,800.00
Jug, #5/floral spray, AO Whittemore...NY, Albany slip int, 15", EX ..350.00
Jug, accents, C Crolius Mfg Manhattan-Wells NY, 1830s, 2-gal, 13" ... 1,485.00

Jug, flower, emb label: NY Stoneware...Fort Edward NY, flakes, 11¾" .. 285.00
Jug, H Heiser Buffalo NY, ovoid, ca 1857, 10½" 355.00
Jug, leaf, AK Ballard Burlington VT, minor damage, 14" 150.00
Jug, Sheehan & Co...Troy NY, strap hdl, 9¼" 230.00
Jug, ½ Gal M Farrell...95 Haverhhill St, eagle w/banner, 1872, 10" ...1,875.00
Meat tenderizer, orig hdl, mk Pat'd Dec 25 1877, 9½" 145.00
Pitcher, cream; tanware, brushed brn flower/accents, 1870s, 7" ...685.00
Pitcher, flower & curled foliage, strap hdl, minor damage, 9½" 700.00
Stein, bl accents, pewter lid w/elf thumb lift, Albany slip int, 15" ..575.00

Water cooler, J. Lambright, Newport, Ohio, 1873, twisted handles, no lid, 16", $7,245.00. (Photo courtesy Garth's Auctions Inc.)

Store

Perhaps more so than any other yesteryear establishment, the country store evokes feelings of nostalgia for folks old enough to remember its charms — barrels for coffee, crackers, and big green pickles; candy in a jar for the grocer to weigh on shiny brass scales; beheaded chickens in the meat case outwardly devoid of nothing but feathers. Today mementos from this segment of Americana are being collected by those who 'lived it' as well as those less fortunate! See also Advertising; Scales.

Barrel, staved wood, red stain, 29½x19" 275.00
Bin, vegetable; 6 wooden compartments on wheels, 50x50x16" .. 600.00
Broom holder, folding wooden fr w/holds for hdls, 34x24x22" 24.00
Ceiling lamp, kerosene type, electrified, 36x22x20" 80.00
Cheese cutter, Dunn, CI w/red pnt, 8x21" 345.00
Counter/potato bin, wood w/3 deep drws at side of tilt-out bin, 32x38"...480.00
Crock, Red Murdoch & Co Pickles, missing top glass, 7x16" dia... 42.50
Display, metal hanger for buggy whips, 46" H 155.00
Display case, Age Combs for Purse or Pocket, 7-drw, 12" H 155.00
Display case, Excelsior, wood & glass, 35x36" 1,550.00
Display case, glass w/oak fr, 42x96x26" 480.00
Dolly, iron w/hard rubber tires, 34", VG 60.00
Footstool, pine w/slanted area for fitting shoes, ca 1900 .... 30.00
Jar, clear glass, slanted top, metal lid, 10" 72.50
Jar, Lance, red & bl pyro on clear glass, red metal lid, 12x8½x7" .. 110.00
Jar, Rich's Crystallized Ginger, label on clear glass, sq sides, 12" 72.50
Jar, Tom's Toasted Peanuts, blk print on glass, red finial, 9½x7" 85.00
Ladder, oak w/store decals, trn top rung, 108x17¼" 110.00
Rack, broom; oak fr w/drilled holes for 12 brooms, 56x30" 85.00
Rack, display; Nat'l Biscuit Co, 4 tiered oak shelves, 60x46x17" ..1,200.00
Rack, sack; wire & strap iron, pyramidal, ca 1910, 31x10x15" 300.00
Rack, shoe; bamboo & brass, folds, 41x64" 60.00
Rack, upright wood fr w/wire loops, holds bolts of cloth, 41x21x18" .. 600.00
String holder, CI ball shape w/hanger, 8x6" 90.00
Tin, Bunte Fine Confections, tin litho, 14x10" dia 110.00
Tin, Laval Sausage Seasoning, hinged lid, 11¼x11¼" 85.00
Token, 101 Ranch, 25¢, pressed metal 110.00

Stoves

Antique stoves' desirability is based on two criteria: their utility and their decorative merit. It's the latter that adds an 'antique' premium to the basic functional value that could be served just as well by a modern stove. Sheer age is usually irrelevant. Decorative features that enhance desirability include fancy, embossed ornamentation (especially with figures such as cherubs, Old Man Winter, gargoyles, etc.) rather than a solely vegetative motif, nickel-plated trim, mica windows, ceramic tiles, and (in cooking stoves) water reservoirs and high warming closets rather than mere high shelves. The less sheet metal and the more cast iron, the better. Look for crisp, sharp designs in preference to those made from worn or damaged and repaired foundry patterns. Stoves with a pastel porcelain finish can be very attractive; blue is a favorite, white is least desirable. Chrome trim, rather than nickel, dates a stove to circa 1933 or later and is a good indicator of a post-antique stove. Though purists prefer the earlier models trimmed in nickel rather than chrome, there is now considerable public interest in these post-antique stoves as well, and some people are willing to pay a good price for these appliance-era 'classics.' (Note: Remember, not all bright metal trim is chrome; it is important to learn to distinguish chrome from the earlier, more desirable nickel plate.)

Among stove types, base burners (with self-feeding coal magazines) are the most desirable. Then come the upright, cylindrical 'oak' stoves, kitchen ranges, and wood parlors. Cannon stoves approach the margin of undesirability; laundries and gasoline stoves plunge through it.

There's a thin but continuing stream of desirable antique stoves going to the high-priced Pacific Coast market. Interest in antique stoves is least in the Deep South. Demand for wood/coal stoves is strongest in areas where firewood is affordable and storage of it is practical. Demand for antique gas ranges has become strong, especially in metropolitan markets, and interest in antique electric ranges is slowly dawning. The market for antique stoves is so limited and the variety so bewildering that a consensus on a going price can hardly emerge. They are only worth something to the right individual, and prices realized depend very greatly on who happens to be in the auction crowd. Even an expert's appraisal will usually miss the realized price by a substantial percent.

In judging condition look out for deep rust pits, warped or burnt-out parts, unsound fire bricks, poorly fitting parts, poor repairs, and empty mounting holes indicating missing trim. Search meticulously for cracks in the cast iron. Our listings reflect auction prices of completely restored, safe, and functional stoves, unless indicated otherwise. Franklin stoves could burn either wood or coal; to determine whether or not a stove originally had a grate, check for mounting points where it would have been attached. Wood-burning Franklin stoves did not require a grate.

Note: Round Oak stoves carrying the words 'Estate of P.D. Beckwith' above the lower door were made prior to 1935. After that date, the company name was changed to Round Oak Company, and the Beckwith reference was no longer used. In our listings, the term 'tea shelf' has been used to describe both drop and swing shelves, as the function of both types was to accommodate teapots and coffeepots.

Key: func — functional

Base Burners

Art Garland #400, Michigan Stove, gargoyles/NP/mica, 1889, rstr ..10,750.00
Faultless, Redway & Burton, Cincinnati O, CI, 1873, 38x34x23" ..475.00
Waverly #12, Thos Caffney, Boston MA, 40x20x22" 6,100.00

Franklin Stoves

Acme Orient #18, 6 tiles, mica windows, fancy, 1890 .... 315.00
Federal style, CI sunburst, ca 1810-20, 38x42" 500.00

Ideal #3, Magee, CI, 2 side trivets, 1892, 32x28" 275.00
Iron Foundry...NH, ornate CI, grate missing, 1820s, 37x26x32" .. 250.00
Unmk, CI w/brass mts, 19th C, 40x49½" 150.00
Villa Franklin, Muzzy & Co, folding doors, 1830s, 30"+4" urn 200.00

Parlor Stoves

The term 'parlor stove' as we use it here is very general and encompasses at least six distinct types recognized by the stove industry: cottage parlor, double-cased airtight, circulator, cylinder, oak, and the fireplace heater.

#2, JH Shear, Albany NY, CI, column style, 56" 950.00
#20, Somersworth, tip-up dome top, 1850s, 39x30x29" 350.00
Barstow #137, Orient tile inserts, CI, 1886, EX 900.00
Crown, Magee, ornate CI, cylindrical w/cabriole legs, urn finial, 63" ... 400.00
Estate Triple Effect #5, gas heater, mica windows, NP, ornate, VG .. 260.00
Grayville Active 1919, blk CI w/ornate urn & doors, 1903, 39" ... 1,100.00
Hot Blast-Air Tight Florence #53, CI w/all-over scrolls, 66x28x28" .. 800.00
IA Sheppard & Co Excelsior, Fern 9, cylindrical, 34½" 250.00
Ideal Garland #200, wood/coal, no urn, ca 1898, rstr 1,300.00
Jewel #214, Detroit, ornate NP CI, urn finial, ca 1903, 54" 2,650.00
Modern Glenwood Wood Parlor, slide top, 1920s, 45x28x24½" .. 360.00
Moore's Heater, Joliet IL, ornate CI outer case, urn finial, 60x22x22" .. 600.00
Neoclassical CI, 4 fluted columns, paw ft, 2 urn sensors, 38x29x18" .. 600.00
Pearl, OH Stove, ornate CI/cabriole legs, scrollwork finial, 33x23x18" .. 500.00
Peerless, Pratt & Wentworth, tip-up dome, 1840s, 37x19x15" 150.00
Railway carriage, CI, 27½x24x18", EX 150.00
Round Oak D-18, 1904, complete, unrstr 300.00
Sylvan Red Cross #31, Co-Op Foundry, tiles, gargoyle legs, Pat 1888-89 .. 350.00
Union Airtight, Warnick & Leibrandt, ornate CI, 1851, 26" 350.00

Ranges (Gas)

Alcazar, Milwaukee, 4-burner/1-oven, 1928, G 50.00
Jewel, Detroit, 4-burner, blk/NP, glass oven door, 1918, VG 550.00
Magic Chef, wht, 6-burner/2-oven, high closet, 1938, rstr, up to .. 12,000.00
Magic Chef, 6-burner/2-oven, high closet, 1932, EX 2,750.00
MUCo, wht enamel, 3-burner, monogram on oven door, 32x26x17" .. 175.00
Quick Meal, 4-burner, bl, cabinet style, 1919, G 925.00
Quick Meal, 4-burner/1-oven, 1928, unrstr 300.00

Ranges (Wood and Coal)

Alpine Bride, CI, blk, ca 1920, rstr 300.00
Ideal Atlantic #8-20, Portland, ornate CI, bk shelf, 1890s 1,675.00
Kalamazoo Peerless, gray & wht, wood/coal/gas, 1920s, G 875.00
Kineo C, Noyes & Nutter, high warming closet, reservoir, 1920s ... 715.00
Quick Meal, bl enamel, high warming closet, rnd shelf, 1920s 800.00
Walker & Pratt, Village Crawford Royal, tea shelves, 1920s 800.00
Wood/Pishop Popular Clarion scrolling tea shelves, 1890s 950.00

Stove Manufacturers' Toy Stoves

Buck's Jr #3, St Louis MO, new body/pnt/recast parts, 26" 850.00
Charter Oak #503, GF Filley, St Louis MO, 14x12x25", EX 2,050.00
Dainty, Reading Stove Works, PA, 7x13x8", VG 150.00
Jersey, Cook & Van Evera, Chicago, ca 1908, 28x15x12", EX .. 6,400.00
Karr Qualified Range, aluminum/tin, dial on door, 21½x13", EX. 775.00
Little Eva, T Southard, NYC, 8½x14x11", VG w/accessories 575.00
Royal American, Bridgeford, Louisville KY, 14x12x10", G 950.00

Toy Manufacturers' Toy Stoves

Electric, Empire, Metal Ware, WI, functional burner+oven, '25, 15", VG .. 50.00
Electric, Hotpoint, Arcade, pnt CI range, tan/gr, non-functional, VG... 150.00
Wood/coal, Bing, bl steel cookstove, brass trim, Germany, 17", VG .. 600.00
Wood/coal, Crescent, 4-hole, plated CI & steel, 11½", EX 230.00
Wood/coal, Eagle, Kenton, CI, heavily scrolled, 4-ft, 11½x10", G... 125.00
Wood/coal, Little Giant, unmk/unidentified, 7½x8½x11", EX orig . 675.00
Wood/coal, Pet, Adams, CI, cooking, ornate, 1857, 8½" W base.. 300.00
Wood/coal, Royal, Kenton, 4-hole, CI & steel, ornate, 10", VG .. 100.00
Wood/coal, Triumph, Kenton OH, 14x8½x19", G 195.00

Stretch Glass

Stretch glass, produced from circa 1916 through 1935, was made in an effort to emulate the fine art glass of Tiffany and Carder. The pressed or blown glassware was sprayed with a metallic salts mix while hot, then reshaped, causing a stretch effect in the iridescent finish. Pieces which were not reshaped had the iridized finish without the stretch, as seen on Fenton's #222 lemonade set and #401 guest set. Northwood, Imperial, Fenton, Diamond, Lancaster, Jeannette, Central, Vineland Flint, and the United States Glass Company were the manufacturers of this type of glass. See also specific companies.

Aquarium bowl, Celeste Blue, Fenton, 6x9¾" 140.00
Ashtray, bl, US Glass, rare, ¾x3x4" 125.00
Basket, Velva Rose, Dmn Optic, Fenton, 6x9" 150.00
Bonbon, gr, ftd, w/lid, Diamond Glass, 5¾x5⅝" 50.00
Bottle, cologne; topaz, flower finial, Fenton, 7" 250.00
Bowl, amber, flared rim, 3-ftd, Jeannette, 3¾x10" 40.00
Bowl, bl, flared rim, US Glass, 1⅞x12" 60.00
Bowl, cobalt, flared, Vineland Flint Glass, 4x7½" 180.00
Bowl, Egyptian Lustre, Diamond Glass, 2⅝x5⅝" 110.00
Bowl, Egyptian Lustre, incurvate rim, Diamond Glass, 4½x8¼" .. 125.00
Bowl, gr, flared, US Glass, 2¾x9⅞" 80.00
Bowl, Green Ice (bl-gr), 16-panel, Imperial, 3¼x10½" 70.00
Bowl, lt bl-gr, flared, crimped, Vineland Flint Glass, 3x9¼" 75.00
Bowl, marigold milk, incurvate rim, Imperial, rare, 3⅝x8⅜" 175.00
Bowl, Pearl Ruby (marigold), crimped, Imperial, 2¼x8" 135.00
Bowl, red, incurvate rim, sm ft, Diamond Glass, 3¾x8" 170.00
Bowl, Russet, flared rim, Northwood, 4½x9¾" 70.00
Bowl, Tangerine, metal base, Fenton, 3⅛x8¾" 110.00
Bowl, topaz, flared, ftd, US Glass, 3⅞x6⅛" 65.00
Bowl, Twilight Wisteria, 3-mold, Diamond Glass, 2½x7½" 85.00
Bowl, Velva Rose, oval, hdls, ftd, Fenton, 4⅝x12¾" 225.00
Cake server, pk, yel flower on rim, ftd, Lancaster, #504, 2½x11"... 125.00
Candlesticks, gr, Central, 9¼", pr 110.00
Candlesticks, Octagon, pk, US Glass, 1½", pr 70.00
Candlesticks, Spindle, bl, Northwood, 8¾", pr 150.00
Candlesticks, Wisteria, Vineland, 6¾", pr 80.00
Cheese & cracker, Blue Ice, Imperial, 2-pc 75.00
Cheese & cracker, Harding Blue, Diamond Glass, 2-pc 90.00
Compote, Florentine Green, flared, oval, Fenton, 3¾x6" 55.00
Compote, marigold, optic ray stem, Diamond Glass, 6x7½" 55.00
Compote, 18 rays, flared/rolled rim, Imperial, 3½x6½" 130.00
Console set, gr w/gold, Central, 3½x9" bowl +pr 7¼" sticks 150.00
Console set, purple w/gold, Central Glass, 10" bowl+pr 7" sticks.... 190.00
Goblet, gr, scarce shape, Diamond Glass, 6½" 80.00
Lamp shade, wht opaque, ribbed, flared, Northwood, 5x5" 80.00
Mug, Adam's Rib, Harding Blue, Diamond Glass, 5⅛" 95.00
Nut cup, Florentine Green, dolphin stem, Fenton, #277, 4⅜x2⅛"... 600.00
Plate, Celeste Blue, Fenton, 9½" 40.00
Plate, Egyptian Lustre (blk opaque), Diamond Glass, 8⅜" 130.00
Plate, gr, pressed star base, Diamond Glass, 7⅝" 35.00
Plate, Iris Ice, floral decor on 2 sides, Lancaster, 6¼" 20.00
Plate, Twilight Wisteria, Diamond Glass, 9⅞" 75.00

Salver, Wisteria (lt purple), Fenton, 2⅝x6½" 60.00
Server, Velva Rose, center dolphin hdl, Fenton, 4½x10¼" 125.00
Sherbet, Green Ice (bl gr), optic panels, Imperial, 3¾x4¾" 50.00
Tumbler, topaz, optic panels, Northwood, 3⅞x2¾" 150.00
Vase, cobalt, scalloped, ftd, Vineland, 6½x3" 95.00
Vase, Pearl (crystal), Diamond Glass, 4x4⅜" 50.00
Vase, Rose Ice (lt marigold), Imperial, 8x6½" 70.00

String Holders

Today, if you want to wrap and secure a package, you have a variety of products to choose from: cellophane tape, staples, etc. But in the 1800s and even well past the advent of Scotch tape in the early 1930s, string was often the only available binder; thus the string holder, either the hanging or counter type, was a common and practical item found in most homes and businesses. Chalkware and ceramic figurals from the 1930s, 1940s, and 1950s contrast with the cast and wrought-iron examples from the 1800s to make for an interesting collection. Our advisor for this category is Larry G. Pogue (L & J Antiques and Collectibles); he is listed in the Directory under Texas. See also Advertising.

Black boy riding alligator, pnt chalkware, 1948, 9" 345.00
Black chef, pnt chalkware, 1950s, 6¼" 195.00
Bonzo, bl dog w/wht & red belly, pnt chalkware, 6½" 185.00
Bozo the clown, face only, pnt chalkware, 1950s, 7½" 295.00
Bride, wide brim hat, gr & wht dress, ceramic, Made in Japan, 6¼" ...110.00
Carrots w/gr tops, pnt chalkware, 1950s, 10" 145.00
Cat w/ball of twine, pnt chalkware, 6½" 95.00
Chef, pnt chalkware, mk Conovers Original 1945, 6x6" 245.00
Coca-Cola Kid w/Coke lid cap, pnt chalkware, 1950s, 8" 695.00
Corn (3 ears) w/gr leaves, pnt chalkware, 5½" 175.00
Donald Duck, face only, pnt chalkware, mk WDP, 8" 395.00
Dutch girl, pnt chalkware, 7½" 165.00
Elmer the Bull, employee's giveaway, pnt chalkware, 7½" 425.00
Emmett Kelly Jr, pnt chalkware, 1940s-50s, 8" 425.00
Fish, Goldie, pnt chalkware, ca 1950s, 6¾" 225.00
Gourd, pnt gr chalkware, Ellis Studios, 7½" 95.00
Howdy Doody, pnt chalkware, c 1950s, 6½" 495.00
Indian w/headband, pnt chalkware, 1950s, 10x7¼" 285.00
Jackie Kennedy, face only, pnt chalkware, 1960s, 8" 295.00
Jester, pnt chalkware, 1950s, 7½" 245.00
JF Kennedy, face only, pnt chalkware, 1960s, 8" 295.00
Lemon w/gr leaves & short stem, pnt chalkware, 1950s, 6¾" 165.00
Little Red Riding Hood, pnt chalkware, Bello, 1941, 9½" 295.00
Mammy, blk face & hands, plaid dress, ceramic, Made in Japan, 6½" ...165.00
Mammy, brn face, plaid dress, pnt chalkware, 1940s, 6½" 245.00
Mammy, scissors holder, rhinestone eyes, pnt chalkware, 1940s, 6¾" ...345.00
Mammy w/yarn ball, red dress w/wht apron, pnt plastic, 1940s, 6½" ..175.00
Marilyn Monroe, pnt chalkware, 7" 265.00
Monkey on ball of twine, pnt chalkware, 7½" 245.00
Monkey on bananas, pnt chalkware, 1950s, 8¼" 295.00
Mutt (dog), pnt chalkware, 1950s-60s, 6½" 185.00
Pineapple w/face, gr top, pnt chalkware, 1950s, 7" 175.00
Pinocchio, face only, pnt chalkware, mk WDP, 7½" 395.00
Pumpkin face, winking, ceramic, Japan, 5" 185.00
Sailor boy, pnt chalkware, Bello, Chicago IL, 8" 225.00
Santa Claus, pnt chalkware, 1940s-50s, 9" 275.00
Senora w/comb in hair, flower at ear, pnt chalkware, 1940s, 8" 250.00
Smokey the Bear, pnt chalkware, c 1957 NM, 6½" 425.00
Strawberry w/gr top, pnt chalkware, 1950s, 6½" 175.00
Tomato face, w/bl hat, pnt chalkware, Japan, 5½" 175.00
Woody Woodpecker, pnt chalkware, 1950s, 9½" 375.00

Sugar Shakers

Sugar shakers (or muffineers, as they were also called) were used during the Victorian era to sprinkle sugar and spice onto breakfast muffins, toast, etc. They were made of art glass, in pressed patterns, and in china. See also specific types and manufacturers (such as Northwood). Our coadvisors for this category are Jeff Bradfield and Dale MacAllister; they are listed in the Directory under Virginia.

Acorn, bl opaque 225.00
Alba, bl opaque, period top, Dithridge, 4¾" 120.00
Argus Swirl, pk (Peach Bloom) 250.00
Block & Fan, clear pattern glass 75.00
Bubble Lattice, bl opal 550.00
Chrysanthemum Base Swirl, cranberry opal 500.00
Coin Spot (9-Panel), cranberry opal (+) 325.00
Cone, bl opaque 150.00
Cone, pk cased, Consolidated, 5¼" 175.00
Consolidated Criss-Cross, wht opal 650.00
Cranberry w/8 panels, metal top, 6" 150.00
Daisy & Fern, cranberry opal, bulbous 450.00
Diamond Quilt on shaded butterscotch MOP, Webb, 4⅝" 500.00
Fern, cranberry opal 650.00
Flat Flower, gr opaque 400.00
Guttate, pk cased (+) 350.00
Guttate, pk satin 280.00
Hobnail (pressed), clear pattern glass 60.00
Leaf Mold, cranberry spatter 475.00
Leaning Pillar, bl opaque 95.00
Medallion Sprig, bl to clear 550.00
Netted Oak, milk glass w/decor, Northwood 125.00
Paneled Sprig, amethyst 275.00

Quilted Phlox, cased blue, $225.00. (Photo courtesy Randy Best, antiquesrbest)

Quilted Phlox, gr cased, Northwood 175.00
Reverse Swirl, bl opal, 4¾" 250.00
Reverse Swirl, cranberry opal 485.00
Reverse Swirl, wht opal 175.00
Ring Neck, cranberry & wht spatter 225.00
Ring Neck Optic, dk gr 250.00
Snail, clear 125.00
Spanish Lace, bl opal, wide waist, 4⅞" 250.00
Swirl, wht opal, bbl shape, 5½" 200.00
Swirl (9 Panel), gr opal 400.00
Twist (blown), gr opal 350.00
Venetian Diamond, cranberry 225.00
Windows (Swirled), bl opal 550.00
Windows (Swirled), wht opal 350.00

Sumida Ware

First made outside Kyoto, Japan, about 1870, Sumida Ware is a whimsical yet serious type of art pottery, easily recognized by its painted backgrounds and applied figures. Though most often painted red, examples with green or black backgrounds may be found as well. Vases and mugs are easier to find than other forms, and most are characterized by the human and animal figures that have been attached to their surfaces. Because these figures are in high relief, it is not unsual to find them chipped; it is important to seek a professional if restoration work is needed. It is not uncommon to find examples with the red background paint missing; collectors generally leave such pieces as they find them. Our advisor for this category is Jeffery Person; he is listed in the Directory under Florida.

Bowl, 12 figures perched on rim/peering inside, red/flambé, 2x7x5"...780.00
Box, boy finial, red/blk flambé, 3½x5" dia.. 65.00
Conch shell w/rabbit & boy, sgn, 5" L..300.00
Figurine, 2 Sumo wrestlers, sgn, ca 1920, 6¾x7", NM 1,440.00
Humidor, children at play appl on red, flambé top, child finial, 7x6"..240.00
Humidor, men appl on ridged red, wht flambé top, man on lid, 7", NM..480.00
Jardiniere, elephants in mtns, ivory/blk, flambé top, appl mk, 12x19"..1,560.00
Mug, elephant pr on cliffs appl on red, Koji/Koni cartouch, 5", NM.....135.00
Mug, sage in bl/wht robe/foliage emb on red, bamboo hdl, 5" 120.00
Pitcher, 3 monkeys, lg 1 pouring water on 2nd, red/blk flambé, 13", EX..360.00
Pitcher, 3-D dragon hdl on blk/red flambé, 6¼" 90.00
Teapot, 2 monkeys sharing peach on red, blk flambé top, rprs, 5", EX. 400.00
Vase, children on branch appl on ridged red, flambé top, 12x6" ..390.00
Vase, dragon/cloud/Ishiguro Koko seal appl on red, flambé top, 15", EX..1,320.00
Vase, lady w/flute/2 servants, moon shape w/house in opening, 12x10"..990.00
Vase, man holding up incense burner on red/blk, drilled for lamp, 10"..90.00
Vase, wht irises on red, blk flambé basket hdl, 8x7" 240.00
Wall pocket, crab figural, claws reach toward open mouth, tan, 9" W..180.00
Wall pocket, floral, wht/dk brn on red, elephant's trunk form, 10"...925.00

Sunderland Lustre

Sunderland lustre was made by various potters in the Sunderland district of England during the eighteenth an nineteenth centuries. It is often characterized by a splashed-on application of the pink lustre, which results in an effect sometimes referred to as the 'cloud' pattern. Some pieces are transfer printed with scenes, ships, florals, or portraits.

Bowl, Ship Caroline transfer, pk border, later production, 10½"..215.00
Bowl, ships & sayings in reserves, pk lustre, 4x11" 660.00
Covered dish, Sailor's Tear, chipped lid, 3½x4½" dia.....................275.00
Jug, Am ship/mariner's compass, blk transfer, 5¾" 180.00
Jug, Garibaldi, pk lustre border, hairlines, 5¼x7"............................85.00
Jug, ship/Peace & Plenty/Sailor's Tear, mc transfer, 9", EX...........600.00
Jug, 3-masted ship/pious verse/motto, pk borders, early 1800s, 7". 515.00
Mug, children at play, blk transfer, pk borders, 4"..........................240.00
Plaque, Duke of Wellington - 131 Guns, pk border, rpr, 8½x9½". 155.00
Plaque, Oriental scene, pk border, gr corners, 1¼x8½", EX......180.00
Plaque, Prepare To Meet Thy God, pk border, 8¼x9¼"................180.00
Plaque, Thou God See'st Me, pk border, ca 1830s, 9¼x8¼" 180.00

Surveying Instruments

The practice of surveying offers a wide variety of precision instruments primarily for field use, most of which are associated with the recording of distance and angular measurements. These instruments were primarily made from brass; the larger examples were fitted with tripods and protective cases. These cases also held accessories for the instruments, and these can sometimes play a key part in their evaluation. Instruments in complete condition and showing little use will have much greater values than those that appear to have had moderate or heavy use. Instruments were never polished during use, and those that have been polished as decorator pieces are of little interest to most avid collectors.

Alidade, Gurley, low post explorer model #580, +cover & case, $400 to. 500.00
Alidade, W&LE Gurley #584, EXIB... 395.00
Circumferentor, T Blunt London, silvered dial/rotating alidade, 9½" ...975.00
Clinometer, Reynolds, Birmingham England, 1767-81, VG 300.00
Compass, Abner Dod, brass, 5" silvered dial, 1800s, 14", +fitted case..2,585.00
Compass, Alex Mabon & Son, miner's dial, polished brass/wood, ca 1870.2,000.00
Compass, D Rittenhouse, 5¼" dial, brass, 8⅜x14½" 19,975.00
Compass, dry; R Merrill NY, gimballed brass case, mtd in 6x10x10" box..285.00
Compass, E Draper, brass, 4" silvered dial, lacquer rubbed/dk, 11" L..700.00
Compass, Edm Blunt, silvered needle ring/6" eng 4-quadrant card, 13"..3,410.00
Compass, J Hanks, 5¾" silvered dial/sights on wide shaped limb, 15"... 2,235.00

Compass, large American Benj Pike's Son, New York, ca 1880, some repairs, with box, $1,200.00. (Photo courtesy Dale Beeks)

Compass, Micheal Rupp, 5" needle, ca 1860, EX......................1,500.00
Compass, T Greenough, eng 4½" HP card, eng 1737, 8"..........2,115.00
Compass, T Kendally, brass, engine-trn medallion, 12", case & tripod ...1,880.00
Compass, table; 5" brass dial w/eng, fruitwood case w/geometric star.. 470.00
Compass, Troughton & Sims, 4" dial, brass arm, 14" telescope, EXIB.. 350.00
Compass, vernier; Benjamin Hanks, 6" dia, mahog/brass, 9x15"+case. 2,585.00
Compass, vernier; BK Hagger & Son, brass w/5½" dial, 10x15"+case.. 1,525.00
Compass, vernier; WE Young, 5" dial, brass hub & lamp, 14"......265.00
Compass, Young & Sons, 3¾" dial, brass, Pat 1875, 6x10"+case.. 585.00
Compass, Ziba Blakslee, brass w/5½" silvered dial, 9x15"+case.5,875.00
Heliotrope, Steinheil; Bausch & Lomb, ca 1910, EX 1,500.00
Level, combination; AS Aloe, ca 1923, 12", EXIB...................... 450.00
Level, dumpy; Buff & Buff, ca 1900, 18", EXIB 800.00
Level, dumpy; Keuffel & Esser, ca 1913, 18", EXIB 500.00
Level, staff; Adie & Sons, 7" telescope/vial/bull's eye level, EXIB...200.00
Level, wye; Buff & Buff, ca 1930, 18", EXIB............................. 600.00
Level, wye; Gurley, aluminum & brass, ca 1948, 18", EXIB 450.00
Level, wye; Keuffel & Esser architect's #5111, ca 1924, EX.......... 450.00
Level, wye; W&LE Gurley, silvered scale, leveling base, 18" L, +case.. 360.00
Miner's dial/theodlite, brass, 4½" dial sgn Willm Wilton, 10½" ... 590.00
Octant, ebony w/bone scale, 10" radius, EXIB............................. 500.00
Octant, Norris & Co, bone scale, ebony w/brass ft, 13"................ 295.00
Protractor, homemade, 12" dia glazed paper circle, sgn/1847, 24" L...650.00
Protractor, Thos Jones, brass, dbl-rotating index arm, 5¾" dia..... 295.00
Quadrant, J Bennett...MA, pewter scale, alidade w/trough, 8½" .. 585.00
Semi-circumferentor, birch w/punched divisions, steel needle, 10" L.. 120.00
Semi-circumferentor, brass, w/trough compass, mahog w/staff mt, 7½" ..355.00
Semi-circumferentor, scale 0-90-0, bubble level alidade w/N mk, 7".. 1,295.00
Sextant, Graham & Parkes, silvered scale, 2 sights, ca 1944, 9" .. 295.00
Sextant, J Sewill, 3 sights, 7 shades, mahog w/brass ft, 8½".........475.00
Sextant, London, oxidized brass w/silvered scale, 9", +case..........300.00
Solar attachment, Gurly, brass, rack & pinon focusing, 8" 765.00
Theodolite, att Benj Cole, 4" silvered dial, 9" telescope, EXIB....825.00

Theodolite, C Leach, sliding mica compass cover, 1792, 6" dia, +case ...2,470.00
Theodolite, E Draper, brass, 3½" dial, 2 verniers, darkened, 13"....2,350.00
Theodolite, eng Dearborne Pocket, brass, 8" dia 1,175.00
Theodolite, FE Brandis & Sons, triangulation w/sliding level, 1906, EX..3,000.00
Theodolite, T Cooke & Sons, ca 1890, EXIB................2,000.00
Transit, Berger, for calibrating aircraft compasses, 1950s, EX.......550.00
Transit, Gurley, Burts Pat Solar attachment, 4¾" dial, 15"+tripod...7,650.00
Transit, Heiseley & Son Harrisburg, plated brass, 6¼" dial, 14" .. 1,075.00
Transit, HM Pool, brass w/silvered dial, 11" telescope, w/tripod ..880.00
Transit, Keuffel & Esser, Y&S #5166 Special Survey, ca 1918, EX...695.00
Transit, Keuffel & Esser #5030, ca 1887, EXIB.........................2,000.00
Transit, Keuffel & Esser #5077, w/9" scope/compass & full circle, EX.875.00
Transit, Troughlon & Simms London, brass, 19th C, 19" in fitted case..350.00
Transit, vernier; Queen & Co, anodized/lacquered brass, 14¾"+tripod..650.00
Tripod, Keuffel & Esser, stiff legs, staff mt for compass, early, VG ...275.00
Tripod, Warren Knight, oak, stiff legs, ca 1920, EX 150.00
Wading rod set, Gurley's Hydraulic Current Meters #612/621/624, EX...225.00
Waywiser, J Beers, 21" dia spoked metal-rim wheel, 1974, 64" L...3,290.00
Wye-level, Sawyer & Hobby, 17" focusing telescope, 9" 210.00

Swastika Keramos

Swastika Keramos was a line of artware made by the Owens China Company of Minerva, Ohio, around 1902 – 1904. It is characterized either by a coralene type of decoration (similar to the Opalesce line made by the J. B. Owens Pottery Company of Zanesville) or by the application of metallic lustres, usually in simple designs. Shapes are often plain and handles squarish and rather thick, suggestive of the Arts and Crafts style. Our advisors for this category are Suzanne Perrault and David Rago; they are listed in the Directory under New Jersey.

Ewer, floral on bronze, flared bottom, #7042, 11"...........................210.00
Vase, birds on branch, wht, bulbous, slim neck, 9" 145.00
Vase, floral gold-tones & red, 3 buttress hdls, 7" 545.00
Vase, floral on gold neck, plain swollen bottom, 8" 200.00
Vase, gr & wht veining on gold, rim-to-hip hdls, 8" 200.00

Syracuse

Syracuse was a line of fine dinnerware and casual ware which was made for nearly a century by the Onondaga Pottery Company of Syracuse, New York. Early patterns were marked O.P. Company. Collectors of American dinnerware are focusing their attention on reassembling some of their many lovely patterns. In 1966 the firm became officially known as the Syracuse China Company in order to better identify with the name of their popular chinaware. Many of the patterns were marked with the shape and color names (Old Ivory, Federal, etc.), not the pattern names. By 1971 dinnerware geared for use in the home was discontinued, and the company turned to the manufacture of hotel, restaurant, and other types of commercial tableware.

Alpine, creamer, ca 1955-70, 7-oz......................................31.50
Alpine, plate, dinner; ca 1955-70, 10½" 24.00
Alpine, platter, ca 1955-70, 15" L 88.00
Bamboo, cup & saucer, ca 1950, 2½" 31.50
Bamboo, gravy boat w/attached underplate, ca 1950....................70.00
Bamboo, sugar bowl, ca 1950, 2¾" 37.00
Carmelita, cup & saucer, ftd, ca 1923, 2½" 36.00
Carmelita, plate, luncheon; ca 1923, 8½" 30.00
Coronet, bowl, rimmed soup; ca 1955, 9" 24.00
Coronet, bowl, vegetable; rnd, ftd, ca 1955, 8½" 56.00
Coronet, plate, dinner; ca 1955, 10" 24.00

Elizabeth, bowl, cereal; 6" 20.00
Elizabeth, creamer...23.00
Greenwood, cup & saucer, ftd, ca 1950, 2½" 31.00
Greenwood, teapot, ca 1950, 4-cup...................................125.00
Honeysuckle, bowl, cereal; 5" 22.00
Honeysuckle, platter, 12" L 64.00
Honeysuckle, sugar bowl..30.00
June Rose, bowl, rimmed soup; 8" 24.00
June Rose, plate, chop; 13" 80.00
June Rose, plate, salad; 8" 10.00
Magnolia, gravy boat w/attached underplate, ca 1960....................75.00
Magnolia, plate, dinner; ca 1960, 10½" 24.00
Milicent, cup, ftd, ca 1949, 2" 27.00
Milicent, platter, ca 1949, 16" L 116.00
Nocturne, saucer...6.25
Nocturne, sugar bowl...39.00
Portland, bowl, rimmed soup; 8" 18.00
Portland, plate, chop; 13" 78.00
Romance, cup & saucer, ftd, 2½" 26.00
Romance, plate, dessert; 7" 15.00
Romance, platter, 14" L 78.00
Romance, teapot, 4-cup..250.00
Royal Court, creamer, ca 1949-70, 3" 44.00
Royal Court, plate, dinner; ca 1949-70, 10"...........................42.50
Royal Court, platter, ca 1949-70, 14" L................................232.00
Selma, bowl, vegetable; 10" 30.00
Selma, plate, pie; 7" 10.50
Selma, saucer..8.00
Suzanne, plate, bread & butter; ca 1950, 6½" 10.00
Suzanne, platter, ca 1950, 14" L 45.00
Victoria, bowl, cream soup; w/underplate, ftd, ca 1949-70 ....36.00
Victoria, cup & saucer, ftd, ca 1949-70, 2".............................30.00

Syrups

Values are for old, original syrups. Beware of reproductions and watch handle area for cracks! See also various manufacturers (such as Northwood) and specific types of glass. Our coadvisors are Jeff Bradfield and Dale MacAllister; they are listed in the Directory under Virginia. See also Pattern Glass.

Acorn, pk opaque..300.00
Arabian Nights, canary opal..1,250.00
Artichoke, clear..75.00
Bubble Lattice, vaseline opal...800.00
Catherine Ann, milk glass...115.00
Coin Spot & Swirl, bl opal, Hobbs, ca 1890, 6"........................250.00
Cone, pk cased, Consolidated 325.00
Cordova, clear...135.00
Dahlia, amber...125.00
Daisy & Button w/Crossbars, bl...225.00
Diamond Spearhead, bl opal..650.00
Flora, bl opal 450.00
Grape & Leaf, bl opaque, 5¾" 325.00
Hobnail, vaseline, Hobbs, pewter top, ca 1883, 7" 325.00
Invt T'print, bl, Hobbs, ca 1883, 8"....................................250.00
Jeweled Heart, bl...350.00
Klondike, clear..200.00
Leaf Umbrella, mauve cased, pewter lid, rare..........................700.00
Loop, clear..90.00
Poinsettia, wht opal..400.00
Reverse Swirl, wht opal, Buckeye, 7¼" 275.00
Ribbed Pillar, pk w/wht spatter...375.00

Ring Band, custard w/EX gold 425.00
Royal Ivy, cased spatter, Northwood 750.00
Spanish Lace, bl opal 500.00
Sunken Honeycomb, ruby stain 275.00
Torpedo, ruby stain 250.00
Tree of Life, bl opaque, Challinor Taylor, ca 1890, 7".... 125.00
Wild Iris, milk glass w/yel & pk decor 200.00
Windows Swirled, bl opal 650.00
Zipper Border, ruby stain, etched.................................... 300.00

Target Balls and Related Memorabilia

Prior to 1880 when the clay pigeon was invented, blown glass target balls were used extensively for shotgun competitions. Approximately 2¾" in diameter, these balls were hand blown into a three-piece mold. All have a ragged hole where the blowpipe was twisted free. Target balls date from approximately 1840 (English) to World War I, although they were most widely used in the 1870 – 1880 period. Common examples are unmarked except for the blower's code — dots, crude numerals, etc. Some balls were embossed in a dot or diamond pattern so they were more likely to shatter when struck by shot, and some have names and/or patent dates. When evaluating condition, bubbles and other minor manufacturing imperfections are acceptable; cracks are not. The prices below are for mint condition examples. Our advisor for this category is C.D. Kilhoffer; he is listed in the Directory under Maryland.

Boers & CR Delft Flesschen Fabriek, lt gr, rare, 2⅝" 470.00
Bogardus' Glass Ball Pat'd April 10 1877, amber, Am, 2¾".......... 400.00
Bogardus' Glass Ball Pat'd April 10 1877, amber, hobnails, 2⅝".. 3,000.00
Bogardus' Glass Ball Pat'd April 10 1877, cobalt, 2¾", $700 to ... 800.00
Bogardus' Glass Ball Pat'd April 10 1877, gr, 4-dot variant, $1,200 to.. 1,475.00
C Newman, Dmn Quilt, amber, rare, 2⅝" 800.00
CTB Co, blk pitch, Pat dates on bottom, Am 175.00
Dmn Quilt w/plain center band, clear, ground top, Am 150.00
Dmn Quilt w/plain center band, cobalt, 2⅝" 210.00
Dmn Quilt w/shooter emb in 2 panels, clear, English 300.00
Dmn Quilt w/shooter emb in 2 panels, cobalt, English 500.00
Dmn Quilt w/shooter emb in 2 panels, deep moss gr, English 500.00
Dmn Quilt w/shooter emb in 2 panels, med gr, English.............. 375.00
Emb dmns, dk amber w/hint of red, 2⅝" 325.00
Emb dmns, dk cobalt, 2¾" 500.00
For Hockey's Pat Trap, gr aqua, 2⅜" 500.00
Glashuttenewotte Un Charlottenburg, clear, emb dmns, 2⅝"...... 500.00
Gurd & Son, London, Ontario, amber, Canadian 500.00
Hockey's Pat Trap, aqua, English, 2½"................................ 650.00
Horizontal bands (7), tobacco amber, 2⅝" 250.00
Horizontal ribs (2) intersect w/2 vertical, cobalt, 2⅝" 150.00
Ilmenau (Thur) Sophiehutte, amber, Dmn Quilt, Germany 320.00
Mauritz Widfords, honey amber, 2⅝", EX 500.00
NB Glass Works Perth, pale gr, English 125.00
Plain, amber w/mold mks.. 65.00
Plain, cobalt w/mold mks.. 125.00
Plain, dk teal gr w/mold mks, 2¾" 250.00
Plain, pk amethyst w/mold mks, 2⅝" 250.00
PMP London, cobalt, chip, 2⅛" 175.00
T Jones, Gunmaker, Blackburn, cobalt, English, 2⅝" 400.00
T Jones, Gunmaker, Blackburn, pale bl, English........................ 125.00
Van Cutsem A St Quentin, cobalt, 2¾"................................ 175.00

Related Memorabilia

Ball thrower, dbl; old red pnt, ME Card, Pat...78, 79, VG............ 800.00
Clay birds, Winchester, Pat May 29 1917, 1 flight in box 100.00

Pitch bird, blk DUVROCK.. 10.00
Shell, dummy, w/single window, any brand 50.00
Shell, dummy shotgun, Winchester, window w/powder, 6" 125.00
Shell set, dummy, Gamble Stores, 2 window shells, 3 cut out 125.00
Shell set, dummy, Winchester, 5 window shells........................ 175.00
Shell set, dummy shotgun, Peters, 6 window shells+full box........ 175.00
Shot-shell loader, rosewood/brass, Parker Bros, Pat 1884 .... 50.00
Target, Am, sheet metal, rod ends mk Pat Feb 8 '21, set 25.00
Target, blk japanned sheet metal, Bussey Patentee, London 50.00
Target, BUST-O, blk or wht breakable wafer 20.00
Thrower, oak wood base, heavy steel spring, leather wrap, ca 1900, EX .1,200.00
Trap, Chamberlain Cartridge...Nov 7th 05...USA, CI, 21½" L, EX.1,300.00
Trap, DUVROCK, w/blk pitch birds....................................... 125.00
Trap, MO-SKEET-O, w/birds.. 100.00

Taylor, Smith & Taylor

Producers of mainly dinnerware and kitchenware, this company operated in Chester, West Virginia, from about 1900 to 1982. Today collectors enjoy reassembling some of their lovely patterns. Some of their most collectible lines are Lu Ray and Vistosa (see also those categories), but many of their decorated lines are popular as well. Reville Rooster features a large colorful red and orange rooster on simple shapes; Pebble Ford is a plain-colored ware with specks of dark and light blue-green, yellow, gray, and tan sprinkled throughout. There are many others. They made advertising pieces and souvenir ware as well.

Autumn Harvest, bowl, vegetable; 8".. 17.50
Autumn Harvest, creamer 12.50
Autumn Harvest, cup & saucer, ftd..7.50
Autumn Harvest, plate, dinner; 10" 7.50
Autumn Harvest, sugar bowl, w/lid 15.00
Blue Bonnet, bowl, coupe cereal 7.50
Blue Bonnet, bowl, vegetable; 9".. 24.00
Blue Bonnet, cup & saucer 8.00
Blue Bonnet, plate, dinner; 10" 8.00
Blue Bonnet, sugar bowl, w/lid 15.00
Boutonniere, casserole, w/lid, 1¼-qt...................................... 24.00
Boutonniere, creamer 8.50
Boutonniere, cup & saucer 5.00
Boutonniere, mug 8.00
Boutonniere, plate, 6¾"...2.50
Boutonniere, platter, 13½" L 14.00
Bridal Wreath, bowl, fruit; 5" 7.50
Bridal Wreath, bowl, vegetable; 9" 22.00
Bridal Wreath, creamer.. 12.00
Bridal Wreath, plate, dinner; 10½".. 12.00
Bridal Wreath, platter, 13¾" L.. 25.00
Cockerel, bowl, rimmed fruit; 5½" 7.00
Cockerel, bowl, vegetable; 9" 20.00
Cockerel, coffeepot, 5-cup 45.00
Cockerel, plate, bread & butter; 6½"......................................4.00
Corinthian, bowl, vegetable; 9½" 22.00
Corinthian, chop plate, 11½" 40.00
Corinthian, cup & saucer 8.00
Corinthian, plate, dinner; 10½" 12.00
Corinthian, platter, 13½" L 24.00
Corinthian, sugar bowl 16.00
Golden Jubilee, bowl, dessert; 5½" 7.00
Golden Jubilee, bowl, vegetable; 9".. 30.00
Golden Jubilee, cup & saucer 15.00
Golden Jubilee, plate, dinner; 10" 14.00
Golden Jubilee, plate, luncheon; 9" 10.00

Melody Lane, bowl, vegetable; 9"...22.00
Melody Lane, creamer 12.00
Melody Lane, cup & saucer 6.00
Melody Lane, plate, dinner; 10" 12.50
Pebbleford, bowl, coupe soup; 6¾" 7.50
Pebbleford, bowl, vegetable; 8½" 12.00
Pebbleford, creamer 9.00
Pebbleford, cup & saucer 8.00
Pebbleford, platter, 11½" L 18.00
Pebbleford, sugar bowl, w/lid 12.00
Reveille Rooster, bowl, vegetable; 8" 18.00
Reveille Rooster, creamer 14.00
Reveille Rooster, cup & saucer 7.50
Reveille Rooster, gravy boat, oval 25.00
Reveille Rooster, plate, dinner; 10" 7.50
Reveille Rooster, platter, 13½" L 20.00
Reveille Rooster, sugar bowl, w/lid 16.00
Silhouette, cup & saucer, ftd 10.00
Silhouette, plate, luncheon; 9" 7.50
Silhouette, tureen, w/lid, 4½"x8" 65.00
Tulip, pitcher, bulbous, 7½" 30.00
Summer Morn, cup & saucer 10.00
Summer Morn, plate, dinner; 10½" 12.00
Summer Morn, plate, salad; 8½" 7.50
Summer Morn, platter, 13½" L 24.00
Summer Morn, sugar bowl, w/lid 18.00
Wheat, bowl, vegetable; 9" 12.50
Wheat, cup & saucer 6.00
Wheat, plate, luncheon; 9" 4.50
Wheat, platter, 13½" L 12.50

Tea Caddies

Because tea was once regarded as a precious commodity, special boxes called caddies were used to store the tea leaves. They were made from various materials: porcelain, carved and inlaid woods, and metals ranging from painted tin or tole to engraved silver.

Turned fruitwood, pear form, England, late eighteenth century, 6¼", $2,115.00.

(Photo courtesy Skinner Inc. Auctioneers & Appraisers of Antiques & Fine Art)

Burl walnut Regency sarcophagus form, domed lid, fitted int, 8x14x8"....865.00
Fruitwood Geo III apple form, lacks stem, SP lining, 1800s, 4½" ..2,000.00
Georgian silvered brass-mtd blk shagreen sarcophagus, 1800s, 6x9½".. 1,000.00
Lacewood vnr w/string inlay, fitted int, bone knobs, rfn, 5x8x5" ...1,950.00
Mahog & rosewood w/inlay, hinged lid w/conch shell reserve, 5x10x5"..765.00
Mahog bombé, inged lid, brass hdl, England, 1760s, 6½x10x6½"..2,100.00
Mahog vnr, brass bail hdl, keyhole escutcheon, 3-compartment, 6x10x5" ..575.00
Mahog vnr w/banded inlay, ivory keyhole escutcheon, 6x10x6" 375.00
Mahog vnr w/geometric inlay, 3-compartment, bone knobs, 6x10x5"....4,400.00
Mahog w/ebony & lt wood inlay, ivory inlay escutcheon, mask hdls, 12"....200.00
Mahog w/gilt quillwork & mini painting on ivory, 1800s, 5x8x4".3,100.00
Mahog w/hinged lid, brass hdl, 3 tin canisters, 5x9x5"......................475.00
Oak w/leaves & acorn cvgs, 3-compartment, Latin inscription, 4x8x4" ..400.00
Oak w/SP mts, sarcophagus form, ball ft, 1880s, 5⅛x7⅛" 600.00
Satinwood & burl w/inlay oval medallions, brass knob, 1790s, 5x5x4" ..650.00

Tea Leaf Ironstone

Tea Leaf Ironstone became popular in the 1880s when middle-class American housewives became bored with the plain white stone china that English potters had been exporting to this country for nearly a century. The original design has been credited to Anthony Shaw of Burslem, who decorated the plain ironstone with a hand-painted copper lustre design of bands and leaves. Originally known as Lustre Band and Sprig, the pattern has since come to be known as Tea Leaf Lustre. It was produced with minor variations by many different firms both in England and the United States. By the early 1900s, it had become so commonplace that it had lost much of its appeal. Items marked Red Cliff are reproductions made from 1950 until 1980 for this distributing and decorating company of Chicago, Illinois. Hall China provided many of the blanks. It is assumed that all pieces listed below are in at least excellent condition. Loss of the lustre, staining, crazing, or damage and wear of any kind will result in a much lower evaluation.

Bone dish, scalloped, Meakin 45.00
Bowl, vegetable; Cable, w/lid, Burgess 140.00
Bowl, vegetable; Fish Hook, bracket ft, Meakin, w/lid, 11x7"......175.00
Bowl, vegetable; Wrapped Sydenham, Shaw, w/lid, ca 1860, sm.... 95.00
Butter dish, Bamboo, Meakin, 4½x6"...165.00
Butter dish, Little Cable, Furnival..200.00
Butter dish, sq, ftd, Burgess 125.00
Butter pat, copper rim, Alfred Meakin 10.00
Cake plate, 8-sided, Adams Microtex, 11⅛x8¾" 65.00
Champer pot, Square Ridged, Mellor-Taylor, EX.........................275.00
Coffeepot, Basketweave, Shaw, 1887 ....295.00
Coffeepot, Lily of the Valley, Shaw, 1860s.................................395.00
Compote, fruit; ped ft, Royal Ironstone, Meakin, 5½x8½", NM ..375.00
Covered dish, ftd, Meakin, 5x6½" 55.00
Creamer, Fish Hook, Meakin, 5x5" 60.00
Creamer, flared, Mellor-Taylor, 3½"...90.00
Creamer, Morning Glory, Elsmore & Forster, lg............................285.00
Cup & saucer, Adams Mircrotex 25.00
Cup & saucer, handleless; Morning Glory, early 1800s..................95.00
Cup & saucer, handleless; Paneled, Shaw 95.00
Dish, Fish Hook, sq, Meakin, 4½" 35.00
Dish, oval, Shaw, 4½x6" 35.00
Gravy boat, ftd, Mellor-Taylor, 4½x7½" 120.00
Gravy boat, Laurel Wreath, Elsmore & Forster............................95.00
Nappy, Red Cliff, ca 1950-80...18.00
Pitcher, milk; Bamboo, Meakin, 7½"...220.00
Pitcher, milk; Lily of the Valley, 1860s.......................................225.00
Plate, Chinese, Shaw, 7⅞" 22.50
Plate, gold lustre, Bridgewood, 7" 12.00
Plate, Red Cliff, ca 1950-80, 8¼" 12.00
Platter, Brocade, Meakin, ca 1879+, 15x10½" 75.00
Platter, rectangular, ribbed, Wedgwood, 12" 75.00
Relish, Lily of the Valley, leaf form, Shaw, 2¼x5¾x8¾" 140.00
Sauce tureen, Bamboo, Meakin, w/lid & ladle.............................275.00
Shaving mug, Meakin, 3¼x3½" 185.00
Soap dish, Cable, Shaw 225.00
Soap dish, plain, Meakin, 3¾x5½" 35.00
Sugar bowl, Crystal, unmk, 1870s 225.00
Sugar bowl, Fish Hook, Meakin, w/lid, 6½" 190.00
Sugar bowl, Lily of the Valley, Shaw, 5½x6½" 145.00
Toothbrush holder, scalloped rim, Meakin, 4½" 60.00
Washbowl & pitcher, Fish Hook, Meakin.....................................300.00
Waste bowl, Burgess, 3x5⅜" 60.00

Teco

Teco artware was made by the American Terra Cotta and Ceramic Company, located near Chicago, Illinois. The firm was established in 1886 and until 1901 produced only brick, sewer tile, and other redware. Their early glaze was inspired by the matt green made popular by Grueby. 'Teco Green,' a smooth microcrystalline glaze, often accented by charcoaling in creases, was made for nearly 10 years. The company was one of the first in the United States to perfect a true crystalline glaze. The only decoration used was through the modeling and glazing techniques; no hand painting was attempted. Favored motifs were naturalistic leaves and flowers. The company broadened their lines to include garden pottery and faience tiles and panels. New matt glazes (browns, yellows, blue, and rose) were added to the green in 1910, as was a bright multicolored crystalline glaze called Aventurine. By 1922 the artware lines were discontinued; the company was sold in 1930.

Values are dictated by size and shape, with architectural and organic forms being more desirable. Teco is almost always marked with a vertical stamp spelling 'Teco.' Our advisors for this category are Suzanne Perrault and David Rago; they are listed in the Directory under New Jersey.

Lamp base, gr, tall leaves, 2-socket fixture, 20¾x9½" **2,645.00**
Pitcher, aventurine, sm nick, 4x5" **300.00**
Vase, bl matt, lobed, 5¼x3½" **900.00**
Vase, brn-gr, integral hdls, 5½x8½" **2,160.00**
Vase, buff, 4 full-height buttresses, rstr chip, 7x4¼" **1,550.00**
Vase, frothy dk brn, 4 buttress hdls, #175, 14x10" **3,000.00**
Vase, gr, beaker shape w/4 buttress hdls, rpr/burst bubble, 7¾" **3,600.00**
Vase, gr, bulbous, #250, 9¼x9¼" **1,680.00**
Vase, gr, calla lillies & ferns, #134, nicks, 13x5½" **3,000.00**
Vase, gr, dbl gourd w/4 hdls, WB Mundie design, 13¼" **14,000.00**
Vase, gr, floriform, 14x6" **4,500.00**
Vase, gr, full-height buttresses, 5½x3", NM **1,150.00**
Vase, gr, gourd shape, #661, prof rstr chip, 10x7" **4,000.00**
Vase, gr, gourd shape, 16¾x8" **4,000.00**
Vase, gr, rtcl narrow folded leaves, 11½x4½" **9,600.00**
Vase, gr, sq top, flared neck, bulbous base, rpr, 16¾x8½" **5,400.00**
Vase, gr, tulip shapes at rim, 12½x6" **6,000.00**
Vase, gr w/4 silver o/l buttresses mk Schreve, 10" **5,500.00**
Vase, gr/ultramarine, floral, 4-ftd, drilled, 18½x7½" **7,800.00**
Vase, mauve, rim-to-hip hdls, WD Gates design, #438, 11½" ... **2,000.00**
Wall pocket, gr, Asian medallion, 6½x5¼" **1,080.00**
Wall pocket, gr, F Albert design, rpr, 15" L **400.00**

Teddy Bear Collectibles

The story of Teddy Roosevelt's encounter with the bear cub has been oft recounted with varying degrees of accuracy, so it will suffice to say that it was as a result of this incident in 1902 that the teddy bear got his name. These appealing little creatures are enjoying renewed popularity with collectors today. To one who has not yet succumbed to their obvious charms, one bear seems to look very much like another. How to tell the older ones? Look for long snouts, jointed limbs, large feet and felt paws, long curving arms, and glass or shoe-button eyes. Most old bears have a humped back and are made of mohair stuffed with straw or excelsior. Cute expressions, original clothes, a nice personality, and, of course, good condition add to their value. Early Steiff bears in mint condition may go for a minimum of $150.00 per inch for a small bear up to $300.00 to $350.00 (sometimes even more) per inch for one 20" high or larger. These are easily recognized by the trademark button within the ear. (Please see Toys, Steiff, for values of later bears.) Unless noted otherwise, values are for bears in excellent condition. For character bears, see also Toys, Steiff.

Key: jtd — jointed

Bing, cinnamon mohair, long arms, 1920s, 17", minimum value.... **3,000.00**
Bing, copper mohair, glass eyes, jtd, excelsior stuffing, 1920s, 18" .. **8,000.00**
Bing, wht mohair, button eyes, key-wind skater, 1907, 8", VG . **5,000.00**
Bruin/BMC, button eyes, very early, 10" **2,000.00**
Chiltern, tan mohair, amber glass eyes, jtd, squeaker, 1947, 16" .. **325.00**
Columbia, Laughing Roosevelt, mohair, jtd mouth w/teeth, 1908, 20".. **2,350.00**
Gund, pk mohair w/lt snout etc, metal shield in chest, 1960, 15".. **250.00**
Hermann, chest tag, mini series from 1950, 5", minimum value.. **500.00**
Ideal, dense mohair, button eyes, growler, 3 claws, 1920s, 22", M .. **5,500.00**
Ideal, gold plush mohair, glass eyes, fabric nose, jtd, 1910s, 20" ... **480.00**
Ideal, tan mohair, button eyes, jtd, 1903, 18" **5,500.00**
Ideal, tan mohair, gutta-percha eyes, felt pads, jtd, 28", VG **900.00**
Russia, brn plush, button eyes, jtd, straw stuffed, 1930s, 16" **700.00**
Schuco, no felt on hands or ft, 1950-60s, 4-5", ea **20.00**
Schuco, skater, mohair key-wind, 1948, 9", minimum value..... **1,500.00**
Schuco, transitional style, 1930s, 12" **1,000.00**
Schuco, yes/no, caramel, glass eyes, 1950s, 5", NM **500.00**
Steiff, beige, glass eyes, 1970s, 9", EX **100.00**
Steiff, beige mohair, button eyes, felt pads, button, 1910s, 17½" .. **6,000.00**
Steiff, blond mohair, button eyes, embr nose, w/button, 1908, 16", VG. **3,600.00**
Steiff, cinnamon mohair, center seam, button eyes, jtd, 1905, 23" .. **14,500.00**
Steiff, glass eyes, 1918-22, 11½", G **1,200.00**
Steiff, gold mohair, button eyes, hump/silent, w/button, '05, 13", VG.. **1,800.00**
Steiff, honey mohair, button eyes, hump/jtd, w/button, 18", VG .. **3,000.00**
Steiff, lt brn mohair, glass eyes, fuzzy pads, 1950s, 9", EX **150.00**
Steiff, lt mohair, button eyes, embr nose, jtd, w/button, 1907, 14" .. **3,600.00**
Steiff, on wheels, brn grizzly type on all 4s, 10½" L, VG **950.00**
Steiff, shoe-button eyes, long-haired, orig button, 24", VG **4,450.00**
Steiff, shoe-button eyes, 1905, 16", G **3,525.00**
Steiff, tan mohair, brn glass eyes, sm hump, jtd, ca 1920, 9" **350.00**
Strunz, lt mohair, hump bk, jtd, jester outfit, ca 1905, 15" **3,350.00**
Uncle Remus, blond mohair, growler, 1906, 20", minimum value . **5,000.00**
Unmk, blond mohair, button eyes, embr nose, jtd, 1930s, 14", VG ... **120.00**
Unmk, brn mohair, glass eyes, sm hump, silent, ca 1900, 21½", VG.. **360.00**
Unmk, gold mohair, glass eyes/embr nose, hump/felt pads, 18" **950.00**
Unmk, tan mohair, bl glass eyes, swivel head/jtd, stock, 18" **600.00**
Unmk Am, tan mohair, glass eyes, orig ribbon, jtd, 1908, 21" **450.00**
Unmk English, silky mohair, glass eyes, squeaker, 1930s, 18", VG .. **475.00**

Telephones

Since Alexander Graham Bell's first successful telephone communication, the phone itself has undergone a complete evolution in style as well as efficiency. Early models, especially those wall types with ornately carved oak boxes, are of special interest to collectors. Also of value are the candlestick phones from the early part of the century and any related memorabilia. Unless otherwise noted, our values reflect the worth of examples that are working and in excellent original condition.

Automatic Electric #18, dial candlestick, 1919, rstr **250.00**
Automatic Electric #40, chrome trim, 1940s **135.00**
Automatic Electric #50, wall mt, aka jukebox phone, rstr **125.00**
Chicago Telephone Supply Co, oak wall mt, 25x9x14" **150.00**
Couch & Seeley, oak wall mt, poor finish/pnt loss, 32" **85.00**
Farr #6, oak wall type, battery operated, ca 1905, 32" **475.00**
Kellogg, cradle style w/rnd base, 1920s, rstr **200.00**
Kellogg, oak wall mt, side crank, dbl bells **200.00**
Kellogg Red Bar desk, rotary dial, bell ringer, 1937-53, rstr **125.00**
Northern Electric #5C, chrome payphone, rstr **225.00**
Stromberg-Carlson, blk candlestick, 10½", w/subset **175.00**
Stromberg-Carlson, oak wall style, working, EX rstr **235.00**

Telephone Pay Station, metal w/red pnt, wall mt, 1960s, 19".......... 260.00
Unknown mfg, desk type, all tin, mc enameling............................ 85.00
Western Bell, blk candlestick, pitting/pnt loss, 20th C 85.00
Western Electric, brass candlestick, blk receiver, 11½" 120.00
Western Electric #102, rnd base, #2 dial, 1920s, rstr 250.00
Western Electric #302, pnt blk metal, 1938-40 .... 125.00
Western Electric Trimline, clear plastic, rotary dial, 1967............ 300.00

Large Original Blue Bell Paperweights

First issued in the early 1900s, bell-shaped glass paperweights were used as 'give-aways' and/or presented to telephone company executives as tokens of appreciation. The paperweights were used to prevent stacks of papers from blowing off the desks in the days of overhead fans. Over the years they have all but vanished — some taken by retiring employees, others accidentally broken. The weights came to be widely used for advertising by individual telephone companies; and as the smaller companies merged to form larger companies, more and more new paperweights were created. They were widely distributed with the opening of the first transcontinental telephone line in 1915. The bell-shaped paperweight embossed 'Opening of Trans-Pacific Service, Dec. 23, 1931,' in peacock blue glass is very rare, and the price is negotiable. (Weights with 'open' in the price field are also rare and impossible to accurately evaluate.) In 1972 the first Pioneer bell paperweights were made to sell to raise funds for the charities the Pioneers support. This has continued to the present day. These bell paperweights have also become 'collectibles.' For further study we recommend *Blue Bell Paperweights, Telephone Pioneers of America Bells and Other Telephone Related Items, 2003 Revised Edition*, by Jacqueline Linscott Barnes; she is listed in the Directory under Florida.

Bell System, Peacock 200.00
Bell System/Central District...Printing Telegraph Company, Peacock ... 500.00
Bell System/Ches & Pot/Telephone...Associated Companies, Peacock . 250.00
Bell System/New York/Telephone/Company, ice bl.................... 130.00
Missouri/and/Kansas/Telephone/Company, Peacock 150.00
Nebraska/Telephone/Company, Peacock 350.00
Opening of Trans-Pacific Service Dec 21, 1931, Peacock .... open

Large Telephone Pioneers of America (TPA) Commemoratives

Bell Atlantic, cobalt w/wht swirls 60.00
Bell of Pennsylvania 1879 - 1979, lt purple .... open
Break-Up of the Bell System, emerald gr 50.00
First 50 Years NJ, Jersey Green 30.00
Laureldale Council 1959 - 1979, Peacock.................................... 25.00
Lucent Technologies, ruby red w/gold emb 50.00
Nevada Bell, blk.. 80.00
Region 10 Assembly, bl.. 100.00
Telephone Centennial 1876 - 1976, carnival................................ 35.00
75 Years of Community Service, pk... open

Small Commemorative Bells

(No emb), amber 125.00
(No emb), clear... 150.00
(No emb), cobalt 95.00
Bell System, cobalt.. 125.00
Bell System The Chesapeake - Potomac Telephone Company &..., ice bl .425.00
Ohio Bell, cobalt.. 75.00
Save Time - Telephone, cobalt... 100.00
Save Time - Telephone, ice bl 75.00
Save Time - Telephone, Peacock... 85.00
The Ohio Bell Telephone Company, cobalt 145.00
Universal Service, ice bl.. 75.00

Telescopes

Antique telescopes were sold in large quantities to sailors, astronomers, voyeurs, and the military but survive in relatively few numbers because their glass lenses and brass tubes were easily damaged. Even scarcer are antique reflecting telescopes, which use a polished metal mirror to magnify the world. Telescopes used for astronomy give an inverted image, but most old telescopes were used for marine purposes and have more complicated optics that show the world right-side up. Spyglasses are smaller, hand-held telescopes that collapse into their tube and focus by drawing out the tube to the correct length. A more compact instrument, with three or four sections, is also more delicate, and sailors usually preferred a single-draw spyglass. They are almost always of brass, occasionally of nickel silver or silver plate, and usually covered with leather, or sometimes a beautiful rosewood veneer. Solid wood barrel spyglasses (with a brass draw tube) tend to be early and rare. Before the middle of the 1800s, makers put their names in elaborate script on the smallest draw tube, but as 1900 approached, most switched to plain block printing. British instruments from World War One made by a variety of makers are commonly found, sharing a format of a 2" objective, 30" long with three draws extended, a tapered main tube, and sometimes having low- and high-power oculars and beautiful leather cases. U.S. Navy WWII spyglasses are quite common but have outstanding optics and focus by twisting the eyepiece, which makes them weather-proof. The Quartermaster (Q.M.) 16x spyglass is 31" long, with a tapered barrel and a 2½" objective. The Officer of the Deck (O.D.D.) is a 23" cylinder with a 1½" objective. Very massive, short, brass telescopes are usually gun sights or ship equipment and have little interest to most collectors. World War II marked the first widespread use of coated optics, which can be recognized by a colored film on the objective lens. Collectible post-WWII telescopes include early refractors by Unitron or Fecker and reflectors by Cave or Questar. Modern spotting scopes often use a prism to erect the image and are of great interest if made by the best makers, including Nikon and Zeiss. Several modern makers still use lacquered brass, and many replica instruments have been produced.

A telescope with no maker's name is much less interesting than a signed instrument, and 'Made in France' is the most common mark on old spyglasses. Dollond of London made instruments for 200 years and this is probably the most common name on antiques; but because of its important technical innovations and very high quality, Dollond telescopes are always valuable. Bardou, Paris, telescopes are also of very high quality. Bardou is another relatively common name, since it was a prolific maker for many years, and its spyglasses were sold by Sears. Alvan Clark and Sons was the most prolific early American makers, in operation from the 1850s to the 1920s, and its astronomical telescopes are of great historical import.

Spyglasses are delicate instruments that were subject to severe use under all weather conditions. Cracked or deeply scratched optics are impossible to repair and lower the value considerably. Most lenses are doublets, two lenses glued together, and deteriorated cement is common. This looks like crazed glaze and is fairly difficult to repair. Dents in the tube and damaged or missing leather covering can usually be fixed. The best test of a telescope is to use it, and the image should be sharp and clear. Any accessories, eyepieces, erecting prisms, or quality cases can add significantly to value. The following prices assume that the telescope is in very good to fine condition and give the objective lens (obj.) diameter, which is the most important measurement of a telescope.

Accessories from vintage astronomical telescopes often have collectible value by themselves. Spectroscope and micrometer attachments for Ziess, Clark, Brashear, Fecker, and Mogey telescopes are rarely seen. Eyepieces alone from many famous makers also may be found. Our advisor for this category is Peter Bealo; he is listed in the Directory under New Hampshire.

Key:
obj — objective lens

Adams, George; 2" reflecting, brass cabriole tripod 3,500.00
Bardou & Son, Paris, 4-draw, 50mm obj, leather, 36" 250.00
Bausch & Lomb, 1-draw, 45mm obj, wrinkled pnt, 17" 90.00
Brashear, 3½" obj, brass, tripod, w/eyepcs 4,500.00
Cary, London (script), 2" obj, tripod, w/3 eyepcs 3,000.00
Clark, Alvan; 4" obj, 48", iron mt on wooden legs 9,000.00
Criterion RV-6 Dynascope, 6" reflector, 1960s 500.00
Dallmeyer, London (script), 5-draw, 2½" obj, SP, 49" 800.00
Dollond, London (block), 2-draw, 2" obj, leather cover 290.00
Dollond, London (script), brass, 3" obj, 40", on tripod 2,900.00
Dollond, London (script), 2-draw, 2" obj, leather cover 450.00
France or Made in France, 3-draw, 30mm obj, lens cap 80.00
McAlister (script), brass, 3½" obj, 45", tripod 3,000.00
Messer, London Day & Night, brass, mahog handgrip, 2-draw, 1860s, EX .. 200.00
Mogey, brass, 3" obj, 40", on tripod, w/4 eyepcs 4,000.00
Negretti & Zambra, 2½" obj, equatorial mt, 36", tripod 2,500.00
Plossl, Wein, 2½" obj, Dialytic optics, 24", tabletop tripod 4,000.00
Queen & Co (script), 6-draw, 70mm obj, wood vnr, 50" 1,000.00
Questar, reflecting, on astro mt, 1950s, 3½" dia 3,000.00
R&J Beck, 2" obj, 24", tabletop tripod w/cabriole legs 2,500.00
Short, James; 3" dia reflecting, brass cabriole tripod 4,000.00
Student's No 52, altazimuth to equatorial, 36" focal length, w/stand .. 125.00
TB Winter...Newcastle on Tyne, brass, 17" on tripod, 42" L, EX . 650.00
Tel Sct Regt Mk 2 S (many maker's names), UK, WWI 120.00
Unitron, 4" obj, wht, 60", on tripod, many accessories............. 3,000.00
Unmk, brass, 2" obj, spyglass, leather cover, from $150 to 300.00
Unmk, brass, 2" obj, stand w/cabriole legs 1,200.00
Unmk floor-standing tripod type, brass, clear optics, EX 525.00
US Military, brass, very heavy, from $100 to............................... 300.00
US Navy, QM Spyglass, 16X, MK II, in box 220.00
Vion, Paris, 40mm obj, 3-draw, 40-power, leather, 21" 110.00
Voigtander & Sohn Wein, brass, 1-draw, tapered bbl, 31", EX..... 275.00
Wollensak Mirroscope, 1950s, 12x2" dia, leather case................. 300.00
Wood bbl, rnd taper, 1½" obj, sgn, 1800s 350.00
Wood bbl, 8-sided, 1½" obj, 1700s, 30" 1,500.00
Yeates & Son Dublin, brass, 2-draw, QA-style stand, 15x38" 575.00
Zeiss, brass, 60mm obj, w/eyepcs & porro prism, tripod............. 1,700.00
Zeiss Asiola, 60mm obj, prism spotting scope, pre-WWII 650.00

Televisions

Many early TVs have escalated in value over the last few years. Pre-1943 sets (usually with only one to five channels) are often worth $500.00 to $5,000.00. Unusually styled small-screen wooden 1940s TVs are 'hot'; but most metal, Bakelite, and large-screen sets are still shunned by collectors. Color TVs from the 1950s with 16" or smaller tubes are valuable; larger color sets are not. One of our advisors for this category is Harry Poster, author of *Poster's Radio & Television Price Guide 1920 – 1990, 2nd Edition*; he is listed in the Directory under New Jersey.

Key: t/t — tabletop

Admiral #19A11, blond wood t/t, 1948, 7" 100.00
Admiral #24A12, Bakelite console, 1949, 12" 85.00
Airline #94WG-3029A, blond wood console, 1949, 12" 60.00
Arvin #3160CM, mahog console, TE-276 chassis, 1949, 16" 40.00
Bendix #2020, mahog t/t, 1950, 12" 80.00
Cape-Farnsworth #3001-M, mahog t/t, 1950, 12" 50.00
Coronado #94TV2-43-8970A, mahog console, 1949, 10" 70.00
Delco #TV-121, blond wood console, 1949, 12" 65.00

DeWald #CT-104, wood t/t, 1949, 10" 100.00
DuMont #RA-109-A6, blond TV-radio console, dbl doors, 1950, 19" .. 70.00
Emerson #620, mahog t/t, 1948, 10" 120.00
Emerson #630, mahog TV-radio-phono console, 1948, 12" 65.00
Garod #10TZ23, blond wood TV-radio console, Catalina, 10" 140.00
Garod #1549G, blond wood console, 1949, 16" 50.00
General Electric #10T1, Bakelite t/t, 1949, 10" 125.00
General Electric #12C108, blond wood console, 1949, 12" 50.00
General Electric #24C101, mahog console, rnd tube, 1950, 24" 70.00
JVC #3100D, wht plastic transistor w/clock, Pyramid, 1978, 6½" .. 400.00
Meck #XB-702, wood t/t 1948, 7" 175.00
Motorola #12T1B, blond wood t/t, TS-53 chassis, 1950, 12" 75.00
Motorola #9L1, red leatherette portable w/lid, TS-18 chassis, 1949, 8". 95.00
National #TV-10T, mahog t/t, 1949, 10" 160.00
Olympic #TV-104, wood t/t, Cruzair, 1948, 10" 80.00
Olympic #TV-944, wood t/t, Beverly, 1949, 12" 75.00
Philco #B-350-HYL, yel plastic transistor t/t, 1982, 9" 75.00
Philco #51-T1-601, metal t/t, 1951, 16" 35.00
Raytheon-Belmont #22AX22, wood console, 1947, 10" 150.00
RCA #21-T-324, wood console, dbl doors, 21" 20.00
RCA #6T84, wood TV-radio/phono console, 1950, 16" 40.00
RCA #630TS, mahog t/t, 1946, 10" 175.00
Sentinel #412, wood t/t, 1949, 10" 60.00
Silvertone #125B, mahog t/t, 1949, 10" 75.00
Silvertone #9114, mahog t/t, 1949, 12" 55.00
Silvertone #9125B, brn Bakelite t/t, 1949, 10" 75.00
Sony #FD-42A, wht plastic LCD transistor, Watchman, 1989, 2" .. 55.00
Sparton, Cosmopolitan, TV-radio/phono console, 1949, 16" 125.00
Sparton #4918, blond wood TV-radio/phono console, 1949, 10" .. 90.00
Stewart-Warner #9054-B, blond oak console, mirror in lid, 1948, 10" . 135.00
Sylvania #1-247-1, mahog console, #1-231 chassis, 1950, 16" 35.00
Tele-King #710, wood console, 1949, 10" 70.00
Templeton Mfg Co, #TV-1776, wood t/t, built-in magnifier, 1948... 500.00
UST #T-507, wood projection TV-radio/phono console, 1949 .... 100.00
Zenith #G2340Z, walnut console, #23G24 chassis, Ensign, 1950, 12" .. 100.00
Zenith #G2420E, blond wood t/t, #24G20 chassis, Wilshire, 1950.. 170.00

Philco Predictas and Related Items

Made in the years between 1958 and 1960, Philco Predictas have become the most sought-after line of televisions in the postwar era. The Predicta line continues to be highly collectible, due mainly to its atom-age styling. Philco Predictas feature a swivel or separate enclosed picture tube and radial cabinet designs. The values given here are for as-found, average, clean, complete, unrestored sets, running or not, that have good picture tubes. Predictas that are missing parts or have damaged viewing screens will have lower values. Those that have the UHF optional tuner will have only slightly higher values. Predictas that have been fully restored in appearance and electronically can bring three or more times the stated values. Collectors should note that some Predictas will have missing parts (knobs, antennas, viewing screen, etc.). These sets and those that have been damaged in shipping will be very costly to restore. This is due to the fact that no new parts are being made and the availability of 'new' old stock is nonexistent. These facts have driven the cost of replacement parts sky high. Collectors will find it better to combine two sets, using the parts from one to complete the better set. Our advisor for Predicta televisions is David Weddington; he is listed in the Directory under Tennessee.

G4242 Holiday 21" t/t, wood cabinet blond finish 475.00
G4242 21" t/t wood cabinet, mahog finish.................................. 425.00
G4654 Barber Pole 21" console, boomerang front leg, blond 725.00
G4710 Tandem 21" separate screen w/25' cable, mahog finish..... 650.00
G4720 Stereo Tandem w/matching 1606S phonoamp, mahog .. 1,200.00
G4720 Stereo Tandem 21" separate screen, 4 brass legs, mahog .. 900.00

H3308 Debutante 17" t/t, cloth grille, w/antenna, charcoal......... 375.00
H3406 Motel 17" t/t, metal cabinet, cloth grille, no antenna 200.00
H3410 Princess 17" t/t, metal grille, plastic tuner window 400.00
H3410 Princess 17" t/t, orig metal stand, red finish 525.00
H3412 Siesta t/t, w/clock-timer above tuner, gold finish 575.00
H4730 Danish Modern 21" console, 4 fin-shaped legs, mahog finish.. 975.00
H4744 Town house 21" room-divider, walnut shelves, brass finish ..1,400.00
17DRP4 picture tube, MIB, replacement for all 17" t/t Predictas.. 275.00
21FDP4, picture tube, MIB, replacement for all 21" t/t Predictas.. 275.00

Terra Cotta

Terra cotta is a type of earthenware or clay used for statuary, architectural facings, or domestic articles. It is unglazed, baked to durable hardness, and characterized by the color of the body which may range from brick red to buff.

Bust, Abraham Lincoln, sgn Davidson, 1945, 10" 75.00
Bust, Dorine Maid of Orleans, Harze, 1880, 20¼" 780.00
Bust, girl w/detailed hair, after Houdon, 15x8x5", on marble plinth ..360.00
Bust, US Grant, c K Gerhart, Goodwin Bros, 1885 .... 425.00
Plaque, 6 putti w/lion, in manner of C Michel, 9½x18" 150.00
Sculpture, African man's head, dk glaze, unsgn, 12", EX 215.00
Sculpture, boy lighting cigarette, mc (fading), 1880s, 30" 1,200.00
Sculpture, Dutch girl w/flowing dress, R Miles, 10" 180.00
Sculpture, eagle on integral socle base, Fr, 19th C, 25x18" 1,950.00
Sculpture, eagle on orb, architectural finial, rpr, 20x29" 240.00
Sculpture, Madonna & Child, molded in full rnd, Austria, 1930s, 16" ..120.00
Sculpture, putto w/basket of goods, marble base, Paris 1735, 14½" ..575.00
Sculpture, seated putto w/fruit/flower basket, 20th C, 14", +wood base .480.00
Sculpture, Sysyphus, nude male, Art Deco, H Bargas, 12x20" ..1,325.00

Thermometers

Many companies have utilitzed thermometers as a means of promoting their products. From gasoline to soda pop, there are scores to choose from. Many were 'button' styles, approximately 12" in diameter with a protective, see-through dome-like cover and a sweep hand. Unless otherwise described, assume that the 12" round examples in our listing are of this design. Advertising thermometers were most often made of painted tin or metal; other materials will be noted in the description. Porcelain paint (abbreviated 'porc' in lines) is a glass material fused to metal by firing.

Decorative thermometers run the gamut from plain tin household varieties to the highly ornate creations of Tiffany and Bradley and Hubbard. They have been manufactured from nearly every conceivable material — oak, sterling, brass, and glass being the favorites — and have tested the artistry and technical skills of some of America's finest craftsmen. Ornamental models can be found in free-hanging, wall-mounted, or desk/mantel versions. American-made thermometers available today as collectors' items were made between 1875 and 1940. The golden age of decoratives ended in the early 1940s as modern manufacturing processes and materials robbed them of their natural distinctiveness. Prices are based on age, ornateness, and whether mercury or alcohol is used as the filler in the tube. A broken or missing tube will cut at least 40% off the value. Our advisor for this category is Richard T. Porter, who holds the Guinness Book of World Records certificate for his collection of over 5,000 thermometers; he is listed in the Directory under Massachusetts.

Key:
Cen — Centigrade   Rea — Reaumer
Fah — Fahrenheit   sc — scale
mrc — mercury in tube

Advertising

AC Spark Plugs, w/Coralox Insulator, glass face, 1940s, 12" dia, EX..310.00
Aunt Jemima's Pancake Flour, diecut cb string-climbing AJ figure, EX+.2,400.00
Barq's Root Beer, bottle center, pnt metal, #117A, 1960s, 26x10", EX.180.00
Borden's Ice Cream, Elsie-in-daisy logo on turq, 26", M.............. 550.00
Buick Motor Cars, Creekmore Motor Co, bl on wht, porc, 1915, 27x7", EX.225.00
Delco Engergizer, battery image w/United Delco, 36x8", EX 130.00
Doan's Kidney Pills, man holding bk at top, die-cut pnt wood, 21", VG .350.00
Dr Chase's Nerve Food, wht letters on bl, porc, 39x8", VG 390.00
Dr Pepper, Frosty Cold, Donasco, tin, 1957, 26x10", EX.............. 230.00
Dr Swett's Root Beer, bottle cap at top, tin litho, 17⅛x5", NM ...200.00

Ed Pinaud's Hair Tonic, extremely rare, 26x9", VG, $1,400.00. (Photo courtesy Wm. Morford Auctions)

EX-Lax Keep Regular, porc, 36x8x1½", EX+ 175.00
Gold Medal Oil, Long Life for Your Car, logo, 1920s, 12" dia, EX ..190.00
Gray-Seal Paint, It Cost Less To Paint With the Best, 12" dia, EX ..130.00
Hire's Root Beer, bottle shape, #BN-16, 1950s, 29", EX.............. 140.00
International Stock Food, livestock graphics on wood, TB Co, 47", VG ..745.00
Kasco Dog Food, It's Dog-licious w/bag, tin, 9" dia, EX 150.00
Keystone Seeds, The Original Legume Inoculator, blk on yel, 27x7", EX .190.00
Koch Bros, arched top/sq bottom, beveled rim, 21x5", EX 350.00
Mail Pouch Tobacco, wht/yel on bl, curved top/bottom, porc, 39x8", NM .250.00
Old German Lager Beer, red/wht/bl face, 1950s, 6" dia, EX+ 100.00
Orange Crush, bottle cap, Pam, 1959, 12" dia, EX 220.00
Ramon's Brownie/Pink Pills, red/gr on wht, arched top, wood, 21x9", EX...475.00
Red Crown Gasoline/Polarine, red/wht/blk, sq corners, porc, 73", VG...2,500.00
Royal Crown Cola, bottle on wht, emb tin, 13½x6x¾", NM 170.00
Royal Crown Cola, Enjoy RC, tin litho, 26x10", NM.................. 110.00
Royal Crown Cola, plaque above bottle, tin, 1960s, 13½x6", EX....180.00
Sauer's Flavoring Extracts, wood, arched top, 24x7", EX+ 1,050.00
Sun Drop Golden Soda, upside-down bottle, 27x7½", EX 140.00
Sylvania Radio Tubes, Radio Service, wht on gr, tin, 38x8", EX.. 130.00
Teem, lemon atop w/Teem, bottle, Donasco, 28x12", EX............. 250.00
Tom's Toasted Peanuts, bag image, metal, 1950s, 16x6", EX 165.00
Trico Wiper Blades, arc shape, red & blk on wht, 9x12½", EX 130.00

Ornamental

Birmingham, desk, cast metal Wm IV w/birds finial, 1836, 3" 360.00
Birmingham, desk, silver floral repoussé, easel bk, 1904, 3½", VG...70.00
Blk Starr & Frost, desk, silver w/emb floral, easel bk, #550, 5"..... 120.00
Desk, CI lion among foliage, Fah sc, mrc, easel bk, 7" 85.00
English, brass w/cast foliage/scrolls, mrc, 19th C, 6" 150.00
Fahr Reau, wall, bronze umbrella form, Fah/Cen sc, mrc, 14" L..... 72.50
FR, desk, lady leaning on ped thermometer, metal w/marble base, 6"...100.00
France, desk, gilt metal w/scrolls & 2 figures at base, 1900-20, 6" ...110.00
Gorham, desk, silver repoussé, Cen/Fah sc, mrc, ca 1891, 5½" 95.00
Grand Tour, desk, brass/CI columns (2) on reeded base, mrc, 8"... 275.00
Kerr, desk, Nouveau silver w/emb florals, rpl card/tube, 1900s, 7"...175.00

Pat Pend LVL (Candlestick Co), pnt CI w/molded flowers, Fah sc, 6" .300.00
Reaumer, after; desk, brass eagle finial, Cen sc, mrc, 11¾x4x2" 85.00
Turnbridge, Cleopatra's needle, cube & tesserae mosaic panels ... 100.00
Unknown, desk, brass columns (2), Fah sc, mrc, 19th C, 7¾" 350.00
Unknown, desk, brass monument form, Fah sc, mrc, 8½" 95.00
Unknown, desk, brass w/lady finial, ped base w/ornate ft, 19th C, 10" ...110.00
Unknown, desk, brass w/malachite panel inserts, 6x5" 235.00
Unknown, desk, metal steeple form w/marble inlay, Cen/Fah sc, 19" ...1,300.00
Unknown, wall, bronze w/cherubs/scrolls, Cen/Fah sc, mrc, 1900s, 10x4" ..215.00
Unknown, wall, rococo scrolls & flowers on gilt metal w/putto, 1920s ..180.00
Wall, brass Gothic Revival quatrefoil, Cen/Fah/Rea sc, 7⅝" 150.00

Thousand Faces

The name of this china arises from the claim that 1,000 faces can be seen on every dinner plate. Though the overall pattern is called Thousand Faces, there are several variations, including Men in Robes and Thousand Geishas. (The Immortals, a Satsuma style of china, is not considered to be Thousand Faces, although many people list it as such.) This china was made in the early part of the century and stayed popular through the 1930s, 1940s, and 1950s. Although few items are marked (many of them were brought into the country by servicemen), the ones that are carry a variety: Made in Japan, Made in Occupied Japan, Kutani, or other Japan marks. The tea/coffee sets are often found to serve four, five, or six people, many having dragon spouts on the teapot and creamer.

The two main colors are gold-face and black-face. As its name suggests, the gold-face pattern is primarily gold; it features rings of multiple colors with gold faces painted on them. This color has always been the most prevalent, and is today the easiest to find and the most popular. The black-face pattern has a background of white with rings of multiple colors; it has black faces painted on the rings. It's not as popular, and it's harder to find — even so, the two patterns command similar prices. Even though the gold-face is easier to find, many think it is the more striking of the two.

The blue and green patterns are rarely seen. In both types, the primary color has rings of the same color in varying shades with gold-painted faces and accents. As expected, these two colors command a higher price (for pieces in mint condition). Complete sets are rarely if ever found, but the component pieces that turn up from time to time vouch for their existence. There are other variations in color, such as the black-face pattern with black or cobalt blue rims, but the more popular variations are Men in Robes and Thousand Geishas.

Men in Robes is a striking variation with bursts of colors coming from the robes instead of the rings of color. There are usually gold accents and a ring of color around the rim. Often the faces are concentrated in one area of the piece while the other section is filled with robes, giving the impression that the men are standing.

Thousand Geishas is a striking variation similar to Men in Robes. The colors come from the kimonos worn by the ladies, all of whom have black hair in the true geisha fashion. The Thousand Geishas pattern may be found in various colors, including lighter shades. EBay is a good source of information regarding Thousand Faces china and its variations. Our advisor for this category is Suzi Hibbard; she is listed in the Directory under California.

Key: MIJ — Made in Japan   MIOJ — Made in Occupied Japan

Biscuit jar, Men in Robes, ftd, 8x6", NM, from $125 to 175.00
Bowl, serving; gold, Kutani, 2½x5", +plate & spoon, from $35 to . 50.00
Bowl, soup; Men in Robes, w/lid, Kutani, from $50 to 75.00
Cup & saucer, coffee; gr, MIJ, from $50 to................................. 125.00
Cup & saucer, coffee; Thousand Geishas, unmk, from $40 to........ 75.00
Dresser set, blk, unmk, tray+hatpin holder+jar+hair receiver, $250 to...550.00
Lamp, gold, unmk, 10½", from $125 to 175.00

Plate, blk, MIJ, 7¼", from $20 to... 45.00
Plate, Men in Robes, Kutani, 7¼", from $30 to 40.00
Plate, Men in Robes, unmk, 9½", from $30 to 45.00
Tea set, demi; gold, unmk, pot+cr/sug+6 c/s+tray, 17-pc, from $125 to..300.00
Tea set, gold, MIJ, 17-pc, from $150 to 275.00
Tea set, gold, rattan hdl, mk, 20-pc, from $175 to 250.00
Tea set, Men in Robes, 24-pc, from $200 to................................. 325.00
Teapot, Men in Robes, Shofu - MIJ, from $35 to........................... 50.00
Teapot, Thousand Geishas, mk, 6x7", from $45 to 85.00
Vase, gold, 5", from $45 to.. 70.00
Vase, Men in Robes, red/blk, mk, 2⅞", from $50 to 125.00

Tiffany

Louis Comfort Tiffany was born in 1848 to Charles Lewis and Harriet Young Tiffany of New York. By the time he was 18, his father's small dry goods and stationery store had grown and developed into the world-renowned Tiffany and Company. Preferring the study of art to joining his father in the family business, Louis spent the next six years under the tutelage of noted artists. He returned to America in 1870 and until 1875 painted canvases that focused on European and North African scenes. Deciding the more lucrative approach was in the application of industrial arts and crafts, he opened a decorating studio called Louis C. Tiffany and Co., Associated Artists. He began seriously experimenting with glass, and eschewing traditionally painted-on details, he instead learned to produce glass with qualities that could suggest natural textures and effects. His experiments broadened, and he soon concentrated his efforts on vases, bowls, etc., that came to be considered the highest achievements of the art. Peacock feathers, leaves and vines, flowers, and abstracts were developed within the plane of the glass as it was blown. Opalescent and metallic lustres were combined with transparent color to produce stunning effects. Tiffany called his glass Favrile, meaning handmade.

In 1900 he established Tiffany Studios and turned his attention full time to producing art glass, leaded-glass lamp shades and windows, and household wares with metal components. He also designed a complete line of jewelry which was sold through his father's store. He became proficiently accomplished in silverwork and produced such articles as hand mirrors embellished with peacock feather designs set with gems and candlesticks with Favrile glass inserts. Tiffany's work exemplified the Art Nouveau style of design and decoration, and through his own flamboyant personality and business acumen he perpetrated his tastes onto the American market to the extent that his name became a household word. Tiffany Studios continued to prosper until the second decade of the twentieth century when, due to changing tastes, his influence began to diminish. By the early 1930s the company had closed.

Serial numbers were assigned to much of Tiffany's work, and letter prefixes indicated the year of manufacture: A – N for 1896 – 1900, P – Z for 1901 – 1905. After that, the letter followed the numbers with A – N in use from 1906 – 1912; P – Z from 1913 – 1920. O-marked pieces were made especially for friends and relatives; X indicated pieces not made for sale.

Our listings are primarily from the auction houses in the East where both Tiffany and Company and Tiffany Studio items sell at a premium. All pieces are signed unless noted otherwise.

Glass

Bowl, centerpc; gold irid w/foliage intaglio, #T-1406, 3¾x12" ..2,300.00
Bowl, gold irid, scalloped, #1561, 2¼x10¼" 1,200.00
Bowl, pastel w/indigo morning glories on trellis, #2132P, 3x12½" ..4,200.00
Butter pat, gold irid, #G1478, 3" 165.00
Candlestick, cobalt irid, twisted stem, 5¼", ea............................1,600.00
Candlestick, thistle form w/brn patina, Engineers Club...1907, 8", ea .. 1,495.00

Candlesticks, gr opal w/opal laurel leaves, clear stem/ft, 4", pr.. 1,725.00
Champagne, Princess, gold irid, 8½" 865.00
Cocktail, moonstone opal, clear stem & ft, 4¼" 635.00
Compote, butterscotch irid, 5-scallop top, saucer ft, #4677, 4x6" ... 700.00
Compote, feathers, gr on opal w/gold int, ruffled, 4¼x5½" 1,675.00
Compote, gold w/gr tendrills, scalloped rim, 3⅛x8½" 2,000.00
Compote, Queen's pattern, gold irid, emb ribs, ruffled, 6x6¼" 750.00
Compote, silvery-bl irid, stretched ruffled rim, #8545E, 5¼x7" .. 2,645.00
Decanter, gold w/purple/red/gold irid, long neck, #1272, 9¼" ... 2,300.00
Finger bowl, gold irid, ribs, scalloped, 2¾x5" 345.00
Finger bowl, leaves & vines, gr on gold irid, #T4129, 2¼x4" 975.00
Finger bowl, Queen's pattern, gold irid, scalloped, +6" underplate... 925.00
Humidor, silver-bl w/cvd floret on lid, #6582J, 7¼" 2,875.00
Medallion, eagle over bell, gold w/rainbow irid, 1918, 2¾" 700.00
Pitcher, vines, gr on gold, cylindrical, #1257, 8¾x7¾" 3,500.00
Plate, turq & wht pastel floriform, 11" 1,025.00
Punch cup, gold irid w/purple int, #1157, 2¼" 285.00
Salt cellar, bl irid, ruffled, master, 1x4" 925.00
Stem, gold irid w/purple irid, 4" 575.00
Toothpick holder, gold irid w/appl tendrils, #W415, 2¼", EX 175.00
Vase, bl, elongated neck, #6578K, paper label, 6" 1,150.00
Vase, bud; hearts & vines, gr on gold irid, #6198E, 6¼" 1,380.00
Vase, feathers, brn on silvery bl, #9288G, 9¾" 10,350.00
Vase, feathers, gold irid on wht frost, slim, #9436M, 14" 1,035.00
Vase, feathers, gold on wht frost, invt trumpet form, #1414K, 10" ... 1,035.00
Vase, feathers, gr on gold irid, rnd shoulders, #Y8, 2¼" 1,325.00
Vase, floriform, feathers, gr w/aventurine on opal, #M2879, 15" .. 17,825.00
Vase, floriform; feathers, gr on clambroth opal, shaped rim, 12" ... 10,350.00
Vase, floriform; feathers, gr on opal, gold irid ft, 15" 9,250.00
Vase, floriform; feathers, rum/gold/opal on yel, bronze stem, 13". 7,000.00
Vase, floriform; gold, #1523-1348K, 7x2¾" 1,700.00
Vase, floriform; gold irid, gold doré saucer ft, #160, 21½" 2,300.00
Vase, floriform; wht opal to gold irid, clear stem/ft, #4536B, 12" ... 7,475.00
Vase, gold irid, trumpet form, #1832, 10" 1,035.00
Vase, gold irid w/pulled ribbon design at shoulder, #K1064, 13¼" ... 925.00
Vase, gold irid w/8 appl tendrils, #K2292, 4" 550.00
Vase, jack-in-pulpit; gold, ruffled rim, #1636H, 1900-10, 19½" .. 20,400.00
Vase, mc irid bands on whitened ground, experimental, ca 1900, 3¼" 3,000.00
Vase, paperweight; leaves, gray/rose/gr on bl-purple, #7989N, 7¾" ... 40,250.00
Vase, paperweight; purple & agate swirl, #7908N, 4" 1,075.00
Vase, peacock bl irid, #2604J, 10", NM 1,450.00
Vase, raspberry to opal, clear knop/ft, trumpet form, #1039P, 1886, 9" 1,600.00
Vase, red, sloped shoulder, #1078A, 5¾x3" 2,200.00
Vase, red, tall neck in Persian taste, blk ft, #2440, 11¾" 9,600.00
Vase, scallops, gold irid on gr, #Q6057, 2½" 2,300.00
Vase, silvery bl, baluster w/2 scroll hdls, #2985E, 9½" 3,750.00
Vase, turq w/olive appl rim, shouldered, #327E, 6½" 1,725.00
Window, transom; 49 in circle/flowers/jewels/border, 15x33¾"+fr ... 2,585.00
Wine, lav w/wht opal ribs, clear stem, ribbed ft, 8¼" 1,725.00
Wine, raspberry cup w/opal stripes, gr stem (hollow) & ft, 9" ... 1,375.00

Lamps

Lamp prices seem to be getting stronger, especially for leaded lamps with brighter colors (red, blue, purple). Bases that are unusual or rare have brought good prices and added to the value of the more common shades that sold on them. Bases with enamel or glass inserts are very much in demand. Our advisor for Tiffany lamps is Carl Heck; he is listed in the Directory under Colorado.

Key: c-b — counterbalance

Base, boudoir; leaves on cushion platform, #822, 10½" 1,600.00
Base, Seccessionist, bronze w/appl swirls, 5 ball ft, 18x13½" 9,000.00
Boudoir, gold 4¼" #13889 tulip shade; bronze std, 15¼" 3,500.00
Boudoir, silver roses shade; matching harp std, rpr, 10" 1,375.00
Candle, gold ruffled/stretched shade; pulled feather twisted std, 12" .. 1,850.00
Candle, tulip-form feather shade; bronze/glass tripod std, 17" ... 6,800.00
Chandelier, copper & mica, circular ceiling plate, 10¼x47" dia.. 2,280.00
Desk, Arabian, 7" etched gold shade; gr std, 14½" 5,400.00
Desk, damascene 7" gold shade; gold doré #418 captain's bell std, 12" 7,475.00
Desk, feathered 6" gold shade; bronze #419 harp std, 13" 3,000.00
Desk, Grapevine 6¾" shade w/blown-in gr glass; #2127 harp std, 13" .. 7,475.00
Desk, ldgl 18" Dogwood #1555-2 shade; bronze #363 std, 24" ... 48,000.00
Desk, Pine Needle 10" domical shade; bronze std, 17¼", EX 4,800.00
Desk, Zodiac bronze cylinder shade; wht glass diffusers, #668, 14" ... 4,000.00
Floor, damascene 11" gr shade; #582 harp std w/table/tray/etc, 57" ... 10,500.00
Floor, damascene 12" gr shade; #423H harp std w/pad ft, 58" ... 20,700.00
Hanging, rtcl 12" shade w/blown-out gr glass body; 3-chain hanger, 30" ... 13,000.00
Lily, 3-light, gold shades, bronze base, #320, 8½x8¼" 6,000.00
Lily, 3-light, gr feathers on opal shades; #28593 telescopic std, 21" .. 6,900.00
Lily, 3-light gold shades; mk bronze base, 12½" 9,000.00
Shade, candlestick; red w/gold irid shoulder, #1235, 7¼", EX ... 3,750.00
Shade, gr feathers w/gold on wht opal, stalagmite form, 13" 3,450.00
Student, dbl; gold irid 9¾" shades; Moorish-style std, 29", EX... 10,000.00
Student, dbl; opal 6¾" ruffled bell shades; bronze #28600 std, 26" ... 9,250.00
Student, dbl; platinum pattern on gold to gr bell shade; #318 std, 25" ... 11,500.00
Student, ldgl 10" acorn shades (2); bronze coiled rope std, 1905, 29" ... 21,600.00
Table, gold waves on yel irid #S3232 shade; organic #7818 std, 24" .. 25,875.00
Table, ldgl 14" brickwork #1421 shade; bronze #615 std, 14" .. 12,500.00
Table, ldgl 14" Sunset Tulip shade; 3-arm bronze Nouveau std, 21½" .. 40,825.00
Table, ldgl 16" acorn shade; bronze std w/3-light swirl cluster, 22" .. 10,000.00
Table, ldgl 16" apple blossom #1455-21 shade; hammered bronze std, 23" .. 25,200.00
Table, ldgl 16" apple blossom shade; 3-arm Grecian std, 22" ... 30,000.00
Table, ldgl 16" pomegranate #1457 shade; bronze #533 std, 22½" ... 19,200.00
Table, ldgl 16" pomegranate shade; jeweled #S1044 std, 22", VG+ 17,250.00
Table, ldgl 16" turtlebk-tile border shade; bronze std, #d font, 23" ... 48,000.00
Table, ldgl 16½" geometric #354 shade; simple stick std, 21", NM.. 12,000.00
Table, ldgl 18" leaf & acorn shade; 3-socket bronze #628 std, 26" ... 36,000.00
Table, ldgl 18" swirling leaves shade; bronze #0533 std, 21", EX... 20,000.00
Table, ldgl 18" swirling leaves shade; bronze #2128 std, 25", NM.. 32,000.00
Table, linen-fold 19" amber 12-panel shade; candelabra std, 22" ... 36,800.00
Table, linen-fold 19" amber 12-panel shade; gold doré #631 std, 22" .. 21,000.00

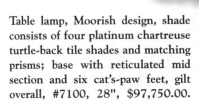

Table lamp, Moorish design, shade consists of four platinum chartreuse turtle-back tile shades and matching prisms; base with reticulated mid section and six cat's-paw feet, gilt overall, #7100, 28", $97,750.00.

(Photo courtesy James D. Julia Inc.)

Table, rvpt 16" acorn #1435-34 shade; Grueby std w/cinquefoils, 21" 29,000.00
Table, 8-panel 9½" shade w/emb floral; harp std w/8-panel ft, 15" 2,000.00

Metal Work

Grapevine and Pine Needle are the most sought-after lines — dependent, of course, on condition. In the following listings, items are bronze unless otherwise noted.

Ashtray, clipper ship emb on center matchbox holder, #303, 5x8" .. 865.00
Blotter, Grapevine, gr glass, 3x6" 360.00
Blotter ends, Pine Needle, #998, 12" L, pr 100.00
Blotter ends, Zodiac, #988, 19" 115.00
Bookends, Zodiac, gold doré, #1092, 6x5", pr 230.00
Box, American Indian, #1192, rare, 6" L 1,100.00
Box, Grapevine w/beading, gold doré, pull-out tray, #823, rstr, 9x6" .. 6,900.00
Box, utility; Grapevine, gr glass, rprs, 4x6½" 515.00
Candlestick, glass mosaic inlay, drilled, #L238, 7½x4½", ea 13,200.00
Candlestick, rtcl cup w/gr blown-out glass, #831D, 14½", ea 4,600.00
Candlesticks, gold doré, slim stem w/padded base, #1213, 17", pr .. 4,885.00
Clip, Zodiac, gold doré patina, #1080, 7¾x2¾" 250.00
Clock, Grapevine, gr glass, Riviere Studios, 5x4½" 550.00
Desk set, Zodiac, 2 inkwells+blotter+clip+2 trays+2 holders+scale .. 2,000.00
Frame, Grapevine, gr glass w/gr-brn patina, 9½x8" 3,450.00
Frame, Zodiac, EX patina, #943, 7x8" 1,550.00
Goblet, Thistle, parcel-gilt, ca 1907, 7¾x4¼" 900.00
Humidor, Pine Needle, gr glass, 2 lids, #1026, 7" 8,000.00
Inkwell, American Indian, #1183, 3½" 800.00
Inkwell, dull gold doré w/abalone, #1167, 2¾x4" 515.00
Inkwell, Zodiac, clear glass insert, #1072, 6½" dia 575.00
Note pad, Zodiac, #1090, rstr finish, 4½x7½" 230.00
Paper clip, Pine Needle, gr glass, #971, 4x2½" 780.00
Paper clip, Zodiac, gr/red/brn patina, #1080, 3½x2" 345.00
Paper rack, Grapevine, gr glass, 3-tier, #1008, 6x10" 800.00
Paper rack, 3-tier, EX patina, #1030, 8x12" 460.00
Paperweight, Pine Needle, caramel glass, 3¾" dia 460.00
Paperweight, Zodiac, #935/S1006, 3½x2¼" 635.00
Plate, flowers/leaves, pk & gr on gilt, #420, 84-11-19, 9¾" 1,150.00
Tray, gold doré w/HP dogwood & foliage, #420, 11" 2,075.00
Tray, Zodiac, #0970, 3¾" W.. 250.00

Pottery

Vase, dogwood blossoms emb on wht bsk, squat, #BP206, 9x14" .. 5,750.00
Vase, gr/amber/brn mottle, #P1233, 16x8½", NM 4,250.00
Vase, leaves emb, sheer amber on wht clay, rstr, 4½x2¾" 800.00
Vase, Nouveau floral w/shaped rim, pastel, 10", NM 1,325.00
Vase, verdigris, gourd shape, hairlines, 16¼x7½" 5,400.00

Silver

Key: t-oz — troy ounces

Basket, rtcl rim w/berries & leaves, 5x11", 39-t-oz 6,615.00
Bowl, floral w/rtcl along rim, ftd, gilt int, 5x12" 2,750.00
Bowl, scalloped & rtcl border, 9" 360.00
Candelabra, 3-branch, repoussé flowers/claw ft, 17", 110-t-oz .. 17,250.00
Candlesticks, cylindrical w/monogram, 1907-47, 5½", pr 235.00
Child's set, knife, spoon & fork w/nursery characters, 5-t-oz 600.00
Flask, flattened oval w/emb floral branch, 5-t-oz 1,550.00
Knife/fork set, 2-tine forks/knives w/serrated saw bks, 1900s, 16-pc .. 1,725.00
Plate, bl fleur-de-lis enameling at rim, 10" 425.00
Salver, appl floral decor at rim, 8½" dia, 14-t-ozs 325.00
Serving dish, acanthus leaves/pineapples, w/lid, 7x14", 51.5-t-oz .. 2,645.00
Tea set, ribbed bodies/scroll hdls, 5¼" pot+cr/sug, 23.7-t-oz 1,035.00
Vase, flower form, slim, ftd, 6", pr... 300.00

Tiffin Glass

The Tiffin Glass Company was founded in 1889 in Tiffin, Ohio, one of the many factories composing the U.S. Glass Company. Its early wares consisted of tablewares and decorative items such as lamps and globes.

Among the most popular of all Tiffin products was the stemware produced there during the 1920s. In 1959 U.S. Glass was sold, and in 1962 the factories closed. The plant was re-opened in 1963 as the Tiffin Art Glass Company. Products from this period were tableware, hand-blown stemware, and other decorative items. Those interested in learning more about Tiffin glass are encouraged to contact the Tiffin Glass Collectors' Club, whose address can be found in the Directory under Clubs, Newsletters, and Catalogs. See also Black Glass; Glass Animals.

Cadena, crystal, cup, #5831... 40.00
Cadena, crystal, decanter... 140.00
Cadena, crystal, finger bowl, ftd, #041 .... 25.00
Cadena, crystal, plate, #8814, 6" 8.00
Cadena, crystal, vase, 9" 115.00
Cadena, pk or yel, bowl, grapefruit; ftd, #251 .... 110.00
Cadena, pk or yel, candlestick, #5831, ea 50.00
Cadena, pk or yel, champagne, 6½" 28.00
Cadena, pk or yel, cocktail, 5¼" 30.00
Cadena, pk or yel, pitcher, ftd, #194 .... 300.00
Cadena, pk or yel, plate, 9¼" 75.00
Cadena, pk or yel, sugar bowl, #5831 .... 35.00
Cadena, pk or yel, tumbler, water; ftd, #065, 5¼" 30.00
Cherokee Rose, crystal, compote, #15082, 6" 52.50
Cherokee Rose, crystal, finger bowl, 5" 28.00
Cherokee Rose, crystal, oyster cocktail, #14198, 4½-oz 23.00
Cherokee Rose, crystal, pitcher, straight top, ftd, #14194, 2-qt .. 500.00
Cherokee Rose, crystal, plate, luncheon; beaded rim, #5902, 8" 15.00
Cherokee Rose, crystal, relish, 3-part, #5902, 6½" 40.00
Cherokee Rose, crystal, shakers, pr 160.00
Cherokee Rose, crystal, vase, bud; flared rim, 6-bead stem, 11" 50.00
Cherokee Rose, crystal, vase, teardrop, 8½" 75.00
Cherokee Rose, crystal, wine, #17399, 3½-oz 30.00
Classic, crystal, bowl, w/hdls, 8x9¼" 140.00
Classic, crystal, cheese & cracker set.. 95.00
Classic, crystal, plate, #8833, 8" 15.00
Classic, pk, creamer, #6... 90.00
Classic, pk, saucer champagne, 7½-oz, 6" 50.00
Classic, pk, tumbler, iced tea; ftd, 13-oz, 6"................................ 75.00
Flanders, crystal, compote, 3½" 40.00
Flanders, crystal, tumbler, ftd, 10-oz, 4¼" 20.00
Flanders, pk, bowl, bonbon; w/hdls 100.00
Flanders, pk, relish, 3-part 125.00
Flanders, yel, candy jar, ftd 185.00
Flanders, yel, plate, dinner; #8818, 10¼" 70.00
Fontaine, amber, gr or pk, cocktail, #033 .... 35.00
Fontaine, amber, gr or pk, plate, dinner; #8818, 10" 75.00
Fontaine, Twilight, plate, luncheon; #8833, 8" 30.00
Fontaine, Twilight, vase, bowed top, #7, 9¼" 250.00
Fuchsia, crystal, bowl, cream soup; ftd, #5831, 6¼" 50.00
Fuchsia, crystal, celery, #5831, 10" L 35.00
Fuchsia, crystal, compote, #5831, 6¼" 30.00
Fuchsia, crystal, nut dish, 6¼" 40.00
Fuchsia, crystal, plate, luncheon; #5902, 8¼" 15.00
Fuchsia, crystal, relish, 3-part, #5902, 6½" 30.00
Fuchsia, crystal, tumbler, old-fashioned; #580, 3½" 50.00
Fuchsia, crystal, whipped cream, 3-ftd, #310 .... 30.00
June Night, crystal, bowl, crimped rim, 12" 75.00
June Night, crystal, creamer 25.00
June Night, crystal, plate, sandwich; 14"..................................... 45.00
June Night, crystal, vase, bud; 10"... 45.00
June Night, crystal, wine, 3½-oz 20.00
Jungle Assortment, colors, bonbon, w/lid, low ft, #330, 5"............ 60.00
Jungle Assortment, colors, candy box, w/lid, 5½" 55.00
Jungle Assortment, colors, cologne bottle, #5722........................ 110.00

Tiffin Glass (continued)

Jungle Assortment, colors, shakers, ftd, #6205, pr 40.00
Jungle Assortment, colors, vase, wall; #320 .... 95.00
Jungle Assortment, colors, vase, 6½" 45.00
Luciana, crystal, bonbon, 5" 75.00
Luciana, crystal, plate, dinner; #8833, 10" 80.00
Luciana, crystal, sugar bowl, #6 .... 65.00
Luciana, crystal, sundae, ftd, #043 .... 22.00
Psyche, crystal, vase, bud 125.00

Miscellaneous

Basket, blk satin w/gold-lined parrot on branch, 1920s-30s, 10¼x4" ...85.00
Bath salt jar/vase, Reflex Green w/emb floral, 5½x6" 225.00
Flower box, pk satin, ladies dancing & w/instruments, 4x9¾x4"... 115.00
Lamp, Girl #E-3, pk, 1923, 10½", from $450 to 500.00
Lamp, Rabbit #E-8, brn on blk base, 1925-26, 8", from $1,400 to.. 1,600.00
Lamp, Santa Claus in chimney, mc fired-on pnt, 1920s, 10x4½" ..1,950.00
Paperweight, deep bl w/clear casing & int bubbles, w/gold label, 6"...125.00
Puff box, dancing girl, pk satin, #9313, 1924, 6", from $150 to.... 175.00
Vase, amberina satin on separate blk ped base, 6½" 60.00
Vase, blk satin w/coralene poppies, bulbous, 5½x5" 125.00
Vase, blk satin w/silver o/l leaf & flower, HP parrot, 6½" 250.00
Vase, Cellini, crown finial on lid, 13½" 175.00
Vase, poppies relief on blk satin, bulbous, 5½", NM 65.00
Wall pocket, bl, morning glory shape w/stem curling over top, 8", pr ..90.00

Tiles

Revival of the ancient art of tile-making dates to mid-nineteenth century England. Following the invention of the dust-pressing process for the manufacturing of buttons, potteries such as Minton and Wedgwood borrowed the technique for mass producing tiles. The Industrial Revolution market thus encouraged replacing the time-consuming medieval encaustic or inlay process for the foolproof press-molding method or the very decorative transfer-print. English tiles adorned American buildings until a good native alternative became available following the Philadelphia Centennial Exposition of 1876. Shortly thereafter, important tile companies sprung up around Boston, Trenton, and East Liverpool, Ohio. By the turn of the century, Victorian aesthetics began to give way to the Arts and Crafts style that was being set forth by John Ruskin and Thomas Carlyle and practiced by William Morris and his Pre-Raphaelite Brotherhood. Tile bodies were once more pressed from wet or faience clay and decorated in bas-relief or in the ancient Spanish techniques of cuenca or cuerda seca. The glazes adorning them became matt and vegetal, reflecting the movement's fondness for medieval and Japanese aesthetics. During the 1920s designs became simpler and more commercialized, but some important artists were still employed by the larger companies (for example, Louis Solon at AETCo), and the California tile industry continued to reflect the love of nature and Spanish Missions well into the 1930s.

Collecting tiles today means purchasing architectural salvage or new old stock. Arts and Crafts pottery and tiles are still extremely collectible. Important and large panels will fetch prices into the six figures. The prices for Victorian tiles have not increased over the last decade, but the value of California tiles, both matt and glossy, has gone through the roof. Catalina pottery and tile collectors are a particularly voracious lot. Larger pieces usually bring more, and condition is paramount. Look for damage and repair, as tiles often will chip or crack during the removal process. Our advisor for this category is Suzanne Perrault; she is listed in the Directory under New Jersey. See also California Faience; Grueby; Newcomb; Rookwood; other specific manufacturers.

AE Tile, Middle Ages man (& lady), gr gloss, 6", pr, EX 195.00

AE Tile, Middle Ages man w/lute (& lady), 3-pc, 19¼x7¼", pr, EX ... 395.00
California Art Tile, mission courtyard, candle sconces, 13½", pr ..1,950.00
Cecil Jones, Diana & Her Quarry, Art Deco, mc, 12x8¾", pr 840.00
Claycraft, CA coastline scene, 7½x3¾"+new Arts & Crafts fr...2,000.00
Claycraft, Conestoga wagon scene, mc, 8x16½"+fr 1,500.00
Claycraft, flowers in bowl in cuenca, mc on blk, sm flecks, 7¾" ... 725.00
Claycraft, landscape w/lg plant & mission beyond, mc matt, 7¾x4"+fr... 960.00
Claycraft, landscape w/tree, modeled, mc matt, 7½x3¾" 1,920.00
Claycraft, mission courtyard w/fountain, mc matt, rstr, 8½x6½" ...1,550.00
Claycraft, pirates on deck of ship, mc matt, 11¾x15¾" 2,150.00
Claycraft, Rocky Mountain road, mc matt, 12x4"+new Arts & Crafts fr.. 1,500.00
De Porceleyne Fles, cat perched on book, 8¾x4¾" 1,325.00
De Porceleyne Fles, deer hunt scene in snow, rstr, 4¾x17¼" 575.00
De Porceleyne Fles, flamingo faces right, chips, 12x4½" 550.00
De Porceleyne Fles, ostrich, mc, 5-color, nicks, 8x4" 360.00
De Porceleyne Fles, parrot, 12¾x4¾" 550.00
De Porceleyne Fles, peacock on brick wall, 13x4¾" 550.00
De Porceleyne Fles, swan facing right in cuenca, 4¾x8¾"+fr 495.00
De Porceleyne Fles, tiger leaping, sm amber border tiles, 5x13½" ...480.00
De Porceleyne Fles, wht rooster w/red comb on bl, 8¾x4¾"+fr ... 600.00
Flint, Arts & Crafts design, 6-color, 6" 90.00
Flint, court servant w/turkey on platter, nicks, 4¼" 265.00
Franklin, swan facing left, gr/bl/wht, sm rstr, 8½"+fr 415.00
Grueby-Pardee, Cheshire Cat perched in tree, 4½" 1,950.00
Grueby-Pardee, chick, yel on bl-gr, flakes, 4¼" 1,025.00
Grueby-Pardee, frog footmen from Alice in Wonderland, nicks, 4¼" .. 1,100.00
Hamilton, deer in forest, brn/gr/cobalt, nicks/rubs, 6x12" 300.00
Harris Strong, harbor scene, 4-tile frieze, 13x30"+fr.................... 165.00
Harris Strong, lady's portrait, 8-tile frieze, 24x12"+fr 645.00
Harris Strong, nobleman w/pointed beard, 6-tile frieze, 24x12"+fr ...195.00
Harris Strong, NY from East River, 12x12+orig fr 195.00
Hartford, eagle in dmn fr among foliage, mottled brn on gr, 6".... 515.00
Hartford, Eventide, pre-Raphaelite lady, mc, 13x7¾"...............6,000.00
Hartford, maiden seated in hilly landscape, mosaic panel in 19x13" fr. 7,800.00

Hartford owl with egg, period wooden box frame, 13x13", EX, $20,000.00.
(Photo courtesy David Rago Auctions)

J&JG Low, Nunovam Satis, old man w/bag, cobalt, plastic sketch, 6"..150.00
J&JG Low, violin player, amber, plastic sketch, 16½x10½" 1,920.00
Mosaic Tile, elephant on ball, advertising pc, chip, 6" 4,800.00
Muller, farmer sowing, mc matt, cvd, 12¼x6" 960.00
Paducah, pine branch, caramel & indigo microcrystalline, 6", pr....780.00
Providential, lady's portrait, amber, 6"+ornate fr 180.00
Rozenburg, Dutch cityscape w/canal, 12-tile panel, chip, 18x24"+fr .. 2,400.00
Rozenburg, mother/children at table, after Artz, 12-tile panel, 24x18" ...2,000.00
San Jose, cactus, mc, Mexican A & C mk, 8" 600.00
San Jose, man serenades lady, cuerda seca, 15-tile panel, 18x30" .. 18,000.00
Trent, cavalier holding flute, amber, 3-tile frieze, chips, 18x6"+fr ...300.00
Trent, girl's portrait facing right, gr-gold, ca 1890, 2⅝" dia............. 85.00
Trent, maidens (3) reclining, brn, 3-tile frieze, 6x18"+fr.............. 900.00

Tinware

In the American household of the seventeenth and eighteenth centuries, tinware items could be found in abundance, from food containers to foot warmers and mirror frames. Although the first settlers brought much of their tinware with them from Europe, by 1798 sheets of tin plate were being imported from England for use by the growing number of American tinsmiths. Tinwares were often decorated either by piercing or painted designs which were both freehand and stenciled. (See Toleware.) By the early 1900s, many homes had replaced their old tinware with the more attractive aluminum and graniteware. In the nineteenth century, tenth wedding anniversaries were traditionally celebrated by gifts of tin. Couples gave big parties, dressed in their wedding clothes, and reaffirmed their vows before their friends and families who arrived bearing (and often wearing) tin gifts, most of which were quite humorous. Anniversary tin items may include hats, cradles, slippers and shoes, rolling pins, etc. See also Primitives and Kitchen Collectibles.

Anniversary pc, hat, corrugated tin band & bow, old pnt, 5" H... 700.00
Anniversary pc, top hat, rust throughout, 6½x12"........................ 635.00
Anniversary pc, top hat, w/tin ribbon, 6".............................. 1,450.00
Candle box, cylinder w/punched stars, wall mt, 6x13" 350.00
Candle box, cylindrical, wall mt, old blk pnt, 6½x10½"............... 240.00
Candle box, cylindrical w/fan bk, wall mk, old gr pnt, 10x11"..... 240.00
Coffee roaster, cylindrical, long iron hdl, 18th C, 44" L............... 400.00
Coffeepot, gooseneck spout, brass finial, punched decor, lt rust, 11"..515.00
Coffeepot, gooseneck spout, padded hdl, punched decor, hinged lid, 11".. 1,450.00
Coffeepot, tapered cylinder, S Culver...1858...NY, 20x13x9".... 1,150.00
Colander, appl hdls, ca 1880-1900s, 5x7" 55.00
Colander, berry; heart shape, 19th C, 4x4" 300.00
Comb case, punched designs w/wood bk & fr mirror, 10" H 200.00
Infant feeder, conical, sm spout & strap hdl, w/cap, 4⅞" 300.00
Sconce, rnd w/crimped edge & emb decor, resoldered, 9⅛" dia, ea .. 480.00
Sconces, crimped arched/pierced bk panels, 19th C, 7⅞", pr 180.00
Sconces, crimped pans w/circular reflectors, 9¼" dia, pr.............. 575.00
Sconces, oval mirrored bks, 19th C, 15¼x7⅝".......................... 3,850.00
Sconces, semicircular base w/raised rings/folded rim, 11x8", pr.. 1,025.00
Strainer, cheese; punched heart shape, 3¼x6x5⅝" 240.00
Strainer, dmn shape, punched tin, possibly slave made, 4¼x9¼" ... 55.00
Strainer, oval w/fine mesh fitted strainer, hdls, 3x9½" 125.00
Teakettle, domed lid, bail hdl, 7½"... 50.00
Tinder box, rnd w/hdl & candle socket on lid, w/damper/striker, 4" ..300.00

Tobacciana

Tobacciana is the generally accepted term used to cover a field of collecting that includes smoking pipes, cigar molds, cigarette lighters, humidors — in short, any article having to do with the practice of using tobacco in any form. Perhaps the most valuable variety of pipes is the meerschaum, hand carved from hydrous magnesium, an opaque white-gray or cream-colored mineral of the soapstone family. (Much of this is today mined in Turkey which has the largest meerschaum deposit in the world, though there are other deposits of lesser significance around the globe.) These figural bowls often portray an elaborately carved mythological character, an animal, or a historical scene. Amber is sometimes used for the stem. Other collectible pipes are corn cob (Missouri Meerschaum) and Indian peace pipes of clay or catlinite. (See American Indian Art.)

Chosen because it was the Indians who first introduced the white man to smoking, the cigar store Indian was a symbol used to identify tobacco stores in the nineteenth century. The majority of them were hand carved between 1830 and 1900 and are today recognized as some of the finest examples of early wood sculptures. When found they command very high prices.

Unless otherwise noted, values are given for examples in undamaged, near mint condition. See also Advertising; Snuff Boxes.

Ashtray, cigar; clear crystal, Dunhill, 1¼x6⅞x4½" 75.00
Ashtray, Deco nude, chrome, at side of bl glass tray, FDC Co #4, 5"..110.00
Ashtray, hunting dogs emb on brass, England, 1930s-40s, 5½x3¼"... 50.00
Ashtray, man's face/wide mouth, ceramic, Down By...Mill Stream, 5½" .. 45.00
Ashtray, nude boys (3), bronze on brn marble tray, 4x6"............. 180.00
Ashtray, nude w/fans, chrome, at side of blk glass tray, 4½x5" 100.00
Ashtray, pheasants (2), mc on bronze, on side of onyx tray, 4½x7"..235.00
Ashtray, smoke glass, triangular w/3 rests, 3x10" 72.50
Ashtray, swordfish figural, metal, Clearwater FL, 6¾".................... 65.00
Ashtray, 3 brass trays remove from base w/SP horse at side, Ronson.. 78.00
Ashtray,laughing man's head, metal w/rhinestone eye/striker, 4½x3" ..60.00
Cigar box, Black boy on lid, wht metal figure on CI, mc pnt, 9" H..2,700.00
Cigar cutter, Amsterdam ship's wheel, brass, wheel turns, 5" 95.00
Cigar cutter, bullet shape, brass, 2"... 90.00
Cigar cutter, Dean's Havanas, pnt CI, clockwork mechanism, 5¼", VG+ ..1,150.00
Cigar cutter, Declarencia Havana Cigars, NP CI w/red enamel, 9"..600.00
Cigar cutter, elephant, bronze, 6½x10" 780.00
Cigar cutter, fish form, silver, US Tobacco, much detail, rare ...6,000.00

Cigar cutter, General Greene, cast iron, inner label, ca. 1890s, 7½x5¼x3¾", EX+, $2,400.00. (Photo courtesy Wm. Morford Auctions)

Cigar cutter, Grand Union Havana Cigars, NP, 1890s, 3x3½x2", VG...140.00
Cigar cutter, hunting dogs w/oak leaves & acorn, bronze, 6½" L... 100.00
Cigar cutter, King Alfred...on rnd CI clock face, ftd base, 13", VG+..2,300.00
Cigar cutter, lady's legs w/high-top shoes, metal w/EX patina, 1¾" ..115.00
Cigar cutter, Manhattan Girl, paper litho/glass dome/wood base, VG..745.00
Cigar cutter, monkey on top hat, brass................................... 120.00
Cigar cutter, padlock form, brass, emb detail, 4¼", EX 200.00
Cigar cutter, padlock form, brass, mk DBGM, 4"........................ 360.00
Cigar cutter, pig figural, Red Clover Havanna..., CI, 4½x8" 350.00
Cigar cutter, The Yankee, CI shield on stand, 7", EX................. 1,035.00
Cigar cutter, TTMA...5¢ Cigar, CI w/milk glass globe, 8½", EX....2,070.00
Cigar cutter, whiskey bbl w/tapper, CI, push lever type, 1910s, 4x5"..150.00
Cigar cutter, woman on chamber pot, brass 120.00
Cigar cutter, 3-hole countertop style, brass, London, 3x6¼" 90.00
Cigar cutter/dispenser, elephant, CI, old rpt, 1880s, 6⅛x11" 600.00
Cigar cutter/lighter, pnt CI elephant figure w/ruby glass lighter, VG ..3,450.00
Cigar cutter/lighter, silver gimbal & boar's tusk, 1870-90............. 725.00
Cigar cutter/lighter, Spanish Maid, pnt CI w/ruby glass lighter, EX ..2,585.00
Cigar holder, 3 joined cylinders w/hinged lid, silver, 2-oz............. 215.00
Cigar lighter, bear figural, NP metal, head removes, rpl base, 4½"..210.00
Cigar lighter, Black man's bust on taloned ft, brass, 10" 2,450.00
Cigar lighter, bulldog, copper-flashed metal, 5x4x2½", EX.......... 160.00
Cigar lighter, cloisonné font w/ft, 2 brass lighters/ruby shade, 11"...345.00
Cigar lighter, gr glass globe on ornate wht metal ftd base, 14", VG..115.00
Cigar lighter, lamp form w/Northwind face, brass, 5x6" 60.00
Cigar lighter, man's bust on claw ft, brass, 9¾" 240.00
Cigar lighter, poodle wearing top hat, CI, kerosene, 4x3x1½", EX..240.00
Cigar lighter, railroad conductor figural, wht metal, 7"................. 150.00
Cigar lighter, 1880s gentleman, metal, kerosene burner, 6½", EX ...300.00
Cigar lighter/holder, Black man sitting, copper-tone wht metal, 6" ..30.00

Cigar/match holder w/ashtray, Black minstrel figural, porc, 1900s, 8".. 150.00
Cigarette box, Nouveau lady w/flowers emb, Sterling silver, 4".... 850.00
Cigarette box, SP w/wood liner, Apollo, 2x7¾x3½" 20.00
Cigarette box, wood w/inlay, pop-out shelves, music box base, 1950s....60.00
Cigarette case, brushed & polished design on 10k rose gold 1,325.00
Cigarette case, diagonal design on 14k yel gold, push-button closure . 1,175.00
Cigarette case, Japanese damascene landscape w/flowers, 3½x2½".... 60.00
Cigarette case, silver w/eng decor, 1850s, 5½" L 215.00
Cigarette dispenser, donkey w/bundle on bk, pnt wht metal, 6"..... 85.00
Cigarette dispenser, man w/bow tie figural, Germany, ca 1925..... 600.00
Cigarette holder, stag figural, cold-pnt spelter, 10x9½", EX............ 36.00
Cigarette holder/music box, carousel form, porc, 15½x6" 180.00
Cigarette lighter, aquarium scene in Lucite, Dunhill, 1950s, 3x4".. 2,000.00
Cigarette lighter, Black Bartender, touch-top, Ronson, 7", NM.. 3,250.00
Cigarette lighter, burl walnut, Dunhill, 3x4¼" 235.00
Cigarette lighter, courting scene HP on silver, 1930s, 2¼x1½".... 660.00
Cigarette lighter, diagonal design on 14k yel gold, Cartier, 1⅞".... 515.00
Cigarette lighter, draped nude figural, electric, 1920s, 6½", VG+ ...275.00
Cigarette lighter, eng silver w/fiery opal inlay, Cartier #F23470... 360.00
Humidor, bear figure, cvd wood, hinged at shoulders, Swiss, 1910, 13"..1,690.00
Humidor, bearded man's head, bl cossack hat, majolica, 6"........... 70.00
Humidor, Black Chef, pnt bsk, #363LM, 1920s, 8½x5"............... 275.00
Humidor, boy's face emerging from tobacco leaves, ceramic, 5"... 155.00
Humidor, burlwood, 6-sided, Alfred Dunhill, 7x7½" 780.00
Humidor, dog's head, ceramic, brn, 6½" 165.00
Humidor, lion's head, majolica, Austria, 5"................................... 48.00
Humidor, man on recumbent camel, majolica, mc, 8¼", EX........ 215.00
Humidor, monk's head, majolica, mc, 9"..................................... 145.00
Humidor, walnut wood, revolving demilune holder/bin, 1900s, 8x12x7".. 725.00
Pipe, meerschaum; baseball player figural, amber stem, 19th C.. 1,450.00
Pipe, meerschaum; galloping horse, amber stem, 3¼x7½", +case .. 275.00
Pipe, meerschaum; nude lady, amber mouthpc, 7½", +case.......2,250.00
Pipe box, brn-pnt cherry wood, dvtl drw, brass knobs, 19th C, 21x5x4"..8,800.00
Pipe box, cherry wood, divided int, NE, early 1800s, 20x7x4"..1,100.00
Pipe box, walnut, scrolled top w/fan-cvd drw, rfn, 1800s, 19x5x4"...6,465.00
Store bin, Sweet Burley Tobacco, letters on yel, 11x8" dia, NM..200.00
Store figure, Indian brave, cvd wood, worn pnt, 57".................... 660.00
Store figure, Indian chief, cvd wood, mc pnt, 72"....................... 875.00
Store figure, Indian chief looking away, cvd wood, mc pnt, 1950s, 75"..1,100.00
Store figure, maiden w/feather headdress, cvd/pnt wood, 19th C, 61"....4,400.00
Store figure, maiden w/feathered headdress, cast lead, mc rpt, 31"...3,450.00
Tobacco blanket, Boston Braves, bright mc, 1914 .... 30.00
Tobacco blanket, Frank Chance, 1914.. 42.50
Tobacco blanket, Larry Doyle of NY Giants, 1914 .... 30.00
Tobacco blanket, NY Yankees, bl infield (rare), 1914................... 30.00
Tobacco blanket, Walter Johnson of Senators, 1914 .... 180.00
Tobacco card, female bull fighter, Honest Long Cut photo series, 1889 ... 18.00
Tobacco card, Hoffman of St Louis, Sweet Caporal #50, 1909....... 36.00
Tobacco card, Robt Byrne of Pittsburgh Pirates, 1911, VG............ 18.00
Tobacco card, Rube Marquard of NY Giants, Polar Bear, 1911.... 100.00
Tobacco card, Yerkes of Boston Red Sox, recruit bk, 1912 .... 24.00
Tobacco cutter, Master Workman, CI, 10½" L................................ 90.00
Tobacco cutter, Shamrock Smoking Plug, CI on wood base, 10¾" .. 120.00
Tobacco rug, University of PA, Fatima, 13x28" 215.00
Tobacco rug, 48-star flag, Federal Shields, 10½x15" 60.00

Toby Jugs

The delightful jug known as the Toby dates back to the eighteenth century, when factories in England produced them for export to the American colonies. Named for the character Toby Philpots in the song *The Little Brown Jug*, the Toby was fashioned in the form of a jolly fellow, usually holding a jug of beer and a glass. The earlier examples were made with strict attention to details such as fingernails and teeth. Originally representing only a non-entity, a trend developed to portray well-known individuals such as George II, Napoleon, and Ben Franklin. Among the most valued Tobies are those produced by Ralph Wood I in the late 1700s. By the mid-1830s Tobies were being made in America. When no manufacturer is given, assume the Toby to have been made in Staffordshire, nineteenth century; unless otherwise described, because of space restrictions, assume the model is of a seated man. See also Occupied Japan; Royal Doulton.

Lord How (sic) seated on sea chest, anchor at ft, Wood type, rprs, 12" ...3,100.00
Lord Howe seated on bbl w/jug, dog & pipe beside, R Wood type, 10"..6,400.00
Seated, holds bl lantern, spout in bk of chair, 9¼", EX................. 425.00
Seated, holds cup/jug, pearlware, red face, caryatid hdl, 10" 1,450.00
Seated, holds empty jug, pearlware, brn face, R Wood type, 10" ...1,650.00
Seated, holds jug, brn coat/blk hat, mk Walton, 10" 1,325.00
Seated, holds jug, defined laces, att Wood, rprs, early 19th C, 10" 1,100.00
Seated, holds jug, pipe at side, pearlware, R Wood type, 18th C, 10" ...900.00
Seated, holds jug & cup, gr coat/yel pants, figurehead hdl, 9" 550.00
Seated, holds jug & cup, pipe at side, R Wood type, 18th C, 9¾" 1,650.00
Seated, man on bbl w/bottle/tumbler, Rockingham w/gr, 13"..................2,100.00
Squire seated w/bulging eyes, arsenic glazes, R Wood, rprs, 11" ...950.00

Toleware

The term 'toleware' originally came from a French term meaning 'sheet iron.' Today it is used to refer to paint-decorated tin items, most popular from 1800 to 1850s. The craft flourished in Pennsylvania, Connecticut, Maine, and New York state. Early toleware has a very distinctive look. The surface is dull and unvarnished; background colors range from black to cream. Geometrics are quite common, but florals and fruits were also favored. Items made after 1850 were often stenciled, and gold trim was sometimes added. American toleware is usually found in practical, everyday forms — trays, boxes, and coffeepots are most common — while French examples might include candlesticks, wine coolers, jardinieres, etc. Be sure to note color and design when determining date and value, but condition of the paint is the most important worth-assessing factor. Unless noted otherwise, values are for very good examples with average wear.

Box, blueberries/strawberries on blk, yel border, 5½x9x5".........3,500.00
Box, deed; floral/foliage on dk japanning, dome lid, worn, 5½x9"...950.00
Box, deed; swags on blk japanning, dome top, 19th C, 6½x10" .. 1,200.00
Canister, chinoiserie/gold bands on blk japanning, 1850s, 13½x11"... 780.00
Canister, floral on blk japanning w/yel bands, press-on lid, 7x6" dia... 300.00
Canister, stenciled landscape/flowers on blk japanning, 18x11" dia.... 480.00
Coffeepot, apples/lt gr foliage on blk, str spout, C-hdl, 9", NM... 6,000.00
Coffeepot, fruit, red/etc on blk, flaring sides, 10½", EX 4,500.00
Coffeepot, fruit/flowers, blk/dk red on red, dome lid, 11" 4,500.00
Coffeepot, pomegranate band, yel on red, 2nd band under dome lid, 11".. 2,700.00
Creamer, stylized balls, red/pk on blk, w/lid, flakes, 4¼" 275.00
Tea caddy, stylized decor, blk/yel on red, 4¼x3½x2¾", EX 1,175.00
Teapot, floral, mc on blk, hinged lid, pnt losses, 5½" 325.00
Teapot, red & blk marbled w/Greek key border, urn form, 1820s, 9½" ...500.00
Tray, bread; floral border/mc on blk japanning, 12½x7⅞"............. 780.00
Tray, bread; floral on blk w/yel band, flaking pnt, 4x12x8" 395.00
Tray, floral on red, 19th C, 26½" dia.. 725.00
Tray, floral/leaf motif, 3-color on blk, wht hdls, 14x8", EX+ 5,100.00
Tray, peacock & flowers on blk japanning w/gold, hdls, 22x16"...230.00

Tools

Before the Civil War, tools for the most part were handmade. Some were primitive to the point of crudeness, while others reflected the skill of those who took pride in their trade. Increasing demand for quality tools and the dawning of the age of industrialization resulted in tools that were mass produced. Factors important in evaluating antique tools are scarcity, usefulness, and portability. Those with a manufacturer's mark are worth more than unmarked items. When no condition is indicated, the items listed here are assumed to be in excellent condition. For more information, we recommend *Antique Tools* by Kathryn McNerney (Collector Books). See also Keen Kutter; Winchester.

Key: tpi — teeth per inch

Adz, carpenter's; True Temper, polled, 4" blade, 10" hdl, VG 75.00
Bevel, sliding T; Stanley #25, gold letters on rosewood hdl, 10", NM..37.50
Chisel, OH Tool Co, ¾-corner, 8" blade, 16½", VG+ 65.00
Chisel, Stanley #50 Everlasting, ½" bevel-edge butt, 8¾", VG 75.00
Chisel, Zenith, 1" bevel-edge socket firmer, 6½" blade, 14", EX..... 50.00
Draw knife, OH Tool Co, laminated blade, folding hdls, 8", EX.... 85.00
Draw knife, Whitherby, laminated blade, ebonized hdls, 6", VG... 35.00
Drill, breast; Millers Falls #120B, 2-speed, 3-jaw chuck, NM......... 55.00
Drill, hand; Goodell Pratt #4½, 3-jaw, Pat Aug 13 1895, VG........ 50.00
Gauge, marking; Stanley #65, boxwood, sweetheart logo, NM...... 32.50
Gouge, Buck Brothers #8, 1/16" med sweep, VG.............................. 32.50
Gouge, Herring Bros #3, ⅝", EX.. 35.00
Hammer, claw; D Maydole, orig hdl, 10-oz, EX 45.00
Hammer, plumb claw; Signature, orig hdl, 13-oz, VG 32.00
Hammer, tack; Capewell, spring-loaded puller, Pat Nov 25 1873, EX...80.00
Hatchet, Stanley, 1¼-lb, 2¾" blade, 13½", VG.............................. 35.00
Level, Goodell Pratt, CI, rnded ends, EX japanning.................... 200.00
Nippers, Sargent & Co, Bernard's Pat, 6", EX+ 32.50
Nippers, W Schollhorn, Bernard's Pat Oct 24 1899, EX NP, EX.... 30.00
Plane, block; Fulton #102, NM japanning...................................... 30.00
Plane, block; Stanley #9½, adjustable throat & cutter, NMIB 90.00
Plane, circular; Stanley #113, Type 1, Pat 1876/1877, VG........... 235.00
Plane, jack; Stanley #5C, type 11, T trademk, rosewood hdl, EX....100.00
Plane, jointer; Stanley #8, full-length cutter, rosewood hdl, EX... 200.00
Plane, jointer; Union Mfg #X-8, mahog hdl, Pat 12/8/(19)03, EX... 285.00
Plane, smooth; Stanley #4, rosewood hdl, Pat 1910, NM japanning..115.00
Plane, smooth; Stanley #4½, type 11, Pat 1902/1910, VG........... 120.00
Plumb bob, K&E #6482, long neck, 16-oz, VG 45.00
Router, Stanley #17, open throat, ebonized hdls, Made in USA, 1950s, M..110.00
Rule, Rabone #1167, boxwood, 4-fold w/rnd joint, 24", M 45.00
Rule, zigzag extension; Lufkin #X46, brass slide, 72", NM............. 32.50
Saw, docking; Disston #498, 4½" tpi, 30", VG............................... 60.00
Saw, rip; Geo Bishop & Co #B-80, 5½ tpi, 28", EX...................... 145.00
Saw set, Morrill's Pat, for handsaws/panel saws, Pats 1887/1890, VG.. 12.50
Saw vice, unmk, 9½" jaws, lt duty, cam-lock jaws, VG.................. 40.00
Scraper, cabinet; Stanley #82, 2 cutters, NM................................. 55.00
Spoke shave, Crescent, flat bottom, loop hdls, VG japanning 45.00
Spoke shave, Phelps Bros, NP brass, flat bottom, 3¾" L, VG 85.00
Spoke shave, Stanley #67 Universal, rnd sole, removable hdls, EX .. 85.00
Square, combo; Fitchburg Tool Co, w/level & scribe, 12", VG 25.00
Square, take-down framing; Eagle Square Mfg, Pat 1894/1899, VG ..175.00
Square, try/miter; Stanley #1, NP, sweetheart mk, 6", VG 25.00
Wrench, buggy; Diamond Wrench Co, Pat Nov 2 80, pitting, 12", G...40.00
Wrench, crescent; Challenger, 4", NM 25.00
Wrench, pipe; Sheffy Mfg Chicago, self-adjust, Pat'd Jan 24 1896, VG. 125.00

Toothbrush Holders

Most of the collectible toothbrush holders were made in prewar Japan and were modeled after popular comic strip, Disney, and nursery rhyme characters. Since many were made of bisque and decorated with unfired paint, it's not uncommon to find them in less-than-perfect paint, a factor you must consider when attempting to assess their values.

Bashful dwarf, mc bsk, holder behind, Disney Foreign mk, EX 65.00
Bellboy w/2 suitcases, mc lustre, unmk Japan, 4½x5", EX 95.00
Bonzo, cold-pnt porc, Occupied Japan, 1945-53, 3¾x3¼"............. 60.00
Boston terrier w/circus collar, ceramic, sm rpt, Germany, 3½" 100.00
Boy stands w/hand in pocket, mc lustre, Made in Germany, 4¼x2⅜"... 825.00
Comic golfer, bag is holder, mc pnt, Germany, #1552, ca 1925, 8½".. 80.00
Dick Whitting sits on marker: To London 10 Miles, Japan, 4¾".... 85.00
Dog, yel & gr, ceramic, Goebel, T718/0, 4x1½x1¾"...................... 60.00
Donald between Mickey & Minnie, base tray, pnt bsk, WD/Japan, EX... 270.00

Donald Duck (long-billed), double figure, $420.00. (Photo courtesy Morphy Auctions/LiveAuctioneers.com)

Fiddler pig in sailor suit, ceramic, Walt Disney Foreign, 1930s?, 4½" .140.00
Genie w/sword & Black face, stands w/toothpaste box behind, 6" ..235.00
Girl w/puzzled look stands by holder, mc lustre, Germany, #176, 4⅜" .. 80.00
Mickey & Minnie Mouse, pnt bsk, W Disney, Japan, 4½x3¾", EX.210.00
Mickey & Minnie Mouse on couch, dog at ft, pnt bsk 220.00
Mickey & Minnie Mouse stand arm-in-arm, pnt bsk, 1930s, 4½", EX ...270.00
Mickey Mouse holds handkerchief to Pluto's nose, ceramic, MIJ, 4¾" ..240.00
Penguin, holds 3 brushes, tray at ft, Made in Japan, 5½"............... 60.00
Pirate, holds 2 brushes, tray at ft, lt wear, Japan, 5¼", EX 60.00
Popeye the Sailor, pnt bsk, King Features/Chein, missing pipe, 1932 ... 120.00
Skeezix, man & boy, mc, ceramic, 5", EX 60.00
Sleepy & Dopey before fence, mc, ceramic, Disney, 1938, EX 215.00
Wire-haired terrier w/bellhop toothpowder shaker hat, Germany, 4½" .. 210.00
3 Little Pigs w/instruments, ceramic, pnt wear, 3" 55.00

Toothpick Holders

Once common on every table, the toothpick holder was relegated to the china cabinet near the turn of the century. Fortunately, this contributed to their survival. As a result, many are available to collectors today. Because they are small and easily displayed, they are very popular collectibles. They come in a wide range of prices to fit every budget. Many have been reproduced and, unfortunately, are being offered for sale right along with the originals. These 'repros' should be priced in the $10.00 to $30.00 range. Unless you're sure of what you're buying, choose a reputable dealer. In addition to pattern glass, you'll find examples in china, bisque, art glass, and various metals. For further information we recommend *Glass Toothpick Holders* by Neila and Tom Bredehoft and Jo and Bob Sanford (Collector Books), and *China Toothpick Holders* by Judy Knauer and Sandra Raymond (Schiffer). Examples in the listings that follow are glass, unless noted otherwise, and clear unless a color is mentioned in the description. See also specific companies (such as Northwood) and types of glassware (such as Burmese, cranberry, etc.).

Glass

Alexis (Fostoria) 50.00
Bead Swag, milk glass 50.00
Bead Swag, vaseline... 85.00
Beaded Grape, gr.. 65.00
Beaumont's Columbia, ruby stain 75.00

Belladonna, ruby stain 55.00
Beveled Diamond & Star, ruby stain 80.00
Britannic, ruby stain 175.00
Chrysanthemum Sprig, custard 175.00
Cord Drapery, amber 450.00
Cord Drapery, bl 500.00
Daisy & Button w/V Ornament, bl or gr 55.00
Delaware, bl or rose 75.00
Esther, ruby stain 135.00
Feather 75.00
Feather, bl or gr 150.00
Flying Swan 35.00
Garland of Roses, vaseline 85.00
Heart Band, ruby stain 60.00
Jefferson #271, bl or gr 55.00
Klondike 150.00
Leaf Mould (Northwood), vaseline 350.00
New Jersey, ruby stain 225.00
Ohio Star 85.00
Pennsylvania, gr 140.00
Royal Crystal, ruby stain 65.00
Scalloped Swirl, bl or gr 60.00
Snow Flake 35.00
Sunken Primrose, ruby stain 60.00
Winged Scroll 65.00
Winged Scroll, custard 115.00

Novelties

Bear bust, clear, Richards & Hartley, ca 1885, 2½x2" 68.00
Bear bust, yel, Richards & Hartley, ca 1885, 2½x2" 150.00
Boot w/spur, blk, ca 1886, 3¼x4" 125.00
Butterfly figure, amber, Buckeye Glass Co, ca 1885, 2¾" 145.00
Dog beside top hat, amber, 1885, 2¾x1¼" 95.00
Frog on lily pad, blk, Co-operative Flint Glass Co, ca 1886, 3½x2" .. 45.00
Horse w/cart, clear, rnd base, Central Glass #1396, 18805, 3x3" ... 65.00
Horse w/cart, yel, rnd base, Central Glass #1396, 1885, 3x3" 95.00
Pig on flat car, amber, 3x5½" 365.00
Pig on flat car, clear, 3x5½" 250.00
Skull, opal, McKee & Bros, 1899, 2½x3½" 150.00

Torquay Pottery

Torquay is a unique type of pottery made in the South Devon area of England as early as 1869. At the height of productivity, at least a dozen companies flourished there, producing simple folk pottery from the area's natural red clay. The ware was both wheel-turned and molded and decorated under the glaze with heavy slip resulting in low-relief nature subjects or simple scrollwork. Three of the best-known of these potteries were Watcombe (1869 – 1962), Aller Vale (in operation from the mid-1800s, producing domestic ware and architectural products), and Longpark (1883 until 1957). Watcombe and Aller Vale merged in 1901 and operated until 1962 under the name of Royal Aller Vale and Watcombe Art Pottery.

A decline in the popularity of the early classical terra-cotta styles (urns, busts, figures, etc.) lead to the introduction of painted and glazed terra-cotta wares. During the late 1880s, white clay wares, both turned and molded, were decorated with colored glazes (Stapleton ware, grotesque molded figures, ornamental vases, large jardinieres, etc.). By the turn of the century, the market for art pottery was diminishing, so the potteries turned to wares decorated in colored slips (Barbotine, Persian, Scrolls, etc.).

Motto wares were introduced in the late nineteenth century by Aller Vale and taken up in the present century by the other Torquay potteries. This eventually became the 'bread and butter' product of the local industry. This was perhaps the most famous type of ware potted in this area because of the verses, proverbs, and quotations that decorated it. This was achieved by the sgraffito technique — scratching the letters through the slip to expose the red clay underneath. The most popular patterns were Cottage, Black Cockerel, Multi-Cockerel, and a scrollwork design called Scandy. Other popular decorations were Kerswell Daisy, ships, kingfishers, applied bird decorations, Art Deco styles, Egyptian ware, and many others. Aller Vale ware may sometimes be found marked 'H.H. and Company,' a firm who assumed ownership from 1897 to 1901. 'Watcombe Torquay' was an impressed mark used from 1884 to 1927. Our advisors for this category are Jerry and Gerry Kline; they are listed in the Directory under Ohio. If you're interested in joining a Torquay club, you'll find the address of The North American Torquay Society under Clubs, Newsletters, and Catalogs.

Art Pottery

Biscuit barrel, parrots on branches on bl, wrapped hdl, 6" 155.00
Bottle, scent; Devon Lavender/lav sprig, crown stopper, 4" 85.00
Bottle, scent; Devon Violets, Made in Great Britian, 2¼" 28.00
Bottle, scent; 3 dimples on purple, crown top, 1924-40 mk, 3½" ... 57.00
Bowl, Blarney Castle, Watcombe, hdls, ftd, 4½x4¼" 75.00
Candlesticks, Scroll, Aller Vale, ca 1900, 6", pr 100.00
Cat, gr, Aller Vale, rpr, 9" 695.00
Chamberstick, Persian, Aller Vale, 1891-1902, 10" 90.00
Hot water jug, Sandringham, Aller Vale, 6½" 225.00
Jam jar, Crocus, Longpark, 1930-40, 4¾" 55.00
Jardiniere, Scroll, Aller Vale, early 1900s, 3¾" 75.00
Jug, Ruins (Tintern Abbey), Longpark, strap hdl, 5½" 125.00
Match holder/striker, boxer dog's head on collar, 1898, rare 335.00
Plate, Terra Cotta, dog w/butterfly, Watcombe, 1900s, 3" 75.00
Tray, dresser; windmill, Aller Vale, 10½x7" 395.00
Urn, sailing ships, Sepia Ware, Watcombe, 1880s, 12½" 395.00
Vase, fan; Kerswell Daisy variant, Aller Vale, 1887-1924, 4½" 125.00
Vase, geometric design (resembling tumbling blocks), 9½" 110.00
Vase, swan on gr tricorn shape, ca 1900, unusual, 4½" 175.00
Wall pocket, flowers on horn shape, Exeter, 6½x4½" 175.00

Devon Motto Ware

Ashtray, Ship, Longpark, 'I'll Take the Ashes,' 4¾x3¼" 40.00
Beaker, Cottage, Dartmouth, 'Daun'ce Be 'Fraid...,' 3" 50.00
Bowl, Cottage, Watcombe, 'Masters Two Will Never...,' 3x4¼" 65.00
Bowl, Sea Gull, Dartmouth, w/motto, 1½x4" 40.00
Bowl, Shamrock, Aller Vale, 'Old Erin's Native Shamrock,' 3" 60.00
Candlestick, Cottage, Watcombe, 2½x5x4" 75.00
Candlestick, Longpark, 'Many Are Called...Few Get Up,' 3½" 89.00
Coffeepot, Black Cockerel, Watcombe, 'Before You Act...' 6¾" .. 150.00
Creamer, Scandy, unmk, 'He Does Much Who Does...,' 3¾" 65.00
Creamer & sugar bowl, Cottage, Watcombe, 'Yu Must' Ave/Du'ee Help'....70.00
Cup, Cottage, Watcombe, 'Speak Little Speak Tongue...,' 2" 30.00
Cup, Cottage, Watcombe, 'Speak Little Speak Well,' child sz, 3½" ..60.00
Egg cup, Cockerel, Longpark, 'Fresh Laid,' 2½" 40.00
Egg cup, Cottage, 'Laid To Day,' 3½x3½" 42.00
Inkwell, Colored Cockerel, Aller Vale, 'Good Morning...,' 2¾" dia... 85.00
Jug, Black Cat, Aller Vale, 'Oh Where Is My Boy Tonight,' 5x4" ...195.00
Jug, Cockerel, St Mary Church Pottery Ltd, w/motto, 4¼" 80.00
Jug, Cottage, 'Help Yourself...,' 5½x4½" 98.00
Jug, Cottage, Devon, 'Time Ripens All Things,' 4" 85.00
Jug, Cottage, Watcombe, 'Better To Sit Still...Fall,' 4" 85.00
Jug, Kerswell Daisy, Aller Vale, 'Freely Drink...,' 4" 85.00
Jug, Kerswell Daisy, Aller Vale, 'There's a Saying Old...,' 8½" 225.00
Jug, Kingfisher, Torquay, 'Time & Tide...,' 1925-30, 5½" 75.00
Jug, Multi-Cockerel, Aller Vale, 'Be Canny Wi...,' mini, 2½" 75.00

Jug, puzzle; Colored Cockerel, 'This Yer Jug Was...,' 3½" 200.00
Jug, puzzle; Primrose, Exeter, 'Within This Jug...' 210.00
Jug, Scandy, 'Say Well Is Good...Better,' sq, 4x4" 105.00
Jug, Scandy, Aller Vale, 'Demsher Craim Yak...,' 2½" 75.00
Jug, Ship, 'A Rolling Stone Gathers...,' Bridlington souvenir, 5" ... 65.00
Jug, Ship, 'Promise Little & Do Much,' conical, 4" 60.00
Mug, Black Cockerel, Longpark, 'For Good Boy,' 3" 75.00
Mug, Cottage, Watcombe, 'From Rocks & Sands...,' 4½x5½" 85.00
Mug, shaving; Cottage, Watcombe, 'Hair on Head Is Worth...'... 175.00
Mug, Thistle, 'There's No Time Like Now,' 3¼" 58.00
Plate, Black Cockerel, Longpark, 'Guide Folks Be...,' 7½" 110.00
Sugar bowl, Scandy, Watcombe, 'Sweeten to Your...,' 2x3½" 35.00
Tray, Black Cockerel, Watcombe, 'There's a Saying...,' 11x7½"... 300.00
Vase, Cottage, Watcombe, no motto, ca 1910, 10x4½" 195.00

Tortoiseshell

The outer shell of several species of land turtles, called tortoises, was once commonly used to make brooches, combs, small boxes, and novelty items. It was often used for inlay as well. The material is easily recognized by its mottled brown and yellow coloring. Because some of these turtles are now on the endangered list, such use is prohibited.

Box, dome lid, rectangular, 1x3½x2" 240.00
Box, jewelry; simple inlay, fitted drw, 8¼x11⅛x8⅛" 600.00
Box, repoussé silver corner mts/medallion, Asian, 19th C, 2½x6x4" 450.00
Box, w/ivory plaque on chamfered hinged lid, bone ft, 1½x2x1½" 325.00
Cape clasp, pin-bk terminals ea w/cameo floral in pearl surround, 6" L. 420.00
Case, calling card; cvd lady w/harp/cherubs/lattice bower, 19th C, 4" .. 540.00
Cigarette case, domed top/base, all-over cvg w/oval reserve, Jpan, 5" ... 550.00
Coin purse, satin lined w/compartments, nickel-silver trim, 3x2". 120.00
Page turner, rococo floral repoussé silver hdl, Geo III, 14½", NM. 390.00
Shell of turtle, 23x24" 600.00

Toys

Toys can be classified into at least two categories: early collectible toys with an established history and the newer toys. The antique toys are easier to evaluate. A great deal of research has been done on them, and much data is available. The newer toys are just beginning to be studied; relative information is only now being published, and the lack of production records makes it difficult to know how many may be available. Often warehouse finds of these newer toys can change the market. This has happened with battery-operated toys and to some extent with robots. Review past issues of this guide. You will see the changing trends for the newer toys. All toys become more important as collectibles when a fixed period of manufacture is known. When we know the numbers produced and documentation of the makers is established, the prices become more predictable.

The best way to learn about toys is to attend toy shows and auctions. This will give you the opportunity to compare prices and condition. The more collectors and dealers you meet, the more you will learn. There is no substitute for holding a toy in your hand and seeing for yourself what they are. If you are going to be a serious collector, buy all the books you can find. Read every article you see. Knowledge is vital to building a good collection. Study all books that are available. These are some of the most helpful: *Schroeder's Collectible Toys, Antique to Modern; Collecting Disneyana* and *Collector's Toy Yearbook* by David Longest; *Breyer Animal Collector's Guide* by Felicia Browell, Kelly Korber-Weimer, and Kelly Kesicki; *Matchbox Toys, 1947 – 2007*, and *Toy Car Collector's Guide*, both by Dana Johnson; *Hot Wheels, The Ultimate Redline Guide, 1968 – 1977*, by Jack Clark and Robert P. Wicker; and *Collector's Guide to Housekeeping Toys* by Margret Wright. All are published by Collector Books. Other in-

formative books are: *Collecting Toys, Collecting Toy Soldiers,* and *Collecting Toy Trains* by Richard O'Brien; and *Toys of the Sixties, A Pictorial Guide,* by Bill Bruegman. In the listings that follow, toys are listed by manufacturer's name if possible, otherwise by type. Measurements are given when appropriate and available; if only one dimension is noted, it is the greater one — height if the toy is vertical, length if it is horizontal. See also Children's Things; Personalities. For toy stoves, see Stoves.

Key:
b/o — battery operated   NP — nickel plated
cl — celluloid   r/c — remote control
jtd — jointed   w/up — windup
loco — locomotive

Toys by Various Manufacturers

Alps, Acrocycle, w/up, clown performs tricks on motorcycle, 6", EXIB ...400.00
Alps, Smiling Sam the Carnival Man, w/up, 9", NM+IB 300.00
Chad Valley, Roadster, w/up, tin, 12½", EX 650.00
Corgi, Austin A-40, red & blk, #216, MIP, from $125 to 150.00
Corgi, Bentley Continental, #224, MIP, from $100 to 125.00
Corgi, Bluebird Record Car, #153, from $125 to 150.00
Corgi, Ford Consul, dual colors, #200, MIP, from $175 to........... 200.00
Corgi, Ford Thunderbird, w/motor, #214m, MIP, from $300 to.... 325.00
Corgi, Japan Air Line Concorde, #651, MIP, from $450 to 500.00
Corgi, Man From UNCLE, wht, #497, MIP, from $650 to 700.00
Corgi, Riley Pathfinder, #205, bl, from $150 to 175.00
Corgi, Rolls Royce Silver Cloud, #273, MIP, from $100 to 125.00
Corgi, Starfighter Jet Dragster, #169, MIP, from $45 to 60.00
Corgi, Starsky & Hutch Ford Torino, #292, MIP, from $85 to 100.00
Corgi, Triumph TR2 Sports Car, MIP, from $150 to 175.00
Dinky, AC Acceca, #167, all cream, MIP, from $275 to.............. 325.00
Dinky, Big Ben Lorry, #408, pk & cream, MIP, from $1,950 to .. 2,350.00
Dinky, Fire Station, #954, MIP, from $425 to 450.00
Dinky, Leyland Cement Lorry, #417, MIP, from $170 to 295.00
Dinky, Morris Mini Traveller, #197, dk gr & brn, MIP, from $400 to.. 450.00
Dinky, Racing Gift Set, #249, MIP, from $1,450 to 1,750.00
Dinky, Volkswagen, #181, MIP, from $210 to 225.00
Ertl, '67 Corvette L-71 Roadster, Sunfire Yel, 1:18 scale, MIP, $35 to.. 40.00
Ertl, Buick GSX (1971), blk & gold, 1:18 scale, MIP, from $30 to...35.00
Girard, Overland Trail Bus, tin, w/up, 1920s, 14", EX+............. 2,200.00
Hot Wheels, GMC Motor Home, Hong Kong, 1977, redlines, orange, EX. 300.00
Hot Wheels, Mod Quad, 1970, redlines, magenta, scarce, M....... 125.00
Hot Wheels, Open Fire, 1972, redlines, magenta, NM+ 225.00
Hubley, Kiddie Toy Convertible, bl, diecast, 7", EXIB 165.00
Johnny Lightning, Custom El Camino, diecast, 1969, MIP 1,250.00
Johnny Lightning, Custom XKE, doors open, diecast, 1969, M ... 125.00
Kingsbury, bus, #788, metal, w/up, VG 550.00
Kingsbury, Fire Chief coupe #243, metal, w/up, b/o lights, 12", VG...450.00
Lehmann, Adam the Porter, w/up, NMIB................................. 1,350.00
Lehmann, Halloh Motorcycle w/Rider, NM 2,400.00
Lehmann, Lo & Li, w/up, NM... 8,000.00
Lehmann, Motor Car, w/up, EXIB.. 1,000.00
Linemar, Mickey Mouse Roller Skater, w/up, 6", NMIB........... 3,550.00
Linemar, Popeye & Olive Oyl Playing Catch w/Ball, w/up, 19" L, EX .900.00
Linemar, Popeye Turnover Tank, w/up, 4", NM+IB 600.00
Linemar, Xylophone Player, w/up, 5", VG 425.00
Lionel, Donald Duck Handcar, w/up, doghouse w/Pluto, 11" L, EXIB..825.00
Lionel, Mickey Mouse Circus Train, w/up, 29", EX 1,325.00
Marx, Auto Transport, metal w/ramp & 2 plastic autos, 22", NMIB..350.00
Marx, Charleston Trio, w/up, 1921, 10", EX 700.00
Marx, Donald Duck Duet, w/up, 10", EXIB 725.00
Marx, Fred Flintstone on Dino, b/o, plush Dino, 14", MIB....... 1,225.00
Marx, Main Street, w/up, EXIB... 475.00

Marx, Mighty Kong, plush, b/o, 11", EXIB..................500.00
Marx, Popeye the Champ, w/up, NMIB......................3,000.00
Marx, Snoopy & Gus Hook & Ladder Truck, w/up, 9", NM+...2,000.00
Marx, Tricky Taxi, w/up, 5", EXIB...............................225.00
Matchbox, Chevy Impala Taxi, #20, 1965, orange w/gray wheels, MIP.1,300.00
Matchbox, Safari Landrover, #12, 1970, Super Fast wheels, 1970, MIP.1,250.00
Matchbox, 8-Wheel Crane Truck, #30, 1965, mint gr, MIP, from $1,000 to...1,250.00
Ny-Lint, Howdy Doody Cart, tin, w/up, 9", VG..................300.00
Ny-Lint, Payloader, pressed steel w/rubber treads, 1950s, 17", VG...125.00
Ny-Lint, Street Sweeper, tin, w/up, 8" L, EXIB..................300.00

Ohio Art, sand pail, Mickey's Garden, Walt Disney Enterprises, 1930s, minimum value, $350.00.

(Photo courtesy David Longest)

Smith-Miller, Dump Truck, GMC, 1950s, crank action, 12", NM...275.00
Smith-Miller, West Coast Fast Freight Truck, L Mack, 1940s, EX..500.00
Steelcraft, Bloomingdale's Delivery Van, b/o lights, open cab, EX...2,975.00
Steelcraft, City Trucking Co Dump Truck, 1940s, metal, 21", VG......350.00
Steelcraft, Inter-City Bus, b/o lights, 24", VG...................650.00
Strauss, Ham & Sam, w/up, NMIB.............................1,200.00
Strauss, Jazzbo Jim (Jigger), w/up, EXIB....................700.00
Strauss, Santee Claus Sleigh, w/up, EXIB....................1,750.00
Structo, Dump Truck, lt gr, wht rubber tires, 22", VG...............350.00
Structo, Guided Missile Launcher Truck, 1960s, 14", EXIB.........200.00
Structo, tank, w/up, gr w/red turret & wheels, w/treads, 11½", EX...450.00
Sturditoy, Coal Truck, metal, 24", VG........................1,100.00
Tonka, Big Mike Hydraulic Dump Truck w/Snow Plow, 1950s, 20", VG..575.00
Tonka, Sanitary System Truck, pressed steel, 17", EX..............500.00
Tootsietoy, Build-A-Truck Set, NMIB.........................425.00
Tootsietoy, Pan American Airport Set, 1950s, NMIB.................300.00
Unique Art, Dandy Jim the Jolly Clown Dancer, w/up, 10", NMIB..1,100.00
Unique Art, GI Joe & His K-9 Pups, w/up, 9", EXIB...................275.00
Unique Art, Li'l Abner & His Dogpatch Band, w/up, 6x9", EXIB...700.00
Unique Art, Lincoln Tunnel, w/up, 24", EXIB....................350.00
Wolverine, carousel, tin, w/up, circus theme, 12" dia, VG...........300.00
Wolverine, Jackie Gleason Bus, tin, press-down action, 14", NMIB..900.00
Wolverine, Sunny Andy Kiddie Campers, tin, 14" L, EXIB.........350.00
Wyandotte, Moto-Fix Towcar, metal, 1950s, 15", EX..............225.00
Wyandotte, Shady Glenn Stock Ranch Cattle Truck, metal, 1950s, 17", EX...150.00

Cast Iron

Airplane, America Tri-Motor Airplane, Hubley, 2 pilots, 17" W, EX...3,500.00
Airplane, Spirit of St Louis, AC Williams, 4" W, EX..................350.00
Bell toy, Captain & the Kids, Gong Bell, 8", VG+.................13,225.00
Bell toy, Mary & Her Little Lamb, Gong Bell, 8", VG...............2,500.00
Boat, Priscilla Side-Wheeler, Dent, 10½", EX....................800.00
Boat, Racing Skull w/Pace Man & 4 Rowers, US Hardware, 9½", EX...4,500.00
Character, Alphone & Gaston Car w/Gloomy Gus Driving, Kenton, 8", NM.13,500.00
Character, Popeye Patrol Motorcycle, Hubley, 8½", G..............1,950.00
Circus, Bandwagon, Hubley, 4 horses & 6 musicians, EX..........3,450.00
Circus, Royal Circus Cage Wagon, Hubley, 2 horses, 12", NM.2,400.00
Construction, Buckeye Ditcher, Kenton, chain treads, 12" L, EX+..1,650.00

Construction, Contractors Dump Truck, Kenton, 3 buckets, 10", EX+..2,100.00
Firefighting, Aherns-Fox Pumper Truck, Hubley, w/driver, 11", NM..4,500.00
Firefighting, Mack Chemical Truck, Arcade, open, 2 ladders, 15", G+..2,750.00
Horse-drawn, Hansom Cab, Dent, lady passenger, 13½", EX....1,500.00
Horse-drawn, Ice Wagon, Arcade, enclosed, 2 horses & driver, 11", VG..500.00
Motor vehicle, Ambulance, Kenton, NP version, 10", VG.......1,700.00
Motor vehicle, Bell Telephone Truck, Hubley, complete, 10", NMIB..3,500.00
Motor vehicle, Crash Car, Hubley, Indian decal, w/driver, 11½", NM....6,325.00
Motor vehicle, Double-Decker Bus, Arcade, 8", NM.............1,500.00
Motor vehicle, Ford Model-T Sedan, Arcade, center door, 6½", NMIB..2,500.00
Motor vehicle, Int'l Red Baby Dump Truck, Arcade, w/driver, 11", EX+....1,100.00
Motor vehicle, Lincoln Zephyr Pulling House Trailer, Hubley, 14", NM.....2,500.00
Motor vehicle, Pierce-Arrow Coupe, Hubley, take-apart body, 6½", NM...2,400.00

Farm Toys

Combine, Case, Vindex, CI, 7½x12", NM.................5,775.00
Combine, Oliver, SLIK, stamped S9830BAR, 1952, 5x12", EX.....25.00
Field cultivator, John Deere, Ertl, #15081, 1/64 scale, MIB..............8.00
Hay loader, John Deer Vindex, CI, very rare, 9", EX.................4,500.00
Hay rake, Arcade, CI w/NP spoke wheels, w/seat, NM.............1,100.00
Hay wagon, Vindex, CI, 8", VG.............................1,425.00
Manure spreader, Case, Vindex, 12", EX.....................1,325.00
Plow, Arcade, 2-bottom, CI, 5½", EX........................400.00
Plow, John Deere 3-Bottom, Vindex, 9", VG....................800.00
Skid steer loader, John Deer Ertl, #569, 1/16 scale, MIB...............18.00
Thrasher, John Deere, Vindex, CI, 15", EX+..........................3,300.00
Tractor, Allis-Chalmers D-21 w/Duals, Ertl #12078, 1/16 scale, MIB..40.00
Tractor, Allis-Chalmers WD-45 Precision #7, Ertl, #13101, MIB...115.00
Tractor, Case L, Vindex, CI w/metal spoke wheels, NP driver, 7", EX+..2,750.00
Tractor, Ford 6640 Row Crop, Ertl, #332, 1/64 scale, MIB...........325.00
Tractor, Fordson, Dent, CI w/metal spoke wheels, NP driver, VG+..3,575.00
Tractor, John Deere D, Vindex, CI, spoke wheels, NP driver, 6", NM..3,300.00
Tractor, McCormick-Deering 10-20, Arcade, CI, 1925, VG........275.00
Tractor, Oliver 70-Row Crop, Arcade, CI, NP driver, 7", EX.......500.00
Tractor, Wallis, Freidag, CI, cast driver, 5", G.........................3,000.00
Wagon, McCormick-Deering Weber, Arcade, CI, 12", EX..........450.00

Guns and Early Cast-Iron Cap Shooters

In years past, virtually every child played with toy guns, and the survival rate of these toys is minimal, at best. The interest in these charming toy guns has recently increased considerably, especially those with western character examples, as collectors discover their scarcity, quality, and value. Toy gun collectibles encompass the early and the very ornate figural toy guns and bombs through the more realistic ones with recognizable character names, gleaming finishes, faux jewels, dummy bullets, engraving, and colorful grips. This section will cover some of the most popular cast-iron and diecast toy guns from the past 100 years. Recent market trends have witnessed a decline of interest in the earlier (1900 – 1940) single-shot cast-iron pistols. The higher collector interest is for known western characters and cap pistols from the 1950 – 1965 era. Generic toy guns such as, Deputy, Pony Boy, Marshal, Ranger, Sheriff, Pirate, Cowboy, Dick, Western, Army, etc., generate only minimal collector interest.

Buck Rogers Sonic Ray Gun, Norton-Horner, plastic, b/o, 7½", NMIB..250.00
Butting Match Cap Shooter, Ives, ca 1885, 5", EX....................1,000.00
Captain Gallant Foreign Legion Holster Outfit, Halco, complete, NMIB..275.00
Daisy No 50 'Golden Eagle' BB Gun, lever action, blk wood stock, EX..150.00
G-Man (Silent Alarm) Gun, Marx, EXIB.........................150.00
Gene Autry Cap Pistol, Leslie-Henry, NP repeater, wht grips, 8", EXIB..250.00
Hopalong Cassidy Gold Plated Single Shot Cap Pistol, Wyandotte, EXIB..500.00
Humpty-Dumpty (2-Prong), Ives, CI, 1882, 5¼", EX................1,300.00
Jupiter 4-Color Signal Gun, Remco, plastic, b/o, 1950s, 9", EXIB..175.00

Lone Ranger Carbine Rifle, Leslie-Henry, plastic, 26", NMIB 350.00
Pioneer Repeating Cap Pistol, Stevens, NP, blk grips, 1950s, 7", NMIB.. 100.00
Rodeo Cap Gun, Hubley, 1950s, 8", MIB 100.00
Space Super Jet Gun, KO, litho tin, 9", MIB............................... 200.00
Texan Double Gun & Holster Set, Halco, unused, MIB 500.00
Uncle Sam Says Cap Shooter, CI, mk Pat 1899 Franklin, 4", EX+ ..8,000.00

Model Kits

Addar, Jaws in a Bottle, 1975, MIB 60.00
Addar, Planet of the Apes, Dr Zaius, 1974, MIB 40.00
AMT, Man From UNCLE Car, MIB.. 225.00
AMT, Star Trek, Spock, 1973, NMIB (sm box).......................... 150.00
AMT/Ertl, Batman (movie), Batwing, 1990, MIB (sealed)............ 30.00
Anubis, Jonny Quest, Turu the Terrible, 1992, MIB.................... 60.00
Aurora, Bride of Frankenstein, 1965, MIB 750.00
Aurora, Captain America, 1966, MIB... 330.00
Aurora, Dracula, 1962, MIB... 300.00
Aurora, Godzilla's Go-Cart, 1966, assembled, NM 750.00
Aurora, Godzilla's Go-Cart, 1966, MIB 3,000.00
Aurora, Green Hornet's Black Beauty, 1966, MIB 500.00
Aurora, Munster's Living Room, 1964, MIB..........................1,200.00
Aurora, Rodan, 1975, Monsters of the Movies, rare, MIB........... 375.00
Aurora, Spider-Man, 1966, MIB 300.00
Aurora, Viking, 1959, Famous Fighters, MIB............................. 250.00
Aurora, Whoozis?, 1966, Denty, MIB... 85.00
Hawk, Freddy Flameout, 1963, Weird-Ohs, MIB........................ 85.00
Horizon, Frankenstein, MIB... 100.00
Monogram, Bathtub Buggy, 1960s, MIB (sealed)....................... 100.00
Monogram, Snoopy as Joe Cool, 1971, MIB.............................. 100.00
MPC, Hogan's Heroes Jeep, 1968, MIB 125.00
MPC, Sweathogs 'Dream Machine,' 1976, MIB 50.00
Pyro, Peacemaker 45, 1960, MIB (sealed)................................. 100.00
Revell, Angel Fink, 1965, Ed 'Big Daddy' Roth, MIB 180.00
Revell, Apollo Columbia/Eagle, 1969, MIB (sealed)................... 100.00
Revell, Beatles, 1965, any, MIB, ea from $200 to 250.00
Revell, Peter Pan Pirate Ship, 1960, MIB.................................. 100.00
Revell, Space Explorer Solaris, 1969, MIB................................ 125.00
Screamin', Friday the 13th's Jason, MIB 125.00
Screamin', Werewolf, MIB 100.00
Tsukuda, Ghostbusters Terror Dog, MIB.................................. 125.00

Pedal Cars and Ride-On Toys

Aero-Flite Wagon, 1930s, electric lights, 47", EX.....................2,350.00
Air Mail CN 67 Plane, Steelcraft, gold w/orange trim, 46", EX . 1,900.00
Buick, Steelcraft, V-shaped windshield, chrome trim, lights, 35", EX... 2,100.00
Casey Jones/Cannon Ball Express Train Engine No 9, 40", EX . 1,500.00
Chevrolet, 1930s, 36", EX rstr..2,500.00
Chrysler (1941), Steelcraft, 37", EX rstr 4,100.00
Earth Mover w/Payload Dump, yel w/blk & wht trim, 47", VG ... 800.00
Fire Chief Car (Deluxe), Toledo, 57", EX rstr..........................2,100.00
Fire Hook & Ladder Pumper 519, 46", EX rstr............................ 550.00
Gilmore Tank Truck, C-style cab, 54", EX rstr............................ 575.00
Gulf 24-hr Service Wrecker, 49", EX rstr 775.00
Hummer, Pioneer, metal & wood, 33", VG 11,200.00
Packard, American National, roof, side spare, running brds, 28", EX... 16,500.00
Pontiac Station Wagon, Murray, 1949, 47", G 600.00
Skippy Airflow Wagon, 1930s, electric lights, 48", EX rstr........1,500.00
Super Sport, Murray, 1953, EX..2,250.00

Penny Toys

Aeroplane w/pilot, Meier, 4 props & wheels, 3" L, G 575.00

Air Plane spinning toy, Einfalt, 2 planes on rods, 7", EX............. 825.00
Camel w/backpack, Meier, non-wheeled version, 2¾", VG+ 350.00
Elephant cart, Fischer, nodding head, 5", VG........................... 225.00
Fieldpost truck, Distler, w/driver, 3¼", NM............................. 700.00
Garage w/limousine & roadster, Kellerman, 3½x3½", EX............ 300.00
Girls (2) in dbl swing, Meier, 3¼", VG+ 275.00
Gunboat, Meier, w/'smoke' coming out of stack, 4¼", VG 250.00
Jigger on ftd box, Distler, hand-crank, 3¾", EX....................... 450.00
Jockey on rocking horse, Meier, 3¾", NM................................ 900.00
Launch, Fischer, railed, w/flag, 3-wheeled, 4½", EX................... 825.00
Ocean liner, Meier, 2 stacks, 4½", EX 375.00
Omnibus, Fischer, 4½", EX.. 200.00
Punch & Judy theatre, Meier, lever action, 3½", EX................... 775.00
Racer, Fischer, 4¾", EX.. 450.00

Playsets by Marx

Alamo, #3543, NMIB.. 250.00
Alamo, #3546, NMIB.. 400.00
Battle of the Blue & Gray, #4744, NMIB.................................. 800.00
Captain Gallant, #4729, NMIB.. 750.00
Daktari, #3718, NMIB... 375.00
Daniel Boone Wilderness Scout, #3442, NMIB......................... 400.00
Davy Crockett at the Alamo, #3530, NMIB............................... 300.00
Flintstones, #5948, EXIB 165.00
Fort Dearborn, #3688, NMIB.. 275.00
Gunsmoke Dodge City, #4268, Series 2000, EXIB 800.00
Jungle Jim, #3705-6, Series 1000, EXIB 350.00
Medieval Castle, #4700, unused, MIB (sealed) 550.00
Rifleman Ranch, #3997-8, EX+IB.. 300.00
Rin Tin Tin Fort Apache, #3628, NMIB.................................... 550.00
Roy Rogers Rodeo Ranch, #3996, NMIB.................................. 425.00
Wagon Train, #4888, Series 5000, NMIB...............................1,000.00
Wyatt Earp Dodge City Western Town, #4228, Series 1000, NMIB... 475.00
Yogi Bear at Jellystone National Park, #4363-4, MIB..............1,200.00
Zorro, #3753, Series 1000, NMIB... 800.00

Pull and Push Toys

Camel on platform, pnt tin, Adolph Bergmann, 9", EX 500.00
Circus wagon, litho tin, Harrison, 11", EX................................ 450.00
Easter bunny truck, litho tin, bunny pulls trailer, Courtland, 12", EX... 150.00
Goat cart, tin, cart emb w/leafy branches, Hull & Stafford, 11", VG.... 600.00
Grasshopper, pnt CI w/aluminum legs, 2 sm front wheels, Hubley, 9", VG.650.00
Horse on platform, pnt tin, George Brown, 8x12", G...............1,000.00
Horse prancing, pnt on gesso, leather ears, wooden base, 15x15"... 350.00
Horse-drawn dray wagon, pnt tin, Adolph Bergmann, G............ 400.00
Horse-drawn menagerie wagon, litho tin & wood, Converse, 13", EX... 300.00
Horse-drawn US Mail cart, litho on wood & tin, Gibbs, 12", EX ...275.00
Lamb (stuffed) on wood base, spoked wheels, 16½x21"............. 925.00
Mallard, head nods, pnt felt/glass eyes/metal ft, wood base, 13x14" ...1,380.00
Ox cart, pnt tin, 2 oxen, George Brown, 10", VG 500.00
Train engine, pnt tin, American Metal Toys, 8", VG 450.00
Trolley #59 (All Cars Transfer to Bloomingdales), Rich Toy, 13", EX. 600.00

Robots

Action Planet Robot, Yoshia, w/up, 1950s, 9", NM+IB 250.00
Battery-Operated Robot, Yonezawa, 6", NMIB.......................2,500.00
Earth Man, TN, r/c, 9", NM+IB..4,875.00
Giant Sonic (Train) Robot, MY, b/o, 15", EX............................2,800.00
Golden Robot, Linemar, r/c, 6½", EXIB....................................1,600.00
Juniper Robot, Yoshiya, w/up, MIB... 300.00
Lantern Robot (Powder Robot), Linemar, r/c, 8", EX.................1,500.00

Mechanical Robot, Yonezawa, w/up, 6", EXIB	1,350.00
Moon Explorer, Alps, b/o, 18", EXIB	2,000.00
Mr Atom the Elctronic Walking Robot, b/o, 18", EXIB	300.00
Mr Mercury, Linemar, r/c, 13", EXIB	750.00
Porthole Spaceman Robot, Linemar, r/c, 8", EX	3,350.00
Ranger Robot, Daiya, b/o, NMIB	3,000.00
Robby Space Patrol, Nomura, b/o, 13", EXIB	6,750.00
Roby Robot, Yonezawa, w/up, 8", EXIB	1,900.00
Rocket Man, Alps, r/c, 16", EX+IB	2,500.00
Space Commando, Nomura, 1956, w/up, 8", EX	275.00
Space Conqueror, Daiya, b/o, 12", EX	600.00
Space Man Robot, Nomura, b/o, MIB	1,250.00
Spaceman Robot, Modern Toys, b/o, 7", NM	1,775.00
Super Robot, Noguchi, w/up, 5", MIB	200.00
Target Robot, Masudaya, b/o, 15", EX	4,500.00
Walking Martian, Hishimo, w/up, 8", EX	5,000.00
Zoomer the Robot, Nomura, b/o, 8", NMIB	725.00

Schoenhut

Our advisor for Schoenhut toys is Keith Kaonis, who has collected these toys for 25 years. Because of his involvement with the publishing industry (currently *Antique DOLL Collector*, and during the '80s, *Collectors' SHOW-CASE*), he has visited collections across the United States, produced several articles on Schoenhut toys, and served a term as president of the Schoenhut Collectors' Club. Keith is listed in the Directory under New York.

The listings below are for Humpty Dumpty Circus pieces. All values are based on rating conditions of good to very good, i.e., very minor scratches and wear, good original finish, no splits or chips, no excessive paint wear or cracked eyes, and of course completeness and condition of clothes (if dressed figures).

Humpty Dumpty Circus Clowns and Other Personel

Clowns with two-part heads (a cast face applied to a wooden head) were made from 1903 to 1912 and are most desirable — condition always is important. There have been nine distinct styles in 14 different costumes recorded. Only eight costume styles apply to the two-part headed clowns. The later clowns had one-part heads whose features were pressed wood, and the costumes on the later ones, circa 1920+, were no longer tied at the wrists and ankles.

Black Dude, 1-part head, purple coat, from $250 to	750.00
Black Dude, 2-part head, blk coat, from $400 to	1,000.00
Chinese Acrobat, 1-part head, from $200 to	900.00
Chinese Acrobat, 2-part head, rare, from $400 to	1,600.00
Clown, reduced sz, from $75 to	125.00
Hobo, reduced sz, from $200 to	400.00
Hobo, 1-part head, from $200 to	400.00
Hobo, 2-part head, curved-up toes, blk coat, from $500 to	1,200.00
Lady Acrobat, bsk head, from $300 to	800.00
Lady Acrobat, 1-part head, from $150 to	400.00
Lady Rider, bsk head, from $250 to	550.00
Lady Rider, 2-part head, very rare, from $500 to	1,000.00
Lion Tamer, 1-part head, from $150 to	700.00
Lion Tamer, 2-part head, early, very rare, from $700 to	1,600.00
Ringmaster, bsk, from $300 to	800.00
Ringmaster, 1-part head, from $200 to	450.00
Ringmaster, 2-part head, blk coat, very rare, from $800 to	1,800.00
Ringmaster, 2-part head, red coat, very rare, from $700 to	1,600.00

Humpty Dumpty Circus Animals

Humpty Dumpty Circus animals with glass eyes, ca. 1903 – 1914, are more desirable and can demand much higher prices than the later painted-eye versions. As a general rule, a glass-eye version is 30% to 40% more than a painted-eye version. (There are exceptions.) The following list suggests values for both GE (glass-eye) and PE (painted-eye) versions and reflects a **low PE price** to a **high GE price**.

There are other variations and nuances of certain figures: Bulldog — white with black spots or Brindle (brown); open- and closed-mouth zebras, camels, and giraffes; ball necks and hemispherical necks on some animals such as the pig, cat, and hippo, to name a few. These points can affect the price and should be judged individually. Condition and rarity affect the price most significantly and the presence of an original box virtually doubles the price.

Alligator, PE/GE, from $250 to	750.00
Arabian camel, 1 hump, PE/GE, from $250 to	750.00
Bactrain camel, 2 humps, PE/GE, from $200 to	1,200.00
Brown bear, PE/GE, from $200 to	800.00
Buffalo, cvd mane, PE/GE, from $200 to	1,200.00
Bulldog, PE/GE, from $400 to	1,500.00
Burro, farm set, PE/GE, no harness/no belly hole for chariot, $300 to	800.00
Burro, made to go w/chariot & clown, PE/GE, w/leather track, $200 to	800.00
Cat, PE/GE, rare, from $500 to	3,000.00
Cow, PE/GE, from $300 to	1,200.00
Deer, PE/GE, from $300 to	1,500.00
Donkey, PE/GE, from $75 to	300.00
Donkey w/blanket, PE/GE, from $100 to	600.00
Elephant, PE/GE, from $75 to	300.00
Gazelle, PE/GE, rare, from $500 to	3,000.00
Giraffe, PE/GE, from $200 to	900.00
Goose, PE only, from $200 to	750.00
Gorilla, PE only, from $1,500 to	4,000.00
Hippo, PE/GE, from $200 to	900.00
Horse, brn, PE/GE, saddle & stirrups, from $250 to	500.00
Horse, dapple, PE/GE, platform, from $250 to	700.00
Hyena, PE/GE, very rare, from $1,000 to	6,000.00
Kangaroo, PE/GE, from $200 to	1,500.00
Lion, cvd mane, PE/GE, from $200 to	1,400.00
Monkey, 1-part head, PE only, from $200 to	600.00
Monkey, 2-part head, wht face, from $300 to	1,000.00
Ostrich, PE/GE, from $200 to	900.00
Pig, 5 versions, PE/GE, from $200 to	800.00
Polar bear, PE/GE, from $200 to	2,000.00
Poodle, PE/GE, from $100 to	300.00
Rabbit, PE/GE, very rare, from $500 to	3,500.00
Rhino, PE/GE, from $250 to	800.00
Sea Lion, PE/GE, from $400 to	1,500.00
Sheep (lamb), PE/GE, w/bell, from $200 to	800.00
Tiger, PE/GE, from $250 to	1,200.00
Wolf, PE/GE, very rare, from $500 to	5,000.00
Zebra, PE/GE, rare, from $500 to	3,000.00

Humpty Dumpty Circus Accessories

There are many accessories: wagons, tents, ladders, chairs, pedestals, tightrope, weights, and more.

Managerie tent, early, ca 1904, from $1,500 to	3,000.00
Menagerie tent, later, 1914-20, from $1,200 to	2,000.00
Oval litho tin, 1920, from $4,000 to	10,000.00
Sideshow panels, 1920, pr from $2,000 to	5,000.00

Steiff

Margaret Steiff began making her stuffed felt toys in Germany in the late 1800s. The animals she made were tagged with an elephant in a circle. Her first teddy bear, made in 1903, became such a popular seller that she changed her tag to a bear. Felt stuffing was replaced with excelsior and wool; when it became available, foam was used. In addition to the tag, look for the 'Steiff' ribbon and the button inside the ear.

Early Steiff bears in mint condition may go for a minimum of $150.00 per inch for a small bear up to $300.00 to $350.00 (sometimes even more) per inch for one 20" high or larger. See also Teddy Bears.

Ali the Alligator, 25", VG.. 125.00
Bear, shoe-button eyes, early 1900s, no tag or button, 23", EX... 7,200.00
Bear hand puppet, glass eyes, 1950s, NM.. 100.00
Coco the Baboon, 8", G... 50.00
Fellow the Airedale dog, 12", EX 270.00
Finch bird, mc mohair w/fiber feathers, wire legs & ft, 3x6", NM ...210.00
Happy Hooligan doll, ca 1915, 15", EX....................................... 2,750.00
Mongo Monkey seated on 4-wheeled cart, 1930s, 8", G............ 1,500.00
Ophelia the Bear, wht mohair, gold button in ear, 1984, 16½", M..110.00
Panda Bear, blk & wht mohair, 6", EX.. 290.00
Peggy Penguin, 21", EX... 450.00
Polar Bear, wht mohair, blk glass eyes, bl collar, 1959-67, 4", NM ..135.00
Poodles (4) in a basket, FAO Schwarz, 1950s-60s, 4-6", EX 500.00
Rabbit seated upright, w/squeaker, 'FF' button, 1930s-40s, 13", EX....275.00
Rooster, 1950s, life sz, 23" H... 130.00
Scotty dog, blk w/brn nose, glass eyes, red collar, 1957, 4x5", NM..150.00
Typos dinosaur, 1954, 17", EX 400.00
Tysus Tyrannosaurus, 1959, 7", NM 350.00

Toy Soldiers and Accessories

Among the better known manufacturers of 'Dimestore' soldiers are American Metal Toys, Barclay, and Manoil, all of whom made hollow cast-lead figures; Grey Iron, who used cast iron; and Auburn, who made figures of rubber. They measured about 3" to 3½" tall, and often accessories such as trucks, tents, tanks, and airplanes were designed to add to the enjoyment of staging mock battles, parades, encampments, and wars. Some figures are very rare and therefore expensive, but condition is just as important in making a value assessment. Percentages in the description lines refer to the amount of original paint remaining. Our advisors for this category are Stan and Sally Alekna; they are listed in the Directory under Pennsylvania.

Am Metal Toys, AA gunner, khaki, rare, 97% 120.00
Am Metal Toys, ammo carrier, khaki, very rare, 96%.................... 375.00
Am Metal Toys, howitzer, rubber tires, rare, 7", 99%..................... 95.00
Am Metal Toys, soldier kneeling firing long rifle, khaki, rare, 95%....125.00
Am Metal Toys, soldier wire cutter, khaki, very rare, 93%-95% ..400.00
Auburn Rubber, collie dog, lg, NM... 25.00
Auburn Rubber, football lineman, red, rare, 97%......................... 57.00
Auburn Rubber, infantry officer, M 35.00
Barclay, ambulance, sm bl cross, wht tires, 3½", 98% 63.00
Barclay, aviator, gr, M 34.00
Barclay, Boy Scout hiking, NM 65.00
Barclay, bride or groom, 98%, ea.. 2,700.00
Barclay, cadet officer w/sword, short stride, wht, 98% 30.00
Barclay, conductor, HO, M 13.00
Barclay, couple on park bench (summer or winter), M, ea 45.00
Barclay, cowboy w/lasso standing, gray, NM 29.00
Barclay, elderly man w/cane, NM... 22.00
Barclay, fireman w/hose, 99% 45.00
Barclay, girl on sled, M.. 2,900.00
Barclay, hobo, HO, 98% 10.00
Barclay, Indian chief w/rifle, pod ft, rare, 98% 40.00
Barclay, Japanese soldier advancing w/rifle, scarce, 95% 45.00
Barclay, knight w/pennant, 99%... 27.00
Barclay, mailman, NM... 22.00
Barclay, marine officer, cast helmet, bl, 88%............................... 86.00

Barclay, cannon, two variations of BC1, Barclay's first toy, ca 1930, rare, M, **$95.00 each.** (Photo courtesy Stan and Sally Alekna)

Barclay, naval officer, long stride, bl, very scarce, 98% 425.00
Barclay, nurse, blk hair, rare, 99% 46.00
Barclay, nurse w/bag, 94%.. 26.00
Barclay, sailor, bl, 99%... 27.00
Barclay, Santa on skis, 97%.. 68.00
Barclay, soldier ammo carrier, silver boxes, 99%.......................... 29.00
Barclay, soldier bomb thrower, gr, M 29.00
Barclay, soldier charging, short stride, tin helmet, 95%................. 28.00
Barclay, soldier drummer, long stride, tin helmet, 97% 38.00
Barclay, soldier kneeling firing, red, very rare, 96% 142.00
Barclay, soldier machine gunner charging, 96%............................ 44.00
Barclay, soldier radio operator, separate antenna, 94%................. 55.00
Barclay, soldier running w/rifle, cast helmet, 93% 36.00
Barclay, soldier w/sentry dog, scarce, 99%................................... 97.00
Barclay, speed skater, 98%... 20.00
Barclay, train conductor, M 22.00
Grey Iron, baseball player, any, very scarce, 1½", NM, ea............. 150.00
Grey Iron, boy w/life preserver, very rare, M................................ 76.00
Grey Iron, cavalryman on brn horse, 97% 46.00
Grey Iron, cowboy (masked) on wht horse, very rare, 96%.......... 475.00
Grey Iron, cowboy on bucking bronc, rare, 96% 73.00
Grey Iron, girl holding cat, 96%... 18.00
Grey Iron, Legion drum major, early version, rare, 97%................. 52.00
Grey Iron, man in traveling suit, aluminum, rare, M...................... 20.00
Grey Iron, policeman, NM 18.00
Grey Iron, Red Cross doctor, 95%.. 46.00
Grey Iron, sailor signalman, rare, 92-94%.................................... 42.00
Grey Iron, soldier machine gunner kneeling, 97% 21.00
Grey Iron, train engineer, 98%... 16.00
Grey Iron, US doughboy charging, postwar, 95%.......................... 21.00
Grey Iron, US infantry officer, early version, 97%......................... 25.00
Grey Iron, wounded soldier on crutches, rare, 98%...................... 77.00
Jones, Annapolis cadet port arms, bl, M 35.00
Jones, Scot Highlander of 1814, 98%... 29.00
Jones, US marine, 1809, no pigtail, rare, 96% 35.00
Lincoln Log, caveman or cavewoman, rare, 97-99%, ea................ 71.00
Lincoln Log, foot soldier of 1918 charging or marching, 99%, ea .. 25.00
Lincoln Log, policeman, NM 20.00
Lincoln Log, train engineer, 98%.. 18.00
Lincoln Log, traveling man, M 21.00
Manoil, boxer, very rare, 98% 125.00
Manoil, cadet marching, dk bl, very scarce, 95%.......................... 175.00
Manoil, cook's helper w/ladle, rare, 97%...................................... 73.00
Manoil, cowboy on galloping horse, scarce, M.............................. 76.00
Manoil, cowboy w/raised postol, 97% 28.00
Manoil, drummer, stocky version, 99%.. 47.00
Manoil, farmer cutting corn, 99% 30.00
Manoil, man carrying door, rare, M... 75.00
Manoil, nurse w/bowl, NM.. 34.00
Manoil, parade soldier, stocky, 98% 29.00
Manoil, parade soldier, thin, 99% 48.00
Manoil, sailor, wht uniform, 2nd version, M.................................. 36.00
Manoil, school teacher, 98% 60.00
Manoil, signalman, hollow base, 93-95%...................................... 67.00

Manoil, soldier firing rifle in air, 95%..................................... 51.00
Manoil, soldier grenade thrower, 99%.................................... 56.00
Manoil, soldier marching w/rifle & pack, 97%.................... 36.00
Manoil, soldier shell loader, 97% 30.00
Manoil, soldier sniper firing carbine at an angle, 98%................... 45.00
Manoil, soldier tommy gunner charging, 96% 48.00
Manoil, soldier w/bazooka kneeling, 97% 41.00
Manoil, soldier wounded, 94% 20.00
Manoil, stretcher bearer, gr cross on pouch, NM 15.00
Marx, cowboy rider, postwar, rare, EX+............................... 23.00
Marx, Indian chief w/spear, rare, EX+ 23.00
Marx, infantry private at attention, tin, M 10.00
Marx, Soldiers of Fortune, set of 8 tin figures, 4", NMIB.............. 100.00

Trains

Electric trains were produced as early as the late nineteenth century. Names to look for are Lionel, Ives, and American Flyer. Identification numbers given in the listings below actually appear on the item.

Am Flyer, boxcar (MKT), #24106, VG... 550.00
Am Flyer, caboose, #484, 10th Anniversary, NM 100.00
Am Flyer, freight station, #91 or #95, EX, ea................................ 200.00
Am Flyer, hopper, #4006, red, EXIB.. 450.00
Am Flyer, loco & tender, #343, VG 350.00
Am Flyer, loco & tender, NYC, #151, MIB (sealed) 400.00
Am Flyer, lumber loader, #751, VGIB.. 175.00
Am Flyer, Macy's Electric Speed Special, red, NMIB 1,300.00
Am Flyer, passenger station, #102, EXIB 350.00
Am Flyer, set, Golden State, loco (#3115) & 3 cars, VGIB 575.00
Am Flyer, switchtower, #108, prewar, VG................................. 450.00
Am Flyer, tank car (Gilbert Chemicals), #910, EXIB.................. 325.00
Lionel, boxcar, #214, yel w/orange roof, prewar, EXIB 525.00
Lionel, boxcar (Mail Express), #9229, modern era, MIB 30.00
Lionel, caboose, #6517, bay window, prewar, EXIB 700.00
Lionel, caboose (Reading), #17605, modern era, MIB 30.00
Lionel, cattle car, #13, prewar, EX... 450.00
Lionel, freight car (Minneapolis & St Louis), modern era, MIB.... 50.00
Lionel, loco, Burlington GP, #2328, prewar, EX+ 475.00
Lionel, loco & tender, Chessie, #18011, modern era, MIB........... 575.00
Lionel, oil drum loader, #12862, EXIB..................................... 100.00
Lionel, power station, #436, prewar, NM+IB.............................. 6,000.00
Lionel, reefer (Hershey billboard), #9867, modern era, NMIB 35.00
Lionel, set, Burlington & Northern Limited, #8585, modern era, NMIB.... 300.00
Lionel, set, Hiawatha, #1000, prewar, MIB................................ 825.00
Lionel, set, Silver Streak (#265E) w/loco, tender & 2 cars, prewar, EX...2,250.00
Lionel, set, SSS Santa Fe Work Train, #1632, modern era, MIB... 275.00
Lionel, snowplow (Rio Grande), #53, VGIB 225.00
Lionel, station, #116, prewar, EX+IB.. 3,100.00
Marklin, freight car, #1929, w/guardhouse, brn, VG................. 150.00
Marklin, loco TNM 65, #1302, #1 gauge, VG 465.00
Marklin, log carrier car w/logs, #1 gauge, VG 150.00
Marklin, passenger car #1888, hinged roof, VG+ 275.00
Marklin, set, loco, tender, 3 cars & rack, pnt & litho tin, EXIB .. 850.00
Marx, set, NY Central Passenger, #35250, 5-pc, VGIB 200.00
Marx, set, Western Pacific Passenger, #44464, 6-pc, MIB 600.00

Trade Signs

Trade signs were popular during the 1800s. They were usually made in an easily recognizable shape that one could mentally associate with the particular type of business it was to represent, especially appropriate in the days when many customers could not read!

Andersons, oval wood panel w/mc pnt, iron brackets, 19th C, 9x56" ..475.00
Blacksmith, horseshoe, cvd/pnt wood, late 19th C, 42½x34" 950.00
Boston American (newspaper), pnt plywood w/appl letters, 1900s, 84" W.7,600.00
Butcher, CI, tools & steer, silver & gold pnt, Pat 1889, 28x33" .. 1,850.00
Fairbanks Scales, pnt wood fr panel, late 1800s, 18x28".............. 450.00
Fishmonger, fish, cvd wood w/worn mc pnt, early 1900s, 21" L.... 550.00
General store, pnt wood panel: Cash Store in fr, 15¾x29", EX, 29".... 550.00
Hardware, handsaw, die-cut, Grinding & Saw Filing on blade, 63" L . 1,500.00
Innkeeper, Heartwellville Inn, pnt wood, 2-sided, 19th C, 25x36" ...1,000.00
Jeweler/watchmaker, pocket watch, pnt metal, EX details, 20x14" dia ...3,450.00
Locksmith, key, cvd wood w/red pnt, weathered, 19th C, 74½" .. 2,750.00
Meat Market, pnt wood, blk letters on wht, pnt molding, 11x49" ...1,650.00
Milk/Sandwiches, pnt galvanized metal, early 1900s, 18x28" 700.00
Optometrist, eye in oval, rvpt glass, 13¼x17¼" 480.00
Pharmacist, mortar & pestle, pnt aluminum w/RX on yel, 32x23x6" ...240.00
Produce market, James Bradley Country Produce, pnt wood, 1900s, 24x58"..4,000.00
Safe-T Cup ice cream cone, paper compo, 3-D, 20th C, rpr, 21" .. 175.00
Shoe repair, boot, cvd wood, made in 2 pcs, worn pnt, ca 1900, 18"..1,175.00
Tailor, scissors, cvd wood w/blk/gold pnt, brass hinge, 38½" L ..5,175.00
Tobacconist, wooden pipe w/long stem, unmk, VG pnt/crack, 33" L .150.00
Tool Co, folding str-edged razor, pnt pine, Dunn Edge Tool Co, 36"..2,700.00
Watchmaker, pocketwatch, metal w/orig pnt, 24x14" dia, EX ..2,400.00
5 & 10 Cent Store..., blk & wht pnt on brds, 59x39"................ 3,000.00
5¢ Counter, tin w/red/wht/blk/gold pnt, early 1900s, 6x27".........200.00

Tramp Art

'Tramp' is considered a type of folk art. In America it was primarily made from the end of the Civil War through the 1930s, though it employs carving and decorating methods which are much older, originating mostly in Germany and Scandinavia. 'Trampen' probably refers to the itinerant stages of Middle Ages craft apprenticeship. The carving techniques were also used for practice. Tramp art was spread by soldiers in the Civil War and primarily practiced where there was a plentiful and free supply of materials such as cigar boxes and fruit crates. The belief that this work was done by tramps and hobos as payment for rooms or meals is generally incorrect. The larger pieces especially would have required a lengthy stay in one place.

There is a great variety of tramp art, from boxes and frames which are most common to large pieces of furniture and intricate objects. The most common method of decoration is chip carving with several layers built one on top of another. There are several variations of that form as well as others such as 'Crown of Thorns,' an interlocking method, which are completely different. The most common finishes were lacquer or stain, although paints were also used. The value of tramp art varies according to size, detail, surface, and complexity. The new collector should be aware that tramp art is being made today. While some sell it as new, others are offering it as old. In addition, many people mistakenly use the term as a catchall phrase to refer to other forms of construction — especially things they are uncertain about. This misuse of the term is growing, and makes a difference in the value of pieces. New collectors need to pay attention to how items are described. For further information we recommend *Tramp Art: A Folk Art Phenomenon* by Helaine Fendelmam, Jonathan Taylor (Photographer)/Stewart Tabori & Chang; *Hobo & Tramp Art Carving: An Authentic American Folk Tradition* by Adolph Vandertie, Patrick Spielman/Sterling Publications; and *Tramp Art, One Notch at a Time*, by Cornish and Wallach. Our advisors for this category are Matt Lippa and Elizabeth Schaff; they are listed in the Directory under Alabama.

Box, chip cvg, 7 layers, covered pine, early 1900s, 8½x20" 500.00
Box, stacked/chip-cvd pyramidal lid/sides/base, gilt ball finial, 18"...1,120.00
Box, stepped pyramid shapes, drw, appl leaves/pnt birds, 7x9" ..1,600.00
Cabinet, drw/dbl doors/gesso molding/mirror bk, 1930s, 41x20x14"..9,000.00

Crucifix on stepped base, wht metal Jesus, 26x13"........................ 300.00
Cupboard, chip-cvd graduated blocks, divided drw, fitted int, 23x17x7" ... 575.00
Desk, slant front w/fitted int & drw, ornate chip cvg, 39x25x15"..4,800.00
Desk/bookcase, drop front, chip-cvd rosettes/leaves, 2-pc, KY, 73x47" ...2,300.00
Fr, chip-cvd hearts/triangles/rnds/teardrops, 19th C, 31x28".....2,700.00
Fr, chip-cvd sawtooth borders/Xs, gold & silver pnt, 19x16"........ 235.00
Frame, cut geometrics/lapped hearts, red pnt, ca 1900, 23x19" .. 1,060.00
Frame, deep cvg & appl rondels & hearts, alligatored varnish, 17x21"...300.00
Frame, oak w/chip-cvd pinwheels & quarter fans, 11x7".............. 300.00
Frame, 5-step chip cvgs w/stylized tulips, rpl mirror, 21x18" 660.00
Lamp base, chip-cvd geometrics, mc pnt, 6-sided, 29½x10¼" 900.00
Medicine cabinet, rpl mirror on door/1 drw, geometric cvgs, 23x17x8"..1,100.00

Traps

Though of interest to collectors for many years, trap collecting has gained in popularity over the past 10 years in particular, causing prices to appreciate rapidly. Traps are usually marked on the pan as to manufacturer, and the condition of these trademarks are important when determining their value. Our advisor for this category is Boyd Nedry; he is listed in the Directory under Michigan. Our values are for traps in fine condition. Grading is as follows:

Good: one-half of pan legible.
Very good: legible in entirety, but light.
Fine: legible in entirety, with strong lettering.
Mint: in like-new, shiny condition.

Ampo, gopher trap.. 20.00
Andirondak, killer, w/trip wire 395.00
Arrow #1½, single under spring.................................... 65.00
Austin Humane, killer 40.00
Bellspring #1¼, single long spring 275.00
Bigelow, killer, 9½" 70.00
Blake-Lamb #0, single under spring............................. 90.00
Blizzard, wood snap rattrap 75.00
Buffalo Bill, wood snap rattrap 75.00
Cabelas #1½, dbl coil spring 35.00
Cannon Ball, wood snap rattrap 70.00
Champion #2, dbl long spring 100.00
Cortland #2, dbl long spring... 165.00
Crago, clutch trap 340.00
Cyclone, wood snap rattrap 40.00
Dahlgren Sur Pelt, 12" 35.00
Dauffer.. 35.00
Diamond #33, dbl coil spring.. 35.00
Dixie, fly trap 45.00
Eclipse #2 .... 180.00

Eel, wicker, light damage, early, $125.00. (Photo courtesy Aston Macek Auctions)

Elenchik #1½, dbl coil spring 25.00
Elgin, metal snap rattrap... 20.00
Fatal, drowner mousetrap.. 225.00
Gabariel, rattrap.. 800.00

Gibbs #4, dope trap 565.00
Good Housekeeping, mousetrap..................................... 15.00
Goshen... 475.00
Half Moon, metal mousetrap.. 250.00
Hawley Norton #4, dbl long spring 40.00
Hector #1, single long spring.. 65.00
Helfrich #750 Eliminator.. 80.00
Herters #2, dbl coil spring 10.00
Iron Cat, metal snap mousetrap.................................... 135.00
IT, metal choker mousetrap.. 350.00
Joker #3, wood snap rattrap.. 45.00
JUJ, gopher trap 35.00
Jumbo, minnow trap 70.00
Ketchem, mousetrap for fruit jar................................... 45.00
Kidds Mouser, fruit jar mousetrap................................ 175.00
Knapp #1½, coil spring 35.00
Knock Em Stiff, wood snap rattrap............................... 50.00
Kompakt #3, under spring.. 175.00
Kubes Killer Trap, unmk.. 400.00
Lightning, wood snap rattrap 40.00
Little Champ, plastic mousetrap.................................... 25.00
Lomar #2, coil spring 35.00
Madams Mouser, wht plastic... 20.00
Magnetic, metal snap mousetrap................................... 65.00
McGill, steel squeeze set 20.00
Nebraska Trail... 875.00
Newhouse #44, dbl long spring.................................... 170.00
Newhouse #91½, single long spring.............................. 60.00
Nisbet #1½, single long spring.....................................1,200.00
Nox, wood snap rattrap.. 75.00
Old Tom, Detroit MI fruit jar mousetrap....................... 45.00
Orbeto #300, dbl under spring...................................... 65.00
Philips Specialty Co, gopher trap 50.00
PS Mfg Co #1½, single long spring............................... 20.00
PS&W #1, single under spring 65.00
Quigley, wood snap mousetrap...................................... 40.00
Roto, PVC plastic mousetrap 40.00
Royal, CI rattrap 450.00
Runway, metal mousetrap 35.00
Sargent #0, single long spring....................................... 80.00
Snappy, mousetrap 28.00
St Louis, killer..7,000.00
Stand-By, wood snap mousetrap.................................... 25.00
Stout Master Grip, killer... 100.00
Terminix, wood snap mousetrap.................................... 15.00
Tomcat, wood snap mousetrap...................................... 40.00
Triple J, 4-jaw killer 75.00
Triumph #34X, dbl coil spring...................................... 525.00
U-Neek, glass live mousetrap 150.00
Unique, plastic coon trap 40.00
Verbail #1, ft snare... 85.00
Victor #1½ over 33, single long spring 35.00
Victor Gladiator, steel snap rattrap 85.00
Victor Louisiana Special, w/teeth.................................. 45.00
Walker, CI rattrap...2,700.00
Webley #4, dbl coil spring 40.00
World's Best, Memphis TN, roach trap 45.00
Zip, metal snap mousetrap.. 35.00

Trenton

Trenton, New Jersey, was an area that supported several pottery companies from the mid-1800s until the late 1960s. A consolidation of several smaller companies that occurred in the 1890s was called Trenton Potteries Company. Each company produced their own types of wares independent of the others.

Vase, bl gloss, spherical, 8x8" 120.00
Vase, bl gloss, triple disk, circular mk, 8½x8⅞" 180.00
Vase, gr semigloss, dbl disk, 5⅞x6¼" 145.00
Vase, wht Deco triple U form, circular mk, 7½x5½" 110.00

Trevaise

In 1907 the vacant Sandwich glasshouse was purchased and refurbished by the Alton Manufacturing Company. They specialized in lighting and fixtures, but under the direction of an ex-Tiffany glassblower and former Sandwich resident James H. Grady, they also produced a line of iridescent art glass called Trevaise, examples of which are very rare today. It was often decorated with pulled feathers, whorls, leaves, and vines similar to the glassware produced by Tiffany, Quezal, and Durand. Examples that surface on today's market range in price from $1,500.00 to $2,000.00 and up. Trevaise was made for less than one year. Due to financial problems, the company closed in 1908. Our advisor for this category is Frank W. Ford; he is listed in the Directory under Massachusetts.

Vase, gr & opal w/pulled & hooked decor, 1907 ....3,500.00

Vase, olive green with eight braided ribs highlighted by greenish black, wavy gray-green spirals under rows of irregular lavender scallops, 9½", $3,000.00. (Photo courtesy Cincinnati Art Galleries/LiveAuctioneers.com)

Trivets

Although strictly a decorative item today, the original purpose of the trivet was much more practical. They were used to protect table tops from hot serving dishes, and irons heated on the kitchen range were placed on trivets during use to protect work surfaces. The first patent date was 1869; many of the earliest trivets bore portraits of famous people or patriotic designs. Florals, birds, animals, and fruit were other favored motifs. Watch for remakes of early original designs. Some of these are marked Wilton, Emig, Wright, Iron Art, and V.M. for Virginia Metalcrafters. However, many of these reproductions are becoming collectible. Expect to pay considerably less for these than for the originals, since they are abundant.

Brass

Bowling Handicap Award, flower center w/openwork, 1945, 7" dia..40.00
Circles interlocking, 3-ftd, w/hdl, ca 1880, 10½x5½" 120.00
Circuler w/lobed edge, rtcl pattern, tripod base, 12x11" dia......... 340.00
Dmn shape w/ped ft (for teapot), 1890-1900s, 8x10" 75.00
East West Hames Best/rtcl thistles, 4-ftd, 1890s, 7x15x9" 285.00
Flatiron shape, punched design, ca 1900, 9x4¼" 95.00
Good luck, pierced rim, tall std w/flared ft, 19th C, 10x8½" dia 90.00

Heart cutouts, Am, 19th C, 10½" L, from $135 to 150.00
Heart cutouts, pierced skirt, iron fr, 4-ftd, 12x17x15" 350.00
Hearts (2) & dmn cutout on spade shape, 3-ftd, 1900, 10x4".......... 130.00
King's arms, w/lions, crown, & unicorn, 4-ftd, CW 10-17, 1957, 6" .. 90.00
Lyre form w/wrought-iron base, wood hdl, 13" H 85.00
Maple leaf in open circle, ca 1900, 4¾" dia................................... 30.00
Owl shape, emb openwork, ca 1900, 8x5½" 65.00
Queen Anne's style, 3-ftd, CW10-10, 1950s, 9½x10½" 45.00
Rectangular, rtcl ship among waves, paw & ball ft, 4x10x6".......... 48.00
Rectangular w/rtcl hunt scene, shaped ft, England, 7x14x8"........ 340.00
Sunburst w/openwork, 7½" dia+11½" stand 95.00
Unicorn, w/openwork, 3-legs, rnd, 3½x6" 25.00

Cast Iron

Art Nouveau floral pattern, 5½" 65.00
Best on Earth.. 25.00
Broom & wheat pattern, Griswold, ca 1900, 8½" L 48.00
Brooms & leaves, Wilton #10, 8½" 15.00
Cherubs holding wreath, w/figural man hdl, JZH, 1948, 8¾x4½" .. 60.00
Circles in heart, emb 1829 on hdl w/heart on end, 3-ftd, 11x6" 60.00
Circular w/heart cutouts, tripod base, 10" H............................... 180.00
Circular w/wavy bars, revolves, 19th C, 53" L 240.00
Colt emb on iron flatiron shape w/openwork, ca 1900, 6½x4" 110.00
Curlicues w/1894 on iron shape, w/hdl, 8¾" L 90.00
Flower (4 petals) center w/cut-out heart design, Wright #270, 6½" ..50.00
Geo Washington medallion on spade shape, 1820s 1,200.00
Golden eagle in wreath, mc pnt, T-13, 5¼x8½" 35.00
Good Luck to All Who Use This Stand, horseshoe shape, 1900s, 8x4½"....30.00
Heart shape, 3-ftd, #262, 4½x9½" 55.00
Heart w/serrated edges, open hearts/dmn, 1¾x8x5⅛" 215.00
I Want U Comfort Iron....PA USA, flatiron shape, 6½" L 25.00
Running dog & fox w/W, 7½" L 35.00
Star in circle w/serrated edges, 5½" dia 36.00

Wrought Iron

Circular, 3-leg, 23" L... 75.00
Circular (very plain), 3-ftd, long hdl, 17x7½" dia......................... 85.00
Circular w/scrollwork, 3-ftd, long hdl, 21½x9¼" dia.................... 300.00
Family Day, Trafford Foundry, mk W, Westinghouse, 1953, 8½x5" ...35.00
Flatiron shape w/PA Dutch motif, 19th C, ftd, 2x9x4¼"............... 36.00
Heart shape, 3 curled ft, sgn Dietrich, 6½" 100.00
Heart shape w/rattail terminal, 3-ftd, 11" L 215.00
Lyre form w/long hdl, 3½x24x10"... 300.00
Rectangle w/7 bars, long hdl, ftd, 20" L, G 25.00
Rnd w/3 dmn-ftd legs, scalloped edges, 2½x4½" 90.00
Triangular, 3 curved legs, curved hdl w/scrolled heart, 3x6x14" .. 1,000.00
4-point star, cabriole legs, penny ft, 18th C, 14" H...................... 600.00

Tuthill

The Tuthill Glass Company operated in Middletown, New York, from 1902 to 1923. Collectors look for signed pieces and those in an identifiable pattern. Condition is of utmost importance, and examples with brilliant cutting and intaglio (natural flowers and fruits) combined fetch the highest prices. Unless noted otherwise, values are for signed items.

Bowl, Gravic Iris, att, deep, 9"... 180.00
Bowl, Rex cutting, several sm chips, 8"..................................... 1,450.00
Bowl, Rex variation cutting, unsgn/att, 8" 900.00
Bowl, wild rose intaglio, 8" 100.00
Bowl, 6-point brilliant-cut star in base, vintage intaglio rim, 2x12" ...525.00

Compote, intaglio flower/berry vine in bowl, star ft, 7x5½", pr.... 150.00
Cruet, Russian cut panel, eng garlands, ped ft, faceted stopper, 9" ..720.00
Pitcher, Thousand Eye & Hobstar cutting, tankard form, 9½" 300.00
Pitcher, vining 5-petal flower intaglio, scalloped rim, tankard, 8" ..100.00
Plate, butterflies/flowers intaglio, serrated star in center, 8" 500.00
Vase, all-over eng vine w/3-lobe leaves, slender, 10" 385.00
Vase, bud; eng leafy band under rim/around ft, slim/ftd, 12" 325.00

Twin Winton

Twin brothers Don and Ross Winton started this California-based company during the mid-1930s while still in high school. In the mid-1940s they shut it down while in the armed forces and started up again in the late 1940s, when older brother Bruce Winton joined them and bought them out in the early 1950s. The company became a major producer of cookie jars, kitchenware, and household items sold nationally until it closed its San Juan Capistrano, location in 1977. They're also well known for their Hillbilly line — mugs, pitchers, bowls, lamps, ashtrays, decanters, and other novelty items, which evolved from the late 1940s through the early 1970s with a variety of decorating methods still being discovered. Don Winton was the only designer for Twin Winton and created literally thousands of designs for them and hundreds of other companies. He is still sculpting in Corona del Mar, California, and collectors and dealers are continuing to find and document new pieces daily. To learn more about this subject, we recommend *Collector's Guide to Don Winton Designs* by our advisor, Mike Ellis; he is listed in the Directory under California.

Ashtray, Hillbilly, 4½x4" 20.00
Bank, Hillbilly, emb Mountain Dew Loot, 7" 75.00
Bank, Teddy Bear, TW-409, 8" 40.00
Bank, Wooly Mammoth, Ford Advertising, 5" 75.00
Bowl, salad; Artist Palette, rare, 13", minimum value 250.00
Candleholder, Aladdin lamp, TW-510, 6½x9½", ea 45.00
Candy jar, Shoe, TW-352, 10x10" 75.00
Canister, Tea Sty, Canister Farm, TW-114, 5x3" 30.00
Cookie jar, Bambi, TW-54, 8x10" 175.00
Cookie jar, Barn, TW-41, 12x8" 80.00
Cookie jar, Butler, wood finish, TW-60, 12x7" 300.00
Cookie jar, Chipmunk, TW-45, 10x10" 75.00
Cookie jar, Cookie Bucket, TW-59, 8x9" 40.00
Cookie jar, Donkey, TW-88, 13x8" 65.00
Cookie jar, Fire Engine, TW-56, 7x12" 85.00
Cookie jar, Flopsy, TW-243 .... 350.00
Cookie jar, Hen on basket, TW-61, 8½x8½" 125.00
Cookie jar, Hobby Horse, TW-239 .... 300.00
Cookie jar, Mother Goose, TW-75, 14x7" 100.00
Cookie jar, Noah's Ark, TW-94, 10x9½" 75.00
Cookie jar, Pirate Fox, TW-246, 8½x11" 225.00
Cookie jar, Pot O' Cookies, TW-58, 8x10" 40.00
Cookie jar, Sheriff, TW-255 .... 200.00
Cookie jar, Snail, wood finish, TW-37, 7½x12" 175.00
Cookie jar, Walrus, TW-63, 10x11" 375.00
Decanter, Bavarian, Schnapps on base, #735, 12" 40.00
Decanter, Irishman, Irish Whiskey on base, #615, 12½" 50.00
Decanter, Japanese, Sake on base, #616, 12"............................ 30.00
Figurine, Black girl holding elephant, T-14, 3½" 125.00
Figurine, boy on stick horse w/dog at feet, 1980s, 6"................. 35.00
Figurine, boy shot putting w/Yale logo on shirt, 3" 150.00
Figurine, boy skier, 7".. 225.00
Figurine, boy standing by mailbox, T-8, 5½" 175.00
Figurine, football player, bl & wht uniform, A-572, 5"............... 15.00
Figurine, football player talking to girl, ca 1950, 5x6"................ 275.00
Figurine, girl playing dress-up, T-19, 5½" 200.00

Figurine, Indian w/shield & quiver, #759, 18" 100.00
Figurine, Kitten Muffy, wht w/yarn ball, A-179, 2" 10.00
Figurine, Mickey the Sorcerer, wand in hand, 8"..................... 150.00
Figurine, seated gnome w/elbows on knees, #587, 8" 20.00
Figurine, wht kitten in brn shoe, A-83, 4x6¾" 15.00
Flowerpot, gnome w/wheelbarrow, A-41, 5" 10.00
Ice bucket, Suspenders, Hillbilly, TW-30, 14x7½"................... 250.00
Lamp, Squirrel, TW-255, 12" 175.00
Miniature, baby duck, yel, #102 ....5.00
Miniature, beaver lying down, #315, 1x2½" 8.00
Miniature, fawn kneeling, #305 ....9.00
Miniature, floppy rabbit, #205 ....7.00
Miniature, kitty, blk & wht, #204 ....6.00
Miniature, swan, blk, #313 ....6.00
Mug, mustache; Bronco Group, 3" 50.00
Mug, stein; Bamboo, 8".. 35.00
Mug, Wood Grain, rope hdl w/spur, 4"................................... 40.00
Napkin holder, elephant, TW-453, 6x4" 150.00
Napkin holder, horse, TW-450, 6x4" 150.00
Napkin holder, Porky Pig, TW-473, 8x5" 75.00
Ornament, Christmas; camel in Santa hat, A-134 ....6.00
Ornament, Christmas; lamb, A-76 ....4.00
Ornament, Christmas; snowman w/broom, hat & scarf, A-54 ....8.00
Pitcher, Hillbilly, 7½" 75.00
Plate, dinner; Wood Grain, 10"... 40.00
Relish tray, Artist Palette, 4x8" 30.00
Shakers, apple, TW-135, pr 75.00
Shakers, bull, TW-195, pr... 40.00
Shakers, cart, TW-148, pr... 50.00
Shakers, duckling, TW-193, pr 75.00
Shakers, jack-in-the-box, TW-148, pr.................................... 125.00
Shakers, owl, TW-191, pr 30.00
Shakers, poodle, TW-164, pr 50.00
Shakers, saddle, B-207, 3", pr 50.00
Spoon rest, cow, TW-23, 5x10".. 40.00
Wall pocket, rabbit head, TW-302, 5½"................................. 100.00

Typewriters

The first commercially successful typewriter was the Sholes and Glidden, introduced in 1874. By 1882 other models appeared, and by the 1890s dozens were on the market. At the time of the First World War, the ranks of typewriter-makers thinned, and by the 1920s only a few survived.

Collectors informally divide typewriter history into the pioneering period, up to about 1890; the classic period, from 1890 to 1920; and the modern period, since 1920. There are two broad classifications of early typewriters: (1) Keyboard machines, in which depression of a key prints a character and via a shift key prints up to three different characters per key; (2) Index machines, in which a chart of all the characters appears on the typewriter; the character is selected by a pointer or dial and is printed by operation of a lever or other device. Even though index typewriters were simpler and more primitive than keyboard machines, they were none-the-less a later development, designed to provide a cheaper alternative to the standard keyboard models that were selling for upwards of $100.00. Eventually second-hand keyboard typewriters supplied the low-price customer, and index typewriters vanished except as toys. Both classes of typewriters appeared in a great many designs.

It is difficult, if not impossible, to assign standard market prices to early typewriters. Over the past decade, competition from a handful of wealthy overseas collectors drastically affected the American market, but now Americans are among the top bidders. This surge in interest has resulted in much higher prices on the rarer models. Some auction-realized prices have been astronomical. We have updated values to reflect current market activity. Bear in mind that condition is a very important factor, and typewriters can vary infinitely in condition. Another factor to consider is that an early typewriter achieves its value mainly through the skill, effort, and patience of the collector who restores it to its original condition, in which case its purchase price is insignificant. Some unusual looking early typewriters are not at all rare or valuable, while some very ordinary looking ones are scarce and could be quite valuable. No general rules apply. See Clubs, Newsletters, and Catalogs in the Directory for information on the Early Typewriter Collectors Association. When no condition is indicated, the items listed below are assumed to be in excellent, unrestored condition.

American, indicator type, M	85.00
Bar-Lock #1, fancy iron front w/'B'	1,000.00
Bennett, w/case	95.00
Blinkensderfer, #6, oak case	200.00
Brooks, 4-row, bk-strike, ca 1895, minimum value	5,000.00
Coffman, index	175.00
Crandall	1,000.00
Crary, circular keyboard/type-bar assembly, ca 1892, minimum value	1,000.00
Daugherty, 4-row, front-strike, elongated profile	350.00
Eagle, Defi, 3-row, swinging sector	800.00
Edison, index	1,000.00
English, curved keyboard, down-strike, Pat 1890, minimum value	3,000.00
Fox Portable #1, 3-row, front-strike, folding	150.00
Gourland, 4-row, front-strike, ca 1920-25	50.00

Hammond E.I., original leather case, 16x13x8½", $265.00. (Photo courtesy Randy Inman Auctions Inc./LiveAuctioneers.com)

Hammond #2, str keyboard, 3-row, type shuttle	75.00
Ingersoll, type-slug index	500.00
Liliput, circular index machine, Germany, ca 1907	1,000.00
McCool #2, 3-row, type wheel, pre-1910	850.00
National	1,200.00
Pearl (Searing), circular index, unpnt base, ca 1891	1,000.00
Remington #4, 4-row, up-strike, caps only	350.00
Royal Grand, 4-row, front-strike, no glass windows on sides	500.00
Standard Folding #2, 3-row, frontstrike, ca 1908	57.00
Wellington Empire #2, 3-row, thrust action	75.00
Yost #1, dbl keyboard, up-strike, grasshopper action, ca 1887	250.00

Uhl Pottery

Founded in Evansville, Indiana, in 1849 by German immigrants, the Uhl Pottery was moved to Huntingburg, Indiana, in 1908 because of the more suitable clay available there. They produced stoneware — Acorn Ware jugs, crocks, and bowls — which were marked with the acorn logo and 'Uhl Pottery.' They also made mugs, pitchers, and vases in simple shapes and solid glazes marked with a circular ink stamp containing the name of the pottery and 'Huntingburg, Indiana.' The pottery closed in the mid-1940s. Those seeking additional information about Uhl pottery

are encouraged to contact the Uhl Collectors' Society, whose address is listed in the Directory under Clubs, Newsletters, and Catalogs. For more information, we recommend *Uhl Pottery* by Anna Mary Feldmeyer and Kara Holtzman (Collector Books).

Ashtray, emb Cannelton Sewer Pipe Co on brn, 6" dia, from $90 to	120.00
Bank, acorn shape, brn, 3", from $125 to	175.00
Bean pot, glossy bl, w/hdls, ½-gal, 6", from $180 to	225.00
Bowl, porridge; yel, w/emb fleur-de-lis hdl, Jane Uhl, 5½", $125 to	175.00
Bowl, salad; red w/wht int, ftd, 11", from $45 to	60.00
Churn, brn & wht, McHenry's, 4-gal, 15", from $200 to	300.00
Cup, dessert; yel, ped, Jane Uhl, 4½", from $150 to	200.00
Cuspidor, sponged bl on wht, 6¾"	150.00
Dog feeder, emb DOG on gr, #146, 3½x6½"	75.00
Dutch pot, brn & wht, 1-gal, from $50 to	75.00
Jar, brn, A&L Uhl, w/hdls, 10-gal, 22", from $700 to	900.00
Jar, clamp; bl, 10-oz, from $50 to	75.00
Jug, canteen; emb cattail scene on bl, 10", from $300 to	450.00
Jug, glossy brn, shouldered, 2-ring hdls, #172, 7½", from $50 to	60.00
Novelty, Liberty Bell w/wood stand, 15", from $175 to	200.00
Pail, butter; sponged bl on yel, bail hdl, w/lid, 2-lb, from $160 to	200.00
Paperweight, jug shaped, brn, w/hdl, 3¼", from $400 to	500.00
Pitcher, ball form, bl w/wht int, 6"	75.00
Pitcher, barrel, red, ¼-gal, from $75 to	125.00
Pitcher, grapes emb on gr & tan, squatty, from $250 to	300.00
Pitcher, stags (3) on gr, stag makes spout, Jane Uhl, 12", $1,200 to	2,000.00
Pitcher & bowl, emb bl & wht, rimmed bowl, from $400 to	500.00
Plate, compartment; orange, 9¾", from $75 to	100.00
Rabbit feeder, wht stoneware, w/ledge rim, 7" dia, from $25 to	40.00
Stein, flagon; yel w/wht int, 16-oz, from $50 to	70.00
Umbrella stand, yel w/red int, #192, 15½", from $200 to	300.00
Vase, bl, flared, ftd, #117, 10", from $60 to	80.00
Vase, bud; yel, #168, 8", from $125 to	150.00
Water cooler, bl & wht, Ice Water 5 on front, 5-gal, w/lid, $450 to	550.00

Unger Brothers

Art Nouveau silver items of the highest quality were produced by Unger Brothers, who operated in Newark, New Jersey, from the early 1880s until 1919. In addition to tableware, they also made brushes, mirrors, powder boxes, and the like for milady's dressing table as well as jewelry and small personal accessories such as match safes and flasks. They often marked their products with a circular seal containing an intertwined 'UB' and '925 fine sterling.' Some Unger pieces contain a patent date near the mark. In addition to sterling, a very limited amount of gold was also used. Note: This company made no pewter items; Unger designs may occasionally be found in pewter, but these are copies. Items with English hallmarks or signed 'Birmingham' are English (not Unger).

Basket, rtcl scrollwork, flared rim, swing hdl, 11½"	225.00
Belt buckle, Egyptian style w/Nouveau florals, 2x3"	100.00
Bowl, floral repoussé border, flared rim, 2½x10"	480.00
Brooch, baby figural, ca 1890, 1⅜"	85.00
Cheese server, ivory (or bone) hdl, ca 1900, 7"	235.00
Fork, Love's Dream, Nouveau design, monogram, 1890s, 7"	25.00
Hand mirror, Nouveau floral, 1903	595.00
Hem measure, silver w/Nouveau lady's head at top, 4" L	160.00
Match safe, Nouveau leaves, rococo, monogram	200.00
Purse, silver mesh, hinged fr, chain-link hdl, sm	145.00
Spoon, grotesque head/Nouveau floral hdl, 5¾"	48.00
Thimble case, pierced silver w/Nouveau scrolls, monogram, 1"	145.00
Thimble case, silver w/Nouveau openwork, ring for chatelaine	145.00
Tray, Nouveau floral, 925 silver, 7"	780.00

University City

Located in University City, Missouri, this pottery was open for only five years (1910 – 1915), but because of the outstanding potters associated with it, notable artware was produced. The company's founder was Edward Gardner Lewis, and among the well-known artists he employed were Adelaide Robineau, Fredrick Rhead, Taxile Doat, and Julian Zsolnay.

Dish, sea life, bl/pk/wht crackle, emb shell, 3 ft w/jewels, TD, 3x5" ...1,200.00
Teapot, gr matt, modeled as bldg, seated figure on dome lid, rstr, 9"...3,500.00
Trivet, Atascadero Nymph of Springs (lady's head), lt bl, Doat, 5" dia...425.00
Vase, stylized cvd blossoms/leaves, unglazed, cylindrical, 9x3"..1,000.00
Vase, wht classic form, sgn TD, mk UC, dtd 1914, 2¼" 500.00

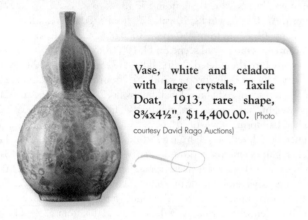

Vase, white and celadon with large crystals, Taxile Doat, 1913, rare shape, 8¾x4½", $14,400.00. (Photo courtesy David Rago Auctions)

Val St. Lambert

Since its inception in Belgium at the turn of the nineteenth century, the Val St. Lambert Cristalleries has been involved in the production of high-quality glass, producing some cameo. The factory is still in production.

Cameo

Goblet, wine; geometric cuttings, citron on crystal, 7", 8 for 240.00
Vase, bud; bumblebees/pussy willows, red & amber to clear, 15"...3,650.00
Vase, chamelion on branch, bl on chartreuse, 4⅝" 1,200.00
Vase, floral, cranberry on frost, cylindrical, 4x1½" 55.00
Vase, flowers/leaves, brn on olive to brn, flared ft, 7½" 200.00
Vase, geometric cuttings, cobalt on clear, 1930, 9x7" 120.00
Vase, geometric floral, cranberry to vaseline, 14".......................1,550.00
Vase, house/trees/water, cut/pnt on pk to bl, sq top, 2¼x2½" 900.00
Vase, mums, chartreuse on frost, cylindrical, 14½" 600.00
Vase, trees/meadow/building, cut/pnt on orange, sq top, 2½x2½" .. 1,150.00

Miscellaneous

Bowl, fruit; cut crystal, 9" 120.00
Candleholders, cranberry cased, twisted form, 3½", pr 85.00
Candlesticks, cut crystal, 12", pr.. 240.00
Caviar server, cut crystal, 2-pc w/SP fr, 4x9¼" 90.00
Decanter, elongated pear shape w/8-sided base, w/stopper, 13¼" ... 85.00
Pitcher, cut crystal, dmns/ribs, 7½"... 100.00
Sculpture, Madonna, Modern style, crystal, 10½x2¾x2"................. 60.00
Sculpture, porpoise, crystal, 4¾x7x3½" 60.00
Sugar bowl, frost, hound finial, 3 hound heads form ft, 8" 360.00
Vase, abstract irid decor on lt bl, squat, S Herman, 6½" 480.00
Vase, bl enamel w/copper o/l, flared rim, slim, 12"...................... 660.00
Vase, crystal w/etched man & women ballet dancers, 6½" 65.00

Valentines

The age-old debate regarding value is still swirling around every antique in the market place today and no doubt will continue to do so. Valentines card values are a prime example. Since the internet put the world at everyone's fingertips, values evolve on a daily basis. It is good to know that some worth-assessing factors will remain constant. It is always important to determine category, condition, size, rarity, and manufacturer. Our advisor for this category is Katherine Kreider, author of *Valentines With Values, One Hundred Years of Valentines,* and *Valentines for the Eclectic Collector.* She is listed in the Directory under Pennsylvania. Values are for valentines in excellent condition, showing no wear, fading, creases, or repair.

Key:
D — dimension
dim — dimensional
HCPP — honeycomb paper puff
PIG — printed/published in Germany

Dim, airplane, crepe-paper wings, PIG, 6x14x4" 125.00
Dim, cat sits in tennis hat before fireplace, 7½x5½x1" 50.00
Dim, cherub w/bow & arrow, PIG, early 1900s, 6½x5x3".............. 35.00
Dim, observation car, Tuck, 8½x5½x3".................................... 150.00
Dim, rowboat, early 1900s, 5x6x1½".. 50.00
Dim, speed boat, Charles Twelvetrees, 10x10x2" 50.00
Dim, Viking ship, PIG, 9¾x9x5".. 75.00
Dim, 3D Cinderella coach, Hallmark, 1960s, 9¾x7½x4½" 15.00
Dim, 4D greeting-card heart w/floral/children, PIG, 4½x4x4½" 40.00
Dim & greeting-card style, A Valentine for My Wife, Hallmark, 1961 .. 15.00
Flat, children drinking ice-cream sodas, felt accent, USA, 1940s, 8x6".. 10.00
Flat, Dutch children, English, Tuck, early 1900s, 8x7" 50.00
Flat, girl w/toy sewing machine, USA, 1950s, 4x2" 6.00
Flat, golfing kitten, USA, 1950s, 4x2" 6.00
Flat, postman, PIG, 1900s, 6½x4".. 15.00
Flat, toaster motif, USA, 1950s, 4x2½"...6.00
Flat, Wizard of Oz, USA, 1960s, 5x4" 25.00
Flat, 3 Blind Mice, USA, 1940s, EX..6.00
Folded-flat, Superman, USA, 1940s, 4½x6½".............................. 50.00
Folded-flat, vanity, 1940s, 5x4" 10.00
Folded-flat, Wonder Woman, 1940s, 6x6" 100.00
Greeting card, boy & girl on scooter, Whitney, 1930s, 5x4" 4.00
Greeting card, Choked to Death, Esther Howland, 1860s, 9½x8" ..350.00
Greeting card, Civil War soldier, 1860s, rare, 7x5"...................... 500.00
Greeting card, To My Wife, Hallmark, 1950s, 9½x7½" 6.00
Greeting card, woman & cherub, litho, hand colored, 1890s, 8x5" ...125.00
HCPP, Dan Cupid, Beistle, USA, 1920s, 6x8x2".......................... 35.00
HCPP, hanging heart, Beistle, USA, 1920s, 8x8x4" 25.00
HCPP, Jack Be Nimble, Beistle, USA, 1920s, 9x6x3" 25.00
HCPP & hold-to-light, fountain, PIG, early 1900s, 11x8x3"....... 125.00
HCPP & hold-to-light, Victorian House, PIG, early 1900s, 10x9x5" ... 175.00
Hold-to-light, steamship, 4D, PIG, early 1900s, 10x6x4"........... 175.00
Hold-to-light, Victorian girl & flowers, 2D, PIG, 1925, 8½x6x3".. 50.00
Hold-to-light, windmill & sailboat, 3D, PIG, 1915, 12x10x4".... 175.00
Hold-to-light postcard, angels & children, undivided bk, early 1900s ...25.00
Mechanical-flat, Army men & tent, Twelvetrees, 1940s, 12x6"...... 45.00
Mechanical-flat, big-eyed children in roadster, PIG, 1924, 7½x9" . 75.00
Mechanical-flat, cat on teeter-totter, PIG, 1920s, 8x11" 75.00
Mechanical-flat, cherub riding dragonfly, PIG, 1930s, 7x6" 40.00
Mechanical-flat, monkey, harmonica, PIG, 1915, 8x5" 15.00
Mechanical-flat, standard poodle, PIG, early 1900s, 9x5" 50.00
Mechanical-flat, Wee-Gee board, hand colored, 1920s, 6½x4"...... 25.00
Novelty, African Am w/Chiclet boxes attached, Rust Craft, 1920s, 10x6"..75.00
Novelty, Cupid's Book, San Francisco, hardbk, 1920s, 9x6".......... 75.00
Novelty, HP satin candy box, 1920s, 8x8" 45.00

Novelty, mechanical, kissing couple, PIG, 1920s, 6x5" 50.00
Postcard, cherub w/human hair & spun glass wings, early 1900s.... 50.00
Postcard, dressed kittens, chromolitho, PIG, mid-1900s 15.00
Postcard, real photo of cherub, Tuck, early 1900s.......................... 25.00
Postcard, real photo w/Victorian lady & heart, early 1900s............ 15.00

Vallerysthal

Fine glassware has been produced in Vallerysthal, France, since the middle of the nineteenth century.

Stem, cameo grapes, cobalt to clear, hexagonal stem/ft, 7¾x3"...... 24.00
Stem, cameo ovals, sapphire to clear, tall stem, 6x2⅝" 20.00
Tumble up, geometric cameo, gr to clear, att, 7½", w/3½" tumbler... 180.00
Vase, cameo fern leaves, blk on gr w/gold, flat pillow shape, 10½" ...1,200.00
Vase, cameo thistles, pk on frost, cylindrical, 6x1½" 155.00

Van Briggle

The Van Briggle Pottery of Colorado Springs, Colorado, was established in 1901 by Artus Van Briggle, whose early career had been shaped by such notables as Karl Langenbeck and Maria Nichols Storer. His quest for several years had been to perfect a completely flat matt glaze, and upon accomplishing his goal, he opened his pottery. His wife, Anne, worked with him, and they, along with George Young, were responsible for the modeling of the wares. Their work typified the flow and form of the Art Nouveau movement, and the shapes they designed played as important a part in their success as their glazes. Some of their most famous pieces were Despondency, Lorelei, and Toast Cup. Increasing demand for their work soon made it necessary to add to their quarters as well as their staff. Although much of the ware was eventually made from molds, each piece was carefully trimmed and refined before the glaze was sprayed on. Their most popular colors were Persian Rose, Ming Blue, and Mustard Yellow.

Van Briggle died in 1904, but the work was continued by his wife. New facilities were built; and by 1908, in addition to their artware, tiles, gardenware, and commercial lines were added. By the '20s the emphasis had shifted from art pottery to novelties and commercial wares. Reproductions of some of the early designs continue to be made. The double AA mark has always been in use, but after 1920 the dates and/or shape numbers were dropped. Mention should be made here as well that the Anna Van Briggle glaze is a later line which was made between 1956 and 1968. Our advisor for this category is Michelle Ross; she is listed in the Directory under Michigan.

Jardiniere, morning glories, raspberry on mustard, #284, 1905, 7", NM..1,200.00
Tile, bird on branch, mc cuenca, chip, unmk, 6" 1,800.00
Tile, blue jay, mc cuenca, unmk, 6" 3,240.00
Tile, kingfisher on branch, 4-color cuenca, unmk, 6" 1,800.00
Tile, sailboats on lake, 4-color cuenca, unmk, 6" 1,450.00
Vase, buds on tall stems, gr, bulbous, #835, 5¼x3¼" 2,200.00
Vase, daffodils, robin's egg bl w/clay showing, 1908-11, 10¼" ...1,560.00
Vase, geese emb on gr to chartreuse, 1903, 6¼x5½" 7,800.00
Vase, jonquils, bright gr on rose, #40, 1905, 10½x4" 2,050.00
Vase, leaves, robin's egg bl, 1915, 3½x4" 660.00
Vase, Lorelei, bl/gr, Colo Springs, 11" 420.00
Vase, Lorelei, Persian Rose, 1920s, 10x4½" 900.00
Vase, morning glories, raspberry w/gr accents, #287, 1905, 7x3¾" 1,225.00
Vase, organic cvgs on swollen form, gr, 1907-12, 4½" 650.00
Vase, organic designs on bulbous form, gr, 1907-12, 3" 325.00
Vase, papyrus, Persian Rose, emb ribs, #20, 1920s, 10½" 960.00
Vase, papyrus, Persian Rose, rtcl at rim, 1916, hairline, 6½x4¾" 1,300.00
Vase, peacock feathers, gr on purple, bronze base, 1904, 13x4¼"... 42,000.00

Vase, peacock feathers, lt bl to sheer wht, 1904, 10¾x3¾", NM 1,200.00
Vase, peacock feathers, sheer gray-gr on brn clay, #598, 1908-11, 9"..1,680.00
Vase, pine cones & needles, Persian Rose, late 1910s, 5x9½" 600.00
Vase, poppy pods, dk gr to med gr, 1916, 7¾x3½"..................... 1,200.00
Vase, trefoils, frothy gr w/clay showing, grinding chip, 17½x3½" ...1,000.00
Vase, trefoils (swirling), gr/bl, #695, 1908-11, 4x4½", NM.......... 350.00
Vase, trefoils indigo to bright gr, hdls, drilled, #172, 1903, 12" ..2,200.00
Vase, yucca plant, Mountain Craig Brown, sm base chip, 1930s, 17½" ..960.00
Vase, yucca plant, yel to gr, #169, 1903, 12½x5" 2,800.00

Van Erp, Dirk

Dirk van Erp was a Leeuwarden, Holland, coppersmith who emigrated to the United States in 1886 and began making decorative objects from artillery shell casings in the San Francisco shipyards. He opened a shop in 1908 in Oakland and in 1910 formed a brief (one year) partnership with D'Arcy Gaw. Apprentices at the studio included his daughter Agatha and Harry Dixon, who was later to open his own shop in San Francisco. Gaw has been assigned design credit for many of the now famous hammered copper and mica lamp shade lamp forms. So popular were the lamps that other San Francisco craftspeople, Lillian Palmer, Fred Brosi, Hans Jauchen, and Old Mission Kopperkraft among them, began producing similar forms. In addition to lamps, he manufactured a broad range of objects including vases, bowls, desk sets, and smoking accessories. Van Erp's work is typically finely hammered with a deep red-brown patina and of good proportions. On rare occasions, van Erp created pieces in a 'warty' finish: an irregular, indeed lumpy, surface with a much redder appearance. Van Erp died in 1933. In 1929 the shop was taken over by his son, William, who produced hammered goods in both brass and copper. Many feature Art Deco style designs and are of considerably lower value than his father's work. The van Erp mark is prominent and takes the form of a windmill above a rectangle that includes his name, sometimes D'Arcy Gaw's name, and sometimes San Francisco.

Please note: Cleaning or scrubbing original patinas diminishes the value of the object. Our prices are for examples with excellent original patina unless noted. Our advisor for this and related Arts and Crafts objects is Bruce Austin, he is listed in the Directory under New York.

Key: h/cp — hammered copper

Ash pan, copper, highly polished, letter P finial, 7x11" 300.00
Ashtray, floor; h/cp, removable tray, 31" 1,400.00
Basket, h/cp, canoe shape w/cutouts in hdl, 7½x11½" 1,200.00
Basket, h/cp, pierced/riveted hdl, some cleaning, 7½x11½" 600.00
Blotter, h/cp w/monogram, 2¾x5½" 120.00
Bookends, h/cp w/enamel flower, 4¼x6x4" 200.00
Bowl, h/cp, flared rim, sm ft, 9" W 650.00
Bowl, sculpted h/cp, 3x10½"... 900.00
Candlestands, 3 nozzles on copper strap base, ca 1925, 3x11x3", pr...900.00
Jardiniere, h/cp, bulbous w/new patina, 7½x16" 6,000.00
Jardiniere, h/cp, new patina, 13x14½" 3,000.00
Jardiniere, h/cp, red/warty, sm dents, 6x7¾" 4,500.00
Jardiniere, h/cp w/warty texture, 6¼x10½" 4,800.00
Lamp, 11" conical copper & mica shade; h/cp base, 11½".........3,950.00
Lamp, 13" 3-panel riveted copper/mica shade; spherical base, 16½"...10,000.00
Lamp, 14" 4-panel h/cp & mica shade; bulbous base, ca 1911, 16"...11,000.00
Lamp, 18" 4-panel h/cp mica shade; 2-socket trumpet-form base, 17"...14,500.00
Lamp, 19½" 3-panel h/cp mica shade; h/cp base, 23" 15,000.00
Vase, bronzed metal, flared cylinder, ca 1901, 11x10" 3,000.00
Vase, h/cp, cylindrical w/incurvate rim, ca 1910, 6½x3¾".........1,550.00
Vase, h/cp, flared rim, open box mk, 3x6"............................... 550.00
Vase, h/cp, warty, rim-to-hip hdls, 10¼"...............................6,600.00
Vase, h/cp shell casing form w/fluted rim, dtd 1903, 25½x14¼" .. 5,750.00
Vase, hammered brass shell casing form, drilled base, 19¼x6½" .. 2,750.00

Vance/Avon Faience

One of the many American potteries to evolve from a commercial ceramics plant, Vance Faience was organized in 1901 in Tiltonsville, Ohio, for the purpose of producing artistic and utilitarian wares. In 1902 the name was changed to The Avon Faience Company, with the talented William Jervis serving as manager and designer. His British colleague, Frederick Rhead, left England at his behest to join him there. Together they completely revamped the design direction of the company, transforming Victorian shapes and motifs into streamlined Arts & Crafts vases with squeezebag and sgraffito decoration.

In yet another reorganization, the company was incorporated at the end of 1902 with three potteries from nearby West Virginia as the Wheeling Potteries Company. This change of management encouraged the rapid manufacture of commercial wares, which hastened the departure of Jervis and Rhead. Artware production stopped altogether in 1905.

Marks include several versions of 'Vance' and 'Avon.' Our advisors for this category are Suzanne Perrault and David Rago; they are listed in the Directory under New Jersey.

Jardiniere & ped, cvd lotus blossoms/leaves, F Rhead, 33x16" .. 9,600.00
Mug, scenic, HP, Avon, ca 1902-05, 5¼" 90.00
Vase, Nouveau mermaid relief, brn tones, #118, ca 1900, 12x12" ... 900.00
Vase, quintal, gnarled branches, earth tones, Vance FC, 9x9 .... 150.00

Vaseline

Vaseline, a greenish-yellow colored glass produced by adding uranium oxide to the batch, was produced during the Victorian era. It was made in smaller quantities than other colors and lost much of its popularity with the advent of the electric light. It was used for pressed tablewares, vases, whimseys, souvenir items, oil lamps, perfume bottles, drawer pulls, and doorknobs. Pieces have been reproduced, and some factories still make it today in small batches. Vaseline glass will fluoresce under an ultraviolet light.

Banana boat, Button & Bows, 8" L, pr 100.00
Butter dish, globular w/molded flowers, floral finial, 4-ftd, 6" 55.00
Cake stand, Buttons & Bows, ftd, 4¾x9½" 145.00
Candlesticks, molded w/flower-form top, 7", pr 350.00
Car vase, orig bracket, 7½" 85.00
Compote, ftd w/pnt leaves at base rim, 6x5" 48.00
Pitcher, Basketweave, 7½" 30.00
Stand, Clark's Teaberry gum, no box, 7" W 85.00
Vase, controlled bubbles, ftd, flared rim, 16" 90.00
Vase, ftd cylinder w/flared top, appl serpentine, 10" 120.00

Verlys

Verlys art glass, produced in France after 1931 by the Holophane Company of Verlys, was made in crystal with acid-finished relief work in the Art Deco style. Colored and opalescent glass was also used. In 1935 an American branch was opened in Newark, Ohio, where very similar wares were produced until the factory ceased production in 1951. French Verlys was signed with one of three mold-impressed script signatures, all containing the company name and country of origin. The American-made glassware was signed 'Verlys' only, either scratched with a diamond-tipped pen or impressed in the mold. There is very little if any difference in value between items produced in France and America. Though some seem to feel that the French should be higher priced (assuming it to be scarce), many prefer the American-made product. In June of 1955, about 16 Verlys molds were leased to the A.H. Heisey Company. Heisey's versions were not signed with the Verlys name, so if an item is unsigned it is almost certainly a Heisey piece. The molds were returned to Verlys of America in July 1957. Fenton now owns all Verlys molds, but all issues are marked Fenton. Our advisor for this category is Don Frost; he is listed in the Directory under Washington.

Bowl, scalloped/rtcl swirled rim, oval, 20x16" 120.00
Charger, birds & bees, clear & frosted, 3 bird ft, 11⅝" 120.00
Charger, lg center flower, clear & frosted, low, 11⅝" 120.00
Charger, roses, clear & frosted, 3x13" 325.00
Charger, thick swirled melon ribs, crystal, 5x8" 120.00
Charger, water lilies, lt amber, 2½x13¾" 390.00
Charger, water lilies, wht opal, 2½x13¾" 200.00
Dish, swirled rim, duck at side, wht opal, brass base, 1940s, 4x6" .. 215.00
Fishbowl, relief goldfish, tails form hdls, amber, 4x18" 350.00
Fishbowl, relief goldfish, tails form hdls, clear satin, 4x18" 300.00
Vase, bumblebees & grass, wht opaque, ovoid, narrow rim, 1930s, 5⅝" ... 150.00
Vase, laurel, amber, 1960s, 10½" 120.00
Vase, laurel, wht opal, 1960s, 10½" 325.00
Vase, lg flower heads, flat rim, opal, 8⅞x4½" 420.00
Vase, Oriental figure w/umbrella, clear & frosted, 1940, 9⅜x5¼" 180.00
Vase, thistle, clear & frosted, 9¾x7" 200.00
Vase, tumbler form w/lg tab hdls emb w/birds, opal, 7⅞" 585.00

Vernon Kilns

Vernon Potteries Ltd. was established by Faye G. Bennison in Vernon, California, in 1931. The name was later changed to Vernon Kilns; until it closed in 1958, dinnerware, specialty plates, artware, and figurines were their primary products. Among its wares most sought after by collectors today are items designed by such famous artists as Rockwell Kent, Walt Disney, Don Blanding, Jane Bennison, and May and Vieve Hamilton. Our advisor for this category is Ray Vlach; he is listed in the Directory under Illinois.

Chatelaine Shape

This designer pattern by Sharon Merrill was made in four color variations: Topaz, Bronze, decorated Platinum, and Jade.

Bowl, chowder; Topaz or Bronze, 6", from $12 to 15.00
Bowl, salad; Platinum or Jade, decor, 12", from $55 to 75.00
Plate, chop; Platinum or Jade, decor, 16", from $50 to 65.00
Plate, salad; Topaz or Bronze, 7½", from $12 to 15.00
Platter, Platinum or Jade, decor, 16", from $65 to 85.00
Shakers, Decorated Platinum or Jade, pr from $25 to 30.00
Sugar bowl, Platinum or Jade, decor, w/lid, from $35 to 40.00
Teapot, Topaz or Bronze, w/lid, from $175 to 200.00

Melinda Shape

Patterns found on this shape are Arcadia, Beverly, Blossom Time, Chintz, Cosmos, Dolores, Fruitdale, Hawaii (Lei Lani on Melinda is two and a half times base value), May Flower, Monterey, Native California, and Philodendron. Two patterns, Rosedale and Wheat, were made for Sears, Roebuck & Co. and marked with Sears Harmony House backstamp. The more elaborate the pattern, the higher the value.

Bowl, lug chowder; 6", from $12 to 18.00
Bowl, rim soup; 8", from $12 to 18.00
Coffeepot, 8-cup, from $55 to 85.00
Creamer, ind; short or tall, ea from $12 to 18.00
Egg cup, from $18 to 25.00
Pitcher, 2-qt, from $35 to 50.00
Plate, dinner; 10½", from $12 to 18.00

Plate, luncheon; 9½", from $12 to.................................... 15.00
Sauceboat, from $20 to 30.00
Teapot, w/lid, 6-cup, from $45 to 85.00

Monticeto Shape (and Coronado)

This was one of the company's most utilized shapes — well over 200 patterns have been documented. Among the most popular are the solid colors, plaids, the florals, westernware, and the Bird and Turnbull series. Bird, Turnbull, and Winchester 73 (Frontier Days) are two to four times base values. Disney hollow ware is seven to eight times base values. Plaids (except Tweed and Calico), solid colors, Brown-eyed Susan are represented by the lower range.

Ashtray, rnd, 5½", from $12 to 20.00
Bowl, mixing; 7", from $22 to.................................... 30.00
Bowl, salad; rnd or angular, 13", ea from $40 to............. 65.00
Bowl, serving; angular, 9", from $20 to.......................... 25.00
Butter pat, 2½", from $15 to...................................... 25.00
Coaster/cup warmer, 4½", from $20 to 25.00
Egg cup, dbl; cupped or str sides, ea from $18 to 25.00
Jam jar, notched lid, 5", from $65 to 95.00
Lemon server, center brass hdl, 6", from $25 to 35.00
Pepper mill, wood encased, 4½", from $45 to 55.00

Pitcher, Winchester Western, 11", $240.00.

Plate, bread & butter; 6½", from $5 to 10.00
Plate, salad; 7½", from $8 to....................................... 15.00
Spoon holder, from $45 to.. 65.00
Teapot, angular or rnd, from $45 .... 95.00

San Clemente (Anytime) Shape

Patterns you will find on this shape include Tickled Pink, Heavenly Days, Anytime, Imperial, Sherwood, Frolic, Young in Heart, Rose-A-Day, and Dis 'N Dot.

Bowl, chowder; 6", from $8 to 12.00
Bowl, vegetable; divided, 9", from $15 to......................... 22.00
Butter pat, 2½", from $15 to....................................... 20.00
Creamer, from $8 to.. 12.00
Gravy boat, from $18 to... 20.00
Mug, 12-oz, from $15 to... 25.00
Plate, chop; 13", from $18 to 25.00
Platter, 11", from $12 to.. 20.00
Sugar bowl, w/lid, from $12 to..................................... 20.00
Teacup & saucer, from $10 to...................................... 15.00
Teapot, from, $35 to... 65.00

San Fernando Shape

Known patterns for this shape are Desert Bloom, Early Days, Hibiscus, R.F.D., Vernon's 1860, and Vernon Rose.

Bowl, fruit; 5½", from $6 to 10.00
Bowl, lug chowder; 6", from $12 to 18.00
Bowl, salad; 10½", from $45 to 65.00
Bowl, serving; rnd, 9", from $18 to 25.00
Coaster, ridged, 3¾", from $15 to 20.00
Creamer, regular, from $12 to 15.00
Mug, 9-oz, from $20 to 25.00
Olive dish, oval, 10", from $20 to 35.00
Plate, dinner; 10½", from $12 to 18.00
Platter, 16", from $50 to.. 75.00
Shakers, pr from $15 to 25.00
Tumbler, style #5, 14-oz, from $20 to 25.00

San Marino Shape

Known patterns for this shape are Barkwood, Bel Air, California Originals, Casual California, Gayety, Hawaiian Coral, Heyday, Lei Lani (two and a half times base values), Mexicana, Pan American Lei (two and a half times base values), Raffia, Seven Seas, Shadow Leaf, Shantung, Sun Garden, and Trade Winds. The Mojave pattern was produced for Montgomery Ward, Wheat Rose for Belmar China Co.

Ashtray, 5½", from $12 to... 20.00
Bowl, mixing; 6", from $19 to...................................... 24.00
Bowl, mixing; 9", from $28 to...................................... 35.00
Casserole, w/lid, 8", from $35 to.................................. 60.00
Coffee server, w/stopper, 10-cup, from $35 to 60.00
Cup, jumbo, from $25 to.. 35.00
Flowerpot, w/saucer, 4", from $35 to 45.00
Plate, bread & butter; 6", from $5 to 8.00
Sauceboat, from $17 to 22.00
Spoon holder, from $30 to.. 45.00
Sugar bowl, w/lid, from $12 to.................................... 17.00

Transitional (Year 'Round) Shape

Patterns on this shape include Country Cousin, Lollipop Tree, Blueberry Hill, and Year 'Round.

Bowl, cereal/soup; from $8 to 10.00
Buffet server, trio, from $35 to.................................... 50.00
Casserole, w/lid, 8", from $25 to.................................. 45.00
Coffeepot, w/lid, 6-cup, from $25 to............................. 45.00
Gravy boat, from $18 to... 25.00
Plate, dinner; 10", from $9 to 13.00
Platter, 11", from $12 to.. 20.00
Teapot, from $25 to.. 50.00

Ultra Shape

More than 50 patterns were issued on this shape. Nearly all the artist-designed lines (Rockwell Kent, Don Blanding, and Disney) utilized Ultra. The shape was developed by Gale Turnbull, and many of the elaborate flower and fruit patterns can be credited to him as well; use the high end of our range as a minimum value for his work. For Frederick Lunning, use the mid range. For other artist patterns, use these formulae based on the high end: Blanding — 3x (Aquarium 5x); Disney, 5 – 7x; Kent — Moby Dick, 2 – 4x; and Our America, 3 – 5x; Salamina, 5 – 7x.

Bowl, cereal; 6", from $10 to 15.00
Bowl, fruit; 5½", from $6 to 12.00
Butter tray, w/lid, from $35 to..................................... 75.00
Casserole, w/lid, 8" (inside dia), from $45 to 95.00
Egg cup, from $18 to 25.00

Pitcher, jug style, 1-pt, 4½", from $35 to 50.00
Plate, chop; 17", from $65 to 95.00
Plate, luncheon; 9½", from $10 to 20.00
Shakers, pr from $20 to 30.00
Teapot, 6-cup, from $45 to 100.00

Fantasia and Disney Figures

Baby Pegasus, from $250 to 300.00
Baby Weems, #37, Disney, from $250 to 350.00
Centurette, #17, from $600 to 800.00
Dumbo, #40 or #41, from $75 to 150.00
Elephant, #25, from $300 to 400.00
Goldfish bowl, #121, hand decor, from $500 to 600.00
Hippo, #33, Disney, from $350 to 400.00
Ostrich, #29, Disney, from $1,200 to 1,500.00
Pegasus, #21, from $200 to 300.00
Sprite, #7, #9, #10, #11 or #12, ea from $250 to 300.00
Sprite, #8, scarce, from $300 to 400.00
Unicorn sitting, #14, from $400 to 500.00
Winged Pegsus vase, lt bl, 7½x12", from $500 to 700.00

Specialty Ware

Ashtray, city & state souvenir, 1-color transfer 20.00
Cup & saucer, demi; souvenir, from $20 to 30.00
Pitcher, state seal, Melinda shape, 1½-pt, from $45 to 50.00
Plate, city &/or state souvenirs, 1-color transfer 20.00
Plate, French Opera Reproductions, 8½", from $18 to 25.00
Plate, historic places, from $25 to 45.00
Plate, Mother Goose 65.00
Plate, Music Masters, 8½", from $18 to 25.00
Plate, presidential or armed services, from $35 to 75.00
Plate, Race Horse, 10½" 75.00
Plate, school or organizations, from $20 to 35.00
Plate, Trader Vic, 9½", minimum value 85.00
Plate, transportation theme, mc, from $65 to 95.00
Plate, transportation theme, 1-color, from $45 to 60.00
Plate, Ye Old Times, 10½", from $35 to 45.00
Spoon rest, souvenir, minimum value 35.00

Villeroy and Boch

The firm of Villeroy and Boch, located in Mettlach, Germany, was brought into being by the 1841 merger of three German factories — the Wallerfangen factory, founded by Nicholas Villeroy in 1787, and two potteries owned by Jean-Francois Boch, the earlier having been in operation there since 1748. Villeroy and Boch produced many varieties of wares, including earthenware with printed under-glaze designs which carried the well-known castle mark with the name 'Mettlach.' See also Mettlach.

Charger, castle scene, Heidelberg Schloss, 12" 75.00
Charger, Japanese lady seated, #355, 20th C, 14" 75.00
Ewer, harvest scenes in relief, German saying on neck, drilled, 15"....240.00
Paperweight, dwarf figural, mc majolica, sm touchups, 3¾x7" 240.00
Pitcher, brn stoneware w/hinged pewter lid, 13¼" 155.00
Planter, scenic transfer, bl on wht, rnd w/shaped rim, hdls, 19th C.. 120.00
Plaque, classical women (2), wht on bl, 8¼x6" 250.00
Plaque, hunting dog in wetlands, 17" dia 300.00
Plaque, lady (stout) drinking, #2626, 7¾" 50.00
Plaque, Muttertag (Mother's Day) 1979, bl & wht, 10x7"+fr 48.00
Plaque, windmill scene, bl on wht Delft style, 8⅞" 36.00
Plate, floral, bl on wht, crazing, 9½" 15.00

Stein, birds & flowers in grid, hinged lid, #1821, 13" 180.00
Stein, figural panels/acorn borders, gr jasper, hinged lid, #147 ..... 155.00
Tray, fish on basket, gr majolica, prof rpr, 25" L 180.00
Vase, bl & sea gr mottle, bulbous, Luxembourg #324, 1950s, 4" .. 100.00
Vase, bl crystalline on cream, bulbous, sm mouth, Luxembourg #321, 5"..275.00
Vase, bl/gr/brn mottle, Luxembourg V&B, #275/3, 7½" 480.00
Vase, ewer form w/boy climbing to spout, worn silver trim, 1840s, 13"...180.00
Vase, floral, mc on cream, shouldered, 9¾x5", pr 125.00

Vistosa

Vistosa was produced from about 1938 through the early 1940s. It was Taylor, Smith, and Taylor's answer to the very successful Fiesta line of their nearby competitor, Homer Laughlin. Vistosa was made in four solid colors: mango red, cobalt blue, light green, and deep yellow. 'Pie crust' edges and a dainty five-petal flower molded into handles and lid finials made for a very attractive yet nevertheless commercially unsuccessful product. Our advisor for this category is Ted Haun; he is listed in the Directory under Indiana.

Bowl, cereal; 6¾" 22.00
Bowl, cream soup; from $22 to 28.00
Bowl, fruit; 5¾", from $15 to 18.00
Bowl, salad; ftd, 12", from $200 to 225.00
Bowl, soup; lug hdl, from $30 to 35.00
Bowl, 3x9¼", from $35 to 40.00
Chop plate, 12", from $35 to 50.00
Chop plate, 15", from $40 to 55.00
Coffee cup, AD; from $40 to 50.00
Coffee saucer, AD; from $10 to 15.00
Creamer, from $20 to 25.00
Egg cup, ftd, from $50 to 70.00
Jug, water; 2-qt, from $120 to 150.00
Plate, 6", cobalt 25.00
Plate, 6", colors other than cobalt, from $12 to 15.00
Plate, 7", from $14 to 18.00
Plate, 9", from $15 to 20.00
Plate, 10", from $35 to 45.00
Platter, 13", from $40 to 50.00
Sauceboat, from $175 to 200.00
Shakers, pr from $25 to 32.00
Sugar bowl, w/lid 25.00
Teacup & saucer, from $18 to 22.00
Teapot, 6-cup, from $190 to 225.00

Volkmar

Charles Volkmar established a workshop in Tremont, New York, in 1882. He produced artware decorated under the glaze in the manner of the early Barbotine work done at the Haviland factory in Limoges, France. He relocated in 1888 in Menlo Park, New Jersey, and together with J.T. Smith established the Menlo Park Ceramic Company for the production of art tile. The partnership was dissolved in 1893. From 1895 until 1902, Volkmar was located in Corona, New York, first under the name Volkmar Ceramic Company, later as Volkmar and Cory, and for the final six years as Crown Point. During the latter period he made art tile, blue under-glaze Delft-type wares, colorful polychrome vases, etc. The Volkmar Kilns were established in 1903 in Metuchen, New Jersey, by Volkmar and his son, Leon. The production in the teens became more stylized, and bold shapes were covered in rich, crackled Persian glazes. The studio won prizes for a special line of enamel-decorated wares, in bright polychrome on Art Deco, Egyptian-Revival patterns. Difficult to find today, these command prices in the tens of thousands of dollars. Wares were marked with various devices consisting of the Volkmar name, initials, 'Durant Kilns,' or 'Crown Point Ware.' Our advisors for this category are Suzanne Perrault and David Rago; they are listed in the Directory under New Jersey.

Bowl, aubergene gloss w/Egyptian Blue matt int, conical, ftd, 9¾"... 240.00
Mug, Pierrot clowns, snake hdl, Salmagundi Club, Chamberlin, 6x5", NM.. 1,550.00
Oil on canvas, dusky landscape, C Volkmar, 14x24" 1,800.00
Panel, landscape, Impressionist style, 3 8" tiles, hairline, +fr 6,600.00
Vase, brn & yel striations, bulbous base, 19th C, 7x11" 275.00
Vase, couple in period dress, Barbotine, pillow form, rstr, 9½x7" . 800.00
Vase, indigo mottle, 3 angle rim-to-hip hdls, 7x6" 960.00
Vase, pastoral scene in Barbotine, hdls, ca 1875, 11x8", NM.... 1,250.00

Volkstedt

Fine porcelain has been produced in the German state of Thuringia since 1760, when the first factory was established. Financed by the prince, the company produced not only dinnerware, but also the lovely figurines for which they are best known. They perfected the technique of using real lace dipped in soft paste porcelain which would burn away during the firing process, leaving a durable porcelain lace which they used extensively on their famous ballerina figurines.

By the 1830s, other small factories began to emerge in the area. One such company was begun by Anton Muller, who marked his wares with a crown over the letters MV (Muller, Volkstedt). Greiner and Holzappel (1804 – 1815) signed some of their pieces with an 'R' accompanied with a series of numbers. Several other marks were used on wares from this area, among them are the 'cross hair' mark with E, N, and S indicated within the pie sections, various marks with a crown over two opposing 'double fish hook' devices, partial crossed swords with a star, crossed forks (variations), a beehive, and a scrolled cartouche containing the crown and the Volkstedt designation. There were others. Later marks may be simply 'Volkstedt Germany.' Both the original Volkstedt factory and the Muller operation continue in production to this day.

Centerpc, cherubs (2) pulling cornucopia w/garland, 1880s, 10" L, pr.. 480.00
Figurine, ballerina w/wide lace skirt, appl flowers, 6½x10", NM .. 350.00
Figurine, Feeding Time, peasant lady w/chickens, ca 1895, 5" 195.00
Figurine, hound dog, brn & wht, recumbent, ca 1900, 5x12½".... 215.00
Figurine, lady seated, much lace & gold, plumed hat, 11x11", NM....900.00
Figurine, man in elegant attire & blk tricorn hat, 5" 120.00
Figurine, nude child w/huge grasshopper, ca 1937-42, 3½x4" L ... 415.00
Figurine, terrier dog seated, brn & wht, 15x12x7" 195.00
Figurines, man w/object in hand, lady w/purse, pastels, 10½", pr . 155.00
Figurines, man w/walking stick, lady w/fan, much lace, 8", pr...... 180.00
Group, ballerinas dancing in ring, appl gold roses, 4¾x4½" 215.00
Group, cellist/paianist/flutist on base, 1915-30, 17x22x16"..........850.00
Group, cherubs (3) at stove w/porridge, 6¾x5"........................... 300.00
Group, man & lady playing chess, 6x9½", NM........................... 325.00
Group, pianist/cellist & dancing couple, 7½x12½"...................... 725.00
Lamps, dancing couple on base, bronze doré mts, 13½x12x4", pr.. 2,650.00
Sculpture, dragon, mc faience, rpr, 39¼x21"...........................8,600.00
Soup tureen, floral sprays, 3-tier form w/rococo, ca 1899, 6½" H .. 165.00
Vase, floral reserves, gilt-bronze mts, early 1900s, 10", pr 660.00

Wade

The Wade Potteries was established in 1867 by George Wade and his partner, a man by the name of Myatt. It was located in Burslem, England, the center of that country's pottery industry. In 1882 George Wade bought out his partner, and the name of the pottery was changed to Wade and Sons. In 1919 the pottery underwent yet another name change and became known as George Wade & Son Ltd. The year 1891 saw the establishment of another Wade Pottery — J & W Wade & Co., which in turn changed its name to A.J. Wade & Co. in 1927. At this time (1927) Wade Heath & Co. Ltd. was also formed.

The three potteries plus a new Irish pottery named Wade (Ireland) Ltd. were incorporated into one company in 1958 and given the name The Wade Group of Potteries. In 1990 the group was taken over by Beauford PLC and became Wade Ceramics Ltd. It sold again in early 1999 to Wade Management and is now a private company.

For those interested in learning more about Wade pottery, we recommend *The World of Wade*, *The World of Wade Book 2*, and *The World of Wade — Figurines and Miniatures*, all by Ian Warner and Mike Posgay; Mr. Warner is listed in the Directory under Canada.

Animal, Asatian, glass eyes, ca 1936, 5¼x7½" 225.00
Animal, Ermine, Faust Lang, 1939, 9¾".................................... 1,400.00
Animal, Giant Panda, 7", MIB.. 550.00
Animal, Lion Cub, paw up, 1935-39, 8x5" 2,000.00
Animal, Mrs Penguin, late 1940s-50s, 3" 175.00
Animal, Panther, underglaze finish, 1935-39, 8x5"...................1,500.00
British Character, Pearly Queen, ca 1959, 2⅞" 150.00
Canadian Red Rose Tea, Fawn, 1967-73...6.00
Disney, Big Bad Wolf & 3 Little Pigs pitcher, non-musical, EX ... 800.00
Disney, Chief, 1981-87, 1⅞" 60.00
Disney, Donald Duck teapot, 7", NM.. 300.00
Disney, Grumpy, 1981-86, 3½".. 200.00
Disney, Merlin as a hare, 1965, 2¼x1⅜"..................................... 200.00
Disney, Sammy the Seal, 6¼".. 450.00
Disney, Scamp, Hat Series Blow-Up, 4" 150.00
Disney, Sgt Tibbs, 1960-64, 2" 100.00
Disney, Si, Siamese cat, Blow-Up, 6" 150.00
Disney, Snow White, 1981-86... 225.00
Disney, Snow White & 7 Dwarfs, 8-pc set 1,500.00
Disney, Thumper, Hatbox series, 5" 70.00
Disney, Thumper Blow-Up, 1961-65, 5¼".................................... 600.00
Dog model, Dalmatian, cellulose finish, 1927-early 1930s, 7x8"..800.00
Drum Box Series, Clara, 1956-59, 2"...90.00
Drum Box Series, Jem, 1956-59, 2" 90.00
Flower, Anemone, Ajax bowl, earthenware....................................40.00
Flower, Anemones, 1930-39, 6"...60.00
Happy Families Series, Frog Parent, 1978-86, ⅞".............................30.00
Happy Families Series, Rabbit Baby, 1978-86, 1⅛"...........................14.00
Nursery Favourite, Boy Blue, 1974, 2⅞"...50.00
Nursery Favourite, Miss Muffet, 1972, 3⅜" 50.00
Nursery Rhyme Character, Butcher, 1949-58, 3¼" 360.00
Nursery Rhyme Character, Soldier, 1949-58, 3" 200.00
Souvenir dish, City of London, 4½x4".. 15.00
Souvenir dish, Tower Bridge, ca 1957, 1½x4x3" 48.00
USA Red Rose Tea, Beaver, 1985, 1¼"...4.00
USA Red Rose Tea, Langur, 1985, 1⅜"..4.00
Whimsey-on-Why Village Set, Greengrocer's Shop, 1981, 1½"..... 15.00
Whimsie, Beagle, 1956, ¾x1"... 62.00
Whimsie, Bison, 1979, 1⅜x1¾"... 10.00
Whimsie, Bluebird, 1979, ⅝"...8.00
Whimsie, Fox Cub, 1955, 1⅜".. 72.00
Whimsie, Husky, 1956, 1¼".. 45.00
Whimsie, Kitten, 1953-59, 1⅜x1¾"... 90.00
Whimsie, Lamb, 1971-84, 2⅜x1⅛"... 10.00
Whimsie, Spaniel, 1953, 2x2¾".. 34.00
Whimsie, Swan, unmk, 1953-59, ⅞x1½"..................................... 200.00
Whimsie - Land Series, Pheasant, 1984-88, 2½x2" 40.00
Whoppa, Brown Bear, 1976-81, 1½" 25.00
Whoppa, Polar Bear, 1976-81, 1½" 20.00

World of Survival Series, African Elephant, 1978-82, 6x10" 650.00
World of Survival Series, American Bison............................. 650.00
World of Survival Series, Polar Bear 650.00

Wallace China

Dinnerware with a western theme was produced by the Wallace China Company, who operated in California from 1931 until 1964. Artist Till Goodan designed three lines, Rodeo, Pioneer Trails, and Boots and Saddle, which they marketed under the package name Westward Ho. When dinnerware with a western theme became so popular just a few years ago, Rodeo was reproduced, but the new trademark includes neither 'California' or 'Wallace China.'

This ware is very heavy and not prone to chips, but be sure to examine it under a strong light to look for knife scratches, which will lessen its value to a considerable extent when excessive.

Note: You'll find cups and saucers with only a border design, which is made up of the lariat and brands. This border was used not only on Rodeo but on Boots 'n Saddle and Little Buckaroo patterns as well. If you'd like to learn more about this company, we recommend *Collector's Encyclopedia of California Pottery* by Jack Chipman.

Boots & Saddle, bowl, cereal; 5¾"................................ 70.00
Boots & Saddle, bowl, fruit; 4⅞", from $50 to 60.00
Boots & Saddle, bowl, oval, 12", from $135 to 175.00
Boots & Saddle, bowl, oval, 9½", from $110 to 120.00
Boots & Saddle, creamer & sugar bowl, 4¾x4⅝", from $210 to ... 225.00
Boots & Saddle, cup & saucer, from $65 to 75.00
Boots & Saddle, pitcher, disk type, 7½", from $225 to 275.00
Boots & Saddle, plate, bread & butter; 7⅛", from $45 to 60.00
Boots & Saddle, plate, dinner; 10½", from $75 to 100.00
Boots & Saddle, platter, 15¼" L, from $200 to 235.00
Boots & Saddle, tumbler, glass, Libby, 4", set of 4............ 50.00
Chuck Wagon, bowl, oval, 1½x8¼" L, from $65 to 85.00
Chuck Wagon, bowl, oval, 10" L, from $120 to............. 130.00
Chuck Wagon, creamer, 2-oz, 2½", from $65 to............... 80.00
Chuck Wagon, cup & saucer, demitasse............................. 110.00
Chuck Wagon, cup & saucer, 2½x3", 5½", from $55 to........ 70.00
Chuck Wagon, platter, 13x9", from $120 to 145.00
Chuck Wagon, sauceboat w/attached undertray, 9½" L 185.00
Dahlia, cup & saucer, from $35 to................................... 40.00
Dahlia, platter, 11½" L.. 40.00
Dahlia, teapot 100.00
El Rancho, bowl, soup; 6½".. 82.50
El Rancho, cup & saucer 45.00
El Rancho, plate, dinner; 10¾", from $70 to..................... 90.00
El Rancho, plate, grill; 9"... 70.00
El Rancho, plate, luncheon; 9½", from $50 to 60.00
El Rancho, plate, salad; 8¼" 45.00
El Rancho, plate, 6½", from $25 to 30.00
El Rancho, platter, 13½" L, from $120 to 135.00
El Rancho, sugar bowl, w/lid, 4", from $50 to 65.00
Longhorn, ashtray, 5½".. 50.00
Longhorn, bowl, mixing; lg... 295.00
Longhorn, creamer, ftd, 3½x6¼", from $125 to 135.00
Longhorn, cup & saucer, from $150 to............................. 165.00
Longhorn, cup & saucer, jumbo; from $240 to.................. 265.00
Longhorn, plate, bread & butter; 7"................................. 75.00
Longhorn, shaker, 5", ea 65.00
Longhorn, shot glass, glass w/fired-on longhorn............... 75.00
Pioneer Trails, bowl, vegetable; oval, 12" L, from $200 to........... 240.00
Pioneer Trails, cup & saucer, 3", 6"................................. 55.00
Pioneer Trails, plate, bread & butter; 7¼", from $50 to 65.00

Pioneer Trails, plate, chop; 13½", from $250 to 270.00
Pioneer Trails, plate, dinner; 10¾", from $85 to 110.00
Rodeo, bowl, int wear, 2¼x4" 65.00
Rodeo, bowl, vegetable; oval, 11⅞" L, from $160 to........ 200.00
Rodeo, creamer, 3½", from $50 to 65.00
Rodeo, cup & saucer, from $50 to 70.00
Rodeo, cup & saucer, jumbo; 3⅝", from $50 to 70.00
Rodeo, pitcher, disk type, 7x7½", from $195 to 225.00
Rodeo, plate, bread & butter; w/center design, 7⅛", from $50 to... 60.00
Rodeo, plate, chop; 13", from $200 to............................ 230.00
Rodeo, plate, dinner; bronco rider, 10¾", from $85 to...... 110.00
Rodeo, platter, 15⅛" L, from $150 to 175.00
Rodeo, shakers, oversz, 4⅞", pr from $90 to 120.00
Rodeo, sugar bowl, open, from $65 to 75.00
Rodeo, sugar bowl, w/lid, 4½" 125.00
Shadowleaf, plate, bread & butter; 7⅛"........................... 30.00
Shadowleaf, plate, dinner; 10½", from $65 to 80.00
Southwest Desert, creamer 65.00
Ye Olde Mill, plate, dinner; 10⅝" 20.00
49ers, bowl, serving; 8" dia 120.00
49ers, bowl (deep plate), 1½x7⅛"................................. 75.00

Walley

The Walley Pottery operated in West Sterling, Massachusetts, from 1898 to 1919. Never more than a one-man operation, William Walley himself handcrafted all his wares from local clay. The majority of his pottery was simple and unadorned and usually glazed in matt green. On occasion, however, you may find high- and semi-gloss green, as well as matt glazes in blue, cream, brown, and red. The rarest and most desirable examples of his work are those with applied or relief-carved decorations. Most pieces are marked 'WJW,' and some, made for the Worcester State Hospital, are stamped 'WSH.' Our advisors for this category are Suzanne Perrault and David Rago; they are listed in the Directory under New Jersey.

Bowl, gr/brn flambé, incurvate rim, WJW, 4x6½" 550.00
Vase, bl slip on yel, bulbous, WJW, flakes, 5¼" 1,200.00
Vase, broad leaves, gr-brn leather texture, bulbous, WJW, 6¾" .9,000.00
Vase, foliage, gr & brn flambé, flecks/nicks, 5¼x3½" 1,325.00
Vase, gr curdled semimatt, WJW, 16½x8" 5,125.00
Vase, gr semimatt w/striations, bottle shape, WJW, 9¾x5½" 900.00
Vase, gr w/striations on red clay, stick neck, WJW, 10" 425.00
Vase, gr/brn flambé, bottle shape, WJW, 7¼x4¼" 725.00
Vase, gr/brn mottle, swollen cylinder w/pinched neck, WJW, 5¾"..575.00
Vase, gr/brn striations, devil's masks in relief, crude rpr, WJW, 12"...2,750.00
Vase, wooded landscape & cabin, mc band on gr, 1915, 7¼x4¼".. 14,500.00
Vase, 2 lizards under frothy gr & brn matt, WJW, 3¼x4¼" 4,200.00

Walrath

Frederick E. Walrath learned his craft as a student of Charles Fergus Binns at Alfred University (1900 – 1904). Walrath worked first, and briefly, at Grueby Faience Company in Boston and then, from 1908 to 1918, as an instructor at the Mechanics Institute in Rochester, New York. He was chief ceramist at Newcomb Pottery (New Orleans) until his death in 1921. A studio potter, Walrath's work bears stylistic similarity to that of Marblehead Pottery, whose founder, Arthur Baggs, was also a student of Binns'. Vases featuring matt glazes of stylized natural motifs (especially florals) are most sought after; sculptural and figural forms (center bowls, flower frogs, various animals) are less desirable. Typically his work is signed with an incised circular signature: Walrath Pottery with conjoined M and

I at the center. Our advisor for this and related Arts & Crafts objects is Bruce A. Austin; he is listed in the Directory under New York.

Bowl, bl matt, ftd, incurvate rim, 1¾x7", EX 120.00
Bowl, stylized floral, pk/gr on café-au-lait, shouldered, 3x7", EX.. 650.00
Cider set, apples, rust on brn, pitcher(7½x8")+ 4 mugs(3½x5").. 4,200.00
Flower frog, swan on pierced base, beige & gr, 3½x4" 75.00
Vase, cabin in wooded landscape at shoulder, mc on gr, 1915, 7¼x4".... 14,400.00
Vase, landscape w/tall trees, gr on gr-brn, hairline, 6¼x4½" 300.00
Vase, stylized floral, tan & lt gr on gray, broad, 5" 6,000.00
Vase, stylized floral, yel & gr on dk gr, bulbous bottom, 11x5½".. 9,000.00
Vase, stylized trees, dk gr on gr matt, hairline crack, 6½x4½" ...3,000.00
Vase, stylized water lilies, mc on gr, shouldered, sm chip, 7x4½" ...6,000.00

Walter, A.

Almaric Walter was employed from 1904 through 1914 at Verreries Artistiques des Freres Daum in Nancy, France. After 1919 he opened his own business where he continued to make the same type of quality objets d'art in pate-de-verre glass as he had earlier. His pieces are signed A. Walter, Nancy H. Berge Sc.

Inkwell, lizard stalking a bumble bee, 3¾", $8,400.00.

(Photo courtesy James D. Julia Inc.)

Encriere, scarabs between 2 posts, brn/blk on orange, 4½x6½" .4,800.00
Paperweight, crab, dk gr & bl, 1¾x2½" 1,100.00
Paperweight, moth, blk/brn/bl/turq on teal, 3¾", NM 425.00
Paperweight, mouse w/nut on outcrop, wht/brn/gr, ca 1900, 3½"..1,450.00
Paperweight, satyr, yel w/gr leaf headband w/purple berries, 3" 780.00
Paperweight, scarab on circular base, gr & bl, 1x2" dia 900.00
Tray, goose & worm at edge, lily pad w/in, 2½x6½" 6,000.00
Tray, moth, gr & aqua mottle, ca 1900, 5" 1,650.00
Vase, blackberries & foliage, mc on yel, flared body, 4½" 3,000.00
Vases, trees/flowers/water, mc, slim, ftd, 12¼", pr, EX................1,950.00

Walters, Carl

Trained as a painter, Walters began designing ceramics about 1921. He is best known for his sculpted and painted animal forms.

Carp, teal bl/gr/blk, iron stand, 24" L................................5,500.00
Rooster vase, red/blk on ivory, 11x8" 280.00

Wannopee

The Wannopee Pottery, established in 1892, developed from the reorganization of the financially insecure New Milford Pottery Company of New Milford, Connecticut. They produced a line of mottled-glazed pottery called 'Duchess' and a similar line in porcelain. Both were marked with the impressed sunburst 'W' with 'porcelain' added to indicate that particular body type. In 1895 semiporcelain pitchers in three sizes were decorated with relief medallion cameos of Beethoven, Mozart, and Napo-

leon. Lettuce-leaf ware was first produced in 1901 and used actual leaves in the modeling. Scarabronze, made in 1895, was their finest artware. It featured simple Egyptian shapes with a coppery glaze. It was marked with a scarab, either impressed or applied. Production ceased in 1903.

Chamberstick, brn, twisted cylinder w/flared ft, 13¼x8¾", ea 450.00
Pitcher, gr gloss, dotted leaves among vertical rows of beads, 8", EX..200.00

Warwick

The Warwick China Company operated in Wheeling, West Virginia, from 1887 until 1951. They produced both hand-painted and decaled plates, vases, teapots, coffeepots, pitchers, bowls, and jardinieres featuring lovely florals or portraits of beautiful ladies done in luscious colors. Backgrounds were usually blendings of brown and beige, but ivory was also used as well as greens and pinks. Various marks were employed, all of which incorporate the Warwick name. For a more thorough study of the subject, we recommend *Warwick, A to W*, a supplement to *Why Not Warwick* by our advisor, Donald C. Hoffmann, Sr.; his address can be found in the Directory under Illinois. In an effort to inform the collector/dealer, Mr. Hoffmann now has a video available that identifies the company's decals and their variations by number.

A-Beauty, vase, floral on brn, A-27, 15" 400.00
A-Beauty, vase, floral on gr, F-2, 15" 425.00
A-Beauty, vase, portrait on pk, H-1, 15" 475.00
Albany, vase, floral on brn, A-27, 7" 300.00
Alexandria, vase, floral on brn, A-27, 12½" 400.00
Bonnie, vase, birds on wht, D-2, 10½" 400.00
Bonnie, vase, floral on brn, A-40, 10½" 370.00
Bouquet #1, vase, floral on brn, A-21, 11¾" 275.00
Bouquet #1, vase, floral on brn, A-27, 11¾" 240.00
Bouquet #1, vase, portrait on brn, A-17, 11¾" 300.00
Bouquet #1, vase, portrait on pk, H-1, 11¾" 440.00
Bouquet #1, vase, portrait on red, E-1, 11¾" 300.00
Bouquet #2, vase, floral on brn, A-16 or A-27, 10½" 220.00
Bouquet #2, vase, portrait on brn, A-17, 10½" 300.00
Bouquet #2, vase, portrait on pk, H-1, 10½" 400.00
Bouquet #2, vase, portrait on red, E-1, 10½" 300.00
Carnation, vase, floral on brn, A-6 or A-23, 10½" 165.00
Carol, vase, floral on brn, A-40, 8" 250.00
Carol, vase, portrait on pk, H-1, 8" 320.00
Chicago, vase, floral on brn, A-22 or A-23, 8", from $250 to....... 260.00
Chrysanthemum, vase, floral on brn, A-16 or A-27, 13½", $180 to...190.00
Chrysanthemum, vase, floral on yel to gr, 13½" 230.00
Clematis, vase, birds on wht, D-1, 11" 320.00
Clematis, vase, floral on brn, A-27, 10½" 220.00
Clematis, vase, portrait on charcoal, C-1, 11" 325.00
Cloverleaf, vase, floral on brn, A-16, 7¼" 330.00
Cloverleaf, vase, floral on matt, M-2, 7¼".....................................350.00
Clytie, vase, floral on brn, A-6, 6½" 400.00
Clytie, vase, floral on red, E-2, 6½" 360.00
Clytie, vase, portrait on red, E-1, 6½" 400.00
Cuba, vase, floral on brn, A-6, 7¼" 360.00
Cuba, vase, floral on matt, M-2, 7¼" 340.00
Cuba, vase, portrait in matt, M-1, 7¼" 350.00
Dahlia, vase, floral (nuts) on brn, A-67, 8½" 220.00
Dahlia, vase, portrait on brn, A-17, 8½" 220.00
Dainty, vase, floral on brn, A-27, 4½" 290.00
Dainty, vase, floral on red, E-2, 4½" 265.00
Dainty, vase, portrait on brn, A-17, 4½" 285.00
Den, vase, floral (nuts) on brn, A-67, 6½" 300.00
Den, vase, floral (nuts) on matt, M-4, 6½"....................................300.00

Den, vase, floral on red, E-2, 6½" 325.00
Duchess, vase, floral on brn, A-16 or A-40, 7½", from $220 to 230.00
Egyptian, vase, floral on brn, A-27, 11¾" 295.00
Egyptian, vase, portrait on charcoal, C-2, 11¾" 295.00
Favorite, vase, floral (nuts) on brn, A-64, 10½" 285.00
Favorite, vase, floral (nuts) on matt, M-2 or M-4, 10½" 285.00
Favorite, vase, portrait on matt, M-1, 10½" 325.00
Favorite, vase, portrait on pk, H-1, 10½" 415.00
Flower, vase, floral on brn, A-6 or A-27, 10", from $200 to 210.00
Flower, vase, portrait on brn, A-17, 10" 295.00

Watch Fobs

Watch fobs have been popular since the last quarter of the nine-teenth century. They were often made by retail companies to feature their products. Souvenir, commemorative, and political fobs were also produced. Of special interest today are those with advertising, heavy equipment in particular. Some of the more pricey fobs are listed here, but most of those currently available were produced in such quantities that they are relatively common and should fall within a price range of $3.00 to $10.00. When no material is mentioned in the description, assume the fob is made of metal.

Anchor, 14k gold, w/thick 15" gold chain, 63.0 dwt 1,325.00
Bloodstone/agate in gold disk/twisted rope fr 245.00
Compass, gold-filled w/14¼" slide chain, ca 1900 .... 180.00
Compass, 14k gold w/15" gold chain, 34.6 dwt 850.00
Cupid's bow/letter seal/lion, blk enameling, 1½x1¼"+chain 145.00
Herakles intaglio on onyx stone w/14k gold mt, oval, 1¾" 335.00
Internat'l Aeor Congress commemorative, 1921, w/vintage stopwatch . 180.00
John Deere, badge logo on brass, w/strap 110.00
John Deere, leaping deer, aqua enamel on metal oval (G), w/strap ... 36.00
John Deere, leaping deer & plow on brass shield form, w/strap 425.00
John Deere, man's portrait on brass, Centennial 36.00
Patriotic beadwork ribbon w/2 Union shields, ca 1865, 4x1½" 425.00
39th Annual Reunion...1929, 2 military portraits, brass 110.00
5-pointed star in shield, mk JWW 1928 .... 120.00

Watch Stands

Watch stands were decorative articles designed with a hook from which to hang a watch. Some displayed the watch as the face of a grand-father clock or as part of an interior scene with figures in period costumes and contemporary furnishings. They were popular products of Stafford-shire potters and silver companies as well.

Ivory, 2 columns w/dome top, 2 armed guards on front, 19th C .. 1,650.00
Lyre form w/swan supports, bronzed metal, Charles X, 19th C, 10½" ... 725.00

Watches

First made in the 1500s in Germany, early watches were actually small clocks, suspended from the neck or belt. By 1700 they had become the approximate shape and size we know today. The first watches produced in America were made in 1810. The well-known Waltham Watch Company was established in 1850. Later, Waterbury produced inexpensive watches which they sold by the thousands.

Open-face and hunting-case watches of the 1890s were often solid gold or gold-filled and were often elaborately decorated in several colors of gold. Gold watches became a status symbol in this decade and were worn by both men and women on chains with fobs or jeweled slides. Ladies

sometimes fastened them to their clothing with pins often set with jewels. The chatelaine watch was worn at the waist, only one of several items such as scissors, coin purses, or needle cases, each attached by small chains. Most turn-of-the-century watch cases were gold-filled; these are plentiful today. Sterling cases, though interest in them is on the increase, are not in great demand. Our advice for this category comes from Maundy International Watches, Antiquarian Horologists, price consultants, and researchers for many watch reference guides and books on horology. Their firm is a leading purveyor of antique watches of all kinds. They are listed in the Directory under Kansas. For character-related watches, see Personalities.

Key:
adj — adjusted		k/s — key set	
brg — bridge plate design		k/w — key wind	
d/s — double sunk dial		l/s — lever set	
fbd — finger bridge design		mvt — movement	
g/f — gold-filled		o/f — open face	
g/j/s — gold jewel setting		p/s — pendant set	
h/c — hunter case		r/g/p — rolled gold plate	
HCI≠P — heat, cold,		s — size	
isochronism & position		s/s — single sunk dial	
adjusted		s/w — stem wind	
j — jewel		w/g/f — white gold-filled	
k — karat		y/g/f — yellow gold-filled	

Am Watch Co, 0s, 7j, #1891, 14k, h/c, Am Watch Co, M 450.00
Am Watch Co, 6s, 7j, #1873, y/g/f, h/c, Am Watch Co, M 275.00
Am Watch Co, 12s, 17j, #1894, 14k, o/f, Royal, M 475.00
Am Watch Co, 12s, 21j, #1894, 14k, h/c, M 800.00
Am Watch Co, 16s, 11j, #1872, silver, p/s, h/c, Park Road, M 325.00
Am Watch Co, 16s, 15j, #1899, y/g/f, h/c, M 375.00
Am Watch Co, 16s, 16j, #1884, 14k, 5-min, Repeater, M 6,595.00
Am Watch Co, 16s, 17j, #1888, Railroader, M 1,695.00
Am Watch Co, 16s, 19j, #1872, 14k, h/c, Am Watch Woerd's Pat, M .. 8,500.00
Am Watch Co, 16s, 21j, #1888, 14k, h/c, Riverside Maximus, M.. 1,950.00
Am Watch Co, 16s, 21j, #1899, y/g/f, o/f, l/s, Crescent St, M 400.00
Am Watch Co, 16s, 21j, #1908, y/g/f, o/f, Grade #645, M 400.00
Am Watch Co, 16s, 23j, #1908, y/g/f, o/f, adj, RR, Vanguard, M. 600.00
Am Watch Co, 16s, 23j, #1908, y/g/f, o/f, Vanguard Up/Down, EX.1,300.00
Am Watch Co, 16s, 23j, #1908, 18k, o/f, Premier Maximus, MIB.. 16,500.00
Am Watch Co, 18s, #1857, silver, h/c, Samuel Curtiss k/w, M .4,275.00
Am Watch Co, 18s, 7j, #1857, silver, k/w, CT Parker, M 4,200.00
Am Watch Co, 18s, 11j, #1857, k/w, 1st run, PS Barlett, M 8,795.00
Am Watch Co, 18s, 11j, #1857, silver, h/c, k/w, DH&D, EX 2,850.00
Am Watch Co, 18s, 11j, #1857, silver, h/c, k/w, s/s, Wm Ellery, EX...250.00
Am Watch Co, 18s, 15j, #1877, k/w, RE Robbins, M 550.00
Am Watch Co, 18s, 15j, #1883, y/g/f, 2-tone, Railroad King, EX ...675.00
Am Watch Co, 18s, 17j, #1883, y/g/f, o/f, Crescent Street, M 325.00
Am Watch Co, 18s, 17j, #1892, h/c, Canadian Pacific Railway, M .2,900.00
Am Watch Co, 18s, 17j, #1892, y/g/f, o/f, Sidereal, rare, M 4,400.00
Am Watch Co, 18s, 17j, 25-yr, y/g/f, o/f, s/s, PS Bartlett, M 350.00
Am Watch Co, 18s, 21j, #1892, y/g/f, o/f, d/s, Crescent St, M 575.00
Am Watch Co, 18s, 21j, #1892, y/g/f, o/f, Grade #845, EX 325.00
Am Watch Co, 18s, 21j, #1892, y/g/f, o/f, Pennsylvania Special, M .3,950.00
Auburndale Watch Co, 18s, 7j, k/w, l/s, Lincoln, M 1,300.00
Aurora Watch Co, 18s, 11j, silver, k/w, h/c, M 475.00
Aurora Watch Co, 18s, 15 ruby j, y/g/f, s/w, 5th pinion, M 1,750.00
Ball (Elgin), 18s, 17j, silver, o/f, Official RR Standard, M 1,050.00
Ball (Hamilton), 16s, 21j, #999, g/f, o/f, l/s, M 1,350.00
Ball (Hamilton), 16s, 23j, #998, y/g/f, o/f, Elinvar, M 3,850.00
Ball (Hamilton), 18s, 17j, #999, g/f, o/f, l/s, EX 550.00
Ball (Hampden), 18s, 17j, o/f, adj, RR, Superior Grade, M 2,200.00
Ball (Illinois), 12s, 19j, w/g/f, o/f, M 325.00
Ball (Waltham), 16s, 17j, y/g/f, o/f, RR, Commercial Std, M 475.00

Ball (Waltham), 16s, 21j, o/f, Official RR Standard, M.............950.00
Columbus, 6s, 11j, y/g/f, h/c, M.............250.00
Columbus, 18s, 11-15j, k/w, k/s, M.............500.00
Columbus, 18s, 15j, o/f, l/s, M.............250.00
Columbus, 18s, 15j, y/g/f, o/f, Jay Gould on dial, M.............2,750.00
Columbus, 18s, 21j, y/g/f, h/c, train on dial, Railway King, M ..2,150.00
Columbus, 18s, 23j, y/g/f, h/c, Columbus King, M.............2,800.00
Cornell, 18s, 15j, s/w, JC Adams, EX.............550.00
Cornell, 18s, 15j, silver, h/c, k/w, John Evans, EX.............425.00
Dudley, 12s, #1, 14k, o/f, flip-bk case, Masonic, M.............3,250.00
Elgin, 6s, 11j, 14k, h/c, M.............500.00
Elgin, 6s, 15j, y/g/f, h/c, s/s, 20-yr, EX.............60.00
Elgin, 10s, 18k, h/c, k/w, k/s, s/s, Gail Borden, M.............750.00
Elgin, 12s, 15j, 14k, h/c, EX.............425.00
Elgin, 12s, 17j, 14k, h/c, GM Wheeler, M.............450.00
Elgin, 16s, 15j, doctor's, 4th model, 18k, h/c, 2nd sweep hand, M..2,400.00
Elgin, 16s, 15j, 14k, h/c, EX.............775.00
Elgin, 16s, 21j, y/g/f, g/j/s, o/f, BW Raymond, EX.............395.00
Elgin, 16s, 21j, y/g/f, g/j/s, 3 fbd, h/c, M.............995.00
Elgin, 16s, 21j, y/g/f, o/f, l/s, RR, Father Time, M.............575.00
Elgin, 16s, 21j, 14k, 3 fbd, grade #91, scarce, M.............4,500.00
Elgin, 16s, 23j, up/down indicator, BW Raymond, EX.............2,300.00
Elgin, 17s, 7j, silver, k/w, Leader, M.............200.00
Elgin, 18s, 11j, silver, h/c, k/w, gilded, MG Odgen, M.............325.00
Elgin, 18s, 15j, silver, h/c, k/w, k/s, HL Culver, M.............425.00
Elgin, 18s, 15j, silver, o/f, d/s, k/w, RR, BW Raymond 1st run, M...1,475.00
Elgin, 18s, 15j, silver h/c, Penn RR dial, BW Raymond k/w mvt, M ..6,200.00
Elgin, 18s, 17j, silveroid, h/c, BW Raymond, M.............300.00
Elgin, 18s, 21j, y/g/f, o/f, Father Time, G.............295.00
Elgin, 18s, 23j, y/g/f, o/f, 5-position, RR, Veritas, M.............1,050.00
Fredonia, 18s, 11j, y/g/f, h/c, k/w, M.............595.00
Hamilton, #910, 12s, 17j, y/g/f, o/f, s/s, 20-yr, EX.............50.00
Hamilton, #912, 12s, 17j, y/g/f, o/f, adj, EX.............50.00
Hamilton, #920, 12s, 23j, 14k, o/f, M.............650.00
Hamilton, #922MP, 12s, 18k, Masterpiece (sgn), M.............1,600.00
Hamilton, #925, 18s, 17j, y/g/f, h/c, s/s, l/s, M.............350.00
Hamilton, #928, 18s, 15j, y/g/f, o/f, s/s, EX.............275.00
Hamilton, #933, 18s, 16j, nickel plate, h/c, low serial #, M.............1,500.00
Hamilton, #938, 18s, 17j, y/g/f, adj, M.............675.00
Hamilton, #940, 18s, 21j, nickel plate, coin silver, o/f, M.............525.00
Hamilton, #946, 18s, 23j, y/g/f, o/f, g/j/s, M.............1,450.00
Hamilton, #947 (mk), 18s, 23j, 14k, h/c, orig/sgn, EX.............5,950.00
Hamilton, #950, 16s, 23j, y/g/f, o/f, l/s, sgn d/s, M.............2,100.00
Hamilton, #965, 16s, 17j, 14k, h/c, p/s, brg, scarce, M.............1,500.00
Hamilton, #972, 16s, 17j, y/g/f, o/f, g/j/s, d/s, l/s, adj, EX.............135.00
Hamilton, #974, 16s, 17j, y/g/f, o/f, 20-yr, s/s, EX.............75.00
Hamilton, #992, 16s, 21j, y/g/f, o/f, adj, d/s, dbl roller, M.............495.00
Hamilton, #992B, 16s, 21j, y/g/f, o/f, l/s, Bar/Crown, M.............700.00
Hamilton, #4992B, 16s, 22j, o/f, steel case, G.............375.00
Hampden, 12s, 17j, w/g/f, o/f, thin model, Aviator, M.............220.00
Hampden, 16s, 7j, gilded, nickel plate, o/f, ¾-mvt, EX.............38.00
Hampden, 16s, 17j, o/f, adj, EX.............40.00
Hampden, 16s, 17j, y/g/f, h/c, s/w, M.............250.00
Hampden, 16s, 21j, g/j/s, y/g/f, NP, h/c, Dueber, ¾-mvt, M.............350.00
Hampden, 16s, 23j, o/f, adj, dbl roller, Special Railway, M.............725.00
Hampden, 18s, 7-11j, gilded, k/w, Springfield Mass, EX.............145.00
Hampden, 18s, 15j, k/w, mk on mvt, Railway, M.............1,550.00
Hampden, 18s, 15j, s/w, gilded, JC Perry, M.............300.00
Hampden, 18s, 15j, silver, h/c, k/w, Hayward, M.............300.00
Hampden, 18s, 15j, y/g/f, damascened, h/c, Dueber, M.............200.00
Hampden, 18s, 21j, y/g/f, g/j/s, h/c, New Railway, M.............625.00
Hampden, 18s, 21j, y/g/f, o/f, d/s, l/s, N Am Railway, M.............525.00
Hampden, 18s, 23j, y/g/f, o/f, d/s, adj, New Railway, M.............650.00
Hampden, 18s, 23j, 14k, h/c, Special Railway, M.............1,300.00

Howard, E; 6s, 15j, 18k, h/c, s/w, Series VIII, G sz, M.............1,500.00
Howard, E; 16s, 15j, 14k, h/c, s/w, L sz, M.............2,250.00
Howard, E; 18s, 15j, silver, h/c, k/w, Series I, N sz, M.............4,500.00
Howard, E; 18s, 15j, 18k h/c, k/w, Series II, N sz, M.............5,500.00
Howard, E; 18s, 17j, 25-yr, y/g/f, o/f, orig case, split plate, M ...1,950.00
Howard (Keystone), 12s, 23j, 14k, h/c, brg, Series 8, M.............775.00
Howard (Keystone), 16s, 17j, y/g/f, o/f, Series 9, M.............325.00
Howard (Keystone), 16s, 21j, y/g/f, o/f, RR Chronometer II, M...975.00
Howard (Keystone), 16s, 23j, y/g/f, o/f, Series 0, jeweled bbl, M ...1,500.00
Illinois, 0s, 7j, 14k, h/c, l/s, EX.............425.00
Illinois, 8s, 13j, ¾-mvt, Rose LeLand, scarce, M.............250.00
Illinois, 12s, 17j, y/g/f, o/f, d/s dial, EX.............38.00
Illinois, 16s, 17j, y/g/f, o/f, d/s, Bunn, EX.............240.00
Illinois, 16s, 21j, o/f, d/s, Santa Fe Special, M.............975.00
Illinois, 16s, 21j, y/g/f, h/c, g/j/s, Burlington, M.............375.00
Illinois, 16s, 21j, y/g/f, o/f, d/s, Bunn Special, M.............625.00
Illinois, 16s, 23j, y/g/f, o/f, d/s, 60-hr, Sangamo Special, mk, M...3,900.00
Illinois, 16s, 23j, y/g/f, o/f, stiff bow, Sangamo Special, EX.............1,100.00
Illinois, 18s, 7j, #3, o/f, Interior, G.............40.00
Illinois, 18s, 7j, #3, silveroid, America, G.............45.00
Illinois, 18s, 9-11j, o/f, k/w, s/s, silveroid case, Hoyt, M.............250.00
Illinois, 18s, 11j, #1, silver, k/w, Alleghany, EX.............135.00
Illinois, 18s, 11j, #3, o/f, s/w, l/s, Comet, G.............70.00
Illinois, 18s, 11j, Forest City, G.............75.00
Illinois, 18s, 15j, #1, adj, y/g/f, h/c, k/w, gilt, Bunn, M.............800.00
Illinois, 18s, 15j, #1, k/w, k/s, silver, h/c, Stuart, M.............875.00
Illinois, 18s, 15j, k/w, k/s, gilt, Railway Regulator, M.............900.00
Illinois, 18s, 15j, silveroid, s/w, G.............37.00
Illinois, 18s, 15j, y/g/f, o/f, s/s, Jay Gould Railroad King, rare 9,750.00
Illinois, 18s, 17j, g/j/s, adj, h/c, B&O RR Special (Hunter), M.2,950.00
Illinois, 18s, 17j, nickel plate, coin silver, h/c, s/w, Bunn, M.........600.00
Illinois, 18s, 17j, o/f, s/w, 5th pinion, Miller, EX.............80.00
Illinois, 18s, 17j, silveroid, o/f, d/s, adj, Lakeshore, G.............60.00
Illinois, 18s, 21j, g/f, g/j/s, o/f, A Lincoln, M.............425.00
Illinois, 18s, 21j, g/j/s, o/f, adj, B&O RR Special, EX.............2,150.00
Illinois, 18s, 21j, 14k, h/c, g/j/s, Bunn Special, M.............2,200.00
Illinois, 18s, 23j, g/j/s, Bunn Special, EX.............1,000.00
Illinois, 18s, 24j, g/j/s, o/f, adj, Chesapeake & Ohio, M.............4,200.00
Illinois, 18s, 24j, g/j/s, o/f, Bunn Special, EX.............1,200.00
Illinois, 18s, 26j, g/j/s, o/f, Ben Franklin USA, M.............6,200.00
Illinois, 18s, 26j, 14k, Penn Special, M.............8,500.00
Ingersoll, 16s, 7j, wht base metal, Reliance, G.............18.00
Lancaster, 18s, 7j, silver, o/f, k/w, k/s, EX.............150.00
Marion US, 18s, h/c, k/w, k/s, ¾-plate, Asa Fuller, M.............450.00
Marion US, 18s, 15j, nickel plate, h/c, s/w, Henry Randel, M......475.00
Melrose Watch Co, 18s, 7j, k/w, k/s, G.............300.00
New York Watch Co, 18s, 7j, silver, h/c, k/w, Geo Sam Rice, EX ...185.00
New York Watch Co, 19j, low sz #, wolf's teeth wind, M.............1,650.00
Patek Philippe, 12s, 18j, 18k, o/f, EX.............2,850.00
Patek Philippe, 16s, 20j, 18k, h/c, M.............3,900.00
Rockford, 16s, 17j, y/g/f, h/c, brg, dbl roller, EX.............65.00
Rockford, 16s, 21j, #515, y/g/f, M.............800.00
Rockford, 16s, 21j, g/j/s, o/f, grade #537, rare, M.............2,200.00
Rockford, 16s, 23j, 14k, o/f, mk Doll on dial/mvt, M.............3,900.00
Rockford, 18s, 15j, silver, o/f, k/w, EX.............150.00
Rockford, 18s, 17j, silveroid, 2-tone, M.............300.00
Rockford, 18s, 17j, y/g/f, o/f, Winnebago, M.............375.00
Rockford, 18s, 21j, o/f, King Edward, M.............450.00
Seth Thomas, 18s, 7j, ¾-mvt, bk: eagle/Liberty model, M.............300.00
Seth Thomas, 18s, 17j, #2, g/j/s, adj, Henry Molineux, EX.............625.00
Seth Thomas, 18s, 17j, Edgemere, G.............25.00
Seth Thomas, 18s, 25j, g/f, g/j/s, Maiden Lane, EX.............2,450.00
South Bend, 12s, 21j, dbl roller, Grade #431, M.............200.00
South Bend, 12s, 21j, orig o/f, d/s, Studebaker, M.............600.00

South Bend, 18s, 21j, g/j/s, h/c, Studebaker, M..........................1,800.00
South Bend, 18s, 21j, 14k, h/c, M 1,500.00
Swiss, 18s, 18k, h/c, 1-min, Repeater, High Grade, M..............6,500.00

Waterford

The Waterford Glass Company operated in Ireland from the late 1700s until 1851 when the factory closed. One hundred years later (in 1951) another Waterford glassworks was instituted that produced glass similar to the eighteenth-century wares — crystal, usually with cut decoration. Today Waterford is a generic term referring to the type of glass first produced there.

Bowl, centerpc; cut boat form on tall ped, att, 9½x13x6½".......... 360.00
Bowl, centerpc; cut panels, scalloped/ftd, sgn M O'Leary, 7x9".... 350.00
Bowl, centerpc; dmn pattern w/vertical cut rim, ped ft, 7¾x11".. 550.00
Bowl, King's; scalloped rim, ped ft, 7x9¾"...................................... 480.00
Candelabra, 3-light, 6-arm, rnd ped, star finial, drops, 30x17", pr.. 12,000.00
Celery vase, dmn-point band, ftd, ca early 19th C, att, 8¾"........ 265.00
Champagne cooler, urn form, deep cuttings, 13x9½", NM.......... 600.00
Chandelier, cut glass column, 12-branch w/bobeches/prisms, 40x36".. 5,150.00
Chandelier, molded crystal, 5-light, w/prisms, 20x24".............. 1,200.00
Christmas ornament, 5 rings on tree shape, 1991 .... 285.00
Decanter, dmn cuttings, 3-notch hdl, ftd, prism ball stopper, 12" ...350.00
Decanter, Kylemore, 12", +9 matching old-fashioned tumblers ... 300.00
Lamps, crystal & brass, 3-candle, wall mt, 18x9" dia, pr.............. 900.00
Stem, champagne; Curraghmore, 5½", 12 for 550.00
Stem, champagne/sherbet; Powerscourt, 5⅜", 6 for 550.00
Stem, flute; Colleen, 6", 6 for.. 300.00
Stem, iced tea; Kelsey, 6 for.. 350.00
Stem, liquor; Lismore, tapered bowl, 4½", 12 for 360.00
Stem, water; Colleen, 5¼", 10 for... 300.00
Stem, water; Curraghmore, 7½", 12 for................................... 780.00
Stem, water; Powerscourt, 7½", 12 for.................................... 660.00
Stem, water; Tramore, 5⅝", 12 for... 360.00
Stem, wine; Curraghmore, 7⅛", 12 for................................... 850.00
Stem, wine; Kenmare, 7½", 12 for.. 725.00
Tumbler, old-fashioned; Lismore, 8 for..................................... 350.00
Tumblers, Colleen, 12-oz, 4¾", 12 for..................................... 480.00
Vase, cut dmns/sqs/panels, scalloped rim, sq, 12"...................... 300.00
Vase, Deco horizontal broken ribs, stepped sq ft, 12½"............. 395.00
Vase, dmn cuttings, slim w/rnd ft, 14"...................................... 350.00
Vase, geometric cuttings, vertical ribs at rim, cylindrical, 12x6".. 350.00
Vase, Millennium, geometric cuttings, 2000, MIB...................... 360.00
Vase, presentation; geometric cuttings/panels, scalloped rim, ftd, 13"...300.00

Watt Pottery

The Watt Pottery Company was established in Crooksville, Ohio, on July 5, 1922. From approximately 1922 until 1935, they manufactured hand-turned stone containers — jars, jugs, milk pans, preserve jars, and various sizes of mixing bowls, usually marked with a cobalt blue acorn stamp. In 1936 production of these items was discontinued, and the company began to produce kitchen utility ware and ovenware such as mixing bowls, spaghetti bowls and plates, canister sets, covered casseroles, salt and pepper shakers, cookie jars, ice buckets, pitchers, bean pots, and salad and dinnerware sets. Most Watt ware is individually hand painted with bold brush strokes of red, green, or blue contrasting with the natural buff color of the glazed body. Several patterns were produced: Apple, Autumn Foliage, Cherry, Dutch Tulip, Morning Glory, Rio Rose, Rooster, Tear Drop, Starflower, and Tulip, to name a few. Much of the ware was made for advertising premiums and is often found stamped with the name of the retail company.

Tragedy struck the Watt Pottery Company on October 4, 1965, when fire completely destroyed the factory and warehouse. Production never resumed, but the ware they made has withstood many years of service in American kitchens and is today highly regarded and prized by collectors. The vivid colors and folksy execution of each cheerful pattern create a homespun ambiance that will make Watt pottery a treasure for years to come.

Apple, canister, #72, 9½x7".. 500.00
Apple, creamer & sugar bowl, very rare sz, 2¾x5" 1,000.00
Apple, ice bucket, w/lid, 7¼x7½".. 275.00
Apple, pitcher, #17, 8x8½"... 275.00
Apple, platter, #49, 12" dia... 400.00
Apple, tumbler, #56, rare, 4½x4".. 1,000.00
Autumn Foliage, platter, #31, 15" dia 110.00
Autumn Foliage, teapot, #505, rare, 5¾x9" 1,600.00
Blue/White Banded, bowl, mixing; 4x7"... 25.00
Blue/White Banded, casserole, 4½x8¾" 45.00
Blue/White Banded, pitcher, 7x7¾"... 95.00
Cherry, bowl, berry; #6, 3x6"... 40.00
Cherry, salt shaker, bbl shaped, 4x2½", ea....................................... 90.00
Cut-Leaf Pansy, platter, 15"... 110.00
Dutch Tulip, cookie jar, #503, 8¼"... 375.00
Kitchen-N-Queen, bowl, mixing; ribbed, #8, 5½x8" 40.00
Pansy (Cut-Leaf), bowl, mixing; 4½x9"... 45.00
Pansy (Cut-Leaf) w/Bull's Eye, plate, 7½" dia 55.00
Pansy (Cut-Leaf) w/Bull's Eye, platter, 15" dia................................ 110.00
Pansy (Old), casserole, #2/48, 4¼x7½"... 75.00
Pansy (Old), platter, #31, 15" dia 100.00
Pansy (Old), platter, cross-hatch pansy pattern, 15" dia.............. 175.00
Raised Pansy, casserole, ind; French hdl, 3¾x7½"............................ 90.00
Rooster, bowl, w/lid, #05, 4x5".. 190.00
Starflower, creamer, #62, 4¼x4½".. 250.00
Starflower, mug, #121, 3¾x3".. 275.00
Starflower, pitcher, refrigerator; #69, 4-petal, sq, 8"..................... 225.00
Starflower (Green-on-Brown), cookie jar, #21, 7½x7" 125.00
Starflower (Pink-on-Black), casserole, w/lid, 4½x8¾"................. 125.00
Starflower (Red-on-White), mug, #121, rare, 3¾x3"................... 400.00
Starflower (standard colors), platter, #31, 15"............................ 110.00
Tear Drop, cheese crock, #80, 8x8¼"... 375.00
Tear Drop, creamer, #62, 4¼".. 275.00
Tear Drop, shakers, bbl shape, 4x2½" dia, pr................................. 350.00
White Banded, bowl, 2½x5"... 25.00
White Banded, bowl, 4½x6"... 25.00
White Banded, pitcher, 7x7¾".. 85.00

Wave Crest

Wave Crest is a line of decorated opal ware (milk glass) patented in 1892 by the C.F. Monroe Co. of Meriden, Connecticut. They made a full line of items for every room of the house, but they are probably best known for their boxes and vases. Most items were hand painted with various levels of decoration, but more transfers were used in the later years prior to the company's demise in 1916. Floral themes are common; items with the scenics and portraits are rarer and more highly prized. Many pieces have ornately scrolled ormolu and brass handles, feet, and rims. Early pieces were unsigned (though they may have had paper labels); later, about 1898, a red banner mark was used. The black mark is probably from about 1902 – 1903. However, the glass is quite distinctive and has not been reproduced, so even unmarked items are easy to recognize. Our advisors for this category are Dolli and Wilfred Cohen; they are listed in the Directory under California. Note: There is no premium for signatures on Wave Crest. Values are given for hand-decorated pieces (unless noted 'transfer') that are *not* worn.

Biscuit jar, Swirl, daisies & leaves, orig mts, 7¼" 450.00
Bowl, zinnias in gold scroll reserve, shouldered/paneled, ormolu ft, 8" .. 450.00
Box, Baroque, damask-like scrolls, 4 repeats around daisy, 7" 950.00
Box, Collars & Cuffs, bl floral, ormolu mts, 7½x7" dia 850.00
Box, glove; daisies, mc on wht opal, ftd ormolu base, 6" 1,000.00
Box, gondolas & canal street, 4¾" W 495.00
Box, Puffy, day lilies, metal mts, sq, 6½x6½" 795.00
Box, Puffy, floral, metal mts, 3x5½x3¼" 250.00
Box, Puffy, floral on burnt orange to yel, ormolu w/lions heads, 7" L .. 635.00
Box, Puffy, mums on amber, rtcl shoulder, 6¾x6¾" 1,750.00
Box, Scroll, daisies on gr, metal mts, 5x7x4" 1,150.00
Box, Scroll, violets on pk, 4¼" dia 200.00
Box, Swirl, blackberries on opal & lt turq w/gold, 5" 500.00
Box, Swirl, Cupid & flowers, sq, 4¼" 300.00
Box, Swirl, holly on crystal satin, 4x7" dia 850.00
Box, Swirl, lilacs, metal mts, 4½x6" 600.00
Box, Swirl, sm bl forget-me-nots, rnd, 2½" H 195.00
Broom holder, floral, ornate gilt fr, missing liner, 7x10½" 975.00
Clock, floral-molded scrolls, gilt fr, Pat Jan 13 1891, easel bk, 7" .. 2,500.00
Cracker jar, Swirl, forget-me-nots, bowl form w/metal mts 495.00
Ferner, Puffy, floral w/gold on ivory, 4 lion's face ft, 5x7" 315.00
Jardiniere, Shell, red & bl mums, 4-ftd metal fr w/emb faces, 8½" ... 550.00
Letter holder, Puffy, silver/gold fern fronds on wht, ormolu rim, 6" L .. 395.00
Shakers, floral, tulip mold, 2½", pr 125.00
Spooner, Swirl, pansies on opal/pk, lg ornate SP hdls, 4" 250.00
Tray, daisies on pk, emb rosebuds/scrolls, 4½" dia 100.00
Tray, Swirl, floral on wht opal, brass collar, 1½x3½" 125.00

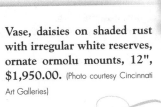

Vase, daisies on shaded rust with irregular white reserves, ornate ormolu mounts, 12", $1,950.00. (Photo courtesy Cincinnati Art Galleries)

Vase, orchids on cobalt, gold mts & hdls, 12½x9½" 1,950.00
Vase, Scroll w/dainty flowers, 9½", NM 650.00

Weapons

Among the varied areas of specialization within the broad category of weapons, guns are by far the most popular. Muskets are among the earliest firearms; they were large-bore shoulder arms, usually firing black powder with separate loading of powder and shot. Some ignited the charge by flintlock or caplock, while later types used a firing pin with a metallic cartridge. Side arms, referred to as such because they were worn at the side, include pistols and revolvers. Pistols range from early single-shot and multiple barrels to modern types with cartridges held in the handle. Revolvers were supplied with a cylinder that turned to feed a fresh round in front of the barrel breech. Other firearms include shotguns, which fired round or conical bullets and had a smooth inner barrel surface, and rifles, so named because the interior of the barrel contained spiral grooves (rifling) which increased accuracy. For further study we recommend *Modern Guns* by Russell Quertermous and Steve Quertermous, available at your local bookstore or from Collector Books. Our advisor for this category is Steve Howard; he is listed the Directory under California. Unless noted otherwise, our values are for examples in excellent condition. See also Militaria.

Key:

bbl — barrel	mod — modified
cal — caliber	oct — octagon
conv — conversion	O/U — over/under
cyl — cylinder	p/b — patch box
f/l — flintlock	perc — percussion
ga — gauge	/s — stock
hdw — hardware	Spec O — Special Order
mag — magazine	

Carbines

Burnside 2nd Model, 54 cal, 21" rnd bbl, walnut/s, w/saddle ring .. 4,600.00
Enfield 1863 Pattern 56, 577 cal, 1863 Tower on lock, orig/complete .. 7,500.00
Ken Walker Confederate, 54 cal, rifled bbl, copper/brass fr/rpl nipple .. 21,850.00
Richmond 1863, 58 cal, 25" bbl, sling swivel w/rpr 7,475.00
Smith Civil War, 50RF cal, Am Machine Works fr, 21⅝" bbl, walnut/s .. 1,265.00
Spencer Belgian Made, 50RF cal, 20" rnd bbl, 1873 on butt stock, VG+ . 1,150.00
Triplett & Scott Repeating, 50RF cal, 30" rnd bbl, 2 swivels, EX+ .. 2,875.00

Muskets

Colt 1861 Special, 58 cal, 39½" rnd bbl, tulip-head ramrod, NM .. 4,315.00
Enfield Pattern 53, 577 cal, Tower 1861 on hammer, 39" bbl, w/bayonet .. 3,165.00
Enfield 1862 Tower Perc, 69 cal, mk lockplate, 3 bbl bands, 39" bbl .. 750.00
Remington Zouave, 58 cal, 33" rnd bbl, mk lockplate, walnut/s 2,875.00
Richmond 1861, 58 cal, mk lockplate, rpr ramrod, correct/s, VG .. 3,450.00
Richmond 1863, 58 cal, bbl dtd 1864, mk lockplate, w/bayonet .. 13,800.00
Springfield 1816, Remington conv, 69 cal, Maynard tape primer, 33" bbl. 1,600.00
Tower 3rd Model Brown Bess, 78 cal, 38⅜" bbl, walnut/s 2,875.00

Pistols

Continental Blunderbus, f/l, 60 cal, 6⅝" part oct oval bore bbl ... 2,000.00
Johnson 1836 Martial, f/l, 54 cal, 8½" rnd bbl, walnut/s, VG 1,100.00
Ketland Light Dragoon, f/l, 66 cal, 9⁹⁄₁₆" rnd bbl, mk lock, G 1,100.00
North 1811 Martial, f/l, 69 cal, 8¾" bbl, mk hammer, VG 16,000.00
North 1819 Martial, f/l, 56 cal, 10" rnd bbl, 1822 on lock plate, VG .. 1,375.00
Remington M1871 Army Rolling Block, 50CF cal, 8" rnd bbl .3,675.00
Trylon, f/l, 54 cal, 8⅝" rnd bbl, mk lock plate, fair reconv, G 1,265.00
Williamson Pocket Derringer, 45RF cal, single shot, 2½" bbl, VG ... 800.00

Revolvers

Allen & Wheelock Sidehammer Navy, 36 cal, 5" oct bbl, 5-shot cyl, G+ .. 1,100.00
Colt 1849 Pocket, 31 cal, 6" oct bbl, 5-shot cyl, walnut grip 2,000.00
Colt 1851 Navy, 36 cal, 7½" oct bbl, brass trigger, rpl grips 1,600.00
Colt 1855 5 Root Sidehammer, perc, 3½" bbl, 5-shot cyl, ivory grips ... 1,265.00
Colt 1860 Army, perc, 44 cal, 7½" rnd bbl, fluted cyl, 4-screw fr .. 4,600.00
Colt 1862 Police, perc, 36 cal, 4½" rnd bbl, 5-shot fluted cyl 1,850.00
Joslyn Navy, perc, 44 cal, 7⅞" oct bbl, 3-pc rammer, walnut grips .. 6,325.00
Kerr, 44 cal, 5-cyl, Kerr's Pat 1493 on fr, low serial # 8,625.99
Remington New Model Army, 44 cal, 8" oct bbl, 2-pc walnut grips, VG .925.00
Tranter Army, 44 cal, 5-cyl, Dean & Son... on fr, minor pitting .. 1,435.00

Rifles

Harper's Ferry 1803, perc conv, rpl M1841 trigger, p/b & ramrod 2,585.00
Henry Gibbs, perc, curly maple full/s w/inlay, p/b, rpl ramrod, 55" ... 2,400.00
J Bishop Warranted, perc, bird's-eye maple half/s w/inlay, p/b, 49" ... 1,500.00
Joseph Tonks Sporting, perc, 38-cal, 28" med oct to rnd bbl 1,550.00
Marlin-Ballard #5 Pacific, 40-85 cal, ring-shaped lever, 32" oct bbl ... 1,750.00
Spencer Navy Repeating, 52 cal, 6-groove rifling, full/s, 30" bbl .. 850.00
US 1888 Trapdoor, 45-70 cal, tool compartment, 23⅝" bbl, G 700.00

Winchester 1866 Lever Action, 44RF cal, 24¼" oct bbl w/full mag ...13,800.00
Winchester 1873, 38CWF cal, mk brass elevator block 4,250.00
Winchester 1876, 45-60 cal, brass elevator block, rnd 28" bbl, G .. 1,000.00
Winchester 1885 Single Shot, 25-20s cal, 28" oct #3 bbl..........3,750.00
Winchester 1894, 30WCF lever-action repeater, 26" rnd bbl 800.00
Winchester 1894 Special O Takedown Lever Action, 50wCF cal, 26" bbl...2,875.00

Shotguns

AH Fox A Grade, 12 ga, 30" steel full choke bbls, walnut/s.......1,150.00
Belgian Browning Grade I Superposed, 12 ga, 30" full/mod choked bbls...2,000.00
Browning Custom Superposed, 12 ga, 27½" full/mod choked bbls, NM..4,600.00
Browning Diana Grade Superposed, 410 cal, 28" choked bbls, NM.14,500.00
Colt 1883 Field Grade, 12 ga, 30" Damascus choked, bbls, NM ... 800.00
English, full/s blunderbuss, rnd brass bbl, f/l w/2¼" bore, 42"...... 1,850.00
Green, perc, 12 cal bore, 27" Damascus bbls, walnut/s, G 300.00
Greener Empire Grade, 12 ga, 32" full choke bbls, dbl triggers, NM..4,600.00
Henry Adkin, 12 ga, 30" dbl bbls w/mod choke, eng, burl/s dtd 1868 .. 7,500.00
Ithaca Field Grade, 10 ga, magnum 10 dbl 34" steel bbls, NM...2,875.00
Ithaca NID Field Model, 28 cal, 26" cyl/open mod choked bbls....3,165.00
LC Smith Monogram Grade, 10 ga, 32" Whitworth bbls, walnut/s, NM .9,775.00
London, walnut full/s blunderbuss, f/l, brass bbl, 2⅜" bore, 41"..2,900.00
Parker AH Grade, 16 ga, #1 fr w/26" Acme steel bbls, mod/cyl choke.. 19,550.00
Parker DH Grade, 28 ga, OO fr w/25½" Titanic steel bbls, NM .. 8,000.00
Remington 32 Skeet Grade Over/Under, 12 ga, 28" bbls, walnut/s....1,725.00
Webley & Scott 712, 12 ga, 28" dbl bbls w/full/mod chokes, walnut/s . 1,500.00
Whitney Phoenix Breechloading, 12 ga, 26¼" rnd bbl (shortened), G..200.00
Williams, 12 ga, 32" nibbed bbls, mk lockplate, VG...................... 235.00
Winchester #21 Skeet Grade, 12 ga, 26" bbls, walnut/s, NM 5,175.00
Winchester Custom 101 Over/Under, 12 ga, 30" vent rib choked bbls..1,265.00
Winchester 101 Superposed, 12 ga, 30" ventilated ribbed bbls .. 1,380.00
Winchester 1887 Lever Action Std Grade, 12 ga, 30" mod choked bbl ..975.00
Winchester 1901 Lever Action, 10 ga, 32" steel bbl, half mag... 1,265.00
Winchester 1901 Lever Action Std Grade, 10 ga, 30" rnd steel bbl, VG ..975.00
Winchester 1901 Lever Action Std Grade, 10 ga, 32" rnd/full choke bbl . 1,265.00

Weather Vanes

The earliest weather vanes were of handmade wrought iron and were generally simple angular silhouettes with a small hole suggesting an eye. Later copper, zinc, and polychromed wood with features in relief were fashioned into more realistic forms. Ships, horses, fish, Indians, roosters, and angels were popular motifs. In the nineteenth century, silhouettes were often made from sheet metal. Wooden figures became highly carved and were painted in vivid colors. E. G. Washburne and Company in New York was one of the most prominent manufacturers of weather vanes during the last half of the century. Two-dimensional sheet metal weather vanes are increasing in value due to the already heady prices of the full-bodied variety. Originality, strength of line and patina help to determine value. When no condition is indicated, the items listed below are assumed to be in excellent condition.

Key: f/fb — flattened full body   f/b — full body

Airplane, sheet copper on wood w/wood propeller, weathered, 17" L...550.00
Am Indian archer, f/fb copper, on arrow, old rpt/holes, 31x38" .. 10,000.00
Arrow, wrought/sheet iron, metal stand, 14¼x35"........................ 825.00
Bull, f/fb wood, iron strap rprs, weathered wht, on arrow, 22x55"... 3,500.00
Cow, f/fb copper, rpr, 19x32".. 7,000.00
Cow, f/fb copper w/zinc head, att Cushing & Wht, on stand, 18x29"..25,850.00
Dog, f/fb copper, mtd on 2 copper rods, att J Davis, 18x27¾" ...5,000.00
Eagle, f/b copper w/spread wings, on orb, layered pnt, 20x18"...... 375.00
Eagle, fb copper, spread wings, EX verdigris/gilt, 10x9¾"+stand.. 1,725.00

Eagle, fb copper, spread wings, on ball, gold pnt, on stand, 37" W ...2,185.00
Eagle, hollow f/b zinc, on orb, weathered gilt, rpr, 17x13"............ 460.00
Finger pointing & banner over directionals, copper, Fiske, 67x37"..8,200.00
Fish, fb copper w/verdigris, some splits, 25½".............................1,725.00
Game cock, f/fb sheet metal, gilt w/red details, on arrow, 16x19".. 2,645.00
Horse, f/fb copper w/CI head, yel/verdigris/gilt, rpr, 28x32" 25,850.00
Horse, f/fb copper w/zinc head, mustard pnt, on rod, 35x31" 5,000.00
Horse, sheet iron, old gray/blk pnt, lt rust/damage, OH, 31" L.. 1,300.00
Horse & driver in lg-wheel sulky, fb copper, post directional, 29" ...400.00
Horse & jockey, f/fb iron w/copper, verdigris/gilt, 19½x31".....15,275.00
Horse running, dbl sheet iron, worn yel over silver, att NH, 24" L...2,100.00
Horse running, f/fb, copper/zinc, Ethan Allen by Fiske, orig gilt, 27".. 6,000.00
Horse running, f/fb copper, Black Hawk, rprs/dents, 17¼x22¾".. 4,400.00
Horse running, f/fb copper, bullet holes, att Jewell, on stand, 25x39".12,650.00
Horse running, f/fb copper, weathered gilt, on rod w/sphere, 17x29".5,590.00
Horse trotting, f/fb copper, old gilt, w/directionals, 19x27".......1,500.00
Man fishing, sheet metal, on directional arrow, iron base, 25x25" ..460.00
Man trumpeting, horizontal figure, 2-D, weathered wood, 39" W..3,000.00
Peacock, copper w/enamel feathers, minor losses, unmk, 25½x20"..4,000.00
Pig silhouette, galvanized sheet metal, ca 1950s, 10½x17"........... 380.00
Pigeon on ball & arrow, f/fb copper/zinc, worn gilt, on stand, 29x34". 1,400.00
Quill pen, copper, on copper rod w/2 spheres, 26x24"...............4,400.00
Ram, pnt wood & sheet iron, 20th C, on stand, 23x35" 1,400.00
Rooster, f/fb copper w/worn gold rpt, on arrow, att Fiske, 26x30"..2,300.00
Rooster, f/fb copper/tin, verdigris/old pnt, Cushing, 45" w/stand...3,900.00
Rooster, fb copper, blk w/gilt traces, bullet holes, on base, 28"..1,035.00
Rooster, fb copper, emb comb/wattle/tail, gilt/verdigris, 39" w/stand..8,800.00
Rooster, fb copper w/riveted comb & ft, EX verdigris, on base, 28"....3,795.00
Rooster, fb copper w/tin comb/tail/wattle, old gilt, 31" on stand...... 11,200.00
Rooster, sheet steel w/old pnt, on plinth & steel flange, 39x25".. 4,600.00
Rooster, zinc f/fb w/copper tail, molded details, J Howard, 25x26".. 14,375.00
Rooster on ball, f/fb copper/zinc, red pnt, on stand, 30x23" 4,400.00
Setter dog, f/fb copper, att Fiske or Washburne, weathered, 36" W...44,000.00
Sperm whale, f/fb copper w/verdigris, McQuarry, 20th C, 36" 450.00
St Julien & sulke, fb copper w/CI horse's head, Fiske, 23x40".23,500.00
1864 Banner, sheet iron, riveted spearheads, blk pnt, on stand, 26x33".825.00

Webb

Thomas Webb and Sons have been glassmakers in Stourbridge, England, since 1837. Besides their fine cameo glass, they have also made enameled ware and pieces heavily decorated with applied glass ornaments. The butterfly is a motif that has been so often featured that it tends to suggest Webb as the manufacturer. Our advisor for this category is Don Williams; he is listed in the Directory under Missouri. See also specific types of glass such as Alexandrite, Burmese, Mother of Pearl, and Peachblow.

Cameo

Bottle, scent; floral, wht on apricot, lay-down, 1884, 10¾".......4,200.00
Bottle, scent; palms & bamboo, wht on lt bl, silver cap, 3¾"....2,700.00
Bottle, scent; swan's head, wht on bl, Gorham silver cap, 5¾"..7,250.00
Bottle, scent; swan's head, wht on citron, silver cap, 6" 6,600.00
Bottle, scent; swan's head, wht on red, threaded top, 9¼".......19,500.00
Bowl, floral sprigs & border, wht on gr, scalloped, 2½x5⅞" 5,000.00
Bowl, floral tapestry, wht on bl, Gem, 3¾x5".............................11,750.00
Bowl, floral/scrolling bands, wht on raisin/apricot, 2¼x3¼" 6,600.00
Bowl, morning-glory vines, wht/red on citron, scalloped, 4x8¼"...5,400.00
Bowl, roses/buds/leaves, wht/purple on bl, Tiffany...1889, Gem, 2½" .. 3,600.00
Bowl, trailing flowers/butterfly, wht on red, 1890s, 5¼" 650.00
Inkwell, fuchsias, wht/red on frost, w/liner, silver lid, 6" 3,500.00
Lamp, floral, pk/opal on frost globe & base, 9¾" w/chimney.....7,800.00

Vase, arabesque floral, olive & wht on lav, 5⅞" 5,350.00
Vase, arabesque floral, wht on canary, dbl gourd, 6⅛" 3,900.00
Vase, arabesque floral, wht on red, stick neck, #957, 10" 7,000.00
Vase, berries/leaves, red on vaseline, vasiform, Gem, 6¼" 3,600.00
Vase, bud; flowers/bee, wht on red, 8¾" 3,400.00
Vase, floral, red & gold on cream, Gem, ca 1888, 5¾" 10,000.00
Vase, floral, wht on bl, slightly bulbous, ftd, Gem, 6¾" 6,900.00
Vase, floral/basketweave/grasses/ferns, wht on raisin, Gem, 8½" ..7,000.00
Vase, floral/insect, wht on rose to honey, stick neck, Gem, 9¼" ..7,800.00
Vase, floral/insects, wht on citron, cylinder neck, Gem, 9" 9,500.00
Vase, fruit/foliage, wht w/purple hints on bl, flared neck, 8¾"...4,600.00
Vase, fuchsias, wht on gr, ovoid, 7" 3,600.00
Vase, lilies/butterfly, wht on citron, decor rim, 6¼" 3,200.00

Vase, morning glories, reverse with red cameo butterfly, semi-transparent purple background with gold and purple bands, Jules Barbe, 5¾", from $15,000.00 to $17,500.00.

(Photo courtesy Early Auction Co.)

Vase, morning glories/moths, wht/red on bl, trumpet neck, 12" .. 7,800.00
Vase, repeating tapestry, red on yel, wht int, 1880s, 3¼" 7,200.00
Vase, roses/butterflies, wht on citron, flared rim, 7¾" 2,650.00
Vase, roses/butterflies, wht/red on citron gr, shouldered, 8¾" 4,200.00
Vase, shells/seaweed, wht on red, scalloped, 6¾x7¼x4" 13,250.00
Vase, sunflowers/grasses, wht on gr, vasiform, Gem, 8⅞" 3,000.00
Vase, trumpet flowers/insects, wht on citron, stick neck, Gem, 15" .7,250.00

Miscellaneous

Urn, intaglio swags/parrots, w/lid, sgn W Fritsche, 10¼" 5,000.00
Vase, cherry blossom branches/insects, gold on yel satin, 9⅝" 480.00
Vase, lily pads/flowers in relief & cut on crystal, ftd, 1906-35, 30" ...350.00
Vase, roses HP on creamy wht, gold trim, #80167, 6½" 1,450.00

Wedgwood

Josiah Wedgwood established his pottery in Burslem, England, in 1759. He produced only molded utilitarian earthenwares until 1770 when new facilities were opened at Etruria for the production of ornamental wares. It was there he introduced his famous Basalt and Jasperware. Jasperware, an unglazed fine stoneware decorated with classic figures in white relief, was usually produced in blues, but it was also made in ground colors of green, lilac, yellow, black, or white. Occasionally three or more colors were used in combination. It has been in continuous production to the present day and is the most easily recognized of all the Wedgwood lines. Jasper-dip is a ware with a solid-color body or a white body that has been dipped in an overlay color. It was introduced in the late 1700s and is the type most often encountered on today's market. (In our listings, all Jasper is of this type unless noted 'solid' color.)

Though Wedgwood's Jasperware was highly acclaimed, on a more practical basis his improved creamware was his greatest success, due to the ease with which it could be potted and because its lighter weight significantly reduced transportation expenses. Wedgwood was able to offer 'chinaware' at afford-

able prices. Queen Charlotte was so pleased with the ware that she allowed it to be called 'Queen's Ware.' Most creamware was marked simply 'WEDGWOOD.' ('Wedgwood & Co.' and 'Wedgewood' are marks of other potters.) From 1769 to 1780, Wedgwood was in partnership with Thomas Bentley; artwares of the highest quality may bear the 'Wedgwood & Bentley' mark indicating this partnership. Moonlight Lustre, an allover splashed-on effect of pink intermingling with gray, brown, or yellow, was made from 1805 to 1815. Porcelain was made, though not to any great extent, from 1812 to 1822. Bone china was produced before 1822 and after 1872. These types of wares were marked 'WEDGWOOD' (with a printed 'Portland Vase' mark after 1872). Stone china and Pearlware were made from about 1820 to 1875. Examples of either may be found with a printed or impressed mark to indicate their body type. During the late 1800s, Wedgwood produced some fine parian and majolica. Creamware, hand painted by Emile Lessore, was sold from about 1860 to 1875. From the twentieth century century, several lines of lustre wares — Butterfly, Dragon, and Fairyland (designed by Daisy Makeig-Jones) — have attracted the collector and, as their prices suggest, are highly sought after and admired. Nearly all of Wedgwood's wares are clearly marked. 'WEDGWOOD' was used before 1891, after which time 'ENGLAND' was added. Most examples marked 'MADE IN ENGLAND' were made after 1905. A detailed study of all marks is recommended for accurate dating. See also Majolica.

Key:
WW — WEDGWOOD   WWMIE — WEDGWOOD Made
WWE — WEDGWOOD England   in England

Barber bottle, Jasper, 3-color, Bacchus heads/ram's heads, 19th C, 10"....2,350.00
Biggin, Caneware, arabesque floral bands, smear glaze, w/lid, 1830, 7"...350.00
Biscuit bbl, Jasper, bl/lav/wht, horses, SP mts, 19th C, 6" 1,300.00
Biscuit bbl, Jasper, blk dip, Egyptian motifs, 20th C, 6¼" 1,000.00
Biscuit bbl, Jasper, dk & lt bl/wht, men/horses, SP mts, 19th C, 6" .. 500.00
Biscuit bbl, Jasper/Dice Ware, 3-color, SP trim, 1870, 5¾" 950.00
Bough pot, wht terra cotta on brn, acanthus leaves, w/lid, 1680s, 6" .. 880.00
Bowl, Butterfly Lustre, Z4832, Oriental motifs, 1920, 8" 765.00
Bowl, chalice; Fairyland Lustre, Twyford Garlands, 1920s, 10¾"....4,700.00
Bowl, Dragon Lustre, Z4829 on bl, MOP int, scalloped/lobed, 1920, 7" ..1,000.00
Bowl, Dragon Lustre, Z4829 on bl mottle, MOP int, 1920, 8¾"...650.00
Bowl, Fairyland Lustre, Castle on Road, Z5115, octagonal, WWE, 9".5,175.00
Bowl, Fairyland Lustre, Castle on Road/Fairy in Cage, MIE, 9" .2,875.00
Bowl, Fairyland Lustre Imperial, Leapfrogging Elves, 1920s, 5½" ..1,000.00
Bowl, Fairyland Lustre Imperial, Woodland Bridge, 1920s, 8⅛" .. 5,580.00
Bowl, Fish Lustre, pattern Z4920 on bl mottle, 1920, 6" 765.00
Bowl, Hummingbird Lustre on bl, 8-sided, 1920s, 8".................... 700.00
Bowl, Queen's Ware, children, Lessore, w/lid, 1870s, 5"............... 350.00
Bowl, Queen's Ware, pierced dome lid, pierced rim, late 18th C, 9¾"..880.00
Bowl, sauce; Caneware, draped ferns, hdls, ca 1800, 7⅛" 1,000.00
Brooch, Butterfly Lustre, butterflies, SP rim, 1930, 2" 300.00
Bulb pot, Pearlware w/sponging, late 18th C, w/lid, 7½"............5,000.00
Bust, Basalt, Geo Washington, after Houdon, late 20th C, 16¼" ..2,000.00
Bust, Basalt, Venus, waisted socle, late 19th C, 10" 700.00
Butter dish, Jasper, dk bl dip, classical figures, 1882, 4⅝" dia........ 700.00
Charger, Earthenware, HP florals, sgn GES, ca 1913, 16¼".......1,650.00
Charger, Queen's Ware, Gariboldi, M Elden, ca 1861, 12¾" 300.00
Coffee can & saucer, Jasper, lav/gr on wht, berries, leaves, 1880, 5"...1,000.00
Compote, Queen's Ware, figures in landscape, 1870s, 9¼" 600.00
Crocus pot, bl smear glaze, hedgehog figural on tray, 1860, 9" L.. 1,000.00
Cup & saucer, coffee; Caneware, hieroglyphs, early 19th C, 4⅞" ... 2,000.00
Deep dish, Earthenware, silver luster/brn foliage, L Powell, 1923, 18".. 1,650.00
Egg stand, Stoneware, w/central salt+6 cups w/bl decor, 1830s, 7" dia..825.00
Figure, Basalt, elephant, glass eyes, E Light, 1915, 3⅜" 385.00
Figure, Basalt, poodle, glass eyes, E Light, 1915, 3" 550.00
Figure, Basalt, Sphinx, seated on sq base, WW, 8¼".................. 1,800.00
Figure, Basalt, squirrel w/nut, E Light, 1935, 5¼" 600.00
Figure, Basalt, Taurus the Bull, after Machin, 1945, 6x15"........... 720.00

Game pie dish, Caneware, grapevine festoons, hare finial, 19th C, 11"..350.00
Inkstand, Drabware, bowl w/insert on 3-dolphin base, 1830s, 4" .. 560.00
Jar, Jasper, lilac dip, foliage, H Barnard, w/lid, 19th C, 3x4", EX ...1,300.00
Jardiniere, Jasper, lilac dip, Muses/festoons, 19th C, 7¾" 880.00
Jardiniere, Jasper, yel dip, classical releif, 1900, 7" 1,000.00
Jardiniere, Redware, mc floral, mask/ring hdls, 19th C, 6" dia, +tray .. 560.00
Jardiniere on stand, Jasper, crimson, classical relief, 1915, 4¼" .. 2,200.00
Jug, basalt, appl mask-head terminal, pear shape, 18th C, 7¾"...2,000.00
Jug, Club; Roso Antico, mc floral w/gold, ca 1830, 7¼" 475.00
Jug, Drabware, Gothic, wht clasical figures, hexagonal, 1830s, 8" ...265.00
Jug, pearlware, floral sprays, strawberry leaf banding, 19th C, 8¼" ..880.00
Jug, Rosso Antico, mc florals, ca 1882, 7" 240.00
Lamp, oil; Rosso Antico, mc floral, squat, scrolled hdl, 19th C, 5"... 440.00
Pie dish, Caneware, acanthus leaves on lid, oval, early 19th c, 14"..350.00
Pitcher, Rockingham, gilt floral, pewter lid, ca 1875, 7½" 650.00
Plaque, Bone China, Man Diagram I, Barton, 1976, 11"...........2,500.00
Plaque, Jasper, bl, classical children, late 19th C, 4¼x5½"+fr ...1,000.00
Plaque, Jasper, lt bl, Bacchanalian boys, 19th C, 22½", +wood fr....825.00
Plaque, Queen's Ware, Peace, Latin inscription, 1919, 16⅞" 2,200.00
Plate, Jasper, blk dip, classical motifs/festoons/flowers, 19th C, 9" .. 1,200.00
Potpourri, Caneware, Rosso Antico grapevines, disk lid, 19th C, 7⅜"..650.00
Punch bowl, Lustre Celtic Ornaments, Z5265, 1920, 11" 3,800.00
Spill vase, Jasper, yel dip, foliate/florets, 19th C, 3⅞" 1,500.00
Spittoon; Basalt, dice banding, globular, mid-19th C, 4⅞" 530.00
Syrup jug, Jasper, yel/wht on gr, trellis, pewter lid, 1890s, 6¾" 300.00
Tankard, Queen's Ware, farmer & horses, Lessore, 1871, 8"......... 450.00
Tea bowl & saucer, Jasper, gr dip, classical figures, 18th C, 5" dia... 1,050.00
Tea canister, Queen's Ware, tea party red transfer, 18th C, 5¼"... 700.00
Tea tray, Queen's Ware, figures in landscape, Lessore, 1864, 17".. 600.00
Teacup & saucer, Jasper, crimson, classical scenes, 1915, 5½" ...1,880.00
Teapot, Rosso Antico, hieroglyphs, crocodile finial, 19th C, 4¼" .. 1,200.00
Tray, lily; Fairyland Lustre, Poplar Tree/Woodland Elves III, MIE, 10". 3,000.00
Vase, Agate/Terra Cotta bands, pierced lid, late 18th C, 9" 1,600.00
Vase, Auro Basalt, gilt/slip foliage & fruits, 1885, 9" 2,350.00
Vase, Basalt, Bacchus head hdls, drapery swags, 19th C, 8¼" 880.00
Vase, Basalt, Classical figures in iron red, Portland shape, 1858, 6"..2,825.00
Vase, Basalt, Classical figures in iron red & wht, 19th C, 7½" ..4,000.00
Vase, Basalt, classical figures w/gilt & bronze, uptrn hdls, 1885, 6"...1,300.00
Vase, Bone China, flowers & cobalt bands on cream, w/lid, 19th C, 7". 150.00
Vase, Daventry Lustre, Oriental scenic panels, 1920s, 8½" 880.00
Vase, Fairyland Lustre, butterfly lady, trumpet form, 1920s, 10" .. 3,100.00

Vase, Fairyland Lustre, Temple on a Rock, Z4968, #2046, with lid, ca 1920, 19", $37,600.00. (Photo courtesy Skinner Inc. Auctioneers & Appraisers of Antiques & Fine Art)

Vase, Jasper, lilac dip, Muses in relief, Portland shape, 1877, 10" ..1,500.00
Vase, Jasper, lt bl dip, Blind Man's Bluff, mid-19th C, 6½" 880.00
Vase, Jasper, wht w/gr medallions, floral festoons, 19th C, 9"....2,650.00
Vase, Porphyry, laurel & berry swags, hdls/Basalt plinth, ca 1775, 11".. 1,650.00
Vase, potpourri; pearl-glazed terra cotta, floral festoons, 18th C, 6" . 530.00
Vase, Queen's Ware, cherubs, Lessore, scrolled hdls, 1863, 8"... 1,100.00
Vase, Rockingham, gilt flowers, bottle form, ca 1875, 12¼" 300.00
Vase, Victoria Ware, Bone China, florals/panels on buff, 19th C, 5"..825.00
Vase, Victoria Ware, gilt florets/wht trophies on cobalt, 1885, 5" ...650.00

Weil Ware

Max Weil came to the United States in the 1940s, settling in California. There he began manufacturing dinnerware, figurines, cookie jars, and wall pockets. American clays were used, and the dinnerware was all hand decorated. Weil died in 1954; the company closed two years later. The last backstamp to be used was the outline of a burro with the words 'Weil Ware — Made in California.' Many unmarked pieces found today originally carried a silver foil label; but you'll often find a four-digit handwritten number series, especially on figurines. For further study we recommend *Collector's Encyclopedia of California Pottery*, by Jack Chipman (Collector Books).

Dinnerware

Birchwood, creamer 15.00
Birchwood, cup & saucer..7.00
Birchwood, plate, salad; 8" 5.00
Birchwood, sugar bowl, w/lid 15.00
Malay Bambu, bowl, divided vegetable; 10½" 37.50
Malay Bambu, bowl, lug cereal 10.00
Malay Bambu, bowl, vegetable; 9⅛" L 30.00
Malay Bambu, butter dish, ¼-lb.. 35.00
Malay Bambu, coffeepot, 6-cup 38.00
Malay Bambu, creamer, 3x5½", from $12 to 15.00
Malay Bambu, cup & saucer, from $9 to 12.00
Malay Bambu, snack plate & cup..7.50
Malay Bambu, tray, sandwich; 11½" 30.00
Malay Blossom, bowl, coupe cereal; 4¾" 7.50
Malay Blossom, bowl, divided vegetable; 10½" L 32.50
Malay Blossom, cup & saucer, from $7 to 10.00
Malay Blossom, plate, 9¾", from $15 to 20.00
Malay Blossom, sugar bowl, w/lid 18.00
Mango, bowl, vegetable; 8½" L.. 20.00
Mango, cup & saucer.. 10.00
Mango, gravy boat, attached underplate 42.50
Mango, plate, dinner; 10" 7.00
Mango, shakers, pr 17.50
Mango, sugar bowl, w/lid 22.50
Rose, coffeepot, 6-cup.. 50.00
Rose, plate, dinner; 10".. 15.00
Rose, relish, 3-part 14.00
Rose, snack plate w/cup 12.00
Rose, sugar bowl, w/lid... 22.50
Rose, tumbler, 4¼" 10.00

Miscellaneous

Figurine, lady in lt gr dress w/matching cap, holds flowers, 11½" ... 70.00
Flower holder, Chinese lady in red w/wht fan behind head, seated, 9x6". 50.00
Flower holder, lady ice skater holds basket, 10" 65.00
Flower holder, lady in purple floral dress, yel shawl, 11" 75.00
Flower holder, lady in yel dress seated between vases, 8½" 45.00
Flower holder, lady pushing cart, 8½"... 35.00
Flower holder, lady w/auburn braids, left hands holds out apron, 11"...35.00
Flower holder, Spanish lady seated w/basket on bk, #180, 8x9x5" ...70.00
Shelf sitters, Oriental boy (& girl) sits between pots, 9½", pr 70.00
Vase, Ming Tree, cylindrical w/slanted top, 11" 45.00
Wall pocket, Oriental girl in bl seated w/flowered pot on ea side, 10"..35.00

Weller

The Weller Pottery Company was established in Zanesville, Ohio, in 1882, the outgrowth of a small one-kiln log cabin works Sam Weller had operated in Fultonham. Through an association with Wm. Long, he entered the art pottery field in 1895, producing the Lonhuda Ware Long had perfected in Steubenville six years earlier. His famous Louwelsa line was merely a continuation of Lonhuda and was made in at least 500 different shapes. Many fine lines of artware followed under the direction of Charles Babcock Upjohn, art director from 1895 to 1904: Dickens Ware (First Line), under-glaze slip decorations on dark backgrounds; Turada, featuring applied ivory bands of delicate openwork on solid dark brown backgrounds; and Aurelian, similar to Louwelsa, but with a brushed-on rather than blended ground. One of their most famous lines was Second Line Dickens, introduced in 1900. Backgrounds, characteristically caramel shading to turquoise matt, were decorated by sgraffito with animals, golfers, monks, Indians, and scenes from Dickens novels. The work is often artist signed. Sicardo, 1902, was a metallic lustre line in tones of blue, green, or purple with flowing Art Nouveau patterns developed within the glaze.

Frederick Hurten Rhead, who worked for Weller from 1903 to mid-1904, created the prestigious Jap Birdimal line decorated with geisha girls, landscapes, storks, etc., accomplished through application of heavy slip forced through the tiny nozzle of a squeeze bag. Other lines to his credit are L'Art Nouveau, produced in both high-gloss brown and matt pastels, and Third Line Dickens, often decorated with Cruikshank's illustrations in relief. Other early artware lines were Eocean, Floretta, Hunter, Perfecto, Dresden, Etched Matt, and Etna.

In 1920 John Lessel was hired as art director, and under his supervision several new lines were created. LaSa, LaMar, Marengo, and Besline attest to his expertise with metallic lustres. The last of the artware lines and one of the most sought after by collectors today is Hudson, first made during the early 1920s. Hudson, a semimatt glazed ware, was beautifully artist decorated on shaded backgrounds with florals, animals, birds, and scenics. Notable artists often signed their work, among them Hester Pillsbury, Dorothy England Laughead, Ruth Axline, Claude Leffler, Sarah Reid McLaughlin, E.L. Pickens, and Mae Timberlake.

During the late 1920s Weller produced a line of gardenware and naturalistic life-sized and larger figures of frogs, dogs, cats, swans, ducks, geese, rabbits, squirrels, and playful gnomes, most of which were sold at the Weller store in Zanesville due to the fragile nature of their designs. The Depression brought a slow, steady decline in sales, and by 1948 the pottery was closed.

Note: Several factors come in to play when evaluating a piece of Hudson: subject matter, artist signature, and size are all important. Artist-signed florals from 5" to 7" range from $300.00 to $800.00; scenics and bud vases from 6" to 8" range from $2,500.00 to $10,000.00, with fine artwork from superior artists at the upper end. Pieces bearing the signatures of Mae Timberlake, Hester Pillsbury, or Sarah Reid McLaughlin bring top prices. Our advisor for this category is Hardy Hudson; he is listed in the Directory under Florida.

Baldin, vase, apples on tan, bulbous bottom, 12"	500.00
Baldin, vase, bl, apple branch on bl, cylindrical, 9x5"	350.00
Barcelona, ewer, 8", from $250 to	300.00
Blue Ware, compote, low ftd, 5½", from $225 to	275.00
Brighton, crow, 9", from $550 to	650.00
Brighton, parrot, 7½", from $650 to	750.00
Brighton, yel butterfly, 2", from $250 to	300.00
Burtwood, jarniniere, birds/flowers, 6½" H, from $175 to	250.00
Cameo Jewel, jardiniere, 11", from $350 to	400.00
Cameo Jewel, umbrella stand, 22", from $1,000 to	1,500.00
Claywood, plate, Wilday Picnic Zanesville, 7", from $175 to	200.00
Claywood, spittoon, floral panels, 4½", from $125 to	150.00
Eocean, candlestick, moonstone leaves, LJB, 9", ea from $400 to	450.00
Eocean, vase, floral, cylindrical, w/sm high hdls, 16", from $800 to	1,000.00
Etna, pitcher, floral, 6½", from $175 to	225.00
Fairfield, bowl, 4½", from $80 to	100.00

Flemish, jardiniere & ped, Deco floral, 2-pc, 26½", from $900 to	1,200.00
Floretta, ewer, emb grapes, 10½", from $250 to	300.00
Forest, window box, 5½x14½", from $550 to	650.00
Fruitone, console bowl, 5", from $150 to	200.00
Glendale, vase, dbl bud; 7", from $300 to	400.00

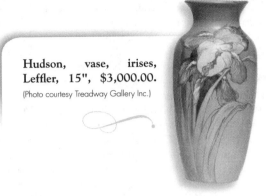

Hudson, vase, irises, Leffler, 15", $3,000.00.
(Photo courtesy Treadway Gallery Inc.)

Hudson, vase, tiger, 8", from $3,500 to	4,000.00
Jap Birdimal, wht bird in flight, 7", from $400 to	450.00
Knifewood, tobacco jar, hunting dog, 7", from $800 to	900.00
L'art Nouveau, ewer, emb floral, 8", from $250 to	300.00
Lorbeek, wall pocket, 8½", from $200 to	250.00
Louwelsa, clock, floral, 10½x12½", from $1,000 to	1,250.00
Louwelsa, ewer, berries, Ferrell, 17", from $1,500 to	2,000.00
Louwelsa, mug, leaves, 4½", from $115 to	140.00
Louwelsa, vase, grapes, Lybarger, 17", from $1,500 to	2,000.00
Malverne, boat bowl, 5½x11", from $150 to	175.00
Mammy, teapot, 8", from $900 to	1,200.00
Marvo, bowl, 5", from $85 to	100.00
Mirror Black, wall vase, 6", from $100 to	125.00
Muskota, geese flower frog, 6", from $400 to	500.00
Parian, wall pocket, 10", from $200 to	250.00
Pearl, basket, 6½", from $200 to	250.00
Perfecto, vase, floral, MH, 14", from $900 to	1,100.00
Roma, bud vase, emb hdls, 6½", from $80 to	100.00
Roma, compote, sm hdls under bowl on high ped, 8½", from $100 to	150.00
Sabrinian, bowl, 2½x9", from $150 to	190.00
Sicardo, vase, shouldered w/flared bottom, 6", from $500 to	750.00
Stellar, vase, 6", from $500 to	600.00
Tutone, basket, 7½", from $150 to	200.00
Velva, bowl, ftd, w/hdls, 3½x12½", from $125 to	150.00
Woodcraft, mug, foxes, 6", from $375 to	475.00
Zona, compote, pastel floral bowl, 5½", from $100 to	125.00

Western Americana

The collecting of Western Americana encompasses a broad spectrum of memorabilia. Examples of various areas within the main stream would include the following fields: weapons, bottles, photographs, mining/railroad artifacts, cowboy paraphernalia, farm and ranch implements, maps, barbed wire, tokens, Indian relics, saloon/gambling items, and branding irons. Some of these areas have their own separate listings in this book. Western Americana is not only a collecting field but is also a collecting era with specific boundries. Depending upon which field the collector decides to specialize in, prices can start at a few dollars and run into the thousands.

Our advisor for this category is Bill Mackin, author of *Cowboy and Gunfighter Collectibles* (order from the author); he is listed in the Directory under Colorado. Values are for examples in excellent original condition, unless otherwise noted in the description.

Bit, C Figueroa, silver inlay, half-breed Santa Barbara style, 1930s ..950.00
Bit, T Hildreth, loose-jaw silver inlaid kissing bird, floral eng...... 600.00
Business card, Dexter Saloon, W Earp/CE Hoxie Proprieters, Nome . 150.00
Chaps, brn leather batwing style w/nickel conchos, some wear ... 240.00
Chaps, SD Myres, 2-tone leather, silver conchos/5-point TX stars...2,400.00
Chaps, unmk tooled leather step-in style w/fringe, ca 1900, VG... 660.00
Coat, horsehair, satin lined, shawl collar, knee length, ca 1900, lg... 450.00
Cuffs, tooled leather, 7" L, pr... 115.00
Hat, Stetson, beaver felt, 1920s, VG... 300.00
Lariat, braided rawhide, 50 ft L 250.00
Lithograph, cowgirl w/gun & rope, Tobin, NY, 1904, 18x14", EX+ ...475.00
Saddle, CP Shipley, sq skirt, nickel conchos, NP horn, 1930s 725.00
Saddle, HT O'Brien, sq skirt/S Stagg rigging/16" seat/conchos, 1880s . 6,000.00
Saddle, Mother Hubbard w/apple horn, attached mochilla, 1880s, VG ..4,800.00
Saddle, RT Frazier Pueblo, sq skirt, 14" seat, nickel horn, 1930s, VG... 2,700.00
Spurs, Buermann, forged steel, 2" 20-point rowels, 1½" conchos, 7" ..300.00
Spurs, Buermann, silver o/l, gold slippers/garters, rowels, 1920s .. 1,200.00
Spurs, Crocket, Paddy Ryan pattern, 5-point rowels, 1930s, lady's sz .1,200.00
Spurs, Mexican silver w/snake/flowers/peso coin, 8-point rowels, 1890s...1,500.00
Trunk, hide-covered, forged hinges/fancy studs, 1850s, 19x39x15", VG ..1,950.00

Western Pottery Manufacturing Company

This pottery was originally founded as the Denver China and Pottery Company; William Long was the owner. The company's assets were sold to a group who in 1905 formed the Western Pottery Manufacturing Company, located at 16th Street and Alcott in Denver, Colorado. By 1926, 186 different items were being produced, including crocks, flowerpots, kitchen items, and other stoneware. The company dissolved in 1936. Seven various marks were used during the years, and values may be higher for items that carry a rare mark. Numbers within the descriptions refer to specific marks, see the line drawings. Prices may vary depending on demand and locale. Our advisors for this category are Cathy Segelke and Pat James; they are listed in the Directory under Colorado.

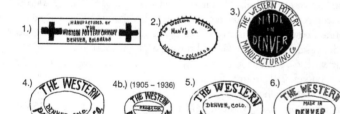

Churn, #2, hdl, 4-gal, M 75.00
Churn, #2, hdl, 5-gal, M 65.00
Churn, #2, no lid, 5-gal, G 80.00
Crock, #4, bail lip, 4-gal, G 55.00
Crock, #4, hdl, no lid, 8-gal, M 90.00
Crock, #4, ice water; bl & wht sponge pnt, 3-gal, NM 30.00
Crock, #4, 6-gal, EX 72.00
Crock, #4b, 15-gal, 22x17½", NM.. 150.00
Crock, #4b, 20-gal, M 200.00
Crock, #5, bail lip, 1½-gal, M 45.00
Crock, #5, no lid, 6-gal, M.. 70.00
Crock, #6, wire hdl, 10-gal, NM 100.00
Crock, #6, 3-gal, M 40.00
Crock, #6, 4-gal, M 50.00
Crock, #6, 5-gal, NM 60.00
Foot warmer, #6, M... 60.00

Jug, #6, brn/wht, 1-gal, EX.. 25.00
Jug, #6, brn/wht, 5-gal, M... 75.00
Rabbit feeder, #1, EX 25.00
Rabbit waterer, #1, M.. 25.00

Western Stoneware Co.

The Western Stoneware Co., Monmouth, Illinois, was formed in 1906 as a merger of seven potteries: Monmouth Pottery Co., Monmouth, Illinois; Weir Pottery Co., Monmouth, Illinois; Macomb Pottery Co. and Macomb Stoneware Co., Macomb, Illinois; D. Culbertson Stoneware Co., Whitehall, Illinois; Clinton Stoneware Co., Clinton, Missouri; and Fort Dodge Stoneware Co., Fort Dodge, Iowa. Western Stoneware Co. manufactured stoneware, gardenware, flowerpots, artware, and dinnerware. Some early crocks, jugs, and churns are found with a plant number in the Maple Leaf logo. Plants 1 through 7 turn up. In 1926 an artware line was introduced as the Monmouth Pottery Artware. One by one each branch of the operation closed, and today one branch remains. Western Stoneware Co. closed in April 2006, after 100 years of stoneware production. Our advisor for this category is Jim Martin; he is listed in the Directory under Illinois. See also Old Sleepy Eye.

Bean pot, souvenir of Monmouth, bl & wht, sm............................ 150.00
Beater jar, bl band on wht w/advertising.................................... 120.00
Beehive jug, brn & wht, 1-gal 100.00
Birdbath, Burntwood glaze, iron perch....................................... 600.00
Book, Monmouth-Western Stoneware, Jim Martin & Bette Cooper, 1983..60.00
Butter jar, #5, bl tint, w/lid & bail... 150.00
Chicken waterer, 1-gal... 130.00
Churn, Maple Leaf mk, mini...1,000.00
Churn, Maple Leaf mk, 2-gal... 150.00
Churn, Maple Leaf mk, 6-gal, Plant 6.. 250.00
Combinet, w/lid & hdl, mini... 700.00

Crock, blue bands (hard to find), two-gallon, $200.00.

(Photo courtesy Jim Martin)

Crock, cake; bl tint, no lid..2,300.00
Crock, Maple Leaf mk, 2-gal, Plant 1, 3 or 4, ea.......................... 80.00
Crock, Maple Leaf mk, 20-gal 125.00
Crock, Maple Leaf mk, 60-gal...1,500.00
Custard cup, Colonial... 350.00
Flowerpot/ashtray, Cardinal, red flowerpot clay, no glaze 150.00
Humidor, Duke of Monmouth, cobalt.. 300.00
Jar, Maple Leaf & oval mk, 2-gal.. 50.00
Jardiniere, Egyptian, brn-glazed int, 7"..................................... 75.00
Jug, Bristol, Plant 3, 3-gal 240.00
Jug, Bristol, Plant 5, 5-gal 240.00
Jug, Monmouth advertising, 1-qt.. 125.00
Monkey jug, brn & wht, 1-gal 150.00
Mug, Cattail, bl tint.. 150.00
Pitcher, band & rivets, bl tint, ½-gal... 200.00
Pitcher, Cattail, bl & wht, 1-qt 150.00

Pitcher, Scroll & Leaf, bl & wht w/advertising 1,000.00
Pitcher & bowl, Memphis, bl & wht 300.00
Rolling pin, bl & wht w/advertising 900.00
Ruler, wooden, 12" 50.00
Stock certificate, 1911 .... 90.00
Sundial, Burntwood 500.00
Vase, Etruscan, gr & wht 45.00
Vase, lotus design, bl, 14" 75.00
Wall pockets, Egyptian ware, brn & gr, pr 450.00
Water cooler, Cupid, bl & wht, 4-gal 1,000.00
Water cooler, emb maple leaves, bl & wht, w/lid & spigot, 4-gal ..2,000.00
Wren house, rnd, Burntwood 125.00

Westmoreland

Originally titled the Specialty Glass Company, Westmoreland began operations in East Liverpool, Ohio, producing utility items as well as tableware in milk glass and crystal. When the company moved to Grapeville, Pennsylvania, in 1890, lamps, vases, covered animal dishes, and decorative plates were introduced. Prior to 1920 Westmoreland was a major manufacturer of carnival glass and soon thereafter added a line of lovely reproduction art glass items. High-quality milk glass became their speciality, accounting for about 90% of their production. Black glass was introduced in the 1940s, and later in the decade ruby-stained pieces and items decorated in the Mary Gregory style became fashionable. By the 1960s colored glassware was being produced, examples of which are very popular with collectors today. Early pieces were marked with a paper label; by the 1960s the ware was embossed with a superimposed 'WG.' The last mark was a circle containing 'Westmoreland' around the perimeter and a large 'W' in the center. The company closed in 1985, and on February 28, 1996, the factory burned to the ground.

Note: Though you may find pieces very similar to Westmoreland's, their Della Robbia has no bananas among the fruits relief. For more information we recommend *Westmoreland Glass, The Popular Years*, by Lorraine Kovar (Collector Books). See *Garage Sale & Flea Market Annual* for a listing of many other items with current market values. Our advisor for this category is Philip Rosso, Jr. He is listed in the Directory under Pennsylvania. See also Animal Dishes with Covers; Carnival Glass; Glass Animals.

American Hobnail, bonbon, gr 45.00
American Hobnail, goblet, iced tea; crystal, 14-oz 25.00
American Hobnail, goblet, water; Golden Sunset, 8-oz 15.00
American Hobnail, pickle dish, milk glass, oval 25.00
American Hobnail, plate, crystal, 11½" 50.00
American Hobnail, shakers, milk glass, pr 20.00
American Hobnail, vase, cylinder, milk glass, 7½" 27.00
Ashburton, goblet, water; any color 12.50
Ashburton, pitcher, any color, ftd, lg 60.00
Ashburton, sherbet, any color, ftd 7.50
Beaded Edge, bowl, fruit; milk glass, 5" 10.00
Beaded Edge, plate, dinner; milk glass w/floral decor, 10½" ... 42.50
Beaded Edge, plate, dinner; milk glass w/fruit decor, 10½" 22.50
Beaded Edge, platter, milk glass w/red rim, w/hdls, 12" 70.00
Beaded Grape, bowl, milk glass, sq, w/lid, 4½" 45.00
Beaded Grape, creamer, milk glass 12.50
Beaded Grape, honey dish, crystal w/ruby stain, ftd, w/lid, 5" 45.00
Beaded Grape, saucer, milk glass 10.00
Beaded Grape, vase, milk glass w/fruit decor, crimped rim, ftd, 9" 90.00
Cherry, bowl, milk glass, ftd, 9" 160.00
Cherry, candlesticks, milk glass, 4", pr 65.00
Colonial, pitcher, crystal, 8" 55.00
Colonial, sherbet, Olive Green, ftd 7.50

Della Robbia, compote, crystal or milk glass, 6½" 17.50
Della Robbia, plate, salad; crystal, 7½" 10.00
Della Robbia, plate, torte; crystal, 14" 35.00
Della Robbia, shakers, crystal w/any stain, ftd, pr 75.00
Della Robbia, shakers, milk glass, ftd, pr 40.00
Della Robbia, tumbler, crystal w/any stain, 5" 35.00
Dolphin & Shell, candy dish, Golden Sunset, 3-ftd, 6" 45.00
Dolphin & Shell, vase, Almond, 3-ftd, 8½" 65.00
English Hobnail, basket, crystal, 9" 50.00
English Hobnail, bowl, crystal or milk glass, 5" 10.00
English Hobnail, bowl, rimmed grapefruit; gr or pk, 6½" 25.00
English Hobnail, cigarette box, crystal, 4½x3½" 17.50
English Hobnail, claret, turq, rnd ft, 5-oz, 6" 20.00
English Hobnail, cocktail, milk glass, rnd ft, 3-oz, 4½" 15.00
English Hobnail, creamer, amber, hexagonal 20.00
English Hobnail, cruet, ruby, w/hdl, 6-oz, 6" 40.00
English Hobnail, goblet, crystal or milk glass, 8-oz, 5" 17.50
English Hobnail, plate, luncheon; crystal, plain rim, 8½" 12.50
English Hobnail, shakers, pk, rnd ftd, pr 27.50
English Hobnail, sugar bowl, ruby, hexagon ft, 4½" 15.00
English Hobnail, tumbler, Belgian Blue, 8-oz, 4" 40.00
English Hobnail, tumbler, crystal, rnd ft, 9-oz 15.00
English Hobnail, vase, gr or pk, pinched rim, 7½x6" 80.00
English Hobnail, whiskey, crystal, ½-oz, 2½" 15.00
English Hobnail, wine, crystal, sq ft, 2-oz, 4½" 17.50
Lattice Edge, bowl, milk glass, flared rim, ftd, 10½" 55.00
Lattice Edge, candlesticks, milk glass, 4", pr 40.00
Lotus, bowl, milk glass, oval, sq ft 155.00
Lotus, mayonnaise, ruby, 4" 25.00
Maple Leaf, creamer, ruby, ftd, w/twig hdl 35.00
Maple Leaf, vase, bud; milk glass, decanter style 45.00
Old Quilt, cake salver, milk glass, skirted, bell ft, 12" 125.00
Old Quilt, cheese dish, Aquamarine 85.00
Old Quilt, cheese dish, crystal 35.00
Old Quilt, compote, milk glass, crimped & ruffled rim 65.00
Old Quilt, cruet, crystal w/ruby stain, 6-oz 35.00
Old Quilt, jardiniere, milk glass, ftd, 6½" 65.00
Old Quilt, perfume bottle, milk glass w/forget-me-not, 5-oz ... 125.00
Old Quilt, pitcher, water; purple marble, 3-pt, 8½" 100.00
Old Quilt, plate, salad; milk glass, 8½" 35.00
Old Quilt, tumbler, cobalt, 9-oz 32.50
Old Quilt, tumbler, juice; milk glass, 5-oz 27.50
Old Quilt, vase, milk glass, fan shape, octagon ft, 9" 25.00
Paneled Grape, bowl, blk, 4½" 20.00
Paneled Grape, cheese dish, purple marble 75.00
Paneled Grape, compote, Brandywine Blue, w/lid, 7x4½" 45.00
Paneled Grape, compote, milk glass w/HP pansy, w/lid, 7x4½" 60.00
Paneled Grape, cruet, amber, 2-oz 27.50
Paneled Grape, cup, any color but milk glass, flared rim 25.00
Paneled Grape, cup, milk glass, flared rim 15.00
Paneled Grape, goblet, Laurel Green, 8-oz, 6" 25.00
Paneled Grape, goblet, Olive Green, 8-oz, 6" 12.50
Paneled Grape, jardinere, milk glass, cupped, ftd, 4" 27.50
Paneled Grape, mayonnaise set, crystal, 3-pc 40.00
Paneled Grape, nut dish, crystal, oval, ftd 25.00
Paneled Grape, parfait, crystal, scalloped ft, 6" 25.00
Paneled Grape, pitcher, Golden Sunset, ftd, 1-qt 65.00
Paneled Grape, plate, torte; milk glass, 14½" 135.00
Paneled Grape, sauceboat, milk glass, w/oval underplate 65.00
Paneled Grape, sherbet, milk glass, high ped ft 40.00
Paneled Grape, sugar bowl, milk glass, lace rim 30.00
Paneled Grape, sugar bowl, Moss Green, lace rim, open 25.00
Paneled Grape, tumbler, juice; crystal or milk glass, 5-oz, 4½" 25.00
Paneled Grape, vase, milk glass w/gold, ftd, 9½" 35.00

Princess Feather, cup & saucer, Golden Sunset 17.50
Princess Feather, pitcher, crystal, 54-oz 95.00
Princess Feather, plate, dinner; Golden Sunset, 10½" 45.00
Princess Feather, punch bowl & base, crystal 195.00
Princess Feather, punch cup, crystal 125.00
Princess Feather, tumbler, ftd, milk glass 25.00
Thousand Eye, creamer, ruby 40.00
Thousand Eye, plate, dinner; crystal w/stain, 10" 75.00
Thousand Eye, relish, crystal, 6-part, 10" 20.00
Thousand Eye, tumbler, iced tea; crystal, ftd, 12-oz, 6¾"............... 20.00
Thousand Eye, wine, crystal, 2-oz, 4¾" 22.50
Waterford, bowl, crystal w/ruby stain, cupped, 6" 40.00
Waterford, candy dish, pk, crimped rim, ftd................................. 45.00
Waterford, plate, bread & butter; crystal, 6" 10.00

Waterford, server with center handle, WF-39, 10½", $55.00. (Photo courtesy Lorraine Kovar)

Wheatley, T. J.

In 1880 after a brief association with the Coultry Works, Thomas J. Wheatley opened his own studio in Cincinnati, Ohio, claiming to have been the first to discover the secret of under-glaze slip decoration on an unbaked clay vessel. He applied for and was granted a patent for his process. Demand for his ware increased to the point that several artists were hired to decorate the ware. The company incorporated in 1880 as the Cincinnati Art Pottery, but until 1882 it continued to operate under Wheatley's name. Ware from this period is marked 'T.J. Wheatley' or 'T.J.W. and Co.,' and it may be dated. The business was reorganized in 1903 as the Wheatley Pottery Company, and its production turned to Arts and Crafts vessels, particularly lamp bases, many of which were copies of Grueby shapes or those of other contemporaries. These were often covered in a thick curdled matt green glaze, although some are found in brown as well. Decorative and collectible, these have been referred to as the 'poor man's Grueby.' An incised or stamped mark reads 'WP' or WPCo' and might be hidden beneath glaze on the bottom.

Jardiniere, medallions/raised bands, gr matt, 12⅛x20¾"............... 780.00
Lamp base, leaves (long), matt brn, Kendrick style, buttressed ft, 13" .. 1,550.00
Pitcher, grapes & vines, gr matt, burst bubbles, 8" 300.00
Pot, thistles, dk gr matt, rstr, 11x10" 2,000.00
Vase, appl thistles, gr, flecks/nicks, 11½x10¼" 780.00
Vase, bird on ground beneath tree, Limoges style, 1880, 10¾", NM ..275.00
Vase, cherry blossoms HP on mc mottle, flaw, 1880, 8x5½" 345.00
Vase, floral, bl on mc earth tones, bulbous, 1880, 8¾x8" 550.00
Vase, geometrics, gr w/3 buttress ft, 4½x6¼" 425.00
Vase, gr (feathered), buttress ft, bowl-like w/long neck, #648, 13" ...2,200.00
Vase, gr (organic), 4 buttress ft, 11" 3,000.00
Vase, gr crackle drip on unglazed clay, sm chips, 30x16" 3,600.00
Vase, gr matt, bulbous, 11½x9½" 850.00
Vase, Greek key band at opening, feathery gr matt, burst bubbles, 7"... 1,175.00
Vase, hibiscus appl on Barbotine, KW, ca 1880, 19x10", NM 960.00
Vase, leaves & buds, gr matt, 4 buttress ft, #609, 10x8½"........... 1,650.00
Vase, leaves & buds, ochre matt, #607, 9x8" 1,800.00
Vase, moths/foliage, gr matt, 8⅛" 3,000.00
Wall pocket, grapes, gr matt, #279, rstr, 11¾" 215.00

Whieldon

Thomas Whieldon was regarded as the finest of the Staffordshire potters of the mid-1700s. He produced marbled and black Egyptian wares as well as tortoise shell, a mottled brown-glazed earthenware accented with touches of blue and yellow. In 1754 he became a partner of Josiah Wedgwood. Other potters produced similar wares, and today the term Whieldon is used generically.

Charger, tortoiseshell, scroll-molded rim, ca 1765, 15" 650.00
Creamer, cow, brn/gray on gr base, w/lid, rstr, 5¼"...................... 400.00
Creamer, cow w/milkmaid at base, 19th C, 9" 1,100.00
Plate, tortoiseshell, molded edge, 18th C, 9" 345.00
Plate, tortoiseshell, 8-sided, ribbed rim, ca 1765, 9" 275.00
Plate, tortoiseshell, 8-sided, tooled rim, 9½" 300.00
Teapot, agate ware, pewter lid, #22, chipped spout, 8x8" 60.00
Teapot, tortoiseshell on soft paste, melon shape, twig spout, 18th C... 950.00
Teapot, tortoiseshell w/molded leaves, 19th C, 9" 300.00

Wicker

Wicker is the basket-like material used in many types of furniture and accessories. It may be made from bamboo cane, rattan, reed, or artificial fibers. It is airy, lightweight, and very popular in hot regions. Imported from the Orient in the eighteenth century, it was first manufactured in the United States in about 1850. The elaborate, closely woven Victorian designs belong to the mid- to late 1800s, and the simple styles with coarse reedings usually indicate a post-1900 production. Art Deco styles followed in the '20s and '30s. The most important consideration in buying wicker is condition — it can be restored, but only by a professional. Age is an important factor, but be aware that 'Victorian-style' furniture is being manufactured today.

Key:
HB — Heywood Bros.   H/W — Heywood Wakefield

Armchair, tubular steel fr, wooden arm rests, Breuer/Thonet, 1928, 33"..575.00
Armchair & ottoman, natural tight weave, uphl seat & cushion, EX...900.00
Baby buggy, curved arms, ft rest, Victorian era, 36x44x21" 400.00
Baby carriage, sleigh front, natural, H/W, 41x54x23".................... 550.00
Chair, continuous arms, tight weave, skirt, Smith & Hawkins, 39" ...120.00
Chair, continuous arms, loose-weave bk, rstr cushion, 1900s, 35"...400.00
Chair, continuous arms, scrolling heart bk, cane seat, 1890s, 31" ...465.00
Chair, continuous arms, tight weave, stick & ball, att H/W, 36x27x26"..480.00
Chair, corner; curlicues, ornate apron, H/W, 1880s, 33" 360.00
Chair, photographer's; single continuous arm, ornate scrolls, 32x34".. 300.00
Chair, tulip; wrought-iron fr, Erwin & Estelle Laverne, 1950s, 49x45"..4,350.00
Chaise lounge, scrolled arm, dmn-weave skirt, att H/W, 72" L 480.00
Daybed, Chinese teakwood fr, rnd mirror in bk, hardstone panels, 72"...3,600.00
Desk, tight weave, drw/letter holders/cubbiess, wht pnt, H/W, +chair..360.00
Desk, 2 oak drws, glass top, raised shelf at bk, Nouveau style, 33x45".850.00
Easel, Victorian scrolls, H/W, ca 1880, 75x25" 850.00
Hall tree, demilune shelf/tall bk w/lg mirror, wht pnt, 73" 850.00
Lamp, floor; natural rattan shade w/rpl liner, 72x20x20"............. 780.00
Lamp, table; tight weave shade & base, H/W, ca 1900, 25".......... 345.00
Rocker, continuous arms, scrolls/fans, att H/W, 44x34x26" 725.00
Screen, mahog fr, 3 hinged panels, Adams style w/HP cherubs, 63x59" .. 950.00
Settee, continuous arms, lattice weave, wht pnt, rpl cushion, 39x54"..425.00
Sewing basket, tight-weave body, scrolled legs, ca 1900, 31" 345.00
Sewing stand, 2 galleried tiers, curved legs, 8-sided, 19th C, 27x18"..550.00
Sofa, tight weave w/pnt sunbursts, rstr cushions, Lloyd, 32x70x27"...425.00
Stand, wrapped/twisted design, 3 oak shelves, H/W, 45x18¾x18¾" ..850.00

Table, leather top, shelf, tight weave, H/W, ca 1900, 29x30x18" .. 345.00
Tea cart, wood top & shelf, lattice sides, Wakefield, 30x32x17", VG ...325.00

Wiener Werkstatte

The Wiener Werkstatte was established in Austria in 1903. It was one of many workshops worldwide that ascribed to the new wave of design and style that was sweeping not only Austria but England and other European countries as well.

Its founders were Josef Hoffmann, Kolo Moser, and Fritz Warndorfer. Hoffmann had for some time been involved in a movement bent toward refining prevailing Art Nouveau trends. He was a primary initiator of the Viennese Secession, and in 1899 he worked as a professor at the Viennese School of Applied Arts. Through his work as an architect, he began to develop his own independent style, preferring and promoting clean rectangular shapes over the more accepted building concepts of the day. His progressive ideas resulted in contemporary designs, completely breaking away from past principles in all medias of art as well as architecture, completely redefining Arts and Crafts. At the Wiener Werkstatte, every object was crafted with exquisite attention to design, workmanship, and materials.

Book, Evolution of Modern Appl Arts 1903-28, hardbound, pnt cover ..4,650.00
Bowl, centerpc; amber glass, ftd, Hoffman design by Mosser, 1917, 4x5" .725.00
Bowl, centerpc; Gold Aurene, Hoffman design, Mosser, 1917, 4x5" ..600.00
Box, geometric overlapping earth tones, paper, 1920s, 3¼x6x6" ..1,325.00
Bust, elegant lady, HP earthenware, C Calm-Wierink, 1920s, 8½" ..3,000.00
Candelabrum, vines w/flowers & leaves, Wieselthier, #0908, 8", NM 2,500.00
Centerpc coupe, hammered/chased brass w/ribbon hdls, Hoffman, 8x12" ..2,650.00
Centerpc figure, lady w/2 baskets, mc, ceramic, Kppriva, 6¼" ...1,100.00
Fashion card, lady in fancy garb w/butterfly, #693, 3x3½" 120.00
Jar, amber glass, 10-panel w/faceted finial, ca 1920, 12" 575.00
Lamp, tabby cat figural, creamic w/glass eyes, Hoffman, rpr, 14" ..425.00
Pitcher, rooster-head spout, gr & yel on red clay, Lotte Calm ...1,200.00
Postcard, girl w/spool & string game, Mela Koehler, #648, NM... 165.00
Postcard, Nicolo, religious figure & children, Mela Kohler, #71 ..780.00
Teapot, brass-washed copper, tin lining, rosewood hdl, Hoffman, 6x10" ..6,600.00
Vase, dk amethyst glass w/melon ribs, Hoffman, 7½" 550.00
Vase, dmn cutouts/abstracts, mc on red clay, Wieselthier, 7⅜", EX ..1,450.00

Vase, three connected cylinders, signed Gudrun Baudisch, #280, 9½", $2,200.00. (Photo courtesy Treadway Gallery Inc.)

Vase, yel/rose flambé, ovoid w/pinched sides, 1920s, 8¼x6x2½" ..500.00
Vessel, amber glass 10-panel cylinder, scalloped lid, 1920s, 12" ...575.00

Will-George

After years of working in the family garage, William and George Climes founded the Will-George company in Los Angeles, California, in 1934. They manufactured high-quality artware, utilizing both porcelain and earthenware clays. Both brothers, motivated by their love

of art pottery, had extensive education and training in manufacturing processes as well as decoration. In 1940 actor Edgar Bergen, a collector of pottery, developed a relationship with the brothers and invested in their business. With this new influx of funds, the company relocated to Pasadena. There they produced an extensive line of art pottery, but they excelled in their creation of bird and animal figurines. In addition, they molded a large line of human figurines similar to Royal Doulton. The brothers, now employing a staff of decorators, precisely molded their pieces with great care and strong emphasis on originality and detail, creating high-quality works of art that were only carried by exclusive gift stores.

In the late 1940s after a split with Bergen, the company moved to San Gabriel to a larger, more modern location and renamed themselves The Claysmiths. Their business flourished and they were able to successfully mass produce many items; but due to the abundance of cheap, postwar imports from Italy and Japan that were then flooding the market, they liquidated the business in 1956.

Bowl, red onion, gr stem finial on lid, 4x4¾" 30.00
Candleholders, upright leaves w/1 curled down, turq w/pk, 6¼", pr ...155.00
Figurine, ballerina girl stands on rnd base, 5⅜" 135.00
Figurine, cockatoo on stump, yel/pk/brn, 12¼", NM 215.00
Figurine, eagle on rock, wht & brn, 10" 150.00
Figurine, flamingo, closed-S neck, wings closed, 12" 335.00
Figurine, flamingo, female preening, dk pk (almost red), 10x6" ...275.00
Figurine, flamingo, floater type w/head & wings up, 3⅝" 300.00
Figurine, flamingo, head down & wings closed, 6½" 175.00
Figurine, flamingo, head up, wings up, 8", from $225 to............. 250.00
Figurine, flamingo, head up, wings up, 15½" 365.00
Figurine, flamingo, in stride/preening, wings partly closed, 10" 75.00
Figurine, giraffe stands w/head up & legs wide, 13" 185.00
Figurine, giraffe w/head trn & legs wide, 14½" 160.00
Figurine, lady in dress w/wht apron, flowered hat, #106, 1956, 5" ...110.00
Figurine, monk, brn bsk, 4½" 50.00
Figurine, robin, detailed pnt, 3" 25.00
Figurine, rooster, wht w/red comb, 4¼" 85.00
Flower holder, bird on stump w/5 openings, 7½" 65.00
Flower holder, bird on stump w/6 openings, 1934-56, 8" 60.00
Martini glass, rooster stem w/clear bowl, 5" 25.00
Planter, Oriental girl seated on wooden bucket planter, 7½" 85.00
Planter, Swiss hiker, flower in left hand, basket on bk, 16" 50.00
Plate, luncheon; red onion, 8½" 15.00
Platter, half red onion shape, 3x11x13" 45.00
Tumbler, rooster, formed by tall tail feathrs, 4½", from $50 to 60.00
Tureen, soup; red onion shape, w/lid & ladle, 7½" 325.00

Willets

The Willets Manufacturing Company of Trenton, New Jersey, produced a type of belleek porcelain during the late 1880s and 1890s. Examples were often marked with a coiled snake that formed a 'W' with 'Willets' below and 'Belleek' above. Not all Willets is factory decorated. Items painted by amateurs outside the factory are worth considerably less. High prices usually equate with fine artwork. In the listings below, all items are Belleek unless noted otherwise. Our advisor for this category is Mary Frank Gaston; she is listed in the Directory under Texas.

Bowl, floral, lt & med gr, 4x6¼" 72.50
Bowl, roses, pk/gr on wht, sgn Zeigler, gold hdls, 1879-1912, 5x13" ...150.00
Chocolate pot, wht w/ornate hdl, slim, 10", +6 wht scalloped c/s ...110.00
Compote, floral reserve & vines, gold hdls, 5⅛x8¾" L 120.00
Hatpin holder, floral silver o/l on wht, 4⅞" 120.00

Jar, Oriental ladies & paper lanterns, fans on lid, 5x4" 360.00
Pitcher, grapes on wht w/gold trim, cylindrical, sgn MMB, 14¼" .. 240.00
Punch bowl, roses on pk to gr, 6⅝x10¼" 275.00
Vase, Biblical scene of lady in garden holding flowers, 15" 1,050.00
Vase, daffodils, yel on gr, swollen cylinder, 14½" 345.00
Vase, landscape, bl/gr/brn, cylindrical, Brischoff, 1910s, 16¼" .. 1,650.00
Vase, Mt Fuji & village scene, flattened ovoid, gold hdls/rim, 8⅞" ... 240.00
Vase, roses, mc on cream, shouldered, 11⅛" 395.00

Winchester

The Winchester Repeating Arms Company lost their important government contract after WWI and of necessity turned to the manufacture of sporting goods, hardware items, tools, etc., to augment their gun production. Between 1920 and 1931, over 7,500 different items, each marked 'Winchester Trademark U.S.A.,' were offered for sale by thousands of Winchester Hardware stores throughout the country. After 1931 the firm became Winchester-Western. Collectors prefer the prewar items, and the majority of our listings are from this era.

Concerning current collecting trends: Oil cans that a short time ago could be purchased for $2.00 to $5.00 now often sell for $25.00, some over $50.00, and demand is high. Good examples of advertising posters and calendars seem to have no upper limits and are difficult to find. Winchester fishing lures are strong, and the presence of original boxes increases values by 25% to 40%. Another current trend concerns the price of 'diecuts' (cardboard stand-ups, signs, or hanging signs). These are out-pricing many other items. A short time ago the average value of a 'diecut' ranged from $25.00 to $45.00. Current values for most are in the $200.00 to $800.00 range, with some approaching $2,500.00.

Unless noted otherwise, our values are for items in excellent condition. Our advisor for this category is James Anderson; he is listed in the Directory under Minnesota. See also Knives; Fishing Collectibles.

Auger bit, VG+ 25.00
Axe, dbl; 10½", w/24" wooden hdl 135.00
Barrel reflector, VG 165.00
Baseball bat, #2408 .... 350.00
Basketball, G 1,200.00
Battery, 3-cell, tubular, rare, VG 135.00
Box, shotshell, Leader 12-Gauge, full box of 10, 3½" L, G- 45.00
Box, 12-gauge shotgun cartridges, stencil on dvtl wood, 9x15x9½" .. 85.00
Calendar, father & son w/ducks, Atlantic Litho, 1920, partial pad .. 1,450.00
Calendar, Western scene after Leigh painting, partial pad, 31x16"+fr .. 7,200.00
Calendar top, man w/gun stands by game animal, 1901, 27x13" .. 425.00
Can, gun oil; gr graphics, #1052, ca 1920, 3-oz, VG+ 185.00
Cannon, signal; 10-gauge, Pat August 20, 1901, VG 1,450.00
Carpet sweeper, G- 600.00
Catalog, bl cover, #89, 1934, EX 85.00
Catalog, Winchester Pocket Catalog of Tools 1923, 6x3", G 115.00
Catalog, Winchester...No 75, March 1909, 182 pgs, G 55.00
Cold chisel, #W12, G- 25.00
Container, No 9114 Split BB Shot, fish on lid, NM 215.00
Drill, breast; #W44 .... 135.00
Fishing reel, #4252, G 150.00
Food chopper, #W12, from $60 to 75.00
Football helmet, blk leather 3,750.00
Garden hoe, VG+ 125.00
Gun case, leather, mks on both lids, broken leather tongues, VG ... 300.00
Hacksaw, G+ 85.00
Hatchet, 5" head, wooden hdl 165.00
Holster, VG 950.00
Knife sharpener, button type, This Side Will Sharpen 48.00
Level, wood & brass, 14", VG 100.00

Level, 2 bubble vials, #W3, 28", VG+ 40.00
Loading tool, 32WCF caliber, pliers shape 100.00
Lure, multi-wobbler #9203, gold foil finish, 2 treble hooks, VG .. 335.00
Lure, 5-hook underwater minnow w/blended red finish, NM in G box .. 1,175.00
Meat cleaver, wooden hdl, #7814 .... 65.00
Meat fork, riveted wood hdl, 13" 45.00
Meat grinder, 3- blade, #W31, from $75 to 85.00
Padlock, cast steel, slide-swing shackle, 2", NMIB 550.00
Paint brush, 4", G- 275.00
Pin-bk button, Wonderful Topperweins, couple portrait, NM 150.00
Pipe wrench, wood hdl, #1022, 10" 80.00
Plane, #3015, 18" 70.00
Plane, router; #3070, ½" cutter 130.00
Pliers, #2489-10, 10" 50.00
Pliers, rnd nose; #2182, from $75 to 110.00
Pocketknife purse, G, from $250 to 275.00
Poster, Repeating Shotguns, man & 2 bird dogs, 30x16½", NM ... 1,850.00
Putty knife, 3½" 95.00
Reel, casting; #2744 .... 90.00
Reel, casting; tubular fr w/screw-off ends, #4250, 80-yd, VG+ 180.00
Reloading tool, #38-55, Pat Feb 13 1894 .... 180.00
Rod cleaning set, 4-pc, for Winchester Henry 1866-1892-1873 .. 180.00
Roller skates, #30, MIB 11.00
Saw, hand; #16, wooden riveted hdl 75.00
Scale, country store type, weighs up to 24 lbs 135.00
Screwdriver, offset; #2815, 6", VG 80.00
Shears, barber's; G 95.00
Sign, bullet graphics, Super Speed 22s, cb die-cut, 1935, 26½x20" .. 1,950.00

Sign, game and trophies with guns, ca. 1914, 36x30", EX, $1,210.00. (Photo courtesy Jackson's International Auctioneers & Appraisers of Fine Art & Antiques)

Sign, Winchester tires, tin litho, red/wht/bl, 18x55", VG 900.00
Sign, Winchester Western, man on horse, 2-sided tin litho, 38" dia, VG .. 950.00
Spatula, #7646, G, from $25 to 45.00
Spoke shave, EX, from $145 to 165.00
Straight razor, #5832 on tang, MIB 300.00
Tennis racket, #W3, G-, from $600 to 650.00
Thermometer, Sporting Ammunition Sold Here, shotshell shape, 26", EXIB .. 120.00
Tin container, After Shave Talc, hunter & dog, red lid, 4¾x3" ... 335.00
Whistle, referee's; NP brass, #1805, 1920s, scarce 400.00

Windmill Weights

Windmill weights made of cast iron were used to protect the windmill's plunger rod from damage during high winds by adding weight that slowed down the speed of the blades. Since they were constantly exposed to the elements, any painted surfaces would be seriously compromised. Our values are for 'as found' examples, as described.

Bull, Fairbury, old rpt, 24½" 1,500.00

Bull, Fairbury, orig brn/wht pnt, ca 1910-20, 18x26" 1,950.00
Bull, Simpson, striding, bell at neck, blk/wht pnt, 14" L 2,100.00
Bull, unmk, CI silhouette, worn blk/wht pnt, 18x25" 1,450.00
Horse, bobtail; Dempster, old blk/wht pnt, 17x17" 550.00
Horse, long tail; Dempster, integral base, brn pnt traces, 19x17"...2,100.00
Horse, long tail; Dempster, 50% wht pnt remains, 18¾x19½" 865.00
Horse, long tail; unmk, 3-D, 15x17" 550.00
Rooster, att Elgin, 20% red/wht pnt remains, 19x18x3½" 2,215.00
Rooster, Elgin, emb #s: 10 ft No 2, old 2-color pnt, 16x16½"+base....1,525.00
Rooster, Elgin Hummer, flat base, incised eye detail, pitted, 12x17" ..1,550.00
Rooster, Elgin Hummer #184, short stem, ball base, no pnt, 20" ...1,300.00
Rooster, Elgin Hummer #184, short stem, worn silver/red pnt, 9"+base...960.00
Rooster, rainbow tail; Elgin, worn 3-color rpt, 18"+wood base .1,500.00
W, Althouse-Wheeler, modern metal base, 9¼x17" 575.00

Wire Ware

Very primitive wire was first made by cutting sheet metal into strips which were shaped with mallet and file. By the late thirteenth century craftsmen in Europe had developed a method of pulling these strips through progressively smaller holes until the desired gauge was obtained. During the Industrial Revolution of the late 1800s, machinery was developed that could produce wire cheaply and easily; and it became a popular commercial commodity. It was used to produce large items such as garden benches and fencing as well as innumerable small pieces for use in the kitchen or on the farm. Beware of reproductions.

Basket, loose weave, crusty old surface, wall mt, 5½x8x8" 48.00
Carrier, 12 compartment w/decorative zigs & zags, arched hdl, 9x14x11" ...155.00
Cradle on stand, brass castors, 1900s, 20x40"+60" H stand.......... 550.00
Egg basket, bulbous, ftd, bail hdl, 10x7" 75.00
Plant stand, 2-tier, arched top, ca 1880, 75x32x18" 275.00
Plant stand, 3-tier, heart designs, 44x39" at base 425.00
Planter, 3-tier, loops & scrolls, Victorian style, 59x24" dia........... 300.00
Rack, looping pattern, 8 hooks, 5x22¾" 48.00
Utensil rack, scrolled top, 6-hook, 21" L... 90.00
Vegetable washer, bulbous, 2-pc, 2 D-form hdls, 4x7x10" 10.00

Wisecarver, Rick

Rick Wisecarver is a contemporary artist from Ohio who is well known not only for his renderings of Indian portraits, animals, cookie jars, and scenics on pottery that is reminiscent of that made by earlier Ohio companies, but for limited edition lithographs as well.

Humidor, buffalo figural, brn w/gr base, 6⅞x8½" 65.00
Jug, Am Indian portrait cvd/incised on free-form, 1981, 9½" 425.00
Jug, cat portrait, Shezane Critters #1130, 1983, 6⅝" 100.00
Jug, whiskey; frontiersman on brn, 1982, 6½x4½" 85.00
Vase, Am Indian brave portrait, collared rim, 1980, 14½" 515.00
Vase, Am Indian chief form, 1986, 7x7½" 240.00
Vase, Am Indian chief on lt purple ground, baluster, 16¾x7½" ... 480.00
Vase, Am Indian elder, Red Cloud, rim-to-hip hdls, slim, 1983, 16¼" ...350.00
Vase, Am Indian Geronimo portrait, 1984, 7⅞x4½" 315.00
Vase, Am Indian lady (Thigh's Wichita), 1984, 13⅛x6¼" 480.00
Vase, Am Indian on horsebk w/crescent moon, 1979, 16¾"......... 600.00
Vase, Am Indian Pontiac portrait, RS 9/15/84 Wihoas..., 12⅜x7¼" ..550.00
Vase, Am Indian warrior, Special, 1982, 14" 325.00
Vase, Am Indian warrior, 1984, 9½x3⅞" 275.00
Vase, Am Indian warrior & horse on lime gr pillow form, 1981, 7⅜" . 240.00
Vase, autumn scene w/canoe & lake on pillow form, 1986, 6⅞x7½" .. 135.00
Vase, buffalo scene on pillow form, 1986, 7x7¼" 235.00
Vase, cat portrait, pastels, 1984, 11⅜x4¼" 300.00
Vase, ear of corn on brn, 1983, 11½" 250.00
Vase, Roseville Harvest scenic, 1986, 8⅛" 425.00
Vase, trees on textured ground, tapered form, 1983, 11x3½"........ 325.00
Watering can, Am Indian chief, 1975, 9x13½" 300.00

Wood, Beatrice

Born in San Francisco in 1893, the young Beatrice was educated in painting and theater in Paris. She worked as an actress in New York through the teens, where she befriended expatriate artists from the Dadist movement and furthered her explorations in fine arts. It was to follow the Theosophist Krishnamurti that Beatrice visited and then moved to California. She studied pottery with several California teachers, including Glen Lukens, Otto and Gertrud Natzler, and Vivika and Otto Heino.

Beatrice Wood taught ceramics and operated a studio in Ojai, becoming well known for her personal interpretation of ancient forms and glazes. Besides throwing vases and plates, she built figural sculptures full of humor and eroticism. Her pieces, signed 'Beato,' are in collections and museums all over the world. She passed away in Ojai in 1998 at the ago of 105.

Bowl, centerpc; bl & wht volcanic crackle, 3x24x14" 6,000.00
Bowl, centerpc; hen form, appl floral, pastel faience, Beato, 12x17" ..3,500.00
Chalice, mc lustre, simple form, prof rstr, 5¼x4¼" 1,450.00
Challice, gold lustre on earthenware, Beato, 8x5" 8,400.00
Figure, mermaid, raspberry & gr lustre, on quartz crystal base, 7" ..5,500.00
Figure, slab style, gray clay w/thin wash, Beato, 8" 1,100.00
Mug, floral on pk, loop hdl, Beato, 5¼"......................................1,200.00
Pencil/watercolor on paper, Superior Masculine Mind, 1925, 10x14"+fr .. 1,950.00
Urn, volcanic brn & burgundy, sm hdls, Beato, 9x8" 3,350.00
Vase, mc metallic finish, gourd shape, rpr, 9x4" 900.00
Vase, thin gr over dk red, near-spherical, Beato, 3" 1,100.00
Vase, volcanic gold & verdigris, cylinder neck, hdls, 7¾x5" 5,300.00

Wood Carvings

Wood sculptures represent an important section of American folk art. Wood carvings were made not only by skilled woodworkers such as cabinetmakers, carpenters, etc., but by amateur 'whittlers' as well. They take the form of circus-wagon figures, carousel animals, decoys, busts, figurines, and cigar store Indians. Oriental artists show themselves to have been as proficient with the medium of wood as they were with ivory or hardstone. See also Carousel Animals; Decoys; Tobacciana.

Owl, walnut with glass eyes, head is hinged to reveal an inner chamber, match receptacle extends from base, Black Forest, ca. 1900, 19", $8,050.00.

(Photo courtesy Jackson's International Auctioneers & Appraisers of Fine Art & Antiques)

Abe Lincoln w/law book & cane, mc pnt, late 19th C, 22" **4,000.00**

Birds (6) in tree, HP w/bead eyes & wire ft, realistic, 23" **1,725.00**

Dog (hunting) & fence, mc pnt, wooden base, ca 1900, 5½x6x1¾" ..**200.00**

Dog seated, blk/wht w/gold collar, May Lancaster/Seattle, 20th C, 8" ..**470.00**

Dove, box, hollowed-out hardwood, realistic pnt, 5x9½" **435.00**

Eagle, fully cvd head & spread wings, mustard/brn pnt, 19th C, 7x50"...**5,875.00**

Eagle w/banner & shield, red/wht/bl pnt w/gold, 27" W, +provenance...**5,175.00**

Eagle w/spread wings/olive branch/flag shield, gesso/pnt, 22x50" .. **88,125.00**

Egret, cvd/pnt, glass eyes/wire legs, on pnt wood base, ca 1900, 22"...**1,750.00**

Goldfinch, scratch-feather cvg, rock base, J Blackstone, 1940s, 2⅝"...**1,400.00**

Great Horned Owl, realistic pnt, glass eyes, F Finney, 26" **3,100.00**

Guinea hens (3) on stump, chip-cvd feathers, brn stain, 14" **545.00**

Heron, gr pnt, glass eyes, wire legs, late 19th C, 7x10" **350.00**

Horse, orig brn pnt, appl fur mane/tail, 6¾" **750.00**

Lady's head, birch, used by milliner, splits, 12½" **465.00**

Madonna seated/holds book, walnut, dk patina, Germany, 22"....**975.00**

Moose on base, brn & blk pnt, tack eyes, rpr, mid-20th C, 9"......**120.00**

Owl on stump, plaster legs/wire ft, orig pnt, 7½" **700.00**

Penguin, appl flippers/tack eyes, old mc pnt, att C Hart, 1936, 5".. **1,900.00**

Puffin, realistic pnt, mtd on driftwood, D Brown, ME, 3½" **175.00**

Rattlesnake, realistic decor, att O Spencer, 31" L **315.00**

Robin, realistic pnt, wire legs, wooden ft, on base, 5x7¾" **265.00**

Robin by fence, realistic pnt, glass eyes, rustic fence, 7x12x4".....**355.00**

Rooster, cvd from 1 block, mc pnt, att Schimmel, PA, 1850s, 7x5"...**1,000.00**

Rooster, glass eyes/antler spurs, E Reed, 15½"+stand.................**1,495.00**

Rooster w/fan tail, simple details, orig pnt, lt wear, 5" **285.00**

Spaniel w/docked tail & feathered front legs, orig pnt, 5½" L......**350.00**

Statue of Liberty bust, nut brn stain, E Reed, age split, 11".......**1,495.00**

Swan, wht pnt, label: Herter's Inc 1893, 14½x28½" **375.00**

Tugboat model, mc pnt, metal furnishings, on stand, 6x4½x2¼" .. **350.00**

Woodenware

    Woodenware (or treenware, as it is sometimes called) generally refers to those wooden items such as spoons, bowls, food molds, etc., that were used in the preparation of food. Common during the eighteenth and nineteenth centuries, these wares were designed from a strictly functional viewpoint and were used on a day-to-day basis. With the advent of the Industrial Revolution which brought with it new materials and products, much of the old woodenware was simply discarded. Today original handcrafted American woodenwares are extremely difficult to find. See also Primitives.

Bowl, ash burl, cvd collar on exterior rim, 19th C, 6x19½" **3,525.00**

Bowl, ash burl, good color & form, flared sides, splits, 3½x8".......**435.00**

Bowl, ash burl, scrubbed, wide trn outside rim, 5x13" **2,075.00**

Bowl, ash burl, steep sides, flat base, primitive, 7x16" **350.00**

Bowl, ash burl, trn w/raised collar, 19th C, 6x14"......................**4,000.00**

Bowl, ash burl, 2 integral cvd hdls, early 1800s 4¾x13½" **4,000.00**

Bowl, ash burl w/coarse grain, EX patina, 7½x17x15" **700.00**

Bowl, ash burl w/good color, damage, 2¼x6½".............................**115.00**

Bowl, ash burl w/good figure & color, red traces, putty, 3x14"......**550.00**

Bowl, ash burl w/loose figure, almond shape, wood patch, 6x16x13".. **1,265.00**

Bowl, ash burl w/tight figure, mellow patina, 1¾x4½" **1,550.00**

Bowl, ash burl w/tight figure, scrubbed, 5x11½x10"...................**2,300.00**

Bowl, bl pnt, well trn, no splits, 21" **1,100.00**

Bowl, curly maple, old rich finish, glued rpr at rim, OH, 17" **435.00**

Bowl, dk brn varnish, w/lid, 8x12½" **1,375.00**

Bowl, dough; oblong, dk bl pnt, 4x20x11¾" **1,000.00**

Bowl, medial incised line, early 1800s, 3⅝x5¾"...........................**850.00**

Bowl, natural form w/EX patina, worn red stain, sgn MP/1872, 4x13x10"...**800.00**

Bowl, soft wood w/old bl-gr pnt, hewn mks, hdls, 5x19x13½"......**400.00**

Bowl, tiger maple, yel-gr pnt, raised collar, 7¼x22" **2,500.00**

Bowl, 3 bands of incised lines, red pnt, rprs, 19th C, 3½x10¼"....**300.00**

Butter paddle, cvd horse-head finial, scrubbed, 9¼" **175.00**

Canister, trn, pnt stylized flowers/etc, on pk, Lehnware, 5½" **2,000.00**

Canteen, bentwood, early nails, orig bl pnt, wooden stopper, 6½" ...**975.00**

Container, red over mustard vinegar pnt, trn finial, 7x7" dia.......**800.00**

Container, trn, wire & wooden bail hdl, Peaseware, 8x9" **575.00**

Container, trn, wood & wire bail hdl, varnish, Peaseware, 3⅝x3½".**230.00**

Covered jars, yellow and ochre putty decorations, ca. 1820 – 1830, cracks and repairs, from 4" to 8½", from $400.00 to $750.00. (Photo courtesy Skinner Inc. Auctioneers & Appraisers of Antiques & Fine Art)

Cup, saffron; strawberries on salmon, Lehnware, 4¼".................**1,800.00**

Inkwell, trn wood w/pottery inset, mellow finish, 3x5" dia...........**400.00**

Jar, squat w/urn finial, Peaseware, sm splits/rpr, 8x7" **375.00**

Jar, yel & ocher plume/earthworm/spots, rprs/cracks, 19th C, 6⅝"...**600.00**

Trencher, walnut, orig bl pnt, age splits, 5¾x25x12" **700.00**

Woodworking Machinery

    Vintage cast-iron woodworking machines are monuments to the highly skilled engineers, foundrymen, and machinists who devised them, thus making possible the mass production of items ranging from clothespins, boxes, and barrels to decorative moldings and furniture. Though attractive from a nostalgic viewpoint, many of these machines are bought by the hobbyist and professional alike, to be put into actual use — at far less cost than new equipment. Many worth-assessing factors must be considered; but as a general rule, a machine in good condition is worth about 65¢ a pound (excluding motors). A machine needing a lot of restoration is not worth more than 35¢ a pound, while one professionally rebuilt and with a warranty can be calculated at $1.10 a pound. Modern, new machinery averages over $3.00 a pound. Two of the best sources of information on purchasing or selling such machines are *Vintage Machines — Searching for the Cast Iron Classics*, by Tom Howell, and *Used Machines and Abused Buyers* by Chuck Seidel from *Fine Woodworking*, November/December 1984. Prices quoted are for machines in good condition, less motors and accessories. Our advisor for this category is Mr. Dana Martin Batory, author of *Vintage Woodworking Machinery, An Illustrated Guide to Four Manufacturers, Volumes I and II*, and *An Illustrated Guide to Four More Manufacturers*. See his listing in the Directory under Ohio for further information. No phone calls, please.

American Wood Working Machinery Company, 1920

Jointer, #1, 16" **1,200.00**

Sander, #2, Columbia, 61" **6,825.00**

Table saw, #0, 12"...**450.00**

Boice-Crane Power Tools, 1937

Band saw, #800, 14" **100.00**

Drill press, #1600, 15" 75.00
Lathe, #1100, gap bed 50.00
Scroll saw, #900, 24" 75.00

Buss Machine Works, ca 1950

Planer, #44, 30" 4,225.00
Planer, #55, dbl surface, 30" 6,175.00
Planer, #88, dbl surface, 30" 7,800.00

Delta Manufacturing Company, 1939

Band saw, #768, 10" 50.00
Disk sander, #1426, belt drive, 12" 35.00
Drill press, #1370-H, high speed, floor, 17" 200.00
Drill press, #645, bench, 11" 30.00
Jointer, #390, ball-bearing, 4" 35.00
Lathe, #930, timken-bearing, 11" 45.00
Lathe, #955, timken-bearing, 9" 35.00
Shaper, #1180, ball-bearing, reversible 30.00
Unisaw, #1450, tilting arbor, 10" 200.00

Duro Metal Products Co., 1935

Band saw, #3020, 12" 55.00
Jigsaw, #3000, 12" 10.00
Scroll saw, #3005, 24" 55.00

F.H. Clement Co., 1896

Band saw, 30" 555.00
Band saw, 36", Patent Improved 815.00
Band saw, 38", Improved 1,040.00
Mortising & boring machine, #1 .... 520.00
Planer, #3, dbl-belted, Improved, 20" 2,015.00
Ripsaw, #2, iron fr, 16" 585.00
Sander, #1, spindle & drum 520.00
Sanding machine, surface; Improved 650.00
Shaper, #3, variety, dbl spindle, heavy 1,300.00
Table saw, #1, variety, 15" 585.00

Gallmeyer & Livingston Company, 1927

Band saw, Union, 20" 390.00
Jointer, Union, motor on arbor, 8" 370.00
Table saw, Union #7, 7" 210.00

G.N. Goodspeed Company, 1876

Boring machine, upright 225.00
Planer, New & Improved, Pony, 24" 900.00
Table saw, 12" 200.00

Hoyt & Brother Company, 1888

Planer, matcher & surfacer, New Combined, #2, 24" 5,200.00
Sand-papering machine, The Boss, #5, 24" 1,600.00
Shingle machine, Grand Mogul, 2-block, automatic feed 2,210.00
Wood shaper, dbl spindle 850.00

J.A. Fay & Egan Company, 1900

Jointer, New #2, 24" 1,700.00
Jointer, New #4, extra heavy, 16" 1,625.00

Molder, #2, 4-sided, 6" 1,500.00
Mortiser, #2, hollow chisel, automatic horizontal 1,500.00
Ripsaw, #2, Improved Standard 1,175.00
Saw, rip; #2, self feed, lg 1,775.00

J.D. Wallace Company, 1940s

Band saw, 16" 210.00
Grinder & sander, disk, Wonder, 16" 165.00
Jointer, 4" 15.00

L. Power & Co., 1888

Mortiser & borer, #2 .... 780.00
Shaper, single spindle, reversible 585.00
Table saw, self-feed, 14" 715.00

Levi Houston Co., 1897

Moulder, new 4", 4-sided 650.00
Saw, new #1, Improved variety, 14" 650.00
Sticker, special, door 520.00
Tenoning machine, new style, #3 .... 585.00

Northfield Foundry & Machine Co., 1950

Band saw, bench; 14" 125.00
Band saw, 32" 1,100.00
Jointer, heavy duty, 16" 1,050.00
Table saw, No 2, 16" 450.00
Table saw, No 3, 16" 525.00

Ober Manufacturing Company, 1889

Ripsaw, self-feed, 14" 725.00
Saw, swing cut-off, 18" 275.00
Shaper, saw & jointer combination 400.00

Parks Ball Bearing Machine Company, 1925

Jointer, H-133, Ideal, 12" 400.00
Sanding machine, H-165, Economy, 24" 230.00
Saw, H-97, swing cut-off, Alert, 12" 225.00

P.B. Yates Machine Company, 1917

Planer, #160, dbl surface, 20" 5,225.00
Saw, #232, swing-cut-off, 16" 260.00

Powermatic, Inc., 1965

Band saw, #81, 20" 500.00
Jointer, #60, 8" 170.00
Lathe, #45, 12" 230.00
Lathe, #90, 12" 360.00
Sander, #300-01, 12" disk & 6" belt combination 95.00
Shaper, #26, single spindle 240.00
Tenoner, #2-A, single end 620.00

Richardson, Meriam & Co., 1865

Band saw, Granite State, 36" 400.00
Mortising & boring machine, lg No 1 .... 1,300.00
Planing & matching machine, #5, single cutter head 4,225.00

Scroll saw, Empire, lg... 400.00
Scroll saw, Patent, common sz.. 330.00

S.A. Woods Machine Company, 1876

Planer, panel; Improved, 20" 520.00
Planer, suface, Pat Improved, 30" 1,430.00
Re-sawing machine, circular, Joslin's Improved, 50" ...2,275.00

The Sidney Machine Tool Co., 1916 (Famous Woodworking Machinery)

Band saw, No 1, 36", new 1,100.00
Jointer, Cyclone, 12".. 525.00
Jointer, Cyclone, 16".. 585.00
Lathe, pattern maker's, 14" 275.00
Mortiser, hollow chisel.. 650.00
Planer, 18" 880.00
Saw, combination; No 5, 16" 525.00
Saw, Variety, No 08, 20" 650.00
Shaper, single spindle.. 650.00
Woodworker, Universal, No 30 or No 31 (5 machines in 1).....2,015.00

Valley City Machine Works, ca 1910

Boring machine, vertical 650.00
Dowel machine, No 2 .... 520.00
Rounding, routing & rosette machine, No 2 .... 910.00
Spiral-twist machine.. 875.00

Williamsport Machine Company, 1897

Band re-saw, New No 4, 40" 2,275.00
Band saw, No 2, 26" 620.00
Mortiser, No 2 Latest Improved.................................... 910.00
Saw & dado machine, No 1 Combined.......................... 585.00
Shaper, single spindle.. 550.00

Worcester Porcelain Company

The Worcester Porcelain Company was deeded in 1751. During the first or Dr. Wall period (so called for one of its proprietors), porcelain with an Oriental influence was decorated in underglaze blue. Useful tablewares represented the largest portion of production, but figurines and decorative items were also made. Very little of the earliest wares were marked and can only be identified by a study of forms, glazes, and the porcelain body, which tends to transmit a greenish cast when held to light. Late in the fifties, a crescent mark was in general use, and rare examples bear a facsimile of the Meissen crossed swords. The first period ended in 1783, and the company went through several changes in ownership during the next 80 years. The years from 1783 – 1792 are referred to as the Flight period. Marks were a small crescent, a crown with 'Royal,' or an impressed 'Flight.' From 1792 to 1807 the company was known as Flight and Barr and used the trademark 'F&B' or 'B,' with or without a small cross. From 1807 to 1813 the company was under the Barr, Flight, and Barr management; this era is recognized as having produced porcelain with the highest quality of artistic decoration. Their mark was 'B.F.B.' From 1813 to 1840 many marks were used, but the most usual was 'F.B.B.' under a crown to indicate Flight, Barr, and Barr. In 1840 the firm merged with Chamberlain, and in 1852 they were succeeded by Kerr and Binns. The firm became known as Royal Worcester in 1862. The production was then marked with a circle with '51' within and a crown on top. The date of manufacture was incised into the bottom or stamped with a letter of the alphabet, just under the circle. In 1891 Royal Worcester England was added to the circle and crown. From that point on, each piece is dated with a code of dots or other symbols. After 1891 most wares had a blush-color ground. Prior to that date it was ivory. Most shapes were marked with a unique number.

During the early years they produced considerable ornamental wares with a Persian influence. This gave way to a Japanesque influence. James Hadley is most responsible for the Victorian look. He is considered the 'best ever' designer and modeller. He was joined by the finest porcelain painters. Together they produced pieces with very fine detail and exquisite painting and decoration. Figures, vases, and tableware were produced in great volume and are highly collectible. During the 1890s they allowed the artists to sign some of their work. Pieces signed on the face by the Stintons, Baldwyn, Davis, Raby, Powell, Sedgley, and Rushton (not a complete list) are in great demand. The company is still in production. There is an outstanding museum on the company grounds in Worcester, England.

Note: Most pieces had lids or tops (if there is a flat area on the top lip, chances are it had one), if missing deduct 30% to 40%.

Candelabra, Greenaway boy & girl, 3-light tree trunk, 1888, 19", pr ... 2,400.00
Creamer, rtcl lattice/floral band, bamboo hdl, G Owen, 19th C, 4¼" . 3,250.00
Dessert set, horse/Festina Lente banner, 1783-1840, 14-pc set..3,500.00
Ewer, birds, wht on bl w/gold, ftd, Baldwin, 1906, 7" 7,750.00
Figurine, Baltimore Oriole (male/female), Doughty, 11", 11½", pr..2,750.00
Figurine, bluebirds & apple blossoms, Doughty, 10", 9", NM, pr ..2,400.00
Figurine, gnatcatchers & dogwood, Doughty, 11¾", 10¼", pr ..2,500.00
Figurine, In the Ring, circus rider, Linder, #3180, 1936, 14½" ..2,150.00
Figurine, Indigo Bunting cock, Doughty, 8¾" 3,800.00
Figurine, Magnolia Warblers/flowers, Doughty, 15½", pr...........6,000.00
Figurine, Parula Warblers, Doughty, 9", 9½", pr........................2,650.00
Figurine, Ruby-Throated Hummingbird & fuchsia, Doughty, 10", pr . 2,350.00
Figurine, Skye terrier, gray/brn, jeweled eyes, 1874, 15x19" 6,600.00
Group, classical lady w/jug & basin, eagle at base, 1870s, 29" ...6,000.00
Jar, potpourri; floral w/gold, #1515, 1891, 10¾" 440.00
Plate, Blarney Castle Near Cork, cobalt & gold rim, ca 1820, 9" ..2,150.00
Potpourri vase, fruit on woodland bank, Aryton, w/lid, pre-1956, 14".. 3,150.00
Sconce, ¾-figure of lady holding vase w/3 flower-form shades, 1895..3,600.00
Spill vase, cattle in mtn landscape, Stanton, gr/gold neck, 1910, 9" ..3,000.00
Sugar bowl, rtcl lattice w/gold, G Owen, w/lid, 19th C, 4⅝".....3,150.00
Sweetmeat dish, Bengal Tiger, 4 compartments remove, 1810s, 9½x8"..3,250.00
Teakettle, Oriental floral panels on turq, majolica, prof rpr lid, 9".. 3,150.00
Teapot, Oriental floral on turq, sq w/dragon hdl, sm chip 6,000.00
Teapot, rtcl lattice design, bambo spout/hdl, G Owens, 19th C, 5x7".. 3,600.00
Urn, bouquets, grapevine hdls, artichoke finial, 1816-40, 12x14", EX . 5,000.00
Vase, castle ruins scene, uptrn hdls, emb masks/swags/etc, 1891, 18".... 3,000.00
Vase, fruit on woodland ground, Freeman, w/lid, #1691, 1950s, 14" ..2,750.00
Vase, lighthouse scenic, dolphin hdls, slim neck, 1890, 18" 2,900.00
Vase, pheasant scene, gold hdls, Stinton, 16", NM....................2,750.00
Vase, sheep scene, H Davis, cylindrical, 1935, 7½" 4,750.00

Vase, pierced honeycomb body with gilt, mask handles, #1552, 9", $31,000.00. (Photo courtesy Skinner Inc. Auctioneers & Appraisers of Antiques & Fine Art)

World's Fairs and Expos

Since 1851 and the Crystal Palace Exhibition in London, world's fairs and expositions have taken place at a steady pace. Many of them commemorate historical events. The 1904 Louisiana Purchase Exposition, commonly known as the St. Louis World's Fair, celebrated the 100th anniversary of the Louisiana Purchase agreement between Thomas Jefferson and Napoleon in 1803. The 1893 Columbian Exposition commemorated the 400th anniversary of the discovery of America by Columbus in 1492. (Both of these fairs were held one year later than originally scheduled.) The multitude of souvenirs from these and similar events have become a growing area of interest to collectors in recent years. Many items have a 'crossover' interest into other fields: i.e., collectors of postcards and souvenir spoons eagerly search for those from various fairs and expositions. Values have fallen somewhat due to eBay sales. Many of the so called common items have come down in value. However 1939 World's Fair items are still hot. For additional information collectors may contact World's Fairs Collectors Society (WFCS), whose address is in the Directory under Clubs, Newsletters, and Catalogs, or our advisor, Herbert Rolfes. His address is listed in the Directory under Florida.

Key:
T&P — Trylon & Perisphere   WF — World's Fair

1876 Centennial, Philadelphia

Book, History of the Centennial Exhibition, JD McCabe, 1876, 874 pgs . 260.00
Bowl, folding; wood, 8 'leaves' w/photos on ftd base, open: 8" dia, EX...55.00
Plate, printing; steel, used to eng Centennial..., #502...New York, 4" . 3,000.00
Platter, glass, Liberty Bell etched in center, scalloped rim, 13" L ... 50.00
Purse, coin; leather w/metal fr, Independence Hall-1776, 2½"....... 35.00
Trade card, Brownell & Ashley & Carriage Mfg/Memorial Hall, 3x5" ..10.00

1893 Columbian, Chicago

Book, History of the World's...Inception, HW Kelley, 1893, 610 pgs, VG ...75.00
Book, World's Fair Photographed, J Shepp & D Shepp, 1893, 528 pgs..50.00
Book, World's Fair Through a Camera, F Todd, 2nd ed, 78 pgs, 5x7", VG...35.00

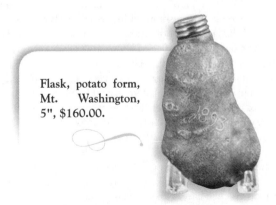

Flask, potato form, Mt. Washington, 5", $160.00.

Medal, brass, Missouri on top bar, Souvenir World's...1893, 1½" ... 26.00
Photo, Ferris Wheel, facts printed on bk, 6½x4¼"........................... 50.00
Plaque, bsk, Liberal Arts Building transfer on moon, w/angel, 5"....100.00
Plate, Administration Building transfer, wht w/bl trim, 7" sq......... 25.00
Postcard, Offical Souvenir Postal, World's Columbian Expo, NM 18.00
Song booklet, Ferris Wheel March, Chas M Stieff, 12 songs.......... 43.00
Spoon, sterling, Manufacturing Pavillion emb in bowl, Leonard Mfg, 6". 11.00
Spoon, sterling, World's Fair Souvenir/Algeria emb in bowl, 4" 10.00
Ticket, admission; Abe Lincoln portrait, American Bank Note Co, M.. 44.00
Ticket, grounds admission, stamped sgn WT Baker, unused, EX.... 45.00

Trivet, ceramic, 1893 World's Fair, Art Building, wht w/gold, 7" 8.00
Watch fob, brass Columbus medallion w/eagle on bk, 3 emb panels.. 36.00

1904 St. Louis

Booklet, 1904 St Louis World's Fair Ceylon Hand Book, 183 pgs, 9x6". 85.00
Box, jewelry; Cascade Gardens 1904 St Louis, w/mirror, gold trim & ft. 90.00
Cup, 1904 Louisiana Purchase Expostion Cup, mc, 3x2¼", VG 20.00
Magazine, The Criterion, St Louis Exposition Number, Oct 1903, VG.......25.00
Paperweight, glass, Festival Hall on front, souvenir write-up on bk .57.00
Plate, General Grant's Log Cabin..., CF Blanke, wht, 9", VG........ 25.00
Playing cards, mc eagle design on bk, 52+joker, EXIB.................. 50.00
Postcard, Manufacturer's Building, Frisco System.......................... 28.00
Shakers, milk glass, Electricity & Government Building transfers, pr.. 25.00
Spoon, sterling, Palace of Transportation emb in bowl, detailed, 5".....55.00
Token, brass, Missouri, Empire State of Louisiana Purchase........... 48.00

1933 Chicago

Bank, cvd wood, barrel, Century of Progress Chicago 1933 .... 25.00
Bracelet, cuff; brass, imp images/A Century in Progress/1933 .... 52.00
Cane, walking; oak, Century News & building images on brass tag, 34" L...45.00
Flag, 48-star, ...Chicago World's Fair & images on box, Marshall Field..57.00

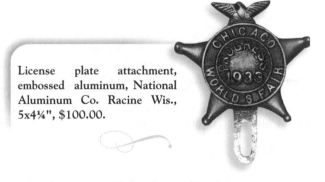

License plate attachment, embossed aluminum, National Aluminum Co. Racine Wis., 5x4¼", $100.00.

Lighter, emb metal label on gr Bakelite, Match King, 1¾x1"......... 28.00
Medal, Research & Industry, bronze w/male in relief, 3", MIB +brochure. 75.00
Mug, Travel Building Century of Progress..., red on wht, 4½"........ 40.00
Paperweight, glass, Sky Ride Chicago World's Fair, 2½x3¾".......... 38.00
Stein, brn, World's...in Progress, nude forms hdl, brn, Haeger, 6½"...35.00
Stereoscope & photographs, Chicago..., Keystone Third Dimension, MIB..50.00
Talking letter, record w/personal message, RCA Victor, in sleeve.. 35.00
Token, brass, Good Luck/World's Fair on front, 1933...Chicago on bk..15.00
Toy, Greyhound Bus, Century of... on top, pnt metal, Arcade, 10" L, VG...58.00

1939 New York

Badge, NY World's Fair Police, enamel center in metal shield shape, 3".. 300.00
Bingo game, The NY World's Fair, Whitman Co, MIB.................. 33.00
Book, comic; NY World's Fair Comics, V Sullivan, DC Comics.. 280.00
Book, Official Guide; orange & bl cover, hardbk, 200 pgs, 7x10" .. 25.00
Book, Official Guide; 3rd ed, w/fold-out map, paperbk.................. 25.00
Brochure, General Electric Television Exhibit, 6x4½" 10.00
Card, identification; Radio, red letters on pk paper, unused........... 50.00
Compact, 1939 NY World's Fair on Lucite lid w/mirror, gold-tone, sq ..65.00
Lighter, glass, T&P shape, emb 1939 World Fair 100.00
Paperweight, metal, elephant figural, trunk up, symbols on side 60.00
Pennant, NY World's Fair 1939, wht letters on purple, gold symbol, 11"... 30.00
Pin, USSR The NY World's Fair, red enamel on gold-tone, 1½x1" .. 45.00
Pin-bk, Lithuanian Day Sept 10th, bl on orange, w/ribbon, 1" dia....... 60.00
Plate, NY World's..., Cronin China, mc on wht, geometric red rim, 10".. 40.00
Plate, NY World's Fair 1930, bright bl images on wht, Adams, 10½"...40.00

Poster, NY World's Fair, World of Tomorrow, 1939, 10½x7", M .. 500.00

Sculpture, Trylon and Perisphere, amber Bakelite, 17x13x6", $800.00. (Photo courtesy David Rago Auctions)

Shakers, metal, T&P on emb tray, WM Rogers Mfg, 3½"...............................38.00
Ticket, preview; admission to Administration Building, May 8, 1938 .48.00
Toy, CI, greyhound bus, Visit the World's Fair..., bl & wht, 9" L.. 400.00

1939 San Francisco

Coasters, plastic, Firestone, red/bl/yel/gr, set of 4, 3", MIB............. 32.00
Map, Official Pictorial; Tony Sarg, mc, closed: 11¼" sq.................. 35.00

1962 Seattle

Bolo tie, leather & copper, emb Seattle... & Space Needle image, 18" L... 25.00
Pen, Space Needle; stands in wood holder, 12", MIB 30.00
Pin-bk, Seattle's World Fair 1962 w/Space Needle, mc enamel on metal......32.00
Pin-bk, Seattle World's...Coliseum 21, mc enamel on metal, Germany 40.00
Plate, Seattle... on wht center, wide pk rim, Frederick & Nelson, 11" ...26.00
Tumblers, Mobil Dealers Century, mc print, set of 8, MIB............. 90.00

1964 New York

Camera, Kodak World's Fair Flash; built-in flash w/AG-1 bulb, w/strap... 44.00
Figurine, ceramic, Pieta, Vatican Pavilion Pieta NY...on base, 6" 35.00
License plate, logo in center, orange/wht/bl.................................. 60.00
License plate, yel on blk, 6x12", NM 86.00
Matchbook, World's Fair Marina, HMS Bounty, mc, unused, 12¾" L...35.00
Plaque, brass, Statue of Liberty & Empire State Building, 7" dia ... 40.00
Poster, New York World's Fair 1964-65, mc, 42x28"...................... 100.00
Trading cards, Official Souvenir...Attractions, set of 24, MIB........ 15.00

Wright, Frank Lloyd

Born in Richland Center, Wisconsin, in 1869, Wright became a pioneer in architectural expression, developing a style referred to as 'prairie.' From early in the century until he died in 1959, he designed houses with rooms that were open, rather than divided by walls in the traditional manner. They exhibited low, horizontal lines and strongly projecting eaves, and he filled them with furnishings whose radical aesthetics complemented the structures. Several of his homes have been preserved to the present day, and collectors who admire his ideas and the unique, striking look he achieved treasure the stained glass windows, furniture, chinaware, lamps, and other decorative accessories designed by Wright. His Taliesin line of furniture was made for a few years in the late 1950s; it was produced by Heritage Henredon, and most pieces were edged with a Green Key design. Our advisor for this category and related Arts and Crafts subjects is Bruce Austin; he is listed in the Directory under New York.

Key: H — Heritage Henredon/Taliesin

Armchair, executive; leather seat & bk, aluminum fr, 36½"....12,000.00
Armchair, H, loose cushions, reuphl, 27x32x34".......................2,750.00
Armchair, H, wood fr w/silk uphl bk & seat, 32x18", pr............1,450.00
Book, In Nature of Materials, sgn 1st edition, 1942, 143-pg, EX...1,200.00
Book, sample; Collection of Wall Coverings..., Schumaker, 18x14" ... 275.00
Book, When Democracy Builds, sgn 1st edition, 132-pg, EX 1,200.00
Bronze, Nakoma, sgn FLW/FLW Foundation, 1975, 12"............2,150.00
Bronze, Nakomis, sgn FLW/FLW Foundation, c 1975, 18" 3,150.00
Cabinet, H, sq top, open shelf, 2-drw, 26x20x20"......................1,600.00
Cabinet, H, 3 drws w/recess hdls, 29x21½x20".......................... 575.00
Chair, H, open wood fr, worn uphl, 32x23x20" 780.00
Chair, side; H, reuphl bk/seat, wood fr, 32½x20", 6 for..............3,450.00
Chairs, dining; H, high-bk, reuphl/rfn, 39", 2 arm+4 side 3,250.00
Chairs, side; H, reuphl seat/bk, 32½", 6 for 800.00
Chest, H, mahog, 10 arranged drws, 33¼x65¼x20"....................1,650.00
Chest, H, 2 doors over 3 drws, 52½x36½x20"............................1,550.00
Coffee table, H, hexagonal, 17x48x41½", +6 triangular stools..9,000.00
Coffee table, H, rectangular w/drop sides, 14x60x19½".............4,500.00
Desk, cypress, 3-drw, triangular top, brass hdls, rfn, 26x58x50" ... 4,000.00
Fabric, run A w/samples showing different colors, 47x26" 660.00
Headbrd, H, full sz, 39x54" 425.00
Hutch, H, open shelves over 6 drws, 2-pc, 80x52x21" 1,800.00

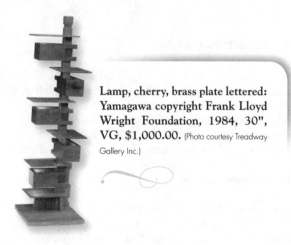

Lamp, cherry, brass plate lettered: Yamagawa copyright Frank Lloyd Wright Foundation, 1984, 30", VG, $1,000.00. (Photo courtesy Treadway Gallery Inc.)

Mirror, H, 31½x43½"... 480.00
Settle, cypress, high bk, orig cushions, minor rstr, 54x121x28".4,250.00
Sideboard, H, 10-drw, recessed hdls, 33x65½x20½" 2,100.00
Sideboard, 9-drw, dbl doors, 35x66½x21" 1,300.00
Sofa, sectional; H, wood fr, reuphl, 3-pc, 72x70", +chair 6,600.00
Stained glass window, geometrics, after Coonley Playhouse, 55x20" .. 1,200.00
Stool, vanity; uphl swivel top on cruciform base, H, 18x18" dia ...1,000.00
Stool, 3 recovered cushions over copper-clad base, 1950s, 20x22x18"....1,325.00
Table, cypress (rfn top), 2-tiered, ca 1950, 23½x55x39½" 5,500.00
Table, dining; H, mahog w/X-base, #2000, 29x48" dia+3 leaves . 1,450.00
Table, dining; H, metal key banding, +3 leaves/6 slipper chairs .. 2,650.00
Table, H, rectangular top, dbl-V base, 29x64x42" w/2 16" leaves..3,950.00
Table, H, slate top, cruciform base, 16x36" dia 2,750.00
Table, H, sq top on cube base, 12½x46½x46½" 1,950.00
Table, H, triangular w/Greek key edge, 15x22x19"...................... 750.00

Wrought Iron

Until the middle of the nineteenth century, almost all the metal hand forged in America was made from a material called wrought iron. When wrought iron rusts it appears grainy, while the mild steel that was used later shows no grain but pits to an orange-peel surface. This is an important aid in determining the age of an ironwork piece. See also Fireplace Implements.

Heart spatula, inlaid touchmark, 1774 on handle, 14½", $575.00; Beetlenut pick, bird-head crest, 5½", $45.00; Wedding spatula, two Distlefinks, incised rosettes, etc., $550.00; Sugar nippers, Continental, late eighteenth century, 7½", $75.00; Pipe tongs, hinged support arm, complete with reamer and tamper, eighteenth century, 18", $625.00. (Photo courtesy Aston Macek Auctions)

Bench, curlicues, wing-like arms, old wht pnt, cushion................150.00
Bracket, sign; griffin form, 37" L..395.00
Garden sculpture, parrot w/long tail, Deco style, mc pnt, 45"......575.00
Gates, vine motif, jester hdl, S Yellin (unmk), 74x30", pr 42,000.00
Pot stand, triangular ladder shape, 55½" 85.00

Yellow Ware

Ranging in color from buff to deep mustard, yellow ware which almost always has a clear glaze can be slip banded, plain, Rockingham decorated, flint enamel glazed, or mocha decorated. Black or red mocha decorated pieces are the most desirable. Although blue mocha decorated pieces are the most common, green decorated pieces command the lowest prices. Pieces having a combination of two colors are the rarest. The majority of pieces are plain and do not bear a manufacturer's mark. Primarily produced in the United States, England, and Canada this utilitarian ware was popular from the mid-nineteenth century until the early twentieth century. Yellow ware was first produced in New York, Pennsylvania, and Vermont. However, the center for yellow ware production was East Liverpool, Ohio, a town which once supported more than 30 potters. Yellow ware is still being produced today in both the United States and England. Because of websites and internet auctions, prices have tended to become uniform throughout the United States. The use of this pottery as accessories in decorating and its exposure in country magazines has caused prices to rise, especially for the more utilitarian forms such as plates and bowls. Note: Because this is a utilitarian ware, it is often found with damage and heavy wear. Damage does have a negative impact on price, especially for the common forms. For further information we recommend *Collector's Guide to Yellow Ware, Book I*, written by our advisor John Michel and Lisa McAllister, and *Collector's Guide to Yellow Ware, Books II* and *III*, by Lisa McAllister. Mr. Michel's address is in the Directory under New York. See also Rockingham.

Coffeepot, streaky brown overglaze, NM, $300.00.

Bowl, batter; plain, 19th C, 6x14¼" to edge of spout 150.00
Bowl, brn & wht slip-trailed bands, late 19th C, 6⅝x15½" 300.00
Bowl, cream w/gr border, scale pattern, 6x12" 240.00
Bowl, wide cream band, flared sides, 7¼x15" 165.00
Bowls, pk w/bl bands, nesting set of 6, largest: 6x10½", VG.........240.00
Pitcher, basketweave, cylindrical, 7¼x6¾", EX 215.00
Pitcher, Peacock at Fountain, rim chip, 9x7½"..............................500.00
Salt box, 3 wht stripes on cream, 5¾x6" 145.00
Salt crock, bl & wht bands, hairline near hanger, 6x5¾" 275.00
Sugar bowl, wht band & sand-textured band, w/lid, 5x4¼", EX...300.00

Zanesville Glass

Glassware was produced in Zanesville, Ohio, from as early as 1815 until 1851. Two companies produced clear and colored hollow ware pieces in five characteristic patterns: 1) diamond faceted, 2) broken swirls, 3) vertical swirls, 4) perpendicular fluting, 5) plain, with scalloped or fluted rims and strap handles. The most readily identified product is perhaps the whiskey bottles made in the vertical swirl pattern, often called globular swirls because of their full, round bodies. Their necks vary in width; some have a ringed rim and some are collared. They were made in several colors; amber, light green, and light aquamarine are the most common. Our advisor for this category is Mark Vuono; he is listed in the Directory under Connecticut.

Bottle, amber, 25-rib, blister, 8"..485.00
Bottle, aqua, 13 swirled ribs on club form, pontil, 9" 235.00
Bottle, aqua, 24 tightly swirled ribs, globular, 7½"........................315.00
Chestnut flask, bl aqua, 24 left-swirl ribs, pontil, 4⅞"..................100.00
Pitkin flask, amber, 24 tightly swirled ribs, pot stones, 5" 460.00
Pitkin flask, lt gr, 20 slightly swirled ribs, sm blisters, 5½" 485.00

Zanesville Stoneware Company

Still in operation at its original location in Zanesville, Ohio, this company is the last surviving pottery dating from Zanesville's golden era of pottery production. They manufactured utilitarian stoneware, art ware vases, jardinieres and pedestals, dinnerware, and large hand-turned vases for use in outdoor gardens. Much of this ware has remained unidentified until today, since they often chose to mark their wares only with item numbers or the names of their various clients. Other items were marked with an impressed circular arrangement containing the company name and location or a three-line embossed device, the bottom line of which contained the letters ZSC. For more information we recommend *Zanesville Stoneware Company* by Jon Rans, Glenn Ralston, and Nate Russell (Collector Books).

Vase, Neptune glaze dripped over blue-gray matt with purple highlights, unmarked, 19", $540.00. (Photo courtesy Cincinnati Art Galleries)

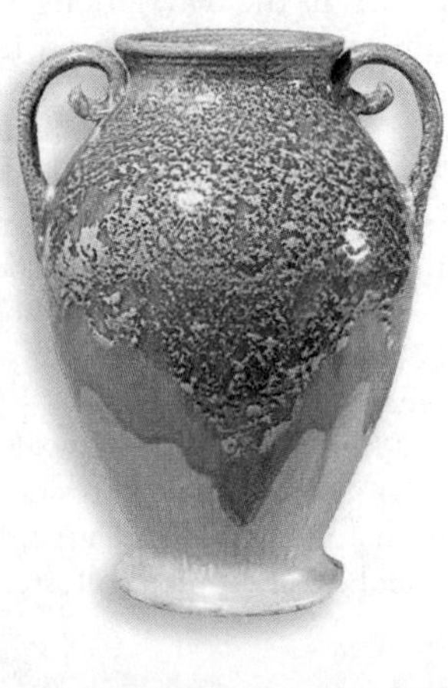

Vase, cobalt drips on speckled beige, chip, 28x18" 1,800.00
Vase, deep mauve matt, horizontal ribs, w/hdls, #521, 12" 155.00
Vase, dk gr w/speckles, 2 angle hdls, squat, 3x7" 660.00
Vase, leaves & stems, gr & lav, ovoid, glaze misses, 9x4" 2,000.00
Vase, Matt Green, shouldered, #102, 8" 65.00
Vase, Matt Green (dk), tapered cylinder w/buttress ft, 9¼x4" 300.00
Vase, Matt Green w/speckles, baluster, 12" 240.00
Vase, Neptune, bl/brn mottle, curled hdls, 18x13" 780.00
Vase, Neptune, mc mottle, twisted hdls, flaw, #106, 24x15" 660.00

Zark

Established circa 1907 in St. Louis, Missouri, the Ozark Pottery made artware which it sold through an outlet called Zark Shops, hence the use of the Zark trademark. Most of their output was earthenware, but high-fired pottery has been reported as well. Some of the decoration was slip painted; other pieces were embossed. It operated for only a few years, perhaps closing as early as 1910. One of its founders and the primary designer was Robert Bringhurst, who was best known as a sculptor. Pieces are marked Zark, either incised or impressed. Our advisors for this category are Suzanne Perrault and David Rago; they are listed in the Directory under New Jersey.

Bowl, Egyptian, cvd gr matt, figural crouching scribes hdls, 5x10", EX. 900.00
Bowl, stylized pattern, lt gr on bl matt, gr gloss int, 3x9" 1,325.00
Bust, maiden, dk bl/gr matt, 8½x11½", EX 660.00

Vase, carved dragon-flies, two-tone matt, incised C.C.B., 4¾x7", $3,900.00. (Photo courtesy Dave Rago Auctions)

Vase, speckled turq & bl matt, 4 buttress hdls, 6x6" 1,925.00
Vase, stylized floral, blk on gr matt, cylindrical, 10x4 12" 2,760.00

Zell

The Georg Schmider United Zell Ceramic Factories has a long and colorful history. Affectionately called 'Zell' by those who are attracted to this charming German-Dutch type tin-glazed earthenware, this type of ware came into production in the latter part of the last century. Zell has created some lovely majolica-like examples (described 'majolica' in the descriptions due to space restrictions) which are beginning to attract their own following, but it is the German-Dutch scenes that are collected with such enthusiasm. Typical scenes are set against a lush green background with windmills on the distant horizon. Into the scenes appear typically garbed girls (long dresses with long white aprons and low-land bonnet head-gear) being teased or admired by little boys attired in pantaloon-type trousers and short rust-colored jackets, all wearing wooden shoes. There are variations on this theme, and occasionally a collector may find an animal theme or even a Kate Greenaway-like scene.

While Zell produced a wide range of wares and even quite recently (1970s) introduced an entirely hand-painted hen/rooster line, it is this early charming German-Dutch theme pottery that is coveted by increasing numbers of devoted collectors.

A similar ware in both theme, technique, and quality but bearing the mark Haag or Made in Austria is included in this listing. Our advisor for this category is Lila Shrader; she is listed in the Directory under California. In the listings that follow, items noted 'Baden' are generally the earlier Zell wares.

Key:
BlkR — Black hen/rooster
hdl/RA — handle at right
    angle to spout
KG — Kate Greenaway style
MIA — Made in Austria

Plate, 9", $85.00; Tumbler, no handle, 4½", $65.00. (Photo courtesy Lila Shrader)

Biscuit jar, BlkR, bbl like, lid w/recessed finial, 5¾" 30.00
Bowl, berries/leaves/vines emb, majolica, 6-sided, 7¾" 55.00
Bowl, birds on branches w/grapes, majolica, Germany, 7½" 48.00
Bowl, rim soup; Dutch boy & girl in eerie woods, Baden, 7½" 95.00
Bowl, water lilies on turq, majolica, rtcl hdls, Germany, 11" 85.00
Butter pat, various Dutch children scenes, Baden, 3", from $30 to .. 60.00
Cake plate, costumed animals party in woods, rtcl hdls, Haag, 9½". 135.00
Cake plate, girls chat on bench, KG, rtcl/emb hdls, Haag, 10½" . 110.00
Cake plate, grapes on basketweave, majolica, ped ft, 3x9" 125.00
Cake set, Nouveau water lilies, majolica, Germany, 11", +5 plates .. 90.00
Candlestick, Dutch boys strolling, flared base, Baden, 7", ea 165.00
Canister, BlkR, Tea, Germany, 5¾" 38.00
Canister, Dutch boys strolling, Sucre, bl & wht, Haag, 6x4x4" 58.00
Chamberstick, hen & rooster, finger ring, 6" dia, ea 72.00
Child's feeding dish, Dutch boy & girl, MIA, 7½x1½" 65.00
Child's feeding dish, Dutch children in forest, Baden, 1½x7½" ... 125.00
Creamer, Dutch clad girl w/stick chasing geese, MIA, hdl/RA, 3". 42.00
Creamer, Dutch girl shakes hands w/dog, Haag & MIA, 4½" 22.00
Creamer, Dutch girls chatting, harbor scene, bl & wht, Haag, 4" .. 62.00
Creamer, Dutch girls w/wagon, hdl/RA, Haag, 3¼" 58.00
Creamer, geese chasing Dutch boy w/golden goose, w/hdl, Haag, 4". 20.00
Cup & saucer, Dutch girls chatting, harbor scene, bl & wht, Haag.. 65.00
Cup & saucer, Dutch girls feeding cats, dk gr, MIA 20.00
Egg cup, Puss 'n Boots, att MIA/Haag, 3¾" 72.00
Mug, Dutch children strolling, harbor scene, Germany, 3½", $18 to. 30.00
Pitcher, cat attracted to fish in basket, MIA, 6½" 145.00
Pitcher, costumed animals party in woods, deep lip, Haag, 6" 135.00
Pitcher, Dutch boys stroll on path, hills beyond, Haag, MIA, 6" ... 58.00
Plate, apples on basketweave, mc majolica, Baden, 9" 40.00
Plate, Cat & Fiddle w/moon, scalloped, MIA, 6½" 65.00
Plate, children at sea in 'dish,' dreamy KG, Baden, 9¾" 345.00
Plate, dandelions & leaves, 3-D, majolica, Baden, 7" 47.00
Plate, Dish Running Away w/Spoon, scalloped, MIA, 6½" 58.00
Plate, Dutch boy w/dog, harbor scene, Baden, 9" 58.00
Plate, kittens w/aprons, Busy Hands Are Happy Hands, MIA, 9" 112.00
Plate, Nouveau water lilies & leaves, majolica, Baden, 9" 60.00
Plate, rag dolls rest under tree, scalloped, MIA, 9½" 98.00
Plate, Tom Thumb w/pie & blkbirds, scalloped, MIA, 6½" 68.00
Plate, woman & child walking/masted ships/windmill, Germany, 9½" .. 40.00

Shakers, Dutch children strolling/dogs/harbor scene, Baden, 3½", pr ..60.00
Stein, Dutch boys tease girls at shore, recessed base, Baden, 6½" .. 95.00
Tankard, Dutch girl watches boatmakers, recessed base, Baden, 11¾"..355.00
Tea tile, Dutch boys tease girls, 3 self-ft pads, Germany, 6" dia 55.00
Teapot, Dutch children walking/harbor/masted ships, Baden, 4½" .285.00
Tumbler, Dutch boys/harbor scene/masted ships, w/hdl, Germany, 4¼"... 30.00
Vase, girls at tea party under tree, KG, squat, Haag, MIA, 6½".... 135.00
Vase, grandma reads to girls/garden, KG, bulbous, Haag, 6" 180.00

Zsolnay

Only until the past decade has the production of the Zsolnay factory become more correctly understood. In the beginning they produced only cement; industrial and kitchen ware manufacture began in the 1850s, and in the early 1870s a line of decorative architectural and art pottery was initiated which has continued to the present time.

The city of Pecs (pronounced Paach) is the major provincial city of southwest Hungary close to the Yugoslav border. The old German name for the city was Funfkirchen, meaning 'Five Churches.' (The 'five-steeple' mark became the factory's logo in 1878.)

Although most Americans only think of Zsolnay in terms of the bizarre, reticulated examples of the 1880s and 1890s and the small 'Eosine' green figures of animals and children that have been produced since the 1920s, the factory went through all the art trends of major international art potteries and produced various types of forms and decorations. The 'golden period,' circa 1895 – 1920, is when its Art Nouveau (Sezession in Austro-Hungarian terms) examples were unequaled. Vilmos Zsolnay was a Renaissance man devoted to innovation, and his children carried on the tradition after his death in 1900. Important sculptors and artists of the day were employed (usually anonymously) and married into the family, creating a dynasty.

Nearly all Zsolnay is marked, either impressed 'Zsolnay Pecs' or with the 'five steeple' stamp. Variations and form numbers can date a piece fairly accurately. For the most part, the earlier ethnic historical-revival pieces do not bring the prices that the later Sezession and second Sezession (Deco) examples do. Our advisors for this category are John Gacher and Federico Santi; they are listed in the Directory under Rhode Island.

Bowl, boat shape w/parrot ea end, red/marbleized lustre, #8805E, 15" L....3,000.00
Figure, maiden w/pitcher, bl-gr lustre, #86?2, 11x4½" 1,200.00
Figure, nude reclining, gold-gr irid, ca 1900, 4½x9x4½" 1,450.00
Figure, owl, Ketupa Ceylonsis, red, #8771, sm chip, 13½x5½"..1,100.00
Jardiniere, weeds & cattails, mc lustre, #4055/#6127B, 8¼x12", NM..11,400.00
Plaque, maiden by pond w/swans, gargoyle fr, prof touchups, 19x18" .31,500.00
Tankard, oak branches/lg beetles, mc lustre, #4115/10/36, 15½x7". 22,800.00

Tankard, spiraling locomotive, Eosin/Labrador glazes, #16, 17" .6,500.00
Tile, classical satyrs & nude, mc lustre, #7893 Zsolnay #6, 8x11"..2,200.00
Tile, maiden medallion flanked w/lotus flowers, 4-color, 3x6" 900.00
Tile, stylized crocus, 3-color lustre, 5¾x5¾" 1,550.00
Tray, figures (2) at rim, mc irid, #7521/partial label, 3x12", NM . 1,175.00
Tray, peacock figural integral to side, gr/gold irid, 7x16" 475.00
Vase, birds of paradise, mc lustre, illegible #, 6¾x8¼" 5,400.00
Vase, daisies etched on gr, 3-spout, #6172M21, 8⅛", NM 2,350.00
Vase, exotic birds in panels, mc lustre, illegible #, 6¾x8¼"........ 5,500.00
Vase, floral, orange/bl/gr Eosin, integral hdls, slim, #8086, 12", NM ..5,750.00
Vase, geranium plant form, red/pk/gr on turq, #6466, 9x5¾", EX.10,800.00
Vase, goddess/putti/trees in relief, bl-gr irid, #3119, bruise, 12x6" .1,200.00
Vase, Limoges-style floral, emb ribs, stick neck, #821, 15x11", NM.1,100.00
Vase, Lovers, Eosin/Labrador glazes, #8068, chip, 15¼" 7,175.00
Vase, maids in relief/swirling waves, gr-platinum irid, #6975, 5x6"...2,400.00
Vase, Nouveau floral, mc on dk red, Karpati, 1910, 7½" 480.00
Vase, Nouveau landscape, mc metallic lustre, #6038M, rpr, 4" 780.00
Vase, Nouveau moths in relief, gold lustre, #3220, 10½", NM ..5,500.00
Vase, Oriental flowering trees/birds, tan-red Eosin, drill rpr, 11" . 3,600.00
Vase, passion flowers, mc on rich bl Eosin, #3939, 12¾", NM ..5,200.00
Vase, red/gr/bl/gold/purple Labrador, slim neck, 12" 900.00
Vase, scarabs/flowers on dead matt, angle shoulder, #8868, 6x8½". 3,500.00
Vase, stylized flowers, mc on wht, #4892, 14⅛", NM................. 4,250.00
Vase, trees & crows in low relief, gr-gold Eosin, scroll hdls, 6¾" . 2,500.00
Vase, tulip form w/mc swirling leaves, mc lustre, #5495, 14x5½", EX ..14,500.00

Vase, doe within reticulated trees, purple, gold, and green lustered glazes, Zsolnay Pecs/M6513A, 18", EX, $15,250.00. (Photo courtesy David Rago Auctions)

Advisory Board

The editors and staff take this opportunity to express our sincere gratitude and appreciation to each person who has in any way contributed to the preparation of this guide. We believe the credibility of our book is greatly enhanced through their efforts. See each advisor's Directory listing for information concerning their specific areas of expertise.

You will notice that at the conclusion of some of the narratives the advisor's name is given. This is optional and up to the discretion of each individual. Simply because no name is mentioned does not indicate that we have no advisor for that subject. Our board grows with each issue and now numbers nearly 425; if you care to correspond with any of them or anyone listed in our Directory, you must send a SASE with your letter. If you are seeking an appraisal, first ask about their fee, since many of these people are professionals who must naturally charge for their services. Because of our huge circulation, every person who allows us to publish their name runs the risk of their privacy being invaded by too many phone calls and letters. We are indebted to every advisor and very much regret losing any one of them. By far, the majority of those we lose give that reason. Please help us retain them on our board by observing the simple rules of common courtesy. Take the differences in time zones into consideration; some of our advisors tell us they often get phone calls in the middle of the night. For suggestions that may help you evaluate your holdings, see the Introduction.

Barbara J. Aaronson
Northridge, California

Charles and Barbara Adams
South Yarmouth, Massachusetts

Ed & Sheri Alcorn
Shady Hills, Florida

Beverly L. Ales
Pleasanton, California

Charles Alexander
Indianapolis, Indiana

Cheryl Anderson
Cedar City, Utah

James Anderson
New Brighton, Minnesota

Suzy McLennan Anderson
Walterboro, South Carolina

Tim Anderson
Provo, Utah

Bruce A. Austin
Pittsford, New York

Bobby Babcock
Austin, Texas

Veldon Badders
Hamlin, New York

Rod Baer
Vienna, Virginia

Wayne and Gale Bailey
Dacula, Georgia

Jacqueline Linscott Barnes
Titusville, Florida

Kit Barry
Brattleboro, Vermont

Dana Martin Batory
Crestline, Ohio

Peter Bealo
Plaistow, New Hampshire

Scott Benjamin
LaGrange, Ohio

Robert Bettinger
Mt. Dora, Florida

William M. Bilsland III
Cedar Rapids, Iowa

Brenda Blake
York Harbor, Maine

Robert and Stan Block
Trumbull, Connecticut

Clarence H. Bodine, Jr.
New Hope, Pennsylvania

Sandra V. Bondhus
Farmington, Connecticut

Phyllis Bess Boone
Tulsa, Oklahoma

Clifford Boram
Monticello, Indiana

Michael and Valarie Bozarth
Williamsville, New York

Jeff Bradfield
Dayton, Virginia

Shane A. Branchcomb
Lovettsville, Virginia

Harold Brandenburg
Wichita, Kansas

Jim Broom
Effingham, Illinois

Dr. Kirby William Brown
Paradise, California

Marcia Brown
White City, Oregon

Rick Brown
Newspaper Collector's Society of
America
Lansing, Michigan

Donald A. Bull
Wirtz, Virginia

Mike Carwile
Lynchburg, Virginia

Gene Cataldo
Huntsville, Alabama

Cerebro
East Prospect, Pennsylvania

Mick and Lorna Chase
Cookeville, Tennessee

Victor J.W. Christie, Ed. D.
Ephrata, Pennsylvania

Lanette Clarke
Antioch, California

John Cobabe
Redondo Beach, California

Debbie and Randy Coe
Hillsboro, Oregon

Wilfred and Dolli Cohen
Santa Ana, California

Ryan Cooper
Yarmouthport, Massachusetts

J.W. Courter
Kevil, Kentucky

John Danis
Rockford, Illinois

Patricia M. Davis
Portland, Oregon

Clive Devenish
Orinda, California

Joe Devine
Council Bluffs, Iowa

David Dilley
Indianapolis, Indiana

Ginny Distel
Tiffin, Ohio

Rod Dockery
Ft. Worth, Texas

L.R. 'Les' Docks
San Antonio, Texas

Rebecca Dodds-Metts
Coral Springs, Florida

Darlene Dommel
Minneapolis, Minnesota

Robert A. Doyle, CAI, ISA, CAGA,
CES
Pleasant Valley, New York

Louise Dumont
Leesburg, Florida

Jeanne Dunay
Camden, South Carolina

Ken and Jackie Durham
Washington, DC

Rita and John Ebner
Columbus, Ohio

Michael L. Ellis
Costa Mesa, California

Dr. Robert Elsner
Boynton Beach, Florida

Bryce Farnsworth
Fargo, North Dakota

Arthur M. Feldman
Tulsa, Oklahoma

Linda Fields
Buchanan, Tennessee

Vicki Flanigan
Winchester, Virginia

Gene Florence
Lexington, Kentucky

Frank W. Ford
Shrewsbury, Massachusetts

Robert Tuggle
New York, New York

Hobart D. Van Deusen
Lakeville, Connecticut

Joan F. Van Patten
Rexford, New York

Linda L. Vines
Torrence, California

Stephen Visakay
Upper Grandview, New York

Ray Vay Vlach
Illinois

Janice and Richard Vogel
Anderson, South Carolina

Mark Vuono
Stamford, Connecticut

John W. Waddell
Mineral Wells, Texas

Ian Warner
Brampton, Ontario, Canada

Marty Webster
Saline, Michigan

David Weddington
Murfreesboro, Tennessee

Robert Weisblut
Ocean Ridge, Florida

Pastor Frederick S. Weiser
New Oxford, Pennsylvania

Stan and Arlene Weitman
Massapequa, New York

BA Wellman
Westminster, Massachusetts

Lonnie Wells
Doe Run, Missouri

David Wendel
Poplar Bluff, Missouri

Kaye and Jim Whitaker
Lynnwood, Washington

Douglass White
Orlando, Florida

Margaret and Kenn Whitmyer
Gahanna, Ohio

Steven Whysel
Tulsa, Oklahoma

Don Williams
Kirksville, Missouri

Linda Williams
Chester, Massachusetts

Ron L. Willis
Ilwaco, Washington

Roy M. Willis
Lebanon Junction, Kentucky

Ralph Winslow
Carl Junction, Missouri

Nancy Winston
Northwood, New Hampshire

Dannie Woodard
Weatherford, Texas

Virginia Woodbury
Rolling Hills Estates, California

Bill Wright
New Albany, Indiana

Darlene Yohe
Stuttgart, Arkansas

Mary Young
Kettering, Ohio

Audrey Zeder
North Bend, Washington

Auction Houses

We wish to thank the following auction houses whose catalogs have been used as sources for pricing information. Many have granted us permission to reproduce their photographs as well.

A-1 Auction Service
2042 N. Rio Grande Ave., Suite 'E,' Orlando, FL 32804; 407-839-0004. Specializing in American antique sales.
a-1auction@cfl.rr.com
www.a-1auction.net

A&B Auctions Inc.
17 Sherman St., Marlboro, MA 01752-3314; 508-480-0006 or fax 508-460-6101. Specializing in English ceramics, flow blue, pottery and Mason's Ironstone. www.aandbauctions.com

Absolute Auction & Realty Inc./
   Absolute Auction Center
Robert Doyle
PO Box 1739, Pleasant Valley, NY 12569. Antique and estate auctions twice a month at Absolute Auction Center; Free calendar of auctions; Specializing in specialty collections.
www.AbsoluteAuctionRealty.com

Allard Auctions Inc.
Col. Doug Allard
PO Box 1030, 419 Flathead St., Ste. 4, Ignatius, MT 59865; 406-745-0500 or fax 406-745-0502. Specializing in American Indian collectibles.
info@allardauctions.com
www.allardauctions.com

America West Archives
Anderson, Cheryl
PO Box 100, Cedar City, UT 84721; 435-586-9497. Has online illustrated catalog that includes auction section of scarce and historical early western documents, letters, autographs, stock certificates, and other important ephemera.
info@americawestarchives.com
www.americawestarchives.com

American Bottle Auctions
1507 21st St., Ste. 203, Sacramento, CA 95814; 800-806-7722. Specializing in antique bottles.
info@americanbottle.com
www.americanbottle.com

Americana Auctions
c/o Glen Rairigh
12633 Sandborn, Sunfield, MI 48890. Specializing in Skookum dolls, art glass and art auctions.

Anderson Auctions/Heritage Antiques
   & Appraisal Services
Suzy McLennan Anderson
Batchelor Hill Antiques & Appraisal Services
246 E Washington St., Walterboro, SC 29488; 843-549-1300. Specializing in American furniture and decorative accessories. andersonauctions@aol.com
www.andersonauctions.net

Andre Ammelounx
The Stein Auction Company
PO Box 136, Palatine, IL 60078-0136; 847-991-5927 or fax 847-991-5947. Specializing in steins, catalogs available.
www.tsaco.com

Bertoia Auctions
2141 DeMarco Dr., Vineland, NJ 08360; 856-692-1881 or fax 856-692-8697. Specializing in toys, dolls, advertising, and related items. bertoiaauctions.com

Bider's
397 Methuen St., Lawrence, MA 01843; 978-688-0923 or 978-475-8336. Antiques appraised, purchased, and sold on consignment. bider@netway.com
www.biders-auction.com

Bonhams & Butterfields
220 San Bruno Ave., San Francisco, CA 94103; 415-861-7500 or fax 415-861-8951. Also located at: 7601 Sunset Blvd., Los Angeles, CA 90046; 323-850-7500 or fax 323-850-5843. Fine art auctioneers and appraisers since 1865. info@butterfields.com
www.butterfields.com

Buffalo Bay Auction Co.
825 Fox Run Trail, Edmond, OK 73034; 405-285-8990. Specializing in advertising, tins and country store items.

buffalobayauction@hotmail.com
buffalobayauction.com

Cerebro
PO Box 327, E. Prospect, PA 17317-0327; 717-252-2400 or 800-69-LABEL. Specializing in antique advertising labels, especially cigar box labels, cigar bands, food labels, firecracker labels; Holds semiannual auction on tobacco ephemera; Consignments accepted.
Cerebro@Cerebro.com
www.cerebro.com

Cincinnati Art Galleries
225 E. Sixth, Cincinnati, OH 45202; 513-381-2128; fax: 513-381-7527. Specializing in American art pottery, American and European fine paintings, watercolors.
www.cincinnatiartgalleries.com

Craftsman Auctions
1485 W Housatonic (Rt 20); Pittsfield, MA 01201; 413-448-8922. Specializing in Arts & Crafts furniture and accessories as well as American art pottery. Color catalogs available.
www.artsncrafts.com or
www.ragoarts.com

Dargate Auction Galleries
214 N. Lexington, Pittsburgh, PA 15208; 412-362-3558. Specializing in estate

auctions featuring fine art, antiques, and collectibles. info@dargate.com
www.dargate.com

David Rago Auctions
333 N. Main, Lambertville, NJ 08530; 609-397-9374 or fax 609-397-9377. Specializing in American art pottery and Arts and Crafts. info@ragoarts.com
www.ragoarts.com

Decoys Unlimited Inc.
West Barnstable, MA; 508-362-2766. Buy, sell, broker, appraise. info@decoysunlimitedinc.net
www.decoysunlimitedinc.net

Du Mouchelles
409 E Jefferson Ave., Detroit, MI 48226-4300; 313-963-6255 or fax 313-963-8199.
info@dumouchelle.com
dumouchelle.com

Dunbar's Gallery
Leila and Howard Dunbar
76 Haven St., Milford, MA 01757; 508-634-8697 or fax 508-634-8698. dunbargallery@comcast.net
www.dunbarsgallery.com

Early American History Auctions
PO Box 3507, Rancho Santa Fe, CA 92067; 858-759-3290 or fax 858-759-1439.
auctions@earlyamerican.com
www.earlyamerican.com

Early Auction Co.
123 Main St., Milford, OH 45150-1121; 513-831-4833 or fax 513-831-1441. info@EarlyAuctionCo.com
EarlyAuctionCo.com

Flying Deuce Auctions & Antiques
14051 W. Chubbuck Rd., Chubbuck ID 83202 208-237-2002 or fax 208-237-4544. Specializing in vintage denim. flying2@ida.net
www.flying2.com

Fontaine's Auction Gallery
1485 W. Housatonic St., Pittsfield, MA 01201; 413-448-8922 or fax 413-442-1550. Specializing in fine quality antiques; important twentieth-century lighting, clocks, art glass. Color catalogs available.
info@fontaineauction.com
www.fontaineauction.com

Frank's Antiques and Auctions
PO Box 516, 551625 U.S. Hwy 1, Hilliard, FL 32046; 1-800-481-6825. Specializing in antique advertising, country store items, rec room and restaurant decor; sporting goods; and nostalgia items. franksauct@aol.com
franksauctions.com

Garth's Auctions Inc.
2690 Stratford Rd., Box 369, Delaware, OH 43015; 740-362-4771.
info@garths.com or www.garths.com

Glass-Works Auctions
102 Jefferson, East Greenville, PA 18041-11623; 215-679-5849 or fax 215-679-3068. America's leading auction company in early American bottles and glass and barber shop memorabilia. glswrk@enter.net
www.glswrk-auction.com

Green Valley Auctions Inc.
2259 Green Valley Lane, Mt. Crawford, VA 22841; 540-434-4532. A leader in the field of Southern decorative and folk art, also pottery, furniture, carpets, fine art and sculpture, silver, jewelry, antique glass and ceramics, textiles, Civil War and militaria, toys and dolls, books, ephemera, advertising, Black Americana, toy trains, railroad material and much more.
info@greenvalleyauctions.com
www.greenvalleyauctions.com

Henry/Pierce Auctioneers
1456 Carson Court, Homewood, IL 60430-4013; 708-798-7508 or fax 708-799-3594. Specializing in bank auctions.

High Noon
9929 Venice Blvd., Los Angeles, CA 90034-5111; 310-202-9010 or fax 310-202-9011. Specializing in cowboy and western collectibles.
info@highnoon.com
www.highnoon.com

History Buff Auction
6031 Winterset, Lansing, MI 48911. Specializing in paper collectibles spanning five centuries.
admin@historybuffauction.com
www.historybuffauction.com

Horst Auctioneers
Horst Auction Center
50 Durlach Rd. (corner of Rt. 322 & Durlach Rd., West of Ephrata), Ephrata, Lancaster County, PA 17522-9741; 717-738-3080. Voices of Experience. sale@horstauction.com
www.horstauction.com

Jackson's, International Auctioneers & Appraisers of Fine Art & Antiques
2229 Lincoln St., Cedar Falls, IA 50613; 319-277-2256 or fax 319-277-1252; Specializing in American and European art pottery and art glass, American and European paintings, Russian works of art, decorative arts, toys and jewelry.
www.jacksonsauction.com

James D. Julia Inc.
PO Box 830, Rt. 201, Skowhegan Rd., Fairfield, ME 04937-0830; 207-453-7125 or fax 207-453-2502.

jjulia@juliaauctions.com or www.juliaauctions.com

John Toomey Gallery
818 North Blvd., Oak Park, IL 60301-1302; 708-383-5234 or fax 708-383-4828. Specializing in furniture and decorative arts of the Arts & Crafts, Art Deco, and Modern Design movements; Modern Design Expert: Richard Wright.
info@johntoomeygallery.com
www.treadwaygallery.com

Joy Luke Fine Art Brokers & Auctioneers The Gallery
300 East Grove St., Bloomington, IL 61701-5290; 309-828-5533 or fax 309-829-2266. robert@joyluke.com
www.joyluke.com

Kit Barry Ephemera Auctions
74 Cotton Mill Hill #A252, VT 05301. Tradecard and ephemera auctions, fully illustrated catalogs with prices realized; Consignment inquiries welcome.
kbarry@surfglobal.net
www.tradecards.com/kb

L.R. 'Les' Docks
Box 691035, San Antonio, TX 78269-1035. Providing occasional mail-order record auctions, rarely consigned; The only consignments considered are exceptionally scarce and unusual records. docks@texas.net
docks.home.texas.net

Lang's Sporting Collectables
633 Pleasant Valley Road; Waterville, NY 13480; 513-841-4623 or fax 315-841-8934. America's Leading Fishing Tackle Auctions.
LangsAuction@aol.com
www.langsauction.com

Leslie Hindman Auctioneers
122 N. Aberdeen St.
Chicago, IL 60607; 312-280-1212; fax 312-280-1211.
www.lesliehindman.com

Lloyd Ralston Gallery Inc.
549 Howe Ave., Shelton, CT 06484; 203-924-5804 or fax 303-924-5834. lrgallery@sbcglobal.net
www.lloydralstontoys.com

Lowe, James Lewis
PO Box 8, Norwood, PA 19074. Specializing in Kate Greenaway, postcards. ClassicPostcards@juno.com

Majolica Auctions
Strawser Auction Group
200 North Main, PO Box 332, Wolcottville, IN 46795-0332; 260-854-2859 or fax 260-854-3979. Issues colored catalog; Also specializing in Fiesta ware. info@strawserauctions.com
strawserauctions.com

Manion's International Auction House Inc.
PO Box 12214, Kansas City, KS 66112-0214; 913-299-6692 or fax 913-299-6792. Specializing in international militaria, particularly the US, Germany and Japan. Extensive catalogs in antiques and collectibles, sports, transportation, political and advertising memorabilia and vintage clothing and denim. Publishes nine catalogs for each of the five categories per year. Request a free sample of past auctions, one issue of current auction for $15.
collecting@manions.com
www.manions.com

Maritime Antiques & Auctions
935 US Rt. 1, PO Box 322, York, ME 03909-0322; 207-363-4247 or fax 353-1416. info@maritiques.com
www.maritiques.com

McMasters Harris Auction Company
PO Box 1755, 5855 Glenn Highway, Cambridge, OH 43725-8768; 740-432-4419 or 800-842-3526. mark@mcmastersharris.com
www.mharrislive.com

Michael Ivankovich Antiques & Auction Company Inc.
PO Box 1536, Doylestown, PA, 18901; 215-345-6094. Specializing in early hand-colored photography and prints. Auction held four times each year, providing opportunity for collectors and dealers to compete for the largest variety of Wallace Nutting, Wallace Nutting-like pictures, Maxfield Parrish, Bessie Pease Gutmann, R. Atkinson Fox, Philip Boileau, Harrison Fisher, etc. ivankovich@wnutting.com
www.wnutting.com

Michael John Verlangieri
PO Box 844, Cambria, CA 93428-0844; 805-927-4428. Specializing in fine California pottery; cataloged auctions (video tapes available).
michael@calpots.com
www.calpots.com

Monsen & Baer, Annual Perfume Bottle Auction
Monsen, Randall; and Baer, Rod
Box 529, Vienna, VA 22183; 703-938-2129 or fax 703-242-1357. Cataloged auctions of perfume bottles; Will purchase, sell, and accept consignments; Specializing in commercial, Czechoslovakian, Lalique, Baccarat, Victorian, crown top, factices, miniatures.

Morphy Auctions
2000 N. Reading Rd., Denver, PA 17517; 717-335-3435 or fax 717-336-7115. A division of Diamond International Galleries; with extensive worldwide media campaigns targeting the most influential antique publications and media venues; specializing

in advertising, Americana, toys, trains, dolls and early holiday items. Hosts three to five consignment sales per year; based in Adamstown Antique Gallery. www.morphyauctions.com

Neal Auction Company
Auctioneers & Appraisers of Antiques
   & Fine Art
4038 Magazine St., New Orleans, LA 70115; 504-899-5329 or 1-800-467-5329; fax: 504-897-3803. customerservice@nealauction.com www.nealauction.com

New England Absentee Auctions
16 Sixth St., Stamford, CT 06905-4610; 203-975-9055. Specializing in Quimper. pottery; neaauction@aol.com www.neabsenteeauctions.com

New Orleans Auction Galleries Inc.
801 Magazine St., New Orleans, LA 70130; 800-501-0277, 504-566-1849. Specializing in American furniture and decorative arts, paintings, prints, and photography. info@neworleansauction.com www.neworleansauction.com

Noel Barrett Antiques & Auctions
PO Box 300, 6183 Carversville Rd., Carversville, PA 18913; 215-297-5109. toys@noelbarrett.com www.noelbarrett.com

Norman C. Heckler & Company
79 Bradford Corner Rd., Woodstock Valley, CT 06282-2002; 860-974-1634 or fax 860-974-2003. Auctioneers and appraisers specializing in early glass and bottles. info@hecklerauction.com www.hecklerauction.com

Past Tyme Pleasures
Steve & Donna Howard
PMB #204, 2491 San Ramon Blvd., #1, San Ramon, CA 94583; 925-484-4488 or fax 925-484-2551. Offers two absentee auction catalogs per year pertaining to old advertising items. pasttyme1@comcast.net www.pasttyme1.com

Perrault-Rago Gallery
333 N. Main St., Lambertville, NJ 08530; 609-397-9374 or fax: 505-687-3592. Specializing in American Art Pottery, Tiles, Arts & Crafts, Moderns, and Bucks County Paintings. www.ragoarts.com

Pettigrew Auction Company
1645 S. Tegon Street
Colorado Springs, Colorado, 80903; 719-633-7963.

Randy Inman Auctions Inc.
PO Box 726; Waterville, ME 04903; 027-872-6900 or fax 207-872-6966.

Specializing in antique toys, advertising, general line. www.inmanauctions.com

R.G. Munn Auction LLC
PO Box 705; Cloudcroft, NM 88317; 505-687-3676. Specializing in American Indian collectibles. rgmunnauc@pvtnetworks.net

Richard Opfer Auctioneering Inc.
1919 Greenspring Dr., Timonium, MD 21093-4113; 410-252-5035; fax: 410-252-5863. info@opferauction.com www.opferauction.com

R.O. Schmitt Fine Arts
PO Box 162; Windham, NH 03087; 603-432-2237. 603-432-2271. Specializing in clocks, music boxes, and scientific instruments; holds catalog auctions. www.roschmittfinearts.com

Roan Inc.
3530 Lycoming Creek Rd., Cogan Station, PA 17728; 570-494-0170. info@roaninc.com; www.roaninc.com

Sandy Rosnick Auctions
7 Big Rock Road, Manchester, MA 01944; 978-526-1093.

Samuel T. Freeman & Co. Est. 1805
1808 Chestnut St., Philadelphia, PA 19103; 215-563-9275 or fax 215-563-8236. info@freemansauction.com www.freemansauction.com

Schoolmaster Auctions and Real Estate
Kenn Norris
PO Box 4830; 513 N. 2nd St., Sanderson, TX 79848; 915-345-2640. Specializing in school-related items, barbed wire and related literature, and L'il Abner.

Skinner Inc.
Auctioneers & Appraisers of Antiques
   and Fine Arts
The Heritage on the Garden, 63 Park Plaza, Boston, MA 02116-3925; 617-350-5400 or fax 617-350-5429. Second address: 357 Main St., Bolton, MA 01740; 978-779-6241 or fax 978-779-5144. www.skinnerinc.com

SoldUSA.com
1418 Industrial Dr., Building 2, Box 11, Matthews, NC 28105; 704-815-1500. Specializing in fine sporting collectibles. support@soldusa.com www.soldUSA.com

Sotheby's
1334 York Ave., New York, NY 10021; 212-606-7000. leiladunbar@sothebys.com www.sothebys.com

Stanton's Auctioneers & Realtors
144 S. Main St., PO Box 146, Vermontville, MI 49096-0146; 517-726-0181. Specializing in all types of property, at auction, anywhere. stanton@voyager.net www.stantons-auctions.com

Stout Auctions, Greg Stout
11 West Third Street; Williamsport, IN 47993-1119; 765-764-6901 or fax 765-764-1516. Specializing in Lionel, American Flyer, Ives, MTH, and other scale and toy trains. stoutauctus@hotmail.com www.stoutauctions.com

Superior Galleries
9478 West Olympic Boulevard, Beverly Hills, CA 90212-4246; 310-203-9855. Specializing in manuscripts, decorative and fine arts, Hollywood memorabilia, sports memorabilia, stamps and coins. info@sgbh.com; www.sgbh.com

Swann Galleries Inc.
104 E. 25th St., New York, NY 10010; 312-254-4710 or fax 212-979-1017. swann@swanngalleries.com www.swanngalleries.com

Three Rivers Collectibles
Wendy and Leo Frese
PO Box 551542, Dallas, TX 75355; 214-341-5165. Annual Red Wing and RumRill pottery and stoneware auctions.

Tom Harris Auctions
203 South 18th Avenue
Marshalltown, IA 50158
614-754-4890 or fax 641-753-0226. Specializing in clocks and watches, high quality antiques and collectibles; estate and lifetime collections, including eBay Live Auctions; Members of NAWCC, NAA, CAI. www.tomharrisauctions.com

Tradewinds Auctions
Henry Taron
PO Box 249, 24 Magnolia Ave., Manchester-By-The-Sea, MA 01944-0249; 978-526-4085. Specializing in antique canes; www.tradewindsantiques.com

Treadway Gallery Inc.
2029 Madison Rd., Cincinnati, OH 45208-3218; 513-321-6742 or fax 513-871-7722. Specializing in American art pottery; American and European art glass; European ceramics; Italian glass; fine American and European paintings and graphics; and furniture and decorative arts of the Arts & Crafts, Art Nouveau, Art Deco and Modern Design Movements. Modern Design expert: Thierry Lorthioir. Members: National Antique Dealers Association, American Art Pottery Association, International Society of Appraisers, American Ceramic Arts

Society, Ohio Decorative Arts Society, Art Gallery Association of Cincinnati. info@treadwaygallery.com www.treadwaygallery.com

Vicki and Bruce Waasdorp Auctions
PO Box 434; 10931 Main St.; Clarence, NY 14031; 716-759-2361. Specializing in decorated stoneware. waasdorp@antiques-stoneware.com www.antiques-stoneware.com

VintagePostcards.Com
Antique Postcards for Collectors
312 Feather Tree Dr. Clearwater FL 33765; 727-467-0555. quality@vintagepostcards.com www.vintagepostcards.com

Weschler's
Adam A. Weschler & Son
905 E. St. N.W., Washington, DC 20004-2006; 202-628-1281. www.weschlers.com

William Doyle Galleries
Auctioneers & Appraisers
175 East 87th St., New York, NY 10128; 212-427-2730. info@DoyleNewYork.com www.doylenewyork.com

Willis Henry Auctions
22 Main St., Marshfield, MA 02050-2808; 781-834-7774 or fax 781-826-3520. wha@willishenry.com www.willishenry.com

Wm. Morford
Investment Grade Collectibles at Auction
RD #2, Cazenovia, NY 13035; 315-662-7625 or fax 315-662-3570. Specializing in antique advertising items and related collectibles; Maxfield Parrish items; rare and unique items at the upper end of the market with a heavy emphasis on quality, rarity and condition. Premier auctions held several times a year. morf2bid@aol.com www.morfauction.com

Directory of Contributors

When contacting any of the buyers/sellers listed in this part of the Directory by mail, you must include an SASE (stamped, self-addressed envelope) if you expect a reply. Many of these people are professional appraisers, and there may be a fee for their time and service. Find out up front. Include a clear photo if you want an item identified. Most items cannot be described clearly enough to make an identification without a photo.

If you call and get their answering machine, when you leave your number so that they can return your call, tell them to call back collect. And please take the differences in time zones into consideration. 7:00 AM in the Midwest is only 4:00 AM in California! And if you're in California, remember that even 7:00 PM is too late to call the east coast. Most people work and are gone during the daytime. Even some of our antique dealers say they prefer after-work phone calls. Don't assume that a person who deals in a particular field will be able to help you with related items. They may seem related to you when they are not.

Please, we need your help. This book sells in such great numbers that allowing their names to be published can create a potential nightmare for each advisor and contributor. Please do your part to help us minimize this, so that we can retain them on our board and in turn pass their experience and knowledge on to you through our book. Their only obligation is to advise us, not to evaluate your holdings.

Alabama

Cataldo, Gene
C.E. Cataldo
4726 Panorama Dr., S.E., Huntsville, 35801; 256-536-6893. Specializing in classic and used cameras.
genecams@aol.com

Lippa, Matt; and Schaaf, Elizabeth
Artisans
PO Box 256, Mentone, 35984; 256-634-4037. Specializing in folk art, quilts, painted and folky furniture, tramp art, whirligigs, windmill weights.
artisans@folkartisans.com
www.folkartisans.com

Arizona

Jackson, Denis
Illustrator Collector's News
PO Box 6433, Kingman, 86401.
ticn@olypen.com

Arkansas

Freyaldenhoven, Tony
1412 S. Tyler St., Little Rock, 72204; 501-352-3559. Specializing in Camark pottery. tonyfrey@conwaycorp.net

Roenigk, Martin
Mechantiques
Crescent Hotel & Spa
75 Prospect Ave., Eureka Springs, 72632; 800-671-6333. Specializing in mechanical musical instruments, music boxes, band organs, musical clocks and watches, coin pianos, orchestrions, monkey organs, automata, mechanical birds and dolls, etc. mroenigk@aol.com
www.mechantiques.com

Yohe, Darlene
Timberview Antiques
1303 S. Prairie St., Stuttgart, 72160-5132; 870-673-3437. Specializing in American pattern glass, historical glass, Victorian pattern glass, carnival glass, and custard glass.

California

Aaronson, Barbara J.
The Victorian Lady
PO Box 7522, Northridge, 91327; 818-368-6052. Specializing in figural napkin rings, pickle castors, American Victorian silver plate.
bjaaronson@aol.com
www.thevictorianlady.com

Ales, Beverly Schell
4046 Graham St., Pleasanton, 94566-5619; 925-846-5297. Specializing in knife rests.
Kniferests@sbcglobal.net

Babcock, Bobby
Jubilation Antiques
1034 Camino Pablo Drive, Pueblo West, 81007; 719-557-1252. Specializing in Maxfield Parrish, Black Americana, and brown Roseville Pine Cone.
jubantique@aol.com

Berg, Paul
PO Box 8895, Newport Beach, 92620. Author of *Nineteenth Century Photographica Cases and Wall Frames.*

Brown, Dr. Kirby William
PO Box 1842, Paradise, 95967; 530-877-2159. Authoring book on history and products of California Faience, West Coast Porcelain, and Potlatch Pottery. Any contribution of information, new pieces, etc., is welcome.
kirbybrownbooks@sbcglobal.net

Clarke, Lanette
5021 Toyon Way, Antioch, 94532; 925-776-7784. Co-founder of *Haeger Pottery Collectors of America.* Specializing in Haeger and Royal Hickman.
Lanette_Clarke@msn.com

Cobabe, John
800 So. Pacific Coast Hwy; Suite 8-301; Redondo Beach 90277; 310-544-8790. Specializing in Amphora, Zsolnay, and Massier. johncobabe@aol.com

Cohen, Wilfred and Dolli
Antiques & Art Glass

PO Box 27151, Santa Ana, 92799; 714-545-5673. Specializing in Kelva, Wave Crest (C.F. Monroe), and Nakara. Please include SASE for reply. A photo is very helpful for identification.
antsandartglass@aol.com

Conroy, Barbara J.
PO Box 2369, Santa Clara, 95055-2369. Specializing in commercial china; author and historian.

Devenish, Clive
PO Box 708, Orinda, 94563; 925-254-8383. Specializing in still and mechanical banks; Buys and sells.

Ellis, Michael L.
266 Rose Lane., Costa Mesa, 92627; 949-646-7112 or fax 949-645-4919. Author (Collector Books) of *Collector's Guide to Don Winton Designs, Identification & Values.* Specializing in Twin Winton

George, Tony
22431-B160 Antonio Parkway., #521, Rancho Santa Margarita, 92688; 949-589-6075. Specializing in watch fobs. Tony@strikezoneinc.com

Gibson, Pat
38280 Guava Dr., Newark, 94560; 510-792-0586. Specializing in R.A. Fox.

Harrison, Gwynneth M.
11566 River Heights Dr., Riverside, 92505; 951-343-0414. Specializing in Autumn Leaf (Jewel Tea).
morgan27@sbcglobal.com

Hibbard, Suzi
WanderWares
Specializing in Dragonware and 1000 Faces china, other Orientalia.
Dragon_Ware@hotmail.com

Howard, Steve
Past Tyme Pleasures
PMB #204, 2491 San Ramon Valley Blvd., #1, San Ramon, 94583; 925-484-6442 or fax 925-484-6427. Specializing in antique American fire-

arms, bowie knives, Western Americana, old advertising, vintage gambling items, barber and saloon items.
pasttyme1@sbcglobal.net
www.pasttyme1.com

Main Street Antique Mall
237 E Main St., El Cajon, 92020; 619-447-0800 or fax 619-447-0815.

The Meadows Collection
Mark and Adela Meadows
PO Box 819, Carnelian Bay, 96140; 530-546-5516. Specializing in Gouda and Quimper; lecturers, authors of *Quimper Pottery, A Guide to Origins, Styles, and Values,* serving on the board of directors of the Associated Antiques Dealers of America; Please include SASE for inquiries.
meadows@meadowscollection.com
www.meadowscollection.com

Needham, Leonard
925-684-9674
screensider@sbcglobal.net

Pardini, Dick
3107 N. El Dorado St., Dept. SAPG, Stockton, 95204-3412; 209-466-5550 (recorder may answer). Specializing in California Perfume Company items dating from 1886 to 1928 and 'go-with' related companies: buyer and information center. Not interested in items that have Avon, Perfection, or Anniversary Keepsake markings. California Perfume Company offerings must be accompanied by a photo, photocopy, or sketching along with a condition report and, most importantly, price wanted. Inquiries require large SASE and must state what information you are seeking; not necessary if offering items for sale.

Sanford, Steve and Martha
230 Harrison Ave., Campbell, 95008; 408-978-8408. Authors of two books on Brush-McCoy and *Sanfords Guide to McCoy Pottery* (available from the authors). www.sanfords.com

Shrader, Lila
Shrader Antiques

2025 Hwy. 199, Crescent City, 95531; 707-458-3525. Specializing in railroad, steamship and other transportation memorabilia; Shelley china (and its predecessor, Wileman/Foley China); Buffalo china and Buffalo Pottery including Deldare; Niloak, and Zell (and Haag); Please include SASE for reply.

Stillwell, Liz
Our Attic Antiques & Belleek
PO Box 1074, Pico Rivera, 90660; 323-257-3879. Specializing in Irish and American Belleek.

Tanner, Joseph and Pamela
Tanner Treasures
5200 Littig Way, Elk Grove, 95757; 916-684-4006. Specializing in handcuffs, leg shackles, balls and chains, restraints and padlocks of all kinds (including railroad), locking and non-locking devices; Also Houdini memorabilia: autographs, photos, posters, books, letters, etc.

Thoerner, Sharon
15549 Ryon Ave., Bellflower, 90706; 562-866-1555. Specializing in covered animal dishes, powder jars with animal and human figures, slag glass.

Thornton, Don
PO Box 57, Moss Beach, 94038; 650-563-9445. Specializing in egg beaters and apple parers; author of *The Eggbeater Chronicles, 2nd Edition* ($50.45 ppd.); and *Apple Parers* ($59 ppd.). dont@thorntonhouse.com

Vines, Linda
2390 Ocean Ave., #144, Torance, 90505-5856; 310-373-9293. Specializing in Snow Babies, Halloween, Steiff, and Santas (all German). lleigh2000@hotmail.com

Webb, Frances Finch
1589 Gretel Lane, Mountain View, 94040. Specializing in Kay Finch ceramics.

Woodbury, Virginia; Past President of the American Hatpin Society
20 Montecillo Dr., Ro 310-326-2196. Quarterly meetings and newsletters; Membership: $30 per year; SASE required when requesting information. HATPINGINIA@aol.com

Canada

Warner, Ian
PO Box 93022, 499 Main St. S., Brampton, Ontario, L6Y 4V8; 905-453-9074. Specializing in Wade porcelain, author of *The World of Wade, The World of Wade Book 2, Wade Price Trends, The World of Wade — Figurines and Miniatures,* and *The World of Wade Head Vase Planters;* Co-author: Mike Posgay. idwarner@rogers.com

Colorado

Heck, Carl
Carl Heck Decorative Arts
Box 8416, Aspen, 81612; phone/fax: 970-925-8011. Specializing in Tiffany lamps, art glass, paintings, windows and chandeliers; Also reverse-painted and leaded-glass table lamps, stained and beveled glass windows, bronzes, paintings, etc.; Buy and sell; Fee for written appraisals; Please include SASE for reply. carlheck5@aol.com www.carlheck.com

Mackin, Bill
Author of *Cowboy and Gunfighter Collectibles,* available from author: 1137 Washington St., Craig, 81625; 970-824-6717, Paperback: $28 ppd.; Other titles available. Specializing in old and fine spurs, guns, gun leather, cowboy gear, Western Americana (Collection in the Museum of Northwest Colorado, Craig).

Segelke, Cathy
970-522-5424. Specializing in crocks, Western Pottery Mfg. Co. (Denver, CO).

Stifter, Craig
0062 Elk Mountain Drive
Redstone, 81623. Specializing in Coca-Cola, Orange Crush, Dr. Pepper, Hires, and other soda-pop brand collectibles. cstifter@gmail.com

Connecticut

Block, Robert and Stan
Block's Box
51 Johnson St., Trumbull, 06611; 203-926-8448. Specializing in marbles. blockschip@aol.com

Bondhus, Sandra V.
16 Salisbury Way, Farmington, 06032; 860-678-1808. Author of *Quimper Pottery: A French Folk Art Faience.* Specializing in Quimper pottery.

Lehrer, Gary
16 Mulberry Road, Woodbridge, 06525-1717. Specializing in pens and pencils; Catalog available. www.gopens.com

Postcards International
Martin J. Shapiro
2321 Whitney Ave., Suite 102, PO Box 185398, Hamden, 06518; 203-248-6621 or fax 203-248-6628. Specializing in vintage picture postcards. www.vintagepostcards.com

Van Deusen, Hoby and Nancy
15 Belgo Road, Lakeville, 06039-1001; 860-435-0088. Specializing in Canton, SASE required when requesting information. rtn.hoby@snet.net

Vuono, Mark
166th St., Stamford, 06905; 203-357-0892 (10 a.m. to 5:30 p.m. E.S.T.). Specializing in historical flasks, blown three-mold glass, blown American glass.

District of Columbia

Durham, Ken and Jackie (by appt.)
909 26 St. N.W., Suite 502, Washington, DC 20037. Specializing in slot machines, jukeboxes, arcade machines, trade stimulators, vending machines, scales, popcorn machines, and service manuals.
www.GameRoomAntiques.com

Florida

Alcorn, Ed and Sheri
Animal Rescue of West Pasco
14945 Harmon Dr., Shady Hills, 34610; 727-856-6762. Specializing in Hagen-Renaker. horsenut@gate.net

Barnes, Jacqueline Linscott
Line Jewels
3557 Nicklaus Dr., Titusville, 32780; 321-267-9170. Specializing in glass insulators, bell paperweights and other telephone items. Author and distributor of 2003 edition of *Bluebell Paperweights, Telephone Pioneers of America Bells, and other Telephone Related Items;* LSASE required for information. bluebellwt@aol.com

Bettinger, Robert
PO Box 333, Mt. Dora, 32756; 352-735-3575. Specializing in American and European art pottery and glass, Arts & Crafts furniture and accessories, fountain pens, marbles, and general antiques. rgbett@aol.com

Dodds-Metts, Rebecca
Silver Flute
PO Box 670664, Coral Springs, 33067. Specializing in jewelry.

Elsner, Dr. Robert
29 Clubhouse Lane, Boynton Beach, 33436; 561-736-1362. Specializing in antique barometers and nautical instruments.

France, Madeleine
9 North Federal Highway, Dania Beach, 33004; 954-921-0022. Specializing in top-quality perfume bottles: Rene Lalique, Steuben, Czechoslovakian, DeVilbiss, Baccarat, Commercials; French doré bronze and decorative arts.

Hastins, Bud
Author of *Bud Hastin's Avon Collector's Encyclopedia,* signed copies available from author for $33.95 postage paid. Write to PO Box 11004, Ft. Lauderdale, 33339; or call 954-566-0691 after 10:00 AM Eastern time.

Hirshman, Susan and Larry
Everyday Antiques
1624 Pine Valley Dr., Ft Myers, 33907. Specializing in china, glassware, kitchenware.

Hudson, Hardy
Antiques on the Avenue
505 Park Ave. N., Winter Park, 32789; 407-657-2100 or cell: 407-963-6093. Specializing in majolica, American art pottery (buying one piece or entire collections); Also buying Weller (garden ornaments, birds, Hudson, Sicard, Sabrinian, Glendale, Knifewoood, or animal related), Roseville, Grueby, Ohr, Newcomb, Overbeck, Pewabic, Teco, Tiffany, Fulper, Rookwood, SEG, etc. Also buying better art glass, paintings and silver. todiefor@mindspring.com

Joyce, Harriet
415 Soft Shadow Lane, DeBary, 32713; 386-668-8006. Specializing in Cracker Jack and Checkers (a competitor) early prizes and Flossie Fisher items.

Kuritzky, Louis
4510 NW 17th Place, Gainesville, 32605; 352-377-3193. Co-author (Collector Books) of *Encyclopedia of Bookends* (2005). lkuritzky@aol.com

Person, Jeffrey M.
727-504-1139. Specializing in Asian art including cloisonné, Sumida Ware, and fine carved furniture, Art Nouveau, and jewelry. Has lectured, written articles, and been doing fine antique shows for 40 years. Person1@tampabay.rr.com

Posner, Judy
PO Box 2194 SC, Englewood, FL 34295, 941-475-1725. Specializing in Disneyana, Black memorabilia, salt and pepper shakers, souvenirs of the USA, character and advertising memorabilia, figural pottery; Buy, sell, collect. judyposner@yahoo.com

Rolfes, Herbert
Yesterday's World
PO Box 398, Mt. Dora, 32756; 352-735-3947. Specializing in World's Fairs and Expositions. NY1939@aol.com

Snyder-Haug, Diane
St. Petersburg, 33705. Specializing in women's clothing, 1850 – 1940.

Supnick, Mark
2771 Oakbrook Manor, Ft. Lauderdale, 33332. Author of *Collecting Hull Pottery's Little Red Riding Hood* ($12.95 ppd.). Specializing in American pottery.

Weisblut, Robert
International Ivory Society
5001 Old Ocean Blvd. #1, Ocean Ridge, 33435; 561-276-5657. Specializing in ivory carvings and utilitarian objects. rweisblut@yahoo.com

White, Douglass
A-1 Auction
2042 N. Rio Grande Ave., Suite E, Orlando, 32804; 407-839-0004. Specializing in Fulper, Arts & Crafts furniture (photos helpful).
a-1auction@cfl.rr.com

Georgia

Bailey, Wayne and Gale
3152 Fence Rd., Dacula, 30019; 770-963-5736. Specializing in Goebels (Friar Tuck).

Glenn, Walter
3420 Sonata Lane, Alpharetta, 30004-7492; 678-624-1298. Specializing in Frankart.

Hoefs, Steven
PO Box 1024, Avalon, 90704; 310-510-2623. Specializing in Catalina Island Pottery; author of book, available from the author.

Joiner, John R.
Aviation Collectors
130 Peninsula Circle, Newnan, 30263; 770-502-9565. Specializing in commercial aviation collectibles. propJJ@bellsouth.net

Jones, Donald
107 Rivers Edge Dr., Savannah, 31406; 912-354-2133. Specializing in vintage tennis collectibles; SASE with inquiries please. Glassman912@comcast.net

Illinois

Broom, Jim
Box 65, Effingham, 62401. Specializing in opalescent pattern glassware.

Danis, John
2929 Sunnyside Dr. #D362, Rockford, 61114; 815-978-0647. Specializing in R. Lalique and Norse pottery.
danis6033@aol.com

Garmon, Lee
1529 Whittier St., Springfield, 62704; 217-789-9574. Specializing in Royal Haeger, Royal Hickman, glass animals.

Hall, Doris and Burdell
210 W. Sassafras Dr., Morton, 61550-1254; 309-263-2988. Authors of *Morton's Potteries: 99 Years* (Vols. I and II). Specializing in Morton pottery, American dinnerware, early American pattern glass, historical items, elegant Depression-era glassware.
bnbhall@mto.com

Hamburg, Mary 'Tootsie'
Charlotte's, Queen Ann's, and Among Friends shops, all in Corner Victorian in Danville; 217-446-2323. Specializing in German Pink Pigs, Bakelite jewelry, general line.

Hastings, Mary Jane
212 West Second South, Mt. Olive, 62069; 217-999-7519 or cell: 618-910-1528. Specializing in Chintz dinnerware. sgh@chaliceantiques.com

Hoffmann, Pat and Don, Sr.
1291 N. Elmwood Dr., Aurora, 60506-1309; 630-859-3435. Authors of *Warwick, A to W*, a supplement to *Why Not Warwick?*; video regarding Warwick decals currently available.
warwick@ntsource.com

Karman, Laurie and Richard; Editors of *The Fenton Flyer*
815 S. Douglas Ave., Springfield, 62704. Specializing in Fenton art glass.

Martin, Jim
1095 215th Ave., Monmouth, 61462; 309-734-2703. Specializing in Old Sleepy Eye, Monmouth pottery, Western Stoneware.

Miller, Larry
218 Devron Circle, E. Peoria, 61611-1605. Specializing in German and Czechoslovakian Erphila.

Ochsner, Grace
Grace Ochsner Doll House
1636 E. County Rd. 2700, Niota, 62358; 217-755-4362. Specializing in piano babies, bisque German dolls and figurines.

Rhoden, Joan and Charles
8693 N. 1950 East Rd., Georgetown, 61846-6264; 217-662-8046. Specializing in Heisey and other Elegant glassware, spice tins, lard tins, and yard-long prints. Co-authors of *Those Wonderful Yard-Long Prints* and *More*, and *More Wonderful Yard-Long Prints, Book II*, and *Yard-Long Prints, Book III*, illustrated value guides.
rhoden@soltec.net

Schwab, Betty and Larry
The Paperweight Shoppe
2507 Newport Dr., Bloomington, 61704; 877-517-6518 and 309-662-1956. Specializing in glass

paperweights; Now buying quality weights, one piece or a collection.
thepaperweightshoppe@verizon.net or paperweightguy@yahoo.com

Spencer, Dick and Pat
Glass and More (Shows only)
1203 N. Yale, O'Fallon, 62269; 618-632-9067. Specializing in Cambridge, Fenton, Fostoria, Heisey, etc.

Spiess, Greg
230 E. Washington, Joliet, 60433; 815-722-5639. Specializing in Odd Fellows lodge items. spiessantq@aol.com

TV Guide Specialists
Box 20, Macomb 61455; 309-833-1809

Vlach, Ray
Specializing in Homer Laughlin, Red Wing, Vernon Kilns, Russel Wright, Eva Zeisel, and childrens's ware china and pottery. rayvlach@hotmail.com

Yester-Daze Glass
c/o Illinois Antique Center
320 S.W. Commercial St., Peoria, 61604; 309-347-1679. Specializing in glass from the 1920's, '30s and '40s; Fiesta; Hall; pie birds; sprinkler bottles; and Florence figurines.

Indiana

Alexander, Charles
221 E. 34th St., Indianapolis, 46205; 317-924-9665. Specializing in Fiesta, Russel Wright, Eva Zeisel.
chasalex1848@charter.net

Boram, Clifford
Antique Stove Information Clearinghouse
Monticello; Free consultation by phone only: 574-583-6465.

Dilley, David
6125 Knyghton Rd., Indianapolis, 46220; 317-251-0575. Specializing in Royal Haeger and Royal Hickman. glazebears@aol.com

Freese, Carol and Warner
House With the Lions Antiques
On the Square, Covington, 47932. General line.

Garrett, Sandi
1807 W. Madison St., Kokomo, 46901. Specializing in Greentown glass, old postcards. sandpiper@iquest.net

Haun, Ted
2426 N. 700 East, Kokomo, 46901. Specializing in American pottery and china, '50s items, Russel Wright designs. Sam17659@cs.com

Highfield, James
1601 Lincolnway East, South Bend, 46613-3418; 574-288-0300. Specializing in relief-style Capo-di-Monte-style porcelain (Doccia, Ginori, and Royal Naples).

Hoover, Dave
1023 Skyview Dr., New Albany, 47150; 812-945-3614 (would rather receive calls than letters). Specializing in fishing collectibles; also miniature boats and motors. lurejockey@aol.com

Keagy, William
PO Box 106, Bloomfield, 47424; 812-384-3471. Co-author of *Those Wonderful Yard-Long Prints* and *More, More Wonderful Yard-Long Prints, Book II*, and *Yard-Long Prints, Book III*, illustrated value guides.

McQuillen, Michael J. and Polly
Political Parade
PO Box 50022, Indianapolis, 46250-0022; 317-845-1721. Writer of column, *Political Parade*, which appears monthly in *AntiqueWeek* other newspapers. Specializing in political advertising, pin-back buttons, and sports memorabilia; Buys and sells.
michael@politicalparade.com
www.politicalparade.com

Miller, Robert
44 Hickory Lane North, Crawfordsville, 47833-7601. Specializing in Dryden pottery.

Pruitt, Ted
3350 W. 700 N., Anderson, 46011. *St. Clair Glass Collector's Guide, Vol. 2*, available for $25 each at above address.

Ricketts, Vicki
Covington Antiques Company
6431 W US Highway 136; Covington 47932. General line.

Sanders, Lisa
8900 Old State Rd., Evansville, 47711. Specializing in MA Hadley.
1dlk@insight.bb.com

Skrobis, Mark J.
4016 Jerelin Dr.
Franklin, WI 53132-8727
414-737-4109. mjskrobis@wi.rr.com

Slater, Thomas D.
Slater's Americana
1325 W. 86th St., Indianapolis, 46260; 317-257-0863. Specializing in political and sports memorabilia.

Taylor, Dr. E.E.
245 N. Oakland Ave., Indianapolis, 46201-3360; 317-638-1641. Specializing in radios; SASE required for replies to inquiries.

Webb's Antique Mall
over 400 Quality Dealers
200 W. Union St., Centerville, 47330;
765-855-2489.
webbsin@antiquelandusa.com

Wright, Bill
325 Shady Dr., New Albany, 47150.
Specializing in knives: Bowie, hunting,
military, and pocketknives.

Iowa

Bilsland, William M., III
PO Box 2671, Cedar Rapids,
52406-2671; 319-368-0658 (message)
or (cell) 714-328-7219. Specializing in
American art pottery.

Devine, Joe
1411 S. 3rd St., Council Bluffs, 51503;
712-328-7305. Specializing in Royal
Copley and other types of pottery
(collector), author of *Collecting Royal
Copley Plus Royal Windsor & Spaulding*.

Jaarsma, Ralph
1220 Broadway, Pella, 50219;
641-628-2824. Specializing in Dutch
antiques; SASE required when requesting information.

Jackson, James and Tatiana
Jackson's, International Auctioneers &
Appraisers of Fine Art and Antiques
2229 Lincoln St., Cedar Falls, 50613;
319-277-2256 or fax 319-277-1252.
Specializing in American and European art pottery and art glass, American
and European paintings, Russian works
of art, decorative arts, toys and jewelry.
www.jacksonsauction.com

Picek, Louis
Main Street Antiques
110 W. Main St., Box 340, West
Branch, 52358; 319-643-2065. Specializing in folk art, country Americana, the unusua.
msantiques@bigplanet.com

Kansas

Brandenburg, Harold
662 Chipper Lane, Wichita, 67212;
316-722-1200. Specializing in Royal
Bayreuth; Charter member of the
Royal Bayreuth Collectors Club; Buys,
sells, and collects.

Maundy International
PO Box 13028-GG, Shawnee Mission,
66282; 1-800-235-2866. Specializing in
watches — antique pocket and vintage
wristwatches. mitime@hotmail.com

Old World Antiques
4436 State Line Rd., Kansas City,
66103; 913-677-4744. Specializing

in 18th- and 19th-century furniture,
paintings, accessories, clocks, chandeliers, sconces, and much more.

Smies, David
Pops Collectibles
Box 522, 315 South 4th, Manhattan,
66502; 785-776-1433. Specializing in
coins, stamps, cards, tokens, Masonic
collectibles.

Street, Patti
Currier & Ives (China) Quarterly newsletter
PO Box 504, Riverton, 66770;
316-848-3529. Subscription: $12 per
year (includes 2 free ads).

Kentucky

Courter, J.W.
3935 Kelley Rd., Kevil, 42053;
270-488-2116. Specializing in Aladdin lamps; Author of *Aladdin — The
Magic Name in Lamps*, Revised Edition,
hardbound, 304 pages; *Aladdin Electric Lamps*, softbound, 229 pages; and
*Angle Lamps Collectors Manual & Price
Guide*, softbound, 48 pages.

Florence, Gene and Cathy
Box 22186, Lexington, 40522. Au-
thors (Collector Books) on Depression
Glass, Occupied Japan; Elegant Glass,
Kitchen Glassware.

Hornback, Betty
707 Sunrise Lane, Elizabethtown,
42701. Specializing in Kentucky Derby
glasses, Detailed Derby, Preakness, Belmont, Breeder's Cup and others; Glass
information and pictures available in a
booklet for $15 ppd.
bettysantiques@kvnet.org;

Ritchie, Roy B.
197 Royhill Rd., Hindman, 41822;
606-785-5796. Co-author of *Standard
Knife Collector's Guide*; *Standard Guide
to Razors*; *Cattaraugus Cutlery, Identification and Values*; and *The Big Knife
Book*. Specializing in razors and knives,
all types of cutlery.

Stewart, Ron
PO Box 2421, Hazard, 41702;
606-436-5917. Co-author of *Standard
Knife Collector's Guide*; *Standard Guide
to Razors*; *Cattaraugus Cutlery, Identification and Values*; *The Big Book of
Pocket Knives*; and *Remington Knives,
Identification and Values*. Specializing in
razors and knives, all types of cutlery.

Willis, Roy M.
Heartland of Kentucky Decanters and
    Steins
PO Box 428, Lebanon Jct., 40150. Huge
selection of limited edition decanters,
beer steins and die-cast collectibles —
open showroom; Call, write or check

our website (www.decantersandsteins.
com) for road directions. Include large
self-addressed envelope (2 stamps) with
correspondence; Fee for appraisals.
heartland@decantersandsteins.com

Louisiana

Langford, Paris
Kollecting Kiddles
415 Dodge Ave., Jefferson, 70121;
504-733-0667. Specializing in all small
vinyl dolls of the '60s and '70s; Author
of *Liddle Kiddles Identification and Value
Guide* (Now out of print). Please include SASE when requesting information; Contact for information concerning Liddle Kiddle convention.
bbean415@aol.com

Maine

Blake, Brenda
Box 555, York Harbor, 03911;
207-363-6566. Specializing in eggcups.
Eggcentric@aol.com

Hathaway, John
Hathaway's Antiques
295 E. Oxford Rd., South Paris, 04281;
207-665-2214. Specializing in fruit
jars; Mail order a specialty.

Hillman, Alma
Antiques at the Hillman's
197 Coles Corner Rd. 04496;
207-223-5656. Co-author (Collector
Books) of *Collector's Encyclopedia of
Old Ivory China, The Mystery Explored,
Identification & Values*. Specializing in
Old Ivory China.
oldivory@roadrunner.com

Rinaldi, John
Nautical Antiques and Related Items
Box 765, Dock Square, Kennebunkport, 04046; 207-967-3218. Specializing in nautical antiques, scrimshaw,
naval items, marine paintings, naval
items, etc.; Fully illustrated catalog: $5.
jfrinaldi@adelphia.net

Simpson, Elizabeth
Elizabeth Simpson Antiques
PO Box 201, Freeport, 04032. Special-
izing in early glass and Sandwich glass.

Zayic, Charles S.
Americana Advertising Art
PO Box 57, Ellsworth, 04605;
207-667-7342. Specializing in early magazines, early advertising art, illustrators.

Maryland

Kilhoffer, C.D.
Churchville, Specializing in glass target balls.

Meadows, John, Jean and Michael
Meadows House Antiques
919 Stiles St., Baltimore, 21202;
410-837-5427. Specializing in antique
wicker furniture (rustic, twig, and old
hickory), quilts, and tramp art.

Screen, Harold and Joyce
2804 Munster Rd., Baltimore, 21234;
410-661-6765. Specializing in soda
fountain 'tools of the trade' and paper:
catalogs, 'Soda Fountain' magazines,
etc. hscreen@comcast.net

Welsh, Joan
7015 Partridge Pl., Hyattsville, 20782;
301-779-6181. Specializing in Chintz;
Author of *Chintz Ceramics*.

Massachusetts

Adams, Charles and Barbara
South Yarmouth, 02664; 508-760-3290
or (business) 508-587-5640. Specializing in Bennington (brown only).
adams_2340@msn.com

Cooper, Ryan
205 White Rock Rd., Yarmouthport,
02675; 508-362-1604. Specializing in
flags of historical significance and exceptional design.
rcmaritime@capecod.net

Dunbar's Gallery
Leila and Howard Dunbar
54 Haven St., Milford, 01757;
508-634-8697 (also fax). Specializing
in advertising and toys.
Dunbarsgallery@comcast.net
www.dunbarsgallery.com

Ford, Frank W.
Shrewsbury, 508-842-6459. Specializing in American iridescent art glass,
ca 1900 – 1930.

Frei, Peter
PO Box 500, Brimfield, 01010;
413-245-4660. Specializing in sewing machines (pre-1875, non-electric
only), adding machines, typewriters,
and hand-powered vacuum cleaners;
SASE required with correspondence.

Hess, John A.
Fine Photographic Americana
PO Box 3062, Andover, 01810. Spe-
cializing in 19th-century photography.

Longo, Paul J.
Paul Longo Americana
Box 5510, Magnolia, 01930;
978-525-2290. Specializing in political
pins, ribbons, banners, autographs, old
stocks and bonds, baseball and sports
memorabilia of all types.

MacLean, Dale
183 Robert Rd., Dedham, 02026;

781-329-1303. Specializing in Dedham and Dorchester pottery. dedham-dorchester@comcast.net

Morin, Albert
668 Robbins Ave. #23, Dracut, 01826; 978-454-7907. Specializing in miscellaneous Akro Agate and Westite. akroal@comcast.net

Porter, Richard T., Curator
Porter Thermometer Museum
Box 944, Onset, 02558; 508-295-5504. Visits (always open) free, with 4,580 thermometers to see; Appraisals, repairs and traveling lecture (over 700 given, ages 8 – 98, all venues). Richard is also vice president of the Thermometer Collectors Club of America. thermometerman@aol.com

Wellman, BA
PO Box 673, Westminster, 01473-0673. Willing to assist in identification through e-mail free of charge. Specializing in **all** areas of American ceramics, dinnerware, figurines, and art pottery. BA@dishinitout.com

Williams, Linda
1 School St. #305, Chester, 01011. Specializing in glass & china, general line antiques; sito1845@hotmail.com

Michigan

Brown, Rick
Newspaper Collector's Society of
    America
Lansing, 517-887-1255. Specializing in newspapers. help@historybuff.com www.historybuff.com

Hogan & Woodworth
Walter P. Hogan and Wendy L.
    Woodworth
520 N. State, Ann Arbor, 48104; 313-930-1913. Specializing in Kellogg Studio. http://people.emich.edu/whogan/kellogg/index.html

Iannotti, Dan
212 W. Hickory Grove Rd., Bloomfield Hills, 48302-1127S. 248-335-5042. Specializing in selling/buying: Reynolds, Sandman, John Wright, Capron, BOK, and other banks; Member of the Mechanical Bank Collectors of America. modernbanks@sbcglobal.net

Krupka, Rod
2641 Echo Lane, Ortonville, 48462; 248-627-6351. Specializing in lightning rod balls. krupka@qix.net

Marsh, Linda K.
1229 Gould Rd., Lansing, 48917. Specializing in Degenhart glass.

Nedry, Boyd W.
728 Buth Dr., Comstock Park, 49321; 616-784-1513. Specializing in traps (including mice, rat, and fly traps) and trap-related items; Please send postage when requesting information.

Nickel, Mike
A Nickel's Worth
PO Box 456, Portland, 48875; 517-647-7646. Specializing in American Art Pottery: Roseville, Van Briggle, Weller, Rookwood, Pillin, Newcomb, Kay Finch, Stangl, and Pennsbury Birds. mandc@voyager.net

Oates, Joan
1107 Deerfield Lane, Marshall, 49068; 269-781-9791. Specializing in Phoenix Bird chinaware. joates120@broadstripe.net

Rairigh, Glen
Americana Auctions
12633 Sandborn, Sunfield, 48890. Specializing in Skookum dolls and antique auctions. www.AmericanAuctions.com

Ross, Michelle
PO Box 94, Berrien Center, 49102; 269-925-6382. Specializing in Van Briggle and American pottery. motherclay2@aol.com

Webster, Marty
6943 Suncrest Drive, Saline, 48176; 313-944-1188. Specializing in California porcelain and pottery, Orientalia.

Minnesota

Anderson, James
Box 120704, New Brighton, 55112; 651-484-3198. Specializing in old fishing lures and reels, also tackle catalogs, posters, calendars, Winchester items.

Dommel, Darlene
PO Box 22493, Minneapolis, 55422. Collector Books author of *Collector's Encyclopedia of Howard Pierce Porcelain, Collector's Encyclopedia of Dakota Potteries,* and *Collector's Encyclopedia of Rosemeade Pottery.* Specializing in Howard Pierce and Dakota potteries.

Harrigan, John
1900 Hennepin, Minneapolis, 55403; 612-991-1271 or (in winter) 561-732-0525. Specializing in Battersea (English enamel) boxes, Moorcroft, Royal Doulton character jugs, and Toby jugs.

Miller, Clark
4444 Garfield Ave., Minneapolis, 55419-1847; 612-827-6062. Specializing in Anton Lang pottery, American art pottery, Tibet postal history.

Putratz, Barb
Spring Lake Park, 763-784-0422. Specializing in Norman Rockwell figurines and plates.

Schoneck, Steve
HG Handicraft Guild, Minneapolis
PO Box 56, Newport, 55055; 651-459-2980. Specializing in American art pottery, Arts & Crafts, HG Handicraft Guild Minneapolis.

Missouri

Gillespie, Steve, Publisher
Goofus Glass Gazette
400 Martin Blvd, Village of the Oaks, 64118; 816-455-5558. Specializing in Goofus Glass, curator of 'Goofus Glass Museum,' had 4,000+ piece collection of goofus glass; Buy, sell and collect goofus for 30+ years; Expert contributor to forums on goofus glass; Contributor to website for goofus glass. stegil@sbcglobal.net

Heuring, Jerry
28450 US Highway 61, Scott City, 63780; 573-264-3947. Specializing in Keen Kutter.

Tarrant, Jenny
Holly Daze Antiques
4 Gardenview, St. Peters, 63376. Holiday for sale. Specializing in early holiday items, Halloween, Christmas, Easter, etc.; Always buying early holiday collectibles and German holiday candy containers. hollydaze@charter.net www.hollydaze@charter.net

Wendel, David
F.E.I., Inc.
PO Box 1187, Poplar Bluff, 63902-1187; 573-686-1926. Specializing in Fraternal Elks collectibles.

Williams, Don
PO Box 147, Kirksville 63501; 660-627-8009 (between 8 a.m. and 6 p.m. only). Specializing in art glass; SASE required with all correspondence.

Winslow, Ralph
PO Box 505, Carl Junction, 64834; 471-627-0258. Specializing in Dryden pottery. justsaya@sbcglobal.net

Nebraska

Johnson, Donald-Brian
3329 South 56th Street, #611; Omaha, NE 68106. Author of numerous Schiffer Publishing Ltd. books on collectibles, including: *Ceramic Arts Studio, The Legacy of Betty Harrington* (in association with Timothy J. Holthaus and James E. Petzold); and with co-

author Leslie Piña, *Higgins, Adventures in Glass; Higgins: Poetry in Glass; Moss Lamps: Lighting the '50s; Specs Appeal: Extravagant 1950s and 1960s Eyewear; Whiting & Davis Purses: The Perfect Mesh; Popular Purses: It's In the Bag!* and a four-volume series on the Chase Brass & Copper Co. Be sure to see Clubs and Newsletters for information on the CAS Collectors club. donaldbrian@webtv.net

New Hampshire

Bealo, Peter
82 Sweet Hill Rd., Plaistow, 03865; 603-882-8023 or (cell) 978-204-9849. Please include SASE with mailed inquiries. pbealo@comcast.net

Holt, Jane
Jane's Collectibles
PO Box 115, Derry, 03038. Specializing in Annalee Mobilitee Dolls.

Winston, Nancy
Willow Hollow Antiques
648 1st N.H. Turnpike, Northwood, 03261; 603-942-5739. Specializing in Shaker smalls, primitives, iron, copper, stoneware, and baskets.

New Jersey

Doorstop Collectors of America
Doorstopper Newsletter
Jeanie Bertoia
2413 Madison Ave., Vineland, 08630; 609-692-4092. Membership: $20 per year, includes two newsletters and convention. Send two-stamp SASE for sample.

George, Dr. Joan M.
ABC Collector's Circle newsletter
67 Stevens Ave., Old Bridge, 08857. Specializing in educational china (particularly ABC plates and mugs). drgeorge@nac.net

Harran, Jim and Susan
A Moment in Time
208 Hemlock Dr., Neptune, 07753. Specializing in English and Continental porcelains with emphasis on antique cups and saucers; Author of *Collectible Cups and Saucers, Identification and Values, Book I, II, III and IV; Dresden Porcelain Studios; Decorative Plates, Identification and Values;* and *Meissen Porcelain,* all published by Collector Books. www.tias.com/stores/amit

Litts, Elyce
Happy Memories Antiques & Collectibles
PO Box 394, Morris Plains, 07950; 201-707-4241. Specializing in general line with special focus on Geisha Girl Porcelain, vintage compacts and

Goebel figurines.
maildepothm@happy-memories.com
www.happy-memories.com

Meschi, Edward J.
129 Pinyard Rd., Monroeville, 08343; 856-358-7293. Specializing in Durand art glass, Icart etchings, Maxfield Parrish prints, Tiffany lamps, Rookwood pottery, occupational shaving mugs, American paintings, and other fine arts; Author of *Durand — The Man and His Glass,* (Antique Publications) available from author for $30 plus postage. ejmeschi@hotmail.com

Perrault, Suzanne
Perrault-Rago Gallery
333 N. Main St., Lambertville, 08530; 609-397-9374. Specializing in Arts and Crafts, art pottery, moderns, and tiles.

Perzel, Robert and Nancy
Popkorn Antiques
505 Route 579, Ringoes, 08551; 908-782-9631. Specializing in Stangl dinnerware, birds, and artware; American pottery and dinnerware.

Poster, Harry
Vintage TVs
Box 1883, S. Hackensack, 07606; 201-794-9606. Writes *Poster's Radio and Television Price Guide.* Specializes in vintage televisions, vintage radios, stereo cameras; Catalog available online. www.harryposter.com

Rago, David
333 N. Main St., Lambertville, 08530; 609-397-6780. Specializing in Arts & Crafts, art pottery.
ragoarts@ragoarts.com
www.ragoarts.com

Rosen, Barbara
6 Shoshone Trail, Wayne, 07470. Specializing in figural bottle openers and antique dollhouses.

Visakay, Stephen
Vintage Cocktail Shakers (by appt.)
Author of book and specializing in vintage cocktail shakers and bar ware.
visakay@optonline.net;

New Mexico

Hardisty, Don
Las Cruces. For information and questions: 505-522-3721 or (cell) 505-649-4191. Specializing in Bossons and Hummels. Don's Collectibles carries a full line of Bossons and Hummel figurines of all marks.
don@donsbossons.com
www.donsbossons.com

Manns, William
PO Box 6459, Santa Fe, 87502;

505-995-0102. Co-author of *Painted Ponies,* hardbound (226 pages), available from author for $47 ppd.. Specializing in carousel art and cowboy. antiques zon@nets.com

Nelson, Scott H.
PO Box 6081, Santa Fe, 87502-6081. Specializing in ethnographic art.

New York

Austin, Bruce A.
1 Hardwood Hill Rd., Pittsford, 14534; 585-387-9820 (evenings); 585-475-2879 (week days). Specializing in clocks and Arts & Crafts furnishings and accessories including metalware, pottery, and lighting. baagll@rit.edu.

Badders, Veldon
692 Martin Rd., Hamlin, 14464; 716-964-3360. Author (Collector Books) of *Collector's Guide to Inkwells, Identification & Values.* Specializing in inkwells.

Bozarth, Michael and Valarie
Beaux Arts USA
Williamsville. Specializing in Cosmos, Audubon prints, and Currier & Ives prints. info@BeauxArtsUSA.com
www.BeauxArtsUSA.com

Doyle, Robert A., CAI, ISA, CAGA, CES
Absolute Auction & Realty, Inc./ Absolute Auction Center
PO Box 1739, Pleasant Valley, 12569; 845-635-3169. Antique and estate auctions twice a month at Absolute Auction Center; Free calendar of auctions available. Specializing in specialty collections. absoluteauction@hvc.rr.com
www.AbsoluteAuctionRealty.com

Gerson, Roselyn
PO Box 40, Lynbrook, 11563; 516-593-8746. Author/collector specializing in unusual, gadgetry, figural compacts, vanity bags and purses, solid perfumes and lipsticks.

Handelsman, Burton
18 Hotel Dr., White Plains, 10605; 914-428-4480 (home) and 914-761-8880 (office). Specializing in occupational shaving mugs, accessories.

Kaonis, Keith; Manager
Antique Doll Collector Magazine
6 Woodside Ave., Suite 300, Northport, 11768 or PO Box 344, Center Port, NY 11721-0344; 631-261-4100 or 631-361-0982 (evenings). Specializing in Schoenhut toys.

Laun, H. Thomas and Patricia
Little Century

215 Paul Ave., Syracuse, 13206; December through March: 315-437-4156; April through December residence: 35109 Country Rte. 7, Cape Vincent, 13618; 315-654-3244. Specializing in firefighting collectibles; **All appraisals are free,** but we will respond only to those who are considerate enough to include a self-addressed stamped envelope (photo is requested for accuracy); We will return phone calls as soon as possible.

Malitz, Lucille
Lucid Antiques
Box KH, Scarsdale, 10583; 914-636-7825. Specializing in lithophanes, kaleidoscopes, stereoscopes, medical and dental antiques.

Michel, John and Barbara
Iron Star Antiques
200 E. 78th St., 18E, New York City, 10021; 212-861-6094. Specializing in yellow ware, cast iron, tramp art, shooting gallery targets and blue feather-edge. jlm58@columbia.edu

Rifken, Blume J.
Author of *Silhouettes in America — 1790 – 1840 — A Collector's Guide.* Specializing in American antique silhouettes from 1790 to 1840.

Russ, William A.
Russ Trading Post
23 William St., Addison 14801-1326. Animal lure manufacture; hunting and trapping supply; catalog $1.

Safir, Charlotte F.
1349 Lexington Ave., 9-B, New York City, 10128-1513; 212-534-7933. Specializing in cookbooks, children's books (out-of-print only).

Schleifman, Roselle
Ed's Collectibles/The Rage
16 Vincent Road, Spring Valley, 10977; 845-356-2121. Specializing in Duncan & Miller, Elegant Glass, Depression Glass.

Sherman, David
President of Phoenix & Consolidated Club
New York. Specializing in Phoenix and Consolidated glass.

Tuggle, Robert
105 W. St., New York City, 10023; 212-595-0514. Specializing in John Bennett, Anglo-Japanese china.

Van Patten, Joan F.
Box 102, Rexford, 12148. Author (Collector Books) of books on Nippon and Noritake.

Weitman, Stan and Arlene
PO Box 1186; 101 Cypress St., N.

Massapequa, 11758. Author of book on crackle glass (Collector Books). scrackled@earthlink.net
www.crackleglass.com

North Carolina

Hussey, Billy Ray
Southern Folk Pottery Collector's Society
220 Washington Street, Bennett, 27208; 336-581-4246. Specializing in historical research and documentation, education and promotion of the traditional folk potter (past and present) to a modern collecting audience. sfpcs@rtmc.net

Kirtley, Charles E.
PO Box 2273, Elizabeth City, 27096; 919-335-1262. Specializing in monthly auctions and bid sales dealing with World's Fair, Civil War, political, advertising, and other American collectibles.

Newbound, Betty
2206 Nob Hill Dr., Sanford, 27330. Author (Collector Books) on Blue Ridge dinnerware, milk glass, wall pockets, figural planters and vases. Specializing in collectible china and glass.

Savage, Jeff
Drexel Grapevine Antiques, 2784 US Highway 70 East, Valdese 28690; 828-437-5938. Specializing in pottery, china, antique fishing tackle, and much more. info@drexelantiques.com
www.drexelantiques.com

Sayers, R.J.
Southeastern Antiques & Appraisals
PO Box 629, Brevard, 28712. Specializing in Boy Scout collectibles, collectibles, Pisgah Forest pottery, primitive American furniture. rjsayers@citcom.net

North Dakota

Farnsworth, Bryce
1334 14½ St. South, Fargo, 58103; 701-237-3597. Specializing in Rosemeade pottery; If writing for information, please send a picture if possible, also phone number and best time to call.

Ohio

Batory, Mr. Dana Martin
402 E. Bucyrus St., Crestline, 44827. Specializing in antique woodworking machinery, old and new woodworking machinery catalogs; Author of *Vintage Woodworking Machinery, an Illustrated Guide to Four Manufacturers* and *Vintage Woodworking Machinery, an Illustrated Guide to Four More Manufactur-*

ers, currently available from Astragal Press, 8075 215th St. W, Lakeville, MN, 55044 for $25.95 and $33 ppd. or signed copies available from author for $30 and $35; In order to prepare a difinitive history on American manufacturers of woodworking machinery, Dana is interested in acquiring (by loan, gift, or photocopy) catalogs, manuals photos, personal reminiscences, etc., pertaining to woodworking machinery and/or their manufacturers. Also available for $7.50 money order: 70+ page list of catalogs, owner's manuals, parts lists, company publications, etc. (updated quarterly). No phone calls please. A third volume devoted to Beach Mfg., C.B. Rogers & Co., DeWalt, Syncro, and H.B. Smith Co. is a work in progress.

Benjamin, Scott
PO Box 556, LaGrange, 44050-0556; 440-355-6608. Specializing in gas globes; Co-author of *Gas Pump Globes* and several other related books, listing nearly 4,000 gas globes with over 2,000 photos, prices, rarity guide, histories, and reproduction information (currently available from author); Also available: *Petroleum Collectibles Monthly* Magazine.
www.oilcollectibles.com or www.gasglobes.com

China Specialties, Inc.
Box 471, Valley City, 44280. Specializing in high-quality reproductions of Homer Laughlin and Hall china, including Autumn Leaf.

Distel, Ginny
Distel's Antiques
4041 S.C.R. 22, Tiffin, 44883; 419-447-5832. Specializing in Tiffin glass.

Ebner, Rita and John
Columbus. Specializing in door knockers, cast-iron bottle openers, Griswold.

Graff, Shirley
4515 Grafton Rd., Brunswick, 44212. Specializing in Pennsbury pottery.

Guenin, Tom
Box 454, Chardon, 44024. Specializing in antique telephones and antique telephone restoration.

Hall, Kathy
Monclova, 43542. Specializing in Labino art glass. kewpieluvin@msn.com

Hamlin, Jack and Treva Jo
145 Township Rd. 1088, Proctorville, 45669; 740-886-7644. Specializing in Currier and Ives by Royal China Co. and Homer Laughlin China (especially Virginia Rose, Priscilla, and Dogwood dinnerware); Call — we carry a large inventory. jacktrevajo@zoominternet.net

Hothem, Sue McClurg
PO Box 458, Lancaster, 43130-0458. Specialing in pencil boxes.

Kao, Fern Larking
PO Box 312, Bowling Green, 43402; 419-352-5928. Specializing in jewelry, sewing implements, ladies' accessories.

Kier, Anne and Don
202 Marengo St., Toledo, 43614-4213; 419-385-8211. Specializing in glass, china, autographs, Brownies, Royal Bayreuth, 19th-century antiques, general line. d.a.k.@worldnet.att.net

Kline, Mr. and Mrs. Jerry and Gerry
Two of the founding members of North American Torquay Society and members of Torquay Pottery Collectors' Society
604 Orchard View Dr., Maumee, 43537; 419-893-1226. Specializing in collecting Torquay pottery; please send SASE for info.

Mangus, Bev and Jim
5147 Broadway NE, Louisville, 44641. Author (Collector Books) of *Shawnee Pottery, an Identification & Value Guide*. Specializing in Shawnee pottery.

Mathes, Richard
PO Box 1408, Springfield, 45501-1408; 513-324-6917. Specializing in buttonhooks.

Moore, Carolyn
Carolyn Moore Antiques
445 N. Prospect, Bowling Green, 43402-2002. Specializing in primitives, yellow ware, graniteware, collecting stoneware.

Murphy, James L.
1023 Neil Ave., Columbus, 43201; 614-297-0746. Specializing in American Radford, Vance Avon. jlmurphy@columbus.rr.com

Otto, Susan
12204 Fox Run Trail, Chesterland, 44026; 440-729-2686. Specializing in nutcrackers, not toy soldier (Steinbach) type. nutsue@roadrunner.com

Pierce, David
PO Box 205, Mt. Vernon, 43022. Specializing in Glidden pottery; Fee for appraisals.

Roberts, Brenda
Specializing in Hull pottery and general line. Author of *Collector's Encyclopedia of Hull Pottery, Roberts' Ultimate Encyclopedia of Hull Pottery, The Companion Guide to Roberts' Ultimate Encyclopedia of Hull Pottery*, and the newly released *The Collector's Ultimate Encyclopedia of Hull Pottery*, all with accompanying price guides.

Schumaker, Debbie Rees
Zanesville. Specializing in Watt, Roseville juvenile and other Roseville pottery, Zanesville area pottery, cookie jars, and Steiff.

Shetlar, David
35 Vandeman Ave., Delaware, 43015; 740-369-1645. Specializing in stretch glass and co-author of *American Iridescent Stretch Glass, Identification & Value Guide* (Collector Books).
stretchglasssociety@columbus.rr.com

Sublette, Tim
Partner, Seeker Antiques
PO Box 10083, Columbus, 43201-0583; 614-291-2203. Specializing in reliefmolded jugs.
seekersantiques@hotmail.com
www.seekersantiques.com

Trainer, Veronica
Bayhouse
Box 40443, Cleveland, 44140; 440-871-8584. Specializing in beaded and enameled mesh purses.

Whitmyer, Margaret and Kenn
Box 30806, Gahanna, 43230. Author (Collector Books) on children's dishes. Specializing in Depression-era collectibles.

Young, Mary
Box 9244, Wright Brothers Branch, Dayton, 45409; 937-298-4838. Specializing in paper dolls; Author of several books.

Oklahoma

Boone, Phyllis Bess
14535 E. 13th St., Tulsa, 74108; 918-437-7776. Author of *Frankoma Treasures*, and *Frankoma and Other Oklahoma Potteries*. Specializing in Frankoma and Oklahoma pottery.

Feldman, Arthur M; Executive Director
The Sherwin Miller Museum of Jewish Art
2021 East 71st St., Tulsa, 74136-5408; 918-492-1818. Specializing in Judaica, fine art, and antiques.
director@jewishmuseum.net
www.jewishmuseum.net

Moore, Art and Shirley
4423 E. 31st St., Tulsa, 74135; 918-747-4164 or 918-744-8020. Specializing in Lu Ray Pastels, Depression glass, Franciscan.

Scott, Roger R.
4250 S. Oswego, Tulsa, 74135; 918-742-8710. Specializing in Victor and RCA Victor trademark items along with Nipper.
Roger13@mindspring.com

Whysel, Steven
24240 S. Utica, Ave, Tulsa, 74114; 9;18-295-8666. Specializing in Art Nouveau, 19th- and 20th-century art and estate sales.

Oregon

Brown, Marcia; author, appraiser, and lecturer
Sparkles
PO Box 2314, White City, 97503; 541-826-3039. Author of *Unsigned Beauties of Costume Jewelry, Signed Beauties of Costume Jewelry, Signed Beauties of Costume Jewelry, Volume II, Coro Jewelry, A Collector's Guide*, and *Rhinestone Jewelry — Figurals, Animals, and Whimsicals* (all Collector Books), Co-author and host of 7 volumes: *Hidden Treasures* videos. Specializing in rhinestone jewelry; Please include SASE if requesting information.

Coe, Debbie and Randy
Coe's Mercantile
PO Box 173, Hillsboro, 97123. Specializing in Elegant and Depression glass, Fenton glass, Liberty Blue, art pottery.

Davis, Patricia Morrison
Antique and personal property appraisals
4326 N.W. Tam-O-Shanter Way, Portland, 97229-8738; 503-645-3084.
pam100davis@comcast.net

Foland, Doug
PO Box 66854, Portland, 97290; 503-772-0471. Author of *The Florence Collectibles, an Era of Elegance*, available at your local bookstore or from Schiffer publishers.

Main Antique Mall
30 N. Riverside, Medford, 97501. Quality products and services for the serious collector, dealer, or those just browsing.
mainantiquemall.com

Medford Antique Mall
Jim & Eileen Pearson, Owners
1 West 6th St., Medford 97501; 541-773-4983. medama11@mind.net

Miller, Don and Robbie
541-535-1231. Specializing in milk bottles, TV Siamese cat lamps, seltzer bottles, red cocktail shakers.

Ringering, David and Angi
Kay Ring Antiques
1395 59th Ave., S.E., Salem, 97301; 503-364-0464 or (cell) 503-930-2247. Specializing in Rowland & Marsellus and other souvenir/historical china dating from the 1890s to the 1930s. Feel free to contact David if you have

questions about Rowland and Marsellus or other souvenir china. AR1480@aol.com

Pennsylvania

Alekna, Stan and Sally
732 Aspen Lane, Lebanon, 17042-9073; 717-228-2361. Specializing in American Dimestore Toy Soldiers. Send SASE for 3 to 4 mail-order lists per year; Always buying 1 or 100 top-quality figures. salekna@bellatlantic.net

Barrett, Noel
Noel Barrett Antiques & Auctions Ltd. PO Box 300, Carversville, 18913; 215-297-5109. Specializing in toys; Appraiser on PBS Antiques Roadshow; Active in toy-related auctions. toys@noelbarrett.com www.noelbarrett.com

Bodine, Clarence H., Jr., Proprietor
East/West Gallery
41B West Ferry St., New Hope, 18938. Specializing in antique Japanese woodblock prints, netsuke, inro, porcelains.

Cerebro
PO Box 327, E. Prospect, 17317-0327; 717-252-2400 or 800-69-LABEL. Specializing in antique advertising labels, especially cigar box labels, cigar bands, food labels, firecracker labels. Cerebro@Cerebro.com www.cerebro.com

Christie, Dr. Victor J.W.; Author/Appraiser/Broker
1050 West Main St., Ephrata, 17522; 717-738-4032. The family-designated biographer of Bessie Pease Gutmann. Specializing in Bessie Pease Gutmann and other Gutmann & Gutmann artists and author of 5 books on these artists, the latest in 2001: *The Gutmann & Gutmann Artists: A Published Works Catalog, Fourth Edition*; a signed copy is available from the author for $20 at the above address. Dr. Christie is an active member of the New England Appraisers Association, The Ephemera Society of America, and the American Revenue Association. thecheshirecat@dejazzd.com

Gottuso, Bob
Bojo
PO Box 1403, Cranberry Township, 16066-0403; phone/fax: 724-776-0621. Specializing in Beatles, Elvis, KISS, Monkees, licensed Rock 'n Roll memorabilia. www.bojoonline.com

Hain, Henry F., III
Antiques & Collectibles
2623 N. Second St., Harrisburg, 17110; 717-238-0534. Lists available of items for sale.

Hinton, Michael C.
246 W. Ashland St., Doylestown, 18901; 215-345-0892. Owns/operates Bucks County Art & Antiques Company and Chem-Clean Furniture Restoration Company. Specializing in quality restorations of art and antiques from colonial to contemporary; Also owns Trading Post Antiques, 532 Durham Rd., Wrightstown, PA, 18940-9615, a 60-dealer antiques co-op with 15,000 square feet — something for everyone in antiques and collectibles. iscsusn@comcast.net

Holland, William
1554 Paoli Pike, West Chester, 19380-6123; 610-344-9848. Specializing in Louis Icart etchings and oils; Tiffany studios lamps, glass, and desk accessories; Maxfield Parrish; Art Nouveau and Art Deco items. Author of *Louis Icart: The Complete Etchings, The Collectible Maxfield Parrish*, and *Louis Icart Erotica*. bill@hollandarts.com

Irons, Dave
Dave Irons Antiques
223 Covered Bridge Rd., Northampton, 18067; 610-262-9335. Author of *Irons by Irons, More Irons by Irons*, and *Even More Irons by Irons*, available from author (each with pictures of over 1,600 irons, current information and price ranges, collecting hints, news of trends, and information for proper care of irons). Specializing in pressing irons, country furniture, primitives, quilts, accessories. www.ironsantiques.com

Ivankovich, Michael
Michael Ivankovich Auctions, Inc.
PO Box 1536, Doylestown, 18901; 215-345-6094. Specializing in 20th-century hand-colored photography and prints; Author of *The Collector's Value Guide to Popular Early 20th Century American Prints 1998* $19.95; *The Collector's Guide to Wallace Nutting Pictures*, $18.95; *The Alphabetical and Numerical Index to Wallace Nutting Pictures*, $14.95; and *The Collectors Guide to Wallace Nutting Furniture*, $19.95. Also available: *Wallace Nutting General Catalog, Supreme Edition* (reprint), $13.95; *Wallace Nutting: A Great American Idea* (reprint), $13.95; and *Wallace Nutting's Windsor's: Correct Windsor Furniture* (reprint), $13.95 (all available at the above address). Shipping is $4.25 for the first item ordered and $1.50 for each additional item. ivankovich@wnutting.com www.wnutting.com

Katz, Jerome R.
Downingtown, 19935; 610-269-7938. Specializing in technological artifacts.

Knauer, Judy A.
National Toothpick Holder Collectors Society

1224 Spring Valley Lane, West Chester, 19380-5112; 610-431-4377. Specializing in toothpick holders and Victorian glass; winkj@comcast.net

Kreider, Katherine
PO Box 7957, Lancaster, 17604-7957; 717-892-3001. Author of *Valentines With Values*, available for $24.70 ppd. ($26.17 PA residents); *One Hundred Years of Valentines*, available for $29.70 ppd. ($31.20 PA residents); and *Valentines for the Eclectic Collector* ($29.70 ppd., $31.20 PA residents); Appraisal fee schedule upon request. Stop by Booth #315 in Stroudt's Black Angus Mall in Adamstown, PA, Sundays only. katherinekreider@valentinesdirect.com www.valentinesdirect.com

Lowe, James Lewis
Kate Greenaway Society
PO Box 8, Norwood, 19074. Specializing in Kate Greenaway. PostcardClassics@juno.com

McManus, Joe
PO Box 153, Connellsville, 15425. Editor of *Purinton News & Views*, a newsletter for Purinton pottery enthusiasts; Subscription: $16 per year; Sample copies available with SASE. Specializing in Blair Ceramics and Purinton Pottery; jmcmanus@hhs.net

Reimert, Leon
121 Highland Dr., Coatesville, 19320; 610-383-9880. Specializing in Boehm porcelain.

Rosso, Philip J. and Philip Jr.
Wholesale Glass Dealers
1815 Trimble Ave., Port Vue, 15133. Specializing in Westmoreland glass.

Scola, Anthony
215-284-8158. Specializing in Planters Peanuts; scolaville@aol.com

Weiser, Pastor Frederick S.
55 Kohler School Rd., New Oxford, 17350-9210; 717-624-4106. Specializing in frakturs and other Pennsylvania German documents; SASE required when requesting information; No telephone appraisals. Must see original or clear colored photocopy.

Rhode Island

Gacher, John; and Santi, Federico
The Drawing Room of Newport
152 Spring St., Newport, 02840; 401-841-5060. Specializing in Zsolnay, Fischer, Amphora, and Austro-Hungarian art pottery. www.drawrm.com

The Occupied Japan Club
c/o Florence Archambault
29 Freeborn St., Newport, 02840-1821.

Publishes bimonthly newsletter, *The Upside Down World of an O.J. Collector*; SASE required when requesting information. florence@aiconnect.com

South Carolina

Anderson, Suzy McLennan
246 E., Washington St., Walterboro, 29488; 843-549-1300. Specializing in American furniture and decorative accessories; Please include photo and SASE when requesting information; appraisals and identification are impossible to do over the phone. andersonauctions@aol.com

Dunay, Jeanne
Bellflower Antiques
Camden. Specializing in historic and Romantic Staffordshire, 1790 – 1850.

Greguire, Helen
Helen's Antiques
79 Lake Lyman Hgts., Lyman, 29365; 864-848-0408. Specializing in graniteware (any color), carnival glass lamps and shades, carnival glass lighting of all kinds; Author (Collector Books) of *The Collector's Encyclopedia of Graniteware, Colors, Shapes & Values, Book 1* (out of print); Second book on graniteware now available (updated 2003, $33.70 ppd.); Also available is *Carnival in Lights*, featuring carnival glass, lamps, shades, etc. ($13.45 ppd.); and *Collector's Guide to Toasters and Accessories, Identification & Values* ($21.95 ppd.); Available from author; Please include SASE when requesting information; Looking for people interested in collecting toasters.

Guthrie, John
1524 Plover Ave., Mount Pleasant, 29464; 843-884-1873. Specializing in Santa Barbara Ceramic Design.

Roerig, Fred and Joyce
1501 Maple Ridge Rd., Walterboro, 29488; 843-538-2487. Specializing in cookie jars; Authors of *Collector's Encyclopedia of Cookie Jars, An Illustrated Value Guide* (three in the series).

Vogel, Janice and Richard
110 Sentry Lane, Anderson, 29621. Authors of *Victorian Trinket Boxes* and *Conta and Boehme Porcelain*. Specializing in Conta and Boehme German porcelain. vogels@contaandboehme.com www.ContaAndBoehme.com

Tennessee

Chase, Mick and Lorna
Dishes Old and New
380 Hawkins Crawford Rd., Cookeville, 38501; 931-372-8333. Specializ-

ing in Fiesta, Harlequin, Riviera, Franciscan, Metlox, Lu Ray, Bauer, Vernon, other American dinnerware.

Fields, Linda
230 Beech Lane, Buchanan, 38222; 731-644-2244 after 6:00 p.m. Specializing in pie birds.
Fpiebird@compu.net

Grist, Everett
PO Box 91375, Chattanooga, 37412-3955; 423-510-8052. Specializing in covered animal dishes and marbles.

Hudson, Murray
Murray Hudson Antiquarian Books,
    Maps, Prints & Globes
109 S. Church St., Box 163, Halls, 38040; 731-836-9057 or 800-748-9946. Specializing in antique maps, globes, and books with maps, atlases, explorations, travel guides, geographies, surveys, and historical prints.
mapman@ecsis.net
www.murrayhudson.com

Kline, Jerry
4546 Winslow, Dr., Strawberry Plains, 37871; 865-932-0182. Specializing in Florence Ceramics of California, Rookwood pottery, English china, art glass, period furniture (small), tea caddies, brass and copper (early), and other quality items.
artpotterynants@bellsouth.net

Weddington, David
Vintage Predicta Service
2702 Albany Ct., Murfreesboro, 37129; 615-890-7498. Specializing in vintage Philco Predicta TVs.
service@50spredicta.com
www.50spredicta.com

Texas

Dockery, Rod
4600 Kemble St., Ft. Worth, 76103; 817-536-2168. Specializing in milk glass; SASE required with correspondence.

Docks, L.R. 'Les'
Shellac Shack; Discollector
PO Box 780218, San Antonio, 78278-0218. Author of American Premium Record Guide. Specializing in vintage records. docks@texas.net
www.docks.home.texas.net

Frese, Leo and Wendy
Three Rivers Collectibles
Box 551542, Dallas, 75355; 214-341-5165. Specializing in Rum-Rill, Red Wing pottery and stoneware.

Gaston, Mary Frank
PO Box 342

Bryan, 77802. Author (Collector Books) on china and metals.

Gibbs, Carl, Jr.
1716 Westheimer Rd., Houston, 77098. Author of Collector's Encyclopedia of Metlox Potteries, Second Edition, autographed copies available from author for $32.95 ppd.. Specializing in American ceramic dinnerware.

Groves, Bonnie
402 North Ave. A, Elgin, 78621. Specializing in boudoir dolls.
www.bonniescatsmeow.com

Koehn, Joanne M.
Temple's Antiques
7209 Seneca Falls Loop, Austin, 78739; 512-288-6086. Specializing in Victorian glass and china.

Nelson, C.L.
4020 N. MacArthur Blvd., Suite 122-109, Irving, 75038. Specializing in English pottery and porcelain, among others: Gaudy Welsh, ABC plates, relief-molded jugs, Staffordshire transfer ware.

Norris, Kenn
Schoolmaster Auctions and Real Estate
PO Box 4830, 513 N. 2nd St., Sanderson, 79848-4830; 915-345-2640. Specializing in school-related items, barbed wire, related literature, and L'il Abner (antique shop in downtown Sanderson).

Pogue, Larry G.
L&J Antiques & Collectibles
8142 Ivan Court, Terrell, 75161-6921; 972-524-8716. Specializing in string holders and head vases.
www.landjantiques.com

Rosen, Kenna
9138 Loma Vista, Dallas, 75243; 972-503-1436. Specializing in Bluebird china. ke-rosen@swbell.net

Tucker, Richard and Valerie
Argyle Antiques
PO Box 262, Argyle, 76226; 940-464-3752. Specializing in windmill weights, shooting gallery targets, figural lawn sprinklers, cast-iron advertising paperweights and other unusual figural cast iron.
lead1234@gte.net or rtucker@jw.com

Turner, Danny and Gretchen
Running Rabbit Video Auctions
PO Box 701, Waverly, 37185; 615-296-3600. Specializing in marbles.

Waddell, John
2903 Stan Terrace, Mineral Wells, 76067. Specializing in buggy steps.

Woodard, Dannie; Publisher
The Aluminist

PO Box 1346, Weatherford, 76086; 817-594-4680. Specializing in aluminum items, books and newsletters about aluminum.

Utah

Anderson, Cheryl
America West Archives
PO Box 100, Cedar City, 84721; 435-586-9497. Specializing in old stock certificates and bonds, western documents and books, financial ephemera, autographs, maps, photos; Author of Owning Western History, with 75+ photos of old documents and recommended reference.
info@americawestarchives.com

Anderson, Tim
Box 461, Provo, 84603. Specializing in autographs; Buys single items or collections — historical, movie stars, US Presidents, sports figures, and pre-1860 correspondence. Autograph questions? Please include photocopies of your autographs if possible and enclose a SASE for guaranteed reply.
www.autographsofamerica.com

Spencer, Rick
Salt Lake City. Specializing in American silverplate and sterling flatware, hollow ware, Shawnee, Van Tellingen, salt and pepper shakers. Appraisals available at reasonable cost.
repousse@hotmail.com

Whysel, Steve
24240 S. Utica Ave.
Tulsa, OK 74114; 918-295-8666
Specializing in Art Nouveau, 19th- and 20th-century art and estate sales.

Vermont

Barry, Kit
74 Cotton Mill Hill #A252, Brattleboro, 05301; 802-254-3634. Author of Reflections 1 and Reflections 2, reference books on ephemera. Specializing in advertising trade cards and ephemera in general.
kbarry@surfglobal.net

Virginia

Bradfield, Jeff
Jeff's Antiques
90 Main St., Dayton, 22821; 540-879-9961. Also located at Rolling Hills Antique Mall, Interstate 81, Exit 247B, Harrisonburg, VA. Specializing in candy containers, toys, postcards, sugar shakers, lamps, furniture, pottery, and advertising items.

Branchcomb, Shane
12031 George Farm Dr., Lovettesville, 20180. Specializing in antique coffee mills, send SASE for reply.
acmeman@erols.com

Bull, Donald A.
PO Box 596, Wirtz, 24184; 540-721-1128. Author of The Ultimate Corkscrew Book, Boxes Full of Corkscrews, Bull's Pocket Guide to Corkscrews, Just for Openers (with John Stanley); Boxes of Corkscrews, Anri Woodcarvings (with Philly Rains); Corkscrew Stories, Vols. 1 and 2; Corkscrew Patents of Japan; Cork Ejectors; and Soda Advertising Openers. Specializing in corkscrews.
corkscrew@bullworks.net
www.corkscrewmuseum.com

Carwile, Mike
180 Cheyenne Dr., Lynchburg, VA 24502; 804-237-4247. Author (Collector Books) on carnival glass.
mcarwile@jeatbroadband.com

Flanigan, Vicki
Flanigan's Antiques
PO Box 1662, Winchester, 22604. Member: Steiff Club, National Antique Doll Dealers Assoc. Specializing in antique dolls, hand fans, and teddy bears; SASE required with correspondence; Fee for appraisals.

Haigh, Richard
PO Box 29562, Richmond 23242; 804-741-5770. Specializing in Locke Art, Steuben, Loetz, Fry, Italian. SASE required for reply.

MacAllister, Dale
PO Box 46, Singers Glen, 22850. Specializing in sugar shakers and syrups.

Monsen, Randall; and Baer, Rod
Monsen & Baer
Box 529, Vienna, 22183; 703-938-2129. Specializing in perfume bottles, Roseville pottery, Art Deco.

Washington

Frost, Donald M.
Country Estate Antiques (appt. only)
14800 N.E. 8th St., Vancouver, 98684; 360-604-8434. Specializing in art glass and earlier 20th-century American glass.

Haase, Don (Mr. Spode)
The Spode Shop at Star Center Mall
225 92nd PL SE, Everett, 98208. Specializing in Spode-Copeland China.
mrspode@aol.com
www.mrspode.com

Jackson, Denis C., Editor
The Illustrator Collector's News
PO Box 1958, Sequim, 98382;
360-452-3810. Copy of recent sample:
$3. Specializing in old magazines & illustrations such as: Rose O'Neill, Maxfield Parrish, pinups, Marilyn Monroe, Norman Rockwell, etc.
ticn@olypen.com

Kelly, Jack
20909 NE 164th Circle, Brush Prairie, 98606; 360-882-8023. Please include SASE with mailed inquiries.
binocs@msn.com

Payne, Sharon A.
Antiquities & Art
Specializing in Cordey.
hotel_california94546@yahoo.com

Peterson, Gerald and Sharon
Sentimental Journeys
315 Deer Park Dr., Aberdeen, 98520; 360-532-4724. Specializing in Lotton glass, Flow Blue, Nippon, carnival glass. journeys@techline.com

Weldin, Bob
Miner's Quest
W. 3015 Weile, Spokane, WA 99208; 509-327-2897. Specializing in mining antiques and collectibles (mail-order business).

Whitaker, Jim and Kaye
Eclectic Antiques
PO Box 475 Dept. S, Lynnwood,

98046. Specializing in Josef Originals and motion lamps; SASE required.
www.eclecticantiques.com

Willis, Ron L.
PO Box 370, Ilwaco, 98624-0370. Specializing in military collectibles.

Zeder, Audrey
1320 S.W. 10th Street #S, North Bend, 98045 (appointment only). Specializing in British Royalty Commemorative souvenirs (mail-order catalog available); Author (Wallace Homestead) of *British Royalty Commemoratives*.

West Virginia

Fostoria Glass Society of America, Inc.
Box 826, Moundsville, 26041. Specializing in Fostoria glass.

Hardy, Roger and Claudia
West End Antiques
10 Bailey St., Clarksburg, 26301; 304-624-7600 (days) or 304-624-4523 (evenings). Authors of *The Complete Line of the Akro Agate Co.* Specializing in Akro Agate.

Wisconsin

Skrobis, Mark J.
Franklin, 53132. Specializing in Currier and Ives dinnerware.

Thomas, Darrell
Sweets & Antiques (mail order)
PO Box 418, New London, 54961. Specializing in art pottery, ceramics, Deco era, Goldscheider, Keramos, and eBay auctions.
wwodenclockworks@msn.com

Thorpe, Donna and John
204 North St., Sun Prairie, 53590; 608-837-7674. Specializing in Chase Brass and Copper Co.

Contributors by Internet Address or eBay User Name

www.dewittco.com
Vintage fabric, feed sacks, sewing patterns and transfers, ephemera and vintage paper of all kinds.

www.gasolinealleyantiques.com
Model kits, scale diecast cars, antique and collectible toys, sports memorabilia, yo-yos, comic character merchandise, boomerbalia.

www.lifeofrileycollectiques.com
American Art Pottery: Weller, Roseville, California, Stangl, Nicodemus, Rookwood, Sascha Brastoff, McCoy, Gort, Villeroy & Boch, and others.

www.retro-redheads.com
Vintage and retro housewares: dinnerware; cocktail and beverage; holiday collectibles; kitchen towels, tablecloths, containers and miscellaneous items; aprons; and souvenir linens.

www.SweetlandForemost.com

www.timewasantiques.net
Shelly china, Cottage Ware, Wedgwood and Adams Jasperware, silver figural knife rests, sugar tongs, napkin rings, teacups, biscuit jars, transferware, Torquay Mottoware.

Randy Best (user name Antiquesrbest)

David Elyea (user name neatstuffdave)

Lori Kalal (user name: dlkunited), poodlegirl@hotmail.com

Christine Padialla (user name frill_frippery_treasures)

Jerry Poarch (user name jerry9645)

Peter L. Smith (user name quarryman.2), quarryman2@ukonline.co.uk

Sandy Truax (user name fastgril)

Clubs, Newsletters, and Catalogs

ABC Collectors' Circle (16-page newsletter, published 3 times a year)
Dr. Joan M. George
67 Stevens Ave., Old Bridge, NJ 08857; fax 732-679-6102. Specializing in ABC plates and mugs.
drjgeorge@nac.net

Abingdon Pottery Collectors Club
To become a member or for further information, contact Nancy Legate at mamaleg@abingdon.net or call 309-462-2547. Dues $8 for single, $10 per couple. Specializing in collecting and preservation of Abingdon pottery.

Akro Agate Collectors Club and *Clarksburg Crow* quarterly newsletter
Claudia and Roger Hardy
10 Bailey St., Clarksburg, WV 26301-2524; 304-624-4523 (evenings) or West End Antiques, 917 W. Pike St., Clarksburg, WV 26301; 304-624-7600 (Tuesday through Saturday). Annual membership fee: $25

The Akro Arsenal, quarterly catalog
Larry D. Wells
5411 Joyce Ave., Ft. Wayne, IN 46818; 219-489-5842

The Aluminist
Dannie Woodard, Publisher
PO Box 1346, Weatherford, TX 76086. Subscription: $20 (includes membership).

America West Archives
Anderson, Cheryl
PO Box 100, Cedar City, UT 84721; 435-586-9497. Illustrated online catalogs; Has both fixed-price and auction sections offering early western documents, letters, stock certificates, autographs, and other important ephemera.
info@americawestarchives.com

American Antique Deck Collectors
52 Plus Joker Club
Clear the Decks, quarterly publication
Clarence Peterson, Membership
12290 W. 18th Drive, Lakewood, CO, 80215. Membership: $20 (US and Canada), $30 (foreign). Specializing in antique playing cards.
denverpete@comcast.net
www.52plusjoker.org

American Cut Glass Association
Kathy Emmerson, Executive Secretary
PO Box 482, Ramona, CA 92065-0482; 760-789-2715. Membership dues (includes subscription to newsletter, *The Hobstar*) $45 (USA bulk mail) or $55 (first class and international).
acgakathy@aol.com

American Hatpin Society
Jodi Lenocker, President
Virginia Woodbury Past President
20 Montecillo Dr., Rolling Hills Estates, CA 90274; 310-326-2196. Newsletter published quarterly; Meetings also quarterly; Membership: $40.
HATPNGINIA@aol.com
www.americanhatpinsociety.com

American Historical Print Collectors Society
PO Box 201, Fairfield, CT 06824; Regular one-year membership: $35.

Antique and Art Glass Salt Shaker Collectors' Society (AAGSSCS)
1775 Lakeview Dr., Zeeland, MI 49464-2018. Membership: $20.
antiques@wmis.net
www.antiquesaltshakers.com

Antique & Collectors Reproduction News News
Antiques Coast to Coast
Mark Chervenka, Editor
PO Box 12130, Des Moines, IA 50312-9403; 515-274-5886 or (subscriptions only) 800-227-5531. Online subscription: $27.
acrn@repronews.com.

Antique Amusements Slot Machine & Jukebox Gazette
Ken Durham, Editor
909 26 St., N.W., Suite 502, Washington, DC 20037. Eight-page newspaper published once a year; Sample: $10.
www.GameRoomAntiques.com

Antique Bottle & Glass Collector Magazine
Jim Hagenbuch, Publisher
102 Jefferson St., PO Box 180, East Greenville, PA 18041; 215-679-5849. Subscription (12 issues): $25 (US); $28 (Canada). glswrk@enter.net

Antique Purses Catalog: $4
Bayhouse
PO Box 40443, Cleveland, OH 44140; 216-871-8584. Includes colored photos of beaded and enameled mesh purses.

Antique Radio Classified (ARC)
PO Box 2, Carlisle, MA 01741; 978-371-0512. ARC@antiqueradio.com

Antique Souvenir Collectors' News News
Gary Leveille, Editor

PO Box 562, Great Barrington, MA 01230

Antique Stove Association
Norm Howe, Treasurer of Newsletter
204 Buckeye Lane, Brownsboro, AL 35741-9302

Antique Stove Exchange
c/o Caroline Royske
PO Box 2101, Waukesha, WI 53187-2101; 262-542-9190 after 6 p.m.

Antique Telephone Collectors Assoc.
PO Box 1252, McPherson, KS 67460; 620-245-9555. An international organization associated with the Museum of Independent Telephony; Membership: $35 (+$5 initiation fee for new membership. office@atcaonline.com
www.atcaonline.com

Antique Trader
700 East State Street, Iola, WI 54990-0001. Featuring news about antiques and collectibles, auctions and events; Listing over 165,000 buyers and sellers in every edition; Subscription: $35 (US) for 52 issues per year.
robyn.austin@fwpubs.com
www.antiquetrader.com

Antique Wireless Association
Ormiston Rd., Breesport, NY 14816

Appraisers National Association
25602 Alicia Parkway, PMB 245, Laguna Hills, CA 92653; 949-349-9179. Founded in 1982, a nonprofit organization dedicated to the professionalism and education of personal property appraiser. All members adhere to a code of ethics and abide by professional standards. ANA also works to develop awareness of the professionalism of appraising, and the service it provides to the public. Free referrals to Accredited Appraisers for antiques, collectibles, art, jewelry, furniture, and residential contents.
info@ana-appraisers.org
www.ana-appraisers.org

Aspen Chamber Resort Assn.; 970-925-1940
www.aspenchamber.org

Association of Coffee Mill Enthusiasts (ACME)
c/o Robert P. Palmer, Treasurer
PO Box 86, Olivet, MI 49076. Quarterly newsletter, annual convention; Dues are $40 ($50 outside the continental US and Canada), covers cost of quarterly newsletter and copy of membership roster.

Auction Times for the West
Michael F. Shores, Publisher
Jeffrey Hill, Editor/General Manager
2329 Santa Clara Ave., Suite 207, Alamedo, CA 94501; 800-791-8592

Autograph Collector newsletter
Odyssey Publications
510-AS Corona Mall, Corona, CA 91719-1420; 909-371-7137
DBTOG@aol.com

Autographs of America
Tim Anderson
PO Box 461, Provo, UT 84603; 801-226-1787 (please call in the afternoon). www.AutographsOfAmerica.com

Automatical Musical Instruments Collector's Association
www.amica.org

Autumn Leaf
Glen Karlgaard Editor
13800 Fernando Ave., Apple Valley, MN 55124; 952-431-1814

Beatlefan
PO Box 33515, Decatur, GA 30033. Subscription: $15 (US) for 6 issues or $19 (Canada and Mexico).

Belleek Collectors International Society
PO Box 1498, Great Falls, VA 22066-8498; 1-800-Belleek; 703-272-6270 (outside the US & Canada). Each new member receives a certificate of membership, a new member/renewal gift, a binder for the Belleek Collectors Society magazines and the opportunity to purchase exclusive limited edition items; US membership: $43; info@belleek.com

Blue & White Pottery Club
224 12th St., NW, Cedar Rapids, IA 52405; Membership: $12 ($17 for spouse).
www.blueandwhitepottery.org

Bojo
PO Box 1403, Cranberry Township, PA 16066-0403. Send $3 for 38 pages of Beatles, toys, dolls, jewelry, autographs, Yellow Submarine items, etc.
www.bojoonline.com

Bookend Collector Club
c/o Louis Kuritzky, M.D.
4510 NW 17th Place, Gainesville, FL 32650; 352-377-3193. Quarterly full-color glossy newsletter, $25 per year.
lkuritzky@aol.com

Bossons Briefs, quarterly newsletter
Requires membership ($45 per year) in the International Bossons Collectors

Society; www/bossons.org
Norman E. Derocher, Exec. Director
8316 Woodlake Place, Tampa FL
33615-1728.
NormanDerocher@verizon.net

British Royal Commemorative Souvenirs Mail Order Catalog
Audrey Zeder
1320 SW 10th St. #S, North Bend,
WA 98045. Catalog issued monthly,
$5 each.

Buckeye Marble Collectors Club
Brian Estepp (info re: membership or
shows)
2206 Mardi Court, Grove City, OH
431251; 614-863-5350. Membership:
$10 (payable to club).
bthomas0725@woway.com
www.buckeyemarble.com

Butter Pat Patter Association
The Patter newsletter
265 Eagle Bend Drive
Bigfork, MT 59911-6235. Subscription
to newsletter: $22 (payable to Mary
Dessoie at above address), includes a
Royal Doulton butter pat; Sample cop-
ies also available by sending $4 and
LLSASE (65¢).

The Buttonhook Society
BHS, PO Box 1089, Maidstone, Kent
ME14 9BA, England
or Box 287, White Marsh, MD
21162-0287, USA. Publishes bimonthly newsletter *The Boutonneur*, which
promotes collecting of buttonhooks
and shares research and information
contributed by members.
buttonhooksociety@tiscali.co.uk
www.buttonhooksociety.com

Candy Container Collectors of America
c/o Jim Olean, 115 Mac Beth Dr., Lower Burrell, PA 15068-2628
or Contact: Jeff Bradfield
90 Main St., Dayton, VA 22821
www.candycontainer.org

Cane Collectors Club
PO Box 1004, Englewood Cliff, NJ
07632; 201-886-8826.
liela@walkingstickworld.com

The Carnival Pump
International Carnival Glass Assoc., Inc.
Lee Markley
Box 306, Mentone, IN 46539; Dues:
$25 per family per year in US and
Canada or $25 overseas.
www.internationalcarnivalglass.com

The Carousel News & Trader
87 Parke Ave. W., Suite 206, Mansfield, OH 44902. A monthly magazine
for the carousel enthusiast. Subscription: $35 per year.
www.carouseltrader.com

The Carousel Shopper Resource Catalog
Box 47, Dept. PC, Millwood, NY
10546. Only $2 (+50¢ postage); A full-
color catalog featuring dealers of antique carousel art offering single figures
or complete carousels, museums, restoration services, organizations, full-size
reproductions, books, cards, posters,
auction services and other hard-to-find
items for carousel enthusiasts.

CAS Collectors
206 Grove St.
Rockton, IL 61072
Established in 1994 as the Ceramic
Arts Studio Collectors Association,
CAS Collectors welcomes all with a
common interest in the work of Ceramic Arts Studio of Madison, Wisconsin. The club publishes a quarterly newsletter and hosts an annual
convention in Madison each August
in conjunction with the Wisconsin
Pottery Association Show & Sale.
Family membership: $25 per year.
Information about the club and its
activities, as well as a complete illustrated CAS history, is included in the
book *Ceramic Arts Studio: The Legacy
of Betty Harrington* by Donald-Brian
Johnson, Timothy J. Holthaus, and
James E. Petzold (Schiffer Publishing, 2003).
www.cascollectors.com or (for history)
www.ceramicartsstudio.org

A Catalog Collection
Kenneth E. Schneringer
271 Sabrina Ct., Woodstock, GA
30188-4228; 770-926-9383. Specializing in catalogs, promochures, view
books, labels, trade cards, special paper
needs. trademan68@aol.com
www.old-paper.com

Central Florida Insulator Collectors
Line Jewels, NIA #1380
3557 Nicklaus Dr., Titusville, FL
32780-5356. Dues: $10 per year for
single or family membership (checks
payable to Jacqueline Barnes); Dues
covers the cost of *Newsnotes,* the club's
monthly newsletter, which informs
members of meetings and shows, articles of interest on insulators and other
collectibles. For club information send
SASE to above address.
bluebellwt@aol.com.

China Specialties, Inc.
Fiesta Collector's Quarterly Newsletter
PO Box 361280, Strongsville, OH
44316-1280
www.chinaspecialties.com

Chintz Connection Newsletter
PO Box 222, Riverdale, MD 20738.
Dedicated to helping collectors share
information and find matchings; Subscription: 4 issues per year for $25.

The Coca-Cola Collectors Club
PMB 609
4780 Ashford-Dunwoody Rd, Suite A
Atlanta, GA 30338. Membership: $30
in US ($35, Canada).
www.cocacolaclub.org

Coin Operated Collectors Association
A club for those who collect antique
coin-operated slot machines, trade
stimulators, arcade machines, vending machines, and related collectibles.
Call 202-338-2471 to join. Membership fee; $33 per year.
www.CoinOpClub.org

The Cola Clan
Alice Fisher, Treasurer
2084 Continental Dr., N.E., Atlanta,
GA 30345

Collector's Life
The World's Foremost Publication for
Steiff Enthusiasts
Beth Savino
PO Box 798; Holland, OH 43528;
1-800-862-8697; fax: 419-531-2730.
info@toystore.net
www.toystorenet.com

Collector Glass News
Promotional Glass Collectors Assoc.
Box 308, Slippery Rock, PA 16057
724-946-2838 or fax 724-946-9012.
An international publication providing
current news to collectors of cartoon,
fast-food, and promotional glassware;
Subscription: $15 per household.
cgn@glassnews.com
www.glassnews.com

Collectors of Findlay Glass
PO Box 256, Findlay, OH 45840. An
organization dedicated to the study and
recognition of Findlay glass; Newsletter
The Melting Pot, published quarterly;
Annual convention; Membership: $10
per year ($15 per couple).

Compact Collectors
Roselyn Gerson
PO Box 40, Lynbrook, NY 11563;
516-593-8746 or fax 516-593-0610.
Publishes *Powder Puff* Newsletter,
which contains articles covering all
aspects of powder and solid perfume
compact collecting, restoration, vintage ads, patents, history, and articles
by members and prominent guest writers; Seeker and sellers column offered
free to members. compactldy@aol.com

Cookie Crumbs
Cookie Cutter Collectors Club
Ruth Capper, Secretary/Treasurer
PO Box 245, Cannon Falls, MN
55009. Subscription $20 per year (4 is-
sues, payable to CCCC).

Cookies
Rosemary Henry

9610 Greenview Lane, Manassas, VA
20109-3320. Subscription: $15 per
year (6 issues); Payable to Cookies.

The Copley Courier
1639 N. Catalina St., Burbank, CA
91505

Cowan Pottery Museum Associates
For information write: CPMA, PO
Box 16765, Rocky River, OH 44116 or
contact Victoria Naumann Peltz, Cu-
ratorial Associate, Cowan Pottery Museum at Rocky River Public Library,
1600 Hampton Rd., Rocky River, OH
44116; 440-333-7610, ext. 214. Membership: $25 ($35 dual) includes subscription to biannual *Cowan Pottery
Journal* Newsletter.
www.cowanpottery.org

Cracker Jack® Collector's Assoc.
The Prize Insider Newsletter
Deb Gunnerson, Membership Chair
3325 Edward St., NE, St. Anthony,
MN 55418. Subscription/membership:
$20 per year (single) or $24 (family).
raegun@comcast.net
www.collectoronline.com/CJCA/

Creamers, quarterly newsletter
Lloyd B. Bindscheattle
PO Box 11, Lake Villa, IL 60046-0011.
Subscription: $5 per year.

(Currier & Ives) C&I Dinnerware
Collector Club
Charles Burgess, Membership
308 Jodi Dr., Brownstown, IN
47220-1523; 812-358-4569. Membership: $15. annmah2@aol.com
www.currierandivesdinnerware.com

Custard Glass Collectors Society
Custard Connection quarterly newsletter
Sarah Coulon, Editor
591 SW Duxbury Ave., Port St. Lucie,
FL 34983; 561-785-9446.
custardsociety@aol.com
www.custardsociety.com

Czechoslovakian Collectors Guild
International
Alan Badia
15006 Meadowlake St., Odessa, FL
33556-3126. Annual membership: $65
in US. ab@czechartglass.com
www.czechartglass.com/ccgi

*The Dedham Pottery Collectors Society
Newsletter*
Jim Kaufman, Publisher
248 Highland St., Dedham, MA
02026-5833; 800-283-8070. $5 per is-
sue. DedhamPottery.com

Docks, L.R. 'Les'
Shellac Shack
Box 691035, San Antonio, TX
78269-1035. Send $2 for an illustrated
booklet of 78s that Docks wants to buy,

the prices he will pay, and shipping instructions. docks@texas.net
http://docks.home.texas.net

Doorstop Collectors of America
Doorstopper Newsletter
Jeanie Bertoia
2413 Madison Ave., Vineland, NJ 08630; 609-692-4092. Membership: $20 per year, includes two newsletters and convention; Send two-stamp SASE for sample.

Dragonware Club
c/o Suzi Hibbard
849 Vintage Ave., Fairfield, CA 94585; Inquiries must be accompanied with LSASE or they will not be responded to; All contributions are welcome. Dragon_Ware@hotmail.com

Drawing Room of Newport
Gacher, John; and Santi, Federico
152 Spring St., Newport, RI 02840; 401-841-5060. Book on Zsolnay available. www.drawrm.com

Early Typewriter Collectors Assoc.
ETCetera newsletter
Chuck Dilts and Rich Cincotta, Co-editors
PO Box 286; Southborough, MA 01772; 508-229-2064.
etcetera@writeme.com

Ed Taylor Radio Museum
245 N. Oakland Ave., Indianapolis, IN 46201-3360; 317-638-1641

Eggcup Collector's Corner
67 Stevens Ave., Old Bridge, NJ 08857. Issued quarterly; Subscription: $20 per year (payable to Joan George); Sample copy: $5.

The Elegance of Old Ivory Newsletter
Box 1004, Wilsonville, OR 97070

Fenton Art Glass Collectors of America, Inc.
Butterfly Net Newsletter
Kay Kenworthy, Editor
PO Box 384, 702 W. 5th St., Williamstown, WV 26187. Dues: $20 per year (full membership +$5 for each associate membership, children under 12 free). faqcainc@wirefire.com
www.fagcainc.wirefire.com

The Fenton Flyer
Laurie & Rich Karman, Editors
815 S. Douglas, Springfield, IL 62704; 217-787-8166

Fiesta Collector's Quarterly Newsletter
PO Box 471, Valley City, OH 44280. Subscription: $12 per year.
www.chinaspecialties.com

Florence Ceramics Collectors Society
1971 Blue Fox Drive; Lansdale, PA

19446-5505. Newsletter and club membership: $35 per year (6 issues in color). FlorenceCeramics@aol.com

Fostoria Glass Society of America, Inc.
PO Box 826, Moundsville, WV 26041. Membership: $18.
www.fostoriaglass.org

Frankoma Family Collectors Assoc.
PO Box 32571, Oklahoma City, OK 73123-0771. Membership dues: $35 (includes newsletters); Annual convention.
www.frankoma.org

Friends of Degenhart
c/o Degenhart Museum
PO Box 186, Cambridge, OH 43725; 740-432-2626. Membership: $5 ($10 for family) includes *Heartbeat* Newsletter (printed quarterly) and free admission to museum.
www.degenhartmuseum.com

H.C. Fry Society
PO Box 41, Beaver, PA 15009. Founded in 1983 for the sole purpose of learning about Fry glass; Publishes *Shards*, quarterly newsletter.

Goofus Glass Gazette
Steve Gillespie, Publisher
400 Martin Blvd., Village of the Oaks, MO 64118; 888-455-5558.
stegil@sbcglobal.net
www.goofus.org

The Gonder Collector
917 Hurl Dr.
Pittsburgh, PA 15236

Haeger Pottery Collectors of America
Lanette Clarke
5021 Toyon Way, Antioch, CA 94509; 925-776-7784. Newsletter published six times per year; Dues: $20.
Lanette-Clarke@msn.com.

Hagen-Renaker Collector's Club
c/o Debra Kerr
2055 Hammock Moss Dr., Orlando, FL 32820. Subscription rate: $24 per year.
wwww.hagenrenaker.com

Hall China Collector's Club Newsletter
Virginia Lee
PO Box 360488, Cleveland, OH 44136; 330-220-7456

Hammered Aluminum Collectors Association (HACA)
Dannie Woodard
PO Box 1346, Weatherford, TX 76086; 817-594-4680

Headhunters Newsletter
c/o Maddy Gordon
PO Box 83H, Scarsdale, NY 10583; 914-472-0227. Subscription: $24 per year for 4 issues; also holds convention.

Homer Laughlin China Collectors Association (HLCCA)
The Dish magazine (a 16-page quarterly included with membership); PO Box 721, North Platte, NE 69103-0721. Membership: $30 (single), $45 (couple/family). info@hlcca.org
www.hlcca.org

The Illustrator Collector's News (*TICN*)
Denis C. Jackson, Editor
PO Box 6433, Kingman, AZ 86401. A free use site on the internet for paper collectors of all kinds, listing paper and magazine-related price guides available for sale only at this site.
www.olypen.com/ticn

Indiana Historical Radio Society
245 N. Oakland Ave., Indianapolis, IN 46201-3360; 317-638-1641. Membership: $15 (US), $19 (overseas) includes *IHRS Bulletin* newsletter.
home.att.net/~indianahistoricalradio

International Assoc. of R.S. Prussia, Inc.
Linn or Leslie Schultz
PO Box 185, Lost Nation, IA 52254. Membership: $30 per household; Yearly convention. lschultz@netins.net
www.rsprussia.com

International Club for Collectors of Hatpins and Hatpin Holders (ICC of H&HH)
Audrae Heath, Managing Editor
PO Box 1009, Bonners Ferry, ID 83805-1009. *Bimonthly Points* newsletter and *Pictorial Journal.*

International Ivory Society
Robert Weisblut, Co-Founder
5001 Old Ocean Blvd. #1, Ocean Ridge, FL 33435; 561-276-5657. Free membership.

International Map Collectors Society
Membership Secretary
104 Church Rd., Watford, WD17 4QB, UK

International Antiquarian Mapsellers Association
www.antiquemapdealers.com

International Match Safe Association
Membership Chairman
PO Box 791, Malaga, NJ, 08328; 856-694-4167. Membership: $50; Quarterly newsletter and annual convention. IMSA@matchsafe.org
www.matchsafe.org

International Nippon Collectors Club (INCC)
Dick Bittner
8 Geoley Ct., Thurmont, MD 21788. Publishes newsletter six times a year; Holds annual convention; Membership: $30.
www.nipponcollectorsclub.com

International Perfume and Scent Bottle Collectors Association
Randall Monsen, PO Box 529, Vienna, VA 22183, or Coleen Abbot, 396 Croton Rd., Wayne, PA 19087-2038. Membership: $45 (USA) or $55 (Foreign); Newsletter published quarterly.
www.perfumebottles.org

International Rose O'Neill Club
Contact Irene Asher
103 W. Locust, Aurora, MO 65605-1416. Publishes quarterly newsletter *Kewpiesta Kourier*. Membership: (includes newsletter) $20 (single) or $25 (family).

International Society of Antique Scale Collectors (ISASC)
Jan Macho, Executive Secretary
3616 Noakes St., Los Angeles, CA 90023; 323-263-6878. Publishes *Equilibrium* Magazine; Quarterly newsletter; Annual membership directory and out-of-print scale catalogs; Annual convention; Please visit the ISASC website to learn more.
www.isasc.org (This site offers a research and reply service for a fee.)

International Vintage Poster Dealers Association (IVPDA)
PO Box 501, Old Chelsea Station, New York, NY 10113-0501. Specializing in posters. info@ivpda.com
www.ivpda.com

John F. Rinaldi
Nautical Antiques and Related Items (Appointment only)
Box 765, Dock Square, Kennebunkport, ME 04046; 207-967-3218; fax 207-967-2918. Illustrated catalog: $5.
jfrinaldi@adelphia.net

Josef Originals Newsletter
Jim and Kaye Whitaker
PO Box 475, Dept. S, Lynnwood, WA 98046. Subscription (4 issues): $10 per year.

Kate Greenaway Society
James Lewis Lowe
PO Box 8, Norwood, 19074
Postcard Classics@juno.com

Knife Rests of Yesterday and Today
Beverly L. Ales
4046 Graham St., Pleasanton, CA 94566-5619. Subscription: $20 per year for six issues.

The Laughlin Eagle
Joan Jasper, Publisher
Richard Racheter, Editor
1270 63rd Terrace S., St. Petersburg, FL 33705; 813-867-3982. Subscription: $18 (four issues) per year; Sample: $4.

Les Amis de Vieux Quimper (Friends of Old Quimper)

c/o Mark and Adela Meadows
PO Box 819, Carnelian Bay, CA
96140. SASE required for written reply. meadows@oldquimper.com
www.oldquimper.com

Liddle Kiddle Konvention
Paris Langford
415 Dodge Ave. Jefferson, LA 70121.
Send SASE for information about upcoming Liddle Kiddle Convention, also
send additional SASE for Liddle Kiddle
Newsletter information.
bbean415@aol.com
liddlekiddlesnewsletter@yahoo.com

Central Florida Insulator Collectors
Line Jewels, NIA #1380
3557 Nicklaus Dr., Titusville, FL
32780

Majolica International Society
Michael Foley, Membership Chairman
77 Wright St., New Bedford, MA
02740. Membership: $50 per year, includes annual meeting and quarterly
newsletter *Majolica Matters*.
www.majolicasociety.com

Marble Collectors' Society of America
Box 222, Trumbull, CT 06611. Publishes *Marble Mania*; Gathers and
disseminates information to further
the hobby of marbles and marble collecting; $12 adds your name to the
contributor mailing list ($21 covers 2
years). blockglss@aol.com

Marble Collectors Unlimited
PO Box 206, Northboro, MA 01532

Midwest Open Salt Society
c/o Ed Bowman
2411 W. 500 North, Hartford City, IN
47348. Dues: $10 ($6 for spouse).

Midwest Sad Iron Collector Club
Jerry Marcus, Secretary
67-10 161st St, Flushing, NY
11365-3163; 718-591-0927. Membership $30 per year. reginabeau.aol.com

Moss Lamps
eBay group site: Moss Lamps of California

Murray Hudson Antiquarian Books,
  Maps & Globes
109 S. Church St., Box 163, Halls, TN
38040; 800-748-9946 or 731-836-9057.
Buyer and seller specializing in antique
maps, globes, and books with maps:
atlases, explorations, travel guides,
geographies, surveys, etc.; Largest ever
catalog of Civil War maps and graphics; Largest selection of wall maps and
world globes. mapman@ecis.com
www.murrayhudson.com

The Museum of the American Cocktail
PO Box 38, Malverne, NY 11565

svisakay@aol.com
www.MuseumOfTheAmericanCocktail.org

Mystic Lights of the Aladdin Knights,
  bimonthly newsletter
c/o J.W. Courter
3935 Kelley Rd., Kevil, KY 40253-9532;
270-488-2116

National Assoc. of Avon Collectors
c/o Connie Clark
PO Box 7006, Dept. P, Kansas City,
MO 64113. Information requires
LSASE.

National Association of Breweriana
  Advertising (NABA)
Publishes *The Breweriana Collector*;
Holds annual convention; Membership information and Directory available on www.nababrew.org

National Association of Warwick
  China and Pottery Collectors
Betty June Wymer
28 Bachmann Drive, Wheeling, WV
26003; 304-232-3031. Annual dues
$15 (single) or $20 (couple), checks
payable to NAWCPA; Publishes quarterly newsletter; Holds annual convention in Wheeling, West Virginia.

National Autumn Leaf Collectors'
  Club
Bill Swanson, President
807 Roaring Springs Dr., Allen, TX
75002-2112; 972-727-5527 or fax
972-727-2107; bescom@nalcc.org
or Gwynne Harrison
PO Box 1, Mira Loma, CA 91752-0001;
909-685-5434 or fax 909-681-1692.
Membership: $20, payable to NALCC,
c/o Dianna Kowales, PO Box 900968,
Palmdale, CA 93590-0968.
morgan99@pe.net
www.nalcc.org

National Blue Ridge Newsletter
Norma Lilly
144 Highland Dr., Blountville, TN
37617. Subscription: $15 per year (6
issues).

National Cambridge Collectors, Inc.
PO Box 416, Cambridge, OH
43725-0416; 740-432-4245. Membership: $20 (Associate member: $3).
NCC-Crystal-Ball@compuserve.com
www.cambridgeglass.org

National Cuff Link Society
c/o Eugene R. Klompus
PO Box 5700, Vernon Hills, IL 60061;
phone/fax: 847-816-0035. $30 annual
dues includes subscription to *The Link*,
a quarterly magazine; write for free
booklet *The Fun of Cuff Link Collecting*.
genek@cufflink.com
ncls@bellsouth.net
www.cufflink.com

National Depression Glass Assoc.
PO Box, 8264, Wichita, KS
67208-0264; Publishes *News and
Views*; Membership: $20 (individual);
$5 (associate).
www.ndga.net

National Fenton Glass Society
PO Box 4008, Marietta, OH 45750;
740-374-3345; fax: 740-376-9708.
Membership: $20, includes *The Fenton
Flyer* newsletter.

National Graniteware Society
PO Box 9248, Cedar Rapids, IA
52409-9248. Membership: $20.
www.graniteware.org

National Greentown Glass Assoc.
PO Box 107, Greentown, IN
46936-0107. Membership: $20.
www.greentownglass.org

National Imperial Glass Collectors'
  Society, Inc.
PO Box 534, Bellaire, OH 43906.
Membership: $18 per year (+$3 for
each associate member); Quarterly
newsletter; Convention every June.
info@nigcs.org; www.imperialglass.org

National Insulator Association
1315 Old Mill Path, Broadview Heights,
OH 44147. Membership: $12.
kwjacob@icsaero.com
www.nia.org

National Milk Glass Collectors' Society and *Opaque News*, quarterly
  newsletter
Membership: $18 (payable to club)
Rick Weymuth, Membership Chair
105 N. Grand, Maryville, MO 64468.
Please include SASE.
membership@nmgsc.org
www.nmgcs.org

National Organization of Open Salt
  Collectors
C/o Ed Bowman
2411 W. 500 N, Hartford City, IN
47348

National Reamer Collectors Assoc.
c/o Wayne Adickes
408 E. Reuss, Cuero, TX 77954. Membership: $27.50 per household.
adickes@sbcglobal.net
www.reamers.org

National Shaving Mug Collectors
  Association
Dick Leidlein
3443 Boston Twp. Line Rd., Richmond,
IN, 47374. To stimulate the study, collection, and preservation of shaving
mugs and all related barbering items;
Provides quarterly newsletter, bibliography, and directory; Holds 2 meetings
per year. dleidlein@parallax.ws
www.nsmca.net

National Shelley China Club
Rochelle Hart, Secretary/Treasurer
591 West 67th Ave., Anchorage, AK
99518-1555; 907-562-2124. Membership: $45 per year, 4 quarterly newsletters plus many other benefits and publications. imahart@alaska.net
www.nationalshelleychinaclub.com

National Toothpick Holder Collectors
  Society
Membership Chairperson
PO Box 852, Archer City, TX 76351.
Dues: $20 (single) or $25 (couple); Foreign dues: $23 (single) or $28 (couple)
in US dollars. Includes 10 *Toothpick
Bulletin* newsletters per year; Annual
convention held in August; Exclusive
toothpick holder annually.
information@nthcs.org
www.nthcs.org

National Valentine Collectors Assoc.
Nancy Rosin
PO Box 1404, Santa Ana, CA 92702;
714-547-1355. Membership: $16. Specializing in Valentines and love tokens.

New England Society of Open Salt
  Collectors
Chuck Keys
21 Overbrook Lane, East Greenwich,
RI 02818. Dues: $7 per year.

Newspaper Collector's Society of
  America
Rick Brown
Lansing, MI, 517-887-1255. An extensive, searchable, 300,000-word reference library of American history with
an emphasis on newspapers publishing
speeches; interactive crossword puzzles;
regular auctions of ephemera, historic
documents, and newspapers; a mall
with over 100 different online catalogs
of paper collectibles; and much, much
more!
help@historybuff.com
www.historybuff.com

Night Light Club/Newsletter
Culver, Bob
3081 Sand Pebble Cove, Pinckney, MI
48169. Specializing in miniature oil
lamps; Membership: $15 per year.

NM (Nelson McCoy) Express
Carol Seman, Editor
8934 Brecksville Rd., Suite 406, Brecksville, OH 44141-2318; 440-526-2094
(voice & fax). Membership: $26 per
year (12 issues). McCjs@aol.com
www.members.aol.com/nmXpress/

North American Torquay Society
Jerry and Gerry Kline, two of the
  founding members
604 Orchard View Dr., Maumee, OH
43537; 419-893-1226. Send SASE for
information.

North American Trap Collectors' Association
c/o Tom Parr
PO Box 94, Galloway, OH 43119-0094. Dues: $25 per year; Publishes bimonthly newsletter.

North Dakota Pottery Collectors Society and Newsletter
c/o Sandy Short, Membership Chair
Box 14, Beach, ND 58621. Membership: $15 (includes spouse); Annual convention in June; Quarterly newsletters. csshortnd@mcn.net
www.ndpcs.org

Novelty Salt & Pepper Shakers Club
Louise Davis
PO Box 416, Gladstone, OR 72037-0416. Publishes quarterly newsletter; Holds annual convention; Dues: $30 per year in US, Canada and Mexico ($5 extra for couple).
dmac925@yahoo.com

Nutcracker Collectors' Club and Newsletter
Susan Otto, Editor
12204 Fox Run Dr., Chesterland, OH 44026; 440-729-2686. Membership: $20 ($25 foreign) includes quarterly newsletters. nutsue@adelphia.net

The Occupied Japan Club
c/o Florence Archambault
29 Freeborn St., Newport, RI 02840-1821. Publishes *The Upside Down World of an O.J. Collector*, a bimonthly newsletter. Information requires SASE. florence@aiconnect.com
www.ojclub.com

Old Sleepy Eye Collectors Club of America, Inc.
PO Box 12, Monmouth, IL 61462. Membership: $10 per year with additional $1 for spouse (if joining).
oseclub@maplecity.com
www.maplecity.com/~MARKoseclub/

Old Stuff
Donna and Ron Miller, Publishers
PO Box 449, McMinnville, OR 97128. Published six times annually; Copies by mail: $3.50 each; Annual subscription: $20 ($30 in Canada).
millers@oldstuffnews.com
www.oldstuffnews.com

On the LIGHTER Side Newsletter (bimonthly publication)
International Lighter Collectors
Judith Sanders, Editor
PO Box 1733, Quitman, TX 75783-1733; 903-763-2795 or fax 903-763-4953. Annual convention held in US; Subscription: $43 (overseas) $40 (US and Canada), $35 (Senior member); $25 (Junior member); Please include SASE when requesting information.

Open Salt Collectors of the Atlantic Regions (O.S.C.A.R.)
Wilbur Rudisill, Treasurer
1844 York Rd., Gettysburg, PA 17325. Dues: $5 per year.

Open Salt Seekers of the West, Northern California Chapter
Sara Conley
84 Margaret Dr., Walnut Creek, CA 94596. Dues: $7 per year.

Open Salt Seekers of the West, Southern California Chapter
Janet Hudson
2525 E. Vassar Court, Visalia, CA 93277. Dues: $5 per year.

Pacific Northwest Fenton Association
c/o Jackie Shirley
PO Box 881, Tillamook, OR 97141. Newsletter subscription: $25 per year (published quarterly, includes annual piece of glass made only for subscribers). jshirley@oregoncoast.com
www.glasscastle.com/pnwfa.htm

Paden City Glass Collectors Guild
Paul Torsiello, Editor
42 Aldine Road, Parsippany, NJ, 07054. Publishes newsletter; for subscription information pcguild1@yahoo.com

Paper & Advertising Collectors' Marketplace
PO Box 128, Scandinavia, WI 54977-0128; 715-467-2379 or fax 715-467-2243. Subscription: $19.95 in US (12 issues).
pacpcm@eagleonline.com
www.engleonline.com

Paper Pile Quarterly Magazine
Paperweight Collectors' Assoc., Inc.
PO Box 4153, Emerald Isle, NC 28594. Sustaining US membership $55 per year (non-US: $35), includes quarterly *PCA Inc. Annual Bulletin* newsletter; Biannual convention.
info@paperweight.org

Past Tyme Pleasures
Steve and Donna Howard
PMB #204, 2491 San Ramon Blvd., #1, San Ramon, 94583; 925-484-6442 or fax 925-484-6427. Offers two absentee auction catalogs per year pertaining to old advertising.
pasttyme@comcast.net
www.pasttyme1.com

Peanut Pals
Publishes *Peanut Papers*; Annual directory sent to members; Annual convention and regional conventions; Primary membership: $20 per year (associate memberships available); More information on www.peanutpals.org; Sample newsletter: $2.

Pen Collectors of America
Roger E. Wooden

PO Box 174, Garden Prairie, IL 61038-0174. Quarterly newsletter, *Pennant*; Annual membership: $40 in US and Canada (includes newsletter and access to reference library).
info@pencollectors.com
www.pencollectors.com

Pepsi-Cola Collectors Club Express
Bob Stoddard, Editor
PO Box 817; Claremont, CA 91711-0817

Perrault-Rago Gallery
333 N. Main St., Lambertville, NJ 08530; 609-397-9374. Specializing in 20th-century decorative arts, particularly art pottery and decorative tiles.
ragoarts@aol.com.

Petroleum Collectibles Monthly
Scott Benjamin and Wayne Henderson, Publishers
PO Box 556, LaGrange, OH 44050-0556; 440-355-6608. Subscription: $35.95 per year (Canada, $44.50; International, $71.95; Samples $5) with over $2,000 subscribers. Scott advises gasoline globes and is devoted to gas and oil collectibles.
www.pcmpublishing.com

Phoenix and Consolidated Glass Collectors' Club
Ruth Ann Davis, Treasurer
PO Box 387, Southington, CT 96489; 860-747-2275. Membership: $25 (single), $35 (family) per year. Please make checks payable to club.
ruthan11@cox.net

Phoenix Bird Collectors of America (PBCA)
1107 Deerfield Lane, Marshall, MI 49068; 269-781-9791. Membership: (payable to Joan Oates) $12 per year, includes *Phoenix Bird Discoveries*, published two times a year; Also available: 1996 updated value guide to be used in conjunction with Books I – IV; now $4.45 ppd; Newly cataloged Phoenix Bird since Book IV of 1989, Book V, published January, 2002, 96 pages (32 in color). joates120@broadstripe.net

Pickard Collectors Club, Ltd.
Membership office: 300 E. Grove St., Bloomington, IL 61701; 309-828-5533 or fax 309-829-2266. Membership (includes newsletter): $30 a year (single) or $40 (family).

Pie Birds Unlimited newsletter
John Lo Bello
1039 NW Hwy. 101, Lincoln City, OR 97367
qps1@earthlink.net

Political Collectors of Indiana Club
Michael McQuillen
PO Box 50022, Indianapolis, IN

46250-0022; 317-845-1721. Official APIC (American Political Items Collectors) Chapter comprised of over 300 collectors of presidential and local political items.
michael@politicalparade.com
www.politicalparade.com

Porcelain Collector's Companion
c/o Dorothy Kamm
PO Box 7460, Port St. Lucie, FL 34985-4760; 561-464-4008

Posner, Judy and Jeff
Specializing in Disneyana, Black memorabilia, salt and pepper shakers, souvenirs of the USA, character and advertising memorabilia, and figural pottery. www.judyposner.com

Powder Puff Compact Collectors' Chronicle
Roselyn Gerson
PO Box 40, Lynbrook, NY 11563; 516-593-8746 or fax 516-593-0610. Author of six books related to figural compacts, vanity bags/purses, solid perfumes, lipsticks, and related gadgetry.
compactlady@aol.com

Purinton News & Views
Joe McManus, Editor
PO Box 153, Connellsville, PA 15425. Newsletter for Purinton pottery enthusiasts; Subscription: $16 per year.

R.A. Fox Collector's Club
c/o Pat Gibson
38280 Guava Dr., Newark, CA, 94560; 510-792-0586

Ribbon Tin News Newsletter (quarterly publication)
Hobart D. Van Deusen, Editor
15 Belgo Rd, Lakeville, CT 06339; 860-435-0088. $30 per year for 24+ color plates. For collectors of typewriters, typewriter ribbon tins and go-withs. Indexed subscribers' list and participation in occasional mail/phone auctions. rtn.hoby@snet.net

Rosevilles of the Past Newsletter
Nancy Bomm, Editor
PO Box 656, Clarcona, FL 32710-0656; 407-294-3980 or fax 407-294-7836. $19.95 per year for 6 newsletters.
rosepast@worldnet.att.net

Schoenhut Collectors Club
c/o Pat Girbach, Secretary
1003 W. Huron St., Ann Arbor, MI 48103-4217 for membership information.

Shawnee Pottery Collectors' Club
PO Box 713, New Smyrna Beach, FL 32170-0713. Monthly nation-wide newsletter. SASE (c/o Pamela Curran) required when requesting information; $3 for sample of current newsletter.

Shot Glass Exchange
PO Box 219, Western Springs, IL 60558; 708-246-1559. Primarily pre-prohibition glasses. Subscription: (includes 2 semi-annual issues, available in US only) $13 per year, single copy $8.

Society of Inkwell Collectors
PO Box 324, Missville, IL, 61552. Membership: $35 per year, includes subscription to *The Stained Finger*, a quarterly publication.
membership@soic.com; www.soic.com

Society for Old Ivory and Ohme Porcelain
Pat Fitzwater Wimkin, Secretary/ Treasurer
1650 S.E. River Ridge Dr., Milwaukie, OR 97222

Southern California Marble Club
18361-1 Strothern St., Reseda, CA 91335

Southern Folk Pottery Collectors Society quarterly newsletter
Society headquarters: 220 Washington St., Bennett, NC 27208; 336-581-4246 (Wednesday through Saturday, 10:00 to 5:00). Specializing in historical research and promotion of the traditional southern folk potter (past and present) to a modern collecting audience. Membership includes biannual absentee auction catalogs (at discounted prices), access to member pieces, opportunities to meet potters, participate in events, newsletter information, and more. The society auctions represent three centuries of productions from all of the southern states. The bi-annual absentee auctions are structured in a personalized format of sales that benefits both the seller and buyer. For more information contact the society.
sfpcs@rtmc.net

Southern Oregon Antiques & Collectibles Club
PO Box 508, Talent, OR 97540; 541-535-1231 or fax 541-535-5109. Meets 1st Wednesday of the month; Promotes two shows a year in Medford, OR. contact@soacc.com
www.soacc.com

Stangl/Fulper Collectors Club
PO Box 538, Flemington, NJ 08822. Annual auction in June; American pottery and dinnerware show and sale in October.
www.stanglfulper.com

Still Bank Collectors Club of America
Membership Chairman
440 Homestead Ave., Metairie, LA 70005. Membership: $35.
contact@stillbankclub.com
www.stillbankclub.com

Stretch Glass Society
Membership: $22 (US); $24 (International), International membership MUST be paid by money order; Quarterly newsletter with color photos; Annual convention.
http://stretchglasssociety.org

Style: 1900 and *Modernism*
David Rago
333 N. Main St., Lambertville, NJ, 08530; 609-397-4104

The Tanner Restraints Collection
6442 Canyon Creek Way, Elk Grove, CA 95758-5431; 916-684-4006. 40-page catalog of magician/escape artist equipment from trick and regulation padlocks, handcuffs, leg shackles, and straight jackets to picks and pick sets; Books on all of the above and much more.

Tarrant, Jenny
Holly Daze Antiques
4 Gardenview, St. Peters, MO 63376. Specializing in Halloween, Christmas, Easter, etc.; Buying & selling Halloween and holiday items; Antique holiday for sale. Jennyjol@aol.com
www.holly-days.com

Tea Leaf Club International
Maxine Johnson, Membership Chair
PO Box 377, Belton, MO 64012. Publishes *Tea Leaf Readings* Newsletter; Membership: $30 per household (up to 2 members).
www.tealeafclub.com

THCKK
The Hardware Companies Kollector's Klub
For information contact Jerry Heuring, 28450 US Highway 61, Scott City, MO 63780; 573-264-3947. Membership: $20 per year; jheuring@charter.net
www.thckk.org

Thermometer Collectors' Club of America
Richard Porter, Vice President
PO Box 944, Onset, MA 02558; 508-295-4405. Visit the Porter Thermometer Museum (world's only, always open) free with 4,900+ thermometers to see. Appraisals, repairs and traveling lecture (600 given, ages 8 – 98, all venues).

Thimble Collectors International
Jina Samulka, Membership Chair
Membership: $25 (US), $30 (International).
membershipVP@thimblecollectors.com
www.thimblecollectors.com

Three Rivers Depression Era Glass Society
Meetings held 1st Monday of each month at 7:00 p.m. at Hoss's Restau-rant, Canonsburg, PA.
info@pghdepressionglass.org

Tiffin Glass Collectors
PO Box 554, Tiffin, OH 44883. Meetings at Seneca County Museum on 2nd Tuesday of each month; Tiffin Glass Museum, 25 S. Washington, Tiffin, OH, Wednesday – Sunday from 1:00 p.m. – 5:00 p.m.; Membership: $15.
www.tiffinglass.org

Tins 'n Signs
Box 440101, Aurora, CO 80044. Subscription: $25 per year.

Toaster Collectors Association
1615 Winding Trail, Springfield, OH 45503. Membership: $30 per year, holds convention, publishes quarterly newsletter.
www.toastercollectors.org

Tops & Bottoms Club (Rene Lalique perfumes only)
c/o Madeleine France
9 N. Federal Highway, Dania Beach, FL 33004

Toy Shop
Mark Williams, Publisher
700 E. State St., Iola, WI 54990-0001; 715-445-2214 or fax 715-445-4087. Subscription $33.98 (26 issues) in US

Trick or Treat Trader
577 Boggs Run Elementary School Benwood, WV 26031; 304-233-1031. Subscription: $15 (four issues).
halloweenqueen@castlehalloween.com
www.castlehalloween.com

TW List (Typewriters)
Rich Cincotta
PO Box 286, Southboro, MA 01772; 508-229-2064
typewriter@writeme.com
http://typewriter.rydia.net

Uhl Collectors' Society
Amy & Sam Busler, Secretary/Treasurer
398 S. Star Dr. Santa Claus, IN 47579; 812-544-2987. Membership: $15 per family.
www.uhlcollectors.org

Vaseline Glass Collectors, Inc.
Squeaker Bootsma, Secretary
14560 Schleisman, Corona, CA 92880. An organization whose sole purpose is to unify vaseline glass collectors; newsletter *Glowing Report* published bimonthly; Convention held annually. Membership: $25.
www.vaselineglass.org

Vetri: Italian Glass News
Howard Lockwood, Publisher
PO Box 191, Fort Lee, NJ 07024; 201-969-0373. Quarterly newsletter about 20th-century Italian glass.

Vintage Fashion & Costume Jewelry Newsletter/Club
PO Box 265, Glen Oaks, NY 11004; 718-939-3095. Subscription (four issues): $20 US, $25 Canada, $25 International. Back issues available at $5 each.
vfck@aol.com; www.lizjewel.com/vf

Vintage TVs
Harry Poster
Box 1883, S. Hackensack, 07606; 201-794-9606. Specializes in vintage TVs, vintage radios, stereo cameras.
www.harryposter.com

The Wallace Nutting Collector's Club
Pam & Bob Franscella, Membership
2944 Ivanhoe Glen, Madison, WI 53711; 608-274-4506. Membership: $20; Established in 1973, holds annual conventions; Generally recognized national center of Wallace Nutting-like activity are Michael Ivankovich's Wallace Nutting & Wallace Nutting-Like Specialty Auctions, which provide the opportunity for collectors and dealers to compete for Wallace Nutting and Wallace Nutting-like pictures as well as giving sellers the opportunity to place items before the country's leading enthusiasts. When requesting information, a close-up photo which includes the picture's frame and a SASE are required.
www.wallacenutting.com

Warwick China Collectors Club
Pat and Don Hoffmann, Sr.
1291 N. Elmwood Dr., Aurora, IL 60506-1309; 630-859-3435
warwick@ntsource.com

Watt Collectors' Association
Watt's News Newsletter, for Watt pottery enthusiasts
PO Box 253, Sussex, WI 53089-0253. Membership includes quarterly newsletter) $20; annual convention.

Wave Crest Collectors Club
c/o Whitney Newland
PO Box 2013, Santa Barbara, CA 93120. Membership dues: $25 (includes quarterly newsletter); Annual convention. whntique@gte.net

The Wedgwood Society of New York
5 Dogwood Court, Glen Head, NY 11545; 516-626-3427. Membership: $30 (single) or $35 (family). Publishes newsletter (six times per year) and a scholarly magazine, *Ars Ceramica*, of original articles published by the Society; six meetings per year.
www.wsny.org

Westmoreland Glass Collector's Newsletter
PO Box 143, North Liberty, IA 52317. Subscription: $16 per year. This publication is dedicated to the purpose of

preserving Westmoreland Glass and its history.

Westmoreland Glass Society
Steve Jensen
PO Box PO Box 2883, Iowa City, IA 52240-2883. Membership: $15 (single) or $25 (household).
www.westmorelandglassclubs.org

The Whimsey Club
c/o Lon Knickerbocker
PO Box 312, Danville, NY, 14437. *Whimsical Notions*, quarterly newsletter with colored photos; Dues: $10 per year; Annual get together.
mountainmonster@mountain.net

The White Ironstone China Assoc., Inc.
Diane Dorman, Membership Chair
PO Box 855, Fairport, NY 14450-0855. Newsletter available for $30.
www.whiteironstonechina.com

Willow Review
PO Box 41312, Nashville, TN 37204. Send SASE for information.

The Zsolnay Store
152 Spring St., Newport, RI 02840; 401-841-5060. Zsolnay book available.
www.drawrm.com

Index